Plumbing Costs with RSMeans Data

Chris Clough, Editor

2024
47th annual edition

Chief Product Officer
Chris Gaudreau

Chief Technology Officer
Chris Gaudreau

Director, Data Operations
Sam Giffin

Engineering and Research
Matthew Doheny, Sr. Manager

Engineers: Architectural Divisions
1, 3, 4, 5, 6, 7, 8, 9, 10, 11, 12, 13, 41
Sam Babbitt
Stephen Bell
Richard Goldin
Scott Keller
Thomas Lane
Melissa Stewart

Engineers: Civil Divisions and Wages
2, 31, 32, 33, 34, 35, 44, 46
Derrick Hale, PE
Christopher Babbitt
Michael Lynch
Elisa Mello
Giles Munyard
David Yazbek

Engineers: Mechanical, Electrical, Plumbing & Conveying Divisions
14, 21, 22, 23, 25, 26, 27, 28, 48
Joseph Kelble
Brian Adams
Michelle Curran
Antonio D'Aulerio
Thomas Lyons
Jake MacDonald
Chris Clough

Contributing Engineers
John Melin, PE, Manager
Paul Cowan
Gerard Lafond, PE
Matthew Sorrentino

Production
Debra Panarelli, Manager
Sheryl Rose
Janice Thalin

Data Quality
Patrice Bruesch
Ellen D'Amico

Cover Design
Blaire Collins

Data Management Ecosystem
Audrey Considine
Kedar Gaikwad
Mike Bruesch
Jonathan Forgit

RSMeans Data from Gordian
Construction Publishers & Consultants
30 Patewood Dr., Suite 350
Greenville, SC 29615
United States of America
1.800.448.8182
rsmeans.com

Copyright 2023 by The Gordian Group Inc.
All rights reserved.
Cover photo © iStock/DenBoma

Printed in the United States of America
ISSN 1537-8411
ISBN 978-1-961006-15-7

Gordian's authors, editors, and engineers apply diligence and judgment in locating and using reliable sources for the information published. However, Gordian makes no express or implied warranty or guarantee in connection with the content of the information contained herein, including the accuracy, correctness, value, sufficiency, or completeness of the data, methods, and other information contained herein. Gordian makes no express or implied warranty of merchantability or fitness for a particular purpose. Gordian shall have no liability to any customer or third party for any loss, expense, or damage, including consequential, incidental, special, or punitive damage, including lost profits or lost revenue, caused directly or indirectly by any error or omission, or arising out of, or in connection with, the information contained herein. For the purposes of this paragraph, "Gordian" shall include The Gordian Group, Inc., and its divisions, subsidiaries, successors, parent companies, and their employees, partners, principals, agents and representatives, and any third-party providers or sources of information or data. Gordian grants the purchaser of this publication limited license to use the cost data contained herein for purchaser's internal business purposes in connection with construction estimating and related work. The publication, and all cost data contained herein, may not be reproduced, integrated into any software or computer program, developed into a database or other electronic compilation, stored in an information storage or retrieval system, or transmitted or distributed to anyone in any form or by any means, electronic or mechanical, including photocopying or scanning, without prior written permission of Gordian. This publication is subject to protection under copyright law, trade secret law and other intellectual property laws of the United States, Canada and other jurisdictions. Gordian and its affiliates exclusively own and retain all rights, title and interest in and to this publication and the cost data contained herein including, without limitation, all copyright, patent, trademark and trade secret rights. Except for the limited license contained herein, your purchase of this publication does not grant you any intellectual property rights in the publication or the cost data.

2124 $420.00 per copy (in United States)
Price is subject to change without prior notice.

Related Data and Services

Our engineers recommend the following products and services to complement *Plumbing Costs with RSMeans Data*:

Annual Cost Data Books
2024 Assemblies Costs with RSMeans Data
2024 Square Foot Costs with RSMeans Data

Reference Books
Estimating Building Costs
RSMeans Estimating Handbook
Green Building: Project Planning & Estimating
How to Estimate with RSMeans Data
Plan Reading & Material Takeoff
Project Scheduling & Management for Construction
Universal Design Ideas for Style, Comfort & Safety

Virtual, Instructor-led & On-site Training Offerings
Introduction to Cost Estimating
Advanced Cost Estimating
Facilities Estimating
Maintenance & Repair Estimating
Mechanical & Electrical Estimating
RSMeans Online Training

RSMeans Data
For access to the latest cost data, an intuitive search, and an easy-to-use estimate builder, take advantage of the time savings available from our online application.

To learn more visit: **RSMeans.com/online**

Enterprise Solutions
Building owners, facility managers, building product manufacturers and attorneys across the public and private sectors engage with RSMeans Data Enterprise to solve unique challenges where trusted construction cost data is critical.

To learn more about our Enterprise Solutions, please call us toll-free at 800.448.8182.

Custom Built Datasets
Building and Space Models: Quickly plan construction costs across multiple locations based on geography, project size, building system component, product options and other variables for precise budgeting and cost control.

Predictive Analytics: Accurately plan future builds with custom graphical interactive dashboards, negotiate future costs of tenant build-outs and identify and compare national account pricing.

Consulting
Building Product Manufacturing Analytics: Validate your claims and assist with new product launches.

Third-Party Legal Resources: Used in cases of construction cost or estimate disputes, construction product failure vs. installation failure, eminent domain, class action construction product liability and more.

API
For resellers or internal application integration, RSMeans Data is offered via API. Deliver Unit, Assembly and Square Foot Model data within your interface. To learn more about our API solutions, please call us toll-free at 800.448.8182.

Table of Contents

Foreword	iv
How the Cost Data Is Built: An Overview	v
Estimating with RSMeans Data: Unit Prices	vii
How to Use the Cost Data: The Details	ix
Unit Price Section	1
RSMeans Data: Unit Prices—How They Work	2
Assemblies Section	471
RSMeans Data: Assemblies—How They Work	472
Reference Section	581
Construction Equipment Rental Costs	583
Crew Listings	595
Historical Cost Indexes	632
City Cost Indexes	633
Location Factors	676
Reference Tables	682
Change Orders	720
Project Costs	723
Abbreviations	728
Index	732
Training Class Options	754
Labor Trade Rates including Overhead & Profit	Inside Back Cover

Foreword

The Value of RSMeans Data from Gordian

Since 1942, RSMeans Data has been the industry-standard materials, labor, and equipment cost information database for contractors, facility owners and managers, architects, engineers and anyone else that requires the latest localized construction cost information. More than 80 years later, the objective remains the same: to provide facility and construction professionals with the most current and comprehensive construction cost database possible.

With the constant influx of new construction methods and materials, in addition to ever-changing labor and material costs, last year's cost data is not reliable for today's designs, estimates or budgets. Gordian's cost engineers apply real-world construction experience to identify and quantify new building products and methodologies, adjust productivity rates and adjust costs to local market conditions across the nation. This adds up to more than 30,000 hours in cost research annually. This unparalleled construction cost expertise is why so many facility and construction professionals rely on RSMeans Data year over year.

About Gordian

Gordian is the leading provider of Building Intelligence™ Solutions, delivering unrivaled insights, robust technology and comprehensive expertise that fuel customers' success during every phase of the building lifecycle. Gordian created Job Order Contracting (JOC) and the industry standard RSMeans Data. We empower organizations to optimize capital investments, improve project performance and minimize long-term operating expenses. We develop and maintain the largest collection of labor, material, and equipment data and associated costs for all areas of construction. Gordian's solutions are accessed through our innovative software platforms and supported by a team of industry experts proven to help clients maximize efficiency, optimize cost savings, and increase building quality.

Our Commitment

At Gordian, we do more than talk about the quality of our data and the usefulness of its application. We stand behind all of our RSMeans Data — from historical cost indexes to construction materials and techniques — to craft current costs and predict future trends. If you have any questions about our products or services, please call us toll-free at 800.448.8182 or visit our website at rsmeans.com.

How the Cost Data Is Built: An Overview

Unit Prices*
All cost data have been divided into 50 divisions according to the MasterFormat® system of classification and numbering.

Assemblies*
The cost data in this section have been organized in an "Assemblies" format. These assemblies are the functional elements of a building and are arranged according to the seven elements of the UNIFORMAT II classification system. For a complete explanation of a typical "Assembly", see "RSMeans Data: Assemblies—How They Work."

Residential Models*
Model buildings for four classes of construction — economy, average, custom, and luxury — are developed and shown with complete costs per square foot.

Commercial/Industrial/Institutional Models*
This section contains complete costs for 77 typical model buildings expressed as costs per square foot.

Green Commercial/Industrial/Institutional Models*
This section contains complete costs for 25 green model buildings expressed as costs per square foot.

References*
This section includes information on Equipment Rental Costs, Crew Listings, Historical Cost Indexes, City Cost Indexes, Location Factors, Reference Tables and Change Orders, as well as a listing of abbreviations.

- **Equipment Rental Costs:** Included are the average costs to rent and operate hundreds of pieces of construction equipment.
- **Crew Listings:** This section lists all the crews referenced in the cost data. A crew is composed of more than one trade classification and/or the addition of power equipment to any trade classification. Power equipment is included in the cost of the crew. Costs are shown both with bare labor rates and with the installing contractor's overhead and profit added. For each, the total crew cost per eight-hour day and the composite cost per labor-hour are listed.

Square Foot Models

- **Historical Cost Indexes:** These indexes provide you with data to adjust construction costs over time.
- **City Cost Indexes:** All costs in this dataset are U.S. national averages. Costs vary by region. You can adjust for this by CSI Division to over 730 cities in 900+ 3-digit zip codes throughout the U.S. and Canada by using this data.
- **Location Factors:** You can adjust total project costs to over 730 cities in 900+ 3-digit zip codes throughout the U.S. and Canada by using the weighted number, which applies across all divisions.
- **Reference Tables:** At the beginning of selected major classifications in the Unit Prices are reference numbers indicators. These numbers refer you to related information in the Reference Section. In this section, you'll find reference tables, explanations and estimating information that support how we develop the unit price data, technical data and estimating procedures.
- **Change Orders:** This section includes information on the factors that influence the pricing of change orders.
- **Abbreviations:** A listing of abbreviations used throughout this information, along with the terms they represent, is included.

Index (printed versions only)
A comprehensive listing of all terms and subjects will help you quickly find what you need when you are not sure where it occurs in MasterFormat®.

Conclusion
This information is designed to be as comprehensive and easy to use as possible.

The Construction Specifications Institute (CSI) and Construction Specifications Canada (CSC) have produced the 2018 edition of MasterFormat®, a system of titles and numbers used extensively to organize construction information.

All unit prices in the RSMeans cost data are now arranged in the 50-division MasterFormat® 2018 system.

---

* Not all information is available in all datasets

Note: The material prices in RSMeans cost data are "contractor's prices." They are the prices that contractors can expect to pay at the lumberyards, suppliers'/distributors' warehouses, etc. Small orders of specialty items would be higher than the costs shown, while very large orders, such as truckload lots, would be less. The variation would depend on the size, timing, and negotiating power of the contractor. The labor costs are primarily for new construction or major renovation rather than repairs or minor alterations. With reasonable exercise of judgment, the figures can be used for any building work.

Estimating with RSMeans Data: Unit Prices

Following these steps will allow you to complete an accurate estimate using RSMeans Data: Unit Prices.

1. Scope Out the Project
- Think through the project and identify the CSI divisions needed in your estimate.
- Identify the individual work tasks that will need to be covered in your estimate.
- The Unit Price data have been divided into 50 divisions according to CSI MasterFormat® 2018.
- In printed versions, the Unit Price Section Table of Contents on page 1 may also be helpful when scoping out your project.
- Experienced estimators find it helpful to begin with Division 2 and continue through completion. Division 1 can be estimated after the full project scope is known.

2. Quantify
- Determine the number of units required for each work task that you identified.
- Experienced estimators include an allowance for waste in their quantities. (Waste is not included in our Unit Price line items unless otherwise stated.)

3. Price the Quantities
- Use the search tools available to locate individual Unit Price line items for your estimate.
- Reference Numbers indicated within a Unit Price section refer to additional information that you may find useful.
- The crew indicates who is performing the work for that task. Crew codes are expanded in the Crew Listings in the Reference Section to include all trades and equipment that comprise the crew.
- The Daily Output is the amount of work the crew is expected to complete in one day.
- The Labor-Hours value is the amount of time it will take for the crew to install one unit of work.
- The abbreviated Unit designation indicates the unit of measure upon which the crew, productivity, and prices are based.
- Bare Costs are shown for materials, labor and equipment needed to complete the Unit Price line item. Bare costs do not include waste, project overhead, payroll insurance, payroll taxes, main office overhead or profit.
- The Total Incl O&P cost is the billing rate or invoice amount of the installing contractor or subcontractor who performs the work for the Unit Price line item.

4. Multiply
- Multiply the total number of units needed for your project by the Total Incl O&P cost for each Unit Price line item.
- Be careful that your take off unit of measure matches the unit of measure in the Unit column.
- The price you calculate is an estimate for a completed item of work.
- Keep scoping individual tasks, determining the number of units required for those tasks, matching each task with individual Unit Price line items and multiplying quantities by Total Incl O&P costs.
- An estimate completed in this manner is priced as if a subcontractor, or set of subcontractors, is performing the work. The estimate does not yet include Project Overhead or Estimate Summary components such as general contractor markups on subcontracted work, general contractor office overhead and profit, contingency and location factors.

5. Project Overhead
- Include project overhead items from Division 1-General Requirements.
- These items are needed to make the job run. They are typically, but not always, provided by the general contractor. Items include, but are not limited to, field personnel, insurance, performance bond, permits, testing, temporary utilities, field office and storage facilities, temporary scaffolding and platforms, equipment mobilization and demobilization, temporary roads and sidewalks, winter protection, temporary barricades and fencing, temporary security, temporary signs, field engineering and layout, final cleaning and commissioning.
- Each item should be quantified and matched to individual Unit Price line items in Division 1, then priced and added to your estimate.
- An alternate method of estimating project overhead costs is to apply a percentage of the total project cost — usually 5% to 15% with an average of 10% (see General Conditions).
- Include other project related expenses in your estimate such as:
  - Rented equipment not itemized in the Crew Listings
  - Rubbish handling throughout the project (see section 02 41 19.19)

6. Estimate Summary
- Include sales tax as required by laws of your state or county.
- Include the general contractor's markup on self-performed work, usually 5% to 15% with an average of 10%.
- Include the general contractor's markup on subcontracted work, usually 5% to 15% with an average of 10%.
- Include the general contractor's main office overhead and profit:
  - RSMeans Data provides general guidelines on the general contractor's main office overhead (see section 01 31 13.60 and Reference Number R013113-50).
  - Markups will depend on the size of the general contractor's operations, projected annual revenue, the level of risk and the level of competition in the local area and for this project in particular.
- Include a contingency, usually 3% to 5%, if appropriate.
- Adjust your estimate to the project's location by using the City Cost Indexes or the Location Factors in the Reference Section:
  - Look at the rules in "How to Use the City Cost Indexes" to see how to apply the Indexes for your location.
  - When the proper Index or Factor has been identified for the project's location, convert it to a multiplier by dividing it by 100, then multiply that multiplier by your estimated total cost. The original estimated total cost will now be adjusted up or down from the national average to a total that is appropriate for your location.

Editors' Note:
We urge you to spend time reading and understanding the supporting material. An accurate estimate requires experience, knowledge, and careful calculation. The more you know about how we at RSMeans developed the data, the more accurate your estimate will be. In addition, it is important to take into consideration the reference material such as Equipment Listings, Crew Listings, City Cost Indexes, Location Factors, and Reference Tables.

How to Use the Cost Data: The Details

What's Behind the Numbers? The Development of Cost Data

RSMeans Data engineers continually monitor developments in the construction industry to ensure reliable, thorough and up-to-date cost information. While overall construction costs may vary relative to general economic conditions, price fluctuations within the industry are dependent upon many factors. Individual price variations may, in fact, be opposite to overall economic trends. Therefore, costs are constantly tracked and complete updates are performed yearly. Also, new items are frequently added in response to changes in materials and methods.

Costs in U.S. Dollars

All costs represent U.S. national averages and are given in U.S. dollars. The City Cost Index (CCI) with RSMeans Data can be used to adjust costs to a particular location. The CCI for Canada can be used to adjust U.S. national averages to local costs in Canadian dollars. No exchange rate conversion is necessary because it has already been factored in.

G The processes or products identified by the green symbol in our publications have been determined to be environmentally responsible and/or resource-efficient solely by RSMeans Data engineering staff. The inclusion of the green symbol does not represent compliance with any specific industry association or standard.

Material Costs

RSMeans Data engineers contact manufacturers, dealers, distributors and contractors all across the U.S. and Canada to determine national average material costs. If you have access to current material costs for your specific location, you may wish to make adjustments to reflect differences from the national average. Included within material costs are fasteners for a normal installation. RSMeans Data engineers use manufacturers' recommendations, written specifications and/or standard construction practices for the sizing and spacing of fasteners. Adjustments to material costs may be required for your specific application or location. The manufacturer's warranty is assumed. Extended warranties are not included in the material costs. **Material costs do not include sales tax.**

Labor Costs

Labor costs are based upon a mathematical average of trade-specific wages in 30 major U.S. cities. The type of wage (union, open shop or residential) is identified on the inside back cover of printed publications or selected by the estimator when using the electronic products. Markups for the wages can also be found on the inside back cover of printed publications and/or under the labor references found in the electronic products.

- If wage rates in your area vary from those used, or if rate increases are expected within a given year, labor costs should be adjusted accordingly.

Labor costs reflect productivity based on actual working conditions. In addition to actual installation, these figures include time spent during a normal weekday on tasks, such as material receiving and handling, mobilization at the site, site movement, breaks and cleanup.

Productivity data is developed over an extended period so as not to be influenced by abnormal variations and reflects a typical average.

Equipment Costs

Equipment costs include not only rental but also operating costs for equipment under normal use. The operating costs include parts and labor for routine servicing, such as the repair and replacement of pumps, filters and worn lines. Normal operating expendables, such as fuel, lubricants, tires and electricity (where applicable) are also included. Extraordinary operating expendables with highly variable wear patterns, such as diamond bits and blades, are excluded. These costs are included under materials. Equipment rental rates are obtained from industry sources throughout North America — contractors, suppliers, dealers, manufacturers and distributors.

Rental rates can also be treated as reimbursement costs for contractor-owned equipment. Owned equipment costs include depreciation, loan payments, interest, taxes, insurance, storage and major repairs.

Equipment costs do not include operators' wages.

Equipment Cost/Day—The cost of equipment required for each crew is included in the Crew Listings in the Reference Section (small tools that are considered essential everyday tools are not listed out separately). The Crew Listings itemize specialized tools and heavy equipment along with labor trades. The daily cost of itemized equipment included in a crew is based on dividing the weekly bare rental rate by five (5) (number of working days per week), then adding the hourly operating cost times eight (8) (the number of hours per day). This Equipment Cost/Day is shown in the last column of the Equipment Rental Costs in the Reference Section.

Mobilization, Demobilization—The cost to move construction equipment from an equipment yard or rental company to the job site and back again is not included in equipment costs. Mobilization (to the site) and demobilization (from the site) costs can be found in the Unit Price Section. If a piece of equipment is already at the job site, it is not appropriate to utilize mobilization or demobilization costs again in an estimate.

Overhead and Profit

Total Cost including O&P for the installing contractor is shown in the last column of the Unit Price and/or Assemblies. This figure is the sum of the bare material cost plus 10% for profit, the bare labor cost plus total overhead and profit, and the bare equipment cost plus 10% for profit. Details for the calculation of overhead and profit on labor are shown on the inside back cover of the printed product and in the Reference Section of the electronic product.

General Conditions

Cost data in this dataset are presented in two ways: Bare Costs and Total Cost including O&P (Overhead and Profit). General Conditions, or General Requirements, of the contract should also be added to the Total Cost including O&P when applicable. Costs for General Conditions are listed in Division 1 of the Unit Price Section and in the Reference Section.

General Conditions for the installing contractor may range from 0% to 10% of the Total Cost including O&P. For the general or prime contractor, costs for General Conditions may range from 5% to 15% of the Total Cost including O&P, with a figure of 10% as the most typical allowance. If applicable, the Assemblies and Models sections use costs that include the installing contractor's overhead and profit (O&P).

Factors Affecting Costs

Costs can vary depending upon a number of variables. Here's a listing of some factors that affect costs and points to consider.

Quality: The prices for materials and the workmanship upon which productivity is based represent sound construction work. They are also in line with industry standard and manufacturer specifications and are frequently used by federal, state and local governments.

Overtime: We have made no allowance for overtime. If you anticipate premium time or work beyond normal working hours, be sure to make an appropriate adjustment to your labor costs.

Productivity: The productivity, daily output and labor-hour figures for each line item are based on an eight-hour work day in daylight hours in moderate temperatures and up to a 14' working height unless otherwise indicated. For work that extends beyond normal work hours or is performed under adverse conditions, productivity may decrease.

Size of Project: The size, scope of work and type of construction project will have a significant impact on cost. Economies of scale can reduce costs for large projects. Unit costs can often run higher for small projects.

Location: Material prices are for metropolitan areas. However, in dense urban areas, traffic and site storage limitations may increase costs. Beyond a 20-mile radius of metropolitan areas, extra trucking or transportation charges may also increase the material costs slightly. On the other hand, lower wage rates may be in effect. Be sure to consider both of these factors when preparing an estimate, particularly if the job site is located in a central city or remote rural location. In addition, highly specialized subcontract items may require travel and per-diem expenses for mechanics.

Other Factors
- Season of year
- Contractor management
- Weather conditions
- Local union restrictions
- Building code requirements
- Availability of:
  - adequate energy
  - skilled labor
  - building materials
- Owner's special requirements/restrictions
- Safety requirements
- Environmental considerations
- Access

Unpredictable Factors: General business conditions influence "in-place" costs of all items. Substitute materials and construction methods may have to be employed. These may affect the installed cost and/or life cycle costs. Such factors may be difficult to evaluate and cannot necessarily be predicted on the basis of the job's location in a particular section of the country. Thus, where these factors apply, you may find significant but unavoidable cost variations for which you will have to apply a measure of judgment to your estimate.

Rounding of Costs

In printed publications only, all unit prices in excess of $5.00 have been rounded to make them easier to use and still maintain adequate precision of the results.

How Subcontracted Items Affect Costs

A considerable portion of all large construction jobs is usually subcontracted. In fact, the percentage done by subcontractors is constantly increasing and may run over 90%. Since the workers employed by these companies do nothing else but install their particular products, they soon become experts in that line. As a result, installation by these firms is accomplished so efficiently that the total in-place cost, even with the general contractor's overhead and profit, is no more, and often less, than if the principal contractor had handled the installation. Companies that deal with construction specialties are anxious to have their products perform well and, consequently, the installation will be the best possible.

Contingencies

The allowance for contingencies generally provides for unforeseen construction difficulties. On alterations or repair jobs, 20% is not too much. If drawings are final and only field contingencies are being considered, 2% or 3% is probably sufficient and often nothing needs to be added. Contractually, changes in plans will be covered by extras. The contractor should consider inflationary price trends and possible material shortages during the course of the job. These escalation factors are dependent upon both economic conditions and the anticipated time between the estimate and actual construction. If drawings are not complete or approved, or a budget cost is wanted, it is wise to add 5% to 10%. Contingencies, then, are a matter of judgment.

Important Estimating Considerations

The productivity, or daily output, of each craftsman or crew assumes a well-managed job where tradesmen with the proper tools and equipment, along with the appropriate construction materials, are present. Included are daily set-up and cleanup time, break time and plan layout time. Unless otherwise indicated, time for material movement on site (for items that can be transported by hand) of up to 200' into the building and to the first or second floor is also included. If material has to be transported by other means, over greater distances or to higher floors, an additional allowance should be considered by the estimator.

While horizontal movement is typically a sole function of distances, vertical transport introduces other variables that can significantly impact productivity. In an occupied building, the use of elevators (assuming access, size and required protective measures are acceptable) must be understood at the time of the estimate. For new construction, hoist wait and cycle times can easily be 15 minutes and may result in scheduled access extending beyond the normal work day. Finally, all vertical transport will impose strict weight limits likely to preclude the use of any motorized material handling.

The productivity, or daily output, also assumes installation that meets manufacturer/designer/standard specifications. A time allowance for quality control checks, minor adjustments and any task required to ensure proper function or operation is also included. For items that require connections to services, time is included for positioning, leveling, securing the unit and making all the necessary connections (and start up where applicable) to ensure a complete installation. Estimating of the services themselves (electrical, plumbing, water, steam, hydraulics, dust collection, etc.) is separate.

In some cases, the estimator must consider the use of a crane and an appropriate crew for the installation of large or heavy items. For those situations where a crane is not included in the assigned crew and as part of the line item cost, then equipment rental costs, mobilization and demobilization costs, and operator and support personnel costs must be considered.

Labor-Hours

The labor-hours expressed in this publication are derived by dividing the total daily labor-hours for the crew by the daily output. Based on average installation time and the assumptions listed above, the labor-hours include: direct labor, indirect labor and nonproductive time. A typical day for a craftsman might include but is not limited to:

- Direct Work
    - Measuring and layout
    - Preparing materials
    - Actual installation
    - Quality assurance/quality control
- Indirect Work
    - Reading plans or specifications
    - Preparing space
    - Receiving materials
    - Material movement
    - Giving or receiving instruction
    - Miscellaneous
- Non-Work
    - Chatting
    - Personal issues
    - Breaks
    - Interruptions (i.e., sickness, weather, material or equipment shortages, etc.)

If any of the items for a typical day do not apply to the particular work or project situation, the estimator should make any necessary adjustments.

Final Checklist

Estimating can be a straightforward process provided you remember the basics. Here's a checklist of some of the steps you should remember to complete before finalizing your estimate.

Did you remember to:

- Factor in the City Cost Index for your locale?
- Take into consideration which items have been marked up and by how much?
- Mark up the entire estimate sufficiently for your purposes?
- Read the background information on techniques and technical matters that could impact your project time span and cost?
- Include all components of your project in the final estimate?
- Double check your figures for accuracy?
- Call RSMeans Data engineers if you have any questions about your estimate or the data you've used? Remember, Gordian stands behind all of our products, including our extensive RSMeans Data solutions. If you have any questions about your estimate, about the costs you've used from our data or even about the technical aspects of the job that may affect your estimate, feel free to call the Gordian RSMeans editors at 800.448.8182.

Save Time. Go Online.

For access to the latest cost data, an intuitive search and pre-calculated location costs, take advantage of the time savings available from our online application.

rsmeans.com/online

Unit Price Section

Table of Contents

Sect. No.		Page
	General Requirements	
01 11	Summary of Work	8
01 21	Allowances	8
01 31	Project Management and Coordination	10
01 32	Construction Progress Documentation	12
01 41	Regulatory Requirements	12
01 51	Temporary Utilities	12
01 52	Construction Facilities	13
01 54	Construction Aids	13
01 55	Vehicular Access and Parking	16
01 56	Temporary Barriers and Enclosures	16
01 57	Temporary Controls	18
01 58	Project Identification	18
01 66	Product Storage and Handling Requirements	18
01 74	Cleaning and Waste Management	18
01 91	Commissioning	19
01 93	Facility Maintenance	19
	Existing Conditions	
02 21	Surveys	22
02 41	Demolition	22
02 65	Underground Storage Tank Rem.	24
02 81	Transportation and Disposal of Hazardous Materials	24
02 82	Asbestos Remediation	25
02 87	Biohazard Remediation	28
	Concrete	
03 11	Concrete Forming	32
03 15	Concrete Accessories	32
03 21	Reinforcement Bars	35
03 22	Fabric and Grid Reinforcing	36
03 30	Cast-In-Place Concrete	36
03 31	Structural Concrete	37
03 35	Concrete Finishing	38
03 63	Epoxy Grouting	38
03 82	Concrete Boring	39
	Metals	
05 05	Common Work Results for Metals	42
05 12	Structural Steel Framing	46
05 54	Metal Floor Plates	46
	Wood, Plastics & Composites	
06 11	Wood Framing	48
06 16	Sheathing	48
	Thermal & Moisture Protection	
07 65	Flexible Flashing	50
07 71	Roof Specialties	51
07 72	Roof Accessories	51
07 76	Roof Pavers	51
07 84	Firestopping	52
07 91	Preformed Joint Seals	53
07 92	Joint Sealants	54
	Finishes	
09 22	Supports for Plaster and Gypsum Board	58
09 91	Painting	58
	Specialties	
10 21	Compartments and Cubicles	62
10 28	Toilet, Bath, and Laundry Accessories	64
10 44	Fire Protection Specialties	66
	Equipment	
11 11	Vehicle Service Equipment	70
11 21	Retail and Service Equipment	70
11 30	Residential Equipment	71
11 32	Unit Kitchens	72
11 41	Foodservice Storage Equipment	73
11 44	Food Cooking Equipment	73
11 46	Food Dispensing Equipment	73
11 48	Foodservice Cleaning and Disposal Equipment	73
11 53	Laboratory Equipment	73
11 71	Medical Sterilizing Equipment	74
11 73	Patient Care Equipment	75
11 74	Dental Equipment	75
11 76	Operating Room Equipment	75
11 78	Mortuary Equipment	76
11 81	Facility Maintenance Equipment	76
11 91	Religious Equipment	76
11 98	Detention Equipment	76
	Furnishings	
12 32	Manufactured Wood Casework	78
	Special Construction	
13 11	Swimming Pools	80
13 12	Fountains	81
13 17	Tubs and Pools	81
13 24	Special Activity Rooms	81
13 34	Fabricated Engineered Structures	82
13 42	Building Modules	82
13 47	Facility Protection	83
	Conveying Equipment	
14 45	Vehicle Lifts	86
	Fire Suppression	
21 05	Common Work Results for Fire Suppression	88
21 11	Facility Fire-Suppression Water-Service Piping	89
21 12	Fire-Suppression Standpipes	96
21 13	Fire-Suppression Sprinkler Systems	100
21 21	Carbon-Dioxide Fire-Extinguishing Systems	103
21 22	Clean-Agent Fire-Extinguishing Systems	103
21 31	Centrifugal Fire Pumps	104
	Plumbing	
22 01	Operation and Maintenance of Plumbing	108
22 05	Common Work Results for Plumbing	109
22 07	Plumbing Insulation	132
22 11	Facility Water Distribution	151
22 12	Facility Potable-Water Storage Tanks	261
22 13	Facility Sanitary Sewerage	261
22 14	Facility Storm Drainage	283
22 15	General Service Compressed-Air Systems	286
22 31	Domestic Water Softeners	287
22 32	Domestic Water Filtration Equipment	288
22 33	Electric Domestic Water Heaters	288
22 34	Fuel-Fired Domestic Water Heaters	290
22 35	Domestic Water Heat Exchangers	291
22 41	Residential Plumbing Fixtures	292
22 42	Commercial Plumbing Fixtures	299
22 43	Healthcare Plumbing Fixtures	304
22 45	Emergency Plumbing Fixtures	305
22 46	Security Plumbing Fixtures	306
22 47	Drinking Fountains and Water Coolers	307
22 51	Swimming Pool Plumbing Systems	309
22 52	Fountain Plumbing Systems	309
22 62	Vacuum Systems for Laboratory and Healthcare Facilities	310
22 63	Gas Systems for Laboratory and Healthcare Facilities	311
22 66	Chemical-Waste Systems for Lab. and Healthcare Facilities	314
	Heating Ventilation Air Conditioning	
23 05	Common Work Results for HVAC	322
23 07	HVAC Insulation	331
23 09	Instrumentation and Control for HVAC	332
23 11	Facility Fuel Piping	335
23 12	Facility Fuel Pumps	337
23 13	Facility Fuel-Storage Tanks	337
23 21	Hydronic Piping and Pumps	340
23 23	Refrigerant Piping	349
23 34	HVAC Fans	349
23 35	Special Exhaust Systems	350
23 38	Ventilation Hoods	352
23 51	Breechings, Chimneys, and Stacks	353
23 52	Heating Boilers	359
23 54	Furnaces	361
23 55	Fuel-Fired Heaters	362
23 56	Solar Energy Heating Equipment	363
23 57	Heat Exchangers for HVAC	365
23 72	Air-to-Air Energy Recovery Equipment	366
23 81	Decentralized Unitary HVAC Equipment	366
23 82	Convection Heating and Cooling Units	368
23 83	Radiant Heating Units	369
23 91	Prefabricated Equipment Supports	374
	Electrical	
26 05	Common Work Results for Electrical	376
26 24	Switchboards and Panelboards	383
26 29	Low-Voltage Controllers	384
	Electronic Safety & Security	
28 31	Intrusion Detection	386
28 42	Gas Detection and Alarm	386
28 46	Fire Detection and Alarm	386
	Earthwork	
31 23	Excavation and Fill	390
	Exterior Improvements	
32 12	Flexible Paving	406
32 84	Planting Irrigation	407
	Utilities	
33 01	Operation and Maintenance of Utilities	412
33 05	Common Work Results for Utilities	417
33 11	Groundwater Sources	419
33 14	Water Utility Transmission and Distribution	421
33 16	Water Utility Storage Tanks	430
33 31	Sanitary Sewerage Piping	431
33 34	Onsite Wastewater Disposal	431
33 41	Subdrainage	433
33 42	Stormwater Conveyance	434
33 52	Hydrocarbon Transmission and Distribution	438
33 61	Hydronic Energy Distribution	455
33 63	Steam Energy Distribution	457
	Material Processing & Handling Equipment	
41 22	Cranes and Hoists	462
	Pollution Control Equipment	
44 11	Particulate Control Equipment	464
	Water and Wastewater Equipment	
46 07	Packaged Water and Wastewater Treatment Equipment	468
46 23	Grit Removal And Handling Equipment	468
46 25	Oil and Grease Separation and Removal Equipment	469

RSMeans Data: Unit Prices—How They Work

All RSMeans Data: Unit Prices are organized in the same way.

03 30 Cast-In-Place Concrete

03 30 53 – Miscellaneous Cast-In-Place Concrete

03 30 53.40 Concrete In Place		Crew	Daily Output	Labor-Hours	Unit	Material	2024 Bare Costs Labor	Equipment	Total	Total Incl O&P
0010	**CONCRETE IN PLACE**									
0020	Including forms (4 uses), Grade 60 rebar, concrete (Portland cement									
0050	Type I), placement and finishing unless otherwise indicated									
3540	Equipment pad (3000 psi), 3' x 3' x 6" thick	C-14H	45	1.067	Ea.	79	63.50	.69	143.19	181
3550	4' x 4' x 6" thick		30	1.600		118	95	1.04	214.04	272
3560	5' x 5' x 8" thick		18	2.667		192	158	1.73	351.73	445
3570	6' x 6' x 8" thick		14	3.429		261	204	2.23	467.23	590
3580	8' x 8' x 10" thick		8	6		595	355	3.90	953.90	1,175
3590	10' x 10' x 12" thick		5	9.600		1,025	570	6.25	1,601.25	1,975
3800	Footings (3000 psi), spread under 1 C.Y.	C-14C	28	4	C.Y.	283	232	1.12	516.12	655
3825	1 C.Y. to 5 C.Y.		43	2.605		350	151	.73	501.73	610
3850	Over 5 C.Y.	R033053-60	75	1.493		330	86.50	.42	416.92	495
3900	Footings, strip (3000 psi), 18" x 9", unreinforced	C-14L	40	2.400		230	136	.79	366.79	455
3920	18" x 9", reinforced	C-14C	35	3.200		263	186	.90	449.90	565

It is important to understand the structure of RSMeans Data: Unit Prices so that you can find information easily and use it correctly.

---

❶ Line Numbers

Line Numbers consist of 12 characters, which identify a unique location in the database for each task. The first six (6) or eight (8) digits conform to the Construction Specifications Institute MasterFormat® 2018. The remainder of the digits are a further breakdown in order to arrange items in understandable groups of similar tasks. Line numbers are consistent across all of our publications, so a line number in any of our products will always refer to the same item of work.

❷ Descriptions

Descriptions are shown in a hierarchical structure to make them readable. In order to read a complete description, read up through the indents to the top of the section. Include everything that is above and to the left that is not contradicted by information below. For instance, the complete description for line 03 30 53.40 3550 is "Concrete in place, including forms (4 uses), Grade 60 rebar, concrete (Portland cement Type 1), placement and finishing unless otherwise indicated; Equipment pad (3,000 psi), 4' × 4' × 6" thick."

❸ RSMeans Data

When using **RSMeans Data**, it is important to read through an entire section to ensure that you use the data that most closely matches your work. Note that sometimes there is additional information shown in the section that may improve your price. There are frequently lines that further describe, add to or adjust data for specific situations.

❹ Reference Information

Gordian's engineers have created **reference** information to assist you in your estimate. **If** there is information that applies to a section, it will be indicated at the start of the section. The Reference Section is located in the back of the dataset.

❺ Crews

Crews include labor and/or equipment necessary to accomplish each task. In this case, Crew C-14H is used. Gordian's staff selects a crew to represent the workers and equipment that are typically used for that task. In this case, Crew C-14H consists of one carpenter foreperson (outside), two carpenters, one rodman, one laborer, one cement finisher and one gas engine vibrator. Details of all crews can be found in the Reference Section.

Crews - Standard

Crew No.	Bare Costs		Incl. Subs O&P		Cost Per Labor-Hour	
Crew C-14H	Hr.	Daily	Hr.	Daily	Bare Costs	Incl. O&P
1 Carpenter Foreman (outside)	$62.55	$500.40	$92.60	$740.80	$59.42	$87.88
2 Carpenters	60.55	968.80	89.65	1434.40		
1 Rodman (reinf.)	67.05	536.40	100.00	800.00		
1 Laborer	49.00	392.00	72.55	580.40		
1 Cement Finisher	56.80	454.40	82.80	662.40		
1 Gas Engine Vibrator		31.20		34.32	.65	.71
48 L.H., Daily Totals		$2883.20		$4252.32	$60.07	$88.59

⑥ Daily Output

The **Daily Output** is the amount of work that the crew can do in a normal 8-hour workday, including mobilization, layout, movement of materials and cleanup. In this case, crew C-14H can install thirty 4' × 4' × 6" thick concrete pads in a day. Daily output is variable and based on many factors, including the size of the job, location and environmental conditions. RSMeans Data represents work done in daylight (or adequate lighting) and temperate conditions.

⑦ Labor-Hours

The figure in the **Labor-Hours** column is the amount of labor required to perform one unit of work—in this case the amount of labor required to construct one 4' × 4' equipment pad. This figure is calculated by dividing the number of hours of labor in the crew by the daily output (48 labor-hours divided by 30 pads = 1.6 hours of labor per pad). Multiply 1.6 times 60 to see the value in minutes: 60 × 1.6 = 96 minutes. Note: The labor-hour figure is not dependent on the crew size. A change in crew size will result in a corresponding change in daily output, but the labor-hours per unit of work will not change.

⑧ Unit of Measure

Unit Prices include the typical **Unit of Measure** used for estimating that item. For concrete-in-place the typical unit is cubic yards (C.Y.) or each (Ea.). For installing broadloom carpet it is square yard and for gypsum board it is square foot. The estimator needs to take special care that the unit in the data matches the unit in the take-off. Unit conversions may be found in the Reference Section.

⑨ Bare Costs

Bare Costs are the costs of materials, labor, and equipment that the installing contractor pays. They represent the cost, in U.S. dollars, for one unit of work. They do not include any markups for profit or labor burden.

⑩ Bare Total

The **Total column** represents the total bare cost for the installing contractor in U.S. dollars. In this case, the sum of $118 for material + $95 for labor + $1.04 for equipment is $214.04.

⑪ Total Incl O&P

The **Total Incl O&P column** is the total cost, including overhead and profit, that the installing contractor will charge the customer. This represents the cost of materials plus 10% profit, the cost of labor plus labor burden and 10% profit, and the cost of equipment plus 10% profit. It does not include the general contractor's overhead and profit. Note: See the inside back cover of the printed product or the Reference Section of the electronic product for details on how the labor burden is calculated.

National Average

The RSMeans Data in our print publications represent a "national average" cost. This data should be modified to the project location using the **City Cost Indexes** or **Location Factors** tables found in the Reference Section. Use the Location Factors to adjust estimate totals if the project covers multiple trades. Use the City Cost Indexes (CCI) for single trade projects or projects where a more detailed analysis is required. All figures in the two tables are derived from the same research. The last row of data in the CCI — the weighted average — is the same as the numbers reported for each location in the location factor table.

RSMeans Data: Unit Prices— How They Work (Continued)

Project Name: Pre-Engineered Steel Building		Architect: As Shown					
Location:	Anywhere, USA					01/01/24	STD
Line Number	Description	Qty	Unit	Material	Labor	Equipment	SubContract	Estimate Total
033053403940	Strip footing, 12" x 24", reinforced	15	C.Y.	$3,705.00	$2,025.00	$9.75	$0.00	
033053403950	Strip footing, 12" x 36", reinforced	34	C.Y.	$8,024.00	$3,672.00	$17.68	$0.00	
031113653000	Concrete slab edge forms	500	L.F.	$335.00	$1,540.00	$0.00	$0.00	
032211100200	Welded wire fabric reinforcing	150	C.S.F.	$6,975.00	$5,175.00	$0.00	$0.00	
033113350300	Ready mix concrete, 4000 psi for slab on grade	278	C.Y.	$53,098.00	$0.00	$0.00	$0.00	
033113704300	Place, strike off & consolidate concrete slab	278	C.Y.	$0.00	$6,116.00	$158.46	$0.00	
033513300250	Machine float & trowel concrete slab	15,000	S.F.	$0.00	$11,400.00	$1,050.00	$0.00	
031516200140	Cut control joints in concrete slab	950	L.F.	$38.00	$475.00	$104.50	$0.00	
033923130300	Sprayed concrete curing membrane	150	C.S.F.	$2,707.50	$1,237.50	$0.00	$0.00	
Division 03	**Subtotal**			$74,882.50	$31,640.50	$1,340.39	$0.00	$107,863.39
083613102650	Manual 10' x 10' steel sectional overhead door	8	Ea.	$16,600.00	$4,320.00	$0.00	$0.00	
083613102860	Insulation and steel back panel for OH door	800	S.F.	$5,560.00	$0.00	$0.00	$0.00	
Division 08	**Subtotal**			$22,160.00	$4,320.00	$0.00	$0.00	$26,480.00
133419501100	Pre-Engineered Steel Building, 100' x 150' x 24'	15,000	SF Flr.	$0.00	$0.00	$0.00	$468,750.00	
133419506050	Framing for PESB door opening, 3' x 7'	4	Opng.	$0.00	$0.00	$0.00	$2,676.00	
133419506100	Framing for PESB door opening, 10' x 10'	8	Opng.	$0.00	$0.00	$0.00	$11,240.00	
133419506200	Framing for PESB window opening, 4' x 3'	6	Opng.	$0.00	$0.00	$0.00	$3,990.00	
133419505750	PESB door, 3' x 7', single leaf	4	Opng.	$3,300.00	$860.00	$0.00	$0.00	
133419507750	PESB sliding window, 4' x 3' with screen	6	Opng.	$3,180.00	$732.00	$75.60	$0.00	
133419506550	PESB gutter, eave type, 26 ga., painted	300	L.F.	$3,420.00	$1,005.00	$0.00	$0.00	
133419508650	PESB roof vent, 12" wide x 10' long	15	Ea.	$750.00	$4,020.00	$0.00	$0.00	
133419506900	PESB insulation, vinyl faced, 4" thick	27,400	S.F.	$51,512.00	$11,508.00	$0.00	$0.00	
Division 13	**Subtotal**			$62,162.00	$18,125.00	$75.60	$486,656.00	$567,018.60
	Subtotal			$159,204.50	$54,085.50	$1,415.99	$486,656.00	$701,361.99
Division 01	General Requirements @ 7%			11,144.32	3,785.99	99.12	34,065.92	
	Estimate Subtotal			$170,348.82	$57,871.49	$1,515.11	$520,721.92	$701,361.99
	Sales Tax @ 5%			8,517.44		75.76	13,018.05	
	Subtotal A			178,866.26	57,871.49	1,590.86	533,739.97	
	GC O & P			17,886.63	28,704.26	159.09	53,374.00	
	Subtotal B			196,752.88	86,575.74	1,749.95	587,113.96	$872,192.54
	Contingency @ 5%							43,609.63
	Subtotal C							$915,802.17
	Bond @ $12/1000 +10% O&P							12,088.59
	Subtotal D							$927,890.75
	Location Adjustment Factor				112.40			115,058.45
	Grand Total							$1,042,949.21

This estimate is based on an interactive spreadsheet. You are free to download it and adjust it to your methodology.
A copy of this spreadsheet is available at RSMeans.com/2024books.

Sample Estimate

This sample demonstrates the elements of an estimate, including a tally of the RSMeans Data lines and a summary of the markups on a contractor's work to arrive at a total cost to the owner. The Location Factor with RSMeans data is added at the bottom of the estimate to adjust the cost of the work to a specific location.

1 Work Performed

The body of the estimate shows the RSMeans Data selected, including the line number, a brief description of each item, its take-off unit and quantity, and the bare costs of materials, labor and equipment. This estimate also includes a column titled "SubContract." This data is taken from the column "Total Incl O&P" and represents the total that a subcontractor would charge a general contractor for the work, including the sub's markup for overhead and profit.

2 Division 1, General Requirements

This is the first division numerically but the last division estimated. Division 1 includes project-wide needs provided by the general contractor. These requirements vary by project but may include temporary facilities and utilities, security, testing, project cleanup, etc. For small projects a percentage can be used — typically between 5% and 15% of project cost. For large projects the costs may be itemized and priced individually.

3 Sales Tax

If the work is subject to state or local sales taxes, the amount must be added to the estimate. Sales tax may be added to material costs, equipment costs and subcontracted work. In this case, sales tax was added in all three categories. It was assumed that approximately half the subcontracted work would be material cost, so the tax was applied to 50% of the subcontract total.

4 GC O&P

This entry represents the general contractor's markup on material, labor, equipment and subcontractor costs. Our standard markup on materials, equipment and subcontracted work is 10%. In this estimate, the markup on the labor performed by the GC's workers uses "Skilled Workers Average" shown in Column F on the table "Installing Contractor's Overhead & Profit," which can be found on the inside back cover of the printed product or in the Reference Section of the electronic product.

5 Contingency

A factor for contingency may be added to any estimate to represent the cost of unknowns that may occur between the time that the estimate is performed and the time the project is constructed. The amount of the allowance will depend on the stage of design at which the estimate is done and the contractor's assessment of the risk involved. Refer to section 01 21 16.50 for contingency allowances.

6 Bonds

Bond costs should be added to the estimate. The figures here represent a typical performance bond, ensuring the owner that if the general contractor does not complete the obligations in the construction contract the bonding company will pay the cost for completion of the work.

7 Location Adjustment

Published prices are based on national average costs. If necessary, adjust the total cost of the project using a location factor from the "Location Factor" table or the "City Cost Index" table. Use location factors if the work is general, covering multiple trades. If the work is by a single trade (e.g., masonry) use the more specific data found in the "City Cost Indexes."

Division 1 General Requirements

Estimating Tips

01 20 00 Price and Payment Procedures
- Allowances that should be added to estimates to cover contingencies and job conditions that are not included in the national average material and labor costs are shown in Section 01 21.
- When estimating historic preservation projects (depending on the condition of the existing structure and the owner's requirements), a 15–20% contingency or allowance is recommended, regardless of the stage of the drawings.

01 30 00 Administrative Requirements
- Before determining a final cost estimate, it is good practice to review all the items listed in Subdivisions 01 31 and 01 32 to make final adjustments for items that may need customizing to specific job conditions.
- Requirements for initial and periodic submittals can represent a significant cost to the General Requirements of a job. Thoroughly check the submittal specifications when estimating a project to determine any costs that should be included.

01 40 00 Quality Requirements
- All projects will require some degree of quality control. This cost is not included in the unit cost of construction listed in each division. Depending upon the terms of the contract, the various costs of inspection and testing can be the responsibility of either the owner or the contractor. Be sure to include the required costs in your estimate.

01 50 00 Temporary Facilities and Controls
- Barricades, access roads, safety nets, scaffolding, security, and many more requirements for the execution of a safe project are elements of direct cost. These costs can easily be overlooked when preparing an estimate. When looking through the major classifications of this subdivision, determine which items apply to each division in your estimate.
- Construction equipment rental costs can be found in the Reference Section in Section 01 54 33. Operators' wages are not included in equipment rental costs.
- Equipment mobilization and demobilization costs are not included in equipment rental costs and must be considered separately.

- The cost of small tools provided by the installing contractor for his workers is covered in the "Overhead" column on the "Installing Contractor's Overhead and Profit" table that lists labor trades, base rates, and markups. Therefore, it is included in the "Total Incl. O&P" cost of any unit price line item.

01 70 00 Execution and Closeout Requirements
- When preparing an estimate, thoroughly read the specifications to determine the requirements for Contract Closeout. Final cleaning, record documentation, operation and maintenance data, warranties and bonds, and spare parts and maintenance materials can all be elements of cost for the completion of a contract. Do not overlook these in your estimate.

Reference Numbers
Reference numbers are shown at the beginning of some major classifications. These numbers refer to related items in the Reference Section. The reference information may be an estimating procedure, an alternate pricing method, or technical information.

Note: Not all subdivisions listed here necessarily appear. ∎

Same Data. Simplified.

Enjoy the convenience and efficiency of accessing your costs anywhere:
- **Skip the multiplier** by setting your location
- **Quickly search,** edit, favorite and share costs
- **Stay on top of price changes** with automatic updates

Discover more at rsmeans.com/online

No part of this cost data may be reproduced, stored in a retrieval system, or transmitted in any form or by any means without prior written permission of Gordian.

01 11 Summary of Work

01 11 31 – Professional Consultants

01 11 31.10 Architectural Fees

	Crew	Daily Output	Labor-Hours	Unit	Material	2024 Bare Costs Labor	Equipment	Total	Total Incl O&P
0010 **ARCHITECTURAL FEES**									
0020 For new construction									
0060 Minimum				Project				4.90%	4.90%
0090 Maximum								16%	16%
0100 For alteration work, to $500,000, minimum								7.35%	7.35%
0125 Maximum								24%	24%
0150 For alteration work, over $500,000, minimum								6.13%	6.13%
0175 Maximum								20%	20%

01 11 31.20 Construction Management Fees

	Crew	Daily Output	Labor-Hours	Unit	Material	Labor	Equipment	Total	Total Incl O&P
0010 **CONSTRUCTION MANAGEMENT FEES**									
0020 $1,000,000 job, minimum				Project				4.50%	4.50%
0050 Maximum								7.50%	7.50%
0300 $50,000,000 job, minimum								2.50%	2.50%
0350 Maximum								4%	4%

01 11 31.30 Engineering Fees

	Crew	Daily Output	Labor-Hours	Unit	Material	Labor	Equipment	Total	Total Incl O&P
0010 **ENGINEERING FEES** R011110-30									
0020 Educational planning consultant, minimum				Project				.50%	.50%
0100 Maximum				"				2.50%	2.50%
0200 Electrical, minimum				Contrct				4.10%	4.10%
0300 Maximum								10.10%	10.10%
0400 Elevator & conveying systems, minimum								2.50%	2.50%
0500 Maximum								5%	5%
0600 Food service & kitchen equipment, minimum								8%	8%
0700 Maximum								12%	12%
0800 Landscaping & site development, minimum								2.50%	2.50%
0900 Maximum								6%	6%
1000 Mechanical (plumbing & HVAC), minimum								4.10%	4.10%
1100 Maximum								10.10%	10.10%
1200 Structural, minimum				Project				1%	1%
1300 Maximum				"				2.50%	2.50%

01 21 Allowances

01 21 16 – Contingency Allowances

01 21 16.50 Contingencies

	Crew	Daily Output	Labor-Hours	Unit	Material	Labor	Equipment	Total	Total Incl O&P
0010 **CONTINGENCIES**, Add to estimate									
0020 Conceptual stage				Project				20%	20%
0050 Schematic stage								15%	15%
0100 Preliminary working drawing stage (Design Dev.)								10%	10%
0150 Final working drawing stage								3%	3%

01 21 53 – Factors Allowance

01 21 53.50 Factors

	Crew	Daily Output	Labor-Hours	Unit	Material	Labor	Equipment	Total	Total Incl O&P
0010 **FACTORS** Cost adjustments R012153-10									
0100 Add to construction costs for particular job requirements									
0500 Cut & patch to match existing construction, add, minimum				Costs	2%	3%			
0550 Maximum					5%	9%			
0800 Dust protection, add, minimum					1%	2%			
0850 Maximum					4%	11%			
1100 Equipment usage curtailment, add, minimum					1%	1%			
1150 Maximum					3%	10%			
1400 Material handling & storage limitation, add, minimum					1%	1%			

01 21 Allowances

01 21 53 – Factors Allowance

01 21 53.50 Factors

		Crew	Daily Output	Labor-Hours	Unit	Material	2024 Bare Costs Labor	Equipment	Total	Total Incl O&P
1450	Maximum				Costs	6%	7%			
1700	Protection of existing work, add, minimum					2%	2%			
1750	Maximum					5%	7%			
2000	Shift work requirements, add, minimum						5%			
2050	Maximum						30%			
2300	Temporary shoring and bracing, add, minimum					2%	5%			
2350	Maximum					5%	12%			

01 21 53.60 Security Factors

		Crew	Daily Output	Labor-Hours	Unit	Material	Labor	Equipment	Total	Total Incl O&P
0010	**SECURITY FACTORS** R012153-60									
0100	Additional costs due to security requirements									
0110	Daily search of personnel, supplies, equipment and vehicles									
0120	Physical search, inventory and doc of assets, at entry				Costs		30%			
0130	At entry and exit						50%			
0140	Physical search, at entry						6.25%			
0150	At entry and exit						12.50%			
0160	Electronic scan search, at entry						2%			
0170	At entry and exit						4%			
0180	Visual inspection only, at entry						.25%			
0190	At entry and exit						.50%			
0200	ID card or display sticker only, at entry						.12%			
0210	At entry and exit						.25%			
0220	Day 1 as described below, then visual only for up to 5 day job duration									
0230	Physical search, inventory and doc of assets, at entry				Costs		5%			
0240	At entry and exit						10%			
0250	Physical search, at entry						1.25%			
0260	At entry and exit						2.50%			
0270	Electronic scan search, at entry						.42%			
0280	At entry and exit						.83%			
0290	Day 1 as described below, then visual only for 6-10 day job duration									
0300	Physical search, inventory and doc of assets, at entry				Costs		2.50%			
0310	At entry and exit						5%			
0320	Physical search, at entry						.63%			
0330	At entry and exit						1.25%			
0340	Electronic scan search, at entry						.21%			
0350	At entry and exit						.42%			
0360	Day 1 as described below, then visual only for 11-20 day job duration									
0370	Physical search, inventory and doc of assets, at entry				Costs		1.25%			
0380	At entry and exit						2.50%			
0390	Physical search, at entry						.31%			
0400	At entry and exit						.63%			
0410	Electronic scan search, at entry						.10%			
0420	At entry and exit						.21%			
0430	Beyond 20 days, costs are negligible									
0440	Escort required to be with tradesperson during work effort				Costs		6.25%			

01 21 53.65 Infectious Disease Precautions

		Crew	Daily Output	Labor-Hours	Unit	Material	Labor	Equipment	Total	Total Incl O&P
0010	**INFECTIOUS DISEASE PRECAUTIONS** R012153-65									
0100	Additional costs due to infectious disease precautions									
0120	Daily temperature checks				Costs		1%			
0130	Donning & doffing masks and gloves						1%			
0140	Washing hands						1%			
0150	Informational meetings						2%			
0160	Maintaining social distance						1%			

01 21 Allowances

01 21 53 – Factors Allowance

01 21 53.65 Infectious Disease Precautions

		Crew	Daily Output	Labor-Hours	Unit	Material	2024 Bare Costs Labor	Equipment	Total	Total Incl O&P
0170	Disinfecting tools or equipment				Costs		3%			
0200	N95 rated masks				Ea.	2.17			2.17	2.38
0210	Surgical masks				"	.24			.24	.27
0220	Black nitrile disposable gloves				Pair	.49			.49	.54
0250	Hand washing station & 2 x weekly service				Week				158	174

01 21 55 – Job Conditions Allowance

01 21 55.50 Job Conditions

0010	**JOB CONDITIONS** Modifications to applicable									
0020	cost summaries									
0100	Economic conditions, favorable, deduct				Project				2%	2%
0200	Unfavorable, add								5%	5%
0300	Hoisting conditions, favorable, deduct								2%	2%
0400	Unfavorable, add								5%	5%
0700	Labor availability, surplus, deduct								1%	1%
0800	Shortage, add								10%	10%
0900	Material storage area, available, deduct								1%	1%
1000	Not available, add								2%	2%
1100	Subcontractor availability, surplus, deduct								5%	5%
1200	Shortage, add								12%	12%
1300	Work space, available, deduct								2%	2%
1400	Not available, add								5%	5%

01 21 57 – Overtime Allowance

01 21 57.50 Overtime

0010	**OVERTIME** for early completion of projects or where	R012909-90								
0020	labor shortages exist, add to usual labor, up to				Costs		100%			

01 21 63 – Taxes

01 21 63.10 Taxes

0010	**TAXES**	R012909-80								
0020	Sales tax, State, average				%	5.08%				
0050	Maximum	R012909-85				7.50%				
0200	Social Security, on first $118,500 of wages						7.65%			
0300	Unemployment, combined Federal and State, minimum	R012909-86					.60%			
0350	Average						9.60%			
0400	Maximum						12%			

01 31 Project Management and Coordination

01 31 13 – Project Coordination

01 31 13.20 Field Personnel

		Crew	Daily Output	Labor-Hours	Unit	Material	Labor	Equipment	Total	Total Incl O&P
0010	**FIELD PERSONNEL**									
0020	Clerk, average				Week		500		500	750
0100	Field engineer, junior engineer						1,700		1,700	2,549
0120	Engineer						2,180		2,180	3,269
0140	Senior engineer						2,660		2,660	3,989
0160	General purpose laborer, average	1 Clab	.20	40			1,950		1,950	2,900
0180	Project manager, minimum						2,175		2,175	3,262
0200	Average						2,500		2,500	3,749
0220	Maximum						2,850		2,850	4,274
0240	Superintendent, minimum						2,150		2,150	3,224
0260	Average						2,325		2,325	3,525

01 31 Project Management and Coordination

01 31 13 – Project Coordination

01 31 13.20 Field Personnel

		Crew	Daily Output	Labor-Hours	Unit	Material	2024 Bare Costs Labor	2024 Bare Costs Equipment	Total	Total Incl O&P
0280	Maximum				Week		2,650		2,650	4,025
0290	Timekeeper, average				"		1,350		1,350	2,050

01 31 13.30 Insurance

0010	**INSURANCE**	R013113-40								
0020	Builders risk, standard, minimum				Job				.24%	.24%
0050	Maximum	R013113-50							.80%	.80%
0200	All-risk type, minimum								.25%	.25%
0250	Maximum	R013113-60							.62%	.62%
0400	Contractor's equipment floater, minimum				Value				.50%	.50%
0450	Maximum				"				1.50%	1.50%
0600	Public liability, average				Job				2.02%	2.02%
0800	Workers' compensation & employer's liability, average									
0850	by trade, carpentry, general				Payroll		8.92%			
1000	Electrical						3.92%			
1150	Insulation						8.13%			
1450	Plumbing						4.42%			
1550	Sheet metal work (HVAC)						5.86%			

01 31 13.50 General Contractor's Mark-Up

0010	**GENERAL CONTRACTOR'S MARK-UP** on Change Orders									
0200	Extra work, by subcontractors, add				%				10%	10%
0250	By General Contractor, add								15%	15%
0400	Omitted work, by subcontractors, deduct all but								5%	5%
0450	By General Contractor, deduct all but								7.50%	7.50%
0600	Overtime work, by subcontractors, add								15%	15%
0650	By General Contractor, add								10%	10%

01 31 13.80 Overhead and Profit

0010	**OVERHEAD & PROFIT** Allowance to add to items in this	R013113-50								
0020	book that do not include Subs O&P, average				%				25%	
0100	Allowance to add to items in this book that	R013113-55								
0110	do include Subs O&P, minimum				%				5%	5%
0150	Average								10%	10%
0200	Maximum								15%	15%
0300	Typical, by size of project, under $100,000								30%	
0350	$500,000 project								25%	
0400	$2,000,000 project								20%	
0450	Over $10,000,000 project								15%	

01 31 13.90 Performance Bond

0010	**PERFORMANCE BOND**	R013113-80								
0020	For buildings, minimum				Job				.60%	.60%
0100	Maximum				"				2.50%	2.50%

01 31 14 – Facilities Services Coordination

01 31 14.20 Lock Out/Tag Out

		Crew	Daily Output	Labor-Hours	Unit	Material	Labor	Equipment	Total	Total Incl O&P
0010	**LOCK OUT/TAG OUT**									
0020	Miniature circuit breaker lock out device	1 Elec	220	.036	Ea.	29	2.61		31.61	35.50
0030	Miniature pin circuit breaker lock out device		220	.036		26	2.61		28.61	32.50
0040	Single circuit breaker lock out device		220	.036		25.50	2.61		28.11	32
0050	Multi-pole circuit breaker lock out device (15 to 225 Amp)		210	.038		25	2.73		27.73	31.50
0060	Large 3 pole circuit breaker lock out device (over 225 Amp)		210	.038		29	2.73		31.73	36
0080	Square D I-Line circuit breaker lock out device		210	.038		92.50	2.73		95.23	106
0090	Lock out disconnect switch, 30 to 100 Amp		330	.024		13.15	1.74		14.89	17.10
0100	100 to 400 Amp		330	.024		13.15	1.74		14.89	17.10

01 31 Project Management and Coordination

01 31 14 – Facilities Services Coordination

01 31 14.20 Lock Out/Tag Out

		Crew	Daily Output	Labor-Hours	Unit	Material	2024 Bare Costs Labor	2024 Bare Costs Equipment	Total	Total Incl O&P
0110	Over 400 Amp	1 Elec	330	.024	Ea.	13.15	1.74		14.89	17.10
0120	Lock out hasp for multiple lockout tags		200	.040		7.40	2.87		10.27	12.40
0130	Electrical cord plug lock out device		220	.036		15.90	2.61		18.51	21.50
0140	Electrical plug prong lock out device (3-wire grounding plug)		220	.036		14.60	2.61		17.21	19.90
0150	Wall switch lock out		200	.040		25	2.87		27.87	32
0160	Fire alarm pull station lock out	1 Stpi	200	.040		23	3.02		26.02	29.50
0170	Sprinkler valve tamper and flow switch lock out device	1 Skwk	220	.036		20.50	2.31		22.81	26
0180	Lock out sign		330	.024		24.50	1.54		26.04	29.50
0190	Lock out tag		440	.018		2.46	1.15		3.61	4.44

01 32 Construction Progress Documentation

01 32 33 – Photographic Documentation

01 32 33.50 Photographs

		Crew	Daily Output	Labor-Hours	Unit	Material	2024 Bare Costs Labor	2024 Bare Costs Equipment	Total	Total Incl O&P
0010	**PHOTOGRAPHS**									
0020	8" x 10", 4 shots, 2 prints ea., std. mounting				Set	595			595	655
0100	Hinged linen mounts					605			605	665
0200	8" x 10", 4 shots, 2 prints each, in color					625			625	690
0300	For I.D. slugs, add to all above					5.55			5.55	6.15
1500	Time lapse equipment, camera and projector, buy				Ea.	2,825			2,825	3,125
1550	Rent per month				"	1,450			1,450	1,600
1700	Cameraman and processing, black & white				Day	1,425			1,425	1,550
1720	Color				"	1,675			1,675	1,825

01 41 Regulatory Requirements

01 41 26 – Permit Requirements

01 41 26.50 Permits

		Crew	Daily Output	Labor-Hours	Unit	Material	2024 Bare Costs Labor	2024 Bare Costs Equipment	Total	Total Incl O&P
0010	**PERMITS**									
0020	Rule of thumb, most cities, minimum				Job				.50%	.50%
0100	Maximum				"				2%	2%

01 51 Temporary Utilities

01 51 13 – Temporary Electricity

01 51 13.80 Temporary Utilities

		Crew	Daily Output	Labor-Hours	Unit	Material	2024 Bare Costs Labor	2024 Bare Costs Equipment	Total	Total Incl O&P
0010	**TEMPORARY UTILITIES**									
0350	Lighting, lamps, wiring, outlets, 40,000 S.F. building, 8 strings	1 Elec	34	.235	CSF Flr	4.02	16.85		20.87	29.50
0360	16 strings	"	17	.471		8.05	33.50		41.55	59
0400	Power for temp lighting only, 6.6 KWH, per month								.92	1.01
0430	11.8 KWH, per month								1.65	1.82
0450	23.6 KWH, per month								3.30	3.63
0600	Power for job duration incl. elevator, etc., minimum								53	58
0650	Maximum								110	121
0675	Temporary cooling				Ea.	1,500			1,500	1,650

01 52 Construction Facilities

01 52 13 – Field Offices and Sheds

01 52 13.20 Office and Storage Space

		Crew	Daily Output	Labor-Hours	Unit	Material	2024 Bare Costs Labor	Equipment	Total	Total Incl O&P
0010	**OFFICE AND STORAGE SPACE**									
0020	Office trailer, furnished, no hookups, 20' x 8', buy	2 Skwk	1	16	Ea.	11,000	1,025		12,025	13,600
0250	Rent per month					340			340	375
0300	32' x 8', buy	2 Skwk	.70	22.857		16,400	1,450		17,850	20,300
0350	Rent per month					266			266	293
0400	50' x 10', buy	2 Skwk	.60	26.667		33,300	1,700		35,000	39,200
0450	Rent per month					385			385	425
0500	50' x 12', buy	2 Skwk	.50	32		28,300	2,025		30,325	34,200
0550	Rent per month					495			495	545
0700	For air conditioning, rent per month, add					58			58	64
0800	For delivery, add per mile				Mile	13.10			13.10	14.40
0900	Bunk house trailer, 8' x 40' duplex dorm with kitchen, no hookups, buy	2 Carp	1	16	Ea.	97,500	970		98,470	109,000
0910	9 man with kitchen and bath, no hookups, buy		1	16		100,000	970		100,970	111,500
0920	18 man sleeper with bath, no hookups, buy		1	16		107,500	970		108,470	120,000
1000	Portable buildings, prefab, on skids, economy, 8' x 8'		265	.060	S.F.	105	3.66		108.66	121
1100	Deluxe, 8' x 12'		150	.107	"	90.50	6.45		96.95	110
1200	Storage boxes, 20' x 8', buy	2 Skwk	1.80	8.889	Ea.	4,075	565		4,640	5,350
1250	Rent per month					132			132	145
1300	40' x 8', buy	2 Skwk	1.40	11.429		7,400	725		8,125	9,200
1350	Rent per month					159			159	175

01 54 Construction Aids

01 54 16 – Temporary Hoists

01 54 16.50 Weekly Forklift Crew

		Crew	Daily Output	Labor-Hours	Unit	Material	Labor	Equipment	Total	Total Incl O&P
0010	**WEEKLY FORKLIFT CREW**									
0100	All-terrain forklift, 45' lift, 35' reach, 9000 lb. capacity	A-3P	.20	40	Week		2,475	3,175	5,650	7,150

01 54 19 – Temporary Cranes

01 54 19.50 Daily Crane Crews

		Crew	Daily Output	Labor-Hours	Unit	Material	Labor	Equipment	Total	Total Incl O&P
0010	**DAILY CRANE CREWS** for small jobs, portal to portal R015433-15									
0100	12-ton truck-mounted hydraulic crane	A-3H	1	8	Day		550	2,175	2,725	3,200
0200	25-ton	A-3I	1	8			550	2,300	2,850	3,350
0300	40-ton	A-3J	1	8			550	2,475	3,025	3,550
0400	55-ton	A-3K	1	16			1,025	2,650	3,675	4,425
0500	80-ton	A-3L	1	16			1,025	2,850	3,875	4,625
0600	100-ton hydraulic crane crew	A-3M	1	16			1,025	2,975	4,000	4,775
0900	If crane is needed on a Saturday, Sunday or Holiday									
0910	At time-and-a-half, add				Day		50%			
0920	At double time, add				"		100%			

01 54 19.60 Monthly Tower Crane Crew

		Crew	Daily Output	Labor-Hours	Unit	Material	Labor	Equipment	Total	Total Incl O&P
0010	**MONTHLY TOWER CRANE CREW**, excludes concrete footing									
0100	Static tower crane, 130' high, 106' jib, 6200 lb. capacity	A-3N	.05	176	Month		12,100	43,200	55,300	65,500

01 54 23 – Temporary Scaffolding and Platforms

01 54 23.70 Scaffolding

		Crew	Daily Output	Labor-Hours	Unit	Material	Labor	Equipment	Total	Total Incl O&P
0010	**SCAFFOLDING** R015423-10									
0015	Steel tube, regular, no plank, labor only to erect & dismantle									
0090	Building exterior, wall face, 1 to 5 stories, 6'-4" x 5' frames	3 Carp	8	3	C.S.F.		182		182	269
0200	6 to 12 stories	4 Carp	8	4			242		242	360
0301	13 to 20 stories	5 Clab	8	5			245		245	365
0460	Building interior, wall face area, up to 16' high	3 Carp	12	2			121		121	179
0560	16' to 40' high		10	2.400			145		145	215

01 54 Construction Aids

01 54 23 – Temporary Scaffolding and Platforms

01 54 23.70 Scaffolding		Crew	Daily Output	Labor-Hours	Unit	Material	2024 Bare Costs Labor	Equipment	Total	Total Incl O&P
0800	Building interior floor area, up to 30' high	3 Carp	150	.160	C.C.F.		9.70		9.70	14.35
0900	Over 30' high	4 Carp	160	.200	"		12.10		12.10	17.95
0906	Complete system for face of walls, no plank, material only rent/mo				C.S.F.	84.50			84.50	93
0908	Interior spaces, no plank, material only rent/mo				C.C.F.	5.70			5.70	6.30
0910	Steel tubular, heavy duty shoring, buy									
0920	Frames 5' high 2' wide				Ea.	71.50			71.50	78.50
0925	5' high 4' wide					84.50			84.50	93
0930	6' high 2' wide					85.50			85.50	94
0935	6' high 4' wide					103			103	113
0940	Accessories									
0945	Cross braces				Ea.	23			23	25.50
0950	U-head, 8" x 8"					15.60			15.60	17.15
0955	J-head, 4" x 8"					12.85			12.85	14.10
0960	Base plate, 7" x 7"					15.45			15.45	17
0965	Leveling jack					22.50			22.50	25
1000	Steel tubular, regular, buy									
1100	Frames 3' high 5' wide				Ea.	85			85	93.50
1150	5' high 5' wide					144			144	158
1200	6'-4" high 5' wide					128			128	141
1350	7'-6" high 6' wide					89.50			89.50	98.50
1500	Accessories, cross braces					17.70			17.70	19.45
1550	Guardrail post					16.30			16.30	17.95
1600	Guardrail 7' section					11.50			11.50	12.65
1650	Screw jacks & plates					19.55			19.55	21.50
1700	Sidearm brackets					13			13	14.30
1750	8" casters					35			35	38.50
1800	Plank 2" x 10" x 16'-0"					78			78	86
1900	Stairway section					360			360	395
1910	Stairway starter bar					12.90			12.90	14.20
1920	Stairway inside handrail					107			107	118
1930	Stairway outside handrail					117			117	128
1940	Walk-thru frame guardrail					53.50			53.50	59
2000	Steel tubular, regular, rent/mo.									
2100	Frames 3' high 5' wide				Ea.	13			13	14.30
2150	5' high 5' wide					13			13	14.30
2200	6'-4" high 5' wide					7.30			7.30	8.05
2250	7'-6" high 6' wide					12.60			12.60	13.90
2500	Accessories, cross braces					3			3	3.30
2550	Guardrail post					3.60			3.60	3.96
2600	Guardrail 7' section					11.40			11.40	12.55
2650	Screw jacks & plates					4.50			4.50	4.95
2700	Sidearm brackets					6			6	6.60
2750	8" casters					10			10	11
2800	Outrigger for rolling tower					18			18	19.80
2850	Plank 2" x 10" x 16'-0"					12.65			12.65	13.90
2900	Stairway section					41			41	45
2940	Walk-thru frame guardrail					10.80			10.80	11.90
3000	Steel tubular, heavy duty shoring, rent/mo.									
3250	5' high 2' & 4' wide				Ea.	10.75			10.75	11.80
3300	6' high 2' & 4' wide					10.75			10.75	11.80
3500	Accessories, cross braces					1.16			1.16	1.28
3600	U-head, 8" x 8"					3.16			3.16	3.48
3650	J-head, 4" x 8"					3.16			3.16	3.48

01 54 Construction Aids

01 54 23 – Temporary Scaffolding and Platforms

01 54 23.70 Scaffolding

		Crew	Daily Output	Labor-Hours	Unit	Material	2024 Bare Costs Labor	2024 Bare Costs Equipment	Total	Total Incl O&P
3700	Base plate, 8" x 8"				Ea.	1.16			1.16	1.28
3750	Leveling jack					3.14			3.14	3.45
5700	Planks, 2" x 10" x 16'-0", labor only to erect & remove to 50' H	3 Carp	72	.333			20		20	30
5800	Over 50' high	4 Carp	80	.400			24		24	36
6000	Heavy duty shoring for elevated slab forms to 8'-2" high, floor area									
6100	Labor only to erect & dismantle	4 Carp	16	2	C.S.F.		121		121	179
6110	Materials only, rent/mo.				"	55.50			55.50	61
6500	To 14'-8" high									
6600	Labor only to erect & dismantle	4 Carp	10	3.200	C.S.F.		194		194	287
6610	Materials only, rent/mo				"	81			81	89.50

01 54 23.75 Scaffolding Specialties

		Crew	Daily Output	Labor-Hours	Unit	Material	2024 Bare Costs Labor	2024 Bare Costs Equipment	Total	Total Incl O&P
0010	**SCAFFOLDING SPECIALTIES**									
1200	Sidewalk bridge, heavy duty steel posts & beams, including									
1210	parapet protection & waterproofing (material cost is rent/month)									
1220	8' to 10' wide, 2 posts	3 Carp	15	1.600	L.F.	153	97		250	310
1230	3 posts	"	10	2.400	"	262	145		407	505
1500	Sidewalk bridge using tubular steel scaffold frames including									
1510	planking (material cost is rent/month)	3 Carp	45	.533	L.F.	11.85	32.50		44.35	61
1600	For 2 uses per month, deduct from all above					50%				
1700	For 1 use every 2 months, add to all above					100%				
1900	Catwalks, 20" wide, no guardrails, 7' span, buy				Ea.	229			229	252
2000	10' span, buy					291			291	320
3720	Putlog, standard, 8' span, with hangers, buy					44			44	48.50
3730	Rent per month					16.10			16.10	17.70
3750	12' span, buy					99			99	109
3755	Rent per month					20			20	22
3760	Trussed type, 16' span, buy					545			545	600
3770	Rent per month					24			24	26.50
3790	22' span, buy					550			550	605
3795	Rent per month					32			32	35
3800	Rolling ladders with handrails, 30" wide, buy, 2 step					296			296	325
4000	7 step					900			900	990
4050	10 step					1,275			1,275	1,400
4100	Rolling towers, buy, 5' wide, 7' long, 10' high					1,525			1,525	1,675
4200	For additional 5' high sections, to buy					325			325	355
4300	Complete incl. wheels, railings, outriggers,									
4350	21' high, to buy				Ea.	2,400			2,400	2,625
4400	Rent/month = 5% of purchase cost				"	120			120	132

01 54 36 – Equipment Mobilization

01 54 36.50 Mobilization

		Crew	Daily Output	Labor-Hours	Unit	Material	2024 Bare Costs Labor	2024 Bare Costs Equipment	Total	Total Incl O&P
0010	**MOBILIZATION** (Use line item again for demobilization) R015436-50									
0015	Up to 25 mi. haul dist. (50 mi. RT for mob/demob crew)									
1200	Small equipment, placed in rear of, or towed by pickup truck	A-3A	4	2	Ea.		124	59	183	249
1300	Equipment hauled on 3-ton capacity towed trailer	A-3Q	2.67	3			186	119	305	405
1400	20-ton capacity	B-34U	2	8			475	257	732	995
1500	40-ton capacity	B-34N	2	8			490	395	885	1,150
1600	50-ton capacity	B-34V	1	24			1,500	1,275	2,775	3,650
1700	Crane, truck-mounted, up to 75 ton (driver only)	1 Eqhv	4	2			137		137	204
1800	Over 75 ton (with chase vehicle)	A-3E	2.50	6.400			405	94.50	499.50	705
2400	Crane, large lattice boom, requiring assembly	B-34W	.50	144			8,650	8,900	17,550	22,700
2500	For each additional 5 miles haul distance, add						10%	10%		
3000	For large pieces of equipment, allow for assembly/knockdown									

01 54 Construction Aids

01 54 36 – Equipment Mobilization

01 54 36.50 Mobilization	Crew	Daily Output	Labor-Hours	Unit	Material	2024 Bare Costs Labor	Equipment	Total	Total Incl O&P
3100 For mob/demob of micro-tunneling equip, see Section 33 05 07.36									

01 55 Vehicular Access and Parking

01 55 23 – Temporary Roads

01 55 23.50 Roads and Sidewalks

		Crew	Daily Output	Labor-Hours	Unit	Material	Labor	Equipment	Total	Total Incl O&P
0010	ROADS AND SIDEWALKS Temporary									
0050	Roads, gravel fill, no surfacing, 4" gravel depth	B-14	715	.067	S.Y.	2.73	3.46	.41	6.60	8.55
0100	8" gravel depth	"	615	.078	"	5.45	4.02	.47	9.94	12.45
1000	Ramp, 3/4" plywood on 2" x 6" joists, 16" OC	2 Carp	300	.053	S.F.	3.27	3.23		6.50	8.40
1100	On 2" x 10" joists, 16" OC	"	275	.058	"	4.38	3.52		7.90	10

01 56 Temporary Barriers and Enclosures

01 56 13 – Temporary Air Barriers

01 56 13.60 Tarpaulins

		Crew	Daily Output	Labor-Hours	Unit	Material	Labor	Equipment	Total	Total Incl O&P
0010	TARPAULINS									
0020	Cotton duck, 10-13.13 oz./S.Y., 6' x 8'				S.F.	.84			.84	.92
0050	30' x 30'					.54			.54	.59
0100	Polyvinyl coated nylon, 14-18 oz., minimum					1.05			1.05	1.16
0150	Maximum					1.27			1.27	1.40
0200	Reinforced polyethylene 3 mils thick, white					.23			.23	.25
0300	4 mils thick, white, clear or black					.11			.11	.12
0400	5.5 mils thick, clear					.11			.11	.12
0500	White, fire retardant					.46			.46	.51
0600	12 mils, oil resistant, fire retardant					.48			.48	.53
0700	8.5 mils, black					.42			.42	.46
0710	Woven polyethylene, 6 mils thick					.08			.08	.09
0730	Polyester reinforced w/integral fastening system, 11 mils thick					.16			.16	.18
0740	Polyethylene, reflective, 23 mils thick					1.26			1.26	1.39

01 56 13.90 Winter Protection

		Crew	Daily Output	Labor-Hours	Unit	Material	Labor	Equipment	Total	Total Incl O&P
0010	WINTER PROTECTION									
0100	Framing to close openings	2 Clab	500	.032	S.F.	1.18	1.57		2.75	3.62
0200	Tarpaulins hung over scaffolding, 8 uses, not incl. scaffolding		1500	.011		.23	.52		.75	1.02
0250	Tarpaulin polyester reinf. w/integral fastening system, 11 mils thick		1600	.010		.20	.49		.69	.95
0300	Prefab fiberglass panels, steel frame, 8 uses		1200	.013		3.16	.65		3.81	4.45

01 56 16 – Temporary Dust Barriers

01 56 16.10 Dust Barriers, Temporary

		Crew	Daily Output	Labor-Hours	Unit	Material	Labor	Equipment	Total	Total Incl O&P
0010	DUST BARRIERS, TEMPORARY, erect and dismantle									
0020	Spring loaded telescoping pole & head, to 12', erect and dismantle	1 Clab	240	.033	Ea.		1.63		1.63	2.42
0025	Cost per day (based upon 250 days)				Day	.58			.58	.64
0030	To 21', erect and dismantle	1 Clab	240	.033	Ea.		1.63		1.63	2.42
0035	Cost per day (based upon 250 days)				Day	1.39			1.39	1.53
0040	Accessories, caution tape reel, erect and dismantle	1 Clab	480	.017	Ea.		.82		.82	1.21
0045	Cost per day (based upon 250 days)				Day	.32			.32	.35
0060	Foam rail and connector, erect and dismantle	1 Clab	240	.033	Ea.		1.63		1.63	2.42
0065	Cost per day (based upon 250 days)				Day	.31			.31	.34
0070	Caution tape	1 Clab	384	.021	C.L.F.	2.32	1.02		3.34	4.06
0080	Zipper, standard duty		60	.133	Ea.	18	6.55		24.55	29.50
0090	Heavy duty		48	.167	"	19	8.15		27.15	33

01 56 Temporary Barriers and Enclosures

01 56 16 – Temporary Dust Barriers

01 56 16.10 Dust Barriers, Temporary

		Crew	Daily Output	Labor-Hours	Unit	Material	2024 Bare Costs Labor	Equipment	Total	Total Incl O&P
0100	Polyethylene sheet, 4 mil	1 Clab	37	.216	Sq.	5.35	10.60		15.95	21.50
0110	6 mil	↓	37	.216	"	19	10.60		29.60	36.50
1000	Dust partition, 6 mil polyethylene, 1" x 3" frame	2 Carp	2000	.008	S.F.	.50	.48		.98	1.26
1080	2" x 4" frame	"	2000	.008	"	.93	.48		1.41	1.75
1085	Negative air machine, 1800 CFM				Ea.	900			900	990
1090	Adhesive strip application, 2" width	1 Clab	192	.042	C.L.F.	13.50	2.04		15.54	17.85
4000	Dust & infectious control partition, adj. to 10' high, obscured, 4' panel	2 Carp	90	.178	Ea.	610	10.75		620.75	685
4010	3' panel		90	.178		575	10.75		585.75	645
4020	2' panel	↓	90	.178		450	10.75		460.75	510
4030	1' panel	1 Carp	90	.089		299	5.40		304.40	340
4040	6" panel	"	90	.089		276	5.40		281.40	315
4050	2' panel with HEPA filtered discharge port	2 Carp	90	.178		525	10.75		535.75	590
4060	3' panel with 32" door		90	.178		945	10.75		955.75	1,075
4070	4' panel with 36" door		90	.178		1,050	10.75		1,060.75	1,175
4080	4'-6" panel with 44" door		90	.178		1,250	10.75		1,260.75	1,400
4090	Hinged corner		80	.200		190	12.10		202.10	227
4100	Outside corner		80	.200		162	12.10		174.10	196
4110	T post		80	.200		162	12.10		174.10	196
4120	Accessories, ceiling grid clip		360	.044		7.10	2.69		9.79	11.80
4130	Panel locking clip		360	.044		4.89	2.69		7.58	9.40
4140	Panel joint closure strip		360	.044		8.55	2.69		11.24	13.40
4150	Screw jack	↓	360	.044		6.30	2.69		8.99	10.95
4160	Digital pressure difference gauge					305			305	335
4180	Combination lockset	1 Carp	13	.615	↓	209	37.50		246.50	285
4185	Sealant tape, 2" wide	1 Clab	192	.042	C.L.F.	13.50	2.04		15.54	17.85
4190	System in place, including door and accessories									
4200	Based upon 25 uses	2 Carp	51	.314	L.F.	10.25	19		29.25	39.50
4210	Based upon 50 uses		51	.314		5.10	19		24.10	33.50
4230	Based upon 100 uses	↓	51	.314	↓	2.56	19		21.56	31

01 56 23 – Temporary Barricades

01 56 23.10 Barricades

		Crew	Daily Output	Labor-Hours	Unit	Material	2024 Bare Costs Labor	Equipment	Total	Total Incl O&P
0010	**BARRICADES**									
0020	5' high, 3 rail @ 2" x 8", fixed	2 Carp	20	.800	L.F.	6.45	48.50		54.95	78.50
0150	Movable		30	.533		5.15	32.50		37.65	53.50
1000	Guardrail, wooden, 3' high, 1" x 6" on 2" x 4" posts		200	.080		2.21	4.84		7.05	9.60
1100	2" x 6" on 4" x 4" posts	↓	165	.097		3.85	5.85		9.70	12.95
1200	Portable metal with base pads, buy					17.05			17.05	18.80
1250	Typical installation, assume 10 reuses	2 Carp	600	.027	↓	2.87	1.61		4.48	5.55
1300	Barricade tape, polyethylene, 7 mil, 3" wide x 300' long roll	1 Clab	128	.063	Ea.	6.95	3.06		10.01	12.20
3000	Detour signs, set up and remove									
3010	Reflective aluminum, MUTCD, 24" x 24", post mounted	1 Clab	20	.400	Ea.	3.85	19.60		23.45	33
4000	Roof edge portable barrier stands and warning flags, 50 uses	1 Rohe	9100	.001	L.F.	.11	.04		.15	.18
4010	100 uses	"	9100	.001	"	.05	.04		.09	.12

01 56 26 – Temporary Fencing

01 56 26.50 Temporary Fencing

		Crew	Daily Output	Labor-Hours	Unit	Material	2024 Bare Costs Labor	Equipment	Total	Total Incl O&P
0010	**TEMPORARY FENCING**									
0020	Chain link, 11 ga., 4' high	2 Clab	400	.040	L.F.	3.02	1.96		4.98	6.20
0100	6' high		300	.053		4.50	2.61		7.11	8.80
0200	Rented chain link, 6' high, to 1000' (up to 12 mo.)		400	.040		3.09	1.96		5.05	6.30
0250	Over 1000' (up to 12 mo.)	↓	300	.053	↓	3.65	2.61		6.26	7.90
0350	Plywood, painted, 2" x 4" frame, 4' high	A-4	135	.178		7.70	10.25		17.95	23.50
0400	4" x 4" frame, 8' high	"	110	.218	↓	15	12.55		27.55	35

01 56 Temporary Barriers and Enclosures

01 56 26 – Temporary Fencing

01 56 26.50 Temporary Fencing

		Crew	Daily Output	Labor-Hours	Unit	Material	2024 Bare Costs Labor	2024 Bare Costs Equipment	Total	Total Incl O&P
0500	Wire mesh on 4" x 4" posts, 4' high	2 Carp	100	.160	L.F.	12.95	9.70		22.65	28.50
0550	8' high	"	80	.200		19.55	12.10		31.65	39.50

01 56 29 – Temporary Protective Walkways

01 56 29.50 Protection

		Crew	Daily Output	Labor-Hours	Unit	Material	Labor	Equipment	Total	Total Incl O&P
0010	**PROTECTION**									
0020	Stair tread, 2" x 12" planks, 1 use	1 Carp	75	.107	Tread	10.15	6.45		16.60	20.50
0100	Exterior plywood, 1/2" thick, 1 use		65	.123		2.30	7.45		9.75	13.60
0200	3/4" thick, 1 use		60	.133		5.40	8.05		13.45	17.85
2200	Sidewalks, 2" x 12" planks, 2 uses		350	.023	S.F.	1.69	1.38		3.07	3.91
2300	Exterior plywood, 2 uses, 1/2" thick		750	.011		.38	.65		1.03	1.38
2400	5/8" thick		650	.012		.56	.75		1.31	1.71
2500	3/4" thick		600	.013		.90	.81		1.71	2.19

01 57 Temporary Controls

01 57 33 – Temporary Security

01 57 33.50 Watchman

		Crew	Daily Output	Labor-Hours	Unit	Material	Labor	Equipment	Total	Total Incl O&P
0010	**WATCHMAN**									
0020	Service, monthly basis, uniformed person, minimum				Hr.				27.65	30.40
0100	Maximum								56	61.62
0200	Person and command dog, minimum								31	34
0300	Maximum								60	65

01 58 Project Identification

01 58 13 – Temporary Project Signage

01 58 13.50 Signs

		Crew	Daily Output	Labor-Hours	Unit	Material	Labor	Equipment	Total	Total Incl O&P
0010	**SIGNS**									
0020	High intensity reflectorized, no posts, buy				Ea.	15.60			15.60	17.15

01 66 Product Storage and Handling Requirements

01 66 19 – Material Handling

01 66 19.10 Material Handling

		Crew	Daily Output	Labor-Hours	Unit	Material	Labor	Equipment	Total	Total Incl O&P
0010	**MATERIAL HANDLING**									
0020	Above 2nd story, via stairs, per C.Y. of material per floor	2 Clab	145	.110	C.Y.		5.40		5.40	8
0030	Via elevator, per C.Y. of material		240	.067			3.27		3.27	4.84
0050	Distances greater than 200', per C.Y. of material per each addl 200'		300	.053			2.61		2.61	3.87

01 74 Cleaning and Waste Management

01 74 13 – Progress Cleaning

01 74 13.20 Cleaning Up

		Crew	Daily Output	Labor-Hours	Unit	Material	Labor	Equipment	Total	Total Incl O&P
0010	**CLEANING UP**									
0020	After job completion, allow, minimum				Job				.30%	.30%
0040	Maximum				"				1%	1%
0050	Cleanup of floor area, continuous, per day, during const.	A-5	24	.750	M.S.F.	4.97	37.50	4.38	46.85	65.50
0100	Final by GC at end of job	"	11.50	1.565	"	5.25	78	9.15	92.40	131

01 91 Commissioning

01 91 13 – General Commissioning Requirements

01 91 13.50 Building Commissioning

		Crew	Daily Output	Labor-Hours	Unit	Material	2024 Bare Costs Labor	Equipment	Total	Total Incl O&P
0010	**BUILDING COMMISSIONING**									
0100	Systems operation and verification during turnover				%				.25%	.25%
0150	Including all systems subcontractors								.50%	.50%
0200	Systems design assistance, operation, verification and training								.50%	.50%
0250	Including all systems subcontractors								1%	1%

01 93 Facility Maintenance

01 93 13 – Facility Maintenance Procedures

01 93 13.15 Mechanical Facilities Maintenance

			Crew	Daily Output	Labor-Hours	Unit	Material	2024 Bare Costs Labor	Equipment	Total	Total Incl O&P
0010	**MECHANICAL FACILITIES MAINTENANCE**										
0100	Air conditioning system maintenance										
0130	Belt, replace		1 Stpi	15	.533	Ea.		40.50		40.50	60
0170	Fan, clean			16	.500			38		38	56
0180	Filter, remove, clean, replace			12	.667			50.50		50.50	75
0190	Flexible coupling alignment, inspect			40	.200			15.10		15.10	22.50
0200	Gas leak, locate and repair			4	2			151		151	225
0250	Pump packing gland, remove and replace			11	.727			55		55	82
0270	Tighten			32	.250			18.90		18.90	28
0290	Pump, disassemble and assemble			4	2			151		151	225
0300	Air pressure regulator, disassemble, clean, assemble		1 Skwk	4	2			127		127	190
0310	Repair or replace part		"	6	1.333			84.50		84.50	127
0320	Purging system		1 Stpi	16	.500			38		38	56
0400	Compressor, air, remove or install fan wheel		1 Skwk	20	.400			25.50		25.50	38
0410	Disassemble or assemble 2 cylinder, 2 stage			4	2			127		127	190
0420	4 cylinder, 4 stage			1	8			510		510	760
0430	Repair or replace part			2	4			254		254	380
0700	Demolition, for mech. demolition see Section 23 05 05.10 or 22 05 05.10										
0800	Ductwork, clean										
0810	Rectangular										
0820	6"	G	1 Shee	187.50	.043	L.F.		3.08		3.08	4.64
0830	8"	G		140.63	.057			4.11		4.11	6.20
0840	10"	G		112.50	.071			5.15		5.15	7.75
0850	12"	G		93.75	.085			6.15		6.15	9.30
0860	14"	G		80.36	.100			7.20		7.20	10.80
0870	16"	G		70.31	.114			8.20		8.20	12.35
0900	Round										
0910	4"	G	1 Shee	358.10	.022	L.F.		1.61		1.61	2.43
0920	6"	G		238.73	.034			2.42		2.42	3.64
0930	8"	G		179.05	.045			3.23		3.23	4.86
0940	10"	G		143.24	.056			4.04		4.04	6.05
0950	12"	G		119.37	.067			4.84		4.84	7.30
0960	16"	G		89.52	.089			6.45		6.45	9.70
1000	Expansion joint, not screwed, install or remove		1 Stpi	3	2.667	Ea.		201		201	300
1010	Repack		"	6	1.333	"		101		101	150
1200	Fire protection equipment										
1220	Fire hydrant, replace		Q-1	3	5.333	Ea.		360		360	535
1230	Service, lubricate, inspect, flush, clean		1 Plum	7	1.143			85.50		85.50	127
1240	Test		"	11	.727			54.50		54.50	81
1310	Inspect valves, pressure, nozzle		1 Spri	4	2	System		149		149	222
1800	Plumbing fixtures, for installation see Section 22 41 00										
1801	Plumbing fixtures										

For customer support on your Plumbing Costs with RSMeans Data call 800.448.8182.

01 93 Facility Maintenance

01 93 13 – Facility Maintenance Procedures

01 93 13.15 Mechanical Facilities Maintenance		Crew	Daily Output	Labor-Hours	Unit	Material	2024 Bare Costs Labor	2024 Bare Costs Equipment	Total	Total Incl O&P
1850	Open drain with toilet auger	1 Plum	16	.500	Ea.		37.50		37.50	55.50
1870	Plaster trap, clean	"	6	1.333			99.50		99.50	148
1881	Clean commode	1 Clab	20	.400		.27	19.60		19.87	29.50
1882	Clean commode seat		48	.167		.14	8.15		8.29	12.25
1884	Clean double sink		20	.400		.27	19.60		19.87	29.50
1886	Clean bathtub		12	.667		.55	32.50		33.05	49
1888	Clean fiberglass tub/shower		8	1		.68	49		49.68	73.50
1889	Clean faucet set		32	.250		.11	12.25		12.36	18.25
1891	Clean shower head		80	.100		.01	4.90		4.91	7.25
1893	Clean water heater	↓	16	.500		.96	24.50		25.46	37.50
1900	Relief valve, test and adjust	1 Stpi	20	.400			30		30	45
1910	Clean pump, heater, or motor for whirlpool	1 Clab	16	.500		.14	24.50		24.64	36.50
1920	Clean thermal cover for whirlpool	"	16	.500		1.37	24.50		25.87	38
2000	Repair or replace, steam trap	1 Stpi	8	1			75.50		75.50	112
2020	Y-type or bell strainer		6	1.333			101		101	150
2040	Water trap or vacuum breaker, screwed joints	↓	13	.615	↓		46.50		46.50	69
2100	Steam specialties, clean									
2120	Air separator with automatic trap, 1" fittings	1 Stpi	12	.667	Ea.		50.50		50.50	75
2130	Bucket trap, 2" pipe		7	1.143			86.50		86.50	128
2150	Drip leg, 2" fitting		45	.178			13.45		13.45	20
2200	Thermodynamic trap, 1" fittings		50	.160			12.10		12.10	18
2210	Thermostatic		65	.123			9.30		9.30	13.85
2240	Screen and seat in Y-type strainer, plug type		25	.320			24		24	36
2242	Screen and seat in Y-type strainer, flange type		12	.667			50.50		50.50	75
2500	Valve, replace broken handwheel	↓	24	.333	↓		25		25	37.50
3000	Valve, overhaul, regulator, relief, flushometer, mixing									
3040	Cold water, gas	1 Stpi	5	1.600	Ea.		121		121	180
3050	Hot water, steam		3	2.667			201		201	300
3080	Globe, gate, check up to 4" cold water, gas		10	.800			60.50		60.50	90
3090	Hot water, steam		5	1.600			121		121	180
3100	Over 4" ID hot or cold line	↓	1.40	5.714			430		430	640
3120	Remove and replace, gate, globe or check up to 4"	Q-5	6	2.667			181		181	270
3130	Over 4"	"	2	8			545		545	810
3150	Repack up to 4"	1 Stpi	13	.615			46.50		46.50	69
3160	Over 4"	"	4	2	↓		151		151	225

Division 2 Existing Conditions

Estimating Tips
02 30 00 Subsurface Investigation
In preparing estimates on structures involving earthwork or foundations, all information concerning soil characteristics should be obtained. Look particularly for hazardous waste, evidence of prior dumping of debris, and previous stream beds.

02 40 00 Demolition and Structure Moving
The costs shown for selective demolition do not include rubbish handling or disposal. These items should be estimated separately using RSMeans data or other sources.

- Historic preservation often requires that the contractor remove materials from the existing structure, rehab them, and replace them. The estimator must be aware of any related measures and precautions that must be taken when doing selective demolition and cutting and patching. Requirements may include special handling and storage, as well as security.
- In addition to Subdivision 02 41 00, you can find selective demolition items in each division. Example: Roofing demolition is in Division 7.
- Absent of any other specific reference, an approximate demolish-in-place cost can be obtained by halving the new-install labor cost. To remove for reuse, allow the entire new-install labor figure.

02 40 00 Building Deconstruction
This section provides costs for the careful dismantling and recycling of most low-rise building materials.

02 50 00 Containment of Hazardous Waste
This section addresses on-site hazardous waste disposal costs.

02 80 00 Hazardous Material Disposal/Remediation
This subdivision includes information on hazardous waste handling, asbestos remediation, lead remediation, and mold remediation. See reference numbers R028213-20 and R028319-60 for further guidance in using these unit price lines.

02 90 00 Monitoring Chemical Sampling, Testing Analysis
This section provides costs for on-site sampling and testing hazardous waste.

Reference Numbers
Reference numbers are shown at the beginning of some major classifications. These numbers refer to related items in the Reference Section. The reference information may be an estimating procedure, an alternate pricing method, or technical information.

Note: Not all subdivisions listed here necessarily appear. ■

Same Data. Simplified.
Enjoy the convenience and efficiency of accessing your costs anywhere:
- **Skip the multiplier** by setting your location
- **Quickly search,** edit, favorite and share costs
- **Stay on top of price changes** with automatic updates

Discover more at rsmeans.com/online

No part of this cost data may be reproduced, stored in a retrieval system, or transmitted in any form or by any means without prior written permission of Gordian.

02 21 Surveys

02 21 13 – Site Surveys

02 21 13.09 Topographical Surveys

		Crew	Daily Output	Labor-Hours	Unit	Material	2024 Bare Costs Labor	2024 Bare Costs Equipment	Total	Total Incl O&P
0010	**TOPOGRAPHICAL SURVEYS**									
0020	Topographical surveying, conventional, minimum	A-7	3.30	7.273	Acre	53	475	11.05	539.05	775
0050	Average	"	1.95	12.308		79.50	805	18.70	903.20	1,300
0100	Maximum	A-8	.60	53.333		106	3,375	61	3,542	5,200

02 21 13.13 Boundary and Survey Markers

		Crew	Daily Output	Labor-Hours	Unit	Material	Labor	Equipment	Total	Total Incl O&P
0010	**BOUNDARY AND SURVEY MARKERS**									
0300	Lot location and lines, large quantities, minimum	A-7	2	12	Acre	36.50	785	18.25	839.75	1,225
0320	Average	"	1.25	19.200		48.50	1,250	29	1,327.50	1,950
0400	Small quantities, maximum	A-8	1	32		73	2,025	36.50	2,134.50	3,150
0600	Monuments, 3' long	A-7	10	2.400	Ea.	46	157	3.65	206.65	288
0800	Property lines, perimeter, cleared land	"	1000	.024	L.F.	.07	1.57	.04	1.68	2.45
0900	Wooded land	A-8	875	.037	"	.10	2.32	.04	2.46	3.61

02 21 13.16 Aerial Surveys

		Crew	Daily Output	Labor-Hours	Unit	Material	Labor	Equipment	Total	Total Incl O&P
0010	**AERIAL SURVEYS**									
1500	Aerial surveying, including ground control, minimum fee, 10 acres				Total				4,700	4,700
1510	100 acres								9,400	9,400
1550	From existing photography, deduct								1,625	1,625
1600	2' contours, 10 acres				Acre				470	470
1850	100 acres								94	94
2000	1000 acres								90	90
2050	10,000 acres								85	85

02 41 Demolition

02 41 13 – Selective Site Demolition

02 41 13.17 Demolish, Remove Pavement and Curb

			Crew	Daily Output	Labor-Hours	Unit	Material	Labor	Equipment	Total	Total Incl O&P
0010	**DEMOLISH, REMOVE PAVEMENT AND CURB**	R024119-10									
5010	Pavement removal, bituminous roads, up to 3" thick		B-38	690	.058	S.Y.		3.20	2.08	5.28	7
5050	4"-6" thick		"	420	.095	"		5.25	3.41	8.66	11.55

02 41 13.23 Utility Line Removal

		Crew	Daily Output	Labor-Hours	Unit	Material	Labor	Equipment	Total	Total Incl O&P
0010	**UTILITY LINE REMOVAL**									
0015	No hauling, abandon catch basin or manhole	B-6	7	3.429	Ea.		183	41.50	224.50	315
0020	Remove existing catch basin or manhole, masonry		4	6			320	73	393	555
0030	Catch basin or manhole frames and covers, stored		13	1.846			98.50	22.50	121	171
0040	Remove and reset		7	3.429			183	41.50	224.50	315
0900	Hydrants, fire, remove only	B-21A	5	8			485	133	618	865
0950	Remove and reset	"	2	20			1,200	330	1,530	2,175
2900	Pipe removal, sewer/water, no excavation, 12" diameter	B-6	175	.137	L.F.		7.30	1.66	8.96	12.70
2930	15"-18" diameter	B-12Z	150	.160			8.90	12	20.90	26.50
2960	21"-24" diameter		120	.200			11.10	15	26.10	33
3000	27"-36" diameter		90	.267			14.80	20	34.80	44
3200	Steel, welded connections, 4" diameter	B-6	160	.150			8	1.82	9.82	13.85
3300	10" diameter	"	80	.300			16	3.64	19.64	27.50

02 41 13.30 Minor Site Demolition

			Crew	Daily Output	Labor-Hours	Unit	Material	Labor	Equipment	Total	Total Incl O&P
0010	**MINOR SITE DEMOLITION**	R024119-10									
4000	Sidewalk removal, bituminous, 2" thick		B-6	350	.069	S.Y.		3.66	.83	4.49	6.30
4010	2-1/2" thick			325	.074			3.94	.90	4.84	6.85
4100	Concrete, plain, 4"			160	.150			8	1.82	9.82	13.85
4110	Plain, 5"			140	.171			9.15	2.08	11.23	15.85
4120	Plain, 6"			120	.200			10.65	2.43	13.08	18.45

02 41 Demolition

02 41 19 – Selective Demolition

02 41 19.19 Selective Demolition

		Crew	Daily Output	Labor-Hours	Unit	Material	2024 Bare Costs Labor	2024 Bare Costs Equipment	Total	Total Incl O&P
0010	**SELECTIVE DEMOLITION**, Rubbish Handling R024119-10									
0020	The following are to be added to the demolition prices									
0600	Dumpster, weekly rental, 1 dump/week, 6 C.Y. capacity (2 tons)				Week	415			415	455
0700	10 C.Y. capacity (3 tons)					480			480	530
0725	20 C.Y. capacity (5 tons) R024119-20					565			565	625
0800	30 C.Y. capacity (7 tons)					730			730	800
0840	40 C.Y. capacity (10 tons)					775			775	850
2000	Load, haul, dump and return, 0'-50' haul, hand carried	2 Clab	24	.667	C.Y.		32.50		32.50	48.50
2005	Wheeled		37	.432			21		21	31.50
2040	0'-100' haul, hand carried		16.50	.970			47.50		47.50	70.50
2045	Wheeled		25	.640			31.50		31.50	46.50
2050	Forklift	A-3R	25	.320			19.85	13.05	32.90	44
2080	Haul and return, add per each extra 100' haul, hand carried	2 Clab	35.50	.451			22		22	32.50
2085	Wheeled		54	.296			14.50		14.50	21.50
2120	For travel in elevators, up to 10 floors, add		140	.114			5.60		5.60	8.30
2130	0'-50' haul, incl. up to 5 riser stairs, hand carried		23	.696			34		34	50.50
2135	Wheeled		35	.457			22.50		22.50	33
2140	6-10 riser stairs, hand carried		22	.727			35.50		35.50	53
2145	Wheeled		34	.471			23		23	34
2150	11-20 riser stairs, hand carried		20	.800			39		39	58
2155	Wheeled		31	.516			25.50		25.50	37.50
2160	21-40 riser stairs, hand carried		16	1			49		49	72.50
2165	Wheeled		24	.667			32.50		32.50	48.50
2170	0'-100' haul, incl. 5 riser stairs, hand carried		15	1.067			52.50		52.50	77.50
2175	Wheeled		23	.696			34		34	50.50
2180	6-10 riser stairs, hand carried		14	1.143			56		56	83
2185	Wheeled		21	.762			37.50		37.50	55.50
2190	11-20 riser stairs, hand carried		12	1.333			65.50		65.50	96.50
2195	Wheeled		18	.889			43.50		43.50	64.50
2200	21-40 riser stairs, hand carried		8	2			98		98	145
2205	Wheeled		12	1.333			65.50		65.50	96.50
2210	Haul and return, add per each extra 100' haul, hand carried		35.50	.451			22		22	32.50
2215	Wheeled		54	.296			14.50		14.50	21.50
2220	For each additional flight of stairs, up to 5 risers, add		550	.029	Flight		1.43		1.43	2.11
2225	6-10 risers, add		275	.058			2.85		2.85	4.22
2230	11-20 risers, add		138	.116			5.70		5.70	8.40
2235	21-40 risers, add		69	.232			11.35		11.35	16.80
3000	Loading & trucking, including 2 mile haul, chute loaded	B-16	45	.711	C.Y.		36.50	22	58.50	78.50
3040	Hand loading truck, 50' haul	"	48	.667			34.50	20.50	55	73.50
3080	Machine loading truck	B-17	120	.267			14.50	6.65	21.15	29
5000	Haul, per mile, up to 8 C.Y. truck	B-34B	1165	.007			.39	.85	1.24	1.51
5100	Over 8 C.Y. truck	"	1550	.005			.30	.64	.94	1.14

02 41 19.20 Selective Demolition, Dump Charges

		Crew	Daily Output	Labor-Hours	Unit	Material	Labor	Equipment	Total	Total Incl O&P
0010	**SELECTIVE DEMOLITION, DUMP CHARGES** R024119-10									
0100	Building construction materials				Ton	74			74	81
0300	Rubbish only					63			63	69.50
0500	Reclamation station, usual charge					74			74	81

02 41 19.27 Selective Demolition, Torch Cutting

		Crew	Daily Output	Labor-Hours	Unit	Material	Labor	Equipment	Total	Total Incl O&P
0010	**SELECTIVE DEMOLITION, TORCH CUTTING** R024119-10									
0020	Steel, 1" thick plate	E-25	333	.024	L.F.	1.53	1.66	.04	3.23	4.28
0040	1" diameter bar	"	600	.013	Ea.	.26	.92	.02	1.20	1.72
1000	Oxygen lance cutting, reinforced concrete walls									

02 41 Demolition

02 41 19 – Selective Demolition

02 41 19.27 Selective Demolition, Torch Cutting		Crew	Daily Output	Labor-Hours	Unit	Material	2024 Bare Costs Labor	Equipment	Total	Total Incl O&P
1040	12"-16" thick walls	1 Clab	10	.800	L.F.		39		39	58
1080	24" thick walls	"	6	1.333	"		65.50		65.50	96.50

02 65 Underground Storage Tank Removal

02 65 10 – Underground Tank and Contaminated Soil Removal

02 65 10.30 Removal of Underground Storage Tanks

			Crew	Daily Output	Labor-Hours	Unit	Material	Labor	Equipment	Total	Total Incl O&P
0010	**REMOVAL OF UNDERGROUND STORAGE TANKS**	R026510-20									
0011	Petroleum storage tanks, non-leaking										
0100	Excavate & load onto trailer										
0110	3,000 gal. to 5,000 gal. tank	G	B-14	4	12	Ea.		620	72.50	692.50	995
0120	6,000 gal. to 8,000 gal. tank	G	B-3A	3	13.333			695	400	1,095	1,475
0130	9,000 gal. to 12,000 gal. tank	G	"	2	20			1,050	595	1,645	2,200
0190	Known leaking tank, add					%				100%	100%
0200	Remove sludge, water and remaining product from bottom										
0201	of tank with vacuum truck										
0300	3,000 gal. to 5,000 gal. tank	G	A-13	5	1.600	Ea.		99	171	270	335
0310	6,000 gal. to 8,000 gal. tank	G		4	2			124	214	338	420
0320	9,000 gal. to 12,000 gal. tank	G		3	2.667			165	285	450	560
0390	Dispose of sludge off-site, average					Gal.				6.25	6.80
0400	Insert inert solid CO_2 "dry ice" into tank										
0401	For cleaning/transporting tanks (1.5 lb./100 gal. cap)	G	1 Clab	500	.016	Lb.	1.35	.78		2.13	2.65
1020	Haul tank to certified salvage dump, 100 miles round trip										
1023	3,000 gal. to 5,000 gal. tank					Ea.				760	830
1026	6,000 gal. to 8,000 gal. tank									880	960
1029	9,000 gal. to 12,000 gal. tank									1,050	1,150
1100	Disposal of contaminated soil to landfill										
1110	Minimum					C.Y.				145	160
1111	Maximum					"				400	440
1120	Disposal of contaminated soil to										
1121	bituminous concrete batch plant										
1130	Minimum					C.Y.				80	88
1131	Maximum					"				115	125
2010	Decontamination of soil on site incl poly tarp on top/bottom										
2011	Soil containment berm and chemical treatment										
2020	Minimum	G	B-11C	100	.160	C.Y.	8.45	9.10	2.91	20.46	26
2021	Maximum	G	"	100	.160		10.95	9.10	2.91	22.96	29
2050	Disposal of decontaminated soil, minimum									135	150
2055	Maximum									400	440

02 81 Transportation and Disposal of Hazardous Materials

02 81 20 – Hazardous Waste Handling

02 81 20.10 Hazardous Waste Cleanup/Pickup/Disposal

		Crew	Daily Output	Labor-Hours	Unit	Material	Labor	Equipment	Total	Total Incl O&P
0010	**HAZARDOUS WASTE CLEANUP/PICKUP/DISPOSAL**									
0100	For contractor rental equipment, i.e., dozer,									
0110	Front end loader, dump truck, etc., see 01 54 33 Reference Section									
1000	Solid pickup									
1100	55 gal. drums				Ea.				240	265
1120	Bulk material, minimum				Ton				190	210
1130	Maximum				"				595	655

02 81 Transportation and Disposal of Hazardous Materials
02 81 20 – Hazardous Waste Handling

02 81 20.10 Hazardous Waste Cleanup/Pickup/Disposal	Crew	Daily Output	Labor-Hours	Unit	Material	2024 Bare Costs Labor	Equipment	Total	Total Incl O&P
1200 Transportation to disposal site									
1220 Truckload = 80 drums or 25 C.Y. or 18 tons									
1260 Minimum				Mile				3.95	4.45
1270 Maximum				"				7.25	7.98
3000 Liquid pickup, vacuum truck, stainless steel tank									
3100 Minimum charge, 4 hours									
3110 1 compartment, 2200 gallon				Hr.				140	155
3120 2 compartment, 5000 gallon				"				200	225
3400 Transportation in 6900 gallon bulk truck				Mile				7.95	8.75
3410 In teflon lined truck				"				10.20	11.25
5000 Heavy sludge or dry vacuumable material				Hr.				140	155
6000 Dumpsite disposal charge, minimum				Ton				140	155
6020 Maximum				"				415	455

02 82 Asbestos Remediation
02 82 13 – Asbestos Abatement
02 82 13.39 Asbestos Remediation Plans and Methods

	Crew	Daily Output	Labor-Hours	Unit	Material	2024 Bare Costs Labor	Equipment	Total	Total Incl O&P
0010 **ASBESTOS REMEDIATION PLANS AND METHODS**									
0100 Building Survey-Commercial Building				Ea.				2,200	2,400
0200 Asbestos Abatement Remediation Plan				"				1,350	1,475

02 82 13.41 Asbestos Abatement Equipment

	Crew	Daily Output	Labor-Hours	Unit	Material	2024 Bare Costs Labor	Equipment	Total	Total Incl O&P
0010 **ASBESTOS ABATEMENT EQUIPMENT** R028213-20									
0011 Equipment and supplies, buy									
0200 Air filtration device, 2000 CFM				Ea.	1,350			1,350	1,475
0250 Large volume air sampling pump, minimum					395			395	435
0260 Maximum					830			830	915
0300 Airless sprayer unit, 2 gun					2,650			2,650	2,900
0350 Light stand, 500 watt					32			32	35.50
0400 Personal respirators									
0410 Negative pressure, 1/2 face, dual operation, minimum				Ea.	28.50			28.50	31
0420 Maximum					33.50			33.50	37
0450 P.A.P.R., full face, minimum					1,025			1,025	1,150
0460 Maximum					1,175			1,175	1,275
0470 Supplied air, full face, including air line, minimum					268			268	294
0480 Maximum					1,200			1,200	1,325
0500 Personnel sampling pump					315			315	345
1500 Power panel, 20 unit, including GFI					610			610	670
1600 Shower unit, including pump and filters					1,175			1,175	1,300
1700 Supplied air system (type C)					4,350			4,350	4,775
1750 Vacuum cleaner, HEPA, 16 gal., stainless steel, wet/dry					1,450			1,450	1,600
1760 55 gallon					1,925			1,925	2,100
1800 Vacuum loader, 9-18 ton/hr.					150,000			150,000	165,000
1900 Water atomizer unit, including 55 gal. drum					315			315	345
2000 Worker protection, whole body, foot, head cover & gloves, plastic					10.80			10.80	11.85
2500 Respirator, single use					2.23			2.23	2.45
2550 Cartridge for respirator					30			30	32.50
2570 Glove bag, 7 mil, 50" x 60"					10.70			10.70	11.80
2580 10 mil, 44" x 60"					10.10			10.10	11.10
2590 6 mil, 44" x 60"					6.20			6.20	6.80
6000 Disposable polyethylene bags, 6 mil, 3 C.F.					1.35			1.35	1.49
6300 Disposable fiber drums, 55gal					31			31	34

02 82 Asbestos Remediation

02 82 13 – Asbestos Abatement

02 82 13.41 Asbestos Abatement Equipment

		Crew	Daily Output	Labor-Hours	Unit	Material	2024 Bare Costs Labor	Equipment	Total	Total Incl O&P
6400	Pressure sensitive caution labels, 3" x 5"				Ea.	3.59			3.59	3.95
6450	11" x 17"					19.45			19.45	21.50
6500	Negative air machine, 1800 CFM					900			900	990

02 82 13.42 Preparation of Asbestos Containment Area

		Crew	Daily Output	Labor-Hours	Unit	Material	Labor	Equipment	Total	Total Incl O&P
0010	**PREPARATION OF ASBESTOS CONTAINMENT AREA** R028213-20									
0100	Pre-cleaning, HEPA vacuum and wet wipe, flat surfaces	A-9	12000	.005	S.F.	.03	.36		.39	.59
0200	Protect carpeted area, 2 layers 6 mil poly on 3/4" plywood	"	1000	.064		3.06	4.30		7.36	9.90
0300	Separation barrier, 2" x 4" @ 16", 1/2" plywood ea. side, 8' high	2 Carp	400	.040		4.38	2.42		6.80	8.40
0310	12' high		320	.050		4.25	3.03		7.28	9.15
0320	16' high		200	.080		4.19	4.84		9.03	11.75
0400	Personnel decontam. chamber, 2" x 4" @ 16", 3/4" ply ea. side		280	.057		6.30	3.46		9.76	12.05
0450	Waste decontam. chamber, 2" x 4" studs @ 16", 3/4" ply ea. side		360	.044		6.30	2.69		8.99	10.95
0500	Cover surfaces with polyethylene sheeting									
0501	Including glue and tape									
0550	Floors, each layer, 6 mil	A-9	8000	.008	S.F.	.20	.54		.74	1.04
0551	4 mil		9000	.007		.06	.48		.54	.79
0560	Walls, each layer, 6 mil		6000	.011		.20	.72		.92	1.31
0561	4 mil		7000	.009		.06	.61		.67	1
0570	For heights above 14', add						20%			
0575	For heights above 20', add						30%			
0580	For fire retardant poly, add					100%				
0590	For large open areas, deduct					10%	20%			
0600	Seal floor penetrations with foam firestop to 36 sq. in.	2 Carp	200	.080	Ea.	21.50	4.84		26.34	30.50
0610	36 sq. in. to 72 sq. in.		125	.128		43	7.75		50.75	59
0615	72 sq. in. to 144 sq. in.		80	.200		86	12.10		98.10	113
0620	Wall penetrations, to 36 sq. in.		180	.089		21.50	5.40		26.90	31.50
0630	36 sq. in. to 72 sq. in.		100	.160		43	9.70		52.70	62
0640	72 sq. in. to 144 sq. in.		60	.267		86	16.15		102.15	119
0800	Caulk seams with latex	1 Carp	230	.035	L.F.	.19	2.11		2.30	3.33
0900	Set up neg. air machine, 1-2k CFM/25 M.C.F. volume	1 Asbe	4.30	1.860	Ea.		125		125	190
0950	Set up and remove portable shower unit	2 Asbe	4	4	"		268		268	410

02 82 13.43 Bulk Asbestos Removal

		Crew	Daily Output	Labor-Hours	Unit	Material	Labor	Equipment	Total	Total Incl O&P
0010	**BULK ASBESTOS REMOVAL**									
0020	Includes disposable tools and 2 suits and 1 respirator filter/day/worker									
0200	Boiler insulation	A-9	480	.133	S.F.	1.03	8.95		9.98	14.80
0210	With metal lath, add				%		50%		50%	50%
0300	Boiler breeching or flue insulation	A-9	520	.123	S.F.	.79	8.25		9.04	13.45
0310	For active boiler, add				%		100%		100%	100%
0400	Duct or AHU insulation	A-10B	440	.073	S.F.	.47	4.89		5.36	7.95
0500	Duct vibration isolation joints, up to 24 sq. in. duct	A-9	56	1.143	Ea.	7.35	77		84.35	125
0520	25 sq. in. to 48 sq. in. duct		48	1.333		8.55	89.50		98.05	145
0530	49 sq. in. to 76 sq. in. duct		40	1.600		10.25	107		117.25	175
0600	Pipe insulation, air cell type, up to 4" diameter pipe		900	.071	L.F.	.46	4.78		5.24	7.80
0610	4" to 8" diameter pipe		800	.080		.51	5.35		5.86	8.75
0620	10" to 12" diameter pipe		700	.091		.59	6.15		6.74	10
0630	14" to 16" diameter pipe		550	.116		.75	7.80		8.55	12.70
0650	Over 16" diameter pipe		650	.098	S.F.	.63	6.60		7.23	10.80
0700	With glove bag up to 3" diameter pipe		200	.320	L.F.	.79	21.50		22.29	34
1000	Pipe fitting insulation up to 4" diameter pipe		320	.200	Ea.	1.28	13.45		14.73	22
1100	6" to 8" diameter pipe		304	.211		1.35	14.15		15.50	23
1110	10" to 12" diameter pipe		192	.333		2.14	22.50		24.64	36.50
1120	14" to 16" diameter pipe		128	.500		3.21	33.50		36.71	54.50

02 82 Asbestos Remediation

02 82 13 – Asbestos Abatement

02 82 13.43 Bulk Asbestos Removal

		Crew	Daily Output	Labor-Hours	Unit	Material	2024 Bare Costs Labor	Equipment	Total	Total Incl O&P
1130	Over 16" diameter pipe	A-9	176	.364	S.F.	2.33	24.50		26.83	39.50
1200	With glove bag, up to 8" diameter pipe		75	.853	L.F.	10	57.50		67.50	98.50
2000	Scrape foam fireproofing from flat surface		2400	.027	S.F.	.17	1.79		1.96	2.92
2100	Irregular surfaces		1200	.053		.34	3.58		3.92	5.85
3000	Remove cementitious material from flat surface		1800	.036		.23	2.39		2.62	3.89
3100	Irregular surface		1000	.064		.29	4.30		4.59	6.85
6000	Remove contaminated soil from crawl space by hand		400	.160	C.F.	1.03	10.75		11.78	17.50
6100	With large production vacuum loader	A-12	700	.091	"	.59	6.15	1.22	7.96	11.35
7000	Radiator backing, not including radiator removal	A-9	1200	.053	S.F.	.34	3.58		3.92	5.85
9000	For type B (supplied air) respirator equipment, add				%				10%	10%

02 82 13.44 Demolition In Asbestos Contaminated Area

		Crew	Daily Output	Labor-Hours	Unit	Material	2024 Bare Costs Labor	Equipment	Total	Total Incl O&P
0010	**DEMOLITION IN ASBESTOS CONTAMINATED AREA**									
0200	Ceiling, including suspension system, plaster and lath	A-9	2100	.030	S.F.	.20	2.05		2.25	3.34
0210	Finished plaster, leaving wire lath		585	.109		.70	7.35		8.05	11.95
0220	Suspended acoustical tile		3500	.018		.12	1.23		1.35	2
0230	Concealed tile grid system		3000	.021		.14	1.43		1.57	2.33
0240	Metal pan grid system		1500	.043		.27	2.87		3.14	4.67
0250	Gypsum board		2500	.026		.16	1.72		1.88	2.80
0260	Lighting fixtures up to 2' x 4'		72	.889	Ea.	5.70	59.50		65.20	97.50
0400	Partitions, non load bearing									
0410	Plaster, lath, and studs	A-9	690	.093	S.F.	1.06	6.25		7.31	10.65
0450	Gypsum board and studs	"	1390	.046	"	.30	3.09		3.39	5.05
9000	For type B (supplied air) respirator equipment, add				%				10%	10%

02 82 13.45 OSHA Testing

		Crew	Daily Output	Labor-Hours	Unit	Material	2024 Bare Costs Labor	Equipment	Total	Total Incl O&P
0010	**OSHA TESTING**									
0100	Certified technician, minimum				Day		340		340	340
0110	Maximum						670		670	670
0121	Industrial hygienist, minimum						385		385	385
0130	Maximum						755		755	755
0200	Asbestos sampling and PCM analysis, NIOSH 7400, minimum	1 Asbe	8	1	Ea.	22.50	67		89.50	127
0210	Maximum		4	2		29.50	134		163.50	238
1000	Cleaned area samples		8	1		22.50	67		89.50	127
1100	PCM air sample analysis, NIOSH 7400, minimum		8	1		22.50	67		89.50	127
1110	Maximum		4	2		29.50	134		163.50	238
1200	TEM air sample analysis, NIOSH 7402, minimum								80	106
1210	Maximum								360	450

02 82 13.46 Decontamination of Asbestos Containment Area

		Crew	Daily Output	Labor-Hours	Unit	Material	2024 Bare Costs Labor	Equipment	Total	Total Incl O&P
0010	**DECONTAMINATION OF ASBESTOS CONTAINMENT AREA**									
0100	Spray exposed substrate with surfactant (bridging)									
0200	Flat surfaces	A-9	6000	.011	S.F.	.05	.72		.77	1.15
0250	Irregular surfaces		4000	.016	"	.06	1.07		1.13	1.71
0300	Pipes, beams, and columns		2000	.032	L.F.	.06	2.15		2.21	3.34
1000	Spray encapsulate polyethylene sheeting		8000	.008	S.F.	.54	.54		1.08	1.41
1100	Roll down polyethylene sheeting		8000	.008	"		.54		.54	.82
1500	Bag polyethylene sheeting		400	.160	Ea.	1.23	10.75		11.98	17.70
2000	Fine clean exposed substrate, with nylon brush		2400	.027	S.F.		1.79		1.79	2.73
2500	Wet wipe substrate		4800	.013			.90		.90	1.36
2600	Vacuum surfaces, fine brush		6400	.010			.67		.67	1.02
3000	Structural demolition									
3100	Wood stud walls	A-9	2800	.023	S.F.		1.54		1.54	2.34
3500	Window manifolds, not incl. window replacement		4200	.015			1.02		1.02	1.56
3600	Plywood carpet protection		2000	.032			2.15		2.15	3.27

02 82 Asbestos Remediation

02 82 13 – Asbestos Abatement

02 82 13.46 Decontamination of Asbestos Containment Area	Crew	Daily Output	Labor-Hours	Unit	Material	2024 Bare Costs Labor	Equipment	Total	Total Incl O&P
4000 Remove custom decontamination facility	A-10A	8	3	Ea.	20	202		222	335
4100 Remove portable decontamination facility	3 Asbe	12	2	"	18.60	134		152.60	226
5000 HEPA vacuum, shampoo carpeting	A-9	4800	.013	S.F.	.15	.90		1.05	1.53
9000 Final cleaning of protected surfaces	A-10A	8000	.003	"		.20		.20	.31
02 82 13.47 Asbestos Waste Pkg., Handling, and Disp.									
0010 ASBESTOS WASTE PACKAGING, HANDLING, AND DISPOSAL									
0100 Collect and bag bulk material, 3 C.F. bags, by hand	A-9	400	.160	Ea.	1.35	10.75		12.10	17.85
0200 Large production vacuum loader	A-12	880	.073		1.75	4.88	.97	7.60	10.45
1000 Double bag and decontaminate	A-9	960	.067		1.35	4.48		5.83	8.30
2000 Containerize bagged material in drums, per 55gal drum	"	800	.080		31	5.35		36.35	42
3000 Cart bags 50' to dumpster	2 Asbe	400	.040			2.68		2.68	4.09
5000 Disposal charges, not including haul, minimum				C.Y.				61	67
5020 Maximum				"				355	395
9000 For type B (supplied air) respirator equipment, add				%				10%	10%
02 82 13.48 Asbestos Encapsulation With Sealants									
0010 ASBESTOS ENCAPSULATION WITH SEALANTS									
0100 Ceilings and walls, minimum	A-9	21000	.003	S.F.	.58	.20		.78	.95
0110 Maximum		10600	.006	"	.70	.41		1.11	1.39
0300 Pipes to 12" diameter including minor repairs, minimum		800	.080	L.F.	.58	5.35		5.93	8.85
0310 Maximum		400	.160	"	.70	10.75		11.45	17.10

02 87 Biohazard Remediation

02 87 13 – Mold Remediation

02 87 13.16 Mold Remediation Preparation and Containment	Crew	Daily Output	Labor-Hours	Unit	Material	2024 Bare Costs Labor	Equipment	Total	Total Incl O&P
0010 MOLD REMEDIATION PREPARATION AND CONTAINMENT									
6010 Preparation of mold containment area									
6100 Pre-cleaning, HEPA vacuum and wet wipe, flat surfaces	A-9	12000	.005	S.F.	.03	.36		.39	.59
6300 Separation barrier, 2" x 4" @ 16", 1/2" plywood ea. side, 8' high	2 Carp	333	.048		5.40	2.91		8.31	10.25
6310 12' high		320	.050		7.10	3.03		10.13	12.30
6320 16' high		200	.080		2.92	4.84		7.76	10.35
6400 Personnel decontam. chamber, 2" x 4" @ 16", 3/4" ply ea. side		280	.057		5.95	3.46		9.41	11.65
6450 Waste decontam. chamber, 2" x 4" studs @ 16", 3/4" ply each side		360	.044		24	2.69		26.69	30
6500 Cover surfaces with polyethylene sheeting									
6501 Including glue and tape									
6550 Floors, each layer, 6 mil	A-9	8000	.008	S.F.	.20	.54		.74	1.04
6551 4 mil		9000	.007		.06	.48		.54	.79
6560 Walls, each layer, 6 mil		6000	.011		.20	.72		.92	1.31
6561 4 mil		7000	.009		.06	.61		.67	1
6570 For heights above 14', add						20%			
6575 For heights above 20', add						30%			
6580 For fire retardant poly, add					100%				
6590 For large open areas, deduct					10%	20%			
6600 Seal floor penetrations with foam firestop to 36 sq. in.	2 Carp	200	.080	Ea.	21.50	4.84		26.34	30.50
6610 36 sq. in. to 72 sq. in.		125	.128		43	7.75		50.75	59
6615 72 sq. in. to 144 sq. in.		80	.200		86	12.10		98.10	113
6620 Wall penetrations, to 36 sq. in.		180	.089		21.50	5.40		26.90	31.50
6630 36 sq. in. to 72 sq. in.		100	.160		43	9.70		52.70	62
6640 72 sq. in. to 144 sq. in.		60	.267		86	16.15		102.15	119
6800 Caulk seams with latex caulk	1 Carp	230	.035	L.F.	.19	2.11		2.30	3.33
6900 Set up neg. air machine, 1-2k CFM/25 M.C.F. volume	1 Asbe	4.30	1.860	Ea.		125		125	190

02 87 Biohazard Remediation

02 87 13 – Mold Remediation

02 87 13.33 Removal and Disposal of Materials With Mold

		Crew	Daily Output	Labor-Hours	Unit	Material	2024 Bare Costs Labor	2024 Bare Costs Equipment	Total	Total Incl O&P
0010	**REMOVAL AND DISPOSAL OF MATERIALS WITH MOLD**									
0015	Demolition in mold contaminated area									
0200	Ceiling, including suspension system, plaster and lath	A-9	2100	.030	S.F.	.20	2.05		2.25	3.34
0210	Finished plaster, leaving wire lath		585	.109		.70	7.35		8.05	11.95
0220	Suspended acoustical tile		3500	.018		.12	1.23		1.35	2
0230	Concealed tile grid system		3000	.021		.14	1.43		1.57	2.33
0240	Metal pan grid system		1500	.043		.27	2.87		3.14	4.67
0250	Gypsum board		2500	.026		.16	1.72		1.88	2.80
0255	Plywood		2500	.026		.16	1.72		1.88	2.80
0260	Lighting fixtures up to 2' x 4'		72	.889	Ea.	5.70	59.50		65.20	97.50
0400	Partitions, non load bearing									
0410	Plaster, lath, and studs	A-9	690	.093	S.F.	1.06	6.25		7.31	10.65
0450	Gypsum board and studs		1390	.046		.30	3.09		3.39	5.05
0465	Carpet & pad		1390	.046		.30	3.09		3.39	5.05
0600	Pipe insulation, air cell type, up to 4" diameter pipe		900	.071	L.F.	.46	4.78		5.24	7.80
0610	4" to 8" diameter pipe		800	.080		.51	5.35		5.86	8.75
0620	10" to 12" diameter pipe		700	.091		.59	6.15		6.74	10
0630	14" to 16" diameter pipe		550	.116		.75	7.80		8.55	12.70
0650	Over 16" diameter pipe		650	.098	S.F.	.63	6.60		7.23	10.80
9000	For type B (supplied air) respirator equipment, add				%				10%	10%

02 87 19 – Bio-Hazard and Infectious Disease Control Remediation

02 87 19.10 Temporary Barriers, Including Ppe

		Crew	Daily Output	Labor-Hours	Unit	Material	2024 Bare Costs Labor	2024 Bare Costs Equipment	Total	Total Incl O&P
0010	**TEMPORARY BARRIERS, including PPE**									
0100	Infectious control partition, adjustable to 10' high, obscured, 4' panel	2 Carp	75	.213	Ea.	610	12.90		622.90	690
0110	3' panel		75	.213		575	12.90		587.90	655
0120	2' panel		75	.213		455	12.90		467.90	520
0130	1' panel	1 Carp	75	.107		300	6.45		306.45	340
0140	6" panel	"	75	.107		277	6.45		283.45	315
0150	2' panel with HEPA filtered discharge port	2 Carp	75	.213		525	12.90		537.90	595
0160	3' panel with 32" door		75	.213		945	12.90		957.90	1,075
0170	4' panel with 36" door		75	.213		1,050	12.90		1,062.90	1,175
0180	4'-6" panel with 44" door		75	.213		1,250	12.90		1,262.90	1,400
0190	Hinged corner		68	.235		192	14.25		206.25	233
0200	Outside corner		68	.235		164	14.25		178.25	201
0210	T post		68	.235		164	14.25		178.25	201
0220	Accessories, ceiling grid clip		300	.053		7.60	3.23		10.83	13.20
0230	Panel locking clip		300	.053		5.45	3.23		8.68	10.75
0240	Panel joint closure strip		300	.053		9.10	3.23		12.33	14.80
0250	Screw jack		300	.053		6.85	3.23		10.08	12.35
0260	Digital pressure difference gauge					305			305	335
0280	Combination lockset	1 Carp	11	.727		216	44		260	305
0285	Sealant tape, 2" wide	1 Clab	165	.048	C.L.F.	14	2.38		16.38	18.90
0290	System in place, including door and accessories									
0300	Based upon 25 uses	2 Carp	43	.372	L.F.	14	22.50		36.50	49
0310	Based upon 50 uses		43	.372		8.90	22.50		31.40	43.50
0330	Based upon 100 uses		43	.372		6.35	22.50		28.85	40.50
0400	Separation barrier, 2" x 4" @ 16" O.C., 1/2" plywood each side, 8' high		340	.047	S.F.	4.85	2.85		7.70	9.55
0410	12' high		275	.058		4.84	3.52		8.36	10.55
0420	16' high		170	.094		5.15	5.70		10.85	14.10
0430	5/8" FR GWB each side, 8' high		290	.055		4.02	3.34		7.36	9.35
0440	12' high		235	.068		3.89	4.12		8.01	10.40
0450	16' high		144	.111		3.83	6.75		10.58	14.15

02 87 Biohazard Remediation

02 87 19 – Bio-Hazard and Infectious Disease Control Remediation

02 87 19.20 Temporary Protection, Including PPE

		Crew	Daily Output	Labor-Hours	Unit	Material	2024 Bare Costs Labor	2024 Bare Costs Equipment	Total	Total Incl O&P
0010	**TEMPORARY PROTECTION, including PPE**									
0100	Infectious control protection, 6 mil plastic sheeting, applied to floors	1 Skwk	1900	.004	S.F.	.19	.27		.46	.61
0110	Applied to walls		1400	.006		.19	.36		.55	.75
0120	Applied to ceilings		1000	.008		.19	.51		.70	.97
0130	Sealant tape, 2" wide	1 Clab	165	.048	C.L.F.	14	2.38		16.38	18.90
0140	Floor covering, 1/8" tempered hardboard	2 Carp	878	.018	S.F.	.82	1.10		1.92	2.53
0150	1/2" CDX		878	.018		1.08	1.10		2.18	2.82
0160	3/4" CDX		755	.021		2.11	1.28		3.39	4.22

02 87 19.30 Infectious Control Equipment and Supplies

		Crew	Daily Output	Labor-Hours	Unit	Material	Labor	Equipment	Total	Total Incl O&P
0010	**INFECTIOUS CONTROL EQUIPMENT AND SUPPLIES**									
0100	Entry/exit decontamination chamber, portable, 10 uses	A-10C	12	2	Ea.	282	134	35	451	555
0105	Negative air machine, 1800 CFM					900			900	990
0110	Disposable polyethylene bags, 6 mil, 3 C.F.					1.35			1.35	1.49
0130	Paper towels, carton of 12, 350' rolls					88.50			88.50	97
0140	Heavy duty wipes, 160 per box					28.50			28.50	31.50
0200	Tent, including frame, weights, roof, walls, 5' x 5'	2 Skwk	32	.500		2,150	32		2,182	2,425
0205	5' x 10'		24	.667		2,500	42.50		2,542.50	2,825
0210	10' x 10'		24	.667		3,125	42.50		3,167.50	3,500
0220	13' x 26'		12	1.333		8,200	84.50		8,284.50	9,150
0230	13' x 26', flat roof infirmary		12	1.333		7,600	84.50		7,684.50	8,475
0240	13' x 26', drive through screening		12	1.333		8,800	84.50		8,884.50	9,800
0242	LED light kit for tents, 15 watt	1 Elec	48	.167		199	11.95		210.95	237
0244	Halogen heating kit, 1500 watt	"	48	.167		500	11.95		511.95	570
0250	Medical partition system, including frame, drapes, 5' x 5'	2 Skwk	48	.333		1,300	21		1,321	1,450

02 87 19.40 Infectious Control Cleaning, Includes PPE

		Crew	Daily Output	Labor-Hours	Unit	Material	Labor	Equipment	Total	Total Incl O&P
0010	**INFECTIOUS CONTROL CLEANING, Includes PPE**									
0100	Infectious control cleaning, including PPE and antimicrobial spray, floors	1 Skwk	3600	.002	S.F.	.07	.14		.21	.29
0110	Walls		3000	.003		.07	.17		.24	.33
0120	Ceilings		2700	.003		.08	.19		.27	.37
0130	Countertops		3300	.002		.07	.15		.22	.31
0140	Other surfaces		2600	.003		.08	.20		.28	.38
0150	Plumbing fixtures		14	.571	Ea.	6.25	36.50		42.75	61.50
0160	Bathroom accessories		30	.267		2.89	16.95		19.84	28.50
0170	Kitchen appliance		9	.889		10.45	56.50		66.95	96
0180	Electrical switches and receptacles		140	.057		.63	3.63		4.26	6.15
0190	Work station		9	.889		10.95	56.50		67.45	96.50
0200	Door and window hardware		88	.091		.97	5.75		6.72	9.70
0250	Supply / return ductwork, up to 2 S.F. cross section		240	.033	L.F.	.63	2.12		2.75	3.86
0260	2 to 4 S.F. cross section		192	.042		.90	2.65		3.55	4.95
0270	4 to 8 S.F. cross section		144	.056		1.14	3.53		4.67	6.55
0280	8 SF cross section		102	.078		1.71	4.98		6.69	9.35
0300	Duct coil		5	1.600	Ea.	18.15	102		120.15	172
0310	Duct damper and vane set		77	.104		2.01	6.60		8.61	12.05
0320	Fan coil unit or VAV box		8	1		11.10	63.50		74.60	107
0330	Air handling unit and coil		2	4		44.50	254		298.50	430
0340	Grill / diffuser or register		32	.250		3.11	15.90		19.01	27.50

Division 3 Concrete

Estimating Tips
General
- Carefully check all the plans and specifications. Concrete often appears on drawings other than structural drawings, including mechanical and electrical drawings for equipment pads. The cost of cutting and patching is often difficult to estimate. See Subdivision 03 81 for Concrete Cutting, Subdivision 02 41 19.16 for Cutout Demolition, Subdivision 03 05 05.10 for Concrete Demolition, and Subdivision 02 41 19.19 for Rubbish Handling (handling, loading, and hauling of debris).
- Always obtain concrete prices from suppliers near the job site. A volume discount can often be negotiated, depending upon competition in the area. Remember to add for waste, particularly for slabs and footings on grade.

03 10 00 Concrete Forming and Accessories
- A primary cost for concrete construction is forming. Most jobs today are constructed with prefabricated forms. The selection of the forms best suited for the job and the total square feet of forms required for efficient concrete forming and placing are key elements in estimating concrete construction. Enough forms must be available for erection to make efficient use of the concrete placing equipment and crew.
- Concrete accessories for forming and placing depend upon the systems used. Study the plans and specifications to ensure that all special accessory requirements have been included in the cost estimate, such as anchor bolts, inserts, and hangers.
- Included within costs for forms-in-place are all necessary bracing and shoring.

03 20 00 Concrete Reinforcing
- Ascertain that the reinforcing steel supplier has included all accessories, cutting, bending, and an allowance for lapping, splicing, and waste. A good rule of thumb is 10% for lapping, splicing, and waste. Also, 10% waste should be allowed for welded wire fabric.
- The unit price items in the subdivisions for Reinforcing In Place, Glass Fiber Reinforcing, and Welded Wire Fabric include the labor to install accessories such as beam and slab bolsters, high chairs, and bar ties and tie wire. The material cost for these accessories is not included; they may be obtained from the Accessories Subdivisions.

03 30 00 Cast-In-Place Concrete
- When estimating structural concrete, pay particular attention to requirements for concrete additives, curing methods, and surface treatments. Special consideration for climate, hot or cold, must be included in your estimate. Be sure to include requirements for concrete placing equipment and concrete finishing.
- For accurate concrete estimating, the estimator must consider each of the following major components individually: forms, reinforcing steel, ready-mix concrete, placement of the concrete, and finishing of the top surface. For faster estimating, Subdivision 03 30 53.40 for Concrete-In-Place can be used; here, various items of concrete work are presented that include the costs of all five major components (unless specifically stated otherwise).

03 40 00 Precast Concrete
03 50 00 Cast Decks and Underlayment
- The cost of hauling precast concrete structural members is often an important factor. For this reason, it is important to get a quote from the nearest supplier. It may become economically feasible to set up precasting beds on the site if the hauling costs are prohibitive.

Reference Numbers
Reference numbers are shown at the beginning of some major classifications. These numbers refer to related items in the Reference Section. The reference information may be an estimating procedure, an alternate pricing method, or technical information.

Note: Not all subdivisions listed here necessarily appear. ■

Same Data. Simplified.

Enjoy the convenience and efficiency of accessing your costs anywhere:
- **Skip the multiplier** by setting your location
- **Quickly search,** edit, favorite and share costs
- **Stay on top of price changes** with automatic updates

Discover more at rsmeans.com/online

No part of this cost data may be reproduced, stored in a retrieval system, or transmitted in any form or by any means without prior written permission of Gordian.

03 11 Concrete Forming

03 11 13 – Structural Cast-In-Place Concrete Forming

03 11 13.40 Forms In Place, Equipment Foundations

		Crew	Daily Output	Labor-Hours	Unit	Material	2024 Bare Costs Labor	Equipment	Total	Total Incl O&P
0010	**FORMS IN PLACE, EQUIPMENT FOUNDATIONS**									
0020	1 use	C-2	160	.300	SFCA	6.20	17.70		23.90	33
0050	2 use		190	.253		3.42	14.90		18.32	26
0100	3 use		200	.240		2.49	14.15		16.64	23.50
0150	4 use		205	.234		2.03	13.80		15.83	22.50

03 11 13.45 Forms In Place, Footings

		Crew	Daily Output	Labor-Hours	Unit	Material	Labor	Equipment	Total	Total Incl O&P
0010	**FORMS IN PLACE, FOOTINGS**									
0020	Continuous wall, plywood, 1 use	C-1	375	.085	SFCA	13.95	4.92		18.87	22.50
0050	2 use		440	.073		7.65	4.19		11.84	14.65
0100	3 use		470	.068		5.55	3.93		9.48	11.95
0150	4 use		485	.066		4.54	3.80		8.34	10.65
5000	Spread footings, job-built lumber, 1 use		305	.105		4.82	6.05		10.87	14.25
5050	2 use		371	.086		2.68	4.97		7.65	10.30
5100	3 use		401	.080		1.93	4.60		6.53	8.90
5150	4 use		414	.077		1.57	4.46		6.03	8.30

03 11 13.65 Forms In Place, Slab On Grade

		Crew	Daily Output	Labor-Hours	Unit	Material	Labor	Equipment	Total	Total Incl O&P
0010	**FORMS IN PLACE, SLAB ON GRADE**									
3000	Edge forms, wood, 4 use, on grade, to 6" high	C-1	600	.053	L.F.	.67	3.08		3.75	5.30
6000	Trench forms in floor, wood, 1 use		160	.200	SFCA	4.44	11.55		15.99	22
6050	2 use		175	.183		2.44	10.55		12.99	18.30
6100	3 use		180	.178		1.78	10.25		12.03	17.15
6150	4 use		185	.173		1.44	9.95		11.39	16.35

03 15 Concrete Accessories

03 15 05 – Concrete Forming Accessories

03 15 05.75 Sleeves and Chases

			Crew	Daily Output	Labor-Hours	Unit	Material	Labor	Equipment	Total	Total Incl O&P
0010	**SLEEVES AND CHASES**										
0100	Plastic, 1 use, 12" long, 2" diameter		1 Carp	100	.080	Ea.	3.99	4.84		8.83	11.55
0150	4" diameter			90	.089		8.45	5.40		13.85	17.25
0200	6" diameter			75	.107		22.50	6.45		28.95	34.50
0250	12" diameter			60	.133		62	8.05		70.05	80.50
5000	Sheet metal, 2" diameter	G		100	.080		4.84	4.84		9.68	12.45
5100	4" diameter	G		90	.089		6.05	5.40		11.45	14.60
5150	6" diameter	G		75	.107		8.60	6.45		15.05	19
5200	12" diameter	G		60	.133		13.40	8.05		21.45	26.50
6000	Steel pipe, 2" diameter	G		100	.080		17.45	4.84		22.29	26.50
6100	4" diameter	G		90	.089		49	5.40		54.40	62
6150	6" diameter	G		75	.107		90	6.45		96.45	109
6200	12" diameter	G		60	.133		159	8.05		167.05	187

03 15 16 – Concrete Construction Joints

03 15 16.20 Control Joints, Saw Cut

		Crew	Daily Output	Labor-Hours	Unit	Material	Labor	Equipment	Total	Total Incl O&P
0010	**CONTROL JOINTS, SAW CUT**									
0100	Sawcut control joints in green concrete									
0120	1" depth	C-27	2000	.008	L.F.	.03	.45	.10	.58	.80
0140	1-1/2" depth		1800	.009		.04	.50	.11	.65	.91
0160	2" depth		1600	.010		.06	.57	.12	.75	1.02
0180	Sawcut joint reservoir in cured concrete									
0182	3/8" wide x 3/4" deep, with single saw blade	C-27	1000	.016	L.F.	.04	.91	.19	1.14	1.58
0184	1/2" wide x 1" deep, with double saw blades		900	.018		.08	1.01	.22	1.31	1.80
0186	3/4" wide x 1-1/2" deep, with double saw blades		800	.020		.17	1.14	.24	1.55	2.11

03 15 Concrete Accessories

03 15 16 – Concrete Construction Joints

03 15 16.20 Control Joints, Saw Cut

		Crew	Daily Output	Labor-Hours	Unit	Material	2024 Bare Costs Labor	Equipment	Total	Total Incl O&P
0190	Water blast joint to wash away laitance, 2 passes	C-29	2500	.003	L.F.		.16	.05	.21	.29
0200	Air blast joint to blow out debris and air dry, 2 passes	C-28	2000	.004	↓		.23	.02	.25	.35
0300	For backer rod, see Section 07 91 23.10									
0342	For joint sealant, see Section 07 92 13.20									

03 15 19 – Cast-In Concrete Anchors

03 15 19.10 Anchor Bolts

			Crew	Daily Output	Labor-Hours	Unit	Material	Labor	Equipment	Total	Total Incl O&P
0010	**ANCHOR BOLTS**										
0015	Made from recycled materials										
0025	Single bolts installed in fresh concrete, no templates										
0030	Hooked w/nut and washer, 1/2" diameter, 8" long	G	1 Carp	132	.061	Ea.	2.77	3.67		6.44	8.50
0040	12" long	G		131	.061		3.08	3.70		6.78	8.85
0050	5/8" diameter, 8" long	G		129	.062		4.63	3.76		8.39	10.65
0060	12" long	G		127	.063		5.70	3.81		9.51	11.90
0070	3/4" diameter, 8" long	G		127	.063		5.70	3.81		9.51	11.90
0080	12" long	G		125	.064	↓	7.10	3.88		10.98	13.60
0090	2-bolt pattern, including job-built 2-hole template, per set										
0100	J-type, incl. hex nut & washer, 1/2" diameter x 6" long	G	1 Carp	21	.381	Set	9.15	23		32.15	44
0110	12" long	G		21	.381		10.40	23		33.40	45.50
0120	18" long	G		21	.381		12.25	23		35.25	47.50
0130	3/4" diameter x 8" long	G		20	.400		15.60	24		39.60	53
0140	12" long	G		20	.400		18.45	24		42.45	56.50
0150	18" long	G		20	.400		22.50	24		46.50	61
0160	1" diameter x 12" long	G		19	.421		49.50	25.50		75	92.50
0170	18" long	G		19	.421		58.50	25.50		84	103
0180	24" long	G		19	.421		70.50	25.50		96	116
0190	36" long	G		18	.444		95	27		122	145
0200	1-1/2" diameter x 18" long	G		17	.471		54.50	28.50		83	102
0210	24" long	G		16	.500		64	30.50		94.50	116
0300	L-type, incl. hex nut & washer, 3/4" diameter x 12" long	G		20	.400		19.35	24		43.35	57.50
0310	18" long	G		20	.400		23.50	24		47.50	62
0320	24" long	G		20	.400		28	24		52	66.50
0330	30" long	G		20	.400		34	24		58	73.50
0340	36" long	G		20	.400		38.50	24		62.50	78.50
0350	1" diameter x 12" long	G		19	.421		39	25.50		64.50	81
0360	18" long	G		19	.421		48	25.50		73.50	90.50
0370	24" long	G		19	.421		58	25.50		83.50	102
0380	30" long	G		19	.421		67.50	25.50		93	113
0390	36" long	G		18	.444		77	27		104	125
0400	42" long	G		18	.444		92.50	27		119.50	142
0410	48" long	G		18	.444		103	27		130	153
0420	1-1/4" diameter x 18" long	G		18	.444		70	27		97	117
0430	24" long	G		18	.444		82.50	27		109.50	131
0440	30" long	G		17	.471		95	28.50		123.50	146
0450	36" long	G	↓	17	.471		107	28.50		135.50	160
0460	42" long	G	2 Carp	32	.500		121	30.50		151.50	178
0470	48" long	G		32	.500		137	30.50		167.50	196
0480	54" long	G		31	.516		161	31.50		192.50	224
0490	60" long	G		31	.516		176	31.50		207.50	241
0500	1-1/2" diameter x 18" long	G		33	.485		83	29.50		112.50	135
0510	24" long	G		32	.500		96	30.50		126.50	151
0520	30" long	G		31	.516		108	31.50		139.50	166
0530	36" long	G	↓	30	.533		124	32.50		156.50	184

03 15 Concrete Accessories

03 15 19 – Cast-In Concrete Anchors

03 15 19.10 Anchor Bolts		Crew	Daily Output	Labor-Hours	Unit	Material	2024 Bare Costs Labor	Equipment	Total	Total Incl O&P
0540	42" long	G 2 Carp	30	.533	Set	140	32.50		172.50	202
0550	48" long	G	29	.552		157	33.50		190.50	223
0560	54" long	G	28	.571		191	34.50		225.50	261
0570	60" long	G	28	.571		208	34.50		242.50	280
0580	1-3/4" diameter x 18" long	G	31	.516		114	31.50		145.50	172
0590	24" long	G	30	.533		133	32.50		165.50	194
0600	30" long	G	29	.552		154	33.50		187.50	219
0610	36" long	G	28	.571		175	34.50		209.50	243
0620	42" long	G	27	.593		196	36		232	268
0630	48" long	G	26	.615		215	37.50		252.50	291
0640	54" long	G	26	.615		265	37.50		302.50	345
0650	60" long	G	25	.640		286	39		325	375
0660	2" diameter x 24" long	G	27	.593		166	36		202	236
0670	30" long	G	27	.593		187	36		223	258
0680	36" long	G	26	.615		205	37.50		242.50	280
0690	42" long	G	25	.640		228	39		267	310
0700	48" long	G	24	.667		261	40.50		301.50	345
0710	54" long	G	23	.696		310	42		352	405
0720	60" long	G	23	.696		335	42		377	430
0730	66" long	G	22	.727		355	44		399	455
0740	72" long	G	21	.762		390	46		436	500
1000	4-bolt pattern, including job-built 4-hole template, per set									
1100	J-type, incl. hex nut & washer, 1/2" diameter x 6" long	G 1 Carp	19	.421	Set	14.10	25.50		39.60	53.50
1110	12" long	G	19	.421		16.55	25.50		42.05	56
1120	18" long	G	18	.444		20.50	27		47.50	62.50
1130	3/4" diameter x 8" long	G	17	.471		27	28.50		55.50	71.50
1140	12" long	G	17	.471		32.50	28.50		61	78
1150	18" long	G	17	.471		41.50	28.50		70	87.50
1160	1" diameter x 12" long	G	16	.500		94.50	30.50		125	149
1170	18" long	G	15	.533		113	32.50		145.50	172
1180	24" long	G	15	.533		137	32.50		169.50	199
1190	36" long	G	15	.533		186	32.50		218.50	253
1200	1-1/2" diameter x 18" long	G	13	.615		105	37.50		142.50	170
1210	24" long	G	12	.667		124	40.50		164.50	197
1300	L-type, incl. hex nut & washer, 3/4" diameter x 12" long	G	17	.471		34.50	28.50		63	80
1310	18" long	G	17	.471		43	28.50		71.50	89.50
1320	24" long	G	17	.471		51.50	28.50		80	98.50
1330	30" long	G	16	.500		64	30.50		94.50	116
1340	36" long	G	16	.500		72.50	30.50		103	125
1350	1" diameter x 12" long	G	16	.500		74	30.50		104.50	127
1360	18" long	G	15	.533		91.50	32.50		124	148
1370	24" long	G	15	.533		112	32.50		144.50	171
1380	30" long	G	15	.533		131	32.50		163.50	192
1390	36" long	G	15	.533		149	32.50		181.50	212
1400	42" long	G	14	.571		181	34.50		215.50	250
1410	48" long	G	14	.571		202	34.50		236.50	273
1420	1-1/4" diameter x 18" long	G	14	.571		136	34.50		170.50	201
1430	24" long	G	14	.571		161	34.50		195.50	228
1440	30" long	G	13	.615		185	37.50		222.50	259
1450	36" long	G	13	.615		210	37.50		247.50	286
1460	42" long	G 2 Carp	25	.640		237	39		276	320
1470	48" long	G	24	.667		270	40.50		310.50	355
1480	54" long	G	23	.696		315	42		357	415

03 15 Concrete Accessories

03 15 19 – Cast-In Concrete Anchors

03 15 19.10 Anchor Bolts

			Crew	Daily Output	Labor-Hours	Unit	Material	2024 Bare Costs Labor	Equipment	Total	Total Incl O&P
1490	60" long	G	2 Carp	23	.696	Set	350	42		392	450
1500	1-1/2" diameter x 18" long	G		25	.640		162	39		201	236
1510	24" long	G		24	.667		188	40.50		228.50	267
1520	30" long	G		23	.696		212	42		254	296
1530	36" long	G		22	.727		243	44		287	330
1540	42" long	G		22	.727		277	44		321	370
1550	48" long	G		21	.762		310	46		356	410
1560	54" long	G		20	.800		375	48.50		423.50	485
1570	60" long	G		20	.800		415	48.50		463.50	525
1580	1-3/4" diameter x 18" long	G		22	.727		223	44		267	310
1590	24" long	G		21	.762		261	46		307	355
1600	30" long	G		21	.762		305	46		351	405
1610	36" long	G		20	.800		345	48.50		393.50	450
1620	42" long	G		19	.842		385	51		436	500
1630	48" long	G		18	.889		425	54		479	550
1640	54" long	G		18	.889		525	54		579	660
1650	60" long	G		17	.941		570	57		627	710
1660	2" diameter x 24" long	G		19	.842		330	51		381	435
1670	30" long	G		18	.889		370	54		424	485
1680	36" long	G		18	.889		405	54		459	525
1690	42" long	G		17	.941		450	57		507	580
1700	48" long	G		16	1		520	60.50		580.50	660
1710	54" long	G		15	1.067		615	64.50		679.50	770
1720	60" long	G		15	1.067		660	64.50		724.50	825
1730	66" long	G		14	1.143		710	69		779	880
1740	72" long	G		14	1.143		775	69		844	955
1990	For galvanized, add					Ea.	75%				

03 15 19.45 Machinery Anchors

			Crew	Daily Output	Labor-Hours	Unit	Material	2024 Bare Costs Labor	Equipment	Total	Total Incl O&P
0010	**MACHINERY ANCHORS**, heavy duty, incl. sleeve, floating base nut,										
0020	lower stud & coupling nut, fiber plug, connecting stud, washer & nut.										
0030	For flush mounted embedment in poured concrete heavy equip. pads.										
0200	Stud & bolt, 1/2" diameter	G	E-16	40	.400	Ea.	95	27	4.10	126.10	151
0300	5/8" diameter	G		35	.457		111	31	4.68	146.68	175
0500	3/4" diameter	G		30	.533		134	36.50	5.45	175.95	210
0600	7/8" diameter	G		25	.640		151	43.50	6.55	201.05	240
0800	1" diameter	G		20	.800		164	54.50	8.20	226.70	274
0900	1-1/4" diameter	G		15	1.067		219	72.50	10.90	302.40	365

03 21 Reinforcement Bars

03 21 11 – Plain Steel Reinforcement Bars

03 21 11.60 Reinforcing In Place

			Crew	Daily Output	Labor-Hours	Unit	Material	2024 Bare Costs Labor	Equipment	Total	Total Incl O&P
0010	**REINFORCING IN PLACE**, 50-60 ton lots, A615 Grade 60										
0020	Includes labor, but not material cost, to install accessories										
0030	Made from recycled materials										
0502	Footings, #4 to #7	G	4 Rodm	4200	.008	Lb.	.69	.51		1.20	1.52
0552	#8 to #18	G		7200	.004		.69	.30		.99	1.20
0602	Slab on grade, #3 to #7	G		4200	.008		.69	.51		1.20	1.52
0900	For other than 50-60 ton lots										
1000	Under 10 ton job, #3 to #7, add						25%	10%			
1010	#8 to #18, add						20%	10%			
1050	10-50 ton job, #3 to #7, add						10%				

03 21 Reinforcement Bars

03 21 11 – Plain Steel Reinforcement Bars

03 21 11.60 Reinforcing In Place		Crew	Daily Output	Labor-Hours	Unit	Material	2024 Bare Costs Labor	Equipment	Total	Total Incl O&P
1060	#8 to #18, add					5%				
1100	60-100 ton job, #3 to #7, deduct					5%				
1110	#8 to #18, deduct					10%				
1150	Over 100 ton job, #3 to #7, deduct					10%				
1160	#8 to #18, deduct					15%				

03 22 Fabric and Grid Reinforcing

03 22 11 – Plain Welded Wire Fabric Reinforcing

03 22 11.10 Plain Welded Wire Fabric

0010	**PLAIN WELDED WIRE FABRIC** ASTM A185									
0020	Includes labor, but not material cost, to install accessories									
0030	Made from recycled materials									
0050	Sheets									
0100	6 x 6 - W1.4 x W1.4 (10 x 10) 21 lb./C.S.F.	G	2 Rodm	35	.457	C.S.F.	34.50	30.50		65	83.50

03 22 13 – Galvanized Welded Wire Fabric Reinforcing

03 22 13.10 Galvanized Welded Wire Fabric

0010	**GALVANIZED WELDED WIRE FABRIC**									
0100	Add to plain welded wire pricing for galvanized welded wire					Lb.	.27			.27	.30

03 22 16 – Epoxy-Coated Welded Wire Fabric Reinforcing

03 22 16.10 Epoxy-Coated Welded Wire Fabric

0010	**EPOXY-COATED WELDED WIRE FABRIC**									
0100	Add to plain welded wire pricing for epoxy-coated welded wire					Lb.	.54			.54	.59

03 30 Cast-In-Place Concrete

03 30 53 – Miscellaneous Cast-In-Place Concrete

03 30 53.40 Concrete In Place

		Crew	Daily Output	Labor-Hours	Unit	Material	Labor	Equipment	Total	Total Incl O&P
0010	**CONCRETE IN PLACE**									
0020	Including forms (4 uses), Grade 60 rebar, concrete (Portland cement									
0050	Type I), placement and finishing unless otherwise indicated									
3540	Equipment pad (3000 psi), 3' x 3' x 6" thick	C-14H	45	1.067	Ea.	79	63.50	.69	143.19	181
3550	4' x 4' x 6" thick		30	1.600		118	95	1.04	214.04	272
3560	5' x 5' x 8" thick		18	2.667		192	158	1.73	351.73	445
3570	6' x 6' x 8" thick		14	3.429		261	204	2.23	467.23	590
3580	8' x 8' x 10" thick		8	6		595	355	3.90	953.90	1,175
3590	10' x 10' x 12" thick		5	9.600		1,025	570	6.25	1,601.25	1,975
3800	Footings (3000 psi), spread under 1 C.Y.	C-14C	28	4	C.Y.	283	232	1.12	516.12	655
3825	1 C.Y. to 5 C.Y.		43	2.605		350	151	.73	501.73	610
3850	Over 5 C.Y.		75	1.493		330	86.50	.42	416.92	495
3900	Footings, strip (3000 psi), 18" x 9", unreinforced	C-14L	40	2.400		230	136	.79	366.79	455
3920	18" x 9", reinforced	C-14C	35	3.200		263	186	.90	449.90	565
3925	20" x 10", unreinforced	C-14L	45	2.133		223	121	.70	344.70	425
3930	20" x 10", reinforced	C-14C	40	2.800		250	163	.78	413.78	515
3935	24" x 12", unreinforced	C-14L	55	1.745		219	98.50	.58	318.08	390
3940	24" x 12", reinforced	C-14C	48	2.333		247	135	.65	382.65	475
3945	36" x 12", unreinforced	C-14L	70	1.371		211	77.50	.45	288.95	345
3950	36" x 12", reinforced	C-14C	60	1.867		236	108	.52	344.52	420
4000	Foundation mat (3000 psi), under 10 C.Y.	"	38.67	2.896		335	168	.81	503.81	615
4650	Slab on grade (3500 psi), not including finish, 4" thick	C-14E	60.75	1.449		231	86.50	.51	318.01	385

03 30 Cast-In-Place Concrete

03 30 53 – Miscellaneous Cast-In-Place Concrete

03 30 53.40 Concrete In Place

		Crew	Daily Output	Labor-Hours	Unit	Material	2024 Bare Costs Labor	Equipment	Total	Total Incl O&P
4700	6" thick	C-14E	92	.957	C.Y.	219	57	.33	276.33	325
4701	Thickened slab edge (3500 psi), for slab on grade poured									
4702	monolithically with slab; depth is in addition to slab thickness;									
4703	formed vertical outside edge, earthen bottom and inside slope									
4705	8" deep x 8" wide bottom, unreinforced	C-14L	2190	.044	L.F.	6.65	2.48	.01	9.14	11.05
4710	8" x 8", reinforced	C-14C	1670	.067		9.90	3.89	.02	13.81	16.65
4715	12" deep x 12" wide bottom, unreinforced	C-14L	1800	.053		13.25	3.02	.02	16.29	19.10
4720	12" x 12", reinforced	C-14C	1310	.086		19.15	4.96	.02	24.13	28.50
4725	16" deep x 16" wide bottom, unreinforced	C-14L	1440	.067		22	3.77	.02	25.79	29.50
4730	16" x 16", reinforced	C-14C	1120	.100		29	5.80	.03	34.83	40.50
4735	20" deep x 20" wide bottom, unreinforced	C-14L	1150	.083		33	4.72	.03	37.75	43.50
4740	20" x 20", reinforced	C-14C	920	.122		42	7.05	.03	49.08	56.50
4745	24" deep x 24" wide bottom, unreinforced	C-14L	930	.103		46.50	5.85	.03	52.38	59.50
4750	24" x 24", reinforced	C-14C	740	.151		58	8.80	.04	66.84	77

03 31 Structural Concrete

03 31 13 – Heavyweight Structural Concrete

03 31 13.35 Heavyweight Concrete, Ready Mix

		Crew	Daily Output	Labor-Hours	Unit	Material	2024 Bare Costs Labor	Equipment	Total	Total Incl O&P
0010	**HEAVYWEIGHT CONCRETE, READY MIX**, delivered									
0012	Includes local aggregate, sand, Portland cement (Type I) and water									
0015	Excludes all additives and treatments									
0020	2000 psi				C.Y.	178			178	196
0100	2500 psi					181			181	199
0150	3000 psi					184			184	202
0200	3500 psi					188			188	206
0300	4000 psi					191			191	210
1000	For high early strength (Portland cement Type III), add					10%				
1300	For winter concrete (hot water), add					8.50			8.50	9.35
1410	For mid-range water reducer, add					6.60			6.60	7.25
1420	For high-range water reducer/superplasticizer, add					8.50			8.50	9.35
1430	For retarder, add					5.10			5.10	5.60
1440	For non-Chloride accelerator, add					9.50			9.50	10.45
1450	For Chloride accelerator, per 1%, add					5			5	5.50
1460	For fiber reinforcing, synthetic (1 lb./C.Y.), add					11.25			11.25	12.40
1500	For Saturday delivery, add					15			15	16.50
1510	For truck holding/waiting time past 1st hour per load, add				Hr.	154			154	169
1520	For short load (less than 4 C.Y.), add per load				Ea.	135			135	149
2000	For all lightweight aggregate, add				C.Y.	45%				

03 31 13.70 Placing Concrete

		Crew	Daily Output	Labor-Hours	Unit	Material	2024 Bare Costs Labor	Equipment	Total	Total Incl O&P
0010	**PLACING CONCRETE**									
0020	Includes labor and equipment to place, level (strike off) and consolidate									
1200	Duct bank, direct chute	C-6	155	.310	C.Y.		15.70	.40	16.10	23.50
1900	Footings, continuous, shallow, direct chute	"	120	.400			20.50	.52	21.02	30.50
1950	Pumped	C-20	150	.427			22.50	6.15	28.65	40
2000	With crane and bucket	C-7	90	.800			42.50	29.50	72	95
2100	Footings, continuous, deep, direct chute	C-6	140	.343			17.35	.45	17.80	26
2150	Pumped	C-20	160	.400			21	5.80	26.80	37.50
2200	With crane and bucket	C-7	110	.655			34.50	24	58.50	77.50
2400	Footings, spread, under 1 C.Y., direct chute	C-6	55	.873			44	1.13	45.13	66.50
2450	Pumped	C-20	65	.985			51.50	14.20	65.70	91.50
2500	With crane and bucket	C-7	45	1.600			84.50	59.50	144	190

03 31 Structural Concrete

03 31 13 – Heavyweight Structural Concrete

03 31 13.70 Placing Concrete

		Crew	Daily Output	Labor-Hours	Unit	Material	2024 Bare Costs Labor	2024 Bare Costs Equipment	Total	Total Incl O&P
2600	Over 5 C.Y., direct chute	C-6	120	.400	C.Y.		20.50	.52	21.02	30.50
2650	Pumped	C-20	150	.427			22.50	6.15	28.65	40
2700	With crane and bucket	C-7	100	.720			38	26.50	64.50	86
2900	Foundation mats, over 20 C.Y., direct chute	C-6	350	.137			6.95	.18	7.13	10.45
2950	Pumped	C-20	400	.160			8.35	2.31	10.66	14.90
3000	With crane and bucket	C-7	300	.240			12.70	8.90	21.60	28.50

03 35 Concrete Finishing

03 35 13 – High-Tolerance Concrete Floor Finishing

03 35 13.30 Finishing Floors, High Tolerance

		Crew	Daily Output	Labor-Hours	Unit	Material	2024 Bare Costs Labor	2024 Bare Costs Equipment	Total	Total Incl O&P
0010	**FINISHING FLOORS, HIGH TOLERANCE**									
0012	Finishing of fresh concrete flatwork requires that concrete									
0013	first be placed, struck off & consolidated									
0015	Basic finishing for various unspecified flatwork									
0100	Bull float only	C-10	4000	.006	S.F.		.33		.33	.48
0125	Bull float & manual float		2000	.012			.65		.65	.95
0150	Bull float, manual float & broom finish, w/edging & joints		1850	.013			.70		.70	1.03
0200	Bull float, manual float & manual steel trowel		1265	.019			1.03		1.03	1.51
0210	For specified Random Access Floors in ACI Classes 1, 2, 3 and 4 to achieve									
0215	Composite Overall Floor Flatness and Levelness values up to FF35/FL25									
0250	Bull float, machine float & machine trowel (walk-behind)	C-10C	1715	.014	S.F.		.76	.07	.83	1.19
0300	Power screed, bull float, machine float & trowel (walk-behind)	C-10D	2400	.010			.54	.09	.63	.89
0350	Power screed, bull float, machine float & trowel (ride-on)	C-10E	4000	.006			.33	.08	.41	.57
0352	For specified Random Access Floors in ACI Classes 5, 6, 7 and 8 to achieve									
0354	Composite Overall Floor Flatness and Levelness values up to FF50/FL50									
0356	Add for two-dimensional restraightening after power float	C-10	6000	.004	S.F.		.22		.22	.32
0358	For specified Random or Defined Access Floors in ACI Class 9 to achieve									
0360	Composite Overall Floor Flatness and Levelness values up to FF100/FL100									
0362	Add for two-dimensional restraightening after bull float & power float	C-10	3000	.008	S.F.		.43		.43	.64
0364	For specified Superflat Defined Access Floors in ACI Class 9 to achieve									
0366	Minimum Floor Flatness and Levelness values of FF100/FL100									
0368	Add for 2-dim'l restraightening after bull float, power float, power trowel	C-10	2000	.012	S.F.		.65		.65	.95

03 63 Epoxy Grouting

03 63 05 – Grouting of Dowels and Fasteners

03 63 05.10 Epoxy Only

		Crew	Daily Output	Labor-Hours	Unit	Material	2024 Bare Costs Labor	2024 Bare Costs Equipment	Total	Total Incl O&P
0010	**EPOXY ONLY**									
1500	Chemical anchoring, epoxy cartridge, excludes layout, drilling, fastener									
1530	For fastener 3/4" diam. x 6" embedment	2 Skwk	72	.222	Ea.	6.05	14.10		20.15	27.50
1535	1" diam. x 8" embedment		66	.242		9.05	15.40		24.45	33
1540	1-1/4" diam. x 10" embedment		60	.267		18.15	16.95		35.10	45.50
1545	1-3/4" diam. x 12" embedment		54	.296		30	18.80		48.80	61.50
1550	14" embedment		48	.333		36.50	21		57.50	71.50
1555	2" diam. x 12" embedment		42	.381		48.50	24		72.50	89
1560	18" embedment		32	.500		60.50	32		92.50	114

03 82 Concrete Boring

03 82 13 – Concrete Core Drilling

03 82 13.10 Core Drilling

		Crew	Daily Output	Labor-Hours	Unit	Material	2024 Bare Costs Labor	2024 Bare Costs Equipment	Total	Total Incl O&P
0010	**CORE DRILLING**									
0015	Includes bit cost, layout and set-up time									
0020	Reinforced concrete slab, up to 6" thick									
0100	1" diameter core	B-89A	17	.941	Ea.	.25	53	9.20	62.45	89.50
0150	For each additional inch of slab thickness in same hole, add		1440	.011		.04	.63	.11	.78	1.10
0200	2" diameter core		16.50	.970		.34	54.50	9.45	64.29	92
0250	For each additional inch of slab thickness in same hole, add		1080	.015		.06	.83	.14	1.03	1.46
0300	3" diameter core		16	1		.50	56.50	9.75	66.75	95.50
0350	For each additional inch of slab thickness in same hole, add		720	.022		.08	1.25	.22	1.55	2.19
0500	4" diameter core		15	1.067		.65	60	10.40	71.05	102
0550	For each additional inch of slab thickness in same hole, add		480	.033		.11	1.88	.33	2.32	3.27
0700	6" diameter core		14	1.143		.91	64.50	11.15	76.56	109
0750	For each additional inch of slab thickness in same hole, add		360	.044		.15	2.50	.43	3.08	4.37
0900	8" diameter core		13	1.231		1.49	69	12	82.49	118
0950	For each additional inch of slab thickness in same hole, add		288	.056		.25	3.13	.54	3.92	5.50
1100	10" diameter core		12	1.333		1.62	75	13	89.62	128
1150	For each additional inch of slab thickness in same hole, add		240	.067		.27	3.75	.65	4.67	6.60
1300	12" diameter core		11	1.455		2.09	82	14.20	98.29	140
1350	For each additional inch of slab thickness in same hole, add		206	.078		.35	4.37	.76	5.48	7.70
1500	14" diameter core		10	1.600		2.58	90	15.60	108.18	154
1550	For each additional inch of slab thickness in same hole, add		180	.089		.43	5	.87	6.30	8.85
1700	18" diameter core		9	1.778		2.98	100	17.35	120.33	171
1750	For each additional inch of slab thickness in same hole, add		144	.111		.50	6.25	1.08	7.83	11.05
1754	24" diameter core		8	2		5.35	113	19.50	137.85	195
1756	For each additional inch of slab thickness in same hole, add		120	.133		.89	7.50	1.30	9.69	13.55
1760	For horizontal holes, add to above						20%	20%		
1770	Prestressed hollow core plank, 8" thick									
1780	1" diameter core	B-89A	17.50	.914	Ea.	.33	51.50	8.90	60.73	86.50
1790	For each additional inch of plank thickness in same hole, add		3840	.004		.04	.23	.04	.31	.44
1794	2" diameter core		17.25	.928		.46	52	9.05	61.51	88
1796	For each additional inch of plank thickness in same hole, add		2880	.006		.06	.31	.05	.42	.59
1800	3" diameter core		17	.941		.67	53	9.20	62.87	90
1810	For each additional inch of plank thickness in same hole, add		1920	.008		.08	.47	.08	.63	.88
1820	4" diameter core		16.50	.970		.86	54.50	9.45	64.81	92.50
1830	For each additional inch of plank thickness in same hole, add		1280	.013		.11	.70	.12	.93	1.30
1840	6" diameter core		15.50	1.032		1.21	58	10.05	69.26	99
1850	For each additional inch of plank thickness in same hole, add		960	.017		.15	.94	.16	1.25	1.75
1860	8" diameter core		15	1.067		1.98	60	10.40	72.38	103
1870	For each additional inch of plank thickness in same hole, add		768	.021		.25	1.17	.20	1.62	2.24
1880	10" diameter core		14	1.143		2.16	64.50	11.15	77.81	111
1890	For each additional inch of plank thickness in same hole, add		640	.025		.27	1.41	.24	1.92	2.66
1900	12" diameter core		13.50	1.185		2.79	66.50	11.55	80.84	115
1910	For each additional inch of plank thickness in same hole, add		548	.029		.35	1.64	.28	2.27	3.14

03 82 16 – Concrete Drilling

03 82 16.10 Concrete Impact Drilling

		Crew	Daily Output	Labor-Hours	Unit	Material	2024 Bare Costs Labor	2024 Bare Costs Equipment	Total	Total Incl O&P
0010	**CONCRETE IMPACT DRILLING**									
0020	Includes bit cost, layout and set-up time, no anchors									
0050	Up to 4" deep in concrete/brick floors/walls									
0100	Holes, 1/4" diameter	1 Carp	75	.107	Ea.	.04	6.45		6.49	9.60
0150	For each additional inch of depth in same hole, add		430	.019		.01	1.13		1.14	1.68
0200	3/8" diameter		63	.127		.04	7.70		7.74	11.45
0250	For each additional inch of depth in same hole, add		340	.024		.01	1.42		1.43	2.12

03 82 Concrete Boring

03 82 16 – Concrete Drilling

03 82 16.10 Concrete Impact Drilling		Crew	Daily Output	Labor-Hours	Unit	Material	2024 Bare Costs Labor	Equipment	Total	Total Incl O&P
0300	1/2" diameter	1 Carp	50	.160	Ea.	.04	9.70		9.74	14.40
0350	For each additional inch of depth in same hole, add		250	.032		.01	1.94		1.95	2.88
0400	5/8" diameter		48	.167		.08	10.10		10.18	15.05
0450	For each additional inch of depth in same hole, add		240	.033		.02	2.02		2.04	3.01
0500	3/4" diameter		45	.178		.09	10.75		10.84	16.05
0550	For each additional inch of depth in same hole, add		220	.036		.02	2.20		2.22	3.28
0600	7/8" diameter		43	.186		.10	11.25		11.35	16.80
0650	For each additional inch of depth in same hole, add		210	.038		.03	2.31		2.34	3.45
0700	1" diameter		40	.200		.15	12.10		12.25	18.10
0750	For each additional inch of depth in same hole, add		190	.042		.04	2.55		2.59	3.81
0800	1-1/4" diameter		38	.211		.28	12.75		13.03	19.15
0850	For each additional inch of depth in same hole, add		180	.044		.07	2.69		2.76	4.06
0900	1-1/2" diameter		35	.229		.43	13.85		14.28	21
0950	For each additional inch of depth in same hole, add	▼	165	.048	▼	.11	2.94		3.05	4.47
1000	For ceiling installations, add						40%			

Estimating Tips

05 05 00 Common Work Results for Metals

- Nuts, bolts, washers, connection angles, and plates can add a significant amount to both the tonnage of a structural steel job and the estimated cost. As a rule of thumb, add 10% to the total weight to account for these accessories.
- Type 2 steel construction, commonly referred to as "simple construction," consists generally of field-bolted connections with lateral bracing supplied by other elements of the building, such as masonry walls or x-bracing. The estimator should be aware, however, that shop connections may be accomplished by welding or bolting. The method may be particular to the fabrication shop and may have an impact on the estimated cost.

05 10 00 Structural Steel

- Steel items can be obtained from two sources: a fabrication shop or a metals service center. Fabrication shops can fabricate items under more controlled conditions than crews in the field can. They are also more efficient and can produce items more economically. Metal service centers serve as a source of long mill shapes to both fabrication shops and contractors.
- Most line items in this structural steel subdivision, and most items in 05 50 00 Metal Fabrications, are indicated as being shop fabricated. The bare material cost for these shop fabricated items is the "Invoice Cost" from the shop and includes the mill base price of steel plus mill extras, transportation to the shop, shop drawings and detailing where warranted, shop fabrication and handling, sandblasting and a shop coat of primer paint, all necessary structural bolts, and delivery to the job site. The bare labor cost and bare equipment cost for these shop fabricated items are for field installation or erection.
- Line items in Subdivision 05 12 23.40 Lightweight Framing, and other items scattered in Division 5, are indicated as being field fabricated. The bare material cost for these field fabricated items is the "Invoice Cost" from the metals service center and includes the mill base price of steel plus mill extras, transportation to the metals service center, material handling, and delivery of long lengths of mill shapes to the job site. Material costs for structural bolts and welding rods should be added to the estimate. The bare labor cost and bare equipment cost for these items are for both field fabrication and field installation or erection, and include time for cutting, welding, and drilling in the fabricated metal items. Drilling into concrete and fasteners to fasten field fabricated items to other work is not included and should be added to the estimate.

05 20 00 Steel Joist Framing

- In any given project the total weight of open web steel joists is determined by the loads to be supported and the design. However, economies can be realized in minimizing the amount of labor used to place the joists. This is done by maximizing the joist spacing and therefore minimizing the number of joists required to be installed on the job. Certain spacings and locations may be required by the design, but in other cases maximizing the spacing and keeping it as uniform as possible will keep the costs down.

05 30 00 Steel Decking

- The takeoff and estimating of a metal deck involve more than the area of the floor or roof and the type of deck specified or shown on the drawings. Many different sizes and types of openings may exist. Small openings for individual pipes or conduits may be drilled after the floor/roof is installed, but larger openings may require special deck lengths as well as reinforcing or structural support. The estimator should determine who will be supplying this reinforcing. Additionally, some deck terminations are part of the deck package, such as screed angles and pour stops, and others will be part of the steel contract, such as angles attached to structural members and cast-in-place angles and plates. The estimator must ensure that all pieces are accounted for in the complete estimate.

05 50 00 Metal Fabrications

- The most economical steel stairs are those that use common materials, standard details, and most importantly, a uniform and relatively simple method of field assembly. Commonly available A36/A992 channels and plates are very good choices for the main stringers of the stairs, as are angles and tees for the carrier members. Risers and treads are usually made by specialty shops, and it is most economical to use a typical detail in as many places as possible. The stairs should be pre-assembled and shipped directly to the site. The field connections should be simple and straightforward enough to be accomplished efficiently, and with minimum equipment and labor.

Reference Numbers

Reference numbers are shown at the beginning of some major classifications. These numbers refer to related items in the Reference Section. The reference information may be an estimating procedure, an alternate pricing method, or technical information.

Note: Not all subdivisions listed here necessarily appear. ■

Division 5 — Metals

Same Data. Simplified.

Enjoy the convenience and efficiency of accessing your costs anywhere:

- **Skip the multiplier** by setting your location
- **Quickly search,** edit, favorite and share costs
- **Stay on top of price changes** with automatic updates

Discover more at rsmeans.com/online

No part of this cost data may be reproduced, stored in a retrieval system, or transmitted in any form or by any means without prior written permission of Gordian.

05 05 Common Work Results for Metals

05 05 19 – Post-Installed Concrete Anchors

05 05 19.10 Chemical Anchors		Crew	Daily Output	Labor-Hours	Unit	Material	2024 Bare Costs Labor	Equipment	Total	Total Incl O&P
0010	**CHEMICAL ANCHORS**									
0020	Includes layout & drilling									
1430	Chemical anchor, w/rod & epoxy cartridge, 3/4" diameter x 9-1/2" long	B-89A	27	.593	Ea.	13.75	33.50	5.80	53.05	71
1435	1" diameter x 11-3/4" long		24	.667		22	37.50	6.50	66	87
1440	1-1/4" diameter x 14" long		21	.762		44.50	43	7.45	94.95	121
1445	1-3/4" diameter x 15" long		20	.800		72	45	7.80	124.80	155
1450	18" long		17	.941		86.50	53	9.20	148.70	185
1455	2" diameter x 18" long		16	1		125	56.50	9.75	191.25	233
1460	24" long		15	1.067		163	60	10.40	233.40	281

05 05 19.20 Expansion Anchors			Crew	Daily Output	Labor-Hours	Unit	Material	2024 Bare Costs Labor	Equipment	Total	Total Incl O&P
0010	**EXPANSION ANCHORS**										
0100	Anchors for concrete, brick or stone, no layout and drilling										
0200	Expansion shields, zinc, 1/4" diameter, 1-5/16" long, single	G	1 Carp	90	.089	Ea.	.64	5.40		6.04	8.65
0300	1-3/8" long, double	G		85	.094		.84	5.70		6.54	9.35
0400	3/8" diameter, 1-1/2" long, single	G		85	.094		1.02	5.70		6.72	9.55
0500	2" long, double	G		80	.100		1.79	6.05		7.84	10.90
0600	1/2" diameter, 2-1/16" long, single	G		80	.100		2.55	6.05		8.60	11.75
0700	2-1/2" long, double	G		75	.107		2.22	6.45		8.67	12
0800	5/8" diameter, 2-5/8" long, single	G		75	.107		2.86	6.45		9.31	12.70
0900	2-3/4" long, double	G		70	.114		4.02	6.90		10.92	14.65
1000	3/4" diameter, 2-3/4" long, single	G		70	.114		6.60	6.90		13.50	17.50
1100	3-15/16" long, double	G		65	.123		6.95	7.45		14.40	18.70
2100	Hollow wall anchors for gypsum wall board, plaster or tile										
2300	1/8" diameter, short	G	1 Carp	160	.050	Ea.	.42	3.03		3.45	4.94
2400	Long	G		150	.053		.36	3.23		3.59	5.20
2500	3/16" diameter, short	G		150	.053		.83	3.23		4.06	5.70
2600	Long	G		140	.057		.94	3.46		4.40	6.15
2700	1/4" diameter, short	G		140	.057		.90	3.46		4.36	6.10
2800	Long	G		130	.062		.94	3.73		4.67	6.55
3000	Toggle bolts, bright steel, 1/8" diameter, 2" long	G		85	.094		.30	5.70		6	8.80
3100	4" long	G		80	.100		.35	6.05		6.40	9.35
3200	3/16" diameter, 3" long	G		80	.100		.39	6.05		6.44	9.40
3300	6" long	G		75	.107		.56	6.45		7.01	10.15
3400	1/4" diameter, 3" long	G		75	.107		.46	6.45		6.91	10.05
3500	6" long	G		70	.114		.68	6.90		7.58	11
3600	3/8" diameter, 3" long	G		70	.114		1.16	6.90		8.06	11.55
3700	6" long	G		60	.133		1.89	8.05		9.94	14.05
3800	1/2" diameter, 4" long	G		60	.133		2.66	8.05		10.71	14.90
3900	6" long	G		50	.160		3.31	9.70		13.01	18
4000	Nailing anchors										
4100	Nylon nailing anchor, 1/4" diameter, 1" long		1 Carp	3.20	2.500	C	16.90	151		167.90	243
4200	1-1/2" long			2.80	2.857		19.40	173		192.40	278
4300	2" long			2.40	3.333		24	202		226	325
4400	Metal nailing anchor, 1/4" diameter, 1" long	G		3.20	2.500		15.10	151		166.10	241
4500	1-1/2" long	G		2.80	2.857		19.30	173		192.30	278
4600	2" long	G		2.40	3.333		23	202		225	325
5000	Screw anchors for concrete, masonry,										
5100	stone & tile, no layout or drilling included										
5700	Lag screw shields, 1/4" diameter, short	G	1 Carp	90	.089	Ea.	.34	5.40		5.74	8.30
5800	Long	G		85	.094		.45	5.70		6.15	8.95
5900	3/8" diameter, short	G		85	.094		.76	5.70		6.46	9.30
6000	Long	G		80	.100		1.05	6.05		7.10	10.10

05 05 Common Work Results for Metals

05 05 19 – Post-Installed Concrete Anchors

05 05 19.20 Expansion Anchors

		Crew	Daily Output	Labor-Hours	Unit	Material	2024 Bare Costs Labor	Equipment	Total	Total Incl O&P
6100	1/2" diameter, short G	1 Carp	80	.100	Ea.	.94	6.05		6.99	10
6200	Long G		75	.107		1.45	6.45		7.90	11.15
6300	5/8" diameter, short G		70	.114		1.40	6.90		8.30	11.80
6400	Long G		65	.123		2.50	7.45		9.95	13.80
6600	Lead, #6 & #8, 3/4" long G		260	.031		.29	1.86		2.15	3.08
6700	#10 - #14, 1-1/2" long G		200	.040		.60	2.42		3.02	4.25
6800	#16 & #18, 1-1/2" long G		160	.050		.89	3.03		3.92	5.45
6900	Plastic, #6 & #8, 3/4" long		260	.031		.03	1.86		1.89	2.79
7000	#8 & #10, 7/8" long		240	.033		.03	2.02		2.05	3.02
7100	#10 & #12, 1" long		220	.036		.06	2.20		2.26	3.33
7200	#14 & #16, 1-1/2" long		160	.050		.09	3.03		3.12	4.58
8000	Wedge anchors, not including layout or drilling									
8050	Carbon steel, 1/4" diameter, 1-3/4" long G	1 Carp	150	.053	Ea.	.33	3.23		3.56	5.15
8100	3-1/4" long G		140	.057		.43	3.46		3.89	5.60
8150	3/8" diameter, 2-1/4" long G		145	.055		.45	3.34		3.79	5.45
8200	5" long G		140	.057		.79	3.46		4.25	5.95
8250	1/2" diameter, 2-3/4" long G		140	.057		1	3.46		4.46	6.20
8300	7" long G		125	.064		1.71	3.88		5.59	7.65
8350	5/8" diameter, 3-1/2" long G		130	.062		1.87	3.73		5.60	7.55
8400	8-1/2" long G		115	.070		3.98	4.21		8.19	10.65
8450	3/4" diameter, 4-1/4" long G		115	.070		3.71	4.21		7.92	10.35
8500	10" long G		95	.084		8.45	5.10		13.55	16.80
8550	1" diameter, 6" long G		100	.080		9.10	4.84		13.94	17.15
8575	9" long G		85	.094		11.80	5.70		17.50	21.50
8600	12" long G		75	.107		12.75	6.45		19.20	23.50
8650	1-1/4" diameter, 9" long G		70	.114		47.50	6.90		54.40	62.50
8700	12" long G		60	.133		60.50	8.05		68.55	78.50
8750	For type 303 stainless steel, add					350%				
8800	For type 316 stainless steel, add					450%				
8950	Self-drilling concrete screw, hex washer head, 3/16" diam. x 1-3/4" long G	1 Carp	300	.027	Ea.	.25	1.61		1.86	2.67
8960	2-1/4" long G		250	.032		.27	1.94		2.21	3.17
8970	Phillips flat head, 3/16" diam. x 1-3/4" long G		300	.027		.20	1.61		1.81	2.61
8980	2-1/4" long G		250	.032		.21	1.94		2.15	3.10

05 05 21 – Fastening Methods for Metal

05 05 21.15 Drilling Steel

		Crew	Daily Output	Labor-Hours	Unit	Material	2024 Bare Costs Labor	Equipment	Total	Total Incl O&P
0010	**DRILLING STEEL**									
1910	Drilling & layout for steel, up to 1/4" deep, no anchor									
1920	Holes, 1/4" diameter	1 Sswk	112	.071	Ea.	.06	4.79		4.85	7.40
1925	For each additional 1/4" depth, add		336	.024		.06	1.60		1.66	2.51
1930	3/8" diameter		104	.077		.06	5.15		5.21	7.95
1935	For each additional 1/4" depth, add		312	.026		.06	1.72		1.78	2.71
1940	1/2" diameter		96	.083		.08	5.60		5.68	8.65
1945	For each additional 1/4" depth, add		288	.028		.08	1.86		1.94	2.94
1950	5/8" diameter		88	.091		.12	6.10		6.22	9.50
1955	For each additional 1/4" depth, add		264	.030		.12	2.03		2.15	3.25
1960	3/4" diameter		80	.100		.13	6.70		6.83	10.45
1965	For each additional 1/4" depth, add		240	.033		.13	2.24		2.37	3.57
1970	7/8" diameter		72	.111		.15	7.45		7.60	11.55
1975	For each additional 1/4" depth, add		216	.037		.15	2.48		2.63	3.97
1980	1" diameter		64	.125		.22	8.40		8.62	13.10
1985	For each additional 1/4" depth, add		192	.042		.22	2.79		3.01	4.52
1990	For drilling up, add						40%			

05 05 Common Work Results for Metals

05 05 21 – Fastening Methods for Metal

05 05 21.90 Welding Steel		Crew	Daily Output	Labor-Hours	Unit	Material	2024 Bare Costs Labor	Equipment	Total	Total Incl O&P
0010	**WELDING STEEL**, Structural	R050521-20								
0020	Field welding, 1/8" E6011, cost per welder, no operating engineer	E-14	8	1	Hr.	8.45	69	20.50	97.95	138
0200	With 1/2 operating engineer	E-13	8	1.500		8.45	100	20.50	128.95	184
0300	With 1 operating engineer	E-12	8	2	↓	8.45	131	20.50	159.95	230
0500	With no operating engineer, 2# weld rod per ton	E-14	8	1	Ton	8.45	69	20.50	97.95	138
0600	8# E6011 per ton	"	2	4		33.50	276	82	391.50	550
0800	With one operating engineer per welder, 2# E6011 per ton	E-12	8	2		8.45	131	20.50	159.95	230
0900	8# E6011 per ton	"	2	8	↓	33.50	525	82	640.50	915
1200	Continuous fillet, down welding									
1300	Single pass, 1/8" thick, 0.1#/L.F.	E-14	150	.053	L.F.	.42	3.68	1.09	5.19	7.30
1400	3/16" thick, 0.2#/L.F.		75	.107		.84	7.35	2.18	10.37	14.65
1500	1/4" thick, 0.3#/L.F.		50	.160		1.27	11.05	3.28	15.60	22
1610	5/16" thick, 0.4#/L.F.		38	.211		1.69	14.55	4.31	20.55	29
1800	3 passes, 3/8" thick, 0.5#/L.F.		30	.267		2.11	18.40	5.45	25.96	36.50
2010	4 passes, 1/2" thick, 0.7#/L.F.		22	.364		2.95	25	7.45	35.40	50
2200	5 to 6 passes, 3/4" thick, 1.3#/L.F.		12	.667		5.50	46	13.65	65.15	91.50
2400	8 to 11 passes, 1" thick, 2.4#/L.F.	↓	6	1.333		10.10	92	27.50	129.60	182
2600	For vertical joint welding, add						20%			
2700	Overhead joint welding, add						300%			
2900	For semi-automatic welding, obstructed joints, deduct						5%			
3000	Exposed joints, deduct				↓		15%			
4000	Cleaning and welding plates, bars, or rods									
4010	to existing beams, columns, or trusses	E-14	12	.667	L.F.	2.11	46	13.65	61.76	88

05 05 23 – Metal Fastenings

05 05 23.30 Lag Screws

			Crew	Daily Output	Labor-Hours	Unit	Material	Labor	Equipment	Total	Total Incl O&P
0010	**LAG SCREWS**										
0020	Steel, 1/4" diameter, 2" long	G	1 Carp	200	.040	Ea.	.14	2.42		2.56	3.74
0100	3/8" diameter, 3" long	G		150	.053		.51	3.23		3.74	5.35
0200	1/2" diameter, 3" long	G		130	.062		1.13	3.73		4.86	6.75
0300	5/8" diameter, 3" long	G	↓	120	.067	↓	1.91	4.04		5.95	8.10

05 05 23.35 Machine Screws

0010	**MACHINE SCREWS**										
0020	Steel, round head, #8 x 1" long	G	1 Carp	4.80	1.667	C	5.55	101		106.55	155
0110	#8 x 2" long	G		2.40	3.333		8.75	202		210.75	310
0200	#10 x 1" long	G		4	2		7.10	121		128.10	187
0300	#10 x 2" long	G	↓	2	4	↓	13.20	242		255.20	375

05 05 23.50 Powder Actuated Tools and Fasteners

0010	**POWDER ACTUATED TOOLS & FASTENERS**										
0020	Stud driver, .22 caliber, single shot					Ea.	96			96	106
0100	.27 caliber, semi automatic, strip					"	740			740	815
0300	Powder load, single shot, .22 cal, power level 2, brown					C	7.30			7.30	8
0400	Strip, .27 cal, power level 4, red						13.15			13.15	14.50
0600	Drive pin, .300 x 3/4" long	G	1 Carp	4.80	1.667		3.95	101		104.95	153
0700	.300 x 3" long with washer	G	"	4	2	↓	13.85	121		134.85	194

05 05 23.55 Rivets

0010	**RIVETS**										
0100	Aluminum rivet & mandrel, 1/2" grip length x 1/8" diameter	G	1 Carp	4.80	1.667	C	3.78	101		104.78	153
0200	3/16" diameter	G		4	2		6.95	121		127.95	187
0300	Aluminum rivet, steel mandrel, 1/8" diameter	G		4.80	1.667		4.11	101		105.11	154
0400	3/16" diameter	G		4	2		6.65	121		127.65	186
0500	Copper rivet, steel mandrel, 1/8" diameter	G	↓	4.80	1.667		9.20	101		110.20	159

05 05 Common Work Results for Metals

05 05 23 – Metal Fastenings

05 05 23.55 Rivets

		Crew	Daily Output	Labor-Hours	Unit	Material	2024 Bare Costs Labor	Equipment	Total	Total Incl O&P
0800	Stainless rivet & mandrel, 1/8" diameter	G 1 Carp	4.80	1.667	C	13.80	101		114.80	164
0900	3/16" diameter	G	4	2		24	121		145	205
1000	Stainless rivet, steel mandrel, 1/8" diameter	G	4.80	1.667		6.95	101		107.95	157
1100	3/16" diameter	G	4	2		19.05	121		140.05	200
1200	Steel rivet and mandrel, 1/8" diameter	G	4.80	1.667		6.20	101		107.20	156
1300	3/16" diameter	G	4	2		8.75	121		129.75	189
1400	Hand riveting tool, standard				Ea.	24			24	26.50
1500	Deluxe					480			480	530
1600	Power riveting tool, standard					625			625	690
1700	Deluxe					1,675			1,675	1,850

05 05 23.70 Structural Blind Bolts

		Crew	Daily Output	Labor-Hours	Unit	Material	Labor	Equipment	Total	Total Incl O&P
0010	**STRUCTURAL BLIND BOLTS**									
0100	1/4" diameter x 1/4" grip	G 1 Sswk	240	.033	Ea.	.93	2.24		3.17	4.45
0150	1/2" grip	G	216	.037		1.07	2.48		3.55	4.99
0200	3/8" diameter x 1/2" grip	G	232	.034		1.94	2.31		4.25	5.65
0250	3/4" grip	G	208	.038		1.87	2.58		4.45	6
0300	1/2" diameter x 1/2" grip	G	224	.036		4.37	2.39		6.76	8.50
0350	3/4" grip	G	200	.040		4.04	2.68		6.72	8.55
0400	5/8" diameter x 3/4" grip	G	216	.037		6.30	2.48		8.78	10.75
0450	1" grip	G	192	.042		6.85	2.79		9.64	11.85

05 05 23.90 Welding Rod

		Crew	Daily Output	Labor-Hours	Unit	Material	Labor	Equipment	Total	Total Incl O&P
0010	**WELDING ROD**									
0020	Steel, type 6011, 1/8" diam., less than 500#				Lb.	4.22			4.22	4.64
0100	500# to 2,000#					3.80			3.80	4.18
0200	2,000# to 5,000#					3.57			3.57	3.93
0300	5/32" diam., less than 500#					4.14			4.14	4.55
0310	500# to 2,000#					3.73			3.73	4.10
0320	2,000# to 5,000#					3.51			3.51	3.86
0400	3/16" diam., less than 500#					4.13			4.13	4.54
0500	500# to 2,000#					3.72			3.72	4.09
0600	2,000# to 5,000#					3.50			3.50	3.85
0620	Steel, type 6010, 1/8" diam., less than 500#					4.38			4.38	4.82
0630	500# to 2,000#					3.95			3.95	4.35
0640	2,000# to 5,000#					3.71			3.71	4.08
0650	Steel, type 7018 Low Hydrogen, 1/8" diam., less than 500#					4.05			4.05	4.46
0660	500# to 2,000#					3.65			3.65	4.02
0670	2,000# to 5,000#					3.43			3.43	3.77
0700	Steel, type 7024 Jet Weld, 1/8" diam., less than 500#					4.23			4.23	4.65
0710	500# to 2,000#					3.81			3.81	4.19
0720	2,000# to 5,000#					3.58			3.58	3.94
1550	Aluminum, type 4043 TIG, 1/8" diam., less than 10#					7.55			7.55	8.30
1560	10# to 60#					6.80			6.80	7.50
1570	Over 60#					6.40			6.40	7.05
1600	Aluminum, type 5356 TIG, 1/8" diam., less than 10#					8			8	8.80
1610	10# to 60#					7.20			7.20	7.90
1620	Over 60#					6.75			6.75	7.45
1900	Cast iron, type 8 Nickel, 1/8" diam., less than 500#					31			31	34.50
1910	500# to 1,000#					28			28	31
1920	Over 1,000#					26.50			26.50	29
2000	Stainless steel, type 316/316L, 1/8" diam., less than 500#					12.70			12.70	13.95
2100	500# to 1,000#					11.40			11.40	12.55
2220	Over 1,000#					10.75			10.75	11.80

05 12 Structural Steel Framing

05 12 23 – Structural Steel for Buildings

05 12 23.40 Lightweight Framing

05 12 23.40 Lightweight Framing		Crew	Daily Output	Labor-Hours	Unit	Material	2024 Bare Costs Labor	Equipment	Total	Total Incl O&P
0010	**LIGHTWEIGHT FRAMING**									
0015	Made from recycled materials									
0400	Angle framing, field fabricated, 4" and larger	G	E-3	440	.055	Lb.	.98	3.69	.37	5.04	7.15
0450	Less than 4" angles	G		265	.091		1.01	6.15	.62	7.78	11.20
0600	Channel framing, field fabricated, 8" and larger	G		500	.048		1.01	3.25	.33	4.59	6.45
0650	Less than 8" channels	G	↓	335	.072		1.01	4.85	.49	6.35	9.10
1000	Continuous slotted channel framing system, shop fab, simple framing	G	2 Sswk	2400	.007		5.25	.45		5.70	6.45
1200	Complex framing	G	"	1600	.010		5.90	.67		6.57	7.55
1250	Plate & bar stock for reinforcing beams and trusses	G					1.86			1.86	2.05
1300	Cross bracing, rods, shop fabricated, 3/4" diameter	G	E-3	700	.034		2.03	2.32	.23	4.58	6.05
1310	7/8" diameter	G		850	.028		2.03	1.91	.19	4.13	5.35
1320	1" diameter	G		1000	.024		2.03	1.63	.16	3.82	4.90
1330	Angle, 5" x 5" x 3/8"	G		2800	.009		2.03	.58	.06	2.67	3.18
1350	Hanging lintels, shop fabricated	G	↓	850	.028		2.03	1.91	.19	4.13	5.35
1380	Roof frames, shop fabricated, 3'-0" square, 5' span	G	E-2	4200	.013		2.03	.88	.66	3.57	4.30
1400	Tie rod, not upset, 1-1/2" to 4" diameter, with turnbuckle	G	2 Sswk	800	.020		2.20	1.34		3.54	4.48
1420	No turnbuckle	G		700	.023		2.11	1.53		3.64	4.67
1500	Upset, 1-3/4" to 4" diameter, with turnbuckle	G		800	.020		2.20	1.34		3.54	4.48
1520	No turnbuckle	G	↓	700	.023	↓	2.11	1.53		3.64	4.67

05 12 23.60 Pipe Support Framing

05 12 23.60 Pipe Support Framing		Crew	Daily Output	Labor-Hours	Unit	Material	Labor	Equipment	Total	Total Incl O&P
0010	**PIPE SUPPORT FRAMING**									
0020	Under 10#/L.F., shop fabricated	G	E-4	3900	.008	Lb.	2.26	.55	.04	2.85	3.39
0200	10.1 to 15#/L.F.	G		4300	.007		2.23	.50	.04	2.77	3.26
0400	15.1 to 20#/L.F.	G		4800	.007		2.20	.45	.03	2.68	3.15
0600	Over 20#/L.F.	G	↓	5400	.006	↓	2.16	.40	.03	2.59	3.02

05 54 Metal Floor Plates

05 54 13 – Floor Plates

05 54 13.20 Checkered Plates

05 54 13.20 Checkered Plates		Crew	Daily Output	Labor-Hours	Unit	Material	Labor	Equipment	Total	Total Incl O&P
0010	**CHECKERED PLATES**, steel, field fabricated									
0015	Made from recycled materials									
0020	1/4" & 3/8", 2000 to 5000 S.F., bolted	G	E-4	2900	.011	Lb.	1.53	.75	.06	2.34	2.88
0100	Welded	G		4400	.007	"	1.53	.49	.04	2.06	2.47
0300	Pit or trench cover and frame, 1/4" plate, 2' to 3' wide	G	↓	100	.320	S.F.	23.50	21.50	1.64	46.64	61
0400	For galvanizing, add	G				Lb.	.35			.35	.39
0500	Platforms, 1/4" plate, no handrails included, rectangular	G	E-4	4200	.008	↓	4.19	.51	.04	4.74	5.45
0600	Circular	G	"	2500	.013	↓	5.25	.86	.07	6.18	7.15

Division 6 — Wood, Plastics & Composites

Estimating Tips

06 05 00 Common Work Results for Wood, Plastics, and Composites

- Common to any wood-framed structure are the accessory connector items such as screws, nails, adhesives, hangers, connector plates, straps, angles, and hold-downs. For typical wood-framed buildings, such as residential projects, the aggregate total for these items can be significant, especially in areas where seismic loading is a concern. For floor and wall framing, the material cost is based on 10 to 25 lbs. of accessory connectors per MBF. Hold-downs, hangers, and other connectors should be taken off by the piece.

  Included with material costs are fasteners for a normal installation. Gordian's RSMeans engineers use manufacturers' recommendations, written specifications, and/or standard construction practice for the sizing and spacing of fasteners. Prices for various fasteners are shown for informational purposes only. Adjustments should be made if unusual fastening conditions exist.

06 10 00 Carpentry

- Lumber is a traded commodity and therefore sensitive to supply and demand in the marketplace. Even with "budgetary" estimating of wood-framed projects, it is advisable to call local suppliers for the latest market pricing.

- The common quantity unit for wood-framed projects is "thousand board feet" (MBF). A board foot is a volume of wood—1" x 1' x 1' or 144 cubic inches. Board-foot quantities are generally calculated using nominal material dimensions—dressed sizes are ignored. Board foot per lineal foot of any stick of lumber can be calculated by dividing the nominal cross-sectional area by 12. As an example, 2,000 lineal feet of 2 x 12 equates to 4 MBF by dividing the nominal area, 2 x 12, by 12, which equals 2, and multiplying that by 2,000 to give 4,000 board feet. This simple rule applies to all nominal dimensioned lumber.

- Waste is an issue of concern at the quantity takeoff for any area of construction. Framing lumber is sold in even foot lengths, i.e., 8', 10', 12', 14', 16', and depending on spans, wall heights, and the grade of lumber, waste is inevitable. A rule of thumb for lumber waste is 5–10% depending on material quality and the complexity of the framing.

- Wood in various forms and shapes is used in many projects, even where the main structural framing is steel, concrete, or masonry. Plywood as a back-up partition material and 2x boards used as blocking and cant strips around roof edges are two common examples. The estimator should ensure that the costs of all wood materials are included in the final estimate.

06 20 00 Finish Carpentry

- It is necessary to consider the grade of workmanship when estimating labor costs for erecting millwork and an interior finish. In practice, there are three grades: premium, custom, and economy. The RSMeans daily output for base and case moldings is in the range of 200 to 250 L.F. per carpenter per day. This is appropriate for most average custom-grade projects. For premium projects, an adjustment to productivity of 25–50% should be made, depending on the complexity of the job.

Reference Numbers

Reference numbers are shown at the beginning of some major classifications. These numbers refer to related items in the Reference Section. The reference information may be an estimating procedure, an alternate pricing method, or technical information.

Note: Not all subdivisions listed here necessarily appear. ■

Same Data. Simplified.

Enjoy the convenience and efficiency of accessing your costs anywhere:

- **Skip the multiplier** by setting your location
- **Quickly search,** edit, favorite and share costs
- **Stay on top of price changes** with automatic updates

Discover more at rsmeans.com/online

No part of this cost data may be reproduced, stored in a retrieval system, or transmitted in any form or by any means without prior written permission of Gordian.

06 11 Wood Framing

06 11 10 – Framing with Dimensional, Engineered or Composite Lumber

06 11 10.24 Miscellaneous Framing		Crew	Daily Output	Labor-Hours	Unit	Material	2024 Bare Costs Labor	Equipment	Total	Total Incl O&P
0010	MISCELLANEOUS FRAMING									
8500	Firestops, 2" x 4"	2 Carp	.51	31.373	M.B.F.	1,525	1,900		3,425	4,500
8505	Pneumatic nailed		.62	25.806		1,500	1,575		3,075	4,000
8520	2" x 6"		.60	26.667		1,525	1,625		3,150	4,075
8525	Pneumatic nailed		.73	21.858		1,500	1,325		2,825	3,600
8540	2" x 8"		.60	26.667		645	1,625		2,270	3,100
8560	2" x 12"		.70	22.857		1,725	1,375		3,100	3,950
8600	Nailers, treated, wood construction, 2" x 4"		.53	30.189		1,300	1,825		3,125	4,125
8605	Pneumatic nailed		.64	25.157		1,275	1,525		2,800	3,650
8620	2" x 6"		.75	21.333		1,075	1,300		2,375	3,125
8625	Pneumatic nailed		.90	17.778		1,075	1,075		2,150	2,775

06 16 Sheathing

06 16 36 – Wood Panel Product Sheathing

06 16 36.10 Sheathing		Crew	Daily Output	Labor-Hours	Unit	Material	2024 Bare Costs Labor	Equipment	Total	Total Incl O&P
0010	SHEATHING									
0012	Plywood on roofs, CDX									
0050	3/8" thick	2 Carp	1525	.010	S.F.	.93	.64		1.57	1.96
0055	Pneumatic nailed		1860	.009		.93	.52		1.45	1.79
0200	5/8" thick		1300	.012		1.12	.75		1.87	2.33
0205	Pneumatic nailed		1586	.010		1.12	.61		1.73	2.13
0300	3/4" thick		1200	.013		1.79	.81		2.60	3.17
0305	Pneumatic nailed		1464	.011		1.79	.66		2.45	2.95
0500	Plywood on walls, with exterior CDX, 3/8" thick		1200	.013		.93	.81		1.74	2.22
0505	Pneumatic nailed		1488	.011		.93	.65		1.58	1.98
0700	5/8" thick		1050	.015		1.12	.92		2.04	2.60
0705	Pneumatic nailed		1302	.012		1.12	.74		1.86	2.33
0800	3/4" thick		975	.016		1.79	.99		2.78	3.44
0805	Pneumatic nailed		1209	.013		1.79	.80		2.59	3.16

Division 7 — Thermal & Moisture Protection

Estimating Tips

07 10 00 Dampproofing and Waterproofing
- Be sure of the job specifications before pricing this subdivision. The difference in cost between waterproofing and dampproofing can be great. Waterproofing will hold back standing water. Dampproofing prevents the transmission of water vapor. Also included in this section are vapor retarding membranes.

07 20 00 Thermal Protection
- Insulation and fireproofing products are measured by area, thickness, volume, or R-value. Specifications may give only what the specific R-value should be in a certain situation. The estimator may need to choose the type of insulation to meet that R-value.

07 30 00 Steep Slope Roofing
07 40 00 Roofing and Siding Panels
- Many roofing and siding products are bought and sold by the square. One square is equal to an area that measures 100 square feet.

  This simple change in unit of measure could create a large error if the estimator is not observant. Accessories necessary for a complete installation must be figured into any calculations for both material and labor.

07 50 00 Membrane Roofing
07 60 00 Flashing and Sheet Metal
07 70 00 Roofing and Wall Specialties and Accessories
- The items in these subdivisions compose a roofing system. No one component completes the installation, and all must be estimated. Built-up or single-ply membrane roofing systems are made up of many products and installation trades. Wood blocking at roof perimeters or penetrations, parapet coverings, reglets, roof drains, gutters, downspouts, sheet metal flashing, skylights, smoke vents, and roof hatches all need to be considered along with the roofing material. Several different installation trades will need to work together on the roofing system. Inherent difficulties in the scheduling and coordination of various trades must be accounted for when estimating labor costs.

07 90 00 Joint Protection
- To complete the weather-tight shell, the sealants and caulkings must be estimated. Where different materials meet—at expansion joints, at flashing penetrations, and at hundreds of other locations throughout a construction project—caulking and sealants provide another line of defense against water penetration. Often, an entire system is based on the proper location and placement of caulking or sealants. The detailed drawings that are included as part of a set of architectural plans show typical locations for these materials. When caulking or sealants are shown at typical locations, this means the estimator must include them for all the locations where this detail is applicable. Be careful to keep different types of sealants separate, and remember to consider backer rods and primers if necessary.

Reference Numbers
Reference numbers are shown at the beginning of some major classifications. These numbers refer to related items in the Reference Section. The reference information may be an estimating procedure, an alternate pricing method, or technical information.

Note: Not all subdivisions listed here necessarily appear. ■

Same Data. Simplified.

Enjoy the convenience and efficiency of accessing your costs anywhere:

- **Skip the multiplier** by setting your location
- **Quickly search**, edit, favorite and share costs
- **Stay on top of price changes** with automatic updates

Discover more at rsmeans.com/online

No part of this cost data may be reproduced, stored in a retrieval system, or transmitted in any form or by any means without prior written permission of Gordian.

07 65 Flexible Flashing

07 65 10 – Sheet Metal Flashing

07 65 10.10 Sheet Metal Flashing and Counter Flashing	Crew	Daily Output	Labor-Hours	Unit	Material	2024 Bare Costs Labor	Equipment	Total	Total Incl O&P
0010 SHEET METAL FLASHING AND COUNTER FLASHING									
0011 Including up to 4 bends									
0020 Aluminum, mill finish, .013" thick	1 Rofc	145	.055	S.F.	1.75	2.96		4.71	6.70
0030 .016" thick		145	.055		.99	2.96		3.95	5.85
0060 .019" thick		145	.055		6.95	2.96		9.91	12.45
0100 .032" thick		145	.055		7.70	2.96		10.66	13.25
0200 .040" thick		145	.055		8.30	2.96		11.26	13.90
0300 .050" thick		145	.055		11.65	2.96		14.61	17.65
0325 Mill finish 5" x 7" step flashing, .016" thick		1920	.004	Ea.	.22	.22		.44	.60
0350 Mill finish 12" x 12" step flashing, .016" thick		1600	.005	"	.81	.27		1.08	1.32
0400 Painted finish, add				S.F.	.42			.42	.46
1000 Mastic-coated 2 sides, .005" thick	1 Rofc	330	.024		1.42	1.30		2.72	3.66
1100 .016" thick		330	.024		2.77	1.30		4.07	5.15
1600 Copper, 16 oz. sheets, under 1000 lb.		115	.070		22	3.74		25.74	30
1700 Over 4000 lb.		155	.052		22	2.77		24.77	28.50
1900 20 oz. sheets, under 1000 lb.		110	.073		30.50	3.91		34.41	40
2000 Over 4000 lb.		145	.055		29	2.96		31.96	37
2200 24 oz. sheets, under 1000 lb.		105	.076		19.65	4.09		23.74	28
2300 Over 4000 lb.		135	.059		18.65	3.18		21.83	25.50
2500 32 oz. sheets, under 1000 lb.		100	.080		36.50	4.30		40.80	47
2600 Over 4000 lb.		130	.062		34.50	3.30		37.80	43.50
5800 Lead, 2.5 lb./S.F., up to 12" wide		135	.059		8.45	3.18		11.63	14.45
5900 Over 12" wide		135	.059		8.80	3.18		11.98	14.85
8900 Stainless steel sheets, 32 ga.		155	.052		4.76	2.77		7.53	9.70
9000 28 ga.		155	.052		12.95	2.77		15.72	18.70
9100 26 ga.		155	.052		9.70	2.77		12.47	15.10
9200 24 ga.		155	.052		11.60	2.77		14.37	17.20
9400 Terne coated stainless steel, .015" thick, 28 ga.		155	.052		10.95	2.77		13.72	16.45
9500 .018" thick, 26 ga.		155	.052		10	2.77		12.77	15.45
9600 Zinc and copper alloy (brass), .020" thick		155	.052		12.15	2.77		14.92	17.80
9700 .027" thick		155	.052		14.30	2.77		17.07	20
9800 .032" thick		155	.052		16.65	2.77		19.42	23
9900 .040" thick		155	.052		22.50	2.77		25.27	29.50

07 65 13 – Laminated Sheet Flashing

07 65 13.10 Laminated Sheet Flashing

	Crew	Daily Output	Labor-Hours	Unit	Material	Labor	Equipment	Total	Total Incl O&P
0010 LAMINATED SHEET FLASHING, Including up to 4 bends									
0500 Aluminum, fabric-backed 2 sides, mill finish, .004" thick	1 Rofc	330	.024	S.F.	2.12	1.30		3.42	4.43
0700 .005" thick		330	.024		2.50	1.30		3.80	4.85
0750 Mastic-backed, self adhesive		460	.017		4.58	.93		5.51	6.55
0800 Mastic-coated 2 sides, .004" thick		330	.024		2.12	1.30		3.42	4.43
2800 Copper, paperbacked 1 side, 2 oz.		330	.024		2.89	1.30		4.19	5.30
2900 3 oz.		330	.024		4.21	1.30		5.51	6.75
3100 Paperbacked 2 sides, 2 oz.		330	.024		3.20	1.30		4.50	5.60
3150 3 oz.		330	.024		3	1.30		4.30	5.40
3200 5 oz.		330	.024		5.20	1.30		6.50	7.85
3250 7 oz.		330	.024		7.05	1.30		8.35	9.90
3400 Mastic-backed 2 sides, copper, 2 oz.		330	.024		3.05	1.30		4.35	5.45
3500 3 oz.		330	.024		3.45	1.30		4.75	5.90
3700 5 oz.		330	.024		5.25	1.30		6.55	7.90
3800 Fabric-backed 2 sides, copper, 2 oz.		330	.024		2.75	1.30		4.05	5.15
4000 3 oz.		330	.024		3.87	1.30		5.17	6.35
4100 5 oz.		330	.024		5.40	1.30		6.70	8.05

07 65 Flexible Flashing

07 65 13 – Laminated Sheet Flashing

07 65 13.10 Laminated Sheet Flashing

		Crew	Daily Output	Labor-Hours	Unit	Material	2024 Bare Costs Labor	Equipment	Total	Total Incl O&P
4300	Copper-clad stainless steel, .015" thick, under 500 lb.	1 Rofc	115	.070	S.F.	9.25	3.74		12.99	16.20
4400	Over 2000 lb.		155	.052		9.10	2.77		11.87	14.50
4600	.018" thick, under 500 lb.		100	.080		10.60	4.30		14.90	18.60
4700	Over 2000 lb.		145	.055		10.95	2.96		13.91	16.85
8550	Shower pan, 3 ply copper and fabric, 3 oz.		155	.052		5.55	2.77		8.32	10.55
8600	7 oz.		155	.052		6.70	2.77		9.47	11.80
9300	Stainless steel, paperbacked 2 sides, .005" thick		330	.024		5.45	1.30		6.75	8.05

07 65 19 – Plastic Sheet Flashing

07 65 19.10 Plastic Sheet Flashing and Counter Flashing

		Crew	Daily Output	Labor-Hours	Unit	Material	Labor	Equipment	Total	Total Incl O&P
0010	**PLASTIC SHEET FLASHING AND COUNTER FLASHING**									
7300	Polyvinyl chloride, black, 10 mil	1 Rofc	285	.028	S.F.	.36	1.51		1.87	2.83
7400	20 mil		285	.028		.35	1.51		1.86	2.82
7600	30 mil		285	.028		.45	1.51		1.96	2.93
7700	60 mil		285	.028		1.19	1.51		2.70	3.74
7900	Black or white for exposed roofs, 60 mil		285	.028		5.30	1.51		6.81	8.25
8060	PVC tape, 5" x 45 mils, for joint covers, 100 L.F./roll				Ea.	150			150	165
8850	Polyvinyl chloride, 30 mil	1 Rofc	160	.050	S.F.	1.07	2.69		3.76	5.50

07 71 Roof Specialties

07 71 16 – Manufactured Counterflashing Systems

07 71 16.20 Pitch Pockets, Variable Sizes

		Crew	Daily Output	Labor-Hours	Unit	Material	Labor	Equipment	Total	Total Incl O&P
0010	**PITCH POCKETS, VARIABLE SIZES**									
0100	Adjustable, 4" to 7", welded corners, 4" deep	1 Rofc	48	.167	Ea.	46	8.95		54.95	65
0200	Side extenders, 6"	"	240	.033	"	4.27	1.79		6.06	7.60

07 72 Roof Accessories

07 72 53 – Snow Guards

07 72 53.10 Snow Guard Options

		Crew	Daily Output	Labor-Hours	Unit	Material	Labor	Equipment	Total	Total Incl O&P
0010	**SNOW GUARD OPTIONS**									
0100	Slate & asphalt shingle roofs, fastened with nails	1 Rofc	160	.050	Ea.	15.35	2.69		18.04	21
0200	Standing seam metal roofs, fastened with set screws		48	.167		22	8.95		30.95	38.50
0300	Surface mount for metal roofs, fastened with solder		48	.167		9.55	8.95		18.50	25
0400	Double rail pipe type, including pipe		130	.062	L.F.	44	3.30		47.30	54

07 76 Roof Pavers

07 76 16 – Roof Decking Pavers

07 76 16.10 Roof Pavers and Supports

		Crew	Daily Output	Labor-Hours	Unit	Material	Labor	Equipment	Total	Total Incl O&P
0010	**ROOF PAVERS AND SUPPORTS**									
1000	Roof decking pavers, concrete blocks, 2" thick, natural	1 Clab	115	.070	S.F.	1.96	3.41		5.37	7.20
1100	Colors		115	.070	"	1.96	3.41		5.37	7.20
1200	Support pedestal, bottom cap		960	.008	Ea.	3.80	.41		4.21	4.78
1300	Top cap		960	.008		6.95	.41		7.36	8.25
1400	Leveling shims, 1/16"		1920	.004		1.72	.20		1.92	2.19
1500	1/8"		1920	.004		1.99	.20		2.19	2.49
1600	Buffer pad		960	.008		8.55	.41		8.96	10
1700	PVC legs (4" SDR 35)		2880	.003	Inch	.42	.14		.56	.66
2000	Alternate pricing method, system in place		101	.079	S.F.	8.85	3.88		12.73	15.50

07 84 Firestopping

07 84 13 – Penetration Firestopping

07 84 13.10 Firestopping		Crew	Daily Output	Labor-Hours	Unit	Material	2024 Bare Costs Labor	Equipment	Total	Total Incl O&P
0010	**FIRESTOPPING**									
0100	Metallic piping, non insulated									
0110	Through walls, 2" diameter	1 Carp	16	.500	Ea.	11.80	30.50		42.30	58
0120	4" diameter		14	.571		20.50	34.50		55	73.50
0130	6" diameter		12	.667		30	40.50		70.50	93
0140	12" diameter		10	.800		26	48.50		74.50	100
0150	Through floors, 2" diameter		32	.250		5.90	15.15		21.05	29
0160	4" diameter		28	.286		10.30	17.30		27.60	37
0170	6" diameter		24	.333		15.10	20		35.10	46.50
0180	12" diameter		20	.400		13.25	24		37.25	50.50
0190	Metallic piping, insulated									
0200	Through walls, 2" diameter	1 Carp	16	.500	Ea.	20.50	30.50		51	67.50
0210	4" diameter		14	.571		30	34.50		64.50	84
0220	6" diameter		12	.667		40.50	40.50		81	105
0230	12" diameter		10	.800		69.50	48.50		118	148
0240	Through floors, 2" diameter		32	.250		10.30	15.15		25.45	34
0250	4" diameter		28	.286		15.10	17.30		32.40	42
0260	6" diameter		24	.333		20.50	20		40.50	52.50
0270	12" diameter		20	.400		34.50	24		58.50	74
0280	Non metallic piping, non insulated									
0290	Through walls, 2" diameter	1 Carp	12	.667	Ea.	71.50	40.50		112	139
0300	4" diameter		10	.800		132	48.50		180.50	217
0310	6" diameter		8	1		252	60.50		312.50	370
0330	Through floors, 2" diameter		16	.500		45.50	30.50		76	95
0340	4" diameter		6	1.333		83	80.50		163.50	211
0350	6" diameter		6	1.333		150	80.50		230.50	285
0370	Ductwork, insulated & non insulated, round									
0380	Through walls, 6" diameter	1 Carp	12	.667	Ea.	40.50	40.50		81	105
0390	12" diameter		10	.800		69.50	48.50		118	148
0400	18" diameter		8	1		84	60.50		144.50	182
0410	Through floors, 6" diameter		16	.500		20.50	30.50		51	67.50
0420	12" diameter		14	.571		15.10	34.50		49.60	67.50
0430	18" diameter		12	.667		18.25	40.50		58.75	80
0440	Ductwork, insulated & non insulated, rectangular									
0450	With stiffener/closure angle, through walls, 6" x 12"	1 Carp	8	1	Ea.	53	60.50		113.50	148
0460	12" x 24"		6	1.333		106	80.50		186.50	237
0470	24" x 48"		4	2		212	121		333	410
0480	With stiffener/closure angle, through floors, 6" x 12"		10	.800		10.75	48.50		59.25	83.50
0490	12" x 24"		8	1		53	60.50		113.50	148
0500	24" x 48"		6	1.333		106	80.50		186.50	237
0510	Multi trade openings									
0520	Through walls, 6" x 12"	1 Carp	2	4	Ea.	81	242		323	450
0530	12" x 24"	"	1	8		218	485		703	955
0540	24" x 48"	2 Carp	1	16		660	970		1,630	2,150
0550	48" x 96"	"	.75	21.333		2,625	1,300		3,925	4,800
0560	Through floors, 6" x 12"	1 Carp	2	4		49.50	242		291.50	415
0570	12" x 24"	"	1	8		66	485		551	790
0580	24" x 48"	2 Carp	.75	21.333		142	1,300		1,442	2,075
0590	48" x 96"	"	.50	32		335	1,950		2,285	3,250
0600	Structural penetrations, through walls									
0610	Steel beams, W8 x 10	1 Carp	8	1	Ea.	76	60.50		136.50	173
0620	W12 x 14		6	1.333		111	80.50		191.50	242
0630	W21 x 44		5	1.600		170	97		267	330

07 84 Firestopping

07 84 13 – Penetration Firestopping

07 84 13.10 Firestopping

	07 84 13.10 Firestopping	Crew	Daily Output	Labor-Hours	Unit	Material	2024 Bare Costs Labor	Equipment	Total	Total Incl O&P
0640	W36 x 135	1 Carp	3	2.667	Ea.	241	161		402	505
0650	Bar joists, 18" deep		6	1.333		44.50	80.50		125	169
0660	24" deep		6	1.333		62.50	80.50		143	189
0670	36" deep		5	1.600		94	97		191	246
0680	48" deep		4	2		136	121		257	330
0690	Construction joints, floor slab at exterior wall									
0700	Precast, brick, block or drywall exterior									
0710	2" wide joint	1 Carp	125	.064	L.F.	11.35	3.88		15.23	18.20
0720	4" wide joint	"	75	.107	"	17.50	6.45		23.95	29
0730	Metal panel, glass or curtain wall exterior									
0740	2" wide joint	1 Carp	40	.200	L.F.	12.90	12.10		25	32
0750	4" wide joint	"	25	.320	"	14.65	19.40		34.05	44.50
0760	Floor slab to drywall partition									
0770	Flat joint	1 Carp	100	.080	L.F.	14.85	4.84		19.69	23.50
0780	Fluted joint		50	.160		17.25	9.70		26.95	33.50
0790	Etched fluted joint		75	.107		20.50	6.45		26.95	32.50
0800	Floor slab to concrete/masonry partition									
0810	Flat joint	1 Carp	75	.107	L.F.	17.30	6.45		23.75	28.50
0820	Fluted joint	"	50	.160	"	18.85	9.70		28.55	35
0830	Concrete/CMU wall joints									
0840	1" wide	1 Carp	100	.080	L.F.	21	4.84		25.84	30
0850	2" wide		75	.107		32.50	6.45		38.95	45.50
0860	4" wide		50	.160		37	9.70		46.70	55
0870	Concrete/CMU floor joints									
0880	1" wide	1 Carp	200	.040	L.F.	22	2.42		24.42	28
0890	2" wide		150	.053		25.50	3.23		28.73	33
0900	4" wide		100	.080		37	4.84		41.84	47.50

07 91 Preformed Joint Seals

07 91 13 – Compression Seals

07 91 13.10 Compression Seals

		Crew	Daily Output	Labor-Hours	Unit	Material	Labor	Equipment	Total	Total Incl O&P
0010	**COMPRESSION SEALS**									
4900	O-ring type cord, 1/4"	1 Bric	472	.017	L.F.	.54	1.01		1.55	2.10
4910	1/2"		440	.018		1.44	1.08		2.52	3.20
4920	3/4"		424	.019		2.89	1.13		4.02	4.86
4930	1"		408	.020		5.80	1.17		6.97	8.15
4940	1-1/4"		384	.021		13.95	1.24		15.19	17.20
4950	1-1/2"		368	.022		17.15	1.30		18.45	21
4960	1-3/4"		352	.023		20	1.36		21.36	24
4970	2"		344	.023		35	1.39		36.39	40.50

07 91 16 – Joint Gaskets

07 91 16.10 Joint Gaskets

		Crew	Daily Output	Labor-Hours	Unit	Material	Labor	Equipment	Total	Total Incl O&P
0010	**JOINT GASKETS**									
4400	Joint gaskets, neoprene, closed cell w/adh, 1/8" x 3/8"	1 Bric	240	.033	L.F.	.19	1.99		2.18	3.18
4500	1/4" x 3/4"		215	.037		.36	2.22		2.58	3.72
4700	1/2" x 1"		200	.040		.73	2.39		3.12	4.36
4800	3/4" x 1-1/2"		165	.048		2.04	2.89		4.93	6.55

For customer support on your Plumbing Costs with RSMeans Data call 800.448.8182.

07 91 Preformed Joint Seals

07 91 23 – Backer Rods

07 91 23.10 Backer Rods

		Crew	Daily Output	Labor-Hours	Unit	Material	2024 Bare Costs Labor	Equipment	Total	Total Incl O&P
0010	**BACKER RODS**									
0030	Backer rod, polyethylene, 1/4" diameter	1 Bric	4.60	1.739	C.L.F.	99	104		203	264
0050	1/2" diameter		4.60	1.739		16	104		120	173
0070	3/4" diameter		4.60	1.739		99	104		203	264
0090	1" diameter	↓	4.60	1.739	↓	99	104		203	264

07 91 26 – Joint Fillers

07 91 26.10 Joint Fillers

		Crew	Daily Output	Labor-Hours	Unit	Material	Labor	Equipment	Total	Total Incl O&P
0010	**JOINT FILLERS**									
4360	Butyl rubber filler, 1/4" x 1/4"	1 Bric	290	.028	L.F.	.39	1.65		2.04	2.88
4365	1/2" x 1/2"		250	.032		1.54	1.91		3.45	4.55
4370	1/2" x 3/4"		210	.038		2.32	2.27		4.59	5.95
4375	3/4" x 3/4"		230	.035		3.47	2.07		5.54	6.90
4380	1" x 1"	↓	180	.044	↓	4.63	2.65		7.28	9.05
4390	For coloring, add					12%				
4980	Polyethylene joint backing, 1/4" x 2"	1 Bric	2.08	3.846	C.L.F.	14.05	229		243.05	360
4990	1/4" x 6"		1.28	6.250	"	150	375		525	720
5600	Silicone, room temp vulcanizing foam seal, 1/4" x 1/2"		1312	.006	L.F.	.39	.36		.75	.97
5610	1/2" x 1/2"		656	.012		.78	.73		1.51	1.95
5620	1/2" x 3/4"		442	.018		1.18	1.08		2.26	2.90
5630	3/4" x 3/4"		328	.024		1.76	1.45		3.21	4.11
5640	1/8" x 1"		1312	.006		.39	.36		.75	.97
5650	1/8" x 3"		442	.018		1.18	1.08		2.26	2.90
5670	1/4" x 3"		295	.027		2.35	1.62		3.97	5
5680	1/4" x 6"		148	.054		4.71	3.22		7.93	10
5690	1/2" x 6"		82	.098		9.40	5.80		15.20	19.05
5700	1/2" x 9"		52.50	.152		14.10	9.10		23.20	29
5710	1/2" x 12"	↓	33	.242	↓	18.85	14.45		33.30	42

07 92 Joint Sealants

07 92 13 – Elastomeric Joint Sealants

07 92 13.20 Caulking and Sealant Options

		Crew	Daily Output	Labor-Hours	Unit	Material	Labor	Equipment	Total	Total Incl O&P
0010	**CAULKING AND SEALANT OPTIONS**									
0050	Latex acrylic based, bulk				Gal.	39			39	43
0055	Bulk in place 1/4" x 1/4" bead	1 Bric	300	.027	L.F.	.12	1.59		1.71	2.52
0060	1/4" x 3/8"		294	.027		.21	1.62		1.83	2.65
0065	1/4" x 1/2"		288	.028		.28	1.66		1.94	2.78
0075	3/8" x 3/8"		284	.028		.31	1.68		1.99	2.85
0080	3/8" x 1/2"		280	.029		.41	1.70		2.11	3
0085	3/8" x 5/8"		276	.029		.52	1.73		2.25	3.15
0095	3/8" x 3/4"		272	.029		.62	1.75		2.37	3.30
0100	1/2" x 1/2"		275	.029		.55	1.74		2.29	3.20
0105	1/2" x 5/8"		269	.030		.69	1.77		2.46	3.41
0110	1/2" x 3/4"		263	.030		.83	1.81		2.64	3.62
0115	1/2" x 7/8"		256	.031		.96	1.86		2.82	3.84
0120	1/2" x 1"		250	.032		1.10	1.91		3.01	4.06
0125	3/4" x 3/4"		244	.033		1.24	1.96		3.20	4.28
0130	3/4" x 1"		225	.036		1.65	2.12		3.77	4.99
0135	1" x 1"	↓	200	.040	↓	2.20	2.39		4.59	6
0190	Cartridges				Gal.	58.50			58.50	64.50
0200	11 fl. oz. cartridge				Ea.	5			5	5.50

07 92 Joint Sealants

07 92 13 – Elastomeric Joint Sealants

07 92 13.20 Caulking and Sealant Options		Crew	Daily Output	Labor-Hours	Unit	Material	2024 Bare Costs Labor	Equipment	Total	Total Incl O&P
0500	1/4" x 1/2"	1 Bric	288	.028	L.F.	.41	1.66		2.07	2.93
0600	1/2" x 1/2"		275	.029		.82	1.74		2.56	3.49
0800	3/4" x 3/4"		244	.033		1.85	1.96		3.81	4.95
0900	3/4" x 1"		225	.036		2.46	2.12		4.58	5.90
1000	1" x 1"	↓	200	.040	↓	3.08	2.39		5.47	6.95
1400	Butyl based, bulk				Gal.	53.50			53.50	58.50
1500	Cartridges				"	53.50			53.50	58.50
1700	1/4" x 1/2", 154 L.F./gal.	1 Bric	288	.028	L.F.	.35	1.66		2.01	2.86
1800	1/2" x 1/2", 77 L.F./gal.	"	275	.029	"	.69	1.74		2.43	3.35
2300	Polysulfide compounds, 1 component, bulk				Gal.	109			109	119
2600	1 or 2 component, in place, 1/4" x 1/4", 308 L.F./gal.	1 Bric	300	.027	L.F.	.35	1.59		1.94	2.77
2700	1/2" x 1/4", 154 L.F./gal.		288	.028		.70	1.66		2.36	3.26
2900	3/4" x 3/8", 68 L.F./gal.		272	.029		1.60	1.75		3.35	4.38
3000	1" x 1/2", 38 L.F./gal.	↓	250	.032	↓	2.86	1.91		4.77	6
3200	Polyurethane, 1 or 2 component				Gal.	70.50			70.50	78
3300	Cartridges				"	84.50			84.50	92.50
3500	Bulk, in place, 1/4" x 1/4"	1 Bric	300	.027	L.F.	.23	1.59		1.82	2.63
3655	1/2" x 1/4"		288	.028		.46	1.66		2.12	2.99
3800	3/4" x 3/8"		272	.029		1.04	1.75		2.79	3.76
3900	1" x 1/2"	↓	250	.032	↓	1.84	1.91		3.75	4.87
4100	Silicone rubber, bulk				Gal.	85			85	93.50
4200	Cartridges				"	57.50			57.50	63.50

07 92 16 – Rigid Joint Sealants

07 92 16.10 Rigid Joint Sealants		Crew	Daily Output	Labor-Hours	Unit	Material	Labor	Equipment	Total	Total Incl O&P
0010	**RIGID JOINT SEALANTS**									
5800	Tapes, sealant, PVC foam adhesive, 1/16" x 1/4"				C.L.F.	3.64			3.64	4
5900	1/16" x 1/2"					8.25			8.25	9.10
5950	1/16" x 1"					15.35			15.35	16.90
6000	1/8" x 1/2"				↓	12			12	13.20

07 92 19 – Acoustical Joint Sealants

07 92 19.10 Acoustical Sealant		Crew	Daily Output	Labor-Hours	Unit	Material	Labor	Equipment	Total	Total Incl O&P
0010	**ACOUSTICAL SEALANT**									
0020	Acoustical sealant, elastomeric, cartridges				Ea.	6.15			6.15	6.75
0025	In place, 1/4" x 1/4"	1 Bric	300	.027	L.F.	.25	1.59		1.84	2.66
0030	1/4" x 1/2"		288	.028		.50	1.66		2.16	3.03
0035	1/2" x 1/2"		275	.029		1	1.74		2.74	3.69
0040	1/2" x 3/4"		263	.030		1.50	1.81		3.31	4.37
0045	3/4" x 3/4"		244	.033		2.26	1.96		4.22	5.40
0050	1" x 1"	↓	200	.040	↓	4.01	2.39		6.40	7.95

Division Notes

	CREW	DAILY OUTPUT	LABOR-HOURS	UNIT	BARE COSTS				TOTAL INCL O&P
					MAT.	LABOR	EQUIP.	TOTAL	

Division 9 Finishes

Estimating Tips
General
- Room Finish Schedule: A complete set of plans should contain a room finish schedule. If one is not available, it would be well worth the time and effort to obtain one.

09 20 00 Plaster and Gypsum Board
- Lath is estimated by the square yard plus a 5% allowance for waste. Furring, channels, and accessories are measured by the linear foot. An extra foot should be allowed for each accessory miter or stop.
- Plaster is also estimated by the square yard. Deductions for openings vary by preference, from zero deduction to 50% of all openings over 2 feet in width. The estimator should allow one extra square foot for each linear foot of horizontal interior or exterior angle located below the ceiling level. Also, double the areas of small radius work.
- Drywall accessories, studs, track, and acoustical caulking are all measured by the linear foot. Drywall taping is figured by the square foot. Gypsum wallboard is estimated by the square foot. No material deductions should be made for door or window openings under 32 S.F.

09 60 00 Flooring
- Tile and terrazzo areas are taken off on a square foot basis. Trim and base materials are measured by the linear foot. Accent tiles are listed per each. Two basic methods of installation are used. Mud set is approximately 30% more expensive than thin set.

The cost of grout is included with tile unit price lines unless otherwise noted. In terrazzo work, be sure to include the linear footage of embedded decorative strips, grounds, machine rubbing, and power cleanup.
- Wood flooring is available in strip, parquet, or block configuration. The latter two types are set in adhesives with quantities estimated by the square foot. The laying pattern will influence labor costs and material waste. In addition to the material and labor for laying wood floors, the estimator must make allowances for sanding and finishing these areas, unless the flooring is prefinished.
- Sheet flooring is measured by the square yard. Roll widths vary, so consideration should be given to use the most economical width, as waste must be figured into the total quantity. Consider also the installation methods available—direct glue down or stretched. Direct glue-down installation is assumed with sheet carpet unit price lines unless otherwise noted.

09 70 00 Wall Finishes
- Wall coverings are estimated by the square foot. The area to be covered is measured—length by height of the wall above the baseboards—to calculate the square footage of each wall. This figure is divided by the number of square feet in the single roll which is being used. Deduct, in full, the areas of openings such as doors and windows. Where a pattern match is required allow 25–30% waste.

09 80 00 Acoustic Treatment
- Acoustical systems fall into several categories. The takeoff of these materials should be by the square foot of area with a 5% allowance for waste. Do not forget about scaffolding, if applicable, when estimating these systems.

09 90 00 Painting and Coating
- New line items created for cut-ins with reference diagram.
- A major portion of the work in painting involves surface preparation. Be sure to include cleaning, sanding, filling, and masking costs in the estimate.
- Protection of adjacent surfaces is not included in painting costs. When considering the method of paint application, an important factor is the amount of protection and masking required. These must be estimated separately and may be the determining factor in choosing the method of application.

Reference Numbers
Reference numbers are shown at the beginning of some major classifications. These numbers refer to related items in the Reference Section. The reference information may be an estimating procedure, an alternate pricing method, or technical information.

Note: Not all subdivisions listed here necessarily appear. ■

Same Data. Simplified.

Enjoy the convenience and efficiency of accessing your costs anywhere:
- **Skip the multiplier** by setting your location
- **Quickly search**, edit, favorite and share costs
- **Stay on top of price changes** with automatic updates

Discover more at rsmeans.com/online

No part of this cost data may be reproduced, stored in a retrieval system, or transmitted in any form or by any means without prior written permission of Gordian.

09 22 Supports for Plaster and Gypsum Board

09 22 03 – Fastening Methods for Finishes

09 22 03.20 Drilling Plaster/Drywall

		Crew	Daily Output	Labor-Hours	Unit	Material	2024 Bare Costs Labor	2024 Bare Costs Equipment	Total	Total Incl O&P
0010	**DRILLING PLASTER/DRYWALL**									
1100	Drilling & layout for drywall/plaster walls, up to 1" deep, no anchor									
1200	Holes, 1/4" diameter	1 Carp	150	.053	Ea.	.01	3.23		3.24	4.79
1300	3/8" diameter		140	.057			3.46		3.46	5.10
1400	1/2" diameter		130	.062		.01	3.73		3.74	5.50
1500	3/4" diameter		120	.067		.01	4.04		4.05	6
1600	1" diameter		110	.073		.02	4.40		4.42	6.50
1700	1-1/4" diameter		100	.080		.04	4.84		4.88	7.20
1800	1-1/2" diameter		90	.089		.05	5.40		5.45	8
1900	For ceiling installations, add						40%			

09 91 Painting

09 91 23 – Interior Painting

09 91 23.52 Miscellaneous, Interior

		Crew	Daily Output	Labor-Hours	Unit	Material	2024 Bare Costs Labor	2024 Bare Costs Equipment	Total	Total Incl O&P
0010	**MISCELLANEOUS, INTERIOR**									
3800	Grilles, per side, oil base, primer coat, brushwork	1 Pord	520	.015	S.F.	.23	.80		1.03	1.43
3850	Spray		1140	.007		.24	.36		.60	.81
3880	Paint 1 coat, brushwork		520	.015		.37	.80		1.17	1.58
3900	Spray		1140	.007		.41	.36		.77	.99
3920	Paint 2 coats, brushwork		325	.025		.72	1.27		1.99	2.67
3940	Spray		650	.012		.82	.64		1.46	1.84
3950	Prime & paint 1 coat		325	.025		.60	1.27		1.87	2.54
3960	Prime & paint 2 coats		270	.030		.59	1.53		2.12	2.91
4500	Louvers, 1 side, primer, brushwork		524	.015		.12	.79		.91	1.29
4520	Paint 1 coat, brushwork		520	.015		1.27	.80		2.07	2.56
4530	Spray		1140	.007		1.41	.36		1.77	2.09
4540	Paint 2 coats, brushwork		325	.025		2.46	1.27		3.73	4.59
4550	Spray		650	.012		2.73	.64		3.37	3.94
4560	Paint 3 coats, brushwork		270	.030		3.65	1.53		5.18	6.30
4570	Spray		500	.016		4.06	.83		4.89	5.70
5000	Pipe, 1"-4" diameter, primer or sealer coat, oil base, brushwork	2 Pord	1250	.013	L.F.	.12	.66		.78	1.12
5100	Spray		2165	.007		.12	.38		.50	.69
5200	Paint 1 coat, brushwork		1250	.013		1.48	.66		2.14	2.61
5300	Spray		2165	.007		1.29	.38		1.67	1.98
5350	Paint 2 coats, brushwork		775	.021		2.58	1.07		3.65	4.42
5400	Spray		1240	.013		2.87	.67		3.54	4.14
5420	Paint 3 coats, brushwork		775	.021		3.84	1.07		4.91	5.80
5450	5"-8" diameter, primer or sealer coat, brushwork		620	.026		.25	1.33		1.58	2.24
5500	Spray		1085	.015		.40	.76		1.16	1.58
5550	Paint 1 coat, brushwork		620	.026		3.93	1.33		5.26	6.30
5600	Spray		1085	.015		4.36	.76		5.12	5.95
5650	Paint 2 coats, brushwork		385	.042		5.15	2.15		7.30	8.85
5700	Spray		620	.026		5.75	1.33		7.08	8.25
5720	Paint 3 coats, brushwork		385	.042		7.65	2.15		9.80	11.60
5750	9"-12" diameter, primer or sealer coat, brushwork		415	.039		.37	1.99		2.36	3.35
5800	Spray		725	.022		4.70	1.14		5.84	6.85
5850	Paint 1 coat, brushwork		415	.039		3.98	1.99		5.97	7.30
6000	Spray		725	.022		4.42	1.14		5.56	6.55
6200	Paint 2 coats, brushwork		260	.062		7.75	3.18		10.93	13.20
6250	Spray		415	.039		8.60	1.99		10.59	12.40
6270	Paint 3 coats, brushwork		260	.062		11.50	3.18		14.68	17.30

09 91 Painting

09 91 23 – Interior Painting

09 91 23.52 Miscellaneous, Interior		Crew	Daily Output	Labor-Hours	Unit	Material	2024 Bare Costs Labor	Equipment	Total	Total Incl O&P
6300	13"-16" diameter, primer or sealer coat, brushwork	2 Pord	310	.052	L.F.	.49	2.67		3.16	4.48
6350	Spray		540	.030		.55	1.53		2.08	2.86
6400	Paint 1 coat, brushwork		310	.052		5.30	2.67		7.97	9.80
6450	Spray		540	.030		5.90	1.53		7.43	8.75
6500	Paint 2 coats, brushwork		195	.082		10.35	4.24		14.59	17.60
6550	Spray		310	.052		11.50	2.67		14.17	16.60
6600	Radiators, per side, primer, brushwork	1 Pord	520	.015	S.F.	.12	.80		.92	1.30
6620	Paint, 1 coat		520	.015		.11	.80		.91	1.29
6640	2 coats		340	.024		2.46	1.22		3.68	4.51
6660	3 coats		283	.028		3.65	1.46		5.11	6.20

Division Notes

	CREW	DAILY OUTPUT	LABOR-HOURS	UNIT	BARE COSTS				TOTAL INCL O&P
					MAT.	LABOR	EQUIP.	TOTAL	

Estimating Tips
General
- The items in this division are usually priced per square foot or each.
- Many items in Division 10 require some type of support system or special anchors that are not usually furnished with the item. The required anchors must be added to the estimate in the appropriate division.
- Some items in Division 10, such as lockers, may require assembly before installation. Verify the amount of assembly required. Assembly can often exceed installation time.

10 20 00 Interior Specialties
- Support angles and blocking are not included in the installation of toilet compartments, shower/dressing compartments, or cubicles. Appropriate line items from Division 5 or 6 may need to be added to support the installations.
- Toilet partitions are priced by the stall. A stall consists of a side wall, pilaster, and door with hardware. Toilet tissue holders and grab bars are extra.
- The required acoustical rating of a folding partition can have a significant impact on costs. Verify the sound transmission coefficient rating of the panel priced against the specification requirements.
- Grab bar installation does not include supplemental blocking or backing to support the required load. When grab bars are installed at an existing facility, provisions must be made to attach the grab bars to a solid structure.

Reference Numbers
Reference numbers are shown at the beginning of some major classifications. These numbers refer to related items in the Reference Section. The reference information may be an estimating procedure, an alternate pricing method, or technical information.

Note: Not all subdivisions listed here necessarily appear. ∎

Same Data. Simplified.

Enjoy the convenience and efficiency of accessing your costs anywhere:
- **Skip the multiplier** by setting your location
- **Quickly search,** edit, favorite and share costs
- **Stay on top of price changes** with automatic updates

Discover more at rsmeans.com/online

No part of this cost data may be reproduced, stored in a retrieval system, or transmitted in any form or by any means without prior written permission of Gordian.

10 21 Compartments and Cubicles

10 21 13 – Toilet Compartments

10 21 13.13 Metal Toilet Compartments

		Crew	Daily Output	Labor-Hours	Unit	Material	2024 Bare Costs Labor	2024 Bare Costs Equipment	Total	Total Incl O&P
0010	**METAL TOILET COMPARTMENTS**									
0110	Cubicles, ceiling hung									
0200	Powder coated steel	2 Carp	4	4	Ea.	520	242		762	930
0500	Stainless steel	"	4	4		2,100	242		2,342	2,650
0600	For handicap units, add					148			148	163
0900	Floor and ceiling anchored									
1000	Powder coated steel	2 Carp	5	3.200	Ea.	1,075	194		1,269	1,450
1300	Stainless steel	"	5	3.200		2,000	194		2,194	2,475
1400	For handicap units, add					146			146	161
1610	Floor anchored									
1700	Powder coated steel	2 Carp	7	2.286	Ea.	770	138		908	1,050
2000	Stainless steel	"	7	2.286		1,250	138		1,388	1,575
2100	For handicap units, add					136			136	150
2200	For juvenile units, deduct					66			66	72.50
2450	Floor anchored, headrail braced									
2500	Powder coated steel	2 Carp	6	2.667	Ea.	750	161		911	1,075
2804	Stainless steel	"	6	2.667		1,350	161		1,511	1,725
2900	For handicap units, add					239			239	263
3000	Wall hung partitions, powder coated steel	2 Carp	7	2.286		615	138		753	885
3300	Stainless steel	"	7	2.286		460	138		598	715
3400	For handicap units, add					985			985	1,075
4000	Screens, entrance, floor mounted, 58" high, 48" wide									
4200	Powder coated steel	2 Carp	15	1.067	Ea.	310	64.50		374.50	440
4500	Stainless steel	"	15	1.067	"	655	64.50		719.50	815
4650	Urinal screen, 18" wide									
4704	Powder coated steel	2 Carp	6.15	2.602	Ea.	330	158		488	600
5004	Stainless steel	"	6.15	2.602	"	675	158		833	980
5100	Floor mounted, headrail braced									
5300	Powder coated steel	2 Carp	8	2	Ea.	330	121		451	545
5600	Stainless steel	"	8	2	"	670	121		791	915
5750	Pilaster, flush									
5800	Powder coated steel	2 Carp	10	1.600	Ea.	355	97		452	540
6100	Stainless steel		10	1.600		233	97		330	400
6300	Post braced, powder coated steel		10	1.600		202	97		299	365
6800	Powder coated steel		10	1.600		149	97		246	305
7800	Wedge type, powder coated steel		10	1.600		202	97		299	365
8100	Stainless steel		10	1.600		920	97		1,017	1,175

10 21 13.16 Plastic-Laminate-Clad Toilet Compartments

		Crew	Daily Output	Labor-Hours	Unit	Material	Labor	Equipment	Total	Total Incl O&P
0010	**PLASTIC-LAMINATE-CLAD TOILET COMPARTMENTS**									
0110	Cubicles, ceiling hung									
0300	Plastic laminate on particle board	2 Carp	4	4	Ea.	650	242		892	1,075
0600	For handicap units, add				"	148			148	163
0900	Floor and ceiling anchored									
1100	Plastic laminate on particle board	2 Carp	5	3.200	Ea.	815	194		1,009	1,175
1400	For handicap units, add				"	146			146	161
1610	Floor mounted									
1800	Plastic laminate on particle board	2 Carp	7	2.286	Ea.	1,075	138		1,213	1,375
2450	Floor mounted, headrail braced									
2600	Plastic laminate on particle board	2 Carp	6	2.667	Ea.	1,125	161		1,286	1,475
3400	For handicap units, add					985			985	1,075
4300	Entrance screen, floor mtd., plas. lam., 58" high, 48" wide	2 Carp	15	1.067		350	64.50		414.50	480
4800	Urinal screen, 18" wide, ceiling braced, plastic laminate		8	2		360	121		481	575

10 21 Compartments and Cubicles

10 21 13 – Toilet Compartments

10 21 13.16 Plastic-Laminate-Clad Toilet Compartments

		Crew	Daily Output	Labor-Hours	Unit	Material	2024 Bare Costs Labor	Equipment	Total	Total Incl O&P
5400	Floor mounted, headrail braced	2 Carp	8	2	Ea.	280	121		401	490
5900	Pilaster, flush, plastic laminate		10	1.600		435	97		532	625
6400	Post braced, plastic laminate	↓	10	1.600	↓	345	97		442	525
6700	Wall hung, bracket supported									
6900	Plastic laminate on particle board	2 Carp	10	1.600	Ea.	168	97		265	330
7450	Flange supported									
7500	Plastic laminate on particle board	2 Carp	10	1.600	Ea.	168	97		265	330

10 21 13.19 Plastic Toilet Compartments

		Crew	Daily Output	Labor-Hours	Unit	Material	Labor	Equipment	Total	Total Incl O&P
0010	**PLASTIC TOILET COMPARTMENTS**									
0110	Cubicles, ceiling hung									
0250	Phenolic	2 Carp	4	4	Ea.	1,625	242		1,867	2,125
0260	Polymer plastic	"	4	4		400	242		642	800
0600	For handicap units, add				↓	148			148	163
0900	Floor and ceiling anchored									
1050	Phenolic	2 Carp	5	3.200	Ea.	1,575	194		1,769	2,025
1060	Polymer plastic	"	5	3.200		1,125	194		1,319	1,500
1400	For handicap units, add				↓	146			146	161
1610	Floor mounted									
1750	Phenolic	2 Carp	7	2.286	Ea.	1,525	138		1,663	1,875
1760	Polymer plastic	"	7	2.286		1,075	138		1,213	1,375
2100	For handicap units, add					136			136	150
2200	For juvenile units, deduct				↓	66			66	72.50
2450	Floor mounted, headrail braced									
2550	Phenolic	2 Carp	6	2.667	Ea.	1,475	161		1,636	1,875
3600	Polymer plastic		6	2.667		380	161		541	660
3810	Entrance screen, polymer plastic, flr. mtd., 48" x 58"		6	2.667		650	161		811	955
3820	Entrance screen, polymer plastic, flr. to clg pilaster, 48" x 58"		6	2.667		650	161		811	955
6110	Urinal screen, polymer plastic, pilaster flush, 18" w		6	2.667		315	161		476	585
7110	Wall hung		6	2.667		142	161		303	395
7710	Flange mounted	↓	6	2.667		315	161		476	585

10 21 13.40 Stone Toilet Compartments

		Crew	Daily Output	Labor-Hours	Unit	Material	Labor	Equipment	Total	Total Incl O&P
0010	**STONE TOILET COMPARTMENTS**									
0100	Cubicles, ceiling hung, marble	2 Marb	2	8	Ea.	2,425	470		2,895	3,375
0600	For handicap units, add					148			148	163
0800	Floor & ceiling anchored, marble	2 Marb	2.50	6.400		2,450	375		2,825	3,275
1400	For handicap units, add					146			146	161
1600	Floor mounted, marble	2 Marb	3	5.333		1,550	315		1,865	2,175
2400	Floor mounted, headrail braced, marble	"	3	5.333		1,775	315		2,090	2,425
2900	For handicap units, add					239			239	263
4100	Entrance screen, floor mounted marble, 58" high, 48" wide	2 Marb	9	1.778		1,075	105		1,180	1,325
4600	Urinal screen, 18" wide, ceiling braced, marble	D-1	6	2.667	↓	1,125	144		1,269	1,450
5100	Floor mounted, headrail braced									
5200	Marble	D-1	6	2.667	Ea.	955	144		1,099	1,275
5700	Pilaster, flush, marble		9	1.778		1,250	96		1,346	1,525
6200	Post braced, marble	↓	9	1.778		1,225	96		1,321	1,500

10 28 Toilet, Bath, and Laundry Accessories

10 28 13 – Toilet Accessories

10 28 13.13 Commercial Toilet Accessories

		Crew	Daily Output	Labor-Hours	Unit	Material	2024 Bare Costs Labor	Equipment	Total	Total Incl O&P
0010	**COMMERCIAL TOILET ACCESSORIES**									
0200	Curtain rod, stainless steel, 5' long, 1" diameter	1 Carp	13	.615	Ea.	57	37.50		94.50	118
0300	1-1/4" diameter	"	13	.615	"	39	37.50		76.50	98
0500	Dispenser units, combined soap & towel dispensers,									
0510	Mirror and shelf, flush mounted	1 Carp	10	.800	Ea.	405	48.50		453.50	515
0600	Towel dispenser and waste receptacle,									
0610	18 gallon capacity	1 Carp	10	.800	Ea.	580	48.50		628.50	705
0800	Grab bar, straight, 1-1/4" diameter, stainless steel, 18" long		24	.333		22	20		42	54
0900	24" long		23	.348		25	21		46	58.50
1000	30" long		22	.364		36	22		58	72
1100	36" long		20	.400		44.50	24		68.50	85
1105	42" long		20	.400		45	24		69	85.50
1120	Corner, 36" long		20	.400		123	24		147	171
1200	1-1/2" diameter, 24" long		23	.348		33.50	21		54.50	67.50
1300	36" long		20	.400		45.50	24		69.50	86.50
1310	42" long		18	.444		48	27		75	92.50
1500	Tub bar, 1-1/4" diameter, 24" x 36"		14	.571		125	34.50		159.50	188
1600	Plus vertical arm		12	.667		221	40.50		261.50	305
1900	End tub bar, 1" diameter, 90° angle, 16" x 32"		12	.667		87	40.50		127.50	156
2300	Hand dryer, surface mounted, electric, 115 volt, 20 amp		4	2		470	121		591	695
2400	230 volt, 10 amp		4	2		635	121		756	880
2450	Hand dryer, touch free, 1400 watt, 81,000 rpm		4	2		1,450	121		1,571	1,775
2600	Hat and coat strip, stainless steel, 4 hook, 36" long		24	.333		85.50	20		105.50	124
2700	6 hook, 60" long		20	.400		117	24		141	165
3000	Mirror, with stainless steel 3/4" square frame, 18" x 24"		20	.400		62	24		86	104
3100	36" x 24"		15	.533		85	32.50		117.50	142
3200	48" x 24"		10	.800		140	48.50		188.50	226
3300	72" x 24"		6	1.333		158	80.50		238.50	294
3500	With 5" stainless steel shelf, 18" x 24"		20	.400		118	24		142	166
3600	36" x 24"		15	.533		156	32.50		188.50	220
3700	48" x 24"		10	.800		247	48.50		295.50	345
3800	72" x 24"		6	1.333		855	80.50		935.50	1,050
4100	Mop holder strip, stainless steel, 5 holders, 48" long		20	.400		60	24		84	102
4200	Napkin/tampon dispenser, recessed		15	.533		435	32.50		467.50	530
4220	Semi-recessed		6.50	1.231		440	74.50		514.50	590
4250	Napkin receptacle, recessed		6.50	1.231		229	74.50		303.50	360
4300	Robe hook, single, regular		96	.083		28	5.05		33.05	38.50
4400	Heavy duty, concealed mounting		56	.143		28	8.65		36.65	44
4600	Soap dispenser, chrome, surface mounted, liquid		20	.400		56	24		80	97.50
5000	Recessed stainless steel, liquid		10	.800		100	48.50		148.50	182
5600	Shelf, stainless steel, 5" wide, 18 ga., 24" long		24	.333		82	20		102	121
5700	48" long		16	.500		124	30.50		154.50	181
5800	8" wide shelf, 18 ga., 24" long		22	.364		69	22		91	109
5900	48" long		14	.571		107	34.50		141.50	168
6000	Toilet seat cover dispenser, stainless steel, recessed		20	.400		221	24		245	279
6050	Surface mounted		15	.533		46	32.50		78.50	98.50
6200	Double roll		24	.333		108	20		128	149
6240	Plastic, twin/jumbo dbl. roll		24	.333		34.50	20		54.50	68
6400	Towel bar, stainless steel, 18" long		23	.348		43.50	21		64.50	79
6500	30" long		21	.381		42	23		65	80.50
6700	Towel dispenser, stainless steel, surface mounted		16	.500		65	30.50		95.50	117
6800	Flush mounted, recessed		10	.800		93	48.50		141.50	174
6900	Plastic, touchless, battery operated		16	.500		156	30.50		186.50	216

10 28 Toilet, Bath, and Laundry Accessories

10 28 13 – Toilet Accessories

10 28 13.13 Commercial Toilet Accessories

		Crew	Daily Output	Labor-Hours	Unit	Material	2024 Bare Costs Labor	Equipment	Total	Total Incl O&P
7000	Towel holder, hotel type, 2 guest size	1 Carp	20	.400	Ea.	83	24		107	128
7200	Towel shelf, stainless steel, 24" long, 8" wide		20	.400		52.50	24		76.50	94
7400	Tumbler holder, for tumbler only		30	.267		18	16.15		34.15	44
7410	Tumbler holder, recessed		20	.400		18.40	24		42.40	56
7500	Soap, tumbler & toothbrush		30	.267		7.10	16.15		23.25	32
7510	Tumbler & toothbrush holder		20	.400		11.05	24		35.05	48
8000	Waste receptacles, stainless steel, with top, 13 gallon		10	.800		465	48.50		513.50	580
8100	36 gallon		8	1		425	60.50		485.50	560
9996	Bathroom access., grab bar, straight, 1-1/2" diam., SS, 42" L install only		18	.444			27		27	40

10 28 16 – Bath Accessories

10 28 16.20 Medicine Cabinets

		Crew	Daily Output	Labor-Hours	Unit	Material	2024 Bare Costs Labor	Equipment	Total	Total Incl O&P
0010	**MEDICINE CABINETS**									
0020	With mirror, sst frame, 16" x 22", unlighted	1 Carp	14	.571	Ea.	259	34.50		293.50	335
0100	Wood frame		14	.571		136	34.50		170.50	201
0300	Sliding mirror doors, 20" x 16" x 4-3/4", unlighted		7	1.143		169	69		238	288
0400	24" x 19" x 8-1/2", lighted		5	1.600		189	97		286	350
0600	Triple door, 30" x 32", unlighted, plywood body		7	1.143		278	69		347	405
0700	Steel body		7	1.143		225	69		294	350
0900	Oak door, wood body, beveled mirror, single door		7	1.143		300	69		369	430
1000	Double door		6	1.333		480	80.50		560.50	645
1200	Hotel cabinets, stainless, with lower shelf, unlighted		10	.800		510	48.50		558.50	630
1300	Lighted		5	1.600		350	97		447	530

10 28 19 – Tub and Shower Enclosures

10 28 19.10 Partitions, Shower

		Crew	Daily Output	Labor-Hours	Unit	Material	2024 Bare Costs Labor	Equipment	Total	Total Incl O&P
0010	**PARTITIONS, SHOWER** floor mounted, no plumbing									
0400	Cabinet, one piece, fiberglass, 32" x 32"	2 Carp	5	3.200	Ea.	665	194		859	1,025
0420	36" x 36"		5	3.200		1,300	194		1,494	1,700
0440	36" x 48"		5	3.200		1,300	194		1,494	1,700
0460	Acrylic, 32" x 32"		5	3.200		277	194		471	590
0480	36" x 36"		5	3.200		670	194		864	1,025
0500	36" x 48"		5	3.200		1,100	194		1,294	1,475
0520	Shower door for above, clear plastic, 24" wide	1 Carp	8	1		111	60.50		171.50	212
0540	28" wide		8	1		505	60.50		565.50	645
0560	Tempered glass, 24" wide		8	1		187	60.50		247.50	296
0580	28" wide		8	1		218	60.50		278.50	330
2400	Glass stalls, with doors, no receptors, chrome on brass	2 Shee	3	5.333		1,225	385		1,610	1,925
2700	Anodized aluminum	"	4	4		865	289		1,154	1,400
2900	Marble shower stall, stock design, with shower door	2 Marb	1.20	13.333		820	785		1,605	2,075
3000	With curtain		1.30	12.308		2,525	725		3,250	3,850
3200	Receptors, precast terrazzo, 32" x 32"		14	1.143		315	67.50		382.50	445
3300	48" x 34"		9.50	1.684		420	99		519	610
3500	Plastic, simulated terrazzo receptor, 32" x 32"		14	1.143		161	67.50		228.50	277
3600	32" x 48"		12	1.333		835	78.50		913.50	1,025
3800	Precast concrete, colors, 32" x 32"		14	1.143		204	67.50		271.50	325
3900	48" x 48"		8	2		890	118		1,008	1,150
4100	Shower doors, economy plastic, 24" wide	1 Shee	9	.889		166	64		230	279
4200	Tempered glass door, economy		8	1		575	72.50		647.50	745
4400	Folding, tempered glass, aluminum frame		6	1.333		600	96.50		696.50	805
4500	Sliding, tempered glass, 48" opening		6	1.333		640	96.50		736.50	850
4700	Deluxe, tempered glass, chrome on brass frame, 42" to 44"		8	1		440	72.50		512.50	595
4800	39" to 48" wide		1	8		940	580		1,520	1,900
4850	On anodized aluminum frame, obscure glass		2	4		730	289		1,019	1,225

10 28 Toilet, Bath, and Laundry Accessories

10 28 19 – Tub and Shower Enclosures

10 28 19.10 Partitions, Shower

		Crew	Daily Output	Labor-Hours	Unit	Material	2024 Bare Costs Labor	Equipment	Total	Total Incl O&P
4900	Clear glass	1 Shee	1	8	Ea.	505	580		1,085	1,425
5100	Shower enclosure, tempered glass, anodized alum. frame									
5120	2 panel & door, corner unit, 32" x 32"	1 Shee	2	4	Ea.	1,275	289		1,564	1,850
5140	Neo-angle corner unit, 16" x 24" x 16"	"	2	4		1,850	289		2,139	2,450
5200	Shower surround, 3 wall, polypropylene, 32" x 32"	1 Carp	4	2		350	121		471	565
5220	PVC, 32" x 32"		4	2		280	121		401	490
5240	Fiberglass		4	2		615	121		736	855
5250	2 wall, polypropylene, 32" x 32"		4	2		820	121		941	1,075
5270	PVC		4	2		820	121		941	1,075
5290	Fiberglass		4	2		375	121		496	590
5300	Tub doors, tempered glass & frame, obscure glass	1 Shee	8	1		228	72.50		300.50	360
5400	Clear glass		6	1.333		695	96.50		791.50	910
5600	Chrome plated, brass frame, obscure glass		8	1		355	72.50		427.50	500
5700	Clear glass		6	1.333		390	96.50		486.50	570
5900	Tub/shower enclosure, temp. glass, alum. frame, obscure glass		2	4		400	289		689	875
6200	Clear glass		1.50	5.333		420	385		805	1,050
6500	On chrome-plated brass frame, obscure glass		2	4		400	289		689	875
6600	Clear glass		1.50	5.333		390	385		775	1,000
6800	Tub surround, 3 wall, polypropylene	1 Carp	4	2		310	121		431	520
6900	PVC		4	2		420	121		541	640
7000	Fiberglass, obscure glass		4	2		1,025	121		1,146	1,300
7100	Clear glass		3	2.667		805	161		966	1,125

10 44 Fire Protection Specialties

10 44 13 – Fire Protection Cabinets

10 44 13.53 Fire Equipment Cabinets

			Crew	Daily Output	Labor-Hours	Unit	Material	2024 Bare Costs Labor	Equipment	Total	Total Incl O&P
0010	**FIRE EQUIPMENT CABINETS**, not equipped, 20 ga. steel box	D4020-310									
0040	Recessed, D.S. glass in door, box size given										
1000	Portable extinguisher, single, 8" x 12" x 27", alum. door & frame		Q-12	8	2	Ea.	186	134		320	405
1100	Steel door and frame			8	2		119	134		253	330
1200	Stainless steel door and frame			8	2		192	134		326	410
2000	Portable extinguisher, large, 8" x 12" x 36", alum. door & frame			8	2		430	134		564	670
2100	Steel door and frame	D4020-330		8	2		375	134		509	615
2200	Stainless steel door and frame			8	2		625	134		759	885
2500	8" x 16" x 38", aluminum door & frame			8	2		121	134		255	335
2600	Steel door and frame			8	2		146	134		280	360
2700	Fire blanket & extinguisher cab, inc blanket, rec stl., 14" x 40" x 8"			7	2.286		325	154		479	590
2800	Fire blanket cab, inc blanket, surf mtd, stl, 15"x10"x5", w/pwdr coat fin			8	2		124	134		258	335
3000	Hose rack assy., 1-1/2" valve & 100' hose, 24" x 40" x 5-1/2"										
3100	Aluminum door and frame		Q-12	6	2.667	Ea.	1,000	179		1,179	1,400
3200	Steel door and frame	D4020-410		6	2.667		1,025	179		1,204	1,400
3300	Stainless steel door and frame			6	2.667		1,375	179		1,554	1,775
4000	Hose rack assy., 2-1/2" x 1-1/2" valve, 100' hose, 24" x 40" x 8"										
4100	Aluminum door and frame		Q-12	6	2.667	Ea.	1,125	179		1,304	1,500
4200	Steel door and frame	R211226-10		6	2.667		1,150	179		1,329	1,525
4300	Stainless steel door and frame			6	2.667		1,575	179		1,754	2,025
5000	Hose rack assy., 2-1/2" x 1-1/2" valve, 100' hose										
5010	and extinguisher, 30" x 40" x 8"										
5100	Aluminum door and frame		Q-12	5	3.200	Ea.	470	215		685	835
5200	Steel door and frame			5	3.200		470	215		685	835
5300	Stainless steel door and frame			5	3.200		1,025	215		1,240	1,450

10 44 Fire Protection Specialties

10 44 13 – Fire Protection Cabinets

10 44 13.53 Fire Equipment Cabinets

		Crew	Daily Output	Labor-Hours	Unit	Material	2024 Bare Costs Labor	Equipment	Total	Total Incl O&P
6000	Hose rack assy., 1-1/2" valve, 100' hose									
6010	and 2-1/2" FD valve, 24" x 44" x 8"									
6100	Aluminum door and frame	Q-12	5	3.200	Ea.	485	215		700	855
6200	Steel door and frame		5	3.200		440	215		655	805
6300	Stainless steel door and frame	↓	5	3.200	↓	770	215		985	1,175
7000	Hose rack assy., 1-1/2" valve & 100' hose, 2-1/2" FD valve	R211226-20								
7010	and extinguisher, 30" x 44" x 8"									
7100	Aluminum door and frame	Q-12	5	3.200	Ea.	460	215		675	825
7200	Steel door and frame		5	3.200		395	215		610	755
7300	Stainless steel door and frame	↓	5	3.200	↓	765	215		980	1,150
8000	Valve cabinet for 2-1/2" FD angle valve, 18" x 18" x 8"									
8100	Aluminum door and frame	Q-12	12	1.333	Ea.	460	89.50		549.50	640
8200	Steel door and frame		12	1.333		410	89.50		499.50	585
8300	Stainless steel door and frame	↓	12	1.333	↓	510	89.50		599.50	695

10 44 16 – Fire Extinguishers

10 44 16.13 Portable Fire Extinguishers

		Crew	Daily Output	Labor-Hours	Unit	Material	2024 Bare Costs Labor	Equipment	Total	Total Incl O&P
0010	**PORTABLE FIRE EXTINGUISHERS**									
0140	CO_2, with hose and "H" horn, 10 lb.				Ea.	400			400	440
0160	15 lb.					490			490	540
0180	20 lb.				↓	625			625	685
1000	Dry chemical, pressurized									
1040	Standard type, portable, painted, 2-1/2 lb.				Ea.	37.50			37.50	41
1060	5 lb.					67			67	73.50
1080	10 lb.					105			105	116
1100	20 lb.					228			228	251
1120	30 lb.					1,075			1,075	1,175
1300	Standard type, wheeled, 150 lb.					2,500			2,500	2,750
2000	ABC all purpose type, portable, 2-1/2 lb.					25.50			25.50	28
2060	5 lb.					46			46	50.50
2080	9-1/2 lb.					79			79	87
2100	20 lb.					135			135	148
5000	Pressurized water, 2-1/2 gallon, stainless steel					112			112	124
5060	With anti-freeze					171			171	188
9400	Installation of extinguishers, 12 or more, on nailable surface	1 Carp	30	.267			16.15		16.15	24
9420	On masonry or concrete	"	15	.533	↓		32.50		32.50	48

10 44 16.16 Wheeled Fire Extinguisher Units

		Crew	Daily Output	Labor-Hours	Unit	Material	2024 Bare Costs Labor	Equipment	Total	Total Incl O&P
0010	**WHEELED FIRE EXTINGUISHER UNITS**									
0350	CO_2, portable, with swivel horn									
0360	Wheeled type, cart mounted, 50 lb.				Ea.	2,050			2,050	2,275
0400	100 lb.				"	3,575			3,575	3,950
2200	ABC all purpose type									
2300	Wheeled, 45 lb.				Ea.	2,475			2,475	2,725
2360	150 lb.				"	3,950			3,950	4,325

Division Notes

	CREW	DAILY OUTPUT	LABOR-HOURS	UNIT	BARE COSTS				TOTAL INCL O&P
					MAT.	LABOR	EQUIP.	TOTAL	

Estimating Tips
General
- The items in this division are usually priced per square foot or each. Many of these items are purchased by the owner for installation by the contractor. Check the specifications for responsibilities and include time for receiving, storage, installation, and mechanical and electrical hookups in the appropriate divisions.
- Many items in Division 11 require some type of support system that is not usually furnished with the item. Examples of these systems include blocking for the attachment of casework and support angles/blocking for ceiling-hung projection screens. The required blocking or supports must be added to the estimate in the appropriate division.
- Some items in Division 11 may require assembly or electrical hookups. Verify the amount of assembly required or the need for a hard electrical connection and add the appropriate costs.

Reference Numbers
Reference numbers are shown at the beginning of some major classifications. These numbers refer to related items in the Reference Section. The reference information may be an estimating procedure, an alternate pricing method, or technical information.

Same Data. Simplified.
Enjoy the convenience and efficiency of accessing your costs anywhere:
- **Skip the multiplier** by setting your location
- **Quickly search**, edit, favorite and share costs
- **Stay on top of price changes** with automatic updates

Discover more at rsmeans.com/online

No part of this cost data may be reproduced, stored in a retrieval system, or transmitted in any form or by any means without prior written permission of Gordian.

11 11 Vehicle Service Equipment

11 11 13 – Compressed-Air Vehicle Service Equipment

11 11 13.10 Compressed Air Equipment

		Crew	Daily Output	Labor-Hours	Unit	Material	2024 Bare Costs Labor	2024 Bare Costs Equipment	Total	Total Incl O&P
0010	**COMPRESSED AIR EQUIPMENT**									
0030	Compressors, electric, 1-1/2 HP, standard controls	L-4	1.50	16	Ea.	1,325	925		2,250	2,875
0550	Dual controls		1.50	16		1,250	925		2,175	2,775
0600	5 HP, 115/230 volt, standard controls		1	24		1,800	1,400		3,200	4,050
0650	Dual controls		1	24		1,975	1,400		3,375	4,250

11 11 19 – Vehicle Lubrication Equipment

11 11 19.10 Lubrication Equipment

		Crew	Daily Output	Labor-Hours	Unit	Material	Labor	Equipment	Total	Total Incl O&P
0010	**LUBRICATION EQUIPMENT**									
3000	Lube equipment, 3 reel type, with pumps, not including piping	L-4	.50	48	Set	12,400	2,775		15,175	17,800
3700	Pump lubrication, pneumatic, not incl. air compressor									
3710	Oil/gear lube	Q-1	9.60	1.667	Ea.	1,300	112		1,412	1,625
3720	Grease	"	9.60	1.667	"	43	112		155	215

11 11 33 – Vehicle Spray Painting Equipment

11 11 33.10 Spray Painting Equipment

		Crew	Daily Output	Labor-Hours	Unit	Material	Labor	Equipment	Total	Total Incl O&P
0010	**SPRAY PAINTING EQUIPMENT**									
4000	Spray painting booth, 26' long, complete	L-4	.40	60	Ea.	26,100	3,475		29,575	33,900

11 21 Retail and Service Equipment

11 21 53 – Barber and Beauty Shop Equipment

11 21 53.10 Barber Equipment

		Crew	Daily Output	Labor-Hours	Unit	Material	Labor	Equipment	Total	Total Incl O&P
0010	**BARBER EQUIPMENT**									
0020	Chair, hydraulic, movable, minimum	1 Carp	24	.333	Ea.	595	20		615	685
0050	Maximum	"	16	.500		1,200	30.50		1,230.50	1,375
0500	Sink, hair washing basin, rough plumbing not incl.	1 Plum	8	1		299	74.50		373.50	440
1000	Sterilizer, liquid solution for tools					22			22	24

11 21 73 – Commercial Laundry and Dry Cleaning Equipment

11 21 73.16 Drying and Conditioning Equipment

		Crew	Daily Output	Labor-Hours	Unit	Material	Labor	Equipment	Total	Total Incl O&P
0010	**DRYING AND CONDITIONING EQUIPMENT**									
0100	Dryers, not including rough-in									
1500	Industrial, 30 lb. capacity	1 Plum	2	4	Ea.	1,650	299		1,949	2,275
1600	50 lb. capacity	"	1.70	4.706	"	8,925	350		9,275	10,400

11 21 73.26 Commercial Washers and Extractors

		Crew	Daily Output	Labor-Hours	Unit	Material	Labor	Equipment	Total	Total Incl O&P
0010	**COMMERCIAL WASHERS AND EXTRACTORS**, not including rough-in									
6000	Combination washer/extractor, 20 lb. capacity	L-6	1.50	8	Ea.	6,600	590		7,190	8,125
6100	30 lb. capacity		.80	15		12,200	1,100		13,300	15,100
6200	50 lb. capacity		.68	17.647		15,400	1,300		16,700	18,800
6300	75 lb. capacity		.30	40		17,600	2,950		20,550	23,800
6350	125 lb. capacity		.16	75		21,800	5,525		27,325	32,100

11 21 73.33 Coin-Operated Laundry Equipment

		Crew	Daily Output	Labor-Hours	Unit	Material	Labor	Equipment	Total	Total Incl O&P
0010	**COIN-OPERATED LAUNDRY EQUIPMENT**									
0990	Dryer, gas fired									
1000	Commercial, 30 lb. capacity, coin operated, single	1 Plum	3	2.667	Ea.	1,425	199		1,624	1,875
1100	Double stacked	"	2	4	"	2,100	299		2,399	2,775
5290	Clothes washer									
5300	Commercial, coin operated, average	1 Plum	3	2.667	Ea.	1,075	199		1,274	1,475

11 21 Retail and Service Equipment

11 21 83 – Photo Processing Equipment

11 21 83.13 Darkroom Equipment

		Crew	Daily Output	Labor-Hours	Unit	Material	2024 Bare Costs Labor	2024 Bare Costs Equipment	Total	Total Incl O&P
0010	DARKROOM EQUIPMENT									
0020	Developing sink, 5" deep, 24" x 48"	Q-1	2	8	Ea.	400	535		935	1,250
0050	48" x 52"		1.70	9.412		990	630		1,620	2,050
0200	10" deep, 24" x 48"		1.70	9.412		1,825	630		2,455	2,950
0250	24" x 108"		1.50	10.667		5,175	715		5,890	6,775

11 30 Residential Equipment

11 30 13 – Residential Appliances

11 30 13.15 Cooking Equipment

		Crew	Daily Output	Labor-Hours	Unit	Material	2024 Bare Costs Labor	2024 Bare Costs Equipment	Total	Total Incl O&P
0010	COOKING EQUIPMENT									
0020	Cooking range, 30" free standing, 1 oven, minimum	2 Clab	10	1.600	Ea.	700	78.50		778.50	885
0050	Maximum		4	4		935	196		1,131	1,325
0150	2 oven, minimum		10	1.600		1,550	78.50		1,628.50	1,825
0200	Maximum		10	1.600		4,700	78.50		4,778.50	5,300

11 30 13.16 Refrigeration Equipment

		Crew	Daily Output	Labor-Hours	Unit	Material	Labor	Equipment	Total	Total Incl O&P
0010	REFRIGERATION EQUIPMENT									
5200	Icemaker, automatic, 20 lbs./day	1 Plum	7	1.143	Ea.	1,725	85.50		1,810.50	2,025
5350	51 lbs./day	"	2	4	"	3,050	299		3,349	3,800

11 30 13.17 Kitchen Cleaning Equipment

		Crew	Daily Output	Labor-Hours	Unit	Material	Labor	Equipment	Total	Total Incl O&P
0010	KITCHEN CLEANING EQUIPMENT									
2750	Dishwasher, built-in, 2 cycles, minimum	L-1	4	4	Ea.	525	293		818	1,000
2800	Maximum		2	8		525	585		1,110	1,450
2950	4 or more cycles, minimum		4	4		650	293		943	1,150
2960	Average		4	4		865	293		1,158	1,375
3000	Maximum		2	8		445	585		1,030	1,350

11 30 13.18 Waste Disposal Equipment

		Crew	Daily Output	Labor-Hours	Unit	Material	Labor	Equipment	Total	Total Incl O&P
0010	WASTE DISPOSAL EQUIPMENT									
3300	Garbage disposal, sink type, minimum	L-1	10	1.600	Ea.	94	117		211	278
3350	Maximum	"	10	1.600	"	255	117		372	455

11 30 13.19 Kitchen Ventilation Equipment

		Crew	Daily Output	Labor-Hours	Unit	Material	Labor	Equipment	Total	Total Incl O&P
0010	KITCHEN VENTILATION EQUIPMENT									
4150	Hood for range, 2 speed, vented, 30" wide, minimum	L-3	5	3.200	Ea.	69	212		281	390
4200	Maximum		3	5.333		1,200	355		1,555	1,850
4300	42" wide, minimum		5	3.200		120	212		332	445
4330	Custom		5	3.200		182	212		394	515
4350	Maximum		3	5.333		222	355		577	770
4500	For ventless hood, 2 speed, add					99			99	109
4650	For vented 1 speed, deduct from maximum					133			133	146

11 30 13.24 Washers

		Crew	Daily Output	Labor-Hours	Unit	Material	Labor	Equipment	Total	Total Incl O&P
0010	WASHERS									
5000	Residential, 4 cycle, average	1 Plum	3	2.667	Ea.	500	199		699	845
6650	Washing machine, automatic, minimum		3	2.667		800	199		999	1,175
6700	Maximum		1	8		2,700	595		3,295	3,875

11 30 13.25 Dryers

		Crew	Daily Output	Labor-Hours	Unit	Material	Labor	Equipment	Total	Total Incl O&P
0010	DRYERS									
0500	Gas fired residential, 16 lb. capacity, average	1 Plum	3	2.667	Ea.	1,000	199		1,199	1,400
7450	Vent kits for dryers	1 Carp	10	.800	"	64	48.50		112.50	142

11 30 Residential Equipment

11 30 15 – Miscellaneous Residential Appliances

11 30 15.13 Sump Pumps

		Crew	Daily Output	Labor-Hours	Unit	Material	2024 Bare Costs Labor	2024 Bare Costs Equipment	Total	Total Incl O&P
0010	**SUMP PUMPS**									
6400	Cellar drainer, pedestal, 1/3 HP, molded PVC base	1 Plum	3	2.667	Ea.	192	199		391	505
6450	Solid brass	"	2	4	"	350	299		649	830
6460	Sump pump, see also Section 22 14 29.16									

11 30 15.23 Water Heaters

		Crew	Daily Output	Labor-Hours	Unit	Material	Labor	Equipment	Total	Incl O&P
0010	**WATER HEATERS**									
6900	Electric, glass lined, 30 gallon, minimum	L-1	5	3.200	Ea.	750	234		984	1,175
6950	Maximum		3	5.333		1,050	390		1,440	1,725
7100	80 gallon, minimum		2	8		1,400	585		1,985	2,425
7150	Maximum		1	16		1,950	1,175		3,125	3,900
7180	Gas, glass lined, 30 gallon, minimum	2 Plum	5	3.200		950	239		1,189	1,400
7220	Maximum		3	5.333		1,325	400		1,725	2,050
7260	50 gallon, minimum		2.50	6.400		905	480		1,385	1,700
7300	Maximum		1.50	10.667		1,250	795		2,045	2,550
7310	Water heater, see also Section 22 33 30.13									

11 30 15.43 Air Quality

		Crew	Daily Output	Labor-Hours	Unit	Material	Labor	Equipment	Total	Incl O&P
0010	**AIR QUALITY**									
2450	Dehumidifier, portable, automatic, 15 pint	1 Elec	4	2	Ea.	193	143		336	425
2550	40 pint		3.75	2.133		345	153		498	605
3550	Heater, electric, built-in, 1250 watt, ceiling type, minimum		4	2		119	143		262	345
3600	Maximum		3	2.667		271	191		462	580
3700	Wall type, minimum		4	2		123	143		266	350
3750	Maximum		3	2.667		142	191		333	440
3900	1500 watt wall type, with blower		4	2		193	143		336	425
3950	3000 watt		3	2.667		235	191		426	540
4850	Humidifier, portable, 8 gallons/day					178			178	196
5000	15 gallons/day					289			289	320

11 32 Unit Kitchens

11 32 13 – Metal Unit Kitchens

11 32 13.10 Commercial Unit Kitchens

		Crew	Daily Output	Labor-Hours	Unit	Material	Labor	Equipment	Total	Incl O&P
0010	**COMMERCIAL UNIT KITCHENS**									
1500	Combination range, refrigerator and sink, 30" wide, minimum	L-1	2	8	Ea.	1,475	585		2,060	2,475
1550	Maximum		1	16		1,450	1,175		2,625	3,350
1570	60" wide, average		1.40	11.429		2,075	835		2,910	3,525
1590	72" wide, average		1.20	13.333		2,175	975		3,150	3,825
1600	Office model, 48" wide		2	8		3,400	585		3,985	4,625
1620	Refrigerator and sink only		2.40	6.667		3,600	490		4,090	4,675
1640	Combination range, refrigerator, sink, microwave									
1660	Oven and ice maker	L-1	.80	20	Ea.	5,925	1,475		7,400	8,700

11 41 Foodservice Storage Equipment

11 41 13 – Refrigerated Food Storage Cases

11 41 13.20 Refrigerated Food Storage Equipment	Crew	Daily Output	Labor-Hours	Unit	Material	2024 Bare Costs Labor	Equipment	Total	Total Incl O&P
0010 **REFRIGERATED FOOD STORAGE EQUIPMENT**									
2350 Cooler, reach-in, beverage, 6' long	Q-1	6	2.667	Ea.	4,075	179		4,254	4,750
4300 Freezers, reach-in, 44 C.F.		4	4		2,550	269		2,819	3,200
4500 68 C.F.	↓	3	5.333	↓	9,000	360		9,360	10,400

11 44 Food Cooking Equipment

11 44 13 – Commercial Ranges

11 44 13.10 Cooking Equipment

	Crew	Daily Output	Labor-Hours	Unit	Material	Labor	Equipment	Total	Total Incl O&P
0010 **COOKING EQUIPMENT**									
0020 Bake oven, gas, one section	Q-1	8	2	Ea.	3,700	134		3,834	4,250
0300 Two sections		7	2.286		9,050	154		9,204	10,200
0600 Three sections	↓	6	2.667		14,700	179		14,879	16,500
0900 Electric convection, single deck	L-7	4	7		16,700	410		17,110	18,900
6350 Kettle, w/steam jacket, tilting, w/positive lock, SS, 20 gallons		7	4		19,500	235		19,735	21,800
6600 60 gallons	↓	6	4.667	↓	24,100	275		24,375	26,900

11 46 Food Dispensing Equipment

11 46 83 – Ice Machines

11 46 83.10 Commercial Ice Equipment

	Crew	Daily Output	Labor-Hours	Unit	Material	Labor	Equipment	Total	Total Incl O&P
0010 **COMMERCIAL ICE EQUIPMENT**									
5800 Ice cube maker, 50 lbs./day	Q-1	6	2.667	Ea.	2,725	179		2,904	3,275
6050 500 lbs./day	"	4	4	"	3,575	269		3,844	4,350

11 48 Foodservice Cleaning and Disposal Equipment

11 48 13 – Commercial Dishwashers

11 48 13.10 Dishwashers

	Crew	Daily Output	Labor-Hours	Unit	Material	Labor	Equipment	Total	Total Incl O&P
0010 **DISHWASHERS**									
2700 Dishwasher, commercial, rack type									
2720 10 to 12 racks/hour	Q-1	3.20	5	Ea.	38,500	335		38,835	42,900
2730 Energy star rated, 35 to 40 racks/hour [G]		1.30	12.308		6,350	825		7,175	8,200
2740 50 to 60 racks/hour [G]	↓	1.30	12.308		10,100	825		10,925	12,300
2800 Automatic, 190 to 230 racks/hour	L-6	.35	34.286		36,200	2,525		38,725	43,700
2820 235 to 275 racks/hour		.25	48		32,100	3,525		35,625	40,600
2840 8,750 to 12,500 dishes/hour	↓	.10	120	↓	54,000	8,850		62,850	72,500

11 53 Laboratory Equipment

11 53 13 – Laboratory Fume Hoods

11 53 13.13 Recirculating Laboratory Fume Hoods

	Crew	Daily Output	Labor-Hours	Unit	Material	Labor	Equipment	Total	Total Incl O&P
0010 **RECIRCULATING LABORATORY FUME HOODS**									
0670 Service fixtures, average				Ea.	1,950			1,950	2,150
0680 For sink assembly with hot and cold water, add	1 Plum	1.40	5.714	"	770	425		1,195	1,475

11 53 Laboratory Equipment

11 53 19 – Laboratory Sterilizers

11 53 19.13 Sterilizers	Crew	Daily Output	Labor-Hours	Unit	Material	2024 Bare Costs Labor	2024 Bare Costs Equipment	Total	Total Incl O&P
0010 **STERILIZERS**									
0700 Glassware washer, undercounter, minimum	L-1	1.80	8.889	Ea.	7,925	650		8,575	9,700
0710 Maximum	"	1	16		17,400	1,175		18,575	20,900
1850 Utensil washer-sanitizer	1 Plum	2	4		7,275	299		7,574	8,450

11 53 23 – Laboratory Refrigerators

11 53 23.13 Refrigerators

	Crew	Daily Output	Labor-Hours	Unit	Material	Labor	Equipment	Total	Total Incl O&P
0010 **REFRIGERATORS**									
1200 Blood bank, 28.6 C.F. emergency signal				Ea.	14,600			14,600	16,100
1210 Reach-in, 16.9 C.F.				"	8,025			8,025	8,825

11 53 33 – Emergency Safety Appliances

11 53 33.13 Emergency Equipment

	Crew	Daily Output	Labor-Hours	Unit	Material	Labor	Equipment	Total	Total Incl O&P
0010 **EMERGENCY EQUIPMENT**									
1400 Safety equipment, eye wash, hand held				Ea.	350			350	385
1450 Deluge shower				"	284			284	315

11 53 43 – Service Fittings and Accessories

11 53 43.13 Fittings

	Crew	Daily Output	Labor-Hours	Unit	Material	Labor	Equipment	Total	Total Incl O&P
0010 **FITTINGS**									
1600 Sink, one piece plastic, flask wash, hose, free standing	1 Plum	1.60	5	Ea.	340	375		715	930
1610 Epoxy resin sink, 25" x 16" x 10"	"	2	4	"	1,700	299		1,999	2,300
8000 Alternate pricing method: as percent of lab furniture									
8050 Installation, not incl. plumbing & duct work				% Furn.				22%	22%
8100 Plumbing, final connections, simple system								10%	10%
8110 Moderately complex system								15%	15%
8120 Complex system								20%	20%
8150 Electrical, simple system								10%	10%
8160 Moderately complex system								20%	20%
8170 Complex system								35%	35%

11 71 Medical Sterilizing Equipment

11 71 10 – Medical Sterilizers & Distillers

11 71 10.10 Sterilizers and Distillers

	Crew	Daily Output	Labor-Hours	Unit	Material	Labor	Equipment	Total	Total Incl O&P
0010 **STERILIZERS AND DISTILLERS**									
0700 Distiller, water, steam heated, 50 gal. capacity	1 Plum	1.40	5.714	Ea.	53,000	425		53,425	59,000
5600 Sterilizers, floor loading, 26" x 62" x 42", single door, steam					67,000			67,000	73,500
5650 Double door, steam					67,000			67,000	73,500
5800 General purpose, 20" x 20" x 38", single door					29,300			29,300	32,200
6000 Portable, counter top, steam, minimum					3,650			3,650	4,000
6020 Maximum					2,200			2,200	2,425
6050 Portable, counter top, gas, 17" x 15" x 32-1/2"					3,650			3,650	4,000
6150 Manual washer/sterilizer, 16" x 16" x 26"	1 Plum	2	4		3,600	299		3,899	4,425
6200 Steam generators, electric 10 kW to 180 kW, freestanding									
6250 Minimum	1 Elec	3	2.667	Ea.	6,850	191		7,041	7,800
6300 Maximum	"	.70	11.429		3,625	820		4,445	5,225
8200 Bed pan washer-sanitizer	1 Plum	2	4		6,550	299		6,849	7,675

11 73 Patient Care Equipment

11 73 10 – Patient Treatment Equipment

11 73 10.10 Treatment Equipment

		Crew	Daily Output	Labor-Hours	Unit	Material	2024 Bare Costs Labor	2024 Bare Costs Equipment	Total	Total Incl O&P
0010	TREATMENT EQUIPMENT									
1800	Heat therapy unit, humidified, 26" x 78" x 28"				Ea.	350			350	385
2100	Hubbard tank with accessories, stainless steel,									
2110	125 GPM at 45 psi water pressure				Ea.	28,100			28,100	30,900
2150	For electric overhead hoist, add					2,725			2,725	3,000
3600	Paraffin bath, 126°F, auto controlled					245			245	270
4600	Station, dietary, medium, with ice					620			620	680
8400	Whirlpool bath, mobile, sst, 18" x 24" x 60"					5,200			5,200	5,725
8450	Fixed, incl. mixing valves	1 Plum	2	4	↓	7,950	299		8,249	9,200

11 74 Dental Equipment

11 74 10 – Dental Office Equipment

11 74 10.10 Diagnostic and Treatment Equipment

		Crew	Daily Output	Labor-Hours	Unit	Material	2024 Bare Costs Labor	2024 Bare Costs Equipment	Total	Total Incl O&P
0010	DIAGNOSTIC AND TREATMENT EQUIPMENT									
0020	Central suction system, minimum	1 Plum	1.20	6.667	Ea.	1,800	500		2,300	2,750
0100	Maximum	"	.90	8.889		4,725	665		5,390	6,150
0300	Air compressor, minimum	1 Skwk	.80	10		4,075	635		4,710	5,425
0400	Maximum		.50	16		10,900	1,025		11,925	13,500
0600	Chair, electric or hydraulic, minimum		.50	16		3,700	1,025		4,725	5,600
0700	Maximum		.25	32		4,325	2,025		6,350	7,800
2000	Light, ceiling mounted, minimum		8	1		940	63.50		1,003.50	1,125
2100	Maximum	↓	8	1		3,425	63.50		3,488.50	3,850
2200	Unit light, minimum	2 Skwk	5.33	3.002		655	191		846	1,000
2210	Maximum		5.33	3.002		2,225	191		2,416	2,725
2220	Track light, minimum		3.20	5		2,475	320		2,795	3,200
2230	Maximum	↓	3.20	5		4,700	320		5,020	5,650
2300	Sterilizers, steam portable, minimum					3,675			3,675	4,050
2350	Maximum					7,600			7,600	8,350
2600	Steam, institutional					3,400			3,400	3,725
2650	Dry heat, electric, portable, 3 trays				↓	1,975			1,975	2,175

11 76 Operating Room Equipment

11 76 10 – Equipment for Operating Rooms

11 76 10.10 Surgical Equipment

		Crew	Daily Output	Labor-Hours	Unit	Material	2024 Bare Costs Labor	2024 Bare Costs Equipment	Total	Total Incl O&P
0010	SURGICAL EQUIPMENT									
5000	Scrub, surgical, stainless steel, single station, minimum	1 Plum	3	2.667	Ea.	2,025	199		2,224	2,525
5100	Maximum				"	14,500			14,500	15,900

11 78 Mortuary Equipment

11 78 13 – Mortuary Refrigerators

11 78 13.10 Mortuary and Autopsy Equipment	Crew	Daily Output	Labor-Hours	Unit	Material	2024 Bare Costs Labor	Equipment	Total	Total Incl O&P
0010 **MORTUARY AND AUTOPSY EQUIPMENT**									
0015 Autopsy table, standard	1 Plum	1	8	Ea.	8,300	595		8,895	10,000
0020 Deluxe	"	.60	13.333	"	3,175	995		4,170	4,975

11 81 Facility Maintenance Equipment

11 81 19 – Vacuum Cleaning Systems

11 81 19.10 Vacuum Cleaning

	Crew	Daily Output	Labor-Hours	Unit	Material	Labor	Equipment	Total	Total Incl O&P
0010 **VACUUM CLEANING**									
0020 Central, 3 inlet, residential	1 Skwk	.90	8.889	Total	1,250	565		1,815	2,225
0200 Commercial		.70	11.429		2,550	725		3,275	3,875
0400 5 inlet system, residential		.50	16		1,975	1,025		3,000	3,675
0600 7 inlet system, commercial		.40	20		1,750	1,275		3,025	3,825
0800 9 inlet system, residential	↓	.30	26.667	↓	4,525	1,700		6,225	7,500

11 91 Religious Equipment

11 91 13 – Baptisteries

11 91 13.10 Baptistry

	Crew	Daily Output	Labor-Hours	Unit	Material	Labor	Equipment	Total	Total Incl O&P
0010 **BAPTISTRY**									
0150 Fiberglass, 3'-6" deep, x 13'-7" long,									
0160 steps at both ends, incl. plumbing, minimum	L-8	1	20	Ea.	3,650	1,275		4,925	5,875
0200 Maximum	"	.70	28.571		4,150	1,800		5,950	7,250
0250 Add for filter, heater and lights				↓	1,550			1,550	1,700

11 91 23 – Sanctuary Equipment

11 91 23.10 Sanctuary Furnishings

	Crew	Daily Output	Labor-Hours	Unit	Material	Labor	Equipment	Total	Total Incl O&P
0010 **SANCTUARY FURNISHINGS**									
0020 Altar, wood, custom design, plain	1 Carp	1.40	5.714	Ea.	505	345		850	1,075
0050 Deluxe	"	.20	40	"	12,100	2,425		14,525	16,900

11 98 Detention Equipment

11 98 30 – Detention Cell Equipment

11 98 30.10 Cell Equipment

	Crew	Daily Output	Labor-Hours	Unit	Material	Labor	Equipment	Total	Total Incl O&P
0010 **CELL EQUIPMENT**									
3000 Toilet apparatus including wash basin, average	L-8	1.50	13.333	Ea.	2,175	845		3,020	3,625

Division 12 Furnishings

Estimating Tips
General
- The items in this division are usually priced per square foot or each. Most of these items are purchased by the owner and installed by the contractor. Do not assume the items in Division 12 will be purchased and installed by the contractor. Check the specifications for responsibilities and include receiving, storage, installation, and mechanical and electrical hookups in the appropriate divisions.
- Some items in this division require some type of support system that is not usually furnished with the item. Examples of these systems include blocking for the attachment of casework and heavy drapery rods. The required blocking must be added to the estimate in the appropriate division.

Reference Numbers
Reference numbers are shown at the beginning of some major classifications. These numbers refer to related items in the Reference Section. The reference information may be an estimating procedure, an alternate pricing method, or technical information.

Same Data. Simplified.

Enjoy the convenience and efficiency of accessing your costs anywhere:
- **Skip the multiplier** by setting your location
- **Quickly search,** edit, favorite and share costs
- **Stay on top of price changes** with automatic updates

Discover more at rsmeans.com/online

No part of this cost data may be reproduced, stored in a retrieval system, or transmitted in any form or by any means without prior written permission of Gordian.

12 32 Manufactured Wood Casework

12 32 23 – Hardwood Casework

12 32 23.10 Manufactured Wood Casework, Stock Units

		Crew	Daily Output	Labor-Hours	Unit	Material	2024 Bare Costs Labor	Equipment	Total	Total Incl O&P
0010	**MANUFACTURED WOOD CASEWORK, STOCK UNITS**									
0700	Kitchen base cabinets, hardwood, not incl. counter tops,									
0710	24" deep, 35" high, prefinished									
0800	One top drawer, one door below, 12" wide	2 Carp	24.80	.645	Ea.	425	39		464	530
0840	18" wide		23.30	.687		465	41.50		506.50	575
0880	24" wide		22.30	.717		545	43.50		588.50	665
1000	Four drawers, 12" wide		24.80	.645		645	39		684	770
1040	18" wide		23.30	.687		690	41.50		731.50	820
1060	24" wide		22.30	.717		750	43.50		793.50	885
1200	Two top drawers, two doors below, 27" wide		22	.727		500	44		544	615
1260	36" wide		20.30	.788		505	47.50		552.50	625
1300	48" wide		18.90	.847		735	51.50		786.50	885
1500	Range or sink base, two doors below, 30" wide		21.40	.748		455	45.50		500.50	565
1540	36" wide		20.30	.788		485	47.50		532.50	600
1580	48" wide		18.90	.847		550	51.50		601.50	680
1800	For sink front units, deduct					211			211	233
9000	For deluxe models of all cabinets, add					40%				
9500	For custom built in place, add					25%	10%			
9558	Rule of thumb, kitchen cabinets not including									
9560	appliances & counter top, minimum	2 Carp	30	.533	L.F.	249	32.50		281.50	320
9600	Maximum	"	25	.640	"	550	39		589	665

12 32 23.30 Manufactured Wood Casework Vanities

		Crew	Daily Output	Labor-Hours	Unit	Material	2024 Bare Costs Labor	Equipment	Total	Total Incl O&P
0010	**MANUFACTURED WOOD CASEWORK VANITIES**									
8000	Vanity bases, 2 doors, 30" high, 21" deep, 24" wide	2 Carp	20	.800	Ea.	540	48.50		588.50	665
8050	30" wide		16	1		595	60.50		655.50	740
8100	36" wide		13.33	1.200		495	72.50		567.50	655
8150	48" wide		11.43	1.400		645	85		730	835
9000	For deluxe models of all vanities, add to above					40%				
9500	For custom built in place, add to above					25%	10%			

Division 13 — Special Construction

Estimating Tips
General
- The items and systems in this division are usually estimated, purchased, supplied, and installed as a unit by one or more subcontractors. The estimator must ensure that all parties are operating from the same set of specifications and assumptions, and that all necessary items are estimated and will be provided. Many times the complex items and systems are covered, but the more common ones, such as excavation or a crane, are overlooked for the very reason that everyone assumes nobody could miss them. The estimator should be the central focus and be able to ensure that all systems are complete.
- It is important to consider factors such as site conditions, weather, shape and size of building, as well as labor availability as they may impact the overall cost of erecting special structures and systems included in this division.
- Another area where problems can develop in this division is at the interface between systems. The estimator must ensure, for instance, that anchor bolts, nuts, and washers are estimated and included for the air-supported structures and pre-engineered buildings to be bolted to their foundations. Utility supply is a common area where essential items or pieces of equipment can be missed or overlooked because each subcontractor may feel it is another's responsibility. The estimator should also be aware of certain items which may be supplied as part of a package but installed by others, and ensure that the installing contractor's estimate includes the cost of installation. Conversely, the estimator must also ensure that items are not costed by two different subcontractors, resulting in an inflated overall estimate.

13 30 00 Special Structures
- The foundations and floor slab, as well as rough mechanical and electrical, should be estimated, as this work is required for the assembly and erection of the structure. Generally, as noted in the data set, the pre-engineered building comes as a shell. Pricing is based on the size and structural design parameters stated in the reference section. Additional features, such as windows and doors with their related structural framing, must also be included by the estimator. Here again, the estimator must have a clear understanding of the scope of each portion of the work and all the necessary interfaces.

Reference Numbers
Reference numbers are shown at the beginning of some major classifications. These numbers refer to related items in the Reference Section. The reference information may be an estimating procedure, an alternate pricing method, or technical information.

Note: Not all subdivisions listed here necessarily appear. ■

Same Data. Simplified.
Enjoy the convenience and efficiency of accessing your costs anywhere:
- **Skip the multiplier** by setting your location
- **Quickly search,** edit, favorite and share costs
- **Stay on top of price changes** with automatic updates

Discover more at rsmeans.com/online

No part of this cost data may be reproduced, stored in a retrieval system, or transmitted in any form or by any means without prior written permission of Gordian.

13 11 Swimming Pools

13 11 13 – Below-Grade Swimming Pools

13 11 13.50 Swimming Pools

		Crew	Daily Output	Labor-Hours	Unit	Material	2024 Bare Costs Labor	2024 Bare Costs Equipment	Total	Total Incl O&P
0010	**SWIMMING POOLS** Residential in-ground, vinyl lined									
0020	Concrete sides, w/equip, sand bottom	B-52	300	.187	SF Surf	44	10.50	2.19	56.69	66.50
0100	Metal or polystyrene sides	B-14	410	.117		92	6.05	.71	98.76	111
0200	Add for vermiculite bottom					3.74			3.74	4.11
0500	Gunite bottom and sides, white plaster finish									
0600	12' x 30' pool	B-52	145	.386	SF Surf	68.50	21.50	4.53	94.53	112
0720	16' x 32' pool		155	.361		62	20.50	4.23	86.73	103
0750	20' x 40' pool		250	.224		55.50	12.55	2.63	70.68	82.50
0810	Concrete bottom and sides, tile finish									
0820	12' x 30' pool	B-52	80	.700	SF Surf	69.50	39.50	8.20	117.20	143
0830	16' x 32' pool		95	.589		57.50	33	6.90	97.40	120
0840	20' x 40' pool		130	.431		45.50	24	5.05	74.55	91.50
1100	Motel, gunite with plaster finish, incl. medium									
1150	capacity filtration & chlorination	B-52	115	.487	SF Surf	84.50	27.50	5.70	117.70	140
1200	Municipal, gunite with plaster finish, incl. high									
1250	capacity filtration & chlorination	B-52	100	.560	SF Surf	109	31.50	6.55	147.05	174
1350	Add for formed gutters				L.F.	161			161	177
1360	Add for stainless steel gutters				"	475			475	525
1600	For water heating system, see Section 23 52 28.10									
1700	Filtration and deck equipment only, as % of total				Total				20%	20%
1800	Automatic vacuum, hand tools, etc., 20' x 40' pool				SF Pool				.56	.62
1900	5,000 S.F. pool				"				.11	.12
3000	Painting pools, preparation + 3 coats, 20' x 40' pool, epoxy	2 Pord	.33	48.485	Total	2,250	2,500		4,750	6,175
3100	Rubber base paint, 18 gallons	"	.33	48.485		1,550	2,500		4,050	5,400
3500	42' x 82' pool, 75 gallons, epoxy paint	3 Pord	.14	171		9,550	8,875		18,425	23,600
3600	Rubber base paint	"	.14	171		6,400	8,875		15,275	20,100

13 11 23 – On-Grade Swimming Pools

13 11 23.50 Swimming Pools

		Crew	Daily Output	Labor-Hours	Unit	Material	Labor	Equipment	Total	Total Incl O&P
0010	**SWIMMING POOLS** Residential above ground, steel construction									
0100	Round, 15' diam.	B-80A	3	8	Ea.	1,100	390	173	1,663	2,000
0120	18' diam.		2.50	9.600		1,175	470	208	1,853	2,225
0140	21' diam.		2	12		1,325	590	260	2,175	2,600
0160	24' diam.		1.80	13.333		1,500	655	289	2,444	2,925
0180	27' diam.		1.50	16		1,875	785	345	3,005	3,575
0200	30' diam.		1	24		2,175	1,175	520	3,870	4,725
0220	Oval, 12' x 24'		2.30	10.435		1,900	510	226	2,636	3,100
0240	15' x 30'		1.80	13.333		4,925	655	289	5,869	6,675
0260	18' x 33'		1	24		3,025	1,175	520	4,720	5,650

13 11 46 – Swimming Pool Accessories

13 11 46.50 Swimming Pool Equipment

		Crew	Daily Output	Labor-Hours	Unit	Material	Labor	Equipment	Total	Total Incl O&P
0010	**SWIMMING POOL EQUIPMENT**									
0020	Diving stand, stainless steel, 3 meter	2 Carp	.40	40	Ea.	18,500	2,425		20,925	23,900
0300	1 meter	"	2.70	5.926		20,700	360		21,060	23,300
2100	Lights, underwater, 12 volt, with transformer, 300 watt	1 Elec	1	8		291	575		866	1,175
2200	110 volt, 500 watt, standard		1	8		385	575		960	1,275
2400	Low water cutoff type		1	8		415	575		990	1,300
2800	Heaters, see Section 23 52 28.10									

13 12 Fountains

13 12 13 – Exterior Fountains

13 12 13.10 Outdoor Fountains		Crew	Daily Output	Labor-Hours	Unit	Material	2024 Bare Costs Labor	Equipment	Total	Total Incl O&P
0010	**OUTDOOR FOUNTAINS**									
0100	Outdoor fountain, 48" high with bowl and figures	2 Clab	2	8	Ea.	410	390		800	1,025
0200	Commercial, concrete or cast stone, 40-60" H, simple		2	8		1,025	390		1,415	1,700
0220	Average		2	8		2,000	390		2,390	2,775
0240	Ornate		2	8		4,550	390		4,940	5,575
0260	Metal, 72" high		2	8		1,600	390		1,990	2,350
0280	90" high		2	8		2,325	390		2,715	3,150
0300	120" high		2	8		5,550	390		5,940	6,675
0320	Resin or fiberglass, 40-60" H, wall type		2	8		730	390		1,120	1,375
0340	Waterfall type		2	8		1,225	390		1,615	1,925

13 12 23 – Interior Fountains

13 12 23.10 Indoor Fountains		Crew	Daily Output	Labor-Hours	Unit	Material	Labor	Equipment	Total	Total Incl O&P
0010	**INDOOR FOUNTAINS**									
0100	Commercial, floor type, resin or fiberglass, lighted, cascade type	2 Clab	2	8	Ea.	645	390		1,035	1,300
0120	Tiered type		2	8		685	390		1,075	1,325
0140	Waterfall type		2	8		1,375	390		1,765	2,075

13 17 Tubs and Pools

13 17 13 – Hot Tubs

13 17 13.10 Redwood Hot Tub System

		Crew	Daily Output	Labor-Hours	Unit	Material	Labor	Equipment	Total	Total Incl O&P
0010	**REDWOOD HOT TUB SYSTEM**									
7050	4' diameter x 4' deep	Q-1	1	16	Ea.	5,725	1,075		6,800	7,900
7100	5' diameter x 4' deep		1	16		6,100	1,075		7,175	8,325
7150	6' diameter x 4' deep		.80	20		7,775	1,350		9,125	10,600
7200	8' diameter x 4' deep		.80	20		11,100	1,350		12,450	14,200

13 17 33 – Whirlpool Tubs

13 17 33.10 Whirlpool Bath

		Crew	Daily Output	Labor-Hours	Unit	Material	Labor	Equipment	Total	Total Incl O&P
0010	**WHIRLPOOL BATH**									
6000	Whirlpool, bath with vented overflow, molded fiberglass									
6100	66" x 36" x 24"	Q-1	1	16	Ea.	2,525	1,075		3,600	4,375
6400	72" x 36" x 21"		1	16		2,150	1,075		3,225	3,975
6500	60" x 34" x 21"		1	16		1,500	1,075		2,575	3,250
6600	72" x 42" x 23"		1	16		1,275	1,075		2,350	3,000
6710	For color, add					10%				
6711	For designer colors and trim, add					25%				

13 24 Special Activity Rooms

13 24 16 – Saunas

13 24 16.50 Saunas and Heaters

		Crew	Daily Output	Labor-Hours	Unit	Material	Labor	Equipment	Total	Total Incl O&P
0010	**SAUNAS AND HEATERS**									
0020	Prefabricated, incl. heater & controls, 7' high, 6' x 4', C/C	L-7	2.20	12.727	Ea.	5,925	750		6,675	7,625
0050	6' x 4', C/P		2	14		4,800	825		5,625	6,525
0400	6' x 5', C/C		2	14		5,975	825		6,800	7,800
0450	6' x 5', C/P		2	14		5,775	825		6,600	7,575
0600	6' x 6', C/C		1.80	15.556		10,800	915		11,715	13,300
0650	6' x 6', C/P		1.80	15.556		6,425	915		7,340	8,425
0800	6' x 9', C/C		1.60	17.500		8,300	1,025		9,325	10,700
0850	6' x 9', C/P		1.60	17.500		6,525	1,025		7,550	8,700

13 24 Special Activity Rooms

13 24 16 – Saunas

13 24 16.50 Saunas and Heaters

		Crew	Daily Output	Labor-Hours	Unit	Material	2024 Bare Costs Labor	Equipment	Total	Total Incl O&P
1000	8' x 12', C/C	L-7	1.10	25.455	Ea.	20,100	1,500		21,600	24,300
1050	8' x 12', C/P		1.10	25.455		23,500	1,500		25,000	28,000
1200	8' x 8', C/C		1.40	20		10,900	1,175		12,075	13,800
1250	8' x 8', C/P		1.40	20		7,950	1,175		9,125	10,500
1400	8' x 10', C/C		1.20	23.333		10,100	1,375		11,475	13,100
1450	8' x 10', C/P		1.20	23.333		9,250	1,375		10,625	12,200
1600	10' x 12', C/C		1	28		15,900	1,650		17,550	20,000
1650	10' x 12', C/P	↓	1	28		16,000	1,650		17,650	20,100
2500	Heaters only (incl. above), wall mounted, to 200 C.F.					1,150			1,150	1,250
2750	To 300 C.F.					1,300			1,300	1,425
3000	Floor standing, to 720 C.F., 10,000 watts, w/controls	1 Elec	3	2.667		3,300	191		3,491	3,900
3250	To 1,000 C.F., 16,000 watts	"	3	2.667	↓	4,525	191		4,716	5,250

13 24 26 – Steam Baths

13 24 26.50 Steam Baths and Components

		Crew	Daily Output	Labor-Hours	Unit	Material	Labor	Equipment	Total	Total Incl O&P
0010	**STEAM BATHS AND COMPONENTS**									
0020	Heater, timer & head, single, to 140 C.F.	1 Plum	1.20	6.667	Ea.	2,400	500		2,900	3,400
0500	To 300 C.F.		1.10	7.273		4,300	545		4,845	5,525
1000	Commercial size, with blow-down assembly, to 800 C.F.		.90	8.889		6,850	665		7,515	8,525
1500	To 2,500 C.F.	↓	.80	10		8,100	745		8,845	10,000
2000	Multiple, motels, apts., 2 baths, w/blow-down assm., 500 C.F.	Q-1	1.30	12.308		7,575	825		8,400	9,550
2500	4 baths	"	.70	22.857		11,400	1,525		12,925	14,900
2700	Conversion unit for residential tub, including door				↓	4,625			4,625	5,100

13 34 Fabricated Engineered Structures

13 34 23 – Fabricated Structures

13 34 23.10 Comfort Stations

		Crew	Daily Output	Labor-Hours	Unit	Material	Labor	Equipment	Total	Total Incl O&P
0010	**COMFORT STATIONS** Prefab., stock, w/doors, windows & fixt.									
0100	Not incl. interior finish or electrical									
0300	Mobile, on steel frame, 2 unit				S.F.	211			211	232
0350	7 unit					335			335	370
0400	Permanent, including concrete slab, 2 unit	B-12J	50	.320		271	18.80	18.40	308.20	345
0500	6 unit	"	43	.372	↓	231	22	21.50	274.50	310
0600	Alternate pricing method, mobile, 2 fixture				fixture	7,225			7,225	7,950
0650	7 fixture					12,500			12,500	13,800
0700	Permanent, 2 unit	B-12J	.70	22.857		22,400	1,350	1,325	25,075	28,100
0750	6 unit	"	.50	32	↓	19,300	1,875	1,850	23,025	26,000

13 42 Building Modules

13 42 63 – Detention Cell Modules

13 42 63.16 Steel Detention Cell Modules

		Crew	Daily Output	Labor-Hours	Unit	Material	Labor	Equipment	Total	Total Incl O&P
0010	**STEEL DETENTION CELL MODULES**									
2000	Cells, prefab., 5' to 6' wide, 7' to 8' high, 7' to 8' deep,									
2010	bar front, cot, not incl. plumbing	E-4	1.50	21.333	Ea.	9,175	1,450	109	10,734	12,400

13 47 Facility Protection

13 47 13 – Cathodic Protection

13 47 13.16 Cathodic Prot. for Underground Storage Tanks	Crew	Daily Output	Labor-Hours	Unit	Material	2024 Bare Costs Labor	Equipment	Total	Total Incl O&P
0010 **CATHODIC PROTECTION FOR UNDERGROUND STORAGE TANKS**									
1000 Anodes, magnesium type, 9 #	R-15	18.50	2.595	Ea.	47	182	18.60	247.60	340
1010 17 #		13	3.692		97	259	26.50	382.50	520
1020 32 #		10	4.800		142	335	34.50	511.50	695
1030 48 #	↓	7.20	6.667		182	470	48	700	950
1100 Graphite type w/epoxy cap, 3" x 60" (32 #)	R-22	8.40	4.438		168	291		459	615
1110 4" x 80" (68 #)		6	6.213		291	410		701	925
1120 6" x 72" (80 #)		5.20	7.169		1,775	470		2,245	2,650
1130 6" x 36" (45 #)	↓	9.60	3.883		890	255		1,145	1,350
2000 Rectifiers, silicon type, air cooled, 28 V/10 A	R-19	3.50	5.714		2,800	410		3,210	3,675
2010 20 V/20 A		3.50	5.714		2,825	410		3,235	3,700
2100 Oil immersed, 28 V/10 A		3	6.667		2,850	480		3,330	3,850
2110 20 V/20 A	↓	3	6.667	↓	3,775	480		4,255	4,850
3000 Anode backfill, coke breeze	R-22	3850	.010	Lb.	.33	.64		.97	1.30
4000 Cable, HMWPE, No. 8		2.40	15.533	M.L.F.	765	1,025		1,790	2,350
4010 No. 6		2.40	15.533		1,225	1,025		2,250	2,850
4020 No. 4		2.40	15.533		1,975	1,025		3,000	3,675
4030 No. 2		2.40	15.533		2,950	1,025		3,975	4,750
4040 No. 1		2.20	16.945		2,375	1,100		3,475	4,250
4050 No. 1/0		2.20	16.945		4,750	1,100		5,850	6,875
4060 No. 2/0		2.20	16.945		5,350	1,100		6,450	7,525
4070 No. 4/0	↓	2	18.640	↓	10,100	1,225		11,325	12,900
5000 Test station, 7 terminal box, flush curb type w/lockable cover	R-19	12	1.667	Ea.	94.50	120		214.50	281
5010 Reference cell, 2" diam. PVC conduit, cplg., plug, set flush	"	4.80	4.167	"	188	299		487	650

Division Notes

		CREW	DAILY OUTPUT	LABOR-HOURS	UNIT	BARE COSTS				TOTAL INCL O&P
						MAT.	LABOR	EQUIP.	TOTAL	

Division 14 Conveying Equipment

Estimating Tips
General
- Many products in Division 14 will require some type of support or blocking for installation not included with the item itself. Examples are supports for conveyors or tube systems, attachment points for lifts, and footings for hoists or cranes. Add these supports in the appropriate division.

14 10 00 Dumbwaiters
14 20 00 Elevators
- Dumbwaiters and elevators are estimated and purchased in a method similar to buying a car. The manufacturer has a base unit with standard features. Added to this base unit price will be whatever options the owner or specifications require. Increased load capacity, additional vertical travel, additional stops, higher speed, and cab finish options are items to be considered. When developing an estimate for dumbwaiters and elevators, remember that some items needed by the installers may have to be included as part of the general contract.

Examples are:
- ☐ shaftway
- ☐ rail support brackets
- ☐ machine room
- ☐ electrical supply
- ☐ sill angles
- ☐ electrical connections
- ☐ pits
- ☐ roof penthouses
- ☐ pit ladders

Check the job specifications and drawings before pricing.

- Installation of elevators and handicapped lifts in historic structures can require significant additional costs. The associated structural requirements may involve cutting into and repairing finishes, moldings, flooring, etc. The estimator must account for these special conditions.

14 30 00 Escalators and Moving Walks
- Escalators and moving walks are specialty items installed by specialty contractors. There are numerous options associated with these items. For specific options, contact a manufacturer or contractor. In a method similar to estimating dumbwaiters and elevators, you should verify the extent of general contract work and add items as necessary.

14 40 00 Lifts
14 90 00 Other Conveying Equipment
- Products such as correspondence lifts, chutes, and pneumatic tube systems, as well as other items specified in this subdivision, may require trained installers. The general contractor might not have any choice as to who will perform the installation or when it will be performed. Long lead times are often required for these products, making early decisions in scheduling necessary.

Reference Numbers
Reference numbers are shown at the beginning of some major classifications. These numbers refer to related items in the Reference Section. The reference information may be an estimating procedure, an alternate pricing method, or technical information.

Note: Not all subdivisions listed here necessarily appear. ∎

Same Data. Simplified.

Enjoy the convenience and efficiency of accessing your costs anywhere:
- **Skip the multiplier** by setting your location
- **Quickly search,** edit, favorite and share costs
- **Stay on top of price changes** with automatic updates

Discover more at rsmeans.com/online

No part of this cost data may be reproduced, stored in a retrieval system, or transmitted in any form or by any means without prior written permission of Gordian.

14 45 Vehicle Lifts

14 45 10 – Hydraulic Vehicle Lifts

14 45 10.10 Hydraulic Lifts	Crew	Daily Output	Labor-Hours	Unit	Material	2024 Bare Costs Labor	2024 Bare Costs Equipment	Total	Total Incl O&P
0010 **HYDRAULIC LIFTS**									
2200 Single post, 8,000 lb. capacity	L-4	.40	60	Ea.	6,675	3,475		10,150	12,500
2810 Double post, 6,000 lb. capacity		2.67	8.989		2,725	520		3,245	3,775
2815 9,000 lb. capacity		2.29	10.480		2,725	605		3,330	3,900
2820 15,000 lb. capacity		2	12		5,500	695		6,195	7,100
2822 Four post, 26,000 lb. capacity		1.80	13.333		21,500	770		22,270	24,800
2825 30,000 lb. capacity		1.60	15		35,600	870		36,470	40,500
2830 Ramp style, 4 post, 25,000 lb. capacity		2	12		19,200	695		19,895	22,200
2835 35,000 lb. capacity		1	24		19,000	1,400		20,400	23,000
2840 50,000 lb. capacity		1	24		92,000	1,400		93,400	103,500
2845 75,000 lb. capacity		1	24		125,000	1,400		126,400	139,000
2850 For drive thru tracks, add, minimum					1,300			1,300	1,425
2855 Maximum					2,225			2,225	2,450
2860 Ramp extensions, 3' (set of 2)					455			455	500
2865 Rolling jack platform					2,025			2,025	2,225
2870 Electric/hydraulic jacking beam					5,150			5,150	5,675
2880 Scissor lift, portable, 6,000 lb. capacity					2,000			2,000	2,200

Division 21 Fire Suppression

Estimating Tips

Pipe for fire protection and all uses is located in Subdivisions 21 11 13 and 22 11 13.

The labor adjustment factors listed in Subdivision 22 01 02.20 also apply to Division 21.

Many, but not all, areas in the U.S. require backflow protection in the fire system. Insurance underwriters may have specific requirements for the type of materials to be installed or design requirements based on the hazard to be protected. Local jurisdictions may have requirements not covered by code. It is advisable to be aware of any special conditions.

For your reference, the following is a list of the most applicable Fire Codes and Standards, which may be purchased from the NFPA, 1 Batterymarch Park, Quincy, MA 02169-7471.

- NFPA 1: Uniform Fire Code
- NFPA 10: Portable Fire Extinguishers
- NFPA 11: Low-, Medium-, and High-Expansion Foam
- NFPA 12: Carbon Dioxide Extinguishing Systems (Also companion 12A)
- NFPA 13: Installation of Sprinkler Systems (Also companion 13D, 13E, and 13R)
- NFPA 14: Installation of Standpipe and Hose Systems
- NFPA 15: Water Spray Fixed Systems for Fire Protection
- NFPA 16: Installation of Foam-Water Sprinkler and Foam-Water Spray Systems
- NFPA 17: Dry Chemical Extinguishing Systems (Also companion 17A)
- NFPA 18: Wetting Agents
- NFPA 20: Installation of Stationary Pumps for Fire Protection
- NFPA 22: Water Tanks for Private Fire Protection
- NFPA 24: Installation of Private Fire Service Mains and their Appurtenances
- NFPA 25: Inspection, Testing and Maintenance of Water-Based Fire Protection

Reference Numbers

Reference numbers are shown at the beginning of some major classifications. These numbers refer to related items in the Reference Section. The reference information may be an estimating procedure, an alternate pricing method, or technical information.

Same Data. Simplified.

Enjoy the convenience and efficiency of accessing your costs anywhere:

- **Skip the multiplier** by setting your location
- **Quickly search,** edit, favorite and share costs
- **Stay on top of price changes** with automatic updates

Discover more at rsmeans.com/online

No part of this cost data may be reproduced, stored in a retrieval system, or transmitted in any form or by any means without prior written permission of Gordian.

Note: "Powered in part by CINX™, based on licensed proprietary information of Harrison Publishing House, Inc."

Note: Trade Service, in part, has been used as a reference source for some of the material prices used in Division 21.

21 05 Common Work Results for Fire Suppression

21 05 23 – General-Duty Valves for Water-Based Fire-Suppression Piping

21 05 23.50 General-Duty Valves		Crew	Daily Output	Labor-Hours	Unit	Material	2024 Bare Costs Labor	Equipment	Total	Total Incl O&P
0010	**GENERAL-DUTY VALVES**, for water-based fire suppression									
6200	Valves and components									
6210	Wet alarm, includes									
6220	retard chamber, trim, gauges, alarm line strainer									
6260	3" size	Q-12	3	5.333	Ea.	2,700	360		3,060	3,475
6280	4" size	"	2	8		2,300	535		2,835	3,325
6300	6" size	Q-13	4	8		3,350	570		3,920	4,550
6320	8" size	"	3	10.667		3,925	760		4,685	5,450
6400	Dry alarm, includes									
6405	retard chamber, trim, gauges, alarm line strainer									
6410	1-1/2" size	Q-12	3	5.333	Ea.	4,225	360		4,585	5,175
6420	2" size		3	5.333		4,225	360		4,585	5,175
6430	3" size		3	5.333		4,225	360		4,585	5,175
6440	4" size		2	8		4,575	535		5,110	5,850
6450	6" size	Q-13	3	10.667		5,275	760		6,035	6,925
6460	8" size	"	3	10.667		7,775	760		8,535	9,675
6500	Check, swing, C.I. body, brass fittings, auto. ball drip									
6520	4" size	Q-12	3	5.333	Ea.	460	360		820	1,050
6540	6" size	Q-13	4	8		850	570		1,420	1,775
6580	8" size	"	3	10.667		2,350	760		3,110	3,725
6800	Check, wafer, butterfly type, C.I. body, bronze fittings									
6820	4" size	Q-12	4	4	Ea.	3,125	269		3,394	3,850
6840	6" size	Q-13	5.50	5.818		4,975	415		5,390	6,100
6860	8" size		5	6.400		5,575	455		6,030	6,800
6880	10" size		4.50	7.111		8,800	505		9,305	10,400
8700	Floor control valve, includes trim and gauges, 2" size	Q-12	6	2.667		1,325	179		1,504	1,725
8710	2-1/2" size		6	2.667		1,075	179		1,254	1,450
8720	3" size		6	2.667		955	179		1,134	1,325
8730	4" size		6	2.667		955	179		1,134	1,325
8740	6" size		5	3.200		955	215		1,170	1,375
8800	Flow control valve, includes trim and gauges, 2" size		2	8		5,650	535		6,185	7,000
8820	3" size		1.50	10.667		6,500	715		7,215	8,225
8840	4" size	Q-13	2.80	11.429		6,475	810		7,285	8,325
8860	6" size	"	2	16		7,675	1,125		8,800	10,100
9200	Pressure operated relief valve, brass body	1 Spri	18	.444		845	33		878	980
9600	Waterflow indicator, vane type, with recycling retard and									
9610	two single pole retard switches, 2" thru 6" pipe size	1 Spri	8	1	Ea.	174	74.50		248.50	300

21 05 53 – Identification For Fire-Suppression Piping and Equipment

21 05 53.50 Identification

		Crew	Daily Output	Labor-Hours	Unit	Material	Labor	Equipment	Total	Total Incl O&P
0010	**IDENTIFICATION**, for fire suppression piping and equipment									
3010	Plates and escutcheons for identification of fire dept. service/connections									
3100	Wall mount, round, aluminum									
3110	4"	1 Plum	96	.083	Ea.	26.50	6.20		32.70	38.50
3120	6"	"	96	.083	"	67.50	6.20		73.70	84
3200	Wall mount, round, cast brass									
3210	2-1/2"	1 Plum	70	.114	Ea.	69.50	8.55		78.05	89
3220	3"		70	.114		134	8.55		142.55	160
3230	4"		70	.114		129	8.55		137.55	155
3240	6"		70	.114		164	8.55		172.55	193
3250	For polished brass, add					25%				
3260	For rough chrome, add					33%				
3270	For polished chrome, add					55%				

21 05 Common Work Results for Fire Suppression

21 05 53 – Identification For Fire-Suppression Piping and Equipment

21 05 53.50 Identification		Crew	Daily Output	Labor-Hours	Unit	Material	2024 Bare Costs Labor	Equipment	Total	Total Incl O&P
3300	Wall mount, square, cast brass									
3310	2-1/2"	1 Plum	70	.114	Ea.	84.50	8.55		93.05	106
3320	3"	"	70	.114	"	134	8.55		142.55	160
3330	For polished brass, add					15%				
3340	For rough chrome, add					25%				
3350	For polished chrome, add					33%				
3400	Wall mount, cast brass, multiple outlets									
3410	rect. 2 way	Q-1	5	3.200	Ea.	116	215		331	450
3420	rect. 3 way		4	4		274	269		543	700
3430	rect. 4 way		4	4		228	269		497	650
3440	square 4 way		4	4		345	269		614	775
3450	rect. 6 way		3	5.333		335	360		695	900
3460	For polished brass, add					10%				
3470	For rough chrome, add					20%				
3480	For polished chrome, add					25%				
3500	Base mount, free standing fdc, cast brass									
3510	4"	1 Plum	60	.133	Ea.	63.50	9.95		73.45	84.50
3520	6"	"	60	.133	"	84.50	9.95		94.45	108
3530	For polished brass, add					25%				
3540	For rough chrome, add					30%				
3550	For polished chrome, add					45%				

21 11 Facility Fire-Suppression Water-Service Piping

21 11 11 – Fire-Suppression, Pipe Fittings, Grooved Joint

21 11 11.05 Corrosion Monitors

		Crew	Daily Output	Labor-Hours	Unit	Material	Labor	Equipment	Total	Total Incl O&P
0010	**CORROSION MONITORS**, pipe, in line spool									
1100	Powder coated, schedule 10									
1140	2"	1 Plum	17	.471	Ea.	216	35		251	291
1150	2-1/2"	Q-1	27	.593		222	40		262	305
1160	3"		22	.727		228	49		277	325
1170	4"		17	.941		240	63		303	360
1180	6"	Q-2	17	1.412		258	98.50		356.50	430
1190	8"	"	14	1.714		276	119		395	485
1200	Powder coated, schedule 40									
1240	2"	1 Plum	17	.471	Ea.	217	35		252	291
1250	2-1/2"	Q-1	27	.593		223	40		263	305
1260	3"		22	.727		229	49		278	325
1270	4"		17	.941		253	63		316	370
1280	6"	Q-2	17	1.412		277	98.50		375.50	450
1290	8"	"	14	1.714		300	119		419	510
1300	Galvanized, schedule 10									
1340	2"	1 Plum	17	.471	Ea.	234	35		269	310
1350	2-1/2"	Q-1	27	.593		246	40		286	330
1360	3"		22	.727		258	49		307	355
1370	4"		17	.941		270	63		333	390
1380	6"	Q-2	17	1.412		288	98.50		386.50	460
1390	8"	"	14	1.714		305	119		424	515
1400	Galvanized, schedule 40									
1440	2"	1 Plum	17	.471	Ea.	235	35		270	310
1450	2-1/2"	Q-1	27	.593		247	40		287	330
1460	3"		22	.727		258	49		307	355

21 11 Facility Fire-Suppression Water-Service Piping

21 11 11 – Fire-Suppression, Pipe Fittings, Grooved Joint

21 11 11.05 Corrosion Monitors		Crew	Daily Output	Labor-Hours	Unit	Material	2024 Bare Costs Labor	2024 Bare Costs Equipment	Total	Total Incl O&P
1470	4"	Q-1	17	.941	Ea.	283	63		346	405
1480	6"	Q-2	17	1.412		305	98.50		403.50	480
1490	8"	"	14	1.714		330	119		449	545
1500	Mechanical tee, painted									
1540	2"	1 Plum	50	.160	Ea.	180	11.95		191.95	216
1550	2-1/2"	Q-1	80	.200		186	13.45		199.45	225
1560	3"		67	.239		192	16.05		208.05	235
1570	4"		50	.320		198	21.50		219.50	250
1580	6"	Q-2	50	.480		204	33.50		237.50	275
1590	8"	"	42	.571		276	40		316	365
1600	Mechanical tee, galvanized									
1640	2"	1 Plum	50	.160	Ea.	192	11.95		203.95	229
1650	2-1/2"	Q-1	80	.200		198	13.45		211.45	238
1660	3"		67	.239		204	16.05		220.05	249
1670	4"		50	.320		210	21.50		231.50	263
1680	6"	Q-2	50	.480		216	33.50		249.50	288
1690	8"	"	42	.571		310	40		350	405

21 11 11.16 Pipe Fittings, Grooved Joint

		Crew	Daily Output	Labor-Hours	Unit	Material	Labor	Equipment	Total	Total Incl O&P
0010	**PIPE FITTINGS, GROOVED JOINT,** For fire-suppression									
0020	Fittings, ductile iron									
0030	Coupling required at joints not incl. in fitting price.									
0034	Add 1 coupling, material only, per joint for installed price.									
0038	For standard grooved joint materials see Div. 22 11 13.48									
0040	90° elbow									
0110	2"	1 Plum	25	.320	Ea.	13.55	24		37.55	50.50
0120	2-1/2"	Q-1	40	.400		18.80	27		45.80	60.50
0130	3"		33	.485		24.50	32.50		57	75.50
0140	4"		25	.640		36	43		79	104
0150	5"		20	.800		87	53.50		140.50	176
0160	6"	Q-2	25	.960		93	67		160	202
0170	8"	"	21	1.143		183	79.50		262.50	320
0200	45° elbow									
0210	2"	1 Plum	25	.320	Ea.	15	24		39	52
0220	2-1/2"	Q-1	40	.400		19.80	27		46.80	62
0230	3"		33	.485		26.50	32.50		59	78
0240	4"		25	.640		36.50	43		79.50	104
0250	5"		20	.800		87.50	53.50		141	177
0260	6"	Q-2	25	.960		98	67		165	208
0270	8"	"	21	1.143		191	79.50		270.50	330
0300	Tee									
0310	2"	1 Plum	17	.471	Ea.	23	35		58	78
0320	2-1/2"	Q-1	27	.593		32.50	40		72.50	94.50
0330	3"		22	.727		43.50	49		92.50	121
0340	4"		17	.941		66.50	63		129.50	167
0350	5"		13	1.231		163	82.50		245.50	300
0360	6"	Q-2	17	1.412		168	98.50		266.50	330
0370	8"	"	14	1.714		340	119		459	555
0400	Cap									
0410	1-1/4"	1 Plum	76	.105	Ea.	5.90	7.85		13.75	18.20
0420	1-1/2"		63	.127		6.95	9.50		16.45	21.50
0430	2"		47	.170		8.80	12.70		21.50	28.50
0440	2-1/2"	Q-1	76	.211		10.85	14.15		25	33

21 11 Facility Fire-Suppression Water-Service Piping

21 11 11 – Fire-Suppression, Pipe Fittings, Grooved Joint

21 11 11.16 Pipe Fittings, Grooved Joint

		Crew	Daily Output	Labor-Hours	Unit	Material	2024 Bare Costs Labor	2024 Bare Costs Equipment	Total	Total Incl O&P
0450	3"	Q-1	63	.254	Ea.	13.85	17.05		30.90	41
0460	4"		47	.340		19.05	23		42.05	55
0470	5"	↓	37	.432		46.50	29		75.50	94
0480	6"	Q-2	47	.511		47.50	35.50		83	106
0490	8"	"	39	.615	↓	87.50	43		130.50	160
0500	Coupling, rigid									
0510	1-1/4"	1 Plum	100	.080	Ea.	17	5.95		22.95	27.50
0520	1-1/2"		67	.119		17.35	8.90		26.25	32.50
0530	2"	↓	50	.160		18.15	11.95		30.10	37.50
0540	2-1/2"	Q-1	80	.200		21	13.45		34.45	43.50
0550	3"		67	.239		24.50	16.05		40.55	51
0560	4"		50	.320		34.50	21.50		56	69.50
0570	5"	↓	40	.400		44.50	27		71.50	89
0580	6"	Q-2	50	.480		55	33.50		88.50	110
0590	8"	"	42	.571	↓	90.50	40		130.50	159
0700	End of run fitting									
0710	1-1/4" x 1/2" NPT	1 Plum	76	.105	Ea.	14.45	7.85		22.30	27.50
0714	1-1/4" x 3/4" NPT		76	.105		14.20	7.85		22.05	27.50
0718	1-1/4" x 1" NPT		76	.105		14.05	7.85		21.90	27
0722	1-1/2" x 1/2" NPT		63	.127		14.45	9.50		23.95	30
0726	1-1/2" x 3/4" NPT		63	.127		14.45	9.50		23.95	30
0730	1-1/2" x 1" NPT		63	.127		14.45	9.50		23.95	30
0734	2" x 1/2" NPT		47	.170		15.05	12.70		27.75	35.50
0738	2" x 3/4" NPT		47	.170		15.60	12.70		28.30	36
0742	2" x 1" NPT		47	.170		15.35	12.70		28.05	36
0746	2-1/2" x 1/2" NPT		40	.200		17.80	14.95		32.75	41.50
0750	2-1/2" x 3/4" NPT		40	.200		19.50	14.95		34.45	43.50
0754	2-1/2" x 1" NPT	↓	40	.200	↓	19.35	14.95		34.30	43.50
0800	Drain elbow									
0820	2-1/2"	Q-1	40	.400	Ea.	35	27		62	78.50
0830	3"		33	.485		47.50	32.50		80	101
0840	4"	↓	25	.640		58	43		101	128
0850	6"	Q-2	25	.960	↓	116	67		183	227
1000	Valves, grooved joint									
1002	Coupling required at joints not incl. in fitting price.									
1004	Add 1 coupling, material only, per joint for installed price.									
1010	Ball valve with weatherproof actuator									
1020	1-1/4"	1 Plum	39	.205	Ea.	162	15.30		177.30	201
1030	1-1/2"		31	.258		192	19.25		211.25	240
1040	2"	↓	24	.333	↓	231	25		256	292
1100	Butterfly valve, high pressure, with actuator									
1110	Supervised open									
1120	2"	1 Plum	23	.348	Ea.	430	26		456	515
1130	2-1/2"	Q-1	38	.421		445	28.50		473.50	530
1140	3"		30	.533		480	36		516	585
1150	4"		22	.727		505	49		554	630
1160	5"		19	.842		755	56.50		811.50	915
1170	6"	Q-2	23	1.043		780	72.50		852.50	965
1180	8"		18	1.333		1,100	93		1,193	1,350
1190	10"		15	1.600		2,650	111		2,761	3,100
1200	12"	↓	12	2	↓	3,800	139		3,939	4,375
1300	Gate valve, OS&Y									
1310	2-1/2"	Q-1	35	.457	Ea.	475	30.50		505.50	565

For customer support on your Plumbing Costs with RSMeans Data call 800.448.8182.

21 11 Facility Fire-Suppression Water-Service Piping

21 11 11 – Fire-Suppression, Pipe Fittings, Grooved Joint

21 11 11.16 Pipe Fittings, Grooved Joint		Crew	Daily Output	Labor-Hours	Unit	Material	2024 Bare Costs Labor	Equipment	Total	Total Incl O&P
1320	3"	Q-1	28	.571	Ea.	365	38.50		403.50	455
1330	4"	▼	20	.800		725	53.50		778.50	880
1340	6"	Q-2	21	1.143		855	79.50		934.50	1,050
1350	8"		16	1.500		1,350	105		1,455	1,650
1360	10"		13	1.846		2,050	129		2,179	2,450
1370	12"	▼	10	2.400	▼	3,300	167		3,467	3,900
1400	Gate valve, non-rising stem									
1410	2-1/2"	Q-1	36	.444	Ea.	500	30		530	595
1420	3"		29	.552		590	37		627	705
1430	4"	▼	21	.762		700	51		751	845
1440	6"	Q-2	22	1.091		900	76		976	1,100
1450	8"		17	1.412		1,750	98.50		1,848.50	2,075
1460	10"		14	1.714		1,825	119		1,944	2,200
1470	12"	▼	11	2.182	▼	2,350	152		2,502	2,800
2000	Alarm check valve, pre-trimmed									
2010	1-1/2"	Q-1	6	2.667	Ea.	108	179		287	385
2020	2"	"	5	3.200		108	215		323	440
2030	2-1/2"	Q-2	7	3.429		126	239		365	495
2040	3"		6	4		1,800	279		2,079	2,400
2050	4"		5	4.800		162	335		497	675
2060	6"		4	6		162	420		582	800
2070	8"	▼	2	12	▼	162	835		997	1,425
2200	Dry valve, pre-trimmed									
2210	1-1/2"	Q-1	5	3.200	Ea.	2,875	215		3,090	3,500
2220	2"	"	4	4		2,875	269		3,144	3,575
2230	2-1/2"	Q-2	6	4		2,925	279		3,204	3,650
2240	3"		5	4.800		2,925	335		3,260	3,725
2250	4"		4	6		3,125	420		3,545	4,075
2260	6"		2	12		3,600	835		4,435	5,200
2270	8"	▼	1	24	▼	5,300	1,675		6,975	8,300
2300	Deluge valve, pre-trimmed, with electric solenoid									
2310	1-1/2"	Q-1	5	3.200	Ea.	4,100	215		4,315	4,850
2320	2"	"	4	4		4,100	269		4,369	4,925
2330	2-1/2"	Q-2	6	4		4,175	279		4,454	5,000
2340	3"		5	4.800		4,175	335		4,510	5,075
2350	4"		4	6		4,975	420		5,395	6,100
2360	6"		2	12		5,925	835		6,760	7,775
2370	8"	▼	1	24	▼	6,700	1,675		8,375	9,850
2400	Preaction valve									
2410	Valve has double interlock,									
2420	pneumatic/electric actuation and trim.									
2430	1-1/2"	Q-1	5	3.200	Ea.	2,600	215		2,815	3,200
2440	2"	"	4	4		2,600	269		2,869	3,275
2450	2-1/2"	Q-2	6	4		2,600	279		2,879	3,300
2460	3"		5	4.800		2,600	335		2,935	3,375
2470	4"		4	6		2,875	420		3,295	3,800
2480	6"		2	12		2,875	835		3,710	4,425
2490	8"	▼	1	24	▼	3,175	1,675		4,850	5,950
3000	Fittings, ductile iron, ready to install									
3010	Includes bolts & grade "E" gaskets									
3012	Add 1 coupling, material only, per joint for installed price.									
3200	90° elbow									
3210	1-1/4"	1 Plum	88	.091	Ea.	63.50	6.80		70.30	79.50

21 11 Facility Fire-Suppression Water-Service Piping

21 11 11 – Fire-Suppression, Pipe Fittings, Grooved Joint

21 11 11.16 Pipe Fittings, Grooved Joint		Crew	Daily Output	Labor-Hours	Unit	Material	2024 Bare Costs Labor	Equipment	Total	Total Incl O&P
3220	1-1/2"	1 Plum	72	.111	Ea.	65.50	8.30		73.80	84.50
3230	2"		60	.133		65.50	9.95		75.45	87.50
3240	2-1/2"	Q-1	85	.188		79	12.65		91.65	106
3300	45° elbow									
3310	1-1/4"	1 Plum	88	.091	Ea.	63.50	6.80		70.30	79.50
3320	1-1/2"		72	.111		65.50	8.30		73.80	84.50
3330	2"		60	.133		65.50	9.95		75.45	87.50
3340	2-1/2"	Q-1	85	.188		79	12.65		91.65	106
3400	Tee									
3410	1-1/4"	1 Plum	60	.133	Ea.	97.50	9.95		107.45	122
3420	1-1/2"		48	.167		101	12.45		113.45	130
3430	2"		38	.211		102	15.70		117.70	136
3440	2-1/2"	Q-1	60	.267		118	17.90		135.90	156
3500	Coupling									
3510	1-1/4"	1 Plum	200	.040	Ea.	9.90	2.99		12.89	15.35
3520	1-1/2"		134	.060		9.95	4.46		14.41	17.60
3530	2"		100	.080		11.15	5.95		17.10	21
3540	2-1/2"	Q-1	160	.100		13.30	6.70		20	24.50
3550	3"		134	.119		15.45	8		23.45	29
3560	4"		100	.160		20.50	10.75		31.25	38.50
3570	5"		80	.200		44	13.45		57.45	68.50
3580	6"	Q-2	100	.240		34	16.70		50.70	62.50
3590	8"	"	84	.286		34	19.90		53.90	67
4000	For seismic bracing, see Section 22 05 48.40									
5000	For hangers and supports, see Section 22 05 29.10									

21 11 13 – Facility Fire Suppression Piping

21 11 13.16 Pipe, Plastic

		Crew	Daily Output	Labor-Hours	Unit	Material	Labor	Equipment	Total	Total Incl O&P
0010	**PIPE, PLASTIC**									
0020	CPVC, fire suppression (C-UL-S, FM, NFPA 13, 13D & 13R)									
0030	Socket joint, no couplings or hangers									
0100	SDR 13.5 (ASTM F442)									
0120	3/4" diameter	Q-12	420	.038	L.F.	1.39	2.56		3.95	5.35
0130	1" diameter		340	.047		2.16	3.16		5.32	7.10
0140	1-1/4" diameter		260	.062		3.37	4.13		7.50	9.85
0150	1-1/2" diameter		190	.084		4.64	5.65		10.29	13.50
0160	2" diameter		140	.114		6.95	7.70		14.65	19.10
0170	2-1/2" diameter		130	.123		10.60	8.25		18.85	24
0180	3" diameter		120	.133		16.10	8.95		25.05	31

21 11 13.18 Pipe Fittings, Plastic

		Crew	Daily Output	Labor-Hours	Unit	Material	Labor	Equipment	Total	Total Incl O&P
0010	**PIPE FITTINGS, PLASTIC**									
0020	CPVC, fire suppression (C-UL-S, FM, NFPA 13, 13D & 13R)									
0030	Socket joint									
0100	90° elbow									
0120	3/4"	1 Plum	26	.308	Ea.	1.87	23		24.87	36
0130	1"		22.70	.352		4.11	26.50		30.61	43.50
0140	1-1/4"		20.20	.396		5.20	29.50		34.70	49.50
0150	1-1/2"		18.20	.440		7.40	33		40.40	57
0160	2"	Q-1	33.10	.483		9.20	32.50		41.70	58.50
0170	2-1/2"		24.20	.661		17.65	44.50		62.15	85.50
0180	3"		20.80	.769		24	51.50		75.50	104
0200	45° elbow									
0210	3/4"	1 Plum	26	.308	Ea.	2.57	23		25.57	37

For customer support on your Plumbing Costs with RSMeans Data call 800.448.8182.

21 11 Facility Fire-Suppression Water-Service Piping

21 11 13 – Facility Fire Suppression Piping

21 11 13.18 Pipe Fittings, Plastic

		Crew	Daily Output	Labor-Hours	Unit	Material	2024 Bare Costs Labor	Equipment	Total	Total Incl O&P
0220	1"	1 Plum	22.70	.352	Ea.	3.02	26.50		29.52	42.50
0230	1-1/4"		20.20	.396		4.37	29.50		33.87	49
0240	1-1/2"	↓	18.20	.440		6.10	33		39.10	55.50
0250	2"	Q-1	33.10	.483		7.60	32.50		40.10	57
0260	2-1/2"		24.20	.661		13.60	44.50		58.10	81
0270	3"	↓	20.80	.769	↓	19.50	51.50		71	98.50
0300	Tee									
0310	3/4"	1 Plum	17.30	.462	Ea.	2.57	34.50		37.07	54.50
0320	1"		15.20	.526		5.05	39.50		44.55	64
0330	1-1/4"		13.50	.593		7.65	44		51.65	74.50
0340	1-1/2"	↓	12.10	.661		11.25	49.50		60.75	86
0350	2"	Q-1	20	.800		16.60	53.50		70.10	98.50
0360	2-1/2"		16.20	.988		27	66.50		93.50	128
0370	3"	↓	13.90	1.151	↓	42	77.50		119.50	162
0400	Tee, reducing x any size									
0420	1"	1 Plum	15.20	.526	Ea.	4.31	39.50		43.81	63
0430	1-1/4"		13.50	.593		7.90	44		51.90	74.50
0440	1-1/2"	↓	12.10	.661		9.55	49.50		59.05	84
0450	2"	Q-1	20	.800		17.20	53.50		70.70	99
0460	2-1/2"		16.20	.988		21	66.50		87.50	122
0470	3"	↓	13.90	1.151		24.50	77.50		102	142
0500	Coupling									
0510	3/4"	1 Plum	26	.308	Ea.	1.80	23		24.80	36
0520	1"		22.70	.352		2.38	26.50		28.88	41.50
0530	1-1/4"		20.20	.396		3.47	29.50		32.97	48
0540	1-1/2"	↓	18.20	.440		4.94	33		37.94	54.50
0550	2"	Q-1	33.10	.483		6.70	32.50		39.20	56
0560	2-1/2"		24.20	.661		10.20	44.50		54.70	77.50
0570	3"	↓	20.80	.769		13.30	51.50		64.80	91.50
0600	Coupling, reducing									
0610	1" x 3/4"	1 Plum	22.70	.352	Ea.	2.38	26.50		28.88	41.50
0620	1-1/4" x 1"		20.20	.396		3.60	29.50		33.10	48
0630	1-1/2" x 3/4"		18.20	.440		5.40	33		38.40	55
0640	1-1/2" x 1"		18.20	.440		5.20	33		38.20	54.50
0650	1-1/2" x 1-1/4"	↓	18.20	.440		4.94	33		37.94	54.50
0660	2" x 1"	Q-1	33.10	.483		6.95	32.50		39.45	56
0670	2" x 1-1/2"	"	33.10	.483	↓	6.70	32.50		39.20	56
0700	Cross									
0720	3/4"	1 Plum	13	.615	Ea.	4.05	46		50.05	73
0730	1"		11.30	.708		5.05	53		58.05	84
0740	1-1/4"		10.10	.792		7	59		66	95.50
0750	1-1/2"	↓	9.10	.879		9.70	65.50		75.20	108
0760	2"	Q-1	16.60	.964		15.80	65		80.80	114
0770	2-1/2"	"	12.10	1.322	↓	34.50	89		123.50	170
0800	Cap									
0820	3/4"	1 Plum	52	.154	Ea.	1.09	11.50		12.59	18.30
0830	1"		45	.178		1.55	13.25		14.80	21.50
0840	1-1/4"		40	.200		2.51	14.95		17.46	25
0850	1-1/2"	↓	36.40	.220		3.47	16.40		19.87	28.50
0860	2"	Q-1	66	.242		5.20	16.30		21.50	29.50
0870	2-1/2"		48.40	.331		7.50	22		29.50	41.50
0880	3"	↓	41.60	.385	↓	12.15	26		38.15	52
0900	Adapter, sprinkler head, female w/metal thd. insert (s x FNPT)									

21 11 Facility Fire-Suppression Water-Service Piping

21 11 13 – Facility Fire Suppression Piping

21 11 13.18 Pipe Fittings, Plastic

		Crew	Daily Output	Labor-Hours	Unit	Material	2024 Bare Costs Labor	Equipment	Total	Total Incl O&P
0920	3/4" x 1/2"	1 Plum	52	.154	Ea.	4.96	11.50		16.46	22.50
0930	1" x 1/2"		45	.178		5.25	13.25		18.50	25.50
0940	1" x 3/4"	↓	45	.178	↓	8.25	13.25		21.50	29

21 11 16 – Facility Fire Hydrants

21 11 16.50 Fire Hydrants for Buildings

		Crew	Daily Output	Labor-Hours	Unit	Material	Labor	Equipment	Total	Total Incl O&P
0010	**FIRE HYDRANTS FOR BUILDINGS**									
3750	Hydrants, wall, w/caps, single, flush, polished brass									
3800	2-1/2" x 2-1/2"	Q-12	5	3.200	Ea.	320	215		535	675
3840	2-1/2" x 3"		5	3.200		355	215		570	710
3860	3" x 3"	↓	4.80	3.333		550	224		774	940
3900	For polished chrome, add					20%				
3950	Double, flush, polished brass									
4000	2-1/2" x 2-1/2" x 4"	Q-12	5	3.200	Ea.	965	215		1,180	1,375
4040	2-1/2" x 2-1/2" x 6"		4.60	3.478		1,425	234		1,659	1,900
4080	3" x 3" x 4"		4.90	3.265		1,475	219		1,694	1,950
4120	3" x 3" x 6"	↓	4.50	3.556		1,425	239		1,664	1,925
4200	For polished chrome, add					10%				
4350	Double, projecting, polished brass									
4400	2-1/2" x 2-1/2" x 4"	Q-12	5	3.200	Ea.	520	215		735	890
4450	2-1/2" x 2-1/2" x 6"	"	4.60	3.478	"	715	234		949	1,125
4460	Valve control, dbl. flush/projecting hydrant, cap &									
4470	chain, extension rod & cplg., escutcheon, polished brass	Q-12	8	2	Ea.	475	134		609	725
4480	Four-way square, flush, polished brass									
4540	2-1/2" (4) x 6"	Q-12	3.60	4.444	Ea.	6,600	299		6,899	7,725

21 11 19 – Fire-Department Connections

21 11 19.50 Connections for the Fire-Department

		Crew	Daily Output	Labor-Hours	Unit	Material	Labor	Equipment	Total	Total Incl O&P
0010	**CONNECTIONS FOR THE FIRE-DEPARTMENT**									
0020	For fire pro. cabinets, see Section 10 44 13.53									
4000	Storz type, with cap and chain									
4100	2-1/2" Storz x 2-1/2" F NPT, silver powder coat	Q-12	4.80	3.333	Ea.	62	224		286	405
4200	4" Storz x 1-1/2" F NPT, silver powder coat		4.80	3.333		119	224		343	465
4300	4" Storz x 2-1/2" F NPT, silver powder coat		4.80	3.333		124	224		348	470
4400	4" Storz x 3" F NPT, silver powder coat		4.80	3.333		133	224		357	480
4500	4" Storz x 4" F NPT, red powder coat		4.80	3.333		149	224		373	500
4600	4" Storz x 4" F NPT, silver powder coat		4.80	3.333		145	224		369	495
4700	4" Storz x 6" F NPT, red powder coat		4.80	3.333		204	224		428	560
4800	4" Storz x 6" F NPT, silver powder coat		4.80	3.333		203	224		427	560
4900	5" Storz x 2-1/2" F NPT, silver powder coat		4.80	3.333		178	224		402	530
5000	5" Storz x 3" F NPT, silver powder coat		4.80	3.333		187	224		411	540
5100	5" Storz x 4" F NPT, red powder coat		4.80	3.333		163	224		387	515
5200	5" Storz x 4" F NPT, silver powder coat		4.80	3.333		1,050	224		1,274	1,475
5300	5" Storz x 6" F NPT, red powder coat		4.80	3.333		246	224		470	605
5400	5" Storz x 6" F NPT, silver powder coat	↓	4.80	3.333	↓	1,475	224		1,699	1,950
6000	Roof manifold, horiz., brass, without valves & caps									
6040	2-1/2" x 2-1/2" x 4"	Q-12	4.80	3.333	Ea.	252	224		476	610
6060	2-1/2" x 2-1/2" x 6"		4.60	3.478		585	234		819	990
6080	2-1/2" x 2-1/2" x 2-1/2" x 4"		4.60	3.478		610	234		844	1,025
6090	2-1/2" x 2-1/2" x 2-1/2" x 6"	↓	4.60	3.478		660	234		894	1,075
7000	Sprinkler line tester, cast brass					56.50			56.50	62
7140	Standpipe connections, wall, w/plugs & chains									
7160	Single, flush, brass, 2-1/2" x 2-1/2", Fire Dept Conn.	Q-12	5	3.200	Ea.	210	215		425	550
7180	2-1/2" x 3"	"	5	3.200	"	219	215		434	560

For customer support on your Plumbing Costs with RSMeans Data call 800.448.8182.

21 11 Facility Fire-Suppression Water-Service Piping

21 11 19 – Fire-Department Connections

21 11 19.50 Connections for the Fire-Department

		Crew	Daily Output	Labor-Hours	Unit	Material	2024 Bare Costs Labor	Equipment	Total	Total Incl O&P
7240	For polished chrome, add					15%				
7280	Double, flush, polished brass									
7300	2-1/2" x 2-1/2" x 4"	Q-12	5	3.200	Ea.	815	215		1,030	1,225
7330	2-1/2" x 2-1/2" x 6"		4.60	3.478		1,050	234		1,284	1,500
7340	3" x 3" x 4"		4.90	3.265		1,150	219		1,369	1,600
7370	3" x 3" x 6"		4.50	3.556		1,500	239		1,739	2,000
7400	For polished chrome, add					15%				
7440	For sill cock combination, add				Ea.	113			113	124
7580	Double projecting, polished brass									
7600	2-1/2" x 2-1/2" x 4"	Q-12	5	3.200	Ea.	430	215		645	795
7630	2-1/2" x 2-1/2" x 6"	"	4.60	3.478	"	975	234		1,209	1,425
7680	For polished chrome, add					15%				
7900	Three way, flush, polished brass									
7920	2-1/2" (3) x 4"	Q-12	4.80	3.333	Ea.	1,625	224		1,849	2,125
7930	2-1/2" (3) x 6"	"	4.60	3.478		3,175	234		3,409	3,850
8000	For polished chrome, add					9%				
8020	Three way, projecting, polished brass									
8040	2-1/2" (3) x 4"	Q-12	4.80	3.333	Ea.	2,150	224		2,374	2,675
8070	2-1/2" (3) x 6"	"	4.60	3.478		2,275	234		2,509	2,850
8100	For polished chrome, add					12%				
8200	Four way, square, flush, polished brass,									
8240	2-1/2" (4) x 6"	Q-12	3.60	4.444	Ea.	2,900	299		3,199	3,650
8300	For polished chrome, add				"	10%				
8550	Wall, vertical, flush, cast brass									
8600	Two way, 2-1/2" x 2-1/2" x 4"	Q-12	5	3.200	Ea.	560	215		775	940
8660	Four way, 2-1/2" (4) x 6"		3.80	4.211		4,050	283		4,333	4,875
8680	Six way, 2-1/2" (6) x 6"		3.40	4.706		2,250	315		2,565	2,950
8700	For polished chrome, add					10%				
8800	Free standing siamese unit, polished brass, two way									
8820	2-1/2" x 2-1/2" x 4"	Q-12	2.50	6.400	Ea.	845	430		1,275	1,575
8850	2-1/2" x 2-1/2" x 6"		2	8		1,350	535		1,885	2,275
8860	3" x 3" x 4"		2.50	6.400		1,175	430		1,605	1,950
8890	3" x 3" x 6"		2	8		1,725	535		2,260	2,700
8940	For polished chrome, add					12%				
9100	Free standing siamese unit, polished brass, three way									
9120	2-1/2" x 2-1/2" x 2-1/2" x 6"	Q-12	2	8	Ea.	1,650	535		2,185	2,600
9160	For polished chrome, add				"	15%				

21 12 Fire-Suppression Standpipes

21 12 13 – Fire-Suppression Hoses and Nozzles

21 12 13.50 Fire Hoses and Nozzles

			Crew	Daily Output	Labor-Hours	Unit	Material	2024 Bare Costs Labor	Equipment	Total	Total Incl O&P
0010	**FIRE HOSES AND NOZZLES**										
0200	Adapters, rough brass, straight hose threads	R211226-10									
0220	One piece, female to male, rocker lugs										
0240	1" x 1"	R211226-20				Ea.	37.50			37.50	41
0260	1-1/2" x 1"						44.50			44.50	49
0280	1-1/2" x 1-1/2"						53.50			53.50	58.50
0300	2" x 1-1/2"						78			78	85.50
0320	2" x 2"						111			111	122
0340	2-1/2" x 1-1/2"						34			34	37.50
0360	3" x 1-1/2"						132			132	145

21 12 Fire-Suppression Standpipes

21 12 13 – Fire-Suppression Hoses and Nozzles

21 12 13.50 Fire Hoses and Nozzles		Crew	Daily Output	Labor-Hours	Unit	Material	2024 Bare Costs Labor	Equipment	Total	Total Incl O&P
0380	2-1/2" x 2-1/2"				Ea.	118			118	130
0400	3" x 2-1/2"					91.50			91.50	101
0420	3" x 3"					154			154	169
0500	For polished brass, add					50%				
0520	For polished chrome, add				▼	75%				
0700	One piece, female to male, hexagon									
0740	1-1/2" x 3/4"				Ea.	102			102	113
0760	2" x 1-1/2"					37.50			37.50	41.50
0780	2-1/2" x 1"					197			197	216
0800	2-1/2" x 1-1/2"					76.50			76.50	84.50
0820	2-1/2" x 2"					53.50			53.50	59
0840	3" x 2-1/2"					126			126	138
0900	For polished chrome, add				▼	75%				
1100	Swivel, female to female, pin lugs									
1120	1-1/2" x 1-1/2"				Ea.	84.50			84.50	93
1200	2-1/2" x 2-1/2"					150			150	165
1260	For polished brass, add					50%				
1280	For polished chrome, add				▼	75%				
1400	Couplings, sngl. & dbl. jacket, pin lug or rocker lug, cast brass									
1410	1-1/2"				Ea.	65			65	71.50
1420	2-1/2"				"	187			187	206
1500	For polished brass, add					20%				
1520	For polished chrome, add					40%				
1580	Reducing, F x M, interior installation, cast brass									
1590	2" x 1-1/2"				Ea.	68			68	75
1600	2-1/2" x 1-1/2"					24			24	26.50
1680	For polished brass, add					50%				
1720	For polished chrome, add				▼	75%				
2200	Hose, less couplings									
2260	Synthetic jacket, lined, 300 lb. test, 1-1/2" diameter	Q-12	2600	.006	L.F.	2.19	.41		2.60	3.03
2270	2" diameter		2200	.007		3.16	.49		3.65	4.21
2280	2-1/2" diameter		2200	.007		4.08	.49		4.57	5.20
2290	3" diameter		2200	.007		6.20	.49		6.69	7.55
2360	High strength, 500 lb. test, 1-1/2" diameter		2600	.006		3.62	.41		4.03	4.60
2380	2-1/2" diameter	▼	2200	.007	▼	6.10	.49		6.59	7.45
5000	Nipples, straight hose to tapered iron pipe, brass									
5060	Female to female, 1-1/2" x 1-1/2"				Ea.	26			26	28.50
5100	2-1/2" x 2-1/2"					64.50			64.50	71
5190	For polished chrome, add					75%				
5200	Double male or male to female, 1" x 1"					34			34	37.50
5220	1-1/2" x 1"					17.40			17.40	19.15
5230	1-1/2" x 1-1/2"					17.45			17.45	19.20
5260	2" x 1-1/2"					93			93	102
5270	2" x 2"					141			141	155
5280	2-1/2" x 1-1/2"					129			129	142
5300	2-1/2" x 2"					55.50			55.50	61
5310	2-1/2" x 2-1/2"					55.50			55.50	61.50
5340	For polished chrome, add				▼	75%				
5600	Nozzles, brass									
5620	Adjustable fog, 3/4" booster line				Ea.	154			154	170
5630	1" booster line					184			184	202
5640	1-1/2" leader line					120			120	132
5660	2-1/2" direct connection				▼	280			280	310

21 12 Fire-Suppression Standpipes

21 12 13 – Fire-Suppression Hoses and Nozzles

21 12 13.50 Fire Hoses and Nozzles		Crew	Daily Output	Labor-Hours	Unit	Material	2024 Bare Costs Labor	Equipment	Total	Total Incl O&P
5680	2-1/2" playpipe nozzle				Ea.	365			365	405
5780	For chrome plated, add					8%				
5850	Electrical fire, adjustable fog, no shock									
5900	1-1/2"				Ea.	194			194	213
5920	2-1/2"					635			635	695
5980	For polished chrome, add					6%				
6200	Heavy duty, comb. adj. fog and str. stream, with handle									
6210	1" booster line				Ea.	325			325	360
6240	1-1/2"					735			735	805
6260	2-1/2", for playpipe					940			940	1,025
6280	2-1/2" direct connection					660			660	730
6300	2-1/2" playpipe combination					1,125			1,125	1,250
6480	For polished chrome, add					7%				
6500	Plain fog, polished brass, 1-1/2"					267			267	293
6540	Chrome plated, 1-1/2"					186			186	204
6700	Plain stream, polished brass, 1-1/2" x 10"					58.50			58.50	64.50
6760	2-1/2" x 15" x 7/8" or 1-1/2"					164			164	180
6860	For polished chrome, add					20%				
7000	Underwriters playpipe, 2-1/2" x 30" with 1-1/8" tip				Ea.	950			950	1,050
9200	Storage house, hose only, primed steel					2,025			2,025	2,225
9220	Aluminum					2,275			2,275	2,500
9280	Hose and hydrant house, primed steel					1,900			1,900	2,100
9300	Aluminum					2,025			2,025	2,250
9340	Tools, crowbar and brackets		1 Carp	12	.667		85.50	40.50		126	154
9360	Combination hydrant wrench and spanner						86			86	94.50
9380	Fire axe and brackets									
9400	6 lb.		1 Carp	12	.667	Ea.	209	40.50		249.50	290
9500	For fire equipment cabinets, Section 10 44 13.53									

21 12 16 – Fire-Suppression Hose Reels

21 12 16.50 Fire-Suppression Hose Reels		Crew	Daily Output	Labor-Hours	Unit	Material	Labor	Equipment	Total	Total Incl O&P
0010	**FIRE-SUPPRESSION HOSE REELS**									
2990	Hose reel, swinging, for 1-1/2" polyester neoprene lined hose									
3000	50' long	Q-12	14	1.143	Ea.	181	77		258	315
3020	100' long		14	1.143		271	77		348	410
3060	For 2-1/2" cotton rubber hose, 75' long		14	1.143		259	77		336	400
3100	150' long		14	1.143		300	77		377	445

21 12 19 – Fire-Suppression Hose Racks

21 12 19.50 Fire Hose Racks		Crew	Daily Output	Labor-Hours	Unit	Material	Labor	Equipment	Total	Total Incl O&P
0010	**FIRE HOSE RACKS**									
2600	Hose rack, swinging, for 1-1/2" diameter hose,									
2620	Enameled steel, 50' and 75' lengths of hose	Q-12	20	.800	Ea.	83.50	53.50		137	172
2640	100' and 125' lengths of hose		20	.800		83.50	53.50		137	172
2680	Chrome plated, 50' and 75' lengths of hose		20	.800		110	53.50		163.50	201
2700	100' and 125' lengths of hose		20	.800		176	53.50		229.50	274
2750	2-1/2" diameter, 100' hose		20	.800		155	53.50		208.50	250
2780	For hose rack nipple, 1-1/2" polished brass, add					32.50			32.50	35.50
2820	2-1/2" polished brass, add					104			104	114
2840	1-1/2" polished chrome, add					41			41	45
2860	2-1/2" polished chrome, add					114			114	126

21 12 Fire-Suppression Standpipes

21 12 23 – Fire-Suppression Hose Valves

21 12 23.70 Fire Hose Valves

			Crew	Daily Output	Labor-Hours	Unit	Material	2024 Bare Costs Labor	2024 Bare Costs Equipment	Total	Total Incl O&P
0010	**FIRE HOSE VALVES**										
0020	Angle, combination pressure adjust/restricting, rough brass	R211226-10									
0030	1-1/2"		1 Spri	12	.667	Ea.	143	50		193	231
0040	2-1/2"	R211226-20	"	7	1.143	"	235	85.50		320.50	385
0042	Nonpressure adjustable/restricting, rough brass										
0044	1-1/2"		1 Spri	12	.667	Ea.	127	50		177	213
0046	2-1/2"		"	7	1.143	"	205	85.50		290.50	350
0050	For polished brass, add						30%				
0060	For polished chrome, add						40%				
0080	Wheel handle, 300 lb., 1-1/2"		1 Spri	12	.667	Ea.	101	50		151	185
0090	2-1/2"		"	7	1.143	"	194	85.50		279.50	340
0100	For polished brass, add						35%				
0110	For polished chrome, add						50%				
1000	Ball drip, automatic, rough brass, 1/2"		1 Spri	20	.400	Ea.	19.80	30		49.80	66.50
1010	3/4"		"	20	.400	"	22.50	30		52.50	69
1100	Ball, 175 lb., sprinkler system, FM/UL, threaded, bronze										
1120	Slow close										
1150	1" size		1 Spri	19	.421	Ea.	305	31.50		336.50	380
1160	1-1/4" size			15	.533		330	40		370	425
1170	1-1/2" size			13	.615		435	46		481	550
1180	2" size			11	.727		530	54.50		584.50	660
1190	2-1/2" size		Q-12	15	1.067		715	71.50		786.50	890
1230	For supervisory switch kit, all sizes										
1240	One circuit, add		1 Spri	48	.167	Ea.	155	12.45		167.45	190
1280	Quarter turn for trim										
1300	1/2" size		1 Spri	22	.364	Ea.	59.50	27		86.50	106
1310	3/4" size			20	.400		64	30		94	115
1320	1" size			19	.421		71	31.50		102.50	125
1330	1-1/4" size			15	.533		117	40		157	188
1340	1-1/2" size			13	.615		146	46		192	230
1350	2" size			11	.727		174	54.50		228.50	273
1400	Caps, polished brass with chain, 3/4"						64.50			64.50	71
1420	1"						72			72	79
1440	1-1/2"						21			21	23.50
1460	2-1/2"						30.50			30.50	33.50
1480	3"						144			144	159
1900	Escutcheon plate, for angle valves, polished brass, 1-1/2"						22			22	24.50
1920	2-1/2"						37.50			37.50	41
1940	3"						45			45	49.50
1980	For polished chrome, add						15%				
2000	Foam, control valve, 3"		1 Spri	6	1.333		4,125	99.50		4,224.50	4,700
2020	Supply valve, 2-1/2"			7	1.143		5,250	85.50		5,335.50	5,900
2040	Proportioner, 8"			2	4		5,775	299		6,074	6,800
2060	Oscillating foam monitor with electric remote control		Q-12	5.33	3.002		26,300	202		26,502	29,300
3000	Gate, hose, wheel handle, N.R.S., rough brass, 1-1/2"		1 Spri	12	.667		180	50		230	272
3040	2-1/2", 300 lb.		"	7	1.143		254	85.50		339.50	405
3080	For polished brass, add						40%				
3090	For polished chrome, add						50%				
3800	Hydrant, screw type, crank handle, brass										
3840	2-1/2" size		Q-12	11	1.455	Ea.	585	97.50		682.50	785
3880	For chrome, same price										
4200	Hydrolator, vent and draining, rough brass, 1-1/2"		1 Spri	12	.667	Ea.	165	50		215	256

For customer support on your Plumbing Costs with RSMeans Data call 800.448.8182.

21 12 Fire-Suppression Standpipes

21 12 23 – Fire-Suppression Hose Valves

21 12 23.70 Fire Hose Valves		Crew	Daily Output	Labor-Hours	Unit	Material	2024 Bare Costs Labor	Equipment	Total	Total Incl O&P
4280	For polished brass, add				Ea.	50%				
4290	For polished chrome, add					90%				
5000	Pressure reducing rough brass, 1-1/2"	1 Spri	12	.667		520	50		570	650
5020	2-1/2"	"	7	1.143		785	85.50		870.50	990
5080	For polished brass, add					105%				
5090	For polished chrome, add				↓	140%				
8000	Wye, leader line, ball type, swivel female x male x male									
8040	2-1/2" x 1-1/2" x 1-1/2" polished brass				Ea.	570			570	630
8060	2-1/2" x 1-1/2" x 1-1/2" polished chrome				"	930			930	1,025

21 13 Fire-Suppression Sprinkler Systems

21 13 13 – Wet-Pipe Sprinkler Systems

21 13 13.50 Wet-Pipe Sprinkler System Components

			Crew	Daily Output	Labor-Hours	Unit	Material	2024 Bare Costs Labor	Equipment	Total	Total Incl O&P
0010	**WET-PIPE SPRINKLER SYSTEM COMPONENTS**										
1100	Alarm, electric pressure switch (circuit closer)	R211313-10	1 Spri	26	.308	Ea.	160	23		183	210
1140	For explosion proof, max 20 psi, contacts close or open			26	.308		700	23		723	805
1220	Water motor gong		↓	4	2		505	149		654	775
1900	Flexible sprinkler head connectors										
1910	Braided stainless steel hose with mounting bracket										
1920	1/2" and 3/4" outlet size										
1940	40" length		1 Spri	30	.267	Ea.	44	19.90		63.90	78
1960	60" length		"	22	.364	"	68.50	27		95.50	116
1982	May replace hard-pipe armovers										
1984	for wet and pre-action systems.										
2000	Release, emergency, manual, for hydraulic or pneumatic system		1 Spri	12	.667	Ea.	267	50		317	365
2060	Release, thermostatic, for hydraulic or pneumatic release line			20	.400		1,125	30		1,155	1,300
2200	Sprinkler cabinets, 6 head capacity			16	.500		59	37.50		96.50	120
2260	12 head capacity			16	.500		79.50	37.50		117	143
2340	Sprinkler head escutcheons, standard, brass tone, 1" size			40	.200		2.28	14.95		17.23	24.50
2360	Chrome, 1" size			40	.200		5.35	14.95		20.30	28
2400	Recessed type, bright brass			40	.200		16.80	14.95		31.75	40.50
2440	Chrome or white enamel		↓	40	.200	↓	3.50	14.95		18.45	26
2600	Sprinkler heads, not including supply piping										
3700	Standard spray, pendent or upright, brass, 135°F to 286°F										
3720	1/2" NPT, K2.8		1 Spri	16	.500	Ea.	39.50	37.50		77	99
3730	1/2" NPT, 7/16" orifice			16	.500		26	37.50		63.50	84
3740	1/2" NPT, K5.6			16	.500		21	37.50		58.50	78.50
3760	1/2" NPT, 17/32" orifice			16	.500		27.50	37.50		65	85.50
3780	3/4" NPT, 17/32" orifice		↓	16	.500	↓	14.75	37.50		52.25	72
3800	For open sprinklers, deduct						15%				
3840	For chrome, add					Ea.	5.85			5.85	6.45
3920	For 360°F, same cost										
3930	For 400°F		1 Spri	16	.500	Ea.	178	37.50		215.50	252
3940	For 500°F		"	16	.500	"	134	37.50		171.50	203
4200	Sidewall, vertical brass, 135°F to 286°F										
4240	1/2" NPT, 1/2" orifice		1 Spri	16	.500	Ea.	42	37.50		79.50	102
4280	3/4" NPT, 17/32" orifice		"	16	.500		141	37.50		178.50	211
4360	For satin chrome, add						6.95			6.95	7.65
4400	For 360°F, same cost										
4500	Sidewall, horizontal, brass, 135°F to 286°F										
4520	1/2" NPT, 1/2" orifice		1 Spri	16	.500	Ea.	28	37.50		65.50	86

21 13 Fire-Suppression Sprinkler Systems

21 13 13 – Wet-Pipe Sprinkler Systems

21 13 13.50 Wet-Pipe Sprinkler System Components

		Crew	Daily Output	Labor-Hours	Unit	Material	2024 Bare Costs Labor	Equipment	Total	Total Incl O&P
4540	For 360°F, same cost									
4800	Recessed pendent, brass, 135°F to 286°F									
4820	1/2" NPT, K2.8	1 Spri	10	.800	Ea.	19.50	59.50		79	111
4830	1/2" NPT, 7/16" orifice		10	.800		20.50	59.50		80	112
4840	1/2" NPT, K5.6		10	.800		22	59.50		81.50	113
4860	1/2" NPT, 17/32" orifice		10	.800		25.50	59.50		85	117
4900	For satin chrome, add					15			15	16.50
5000	Recessed-vertical sidewall, brass, 135°F to 286°F									
5020	1/2" NPT, K2.8	1 Spri	10	.800	Ea.	52	59.50		111.50	147
5030	1/2" NPT, 7/16" orifice		10	.800		52	59.50		111.50	147
5040	1/2" NPT, K5.6		10	.800		52	59.50		111.50	147
5100	For bright nickel, same cost									
5600	Concealed, complete with cover plate									
5620	1/2" NPT, 1/2" orifice, 135°F to 212°F	1 Spri	9	.889	Ea.	26.50	66.50		93	128
5800	Window, brass, 1/2" NPT, 1/4" orifice		16	.500		59.50	37.50		97	121
5810	1/2" NPT, 5/16" orifice		16	.500		59.50	37.50		97	121
5820	1/2" NPT, 3/8" orifice		16	.500		58.50	37.50		96	120
5830	1/2" NPT, 7/16" orifice		16	.500		59.50	37.50		97	121
5840	1/2" NPT, 1/2" orifice		16	.500		59	37.50		96.50	121
5860	For polished chrome, add					4			4	4.40
5880	3/4" NPT, 5/8" orifice	1 Spri	16	.500		61.50	37.50		99	124
5890	3/4" NPT, 3/4" orifice	"	16	.500		68	37.50		105.50	131
6000	Sprinkler head guards, bright zinc, 1/2" NPT					9.95			9.95	10.95
6020	Bright zinc, 3/4" NPT					7.70			7.70	8.45
6025	Residential sprinkler components (one and two family)									
6026	Water motor alarm with strainer	1 Spri	4	2	Ea.	610	149		759	890
6027	Fast response, glass bulb, 135°F to 155°F									
6028	1/2" NPT, pendent, brass	1 Spri	16	.500	Ea.	17	37.50		54.50	74
6029	1/2" NPT, sidewall, brass		16	.500		55.50	37.50		93	117
6030	1/2" NPT, pendent, brass, extended coverage		16	.500		42	37.50		79.50	102
6031	1/2" NPT, sidewall, brass, extended coverage		16	.500		38	37.50		75.50	97
6032	3/4" NPT sidewall, brass, extended coverage		16	.500		41.50	37.50		79	101
6033	For chrome, add					15%				
6034	For polyester/teflon coating, add					20%				
6100	Sprinkler head wrenches, standard head				Ea.	59.50			59.50	65.50
6120	Recessed head					125			125	138
6160	Tamper switch (valve supervisory switch)	1 Spri	16	.500		267	37.50		304.50	350
6165	Flow switch (valve supervisory switch)	"	16	.500		267	37.50		304.50	350

21 13 16 – Dry-Pipe Sprinkler Systems

21 13 16.50 Dry-Pipe Sprinkler System Components

		Crew	Daily Output	Labor-Hours	Unit	Material	Labor	Equipment	Total	Total Incl O&P
0010	**DRY-PIPE SPRINKLER SYSTEM COMPONENTS**									
0600	Accelerator	1 Spri	8	1	Ea.	1,125	74.50		1,199.50	1,350
0800	Air compressor for dry pipe system, automatic, complete									
0820	30 gal. system capacity, 3/4 HP	1 Spri	1.30	6.154	Ea.	2,075	460		2,535	2,950
0860	30 gal. system capacity, 1 HP		1.30	6.154		1,650	460		2,110	2,500
0910	30 gal. system capacity, 1-1/2 HP		1.30	6.154		1,775	460		2,235	2,625
0920	30 gal. system capacity, 2 HP		1.30	6.154		1,925	460		2,385	2,800
0960	Air pressure maintenance control		24	.333		520	25		545	605
1600	Dehydrator package, incl. valves and nipples R211313-20		12	.667		785	50		835	940
2600	Sprinkler heads, not including supply piping									
2640	Dry, pendent, 1/2" orifice, 3/4" or 1" NPT									
2660	3" to 6" length	1 Spri	14	.571	Ea.	132	42.50		174.50	209

21 13 Fire-Suppression Sprinkler Systems

21 13 16 – Dry-Pipe Sprinkler Systems

21 13 16.50 Dry-Pipe Sprinkler System Components

		Crew	Daily Output	Labor-Hours	Unit	Material	2024 Bare Costs Labor	Equipment	Total	Total Incl O&P
2670	6-1/4" to 8" length	1 Spri	14	.571	Ea.	138	42.50		180.50	215
2680	8-1/4" to 12" length		14	.571		145	42.50		187.50	223
2690	12-1/4" to 15" length		14	.571		155	42.50		197.50	234
2700	15-1/4" to 18" length		14	.571		164	42.50		206.50	244
2710	18-1/4" to 21" length		13	.615		174	46		220	261
2720	21-1/4" to 24" length		13	.615		185	46		231	273
2730	24-1/4" to 27" length		13	.615		196	46		242	285
2740	27-1/4" to 30" length		13	.615		305	46		351	405
2750	30-1/4" to 33" length		13	.615		215	46		261	305
2760	33-1/4" to 36" length		13	.615		224	46		270	315
2780	36-1/4" to 39" length		12	.667		214	50		264	310
2790	39-1/4" to 42" length	▼	12	.667		222	50		272	320
2800	For each inch or fraction, add				▼	2.85			2.85	3.14
6330	Valves and components									
6340	Alarm test/shut off valve, 1/2"	1 Spri	20	.400	Ea.	19.35	30		49.35	66
8000	Dry pipe air check valve, 3" size	Q-12	2	8		2,450	535		2,985	3,500
8200	Dry pipe valve, incl. trim and gauges, 3" size		2	8		4,125	535		4,660	5,325
8220	4" size	▼	1	16		3,850	1,075		4,925	5,850
8240	6" size	Q-13	2	16		5,175	1,125		6,300	7,400
8280	For accelerator trim with gauges, add	1 Spri	8	1	▼	400	74.50		474.50	555

21 13 19 – Preaction Sprinkler Systems

21 13 19.50 Preaction Sprinkler System Components

		Crew	Daily Output	Labor-Hours	Unit	Material	2024 Bare Costs Labor	Equipment	Total	Total Incl O&P
0010	**PREACTION SPRINKLER SYSTEM COMPONENTS**									
3000	Preaction valve cabinet									
3100	Single interlock, pneum. release, panel, 1/2 HP comp. regul. air trim									
3110	1-1/2"	Q-12	3	5.333	Ea.	30,200	360		30,560	33,700
3120	2"		3	5.333		30,300	360		30,660	33,800
3130	2-1/2"		3	5.333		30,900	360		31,260	34,500
3140	3"		3	5.333		30,500	360		30,860	34,000
3150	4"		2	8		31,900	535		32,435	35,900
3160	6"	Q-13	4	8	▼	34,000	570		34,570	38,200
3200	Double interlock, pneum. release, panel, 1/2 HP comp. regul. air trim									
3210	1-1/2"	Q-12	3	5.333	Ea.	31,400	360		31,760	35,000
3220	2"		3	5.333		31,500	360		31,860	35,200
3230	2-1/2"		3	5.333		31,400	360		31,760	35,100
3240	3"		3	5.333		31,700	360		32,060	35,400
3250	4"	▼	2	8		34,800	535		35,335	39,100
3260	6"	Q-13	4	8		36,400	570		36,970	40,900

21 13 20 – On-Off Multicycle Sprinkler System

21 13 20.50 On-Off Multicycle Fire-Suppression Sprinkler Systems

		Crew	Daily Output	Labor-Hours	Unit	Material	2024 Bare Costs Labor	Equipment	Total	Total Incl O&P
0010	**ON-OFF MULTICYCLE FIRE-SUPPRESSION SPRINKLER SYSTEMS**									
8400	On-off multicycle package, includes swing check									
8420	and flow control valves with required trim									
8440	2" size	Q-12	2	8	Ea.	6,375	535		6,910	7,825
8460	3" size		1.50	10.667		7,025	715		7,740	8,800
8480	4" size	▼	1	16		7,850	1,075		8,925	10,200
8500	6" size	Q-13	1.40	22.857		9,075	1,625		10,700	12,400

21 13 Fire-Suppression Sprinkler Systems

21 13 26 – Deluge Fire-Suppression Sprinkler Systems

21 13 26.50 Deluge Fire-Suppression Sprinkler Sys. Comp.	Crew	Daily Output	Labor-Hours	Unit	Material	2024 Bare Costs Labor	2024 Bare Costs Equipment	Total	Total Incl O&P
0010 **DELUGE FIRE-SUPPRESSION SPRINKLER SYSTEM COMPONENTS**									
1400　Deluge system, monitoring panel w/deluge valve & trim	1 Spri	18	.444	Ea.	26,100	33		26,133	28,700
6200　Valves and components									
7000　　Deluge, assembly, incl. trim, pressure									
7020　　　operated relief, emergency release, gauges									
7040　　　　2" size	Q-12	2	8	Ea.	5,750	535		6,285	7,125
7060　　　　3" size		1.50	10.667		6,950	715		7,665	8,700
7080　　　　4" size	↓	1	16		7,575	1,075		8,650	9,950
7100　　　　6" size	Q-13	1.80	17.778	↓	8,225	1,275		9,500	10,900
7800　　Pneumatic actuator, bronze, required on all									
7820　　　pneumatic release systems, any size deluge	1 Spri	18	.444	Ea.	430	33		463	520

21 13 39 – Foam-Water Systems

21 13 39.50 Foam-Water System Components

	Crew	Daily Output	Labor-Hours	Unit	Material	Labor	Equipment	Total	Total Incl O&P
0010 **FOAM-WATER SYSTEM COMPONENTS**									
2600　Sprinkler heads, not including supply piping									
3600　　Foam-water, pendent or upright, 1/2" NPT	1 Spri	12	.667	Ea.	390	50		440	505

21 21 Carbon-Dioxide Fire-Extinguishing Systems

21 21 16 – Carbon-Dioxide Fire-Extinguishing Equipment

21 21 16.50 CO2 Fire Extinguishing System

	Crew	Daily Output	Labor-Hours	Unit	Material	Labor	Equipment	Total	Total Incl O&P
0010 **CO$_2$ FIRE EXTINGUISHING SYSTEM**									
0042　For detectors and control stations, see Section 28 31 23.50									
0100　Control panel, single zone with batteries (2 zones det., 1 suppr.)	1 Elec	1	8	Ea.	1,825	575		2,400	2,875
0150　　Multizone (4) with batteries (8 zones det., 4 suppr.)	"	.50	16		3,575	1,150		4,725	5,625
1000　Dispersion nozzle, CO$_2$, 3" x 5"	1 Plum	18	.444		185	33		218	253
2000　Extinguisher, CO$_2$ system, high pressure, 75 lb. cylinder	Q-1	6	2.667		1,650	179		1,829	2,075
2100　　100 lb. cylinder	"	5	3.200		2,500	215		2,715	3,075
3000　Electro/mechanical release	L-1	4	4		1,225	293		1,518	1,775
3400　Manual pull station	1 Plum	6	1.333		117	99.50		216.50	277
4000　Pneumatic damper release	"	8	1	↓	380	74.50		454.50	530

21 22 Clean-Agent Fire-Extinguishing Systems

21 22 16 – Clean-Agent Fire-Extinguishing Equipment

21 22 16.50 Clean-Agent Extinguishing Systems

	Crew	Daily Output	Labor-Hours	Unit	Material	Labor	Equipment	Total	Total Incl O&P
0010 **CLEAN-AGENT EXTINGUISHING SYSTEMS**									
0020　FM200 fire extinguishing system									
1100　Dispersion nozzle FM200, 1-1/2"	1 Plum	14	.571	Ea.	294	42.50		336.50	390
2400　Extinguisher, FM200 system, filled, with mounting bracket									
2460　　26 lb. container	Q-1	8	2	Ea.	2,750	134		2,884	3,225
2480　　44 lb. container		7	2.286		3,575	154		3,729	4,150
2500　　63 lb. container		6	2.667		5,075	179		5,254	5,850
2520　　101 lb. container		5	3.200		7,325	215		7,540	8,375
2540　　196 lb. container	↓	4	4	↓	8,850	269		9,119	10,100
6000　FM200 system, simple nozzle layout, with broad dispersion				C.F.	2.40			2.40	2.64
6010　Extinguisher, FM200 system, filled, with mounting bracket									
6020　　Complex nozzle layout and/or including underfloor dispersion				C.F.	4.78			4.78	5.25
6100　　20,000 C.F. 2 exits, 8' clng					2.67			2.67	2.94
6200　　100,000 C.F. 4 exits, 8' clng					2.42			2.42	2.66

21 22 Clean-Agent Fire-Extinguishing Systems

21 22 16 – Clean-Agent Fire-Extinguishing Equipment

21 22 16.50 Clean-Agent Extinguishing Systems		Crew	Daily Output	Labor-Hours	Unit	Material	2024 Bare Costs Labor	2024 Bare Costs Equipment	Total	Total Incl O&P
6300	250,000 C.F. 6 exits, 8' clng				C.F.	2.04			2.04	2.24
7010	HFC-227ea fire extinguishing system									
7100	Cylinders with clean-agent									
7110	Does not include pallet jack/fork lift rental fees									
7120	70 lb. cyl, w/35 lb. agent, no solenoid	Q-12	14	1.143	Ea.	5,175	77		5,252	5,800
7130	70 lb. cyl w/70 lb. agent, no solenoid		10	1.600		6,775	107		6,882	7,625
7140	70 lb. cyl w/35 lb. agent, w/solenoid		14	1.143		4,650	77		4,727	5,225
7150	70 lb. cyl w/70 lb. agent, w/solenoid		10	1.600		5,875	107		5,982	6,600
7220	250 lb. cyl, w/125 lb. agent, no solenoid		8	2		12,000	134		12,134	13,300
7230	250 lb. cyl, w/250 lb. agent, no solenoid		5	3.200		12,000	215		12,215	13,400
7240	250 lb. cyl, w/125 lb. agent, w/solenoid		8	2		10,000	134		10,134	11,300
7250	250 lb. cyl, w/250 lb. agent, w/solenoid		5	3.200		14,400	215		14,615	16,200
7320	560 lb. cyl, w/300 lb. agent, no solenoid		4	4		22,900	269		23,169	25,500
7330	560 lb. cyl, w/560 lb. agent, no solenoid		2.50	6.400		34,900	430		35,330	39,000
7340	560 lb. cyl, w/300 lb. agent, w/solenoid		4	4		18,600	269		18,869	20,900
7350	560 lb. cyl, w/560 lb. agent, w/solenoid		2.50	6.400		27,700	430		28,130	31,100
7420	1,200 lb. cyl, w/600 lb. agent, no solenoid	Q-13	4	8		43,500	570		44,070	48,700
7430	1,200 lb. cyl, w/1,200 lb. agent, no solenoid		3	10.667		71,500	760		72,260	79,500
7440	1,200 lb. cyl, w/600 lb. agent, w/solenoid		4	8		64,500	570		65,070	72,000
7450	1,200 lb. cyl, w/1,200 lb. agent, w/solenoid		3	10.667		101,500	760		102,260	112,500
7500	Accessories									
7510	Dispersion nozzle	1 Spri	16	.500	Ea.	197	37.50		234.50	273
7520	Agent release panel	1 Elec	4	2		117	143		260	340
7530	Maintenance switch	"	6	1.333		420	95.50		515.50	600
7540	Solenoid valve, 12v dc	1 Spri	8	1		273	74.50		347.50	410
7550	12v ac		8	1		670	74.50		744.50	845
7560	12v dc, explosion proof		8	1		705	74.50		779.50	885

21 31 Centrifugal Fire Pumps

21 31 13 – Electric-Drive, Centrifugal Fire Pumps

21 31 13.50 Electric-Drive Fire Pumps

		Crew	Daily Output	Labor-Hours	Unit	Material	2024 Bare Costs Labor	2024 Bare Costs Equipment	Total	Total Incl O&P
0010	**ELECTRIC-DRIVE FIRE PUMPS** Including controller, fittings and relief valve									
3100	250 GPM, 55 psi, 15 HP, 3550 RPM, 2" pump	Q-13	.70	45.714	Ea.	17,900	3,250		21,150	24,500
3200	500 GPM, 50 psi, 27 HP, 1770 RPM, 4" pump		.68	47.059		22,200	3,350		25,550	29,400
3250	500 GPM, 100 psi, 47 HP, 3550 RPM, 3" pump		.66	48.485		26,900	3,450		30,350	34,700
3300	500 GPM, 125 psi, 64 HP, 3550 RPM, 3" pump		.62	51.613		29,500	3,675		33,175	37,900
3350	750 GPM, 50 psi, 44 HP, 1770 RPM, 5" pump		.64	50		32,400	3,550		35,950	41,000
3400	750 GPM, 100 psi, 66 HP, 3550 RPM, 4" pump		.58	55.172		28,700	3,925		32,625	37,400
3450	750 GPM, 165 psi, 120 HP, 3550 RPM, 4" pump		.56	57.143		37,400	4,050		41,450	47,300
3500	1000 GPM, 50 psi, 48 HP, 1770 RPM, 5" pump		.60	53.333		32,400	3,800		36,200	41,400
3550	1000 GPM, 100 psi, 86 HP, 3550 RPM, 5" pump		.54	59.259		36,300	4,200		40,500	46,300
3600	1000 GPM, 150 psi, 142 HP, 3550 RPM, 5" pump		.50	64		41,200	4,550		45,750	52,000
3650	1000 GPM, 200 psi, 245 HP, 1770 RPM, 6" pump		.36	88.889		54,500	6,325		60,825	69,500
3660	1250 GPM, 75 psi, 75 HP, 1770 RPM, 5" pump		.55	58.182		33,300	4,125		37,425	42,800
3700	1500 GPM, 50 psi, 66 HP, 1770 RPM, 6" pump		.50	64		35,000	4,550		39,550	45,300
3750	1500 GPM, 100 psi, 139 HP, 1770 RPM, 6" pump		.46	69.565		39,500	4,950		44,450	51,000
3800	1500 GPM, 150 psi, 200 HP, 1770 RPM, 6" pump		.36	88.889		48,500	6,325		54,825	63,000
3850	1500 GPM, 200 psi, 279 HP, 1770 RPM, 6" pump		.32	100		52,000	7,100		59,100	68,000
3900	2000 GPM, 100 psi, 167 HP, 1770 RPM, 6" pump		.34	94.118		47,400	6,675		54,075	62,000
3950	2000 GPM, 150 psi, 292 HP, 1770 RPM, 6" pump		.28	114		59,000	8,125		67,125	77,000
4000	2500 GPM, 100 psi, 213 HP, 1770 RPM, 8" pump		.30	107		55,000	7,575		62,575	72,500

21 31 Centrifugal Fire Pumps

21 31 13 – Electric-Drive, Centrifugal Fire Pumps

21 31 13.50 Electric-Drive Fire Pumps		Crew	Daily Output	Labor-Hours	Unit	Material	2024 Bare Costs Labor	Equipment	Total	Total Incl O&P
4040	2500 GPM, 135 psi, 339 HP, 1770 RPM, 8" pump	Q-13	.26	123	Ea.	79,000	8,750		87,750	100,000
4100	3000 GPM, 100 psi, 250 HP, 1770 RPM, 8" pump		.28	114		66,000	8,125		74,125	85,000
4150	3000 GPM, 140 psi, 428 HP, 1770 RPM, 10" pump		.24	133		105,000	9,475		114,475	129,500
4200	3500 GPM, 100 psi, 300 HP, 1770 RPM, 10" pump		.26	123		82,000	8,750		90,750	103,500
4250	3500 GPM, 140 psi, 450 HP, 1770 RPM, 10" pump		.24	133		105,000	9,475		114,475	129,500
5000	For jockey pump 1", 3 HP, with control, add	Q-12	2	8		4,200	535		4,735	5,425

21 31 16 – Diesel-Drive, Centrifugal Fire Pumps

21 31 16.50 Diesel-Drive Fire Pumps		Crew	Daily Output	Labor-Hours	Unit	Material	2024 Bare Costs Labor	Equipment	Total	Total Incl O&P
0010	**DIESEL-DRIVE FIRE PUMPS** Including controller, fittings and relief valve									
0050	500 GPM, 50 psi, 27 HP, 4" pump	Q-13	.64	50	Ea.	71,500	3,550		75,050	84,000
0100	500 GPM, 100 psi, 62 HP, 4" pump		.60	53.333		75,500	3,800		79,300	88,500
0150	500 GPM, 125 psi, 78 HP, 4" pump		.56	57.143		76,500	4,050		80,550	90,000
0200	750 GPM, 50 psi, 44 HP, 5" pump		.60	53.333		76,000	3,800		79,800	89,500
0250	750 GPM, 100 psi, 80 HP, 4" pump		.56	57.143		79,500	4,050		83,550	93,500
0300	750 GPM, 165 psi, 203 HP, 5" pump		.52	61.538		82,500	4,375		86,875	97,000
0350	1000 GPM, 50 psi, 48 HP, 5" pump		.58	55.172		76,500	3,925		80,425	90,500
0400	1000 GPM, 100 psi, 89 HP, 4" pump		.56	57.143		81,500	4,050		85,550	96,000
0450	1000 GPM, 150 psi, 148 HP, 4" pump		.48	66.667		80,500	4,725		85,225	95,500
0470	1000 GPM, 200 psi, 280 HP, 5" pump		.40	80		101,500	5,675		107,175	120,000
0480	1250 GPM, 75 psi, 75 HP, 5" pump		.54	59.259		77,500	4,200		81,700	92,000
0500	1500 GPM, 50 psi, 66 HP, 6" pump		.50	64		82,500	4,550		87,050	98,000
0550	1500 GPM, 100 psi, 140 HP, 6" pump		.46	69.565		84,500	4,950		89,450	100,500
0600	1500 GPM, 150 psi, 228 HP, 6" pump		.42	76.190		95,500	5,425		100,925	113,000
0650	1500 GPM, 200 psi, 279 HP, 6" pump		.38	84.211		149,500	5,975		155,475	173,500
0700	2000 GPM, 100 psi, 167 HP, 6" pump		.34	94.118		86,500	6,675		93,175	105,000
0750	2000 GPM, 150 psi, 284 HP, 6" pump		.30	107		117,000	7,575		124,575	140,500
0800	2500 GPM, 100 psi, 213 HP, 8" pump		.32	100		110,500	7,100		117,600	132,000
0820	2500 GPM, 150 psi, 365 HP, 8" pump		.26	123		129,500	8,750		138,250	155,500
0850	3000 GPM, 100 psi, 250 HP, 8" pump		.28	114		127,500	8,125		135,625	152,500
0900	3000 GPM, 150 psi, 384 HP, 10" pump		.20	160		148,500	11,400		159,900	180,500
0950	3500 GPM, 100 psi, 300 HP, 10" pump		.24	133		152,500	9,475		161,975	181,500
1000	3500 GPM, 150 psi, 518 HP, 10" pump		.20	160		215,500	11,400		226,900	254,000

Division Notes

		CREW	DAILY OUTPUT	LABOR-HOURS	UNIT	BARE COSTS				TOTAL INCL O&P
						MAT.	LABOR	EQUIP.	TOTAL	

Estimating Tips
22 10 00 Plumbing Piping and Pumps
This subdivision is primarily basic pipe and related materials. The pipe may be used by any of the mechanical disciplines, i.e., plumbing, fire protection, heating, and air conditioning.

Note: CPVC plastic piping approved for fire protection is located in 21 11 13.

- The labor adjustment factors listed in Subdivision 22 01 02.20 apply throughout Divisions 21, 22, and 23. CAUTION: the correct percentage may vary for the same items. For example, the percentage add for the basic pipe installation should be based on the maximum height that the installer must install for that particular section. If the pipe is to be located 14' above the floor but it is suspended on threaded rod from beams, the bottom flange of which is 18' high (4' rods), then the height is actually 18' and the add is 20%. The pipe cover, however, does not have to go above the 14' and so the add should be 10%.
- Most pipe is priced first as straight pipe with a joint (coupling, weld, etc.) every 10' and a hanger usually every 10'. There are exceptions with hanger spacing such as for cast iron pipe (5') and plastic pipe (3 per 10'). Following each type of pipe there are several lines listing sizes and the amount to be subtracted to delete couplings and hangers. This is for pipe that is to be buried or supported together on trapeze hangers. The reason that the couplings are deleted is that these runs are usually long, and frequently longer lengths of pipe are used. By deleting the couplings, the estimator is expected to look up and add back the correct reduced number of couplings.
- When preparing an estimate, it may be necessary to approximate the fittings. Fittings usually run between 25% and 50% of the cost of the pipe. The lower percentage is for simpler runs, and the higher number is for complex areas, such as mechanical rooms.
- For historic restoration projects, the systems must be as invisible as possible, and pathways must be sought for pipes, conduit, and ductwork. While installations in accessible spaces (such as basements and attics) are relatively straightforward to estimate, labor costs may be more difficult to determine when delivery systems must be concealed.

22 40 00 Plumbing Fixtures
- Plumbing fixture costs usually require two lines: the fixture itself and its "rough-in, supply, and waste."
- In the Assemblies Section (Plumbing D2010) for the desired fixture, the System Components Group at the center of the page shows the fixture on the first line. The rest of the list (fittings, pipe, tubing, etc.) will total up to what we refer to in the Unit Price section as "Rough-in, supply, waste, and vent." Note that for most fixtures we allow a nominal 5' of tubing to reach from the fixture to a main or riser.
- Remember that gas- and oil-fired units need venting.

Reference Numbers
Reference numbers are shown at the beginning of some major classifications. These numbers refer to related items in the Reference Section. The reference information may be an estimating procedure, an alternate pricing method, or technical information.

Note: Not all subdivisions listed here necessarily appear. ■

Same Data. Simplified.
Enjoy the convenience and efficiency of accessing your costs anywhere:
- **Skip the multiplier** by setting your location
- **Quickly search**, edit, favorite and share costs
- **Stay on top of price changes** with automatic updates

Discover more at rsmeans.com/online

No part of this cost data may be reproduced, stored in a retrieval system, or transmitted in any form or by any means without prior written permission of Gordian.

Note: "Powered in part by CINX™, based on licensed proprietary information of Harrison Publishing House, Inc."

Note: Trade Service, in part, has been used as a reference source for some of the material prices used in Division 22.

22 01 Operation and Maintenance of Plumbing

22 01 02 – Labor Adjustments

22 01 02.10 Boilers, General

		Crew	Daily Output	Labor-Hours	Unit	Material	2024 Bare Costs Labor	2024 Bare Costs Equipment	Total	Total Incl O&P
0010	**BOILERS, GENERAL**, Prices do not include flue piping, elec. wiring,									
0020	gas or oil piping, boiler base, pad, or tankless unless noted									
0100	Boiler H.P.: 10 KW = 34 lb./steam/hr. = 33,475 BTU/hr.									
0150	To convert SFR to BTU rating: Hot water, 150 x SFR;									
0160	Forced hot water, 180 x SFR; steam, 240 x SFR									

22 01 02.20 Labor Adjustment Factors

0010	**LABOR ADJUSTMENT FACTORS** (For Div. 21, 22 and 23) R220102-20									
0100	Labor factors: The below are reasonable suggestions, but									
0110	each project must be evaluated for its own peculiarities, and									
0120	the adjustments be increased or decreased depending on the									
0130	severity of the special conditions.									
1000	Add to labor for elevated installation (Above floor level)									
1080	10' to 14.5' high R221113-70						10%			
1100	15' to 19.5' high						20%			
1120	20' to 24.5' high						25%			
1140	25' to 29.5' high						35%			
1160	30' to 34.5' high						40%			
1180	35' to 39.5' high						50%			
1200	40' and higher						55%			
2000	Add to labor for crawl space									
2100	3' high						40%			
2140	4' high						30%			
3000	Add to labor for multi-story building									
3010	For new construction (No elevator available)									
3100	Add for floors 3 thru 10						5%			
3110	Add for floors 11 thru 15						10%			
3120	Add for floors 16 thru 20						15%			
3130	Add for floors 21 thru 30						20%			
3140	Add for floors 31 and up						30%			
3170	For existing structure (Elevator available)									
3180	Add for work on floor 3 and above						2%			
4000	Add to labor for working in existing occupied buildings									
4100	Hospital						35%			
4140	Office building						25%			
4180	School						20%			
4220	Factory or warehouse						15%			
4260	Multi dwelling						15%			
5000	Add to labor, miscellaneous									
5100	Cramped shaft						35%			
5140	Congested area						15%			
5180	Excessive heat or cold						30%			
9000	Labor factors: The above are reasonable suggestions, but									
9010	each project should be evaluated for its own peculiarities.									
9100	Other factors to be considered are:									
9140	Movement of material and equipment through finished areas									
9180	Equipment room									
9220	Attic space									
9260	No service road									
9300	Poor unloading/storage area									
9340	Congested site area/heavy traffic									

22 05 Common Work Results for Plumbing

22 05 05 – Selective Demolition for Plumbing

22 05 05.10 Plumbing Demolition

		Crew	Daily Output	Labor-Hours	Unit	Material	2024 Bare Costs Labor	2024 Bare Costs Equipment	Total	Total Incl O&P
0010	**PLUMBING DEMOLITION** R220105-10									
0400	Air compressor, up thru 2 HP	Q-1	10	1.600	Ea.		107		107	160
0410	3 HP thru 7-1/2 HP R024119-10		5.60	2.857			192		192	286
0420	10 HP thru 15 HP	↓	1.40	11.429			770		770	1,150
0430	20 HP thru 30 HP	Q-2	1.30	18.462			1,275		1,275	1,925
0500	Backflow preventer, up thru 2" diameter	1 Plum	17	.471			35		35	52.50
0510	2-1/2" thru 3" diameter	Q-1	10	1.600			107		107	160
0520	4" thru 6" diameter	"	5	3.200			215		215	320
0530	8" thru 10" diameter	Q-2	3	8	↓		555		555	830
0700	Carriers and supports									
0710	Fountains, sinks, lavatories and urinals	1 Plum	14	.571	Ea.		42.50		42.50	63.50
0720	Water closets	"	12	.667	"		50		50	74
0730	Grinder pump or sewage ejector system									
0732	Simplex	Q-1	7	2.286	Ea.		154		154	228
0734	Duplex	"	2.80	5.714			385		385	570
0738	Hot water dispenser	1 Plum	36	.222			16.60		16.60	24.50
0740	Hydrant, wall		26	.308			23		23	34
0744	Ground		12	.667			50		50	74
0760	Cleanouts and drains, up thru 4" pipe diameter	↓	10	.800			59.50		59.50	89
0764	5" thru 8" pipe diameter	Q-1	10	1.600			107		107	160
0780	Industrial safety fixtures	1 Plum	8	1	↓		74.50		74.50	111
1020	Fixtures, including 10' piping									
1100	Bathtubs, cast iron	1 Plum	4	2	Ea.		149		149	222
1120	Fiberglass		6	1.333			99.50		99.50	148
1140	Steel	↓	5	1.600			119		119	178
1150	Bidet	Q-1	7	2.286			154		154	228
1200	Lavatory, wall hung	1 Plum	10	.800			59.50		59.50	89
1220	Counter top		8	1			74.50		74.50	111
1300	Sink, single compartment		8	1			74.50		74.50	111
1320	Double compartment	↓	7	1.143			85.50		85.50	127
1340	Shower, stall and receptor	Q-1	6	2.667			179		179	266
1350	Group	"	7	2.286			154		154	228
1400	Water closet, floor mounted	1 Plum	8	1			74.50		74.50	111
1420	Wall mounted	"	7	1.143			85.50		85.50	127
1440	Wash fountain, 36" diameter	Q-2	8	3			209		209	310
1442	54" diameter	"	7	3.429			239		239	355
1500	Urinal, floor mounted	1 Plum	4	2			149		149	222
1520	Wall mounted	"	7	1.143			85.50		85.50	127
1590	Whirl pool or hot tub	Q-1	2.60	6.154			415		415	615
1600	Water fountains, free standing	1 Plum	8	1			74.50		74.50	111
1620	Wall or deck mounted		6	1.333			99.50		99.50	148
1800	Medical gas specialties		8	1			74.50		74.50	111
1810	Plumbing demo, floor drain, remove		12	.667			50		50	74
1820	Plumbing demo, roof drain, remove		9	.889			66.50		66.50	98.50
1900	Piping fittings, single connection, up thru 1-1/2" diameter		30	.267			19.90		19.90	29.50
1910	2" thru 4" diameter		14	.571			42.50		42.50	63.50
1980	Pipe hanger/support removal		80	.100	↓		7.45		7.45	11.10
1990	Glass pipe with fittings, 1" thru 3" diameter		200	.040	L.F.		2.99		2.99	4.44
1992	4" thru 6" diameter		150	.053			3.98		3.98	5.90
2000	Piping, metal, up thru 1-1/2" diameter		200	.040			2.99		2.99	4.44
2050	2" thru 3-1/2" diameter	↓	150	.053			3.98		3.98	5.90
2100	4" thru 6" diameter	2 Plum	100	.160			11.95		11.95	17.75
2150	8" thru 14" diameter	"	60	.267	↓		19.90		19.90	29.50

22 05 Common Work Results for Plumbing

22 05 05 – Selective Demolition for Plumbing

22 05 05.10 Plumbing Demolition		Crew	Daily Output	Labor-Hours	Unit	Material	2024 Bare Costs Labor	2024 Bare Costs Equipment	Total	Total Incl O&P
2153	16" thru 20" diameter	Q-18	70	.343	L.F.		24	1.03	25.03	37
2155	24" thru 26" diameter		55	.436			31	1.30	32.30	47.50
2156	30" thru 36" diameter		40	.600			42.50	1.79	44.29	65
2160	Plastic pipe with fittings, up thru 1-1/2" diameter	1 Plum	250	.032			2.39		2.39	3.55
2162	2" thru 3" diameter	"	200	.040			2.99		2.99	4.44
2164	4" thru 6" diameter	Q-1	200	.080			5.35		5.35	8
2166	8" thru 14" diameter		150	.107			7.15		7.15	10.65
2168	16" diameter		100	.160			10.75		10.75	16
2170	Prison fixtures, lavatory or sink		18	.889	Ea.		59.50		59.50	89
2172	Shower		5.60	2.857			192		192	286
2174	Urinal or water closet		13	1.231			82.50		82.50	123
2180	Pumps, all fractional horse-power		12	1.333			89.50		89.50	133
2184	1 HP thru 5 HP		6	2.667			179		179	266
2186	7-1/2 HP thru 15 HP		2.50	6.400			430		430	640
2188	20 HP thru 25 HP	Q-2	4	6			420		420	620
2190	30 HP thru 60 HP		.80	30			2,100		2,100	3,100
2192	75 HP thru 100 HP		.60	40			2,775		2,775	4,150
2194	150 HP		.50	48			3,350		3,350	4,975
2198	Pump, sump or submersible	1 Plum	12	.667			50		50	74
2200	Receptors and interceptors, up thru 20 GPM	"	8	1			74.50		74.50	111
2204	25 thru 100 GPM	Q-1	6	2.667			179		179	266
2208	125 thru 300 GPM	"	2.40	6.667			450		450	665
2211	325 thru 500 GPM	Q-2	2.60	9.231			645		645	955
2212	Deduct for salvage, aluminum scrap				Ton	780			780	860
2214	Brass scrap					3,375			3,375	3,725
2216	Copper scrap					4,850			4,850	5,350
2218	Lead scrap					835			835	920
2220	Steel scrap								204	224
2230	Temperature maintenance cable	1 Plum	1200	.007	L.F.		.50		.50	.74
2240	Toilet partitions, see Section 10 21 13									
2250	Water heater, 40 gal.	1 Plum	6	1.333	Ea.		99.50		99.50	148
3100	Tanks, water heaters and liquid containers									
3110	Up thru 45 gallons	Q-1	22	.727	Ea.		49		49	72.50
3120	50 thru 120 gallons		14	1.143			77		77	114
3130	130 thru 240 gallons		7.60	2.105			141		141	210
3140	250 thru 500 gallons		5.40	2.963			199		199	296
3150	600 thru 1,000 gallons	Q-2	1.60	15			1,050		1,050	1,550
3160	1,100 thru 2,000 gallons		.70	34.286			2,400		2,400	3,550
3170	2,100 thru 4,000 gallons		.50	48			3,350		3,350	4,975
6000	Remove and reset fixtures, easy access	1 Plum	6	1.333			99.50		99.50	148
6100	Difficult access	"	4	2			149		149	222
6500	Solar heating system									
6510	Solar panel, hot water system	1 Plum	304	.026	S.F.		1.96		1.96	2.92
7910	Solar panel for pool	"	300	.027	"		1.99		1.99	2.96
8000	Sprinkler system									
8100	Exposed wet/dry	1 Plum	2500	.003	SF Flr.		.24		.24	.36
8200	Concealed wet/dry	"	1250	.006	"		.48		.48	.71
9100	Valve, metal valves or strainers and similar, up thru 1-1/2" diameter	1 Stpi	28	.286	Ea.		21.50		21.50	32
9110	2" thru 3" diameter	Q-1	11	1.455			97.50		97.50	145
9120	4" thru 6" diameter	"	8	2			134		134	200
9130	8" thru 14" diameter	Q-2	8	3			209		209	310
9140	16" thru 20" diameter		2	12			835		835	1,250
9150	24" diameter		1.20	20			1,400		1,400	2,075

22 05 Common Work Results for Plumbing

22 05 05 – Selective Demolition for Plumbing

22 05 05.10 Plumbing Demolition		Crew	Daily Output	Labor-Hours	Unit	Material	2024 Bare Costs Labor	2024 Bare Costs Equipment	Total	Total Incl O&P
9200	Valve, plastic, up thru 1-1/2" diameter	1 Plum	42	.190	Ea.		14.20		14.20	21
9210	2" thru 3" diameter		15	.533			40		40	59
9220	4" thru 6" diameter		12	.667			50		50	74
9300	Vent flashing and caps		55	.145			10.85		10.85	16.15
9350	Water filter, commercial, 1" thru 1-1/2"	Q-1	2	8			535		535	800
9360	2" thru 2-1/2"	"	1.60	10			670		670	1,000
9400	Water heaters									
9410	Up thru 245 GPH	Q-1	2.40	6.667	Ea.		450		450	665
9420	250 thru 756 GPH		1.60	10			670		670	1,000
9430	775 thru 1,640 GPH		.80	20			1,350		1,350	2,000
9440	1,650 thru 4,000 GPH	Q-2	.50	48			3,350		3,350	4,975
9470	Water softener	Q-1	2	8			535		535	800

22 05 23 – General-Duty Valves for Plumbing Piping

22 05 23.10 Valves, Brass

		Crew	Daily Output	Labor-Hours	Unit	Material	Labor	Equipment	Total	Incl O&P
0010	**VALVES, BRASS**									
0032	For motorized valves, see Section 23 09 53.10									
0500	Gas cocks, threaded									
0510	1/4"	1 Plum	26	.308	Ea.	32	23		55	69.50
0520	3/8"		24	.333		32	25		57	72.50
0530	1/2"		24	.333		33	25		58	73
0540	3/4"		22	.364		37.50	27		64.50	82
0550	1"		19	.421		59.50	31.50		91	113
0560	1-1/4"		15	.533		73.50	40		113.50	140
0570	1-1/2"		13	.615		113	46		159	194
0580	2"		11	.727		186	54.50		240.50	285
0672	For larger sizes use lubricated plug valve, Section 23 05 23.70									

22 05 23.20 Valves, Bronze

			Crew	Daily Output	Labor-Hours	Unit	Material	Labor	Equipment	Total	Incl O&P
0010	**VALVES, BRONZE**	R220523-80									
1020	Angle, 150 lb., rising stem, threaded										
1030	1/8"	R220523-90	1 Plum	24	.333	Ea.	274	25		299	335
1040	1/4"			24	.333		274	25		299	335
1050	3/8"			24	.333		255	25		280	315
1060	1/2"			22	.364		255	27		282	320
1070	3/4"			20	.400		350	30		380	430
1080	1"			19	.421		490	31.50		521.50	585
1090	1-1/4"			15	.533		525	40		565	635
1100	1-1/2"			13	.615		830	46		876	980
1102	Soldered same price as threaded										
1110	2"		1 Plum	11	.727	Ea.	1,300	54.50		1,354.50	1,525
1300	Ball										
1304	Soldered										
1312	3/8"		1 Plum	21	.381	Ea.	27	28.50		55.50	72
1316	1/2"			18	.444		24	33		57	75.50
1320	3/4"			17	.471		46	35		81	103
1324	1"			15	.533		58	40		98	123
1328	1-1/4"			13	.615		104	46		150	183
1332	1-1/2"			11	.727		132	54.50		186.50	226
1336	2"			9	.889		213	66.50		279.50	335
1340	2-1/2"			7	1.143		158	85.50		243.50	300
1344	3"			5	1.600		236	119		355	435
1350	Single union end										
1358	3/8"		1 Plum	21	.381	Ea.	43	28.50		71.50	89.50

22 05 Common Work Results for Plumbing

22 05 23 – General-Duty Valves for Plumbing Piping

22 05 23.20 Valves, Bronze		Crew	Daily Output	Labor-Hours	Unit	Material	2024 Bare Costs Labor	2024 Bare Costs Equipment	Total	Total Incl O&P
1362	1/2"	1 Plum	18	.444	Ea.	44	33		77	98
1366	3/4"		17	.471		79	35		114	139
1370	1"		15	.533		91	40		131	159
1374	1-1/4"		13	.615		126	46		172	207
1378	1-1/2"		11	.727		100	54.50		154.50	191
1382	2"		9	.889		224	66.50		290.50	345
1398	Threaded, 150 psi									
1400	1/4"	1 Plum	24	.333	Ea.	23.50	25		48.50	63
1430	3/8"		24	.333		23.50	25		48.50	62.50
1450	1/2"		22	.364		21.50	27		48.50	64
1460	3/4"		20	.400		37.50	30		67.50	85.50
1470	1"		19	.421		59.50	31.50		91	113
1480	1-1/4"		15	.533		71	40		111	137
1490	1-1/2"		13	.615		85	46		131	162
1500	2"		11	.727		114	54.50		168.50	206
1510	2-1/2"		9	.889		152	66.50		218.50	267
1520	3"		8	1		129	74.50		203.50	253
1522	Solder the same price as threaded									
1600	Butterfly, 175 psi, full port, solder or threaded ends									
1610	Stainless steel disc and stem									
1620	1/4"	1 Plum	24	.333	Ea.	31.50	25		56.50	71.50
1630	3/8"		24	.333		37	25		62	77.50
1640	1/2"		22	.364		37	27		64	81
1650	3/4"		20	.400		59.50	30		89.50	110
1660	1"		19	.421		76.50	31.50		108	132
1670	1-1/4"		15	.533		117	40		157	188
1680	1-1/2"		13	.615		136	46		182	219
1690	2"		11	.727		190	54.50		244.50	290
1750	Check, swing, class 150, regrinding disc, threaded									
1800	1/8"	1 Plum	24	.333	Ea.	106	25		131	154
1830	1/4"		24	.333		128	25		153	178
1840	3/8"		24	.333		137	25		162	188
1850	1/2"		24	.333		146	25		171	198
1860	3/4"		20	.400		194	30		224	258
1870	1"		19	.421		279	31.50		310.50	350
1880	1-1/4"		15	.533		410	40		450	510
1890	1-1/2"		13	.615		430	46		476	540
1900	2"		11	.727		625	54.50		679.50	765
1910	2-1/2"	Q-1	15	1.067		1,550	71.50		1,621.50	1,800
1920	3"	"	13	1.231		2,050	82.50		2,132.50	2,400
2000	For 200 lb., add					5%	10%			
2040	For 300 lb., add					15%	15%			
2060	Check swing, 300 lb., lead free unless noted, sweat, 3/8" size	1 Plum	24	.333	Ea.	227	25		252	287
2070	1/2"		24	.333		250	25		275	310
2080	3/4"		20	.400		375	30		405	460
2090	1"		19	.421		555	31.50		586.50	655
2100	1-1/4"		15	.533		555	40		595	670
2110	1-1/2"		13	.615		600	46		646	730
2120	2"		11	.727		1,075	54.50		1,129.50	1,275
2130	2-1/2", not lead free	Q-1	15	1.067		455	71.50		526.50	605
2140	3", not lead free	"	13	1.231		550	82.50		632.50	730
2850	Gate, N.R.S., soldered, 125 psi									
2900	3/8"	1 Plum	24	.333	Ea.	111	25		136	159

22 05 Common Work Results for Plumbing

22 05 23 – General-Duty Valves for Plumbing Piping

22 05 23.20 Valves, Bronze		Crew	Daily Output	Labor-Hours	Unit	Material	2024 Bare Costs Labor	Equipment	Total	Total Incl O&P
2920	1/2"	1 Plum	24	.333	Ea.	111	25		136	159
2940	3/4"		20	.400		123	30		153	180
2950	1"		19	.421		177	31.50		208.50	241
2960	1-1/4"		15	.533		271	40		311	355
2970	1-1/2"		13	.615		300	46		346	400
2980	2"		11	.727		425	54.50		479.50	550
2990	2-1/2"	Q-1	15	1.067		1,075	71.50		1,146.50	1,275
3000	3"	"	13	1.231		1,400	82.50		1,482.50	1,650
3350	Threaded, class 150									
3410	1/4"	1 Plum	24	.333	Ea.	166	25		191	220
3420	3/8"		24	.333		166	25		191	220
3430	1/2"		24	.333		177	25		202	231
3440	3/4"		20	.400		173	30		203	235
3450	1"		19	.421		248	31.50		279.50	320
3460	1-1/4"		15	.533		293	40		333	380
3470	1-1/2"		13	.615		450	46		496	565
3480	2"		11	.727		500	54.50		554.50	630
3490	2-1/2"	Q-1	15	1.067		1,175	71.50		1,246.50	1,375
3500	3"	"	13	1.231		1,875	82.50		1,957.50	2,175
3600	Gate, flanged, 150 lb.									
3610	1"	1 Plum	7	1.143	Ea.	2,250	85.50		2,335.50	2,600
3620	1-1/2"		6	1.333		2,825	99.50		2,924.50	3,250
3630	2"		5	1.600		4,150	119		4,269	4,750
3634	2-1/2"	Q-1	5	3.200		6,400	215		6,615	7,375
3640	3"	"	4.50	3.556		7,275	239		7,514	8,375
3850	Rising stem, soldered, 300 psi									
3900	3/8"	1 Plum	24	.333	Ea.	226	25		251	286
3920	1/2"		24	.333		221	25		246	280
3940	3/4"		20	.400		252	30		282	320
3950	1"		19	.421		340	31.50		371.50	420
3960	1-1/4"		15	.533		475	40		515	580
3970	1-1/2"		13	.615		575	46		621	700
3980	2"		11	.727		920	54.50		974.50	1,075
3990	2-1/2"	Q-1	15	1.067		1,950	71.50		2,021.50	2,250
4000	3"	"	13	1.231		3,025	82.50		3,107.50	3,450
4250	Threaded, class 150									
4310	1/4"	1 Plum	24	.333	Ea.	152	25		177	204
4320	3/8"		24	.333		152	25		177	204
4330	1/2"		24	.333		154	25		179	207
4340	3/4"		20	.400		178	30		208	241
4350	1"		19	.421		208	31.50		239.50	276
4360	1-1/4"		15	.533		282	40		322	370
4370	1-1/2"		13	.615		355	46		401	460
4380	2"		11	.727		480	54.50		534.50	605
4390	2-1/2"	Q-1	15	1.067		1,125	71.50		1,196.50	1,325
4400	3"	"	13	1.231		1,550	82.50		1,632.50	1,825
4500	For 300 psi, threaded, add					100%	15%			
4540	For chain operated type, add					15%				
4850	Globe, class 150, rising stem, threaded									
4920	1/4"	1 Plum	24	.333	Ea.	209	25		234	267
4940	3/8"		24	.333		206	25		231	263
4950	1/2"		24	.333		206	25		231	263
4960	3/4"		20	.400		274	30		304	345

22 05 Common Work Results for Plumbing
22 05 23 – General-Duty Valves for Plumbing Piping

22 05 23.20 Valves, Bronze		Crew	Daily Output	Labor-Hours	Unit	Material	2024 Bare Costs Labor	Equipment	Total	Total Incl O&P
4970	1"	1 Plum	19	.421	Ea.	430	31.50		461.50	520
4980	1-1/4"		15	.533		580	40		620	700
4990	1-1/2"		13	.615		835	46		881	985
5000	2"	↓	11	.727		1,250	54.50		1,304.50	1,450
5010	2-1/2"	Q-1	15	1.067		2,500	71.50		2,571.50	2,850
5020	3"	"	13	1.231	↓	3,575	82.50		3,657.50	4,050
5120	For 300 lb. threaded, add					50%	15%			
5600	Relief, pressure & temperature, self-closing, ASME, threaded									
5640	3/4"	1 Plum	28	.286	Ea.	270	21.50		291.50	330
5650	1"		24	.333		415	25		440	495
5660	1-1/4"		20	.400		1,250	30		1,280	1,425
5670	1-1/2"		18	.444		2,675	33		2,708	2,975
5680	2"	↓	16	.500	↓	2,825	37.50		2,862.50	3,150
5950	Pressure, poppet type, threaded									
6000	1/2"	1 Plum	30	.267	Ea.	49.50	19.90		69.40	84
6040	3/4"	"	28	.286	"	111	21.50		132.50	154
6400	Pressure, water, ASME, threaded									
6440	3/4"	1 Plum	28	.286	Ea.	90.50	21.50		112	131
6450	1"		24	.333		214	25		239	273
6460	1-1/4"		20	.400		530	30		560	625
6470	1-1/2"		18	.444		1,250	33		1,283	1,425
6480	2"		16	.500		1,600	37.50		1,637.50	1,825
6490	2-1/2"		15	.533		6,550	40		6,590	7,250
6900	Reducing, water pressure									
6920	300 psi to 25-75 psi, threaded or sweat									
6940	1/2"	1 Plum	24	.333	Ea.	248	25		273	310
6950	3/4"		20	.400		970	30		1,000	1,125
6960	1"		19	.421		1,500	31.50		1,531.50	1,700
6970	1-1/4"		15	.533		1,725	40		1,765	1,950
6980	1-1/2"		13	.615		1,250	46		1,296	1,450
6990	2"	↓	11	.727		5,825	54.50		5,879.50	6,500
7100	For built-in by-pass or 10-35 psi, add					72.50			72.50	80
7700	High capacity, 250 psi to 25-75 psi, threaded									
7740	1/2"	1 Plum	24	.333	Ea.	1,550	25		1,575	1,725
7780	3/4"		20	.400		1,125	30		1,155	1,300
7790	1"		19	.421		1,625	31.50		1,656.50	1,825
7800	1-1/4"		15	.533		3,125	40		3,165	3,475
7810	1-1/2"		13	.615		4,075	46		4,121	4,575
7820	2"		11	.727		6,650	54.50		6,704.50	7,375
7830	2-1/2"		9	.889		9,500	66.50		9,566.50	10,600
7840	3"	↓	8	1		11,400	74.50		11,474.50	12,600
7850	3" flanged (iron body)	Q-1	10	1.600		9,075	107		9,182	10,100
7860	4" flanged (iron body)	"	8	2	↓	14,600	134		14,734	16,300
7920	For higher pressure, add					25%				
8000	Silent check, bronze trim									
8010	Compact wafer type, for 125 or 150 lb. flanges									
8020	1-1/2"	1 Plum	11	.727	Ea.	615	54.50		669.50	755
8021	2"	"	9	.889		650	66.50		716.50	815
8022	2-1/2"	Q-1	9	1.778		700	119		819	950
8023	3"		8	2		780	134		914	1,050
8024	4"	↓	5	3.200		1,300	215		1,515	1,750
8025	5"	Q-2	6	4		1,400	279		1,679	1,950
8026	6"	"	5	4.800	↓	1,500	335		1,835	2,150

22 05 Common Work Results for Plumbing

22 05 23 – General-Duty Valves for Plumbing Piping

22 05 23.20 Valves, Bronze

		Crew	Daily Output	Labor-Hours	Unit	Material	2024 Bare Costs Labor	2024 Bare Costs Equipment	Total	Total Incl O&P
8050	For 250 or 300 lb. flanges, thru 6" no change									
8060	Full flange wafer type, 150 lb.									
8063	1-1/2"	1 Plum	11	.727	Ea.	70.50	54.50		125	159
8064	2"	"	9	.889		78.50	66.50		145	185
8065	2-1/2"	Q-1	9	1.778		104	119		223	293
8066	3"		8	2		155	134		289	370
8067	4"	↓	5	3.200		224	215		439	565
8068	5"	Q-2	6	4		375	279		654	825
8069	6"	"	5	4.800	↓	510	335		845	1,050
8080	For 300 lb., add					40%	10%			
8100	Globe type, 150 lb.									
8110	2"	1 Plum	9	.889	Ea.	830	66.50		896.50	1,000
8111	2-1/2"	Q-1	9	1.778		1,025	119		1,144	1,325
8112	3"		8	2		1,250	134		1,384	1,575
8113	4"	↓	5	3.200		1,725	215		1,940	2,200
8114	5"	Q-2	6	4		2,100	279		2,379	2,725
8115	6"	"	5	4.800	↓	2,925	335		3,260	3,725
8130	For 300 lb., add					20%	10%			
8140	Screwed end type, 250 lb.									
8141	1/2"	1 Plum	24	.333	Ea.	75.50	25		100.50	120
8142	3/4"		20	.400		75.50	30		105.50	128
8143	1"		19	.421		86	31.50		117.50	142
8144	1-1/4"		15	.533		119	40		159	190
8145	1-1/2"		13	.615		133	46		179	216
8146	2"	↓	11	.727	↓	180	54.50		234.50	279
8350	Tempering, water, sweat connections									
8400	1/2"	1 Plum	24	.333	Ea.	157	25		182	210
8440	3/4"	"	20	.400	"	224	30		254	291
8650	Threaded connections									
8700	1/2"	1 Plum	24	.333	Ea.	268	25		293	330
8740	3/4"		20	.400		1,775	30		1,805	2,000
8750	1"		19	.421		2,000	31.50		2,031.50	2,250
8760	1-1/4"		15	.533		3,075	40		3,115	3,425
8770	1-1/2"		13	.615		3,350	46		3,396	3,775
8780	2"	↓	11	.727		5,025	54.50		5,079.50	5,600
8800	Water heater water & gas safety shut off									
8810	Protection against a leaking water heater									
8814	Shut off valve	1 Plum	16	.500	Ea.	204	37.50		241.50	281
8818	Water heater dam		32	.250		55	18.65		73.65	88.50
8822	Gas control wiring harness	↓	32	.250	↓	25.50	18.65		44.15	56
8830	Whole house flood safety shut off									
8834	Connections									
8838	3/4" NPT	1 Plum	12	.667	Ea.	1,100	50		1,150	1,275
8842	1" NPT		11	.727		1,125	54.50		1,179.50	1,300
8846	1-1/4" NPT	↓	10	.800	↓	1,150	59.50		1,209.50	1,375

22 05 23.40 Valves, Lined, Corrosion Resistant/High Purity

		Crew	Daily Output	Labor-Hours	Unit	Material	2024 Bare Costs Labor	2024 Bare Costs Equipment	Total	Total Incl O&P
0010	**VALVES, LINED, CORROSION RESISTANT/HIGH PURITY**									
3500	Check lift, 125 lb., cast iron flanged									
3510	Horizontal PPL or SL lined									
3530	1"	1 Plum	14	.571	Ea.	880	42.50		922.50	1,025
3540	1-1/2"		11	.727		1,075	54.50		1,129.50	1,250
3550	2"	↓	8	1		1,250	74.50		1,324.50	1,475

22 05 Common Work Results for Plumbing

22 05 23 – General-Duty Valves for Plumbing Piping

22 05 23.40	Valves, Lined, Corrosion Resistant/High Purity	Crew	Daily Output	Labor-Hours	Unit	Material	2024 Bare Costs Labor	Equipment	Total	Total Incl O&P
3560	2-1/2"	Q-1	5	3.200	Ea.	1,600	215		1,815	2,100
3570	3"		4.50	3.556		2,025	239		2,264	2,575
3590	4"	↓	3	5.333		2,675	360		3,035	3,475
3610	6"	Q-2	3	8		4,550	555		5,105	5,825
3620	8"	"	2.50	9.600	↓	10,000	670		10,670	12,000
4250	Vertical PPL or SL lined									
4270	1"	1 Plum	14	.571	Ea.	835	42.50		877.50	985
4290	1-1/2"		11	.727		1,050	54.50		1,104.50	1,225
4300	2"	↓	8	1		1,225	74.50		1,299.50	1,450
4310	2-1/2"	Q-1	5	3.200		1,825	215		2,040	2,325
4320	3"		4.50	3.556		1,825	239		2,064	2,375
4340	4"	↓	3	5.333		2,550	360		2,910	3,325
4360	6"	Q-2	3	8		3,800	555		4,355	5,000
4370	8"	"	2.50	9.600	↓	7,425	670		8,095	9,175
5000	Clamp type, ductile iron, 150 lb. flanged									
5010	TFE lined									
5030	1" size, lever handle	1 Plum	9	.889	Ea.	1,750	66.50		1,816.50	2,025
5050	1-1/2" size, lever handle		6	1.333		2,300	99.50		2,399.50	2,675
5060	2" size, lever handle	↓	5	1.600		2,875	119		2,994	3,350
5080	3" size, lever handle	Q-1	4.50	3.556		3,650	239		3,889	4,375
5100	4" size, gear operated	"	3	5.333		5,025	360		5,385	6,050
5120	6" size, gear operated	Q-2	3	8		17,600	555		18,155	20,100
5130	8" size, gear operated	"	2.50	9.600	↓	20,800	670		21,470	23,900
6000	Diaphragm type, cast iron, 125 lb. flanged									
6010	PTFE or VITON, lined									
6030	1" size, handwheel operated	1 Plum	9	.889	Ea.	440	66.50		506.50	580
6050	1-1/2" size, handwheel operated		6	1.333		515	99.50		614.50	720
6060	2" size, handwheel operated	↓	5	1.600		595	119		714	835
6080	3" size, handwheel operated	Q-1	4.50	3.556		985	239		1,224	1,425
6100	4" size, handwheel operated	"	3	5.333		1,950	360		2,310	2,675
6120	6" size, handwheel operated	Q-2	3	8		3,050	555		3,605	4,175
6130	8" size, handwheel operated	"	2.50	9.600		6,150	670		6,820	7,750

22 05 23.60 Valves, Plastic

		Crew	Daily Output	Labor-Hours	Unit	Material	Labor	Equipment	Total	Total Incl O&P
0010	**VALVES, PLASTIC** R220523-90									
1100	Angle, PVC, threaded									
1110	1/4"	1 Plum	26	.308	Ea.	72	23		95	114
1120	1/2"		26	.308		103	23		126	147
1130	3/4"		25	.320		122	24		146	170
1140	1"	↓	23	.348		148	26		174	202
1150	Ball, PVC, socket or threaded, true union									
1230	1/2"	1 Plum	26	.308	Ea.	45	23		68	83.50
1240	3/4"		25	.320		53	24		77	94
1250	1"		23	.348		63.50	26		89.50	108
1260	1-1/4"		21	.381		101	28.50		129.50	154
1270	1-1/2"		20	.400		101	30		131	156
1280	2"	↓	17	.471		182	35		217	253
1290	2-1/2"	Q-1	26	.615		257	41.50		298.50	345
1300	3"		24	.667		320	45		365	415
1310	4"	↓	20	.800		540	53.50		593.50	675
1360	For PVC, flanged, add					100%	15%			
1450	Double union 1/2"	1 Plum	26	.308		68	23		91	109
1460	3/4"	↓	25	.320		80.50	24		104.50	124

22 05 Common Work Results for Plumbing

22 05 23 – General-Duty Valves for Plumbing Piping

	22 05 23.60 Valves, Plastic	Crew	Daily Output	Labor-Hours	Unit	Material	2024 Bare Costs Labor	Equipment	Total	Total Incl O&P
1470	1"	1 Plum	23	.348	Ea.	81.50	26		107.50	128
1480	1-1/4"		21	.381		133	28.50		161.50	189
1490	1-1/2"		20	.400		136	30		166	195
1500	2"	↓	17	.471	↓	210	35		245	285
1650	CPVC, socket or threaded, single union									
1700	1/2"	1 Plum	26	.308	Ea.	69.50	23		92.50	111
1720	3/4"		25	.320		88	24		112	132
1730	1"		23	.348		105	26		131	155
1750	1-1/4"		21	.381		168	28.50		196.50	228
1760	1-1/2"		20	.400		168	30		198	230
1770	2"	↓	17	.471		231	35		266	305
1780	3"	Q-1	24	.667		690	45		735	820
1840	For CPVC, flanged, add					65%	15%			
1880	For true union, socket or threaded, add				↓	50%	5%			
2050	Polypropylene, threaded									
2100	1/4"	1 Plum	26	.308	Ea.	60	23		83	99.50
2120	3/8"		26	.308		61.50	23		84.50	102
2130	1/2"		26	.308		49	23		72	88
2140	3/4"		25	.320		59	24		83	101
2150	1"		23	.348		69	26		95	115
2160	1-1/4"		21	.381		91.50	28.50		120	144
2170	1-1/2"		20	.400		114	30		144	170
2180	2"	↓	17	.471		152	35		187	220
2190	3"	Q-1	24	.667		345	45		390	445
2200	4"	"	20	.800	↓	610	53.50		663.50	750
2550	PVC, three way, socket or threaded									
2600	1/2"	1 Plum	26	.308	Ea.	84.50	23		107.50	127
2640	3/4"		25	.320		102	24		126	148
2650	1"		23	.348		121	26		147	173
2660	1-1/2"		20	.400		171	30		201	233
2670	2"	↓	17	.471		224	35		259	300
2680	3"	Q-1	24	.667		690	45		735	825
2740	For flanged, add				↓	60%	15%			
3150	Ball check, PVC, socket or threaded									
3200	1/4"	1 Plum	26	.308	Ea.	64.50	23		87.50	105
3220	3/8"		26	.308		64.50	23		87.50	105
3240	1/2"		26	.308		68.50	23		91.50	110
3250	3/4"		25	.320		76.50	24		100.50	120
3260	1"		23	.348		96	26		122	145
3270	1-1/4"		21	.381		145	28.50		173.50	203
3280	1-1/2"		20	.400		161	30		191	222
3290	2"	↓	17	.471		219	35		254	294
3310	3"	Q-1	24	.667		610	45		655	735
3320	4"	"	20	.800		860	53.50		913.50	1,025
3360	For PVC, flanged, add				↓	50%	15%			
3750	CPVC, socket or threaded									
3800	1/2"	1 Plum	26	.308	Ea.	123	23		146	169
3840	3/4"		25	.320		126	24		150	174
3850	1"		23	.348		149	26		175	203
3860	1-1/2"		20	.400		256	30		286	325
3870	2"	↓	17	.471		345	35		380	435
3880	3"	Q-1	24	.667		930	45		975	1,100
3920	4"	"	20	.800		1,250	53.50		1,303.50	1,450

22 05 Common Work Results for Plumbing

22 05 23 – General-Duty Valves for Plumbing Piping

22 05 23.60 Valves, Plastic		Crew	Daily Output	Labor-Hours	Unit	Material	2024 Bare Costs Labor	Equipment	Total	Total Incl O&P
3930	For CPVC, flanged, add				Ea.	40%	15%			
4340	Polypropylene, threaded									
4360	1/2"	1 Plum	26	.308	Ea.	106	23		129	150
4400	3/4"		25	.320		100	24		124	146
4440	1"		23	.348		134	26		160	186
4450	1-1/2"		20	.400		178	30		208	241
4460	2"		17	.471		320	35		355	405
4500	For polypropylene flanged, add					200%	15%			
4850	Foot valve, PVC, socket or threaded									
4900	1/2"	1 Plum	34	.235	Ea.	73	17.55		90.55	107
4930	3/4"		32	.250		83	18.65		101.65	120
4940	1"		28	.286		109	21.50		130.50	151
4950	1-1/4"		27	.296		244	22		266	300
4960	1-1/2"		26	.308		209	23		232	264
4970	2"		24	.333		242	25		267	305
4980	3"		20	.400		580	30		610	680
4990	4"		18	.444		1,025	33		1,058	1,175
5000	For flanged, add					25%	10%			
5050	CPVC, socket or threaded									
5060	1/2"	1 Plum	34	.235	Ea.	102	17.55		119.55	138
5070	3/4"		32	.250		142	18.65		160.65	184
5080	1"		28	.286		174	21.50		195.50	224
5090	1-1/4"		27	.296		265	22		287	325
5100	1-1/2"		26	.308		265	23		288	325
5110	2"		24	.333		330	25		355	400
5120	3"		20	.400		675	30		705	785
5130	4"		18	.444		1,225	33		1,258	1,400
5140	For flanged, add					25%	10%			
5280	Needle valve, PVC, threaded									
5300	1/4"	1 Plum	26	.308	Ea.	94.50	23		117.50	138
5340	3/8"		26	.308		108	23		131	153
5360	1/2"		26	.308		107	23		130	152
5380	For polypropylene, add					10%				
5800	Y check, PVC, socket or threaded									
5820	1/2"	1 Plum	26	.308	Ea.	96.50	23		119.50	140
5840	3/4"		25	.320		104	24		128	151
5850	1"		23	.348		113	26		139	163
5860	1-1/4"		21	.381		178	28.50		206.50	239
5870	1-1/2"		20	.400		194	30		224	258
5880	2"		17	.471		241	35		276	320
5890	2-1/2"		15	.533		515	40		555	625
5900	3"	Q-1	24	.667		515	45		560	630
5910	4"	"	20	.800		840	53.50		893.50	1,000
5960	For PVC flanged, add					45%	15%			
6350	Y sediment strainer, PVC, socket or threaded									
6400	1/2"	1 Plum	26	.308	Ea.	64.50	23		87.50	105
6440	3/4"		24	.333		69.50	25		94.50	114
6450	1"		23	.348		82.50	26		108.50	129
6460	1-1/4"		21	.381		256	28.50		284.50	325
6470	1-1/2"		20	.400		170	30		200	232
6480	2"		17	.471		170	35		205	240
6490	2-1/2"		15	.533		490	40		530	600
6500	3"	Q-1	24	.667		410	45		455	520

22 05 Common Work Results for Plumbing

22 05 23 – General-Duty Valves for Plumbing Piping

22 05 23.60 Valves, Plastic		Crew	Daily Output	Labor-Hours	Unit	Material	2024 Bare Costs Labor	Equipment	Total	Total Incl O&P
6510	4"	Q-1	20	.800	Ea.	685	53.50		738.50	835
6560	For PVC, flanged, add					55%	15%			

22 05 29 – Hangers and Supports for Plumbing Piping and Equipment

22 05 29.10 Hangers & Supp. for Plumb'g/HVAC Pipe/Equip.

		Crew	Daily Output	Labor-Hours	Unit	Material	2024 Bare Costs Labor	Equipment	Total	Total Incl O&P
0010	**HANGERS AND SUPPORTS FOR PLUMB'G/HVAC PIPE/EQUIP.**									
0011	TYPE numbers per MSS-SP58									
0050	Brackets									
0060	Beam side or wall, malleable iron, TYPE 34									
0070	3/8" threaded rod size	1 Plum	48	.167	Ea.	5.15	12.45		17.60	24
0080	1/2" threaded rod size		48	.167		9.25	12.45		21.70	28.50
0090	5/8" threaded rod size		48	.167		22	12.45		34.45	43
0100	3/4" threaded rod size		48	.167		23	12.45		35.45	43.50
0110	7/8" threaded rod size		48	.167		25	12.45		37.45	46
0120	For concrete installation, add						30%			
0150	Wall, welded steel, medium, TYPE 32									
0160	0 size, 12" wide, 18" deep	1 Plum	34	.235	Ea.	430	17.55		447.55	495
0170	1 size, 18" wide, 24" deep		34	.235		510	17.55		527.55	585
0180	2 size, 24" wide, 30" deep		34	.235		675	17.55		692.55	765
0200	Beam attachment, welded, TYPE 22									
0202	3/8"	Q-15	80	.200	Ea.	14.55	13.45	.90	28.90	37
0203	1/2"		76	.211		14.10	14.15	.95	29.20	37.50
0204	5/8"		72	.222		14.85	14.95	1	30.80	39.50
0205	3/4"		68	.235		17.15	15.80	1.06	34.01	43.50
0206	7/8"		64	.250		25.50	16.80	1.12	43.42	54
0207	1"		56	.286		65.50	19.20	1.28	85.98	102
0300	Clamps									
0310	C-clamp, for mounting on steel beam flange, w/locknut, TYPE 23									
0320	3/8" threaded rod size	1 Plum	160	.050	Ea.	3.88	3.73		7.61	9.80
0330	1/2" threaded rod size		160	.050		4.82	3.73		8.55	10.85
0340	5/8" threaded rod size		160	.050		6.40	3.73		10.13	12.60
0350	3/4" threaded rod size		160	.050		8.35	3.73		12.08	14.75
0352	7/8" threaded rod size		140	.057		22	4.27		26.27	30.50
0400	High temperature to 1050°F, alloy steel									
0410	4" pipe size	Q-1	106	.151	Ea.	62.50	10.15		72.65	83.50
0420	6" pipe size		106	.151		90.50	10.15		100.65	115
0430	8" pipe size		97	.165		103	11.10		114.10	130
0440	10" pipe size		84	.190		132	12.80		144.80	165
0450	12" pipe size		72	.222		174	14.95		188.95	214
0460	14" pipe size		64	.250		305	16.80		321.80	360
0470	16" pipe size		56	.286		340	19.20		359.20	405
0480	Beam clamp, flange type, TYPE 25									
0482	For 3/8" bolt	1 Plum	48	.167	Ea.	11.15	12.45		23.60	31
0483	For 1/2" bolt		44	.182		14.30	13.55		27.85	35.50
0484	For 5/8" bolt		40	.200		22	14.95		36.95	46.50
0485	For 3/4" bolt		36	.222		29.50	16.60		46.10	57
0486	For 1" bolt		32	.250		9	18.65		27.65	38
0500	I-beam, for mounting on bottom flange, strap iron, TYPE 21									
0530	4" flange size	1 Plum	93	.086	Ea.	21	6.40		27.40	33
0540	5" flange size		92	.087		23	6.50		29.50	35
0550	6" flange size		90	.089		26	6.65		32.65	38.50
0560	7" flange size		88	.091		28.50	6.80		35.30	41.50
0570	8" flange size		86	.093		30.50	6.95		37.45	44

For customer support on your Plumbing Costs with RSMeans Data call 800.448.8182.

22 05 Common Work Results for Plumbing

22 05 29 – Hangers and Supports for Plumbing Piping and Equipment

22 05 29.10 Hangers & Supp. for Plumb'g/HVAC Pipe/Equip.		Crew	Daily Output	Labor-Hours	Unit	Material	2024 Bare Costs Labor	Equipment	Total	Total Incl O&P
0600	One hole, vertical mounting, malleable iron									
0610	1/2" pipe size	1 Plum	160	.050	Ea.	2.94	3.73		6.67	8.80
0620	3/4" pipe size		145	.055		3.77	4.12		7.89	10.30
0630	1" pipe size		136	.059		4.01	4.39		8.40	10.95
0640	1-1/4" pipe size		128	.063		5.90	4.67		10.57	13.45
0650	1-1/2" pipe size		120	.067		6.90	4.98		11.88	15
0660	2" pipe size		112	.071		9.05	5.35		14.40	17.95
0670	2-1/2" pipe size		104	.077		17.75	5.75		23.50	28
0680	3" pipe size		96	.083		24	6.20		30.20	35.50
0690	3-1/2" pipe size		90	.089		13.80	6.65		20.45	25
0700	4" pipe size		84	.095		24	7.10		31.10	37
0750	Riser or extension pipe, carbon steel, TYPE 8									
0756	1/2" pipe size	1 Plum	52	.154	Ea.	6.35	11.50		17.85	24
0760	3/4" pipe size		48	.167		6.35	12.45		18.80	25.50
0770	1" pipe size		47	.170		6.95	12.70		19.65	26.50
0780	1-1/4" pipe size		46	.174		8.10	13		21.10	28
0790	1-1/2" pipe size		45	.178		8.25	13.25		21.50	29
0800	2" pipe size		43	.186		8.50	13.90		22.40	30
0810	2-1/2" pipe size		41	.195		9.40	14.55		23.95	32
0820	3" pipe size		40	.200		9.95	14.95		24.90	33
0830	3-1/2" pipe size		39	.205		12.70	15.30		28	37
0840	4" pipe size		38	.211		12.40	15.70		28.10	37
0850	5" pipe size		37	.216		17.60	16.15		33.75	43.50
0860	6" pipe size		36	.222		20.50	16.60		37.10	47
0870	8" pipe size		34	.235		37.50	17.55		55.05	67.50
0880	10" pipe size		32	.250		50.50	18.65		69.15	83.50
0890	12" pipe size		28	.286		76.50	21.50		98	116
0900	For plastic coating 3/4" to 4", add					190%				
0910	For copper plating 3/4" to 4", add					58%				
0950	Two piece, complete, carbon steel, medium weight, TYPE 4									
0960	1/2" pipe size	Q-1	137	.117	Ea.	6.25	7.85		14.10	18.55
0970	3/4" pipe size		134	.119		6.50	8		14.50	19.10
0980	1" pipe size		132	.121		6.15	8.15		14.30	18.85
0990	1-1/4" pipe size		130	.123		7.05	8.25		15.30	20
1000	1-1/2" pipe size		126	.127		7.50	8.55		16.05	21
1010	2" pipe size		124	.129		11.75	8.65		20.40	26
1020	2-1/2" pipe size		120	.133		12.80	8.95		21.75	27.50
1030	3" pipe size		117	.137		14	9.20		23.20	29
1040	3-1/2" pipe size		114	.140		19.95	9.45		29.40	36
1050	4" pipe size		110	.145		22.50	9.75		32.25	39.50
1060	5" pipe size		106	.151		37.50	10.15		47.65	56.50
1070	6" pipe size		104	.154		42	10.35		52.35	61.50
1080	8" pipe size		100	.160		50	10.75		60.75	71
1090	10" pipe size		96	.167		95	11.20		106.20	121
1100	12" pipe size		89	.180		116	12.10		128.10	145
1110	14" pipe size		82	.195		189	13.10		202.10	228
1120	16" pipe size		68	.235		205	15.80		220.80	249
1130	For galvanized, add					45%				
1150	Insert, concrete									
1160	Wedge type, carbon steel body, malleable iron nut, galvanized									
1170	1/4" threaded rod size	1 Plum	96	.083	Ea.	5.70	6.20		11.90	15.55
1180	3/8" threaded rod size		96	.083		5.70	6.20		11.90	15.55
1190	1/2" threaded rod size		96	.083		5.70	6.20		11.90	15.55

22 05 Common Work Results for Plumbing

22 05 29 – Hangers and Supports for Plumbing Piping and Equipment

22 05 29.10 Hangers & Supp. for Plumb'g/HVAC Pipe/Equip.		Crew	Daily Output	Labor-Hours	Unit	Material	2024 Bare Costs Labor	2024 Bare Costs Equipment	Total	Total Incl O&P
1200	5/8" threaded rod size	1 Plum	96	.083	Ea.	5.70	6.20		11.90	15.55
1210	3/4" threaded rod size		96	.083		5.70	6.20		11.90	15.55
1220	7/8" threaded rod size		96	.083		6.55	6.20		12.75	16.45
1250	Pipe guide sized for insulation									
1260	No. 1, 1" pipe size, 1" thick insulation	1 Stpi	26	.308	Ea.	435	23.50		458.50	515
1270	No. 2, 1-1/4"-2" pipe size, 1" thick insulation		23	.348		305	26.50		331.50	380
1280	No. 3, 1-1/4"-2" pipe size, 1-1/2" thick insulation		21	.381		305	29		334	385
1290	No. 4, 2-1/2"-3-1/2" pipe size, 1-1/2" thick insulation		18	.444		345	33.50		378.50	430
1300	No. 5, 4"-5" pipe size, 1-1/2" thick insulation		16	.500		360	38		398	455
1310	No. 6, 5"-6" pipe size, 2" thick insulation	Q-5	21	.762		415	52		467	535
1320	No. 7, 8" pipe size, 2" thick insulation		16	1		545	68		613	695
1330	No. 8, 10" pipe size, 2" thick insulation		12	1.333		810	90.50		900.50	1,025
1340	No. 9, 12" pipe size, 2" thick insulation	Q-6	17	1.412		810	99.50		909.50	1,050
1350	No. 10, 12"-14" pipe size, 2-1/2" thick insulation		16	1.500		975	106		1,081	1,225
1360	No. 11, 16" pipe size, 2-1/2" thick insulation		10.50	2.286		975	161		1,136	1,325
1370	No. 12, 16"-18" pipe size, 3" thick insulation		9	2.667		1,375	188		1,563	1,775
1380	No. 13, 20" pipe size, 3" thick insulation		7.50	3.200		1,375	226		1,601	1,825
1390	No. 14, 24" pipe size, 3" thick insulation		7	3.429		1,950	242		2,192	2,500
1400	Bands									
1410	Adjustable band, carbon steel, for non-insulated pipe, TYPE 7									
1420	1/2" pipe size	Q-1	142	.113	Ea.	1.26	7.55		8.81	12.65
1430	3/4" pipe size		140	.114		1.34	7.70		9.04	12.85
1440	1" pipe size		137	.117		1.34	7.85		9.19	13.10
1450	1-1/4" pipe size		134	.119		1.28	8		9.28	13.35
1460	1-1/2" pipe size		131	.122		1.39	8.20		9.59	13.75
1470	2" pipe size		129	.124		1.39	8.35		9.74	13.95
1480	2-1/2" pipe size		125	.128		2.01	8.60		10.61	15
1490	3" pipe size		122	.131		2.65	8.80		11.45	16
1500	3-1/2" pipe size		119	.134		4.81	9.05		13.86	18.75
1510	4" pipe size		114	.140		5.10	9.45		14.55	19.65
1520	5" pipe size		110	.145		5.45	9.75		15.20	20.50
1530	6" pipe size		108	.148		6.40	9.95		16.35	22
1540	8" pipe size		104	.154		9.50	10.35		19.85	26
1550	For copper plated, add					50%				
1560	For galvanized, add					30%				
1570	For plastic coating, add					30%				
1600	Adjusting nut malleable iron, steel band, TYPE 9									
1610	1/2" pipe size, galvanized band	Q-1	137	.117	Ea.	9.30	7.85		17.15	22
1620	3/4" pipe size, galvanized band		135	.119		1.99	7.95		9.94	14.05
1630	1" pipe size, galvanized band		132	.121		9.60	8.15		17.75	22.50
1640	1-1/4" pipe size, galvanized band		129	.124		9.65	8.35		18	23
1650	1-1/2" pipe size, galvanized band		126	.127		9.95	8.55		18.50	23.50
1660	2" pipe size, galvanized band		124	.129		10.40	8.65		19.05	24.50
1670	2-1/2" pipe size, galvanized band		120	.133		16.45	8.95		25.40	31.50
1680	3" pipe size, galvanized band		117	.137		17.15	9.20		26.35	32.50
1690	3-1/2" pipe size, galvanized band		114	.140		5.10	9.45		14.55	19.65
1700	4" pipe size, cadmium plated band		110	.145		43.50	9.75		53.25	62.50
1740	For plastic coated band, add					35%				
1750	For completely copper coated, add					45%				
1800	Clevis, adjustable, carbon steel, for non-insulated pipe, TYPE 1									
1810	1/2" pipe size	Q-1	137	.117	Ea.	2.23	7.85		10.08	14.10
1820	3/4" pipe size		135	.119		2.19	7.95		10.14	14.25
1830	1" pipe size		132	.121		2.25	8.15		10.40	14.60

22 05 Common Work Results for Plumbing

22 05 29 – Hangers and Supports for Plumbing Piping and Equipment

22 05 29.10 Hangers & Supp. for Plumb'g/HVAC Pipe/Equip.		Crew	Daily Output	Labor-Hours	Unit	Material	2024 Bare Costs Labor	Equipment	Total	Total Incl O&P
1840	1-1/4" pipe size	Q-1	129	.124	Ea.	2.44	8.35		10.79	15.10
1850	1-1/2" pipe size		126	.127		2.30	8.55		10.85	15.25
1860	2" pipe size		124	.129		2.78	8.65		11.43	15.95
1870	2-1/2" pipe size		120	.133		4.31	8.95		13.26	18.05
1880	3" pipe size		117	.137		5.15	9.20		14.35	19.30
1890	3-1/2" pipe size		114	.140		5.70	9.45		15.15	20.50
1900	4" pipe size		110	.145		6.70	9.75		16.45	22
1910	5" pipe size		106	.151		8.60	10.15		18.75	24.50
1920	6" pipe size		104	.154		11.50	10.35		21.85	28
1930	8" pipe size		100	.160		17.75	10.75		28.50	35.50
1940	10" pipe size		96	.167		33.50	11.20		44.70	53.50
1950	12" pipe size		89	.180		49	12.10		61.10	72
1960	14" pipe size		82	.195		72	13.10		85.10	98.50
1970	16" pipe size		68	.235		110	15.80		125.80	145
1971	18" pipe size		54	.296		142	19.90		161.90	187
1972	20" pipe size		38	.421		259	28.50		287.50	325
1980	For galvanized, add					66%				
1990	For copper plated 1/2" to 4", add					77%				
2000	For light weight 1/2" to 4", deduct					13%				
2010	Insulated pipe type, 3/4" to 12" pipe, add					180%				
2020	Insulated pipe type, chrome-moly U-strap, add					530%				
2250	Split ring, malleable iron, for non-insulated pipe, TYPE 11									
2260	1/2" pipe size	Q-1	137	.117	Ea.	10.65	7.85		18.50	23.50
2270	3/4" pipe size		135	.119		10.75	7.95		18.70	23.50
2280	1" pipe size		132	.121		11.40	8.15		19.55	24.50
2290	1-1/4" pipe size		129	.124		14.10	8.35		22.45	28
2300	1-1/2" pipe size		126	.127		17.15	8.55		25.70	31.50
2310	2" pipe size		124	.129		19.40	8.65		28.05	34.50
2320	2-1/2" pipe size		120	.133		28	8.95		36.95	44.50
2330	3" pipe size		117	.137		35	9.20		44.20	52
2340	3-1/2" pipe size		114	.140		24	9.45		33.45	40.50
2350	4" pipe size		110	.145		36.50	9.75		46.25	54.50
2360	5" pipe size		106	.151		70.50	10.15		80.65	92.50
2370	6" pipe size		104	.154		158	10.35		168.35	189
2380	8" pipe size		100	.160		232	10.75		242.75	271
2390	For copper plated, add					8%				
2400	Channels, steel, 3/4" x 1-1/2"	1 Plum	80	.100	L.F.	7.70	7.45		15.15	19.60
2404	1-1/2" x 1-1/2"		70	.114		8.60	8.55		17.15	22
2408	1-7/8" x 1-1/2"		60	.133		52	9.95		61.95	72
2412	3" x 1-1/2"		50	.160		39.50	11.95		51.45	61.50
2416	Hangers, trapeze channel support, 12 ga. 1-1/2" x 1-1/2", 12" wide, steel		8.80	.909	Ea.	60	68		128	167
2418	18" wide, steel		8.30	.964		64.50	72		136.50	178
2430	Spring nuts, long, 1/4"		120	.067		.78	4.98		5.76	8.25
2432	3/8"		100	.080		1.19	5.95		7.14	10.20
2434	1/2"		80	.100		1.13	7.45		8.58	12.35
2436	5/8"		80	.100		6.85	7.45		14.30	18.60
2438	3/4"		75	.107		9.15	7.95		17.10	22
2440	Spring nuts, short, 1/4"		120	.067		2.12	4.98		7.10	9.75
2442	3/8"		100	.080		2.21	5.95		8.16	11.35
2444	1/2"		80	.100		3.23	7.45		10.68	14.65
2500	Washer, flat steel									
2502	3/8"	1 Plum	240	.033	Ea.	.06	2.49		2.55	3.77
2503	1/2"		220	.036		.21	2.71		2.92	4.27

22 05 Common Work Results for Plumbing

22 05 29 – Hangers and Supports for Plumbing Piping and Equipment

22 05 29.10 Hangers & Supp. for Plumb'g/HVAC Pipe/Equip.		Crew	Daily Output	Labor-Hours	Unit	Material	2024 Bare Costs Labor	Equipment	Total	Total Incl O&P
2504	5/8"	1 Plum	200	.040	Ea.	.07	2.99		3.06	4.52
2505	3/4"		180	.044		.21	3.32		3.53	5.15
2506	7/8"		160	.050		.90	3.73		4.63	6.55
2507	1"		140	.057		.97	4.27		5.24	7.40
2508	1-1/4"		120	.067		1.51	4.98		6.49	9.05
2520	Nut, steel, hex									
2522	3/8"	1 Plum	200	.040	Ea.	.22	2.99		3.21	4.68
2523	1/2"		180	.044		.53	3.32		3.85	5.50
2524	5/8"		160	.050		.85	3.73		4.58	6.50
2525	3/4"		140	.057		1.42	4.27		5.69	7.90
2526	7/8"		120	.067		2.28	4.98		7.26	9.90
2527	1"		100	.080		3.15	5.95		9.10	12.35
2528	1-1/4"		80	.100		7.85	7.45		15.30	19.75
2532	Turnbuckle, TYPE 13									
2534	3/8"	1 Plum	80	.100	Ea.	22	7.45		29.45	35.50
2535	1/2"		72	.111		28.50	8.30		36.80	43.50
2536	5/8"		64	.125		29.50	9.35		38.85	46.50
2537	3/4"		56	.143		40.50	10.65		51.15	60.50
2538	7/8"		48	.167		55	12.45		67.45	78.50
2539	1"		40	.200		73.50	14.95		88.45	103
2540	1-1/4"		32	.250		93	18.65		111.65	131
2650	Rods, carbon steel									
2660	Continuous thread									
2670	1/4" thread size	1 Plum	144	.056	L.F.	.40	4.15		4.55	6.60
2680	3/8" thread size		144	.056		.58	4.15		4.73	6.80
2690	1/2" thread size		144	.056		.97	4.15		5.12	7.20
2700	5/8" thread size		144	.056		1.93	4.15		6.08	8.25
2710	3/4" thread size		144	.056		3	4.15		7.15	9.45
2720	7/8" thread size		144	.056		4.66	4.15		8.81	11.30
2721	1" thread size	Q-1	160	.100		6.90	6.70		13.60	17.60
2722	1-1/8" thread size	"	120	.133		14.25	8.95		23.20	29
2725	1/4" thread size, bright finish	1 Plum	144	.056		.47	4.15		4.62	6.65
2726	1/2" thread size, bright finish	"	144	.056		1.29	4.15		5.44	7.55
2730	For galvanized, add					40%				
2820	Rod couplings									
2821	3/8"	1 Plum	60	.133	Ea.	2.48	9.95		12.43	17.55
2822	1/2"		54	.148		3.85	11.05		14.90	20.50
2823	5/8"		48	.167		4.70	12.45		17.15	23.50
2824	3/4"		44	.182		6.10	13.55		19.65	26.50
2825	7/8"		40	.200		10.20	14.95		25.15	33.50
2826	1"		34	.235		14.45	17.55		32	42
2827	1-1/8"		30	.267		77.50	19.90		97.40	115
2860	Pipe hanger assy, adj. clevis, saddle, rod, clamp, insul. allowance									
2864	1/2" pipe size	Q-5	35	.457	Ea.	53	31		84	105
2866	3/4" pipe size		34.80	.460		56.50	31.50		88	109
2868	1" pipe size		34.60	.462		57.50	31.50		89	110
2869	1-1/4" pipe size		34.30	.466		58	31.50		89.50	111
2870	1-1/2" pipe size		33.90	.472		59	32		91	113
2872	2" pipe size		33.30	.480		66	32.50		98.50	121
2874	2-1/2" pipe size		32.30	.495		75.50	33.50		109	134
2876	3" pipe size		31.20	.513		85.50	35		120.50	146
2880	4" pipe size		30.70	.521		92.50	35.50		128	155
2884	6" pipe size		29.80	.537		119	36.50		155.50	186

22 05 Common Work Results for Plumbing

22 05 29 – Hangers and Supports for Plumbing Piping and Equipment

	22 05 29.10 Hangers & Supp. for Plumb'g/HVAC Pipe/Equip.	Crew	Daily Output	Labor-Hours	Unit	Material	2024 Bare Costs Labor	Equipment	Total	Total Incl O&P
2888	8" pipe size	Q-5	28	.571	Ea.	142	39		181	214
2892	10" pipe size		25.20	.635		146	43		189	225
2896	12" pipe size	↓	23.20	.690	↓	221	47		268	315
2900	Rolls									
2910	Adjustable yoke, carbon steel with CI roll, TYPE 43									
2918	2" pipe size	Q-1	140	.114	Ea.	16.40	7.70		24.10	29.50
2920	2-1/2" pipe size		137	.117		19.75	7.85		27.60	33
2930	3" pipe size		131	.122		23	8.20		31.20	37.50
2940	3-1/2" pipe size		124	.129		30	8.65		38.65	46
2950	4" pipe size		117	.137		29.50	9.20		38.70	45.50
2960	5" pipe size		110	.145		34	9.75		43.75	52
2970	6" pipe size		104	.154		44	10.35		54.35	64
2980	8" pipe size		96	.167		62	11.20		73.20	84.50
2990	10" pipe size		80	.200		82.50	13.45		95.95	111
3000	12" pipe size		68	.235		124	15.80		139.80	160
3010	14" pipe size		56	.286		290	19.20		309.20	350
3020	16" pipe size	↓	48	.333	↓	530	22.50		552.50	615
3050	Chair, carbon steel with CI roll									
3060	2" pipe size	1 Plum	68	.118	Ea.	26.50	8.80		35.30	42
3070	2-1/2" pipe size		65	.123		28.50	9.20		37.70	45
3080	3" pipe size		62	.129		29.50	9.65		39.15	47
3090	3-1/2" pipe size		60	.133		36	9.95		45.95	55
3100	4" pipe size		58	.138		37.50	10.30		47.80	57
3110	5" pipe size		56	.143		41.50	10.65		52.15	61.50
3120	6" pipe size		53	.151		58	11.25		69.25	80.50
3130	8" pipe size		50	.160		78	11.95		89.95	104
3140	10" pipe size		48	.167		98	12.45		110.45	127
3150	12" pipe size	↓	46	.174		147	13		160	180
3170	Single pipe roll (see line 2650 for rods), TYPE 41, 1" pipe size	Q-1	137	.117		25.50	7.85		33.35	39.50
3180	1-1/4" pipe size		131	.122		19.10	8.20		27.30	33
3190	1-1/2" pipe size		129	.124		27	8.35		35.35	42
3200	2" pipe size		124	.129		27	8.65		35.65	42.50
3210	2-1/2" pipe size		118	.136		29	9.10		38.10	45
3220	3" pipe size		115	.139		30.50	9.35		39.85	47.50
3230	3-1/2" pipe size		113	.142		34	9.50		43.50	51
3240	4" pipe size		112	.143		33.50	9.60		43.10	51.50
3250	5" pipe size		110	.145		40	9.75		49.75	58.50
3260	6" pipe size		101	.158		46	10.65		56.65	66.50
3270	8" pipe size		90	.178		57	11.95		68.95	80.50
3280	10" pipe size		80	.200		105	13.45		118.45	136
3290	12" pipe size	↓	68	.235	↓	163	15.80		178.80	203
3300	Saddles (add vertical pipe riser, usually 3" diameter)									
3310	Pipe support, complete, adjust., CI saddle, TYPE 36									
3320	2-1/2" pipe size	1 Plum	96	.083	Ea.	177	6.20		183.20	204
3330	3" pipe size		88	.091		180	6.80		186.80	208
3340	3-1/2" pipe size		79	.101		191	7.55		198.55	221
3350	4" pipe size		68	.118		267	8.80		275.80	305
3360	5" pipe size		64	.125		259	9.35		268.35	299
3370	6" pipe size		59	.136		284	10.10		294.10	325
3380	8" pipe size		53	.151		310	11.25		321.25	355
3390	10" pipe size		50	.160		315	11.95		326.95	365
3400	12" pipe size	↓	48	.167	↓	325	12.45		337.45	380
3450	For standard pipe support, one piece, CI, deduct					34%				

22 05 Common Work Results for Plumbing

22 05 29 – Hangers and Supports for Plumbing Piping and Equipment

22 05 29.10 Hangers & Supp. for Plumb'g/HVAC Pipe/Equip.		Crew	Daily Output	Labor-Hours	Unit	Material	2024 Bare Costs Labor	Equipment	Total	Total Incl O&P
3460	For stanchion support, CI with steel yoke, deduct					60%				
3550	Insulation shield 1" thick, 1/2" pipe size, TYPE 40	1 Asbe	100	.080	Ea.	3.53	5.35		8.88	12.10
3560	3/4" pipe size		100	.080		3.53	5.35		8.88	12.10
3570	1" pipe size		98	.082		4.39	5.50		9.89	13.20
3580	1-1/4" pipe size		98	.082		4.39	5.50		9.89	13.20
3590	1-1/2" pipe size		96	.083		5.70	5.60		11.30	14.75
3600	2" pipe size		96	.083		11.75	5.60		17.35	21.50
3610	2-1/2" pipe size		94	.085		12.10	5.70		17.80	22
3620	3" pipe size		94	.085		14.60	5.70		20.30	25
3630	2" thick, 3-1/2" pipe size		92	.087		15.55	5.85		21.40	26
3640	4" pipe size		92	.087		21.50	5.85		27.35	33
3650	5" pipe size		90	.089		29.50	5.95		35.45	41.50
3660	6" pipe size		90	.089		33.50	5.95		39.45	46
3670	8" pipe size		88	.091		53.50	6.10		59.60	68.50
3680	10" pipe size		88	.091		67.50	6.10		73.60	83.50
3690	12" pipe size		86	.093		77	6.25		83.25	94.50
3700	14" pipe size		86	.093		129	6.25		135.25	151
3710	16" pipe size		84	.095		135	6.40		141.40	159
3720	18" pipe size		84	.095		152	6.40		158.40	177
3730	20" pipe size		82	.098		167	6.55		173.55	194
3732	24" pipe size	↓	80	.100	↓	196	6.70		202.70	226
3750	Covering protection saddle, TYPE 39									
3760	1" covering size									
3770	3/4" pipe size	1 Plum	68	.118	Ea.	14.55	8.80		23.35	29
3780	1" pipe size		68	.118		14.55	8.80		23.35	29
3790	1-1/4" pipe size		68	.118		14.55	8.80		23.35	29
3800	1-1/2" pipe size		66	.121		15.50	9.05		24.55	30.50
3810	2" pipe size		66	.121		15.50	9.05		24.55	30.50
3820	2-1/2" pipe size		64	.125		15.50	9.35		24.85	31
3830	3" pipe size		64	.125		21	9.35		30.35	37
3840	3-1/2" pipe size		62	.129		23	9.65		32.65	40
3850	4" pipe size		62	.129		23	9.65		32.65	40
3860	5" pipe size		60	.133		23	9.95		32.95	40.50
3870	6" pipe size	↓	60	.133	↓	27.50	9.95		37.45	45.50
3900	1-1/2" covering size									
3910	3/4" pipe size	1 Plum	68	.118	Ea.	17.35	8.80		26.15	32
3920	1" pipe size		68	.118		17.35	8.80		26.15	32
3930	1-1/4" pipe size		68	.118		10.80	8.80		19.60	25
3940	1-1/2" pipe size		66	.121		17.35	9.05		26.40	32.50
3950	2" pipe size		66	.121		18.85	9.05		27.90	34
3960	2-1/2" pipe size		64	.125		22.50	9.35		31.85	39
3970	3" pipe size		64	.125		22.50	9.35		31.85	39
3980	3-1/2" pipe size		62	.129		24	9.65		33.65	41
3990	4" pipe size		62	.129		24	9.65		33.65	41
4000	5" pipe size		60	.133		24	9.95		33.95	41.50
4010	6" pipe size		60	.133		32.50	9.95		42.45	50.50
4020	8" pipe size		58	.138		46.50	10.30		56.80	67
4022	10" pipe size		56	.143		46.50	10.65		57.15	67.50
4024	12" pipe size	↓	54	.148	↓	101	11.05		112.05	127
4028	2" covering size									
4029	2-1/2" pipe size	1 Plum	62	.129	Ea.	22.50	9.65		32.15	39.50
4032	3" pipe size		60	.133		26.50	9.95		36.45	44
4033	4" pipe size	↓	58	.138		26.50	10.30		36.80	44.50

For customer support on your Plumbing Costs with RSMeans Data call 800.448.8182.

22 05 Common Work Results for Plumbing

22 05 29 – Hangers and Supports for Plumbing Piping and Equipment

	22 05 29.10 Hangers & Supp. for Plumb'g/HVAC Pipe/Equip.	Crew	Daily Output	Labor-Hours	Unit	Material	2024 Bare Costs Labor	Equipment	Total	Total Incl O&P
4034	6" pipe size	1 Plum	56	.143	Ea.	43.50	10.65		54.15	64
4035	8" pipe size		54	.148		51.50	11.05		62.55	73
4080	10" pipe size		58	.138		55	10.30		65.30	76
4090	12" pipe size		56	.143		114	10.65		124.65	141
4100	14" pipe size		56	.143		114	10.65		124.65	141
4110	16" pipe size		54	.148		147	11.05		158.05	178
4120	18" pipe size		54	.148		147	11.05		158.05	178
4130	20" pipe size		52	.154		164	11.50		175.50	197
4150	24" pipe size		50	.160		192	11.95		203.95	229
4160	30" pipe size		48	.167		211	12.45		223.45	251
4180	36" pipe size		45	.178		280	13.25		293.25	330
4186	2-1/2" covering size									
4187	3" pipe size	1 Plum	58	.138	Ea.	27.50	10.30		37.80	45.50
4188	4" pipe size		56	.143		29.50	10.65		40.15	48.50
4189	6" pipe size		52	.154		52	11.50		63.50	74
4190	8" pipe size		48	.167		57.50	12.45		69.95	82
4191	10" pipe size		44	.182		63	13.55		76.55	89.50
4192	12" pipe size		40	.200		121	14.95		135.95	155
4193	14" pipe size		36	.222		121	16.60		137.60	158
4194	16" pipe size		32	.250		155	18.65		173.65	198
4195	18" pipe size		28	.286		173	21.50		194.50	222
4200	Sockets									
4210	Rod end, malleable iron, TYPE 16									
4220	1/4" thread size	1 Plum	240	.033	Ea.	3.57	2.49		6.06	7.65
4230	3/8" thread size		240	.033		3.58	2.49		6.07	7.65
4240	1/2" thread size		230	.035		4.73	2.60		7.33	9.05
4250	5/8" thread size		225	.036		8.85	2.65		11.50	13.65
4260	3/4" thread size		220	.036		12.05	2.71		14.76	17.30
4270	7/8" thread size		210	.038		17.40	2.84		20.24	23.50
4290	Strap, 1/2" pipe size, TYPE 26	Q-1	142	.113		2.20	7.55		9.75	13.65
4300	3/4" pipe size		140	.114		5.20	7.70		12.90	17.10
4310	1" pipe size		137	.117		6.50	7.85		14.35	18.80
4320	1-1/4" pipe size		134	.119		6.50	8		14.50	19.10
4330	1-1/2" pipe size		131	.122		6.85	8.20		15.05	19.75
4340	2" pipe size		129	.124		7.55	8.35		15.90	20.50
4350	2-1/2" pipe size		125	.128		11.55	8.60		20.15	25.50
4360	3" pipe size		122	.131		15.10	8.80		23.90	29.50
4370	3-1/2" pipe size		119	.134		16.50	9.05		25.55	31.50
4380	4" pipe size		114	.140		15.45	9.45		24.90	31
4400	U-bolt, carbon steel									
4410	Standard, with nuts, TYPE 42									
4420	1/2" pipe size	1 Plum	160	.050	Ea.	2.56	3.73		6.29	8.35
4430	3/4" pipe size		158	.051		2.56	3.78		6.34	8.40
4450	1" pipe size		152	.053		2.92	3.93		6.85	9.05
4460	1-1/4" pipe size		148	.054		3.17	4.04		7.21	9.50
4470	1-1/2" pipe size		143	.056		3.38	4.18		7.56	9.90
4480	2" pipe size		139	.058		3.70	4.30		8	10.45
4490	2-1/2" pipe size		134	.060		6.15	4.46		10.61	13.40
4500	3" pipe size		128	.063		6.40	4.67		11.07	14
4510	3-1/2" pipe size		122	.066		6.75	4.90		11.65	14.75
4520	4" pipe size		117	.068		6.95	5.10		12.05	15.25
4530	5" pipe size		114	.070		7.20	5.25		12.45	15.75
4540	6" pipe size		111	.072		14.95	5.40		20.35	24.50

22 05 Common Work Results for Plumbing

22 05 29 – Hangers and Supports for Plumbing Piping and Equipment

22 05 29.10 Hangers & Supp. for Plumb'g/HVAC Pipe/Equip.		Crew	Daily Output	Labor-Hours	Unit	Material	2024 Bare Costs Labor	Equipment	Total	Total Incl O&P
4550	8" pipe size	1 Plum	109	.073	Ea.	17.75	5.50		23.25	27.50
4560	10" pipe size		107	.075		32	5.60		37.60	43.50
4570	12" pipe size	↓	104	.077	↓	42.50	5.75		48.25	55.50
4580	For plastic coating on 1/2" thru 6" size, add					150%				
4700	U-hook, carbon steel, requires mounting screws or bolts									
4710	3/4" thru 2" pipe size									
4720	6" long	1 Plum	96	.083	Ea.	1.67	6.20		7.87	11.10
4730	8" long		96	.083		1.81	6.20		8.01	11.25
4740	10" long		96	.083		2.13	6.20		8.33	11.60
4750	12" long	↓	96	.083	↓	2.81	6.20		9.01	12.35
4760	For copper plated, add					50%				
7000	Roof supports									
7006	Duct									
7010	Rectangular, open, 12" off roof									
7020	To 18" wide	Q-9	26	.615	Ea.	248	40		288	335
7030	To 24" wide	"	22	.727		289	47.50		336.50	390
7040	To 36" wide	Q-10	30	.800		330	54		384	445
7050	To 48" wide		28	.857		370	58		428	495
7060	To 60" wide	↓	24	1	↓	415	67.50		482.50	555
7100	Equipment									
7120	Equipment support	Q-5	20	.800	Ea.	109	54.50		163.50	201
7300	Pipe									
7310	Roller type									
7320	Up to 2-1/2" diam. pipe									
7324	3-1/2" off roof	Q-5	24	.667	Ea.	19.40	45.50		64.90	89
7326	Up to 10" off roof	"	20	.800	"	42	54.50		96.50	128
7340	2-1/2" to 3-1/2" diam. pipe									
7342	Up to 16" off roof	Q-5	18	.889	Ea.	75.50	60.50		136	173
7360	4" to 5" diam. pipe									
7362	Up to 12" off roof	Q-5	16	1	Ea.	107	68		175	219
7400	Strut/channel type									
7410	Up to 2-1/2" diam. pipe									
7424	3-1/2" off roof	Q-5	24	.667	Ea.	18.60	45.50		64.10	88
7426	Up to 10" off roof	"	20	.800	"	56.50	54.50		111	143
7440	Strut and roller type									
7452	2-1/2" to 3-1/2" diam. pipe									
7454	Up to 16" off roof	Q-5	18	.889	Ea.	108	60.50		168.50	209
7460	Strut and hanger type									
7470	Up to 3" diam. pipe									
7474	Up to 8" off roof	Q-5	19	.842	Ea.	68.50	57.50		126	161
8000	Pipe clamp, plastic, 1/2" CTS	1 Plum	80	.100		.27	7.45		7.72	11.40
8010	3/4" CTS		73	.110		.27	8.20		8.47	12.45
8020	1" CTS		68	.118		.66	8.80		9.46	13.80
8080	Economy clamp, 1/4" CTS		175	.046		.08	3.41		3.49	5.20
8090	3/8" CTS		168	.048		.08	3.55		3.63	5.40
8100	1/2" CTS		160	.050		.08	3.73		3.81	5.65
8110	3/4" CTS		145	.055		.08	4.12		4.20	6.25
8200	Half clamp, 1/2" CTS		80	.100		.09	7.45		7.54	11.20
8210	3/4" CTS		73	.110		.14	8.20		8.34	12.30
8300	Suspension clamp, 1/2" CTS		80	.100		.27	7.45		7.72	11.40
8310	3/4" CTS		73	.110		.27	8.20		8.47	12.45
8320	1" CTS		68	.118		.62	8.80		9.42	13.75
8400	Insulator, 1/2" CTS		80	.100		.40	7.45		7.85	11.55

22 05 Common Work Results for Plumbing

22 05 29 – Hangers and Supports for Plumbing Piping and Equipment

22 05 29.10 Hangers & Supp. for Plumb'g/HVAC Pipe/Equip.		Crew	Daily Output	Labor-Hours	Unit	Material	2024 Bare Costs Labor	Equipment	Total	Total Incl O&P
8410	3/4" CTS	1 Plum	73	.110	Ea.	.41	8.20		8.61	12.60
8420	1" CTS		68	.118		.42	8.80		9.22	13.50
8500	J hook clamp with nail, 1/2" CTS		240	.033		.13	2.49		2.62	3.84
8501	3/4" CTS	▼	240	.033	▼	.14	2.49		2.63	3.85
8800	Wire cable support system									
8810	Cable with hook terminal and locking device									
8830	2 mm (.079") diam. cable (100 lb. cap.)									
8840	1 m (3.3') length, with hook	1 Shee	96	.083	Ea.	5.55	6		11.55	15.15
8850	2 m (6.6') length, with hook		84	.095		6.55	6.90		13.45	17.60
8860	3 m (9.9') length, with hook	▼	72	.111		7.35	8.05		15.40	20
8870	5 m (16.4') length, with hook	Q-9	60	.267		9	17.35		26.35	36
8880	10 m (32.8') length, with hook	"	30	.533		12.90	34.50		47.40	66
8900	3 mm (.118") diam. cable (200 lb. cap.)									
8910	1 m (3.3') length, with hook	1 Shee	96	.083	Ea.	16.15	6		22.15	27
8920	2 m (6.6') length, with hook		84	.095		21.50	6.90		28.40	34
8930	3 m (9.9') length, with hook		72	.111		19.85	8.05		27.90	34
8940	5 m (16.4') length, with hook	Q-9	60	.267		28.50	17.35		45.85	57
8950	10 m (32.8') length, with hook	"	30	.533		28.50	34.50		63	83.50
9000	Cable system accessories									
9010	Anchor bolt, 3/8", with nut	1 Shee	140	.057	Ea.	3.96	4.13		8.09	10.55
9020	Air duct corner protector		160	.050		1.88	3.61		5.49	7.50
9030	Air duct support attachment	▼	140	.057	▼	3.52	4.13		7.65	10.05
9040	Flange clip, hammer-on style									
9044	For flange thickness 3/32"-9/64", 160 lb. cap.	1 Shee	180	.044	Ea.	.94	3.21		4.15	5.85
9048	For flange thickness 1/8"-1/4", 200 lb. cap.		160	.050		1.05	3.61		4.66	6.60
9052	For flange thickness 5/16"-1/2", 200 lb. cap.		150	.053		2.21	3.85		6.06	8.25
9056	For flange thickness 9/16"-3/4", 200 lb. cap.		140	.057	▼	3.05	4.13		7.18	9.55
9060	Wire insulation protection tube	▼	180	.044	L.F.	.84	3.21		4.05	5.75
9070	Wire cutter				Ea.	132			132	145

22 05 33 – Heat Tracing for Plumbing Piping

22 05 33.20 Temperature Maintenance Cable

		Crew	Daily Output	Labor-Hours	Unit	Material	Labor	Equipment	Total	Total Incl O&P
0010	**TEMPERATURE MAINTENANCE CABLE**									
0040	Components									
0080	Heating cable									
0100	208 V									
0150	140°F	Q-1	1060.80	.015	L.F.	15.35	1.01		16.36	18.40
0200	120 V									
0220	125°F	Q-1	1060.80	.015	L.F.	6.85	1.01		7.86	9
0300	Power kit w/1 end seal	1 Elec	48.80	.164	Ea.	178	11.75		189.75	213
0310	Splice kit		35.50	.225		276	16.15		292.15	330
0320	End seal		160	.050		19.10	3.59		22.69	26.50
0330	Tee kit w/1 end seal		26.80	.299		263	21.50		284.50	320
0340	Powered splice w/2 end seals		20	.400		217	28.50		245.50	282
0350	Powered tee kit w/3 end seals		18	.444		279	32		311	350
0360	Cross kit w/2 end seals	▼	18.60	.430	▼	287	31		318	360
0500	Recommended thickness of fiberglass insulation									
0510	Pipe size									
0520	1/2" to 1" use 1" insulation									
0530	1-1/4" to 2" use 1-1/2" insulation									
0540	2-1/2" to 6" use 2" insulation									
0560	NOTE: For pipe sizes 1-1/4" and smaller use 1/4" larger diameter									
0570	insulation to allow room for installation over cable.									

22 05 Common Work Results for Plumbing

22 05 48 – Vibration and Seismic Controls for Plumbing Piping and Equipment

22 05 48.40 Vibration Absorbers		Crew	Daily Output	Labor-Hours	Unit	Material	2024 Bare Costs Labor	Equipment	Total	Total Incl O&P
0010	**VIBRATION ABSORBERS**									
0100	Hangers, neoprene flex									
0200	10-120 lb. capacity				Ea.	24.50			24.50	27
0220	75-550 lb. capacity					41			41	45.50
0240	250-1,100 lb. capacity					86			86	94.50
0260	1,000-4,000 lb. capacity					139			139	153
0500	Spring flex, 60 lb. capacity					38			38	42
0520	450 lb. capacity					59			59	65
0540	900 lb. capacity					86			86	94.50
0560	1,100-1,300 lb. capacity					86			86	94.50
0600	Rubber in shear									
0610	45-340 lb., up to 1/2" rod size	1 Stpi	22	.364	Ea.	24	27.50		51.50	67.50
0620	130-700 lb., up to 3/4" rod size		20	.400		51.50	30		81.50	102
0630	50-1,000 lb., up to 3/4" rod size		18	.444		68	33.50		101.50	125
1000	Mounts, neoprene, 45-380 lb. capacity					18.30			18.30	20
1020	250-1,100 lb. capacity					59			59	65
1040	1,000-4,000 lb. capacity					115			115	127
1100	Spring flex, 60 lb. capacity					75			75	82.50
1120	165 lb. capacity					77			77	84.50
1140	260 lb. capacity					92			92	101
1160	450 lb. capacity					94			94	103
1180	600 lb. capacity					97.50			97.50	107
1200	750 lb. capacity					158			158	174
1220	900 lb. capacity					155			155	171
1240	1,100 lb. capacity					191			191	210
1260	1,300 lb. capacity					207			207	228
1280	1,500 lb. capacity					207			207	228
1300	1,800 lb. capacity					253			253	279
1320	2,200 lb. capacity					320			320	350
1340	2,600 lb. capacity					320			320	350
1399	Spring type									
1400	2 piece									
1410	50-1,000 lb.	1 Stpi	12	.667	Ea.	217	50.50		267.50	315
1420	1,100-1,600 lb.	"	12	.667	"	258	50.50		308.50	360
1500	Double spring open									
1510	150-450 lb.	1 Stpi	24	.333	Ea.	149	25		174	202
1520	500-1,000 lb.		24	.333		165	25		190	220
1530	1,100-1,600 lb.		24	.333		165	25		190	220
1540	1,700-2,400 lb.		24	.333		162	25		187	216
1550	2,500-3,400 lb.		24	.333		276	25		301	345
2000	Pads, cork rib, 18" x 18" x 1", 10-50 psi					169			169	186
2020	18" x 36" x 1", 10-50 psi					320			320	350
2100	Shear flexible pads, 18" x 18" x 3/8", 20-70 psi					68			68	74.50
2120	18" x 36" x 3/8", 20-70 psi					160			160	176
2150	Laminated neoprene and cork									
2160	1" thick	1 Stpi	16	.500	S.F.	83	38		121	148
2200	Neoprene elastomer isolation bearing pad									
2230	464 psi, 5/8" x 19-11/16" x 39-3/8"	1 Stpi	16	.500	Ea.	65.50	38		103.50	128
3000	Note overlap in capacities due to deflections									

22 05 Common Work Results for Plumbing

22 05 53 – Identification for Plumbing Piping and Equipment

22 05 53.10 Piping System Identification Labels

		Crew	Daily Output	Labor-Hours	Unit	Material	2024 Bare Costs Labor	2024 Bare Costs Equipment	Total	Total Incl O&P
0010	**PIPING SYSTEM IDENTIFICATION LABELS**									
0100	Indicate contents and flow direction									
0106	Pipe markers									
0110	Plastic snap around									
0114	1/2" pipe	1 Plum	80	.100	Ea.	2.24	7.45		9.69	13.55
0116	3/4" pipe		80	.100		2.71	7.45		10.16	14.10
0118	1" pipe		80	.100		2.71	7.45		10.16	14.10
0120	2" pipe		75	.107		3.51	7.95		11.46	15.70
0122	3" pipe		70	.114		7.10	8.55		15.65	20.50
0124	4" pipe		60	.133		7.80	9.95		17.75	23.50
0126	6" pipe		60	.133		7.95	9.95		17.90	23.50
0128	8" pipe		56	.143		11	10.65		21.65	28
0130	10" pipe		56	.143		11	10.65		21.65	28
0200	Over 10" pipe size		50	.160		15.20	11.95		27.15	34.50
1110	Self adhesive									
1114	1" pipe	1 Plum	80	.100	Ea.	1.02	7.45		8.47	12.20
1116	2" pipe		75	.107		1.08	7.95		9.03	13.05
1118	3" pipe		70	.114		1.66	8.55		10.21	14.55
1120	4" pipe		60	.133		1.63	9.95		11.58	16.60
1122	6" pipe		60	.133		1.63	9.95		11.58	16.60
1124	8" pipe		56	.143		3.09	10.65		13.74	19.25
1126	10" pipe		56	.143		3.66	10.65		14.31	19.90
1200	Over 10" pipe size		50	.160		4.63	11.95		16.58	23
2000	Valve tags									
2010	Numbered plus identifying legend									
2100	Brass, 2" diameter	1 Plum	40	.200	Ea.	2.65	14.95		17.60	25
2200	Plastic, 1-1/2" diameter	"	40	.200	"	2.15	14.95		17.10	24.50

22 05 76 – Facility Drainage Piping Cleanouts

22 05 76.10 Cleanouts

		Crew	Daily Output	Labor-Hours	Unit	Material	2024 Bare Costs Labor	2024 Bare Costs Equipment	Total	Total Incl O&P
0010	**CLEANOUTS**									
0060	Floor type									
0080	Round or square, scoriated nickel bronze top									
0100	2" pipe size	1 Plum	10	.800	Ea.	310	59.50		369.50	430
0120	3" pipe size		8	1		335	74.50		409.50	480
0140	4" pipe size		6	1.333		440	99.50		539.50	635
0160	5" pipe size		4	2		655	149		804	940
0180	6" pipe size	Q-1	6	2.667		775	179		954	1,125
0200	8" pipe size	"	4	4		415	269		684	860
0340	Recessed for tile, same price									
0980	Round top, recessed for terrazzo									
1000	2" pipe size	1 Plum	9	.889	Ea.	195	66.50		261.50	315
1080	3" pipe size		6	1.333		340	99.50		439.50	525
1100	4" pipe size		4	2		223	149		372	465
1120	5" pipe size	Q-1	6	2.667		790	179		969	1,125
1140	6" pipe size		5	3.200		835	215		1,050	1,250
1160	8" pipe size		4	4		610	269		879	1,075
2000	Round scoriated nickel bronze top, extra heavy duty									
2060	2" pipe size	1 Plum	9	.889	Ea.	283	66.50		349.50	410
2080	3" pipe size		6	1.333		191	99.50		290.50	360
2100	4" pipe size		4	2		580	149		729	860
2120	5" pipe size	Q-1	6	2.667		580	179		759	900
2140	6" pipe size		5	3.200		395	215		610	755

22 05 Common Work Results for Plumbing

22 05 76 – Facility Drainage Piping Cleanouts

22 05 76.10 Cleanouts

		Crew	Daily Output	Labor-Hours	Unit	Material	2024 Bare Costs Labor	Equipment	Total	Total Incl O&P
2160	8" pipe size	Q-1	4	4	Ea.	675	269		944	1,150
4000	Wall type, square smooth cover, over wall frame									
4060	2" pipe size	1 Plum	14	.571	Ea.	298	42.50		340.50	390
4080	3" pipe size		12	.667		315	50		365	420
4100	4" pipe size		10	.800		325	59.50		384.50	450
4120	5" pipe size		9	.889		480	66.50		546.50	630
4140	6" pipe size		8	1		685	74.50		759.50	860
4160	8" pipe size	Q-1	11	1.455		725	97.50		822.50	940
5000	Extension, CI; bronze countersunk plug, 8" long									
5040	2" pipe size	1 Plum	16	.500	Ea.	126	37.50		163.50	195
5060	3" pipe size		14	.571		197	42.50		239.50	280
5080	4" pipe size		13	.615		149	46		195	232
5100	5" pipe size		12	.667		264	50		314	365
5120	6" pipe size		11	.727		465	54.50		519.50	590

22 05 76.20 Cleanout Tees

		Crew	Daily Output	Labor-Hours	Unit	Material	2024 Bare Costs Labor	Equipment	Total	Total Incl O&P
0010	**CLEANOUT TEES**									
0100	Cast iron, B&S, with countersunk plug									
0200	2" pipe size	1 Plum	4	2	Ea.	75	149		224	305
0220	3" pipe size		3.60	2.222		81.50	166		247.50	335
0240	4" pipe size		3.30	2.424		130	181		311	410
0260	5" pipe size	Q-1	5.50	2.909		945	195		1,140	1,350
0280	6" pipe size	"	5	3.200		360	215		575	720
0300	8" pipe size	Q-3	5	6.400		1,925	455		2,380	2,775
0500	For round smooth access cover, same price									
0600	For round scoriated access cover, same price									
0700	For square smooth access cover, add				Ea.	60%				
2000	Cast iron, no hub									
2010	Cleanout tee, with 2 couplings									
2012	2"	Q-1	22	.727	Ea.	59.50	49		108.50	138
2014	3"		19	.842		84.50	56.50		141	177
2016	4"		16.50	.970		130	65		195	240
2018	6"	Q-2	20	1.200		305	83.50		388.50	460
2040	Cleanout plug, no hub, with 1 coupling									
2042	2"	Q-1	44	.364	Ea.	9.85	24.50		34.35	47.50
2046	3"		38	.421		15.30	28.50		43.80	59
2048	4"		33	.485		19.75	32.50		52.25	70
2050	6"	Q-2	40	.600		91	42		133	162
2052	8"	"	33	.727		127	50.50		177.50	216
4000	Plastic, tees and adapters. Add plugs									
4010	ABS, DWV									
4020	Cleanout tee, 1-1/2" pipe size	1 Plum	15	.533	Ea.	69.50	40		109.50	136
4030	2" pipe size	Q-1	27	.593		65	40		105	131
4040	3" pipe size		21	.762		142	51		193	232
4050	4" pipe size		16	1		310	67		377	440
4100	Cleanout plug, 1-1/2" pipe size	1 Plum	32	.250		12.35	18.65		31	41.50
4110	2" pipe size	Q-1	56	.286		13.50	19.20		32.70	43.50
4120	3" pipe size		36	.444		22	30		52	68.50
4130	4" pipe size		30	.533		38	36		74	95.50
4180	Cleanout adapter fitting, 1-1/2" pipe size	1 Plum	32	.250		18.30	18.65		36.95	48
4190	2" pipe size	Q-1	56	.286		25.50	19.20		44.70	56.50
4200	3" pipe size		36	.444		64	30		94	115
4210	4" pipe size		30	.533		120	36		156	186

22 05 Common Work Results for Plumbing

22 05 76 – Facility Drainage Piping Cleanouts

22 05 76.20 Cleanout Tees		Crew	Daily Output	Labor-Hours	Unit	Material	2024 Bare Costs Labor	Equipment	Total	Total Incl O&P
5000	PVC, DWV									
5010	Cleanout tee, 1-1/2" pipe size	1 Plum	15	.533	Ea.	49	40		89	113
5020	2" pipe size	Q-1	27	.593		57	40		97	122
5030	3" pipe size		21	.762		110	51		161	198
5040	4" pipe size	↓	16	1		197	67		264	315
5090	Cleanout plug, 1-1/2" pipe size	1 Plum	32	.250		11.45	18.65		30.10	40.50
5100	2" pipe size	Q-1	56	.286		12.85	19.20		32.05	42.50
5110	3" pipe size		36	.444		23	30		53	69.50
5120	4" pipe size		30	.533		34	36		70	91
5130	6" pipe size	↓	24	.667		108	45		153	185
5170	Cleanout adapter fitting, 1-1/2" pipe size	1 Plum	32	.250		16.50	18.65		35.15	46
5180	2" pipe size	Q-1	56	.286		22	19.20		41.20	53
5190	3" pipe size		36	.444		59.50	30		89.50	110
5200	4" pipe size		30	.533		97.50	36		133.50	161
5210	6" pipe size	↓	24	.667		292	45		337	385
5300	Cleanout tee, with plug									
5310	4"	Q-1	14	1.143	Ea.	184	77		261	315
5320	6"	"	8	2		209	134		343	430
5330	8"	Q-2	11	2.182		400	152		552	665
5340	12"	"	10	2.400		1,125	167		1,292	1,500
5400	Polypropylene, Schedule 40									
5410	Cleanout tee with plug									
5420	1-1/2"	1 Plum	10	.800	Ea.	35	59.50		94.50	128
5430	2"	Q-1	17	.941		33	63		96	131
5440	3"		11	1.455		74.50	97.50		172	227
5450	4"	↓	9	1.778	↓	101	119		220	289

22 07 Plumbing Insulation

22 07 16 – Plumbing Equipment Insulation

22 07 16.10 Insulation for Plumbing Equipment

			Crew	Daily Output	Labor-Hours	Unit	Material	Labor	Equipment	Total	Total Incl O&P
0010	**INSULATION FOR PLUMBING EQUIPMENT**										
2900	Domestic water heater wrap kit										
2920	1-1/2" with vinyl jacket, 20 to 60 gal.	G	1 Plum	8	1	Ea.	30	74.50		104.50	144
2925	50 to 80 gal.	G	"	8	1	"	45	74.50		119.50	161

22 07 19 – Plumbing Piping Insulation

22 07 19.10 Piping Insulation

		Crew	Daily Output	Labor-Hours	Unit	Material	Labor	Equipment	Total	Total Incl O&P
0010	**PIPING INSULATION**									
0110	Insulation req'd. is based on the surface size/area to be covered									
0230	Insulated protectors (ADA)									
0235	For exposed piping under sinks or lavatories									
0240	Vinyl coated foam, velcro tabs									
0245	P Trap, 1-1/4" or 1-1/2"	1 Plum	32	.250	Ea.	18.80	18.65		37.45	48.50
0260	Valve and supply cover									
0265	1/2", 3/8", and 7/16" pipe size	1 Plum	32	.250	Ea.	18.50	18.65		37.15	48.50
0280	Tailpiece offset (wheelchair)									
0285	1-1/4" pipe size	1 Plum	32	.250	Ea.	15.35	18.65		34	45
0600	Pipe covering (price copper tube one size less than IPS)									
1000	Mineral wool									
1010	Preformed, 1200°F, plain									
1014	1" wall									

22 07 Plumbing Insulation

22 07 19 – Plumbing Piping Insulation

22 07 19.10 Piping Insulation		Crew	Daily Output	Labor-Hours	Unit	Material	2024 Bare Costs Labor	Equipment	Total	Total Incl O&P
1016	1/2" iron pipe size G	Q-14	230	.070	L.F.	8.15	4.20		12.35	15.40
1018	3/4" iron pipe size G		220	.073		8.60	4.39		12.99	16.15
1022	1" iron pipe size G		210	.076		8.75	4.60		13.35	16.65
1024	1-1/4" iron pipe size G		205	.078		8.90	4.71		13.61	17
1026	1-1/2" iron pipe size G		205	.078		9.40	4.71		14.11	17.55
1028	2" iron pipe size G		200	.080		11.40	4.83		16.23	19.90
1030	2-1/2" iron pipe size G		190	.084		11.95	5.10		17.05	21
1032	3" iron pipe size G		180	.089		12.75	5.35		18.10	22
1034	4" iron pipe size G		150	.107		14.55	6.45		21	26
1036	5" iron pipe size G		140	.114		16.25	6.90		23.15	28.50
1038	6" iron pipe size G		120	.133		17.80	8.05		25.85	32
1040	7" iron pipe size G		110	.145		7.65	8.80		16.45	22
1042	8" iron pipe size G		100	.160		10.55	9.65		20.20	26.50
1044	9" iron pipe size G		90	.178		11.10	10.75		21.85	28.50
1046	10" iron pipe size G		90	.178		12.55	10.75		23.30	30
1050	1-1/2" wall									
1052	1/2" iron pipe size G	Q-14	225	.071	L.F.	14.05	4.30		18.35	22
1054	3/4" iron pipe size G		215	.074		14.55	4.49		19.04	23
1056	1" iron pipe size G		205	.078		13.75	4.71		18.46	22.50
1058	1-1/4" iron pipe size G		200	.080		15	4.83		19.83	24
1060	1-1/2" iron pipe size G		200	.080		15.65	4.83		20.48	24.50
1062	2" iron pipe size G		190	.084		15.95	5.10		21.05	25.50
1064	2-1/2" iron pipe size G		180	.089		18.40	5.35		23.75	28
1066	3" iron pipe size G		165	.097		18.65	5.85		24.50	29.50
1068	4" iron pipe size G		140	.114		21	6.90		27.90	33.50
1070	5" iron pipe size G		130	.123		22.50	7.45		29.95	36
1072	6" iron pipe size G		110	.145		23.50	8.80		32.30	39.50
1074	7" iron pipe size G		100	.160		10.15	9.65		19.80	26
1076	8" iron pipe size G		90	.178		27.50	10.75		38.25	46.50
1078	9" iron pipe size G		85	.188		13	11.35		24.35	31.50
1080	10" iron pipe size G		80	.200		33	12.10		45.10	55
1082	12" iron pipe size G		75	.213		16.35	12.90		29.25	37.50
1084	14" iron pipe size G		70	.229		18.70	13.80		32.50	41.50
1086	16" iron pipe size G		65	.246		20.50	14.85		35.35	45
1088	18" iron pipe size G		60	.267		24	16.10		40.10	51
1090	20" iron pipe size G		55	.291		25.50	17.55		43.05	55
1092	22" iron pipe size G		50	.320		29	19.35		48.35	61.50
1094	24" iron pipe size G		45	.356		31	21.50		52.50	67
1100	2" wall									
1102	1/2" iron pipe size G	Q-14	220	.073	L.F.	6.30	4.39		10.69	13.60
1104	3/4" iron pipe size G		210	.076		6.55	4.60		11.15	14.20
1106	1" iron pipe size G		200	.080		6.95	4.83		11.78	14.95
1108	1-1/4" iron pipe size G		190	.084		7.45	5.10		12.55	15.90
1110	1-1/2" iron pipe size G		190	.084		7.70	5.10		12.80	16.25
1112	2" iron pipe size G		180	.089		8.15	5.35		13.50	17.15
1114	2-1/2" iron pipe size G		170	.094		9.20	5.70		14.90	18.75
1116	3" iron pipe size G		160	.100		9.80	6.05		15.85	20
1118	4" iron pipe size G		130	.123		11.45	7.45		18.90	24
1120	5" iron pipe size G		120	.133		12.70	8.05		20.75	26
1122	6" iron pipe size G		100	.160		13.20	9.65		22.85	29
1124	8" iron pipe size G		80	.200		16	12.10		28.10	36
1126	10" iron pipe size G		70	.229		19.55	13.80		33.35	42.50
1128	12" iron pipe size G		65	.246		21.50	14.85		36.35	46.50

For customer support on your Plumbing Costs with RSMeans Data call 800.448.8182.

22 07 Plumbing Insulation

22 07 19 – Plumbing Piping Insulation

22 07 19.10 Piping Insulation		Crew	Daily Output	Labor-Hours	Unit	Material	2024 Bare Costs Labor	Equipment	Total	Total Incl O&P
1130	14" iron pipe size	G Q-14	60	.267	L.F.	24.50	16.10		40.60	51
1132	16" iron pipe size	G	55	.291		27.50	17.55		45.05	57
1134	18" iron pipe size	G	50	.320		29.50	19.35		48.85	62
1136	20" iron pipe size	G	45	.356		34	21.50		55.50	70
1138	22" iron pipe size	G	45	.356		37	21.50		58.50	73.50
1140	24" iron pipe size	G	40	.400		39	24		63	80
1150	4" wall									
1152	1-1/4" iron pipe size	G Q-14	170	.094	L.F.	20	5.70		25.70	30.50
1154	1-1/2" iron pipe size	G	165	.097		21	5.85		26.85	32
1156	2" iron pipe size	G	155	.103		21	6.25		27.25	33
1158	4" iron pipe size	G	105	.152		27	9.20		36.20	43.50
1160	6" iron pipe size	G	75	.213		31.50	12.90		44.40	54.50
1162	8" iron pipe size	G	60	.267		35.50	16.10		51.60	64
1164	10" iron pipe size	G	50	.320		43.50	19.35		62.85	77
1166	12" iron pipe size	G	45	.356		47.50	21.50		69	84.50
1168	14" iron pipe size	G	40	.400		51	24		75	93
1170	16" iron pipe size	G	35	.457		57	27.50		84.50	105
1172	18" iron pipe size	G	32	.500		62	30		92	114
1174	20" iron pipe size	G	30	.533		66.50	32		98.50	122
1176	22" iron pipe size	G	28	.571		74.50	34.50		109	135
1178	24" iron pipe size	G	26	.615		79	37		116	144
4280	Cellular glass, closed cell foam, all service jacket, sealant,									
4281	working temp. (-450°F to +900°F), 0 water vapor transmission									
4284	1" wall									
4286	1/2" iron pipe size	G Q-14	120	.133	L.F.	8.65	8.05		16.70	22
4300	1-1/2" wall									
4301	1" iron pipe size	G Q-14	105	.152	L.F.	17.05	9.20		26.25	33
4304	2-1/2" iron pipe size	G	90	.178		30	10.75		40.75	49.50
4306	3" iron pipe size	G	85	.188		29	11.35		40.35	49.50
4308	4" iron pipe size	G	70	.229		32.50	13.80		46.30	56.50
4310	5" iron pipe size	G	65	.246		33	14.85		47.85	58.50
4320	2" wall									
4322	1" iron pipe size	G Q-14	100	.160	L.F.	24.50	9.65		34.15	41.50
4324	2-1/2" iron pipe size	G	85	.188		39	11.35		50.35	60.50
4326	3" iron pipe size	G	80	.200		39	12.10		51.10	61.50
4328	4" iron pipe size	G	65	.246		39.50	14.85		54.35	66
4330	5" iron pipe size	G	60	.267		59.50	16.10		75.60	90
4332	6" iron pipe size	G	50	.320		49	19.35		68.35	83.50
4336	8" iron pipe size	G	40	.400		72.50	24		96.50	117
4338	10" iron pipe size	G	35	.457		97	27.50		124.50	148
4350	2-1/2" wall									
4360	12" iron pipe size	G Q-14	32	.500	L.F.	74	30		104	128
4362	14" iron pipe size	G	"	28	.571	"	105	34.50		139.50	169
4370	3" wall									
4378	6" iron pipe size	G Q-14	48	.333	L.F.	53	20		73	89
4380	8" iron pipe size	G	38	.421		66.50	25.50		92	113
4382	10" iron pipe size	G	33	.485		79.50	29.50		109	132
4384	16" iron pipe size	G	25	.640		113	38.50		151.50	184
4386	18" iron pipe size	G	22	.727		125	44		169	205
4388	20" iron pipe size	G	20	.800		174	48.50		222.50	265
4400	3-1/2" wall									
4412	12" iron pipe size	G Q-14	27	.593	L.F.	102	36		138	167
4414	14" iron pipe size	G	"	25	.640	"	131	38.50		169.50	203

Note: Row 4362 actual columns — | 4362 | 14" iron pipe size | G | " | 28 | .571 | " | 105 | 34.50 | | 139.50 | 169 |

22 07 Plumbing Insulation

22 07 19 – Plumbing Piping Insulation

22 07 19.10 Piping Insulation		Crew	Daily Output	Labor-Hours	Unit	Material	2024 Bare Costs Labor	Equipment	Total	Total Incl O&P
4430	4" wall									
4446	16" iron pipe size	G Q-14	22	.727	L.F.	151	44		195	233
4448	18" iron pipe size	G	20	.800		149	48.50		197.50	238
4450	20" iron pipe size	G ↓	18	.889	↓	217	53.50		270.50	320
4480	Fittings, average with fabric and mastic									
4484	1" wall									
4486	1/2" iron pipe size	G 1 Asbe	40	.200	Ea.	15.05	13.40		28.45	37
4500	1-1/2" wall									
4502	1" iron pipe size	G 1 Asbe	38	.211	Ea.	23.50	14.15		37.65	47
4504	2-1/2" iron pipe size	G	32	.250		43.50	16.80		60.30	73.50
4506	3" iron pipe size	G	30	.267		59	17.90		76.90	92.50
4508	4" iron pipe size	G	28	.286		58.50	19.15		77.65	93.50
4510	5" iron pipe size	G ↓	24	.333	↓	76	22.50		98.50	118
4520	2" wall									
4522	1" iron pipe size	G 1 Asbe	36	.222	Ea.	33.50	14.90		48.40	59.50
4524	2-1/2" iron pipe size	G	30	.267		62	17.90		79.90	96
4526	3" iron pipe size	G	28	.286		65.50	19.15		84.65	101
4528	4" iron pipe size	G	24	.333		68	22.50		90.50	109
4530	5" iron pipe size	G	22	.364		92	24.50		116.50	138
4532	6" iron pipe size	G	20	.400		117	27		144	170
4536	8" iron pipe size	G	12	.667		169	44.50		213.50	254
4538	10" iron pipe size	G ↓	8	1	↓	238	67		305	365
4550	2-1/2" wall									
4560	12" iron pipe size	G 1 Asbe	6	1.333	Ea.	310	89.50		399.50	475
4562	14" iron pipe size	G "	4	2	"	345	134		479	585
4570	3" wall									
4578	6" iron pipe size	G 1 Asbe	16	.500	Ea.	136	33.50		169.50	201
4580	8" iron pipe size	G	10	.800		157	53.50		210.50	255
4582	10" iron pipe size	G ↓	6	1.333	↓	211	89.50		300.50	370
4900	Calcium silicate, with 8 oz. canvas cover									
5100	1" wall, 1/2" iron pipe size	G Q-14	170	.094	L.F.	3.12	5.70		8.82	12.10
5130	3/4" iron pipe size	G	170	.094		3.12	5.70		8.82	12.10
5140	1" iron pipe size	G	170	.094		2.98	5.70		8.68	11.95
5150	1-1/4" iron pipe size	G	165	.097		3.04	5.85		8.89	12.25
5160	1-1/2" iron pipe size	G	165	.097		3.07	5.85		8.92	12.30
5170	2" iron pipe size	G	160	.100		3.55	6.05		9.60	13.10
5180	2-1/2" iron pipe size	G	160	.100		3.74	6.05		9.79	13.30
5190	3" iron pipe size	G	150	.107		4.02	6.45		10.47	14.20
5200	4" iron pipe size	G	140	.114		5	6.90		11.90	16
5210	5" iron pipe size	G	135	.119		5.20	7.15		12.35	16.60
5220	6" iron pipe size	G	130	.123		5.50	7.45		12.95	17.40
5280	1-1/2" wall, 1/2" iron pipe size	G	150	.107		3.29	6.45		9.74	13.40
5310	3/4" iron pipe size	G	150	.107		3.34	6.45		9.79	13.45
5320	1" iron pipe size	G	150	.107		3.65	6.45		10.10	13.80
5330	1-1/4" iron pipe size	G	145	.110		3.93	6.65		10.58	14.45
5340	1-1/2" iron pipe size	G	145	.110		4.23	6.65		10.88	14.80
5350	2" iron pipe size	G	140	.114		4.66	6.90		11.56	15.65
5360	2-1/2" iron pipe size	G	140	.114		5.10	6.90		12	16.10
5370	3" iron pipe size	G	135	.119		5.30	7.15		12.45	16.75
5380	4" iron pipe size	G	125	.128		6.15	7.75		13.90	18.60
5390	5" iron pipe size	G	120	.133		6.95	8.05		15	19.90
5400	6" iron pipe size	G	110	.145		16.45	8.80		25.25	31.50
5460	2" wall, 1/2" iron pipe size	G ↓	135	.119	↓	11.65	7.15		18.80	24

22 07 Plumbing Insulation

22 07 19 – Plumbing Piping Insulation

22 07 19.10 Piping Insulation			Crew	Daily Output	Labor-Hours	Unit	Material	2024 Bare Costs Labor	Equipment	Total	Total Incl O&P
5490	3/4" iron pipe size	G	Q-14	135	.119	L.F.	12.25	7.15		19.40	24.50
5500	1" iron pipe size	G		135	.119		12.90	7.15		20.05	25
5510	1-1/4" iron pipe size	G		130	.123		13.80	7.45		21.25	26.50
5520	1-1/2" iron pipe size	G		130	.123		14.45	7.45		21.90	27
5530	2" iron pipe size	G		125	.128		15.30	7.75		23.05	28.50
5540	2-1/2" iron pipe size	G		125	.128		18.05	7.75		25.80	31.50
5550	3" iron pipe size	G		120	.133		9	8.05		17.05	22
5560	4" iron pipe size	G		115	.139		21	8.40		29.40	36
5570	5" iron pipe size	G		110	.145		24	8.80		32.80	40
5580	6" iron pipe size	G		105	.152		13	9.20		22.20	28.50
5600	Calcium silicate, no cover										
5720	1" wall, 1/2" iron pipe size	G	Q-14	180	.089	L.F.	3.12	5.35		8.47	11.65
5740	3/4" iron pipe size	G		180	.089		3.12	5.35		8.47	11.65
5750	1" iron pipe size	G		180	.089		2.98	5.35		8.33	11.50
5760	1-1/4" iron pipe size	G		175	.091		3.04	5.50		8.54	11.75
5770	1-1/2" iron pipe size	G		175	.091		3.07	5.50		8.57	11.80
5780	2" iron pipe size	G		170	.094		3.55	5.70		9.25	12.55
5790	2-1/2" iron pipe size	G		170	.094		3.74	5.70		9.44	12.75
5800	3" iron pipe size	G		160	.100		4.02	6.05		10.07	13.60
5810	4" iron pipe size	G		150	.107		5	6.45		11.45	15.30
5820	5" iron pipe size	G		145	.110		5.20	6.65		11.85	15.85
5830	6" iron pipe size	G		140	.114		5.50	6.90		12.40	16.55
5900	1-1/2" wall, 1/2" iron pipe size	G		160	.100		3.29	6.05		9.34	12.80
5920	3/4" iron pipe size	G		160	.100		3.34	6.05		9.39	12.85
5930	1" iron pipe size	G		160	.100		3.65	6.05		9.70	13.20
5940	1-1/4" iron pipe size	G		155	.103		3.93	6.25		10.18	13.80
5950	1-1/2" iron pipe size	G		155	.103		4.23	6.25		10.48	14.15
5960	2" iron pipe size	G		150	.107		4.66	6.45		11.11	14.95
5970	2-1/2" iron pipe size	G		150	.107		5.10	6.45		11.55	15.40
5980	3" iron pipe size	G		145	.110		5.30	6.65		11.95	16
5990	4" iron pipe size	G		135	.119		6.15	7.15		13.30	17.70
6000	5" iron pipe size	G		130	.123		6.95	7.45		14.40	19
6010	6" iron pipe size	G		120	.133		7.10	8.05		15.15	20
6020	7" iron pipe size	G		115	.139		8.30	8.40		16.70	22
6030	8" iron pipe size	G		105	.152		9.40	9.20		18.60	24.50
6040	9" iron pipe size	G		100	.160		11.25	9.65		20.90	27
6050	10" iron pipe size	G		95	.168		12.45	10.15		22.60	29
6060	12" iron pipe size	G		90	.178		14.75	10.75		25.50	32.50
6070	14" iron pipe size	G		85	.188		16.65	11.35		28	35.50
6080	16" iron pipe size	G		80	.200		18.65	12.10		30.75	39
6090	18" iron pipe size	G		75	.213		20.50	12.90		33.40	42
6120	2" wall, 1/2" iron pipe size	G		145	.110		5.20	6.65		11.85	15.90
6140	3/4" iron pipe size	G		145	.110		5.50	6.65		12.15	16.20
6150	1" iron pipe size	G		145	.110		5.80	6.65		12.45	16.50
6160	1-1/4" iron pipe size	G		140	.114		6.20	6.90		13.10	17.35
6170	1-1/2" iron pipe size	G		140	.114		7.10	6.90		14	18.30
6180	2" iron pipe size	G		135	.119		7.45	7.15		14.60	19.10
6190	2-1/2" iron pipe size	G		135	.119		8.95	7.15		16.10	21
6200	3" iron pipe size	G		130	.123		8.20	7.45		15.65	20.50
6210	4" iron pipe size	G		125	.128		9.50	7.75		17.25	22.50
6220	5" iron pipe size	G		120	.133		11.90	8.05		19.95	25.50
6230	6" iron pipe size	G		115	.139		11.80	8.40		20.20	26
6240	7" iron pipe size	G		110	.145		12.80	8.80		21.60	27.50

22 07 Plumbing Insulation

22 07 19 – Plumbing Piping Insulation

22 07 19.10 Piping Insulation		Crew	Daily Output	Labor-Hours	Unit	Material	2024 Bare Costs Labor	Equipment	Total	Total Incl O&P
6250	8" iron pipe size	Q-14 G	105	.152	L.F.	15.45	9.20		24.65	31
6260	9" iron pipe size	G	100	.160		15.95	9.65		25.60	32.50
6270	10" iron pipe size	G	95	.168		17.70	10.15		27.85	35
6280	12" iron pipe size	G	90	.178		19.65	10.75		30.40	38
6290	14" iron pipe size	G	85	.188		21.50	11.35		32.85	41.50
6300	16" iron pipe size	G	80	.200		24	12.10		36.10	44.50
6310	18" iron pipe size	G	75	.213		26	12.90		38.90	48
6320	20" iron pipe size	G	65	.246		32	14.85		46.85	57.50
6330	22" iron pipe size	G	60	.267		35.50	16.10		51.60	63.50
6340	24" iron pipe size	G	55	.291		36	17.55		53.55	67
6360	3" wall, 1/2" iron pipe size	G	115	.139		19.25	8.40		27.65	34
6380	3/4" iron pipe size	G	115	.139		19.35	8.40		27.75	34.50
6390	1" iron pipe size	G	115	.139		19.50	8.40		27.90	34.50
6400	1-1/4" iron pipe size	G	110	.145		19.80	8.80		28.60	35.50
6410	1-1/2" iron pipe size	G	110	.145		19.80	8.80		28.60	35.50
6420	2" iron pipe size	G	105	.152		20.50	9.20		29.70	36.50
6430	2-1/2" iron pipe size	G	105	.152		24	9.20		33.20	40.50
6440	3" iron pipe size	G	100	.160		24.50	9.65		34.15	41.50
6450	4" iron pipe size	G	95	.168		31	10.15		41.15	50
6460	5" iron pipe size	G	90	.178		34	10.75		44.75	53.50
6470	6" iron pipe size	G	90	.178		38	10.75		48.75	58.50
6480	7" iron pipe size	G	85	.188		42	11.35		53.35	64
6490	8" iron pipe size	G	85	.188		8.20	11.35		19.55	26.50
6500	9" iron pipe size	G	80	.200		51.50	12.10		63.60	75
6510	10" iron pipe size	G	75	.213		54.50	12.90		67.40	79.50
6520	12" iron pipe size	G	70	.229		60.50	13.80		74.30	87.50
6530	14" iron pipe size	G	65	.246		67.50	14.85		82.35	97
6540	16" iron pipe size	G	60	.267		75	16.10		91.10	107
6550	18" iron pipe size	G	55	.291		82	17.55		99.55	118
6560	20" iron pipe size	G	50	.320		98	19.35		117.35	138
6570	22" iron pipe size	G	45	.356		106	21.50		127.50	149
6580	24" iron pipe size	G	40	.400		114	24		138	162
6600	Fiberglass, with all service jacket									
6640	1/2" wall, 1/2" iron pipe size	Q-14 G	250	.064	L.F.	1.87	3.87		5.74	7.95
6660	3/4" iron pipe size	G	240	.067		2.16	4.03		6.19	8.55
6670	1" iron pipe size	G	230	.070		2.24	4.20		6.44	8.85
6680	1-1/4" iron pipe size	G	220	.073		2.37	4.39		6.76	9.30
6690	1-1/2" iron pipe size	G	220	.073		2.75	4.39		7.14	9.75
6700	2" iron pipe size	G	210	.076		2.93	4.60		7.53	10.20
6710	2-1/2" iron pipe size	G	200	.080		3.08	4.83		7.91	10.75
6840	1" wall, 1/2" iron pipe size	G	240	.067		2.31	4.03		6.34	8.70
6860	3/4" iron pipe size	G	230	.070		2.54	4.20		6.74	9.20
6870	1" iron pipe size	G	220	.073		2.66	4.39		7.05	9.65
6880	1-1/4" iron pipe size	G	210	.076		2.94	4.60		7.54	10.25
6890	1-1/2" iron pipe size	G	210	.076		3.17	4.60		7.77	10.50
6900	2" iron pipe size	G	200	.080		3.40	4.83		8.23	11.10
6910	2-1/2" iron pipe size	G	190	.084		3.83	5.10		8.93	11.95
6920	3" iron pipe size	G	180	.089		4.11	5.35		9.46	12.70
6930	3-1/2" iron pipe size	G	170	.094		4.11	5.70		9.81	13.15
6940	4" iron pipe size	G	150	.107		5.20	6.45		11.65	15.50
6950	5" iron pipe size	G	140	.114		5.85	6.90		12.75	16.95
6960	6" iron pipe size	G	120	.133		6.30	8.05		14.35	19.15
6970	7" iron pipe size	G	110	.145		8.75	8.80		17.55	23

22 07 Plumbing Insulation

22 07 19 – Plumbing Piping Insulation

22 07 19.10 Piping Insulation		Crew	Daily Output	Labor-Hours	Unit	Material	2024 Bare Costs Labor	Equipment	Total	Total Incl O&P
6980	8" iron pipe size	Q-14	100	.160	L.F.	10.40	9.65		20.05	26
6990	9" iron pipe size	G	90	.178		11.40	10.75		22.15	29
7000	10" iron pipe size	G	90	.178		11.65	10.75		22.40	29
7010	12" iron pipe size	G	80	.200		12.95	12.10		25.05	32.50
7020	14" iron pipe size	G	80	.200		14.45	12.10		26.55	34.50
7030	16" iron pipe size	G	70	.229		19.55	13.80		33.35	42.50
7040	18" iron pipe size	G	70	.229		22	13.80		35.80	45
7050	20" iron pipe size	G	60	.267		26.50	16.10		42.60	53.50
7060	24" iron pipe size	G	60	.267		34.50	16.10		50.60	62.50
7080	1-1/2" wall, 1/2" iron pipe size	G	230	.070		4.14	4.20		8.34	10.95
7100	3/4" iron pipe size	G	220	.073		4.24	4.39		8.63	11.35
7110	1" iron pipe size	G	210	.076		4.49	4.60		9.09	11.95
7120	1-1/4" iron pipe size	G	200	.080		4.91	4.83		9.74	12.75
7130	1-1/2" iron pipe size	G	200	.080		5.10	4.83		9.93	12.95
7140	2" iron pipe size	G	190	.084		5.65	5.10		10.75	14
7150	2-1/2" iron pipe size	G	180	.089		6.05	5.35		11.40	14.85
7160	3" iron pipe size	G	170	.094		6.30	5.70		12	15.55
7170	3-1/2" iron pipe size	G	160	.100		7.40	6.05		13.45	17.35
7180	4" iron pipe size	G	140	.114		7.10	6.90		14	18.30
7190	5" iron pipe size	G	130	.123		7.85	7.45		15.30	20
7200	6" iron pipe size	G	110	.145		8.40	8.80		17.20	22.50
7210	7" iron pipe size	G	100	.160		11.40	9.65		21.05	27.50
7220	8" iron pipe size	G	90	.178		12.45	10.75		23.20	30
7230	9" iron pipe size	G	85	.188		13.35	11.35		24.70	32
7240	10" iron pipe size	G	80	.200		13.85	12.10		25.95	33.50
7250	12" iron pipe size	G	75	.213		16.05	12.90		28.95	37.50
7260	14" iron pipe size	G	70	.229		17.95	13.80		31.75	41
7270	16" iron pipe size	G	65	.246		24	14.85		38.85	48.50
7280	18" iron pipe size	G	60	.267		30	16.10		46.10	57.50
7290	20" iron pipe size	G	55	.291		31.50	17.55		49.05	62
7300	24" iron pipe size	G	50	.320		38.50	19.35		57.85	72
7320	2" wall, 1/2" iron pipe size	G	220	.073		6.40	4.39		10.79	13.75
7340	3/4" iron pipe size	G	210	.076		6.65	4.60		11.25	14.35
7350	1" iron pipe size	G	200	.080		7.15	4.83		11.98	15.20
7360	1-1/4" iron pipe size	G	190	.084		7.55	5.10		12.65	16.05
7370	1-1/2" iron pipe size	G	190	.084		7.45	5.10		12.55	15.95
7380	2" iron pipe size	G	180	.089		7.85	5.35		13.20	16.85
7390	2-1/2" iron pipe size	G	170	.094		8.50	5.70		14.20	18
7400	3" iron pipe size	G	160	.100		8.95	6.05		15	19.05
7410	3-1/2" iron pipe size	G	150	.107		8.95	6.45		15.40	19.65
7420	4" iron pipe size	G	130	.123		10.45	7.45		17.90	23
7430	5" iron pipe size	G	120	.133		11.95	8.05		20	25.50
7440	6" iron pipe size	G	100	.160		10.20	9.65		19.85	26
7450	7" iron pipe size	G	90	.178		15	10.75		25.75	33
7460	8" iron pipe size	G	80	.200		15	12.10		27.10	35
7470	9" iron pipe size	G	75	.213		15.70	12.90		28.60	37
7480	10" iron pipe size	G	70	.229		18	13.80		31.80	41
7490	12" iron pipe size	G	65	.246		20.50	14.85		35.35	45
7500	14" iron pipe size	G	60	.267		26.50	16.10		42.60	53.50
7510	16" iron pipe size	G	55	.291		38.50	17.55		56.05	69.50
7520	18" iron pipe size	G	50	.320		63.50	19.35		82.85	99.50
7530	20" iron pipe size	G	45	.356		46.50	21.50		68	83.50
7540	24" iron pipe size	G	40	.400		52	24		76	94.50

22 07 Plumbing Insulation

22 07 19 – Plumbing Piping Insulation

22 07 19.10 Piping Insulation		Crew	Daily Output	Labor-Hours	Unit	Material	2024 Bare Costs Labor	Equipment	Total	Total Incl O&P
7560	2-1/2" wall, 1/2" iron pipe size G	Q-14	210	.076	L.F.	6.95	4.60		11.55	14.65
7562	3/4" iron pipe size G		200	.080		10.10	4.83		14.93	18.45
7564	1" iron pipe size G		190	.084		10.55	5.10		15.65	19.35
7566	1-1/4" iron pipe size G		185	.086		13.85	5.20		19.05	23
7568	1-1/2" iron pipe size G		180	.089		17	5.35		22.35	27
7570	2" iron pipe size G		170	.094		9.10	5.70		14.80	18.65
7572	2-1/2" iron pipe size G		160	.100		10.45	6.05		16.50	20.50
7574	3" iron pipe size G		150	.107		14.60	6.45		21.05	26
7576	3-1/2" iron pipe size G		140	.114		11.45	6.90		18.35	23
7578	4" iron pipe size G		120	.133		12.65	8.05		20.70	26
7580	5" iron pipe size G		110	.145		8.35	8.80		17.15	22.50
7582	6" iron pipe size G		90	.178		18.15	10.75		28.90	36.50
7584	7" iron pipe size G		80	.200		24	12.10		36.10	45
7586	8" iron pipe size G		70	.229		25.50	13.80		39.30	49
7588	9" iron pipe size G		65	.246		20	14.85		34.85	45
7590	10" iron pipe size G		60	.267		22	16.10		38.10	48.50
7592	12" iron pipe size G		55	.291		26.50	17.55		44.05	56.50
7594	14" iron pipe size G		50	.320		31.50	19.35		50.85	64.50
7596	16" iron pipe size G		45	.356		36.50	21.50		58	72.50
7598	18" iron pipe size G		40	.400		39.50	24		63.50	80.50
7602	24" iron pipe size G		30	.533		52	32		84	107
7620	3" wall, 1/2" iron pipe size G		200	.080		12.40	4.83		17.23	21
7622	3/4" iron pipe size G		190	.084		13.05	5.10		18.15	22
7624	1" iron pipe size G		180	.089		14.55	5.35		19.90	24
7626	1-1/4" iron pipe size G		175	.091		17.15	5.50		22.65	27.50
7628	1-1/2" iron pipe size G		170	.094		14.75	5.70		20.45	25
7630	2" iron pipe size G		160	.100		15.80	6.05		21.85	26.50
7632	2-1/2" iron pipe size G		150	.107		16.45	6.45		22.90	28
7634	3" iron pipe size G		140	.114		13.35	6.90		20.25	25
7636	3-1/2" iron pipe size G		130	.123		20.50	7.45		27.95	34
7638	4" iron pipe size G		110	.145		15.80	8.80		24.60	31
7640	5" iron pipe size G		100	.160		17.90	9.65		27.55	34.50
7642	6" iron pipe size G		80	.200		19.15	12.10		31.25	39.50
7644	7" iron pipe size G		70	.229		21	13.80		34.80	44
7646	8" iron pipe size G		60	.267		24	16.10		40.10	51
7648	9" iron pipe size G		55	.291		24.50	17.55		42.05	54
7650	10" iron pipe size G		50	.320		28	19.35		47.35	60.50
7652	12" iron pipe size G		45	.356		35	21.50		56.50	71
7654	14" iron pipe size G		40	.400		79	24		103	124
7656	16" iron pipe size G		35	.457		60.50	27.50		88	109
7658	18" iron pipe size G		32	.500		65	30		95	118
7660	20" iron pipe size G		30	.533		50.50	32		82.50	105
7662	24" iron pipe size G		28	.571		108	34.50		142.50	171
7664	26" iron pipe size G		26	.615		70.50	37		107.50	134
7666	30" iron pipe size G		24	.667		73.50	40.50		114	143
7800	For fiberglass with standard canvas jacket, deduct					5%				
7802	For fittings, add 3 L.F. for each fitting									
7804	plus 4 L.F. for each flange of the fitting									
7820	Polyethylene tubing flexible closed cell foam, UV resistant									
7828	Standard temperature (-90°F to +212°F)									
7830	3/8" wall, 1/8" iron pipe size G	1 Asbe	130	.062	L.F.	.52	4.13		4.65	6.85
7831	1/4" iron pipe size G		130	.062		.53	4.13		4.66	6.90
7832	3/8" iron pipe size G		130	.062		.49	4.13		4.62	6.85

22 07 Plumbing Insulation

22 07 19 – Plumbing Piping Insulation

22 07 19.10 Piping Insulation		Crew	Daily Output	Labor-Hours	Unit	Material	2024 Bare Costs Labor	Equipment	Total	Total Incl O&P
7833	1/2" iron pipe size G	1 Asbe	126	.063	L.F.	.68	4.26		4.94	7.25
7834	3/4" iron pipe size G		122	.066		.67	4.40		5.07	7.45
7835	1" iron pipe size G		120	.067		.86	4.47		5.33	7.75
7836	1-1/4" iron pipe size G		118	.068		1.09	4.55		5.64	8.15
7837	1-1/2" iron pipe size G		118	.068		1.13	4.55		5.68	8.20
7838	2" iron pipe size G		116	.069		1.80	4.63		6.43	9.05
7839	2-1/2" iron pipe size G		114	.070		1.74	4.71		6.45	9.10
7840	3" iron pipe size G		112	.071		3.54	4.79		8.33	11.20
7842	1/2" wall, 1/8" iron pipe size G		120	.067		.61	4.47		5.08	7.45
7843	1/4" iron pipe size G		120	.067		.81	4.47		5.28	7.70
7844	3/8" iron pipe size G		120	.067		.86	4.47		5.33	7.75
7845	1/2" iron pipe size G		118	.068		.99	4.55		5.54	8.05
7846	3/4" iron pipe size G		116	.069		1.01	4.63		5.64	8.15
7847	1" iron pipe size G		114	.070		1.05	4.71		5.76	8.35
7848	1-1/4" iron pipe size G		112	.071		1.22	4.79		6.01	8.65
7849	1-1/2" iron pipe size G		110	.073		1.34	4.88		6.22	8.90
7850	2" iron pipe size G		108	.074		2.54	4.97		7.51	10.35
7851	2-1/2" iron pipe size G		106	.075		3.27	5.05		8.32	11.30
7852	3" iron pipe size G		104	.077		4.27	5.15		9.42	12.55
7853	3-1/2" iron pipe size G		102	.078		4.78	5.25		10.03	13.25
7854	4" iron pipe size G		100	.080		5.70	5.35		11.05	14.45
7855	3/4" wall, 1/8" iron pipe size G		110	.073		.93	4.88		5.81	8.45
7856	1/4" iron pipe size G		110	.073		1.01	4.88		5.89	8.55
7857	3/8" iron pipe size G		108	.074		1.42	4.97		6.39	9.10
7858	1/2" iron pipe size G		106	.075		1.68	5.05		6.73	9.55
7859	3/4" iron pipe size G		104	.077		1.99	5.15		7.14	10.05
7860	1" iron pipe size G		102	.078		2.34	5.25		7.59	10.55
7861	1-1/4" iron pipe size G		100	.080		2.59	5.35		7.94	11.05
7862	1-1/2" iron pipe size G		100	.080		3.28	5.35		8.63	11.80
7863	2" iron pipe size G		98	.082		4.50	5.50		10	13.30
7864	2-1/2" iron pipe size G		96	.083		5.70	5.60		11.30	14.75
7865	3" iron pipe size G		94	.085		5.60	5.70		11.30	14.85
7866	3-1/2" iron pipe size G		92	.087		8	5.85		13.85	17.70
7867	4" iron pipe size G		90	.089		8.95	5.95		14.90	18.95
7868	1" wall, 1/4" iron pipe size G		100	.080		2.45	5.35		7.80	10.90
7869	3/8" iron pipe size G		98	.082		2.31	5.50		7.81	10.90
7870	1/2" iron pipe size G		96	.083		3.10	5.60		8.70	11.90
7871	3/4" iron pipe size G		94	.085		3.54	5.70		9.24	12.60
7872	1" iron pipe size G		92	.087		4.33	5.85		10.18	13.65
7873	1-1/4" iron pipe size G		90	.089		4.90	5.95		10.85	14.50
7874	1-1/2" iron pipe size G		90	.089		6.05	5.95		12	15.75
7875	2" iron pipe size G		88	.091		7.25	6.10		13.35	17.30
7876	2-1/2" iron pipe size G		86	.093		10.05	6.25		16.30	20.50
7877	3" iron pipe size G		84	.095		10.85	6.40		17.25	21.50
7878	Contact cement, quart can G				Ea.	18.10			18.10	19.95
7879	Rubber tubing, flexible closed cell foam									
7880	3/8" wall, 1/4" iron pipe size G	1 Asbe	120	.067	L.F.	.70	4.47		5.17	7.55
7900	3/8" iron pipe size G		120	.067		.75	4.47		5.22	7.65
7910	1/2" iron pipe size G		115	.070		.87	4.67		5.54	8.05
7920	3/4" iron pipe size G		115	.070		.96	4.67		5.63	8.15
7930	1" iron pipe size G		110	.073		1.09	4.88		5.97	8.65
7940	1-1/4" iron pipe size G		110	.073		1.36	4.88		6.24	8.95
7950	1-1/2" iron pipe size G		110	.073		1.53	4.88		6.41	9.15

22 07 Plumbing Insulation

22 07 19 – Plumbing Piping Insulation

22 07 19.10 Piping Insulation		Crew	Daily Output	Labor-Hours	Unit	Material	2024 Bare Costs Labor	Equipment	Total	Total Incl O&P
8100	1/2" wall, 1/4" iron pipe size G	1 Asbe	90	.089	L.F.	1.06	5.95		7.01	10.25
8120	3/8" iron pipe size G		90	.089		1.13	5.95		7.08	10.35
8130	1/2" iron pipe size G		89	.090		1.25	6.05		7.30	10.60
8140	3/4" iron pipe size G		89	.090		1.43	6.05		7.48	10.75
8150	1" iron pipe size G		88	.091		1.56	6.10		7.66	11
8160	1-1/4" iron pipe size G		87	.092		1.72	6.15		7.87	11.30
8170	1-1/2" iron pipe size G		87	.092		1.97	6.15		8.12	11.55
8180	2" iron pipe size G		86	.093		2.52	6.25		8.77	12.25
8190	2-1/2" iron pipe size G		86	.093		4.80	6.25		11.05	14.80
8200	3" iron pipe size G		85	.094		5.65	6.30		11.95	15.85
8210	3-1/2" iron pipe size G		85	.094		7.15	6.30		13.45	17.50
8220	4" iron pipe size G		80	.100		7.80	6.70		14.50	18.85
8230	5" iron pipe size G		80	.100		9.95	6.70		16.65	21
8240	6" iron pipe size G		75	.107		9.95	7.15		17.10	22
8300	3/4" wall, 1/4" iron pipe size G		90	.089		1.76	5.95		7.71	11.05
8320	3/8" iron pipe size G		90	.089		1.74	5.95		7.69	11
8330	1/2" iron pipe size G		89	.090		1.90	6.05		7.95	11.30
8340	3/4" iron pipe size G		89	.090		2.28	6.05		8.33	11.70
8350	1" iron pipe size G		88	.091		3.04	6.10		9.14	12.65
8360	1-1/4" iron pipe size G		87	.092		3.17	6.15		9.32	12.90
8370	1-1/2" iron pipe size G		87	.092		4.21	6.15		10.36	14.05
8380	2" iron pipe size G		86	.093		5.10	6.25		11.35	15.15
8390	2-1/2" iron pipe size G		86	.093		6.25	6.25		12.50	16.40
8400	3" iron pipe size G		85	.094		6.95	6.30		13.25	17.25
8410	3-1/2" iron pipe size G		85	.094		7.75	6.30		14.05	18.10
8420	4" iron pipe size G		80	.100		8.85	6.70		15.55	20
8430	5" iron pipe size G		80	.100		15.20	6.70		21.90	27
8440	6" iron pipe size G		80	.100		21	6.70		27.70	33.50
8444	1" wall, 1/2" iron pipe size G		86	.093		3.73	6.25		9.98	13.60
8445	3/4" iron pipe size G		84	.095		4.60	6.40		11	14.80
8446	1" iron pipe size G		84	.095		5.10	6.40		11.50	15.35
8447	1-1/4" iron pipe size G		82	.098		5.90	6.55		12.45	16.50
8448	1-1/2" iron pipe size G		82	.098		6.55	6.55		13.10	17.20
8449	2" iron pipe size G		80	.100		7.85	6.70		14.55	18.90
8450	2-1/2" iron pipe size G	▼	80	.100	▼	8.50	6.70		15.20	19.60
8456	Rubber insulation tape, 1/8" x 2" x 30' G				Ea.	16.25			16.25	17.85
8460	Polyolefin tubing, flexible closed cell foam, UV stabilized, work									
8462	temp. -165°F to +210°F, 0 water vapor transmission									
8464	3/8" wall, 1/8" iron pipe size G	1 Asbe	140	.057	L.F.	.48	3.83		4.31	6.40
8466	1/4" iron pipe size G		140	.057		.50	3.83		4.33	6.40
8468	3/8" iron pipe size G		140	.057		.56	3.83		4.39	6.45
8470	1/2" iron pipe size G		136	.059		.62	3.95		4.57	6.70
8472	3/4" iron pipe size G		132	.061		.62	4.07		4.69	6.90
8474	1" iron pipe size G		130	.062		.83	4.13		4.96	7.20
8476	1-1/4" iron pipe size G		128	.063		1.02	4.19		5.21	7.50
8478	1-1/2" iron pipe size G		128	.063		1.24	4.19		5.43	7.75
8480	2" iron pipe size G		126	.063		1.50	4.26		5.76	8.15
8482	2-1/2" iron pipe size G		123	.065		2.18	4.36		6.54	9.05
8484	3" iron pipe size G		121	.066		2.42	4.44		6.86	9.40
8486	4" iron pipe size G		118	.068		6.40	4.55		10.95	14
8500	1/2" wall, 1/8" iron pipe size G		130	.062		.70	4.13		4.83	7.05
8502	1/4" iron pipe size G		130	.062		.76	4.13		4.89	7.15
8504	3/8" iron pipe size G	▼	130	.062	▼	.82	4.13		4.95	7.20

For customer support on your Plumbing Costs with RSMeans Data call 800.448.8182.

22 07 Plumbing Insulation

22 07 19 – Plumbing Piping Insulation

22 07 19.10 Piping Insulation		Crew	Daily Output	Labor-Hours	Unit	Material	2024 Bare Costs Labor	2024 Bare Costs Equipment	Total	Total Incl O&P
8506	1/2" iron pipe size G	1 Asbe	128	.063	L.F.	.88	4.19		5.07	7.35
8508	3/4" iron pipe size G		126	.063		1.03	4.26		5.29	7.65
8510	1" iron pipe size G		123	.065		1.18	4.36		5.54	7.95
8512	1-1/4" iron pipe size G		121	.066		1.39	4.44		5.83	8.30
8514	1-1/2" iron pipe size G		119	.067		1.67	4.51		6.18	8.70
8516	2" iron pipe size G		117	.068		2.11	4.59		6.70	9.30
8518	2-1/2" iron pipe size G		114	.070		2.86	4.71		7.57	10.35
8520	3" iron pipe size G		112	.071		3.72	4.79		8.51	11.40
8522	4" iron pipe size G		110	.073		5.15	4.88		10.03	13.10
8534	3/4" wall, 1/8" iron pipe size G		120	.067		1.08	4.47		5.55	8
8536	1/4" iron pipe size G		120	.067		1.14	4.47		5.61	8.05
8538	3/8" iron pipe size G		117	.068		1.31	4.59		5.90	8.45
8540	1/2" iron pipe size G		114	.070		1.45	4.71		6.16	8.80
8542	3/4" iron pipe size G		112	.071		1.57	4.79		6.36	9.05
8544	1" iron pipe size G		110	.073		2.20	4.88		7.08	9.85
8546	1-1/4" iron pipe size G		108	.074		2.94	4.97		7.91	10.80
8548	1-1/2" iron pipe size G		108	.074		3.44	4.97		8.41	11.35
8550	2" iron pipe size G		106	.075		4.35	5.05		9.40	12.50
8552	2-1/2" iron pipe size G		104	.077		5.50	5.15		10.65	13.90
8554	3" iron pipe size G		102	.078		6.85	5.25		12.10	15.50
8556	4" iron pipe size G		100	.080		9	5.35		14.35	18.10
8570	1" wall, 1/8" iron pipe size G		110	.073		1.95	4.88		6.83	9.60
8572	1/4" iron pipe size G		108	.074		3.89	4.97		8.86	11.85
8574	3/8" iron pipe size G		106	.075		2.24	5.05		7.29	10.15
8576	1/2" iron pipe size G		104	.077		2.16	5.15		7.31	10.25
8578	3/4" iron pipe size G		102	.078		3.02	5.25		8.27	11.30
8580	1" iron pipe size G		100	.080		3.27	5.35		8.62	11.80
8582	1-1/4" iron pipe size G		97	.082		4.08	5.55		9.63	12.95
8584	1-1/2" iron pipe size G		97	.082		4.25	5.55		9.80	13.15
8586	2" iron pipe size G		95	.084		6	5.65		11.65	15.20
8588	2-1/2" iron pipe size G		93	.086		7.85	5.75		13.60	17.40
8590	3" iron pipe size G		91	.088		9.55	5.90		15.45	19.50
8606	Contact adhesive (R-320) G				Qt.	28.50			28.50	31.50
8608	Contact adhesive (R-320) G				Gal.	114			114	125
8610	NOTE: Preslit/preglued vs. unslit, same price									

22 07 19.30 Piping Insulation Protective Jacketing, PVC

0010	**PIPING INSULATION PROTECTIVE JACKETING, PVC**									
0100	PVC, white, 48" lengths cut from roll goods									
0120	20 mil thick									
0140	Size based on OD of insulation									
0150	1-1/2" ID	Q-14	270	.059	L.F.	2.23	3.58		5.81	7.90
0152	2" ID		260	.062		2.31	3.72		6.03	8.20
0154	2-1/2" ID		250	.064		2.43	3.87		6.30	8.55
0156	3" ID		240	.067		2.49	4.03		6.52	8.90
0158	3-1/2" ID		230	.070		2.65	4.20		6.85	9.30
0160	4" ID		220	.073		3	4.39		7.39	10
0162	4-1/2" ID		210	.076		3.20	4.60		7.80	10.50
0164	5" ID		200	.080		3.42	4.83		8.25	11.10
0166	5-1/2" ID		190	.084		3.68	5.10		8.78	11.80
0168	6" ID		180	.089		3.68	5.35		9.03	12.25
0170	6-1/2" ID		175	.091		4.21	5.50		9.71	13.05
0172	7" ID		170	.094		4.21	5.70		9.91	13.30

22 07 Plumbing Insulation

22 07 19 – Plumbing Piping Insulation

22 07 19.30 Piping Insulation Protective Jacketing, PVC		Crew	Daily Output	Labor-Hours	Unit	Material	2024 Bare Costs Labor	Equipment	Total	Total Incl O&P
0174	7-1/2" ID	Q-14	164	.098	L.F.	4.72	5.90		10.62	14.20
0176	8" ID		161	.099		4.72	6		10.72	14.35
0178	8-1/2" ID		158	.101		5.10	6.10		11.20	14.95
0180	9" ID		155	.103		5.10	6.25		11.35	15.15
0182	9-1/2" ID		152	.105		5.55	6.35		11.90	15.80
0184	10" ID		149	.107		5.55	6.50		12.05	16
0186	10-1/2" ID		146	.110		5.85	6.60		12.45	16.55
0188	11" ID		143	.112		5.85	6.75		12.60	16.75
0190	11-1/2" ID		140	.114		6.15	6.90		13.05	17.25
0192	12" ID		137	.117		6.15	7.05		13.20	17.50
0194	12-1/2" ID		134	.119		7.10	7.20		14.30	18.80
0195	13" ID		132	.121		7.10	7.30		14.40	18.95
0196	13-1/2" ID		132	.121		7.30	7.30		14.60	19.20
0198	14" ID		130	.123		7.30	7.45		14.75	19.40
0200	15" ID		128	.125		7.70	7.55		15.25	20
0202	16" ID		126	.127		8.15	7.65		15.80	20.50
0204	17" ID		124	.129		9.20	7.80		17	22
0206	18" ID		122	.131		8.80	7.90		16.70	21.50
0208	19" ID		120	.133		9.05	8.05		17.10	22
0210	20" ID		118	.136		9.60	8.20		17.80	23
0212	21" ID		116	.138		9.95	8.35		18.30	23.50
0214	22" ID		114	.140		10.60	8.50		19.10	24.50
0216	23" ID		112	.143		11.25	8.65		19.90	25.50
0218	24" ID		110	.145		12.05	8.80		20.85	26.50
0220	25" ID		108	.148		12.90	8.95		21.85	28
0222	26" ID		106	.151		13.80	9.10		22.90	29
0224	27" ID		104	.154		6	9.30		15.30	21
0226	28" ID		102	.157		6.20	9.45		15.65	21.50
0228	29" ID		100	.160		6.45	9.65		16.10	22
0230	30" ID	▼	98	.163	▼	6.65	9.85		16.50	22.50
0300	For colors, add				Ea.	10%				
1000	30 mil thick									
1010	Size based on OD of insulation									
1020	2" ID	Q-14	260	.062	L.F.	2.48	3.72		6.20	8.40
1022	2-1/2" ID		250	.064		2.82	3.87		6.69	9
1024	3" ID		240	.067		3.10	4.03		7.13	9.55
1026	3-1/2" ID		230	.070		3.51	4.20		7.71	10.25
1028	4" ID		220	.073		3.88	4.39		8.27	10.95
1030	4-1/2" ID		210	.076		4.24	4.60		8.84	11.65
1032	5" ID		200	.080		4.75	4.83		9.58	12.60
1034	5-1/2" ID		190	.084		5.05	5.10		10.15	13.35
1036	6" ID		180	.089		5.50	5.35		10.85	14.25
1038	6-1/2" ID		175	.091		5.95	5.50		11.45	14.90
1040	7" ID		170	.094		6.45	5.70		12.15	15.70
1042	7-1/2" ID		164	.098		6.55	5.90		12.45	16.20
1044	8" ID		161	.099		7.05	6		13.05	16.95
1046	8-1/2" ID		158	.101		7.35	6.10		13.45	17.35
1048	9" ID		155	.103		7.75	6.25		14	18.05
1050	9-1/2" ID		152	.105		8	6.35		14.35	18.50
1052	10" ID		149	.107		8.55	6.50		15.05	19.30
1054	10-1/2" ID		146	.110		8.80	6.60		15.40	19.80
1056	11" ID		143	.112		9.30	6.75		16.05	20.50
1058	11-1/2" ID	▼	140	.114	▼	9.90	6.90		16.80	21.50

22 07 Plumbing Insulation

22 07 19 – Plumbing Piping Insulation

22 07 19.30 Piping Insulation Protective Jacketing, PVC		Crew	Daily Output	Labor-Hours	Unit	Material	2024 Bare Costs Labor	Equipment	Total	Total Incl O&P
1060	12" ID	Q-14	137	.117	L.F.	10.20	7.05		17.25	22
1062	12-1/2" ID		134	.119		10.35	7.20		17.55	22.50
1063	13" ID		132	.121		10.70	7.30		18	23
1064	13-1/2" ID		132	.121		10.75	7.30		18.05	23
1066	14" ID		130	.123		10.95	7.45		18.40	23.50
1068	15" ID		128	.125		11.50	7.55		19.05	24
1070	16" ID		126	.127		13.10	7.65		20.75	26
1072	17" ID		124	.129		14.35	7.80		22.15	27.50
1074	18" ID		122	.131		14.65	7.90		22.55	28
1076	19" ID		120	.133		15.40	8.05		23.45	29
1078	20" ID		118	.136		15.75	8.20		23.95	30
1080	21" ID		116	.138		16.75	8.35		25.10	31
1082	22" ID		114	.140		17.85	8.50		26.35	32.50
1084	23" ID		112	.143		19.05	8.65		27.70	34
1086	24" ID		110	.145		20.50	8.80		29.30	36
1088	25" ID		108	.148		22	8.95		30.95	37.50
1090	26" ID		106	.151		23.50	9.10		32.60	40
1092	27" ID		104	.154		9.05	9.30		18.35	24
1094	28" ID		102	.157		9.35	9.45		18.80	25
1096	29" ID		100	.160		9.70	9.65		19.35	25.50
1098	30" ID		98	.163		10	9.85		19.85	26
1300	For colors, add				Ea.	10%				
2000	PVC, white, fitting covers									
2020	Fiberglass insulation inserts included with sizes 1-3/4" thru 9-3/4"									
2030	Size is based on OD of insulation									
2040	90° elbow fitting									
2060	1-3/4"	Q-14	135	.119	Ea.	1.59	7.15		8.74	12.65
2062	2"		130	.123		1.59	7.45		9.04	13.10
2064	2-1/4"		128	.125		1.82	7.55		9.37	13.50
2068	2-1/2"		126	.127		1.82	7.65		9.47	13.70
2070	2-3/4"		123	.130		2.33	7.85		10.18	14.50
2072	3"		120	.133		2.33	8.05		10.38	14.80
2074	3-3/8"		116	.138		2.91	8.35		11.26	15.90
2076	3-3/4"		113	.142		2.91	8.55		11.46	16.25
2078	4-1/8"		110	.145		3.23	8.80		12.03	16.95
2080	4-3/4"		105	.152		4.11	9.20		13.31	18.50
2082	5-1/4"		100	.160		5.40	9.65		15.05	20.50
2084	5-3/4"		95	.168		9.50	10.15		19.65	26
2086	6-1/4"		90	.178		9.50	10.75		20.25	27
2088	6-3/4"		87	.184		12.50	11.10		23.60	30.50
2090	7-1/4"		85	.188		12.50	11.35		23.85	31
2092	7-3/4"		83	.193		16.05	11.65		27.70	35.50
2094	8-3/4"		80	.200		21.50	12.10		33.60	42
2096	9-3/4"		77	.208		29	12.55		41.55	51
2098	10-7/8"		74	.216		27	13.05		40.05	50
2100	11-7/8"		71	.225		34	13.60		47.60	58
2102	12-7/8"		68	.235		39	14.20		53.20	64.50
2104	14-1/8"		66	.242		48	14.65		62.65	75.50
2106	15-1/8"		64	.250		62	15.10		77.10	91
2108	16-1/8"		63	.254		63	15.35		78.35	93
2110	17-1/8"		62	.258		78	15.60		93.60	110
2112	18-1/8"		61	.262		112	15.85		127.85	148
2114	19-1/8"		60	.267		143	16.10		159.10	182

22 07 Plumbing Insulation

22 07 19 – Plumbing Piping Insulation

22 07 19.30 Piping Insulation Protective Jacketing, PVC

		Crew	Daily Output	Labor-Hours	Unit	Material	2024 Bare Costs Labor	Equipment	Total	Total Incl O&P
2116	20-1/8"	Q-14	59	.271	Ea.	159	16.40		175.40	200
2200	45° elbow fitting									
2220	1-3/4" thru 9-3/4" same price as 90° elbow fitting									
2320	10-7/8"	Q-14	74	.216	Ea.	14.40	13.05		27.45	36
2322	11-7/8"		71	.225		15.90	13.60		29.50	38
2324	12-7/8"		68	.235		17.75	14.20		31.95	41
2326	14-1/8"		66	.242		20.50	14.65		35.15	45
2328	15-1/8"		64	.250		22	15.10		37.10	47
2330	16-1/8"		63	.254		25	15.35		40.35	51
2332	17-1/8"		62	.258		28	15.60		43.60	55
2334	18-1/8"		61	.262		34	15.85		49.85	61.50
2336	19-1/8"		60	.267		46.50	16.10		62.60	76
2338	20-1/8"		59	.271		53	16.40		69.40	83
2400	Tee fitting									
2410	1-3/4"	Q-14	96	.167	Ea.	1.19	10.05		11.24	16.65
2412	2"		94	.170		1.35	10.30		11.65	17.15
2414	2-1/4"		91	.176		1.46	10.60		12.06	17.80
2416	2-1/2"		88	.182		1.59	11		12.59	18.50
2418	2-3/4"		85	.188		1.76	11.35		13.11	19.25
2420	3"		82	.195		3.73	11.80		15.53	22
2422	3-3/8"		79	.203		2.19	12.25		14.44	21
2424	3-3/4"		76	.211		2.72	12.70		15.42	22.50
2426	4-1/8"		73	.219		2.95	13.25		16.20	23.50
2428	4-3/4"		70	.229		3.66	13.80		17.46	25
2430	5-1/4"		67	.239		4.40	14.40		18.80	27
2432	5-3/4"		63	.254		5.85	15.35		21.20	30
2434	6-1/4"		60	.267		7.70	16.10		23.80	33
2436	6-3/4"		59	.271		9.50	16.40		25.90	35.50
2438	7-1/4"		57	.281		15.35	16.95		32.30	43
2440	7-3/4"		54	.296		16.85	17.90		34.75	46
2442	8-3/4"		52	.308		20.50	18.60		39.10	51
2444	9-3/4"		50	.320		24	19.35		43.35	56
2446	10-7/8"		48	.333		24.50	20		44.50	57.50
2448	11-7/8"		47	.340		27	20.50		47.50	61.50
2450	12-7/8"		46	.348		30	21		51	65
2452	14-1/8"		45	.356		32.50	21.50		54	68.50
2454	15-1/8"		44	.364		35.50	22		57.50	72.50
2456	16-1/8"		43	.372		38	22.50		60.50	76
2458	17-1/8"		42	.381		40.50	23		63.50	80
2460	18-1/8"		41	.390		45	23.50		68.50	85.50
2462	19-1/8"		40	.400		49	24		73	91
2464	20-1/8"		39	.410		54	25		79	97.50
4000	Mechanical grooved fitting cover, including insert									
4020	90° elbow fitting									
4030	3/4" & 1"	Q-14	140	.114	Ea.	6.15	6.90		13.05	17.25
4040	1-1/4" & 1-1/2"		135	.119		7.75	7.15		14.90	19.45
4042	2"		130	.123		9.90	7.45		17.35	22
4044	2-1/2"		125	.128		11	7.75		18.75	24
4046	3"		120	.133		12.30	8.05		20.35	26
4048	3-1/2"		115	.139		14.25	8.40		22.65	28.50
4050	4"		110	.145		15.90	8.80		24.70	31
4052	5"		100	.160		19.75	9.65		29.40	36
4054	6"		90	.178		29.50	10.75		40.25	49

22 07 Plumbing Insulation

22 07 19 – Plumbing Piping Insulation

22 07 19.30 Piping Insulation Protective Jacketing, PVC

		Crew	Daily Output	Labor-Hours	Unit	Material	2024 Bare Costs Labor	2024 Bare Costs Equipment	Total	Total Incl O&P
4056	8"	Q-14	80	.200	Ea.	32	12.10		44.10	53.50
4058	10"		75	.213		40.50	12.90		53.40	64
4060	12"		68	.235		58.50	14.20		72.70	86
4062	14"		65	.246		86.50	14.85		101.35	118
4064	16"		63	.254		118	15.35		133.35	154
4066	18"		61	.262		162	15.85		177.85	202
4100	45° elbow fitting									
4120	3/4" & 1"	Q-14	140	.114	Ea.	5.55	6.90		12.45	16.60
4130	1-1/4" & 1-1/2"		135	.119		7.05	7.15		14.20	18.65
4140	2"		130	.123		9.65	7.45		17.10	22
4142	2-1/2"		125	.128		10.75	7.75		18.50	23.50
4144	3"		120	.133		11	8.05		19.05	24.50
4146	3-1/2"		115	.139		14.75	8.40		23.15	29
4148	4"		110	.145		18.10	8.80		26.90	33.50
4150	5"		100	.160		19.25	9.65		28.90	35.50
4152	6"		90	.178		27	10.75		37.75	46
4154	8"		80	.200		28.50	12.10		40.60	49.50
4156	10"		75	.213		36.50	12.90		49.40	59.50
4158	12"		68	.235		54.50	14.20		68.70	81.50
4160	14"		65	.246		74.50	14.85		89.35	105
4162	16"		63	.254		90	15.35		105.35	123
4164	18"		61	.262		143	15.85		158.85	182
4200	Tee fitting									
4220	3/4" & 1"	Q-14	93	.172	Ea.	8.10	10.40		18.50	25
4230	1-1/4" & 1-1/2"		90	.178		10.25	10.75		21	27.50
4240	2"		87	.184		16.50	11.10		27.60	35
4242	2-1/2"		84	.190		18.35	11.50		29.85	37.50
4244	3"		80	.200		19.70	12.10		31.80	40
4246	3-1/2"		77	.208		21	12.55		33.55	42
4248	4"		73	.219		26	13.25		39.25	49
4250	5"		67	.239		32.50	14.40		46.90	58
4252	6"		60	.267		43.50	16.10		59.60	72
4254	8"		54	.296		47	17.90		64.90	79
4256	10"		50	.320		53.50	19.35		72.85	88
4258	12"		46	.348		81.50	21		102.50	122
4260	14"		43	.372		118	22.50		140.50	164
4262	16"		42	.381		121	23		144	168
4264	18"		41	.390		180	23.50		203.50	233

22 07 19.40 Pipe Insulation Protective Jacketing, Aluminum

		Crew	Daily Output	Labor-Hours	Unit	Material	2024 Bare Costs Labor	2024 Bare Costs Equipment	Total	Total Incl O&P
0010	**PIPE INSULATION PROTECTIVE JACKETING, ALUMINUM**									
0100	Metal roll jacketing									
0120	Aluminum with polykraft moisture barrier									
0140	Smooth, based on OD of insulation, .016" thick									
0180	1/2" ID	Q-14	220	.073	L.F.	.37	4.39		4.76	7.10
0190	3/4" ID		215	.074		.48	4.49		4.97	7.40
0200	1" ID		210	.076		.58	4.60		5.18	7.65
0210	1-1/4" ID		205	.078		2.83	4.71		7.54	10.30
0220	1-1/2" ID		202	.079		2.83	4.78		7.61	10.40
0230	1-3/4" ID		199	.080		1.01	4.86		5.87	8.50
0240	2" ID		195	.082		2.74	4.96		7.70	10.55
0250	2-1/4" ID		191	.084		2.74	5.05		7.79	10.70
0260	2-1/2" ID		187	.086		2.74	5.15		7.89	10.85

22 07 Plumbing Insulation

22 07 19 – Plumbing Piping Insulation

22 07 19.40 Pipe Insulation Protective Jacketing, Aluminum		Crew	Daily Output	Labor-Hours	Unit	Material	2024 Bare Costs Labor	Equipment	Total	Total Incl O&P
0270	2-3/4" ID	Q-14	184	.087	L.F.	2.74	5.25		7.99	11
0280	3" ID		180	.089		3.14	5.35		8.49	11.65
0290	3-1/4" ID		176	.091		3.14	5.50		8.64	11.80
0300	3-1/2" ID		172	.093		3.41	5.60		9.01	12.30
0310	3-3/4" ID		169	.095		3.41	5.70		9.11	12.45
0320	4" ID		165	.097		3.75	5.85		9.60	13.05
0330	4-1/4" ID		161	.099		3.90	6		9.90	13.45
0340	4-1/2" ID		157	.102		3.90	6.15		10.05	13.70
0350	4-3/4" ID		154	.104		3.90	6.30		10.20	13.85
0360	5" ID		150	.107		4.32	6.45		10.77	14.55
0370	5-1/4" ID		146	.110		4.32	6.60		10.92	14.85
0380	5-1/2" ID		143	.112		4.99	6.75		11.74	15.80
0390	5-3/4" ID		139	.115		4.99	6.95		11.94	16.10
0400	6" ID		135	.119		4.99	7.15		12.14	16.40
0410	6-1/4" ID		133	.120		4.99	7.25		12.24	16.55
0420	6-1/2" ID		131	.122		5.65	7.40		13.05	17.50
0430	7" ID		128	.125		5.70	7.55		13.25	17.75
0440	7-1/4" ID		125	.128		5.65	7.75		13.40	18.05
0450	7-1/2" ID		123	.130		6.40	7.85		14.25	19
0460	8" ID		121	.132		6.40	8		14.40	19.20
0470	8-1/2" ID		119	.134		7.05	8.10		15.15	20
0480	9" ID		116	.138		7.05	8.35		15.40	20.50
0490	9-1/2" ID		114	.140		7.80	8.50		16.30	21.50
0500	10" ID		112	.143		7.80	8.65		16.45	21.50
0510	10-1/2" ID		110	.145		8.50	8.80		17.30	23
0520	11" ID		107	.150		8.50	9.05		17.55	23
0530	11-1/2" ID		105	.152		9.15	9.20		18.35	24
0540	12" ID		103	.155		9.15	9.40		18.55	24.50
0550	12-1/2" ID		100	.160		10	9.65		19.65	25.50
0560	13" ID		99	.162		10	9.75		19.75	26
0570	14" ID		98	.163		10.70	9.85		20.55	27
0580	15" ID		96	.167		11.40	10.05		21.45	28
0590	16" ID		95	.168		12.25	10.15		22.40	29
0600	17" ID		93	.172		12.30	10.40		22.70	29.50
0610	18" ID		92	.174		13.55	10.50		24.05	31
0620	19" ID		90	.178		13.55	10.75		24.30	31.50
0630	20" ID		89	.180		8.95	10.85		19.80	26.50
0640	21" ID		87	.184		9.40	11.10		20.50	27.50
0650	22" ID		86	.186		9.85	11.25		21.10	28
0660	23" ID		84	.190		10.30	11.50		21.80	29
0670	24" ID	▼	83	.193		10.70	11.65		22.35	29.50
0710	For smooth .020" thick, add					27%	10%			
0720	For smooth .024" thick, add					52%	20%			
0730	For smooth .032" thick, add					104%	33%			
0800	For stucco embossed, add					1%				
0820	For corrugated, add				▼	2.50%				
0900	White aluminum with polysurlyn moisture barrier									
0910	Smooth, % is an add to polykraft lines of same thickness									
0940	For smooth .016" thick, add				L.F.	35%				
0960	For smooth .024" thick, add				"	22%				
1000	Aluminum fitting covers									
1010	Size is based on OD of insulation									
1020	90° LR elbow, 2 piece									

22 07 Plumbing Insulation

22 07 19 – Plumbing Piping Insulation

22 07 19.40 Pipe Insulation Protective Jacketing, Aluminum		Crew	Daily Output	Labor-Hours	Unit	Material	2024 Bare Costs Labor	Equipment	Total	Total Incl O&P
1100	1-1/2"	Q-14	140	.114	Ea.	8.80	6.90		15.70	20
1110	1-3/4"		135	.119		8.80	7.15		15.95	20.50
1120	2"		130	.123		11.10	7.45		18.55	23.50
1130	2-1/4"		128	.125		11.10	7.55		18.65	23.50
1140	2-1/2"		126	.127		11.10	7.65		18.75	24
1150	2-3/4"		123	.130		11.10	7.85		18.95	24
1160	3"		120	.133		12.10	8.05		20.15	25.50
1170	3-1/4"		117	.137		12.10	8.25		20.35	26
1180	3-1/2"		115	.139		14.35	8.40		22.75	28.50
1190	3-3/4"		113	.142		13.95	8.55		22.50	28.50
1200	4"		110	.145		15.80	8.80		24.60	31
1210	4-1/4"		108	.148		15.75	8.95		24.70	31
1220	4-1/2"		106	.151		15.75	9.10		24.85	31
1230	4-3/4"		104	.154		15.75	9.30		25.05	31.50
1240	5"		102	.157		17.70	9.45		27.15	34
1250	5-1/4"		100	.160		20.50	9.65		30.15	37
1260	5-1/2"		97	.165		21	9.95		30.95	38
1270	5-3/4"		95	.168		21	10.15		31.15	38.50
1280	6"		92	.174		21.50	10.50		32	40
1290	6-1/4"		90	.178		21.50	10.75		32.25	40.50
1300	6-1/2"		87	.184		26	11.10		37.10	45.50
1310	7"		85	.188		28	11.35		39.35	48.50
1320	7-1/4"		84	.190		28	11.50		39.50	48.50
1330	7-1/2"		83	.193		31.50	11.65		43.15	52.50
1340	8"		82	.195		31.50	11.80		43.30	52.50
1350	8-1/2"		80	.200		64	12.10		76.10	89
1360	9"		78	.205		64	12.40		76.40	89.50
1370	9-1/2"		77	.208		47.50	12.55		60.05	71
1380	10"		76	.211		47.50	12.70		60.20	71.50
1390	10-1/2"		75	.213		48	12.90		60.90	72.50
1400	11"		74	.216		48	13.05		61.05	73
1410	11-1/2"		72	.222		63.50	13.40		76.90	90.50
1420	12"		71	.225		54.50	13.60		68.10	80.50
1430	12-1/2"		69	.232		77.50	14		91.50	107
1440	13"		68	.235		77.50	14.20		91.70	107
1450	14"		66	.242		94	14.65		108.65	126
1460	15"		64	.250		111	15.10		126.10	145
1470	16"		63	.254		111	15.35		126.35	146
2000	45° elbow, 2 piece									
2010	2-1/2"	Q-14	126	.127	Ea.	9.15	7.65		16.80	22
2020	2-3/4"		123	.130		9.15	7.85		17	22
2030	3"		120	.133		10.45	8.05		18.50	24
2040	3-1/4"		117	.137		10.45	8.25		18.70	24
2050	3-1/2"		115	.139		11.75	8.40		20.15	26
2060	3-3/4"		113	.142		11.75	8.55		20.30	26
2070	4"		110	.145		12.15	8.80		20.95	27
2080	4-1/4"		108	.148		13.65	8.95		22.60	28.50
2090	4-1/2"		106	.151		13.65	9.10		22.75	29
2100	4-3/4"		104	.154		13.65	9.30		22.95	29
2110	5"		102	.157		16.20	9.45		25.65	32.50
2120	5-1/4"		100	.160		16.20	9.65		25.85	32.50
2130	5-1/2"		97	.165		17	9.95		26.95	34
2140	6"		92	.174		17	10.50		27.50	34.50

22 07 Plumbing Insulation

22 07 19 – Plumbing Piping Insulation

22 07 19.40 Pipe Insulation Protective Jacketing, Aluminum		Crew	Daily Output	Labor-Hours	Unit	Material	2024 Bare Costs Labor	Equipment	Total	Total Incl O&P
2150	6-1/2"	Q-14	87	.184	Ea.	23.50	11.10		34.60	42.50
2160	7"		85	.188		23.50	11.35		34.85	43
2170	7-1/2"		83	.193		23.50	11.65		35.15	44
2180	8"		82	.195		23.50	11.80		35.30	44
2190	8-1/2"		80	.200		29.50	12.10		41.60	50.50
2200	9"		78	.205		29.50	12.40		41.90	51
2210	9-1/2"		77	.208		41	12.55		53.55	64
2220	10"		76	.211		41	12.70		53.70	64.50
2230	10-1/2"		75	.213		38	12.90		50.90	61.50
2240	11"		74	.216		38	13.05		51.05	62
2250	11-1/2"		72	.222		45.50	13.40		58.90	70.50
2260	12"		71	.225		45.50	13.60		59.10	70.50
2270	13"		68	.235		53.50	14.20		67.70	80.50
2280	14"		66	.242		65.50	14.65		80.15	94.50
2290	15"		64	.250		65	15.10		80.10	94.50
2300	16"		63	.254		70.50	15.35		85.85	101
2310	17"		62	.258		69	15.60		84.60	99.50
2320	18"		61	.262		78.50	15.85		94.35	111
2330	19"		60	.267		96	16.10		112.10	131
2340	20"		59	.271		93	16.40		109.40	127
2350	21"		58	.276		100	16.65		116.65	136
3000	Tee, 4 piece									
3010	2-1/2"	Q-14	88	.182	Ea.	72	11		83	96
3020	2-3/4"		86	.186		72	11.25		83.25	96
3030	3"		84	.190		81	11.50		92.50	107
3040	3-1/4"		82	.195		81	11.80		92.80	107
3050	3-1/2"		80	.200		85	12.10		97.10	112
3060	4"		78	.205		86	12.40		98.40	113
3070	4-1/4"		76	.211		90	12.70		102.70	118
3080	4-1/2"		74	.216		90	13.05		103.05	119
3090	4-3/4"		72	.222		90	13.40		103.40	120
3100	5"		70	.229		93	13.80		106.80	123
3110	5-1/4"		68	.235		93	14.20		107.20	124
3120	5-1/2"		66	.242		97.50	14.65		112.15	130
3130	6"		64	.250		97.50	15.10		112.60	130
3140	6-1/2"		60	.267		107	16.10		123.10	142
3150	7"		58	.276		107	16.65		123.65	143
3160	7-1/2"		56	.286		119	17.25		136.25	158
3170	8"		54	.296		119	17.90		136.90	159
3180	8-1/2"		52	.308		123	18.60		141.60	164
3190	9"		50	.320		123	19.35		142.35	165
3200	9-1/2"		49	.327		142	19.70		161.70	187
3210	10"		48	.333		142	20		162	188
3220	10-1/2"		47	.340		147	20.50		167.50	193
3230	11"		46	.348		147	21		168	193
3240	11-1/2"		45	.356		151	21.50		172.50	199
3250	12"		44	.364		151	22		173	200
3260	13"		43	.372		157	22.50		179.50	207
3270	14"		42	.381		162	23		185	213
3280	15"		41	.390		190	23.50		213.50	245
3290	16"		40	.400		64.50	24		88.50	108
3300	17"		39	.410		74	25		99	120
3310	18"		38	.421		77	25.50		102.50	124

For customer support on your Plumbing Costs with RSMeans Data call 800.448.8182.

22 07 Plumbing Insulation

22 07 19 – Plumbing Piping Insulation

22 07 19.40 Pipe Insulation Protective Jacketing, Aluminum

		Crew	Daily Output	Labor-Hours	Unit	Material	2024 Bare Costs Labor	Equipment	Total	Total Incl O&P
3320	19"	Q-14	37	.432	Ea.	85	26		111	134
3330	20"		36	.444		86.50	27		113.50	137
3340	22"		35	.457		110	27.50		137.50	163
3350	23"		34	.471		113	28.50		141.50	169
3360	24"		31	.516		116	31		147	176

22 07 19.50 Pipe Insulation Protective Jacketing, St. Stl.

		Crew	Daily Output	Labor-Hours	Unit	Material	2024 Bare Costs Labor	Equipment	Total	Total Incl O&P
0010	**PIPE INSULATION PROTECTIVE JACKETING, STAINLESS STEEL**									
0100	Metal roll jacketing									
0120	Type 304 with moisture barrier									
0140	Smooth, based on OD of insulation, .010" thick									
0260	2-1/2" ID	Q-14	250	.064	L.F.	4.90	3.87		8.77	11.30
0270	2-3/4" ID		245	.065		3.86	3.94		7.80	10.25
0280	3" ID		240	.067		4.17	4.03		8.20	10.75
0290	3-1/4" ID		235	.068		4.53	4.11		8.64	11.25
0300	3-1/2" ID		230	.070		4.80	4.20		9	11.70
0310	3-3/4" ID		225	.071		5.15	4.30		9.45	12.25
0320	4" ID		220	.073		5.45	4.39		9.84	12.70
0330	4-1/4" ID		215	.074		5.75	4.49		10.24	13.20
0340	4-1/2" ID		210	.076		6.05	4.60		10.65	13.70
0350	5" ID		200	.080		6.70	4.83		11.53	14.70
0360	5-1/2" ID		190	.084		7.30	5.10		12.40	15.80
0370	6" ID		180	.089		7.95	5.35		13.30	16.95
0380	6-1/2" ID		175	.091		8.60	5.50		14.10	17.85
0390	7" ID		170	.094		9.25	5.70		14.95	18.80
0400	7-1/2" ID		164	.098		9.85	5.90		15.75	19.80
0410	8" ID		161	.099		10.45	6		16.45	20.50
0420	8-1/2" ID		158	.101		11.10	6.10		17.20	21.50
0430	9" ID		155	.103		11.75	6.25		18	22.50
0440	9-1/2" ID		152	.105		12.35	6.35		18.70	23.50
0450	10" ID		149	.107		13	6.50		19.50	24
0460	10-1/2" ID		146	.110		13.65	6.60		20.25	25
0470	11" ID		143	.112		14.25	6.75		21	26
0480	12" ID		137	.117		15.50	7.05		22.55	28
0490	13" ID		132	.121		16.75	7.30		24.05	29.50
0500	14" ID		130	.123		18	7.45		25.45	31
0700	For smooth .016" thick, add					45%	33%			
1000	Stainless steel, Type 316, fitting covers									
1010	Size is based on OD of insulation									
1020	90° LR elbow, 2 piece									
1100	1-1/2"	Q-14	126	.127	Ea.	14.80	7.65		22.45	28
1110	2-3/4"		123	.130		15.45	7.85		23.30	29
1120	3"		120	.133		16.15	8.05		24.20	30
1130	3-1/4"		117	.137		16.15	8.25		24.40	30.50
1140	3-1/2"		115	.139		16.95	8.40		25.35	31.50
1150	3-3/4"		113	.142		17.95	8.55		26.50	33
1160	4"		110	.145		19.70	8.80		28.50	35
1170	4-1/4"		108	.148		26	8.95		34.95	42.50
1180	4-1/2"		106	.151		26	9.10		35.10	43
1190	5"		102	.157		27	9.45		36.45	44
1200	5-1/2"		97	.165		40	9.95		49.95	59
1210	6"		92	.174		44	10.50		54.50	64
1220	6-1/2"		87	.184		60.50	11.10		71.60	83.50

22 07 Plumbing Insulation

22 07 19 – Plumbing Piping Insulation

22 07 19.50 Pipe Insulation Protective Jacketing, St. Stl.

		Crew	Daily Output	Labor-Hours	Unit	Material	2024 Bare Costs Labor	Equipment	Total	Total Incl O&P
1230	7"	Q-14	85	.188	Ea.	60.50	11.35		71.85	84
1240	7-1/2"		83	.193		70.50	11.65		82.15	95.50
1250	8"		80	.200		70.50	12.10		82.60	96
1260	8-1/2"		80	.200		73	12.10		85.10	98.50
1270	9"		78	.205		111	12.40		123.40	141
1280	9-1/2"		77	.208		109	12.55		121.55	139
1290	10"		76	.211		109	12.70		121.70	139
1300	10-1/2"		75	.213		130	12.90		142.90	163
1310	11"		74	.216		124	13.05		137.05	157
1320	12"		71	.225		141	13.60		154.60	176
1330	13"		68	.235		196	14.20		210.20	237
1340	14"		66	.242		197	14.65		211.65	240
2000	45° elbow, 2 piece									
2010	2-1/2"	Q-14	126	.127	Ea.	12.85	7.65		20.50	26
2020	2-3/4"		123	.130		12.85	7.85		20.70	26
2030	3"		120	.133		13.80	8.05		21.85	27.50
2040	3-1/4"		117	.137		13.80	8.25		22.05	28
2050	3-1/2"		115	.139		14	8.40		22.40	28
2060	3-3/4"		113	.142		14	8.55		22.55	28.50
2070	4"		110	.145		18	8.80		26.80	33
2080	4-1/4"		108	.148		25.50	8.95		34.45	41.50
2090	4-1/2"		106	.151		25.50	9.10		34.60	42
2100	4-3/4"		104	.154		25.50	9.30		34.80	42
2110	5"		102	.157		25.50	9.45		34.95	43
2120	5-1/2"		97	.165		25.50	9.95		35.45	43.50
2130	6"		92	.174		30.50	10.50		41	49.50
2140	6-1/2"		87	.184		30.50	11.10		41.60	50.50
2150	7"		85	.188		51.50	11.35		62.85	74.50
2160	7-1/2"		83	.193		52.50	11.65		64.15	76
2170	8"		82	.195		52.50	11.80		64.30	76
2180	8-1/2"		80	.200		61.50	12.10		73.60	86.50
2190	9"		78	.205		61.50	12.40		73.90	87
2200	9-1/2"		77	.208		72.50	12.55		85.05	98.50
2210	10"		76	.211		72.50	12.70		85.20	99
2220	10-1/2"		75	.213		87	12.90		99.90	115
2230	11"		74	.216		87	13.05		100.05	115
2240	12"		71	.225		94.50	13.60		108.10	125
2250	13"		68	.235		111	14.20		125.20	144

22 11 Facility Water Distribution

22 11 13 – Facility Water Distribution Piping

22 11 13.14 Pipe, Brass

		Crew	Daily Output	Labor-Hours	Unit	Material	2024 Bare Costs Labor	Equipment	Total	Total Incl O&P
0010	**PIPE, BRASS**, Plain end									
0900	Field threaded, coupling & clevis hanger assembly 10' OC									
0920	Regular weight									
1120	1/2" diameter	1 Plum	48	.167	L.F.	18.10	12.45		30.55	38.50
1140	3/4" diameter		46	.174		24.50	13		37.50	46.50
1160	1" diameter		43	.186		35.50	13.90		49.40	59.50
1180	1-1/4" diameter	Q-1	72	.222		53.50	14.95		68.45	81
1200	1-1/2" diameter		65	.246		65.50	16.55		82.05	96.50
1220	2" diameter		53	.302		92	20.50		112.50	131

22 11 Facility Water Distribution

22 11 13 – Facility Water Distribution Piping

22 11 13.14 Pipe, Brass

		Crew	Daily Output	Labor-Hours	Unit	Material	2024 Bare Costs Labor	2024 Bare Costs Equipment	Total	Total Incl O&P
1240	2-1/2" diameter	Q-1	41	.390	L.F.	141	26		167	195
1260	3" diameter		31	.516		199	34.50		233.50	271
1300	4" diameter	Q-2	37	.649		340	45		385	435
1930	To delete coupling & hanger, subtract									
1940	1/2" diam.					40%	46%			
1950	3/4" diam. to 1-1/2" diam.					39%	39%			
1960	2" diam. to 4" diam.					48%	35%			

22 11 13.16 Pipe Fittings, Brass

		Crew	Daily Output	Labor-Hours	Unit	Material	2024 Bare Costs Labor	2024 Bare Costs Equipment	Total	Total Incl O&P
0010	**PIPE FITTINGS, BRASS**, Rough bronze, threaded, lead free.									
1000	Standard wt., 90° elbow									
1040	1/8"	1 Plum	13	.615	Ea.	43	46		89	116
1060	1/4"		13	.615		43	46		89	116
1080	3/8"		13	.615		43	46		89	116
1100	1/2"		12	.667		43	50		93	122
1120	3/4"		11	.727		57.50	54.50		112	145
1140	1"		10	.800		93.50	59.50		153	192
1160	1-1/4"	Q-1	17	.941		151	63		214	260
1180	1-1/2"		16	1		221	67		288	345
1200	2"		14	1.143		330	77		407	475
1220	2-1/2"		11	1.455		730	97.50		827.50	950
1240	3"		8	2		1,125	134		1,259	1,425
1260	4"	Q-2	11	2.182		2,250	152		2,402	2,700
1280	5"		8	3		4,925	209		5,134	5,700
1300	6"		7	3.429		9,225	239		9,464	10,500
1500	45° elbow, 1/8"	1 Plum	13	.615		53	46		99	127
1540	1/4"		13	.615		53	46		99	127
1560	3/8"		13	.615		53	46		99	127
1580	1/2"		12	.667		53	50		103	132
1600	3/4"		11	.727		75	54.50		129.50	164
1620	1"		10	.800		128	59.50		187.50	230
1640	1-1/4"	Q-1	17	.941		203	63		266	320
1660	1-1/2"		16	1		256	67		323	380
1680	2"		14	1.143		415	77		492	570
1700	2-1/2"		11	1.455		790	97.50		887.50	1,025
1720	3"		8	2		960	134		1,094	1,250
1740	4"	Q-2	11	2.182		2,150	152		2,302	2,575
1760	5"		8	3		4,000	209		4,209	4,700
1780	6"		7	3.429		5,550	239		5,789	6,450
2000	Tee, 1/8"	1 Plum	9	.889		50.50	66.50		117	154
2040	1/4"		9	.889		50.50	66.50		117	154
2060	3/8"		9	.889		61	66.50		127.50	166
2080	1/2"		8	1		52.50	74.50		127	169
2100	3/4"		7	1.143		72	85.50		157.50	206
2120	1"		6	1.333		150	99.50		249.50	310
2140	1-1/4"	Q-1	10	1.600		223	107		330	405
2160	1-1/2"		9	1.778		252	119		371	455
2180	2"		8	2		420	134		554	660
2200	2-1/2"		7	2.286		995	154		1,149	1,325
2220	3"		5	3.200		1,525	215		1,740	2,000
2240	4"	Q-2	7	3.429		3,775	239		4,014	4,500
2260	5"		5	4.800		5,875	335		6,210	6,975
2280	6"		4	6		9,675	420		10,095	11,300

22 11 Facility Water Distribution

22 11 13 – Facility Water Distribution Piping

22 11 13.16 Pipe Fittings, Brass

		Crew	Daily Output	Labor-Hours	Unit	Material	2024 Bare Costs Labor	Equipment	Total	Total Incl O&P
2500	Coupling, 1/8"	1 Plum	26	.308	Ea.	36	23		59	73.50
2540	1/4"		22	.364		36	27		63	80
2560	3/8"		18	.444		36	33		69	89
2580	1/2"		15	.533		36	40		76	98.50
2600	3/4"		14	.571		50.50	42.50		93	119
2620	1"		13	.615		86	46		132	164
2640	1-1/4"	Q-1	22	.727		144	49		193	231
2660	1-1/2"		20	.800		187	53.50		240.50	286
2680	2"		18	.889		310	59.50		369.50	430
2700	2-1/2"		14	1.143		525	77		602	695
2720	3"		10	1.600		730	107		837	965
2740	4"	Q-2	12	2		1,500	139		1,639	1,850
2760	5"		10	2.400		2,750	167		2,917	3,275
2780	6"		9	2.667		3,950	186		4,136	4,625
3000	Union, 125 lb.									
3020	1/8"	1 Plum	12	.667	Ea.	67.50	50		117.50	149
3040	1/4"		12	.667		71.50	50		121.50	153
3060	3/8"		12	.667		67.50	50		117.50	149
3080	1/2"		11	.727		71.50	54.50		126	160
3100	3/4"		10	.800		98	59.50		157.50	197
3120	1"		9	.889		148	66.50		214.50	262
3140	1-1/4"	Q-1	16	1		214	67		281	335
3160	1-1/2"		15	1.067		255	71.50		326.50	385
3180	2"		13	1.231		345	82.50		427.50	505
3200	2-1/2"		10	1.600		1,275	107		1,382	1,550
3220	3"		7	2.286		1,525	154		1,679	1,900
3240	4"	Q-2	10	2.400		4,750	167		4,917	5,475

22 11 13.23 Pipe/Tube, Copper

		Crew	Daily Output	Labor-Hours	Unit	Material	2024 Bare Costs Labor	Equipment	Total	Total Incl O&P
0010	**PIPE/TUBE, COPPER**, Solder joints R221113-50									
0100	Solder									
0120	Solder, lead free, roll				Lb.	57			57	62.50
1000	Type K tubing, couplings & clevis hanger assemblies 10' OC									
1100	1/4" diameter R221113-70	1 Plum	84	.095	L.F.	2.64	7.10		9.74	13.50
1120	3/8" diameter		82	.098		3.89	7.30		11.19	15.15
1140	1/2" diameter		78	.103		4.25	7.65		11.90	16.10
1160	5/8" diameter		77	.104		6.30	7.75		14.05	18.45
1180	3/4" diameter		74	.108		7.15	8.05		15.20	19.85
1200	1" diameter		66	.121		9.60	9.05		18.65	24
1220	1-1/4" diameter		56	.143		12.15	10.65		22.80	29.50
1240	1-1/2" diameter		50	.160		16	11.95		27.95	35.50
1260	2" diameter		40	.200		24.50	14.95		39.45	48.50
1280	2-1/2" diameter	Q-1	60	.267		36.50	17.90		54.40	67
1300	3" diameter		54	.296		54	19.90		73.90	88.50
1320	3-1/2" diameter		42	.381		72	25.50		97.50	117
1330	4" diameter		38	.421		101	28.50		129.50	153
1340	5" diameter		32	.500		172	33.50		205.50	239
1360	6" diameter	Q-2	38	.632		268	44		312	360
1380	8" diameter	"	34	.706		390	49		439	505
1390	For other than full hard temper, add					13%				
1440	For silver solder, add						15%			
1800	For medical clean (oxygen class), add					12%				
1950	To delete cplgs. & hngrs., 1/4"-1" pipe, subtract					27%	60%			

For customer support on your Plumbing Costs with RSMeans Data call 800.448.8182.

22 11 Facility Water Distribution

22 11 13 – Facility Water Distribution Piping

22 11 13.23 Pipe/Tube, Copper		Crew	Daily Output	Labor-Hours	Unit	Material	2024 Bare Costs Labor	Equipment	Total	Total Incl O&P
1960	1-1/4"-3" pipe, subtract					14%	52%			
1970	3-1/2"-5" pipe, subtract					10%	60%			
1980	6"-8" pipe, subtract					19%	53%			
2000	Type L tubing, couplings & clevis hanger assemblies 10' OC									
2100	1/4" diameter	1 Plum	88	.091	L.F.	2.48	6.80		9.28	12.85
2120	3/8" diameter		84	.095		2.97	7.10		10.07	13.85
2140	1/2" diameter		81	.099		3.69	7.35		11.04	15
2160	5/8" diameter		79	.101		4.99	7.55		12.54	16.75
2180	3/4" diameter		76	.105		5.40	7.85		13.25	17.65
2200	1" diameter		68	.118		7.80	8.80		16.60	21.50
2220	1-1/4" diameter		58	.138		10.90	10.30		21.20	27.50
2240	1-1/2" diameter		52	.154		13.75	11.50		25.25	32.50
2260	2" diameter		42	.190		22	14.20		36.20	45
2280	2-1/2" diameter	Q-1	62	.258		34.50	17.35		51.85	64
2300	3" diameter		56	.286		47.50	19.20		66.70	81
2320	3-1/2" diameter		43	.372		70	25		95	114
2340	4" diameter		39	.410		88	27.50		115.50	138
2360	5" diameter		34	.471		151	31.50		182.50	214
2380	6" diameter	Q-2	40	.600		228	42		270	315
2400	8" diameter	"	36	.667		315	46.50		361.50	415
2410	For other than full hard temper, add					21%				
2590	For silver solder, add						15%			
2900	For medical clean (oxygen class), add					12%				
2940	To delete cplgs. & hngrs., 1/4"-1" pipe, subtract					37%	63%			
2960	1-1/4"-3" pipe, subtract					12%	53%			
2970	3-1/2"-5" pipe, subtract					12%	63%			
2980	6"-8" pipe, subtract					24%	55%			
3000	Type M tubing, couplings & clevis hanger assemblies 10' OC									
3100	1/4" diameter	1 Plum	90	.089	L.F.	3.95	6.65		10.60	14.20
3120	3/8" diameter		87	.092		2.87	6.85		9.72	13.35
3140	1/2" diameter		84	.095		2.95	7.10		10.05	13.85
3160	5/8" diameter		81	.099		4.06	7.35		11.41	15.40
3180	3/4" diameter		78	.103		4.40	7.65		12.05	16.25
3200	1" diameter		70	.114		6.60	8.55		15.15	19.95
3220	1-1/4" diameter		60	.133		9.75	9.95		19.70	25.50
3240	1-1/2" diameter		54	.148		12.90	11.05		23.95	30.50
3260	2" diameter		44	.182		20	13.55		33.55	42
3280	2-1/2" diameter	Q-1	64	.250		32.50	16.80		49.30	60.50
3300	3" diameter		58	.276		43	18.55		61.55	75
3320	3-1/2" diameter		45	.356		62	24		86	104
3340	4" diameter		40	.400		84.50	27		111.50	133
3360	5" diameter		36	.444		142	30		172	201
3370	6" diameter	Q-2	42	.571		226	40		266	310
3380	8" diameter	"	38	.632		300	44		344	395
3440	For silver solder, add						15%			
3960	To delete cplgs. & hngrs., 1/4"-1" pipe, subtract					35%	65%			
3970	1-1/4"-3" pipe, subtract					19%	56%			
3980	3-1/2"-5" pipe, subtract					13%	65%			
3990	6"-8" pipe, subtract					28%	58%			
4000	Type DWV tubing, couplings & clevis hanger assemblies 10' OC									
4100	1-1/4" diameter	1 Plum	60	.133	L.F.	10.55	9.95		20.50	26.50
4120	1-1/2" diameter		54	.148		13.20	11.05		24.25	31
4140	2" diameter		44	.182		18.45	13.55		32	40.50

22 11 Facility Water Distribution

22 11 13 – Facility Water Distribution Piping

22 11 13.23 Pipe/Tube, Copper		Crew	Daily Output	Labor-Hours	Unit	Material	2024 Bare Costs Labor	Equipment	Total	Total Incl O&P
4160	3" diameter	Q-1	58	.276	L.F.	38	18.55		56.55	69.50
4180	4" diameter		40	.400		105	27		132	155
4200	5" diameter		36	.444		181	30		211	244
4220	6" diameter	Q-2	42	.571		276	40		316	365
4240	8" diameter	"	38	.632		875	44		919	1,025
4730	To delete cplgs. & hngrs., 1-1/4"-2" pipe, subtract					16%	53%			
4740	3"-4" pipe, subtract					13%	60%			
4750	5"-8" pipe, subtract					23%	58%			
5200	ACR tubing, type L, hard temper, cleaned and									
5220	capped, no couplings or hangers									
5240	3/8" OD				L.F.	.94			.94	1.03
5250	1/2" OD					1.42			1.42	1.56
5260	5/8" OD					1.83			1.83	2.01
5270	3/4" OD					2.45			2.45	2.70
5280	7/8" OD					2.92			2.92	3.21
5290	1-1/8" OD					4.19			4.19	4.61
5300	1-3/8" OD					7.95			7.95	8.75
5310	1-5/8" OD					9.05			9.05	9.95
5320	2-1/8" OD					13.80			13.80	15.15
5330	2-5/8" OD					19.85			19.85	22
5340	3-1/8" OD					27			27	29.50
5350	3-5/8" OD					50			50	55
5360	4-1/8" OD					51.50			51.50	57
5380	ACR tubing, type L, hard, cleaned and capped									
5381	No couplings or hangers									
5384	3/8"	1 Stpi	160	.050	L.F.	.94	3.78		4.72	6.65
5385	1/2"		160	.050		1.42	3.78		5.20	7.15
5386	5/8"		160	.050		1.83	3.78		5.61	7.60
5387	3/4"		130	.062		2.45	4.65		7.10	9.60
5388	7/8"		130	.062		2.92	4.65		7.57	10.10
5389	1-1/8"		115	.070		4.19	5.25		9.44	12.40
5390	1-3/8"		100	.080		7.95	6.05		14	17.75
5391	1-5/8"		90	.089		9.05	6.70		15.75	19.95
5392	2-1/8"		80	.100		13.80	7.55		21.35	26.50
5393	2-5/8"	Q-5	125	.128		19.85	8.70		28.55	35
5394	3-1/8"		105	.152		27	10.35		37.35	45
5395	4-1/8"		95	.168		51.50	11.45		62.95	74
5800	Refrigeration tubing, dryseal, 50' coils									
5840	1/8" OD				Coil	33.50			33.50	36.50
5850	3/16" OD					46			46	50.50
5860	1/4" OD					46.50			46.50	51
5870	5/16" OD					77			77	85
5880	3/8" OD					64.50			64.50	70.50
5890	1/2" OD					79			79	87
5900	5/8" OD					106			106	117
5910	3/4" OD					127			127	139
5920	7/8" OD					188			188	207
5930	1-1/8" OD					277			277	305
5940	1-3/8" OD					460			460	505
5950	1-5/8" OD					585			585	645

22 11 Facility Water Distribution

22 11 13 – Facility Water Distribution Piping

22 11 13.25 Pipe/Tube Fittings, Copper		Crew	Daily Output	Labor-Hours	Unit	Material	2024 Bare Costs Labor	Equipment	Total	Total Incl O&P
0010	**PIPE/TUBE FITTINGS, COPPER**, Wrought unless otherwise noted									
0020	For silver solder, add						15%			
0040	Solder joints, copper x copper									
0070	90° elbow, 1/4"	1 Plum	22	.364	Ea.	7.15	27		34.15	48.50
0090	3/8"		22	.364		6.90	27		33.90	48
0100	1/2"		20	.400		2.49	30		32.49	47
0110	5/8"		19	.421		5.10	31.50		36.60	52.50
0120	3/4"		19	.421		5.50	31.50		37	53
0130	1"		16	.500		13.45	37.50		50.95	70.50
0140	1-1/4"		15	.533		19.95	40		59.95	81
0150	1-1/2"		13	.615		31	46		77	103
0160	2"		11	.727		56.50	54.50		111	144
0170	2-1/2"	Q-1	13	1.231		103	82.50		185.50	237
0180	3"		11	1.455		147	97.50		244.50	305
0190	3-1/2"		10	1.600		410	107		517	610
0200	4"		9	1.778		320	119		439	535
0210	5"		6	2.667		1,150	179		1,329	1,525
0220	6"	Q-2	9	2.667		1,675	186		1,861	2,125
0230	8"	"	8	3		5,625	209		5,834	6,475
0250	45° elbow, 1/4"	1 Plum	22	.364		12.70	27		39.70	54.50
0270	3/8"		22	.364		10.85	27		37.85	52.50
0280	1/2"		20	.400		3.71	30		33.71	48.50
0290	5/8"		19	.421		17.15	31.50		48.65	66
0300	3/4"		19	.421		7.60	31.50		39.10	55.50
0310	1"		16	.500		19.15	37.50		56.65	76.50
0320	1-1/4"		15	.533		25.50	40		65.50	87
0330	1-1/2"		13	.615		31.50	46		77.50	103
0340	2"		11	.727		52.50	54.50		107	139
0350	2-1/2"	Q-1	13	1.231		102	82.50		184.50	235
0360	3"		13	1.231		143	82.50		225.50	280
0370	3-1/2"		10	1.600		221	107		328	405
0380	4"		9	1.778		294	119		413	505
0390	5"		6	2.667		965	179		1,144	1,325
0400	6"	Q-2	9	2.667		1,675	186		1,861	2,125
0410	8"	"	8	3		6,625	209		6,834	7,600
0450	Tee, 1/4"	1 Plum	14	.571		14.25	42.50		56.75	79
0470	3/8"		14	.571		11.40	42.50		53.90	76
0480	1/2"		13	.615		3.47	46		49.47	72.50
0490	5/8"		12	.667		26	50		76	103
0500	3/4"		12	.667		10.10	50		60.10	85
0510	1"		10	.800		14.55	59.50		74.05	105
0520	1-1/4"		9	.889		41.50	66.50		108	145
0530	1-1/2"		8	1		63	74.50		137.50	180
0540	2"		7	1.143		100	85.50		185.50	237
0550	2-1/2"	Q-1	8	2		184	134		318	405
0560	3"		7	2.286		265	154		419	520
0570	3-1/2"		6	2.667		695	179		874	1,025
0580	4"		5	3.200		620	215		835	1,000
0590	5"		4	4		1,700	269		1,969	2,275
0600	6"	Q-2	6	4		2,350	279		2,629	3,000
0610	8"	"	5	4.800		9,025	335		9,360	10,400
0612	Tee, reducing on the outlet, 1/4"	1 Plum	15	.533		55.50	40		95.50	120

22 11 Facility Water Distribution

22 11 13 – Facility Water Distribution Piping

22 11 13.25 Pipe/Tube Fittings, Copper

		Crew	Daily Output	Labor-Hours	Unit	Material	2024 Bare Costs Labor	Equipment	Total	Total Incl O&P
0613	3/8"	1 Plum	15	.533	Ea.	47	40		87	111
0614	1/2"		14	.571		43.50	42.50		86	112
0615	5/8"		13	.615		88	46		134	165
0616	3/4"		12	.667		20	50		70	96
0617	1"		11	.727		95	54.50		149.50	186
0618	1-1/4"		10	.800		94	59.50		153.50	192
0619	1-1/2"		9	.889		100	66.50		166.50	209
0620	2"		8	1		163	74.50		237.50	290
0621	2-1/2"	Q-1	9	1.778		450	119		569	675
0622	3"		8	2		510	134		644	760
0623	4"		6	2.667		920	179		1,099	1,275
0624	5"		5	3.200		3,975	215		4,190	4,675
0625	6"	Q-2	7	3.429		6,975	239		7,214	8,025
0626	8"	"	6	4		26,900	279		27,179	30,000
0630	Tee, reducing on the run, 1/4"	1 Plum	15	.533		63	40		103	128
0631	3/8"		15	.533		71.50	40		111.50	138
0632	1/2"		14	.571		60	42.50		102.50	130
0633	5/8"		13	.615		88.50	46		134.50	166
0634	3/4"		12	.667		48.50	50		98.50	128
0635	1"		11	.727		77	54.50		131.50	166
0636	1-1/4"		10	.800		123	59.50		182.50	225
0637	1-1/2"		9	.889		213	66.50		279.50	335
0638	2"		8	1		272	74.50		346.50	410
0639	2-1/2"	Q-1	9	1.778		580	119		699	820
0640	3"		8	2		805	134		939	1,075
0641	4"		6	2.667		1,725	179		1,904	2,175
0642	5"		5	3.200		4,850	215		5,065	5,650
0643	6"	Q-2	7	3.429		7,350	239		7,589	8,450
0644	8"	"	6	4		19,000	279		19,279	21,300
0650	Coupling, 1/4"	1 Plum	24	.333		3.57	25		28.57	41
0670	3/8"		24	.333		4.66	25		29.66	42
0680	1/2"		22	.364		3.85	27		30.85	44.50
0690	5/8"		21	.381		10.15	28.50		38.65	53.50
0700	3/4"		21	.381		7.75	28.50		36.25	51
0710	1"		18	.444		15.40	33		48.40	66.50
0715	1-1/4"		17	.471		27	35		62	82
0716	1-1/2"		15	.533		35.50	40		75.50	98.50
0718	2"		13	.615		59.50	46		105.50	134
0721	2-1/2"	Q-1	15	1.067		122	71.50		193.50	241
0722	3"		13	1.231		167	82.50		249.50	305
0724	3-1/2"		8	2		310	134		444	545
0726	4"		7	2.286		365	154		519	635
0728	5"		6	2.667		765	179		944	1,100
0731	6"	Q-2	8	3		1,275	209		1,484	1,700
0732	8"	"	7	3.429		4,100	239		4,339	4,850
0741	Coupling, reducing, concentric									
0743	1/2"	1 Plum	23	.348	Ea.	8.90	26		34.90	48.50
0745	3/4"		21.50	.372		13.45	28		41.45	56.50
0747	1"		19.50	.410		21	30.50		51.50	68.50
0748	1-1/4"		18	.444		38.50	33		71.50	91.50
0749	1-1/2"		16	.500		49	37.50		86.50	110
0751	2"		14	.571		92.50	42.50		135	166
0752	2-1/2"		13	.615		171	46		217	257

22 11 Facility Water Distribution

22 11 13 – Facility Water Distribution Piping

22 11 13.25 Pipe/Tube Fittings, Copper		Crew	Daily Output	Labor-Hours	Unit	Material	2024 Bare Costs Labor	Equipment	Total	Total Incl O&P
0753	3"	Q-1	14	1.143	Ea.	206	77		283	340
0755	4"	"	8	2		420	134		554	660
0757	5"	Q-2	7.50	3.200		2,275	223		2,498	2,825
0759	6"		7	3.429		3,625	239		3,864	4,350
0761	8"	↓	6.50	3.692	↓	9,675	257		9,932	11,100
0771	Cap, sweat									
0773	1/2"	1 Plum	40	.200	Ea.	3.75	14.95		18.70	26
0775	3/4"		38	.211		6.95	15.70		22.65	31
0777	1"		32	.250		16.25	18.65		34.90	46
0778	1-1/4"		29	.276		21.50	20.50		42	54
0779	1-1/2"		26	.308		31.50	23		54.50	68.50
0781	2"	↓	22	.364	↓	58	27		85	105
0791	Flange, sweat									
0793	3"	Q-1	22	.727	Ea.	785	49		834	940
0795	4"		18	.889		1,100	59.50		1,159.50	1,300
0797	5"	↓	12	1.333		2,050	89.50		2,139.50	2,375
0799	6"	Q-2	18	1.333		2,150	93		2,243	2,525
0801	8"	"	16	1.500		4,100	105		4,205	4,650
0850	Unions, 1/4"	1 Plum	21	.381		119	28.50		147.50	174
0870	3/8"		21	.381		119	28.50		147.50	174
0880	1/2"		19	.421		70	31.50		101.50	124
0890	5/8"		18	.444		271	33		304	350
0900	3/4"		18	.444		88	33		121	146
0910	1"		15	.533		137	40		177	210
0920	1-1/4"		14	.571		225	42.50		267.50	310
0930	1-1/2"		12	.667		297	50		347	400
0940	2"		10	.800		505	59.50		564.50	645
0950	2-1/2"	Q-1	12	1.333		1,100	89.50		1,189.50	1,350
0960	3"	"	10	1.600		2,875	107		2,982	3,300
0980	Adapter, copper x male IPS, 1/4"	1 Plum	20	.400		50	30		80	99.50
0990	3/8"		20	.400		25	30		55	72
1000	1/2"		18	.444		10.75	33		43.75	61.50
1010	3/4"		17	.471		17.95	35		52.95	72.50
1020	1"		15	.533		46	40		86	110
1030	1-1/4"		13	.615		66	46		112	141
1040	1-1/2"		12	.667		77.50	50		127.50	159
1050	2"	↓	11	.727		131	54.50		185.50	225
1060	2-1/2"	Q-1	10.50	1.524		455	102		557	650
1070	3"		10	1.600		570	107		677	785
1080	3-1/2"		9	1.778		395	119		514	615
1090	4"		8	2		745	134		879	1,025
1200	5", cast		6	2.667		3,300	179		3,479	3,900
1210	6", cast	Q-2	8.50	2.824	↓	3,725	197		3,922	4,400
1214	Adapter, copper x female IPS									
1216	1/2"	1 Plum	18	.444	Ea.	17	33		50	68
1218	3/4"		17	.471		23.50	35		58.50	78
1220	1"		15	.533		53	40		93	118
1221	1-1/4"		13	.615		77.50	46		123.50	154
1222	1-1/2"		12	.667		121	50		171	207
1224	2"		11	.727		164	54.50		218.50	261
1250	Cross, 1/2"		10	.800		81.50	59.50		141	179
1260	3/4"		9.50	.842		158	63		221	268
1270	1"	↓	8	1	↓	269	74.50		343.50	405

22 11 Facility Water Distribution

22 11 13 – Facility Water Distribution Piping

22 11 13.25 Pipe/Tube Fittings, Copper

		Crew	Daily Output	Labor-Hours	Unit	Material	2024 Bare Costs Labor	Equipment	Total	Total Incl O&P
1280	1-1/4"	1 Plum	7.50	1.067	Ea.	390	79.50		469.50	545
1290	1-1/2"		6.50	1.231		550	92		642	740
1300	2"	▼	5.50	1.455		1,050	109		1,159	1,300
1310	2-1/2"	Q-1	6.50	2.462		2,400	165		2,565	2,900
1320	3"	"	5.50	2.909	▼	1,350	195		1,545	1,775
1500	Tee fitting, mechanically formed (Type 1, 'branch sizes up to 2 in.')									
1520	1/2" run size, 3/8" to 1/2" branch size	1 Plum	80	.100	Ea.		7.45		7.45	11.10
1530	3/4" run size, 3/8" to 3/4" branch size		60	.133			9.95		9.95	14.80
1540	1" run size, 3/8" to 1" branch size		54	.148			11.05		11.05	16.45
1550	1-1/4" run size, 3/8" to 1-1/4" branch size		48	.167			12.45		12.45	18.50
1560	1-1/2" run size, 3/8" to 1-1/2" branch size		40	.200			14.95		14.95	22
1570	2" run size, 3/8" to 2" branch size		35	.229			17.05		17.05	25.50
1580	2-1/2" run size, 1/2" to 2" branch size		32	.250			18.65		18.65	28
1590	3" run size, 1" to 2" branch size		26	.308			23		23	34
1600	4" run size, 1" to 2" branch size	▼	24	.333	▼		25		25	37
1640	Tee fitting, mechanically formed (Type 2, branches 2-1/2" thru 4")									
1650	2-1/2" run size, 2-1/2" branch size	1 Plum	12.50	.640	Ea.		48		48	71
1660	3" run size, 2-1/2" to 3" branch size		12	.667			50		50	74
1670	3-1/2" run size, 2-1/2" to 3-1/2" branch size		11	.727			54.50		54.50	81
1680	4" run size, 2-1/2" to 4" branch size		10.50	.762			57		57	84.50
1698	5" run size, 2" to 4" branch size		9.50	.842			63		63	93.50
1700	6" run size, 2" to 4" branch size		8.50	.941			70.50		70.50	105
1710	8" run size, 2" to 4" branch size	▼	7	1.143	▼		85.50		85.50	127
1800	ACR fittings, OD size									
1802	Tee, straight									
1808	5/8"	1 Stpi	12	.667	Ea.	3.85	50.50		54.35	79
1810	3/4"		12	.667		24	50.50		74.50	102
1812	7/8"		10	.800		9.30	60.50		69.80	100
1813	1"		10	.800		66	60.50		126.50	163
1814	1-1/8"		10	.800		28	60.50		88.50	121
1816	1-3/8"		9	.889		38.50	67		105.50	142
1818	1-5/8"		8	1		58	75.50		133.50	176
1820	2-1/8"	▼	7	1.143		92	86.50		178.50	229
1822	2-5/8"	Q-5	8	2		169	136		305	390
1824	3-1/8"		7	2.286		244	155		399	500
1826	4-1/8"	▼	5	3.200	▼	360	218		578	720
1830	90° elbow									
1836	5/8"	1 Stpi	19	.421	Ea.	18.80	32		50.80	68
1838	3/4"		19	.421		2.50	32		34.50	50.50
1840	7/8"		16	.500		13.70	38		51.70	71
1842	1-1/8"		16	.500		9.20	38		47.20	66
1844	1-3/8"		15	.533		18.35	40.50		58.85	80
1846	1-5/8"		13	.615		41.50	46.50		88	115
1848	2-1/8"	▼	11	.727		52	55		107	140
1850	2-5/8"	Q-5	13	1.231		95	83.50		178.50	230
1852	3-1/8"		11	1.455		135	99		234	296
1854	4-1/8"	▼	9	1.778	▼	187	121		308	385
1860	Coupling									
1866	5/8"	1 Stpi	21	.381	Ea.	1.70	29		30.70	45
1868	3/4"		21	.381		4.47	29		33.47	48
1870	7/8"		18	.444		3.41	33.50		36.91	54
1871	1"		18	.444		11.65	33.50		45.15	63
1872	1-1/8"		18	.444		6.80	33.50		40.30	57.50

22 11 Facility Water Distribution

22 11 13 – Facility Water Distribution Piping

22 11 13.25 Pipe/Tube Fittings, Copper

		Crew	Daily Output	Labor-Hours	Unit	Material	2024 Bare Costs Labor	Equipment	Total	Total Incl O&P
1874	1-3/8"	1 Stpi	17	.471	Ea.	11.90	35.50		47.40	66
1876	1-5/8"		15	.533		15.70	40.50		56.20	77.50
1878	2-1/8"		13	.615		26	46.50		72.50	98
1880	2-5/8"	Q-5	15	1.067		54	72.50		126.50	167
1882	3-1/8"		13	1.231		73.50	83.50		157	206
1884	4-1/8"		7	2.286		162	155		317	410
2000	DWV, solder joints, copper x copper									
2030	90° elbow, 1-1/4"	1 Plum	13	.615	Ea.	55.50	46		101.50	130
2050	1-1/2"		12	.667		73.50	50		123.50	155
2070	2"		10	.800		118	59.50		177.50	218
2090	3"	Q-1	10	1.600		284	107		391	475
2100	4"	"	9	1.778		1,275	119		1,394	1,575
2150	45° elbow, 1-1/4"	1 Plum	13	.615		45	46		91	118
2170	1-1/2"		12	.667		42	50		92	121
2180	2"		10	.800		86	59.50		145.50	184
2190	3"	Q-1	10	1.600		193	107		300	375
2200	4"	"	9	1.778		174	119		293	370
2250	Tee, sanitary, 1-1/4"	1 Plum	9	.889		97	66.50		163.50	206
2270	1-1/2"		8	1		121	74.50		195.50	244
2290	2"		7	1.143		165	85.50		250.50	310
2310	3"	Q-1	7	2.286		695	154		849	995
2330	4"	"	6	2.667		1,525	179		1,704	1,975
2400	Coupling, 1-1/4"	1 Plum	14	.571		23	42.50		65.50	89
2420	1-1/2"		13	.615		28.50	46		74.50	100
2440	2"		11	.727		39.50	54.50		94	125
2460	3"	Q-1	11	1.455		92	97.50		189.50	246
2480	4"	"	10	1.600		203	107		310	385
2602	Traps, see Section 22 13 16.60									
3500	Compression joint fittings									
3510	As used for plumbing and oil burner work									
3520	Fitting price includes nuts and sleeves									
3540	Sleeve, 1/8"				Ea.	.36			.36	.40
3550	3/16"					.36			.36	.40
3560	1/4"					.08			.08	.09
3570	5/16"					.21			.21	.23
3580	3/8"					.75			.75	.83
3600	1/2"					.99			.99	1.09
3620	Nut, 1/8"					.32			.32	.35
3630	3/16"					.56			.56	.62
3640	1/4"					.55			.55	.61
3650	5/16"					.55			.55	.61
3660	3/8"					.89			.89	.98
3670	1/2"					1.55			1.55	1.71
3710	Union, 1/8"	1 Plum	26	.308		2.22	23		25.22	36.50
3720	3/16"		24	.333		2.11	25		27.11	39.50
3730	1/4"		24	.333		4.27	25		29.27	41.50
3740	5/16"		23	.348		4.97	26		30.97	44
3750	3/8"		22	.364		2.75	27		29.75	43.50
3760	1/2"		22	.364		8.50	27		35.50	50
3780	5/8"		21	.381		4.69	28.50		33.19	47.50
3820	Union tee, 1/8"		17	.471		8.40	35		43.40	62
3830	3/16"		16	.500		4.84	37.50		42.34	61
3840	1/4"		15	.533		8.50	40		48.50	68.50

22 11 Facility Water Distribution

22 11 13 – Facility Water Distribution Piping

22 11 13.25 Pipe/Tube Fittings, Copper

		Crew	Daily Output	Labor-Hours	Unit	Material	2024 Bare Costs Labor	Equipment	Total	Total Incl O&P
3850	5/16"	1 Plum	15	.533	Ea.	6.15	40		46.15	66
3860	3/8"		15	.533		12.15	40		52.15	72.50
3870	1/2"		15	.533		18.55	40		58.55	79.50
3910	Union elbow, 1/4"		24	.333		2.61	25		27.61	40
3920	5/16"		23	.348		4.40	26		30.40	43.50
3930	3/8"		22	.364		8.90	27		35.90	50.50
3940	1/2"		22	.364		13.20	27		40.20	55
3980	Female connector, 1/8"		26	.308		1.64	23		24.64	36
4000	3/16" x 1/8"		24	.333		2.17	25		27.17	39.50
4010	1/4" x 1/8"		24	.333		3.38	25		28.38	40.50
4020	1/4"		24	.333		5	25		30	42.50
4030	3/8" x 1/4"		22	.364		4.53	27		31.53	45.50
4040	1/2" x 3/8"		22	.364		7.20	27		34.20	48.50
4050	5/8" x 1/2"		21	.381		10.20	28.50		38.70	53.50
4090	Male connector, 1/8"		26	.308		1.16	23		24.16	35.50
4100	3/16" x 1/8"		24	.333		1.42	25		26.42	38.50
4110	1/4" x 1/8"		24	.333		1.37	25		26.37	38.50
4120	1/4"		24	.333		1.37	25		26.37	38.50
4130	5/16" x 1/8"		23	.348		3.36	26		29.36	42
4140	5/16" x 1/4"		23	.348		1.97	26		27.97	40.50
4150	3/8" x 1/8"		22	.364		3.62	27		30.62	44.50
4160	3/8" x 1/4"		22	.364		4.58	27		31.58	45.50
4170	3/8"		22	.364		4.58	27		31.58	45.50
4180	3/8" x 1/2"		22	.364		6.25	27		33.25	47.50
4190	1/2" x 3/8"		22	.364		6.05	27		33.05	47
4200	1/2"		22	.364		6.80	27		33.80	48
4210	5/8" x 1/2"		21	.381		7.85	28.50		36.35	51
4240	Male elbow, 1/8"		26	.308		5.50	23		28.50	40
4250	3/16" x 1/8"		24	.333		3.11	25		28.11	40.50
4260	1/4" x 1/8"		24	.333		3.20	25		28.20	40.50
4270	1/4"		24	.333		3.80	25		28.80	41
4280	3/8" x 1/4"		22	.364		6.60	27		33.60	48
4290	3/8"		22	.364		11.30	27		38.30	53
4300	1/2" x 1/4"		22	.364		10.95	27		37.95	52.50
4310	1/2" x 3/8"		22	.364		17.20	27		44.20	59.50
4340	Female elbow, 1/8"		26	.308		6.10	23		29.10	41
4350	1/4" x 1/8"		24	.333		6.65	25		31.65	44.50
4360	1/4"		24	.333		7.95	25		32.95	46
4370	3/8" x 1/4"		22	.364		7.85	27		34.85	49
4380	1/2" x 3/8"		22	.364		7.65	27		34.65	49
4390	1/2"		22	.364		10.30	27		37.30	52
4420	Male run tee, 1/4" x 1/8"		15	.533		8.20	40		48.20	68
4430	5/16" x 1/8"		15	.533		8.15	40		48.15	68
4440	3/8" x 1/4"		15	.533		12.65	40		52.65	73
4480	Male branch tee, 1/4" x 1/8"		15	.533		9.50	40		49.50	69.50
4490	1/4"		15	.533		9.25	40		49.25	69
4500	3/8" x 1/4"		15	.533		6.15	40		46.15	66
4510	1/2" x 3/8"		15	.533		9.60	40		49.60	69.50
4520	1/2"		15	.533		15.35	40		55.35	76
4800	Flare joint fittings									
4810	Refrigeration fittings									
4820	Flare joint nuts and labor not incl. in price. Add 1 nut per jnt.									
4830	90° elbow, 1/4"				Ea.	3.79			3.79	4.17

For customer support on your Plumbing Costs with RSMeans Data call 800.448.8182.

22 11 Facility Water Distribution

22 11 13 – Facility Water Distribution Piping

22 11 13.25 Pipe/Tube Fittings, Copper		Crew	Daily Output	Labor-Hours	Unit	Material	2024 Bare Costs Labor	Equipment	Total	Total Incl O&P
4840	3/8"				Ea.	3.12			3.12	3.43
4850	1/2"					4.01			4.01	4.41
4860	5/8"					5.50			5.50	6.05
4870	3/4"					12.50			12.50	13.75
5030	Tee, 1/4"					4.45			4.45	4.90
5040	5/16"					5.85			5.85	6.40
5050	3/8"					5.10			5.10	5.60
5060	1/2"					8.15			8.15	8.95
5070	5/8"					7.35			7.35	8.10
5080	3/4"					10.85			10.85	11.95
5140	Union, 3/16"					2.23			2.23	2.45
5150	1/4"					1.40			1.40	1.54
5160	5/16"					2.09			2.09	2.30
5170	3/8"					1.46			1.46	1.61
5180	1/2"					2.12			2.12	2.33
5190	5/8"					3.74			3.74	4.11
5200	3/4"					17.20			17.20	18.95
5260	Long flare nut, 3/16"	1 Stpi	42	.190		.48	14.40		14.88	22
5270	1/4"		41	.195		1.56	14.75		16.31	23.50
5280	5/16"		40	.200		2.85	15.10		17.95	25.50
5290	3/8"		39	.205		2.66	15.50		18.16	26
5300	1/2"		38	.211		3.25	15.90		19.15	27
5310	5/8"		37	.216		9.90	16.35		26.25	35.50
5320	3/4"		34	.235		21	17.80		38.80	49.50
5380	Short flare nut, 3/16"		42	.190		6.90	14.40		21.30	29
5390	1/4"		41	.195		1.10	14.75		15.85	23
5400	5/16"		40	.200		1.32	15.10		16.42	24
5410	3/8"		39	.205		.34	15.50		15.84	23.50
5420	1/2"		38	.211		3.18	15.90		19.08	27
5430	5/8"		36	.222		2.03	16.80		18.83	27
5440	3/4"		34	.235		10.90	17.80		28.70	38.50
5500	90° elbow flare by MIPS, 1/4"					4.17			4.17	4.59
5510	3/8"					5.10			5.10	5.60
5520	1/2"					8.10			8.10	8.95
5530	5/8"					9.95			9.95	10.95
5540	3/4"					15			15	16.50
5600	Flare by FIPS, 1/4"					7.70			7.70	8.50
5610	3/8"					7.60			7.60	8.35
5620	1/2"					10.90			10.90	12
5670	Flare by sweat, 1/4"					3.47			3.47	3.82
5680	3/8"					6.50			6.50	7.15
5690	1/2"					7.40			7.40	8.15
5700	5/8"					19.70			19.70	21.50
5760	Tee flare by IPS, 1/4"					4.34			4.34	4.77
5770	3/8"					9.80			9.80	10.80
5780	1/2"					16.45			16.45	18.10
5790	5/8"					11.80			11.80	13
5850	Connector, 1/4"					1.67			1.67	1.84
5860	3/8"					2.49			2.49	2.74
5870	1/2"					3.04			3.04	3.34
5880	5/8"					6.05			6.05	6.65
5890	3/4"					8.35			8.35	9.15
5950	Seal cap, 1/4"					.20			.20	.22

22 11 Facility Water Distribution

22 11 13 – Facility Water Distribution Piping

22 11 13.25 Pipe/Tube Fittings, Copper

		Crew	Daily Output	Labor-Hours	Unit	Material	2024 Bare Costs Labor	Equipment	Total	Total Incl O&P
5960	3/8"				Ea.	.33			.33	.36
5970	1/2"					1.21			1.21	1.33
5980	5/8"					2.58			2.58	2.84
5990	3/4"					9.45			9.45	10.35
6000	Water service fittings									
6010	Flare joints nut and labor are included in the fitting price.									
6020	90° elbow, C x C, 3/8"	1 Plum	19	.421	Ea.	107	31.50		138.50	164
6030	1/2"		18	.444		202	33		235	273
6040	3/4"		16	.500		258	37.50		295.50	340
6050	1"		15	.533		276	40		316	365
6080	2"		10	.800		1,775	59.50		1,834.50	2,050
6090	90° elbow, C x MPT, 3/8"		19	.421		81	31.50		112.50	136
6100	1/2"		18	.444		154	33		187	219
6110	3/4"		16	.500		178	37.50		215.50	252
6120	1"		15	.533		485	40		525	595
6130	1-1/4"		13	.615		680	46		726	820
6140	1-1/2"		12	.667		445	50		495	565
6150	2"		10	.800		580	59.50		639.50	725
6160	90° elbow, C x FPT, 3/8"		19	.421		87	31.50		118.50	143
6170	1/2"		18	.444		165	33		198	232
6180	3/4"		16	.500		205	37.50		242.50	281
6190	1"		15	.533		470	40		510	580
6200	1-1/4"		13	.615		234	46		280	325
6210	1-1/2"		12	.667		900	50		950	1,075
6220	2"		10	.800		1,300	59.50		1,359.50	1,525
6230	Tee, C x C x C, 3/8"		13	.615		172	46		218	258
6240	1/2"		12	.667		296	50		346	400
6250	3/4"		11	.727		233	54.50		287.50	335
6260	1"		10	.800		350	59.50		409.50	475
6330	Tube nut, C x nut seat, 3/8"		40	.200		31	14.95		45.95	56.50
6340	1/2"		38	.211		31	15.70		46.70	58
6350	3/4"		34	.235		60	17.55		77.55	92
6360	1"		32	.250		109	18.65		127.65	148
6380	Coupling, C x C, 3/8"		19	.421		105	31.50		136.50	162
6390	1/2"		18	.444		181	33		214	249
6400	3/4"		16	.500		230	37.50		267.50	310
6410	1"		15	.533		425	40		465	525
6420	1-1/4"		12	.667		685	50		735	830
6430	1-1/2"		12	.667		1,050	50		1,100	1,225
6440	2"		10	.800		1,575	59.50		1,634.50	1,825
6450	Adapter, C x FPT, 3/8"		19	.421		79	31.50		110.50	134
6460	1/2"		18	.444		137	33		170	201
6470	3/4"		16	.500		166	37.50		203.50	239
6480	1"		15	.533		355	40		395	450
6490	1-1/4"		13	.615		207	46		253	297
6500	1-1/2"		12	.667		750	50		800	900
6510	2"		10	.800		550	59.50		609.50	695
6520	Adapter, C x MPT, 3/8"		19	.421		64.50	31.50		96	118
6530	1/2"		18	.444		123	33		156	185
6540	3/4"		16	.500		169	37.50		206.50	242
6550	1"		15	.533		299	40		339	390
6560	1-1/4"		13	.615		435	46		481	545
6570	1-1/2"		12	.667		750	50		800	900

22 11 Facility Water Distribution

22 11 13 – Facility Water Distribution Piping

22 11 13.25 Pipe/Tube Fittings, Copper

		Crew	Daily Output	Labor-Hours	Unit	Material	2024 Bare Costs Labor	Equipment	Total	Total Incl O&P
6580	2"	1 Plum	10	.800	Ea.	1,000	59.50		1,059.50	1,200
6992	Tube connector fittings, See Section 22 11 13.76 for plastic ftng.									
7000	Insert type brass/copper, 100 psi @ 180°F, CTS									
7010	Adapter MPT 3/8" x 1/2" CTS	1 Plum	29	.276	Ea.	4.58	20.50		25.08	35.50
7020	1/2" x 1/2"		26	.308		4.57	23		27.57	39
7030	3/4" x 1/2"		26	.308		8.55	23		31.55	43.50
7040	3/4" x 3/4"		25	.320		4.67	24		28.67	40.50
7050	Adapter CTS 1/2" x 1/2" sweat		24	.333		5.65	25		30.65	43
7060	3/4" x 3/4" sweat		22	.364		2.26	27		29.26	43
7070	Coupler center set 3/8" CTS		25	.320		1.98	24		25.98	37.50
7080	1/2" CTS		23	.348		1.74	26		27.74	40.50
7090	3/4" CTS		22	.364		2.18	27		29.18	43
7100	Elbow 90°, copper 3/8"		25	.320		4.34	24		28.34	40.50
7110	1/2" CTS		23	.348		3.04	26		29.04	42
7120	3/4" CTS		22	.364		8.45	27		35.45	50
7130	Tee copper 3/8" CTS		17	.471		5.60	35		40.60	58.50
7140	1/2" CTS		15	.533		3.98	40		43.98	63.50
7150	3/4" CTS		14	.571		6.15	42.50		48.65	70.50
7160	3/8" x 3/8" x 1/2"		16	.500		7.20	37.50		44.70	63.50
7170	1/2" x 3/8" x 1/2"		15	.533		4.64	40		44.64	64
7180	3/4" x 1/2" x 3/4"		14	.571		5.85	42.50		48.35	70

22 11 13.27 Pipe/Tube, Grooved Joint for Copper

		Crew	Daily Output	Labor-Hours	Unit	Material	2024 Bare Costs Labor	Equipment	Total	Total Incl O&P
0010	**PIPE/TUBE, GROOVED JOINT FOR COPPER**									
4000	Fittings: coupling material required at joints not incl. in fitting price.									
4001	Add 1 selected coupling, material only, per joint for installed price.									
4010	Coupling, rigid style									
4018	2" diameter	1 Plum	50	.160	Ea.	50	11.95		61.95	73
4020	2-1/2" diameter	Q-1	80	.200		55	13.45		68.45	80.50
4022	3" diameter		67	.239		62	16.05		78.05	92
4024	4" diameter		50	.320		92.50	21.50		114	134
4026	5" diameter		40	.400		154	27		181	210
4028	6" diameter	Q-2	50	.480		203	33.50		236.50	274
4100	Elbow, 90° or 45°									
4108	2" diameter	1 Plum	25	.320	Ea.	84.50	24		108.50	129
4110	2-1/2" diameter	Q-1	40	.400		91	27		118	140
4112	3" diameter		33	.485		127	32.50		159.50	189
4114	4" diameter		25	.640		291	43		334	385
4116	5" diameter		20	.800		820	53.50		873.50	985
4118	6" diameter	Q-2	25	.960		1,300	67		1,367	1,550
4200	Tee									
4208	2" diameter	1 Plum	17	.471	Ea.	137	35		172	204
4210	2-1/2" diameter	Q-1	27	.593		146	40		186	219
4212	3" diameter		22	.727		217	49		266	310
4214	4" diameter		17	.941		475	63		538	615
4216	5" diameter		13	1.231		1,325	82.50		1,407.50	1,575
4218	6" diameter	Q-2	17	1.412		1,625	98.50		1,723.50	1,950
4300	Reducer, concentric									
4310	3" x 2-1/2" diameter	Q-1	35	.457	Ea.	121	30.50		151.50	179
4312	4" x 2-1/2" diameter		32	.500		245	33.50		278.50	320
4314	4" x 3" diameter		29	.552		245	37		282	325
4316	5" x 3" diameter		25	.640		685	43		728	820
4318	5" x 4" diameter		22	.727		685	49		734	830

22 11 Facility Water Distribution

22 11 13 – Facility Water Distribution Piping

22 11 13.27 Pipe/Tube, Grooved Joint for Copper

		Crew	Daily Output	Labor-Hours	Unit	Material	2024 Bare Costs Labor	Equipment	Total	Total Incl O&P
4320	6" x 3" diameter	Q-2	28	.857	Ea.	745	59.50		804.50	910
4322	6" x 4" diameter		26	.923		745	64.50		809.50	915
4324	6" x 5" diameter		24	1		745	69.50		814.50	925
4350	Flange, w/groove gasket									
4351	ANSI class 125 and 150									
4355	2" diameter	1 Plum	23	.348	Ea.	410	26		436	490
4356	2-1/2" diameter	Q-1	37	.432		425	29		454	515
4358	3" diameter		31	.516		450	34.50		484.50	540
4360	4" diameter		23	.696		490	46.50		536.50	610
4362	5" diameter		19	.842		660	56.50		716.50	810
4364	6" diameter	Q-2	23	1.043		715	72.50		787.50	900

22 11 13.29 Pipe, Fittings and Valves, Copper, Pressed-Joint

		Crew	Daily Output	Labor-Hours	Unit	Material	2024 Bare Costs Labor	Equipment	Total	Total Incl O&P
0010	**PIPE, FITTINGS AND VALVES, COPPER, PRESSED-JOINT**									
0040	Pipe/tube includes coupling & clevis type hanger assy's, 10' OC									
0120	Type K									
0130	1/2" diameter	1 Plum	78	.103	L.F.	4.37	7.65		12.02	16.20
0134	3/4" diameter		74	.108		7.15	8.05		15.20	19.85
0138	1" diameter		66	.121		9.60	9.05		18.65	24
0142	1-1/4" diameter		56	.143		11.45	10.65		22.10	28.50
0146	1-1/2" diameter		50	.160		16.10	11.95		28.05	35.50
0150	2" diameter		40	.200		23	14.95		37.95	47.50
0154	2-1/2" diameter	Q-1	60	.267		38.50	17.90		56.40	68.50
0158	3" diameter		54	.296		55	19.90		74.90	89.50
0162	4" diameter		38	.421		89	28.50		117.50	140
0180	To delete cplgs. & hngrs., 1/2" pipe, subtract					19%	48%			
0184	3/4"-2" pipe, subtract					14%	46%			
0186	2-1/2"-4" pipe, subtract					24%	34%			
0220	Type L									
0230	1/2" diameter	1 Plum	81	.099	L.F.	3.81	7.35		11.16	15.15
0234	3/4" diameter		76	.105		5.40	7.85		13.25	17.65
0238	1" diameter		68	.118		7.80	8.80		16.60	21.50
0242	1-1/4" diameter		58	.138		10.20	10.30		20.50	26.50
0246	1-1/2" diameter		52	.154		13.85	11.50		25.35	32.50
0250	2" diameter		42	.190		20.50	14.20		34.70	43.50
0254	2-1/2" diameter	Q-1	62	.258		36.50	17.35		53.85	66
0258	3" diameter		56	.286		48.50	19.20		67.70	82
0262	4" diameter		39	.410		76	27.50		103.50	125
0280	To delete cplgs. & hngrs., 1/2" pipe, subtract					21%	52%			
0284	3/4"-2" pipe, subtract					17%	46%			
0286	2-1/2"-4" pipe, subtract					23%	35%			
0320	Type M									
0330	1/2" diameter	1 Plum	84	.095	L.F.	3.07	7.10		10.17	14
0334	3/4" diameter		78	.103		4.39	7.65		12.04	16.25
0338	1" diameter		70	.114		6.60	8.55		15.15	19.95
0342	1-1/4" diameter		60	.133		9	9.95		18.95	25
0346	1-1/2" diameter		54	.148		12.95	11.05		24	30.50
0350	2" diameter		44	.182		18.65	13.55		32.20	40.50
0354	2-1/2" diameter	Q-1	64	.250		34	16.80		50.80	62.50
0358	3" diameter		58	.276		44	18.55		62.55	76
0362	4" diameter		40	.400		73	27		100	120
0380	To delete cplgs. & hngrs., 1/2" pipe, subtract					32%	49%			
0384	3/4"-2" pipe, subtract					21%	46%			

22 11 Facility Water Distribution

22 11 13 – Facility Water Distribution Piping

22 11 13.29 Pipe, Fittings and Valves, Copper, Pressed-Joint		Crew	Daily Output	Labor-Hours	Unit	Material	2024 Bare Costs Labor	Equipment	Total	Total Incl O&P
0386	2-1/2"-4" pipe, subtract					25%	36%			
1600	Fittings									
1610	Press joints, copper x copper									
1620	Note: Reducing fittings show most expensive size combination.									
1800	90° elbow, 1/2"	1 Plum	36.60	.219	Ea.	6.80	16.30		23.10	32
1810	3/4"		27.50	.291		6.15	21.50		27.65	39.50
1820	1"		25.90	.309		18.20	23		41.20	54.50
1830	1-1/4"		20.90	.383		19.50	28.50		48	64
1840	1-1/2"		18.30	.437		69.50	32.50		102	125
1850	2"	↓	15.70	.510		77.50	38		115.50	142
1860	2-1/2"	Q-1	25.90	.618		278	41.50		319.50	365
1870	3"		22	.727		350	49		399	460
1880	4"	↓	16.30	.982		410	66		476	555
2000	45° elbow, 1/2"	1 Plum	36.60	.219		6.35	16.30		22.65	31.50
2010	3/4"		27.50	.291		8	21.50		29.50	41.50
2020	1"		25.90	.309		25.50	23		48.50	62.50
2030	1-1/4"		20.90	.383		34.50	28.50		63	80.50
2040	1-1/2"		18.30	.437		59.50	32.50		92	114
2050	2"	↓	15.70	.510		82.50	38		120.50	147
2060	2-1/2"	Q-1	25.90	.618		178	41.50		219.50	258
2070	3"		22	.727		249	49		298	345
2080	4"	↓	16.30	.982		355	66		421	490
2200	Tee, 1/2"	1 Plum	27.50	.291		8.60	21.50		30.10	42
2210	3/4"		20.70	.386		15.10	29		44.10	59.50
2220	1"		19.40	.412		27.50	31		58.50	76.50
2230	1-1/4"		15.70	.510		47.50	38		85.50	109
2240	1-1/2"		13.80	.580		90.50	43.50		134	164
2250	2"	↓	11.80	.678		112	50.50		162.50	199
2260	2-1/2"	Q-1	19.40	.825		335	55.50		390.50	450
2270	3"		16.50	.970		410	65		475	545
2280	4"	↓	12.20	1.311	↓	585	88		673	770
2400	Tee, reducing on the outlet									
2410	3/4"	1 Plum	20.70	.386	Ea.	12.30	29		41.30	56.50
2420	1"		19.40	.412		30	31		61	79
2430	1-1/4"		15.70	.510		44	38		82	105
2440	1-1/2"		13.80	.580		92	43.50		135.50	166
2450	2"	↓	11.80	.678		144	50.50		194.50	234
2460	2-1/2"	Q-1	19.40	.825		430	55.50		485.50	555
2470	3"		16.50	.970		535	65		600	685
2480	4"	↓	12.20	1.311		645	88		733	840
2600	Tee, reducing on the run									
2610	3/4"	1 Plum	20.70	.386	Ea.	24.50	29		53.50	69.50
2620	1"		19.40	.412		47	31		78	97.50
2630	1-1/4"		15.70	.510		92.50	38		130.50	159
2640	1-1/2"		13.80	.580		141	43.50		184.50	221
2650	2"	↓	11.80	.678		156	50.50		206.50	247
2660	2-1/2"	Q-1	19.40	.825		500	55.50		555.50	635
2670	3"		16.50	.970		600	65		665	755
2680	4"	↓	12.20	1.311		750	88		838	955
2800	Coupling, 1/2"	1 Plum	36.60	.219		5.10	16.30		21.40	30
2810	3/4"		27.50	.291		7.70	21.50		29.20	41
2820	1"		25.90	.309		15.45	23		38.45	51.50
2830	1-1/4"	↓	20.90	.383		19.90	28.50		48.40	64.50

22 11 Facility Water Distribution

22 11 13 – Facility Water Distribution Piping

22 11 13.29 Pipe, Fittings and Valves, Copper, Pressed-Joint

		Crew	Daily Output	Labor-Hours	Unit	Material	2024 Bare Costs Labor	Equipment	Total	Total Incl O&P
2840	1-1/2"	1 Plum	18.30	.437	Ea.	36.50	32.50		69	88.50
2850	2"		15.70	.510		46.50	38		84.50	108
2860	2-1/2"	Q-1	25.90	.618		138	41.50		179.50	214
2870	3"		22	.727		176	49		225	267
2880	4"		16.30	.982		249	66		315	370
3000	Union, 1/2"	1 Plum	36.60	.219		26.50	16.30		42.80	54
3010	3/4"		27.50	.291		32.50	21.50		54	68
3020	1"		25.90	.309		53.50	23		76.50	93.50
3030	1-1/4"		20.90	.383		124	28.50		152.50	179
3040	1-1/2"		18.30	.437		162	32.50		194.50	227
3050	2"		15.70	.510		260	38		298	345
3200	Adapter, tube to MPT									
3210	1/2"	1 Plum	15.10	.530	Ea.	6.20	39.50		45.70	66
3220	3/4"		13.60	.588		9.60	44		53.60	76
3230	1"		11.60	.690		16.40	51.50		67.90	94.50
3240	1-1/4"		9.90	.808		44.50	60.50		105	139
3250	1-1/2"		9	.889		45.50	66.50		112	149
3260	2"		7.90	1.013		126	75.50		201.50	251
3270	2-1/2"	Q-1	13.40	1.194		269	80		349	415
3280	3"		10.60	1.509		340	101		441	525
3290	4"		7.70	2.078		415	140		555	665
3400	Adapter, tube to FPT									
3410	1/2"	1 Plum	15.10	.530	Ea.	7.70	39.50		47.20	67.50
3420	3/4"		13.60	.588		12.05	44		56.05	79
3430	1"		11.60	.690		23	51.50		74.50	102
3440	1-1/4"		9.90	.808		53	60.50		113.50	148
3450	1-1/2"		9	.889		74.50	66.50		141	180
3460	2"		7.90	1.013		124	75.50		199.50	248
3470	2-1/2"	Q-1	13.40	1.194		305	80		385	455
3480	3"		10.60	1.509		500	101		601	700
3490	4"		7.70	2.078		640	140		780	915
3600	Flange									
3620	1"	1 Plum	36.20	.221	Ea.	227	16.50		243.50	275
3630	1-1/4"		29.30	.273		325	20.50		345.50	385
3640	1-1/2"		25.60	.313		360	23.50		383.50	430
3650	2"		22	.364		400	27		427	480
3660	2-1/2"	Q-1	36.20	.442		405	29.50		434.50	490
3670	3"		30.80	.519		490	35		525	590
3680	4"		22.80	.702		550	47		597	675
3800	Cap, 1/2"	1 Plum	53.10	.151		10.80	11.25		22.05	28.50
3810	3/4"		39.80	.201		17.30	15		32.30	41.50
3820	1"		37.50	.213		28.50	15.95		44.45	55
3830	1-1/4"		30.40	.263		32	19.65		51.65	64
3840	1-1/2"		26.60	.301		49.50	22.50		72	88
3850	2"		22.80	.351		60	26		86	105
3860	2-1/2"	Q-1	37.50	.427		186	28.50		214.50	248
3870	3"		31.90	.502		236	33.50		269.50	310
3880	4"		23.60	.678		275	45.50		320.50	370
4000	Reducer									
4010	3/4"	1 Plum	27.50	.291	Ea.	23.50	21.50		45	58
4020	1"		25.90	.309		43	23		66	82
4030	1-1/4"		20.90	.383		59.50	28.50		88	108
4040	1-1/2"		18.30	.437		76	32.50		108.50	132

For customer support on your Plumbing Costs with RSMeans Data call 800.448.8182.

22 11 Facility Water Distribution

22 11 13 – Facility Water Distribution Piping

22 11 13.29 Pipe, Fittings and Valves, Copper, Pressed-Joint		Crew	Daily Output	Labor-Hours	Unit	Material	2024 Bare Costs Labor	Equipment	Total	Total Incl O&P
4050	2"	1 Plum	15.70	.510	Ea.	105	38		143	173
4060	2-1/2"	Q-1	25.90	.618		266	41.50		307.50	355
4070	3"		22	.727		365	49		414	475
4080	4"		16.30	.982		470	66		536	615
4100	Stub out, 1/2"	1 Plum	50	.160		15.75	11.95		27.70	35
4110	3/4"		35	.229		28.50	17.05		45.55	56.50
4120	1"		30	.267		31	19.90		50.90	63.50
6000	Valves									
6200	Ball valve									
6210	1/2"	1 Plum	25.60	.313	Ea.	44.50	23.50		68	83.50
6220	3/4"		19.20	.417		53.50	31		84.50	105
6230	1"		18.10	.442		75	33		108	132
6240	1-1/4"		14.70	.544		141	40.50		181.50	217
6250	1-1/2"		12.80	.625		164	46.50		210.50	250
6260	2"		11	.727		305	54.50		359.50	415
6400	Check valve									
6410	1/2"	1 Plum	30	.267	Ea.	49	19.90		68.90	83
6420	3/4"		22.50	.356		62.50	26.50		89	109
6430	1"		21.20	.377		34.50	28		62.50	80
6440	1-1/4"		17.20	.465		104	34.50		138.50	167
6450	1-1/2"		15	.533		148	40		188	222
6460	2"		12.90	.620		133	46.50		179.50	215
6600	Butterfly valve, lug type									
6660	2-1/2"	Q-1	9	1.778	Ea.	230	119		349	430
6670	3"		8	2		282	134		416	510
6680	4"		5	3.200		350	215		565	705

22 11 13.44 Pipe, Steel

		Crew	Daily Output	Labor-Hours	Unit	Material	2024 Bare Costs Labor	Equipment	Total	Total Incl O&P
0010	**PIPE, STEEL**									
0020	All pipe sizes are to Spec. A-53 unless noted otherwise									
0032	Schedule 10, see Line 22 11 13.48 0500									
0050	Schedule 40, threaded, with couplings, and clevis hanger									
0060	assemblies sized for covering, 10' OC									
0540	Black, 1/4" diameter	1 Plum	66	.121	L.F.	11.60	9.05		20.65	26
0550	3/8" diameter		65	.123		15.10	9.20		24.30	30.50
0560	1/2" diameter		63	.127		6	9.50		15.50	20.50
0570	3/4" diameter		61	.131		7.40	9.80		17.20	22.50
0580	1" diameter		53	.151		10.10	11.25		21.35	28
0590	1-1/4" diameter	Q-1	89	.180		13.25	12.10		25.35	32.50
0600	1-1/2" diameter		80	.200		15.70	13.45		29.15	37.50
0610	2" diameter		64	.250		21	16.80		37.80	48
0620	2-1/2" diameter		50	.320		35	21.50		56.50	70.50
0630	3" diameter		43	.372		42	25		67	83.50
0640	3-1/2" diameter		40	.400		65.50	27		92.50	112
0650	4" diameter		36	.444		67	30		97	118
0809	A-106, gr. A/B, seamless w/cplgs. & clevis hanger assemblies									
0811	1/4" diameter	1 Plum	66	.121	L.F.	7.15	9.05		16.20	21.50
0812	3/8" diameter		65	.123		7.10	9.20		16.30	21.50
0813	1/2" diameter		63	.127		6.35	9.50		15.85	21
0814	3/4" diameter		61	.131		7.40	9.80		17.20	22.50
0815	1" diameter		53	.151		8.90	11.25		20.15	26.50
0816	1-1/4" diameter	Q-1	89	.180		11.50	12.10		23.60	30.50
0817	1-1/2" diameter		80	.200		13.55	13.45		27	35

22 11 Facility Water Distribution

22 11 13 – Facility Water Distribution Piping

22 11 13.44 Pipe, Steel

		Crew	Daily Output	Labor-Hours	Unit	Material	2024 Bare Costs Labor	Equipment	Total	Total Incl O&P
0819	2" diameter	Q-1	64	.250	L.F.	16.75	16.80		33.55	43.50
0821	2-1/2" diameter		50	.320		30.50	21.50		52	65.50
0822	3" diameter		43	.372		38	25		63	79
0823	4" diameter	▼	36	.444	▼	58	30		88	108
1220	To delete coupling & hanger, subtract									
1230	1/4" diam. to 3/4" diam.					31%	56%			
1240	1" diam. to 1-1/2" diam.					23%	51%			
1250	2" diam. to 4" diam.					23%	41%			
1280	All pipe sizes are to Spec. A-53 unless noted otherwise									
1281	Schedule 40, threaded, with couplings and clevis hanger									
1282	assemblies sized for covering, 10' OC									
1290	Galvanized, 1/4" diameter	1 Plum	66	.121	L.F.	16	9.05		25.05	31
1300	3/8" diameter		65	.123		21	9.20		30.20	36.50
1310	1/2" diameter		63	.127		6.95	9.50		16.45	22
1320	3/4" diameter		61	.131		8.70	9.80		18.50	24
1330	1" diameter	▼	53	.151		11.75	11.25		23	29.50
1340	1-1/4" diameter	Q-1	89	.180		15.50	12.10		27.60	35
1350	1-1/2" diameter		80	.200		18.35	13.45		31.80	40
1360	2" diameter		64	.250		24.50	16.80		41.30	52
1370	2-1/2" diameter		50	.320		40	21.50		61.50	76
1380	3" diameter		43	.372		52.50	25		77.50	94.50
1390	3-1/2" diameter		40	.400		49	27		76	94
1400	4" diameter	▼	36	.444	▼	71.50	30		101.50	123
1750	To delete coupling & hanger, subtract									
1760	1/4" diam. to 3/4" diam.					31%	56%			
1770	1" diam. to 1-1/2" diam.					23%	51%			
1780	2" diam. to 4" diam.					23%	41%			
1900	Pipe nipple std black 2" long, 1/2" diameter	1 Plum	19	.421	Ea.	2.27	31.50		33.77	49.50
1910	Pipe nipple std black 2" long, 1" diameter	"	15	.533		2.66	40		42.66	62
1920	3" long, 2-1/2" diameter	Q-1	16	1	▼	23	67		90	125
2000	Welded, sch. 40, on yoke & roll hanger assy's, sized for covering, 10' OC									
2040	Black, 1" diameter	Q-15	93	.172	L.F.	11.05	11.55	.77	23.37	30.50
2050	1-1/4" diameter		84	.190		14.55	12.80	.86	28.21	36
2060	1-1/2" diameter		76	.211		16.70	14.15	.95	31.80	40.50
2070	2" diameter		61	.262		21.50	17.60	1.18	40.28	51
2080	2-1/2" diameter		47	.340		30.50	23	1.53	55.03	69
2090	3" diameter		43	.372		39	25	1.67	65.67	81.50
2100	3-1/2" diameter		39	.410		47	27.50	1.84	76.34	94.50
2110	4" diameter		37	.432		54.50	29	1.94	85.44	105
2120	5" diameter	▼	32	.500		34	33.50	2.25	69.75	90
2130	6" diameter	Q-16	36	.667		97.50	46.50	1.99	145.99	178
2140	8" diameter		29	.828		123	57.50	2.47	182.97	225
2150	10" diameter		24	1		156	69.50	2.99	228.49	279
2160	12" diameter		19	1.263		189	88	3.78	280.78	345
2170	14" diameter (two rod roll type hanger for 14" diam. and up)		15	1.600		198	111	4.78	313.78	390
2180	16" diameter (two rod roll type hanger)		13	1.846		293	129	5.50	427.50	515
2190	18" diameter (two rod roll type hanger)		11	2.182		276	152	6.50	434.50	540
2200	20" diameter (two rod roll type hanger)		9	2.667		305	186	7.95	498.95	620
2220	24" diameter (two rod roll type hanger)	▼	8	3	▼	395	209	8.95	612.95	755
2560	To delete hanger, subtract									
2570	1" diam. to 1-1/2" diam.					15%	34%			
2580	2" diam. to 3-1/2" diam.					9%	21%			
2590	4" diam. to 12" diam.					5%	12%			

22 11 Facility Water Distribution

22 11 13 – Facility Water Distribution Piping

22 11 13.44 Pipe, Steel

		Crew	Daily Output	Labor-Hours	Unit	Material	2024 Bare Costs Labor	Equipment	Total	Total Incl O&P
2596	14" diam. to 24" diam.					3%	10%			
3250	Flanged, 150 lb. weld neck, on yoke & roll hangers									
3260	sized for covering, 10' OC									
3290	Black, 1" diameter	Q-15	70	.229	L.F.	19	15.35	1.03	35.38	45
3300	1-1/4" diameter		64	.250		21.50	16.80	1.12	39.42	49.50
3310	1-1/2" diameter		58	.276		24	18.55	1.24	43.79	55.50
3320	2" diameter		45	.356		28	24	1.60	53.60	68.50
3330	2-1/2" diameter		36	.444		38	30	2	70	88.50
3340	3" diameter		32	.500		47	33.50	2.25	82.75	104
3350	3-1/2" diameter		29	.552		58	37	2.48	97.48	121
3360	4" diameter		26	.615		64.50	41.50	2.76	108.76	136
3370	5" diameter		21	.762		56	51	3.42	110.42	141
3380	6" diameter	Q-16	25	.960		115	67	2.87	184.87	229
3390	8" diameter		19	1.263		152	88	3.78	243.78	300
3400	10" diameter		16	1.500		215	105	4.49	324.49	395
3410	12" diameter		14	1.714		282	119	5.15	406.15	495
3470	For 300 lb. flanges, add					63%				
3480	For 600 lb. flanges, add					310%				
3960	To delete flanges & hanger, subtract									
3970	1" diam. to 2" diam.					76%	65%			
3980	2-1/2" diam. to 4" diam.					62%	59%			
3990	5" diam. to 12" diam.					60%	46%			
4750	Schedule 80, threaded, with couplings, and clevis hanger assemblies									
4760	sized for covering, 10' OC									
4790	Black, 1/4" diameter	1 Plum	54	.148	L.F.	10	11.05		21.05	27.50
4800	3/8" diameter		53	.151		13.20	11.25		24.45	31.50
4810	1/2" diameter		52	.154		8.15	11.50		19.65	26
4820	3/4" diameter		50	.160		10	11.95		21.95	29
4830	1" diameter		45	.178		13.45	13.25		26.70	34.50
4840	1-1/4" diameter	Q-1	75	.213		18.55	14.35		32.90	42
4850	1-1/2" diameter		69	.232		21.50	15.60		37.10	47
4860	2" diameter		56	.286		29	19.20		48.20	60.50
4870	2-1/2" diameter		44	.364		40.50	24.50		65	81
4880	3" diameter		38	.421		53	28.50		81.50	100
4890	3-1/2" diameter		35	.457		45	30.50		75.50	95
4900	4" diameter		32	.500		53.50	33.50		87	109
5430	To delete coupling & hanger, subtract									
5440	1/4" diam. to 1/2" diam.					31%	54%			
5450	3/4" diam. to 1-1/2" diam.					28%	49%			
5460	2" diam. to 4" diam.					21%	40%			
5510	Galvanized, 1/4" diameter	1 Plum	54	.148	L.F.	17.55	11.05		28.60	36
5520	3/8" diameter		53	.151		19.10	11.25		30.35	38
5530	1/2" diameter		52	.154		6.45	11.50		17.95	24
5540	3/4" diameter		50	.160		7.80	11.95		19.75	26.50
5550	1" diameter		45	.178		9.25	13.25		22.50	30
5560	1-1/4" diameter	Q-1	75	.213		12.75	14.35		27.10	35.50
5570	1-1/2" diameter		69	.232		14.60	15.60		30.20	39
5580	2" diameter		56	.286		20	19.20		39.20	50.50
5590	2-1/2" diameter		44	.364		32	24.50		56.50	71.50
5600	3" diameter		38	.421		41	28.50		69.50	87.50
5610	3-1/2" diameter		35	.457		48	30.50		78.50	98.50
5620	4" diameter		32	.500		61	33.50		94.50	117
5930	To delete coupling & hanger, subtract									

22 11 Facility Water Distribution

22 11 13 – Facility Water Distribution Piping

22 11 13.44 Pipe, Steel

		Crew	Daily Output	Labor-Hours	Unit	Material	2024 Bare Costs Labor	2024 Bare Costs Equipment	Total	Total Incl O&P
5940	1/4" diam. to 1/2" diam.					31%	54%			
5950	3/4" diam. to 1-1/2" diam.					28%	49%			
5960	2" diam. to 4" diam.					21%	40%			
6000	Welded, on yoke & roller hangers									
6010	sized for covering, 10' OC									
6040	Black, 1" diameter	Q-15	85	.188	L.F.	13.55	12.65	.85	27.05	34.50
6050	1-1/4" diameter		79	.203		18.20	13.60	.91	32.71	41
6060	1-1/2" diameter		72	.222		21.50	14.95	1	37.45	46.50
6070	2" diameter		57	.281		27	18.85	1.26	47.11	59.50
6080	2-1/2" diameter		44	.364		37	24.50	1.63	63.13	79
6090	3" diameter		40	.400		48	27	1.80	76.80	95
6100	3-1/2" diameter		34	.471		38	31.50	2.11	71.61	91.50
6110	4" diameter		33	.485		45	32.50	2.18	79.68	100
6120	5" diameter, A-106B	▼	26	.615		80	41.50	2.76	124.26	153
6130	6" diameter, A-106B	Q-16	30	.800		159	55.50	2.39	216.89	260
6140	8" diameter, A-106B		25	.960		185	67	2.87	254.87	305
6150	10" diameter, A-106B		20	1.200		450	83.50	3.59	537.09	625
6160	12" diameter, A-106B	▼	15	1.600	▼	720	111	4.78	835.78	960
6540	To delete hanger, subtract									
6550	1" diam. to 1-1/2" diam.					30%	14%			
6560	2" diam. to 3" diam.					23%	9%			
6570	3-1/2" diam. to 5" diam.					12%	6%			
6580	6" diam. to 12" diam.					10%	4%			
7250	Flanged, 300 lb. weld neck, on yoke & roll hangers									
7260	sized for covering, 10' OC									
7290	Black, 1" diameter	Q-15	66	.242	L.F.	24.50	16.30	1.09	41.89	52
7300	1-1/4" diameter		61	.262		29	17.60	1.18	47.78	59.50
7310	1-1/2" diameter		54	.296		32	19.90	1.33	53.23	66.50
7320	2" diameter		42	.381		37	25.50	1.71	64.21	80.50
7330	2-1/2" diameter		33	.485		51	32.50	2.18	85.68	107
7340	3" diameter		29	.552		62	37	2.48	101.48	126
7350	3-1/2" diameter		24	.667		53	45	2.99	100.99	128
7360	4" diameter		23	.696		58.50	46.50	3.12	108.12	137
7370	5" diameter	▼	19	.842		116	56.50	3.78	176.28	216
7380	6" diameter	Q-16	23	1.043		194	72.50	3.12	269.62	325
7390	8" diameter		17	1.412		244	98.50	4.22	346.72	420
7400	10" diameter		14	1.714		560	119	5.15	684.15	800
7410	12" diameter	▼	12	2	▼	860	139	6	1,005	1,150
7470	For 600 lb. flanges, add					100%				
7940	To delete flanges & hanger, subtract									
7950	1" diam. to 1-1/2" diam.					75%	66%			
7960	2" diam. to 3" diam.					62%	60%			
7970	3-1/2" diam. to 5" diam.					54%	66%			
7980	6" diam. to 12" diam.					55%	62%			
9000	Threading pipe labor, one end, all schedules through 80									
9010	1/4" through 3/4" pipe size	1 Plum	80	.100	Ea.		7.45		7.45	11.10
9020	1" through 2" pipe size		73	.110			8.20		8.20	12.15
9030	2-1/2" pipe size		53	.151			11.25		11.25	16.75
9040	3" pipe size	▼	50	.160			11.95		11.95	17.75
9050	3-1/2" pipe size	Q-1	89	.180			12.10		12.10	17.95
9060	4" pipe size		73	.219			14.70		14.70	22
9070	5" pipe size		53	.302			20.50		20.50	30
9080	6" pipe size	▼	46	.348	▼		23.50		23.50	35

22 11 Facility Water Distribution

22 11 13 – Facility Water Distribution Piping

22 11 13.44 Pipe, Steel

		Crew	Daily Output	Labor-Hours	Unit	Material	2024 Bare Costs Labor	2024 Bare Costs Equipment	Total	Total Incl O&P
9090	8" pipe size	Q-1	29	.552	Ea.		37		37	55
9100	10" pipe size		21	.762			51		51	76
9110	12" pipe size	↓	13	1.231			82.50		82.50	123
9120	Cutting pipe labor, one cut									
9124	Shop fabrication, machine cut									
9126	Schedule 40, straight pipe									
9128	2" pipe size or less	1 Stpi	62	.129	Ea.		9.75		9.75	14.50
9130	2-1/2" pipe size		56	.143			10.80		10.80	16.05
9132	3" pipe size		42	.190			14.40		14.40	21.50
9134	4" pipe size		31	.258			19.50		19.50	29
9136	5" pipe size		26	.308			23.50		23.50	34.50
9138	6" pipe size		19	.421			32		32	47.50
9140	8" pipe size		14	.571			43		43	64
9142	10" pipe size		10	.800			60.50		60.50	90
9144	12" pipe size	↓	7	1.143			86.50		86.50	128
9146	14" pipe size	Q-5	10.50	1.524			104		104	154
9148	16" pipe size		8.60	1.860			127		127	188
9150	18" pipe size		7	2.286			155		155	231
9152	20" pipe size		5.80	2.759			188		188	279
9154	24" pipe size	↓	4	4			272		272	405
9160	Schedule 80, straight pipe									
9164	2" pipe size or less	1 Stpi	42	.190	Ea.		14.40		14.40	21.50
9166	2-1/2" pipe size		37	.216			16.35		16.35	24.50
9168	3" pipe size		31	.258			19.50		19.50	29
9170	4" pipe size		23	.348			26.50		26.50	39
9172	5" pipe size		18	.444			33.50		33.50	50
9174	6" pipe size		14.60	.548			41.50		41.50	61.50
9176	8" pipe size	↓	10	.800			60.50		60.50	90
9178	10" pipe size	Q-5	14	1.143			77.50		77.50	116
9180	12" pipe size	"	10	1.600	↓		109		109	162
9200	Welding labor per joint									
9210	Schedule 40									
9230	1/2" pipe size	Q-15	32	.500	Ea.		33.50	2.25	35.75	52.50
9240	3/4" pipe size		27	.593			40	2.66	42.66	62
9250	1" pipe size		23	.696			46.50	3.12	49.62	73
9260	1-1/4" pipe size		20	.800			53.50	3.59	57.09	84
9270	1-1/2" pipe size		19	.842			56.50	3.78	60.28	88
9280	2" pipe size		16	1			67	4.49	71.49	105
9290	2-1/2" pipe size		13	1.231			82.50	5.55	88.05	129
9300	3" pipe size		12	1.333			89.50	6	95.50	140
9310	4" pipe size		10	1.600			107	7.20	114.20	168
9320	5" pipe size		9	1.778			119	8	127	187
9330	6" pipe size		8	2			134	9	143	210
9340	8" pipe size		5	3.200			215	14.35	229.35	335
9350	10" pipe size		4	4			269	17.95	286.95	420
9360	12" pipe size		3	5.333			360	24	384	560
9370	14" pipe size		2.60	6.154			415	27.50	442.50	645
9380	16" pipe size		2.20	7.273			490	32.50	522.50	760
9390	18" pipe size		2	8			535	36	571	840
9400	20" pipe size		1.80	8.889			595	40	635	935
9410	22" pipe size		1.70	9.412			630	42.50	672.50	985
9420	24" pipe size	↓	1.50	10.667	↓		715	48	763	1,125
9450	Schedule 80									

22 11 Facility Water Distribution

22 11 13 – Facility Water Distribution Piping

22 11 13.44 Pipe, Steel

		Crew	Daily Output	Labor-Hours	Unit	Material	2024 Bare Costs Labor	2024 Bare Costs Equipment	Total	Total Incl O&P
9460	1/2" pipe size	Q-15	27	.593	Ea.		40	2.66	42.66	62
9470	3/4" pipe size		23	.696			46.50	3.12	49.62	73
9480	1" pipe size		20	.800			53.50	3.59	57.09	84
9490	1-1/4" pipe size		19	.842			56.50	3.78	60.28	88
9500	1-1/2" pipe size		18	.889			59.50	3.99	63.49	93.50
9510	2" pipe size		15	1.067			71.50	4.79	76.29	112
9520	2-1/2" pipe size		12	1.333			89.50	6	95.50	140
9530	3" pipe size		11	1.455			97.50	6.55	104.05	152
9540	4" pipe size		8	2			134	9	143	210
9550	5" pipe size		6	2.667			179	11.95	190.95	279
9560	6" pipe size		5	3.200			215	14.35	229.35	335
9570	8" pipe size		4	4			269	17.95	286.95	420
9580	10" pipe size		3	5.333			360	24	384	560
9590	12" pipe size		2	8			535	36	571	840
9600	14" pipe size	Q-16	2.60	9.231			645	27.50	672.50	985
9610	16" pipe size		2.30	10.435			725	31	756	1,100
9620	18" pipe size		2	12			835	36	871	1,300
9630	20" pipe size		1.80	13.333			930	40	970	1,425
9640	22" pipe size		1.60	15			1,050	45	1,095	1,600
9650	24" pipe size		1.50	16			1,125	48	1,173	1,700

22 11 13.45 Pipe Fittings, Steel, Threaded

		Crew	Daily Output	Labor-Hours	Unit	Material	2024 Bare Costs Labor	2024 Bare Costs Equipment	Total	Total Incl O&P
0010	**PIPE FITTINGS, STEEL, THREADED**									
0020	Cast iron									
0040	Standard weight, black									
0060	90° elbow, straight									
0070	1/4"	1 Plum	16	.500	Ea.	7.55	37.50		45.05	64
0080	3/8"		16	.500		10.90	37.50		48.40	67.50
0090	1/2"		15	.533		4.77	40		44.77	64.50
0100	3/4"		14	.571		4.97	42.50		47.47	69
0110	1"		13	.615		5.90	46		51.90	75
0120	1-1/4"	Q-1	22	.727		8.35	49		57.35	81.50
0130	1-1/2"		20	.800		11.55	53.50		65.05	92.50
0140	2"		18	.889		18.10	59.50		77.60	109
0150	2-1/2"		14	1.143		43.50	77		120.50	162
0160	3"		10	1.600		71	107		178	238
0170	3-1/2"		8	2		193	134		327	410
0180	4"		6	2.667		131	179		310	410
0250	45° elbow, straight									
0260	1/4"	1 Plum	16	.500	Ea.	9.70	37.50		47.20	66
0270	3/8"		16	.500		10.45	37.50		47.95	67
0280	1/2"		15	.533		7.30	40		47.30	67
0300	3/4"		14	.571		7.35	42.50		49.85	71.50
0320	1"		13	.615		8.60	46		54.60	78
0330	1-1/4"	Q-1	22	.727		11.60	49		60.60	85.50
0340	1-1/2"		20	.800		19.20	53.50		72.70	101
0350	2"		18	.889		22	59.50		81.50	114
0360	2-1/2"		14	1.143		141	77		218	269
0370	3"		10	1.600		223	107		330	405
0380	3-1/2"		8	2		550	134		684	805
0400	4"		6	2.667		465	179		644	775
0500	Tee, straight									
0510	1/4"	1 Plum	10	.800	Ea.	30	59.50		89.50	122

For customer support on your Plumbing Costs with RSMeans Data call 800.448.8182.

22 11 Facility Water Distribution

22 11 13 – Facility Water Distribution Piping

22 11 13.45 Pipe Fittings, Steel, Threaded

		Crew	Daily Output	Labor-Hours	Unit	Material	2024 Bare Costs Labor	Equipment	Total	Total Incl O&P
0520	3/8"	1 Plum	10	.800	Ea.	28	59.50		87.50	120
0530	1/2"		9	.889		18.20	66.50		84.70	119
0540	3/4"		9	.889		21	66.50		87.50	122
0550	1"		8	1		18.90	74.50		93.40	132
0560	1-1/4"	Q-1	14	1.143		34.50	77		111.50	152
0570	1-1/2"		13	1.231		45	82.50		127.50	173
0580	2"		11	1.455		62.50	97.50		160	214
0590	2-1/2"		9	1.778		162	119		281	355
0600	3"		6	2.667		249	179		428	540
0610	3-1/2"		5	3.200		500	215		715	870
0620	4"		4	4		485	269		754	935
0660	Tee, reducing, run or outlet									
0661	1/2"	1 Plum	9	.889	Ea.	47	66.50		113.50	151
0662	3/4"		9	.889		29.50	66.50		96	131
0663	1"		8	1		25.50	74.50		100	139
0664	1-1/4"	Q-1	14	1.143		34	77		111	152
0665	1-1/2"		13	1.231		63	82.50		145.50	193
0666	2"		11	1.455		75	97.50		172.50	228
0667	2-1/2"		9	1.778		184	119		303	380
0668	3"		6	2.667		320	179		499	620
0669	3-1/2"		5	3.200		810	215		1,025	1,200
0670	4"		4	4		625	269		894	1,100
0674	Reducer, concentric									
0675	3/4"	1 Plum	18	.444	Ea.	32.50	33		65.50	85.50
0676	1"	"	15	.533		22	40		62	83.50
0677	1-1/4"	Q-1	26	.615		57.50	41.50		99	125
0678	1-1/2"		24	.667		81	45		126	156
0679	2"		21	.762		106	51		157	193
0680	2-1/2"		18	.889		151	59.50		210.50	255
0681	3"		14	1.143		251	77		328	390
0682	3-1/2"		12	1.333		555	89.50		644.50	745
0683	4"		10	1.600		515	107		622	725
0687	Reducer, eccentric									
0688	3/4"	1 Plum	16	.500	Ea.	68.50	37.50		106	131
0689	1"	"	14	.571		74	42.50		116.50	145
0690	1-1/4"	Q-1	25	.640		111	43		154	186
0691	1-1/2"		22	.727		150	49		199	238
0692	2"		20	.800		199	53.50		252.50	299
0693	2-1/2"		16	1		305	67		372	435
0694	3"		12	1.333		475	89.50		564.50	655
0695	3-1/2"		10	1.600		785	107		892	1,025
0696	4"		9	1.778		955	119		1,074	1,225
0700	Standard weight, galvanized cast iron									
0720	90° elbow, straight									
0730	1/4"	1 Plum	16	.500	Ea.	27.50	37.50		65	85.50
0740	3/8"		16	.500		27.50	37.50		65	85.50
0750	1/2"		15	.533		34.50	40		74.50	97
0760	3/4"		14	.571		26.50	42.50		69	93
0770	1"		13	.615		35.50	46		81.50	108
0780	1-1/4"	Q-1	22	.727		47.50	49		96.50	125
0790	1-1/2"		20	.800		75.50	53.50		129	163
0800	2"		18	.889		96.50	59.50		156	195
0810	2-1/2"		14	1.143		198	77		275	330

22 11 Facility Water Distribution

22 11 13 – Facility Water Distribution Piping

22 11 13.45 Pipe Fittings, Steel, Threaded

		Crew	Daily Output	Labor-Hours	Unit	Material	2024 Bare Costs Labor	Equipment	Total	Total Incl O&P
0820	3"	Q-1	10	1.600	Ea.	300	107		407	490
0830	3-1/2"		8	2		480	134		614	730
0840	4"		6	2.667		550	179		729	870
0900	45° elbow, straight									
0910	1/4"	1 Plum	16	.500	Ea.	37.50	37.50		75	96.50
0920	3/8"		16	.500		33	37.50		70.50	91.50
0930	1/2"		15	.533		27	40		67	88.50
0940	3/4"		14	.571		30.50	42.50		73	97.50
0950	1"		13	.615		60.50	46		106.50	135
0960	1-1/4"	Q-1	22	.727		89	49		138	171
0970	1-1/2"		20	.800		105	53.50		158.50	195
0980	2"		18	.889		147	59.50		206.50	251
0990	2-1/2"		14	1.143		221	77		298	360
1000	3"		10	1.600		460	107		567	670
1010	3-1/2"		8	2		855	134		989	1,150
1020	4"		6	2.667		805	179		984	1,150
1100	Tee, straight									
1110	1/4"	1 Plum	10	.800	Ea.	33	59.50		92.50	126
1120	3/8"		10	.800		29	59.50		88.50	121
1130	1/2"		9	.889		46.50	66.50		113	150
1140	3/4"		9	.889		44	66.50		110.50	147
1150	1"		8	1		41.50	74.50		116	157
1160	1-1/4"	Q-1	14	1.143		72	77		149	194
1170	1-1/2"		13	1.231		95.50	82.50		178	228
1180	2"		11	1.455		119	97.50		216.50	276
1190	2-1/2"		9	1.778		245	119		364	445
1200	3"		6	2.667		800	179		979	1,150
1210	3-1/2"		5	3.200		680	215		895	1,075
1220	4"		4	4		940	269		1,209	1,425
1300	Extra heavy weight, black									
1310	Couplings, steel straight									
1320	1/4"	1 Plum	19	.421	Ea.	8.60	31.50		40.10	56.50
1330	3/8"		19	.421		9.35	31.50		40.85	57.50
1340	1/2"		19	.421		12.65	31.50		44.15	61
1350	3/4"		18	.444		13.55	33		46.55	64.50
1360	1"		15	.533		17.20	40		57.20	78
1370	1-1/4"	Q-1	26	.615		27.50	41.50		69	92
1380	1-1/2"		24	.667		27.50	45		72.50	97
1390	2"		21	.762		42	51		93	123
1400	2-1/2"		18	.889		62.50	59.50		122	158
1410	3"		14	1.143		74.50	77		151.50	196
1420	3-1/2"		12	1.333		100	89.50		189.50	243
1430	4"		10	1.600		117	107		224	289
1510	90° elbow, straight									
1520	1/2"	1 Plum	15	.533	Ea.	63	40		103	129
1530	3/4"		14	.571		64	42.50		106.50	134
1540	1"		13	.615		77.50	46		123.50	154
1550	1-1/4"	Q-1	22	.727		116	49		165	200
1560	1-1/2"		20	.800		143	53.50		196.50	238
1580	2"		18	.889		177	59.50		236.50	284
1590	2-1/2"		14	1.143		410	77		487	565
1600	3"		10	1.600		580	107		687	795
1610	4"		6	2.667		1,350	179		1,529	1,775

22 11 Facility Water Distribution

22 11 13 – Facility Water Distribution Piping

22 11 13.45 Pipe Fittings, Steel, Threaded

		Crew	Daily Output	Labor-Hours	Unit	Material	2024 Bare Costs Labor	Equipment	Total	Total Incl O&P
1650	45° elbow, straight									
1660	1/2"	1 Plum	15	.533	Ea.	86	40		126	154
1670	3/4"		14	.571		86.50	42.50		129	159
1680	1"		13	.615		104	46		150	184
1690	1-1/4"	Q-1	22	.727		172	49		221	262
1700	1-1/2"		20	.800		189	53.50		242.50	288
1710	2"		18	.889		268	59.50		327.50	385
1720	2-1/2"		14	1.143		475	77		552	635
1800	Tee, straight									
1810	1/2"	1 Plum	9	.889	Ea.	98.50	66.50		165	207
1820	3/4"		9	.889		98.50	66.50		165	207
1830	1"		8	1		119	74.50		193.50	242
1840	1-1/4"	Q-1	14	1.143		177	77		254	310
1850	1-1/2"		13	1.231		228	82.50		310.50	375
1860	2"		11	1.455		283	97.50		380.50	455
1870	2-1/2"		9	1.778		675	119		794	920
1880	3"		6	2.667		790	179		969	1,125
1890	4"		4	4		790	269		1,059	1,275
4000	Standard weight, black									
4010	Couplings, steel straight, merchants									
4030	1/4"	1 Plum	19	.421	Ea.	2.31	31.50		33.81	49.50
4040	3/8"		19	.421		2.78	31.50		34.28	50
4050	1/2"		19	.421		2.95	31.50		34.45	50.50
4060	3/4"		18	.444		3.77	33		36.77	53.50
4070	1"		15	.533		5.25	40		45.25	65
4080	1-1/4"	Q-1	26	.615		6.75	41.50		48.25	69
4090	1-1/2"		24	.667		8.50	45		53.50	76
4100	2"		21	.762		12.20	51		63.20	89.50
4110	2-1/2"		18	.889		43.50	59.50		103	137
4120	3"		14	1.143		27	77		104	144
4130	3-1/2"		12	1.333		108	89.50		197.50	252
4140	4"		10	1.600		108	107		215	279
4166	Plug, 1/4"	1 Plum	38	.211		5.85	15.70		21.55	30
4167	3/8"		38	.211		4.85	15.70		20.55	29
4168	1/2"		38	.211		5.20	15.70		20.90	29
4169	3/4"		32	.250		14.50	18.65		33.15	44
4170	1"		30	.267		16.70	19.90		36.60	48
4171	1-1/4"	Q-1	52	.308		19.25	20.50		39.75	52
4172	1-1/2"		48	.333		27.50	22.50		50	63.50
4173	2"		42	.381		35	25.50		60.50	76.50
4176	2-1/2"		36	.444		52	30		82	102
4180	4"		20	.800		108	53.50		161.50	199
4200	Standard weight, galvanized									
4210	Couplings, steel straight, merchants									
4230	1/4"	1 Plum	19	.421	Ea.	2.66	31.50		34.16	50
4240	3/8"		19	.421		3.40	31.50		34.90	50.50
4250	1/2"		19	.421		3.61	31.50		35.11	51
4260	3/4"		18	.444		4.53	33		37.53	54.50
4270	1"		15	.533		6.35	40		46.35	66
4280	1-1/4"	Q-1	26	.615		8.10	41.50		49.60	70.50
4290	1-1/2"		24	.667		10.05	45		55.05	77.50
4300	2"		21	.762		15.05	51		66.05	92.50
4310	2-1/2"		18	.889		40.50	59.50		100	134

22 11 Facility Water Distribution

22 11 13 – Facility Water Distribution Piping

22 11 13.45 Pipe Fittings, Steel, Threaded

		Crew	Daily Output	Labor-Hours	Unit	Material	2024 Bare Costs Labor	Equipment	Total	Total Incl O&P
4320	3"	Q-1	14	1.143	Ea.	58	77		135	178
4330	3-1/2"		12	1.333		125	89.50		214.50	270
4340	4"	↓	10	1.600	↓	52.50	107		159.50	218
4370	Plug, galvanized, square head									
4374	1/2"	1 Plum	38	.211	Ea.	15.15	15.70		30.85	40
4375	3/4"		32	.250		12.55	18.65		31.20	42
4376	1"	↓	30	.267		12.55	19.90		32.45	43.50
4377	1-1/4"	Q-1	52	.308		21	20.50		41.50	54
4378	1-1/2"		48	.333		28.50	22.50		51	64.50
4379	2"		42	.381		35	25.50		60.50	76.50
4380	2-1/2"		36	.444		74	30		104	126
4381	3"		28	.571		95	38.50		133.50	162
4382	4"		20	.800		261	53.50		314.50	365
4385	8"	↓	20	.800		207	53.50		260.50	310
4700	Nipple, black									
4710	1/2" x 4" long	1 Plum	19	.421	Ea.	5.90	31.50		37.40	53.50
4712	3/4" x 4" long		18	.444		7.10	33		40.10	57.50
4714	1" x 4" long		15	.533		9.90	40		49.90	70
4716	1-1/4" x 4" long	Q-1	26	.615		12.35	41.50		53.85	75
4718	1-1/2" x 4" long		24	.667		14.55	45		59.55	82.50
4720	2" x 4" long		21	.762		20.50	51		71.50	98.50
4722	2-1/2" x 4" long		18	.889		55	59.50		114.50	150
4724	3" x 4" long		14	1.143		70	77		147	191
4726	4" x 4" long	↓	10	1.600		94.50	107		201.50	264
4800	Nipple, galvanized									
4810	1/2" x 4" long	1 Plum	19	.421	Ea.	7.20	31.50		38.70	55
4812	3/4" x 4" long		18	.444		8.95	33		41.95	59.50
4814	1" x 4" long	↓	15	.533		12	40		52	72
4816	1-1/4" x 4" long	Q-1	26	.615		14.70	41.50		56.20	77.50
4818	1-1/2" x 4" long		24	.667		18.60	45		63.60	87
4820	2" x 4" long		21	.762		23.50	51		74.50	102
4822	2-1/2" x 4" long		18	.889		62	59.50		121.50	158
4824	3" x 4" long		14	1.143		82.50	77		159.50	205
4826	4" x 4" long	↓	10	1.600		111	107		218	282
5000	Malleable iron, 150 lb.									
5020	Black									
5040	90° elbow, straight									
5060	1/4"	1 Plum	16	.500	Ea.	9.10	37.50		46.60	65.50
5070	3/8"		16	.500		9.10	37.50		46.60	65.50
5080	1/2"		15	.533		6.30	40		46.30	66
5090	3/4"		14	.571		7.55	42.50		50.05	72
5100	1"	↓	13	.615		13.20	46		59.20	83
5110	1-1/4"	Q-1	22	.727		21.50	49		70.50	96.50
5120	1-1/2"		20	.800		28.50	53.50		82	112
5130	2"		18	.889		49.50	59.50		109	143
5140	2-1/2"		14	1.143		110	77		187	235
5150	3"		10	1.600		161	107		268	335
5160	3-1/2"		8	2		465	134		599	710
5170	4"	↓	6	2.667	↓	345	179		524	645
5250	45° elbow, straight									
5270	1/4"	1 Plum	16	.500	Ea.	13.70	37.50		51.20	70.50
5280	3/8"		16	.500		13.70	37.50		51.20	70.50
5290	1/2"		15	.533		10.35	40		50.35	70.50

22 11 Facility Water Distribution

22 11 13 – Facility Water Distribution Piping

22 11 13.45 Pipe Fittings, Steel, Threaded

		Crew	Daily Output	Labor-Hours	Unit	Material	2024 Bare Costs Labor	Equipment	Total	Total Incl O&P
5300	3/4"	1 Plum	14	.571	Ea.	12.85	42.50		55.35	77.50
5310	1"	↓	13	.615		16.15	46		62.15	86.50
5320	1-1/4"	Q-1	22	.727		28.50	49		77.50	104
5330	1-1/2"		20	.800		35.50	53.50		89	119
5340	2"		18	.889		53.50	59.50		113	148
5350	2-1/2"		14	1.143		155	77		232	284
5360	3"		10	1.600		201	107		308	380
5370	3-1/2"		8	2		395	134		529	635
5380	4"	↓	6	2.667	↓	395	179		574	700
5450	Tee, straight									
5470	1/4"	1 Plum	10	.800	Ea.	13.20	59.50		72.70	104
5480	3/8"		10	.800		13.20	59.50		72.70	104
5490	1/2"		9	.889		8.40	66.50		74.90	108
5500	3/4"		9	.889		12.10	66.50		78.60	112
5510	1"	↓	8	1		20.50	74.50		95	134
5520	1-1/4"	Q-1	14	1.143		33.50	77		110.50	151
5530	1-1/2"		13	1.231		41.50	82.50		124	169
5540	2"		11	1.455		71	97.50		168.50	223
5550	2-1/2"		9	1.778		153	119		272	345
5560	3"		6	2.667		225	179		404	515
5570	3-1/2"		5	3.200		545	215		760	920
5580	4"	↓	4	4	↓	545	269		814	1,000
5601	Tee, reducing, on outlet									
5602	1/2"	1 Plum	9	.889	Ea.	14.30	66.50		80.80	114
5603	3/4"		9	.889		18.65	66.50		85.15	119
5604	1"	↓	8	1		23.50	74.50		98	137
5605	1-1/4"	Q-1	14	1.143		41	77		118	159
5606	1-1/2"		13	1.231		58.50	82.50		141	188
5607	2"		11	1.455		56.50	97.50		154	207
5608	2-1/2"		9	1.778		199	119		318	395
5609	3"		6	2.667		315	179		494	610
5610	3-1/2"		5	3.200		760	215		975	1,150
5611	4"	↓	4	4	↓	645	269		914	1,100
5650	Coupling									
5670	1/4"	1 Plum	19	.421	Ea.	11.25	31.50		42.75	59.50
5680	3/8"		19	.421		11.25	31.50		42.75	59.50
5690	1/2"		19	.421		8.70	31.50		40.20	56.50
5700	3/4"		18	.444		10.20	33		43.20	60.50
5710	1"	↓	15	.533		15.25	40		55.25	76
5720	1-1/4"	Q-1	26	.615		18.25	41.50		59.75	81.50
5730	1-1/2"		24	.667		24.50	45		69.50	93.50
5740	2"		21	.762		36.50	51		87.50	116
5750	2-1/2"		18	.889		101	59.50		160.50	200
5760	3"		14	1.143		136	77		213	264
5770	3-1/2"		12	1.333		279	89.50		368.50	440
5780	4"	↓	10	1.600		275	107		382	460
5840	Reducer, concentric, 1/4"	1 Plum	19	.421		11.90	31.50		43.40	60
5850	3/8"		19	.421		11.90	31.50		43.40	60
5860	1/2"		19	.421		10.20	31.50		41.70	58
5870	3/4"		16	.500		11.40	37.50		48.90	68
5880	1"	↓	15	.533		17.75	40		57.75	78.50
5890	1-1/4"	Q-1	26	.615		23	41.50		64.50	86.50
5900	1-1/2"	↓	24	.667		29	45		74	98.50

22 11 Facility Water Distribution

22 11 13 – Facility Water Distribution Piping

22 11 13.45 Pipe Fittings, Steel, Threaded

		Crew	Daily Output	Labor-Hours	Unit	Material	2024 Bare Costs Labor	Equipment	Total	Total Incl O&P
5910	2"	Q-1	21	.762	Ea.	42	51		93	122
5911	2-1/2"		18	.889		96.50	59.50		156	195
5912	3"		14	1.143		146	77		223	274
5913	3-1/2"		12	1.333		500	89.50		589.50	685
5914	4"		10	1.600		475	107		582	685
5981	Bushing, 1/4"	1 Plum	19	.421		1.78	31.50		33.28	49
5982	3/8"		19	.421		2.11	31.50		33.61	49.50
5983	1/2"		19	.421		9.40	31.50		40.90	57.50
5984	3/4"		16	.500		10.20	37.50		47.70	66.50
5985	1"		15	.533		10.75	40		50.75	71
5986	1-1/4"	Q-1	26	.615		14	41.50		55.50	77
5987	1-1/2"		24	.667		17.75	45		62.75	86
5988	2"		21	.762		22.50	51		73.50	101
5989	Cap, 1/4"	1 Plum	38	.211		11.35	15.70		27.05	36
5991	3/8"		38	.211		10.80	15.70		26.50	35.50
5992	1/2"		38	.211		6.35	15.70		22.05	30.50
5993	3/4"		32	.250		8.60	18.65		27.25	37.50
5994	1"		30	.267		10.40	19.90		30.30	41
5995	1-1/4"	Q-1	52	.308		13.70	20.50		34.20	46
5996	1-1/2"		48	.333		18.85	22.50		41.35	54.50
5997	2"		42	.381		27.50	25.50		53	68.50
6000	For galvanized elbows, tees, and couplings, add					20%				
6058	For galvanized reducers, caps and bushings, add					20%				
6100	90° elbow, galvanized, 150 lb., reducing									
6110	3/4" x 1/2"	1 Plum	15.40	.519	Ea.	18.10	39		57.10	77.50
6112	1" x 3/4"		14	.571		23	42.50		65.50	89
6114	1" x 1/2"		14.50	.552		24.50	41		65.50	88.50
6116	1-1/4" x 1"	Q-1	24.20	.661		39	44.50		83.50	109
6118	1-1/4" x 3/4"		25.40	.630		46.50	42.50		89	115
6120	1-1/4" x 1/2"		26.20	.611		49.50	41		90.50	116
6122	1-1/2" x 1-1/4"		21.60	.741		62	50		112	143
6124	1-1/2" x 1"		23.50	.681		62	45.50		107.50	137
6126	1-1/2" x 3/4"		24.60	.650		62	43.50		105.50	134
6128	2" x 1-1/2"		20.50	.780		72.50	52.50		125	158
6130	2" x 1-1/4"		21	.762		83	51		134	168
6132	2" x 1"		22.80	.702		86.50	47		133.50	165
6134	2" x 3/4"		23.90	.669		88	45		133	164
6136	2-1/2" x 2"		12.30	1.301		246	87.50		333.50	400
6138	2-1/2" x 1-1/2"		12.50	1.280		274	86		360	430
6140	3" x 2-1/2"		8.60	1.860		445	125		570	675
6142	3" x 2"		11.80	1.356		390	91		481	560
6144	4" x 3"		8.20	1.951		1,000	131		1,131	1,325
6160	90° elbow, black, 150 lb., reducing									
6170	1" x 3/4"	1 Plum	14	.571	Ea.	15.85	42.50		58.35	81
6174	1-1/2" x 1"	Q-1	23.50	.681		37.50	45.50		83	110
6178	1-1/2" x 3/4"		24.60	.650		43	43.50		86.50	113
6182	2" x 1-1/2"		20.50	.780		54.50	52.50		107	138
6186	2" x 1"		22.80	.702		62	47		109	138
6190	2" x 3/4"		23.90	.669		65.50	45		110.50	139
6194	2-1/2" x 2"		12.30	1.301		149	87.50		236.50	294
7000	Union, with brass seat									
7010	1/4"	1 Plum	15	.533	Ea.	47	40		87	111
7020	3/8"		15	.533		32.50	40		72.50	94.50

22 11 Facility Water Distribution
22 11 13 – Facility Water Distribution Piping

22 11 13.45 Pipe Fittings, Steel, Threaded	Crew	Daily Output	Labor-Hours	Unit	Material	2024 Bare Costs Labor	Equipment	Total	Total Incl O&P
7030 1/2"	1 Plum	14	.571	Ea.	29.50	42.50		72	96
7040 3/4"		13	.615		34	46		80	106
7050 1"		12	.667		44	50		94	123
7060 1-1/4"	Q-1	21	.762		63	51		114	146
7070 1-1/2"		19	.842		78.50	56.50		135	171
7080 2"		17	.941		91.50	63		154.50	195
7090 2-1/2"		13	1.231		272	82.50		354.50	425
7100 3"		9	1.778		330	119		449	540
7120 Union, galvanized									
7124 1/2"	1 Plum	14	.571	Ea.	39	42.50		81.50	107
7125 3/4"		13	.615		45	46		91	118
7126 1"		12	.667		58.50	50		108.50	139
7127 1-1/4"	Q-1	21	.762		85	51		136	170
7128 1-1/2"		19	.842		103	56.50		159.50	197
7129 2"		17	.941		118	63		181	224
7130 2-1/2"		13	1.231		410	82.50		492.50	575
7131 3"		9	1.778		575	119		694	810
7500 Malleable iron, 300 lb.									
7520 Black									
7540 90° elbow, straight, 1/4"	1 Plum	16	.500	Ea.	32	37.50		69.50	90.50
7560 3/8"		16	.500		28.50	37.50		66	86.50
7570 1/2"		15	.533		38.50	40		78.50	101
7580 3/4"		14	.571		41.50	42.50		84	109
7590 1"		13	.615		53	46		99	127
7600 1-1/4"	Q-1	22	.727		77	49		126	158
7610 1-1/2"		20	.800		91	53.50		144.50	180
7620 2"		18	.889		131	59.50		190.50	233
7630 2-1/2"		14	1.143		340	77		417	490
7640 3"		10	1.600		390	107		497	590
7650 4"		6	2.667		1,000	179		1,179	1,375
7700 45° elbow, straight, 1/4"	1 Plum	16	.500		47.50	37.50		85	108
7720 3/8"		16	.500		47.50	37.50		85	108
7730 1/2"		15	.533		52.50	40		92.50	117
7740 3/4"		14	.571		58.50	42.50		101	128
7750 1"		13	.615		65	46		111	140
7760 1-1/4"	Q-1	22	.727		104	49		153	187
7770 1-1/2"		20	.800		136	53.50		189.50	229
7780 2"		18	.889		205	59.50		264.50	315
7790 2-1/2"		14	1.143		480	77		557	640
7800 3"		10	1.600		630	107		737	855
7810 4"		6	2.667		1,425	179		1,604	1,850
7850 Tee, straight, 1/4"	1 Plum	10	.800		40	59.50		99.50	133
7870 3/8"		10	.800		42.50	59.50		102	136
7880 1/2"		9	.889		54	66.50		120.50	158
7890 3/4"		9	.889		58.50	66.50		125	163
7900 1"		8	1		70	74.50		144.50	188
7910 1-1/4"	Q-1	14	1.143		101	77		178	225
7920 1-1/2"		13	1.231		117	82.50		199.50	252
7930 2"		11	1.455		173	97.50		270.50	335
7940 2-1/2"		9	1.778		440	119		559	665
7950 3"		6	2.667		600	179		779	925
7960 4"		4	4		1,800	269		2,069	2,375
8050 Couplings, straight, 1/4"	1 Plum	19	.421		28.50	31.50		60	78.50

22 11 Facility Water Distribution

22 11 13 – Facility Water Distribution Piping

22 11 13.45 Pipe Fittings, Steel, Threaded		Crew	Daily Output	Labor-Hours	Unit	Material	2024 Bare Costs Labor	Equipment	Total	Total Incl O&P
8070	3/8"	1 Plum	19	.421	Ea.	28.50	31.50		60	78.50
8080	1/2"		19	.421		32	31.50		63.50	82
8090	3/4"		18	.444		37	33		70	90
8100	1"	▼	15	.533		42	40		82	106
8110	1-1/4"	Q-1	26	.615		50	41.50		91.50	117
8120	1-1/2"		24	.667		75	45		120	149
8130	2"		21	.762		108	51		159	195
8140	2-1/2"		18	.889		209	59.50		268.50	320
8150	3"		14	1.143		300	77		377	445
8160	4"		10	1.600		610	107		717	830
8162	6"	▼	10	1.600	▼	610	107		717	830
8200	Galvanized									
8220	90° elbow, straight, 1/4"	1 Plum	16	.500	Ea.	57	37.50		94.50	118
8222	3/8"		16	.500		58	37.50		95.50	120
8224	1/2"		15	.533		69	40		109	135
8226	3/4"		14	.571		77.50	42.50		120	149
8228	1"	▼	13	.615		99.50	46		145.50	179
8230	1-1/4"	Q-1	22	.727		157	49		206	245
8232	1-1/2"		20	.800		170	53.50		223.50	267
8234	2"		18	.889		285	59.50		344.50	405
8236	2-1/2"		14	1.143		635	77		712	815
8238	3"		10	1.600		750	107		857	985
8240	4"	▼	6	2.667	▼	2,350	179		2,529	2,850
8280	45° elbow, straight									
8282	1/2"	1 Plum	15	.533	Ea.	103	40		143	172
8284	3/4"		14	.571		119	42.50		161.50	195
8286	1"	▼	13	.615		130	46		176	212
8288	1-1/4"	Q-1	22	.727		202	49		251	295
8290	1-1/2"		20	.800		261	53.50		314.50	365
8292	2"	▼	18	.889		360	59.50		419.50	490
8310	Tee, straight, 1/4"	1 Plum	10	.800		81	59.50		140.50	178
8312	3/8"		10	.800		82.50	59.50		142	180
8314	1/2"		9	.889		103	66.50		169.50	213
8316	3/4"		9	.889		114	66.50		180.50	224
8318	1"	▼	8	1		140	74.50		214.50	266
8320	1-1/4"	Q-1	14	1.143		200	77		277	335
8322	1-1/2"		13	1.231		208	82.50		290.50	350
8324	2"		11	1.455		335	97.50		432.50	510
8326	2-1/2"		9	1.778		1,125	119		1,244	1,400
8328	3"		6	2.667		1,300	179		1,479	1,700
8330	4"	▼	4	4		3,225	269		3,494	3,925
8380	Couplings, straight, 1/4"	1 Plum	19	.421		37.50	31.50		69	88
8382	3/8"		19	.421		54	31.50		85.50	106
8384	1/2"		19	.421		55	31.50		86.50	108
8386	3/4"		18	.444		62.50	33		95.50	118
8388	1"	▼	15	.533		82.50	40		122.50	150
8390	1-1/4"	Q-1	26	.615		108	41.50		149.50	180
8392	1-1/2"		24	.667		152	45		197	234
8394	2"		21	.762		184	51		235	278
8396	2-1/2"		18	.889		505	59.50		564.50	645
8398	3"		14	1.143		605	77		682	780
8399	4"	▼	10	1.600		1,075	107		1,182	1,325
8529	Black									

22 11 Facility Water Distribution

22 11 13 – Facility Water Distribution Piping

22 11 13.45 Pipe Fittings, Steel, Threaded		Crew	Daily Output	Labor-Hours	Unit	Material	2024 Bare Costs Labor	2024 Bare Costs Equipment	Total	Total Incl O&P
8530	Reducer, concentric, 1/4"	1 Plum	19	.421	Ea.	43	31.50		74.50	94
8531	3/8"		19	.421		38	31.50		69.50	89
8532	1/2"		17	.471		45.50	35		80.50	103
8533	3/4"		16	.500		46.50	37.50		84	107
8534	1"		15	.533		56	40		96	121
8535	1-1/4"	Q-1	26	.615		73.50	41.50		115	143
8536	1-1/2"		24	.667		115	45		160	193
8537	2"		21	.762		145	51		196	235
8550	Cap, 1/4"	1 Plum	38	.211		29.50	15.70		45.20	56
8551	3/8"		38	.211		29.50	15.70		45.20	56
8552	1/2"		34	.235		29	17.55		46.55	58
8553	3/4"		32	.250		37	18.65		55.65	68.50
8554	1"		30	.267		48.50	19.90		68.40	82.50
8555	1-1/4"	Q-1	52	.308		53.50	20.50		74	90
8556	1-1/2"		48	.333		78.50	22.50		101	120
8557	2"		42	.381		109	25.50		134.50	158
8570	Plug, 1/4"	1 Plum	38	.211		6.40	15.70		22.10	30.50
8571	3/8"		38	.211		6.70	15.70		22.40	31
8572	1/2"		34	.235		7	17.55		24.55	33.50
8573	3/4"		32	.250		8.75	18.65		27.40	37.50
8574	1"		30	.267		13.40	19.90		33.30	44.50
8575	1-1/4"	Q-1	52	.308		27.50	20.50		48	61.50
8576	1-1/2"		48	.333		31.50	22.50		54	68
8577	2"		42	.381		50	25.50		75.50	93
9500	Union with brass seat, 1/4"	1 Plum	15	.533		68.50	40		108.50	135
9530	3/8"		15	.533		69.50	40		109.50	136
9540	1/2"		14	.571		56.50	42.50		99	126
9550	3/4"		13	.615		62.50	46		108.50	137
9560	1"		12	.667		81.50	50		131.50	164
9570	1-1/4"	Q-1	21	.762		133	51		184	222
9580	1-1/2"		19	.842		139	56.50		195.50	237
9590	2"		17	.941		172	63		235	283
9600	2-1/2"		13	1.231		555	82.50		637.50	735
9610	3"		9	1.778		720	119		839	970
9620	4"		5	3.200		2,525	215		2,740	3,100
9630	Union, all iron, 1/4"	1 Plum	15	.533		37.50	40		77.50	100
9650	3/8"		15	.533		39	40		79	102
9660	1/2"		14	.571		39.50	42.50		82	107
9670	3/4"		13	.615		42.50	46		88.50	115
9680	1"		12	.667		52	50		102	131
9690	1-1/4"	Q-1	21	.762		80	51		131	164
9700	1-1/2"		19	.842		97.50	56.50		154	191
9710	2"		17	.941		123	63		186	230
9720	2-1/2"		13	1.231		218	82.50		300.50	365
9730	3"		9	1.778		415	119		534	635
9750	For galvanized unions, add					15%				
9757	Forged steel, 3000 lb.									
9758	Black									
9760	90° elbow, 1/4"	1 Plum	16	.500	Ea.	37.50	37.50		75	97
9761	3/8"		16	.500		37.50	37.50		75	97
9762	1/2"		15	.533		29	40		69	90.50
9763	3/4"		14	.571		36	42.50		78.50	104
9764	1"		13	.615		54	46		100	128

22 11 Facility Water Distribution

22 11 13 – Facility Water Distribution Piping

22 11 13.45 Pipe Fittings, Steel, Threaded		Crew	Daily Output	Labor-Hours	Unit	Material	2024 Bare Costs Labor	Equipment	Total	Total Incl O&P
9765	1-1/4"	Q-1	22	.727	Ea.	102	49		151	185
9766	1-1/2"		20	.800		132	53.50		185.50	225
9767	2"	↓	18	.889		160	59.50		219.50	265
9780	45° elbow, 1/4"	1 Plum	16	.500		48	37.50		85.50	108
9781	3/8"		16	.500		48	37.50		85.50	108
9782	1/2"		15	.533		47	40		87	111
9783	3/4"		14	.571		54.50	42.50		97	124
9784	1"	↓	13	.615		74	46		120	150
9785	1-1/4"	Q-1	22	.727		103	49		152	186
9786	1-1/2"		20	.800		147	53.50		200.50	242
9787	2"	↓	18	.889		203	59.50		262.50	310
9800	Tee, 1/4"	1 Plum	10	.800		45.50	59.50		105	140
9801	3/8"		10	.800		45.50	59.50		105	140
9802	1/2"		9	.889		41	66.50		107.50	144
9803	3/4"		9	.889		55.50	66.50		122	160
9804	1"	↓	8	1		73.50	74.50		148	192
9805	1-1/4"	Q-1	14	1.143		142	77		219	270
9806	1-1/2"		13	1.231		166	82.50		248.50	305
9807	2"	↓	11	1.455		214	97.50		311.50	380
9820	Reducer, concentric, 1/4"	1 Plum	19	.421		23	31.50		54.50	72.50
9821	3/8"		19	.421		24	31.50		55.50	73.50
9822	1/2"		17	.471		24	35		59	79
9823	3/4"		16	.500		28.50	37.50		66	87
9824	1"	↓	15	.533		37	40		77	100
9825	1-1/4"	Q-1	26	.615		65	41.50		106.50	133
9826	1-1/2"		24	.667		70.50	45		115.50	144
9827	2"	↓	21	.762		102	51		153	189
9840	Cap, 1/4"	1 Plum	38	.211		14.15	15.70		29.85	39
9841	3/8"		38	.211		14.15	15.70		29.85	39
9842	1/2"		34	.235		13.75	17.55		31.30	41
9843	3/4"		32	.250		19.15	18.65		37.80	49
9844	1"	↓	30	.267		29.50	19.90		49.40	62
9845	1-1/4"	Q-1	52	.308		47.50	20.50		68	83
9846	1-1/2"		48	.333		56.50	22.50		79	96
9847	2"	↓	42	.381		81.50	25.50		107	128
9860	Plug, 1/4"	1 Plum	38	.211		5.30	15.70		21	29.50
9861	3/8"		38	.211		6.85	15.70		22.55	31
9862	1/2"		34	.235		5.70	17.55		23.25	32.50
9863	3/4"		32	.250		7.20	18.65		25.85	36
9864	1"	↓	30	.267		11.05	19.90		30.95	41.50
9865	1-1/4"	Q-1	52	.308		26	20.50		46.50	59.50
9866	1-1/2"		48	.333		34.50	22.50		57	71.50
9867	2"	↓	42	.381		54.50	25.50		80	98
9880	Union, bronze seat, 1/4"	1 Plum	15	.533		104	40		144	174
9881	3/8"		15	.533		104	40		144	174
9882	1/2"		14	.571		100	42.50		142.50	174
9883	3/4"		13	.615		134	46		180	216
9884	1"	↓	12	.667		151	50		201	241
9885	1-1/4"	Q-1	21	.762		294	51		345	400
9886	1-1/2"		19	.842		305	56.50		361.50	420
9887	2"	↓	17	.941		415	63		478	550
9900	Coupling, 1/4"	1 Plum	19	.421		14.65	31.50		46.15	63
9901	3/8"		19	.421		14.65	31.50		46.15	63

22 11 Facility Water Distribution

22 11 13 – Facility Water Distribution Piping

22 11 13.45 Pipe Fittings, Steel, Threaded		Crew	Daily Output	Labor-Hours	Unit	Material	2024 Bare Costs Labor	Equipment	Total	Total Incl O&P
9902	1/2"	1 Plum	17	.471	Ea.	12.05	35		47.05	66
9903	3/4"		16	.500		15.70	37.50		53.20	73
9904	1"		15	.533		27.50	40		67.50	89
9905	1-1/4"	Q-1	26	.615		45.50	41.50		87	112
9906	1-1/2"		24	.667		59	45		104	132
9907	2"		21	.762		73.50	51		124.50	157

22 11 13.47 Pipe Fittings, Steel

		Crew	Daily Output	Labor-Hours	Unit	Material	Labor	Equipment	Total	Total Incl O&P
0010	**PIPE FITTINGS, STEEL**, flanged, welded & special									
0020	Flanged joints, CI, standard weight, black. One gasket & bolt									
0040	set, mat'l only, required at each joint, not included (see line 0620)									
0060	90° elbow, straight, 1-1/2" pipe size	Q-1	14	1.143	Ea.	435	77		512	590
0080	2" pipe size		13	1.231		267	82.50		349.50	415
0090	2-1/2" pipe size		12	1.333		297	89.50		386.50	460
0100	3" pipe size		11	1.455		259	97.50		356.50	430
0110	4" pipe size		8	2		320	134		454	550
0120	5" pipe size		7	2.286		645	154		799	935
0130	6" pipe size	Q-2	9	2.667		485	186		671	810
0140	8" pipe size		8	3		830	209		1,039	1,225
0150	10" pipe size		7	3.429		1,675	239		1,914	2,175
0160	12" pipe size		6	4		3,450	279		3,729	4,200
0171	90° elbow, reducing									
0172	2-1/2" by 2" pipe size	Q-1	12	1.333	Ea.	925	89.50		1,014.50	1,150
0173	3" by 2-1/2" pipe size		11	1.455		875	97.50		972.50	1,100
0174	4" by 3" pipe size		8	2		650	134		784	915
0175	5" by 3" pipe size		7	2.286		4,400	154		4,554	5,075
0176	6" by 4" pipe size	Q-2	9	2.667		875	186		1,061	1,225
0177	8" by 6" pipe size		8	3		1,175	209		1,384	1,600
0178	10" by 8" pipe size		7	3.429		2,225	239		2,464	2,800
0179	12" by 10" pipe size		6	4		4,250	279		4,529	5,100
0200	45° elbow, straight, 1-1/2" pipe size	Q-1	14	1.143		1,700	77		1,777	2,000
0220	2" pipe size		13	1.231		400	82.50		482.50	565
0230	2-1/2" pipe size		12	1.333		450	89.50		539.50	630
0240	3" pipe size		11	1.455		395	97.50		492.50	580
0250	4" pipe size		8	2		445	134		579	690
0260	5" pipe size		7	2.286		1,050	154		1,204	1,400
0270	6" pipe size	Q-2	9	2.667		725	186		911	1,075
0280	8" pipe size		8	3		1,175	209		1,384	1,600
0290	10" pipe size		7	3.429		2,225	239		2,464	2,800
0300	12" pipe size		6	4		3,325	279		3,604	4,075
0310	Cross, straight									
0311	2-1/2" pipe size	Q-1	6	2.667	Ea.	2,575	179		2,754	3,125
0312	3" pipe size		5	3.200		955	215		1,170	1,375
0313	4" pipe size		4	4		1,250	269		1,519	1,775
0314	5" pipe size		3	5.333		7,650	360		8,010	8,925
0315	6" pipe size	Q-2	5	4.800		2,675	335		3,010	3,425
0316	8" pipe size		4	6		2,225	420		2,645	3,075
0317	10" pipe size		3	8		1,650	555		2,205	2,625
0318	12" pipe size		2	12		1,875	835		2,710	3,325
0350	Tee, straight, 1-1/2" pipe size	Q-1	10	1.600		505	107		612	715
0370	2" pipe size		9	1.778		305	119		424	515
0380	2-1/2" pipe size		8	2		435	134		569	675
0390	3" pipe size		7	2.286		305	154		459	570

22 11 Facility Water Distribution

22 11 13 – Facility Water Distribution Piping

22 11 13.47 Pipe Fittings, Steel		Crew	Daily Output	Labor-Hours	Unit	Material	2024 Bare Costs Labor	Equipment	Total	Total Incl O&P
0400	4" pipe size	Q-1	5	3.200	Ea.	425	215		640	790
0410	5" pipe size	↓	4	4		1,175	269		1,444	1,700
0420	6" pipe size	Q-2	6	4		705	279		984	1,200
0430	8" pipe size		5	4.800		1,250	335		1,585	1,850
0440	10" pipe size		4	6		3,125	420		3,545	4,075
0450	12" pipe size	↓	3	8	↓	5,525	555		6,080	6,900
0459	Tee, reducing on outlet									
0460	2-1/2" by 2" pipe size	Q-1	8	2	Ea.	520	134		654	770
0461	3" by 2-1/2" pipe size		7	2.286		266	154		420	520
0462	4" by 3" pipe size		5	3.200		1,050	215		1,265	1,475
0463	5" by 4" pipe size	↓	4	4		850	269		1,119	1,325
0464	6" by 4" pipe size	Q-2	6	4		930	279		1,209	1,450
0465	8" by 6" pipe size		5	4.800		2,075	335		2,410	2,775
0466	10" by 8" pipe size		4	6		3,325	420		3,745	4,275
0467	12" by 10" pipe size		3	8	↓	1,575	555		2,130	2,575
0476	Reducer, concentric									
0477	3" by 2-1/2"	Q-1	12	1.333	Ea.	580	89.50		669.50	775
0478	4" by 3"		9	1.778		640	119		759	885
0479	5" by 4"	↓	8	2		1,000	134		1,134	1,300
0480	6" by 4"	Q-2	10	2.400		960	167		1,127	1,300
0481	8" by 6"		9	2.667		1,100	186		1,286	1,475
0482	10" by 8"		8	3		2,175	209		2,384	2,675
0483	12" by 10"	↓	7	3.429	↓	3,525	239		3,764	4,225
0492	Reducer, eccentric									
0493	4" by 3"	Q-1	8	2	Ea.	1,025	134		1,159	1,325
0494	5" by 4"	"	7	2.286		1,600	154		1,754	1,975
0495	6" by 4"	Q-2	9	2.667		1,025	186		1,211	1,400
0496	8" by 6"		8	3		1,250	209		1,459	1,700
0497	10" by 8"		7	3.429		3,275	239		3,514	3,950
0498	12" by 10"	↓	6	4		2,200	279		2,479	2,825
0500	For galvanized elbows and tees, add					100%				
0520	For extra heavy weight elbows and tees, add					140%				
0620	Gasket and bolt set, 150 lb., 1/2" pipe size	1 Plum	20	.400		8	30		38	53.50
0622	3/4" pipe size		19	.421		6.95	31.50		38.45	54.50
0624	1" pipe size		18	.444		9.50	33		42.50	60
0626	1-1/4" pipe size		17	.471		10.85	35		45.85	64.50
0628	1-1/2" pipe size		15	.533		10.15	40		50.15	70
0630	2" pipe size		13	.615		10.95	46		56.95	80.50
0640	2-1/2" pipe size		12	.667		11.40	50		61.40	86.50
0650	3" pipe size		11	.727		10.50	54.50		65	92.50
0660	3-1/2" pipe size		9	.889		28.50	66.50		95	130
0670	4" pipe size		8	1		17.25	74.50		91.75	130
0680	5" pipe size		7	1.143		27	85.50		112.50	157
0690	6" pipe size		6	1.333		34	99.50		133.50	186
0700	8" pipe size		5	1.600		33	119		152	214
0710	10" pipe size		4.50	1.778		71.50	133		204.50	276
0720	12" pipe size		4.20	1.905		80.50	142		222.50	300
0730	14" pipe size		4	2		102	149		251	335
0740	16" pipe size		3	2.667		123	199		322	430
0750	18" pipe size		2.70	2.963		185	221		406	535
0760	20" pipe size		2.30	3.478		278	260		538	690
0780	24" pipe size		1.90	4.211		365	315		680	870
0790	26" pipe size		1.60	5		675	375		1,050	1,300

22 11 Facility Water Distribution

22 11 13 – Facility Water Distribution Piping

22 11 13.47 Pipe Fittings, Steel		Crew	Daily Output	Labor-Hours	Unit	Material	2024 Bare Costs Labor	2024 Bare Costs Equipment	Total	Total Incl O&P
0810	30" pipe size	1 Plum	1.40	5.714	Ea.	895	425		1,320	1,625
0830	36" pipe size	▼	1.10	7.273	▼	1,100	545		1,645	2,000
0850	For 300 lb. gasket set, add					40%				
2000	Flanged unions, 125 lb., black, 1/2" pipe size	1 Plum	17	.471	Ea.	55.50	35		90.50	114
2040	3/4" pipe size		17	.471		107	35		142	171
2050	1" pipe size	▼	16	.500		101	37.50		138.50	167
2060	1-1/4" pipe size	Q-1	28	.571		119	38.50		157.50	188
2070	1-1/2" pipe size		27	.593		107	40		147	176
2080	2" pipe size		26	.615		126	41.50		167.50	200
2090	2-1/2" pipe size		24	.667		170	45		215	254
2100	3" pipe size		22	.727		192	49		241	285
2110	3-1/2" pipe size		18	.889		330	59.50		389.50	450
2120	4" pipe size		16	1		263	67		330	390
2130	5" pipe size	▼	14	1.143		610	77		687	785
2140	6" pipe size	Q-2	19	1.263		570	88		658	760
2150	8" pipe size	"	16	1.500	▼	1,300	105		1,405	1,600
2200	For galvanized unions, add					150%				
2290	Threaded flange									
2300	Cast iron									
2310	Black, 125 lb., per flange									
2320	1" pipe size	1 Plum	27	.296	Ea.	46	22		68	84
2330	1-1/4" pipe size	Q-1	44	.364		50	24.50		74.50	91
2340	1-1/2" pipe size		40	.400		57.50	27		84.50	104
2350	2" pipe size		36	.444		49	30		79	98
2360	2-1/2" pipe size		28	.571		57	38.50		95.50	120
2370	3" pipe size		20	.800		72.50	53.50		126	160
2380	3-1/2" pipe size		16	1		93	67		160	202
2390	4" pipe size		12	1.333		104	89.50		193.50	247
2400	5" pipe size	▼	10	1.600		134	107		241	310
2410	6" pipe size	Q-2	14	1.714		155	119		274	350
2420	8" pipe size		12	2		245	139		384	475
2430	10" pipe size		10	2.400		415	167		582	705
2440	12" pipe size	▼	8	3	▼	985	209		1,194	1,375
2460	For galvanized flanges, add					95%				
2490	Blind flange									
2492	Cast iron									
2494	Black, 125 lb., per flange									
2496	1" pipe size	1 Plum	27	.296	Ea.	64	22		86	104
2500	1-1/2" pipe size	Q-1	40	.400		71.50	27		98.50	119
2502	2" pipe size		36	.444		81	30		111	134
2504	2-1/2" pipe size		28	.571		89	38.50		127.50	155
2506	3" pipe size		20	.800		107	53.50		160.50	197
2508	4" pipe size		12	1.333		137	89.50		226.50	283
2510	5" pipe size	▼	10	1.600		222	107		329	405
2512	6" pipe size	Q-2	14	1.714		241	119		360	445
2514	8" pipe size		12	2		380	139		519	620
2516	10" pipe size		10	2.400		560	167		727	865
2518	12" pipe size	▼	8	3	▼	1,125	209		1,334	1,550
2520	For galvanized flanges, add					80%				
2570	Threaded flange									
2580	Forged steel									
2590	Black, 150 lb., per flange									
2600	1/2" pipe size	1 Plum	30	.267	Ea.	44	19.90		63.90	78

22 11 Facility Water Distribution

22 11 13 – Facility Water Distribution Piping

22 11 13.47 Pipe Fittings, Steel

		Crew	Daily Output	Labor-Hours	Unit	Material	2024 Bare Costs Labor	Equipment	Total	Total Incl O&P
2610	3/4" pipe size	1 Plum	28	.286	Ea.	32.50	21.50		54	67
2620	1" pipe size		27	.296		37	22		59	74
2630	1-1/4" pipe size	Q-1	44	.364		38.50	24.50		63	78.50
2640	1-1/2" pipe size		40	.400		37.50	27		64.50	81
2650	2" pipe size		36	.444		41	30		71	90
2660	2-1/2" pipe size		28	.571		55	38.50		93.50	118
2670	3" pipe size		20	.800		52	53.50		105.50	138
2690	4" pipe size		12	1.333		63	89.50		152.50	203
2700	5" pipe size		10	1.600		81	107		188	249
2710	6" pipe size	Q-2	14	1.714		129	119		248	320
2720	8" pipe size		12	2		178	139		317	405
2730	10" pipe size		10	2.400		266	167		433	540
2860	Black, 300 lb., per flange									
2870	1/2" pipe size	1 Plum	30	.267	Ea.	48	19.90		67.90	82
2880	3/4" pipe size		28	.286		49	21.50		70.50	85.50
2890	1" pipe size		27	.296		49	22		71	87
2900	1-1/4" pipe size	Q-1	44	.364		49	24.50		73.50	90.50
2910	1-1/2" pipe size		40	.400		49	27		76	94
2920	2" pipe size		36	.444		55.50	30		85.50	106
2930	2-1/2" pipe size		28	.571		92.50	38.50		131	159
2940	3" pipe size		20	.800		83	53.50		136.50	172
2960	4" pipe size		12	1.333		119	89.50		208.50	264
2970	6" pipe size	Q-2	14	1.714		223	119		342	425
3000	Weld joint, butt, carbon steel, standard weight									
3040	90° elbow, long radius									
3050	1/2" pipe size	Q-15	16	1	Ea.	15.20	67	4.49	86.69	122
3060	3/4" pipe size		16	1		16.45	67	4.49	87.94	123
3070	1" pipe size		16	1		16.90	67	4.49	88.39	124
3080	1-1/4" pipe size		14	1.143		19.40	77	5.15	101.55	141
3090	1-1/2" pipe size		13	1.231		16.90	82.50	5.55	104.95	148
3100	2" pipe size		10	1.600		16.95	107	7.20	131.15	187
3110	2-1/2" pipe size		8	2		25.50	134	9	168.50	238
3120	3" pipe size		7	2.286		30.50	154	10.25	194.75	273
3130	4" pipe size		5	3.200		53.50	215	14.35	282.85	395
3136	5" pipe size		4	4		104	269	17.95	390.95	535
3140	6" pipe size	Q-16	5	4.800		105	335	14.35	454.35	625
3150	8" pipe size		3.75	6.400		202	445	19.15	666.15	910
3160	10" pipe size		3	8		400	555	24	979	1,300
3170	12" pipe size		2.50	9.600		575	670	28.50	1,273.50	1,650
3180	14" pipe size		2	12		870	835	36	1,741	2,250
3190	16" pipe size		1.50	16		1,050	1,125	48	2,223	2,850
3191	18" pipe size		1.25	19.200		1,250	1,350	57.50	2,657.50	3,450
3192	20" pipe size		1.15	20.870		2,075	1,450	62.50	3,587.50	4,525
3194	24" pipe size		1.02	23.529		2,850	1,650	70.50	4,570.50	5,675
3200	45° elbow, long									
3210	1/2" pipe size	Q-15	16	1	Ea.	17.35	67	4.49	88.84	124
3220	3/4" pipe size		16	1		17.35	67	4.49	88.84	124
3230	1" pipe size		16	1		17.35	67	4.49	88.84	124
3240	1-1/4" pipe size		14	1.143		17.35	77	5.15	99.50	139
3250	1-1/2" pipe size		13	1.231		17.35	82.50	5.55	105.40	148
3260	2" pipe size		10	1.600		18.55	107	7.20	132.75	188
3270	2-1/2" pipe size		8	2		21.50	134	9	164.50	233
3280	3" pipe size		7	2.286		21.50	154	10.25	185.75	263

For customer support on your Plumbing Costs with RSMeans Data call 800.448.8182.

22 11 Facility Water Distribution

22 11 13 – Facility Water Distribution Piping

22 11 13.47 Pipe Fittings, Steel		Crew	Daily Output	Labor-Hours	Unit	Material	2024 Bare Costs Labor	Equipment	Total	Total Incl O&P
3290	4" pipe size	Q-15	5	3.200	Ea.	38	215	14.35	267.35	380
3296	5" pipe size	↓	4	4		57	269	17.95	343.95	485
3300	6" pipe size	Q-16	5	4.800		78.50	335	14.35	427.85	595
3310	8" pipe size		3.75	6.400		131	445	19.15	595.15	830
3320	10" pipe size		3	8		261	555	24	840	1,150
3330	12" pipe size		2.50	9.600		370	670	28.50	1,068.50	1,425
3340	14" pipe size		2	12		495	835	36	1,366	1,825
3341	16" pipe size		1.50	16		890	1,125	48	2,063	2,675
3342	18" pipe size		1.25	19.200		1,250	1,350	57.50	2,657.50	3,450
3343	20" pipe size		1.15	20.870		1,300	1,450	62.50	2,812.50	3,675
3345	24" pipe size		1.05	22.857		1,975	1,600	68.50	3,643.50	4,625
3346	26" pipe size		.85	28.235		4,800	1,975	84.50	6,859.50	8,300
3347	30" pipe size		.45	53.333		5,275	3,725	159	9,159	11,500
3349	36" pipe size	↓	.38	63.158	↓	5,800	4,400	189	10,389	13,100
3350	Tee, straight									
3352	For reducing tees and concentrics see starting line 4600									
3360	1/2" pipe size	Q-15	10	1.600	Ea.	48	107	7.20	162.20	221
3370	3/4" pipe size		10	1.600		49.50	107	7.20	163.70	222
3380	1" pipe size		10	1.600		49.50	107	7.20	163.70	222
3390	1-1/4" pipe size		9	1.778		49.50	119	8	176.50	241
3400	1-1/2" pipe size		8	2		49.50	134	9	192.50	264
3410	2" pipe size		6	2.667		50.50	179	11.95	241.45	335
3420	2-1/2" pipe size		5	3.200		61	215	14.35	290.35	405
3430	3" pipe size		4	4		67.50	269	17.95	354.45	495
3440	4" pipe size		3	5.333		95.50	360	24	479.50	665
3446	5" pipe size	↓	2.50	6.400		157	430	28.50	615.50	845
3450	6" pipe size	Q-16	3	8		163	555	24	742	1,025
3460	8" pipe size		2.50	9.600		285	670	28.50	983.50	1,350
3470	10" pipe size		2	12		560	835	36	1,431	1,900
3480	12" pipe size		1.60	15		785	1,050	45	1,880	2,475
3481	14" pipe size		1.30	18.462		1,375	1,275	55	2,705	3,500
3482	16" pipe size		1	24		1,550	1,675	72	3,297	4,250
3483	18" pipe size		.80	30		2,450	2,100	89.50	4,639.50	5,900
3484	20" pipe size		.75	32		3,550	2,225	95.50	5,870.50	7,325
3486	24" pipe size		.70	34.286		4,950	2,400	103	7,453	9,125
3487	26" pipe size		.55	43.636		12,000	3,050	130	15,180	17,900
3488	30" pipe size		.30	80		13,200	5,575	239	19,014	23,100
3490	36" pipe size	↓	.25	96		14,500	6,700	287	21,487	26,300
3491	Eccentric reducer, 1-1/2" pipe size	Q-15	14	1.143		67	77	5.15	149.15	194
3492	2" pipe size		11	1.455		36.50	97.50	6.55	140.55	192
3493	2-1/2" pipe size		9	1.778		42.50	119	8	169.50	233
3494	3" pipe size		8	2		46.50	134	9	189.50	261
3495	4" pipe size	↓	6	2.667		61	179	11.95	251.95	345
3496	6" pipe size	Q-16	5	4.800		89.50	335	14.35	438.85	610
3497	8" pipe size		4	6		159	420	17.95	596.95	815
3498	10" pipe size		3	8		208	555	24	787	1,075
3499	12" pipe size		2.50	9.600		325	670	28.50	1,023.50	1,375
3501	Cap, 1-1/2" pipe size	Q-15	28	.571		18.70	38.50	2.57	59.77	80.50
3502	2" pipe size		22	.727		23.50	49	3.27	75.77	102
3503	2-1/2" pipe size		18	.889		24.50	59.50	3.99	87.99	120
3504	3" pipe size		16	1		24.50	67	4.49	95.99	132
3505	4" pipe size	↓	12	1.333		36	89.50	6	131.50	179
3506	6" pipe size	Q-16	10	2.400		61.50	167	7.20	235.70	325

22 11 Facility Water Distribution

22 11 13 – Facility Water Distribution Piping

22 11 13.47 Pipe Fittings, Steel		Crew	Daily Output	Labor-Hours	Unit	Material	2024 Bare Costs Labor	Equipment	Total	Total Incl O&P
3507	8" pipe size	Q-16	8	3	Ea.	96.50	209	8.95	314.45	425
3508	10" pipe size		6	4		188	279	11.95	478.95	635
3509	12" pipe size		5	4.800		263	335	14.35	612.35	800
3511	14" pipe size		4	6		350	420	17.95	787.95	1,025
3512	16" pipe size		4	6		410	420	17.95	847.95	1,100
3513	18" pipe size	↓	3	8	↓	540	555	24	1,119	1,450
3517	Weld joint, butt, carbon steel, extra strong									
3519	90° elbow, long									
3520	1/2" pipe size	Q-15	13	1.231	Ea.	20	82.50	5.55	108.05	151
3530	3/4" pipe size		12	1.333		20	89.50	6	115.50	162
3540	1" pipe size		11	1.455		20	97.50	6.55	124.05	174
3550	1-1/4" pipe size		10	1.600		20	107	7.20	134.20	190
3560	1-1/2" pipe size		9	1.778		20	119	8	147	209
3570	2" pipe size		8	2		22	134	9	165	234
3580	2-1/2" pipe size		7	2.286		31	154	10.25	195.25	273
3590	3" pipe size		6	2.667		40	179	11.95	230.95	325
3600	4" pipe size		4	4		65.50	269	17.95	352.45	490
3606	5" pipe size	↓	3.50	4.571		156	305	20.50	481.50	650
3610	6" pipe size	Q-16	4.50	5.333		166	370	15.95	551.95	755
3620	8" pipe size		3.50	6.857		315	480	20.50	815.50	1,075
3630	10" pipe size		2.50	9.600		665	670	28.50	1,363.50	1,750
3640	12" pipe size	↓	2.25	10.667	↓	815	745	32	1,592	2,025
3650	45° elbow, long									
3660	1/2" pipe size	Q-15	13	1.231	Ea.	21	82.50	5.55	109.05	153
3670	3/4" pipe size		12	1.333		21	89.50	6	116.50	163
3680	1" pipe size		11	1.455		21	97.50	6.55	125.05	176
3690	1-1/4" pipe size		10	1.600		21	107	7.20	135.20	191
3700	1-1/2" pipe size		9	1.778		21	119	8	148	210
3710	2" pipe size		8	2		23	134	9	166	235
3720	2-1/2" pipe size		7	2.286		51.50	154	10.25	215.75	296
3730	3" pipe size		6	2.667		30	179	11.95	220.95	310
3740	4" pipe size		4	4		47	269	17.95	333.95	470
3746	5" pipe size	↓	3.50	4.571		112	305	20.50	437.50	600
3750	6" pipe size	Q-16	4.50	5.333		129	370	15.95	514.95	715
3760	8" pipe size		3.50	6.857		222	480	20.50	722.50	980
3770	10" pipe size		2.50	9.600		430	670	28.50	1,128.50	1,500
3780	12" pipe size	↓	2.25	10.667	↓	635	745	32	1,412	1,825
3800	Tee, straight									
3810	1/2" pipe size	Q-15	9	1.778	Ea.	40	119	8	167	231
3820	3/4" pipe size		8.50	1.882		40	126	8.45	174.45	241
3830	1" pipe size		8	2		40	134	9	183	254
3840	1-1/4" pipe size		7	2.286		40	154	10.25	204.25	283
3850	1-1/2" pipe size		6	2.667		40	179	11.95	230.95	325
3860	2" pipe size		5	3.200		45.50	215	14.35	274.85	385
3870	2-1/2" pipe size		4	4		76	269	17.95	362.95	505
3880	3" pipe size		3.50	4.571		70.50	305	20.50	396	555
3890	4" pipe size		2.50	6.400		114	430	28.50	572.50	800
3896	5" pipe size	↓	2.25	7.111		259	480	32	771	1,025
3900	6" pipe size	Q-16	2.25	10.667		219	745	32	996	1,375
3910	8" pipe size		2	12		430	835	36	1,301	1,750
3920	10" pipe size		1.75	13.714		645	955	41	1,641	2,175
3930	12" pipe size	↓	1.50	16	↓	995	1,125	48	2,168	2,800
4000	Eccentric reducer, 1-1/2" pipe size	Q-15	10	1.600		55.50	107	7.20	169.70	229

22 11 Facility Water Distribution

22 11 13 – Facility Water Distribution Piping

22 11 13.47 Pipe Fittings, Steel		Crew	Daily Output	Labor-Hours	Unit	Material	2024 Bare Costs Labor	Equipment	Total	Total Incl O&P
4010	2" pipe size	Q-15	9	1.778	Ea.	40	119	8	167	231
4020	2-1/2" pipe size		8	2		60	134	9	203	276
4030	3" pipe size		7	2.286		49.50	154	10.25	213.75	294
4040	4" pipe size		5	3.200		77.50	215	14.35	306.85	420
4046	5" pipe size		4.70	3.404		179	229	15.30	423.30	555
4050	6" pipe size	Q-16	4.50	5.333		206	370	15.95	591.95	800
4060	8" pipe size		3.50	6.857		236	480	20.50	736.50	995
4070	10" pipe size		2.50	9.600		380	670	28.50	1,078.50	1,450
4080	12" pipe size		2.25	10.667		545	745	32	1,322	1,725
4090	14" pipe size		2.10	11.429		1,250	795	34	2,079	2,600
4100	16" pipe size		1.90	12.632		1,225	880	38	2,143	2,675
4151	Cap, 1-1/2" pipe size	Q-15	24	.667		20.50	45	2.99	68.49	92.50
4152	2" pipe size		18	.889		19.60	59.50	3.99	83.09	115
4153	2-1/2" pipe size		16	1		27	67	4.49	98.49	134
4154	3" pipe size		14	1.143		30	77	5.15	112.15	153
4155	4" pipe size		10	1.600		40.50	107	7.20	154.70	213
4156	6" pipe size	Q-16	9	2.667		83	186	7.95	276.95	375
4157	8" pipe size		7	3.429		124	239	10.25	373.25	505
4158	10" pipe size		5	4.800		191	335	14.35	540.35	720
4159	12" pipe size		4	6		255	420	17.95	692.95	920
4190	Weld fittings, reducing, standard weight									
4200	Welding ring w/spacer pins, 2" pipe size				Ea.	5.15			5.15	5.70
4210	2-1/2" pipe size					4.23			4.23	4.65
4220	3" pipe size					4.09			4.09	4.50
4230	4" pipe size					4.56			4.56	5
4236	5" pipe size					5.65			5.65	6.25
4240	6" pipe size					5.90			5.90	6.50
4250	8" pipe size					6.55			6.55	7.20
4260	10" pipe size					9.50			9.50	10.45
4270	12" pipe size					9.95			9.95	10.90
4280	14" pipe size					10.10			10.10	11.10
4290	16" pipe size					11.80			11.80	12.95
4300	18" pipe size					13.20			13.20	14.50
4310	20" pipe size					15			15	16.50
4330	24" pipe size					24.50			24.50	27
4340	26" pipe size					29.50			29.50	32.50
4350	30" pipe size					33.50			33.50	37
4370	36" pipe size					41.50			41.50	45.50
4600	Tee, reducing on outlet									
4601	2-1/2" x 2" pipe size	Q-15	5	3.200	Ea.	63.50	215	14.35	292.85	405
4602	3" x 2-1/2" pipe size		4	4		62	269	17.95	348.95	490
4604	4" x 3" pipe size		3	5.333		78.50	360	24	462.50	650
4605	5" x 4" pipe size		2.50	6.400		170	430	28.50	628.50	860
4606	6" x 5" pipe size	Q-16	3	8		153	555	24	732	1,025
4607	8" x 6" pipe size		2.50	9.600		292	670	28.50	990.50	1,350
4608	10" x 8" pipe size		2	12		540	835	36	1,411	1,875
4609	12" x 10" pipe size		1.60	15		795	1,050	45	1,890	2,475
4610	16" x 12" pipe size		1.50	16		4,225	1,125	48	5,398	6,350
4611	14" x 12" pipe size		1.52	15.789		1,200	1,100	47	2,347	3,000
4618	Reducer, concentric									
4619	2-1/2" by 2" pipe size	Q-15	10	1.600	Ea.	71	107	7.20	185.20	246
4620	3" by 2-1/2" pipe size		9	1.778		23.50	119	8	150.50	213
4621	3-1/2" by 3" pipe size		8	2		60.50	134	9	203.50	276

22 11 Facility Water Distribution

22 11 13 – Facility Water Distribution Piping

22 11 13.47 Pipe Fittings, Steel

		Crew	Daily Output	Labor-Hours	Unit	Material	2024 Bare Costs Labor	Equipment	Total	Total Incl O&P
4622	4" by 2-1/2" pipe size	Q-15	7	2.286	Ea.	36.50	154	10.25	200.75	280
4623	5" by 3" pipe size	↓	7	2.286		244	154	10.25	408.25	505
4624	6" by 4" pipe size	Q-16	6	4		63	279	11.95	353.95	500
4625	8" by 6" pipe size		5	4.800		82.50	335	14.35	431.85	600
4626	10" by 8" pipe size		4	6		160	420	17.95	597.95	815
4627	12" by 10" pipe size	↓	3	8	↓	495	555	24	1,074	1,400
4660	Reducer, eccentric									
4662	3" x 2" pipe size	Q-15	8	2	Ea.	39.50	134	9	182.50	253
4664	4" x 3" pipe size		6	2.667		154	179	11.95	344.95	450
4666	4" x 2" pipe size	↓	6	2.667		58.50	179	11.95	249.45	345
4670	6" x 4" pipe size	Q-16	5	4.800		99	335	14.35	448.35	620
4672	6" x 3" pipe size		5	4.800		155	335	14.35	504.35	680
4676	8" x 6" pipe size		4	6		405	420	17.95	842.95	1,075
4678	8" x 4" pipe size		4	6		230	420	17.95	667.95	895
4682	10" x 8" pipe size		3	8		365	555	24	944	1,250
4684	10" x 6" pipe size		3	8		640	555	24	1,219	1,550
4688	12" x 10" pipe size		2.50	9.600		565	670	28.50	1,263.50	1,650
4690	12" x 8" pipe size		2.50	9.600		890	670	28.50	1,588.50	2,000
4691	14" x 12" pipe size		2.20	10.909		995	760	32.50	1,787.50	2,250
4693	16" x 14" pipe size		1.80	13.333		1,525	930	40	2,495	3,100
4694	16" x 12" pipe size		2	12		2,025	835	36	2,896	3,525
4696	18" x 16" pipe size	↓	1.60	15	↓	2,750	1,050	45	3,845	4,625
5000	Weld joint, socket, forged steel, 3000 lb., schedule 40 pipe									
5010	90° elbow, straight									
5020	1/4" pipe size	Q-15	22	.727	Ea.	9.25	49	3.27	61.52	86.50
5030	3/8" pipe size		22	.727		11	49	3.27	63.27	88
5040	1/2" pipe size		20	.800		19.35	53.50	3.59	76.44	105
5050	3/4" pipe size		20	.800		27.50	53.50	3.59	84.59	114
5060	1" pipe size		20	.800		41.50	53.50	3.59	98.59	129
5070	1-1/4" pipe size		18	.889		66.50	59.50	3.99	129.99	166
5080	1-1/2" pipe size		16	1		77	67	4.49	148.49	190
5090	2" pipe size		12	1.333		114	89.50	6	209.50	265
5100	2-1/2" pipe size		10	1.600		395	107	7.20	509.20	605
5110	3" pipe size		8	2		620	134	9	763	890
5120	4" pipe size	↓	6	2.667	↓	1,475	179	11.95	1,665.95	1,900
5130	45° elbow, straight									
5134	1/4" pipe size	Q-15	22	.727	Ea.	46.50	49	3.27	98.77	128
5135	3/8" pipe size		22	.727		46.50	49	3.27	98.77	128
5136	1/2" pipe size		20	.800		34.50	53.50	3.59	91.59	122
5137	3/4" pipe size		20	.800		40	53.50	3.59	97.09	128
5140	1" pipe size		20	.800		34.50	53.50	3.59	91.59	122
5150	1-1/4" pipe size		18	.889		72	59.50	3.99	135.49	172
5160	1-1/2" pipe size		16	1		88	67	4.49	159.49	202
5170	2" pipe size		12	1.333		142	89.50	6	237.50	296
5180	2-1/2" pipe size		10	1.600		370	107	7.20	484.20	580
5190	3" pipe size		8	2		660	134	9	803	935
5200	4" pipe size	↓	6	2.667	↓	1,275	179	11.95	1,465.95	1,675
5250	Tee, straight									
5254	1/4" pipe size	Q-15	15	1.067	Ea.	51.50	71.50	4.79	127.79	169
5255	3/8" pipe size		15	1.067		51.50	71.50	4.79	127.79	169
5256	1/2" pipe size		13	1.231		32	82.50	5.55	120.05	165
5257	3/4" pipe size		13	1.231		39	82.50	5.55	127.05	172
5260	1" pipe size	↓	13	1.231		53	82.50	5.55	141.05	188

For customer support on your Plumbing Costs with RSMeans Data call 800.448.8182.

22 11 Facility Water Distribution

22 11 13 – Facility Water Distribution Piping

22 11 13.47 Pipe Fittings, Steel		Crew	Daily Output	Labor-Hours	Unit	Material	2024 Bare Costs Labor	Equipment	Total	Total Incl O&P
5270	1-1/4" pipe size	Q-15	12	1.333	Ea.	82	89.50	6	177.50	230
5280	1-1/2" pipe size		11	1.455		108	97.50	6.55	212.05	271
5290	2" pipe size		8	2		156	134	9	299	380
5300	2-1/2" pipe size		6	2.667		450	179	11.95	640.95	775
5310	3" pipe size		5	3.200		1,075	215	14.35	1,304.35	1,500
5320	4" pipe size	↓	4	4	↓	1,725	269	17.95	2,011.95	2,325
5350	For reducing sizes, add					60%				
5450	Couplings									
5451	1/4" pipe size	Q-15	23	.696	Ea.	29.50	46.50	3.12	79.12	105
5452	3/8" pipe size		23	.696		5.35	46.50	3.12	54.97	79
5453	1/2" pipe size		21	.762		5.30	51	3.42	59.72	85.50
5454	3/4" pipe size		21	.762		5.85	51	3.42	60.27	86
5460	1" pipe size		20	.800		7.55	53.50	3.59	64.64	92.50
5470	1-1/4" pipe size		20	.800		12.60	53.50	3.59	69.69	98
5480	1-1/2" pipe size		18	.889		13.15	59.50	3.99	76.64	108
5490	2" pipe size		14	1.143		21	77	5.15	103.15	143
5500	2-1/2" pipe size		12	1.333		41.50	89.50	6	137	185
5510	3" pipe size		9	1.778		68.50	119	8	195.50	262
5520	4" pipe size		7	2.286		156	154	10.25	320.25	410
5570	Union, 1/4" pipe size		21	.762		101	51	3.42	155.42	191
5571	3/8" pipe size		21	.762		101	51	3.42	155.42	191
5572	1/2" pipe size		19	.842		92.50	56.50	3.78	152.78	190
5573	3/4" pipe size		19	.842		148	56.50	3.78	208.28	251
5574	1" pipe size		19	.842		28.50	56.50	3.78	88.78	120
5575	1-1/4" pipe size		17	.941		257	63	4.23	324.23	380
5576	1-1/2" pipe size		15	1.067		291	71.50	4.79	367.29	430
5577	2" pipe size		11	1.455		370	97.50	6.55	474.05	555
5600	Reducer, 1/4" pipe size		23	.696		75.50	46.50	3.12	125.12	156
5601	3/8" pipe size		23	.696		79.50	46.50	3.12	129.12	160
5602	1/2" pipe size		21	.762		48.50	51	3.42	102.92	133
5603	3/4" pipe size		21	.762		48.50	51	3.42	102.92	133
5604	1" pipe size		21	.762		67.50	51	3.42	121.92	154
5605	1-1/4" pipe size		19	.842		86.50	56.50	3.78	146.78	183
5607	1-1/2" pipe size		17	.941		92.50	63	4.23	159.73	201
5608	2" pipe size		13	1.231		102	82.50	5.55	190.05	241
5612	Cap, 1/4" pipe size		46	.348		28	23.50	1.56	53.06	67.50
5613	3/8" pipe size		46	.348		28	23.50	1.56	53.06	67.50
5614	1/2" pipe size		42	.381		17.15	25.50	1.71	44.36	58.50
5615	3/4" pipe size		42	.381		20.50	25.50	1.71	47.71	63
5616	1" pipe size		42	.381		30.50	25.50	1.71	57.71	73.50
5617	1-1/4" pipe size		38	.421		35.50	28.50	1.89	65.89	83.50
5618	1-1/2" pipe size		34	.471		14.70	31.50	2.11	48.31	65.50
5619	2" pipe size		26	.615		79	41.50	2.76	123.26	152
5630	T-O-L, 1/4" pipe size, nozzle		23	.696		14.85	46.50	3.12	64.47	89.50
5631	3/8" pipe size, nozzle		23	.696		15.30	46.50	3.12	64.92	90
5632	1/2" pipe size, nozzle		22	.727		5.30	49	3.27	57.57	82
5633	3/4" pipe size, nozzle		21	.762		5.60	51	3.42	60.02	86
5634	1" pipe size, nozzle		20	.800		7.70	53.50	3.59	64.79	92.50
5635	1-1/4" pipe size, nozzle		18	.889		12.20	59.50	3.99	75.69	107
5636	1-1/2" pipe size, nozzle		16	1		11.30	67	4.49	82.79	117
5637	2" pipe size, nozzle		12	1.333		12.85	89.50	6	108.35	154
5638	2-1/2" pipe size, nozzle		10	1.600		121	107	7.20	235.20	300
5639	4" pipe size, nozzle	↓	6	2.667		89	179	11.95	279.95	375

22 11 Facility Water Distribution

22 11 13 – Facility Water Distribution Piping

22 11 13.47 Pipe Fittings, Steel		Crew	Daily Output	Labor-Hours	Unit	Material	2024 Bare Costs Labor	Equipment	Total	Total Incl O&P
5640	W-O-L, 1/4" pipe size, nozzle	Q-15	23	.696	Ea.	37.50	46.50	3.12	87.12	114
5641	3/8" pipe size, nozzle		23	.696		30.50	46.50	3.12	80.12	106
5642	1/2" pipe size, nozzle		22	.727		31	49	3.27	83.27	110
5643	3/4" pipe size, nozzle		21	.762		13.85	51	3.42	68.27	95
5644	1" pipe size, nozzle		20	.800		11.10	53.50	3.59	68.19	96
5645	1-1/4" pipe size, nozzle		18	.889		39	59.50	3.99	102.49	136
5646	1-1/2" pipe size, nozzle		16	1		40.50	67	4.49	111.99	149
5647	2" pipe size, nozzle		12	1.333		40.50	89.50	6	136	185
5648	2-1/2" pipe size, nozzle		10	1.600		93	107	7.20	207.20	270
5649	3" pipe size, nozzle		8	2		53.50	134	9	196.50	269
5650	4" pipe size, nozzle		6	2.667		129	179	11.95	319.95	420
5651	5" pipe size, nozzle		5	3.200		320	215	14.35	549.35	685
5652	6" pipe size, nozzle		4	4		355	269	17.95	641.95	815
5653	8" pipe size, nozzle		3	5.333		1,025	360	24	1,409	1,675
5654	10" pipe size, nozzle		2.60	6.154		960	415	27.50	1,402.50	1,700
5655	12" pipe size, nozzle		2.20	7.273		1,825	490	32.50	2,347.50	2,750
5674	S-O-L, 1/4" pipe size, outlet		23	.696		18.40	46.50	3.12	68.02	93.50
5675	3/8" pipe size, outlet		23	.696		18.40	46.50	3.12	68.02	93.50
5676	1/2" pipe size, outlet		22	.727		18.45	49	3.27	70.72	96.50
5677	3/4" pipe size, outlet		21	.762		8.45	51	3.42	62.87	89
5678	1" pipe size, outlet		20	.800		11.95	53.50	3.59	69.04	97
5679	1-1/4" pipe size, outlet		18	.889		34.50	59.50	3.99	97.99	131
5680	1-1/2" pipe size, outlet		16	1		34.50	67	4.49	105.99	143
5681	2" pipe size, outlet	▼	12	1.333	▼	36	89.50	6	131.50	179
6000	Weld-on flange, forged steel									
6020	Slip-on, 150 lb. flange (welded front and back)									
6050	1/2" pipe size	Q-15	18	.889	Ea.	28.50	59.50	3.99	91.99	125
6060	3/4" pipe size		18	.889		28.50	59.50	3.99	91.99	125
6070	1" pipe size		17	.941		28.50	63	4.23	95.73	130
6080	1-1/4" pipe size		16	1		28.50	67	4.49	99.99	136
6090	1-1/2" pipe size		15	1.067		28.50	71.50	4.79	104.79	144
6100	2" pipe size		12	1.333		31	89.50	6	126.50	174
6110	2-1/2" pipe size		10	1.600		46	107	7.20	160.20	218
6120	3" pipe size		9	1.778		38.50	119	8	165.50	229
6130	3-1/2" pipe size		7	2.286		49	154	10.25	213.25	293
6140	4" pipe size		6	2.667		49	179	11.95	239.95	335
6150	5" pipe size		5	3.200		88.50	215	14.35	317.85	435
6160	6" pipe size	Q-16	6	4		81	279	11.95	371.95	515
6170	8" pipe size		5	4.800		122	335	14.35	471.35	645
6180	10" pipe size		4	6		207	420	17.95	644.95	870
6190	12" pipe size		3	8		173	555	24	752	1,050
6191	14" pipe size		2.50	9.600		405	670	28.50	1,103.50	1,475
6192	16" pipe size	▼	1.80	13.333	▼	655	930	40	1,625	2,150
6200	300 lb. flange									
6210	1/2" pipe size	Q-15	17	.941	Ea.	38.50	63	4.23	105.73	141
6220	3/4" pipe size		17	.941		38.50	63	4.23	105.73	141
6230	1" pipe size		16	1		38.50	67	4.49	109.99	147
6240	1-1/4" pipe size		13	1.231		38.50	82.50	5.55	126.55	171
6250	1-1/2" pipe size		12	1.333		38.50	89.50	6	134	182
6260	2" pipe size		11	1.455		45.50	97.50	6.55	149.55	202
6270	2-1/2" pipe size		9	1.778		51	119	8	178	243
6280	3" pipe size		7	2.286		58.50	154	10.25	222.75	305
6290	4" pipe size	▼	6	2.667		83	179	11.95	273.95	370

For customer support on your Plumbing Costs with RSMeans Data call 800.448.8182.

22 11 Facility Water Distribution

22 11 13 – Facility Water Distribution Piping

22 11 13.47 Pipe Fittings, Steel

		Crew	Daily Output	Labor-Hours	Unit	Material	2024 Bare Costs Labor	Equipment	Total	Total Incl O&P
6300	5" pipe size	Q-15	4	4	Ea.	135	269	17.95	421.95	570
6310	6" pipe size	Q-16	5	4.800		141	335	14.35	490.35	665
6320	8" pipe size		4	6		237	420	17.95	674.95	900
6330	10" pipe size		3.40	7.059		405	490	21	916	1,200
6340	12" pipe size	↓	2.80	8.571	↓	510	595	25.50	1,130.50	1,475
6400	Welding neck, 150 lb. flange									
6410	1/2" pipe size	Q-15	40	.400	Ea.	36	27	1.80	64.80	81.50
6420	3/4" pipe size		36	.444		36	30	2	68	86
6430	1" pipe size		32	.500		36	33.50	2.25	71.75	92
6440	1-1/4" pipe size		29	.552		31	37	2.48	70.48	91.50
6450	1-1/2" pipe size		26	.615		33	41.50	2.76	77.26	101
6460	2" pipe size		20	.800		30	53.50	3.59	87.09	117
6470	2-1/2" pipe size		16	1		32	67	4.49	103.49	140
6480	3" pipe size		14	1.143		36.50	77	5.15	118.65	160
6500	4" pipe size		10	1.600		42	107	7.20	156.20	214
6510	5" pipe size	↓	8	2		97	134	9	240	315
6520	6" pipe size	Q-16	10	2.400		61	167	7.20	235.20	325
6530	8" pipe size		7	3.429		107	239	10.25	356.25	485
6540	10" pipe size		6	4		172	279	11.95	462.95	620
6550	12" pipe size		5	4.800		305	335	14.35	654.35	845
6551	14" pipe size		4.50	5.333		550	370	15.95	935.95	1,175
6552	16" pipe size		3	8		865	555	24	1,444	1,800
6553	18" pipe size		2.50	9.600		1,175	670	28.50	1,873.50	2,300
6554	20" pipe size		2.30	10.435		1,425	725	31	2,181	2,650
6556	24" pipe size		2	12		1,900	835	36	2,771	3,400
6557	26" pipe size		1.70	14.118		2,500	985	42	3,527	4,275
6558	30" pipe size		.90	26.667		2,875	1,850	79.50	4,804.50	6,050
6559	36" pipe size	↓	.75	32	↓	3,300	2,225	95.50	5,620.50	7,075
6560	300 lb. flange									
6570	1/2" pipe size	Q-15	36	.444	Ea.	50.50	30	2	82.50	102
6580	3/4" pipe size		34	.471		50.50	31.50	2.11	84.11	105
6590	1" pipe size		30	.533		50.50	36	2.39	88.89	112
6600	1-1/4" pipe size		28	.571		50.50	38.50	2.57	91.57	115
6610	1-1/2" pipe size		24	.667		50.50	45	2.99	98.49	125
6620	2" pipe size		18	.889		44	59.50	3.99	107.49	141
6630	2-1/2" pipe size		14	1.143		64.50	77	5.15	146.65	191
6640	3" pipe size		12	1.333		65.50	89.50	6	161	212
6650	4" pipe size		8	2		59	134	9	202	275
6660	5" pipe size	↓	7	2.286		168	154	10.25	332.25	425
6670	6" pipe size	Q-16	9	2.667		172	186	7.95	365.95	475
6680	8" pipe size		6	4		289	279	11.95	579.95	745
6690	10" pipe size		5	4.800		515	335	14.35	864.35	1,075
6700	12" pipe size	↓	4	6	↓	660	420	17.95	1,097.95	1,375
7740	Plain ends for plain end pipe, mechanically coupled									
7750	Cplg. & labor required at joints not included, add 1 per									
7760	joint for installed price, see line 9180									
7770	Malleable iron, painted, unless noted otherwise									
7800	90° elbow, 1"				Ea.	239			239	263
7810	1-1/2"					282			282	310
7820	2"					420			420	460
7830	2-1/2"					490			490	540
7840	3"					510			510	560
7860	4"				↓	575			575	635

22 11 Facility Water Distribution

22 11 13 – Facility Water Distribution Piping

22 11 13.47 Pipe Fittings, Steel		Crew	Daily Output	Labor-Hours	Unit	Material	2024 Bare Costs Labor	Equipment	Total	Total Incl O&P
7870	5" welded steel				Ea.	665			665	730
7880	6"					840			840	920
7890	8" welded steel					1,575			1,575	1,725
7900	10" welded steel					2,000			2,000	2,200
7910	12" welded steel					2,225			2,225	2,450
7970	45° elbow, 1"					144			144	158
7980	1-1/2"					213			213	234
7990	2"					445			445	490
8000	2-1/2"					445			445	490
8010	3"					510			510	560
8030	4"					530			530	585
8040	5" welded steel					665			665	730
8050	6"					760			760	835
8060	8"					890			890	980
8070	10" welded steel					920			920	1,000
8080	12" welded steel					1,650			1,650	1,825
8140	Tee, straight 1"					267			267	293
8150	1-1/2"					345			345	380
8160	2"					345			345	380
8170	2-1/2"					445			445	490
8180	3"					685			685	755
8200	4"					980			980	1,075
8210	5" welded steel					1,350			1,350	1,475
8220	6"					1,175			1,175	1,275
8230	8" welded steel					1,675			1,675	1,850
8240	10" welded steel					3,550			3,550	3,925
8250	12" welded steel					3,075			3,075	3,400
8340	Segmentally welded steel, painted									
8390	Wye 2"				Ea.	525			525	575
8400	2-1/2"					525			525	575
8410	3"					630			630	695
8430	4"					680			680	745
8440	5"					1,200			1,200	1,300
8450	6"					1,450			1,450	1,600
8460	8"					2,125			2,125	2,325
8470	10"					3,275			3,275	3,600
8480	12"					2,975			2,975	3,275
8540	Wye, lateral 2"					465			465	510
8550	2-1/2"					530			530	585
8560	3"					630			630	695
8580	4"					870			870	955
8590	5"					1,475			1,475	1,625
8600	6"					1,525			1,525	1,675
8610	8"					2,550			2,550	2,800
8620	10"					2,550			2,550	2,800
8630	12"					4,675			4,675	5,150
8690	Cross, 2"					320			320	350
8700	2-1/2"					320			320	350
8710	3"					380			380	415
8730	4"					800			800	880
8740	5"					1,200			1,200	1,325
8750	6"					1,250			1,250	1,375
8760	8"					1,800			1,800	2,000

For customer support on your Plumbing Costs with RSMeans Data call 800.448.8182.

22 11 Facility Water Distribution

22 11 13 – Facility Water Distribution Piping

22 11 13.47 Pipe Fittings, Steel		Crew	Daily Output	Labor-Hours	Unit	Material	2024 Bare Costs Labor	Equipment	Total	Total Incl O&P
8770	10"				Ea.	3,075			3,075	3,400
8780	12"					3,250			3,250	3,575
8800	Tees, reducing 2" x 1"					430			430	470
8810	2" x 1-1/2"					430			430	470
8820	3" x 1"					425			425	470
8830	3" x 1-1/2"					294			294	325
8840	3" x 2"					425			425	470
8850	4" x 1"					630			630	690
8860	4" x 1-1/2"					630			630	690
8870	4" x 2"					425			425	470
8880	4" x 2-1/2"					265			265	291
8890	4" x 3"					435			435	480
8900	6" x 2"					655			655	720
8910	6" x 3"					745			745	815
8920	6" x 4"					620			620	680
8930	8" x 2"					1,175			1,175	1,275
8940	8" x 3"					960			960	1,050
8950	8" x 4"					1,425			1,425	1,550
8960	8" x 5"					825			825	905
8970	8" x 6"					990			990	1,100
8980	10" x 4"					930			930	1,025
8990	10" x 6"					955			955	1,050
9000	10" x 8"					1,500			1,500	1,650
9010	12" x 6"					2,475			2,475	2,725
9020	12" x 8"					1,850			1,850	2,025
9030	12" x 10"				↓	1,825			1,825	2,025
9080	Adapter nipples 3" long									
9090	1"				Ea.	33			33	36
9100	1-1/2"					42.50			42.50	47
9110	2"					42.50			42.50	47
9120	2-1/2"					49			49	54
9130	3"					59			59	65
9140	4"					95.50			95.50	105
9150	6"				↓	250			250	275
9180	Coupling, mechanical, plain end pipe to plain end pipe or fitting									
9190	1"	Q-1	29	.552	Ea.	145	37		182	214
9200	1-1/2"		28	.571		145	38.50		183.50	216
9210	2"		27	.593		145	40		185	218
9220	2-1/2"		26	.615		145	41.50		186.50	221
9230	3"		25	.640		211	43		254	296
9240	3-1/2"		24	.667		244	45		289	335
9250	4"	↓	22	.727		244	49		293	340
9260	5"	Q-2	28	.857		345	59.50		404.50	470
9270	6"		24	1		420	69.50		489.50	570
9280	8"		19	1.263		745	88		833	945
9290	10"		16	1.500		965	105		1,070	1,200
9300	12"	↓	12	2	↓	1,200	139		1,339	1,525
9310	Outlets for precut holes through pipe wall									
9331	Strapless type, with gasket									
9332	4" to 8" pipe x 1/2"	1 Plum	13	.615	Ea.	158	46		204	243
9333	4" to 8" pipe x 3/4"		13	.615		169	46		215	255
9334	10" pipe and larger x 1/2"		11	.727		158	54.50		212.50	255
9335	10" pipe and larger x 3/4"	↓	11	.727		169	54.50		223.50	267

22 11 Facility Water Distribution

22 11 13 – Facility Water Distribution Piping

22 11 13.47 Pipe Fittings, Steel		Crew	Daily Output	Labor-Hours	Unit	Material	2024 Bare Costs Labor	Equipment	Total	Total Incl O&P
9341	Thermometer wells with gasket									
9342	4" to 8" pipe, 6" stem	1 Plum	14	.571	Ea.	237	42.50		279.50	325
9343	8" pipe and larger, 6" stem	"	13	.615	"	237	46		283	330
9800	Mech. tee, cast iron, grooved or threaded, w/nuts and bolts									
9805	2" x 1"	1 Plum	50	.160	Ea.	193	11.95		204.95	230
9810	2" x 1-1/4"		50	.160		226	11.95		237.95	266
9815	2" x 1-1/2"	↓	50	.160		234	11.95		245.95	276
9820	2-1/2" x 1"	Q-1	80	.200		202	13.45		215.45	242
9825	2-1/2" x 1-1/4"		80	.200		297	13.45		310.45	345
9830	2-1/2" x 1-1/2"		80	.200		297	13.45		310.45	345
9835	2-1/2" x 2"		80	.200		202	13.45		215.45	242
9840	3" x 1"		80	.200		219	13.45		232.45	260
9845	3" x 1-1/4"		80	.200		284	13.45		297.45	335
9850	3" x 1-1/2"		80	.200		284	13.45		297.45	335
9852	3" x 2"		80	.200		345	13.45		358.45	400
9856	4" x 1"		67	.239		271	16.05		287.05	320
9858	4" x 1-1/4"		67	.239		355	16.05		371.05	415
9860	4" x 1-1/2"		67	.239		360	16.05		376.05	420
9862	4" x 2"		67	.239		370	16.05		386.05	435
9864	4" x 2-1/2"		67	.239		385	16.05		401.05	445
9866	4" x 3"	↓	67	.239		385	16.05		401.05	445
9870	6" x 1-1/2"	Q-2	50	.480		450	33.50		483.50	545
9872	6" x 2"		50	.480		455	33.50		488.50	550
9874	6" x 2-1/2"		50	.480		455	33.50		488.50	550
9876	6" x 3"		50	.480		515	33.50		548.50	620
9878	6" x 4"		50	.480		575	33.50		608.50	685
9880	8" x 2"		42	.571		775	40		815	915
9882	8" x 2-1/2"		42	.571		775	40		815	915
9884	8" x 3"		42	.571		820	40		860	960
9886	8" x 4"	↓	42	.571	↓	1,675	40		1,715	1,875
9940	For galvanized fittings for plain end pipe, add					20%				

22 11 13.48 Pipe, Fittings and Valves, Steel, Grooved-Joint

		Crew	Daily Output	Labor-Hours	Unit	Material	Labor	Equipment	Total	Total Incl O&P
0010	**PIPE, FITTINGS AND VALVES, STEEL, GROOVED-JOINT** R221113-70									
0012	Fittings are ductile iron. Steel fittings noted.									
0020	Pipe includes coupling & clevis type hanger assemblies, 10' OC									
0500	Schedule 10, black									
0550	2" diameter	1 Plum	43	.186	L.F.	11.20	13.90		25.10	33
0560	2-1/2" diameter	Q-1	61	.262		13.85	17.60		31.45	41
0570	3" diameter		55	.291		15.90	19.55		35.45	46.50
0580	3-1/2" diameter		53	.302		23	20.50		43.50	55.50
0590	4" diameter		49	.327		21.50	22		43.50	56.50
0600	5" diameter	↓	40	.400		27.50	27		54.50	70
0610	6" diameter	Q-2	46	.522		34.50	36.50		71	91.50
0620	8" diameter	"	41	.585	↓	49.50	41		90.50	115
0700	To delete couplings & hangers, subtract									
0710	2" diam. to 5" diam.					25%	20%			
0720	6" diam. to 8" diam.					27%	15%			
1000	Schedule 40, black									
1040	3/4" diameter	1 Plum	71	.113	L.F.	10.95	8.40		19.35	24.50
1050	1" diameter		63	.127		12.90	9.50		22.40	28.50
1060	1-1/4" diameter		58	.138		16.85	10.30		27.15	34
1070	1-1/2" diameter	↓	51	.157		19.45	11.70		31.15	39

22 11 Facility Water Distribution

22 11 13 – Facility Water Distribution Piping

22 11 13.48 Pipe, Fittings and Valves, Steel, Grooved-Joint		Crew	Daily Output	Labor-Hours	Unit	Material	2024 Bare Costs Labor	Equipment	Total	Total Incl O&P
1080	2" diameter	1 Plum	40	.200	L.F.	24.50	14.95		39.45	49
1090	2-1/2" diameter	Q-1	57	.281		34.50	18.85		53.35	66
1100	3" diameter		50	.320		43.50	21.50		65	79.50
1110	4" diameter		45	.356		61.50	24		85.50	104
1120	5" diameter	↓	37	.432		44.50	29		73.50	92
1130	6" diameter	Q-2	42	.571		112	40		152	182
1140	8" diameter		37	.649		148	45		193	229
1150	10" diameter		31	.774		198	54		252	298
1160	12" diameter		27	.889		223	62		285	335
1170	14" diameter		20	1.200		240	83.50		323.50	390
1180	16" diameter		17	1.412		360	98.50		458.50	540
1190	18" diameter		14	1.714		355	119		474	570
1200	20" diameter		12	2		430	139		569	680
1210	24" diameter	↓	10	2.400	↓	475	167		642	770
1740	To delete coupling & hanger, subtract									
1750	3/4" diam. to 2" diam.					65%	27%			
1760	2-1/2" diam. to 5" diam.					41%	18%			
1770	6" diam. to 12" diam.					31%	13%			
1780	14" diam. to 24" diam.					35%	10%			
1800	Galvanized									
1840	3/4" diameter	1 Plum	71	.113	L.F.	12.15	8.40		20.55	26
1850	1" diameter		63	.127		10.60	9.50		20.10	26
1860	1-1/4" diameter		58	.138		11.50	10.30		21.80	28
1870	1-1/2" diameter		51	.157		15.85	11.70		27.55	35
1880	2" diameter	↓	40	.200		20.50	14.95		35.45	44.50
1890	2-1/2" diameter	Q-1	57	.281		29	18.85		47.85	60
1900	3" diameter		50	.320		35.50	21.50		57	71.50
1910	4" diameter		45	.356		51	24		75	91.50
1920	5" diameter	↓	37	.432		70	29		99	120
1930	6" diameter	Q-2	42	.571		88.50	40		128.50	157
1940	8" diameter		37	.649		141	45		186	222
1950	10" diameter		31	.774		220	54		274	320
1960	12" diameter	↓	27	.889	↓	246	62		308	365
2540	To delete coupling & hanger, subtract									
2550	3/4" diam. to 2" diam.					36%	27%			
2560	2-1/2" diam. to 5" diam.					19%	18%			
2570	6" diam. to 12" diam.					14%	13%			
2600	Schedule 80, black									
2610	3/4" diameter	1 Plum	65	.123	L.F.	12.55	9.20		21.75	27.50
2650	1" diameter		61	.131		15.40	9.80		25.20	31.50
2660	1-1/4" diameter		55	.145		20.50	10.85		31.35	38.50
2670	1-1/2" diameter		49	.163		24	12.20		36.20	44.50
2680	2" diameter	↓	38	.211		30.50	15.70		46.20	57
2690	2-1/2" diameter	Q-1	54	.296		41	19.90		60.90	74.50
2700	3" diameter		48	.333		52.50	22.50		75	91.50
2710	4" diameter		44	.364		52	24.50		76.50	93.50
2720	5" diameter	↓	35	.457		91	30.50		121.50	146
2730	6" diameter	Q-2	40	.600		169	42		211	247
2740	8" diameter		35	.686		203	48		251	295
2750	10" diameter		29	.828		475	57.50		532.50	605
2760	12" diameter	↓	24	1	↓	730	69.50		799.50	910
3240	To delete coupling & hanger, subtract									
3250	3/4" diam. to 2" diam.					30%	25%			

22 11 Facility Water Distribution

22 11 13 – Facility Water Distribution Piping

22 11 13.48 Pipe, Fittings and Valves, Steel, Grooved-Joint	Crew	Daily Output	Labor-Hours	Unit	Material	2024 Bare Costs Labor	Equipment	Total	Total Incl O&P
3260 2-1/2" diam. to 5" diam.					14%	17%			
3270 6" diam. to 12" diam.					12%	12%			
3300 Galvanized									
3310 3/4" diameter	1 Plum	65	.123	L.F.	10.35	9.20		19.55	25
3350 1" diameter		61	.131		11.20	9.80		21	27
3360 1-1/4" diameter		55	.145		14.75	10.85		25.60	32.50
3370 1-1/2" diameter		46	.174		17	13		30	38
3380 2" diameter		38	.211		22.50	15.70		38.20	48
3390 2-1/2" diameter	Q-1	54	.296		33	19.90		52.90	66
3400 3" diameter		48	.333		42.50	22.50		65	80
3410 4" diameter		44	.364		61	24.50		85.50	104
3420 5" diameter		35	.457		68	30.50		98.50	121
3430 6" diameter	Q-2	40	.600		92	42		134	163
3440 8" diameter		35	.686		243	48		291	340
3450 10" diameter		29	.828		420	57.50		477.50	545
3460 12" diameter		24	1		1,175	69.50		1,244.50	1,375
3920 To delete coupling & hanger, subtract									
3930 3/4" diam. to 2" diam.					30%	25%			
3940 2-1/2" diam. to 5" diam.					15%	17%			
3950 6" diam. to 12" diam.					11%	12%			
3990 Fittings: coupling material required at joints not incl. in fitting price.									
3994 Add 1 selected coupling, material only, per joint for installed price.									
4000 Elbow, 90° or 45°, painted									
4030 3/4" diameter	1 Plum	50	.160	Ea.	129	11.95		140.95	159
4040 1" diameter		50	.160		69	11.95		80.95	94
4050 1-1/4" diameter		40	.200		69	14.95		83.95	98
4060 1-1/2" diameter		33	.242		69	18.10		87.10	103
4070 2" diameter		25	.320		69	24		93	112
4080 2-1/2" diameter	Q-1	40	.400		69	27		96	116
4090 3" diameter		33	.485		121	32.50		153.50	182
4100 4" diameter		25	.640		131	43		174	209
4110 5" diameter		20	.800		310	53.50		363.50	420
4120 6" diameter	Q-2	25	.960		365	67		432	500
4130 8" diameter		21	1.143		760	79.50		839.50	955
4140 10" diameter		18	1.333		1,400	93		1,493	1,700
4150 12" diameter		15	1.600		1,550	111		1,661	1,875
4170 14" diameter		12	2		1,300	139		1,439	1,650
4180 16" diameter		11	2.182		1,700	152		1,852	2,100
4190 18" diameter	Q-3	14	2.286		2,150	162		2,312	2,625
4200 20" diameter		12	2.667		2,850	189		3,039	3,400
4210 24" diameter		10	3.200		4,125	227		4,352	4,875
4250 For galvanized elbows, add					26%				
4690 Tee, painted									
4700 3/4" diameter	1 Plum	38	.211	Ea.	138	15.70		153.70	175
4740 1" diameter		33	.242		106	18.10		124.10	144
4750 1-1/4" diameter		27	.296		106	22		128	150
4760 1-1/2" diameter		22	.364		106	27		133	158
4770 2" diameter		17	.471		106	35		141	170
4780 2-1/2" diameter	Q-1	27	.593		106	40		146	176
4790 3" diameter		22	.727		145	49		194	233
4800 4" diameter		17	.941		220	63		283	335
4810 5" diameter		13	1.231		510	82.50		592.50	685
4820 6" diameter	Q-2	17	1.412		590	98.50		688.50	795

22 11 Facility Water Distribution

22 11 13 – Facility Water Distribution Piping

22 11 13.48 Pipe, Fittings and Valves, Steel, Grooved-Joint		Crew	Daily Output	Labor-Hours	Unit	Material	2024 Bare Costs Labor	Equipment	Total	Total Incl O&P
4830	8" diameter	Q-2	14	1.714	Ea.	1,300	119		1,419	1,600
4840	10" diameter		12	2		1,675	139		1,814	2,050
4850	12" diameter		10	2.400		2,175	167		2,342	2,650
4851	14" diameter		9	2.667		1,650	186		1,836	2,100
4852	16" diameter		8	3		1,875	209		2,084	2,350
4853	18" diameter	Q-3	10	3.200		2,350	227		2,577	2,925
4854	20" diameter		9	3.556		3,350	253		3,603	4,050
4855	24" diameter		8	4		5,100	284		5,384	6,050
4900	For galvanized tees, add					24%				
4906	Couplings, rigid style, painted									
4908	1" diameter	1 Plum	100	.080	Ea.	53.50	5.95		59.45	68
4909	1-1/4" diameter		100	.080		50	5.95		55.95	64
4910	1-1/2" diameter		67	.119		53.50	8.90		62.40	72.50
4912	2" diameter		50	.160		68.50	11.95		80.45	93.50
4914	2-1/2" diameter	Q-1	80	.200		77.50	13.45		90.95	105
4916	3" diameter		67	.239		90	16.05		106.05	123
4918	4" diameter		50	.320		124	21.50		145.50	168
4920	5" diameter		40	.400		160	27		187	216
4922	6" diameter	Q-2	50	.480		211	33.50		244.50	282
4924	8" diameter		42	.571		330	40		370	425
4926	10" diameter		35	.686		640	48		688	775
4928	12" diameter		32	.750		715	52.50		767.50	870
4930	14" diameter		24	1		630	69.50		699.50	795
4931	16" diameter		20	1.200		670	83.50		753.50	865
4932	18" diameter		18	1.333		775	93		868	995
4933	20" diameter		16	1.500		1,050	105		1,155	1,325
4934	24" diameter		13	1.846		1,350	129		1,479	1,700
4940	Flexible, standard, painted									
4950	3/4" diameter	1 Plum	100	.080	Ea.	39.50	5.95		45.45	52.50
4960	1" diameter		100	.080		39.50	5.95		45.45	52.50
4970	1-1/4" diameter		80	.100		51	7.45		58.45	67
4980	1-1/2" diameter		67	.119		55.50	8.90		64.40	74.50
4990	2" diameter		50	.160		59	11.95		70.95	83
5000	2-1/2" diameter	Q-1	80	.200		69	13.45		82.45	95.50
5010	3" diameter		67	.239		75.50	16.05		91.55	107
5020	3-1/2" diameter		57	.281		108	18.85		126.85	147
5030	4" diameter		50	.320		109	21.50		130.50	152
5040	5" diameter		40	.400		163	27		190	220
5050	6" diameter	Q-2	50	.480		193	33.50		226.50	262
5070	8" diameter		42	.571		310	40		350	405
5090	10" diameter		35	.686		510	48		558	630
5110	12" diameter		32	.750		575	52.50		627.50	715
5120	14" diameter		24	1		825	69.50		894.50	1,000
5130	16" diameter		20	1.200		1,075	83.50		1,158.50	1,325
5140	18" diameter		18	1.333		1,275	93		1,368	1,550
5150	20" diameter		16	1.500		1,975	105		2,080	2,325
5160	24" diameter		13	1.846		2,175	129		2,304	2,600
5176	Lightweight style, painted									
5178	1-1/2" diameter	1 Plum	67	.119	Ea.	49	8.90		57.90	67.50
5180	2" diameter	"	50	.160		59	11.95		70.95	83
5182	2-1/2" diameter	Q-1	80	.200		69	13.45		82.45	95.50
5184	3" diameter		67	.239		75.50	16.05		91.55	107
5186	3-1/2" diameter		57	.281		91	18.85		109.85	128

22 11 Facility Water Distribution

22 11 13 – Facility Water Distribution Piping

22 11 13.48 Pipe, Fittings and Valves, Steel, Grooved-Joint		Crew	Daily Output	Labor-Hours	Unit	Material	2024 Bare Costs Labor	Equipment	Total	Total Incl O&P
5188	4" diameter	Q-1	50	.320	Ea.	109	21.50		130.50	152
5190	5" diameter	▼	40	.400		163	27		190	220
5192	6" diameter	Q-2	50	.480		193	33.50		226.50	262
5194	8" diameter		42	.571		310	40		350	405
5196	10" diameter		35	.686		635	48		683	765
5198	12" diameter	▼	32	.750		705	52.50		757.50	855
5200	For galvanized couplings, add				▼	33%				
5220	Tee, reducing, painted									
5225	2" x 1-1/2" diameter	Q-1	38	.421	Ea.	223	28.50		251.50	287
5226	2-1/2" x 2" diameter		28	.571		223	38.50		261.50	300
5227	3" x 2-1/2" diameter		23	.696		197	46.50		243.50	286
5228	4" x 3" diameter		18	.889		265	59.50		324.50	380
5229	5" x 4" diameter	▼	15	1.067		565	71.50		636.50	725
5230	6" x 4" diameter	Q-2	18	1.333		620	93		713	820
5231	8" x 6" diameter		15	1.600		1,300	111		1,411	1,600
5232	10" x 8" diameter		13	1.846		1,425	129		1,554	1,775
5233	12" x 10" diameter		11	2.182		1,800	152		1,952	2,200
5234	14" x 12" diameter		10	2.400		1,750	167		1,917	2,150
5235	16" x 12" diameter	▼	9	2.667		1,500	186		1,686	1,925
5236	18" x 12" diameter	Q-3	12	2.667		1,800	189		1,989	2,250
5237	18" x 16" diameter		11	2.909		2,275	207		2,482	2,800
5238	20" x 16" diameter		10	3.200		2,950	227		3,177	3,600
5239	24" x 20" diameter	▼	9	3.556	▼	4,675	253		4,928	5,500
5240	Reducer, concentric, painted									
5241	2-1/2" x 2" diameter	Q-1	43	.372	Ea.	80.50	25		105.50	126
5242	3" x 2-1/2" diameter		35	.457		97	30.50		127.50	152
5243	4" x 3" diameter		29	.552		117	37		154	183
5244	5" x 4" diameter	▼	22	.727		160	49		209	249
5245	6" x 4" diameter	Q-2	26	.923		186	64.50		250.50	300
5246	8" x 6" diameter		23	1.043		475	72.50		547.50	635
5247	10" x 8" diameter		20	1.200		935	83.50		1,018.50	1,150
5248	12" x 10" diameter	▼	16	1.500	▼	1,675	105		1,780	1,975
5255	Eccentric, painted									
5256	2-1/2" x 2" diameter	Q-1	42	.381	Ea.	166	25.50		191.50	221
5257	3" x 2-1/2" diameter		34	.471		190	31.50		221.50	256
5258	4" x 3" diameter		28	.571		231	38.50		269.50	310
5259	5" x 4" diameter	▼	21	.762		315	51		366	420
5260	6" x 4" diameter	Q-2	25	.960		365	67		432	500
5261	8" x 6" diameter		22	1.091		735	76		811	920
5262	10" x 8" diameter		19	1.263		1,925	88		2,013	2,250
5263	12" x 10" diameter	▼	15	1.600	▼	2,650	111		2,761	3,100
5270	Coupling, reducing, painted									
5272	2" x 1-1/2" diameter	1 Plum	52	.154	Ea.	78	11.50		89.50	103
5274	2-1/2" x 2" diameter	Q-1	82	.195		100	13.10		113.10	130
5276	3" x 2" diameter		69	.232		113	15.60		128.60	148
5278	4" x 2" diameter		52	.308		179	20.50		199.50	228
5280	5" x 4" diameter	▼	42	.381		201	25.50		226.50	260
5282	6" x 4" diameter	Q-2	52	.462		305	32		337	385
5284	8" x 6" diameter	"	44	.545	▼	450	38		488	550
5290	Outlet coupling, painted									
5294	1-1/2" x 1" pipe size	1 Plum	65	.123	Ea.	103	9.20		112.20	127
5296	2" x 1" pipe size	"	48	.167		104	12.45		116.45	134
5298	2-1/2" x 1" pipe size	Q-1	78	.205	▼	160	13.80		173.80	197

22 11 Facility Water Distribution

22 11 13 – Facility Water Distribution Piping

22 11 13.48 Pipe, Fittings and Valves, Steel, Grooved-Joint		Crew	Daily Output	Labor-Hours	Unit	Material	2024 Bare Costs Labor	2024 Bare Costs Equipment	Total	Total Incl O&P
5300	2-1/2" x 1-1/4" pipe size	Q-1	70	.229	Ea.	179	15.35		194.35	220
5302	3" x 1" pipe size		65	.246		203	16.55		219.55	249
5304	4" x 3/4" pipe size		48	.333		225	22.50		247.50	281
5306	4" x 1-1/2" pipe size		46	.348		320	23.50		343.50	385
5308	6" x 1-1/2" pipe size	Q-2	44	.545		450	38		488	550
5320	Outlet, strap-on T, painted									
5324	Threaded female branch									
5330	2" pipe x 1-1/2" branch size	1 Plum	50	.160	Ea.	74	11.95		85.95	99.50
5334	2-1/2" pipe x 1-1/2" branch size	Q-1	80	.200		90	13.45		103.45	119
5338	3" pipe x 1-1/2" branch size		67	.239		93	16.05		109.05	126
5342	3" pipe x 2" branch size		59	.271		107	18.20		125.20	144
5346	4" pipe x 2" branch size		50	.320		112	21.50		133.50	155
5350	4" pipe x 2-1/2" branch size		47	.340		117	23		140	163
5354	4" pipe x 3" branch size		43	.372		125	25		150	174
5358	5" pipe x 3" branch size		40	.400		153	27		180	209
5362	6" pipe x 2" branch size	Q-2	50	.480		140	33.50		173.50	204
5366	6" pipe x 3" branch size		47	.511		160	35.50		195.50	229
5370	6" pipe x 4" branch size		44	.545		178	38		216	252
5374	8" pipe x 2-1/2" branch size		42	.571		244	40		284	325
5378	8" pipe x 4" branch size		38	.632		265	44		309	355
5390	Grooved branch									
5394	2" pipe x 1-1/4" branch size	1 Plum	78	.103	Ea.	74	7.65		81.65	93
5398	2" pipe x 1-1/2" branch size	"	50	.160		74	11.95		85.95	99.50
5402	2-1/2" pipe x 1-1/2" branch size	Q-1	80	.200		90	13.45		103.45	119
5406	3" pipe x 1-1/2" branch size		67	.239		93	16.05		109.05	126
5410	3" pipe x 2" branch size		59	.271		107	18.20		125.20	144
5414	4" pipe x 2" branch size		50	.320		112	21.50		133.50	155
5418	4" pipe x 2-1/2" branch size		47	.340		117	23		140	163
5422	4" pipe x 3" branch size		43	.372		125	25		150	174
5426	5" pipe x 3" branch size		40	.400		153	27		180	209
5430	6" pipe x 2" branch size	Q-2	50	.480		140	33.50		173.50	204
5434	6" pipe x 3" branch size		47	.511		160	35.50		195.50	229
5438	6" pipe x 4" branch size		44	.545		178	38		216	252
5442	8" pipe x 2-1/2" branch size		42	.571		244	40		284	325
5446	8" pipe x 4" branch size		38	.632		265	44		309	355
5750	Flange, w/groove gasket, black steel									
5754	See Line 22 11 13.47 0620 for gasket & bolt set									
5760	ANSI class 125 and 150, painted									
5780	2" pipe size	1 Plum	23	.348	Ea.	225	26		251	287
5790	2-1/2" pipe size	Q-1	37	.432		279	29		308	350
5800	3" pipe size		31	.516		300	34.50		334.50	380
5820	4" pipe size		23	.696		400	46.50		446.50	510
5830	5" pipe size		19	.842		465	56.50		521.50	600
5840	6" pipe size	Q-2	23	1.043		510	72.50		582.50	670
5850	8" pipe size		17	1.412		575	98.50		673.50	775
5860	10" pipe size		14	1.714		905	119		1,024	1,175
5870	12" pipe size		12	2		1,175	139		1,314	1,500
5880	14" pipe size		10	2.400		2,050	167		2,217	2,525
5890	16" pipe size		9	2.667		2,400	186		2,586	2,900
5900	18" pipe size		6	4		2,950	279		3,229	3,650
5910	20" pipe size		5	4.800		3,550	335		3,885	4,400
5920	24" pipe size		4.50	5.333		4,525	370		4,895	5,525
5940	ANSI class 350, painted									

22 11 Facility Water Distribution

22 11 13 – Facility Water Distribution Piping

22 11 13.48 Pipe, Fittings and Valves, Steel, Grooved-Joint

		Crew	Daily Output	Labor-Hours	Unit	Material	2024 Bare Costs Labor	Equipment	Total	Total Incl O&P
7818	4" pipe size	Q-1	23	.696	Ea.	1,650	46.50		1,696.50	1,875
7820	6" pipe size	Q-2	24	1		5,025	69.50		5,094.50	5,625
7830	With gear operator									
7834	2-1/2" pipe size	Q-1	38	.421	Ea.	1,325	28.50		1,353.50	1,500
7836	3" pipe size		31	.516		1,875	34.50		1,909.50	2,125
7838	4" pipe size		23	.696		2,400	46.50		2,446.50	2,700
7840	6" pipe size	Q-2	24	1		5,650	69.50		5,719.50	6,325
7870	Check valve									
7874	2-1/2" pipe size	Q-1	38	.421	Ea.	580	28.50		608.50	680
7876	3" pipe size		31	.516		685	34.50		719.50	805
7878	4" pipe size		23	.696		725	46.50		771.50	865
7880	5" pipe size		18	.889		1,200	59.50		1,259.50	1,425
7882	6" pipe size	Q-2	24	1		1,425	69.50		1,494.50	1,675
7884	8" pipe size		19	1.263		1,950	88		2,038	2,275
7886	10" pipe size		16	1.500		5,200	105		5,305	5,875
7888	12" pipe size		13	1.846		6,175	129		6,304	6,975
7900	Plug valve, balancing, w/lever operator									
7906	3" pipe size	Q-1	31	.516	Ea.	1,200	34.50		1,234.50	1,350
7908	4" pipe size	"	23	.696		1,450	46.50		1,496.50	1,675
7909	6" pipe size	Q-2	24	1		2,250	69.50		2,319.50	2,575
7916	With gear operator									
7920	3" pipe size	Q-1	31	.516	Ea.	2,250	34.50		2,284.50	2,525
7922	4" pipe size	"	23	.696		2,325	46.50		2,371.50	2,650
7924	6" pipe size	Q-2	24	1		3,150	69.50		3,219.50	3,550
7926	8" pipe size		19	1.263		4,850	88		4,938	5,450
7928	10" pipe size		16	1.500		6,100	105		6,205	6,850
7930	12" pipe size		13	1.846		9,300	129		9,429	10,400
8000	Butterfly valve, 2 position handle, with standard trim									
8010	1-1/2" pipe size	1 Plum	30	.267	Ea.	505	19.90		524.90	585
8020	2" pipe size	"	23	.348		505	26		531	595
8030	3" pipe size	Q-1	30	.533		725	36		761	850
8050	4" pipe size	"	22	.727		795	49		844	950
8070	6" pipe size	Q-2	23	1.043		1,600	72.50		1,672.50	1,875
8080	8" pipe size		18	1.333		2,325	93		2,418	2,725
8090	10" pipe size		15	1.600		3,825	111		3,936	4,375
8200	With stainless steel trim									
8240	1-1/2" pipe size	1 Plum	30	.267	Ea.	640	19.90		659.90	735
8250	2" pipe size	"	23	.348		640	26		666	745
8270	3" pipe size	Q-1	30	.533		860	36		896	1,000
8280	4" pipe size	"	22	.727		935	49		984	1,100
8300	6" pipe size	Q-2	23	1.043		1,750	72.50		1,822.50	2,025
8310	8" pipe size		18	1.333		4,650	93		4,743	5,250
8320	10" pipe size		15	1.600		7,750	111		7,861	8,700
8322	12" pipe size		12	2		8,900	139		9,039	10,000
8324	14" pipe size		10	2.400		11,400	167		11,567	12,700
8326	16" pipe size		9	2.667		19,000	186		19,186	21,100
8328	18" pipe size	Q-3	12	2.667		20,300	189		20,489	22,600
8330	20" pipe size		10	3.200		25,000	227		25,227	27,800
8332	24" pipe size		9	3.556		33,400	253		33,653	37,200
8336	Note: sizes 8" up w/manual gear operator									
9000	Cut one groove, labor									
9010	3/4" pipe size	Q-1	152	.105	Ea.		7.05		7.05	10.50
9020	1" pipe size		140	.114			7.70		7.70	11.40

22 11 Facility Water Distribution

22 11 13 – Facility Water Distribution Piping

22 11 13.48 Pipe, Fittings and Valves, Steel, Grooved-Joint

		Crew	Daily Output	Labor-Hours	Unit	Material	2024 Bare Costs Labor	Equipment	Total	Total Incl O&P
5946	2" pipe size	1 Plum	23	.348	Ea.	282	26		308	350
5948	2-1/2" pipe size	Q-1	37	.432		325	29		354	405
5950	3" pipe size		31	.516		445	34.50		479.50	540
5952	4" pipe size		23	.696		590	46.50		636.50	720
5954	5" pipe size		19	.842		670	56.50		726.50	825
5956	6" pipe size	Q-2	23	1.043		780	72.50		852.50	970
5958	8" pipe size		17	1.412		895	98.50		993.50	1,125
5960	10" pipe size		14	1.714		1,425	119		1,544	1,750
5962	12" pipe size		12	2		1,525	139		1,664	1,875
6100	Cross, painted									
6110	2" diameter	1 Plum	12.50	.640	Ea.	188	48		236	278
6112	2-1/2" diameter	Q-1	20	.800		188	53.50		241.50	287
6114	3" diameter		15.50	1.032		335	69.50		404.50	475
6116	4" diameter		12.50	1.280		550	86		636	740
6118	6" diameter	Q-2	12.50	1.920		1,450	134		1,584	1,775
6120	8" diameter		10.50	2.286		1,900	159		2,059	2,325
6122	10" diameter		9	2.667		3,125	186		3,311	3,700
6124	12" diameter		7.50	3.200		4,500	223		4,723	5,275
7400	Suction diffuser									
7402	Grooved end inlet x flanged outlet									
7410	3" x 3"	Q-1	27	.593	Ea.	1,825	40		1,865	2,050
7412	4" x 4"		19	.842		2,450	56.50		2,506.50	2,775
7414	5" x 5"		14	1.143		2,875	77		2,952	3,300
7416	6" x 6"	Q-2	20	1.200		3,625	83.50		3,708.50	4,125
7418	8" x 8"		15	1.600		6,750	111		6,861	7,600
7420	10" x 10"		12	2		9,175	139		9,314	10,300
7422	12" x 12"		9	2.667		15,100	186		15,286	16,900
7424	14" x 14"		7	3.429		14,000	239		14,239	15,800
7426	16" x 14"		6	4		14,400	279		14,679	16,200
7500	Strainer, tee type, painted									
7506	2" pipe size	1 Plum	21	.381	Ea.	1,200	28.50		1,228.50	1,375
7508	2-1/2" pipe size	Q-1	30	.533		1,275	36		1,311	1,450
7510	3" pipe size		28	.571		1,425	38.50		1,463.50	1,625
7512	4" pipe size		20	.800		1,625	53.50		1,678.50	1,850
7514	5" pipe size		15	1.067		2,350	71.50		2,421.50	2,675
7516	6" pipe size	Q-2	23	1.043		2,550	72.50		2,622.50	2,900
7518	8" pipe size		16	1.500		3,900	105		4,005	4,425
7520	10" pipe size		13	1.846		5,725	129		5,854	6,475
7522	12" pipe size		10	2.400		7,350	167		7,517	8,350
7524	14" pipe size		8	3		18,900	209		19,109	21,100
7526	16" pipe size		7	3.429		23,500	239		23,739	26,200
7570	Expansion joint, max. 3" travel									
7572	2" diameter	1 Plum	24	.333	Ea.	1,525	25		1,550	1,700
7574	3" diameter	Q-1	31	.516		1,750	34.50		1,784.50	1,975
7576	4" diameter	"	23	.696		2,300	46.50		2,346.50	2,625
7578	6" diameter	Q-2	38	.632		3,600	44		3,644	4,025
7790	Valves: coupling material required at joints not incl. in valve price.									
7794	Add 1 selected coupling, material only, per joint for installed price.									
7800	Ball valve w/handle, carbon steel trim									
7810	1-1/2" pipe size	1 Plum	31	.258	Ea.	273	19.25		292.25	330
7812	2" pipe size	"	24	.333		300	25		325	370
7814	2-1/2" pipe size	Q-1	38	.421		660	28.50		688.50	765
7816	3" pipe size		31	.516		1,050	34.50		1,084.50	1,225

22 11 Facility Water Distribution

22 11 13 – Facility Water Distribution Piping

22 11 13.48 Pipe, Fittings and Valves, Steel, Grooved-Joint

		Crew	Daily Output	Labor-Hours	Unit	Material	2024 Bare Costs Labor	Equipment	Total	Total Incl O&P
9030	1-1/4" pipe size	Q-1	124	.129	Ea.		8.65		8.65	12.90
9040	1-1/2" pipe size		114	.140			9.45		9.45	14.05
9050	2" pipe size		104	.154			10.35		10.35	15.35
9060	2-1/2" pipe size		96	.167			11.20		11.20	16.65
9070	3" pipe size		88	.182			12.20		12.20	18.15
9080	3-1/2" pipe size		83	.193			12.95		12.95	19.25
9090	4" pipe size		78	.205			13.80		13.80	20.50
9100	5" pipe size		72	.222			14.95		14.95	22
9110	6" pipe size		70	.229			15.35		15.35	23
9120	8" pipe size		54	.296			19.90		19.90	29.50
9130	10" pipe size		38	.421			28.50		28.50	42
9140	12" pipe size		30	.533			36		36	53.50
9150	14" pipe size		20	.800			53.50		53.50	80
9160	16" pipe size		19	.842			56.50		56.50	84
9170	18" pipe size		18	.889			59.50		59.50	89
9180	20" pipe size		17	.941			63		63	94
9190	24" pipe size		15	1.067			71.50		71.50	107
9210	Roll one groove									
9220	3/4" pipe size	Q-1	266	.060	Ea.		4.04		4.04	6
9230	1" pipe size		228	.070			4.71		4.71	7
9240	1-1/4" pipe size		200	.080			5.35		5.35	8
9250	1-1/2" pipe size		178	.090			6.05		6.05	9
9260	2" pipe size		116	.138			9.25		9.25	13.80
9270	2-1/2" pipe size		110	.145			9.75		9.75	14.55
9280	3" pipe size		100	.160			10.75		10.75	16
9290	3-1/2" pipe size		94	.170			11.45		11.45	17
9300	4" pipe size		86	.186			12.50		12.50	18.60
9310	5" pipe size		84	.190			12.80		12.80	19.05
9320	6" pipe size		80	.200			13.45		13.45	20
9330	8" pipe size		66	.242			16.30		16.30	24
9340	10" pipe size		58	.276			18.55		18.55	27.50
9350	12" pipe size		46	.348			23.50		23.50	35
9360	14" pipe size		30	.533			36		36	53.50
9370	16" pipe size		28	.571			38.50		38.50	57
9380	18" pipe size		27	.593			40		40	59
9390	20" pipe size		25	.640			43		43	64
9400	24" pipe size		23	.696			46.50		46.50	69.50

22 11 13.60 Tubing, Stainless Steel

		Crew	Daily Output	Labor-Hours	Unit	Material	2024 Bare Costs Labor	Equipment	Total	Total Incl O&P
0010	**TUBING, STAINLESS STEEL**									
5000	Tubing									
5010	Type 304, no joints, no hangers									
5020	.035 wall									
5021	1/4"	1 Plum	160	.050	L.F.	4.88	3.73		8.61	10.90
5022	3/8"		160	.050		6.15	3.73		9.88	12.30
5023	1/2"		160	.050		7.90	3.73		11.63	14.25
5024	5/8"		160	.050		9.70	3.73		13.43	16.20
5025	3/4"		133	.060		11.70	4.49		16.19	19.55
5026	7/8"		133	.060		12.35	4.49		16.84	20.50
5027	1"		114	.070		13.55	5.25		18.80	23
5040	.049 wall									
5041	1/4"	1 Plum	160	.050	L.F.	5.70	3.73		9.43	11.85
5042	3/8"		160	.050		7.90	3.73		11.63	14.25

22 11 Facility Water Distribution

22 11 13 – Facility Water Distribution Piping

22 11 13.60 Tubing, Stainless Steel

		Crew	Daily Output	Labor-Hours	Unit	Material	2024 Bare Costs Labor	Equipment	Total	Total Incl O&P
5043	1/2"	1 Plum	160	.050	L.F.	8.75	3.73		12.48	15.20
5044	5/8"		160	.050		11.85	3.73		15.58	18.60
5045	3/4"		133	.060		12.65	4.49		17.14	20.50
5046	7/8"		133	.060		13.15	4.49		17.64	21
5047	1"		114	.070		14	5.25		19.25	23
5060	.065 wall									
5061	1/4"	1 Plum	160	.050	L.F.	6.40	3.73		10.13	12.60
5062	3/8"		160	.050		8.85	3.73		12.58	15.30
5063	1/2"		160	.050		10.70	3.73		14.43	17.30
5064	5/8"		160	.050		13	3.73		16.73	19.85
5065	3/4"		133	.060		13.80	4.49		18.29	22
5066	7/8"		133	.060		15.85	4.49		20.34	24
5067	1"		114	.070		15.50	5.25		20.75	25
5210	Type 316									
5220	.035 wall									
5221	1/4"	1 Plum	160	.050	L.F.	7.05	3.73		10.78	13.30
5222	3/8"		160	.050		10.05	3.73		13.78	16.60
5223	1/2"		160	.050		15.25	3.73		18.98	22.50
5224	5/8"		160	.050		13.85	3.73		17.58	21
5225	3/4"		133	.060		29	4.49		33.49	38.50
5226	7/8"		133	.060		23.50	4.49		27.99	32
5227	1"		114	.070		18.55	5.25		23.80	28.50
5240	.049 wall									
5241	1/4"	1 Plum	160	.050	L.F.	8.60	3.73		12.33	15
5242	3/8"		160	.050		8.60	3.73		12.33	15
5243	1/2"		160	.050		14.40	3.73		18.13	21.50
5244	5/8"		160	.050		17.75	3.73		21.48	25
5245	3/4"		133	.060		26	4.49		30.49	35
5246	7/8"		133	.060		21	4.49		25.49	29.50
5247	1"		114	.070		19.10	5.25		24.35	29
5260	.065 wall									
5261	1/4"	1 Plum	160	.050	L.F.	8.90	3.73		12.63	15.35
5262	3/8"		160	.050		15.15	3.73		18.88	22.50
5263	1/2"		160	.050		13.80	3.73		17.53	21
5264	5/8"		160	.050		14.30	3.73		18.03	21.50
5265	3/4"		133	.060		15	4.49		19.49	23
5266	7/8"		133	.060		24.50	4.49		28.99	33.50
5267	1"		114	.070		23.50	5.25		28.75	34

22 11 13.61 Tubing Fittings, Stainless Steel

		Crew	Daily Output	Labor-Hours	Unit	Material	2024 Bare Costs Labor	Equipment	Total	Total Incl O&P
0010	**TUBING FITTINGS, STAINLESS STEEL**									
8200	Tube fittings, compression type									
8202	Type 316									
8204	90° elbow									
8206	1/4"	1 Plum	24	.333	Ea.	32	25		57	72.50
8207	3/8"		22	.364		39.50	27		66.50	84
8208	1/2"		22	.364		65	27		92	112
8209	5/8"		21	.381		73	28.50		101.50	123
8210	3/4"		21	.381		115	28.50		143.50	169
8211	7/8"		20	.400		177	30		207	239
8212	1"		20	.400		220	30		250	287
8220	Union tee									
8222	1/4"	1 Plum	15	.533	Ea.	45.50	40		85.50	109

22 11 Facility Water Distribution

22 11 13 – Facility Water Distribution Piping

22 11 13.61 Tubing Fittings, Stainless Steel

		Crew	Daily Output	Labor-Hours	Unit	Material	2024 Bare Costs Labor	2024 Bare Costs Equipment	Total	Total Incl O&P
8224	3/8"	1 Plum	15	.533	Ea.	58.50	40		98.50	124
8225	1/2"		15	.533		90	40		130	158
8226	5/8"		14	.571		102	42.50		144.50	176
8227	3/4"		14	.571		135	42.50		177.50	213
8228	7/8"		13	.615		265	46		311	360
8229	1"		13	.615		290	46		336	390
8234	Union									
8236	1/4"	1 Plum	24	.333	Ea.	22.50	25		47.50	61.50
8237	3/8"		22	.364		31.50	27		58.50	75.50
8238	1/2"		22	.364		47	27		74	92.50
8239	5/8"		21	.381		61.50	28.50		90	111
8240	3/4"		21	.381		76.50	28.50		105	127
8241	7/8"		20	.400		126	30		156	183
8242	1"		20	.400		133	30		163	191
8250	Male connector									
8252	1/4" x 1/4"	1 Plum	24	.333	Ea.	14.30	25		39.30	52.50
8253	3/8" x 3/8"		22	.364		22.50	27		49.50	65
8254	1/2" x 1/2"		22	.364		33	27		60	76.50
8256	3/4" x 3/4"		21	.381		50.50	28.50		79	98
8258	1" x 1"		20	.400		88	30		118	142

22 11 13.64 Pipe, Stainless Steel

		Crew	Daily Output	Labor-Hours	Unit	Material	2024 Bare Costs Labor	2024 Bare Costs Equipment	Total	Total Incl O&P
0010	**PIPE, STAINLESS STEEL** R221113-70									
0020	Welded, with clevis type hanger assemblies, 10' OC									
0500	Schedule 5, type 304									
0540	1/2" diameter	Q-15	128	.125	L.F.	9.45	8.40	.56	18.41	23.50
0550	3/4" diameter		116	.138		11.15	9.25	.62	21.02	26.50
0560	1" diameter		103	.155		14.30	10.45	.70	25.45	32
0570	1-1/4" diameter		93	.172		16.55	11.55	.77	28.87	36.50
0580	1-1/2" diameter		85	.188		18.95	12.65	.85	32.45	40.50
0590	2" diameter		69	.232		26.50	15.60	1.04	43.14	53
0600	2-1/2" diameter		53	.302		32	20.50	1.36	53.86	67
0610	3" diameter		48	.333		26.50	22.50	1.50	50.50	64
0620	4" diameter		44	.364		31.50	24.50	1.63	57.63	73.50
0630	5" diameter		36	.444		74.50	30	2	106.50	129
0640	6" diameter	Q-16	42	.571		200	40	1.71	241.71	281
0650	8" diameter		34	.706		259	49	2.11	310.11	360
0660	10" diameter		26	.923		90	64.50	2.76	157.26	198
0670	12" diameter		21	1.143		575	79.50	3.42	657.92	750
0700	To delete hangers, subtract									
0710	1/2" diam. to 1-1/2" diam.					8%	19%			
0720	2" diam. to 5" diam.					4%	9%			
0730	6" diam. to 12" diam.					3%	4%			
0750	For small quantities, add				L.F.	10%				
1250	Schedule 5, type 316									
1290	1/2" diameter	Q-15	128	.125	L.F.	12.30	8.40	.56	21.26	26.50
1300	3/4" diameter		116	.138		13.85	9.25	.62	23.72	29.50
1310	1" diameter		103	.155		22.50	10.45	.70	33.65	41
1320	1-1/4" diameter		93	.172		30.50	11.55	.77	42.82	51.50
1330	1-1/2" diameter		85	.188		41.50	12.65	.85	55	65.50
1340	2" diameter		69	.232		65	15.60	1.04	81.64	95
1350	2-1/2" diameter		53	.302		126	20.50	1.36	147.86	169
1360	3" diameter		48	.333		160	22.50	1.50	184	211

22 11 Facility Water Distribution

22 11 13 – Facility Water Distribution Piping

22 11 13.64 Pipe, Stainless Steel

		Crew	Daily Output	Labor-Hours	Unit	Material	2024 Bare Costs Labor	Equipment	Total	Total Incl O&P
1370	4" diameter	Q-15	44	.364	L.F.	199	24.50	1.63	225.13	257
1380	5" diameter	↓	36	.444		228	30	2	260	298
1390	6" diameter	Q-16	42	.571		271	40	1.71	312.71	360
1400	8" diameter		34	.706		410	49	2.11	461.11	525
1410	10" diameter		26	.923		480	64.50	2.76	547.26	625
1420	12" diameter	↓	21	1.143	↓	162	79.50	3.42	244.92	300
1490	For small quantities, add					10%				
1940	To delete hanger, subtract									
1950	1/2" diam. to 1-1/2" diam.					5%	19%			
1960	2" diam. to 5" diam.					3%	9%			
1970	6" diam. to 12" diam.					2%	4%			
2000	Schedule 10, type 304									
2040	1/4" diameter	Q-15	131	.122	L.F.	12.85	8.20	.55	21.60	27
2050	3/8" diameter		128	.125		10.40	8.40	.56	19.36	24.50
2060	1/2" diameter		125	.128		9.25	8.60	.57	18.42	23.50
2070	3/4" diameter		113	.142		10.85	9.50	.64	20.99	27
2080	1" diameter		100	.160		16.15	10.75	.72	27.62	34.50
2090	1-1/4" diameter		91	.176		18.50	11.80	.79	31.09	39
2100	1-1/2" diameter		83	.193		18.80	12.95	.87	32.62	40.50
2110	2" diameter		67	.239		25.50	16.05	1.07	42.62	53
2120	2-1/2" diameter		51	.314		32.50	21	1.41	54.91	69
2130	3" diameter		46	.348		39.50	23.50	1.56	64.56	80
2140	4" diameter		42	.381		51	25.50	1.71	78.21	96
2150	5" diameter	↓	35	.457		130	30.50	2.05	162.55	191
2160	6" diameter	Q-16	40	.600		82	42	1.79	125.79	154
2170	8" diameter		33	.727		87	50.50	2.17	139.67	174
2180	10" diameter		25	.960		84.50	67	2.87	154.37	196
2190	12" diameter	↓	21	1.143	↓	118	79.50	3.42	200.92	252
2250	For small quantities, add					10%				
2650	To delete hanger, subtract									
2660	1/4" diam. to 3/4" diam.					9%	22%			
2670	1" diam. to 2" diam.					4%	15%			
2680	2-1/2" diam. to 5" diam.					3%	8%			
2690	6" diam. to 12" diam.					3%	4%			
2750	Schedule 10, type 316									
2790	1/4" diameter	Q-15	131	.122	L.F.	9	8.20	.55	17.75	22.50
2800	3/8" diameter		128	.125		11.15	8.40	.56	20.11	25.50
2810	1/2" diameter		125	.128		8.90	8.60	.57	18.07	23
2820	3/4" diameter		113	.142		10.45	9.50	.64	20.59	26.50
2830	1" diameter		100	.160		15.50	10.75	.72	26.97	34
2840	1-1/4" diameter		91	.176		18.70	11.80	.79	31.29	39
2850	1-1/2" diameter		83	.193		23.50	12.95	.87	37.32	45.50
2860	2" diameter		67	.239		26.50	16.05	1.07	43.62	54
2870	2-1/2" diameter		51	.314		39.50	21	1.41	61.91	76
2880	3" diameter		46	.348		45	23.50	1.56	70.06	86
2890	4" diameter		42	.381		61	25.50	1.71	88.21	107
2900	5" diameter	↓	35	.457		81.50	30.50	2.05	114.05	137
2910	6" diameter	Q-16	40	.600		93	42	1.79	136.79	166
2920	8" diameter		33	.727		88	50.50	2.17	140.67	174
2930	10" diameter		25	.960		102	67	2.87	171.87	216
2940	12" diameter	↓	21	1.143	↓	143	79.50	3.42	225.92	279
2990	For small quantities, add					10%				
3430	To delete hanger, subtract									

22 11 Facility Water Distribution

22 11 13 – Facility Water Distribution Piping

22 11 13.64 Pipe, Stainless Steel

		Crew	Daily Output	Labor-Hours	Unit	Material	2024 Bare Costs Labor	Equipment	Total	Total Incl O&P
3440	1/4" diam. to 3/4" diam.					6%	22%			
3450	1" diam. to 2" diam.					3%	15%			
3460	2-1/2" diam. to 5" diam.					2%	8%			
3470	6" diam. to 12" diam.					2%	4%			
3500	Threaded, couplings and clevis hanger assemblies, 10' OC									
3520	Schedule 40, type 304									
3540	1/4" diameter	1 Plum	54	.148	L.F.	6.60	11.05		17.65	23.50
3550	3/8" diameter		53	.151		7.45	11.25		18.70	25
3560	1/2" diameter		52	.154		7.90	11.50		19.40	26
3570	3/4" diameter		51	.157		10.85	11.70		22.55	29.50
3580	1" diameter	↓	45	.178		15.20	13.25		28.45	36.50
3590	1-1/4" diameter	Q-1	76	.211		20.50	14.15		34.65	43.50
3600	1-1/2" diameter		69	.232		26.50	15.60		42.10	52
3610	2" diameter		57	.281		35.50	18.85		54.35	67
3620	2-1/2" diameter		44	.364		47	24.50		71.50	88
3630	3" diameter	↓	38	.421		56	28.50		84.50	104
3640	4" diameter	Q-2	51	.471		88	33		121	146
3740	For small quantities, add					10%				
4200	To delete couplings & hangers, subtract				↓					
4210	1/4" diam. to 3/4" diam.					15%	56%			
4220	1" diam. to 2" diam.					18%	49%			
4230	2-1/2" diam. to 4" diam.					34%	40%			
4250	Schedule 40, type 316									
4290	1/4" diameter	1 Plum	54	.148	L.F.	13.55	11.05		24.60	31.50
4300	3/8" diameter		53	.151		13.85	11.25		25.10	32
4310	1/2" diameter		52	.154		14	11.50		25.50	32.50
4320	3/4" diameter		51	.157		17.40	11.70		29.10	36.50
4330	1" diameter	↓	45	.178		24	13.25		37.25	46.50
4340	1-1/4" diameter	Q-1	76	.211		33.50	14.15		47.65	58
4350	1-1/2" diameter		69	.232		37.50	15.60		53.10	64.50
4360	2" diameter		57	.281		48.50	18.85		67.35	81.50
4370	2-1/2" diameter		44	.364		78	24.50		102.50	123
4380	3" diameter	↓	38	.421		75	28.50		103.50	125
4390	4" diameter	Q-2	51	.471		135	33		168	197
4490	For small quantities, add					10%				
4900	To delete couplings & hangers, subtract				↓					
4910	1/4" diam. to 3/4" diam.					12%	56%			
4920	1" diam. to 2" diam.					14%	49%			
4930	2-1/2" diam. to 4" diam.					27%	40%			
5000	Schedule 80, type 304									
5040	1/4" diameter	1 Plum	53	.151	L.F.	20.50	11.25		31.75	39.50
5050	3/8" diameter		52	.154		25.50	11.50		37	45.50
5060	1/2" diameter		51	.157		27	11.70		38.70	47.50
5070	3/4" diameter		48	.167		31	12.45		43.45	52.50
5080	1" diameter	↓	43	.186		40	13.90		53.90	64.50
5090	1-1/4" diameter	Q-1	73	.219		39	14.70		53.70	65
5100	1-1/2" diameter		67	.239		64	16.05		80.05	94.50
5110	2" diameter		54	.296		75	19.90		94.90	112
5190	For small quantities, add				↓	10%				
5700	To delete couplings & hangers, subtract									
5710	1/4" diam. to 3/4" diam.					10%	53%			
5720	1" diam. to 2" diam.					14%	47%			
5750	Schedule 80, type 316									

22 11 Facility Water Distribution

22 11 13 – Facility Water Distribution Piping

22 11 13.64 Pipe, Stainless Steel

		Crew	Daily Output	Labor-Hours	Unit	Material	2024 Bare Costs Labor	Equipment	Total	Total Incl O&P
5790	1/4" diameter	1 Plum	53	.151	L.F.	20.50	11.25		31.75	39.50
5800	3/8" diameter		52	.154		27.50	11.50		39	47.50
5810	1/2" diameter		51	.157		33.50	11.70		45.20	54
5820	3/4" diameter		48	.167		36	12.45		48.45	58.50
5830	1" diameter	▼	43	.186		47	13.90		60.90	72
5840	1-1/4" diameter	Q-1	73	.219		43.50	14.70		58.20	70
5850	1-1/2" diameter		67	.239		72.50	16.05		88.55	104
5860	2" diameter	▼	54	.296		91	19.90		110.90	130
5950	For small quantities, add					10%				
7000	To delete couplings & hangers, subtract									
7010	1/4" diam. to 3/4" diam.					9%	53%			
7020	1" diam. to 2" diam.					14%	47%			
8000	Weld joints with clevis type hanger assemblies, 10' OC									
8010	Schedule 40, type 304									
8050	1/8" pipe size	Q-15	126	.127	L.F.	6.20	8.55	.57	15.32	20
8060	1/4" pipe size		125	.128		6.15	8.60	.57	15.32	20
8070	3/8" pipe size		122	.131		7	8.80	.59	16.39	21.50
8080	1/2" pipe size		118	.136		7.20	9.10	.61	16.91	22
8090	3/4" pipe size		109	.147		9.90	9.85	.66	20.41	26.50
8100	1" pipe size		95	.168		13.80	11.30	.76	25.86	33
8110	1-1/4" pipe size		86	.186		18.25	12.50	.84	31.59	39.50
8120	1-1/2" pipe size		78	.205		24	13.80	.92	38.72	48
8130	2" pipe size		62	.258		32	17.35	1.16	50.51	63
8140	2-1/2" pipe size		49	.327		39	22	1.47	62.47	77
8150	3" pipe size		44	.364		45.50	24.50	1.63	71.63	88.50
8160	3-1/2" pipe size		44	.364		107	24.50	1.63	133.13	155
8170	4" pipe size		39	.410		71.50	27.50	1.84	100.84	122
8180	5" pipe size	▼	32	.500		116	33.50	2.25	151.75	180
8190	6" pipe size	Q-16	37	.649		122	45	1.94	168.94	204
8191	6" pipe size		37	.649		120	45	1.94	166.94	201
8200	8" pipe size		29	.828		198	57.50	2.47	257.97	305
8210	10" pipe size		24	1		535	69.50	2.99	607.49	695
8220	12" pipe size	▼	20	1.200	▼	650	83.50	3.59	737.09	845
8300	Schedule 40, type 316									
8310	1/8" pipe size	Q-15	126	.127	L.F.	17.80	8.55	.57	26.92	33
8320	1/4" pipe size		125	.128		13.05	8.60	.57	22.22	28
8330	3/8" pipe size		122	.131		13.25	8.80	.59	22.64	28.50
8340	1/2" pipe size		118	.136		13.20	9.10	.61	22.91	28.50
8350	3/4" pipe size		109	.147		16.25	9.85	.66	26.76	33
8360	1" pipe size		95	.168		22.50	11.30	.76	34.56	42.50
8370	1-1/4" pipe size		86	.186		31	12.50	.84	44.34	53.50
8380	1-1/2" pipe size		78	.205		34.50	13.80	.92	49.22	59.50
8390	2" pipe size		62	.258		44.50	17.35	1.16	63.01	76.50
8400	2-1/2" pipe size		49	.327		69	22	1.47	92.47	110
8410	3" pipe size		44	.364		62.50	24.50	1.63	88.63	107
8420	3-1/2" pipe size		44	.364		99.50	24.50	1.63	125.63	147
8430	4" pipe size		39	.410		115	27.50	1.84	144.34	170
8440	5" pipe size	▼	32	.500		161	33.50	2.25	196.75	230
8450	6" pipe size	Q-16	37	.649		178	45	1.94	224.94	264
8460	8" pipe size		29	.828		365	57.50	2.47	424.97	490
8470	10" pipe size		24	1		435	69.50	2.99	507.49	585
8480	12" pipe size	▼	20	1.200	▼	520	83.50	3.59	607.09	700
8500	Schedule 80, type 304									

22 11 Facility Water Distribution

22 11 13 – Facility Water Distribution Piping

22 11 13.64 Pipe, Stainless Steel

		Crew	Daily Output	Labor-Hours	Unit	Material	2024 Bare Costs Labor	2024 Bare Costs Equipment	Total	Total Incl O&P
8510	1/4" pipe size	Q-15	110	.145	L.F.	16.45	9.75	.65	26.85	33.50
8520	3/8" pipe size		109	.147		21.50	9.85	.66	32.01	39
8530	1/2" pipe size		106	.151		23	10.15	.68	33.83	41.50
8540	3/4" pipe size		96	.167		25	11.20	.75	36.95	45
8550	1" pipe size		87	.184		32	12.35	.83	45.18	54.50
8560	1-1/4" pipe size		81	.198		23.50	13.25	.89	37.64	46.50
8570	1-1/2" pipe size		74	.216		47.50	14.55	.97	63.02	75
8580	2" pipe size		58	.276		51.50	18.55	1.24	71.29	85.50
8590	2-1/2" pipe size		46	.348		62.50	23.50	1.56	87.56	106
8600	3" pipe size		41	.390		108	26	1.75	135.75	160
8610	4" pipe size		33	.485		139	32.50	2.18	173.68	204
8630	6" pipe size	Q-16	30	.800		258	55.50	2.39	315.89	370
8640	Schedule 80, type 316									
8650	1/4" pipe size	Q-15	110	.145	L.F.	19.25	9.75	.65	29.65	36.50
8660	3/8" pipe size		109	.147		26	9.85	.66	36.51	44.50
8670	1/2" pipe size		106	.151		31	10.15	.68	41.83	50
8680	3/4" pipe size		96	.167		33	11.20	.75	44.95	54
8690	1" pipe size		87	.184		42	12.35	.83	55.18	65.50
8700	1-1/4" pipe size		81	.198		33	13.25	.89	47.14	57
8710	1-1/2" pipe size		74	.216		59.50	14.55	.97	75.02	87.50
8720	2" pipe size		58	.276		75	18.55	1.24	94.79	111
8730	2-1/2" pipe size		46	.348		95.50	23.50	1.56	120.56	142
8740	3" pipe size		41	.390		127	26	1.75	154.75	181
8760	4" pipe size		33	.485		171	32.50	2.18	205.68	239
8770	6" pipe size	Q-16	30	.800		335	55.50	2.39	392.89	455
9100	Threading pipe labor, sst, one end, schedules 40 & 80									
9110	1/4" through 3/4" pipe size	1 Plum	61.50	.130	Ea.		9.70		9.70	14.45
9120	1" through 2" pipe size		55.90	.143			10.70		10.70	15.90
9130	2-1/2" pipe size		41.50	.193			14.40		14.40	21.50
9140	3" pipe size		38.50	.208			15.50		15.50	23
9150	3-1/2" pipe size	Q-1	68.40	.234			15.70		15.70	23.50
9160	4" pipe size		73	.219			14.70		14.70	22
9170	5" pipe size		40.70	.393			26.50		26.50	39.50
9180	6" pipe size		35.40	.452			30.50		30.50	45
9190	8" pipe size		22.30	.717			48		48	71.50
9200	10" pipe size		16.10	.994			67		67	99.50
9210	12" pipe size		12.30	1.301			87.50		87.50	130
9250	Welding labor per joint for stainless steel									
9260	Schedule 5 and 10									
9270	1/4" pipe size	Q-15	36	.444	Ea.		30	2	32	46.50
9280	3/8" pipe size		35	.457			30.50	2.05	32.55	48
9290	1/2" pipe size		35	.457			30.50	2.05	32.55	48
9300	3/4" pipe size		28	.571			38.50	2.57	41.07	60
9310	1" pipe size		25	.640			43	2.87	45.87	67
9320	1-1/4" pipe size		22	.727			49	3.27	52.27	76
9330	1-1/2" pipe size		21	.762			51	3.42	54.42	80
9340	2" pipe size		18	.889			59.50	3.99	63.49	93.50
9350	2-1/2" pipe size		12	1.333			89.50	6	95.50	140
9360	3" pipe size		9.73	1.644			110	7.40	117.40	172
9370	4" pipe size		7.37	2.171			146	9.75	155.75	228
9380	5" pipe size		6.15	2.602			175	11.70	186.70	273
9390	6" pipe size		5.71	2.802			188	12.60	200.60	294
9400	8" pipe size		3.69	4.336			291	19.45	310.45	455

For customer support on your Plumbing Costs with RSMeans Data call 800.448.8182.

22 11 Facility Water Distribution
22 11 13 – Facility Water Distribution Piping

22 11 13.64 Pipe, Stainless Steel		Crew	Daily Output	Labor-Hours	Unit	Material	2024 Bare Costs Labor	Equipment	Total	Total Incl O&P
9410	10" pipe size	Q-15	2.91	5.498	Ea.		370	24.50	394.50	575
9420	12" pipe size	↓	2.31	6.926	↓		465	31	496	725
9500	Schedule 40									
9510	1/4" pipe size	Q-15	28	.571	Ea.		38.50	2.57	41.07	60
9520	3/8" pipe size		27	.593			40	2.66	42.66	62
9530	1/2" pipe size		25.40	.630			42.50	2.83	45.33	66
9540	3/4" pipe size		22.22	.720			48.50	3.23	51.73	75.50
9550	1" pipe size		20.25	.790			53	3.55	56.55	83
9560	1-1/4" pipe size		18.82	.850			57	3.82	60.82	89
9570	1-1/2" pipe size		17.78	.900			60.50	4.04	64.54	94.50
9580	2" pipe size		15.09	1.060			71	4.76	75.76	111
9590	2-1/2" pipe size		7.96	2.010			135	9.05	144.05	211
9600	3" pipe size		6.43	2.488			167	11.15	178.15	261
9610	4" pipe size		4.88	3.279			220	14.70	234.70	345
9620	5" pipe size		4.26	3.756			252	16.85	268.85	395
9630	6" pipe size		3.77	4.244			285	19.05	304.05	445
9640	8" pipe size		2.44	6.557			440	29.50	469.50	690
9650	10" pipe size		1.92	8.333			560	37.50	597.50	875
9660	12" pipe size	↓	1.52	10.526	↓		705	47.50	752.50	1,100
9750	Schedule 80									
9760	1/4" pipe size	Q-15	21.55	.742	Ea.		50	3.33	53.33	77.50
9770	3/8" pipe size		20.75	.771			52	3.46	55.46	81
9780	1/2" pipe size		19.54	.819			55	3.68	58.68	86
9790	3/4" pipe size		17.09	.936			63	4.20	67.20	98
9800	1" pipe size		15.58	1.027			69	4.61	73.61	108
9810	1-1/4" pipe size		14.48	1.105			74	4.96	78.96	115
9820	1-1/2" pipe size		13.68	1.170			78.50	5.25	83.75	123
9830	2" pipe size		11.61	1.378			92.50	6.20	98.70	145
9840	2-1/2" pipe size		6.12	2.614			176	11.75	187.75	274
9850	3" pipe size		4.94	3.239			218	14.55	232.55	340
9860	4" pipe size		3.75	4.267			287	19.15	306.15	445
9870	5" pipe size		3.27	4.893			330	22	352	515
9880	6" pipe size		2.90	5.517			370	25	395	575
9890	8" pipe size		1.87	8.556			575	38.50	613.50	895
9900	10" pipe size		1.48	10.811			725	48.50	773.50	1,125
9910	12" pipe size		1.17	13.675			920	61.50	981.50	1,450
9920	Schedule 160, 1/2" pipe size		17	.941			63	4.23	67.23	98.50
9930	3/4" pipe size		14.81	1.080			72.50	4.85	77.35	113
9940	1" pipe size		13.50	1.185			79.50	5.30	84.80	124
9950	1-1/4" pipe size		12.55	1.275			85.50	5.70	91.20	133
9960	1-1/2" pipe size		11.85	1.350			90.50	6.05	96.55	142
9970	2" pipe size		10	1.600			107	7.20	114.20	168
9980	3" pipe size		4.28	3.738			251	16.80	267.80	395
9990	4" pipe size	↓	3.25	4.923	↓		330	22	352	515

22 11 13.66 Pipe Fittings, Stainless Steel

		Crew	Daily Output	Labor-Hours	Unit	Material	2024 Bare Costs Labor	Equipment	Total	Total Incl O&P
0010	**PIPE FITTINGS, STAINLESS STEEL**									
0100	Butt weld joint, schedule 5, type 304									
0120	90° elbow, long									
0140	1/2"	Q-15	17.50	.914	Ea.	32.50	61.50	4.11	98.11	132
0150	3/4"		14	1.143		32.50	77	5.15	114.65	155
0160	1"		12.50	1.280		34.50	86	5.75	126.25	172
0170	1-1/4"		11	1.455		47	97.50	6.55	151.05	204

22 11 Facility Water Distribution

22 11 13 – Facility Water Distribution Piping

22 11 13.66 Pipe Fittings, Stainless Steel

		Crew	Daily Output	Labor-Hours	Unit	Material	2024 Bare Costs Labor	Equipment	Total	Total Incl O&P
0180	1-1/2"	Q-15	10.50	1.524	Ea.	39.50	102	6.85	148.35	203
0190	2"		9	1.778		47	119	8	174	238
0200	2-1/2"		6	2.667		108	179	11.95	298.95	400
0210	3"		4.86	3.292		101	221	14.80	336.80	455
0220	3-1/2"		4.27	3.747		298	252	16.80	566.80	720
0230	4"		3.69	4.336		169	291	19.45	479.45	645
0240	5"		3.08	5.195		630	350	23.50	1,003.50	1,250
0250	6"	Q-16	4.29	5.594		485	390	16.75	891.75	1,125
0260	8"		2.76	8.696		1,025	605	26	1,656	2,050
0270	10"		2.18	11.009		1,575	765	33	2,373	2,925
0280	12"		1.73	13.873		2,250	965	41.50	3,256.50	3,975
0320	For schedule 5, type 316, add					30%				
0600	45° elbow, long									
0620	1/2"	Q-15	17.50	.914	Ea.	32.50	61.50	4.11	98.11	132
0630	3/4"		14	1.143		32.50	77	5.15	114.65	155
0640	1"		12.50	1.280		34.50	86	5.75	126.25	172
0650	1-1/4"		11	1.455		47	97.50	6.55	151.05	204
0660	1-1/2"		10.50	1.524		39.50	102	6.85	148.35	203
0670	2"		9	1.778		47	119	8	174	238
0680	2-1/2"		6	2.667		108	179	11.95	298.95	400
0690	3"		4.86	3.292		81	221	14.80	316.80	435
0700	3-1/2"		4.27	3.747		298	252	16.80	566.80	720
0710	4"		3.69	4.336		137	291	19.45	447.45	610
0720	5"		3.08	5.195		505	350	23.50	878.50	1,100
0730	6"	Q-16	4.29	5.594		345	390	16.75	751.75	975
0740	8"		2.76	8.696		720	605	26	1,351	1,725
0750	10"		2.18	11.009		1,250	765	33	2,048	2,575
0760	12"		1.73	13.873		1,575	965	41.50	2,581.50	3,225
0800	For schedule 5, type 316, add					25%				
1100	Tee, straight									
1130	1/2"	Q-15	11.66	1.372	Ea.	97.50	92	6.15	195.65	251
1140	3/4"		9.33	1.715		97.50	115	7.70	220.20	286
1150	1"		8.33	1.921		103	129	8.60	240.60	315
1160	1-1/4"		7.33	2.183		83	147	9.80	239.80	320
1170	1-1/2"		7	2.286		81	154	10.25	245.25	330
1180	2"		6	2.667		85	179	11.95	275.95	370
1190	2-1/2"		4	4		204	269	17.95	490.95	645
1200	3"		3.24	4.938		149	330	22	501	685
1210	3-1/2"		2.85	5.614		425	375	25	825	1,050
1220	4"		2.46	6.504		231	435	29	695	935
1230	5"		2	8		730	535	36	1,301	1,650
1240	6"	Q-16	2.85	8.421		575	585	25	1,185	1,550
1250	8"		1.84	13.043		1,225	910	39	2,174	2,750
1260	10"		1.45	16.552		1,975	1,150	49.50	3,174.50	3,950
1270	12"		1.15	20.870		2,750	1,450	62.50	4,262.50	5,275
1320	For schedule 5, type 316, add					25%				
2000	Butt weld joint, schedule 10, type 304									
2020	90° elbow, long									
2040	1/2"	Q-15	17	.941	Ea.	9.90	63	4.23	77.13	110
2050	3/4"		14	1.143		10.10	77	5.15	92.25	131
2060	1"		12.50	1.280		11.30	86	5.75	103.05	147
2070	1-1/4"		11	1.455		17.35	97.50	6.55	121.40	171
2080	1-1/2"		10.50	1.524		14.15	102	6.85	123	175

For customer support on your Plumbing Costs with RSMeans Data call 800.448.8182.

22 11 Facility Water Distribution

22 11 13 – Facility Water Distribution Piping

22 11 13.66 Pipe Fittings, Stainless Steel

		Crew	Daily Output	Labor-Hours	Unit	Material	2024 Bare Costs Labor	Equipment	Total	Total Incl O&P
2090	2"	Q-15	9	1.778	Ea.	17	119	8	144	205
2100	2-1/2"		6	2.667		30.50	179	11.95	221.45	315
2110	3"		4.86	3.292		36.50	221	14.80	272.30	385
2120	3-1/2"		4.27	3.747		295	252	16.80	563.80	720
2130	4"		3.69	4.336		60.50	291	19.45	370.95	525
2140	5"		3.08	5.195		161	350	23.50	534.50	725
2150	6"	Q-16	4.29	5.594		162	390	16.75	568.75	775
2160	8"		2.76	8.696		268	605	26	899	1,225
2170	10"		2.18	11.009		665	765	33	1,463	1,925
2180	12"		1.73	13.873		1,025	965	41.50	2,031.50	2,625
2500	45° elbow, long									
2520	1/2"	Q-15	17.50	.914	Ea.	12.65	61.50	4.11	78.26	110
2530	3/4"		14	1.143		12.90	77	5.15	95.05	134
2540	1"		12.50	1.280		14.25	86	5.75	106	150
2550	1-1/4"		11	1.455		24	97.50	6.55	128.05	179
2560	1-1/2"		10.50	1.524		14.55	102	6.85	123.40	176
2570	2"		9	1.778		17.35	119	8	144.35	206
2580	2-1/2"		6	2.667		27.50	179	11.95	218.45	310
2590	3"		4.86	3.292		31.50	221	14.80	267.30	380
2600	3-1/2"		4.27	3.747		295	252	16.80	563.80	720
2610	4"		3.69	4.336		50.50	291	19.45	360.95	510
2620	5"		3.08	5.195		248	350	23.50	621.50	820
2630	6"	Q-16	4.29	5.594		109	390	16.75	515.75	720
2640	8"		2.76	8.696		194	605	26	825	1,150
2650	10"		2.18	11.009		480	765	33	1,278	1,725
2660	12"		1.73	13.873		730	965	41.50	1,736.50	2,300
2670	Reducer, concentric									
2674	1" x 3/4"	Q-15	13.25	1.208	Ea.	26.50	81	5.40	112.90	156
2676	2" x 1-1/2"	"	9.75	1.641		19.40	110	7.35	136.75	194
2678	6" x 4"	Q-16	4.91	4.888		48.50	340	14.60	403.10	575
2680	Caps									
2682	1"	Q-15	25	.640	Ea.	30	43	2.87	75.87	100
2684	1-1/2"		21	.762		32.50	51	3.42	86.92	115
2685	2"		18	.889		28.50	59.50	3.99	91.99	124
2686	4"		7.38	2.168		44.50	146	9.75	200.25	277
2687	6"	Q-16	8.58	2.797		73	195	8.35	276.35	380
3000	Tee, straight									
3030	1/2"	Q-15	11.66	1.372	Ea.	35	92	6.15	133.15	182
3040	3/4"		9.33	1.715		35.50	115	7.70	158.20	218
3050	1"		8.33	1.921		35.50	129	8.60	173.10	241
3060	1-1/4"		7.33	2.183		55	147	9.80	211.80	289
3070	1-1/2"		7	2.286		36	154	10.25	200.25	279
3080	2"		6	2.667		39	179	11.95	229.95	320
3090	2-1/2"		4	4		101	269	17.95	387.95	530
3100	3"		3.24	4.938		71	330	22	423	600
3110	3-1/2"		2.85	5.614		234	375	25	634	845
3120	4"		2.46	6.504		107	435	29	571	800
3130	5"		2	8		725	535	36	1,296	1,625
3140	6"	Q-16	2.85	8.421		244	585	25	854	1,175
3150	8"		1.84	13.043		500	910	39	1,449	1,950
3151	10"		1.45	16.552		625	1,150	49.50	1,824.50	2,475
3152	12"		1.15	20.870		1,425	1,450	62.50	2,937.50	3,825
3154	For schedule 10, type 316, add					25%				

22 11 Facility Water Distribution

22 11 13 – Facility Water Distribution Piping

22 11 13.66 Pipe Fittings, Stainless Steel

		Crew	Daily Output	Labor-Hours	Unit	Material	2024 Bare Costs Labor	2024 Bare Costs Equipment	Total	Total Incl O&P
3281	Butt weld joint, schedule 40, type 304									
3284	90° elbow, long, 1/2"	Q-15	12.70	1.260	Ea.	11.05	84.50	5.65	101.20	144
3288	3/4"		11.10	1.441		11.25	97	6.45	114.70	164
3289	1"		10.13	1.579		12.80	106	7.10	125.90	180
3290	1-1/4"		9.40	1.702		19.05	114	7.65	140.70	199
3300	1-1/2"		8.89	1.800		15.15	121	8.10	144.25	206
3310	2"		7.55	2.119		21	142	9.50	172.50	245
3320	2-1/2"		3.98	4.020		44.50	270	18.05	332.55	470
3330	3"		3.21	4.984		56.50	335	22.50	414	585
3340	3-1/2"		2.83	5.654		535	380	25.50	940.50	1,175
3350	4"		2.44	6.557		105	440	29.50	574.50	805
3360	5"		2.13	7.512		840	505	33.50	1,378.50	1,700
3370	6"	Q-16	2.83	8.481		287	590	25.50	902.50	1,225
3380	8"		1.83	13.115		520	915	39	1,474	1,975
3390	10"		1.44	16.667		1,225	1,150	50	2,425	3,125
3400	12"		1.14	21.053		3,200	1,475	63	4,738	5,775
3410	For schedule 40, type 316, add					25%				
3460	45° elbow, long, 1/2"	Q-15	12.70	1.260	Ea.	15.25	84.50	5.65	105.40	149
3470	3/4"		11.10	1.441		15.40	97	6.45	118.85	168
3480	1"		10.13	1.579		15.55	106	7.10	128.65	183
3490	1-1/4"		9.40	1.702		22.50	114	7.65	144.15	203
3500	1-1/2"		8.89	1.800		17.50	121	8.10	146.60	208
3510	2"		7.55	2.119		22	142	9.50	173.50	246
3520	2-1/2"		3.98	4.020		44.50	270	18.05	332.55	470
3530	3"		3.21	4.984		41	335	22.50	398.50	570
3540	3-1/2"		2.83	5.654		535	380	25.50	940.50	1,175
3550	4"		2.44	6.557		73.50	440	29.50	543	770
3560	5"		2.13	7.512		590	505	33.50	1,128.50	1,425
3570	6"	Q-16	2.83	8.481		184	590	25.50	799.50	1,100
3580	8"		1.83	13.115		360	915	39	1,314	1,800
3590	10"		1.44	16.667		1,750	1,150	50	2,950	3,700
3600	12"		1.14	21.053		995	1,475	63	2,533	3,350
3610	For schedule 40, type 316, add					25%				
3660	Tee, straight 1/2"	Q-15	8.46	1.891	Ea.	36.50	127	8.50	172	239
3670	3/4"		7.40	2.162		37	145	9.70	191.70	267
3680	1"		6.74	2.374		37.50	159	10.65	207.15	290
3690	1-1/4"		6.27	2.552		62.50	171	11.45	244.95	335
3700	1-1/2"		5.92	2.703		37.50	182	12.15	231.65	325
3710	2"		5.03	3.181		40.50	214	14.30	268.80	380
3720	2-1/2"		2.65	6.038		101	405	27	533	745
3730	3"		2.14	7.477		81.50	500	33.50	615	870
3740	3-1/2"		1.88	8.511		390	570	38	998	1,325
3750	4"		1.62	9.877		117	665	44.50	826.50	1,150
3760	5"		1.42	11.268		905	755	50.50	1,710.50	2,175
3770	6"	Q-16	1.88	12.766		263	890	38	1,191	1,650
3780	8"		1.22	19.672		770	1,375	59	2,204	2,950
3790	10"		.96	25		2,775	1,750	75	4,600	5,725
3800	12"		.76	31.579		1,200	2,200	94.50	3,494.50	4,675
3810	For schedule 40, type 316, add					25%				
3820	Tee, reducing on outlet, 3/4" x 1/2"	Q-15	7.73	2.070	Ea.	112	139	9.30	260.30	340
3822	1" x 1/2"		7.24	2.210		139	148	9.90	296.90	385
3824	1" x 3/4"		6.96	2.299		129	154	10.30	293.30	380
3826	1-1/4" x 1"		6.43	2.488		315	167	11.15	493.15	605

22 11 Facility Water Distribution

22 11 13 – Facility Water Distribution Piping

22 11 13.66 Pipe Fittings, Stainless Steel		Crew	Daily Output	Labor-Hours	Unit	Material	2024 Bare Costs Labor	Equipment	Total	Total Incl O&P
3828	1-1/2" x 1/2"	Q-15	6.58	2.432	Ea.	189	163	10.90	362.90	465
3830	1-1/2" x 3/4"		6.35	2.520		177	169	11.30	357.30	460
3832	1-1/2" x 1"		6.18	2.589		136	174	11.60	321.60	420
3834	2" x 1"		5.50	2.909		243	195	13.05	451.05	570
3836	2" x 1-1/2"		5.30	3.019		204	203	13.55	420.55	540
3838	2-1/2" x 2"		3.15	5.079		305	340	23	668	875
3840	3" x 1-1/2"		2.72	5.882		310	395	26.50	731.50	960
3842	3" x 2"		2.65	6.038		259	405	27	691	920
3844	4" x 2"		2.10	7.619		126	510	34	670	935
3846	4" x 3"		1.77	9.040		470	605	40.50	1,115.50	1,475
3848	5" x 4"		1.48	10.811		1,075	725	48.50	1,848.50	2,325
3850	6" x 3"	Q-16	2.19	10.959		1,200	765	33	1,998	2,475
3852	6" x 4"		2.04	11.765		1,025	820	35	1,880	2,425
3854	8" x 4"		1.46	16.438		2,425	1,150	49	3,624	4,400
3856	10" x 8"		.69	34.783		4,075	2,425	104	6,604	8,225
3858	12" x 10"		.55	43.636		5,450	3,050	130	8,630	10,600
3950	Reducer, concentric, 3/4" x 1/2"	Q-15	11.85	1.350		25	90.50	6.05	121.55	169
3952	1" x 3/4"		10.60	1.509		29	101	6.80	136.80	190
3954	1-1/4" x 3/4"		10.19	1.570		85.50	105	7.05	197.55	259
3956	1-1/4" x 1"		9.76	1.639		41	110	7.35	158.35	218
3958	1-1/2" x 3/4"		9.88	1.619		72.50	109	7.25	188.75	250
3960	1-1/2" x 1"		9.47	1.690		125	114	7.60	246.60	315
3962	2" x 1"		8.65	1.850		27	124	8.30	159.30	224
3964	2" x 1-1/2"		8.16	1.961		22	132	8.80	162.80	230
3966	2-1/2" x 1"		5.71	2.802		125	188	12.60	325.60	430
3968	2-1/2" x 2"		5.21	3.071		97.50	206	13.80	317.30	425
3970	3" x 1"		4.88	3.279		85.50	220	14.70	320.20	440
3972	3" x 1-1/2"		4.72	3.390		39	228	15.20	282.20	400
3974	3" x 2"		4.51	3.548		35	238	15.95	288.95	410
3976	4" x 2"		3.69	4.336		50.50	291	19.45	360.95	510
3978	4" x 3"		2.77	5.776		39	390	26	455	645
3980	5" x 3"		2.56	6.250		565	420	28	1,013	1,275
3982	5" x 4"		2.27	7.048		455	475	31.50	961.50	1,250
3984	6" x 3"	Q-16	3.57	6.723		135	470	20	625	865
3986	6" x 4"		3.19	7.524		101	525	22.50	648.50	915
3988	8" x 4"		2.44	9.836		330	685	29.50	1,044.50	1,425
3990	8" x 6"		2.22	10.811		229	755	32.50	1,016.50	1,425
3992	10" x 6"		1.91	12.565		850	875	37.50	1,762.50	2,275
3994	10" x 8"		1.61	14.907		705	1,050	44.50	1,799.50	2,375
3995	12" x 6"		1.63	14.724		1,600	1,025	44	2,669	3,350
3996	12" x 8"		1.41	17.021		1,200	1,175	51	2,426	3,150
3997	12" x 10"		1.27	18.898		845	1,325	56.50	2,226.50	2,950
4000	Socket weld joint, 3,000 lb., type 304									
4100	90° elbow									
4140	1/4"	Q-15	13.47	1.188	Ea.	12.35	80	5.35	97.70	138
4150	3/8"		12.97	1.234		16.05	83	5.55	104.60	147
4160	1/2"		12.21	1.310		17.60	88	5.90	111.50	157
4170	3/4"		10.68	1.498		22	101	6.75	129.75	182
4180	1"		9.74	1.643		33.50	110	7.40	150.90	209
4190	1-1/4"		9.05	1.768		44	119	7.95	170.95	234
4200	1-1/2"		8.55	1.871		75	126	8.40	209.40	279
4210	2"		7.26	2.204		107	148	9.90	264.90	350
4300	45° elbow									

22 11 Facility Water Distribution

22 11 13 – Facility Water Distribution Piping

	22 11 13.66 Pipe Fittings, Stainless Steel	Crew	Daily Output	Labor-Hours	Unit	Material	2024 Bare Costs Labor	Equipment	Total	Total Incl O&P
4340	1/4"	Q-15	13.47	1.188	Ea.	17.10	80	5.35	102.45	144
4350	3/8"		12.97	1.234		17.30	83	5.55	105.85	148
4360	1/2"		12.21	1.310		17.55	88	5.90	111.45	157
4370	3/4"		10.68	1.498		20.50	101	6.75	128.25	180
4380	1"		9.74	1.643		29.50	110	7.40	146.90	205
4390	1-1/4"		9.05	1.768		47.50	119	7.95	174.45	238
4400	1-1/2"		8.55	1.871		57.50	126	8.40	191.90	260
4410	2"		7.26	2.204		93	148	9.90	250.90	335
4500	Tee									
4540	1/4"	Q-15	8.97	1.784	Ea.	108	120	8	236	305
4550	3/8"		8.64	1.852		129	124	8.30	261.30	335
4560	1/2"		8.13	1.968		121	132	8.85	261.85	340
4570	3/4"		7.12	2.247		139	151	10.10	300.10	390
4580	1"		6.48	2.469		187	166	11.10	364.10	465
4590	1-1/4"		6.03	2.653		440	178	11.90	629.90	760
4600	1-1/2"		5.69	2.812		425	189	12.65	626.65	760
4610	2"		4.83	3.313		545	223	14.85	782.85	945
5000	Socket weld joint, 3,000 lb., type 316									
5100	90° elbow									
5140	1/4"	Q-15	13.47	1.188	Ea.	101	80	5.35	186.35	236
5150	3/8"		12.97	1.234		118	83	5.55	206.55	258
5160	1/2"		12.21	1.310		108	88	5.90	201.90	255
5170	3/4"		10.68	1.498		142	101	6.75	249.75	315
5180	1"		9.74	1.643		201	110	7.40	318.40	395
5190	1-1/4"		9.05	1.768		470	119	7.95	596.95	705
5200	1-1/2"		8.55	1.871		360	126	8.40	494.40	595
5210	2"		7.26	2.204		520	148	9.90	677.90	800
5300	45° elbow									
5340	1/4"	Q-15	13.47	1.188	Ea.	203	80	5.35	288.35	350
5350	3/8"		12.97	1.234		203	83	5.55	291.55	350
5360	1/2"		12.21	1.310		154	88	5.90	247.90	305
5370	3/4"		10.68	1.498		171	101	6.75	278.75	345
5380	1"		9.74	1.643		243	110	7.40	360.40	440
5390	1-1/4"		9.05	1.768		485	119	7.95	611.95	720
5400	1-1/2"		8.55	1.871		370	126	8.40	504.40	600
5410	2"		7.26	2.204		550	148	9.90	707.90	835
5500	Tee									
5540	1/4"	Q-15	8.97	1.784	Ea.	137	120	8	265	335
5550	3/8"		8.64	1.852		167	124	8.30	299.30	375
5560	1/2"		8.13	1.968		141	132	8.85	281.85	360
5570	3/4"		7.12	2.247		175	151	10.10	336.10	430
5580	1"		6.48	2.469		251	166	11.10	428.10	535
5590	1-1/4"		6.03	2.653		560	178	11.90	749.90	895
5600	1-1/2"		5.69	2.812		490	189	12.65	691.65	830
5610	2"		4.83	3.313		720	223	14.85	957.85	1,125
5700	For socket weld joint, 6,000 lb., type 304 and 316, add					100%				
6000	Threaded companion flange									
6010	Stainless steel, 150 lb., type 304									
6020	1/2" diam.	1 Plum	30	.267	Ea.	38.50	19.90		58.40	71.50
6030	3/4" diam.		28	.286		44.50	21.50		66	80.50
6040	1" diam.		27	.296		49	22		71	87
6050	1-1/4" diam.	Q-1	44	.364		63	24.50		87.50	106
6060	1-1/2" diam.		40	.400		65	27		92	112

22 11 Facility Water Distribution

22 11 13 – Facility Water Distribution Piping

22 11 13.66 Pipe Fittings, Stainless Steel		Crew	Daily Output	Labor-Hours	Unit	Material	2024 Bare Costs Labor	Equipment	Total	Total Incl O&P
6070	2" diam.	Q-1	36	.444	Ea.	83.50	30		113.50	136
6080	2-1/2" diam.		28	.571		132	38.50		170.50	202
6090	3" diam.		20	.800		127	53.50		180.50	220
6110	4" diam.	↓	12	1.333		176	89.50		265.50	325
6130	6" diam.	Q-2	14	1.714		305	119		424	515
6140	8" diam.	"	12	2	↓	545	139		684	805
6150	For type 316, add					40%				
6260	Weld flanges, stainless steel, type 304									
6270	Slip on, 150 lb. (welded, front and back)									
6280	1/2" diam.	Q-15	12.70	1.260	Ea.	37	84.50	5.65	127.15	173
6290	3/4" diam.		11.11	1.440		39	97	6.45	142.45	194
6300	1" diam.		10.13	1.579		42.50	106	7.10	155.60	212
6310	1-1/4" diam.		9.41	1.700		59	114	7.65	180.65	243
6320	1-1/2" diam.		8.89	1.800		58	121	8.10	187.10	253
6330	2" diam.		7.55	2.119		73	142	9.50	224.50	305
6340	2-1/2" diam.		3.98	4.020		107	270	18.05	395.05	540
6350	3" diam.		3.21	4.984		115	335	22.50	472.50	650
6370	4" diam.	↓	2.44	6.557		152	440	29.50	621.50	855
6390	6" diam.	Q-16	1.89	12.698		233	885	38	1,156	1,625
6400	8" diam.	"	1.22	19.672	↓	410	1,375	59	1,844	2,575
6410	For type 316, add					40%				
6530	Weld neck 150 lb.									
6540	1/2" diam.	Q-15	25.40	.630	Ea.	47	42.50	2.83	92.33	118
6550	3/4" diam.		22.22	.720		55	48.50	3.23	106.73	136
6560	1" diam.		20.25	.790		62	53	3.55	118.55	151
6570	1-1/4" diam.		18.82	.850		95.50	57	3.82	156.32	194
6580	1-1/2" diam.		17.78	.900		85.50	60.50	4.04	150.04	188
6590	2" diam.		15.09	1.060		92.50	71	4.76	168.26	213
6600	2-1/2" diam.		7.96	2.010		150	135	9.05	294.05	375
6610	3" diam.		6.43	2.488		148	167	11.15	326.15	425
6630	4" diam.		4.88	3.279		229	220	14.70	463.70	600
6640	5" diam.	↓	4.26	3.756		241	252	16.85	509.85	660
6650	6" diam.	Q-16	5.66	4.240		330	295	12.70	637.70	820
6652	8" diam.		3.65	6.575		585	460	19.65	1,064.65	1,350
6654	10" diam.		2.88	8.333		675	580	25	1,280	1,625
6656	12" diam.	↓	2.28	10.526	↓	835	735	31.50	1,601.50	2,050
6670	For type 316, add					23%				
7000	Threaded joint, 150 lb., type 304									
7030	90° elbow									
7040	1/8"	1 Plum	13	.615	Ea.	6.05	46		52.05	75
7050	1/4"		13	.615		6.10	46		52.10	75
7070	3/8"		13	.615		7.45	46		53.45	76.50
7080	1/2"		12	.667		8	50		58	83
7090	3/4"		11	.727		11.45	54.50		65.95	93.50
7100	1"	↓	10	.800		16.30	59.50		75.80	107
7110	1-1/4"	Q-1	17	.941		30.50	63		93.50	128
7120	1-1/2"		16	1		38.50	67		105.50	142
7130	2"		14	1.143		48.50	77		125.50	167
7140	2-1/2"		11	1.455		100	97.50		197.50	255
7150	3"	↓	8	2		127	134		261	340
7160	4"	Q-2	11	2.182	↓	213	152		365	460
7180	45° elbow									
7190	1/8"	1 Plum	13	.615	Ea.	8	46		54	77.50

22 11 Facility Water Distribution

22 11 13 – Facility Water Distribution Piping

22 11 13.66 Pipe Fittings, Stainless Steel		Crew	Daily Output	Labor-Hours	Unit	Material	2024 Bare Costs Labor	Equipment	Total	Total Incl O&P
7200	1/4"	1 Plum	13	.615	Ea.	8	46		54	77.50
7210	3/8"		13	.615		9.55	46		55.55	79
7220	1/2"		12	.667		10.45	50		60.45	85.50
7230	3/4"		11	.727		15.25	54.50		69.75	98
7240	1"		10	.800		18.75	59.50		78.25	110
7250	1-1/4"	Q-1	17	.941		30	63		93	127
7260	1-1/2"		16	1		35.50	67		102.50	139
7270	2"		14	1.143		50	77		127	169
7280	2-1/2"		11	1.455		118	97.50		215.50	275
7290	3"		8	2		163	134		297	380
7300	4"	Q-2	11	2.182		217	152		369	465
7320	Tee, straight									
7330	1/8"	1 Plum	9	.889	Ea.	8.65	66.50		75.15	108
7340	1/4"		9	.889		8.60	66.50		75.10	108
7350	3/8"		9	.889		11	66.50		77.50	111
7360	1/2"		8	1		11.45	74.50		85.95	124
7370	3/4"		7	1.143		18.30	85.50		103.80	147
7380	1"		6.50	1.231		23.50	92		115.50	163
7390	1-1/4"	Q-1	11	1.455		46.50	97.50		144	196
7400	1-1/2"		10	1.600		57.50	107		164.50	224
7410	2"		9	1.778		74	119		193	260
7420	2-1/2"		7	2.286		136	154		290	380
7430	3"		5	3.200		196	215		411	535
7440	4"	Q-2	7	3.429		266	239		505	650
7460	Coupling, straight									
7470	1/8"	1 Plum	19	.421	Ea.	3.54	31.50		35.04	51
7480	1/4"		19	.421		4.20	31.50		35.70	51.50
7490	3/8"		19	.421		4.87	31.50		36.37	52.50
7500	1/2"		19	.421		6.95	31.50		38.45	54.50
7510	3/4"		18	.444		9.65	33		42.65	60
7520	1"		15	.533		14.15	40		54.15	74.50
7530	1-1/4"	Q-1	26	.615		21	41.50		62.50	84.50
7540	1-1/2"		24	.667		25	45		70	94
7550	2"		21	.762		35	51		86	115
7560	2-1/2"		18	.889		77	59.50		136.50	174
7570	3"		14	1.143		105	77		182	229
7580	4"	Q-2	16	1.500		163	105		268	335
7600	Reducer, concentric, 1/2"	1 Plum	12	.667		42.50	50		92.50	121
7610	3/4"		11	.727		54.50	54.50		109	141
7612	1"		10	.800		90.50	59.50		150	189
7614	1-1/4"	Q-1	17	.941		193	63		256	305
7616	1-1/2"		16	1		211	67		278	330
7618	2"		14	1.143		330	77		407	475
7620	2-1/2"		11	1.455		865	97.50		962.50	1,100
7622	3"		8	2		960	134		1,094	1,250
7624	4"	Q-2	11	2.182		1,600	152		1,752	1,975
7710	Union									
7720	1/8"	1 Plum	12	.667	Ea.	16.95	50		66.95	92.50
7730	1/4"		12	.667		19.85	50		69.85	96
7740	3/8"		12	.667		18.55	50		68.55	94.50
7750	1/2"		11	.727		18.60	54.50		73.10	102
7760	3/4"		10	.800		23.50	59.50		83	115
7770	1"		9	.889		35.50	66.50		102	138

22 11 Facility Water Distribution

22 11 13 – Facility Water Distribution Piping

22 11 13.66 Pipe Fittings, Stainless Steel

		Crew	Daily Output	Labor-Hours	Unit	Material	2024 Bare Costs Labor	Equipment	Total	Total Incl O&P
7780	1-1/4"	Q-1	16	1	Ea.	62	67		129	168
7790	1-1/2"		15	1.067		70	71.50		141.50	184
7800	2"		13	1.231		88.50	82.50		171	220
7810	2-1/2"		10	1.600		206	107		313	385
7820	3"		7	2.286		258	154		412	510
7830	4"	Q-2	10	2.400		360	167		527	645
7838	Caps									
7840	1/2"	1 Plum	24	.333	Ea.	13.40	25		38.40	52
7841	3/4"		22	.364		16.75	27		43.75	59
7842	1"		20	.400		31.50	30		61.50	79
7843	1-1/2"	Q-1	32	.500		55	33.50		88.50	110
7844	2"	"	28	.571		74.50	38.50		113	139
7845	4"	Q-2	22	1.091		770	76		846	965
7850	For 150 lb., type 316, add					25%				

22 11 13.74 Pipe, Plastic

		Crew	Daily Output	Labor-Hours	Unit	Material	2024 Bare Costs Labor	Equipment	Total	Total Incl O&P
0010	**PIPE, PLASTIC** R221113-70									
0020	Fiberglass reinforced, couplings 10' OC, clevis hanger assy's, 3 per 10'									
0080	General service									
0120	2" diameter	Q-1	59	.271	L.F.	24	18.20		42.20	53
0140	3" diameter		52	.308		35	20.50		55.50	69.50
0150	4" diameter		48	.333		46	22.50		68.50	84
0160	6" diameter		39	.410		49.50	27.50		77	95.50
0170	8" diameter	Q-2	49	.490		67.50	34		101.50	125
0180	10" diameter		41	.585		101	41		142	172
0190	12" diameter		36	.667		133	46.50		179.50	215
0600	PVC, high impact/pressure, cplgs. 10' OC, clevis hanger assy's, 3 per 10'									
1020	Schedule 80									
1070	1/2" diameter	1 Plum	50	.160	L.F.	4.37	11.95		16.32	22.50
1080	3/4" diameter		47	.170		5	12.70		17.70	24.50
1090	1" diameter		43	.186		5.60	13.90		19.50	26.50
1100	1-1/4" diameter		39	.205		7.55	15.30		22.85	31.50
1110	1-1/2" diameter		34	.235		7.85	17.55		25.40	34.50
1120	2" diameter	Q-1	55	.291		9.45	19.55		29	39.50
1140	3" diameter		50	.320		18.95	21.50		40.45	53
1150	4" diameter		46	.348		26	23.50		49.50	63.50
1170	6" diameter		38	.421		52.50	28.50		81	99.50
1730	To delete coupling & hangers, subtract									
1740	1/2" diam.					62%	80%			
1750	3/4" diam. to 1-1/4" diam.					58%	73%			
1760	1-1/2" diam. to 6" diam.					40%	57%			
1800	PVC, couplings 10' OC, clevis hanger assemblies, 3 per 10'									
1820	Schedule 40									
1860	1/2" diameter	1 Plum	54	.148	L.F.	5.20	11.05		16.25	22
1870	3/4" diameter		51	.157		5.75	11.70		17.45	24
1880	1" diameter		46	.174		5.40	13		18.40	25
1890	1-1/4" diameter		42	.190		7.90	14.20		22.10	29.50
1900	1-1/2" diameter		36	.222		8.20	16.60		24.80	33.50
1910	2" diameter	Q-1	59	.271		9.15	18.20		27.35	37
1920	2-1/2" diameter		56	.286		11.90	19.20		31.10	41.50
1930	3" diameter		53	.302		16.25	20.50		36.75	48
1940	4" diameter		48	.333		21.50	22.50		44	57
1950	5" diameter		43	.372		38	25		63	79

22 11 Facility Water Distribution

22 11 13 – Facility Water Distribution Piping

22 11 13.74 Pipe, Plastic

		Crew	Daily Output	Labor-Hours	Unit	Material	2024 Bare Costs Labor	Equipment	Total	Total Incl O&P
1960	6" diameter	Q-1	39	.410	L.F.	46	27.50		73.50	91.50
1970	8" diameter	Q-2	48	.500		66	35		101	125
1980	10" diameter		43	.558		104	39		143	173
1990	12" diameter		42	.571		130	40		170	202
2000	14" diameter		31	.774		229	54		283	330
2010	16" diameter		23	1.043		315	72.50		387.50	460
2340	To delete coupling & hangers, subtract									
2360	1/2" diam. to 1-1/4" diam.					65%	74%			
2370	1-1/2" diam. to 6" diam.					44%	57%			
2380	8" diam. to 12" diam.					41%	53%			
2390	14" diam. to 16" diam.					48%	45%			
2420	Schedule 80									
2440	1/4" diameter	1 Plum	58	.138	L.F.	3.36	10.30		13.66	19
2450	3/8" diameter		55	.145		3.36	10.85		14.21	19.85
2460	1/2" diameter		50	.160		4.92	11.95		16.87	23
2470	3/4" diameter		47	.170		5.80	12.70		18.50	25.50
2480	1" diameter		43	.186		5.70	13.90		19.60	27
2490	1-1/4" diameter		39	.205		9.15	15.30		24.45	33
2500	1-1/2" diameter		34	.235		9	17.55		26.55	36
2510	2" diameter	Q-1	55	.291		8.05	19.55		27.60	38
2520	2-1/2" diameter		52	.308		15.15	20.50		35.65	47.50
2530	3" diameter		50	.320		24	21.50		45.50	58.50
2540	4" diameter		46	.348		33	23.50		56.50	71.50
2550	5" diameter		42	.381		41	25.50		66.50	83
2560	6" diameter		38	.421		64	28.50		92.50	113
2570	8" diameter	Q-2	47	.511		90	35.50		125.50	152
2580	10" diameter		42	.571		110	40		150	180
2590	12" diameter		38	.632		149	44		193	230
2830	To delete coupling & hangers, subtract									
2840	1/4" diam. to 1/2" diam.					66%	80%			
2850	3/4" diam. to 1-1/4" diam.					61%	73%			
2860	1-1/2" diam. to 6" diam.					41%	57%			
2870	8" diam. to 12" diam.					31%	50%			
2900	Schedule 120									
2910	1/2" diameter	1 Plum	50	.160	L.F.	5.65	11.95		17.60	24
2950	3/4" diameter		47	.170		6.75	12.70		19.45	26.50
2960	1" diameter		43	.186		8.35	13.90		22.25	29.50
2970	1-1/4" diameter		39	.205		11.20	15.30		26.50	35.50
2980	1-1/2" diameter		33	.242		12.15	18.10		30.25	40.50
2990	2" diameter	Q-1	54	.296		16.10	19.90		36	47
3000	2-1/2" diameter		52	.308		25.50	20.50		46	59
3010	3" diameter		49	.327		49.50	22		71.50	87
3020	4" diameter		45	.356		46	24		70	86.50
3030	6" diameter		37	.432		120	29		149	175
3240	To delete coupling & hangers, subtract									
3250	1/2" diam. to 1-1/4" diam.					52%	74%			
3260	1-1/2" diam. to 4" diam.					30%	57%			
3270	6" diam.					17%	50%			
3300	PVC, pressure, couplings 10' OC, clevis hanger assy's, 3 per 10'									
3310	SDR 26, 160 psi									
3350	1-1/4" diameter	1 Plum	42	.190	L.F.	5.50	14.20		19.70	27
3360	1-1/2" diameter	"	36	.222		5.70	16.60		22.30	31
3370	2" diameter	Q-1	59	.271		8.95	18.20		27.15	37

22 11 Facility Water Distribution

22 11 13 – Facility Water Distribution Piping

22 11 13.74 Pipe, Plastic

		Crew	Daily Output	Labor-Hours	Unit	Material	2024 Bare Costs Labor	Equipment	Total	Total Incl O&P
3380	2-1/2" diameter	Q-1	56	.286	L.F.	12.85	19.20		32.05	42.50
3390	3" diameter		53	.302		18.60	20.50		39.10	50.50
3400	4" diameter		48	.333		27.50	22.50		50	63.50
3420	6" diameter		39	.410		51.50	27.50		79	97.50
3430	8" diameter	Q-2	48	.500		73	35		108	132
3660	To delete coupling & clevis hanger assy's, subtract									
3670	1-1/4" diam.					63%	68%			
3680	1-1/2" diam. to 4" diam.					48%	57%			
3690	6" diam. to 8" diam.					60%	54%			
3720	SDR 21, 200 psi, 1/2" diameter	1 Plum	54	.148	L.F.	5	11.05		16.05	22
3740	3/4" diameter		51	.157		5.95	11.70		17.65	24
3750	1" diameter		46	.174		6.75	13		19.75	27
3760	1-1/4" diameter		42	.190		8.75	14.20		22.95	30.50
3770	1-1/2" diameter		36	.222		8.05	16.60		24.65	33.50
3780	2" diameter	Q-1	59	.271		9.90	18.20		28.10	38
3790	2-1/2" diameter		56	.286		11.55	19.20		30.75	41
3800	3" diameter		53	.302		12.60	20.50		33.10	44
3810	4" diameter		48	.333		17.35	22.50		39.85	52.50
3830	6" diameter		39	.410		33	27.50		60.50	77
3840	8" diameter	Q-2	48	.500		48	35		83	105
4000	To delete coupling & hangers, subtract									
4010	1/2" diam. to 3/4" diam.					71%	77%			
4020	1" diam. to 1-1/4" diam.					63%	70%			
4030	1-1/2" diam. to 6" diam.					44%	57%			
4040	8" diam.					46%	54%			
4100	DWV type, schedule 40, couplings 10' OC, clevis hanger assy's, 3 per 10'									
4210	ABS, schedule 40, foam core type									
4212	Plain end black									
4214	1-1/2" diameter	1 Plum	39	.205	L.F.	6.75	15.30		22.05	30.50
4216	2" diameter	Q-1	62	.258		8.45	17.35		25.80	35.50
4218	3" diameter		56	.286		16.15	19.20		35.35	46.50
4220	4" diameter		51	.314		23.50	21		44.50	57.50
4222	6" diameter		42	.381		70.50	25.50		96	116
4240	To delete coupling & hangers, subtract									
4244	1-1/2" diam. to 6" diam.					43%	48%			
4400	PVC									
4410	1-1/4" diameter	1 Plum	42	.190	L.F.	8.30	14.20		22.50	30
4420	1-1/2" diameter	"	36	.222		5.45	16.60		22.05	30.50
4460	2" diameter	Q-1	59	.271		6.30	18.20		24.50	34
4470	3" diameter		53	.302		12.45	20.50		32.95	43.50
4480	4" diameter		48	.333		17.60	22.50		40.10	53
4490	6" diameter		39	.410		38.50	27.50		66	83.50
4500	8" diameter	Q-2	48	.500		63	35		98	122
4510	To delete coupling & hangers, subtract									
4520	1-1/4" diam. to 1-1/2" diam.					48%	60%			
4530	2" diam. to 8" diam.					42%	54%			
4550	PVC, schedule 40, foam core type									
4552	Plain end, white									
4554	1-1/2" diameter	1 Plum	39	.205	L.F.	7.20	15.30		22.50	31
4556	2" diameter	Q-1	62	.258		8.85	17.35		26.20	36
4558	3" diameter		56	.286		16.65	19.20		35.85	47
4560	4" diameter		51	.314		20.50	21		41.50	54
4562	6" diameter		42	.381		44.50	25.50		70	87

22 11 Facility Water Distribution

22 11 13 – Facility Water Distribution Piping

22 11 13.74 Pipe, Plastic

		Crew	Daily Output	Labor-Hours	Unit	Material	2024 Bare Costs Labor	Equipment	Total	Total Incl O&P
4564	8" diameter	Q-2	51	.471	L.F.	80.50	33		113.50	138
4568	10" diameter	↓	48	.500		109	35		144	172
4570	12" diameter	↓	46	.522	↓	134	36.50		170.50	201
4580	To delete coupling & hangers, subtract									
4582	1-1/2" diam. to 2" diam.					58%	54%			
4584	3" diam. to 12" diam.					46%	42%			
4800	PVC, clear pipe, cplgs. 10' OC, clevis hanger assy's 3 per 10', Sched. 40									
4840	1/4" diameter	1 Plum	59	.136	L.F.	4.06	10.10		14.16	19.50
4850	3/8" diameter		56	.143		4.55	10.65		15.20	21
4860	1/2" diameter		54	.148		5.55	11.05		16.60	22.50
4870	3/4" diameter		51	.157		6.55	11.70		18.25	24.50
4880	1" diameter		46	.174		8.55	13		21.55	28.50
4890	1-1/4" diameter		42	.190		10.75	14.20		24.95	33
4900	1-1/2" diameter	↓	36	.222		12.25	16.60		28.85	38
4910	2" diameter	Q-1	59	.271		15.75	18.20		33.95	44.50
4920	2-1/2" diameter		56	.286		24	19.20		43.20	55
4930	3" diameter		53	.302		30.50	20.50		51	63.50
4940	3-1/2" diameter		50	.320		38.50	21.50		60	74.50
4950	4" diameter	↓	48	.333		45	22.50		67.50	83
5250	To delete coupling & hangers, subtract									
5260	1/4" diam. to 3/8" diam.					60%	81%			
5270	1/2" diam. to 3/4" diam.					41%	77%			
5280	1" diam. to 1-1/2" diam.					26%	67%			
5290	2" diam. to 4" diam.					16%	58%			
5300	CPVC, socket joint, couplings 10' OC, clevis hanger assemblies, 3 per 10'									
5302	Schedule 40									
5304	1/2" diameter	1 Plum	54	.148	L.F.	5.10	11.05		16.15	22
5305	3/4" diameter		51	.157		6.45	11.70		18.15	24.50
5306	1" diameter		46	.174		9.50	13		22.50	30
5307	1-1/4" diameter		42	.190		10.25	14.20		24.45	32.50
5308	1-1/2" diameter	↓	36	.222		11.85	16.60		28.45	37.50
5309	2" diameter	Q-1	59	.271		15.85	18.20		34.05	44.50
5310	2-1/2" diameter		56	.286		22.50	19.20		41.70	53.50
5311	3" diameter		53	.302		32.50	20.50		53	66
5312	4" diameter		48	.333		44.50	22.50		67	82.50
5314	6" diameter	↓	43	.372	↓	78.50	25		103.50	123
5318	To delete coupling & hangers, subtract									
5319	1/2" diam. to 3/4" diam.					37%	77%			
5320	1" diam. to 1-1/4" diam.					27%	70%			
5321	1-1/2" diam. to 3" diam.					21%	57%			
5322	4" diam. to 6" diam.					16%	57%			
5324	Schedule 80									
5325	1/2" diameter	1 Plum	50	.160	L.F.	7.55	11.95		19.50	26
5326	3/4" diameter		47	.170		8.35	12.70		21.05	28
5327	1" diameter		43	.186		10.25	13.90		24.15	32
5328	1-1/4" diameter		39	.205		12.45	15.30		27.75	36.50
5329	1-1/2" diameter	↓	34	.235		15.55	17.55		33.10	43
5330	2" diameter	Q-1	55	.291		19.40	19.55		38.95	50.50
5331	2-1/2" diameter		52	.308		30	20.50		50.50	64
5332	3" diameter		50	.320		37.50	21.50		59	73
5333	4" diameter		46	.348		52.50	23.50		76	93
5334	6" diameter	↓	38	.421		95	28.50		123.50	146
5335	8" diameter	Q-2	47	.511	↓	133	35.50		168.50	199

For customer support on your Plumbing Costs with RSMeans Data call 800.448.8182.

22 11 Facility Water Distribution

22 11 13 – Facility Water Distribution Piping

22 11 13.74 Pipe, Plastic		Crew	Daily Output	Labor-Hours	Unit	Material	2024 Bare Costs Labor	2024 Bare Costs Equipment	Total	Total Incl O&P
5339	To delete couplings & hangers, subtract									
5340	1/2" diam. to 3/4" diam.					44%	77%			
5341	1" diam. to 1-1/4" diam.					32%	71%			
5342	1-1/2" diam. to 4" diam.					25%	58%			
5343	6" diam. to 8" diam.					20%	53%			
5360	CPVC, threaded, couplings 10' OC, clevis hanger assemblies, 3 per 10'									
5380	Schedule 40									
5460	1/2" diameter	1 Plum	54	.148	L.F.	5.75	11.05		16.80	23
5470	3/4" diameter		51	.157		7.60	11.70		19.30	26
5480	1" diameter		46	.174		10.70	13		23.70	31
5490	1-1/4" diameter		42	.190		11.20	14.20		25.40	33.50
5500	1-1/2" diameter		36	.222		12.65	16.60		29.25	38.50
5510	2" diameter	Q-1	59	.271		16.80	18.20		35	45.50
5520	2-1/2" diameter		56	.286		24	19.20		43.20	54.50
5530	3" diameter		53	.302		34.50	20.50		55	68
5540	4" diameter		48	.333		51.50	22.50		74	90
5550	6" diameter		43	.372		90	25		115	136
5730	To delete coupling & hangers, subtract									
5740	1/2" diam. to 3/4" diam.					37%	77%			
5750	1" diam. to 1-1/4" diam.					27%	70%			
5760	1-1/2" diam. to 3" diam.					21%	57%			
5770	4" diam. to 6" diam.					16%	57%			
5800	Schedule 80									
5860	1/2" diameter	1 Plum	50	.160	L.F.	8.20	11.95		20.15	27
5870	3/4" diameter		47	.170		9.50	12.70		22.20	29.50
5880	1" diameter		43	.186		11.45	13.90		25.35	33
5890	1-1/4" diameter		39	.205		13.40	15.30		28.70	38
5900	1-1/2" diameter		34	.235		16.35	17.55		33.90	44
5910	2" diameter	Q-1	55	.291		20.50	19.55		40.05	51.50
5920	2-1/2" diameter		52	.308		31	20.50		51.50	65.50
5930	3" diameter		50	.320		39.50	21.50		61	75.50
5940	4" diameter		46	.348		59.50	23.50		83	101
5950	6" diameter		38	.421		107	28.50		135.50	159
5960	8" diameter	Q-2	47	.511		150	35.50		185.50	218
6060	To delete couplings & hangers, subtract									
6070	1/2" diam. to 3/4" diam.					44%	77%			
6080	1" diam. to 1-1/4" diam.					32%	71%			
6090	1-1/2" diam. to 4" diam.					25%	58%			
6100	6" diam. to 8" diam.					20%	53%			
6240	CTS, 1/2" diameter	1 Plum	54	.148	L.F.	3.43	11.05		14.48	20
6250	3/4" diameter		51	.157		4.24	11.70		15.94	22
6260	1" diameter		46	.174		6.15	13		19.15	26
6270	1-1/4" diameter		42	.190		8.70	14.20		22.90	30.50
6280	1-1/2" diameter		36	.222		10.65	16.60		27.25	36
6290	2" diameter	Q-1	59	.271		16.45	18.20		34.65	45
6370	To delete coupling & hangers, subtract									
6380	1/2" diam.					51%	79%			
6390	3/4" diam.					40%	76%			
6392	1" thru 2" diam.					72%	68%			
6500	Residential installation, plastic pipe									
6510	Couplings 10' OC, strap hangers 3 per 10'									
6520	PVC, Schedule 40									
6530	1/2" diameter	1 Plum	138	.058	L.F.	2.52	4.33		6.85	9.20

22 11 Facility Water Distribution

22 11 13 – Facility Water Distribution Piping

22 11 13.74 Pipe, Plastic

		Crew	Daily Output	Labor-Hours	Unit	Material	2024 Bare Costs Labor	Equipment	Total	Total Incl O&P
6540	3/4" diameter	1 Plum	128	.063	L.F.	3.70	4.67		8.37	11
6550	1" diameter		119	.067		3.62	5		8.62	11.45
6560	1-1/4" diameter		111	.072		5.35	5.40		10.75	13.85
6570	1-1/2" diameter		104	.077		5.65	5.75		11.40	14.80
6580	2" diameter	Q-1	197	.081		6.40	5.45		11.85	15.15
6590	2-1/2" diameter		162	.099		9	6.65		15.65	19.75
6600	4" diameter		123	.130		13.90	8.75		22.65	28.50
6700	PVC, DWV, Schedule 40									
6720	1-1/4" diameter	1 Plum	100	.080	L.F.	7.50	5.95		13.45	17.20
6730	1-1/2" diameter	"	94	.085		4.83	6.35		11.18	14.75
6740	2" diameter	Q-1	178	.090		5.75	6.05		11.80	15.35
6760	4" diameter	"	110	.145		17.65	9.75		27.40	34
7280	PEX, flexible, no couplings or hangers									
7282	Note: For labor costs add 25% to the couplings and fittings labor total.									
7285	For fittings see section 23 83 16.10 7000									
7300	Non-barrier type, hot/cold tubing rolls									
7310	1/4" diameter x 100'				L.F.	.47			.47	.52
7350	3/8" diameter x 100'					.52			.52	.57
7360	1/2" diameter x 100'					.47			.47	.52
7370	1/2" diameter x 500'					.56			.56	.62
7380	1/2" diameter x 1000'					.48			.48	.53
7400	3/4" diameter x 100'					.86			.86	.95
7410	3/4" diameter x 500'					.91			.91	1
7420	3/4" diameter x 1000'					.93			.93	1.02
7460	1" diameter x 100'					1.55			1.55	1.71
7470	1" diameter x 300'					1.62			1.62	1.78
7480	1" diameter x 500'					1.81			1.81	1.99
7500	1-1/4" diameter x 100'					4.60			4.60	5.05
7510	1-1/4" diameter x 300'					4.40			4.40	4.84
7540	1-1/2" diameter x 100'					5.10			5.10	5.60
7550	1-1/2" diameter x 300'					4.99			4.99	5.50
7596	Most sizes available in red or blue									
7700	Non-barrier type, hot/cold tubing straight lengths									
7710	1/2" diameter x 20'				L.F.	.66			.66	.73
7750	3/4" diameter x 20'					1.13			1.13	1.24
7760	1" diameter x 20'					2.03			2.03	2.23
7770	1-1/4" diameter x 20'					4.79			4.79	5.25
7780	1-1/2" diameter x 20'					5.55			5.55	6.15
7790	2" diameter					13.10			13.10	14.40
7796	Most sizes available in red or blue									
9000	Polypropylene pipe									
9002	For fusion weld fittings and accessories see line 22 11 13.76 9400									
9004	Note: sizes 1/2" thru 4" use socket fusion									
9005	Sizes 6" thru 10" use butt fusion									
9010	SDR 7.4 (domestic hot water piping)									
9011	Enhanced to minimize thermal expansion and high temperature life									
9016	13' lengths, size is ID, includes joints 13' OC and hangers 3 per 10'									
9020	3/8" diameter	1 Plum	53	.151	L.F.	3.34	11.25		14.59	20.50
9022	1/2" diameter		52	.154		4.26	11.50		15.76	22
9024	3/4" diameter		50	.160		5.60	11.95		17.55	24
9026	1" diameter		45	.178		7.35	13.25		20.60	28
9028	1-1/4" diameter		40	.200		11.35	14.95		26.30	34.50
9030	1-1/2" diameter		35	.229		16.90	17.05		33.95	44

22 11 Facility Water Distribution

22 11 13 – Facility Water Distribution Piping

22 11 13.74 Pipe, Plastic

		Crew	Daily Output	Labor-Hours	Unit	Material	2024 Bare Costs Labor	Equipment	Total	Total Incl O&P
9032	2" diameter	Q-1	58	.276	L.F.	22.50	18.55		41.05	52.50
9034	2-1/2" diameter		55	.291		32	19.55		51.55	64
9036	3" diameter		52	.308		42.50	20.50		63	77.50
9038	3-1/2" diameter		49	.327		65	22		87	104
9040	4" diameter		46	.348		68	23.50		91.50	110
9042	6" diameter		39	.410		102	27.50		129.50	153
9044	8" diameter	Q-2	48	.500		156	35		191	224
9046	10" diameter	"	43	.558		247	39		286	330
9050	To delete joint & hangers, subtract									
9052	3/8" diam. to 1" diam.					45%	65%			
9054	1-1/4" diam. to 4" diam.					15%	45%			
9056	6" diam. to 10" diam.					5%	24%			
9060	SDR 11 (domestic cold water piping)									
9062	13' lengths, size is ID, includes joints 13' OC and hangers 3 per 10'									
9064	1/2" diameter	1 Plum	57	.140	L.F.	3.75	10.50		14.25	19.75
9066	3/4" diameter		54	.148		4.45	11.05		15.50	21.50
9068	1" diameter		49	.163		5.75	12.20		17.95	24.50
9070	1-1/4" diameter		45	.178		8.25	13.25		21.50	29
9072	1-1/2" diameter		40	.200		11.50	14.95		26.45	34.50
9074	2" diameter	Q-1	62	.258		17.05	17.35		34.40	45
9076	2-1/2" diameter		59	.271		23	18.20		41.20	52.50
9078	3" diameter		56	.286		31.50	19.20		50.70	63
9080	3-1/2" diameter		53	.302		46.50	20.50		67	81
9082	4" diameter		50	.320		53	21.50		74.50	90.50
9084	6" diameter		47	.340		68.50	23		91.50	110
9086	8" diameter	Q-2	51	.471		106	33		139	166
9088	10" diameter	"	46	.522		162	36.50		198.50	232
9090	To delete joint & hangers, subtract									
9092	1/2" diam. to 1" diam.					45%	65%			
9094	1-1/4" diam. to 4" diam.					15%	45%			
9096	6" diam. to 10" diam.					5%	24%			

22 11 13.76 Pipe Fittings, Plastic

		Crew	Daily Output	Labor-Hours	Unit	Material	2024 Bare Costs Labor	Equipment	Total	Total Incl O&P
0010	**PIPE FITTINGS, PLASTIC**									
0030	Epoxy resin, fiberglass reinforced, general service									
0100	3"	Q-1	20.80	.769	Ea.	129	51.50		180.50	219
0110	4"		16.50	.970		139	65		204	250
0120	6"		10.10	1.584		258	106		364	440
0130	8"	Q-2	9.30	2.581		475	180		655	785
0140	10"		8.50	2.824		595	197		792	950
0150	12"		7.60	3.158		855	220		1,075	1,275
0170	Elbow, 90°, flanged									
0172	2"	Q-1	23	.696	Ea.	296	46.50		342.50	395
0173	3"		16	1		340	67		407	470
0174	4"		13	1.231		440	82.50		522.50	610
0176	6"		8	2		800	134		934	1,075
0177	8"	Q-2	9	2.667		1,450	186		1,636	1,875
0178	10"		7	3.429		1,975	239		2,214	2,525
0179	12"		5	4.800		2,650	335		2,985	3,425
0186	Elbow, 45°, flanged									
0188	2"	Q-1	23	.696	Ea.	296	46.50		342.50	395
0189	3"		16	1		340	67		407	470
0190	4"		13	1.231		440	82.50		522.50	610

22 11 Facility Water Distribution

22 11 13 – Facility Water Distribution Piping

22 11 13.76 Pipe Fittings, Plastic

		Crew	Daily Output	Labor-Hours	Unit	Material	2024 Bare Costs Labor	Equipment	Total	Total Incl O&P
0192	6"	Q-1	8	2	Ea.	800	134		934	1,075
0193	8"	Q-2	9	2.667		1,475	186		1,661	1,900
0194	10"		7	3.429		2,050	239		2,289	2,600
0195	12"		5	4.800		2,775	335		3,110	3,550
0352	Tee, flanged									
0354	2"	Q-1	17	.941	Ea.	400	63		463	535
0355	3"		10	1.600		530	107		637	740
0356	4"		8	2		595	134		729	850
0358	6"		5	3.200		1,025	215		1,240	1,450
0359	8"	Q-2	6	4		1,925	279		2,204	2,550
0360	10"		5	4.800		2,800	335		3,135	3,575
0361	12"		4	6		3,875	420		4,295	4,875
0365	Wye, flanged									
0367	2"	Q-1	17	.941	Ea.	790	63		853	965
0368	3"		10	1.600		1,100	107		1,207	1,350
0369	4"		8	2		1,450	134		1,584	1,800
0371	6"		5	3.200		2,050	215		2,265	2,600
0372	8"	Q-2	6	4		3,350	279		3,629	4,125
0373	10"		5	4.800		5,225	335		5,560	6,225
0374	12"		4	6		7,600	420		8,020	8,975
0380	Couplings									
0410	2"	Q-1	33.10	.483	Ea.	33	32.50		65.50	85
0420	3"		20.80	.769		42	51.50		93.50	123
0430	4"		16.50	.970		56	65		121	159
0440	6"		10.10	1.584		63.50	106		169.50	228
0450	8"	Q-2	9.30	2.581		107	180		287	385
0460	10"		8.50	2.824		274	197		471	595
0470	12"		7.60	3.158		390	220		610	755
0473	High corrosion resistant couplings, add					30%				
0474	Reducer, concentric, flanged									
0475	2" x 1-1/2"	Q-1	30	.533	Ea.	765	36		801	900
0476	3" x 2"		24	.667		835	45		880	985
0477	4" x 3"		19	.842		940	56.50		996.50	1,100
0479	6" x 4"		15	1.067		940	71.50		1,011.50	1,125
0480	8" x 6"	Q-2	16	1.500		1,550	105		1,655	1,850
0481	10" x 8"		13	1.846		1,425	129		1,554	1,775
0482	12" x 10"		11	2.182		2,225	152		2,377	2,650
0486	Adapter, bell x male or female									
0488	2"	Q-1	28	.571	Ea.	39	38.50		77.50	100
0489	3"		20	.800		59	53.50		112.50	145
0491	4"		17	.941		70	63		133	171
0492	6"		12	1.333		161	89.50		250.50	310
0493	8"	Q-2	15	1.600		231	111		342	420
0494	10"	"	11	2.182		330	152		482	590
0528	Flange									
0532	2"	Q-1	46	.348	Ea.	51.50	23.50		75	91.50
0533	3"		32	.500		71.50	33.50		105	129
0534	4"		26	.615		90.50	41.50		132	161
0536	6"		16	1		148	67		215	263
0537	8"	Q-2	18	1.333		263	93		356	425
0538	10"		14	1.714		370	119		489	590
0539	12"		10	2.400		465	167		632	765

22 11 Facility Water Distribution

22 11 13 – Facility Water Distribution Piping

22 11 13.76 Pipe Fittings, Plastic		Crew	Daily Output	Labor-Hours	Unit	Material	2024 Bare Costs Labor	Equipment	Total	Total Incl O&P
2100	PVC schedule 80, socket joint									
2110	90° elbow, 1/2"	1 Plum	30.30	.264	Ea.	2.23	19.70		21.93	32
2130	3/4"		26	.308		5.55	23		28.55	40
2140	1"		22.70	.352		8.95	26.50		35.45	49
2150	1-1/4"		20.20	.396		11.95	29.50		41.45	57
2160	1-1/2"		18.20	.440		12.80	33		45.80	63
2170	2"	Q-1	33.10	.483		15.45	32.50		47.95	65.50
2180	3"		20.80	.769		40.50	51.50		92	122
2190	4"		16.50	.970		62	65		127	165
2200	6"		10.10	1.584		176	106		282	350
2210	8"	Q-2	9.30	2.581		485	180		665	800
2250	45° elbow, 1/2"	1 Plum	30.30	.264		8.25	19.70		27.95	38.50
2270	3/4"		26	.308		12.45	23		35.45	47.50
2280	1"		22.70	.352		18.65	26.50		45.15	59.50
2290	1-1/4"		20.20	.396		27.50	29.50		57	74.50
2300	1-1/2"		18.20	.440		28	33		61	80
2310	2"	Q-1	33.10	.483		36.50	32.50		69	88.50
2320	3"		20.80	.769		108	51.50		159.50	195
2330	4"		16.50	.970		168	65		233	282
2340	6"		10.10	1.584		212	106		318	390
2350	8"	Q-2	9.30	2.581		460	180		640	770
2400	Tee, 1/2"	1 Plum	20.20	.396		12.20	29.50		41.70	57.50
2420	3/4"		17.30	.462		12.80	34.50		47.30	65.50
2430	1"		15.20	.526		16.05	39.50		55.55	76
2440	1-1/4"		13.50	.593		43	44		87	114
2450	1-1/2"		12.10	.661		44	49.50		93.50	122
2460	2"	Q-1	20	.800		55	53.50		108.50	141
2470	3"		13.90	1.151		73	77.50		150.50	196
2480	4"		11	1.455		86.50	97.50		184	241
2490	6"		6.70	2.388		295	160		455	565
2500	8"	Q-2	6.20	3.871		690	270		960	1,150
2510	Flange, socket, 150 lb., 1/2"	1 Plum	55.60	.144		30	10.75		40.75	49
2514	3/4"		47.60	.168		32	12.55		44.55	54
2518	1"		41.70	.192		36	14.30		50.30	61
2522	1-1/2"		33.30	.240		38	17.95		55.95	68
2526	2"	Q-1	60.60	.264		59.50	17.75		77.25	92
2530	4"		30.30	.528		128	35.50		163.50	194
2534	6"		18.50	.865		202	58		260	310
2538	8"	Q-2	17.10	1.404		305	98		403	480
2550	Coupling, 1/2"	1 Plum	30.30	.264		7.95	19.70		27.65	38.50
2570	3/4"		26	.308		10.90	23		33.90	46
2580	1"		22.70	.352		11.25	26.50		37.75	51.50
2590	1-1/4"		20.20	.396		19.20	29.50		48.70	65
2600	1-1/2"		18.20	.440		20.50	33		53.50	71.50
2610	2"	Q-1	33.10	.483		22	32.50		54.50	72.50
2620	3"		20.80	.769		63	51.50		114.50	146
2630	4"		16.50	.970		84	65		149	190
2640	6"		10.10	1.584		169	106		275	345
2650	8"	Q-2	9.30	2.581		230	180		410	520
2660	10"		8.50	2.824		430	197		627	765
2670	12"		7.60	3.158		495	220		715	870
2700	PVC (white), schedule 40, socket joints									
2760	90° elbow, 1/2"	1 Plum	33.30	.240	Ea.	.47	17.95		18.42	27

22 11 Facility Water Distribution

22 11 13 – Facility Water Distribution Piping

22 11 13.76 Pipe Fittings, Plastic		Crew	Daily Output	Labor-Hours	Unit	Material	2024 Bare Costs Labor	Equipment	Total	Total Incl O&P
2770	3/4"	1 Plum	28.60	.280	Ea.	.54	21		21.54	31.50
2780	1"		25	.320		.98	24		24.98	36.50
2790	1-1/4"		22.20	.360		1.74	27		28.74	42
2800	1-1/2"	▼	20	.400		2	30		32	46.50
2810	2"	Q-1	36.40	.440		2.80	29.50		32.30	47
2820	2-1/2"		26.70	.599		8	40.50		48.50	69
2830	3"		22.90	.699		9.55	47		56.55	80.50
2840	4"		18.20	.879		17.10	59		76.10	107
2850	5"		12.10	1.322		39	89		128	175
2860	6"	▼	11.10	1.441		54.50	97		151.50	204
2870	8"	Q-2	10.30	2.330		140	162		302	395
2980	45° elbow, 1/2"	1 Plum	33.30	.240		.73	17.95		18.68	27.50
2990	3/4"		28.60	.280		1.13	21		22.13	32
3000	1"		25	.320		1.34	24		25.34	37
3010	1-1/4"		22.20	.360		1.85	27		28.85	42
3020	1-1/2"	▼	20	.400		2.35	30		32.35	47
3030	2"	Q-1	36.40	.440		3.08	29.50		32.58	47.50
3040	2-1/2"		26.70	.599		8	40.50		48.50	69
3050	3"		22.90	.699		12.20	47		59.20	83.50
3060	4"		18.20	.879		22.50	59		81.50	113
3070	5"		12.10	1.322		43.50	89		132.50	180
3080	6"	▼	11.10	1.441		55	97		152	205
3090	8"	Q-2	10.30	2.330		132	162		294	385
3180	Tee, 1/2"	1 Plum	22.20	.360		.54	27		27.54	40.50
3190	3/4"		19	.421		.67	31.50		32.17	47.50
3200	1"		16.70	.479		1.15	36		37.15	54.50
3210	1-1/4"		14.80	.541		2.05	40.50		42.55	62.50
3220	1-1/2"	▼	13.30	.602		2.42	45		47.42	69.50
3230	2"	Q-1	24.20	.661		3.52	44.50		48.02	70
3240	2-1/2"		17.80	.899		10.55	60.50		71.05	102
3250	3"		15.20	1.053		12	70.50		82.50	118
3260	4"		12.10	1.322		25.50	89		114.50	160
3270	5"		8.10	1.975		60	133		193	263
3280	6"	▼	7.40	2.162		82.50	145		227.50	305
3290	8"	Q-2	6.80	3.529		198	246		444	585
3380	Coupling, 1/2"	1 Plum	33.30	.240		.28	17.95		18.23	27
3390	3/4"		28.60	.280		.40	21		21.40	31.50
3400	1"		25	.320		.69	24		24.69	36.50
3410	1-1/4"		22.20	.360		.96	27		27.96	41
3420	1-1/2"	▼	20	.400		1.03	30		31.03	45.50
3430	2"	Q-1	36.40	.440		1.57	29.50		31.07	45.50
3440	2-1/2"		26.70	.599		3.46	40.50		43.96	64
3450	3"		22.90	.699		5.40	47		52.40	76
3460	4"		18.20	.879		7.85	59		66.85	96.50
3470	5"		12.10	1.322		14.10	89		103.10	148
3480	6"	▼	11.10	1.441		40	97		137	188
3490	8"	Q-2	10.30	2.330		45.50	162		207.50	291
3600	Cap, schedule 40, PVC socket 1/2"	1 Plum	60.60	.132		.40	9.85		10.25	15.10
3610	3/4"		51.90	.154		.46	11.50		11.96	17.60
3620	1"		45.50	.176		.73	13.15		13.88	20.50
3630	1-1/4"		40.40	.198		1	14.80		15.80	23
3640	1-1/2"	▼	36.40	.220		1.13	16.40		17.53	25.50
3650	2"	Q-1	66.10	.242		1.34	16.25		17.59	25.50

22 11 Facility Water Distribution

22 11 13 – Facility Water Distribution Piping

22 11 13.76	Pipe Fittings, Plastic	Crew	Daily Output	Labor-Hours	Unit	Material	2024 Bare Costs Labor	Equipment	Total	Total Incl O&P
3660	2-1/2"	Q-1	48.50	.330	Ea.	4.22	22		26.22	37.50
3670	3"		41.60	.385		4.60	26		30.60	43.50
3680	4"		33.10	.483		10.70	32.50		43.20	60.50
3690	6"	↓	20.20	.792		25.50	53		78.50	107
3700	8"	Q-2	18.60	1.290	↓	64.50	90		154.50	205
3710	Reducing insert, schedule 40, socket weld									
3712	3/4"	1 Plum	31.50	.254	Ea.	.46	18.95		19.41	28.50
3713	1"		27.50	.291		.83	21.50		22.33	33.50
3715	1-1/2"	↓	22	.364		1.19	27		28.19	42
3716	2"	Q-1	40	.400		1.96	27		28.96	42
3717	4"		20	.800		10.35	53.50		63.85	91.50
3718	6"	↓	12.20	1.311		25.50	88		113.50	160
3719	8"	Q-2	11.30	2.124	↓	95.50	148		243.50	325
3730	Reducing insert, socket weld x female/male thread									
3732	1/2"	1 Plum	38.30	.209	Ea.	2.04	15.60		17.64	25
3733	3/4"		32.90	.243		1.26	18.15		19.41	28.50
3734	1"		28.80	.278		1.76	20.50		22.26	33
3736	1-1/2"	↓	23	.348		3.18	26		29.18	42
3737	2"	Q-1	41.90	.382		3.40	25.50		28.90	41.50
3738	4"	"	20.90	.766	↓	12.70	51.50		64.20	90.50
3742	Male adapter, socket weld x male thread									
3744	1/2"	1 Plum	38.30	.209	Ea.	.40	15.60		16	23.50
3745	3/4"		32.90	.243		.44	18.15		18.59	27.50
3746	1"		28.80	.278		.78	20.50		21.28	32
3748	1-1/2"	↓	23	.348		1.40	26		27.40	40
3749	2"	Q-1	41.90	.382		1.68	25.50		27.18	40
3750	4"	"	20.90	.766	↓	9.30	51.50		60.80	86.50
3754	Female adapter, socket weld x female thread									
3756	1/2"	1 Plum	38.30	.209	Ea.	.49	15.60		16.09	23.50
3757	3/4"		32.90	.243		.62	18.15		18.77	27.50
3758	1"		28.80	.278		.73	20.50		21.23	32
3760	1-1/2"	↓	23	.348		1.28	26		27.28	40
3761	2"	Q-1	41.90	.382		1.72	25.50		27.22	40
3762	4"	"	20.90	.766		9.70	51.50		61.20	87
3800	PVC, schedule 80, socket joints									
3810	Reducing insert									
3812	3/4"	1 Plum	28.60	.280	Ea.	1.29	21		22.29	32.50
3813	1"		25	.320		3.70	24		27.70	39.50
3815	1-1/2"	↓	20	.400		7.90	30		37.90	53
3816	2"	Q-1	36.40	.440		11.25	29.50		40.75	56.50
3817	4"		18.20	.879		43	59		102	135
3818	6"	↓	11.10	1.441		59.50	97		156.50	210
3819	8"	Q-2	10.20	2.353	↓	805	164		969	1,125
3830	Reducing insert, socket weld x female/male thread									
3832	1/2"	1 Plum	34.80	.230	Ea.	8.05	17.15		25.20	34.50
3833	3/4"		29.90	.268		4.94	19.95		24.89	35
3834	1"		26.10	.307		7.75	23		30.75	42.50
3836	1-1/2"	↓	20.90	.383		9.75	28.50		38.25	53
3837	2"	Q-1	38	.421		14.25	28.50		42.75	57.50
3838	4"	"	19	.842		69	56.50		125.50	160
3844	Adapter, male socket x male thread									
3846	1/2"	1 Plum	34.80	.230	Ea.	4.68	17.15		21.83	30.50
3847	3/4"	↓	29.90	.268	↓	5.15	19.95		25.10	35

22 11 Facility Water Distribution

22 11 13 – Facility Water Distribution Piping

22 11 13.76 Pipe Fittings, Plastic

		Crew	Daily Output	Labor-Hours	Unit	Material	2024 Bare Costs Labor	Equipment	Total	Total Incl O&P
3848	1"	1 Plum	26.10	.307	Ea.	8.90	23		31.90	44
3850	1-1/2"		20.90	.383		15	28.50		43.50	59
3851	2"	Q-1	38	.421		21.50	28.50		50	66
3852	4"	"	19	.842		48.50	56.50		105	138
3860	Adapter, female socket x female thread									
3862	1/2"	1 Plum	34.80	.230	Ea.	3.74	17.15		20.89	29.50
3863	3/4"		29.90	.268		5.55	19.95		25.50	35.50
3864	1"		26.10	.307		8.20	23		31.20	43
3866	1-1/2"		20.90	.383		16.30	28.50		44.80	60.50
3867	2"	Q-1	38	.421		28.50	28.50		57	73.50
3868	4"	"	19	.842		87	56.50		143.50	180
3872	Union, socket joints									
3874	1/2"	1 Plum	25.80	.310	Ea.	8.20	23		31.20	43.50
3875	3/4"		22.10	.362		10.45	27		37.45	51.50
3876	1"		19.30	.415		11.90	31		42.90	59
3878	1-1/2"		15.50	.516		26.50	38.50		65	87
3879	2"	Q-1	28.10	.569		36.50	38.50		75	97
3888	Cap									
3890	1/2"	1 Plum	54.50	.147	Ea.	3.91	10.95		14.86	20.50
3891	3/4"		46.70	.171		4.13	12.80		16.93	23.50
3892	1"		41	.195		7.35	14.55		21.90	29.50
3894	1-1/2"		32.80	.244		8.85	18.20		27.05	36.50
3895	2"	Q-1	59.50	.269		17.45	18.05		35.50	46
3896	4"		30	.533		70.50	36		106.50	131
3897	6"		18.20	.879		175	59		234	280
3898	8"	Q-2	16.70	1.437		225	100		325	395
4500	DWV, ABS, non pressure, socket joints									
4540	1/4 bend, 1-1/4"	1 Plum	20.20	.396	Ea.	27	29.50		56.50	74
4560	1-1/2"	"	18.20	.440		21	33		54	72
4570	2"	Q-1	33.10	.483		22.50	32.50		55	73.50
4580	3"		20.80	.769		81.50	51.50		133	167
4590	4"		16.50	.970		167	65		232	281
4600	6"		10.10	1.584		715	106		821	945
4650	1/8 bend, same as 1/4 bend									
4800	Tee, sanitary									
4820	1-1/4"	1 Plum	13.50	.593	Ea.	36	44		80	106
4830	1-1/2"	"	12.10	.661		31	49.50		80.50	108
4840	2"	Q-1	20	.800		48	53.50		101.50	133
4850	3"		13.90	1.151		130	77.50		207.50	258
4860	4"		11	1.455		232	97.50		329.50	400
4862	Tee, sanitary, reducing, 2" x 1-1/2"		22	.727		41.50	49		90.50	119
4864	3" x 2"		15.30	1.046		104	70.50		174.50	219
4868	4" x 3"		12.10	1.322		233	89		322	390
4870	Combination Y and 1/8 bend									
4872	1-1/2"	1 Plum	12.10	.661	Ea.	81	49.50		130.50	163
4874	2"	Q-1	20	.800		82.50	53.50		136	171
4876	3"		13.90	1.151		195	77.50		272.50	330
4878	4"		11	1.455		410	97.50		507.50	595
4880	3" x 1-1/2"		15.50	1.032		221	69.50		290.50	345
4882	4" x 3"		12.10	1.322		293	89		382	455
4900	Wye, 1-1/4"	1 Plum	13.50	.593		41.50	44		85.50	112
4902	1-1/2"	"	12.10	.661		51.50	49.50		101	130
4904	2"	Q-1	20	.800		67.50	53.50		121	154

For customer support on your Plumbing Costs with RSMeans Data call 800.448.8182.

22 11 Facility Water Distribution

22 11 13 – Facility Water Distribution Piping

22 11 13.76 Pipe Fittings, Plastic

		Crew	Daily Output	Labor-Hours	Unit	Material	2024 Bare Costs Labor	Equipment	Total	Total Incl O&P
4906	3"	Q-1	13.90	1.151	Ea.	145	77.50		222.50	274
4908	4"		11	1.455		295	97.50		392.50	470
4910	6"		6.70	2.388		885	160		1,045	1,225
4918	3" x 1-1/2"		15.50	1.032		128	69.50		197.50	244
4920	4" x 3"		12.10	1.322		254	89		343	410
4922	6" x 4"		6.90	2.319		805	156		961	1,125
4930	Double wye, 1-1/2"	1 Plum	9.10	.879		159	65.50		224.50	272
4932	2"	Q-1	16.60	.964		189	65		254	305
4934	3"		10.40	1.538		425	103		528	620
4936	4"		8.25	1.939		830	130		960	1,100
4940	2" x 1-1/2"		16.80	.952		180	64		244	293
4942	3" x 2"		10.60	1.509		296	101		397	475
4944	4" x 3"		8.45	1.893		690	127		817	950
4946	6" x 4"		7.25	2.207		945	148		1,093	1,275
4950	Reducer bushing, 2" x 1-1/2"		36.40	.440		16.55	29.50		46.05	62
4952	3" x 1-1/2"		27.30	.586		72.50	39.50		112	138
4954	4" x 2"		18.20	.879		134	59		193	236
4956	6" x 4"		11.10	1.441		375	97		472	560
4960	Couplings, 1-1/2"	1 Plum	18.20	.440		10.80	33		43.80	61
4962	2"	Q-1	33.10	.483		13.55	32.50		46.05	63.50
4963	3"		20.80	.769		40.50	51.50		92	122
4964	4"		16.50	.970		68	65		133	172
4966	6"		10.10	1.584		285	106		391	475
4970	2" x 1-1/2"		33.30	.480		29	32.50		61.50	80
4972	3" x 1-1/2"		21	.762		86	51		137	171
4974	4" x 3"		16.70	.958		128	64.50		192.50	237
4978	Closet flange, 4"	1 Plum	32	.250		77.50	18.65		96.15	113
4980	4" x 3"	"	34	.235		84.50	17.55		102.05	119
5000	DWV, PVC, schedule 40, socket joints									
5040	1/4 bend, 1-1/4"	1 Plum	20.20	.396	Ea.	56.50	29.50		86	106
5060	1-1/2"	"	18.20	.440		16.20	33		49.20	67
5070	2"	Q-1	33.10	.483		25.50	32.50		58	76.50
5080	3"		20.80	.769		75	51.50		126.50	160
5090	4"		16.50	.970		148	65		213	260
5100	6"		10.10	1.584		355	106		461	550
5105	8"	Q-2	9.30	2.581		520	180		700	835
5106	10"	"	8.50	2.824		695	197		892	1,050
5110	1/4 bend, long sweep, 1-1/2"	1 Plum	18.20	.440		37.50	33		70.50	90.50
5112	2"	Q-1	33.10	.483		28.50	32.50		61	80
5114	3"		20.80	.769		96.50	51.50		148	183
5116	4"		16.50	.970		182	65		247	298
5150	1/8 bend, 1-1/4"	1 Plum	20.20	.396		5.15	29.50		34.65	49.50
5170	1-1/2"	"	18.20	.440		1.97	33		34.97	51
5180	2"	Q-1	33.10	.483		2.93	32.50		35.43	51.50
5190	3"		20.80	.769		8.35	51.50		59.85	86
5200	4"		16.50	.970		15.15	65		80.15	114
5210	6"		10.10	1.584		55.50	106		161.50	219
5215	8"	Q-2	9.30	2.581		75.50	180		255.50	350
5216	10"		8.50	2.824		455	197		652	795
5217	12"		7.60	3.158		460	220		680	830
5250	Tee, sanitary 1-1/4"	1 Plum	13.50	.593		60.50	44		104.50	133
5254	1-1/2"	"	12.10	.661		28	49.50		77.50	105
5255	2"	Q-1	20	.800		41.50	53.50		95	126

22 11 Facility Water Distribution

22 11 13 – Facility Water Distribution Piping

22 11 13.76 Pipe Fittings, Plastic

		Crew	Daily Output	Labor-Hours	Unit	Material	2024 Bare Costs Labor	Equipment	Total	Total Incl O&P
5256	3"	Q-1	13.90	1.151	Ea.	110	77.50		187.50	236
5257	4"		11	1.455		200	97.50		297.50	365
5259	6"		6.70	2.388		805	160		965	1,125
5261	8"	Q-2	6.20	3.871		1,775	270		2,045	2,350
5276	Tee, sanitary, reducing									
5281	2" x 1-1/2" x 1-1/2"	Q-1	23	.696	Ea.	17.30	46.50		63.80	88.50
5282	2" x 1-1/2" x 2"		22	.727		21	49		70	95.50
5283	2" x 2" x 1-1/2"		22	.727		17.35	49		66.35	91.50
5284	3" x 3" x 1-1/2"		15.50	1.032		37.50	69.50		107	145
5285	3" x 3" x 2"		15.30	1.046		39	70.50		109.50	148
5286	4" x 4" x 1-1/2"		12.30	1.301		99	87.50		186.50	239
5287	4" x 4" x 2"		12.20	1.311		81.50	88		169.50	221
5288	4" x 4" x 3"		12.10	1.322		110	89		199	253
5291	6" x 6" x 4"		6.90	2.319		365	156		521	635
5294	Tee, double sanitary									
5295	1-1/2"	1 Plum	9.10	.879	Ea.	29.50	65.50		95	130
5296	2"	Q-1	16.60	.964		39.50	65		104.50	140
5297	3"		10.40	1.538		111	103		214	276
5298	4"		8.25	1.939		179	130		309	390
5303	Wye, reducing									
5304	2" x 1-1/2" x 1-1/2"	Q-1	23	.696	Ea.	71	46.50		117.50	148
5305	2" x 2" x 1-1/2"		22	.727		62	49		111	141
5306	3" x 3" x 2"		15.30	1.046		202	70.50		272.50	330
5307	4" x 4" x 2"		12.20	1.311		149	88		237	295
5309	4" x 4" x 3"		12.10	1.322		202	89		291	355
5314	Combination Y & 1/8 bend, 1-1/2"	1 Plum	12.10	.661		68.50	49.50		118	149
5315	2"	Q-1	20	.800		85.50	53.50		139	174
5317	3"		13.90	1.151		188	77.50		265.50	320
5318	4"		11	1.455		370	97.50		467.50	555
5319	6"		6.70	2.388		1,375	160		1,535	1,750
5320	8"	Q-2	6.20	3.871		2,075	270		2,345	2,675
5321	10"		5.70	4.211		3,300	293		3,593	4,050
5322	12"		5.10	4.706		3,875	330		4,205	4,775
5324	Combination Y & 1/8 bend, reducing									
5325	2" x 2" x 1-1/2"	Q-1	22	.727	Ea.	96.50	49		145.50	179
5327	3" x 3" x 1-1/2"		15.50	1.032		172	69.50		241.50	292
5328	3" x 3" x 2"		15.30	1.046		129	70.50		199.50	247
5329	4" x 4" x 2"		12.20	1.311		194	88		282	345
5331	Wye, 1-1/4"	1 Plum	13.50	.593		76	44		120	150
5332	1-1/2"	"	12.10	.661		50.50	49.50		100	129
5333	2"	Q-1	20	.800		49.50	53.50		103	135
5334	3"		13.90	1.151		134	77.50		211.50	263
5335	4"		11	1.455		244	97.50		341.50	415
5336	6"		6.70	2.388		705	160		865	1,025
5337	8"	Q-2	6.20	3.871		1,250	270		1,520	1,775
5338	10"		5.70	4.211		1,550	293		1,843	2,125
5339	12"		5.10	4.706		2,525	330		2,855	3,275
5341	2" x 1-1/2"	Q-1	22	.727		12.15	49		61.15	86
5342	3" x 1-1/2"		15.50	1.032		18	69.50		87.50	123
5343	4" x 3"		12.10	1.322		39.50	89		128.50	176
5344	6" x 4"		6.90	2.319		107	156		263	350
5345	8" x 6"	Q-2	6.40	3.750		260	261		521	675
5347	Double wye, 1-1/2"	1 Plum	9.10	.879		116	65.50		181.50	226

22 11 Facility Water Distribution

22 11 13 – Facility Water Distribution Piping

22 11 13.76 Pipe Fittings, Plastic		Crew	Daily Output	Labor-Hours	Unit	Material	2024 Bare Costs Labor	Equipment	Total	Total Incl O&P
5348	2"	Q-1	16.60	.964	Ea.	138	65		203	248
5349	3"		10.40	1.538		269	103		372	450
5350	4"		8.25	1.939		580	130		710	830
5353	Double wye, reducing									
5354	2" x 2" x 1-1/2" x 1-1/2"	Q-1	16.80	.952	Ea.	118	64		182	225
5355	3" x 3" x 2" x 2"		10.60	1.509		200	101		301	370
5356	4" x 4" x 3" x 3"		8.45	1.893		430	127		557	665
5357	6" x 6" x 4" x 4"		7.25	2.207		1,525	148		1,673	1,900
5374	Coupling, 1-1/4"	1 Plum	20.20	.396		36.50	29.50		66	84
5376	1-1/2"	"	18.20	.440		7.60	33		40.60	57.50
5378	2"	Q-1	33.10	.483		10.40	32.50		42.90	60
5380	3"		20.80	.769		36.50	51.50		88	117
5390	4"		16.50	.970		62	65		127	165
5400	6"		10.10	1.584		203	106		309	380
5402	8"	Q-2	9.30	2.581		335	180		515	635
5404	2" x 1-1/2"	Q-1	33.30	.480		23	32.50		55.50	73.50
5406	3" x 1-1/2"		21	.762		68	51		119	151
5408	4" x 3"		16.70	.958		111	64.50		175.50	218
5410	Reducer bushing, 2" x 1-1/4"		36.50	.438		6.30	29.50		35.80	51
5411	2" x 1-1/2"		36.40	.440		13.20	29.50		42.70	58.50
5412	3" x 1-1/2"		27.30	.586		59	39.50		98.50	124
5413	3" x 2"		27.10	.590		33.50	39.50		73	96
5414	4" x 2"		18.20	.879		110	59		169	210
5415	4" x 3"		16.70	.958		57	64.50		121.50	159
5416	6" x 4"		11.10	1.441		284	97		381	455
5418	8" x 6"	Q-2	10.20	2.353		555	164		719	855
5425	Closet flange 4"	Q-1	32	.500		95	33.50		128.50	155
5426	4" x 3"	"	34	.471		101	31.50		132.50	159
5450	Solvent cement for PVC, industrial grade, per quart				Qt.	32			32	35
5500	CPVC, Schedule 80, threaded joints									
5540	90° elbow, 1/4"	1 Plum	32	.250	Ea.	7.95	18.65		26.60	37
5560	1/2"		30.30	.264		5.90	19.70		25.60	36
5570	3/4"		26	.308		8.85	23		31.85	43.50
5580	1"		22.70	.352		12.40	26.50		38.90	52.50
5590	1-1/4"		20.20	.396		24	29.50		53.50	70.50
5600	1-1/2"		18.20	.440		25.50	33		58.50	77.50
5610	2"	Q-1	33.10	.483		34.50	32.50		67	86.50
5620	2-1/2"		24.20	.661		107	44.50		151.50	184
5630	3"		20.80	.769		115	51.50		166.50	203
5640	4"		16.50	.970		179	65		244	294
5650	6"		10.10	1.584		330	106		436	520
5660	45° elbow same as 90° elbow									
5700	Tee, 1/4"	1 Plum	22	.364	Ea.	19.75	27		46.75	62.50
5702	1/2"		20.20	.396		19.75	29.50		49.25	66
5704	3/4"		17.30	.462		28.50	34.50		63	83
5706	1"		15.20	.526		30.50	39.50		70	92.50
5708	1-1/4"		13.50	.593		31	44		75	100
5710	1-1/2"		12.10	.661		32.50	49.50		82	109
5712	2"	Q-1	20	.800		36	53.50		89.50	120
5714	2-1/2"		16.20	.988		177	66.50		243.50	294
5716	3"		13.90	1.151		205	77.50		282.50	340
5718	4"		11	1.455		485	97.50		582.50	680
5720	6"		6.70	2.388		865	160		1,025	1,200

22 11 Facility Water Distribution

22 11 13 – Facility Water Distribution Piping

22 11 13.76 Pipe Fittings, Plastic

		Crew	Daily Output	Labor-Hours	Unit	Material	2024 Bare Costs Labor	Equipment	Total	Total Incl O&P
5730	Coupling, 1/4"	1 Plum	32	.250	Ea.	12.95	18.65		31.60	42.50
5732	1/2"		30.30	.264		10.65	19.70		30.35	41.50
5734	3/4"		26	.308		17.20	23		40.20	53
5736	1"		22.70	.352		19.55	26.50		46.05	60.50
5738	1-1/4"		20.20	.396		20.50	29.50		50	67
5740	1-1/2"		18.20	.440		22.50	33		55.50	73.50
5742	2"	Q-1	33.10	.483		26.50	32.50		59	77.50
5744	2-1/2"		24.20	.661		47	44.50		91.50	118
5746	3"		20.80	.769		60.50	51.50		112	144
5748	4"		16.50	.970		123	65		188	232
5750	6"		10.10	1.584		242	106		348	425
5752	8"	Q-2	9.30	2.581		505	180		685	820
5900	CPVC, Schedule 80, socket joints									
5904	90° elbow, 1/4"	1 Plum	32	.250	Ea.	9.70	18.65		28.35	38.50
5906	1/2"		30.30	.264		3.79	19.70		23.49	33.50
5908	3/4"		26	.308		4.85	23		27.85	39.50
5910	1"		22.70	.352		7.70	26.50		34.20	47.50
5912	1-1/4"		20.20	.396		16.65	29.50		46.15	62.50
5914	1-1/2"		18.20	.440		18.55	33		51.55	69.50
5916	2"	Q-1	33.10	.483		22.50	32.50		55	73
5918	2-1/2"		24.20	.661		51.50	44.50		96	123
5920	3"		20.80	.769		58.50	51.50		110	142
5922	4"		16.50	.970		105	65		170	213
5924	6"		10.10	1.584		211	106		317	390
5926	8"		9.30	1.720		520	116		636	740
5930	45° elbow, 1/4"	1 Plum	32	.250		14.40	18.65		33.05	44
5932	1/2"		30.30	.264		4.64	19.70		24.34	34.50
5934	3/4"		26	.308		6.70	23		29.70	41.50
5936	1"		22.70	.352		10.65	26.50		37.15	51
5938	1-1/4"		20.20	.396		21	29.50		50.50	67
5940	1-1/2"		18.20	.440		21.50	33		54.50	72.50
5942	2"	Q-1	33.10	.483		24	32.50		56.50	75
5944	2-1/2"		24.20	.661		49.50	44.50		94	120
5946	3"		20.80	.769		63.50	51.50		115	147
5948	4"		16.50	.970		87	65		152	193
5950	6"		10.10	1.584		268	106		374	455
5952	8"		9.30	1.720		555	116		671	785
5960	Tee, 1/4"	1 Plum	22	.364		8.90	27		35.90	50.50
5962	1/2"		20.20	.396		8.90	29.50		38.40	54
5964	3/4"		17.30	.462		9.05	34.50		43.55	61.50
5966	1"		15.20	.526		11.10	39.50		50.60	70.50
5968	1-1/4"		13.50	.593		23.50	44		67.50	92
5970	1-1/2"		12.10	.661		27	49.50		76.50	103
5972	2"	Q-1	20	.800		30	53.50		83.50	113
5974	2-1/2"		16.20	.988		76	66.50		142.50	182
5976	3"		13.90	1.151		76	77.50		153.50	199
5978	4"		11	1.455		101	97.50		198.50	256
5980	6"		6.70	2.388		263	160		423	530
5982	8"	Q-2	6.20	3.871		755	270		1,025	1,225
5990	Coupling, 1/4"	1 Plum	32	.250		10.30	18.65		28.95	39.50
5992	1/2"		30.30	.264		4	19.70		23.70	34
5994	3/4"		26	.308		5.60	23		28.60	40
5996	1"		22.70	.352		7.55	26.50		34.05	47.50

22 11 Facility Water Distribution

22 11 13 – Facility Water Distribution Piping

22 11 13.76 Pipe Fittings, Plastic		Crew	Daily Output	Labor-Hours	Unit	Material	2024 Bare Costs Labor	Equipment	Total	Total Incl O&P
5998	1-1/4"	1 Plum	20.20	.396	Ea.	11.30	29.50		40.80	56.50
6000	1-1/2"	↓	18.20	.440		14.25	33		47.25	64.50
6002	2"	Q-1	33.10	.483		16.55	32.50		49.05	66.50
6004	2-1/2"		24.20	.661		37	44.50		81.50	107
6006	3"		20.80	.769		40	51.50		91.50	121
6008	4"		16.50	.970		52.50	65		117.50	155
6010	6"	↓	10.10	1.584		123	106		229	294
6012	8"	Q-2	9.30	2.581		335	180		515	630
6200	CTS, 100 psi at 180°F, hot and cold water									
6230	90° elbow, 1/2"	1 Plum	20	.400	Ea.	.47	30		30.47	45
6250	3/4"		19	.421		.78	31.50		32.28	48
6251	1"		16	.500		2.27	37.50		39.77	58
6252	1-1/4"		15	.533		4.53	40		44.53	64
6253	1-1/2"	↓	14	.571		8.15	42.50		50.65	72.50
6254	2"	Q-1	23	.696		15.70	46.50		62.20	87
6260	45° elbow, 1/2"	1 Plum	20	.400		.60	30		30.60	45
6280	3/4"		19	.421		1.04	31.50		32.54	48
6281	1"		16	.500		2.63	37.50		40.13	58.50
6282	1-1/4"		15	.533		5.60	40		45.60	65
6283	1-1/2"	↓	14	.571		8.10	42.50		50.60	72.50
6284	2"	Q-1	23	.696		16.95	46.50		63.45	88
6290	Tee, 1/2"	1 Plum	13	.615		.61	46		46.61	69
6310	3/4"		12	.667		1.13	50		51.13	75
6311	1"		11	.727		5.70	54.50		60.20	87.50
6312	1-1/4"		10	.800		8.75	59.50		68.25	98.50
6313	1-1/2"	↓	10	.800		12.45	59.50		71.95	103
6314	2"	Q-1	17	.941		18.45	63		81.45	115
6320	Coupling, 1/2"	1 Plum	22	.364		.38	27		27.38	41
6340	3/4"		21	.381		.80	28.50		29.30	43.50
6341	1"		18	.444		2.68	33		35.68	52.50
6342	1-1/4"		17	.471		3.26	35		38.26	56
6343	1-1/2"	↓	16	.500		4.60	37.50		42.10	60.50
6344	2"	Q-1	28	.571	↓	8.75	38.50		47.25	66.50
6360	Solvent cement for CPVC, commercial grade, per quart				Qt.	38			38	41.50
7340	PVC flange, slip-on, Sch 80 std., 1/2"	1 Plum	22	.364	Ea.	11.85	27		38.85	53.50
7350	3/4"		21	.381		12.65	28.50		41.15	56.50
7360	1"		18	.444		14.15	33		47.15	65
7370	1-1/4"		17	.471		14.65	35		49.65	68.50
7380	1-1/2"	↓	16	.500		14.95	37.50		52.45	72
7390	2"	Q-1	26	.615		20.50	41.50		62	84
7400	2-1/2"		24	.667		29	45		74	98
7410	3"		18	.889		34	59.50		93.50	127
7420	4"		15	1.067		40	71.50		111.50	152
7430	6"	↓	10	1.600		67.50	107		174.50	234
7440	8"	Q-2	11	2.182		189	152		341	435
7550	Union, schedule 40, socket joints, 1/2"	1 Plum	19	.421		4.30	31.50		35.80	51.50
7560	3/4"		18	.444		4.88	33		37.88	55
7570	1"		15	.533		5.05	40		45.05	64.50
7580	1-1/4"		14	.571		15.90	42.50		58.40	81
7590	1-1/2"	↓	13	.615		16.90	46		62.90	87
7600	2"	Q-1	20	.800		23	53.50		76.50	105
7992	Polybutyl/polyethyl pipe, for copper fittings see Line 22 11 13.25 7000									
8000	Compression type, PVC, 160 psi cold water									

22 11 Facility Water Distribution

22 11 13 – Facility Water Distribution Piping

22 11 13.76	Pipe Fittings, Plastic	Crew	Daily Output	Labor-Hours	Unit	Material	2024 Bare Costs Labor	Equipment	Total	Total Incl O&P
8010	Coupling, 3/4" CTS	1 Plum	21	.381	Ea.	2.94	28.50		31.44	45.50
8020	1" CTS		18	.444		3.66	33		36.66	53.50
8030	1-1/4" CTS		17	.471		5.15	35		40.15	58
8040	1-1/2" CTS		16	.500		7.05	37.50		44.55	63.50
8050	2" CTS		15	.533		9.75	40		49.75	70
8060	Female adapter, 3/4" FPT x 3/4" CTS		23	.348		11.25	26		37.25	51
8070	3/4" FPT x 1" CTS		21	.381		9.25	28.50		37.75	52.50
8080	1" FPT x 1" CTS		20	.400		8.10	30		38.10	53.50
8090	1-1/4" FPT x 1-1/4" CTS		18	.444		11.45	33		44.45	62
8100	1-1/2" FPT x 1-1/2" CTS		16	.500		13.05	37.50		50.55	70
8110	2" FPT x 2" CTS		13	.615		24.50	46		70.50	95
8130	Male adapter, 3/4" MPT x 3/4" CTS		23	.348		9.35	26		35.35	49
8140	3/4" MPT x 1" CTS		21	.381		7.85	28.50		36.35	51
8150	1" MPT x 1" CTS		20	.400		11.15	30		41.15	57
8160	1-1/4" MPT x 1-1/4" CTS		18	.444		15	33		48	66
8170	1-1/2" MPT x 1-1/2" CTS		16	.500		18.05	37.50		55.55	75.50
8180	2" MPT x 2" CTS		13	.615		23.50	46		69.50	94.50
8200	Spigot adapter, 3/4" IPS x 3/4" CTS		23	.348		1.98	26		27.98	40.50
8210	3/4" IPS x 1" CTS		21	.381		3.02	28.50		31.52	46
8220	1" IPS x 1" CTS		20	.400		2.42	30		32.42	47
8230	1-1/4" IPS x 1-1/4" CTS		18	.444		3.65	33		36.65	53.50
8240	1-1/2" IPS x 1-1/2" CTS		16	.500		3.82	37.50		41.32	59.50
8250	2" IPS x 2" CTS		13	.615		4.73	46		50.73	73.50
8270	Price includes insert stiffeners									
8280	250 psi is same price as 160 psi									
8300	Insert type, nylon, 160 & 250 psi, cold water									
8310	Clamp ring stainless steel, 3/4" IPS	1 Plum	115	.070	Ea.	3.24	5.20		8.44	11.30
8320	1" IPS		107	.075		3.90	5.60		9.50	12.60
8330	1-1/4" IPS		101	.079		3.33	5.90		9.23	12.45
8340	1-1/2" IPS		95	.084		4.63	6.30		10.93	14.45
8350	2" IPS		85	.094		6.05	7.05		13.10	17.10
8370	Coupling, 3/4" IPS		22	.364		.79	27		27.79	41.50
8380	1" IPS		19	.421		.83	31.50		32.33	48
8390	1-1/4" IPS		18	.444		1.22	33		34.22	51
8400	1-1/2" IPS		17	.471		1.44	35		36.44	54
8410	2" IPS		16	.500		2.73	37.50		40.23	58.50
8430	Elbow, 90°, 3/4" IPS		22	.364		1.58	27		28.58	42
8440	1" IPS		19	.421		1.74	31.50		33.24	49
8450	1-1/4" IPS		18	.444		1.95	33		34.95	51.50
8460	1-1/2" IPS		17	.471		2.30	35		37.30	55
8470	2" IPS		16	.500		3.21	37.50		40.71	59
8490	Male adapter, 3/4" IPS x 3/4" MPT		25	.320		.79	24		24.79	36.50
8500	1" IPS x 1" MPT		21	.381		.81	28.50		29.31	43.50
8510	1-1/4" IPS x 1-1/4" MPT		20	.400		1.29	30		31.29	46
8520	1-1/2" IPS x 1-1/2" MPT		18	.444		1.44	33		34.44	51
8530	2" IPS x 2" MPT		15	.533		2.77	40		42.77	62
8550	Tee, 3/4" IPS		14	.571		1.53	42.50		44.03	65
8560	1" IPS		13	.615		1.98	46		47.98	70.50
8570	1-1/4" IPS		12	.667		3.10	50		53.10	77.50
8580	1-1/2" IPS		11	.727		3.52	54.50		58.02	85
8590	2" IPS		10	.800		6.95	59.50		66.45	96.50
8610	Insert type, PVC, 100 psi @ 180°F, hot & cold water									
8620	Coupler, male, 3/8" CTS x 3/8" MPT	1 Plum	29	.276	Ea.	.88	20.50		21.38	31.50

22 11 Facility Water Distribution

22 11 13 – Facility Water Distribution Piping

22 11 13.76	Pipe Fittings, Plastic	Crew	Daily Output	Labor-Hours	Unit	Material	2024 Bare Costs Labor	Equipment	Total	Total Incl O&P
8630	3/8" CTS x 1/2" MPT	1 Plum	28	.286	Ea.	.88	21.50		22.38	32.50
8640	1/2" CTS x 1/2" MPT		27	.296		.89	22		22.89	34
8650	1/2" CTS x 3/4" MPT		26	.308		2.04	23		25.04	36
8660	3/4" CTS x 1/2" MPT		25	.320		1.85	24		25.85	37.50
8670	3/4" CTS x 3/4" MPT		25	.320		1.19	24		25.19	37
8700	Coupling, 3/8" CTS x 1/2" CTS		25	.320		4.76	24		28.76	41
8710	1/2" CTS		23	.348		6.35	26		32.35	45.50
8730	3/4" CTS		22	.364		14.60	27		41.60	56.50
8750	Elbow 90°, 3/8" CTS		25	.320		4.65	24		28.65	40.50
8760	1/2" CTS		23	.348		6.30	26		32.30	45.50
8770	3/4" CTS		22	.364		8.60	27		35.60	50
8800	Rings, crimp, copper, 3/8" CTS		120	.067		.24	4.98		5.22	7.65
8810	1/2" CTS		117	.068		.25	5.10		5.35	7.90
8820	3/4" CTS		115	.070		.33	5.20		5.53	8.10
8850	Reducer tee, bronze, 3/8" x 3/8" x 1/2" CTS		17	.471		5.50	35		40.50	58.50
8860	1/2" x 1/2" x 3/4" CTS		15	.533		11.95	40		51.95	72
8870	3/4" x 1/2" x 1/2" CTS		14	.571		11.80	42.50		54.30	76.50
8890	3/4" x 3/4" x 1/2" CTS		14	.571		11.85	42.50		54.35	76.50
8900	1" x 1/2" x 1/2" CTS		14	.571		20	42.50		62.50	85.50
8930	Tee, 3/8" CTS		17	.471		3.48	35		38.48	56.50
8940	1/2" CTS		15	.533		3.22	40		43.22	62.50
8950	3/4" CTS		14	.571		4.06	42.50		46.56	68
8960	Copper rings included in fitting price									
9000	Flare type, assembled, acetal, hot & cold water									
9010	Coupling, 1/4" & 3/8" CTS	1 Plum	24	.333	Ea.	3.98	25		28.98	41.50
9020	1/2" CTS		22	.364		4.55	27		31.55	45.50
9030	3/4" CTS		21	.381		6.75	28.50		35.25	50
9040	1" CTS		18	.444		8.60	33		41.60	59
9050	Elbow 90°, 1/4" CTS		26	.308		4.41	23		27.41	39
9060	3/8" CTS		24	.333		4.73	25		29.73	42
9070	1/2" CTS		22	.364		5.60	27		32.60	46.50
9080	3/4" CTS		21	.381		8.60	28.50		37.10	52
9090	1" CTS		18	.444		12.40	33		45.40	63
9110	Tee, 1/4" CTS		16	.500		4.68	37.50		42.18	60.50
9114	3/8" CTS		15	.533		5.25	40		45.25	65
9120	1/2" CTS		14	.571		6.25	42.50		48.75	70.50
9130	3/4" CTS		13	.615		9.75	46		55.75	79.50
9140	1" CTS		12	.667		13.10	50		63.10	88.50
9400	Polypropylene, fittings and accessories									
9404	Fittings fusion welded, sizes are ID									
9408	Note: sizes 1/2" thru 4" use socket fusion									
9410	Sizes 6" thru 10" use butt fusion									
9416	Coupling									
9420	3/8"	1 Plum	39	.205	Ea.	1.07	15.30		16.37	24
9422	1/2"		37.40	.214		1.21	15.95		17.16	25.50
9424	3/4"		35.40	.226		1.34	16.85		18.19	26.50
9426	1"		29.70	.269		1.77	20		21.77	32
9428	1-1/4"		27.60	.290		2.12	21.50		23.62	34.50
9430	1-1/2"		24.80	.323		4.45	24		28.45	41
9432	2"	Q-1	43	.372		8.90	25		33.90	47
9434	2-1/2"		35.60	.449		9.95	30		39.95	56
9436	3"		30.90	.518		22	35		57	75.50
9438	3-1/2"		27.80	.576		35.50	38.50		74	96.50

22 11 Facility Water Distribution

22 11 13 – Facility Water Distribution Piping

22 11 13.76 Pipe Fittings, Plastic

		Crew	Daily Output	Labor-Hours	Unit	Material	2024 Bare Costs Labor	Equipment	Total	Total Incl O&P
9440	4"	Q-1	25	.640	Ea.	47	43		90	116
9442	Reducing coupling, female to female									
9446	2" to 1-1/2"	Q-1	49	.327	Ea.	17.10	22		39.10	51.50
9448	2-1/2" to 2"		41.20	.388		18.80	26		44.80	59.50
9450	3" to 2-1/2"	▼	33.10	.483	▼	19	32.50		51.50	69.50
9470	Reducing bushing, female to female									
9472	1/2" to 3/8"	1 Plum	38.20	.209	Ea.	1.43	15.65		17.08	25
9474	3/4" to 3/8" or 1/2"		36.50	.219		1.79	16.35		18.14	26.50
9476	1" to 3/4" or 1/2"		33.10	.242		2.39	18.05		20.44	29.50
9478	1-1/4" to 3/4" or 1"		28.70	.279		3.68	21		24.68	35
9480	1-1/2" to 1/2" thru 1-1/4"	▼	26.20	.305		6.10	23		29.10	40.50
9482	2" to 1/2" thru 1-1/2"	Q-1	43	.372		12.20	25		37.20	50.50
9484	2-1/2" to 1/2" thru 2"		41.20	.388		13.65	26		39.65	54
9486	3" to 1-1/2" thru 2-1/2"		33.10	.483		22.50	32.50		55	73.50
9488	3-1/2" to 2" thru 3"		29.20	.548		48.50	37		85.50	109
9490	4" to 2-1/2" thru 3-1/2"		26.20	.611		57	41		98	124
9491	6" to 4" SDR 7.4		16.50	.970		90.50	65		155.50	197
9492	6" to 4" SDR 11		16.50	.970		76	65		141	181
9493	8" to 6" SDR 7.4		10.10	1.584		134	106		240	305
9494	8" to 6" SDR 11		10.10	1.584		85.50	106		191.50	252
9495	10" to 8" SDR 7.4		7.80	2.051		183	138		321	405
9496	10" to 8" SDR 11	▼	7.80	2.051	▼	126	138		264	345
9500	90° elbow									
9504	3/8"	1 Plum	39	.205	Ea.	1.43	15.30		16.73	24.50
9506	1/2"		37.40	.214		1.72	15.95		17.67	26
9508	3/4"		35.40	.226		2.21	16.85		19.06	27.50
9510	1"		29.70	.269		2.39	20		22.39	32.50
9512	1-1/4"		27.60	.290		4.91	21.50		26.41	37.50
9514	1-1/2"	▼	24.80	.323		10.55	24		34.55	47.50
9516	2"	Q-1	43	.372		16.25	25		41.25	55
9518	2-1/2"		35.60	.449		36	30		66	84.50
9520	3"		30.90	.518		60	35		95	118
9522	3-1/2"		27.80	.576		85	38.50		123.50	151
9524	4"		25	.640		98	43		141	172
9526	6" SDR 7.4		5.55	2.883		189	194		383	495
9528	6" SDR 11	▼	5.55	2.883		157	194		351	460
9530	8" SDR 7.4	Q-2	8.10	2.963		360	206		566	700
9532	8" SDR 11		8.10	2.963		262	206		468	595
9534	10" SDR 7.4		7.50	3.200		485	223		708	865
9536	10" SDR 11	▼	7.50	3.200	▼	355	223		578	720
9551	45° elbow									
9554	3/8"	1 Plum	39	.205	Ea.	1.43	15.30		16.73	24.50
9556	1/2"		37.40	.214		1.72	15.95		17.67	26
9558	3/4"		35.40	.226		2.21	16.85		19.06	27.50
9564	1"		29.70	.269		3.19	20		23.19	33.50
9566	1-1/4"		27.60	.290		4.91	21.50		26.41	37.50
9568	1-1/2"	▼	24.80	.323		10.55	24		34.55	47.50
9570	2"	Q-1	43	.372		16.05	25		41.05	54.50
9572	2-1/2"		35.60	.449		35.50	30		65.50	84
9574	3"		30.90	.518		65.50	35		100.50	124
9576	3-1/2"		27.80	.576		93.50	38.50		132	161
9578	4"		25	.640		144	43		187	222
9580	6" SDR 7.4		5.55	2.883	▼	161	194		355	465

22 11 Facility Water Distribution

22 11 13 – Facility Water Distribution Piping

22 11 13.76 Pipe Fittings, Plastic

		Crew	Daily Output	Labor-Hours	Unit	Material	2024 Bare Costs Labor	Equipment	Total	Total Incl O&P
9582	6" SDR 11	Q-1	5.55	2.883	Ea.	154	194		348	455
9584	8" SDR 7.4	Q-2	8.10	2.963		325	206		531	665
9586	8" SDR 11		8.10	2.963		247	206		453	575
9588	10" SDR 7.4		7.50	3.200		525	223		748	910
9590	10" SDR 11		7.50	3.200		325	223		548	690
9600	Tee									
9604	3/8"	1 Plum	26	.308	Ea.	1.91	23		24.91	36
9606	1/2"		24.90	.321		2.32	24		26.32	38
9608	3/4"		23.70	.338		3.19	25		28.19	41
9610	1"		19.90	.402		2.93	30		32.93	47.50
9612	1-1/4"		18.50	.432		6.20	32.50		38.70	55
9614	1-1/2"		16.60	.482		17.70	36		53.70	73
9616	2"	Q-1	26.80	.597		18.95	40		58.95	80.50
9618	2-1/2"		23.80	.672		32	45		77	102
9620	3"		20.60	.777		52.50	52		104.50	135
9622	3-1/2"		18.40	.870		109	58.50		167.50	207
9624	4"		16.70	.958		145	64.50		209.50	256
9626	6" SDR 7.4		3.70	4.324		200	291		491	650
9628	6" SDR 11		3.70	4.324		160	291		451	605
9630	8" SDR 7.4	Q-2	5.40	4.444		435	310		745	940
9632	8" SDR 11		5.40	4.444		325	310		635	815
9634	10" SDR 7.4		5	4.800		755	335		1,090	1,325
9636	10" SDR 11		5	4.800		510	335		845	1,050
9638	For reducing tee use same tee price									
9660	End cap									
9662	3/8"	1 Plum	78	.103	Ea.	2.03	7.65		9.68	13.65
9664	1/2"		74.60	.107		2.52	8		10.52	14.65
9666	3/4"		71.40	.112		3.19	8.35		11.54	15.95
9668	1"		59.50	.134		3.87	10.05		13.92	19.20
9670	1-1/4"		55.60	.144		6.10	10.75		16.85	22.50
9672	1-1/2"		49.50	.162		6.30	12.05		18.35	25
9674	2"	Q-1	80	.200		10.55	13.45		24	31.50
9676	2-1/2"		71.40	.224		20.50	15.05		35.55	45
9678	3"		61.70	.259		46	17.40		63.40	76.50
9680	3-1/2"		55.20	.290		55.50	19.45		74.95	90
9682	4"		50	.320		84.50	21.50		106	125
9684	6" SDR 7.4		26.50	.604		116	40.50		156.50	188
9686	6" SDR 11		26.50	.604		89.50	40.50		130	159
9688	8" SDR 7.4	Q-2	16.30	1.472		116	103		219	281
9690	8" SDR 11		16.30	1.472		96.50	103		199.50	259
9692	10" SDR 7.4		14.90	1.611		174	112		286	360
9694	10" SDR 11		14.90	1.611		119	112		231	298
9800	Accessories and tools									
9802	Pipe clamps for suspension, not including rod or beam clamp									
9804	3/8"	1 Plum	74	.108	Ea.	2.63	8.05		10.68	14.90
9805	1/2"		70	.114		3.29	8.55		11.84	16.30
9806	3/4"		68	.118		3.34	8.80		12.14	16.70
9807	1"		66	.121		4.14	9.05		13.19	18
9808	1-1/4"		64	.125		4.23	9.35		13.58	18.55
9809	1-1/2"		62	.129		5.70	9.65		15.35	20.50
9810	2"	Q-1	110	.145		5.75	9.75		15.50	21
9811	2-1/2"		104	.154		7.40	10.35		17.75	23.50
9812	3"		98	.163		8.60	10.95		19.55	26

22 11 Facility Water Distribution

22 11 13 – Facility Water Distribution Piping

22 11 13.76 Pipe Fittings, Plastic

		Crew	Daily Output	Labor-Hours	Unit	Material	2024 Bare Costs Labor	2024 Bare Costs Equipment	Total	Total Incl O&P
9813	3-1/2"	Q-1	92	.174	Ea.	8.70	11.70		20.40	27
9814	4"		86	.186		16.70	12.50		29.20	37
9815	6"	↓	70	.229		11.90	15.35		27.25	36
9816	8"	Q-2	100	.240		42.50	16.70		59.20	72
9817	10"	"	94	.255	↓	48.50	17.80		66.30	80
9820	Pipe cutter									
9822	For 3/8" thru 1-1/4"				Ea.	132			132	145
9824	For 1-1/2" thru 4"				"	189			189	208
9826	Note: Pipes may be cut with standard									
9827	iron saw with blades for plastic.									
9982	For plastic hangers see Line 22 05 29.10 8000									
9986	For copper/brass fittings see Line 22 11 13.25 7000									

22 11 13.78 Pipe, High Density Polyethylene Plastic (HDPE)

		Crew	Daily Output	Labor-Hours	Unit	Material	2024 Bare Costs Labor	2024 Bare Costs Equipment	Total	Total Incl O&P
0010	**PIPE, HIGH DENSITY POLYETHYLENE PLASTIC (HDPE)**									
0020	Not incl. hangers, trenching, backfill, hoisting or digging equipment.									
0030	Standard length is 40', add a weld for each joint									
0035	For HDPE weld machine see 015433401685 in equipment rental									
0040	Single wall									
0050	Straight									
0054	1" diameter DR 11				L.F.	.86			.86	.95
0058	1-1/2" diameter DR 11					1.48			1.48	1.63
0062	2" diameter DR 11					2.15			2.15	2.37
0066	3" diameter DR 11					4.57			4.57	5.05
0070	3" diameter DR 17					2.59			2.59	2.85
0074	4" diameter DR 11					5.35			5.35	5.90
0078	4" diameter DR 17					3.62			3.62	3.98
0082	6" diameter DR 11					10.50			10.50	11.55
0086	6" diameter DR 17					7.20			7.20	7.90
0090	8" diameter DR 11					18.40			18.40	20
0094	8" diameter DR 26					7.35			7.35	8.05
0098	10" diameter DR 11					27.50			27.50	30.50
0102	10" diameter DR 26					21.50			21.50	23.50
0106	12" diameter DR 11					39			39	43
0110	12" diameter DR 26					32			32	35
0114	16" diameter DR 11					103			103	113
0118	16" diameter DR 26					46			46	50.50
0122	18" diameter DR 11					131			131	144
0126	18" diameter DR 26					60.50			60.50	66.50
0130	20" diameter DR 11					160			160	176
0134	20" diameter DR 26					71			71	78
0138	22" diameter DR 11					195			195	215
0142	22" diameter DR 26					88.50			88.50	97.50
0146	24" diameter DR 11					231			231	254
0150	24" diameter DR 26					103			103	113
0154	28" diameter DR 17					213			213	234
0158	28" diameter DR 26					142			142	156
0162	30" diameter DR 21					199			199	219
0166	30" diameter DR 26					163			163	179
0170	36" diameter DR 26					163			163	179
0174	42" diameter DR 26					315			315	345
0178	48" diameter DR 26					415			415	455
0182	54" diameter DR 26				↓	520			520	575

22 11 Facility Water Distribution

22 11 13 – Facility Water Distribution Piping

22 11 13.78 Pipe, High Density Polyethylene Plastic (HDPE)		Crew	Daily Output	Labor-Hours	Unit	Material	2024 Bare Costs Labor	Equipment	Total	Total Incl O&P
0300	90° elbow									
0304	1" diameter DR 11				Ea.	7.30			7.30	8
0308	1-1/2" diameter DR 11					12.15			12.15	13.35
0312	2" diameter DR 11					11.95			11.95	13.15
0316	3" diameter DR 11					19.20			19.20	21
0320	3" diameter DR 17					21			21	23
0324	4" diameter DR 11					25			25	27.50
0328	4" diameter DR 17					24.50			24.50	27
0332	6" diameter DR 11					77			77	84.50
0336	6" diameter DR 17					71.50			71.50	78.50
0340	8" diameter DR 11					197			197	217
0344	8" diameter DR 26					180			180	198
0348	10" diameter DR 11					540			540	595
0352	10" diameter DR 26					700			700	770
0356	12" diameter DR 11					625			625	685
0360	12" diameter DR 26					725			725	795
0364	16" diameter DR 11					950			950	1,050
0368	16" diameter DR 26					935			935	1,025
0372	18" diameter DR 11					1,200			1,200	1,300
0376	18" diameter DR 26					1,125			1,125	1,225
0380	20" diameter DR 11					1,400			1,400	1,550
0384	20" diameter DR 26					1,350			1,350	1,500
0388	22" diameter DR 11					1,450			1,450	1,600
0392	22" diameter DR 26					1,400			1,400	1,550
0396	24" diameter DR 11					1,625			1,625	1,800
0400	24" diameter DR 26					1,600			1,600	1,750
0404	28" diameter DR 17					1,975			1,975	2,175
0408	28" diameter DR 26					1,875			1,875	2,050
0412	30" diameter DR 17					2,800			2,800	3,075
0416	30" diameter DR 26					2,575			2,575	2,825
0420	36" diameter DR 26					3,275			3,275	3,600
0424	42" diameter DR 26					4,200			4,200	4,625
0428	48" diameter DR 26					4,900			4,900	5,400
0432	54" diameter DR 26					11,700			11,700	12,900
0500	45° elbow									
0512	2" diameter DR 11				Ea.	10.30			10.30	11.35
0516	3" diameter DR 11					25.50			25.50	28.50
0520	3" diameter DR 17					25.50			25.50	28.50
0524	4" diameter DR 11					36			36	39.50
0528	4" diameter DR 17					36			36	39.50
0532	6" diameter DR 11					82			82	90.50
0536	6" diameter DR 17					82			82	90.50
0540	8" diameter DR 11					203			203	223
0544	8" diameter DR 26					118			118	130
0548	10" diameter DR 11					760			760	835
0552	10" diameter DR 26					700			700	770
0556	12" diameter DR 11					800			800	880
0560	12" diameter DR 26					725			725	795
0564	16" diameter DR 11					420			420	465
0568	16" diameter DR 26					395			395	435
0572	18" diameter DR 11					445			445	490
0576	18" diameter DR 26					410			410	450
0580	20" diameter DR 11					680			680	745

22 11 Facility Water Distribution

22 11 13 – Facility Water Distribution Piping

22 11 13.78 Pipe, High Density Polyethylene Plastic (HDPE)		Crew	Daily Output	Labor-Hours	Unit	Material	2024 Bare Costs Labor	Equipment	Total	Total Incl O&P
0584	20" diameter DR 26				Ea.	645			645	705
0588	22" diameter DR 11					935			935	1,025
0592	22" diameter DR 26					890			890	975
0596	24" diameter DR 11					1,150			1,150	1,250
0600	24" diameter DR 26					1,100			1,100	1,200
0604	28" diameter DR 17					1,300			1,300	1,425
0608	28" diameter DR 26					1,250			1,250	1,400
0612	30" diameter DR 17					1,600			1,600	1,775
0616	30" diameter DR 26					1,575			1,575	1,725
0620	36" diameter DR 26					2,000			2,000	2,200
0624	42" diameter DR 26					2,550			2,550	2,800
0628	48" diameter DR 26					2,775			2,775	3,050
0632	54" diameter DR 26				▼	3,725			3,725	4,075
0700	Tee									
0704	1" diameter DR 11				Ea.	13.40			13.40	14.75
0708	1-1/2" diameter DR 11					18.80			18.80	20.50
0712	2" diameter DR 11					16.10			16.10	17.75
0716	3" diameter DR 11					29.50			29.50	32.50
0720	3" diameter DR 17					29.50			29.50	32.50
0724	4" diameter DR 11					43			43	47.50
0728	4" diameter DR 17					43			43	47.50
0732	6" diameter DR 11					107			107	118
0736	6" diameter DR 17					107			107	118
0740	8" diameter DR 11					266			266	293
0744	8" diameter DR 17					266			266	293
0748	10" diameter DR 11					790			790	870
0752	10" diameter DR 17					790			790	870
0756	12" diameter DR 11					1,050			1,050	1,175
0760	12" diameter DR 17					1,050			1,050	1,175
0764	16" diameter DR 11					560			560	615
0768	16" diameter DR 17					460			460	505
0772	18" diameter DR 11					785			785	865
0776	18" diameter DR 17					645			645	710
0780	20" diameter DR 11					965			965	1,050
0784	20" diameter DR 17					785			785	865
0788	22" diameter DR 11					1,225			1,225	1,350
0792	22" diameter DR 17					975			975	1,075
0796	24" diameter DR 11					1,525			1,525	1,675
0800	24" diameter DR 17					1,300			1,300	1,425
0804	28" diameter DR 17					2,500			2,500	2,750
0812	30" diameter DR 17					2,850			2,850	3,150
0820	36" diameter DR 17					4,725			4,725	5,200
0824	42" diameter DR 26					5,250			5,250	5,775
0828	48" diameter DR 26				▼	5,650			5,650	6,200
1000	Flange adptr, w/back-up ring and 1/2 cost of plated bolt set									
1004	1" diameter DR 11				Ea.	51			51	56
1008	1-1/2" diameter DR 11					51			51	56
1012	2" diameter DR 11					22			22	24
1016	3" diameter DR 11					37.50			37.50	41.50
1020	3" diameter DR 17					37.50			37.50	41.50
1024	4" diameter DR 11					51			51	56
1028	4" diameter DR 17					51			51	56
1032	6" diameter DR 11				▼	72.50			72.50	80

22 11 Facility Water Distribution

22 11 13 – Facility Water Distribution Piping

22 11 13.78 Pipe, High Density Polyethylene Plastic (HDPE)

		Crew	Daily Output	Labor-Hours	Unit	Material	2024 Bare Costs Labor	Equipment	Total	Total Incl O&P
1036	6" diameter DR 17				Ea.	72.50			72.50	80
1040	8" diameter DR 11					105			105	115
1044	8" diameter DR 26					105			105	115
1048	10" diameter DR 11					103			103	113
1052	10" diameter DR 26					167			167	183
1056	12" diameter DR 11					245			245	269
1060	12" diameter DR 26					245			245	269
1064	16" diameter DR 11					525			525	575
1068	16" diameter DR 26					525			525	575
1072	18" diameter DR 11					680			680	750
1076	18" diameter DR 26					680			680	750
1080	20" diameter DR 11					945			945	1,025
1084	20" diameter DR 26					945			945	1,025
1088	22" diameter DR 11					1,025			1,025	1,125
1092	22" diameter DR 26					1,025			1,025	1,125
1096	24" diameter DR 17					1,100			1,100	1,225
1100	24" diameter DR 32.5					1,100			1,100	1,225
1104	28" diameter DR 15.5					1,500			1,500	1,650
1108	28" diameter DR 32.5					1,500			1,500	1,650
1112	30" diameter DR 11					1,750			1,750	1,925
1116	30" diameter DR 21					1,750			1,750	1,925
1120	36" diameter DR 26					1,900			1,900	2,100
1124	42" diameter DR 26					2,175			2,175	2,400
1128	48" diameter DR 26					2,650			2,650	2,925
1132	54" diameter DR 26					3,225			3,225	3,550
1200	Reducer									
1208	2" x 1-1/2" diameter DR 11				Ea.	15.45			15.45	17
1212	3" x 2" diameter DR 11					15.45			15.45	17
1216	4" x 2" diameter DR 11					18			18	19.80
1220	4" x 3" diameter DR 11					23			23	25.50
1224	6" x 4" diameter DR 11					54			54	59.50
1228	8" x 6" diameter DR 11					82			82	90.50
1232	10" x 8" diameter DR 11					141			141	156
1236	12" x 8" diameter DR 11					231			231	254
1240	12" x 10" diameter DR 11					185			185	204
1244	14" x 12" diameter DR 11					206			206	226
1248	16" x 14" diameter DR 11					262			262	288
1252	18" x 16" diameter DR 11					320			320	350
1256	20" x 18" diameter DR 11					630			630	695
1260	22" x 20" diameter DR 11					775			775	855
1264	24" x 22" diameter DR 11					875			875	960
1268	26" x 24" diameter DR 11					1,025			1,025	1,125
1272	28" x 24" diameter DR 11					1,300			1,300	1,450
1276	32" x 28" diameter DR 17					1,700			1,700	1,875
1280	36" x 32" diameter DR 17					2,325			2,325	2,550
4000	Welding labor per joint, not including welding machine									
4010	Pipe joint size (cost based on thickest wall for each diam.)									
4030	1" pipe size	4 Skwk	273	.117	Ea.		7.45		7.45	11.15
4040	1-1/2" pipe size		175	.183			11.60		11.60	17.35
4050	2" pipe size		128	.250			15.90		15.90	24
4060	3" pipe size		100	.320			20.50		20.50	30.50
4070	4" pipe size		77	.416			26.50		26.50	39.50
4080	6" pipe size	5 Skwk	63	.635			40.50		40.50	60.50

22 11 Facility Water Distribution

22 11 13 - Facility Water Distribution Piping

22 11 13.78 Pipe, High Density Polyethylene Plastic (HDPE)

		Crew	Daily Output	Labor-Hours	Unit	Material	2024 Bare Costs Labor	2024 Bare Costs Equipment	Total	Total Incl O&P
4090	8" pipe size	5 Skwk	48	.833	Ea.		53		53	79
4100	10" pipe size	↓	40	1			63.50		63.50	95
4110	12" pipe size	6 Skwk	41	1.171			74.50		74.50	111
4120	16" pipe size		34	1.412			89.50		89.50	134
4130	18" pipe size	↓	32	1.500			95.50		95.50	143
4140	20" pipe size	8 Skwk	37	1.730			110		110	164
4150	22" pipe size		35	1.829			116		116	174
4160	24" pipe size		34	1.882			120		120	179
4170	28" pipe size		33	1.939			123		123	184
4180	30" pipe size		32	2			127		127	190
4190	36" pipe size		31	2.065			131		131	196
4200	42" pipe size	↓	30	2.133			135		135	203
4210	48" pipe size	9 Skwk	33	2.182			139		139	207
4220	54" pipe size	"	31	2.323	↓		147		147	221
5000	Dual wall contained pipe									
5040	Straight									
5054	1" DR 11 x 3" DR 11				L.F.	9.70			9.70	10.65
5058	1" DR 11 x 4" DR 11					10.25			10.25	11.25
5062	1-1/2" DR 11 x 4" DR 17					11.30			11.30	12.40
5066	2" DR 11 x 4" DR 17					11.90			11.90	13.10
5070	2" DR 11 x 6" DR 17					18			18	19.80
5074	3" DR 11 x 6" DR 17					20			20	22
5078	3" DR 11 x 6" DR 26					17.25			17.25	18.95
5086	3" DR 17 x 8" DR 17					22			22	24
5090	4" DR 11 x 8" DR 17					30.50			30.50	33.50
5094	4" DR 17 x 8" DR 26					24			24	26
5098	6" DR 11 x 10" DR 17					47.50			47.50	52
5102	6" DR 17 x 10" DR 26					32			32	35.50
5106	6" DR 26 x 10" DR 26					30			30	33
5110	8" DR 17 x 12" DR 26					46.50			46.50	51
5114	8" DR 26 x 12" DR 32.5					42.50			42.50	46.50
5118	10" DR 17 x 14" DR 26					69.50			69.50	76
5122	10" DR 17 x 16" DR 26					49.50			49.50	54.50
5126	10" DR 26 x 16" DR 26					66			66	72.50
5130	12" DR 26 x 16" DR 26					69.50			69.50	76.50
5134	12" DR 17 x 18" DR 26					96.50			96.50	106
5138	12" DR 26 x 18" DR 26					91.50			91.50	101
5142	14" DR 26 x 20" DR 32.5					93.50			93.50	103
5146	16" DR 26 x 22" DR 32.5					103			103	113
5150	18" DR 26 x 24" DR 32.5					128			128	141
5154	20" DR 32.5 x 28" DR 32.5					145			145	160
5158	22" DR 32.5 x 30" DR 32.5					145			145	160
5162	24" DR 32.5 x 32" DR 32.5					151			151	166
5166	36" DR 32.5 x 42" DR 32.5				↓	176			176	194
5300	Force transfer coupling									
5354	1" DR 11 x 3" DR 11				Ea.	335			335	370
5358	1" DR 11 x 4" DR 17					395			395	435
5362	1-1/2" DR 11 x 4" DR 17					380			380	415
5366	2" DR 11 x 4" DR 17					380			380	415
5370	2" DR 11 x 6" DR 17					650			650	715
5374	3" DR 11 x 6" DR 17					695			695	760
5378	3" DR 11 x 6" DR 26					695			695	760
5382	3" DR 11 x 8" DR 11				↓	695			695	765

22 11 Facility Water Distribution

22 11 13 – Facility Water Distribution Piping

22 11 13.78 Pipe, High Density Polyethylene Plastic (HDPE)		Crew	Daily Output	Labor-Hours	Unit	Material	2024 Bare Costs Labor	Equipment	Total	Total Incl O&P
5386	3" DR 11 x 8" DR 17				Ea.	760			760	835
5390	4" DR 11 x 8" DR 17					775			775	850
5394	4" DR 17 x 8" DR 26					780			780	860
5398	6" DR 11 x 10" DR 17					930			930	1,025
5402	6" DR 17 x 10" DR 26					885			885	970
5406	6" DR 26 x 10" DR 26					1,200			1,200	1,325
5410	8" DR 17 x 12" DR 26					1,275			1,275	1,425
5414	8" DR 26 x 12" DR 32.5					1,475			1,475	1,625
5418	10" DR 17 x 14" DR 26					1,750			1,750	1,925
5422	10" DR 17 x 16" DR 26					1,775			1,775	1,950
5426	10" DR 26 x 16" DR 26					1,975			1,975	2,175
5430	12" DR 26 x 16" DR 26					2,400			2,400	2,625
5434	12" DR 17 x 18" DR 26					2,400			2,400	2,650
5438	12" DR 26 x 18" DR 26					2,650			2,650	2,925
5442	14" DR 26 x 20" DR 32.5					2,925			2,925	3,225
5446	16" DR 26 x 22" DR 32.5					3,250			3,250	3,575
5450	18" DR 26 x 24" DR 32.5					3,575			3,575	3,950
5454	20" DR 32.5 x 28" DR 32.5					3,925			3,925	4,325
5458	22" DR 32.5 x 30" DR 32.5					4,325			4,325	4,775
5462	24" DR 32.5 x 32" DR 32.5					4,800			4,800	5,275
5466	36" DR 32.5 x 42" DR 32.5				↓	5,150			5,150	5,650
5600	90° elbow									
5654	1" DR 11 x 3" DR 11				Ea.	370			370	405
5658	1" DR 11 x 4" DR 17					435			435	475
5662	1-1/2" DR 11 x 4" DR 17					445			445	490
5666	2" DR 11 x 4" DR 17					435			435	480
5670	2" DR 11 x 6" DR 17					630			630	695
5674	3" DR 11 x 6" DR 17					685			685	750
5678	3" DR 17 x 6" DR 26					695			695	760
5682	3" DR 17 x 8" DR 11					930			930	1,025
5686	3" DR 17 x 8" DR 17					990			990	1,100
5690	4" DR 11 x 8" DR 17					840			840	925
5694	4" DR 17 x 8" DR 26					810			810	890
5698	6" DR 11 x 10" DR 17					1,475			1,475	1,625
5702	6" DR 17 x 10" DR 26					1,500			1,500	1,650
5706	6" DR 26 x 10" DR 26					1,450			1,450	1,600
5710	8" DR 17 x 12" DR 26					1,950			1,950	2,150
5714	8" DR 26 x 12" DR 32.5					1,625			1,625	1,775
5718	10" DR 17 x 14" DR 26					1,925			1,925	2,100
5722	10" DR 17 x 16" DR 26					1,850			1,850	2,050
5726	10" DR 26 x 16" DR 26					1,850			1,850	2,025
5730	12" DR 26 x 16" DR 26					1,900			1,900	2,075
5734	12" DR 17 x 18" DR 26					2,075			2,075	2,275
5738	12" DR 26 x 18" DR 26					2,100			2,100	2,300
5742	14" DR 26 x 20" DR 32.5					2,250			2,250	2,475
5746	16" DR 26 x 22" DR 32.5					2,350			2,350	2,575
5750	18" DR 26 x 24" DR 32.5					2,425			2,425	2,675
5754	20" DR 32.5 x 28" DR 32.5					2,525			2,525	2,775
5758	22" DR 32.5 x 30" DR 32.5					2,625			2,625	2,875
5762	24" DR 32.5 x 32" DR 32.5					2,700			2,700	2,975
5766	36" DR 32.5 x 42" DR 32.5				↓	2,800			2,800	3,075
5800	45° elbow									
5804	1" DR 11 x 3" DR 11				Ea.	425			425	470

22 11 Facility Water Distribution

22 11 13 – Facility Water Distribution Piping

22 11 13.78 Pipe, High Density Polyethylene Plastic (HDPE)	Crew	Daily Output	Labor-Hours	Unit	Material	2024 Bare Costs Labor	Equipment	Total	Total Incl O&P
5808	1" DR 11 x 4" DR 17				Ea.	350			350	385
5812	1-1/2" DR 11 x 4" DR 17					355			355	390
5816	2" DR 11 x 4" DR 17					340			340	375
5820	2" DR 11 x 6" DR 17					485			485	535
5824	3" DR 11 x 6" DR 17					520			520	575
5828	3" DR 17 x 6" DR 26					525			525	580
5832	3" DR 17 x 8" DR 11					670			670	735
5836	3" DR 17 x 8" DR 17					750			750	825
5840	4" DR 11 x 8" DR 17					620			620	680
5844	4" DR 17 x 8" DR 26					625			625	690
5848	6" DR 11 x 10" DR 17					975			975	1,075
5852	6" DR 17 x 10" DR 26					990			990	1,100
5856	6" DR 26 x 10" DR 26					1,125			1,125	1,225
5860	8" DR 17 x 12" DR 26					1,325			1,325	1,450
5864	8" DR 26 x 12" DR 32.5					1,250			1,250	1,375
5868	10" DR 17 x 14" DR 26					1,400			1,400	1,550
5872	10" DR 17 x 16" DR 26					1,350			1,350	1,475
5876	10" DR 26 x 16" DR 26					1,425			1,425	1,575
5880	12" DR 26 x 16" DR 26					1,300			1,300	1,425
5884	12" DR 17 x 18" DR 26					1,825			1,825	2,000
5888	12" DR 26 x 18" DR 26					1,625			1,625	1,800
5892	14" DR 26 x 20" DR 32.5					1,775			1,775	1,950
5896	16" DR 26 x 22" DR 32.5					1,850			1,850	2,025
5900	18" DR 26 x 24" DR 32.5					1,950			1,950	2,150
5904	20" DR 32.5 x 28" DR 32.5					1,925			1,925	2,125
5908	22" DR 32.5 x 30" DR 32.5					2,000			2,000	2,200
5912	24" DR 32.5 x 32" DR 32.5					2,075			2,075	2,275
5916	36" DR 32.5 x 42" DR 32.5					2,150			2,150	2,350
6000	Access port with 4" riser									
6050	1" DR 11 x 4" DR 17				Ea.	505			505	560
6054	1-1/2" DR 11 x 4" DR 17					510			510	565
6058	2" DR 11 x 6" DR 17					625			625	685
6062	3" DR 11 x 6" DR 17					635			635	695
6066	3" DR 17 x 6" DR 26					615			615	675
6070	3" DR 17 x 8" DR 11					635			635	695
6074	3" DR 17 x 8" DR 17					655			655	720
6078	4" DR 11 x 8" DR 17					675			675	745
6082	4" DR 17 x 8" DR 26					645			645	710
6086	6" DR 11 x 10" DR 17					790			790	870
6090	6" DR 17 x 10" DR 26					720			720	790
6094	6" DR 26 x 10" DR 26					755			755	830
6098	8" DR 17 x 12" DR 26					810			810	895
6102	8" DR 26 x 12" DR 32.5					795			795	875
6200	End termination with vent plug									
6204	1" DR 11 x 3" DR 11				Ea.	172			172	189
6208	1" DR 11 x 4" DR 17					252			252	277
6212	1-1/2" DR 11 x 4" DR 17					252			252	277
6216	2" DR 11 x 4" DR 17					252			252	277
6220	2" DR 11 x 6" DR 17					510			510	560
6224	3" DR 11 x 6" DR 17					510			510	560
6228	3" DR 17 x 6" DR 26					510			510	560
6232	3" DR 17 x 8" DR 11					495			495	540
6236	3" DR 17 x 8" DR 17					550			550	605

22 11 Facility Water Distribution

22 11 13 – Facility Water Distribution Piping

22 11 13.78 Pipe, High Density Polyethylene Plastic (HDPE)		Crew	Daily Output	Labor-Hours	Unit	Material	2024 Bare Costs Labor	Equipment	Total	Total Incl O&P
6240	4" DR 11 x 8" DR 17				Ea.	660			660	725
6244	4" DR 17 x 8" DR 26					620			620	680
6248	6" DR 11 x 10" DR 17					715			715	790
6252	6" DR 17 x 10" DR 26					660			660	730
6256	6" DR 26 x 10" DR 26					965			965	1,050
6260	8" DR 17 x 12" DR 26					1,025			1,025	1,125
6264	8" DR 26 x 12" DR 32.5					1,225			1,225	1,325
6268	10" DR 17 x 14" DR 26					1,600			1,600	1,775
6272	10" DR 17 x 16" DR 26					1,525			1,525	1,675
6276	10" DR 26 x 16" DR 26					1,700			1,700	1,875
6280	12" DR 26 x 16" DR 26					1,900			1,900	2,075
6284	12" DR 17 x 18" DR 26					2,200			2,200	2,425
6288	12" DR 26 x 18" DR 26					2,400			2,400	2,650
6292	14" DR 26 x 20" DR 32.5					2,700			2,700	2,975
6296	16" DR 26 x 22" DR 32.5					3,025			3,025	3,325
6300	18" DR 26 x 24" DR 32.5					3,400			3,400	3,725
6304	20" DR 32.5 x 28" DR 32.5					3,775			3,775	4,150
6308	22" DR 32.5 x 30" DR 32.5					4,225			4,225	4,650
6312	24" DR 32.5 x 32" DR 32.5					4,750			4,750	5,225
6316	36" DR 32.5 x 42" DR 32.5					5,225			5,225	5,750
6600	Tee									
6604	1" DR 11 x 3" DR 11				Ea.	430			430	470
6608	1" DR 11 x 4" DR 17					465			465	510
6612	1-1/2" DR 11 x 4" DR 17					480			480	530
6616	2" DR 11 x 4" DR 17					435			435	480
6620	2" DR 11 x 6" DR 17					695			695	765
6624	3" DR 11 x 6" DR 17					825			825	905
6628	3" DR 17 x 6" DR 26					780			780	855
6632	3" DR 17 x 8" DR 11					955			955	1,050
6636	3" DR 17 x 8" DR 17					1,050			1,050	1,150
6640	4" DR 11 x 8" DR 17					1,250			1,250	1,375
6644	4" DR 17 x 8" DR 26					1,250			1,250	1,375
6648	6" DR 11 x 10" DR 17					1,625			1,625	1,800
6652	6" DR 17 x 10" DR 26					1,625			1,625	1,800
6656	6" DR 26 x 10" DR 26					2,000			2,000	2,200
6660	8" DR 17 x 12" DR 26					2,000			2,000	2,200
6664	8" DR 26 x 12" DR 32.5					2,575			2,575	2,850
6668	10" DR 17 x 14" DR 26					3,025			3,025	3,325
6672	10" DR 17 x 16" DR 26					3,350			3,350	3,675
6676	10" DR 26 x 16" DR 26					3,350			3,350	3,675
6680	12" DR 26 x 16" DR 26					3,800			3,800	4,175
6684	12" DR 17 x 18" DR 26					3,800			3,800	4,175
6688	12" DR 26 x 18" DR 26					4,325			4,325	4,750
6692	14" DR 26 x 20" DR 32.5					4,875			4,875	5,350
6696	16" DR 26 x 22" DR 32.5					5,500			5,500	6,050
6700	18" DR 26 x 24" DR 32.5					6,275			6,275	6,900
6704	20" DR 32.5 x 28" DR 32.5					7,075			7,075	7,775
6708	22" DR 32.5 x 30" DR 32.5					8,000			8,000	8,800
6712	24" DR 32.5 x 32" DR 32.5					9,050			9,050	9,975
6716	36" DR 32.5 x 42" DR 32.5					10,400			10,400	11,400
6800	Wye									
6816	2" DR 11 x 4" DR 17				Ea.	1,050			1,050	1,175
6820	2" DR 11 x 6" DR 17					1,300			1,300	1,450

22 11 Facility Water Distribution

22 11 13 – Facility Water Distribution Piping

22 11 13.78 Pipe, High Density Polyethylene Plastic (HDPE)		Crew	Daily Output	Labor-Hours	Unit	Material	2024 Bare Costs Labor	Equipment	Total	Total Incl O&P
6824	3" DR 11 x 6" DR 17				Ea.	1,400			1,400	1,525
6828	3" DR 17 x 6" DR 26					375			375	410
6832	3" DR 17 x 8" DR 11					1,475			1,475	1,625
6836	3" DR 17 x 8" DR 17					1,600			1,600	1,775
6840	4" DR 11 x 8" DR 17					1,775			1,775	1,950
6844	4" DR 17 x 8" DR 26					1,125			1,125	1,225
6848	6" DR 11 x 10" DR 17					695			695	765
6852	6" DR 17 x 10" DR 26					1,700			1,700	1,875
6856	6" DR 26 x 10" DR 26					2,350			2,350	2,600
6860	8" DR 17 x 12" DR 26					3,300			3,300	3,625
6864	8" DR 26 x 12" DR 32.5					2,725			2,725	3,000
6868	10" DR 17 x 14" DR 26					2,925			2,925	3,200
6872	10" DR 17 x 16" DR 26					3,150			3,150	3,450
6876	10" DR 26 x 16" DR 26					3,400			3,400	3,750
6880	12" DR 26 x 16" DR 26					3,675			3,675	4,025
6884	12" DR 17 x 18" DR 26					3,950			3,950	4,350
6888	12" DR 26 x 18" DR 26					4,275			4,275	4,700
6892	14" DR 26 x 20" DR 32.5					4,575			4,575	5,025
6896	16" DR 26 x 22" DR 32.5					4,825			4,825	5,300
6900	18" DR 26 x 24" DR 32.5					5,525			5,525	6,075
6904	20" DR 32.5 x 28" DR 32.5					5,775			5,775	6,350
6908	22" DR 32.5 x 30" DR 32.5					6,225			6,225	6,850
6912	24" DR 32.5 x 32" DR 32.5					6,725			6,725	7,400
9000	Welding labor per joint, not including welding machine									
9010	Pipe joint size, outer pipe (cost based on the thickest walls)									
9020	Straight pipe									
9050	3" pipe size	4 Skwk	96	.333	Ea.		21		21	31.50
9060	4" pipe size	"	77	.416			26.50		26.50	39.50
9070	6" pipe size	5 Skwk	60	.667			42.50		42.50	63.50
9080	8" pipe size	"	40	1			63.50		63.50	95
9090	10" pipe size	6 Skwk	41	1.171			74.50		74.50	111
9100	12" pipe size		39	1.231			78		78	117
9110	14" pipe size		38	1.263			80		80	120
9120	16" pipe size		35	1.371			87		87	130
9130	18" pipe size	8 Skwk	45	1.422			90.50		90.50	135
9140	20" pipe size		42	1.524			97		97	145
9150	22" pipe size		40	1.600			102		102	152
9160	24" pipe size		38	1.684			107		107	160
9170	28" pipe size		37	1.730			110		110	164
9180	30" pipe size		36	1.778			113		113	169
9190	32" pipe size		35	1.829			116		116	174
9200	42" pipe size		32	2			127		127	190

22 11 19 – Domestic Water Piping Specialties

22 11 19.10 Flexible Connectors

		Crew	Daily Output	Labor-Hours	Unit	Material	Labor	Equipment	Total	Total Incl O&P
0010	**FLEXIBLE CONNECTORS**, Corrugated, 5/8" OD, 3/4" ID									
0050	Gas, seamless brass, steel fittings									
0200	12" long	1 Plum	36	.222	Ea.	30	16.60		46.60	58
0220	18" long		36	.222		37.50	16.60		54.10	66
0240	24" long		34	.235		44.50	17.55		62.05	75
0260	30" long		34	.235		48	17.55		65.55	78.50
0280	36" long		32	.250		53	18.65		71.65	86.50
0320	48" long		30	.267		67	19.90		86.90	104

22 11 Facility Water Distribution

22 11 19 – Domestic Water Piping Specialties

22 11 19.10 Flexible Connectors

		Crew	Daily Output	Labor-Hours	Unit	Material	2024 Bare Costs Labor	Equipment	Total	Total Incl O&P
0340	60" long	1 Plum	30	.267	Ea.	80	19.90		99.90	118
0360	72" long	↓	30	.267	↓	92.50	19.90		112.40	132
2000	Water, copper tubing, dielectric separators									
2100	12" long	1 Plum	36	.222	Ea.	14.95	16.60		31.55	41
2220	15" long		36	.222		16.65	16.60		33.25	43
2240	18" long		36	.222		15.35	16.60		31.95	41.50
2260	24" long	↓	34	.235	↓	22	17.55		39.55	50.50

22 11 19.14 Flexible Metal Hose

		Crew	Daily Output	Labor-Hours	Unit	Material	Labor	Equipment	Total	Total Incl O&P
0010	**FLEXIBLE METAL HOSE**, Connectors, standard lengths									
0100	Bronze braided, bronze ends									
0120	3/8" diameter x 12"	1 Stpi	26	.308	Ea.	40.50	23.50		64	79
0140	1/2" diameter x 12"		24	.333		50	25		75	92.50
0160	3/4" diameter x 12"		20	.400		84	30		114	138
0180	1" diameter x 18"		19	.421		100	32		132	158
0200	1-1/2" diameter x 18"		13	.615		136	46.50		182.50	219
0220	2" diameter x 18"	↓	11	.727		174	55		229	274
1000	Carbon steel ends									
1020	1/4" diameter x 12"	1 Stpi	28	.286	Ea.	69.50	21.50		91	109
1040	3/8" diameter x 12"		26	.308		46	23.50		69.50	85
1060	1/2" diameter x 12"		24	.333		62.50	25		87.50	106
1080	1/2" diameter x 24"		24	.333		72.50	25		97.50	117
1120	3/4" diameter x 12"		20	.400		85.50	30		115.50	139
1140	3/4" diameter x 24"		20	.400		102	30		132	157
1160	3/4" diameter x 36"		20	.400		116	30		146	172
1180	1" diameter x 18"		19	.421		102	32		134	161
1200	1" diameter x 30"		19	.421		106	32		138	165
1220	1" diameter x 36"		19	.421		114	32		146	173
1240	1-1/4" diameter x 18"		15	.533		360	40.50		400.50	455
1260	1-1/4" diameter x 36"		15	.533		161	40.50		201.50	237
1280	1-1/2" diameter x 18"		13	.615		183	46.50		229.50	271
1300	1-1/2" diameter x 36"		13	.615		159	46.50		205.50	244
1320	2" diameter x 24"		11	.727		206	55		261	310
1340	2" diameter x 36"		11	.727		228	55		283	335
1360	2-1/2" diameter x 24"		9	.889		400	67		467	540
1380	2-1/2" diameter x 36"		9	.889		232	67		299	355
1400	3" diameter x 24"		7	1.143		820	86.50		906.50	1,025
1420	3" diameter x 36"	↓	7	1.143	↓	1,875	86.50		1,961.50	2,200
2000	Carbon steel braid, carbon steel solid ends									
2100	1/2" diameter x 12"	1 Stpi	24	.333	Ea.	66.50	25		91.50	111
2120	3/4" diameter x 12"		20	.400		73	30		103	126
2140	1" diameter x 12"		19	.421		136	32		168	197
2160	1-1/4" diameter x 12"		15	.533		106	40.50		146.50	177
2180	1-1/2" diameter x 12"	↓	13	.615		117	46.50		163.50	198
3000	Stainless steel braid, welded on carbon steel ends									
3100	1/2" diameter x 12"	1 Stpi	24	.333	Ea.	82	25		107	128
3120	3/4" diameter x 12"		20	.400		96.50	30		126.50	151
3140	3/4" diameter x 24"		20	.400		101	30		131	156
3160	3/4" diameter x 36"		20	.400		140	30		170	199
3180	1" diameter x 12"		19	.421		142	32		174	205
3200	1" diameter x 24"		19	.421		171	32		203	236
3220	1" diameter x 36"		19	.421		146	32		178	209
3240	1-1/4" diameter x 12"	↓	15	.533	↓	190	40.50		230.50	268

22 11 Facility Water Distribution

22 11 19 – Domestic Water Piping Specialties

22 11 19.14 Flexible Metal Hose

		Crew	Daily Output	Labor-Hours	Unit	Material	2024 Bare Costs Labor	2024 Bare Costs Equipment	Total	Total Incl O&P
3260	1-1/4" diameter x 24"	1 Stpi	15	.533	Ea.	170	40.50		210.50	247
3280	1-1/4" diameter x 36"		15	.533		193	40.50		233.50	272
3300	1-1/2" diameter x 12"		13	.615		122	46.50		168.50	204
3320	1-1/2" diameter x 24"		13	.615		211	46.50		257.50	300
3340	1-1/2" diameter x 36"		13	.615		140	46.50		186.50	223
3400	Metal stainless steel braid, over corrugated stainless steel, flanged ends									
3410	150 psi									
3420	1/2" diameter x 12"	1 Stpi	24	.333	Ea.	107	25		132	156
3430	1" diameter x 12"		20	.400		179	30		209	242
3440	1-1/2" diameter x 12"		15	.533		116	40.50		156.50	188
3450	2-1/2" diameter x 9"		12	.667		195	50.50		245.50	290
3460	3" diameter x 9"		9	.889		196	67		263	315
3470	4" diameter x 9"		7	1.143		255	86.50		341.50	410
3480	4" diameter x 30"		5	1.600		525	121		646	755
3490	4" diameter x 36"		4.80	1.667		525	126		651	760
3500	6" diameter x 11"		5	1.600		455	121		576	680
3510	6" diameter x 36"		3.80	2.105		805	159		964	1,125
3520	8" diameter x 12"		4	2		705	151		856	1,000
3530	10" diameter x 13"		3	2.667		875	201		1,076	1,250
3540	12" diameter x 14"	Q-5	4	4		1,600	272		1,872	2,150
6000	Molded rubber with helical wire reinforcement									
6010	150 psi									
6020	1-1/2" diameter x 12"	1 Stpi	15	.533	Ea.	56	40.50		96.50	122
6030	2" diameter x 12"		12	.667		182	50.50		232.50	275
6040	3" diameter x 12"		8	1		190	75.50		265.50	320
6050	4" diameter x 12"		6	1.333		241	101		342	415
6060	6" diameter x 18"		4	2		360	151		511	620
6070	8" diameter x 24"		3	2.667		505	201		706	855
6080	10" diameter x 24"		2	4		615	300		915	1,125
6090	12" diameter x 24"	Q-5	3	5.333		700	365		1,065	1,300
7000	Molded teflon with stainless steel flanges									
7010	150 psi									
7020	2-1/2" diameter x 3-3/16"	Q-1	7.80	2.051	Ea.	1,075	138		1,213	1,375
7030	3" diameter x 3-5/8"		6.50	2.462		1,000	165		1,165	1,350
7040	4" diameter x 3-5/8"		5	3.200		1,275	215		1,490	1,725
7050	6" diameter x 4"		4.30	3.721		1,775	250		2,025	2,325
7060	8" diameter x 6"		3.80	4.211		2,825	283		3,108	3,525

22 11 19.18 Mixing Valve

		Crew	Daily Output	Labor-Hours	Unit	Material	Labor	Equipment	Total	Total Incl O&P
0010	**MIXING VALVE**, Automatic, water tempering.									
0040	1/2" size	1 Stpi	19	.421	Ea.	540	32		572	645
0050	3/4" size		18	.444		635	33.50		668.50	750
0100	1" size		16	.500		995	38		1,033	1,150
0120	1-1/4" size		13	.615		1,350	46.50		1,396.50	1,550
0140	1-1/2" size		10	.800		1,650	60.50		1,710.50	1,925
0160	2" size		8	1		2,075	75.50		2,150.50	2,375
0170	2-1/2" size		6	1.333		2,075	101		2,176	2,425
0180	3" size		4	2		4,875	151		5,026	5,600
0190	4" size		3	2.667		4,875	201		5,076	5,675

22 11 Facility Water Distribution

22 11 19 – Domestic Water Piping Specialties

22 11 19.22 Pressure Reducing Valve		Crew	Daily Output	Labor-Hours	Unit	Material	2024 Bare Costs Labor	Equipment	Total	Total Incl O&P
0010	**PRESSURE REDUCING VALVE**, Steam, pilot operated.									
0100	Threaded, iron body									
0200	1-1/2" size	1 Stpi	8	1	Ea.	3,075	75.50		3,150.50	3,500
0220	2" size	"	5	1.600	"	4,450	121		4,571	5,050
1000	Flanged, iron body, 125 lb. flanges									
1020	2" size	1 Stpi	8	1	Ea.	6,025	75.50		6,100.50	6,750
1040	2-1/2" size	"	4	2		4,725	151		4,876	5,425
1060	3" size	Q-5	4.50	3.556		5,275	242		5,517	6,150
1080	4" size	"	3	5.333		6,325	365		6,690	7,500
1500	For 250 lb. flanges, add					5%				

22 11 19.26 Pressure Regulators		Crew	Daily Output	Labor-Hours	Unit	Material	2024 Bare Costs Labor	Equipment	Total	Total Incl O&P
0010	**PRESSURE REGULATORS**									
0100	Gas appliance regulators									
0106	Main burner and pilot applications									
0108	Rubber seat poppet type									
0109	1/8" pipe size	1 Stpi	24	.333	Ea.	20.50	25		45.50	60
0110	1/4" pipe size		24	.333		19.50	25		44.50	59
0112	3/8" pipe size		24	.333		25	25		50	64.50
0113	1/2" pipe size		24	.333		28	25		53	68.50
0114	3/4" pipe size		20	.400		35	30		65	83.50
0122	Lever action type									
0123	3/8" pipe size	1 Stpi	24	.333	Ea.	53.50	25		78.50	96.50
0124	1/2" pipe size		24	.333		25	25		50	65
0125	3/4" pipe size		20	.400		60	30		90	111
0126	1" pipe size		19	.421		66.50	32		98.50	121
0132	Double diaphragm type									
0133	3/8" pipe size	1 Stpi	24	.333	Ea.	83	25		108	129
0134	1/2" pipe size		24	.333		104	25		129	153
0135	3/4" pipe size		20	.400		172	30		202	234
0136	1" pipe size		19	.421		143	32		175	205
0137	1-1/4" pipe size		15	.533		445	40.50		485.50	550
0138	1-1/2" pipe size		13	.615		1,275	46.50		1,321.50	1,475
0139	2" pipe size		11	.727		755	55		810	910
0140	2-1/2" pipe size	Q-5	15	1.067		2,475	72.50		2,547.50	2,825
0141	3" pipe size		13	1.231		1,550	83.50		1,633.50	1,825
0142	4" pipe size (flanged)		8	2		3,375	136		3,511	3,900
0160	Main burner only									
0162	Straight-thru-flow design									
0163	1/2" pipe size	1 Stpi	24	.333	Ea.	63	25		88	107
0164	3/4" pipe size		20	.400		63	30		93	115
0165	1" pipe size		19	.421		114	32		146	173
0166	1-1/4" pipe size		15	.533		88	40.50		128.50	157
0200	Oil, light, hot water, ordinary steam, threaded									
0220	Bronze body, 1/4" size	1 Stpi	24	.333	Ea.	355	25		380	430
0230	3/8" size		24	.333		365	25		390	440
0240	1/2" size		24	.333		460	25		485	545
0250	3/4" size		20	.400		510	30		540	605
0260	1" size		19	.421		900	32		932	1,050
0270	1-1/4" size		15	.533		1,050	40.50		1,090.50	1,200
0320	Iron body, 1/4" size		24	.333		235	25		260	296
0330	3/8" size		24	.333		430	25		455	510
0340	1/2" size		24	.333		455	25		480	540

22 11 Facility Water Distribution

22 11 19 – Domestic Water Piping Specialties

22 11 19.26 Pressure Regulators

		Crew	Daily Output	Labor-Hours	Unit	Material	2024 Bare Costs Labor	Equipment	Total	Total Incl O&P
0350	3/4" size	1 Stpi	20	.400	Ea.	450	30		480	540
0360	1" size		19	.421		590	32		622	695
0370	1-1/4" size		15	.533		620	40.50		660.50	740
9002	For water pressure regulators, see Section 22 05 23.20									

22 11 19.30 Pressure and Temperature Safety Plug

		Crew	Daily Output	Labor-Hours	Unit	Material	2024 Bare Costs Labor	Equipment	Total	Total Incl O&P
0010	**PRESSURE & TEMPERATURE SAFETY PLUG**									
1000	3/4" external thread, 3/8" diam. element									
1020	Carbon steel									
1050	7-1/2" insertion	1 Stpi	32	.250	Ea.	91	18.90		109.90	128
1120	304 stainless steel									
1150	7-1/2" insertion	1 Stpi	32	.250	Ea.	71.50	18.90		90.40	107
1220	316 stainless steel									
1250	7-1/2" insertion	1 Stpi	32	.250	Ea.	129	18.90		147.90	169

22 11 19.32 Pressure and Temperature Measurement Plug

		Crew	Daily Output	Labor-Hours	Unit	Material	2024 Bare Costs Labor	Equipment	Total	Total Incl O&P
0010	**PRESSURE & TEMPERATURE MEASUREMENT PLUG**									
0020	A permanent access port for insertion of									
0030	a pressure or temperature measuring probe									
0100	Plug, brass									
0110	1/4" MNPT, 1-1/2" long	1 Stpi	32	.250	Ea.	24.50	18.90		43.40	55
0120	3" long		31	.258		23	19.50		42.50	54
0140	1/2" MNPT, 1-1/2" long		30	.267		24	20		44	56.50
0150	3" long		29	.276		28	21		49	61.50
0200	Pressure gauge probe adapter									
0210	1/8" diameter, 1-1/2" probe				Ea.	22.50			22.50	25
0220	3" probe				"	32.50			32.50	36
0300	Temperature gauge, 5" stem									
0310	Analog				Ea.	20.50			20.50	22.50
0330	Digital				"	55.50			55.50	61.50
0400	Pressure gauge, compound									
0410	1/4" MNPT				Ea.	31.50			31.50	34.50
0500	Pressure and temperature test kit									
0510	Contains 2 thermometers and 2 pressure gauges									
0520	Kit				Ea.	665			665	730

22 11 19.34 Sleeves and Escutcheons

		Crew	Daily Output	Labor-Hours	Unit	Material	2024 Bare Costs Labor	Equipment	Total	Total Incl O&P
0010	**SLEEVES & ESCUTCHEONS**									
0100	Pipe sleeve									
0110	Steel, w/water stop, 12" long, with link seal									
0120	2" diam. for 1/2" carrier pipe	1 Plum	8.40	.952	Ea.	135	71		206	254
0130	2-1/2" diam. for 3/4" carrier pipe		8	1		151	74.50		225.50	277
0140	2-1/2" diam. for 1" carrier pipe		8	1		144	74.50		218.50	269
0150	3" diam. for 1-1/4" carrier pipe		7.20	1.111		183	83		266	325
0160	3-1/2" diam. for 1-1/2" carrier pipe		6.80	1.176		216	88		304	370
0170	4" diam. for 2" carrier pipe		6	1.333		205	99.50		304.50	375
0180	4" diam. for 2-1/2" carrier pipe		6	1.333		202	99.50		301.50	370
0190	5" diam. for 3" carrier pipe		5.40	1.481		235	111		346	425
0200	6" diam. for 4" carrier pipe		4.80	1.667		257	124		381	465
0210	10" diam. for 6" carrier pipe	Q-1	8	2		505	134		639	755
0220	12" diam. for 8" carrier pipe		7.20	2.222		700	149		849	995
0230	14" diam. for 10" carrier pipe		6.40	2.500		720	168		888	1,050
0240	16" diam. for 12" carrier pipe		5.80	2.759		800	185		985	1,150
0250	18" diam. for 14" carrier pipe		5.20	3.077		1,400	207		1,607	1,850
0260	24" diam. for 18" carrier pipe		4	4		2,100	269		2,369	2,700

22 11 Facility Water Distribution

22 11 19 – Domestic Water Piping Specialties

22 11 19.34 Sleeves and Escutcheons

		Crew	Daily Output	Labor-Hours	Unit	Material	2024 Bare Costs Labor	Equipment	Total	Total Incl O&P
0270	24" diam. for 20" carrier pipe	Q-1	4	4	Ea.	1,825	269		2,094	2,400
0280	30" diam. for 24" carrier pipe	↓	3.20	5	↓	2,375	335		2,710	3,125
0500	Wall sleeve									
0510	Ductile iron with rubber gasket seal									
0520	3"	1 Plum	8.40	.952	Ea.	385	71		456	525
0530	4"		7.20	1.111		410	83		493	575
0540	6"		6	1.333		500	99.50		599.50	695
0550	8"		4	2		2,200	149		2,349	2,650
0560	10"		3	2.667		2,675	199		2,874	3,250
0570	12"	↓	2.40	3.333	↓	3,150	249		3,399	3,850
5000	Escutcheon									
5100	Split ring, pipe									
5110	Chrome plated									
5120	1/2"	1 Plum	160	.050	Ea.	1.24	3.73		4.97	6.90
5130	3/4"		160	.050		1.37	3.73		5.10	7.05
5140	1"		135	.059		1.47	4.42		5.89	8.20
5150	1-1/2"		115	.070		2.06	5.20		7.26	10
5160	2"		100	.080		2.29	5.95		8.24	11.40
5170	4"		80	.100		9.40	7.45		16.85	21.50
5180	6"	↓	68	.118	↓	14.80	8.80		23.60	29.50
5400	Shallow flange type									
5410	Chrome plated steel									
5420	1/2" CTS	1 Plum	180	.044	Ea.	.40	3.32		3.72	5.40
5430	3/4" CTS		180	.044		.43	3.32		3.75	5.40
5440	1/2" IPS		180	.044		.49	3.32		3.81	5.50
5450	3/4" IPS		180	.044		.49	3.32		3.81	5.50
5460	1" IPS		175	.046		.57	3.41		3.98	5.75
5470	1-1/2" IPS		170	.047		.93	3.51		4.44	6.25
5480	2" IPS	↓	160	.050		1.13	3.73		4.86	6.80

22 11 19.38 Water Supply Meters

		Crew	Daily Output	Labor-Hours	Unit	Material	Labor	Equipment	Total	Total Incl O&P
0010	**WATER SUPPLY METERS**									
1000	Detector, serves dual systems such as fire and domestic or									
1020	process water, wide range cap., UL and FM approved									
1100	3" mainline x 2" by-pass, 400 GPM	Q-1	3.60	4.444	Ea.	15,200	299		15,499	17,200
1140	4" mainline x 2" by-pass, 700 GPM	"	2.50	6.400		15,200	430		15,630	17,400
1180	6" mainline x 3" by-pass, 1,600 GPM	Q-2	2.60	9.231		23,300	645		23,945	26,600
1220	8" mainline x 4" by-pass, 2,800 GPM		2.10	11.429		34,500	795		35,295	39,200
1260	10" mainline x 6" by-pass, 4,400 GPM		2	12		49,400	835		50,235	56,000
1300	10" x 12" mainlines x 6" by-pass, 5,400 GPM	↓	1.70	14.118	↓	67,000	985		67,985	75,000
2000	Domestic/commercial, bronze									
2020	Threaded									
2060	5/8" diameter, to 20 GPM	1 Plum	16	.500	Ea.	216	37.50		253.50	293
2080	3/4" diameter, to 30 GPM		14	.571		385	42.50		427.50	490
2100	1" diameter, to 50 GPM	↓	12	.667		700	50		750	845
2300	Threaded/flanged									
2340	1-1/2" diameter, to 100 GPM	1 Plum	8	1	Ea.	795	74.50		869.50	985
2360	2" diameter, to 160 GPM	"	6	1.333	"	2,000	99.50		2,099.50	2,350
2600	Flanged, compound									
2640	3" diameter, 320 GPM	Q-1	3	5.333	Ea.	2,575	360		2,935	3,350
2660	4" diameter, to 500 GPM		1.50	10.667		3,800	715		4,515	5,275
2680	6" diameter, to 1,000 GPM		1	16		9,575	1,075		10,650	12,100
2700	8" diameter, to 1,800 GPM	↓	.80	20	↓	11,100	1,350		12,450	14,300

22 11 Facility Water Distribution

22 11 19 – Domestic Water Piping Specialties

22 11 19.38 Water Supply Meters

		Crew	Daily Output	Labor-Hours	Unit	Material	2024 Bare Costs Labor	Equipment	Total	Total Incl O&P
7000	Turbine									
7260	Flanged									
7300	2" diameter, to 160 GPM	1 Plum	7	1.143	Ea.	1,175	85.50		1,260.50	1,400
7320	3" diameter, to 450 GPM	Q-1	3.60	4.444		2,000	299		2,299	2,650
7340	4" diameter, to 650 GPM	"	2.50	6.400		3,300	430		3,730	4,275
7360	6" diameter, to 1,800 GPM	Q-2	2.60	9.231		5,450	645		6,095	6,950
7380	8" diameter, to 2,500 GPM		2.10	11.429		9,350	795		10,145	11,500
7400	10" diameter, to 5,500 GPM		1.70	14.118		12,600	985		13,585	15,300

22 11 19.42 Backflow Preventers

		Crew	Daily Output	Labor-Hours	Unit	Material	Labor	Equipment	Total	Total Incl O&P
0010	**BACKFLOW PREVENTERS**, Includes valves									
0020	and four test cocks, corrosion resistant, automatic operation									
1000	Double check principle									
1010	Threaded, with ball valves									
1020	3/4" pipe size	1 Plum	16	.500	Ea.	278	37.50		315.50	360
1030	1" pipe size		14	.571		455	42.50		497.50	565
1040	1-1/2" pipe size		10	.800		900	59.50		959.50	1,075
1050	2" pipe size		7	1.143		1,225	85.50		1,310.50	1,475
1080	Threaded, with gate valves									
1100	3/4" pipe size	1 Plum	16	.500	Ea.	2,300	37.50		2,337.50	2,575
1120	1" pipe size		14	.571		2,350	42.50		2,392.50	2,650
1140	1-1/2" pipe size		10	.800		2,075	59.50		2,134.50	2,375
1160	2" pipe size		7	1.143		3,700	85.50		3,785.50	4,175
1200	Flanged, valves are gate									
1210	3" pipe size	Q-1	4.50	3.556	Ea.	2,300	239		2,539	2,875
1220	4" pipe size	"	3	5.333		2,850	360		3,210	3,675
1230	6" pipe size	Q-2	3	8		4,150	555		4,705	5,375
1240	8" pipe size		2	12		7,825	835		8,660	9,875
1250	10" pipe size		1	24		10,400	1,675		12,075	13,900
1300	Flanged, valves are OS&Y									
1370	1" pipe size	1 Plum	5	1.600	Ea.	2,450	119		2,569	2,850
1374	1-1/2" pipe size		5	1.600		2,200	119		2,319	2,600
1378	2" pipe size		4.80	1.667		3,800	124		3,924	4,375
1380	3" pipe size	Q-1	4.50	3.556		3,625	239		3,864	4,325
1400	4" pipe size	"	3	5.333		3,750	360		4,110	4,625
1420	6" pipe size	Q-2	3	8		5,675	555		6,230	7,075
1430	8" pipe size	"	2	12		7,875	835		8,710	9,900
4000	Reduced pressure principle									
4100	Threaded, bronze, valves are ball									
4120	3/4" pipe size	1 Plum	16	.500	Ea.	283	37.50		320.50	365
4140	1" pipe size		14	.571		480	42.50		522.50	590
4150	1-1/4" pipe size		12	.667		2,125	50		2,175	2,400
4160	1-1/2" pipe size		10	.800		1,750	59.50		1,809.50	2,025
4180	2" pipe size		7	1.143		680	85.50		765.50	875
5000	Flanged, bronze, valves are OS&Y									
5060	2-1/2" pipe size	Q-1	5	3.200	Ea.	5,050	215		5,265	5,875
5080	3" pipe size		4.50	3.556		5,500	239		5,739	6,400
5100	4" pipe size		3	5.333		6,700	360		7,060	7,900
5120	6" pipe size	Q-2	3	8		10,200	555		10,755	12,000
5200	Flanged, iron, valves are gate									
5210	2-1/2" pipe size	Q-1	5	3.200	Ea.	5,350	215		5,565	6,225
5220	3" pipe size		4.50	3.556		4,850	239		5,089	5,675
5230	4" pipe size		3	5.333		6,700	360		7,060	7,900

22 11 Facility Water Distribution

22 11 19 – Domestic Water Piping Specialties

22 11 19.42 Backflow Preventers

		Crew	Daily Output	Labor-Hours	Unit	Material	2024 Bare Costs Labor	2024 Bare Costs Equipment	Total	Total Incl O&P
5240	6" pipe size	Q-2	3	8	Ea.	10,200	555		10,755	12,000
5250	8" pipe size		2	12		13,800	835		14,635	16,500
5260	10" pipe size	↓	1	24	↓	18,900	1,675		20,575	23,300
5600	Flanged, iron, valves are OS&Y									
5660	2-1/2" pipe size	Q-1	5	3.200	Ea.	5,050	215		5,265	5,875
5680	3" pipe size		4.50	3.556		5,175	239		5,414	6,050
5700	4" pipe size	↓	3	5.333		6,700	360		7,060	7,900
5720	6" pipe size	Q-2	3	8		10,200	555		10,755	12,000
5740	8" pipe size		2	12		18,000	835		18,835	21,100
5760	10" pipe size	↓	1	24	↓	21,500	1,675		23,175	26,200

22 11 19.50 Vacuum Breakers

		Crew	Daily Output	Labor-Hours	Unit	Material	2024 Bare Costs Labor	2024 Bare Costs Equipment	Total	Total Incl O&P
0010	**VACUUM BREAKERS**									
0013	See also backflow preventers Section 22 11 19.42 R221113-40									
1000	Anti-siphon continuous pressure type									
1010	Max. 150 psi - 210°F									
1020	Bronze body									
1030	1/2" size	1 Stpi	24	.333	Ea.	400	25		425	480
1040	3/4" size		20	.400		400	30		430	485
1050	1" size		19	.421		410	32		442	500
1060	1-1/4" size		15	.533		815	40.50		855.50	955
1070	1-1/2" size		13	.615		980	46.50		1,026.50	1,150
1080	2" size	↓	11	.727		625	55		680	770
1200	Max. 125 psi with atmospheric vent									
1210	Brass, in-line construction									
1220	1/4" size	1 Stpi	24	.333	Ea.	272	25		297	340
1230	3/8" size	"	24	.333		272	25		297	340
1260	For polished chrome finish, add				↓	13%				
2000	Anti-siphon, non-continuous pressure type									
2010	Hot or cold water 125 psi - 210°F									
2020	Bronze body									
2030	1/4" size	1 Stpi	24	.333	Ea.	166	25		191	221
2040	3/8" size		24	.333		166	25		191	221
2050	1/2" size		24	.333		187	25		212	243
2060	3/4" size		20	.400		223	30		253	291
2070	1" size		19	.421		345	32		377	430
2080	1-1/4" size		15	.533		605	40.50		645.50	725
2090	1-1/2" size		13	.615		670	46.50		716.50	805
2100	2" size		11	.727		1,100	55		1,155	1,300
2110	2-1/2" size		8	1		3,175	75.50		3,250.50	3,575
2120	3" size	↓	6	1.333	↓	4,200	101		4,301	4,775
2150	For polished chrome finish, add					50%				
3000	Air gap fitting									
3020	1/2" NPT size	1 Plum	19	.421	Ea.	126	31.50		157.50	185
3030	1" NPT size	"	15	.533		120	40		160	191
3040	2" NPT size	Q-1	21	.762		190	51		241	284
3050	3" NPT size		14	1.143		500	77		577	665
3060	4" NPT size	↓	10	1.600	↓	315	107		422	510

22 11 19.54 Water Hammer Arresters/Shock Absorbers

		Crew	Daily Output	Labor-Hours	Unit	Material	2024 Bare Costs Labor	2024 Bare Costs Equipment	Total	Total Incl O&P
0010	**WATER HAMMER ARRESTERS/SHOCK ABSORBERS**									
0490	Copper									
0500	3/4" male IPS for 1 to 11 fixtures	1 Plum	12	.667	Ea.	51.50	50		101.50	131
0600	1" male IPS for 12 to 32 fixtures	↓	8	1	↓	86.50	74.50		161	206

22 11 Facility Water Distribution

22 11 19 – Domestic Water Piping Specialties

22 11 19.54 Water Hammer Arresters/Shock Absorbers

		Crew	Daily Output	Labor-Hours	Unit	Material	2024 Bare Costs Labor	Equipment	Total	Total Incl O&P
0700	1-1/4" male IPS for 33 to 60 fixtures	1 Plum	8	1	Ea.	84.50	74.50		159	204
0800	1-1/2" male IPS for 61 to 113 fixtures		8	1		123	74.50		197.50	246
0900	2" male IPS for 114 to 154 fixtures		8	1		181	74.50		255.50	310
1000	2-1/2" male IPS for 155 to 330 fixtures		4	2		515	149		664	790
4000	Bellows type									
4010	3/4" FNPT, to 11 fixture units	1 Plum	10	.800	Ea.	495	59.50		554.50	635
4020	1" FNPT, to 32 fixture units		8.80	.909		1,000	68		1,068	1,200
4030	1" FNPT, to 60 fixture units		8.80	.909		1,500	68		1,568	1,750
4040	1" FNPT, to 113 fixture units		8.80	.909		3,775	68		3,843	4,250
4050	1" FNPT, to 154 fixture units		6.60	1.212		4,250	90.50		4,340.50	4,800
4060	1-1/2" FNPT, to 300 fixture units		5	1.600		5,225	119		5,344	5,925

22 11 19.64 Hydrants

		Crew	Daily Output	Labor-Hours	Unit	Material	2024 Bare Costs Labor	Equipment	Total	Total Incl O&P
0010	**HYDRANTS**									
0050	Wall type, moderate climate, bronze, encased									
0200	3/4" IPS connection	1 Plum	16	.500	Ea.	2,000	37.50		2,037.50	2,250
0300	1" IPS connection		14	.571		4,225	42.50		4,267.50	4,725
0500	Anti-siphon type, 3/4" connection		16	.500		1,550	37.50		1,587.50	1,775
1000	Non-freeze, bronze, exposed									
1100	3/4" IPS connection, 4" to 9" thick wall	1 Plum	14	.571	Ea.	955	42.50		997.50	1,125
1120	10" to 14" thick wall		12	.667		840	50		890	995
1140	15" to 19" thick wall		12	.667		1,075	50		1,125	1,250
1160	20" to 24" thick wall		10	.800		1,450	59.50		1,509.50	1,700
1200	For 1" IPS connection, add					15%	10%			
1240	For 3/4" adapter type vacuum breaker, add				Ea.	169			169	186
1280	For anti-siphon type, add				"	360			360	395
2000	Non-freeze bronze, encased, anti-siphon type									
2100	3/4" IPS connection, 5" to 9" thick wall	1 Plum	14	.571	Ea.	2,400	42.50		2,442.50	2,725
2120	10" to 14" thick wall		12	.667		3,125	50		3,175	3,525
2140	15" to 19" thick wall		12	.667		3,325	50		3,375	3,725
2160	20" to 24" thick wall		10	.800		3,450	59.50		3,509.50	3,875
2200	For 1" IPS connection, add					10%	10%			
3000	Ground box type, bronze frame, 3/4" IPS connection									
3080	Non-freeze, all bronze, polished face, set flush									
3100	2' depth of bury	1 Plum	8	1	Ea.	2,200	74.50		2,274.50	2,500
3120	3' depth of bury		8	1		1,000	74.50		1,074.50	1,200
3140	4' depth of bury		8	1		1,500	74.50		1,574.50	1,750
3160	5' depth of bury		7	1.143		1,600	85.50		1,685.50	1,875
3180	6' depth of bury		7	1.143		590	85.50		675.50	770
3200	7' depth of bury		6	1.333		3,250	99.50		3,349.50	3,725
3220	8' depth of bury		5	1.600		685	119		804	935
3240	9' depth of bury		4	2		3,600	149		3,749	4,175
3260	10' depth of bury		4	2		2,100	149		2,249	2,525
3400	For 1" IPS connection, add					15%	10%			
3450	For 1-1/4" IPS connection, add					325%	14%			
3500	For 1-1/2" IPS connection, add					370%	18%			
3550	For 2" IPS connection, add					445%	24%			
3600	For tapped drain port in box, add					206			206	226
4000	Non-freeze, CI body, bronze frame & scoriated cover									
4010	with hose storage									
4100	2' depth of bury	1 Plum	7	1.143	Ea.	4,225	85.50		4,310.50	4,775
4120	3' depth of bury		7	1.143		4,425	85.50		4,510.50	5,000
4140	4' depth of bury		7	1.143		4,550	85.50		4,635.50	5,150

22 11 Facility Water Distribution

22 11 19 – Domestic Water Piping Specialties

22 11 19.64 Hydrants		Crew	Daily Output	Labor-Hours	Unit	Material	2024 Bare Costs Labor	2024 Bare Costs Equipment	Total	Total Incl O&P
4160	5' depth of bury	1 Plum	6.50	1.231	Ea.	3,175	92		3,267	3,625
4180	6' depth of bury		6	1.333		2,825	99.50		2,924.50	3,250
4200	7' depth of bury		5.50	1.455		4,900	109		5,009	5,525
4220	8' depth of bury		5	1.600		5,025	119		5,144	5,700
4240	9' depth of bury		4.50	1.778		4,675	133		4,808	5,350
4260	10' depth of bury		4	2		5,400	149		5,549	6,150
4280	For 1" IPS connection, add					1,025			1,025	1,125
4300	For tapped drain port in box, add					206			206	226
5000	Moderate climate, all bronze, polished face									
5020	and scoriated cover, set flush									
5100	3/4" IPS connection	1 Plum	16	.500	Ea.	1,600	37.50		1,637.50	1,800
5120	1" IPS connection	"	14	.571		3,625	42.50		3,667.50	4,075
5200	For tapped drain port in box, add					228			228	251
6000	Ground post type, all non-freeze, all bronze, aluminum casing									
6010	guard, exposed head, 3/4" IPS connection									
6100	2' depth of bury	1 Plum	8	1	Ea.	2,150	74.50		2,224.50	2,475
6120	3' depth of bury		8	1		1,450	74.50		1,524.50	1,700
6140	4' depth of bury		8	1		2,525	74.50		2,599.50	2,875
6160	5' depth of bury		7	1.143		1,600	85.50		1,685.50	1,875
6180	6' depth of bury		7	1.143		2,900	85.50		2,985.50	3,300
6200	7' depth of bury		6	1.333		1,925	99.50		2,024.50	2,250
6220	8' depth of bury		5	1.600		1,700	119		1,819	2,025
6240	9' depth of bury		4	2		3,600	149		3,749	4,200
6260	10' depth of bury		4	2		3,825	149		3,974	4,425
6300	For 1" IPS connection, add					40%	10%			
6350	For 1-1/4" IPS connection, add					140%	14%			
6400	For 1-1/2" IPS connection, add					225%	18%			
6450	For 2" IPS connection, add					315%	24%			

22 11 23 – Domestic Water Pumps

22 11 23.10 General Utility Pumps

		Crew	Daily Output	Labor-Hours	Unit	Material	Labor	Equipment	Total	Total Incl O&P
0010	**GENERAL UTILITY PUMPS**									
2000	Single stage									
3000	Double suction,									
3140	50 HP, 5" D x 6" S	Q-2	.33	72.727	Ea.	11,000	5,075		16,075	19,600
3180	60 HP, 6" D x 8" S	Q-3	.30	107		31,800	7,575		39,375	46,300
3190	75 HP, to 2,500 GPM		.28	114		38,600	8,125		46,725	54,500
3220	100 HP, to 3,000 GPM		.26	123		49,600	8,750		58,350	67,500
3240	150 HP, to 4,000 GPM		.24	133		52,000	9,475		61,475	71,000
4000	Centrifugal, end suction, mounted on base									
4010	Horizontal mounted, with drip proof motor, rated @ 100' head									
4020	Vertical split case, single stage									
4040	100 GPM, 5 HP, 1-1/2" discharge	Q-1	1.70	9.412	Ea.	8,450	630		9,080	10,200
4050	200 GPM, 10 HP, 2" discharge		1.30	12.308		9,225	825		10,050	11,400
4060	250 GPM, 10 HP, 3" discharge		1.28	12.500		10,100	840		10,940	12,500
4070	300 GPM, 15 HP, 2" discharge	Q-2	1.56	15.385		11,400	1,075		12,475	14,200
4080	500 GPM, 20 HP, 4" discharge		1.44	16.667		14,300	1,150		15,450	17,400
4090	750 GPM, 30 HP, 4" discharge		1.20	20		15,100	1,400		16,500	18,700
4100	1,050 GPM, 40 HP, 5" discharge		1	24		11,000	1,675		12,675	14,600
4110	1,500 GPM, 60 HP, 6" discharge		.60	40		31,800	2,775		34,575	39,200
4120	2,000 GPM, 75 HP, 6" discharge		.50	48		21,400	3,350		24,750	28,600
4130	3,000 GPM, 100 HP, 8" discharge		.40	60		43,300	4,175		47,475	54,000
4200	Horizontal split case, single stage									

22 11 Facility Water Distribution

22 11 23 – Domestic Water Pumps

22 11 23.10 General Utility Pumps

		Crew	Daily Output	Labor-Hours	Unit	Material	2024 Bare Costs Labor	2024 Bare Costs Equipment	Total	Total Incl O&P
4210	100 GPM, 7.5 HP, 1-1/2" discharge	Q-1	1.70	9.412	Ea.	9,700	630		10,330	11,600
4220	250 GPM, 15 HP, 2-1/2" discharge	"	1.30	12.308		11,300	825		12,125	13,700
4230	500 GPM, 20 HP, 4" discharge	Q-2	1.60	15		14,000	1,050		15,050	17,000
4240	750 GPM, 25 HP, 5" discharge		1.54	15.584		16,900	1,075		17,975	20,200
4250	1,000 GPM, 40 HP, 5" discharge		1.20	20		16,900	1,400		18,300	20,700
4260	1,500 GPM, 50 HP, 6" discharge	Q-3	1.42	22.535		22,900	1,600		24,500	27,600
4270	2,000 GPM, 75 HP, 8" discharge		1.14	28.070		29,700	2,000		31,700	35,700
4280	3,000 GPM, 100 HP, 10" discharge		.96	33.333		41,700	2,375		44,075	49,400
4290	3,500 GPM, 150 HP, 10" discharge		.86	37.209		52,000	2,650		54,650	61,000
4300	4,000 GPM, 200 HP, 10" discharge		.66	48.485		44,700	3,450		48,150	54,500
4330	Horizontal split case, two stage, 500' head									
4340	100 GPM, 40 HP, 1-1/2" discharge	Q-2	1.70	14.118	Ea.	34,200	985		35,185	39,100
4350	200 GPM, 50 HP, 1-1/2" discharge	"	1.44	16.667		36,900	1,150		38,050	42,200
4360	300 GPM, 75 HP, 2" discharge	Q-3	1.57	20.382		49,200	1,450		50,650	56,000
4370	400 GPM, 100 HP, 3" discharge		1.14	28.070		57,000	2,000		59,000	65,500
4380	800 GPM, 200 HP, 4" discharge		.86	37.209		79,000	2,650		81,650	91,000
5000	Centrifugal, in-line									
5006	Vertical mount, iron body, 125 lb. flgd, 1,800 RPM TEFC mtr									
5010	Single stage									
5012	.5 HP, 1-1/2" suction & discharge	Q-1	3.20	5	Ea.	950	335		1,285	1,550
5014	.75 HP, 2" suction & discharge		2.80	5.714		990	385		1,375	1,675
5015	1 HP, 3" suction & discharge		2.50	6.400		2,000	430		2,430	2,850
5016	1.5 HP, 3" suction & discharge		2.30	6.957		2,050	465		2,515	2,950
5018	2 HP, 4" suction & discharge		2.10	7.619		3,550	510		4,060	4,675
5020	3 HP, 5" suction & discharge		1.90	8.421		5,825	565		6,390	7,250
5030	5 HP, 6" suction & discharge		1.60	10		6,850	670		7,520	8,525
5040	7.5 HP, 6" suction & discharge		1.30	12.308		7,925	825		8,750	9,950
5050	10 HP, 8" suction & discharge	Q-2	1.80	13.333		8,625	930		9,555	10,900
5060	15 HP, 8" suction & discharge		1.70	14.118		10,200	985		11,185	12,700
5064	20 HP, 8" suction & discharge		1.60	15		12,200	1,050		13,250	15,000
5070	30 HP, 8" suction & discharge		1.50	16		26,200	1,125		27,325	30,500
5080	40 HP, 8" suction & discharge		1.40	17.143		31,400	1,200		32,600	36,400
5090	50 HP, 8" suction & discharge		1.30	18.462		32,000	1,275		33,275	37,100
5094	60 HP, 8" suction & discharge		.90	26.667		38,500	1,850		40,350	45,100
5100	75 HP, 8" suction & discharge	Q-3	.60	53.333		38,500	3,800		42,300	47,900
5110	100 HP, 8" suction & discharge	"	.50	64		27,200	4,550		31,750	36,700

22 11 23.11 Miscellaneous Pumps

		Crew	Daily Output	Labor-Hours	Unit	Material	2024 Bare Costs Labor	2024 Bare Costs Equipment	Total	Total Incl O&P
0010	**MISCELLANEOUS PUMPS**									
0020	Water pump, portable, gasoline powered									
0100	170 GPH, 2" discharge	Q-1	11	1.455	Ea.	1,425	97.50		1,522.50	1,725
0110	343 GPH, 3" discharge		10.50	1.524		1,325	102		1,427	1,600
0120	608 GPH, 4" discharge		10	1.600		2,975	107		3,082	3,425
0500	Pump, propylene body, housing and impeller									
0510	22 GPM, 1/3 HP, 40' HD	1 Plum	5	1.600	Ea.	775	119		894	1,025
0520	33 GPM, 1/2 HP, 40' HD	Q-1	5	3.200		750	215		965	1,150
0530	53 GPM, 3/4 HP, 40' HD	"	4	4		1,475	269		1,744	2,025
0600	Rotary pump, CI									
0614	282 GPH, 3/4 HP, 1" discharge	Q-1	4.50	3.556	Ea.	2,150	239		2,389	2,725
0618	277 GPH, 1 HP, 1" discharge		4	4		2,150	269		2,419	2,775
0624	1,100 GPH, 1.5 HP, 1-1/4" discharge		3.60	4.444		5,950	299		6,249	6,975
0628	1,900 GPH, 2 HP, 1-1/4" discharge		3.20	5		7,975	335		8,310	9,275
1000	Turbine pump, CI									

22 11 Facility Water Distribution

22 11 23 – Domestic Water Pumps

22 11 23.11 Miscellaneous Pumps

		Crew	Daily Output	Labor-Hours	Unit	Material	2024 Bare Costs Labor	Equipment	Total	Total Incl O&P
1010	50 GPM, 2 HP, 3" discharge	Q-1	.80	20	Ea.	6,875	1,350		8,225	9,550
1020	100 GPM, 3 HP, 4" discharge	Q-2	.96	25		13,000	1,750		14,750	16,900
1030	250 GPM, 15 HP, 6" discharge	"	.94	25.532		16,100	1,775		17,875	20,400
1040	500 GPM, 25 HP, 6" discharge	Q-3	1.22	26.230		16,200	1,875		18,075	20,600
1050	1,000 GPM, 50 HP, 8" discharge		1.14	28.070		22,400	2,000		24,400	27,600
1060	2,000 GPM, 100 HP, 10" discharge		1	32		26,500	2,275		28,775	32,600
1070	3,000 GPM, 150 HP, 10" discharge		.80	40		42,700	2,850		45,550	51,000
1080	4,000 GPM, 200 HP, 12" discharge		.70	45.714		46,700	3,250		49,950	56,500
1090	6,000 GPM, 300 HP, 14" discharge		.60	53.333		71,000	3,800		74,800	84,000
1100	10,000 GPM, 300 HP, 18" discharge	↓	.58	55.172	↓	82,000	3,925		85,925	96,500
2000	Centrifugal stainless steel pumps									
2100	100 GPM, 100' TDH, 3 HP	Q-1	1.80	8.889	Ea.	23,200	595		23,795	26,400
2130	250 GPM, 100' TDH, 10 HP	"	1.28	12.500		32,500	840		33,340	37,100
2160	500 GPM, 100' TDH, 20 HP	Q-2	1.44	16.667	↓	37,200	1,150		38,350	42,600
2200	Vertical turbine stainless steel pumps									
2220	100 GPM, 100' TDH, 7.5 HP	Q-2	.95	25.263	Ea.	130,000	1,750		131,750	145,500
2240	250 GPM, 100' TDH, 15 HP		.94	25.532		144,000	1,775		145,775	161,000
2260	500 GPM, 100' TDH, 20 HP	↓	.93	25.806		158,000	1,800		159,800	176,000
2280	750 GPM, 100' TDH, 30 HP	Q-3	1.19	26.891		172,000	1,900		173,900	192,000
2300	1,000 GPM, 100' TDH, 40 HP	"	1.16	27.586		186,000	1,950		187,950	207,500
2320	100 GPM, 200' TDH, 15 HP	Q-2	.94	25.532		199,500	1,775		201,275	222,000
2340	250 GPM, 200' TDH, 25 HP	Q-3	1.22	26.230		213,500	1,875		215,375	238,000
2360	500 GPM, 200' TDH, 40 HP		1.16	27.586		227,500	1,950		229,450	253,500
2380	750 GPM, 200' TDH, 60 HP		1.13	28.319		215,500	2,000		217,500	240,000
2400	1,000 GPM, 200' TDH, 75 HP	↓	1.12	28.571	↓	236,500	2,025		238,525	263,000

22 11 23.13 Domestic-Water Packaged Booster Pumps

		Crew	Daily Output	Labor-Hours	Unit	Material	Labor	Equipment	Total	Total Incl O&P
0010	**DOMESTIC-WATER PACKAGED BOOSTER PUMPS**									
0200	Pump system, with diaphragm tank, control, press. switch									
0300	1 HP pump	Q-1	1.30	12.308	Ea.	13,700	825		14,525	16,300
0400	1-1/2 HP pump		1.25	12.800		13,900	860		14,760	16,500
0420	2 HP pump		1.20	13.333		13,100	895		13,995	15,700
0440	3 HP pump	↓	1.10	14.545		14,400	975		15,375	17,400
0460	5 HP pump	Q-2	1.50	16		14,700	1,125		15,825	17,800
0480	7-1/2 HP pump		1.42	16.901		17,800	1,175		18,975	21,300
0500	10 HP pump	↓	1.34	17.910	↓	18,500	1,250		19,750	22,300
2000	Pump system, variable speed, base, controls, starter									
2010	Duplex, 100' head									
2020	400 GPM, 7-1/2 HP, 4" discharge	Q-2	.70	34.286	Ea.	83,000	2,400		85,400	95,000
2025	Triplex, 100' head									
2030	1,000 GPM, 15 HP, 6" discharge	Q-2	.50	48	Ea.	89,000	3,350		92,350	103,000
2040	1,700 GPM, 30 HP, 6" discharge	"	.30	80		133,000	5,575		138,575	155,000
0020	Chlorinator Injector, sewer, gas injected w/booster pump	Q-1	1.30	12.308	↓	2,850	825		3,675	4,375

22 12 Facility Potable-Water Storage Tanks

22 12 21 – Facility Underground Potable-Water Storage Tanks

22 12 21.13 Fiberglass, Undrgrnd Pot.-Water Storage Tanks

		Crew	Daily Output	Labor-Hours	Unit	Material	2024 Bare Costs Labor	Equipment	Total	Total Incl O&P
0010	**FIBERGLASS, UNDERGROUND POTABLE-WATER STORAGE TANKS**									
0020	Excludes excavation, backfill & piping									
0030	Single wall									
2000	600 gallon capacity	B-21B	3.75	10.667	Ea.	1,400	570	595	2,565	3,025
2010	1,000 gallon capacity		3.50	11.429		2,775	610	635	4,020	4,650
2020	2,000 gallon capacity		3.25	12.308		4,425	655	685	5,765	6,575
2030	4,000 gallon capacity		3	13.333		8,325	710	740	9,775	11,000
2040	6,000 gallon capacity		2.65	15.094		22,000	805	840	23,645	26,300
2050	8,000 gallon capacity		2.30	17.391		22,400	925	965	24,290	27,100
2060	10,000 gallon capacity		2	20		22,600	1,075	1,100	24,775	27,600
2070	12,000 gallon capacity		1.50	26.667		21,100	1,425	1,475	24,000	26,900
2080	15,000 gallon capacity		1	40		26,800	2,125	2,225	31,150	35,100
2090	20,000 gallon capacity		.75	53.333		37,700	2,850	2,975	43,525	49,000
2100	25,000 gallon capacity		.50	80		54,000	4,275	4,450	62,725	70,000
2110	30,000 gallon capacity		.35	114		65,000	6,100	6,350	77,450	87,500
2120	40,000 gallon capacity		.30	133		88,500	7,100	7,425	103,025	116,000

22 12 23 – Facility Indoor Potable-Water Storage Tanks

22 12 23.13 Facility Steel, Indoor Pot.-Water Storage Tanks

		Crew	Daily Output	Labor-Hours	Unit	Material	2024 Bare Costs Labor	Equipment	Total	Total Incl O&P
0010	**FACILITY STEEL, INDOOR POT.-WATER STORAGE TANKS**									
2000	Galvanized steel, 15 gal., 14" diam. x 26" LOA	1 Plum	12	.667	Ea.	1,125	50		1,175	1,300
2060	30 gal., 14" diam. x 49" LOA		11	.727		1,250	54.50		1,304.50	1,450
2080	80 gal., 20" diam. x 64" LOA		9	.889		1,850	66.50		1,916.50	2,125
2100	135 gal., 24" diam. x 75" LOA		6	1.333		2,750	99.50		2,849.50	3,175
2120	240 gal., 30" diam. x 86" LOA		4	2		5,100	149		5,249	5,850
2140	300 gal., 36" diam. x 76" LOA		3	2.667		7,175	199		7,374	8,175
2160	400 gal., 36" diam. x 100" LOA	Q-1	4	4		8,725	269		8,994	10,000
2180	500 gal., 36" diam. x 126" LOA	"	3	5.333		10,900	360		11,260	12,500
3000	Glass lined, P.E., 80 gal., 20" diam. x 60" LOA	1 Plum	9	.889		4,550	66.50		4,616.50	5,125
3060	140 gal., 24" diam. x 75" LOA		6	1.333		6,275	99.50		6,374.50	7,050
3080	200 gal., 30" diam. x 71" LOA		4	2		8,525	149		8,674	9,600
3100	350 gal., 36" diam. x 86" LOA		3	2.667		10,300	199		10,499	11,600
3120	450 gal., 42" diam. x 79" LOA	Q-1	4	4		14,000	269		14,269	15,800
3140	600 gal., 48" diam. x 81" LOA		3	5.333		17,100	360		17,460	19,300
3160	750 gal., 48" diam. x 105" LOA		3	5.333		19,200	360		19,560	21,600
3180	900 gal., 54" diam. x 95" LOA		2.50	6.400		26,700	430		27,130	30,000
3200	1,500 gal., 54" diam. x 153" LOA		2	8		34,400	535		34,935	38,600
3220	1,800 gal., 54" diam. x 181" LOA		1.50	10.667		38,400	715		39,115	43,400
3240	2,000 gal., 60" diam. x 165" LOA		1	16		44,100	1,075		45,175	50,000
3260	3,500 gal., 72" diam. x 201" LOA	Q-2	1.50	16		56,000	1,125		57,125	63,000

22 13 Facility Sanitary Sewerage

22 13 16 – Sanitary Waste and Vent Piping

22 13 16.20 Pipe, Cast Iron

			Crew	Daily Output	Labor-Hours	Unit	Material	2024 Bare Costs Labor	Equipment	Total	Total Incl O&P
0010	**PIPE, CAST IRON**, Soil, on clevis hanger assemblies, 5' OC	R221113-70									
0020	Single hub, service wt., lead & oakum joints 10' OC										
2120	2" diameter	R221316-10	Q-1	63	.254	L.F.	11	17.05		28.05	37.50
2140	3" diameter			60	.267		14.45	17.90		32.35	42.50
2160	4" diameter	R221316-20		55	.291		18.65	19.55		38.20	49.50
2180	5" diameter		Q-2	76	.316		37	22		59	73.50
2200	6" diameter		"	73	.329		31	23		54	68.50

22 13 Facility Sanitary Sewerage

22 13 16 – Sanitary Waste and Vent Piping

22 13 16.20 Pipe, Cast Iron		Crew	Daily Output	Labor-Hours	Unit	Material	2024 Bare Costs Labor	Equipment	Total	Total Incl O&P
2220	8" diameter	Q-3	59	.542	L.F.	48	38.50		86.50	111
2240	10" diameter		54	.593		60.50	42		102.50	129
2260	12" diameter		48	.667		113	47.50		160.50	196
2261	15" diameter	↓	40	.800		172	57		229	274
2320	For service weight, double hub, add					10%				
2340	For extra heavy, single hub, add					48%	4%			
2360	For extra heavy, double hub, add				↓	71%	4%			
2400	Lead for caulking (1#/diam. in.)	Q-1	160	.100	Lb.	6.65	6.70		13.35	17.30
2420	Oakum for caulking (1/8#/diam. in.)	"	40	.400	"	14.95	27		41.95	56.50
2960	To delete hangers, subtract									
2970	2" diam. to 4" diam.					16%	19%			
2980	5" diam. to 8" diam.					14%	14%			
2990	10" diam. to 15" diam.					13%	19%			
3000	Single hub, service wt., push-on gasket joints 10' OC									
3010	2" diameter	Q-1	66	.242	L.F.	12.30	16.30		28.60	37.50
3020	3" diameter		63	.254		16.10	17.05		33.15	43.50
3030	4" diameter	↓	57	.281		21	18.85		39.85	51
3040	5" diameter	Q-2	79	.304		40.50	21		61.50	76
3050	6" diameter	"	75	.320		34.50	22.50		57	71
3060	8" diameter	Q-3	62	.516		55.50	36.50		92	116
3070	10" diameter		56	.571		73.50	40.50		114	142
3080	12" diameter		49	.653		130	46.50		176.50	212
3082	15" diameter	↓	40	.800	↓	192	57		249	296
3100	For service weight, double hub, add					65%				
3110	For extra heavy, single hub, add					48%	4%			
3120	For extra heavy, double hub, add					29%	4%			
3130	To delete hangers, subtract									
3140	2" diam. to 4" diam.					12%	21%			
3150	5" diam. to 8" diam.					10%	16%			
3160	10" diam. to 15" diam.					9%	21%			
4000	No hub, couplings 10' OC									
4100	1-1/2" diameter	Q-1	71	.225	L.F.	10.75	15.15		25.90	34.50
4120	2" diameter		67	.239		11.25	16.05		27.30	36.50
4140	3" diameter		64	.250		20	16.80		36.80	47
4160	4" diameter	↓	58	.276		26	18.55		44.55	56
4180	5" diameter	Q-2	83	.289		28	20		48	60.50
4200	6" diameter	"	79	.304		40.50	21		61.50	76.50
4220	8" diameter	Q-3	69	.464		78.50	33		111.50	135
4240	10" diameter		61	.525		125	37.50		162.50	193
4244	12" diameter		58	.552		175	39		214	251
4248	15" diameter	↓	52	.615	↓	259	43.50		302.50	350
4280	To delete hangers, subtract									
4290	1-1/2" diam. to 6" diam.					22%	47%			
4300	8" diam. to 10" diam.					21%	44%			
4310	12" diam. to 15" diam.					19%	40%			

22 13 16.30 Pipe Fittings, Cast Iron

22 13 16.30 Pipe Fittings, Cast Iron		Crew	Daily Output	Labor-Hours	Unit	Material	2024 Bare Costs Labor	Equipment	Total	Total Incl O&P
0010	**PIPE FITTINGS, CAST IRON**, Soil									
0040	Hub and spigot, service weight, lead & oakum joints									
0080	1/4 bend, 2"	Q-1	16	1	Ea.	45	67		112	150
0120	3"		14	1.143		57	77		134	177
0140	4"	↓	13	1.231		89.50	82.50		172	222
0160	5"	Q-2	18	1.333	↓	125	93		218	275

22 13 Facility Sanitary Sewerage

22 13 16 – Sanitary Waste and Vent Piping

22 13 16.30 Pipe Fittings, Cast Iron		Crew	Daily Output	Labor-Hours	Unit	Material	2024 Bare Costs Labor	Equipment	Total	Total Incl O&P
0180	6"	Q-2	17	1.412	Ea.	155	98.50		253.50	315
0200	8"	Q-3	11	2.909		470	207		677	820
0220	10"		10	3.200		685	227		912	1,100
0224	12"		9	3.556		925	253		1,178	1,400
0226	15"	↓	7	4.571		3,325	325		3,650	4,125
0242	Short sweep, CI, 90°, 2"	Q-1	16	1		41.50	67		108.50	146
0243	3"		14	1.143		74.50	77		151.50	196
0244	4"	↓	13	1.231		114	82.50		196.50	249
0245	6"	Q-2	17	1.412		232	98.50		330.50	400
0246	8"	Q-3	11	2.909		505	207		712	860
0247	10"		10	3.200		1,025	227		1,252	1,475
0248	12"		9	3.556		2,400	253		2,653	3,025
0251	Long sweep elbow									
0252	2"	Q-1	16	1	Ea.	65	67		132	172
0253	3"		14	1.143		92.50	77		169.50	216
0254	4"	↓	13	1.231		136	82.50		218.50	272
0255	6"	Q-2	17	1.412		273	98.50		371.50	445
0256	8"	Q-3	11	2.909		615	207		822	985
0257	10"		10	3.200		1,050	227		1,277	1,500
0258	12"		9	3.556		1,700	253		1,953	2,225
0259	15"	↓	7	4.571		4,575	325		4,900	5,525
0266	Closet bend, 3" diameter with flange 10" x 16"	Q-1	14	1.143		235	77		312	375
0268	16" x 16"		12	1.333		263	89.50		352.50	420
0270	Closet bend, 4" diameter, 2-1/2" x 4" ring, 6" x 16"		13	1.231		205	82.50		287.50	350
0280	8" x 16"		13	1.231		179	82.50		261.50	320
0290	10" x 12"		12	1.333		167	89.50		256.50	315
0300	10" x 18"		11	1.455		246	97.50		343.50	415
0310	12" x 16"		11	1.455		207	97.50		304.50	375
0330	16" x 16"		10	1.600		270	107		377	455
0340	1/8 bend, 2"		16	1		30.50	67		97.50	134
0350	3"		14	1.143		47.50	77		124.50	167
0360	4"	↓	13	1.231		69.50	82.50		152	200
0380	5"	Q-2	18	1.333		98	93		191	246
0400	6"	"	17	1.412		118	98.50		216.50	276
0420	8"	Q-3	11	2.909		355	207		562	695
0440	10"		10	3.200		505	227		732	895
0460	12"		9	3.556		960	253		1,213	1,425
0461	15"	↓	7	4.571		2,325	325		2,650	3,025
0500	Sanitary tee, 2"	Q-1	10	1.600		59.50	107		166.50	226
0540	3"		9	1.778		96.50	119		215.50	284
0620	4"	↓	8	2		118	134		252	330
0700	5"	Q-2	12	2		235	139		374	465
0800	6"	"	11	2.182		266	152		418	520
0880	8"	Q-3	7	4.571		705	325		1,030	1,250
0881	10"		7	4.571		1,300	325		1,625	1,900
0882	12"		6	5.333		2,300	380		2,680	3,100
0883	15"	↓	4	8	↓	4,775	570		5,345	6,100
0900	Sanitary tee, tapped									
0901	2" x 2"	Q-1	9	1.778	Ea.	80	119		199	266
0902	3" x 2"		8	2		89.50	134		223.50	299
0903	4" x 2"	↓	7	2.286	↓	146	154		300	390
0910	Sanitary cross, tapped (double tapped sanitary tee)									
0911	2" x 2"	Q-1	7	2.286	Ea.	85.50	154		239.50	320

22 13 Facility Sanitary Sewerage
22 13 16 – Sanitary Waste and Vent Piping

22 13 16.30 Pipe Fittings, Cast Iron		Crew	Daily Output	Labor-Hours	Unit	Material	2024 Bare Costs Labor	Equipment	Total	Total Incl O&P
0912	3" x 2"	Q-1	6	2.667	Ea.	158	179		337	440
0913	4" x 2"	↓	5	3.200	↓	154	215		369	490
0940	Sanitary tee, reducing									
0942	3" x 2"	Q-1	10	1.600	Ea.	83	107		190	251
0943	4" x 3"		9	1.778		108	119		227	297
0944	4" x 2"		9	1.778		101	119		220	289
0945	5" x 3"	Q-2	12.50	1.920		210	134		344	430
0946	6" x 4"		10	2.400		300	167		467	580
0947	6" x 3"		11	2.182		216	152		368	465
0948	6" x 2"	↓	12.50	1.920		209	134		343	430
0949	8" x 6"	Q-3	9	3.556		595	253		848	1,025
0950	8" x 5"		9	3.556		415	253		668	835
0951	8" x 4"		10	3.200		450	227		677	835
0954	10" x 6"		8	4		1,025	284		1,309	1,550
0958	12" x 8"		7	4.571		1,850	325		2,175	2,500
0962	15" x 10"	↓	5	6.400		2,025	455		2,480	2,925
1000	Tee, 2"	Q-1	10	1.600		86	107		193	255
1060	3"		9	1.778		128	119		247	320
1120	4"	↓	8	2		165	134		299	380
1200	5"	Q-2	12	2		350	139		489	590
1300	6"	"	11	2.182		345	152		497	605
1380	8"	Q-3	7	4.571	↓	370	325		695	890
1400	Combination Y and 1/8 bend									
1420	2"	Q-1	10	1.600	Ea.	74.50	107		181.50	242
1460	3"		9	1.778		113	119		232	305
1520	4"	↓	8	2		156	134		290	370
1540	5"	Q-2	12	2		297	139		436	530
1560	6"		11	2.182		375	152		527	640
1580	8"	↓	7	3.429		925	239		1,164	1,375
1582	12"	Q-3	6	5.333		1,325	380		1,705	2,050
1584	Combination Y & 1/8 bend, reducing									
1586	3" x 2"	Q-1	10	1.600	Ea.	86	107		193	255
1587	4" x 2"		9.50	1.684		116	113		229	295
1588	4" x 3"	↓	9	1.778		136	119		255	330
1589	6" x 2"	Q-2	12.50	1.920		242	134		376	465
1590	6" x 3"		12	2		258	139		397	490
1591	6" x 4"		11	2.182		271	152		423	525
1592	8" x 2"	Q-3	11	2.909		510	207		717	865
1593	8" x 4"		10	3.200		450	227		677	835
1594	8" x 6"	↓	9	3.556		620	253		873	1,050
1600	Double Y, 2"	Q-1	8	2		133	134		267	345
1610	3"		7	2.286		165	154		319	410
1620	4"	↓	6.50	2.462		216	165		381	485
1630	5"	Q-2	9	2.667		415	186		601	735
1640	6"	"	8	3		565	209		774	930
1650	8"	Q-3	5.50	5.818		1,350	415		1,765	2,125
1660	10"		5	6.400		3,275	455		3,730	4,275
1670	12"	↓	4.50	7.111		3,750	505		4,255	4,875
1676	Combination double Y & 1/8 bend									
1678	2"	Q-1	8	2	Ea.	153	134		287	370
1680	3"		7	2.286		196	154		350	445
1682	4"	↓	6.50	2.462		320	165		485	600
1684	6"	Q-2	8	3	↓	1,100	209		1,309	1,525

22 13 Facility Sanitary Sewerage

22 13 16 – Sanitary Waste and Vent Piping

22 13 16.30 Pipe Fittings, Cast Iron

		Crew	Daily Output	Labor-Hours	Unit	Material	2024 Bare Costs Labor	Equipment	Total	Total Incl O&P
1690	Combination double Y & 1/8 bend, CI, reducing									
1692	3" x 2"	Q-1	8	2	Ea.	170	134		304	385
1694	4" x 2"		7	2.286		198	154		352	445
1696	4" x 3"	▼	7	2.286		226	154		380	475
1698	6" x 4"	Q-2	9	2.667	▼	725	186		911	1,075
1700	Double Y, CI, reducing									
1702	3" x 2"	Q-1	8	2	Ea.	141	134		275	355
1703	4" x 2"		7	2.286		170	154		324	415
1704	4" x 3"	▼	7	2.286		179	154		333	425
1706	6" x 3"	Q-2	9.50	2.526		430	176		606	735
1707	6" x 4"	"	9	2.667		440	186		626	755
1708	8" x 4"	Q-3	8.50	3.765		945	267		1,212	1,450
1709	8" x 6"		8	4		970	284		1,254	1,500
1711	10" x 6"		8	4		2,075	284		2,359	2,700
1712	10" x 8"		6.50	4.923		3,175	350		3,525	4,000
1713	12" x 6"		7.50	4.267		3,825	305		4,130	4,675
1714	12" x 8"	▼	6	5.333		3,775	380		4,155	4,725
1740	Reducer, 3" x 2"	Q-1	15	1.067		41.50	71.50		113	153
1750	4" x 2"		14.50	1.103		47.50	74		121.50	163
1760	4" x 3"		14	1.143		54.50	77		131.50	174
1770	5" x 2"		14	1.143		115	77		192	241
1780	5" x 3"		13.50	1.185		122	79.50		201.50	252
1790	5" x 4"		13	1.231		70	82.50		152.50	200
1800	6" x 2"		13.50	1.185		114	79.50		193.50	243
1810	6" x 3"		13	1.231		111	82.50		193.50	245
1830	6" x 4"		12.50	1.280		110	86		196	249
1840	6" x 5"	▼	11	1.455		118	97.50		215.50	275
1880	8" x 3"	Q-2	13.50	1.778		213	124		337	420
1900	8" x 4"		13	1.846		183	129		312	390
1920	8" x 5"		12	2		193	139		332	420
1940	8" x 6"		12	2		188	139		327	415
1942	10" x 4"		12.50	1.920		276	134		410	505
1943	10" x 6"		11.50	2.087		310	145		455	555
1944	10" x 8"		9.50	2.526		310	176		486	600
1945	12" x 4"		11.50	2.087		450	145		595	710
1946	12" x 6"		11	2.182		480	152		632	755
1947	12" x 8"		9	2.667		495	186		681	820
1948	12" x 10"		8.50	2.824		505	197		702	850
1949	15" x 6"	Q-3	12	2.667		940	189		1,129	1,300
1950	15" x 8"		10	3.200		1,025	227		1,252	1,475
1951	15" x 10"		9.50	3.368		1,050	239		1,289	1,525
1952	15" x 12"	▼	9	3.556		1,075	253		1,328	1,550
1960	Increaser, 2" x 3"	Q-1	15	1.067		72.50	71.50		144	187
1980	2" x 4"		14	1.143		100	77		177	224
2000	2" x 5"		13	1.231		76	82.50		158.50	207
2020	3" x 4"		13	1.231		110	82.50		192.50	244
2040	3" x 5"		13	1.231		76	82.50		158.50	207
2060	3" x 6"		12	1.333		101	89.50		190.50	245
2070	4" x 5"		13	1.231		131	82.50		213.50	267
2080	4" x 6"	▼	12	1.333		149	89.50		238.50	297
2090	4" x 8"	Q-2	13	1.846		310	129		439	530
2100	5" x 6"	Q-1	11	1.455		221	97.50		318.50	390
2110	5" x 8"	Q-2	12	2	▼	240	139		379	470

22 13 Facility Sanitary Sewerage
22 13 16 – Sanitary Waste and Vent Piping

22 13 16.30 Pipe Fittings, Cast Iron		Crew	Daily Output	Labor-Hours	Unit	Material	2024 Bare Costs Labor	Equipment	Total	Total Incl O&P
2120	6" x 8"	Q-2	12	2	Ea.	355	139		494	600
2130	6" x 10"		8	3		440	209		649	795
2140	8" x 10"		6.50	3.692		655	257		912	1,100
2150	10" x 12"		5.50	4.364		805	305		1,110	1,325
2500	Y, 2"	Q-1	10	1.600		54.50	107		161.50	220
2510	3"		9	1.778		101	119		220	289
2520	4"		8	2		135	134		269	350
2530	5"	Q-2	12	2		239	139		378	470
2540	6"	"	11	2.182		310	152		462	565
2550	8"	Q-3	7	4.571		760	325		1,085	1,325
2560	10"		6	5.333		1,225	380		1,605	1,925
2570	12"		5	6.400		3,100	455		3,555	4,075
2580	15"		4	8		6,325	570		6,895	7,825
2581	Y, reducing									
2582	3" x 2"	Q-1	10	1.600	Ea.	78	107		185	246
2584	4" x 2"		9.50	1.684		105	113		218	283
2586	4" x 3"		9	1.778		116	119		235	305
2588	6" x 2"	Q-2	12.50	1.920		207	134		341	425
2590	6" x 3"		12.25	1.959		211	137		348	435
2592	6" x 4"		12	2		209	139		348	435
2594	8" x 2"	Q-3	11	2.909		465	207		672	815
2596	8" x 3"		10.50	3.048		465	217		682	830
2598	8" x 4"		10	3.200		400	227		627	780
2600	8" x 6"		9	3.556		495	253		748	920
2602	10" x 3"		10	3.200		695	227		922	1,100
2604	10" x 4"		9.50	3.368		685	239		924	1,100
2606	10" x 6"		8	4		745	284		1,029	1,250
2608	10" x 8"		8	4		1,025	284		1,309	1,550
2610	12" x 4"		9	3.556		1,150	253		1,403	1,650
2612	12" x 6"		8.50	3.765		1,200	267		1,467	1,700
2614	12" x 8"		8	4		1,475	284		1,759	2,050
2616	12" x 10"		7.50	4.267		2,725	305		3,030	3,450
2618	15" x 4"		7	4.571		3,875	325		4,200	4,725
2620	15" x 6"		6.50	4.923		4,025	350		4,375	4,975
2622	15" x 8"		6.50	4.923		4,100	350		4,450	5,050
2624	15" x 10"		5	6.400		4,275	455		4,730	5,375
2626	15" x 12"		4.50	7.111		4,350	505		4,855	5,525
3000	For extra heavy, add					44%	4%			
3600	Hub and spigot, service weight gasket joint									
3605	Note: gaskets and joint labor have									
3606	been included with all listed fittings.									
3610	1/4 bend, 2"	Q-1	20	.800	Ea.	58	53.50		111.50	144
3620	3"		17	.941		73.50	63		136.50	175
3630	4"		15	1.067		110	71.50		181.50	228
3640	5"	Q-2	21	1.143		158	79.50		237.50	291
3650	6"	"	19	1.263		189	88		277	340
3660	8"	Q-3	12	2.667		540	189		729	875
3670	10"		11	2.909		815	207		1,022	1,200
3680	12"		10	3.200		1,100	227		1,327	1,550
3690	15"		8	4		3,525	284		3,809	4,300
3692	Short sweep, CI, 90°, 2"	Q-1	20	.800		54.50	53.50		108	140
3693	3"		17	.941		91	63		154	194
3694	4"		15	1.067		135	71.50		206.50	256

22 13 Facility Sanitary Sewerage

22 13 16 – Sanitary Waste and Vent Piping

22 13 16.30 Pipe Fittings, Cast Iron

		Crew	Daily Output	Labor-Hours	Unit	Material	2024 Bare Costs Labor	Equipment	Total	Total Incl O&P
3695	6"	Q-2	19	1.263	Ea.	266	88		354	425
3696	8"	Q-3	12	2.667		575	189		764	915
3697	10"		11	2.909		1,150	207		1,357	1,575
3698	12"		10	3.200		2,575	227		2,802	3,175
3700	Closet bend, 3" diameter with ring 10" x 16"	Q-1	17	.941		252	63		315	370
3710	16" x 16"		15	1.067		279	71.50		350.50	410
3730	Closet bend, 4" diameter, 1" x 4" ring, 6" x 16"		15	1.067		226	71.50		297.50	355
3740	8" x 16"		15	1.067		200	71.50		271.50	325
3750	10" x 12"		14	1.143		188	77		265	320
3760	10" x 18"		13	1.231		267	82.50		349.50	415
3770	12" x 16"		13	1.231		228	82.50		310.50	375
3780	16" x 16"		12	1.333		291	89.50		380.50	455
3786	Long sweep elbow									
3787	2"	Q-1	20	.800	Ea.	78	53.50		131.50	166
3788	3"		17	.941		109	63		172	214
3789	4"		15	1.067		157	71.50		228.50	279
3790	6"	Q-2	19	1.263		305	88		393	470
3791	8"	Q-3	12	2.667		690	189		879	1,050
3792	10"		11	2.909		1,175	207		1,382	1,600
3793	12"		10	3.200		1,850	227		2,077	2,400
3794	15"		8	4		4,775	284		5,059	5,675
3800	1/8 bend, 2"	Q-1	20	.800		43.50	53.50		97	128
3810	3"		17	.941		64	63		127	165
3820	4"		15	1.067		90.50	71.50		162	207
3830	5"	Q-2	21	1.143		131	79.50		210.50	262
3840	6"	"	19	1.263		152	88		240	298
3850	8"	Q-3	12	2.667		425	189		614	750
3860	10"		11	2.909		635	207		842	1,000
3870	12"		10	3.200		1,125	227		1,352	1,600
3880	15"		8	4		2,525	284		2,809	3,200
3882	Sanitary tee, tapped									
3884	2" x 2"	Q-1	11	1.455	Ea.	106	97.50		203.50	262
3886	3" x 2"		10	1.600		119	107		226	291
3888	4" x 2"		9	1.778		180	119		299	375
3890	Sanitary cross, tapped (double tapped sanitary tee)									
3892	2" x 2"	Q-1	9	1.778	Ea.	111	119		230	300
3894	3" x 2"		8	2		187	134		321	405
3896	4" x 2"		7	2.286		188	154		342	435
3900	Sanitary tee, 2"		12	1.333		85.50	89.50		175	228
3910	3"		10	1.600		129	107		236	300
3920	4"		9	1.778		160	119		279	355
3930	5"	Q-2	13	1.846		300	129		429	520
3940	6"	"	11	2.182		335	152		487	595
3950	8"	Q-3	8.50	3.765		855	267		1,122	1,350
3952	10"		8	4		1,550	284		1,834	2,125
3954	12"		7	4.571		2,625	325		2,950	3,350
3956	15"		6	5.333		5,175	380		5,555	6,275
3960	Sanitary tee, reducing									
3961	3" x 2"	Q-1	10.50	1.524	Ea.	112	102		214	276
3962	4" x 2"		10	1.600		135	107		242	310
3963	4" x 3"		9.50	1.684		146	113		259	330
3964	5" x 3"	Q-2	13.50	1.778		260	124		384	470
3965	6" x 2"		13	1.846		256	129		385	470

22 13 Facility Sanitary Sewerage
22 13 16 – Sanitary Waste and Vent Piping

22 13 16.30 Pipe Fittings, Cast Iron		Crew	Daily Output	Labor-Hours	Unit	Material	2024 Bare Costs Labor	Equipment	Total	Total Incl O&P
3966	6" x 3"	Q-2	12.50	1.920	Ea.	267	134		401	490
3967	6" x 4"	”	12	2		355	139		494	595
3968	8" x 4"	Q-3	10.50	3.048		545	217		762	920
3969	8" x 5"		10	3.200		525	227		752	915
3970	8" x 6"		9.50	3.368		705	239		944	1,125
3971	10" x 6"		9	3.556		1,175	253		1,428	1,675
3972	12" x 8"		8.50	3.765		2,075	267		2,342	2,700
3973	15" x 10"		6	5.333		2,350	380		2,730	3,175
3980	Tee, 2"	Q-1	12	1.333		112	89.50		201.50	256
3990	3"		10	1.600		161	107		268	340
4000	4"		9	1.778		207	119		326	405
4010	5"	Q-2	13	1.846		415	129		544	645
4020	6"	”	11	2.182		410	152		562	680
4030	8"	Q-3	8	4		515	284		799	995
4060	Combination Y and 1/8 bend									
4070	2"	Q-1	12	1.333	Ea.	101	89.50		190.50	244
4080	3"		10	1.600		147	107		254	320
4090	4"		9	1.778		198	119		317	395
4100	5"	Q-2	13	1.846		360	129		489	590
4110	6"	”	11	2.182		445	152		597	715
4120	8"	Q-3	8	4		1,075	284		1,359	1,600
4121	12"	”	7	4.571		1,675	325		2,000	2,300
4130	Combination Y & 1/8 bend, reducing									
4132	3" x 2"	Q-1	10.50	1.524	Ea.	115	102		217	279
4134	4" x 2"		10	1.600		150	107		257	325
4136	4" x 3"		9.50	1.684		174	113		287	360
4138	6" x 2"	Q-2	13	1.846		289	129		418	510
4140	6" x 3"		12.50	1.920		310	134		444	540
4142	6" x 4"		12	2		325	139		464	565
4144	8" x 2"	Q-3	11	2.909		620	207		827	985
4146	8" x 4"		10.50	3.048		545	217		762	920
4148	8" x 6"		9.50	3.368		725	239		964	1,150
4160	Double Y, 2"	Q-1	10	1.600		172	107		279	350
4170	3"		8	2		215	134		349	435
4180	4"		7	2.286		279	154		433	535
4190	5"	Q-2	10	2.400		515	167		682	815
4200	6"	”	9	2.667		665	186		851	1,000
4210	8"	Q-3	6	5.333		1,575	380		1,955	2,325
4220	10"		5	6.400		3,675	455		4,130	4,700
4230	12"		4.50	7.111		4,250	505		4,755	5,425
4234	Combination double Y & 1/8 bend									
4235	2"	Q-1	10	1.600	Ea.	192	107		299	370
4236	3"		8	2		246	134		380	470
4237	4"		7	2.286		385	154		539	655
4238	6"	Q-2	9	2.667		1,225	186		1,411	1,600
4242	Combination double Y & 1/8 bend, CI, reducing									
4243	3" x 2"	Q-1	9	1.778	Ea.	212	119		331	410
4244	4" x 2"		8	2		245	134		379	470
4245	4" x 3"		7.50	2.133		280	143		423	525
4246	6" x 4"	Q-2	10	2.400		805	167		972	1,125
4248	Double Y, CI, reducing									
4249	3" x 2"	Q-1	9	1.778	Ea.	183	119		302	380
4250	4" x 2"		8	2		217	134		351	440

22 13 Facility Sanitary Sewerage

22 13 16 – Sanitary Waste and Vent Piping

22 13 16.30 Pipe Fittings, Cast Iron

		Crew	Daily Output	Labor-Hours	Unit	Material	2024 Bare Costs Labor	Equipment	Total	Total Incl O&P
4251	4" x 3"	Q-1	7.50	2.133	Ea.	216	143		359	450
4252	6" x 3"	Q-2	10.50	2.286		500	159		659	785
4253	6" x 4"	"	10	2.400		515	167		682	815
4254	8" x 4"	Q-3	9.50	3.368		1,050	239		1,289	1,525
4255	8" x 6"		9	3.556		1,100	253		1,353	1,600
4256	10" x 6"		8.50	3.765		2,275	267		2,542	2,900
4257	10" x 8"		7.50	4.267		3,450	305		3,755	4,250
4258	12" x 6"		8	4		4,075	284		4,359	4,900
4259	12" x 8"	▼	7	4.571		4,075	325		4,400	4,950
4260	Reducer, 3" x 2"	Q-1	17	.941		71.50	63		134.50	173
4270	4" x 2"		16.50	.970		81.50	65		146.50	187
4280	4" x 3"		16	1		92	67		159	201
4290	5" x 2"		16	1		161	67		228	277
4300	5" x 3"		15.50	1.032		171	69.50		240.50	291
4310	5" x 4"		15	1.067		124	71.50		195.50	243
4320	6" x 2"		15.50	1.032		161	69.50		230.50	280
4330	6" x 3"		15	1.067		162	71.50		233.50	285
4336	6" x 4"		14	1.143		165	77		242	295
4340	6" x 5"	▼	13	1.231		185	82.50		267.50	325
4360	8" x 3"	Q-2	15	1.600		305	111		416	500
4370	8" x 4"		15	1.600		278	111		389	470
4380	8" x 5"		14	1.714		300	119		419	510
4390	8" x 6"		14	1.714		296	119		415	505
4394	10" x 4"		13.50	1.778		425	124		549	655
4395	10" x 6"		13	1.846		470	129		599	710
4396	10" x 8"		12.50	1.920		510	134		644	765
4397	12" x 4"		12	2		635	139		774	905
4398	12" x 6"		11.50	2.087		680	145		825	965
4399	12" x 8"		11	2.182		735	152		887	1,025
4400	12" x 10"	▼	10.50	2.286		795	159		954	1,100
4401	15" x 6"	Q-3	13	2.462		1,175	175		1,350	1,525
4402	15" x 8"		12	2.667		1,300	189		1,489	1,700
4403	15" x 10"		11	2.909		1,375	207		1,582	1,825
4404	15" x 12"	▼	10	3.200		1,425	227		1,652	1,925
4430	Increaser, 2" x 3"	Q-1	17	.941		89	63		152	192
4440	2" x 4"		16	1		121	67		188	233
4450	2" x 5"		15	1.067		109	71.50		180.50	227
4460	3" x 4"		15	1.067		131	71.50		202.50	251
4470	3" x 5"		15	1.067		109	71.50		180.50	227
4480	3" x 6"		14	1.143		135	77		212	263
4490	4" x 5"		15	1.067		164	71.50		235.50	287
4500	4" x 6"	▼	14	1.143		183	77		260	315
4510	4" x 8"	Q-2	15	1.600		385	111		496	585
4520	5" x 6"	Q-1	13	1.231		255	82.50		337.50	405
4530	5" x 8"	Q-2	14	1.714		315	119		434	525
4540	6" x 8"		14	1.714		430	119		549	655
4550	6" x 10"		10	2.400		570	167		737	875
4560	8" x 10"		8.50	2.824		785	197		982	1,150
4570	10" x 12"	▼	7.50	3.200		970	223		1,193	1,400
4600	Y, 2"	Q-1	12	1.333		80.50	89.50		170	222
4610	3"		10	1.600		134	107		241	305
4620	4"	▼	9	1.778		177	119		296	370
4630	5"	Q-2	13	1.846		305	129		434	525

22 13 Facility Sanitary Sewerage
22 13 16 – Sanitary Waste and Vent Piping

22 13 16.30 Pipe Fittings, Cast Iron		Crew	Daily Output	Labor-Hours	Unit	Material	2024 Bare Costs Labor	Equipment	Total	Total Incl O&P
4640	6"	Q-2	11	2.182	Ea.	380	152		532	640
4650	8"	Q-3	8	4		905	284		1,189	1,425
4660	10"		7	4.571		1,475	325		1,800	2,100
4670	12"		6	5.333		3,425	380		3,805	4,350
4672	15"	↓	5	6.400	↓	6,725	455		7,180	8,075
4680	Y, reducing									
4681	3" x 2"	Q-1	10.50	1.524	Ea.	108	102		210	271
4682	4" x 2"		10	1.600		139	107		246	315
4683	4" x 3"	↓	9.50	1.684		153	113		266	335
4684	6" x 2"	Q-2	13	1.846		254	129		383	470
4685	6" x 3"		12.50	1.920		262	134		396	485
4686	6" x 4"	↓	12	2		264	139		403	500
4687	8" x 2"	Q-3	11	2.909		555	207		762	915
4688	8" x 3"		10.75	2.977		555	211		766	925
4689	8" x 4"		10.50	3.048		495	217		712	865
4690	8" x 6"		9.50	3.368		605	239		844	1,025
4691	10" x 3"		10	3.200		840	227		1,067	1,275
4692	10" x 4"		9.50	3.368		835	239		1,074	1,275
4693	10" x 6"		9	3.556		910	253		1,163	1,375
4694	10" x 8"		8.80	3.636		1,225	258		1,483	1,725
4695	12" x 4"		9.50	3.368		1,350	239		1,589	1,825
4696	12" x 6"		9	3.556		1,400	253		1,653	1,900
4697	12" x 8"		8.50	3.765		1,725	267		1,992	2,300
4698	12" x 10"		8	4		3,025	284		3,309	3,750
4699	15" x 4"		8	4		4,075	284		4,359	4,925
4700	15" x 6"		7.50	4.267		4,275	305		4,580	5,150
4701	15" x 8"		7	4.571		4,375	325		4,700	5,300
4702	15" x 10"		6	5.333		4,600	380		4,980	5,625
4703	15" x 12"	↓	5	6.400	↓	4,700	455		5,155	5,850
4900	For extra heavy, add					44%	4%			
4940	Gasket and making push-on joint									
4950	2"	Q-1	40	.400	Ea.	13	27		40	54.50
4960	3"		35	.457		16.60	30.50		47.10	64
4970	4"	↓	32	.500		21	33.50		54.50	73
4980	5"	Q-2	43	.558		33	39		72	94.50
4990	6"	"	40	.600		34	42		76	99.50
5000	8"	Q-3	32	1		74.50	71		145.50	188
5010	10"		29	1.103		129	78.50		207.50	259
5020	12"		25	1.280		165	91		256	315
5022	15"	↓	21	1.524	↓	197	108		305	380
5030	Note: gaskets and joint labor have									
5040	been included with all listed fittings.									
5990	No hub									
6000	Cplg. & labor required at joints not incl. in fitting									
6010	price. Add 1 coupling per joint for installed price									
6020	1/4 bend, 1-1/2"				Ea.	22			22	24
6060	2"					24			24	26.50
6080	3"					33.50			33.50	37
6120	4"					49.50			49.50	54.50
6140	5"					111			111	123
6160	6"					123			123	136
6180	8"					335			335	370
6181	10"				↓	670			670	740

22 13 Facility Sanitary Sewerage

22 13 16 – Sanitary Waste and Vent Piping

22 13 16.30 Pipe Fittings, Cast Iron

		Crew	Daily Output	Labor-Hours	Unit	Material	2024 Bare Costs Labor	Equipment	Total	Total Incl O&P
6182	12"				Ea.	2,100			2,100	2,300
6183	15"					2,750			2,750	3,025
6184	1/4 bend, long sweep, 1-1/2"					56			56	61.50
6186	2"					52.50			52.50	57.50
6188	3"					63.50			63.50	69.50
6189	4"					101			101	111
6190	5"					182			182	200
6191	6"					223			223	245
6192	8"					400			400	440
6193	10"					770			770	850
6200	1/8 bend, 1-1/2"					18.25			18.25	20
6210	2"					20.50			20.50	22.50
6212	3"					27.50			27.50	30.50
6214	4"					36.50			36.50	40
6216	5"					75.50			75.50	83
6218	6"					80.50			80.50	88.50
6220	8"					231			231	255
6222	10"					440			440	485
6364	Closet flange									
6366	4"				Ea.	33.50			33.50	37
6370	Closet bend, no hub									
6376	4" x 16"				Ea.	178			178	195
6380	Sanitary tee, tapped, 1-1/2"					40.50			40.50	45
6382	2" x 1-1/2"					36			36	39.50
6384	2"					41.50			41.50	45.50
6386	3" x 2"					57.50			57.50	63.50
6388	3"					106			106	117
6390	4" x 1-1/2"					51			51	56
6392	4" x 2"					58			58	63.50
6393	4"					58			58	63.50
6394	6" x 1-1/2"					137			137	151
6396	6" x 2"					145			145	160
6459	Sanitary tee, 1-1/2"					31			31	34
6460	2"					33			33	36.50
6470	3"					40.50			40.50	45
6472	4"					77			77	85
6474	5"					180			180	198
6476	6"					184			184	202
6478	8"					745			745	820
6480	10"					590			590	650
6724	Sanitary tee, reducing									
6725	3" x 2"				Ea.	36			36	39.50
6726	4" x 3"					59.50			59.50	65
6727	5" x 4"					139			139	153
6728	6" x 3"					135			135	149
6729	8" x 4"					395			395	430
6730	Y, 1-1/2"					31			31	34.50
6740	2"					30.50			30.50	33.50
6750	3"					44.50			44.50	49
6760	4"					71.50			71.50	78.50
6762	5"					169			169	186
6764	6"					189			189	208
6768	8"					445			445	490

22 13 Facility Sanitary Sewerage

22 13 16 – Sanitary Waste and Vent Piping

22 13 16.30 Pipe Fittings, Cast Iron		Crew	Daily Output	Labor-Hours	Unit	Material	2024 Bare Costs Labor	Equipment	Total	Total Incl O&P
6769	10"				Ea.	990			990	1,100
6770	12"					1,950			1,950	2,150
6771	15"					4,525			4,525	5,000
6791	Y, reducing, 3" x 2"					33			33	36.50
6792	4" x 2"					47.50			47.50	52
6793	5" x 2"					105			105	115
6794	6" x 2"					116			116	128
6795	6" x 4"					151			151	166
6796	8" x 4"					260			260	286
6797	8" x 6"					320			320	350
6798	10" x 6"					720			720	790
6799	10" x 8"					860			860	950
6800	Double Y, 2"					48.50			48.50	53.50
6920	3"					89.50			89.50	98.50
7000	4"					182			182	200
7100	6"					320			320	355
7120	8"					945			945	1,050
7200	Combination Y and 1/8 bend									
7220	1-1/2"				Ea.	33.50			33.50	36.50
7260	2"					35			35	38.50
7320	3"					55			55	60.50
7400	4"					106			106	117
7480	5"					216			216	238
7500	6"					290			290	320
7520	8"					680			680	745
7800	Reducer, 3" x 2"					17.20			17.20	18.95
7820	4" x 2"					26			26	28.50
7840	4" x 3"					26			26	28.50
7842	6" x 3"					70			70	77
7844	6" x 4"					70			70	77
7846	6" x 5"					72			72	79
7848	8" x 2"					111			111	122
7850	8" x 3"					103			103	113
7852	8" x 4"					108			108	119
7854	8" x 5"					122			122	134
7856	8" x 6"					120			120	132
7858	10" x 4"					212			212	234
7860	10" x 6"					225			225	247
7862	10" x 8"					263			263	290
7864	12" x 4"					440			440	485
7866	12" x 6"					470			470	520
7868	12" x 8"					485			485	535
7870	12" x 10"					490			490	540
7872	15" x 4"					950			950	1,050
7874	15" x 6"					895			895	985
7876	15" x 8"					1,025			1,025	1,125
7878	15" x 10"					1,075			1,075	1,175
7880	15" x 12"					1,050			1,050	1,150
8000	Coupling, standard (by CISPI Mfrs.)									
8020	1-1/2"	Q-1	48	.333	Ea.	16.05	22.50		38.55	51
8040	2"		44	.364		17.90	24.50		42.40	56
8080	3"		38	.421		21	28.50		49.50	65
8120	4"		33	.485		27.50	32.50		60	79

22 13 Facility Sanitary Sewerage

22 13 16 – Sanitary Waste and Vent Piping

22 13 16.30 Pipe Fittings, Cast Iron

		Crew	Daily Output	Labor-Hours	Unit	Material	2024 Bare Costs Labor	Equipment	Total	Total Incl O&P
8160	5"	Q-2	44	.545	Ea.	69.50	38		107.50	133
8180	6"	"	40	.600		70.50	42		112.50	140
8200	8"	Q-3	33	.970		116	69		185	229
8220	10"	"	26	1.231		143	87.50		230.50	287
8300	Coupling, cast iron clamp & neoprene gasket (by MG)									
8310	1-1/2"	Q-1	48	.333	Ea.	11.20	22.50		33.70	46
8320	2"		44	.364		15.05	24.50		39.55	53
8330	3"		38	.421		14.75	28.50		43.25	58
8340	4"		33	.485		22.50	32.50		55	73
8350	5"	Q-2	44	.545		41.50	38		79.50	102
8360	6"	"	40	.600		40	42		82	106
8380	8"	Q-3	33	.970		129	69		198	243
8400	10"	"	26	1.231		202	87.50		289.50	350
8410	Reducing, no hub									
8416	2" x 1-1/2"	Q-1	44	.364	Ea.	12.45	24.50		36.95	50
8600	Coupling, stainless steel, heavy duty									
8620	1-1/2"	Q-1	48	.333	Ea.	10.80	22.50		33.30	45.50
8630	2"		44	.364		12.60	24.50		37.10	50.50
8640	2" x 1-1/2"		44	.364		13.35	24.50		37.85	51
8650	3"		38	.421		15.40	28.50		43.90	59
8660	4"		33	.485		17.25	32.50		49.75	67.50
8670	4" x 3"		33	.485		20.50	32.50		53	71
8680	5"	Q-2	44	.545		26.50	38		64.50	85.50
8690	6"	"	40	.600		37.50	42		79.50	103
8700	8"	Q-3	33	.970		54.50	69		123.50	162
8710	10"		26	1.231		68	87.50		155.50	205
8712	12"		22	1.455		159	103		262	330
8715	15"		18	1.778		215	126		341	425

22 13 16.40 Pipe Fittings, Cast Iron for Drainage

		Crew	Daily Output	Labor-Hours	Unit	Material	2024 Bare Costs Labor	Equipment	Total	Total Incl O&P
0010	**PIPE FITTINGS, CAST IRON FOR DRAINAGE**, Special									
0020	Cast iron, drainage, threaded, black									
0030	90° elbow, straight									
0031	1-1/2" pipe size	Q-1	20	.800	Ea.	70	53.50		123.50	157
0032	2" pipe size		18	.889		106	59.50		165.50	205
0033	3" pipe size		10	1.600		395	107		502	595
0034	4" pipe size		6	2.667		630	179		809	955
0040	90° long turn elbow, straight									
0041	1-1/2" pipe size	Q-1	20	.800	Ea.	98	53.50		151.50	188
0042	2" pipe size		18	.889		146	59.50		205.50	250
0043	3" pipe size		10	1.600		535	107		642	745
0044	4" pipe size		6	2.667		980	179		1,159	1,350
0050	90° street elbow, straight									
0051	1-1/2" pipe size	Q-1	20	.800	Ea.	100	53.50		153.50	190
0052	2" pipe size	"	18	.889	"	133	59.50		192.50	235
0060	45° elbow									
0061	1-1/2" pipe size	Q-1	20	.800	Ea.	68.50	53.50		122	156
0062	2" pipe size		18	.889		99	59.50		158.50	198
0063	3" pipe size		10	1.600		390	107		497	585
0064	4" pipe size		6	2.667		605	179		784	930
0070	45° street elbow									
0071	1-1/2" pipe size	Q-1	20	.800	Ea.	93.50	53.50		147	183
0072	2" pipe size	"	18	.889	"	151	59.50		210.50	255

22 13 Facility Sanitary Sewerage
22 13 16 – Sanitary Waste and Vent Piping

22 13 16.40 Pipe Fittings, Cast Iron for Drainage		Crew	Daily Output	Labor-Hours	Unit	Material	2024 Bare Costs Labor	Equipment	Total	Total Incl O&P
0092	Tees, straight									
0093	1-1/2" pipe size	Q-1	13	1.231	Ea.	115	82.50		197.50	250
0094	2" pipe size	"	11	1.455	"	191	97.50		288.50	355
0100	TY's, straight									
0101	1-1/2" pipe size	Q-1	13	1.231	Ea.	113	82.50		195.50	248
0102	2" pipe size		11	1.455		187	97.50		284.50	350
0103	3" pipe size		6	2.667		740	179		919	1,075
0104	4" pipe size		4	4		1,025	269		1,294	1,525
0120	45° Y branch, straight									
0121	1-1/2" pipe size	Q-1	13	1.231	Ea.	139	82.50		221.50	276
0122	2" pipe size		11	1.455		259	97.50		356.50	430
0123	3" pipe size		6	2.667		890	179		1,069	1,250
0124	4" pipe size		4	4		1,325	269		1,594	1,875
0147	Double Y branch, straight									
0148	1-1/2" pipe size	Q-1	10	1.600	Ea.	375	107		482	570
0149	2" pipe size	"	7	2.286	"	300	154		454	560
0160	P trap									
0161	1-1/2" pipe size	Q-1	15	1.067	Ea.	206	71.50		277.50	335
0162	2" pipe size		13	1.231		340	82.50		422.50	500
0163	3" pipe size		7	2.286		1,150	154		1,304	1,500
0164	4" pipe size		5	3.200		2,450	215		2,665	3,025
0180	Tucker connection									
0181	1-1/2" pipe size	Q-1	24	.667	Ea.	214	45		259	305
0182	2" pipe size	"	21	.762	"	264	51		315	365
0205	Cast iron, drainage, threaded, galvanized									
0206	90° elbow, straight									
0207	1-1/2" pipe size	Q-1	20	.800	Ea.	104	53.50		157.50	194
0208	2" pipe size		18	.889		157	59.50		216.50	262
0209	3" pipe size		10	1.600		595	107		702	815
0210	4" pipe size		6	2.667		1,150	179		1,329	1,550
0216	90° long turn elbow, straight									
0217	1-1/2" pipe size	Q-1	20	.800	Ea.	118	53.50		171.50	210
0218	2" pipe size		18	.889		203	59.50		262.50	310
0219	3" pipe size		10	1.600		530	107		637	740
0220	4" pipe size		6	2.667		745	179		924	1,075
0226	90° street elbow, straight									
0227	1-1/2" pipe size	Q-1	20	.800	Ea.	132	53.50		185.50	225
0228	2" pipe size	"	18	.889	"	216	59.50		275.50	325
0236	45° elbow									
0237	1-1/2" pipe size	Q-1	20	.800	Ea.	103	53.50		156.50	193
0238	2" pipe size		18	.889		147	59.50		206.50	251
0239	3" pipe size		10	1.600		510	107		617	725
0240	4" pipe size		6	2.667		835	179		1,014	1,175
0246	45° street elbow									
0247	1-1/2" pipe size	Q-1	20	.800	Ea.	136	53.50		189.50	230
0248	2" pipe size	"	18	.889	"	210	59.50		269.50	320
0268	Tees, straight									
0269	1-1/2" pipe size	Q-1	13	1.231	Ea.	156	82.50		238.50	295
0270	2" pipe size	"	11	1.455	"	262	97.50		359.50	435
0276	TY's, straight									
0277	1-1/2" pipe size	Q-1	13	1.231	Ea.	158	82.50		240.50	297
0278	2" pipe size		11	1.455		259	97.50		356.50	430
0279	3" pipe size		6	2.667		1,100	179		1,279	1,500

22 13 Facility Sanitary Sewerage

22 13 16 – Sanitary Waste and Vent Piping

22 13 16.40 Pipe Fittings, Cast Iron for Drainage		Crew	Daily Output	Labor-Hours	Unit	Material	2024 Bare Costs Labor	Equipment	Total	Total Incl O&P
0280	4" pipe size	Q-1	4	4	Ea.	1,250	269		1,519	1,775
0296	45° Y branch, straight									
0297	1-1/2" pipe size	Q-1	13	1.231	Ea.	176	82.50		258.50	315
0298	2" pipe size		11	1.455		350	97.50		447.50	530
0299	3" pipe size		6	2.667		1,300	179		1,479	1,725
0300	4" pipe size	↓	4	4	↓	1,925	269		2,194	2,500
0323	Double Y branch, straight									
0324	1-1/2" pipe size	Q-1	10	1.600	Ea.	225	107		332	405
0325	2" pipe size	"	7	2.286	"	570	154		724	860
0336	P trap									
0337	1-1/2" pipe size	Q-1	15	1.067	Ea.	284	71.50		355.50	415
0338	2" pipe size		13	1.231		340	82.50		422.50	500
0339	3" pipe size		7	2.286		1,700	154		1,854	2,075
0340	4" pipe size	↓	5	3.200	↓	2,425	215		2,640	3,000
0356	Tucker connection									
0357	1-1/2" pipe size	Q-1	24	.667	Ea.	310	45		355	405
0358	2" pipe size	"	21	.762	"	470	51		521	590
1000	Drip pan elbow (safety valve discharge elbow)									
1010	Cast iron, threaded inlet									
1014	2-1/2"	Q-1	8	2	Ea.	2,650	134		2,784	3,100
1015	3"		6.40	2.500		2,850	168		3,018	3,375
1017	4"	↓	4.80	3.333	↓	3,825	224		4,049	4,550
1018	Cast iron, flanged inlet									
1019	6"	Q-2	3.60	6.667	Ea.	3,100	465		3,565	4,100
1020	8"	"	2.60	9.231	"	3,850	645		4,495	5,175

22 13 16.50 Shower Drains

		Crew	Daily Output	Labor-Hours	Unit	Material	Labor	Equipment	Total	Total Incl O&P
0010	**SHOWER DRAINS**									
2780	Shower, with strainer, uniform diam. trap, bronze top									
2800	2" and 3" pipe size	Q-1	8	2	Ea.	550	134		684	800
2820	4" pipe size	"	7	2.286		625	154		779	915
2840	For galvanized body, add				↓	330			330	365
2860	With strainer, backwater valve, drum trap									
2880	1-1/2", 2" & 3" pipe size	Q-1	8	2	Ea.	545	134		679	800
2890	4" pipe size	"	7	2.286		755	154		909	1,050
2900	For galvanized body, add				↓	261			261	287

22 13 16.60 Traps

		Crew	Daily Output	Labor-Hours	Unit	Material	Labor	Equipment	Total	Total Incl O&P
0010	**TRAPS**									
0030	Cast iron, service weight									
0050	Running P trap, without vent									
1100	2"	Q-1	16	1	Ea.	227	67		294	350
1140	3"		14	1.143		227	77		304	365
1150	4"	↓	13	1.231		287	82.50		369.50	440
1160	6"	Q-2	17	1.412	↓	1,275	98.50		1,373.50	1,550
1180	Running trap, single hub, with vent									
2080	3" pipe size, 3" vent	Q-1	14	1.143	Ea.	227	77		304	365
2120	4" pipe size, 4" vent	"	13	1.231		310	82.50		392.50	465
2140	5" pipe size, 4" vent	Q-2	11	2.182		495	152		647	765
2160	6" pipe size, 4" vent		10	2.400		1,325	167		1,492	1,700
2180	6" pipe size, 6" vent	↓	8	3		1,200	209		1,409	1,625
2200	8" pipe size, 4" vent	Q-3	10	3.200		6,125	227		6,352	7,100
2220	8" pipe size, 6" vent	"	8	4	↓	4,750	284		5,034	5,625
2300	For double hub, vent, add					10%	20%			

For customer support on your Plumbing Costs with RSMeans Data call 800.448.8182.

22 13 Facility Sanitary Sewerage

22 13 16 – Sanitary Waste and Vent Piping

22 13 16.60 Traps		Crew	Daily Output	Labor-Hours	Unit	Material	2024 Bare Costs Labor	Equipment	Total	Total Incl O&P
2800	S trap,									
2850	4" pipe size	Q-1	13	1.231	Ea.	116	82.50		198.50	250
3000	P trap, B&S, 2" pipe size		16	1		68	67		135	175
3040	3" pipe size		14	1.143		102	77		179	226
3060	4" pipe size		13	1.231		146	82.50		228.50	284
3080	5" pipe size	Q-2	18	1.333		365	93		458	540
3100	6" pipe size	"	17	1.412		450	98.50		548.50	640
3120	8" pipe size	Q-3	11	2.909		1,350	207		1,557	1,800
3130	10" pipe size	"	10	3.200		2,200	227		2,427	2,775
3150	P trap, no hub, 1-1/2" pipe size	Q-1	17	.941		37	63		100	135
3160	2" pipe size		16	1		35	67		102	139
3170	3" pipe size		14	1.143		76.50	77		153.50	198
3180	4" pipe size		13	1.231		135	82.50		217.50	272
3190	6" pipe size	Q-2	17	1.412		330	98.50		428.50	505
3350	Deep seal trap, B&S									
3400	1-1/4" pipe size	Q-1	14	1.143	Ea.	95.50	77		172.50	219
3410	1-1/2" pipe size		14	1.143		95.50	77		172.50	219
3420	2" pipe size		14	1.143		121	77		198	247
3440	3" pipe size		12	1.333		149	89.50		238.50	297
3460	4" pipe size		11	1.455		236	97.50		333.50	405
3500	For trap primer connection, add					178			178	196
3540	For trap with floor cleanout, add					70%	5%			
3580	For trap with adjustable cleanout, add	Q-1	10	1.600	Ea.	223	107		330	405
4700	Copper, drainage, drum trap									
4800	3" x 5" solid, 1-1/2" pipe size	1 Plum	16	.500	Ea.	405	37.50		442.50	500
4840	3" x 6" swivel, 1-1/2" pipe size	"	16	.500	"	900	37.50		937.50	1,050
5100	P trap, standard pattern									
5200	1-1/4" pipe size	1 Plum	18	.444	Ea.	267	33		300	345
5240	1-1/2" pipe size		17	.471		204	35		239	277
5260	2" pipe size		15	.533		315	40		355	405
5280	3" pipe size		11	.727		895	54.50		949.50	1,075
5340	With cleanout, swivel joint and slip joint									
5360	1-1/4" pipe size	1 Plum	18	.444	Ea.	186	33		219	254
5400	1-1/2" pipe size		17	.471		530	35		565	635
5420	2" pipe size		15	.533		455	40		495	560
5750	Chromed brass, tubular, P trap, without cleanout, 20 ga.									
5800	1-1/4" pipe size	1 Plum	18	.444	Ea.	21	33		54	72.50
5840	1-1/2" pipe size	"	17	.471	"	19.95	35		54.95	74.50
5900	With cleanout, 20 ga.									
5940	1-1/4" pipe size	1 Plum	18	.444	Ea.	35.50	33		68.50	88.50
6000	1-1/2" pipe size	"	17	.471	"	38.50	35		73.50	95
6350	S trap, without cleanout, 20 ga.									
6400	1-1/4" pipe size	1 Plum	18	.444	Ea.	54.50	33		87.50	110
6440	1-1/2" pipe size	"	17	.471	"	52	35		87	110
6550	With cleanout, 20 ga.									
6600	1-1/4" pipe size	1 Plum	18	.444	Ea.	45	33		78	99
6640	1-1/2" pipe size	"	17	.471		58	35		93	117
6660	Corrosion resistant, glass, P trap, 1-1/2" pipe size	Q-1	17	.941		124	63		187	230
6670	2" pipe size		16	1		162	67		229	278
6680	3" pipe size		14	1.143		330	77		407	480
6690	4" pipe size		13	1.231		495	82.50		577.50	670
6700	6" pipe size	Q-2	17	1.412		1,900	98.50		1,998.50	2,250
6710	ABS DWV P trap, solvent weld joint									

22 13 Facility Sanitary Sewerage

22 13 16 – Sanitary Waste and Vent Piping

22 13 16.60 Traps

		Crew	Daily Output	Labor-Hours	Unit	Material	2024 Bare Costs Labor	Equipment	Total	Total Incl O&P
6720	1-1/2" pipe size	1 Plum	18	.444	Ea.	68.50	33		101.50	125
6722	2" pipe size		17	.471		83	35		118	144
6724	3" pipe size		15	.533		355	40		395	450
6726	4" pipe size		14	.571		655	42.50		697.50	785
6732	PVC DWV P trap, solvent weld joint									
6733	1-1/2" pipe size	1 Plum	18	.444	Ea.	60	33		93	116
6734	2" pipe size		17	.471		73	35		108	133
6735	3" pipe size		15	.533		247	40		287	330
6736	4" pipe size		14	.571		595	42.50		637.50	720
6760	PP DWV, dilution trap, 1-1/2" pipe size		16	.500		395	37.50		432.50	490
6770	P trap, 1-1/2" pipe size		17	.471		99	35		134	162
6780	2" pipe size		16	.500		146	37.50		183.50	217
6790	3" pipe size		14	.571		269	42.50		311.50	360
6800	4" pipe size		13	.615		450	46		496	565
6830	S trap, 1-1/2" pipe size		16	.500		70	37.50		107.50	133
6840	2" pipe size		15	.533		105	40		145	174
6850	Universal trap, 1-1/2" pipe size		14	.571		139	42.50		181.50	217
6860	PVC DWV hub x hub, basin trap, 1-1/4" pipe size		18	.444		35.50	33		68.50	88.50
6870	Sink P trap, 1-1/2" pipe size		18	.444		13.30	33		46.30	64
6880	Tubular S trap, 1-1/2" pipe size		17	.471		38.50	35		73.50	95
6890	PVC sch. 40 DWV, drum trap									
6900	1-1/2" pipe size	1 Plum	16	.500	Ea.	29	37.50		66.50	87.50
6910	P trap, 1-1/2" pipe size		18	.444		7.80	33		40.80	58
6920	2" pipe size		17	.471		9.40	35		44.40	63
6930	3" pipe size		15	.533		32	40		72	94.50
6940	4" pipe size		14	.571		72.50	42.50		115	143
6950	P trap w/clean out, 1-1/2" pipe size		18	.444		15.70	33		48.70	67
6960	2" pipe size		17	.471		12.15	35		47.15	66
6970	P trap adjustable, 1-1/2" pipe size		17	.471		14.40	35		49.40	68.50
6980	P trap adj. w/union & cleanout, 1-1/2" pipe size		16	.500		22	37.50		59.50	79.50
7000	Trap primer, flow through type, 1/2" diameter		24	.333		80	25		105	125
7100	With sediment strainer		22	.364		85	27		112	134
7450	Trap primer distribution unit									
7500	2 openings	1 Plum	18	.444	Ea.	46	33		79	100
7540	3 openings		17	.471		50.50	35		85.50	108
7560	4 openings		16	.500		69	37.50		106.50	132
7850	Trap primer manifold									
7900	2 outlet	1 Plum	18	.444	Ea.	97.50	33		130.50	157
7940	4 outlet		16	.500		157	37.50		194.50	229
7960	6 outlet		15	.533		218	40		258	299
7980	8 outlet		13	.615		280	46		326	380

22 13 16.80 Vent Flashing and Caps

		Crew	Daily Output	Labor-Hours	Unit	Material	Labor	Equipment	Total	Total Incl O&P
0010	**VENT FLASHING AND CAPS**									
0120	Vent caps									
0140	Cast iron									
0160	1-1/4" to 1-1/2" pipe	1 Plum	23	.348	Ea.	129	26		155	181
0170	2" to 2-1/8" pipe		22	.364		133	27		160	187
0180	2-1/2" to 3-5/8" pipe		21	.381		140	28.50		168.50	197
0190	4" to 4-1/8" pipe		19	.421		161	31.50		192.50	224
0200	5" to 6" pipe		17	.471		201	35		236	274
0300	PVC									
0320	1-1/4" to 1-1/2" pipe	1 Plum	24	.333	Ea.	11.10	25		36.10	49

22 13 Facility Sanitary Sewerage

22 13 16 – Sanitary Waste and Vent Piping

22 13 16.80 Vent Flashing and Caps		Crew	Daily Output	Labor-Hours	Unit	Material	2024 Bare Costs Labor	Equipment	Total	Total Incl O&P
0330	2" to 2-1/8" pipe	1 Plum	23	.348	Ea.	17.85	26		43.85	58
0900	Vent flashing									
1000	Aluminum with lead ring									
1020	1-1/4" pipe	1 Plum	20	.400	Ea.	8.40	30		38.40	54
1030	1-1/2" pipe		20	.400		8.40	30		38.40	54
1040	2" pipe		18	.444		8.70	33		41.70	59
1050	3" pipe		17	.471		9.90	35		44.90	63.50
1060	4" pipe		16	.500		11.30	37.50		48.80	68
1350	Copper with neoprene ring									
1400	1-1/4" pipe	1 Plum	20	.400	Ea.	50.50	30		80.50	100
1430	1-1/2" pipe		20	.400		64.50	30		94.50	116
1440	2" pipe		18	.444		64.50	33		97.50	121
1450	3" pipe		17	.471		75	35		110	135
1460	4" pipe		16	.500		76	37.50		113.50	139
2000	Galvanized with neoprene ring									
2020	1-1/4" pipe	1 Plum	20	.400	Ea.	11.10	30		41.10	56.50
2030	1-1/2" pipe		20	.400		11.30	30		41.30	57
2040	2" pipe		18	.444		22	33		55	73.50
2050	3" pipe		17	.471		24	35		59	79
2060	4" pipe		16	.500		28	37.50		65.50	86
2980	Neoprene, one piece									
3000	1-1/4" pipe	1 Plum	24	.333	Ea.	5.85	25		30.85	43.50
3030	1-1/2" pipe		24	.333		6.10	25		31.10	44
3040	2" pipe		23	.348		5.30	26		31.30	44.50
3050	3" pipe		21	.381		5.90	28.50		34.40	49
3060	4" pipe		20	.400		10.05	30		40.05	55.50
4000	Lead, 4#, 8" skirt, vent through roof									
4100	2" pipe	1 Plum	18	.444	Ea.	45.50	33		78.50	99.50
4110	3" pipe		17	.471		69.50	35		104.50	129
4120	4" pipe		16	.500		79	37.50		116.50	143
4130	6" pipe		14	.571		118	42.50		160.50	194

22 13 19 – Sanitary Waste Piping Specialties

22 13 19.13 Sanitary Drains

		Crew	Daily Output	Labor-Hours	Unit	Material	2024 Bare Costs Labor	Equipment	Total	Total Incl O&P
0010	**SANITARY DRAINS**									
0400	Deck, auto park, CI, 13" top									
0440	3", 4", 5", and 6" pipe size	Q-1	8	2	Ea.	2,500	134		2,634	2,950
0480	For galvanized body, add				"	1,550			1,550	1,700
0800	Promenade, heelproof grate, CI, 14" top									
0840	2", 3", and 4" pipe size	Q-1	10	1.600	Ea.	1,075	107		1,182	1,350
0860	5" and 6" pipe size		9	1.778		1,350	119		1,469	1,675
0880	8" pipe size		8	2		1,400	134		1,534	1,750
0940	For galvanized body, add					800			800	880
0960	With polished bronze top, 2"-3"-4" diam.					1,825			1,825	2,000
1200	Promenade, heelproof grate, CI, lateral, 14" top									
1240	2", 3" and 4" pipe size	Q-1	10	1.600	Ea.	1,275	107		1,382	1,550
1260	5" and 6" pipe size		9	1.778		1,475	119		1,594	1,800
1280	8" pipe size		8	2		1,700	134		1,834	2,075
1340	For galvanized body, add					655			655	720
1360	For polished bronze top, add					1,250			1,250	1,400
1500	Promenade, slotted grate, CI, 11" top									
1540	2", 3", 4", 5", and 6" pipe size	Q-1	12	1.333	Ea.	660	89.50		749.50	860
1600	For galvanized body, add					460			460	505

22 13 Facility Sanitary Sewerage

22 13 19 – Sanitary Waste Piping Specialties

22 13 19.13 Sanitary Drains	Crew	Daily Output	Labor-Hours	Unit	Material	2024 Bare Costs Labor	2024 Bare Costs Equipment	Total	Total Incl O&P
1640	With polished bronze top				Ea.	1,325			1,325	1,475
2000	Floor, medium duty, CI, deep flange, 7" diam. top									
2040	2" and 3" pipe size	Q-1	12	1.333	Ea.	510	89.50		599.50	695
2080	For galvanized body, add					192			192	212
2120	With polished bronze top					525			525	575
2160	Heavy duty, CI, 12" diam. anti-tilt grate									
2180	2", 3", 4", 5" and 6" pipe size	Q-1	10	1.600	Ea.	1,150	107		1,257	1,400
2220	For galvanized body, add					585			585	645
2240	With polished bronze top					1,450			1,450	1,600
2300	Extra-heavy duty, CI, 15" anti-tilt grate									
2320	4", 5", 6", and 8" pipe size	Q-1	8	2	Ea.	2,150	134		2,284	2,575
2360	For galvanized body, add					960			960	1,050
2380	With polished bronze top					3,025			3,025	3,325
2400	Heavy duty, with sediment bucket, CI, 12" diam. loose grate									
2420	2", 3", 4", 5" and 6" pipe size	Q-1	9	1.778	Ea.	1,400	119		1,519	1,725
2440	For galvanized body, add					870			870	960
2460	With polished bronze top					2,075			2,075	2,300
2500	Heavy duty, cleanout & trap w/bucket, CI, 15" top									
2540	2", 3", and 4" pipe size	Q-1	6	2.667	Ea.	8,225	179		8,404	9,325
2560	For galvanized body, add					3,325			3,325	3,675
2580	With polished bronze top					13,300			13,300	14,600
2600	Medium duty, with perforated SS basket, CI, body,									
2610	18" top for refuse container washing area									
2620	2" thru 6" pipe size	Q-1	4	4	Ea.	5,600	269		5,869	6,550
2630	Acid resistant									
2638	PVC									
2640	2", 3" and 4" pipe size	Q-1	16	1	Ea.	520	67		587	675
2644	Cast iron, epoxy coated									
2646	2", 3" and 4" pipe size	Q-1	14	1.143	Ea.	1,025	77		1,102	1,250
2650	PVC or ABS thermoplastic									
2660	3" and 4" pipe size	Q-1	16	1	Ea.	565	67		632	720
2680	Extra heavy duty, oil intercepting, gas seal cone,									
2690	with cleanout, loose grate, CI, body 16" top									
2700	3" and 4" diameter outlet, 4" slab depth	Q-1	4	4	Ea.	12,400	269		12,669	14,000
2720	4" diameter outlet, 8" slab depth		3	5.333		10,200	360		10,560	11,700
2740	4" diam. outlet, 10"-12" slab depth, 16" top		2	8		15,900	535		16,435	18,300
2910	Prison cell, vandal-proof, 1-1/2", and 2" diam. pipe		12	1.333		670	89.50		759.50	870
2920	3" pipe size		10	1.600		635	107		742	860
2930	Trap drain, light duty, backwater valve CI top									
2950	8" diameter top, 2" pipe size	Q-1	12	1.333	Ea.	605	89.50		694.50	800
2960	10" diameter top, 3" pipe size		10	1.600		830	107		937	1,075
2970	12" diameter top, 4" pipe size		8	2		1,150	134		1,284	1,475

22 13 19.14 Floor Receptors

		Crew	Daily Output	Labor-Hours	Unit	Material	Labor	Equipment	Total	Total Incl O&P
0010	**FLOOR RECEPTORS**, For connection to 2", 3" & 4" diameter pipe									
0200	12-1/2" square top, 25 sq. in. open area	Q-1	10	1.600	Ea.	2,250	107		2,357	2,625
0300	For grate with 4" diameter x 3-3/4" high funnel, add					2,825			2,825	3,100
0400	For grate with 6" diameter x 6" high funnel, add					290			290	320
0500	For full hinged grate with open center, add					128			128	141
0600	For aluminum bucket, add					253			253	278
0700	For acid-resisting bucket, add					370			370	405
0900	For stainless steel mesh bucket liner, add					375			375	415
1000	For bronze antisplash dome strainer, add					180			180	198

22 13 Facility Sanitary Sewerage

22 13 19 – Sanitary Waste Piping Specialties

22 13 19.14 Floor Receptors		Crew	Daily Output	Labor-Hours	Unit	Material	2024 Bare Costs Labor	Equipment	Total	Total Incl O&P
1100	For partial solid cover, add				Ea.	92			92	101
1200	For trap primer connection, add					144			144	159
2000	12-5/8" diameter top, 40 sq. in. open area	Q-1	10	1.600		965	107		1,072	1,200
2100	For options, add same prices as square top									
3000	8" x 4" rectangular top, 7.5 sq. in. open area	Q-1	14	1.143	Ea.	1,175	77		1,252	1,425
3100	For trap primer connections, add					117			117	128
4000	24" x 16" rectangular top, 70 sq. in. open area	Q-1	4	4		6,775	269		7,044	7,850
4100	For trap primer connection, add					300			300	330

22 13 19.15 Sink Waste Treatment

		Crew	Daily Output	Labor-Hours	Unit	Material	Labor	Equipment	Total	Total Incl O&P
0010	**SINK WASTE TREATMENT**, System for commercial kitchens									
0100	includes clock timer & fittings									
0200	System less chemical, wall mounted cabinet	1 Plum	16	.500	Ea.	480	37.50		517.50	585
2000	Chemical, 1 gallon, add					50			50	55
2100	6 gallons, add					226			226	249
2200	15 gallons, add					615			615	675
2300	30 gallons, add					1,150			1,150	1,275
2400	55 gallons, add					1,950			1,950	2,150

22 13 19.39 Floor Drain Trap Seal

		Crew	Daily Output	Labor-Hours	Unit	Material	Labor	Equipment	Total	Total Incl O&P
0010	**FLOOR DRAIN TRAP SEAL**									
0100	Inline									
0110	2"	1 Plum	20	.400	Ea.	53	30		83	103
0120	3"		16	.500		51.50	37.50		89	113
0130	3.5"		14	.571		68.50	42.50		111	139
0140	4"		10	.800		63	59.50		122.50	159

22 13 23 – Sanitary Waste Interceptors

22 13 23.10 Interceptors

		Crew	Daily Output	Labor-Hours	Unit	Material	Labor	Equipment	Total	Total Incl O&P
0010	**INTERCEPTORS**									
0150	Grease, fabricated steel, 4 GPM, 8 lb. fat capacity	1 Plum	4	2	Ea.	2,275	149		2,424	2,725
0200	7 GPM, 14 lb. fat capacity		4	2		2,725	149		2,874	3,225
1000	10 GPM, 20 lb. fat capacity		4	2		3,700	149		3,849	4,300
1040	15 GPM, 30 lb. fat capacity		4	2		4,750	149		4,899	5,475
1060	20 GPM, 40 lb. fat capacity		3	2.667		6,700	199		6,899	7,675
1080	25 GPM, 50 lb. fat capacity	Q-1	3.50	4.571		6,550	305		6,855	7,650
1100	35 GPM, 70 lb. fat capacity		3	5.333		9,300	360		9,660	10,700
1120	50 GPM, 100 lb. fat capacity		2	8		10,700	535		11,235	12,600
1140	75 GPM, 150 lb. fat capacity		2	8		24,800	535		25,335	28,100
1160	100 GPM, 200 lb. fat capacity		2	8		27,900	535		28,435	31,500
1180	150 GPM, 300 lb. fat capacity		2	8		28,600	535		29,135	32,300
1200	200 GPM, 400 lb. fat capacity		1.50	10.667		40,400	715		41,115	45,500
1220	250 GPM, 500 lb. fat capacity		1.30	12.308		45,600	825		46,425	51,000
1240	300 GPM, 600 lb. fat capacity		1	16		53,500	1,075		54,575	60,500
1260	400 GPM, 800 lb. fat capacity	Q-2	1.20	20		47,100	1,400		48,500	54,000
1280	500 GPM, 1,000 lb. fat capacity	"	1	24		78,000	1,675		79,675	88,000
1580	For seepage pan, add					7%				
3000	Hair, cast iron, 1-1/4" and 1-1/2" pipe connection	1 Plum	8	1	Ea.	740	74.50		814.50	925
3100	For chrome-plated cast iron, add					560			560	615
3200	For polished bronze, add					1,300			1,300	1,425
3400	Lint interceptor, fabricated steel									
3410	Size based on 10 GPM per machine									
3420	30 GPM, 2" pipe size	Q-1	3	5.333	Ea.	8,650	360		9,010	10,100
3430	70 GPM, 3" pipe size		2.50	6.400		10,100	430		10,530	11,700
3440	100 GPM, 4" pipe size		2	8		11,800	535		12,335	13,800

22 13 Facility Sanitary Sewerage

22 13 23 – Sanitary Waste Interceptors

22 13 23.10 Interceptors

		Crew	Daily Output	Labor-Hours	Unit	Material	2024 Bare Costs Labor	Equipment	Total	Total Incl O&P
3450	200 GPM, 4" pipe size	Q-1	1.50	10.667	Ea.	12,600	715		13,315	15,000
3460	300 GPM, 6" pipe size		1	16		16,700	1,075		17,775	19,900
3470	400 GPM, 6" pipe size	Q-2	1.20	20		19,000	1,400		20,400	23,000
3480	500 GPM, 6" pipe size	"	1	24		19,400	1,675		21,075	23,800
4000	Oil, fabricated steel, 10 GPM, 2" pipe size	1 Plum	4	2		4,400	149		4,549	5,050
4100	15 GPM, 2" or 3" pipe size		4	2		6,025	149		6,174	6,850
4120	20 GPM, 2" or 3" pipe size		3	2.667		7,950	199		8,149	9,025
4140	25 GPM, 2" or 3" pipe size	Q-1	3.50	4.571		7,900	305		8,205	9,150
4160	35 GPM, 2", 3", or 4" pipe size		3	5.333		9,625	360		9,985	11,100
4180	50 GPM, 2", 3", or 4" pipe size		2	8		12,900	535		13,435	15,000
4200	75 GPM, 3" pipe size		2	8		24,500	535		25,035	27,700
4220	100 GPM, 3" pipe size		2	8		24,300	535		24,835	27,500
4240	150 GPM, 4" pipe size		2	8		30,100	535		30,635	33,900
4260	200 GPM, 4" pipe size		1.50	10.667		42,500	715		43,215	47,900
4280	250 GPM, 5" pipe size		1.30	12.308		49,200	825		50,025	55,000
4300	300 GPM, 5" pipe size		1	16		55,500	1,075		56,575	63,000
4320	400 GPM, 6" pipe size	Q-2	1.20	20		71,500	1,400		72,900	80,500
4340	500 GPM, 6" pipe size	"	1	24		90,500	1,675		92,175	102,000
5000	Sand interceptor, fabricated steel									
5020	20 GPM, 4" pipe size	Q-1	3	5.333	Ea.	13,500	360		13,860	15,400
5030	50 GPM, 4" pipe size		2.50	6.400		14,300	430		14,730	16,400
5040	150 GPM, 4" pipe size		2	8		43,300	535		43,835	48,400
5050	250 GPM, 6" pipe size		1.30	12.308		45,000	825		45,825	51,000
5060	500 GPM, 6" pipe size	Q-2	1	24		58,000	1,675		59,675	66,000
6000	Solids, precious metals recovery, CI, 1-1/4" to 2" pipe	1 Plum	4	2		865	149		1,014	1,175
6100	Dental lab., large, CI, 1-1/2" to 2" pipe	"	3	2.667		3,025	199		3,224	3,650

22 13 26 – Sanitary Waste Separators

22 13 26.10 Separators

		Crew	Daily Output	Labor-Hours	Unit	Material	2024 Bare Costs Labor	Equipment	Total	Total Incl O&P
0010	**SEPARATORS**, Entrainment eliminator, steel body, 150 PSIG									
0100	1/4" size	1 Stpi	24	.333	Ea.	345	25		370	420
0120	1/2" size		24	.333		284	25		309	355
0140	3/4" size		20	.400		290	30		320	365
0160	1" size		19	.421		370	32		402	460
0180	1-1/4" size		15	.533		395	40.50		435.50	495
0200	1-1/2" size		13	.615		435	46.50		481.50	550
0220	2" size		11	.727		485	55		540	610

22 13 29 – Sanitary Sewerage Pumps

22 13 29.13 Wet-Pit-Mounted, Vertical Sewerage Pumps

		Crew	Daily Output	Labor-Hours	Unit	Material	2024 Bare Costs Labor	Equipment	Total	Total Incl O&P
0010	**WET-PIT-MOUNTED, VERTICAL SEWERAGE PUMPS**									
0020	Controls incl. alarm/disconnect panel w/wire. Excavation not included									
0260	Simplex, 9 GPM at 60 PSIG, 91 gal. tank				Ea.	4,425			4,425	4,875
0300	Unit with manway, 26" ID, 18" high					4,900			4,900	5,400
0340	26" ID, 36" high					4,825			4,825	5,300
0380	43" ID, 4' high					5,125			5,125	5,650
0600	Simplex, 9 GPM at 60 PSIG, 150 gal. tank, indoor					5,150			5,150	5,675
0700	Unit with manway, 26" ID, 36" high					5,900			5,900	6,475
0740	26" ID, 4' high					6,050			6,050	6,675
2000	Duplex, 18 GPM at 60 PSIG, 150 gal. tank, indoor					9,525			9,525	10,500
2060	Unit with manway, 43" ID, 4' high					11,300			11,300	12,500
2400	For core only					2,400			2,400	2,625
3000	Indoor residential type installation									
3020	Simplex, 9 GPM at 60 PSIG, 91 gal. HDPE tank				Ea.	4,450			4,450	4,900

22 13 Facility Sanitary Sewerage

22 13 29 – Sanitary Sewerage Pumps

22 13 29.14 Sewage Ejector Pumps		Crew	Daily Output	Labor-Hours	Unit	Material	2024 Bare Costs Labor	2024 Bare Costs Equipment	Total	Total Incl O&P
0010	**SEWAGE EJECTOR PUMPS**, With operating and level controls									
0100	Simplex system incl. tank, cover, pump 15' head									
0500	37 gal. PE tank, 12 GPM, 1/2 HP, 2" discharge	Q-1	3.20	5	Ea.	610	335		945	1,175
0510	3" discharge		3.10	5.161		650	345		995	1,225
0530	87 GPM, .7 HP, 2" discharge		3.20	5		940	335		1,275	1,525
0540	3" discharge		3.10	5.161		1,025	345		1,370	1,650
0600	45 gal. coated stl. tank, 12 GPM, 1/2 HP, 2" discharge		3	5.333		1,100	360		1,460	1,725
0610	3" discharge		2.90	5.517		1,150	370		1,520	1,800
0630	87 GPM, .7 HP, 2" discharge		3	5.333		1,400	360		1,760	2,075
0640	3" discharge		2.90	5.517		1,475	370		1,845	2,175
0660	134 GPM, 1 HP, 2" discharge		2.80	5.714		1,525	385		1,910	2,250
0680	3" discharge		2.70	5.926		1,600	400		2,000	2,350
0700	70 gal. PE tank, 12 GPM, 1/2 HP, 2" discharge		2.60	6.154		1,175	415		1,590	1,925
0710	3" discharge		2.40	6.667		1,275	450		1,725	2,075
0730	87 GPM, .7 HP, 2" discharge		2.50	6.400		1,575	430		2,005	2,375
0740	3" discharge		2.30	6.957		1,625	465		2,090	2,475
0760	134 GPM, 1 HP, 2" discharge		2.20	7.273		1,650	490		2,140	2,550
0770	3" discharge		2	8		1,775	535		2,310	2,750
0800	75 gal. coated stl. tank, 12 GPM, 1/2 HP, 2" discharge		2.40	6.667		1,325	450		1,775	2,125
0810	3" discharge		2.20	7.273		1,375	490		1,865	2,225
0830	87 GPM, .7 HP, 2" discharge		2.30	6.957		1,650	465		2,115	2,525
0840	3" discharge		2.10	7.619		1,725	510		2,235	2,650
0860	134 GPM, 1 HP, 2" discharge		2	8		1,775	535		2,310	2,750
0880	3" discharge		1.80	8.889		1,850	595		2,445	2,950
1040	Duplex system incl. tank, covers, pumps									
1060	110 gal. fiberglass tank, 24 GPM, 1/2 HP, 2" discharge	Q-1	1.60	10	Ea.	2,375	670		3,045	3,600
1080	3" discharge		1.40	11.429		2,475	770		3,245	3,875
1100	174 GPM, .7 HP, 2" discharge		1.50	10.667		3,050	715		3,765	4,450
1120	3" discharge		1.30	12.308		3,175	825		4,000	4,725
1140	268 GPM, 1 HP, 2" discharge		1.20	13.333		3,325	895		4,220	5,000
1160	3" discharge		1	16		3,450	1,075		4,525	5,375
1260	135 gal. coated stl. tank, 24 GPM, 1/2 HP, 2" discharge	Q-2	1.70	14.118		2,450	985		3,435	4,150
2000	3" discharge		1.60	15		2,600	1,050		3,650	4,400
2640	174 GPM, .7 HP, 2" discharge		1.60	15		3,200	1,050		4,250	5,075
2660	3" discharge		1.50	16		3,375	1,125		4,500	5,350
2700	268 GPM, 1 HP, 2" discharge		1.30	18.462		3,475	1,275		4,750	5,750
3040	3" discharge		1.10	21.818		3,700	1,525		5,225	6,325
3060	275 gal. coated stl. tank, 24 GPM, 1/2 HP, 2" discharge		1.50	16		3,050	1,125		4,175	5,025
3080	3" discharge		1.40	17.143		3,100	1,200		4,300	5,175
3100	174 GPM, .7 HP, 2" discharge		1.40	17.143		3,950	1,200		5,150	6,100
3120	3" discharge		1.30	18.462		4,250	1,275		5,525	6,600
3140	268 GPM, 1 HP, 2" discharge		1.10	21.818		4,325	1,525		5,850	7,000
3160	3" discharge		.90	26.667		4,550	1,850		6,400	7,800
3260	Pump system accessories, add									
3300	Alarm horn and lights, 115 V mercury switch	Q-1	8	2	Ea.	120	134		254	330
3340	Switch, mag. contactor, alarm bell, light, 3 level control		5	3.200		615	215		830	995
3380	Alternator, mercury switch activated		4	4		1,100	269		1,369	1,625

22 14 Facility Storm Drainage

22 14 23 – Storm Drainage Piping Specialties

22 14 23.33 Backwater Valves

		Crew	Daily Output	Labor-Hours	Unit	Material	2024 Bare Costs Labor	2024 Bare Costs Equipment	Total	Total Incl O&P
0010	**BACKWATER VALVES**, CI Body									
6980	Bronze gate and automatic flapper valves									
7000	3" and 4" pipe size	Q-1	13	1.231	Ea.	3,175	82.50		3,257.50	3,625
7100	5" and 6" pipe size	"	13	1.231	"	4,875	82.50		4,957.50	5,475
7240	Bronze flapper valve, bolted cover									
7260	2" pipe size	Q-1	16	1	Ea.	930	67		997	1,125
7280	3" pipe size		14.50	1.103		1,450	74		1,524	1,700
7300	4" pipe size	↓	13	1.231		1,375	82.50		1,457.50	1,625
7320	5" pipe size	Q-2	18	1.333		2,150	93		2,243	2,500
7340	6" pipe size	"	17	1.412		3,025	98.50		3,123.50	3,475
7360	8" pipe size	Q-3	10	3.200		4,325	227		4,552	5,125
7380	10" pipe size	"	9	3.556	↓	7,075	253		7,328	8,150
7500	For threaded cover, same cost									
7540	Revolving disk type, same cost as flapper type									

22 14 26 – Facility Storm Drains

22 14 26.13 Roof Drains

		Crew	Daily Output	Labor-Hours	Unit	Material	2024 Bare Costs Labor	2024 Bare Costs Equipment	Total	Total Incl O&P
0010	**ROOF DRAINS**									
0140	Cornice, CI, 45° or 90° outlet									
0200	3" and 4" pipe size	Q-1	12	1.333	Ea.	190	89.50		279.50	340
0260	For galvanized body, add					49.50			49.50	54
0280	For polished bronze dome, add				↓	65.50			65.50	72
3860	Roof, flat metal deck, CI body, 12" CI dome									
3880	2" pipe size	Q-1	15	1.067	Ea.	395	71.50		466.50	540
3890	3" pipe size		14	1.143		555	77		632	725
3900	4" pipe size		13	1.231		865	82.50		947.50	1,075
3910	5" pipe size		12	1.333		865	89.50		954.50	1,100
3920	6" pipe size	↓	10	1.600	↓	1,100	107		1,207	1,375
4280	Integral expansion joint, CI body, 12" CI dome									
4300	2" pipe size	Q-1	8	2	Ea.	710	134		844	980
4320	3" pipe size		7	2.286		710	154		864	1,000
4340	4" pipe size		6	2.667		710	179		889	1,050
4360	5" pipe size		4	4		710	269		979	1,175
4380	6" pipe size		3	5.333		710	360		1,070	1,325
4400	8" pipe size	↓	3	5.333		1,975	360		2,335	2,700
4440	For galvanized body, add				↓	505			505	555
4620	Main, all aluminum, 12" low profile dome									
4640	2", 3" and 4" pipe size	Q-1	14	1.143	Ea.	855	77		932	1,050
4660	5" and 6" pipe size		13	1.231		1,125	82.50		1,207.50	1,375
4680	8" pipe size		10	1.600		975	107		1,082	1,225
4690	Main, CI body, 12" poly. dome, 2", 3" & 4" pipe		8	2		745	134		879	1,025
4710	5" and 6" pipe size		6	2.667		1,025	179		1,204	1,400
4720	8" pipe size		4	4		1,100	269		1,369	1,600
4730	For underdeck clamp, add		22	.727		410	49		459	525
4740	For vandalproof dome, add					102			102	113
4750	For galvanized body, add					860			860	945
4760	Main, ABS body and dome, 2" pipe size	Q-1	14	1.143		166	77		243	296
4780	3" pipe size		14	1.143		173	77		250	305
4800	4" pipe size		14	1.143		166	77		243	296
4820	For underdeck clamp, add	↓	24	.667	↓	62	45		107	135
4900	Terrace planting area, with perforated overflow, CI									
4920	2", 3" and 4" pipe size	Q-1	8	2	Ea.	965	134		1,099	1,275

22 14 Facility Storm Drainage

22 14 26 – Facility Storm Drains

22 14 26.16 Facility Area Drains

		Crew	Daily Output	Labor-Hours	Unit	Material	2024 Bare Costs Labor	Equipment	Total	Total Incl O&P
0010	**FACILITY AREA DRAINS**									
4980	Scupper floor, oblique strainer, CI									
5000	6" x 7" top, 2", 3" and 4" pipe size	Q-1	16	1	Ea.	500	67		567	650
5100	8" x 12" top, 5" and 6" pipe size	"	14	1.143		970	77		1,047	1,200
5160	For galvanized body, add					40%				
5200	For polished bronze strainer, add					85%				

22 14 26.19 Facility Trench Drains

		Crew	Daily Output	Labor-Hours	Unit	Material	Labor	Equipment	Total	Total Incl O&P
0010	**FACILITY TRENCH DRAINS**									
5980	Trench, floor, heavy duty, modular, CI, 12" x 12" top									
6000	2", 3", 4", 5" & 6" pipe size	Q-1	8	2	Ea.	1,400	134		1,534	1,725
6100	For unit with polished bronze top		8	2		2,050	134		2,184	2,450
6200	For 12" extension section, CI top		8	2		1,400	134		1,534	1,750
6240	For 12" extension section, polished bronze top		8	2		2,250	134		2,384	2,675
6600	Trench, floor, for cement concrete encasement									
6610	Not including trenching or concrete									
6640	Polyester polymer concrete									
6650	4" internal width, with grate									
6660	Light duty steel grate	Q-1	120	.133	L.F.	82.50	8.95		91.45	104
6670	Medium duty steel grate		115	.139		148	9.35		157.35	176
6680	Heavy duty iron grate		110	.145		146	9.75		155.75	176
6700	12" internal width, with grate									
6770	Heavy duty galvanized grate	Q-1	80	.200	L.F.	199	13.45		212.45	239
6800	Fiberglass									
6810	8" internal width, with grate									
6820	Medium duty galvanized grate	Q-1	115	.139	L.F.	134	9.35		143.35	162
6830	Heavy duty iron grate	"	110	.145	"	236	9.75		245.75	275

22 14 29 – Sump Pumps

22 14 29.13 Wet-Pit-Mounted, Vertical Sump Pumps

		Crew	Daily Output	Labor-Hours	Unit	Material	Labor	Equipment	Total	Total Incl O&P
0010	**WET-PIT-MOUNTED, VERTICAL SUMP PUMPS**									
0400	Molded PVC base, 21 GPM at 15' head, 1/3 HP	1 Plum	5	1.600	Ea.	192	119		311	390
0800	Iron base, 21 GPM at 15' head, 1/3 HP		5	1.600		216	119		335	415
1200	Solid brass, 21 GPM at 15' head, 1/3 HP		5	1.600		350	119		469	565
2000	Sump pump, single stage									
2010	25 GPM, 1 HP, 1-1/2" discharge	Q-1	1.80	8.889	Ea.	5,550	595		6,145	7,025
2020	75 GPM, 1-1/2 HP, 2" discharge		1.50	10.667		5,875	715		6,590	7,550
2030	100 GPM, 2 HP, 2-1/2" discharge		1.30	12.308		1,975	825		2,800	3,400
2040	150 GPM, 3 HP, 3" discharge		1.10	14.545		5,975	975		6,950	8,025
2050	200 GPM, 3 HP, 3" discharge		1	16		6,350	1,075		7,425	8,575
2060	300 GPM, 10 HP, 4" discharge	Q-2	1.20	20		6,850	1,400		8,250	9,600
2070	500 GPM, 15 HP, 5" discharge		1.10	21.818		5,075	1,525		6,600	7,825
2080	800 GPM, 20 HP, 6" discharge		1	24		9,200	1,675		10,875	12,600
2090	1,000 GPM, 30 HP, 6" discharge		.85	28.235		10,100	1,975		12,075	14,000
2100	1,600 GPM, 50 HP, 8" discharge		.72	33.333		15,800	2,325		18,125	20,800
2110	2,000 GPM, 60 HP, 8" discharge	Q-3	.85	37.647		16,100	2,675		18,775	21,700
2202	For general purpose float switch, copper coated float, add	Q-1	5	3.200		166	215		381	505

22 14 Facility Storm Drainage

22 14 29 – Sump Pumps

22 14 29.16 Submersible Sump Pumps

		Crew	Daily Output	Labor-Hours	Unit	Material	2024 Bare Costs Labor	2024 Bare Costs Equipment	Total	Total Incl O&P
0010	**SUBMERSIBLE SUMP PUMPS**									
1000	Elevator sump pumps, automatic									
1010	Complete systems, pump, oil detector, controls and alarm									
1020	1-1/2" discharge, does not include the sump pit/tank									
1040	1/3 HP, 115 V	1 Plum	4.40	1.818	Ea.	2,400	136		2,536	2,850
1050	1/2 HP, 115 V		4	2		2,500	149		2,649	2,975
1060	1/2 HP, 230 V		4	2		2,550	149		2,699	3,025
1070	3/4 HP, 115 V		3.60	2.222		2,600	166		2,766	3,125
1080	3/4 HP, 230 V	↓	3.60	2.222	↓	2,675	166		2,841	3,175
1100	Sump pump only									
1110	1/3 HP, 115 V	1 Plum	6.40	1.250	Ea.	239	93.50		332.50	400
1120	1/2 HP, 115 V		5.80	1.379		335	103		438	525
1130	1/2 HP, 230 V		5.80	1.379		395	103		498	590
1140	3/4 HP, 115 V		5.40	1.481		450	111		561	660
1150	3/4 HP, 230 V	↓	5.40	1.481	↓	515	111		626	730
1200	Oil detector, control and alarm only									
1210	115 V	1 Plum	8	1	Ea.	2,175	74.50		2,249.50	2,500
1220	230 V	"	8	1	"	2,175	74.50		2,249.50	2,500
7000	Sump pump, automatic									
7100	Plastic, 1-1/4" discharge, 1/4 HP	1 Plum	6.40	1.250	Ea.	182	93.50		275.50	340
7140	1/3 HP		6	1.333		185	99.50		284.50	350
7160	1/2 HP		5.40	1.481		274	111		385	465
7180	1-1/2" discharge, 1/2 HP		5.20	1.538		144	115		259	330
7500	Cast iron, 1-1/4" discharge, 1/4 HP		6	1.333		213	99.50		312.50	385
7540	1/3 HP		6	1.333		224	99.50		323.50	395
7560	1/2 HP	↓	5	1.600	↓	345	119		464	560

22 14 53 – Rainwater Storage Tanks

22 14 53.13 Fiberglass, Rainwater Storage Tank

		Crew	Daily Output	Labor-Hours	Unit	Material	2024 Bare Costs Labor	2024 Bare Costs Equipment	Total	Total Incl O&P
0010	**FIBERGLASS, RAINWATER STORAGE TANK**									
2000	600 gallon	B-21B	3.75	10.667	Ea.	1,400	570	595	2,565	3,025
2010	1,000 gallon		3.50	11.429		2,775	610	635	4,020	4,650
2020	2,000 gallon		3.25	12.308		4,425	655	685	5,765	6,575
2030	4,000 gallon		3	13.333		8,325	710	740	9,775	11,000
2040	6,000 gallon		2.65	15.094		22,000	805	840	23,645	26,300
2050	8,000 gallon		2.30	17.391		22,400	925	965	24,290	27,100
2060	10,000 gallon		2	20		22,600	1,075	1,100	24,775	27,600
2070	12,000 gallon		1.50	26.667		21,100	1,425	1,475	24,000	26,900
2080	15,000 gallon		1	40		26,800	2,125	2,225	31,150	35,100
2090	20,000 gallon		.75	53.333		37,700	2,850	2,975	43,525	49,000
2100	25,000 gallon		.50	80		54,000	4,275	4,450	62,725	70,000
2110	30,000 gallon		.35	114		65,000	6,100	6,350	77,450	87,500
2120	40,000 gallon	↓	.30	133	↓	88,500	7,100	7,425	103,025	116,000

22 15 General Service Compressed-Air Systems

22 15 13 – General Service Compressed-Air Piping

22 15 13.10 Compressor Accessories		Crew	Daily Output	Labor-Hours	Unit	Material	2024 Bare Costs Labor	Equipment	Total	Total Incl O&P
0010	**COMPRESSOR ACCESSORIES**									
3460	Air filter, regulator, lubricator combination									
3470	Flush mount									
3480	Adjustable range 0-140 psi									
3500	1/8" NPT, 34 SCFM	1 Stpi	17	.471	Ea.	136	35.50		171.50	203
3510	1/4" NPT, 61 SCFM		17	.471		246	35.50		281.50	325
3520	3/8" NPT, 85 SCFM		16	.500		250	38		288	330
3530	1/2" NPT, 150 SCFM		15	.533		269	40.50		309.50	355
3540	3/4" NPT, 171 SCFM		14	.571		330	43		373	430
3550	1" NPT, 150 SCFM	↓	13	.615	↓	530	46.50		576.50	650
4000	Couplers, air line, sleeve type									
4010	Female, connection size NPT									
4020	1/4"	1 Stpi	38	.211	Ea.	11.15	15.90		27.05	36
4030	3/8"		36	.222		8.65	16.80		25.45	34.50
4040	1/2"		35	.229		19.75	17.25		37	47
4050	3/4"	↓	34	.235	↓	24	17.80		41.80	53
4100	Male									
4110	1/4"	1 Stpi	38	.211	Ea.	6.95	15.90		22.85	31
4120	3/8"		36	.222		10.95	16.80		27.75	37
4130	1/2"		35	.229		20.50	17.25		37.75	48
4140	3/4"	↓	34	.235		17.55	17.80		35.35	46
4150	Coupler, combined male and female halves									
4160	1/2"	1 Stpi	17	.471	Ea.	40.50	35.50		76	97.50
4170	3/4"	"	15	.533	"	42	40.50		82.50	106

22 15 19 – General Service Packaged Air Compressors and Receivers

22 15 19.10 Air Compressors		Crew	Daily Output	Labor-Hours	Unit	Material	2024 Bare Costs Labor	Equipment	Total	Total Incl O&P
0010	**AIR COMPRESSORS**									
5250	Air, reciprocating air cooled, splash lubricated, tank mounted									
5300	Single stage, 1 phase, 140 psi									
5303	1/2 HP, 17 gal. tank	1 Stpi	3	2.667	Ea.	2,300	201		2,501	2,825
5305	3/4 HP, 30 gal. tank		2.60	3.077		1,875	232		2,107	2,425
5307	1 HP, 30 gal. tank	↓	2.20	3.636		2,775	275		3,050	3,450
5309	2 HP, 30 gal. tank	Q-5	4	4		3,325	272		3,597	4,050
5310	3 HP, 30 gal. tank		3.60	4.444		3,650	300		3,950	4,475
5314	3 HP, 60 gal. tank		3.50	4.571		4,675	310		4,985	5,625
5320	5 HP, 60 gal. tank		3.20	5		4,025	340		4,365	4,925
5330	5 HP, 80 gal. tank		3	5.333		7,525	365		7,890	8,825
5340	7.5 HP, 80 gal. tank	↓	2.60	6.154	↓	6,050	420		6,470	7,300
5600	2 stage pkg., 3 phase									
5650	6 CFM at 125 psi, 1-1/2 HP, 60 gal. tank	Q-5	3	5.333	Ea.	3,225	365		3,590	4,100
5670	10.9 CFM at 125 psi, 3 HP, 80 gal. tank		1.50	10.667		6,550	725		7,275	8,275
5680	38.7 CFM at 125 psi, 10 HP, 120 gal. tank	↓	.60	26.667		11,400	1,825		13,225	15,200
5690	105 CFM at 125 psi, 25 HP, 250 gal. tank	Q-6	.60	40	↓	20,500	2,825		23,325	26,700
5800	With single stage pump									
5850	8.3 CFM at 125 psi, 2 HP, 80 gal. tank	Q-6	3.50	6.857	Ea.	3,475	485		3,960	4,550
5860	38.7 CFM at 125 psi, 10 HP, 120 gal. tank	"	.90	26.667	"	6,525	1,875		8,400	9,975
6000	Reciprocating, 2 stage, tank mtd, 3 ph, cap rated @ 175 PSIG									
6050	Pressure lubricated, hvy. duty, 9.7 CFM, 3 HP, 120 gal. tank	Q-5	1.30	12.308	Ea.	5,850	835		6,685	7,700
6054	5 CFM, 1-1/2 HP, 80 gal. tank		2.80	5.714		3,325	390		3,715	4,225
6056	6.4 CFM, 2 HP, 80 gal. tank		2	8		3,475	545		4,020	4,625
6058	8.1 CFM, 3 HP, 80 gal. tank		1.70	9.412		4,050	640		4,690	5,400
6059	14.8 CFM, 5 HP, 80 gal. tank	↓	1	16		4,025	1,100		5,125	6,050

22 15 General Service Compressed-Air Systems

22 15 19 – General Service Packaged Air Compressors and Receivers

22 15 19.10 Air Compressors

		Crew	Daily Output	Labor-Hours	Unit	Material	2024 Bare Costs Labor	2024 Bare Costs Equipment	Total	Total Incl O&P
6060	16.5 CFM, 5 HP, 120 gal. tank	Q-5	1	16	Ea.	5,600	1,100		6,700	7,775
6063	13 CFM, 6 HP, 80 gal. tank		.90	17.778		6,150	1,200		7,350	8,550
6066	19.8 CFM, 7.5 HP, 80 gal. tank		.80	20		7,225	1,350		8,575	9,975
6070	25.8 CFM, 7-1/2 HP, 120 gal. tank		.80	20		5,925	1,350		7,275	8,550
6078	34.8 CFM, 10 HP, 80 gal. tank		.70	22.857		8,425	1,550		9,975	11,600
6080	34.8 CFM, 10 HP, 120 gal. tank		.60	26.667		9,425	1,825		11,250	13,100
6090	53.7 CFM, 15 HP, 120 gal. tank	Q-6	.80	30		8,825	2,125		10,950	12,900
6100	76.7 CFM, 20 HP, 120 gal. tank		.70	34.286		11,500	2,425		13,925	16,300
6104	76.7 CFM, 20 HP, 240 gal. tank		.68	35.294		14,500	2,500		17,000	19,700
6110	90.1 CFM, 25 HP, 120 gal. tank		.63	38.095		14,500	2,675		17,175	19,900
6120	101 CFM, 30 HP, 120 gal. tank		.57	42.105		12,600	2,975		15,575	18,200
6130	101 CFM, 30 HP, 250 gal. tank		.52	46.154		15,000	3,250		18,250	21,400
6200	Oil-less, 13.6 CFM, 5 HP, 120 gal. tank	Q-5	.88	18.182		15,900	1,225		17,125	19,400
6210	13.6 CFM, 5 HP, 250 gal. tank		.80	20		17,000	1,350		18,350	20,700
6220	18.2 CFM, 7.5 HP, 120 gal. tank		.73	21.918		15,900	1,500		17,400	19,600
6230	18.2 CFM, 7.5 HP, 250 gal. tank		.67	23.881		17,000	1,625		18,625	21,100
6250	30.5 CFM, 10 HP, 120 gal. tank		.57	28.070		18,700	1,900		20,600	23,500
6260	30.5 CFM, 10 HP, 250 gal. tank		.53	30.189		19,900	2,050		21,950	25,000
6270	41.3 CFM, 15 HP, 120 gal. tank	Q-6	.70	34.286		20,300	2,425		22,725	26,000
6280	41.3 CFM, 15 HP, 250 gal. tank	"	.67	35.821		21,500	2,525		24,025	27,500

22 31 Domestic Water Softeners

22 31 13 – Residential Domestic Water Softeners

22 31 13.10 Residential Water Softeners

		Crew	Daily Output	Labor-Hours	Unit	Material	Labor	Equipment	Total	Total Incl O&P
0010	**RESIDENTIAL WATER SOFTENERS**									
7350	Water softener, automatic, to 30 grains per gallon	2 Plum	5	3.200	Ea.	620	239		859	1,025
7400	To 100 grains per gallon	"	4	4	"	560	299		859	1,050

22 31 16 – Commercial Domestic Water Softeners

22 31 16.10 Water Softeners

		Crew	Daily Output	Labor-Hours	Unit	Material	Labor	Equipment	Total	Total Incl O&P
0010	**WATER SOFTENERS**									
5800	Softener systems, automatic, intermediate sizes									
5820	available, may be used in multiples.									
6000	Hardness capacity between regenerations and flow									
6060	40,000 grains, 14 GPM	Q-1	4	4	Ea.	5,525	269		5,794	6,475
6070	50,000 grains, 17 GPM		3.60	4.444		6,625	299		6,924	7,725
6080	90,000 grains, 25 GPM		2.80	5.714		6,200	385		6,585	7,375
6100	150,000 grains, 37 GPM cont., 51 GPM peak		1.20	13.333		11,200	895		12,095	13,600
6200	300,000 grains, 81 GPM cont., 113 GPM peak		1	16		8,225	1,075		9,300	10,700
6300	750,000 grains, 160 GPM cont., 230 GPM peak		.80	20		11,900	1,350		13,250	15,100
6400	900,000 grains, 185 GPM cont., 270 GPM peak		.70	22.857		19,200	1,525		20,725	23,400
8000	Water treatment, salts, 50 lb. bag									
8020	Salt, water softener, bag, pelletized				Lb.	.53			.53	.58
8030	Salt, water softener, bag, crystal rock salt				"	.21			.21	.23

22 32 Domestic Water Filtration Equipment

22 32 19 – Domestic-Water Off-Floor Cartridge Filters

22 32 19.10 Water Filters		Crew	Daily Output	Labor-Hours	Unit	Material	2024 Bare Costs Labor	Equipment	Total	Total Incl O&P
0010	**WATER FILTERS**, Purification and treatment									
1000	Cartridge style, dirt and rust type	1 Plum	12	.667	Ea.	191	50		241	284
1200	Replacement cartridge		32	.250		25.50	18.65		44.15	56
1600	Taste and odor type		12	.667		173	50		223	264
1700	Replacement cartridge		32	.250		81	18.65		99.65	118
3000	Central unit, dirt/rust/odor/taste/scale		4	2		700	149		849	990
3100	Replacement cartridge, standard		20	.400		123	30		153	181
3600	Replacement cartridge, heavy duty		20	.400		102	30		132	157
8000	Commercial, fully automatic or push button automatic									
8200	Iron removal, 660 GPH, 1" pipe size	Q-1	1.50	10.667	Ea.	2,075	715		2,790	3,375
8240	1,500 GPH, 1-1/4" pipe size		1	16		3,700	1,075		4,775	5,675
8280	2,340 GPH, 1-1/2" pipe size		.80	20		4,050	1,350		5,400	6,475
8320	3,420 GPH, 2" pipe size		.60	26.667		7,475	1,800		9,275	10,900
8360	4,620 GPH, 2-1/2" pipe size		.50	32		11,900	2,150		14,050	16,300
8500	Neutralizer for acid water, 780 GPH, 1" pipe size		1.50	10.667		2,125	715		2,840	3,400
8540	1,140 GPH, 1-1/4" pipe size		1	16		2,375	1,075		3,450	4,225
8580	1,740 GPH, 1-1/2" pipe size		.80	20		3,475	1,350		4,825	5,800
8620	2,520 GPH, 2" pipe size		.60	26.667		4,500	1,800		6,300	7,625
8660	3,480 GPH, 2-1/2" pipe size		.50	32		7,475	2,150		9,625	11,400
8800	Sediment removal, 780 GPH, 1" pipe size		1.50	10.667		2,025	715		2,740	3,300
8840	1,140 GPH, 1-1/4" pipe size		1	16		2,425	1,075		3,500	4,250
8880	1,740 GPH, 1-1/2" pipe size		.80	20		3,200	1,350		4,550	5,525
8920	2,520 GPH, 2" pipe size		.60	26.667		4,625	1,800		6,425	7,775
8960	3,480 GPH, 2-1/2" pipe size		.50	32		7,275	2,150		9,425	11,200
9200	Taste and odor removal, 660 GPH, 1" pipe size		1.50	10.667		2,825	715		3,540	4,175
9240	1,500 GPH, 1-1/4" pipe size		1	16		4,850	1,075		5,925	6,925
9280	2,340 GPH, 1-1/2" pipe size		.80	20		5,525	1,350		6,875	8,075
9320	3,420 GPH, 2" pipe size		.60	26.667		8,475	1,800		10,275	12,000
9360	4,620 GPH, 2-1/2" pipe size		.50	32		11,300	2,150		13,450	15,700

22 33 Electric Domestic Water Heaters

22 33 13 – Instantaneous Electric Domestic Water Heaters

22 33 13.10 Hot Water Dispensers

		Crew	Daily Output	Labor-Hours	Unit	Material	Labor	Equipment	Total	Incl O&P
0010	**HOT WATER DISPENSERS**									
0160	Commercial, 100 cup, 11.3 amp	1 Plum	14	.571	Ea.	455	42.50		497.50	570
3180	Household, 60 cup	"	14	.571	"	240	42.50		282.50	330

22 33 13.20 Instantaneous Elec. Point-Of-Use Water Heaters

			Crew	Daily Output	Labor-Hours	Unit	Material	Labor	Equipment	Total	Incl O&P
0010	**INSTANTANEOUS ELECTRIC POINT-OF-USE WATER HEATERS**										
8965	Point of use, electric, glass lined										
8969	Energy saver										
8970	2.5 gal. single element	G	1 Plum	2.80	2.857	Ea.	252	213		465	590
8971	4 gal. single element	G		2.80	2.857		280	213		493	625
8974	6 gal. single element	G		2.50	3.200		325	239		564	715
8975	10 gal. single element	G		2.50	3.200		560	239		799	970
8976	15 gal. single element	G		2.40	3.333		650	249		899	1,075
8977	20 gal. single element	G		2.40	3.333		650	249		899	1,075
8978	30 gal. single element	G		2.30	3.478		1,125	260		1,385	1,625
8979	40 gal. single element	G		2.20	3.636		995	271		1,266	1,500
8988	Commercial (ASHRAE energy std. 90)										
8989	6 gallon	G	1 Plum	2.50	3.200	Ea.	920	239		1,159	1,350
8990	10 gallon	G		2.50	3.200		805	239		1,044	1,250

22 33 Electric Domestic Water Heaters

22 33 13 – Instantaneous Electric Domestic Water Heaters

22 33 13.20 Instantaneous Elec. Point-Of-Use Water Heaters		Crew	Daily Output	Labor-Hours	Unit	Material	2024 Bare Costs Labor	Equipment	Total	Total Incl O&P
8991	15 gallon	1 Plum G	2.40	3.333	Ea.	865	249		1,114	1,325
8992	20 gallon	G	2.40	3.333		1,075	249		1,324	1,575
8993	30 gallon	G	2.30	3.478		2,025	260		2,285	2,600
8995	Under the sink, copper, w/bracket									
8996	2.5 gallon	1 Plum G	4	2	Ea.	395	149		544	655

22 33 30 – Residential, Electric Domestic Water Heaters

22 33 30.13 Residential, Small-Capacity Elec. Water Heaters

0010	**RESIDENTIAL, SMALL-CAPACITY ELECTRIC DOMESTIC WATER HEATERS**									
1000	Residential, electric, glass lined tank, 5 yr., 10 gal., single element	D2020-210 1 Plum	2.30	3.478	Ea.	485	260		745	920
1040	20 gallon, single element		2.20	3.636		530	271		801	990
1060	30 gallon, double element		2.20	3.636		835	271		1,106	1,325
1080	40 gallon, double element		2	4		715	299		1,014	1,225
1100	52 gallon, double element		2	4		935	299		1,234	1,475
1120	66 gallon, double element		1.80	4.444		1,500	330		1,830	2,150
1140	80 gallon, double element		1.60	5		1,575	375		1,950	2,275
1180	120 gallon, double element		1.40	5.714		1,700	425		2,125	2,500

22 33 33 – Light-Commercial Electric Domestic Water Heaters

22 33 33.10 Commercial Electric Water Heaters

0010	**COMMERCIAL ELECTRIC WATER HEATERS**									
4000	Commercial, 100° rise. NOTE: for each size tank, a range of									
4010	heaters between the ones shown is available									
4020	Electric									
4100	5 gal., 3 kW, 12 GPH, 208 volt	1 Plum	2	4	Ea.	4,750	299		5,049	5,675
4120	10 gal., 6 kW, 25 GPH, 208 volt		2	4		5,200	299		5,499	6,150
4130	30 gal., 24 kW, 98 GPH, 208 volt		1.92	4.167		8,325	310		8,635	9,625
4136	40 gal., 36 kW, 148 GPH, 208 volt		1.88	4.255		7,075	320		7,395	8,250
4140	50 gal., 9 kW, 37 GPH, 208 volt		1.80	4.444		5,300	330		5,630	6,325
4160	50 gal., 36 kW, 148 GPH, 208 volt		1.80	4.444		11,000	330		11,330	12,600
4180	80 gal., 12 kW, 49 GPH, 208 volt		1.50	5.333		6,525	400		6,925	7,775
4200	80 gal., 36 kW, 148 GPH, 208 volt		1.50	5.333		12,500	400		12,900	14,300
4220	100 gal., 36 kW, 148 GPH, 208 volt		1.20	6.667		13,400	500		13,900	15,400
4240	120 gal., 36 kW, 148 GPH, 208 volt		1.20	6.667		13,900	500		14,400	16,000
4260	150 gal., 15 kW, 61 GPH, 480 volt		1	8		36,200	595		36,795	40,700
4280	150 gal., 120 kW, 490 GPH, 480 volt		1	8		49,200	595		49,795	55,000
4300	200 gal., 15 kW, 61 GPH, 480 volt	Q-1	1.70	9.412		38,400	630		39,030	43,100
4320	200 gal., 120 kW, 490 GPH, 480 volt		1.70	9.412		51,500	630		52,130	58,000
4340	250 gal., 15 kW, 61 GPH, 480 volt		1.50	10.667		39,700	715		40,415	44,800
4360	250 gal., 150 kW, 615 GPH, 480 volt		1.50	10.667		48,600	715		49,315	54,500
4380	300 gal., 30 kW, 123 GPH, 480 volt		1.30	12.308		43,700	825		44,525	49,300
4400	300 gal., 180 kW, 738 GPH, 480 volt		1.30	12.308		75,500	825		76,325	84,000
4420	350 gal., 30 kW, 123 GPH, 480 volt		1.10	14.545		38,800	975		39,775	44,200
4440	350 gal., 180 kW, 738 GPH, 480 volt		1.10	14.545		54,500	975		55,475	61,500
4460	400 gal., 30 kW, 123 GPH, 480 volt		1	16		53,000	1,075		54,075	60,000
4480	400 gal., 210 kW, 860 GPH, 480 volt		1	16		88,500	1,075		89,575	99,000
4500	500 gal., 30 kW, 123 GPH, 480 volt		.80	20		62,000	1,350		63,350	70,500
4520	500 gal., 240 kW, 984 GPH, 480 volt		.80	20		103,500	1,350		104,850	116,000
4540	600 gal., 30 kW, 123 GPH, 480 volt	Q-2	1.20	20		69,500	1,400		70,900	78,500
4560	600 gal., 300 kW, 1,230 GPH, 480 volt		1.20	20		122,000	1,400		123,400	136,500
4580	700 gal., 30 kW, 123 GPH, 480 volt		1	24		61,500	1,675		63,175	70,500
4600	700 gal., 300 kW, 1,230 GPH, 480 volt		1	24		93,000	1,675		94,675	104,500
4620	800 gal., 60 kW, 245 GPH, 480 volt		.90	26.667		83,500	1,850		85,350	95,000
4640	800 gal., 300 kW, 1,230 GPH, 480 volt		.90	26.667		95,000	1,850		96,850	107,500

22 33 Electric Domestic Water Heaters

22 33 33 – Light-Commercial Electric Domestic Water Heaters

22 33 33.10 Commercial Electric Water Heaters		Crew	Daily Output	Labor-Hours	Unit	Material	2024 Bare Costs Labor	2024 Bare Costs Equipment	Total	Total Incl O&P
4660	1,000 gal., 60 kW, 245 GPH, 480 volt	Q-2	.70	34.286	Ea.	73,000	2,400		75,400	84,000
4680	1,000 gal., 480 kW, 1,970 GPH, 480 volt		.70	34.286		121,500	2,400		123,900	137,000
4700	1,200 gal., 60 kW, 245 GPH, 480 volt		.60	40		82,500	2,775		85,275	95,000
4720	1,200 gal., 480 kW, 1,970 GPH, 480 volt		.60	40		125,500	2,775		128,275	142,000
4740	1,500 gal., 60 kW, 245 GPH, 480 volt		.50	48		109,000	3,350		112,350	125,000
4760	1,500 gal., 480 kW, 1,970 GPH, 480 volt		.50	48		151,000	3,350		154,350	171,000
5400	Modulating step control for under 90 kW, 2-5 steps	1 Elec	5.30	1.509		960	108		1,068	1,200
5440	For above 90 kW, 1 through 5 steps beyond standard, add		3.20	2.500		257	179		436	550
5460	For above 90 kW, 6 through 10 steps beyond standard, add		2.70	2.963		570	212		782	945
5480	For above 90 kW, 11 through 18 steps beyond standard, add		1.60	5		850	360		1,210	1,475

22 34 Fuel-Fired Domestic Water Heaters

22 34 13 – Instantaneous, Tankless, Gas Domestic Water Heaters

22 34 13.10 Instantaneous, Tankless, Gas Water Heaters

			Crew	Daily Output	Labor-Hours	Unit	Material	Labor	Equipment	Total	Total Incl O&P
0010	**INSTANTANEOUS, TANKLESS, GAS WATER HEATERS**										
9410	Natural gas/propane, 3.2 GPM	G	1 Plum	2	4	Ea.	580	299		879	1,075
9420	6.4 GPM	G		1.90	4.211		815	315		1,130	1,375
9430	8.4 GPM	G		1.80	4.444		1,200	330		1,530	1,800
9440	9.5 GPM	G		1.60	5		1,250	375		1,625	1,925

22 34 30 – Residential Gas Domestic Water Heaters

22 34 30.13 Residential, Atmos, Gas Domestic Wtr Heaters

		Crew	Daily Output	Labor-Hours	Unit	Material	Labor	Equipment	Total	Total Incl O&P
0010	**RESIDENTIAL, ATMOSPHERIC, GAS DOMESTIC WATER HEATERS**									
2000	Gas fired, foam lined tank, 10 yr., vent not incl.									
2040	30 gallon	1 Plum	2	4	Ea.	1,050	299		1,349	1,600
2060	40 gallon		1.90	4.211		980	315		1,295	1,550
2080	50 gallon		1.80	4.444		1,000	330		1,330	1,600
2090	60 gallon		1.70	4.706		1,800	350		2,150	2,500
2100	75 gallon		1.50	5.333		1,550	400		1,950	2,300
2120	100 gallon		1.30	6.154		3,100	460		3,560	4,075
2900	Water heater, safety-drain pan, 26" round		20	.400		17.85	30		47.85	64
3000	Tank leak safety, water & gas shut off see 22 05 23.20 8800									

22 34 36 – Commercial Gas Domestic Water Heaters

22 34 36.13 Commercial, Atmos., Gas Domestic Water Htrs.

		Crew	Daily Output	Labor-Hours	Unit	Material	Labor	Equipment	Total	Total Incl O&P
0010	**COMMERCIAL, ATMOSPHERIC, GAS DOMESTIC WATER HEATERS**									
6000	Gas fired, flush jacket, std. controls, vent not incl.									
6040	75 MBH input, 73 GPH	1 Plum	1.40	5.714	Ea.	3,000	425		3,425	3,925
6060	98 MBH input, 95 GPH		1.40	5.714		5,175	425		5,600	6,325
6080	120 MBH input, 110 GPH		1.20	6.667		6,125	500		6,625	7,500
6100	120 MBH input, 115 GPH		1.10	7.273		6,050	545		6,595	7,450
6120	140 MBH input, 130 GPH		1	8		7,725	595		8,320	9,400
6140	155 MBH input, 150 GPH		.80	10		7,075	745		7,820	8,875
6160	180 MBH input, 170 GPH		.70	11.429		8,300	855		9,155	10,400
6180	200 MBH input, 192 GPH		.60	13.333		8,650	995		9,645	11,000
6200	250 MBH input, 245 GPH		.50	16		9,075	1,200		10,275	11,800
6220	260 MBH input, 250 GPH	Q-1	.80	20		9,225	1,350		10,575	12,100
6240	360 MBH input, 360 GPH		.80	20		10,500	1,350		11,850	13,500
6260	500 MBH input, 480 GPH		.70	22.857		14,800	1,525		16,325	18,600
6280	725 MBH input, 690 GPH		.60	26.667		21,900	1,800		23,700	26,800
6900	For low water cutoff, add	1 Plum	8	1		450	74.50		524.50	605
6960	For bronze body hot water circulator, add	"	4	2		2,250	149		2,399	2,700

22 34 Fuel-Fired Domestic Water Heaters

22 34 46 – Oil-Fired Domestic Water Heaters

22 34 46.10 Residential Oil-Fired Water Heaters

		Crew	Daily Output	Labor-Hours	Unit	Material	2024 Bare Costs Labor	Equipment	Total	Total Incl O&P
0010	**RESIDENTIAL OIL-FIRED WATER HEATERS**									
3000	Oil fired, glass lined tank, 5 yr., vent not included, 30 gallon D2020-260	1 Plum	2	4	Ea.	2,275	299		2,574	2,975
3040	50 gallon		1.80	4.444		2,950	330		3,280	3,725
3060	70 gallon		1.50	5.333		4,400	400		4,800	5,425

22 34 46.20 Commercial Oil-Fired Water Heaters

		Crew	Daily Output	Labor-Hours	Unit	Material	Labor	Equipment	Total	Total Incl O&P
0010	**COMMERCIAL OIL-FIRED WATER HEATERS**									
8000	Oil fired, glass lined, UL listed, std. controls, vent not incl.									
8060	140 gal., 140 MBH input, 134 GPH	Q-1	2.13	7.512	Ea.	23,900	505		24,405	27,000
8080	140 gal., 199 MBH input, 191 GPH		2	8		4,975	535		5,510	6,250
8100	140 gal., 255 MBH input, 247 GPH		1.60	10		25,400	670		26,070	28,900
8120	140 gal., 270 MBH input, 259 GPH		1.20	13.333		31,400	895		32,295	35,800
8140	140 gal., 400 MBH input, 384 GPH		1	16		32,200	1,075		33,275	37,100
8160	140 gal., 540 MBH input, 519 GPH		.96	16.667		33,700	1,125		34,825	38,700
8180	140 gal., 720 MBH input, 691 GPH		.92	17.391		34,300	1,175		35,475	39,500
8200	221 gal., 300 MBH input, 288 GPH		.88	18.182		45,400	1,225		46,625	51,500
8220	221 gal., 600 MBH input, 576 GPH		.86	18.605		59,000	1,250		60,250	67,000
8240	221 gal., 800 MBH input, 768 GPH		.82	19.512		51,000	1,300		52,300	58,000
8260	201 gal., 1,000 MBH input, 960 GPH	Q-2	1.26	19.048		52,000	1,325		53,325	59,500
8280	201 gal., 1,250 MBH input, 1,200 GPH		1.22	19.672		53,000	1,375		54,375	60,500
8300	201 gal., 1,500 MBH input, 1,441 GPH		1.16	20.690		57,500	1,450		58,950	65,000
8320	411 gal., 600 MBH input, 576 GPH		1.12	21.429		58,000	1,500		59,500	65,500
8340	411 gal., 800 MBH input, 768 GPH		1.08	22.222		60,000	1,550		61,550	68,500
8360	411 gal., 1,000 MBH input, 960 GPH		1.04	23.077		61,000	1,600		62,600	70,000
8380	411 gal., 1,250 MBH input, 1,200 GPH		.98	24.490		62,500	1,700		64,200	71,500
8400	397 gal., 1,500 MBH input, 1,441 GPH		.92	26.087		66,000	1,825		67,825	75,500
8420	397 gal., 1,750 MBH input, 1,681 GPH		.86	27.907		68,500	1,950		70,450	78,000
8430	397 gal., 2,000 MBH input, 1,921 GPH		.82	29.268		74,000	2,050		76,050	84,500
8440	375 gal., 2,250 MBH input, 2,161 GPH		.76	31.579		76,000	2,200		78,200	87,000
8450	375 gal., 2,500 MBH input, 2,401 GPH		.82	29.268		79,000	2,050		81,050	90,000
8500	Oil fired, polymer lined									
8510	400 MBH, 125 gallon	Q-2	1	24	Ea.	38,200	1,675		39,875	44,500
8520	400 MBH, 600 gallon		.80	30		70,500	2,100		72,600	80,500
8530	800 MBH, 400 gallon		.67	35.821		63,500	2,500		66,000	73,500
8540	800 MBH, 600 gallon		.60	40		96,500	2,775		99,275	110,000
8550	1,000 MBH, 600 gallon		.50	48		85,500	3,350		88,850	99,500
8560	1,200 MBH, 900 gallon		.40	60		94,500	4,175		98,675	110,000
8900	For low water cutoff, add	1 Plum	8	1		440	74.50		514.50	595
8960	For bronze body hot water circulator, add	"	4	2		2,350	149		2,499	2,800

22 35 Domestic Water Heat Exchangers

22 35 30 – Water Heating by Steam

22 35 30.10 Water Heating Transfer Package

		Crew	Daily Output	Labor-Hours	Unit	Material	Labor	Equipment	Total	Total Incl O&P
0010	**WATER HEATING TRANSFER PACKAGE**, Complete controls,									
0020	expansion tank, converter, air separator									
1000	Hot water, 180°F enter, 200°F exit, 15# steam									
1010	One pump system, 28 GPM	Q-6	.75	32	Ea.	24,900	2,250		27,150	30,800
1020	35 GPM		.70	34.286		28,500	2,425		30,925	34,900
1040	55 GPM		.65	36.923		32,000	2,600		34,600	39,100
1060	130 GPM		.55	43.636		40,600	3,075		43,675	49,300
1080	255 GPM		.40	60		53,000	4,225		57,225	65,000

22 35 Domestic Water Heat Exchangers

22 35 30 – Water Heating by Steam

22 35 30.10 Water Heating Transfer Package		Crew	Daily Output	Labor-Hours	Unit	Material	2024 Bare Costs Labor	Equipment	Total	Total Incl O&P
1100	550 GPM	Q-6	.30	80	Ea.	81,500	5,650		87,150	98,000
1120	800 GPM		.25	96		83,000	6,775		89,775	101,500
1220	Two pump system, 28 GPM		.70	34.286		33,900	2,425		36,325	40,800
1240	35 GPM		.65	36.923		41,700	2,600		44,300	49,800
1260	55 GPM		.60	40		42,900	2,825		45,725	51,500
1280	130 GPM		.50	48		56,500	3,375		59,875	67,000
1300	255 GPM		.35	68.571		74,500	4,825		79,325	89,000
1320	550 GPM		.25	96		90,500	6,775		97,275	109,500
1340	800 GPM		.20	120		109,000	8,450		117,450	132,500

22 35 43 – Domestic Water Heat Reclaimers

22 35 43.10 Drainwater Heat Recovery

		Crew	Daily Output	Labor-Hours	Unit	Material	Labor	Equipment	Total	Total Incl O&P
0010	**DRAINWATER HEAT RECOVERY**									
9005	Drainwater heat recov unit, copp coil type, for 1/2" supply, 3" waste	1 Plum	3	2.667	Ea.	520	199		719	865
9010	For 1/2" supply, 4" waste		3	2.667		820	199		1,019	1,200
9020	For 3/4" supply, 3" waste		3	2.667		605	199		804	960
9030	For 3/4" supply, 4" waste		3	2.667		770	199		969	1,150
9040	For 1" supply, 4" waste, double manifold		3	2.667		1,425	199		1,624	1,850

22 41 Residential Plumbing Fixtures

22 41 06 – Plumbing Fixtures General

22 41 06.10 Plumbing Fixture Notes

		Crew	Daily Output	Labor-Hours	Unit	Material	Labor	Equipment	Total	Total Incl O&P
0010	**PLUMBING FIXTURE NOTES**, Incl. trim fittings unless otherwise noted R224000-30									
0080	For rough-in, supply, waste, and vent, see add for each type									
0122	For electric water coolers, see Section 22 47 16.10									
0160	For color, unless otherwise noted, add				Ea.	20%				

22 41 13 – Residential Water Closets, Urinals, and Bidets

22 41 13.13 Water Closets

		Crew	Daily Output	Labor-Hours	Unit	Material	Labor	Equipment	Total	Total Incl O&P
0010	**WATER CLOSETS** D2010-110									
0022	For seats, see Section 22 41 13.44									
0032	For automatic flush, see Line 22 42 39.10 0972									
0150	Tank type, vitreous china, incl. seat, supply pipe w/stop, 1.6 gpf or noted									
0200	Wall hung R224000-30									
0400	Two piece, close coupled	Q-1	5.30	3.019	Ea.	460	203		663	810
0960	For rough-in, supply, waste, vent and carrier	"	2.73	5.861	"	1,650	395		2,045	2,400
0999	Floor mounted									
1020	One piece, low profile	Q-1	5.30	3.019	Ea.	895	203		1,098	1,275
1050	One piece		5.30	3.019		910	203		1,113	1,300
1100	Two piece, close coupled		5.30	3.019		251	203		454	575
1102	Economy		5.30	3.019		141	203		344	455
1110	Two piece, close coupled, dual flush		5.30	3.019		284	203		487	610
1140	Two piece, close coupled, 1.28 gpf, ADA [G]		5.30	3.019		276	203		479	605
1960	For color, add					30%				
1961	For designer colors and trim, add					55%				
1980	For rough-in, supply, waste and vent	Q-1	3.05	5.246	Ea.	570	350		920	1,150

22 41 13.19 Bidets

		Crew	Daily Output	Labor-Hours	Unit	Material	Labor	Equipment	Total	Total Incl O&P
0010	**BIDETS**									
0180	Vitreous china, with trim on fixture	Q-1	5	3.200	Ea.	730	215		945	1,125
0200	With trim for wall mounting	"	5	3.200		865	215		1,080	1,275
9590	For color, add					40%				
9591	For designer colors and trim, add					50%				

22 41 Residential Plumbing Fixtures

22 41 13 – Residential Water Closets, Urinals, and Bidets

22 41 13.19 Bidets		Crew	Daily Output	Labor-Hours	Unit	Material	2024 Bare Costs Labor	Equipment	Total	Total Incl O&P
9600	For rough-in, supply, waste and vent, add	Q-1	1.78	8.989	Ea.	530	605		1,135	1,475

22 41 13.44 Toilet Seats

		Crew	Daily Output	Labor-Hours	Unit	Material	Labor	Equipment	Total	Total Incl O&P
0010	**TOILET SEATS**									
0100	Molded composition, white									
0150	Industrial, w/o cover, open front, regular bowl	1 Plum	24	.333	Ea.	25	25		50	64.50
0200	With self-sustaining hinge		24	.333		26.50	25		51.50	66
0220	With self-sustaining check hinge		24	.333		26	25		51	65.50
0240	Extra heavy, with check hinge		24	.333		30	25		55	70
0260	Elongated bowl, same price									
0300	Junior size, w/o cover, open front	1 Plum	24	.333	Ea.	50	25		75	92
0320	Regular primary bowl, open front		24	.333		43.50	25		68.50	85
0340	Regular baby bowl, open front, check hinge		24	.333		42.50	25		67.50	83.50
0380	Open back & front, w/o cover, reg. or elongated bowl		24	.333		20.50	25		45.50	59.50
0400	Residential									
0420	Regular bowl, w/cover, closed front	1 Plum	24	.333	Ea.	37.50	25		62.50	78.50
0440	Open front	"	24	.333	"	30	25		55	70
0460	Elongated bowl, add					25%				
0500	Self-raising hinge, w/o cover, open front									
0520	Regular bowl	1 Plum	24	.333	Ea.	118	25		143	167
0540	Elongated bowl	"	24	.333	"	29	25		54	68.50
0700	Molded wood, white, with cover									
0720	Closed front, regular bowl, square back	1 Plum	24	.333	Ea.	11.55	25		36.55	49.50
0740	Extended back		24	.333		16.15	25		41.15	55
0780	Elongated bowl, square back		24	.333		15.35	25		40.35	54
0800	Open front		24	.333		16.20	25		41.20	55
0850	Decorator styles									
0890	Vinyl top, patterned	1 Plum	24	.333	Ea.	24.50	25		49.50	64
0900	Vinyl padded, plain colors, regular bowl		24	.333		24.50	25		49.50	64
0930	Elongated bowl		24	.333		28.50	25		53.50	68.50
1000	Solid plastic, white									
1030	Industrial, w/o cover, open front, regular bowl	1 Plum	24	.333	Ea.	30.50	25		55.50	70.50
1080	Extra heavy, concealed check hinge		24	.333		25.50	25		50.50	65
1100	Self-sustaining hinge		24	.333		29	25		54	68.50
1150	Elongated bowl		24	.333		26.50	25		51.50	66
1170	Concealed check		24	.333		20	25		45	59
1190	Self-sustaining hinge, concealed check		24	.333		64	25		89	107
1220	Residential, with cover, closed front, regular bowl		24	.333		44.50	25		69.50	86
1240	Elongated bowl		24	.333		56.50	25		81.50	99.50
1260	Open front, regular bowl		24	.333		45.50	25		70.50	87
1280	Elongated bowl		24	.333		61.50	25		86.50	105

22 41 16 – Residential Lavatories and Sinks

22 41 16.13 Lavatories

			Crew	Daily Output	Labor-Hours	Unit	Material	Labor	Equipment	Total	Total Incl O&P
0010	**LAVATORIES**, With trim, white unless noted otherwise	D2010-310									
0500	Vanity top, porcelain enamel on cast iron										
0600	20" x 18"	R224000-30	Q-1	6.40	2.500	Ea.	445	168		613	740
0640	33" x 19" oval			6.40	2.500		605	168		773	915
0680	20" x 17" oval			6.40	2.500		284	168		452	560
0720	19" round			6.40	2.500		705	168		873	1,025
0760	20" x 12" triangular bowl			6.40	2.500		550	168		718	855
0860	For color, add						25%				
0861	For designer colors and trim, add						70%				
1000	Cultured marble, 19" x 17", single bowl		Q-1	6.40	2.500	Ea.	192	168		360	460

22 41 Residential Plumbing Fixtures

22 41 16 – Residential Lavatories and Sinks

22 41 16.13 Lavatories		Crew	Daily Output	Labor-Hours	Unit	Material	2024 Bare Costs Labor	2024 Bare Costs Equipment	Total	Total Incl O&P
1040	25" x 19", single bowl	Q-1	6.40	2.500	Ea.	221	168		389	495
1080	31" x 19", single bowl		6.40	2.500		237	168		405	510
1120	25" x 22", single bowl		6.40	2.500		236	168		404	510
1160	37" x 22", single bowl		6.40	2.500		282	168		450	560
1200	49" x 22", single bowl		6.40	2.500		350	168		518	635
1580	For color, same price									
1900	Stainless steel, self-rimming, 25" x 22", single bowl, ledge	Q-1	6.40	2.500	Ea.	216	168		384	485
1960	17" x 22", single bowl		6.40	2.500		325	168		493	610
2040	18-3/4" round		6.40	2.500		725	168		893	1,050
2600	Steel, enameled, 20" x 17", single bowl		5.80	2.759		162	185		347	455
2660	19" round		5.80	2.759		159	185		344	450
2720	18" round		5.80	2.759		162	185		347	455
2860	For color, add					10%				
2861	For designer colors and trim, add					20%				
2900	Vitreous china, 20" x 16", single bowl	Q-1	5.40	2.963	Ea.	203	199		402	520
2960	20" x 17", single bowl		5.40	2.963		170	199		369	485
3020	19" round, single bowl		5.40	2.963		165	199		364	475
3080	19" x 16", single bowl		5.40	2.963		150	199		349	460
3140	17" x 14", single bowl		5.40	2.963		215	199		414	530
3200	22" x 13", single bowl		5.40	2.963		213	199		412	530
3560	For color, add					50%				
3561	For designer colors and trim, add					100%				
3580	Rough-in, supply, waste and vent for all above lavatories	Q-1	2.30	6.957	Ea.	545	465		1,010	1,300
4000	Wall hung									
4040	Porcelain enamel on cast iron, 16" x 14", single bowl	Q-1	8	2	Ea.	560	134		694	820
4060	18" x 15", single bowl		8	2		375	134		509	615
4120	19" x 17", single bowl		8	2		465	134		599	715
4180	20" x 18", single bowl		8	2		475	134		609	725
4240	22" x 19", single bowl		8	2		560	134		694	815
4580	For color, add					30%				
4581	For designer colors and trim, add					75%				
6000	Vitreous china, 18" x 15", single bowl with backsplash	Q-1	7	2.286	Ea.	242	154		396	495
6060	19" x 17", single bowl		7	2.286		178	154		332	425
6120	20" x 18", single bowl		7	2.286		190	154		344	435
6210	27" x 20", ADA compliant		7	2.286		510	154		664	790
6500	For color, add					30%				
6501	For designer colors and trim, add					50%				
6960	Rough-in, supply, waste and vent for above lavatories	Q-1	1.66	9.639	Ea.	630	650		1,280	1,650
7000	Pedestal type									
7600	Vitreous china, 27" x 21", white	Q-1	6.60	2.424	Ea.	1,050	163		1,213	1,400
7610	27" x 21", colored		6.60	2.424		1,350	163		1,513	1,725
7620	27" x 21", premium color		6.60	2.424		1,525	163		1,688	1,925
7660	26" x 20", white		6.60	2.424		780	163		943	1,100
7670	26" x 20", colored		6.60	2.424		980	163		1,143	1,325
7680	26" x 20", premium color		6.60	2.424		1,175	163		1,338	1,550
7700	24" x 20", white		6.60	2.424		485	163		648	775
7710	24" x 20", colored		6.60	2.424		600	163		763	900
7720	24" x 20", premium color		6.60	2.424		675	163		838	985
7760	21" x 18", white		6.60	2.424		370	163		533	645
7770	21" x 18", colored		6.60	2.424		390	163		553	670
7990	Rough-in, supply, waste and vent for pedestal lavatories		1.66	9.639		630	650		1,280	1,650

22 41 Residential Plumbing Fixtures

22 41 16 – Residential Lavatories and Sinks

22 41 16.16 Sinks

		Crew	Daily Output	Labor-Hours	Unit	Material	2024 Bare Costs Labor	2024 Bare Costs Equipment	Total	Total Incl O&P
0010	**SINKS**, With faucets and drain D2010-410									
2000	Kitchen, counter top style, PE on CI, 24" x 21" single bowl	Q-1	5.60	2.857	Ea.	555	192		747	895
2100	31" x 22" single bowl		5.60	2.857		1,050	192		1,242	1,425
2200	32" x 21" double bowl		4.80	3.333		430	224		654	810
2310	For color, add					20%				
2311	For designer colors and trim, add					50%				
3000	Stainless steel, self rimming, 19" x 18" single bowl	Q-1	5.60	2.857	Ea.	685	192		877	1,050
3100	25" x 22" single bowl		5.60	2.857		760	192		952	1,125
3200	33" x 22" double bowl		4.80	3.333		1,100	224		1,324	1,525
3300	43" x 22" double bowl		4.80	3.333		1,275	224		1,499	1,725
3400	22" x 43" triple bowl		4.40	3.636		1,175	244		1,419	1,675
3500	Corner double bowl each 14" x 16"		4.80	3.333		850	224		1,074	1,275
4000	Steel, enameled, with ledge, 24" x 21" single bowl		5.60	2.857		525	192		717	865
4100	32" x 21" double bowl		4.80	3.333		530	224		754	920
4960	For color sinks except stainless steel, add					10%				
4961	For designer colors and trim, add					20%				
4980	For rough-in, supply, waste and vent, counter top sinks	Q-1	2.14	7.477		540	500		1,040	1,350
5000	Kitchen, raised deck, PE on CI									
5100	32" x 21", dual level, double bowl	Q-1	2.60	6.154	Ea.	535	415		950	1,200
5200	42" x 21", double bowl & disposer well	"	2.20	7.273		1,075	490		1,565	1,925
5700	For color, add					20%				
5701	For designer colors and trim, add					50%				
5790	For rough-in, supply, waste & vent, sinks	Q-1	1.85	8.649		540	580		1,120	1,450

22 41 19 – Residential Bathtubs

22 41 19.10 Baths

		Crew	Daily Output	Labor-Hours	Unit	Material	2024 Bare Costs Labor	2024 Bare Costs Equipment	Total	Total Incl O&P
0010	**BATHS** D2010-510									
0100	Tubs, recessed porcelain enamel on cast iron, with trim									
0180	48" x 42"	Q-1	4	4	Ea.	3,800	269		4,069	4,600
0220	72" x 36"	"	3	5.333	"	5,375	360		5,735	6,425
0300	Mat bottom									
0340	4'-6" long	Q-1	5	3.200	Ea.	2,525	215		2,740	3,100
0380	5' long		4.40	3.636		1,800	244		2,044	2,350
0420	5'-6" long		4	4		2,200	269		2,469	2,825
0480	Above floor drain, 5' long		4	4		1,375	269		1,644	1,925
0560	Corner 48" x 44"		4.40	3.636		3,475	244		3,719	4,200
0750	For color, add					30%				
0760	For designer colors & trim, add					60%				
2000	Enameled formed steel, 4'-6" long	Q-1	5.80	2.759	Ea.	765	185		950	1,125
2300	Above floor drain, 5' long	"	5.50	2.909	"	805	195		1,000	1,175
2350	For color, add					10%				
4000	Soaking, acrylic, w/pop-up drain 66" x 36" x 20" deep	Q-1	5.50	2.909	Ea.	1,575	195		1,770	2,025
4100	60" x 42" x 20" deep		5	3.200		1,625	215		1,840	2,100
4200	72" x 42" x 23" deep		4.80	3.333		2,650	224		2,874	3,250
4310	For color, add					5%				
4311	For designer colors & trim, add					20%				
4600	Module tub & showerwall surround, molded fiberglass									
4610	5' long x 34" wide x 76" high	Q-1	4	4	Ea.	1,100	269		1,369	1,600
4620	For color, add					10%				
4621	For designer colors and trim, add					25%				
4750	ADA compliant with 1-1/2" OD grab bar, antiskid bottom									
4760	60" x 32-3/4" x 72" high	Q-1	4	4	Ea.	830	269		1,099	1,300
4770	60" x 30" x 71" high with molded seat		3.50	4.571		1,000	305		1,305	1,550

22 41 Residential Plumbing Fixtures

22 41 19 – Residential Bathtubs

22 41 19.10 Baths

		Crew	Daily Output	Labor-Hours	Unit	Material	2024 Bare Costs Labor	2024 Bare Costs Equipment	Total	Total Incl O&P
9600	Rough-in, supply, waste and vent, for all above tubs, add	Q-1	2.07	7.729	Ea.	640	520		1,160	1,475

22 41 23 – Residential Showers

22 41 23.20 Showers

			Crew	Daily Output	Labor-Hours	Unit	Material	Labor	Equipment	Total	Total Incl O&P
0010	**SHOWERS**	D2010-710									
1500	Stall, with drain only. Add for valve and door/curtain										
1510	Baked enamel, molded stone receptor, 30" square		Q-1	5.20	3.077	Ea.	1,550	207		1,757	2,000
1520	32" square			5	3.200		1,300	215		1,515	1,775
1530	36" square			4.80	3.333		3,500	224		3,724	4,175
1540	Terrazzo receptor, 32" square			5	3.200		1,525	215		1,740	2,000
1560	36" square			4.80	3.333		2,000	224		2,224	2,525
1580	36" corner angle			4.80	3.333		2,500	224		2,724	3,075
1600	For color, add						10%				
1601	For designer colors and trim, add						15%				
1604	For thermostatic valve, add					Ea.	1,350			1,350	1,475
3000	Fiberglass, one piece, with 3 walls, 32" x 32" square		Q-1	5.50	2.909		560	195		755	905
3100	36" x 36" square		"	5.50	2.909		610	195		805	965
3200	ADA compliant, 1-1/2" OD grab bars, nonskid floor										
3210	48" x 34-1/2" x 72" corner seat		Q-1	5	3.200	Ea.	795	215		1,010	1,200
3220	60" x 34-1/2" x 72" corner seat			4	4		945	269		1,214	1,425
3230	48" x 34-1/2" x 72" fold up seat			5	3.200		1,375	215		1,590	1,825
3250	64" x 65-3/4" x 81-1/2" fold. seat, ADA			3.80	4.211		1,675	283		1,958	2,275
3260	For thermostatic valve, add						1,350			1,350	1,475
4000	Polypropylene, stall only, w/molded-stone floor, 30" x 30"		Q-1	2	8		865	535		1,400	1,750
4100	32" x 32"		"	2	8		880	535		1,415	1,775
4110	For thermostatic valve, add						1,350			1,350	1,475
4200	Rough-in, supply, waste and vent for above showers		Q-1	2.05	7.805		615	525		1,140	1,450

22 41 23.40 Shower System Components

		Crew	Daily Output	Labor-Hours	Unit	Material	Labor	Equipment	Total	Total Incl O&P
0010	**SHOWER SYSTEM COMPONENTS**									
4500	Receptor only									
4510	For tile, 36" x 36"	1 Plum	4	2	Ea.	455	149		604	720
4520	Fiberglass receptor only, 32" x 32"		8	1		149	74.50		223.50	275
4530	34" x 34"		7.80	1.026		278	76.50		354.50	420
4540	36" x 36"		7.60	1.053		174	78.50		252.50	310
4600	Rectangular									
4620	32" x 48"	1 Plum	7.40	1.081	Ea.	207	80.50		287.50	350
4630	34" x 54"		7.20	1.111		249	83		332	395
4640	34" x 60"		7	1.143		263	85.50		348.50	415
5000	Built-in, head, arm, 2.5 GPM valve		4	2		105	149		254	340
5200	Head, arm, by-pass, integral stops, handles		3.60	2.222		345	166		511	625
5500	Head, water economizer, 1.6 GPM	G	24	.333		32	25		57	72
5800	Mixing valve, built-in		6	1.333		84	99.50		183.50	241
5900	Exposed		6	1.333		930	99.50		1,029.50	1,175

22 41 36 – Residential Laundry Trays

22 41 36.10 Laundry Sinks

			Crew	Daily Output	Labor-Hours	Unit	Material	Labor	Equipment	Total	Total Incl O&P
0010	**LAUNDRY SINKS**, With trim	D2010-420									
0020	Porcelain enamel on cast iron, black iron frame										
0050	24" x 21", single compartment		Q-1	6	2.667	Ea.	695	179		874	1,025
0100	26" x 21", single compartment			6	2.667		765	179		944	1,100
0200	48" x 20", double compartment			5	3.200		895	215		1,110	1,300
2000	Molded stone, on wall hanger or legs										
2020	22" x 23", single compartment		Q-1	6	2.667	Ea.	199	179		378	485

22 41 Residential Plumbing Fixtures

22 41 36 – Residential Laundry Trays

22 41 36.10 Laundry Sinks

		Crew	Daily Output	Labor-Hours	Unit	Material	2024 Bare Costs Labor	Equipment	Total	Total Incl O&P
2100	45" x 21", double compartment	Q-1	5	3.200	Ea.	410	215		625	770
3000	Plastic, on wall hanger or legs									
3020	18" x 23", single compartment	Q-1	6.50	2.462	Ea.	162	165		327	425
3100	20" x 24", single compartment		6.50	2.462		182	165		347	445
3200	36" x 23", double compartment		5.50	2.909		242	195		437	555
3300	40" x 24", double compartment		5.50	2.909		320	195		515	640
5000	Stainless steel, counter top, 22" x 17" single compartment		6	2.667		84	179		263	360
5200	33" x 22", double compartment		5	3.200		102	215		317	430
9600	Rough-in, supply, waste and vent, for all laundry sinks		2.14	7.477		540	500		1,040	1,350

22 41 39 – Residential Faucets, Supplies and Trim

22 41 39.10 Faucets and Fittings

		Crew	Daily Output	Labor-Hours	Unit	Material	Labor	Equipment	Total	Total Incl O&P
0010	**FAUCETS AND FITTINGS**									
0150	Bath, faucets, diverter spout combination, sweat	1 Plum	8	1	Ea.	99	74.50		173.50	220
0200	For integral stops, IPS unions, add					126			126	139
0300	Three valve combinations, spout, head, arm, flange, sweat	1 Plum	6	1.333		114	99.50		213.50	274
0400	For integral stops, IPS unions, add				Pair	76			76	83.50
0420	Bath, press-bal mix valve w/diverter, spout, shower head, arm/flange	1 Plum	8	1	Ea.	305	74.50		379.50	450
0500	Drain, central lift, 1-1/2" IPS male		20	.400		133	30		163	191
0600	Trip lever, 1-1/2" IPS male		20	.400		68.50	30		98.50	120
0700	Pop up, 1-1/2" IPS male		18	.444		82	33		115	140
0800	Chain and stopper, 1-1/2" IPS male		24	.333		37.50	25		62.50	78
0810	Bidet									
0812	Fitting, over the rim, swivel spray/pop-up drain	1 Plum	8	1	Ea.	261	74.50		335.50	400
1000	Kitchen sink faucets, top mount, cast spout		10	.800		100	59.50		159.50	199
1100	For spray, add		24	.333		19.45	25		44.45	58.50
1110	For basket strainer w/tail piece, add		24	.333		17.65	25		42.65	56.50
1200	Wall type, swing tube spout		10	.800		82.50	59.50		142	180
1240	For soap dish, add					4.15			4.15	4.57
1250	For basket strainer w/tail piece, add					52.50			52.50	57.50
1300	Single control lever handle									
1310	With pull out spray									
1320	Polished chrome	1 Plum	10	.800	Ea.	187	59.50		246.50	294
2000	Laundry faucets, shelf type, IPS or copper unions		12	.667		66.50	50		116.50	147
2100	Lavatory faucet, centerset, without drain		10	.800		80	59.50		139.50	177
2120	With pop-up drain		6.66	1.201		102	89.50		191.50	245
2130	For acrylic handles, add					5.95			5.95	6.55
2150	Concealed, 12" centers	1 Plum	10	.800		106	59.50		165.50	206
2160	With pop-up drain	"	6.66	1.201		127	89.50		216.50	273
2210	Porcelain cross handles and pop-up drain									
2220	Polished chrome	1 Plum	6.66	1.201	Ea.	242	89.50		331.50	400
2230	Polished brass	"	6.66	1.201	"	320	89.50		409.50	490
2260	Single lever handle and pop-up drain									
2280	Satin nickel	1 Plum	6.66	1.201	Ea.	400	89.50		489.50	575
2290	Polished chrome		6.66	1.201		286	89.50		375.50	450
2600	Shelfback, 4" to 6" centers, 17 ga. tailpiece		10	.800		96.50	59.50		156	195
2650	With pop-up drain		6.66	1.201		118	89.50		207.50	263
2700	Shampoo faucet with supply tube		24	.333		51.50	25		76.50	94
2800	Self-closing, center set		10	.800		158	59.50		217.50	263
2810	Automatic sensor and operator, with faucet head		6.15	1.301		670	97		767	880
4000	Shower by-pass valve with union		18	.444		66.50	33		99.50	123
4100	Shower arm with flange and head		22	.364		21.50	27		48.50	64.50
4140	Shower, hand held, pin mount, massage action, chrome		22	.364		83.50	27		110.50	132

22 41 Residential Plumbing Fixtures

22 41 39 – Residential Faucets, Supplies and Trim

22 41 39.10 Faucets and Fittings

		Crew	Daily Output	Labor-Hours	Unit	Material	2024 Bare Costs Labor	Equipment	Total	Total Incl O&P
4142	Polished brass	1 Plum	22	.364	Ea.	181	27		208	240
4144	Shower, hand held, wall mtd, adj. spray, 2 wall mounts, chrome		20	.400		130	30		160	188
4146	Polished brass		20	.400		278	30		308	350
4148	Shower, hand held head, bar mounted 24", adj. spray, chrome		20	.400		208	30		238	274
4150	Polished brass		20	.400		430	30		460	515
4200	Shower thermostatic mixing valve, concealed, with shower head trim kit		8	1		410	74.50		484.50	560
4220	Shower pressure balancing mixing valve									
4230	With shower head, arm, flange and diverter tub spout									
4240	Chrome	1 Plum	6.14	1.303	Ea.	475	97.50		572.50	670
4250	Satin nickel		6.14	1.303		620	97.50		717.50	825
4260	Polished graphite		6.14	1.303		605	97.50		702.50	815
5000	Sillcock, compact, brass, IPS or copper to hose		24	.333		20	25		45	59
6000	Stop and waste valves, bronze									
6100	Angle, solder end 1/2"	1 Plum	24	.333	Ea.	61.50	25		86.50	105
6110	3/4"		20	.400		71	30		101	123
6300	Straightway, solder end 3/8"		24	.333		22	25		47	61
6310	1/2"		24	.333		24	25		49	63
6320	3/4"		20	.400		27.50	30		57.50	74.50
6410	Straightway, threaded 1/2"		24	.333		41	25		66	82
6420	3/4"		20	.400		45.50	30		75.50	95
6430	1"		19	.421		24.50	31.50		56	74
7800	Water closet, wax gasket		96	.083		1.42	6.20		7.62	10.80
7820	Gasket toilet tank to bowl		32	.250		3.26	18.65		21.91	31.50
7830	Replacement diaphragm washer assy for ballcock valve		12	.667		3.26	50		53.26	77.50
7850	Dual flush valve		12	.667		125	50		175	212
8000	Water supply stops, polished chrome plate									
8200	Angle, 3/8"	1 Plum	24	.333	Ea.	12.80	25		37.80	51
8300	1/2"		22	.364		14.65	27		41.65	56.50
8400	Straight, 3/8"		26	.308		17.45	23		40.45	53
8500	1/2"		24	.333		13.40	25		38.40	52
8600	Water closet, angle, w/flex riser, 3/8"		24	.333		45.50	25		70.50	87
9100	Miscellaneous									
9720	Teflon tape, 1/2" x 520" roll				Ea.	1.17			1.17	1.29

22 41 39.70 Washer/Dryer Accessories

		Crew	Daily Output	Labor-Hours	Unit	Material	2024 Bare Costs Labor	Equipment	Total	Total Incl O&P
0010	**WASHER/DRYER ACCESSORIES**									
1020	Valves ball type single lever									
1030	1/2" diam., IPS	1 Plum	21	.381	Ea.	59	28.50		87.50	108
1040	1/2" diam., solder	"	21	.381	"	59	28.50		87.50	108
1050	Recessed box, 16 ga., two hose valves and drain									
1060	1/2" size, 1-1/2" drain	1 Plum	18	.444	Ea.	132	33		165	195
1070	1/2" size, 2" drain	"	17	.471	"	118	35		153	183
1080	With grounding electric receptacle									
1090	1/2" size, 1-1/2" drain	1 Plum	18	.444	Ea.	160	33		193	226
1100	1/2" size, 2" drain	"	17	.471	"	156	35		191	225
1110	With grounding and dryer receptacle									
1120	1/2" size, 1-1/2" drain	1 Plum	18	.444	Ea.	179	33		212	246
1130	1/2" size, 2" drain	"	17	.471	"	180	35		215	251
1140	Recessed box, 16 ga., ball valves with single lever and drain									
1150	1/2" size, 1-1/2" drain	1 Plum	19	.421	Ea.	249	31.50		280.50	320
1160	1/2" size, 2" drain	"	18	.444	"	216	33		249	287
1170	With grounding electric receptacle									
1180	1/2" size, 1-1/2" drain	1 Plum	19	.421	Ea.	295	31.50		326.50	370

22 41 Residential Plumbing Fixtures

22 41 39 – Residential Faucets, Supplies and Trim

22 41 39.70 Washer/Dryer Accessories

		Crew	Daily Output	Labor-Hours	Unit	Material	2024 Bare Costs Labor	Equipment	Total	Total Incl O&P
1190	1/2" size, 2" drain	1 Plum	18	.444	Ea.	240	33		273	315
1200	With grounding and dryer receptacles									
1210	1/2" size, 1-1/2" drain	1 Plum	19	.421	Ea.	261	31.50		292.50	335
1220	1/2" size, 2" drain	"	18	.444	"	262	33		295	340
1300	Recessed box, 20 ga., two hose valves and drain (economy type)									
1310	1/2" size, 1-1/2" drain	1 Plum	19	.421	Ea.	103	31.50		134.50	160
1320	1/2" size, 2" drain		18	.444		96	33		129	156
1330	Box with drain only		24	.333		59.50	25		84.50	103
1340	1/2" size, 1-1/2" ABS/PVC drain		19	.421		128	31.50		159.50	188
1350	1/2" size, 2" ABS/PVC drain		18	.444		156	33		189	222
1352	Box with drain and 15 A receptacle		24	.333		117	25		142	166
1360	1/2" size, 2" drain ABS/PVC, 15 A receptacle		24	.333		93	25		118	139
1400	Wall mounted									
1410	1/2" size, 1-1/2" plastic drain	1 Plum	19	.421	Ea.	31.50	31.50		63	82
1420	1/2" size, 2" plastic drain	"	18	.444		18.75	33		51.75	70
1500	Dryer vent kit									
1510	8' flex duct, clamps and outside hood	1 Plum	20	.400	Ea.	14.75	30		44.75	60.50
1980	Rough-in, supply, waste, and vent for washer boxes	"	3.46	2.310	"	585	172		757	900

22 42 Commercial Plumbing Fixtures

22 42 13 – Commercial Water Closets, Urinals, and Bidets

22 42 13.13 Water Closets

		Crew	Daily Output	Labor-Hours	Unit	Material	2024 Bare Costs Labor	Equipment	Total	Total Incl O&P
0010	**WATER CLOSETS**									
3000	Bowl only, with flush valve, seat, 1.6 gpf unless noted									
3100	Wall hung	Q-1	5.80	2.759	Ea.	1,050	185		1,235	1,450
3200	For rough-in, supply, waste and vent, single WC		2.56	6.250		1,700	420		2,120	2,500
3300	Floor mounted		5.80	2.759		375	185		560	690
3350	With wall outlet		5.80	2.759		620	185		805	960
3360	With floor outlet, 1.28 gpf G		5.80	2.759		615	185		800	950
3362	With floor outlet, 1.28 gpf, ADA G		5.80	2.759		640	185		825	980
3370	For rough-in, supply, waste and vent, single WC		2.84	5.634		620	380		1,000	1,250
3390	Floor mounted children's size, 10-3/4" high									
3392	With automatic flush sensor, 1.6 gpf	Q-1	6.20	2.581	Ea.	725	173		898	1,050
3396	With automatic flush sensor, 1.28 gpf		6.20	2.581		670	173		843	995
3400	For rough-in, supply, waste and vent, single WC		2.84	5.634		620	380		1,000	1,250
3500	Gang side by side carrier system, rough-in, supply, waste & vent									
3510	For single hook-up	Q-1	1.97	8.122	Ea.	2,050	545		2,595	3,050
3520	For each additional hook-up, add	"	2.14	7.477	"	1,900	500		2,400	2,850
3550	Gang back to back carrier system, rough-in, supply, waste & vent									
3560	For pair hook-up	Q-1	1.76	9.091	Pair	3,325	610		3,935	4,550
3570	For each additional pair hook-up, add	"	1.81	8.840	"	3,175	595		3,770	4,375

22 42 13.16 Urinals

		Crew	Daily Output	Labor-Hours	Unit	Material	2024 Bare Costs Labor	Equipment	Total	Total Incl O&P
0010	**URINALS** D2010-210									
0102	For automatic flush see Line 22 42 39.10 0972									
3000	Wall hung, vitreous china, with self-closing valve R224000-30									
3100	Siphon jet type	Q-1	3	5.333	Ea.	430	360		790	1,000
3120	Blowout type		3	5.333		655	360		1,015	1,250
3140	Water saving .5 gpf G		3	5.333		680	360		1,040	1,275
3300	Rough-in, supply, waste & vent		2.83	5.654		1,400	380		1,780	2,100
5000	Stall type, vitreous china, includes valve		2.50	6.400		1,025	430		1,455	1,775
6980	Rough-in, supply, waste and vent		1.99	8.040		695	540		1,235	1,575

22 42 Commercial Plumbing Fixtures

22 42 13 – Commercial Water Closets, Urinals, and Bidets

22 42 13.16 Urinals

			Crew	Daily Output	Labor-Hours	Unit	Material	2024 Bare Costs Labor	2024 Bare Costs Equipment	Total	Total Incl O&P
8000	Waterless (no flush) urinal										
8010	Wall hung										
8014	Fiberglass reinforced polyester										
8020	Standard unit	G	Q-1	21.30	.751	Ea.	625	50.50		675.50	765
8030	ADA compliant unit	G	"	21.30	.751		570	50.50		620.50	705
8070	For solid color, add	G					97			97	107
8080	For 2" brass flange (new const.), add	G	Q-1	96	.167		22.50	11.20		33.70	41
8200	Vitreous china										
8220	ADA compliant unit, 14"	G	Q-1	21.30	.751	Ea.	315	50.50		365.50	420
8250	ADA compliant unit, 15.5"		"	21.30	.751		570	50.50		620.50	705
8270	For solid color, add	G					97			97	107
8290	Rough-in, supply, waste & vent	G	Q-1	2.92	5.479		1,350	370		1,720	2,025
8400	Trap liquid										
8410	1 quart	G				Ea.	27			27	29.50
8420	1 gallon	G				"	95			95	104

22 42 16 – Commercial Lavatories and Sinks

22 42 16.13 Lavatories

0010	**LAVATORIES**, With trim, white unless noted otherwise										
0020	Commercial lavatories same as residential. See Section 22 41 16										

22 42 16.16 Commercial Sinks

			Crew	Daily Output	Labor-Hours	Unit	Material	Labor	Equipment	Total	Total Incl O&P
0010	**COMMERCIAL SINKS**										
5900	Scullery sink, stainless steel										
5910	1 bowl and drain board, 43" x 22" OD		Q-1	5.40	2.963	Ea.	2,075	199		2,274	2,575
5920	2 bowls and drain board, 49" x 22" OD			4.60	3.478		2,425	234		2,659	3,025
5930	3 bowls and drain board, 43" x 22" OD			4.20	3.810		5,050	256		5,306	5,925
5940	1 bowl and drain board, 50" x 28" OD, with legs			5.40	2.963		1,875	199		2,074	2,375

22 42 16.30 Classroom Sinks

0010	**CLASSROOM SINKS**										
6020	Countertop, stainless steel										
6024	with faucet, bubbler and strainer, ADA compliant										
6036	25" x 17" single bowl		Q-1	5.20	3.077	Ea.	1,825	207		2,032	2,325
6040	28" x 22" single bowl			5.20	3.077		1,375	207		1,582	1,825
6044	31" x 19" single bowl			5.20	3.077		1,450	207		1,657	1,900
6070	37" x 17" double bowl			4.40	3.636		2,100	244		2,344	2,700
6100	For rough-in, supply, waste and vent, counter top classroom sinks			2.14	7.477		540	500		1,040	1,350

22 42 16.34 Laboratory Countertops and Sinks

0010	**LABORATORY COUNTERTOPS AND SINKS**										
0050	Laboratory sinks, corrosion resistant										
1000	Stainless steel sink, bench mounted, with										
1020	plug & waste fitting with 1-1/2" straight threads										
1030	Single bowl, 2 drainboards, backnut & strainer										
1050	18-1/2" x 15-1/2" x 12-1/2" sink, 54" x 24" OD		Q-1	3	5.333	Ea.	1,450	360		1,810	2,125
1100	Single bowl, single drainboard, backnut & strainer										
1130	18-1/2" x 15-1/2" x 12-1/2" sink, 47" x 24" OD		Q-1	3	5.333	Ea.	1,075	360		1,435	1,700
1146	Double bowl, single drainboard, backnut & strainer										
1150	18-1/2" x 15-1/2" x 12-1/2" sink, 70" x 24" OD		Q-1	3	5.333	Ea.	1,600	360		1,960	2,300
1280	Polypropylene										
1290	Flanged 1-1/4" wide, rectangular with strainer										
1300	plug & waste fitting, 1-1/2" straight threads										
1320	12" x 12" x 8" sink, 14-1/2" x 14-1/2" OD		Q-1	4	4	Ea.	295	269		564	725
1340	16" x 16" x 8" sink, 18-1/2" x 18-1/2" OD			4	4		415	269		684	855

22 42 Commercial Plumbing Fixtures

22 42 16 – Commercial Lavatories and Sinks

22 42 16.34 Laboratory Countertops and Sinks

		Crew	Daily Output	Labor-Hours	Unit	Material	2024 Bare Costs Labor	Equipment	Total	Total Incl O&P
1360	21" x 18" x 10" sink, 23-1/2" x 20-1/2" OD	Q-1	4	4	Ea.	425	269		694	870
1490	For rough-in, supply, waste & vent, add	↓	2.02	7.921	↓	380	530		910	1,200
1600	Polypropylene									
1620	Cup sink, oval, integral strainers									
1640	6" x 3" I.D., 7" x 4" OD	Q-1	6	2.667	Ea.	185	179		364	470
1660	9" x 3" I.D., 10" x 4-1/2" OD	"	6	2.667		220	179		399	510
1740	1-1/2" diam. x 11" long					48			48	53
1980	For rough-in, supply, waste & vent, add	Q-1	1.70	9.412	↓	405	630		1,035	1,375

22 42 16.40 Service Sinks

		Crew	Daily Output	Labor-Hours	Unit	Material	Labor	Equipment	Total	Total Incl O&P
0010	**SERVICE SINKS**									
6650	Service, floor, corner, PE on CI, 28" x 28"	Q-1	4.40	3.636	Ea.	1,575	244		1,819	2,125
6750	Vinyl coated rim guard, add					71			71	78.50
6755	Mop sink, molded stone, 22" x 18"	1 Plum	3.33	2.402		980	179		1,159	1,350
6760	Mop sink, molded stone, 24" x 36"		3.33	2.402		235	179		414	525
6770	Mop sink, molded stone, 24" x 36", w/rim 3 sides	↓	3.33	2.402		294	179		473	590
6790	For rough-in, supply, waste & vent, floor service sinks	Q-1	1.64	9.756		2,000	655		2,655	3,175
7000	Service, wall, PE on CI, roll rim, 22" x 18"		4	4		1,100	269		1,369	1,625
7100	24" x 20"	↓	4	4		1,625	269		1,894	2,175
7600	For stainless steel rim guard, two sides only, add					56			56	62
7800	For stainless steel rim guard, front only, add					62			62	68.50
8600	Vitreous china, 22" x 20"	Q-1	4	4		1,100	269		1,369	1,625
8960	For stainless steel rim guard, front or one side, add					88			88	97
8980	For rough-in, supply, waste & vent, wall service sinks	Q-1	1.30	12.308	↓	3,225	825		4,050	4,750

22 42 23 – Commercial Showers

22 42 23.30 Group Showers

		Crew	Daily Output	Labor-Hours	Unit	Material	Labor	Equipment	Total	Total Incl O&P
0010	**GROUP SHOWERS**									
6000	Group, w/pressure balancing valve, rough-in and rigging not included									
6800	Column, 6 heads, no receptors, less partitions	Q-1	3	5.333	Ea.	11,000	360		11,360	12,600
6900	With stainless steel partitions		1	16		14,500	1,075		15,575	17,600
7600	5 heads, no receptors, less partitions		3	5.333		7,525	360		7,885	8,800
7620	4 heads (1 ADA compliant) no receptors, less partitions		3	5.333		6,975	360		7,335	8,200
7700	With stainless steel partitions		1	16		7,525	1,075		8,600	9,875
8000	Wall, 2 heads, no receptors, less partitions		4	4		3,200	269		3,469	3,900
8100	With stainless steel partitions	↓	2	8	↓	7,000	535		7,535	8,500

22 42 33 – Wash Fountains

22 42 33.20 Commercial Wash Fountains

		Crew	Daily Output	Labor-Hours	Unit	Material	Labor	Equipment	Total	Total Incl O&P
0010	**COMMERCIAL WASH FOUNTAINS** D2010-610									
1900	Group, foot control									
2000	Precast terrazzo, circular, 36" diam., 5 or 6 persons	Q-2	3	8	Ea.	8,175	555		8,730	9,800
2100	54" diam. for 8 or 10 persons		2.50	9.600		11,900	670		12,570	14,100
2400	Semi-circular, 36" diam. for 3 persons		3	8		6,675	555		7,230	8,150
2500	54" diam. for 4 or 5 persons		2.50	9.600		12,300	670		12,970	14,500
2700	Quarter circle (corner), 54" diam. for 3 persons		3.50	6.857		8,025	480		8,505	9,525
3000	Stainless steel, circular, 36" diameter		3.50	6.857		7,175	480		7,655	8,600
3100	54" diameter		2.80	8.571		8,975	595		9,570	10,700
3400	Semi-circular, 36" diameter		3.50	6.857		5,875	480		6,355	7,150
3500	54" diameter		2.80	8.571		6,300	595		6,895	7,825
5000	Thermoplastic, pre-assembled, circular, 36" diameter		6	4		5,000	279		5,279	5,925
5100	54" diameter		4	6		4,775	420		5,195	5,900
5400	Semi-circular, 36" diameter		6	4		5,400	279		5,679	6,375
5600	54" diameter	↓	4	6	↓	5,475	420		5,895	6,650

22 42 Commercial Plumbing Fixtures

22 42 33 – Wash Fountains

22 42 33.20 Commercial Wash Fountains

		Crew	Daily Output	Labor-Hours	Unit	Material	2024 Bare Costs Labor	Equipment	Total	Total Incl O&P
5610	Group, infrared control, barrier free									
5614	Precast terrazzo									
5620	Semi-circular 36" diam. for 3 persons	Q-2	3	8	Ea.	8,175	555		8,730	9,825
5630	46" diam. for 4 persons		2.80	8.571		8,875	595		9,470	10,700
5640	Circular, 54" diam. for 8 persons, button control		2.50	9.600		10,600	670		11,270	12,700
5700	Rough-in, supply, waste and vent for above wash fountains	Q-1	1.82	8.791		750	590		1,340	1,700
6200	Duo for small washrooms, stainless steel		2	8		3,600	535		4,135	4,775
6400	Bowl with backsplash		2	8		2,625	535		3,160	3,675
6500	Rough-in, supply, waste & vent for duo fountains		2.02	7.921		455	530		985	1,300

22 42 39 – Commercial Faucets, Supplies, and Trim

22 42 39.10 Faucets and Fittings

		Crew	Daily Output	Labor-Hours	Unit	Material	Labor	Equipment	Total	Total Incl O&P
0010	**FAUCETS AND FITTINGS**									
0840	Flush valves, with vacuum breaker									
0850	Water closet									
0860	Exposed, rear spud	1 Plum	8	1	Ea.	172	74.50		246.50	300
0870	Top spud		8	1		224	74.50		298.50	355
0880	Concealed, rear spud		8	1		257	74.50		331.50	395
0890	Top spud		8	1		243	74.50		317.50	380
0900	Wall hung		8	1		257	74.50		331.50	395
0910	Dual flush flushometer		12	.667		269	50		319	370
0912	Flushometer retrofit kit		18	.444		20	33		53	71.50
0920	Urinal									
0930	Exposed, stall	1 Plum	8	1	Ea.	224	74.50		298.50	355
0940	Wall (washout)		8	1		183	74.50		257.50	310
0950	Pedestal, top spud		8	1		196	74.50		270.50	325
0960	Concealed, stall		8	1		191	74.50		265.50	320
0970	Wall (washout)		8	1		206	74.50		280.50	340
0971	Automatic flush sensor and operator for									
0972	urinals or water closets, standard	1 Plum	8	1	Ea.	635	74.50		709.50	810
0980	High efficiency water saving									
0984	Water closets, 1.28 gpf	1 Plum	8	1	Ea.	495	74.50		569.50	650
0988	Urinals, .5 gpf	"	8	1	"	495	74.50		569.50	650
2790	Faucets for lavatories									
2800	Self-closing, center set	1 Plum	10	.800	Ea.	158	59.50		217.50	263
2810	Automatic sensor and operator, with faucet head		6.15	1.301		670	97		767	880
3000	Service sink faucet, cast spout, pail hook, hose end		14	.571		82	42.50		124.50	154

22 42 39.30 Carriers and Supports

		Crew	Daily Output	Labor-Hours	Unit	Material	Labor	Equipment	Total	Total Incl O&P
0010	**CARRIERS AND SUPPORTS**, For plumbing fixtures									
0500	Drinking fountain, wall mounted									
0600	Plate type with studs, top back plate	1 Plum	7	1.143	Ea.	61.50	85.50		147	195
0700	Top front and back plate		7	1.143		660	85.50		745.50	850
0800	Top & bottom, front & back plates, w/bearing jacks		7	1.143		1,050	85.50		1,135.50	1,275
3000	Lavatory, concealed arm									
3050	Floor mounted, single									
3100	High back fixture	1 Plum	6	1.333	Ea.	1,900	99.50		1,999.50	2,225
3200	Flat slab fixture		6	1.333		1,550	99.50		1,649.50	1,850
3220	ADA compliant		6	1.333		291	99.50		390.50	470
3250	Floor mounted, back to back									
3300	High back fixtures	1 Plum	5	1.600	Ea.	1,150	119		1,269	1,425
3400	Flat slab fixtures		5	1.600		1,400	119		1,519	1,725
3430	ADA compliant		5	1.600		370	119		489	585
3500	Wall mounted, in stud or masonry									

22 42 Commercial Plumbing Fixtures

22 42 39 – Commercial Faucets, Supplies, and Trim

22 42 39.30 Carriers and Supports

		Crew	Daily Output	Labor-Hours	Unit	Material	2024 Bare Costs Labor	2024 Bare Costs Equipment	Total	Total Incl O&P
3600	High back fixture	1 Plum	6	1.333	Ea.	790	99.50		889.50	1,025
3700	Flat slab fixture	"	6	1.333	"	320	99.50		419.50	500
4000	Exposed arm type, floor mounted									
4100	Single high back or flat slab fixture	1 Plum	6	1.333	Ea.	1,150	99.50		1,249.50	1,400
4200	Back to back, high back or flat slab fixtures		5	1.600		1,800	119		1,919	2,150
4300	Wall mounted, high back or flat slab lavatory	↓	6	1.333	↓	790	99.50		889.50	1,025
4600	Sink, floor mounted									
4650	Exposed arm system									
4700	Single heavy fixture	1 Plum	5	1.600	Ea.	2,125	119		2,244	2,500
4750	Single heavy sink with slab		5	1.600		3,425	119		3,544	3,925
4800	Back to back, standard fixtures		5	1.600		3,425	119		3,544	3,925
4850	Back to back, heavy fixtures		5	1.600		3,425	119		3,544	3,925
4900	Back to back, heavy sink with slab	↓	5	1.600	↓	2,325	119		2,444	2,725
4950	Exposed offset arm system									
5000	Single heavy deep fixture	1 Plum	5	1.600	Ea.	3,425	119		3,544	3,925
5100	Plate type system									
5200	With bearing jacks, single fixture	1 Plum	5	1.600	Ea.	1,475	119		1,594	1,775
5300	With exposed arms, single heavy fixture		5	1.600		1,275	119		1,394	1,575
5400	Wall mounted, exposed arms, single heavy fixture		5	1.600		1,325	119		1,444	1,625
6000	Urinal, floor mounted, 2" or 3" coupling, blowout type		6	1.333		1,425	99.50		1,524.50	1,700
6100	With fixture or hanger bolts, blowout or washout		6	1.333		610	99.50		709.50	820
6200	With bearing plate		6	1.333		1,125	99.50		1,224.50	1,400
6300	Wall mounted, plate type system	↓	6	1.333	↓	1,000	99.50		1,099.50	1,250
6980	Water closet, siphon jet									
7000	Horizontal, adjustable, caulk									
7040	Single, 4" pipe size	1 Plum	5.33	1.501	Ea.	1,425	112		1,537	1,750
7050	4" pipe size, ADA compliant		5.33	1.501		2,125	112		2,237	2,525
7060	5" pipe size		5.33	1.501		1,225	112		1,337	1,525
7100	Double, 4" pipe size		5	1.600		2,675	119		2,794	3,125
7110	4" pipe size, ADA compliant		5	1.600		1,225	119		1,344	1,525
7120	5" pipe size	↓	5	1.600	↓	1,800	119		1,919	2,150
7160	Horizontal, adjustable, extended, caulk									
7180	Single, 4" pipe size	1 Plum	5.33	1.501	Ea.	1,850	112		1,962	2,200
7200	5" pipe size		5.33	1.501		2,300	112		2,412	2,700
7240	Double, 4" pipe size		5	1.600		5,600	119		5,719	6,325
7260	5" pipe size	↓	5	1.600	↓	3,200	119		3,319	3,700
7400	Vertical, adjustable, caulk or thread									
7440	Single, 4" pipe size	1 Plum	5.33	1.501	Ea.	2,275	112		2,387	2,675
7460	5" pipe size		5.33	1.501		2,000	112		2,112	2,375
7480	6" pipe size		5	1.600		2,075	119		2,194	2,450
7520	Double, 4" pipe size		5	1.600		5,600	119		5,719	6,325
7540	5" pipe size		5	1.600		2,575	119		2,694	3,000
7560	6" pipe size	↓	4	2	↓	2,825	149		2,974	3,350
7600	Vertical, adjustable, extended, caulk									
7620	Single, 4" pipe size	1 Plum	5.33	1.501	Ea.	1,500	112		1,612	1,825
7640	5" pipe size		5.33	1.501		1,175	112		1,287	1,450
7680	6" pipe size		5	1.600		2,250	119		2,369	2,650
7720	Double, 4" pipe size		5	1.600		1,600	119		1,719	1,925
7740	5" pipe size		5	1.600		1,375	119		1,494	1,675
7760	6" pipe size	↓	4	2	↓	1,500	149		1,649	1,875
7780	Water closet, blow out									
7800	Vertical offset, caulk or thread									
7820	Single, 4" pipe size	1 Plum	5.33	1.501	Ea.	1,925	112		2,037	2,275

22 42 Commercial Plumbing Fixtures

22 42 39 – Commercial Faucets, Supplies, and Trim

22 42 39.30 Carriers and Supports

		Crew	Daily Output	Labor-Hours	Unit	Material	2024 Bare Costs Labor	2024 Bare Costs Equipment	Total	Total Incl O&P
7840	Double, 4" pipe size	1 Plum	5	1.600	Ea.	3,300	119		3,419	3,800
7880	Vertical offset, extended, caulk									
7900	Single, 4" pipe size	1 Plum	5.33	1.501	Ea.	2,400	112		2,512	2,825
7920	Double, 4" pipe size	"	5	1.600	"	3,775	119		3,894	4,325
7960	Vertical, for floor mounted back-outlet									
7980	Single, 4" thread, 2" vent	1 Plum	5.33	1.501	Ea.	3,750	112		3,862	4,300
8000	Double, 4" thread, 2" vent	"	6	1.333	"	5,600	99.50		5,699.50	6,300
8040	Vertical, for floor mounted back-outlet, extended									
8060	Single, 4" caulk, 2" vent	1 Plum	6	1.333	Ea.	8,250	99.50		8,349.50	9,225
8080	Double, 4" caulk, 2" vent	"	6	1.333	"	2,900	99.50		2,999.50	3,325
8200	Water closet, residential									
8220	Vertical centerline, floor mount									
8240	Single, 3" caulk, 2" or 3" vent	1 Plum	6	1.333	Ea.	1,525	99.50		1,624.50	1,850
8260	4" caulk, 2" or 4" vent		6	1.333		1,300	99.50		1,399.50	1,575
8280	3" copper sweat, 3" vent		6	1.333		910	99.50		1,009.50	1,150
8300	4" copper sweat, 4" vent		6	1.333		1,100	99.50		1,199.50	1,350
8400	Vertical offset, floor mount									
8420	Single, 3" or 4" caulk, vent	1 Plum	4	2	Ea.	1,150	149		1,299	1,500
8440	3" or 4" copper sweat, vent		5	1.600		1,150	119		1,269	1,450
8460	Double, 3" or 4" caulk, vent		4	2		1,975	149		2,124	2,400
8480	3" or 4" copper sweat, vent		5	1.600		1,975	119		2,094	2,350
9000	Water cooler (electric), floor mounted									
9100	Plate type with bearing plate, single	1 Plum	6	1.333	Ea.	1,125	99.50		1,224.50	1,400
9140	Plate type with bearing plate, back to back	"	4	2	"	1,125	149		1,274	1,475

22 43 Healthcare Plumbing Fixtures

22 43 13 – Healthcare Water Closets

22 43 13.40 Water Closets

		Crew	Daily Output	Labor-Hours	Unit	Material	2024 Bare Costs Labor	2024 Bare Costs Equipment	Total	Total Incl O&P
0010	**WATER CLOSETS**									
1000	Bowl only, 1 piece, w/seat and flush valve, ADA compliant, 18" high									
1030	Floor mounted									
1150	With wall outlet	Q-1	5.30	3.019	Ea.	355	203		558	690
1180	For rough-in, supply, waste and vent		2.84	5.634		620	380		1,000	1,250
1200	With floor outlet		5.30	3.019		410	203		613	750
1800	For rough-in, supply, waste and vent		3.05	5.246		570	350		920	1,150
3100	Wall hung		5.80	2.759		1,050	185		1,235	1,450
3150	Hospital type, slotted rim for bed pan									
3156	Elongated bowl, top spud	Q-1	5.80	2.759	Ea.	670	185		855	1,000
3160	Elongated bowl, rear spud		5.80	2.759		415	185		600	730
3200	For rough-in, supply, waste and vent, single WC		2.56	6.250		1,700	420		2,120	2,500
3300	Floor mounted									
3320	Bariatric (1,200 lb. capacity), elongated bowl, ADA compliant	Q-1	4.60	3.478	Ea.	3,025	234		3,259	3,675
3360	Hospital type, slotted rim for bed pan									
3370	Elongated bowl, top spud	Q-1	5	3.200	Ea.	395	215		610	755
3380	Elongated bowl, rear spud		5	3.200		455	215		670	820
3500	For rough-in, supply, waste and vent		3.05	5.246		570	350		920	1,150

22 43 Healthcare Plumbing Fixtures

22 43 16 – Healthcare Sinks

22 43 16.10 Sinks

		Crew	Daily Output	Labor-Hours	Unit	Material	2024 Bare Costs Labor	2024 Bare Costs Equipment	Total	Total Incl O&P
0010	**SINKS**									
0020	Vitreous china									
6702	Hospital type, without trim (see Section 22 41 39.10)									
6710	20" x 18", contoured splash shield	Q-1	8	2	Ea.	70.50	134		204.50	278
6730	28" x 20", surgeon, side decks		8	2		730	134		864	1,000
6740	28" x 22", surgeon scrub-up, deep bowl		8	2		855	134		989	1,150
6750	20" x 27", patient, ADA compliant		7	2.286		615	154		769	910
6760	30" x 22", all purpose		7	2.286		1,675	154		1,829	2,050
6770	30" x 22", plaster work		7	2.286		1,675	154		1,829	2,050
6820	20" x 24" clinic service, liquid/solid waste		6	2.667		600	179		779	925

22 43 19 – Healthcare Bathtubs

22 43 19.10 Bathtubs

		Crew	Daily Output	Labor-Hours	Unit	Material	Labor	Equipment	Total	Total Incl O&P
0010	**BATHTUBS**									
5002	Hospital type, with trim, see Section 22 41 39.10									
5050	Bathing pool, porcelain enamel on cast iron, grab bars									
5060	pop-up drain, 72" x 36"	Q-1	3	5.333	Ea.	5,875	360		6,235	6,975
5100	Perineal (sitz), vitreous china		3	5.333		1,900	360		2,260	2,625
5120	For pedestal, vitreous china, add		8	2		365	134		499	600
5300	Whirlpool, porcelain enamel on cast iron, 72" x 36"		1	16		6,525	1,075		7,600	8,775
5310	For color, add					5%				
5311	For designer colors and trim, add					15%				

22 43 23 – Healthcare Showers

22 43 23.10 Showers

		Crew	Daily Output	Labor-Hours	Unit	Material	Labor	Equipment	Total	Total Incl O&P
0010	**SHOWERS**									
5950	Module, ADA compl, SS panel, fixed & hand held head, control									
5960	valves, grab bar, curtain & rod, folding seat	1 Plum	4	2	Ea.	1,775	149		1,924	2,200

22 43 39 – Healthcare Faucets

22 43 39.10 Faucets and Fittings

		Crew	Daily Output	Labor-Hours	Unit	Material	Labor	Equipment	Total	Total Incl O&P
0010	**FAUCETS AND FITTINGS**									
2850	Medical, bedpan cleanser, with pedal valve,	1 Plum	12	.667	Ea.	985	50		1,035	1,150
2860	With screwdriver stop valve		12	.667		510	50		560	635
2870	With self-closing spray valve		12	.667		370	50		420	480
2900	Faucet, gooseneck spout, wrist handles, grid drain		10	.800		209	59.50		268.50	320
2940	Mixing valve, knee action, screwdriver stops		4	2		550	149		699	825

22 45 Emergency Plumbing Fixtures

22 45 13 – Emergency Showers

22 45 13.10 Emergency Showers

		Crew	Daily Output	Labor-Hours	Unit	Material	Labor	Equipment	Total	Total Incl O&P
0010	**EMERGENCY SHOWERS**, Rough-in not included									
5000	Shower, single head, drench, ball valve, pull, freestanding	Q-1	4	4	Ea.	475	269		744	925
5200	Horizontal or vertical supply		4	4		785	269		1,054	1,250
6000	Multi-nozzle, eye/face wash combination		4	4		1,050	269		1,319	1,550
6400	Multi-nozzle, 12 spray, shower only		4	4		2,550	269		2,819	3,200
6600	For freeze-proof, add		6	2.667		645	179		824	975
8000	Walk-thru decontamination with eye-face wash		2	8		5,325	535		5,860	6,650
8200	For freeze proof, add		4	4		755	269		1,024	1,225

22 45 Emergency Plumbing Fixtures

22 45 16 – Eyewash Equipment

22 45 16.10 Eyewash Safety Equipment

		Crew	Daily Output	Labor-Hours	Unit	Material	2024 Bare Costs Labor	2024 Bare Costs Equipment	Total	Total Incl O&P
0010	**EYEWASH SAFETY EQUIPMENT**, Rough-in not included									
1000	Eye wash fountain									
1400	Plastic bowl, pedestal mounted	Q-1	4	4	Ea.	625	269		894	1,075
1600	Unmounted		4	4		445	269		714	890
1800	Wall mounted		4	4		228	269		497	650
2000	Stainless steel, pedestal mounted		4	4		515	269		784	965
2200	Unmounted		4	4		345	269		614	780
2400	Wall mounted		4	4		320	269		589	755

22 45 19 – Self-Contained Eyewash Equipment

22 45 19.10 Self-Contained Eyewash Safety Equipment

		Crew	Daily Output	Labor-Hours	Unit	Material	Labor	Equipment	Total	Total Incl O&P
0010	**SELF-CONTAINED EYEWASH SAFETY EQUIPMENT**									
3000	Eye wash, portable, self-contained				Ea.	1,400			1,400	1,525

22 45 26 – Eye/Face Wash Equipment

22 45 26.10 Eye/Face Wash Safety Equipment

		Crew	Daily Output	Labor-Hours	Unit	Material	Labor	Equipment	Total	Total Incl O&P
0010	**EYE/FACE WASH SAFETY EQUIPMENT**, Rough-in not included									
4000	Eye and face wash, combination fountain									
4200	Stainless steel, pedestal mounted	Q-1	4	4	Ea.	2,225	269		2,494	2,850
4400	Unmounted		4	4		375	269		644	810
4600	Wall mounted		4	4		530	269		799	985

22 46 Security Plumbing Fixtures

22 46 13 – Security Water Closets and Urinals

22 46 13.10 Security Water Closets and Urinals

		Crew	Daily Output	Labor-Hours	Unit	Material	Labor	Equipment	Total	Total Incl O&P
0010	**SECURITY WATER CLOSETS AND URINALS**, Stainless steel									
2000	Urinal, back supply and flush									
2200	Wall hung	Q-1	4	4	Ea.	2,000	269		2,269	2,600
2240	Stall		2.50	6.400		2,650	430		3,080	3,575
2300	For urinal rough-in, supply, waste and vent		1.49	10.738		465	720		1,185	1,600
3000	Water closet, integral seat, back supply and flush									
3300	Wall hung, wall outlet	Q-1	5.80	2.759	Ea.	1,150	185		1,335	1,525
3400	Floor mount, wall outlet		5.80	2.759		1,475	185		1,660	1,900
3440	Floor mount, floor outlet		5.80	2.759		1,500	185		1,685	1,925
3480	For recessed tissue holder, add					104			104	114
3500	For water closet rough-in, supply, waste and vent	Q-1	1.19	13.445		585	905		1,490	2,000
5000	Water closet and lavatory units, push button filler valves,									
5010	soap & paper holders, seat									
5300	Wall hung	Q-1	5	3.200	Ea.	2,275	215		2,490	2,825
5400	Floor mount		5	3.200		2,275	215		2,490	2,825
6300	For unit rough-in, supply, waste and vent		1	16		660	1,075		1,735	2,325

22 46 16 – Security Lavatories and Sinks

22 46 16.13 Security Lavatories

		Crew	Daily Output	Labor-Hours	Unit	Material	Labor	Equipment	Total	Total Incl O&P
0010	**SECURITY LAVATORIES**, Stainless steel									
1000	Lavatory, wall hung, push button filler valve									
1100	Rectangular bowl	Q-1	8	2	Ea.	815	134		949	1,100
1200	Oval bowl		8	2		830	134		964	1,125
1240	Oval bowl, corner mount		8	2		970	134		1,104	1,275
1300	For lavatory rough-in, supply, waste and vent		1.50	10.667		680	715		1,395	1,825

22 46 Security Plumbing Fixtures

22 46 63 – Security Service Sink

22 46 63.10 Security Service Sink	Crew	Daily Output	Labor-Hours	Unit	Material	2024 Bare Costs Labor	Equipment	Total	Total Incl O&P
0010 **SECURITY SERVICE SINK**, Stainless steel									
1700 Service sink, with soap dish									
1740 24" x 19" size	Q-1	3	5.333	Ea.	2,475	360		2,835	3,250
1790 For sink rough-in, supply, waste and vent	"	.89	17.978	"	1,575	1,200		2,775	3,550

22 46 73 – Security Shower

22 46 73.10 Security Shower	Crew	Daily Output	Labor-Hours	Unit	Material	2024 Bare Costs Labor	Equipment	Total	Total Incl O&P
0010 **SECURITY SHOWER**, Stainless steel									
1800 Shower cabinet, unitized									
1840 36" x 36" x 88"	Q-1	2.20	7.273	Ea.	6,125	490		6,615	7,475
1900 Shower package for built-in									
1940 Hot & cold valves, recessed soap dish	Q-1	6	2.667	Ea.	266	179		445	560

22 47 Drinking Fountains and Water Coolers

22 47 13 – Drinking Fountains

22 47 13.10 Drinking Water Fountains	Crew	Daily Output	Labor-Hours	Unit	Material	2024 Bare Costs Labor	Equipment	Total	Total Incl O&P
0010 **DRINKING WATER FOUNTAINS**, For connection to cold water supply									
0802 For remote water chiller, see Section 22 47 23.10									
1000 Wall mounted, non-recessed									
1200 Aluminum,									
1280 Dual bubbler type	1 Plum	3.20	2.500	Ea.	2,900	187		3,087	3,450
1400 Bronze, with no back		4	2		3,400	149		3,549	3,950
1600 Cast iron, enameled, low back, single bubbler		4	2		1,550	149		1,699	1,950
1640 Dual bubbler type		3.20	2.500		2,175	187		2,362	2,675
1680 Triple bubbler type		3.20	2.500		2,900	187		3,087	3,475
1800 Cast aluminum, enameled, for correctional institutions		4	2		1,850	149		1,999	2,250
2000 Fiberglass, 12" back, single bubbler unit		4	2		3,425	149		3,574	3,975
2040 Dual bubbler		3.20	2.500		3,250	187		3,437	3,850
2080 Triple bubbler		3.20	2.500		3,575	187		3,762	4,200
2200 Polymarble, no back, single bubbler		4	2		1,100	149		1,249	1,450
2240 Dual bubbler		3.20	2.500		2,950	187		3,137	3,525
2280 Triple bubbler		3.20	2.500		2,925	187		3,112	3,500
2400 Precast stone, no back		4	2		1,325	149		1,474	1,675
2700 Stainless steel, single bubbler, no back		4	2		1,025	149		1,174	1,350
2740 With back		4	2		1,325	149		1,474	1,675
2780 Dual handle, ADA compliant		4	2		1,000	149		1,149	1,350
2820 Dual level, ADA compliant		3.20	2.500		2,200	187		2,387	2,700
2840 Vandal resistant type		4	2		1,225	149		1,374	1,575
3300 Vitreous china									
3340 7" back	1 Plum	4	2	Ea.	1,025	149		1,174	1,350
3940 For vandal-resistant bottom plate, add					144			144	159
3960 For freeze-proof valve system, add	1 Plum	2	4		1,475	299		1,774	2,075
3980 For rough-in, supply and waste, add	"	2.21	3.620		460	270		730	905
4000 Wall mounted, semi-recessed									
4200 Poly-marble, single bubbler	1 Plum	4	2	Ea.	1,350	149		1,499	1,700
4600 Stainless steel, satin finish, single bubbler		4	2		2,000	149		2,149	2,425
4900 Vitreous china, single bubbler		4	2		1,500	149		1,649	1,875
5980 For rough-in, supply and waste, add		1.83	4.372		460	325		785	990
6000 Wall mounted, fully recessed									
6400 Poly-marble, single bubbler	1 Plum	4	2	Ea.	2,475	149		2,624	2,950
6440 For water glass filler, add					122			122	134

22 47 Drinking Fountains and Water Coolers

22 47 13 – Drinking Fountains

22 47 13.10 Drinking Water Fountains

		Crew	Daily Output	Labor-Hours	Unit	Material	2024 Bare Costs Labor	2024 Bare Costs Equipment	Total	Total Incl O&P
6800	Stainless steel, single bubbler	1 Plum	4	2	Ea.	1,900	149		2,049	2,300
6900	Fountain and cuspidor combination		2	4		3,700	299		3,999	4,525
7560	For freeze-proof valve system, add		2	4		1,900	299		2,199	2,525
7580	For rough-in, supply and waste, add	↓	1.83	4.372	↓	460	325		785	990
7600	Floor mounted, pedestal type									
7700	Aluminum, architectural style, CI base	1 Plum	2	4	Ea.	3,325	299		3,624	4,100
7780	ADA compliant unit		2	4		3,150	299		3,449	3,925
8000	Bronze, architectural style		2	4		3,950	299		4,249	4,800
8040	Enameled steel cylindrical column style		2	4		3,175	299		3,474	3,950
8200	Precast stone/concrete, cylindrical column		1	8		2,650	595		3,245	3,825
8240	ADA compliant unit		1	8		4,325	595		4,920	5,650
8400	Stainless steel, architectural style		2	4		2,800	299		3,099	3,525
8600	Enameled iron, heavy duty service, 2 bubblers		2	4		4,075	299		4,374	4,925
8660	4 bubblers		2	4		5,875	299		6,174	6,925
8880	For freeze-proof valve system, add		2	4		1,475	299		1,774	2,075
8900	For rough-in, supply and waste, add	↓	1.83	4.372		460	325		785	990
9100	Deck mounted									
9500	Stainless steel, circular receptor	1 Plum	4	2	Ea.	640	149		789	925
9540	14" x 9" receptor		4	2		530	149		679	800
9580	25" x 17" deep receptor, with water glass filler		3	2.667		415	199		614	755
9760	White enameled steel, 14" x 9" receptor		4	2		560	149		709	835
9860	White enameled cast iron, 24" x 16" receptor		3	2.667		730	199		929	1,100
9980	For rough-in, supply and waste, add	↓	1.83	4.372		460	325		785	990

22 47 16 – Pressure Water Coolers

22 47 16.10 Electric Water Coolers

		Crew	Daily Output	Labor-Hours	Unit	Material	2024 Bare Costs Labor	2024 Bare Costs Equipment	Total	Total Incl O&P
0010	**ELECTRIC WATER COOLERS**	D2010-820								
0100	Wall mounted, non-recessed									
0140	4 GPH	Q-1	4	4	Ea.	910	269		1,179	1,400
0160	8 GPH, barrier free, sensor operated		4	4		2,050	269		2,319	2,650
0180	8.2 GPH		4	4		1,300	269		1,569	1,825
0220	14.3 GPH		4	4		1,375	269		1,644	1,925
0600	8 GPH hot and cold water	↓	4	4		1,775	269		2,044	2,350
0640	For stainless steel cabinet, add					155			155	171
1000	Dual height, 8.2 GPH	Q-1	3.80	4.211		4,275	283		4,558	5,125
1040	14.3 GPH	"	3.80	4.211		2,875	283		3,158	3,575
1240	For stainless steel cabinet, add					297			297	325
2600	ADA compliant, 8 GPH	Q-1	4	4		1,350	269		1,619	1,875
3000	Simulated recessed, 8 GPH		4	4		1,050	269		1,319	1,550
3040	11.5 GPH	↓	4	4		1,450	269		1,719	2,000
3200	For glass filler, add					142			142	157
3240	For stainless steel cabinet, add					123			123	135
3300	Semi-recessed, 8.1 GPH	Q-1	4	4		1,175	269		1,444	1,700
3320	12 GPH	"	4	4		1,350	269		1,619	1,900
3340	For glass filler, add					231			231	254
3360	For stainless steel cabinet, add					206			206	226
3400	Full recessed, stainless steel, 8 GPH	Q-1	3.50	4.571		2,875	305		3,180	3,625
3420	11.5 GPH	"	3.50	4.571		2,575	305		2,880	3,275
3460	For glass filler, add					281			281	310
3600	For mounting can only				↓	310			310	340
4600	Floor mounted, flush-to-wall									
4640	4 GPH	1 Plum	3	2.667	Ea.	1,150	199		1,349	1,550
4680	8.2 GPH		3	2.667		1,200	199		1,399	1,625

22 47 Drinking Fountains and Water Coolers

22 47 16 – Pressure Water Coolers

22 47 16.10 Electric Water Coolers		Crew	Daily Output	Labor-Hours	Unit	Material	2024 Bare Costs Labor	Equipment	Total	Total Incl O&P
4720	14.3 GPH	1 Plum	3	2.667	Ea.	1,375	199		1,574	1,825
4960	14 GPH hot and cold water	↓	3	2.667		1,425	199		1,624	1,875
4980	For stainless steel cabinet, add					199			199	219
5000	Dual height, 8.2 GPH	1 Plum	2	4		1,700	299		1,999	2,300
5040	14.3 GPH	"	2	4		1,750	299		2,049	2,375
5120	For stainless steel cabinet, add					291			291	320
5600	Explosion proof, 16 GPH	1 Plum	3	2.667		3,225	199		3,424	3,850
6000	Refrigerator compartment type, 4.5 GPH		3	2.667		2,175	199		2,374	2,675
6600	Bottle supply type, 1.0 GPH		4	2		1,400	149		1,549	1,775
6640	Hot and cold, 1.0 GPH		4	2		800	149		949	1,100
9800	For supply, waste & vent, all coolers	↓	2.21	3.620	↓	460	270		730	905

22 47 23 – Remote Water Coolers

22 47 23.10 Remote Water Coolers

		Crew	Daily Output	Labor-Hours	Unit	Material	Labor	Equipment	Total	Total Incl O&P
0010	**REMOTE WATER COOLERS**, 80°F inlet									
0100	Air cooled, 50°F outlet, 115 V, 4.1 GPH	1 Plum	6	1.333	Ea.	780	99.50		879.50	1,000
0200	5.7 GPH		5.50	1.455		1,325	109		1,434	1,625
0300	8.0 GPH		5	1.600		860	119		979	1,125
0400	10.0 GPH		4.50	1.778		1,400	133		1,533	1,750
0500	13.4 GPH	↓	4	2		2,250	149		2,399	2,700
0700	29 GPH	Q-1	5	3.200		2,625	215		2,840	3,200
1000	230 V, 32 GPH	"	5	3.200	↓	2,600	215		2,815	3,200

22 51 Swimming Pool Plumbing Systems

22 51 19 – Swimming Pool Water Treatment Equipment

22 51 19.50 Swimming Pool Filtration Equipment

		Crew	Daily Output	Labor-Hours	Unit	Material	Labor	Equipment	Total	Total Incl O&P
0010	**SWIMMING POOL FILTRATION EQUIPMENT**									
0900	Filter system, sand or diatomite type, incl. pump, 6,000 gal./hr.	2 Plum	1.80	8.889	Total	1,250	665		1,915	2,350
1020	Add for chlorination system, 800 S.F. pool		3	5.333	Ea.	171	400		571	780
1040	5,000 S.F. pool	↓	3	5.333	"	2,975	400		3,375	3,875

22 52 Fountain Plumbing Systems

22 52 16 – Fountain Pumps

22 52 16.10 Fountain Water Pumps

		Crew	Daily Output	Labor-Hours	Unit	Material	Labor	Equipment	Total	Total Incl O&P
0010	**FOUNTAIN WATER PUMPS**									
0100	Pump w/controls									
0200	Single phase, 100' cord, 1/2 HP pump	2 Skwk	4.40	3.636	Ea.	1,800	231		2,031	2,325
0300	3/4 HP pump		4.30	3.721		1,900	236		2,136	2,425
0400	1 HP pump		4.20	3.810		2,200	242		2,442	2,775
0500	1-1/2 HP pump		4.10	3.902		2,500	248		2,748	3,125
0600	2 HP pump		4	4		6,000	254		6,254	6,975
0700	Three phase, 200' cord, 5 HP pump		3.90	4.103		9,125	261		9,386	10,400
0800	7-1/2 HP pump		3.80	4.211		16,200	267		16,467	18,200
0900	10 HP pump		3.70	4.324		18,100	275		18,375	20,300
1000	15 HP pump	↓	3.60	4.444	↓	25,300	282		25,582	28,200
2000	DESIGN NOTE: Use two horsepower per surface acre.									

22 52 Fountain Plumbing Systems

22 52 33 – Fountain Ancillary

22 52 33.10 Fountain Miscellaneous		Crew	Daily Output	Labor-Hours	Unit	Material	2024 Bare Costs Labor	2024 Bare Costs Equipment	Total	Total Incl O&P
0010	FOUNTAIN MISCELLANEOUS									
1300	Lights w/mounting kits, 200 watt	2 Skwk	18	.889	Ea.	1,275	56.50		1,331.50	1,475
1400	300 watt		18	.889		1,475	56.50		1,531.50	1,700
1500	500 watt		18	.889		1,725	56.50		1,781.50	1,950
1600	Color blender	↓	12	1.333	↓	655	84.50		739.50	845

22 62 Vacuum Systems for Laboratory and Healthcare Facilities

22 62 19 – Vacuum Equipment for Laboratory and Healthcare Facilities

22 62 19.70 Healthcare Vacuum Equipment		Crew	Daily Output	Labor-Hours	Unit	Material	2024 Bare Costs Labor	2024 Bare Costs Equipment	Total	Total Incl O&P
0010	HEALTHCARE VACUUM EQUIPMENT									
0300	Dental oral									
0310	Duplex									
0330	165 SCFM with 77 gal. separator	Q-2	1.30	18.462	Ea.	56,000	1,275		57,275	64,000
1100	Vacuum system									
1110	Vacuum outlet alarm panel	1 Plum	3.20	2.500	Ea.	1,050	187		1,237	1,450
2000	Medical, with receiver									
2100	Rotary vane type, lubricated, with controls									
2110	Simplex									
2120	1.5 HP, 80 gal. tank	Q-1	8	2	Ea.	7,200	134		7,334	8,125
2130	2 HP, 80 gal. tank		7	2.286		7,450	154		7,604	8,425
2140	3 HP, 80 gal. tank		6.60	2.424		7,850	163		8,013	8,900
2150	5 HP, 80 gal. tank	↓	6	2.667	↓	8,575	179		8,754	9,700
2200	Duplex									
2210	1 HP, 80 gal. tank	Q-1	8.40	1.905	Ea.	11,500	128		11,628	12,900
2220	1.5 HP, 80 gal. tank		7.80	2.051		11,800	138		11,938	13,200
2230	2 HP, 80 gal. tank		6.80	2.353		12,800	158		12,958	14,200
2240	3 HP, 120 gal. tank		6	2.667		13,900	179		14,079	15,600
2250	5 HP, 120 gal. tank	↓	5.40	2.963		15,700	199		15,899	17,600
2260	7.5 HP, 200 gal. tank	Q-2	7	3.429		22,500	239		22,739	25,200
2270	10 HP, 200 gal. tank		6.40	3.750		26,000	261		26,261	29,000
2280	15 HP, 200 gal. tank		5.80	4.138		46,600	288		46,888	51,500
2290	20 HP, 200 gal. tank		5	4.800		53,000	335		53,335	59,000
2300	25 HP, 200 gal. tank	↓	4	6	↓	62,000	420		62,420	68,500
2400	Triplex									
2410	7.5 HP, 200 gal. tank	Q-2	6.40	3.750	Ea.	35,800	261		36,061	39,700
2420	10 HP, 200 gal. tank		5.70	4.211		41,600	293		41,893	46,200
2430	15 HP, 200 gal. tank		4.90	4.898		70,500	340		70,840	78,000
2440	20 HP, 200 gal. tank		4	6		80,500	420		80,920	89,000
2450	25 HP, 200 gal. tank	↓	3.70	6.486	↓	93,000	450		93,450	102,500
2500	Quadruplex									
2510	7.5 HP, 200 gal. tank	Q-2	5.30	4.528	Ea.	44,600	315		44,915	49,500
2520	10 HP, 200 gal. tank		4.70	5.106		51,500	355		51,855	57,000
2530	15 HP, 200 gal. tank		4	6		93,000	420		93,420	102,500
2540	20 HP, 200 gal. tank		3.60	6.667		105,500	465		105,965	116,500
2550	25 HP, 200 gal. tank	↓	3.20	7.500	↓	123,000	525		123,525	136,000
4000	Liquid ring type, water sealed, with controls									
4200	Duplex									
4210	1.5 HP, 120 gal. tank	Q-1	6	2.667	Ea.	22,700	179		22,879	25,300
4220	3 HP, 120 gal. tank	"	5.50	2.909		23,700	195		23,895	26,400
4230	4 HP, 120 gal. tank	Q-2	6.80	3.529		25,300	246		25,546	28,200

22 62 Vacuum Systems for Laboratory and Healthcare Facilities

22 62 19 – Vacuum Equipment for Laboratory and Healthcare Facilities

22 62 19.70	Healthcare Vacuum Equipment	Crew	Daily Output	Labor-Hours	Unit	Material	2024 Bare Costs Labor	Equipment	Total	Total Incl O&P
4240	5 HP, 120 gal. tank	Q-2	6.50	3.692	Ea.	26,700	257		26,957	29,800
4250	7.5 HP, 200 gal. tank		6.20	3.871		32,500	270		32,770	36,100
4260	10 HP, 200 gal. tank		5.80	4.138		40,500	288		40,788	44,900
4270	15 HP, 200 gal. tank		5.10	4.706		49,100	330		49,430	54,500
4280	20 HP, 200 gal. tank		4.60	5.217		63,500	365		63,865	70,500
4290	30 HP, 200 gal. tank	↓	4	6	↓	76,000	420		76,420	84,000

22 63 Gas Systems for Laboratory and Healthcare Facilities

22 63 13 – Gas Piping for Laboratory and Healthcare Facilities

22 63 13.70	Healthcare Gas Piping	Crew	Daily Output	Labor-Hours	Unit	Material	2024 Bare Costs Labor	Equipment	Total	Total Incl O&P
0010	**HEALTHCARE GAS PIPING**									
0030	Air compressor intake filter									
0034	Rooftop									
0036	Filter/silencer									
0040	1"	1 Stpi	10	.800	Ea.	260	60.50		320.50	375
0044	1-1/4"		9.60	.833		268	63		331	390
0048	1-1/2"		9.20	.870		287	65.50		352.50	415
0052	2"		8.80	.909		287	68.50		355.50	415
0056	2-1/2"		8.40	.952		385	72		457	525
0060	3"		8	1		460	75.50		535.50	615
0064	4"		7.60	1.053		480	79.50		559.50	645
0068	5"	↓	7.40	1.081	↓	670	81.50		751.50	855
0076	Inline									
0080	Filter/silencer									
0084	2"	1 Stpi	8.20	.976	Ea.	870	73.50		943.50	1,075
0088	2-1/2"		8	1		895	75.50		970.50	1,100
0090	3"		7.60	1.053		990	79.50		1,069.50	1,200
0092	4"		7.20	1.111		1,150	84		1,234	1,400
0094	5"		6.80	1.176		1,250	89		1,339	1,500
0096	6"	↓	6.40	1.250	↓	1,400	94.50		1,494.50	1,700
1000	Nitrogen or oxygen system									
1010	Cylinder manifold									
1020	5 cylinder	1 Plum	.80	10	Ea.	1,650	745		2,395	2,900
1026	10 cylinder	"	.40	20		3,500	1,500		5,000	6,075
1050	Nitrogen generator, 30 LPM	Q-5	.40	40	↓	26,900	2,725		29,625	33,700
1900	Vaporizers									
1910	LOX vaporizers									
1920	Nominal capacity									
1930	1410 SCFM	Q-1	2	8	Ea.	1,950	535		2,485	2,950
1940	5650 SCFM		1.40	11.429		4,500	770		5,270	6,100
1950	12,703 SCFM	↓	.80	20	↓	6,925	1,350		8,275	9,625
1980	Removal of LOX vaporizers									
1982	Nominal capacity									
1986	1410 SCFM	Q-1	4	4	Ea.		269		269	400
1990	5650 SCFM		2.80	5.714			385		385	570
1994	12,703 SCFM		1.60	10	↓		670		670	1,000
3000	Outlets and valves									
3010	Recessed, wall mounted									
3012	Single outlet	1 Plum	3.20	2.500	Ea.	46.50	187		233.50	330
3100	Ceiling outlet									
3190	Zone valve with box									

22 63 Gas Systems for Laboratory and Healthcare Facilities

22 63 13 – Gas Piping for Laboratory and Healthcare Facilities

22 63 13.70 Healthcare Gas Piping		Crew	Daily Output	Labor-Hours	Unit	Material	2024 Bare Costs Labor	2024 Bare Costs Equipment	Total	Total Incl O&P
3192	Cleaned for oxygen service, not including gauges									
3194	1/2" valve size	1 Plum	4.60	1.739	Ea.	225	130		355	440
3196	3/4" valve size		4.30	1.860		242	139		381	475
3198	1" valve size		4	2		248	149		397	495
3202	1-1/4" valve size		3.80	2.105		285	157		442	550
3206	1-1/2" valve size		3.60	2.222		335	166		501	615
3210	2" valve size		3.20	2.500		400	187		587	720
3214	2-1/2" valve size		3.10	2.581		775	193		968	1,125
3218	3" valve size	↓	3	2.667	↓	1,200	199		1,399	1,625
3224	Gauges for zone valve box									
3226	0-100 psi (O_2, air, N_2, CO_2)	1 Plum	16	.500	Ea.	17.15	37.50		54.65	74.50
3228	Vacuum, WAGD (Waste Anesthesia Gas)		16	.500		17.15	37.50		54.65	74.50
3230	0-300 psi (Nitrogen)	↓	16	.500	↓	17.15	37.50		54.65	74.50
4000	Alarm panel, medical gases and vacuum									
4010	Alarm panel	1 Plum	3.20	2.500	Ea.	825	187		1,012	1,175
4030	Master alarm panel									
4034	Can also monitor area alarms									
4038	and communicate with PC-based alarm monitor.									
4040	10 signal	1 Elec	3.20	2.500	Ea.	1,050	179		1,229	1,425
4044	20 signal		3	2.667		1,200	191		1,391	1,600
4048	30 signal		2.80	2.857		1,600	205		1,805	2,075
4052	40 signal		2.60	3.077		1,825	221		2,046	2,325
4056	50 signal		2.40	3.333		1,950	239		2,189	2,500
4060	60 signal	↓	2.20	3.636	↓	2,275	261		2,536	2,875
4100	Area alarm panel									
4104	Does not include specific gas transducers.									
4108	3 module alarm panel									
4112	P-P-P	1 Elec	2.80	2.857	Ea.	1,400	205		1,605	1,850
4116	P-P-V		2.80	2.857		955	205		1,160	1,350
4120	D-D-D	↓	2.80	2.857		1,050	205		1,255	1,450
4130	6 module alarm panel									
4132	4-P, 3-V	1 Elec	2.20	3.636	Ea.	1,500	261		1,761	2,025
4136	3-P, 2-V, B		2.20	3.636		1,150	261		1,411	1,650
4140	5-D, B		2.20	3.636		1,450	261		1,711	1,975
4144	6-D		2.20	3.636		1,950	261		2,211	2,525
4148	3-P, 3-V	↓	2.20	3.636	↓	1,800	261		2,061	2,350
4170	Note: P=pressure, V=vacuum, B=blank, D=dual display									
4180	Alarm transducers, gas specific									
4182	Oxygen	1 Elec	24	.333	Ea.	232	24		256	291
4184	Vacuum		24	.333		221	24		245	280
4186	Nitrous oxide		24	.333		203	24		227	259
4188	Medical air		24	.333		220	24		244	278
4190	Carbon dioxide		24	.333		203	24		227	259
4192	Nitrogen		24	.333		220	24		244	278
4194	WAGD	↓	24	.333	↓	216	24		240	274
4300	Ball valves cleaned for oxygen service									
4310	with copper extensions and gauge port									
4320	1/4" diam.	1 Plum	24	.333	Ea.	65	25		90	109
4330	1/2" diam.		22	.364		64	27		91	111
4334	3/4" diam.		20	.400		77	30		107	129
4338	1" diam.		19	.421		94	31.50		125.50	150
4342	1-1/4" diam.		15	.533		128	40		168	200
4346	1-1/2" diam.	↓	13	.615	↓	175	46		221	261

22 63 Gas Systems for Laboratory and Healthcare Facilities

22 63 13 – Gas Piping for Laboratory and Healthcare Facilities

22 63 13.70 Healthcare Gas Piping

		Crew	Daily Output	Labor-Hours	Unit	Material	2024 Bare Costs Labor	2024 Bare Costs Equipment	Total	Total Incl O&P
4350	2" diam.	1 Plum	11	.727	Ea.	238	54.50		292.50	345
4354	2-1/2" diam.	Q-1	15	1.067		665	71.50		736.50	835
4358	3" diam.		13	1.231		1,275	82.50		1,357.50	1,525
4362	4" diam.	↓	10	1.600	↓	2,175	107		2,282	2,550
5000	Manifold									
5010	Automatic switchover type									
5020	Note: Both a control panel and header assembly are required									
5030	Control panel									
5040	Oxygen	Q-1	4	4	Ea.	4,950	269		5,219	5,850
5060	Header assembly									
5066	Oxygen									
5070	2 x 2	Q-1	6	2.667	Ea.	810	179		989	1,150
5074	3 x 3		5.50	2.909		950	195		1,145	1,350
5078	4 x 4		5	3.200		1,250	215		1,465	1,700
5082	5 x 5		4.50	3.556		1,375	239		1,614	1,875
5086	6 x 6		4	4		1,750	269		2,019	2,325
5090	7 x 7	↓	3.50	4.571	↓	1,875	305		2,180	2,525
7000	Medical air compressors									
7020	Oil-less with inlet filter, duplexed dryers and aftercoolers									
7030	Duplex systems, horizontal tank, 208/230/460/575 V, 3 Ph.									
7040	1 HP, 80 gal. tank, 3.8 ACFM @50PSIG, 2.7 ACFM @100PSIG	Q-5	4	4	Ea.	30,400	272		30,672	33,900
7050	1.5 HP, 80 gal. tank, 6.8 ACFM @50PSIG, 4.5 ACFM @100PSIG		3.80	4.211		37,900	286		38,186	42,100
7060	2 HP, 80 gal. tank, 8.2 ACFM @50PSIG, 6.3 ACFM @100PSIG		3.60	4.444		38,000	300		38,300	42,400
7070	3 HP, 120 gal. tank, 11.2 ACFM @50PSIG, 9.4 ACFM @100PSIG		3.20	5		29,500	340		29,840	33,000
7080	5 HP, 120 gal. tank, 17.4 ACFM @50PSIG, 15.6 ACFM @100PSIG		2.80	5.714		49,200	390		49,590	54,500
7090	7.5 HP, 250 gal. tank, 31.6 ACFM @50PSIG, 25.9 ACFM @100PSIG		2.40	6.667		65,000	455		65,455	72,500
7100	10 HP, 250 gal. tank, 43 ACFM @50PSIG, 35.2 ACFM @100PSIG		2	8		70,500	545		71,045	78,500
7110	15 HP, 250 gal. tank, 69 ACFM @50PSIG, 56.5 ACFM @100PSIG	↓	1.80	8.889	↓	85,000	605		85,605	94,500
7200	Aftercooler, air-cooled									
7210	Steel manifold, copper tube, aluminum fins									
7220	35 SCFM @ 100PSIG	Q-5	4	4	Ea.	1,050	272		1,322	1,550
7300	Air dryer system									
7310	Refrigerated type									
7320	Flow @ 125 psi									
7330	20 SCFM	Q-5	6	2.667	Ea.	1,575	181		1,756	2,000
7332	25 SCFM		5.80	2.759		1,625	188		1,813	2,075
7334	35 SCFM		5.40	2.963		2,000	201		2,201	2,500
7336	50 SCFM		5	3.200		2,475	218		2,693	3,050
7338	75 SCFM		4.60	3.478		3,100	237		3,337	3,775
7340	100 SCFM		4.30	3.721		3,725	253		3,978	4,475
7342	125 SCFM	↓	4	4	↓	4,800	272		5,072	5,675
7360	Desiccant type									
7362	Flow with energy saving controls									
7366	40 SCFM	Q-5	3.60	4.444	Ea.	6,350	300		6,650	7,425
7368	60 SCFM		3.40	4.706		6,925	320		7,245	8,075
7370	90 SCFM		3.20	5		8,225	340		8,565	9,550
7372	115 SCFM		3	5.333		8,825	365		9,190	10,200
7374	165 SCFM	↓	2.90	5.517		9,500	375		9,875	11,000
7378	260 SCFM	Q-6	3.60	6.667		11,200	470		11,670	13,000
7382	370 SCFM		3.40	7.059		13,100	500		13,600	15,100
7386	590 SCFM		3.20	7.500		16,100	530		16,630	18,500
7390	1130 SCFM	↓	3	8	↓	25,000	565		25,565	28,300
7460	Dew point monitor									

22 63 Gas Systems for Laboratory and Healthcare Facilities

22 63 13 – Gas Piping for Laboratory and Healthcare Facilities

22 63 13.70 Healthcare Gas Piping		Crew	Daily Output	Labor-Hours	Unit	Material	2024 Bare Costs Labor	Equipment	Total	Total Incl O&P
7466	LCD readout, high dew point alarm, probe included									
7470	Monitor	1 Stpi	2	4	Ea.	3,325	300		3,625	4,100

22 66 Chemical-Waste Systems for Lab. and Healthcare Facilities

22 66 53 – Laboratory Chemical-Waste and Vent Piping

22 66 53.30 Glass Pipe

		Crew	Daily Output	Labor-Hours	Unit	Material	Labor	Equipment	Total	Total Incl O&P
0010	**GLASS PIPE**, Borosilicate, couplings & clevis hanger assemblies, 10' OC R221113-70									
0020	Drainage									
1100	1-1/2" diameter	Q-1	52	.308	L.F.	32.50	20.50		53	67
1120	2" diameter		44	.364		43.50	24.50		68	84.50
1140	3" diameter		39	.410		60	27.50		87.50	107
1160	4" diameter		30	.533		101	36		137	165
1180	6" diameter		26	.615		230	41.50		271.50	315
1870	To delete coupling & hanger, subtract									
1880	1-1/2" diam. to 2" diam.					19%	22%			
1890	3" diam. to 6" diam.					20%	17%			
2000	Process supply (pressure), beaded joints									
2040	1/2" diameter	1 Plum	36	.222	L.F.	10.45	16.60		27.05	36
2060	3/4" diameter		31	.258		11.80	19.25		31.05	41.50
2080	1" diameter		27	.296		29	22		51	65
2100	1-1/2" diameter	Q-1	47	.340		17.95	23		40.95	54
2120	2" diameter		39	.410		24	27.50		51.50	67
2140	3" diameter		34	.471		32	31.50		63.50	82.50
2160	4" diameter		25	.640		53	43		96	123
2180	6" diameter		21	.762		130	51		181	218
2860	To delete coupling & hanger, subtract									
2870	1/2" diam. to 1" diam.					25%	33%			
2880	1-1/2" diam. to 3" diam.					22%	21%			
2890	4" diam. to 6" diam.					23%	15%			
3800	Conical joint, transparent									
3980	6" diameter	Q-1	21	.762	L.F.	194	51		245	289
4500	To delete couplings & hangers, subtract									
4530	6" diam.					22%	26%			

22 66 53.40 Pipe Fittings, Glass

		Crew	Daily Output	Labor-Hours	Unit	Material	Labor	Equipment	Total	Total Incl O&P
0010	**PIPE FITTINGS, GLASS**									
0020	Drainage, beaded ends									
0040	Coupling & labor required at joints not incl. in fitting									
0050	price. Add 1 per joint for installed price									
0070	90° bend or sweep, 1-1/2"				Ea.	54.50			54.50	60
0090	2"					69			69	76
0100	3"					102			102	112
0110	4"					182			182	200
0120	6" (sweep only)					440			440	480
0200	45° bend or sweep same as 90°									
0350	Tee, single sanitary, 1-1/2"				Ea.	79.50			79.50	87.50
0370	2"					133			133	146
0380	3"					114			114	126
0390	4"					211			211	232
0400	6"					395			395	435
0410	Tee, straight, 1-1/2"					91.50			91.50	100
0430	2"					98			98	108

22 66 Chemical-Waste Systems for Lab. and Healthcare Facilities

22 66 53 – Laboratory Chemical-Waste and Vent Piping

22 66 53.40 Pipe Fittings, Glass		Crew	Daily Output	Labor-Hours	Unit	Material	2024 Bare Costs Labor	Equipment	Total	Total Incl O&P
0440	3"				Ea.	136			136	150
0450	4"					195			195	215
0460	6"					610			610	670
0500	Coupling, stainless steel, TFE seal ring									
0520	1-1/2"	Q-1	32	.500	Ea.	43	33.50		76.50	97
0530	2"		30	.533		54	36		90	113
0540	3"		25	.640		72.50	43		115.50	144
0550	4"		23	.696		125	46.50		171.50	208
0560	6"		20	.800		281	53.50		334.50	390
0600	Coupling, stainless steel, bead to plain end									
0610	1-1/2"	Q-1	36	.444	Ea.	46	30		76	95
0620	2"		34	.471		66.50	31.50		98	120
0630	3"		29	.552		101	37		138	166
0640	4"		27	.593		169	40		209	244
0650	6"		24	.667		570	45		615	690
2350	Coupling, Viton liner, for temperatures to 400°F									
2370	1/2"	Q-1	40	.400	Ea.	96.50	27		123.50	146
2380	3/4"		37	.432		110	29		139	164
2390	1"		35	.457		190	30.50		220.50	255
2400	1-1/2"		32	.500		43	33.50		76.50	97
2410	2"		30	.533		54	36		90	113
2420	3"		25	.640		72.50	43		115.50	144
2430	4"		23	.696		125	46.50		171.50	208
2440	6"		20	.800		281	53.50		334.50	390
2550	For beaded joint armored fittings, add					200%				
2600	Conical ends. Flange set, gasket & labor not incl. in fitting									
2620	price. Add 1 per joint for installed price.									
2650	90° sweep elbow, 1"				Ea.	164			164	180
2670	1-1/2"					390			390	430
2680	2"					340			340	375
2690	3"					625			625	690
2700	4"					1,125			1,125	1,250
2710	6"					1,650			1,650	1,800
2750	Cross (straight), add					55%				
2850	Tee, add					20%				

22 66 53.60 Corrosion Resistant Pipe

		Crew	Daily Output	Labor-Hours	Unit	Material	Labor	Equipment	Total	Total Incl O&P
0010	**CORROSION RESISTANT PIPE**, No couplings or hangers	R221113-70								
0020	Iron alloy, drain, mechanical joint									
1000	1-1/2" diameter	Q-1	70	.229	L.F.	103	15.35		118.35	137
1100	2" diameter		66	.242		107	16.30		123.30	141
1120	3" diameter		60	.267		117	17.90		134.90	155
1140	4" diameter		52	.308		148	20.50		168.50	194
1980	Iron alloy, drain, B&S joint									
2000	2" diameter	Q-1	54	.296	L.F.	125	19.90		144.90	167
2100	3" diameter		52	.308		121	20.50		141.50	164
2120	4" diameter		48	.333		147	22.50		169.50	196
2140	6" diameter	Q-2	59	.407		222	28.50		250.50	286
2160	8" diameter	"	54	.444		455	31		486	545
2980	Plastic, epoxy, fiberglass filament wound, B&S joint									
3000	2" diameter	Q-1	62	.258	L.F.	16.50	17.35		33.85	44
3100	3" diameter		51	.314		19.30	21		40.30	52.50
3120	4" diameter		45	.356		27.50	24		51.50	66

22 66 Chemical-Waste Systems for Lab. and Healthcare Facilities

22 66 53 – Laboratory Chemical-Waste and Vent Piping

22 66 53.60 Corrosion Resistant Pipe		Crew	Daily Output	Labor-Hours	Unit	Material	2024 Bare Costs Labor	Equipment	Total	Total Incl O&P
3140	6" diameter	Q-1	32	.500	L.F.	38.50	33.50		72	92.50
3160	8" diameter	Q-2	38	.632		60.50	44		104.50	133
3180	10" diameter		32	.750		83	52.50		135.50	169
3200	12" diameter		28	.857		101	59.50		160.50	200
3980	Polyester, fiberglass filament wound, B&S joint									
4000	2" diameter	Q-1	62	.258	L.F.	17.90	17.35		35.25	45.50
4100	3" diameter		51	.314		23.50	21		44.50	57.50
4120	4" diameter		45	.356		34.50	24		58.50	73.50
4140	6" diameter		32	.500		50.50	33.50		84	106
4160	8" diameter	Q-2	38	.632		119	44		163	197
4180	10" diameter		32	.750		159	52.50		211.50	253
4200	12" diameter		28	.857		174	59.50		233.50	281
4980	Polypropylene, acid resistant, fire retardant, Schedule 40									
5000	1-1/2" diameter	Q-1	68	.235	L.F.	16.50	15.80		32.30	41.50
5100	2" diameter		62	.258		11.30	17.35		28.65	38.50
5120	3" diameter		51	.314		16.45	21		37.45	49.50
5140	4" diameter		45	.356		14.45	24		38.45	51.50
5160	6" diameter		32	.500		71.50	33.50		105	129
5980	Proxylene, fire retardant, Schedule 40									
6000	1-1/2" diameter	Q-1	68	.235	L.F.	12.80	15.80		28.60	37.50
6100	2" diameter		62	.258		11.30	17.35		28.65	38.50
6120	3" diameter		51	.314		17.20	21		38.20	50.50
6140	4" diameter		45	.356		19.15	24		43.15	56.50
6160	6" diameter		32	.500		45	33.50		78.50	99
6820	For Schedule 80, add					35%	2%			

22 66 53.70 Pipe Fittings, Corrosion Resistant

		Crew	Daily Output	Labor-Hours	Unit	Material	Labor	Equipment	Total	Total Incl O&P
0010	**PIPE FITTINGS, CORROSION RESISTANT**									
0030	Iron alloy									
0050	Mechanical joint									
0060	1/4 bend, 1-1/2"	Q-1	12	1.333	Ea.	181	89.50		270.50	330
0080	2"		10	1.600		297	107		404	485
0090	3"		9	1.778		355	119		474	570
0100	4"		8	2		410	134		544	650
0110	1/8 bend, 1-1/2"		12	1.333		115	89.50		204.50	260
0130	2"		10	1.600		198	107		305	380
0140	3"		9	1.778		264	119		383	470
0150	4"		8	2		355	134		489	590
0160	Tee and Y, sanitary, straight									
0170	1-1/2"	Q-1	8	2	Ea.	198	134		332	420
0180	2"		7	2.286		264	154		418	520
0190	3"		6	2.667		410	179		589	715
0200	4"		5	3.200		750	215		965	1,150
0360	Coupling, 1-1/2"		14	1.143		95	77		172	218
0380	2"		12	1.333		107	89.50		196.50	251
0390	3"		11	1.455		113	97.50		210.50	269
0400	4"		10	1.600		128	107		235	300
0500	Bell & Spigot									
0510	1/4 and 1/16 bend, 2"	Q-1	16	1	Ea.	171	67		238	288
0520	3"		14	1.143		400	77		477	555
0530	4"		13	1.231		410	82.50		492.50	575
0540	6"	Q-2	17	1.412		810	98.50		908.50	1,050
0550	8"	"	12	2		3,350	139		3,489	3,875

22 66 Chemical-Waste Systems for Lab. and Healthcare Facilities

22 66 53 – Laboratory Chemical-Waste and Vent Piping

22 66 53.70 Pipe Fittings, Corrosion Resistant

		Crew	Daily Output	Labor-Hours	Unit	Material	2024 Bare Costs Labor	Equipment	Total	Total Incl O&P
0620	1/8 bend, 2"	Q-1	16	1	Ea.	193	67		260	310
0640	3"		14	1.143		355	77		432	505
0650	4"	↓	13	1.231		355	82.50		437.50	515
0660	6"	Q-2	17	1.412		680	98.50		778.50	895
0680	8"	"	12	2		2,650	139		2,789	3,125
0700	Tee, sanitary, 2"	Q-1	10	1.600		365	107		472	565
0710	3"		9	1.778		1,175	119		1,294	1,475
0720	4"	↓	8	2		985	134		1,119	1,275
0730	6"	Q-2	11	2.182		1,225	152		1,377	1,575
0740	8"	"	8	3		3,375	209		3,584	4,025
1800	Y, sanitary, 2"	Q-1	10	1.600		385	107		492	585
1820	3"		9	1.778		690	119		809	940
1830	4"	↓	8	2		620	134		754	880
1840	6"	Q-2	11	2.182		2,050	152		2,202	2,475
1850	8"	"	8	3	↓	5,675	209		5,884	6,550
3000	Epoxy, filament wound									
3030	Quick-lock joint									
3040	90° elbow, 2"	Q-1	28	.571	Ea.	140	38.50		178.50	211
3060	3"		16	1		160	67		227	276
3070	4"		13	1.231		219	82.50		301.50	365
3080	6"	↓	8	2		320	134		454	550
3090	8"	Q-2	9	2.667		585	186		771	920
3100	10"		7	3.429		740	239		979	1,175
3110	12"	↓	6	4		1,050	279		1,329	1,600
3120	45° elbow, 2"	Q-1	28	.571		107	38.50		145.50	175
3130	3"		16	1		166	67		233	283
3140	4"		13	1.231		177	82.50		259.50	315
3150	6"	↓	8	2		320	134		454	550
3160	8"	Q-2	9	2.667		585	186		771	920
3170	10"		7	3.429		740	239		979	1,175
3180	12"		6	4		1,050	279		1,329	1,600
3190	Tee, 2"	Q-1	19	.842		330	56.50		386.50	450
3200	3"		11	1.455		400	97.50		497.50	585
3210	4"		9	1.778		485	119		604	715
3220	6"	↓	5	3.200		795	215		1,010	1,200
3230	8"	Q-2	6	4		920	279		1,199	1,425
3240	10"		5	4.800		1,275	335		1,610	1,925
3250	12"	↓	4	6	↓	2,000	420		2,420	2,825
4000	Polypropylene, acid resistant									
4020	Non-pressure, electrofusion joints									
4050	1/4 bend, 1-1/2"	1 Plum	16	.500	Ea.	41	37.50		78.50	101
4060	2"	Q-1	28	.571		63.50	38.50		102	127
4080	3"		17	.941		97	63		160	201
4090	4"		14	1.143		137	77		214	265
4110	6"	↓	8	2	↓	325	134		459	560
4150	1/4 bend, long sweep									
4170	1-1/2"	1 Plum	16	.500	Ea.	45.50	37.50		83	106
4180	2"	Q-1	28	.571		78	38.50		116.50	143
4200	3"		17	.941		99.50	63		162.50	203
4210	4"		14	1.143		141	77		218	269
4250	1/8 bend, 1-1/2"	1 Plum	16	.500		39	37.50		76.50	98.50
4260	2"	Q-1	28	.571		33	38.50		71.50	93
4280	3"	↓	17	.941	↓	70.50	63		133.50	172

22 66 Chemical-Waste Systems for Lab. and Healthcare Facilities
22 66 53 – Laboratory Chemical-Waste and Vent Piping

22 66 53.70 Pipe Fittings, Corrosion Resistant		Crew	Daily Output	Labor-Hours	Unit	Material	2024 Bare Costs Labor	Equipment	Total	Total Incl O&P
4290	4"	Q-1	14	1.143	Ea.	101	77		178	225
4310	6"	↓	8	2	↓	281	134		415	510
4400	Tee, sanitary									
4420	1-1/2"	1 Plum	10	.800	Ea.	50.50	59.50		110	145
4430	2"	Q-1	17	.941		60.50	63		123.50	161
4450	3"		11	1.455		118	97.50		215.50	275
4460	4"		9	1.778		181	119		300	380
4480	6"		5	3.200		1,200	215		1,415	1,650
4490	Tee, sanitary reducing, 2" x 2" x 1-1/2"		17	.941		60.50	63		123.50	161
4491	3" x 3" x 1-1/2"		11	1.455		121	97.50		218.50	278
4492	3" x 3" x 2"		11	1.455		108	97.50		205.50	264
4493	4" x 4" x 2"		10	1.600		163	107		270	340
4494	4" x 4" x 3"		9	1.778		177	119		296	375
4496	6" x 6" x 4"	↓	5	3.200		590	215		805	970
4650	Wye 45°, 1-1/2"	1 Plum	10	.800		56	59.50		115.50	151
4652	2"	Q-1	17	.941		77.50	63		140.50	180
4653	3"		11	1.455		126	97.50		223.50	284
4654	4"		9	1.778		188	119		307	385
4656	6"	↓	5	3.200	↓	475	215		690	840
4660	Wye, reducing									
4662	2" x 2" x 1-1/2"	Q-1	17	.941	Ea.	73.50	63		136.50	175
4666	3" x 3" x 2"		11	1.455		147	97.50		244.50	305
4668	4" x 4" x 2"		10	1.600		174	107		281	350
4669	4" x 4" x 3"		9	1.778		179	119		298	375
4671	6" x 6" x 2"		6	2.667		293	179		472	585
4673	6" x 6" x 3"		5.50	2.909		325	195		520	645
4675	6" x 6" x 4"	↓	5	3.200	↓	335	215		550	690
4678	Combination Y & 1/8 bend									
4681	1-1/2"	1 Plum	10	.800	Ea.	68	59.50		127.50	164
4683	2"	Q-1	17	.941		84.50	63		147.50	187
4684	3"		11	1.455		147	97.50		244.50	305
4685	4"	↓	9	1.778	↓	202	119		321	400
4689	Combination Y & 1/8 bend, reducing									
4692	2" x 2" x 1-1/2"	Q-1	17	.941	Ea.	82	63		145	184
4694	3" x 3" x 1-1/2"		12	1.333		123	89.50		212.50	268
4695	3" x 3" x 2"		11	1.455		129	97.50		226.50	287
4697	4" x 4" x 2"		10	1.600		183	107		290	360
4699	4" x 4" x 3"	↓	9	1.778	↓	191	119		310	390
4710	Hub adapter									
4712	1-1/2"	1 Plum	16	.500	Ea.	95	37.50		132.50	160
4713	2"	Q-1	28	.571		108	38.50		146.50	176
4714	3"		17	.941		136	63		199	243
4715	4"	↓	14	1.143	↓	177	77		254	310
4719	Mechanical joint adapter									
4721	1-1/2"	1 Plum	16	.500	Ea.	58.50	37.50		96	120
4722	2"	Q-1	28	.571		60.50	38.50		99	124
4723	3"		17	.941		86.50	63		149.50	189
4724	4"	↓	14	1.143	↓	129	77		206	256
4728	Couplings									
4731	1-1/2"	1 Plum	16	.500	Ea.	32.50	37.50		70	91.50
4732	2"	Q-1	28	.571		41	38.50		79.50	102
4733	3"		17	.941		50.50	63		113.50	150
4734	4"	↓	14	1.143	↓	73.50	77		150.50	195

22 66 Chemical-Waste Systems for Lab. and Healthcare Facilities

22 66 53 – Laboratory Chemical-Waste and Vent Piping

22 66 53.70 Pipe Fittings, Corrosion Resistant		Crew	Daily Output	Labor-Hours	Unit	Material	2024 Bare Costs Labor	Equipment	Total	Total Incl O&P
4736	6"	Q-1	8	2	Ea.	116	134		250	330

22 66 83 – Chemical-Waste Tanks

22 66 83.13 Chemical-Waste Dilution Tanks

		Crew	Daily Output	Labor-Hours	Unit	Material	Labor	Equipment	Total	Total Incl O&P
0010	**CHEMICAL-WASTE DILUTION TANKS**									
7000	Tanks, covers included									
7800	Polypropylene									
7810	Continuous service to 200°F									
7830	2 gallon, 8" x 8" x 8"	Q-1	20	.800	Ea.	305	53.50		358.50	415
7850	7 gallon, 12" x 12" x 12"		20	.800		365	53.50		418.50	485
7870	16 gallon, 18" x 12" x 18"		17	.941		645	63		708	805
8010	33 gallon, 24" x 18" x 18"		12	1.333		880	89.50		969.50	1,100
8070	44 gallon, 24" x 18" x 24"		10	1.600		460	107		567	665
8080	89 gallon, 36" x 24" x 24"		8	2		955	134		1,089	1,250
8150	Polyethylene, heavy duty walls									
8160	Continuous service to 180°F									
8180	5 gallon, 12" x 6" x 18"	Q-1	20	.800	Ea.	56	53.50		109.50	142
8210	15 gallon, 14" I.D. x 27" deep		17	.941		97	63		160	201
8230	55 gallon, 22" I.D. x 36" deep		10	1.600		270	107		377	455
8250	100 gallon, 28" I.D. x 42" deep		8	2		525	134		659	780
8270	200 gallon, 36" I.D. x 48" deep		6	2.667		670	179		849	1,000
8290	360 gallon, 48" I.D. x 48" deep		5	3.200		895	215		1,110	1,300

Division Notes

	CREW	DAILY OUTPUT	LABOR-HOURS	UNIT	BARE COSTS				TOTAL INCL O&P
					MAT.	LABOR	EQUIP.	TOTAL	

Division 23 — Heating, Ventilating & Air Conditioning

Estimating Tips
The labor adjustment factors listed in Subdivision 22 01 02.20 also apply to Division 23.

23 10 00 Facility Fuel Systems
- The prices in this subdivision for above- and below-ground storage tanks do not include foundations or hold-down slabs, unless noted. The estimator should refer to Divisions 3 and 31 for foundation system pricing. In addition to the foundations, required tank accessories, such as tank gauges, leak detection devices, and additional manholes and piping, must be added to the tank prices.

23 50 00 Central Heating Equipment
- When estimating the cost of an HVAC system, check to see who is responsible for providing and installing the temperature control system. It is possible to overlook controls, assuming that they would be included in the electrical estimate.
- When looking up a boiler, be careful on specified capacity. Some manufacturers rate their products on output while others use input.
- Include HVAC insulation for pipe, boiler, and duct (wrap and liner).
- Be careful when looking up mechanical items to get the correct pressure rating and connection type (thread, weld, flange).

23 70 00 Central HVAC Equipment
- Combination heating and cooling units are sized by the air conditioning requirements. (See Reference No. R236000-20 for the preliminary sizing guide.)
- A ton of air conditioning is nominally 400 CFM.
- Rectangular duct is taken off by the linear foot for each size, but its cost is usually estimated by the pound. Remember that SMACNA standards now base duct on internal pressure.
- Prefabricated duct is estimated and purchased like pipe: straight sections and fittings.
- Note that cranes or other lifting equipment are not included on any lines in Division 23. For example, if a crane is required to lift a heavy piece of pipe into place high above a gym floor, or to put a rooftop unit on the roof of a four-story building, etc., it must be added. Due to the potential for extreme variation—from nothing additional required to a major crane or helicopter—we feel that including a nominal amount for "lifting contingency" would be useless and detract from the accuracy of the estimate. When using equipment rental cost data from RSMeans, do not forget to include the cost of the operator(s).

Reference Numbers
Reference numbers are shown at the beginning of some major classifications. These numbers refer to related items in the Reference Section. The reference information may be an estimating procedure, an alternate pricing method, or technical information.

Note: Not all subdivisions listed here necessarily appear. ■

Same Data. Simplified.
Enjoy the convenience and efficiency of accessing your costs anywhere:
- **Skip the multiplier** by setting your location
- **Quickly search,** edit, favorite and share costs
- **Stay on top of price changes** with automatic updates

Discover more at rsmeans.com/online

No part of this cost data may be reproduced, stored in a retrieval system, or transmitted in any form or by any means without prior written permission of Gordian.

Note: "Powered in part by CINX™, based on licensed proprietary information of Harrison Publishing House, Inc."

Note: Trade Service, in part, has been used as a reference source for some of the material prices used in Division 23.

23 05 Common Work Results for HVAC

23 05 02 – HVAC General

23 05 02.10 Air Conditioning, General		Crew	Daily Output	Labor-Hours	Unit	Material	2024 Bare Costs Labor	2024 Bare Costs Equipment	Total	Total Incl O&P
0010	**AIR CONDITIONING, GENERAL** Prices are for standard efficiencies (SEER 13)									
0020	for upgrade to SEER 14 add					10%				

23 05 05 – Selective Demolition for HVAC

23 05 05.10 HVAC Demolition

			Crew	Daily Output	Labor-Hours	Unit	Material	2024 Bare Costs Labor	2024 Bare Costs Equipment	Total	Total Incl O&P
0010	**HVAC DEMOLITION**	R220105-10									
0100	Air conditioner, split unit, 3 ton		Q-5	2	8	Ea.		545		545	810
0150	Package unit, 3 ton	R024119-10	Q-6	3	8			565		565	840
0190	Rooftop, self contained, up to 5 ton		1 Plum	1.20	6.667			500		500	740
0250	Air curtain		Q-9	20	.800	L.F.		52		52	78.50
0254	Air filters, up thru 16,000 CFM			20	.800	Ea.		52		52	78.50
0256	20,000 thru 60,000 CFM			16	1			65		65	98
0297	Boiler blowdown		Q-5	8	2			136		136	202
0298	Boilers										
0300	Electric, up thru 148 kW		Q-19	2	12	Ea.		830		830	1,225
0310	150 thru 518 kW		"	1	24			1,650		1,650	2,475
0320	550 thru 2,000 kW		Q-21	.40	80			5,675		5,675	8,425
0330	2,070 kW and up		"	.30	107			7,550		7,550	11,200
0340	Gas and/or oil, up thru 150 MBH		Q-7	2.20	14.545			1,050		1,050	1,550
0350	160 thru 2,000 MBH			.80	40			2,875		2,875	4,275
0360	2,100 thru 4,500 MBH			.50	64			4,600		4,600	6,850
0370	4,600 thru 7,000 MBH			.30	107			7,675		7,675	11,400
0380	7,100 thru 12,000 MBH			.16	200			14,400		14,400	21,400
0390	12,200 thru 25,000 MBH			.12	267			19,200		19,200	28,500
0400	Central station air handler unit, up thru 15 ton		Q-5	1.60	10			680		680	1,000
0410	17.5 thru 30 ton		"	.80	20			1,350		1,350	2,025
0430	Computer room unit										
0434	Air cooled split, up thru 10 ton		Q-5	.67	23.881	Ea.		1,625		1,625	2,425
0436	12 thru 23 ton			.53	30.189			2,050		2,050	3,050
0440	Chilled water, up thru 10 ton			1.30	12.308			835		835	1,250
0444	12 thru 23 ton			1	16			1,100		1,100	1,625
0450	Glycol system, up thru 10 ton			.53	30.189			2,050		2,050	3,050
0454	12 thru 23 ton			.40	40			2,725		2,725	4,050
0460	Water cooled, not including condenser, up thru 10 ton			.80	20			1,350		1,350	2,025
0464	12 thru 23 ton			.60	26.667			1,825		1,825	2,700
0600	Condenser, up thru 50 ton			1	16			1,100		1,100	1,625
0610	51 thru 100 ton		Q-6	.90	26.667			1,875		1,875	2,800
0620	101 thru 1,000 ton		"	.70	34.286			2,425		2,425	3,600
0660	Condensing unit, up thru 10 ton		Q-5	1.25	12.800			870		870	1,300
0670	11 thru 50 ton		"	.40	40			2,725		2,725	4,050
0680	60 thru 100 ton		Q-6	.30	80			5,650		5,650	8,400
0700	Cooling tower, up thru 400 ton			.80	30			2,125		2,125	3,150
0710	450 thru 600 ton			.53	45.283			3,200		3,200	4,750
0720	700 thru 1,300 ton			.40	60			4,225		4,225	6,300
0780	Dehumidifier, up thru 155 lb./hr.		Q-1	8	2			134		134	200
0790	240 lb./hr. and up		"	2	8			535		535	800
1560	Ductwork										
1570	Metal, steel, sst, fabricated		Q-9	1000	.016	Lb.		1.04		1.04	1.57
1580	Aluminum, fabricated			485	.033	"		2.15		2.15	3.23
1590	Spiral, prefabricated			400	.040	L.F.		2.60		2.60	3.91
1600	Fiberglass, prefabricated			400	.040			2.60		2.60	3.91
1610	Flex, prefabricated			500	.032			2.08		2.08	3.13
1620	Glass fiber reinforced plastic, prefabricated			280	.057			3.72		3.72	5.60

23 05 Common Work Results for HVAC

23 05 05 – Selective Demolition for HVAC

23 05 05.10 HVAC Demolition		Crew	Daily Output	Labor-Hours	Unit	Material	2024 Bare Costs Labor	Equipment	Total	Total Incl O&P
1630	Diffusers, registers or grills, up thru 20" max dimension	1 Shee	50	.160	Ea.		11.55		11.55	17.40
1640	21 thru 36" max dimension	"	36	.222			16.05		16.05	24
1650	Above 36" max dimension	"	30	.267			19.25		19.25	29
1700	Evaporator, up thru 12,000 BTUH	Q-5	5.30	3.019			205		205	305
1710	12,500 thru 30,000 BTUH	"	2.70	5.926			405		405	600
1720	31,000 BTUH and up	Q-6	1.50	16			1,125		1,125	1,675
1730	Evaporative cooler, up thru 5 HP	Q-9	2.70	5.926			385		385	580
1740	10 thru 30 HP	"	.67	23.881			1,550		1,550	2,325
1750	Exhaust systems									
1760	Exhaust components	1 Shee	8	1	System		72.50		72.50	109
1770	Weld fume hoods	"	20	.400	Ea.		29		29	43.50
2120	Fans, up thru 1 HP or 2,000 CFM	Q-9	8	2			130		130	196
2124	1-1/2 thru 10 HP or 20,000 CFM	"	5.30	3.019			196		196	295
2128	15 thru 30 HP or above 20,000 CFM	"	4	4			260		260	390
2150	Fan coil air conditioner, chilled water, up thru 7.5 ton	Q-5	14	1.143			77.50		77.50	116
2154	Direct expansion, up thru 10 ton	"	8	2			136		136	202
2158	11 thru 30 ton	"	2	8			545		545	810
2170	Flue shutter damper	Q-9	8	2			130		130	196
2200	Furnace, electric	Q-20	2	10			665		665	995
2300	Gas or oil, under 120 MBH	Q-9	4	4			260		260	390
2340	Over 120 MBH	"	3	5.333			345		345	520
2730	Heating and ventilating unit	Q-5	2.70	5.926			405		405	600
2740	Heater, electric, wall, baseboard and quartz	1 Elec	10	.800			57.50		57.50	85
2750	Heater, electric, unit, cabinet, fan and convector	"	8	1			71.50		71.50	106
2760	Heat exchanger, shell and tube type	Q-5	1.60	10			680		680	1,000
2770	Plate type	Q-6	.60	40			2,825		2,825	4,200
2810	Heat pump									
2820	Air source, split, 4 thru 10 ton	Q-5	.90	17.778	Ea.		1,200		1,200	1,800
2830	15 thru 25 ton	Q-6	.80	30			2,125		2,125	3,150
2850	Single package, up thru 12 ton	Q-5	1	16			1,100		1,100	1,625
2860	Water source, up thru 15 ton	"	.90	17.778			1,200		1,200	1,800
2870	20 thru 50 ton	Q-6	.80	30			2,125		2,125	3,150
2910	Heat recovery package, up thru 20,000 CFM	Q-5	2	8			545		545	810
2920	25,000 CFM and up	"	1.20	13.333			905		905	1,350
2930	Heat transfer package, up thru 130 GPM	"	.80	20			1,350		1,350	2,025
2934	255 thru 800 GPM	"	.42	38.095			2,600		2,600	3,850
2940	Humidifier	"	10.60	1.509			103		103	153
2961	Hydronic unit heaters, up thru 200 MBH	"	14	1.143			77.50		77.50	116
2962	Above 200 MBH	"	8	2			136		136	202
2964	Valance units	"	32	.500			34		34	50.50
2966	Radiant floor heating									
2967	System valves, controls, manifolds	Q-5	16	1	Ea.		68		68	101
2968	Per room distribution	"	8	2			136		136	202
2970	Hydronic heating, baseboard radiation	"	16	1			68		68	101
2976	Convectors and free standing radiators	"	18	.889			60.50		60.50	90
2980	Induced draft fan, up thru 1 HP	Q-9	4.60	3.478			226		226	340
2984	1-1/2 HP thru 7-1/2 HP	"	2.20	7.273			475		475	710
2988	Infrared unit	Q-5	16	1			68		68	101
2992	Louvers	1 Shee	46	.174	S.F.		12.55		12.55	18.90
3000	Mechanical equipment, light items. Unit is weight, not cooling.	Q-5	.90	17.778	Ton		1,200		1,200	1,800
3600	Heavy items	"	1.10	14.545	"		990		990	1,475
3720	Make-up air unit, up thru 6,000 CFM	"	3	5.333	Ea.		365		365	540
3730	6,500 thru 30,000 CFM	"	1.60	10			680		680	1,000

23 05 Common Work Results for HVAC

23 05 05 – Selective Demolition for HVAC

23 05 05.10 HVAC Demolition

		Crew	Daily Output	Labor-Hours	Unit	Material	2024 Bare Costs Labor	Equipment	Total	Total Incl O&P
3740	35,000 thru 75,000 CFM	Q-6	1	24	Ea.		1,700		1,700	2,525
3800	Mixing boxes, constant and VAV	Q-9	18	.889			58		58	87
4000	Packaged terminal air conditioner, up thru 18,000 BTUH	Q-5	8	2			136		136	202
4010	24,000 thru 48,000 BTUH	"	2.80	5.714			390		390	580
5000	Refrigerant compressor, reciprocating or scroll									
5010	Up thru 5 ton	1 Stpi	6	1.333	Ea.		101		101	150
5020	5.08 thru 10 ton	Q-5	6	2.667			181		181	270
5030	15 thru 50 ton	"	3	5.333			365		365	540
5040	60 thru 130 ton	Q-6	2.80	8.571			605		605	900
5090	Remove refrigerant from system	1 Stpi	40	.200	Lb.		15.10		15.10	22.50
5100	Rooftop air conditioner, up thru 10 ton	Q-5	1.40	11.429	Ea.		775		775	1,150
5110	12 thru 40 ton	Q-6	1	24			1,700		1,700	2,525
5120	50 thru 140 ton		.50	48			3,375		3,375	5,025
5130	150 thru 300 ton		.30	80			5,650		5,650	8,400
6000	Self contained single package air conditioner, up thru 10 ton	Q-5	1.60	10			680		680	1,000
6010	15 thru 60 ton	Q-6	1.20	20			1,400		1,400	2,100
6100	Space heaters, up thru 200 MBH	Q-5	10	1.600			109		109	162
6110	Over 200 MBH		5	3.200			218		218	325
6200	Split ductless, both sections		8	2			136		136	202
6300	Steam condensate meter	1 Stpi	11	.727			55		55	82
6600	Thru-the-wall air conditioner	L-2	8	2			107		107	160
7000	Vent chimney, prefabricated, up thru 12" diameter	Q-9	94	.170	V.L.F.		11.05		11.05	16.65
7010	14" thru 36" diameter		40	.400			26		26	39
7020	38" thru 48" diameter		32	.500			32.50		32.50	49
7030	54" thru 60" diameter	Q-10	14	1.714			116		116	174
7400	Ventilators, up thru 14" neck diameter	Q-9	58	.276	Ea.		17.95		17.95	27
7410	16" thru 50" neck diameter		40	.400			26		26	39
7450	Relief vent, up thru 24" x 96"		22	.727			47.50		47.50	71
7460	48" x 60" thru 96" x 144"		10	1.600			104		104	157
8000	Water chiller up thru 10 ton	Q-5	2.50	6.400			435		435	650
8010	15 thru 100 ton	Q-6	.48	50			3,525		3,525	5,250
8020	110 thru 500 ton	Q-7	.29	110			7,925		7,925	11,800
8030	600 thru 1000 ton		.23	139			10,000		10,000	14,900
8040	1100 ton and up		.20	160			11,500		11,500	17,100
8041	Absorption Chiller		.02	1600			115,000		115,000	171,000
8042	HVAC demo, water chiller plant		.01	4571			328,500		328,500	489,000
8400	Window air conditioner	1 Carp	16	.500			30.50		30.50	45
8401	HVAC demo, water chiller, 1100 ton and up	"	12	.667	Ton		40.50		40.50	60

23 05 23 – General-Duty Valves for HVAC Piping

23 05 23.20 Valves, Bronze/Brass

		Crew	Daily Output	Labor-Hours	Unit	Material	Labor	Equipment	Total	Total Incl O&P
0010	**VALVES, BRONZE/BRASS**									
0020	Brass									
1300	Ball combination valves, shut-off and union									
1310	Solder, with strainer, drain and PT ports									
1320	1/2"	1 Stpi	17	.471	Ea.	114	35.50		149.50	178
1330	3/4"		16	.500		125	38		163	193
1340	1"		14	.571		168	43		211	248
1350	1-1/4"		12	.667		217	50.50		267.50	315
1360	1-1/2"		10	.800		320	60.50		380.50	440
1370	2"		8	1		400	75.50		475.50	550
1410	Threaded, with strainer, drain and PT ports									
1420	1/2"	1 Stpi	20	.400	Ea.	114	30		144	170

23 05 Common Work Results for HVAC

23 05 23 – General-Duty Valves for HVAC Piping

23 05 23.20 Valves, Bronze/Brass

		Crew	Daily Output	Labor-Hours	Unit	Material	2024 Bare Costs Labor	Equipment	Total	Total Incl O&P
1430	3/4"	1 Stpi	18	.444	Ea.	125	33.50		158.50	187
1440	1"		17	.471		168	35.50		203.50	237
1450	1-1/4"		12	.667		217	50.50		267.50	315
1460	1-1/2"		11	.727		320	55		375	430
1470	2"		9	.889		400	67		467	540

23 05 23.30 Valves, Iron Body

		Crew	Daily Output	Labor-Hours	Unit	Material	2024 Bare Costs Labor	Equipment	Total	Total Incl O&P
0010	**VALVES, IRON BODY** R220523-90									
0022	For grooved joint, see Section 22 11 13.48									
0100	Angle, 125 lb.									
0110	Flanged									
0116	2"	1 Plum	5	1.600	Ea.	2,450	119		2,569	2,875
0118	4"	Q-1	3	5.333		4,050	360		4,410	4,975
0120	6"	Q-2	3	8		8,750	555		9,305	10,500
0122	8"	"	2.50	9.600		14,200	670		14,870	16,600
1020	Butterfly, wafer type, gear actuator, 200 lb.									
1030	2"	1 Plum	14	.571	Ea.	118	42.50		160.50	194
1040	2-1/2"	Q-1	9	1.778		120	119		239	310
1050	3"		8	2		124	134		258	335
1060	4"		5	3.200		138	215		353	470
1070	5"	Q-2	5	4.800		155	335		490	665
1080	6"		5	4.800		176	335		511	690
1090	8"		4.50	5.333		219	370		589	795
1100	10"		4	6		294	420		714	945
1110	12"		3	8		725	555		1,280	1,625
1200	Wafer type, lever actuator, 200 lb.									
1220	2"	1 Plum	14	.571	Ea.	315	42.50		357.50	415
1230	2-1/2"	Q-1	9	1.778		325	119		444	540
1240	3"		8	2		345	134		479	580
1250	4"		5	3.200		420	215		635	780
1260	5"	Q-2	5	4.800		585	335		920	1,125
1270	6"		5	4.800		705	335		1,040	1,275
1280	8"		4.50	5.333		1,100	370		1,470	1,750
1290	10"		4	6		905	420		1,325	1,625
1300	12"		3	8		2,000	555		2,555	3,025
1650	Gate, 125 lb., N.R.S.									
2150	Flanged									
2200	2"	1 Plum	5	1.600	Ea.	1,350	119		1,469	1,650
2240	2-1/2"	Q-1	5	3.200		1,375	215		1,590	1,850
2260	3"		4.50	3.556		2,550	239		2,789	3,150
2280	4"		3	5.333		3,025	360		3,385	3,850
2290	5"	Q-2	3.40	7.059		3,775	490		4,265	4,875
2300	6"		3	8		3,625	555		4,180	4,800
2320	8"		2.50	9.600		6,225	670		6,895	7,850
2340	10"		2.20	10.909		10,900	760		11,660	13,100
2360	12"		1.70	14.118		15,000	985		15,985	18,000
2420	For 250 lb. flanged, add					200%	10%			
3550	OS&Y, 125 lb., flanged									
3600	2"	1 Plum	5	1.600	Ea.	1,125	119		1,244	1,400
3640	2-1/2"	Q-1	5	3.200		1,125	215		1,340	1,550
3660	3"		4.50	3.556		1,225	239		1,464	1,700
3670	3-1/2"		3	5.333		1,425	360		1,785	2,100
3680	4"		3	5.333		1,800	360		2,160	2,500

23 05 Common Work Results for HVAC

23 05 23 – General-Duty Valves for HVAC Piping

23 05 23.30 Valves, Iron Body		Crew	Daily Output	Labor-Hours	Unit	Material	2024 Bare Costs Labor	Equipment	Total	Total Incl O&P
3690	5"	Q-2	3.40	7.059	Ea.	2,975	490		3,465	3,975
3700	6"		3	8		2,975	555		3,530	4,075
3720	8"		2.50	9.600		5,275	670		5,945	6,800
3740	10"		2.20	10.909		9,625	760		10,385	11,700
3760	12"		1.70	14.118		13,100	985		14,085	15,900
3900	For 175 lb., flanged, add					200%	10%			
4350	Globe, OS&Y									
4540	Class 125, flanged									
4550	2"	1 Plum	5	1.600	Ea.	2,225	119		2,344	2,625
4560	2-1/2"	Q-1	5	3.200		2,250	215		2,465	2,800
4570	3"		4.50	3.556		2,725	239		2,964	3,350
4580	4"		3	5.333		3,900	360		4,260	4,825
4590	5"	Q-2	3.40	7.059		7,125	490		7,615	8,550
4600	6"		3	8		7,125	555		7,680	8,650
4610	8"		2.50	9.600		13,900	670		14,570	16,300
4612	10"		2.20	10.909		21,800	760		22,560	25,000
4614	12"		1.70	14.118		15,300	985		16,285	18,400
5040	Class 250, flanged									
5050	2"	1 Plum	4.50	1.778	Ea.	3,650	133		3,783	4,200
5060	2-1/2"	Q-1	4.50	3.556		4,600	239		4,839	5,400
5070	3"		4	4		4,850	269		5,119	5,725
5080	4"		2.70	5.926		7,100	400		7,500	8,425
5090	5"	Q-2	3	8		12,500	555		13,055	14,500
5100	6"		2.70	8.889		12,600	620		13,220	14,700
5110	8"		2.20	10.909		21,400	760		22,160	24,600
5120	10"		2	12		17,500	835		18,335	20,500
5130	12"		1.60	15		26,200	1,050		27,250	30,500
5240	Valve sprocket rim w/chain, for 2" valve	1 Stpi	30	.267		365	20		385	435
5250	2-1/2" valve		27	.296		430	22.50		452.50	510
5260	3-1/2" valve		25	.320		575	24		599	670
5270	6" valve		20	.400		430	30		460	520
5280	8" valve		18	.444		770	33.50		803.50	895
5290	12" valve		16	.500		805	38		843	940
5300	16" valve		12	.667		1,800	50.50		1,850.50	2,050
5310	20" valve		10	.800		1,800	60.50		1,860.50	2,075
5320	36" valve		8	1		745	75.50		820.50	930
5450	Swing check, 125 lb., threaded									
5500	2"	1 Plum	11	.727	Ea.	325	54.50		379.50	435
5540	2-1/2"	Q-1	15	1.067		405	71.50		476.50	550
5550	3"		13	1.231		445	82.50		527.50	610
5560	4"		10	1.600		700	107		807	930
5950	Flanged									
5994	1"	1 Plum	7	1.143	Ea.	415	85.50		500.50	585
5998	1-1/2"		6	1.333		740	99.50		839.50	965
6000	2"		5	1.600		980	119		1,099	1,250
6040	2-1/2"	Q-1	5	3.200		995	215		1,210	1,425
6050	3"		4.50	3.556		1,075	239		1,314	1,525
6060	4"		3	5.333		1,675	360		2,035	2,375
6070	6"	Q-2	3	8		2,875	555		3,430	3,975
6080	8"		2.50	9.600		5,400	670		6,070	6,950
6090	10"		2.20	10.909		9,225	760		9,985	11,200
6100	12"		1.70	14.118		12,500	985		13,485	15,200
6102	14"		1.55	15.484		23,300	1,075		24,375	27,300

23 05 Common Work Results for HVAC

23 05 23 – General-Duty Valves for HVAC Piping

23 05 23.30 Valves, Iron Body

		Crew	Daily Output	Labor-Hours	Unit	Material	2024 Bare Costs Labor	Equipment	Total	Total Incl O&P
6104	16"	Q-2	1.40	17.143	Ea.	36,400	1,200		37,600	41,800
6110	18"		1.30	18.462		47,300	1,275		48,575	54,000
6112	20"		1	24		75,000	1,675		76,675	85,000
6114	24"		.75	32		60,000	2,225		62,225	69,500
6160	For 250 lb. flanged, add					200%	20%			
6600	Silent check, bronze trim									
6610	Compact wafer type, for 125 or 150 lb. flanges									
6630	1-1/2"	1 Plum	11	.727	Ea.	163	54.50		217.50	261
6640	2"	"	9	.889		720	66.50		786.50	890
6650	2-1/2"	Q-1	9	1.778		820	119		939	1,075
6660	3"		8	2		895	134		1,029	1,175
6670	4"		5	3.200		1,200	215		1,415	1,650
6680	5"	Q-2	6	4		1,600	279		1,879	2,175
6690	6"		6	4		2,075	279		2,354	2,700
6700	8"		4.50	5.333		3,700	370		4,070	4,625
6710	10"		4	6		5,725	420		6,145	6,925
6720	12"		3	8		2,900	555		3,455	4,025
6740	For 250 or 300 lb. flanges, thru 6" no change									
6741	For 8" and 10", add				Ea.	11%	10%			
6750	Twin disc									
6752	2"	1 Plum	9	.889	Ea.	740	66.50		806.50	915
6754	4"	Q-1	5	3.200		1,200	215		1,415	1,650
6756	6"	Q-2	5	4.800		1,800	335		2,135	2,475
6758	8"		4.50	5.333		2,750	370		3,120	3,575
6760	10"		4	6		4,400	420		4,820	5,450
6762	12"		3	8		5,700	555		6,255	7,100
6764	18"		1.50	16		24,600	1,125		25,725	28,800
6766	24"		.75	32		34,700	2,225		36,925	41,400
6800	Full flange type, 150 lb.									
6900	Globe type, 125 lb.									
6911	2-1/2"	Q-1	9	1.778	Ea.	485	119		604	715
6912	3"		8	2		430	134		564	675
6913	4"		5	3.200		770	215		985	1,175
6914	5"	Q-2	6	4		1,075	279		1,354	1,600
6915	6"		5	4.800		1,350	335		1,685	1,975
6916	8"		4.50	5.333		2,450	370		2,820	3,250
6917	10"		4	6		3,100	420		3,520	4,025
6918	12"		3	8		5,350	555		5,905	6,700
6940	For 250 lb., add					40%	10%			
6980	Screwed end type, 125 lb.									
6981	1"	1 Plum	19	.421	Ea.	208	31.50		239.50	276
6982	1-1/4"		15	.533		275	40		315	360
6983	1-1/2"		13	.615		335	46		381	435
6984	2"		11	.727		455	54.50		509.50	585

23 05 23.70 Valves, Semi-Steel

		Crew	Daily Output	Labor-Hours	Unit	Material	2024 Bare Costs Labor	Equipment	Total	Total Incl O&P
0010	**VALVES, SEMI-STEEL** R220523-90									
1020	Lubricated plug valve, threaded, 200 psi									
1030	1/2"	1 Plum	18	.444	Ea.	167	33		200	234
1040	3/4"		16	.500		211	37.50		248.50	288
1050	1"		14	.571		239	42.50		281.50	325
1060	1-1/4"		12	.667		211	50		261	305
1070	1-1/2"		11	.727		250	54.50		304.50	355

23 05 Common Work Results for HVAC
23 05 23 – General-Duty Valves for HVAC Piping

23 05 23.70 Valves, Semi-Steel

		Crew	Daily Output	Labor-Hours	Unit	Material	2024 Bare Costs Labor	Equipment	Total	Total Incl O&P
1080	2"	1 Plum	8	1	Ea.	775	74.50		849.50	965
1090	2-1/2"	Q-1	5	3.200		850	215		1,065	1,250
1100	3"	"	4.50	3.556	↓	390	239		629	780
6990	Flanged, 200 psi									
7000	2"	1 Plum	8	1	Ea.	765	74.50		839.50	950
7010	2-1/2"	Q-1	5	3.200		1,125	215		1,340	1,575
7020	3"		4.50	3.556		1,425	239		1,664	1,925
7030	4"		3	5.333		1,950	360		2,310	2,675
7036	5"	↓	2.50	6.400		1,200	430		1,630	1,975
7040	6"	Q-2	3	8		1,575	555		2,130	2,550
7050	8"		2.50	9.600		2,825	670		3,495	4,125
7060	10"		2.20	10.909		4,725	760		5,485	6,325
7070	12"	↓	1.70	14.118	↓	7,675	985		8,660	9,900

23 05 23.90 Valves, Stainless Steel

		Crew	Daily Output	Labor-Hours	Unit	Material	2024 Bare Costs Labor	Equipment	Total	Total Incl O&P
0010	**VALVES, STAINLESS STEEL**		R220523-90							
1700	Check, 200 lb., threaded									
1710	1/4"	1 Plum	24	.333	Ea.	97.50	25		122.50	144
1720	1/2"		22	.364		87	27		114	136
1730	3/4"		20	.400		132	30		162	190
1750	1"		19	.421		172	31.50		203.50	237
1760	1-1/2"		13	.615		445	46		491	560
1770	2"	↓	11	.727	↓	655	54.50		709.50	800
1800	150 lb., flanged									
1810	2-1/2"	Q-1	5	3.200	Ea.	1,725	215		1,940	2,225
1820	3"		4.50	3.556		3,150	239		3,389	3,825
1830	4"	↓	3	5.333		4,700	360		5,060	5,700
1840	6"	Q-2	3	8		8,325	555		8,880	9,975
1850	8"	"	2.50	9.600	↓	17,000	670		17,670	19,700
2100	Gate, OS&Y, 150 lb., flanged									
2120	1/2"	1 Plum	18	.444	Ea.	710	33		743	830
2140	3/4"		16	.500		685	37.50		722.50	805
2150	1"		14	.571		865	42.50		907.50	1,025
2160	1-1/2"		11	.727		1,675	54.50		1,729.50	1,900
2170	2"	↓	8	1		1,975	74.50		2,049.50	2,275
2180	2-1/2"	Q-1	5	3.200		2,800	215		3,015	3,400
2190	3"		4.50	3.556		2,800	239		3,039	3,425
2200	4"		3	5.333		4,150	360		4,510	5,100
2205	5"	↓	2.80	5.714		7,225	385		7,610	8,525
2210	6"	Q-2	3	8		7,750	555		8,305	9,350
2220	8"		2.50	9.600		13,500	670		14,170	15,800
2230	10"		2.30	10.435		23,400	725		24,125	26,800
2240	12"	↓	1.90	12.632	↓	31,300	880		32,180	35,700
2260	For 300 lb., flanged, add					120%	15%			
2600	600 lb., flanged									
2620	1/2"	1 Plum	16	.500	Ea.	222	37.50		259.50	300
2640	3/4"		14	.571		240	42.50		282.50	330
2650	1"		12	.667		289	50		339	390
2660	1-1/2"		10	.800		460	59.50		519.50	600
2670	2"	↓	7	1.143		635	85.50		720.50	825
2680	2-1/2"	Q-1	4	4		10,200	269		10,469	11,700
2690	3"	"	3.60	4.444	↓	10,200	299		10,499	11,700
3100	Globe, OS&Y, 150 lb., flanged									

23 05 Common Work Results for HVAC

23 05 23 – General-Duty Valves for HVAC Piping

23 05 23.90 Valves, Stainless Steel

		Crew	Daily Output	Labor-Hours	Unit	Material	2024 Bare Costs Labor	Equipment	Total	Total Incl O&P
3120	1/2"	1 Plum	18	.444	Ea.	680	33		713	795
3140	3/4"		16	.500		735	37.50		772.50	865
3150	1"		14	.571		960	42.50		1,002.50	1,125
3160	1-1/2"		11	.727		1,500	54.50		1,554.50	1,725
3170	2"		8	1		1,975	74.50		2,049.50	2,275
3180	2-1/2"	Q-1	5	3.200		4,750	215		4,965	5,550
3190	3"		4.50	3.556		4,750	239		4,989	5,575
3200	4"		3	5.333		7,600	360		7,960	8,900
3210	6"	Q-2	3	8		12,800	555		13,355	14,900

23 05 23.94 Hospital Type Valves

		Crew	Daily Output	Labor-Hours	Unit	Material	2024 Bare Costs Labor	Equipment	Total	Total Incl O&P
0010	**HOSPITAL TYPE VALVES**									
0300	Chiller valves									
0330	Manual operation balancing valve									
0340	2-1/2" line size	Q-1	9	1.778	Ea.	975	119		1,094	1,250
0350	3" line size		8	2		1,000	134		1,134	1,300
0360	4" line size		5	3.200		1,450	215		1,665	1,925
0370	5" line size	Q-2	5	4.800		1,825	335		2,160	2,500
0380	6" line size		5	4.800		2,275	335		2,610	3,000
0390	8" line size		4.50	5.333		5,050	370		5,420	6,100
0400	10" line size		4	6		8,225	420		8,645	9,675
0410	12" line size		3	8		10,800	555		11,355	12,700
0600	Automatic flow limiting valve									
0620	2-1/2" line size	Q-1	8	2	Ea.	555	134		689	810
0630	3" line size		7	2.286		875	154		1,029	1,200
0640	4" line size		6	2.667		1,250	179		1,429	1,650
0645	5" line size	Q-2	5	4.800		1,675	335		2,010	2,350
0650	6" line size		5	4.800		2,075	335		2,410	2,775
0660	8" line size		4.50	5.333		3,150	370		3,520	4,025
0670	10" line size		4	6		5,050	420		5,470	6,175
0680	12" line size		3	8		8,400	555		8,955	10,100

23 05 93 – Testing, Adjusting, and Balancing for HVAC

23 05 93.10 Balancing, Air

		Crew	Daily Output	Labor-Hours	Unit	Material	2024 Bare Costs Labor	Equipment	Total	Total Incl O&P
0010	**BALANCING, AIR** (Subcontractor's quote incl. material and labor)									
0900	Heating and ventilating equipment									
1000	Centrifugal fans, utility sets				Ea.				420	420
1100	Heating and ventilating unit								630	630
1200	In-line fan								630	630
1300	Propeller and wall fan								119	119
1400	Roof exhaust fan								280	280
2000	Air conditioning equipment, central station								910	910
2100	Built-up low pressure unit								840	840
2200	Built-up high pressure unit								980	980
2300	Built-up high pressure dual duct								1,550	1,550
2400	Built-up variable volume								1,825	1,825
2500	Multi-zone A.C. and heating unit								630	630
2600	For each zone over one, add								140	140
2700	Package A.C. unit								350	350
2800	Rooftop heating and cooling unit								490	490
3000	Supply, return, exhaust, registers & diffusers, avg. height ceiling								84	84
3100	High ceiling								126	126
3200	Floor height								70	70
3300	Off mixing box								56	56

23 05 Common Work Results for HVAC

23 05 93 – Testing, Adjusting, and Balancing for HVAC

23 05 93.10 Balancing, Air

		Crew	Daily Output	Labor-Hours	Unit	Material	2024 Bare Costs Labor	Equipment	Total	Total Incl O&P
3500	Induction unit				Ea.				91	91
3600	Lab fume hood								420	420
3700	Linear supply								210	210
3800	Linear supply high								245	245
4000	Linear return								70	70
4100	Light troffers								84	84
4200	Moduline - master								84	84
4300	Moduline - slaves								42	42
4400	Regenerators								560	560
4500	Taps into ceiling plenums								105	105
4600	Variable volume boxes								84	84

23 05 93.20 Balancing, Water

		Crew	Daily Output	Labor-Hours	Unit	Material	Labor	Equipment	Total	Total Incl O&P
0010	**BALANCING, WATER** (Subcontractor's quote incl. material and labor)									
0050	Air cooled condenser				Ea.				256	256
0080	Boiler								515	515
0100	Cabinet unit heater								88	88
0200	Chiller								620	620
0300	Convector								73	73
0400	Converter								365	365
0500	Cooling tower								475	475
0600	Fan coil unit, unit ventilator								132	132
0700	Fin tube and radiant panels								146	146
0800	Main and duct re-heat coils								135	135
0810	Heat exchanger								135	135
0900	Main balancing cocks								110	110
1000	Pumps								320	320
1100	Unit heater								102	102

23 05 93.50 Piping, Testing

		Crew	Daily Output	Labor-Hours	Unit	Material	Labor	Equipment	Total	Total Incl O&P
0010	**PIPING, TESTING**									
0100	Nondestructive testing									
0110	Nondestructive hydraulic pressure test, isolate & 1 hr. hold									
0120	1" - 4" pipe									
0140	0-250 L.F.	1 Stpi	1.33	6.015	Ea.		455		455	675
0160	250-500 L.F.	"	.80	10			755		755	1,125
0180	500-1000 L.F.	Q-5	1.14	14.035			955		955	1,425
0200	1000-2000 L.F.		.80	20			1,350		1,350	2,025
0320	0-250 L.F.		1	16			1,100		1,100	1,625
0340	250-500 L.F.		.73	21.918			1,500		1,500	2,225
0360	500-1000 L.F.		.53	30.189			2,050		2,050	3,050
0380	1000-2000 L.F.		.38	42.105			2,875		2,875	4,250
1000	Pneumatic pressure test, includes soaping joints									
1120	1" - 4" pipe									
1140	0-250 L.F.	Q-5	2.67	5.993	Ea.	14.40	405		419.40	620
1160	250-500 L.F.		1.33	12.030		29	820		849	1,250
1180	500-1000 L.F.		.80	20		43	1,350		1,393	2,075
1200	1000-2000 L.F.		.50	32		57.50	2,175		2,232.50	3,325
1300	6" - 10" pipe									
1320	0-250 L.F.	Q-5	1.33	12.030	Ea.	14.40	820		834.40	1,250
1340	250-500 L.F.		.67	23.881		29	1,625		1,654	2,450
1360	500-1000 L.F.		.40	40		57.50	2,725		2,782.50	4,125
1380	1000-2000 L.F.		.25	64		72	4,350		4,422	6,550
2110	2" diam.	1 Stpi	8	1		22.50	75.50		98	137

23 05 Common Work Results for HVAC

23 05 93 – Testing, Adjusting, and Balancing for HVAC

23 05 93.50 Piping, Testing		Crew	Daily Output	Labor-Hours	Unit	Material	2024 Bare Costs Labor	Equipment	Total	Total Incl O&P
2120	3" diam.	1 Stpi	8	1	Ea.	22.50	75.50		98	137
2130	4" diam.		8	1		34	75.50		109.50	150
2140	6" diam.		8	1		34	75.50		109.50	150
2150	8" diam.		6.60	1.212		34	91.50		125.50	174
2160	10" diam.	↓	6	1.333	↓	45.50	101		146.50	200
3000	Liquid penetration of welds									
3110	2" diam.	1 Stpi	14	.571	Ea.	15.50	43		58.50	81
3120	3" diam.		13.60	.588		15.50	44.50		60	83
3130	4" diam.		13.40	.597		15.50	45		60.50	84
3140	6" diam.		13.20	.606		15.50	46		61.50	85
3150	8" diam.		13	.615		23.50	46.50		70	94.50
3160	10" diam.	↓	12.80	.625	↓	23.50	47		70.50	96

23 07 HVAC Insulation

23 07 13 – Duct Insulation

23 07 13.10 Duct Thermal Insulation

			Crew	Daily Output	Labor-Hours	Unit	Material	Labor	Equipment	Total	Total Incl O&P
0010	**DUCT THERMAL INSULATION**										
0110	Insulation req'd. is based on the surface size/area to be covered										
3730	Sheet insulation										
3760	Polyethylene foam, closed cell, UV resistant										
3770	Standard temperature (-90°F to +212°F)										
3771	1/4" thick	G	Q-14	450	.036	S.F.	2.54	2.15		4.69	6.05
3772	3/8" thick	G		440	.036		3.63	2.20		5.83	7.35
3773	1/2" thick	G		420	.038		4.44	2.30		6.74	8.40
3774	3/4" thick	G		400	.040		6.35	2.42		8.77	10.70
3775	1" thick	G		380	.042		8.60	2.54		11.14	13.30
3776	1-1/2" thick	G		360	.044		13.55	2.68		16.23	19.05
3777	2" thick	G		340	.047		17.95	2.84		20.79	24
3778	2-1/2" thick	G	↓	320	.050	↓	23	3.02		26.02	30
3779	Adhesive (see line 7878)										
3780	Foam, rubber										
3782	1" thick	G	1 Stpi	50	.160	S.F.	5.90	12.10		18	24.50
7000	Board insulation										
7020	Mineral wool, 1200° F										
7022	6 lb. density, plain										
7024	1" thick	G	Q-14	370	.043	S.F.	1.40	2.61		4.01	5.50
7026	1-1/2" thick	G		350	.046		.47	2.76		3.23	4.73
7028	2" thick	G		330	.048		.61	2.93		3.54	5.15
7030	3" thick	G		300	.053		.76	3.22		3.98	5.75
7032	4" thick	G	↓	280	.057	↓	1.24	3.45		4.69	6.60
7038	8 lb. density, plain										
7040	1" thick	G	Q-14	360	.044	S.F.	.38	2.68		3.06	4.51
7042	1-1/2" thick	G		340	.047		.55	2.84		3.39	4.94
7044	2" thick	G		320	.050		.75	3.02		3.77	5.45
7046	3" thick	G		290	.055		1.12	3.33		4.45	6.35
7048	4" thick	G	↓	270	.059	↓	1.47	3.58		5.05	7.05
7060	10 lb. density, plain										
7062	1" thick	G	Q-14	350	.046	S.F.	.52	2.76		3.28	4.78
7064	1-1/2" thick	G		330	.048		.78	2.93		3.71	5.30
7066	2" thick	G		310	.052		1.05	3.12		4.17	5.90
7068	3" thick	G		280	.057		1.58	3.45		5.03	7

23 07 HVAC Insulation

23 07 13 – Duct Insulation

23 07 13.10 Duct Thermal Insulation

		Crew	Daily Output	Labor-Hours	Unit	Material	2024 Bare Costs Labor	Equipment	Total	Total Incl O&P
7070	4" thick	G Q-14	260	.062	S.F.	2.01	3.72		5.73	7.85
7878	Contact cement, quart can				Ea.	18.10			18.10	19.95

23 07 16 – HVAC Equipment Insulation

23 07 16.10 HVAC Equipment Thermal Insulation

		Crew	Daily Output	Labor-Hours	Unit	Material	Labor	Equipment	Total	Incl O&P
0010	**HVAC EQUIPMENT THERMAL INSULATION**									
0110	Insulation req'd. is based on the surface size/area to be covered									
1000	Boiler, 1-1/2" calcium silicate only	G Q-14	110	.145	S.F.	7.40	8.80		16.20	21.50
1020	Plus 2" fiberglass	G "	80	.200	"	9.95	12.10		22.05	29.50
2000	Breeching, 2" calcium silicate									
2020	Rectangular	G Q-14	42	.381	S.F.	8.20	23		31.20	44
2040	Round	G "	38.70	.413	"	8.20	25		33.20	47
2300	Calcium silicate block, +200°F to +1,200°F									
2310	On irregular surfaces, valves and fittings									
2340	1" thick	G Q-14	30	.533	S.F.	21	32		53	72
2360	1-1/2" thick	G	25	.640		7.40	38.50		45.90	67
2380	2" thick	G	22	.727		8.20	44		52.20	76
2400	3" thick	G	18	.889		6.40	53.50		59.90	89
2410	On plane surfaces									
2420	1" thick	G Q-14	126	.127	S.F.	21	7.65		28.65	34.50
2430	1-1/2" thick	G	120	.133		7.40	8.05		15.45	20.50
2440	2" thick	G	100	.160		8.20	9.65		17.85	23.50
2450	3" thick	G	70	.229		6.40	13.80		20.20	28

23 09 Instrumentation and Control for HVAC

23 09 13 – Instrumentation and Control Devices for HVAC

23 09 13.60 Water Level Controls

		Crew	Daily Output	Labor-Hours	Unit	Material	Labor	Equipment	Total	Incl O&P
0010	**WATER LEVEL CONTROLS**									
3000	Low water cut-off for hot water boiler, 50 psi maximum									
3100	1" top & bottom equalizing pipes, manual reset	1 Stpi	14	.571	Ea.	790	43		833	935
3200	1" top & bottom equalizing pipes		14	.571		605	43		648	730
3300	2-1/2" side connection for nipple-to-boiler		14	.571		630	43		673	760

23 09 23 – Direct-Digital Control System for HVAC

23 09 23.10 Control Components/DDC Systems

		Crew	Daily Output	Labor-Hours	Unit	Material	Labor	Equipment	Total	Incl O&P
0010	**CONTROL COMPONENTS/DDC SYSTEMS** (Sub's quote incl. M & L)									
0100	Analog inputs									
0110	Sensors (avg. 50' run in 1/2" EMT)									
0120	Duct temperature	2 Elec	3	5.333	Ea.	395	380		775	1,000
0130	Space temperature		3	5.333		860	380		1,240	1,500
0140	Duct humidity, +/- 3%		3	5.333		590	380		970	1,200
0150	Space humidity, +/- 2%		3	5.333		800	380		1,180	1,450
0160	Duct static pressure		3	5.333		205	380		585	790
0170	CFM/transducer		3	5.333		325	380		705	920
0172	Water temperature		3	5.333		810	380		1,190	1,450
0174	Water flow		3	5.333		2,500	380		2,880	3,325
0176	Water pressure differential		3	5.333		252	380		632	840
0177	Steam flow		3	5.333		5,375	380		5,755	6,500
0178	Steam pressure		3	5.333		1,550	380		1,930	2,275
0180	KW/transducer		3	5.333		410	380		790	1,025
0182	KWH totalization (not incl.elec.meter pulse xmtr.)		3	5.333		217	380		597	805
0190	Space static pressure		3	5.333		65	380		445	635

23 09 Instrumentation and Control for HVAC

23 09 23 – Direct-Digital Control System for HVAC

23 09 23.10 Control Components/DDC Systems		Crew	Daily Output	Labor-Hours	Unit	Material	2024 Bare Costs Labor	Equipment	Total	Total Incl O&P
1000	Analog outputs (avg. 50' run in 1/2" EMT)									
1010	P/I transducer	2 Elec	3	5.333	Ea.	445	380		825	1,050
1020	Analog output, matl.in MUX		3	5.333		365	380		745	965
1030	Pneumatic (not incl.control device)		3	5.333		550	380		930	1,175
1040	Electric (not incl.control device)		3	5.333		250	380		630	840
2000	Status (alarms)									
2100	Digital inputs (avg. 50' run in 1/2" EMT)									
2110	Freeze	2 Elec	3	5.333	Ea.	171	380		551	755
2120	Fire		3	5.333		238	380		618	825
2130	Differential pressure (air)		3	5.333		310	380		690	905
2140	Differential pressure (water)		3	5.333		1,275	380		1,655	1,975
2150	Current sensor		3	5.333		263	380		643	855
2160	Duct high temperature thermostat		3	5.333		450	380		830	1,075
2170	Duct smoke detector		3	5.333		555	380		935	1,175
2200	Digital output (avg. 50' run in 1/2" EMT)									
2210	Start/stop	2 Elec	3	5.333	Ea.	279	380		659	870
2220	On/off (maintained contact)	"	3	5.333	"	148	380		528	730
3000	Controller MUX panel, incl. function boards									
3100	48 point	2 Elec	.44	36.364	Ea.	6,650	2,600		9,250	11,200
3110	128 point	"	.22	72.727	"	4,775	5,225		10,000	13,000
3200	DDC controller (avg. 50' run in conduit)									
3210	Mechanical room									
3214	16 point controller (incl.120 volt/1 phase power supply)	2 Elec	.72	22.222	Ea.	2,300	1,600		3,900	4,875
3229	32 point controller (incl.120 volt/1 phase power supply)	"	.64	25	"	6,050	1,800		7,850	9,300
3230	Includes software programming and checkout									
3260	Space									
3266	VAV terminal box (incl.space temp.sensor)	2 Elec	3	5.333	Ea.	615	380		995	1,250
3280	Host computer (avg. 50' run in conduit)									
3281	Package complete with PC, keyboard,									
3282	printer, monitor, basic software	2 Elec	1.16	13.793	Ea.	3,150	990		4,140	4,950
4000	Front end costs									
4100	Computer (P.C.) with software program	2 Elec	1.16	13.793	Ea.	8,775	990		9,765	11,200
4200	Color graphics software		2.22	7.207		6,275	515		6,790	7,675
4300	Color graphics slides		1.16	13.793			990		990	1,475
4350	Additional printer					120			120	132
4400	Communications trunk cable	2 Elec	720	.022	L.F.	3.46	1.59		5.05	6.15
4500	Engineering labor (not incl.dftg.)	1 Enme	1	8	Point		345		345	500
4600	Calibration labor	2 Elec	10.36	1.544			111		111	164
4700	Start-up, checkout labor	"	10.36	1.544			111		111	164
4800	Programming labor, as req'd									
5000	Communications bus (data transmission cable)									
5010	#18 twisted shielded pair in 1/2" EMT conduit	2 Elec	6.01	2.662	C.L.F.	310	191		501	625
8000	Applications software									
8050	Basic maintenance manager software (not incl.data base entry)	2 Elec	1.75	9.143	Ea.	2,250	655		2,905	3,450
8100	Time program		1.16	13.793	Point	12.45	990		1,002.45	1,500
8120	Duty cycle		1.16	13.793		25	990		1,015	1,500
8140	Optimum start/stop		3	5.333		74.50	380		454.50	645
8160	Demand limiting		3	5.333		6,000	380		6,380	7,175
8180	Enthalpy program		3	5.333		6,000	380		6,380	7,175
8200	Boiler optimization		3	5.333	Ea.	6,000	380		6,380	7,175
8220	Chiller optimization		3	5.333	"	6,000	380		6,380	7,175
8240	Custom applications									
8260	Cost varies with complexity									

23 09 Instrumentation and Control for HVAC

23 09 53 – Pneumatic and Electric Control System for HVAC

23 09 53.10 Control Components

		Crew	Daily Output	Labor-Hours	Unit	Material	2024 Bare Costs Labor	2024 Bare Costs Equipment	Total	Total Incl O&P
0010	**CONTROL COMPONENTS**				R230500-10					
0680	Controller for VAV box, includes actuator	1 Stpi	7.30	1.096	Ea.	620	83		703	805
2000	Gauges, pressure or vacuum									
2100	2" diameter dial	1 Stpi	32	.250	Ea.	12.40	18.90		31.30	41.50
2200	2-1/2" diameter dial		32	.250		15.35	18.90		34.25	45
2300	3-1/2" diameter dial		32	.250		42	18.90		60.90	74.50
2400	4-1/2" diameter dial		32	.250		48	18.90		66.90	80.50
2700	Flanged iron case, black ring									
2800	3-1/2" diameter dial	1 Stpi	32	.250	Ea.	224	18.90		242.90	275
2900	4-1/2" diameter dial		32	.250		202	18.90		220.90	250
3000	6" diameter dial		32	.250		320	18.90		338.90	380
3010	Steel case, 0-300 psi									
3012	2" diameter dial	1 Stpi	16	.500	Ea.	8.80	38		46.80	65.50
3014	4" diameter dial	"	16	.500	"	24	38		62	82.50
3020	Aluminum case, 0-300 psi									
3022	3-1/2" diameter dial	1 Stpi	16	.500	Ea.	21	38		59	79.50
3024	4-1/2" diameter dial		16	.500		24.50	38		62.50	83
3026	6" diameter dial		16	.500		310	38		348	400
3028	8-1/2" diameter dial		16	.500		635	38		673	755
3030	Brass case, 0-300 psi									
3032	2" diameter dial	1 Stpi	16	.500	Ea.	40.50	38		78.50	101
3034	4-1/2" diameter dial	"	16	.500	"	186	38		224	260
3040	Steel case, high pressure, 0-10,000 psi									
3042	4-1/2" diameter dial	1 Stpi	16	.500	Ea.	335	38		373	425
3044	6-1/2" diameter dial		16	.500		229	38		267	310
3046	8-1/2" diameter dial		16	.500		755	38		793	890
3080	Pressure gauge, differential, magnehelic									
3084	0-2" W.C., with air filter kit	1 Stpi	6	1.333	Ea.	46	101		147	201
3300	For compound pressure-vacuum, add					18%				
4000	Thermometers									
4100	Dial type, 3-1/2" diameter, vapor type, union connection	1 Stpi	32	.250	Ea.	290	18.90		308.90	350
4120	Liquid type, union connection		32	.250		435	18.90		453.90	510
4500	Stem type, 6-1/2" case, 2" stem, 1/2" NPT		32	.250		60	18.90		78.90	94
4520	4" stem, 1/2" NPT		32	.250		73.50	18.90		92.40	109
4600	9" case, 3-1/2" stem, 3/4" NPT		28	.286		48	21.50		69.50	85
4620	6" stem, 3/4" NPT		28	.286		57.50	21.50		79	95.50
4640	8" stem, 3/4" NPT		28	.286		192	21.50		213.50	243
4660	12" stem, 1" NPT		26	.308		188	23.50		211.50	242
4670	Bi-metal, dial type, steel case brass stem									
4672	2" dial, 4" - 9" stem	1 Stpi	16	.500	Ea.	58.50	38		96.50	121
4673	2-1/2" dial, 4" - 9" stem		16	.500		58.50	38		96.50	121
4674	3-1/2" dial, 4" - 9" stem		16	.500		60	38		98	122
4680	Mercury filled, industrial, union connection type									
4682	Angle stem, 7" scale	1 Stpi	16	.500	Ea.	61.50	38		99.50	124
4683	9" scale		16	.500		170	38		208	243
4684	12" scale		16	.500		218	38		256	295
4686	Straight stem, 7" scale		16	.500		166	38		204	239
4687	9" scale		16	.500		278	38		316	360
4688	12" scale		16	.500		335	38		373	425
4690	Mercury filled, industrial, separable socket type, with well									
4692	Angle stem, with socket, 7" scale	1 Stpi	16	.500	Ea.	200	38		238	276
4693	9" scale		16	.500		200	38		238	276

23 09 Instrumentation and Control for HVAC

23 09 53 – Pneumatic and Electric Control System for HVAC

23 09 53.10 Control Components

		Crew	Daily Output	Labor-Hours	Unit	Material	2024 Bare Costs Labor	Equipment	Total	Total Incl O&P
4694	12" scale	1 Stpi	16	.500	Ea.	237	38		275	315
4696	Straight stem, with socket, 7" scale		16	.500		156	38		194	228
4697	9" scale		16	.500		156	38		194	228
4698	12" scale	↓	16	.500	↓	192	38		230	267
6000	Valves, motorized zone									
6100	Sweat connections, 1/2" C x C	1 Stpi	20	.400	Ea.	153	30		183	213
6110	3/4" C x C		20	.400		154	30		184	214
6120	1" C x C		19	.421		201	32		233	269
6140	1/2" C x C, with end switch, 2 wire		20	.400		151	30		181	211
6150	3/4" C x C, with end switch, 2 wire		20	.400		160	30		190	221
6160	1" C x C, with end switch, 2 wire	↓	19	.421	↓	187	32		219	254

23 11 Facility Fuel Piping

23 11 13 – Facility Fuel-Oil Piping

23 11 13.10 Fuel Oil Specialties

		Crew	Daily Output	Labor-Hours	Unit	Material	Labor	Equipment	Total	Total Incl O&P
0010	**FUEL OIL SPECIALTIES**									
0020	Foot valve, single poppet, metal to metal construction									
0040	Bevel seat, 1/2" diameter	1 Stpi	20	.400	Ea.	133	30		163	191
0060	3/4" diameter		18	.444		82	33.50		115.50	140
1000	Oil filters, 3/8" IPT, 20 gal. per hour	↓	20	.400	↓	36	30		66	84.50
2000	Remote tank gauging system, self contained									
3000	Valve, ball check, globe type, 3/8" diameter	1 Stpi	24	.333	Ea.	17.50	25		42.50	57
3500	Fusible, 3/8" diameter		24	.333		35	25		60	76
3600	1/2" diameter		24	.333		92	25		117	139
3610	3/4" diameter		20	.400		191	30		221	255
3620	1" diameter		19	.421		515	32		547	615
4000	Nonfusible, 3/8" diameter	↓	24	.333	↓	35.50	25		60.50	76.50
4500	Shutoff, gate type, lever handle, spring-fusible kit									
4520	1/4" diameter	1 Stpi	14	.571	Ea.	40	43		83	108
4540	3/8" diameter		12	.667		87	50.50		137.50	171
4560	1/2" diameter		10	.800		128	60.50		188.50	231
4570	3/4" diameter	↓	8	1		153	75.50		228.50	280
5000	Vent alarm, whistling signal					49			49	54
5500	Vent protector/breather, 1-1/4" diameter	1 Stpi	32	.250	↓	30	18.90		48.90	61

23 11 23 – Facility Natural-Gas Piping

23 11 23.10 Gas Meters

		Crew	Daily Output	Labor-Hours	Unit	Material	Labor	Equipment	Total	Total Incl O&P
0010	**GAS METERS**									
4000	Residential									
4010	Gas meter, residential, 3/4" pipe size	1 Plum	14	.571	Ea.	395	42.50		437.50	500
4020	Gas meter, residential, 1" pipe size		12	.667		400	50		450	515
4030	Gas meter, residential, 1-1/4" pipe size	↓	10	.800	↓	360	59.50		419.50	490

23 11 23.20 Gas Piping, Flexible (Csst)

		Crew	Daily Output	Labor-Hours	Unit	Material	Labor	Equipment	Total	Total Incl O&P
0010	**GAS PIPING, FLEXIBLE (CSST)**									
0100	Tubing with lightning protection									
0110	3/8"	1 Stpi	65	.123	L.F.	4.59	9.30		13.89	18.90
0120	1/2"		62	.129		5.15	9.75		14.90	20
0130	3/4"		60	.133		6.65	10.05		16.70	22.50
0140	1"		55	.145		9.55	11		20.55	27
0150	1-1/4"		50	.160		11.95	12.10		24.05	31
0160	1-1/2"	↓	45	.178	↓	29.50	13.45		42.95	52.50

23 11 Facility Fuel Piping

23 11 23 – Facility Natural-Gas Piping

23 11 23.20 Gas Piping, Flexible (Csst)		Crew	Daily Output	Labor-Hours	Unit	Material	2024 Bare Costs Labor	2024 Bare Costs Equipment	Total	Total Incl O&P
0170	2"	1 Stpi	40	.200	L.F.	30	15.10		45.10	55.50
0200	Tubing for underground/underslab burial									
0210	3/8"	1 Stpi	65	.123	L.F.	6.35	9.30		15.65	21
0220	1/2"		62	.129		7.25	9.75		17	22.50
0230	3/4"		60	.133		14.30	10.05		24.35	31
0240	1"		55	.145		12.40	11		23.40	30
0250	1-1/4"		50	.160		16.65	12.10		28.75	36.50
0260	1-1/2"		45	.178		31	13.45		44.45	54.50
0270	2"	▼	40	.200	▼	37	15.10		52.10	63.50
3000	Fittings									
3010	Straight									
3100	Tube to NPT									
3110	3/8"	1 Stpi	29	.276	Ea.	19.85	21		40.85	53
3120	1/2"		27	.296		21	22.50		43.50	56.50
3130	3/4"		25	.320		28.50	24		52.50	67.50
3140	1"		23	.348		44	26.50		70.50	87.50
3150	1-1/4"		20	.400		98	30		128	153
3160	1-1/2"		17	.471		202	35.50		237.50	275
3170	2"	▼	15	.533	▼	345	40.50		385.50	440
3200	Coupling									
3210	3/8"	1 Stpi	29	.276	Ea.	39	21		60	73.50
3220	1/2"		27	.296		38.50	22.50		61	76
3230	3/4"		25	.320		53	24		77	94.50
3240	1"		23	.348		84	26.50		110.50	131
3250	1-1/4"		20	.400		186	30		216	250
3260	1-1/2"		17	.471		380	35.50		415.50	475
3270	2"	▼	15	.533	▼	655	40.50		695.50	780
3300	Flange fitting									
3310	3/8"	1 Stpi	25	.320	Ea.	24.50	24		48.50	63
3320	1/2"		22	.364		26	27.50		53.50	69.50
3330	3/4"		19	.421		33.50	32		65.50	84.50
3340	1"		16	.500		46	38		84	107
3350	1-1/4"	▼	12	.667	▼	107	50.50		157.50	193
3400	90° flange valve									
3410	3/8"	1 Stpi	25	.320	Ea.	42	24		66	82
3420	1/2"		22	.364		52.50	27.50		80	99
3430	3/4"	▼	19	.421	▼	70.50	32		102.50	125
4000	Tee									
4120	1/2"	1 Stpi	20.50	.390	Ea.	73.50	29.50		103	125
4130	3/4"		19	.421		72.50	32		104.50	128
4140	1"	▼	17.50	.457	▼	175	34.50		209.50	245
5000	Reducing									
5110	Tube to NPT									
5120	3/4" to 1/2" NPT	1 Stpi	26	.308	Ea.	30.50	23.50		54	68.50
5130	1" to 3/4" NPT	"	24	.333	"	47.50	25		72.50	90
5200	Reducing tee									
5210	1/2" x 3/8" x 3/8"	1 Stpi	21	.381	Ea.	80.50	29		109.50	132
5220	3/4" x 1/2" x 1/2"		20	.400		75.50	30		105.50	128
5230	1" x 3/4" x 1/2"		18	.444		125	33.50		158.50	188
5240	1-1/4" x 1-1/4" x 1"		15.60	.513		335	38.50		373.50	425
5250	1-1/2" x 1-1/2" x 1-1/4"		13.30	.602		510	45.50		555.50	630
5260	2" x 2" x 1-1/2"		11.80	.678		765	51		816	915
5300	Manifold with four ports and mounting bracket									

23 11 Facility Fuel Piping

23 11 23 – Facility Natural-Gas Piping

23 11 23.20 Gas Piping, Flexible (Csst)

		Crew	Daily Output	Labor-Hours	Unit	Material	2024 Bare Costs Labor	Equipment	Total	Total Incl O&P
5302	Labor to mount manifold does not include making pipe									
5304	connections which are included in fitting labor.									
5310	3/4" x 1/2" x 1/2" (4)	1 Stpi	76	.105	Ea.	59	7.95		66.95	77
5330	1-1/4" x 1" x 3/4" (4)		72	.111		85	8.40		93.40	106
5350	2" x 1-1/2" x 1" (4)		68	.118		106	8.90		114.90	130
5600	Protective striker plate									
5610	Quarter plate, 3" x 2"	1 Stpi	88	.091	Ea.	1.36	6.85		8.21	11.70
5620	Half plate, 3" x 7"		82	.098		3.20	7.35		10.55	14.45
5630	Full plate, 3" x 12"		78	.103		5.50	7.75		13.25	17.60

23 12 Facility Fuel Pumps

23 12 13 – Facility Fuel-Oil Pumps

23 12 13.10 Pump and Motor Sets

		Crew	Daily Output	Labor-Hours	Unit	Material	2024 Bare Costs Labor	Equipment	Total	Total Incl O&P
0010	**PUMP AND MOTOR SETS**									
1810	Light fuel and diesel oils									
1820	20 GPH, 1/3 HP	Q-5	6	2.667	Ea.	2,150	181		2,331	2,650
1850	145 GPH, 1/2 HP	"	4	4	"	2,275	272		2,547	2,900

23 13 Facility Fuel-Storage Tanks

23 13 13 – Facility Underground Fuel-Oil, Storage Tanks

23 13 13.09 Single-Wall Steel Fuel-Oil Tanks

		Crew	Daily Output	Labor-Hours	Unit	Material	2024 Bare Costs Labor	Equipment	Total	Total Incl O&P
0010	**SINGLE-WALL STEEL FUEL-OIL TANKS**									
5000	Tanks, steel ugnd., sti-p3, not incl. hold-down bars									
5500	Excavation, pad, pumps and piping not included									
5510	Single wall, 500 gallon capacity, 7 ga. shell	Q-5	2.70	5.926	Ea.	2,625	405		3,030	3,475
5520	1,000 gallon capacity, 7 ga. shell	"	2.50	6.400		3,800	435		4,235	4,825
5530	2,000 gallon capacity, 1/4" thick shell	Q-7	4.60	6.957		5,450	500		5,950	6,750
5535	2,500 gallon capacity, 7 ga. shell	Q-5	3	5.333		7,350	365		7,715	8,625
5540	5,000 gallon capacity, 1/4" thick shell	Q-7	3.20	10		17,200	720		17,920	20,000
5560	10,000 gallon capacity, 1/4" thick shell		2	16		14,100	1,150		15,250	17,200
5580	15,000 gallon capacity, 5/16" thick shell		1.70	18.824		14,500	1,350		15,850	17,900
5600	20,000 gallon capacity, 5/16" thick shell		1.50	21.333		35,300	1,525		36,825	41,100
5610	25,000 gallon capacity, 3/8" thick shell		1.30	24.615		40,500	1,775		42,275	47,100
5620	30,000 gallon capacity, 3/8" thick shell		1.10	29.091		45,500	2,100		47,600	53,000
5630	40,000 gallon capacity, 3/8" thick shell		.90	35.556		59,000	2,550		61,550	69,000
5640	50,000 gallon capacity, 3/8" thick shell		.80	40		67,500	2,875		70,375	78,500

23 13 13.13 Dbl-Wall Steel, Undrgrnd Fuel-Oil, Stor. Tanks

		Crew	Daily Output	Labor-Hours	Unit	Material	2024 Bare Costs Labor	Equipment	Total	Total Incl O&P
0010	**DOUBLE-WALL STEEL, UNDERGROUND FUEL-OIL, STORAGE TANKS**									
6200	Steel, underground, 360°, double wall, UL listed,									
6210	with sti-P3 corrosion protection,									
6220	(dielectric coating, cathodic protection, electrical									
6230	isolation) 30 year warranty,									
6240	not incl. manholes or hold-downs.									
6250	500 gallon capacity	Q-5	2.40	6.667	Ea.	4,650	455		5,105	5,800
6260	1,000 gallon capacity	"	2.25	7.111		5,075	485		5,560	6,300
6270	2,000 gallon capacity	Q-7	4.16	7.692		6,700	555		7,255	8,175
6280	3,000 gallon capacity		3.90	8.205		9,650	590		10,240	11,500
6290	4,000 gallon capacity		3.64	8.791		11,400	630		12,030	13,400
6300	5,000 gallon capacity		2.91	10.997		12,200	790		12,990	14,600

23 13 Facility Fuel-Storage Tanks

23 13 13 – Facility Underground Fuel-Oil, Storage Tanks

23 13 13.13 Dbl-Wall Steel, Undrgrnd Fuel-Oil, Stor. Tanks		Crew	Daily Output	Labor-Hours	Unit	Material	2024 Bare Costs Labor	Equipment	Total	Total Incl O&P
6310	6,000 gallon capacity	Q-7	2.42	13.223	Ea.	15,600	950		16,550	18,600
6320	8,000 gallon capacity		2.08	15.385		15,500	1,100		16,600	18,700
6330	10,000 gallon capacity		1.82	17.582		19,200	1,275		20,475	23,100
6340	12,000 gallon capacity		1.70	18.824		21,500	1,350		22,850	25,600
6350	15,000 gallon capacity		1.33	24.060		28,700	1,725		30,425	34,200
6360	20,000 gallon capacity		1.33	24.060		47,500	1,725		49,225	54,500
6370	25,000 gallon capacity		1.16	27.586		56,500	1,975		58,475	65,500
6380	30,000 gallon capacity		1.03	31.068		52,500	2,225		54,725	61,000
6390	40,000 gallon capacity		.80	40		177,000	2,875		179,875	199,000
6395	50,000 gallon capacity		.73	43.836		214,500	3,150		217,650	240,500
6400	For hold-downs 500-2,000 gal., add		16	2	Set	281	144		425	525
6410	For hold-downs 3,000-6,000 gal., add		12	2.667		485	192		677	820
6420	For hold-downs 8,000-12,000 gal., add		11	2.909		695	209		904	1,075
6430	For hold-downs 15,000 gal., add		9	3.556		945	256		1,201	1,425
6440	For hold-downs 20,000 gal., add		8	4		1,100	288		1,388	1,625
6450	For hold-downs 20,000 gal. plus, add		6	5.333		1,300	385		1,685	2,025
6500	For manways, add				Ea.	1,550			1,550	1,725
6600	In place with hold-downs									
6652	550 gallon capacity	Q-5	1.84	8.696	Ea.	4,925	590		5,515	6,300

23 13 13.23 Glass-Fiber-Reinfcd-Plastic, Fuel-Oil, Storage

		Crew	Daily Output	Labor-Hours	Unit	Material	Labor	Equipment	Total	Total Incl O&P
0010	**GLASS-FIBER-REINFCD-PLASTIC, UNDERGRND. FUEL-OIL, STORAGE**									
0210	Fiberglass, underground, single wall, UL listed, not including									
0220	manway or hold-down strap									
0225	550 gallon capacity	Q-5	2.67	5.993	Ea.	5,525	405		5,930	6,675
0230	1,000 gallon capacity	"	2.46	6.504		7,125	440		7,565	8,475
0240	2,000 gallon capacity	Q-7	4.57	7.002		11,400	505		11,905	13,300
0245	3,000 gallon capacity		3.90	8.205		11,600	590		12,190	13,600
0250	4,000 gallon capacity		3.55	9.014		15,400	650		16,050	18,000
0255	5,000 gallon capacity		3.20	10		14,100	720		14,820	16,600
0260	6,000 gallon capacity		2.67	11.985		13,200	860		14,060	15,800
0270	8,000 gallon capacity		2.29	13.974		20,600	1,000		21,600	24,200
0280	10,000 gallon capacity		2	16		20,800	1,150		21,950	24,600
0282	12,000 gallon capacity		1.88	17.021		22,000	1,225		23,225	26,000
0284	15,000 gallon capacity		1.68	19.048		31,800	1,375		33,175	37,100
0290	20,000 gallon capacity		1.45	22.069		44,200	1,575		45,775	51,000
0300	25,000 gallon capacity		1.28	25		76,000	1,800		77,800	86,000
0320	30,000 gallon capacity		1.14	28.070		114,500	2,025		116,525	129,000
0340	40,000 gallon capacity		.89	35.955		163,000	2,575		165,575	183,500
0360	48,000 gallon capacity		.81	39.506		242,000	2,850		244,850	270,000
0500	For manway, fittings and hold-downs, add					20%	15%			
0600	For manways, add					3,725			3,725	4,100
1000	For helical heating coil, add	Q-5	2.50	6.400		7,350	435		7,785	8,750
1020	Fiberglass, underground, double wall, UL listed									
1030	includes manways, not incl. hold-down straps									
1040	600 gallon capacity	Q-5	2.42	6.612	Ea.	12,100	450		12,550	14,000
1050	1,000 gallon capacity	"	2.25	7.111		16,600	485		17,085	19,000
1060	2,500 gallon capacity	Q-7	4.16	7.692		23,000	555		23,555	26,100
1070	3,000 gallon capacity		3.90	8.205		25,700	590		26,290	29,200
1080	4,000 gallon capacity		3.64	8.791		26,900	630		27,530	30,500
1090	6,000 gallon capacity		2.42	13.223		33,400	950		34,350	38,100
1100	8,000 gallon capacity		2.08	15.385		42,400	1,100		43,500	48,400
1110	10,000 gallon capacity		1.82	17.582		51,500	1,275		52,775	58,500

23 13 Facility Fuel-Storage Tanks

23 13 13 – Facility Underground Fuel-Oil, Storage Tanks

23 13 13.23 Glass-Fiber-Reinfcd-Plastic, Fuel-Oil, Storage

		Crew	Daily Output	Labor-Hours	Unit	Material	2024 Bare Costs Labor	Equipment	Total	Total Incl O&P
1120	12,000 gallon capacity	Q-7	1.70	18.824	Ea.	53,500	1,350		54,850	60,500
1122	15,000 gallon capacity		1.52	21.053		95,500	1,525		97,025	107,500
1124	20,000 gallon capacity		1.33	24.060		102,500	1,725		104,225	115,500
1126	25,000 gallon capacity		1.16	27.586		118,500	1,975		120,475	133,500
1128	30,000 gallon capacity	↓	1.03	31.068		142,500	2,225		144,725	160,500
1140	For hold-down straps, add					2%	10%			
1150	For hold-downs 500-4,000 gal., add	Q-7	16	2	Set	590	144		734	865
1160	For hold-downs 5,000-15,000 gal., add		8	4		1,175	288		1,463	1,725
1170	For hold-downs 20,000 gal., add		5.33	6.004		1,775	430		2,205	2,600
1180	For hold-downs 25,000 gal., add		4	8		2,375	575		2,950	3,450
1190	For hold-downs 30,000 gal., add	↓	2.60	12.308	↓	3,550	885		4,435	5,225
2210	Fiberglass, underground, single wall, UL listed, including									
2220	hold-down straps, no manways									
2225	550 gallon capacity	Q-5	2	8	Ea.	6,125	545		6,670	7,525
2230	1,000 gallon capacity	"	1.88	8.511		7,700	580		8,280	9,325
2240	2,000 gallon capacity	Q-7	3.55	9.014		12,000	650		12,650	14,200
2250	4,000 gallon capacity		2.90	11.034		16,000	795		16,795	18,800
2260	6,000 gallon capacity		2	16		14,400	1,150		15,550	17,500
2270	8,000 gallon capacity		1.78	17.978		21,800	1,300		23,100	25,900
2280	10,000 gallon capacity		1.60	20		22,000	1,450		23,450	26,400
2282	12,000 gallon capacity		1.52	21.053		23,200	1,525		24,725	27,800
2284	15,000 gallon capacity		1.39	23.022		33,000	1,650		34,650	38,800
2290	20,000 gallon capacity		1.14	28.070		46,000	2,025		48,025	53,500
2300	25,000 gallon capacity		.96	33.333		78,500	2,400		80,900	89,500
2320	30,000 gallon capacity	↓	.80	40	↓	118,500	2,875		121,375	134,500
3020	Fiberglass, underground, double wall, UL listed									
3030	includes manways and hold-down straps									
3040	600 gallon capacity	Q-5	1.86	8.602	Ea.	12,700	585		13,285	14,900
3050	1,000 gallon capacity	"	1.70	9.412		17,200	640		17,840	20,000
3060	2,500 gallon capacity	Q-7	3.29	9.726		23,500	700		24,200	27,000
3070	3,000 gallon capacity		3.13	10.224		26,300	735		27,035	30,000
3080	4,000 gallon capacity		2.93	10.922		27,500	785		28,285	31,400
3090	6,000 gallon capacity		1.86	17.204		34,500	1,225		35,725	39,900
3100	8,000 gallon capacity		1.65	19.394		43,600	1,400		45,000	50,000
3110	10,000 gallon capacity		1.48	21.622		52,500	1,550		54,050	60,500
3120	12,000 gallon capacity		1.40	22.857		54,500	1,650		56,150	62,500
3122	15,000 gallon capacity		1.28	25		96,500	1,800		98,300	108,500
3124	20,000 gallon capacity		1.06	30.189		104,500	2,175		106,675	117,500
3126	25,000 gallon capacity		.90	35.556		121,000	2,550		123,550	137,000
3128	30,000 gallon capacity	↓	.74	43.243	↓	146,000	3,100		149,100	165,500

23 13 23 – Facility Aboveground Fuel-Oil, Storage Tanks

23 13 23.16 Horizontal, Stl, Abvgrd Fuel-Oil, Storage Tanks

		Crew	Daily Output	Labor-Hours	Unit	Material	2024 Bare Costs Labor	Equipment	Total	Total Incl O&P
0010	**HORIZONTAL, STEEL, ABOVEGROUND FUEL-OIL, STORAGE TANKS**									
3000	Steel, storage, aboveground, including cradles, coating,									
3020	fittings, not including foundation, pumps or piping									
3040	Single wall, 275 gallon	Q-5	5	3.200	Ea.	1,450	218		1,668	1,925
3060	550 gallon	"	2.70	5.926		7,575	405		7,980	8,950
3080	1,000 gallon	Q-7	5	6.400		12,700	460		13,160	14,700
3100	1,500 gallon		4.75	6.737		19,400	485		19,885	22,100
3120	2,000 gallon	↓	4.60	6.957		18,800	500		19,300	21,400
3320	Double wall, 500 gallon capacity	Q-5	2.40	6.667		4,150	455		4,605	5,225
3330	2,000 gallon capacity	Q-7	4.15	7.711	↓	7,325	555		7,880	8,875

23 13 Facility Fuel-Storage Tanks

23 13 23 – Facility Aboveground Fuel-Oil, Storage Tanks

23 13 23.16 Horizontal, Stl, Abvgrd Fuel-Oil, Storage Tanks		Crew	Daily Output	Labor-Hours	Unit	Material	2024 Bare Costs Labor	2024 Bare Costs Equipment	Total	Total Incl O&P
3340	4,000 gallon capacity	Q-7	3.60	8.889	Ea.	15,600	640		16,240	18,200
3350	6,000 gallon capacity		2.40	13.333		44,100	960		45,060	49,900
3360	8,000 gallon capacity		2	16		51,500	1,150		52,650	58,500
3370	10,000 gallon capacity		1.80	17.778		60,500	1,275		61,775	68,500
3380	15,000 gallon capacity		1.50	21.333		83,500	1,525		85,025	94,500
3390	20,000 gallon capacity		1.30	24.615		101,000	1,775		102,775	113,500
3400	25,000 gallon capacity		1.15	27.826		95,500	2,000		97,500	108,000
3410	30,000 gallon capacity		1	32		130,000	2,300		132,300	146,500

23 13 23.26 Horizontal, Conc., Abvgrd Fuel-Oil, Stor. Tanks

		Crew	Daily Output	Labor-Hours	Unit	Material	Labor	Equipment	Total	Total Incl O&P
0010	**HORIZONTAL, CONCRETE, ABOVEGROUND FUEL-OIL, STORAGE TANKS**									
0050	Concrete, storage, aboveground, including pad & pump									
0100	500 gallon	F-3	2	20	Ea.	14,500	1,250	1,100	16,850	19,100
0200	1,000 gallon	"	2	20		20,400	1,250	1,100	22,750	25,500
0300	2,000 gallon	F-4	2	24		26,200	1,475	1,275	28,950	32,400

23 21 Hydronic Piping and Pumps

23 21 20 – Hydronic HVAC Piping Specialties

23 21 20.10 Air Control

		Crew	Daily Output	Labor-Hours	Unit	Material	Labor	Equipment	Total	Total Incl O&P
0010	**AIR CONTROL**									
0030	Air separator, with strainer									
0040	2" diameter	Q-5	6	2.667	Ea.	1,775	181		1,956	2,225
0080	2-1/2" diameter		5	3.200		1,975	218		2,193	2,500
0100	3" diameter		4	4		3,050	272		3,322	3,750
1000	Micro-bubble separator for total air removal, closed loop system									
1010	Requires bladder type tank in system.									
1020	Water (hot or chilled) or glycol system									
1030	Threaded									
1040	3/4" diameter	1 Stpi	20	.400	Ea.	101	30		131	156
1050	1" diameter		19	.421		117	32		149	177
1060	1-1/4" diameter		16	.500		154	38		192	226
1070	1-1/2" diameter		13	.615		205	46.50		251.50	294
1080	2" diameter		11	.727		1,400	55		1,455	1,600
1090	2-1/2" diameter	Q-5	15	1.067		1,650	72.50		1,722.50	1,925
1100	3" diameter		13	1.231		2,225	83.50		2,308.50	2,575
1110	4" diameter		10	1.600		2,475	109		2,584	2,875
1800	With drain/dismantle/cleaning access flange									
1810	Flanged									
1820	2" diameter	Q-5	4.60	3.478	Ea.	3,925	237		4,162	4,675
1830	2-1/2" diameter		4	4		4,250	272		4,522	5,075
1840	3" diameter		3.60	4.444		5,200	300		5,500	6,175
1850	4" diameter		2.50	6.400		5,950	435		6,385	7,200
1860	5" diameter	Q-6	2.80	8.571		10,900	605		11,505	12,900
1870	6" diameter	"	2.60	9.231		14,100	650		14,750	16,500

23 21 20.14 Air Purging Scoop

		Crew	Daily Output	Labor-Hours	Unit	Material	Labor	Equipment	Total	Total Incl O&P
0010	**AIR PURGING SCOOP**, With tappings.									
0020	For air vent and expansion tank connection									
0100	1" pipe size, threaded	1 Stpi	19	.421	Ea.	39	32		71	90
0110	1-1/4" pipe size, threaded		15	.533		39	40.50		79.50	103
0120	1-1/2" pipe size, threaded		13	.615		85	46.50		131.50	163
0130	2" pipe size, threaded		11	.727		97	55		152	189

23 21 Hydronic Piping and Pumps

23 21 20 – Hydronic HVAC Piping Specialties

23 21 20.18 Automatic Air Vent

		Crew	Daily Output	Labor-Hours	Unit	Material	2024 Bare Costs Labor	Equipment	Total	Total Incl O&P
0010	**AUTOMATIC AIR VENT**									
0020	Cast iron body, stainless steel internals, float type									
0180	1/2" NPT inlet, 250 psi	1 Stpi	10	.800	Ea.	370	60.50		430.50	495
0220	3/4" NPT inlet, 250 psi	"	10	.800	"	370	60.50		430.50	495
0600	Forged steel body, stainless steel internals, float type									
0640	1/2" NPT inlet, 750 psi	1 Stpi	12	.667	Ea.	1,225	50.50		1,275.50	1,425
0680	3/4" NPT inlet, 750 psi	"	12	.667	"	1,225	50.50		1,275.50	1,425
1100	Formed steel body, noncorrosive									
1110	1/8" NPT inlet, 150 psi	1 Stpi	32	.250	Ea.	19.95	18.90		38.85	50
1120	1/4" NPT inlet, 150 psi		32	.250		67	18.90		85.90	102
1130	3/4" NPT inlet, 150 psi	↓	32	.250	↓	67	18.90		85.90	102
1300	Chrome plated brass, automatic/manual, for radiators									
1310	1/8" NPT inlet, nickel plated brass	1 Stpi	32	.250	Ea.	11.60	18.90		30.50	41

23 21 20.26 Circuit Setter

		Crew	Daily Output	Labor-Hours	Unit	Material	Labor	Equipment	Total	Total Incl O&P
0010	**CIRCUIT SETTER**, Balance valve									
0018	Threaded									
0019	1/2" pipe size	1 Stpi	22	.364	Ea.	111	27.50		138.50	163
0020	3/4" pipe size	"	20	.400	"	118	30		148	175

23 21 20.30 Cocks, Drains and Specialties

		Crew	Daily Output	Labor-Hours	Unit	Material	Labor	Equipment	Total	Total Incl O&P
0010	**COCKS, DRAINS AND SPECIALTIES**									
1000	Boiler drain									
1010	Pipe thread to hose									
1020	Bronze									
1030	1/2" size	1 Stpi	36	.222	Ea.	23.50	16.80		40.30	50.50
1040	3/4" size	"	34	.235	"	25.50	17.80		43.30	54.50
1100	Solder to hose									
1110	Bronze									
1120	1/2" size	1 Stpi	46	.174	Ea.	27	13.15		40.15	49.50
1130	3/4" size	"	44	.182	"	29.50	13.75		43.25	53
1600	With built-in vacuum breaker									
1610	1/2" I.P. or solder	1 Stpi	36	.222	Ea.	34.50	16.80		51.30	63
1630	With tamper proof vacuum breaker									
1640	1/2" I.P. or solder	1 Stpi	36	.222	Ea.	89.50	16.80		106.30	124
1650	3/4" I.P. or solder	"	34	.235	"	78	17.80		95.80	113
3000	Cocks									
3010	Air, lever or tee handle									
3020	Bronze, single thread									
3030	1/8" size	1 Stpi	52	.154	Ea.	15.65	11.60		27.25	34.50
3040	1/4" size		46	.174		16.55	13.15		29.70	38
3050	3/8" size		40	.200		17.05	15.10		32.15	41.50
3060	1/2" size	↓	36	.222	↓	20	16.80		36.80	47
3100	Bronze, double thread									
3110	1/8" size	1 Stpi	26	.308	Ea.	20	23.50		43.50	56.50
3120	1/4" size		22	.364		21	27.50		48.50	64
3130	3/8" size		18	.444		22	33.50		55.50	74
3140	1/2" size	↓	15	.533	↓	26.50	40.50		67	89.50
4500	Gauge cock, brass									
4510	1/4" FPT	1 Stpi	24	.333	Ea.	16.55	25		41.55	55.50
4512	1/4" MPT	"	24	.333	"	21	25		46	61
4600	Pigtail, steam syphon									
4604	1/4"	1 Stpi	24	.333	Ea.	33.50	25		58.50	74
4650	Snubber valve									

23 21 Hydronic Piping and Pumps

23 21 20 – Hydronic HVAC Piping Specialties

23 21 20.30 Cocks, Drains and Specialties

		Crew	Daily Output	Labor-Hours	Unit	Material	2024 Bare Costs Labor	Equipment	Total	Total Incl O&P
4654	1/4"	1 Stpi	22	.364	Ea.	5.75	27.50		33.25	47.50
4660	Nipple, black steel									
4664	1/4" x 3"	1 Stpi	37	.216	Ea.	6.35	16.35		22.70	31.50

23 21 20.34 Dielectric Unions

		Crew	Daily Output	Labor-Hours	Unit	Material	Labor	Equipment	Total	Total Incl O&P
0010	**DIELECTRIC UNIONS**, Standard gaskets for water and air									
0020	250 psi maximum pressure									
0280	Female IPT to sweat, straight									
0300	1/2" pipe size	1 Plum	24	.333	Ea.	10.45	25		35.45	48.50
0340	3/4" pipe size		20	.400		11.60	30		41.60	57.50
0360	1" pipe size		19	.421		15.65	31.50		47.15	64.50
0380	1-1/4" pipe size		15	.533		17.95	40		57.95	78.50
0400	1-1/2" pipe size		13	.615		36.50	46		82.50	109
0420	2" pipe size		11	.727		49.50	54.50		104	136
0580	Female IPT to brass pipe thread, straight									
0600	1/2" pipe size	1 Plum	24	.333	Ea.	22.50	25		47.50	61.50
0640	3/4" pipe size		20	.400		24.50	30		54.50	71.50
0660	1" pipe size		19	.421		45.50	31.50		77	97
0680	1-1/4" pipe size		15	.533		45	40		85	109
0700	1-1/2" pipe size		13	.615		65.50	46		111.50	141
0720	2" pipe size		11	.727		113	54.50		167.50	205
0780	Female IPT to female IPT, straight									
0800	1/2" pipe size	1 Plum	24	.333	Ea.	29	25		54	69
0840	3/4" pipe size		20	.400		34	30		64	82
0860	1" pipe size		19	.421		44	31.50		75.50	95.50
0880	1-1/4" pipe size		15	.533		59	40		99	124
0900	1-1/2" pipe size		13	.615		88.50	46		134.50	166
0920	2" pipe size		11	.727		131	54.50		185.50	225
2000	175 psi maximum pressure									
2180	Female IPT to sweat									
2240	2" pipe size	1 Plum	9	.889	Ea.	244	66.50		310.50	365
2260	2-1/2" pipe size	Q-1	15	1.067		320	71.50		391.50	455
2280	3" pipe size		14	1.143		440	77		517	600
2300	4" pipe size		11	1.455		1,175	97.50		1,272.50	1,450
2480	Female IPT to brass pipe									
2500	1-1/2" pipe size	1 Plum	11	.727	Ea.	325	54.50		379.50	435
2540	2" pipe size	"	9	.889		340	66.50		406.50	475
2560	2-1/2" pipe size	Q-1	15	1.067		380	71.50		451.50	520
2580	3" pipe size		14	1.143		380	77		457	530
2600	4" pipe size		11	1.455		540	97.50		637.50	735

23 21 20.42 Expansion Joints

		Crew	Daily Output	Labor-Hours	Unit	Material	Labor	Equipment	Total	Total Incl O&P
0010	**EXPANSION JOINTS**									
0100	Bellows type, neoprene cover, flanged spool									
0140	6" face to face, 1-1/4" diameter	1 Stpi	11	.727	Ea.	410	55		465	530
0160	1-1/2" diameter	"	10.60	.755		410	57		467	535
0180	2" diameter	Q-5	13.30	1.203		415	82		497	580
0190	2-1/2" diameter		12.40	1.290		430	87.50		517.50	605
0200	3" diameter		11.40	1.404		480	95.50		575.50	670
0210	4" diameter		8.40	1.905		520	130		650	770
0220	5" diameter		7.60	2.105		635	143		778	915
0230	6" diameter		6.80	2.353		655	160		815	960
0240	8" diameter		5.40	2.963		765	201		966	1,150
0250	10" diameter		5	3.200		1,050	218		1,268	1,475

23 21 Hydronic Piping and Pumps

23 21 20 – Hydronic HVAC Piping Specialties

23 21 20.42 Expansion Joints

		Crew	Daily Output	Labor-Hours	Unit	Material	2024 Bare Costs Labor	Equipment	Total	Total Incl O&P
0260	12" diameter	Q-5	4.60	3.478	Ea.	1,200	237		1,437	1,675
0480	10" face to face, 2" diameter		13	1.231		600	83.50		683.50	785
0500	2-1/2" diameter		12	1.333		630	90.50		720.50	830
0520	3" diameter		11	1.455		640	99		739	850
0540	4" diameter		8	2		730	136		866	1,000
0560	5" diameter		7	2.286		875	155		1,030	1,200
0580	6" diameter		6	2.667		900	181		1,081	1,250
0600	8" diameter		5	3.200		1,075	218		1,293	1,500
0620	10" diameter		4.60	3.478		1,175	237		1,412	1,650
0640	12" diameter		4	4		1,475	272		1,747	2,025
0660	14" diameter		3.80	4.211		1,825	286		2,111	2,425
0680	16" diameter		2.90	5.517		2,100	375		2,475	2,875
0700	18" diameter		2.50	6.400		2,375	435		2,810	3,250
0720	20" diameter		2.10	7.619		2,475	520		2,995	3,500
0740	24" diameter		1.80	8.889		2,900	605		3,505	4,100
0760	26" diameter		1.40	11.429		3,250	775		4,025	4,725
0780	30" diameter		1.20	13.333		3,625	905		4,530	5,350
0800	36" diameter		1	16		4,150	1,100		5,250	6,200

23 21 20.46 Expansion Tanks

		Crew	Daily Output	Labor-Hours	Unit	Material	Labor	Equipment	Total	Total Incl O&P
0010	**EXPANSION TANKS**									
1502	Plastic, corrosion resistant, see Section 22 66 83.13									
1505	Aboveground fuel-oil, storage tanks, see Section 23 13 23									
1507	Underground fuel-oil storage tanks, see Section 23 13 13									
1512	Tank leak detection systems, see Section 28 33 33.50									
2000	Steel, liquid expansion, ASME, painted, 15 gallon capacity	Q-5	17	.941	Ea.	980	64		1,044	1,175
2020	24 gallon capacity		14	1.143		820	77.50		897.50	1,025
2040	30 gallon capacity		12	1.333		1,175	90.50		1,265.50	1,425
2060	40 gallon capacity		10	1.600		1,375	109		1,484	1,650
2360	Galvanized									
2370	15 gallon capacity	Q-5	17	.941	Ea.	1,575	64		1,639	1,825
2380	24 gallon capacity		14	1.143		1,700	77.50		1,777.50	2,000
2390	30 gallon capacity		12	1.333		1,775	90.50		1,865.50	2,075
3000	Steel ASME expansion, rubber diaphragm, 19 gal. cap. accept.		12	1.333		3,750	90.50		3,840.50	4,250
3020	31 gallon capacity		8	2		4,150	136		4,286	4,775
3040	61 gallon capacity		6	2.667		6,250	181		6,431	7,150

23 21 20.50 Float Valves

		Crew	Daily Output	Labor-Hours	Unit	Material	Labor	Equipment	Total	Total Incl O&P
0010	**FLOAT VALVES**									
0020	With ball and bracket									
0030	Single seat, threaded									
0040	Brass body									
0050	1/2"	1 Stpi	11	.727	Ea.	107	55		162	199
0060	3/4"		9	.889		120	67		187	232
0070	1"		7	1.143		214	86.50		300.50	365
0080	1-1/2"		4.50	1.778		293	134		427	520
0090	2"		3.60	2.222		310	168		478	595
0300	For condensate receivers, CI, in-line mount									
0320	1" inlet	1 Stpi	7	1.143	Ea.	194	86.50		280.50	340
0360	For condensate receiver, CI, external float, flanged tank mount									
0370	3/4" inlet	1 Stpi	5	1.600	Ea.	120	121		241	310

23 21 Hydronic Piping and Pumps

23 21 20 – Hydronic HVAC Piping Specialties

23 21 20.54 Flow Check Control

		Crew	Daily Output	Labor-Hours	Unit	Material	2024 Bare Costs Labor	Equipment	Total	Total Incl O&P
0010	**FLOW CHECK CONTROL**									
0100	Bronze body, soldered									
0110	3/4" size	1 Stpi	20	.400	Ea.	96	30		126	150
0120	1" size	"	19	.421	"	115	32		147	175
0200	Cast iron body, threaded									
0210	3/4" size	1 Stpi	20	.400	Ea.	74	30		104	126
0220	1" size		19	.421		84	32		116	140
0230	1-1/4" size		15	.533		101	40.50		141.50	171
0240	1-1/2" size		13	.615		155	46.50		201.50	240
0250	2" size		11	.727		223	55		278	325

23 21 20.58 Hydronic Heating Control Valves

		Crew	Daily Output	Labor-Hours	Unit	Material	2024 Bare Costs Labor	Equipment	Total	Total Incl O&P
0010	**HYDRONIC HEATING CONTROL VALVES**									
0050	Hot water, nonelectric, thermostatic									
0100	Radiator supply, 1/2" diameter	1 Stpi	24	.333	Ea.	53.50	25		78.50	96.50
0120	3/4" diameter	"	20	.400	"	61	30		91	112
1000	Manual, radiator supply									
1010	1/2" pipe size, angle union	1 Stpi	24	.333	Ea.	117	25		142	167
1020	3/4" pipe size, angle union	"	20	.400	"	148	30		178	207
1100	Radiator, balancing, straight, sweat connections									
1110	1/2" pipe size	1 Stpi	24	.333	Ea.	44	25		69	86
1120	3/4" pipe size	"	20	.400		61.50	30		91.50	113
1200	Steam, radiator, supply									
1210	1/2" pipe size, angle union	1 Stpi	24	.333	Ea.	127	25		152	178
1220	3/4" pipe size, angle union	"	20	.400	"	138	30		168	197
8000	System balancing and shut-off									
8020	Butterfly, quarter turn, calibrated, threaded or solder									
8040	Bronze, -30°F to +350°F, pressure to 175 psi									
8060	1/2" size	1 Stpi	22	.364	Ea.	37	27.50		64.50	81.50
8070	3/4" size	"	20	.400	"	59.50	30		89.50	111

23 21 20.66 Monoflow Tee Fitting

		Crew	Daily Output	Labor-Hours	Unit	Material	2024 Bare Costs Labor	Equipment	Total	Total Incl O&P
0010	**MONOFLOW TEE FITTING**									
1100	For one pipe hydronic, supply and return									
1110	Copper, soldered									
1120	3/4" x 1/2" size	1 Stpi	13	.615	Ea.	30	46.50		76.50	102

23 21 20.74 Strainers, Basket Type

		Crew	Daily Output	Labor-Hours	Unit	Material	2024 Bare Costs Labor	Equipment	Total	Total Incl O&P
0010	**STRAINERS, BASKET TYPE**, Perforated stainless steel basket									
0100	Brass or monel available									
2000	Simplex style									
2300	Bronze body									
2320	Screwed, 3/8" pipe size	1 Stpi	22	.364	Ea.	41.50	27.50		69	86.50
2340	1/2" pipe size		20	.400		47.50	30		77.50	97
2360	3/4" pipe size		17	.471		60	35.50		95.50	119
2380	1" pipe size		15	.533		87.50	40.50		128	157
2400	1-1/4" pipe size		13	.615		106	46.50		152.50	186
2420	1-1/2" pipe size		12	.667		188	50.50		238.50	282
2440	2" pipe size		10	.800		224	60.50		284.50	335
2460	2-1/2" pipe size	Q-5	15	1.067		335	72.50		407.50	480
2480	3" pipe size	"	14	1.143		445	77.50		522.50	605
2600	Flanged, 2" pipe size	1 Stpi	6	1.333		1,900	101		2,001	2,225
2620	2-1/2" pipe size	Q-5	4.50	3.556		2,950	242		3,192	3,600
2640	3" pipe size		3.50	4.571		3,575	310		3,885	4,400

23 21 Hydronic Piping and Pumps

23 21 20 – Hydronic HVAC Piping Specialties

23 21 20.74 Strainers, Basket Type		Crew	Daily Output	Labor-Hours	Unit	Material	2024 Bare Costs Labor	2024 Bare Costs Equipment	Total	Total Incl O&P
2660	4" pipe size	Q-5	3	5.333	Ea.	5,925	365		6,290	7,075
2680	5" pipe size	Q-6	3.40	7.059		7,875	500		8,375	9,425
2700	6" pipe size		3	8		10,800	565		11,365	12,700
2710	8" pipe size		2.50	9.600		20,100	675		20,775	23,100
3600	Iron body									
3700	Screwed, 3/8" pipe size	1 Stpi	22	.364	Ea.	201	27.50		228.50	262
3720	1/2" pipe size		20	.400		215	30		245	281
3740	3/4" pipe size		17	.471		276	35.50		311.50	360
3760	1" pipe size		15	.533		292	40.50		332.50	380
3780	1-1/4" pipe size		13	.615		370	46.50		416.50	475
3800	1-1/2" pipe size		12	.667		530	50.50		580.50	660
3820	2" pipe size		10	.800		480	60.50		540.50	620
3840	2-1/2" pipe size	Q-5	15	1.067		660	72.50		732.50	835
3860	3" pipe size	"	14	1.143		840	77.50		917.50	1,025
4000	Flanged, 2" pipe size	1 Stpi	6	1.333		790	101		891	1,025
4020	2-1/2" pipe size	Q-5	4.50	3.556		1,075	242		1,317	1,525
4040	3" pipe size		3.50	4.571		1,125	310		1,435	1,700
4060	4" pipe size		3	5.333		1,825	365		2,190	2,550
4080	5" pipe size	Q-6	3.40	7.059		2,700	500		3,200	3,700
4100	6" pipe size		3	8		3,400	565		3,965	4,600
4120	8" pipe size		2.50	9.600		6,175	675		6,850	7,800
4140	10" pipe size		2.20	10.909		16,300	770		17,070	19,200
7000	Stainless steel body									
7200	Screwed, 1" pipe size	1 Stpi	15	.533	Ea.	810	40.50		850.50	950
7210	1-1/4" pipe size		13	.615		1,200	46.50		1,246.50	1,400
7220	1-1/2" pipe size		12	.667		1,200	50.50		1,250.50	1,400
7240	2" pipe size		10	.800		1,775	60.50		1,835.50	2,050
7260	2-1/2" pipe size	Q-5	15	1.067		2,725	72.50		2,797.50	3,100
7280	3" pipe size	"	14	1.143		3,800	77.50		3,877.50	4,300
7400	Flanged, 2" pipe size	1 Stpi	6	1.333		3,975	101		4,076	4,525
7420	2-1/2" pipe size	Q-5	4.50	3.556		4,800	242		5,042	5,625
7440	3" pipe size		3.50	4.571		4,875	310		5,185	5,825
7460	4" pipe size		3	5.333		7,675	365		8,040	9,000
7480	6" pipe size	Q-6	3	8		18,200	565		18,765	20,800
7500	8" pipe size	"	2.50	9.600		26,500	675		27,175	30,100
8100	Duplex style									
8200	Bronze body									
8240	Screwed, 3/4" pipe size	1 Stpi	16	.500	Ea.	3,075	38		3,113	3,450
8260	1" pipe size		14	.571		3,075	43		3,118	3,450
8280	1-1/4" pipe size		12	.667		6,075	50.50		6,125.50	6,775
8300	1-1/2" pipe size		11	.727		3,225	55		3,280	3,625
8320	2" pipe size		9	.889		6,275	67		6,342	7,000
8340	2-1/2" pipe size	Q-5	14	1.143		7,800	77.50		7,877.50	8,725
8420	Flanged, 2" pipe size	1 Stpi	6	1.333		7,425	101		7,526	8,325
8440	2-1/2" pipe size	Q-5	4.50	3.556		10,300	242		10,542	11,700
8460	3" pipe size		3.50	4.571		11,200	310		11,510	12,800
8480	4" pipe size		3	5.333		15,200	365		15,565	17,200
8500	5" pipe size	Q-6	3.40	7.059		36,900	500		37,400	41,200
8520	6" pipe size	"	3	8		35,800	565		36,365	40,200
8700	Iron body									
8740	Screwed, 3/4" pipe size	1 Stpi	16	.500	Ea.	2,075	38		2,113	2,325
8760	1" pipe size		14	.571		2,075	43		2,118	2,350
8780	1-1/4" pipe size		12	.667		2,675	50.50		2,725.50	3,025

23 21 Hydronic Piping and Pumps

23 21 20 – Hydronic HVAC Piping Specialties

23 21 20.74 Strainers, Basket Type

		Crew	Daily Output	Labor-Hours	Unit	Material	2024 Bare Costs Labor	Equipment	Total	Total Incl O&P
8800	1-1/2" pipe size	1 Stpi	11	.727	Ea.	2,675	55		2,730	3,025
8820	2" pipe size	↓	9	.889		3,800	67		3,867	4,275
8840	2-1/2" pipe size	Q-5	14	1.143		4,800	77.50		4,877.50	5,400
9000	Flanged, 2" pipe size	1 Stpi	6	1.333		4,825	101		4,926	5,450
9020	2-1/2" pipe size	Q-5	4.50	3.556		5,150	242		5,392	6,000
9040	3" pipe size		3.50	4.571		5,950	310		6,260	7,025
9060	4" pipe size	↓	3	5.333		9,500	365		9,865	10,900
9080	5" pipe size	Q-6	3.40	7.059		25,000	500		25,500	28,200
9100	6" pipe size		3	8		25,000	565		25,565	28,300
9120	8" pipe size		2.50	9.600		49,700	675		50,375	55,500
9140	10" pipe size		2.20	10.909		71,000	770		71,770	79,000
9160	12" pipe size		1.70	14.118		78,000	995		78,995	87,500
9170	14" pipe size		1.40	17.143		92,000	1,200		93,200	103,500
9180	16" pipe size	↓	1	24		113,500	1,700		115,200	127,000
9700	Stainless steel body									
9740	Screwed, 1" pipe size	1 Stpi	14	.571	Ea.	4,950	43		4,993	5,525
9760	1-1/2" pipe size		11	.727		6,275	55		6,330	7,000
9780	2" pipe size		9	.889		9,475	67		9,542	10,500
9860	Flanged, 2" pipe size	↓	6	1.333		12,100	101		12,201	13,500
9880	2-1/2" pipe size	Q-5	4.50	3.556		20,300	242		20,542	22,700
9900	3" pipe size		3.50	4.571		22,100	310		22,410	24,800
9920	4" pipe size	↓	3	5.333		28,800	365		29,165	32,100
9940	6" pipe size	Q-6	3	8		43,900	565		44,465	49,100
9960	8" pipe size	"	2.50	9.600	↓	95,500	675		96,175	106,000

23 21 20.76 Strainers, Y Type, Bronze Body

		Crew	Daily Output	Labor-Hours	Unit	Material	2024 Bare Costs Labor	Equipment	Total	Total Incl O&P
0010	**STRAINERS, Y TYPE, BRONZE BODY**									
0050	Screwed, 125 lb., 1/4" pipe size	1 Stpi	24	.333	Ea.	76	25		101	121
0070	3/8" pipe size		24	.333		76	25		101	121
0100	1/2" pipe size		20	.400		55	30		85	106
0120	3/4" pipe size		19	.421		93	32		125	150
0140	1" pipe size		17	.471		137	35.50		172.50	204
0150	1-1/4" pipe size		15	.533		218	40.50		258.50	300
0160	1-1/2" pipe size		14	.571		294	43		337	390
0180	2" pipe size		13	.615		385	46.50		431.50	495
0182	3" pipe size	↓	12	.667		2,575	50.50		2,625.50	2,900
0200	300 lb., 2-1/2" pipe size	Q-5	17	.941		1,450	64		1,514	1,700
0220	3" pipe size		16	1		1,600	68		1,668	1,850
0240	4" pipe size	↓	15	1.067	↓	2,950	72.50		3,022.50	3,325
0500	For 300 lb. rating 1/4" thru 2", add					15%				
1000	Flanged, 150 lb., 1-1/2" pipe size	1 Stpi	11	.727	Ea.	680	55		735	830
1020	2" pipe size	"	8	1		835	75.50		910.50	1,025
1030	2-1/2" pipe size	Q-5	5	3.200		1,400	218		1,618	1,875
1040	3" pipe size		4.50	3.556		1,725	242		1,967	2,250
1060	4" pipe size	↓	3	5.333		2,650	365		3,015	3,475
1080	5" pipe size	Q-6	3.40	7.059		3,800	500		4,300	4,925
1100	6" pipe size		3	8		5,100	565		5,665	6,475
1106	8" pipe size	↓	2.60	9.231	↓	5,550	650		6,200	7,075
1500	For 300 lb. rating, add					40%				

23 21 20.78 Strainers, Y Type, Iron Body

		Crew	Daily Output	Labor-Hours	Unit	Material	2024 Bare Costs Labor	Equipment	Total	Total Incl O&P
0010	**STRAINERS, Y TYPE, IRON BODY**									
0050	Screwed, 250 lb., 1/4" pipe size	1 Stpi	20	.400	Ea.	34.50	30		64.50	83
0070	3/8" pipe size	↓	20	.400	↓	34.50	30		64.50	83

23 21 Hydronic Piping and Pumps

23 21 20 – Hydronic HVAC Piping Specialties

	23 21 20.78 Strainers, Y Type, Iron Body	Crew	Daily Output	Labor-Hours	Unit	Material	2024 Bare Costs Labor	Equipment	Total	Total Incl O&P
0100	1/2" pipe size	1 Stpi	20	.400	Ea.	34.50	30		64.50	83
0120	3/4" pipe size		18	.444		40	33.50		73.50	94
0140	1" pipe size		16	.500		52.50	38		90.50	114
0150	1-1/4" pipe size		15	.533		73.50	40.50		114	141
0160	1-1/2" pipe size		12	.667		100	50.50		150.50	185
0180	2" pipe size	▼	8	1		150	75.50		225.50	277
0200	2-1/2" pipe size	Q-5	12	1.333		610	90.50		700.50	805
0220	3" pipe size		11	1.455		660	99		759	870
0240	4" pipe size	▼	5	3.200	▼	1,125	218		1,343	1,550
0500	For galvanized body, add					50%				
1000	Flanged, 125 lb., 1-1/2" pipe size	1 Stpi	11	.727	Ea.	465	55		520	595
1020	2" pipe size	"	8	1		325	75.50		400.50	465
1030	2-1/2" pipe size	Q-5	5	3.200		294	218		512	650
1040	3" pipe size		4.50	3.556		425	242		667	825
1060	4" pipe size	▼	3	5.333		700	365		1,065	1,300
1080	5" pipe size	Q-6	3.40	7.059		850	500		1,350	1,675
1100	6" pipe size		3	8		1,400	565		1,965	2,400
1120	8" pipe size		2.50	9.600		2,350	675		3,025	3,600
1140	10" pipe size		2	12		4,300	845		5,145	5,975
1160	12" pipe size		1.70	14.118		6,450	995		7,445	8,575
1170	14" pipe size		1.30	18.462		11,900	1,300		13,200	15,000
1180	16" pipe size	▼	1	24	▼	16,900	1,700		18,600	21,100
1500	For 250 lb. rating, add					20%				
2000	For galvanized body, add					50%				
2500	For steel body, add					40%				

23 21 20.80 Suction Diffusers

		Crew	Daily Output	Labor-Hours	Unit	Material	Labor	Equipment	Total	Total Incl O&P
0010	**SUCTION DIFFUSERS**									
0100	Cast iron body with integral straightening vanes, strainer									
1000	Flanged									
1010	2" inlet, 1-1/2" pump side	1 Stpi	6	1.333	Ea.	370	101		471	555
1020	2" pump side	"	5	1.600		500	121		621	730
1030	3" inlet, 2" pump side	Q-5	6.50	2.462	▼	460	167		627	760

23 21 20.84 Thermoflo Indicator

		Crew	Daily Output	Labor-Hours	Unit	Material	Labor	Equipment	Total	Total Incl O&P
0010	**THERMOFLO INDICATOR**, For balancing									
1000	Sweat connections, 1-1/4" pipe size	1 Stpi	12	.667	Ea.	1,000	50.50		1,050.50	1,175
1020	1-1/2" pipe size	"	10	.800	"	1,025	60.50		1,085.50	1,225

23 21 20.88 Venturi Flow

		Crew	Daily Output	Labor-Hours	Unit	Material	Labor	Equipment	Total	Total Incl O&P
0010	**VENTURI FLOW**, Measuring device									
0050	1/2" diameter	1 Stpi	24	.333	Ea.	355	25		380	430
0100	3/4" diameter		20	.400		325	30		355	400
0120	1" diameter		19	.421		345	32		377	430
0140	1-1/4" diameter		15	.533		430	40.50		470.50	535
0160	1-1/2" diameter		13	.615		430	46.50		476.50	545
0180	2" diameter	▼	11	.727		460	55		515	585
0200	2-1/2" diameter	Q-5	16	1		630	68		698	795
0220	3" diameter		14	1.143		650	77.50		727.50	830
0240	4" diameter	▼	11	1.455		970	99		1,069	1,225
0260	5" diameter	Q-6	4	6		1,275	425		1,700	2,025
0280	6" diameter		3.50	6.857		1,425	485		1,910	2,300
0300	8" diameter		3	8		1,825	565		2,390	2,850
0320	10" diameter		2	12		4,300	845		5,145	5,975
0330	12" diameter	▼	1.80	13.333	▼	6,100	940		7,040	8,125

23 21 Hydronic Piping and Pumps

23 21 20 – Hydronic HVAC Piping Specialties

23 21 20.88 Venturi Flow		Crew	Daily Output	Labor-Hours	Unit	Material	2024 Bare Costs Labor	Equipment	Total	Total Incl O&P
0340	14" diameter	Q-6	1.60	15	Ea.	6,925	1,050		7,975	9,200
0350	16" diameter	↓	1.40	17.143		7,925	1,200		9,125	10,500
0500	For meter, add				↓	2,950			2,950	3,250

23 21 23 – Hydronic Pumps

23 21 23.13 In-Line Centrifugal Hydronic Pumps

		Crew	Daily Output	Labor-Hours	Unit	Material	Labor	Equipment	Total	Total Incl O&P
0010	**IN-LINE CENTRIFUGAL HYDRONIC PUMPS**									
0600	Bronze, sweat connections, 1/40 HP, in line									
0640	3/4" size	Q-1	16	1	Ea.	385	67		452	520
1000	Flange connection, 3/4" to 1-1/2" size									
1040	1/12 HP	Q-1	6	2.667	Ea.	840	179		1,019	1,200
1060	1/8 HP		6	2.667		1,850	179		2,029	2,300
1100	1/3 HP		6	2.667		2,075	179		2,254	2,550
1140	2" size, 1/6 HP		5	3.200		2,650	215		2,865	3,250
1180	2-1/2" size, 1/4 HP		5	3.200		2,425	215		2,640	2,975
1220	3" size, 1/4 HP		4	4		2,675	269		2,944	3,350
1260	1/3 HP		4	4		3,100	269		3,369	3,800
1300	1/2 HP		4	4		3,175	269		3,444	3,875
1340	3/4 HP		4	4		2,925	269		3,194	3,625
1380	1 HP	↓	4	4	↓	4,575	269		4,844	5,425
2000	Cast iron, flange connection									
2040	3/4" to 1-1/2" size, in line, 1/12 HP	Q-1	6	2.667	Ea.	730	179		909	1,075
2060	1/8 HP		6	2.667		1,175	179		1,354	1,550
2100	1/3 HP		6	2.667		1,300	179		1,479	1,700
2140	2" size, 1/6 HP		5	3.200		1,425	215		1,640	1,875
2180	2-1/2" size, 1/4 HP		5	3.200		1,150	215		1,365	1,575
2220	3" size, 1/4 HP		4	4		1,125	269		1,394	1,625
2260	1/3 HP		4	4		1,425	269		1,694	1,975
2300	1/2 HP		4	4		1,475	269		1,744	2,025
2340	3/4 HP		4	4		1,725	269		1,994	2,275
2380	1 HP	↓	4	4	↓	2,475	269		2,744	3,125
2600	For nonferrous impeller, add					3%				
3000	High head, bronze impeller									
3030	1-1/2" size, 1/2 HP	Q-1	5	3.200	Ea.	1,300	215		1,515	1,750
3040	1-1/2" size, 3/4 HP		5	3.200		1,800	215		2,015	2,300
3050	2" size, 1 HP		4	4		2,175	269		2,444	2,800
3090	2" size, 1-1/2 HP	↓	4	4	↓	2,550	269		2,819	3,200
4000	Close coupled, end suction, bronze impeller									
4040	1-1/2" size, 1-1/2 HP, to 40 GPM	Q-1	3	5.333	Ea.	3,375	360		3,735	4,250
4090	2" size, 2 HP, to 50 GPM		3	5.333		3,700	360		4,060	4,600
4100	2" size, 3 HP, to 90 GPM		2.30	6.957		3,000	465		3,465	4,000
4190	2-1/2" size, 3 HP, to 150 GPM		2	8		4,775	535		5,310	6,050
4300	3" size, 5 HP, to 225 GPM		1.80	8.889		5,000	595		5,595	6,400
4410	3" size, 10 HP, to 350 GPM		1.60	10		8,650	670		9,320	10,500
4420	4" size, 7-1/2 HP, to 350 GPM	↓	1.60	10		5,975	670		6,645	7,575
4520	4" size, 10 HP, to 600 GPM	Q-2	1.70	14.118		9,225	985		10,210	11,600
4530	5" size, 15 HP, to 1,000 GPM		1.70	14.118		5,975	985		6,960	8,025
4610	5" size, 20 HP, to 1,350 GPM		1.50	16		7,375	1,125		8,500	9,750
4620	5" size, 25 HP, to 1,550 GPM	↓	1.50	16	↓	11,800	1,125		12,925	14,700
5000	Base mounted, bronze impeller, coupling guard									
5040	1-1/2" size, 1-1/2 HP, to 40 GPM	Q-1	2.30	6.957	Ea.	9,450	465		9,915	11,100
5090	2" size, 2 HP, to 50 GPM		2.30	6.957		10,600	465		11,065	12,400
5100	2" size, 3 HP, to 90 GPM	↓	2	8	↓	10,500	535		11,035	12,300

23 21 Hydronic Piping and Pumps

23 21 23 – Hydronic Pumps

23 21 23.13 In-Line Centrifugal Hydronic Pumps

		Crew	Daily Output	Labor-Hours	Unit	Material	2024 Bare Costs Labor	Equipment	Total	Total Incl O&P
5190	2-1/2" size, 3 HP, to 150 GPM	Q-1	1.80	8.889	Ea.	12,500	595		13,095	14,600
5300	3" size, 5 HP, to 225 GPM		1.60	10		15,300	670		15,970	17,800
5410	4" size, 5 HP, to 350 GPM		1.50	10.667		15,600	715		16,315	18,300
5420	4" size, 7-1/2 HP, to 350 GPM	↓	1.50	10.667		14,800	715		15,515	17,300
5520	5" size, 10 HP, to 600 GPM	Q-2	1.60	15		18,700	1,050		19,750	22,200
5530	5" size, 15 HP, to 1,000 GPM		1.60	15		20,000	1,050		21,050	23,600
5610	6" size, 20 HP, to 1,350 GPM		1.40	17.143		31,800	1,200		33,000	36,800
5620	6" size, 25 HP, to 1,550 GPM	↓	1.40	17.143	↓	25,600	1,200		26,800	29,900
5800	The above pump capacities are based on 1,800 RPM,									
5810	at a 60' head. Increasing the RPM									
5820	or decreasing the head will increase the GPM.									

23 21 29 – Automatic Condensate Pump Units

23 21 29.10 Condensate Removal Pump System

			Crew	Daily Output	Labor-Hours	Unit	Material	Labor	Equipment	Total	Total Incl O&P
0010	**CONDENSATE REMOVAL PUMP SYSTEM**										
0020	Pump with 1 gal. ABS tank										
0100	115 V										
0120	1/50 HP, 200 GPH	G	1 Stpi	12	.667	Ea.	244	50.50		294.50	345
0140	1/18 HP, 270 GPH	G		10	.800		254	60.50		314.50	370
0160	1/5 HP, 450 GPH	G	↓	8	1	↓	565	75.50		640.50	730
0200	230 V										
0240	1/18 HP, 270 GPH		1 Stpi	10	.800	Ea.	270	60.50		330.50	390
0260	1/5 HP, 450 GPH	G	"	8	1	"	655	75.50		730.50	830

23 23 Refrigerant Piping

23 23 23 – Refrigerants

23 23 23.10 Anti-Freeze

		Crew	Daily Output	Labor-Hours	Unit	Material	Labor	Equipment	Total	Total Incl O&P
0010	**ANTI-FREEZE**, Inhibited									
0900	Ethylene glycol concentrated									
1000	55 gallon drums, small quantities				Gal.	16.40			16.40	18.05
1200	Large quantities					12.80			12.80	14.05
2000	Propylene glycol, for solar heat, small quantities					27.50			27.50	30
2100	Large quantities				↓	14.25			14.25	15.70

23 34 HVAC Fans

23 34 14 – Blower HVAC Fans

23 34 14.10 Blower Type HVAC Fans

		Crew	Daily Output	Labor-Hours	Unit	Material	Labor	Equipment	Total	Total Incl O&P
0010	**BLOWER TYPE HVAC FANS**									
2500	Ceiling fan, right angle, extra quiet, 0.10" S.P.									
2520	95 CFM	Q-20	20	1	Ea.	350	66.50		416.50	485
2540	210 CFM		19	1.053		415	70		485	560
2560	385 CFM	↓	18	1.111		485	73.50		558.50	645
2640	For wall or roof cap, add	1 Shee	16	.500		315	36		351	405
2660	For straight thru fan, add					10%				
2680	For speed control switch, add	1 Elec	16	.500	↓	173	36		209	243

23 34 HVAC Fans

23 34 23 – HVAC Power Ventilators

23 34 23.10 HVAC Power Circulators and Ventilators		Crew	Daily Output	Labor-Hours	Unit	Material	2024 Bare Costs Labor	2024 Bare Costs Equipment	Total	Total Incl O&P
0010	**HVAC POWER CIRCULATORS AND VENTILATORS**									
6650	Residential, bath exhaust, grille, back draft damper									
6660	50 CFM	Q-20	24	.833	Ea.	52.50	55.50		108	141
6670	110 CFM		22	.909		110	60.50		170.50	212
6680	Light combination, squirrel cage, 100 watt, 70 CFM	↓	24	.833	↓	129	55.50		184.50	224
6700	Light/heater combination, ceiling mounted									
6710	70 CFM, 1,450 watt	Q-20	24	.833	Ea.	204	55.50		259.50	310
6800	Heater combination, recessed, 70 CFM		24	.833		94.50	55.50		150	187
6820	With 2 infrared bulbs	↓	23	.870	↓	106	57.50		163.50	203
6940	Residential roof jacks and wall caps									
6944	Wall cap with back draft damper									
6946	3" & 4" diam. round duct	1 Shee	11	.727	Ea.	25	52.50		77.50	107
6948	6" diam. round duct	"	11	.727	"	59.50	52.50		112	144
6958	Roof jack with bird screen and back draft damper									
6960	3" & 4" diam. round duct	1 Shee	11	.727	Ea.	29	52.50		81.50	111
6962	3-1/4" x 10" rectangular duct	"	10	.800	"	35	58		93	126
6980	Transition									
6982	3-1/4" x 10" to 6" diam. round	1 Shee	20	.400	Ea.	28	29		57	74.50

23 35 Special Exhaust Systems

23 35 16 – Engine Exhaust Systems

23 35 16.10 Engine Exhaust Removal Systems

		Crew	Daily Output	Labor-Hours	Unit	Material	2024 Bare Costs Labor	2024 Bare Costs Equipment	Total	Total Incl O&P
0010	**ENGINE EXHAUST REMOVAL SYSTEMS** D3090-320									
0500	Engine exhaust, garage, in-floor system									
0510	Single tube outlet assemblies									
0520	For transite pipe ducting, self-storing tube									
0530	3" tubing adapter plate	1 Shee	16	.500	Ea.	320	36		356	410
0540	4" tubing adapter plate		16	.500		325	36		361	415
0550	5" tubing adapter plate	↓	16	.500	↓	325	36		361	410
0600	For vitrified tile ducting									
0610	3" tubing adapter plate, self-storing tube	1 Shee	16	.500	Ea.	320	36		356	405
0620	4" tubing adapter plate, self-storing tube		16	.500		325	36		361	415
0660	5" tubing adapter plate, self-storing tube	↓	16	.500	↓	325	36		361	415
0800	Two tube outlet assemblies									
0810	For transite pipe ducting, self-storing tube									
0820	3" tubing, dual exhaust adapter plate	1 Shee	16	.500	Ea.	330	36		366	415
0850	For vitrified tile ducting									
0860	3" tubing, dual exhaust, self-storing tube	1 Shee	16	.500	Ea.	360	36		396	450
0870	3" tubing, double outlet, non-storing tubes	"	16	.500	"	360	36		396	450
0900	Accessories for metal tubing (overhead systems also)									
0910	Adapters, for metal tubing end									
0920	3" tail pipe type				Ea.	62.50			62.50	68.50
0930	4" tail pipe type					69			69	76
0940	5" tail pipe type					70			70	77
0990	5" diesel stack type					370			370	405
1000	6" diesel stack type				↓	435			435	480
1100	Bullnose (guide) required for in-floor assemblies									
1110	3" tubing size				Ea.	37.50			37.50	41
1120	4" tubing size					38.50			38.50	42.50
1130	5" tubing size				↓	41			41	45

23 35 Special Exhaust Systems

23 35 16 – Engine Exhaust Systems

23 35 16.10 Engine Exhaust Removal Systems

		Crew	Daily Output	Labor-Hours	Unit	Material	2024 Bare Costs Labor	Equipment	Total	Total Incl O&P
1150	Plain rings, for tubing end									
1160	3" tubing size				Ea.	26.50			26.50	29
1170	4" tubing size				"	44.50			44.50	48.50
1200	Tubing, galvanized, flexible (for overhead systems also)									
1210	3" ID				L.F.	12.60			12.60	13.85
1220	4" ID					15.40			15.40	16.95
1230	5" ID					18.15			18.15	19.95
1240	6" ID					21			21	23
1250	Stainless steel, flexible (for overhead system also)									
1260	3" ID				L.F.	25.50			25.50	28
1270	4" ID					35			35	38
1280	5" ID					39.50			39.50	43.50
1290	6" ID					46			46	50.50
1500	Engine exhaust, garage, overhead components, for neoprene tubing									
1510	Alternate metal tubing & accessories see above									
1550	Adapters, for neoprene tubing end									
1560	3" tail pipe, adjustable, neoprene				Ea.	73.50			73.50	81
1570	3" tail pipe, heavy wall neoprene					83			83	91.50
1580	4" tail pipe, heavy wall neoprene					122			122	135
1590	5" tail pipe, heavy wall neoprene					145			145	159
1650	Connectors, tubing									
1660	3" interior, aluminum				Ea.	26.50			26.50	29.50
1670	4" interior, aluminum					44.50			44.50	48.50
1710	5" interior, neoprene					69.50			69.50	76.50
1750	3" spiralock, neoprene					26.50			26.50	29
1760	4" spiralock, neoprene					44.50			44.50	48.50
1780	Y for 3" ID tubing, neoprene, dual exhaust					248			248	273
1790	Y for 4" ID tubing, aluminum, dual exhaust					196			196	216
1850	Elbows, aluminum, splice into tubing for strap									
1860	3" neoprene tubing size				Ea.	67			67	73.50
1870	4" neoprene tubing size					47			47	52
1900	Flange assemblies, connect tubing to overhead duct					84			84	92.50
2000	Hardware and accessories									
2020	Cable, galvanized, 1/8" diameter				L.F.	.62			.62	.68
2040	Cleat, tie down cable or rope				Ea.	6.40			6.40	7.05
2060	Pulley					8.85			8.85	9.75
2080	Pulley hook, universal					6.40			6.40	7.05
2100	Rope, nylon, 1/4" diameter				L.F.	.45			.45	.50
2120	Winch, 1" diameter				Ea.	130			130	143
2150	Lifting strap, mounts on neoprene									
2160	3" tubing size				Ea.	32			32	35.50
2170	4" tubing size					32			32	35.50
2180	5" tubing size					32			32	35.50
2190	6" tubing size					32			32	35.50
2200	Tubing, neoprene, 11' lengths									
2210	3" ID				L.F.	15.05			15.05	16.60
2220	4" ID					19.70			19.70	21.50
2230	5" ID					36			36	39.50
2500	Engine exhaust, thru-door outlet									
2510	3" tube size	1 Carp	16	.500	Ea.	78.50	30.50		109	132
2530	4" tube size	"	16	.500	"	68.50	30.50		99	121
3000	Tubing, exhaust, flex hose, with									
3010	coupler, damper and tail pipe adapter									

23 35 Special Exhaust Systems

23 35 16 – Engine Exhaust Systems

23 35 16.10 Engine Exhaust Removal Systems		Crew	Daily Output	Labor-Hours	Unit	Material	2024 Bare Costs Labor	2024 Bare Costs Equipment	Total	Total Incl O&P
3020	Neoprene									
3040	3" x 20'	1 Shee	6	1.333	Ea.	445	96.50		541.50	635
3050	4" x 15'		5.40	1.481		495	107		602	705
3060	4" x 20'		5	1.600		595	116		711	830
3070	5" x 15'	↓	4.40	1.818	↓	790	131		921	1,075
3100	Galvanized									
3110	3" x 20'	1 Shee	6	1.333	Ea.	375	96.50		471.50	555
3120	4" x 17'		5.60	1.429		410	103		513	605
3130	4" x 20'		5	1.600		455	116		571	675
3140	5" x 17'	↓	4.60	1.739	↓	485	126		611	725

23 35 43 – Welding Fume Elimination Systems

23 35 43.10 Welding Fume Elimination System Components

		Crew	Daily Output	Labor-Hours	Unit	Material	Labor	Equipment	Total	Total Incl O&P
0010	**WELDING FUME ELIMINATION SYSTEM COMPONENTS**									
7500	Welding fume elimination accessories for garage exhaust systems									
7600	Cut off (blast gate)									
7610	3" tubing size, 3" x 6" opening	1 Shee	24	.333	Ea.	33.50	24		57.50	73
7620	4" tubing size, 4" x 8" opening		24	.333		34.50	24		58.50	74
7630	5" tubing size, 5" x 10" opening		24	.333		39	24		63	79
7640	6" tubing size		24	.333		43	24		67	83.50
7650	8" tubing size	↓	24	.333	↓	56	24		80	97.50
7700	Hoods, magnetic, with handle & screen									
7710	3" tubing size, 3" x 6" opening	1 Shee	24	.333	Ea.	125	24		149	173
7720	4" tubing size, 4" x 8" opening		24	.333		111	24		135	158
7730	5" tubing size, 5" x 10" opening	↓	24	.333		111	24		135	158

23 38 Ventilation Hoods

23 38 13 – Commercial-Kitchen Hoods

23 38 13.10 Hood and Ventilation Equipment

		Crew	Daily Output	Labor-Hours	Unit	Material	Labor	Equipment	Total	Total Incl O&P
0010	**HOOD AND VENTILATION EQUIPMENT**									
2970	Exhaust hood, sst, gutter on all sides, 4' x 4' x 2'	1 Carp	1.80	4.444	Ea.	2,925	269		3,194	3,625
2980	4' x 4' x 7'	"	1.60	5		2,800	305		3,105	3,550
7800	Vent hood, wall canopy with fire protection, 30"	L-3A	9	1.333		112	87.50		199.50	254
7810	Without fire protection, 36"		10	1.200		99	79		178	227
7820	Island canopy with fire protection, 30"		7	1.714		845	113		958	1,100
7830	Without fire protection, 36"		8	1.500		805	98.50		903.50	1,025
7840	Back shelf with fire protection, 30"		11	1.091		415	72		487	560
7850	Without fire protection, black, 36"		12	1		475	66		541	625
7852	Without fire protection, stainless steel, 36"	↓	12	1		485	66		551	630
7860	Range hood & CO_2 system, 30"	1 Carp	2.50	3.200		4,875	194		5,069	5,650
7950	Hood fire protection system, electric stove	Q-1	3	5.333		2,025	360		2,385	2,750
7952	Hood fire protection system, gas stove	"	3	5.333		2,425	360		2,785	3,175

23 51 Breechings, Chimneys, and Stacks

23 51 13 – Draft Control Devices

23 51 13.16 Vent Dampers

		Crew	Daily Output	Labor-Hours	Unit	Material	2024 Bare Costs Labor	2024 Bare Costs Equipment	Total	Total Incl O&P
0010	**VENT DAMPERS**									
5000	Vent damper, bi-metal, gas, 3" diameter	Q-9	24	.667	Ea.	102	43.50		145.50	177
5010	4" diameter	"	24	.667	"	73.50	43.50		117	146

23 51 13.19 Barometric Dampers

		Crew	Daily Output	Labor-Hours	Unit	Material	Labor	Equipment	Total	Total Incl O&P
0010	**BAROMETRIC DAMPERS**									
1000	Barometric, gas fired system only, 6" size for 5" and 6" pipes	1 Shee	20	.400	Ea.	155	29		184	214
1020	7" size, for 6" and 7" pipes		19	.421		165	30.50		195.50	228
1040	8" size, for 7" and 8" pipes		18	.444		214	32		246	284
1060	9" size, for 8" and 9" pipes		16	.500		240	36		276	320
2000	All fuel, oil, oil/gas, coal									
2020	10" for 9" and 10" pipes	1 Shee	15	.533	Ea.	360	38.50		398.50	455
2040	12" for 11" and 12" pipes		15	.533		465	38.50		503.50	575
2060	14" for 13" and 14" pipes		14	.571		605	41.50		646.50	725
2080	16" for 15" and 16" pipes		13	.615		850	44.50		894.50	1,000
2100	18" for 17" and 18" pipes		12	.667		1,125	48		1,173	1,325
2120	20" for 19" and 21" pipes		10	.800		1,350	58		1,408	1,550
2140	24" for 22" and 25" pipes	Q-9	12	1.333		1,650	86.50		1,736.50	1,950
2160	28" for 26" and 30" pipes		10	1.600		2,050	104		2,154	2,400
2180	32" for 31" and 34" pipes		8	2		2,625	130		2,755	3,075
3260	For thermal switch for above, add	1 Shee	24	.333		140	24		164	190

23 51 23 – Gas Vents

23 51 23.10 Gas Chimney Vents

		Crew	Daily Output	Labor-Hours	Unit	Material	Labor	Equipment	Total	Total Incl O&P
0010	**GAS CHIMNEY VENTS**, Prefab metal, UL listed									
0020	Gas, double wall, galvanized steel									
0080	3" diameter	Q-9	72	.222	V.L.F.	12.85	14.45		27.30	35.50
0100	4" diameter		68	.235		15.90	15.30		31.20	40.50
0120	5" diameter		64	.250		18.05	16.25		34.30	44.50
0140	6" diameter		60	.267		21.50	17.35		38.85	49.50
0160	7" diameter		56	.286		41	18.60		59.60	73
0180	8" diameter		52	.308		44	20		64	78
0200	10" diameter		48	.333		84	21.50		105.50	125
0220	12" diameter		44	.364		100	23.50		123.50	146
0240	14" diameter		42	.381		166	25		191	221
0260	16" diameter		40	.400		239	26		265	300
0280	18" diameter		38	.421		885	27.50		912.50	1,025
0300	20" diameter	Q-10	36	.667		350	45		395	455
0320	22" diameter		34	.706		440	47.50		487.50	555
0340	24" diameter		32	.750		545	50.50		595.50	675
0600	For 4", 5" and 6" oval, add					50%				
0650	Gas, double wall, galvanized steel, fittings									
0660	Elbow 45°, 3" diameter	Q-9	36	.444	Ea.	22.50	29		51.50	68.50
0670	4" diameter		34	.471		27.50	30.50		58	76
0680	5" diameter		32	.500		32	32.50		64.50	84
0690	6" diameter		30	.533		39.50	34.50		74	95.50
0700	7" diameter		28	.571		63	37		100	126
0710	8" diameter		26	.615		84	40		124	153
0720	10" diameter		24	.667		179	43.50		222.50	262
0730	12" diameter		22	.727		191	47.50		238.50	281
0740	14" diameter		21	.762		300	49.50		349.50	405
0750	16" diameter		20	.800		390	52		442	510
0760	18" diameter		19	.842		510	55		565	650
0770	20" diameter	Q-10	18	1.333		570	90		660	765

23 51 Breechings, Chimneys, and Stacks

23 51 23 – Gas Vents

23 51 23.10 Gas Chimney Vents		Crew	Daily Output	Labor-Hours	Unit	Material	2024 Bare Costs Labor	Equipment	Total	Total Incl O&P
0780	22" diameter	Q-10	17	1.412	Ea.	910	95		1,005	1,150
0790	24" diameter	↓	16	1.500	↓	1,175	101		1,276	1,425
0916	Adjustable length									
0918	3" diameter, to 12"	Q-9	36	.444	Ea.	29	29		58	75
0920	4" diameter, to 12"		34	.471		33.50	30.50		64	83
0924	6" diameter, to 12"		30	.533		43	34.50		77.50	99.50
0928	8" diameter, to 12"		26	.615		81	40		121	150
0930	10" diameter, to 18"		24	.667		250	43.50		293.50	340
0932	12" diameter, to 18"		22	.727		254	47.50		301.50	350
0936	16" diameter, to 18"		20	.800		515	52		567	645
0938	18" diameter, to 18"	↓	19	.842		590	55		645	730
0944	24" diameter, to 18"	Q-10	16	1.500		1,125	101		1,226	1,375
0950	Elbow 90°, adjustable, 3" diameter	Q-9	36	.444		38.50	29		67.50	86
0960	4" diameter		34	.471		45.50	30.50		76	96
0970	5" diameter		32	.500		54	32.50		86.50	109
0980	6" diameter		30	.533		65.50	34.50		100	124
0990	7" diameter		28	.571		113	37		150	180
1010	8" diameter		26	.615		114	40		154	186
1020	Wall thimble, 4 to 7" adjustable, 3" diameter		36	.444		24	29		53	70
1022	4" diameter		34	.471		27	30.50		57.50	76
1024	5" diameter		32	.500		33	32.50		65.50	85.50
1026	6" diameter		30	.533		34	34.50		68.50	89.50
1028	7" diameter		28	.571		70.50	37		107.50	134
1030	8" diameter		26	.615		87	40		127	156
1040	Roof flashing, 3" diameter		36	.444		13.30	29		42.30	58
1050	4" diameter		34	.471		15.45	30.50		45.95	63
1060	5" diameter		32	.500		34	32.50		66.50	86
1070	6" diameter		30	.533		37	34.50		71.50	92.50
1080	7" diameter		28	.571		49	37		86	110
1090	8" diameter		26	.615		52	40		92	118
1100	10" diameter		24	.667		70	43.50		113.50	142
1110	12" diameter		22	.727		98	47.50		145.50	179
1120	14" diameter		20	.800		223	52		275	325
1130	16" diameter		18	.889		260	58		318	370
1140	18" diameter	↓	16	1		370	65		435	505
1150	20" diameter	Q-10	18	1.333		485	90		575	670
1160	22" diameter		14	1.714		605	116		721	840
1170	24" diameter	↓	12	2		705	135		840	980
1200	Tee, 3" diameter	Q-9	27	.593		59	38.50		97.50	123
1210	4" diameter		26	.615		64	40		104	131
1220	5" diameter		25	.640		67	41.50		108.50	136
1230	6" diameter		24	.667		76.50	43.50		120	149
1240	7" diameter		23	.696		110	45		155	189
1250	8" diameter		22	.727		120	47.50		167.50	203
1260	10" diameter		21	.762		320	49.50		369.50	425
1270	12" diameter		20	.800		330	52		382	440
1280	14" diameter		18	.889		585	58		643	725
1290	16" diameter		16	1		865	65		930	1,050
1300	18" diameter	↓	14	1.143		1,050	74.50		1,124.50	1,250
1310	20" diameter	Q-10	17	1.412		1,425	95		1,520	1,725
1320	22" diameter		13	1.846		1,850	124		1,974	2,200
1330	24" diameter	↓	12	2		2,125	135		2,260	2,525
1460	Tee cap, 3" diameter	Q-9	45	.356		3.96	23		26.96	39.50

23 51 Breechings, Chimneys, and Stacks

23 51 23 – Gas Vents

	23 51 23.10 Gas Chimney Vents	Crew	Daily Output	Labor-Hours	Unit	Material	2024 Bare Costs Labor	Equipment	Total	Total Incl O&P
1470	4" diameter	Q-9	42	.381	Ea.	4.26	25		29.26	42
1480	5" diameter		40	.400		5.45	26		31.45	45
1490	6" diameter		37	.432		7.95	28		35.95	51.50
1500	7" diameter		35	.457		13.30	29.50		42.80	59
1510	8" diameter		34	.471		14.55	30.50		45.05	62
1520	10" diameter		32	.500		117	32.50		149.50	178
1530	12" diameter		30	.533		117	34.50		151.50	181
1540	14" diameter		28	.571		122	37		159	190
1550	16" diameter		25	.640		125	41.50		166.50	200
1560	18" diameter	▼	24	.667		148	43.50		191.50	227
1570	20" diameter	Q-10	27	.889		167	60		227	273
1580	22" diameter		22	1.091		160	73.50		233.50	287
1590	24" diameter	▼	21	1.143		189	77		266	325
1750	Top, 3" diameter	Q-9	46	.348		30	22.50		52.50	67
1760	4" diameter		44	.364		32	23.50		55.50	70.50
1770	5" diameter		42	.381		29.50	25		54.50	70
1780	6" diameter		40	.400		39.50	26		65.50	82
1790	7" diameter		38	.421		87	27.50		114.50	137
1800	8" diameter		36	.444		107	29		136	162
1810	10" diameter		34	.471		176	30.50		206.50	240
1820	12" diameter		32	.500		214	32.50		246.50	285
1830	14" diameter		30	.533		345	34.50		379.50	430
1840	16" diameter		28	.571		440	37		477	540
1850	18" diameter	▼	26	.615		610	40		650	730
1860	20" diameter	Q-10	28	.857		920	58		978	1,100
1870	22" diameter		22	1.091		1,400	73.50		1,473.50	1,650
1880	24" diameter	▼	20	1.200	▼	1,750	81		1,831	2,050
1900	Gas, double wall, galvanized steel, oval									
1904	4" x 1'	Q-9	68	.235	V.L.F.	23	15.30		38.30	48
1906	5" x 1'		64	.250		41	16.25		57.25	69.50
1908	5"/6" x 1'	▼	60	.267	▼	56	17.35		73.35	87.50
1910	Oval fittings									
1912	Adjustable length									
1914	4" diameter to 12" long	Q-9	34	.471	Ea.	23.50	30.50		54	72
1916	5" diameter to 12" long		32	.500		35	32.50		67.50	87.50
1918	5"/6" diameter to 12" long	▼	30	.533	▼	34	34.50		68.50	89.50
1920	Elbow 45°									
1922	4"	Q-9	34	.471	Ea.	55	30.50		85.50	107
1924	5"		32	.500		110	32.50		142.50	170
1926	5"/6"	▼	30	.533	▼	113	34.50		147.50	176
1930	Elbow 45°, flat									
1932	4"	Q-9	34	.471	Ea.	55	30.50		85.50	107
1934	5"		32	.500		110	32.50		142.50	170
1936	5"/6"	▼	30	.533		113	34.50		147.50	176
1940	Top									
1942	4"	Q-9	44	.364	Ea.	42.50	23.50		66	82.50
1944	5"		42	.381		38	25		63	79.50
1946	5"/6"	▼	40	.400	▼	49	26		75	93
1950	Adjustable flashing									
1952	4"	Q-9	34	.471	Ea.	23	30.50		53.50	71.50
1954	5"		32	.500		67.50	32.50		100	124
1956	5"/6"	▼	30	.533		73.50	34.50		108	133
1960	Tee									

23 51 Breechings, Chimneys, and Stacks

23 51 23 – Gas Vents

23 51 23.10 Gas Chimney Vents

		Crew	Daily Output	Labor-Hours	Unit	Material	2024 Bare Costs Labor	Equipment	Total	Total Incl O&P
1962	4"	Q-9	26	.615	Ea.	81.50	40		121.50	150
1964	5"		25	.640		166	41.50		207.50	245
1966	5"/6"	↓	24	.667	↓	169	43.50		212.50	251
1970	Tee with short snout									
1972	4"	Q-9	26	.615	Ea.	60	40		100	127

23 51 26 – All-Fuel Vent Chimneys

23 51 26.10 All-Fuel Vent Chimneys, Press. Tight, Dbl. Wall

		Crew	Daily Output	Labor-Hours	Unit	Material	Labor	Equipment	Total	Total Incl O&P
0010	**ALL-FUEL VENT CHIMNEYS, PRESSURE TIGHT, DOUBLE WALL**									
3200	All fuel, pressure tight, double wall, 1" insulation, UL listed, 1,400°F.									
3210	304 stainless steel liner, aluminized steel outer jacket									
3220	6" diameter	Q-9	60	.267	L.F.	102	17.35		119.35	138
3221	8" diameter		52	.308		104	20		124	145
3222	10" diameter		48	.333		156	21.50		177.50	205
3223	12" diameter		44	.364		320	23.50		343.50	385
3224	14" diameter		42	.381		330	25		355	400
3225	16" diameter		40	.400		128	26		154	180
3226	18" diameter	↓	38	.421		113	27.50		140.50	166
3227	20" diameter	Q-10	36	.667		164	45		209	249
3228	24" diameter	"	32	.750		204	50.50		254.50	300
3260	For 316 stainless steel liner, add				↓	30%				
3280	All fuel, pressure tight, double wall fittings									
3284	304 stainless steel inner, aluminized steel jacket									
3288	Adjustable 20"/29" section									
3292	6" diameter	Q-9	30	.533	Ea.	234	34.50		268.50	310
3293	8" diameter		26	.615		265	40		305	350
3294	10" diameter		24	.667		305	43.50		348.50	400
3295	12" diameter		22	.727		340	47.50		387.50	440
3296	14" diameter		21	.762		292	49.50		341.50	395
3297	16" diameter		20	.800		390	52		442	510
3298	18" diameter	↓	19	.842		475	55		530	610
3299	20" diameter	Q-10	18	1.333		500	90		590	685
3300	24" diameter	"	16	1.500	↓	640	101		741	855
3350	Elbow 90° fixed									
3354	6" diameter	Q-9	30	.533	Ea.	480	34.50		514.50	580
3355	8" diameter		26	.615		540	40		580	655
3356	10" diameter		24	.667		615	43.50		658.50	740
3357	12" diameter		22	.727		695	47.50		742.50	835
3358	14" diameter		21	.762		790	49.50		839.50	945
3359	16" diameter		20	.800		890	52		942	1,050
3360	18" diameter	↓	19	.842		1,000	55		1,055	1,175
3361	20" diameter	Q-10	18	1.333		1,150	90		1,240	1,375
3362	24" diameter	"	16	1.500		1,450	101		1,551	1,750
3380	For 316 stainless steel liner, add				↓	30%				
3400	Elbow 45°									
3404	6" diameter	Q-9	30	.533	Ea.	241	34.50		275.50	315
3405	8" diameter		26	.615		288	40		328	375
3406	10" diameter		24	.667		310	43.50		353.50	405
3407	12" diameter		22	.727		350	47.50		397.50	455
3408	14" diameter		21	.762		420	49.50		469.50	540
3409	16" diameter		20	.800		475	52		527	600
3410	18" diameter	↓	19	.842		540	55		595	675
3411	20" diameter	Q-10	18	1.333	↓	630	90		720	830

23 51 Breechings, Chimneys, and Stacks

23 51 26 – All-Fuel Vent Chimneys

	23 51 26.10 All-Fuel Vent Chimneys, Press. Tight, Dbl. Wall	Crew	Daily Output	Labor-Hours	Unit	Material	2024 Bare Costs Labor	Equipment	Total	Total Incl O&P
3412	24" diameter	Q-10	16	1.500	Ea.	805	101		906	1,050
3430	For 316 stainless steel liner, add				↓	30%				
3450	Tee 90°									
3454	6" diameter	Q-9	24	.667	Ea.	290	43.50		333.50	385
3455	8" diameter		22	.727		315	47.50		362.50	415
3456	10" diameter		21	.762		350	49.50		399.50	460
3457	12" diameter		20	.800		405	52		457	525
3458	14" diameter		18	.889		490	58		548	625
3459	16" diameter		16	1		555	65		620	710
3460	18" diameter	↓	14	1.143		655	74.50		729.50	830
3461	20" diameter	Q-10	17	1.412		735	95		830	955
3462	24" diameter	"	12	2		865	135		1,000	1,150
3480	For tee cap, add					35%	20%			
3500	For 316 stainless steel liner, add				↓	30%				
3520	Plate support, galvanized									
3524	6" diameter	Q-9	26	.615	Ea.	144	40		184	218
3525	8" diameter		22	.727		169	47.50		216.50	257
3526	10" diameter		20	.800		184	52		236	281
3527	12" diameter		18	.889		193	58		251	300
3528	14" diameter		17	.941		229	61		290	345
3529	16" diameter		16	1		242	65		307	365
3530	18" diameter	↓	15	1.067		254	69.50		323.50	385
3531	20" diameter	Q-10	16	1.500		264	101		365	445
3532	24" diameter	"	14	1.714	↓	275	116		391	480
3570	Bellows, lined									
3574	6" diameter	Q-9	30	.533	Ea.	1,775	34.50		1,809.50	2,000
3575	8" diameter		26	.615		1,825	40		1,865	2,075
3576	10" diameter		24	.667		1,850	43.50		1,893.50	2,100
3577	12" diameter		22	.727		1,900	47.50		1,947.50	2,150
3578	14" diameter		21	.762		1,525	49.50		1,574.50	1,750
3579	16" diameter		20	.800		1,975	52		2,027	2,250
3580	18" diameter	↓	19	.842		2,025	55		2,080	2,300
3581	20" diameter	Q-10	18	1.333		2,075	90		2,165	2,400
3590	For all 316 stainless steel construction, add				↓	55%				
3600	Ventilated roof thimble, 304 stainless steel									
3620	6" diameter	Q-9	26	.615	Ea.	310	40		350	400
3624	8" diameter		22	.727		300	47.50		347.50	400
3625	10" diameter		20	.800		300	52		352	410
3626	12" diameter		18	.889		340	58		398	460
3627	14" diameter		17	.941		360	61		421	485
3628	16" diameter		16	1		400	65		465	540
3629	18" diameter	↓	15	1.067		430	69.50		499.50	575
3630	20" diameter	Q-10	16	1.500		440	101		541	630
3631	24" diameter	"	14	1.714	↓	485	116		601	710
3650	For 316 stainless steel, add					30%				
3670	Exit cone, 316 stainless steel only									
3674	6" diameter	Q-9	46	.348	Ea.	227	22.50		249.50	284
3675	8" diameter		42	.381		233	25		258	294
3676	10" diameter		40	.400		230	26		256	292
3677	12" diameter		38	.421		262	27.50		289.50	330
3678	14" diameter		37	.432		258	28		286	325
3679	16" diameter		36	.444		287	29		316	360
3680	18" diameter	↓	35	.457		350	29.50		379.50	430

23 51 Breechings, Chimneys, and Stacks

23 51 26 – All-Fuel Vent Chimneys

23 51 26.10 All-Fuel Vent Chimneys, Press. Tight, Dbl. Wall

		Crew	Daily Output	Labor-Hours	Unit	Material	2024 Bare Costs Labor	Equipment	Total	Total Incl O&P
3681	20" diameter	Q-10	28	.857	Ea.	415	58		473	545
3682	24" diameter	"	26	.923		560	62		622	710
3720	Roof guide, 304 stainless steel									
3724	6" diameter	Q-9	25	.640	Ea.	114	41.50		155.50	188
3725	8" diameter		21	.762		132	49.50		181.50	220
3726	10" diameter		19	.842		145	55		200	242
3727	12" diameter		17	.941		150	61		211	257
3728	14" diameter		16	1		174	65		239	290
3729	16" diameter		15	1.067		184	69.50		253.50	305
3730	18" diameter		14	1.143		196	74.50		270.50	325
3731	20" diameter	Q-10	15	1.600		206	108		314	390
3732	24" diameter	"	13	1.846		215	124		339	425
3750	For 316 stainless steel, add					30%				
3770	Rain cap with bird screen									
3774	6" diameter	Q-9	46	.348	Ea.	345	22.50		367.50	415
3775	8" diameter		42	.381		400	25		425	480
3776	10" diameter		40	.400		470	26		496	555
3777	12" diameter		38	.421		540	27.50		567.50	635
3778	14" diameter		37	.432		625	28		653	735
3779	16" diameter		36	.444		710	29		739	830
3780	18" diameter		35	.457		810	29.50		839.50	935
3781	20" diameter	Q-10	28	.857		920	58		978	1,075
3782	24" diameter	"	26	.923		1,100	62		1,162	1,325

23 51 26.30 All-Fuel Vent Chimneys, Double Wall, St. Stl.

		Crew	Daily Output	Labor-Hours	Unit	Material	Labor	Equipment	Total	Total Incl O&P
0010	**ALL-FUEL VENT CHIMNEYS, DOUBLE WALL, STAINLESS STEEL**									
7780	All fuel, pressure tight, double wall, 4" insulation, UL listed, 1,400°F.									
7790	304 stainless steel liner, aluminized steel outer jacket									
7800	6" diameter	Q-9	60	.267	V.L.F.	63	17.35		80.35	95.50
7804	8" diameter		52	.308		91.50	20		111.50	131
7806	10" diameter		48	.333		105	21.50		126.50	148
7808	12" diameter		44	.364		122	23.50		145.50	170
7810	14" diameter		42	.381		137	25		162	188
7880	For 316 stainless steel liner, add				L.F.	30%				
8000	All fuel, double wall, stainless steel fittings									
8010	Roof support, 6" diameter	Q-9	30	.533	Ea.	141	34.50		175.50	208
8030	8" diameter		26	.615		149	40		189	223
8040	10" diameter		24	.667		177	43.50		220.50	260
8050	12" diameter		22	.727		186	47.50		233.50	276
8060	14" diameter		21	.762		200	49.50		249.50	295
8100	Elbow 45°, 6" diameter		30	.533		288	34.50		322.50	365
8140	8" diameter		26	.615		330	40		370	420
8160	10" diameter		24	.667		400	43.50		443.50	505
8180	12" diameter		22	.727		425	47.50		472.50	540
8200	14" diameter		21	.762		495	49.50		544.50	620
8300	Insulated tee, 6" diameter		30	.533		365	34.50		399.50	450
8360	8" diameter		26	.615		380	40		420	480
8380	10" diameter		24	.667		410	43.50		453.50	515
8400	12" diameter		22	.727		495	47.50		542.50	615
8420	14" diameter		20	.800		585	52		637	725
8500	Boot tee, 6" diameter		28	.571		825	37		862	960
8520	8" diameter		24	.667		880	43.50		923.50	1,025
8530	10" diameter		22	.727		995	47.50		1,042.50	1,175

23 51 Breechings, Chimneys, and Stacks

23 51 26 – All-Fuel Vent Chimneys

23 51 26.30 All-Fuel Vent Chimneys, Double Wall, St. Stl.

		Crew	Daily Output	Labor-Hours	Unit	Material	2024 Bare Costs Labor	Equipment	Total	Total Incl O&P
8540	12" diameter	Q-9	20	.800	Ea.	1,150	52		1,202	1,350
8550	14" diameter		18	.889		1,200	58		1,258	1,400
8600	Rain cap with bird screen, 6" diameter		30	.533		370	34.50		404.50	460
8640	8" diameter		26	.615		405	40		445	505
8660	10" diameter		24	.667		410	43.50		453.50	515
8680	12" diameter		22	.727		580	47.50		627.50	710
8700	14" diameter		21	.762		610	49.50		659.50	745
8800	Flat roof flashing, 6" diameter		30	.533		135	34.50		169.50	201
8840	8" diameter		26	.615		138	40		178	212
8860	10" diameter		24	.667		148	43.50		191.50	228
8880	12" diameter		22	.727		166	47.50		213.50	253
8900	14" diameter		21	.762		174	49.50		223.50	267

23 52 Heating Boilers

23 52 13 – Electric Boilers

23 52 13.10 Electric Boilers, ASME

			Crew	Daily Output	Labor-Hours	Unit	Material	2024 Bare Costs Labor	Equipment	Total	Total Incl O&P
0010	**ELECTRIC BOILERS, ASME**, Standard controls and trim	D3020-102									
1000	Steam, 6 KW, 20.5 MBH		Q-19	1.20	20	Ea.	4,625	1,375		6,000	7,150
1040	9 KW, 30.7 MBH			1.20	20		4,450	1,375		5,825	6,950
1060	18 KW, 61.4 MBH			1.20	20		4,575	1,375		5,950	7,075
1080	24 KW, 81.8 MBH			1.10	21.818		5,300	1,500		6,800	8,075
1120	36 KW, 123 MBH			1.10	21.818		5,875	1,500		7,375	8,700
2000	Hot water, 7.5 KW, 25.6 MBH			1.30	18.462		5,275	1,275		6,550	7,700
2020	15 KW, 51.2 MBH			1.30	18.462		5,575	1,275		6,850	8,025
2040	30 KW, 102 MBH			1.20	20		5,675	1,375		7,050	8,300
2060	45 KW, 164 MBH			1.20	20		5,550	1,375		6,925	8,150
2070	60 KW, 205 MBH			1.20	20		5,925	1,375		7,300	8,575
2080	75 KW, 256 MBH			1.10	21.818		6,275	1,500		7,775	9,150

23 52 16 – Condensing Boilers

23 52 16.24 Condensing Boilers

			Crew	Daily Output	Labor-Hours	Unit	Material	2024 Bare Costs Labor	Equipment	Total	Total Incl O&P
0010	**CONDENSING BOILERS**, Cast iron, high efficiency										
0020	Packaged with standard controls, circulator and trim										
0030	Intermittent (spark) pilot, natural or LP gas										
0040	Hot water, DOE MBH output (AFUE %)										
0100	42 MBH (84.0%)	G	Q-5	1.80	8.889	Ea.	2,100	605		2,705	3,225
0120	57 MBH (84.3%)	G		1.60	10		2,300	680		2,980	3,550
0140	85 MBH (84.0%)	G		1.40	11.429		2,575	775		3,350	3,975
0160	112 MBH (83.7%)	G		1.20	13.333		2,900	905		3,805	4,550
0180	140 MBH (83.3%)	G	Q-6	1.60	15		3,250	1,050		4,300	5,150
0200	167 MBH (83.0%)	G		1.40	17.143		4,000	1,200		5,200	6,200
0220	194 MBH (82.7%)	G		1.20	20		4,050	1,400		5,450	6,550

23 52 19 – Pulse Combustion Boilers

23 52 19.20 Pulse Type Combustion Boilers

			Crew	Daily Output	Labor-Hours	Unit	Material	2024 Bare Costs Labor	Equipment	Total	Total Incl O&P
0010	**PULSE TYPE COMBUSTION BOILERS**, High efficiency										
7990	Special feature gas fired boilers										
8000	Pulse combustion, standard controls/trim										
8010	Hot water, DOE MBH output (AFUE %)										
8030	71 MBH (95.2%)		Q-5	1.60	10	Ea.	4,025	680		4,705	5,425
8050	94 MBH (95.3%)	G		1.40	11.429		4,450	775		5,225	6,050
8080	139 MBH (95.6%)	G		1.20	13.333		5,000	905		5,905	6,850

23 52 Heating Boilers

23 52 19 – Pulse Combustion Boilers

23 52 19.20 Pulse Type Combustion Boilers		Crew	Daily Output	Labor-Hours	Unit	Material	2024 Bare Costs Labor	Equipment	Total	Total Incl O&P
8090	207 MBH (95.4%)	Q-5	1.16	13.793	Ea.	5,650	940		6,590	7,625
8120	270 MBH (96.4%)		1.12	14.286		7,825	970		8,795	10,100
8130	365 MBH (91.7%)		1.07	14.953		8,850	1,025		9,875	11,300

23 52 23 – Cast-Iron Boilers

23 52 23.20 Gas-Fired Boilers

		Crew	Daily Output	Labor-Hours	Unit	Material	Labor	Equipment	Total	Total Incl O&P
0010	**GAS-FIRED BOILERS**, Natural or propane, standard controls, packaged									
1000	Cast iron, with insulated jacket									
2000	Steam, gross output, 81 MBH	Q-7	1.40	22.857	Ea.	3,225	1,650		4,875	6,000
2020	102 MBH		1.30	24.615		2,675	1,775		4,450	5,550
2040	122 MBH		1	32		3,525	2,300		5,825	7,300
2060	163 MBH		.90	35.556		3,525	2,550		6,075	7,675
2080	203 MBH		.90	35.556		4,225	2,550		6,775	8,450
2100	240 MBH		.85	37.647		4,325	2,700		7,025	8,800
2120	280 MBH		.80	40		4,600	2,875		7,475	9,325
2140	320 MBH		.70	45.714		4,800	3,275		8,075	10,200
3000	Hot water, gross output, 80 MBH		1.46	21.918		3,325	1,575		4,900	6,000
3020	100 MBH		1.35	23.704		3,250	1,700		4,950	6,100
3040	122 MBH		1.10	29.091		3,525	2,100		5,625	6,975
3060	163 MBH		1	32		4,125	2,300		6,425	7,975
3080	203 MBH		1	32		4,825	2,300		7,125	8,725
3100	240 MBH		.95	33.684		4,950	2,425		7,375	9,050
3120	280 MBH		.90	35.556		3,850	2,550		6,400	8,050
3140	320 MBH		.80	40		4,225	2,875		7,100	8,925
7000	For tankless water heater, add					10%				
7050	For additional zone valves up to 312 MBH, add					205			205	225

23 52 23.40 Oil-Fired Boilers

		Crew	Daily Output	Labor-Hours	Unit	Material	Labor	Equipment	Total	Total Incl O&P
0010	**OIL-FIRED BOILERS**, Standard controls, flame retention burner, packaged									
1000	Cast iron, with insulated flush jacket									
2000	Steam, gross output, 109 MBH	Q-7	1.20	26.667	Ea.	2,550	1,925		4,475	5,650
2020	144 MBH		1.10	29.091		2,875	2,100		4,975	6,250
2040	173 MBH		1	32		3,250	2,300		5,550	7,000
2060	207 MBH		.90	35.556		3,475	2,550		6,025	7,625
3000	Hot water, same price as steam									
4000	For tankless coil in smaller sizes, add				Ea.	15%				

23 52 26 – Steel Boilers

23 52 26.40 Oil-Fired Boilers

		Crew	Daily Output	Labor-Hours	Unit	Material	Labor	Equipment	Total	Total Incl O&P
0010	**OIL-FIRED BOILERS**, Standard controls, flame retention burner									
5000	Steel, with insulated flush jacket									
7000	Hot water, gross output, 103 MBH	Q-6	1.60	15	Ea.	2,275	1,050		3,325	4,075
7020	122 MBH		1.45	16.506		2,175	1,175		3,350	4,100
7040	137 MBH		1.36	17.595		2,925	1,250		4,175	5,075
7060	168 MBH		1.30	18.405		2,875	1,300		4,175	5,075
7080	225 MBH		1.22	19.704		4,400	1,400		5,800	6,925
7340	For tankless coil in steam or hot water, add					7%				

23 52 28 – Swimming Pool Boilers

23 52 28.10 Swimming Pool Heaters

		Crew	Daily Output	Labor-Hours	Unit	Material	Labor	Equipment	Total	Total Incl O&P
0010	**SWIMMING POOL HEATERS**, Not including wiring, external									
0020	piping, base or pad									
0160	Gas fired, input, 155 MBH	Q-6	1.50	16	Ea.	1,900	1,125		3,025	3,775
0200	199 MBH		1	24		2,050	1,700		3,750	4,800
0220	250 MBH		.70	34.286		2,250	2,425		4,675	6,075

23 52 Heating Boilers

23 52 28 – Swimming Pool Boilers

23 52 28.10 Swimming Pool Heaters

		Crew	Daily Output	Labor-Hours	Unit	Material	2024 Bare Costs Labor	Equipment	Total	Total Incl O&P
0240	300 MBH	Q-6	.60	40	Ea.	2,350	2,825		5,175	6,775
0260	399 MBH		.50	48		2,650	3,375		6,025	7,925
0280	500 MBH		.40	60		7,550	4,225		11,775	14,600
0300	650 MBH		.35	68.571		8,025	4,825		12,850	16,000
0320	750 MBH		.33	72.727		8,775	5,125		13,900	17,300
0360	990 MBH		.22	109		11,800	7,700		19,500	24,300
0370	1,260 MBH		.21	114		18,100	8,050		26,150	31,900
0380	1,440 MBH		.19	126		20,000	8,900		28,900	35,300
0400	1,800 MBH		.14	171		21,300	12,100		33,400	41,500
0410	2,070 MBH	↓	.13	185		25,200	13,000		38,200	47,100
2000	Electric, 12 KW, 4,800 gallon pool	Q-19	3	8		3,025	555		3,580	4,150
2020	15 KW, 7,200 gallon pool		2.80	8.571		3,250	595		3,845	4,450
2040	24 KW, 9,600 gallon pool		2.40	10		3,650	690		4,340	5,025
2060	30 KW, 12,000 gallon pool		2	12		3,700	830		4,530	5,300
2080	36 KW, 14,400 gallon pool		1.60	15		4,325	1,050		5,375	6,300
2100	57 KW, 24,000 gallon pool	↓	1.20	20	↓	5,400	1,375		6,775	7,975
9000	To select pool heater: 12 BTUH x S.F. pool area									
9010	X temperature differential = required output									
9050	For electric, KW = gallons x 2.5 divided by 1,000									
9100	For family home type pool, double the									
9110	Rated gallon capacity = 1/2°F rise per hour									

23 52 88 – Burners

23 52 88.10 Replacement Type Burners

		Crew	Daily Output	Labor-Hours	Unit	Material	2024 Bare Costs Labor	Equipment	Total	Total Incl O&P
0010	**REPLACEMENT TYPE BURNERS**									
0990	Residential, conversion, gas fired, LP or natural									
1000	Gun type, atmospheric input 50 to 225 MBH	Q-1	2.50	6.400	Ea.	1,725	430		2,155	2,550
1020	100 to 400 MBH	"	2	8	"	2,875	535		3,410	3,950
3000	Flame retention oil fired assembly, input									
3020	.50 to 2.25 GPH	Q-1	2.40	6.667	Ea.	370	450		820	1,075
3040	2.0 to 5.0 GPH	"	2	8		345	535		880	1,175
4600	Gas safety, shut off valve, 3/4" threaded	1 Stpi	20	.400		197	30		227	262
4610	1" threaded		19	.421		191	32		223	258
4620	1-1/4" threaded		15	.533		215	40.50		255.50	296
4630	1-1/2" threaded		13	.615		232	46.50		278.50	325
4640	2" threaded	↓	11	.727		260	55		315	370
4650	2-1/2" threaded	Q-1	15	1.067		298	71.50		369.50	430
4660	3" threaded		13	1.231		590	82.50		672.50	775
4670	4" flanged	↓	3	5.333		2,925	360		3,285	3,725
4680	6" flanged	Q-2	3	8	↓	6,500	555		7,055	8,000

23 54 Furnaces

23 54 16 – Fuel-Fired Furnaces

23 54 16.14 Condensing Furnaces

		Crew	Daily Output	Labor-Hours	Unit	Material	2024 Bare Costs Labor	Equipment	Total	Total Incl O&P
0010	**CONDENSING FURNACES**, High efficiency									
0020	Oil fired, packaged, complete									
0030	Upflow									
0040	Output @ 95% A.F.U.E.									
0100	49 MBH @ 1,000 CFM	Q-9	3.70	4.324	Ea.	7,875	281		8,156	9,075
0110	73.5 MBH @ 2,000 CFM		3.60	4.444		8,225	289		8,514	9,475
0120	96 MBH @ 2,000 CFM	↓	3.40	4.706	↓	8,225	305		8,530	9,500

23 54 Furnaces

23 54 16 – Fuel-Fired Furnaces

23 54 16.14 Condensing Furnaces

		Crew	Daily Output	Labor-Hours	Unit	Material	2024 Bare Costs Labor	2024 Bare Costs Equipment	Total	Total Incl O&P
0130	115.6 MBH @ 2,000 CFM	Q-9	3.40	4.706	Ea.	8,225	305		8,530	9,500
0140	147 MBH @ 2,000 CFM		3.30	4.848		18,800	315		19,115	21,200
0150	192 MBH @ 4,000 CFM		2.60	6.154		19,500	400		19,900	22,000
0170	231.5 MBH @ 4,000 CFM		2.30	6.957		19,500	450		19,950	22,100
0260	For variable speed motor, add					765			765	840
0270	Note: Also available in horizontal, counterflow and lowboy configurations.									

23 55 Fuel-Fired Heaters

23 55 23 – Gas-Fired Radiant Heaters

23 55 23.10 Infrared Type Heating Units

		Crew	Daily Output	Labor-Hours	Unit	Material	2024 Bare Costs Labor	2024 Bare Costs Equipment	Total	Total Incl O&P
0010	**INFRARED TYPE HEATING UNITS**									
0020	Gas fired, unvented, electric ignition, 100% shutoff.									
0030	Piping and wiring not included									
0100	Input, 30 MBH	Q-5	6	2.667	Ea.	1,550	181		1,731	1,975
0120	45 MBH		5	3.200		1,450	218		1,668	1,900
0140	50 MBH		4.50	3.556		1,475	242		1,717	1,975
0160	60 MBH		4	4		2,050	272		2,322	2,650
0180	75 MBH		3	5.333		1,475	365		1,840	2,175
0200	90 MBH		2.50	6.400		2,150	435		2,585	3,000
0220	105 MBH		2	8		2,150	545		2,695	3,150
0240	120 MBH		2	8		2,575	545		3,120	3,625
1000	Gas fired, vented, electric ignition, tubular									
1020	Piping and wiring not included, 20' to 80' lengths									
1030	Single stage, input, 60 MBH	Q-6	4.50	5.333	Ea.	1,950	375		2,325	2,700
1040	80 MBH		3.90	6.154		1,850	435		2,285	2,675
1050	100 MBH		3.40	7.059		1,975	500		2,475	2,925
1060	125 MBH		2.90	8.276		1,875	585		2,460	2,950
1070	150 MBH		2.70	8.889		2,550	625		3,175	3,725
1080	170 MBH		2.50	9.600		1,800	675		2,475	2,975
1090	200 MBH		2.20	10.909		2,525	770		3,295	3,925
1100	Note: Final pricing may vary due to									
1110	tube length and configuration package selected									
1130	Two stage, input, 60 MBH high, 45 MBH low	Q-6	4.50	5.333	Ea.	2,250	375		2,625	3,025
1140	80 MBH high, 60 MBH low		3.90	6.154		2,250	435		2,685	3,125
1150	100 MBH high, 65 MBH low		3.40	7.059		2,250	500		2,750	3,225
1160	125 MBH high, 95 MBH low		2.90	8.276		2,275	585		2,860	3,375
1170	150 MBH high, 100 MBH low		2.70	8.889		2,275	625		2,900	3,425
1180	170 MBH high, 125 MBH low		2.50	9.600		2,525	675		3,200	3,775
1190	200 MBH high, 150 MBH low		2.20	10.909		3,375	770		4,145	4,875
1220	Note: Final pricing may vary due to									
1230	tube length and configuration package selected									

23 56 Solar Energy Heating Equipment

23 56 16 – Packaged Solar Heating Equipment

23 56 16.40 Solar Heating Systems

			Crew	Daily Output	Labor-Hours	Unit	Material	2024 Bare Costs Labor	Equipment	Total	Total Incl O&P
0010	**SOLAR HEATING SYSTEMS**	D2020-265									
0020	System/package prices, not including connecting										
0030	pipe, insulation, or special heating/plumbing fixtures	D2020-270									
0152	For solar ultraviolet pipe insulation see Section 22 07 19.10										
0500	Hot water, standard package, low temperature	D2020-275									
0540	1 collector, circulator, fittings, 65 gal. tank	G	Q-1	.50	32	Ea.	5,650	2,150		7,800	9,425
0580	2 collectors, circulator, fittings, 120 gal. tank	D2020-280 G		.40	40		5,650	2,675		8,325	10,200
0620	3 collectors, circulator, fittings, 120 gal. tank	G		.34	47.059		9,050	3,150		12,200	14,700
0700	Medium temperature package	D2020-285									
0720	1 collector, circulator, fittings, 80 gal. tank	G	Q-1	.50	32	Ea.	5,300	2,150		7,450	9,050
0740	2 collectors, circulator, fittings, 120 gal. tank	D2020-290 G		.40	40		8,450	2,675		11,125	13,300
0780	3 collectors, circulator, fittings, 120 gal. tank	G		.30	53.333		9,200	3,575		12,775	15,400
0980	For each additional 120 gal. tank, add	D2020-295 G					1,850			1,850	2,050

23 56 19 – Solar Heating Components

23 56 19.50 Solar Heating Ancillary

			Crew	Daily Output	Labor-Hours	Unit	Material	Labor	Equipment	Total	Total Incl O&P
0010	**SOLAR HEATING ANCILLARY**										
2300	Circulators, air	D3010-650									
2310	Blowers										
2330	100-300 S.F. system, 1/10 HP	D3010-660 G	Q-9	16	1	Ea.	279	65		344	405
2340	300-500 S.F. system, 1/5 HP	G		15	1.067		370	69.50		439.50	515
2350	Two speed, 100-300 S.F., 1/10 HP	D3010-675 G		14	1.143		152	74.50		226.50	280
2400	Reversible fan, 20" diameter, 2 speed	G		18	.889		120	58		178	219
2550	Booster fan 6" diameter, 120 CFM	G		16	1		39	65		104	141
2570	6" diameter, 225 CFM	G		16	1		48	65		113	151
2580	8" diameter, 150 CFM	G		16	1		44	65		109	147
2590	8" diameter, 310 CFM	G		14	1.143		67.50	74.50		142	187
2600	8" diameter, 425 CFM	G		14	1.143		76	74.50		150.50	196
2650	Rheostat	G		32	.500		16.50	32.50		49	67
2660	Shutter/damper	G		12	1.333		61	86.50		147.50	197
2670	Shutter motor	G		16	1		152	65		217	265
2800	Circulators, liquid, 1/25 HP, 5.3 GPM	G	Q-1	14	1.143		215	77		292	350
2820	1/20 HP, 17 GPM	G		12	1.333		320	89.50		409.50	485
2850	1/20 HP, 17 GPM, stainless steel	G		12	1.333		271	89.50		360.50	430
2870	1/12 HP, 30 GPM	G		10	1.600		370	107		477	565
3000	Collector panels, air with aluminum absorber plate										
3010	Wall or roof mount										
3040	Flat black, plastic glazing										
3080	4' x 8'	G	Q-9	6	2.667	Ea.	710	173		883	1,050
3100	4' x 10'	G		5	3.200	"	870	208		1,078	1,275
3200	Flush roof mount, 10' to 16' x 22" wide	G		96	.167	L.F.	188	10.85		198.85	223
3210	Manifold, by L.F. width of collectors	G		160	.100	"	155	6.50		161.50	181
3300	Collector panels, liquid with copper absorber plate										
3320	Black chrome, tempered glass glazing										
3330	Alum. frame, 4' x 8', 5/32" single glazing	G	Q-1	9.50	1.684	Ea.	1,075	113		1,188	1,375
3390	Alum. frame, 4' x 10', 5/32" single glazing	G		6	2.667		1,250	179		1,429	1,650
3450	Flat black, alum. frame, 3.5' x 7.5'	G		9	1.778		790	119		909	1,050
3500	4' x 8'	G		5.50	2.909		955	195		1,150	1,350
3520	4' x 10'	G		10	1.600		1,175	107		1,282	1,450
3540	4' x 12.5'	G		5	3.200		1,300	215		1,515	1,750
3550	Liquid with fin tube absorber plate										
3560	Alum. frame 4' x 8' tempered glass	G	Q-1	10	1.600	Ea.	600	107		707	820
3580	Liquid with vacuum tubes, 4' x 6'-10"	G		9	1.778		980	119		1,099	1,250

23 56 Solar Energy Heating Equipment

23 56 19 – Solar Heating Components

23 56 19.50 Solar Heating Ancillary

		Crew	Daily Output	Labor-Hours	Unit	Material	2024 Bare Costs Labor	Equipment	Total	Total Incl O&P
3600	Liquid, full wetted, plastic, alum. frame, 4' x 10'	G Q-1	5	3.200	Ea.	340	215		555	695
3650	Collector panel mounting, flat roof or ground rack	G	7	2.286		275	154		429	530
3670	Roof clamps	G	70	.229	Set	3.68	15.35		19.03	27
3700	Roof strap, teflon	G 1 Plum	205	.039	L.F.	35	2.91		37.91	43
3900	Differential controller with two sensors									
3930	Thermostat, hard wired	G 1 Plum	8	1	Ea.	119	74.50		193.50	241
3950	Line cord and receptacle	G	12	.667		249	50		299	350
4050	Pool valve system	G	2.50	3.200		199	239		438	575
4070	With 12 VAC actuator	G	2	4		340	299		639	820
4080	Pool pump system, 2" pipe size	G	6	1.333		206	99.50		305.50	375
4100	Five station with digital read-out	G	3	2.667		287	199		486	610
4150	Sensors									
4200	Brass plug, 1/2" MPT	G 1 Plum	32	.250	Ea.	15.85	18.65		34.50	45.50
4210	Brass plug, reversed	G	32	.250		30.50	18.65		49.15	62
4220	Freeze prevention	G	32	.250		27	18.65		45.65	57.50
4240	Screw attached	G	32	.250		19.50	18.65		38.15	49.50
4250	Brass, immersion	G	32	.250		19.50	18.65		38.15	49.50
4300	Heat exchanger									
4315	includes coil, blower, circulator									
4316	and controller for DHW and space hot air									
4330	Fluid to air coil, up flow, 45 MBH	G Q-1	4	4	Ea.	345	269		614	780
4380	70 MBH	G	3.50	4.571		390	305		695	885
4400	80 MBH	G	3	5.333		515	360		875	1,100
4580	Fluid to fluid package includes two circulating pumps									
4590	expansion tank, check valve, relief valve									
4600	controller, high temperature cutoff and sensors	G Q-1	2.50	6.400	Ea.	810	430		1,240	1,525
4650	Heat transfer fluid									
4700	Propylene glycol, inhibited anti-freeze	G 1 Plum	28	.286	Gal.	27.50	21.50		49	61.50
4800	Solar storage tanks, knocked down									
4810	Air, galvanized steel clad, double wall, 4" fiberglass insulation									
5120	45 mil reinforced polypropylene lining,									
5140	4' high, 4' x 4' = 64 C.F./450 gallons	G Q-9	2	8	Ea.	3,075	520		3,595	4,150
5150	4' x 8' = 128 C.F./900 gallons	G	1.50	10.667		4,900	695		5,595	6,450
5160	4' x 12' = 190 C.F./1,300 gallons	G	1.30	12.308		6,150	800		6,950	7,975
5170	8' x 8' = 250 C.F./1,700 gallons	G	1	16		7,800	1,050		8,850	10,200
5190	6'-3" high, 7' x 7' = 306 C.F./2,000 gallons	G Q-10	1.20	20		14,400	1,350		15,750	17,800
5200	7' x 10'-6" = 459 C.F./3,000 gallons	G	.80	30		17,900	2,025		19,925	22,800
5210	7' x 14' = 613 C.F./4,000 gallons	G	.60	40		22,800	2,700		25,500	29,200
5220	10'-6" x 10'-6" = 689 C.F./4,500 gallons	G	.50	48		21,500	3,225		24,725	28,500
5230	10'-6" x 14' = 919 C.F./6,000 gallons	G	.40	60		25,000	4,050		29,050	33,600
5240	14' x 14' = 1,225 C.F./8,000 gallons	G Q-11	.40	80		30,000	5,500		35,500	41,300
5250	14' x 17'-6" = 1,531 C.F./10,000 gallons	G	.30	107		32,400	7,325		39,725	46,700
5260	17'-6" x 17'-6" = 1,914 C.F./12,500 gallons	G	.25	128		44,500	8,800		53,300	62,000
5270	17'-6" x 21' = 2,297 C.F./15,000 gallons	G	.20	160		41,700	11,000		52,700	62,500
5280	21' x 21' = 2,756 C.F./18,000 gallons	G	.18	178		44,100	12,200		56,300	67,000
5290	30 mil reinforced Hypalon lining, add					.02%				
7000	Solar control valves and vents									
7050	Air purger, 1" pipe size	G 1 Plum	12	.667	Ea.	54	50		104	134
7070	Air eliminator, automatic 3/4" size	G	32	.250		32	18.65		50.65	63
7090	Air vent, automatic, 1/8" fitting	G	32	.250		16.45	18.65		35.10	46
7100	Manual, 1/8" NPT	G	32	.250		3.41	18.65		22.06	32
7120	Backflow preventer, 1/2" pipe size	G	16	.500		91.50	37.50		129	157
7130	3/4" pipe size	G	16	.500		76.50	37.50		114	140

23 56 Solar Energy Heating Equipment

23 56 19 – Solar Heating Components

23 56 19.50 Solar Heating Ancillary

		Crew	Daily Output	Labor-Hours	Unit	Material	2024 Bare Costs Labor	2024 Bare Costs Equipment	Total	Total Incl O&P
7150	Balancing valve, 3/4" pipe size G	1 Plum	20	.400	Ea.	57.50	30		87.50	108
7180	Draindown valve, 1/2" copper tube G		9	.889		226	66.50		292.50	350
7200	Flow control valve, 1/2" pipe size G		22	.364		147	27		174	203
7220	Expansion tank, up to 5 gal. G		32	.250		67.50	18.65		86.15	103
7250	Hydronic controller (aquastat) G		8	1		227	74.50		301.50	360
7400	Pressure gauge, 2" dial G		32	.250		26	18.65		44.65	56.50
7450	Relief valve, temp. and pressure 3/4" pipe size G		30	.267		27.50	19.90		47.40	59.50
7500	Solenoid valve, normally closed									
7520	Brass, 3/4" NPT, 24V G	1 Plum	9	.889	Ea.	178	66.50		244.50	295
7530	1" NPT, 24V G		9	.889		281	66.50		347.50	410
7750	Vacuum relief valve, 3/4" pipe size G		32	.250		32	18.65		50.65	63
7800	Thermometers									
7820	Digital temperature monitoring, 4 locations G	1 Plum	2.50	3.200	Ea.	172	239		411	545
7900	Upright, 1/2" NPT G		8	1		59	74.50		133.50	176
7970	Remote probe, 2" dial G		8	1		36	74.50		110.50	151
7990	Stem, 2" dial, 9" stem G		16	.500		23.50	37.50		61	81.50
8250	Water storage tank with heat exchanger and electric element									
8270	66 gal. with 2" x 2 lb. density insulation G	1 Plum	1.60	5	Ea.	2,150	375		2,525	2,925
8300	80 gal. with 2" x 2 lb. density insulation G		1.60	5		1,850	375		2,225	2,575
8380	120 gal. with 2" x 2 lb. density insulation G		1.40	5.714		1,800	425		2,225	2,600
8400	120 gal. with 2" x 2 lb. density insul., 40 S.F. heat coil G		1.40	5.714		2,675	425		3,100	3,575
8500	Water storage module, plastic									
8600	Tubular, 12" diameter, 4' high G	1 Carp	48	.167	Ea.	104	10.10		114.10	130
8610	12" diameter, 8' high G		40	.200		164	12.10		176.10	199
8620	18" diameter, 5' high G		38	.211		184	12.75		196.75	222
8630	18" diameter, 10' high G		32	.250		270	15.15		285.15	320
8640	58" diameter, 5' high G	2 Carp	32	.500		885	30.50		915.50	1,025
8650	Cap, 12" diameter G					21			21	23
8660	18" diameter G					26.50			26.50	29

23 57 Heat Exchangers for HVAC

23 57 16 – Steam-to-Water Heat Exchangers

23 57 16.10 Shell/Tube Type Steam-to-Water Heat Exch.

		Crew	Daily Output	Labor-Hours	Unit	Material	Labor	Equipment	Total	Total Incl O&P
0010	**SHELL AND TUBE TYPE STEAM-TO-WATER HEAT EXCHANGERS**									
0016	Shell & tube type, 2 or 4 pass, 3/4" OD copper tubes,									
0020	C.I. heads, C.I. tube sheet, steel shell									
0100	Hot water 40°F to 180°F, by steam at 10 psi									
0120	8 GPM	Q-5	6	2.667	Ea.	2,750	181		2,931	3,300
0140	10 GPM		5	3.200		4,125	218		4,343	4,875
0160	40 GPM		4	4		6,375	272		6,647	7,425
0500	For bronze head and tube sheet, add					50%				

23 57 19 – Liquid-to-Liquid Heat Exchangers

23 57 19.13 Plate-Type, Liquid-to-Liquid Heat Exchangers

		Crew	Daily Output	Labor-Hours	Unit	Material	Labor	Equipment	Total	Total Incl O&P
0010	**PLATE-TYPE, LIQUID-TO-LIQUID HEAT EXCHANGERS**									
3000	Plate type,									
3100	400 GPM	Q-6	.80	30	Ea.	47,100	2,125		49,225	55,000
3120	800 GPM	"	.50	48		81,000	3,375		84,375	94,500
3140	1,200 GPM	Q-7	.34	94.118		120,500	6,775		127,275	143,000
3160	1,800 GPM	"	.24	133		160,000	9,575		169,575	190,500

23 57 Heat Exchangers for HVAC

23 57 19 – Liquid-to-Liquid Heat Exchangers

23 57 19.16 Shell-Type, Liquid-to-Liquid Heat Exchangers

		Crew	Daily Output	Labor-Hours	Unit	Material	2024 Bare Costs Labor	Equipment	Total	Total Incl O&P
0010	**SHELL-TYPE, LIQUID-TO-LIQUID HEAT EXCHANGERS**									
1000	Hot water 40°F to 140°F, by water at 200°F									
1020	7 GPM	Q-5	6	2.667	Ea.	12,200	181		12,381	13,800
1040	16 GPM		5	3.200		18,000	218		18,218	20,100
1060	34 GPM		4	4		26,700	272		26,972	29,700
1080	55 GPM		3	5.333		37,900	365		38,265	42,200
1100	74 GPM		1.50	10.667		48,900	725		49,625	55,000
1120	86 GPM		1.40	11.429		64,000	775		64,775	71,500
1140	112 GPM	Q-6	2	12		79,500	845		80,345	89,000
1160	126 GPM		1.80	13.333		99,500	940		100,440	111,000
1180	152 GPM		1	24		38,900	1,700		40,600	45,300

23 72 Air-to-Air Energy Recovery Equipment

23 72 16 – Heat-Pipe Air-To-Air Energy-Recovery Equipment

23 72 16.10 Heat Pipes

		Crew	Daily Output	Labor-Hours	Unit	Material	Labor	Equipment	Total	Total Incl O&P
0010	**HEAT PIPES**									
8000	Heat pipe type, glycol, 50% efficient									
8010	100 MBH, 1,700 CFM	1 Stpi	.80	10	Ea.	4,775	755		5,530	6,375
8020	160 MBH, 2,700 CFM		.60	13.333		6,425	1,000		7,425	8,550
8030	620 MBH, 4,000 CFM		.40	20		9,675	1,500		11,175	13,000

23 81 Decentralized Unitary HVAC Equipment

23 81 13 – Packaged Terminal Air-Conditioners

23 81 13.10 Packaged Cabinet Type Air-Conditioners

		Crew	Daily Output	Labor-Hours	Unit	Material	Labor	Equipment	Total	Total Incl O&P
0010	**PACKAGED CABINET TYPE AIR-CONDITIONERS**, Cabinet, wall sleeve,									
0100	louver, electric heat, thermostat, manual changeover, 208 V									
0200	6,000 BTUH cooling, 8,800 BTU heat	Q-5	6	2.667	Ea.	1,175	181		1,356	1,575
0220	9,000 BTUH cooling, 13,900 BTU heat		5	3.200		3,475	218		3,693	4,150
0240	12,000 BTUH cooling, 13,900 BTU heat		4	4		3,975	272		4,247	4,775
0260	15,000 BTUH cooling, 13,900 BTU heat		3	5.333		1,925	365		2,290	2,675

23 81 19 – Self-Contained Air-Conditioners

23 81 19.10 Window Unit Air Conditioners

		Crew	Daily Output	Labor-Hours	Unit	Material	Labor	Equipment	Total	Total Incl O&P
0010	**WINDOW UNIT AIR CONDITIONERS**									
4000	Portable/window, 15 amp, 125 V grounded receptacle required									
4060	5,000 BTUH	1 Carp	8	1	Ea.	355	60.50		415.50	480
4340	6,000 BTUH		8	1		360	60.50		420.50	490
4480	8,000 BTUH		6	1.333		435	80.50		515.50	600
4500	10,000 BTUH		6	1.333		535	80.50		615.50	710
4520	12,000 BTUH	L-2	8	2		760	107		867	995
4600	Window/thru-the-wall, 15 amp, 230 V grounded receptacle required									
4780	18,000 BTUH	L-2	6	2.667	Ea.	1,175	143		1,318	1,525
4940	25,000 BTUH		4	4		2,475	215		2,690	3,050
4960	29,000 BTUH		4	4		1,500	215		1,715	1,975

23 81 Decentralized Unitary HVAC Equipment

23 81 43 – Air-Source Unitary Heat Pumps

23 81 43.10 Air-Source Heat Pumps

		Crew	Daily Output	Labor-Hours	Unit	Material	2024 Bare Costs Labor	Equipment	Total	Total Incl O&P
0010	**AIR-SOURCE HEAT PUMPS**, Not including interconnecting tubing									
1000	Air to air, split system, not including curbs, pads, fan coil and ductwork									
1010	For curbs/pads see Section 23 91 10									
1012	Outside condensing unit only, for fan coil see Section 23 82 19.10									
1015	1.5 ton cooling, 7 MBH heat @ 0°F	Q-5	2.40	6.667	Ea.	1,625	455		2,080	2,450
1020	2 ton cooling, 8.5 MBH heat @ 0°F		2	8		1,750	545		2,295	2,725
1030	2.5 ton cooling, 10 MBH heat @ 0°F		1.60	10		1,950	680		2,630	3,125
1040	3 ton cooling, 13 MBH heat @ 0°F		1.20	13.333		2,150	905		3,055	3,725
1050	3.5 ton cooling, 18 MBH heat @ 0°F		1	16		2,300	1,100		3,400	4,150
1054	4 ton cooling, 24 MBH heat @ 0°F		.80	20		2,475	1,350		3,825	4,750
1060	5 ton cooling, 27 MBH heat @ 0°F		.50	32		2,700	2,175		4,875	6,225
1500	Single package, not including curbs, pads, or plenums									
1502	0.5 ton cooling, supplementary heat included	Q-5	8	2	Ea.	3,025	136		3,161	3,525
1504	0.75 ton cooling, supplementary heat included		6	2.667		3,200	181		3,381	3,775
1506	1 ton cooling, supplementary heat included		4	4		4,125	272		4,397	4,950
1510	1.5 ton cooling, 5 MBH heat @ 0°F		1.55	10.323		3,625	700		4,325	5,025
1520	2 ton cooling, 6.5 MBH heat @ 0°F		1.50	10.667		3,675	725		4,400	5,100
1540	2.5 ton cooling, 8 MBH heat @ 0°F		1.40	11.429		3,550	775		4,325	5,050
1560	3 ton cooling, 10 MBH heat @ 0°F		1.20	13.333		4,075	905		4,980	5,850
1570	3.5 ton cooling, 11 MBH heat @ 0°F		1	16		4,525	1,100		5,625	6,625
1580	4 ton cooling, 13 MBH heat @ 0°F		.96	16.667		4,875	1,125		6,000	7,050
1620	5 ton cooling, 27 MBH heat @ 0°F		.65	24.615		5,525	1,675		7,200	8,575
1640	7.5 ton cooling, 35 MBH heat @ 0°F		.40	40		8,475	2,725		11,200	13,400
6000	Air to water, single package, excluding storage tank and ductwork									
6010	Includes circulating water pump, air duct connections, digital temperature									
6020	controller with remote tank temp. probe and sensor for storage tank.									
6040	Water heating - air cooling capacity									
6110	35.5 MBH heat water, 2.3 ton cool air	Q-5	1.60	10	Ea.	18,400	680		19,080	21,300
6120	58 MBH heat water, 3.8 ton cool air		1.10	14.545		21,000	990		21,990	24,600
6130	76 MBH heat water, 4.9 ton cool air		.87	18.391		25,100	1,250		26,350	29,500
6140	98 MBH heat water, 6.5 ton cool air		.62	25.806		32,400	1,750		34,150	38,200
6150	113 MBH heat water, 7.4 ton cool air		.59	27.119		35,500	1,850		37,350	41,900
6160	142 MBH heat water, 9.2 ton cool air		.52	30.769		43,100	2,100		45,200	50,500
6170	171 MBH heat water, 11.1 ton cool air		.49	32.653		50,500	2,225		52,725	59,500

23 81 46 – Water-Source Unitary Heat Pumps

23 81 46.10 Water Source Heat Pumps

		Crew	Daily Output	Labor-Hours	Unit	Material	Labor	Equipment	Total	Total Incl O&P
0010	**WATER SOURCE HEAT PUMPS**, Not incl. connecting tubing or water source									
2000	Water source to air, single package									
2100	1 ton cooling, 13 MBH heat @ 75°F	Q-5	2	8	Ea.	2,300	545		2,845	3,325
2120	1.5 ton cooling, 17 MBH heat @ 75°F		1.80	8.889		2,100	605		2,705	3,225
2140	2 ton cooling, 19 MBH heat @ 75°F		1.70	9.412		2,525	640		3,165	3,725
2160	2.5 ton cooling, 25 MBH heat @ 75°F		1.60	10		7,050	680		7,730	8,750
2180	3 ton cooling, 27 MBH heat @ 75°F		1.40	11.429		7,325	775		8,100	9,200
2190	3.5 ton cooling, 29 MBH heat @ 75°F		1.30	12.308		3,050	835		3,885	4,625
2200	4 ton cooling, 31 MBH heat @ 75°F		1.20	13.333		3,525	905		4,430	5,225
2220	5 ton cooling, 29 MBH heat @ 75°F		.90	17.778		3,675	1,200		4,875	5,850
3960	For supplementary heat coil, add					10%				

23 82 Convection Heating and Cooling Units

23 82 19 – Fan Coil Units

23 82 19.10 Fan Coil Air Conditioning

		Crew	Daily Output	Labor-Hours	Unit	Material	2024 Bare Costs Labor	2024 Bare Costs Equipment	Total	Total Incl O&P
0010	**FAN COIL AIR CONDITIONING**									
0030	Fan coil AC, cabinet mounted, filters and controls									
0320	1 ton cooling	Q-5	6	2.667	Ea.	2,125	181		2,306	2,625
0940	Direct expansion, for use w/air cooled condensing unit, 1-1/2 ton cooling		5	3.200		825	218		1,043	1,225
0950	2 ton cooling		4.80	3.333		805	227		1,032	1,225
0960	2-1/2 ton cooling		4.40	3.636		945	247		1,192	1,425
0970	3 ton cooling		3.80	4.211		1,150	286		1,436	1,700
0980	3-1/2 ton cooling		3.60	4.444		1,175	300		1,475	1,750
0990	4 ton cooling		3.40	4.706		1,150	320		1,470	1,725
1000	5 ton cooling		3	5.333		1,475	365		1,840	2,175
1500	For hot water coil, add					40%	10%			

23 82 29 – Radiators

23 82 29.10 Hydronic Heating

		Crew	Daily Output	Labor-Hours	Unit	Material	Labor	Equipment	Total	Total Incl O&P
0010	**HYDRONIC HEATING**, Terminal units, not incl. main supply pipe									
1000	Radiation									
1100	Panel, baseboard, C.I., including supports, no covers	Q-5	46	.348	L.F.	73	23.50		96.50	115
3000	Radiators, cast iron									
3100	Free standing or wall hung, 6 tube, 25" high	Q-5	96	.167	Section	70.50	11.35		81.85	94.50
3150	4 tube, 25" high		96	.167		52.50	11.35		63.85	75
3200	4 tube, 19" high		96	.167		49	11.35		60.35	71
3250	Adj. brackets, 2 per wall radiator up to 30 sections	1 Stpi	32	.250	Ea.	64	18.90		82.90	98.50
3500	Recessed, 20" high x 5" deep, without grille	Q-5	60	.267	Section	58	18.15		76.15	91
3525	Free standing or wall hung, 30" high	"	60	.267		49.50	18.15		67.65	81
3600	For inlet grille, add					6.90			6.90	7.55
9500	To convert SFR to BTU rating: Hot water, 150 x SFR									
9510	Forced hot water, 180 x SFR; steam, 240 x SFR									

23 82 33 – Convectors

23 82 33.10 Convector Units

		Crew	Daily Output	Labor-Hours	Unit	Material	Labor	Equipment	Total	Total Incl O&P
0010	**CONVECTOR UNITS**, Terminal units, not incl. main supply pipe									
2204	Convector, multifin, 2 pipe w/cabinet									
2210	17" H x 24" L	Q-5	10	1.600	Ea.	117	109		226	290
2214	17" H x 36" L		8.60	1.860		175	127		302	380
2218	17" H x 48" L		7.40	2.162		233	147		380	475
2222	21" H x 24" L		9	1.778		130	121		251	325
2228	21" H x 48" L		6.80	2.353		261	160		421	525
2240	For knob operated damper, add					140%				
2241	For metal trim strips, add	Q-5	64	.250	Ea.	6.55	17		23.55	32.50
2243	For snap-on inlet grille, add					10%	10%			
2245	For hinged access door, add	Q-5	64	.250	Ea.	42	17		59	71.50
2246	For air chamber, auto-venting, add	"	58	.276	"	9.10	18.75		27.85	38

23 82 36 – Finned-Tube Radiation Heaters

23 82 36.10 Finned Tube Radiation

		Crew	Daily Output	Labor-Hours	Unit	Material	Labor	Equipment	Total	Total Incl O&P
0010	**FINNED TUBE RADIATION**, Terminal units, not incl. main supply pipe									
1310	Baseboard, pkgd, 1/2" copper tube, alum. fin, 7" high	Q-5	60	.267	L.F.	12.40	18.15		30.55	40.50
1320	3/4" copper tube, alum. fin, 7" high	"	58	.276	"	8.25	18.75		27	37
1381	Rough in baseboard panel & fin tube, supply & balance valves	1 Stpi	1.06	7.547	Ea.	410	570		980	1,300
1500	Note: fin tube may also require corners, caps, etc.									

23 83 Radiant Heating Units

23 83 16 – Radiant-Heating Hydronic Piping

23 83 16.10 Radiant Floor Heating

		Crew	Daily Output	Labor-Hours	Unit	Material	2024 Bare Costs Labor	Equipment	Total	Total Incl O&P
0010	**RADIANT FLOOR HEATING**									
0100	Tubing, PEX (cross-linked polyethylene)									
0110	Oxygen barrier type for systems with ferrous materials									
0120	1/2"	Q-5	800	.020	L.F.	1.19	1.36		2.55	3.33
0130	3/4"		535	.030		1.69	2.03		3.72	4.89
0140	1"	↓	400	.040	↓	2.64	2.72		5.36	6.95
0200	Non barrier type for ferrous free systems									
0210	1/2"	Q-5	800	.020	L.F.	.66	1.36		2.02	2.75
0220	3/4"		535	.030		1.20	2.03		3.23	4.35
0230	1"	↓	400	.040	↓	2.06	2.72		4.78	6.30
1000	Manifolds									
1110	Brass									
1120	With supply and return valves, flow meter, thermometer,									
1122	auto air vent and drain/fill valve.									
1130	1", 2 circuit	Q-5	14	1.143	Ea.	385	77.50		462.50	540
1140	1", 3 circuit		13.50	1.185		440	80.50		520.50	605
1150	1", 4 circuit		13	1.231		480	83.50		563.50	650
1154	1", 5 circuit		12.50	1.280		570	87		657	760
1158	1", 6 circuit		12	1.333		620	90.50		710.50	820
1162	1", 7 circuit		11.50	1.391		680	94.50		774.50	890
1166	1", 8 circuit		11	1.455		755	99		854	975
1172	1", 9 circuit		10.50	1.524		810	104		914	1,050
1174	1", 10 circuit		10	1.600		870	109		979	1,125
1178	1", 11 circuit		9.50	1.684		905	115		1,020	1,175
1182	1", 12 circuit	↓	9	1.778	↓	1,000	121		1,121	1,275
1610	Copper manifold header (cut to size)									
1620	1" header, 12 circuit 1/2" sweat outlets	Q-5	3.33	4.805	Ea.	140	325		465	640
1630	1-1/4" header, 12 circuit 1/2" sweat outlets		3.20	5		162	340		502	685
1640	1-1/4" header, 12 circuit 3/4" sweat outlets		3	5.333		175	365		540	735
1650	1-1/2" header, 12 circuit 3/4" sweat outlets		3.10	5.161		210	350		560	750
1660	2" header, 12 circuit 3/4" sweat outlets	↓	2.90	5.517		310	375		685	900
3000	Valves									
3110	Thermostatic zone valve actuator with end switch	Q-5	40	.400	Ea.	58	27		85	104
3114	Thermostatic zone valve actuator	"	36	.444	"	110	30		140	166
3120	Motorized straight zone valve with operator complete									
3130	3/4"	Q-5	35	.457	Ea.	179	31		210	244
3140	1"		32	.500		194	34		228	264
3150	1-1/4"	↓	29.60	.541	↓	247	37		284	325
3500	4 way mixing valve, manual, brass									
3530	1"	Q-5	13.30	1.203	Ea.	256	82		338	405
3540	1-1/4"		11.40	1.404		278	95.50		373.50	445
3550	1-1/2"		11	1.455		355	99		454	535
3560	2"		10.60	1.509		500	103		603	710
3800	Mixing valve motor, 4 way for valves, 1" and 1-1/4"		34	.471		420	32		452	515
3810	Mixing valve motor, 4 way for valves, 1-1/2" and 2"	↓	30	.533	↓	490	36.50		526.50	595
5000	Radiant floor heating, zone control panel									
5120	4 zone actuator valve control, expandable	Q-5	20	.800	Ea.	164	54.50		218.50	262
5130	6 zone actuator valve control, expandable		18	.889		305	60.50		365.50	425
6070	Thermal track, straight panel for long continuous runs, 5.333 S.F.		40	.400		40	27		67	84.50
6080	Thermal track, utility panel, for direction reverse at run end, 5.333 S.F.		40	.400		40	27		67	84.50
6090	Combination panel, for direction reverse plus straight run, 5.333 S.F.	↓	40	.400		40	27		67	84.50
7000	PEX tubing fittings									
7100	Compression type									

23 83 Radiant Heating Units

23 83 16 – Radiant-Heating Hydronic Piping

23 83 16.10 Radiant Floor Heating		Crew	Daily Output	Labor-Hours	Unit	Material	2024 Bare Costs Labor	Equipment	Total	Total Incl O&P
7116	Coupling									
7120	1/2" x 1/2"	1 Stpi	27	.296	Ea.	7.65	22.50		30.15	42
7124	3/4" x 3/4"	"	23	.348	"	18.45	26.50		44.95	59.50
7130	Adapter									
7132	1/2" x female sweat 1/2"	1 Stpi	27	.296	Ea.	4.97	22.50		27.47	39
7134	1/2" x female sweat 3/4"		26	.308		5.55	23.50		29.05	40.50
7136	5/8" x female sweat 3/4"	↓	24	.333	↓	7.95	25		32.95	46.50
7140	Elbow									
7142	1/2" x female sweat 1/2"	1 Stpi	27	.296	Ea.	7.60	22.50		30.10	42
7144	1/2" x female sweat 3/4"		26	.308		8.90	23.50		32.40	44.50
7146	5/8" x female sweat 3/4"	↓	24	.333	↓	9.95	25		34.95	48.50
7200	Insert type									
7206	PEX x male NPT									
7210	1/2" x 1/2"	1 Stpi	29	.276	Ea.	3.54	21		24.54	35
7220	3/4" x 3/4"		27	.296		5.20	22.50		27.70	39.50
7230	1" x 1"		26	.308		8.80	23.50		32.30	44
7300	PEX coupling									
7310	1/2" x 1/2"	1 Stpi	30	.267	Ea.	1.34	20		21.34	31.50
7320	3/4" x 3/4"		29	.276		2.02	21		23.02	33
7330	1" x 1"		28	.286		3.13	21.50		24.63	35.50
7400	PEX stainless crimp ring									
7410	1/2" x 1/2"	1 Stpi	86	.093	Ea.	.64	7.05		7.69	11.15
7420	3/4" x 3/4"		84	.095		.87	7.20		8.07	11.65
7430	1" x 1"	↓	82	.098	↓	1.25	7.35		8.60	12.35

23 83 33 – Electric Radiant Heaters

23 83 33.10 Electric Heating

		Crew	Daily Output	Labor-Hours	Unit	Material	Labor	Equipment	Total	Total Incl O&P
0010	**ELECTRIC HEATING**, not incl. conduit or feed wiring									
1100	Rule of thumb: Baseboard units, including control	1 Elec	4.40	1.818	KW	144	130		274	350
1300	Baseboard heaters, 2' long, 350 watt		8	1	Ea.	40.50	71.50		112	151
1400	3' long, 750 watt		8	1		48	71.50		119.50	159
1600	4' long, 1,000 watt		6.70	1.194		57.50	85.50		143	191
1800	5' long, 935 watt		5.70	1.404		69.50	101		170.50	226
2000	6' long, 1,500 watt		5	1.600		78	115		193	256
2200	7' long, 1,310 watt		4.40	1.818		77.50	130		207.50	278
2400	8' long, 2,000 watt		4	2		92	143		235	315
2600	9' long, 1,680 watt		3.60	2.222		104	159		263	350
2800	10' long, 1,875 watt	↓	3.30	2.424	↓	102	174		276	370
2950	Wall heaters with fan, 120 to 277 volt									
3160	Recessed, residential, 750 watt	1 Elec	6	1.333	Ea.	101	95.50		196.50	253
3170	1,000 watt		6	1.333		405	95.50		500.50	585
3180	1,250 watt		5	1.600		138	115		253	320
3190	1,500 watt		4	2		435	143		578	695
3600	Thermostats, integral		16	.500		35.50	36		71.50	92
3800	Line voltage, 1 pole		8	1		32	71.50		103.50	141
3810	2 pole	↓	8	1	↓	28	71.50		99.50	137
4000	Heat trace system, 400 degree									
4020	115 V, 2.5 watts/L.F.	1 Elec	530	.015	L.F.	12.25	1.08		13.33	15.05
4030	5 watts/L.F.		530	.015		12.25	1.08		13.33	15.05
4050	10 watts/L.F.		530	.015		10.95	1.08		12.03	13.60
4060	208 V, 5 watts/L.F.		530	.015		12.25	1.08		13.33	15.05
4080	480 V, 8 watts/L.F.		530	.015		12.25	1.08		13.33	15.05
4200	Heater raceway									

23 83 Radiant Heating Units

23 83 33 – Electric Radiant Heaters

23 83 33.10 Electric Heating		Crew	Daily Output	Labor-Hours	Unit	Material	2024 Bare Costs Labor	Equipment	Total	Total Incl O&P
4260	Heat transfer cement									
4280	1 gallon				Ea.	106			106	117
4300	5 gallon				"	296			296	325
4320	Cable tie									
4340	3/4" pipe size	1 Elec	470	.017	Ea.	.03	1.22		1.25	1.84
4360	1" pipe size		444	.018		.03	1.29		1.32	1.95
4380	1-1/4" pipe size		400	.020		.03	1.43		1.46	2.16
4400	1-1/2" pipe size		355	.023		.03	1.62		1.65	2.43
4420	2" pipe size		320	.025		.02	1.79		1.81	2.68
4440	3" pipe size		160	.050		.02	3.59		3.61	5.30
4460	4" pipe size		100	.080		.07	5.75		5.82	8.60
4480	Thermostat NEMA 3R, 22 amp, 0-150 degree, 10' cap.		8	1		234	71.50		305.50	365
4500	Thermostat NEMA 4X, 25 amp, 40 degree, 5-1/2' cap.		7	1.143		241	82		323	385
4520	Thermostat NEMA 4X, 22 amp, 25-325 degree, 10' cap.		7	1.143		630	82		712	810
4540	Thermostat NEMA 4X, 22 amp, 15-140 degree		6	1.333		530	95.50		625.50	725
4580	Thermostat NEMA 4, 7, 9, 22 amp, 25-325 degree, 10' cap.		3.60	2.222		790	159		949	1,100
4600	Thermostat NEMA 4, 7, 9, 22 amp, 15-140 degree		3	2.667		720	191		911	1,075
4720	Fiberglass application tape, 36 yard roll		11	.727		66.50	52		118.50	151
5000	Radiant heating ceiling panels, 2' x 4', 500 watt		16	.500		320	36		356	405
5050	750 watt		16	.500		355	36		391	445
5200	For recessed plaster frame, add		32	.250		155	17.95		172.95	198
5300	Infrared quartz heaters, 120 volts, 1,000 watt		6.70	1.194		335	85.50		420.50	495
5350	1,500 watt		5	1.600		330	115		445	530
5400	240 volts, 1,500 watt		5	1.600		340	115		455	545
5450	2,000 watt		4	2		335	143		478	585
5500	3,000 watt		3	2.667		380	191		571	700
5550	4,000 watt		2.60	3.077		385	221		606	750
5570	Modulating control		.80	10		172	715		887	1,275
5600	Unit heaters, heavy duty, with fan & mounting bracket									
5650	Single phase, 208-240-277 volt, 3 kW	1 Elec	6	1.333	Ea.	600	95.50		695.50	800
5750	5 kW		5.50	1.455		620	104		724	840
5800	7 kW		5	1.600		875	115		990	1,125
5850	10 kW		4	2		1,250	143		1,393	1,600
5950	15 kW		3.80	2.105		2,125	151		2,276	2,550
6000	480 volt, 3 kW		6	1.333		715	95.50		810.50	925
6020	4 kW		5.80	1.379		365	99		464	550
6040	5 kW		5.50	1.455		585	104		689	800
6060	7 kW		5	1.600		760	115		875	1,000
6080	10 kW		4	2		1,050	143		1,193	1,400
6100	13 kW		3.80	2.105		2,250	151		2,401	2,700
6120	15 kW		3.70	2.162		1,400	155		1,555	1,750
6140	20 kW		3.50	2.286		2,450	164		2,614	2,925
6300	3 phase, 208-240 volt, 5 kW		5.50	1.455		565	104		669	775
6320	7 kW		5	1.600		905	115		1,020	1,175
6340	10 kW		4	2		945	143		1,088	1,250
6360	15 kW		3.70	2.162		1,650	155		1,805	2,025
6380	20 kW		3.50	2.286		2,375	164		2,539	2,875
6400	25 kW		3.30	2.424		3,400	174		3,574	4,000
6500	480 volt, 5 kW		5.50	1.455		770	104		874	1,000
6520	7 kW		5	1.600		1,100	115		1,215	1,375
6540	10 kW		4	2		1,050	143		1,193	1,375
6560	13 kW		3.80	2.105		1,875	151		2,026	2,275
6580	15 kW		3.70	2.162		1,675	155		1,830	2,050

23 83 Radiant Heating Units

23 83 33 – Electric Radiant Heaters

23 83 33.10 Electric Heating		Crew	Daily Output	Labor-Hours	Unit	Material	2024 Bare Costs Labor	2024 Bare Costs Equipment	Total	Total Incl O&P
6600	20 kW	1 Elec	3.50	2.286	Ea.	2,575	164		2,739	3,100
6800	Vertical discharge heaters, with fan									
6820	Single phase, 208-240-277 volt, 10 kW	1 Elec	4	2	Ea.	970	143		1,113	1,300
6840	15 kW		3.70	2.162		1,725	155		1,880	2,125
6900	3 phase, 208-240 volt, 10 kW		4	2		1,175	143		1,318	1,525
6920	15 kW		3.70	2.162		1,825	155		1,980	2,225
6940	20 kW		3.50	2.286		3,375	164		3,539	3,975
7100	480 volt, 10 kW		4	2		1,375	143		1,518	1,750
7120	15 kW		3.70	2.162		2,250	155		2,405	2,700
7140	20 kW		3.50	2.286		3,100	164		3,264	3,650
7160	25 kW		3.30	2.424		4,050	174		4,224	4,700
7900	Cabinet convector heaters, 240 volt, three phase,									
7920	3' long, 2,000 watt	1 Elec	5.30	1.509	Ea.		108		108	160
7940	3,000 watt		5.30	1.509		2,000	108		2,108	2,350
7960	4,000 watt		5.30	1.509		2,050	108		2,158	2,425
7980	6,000 watt		4.60	1.739		2,150	125		2,275	2,525
8000	8,000 watt		4.60	1.739		2,225	125		2,350	2,625
8020	4' long, 4,000 watt		4.60	1.739		1,925	125		2,050	2,300
8040	6,000 watt		4	2		2,000	143		2,143	2,425
8060	8,000 watt		4	2		2,125	143		2,268	2,575
8080	10,000 watt		4	2		2,150	143		2,293	2,575
8100	Available also in 208 or 277 volt									
8200	Cabinet unit heaters, 120 to 277 volt, 1 pole,									
8220	wall mounted, 2 kW	1 Elec	4.60	1.739	Ea.	1,925	125		2,050	2,300
8230	3 kW		4.60	1.739		2,000	125		2,125	2,375
8240	4 kW		4.40	1.818		2,050	130		2,180	2,475
8250	5 kW		4.40	1.818		2,125	130		2,255	2,550
8260	6 kW		4.20	1.905		2,150	137		2,287	2,550
8270	8 kW		4	2		2,225	143		2,368	2,675
8280	10 kW		3.80	2.105		2,150	151		2,301	2,575
8290	12 kW		3.50	2.286		2,050	164		2,214	2,500
8300	13.5 kW		2.90	2.759		2,225	198		2,423	2,750
8310	16 kW		2.70	2.963		2,275	212		2,487	2,825
8320	20 kW		2.30	3.478		3,450	249		3,699	4,175
8330	24 kW		1.90	4.211		3,500	300		3,800	4,300
8350	Recessed, 2 kW		4.40	1.818		2,500	130		2,630	2,950
8370	3 kW		4.40	1.818		2,575	130		2,705	3,050
8380	4 kW		4.20	1.905		2,625	137		2,762	3,100
8390	5 kW		4.20	1.905		2,700	137		2,837	3,175
8400	6 kW		4	2		2,100	143		2,243	2,550
8410	8 kW		3.80	2.105		2,225	151		2,376	2,675
8420	10 kW		3.50	2.286		3,250	164		3,414	3,825
8430	12 kW		2.90	2.759		3,275	198		3,473	3,900
8440	13.5 kW		2.70	2.963		3,300	212		3,512	3,950
8450	16 kW		2.30	3.478		3,300	249		3,549	4,025
8460	20 kW		1.90	4.211		3,375	300		3,675	4,175
8470	24 kW		1.60	5		3,425	360		3,785	4,300
8490	Ceiling mounted, 2 kW		3.20	2.500		2,500	179		2,679	3,025
8510	3 kW		3.20	2.500		2,575	179		2,754	3,125
8520	4 kW		3	2.667		2,625	191		2,816	3,175
8530	5 kW		3	2.667		2,700	191		2,891	3,250
8540	6 kW		2.80	2.857		2,725	205		2,930	3,300
8550	8 kW		2.40	3.333		2,800	239		3,039	3,425

23 83 Radiant Heating Units

23 83 33 – Electric Radiant Heaters

23 83 33.10 Electric Heating		Crew	Daily Output	Labor-Hours	Unit	Material	2024 Bare Costs Labor	Equipment	Total	Total Incl O&P
8560	10 kW	1 Elec	2.20	3.636	Ea.	2,250	261		2,511	2,850
8570	12 kW		2	4		2,275	287		2,562	2,950
8580	13.5 kW		1.50	5.333		2,325	380		2,705	3,125
8590	16 kW		1.30	6.154		2,375	440		2,815	3,250
8600	20 kW		.90	8.889		3,375	635		4,010	4,675
8610	24 kW		.60	13.333		3,425	955		4,380	5,200
8630	208 to 480 V, 3 pole									
8650	Wall mounted, 2 kW	1 Elec	4.60	1.739	Ea.	2,500	125		2,625	2,925
8670	3 kW		4.60	1.739		2,000	125		2,125	2,375
8680	4 kW		4.40	1.818		2,050	130		2,180	2,475
8690	5 kW		4.40	1.818		2,125	130		2,255	2,550
8700	6 kW		4.20	1.905		2,150	137		2,287	2,550
8710	8 kW		4	2		2,225	143		2,368	2,675
8720	10 kW		3.80	2.105		2,150	151		2,301	2,575
8730	12 kW		3.50	2.286		2,175	164		2,339	2,650
8740	13.5 kW		2.90	2.759		2,225	198		2,423	2,750
8750	16 kW		2.70	2.963		2,275	212		2,487	2,825
8760	20 kW		2.30	3.478		3,250	249		3,499	3,950
8770	24 kW		1.90	4.211		3,500	300		3,800	4,300
8790	Recessed, 2 kW		4.40	1.818		2,500	130		2,630	2,950
8810	3 kW		4.40	1.818		2,575	130		2,705	3,050
8820	4 kW		4.20	1.905		2,625	137		2,762	3,100
8830	5 kW		4.20	1.905		2,700	137		2,837	3,175
8840	6 kW		4	2		2,725	143		2,868	3,225
8850	8 kW		3.80	2.105		2,800	151		2,951	3,300
8860	10 kW		3.50	2.286		2,250	164		2,414	2,725
8870	12 kW		2.90	2.759		2,275	198		2,473	2,825
8880	13.5 kW		2.70	2.963		2,325	212		2,537	2,875
8890	16 kW		2.30	3.478		3,550	249		3,799	4,275
8900	20 kW		1.90	4.211		3,600	300		3,900	4,425
8920	24 kW		1.60	5		3,650	360		4,010	4,550
8940	Ceiling mount, 2 kW		3.20	2.500		2,500	179		2,679	3,025
8950	3 kW		3.20	2.500		2,575	179		2,754	3,125
8960	4 kW		3	2.667		2,625	191		2,816	3,175
8970	5 kW		3	2.667		2,700	191		2,891	3,250
8980	6 kW		2.80	2.857		2,725	205		2,930	3,300
8990	8 kW		2.40	3.333		2,225	239		2,464	2,800
9000	10 kW		2.20	3.636		3,250	261		3,511	3,950
9020	13.5 kW		1.50	5.333		3,300	380		3,680	4,200
9030	16 kW		1.30	6.154		3,550	440		3,990	4,550
9040	20 kW		.90	8.889		3,600	635		4,235	4,925
9060	24 kW		.60	13.333		3,425	955		4,380	5,200
9230	13.5 kW, 40,956 BTU		2.20	3.636		2,250	261		2,511	2,850
9250	24 kW, 81,912 BTU		2	4		2,475	287		2,762	3,150

23 91 Prefabricated Equipment Supports

23 91 10 – Prefabricated Curbs, Pads and Stands

23 91 10.10 Prefabricated Pads and Stands	Crew	Daily Output	Labor-Hours	Unit	Material	2024 Bare Costs Labor	2024 Bare Costs Equipment	Total	Total Incl O&P
0010 **PREFABRICATED PADS AND STANDS**									
6000 Pad, fiberglass reinforced concrete with polystyrene foam core									
6220 30" x 36"	1 Shee	8	1	Ea.	129	72.50		201.50	251
6340 36" x 54"	Q-9	6	2.667	"	144	173		317	420

Estimating Tips

26 05 00 Common Work Results for Electrical

- Conduit should be taken off in three main categories—power distribution, branch power, and branch lighting—so the estimator can concentrate on systems and components, therefore making it easier to ensure all items have been accounted for.
- For cost modifications for elevated conduit installation, add the percentages to labor according to the height of installation and only to the quantities exceeding the different height levels, not to the total conduit quantities. Refer to subdivision 26 01 02.20 for labor adjustment factors.
- Remember that aluminum wiring of equal ampacity is larger in diameter than copper and may require larger conduit.
- If more than three wires at a time are being pulled, deduct percentages from the labor hours of that grouping of wires.
- When taking off grounding systems, identify separately the type and size of wire, and list each unique type of ground connection.
- The estimator should take the weights of materials into consideration when completing a takeoff. Topics to consider include: How will the materials be supported? What methods of support are available? How high will the support structure have to reach? Will the final support structure be able to withstand the total burden? Is the support material included or separate from the fixture, equipment, and material specified?
- Do not overlook the costs for equipment used in the installation. If scaffolding or highlifts are available in the field, contractors may use them in lieu of the proposed ladders and rolling staging.

26 20 00 Low-Voltage Electrical Transmission

- Supports and concrete pads may be shown on drawings for the larger equipment, or the support system may be only a piece of plywood for the back of a panelboard. In either case, they must be included in the costs.

26 40 00 Electrical and Cathodic Protection

- When taking off cathodic protection systems, identify the type and size of cable, and list each unique type of anode connection.

26 50 00 Lighting

- Fixtures should be taken off room by room using the fixture schedule, specifications, and the ceiling plan. For large concentrations of lighting fixtures in the same area, deduct the percentages from labor hours.

Reference Numbers

Reference numbers are shown at the beginning of some major classifications. These numbers refer to related items in the Reference Section. The reference information may be an estimating procedure, an alternate pricing method, or technical information.

Note: Not all subdivisions listed here necessarily appear. ■

Same Data. Simplified.

Enjoy the convenience and efficiency of accessing your costs anywhere:

- **Skip the multiplier** by setting your location
- **Quickly search,** edit, favorite and share costs
- **Stay on top of price changes** with automatic updates

Discover more at rsmeans.com/online

No part of this cost data may be reproduced, stored in a retrieval system, or transmitted in any form or by any means without prior written permission of Gordian.

Note: "Powered in part by CINX™, based on licensed proprietary information of Harrison Publishing House, Inc."

Note: The following companies, in part, have been used as a reference source for some of the material prices used in Division 26:

Electriflex

Trade Service

26 05 Common Work Results for Electrical

26 05 33 – Raceway and Boxes for Electrical Systems

26 05 33.95 Cutting and Drilling		Crew	Daily Output	Labor-Hours	Unit	Material	2024 Bare Costs Labor	Equipment	Total	Total Incl O&P
0010	**CUTTING AND DRILLING**									
0100	Hole drilling to 10' high, concrete wall									
0110	8" thick, 1/2" pipe size	R-31	12	.667	Ea.	.33	48	5.30	53.63	77
0120	3/4" pipe size		12	.667		.33	48	5.30	53.63	77
0130	1" pipe size		9.50	.842		.46	60.50	6.70	67.66	97.50
0140	1-1/4" pipe size		9.50	.842		.46	60.50	6.70	67.66	97.50
0150	1-1/2" pipe size		9.50	.842		.46	60.50	6.70	67.66	97.50
0160	2" pipe size		4.40	1.818		.67	130	14.50	145.17	210
0170	2-1/2" pipe size		4.40	1.818		.67	130	14.50	145.17	210
0180	3" pipe size		4.40	1.818		.67	130	14.50	145.17	210
0190	3-1/2" pipe size		3.30	2.424		.86	174	19.30	194.16	280
0200	4" pipe size		3.30	2.424		.86	174	19.30	194.16	280
0500	12" thick, 1/2" pipe size		9.40	.851		.50	61	6.80	68.30	98.50
0520	3/4" pipe size		9.40	.851		.50	61	6.80	68.30	98.50
0540	1" pipe size		7.30	1.096		.69	78.50	8.75	87.94	126
0560	1-1/4" pipe size		7.30	1.096		.69	78.50	8.75	87.94	126
0570	1-1/2" pipe size		7.30	1.096		.69	78.50	8.75	87.94	126
0580	2" pipe size		3.60	2.222		1	159	17.70	177.70	257
0590	2-1/2" pipe size		3.60	2.222		1	159	17.70	177.70	257
0600	3" pipe size		3.60	2.222		1	159	17.70	177.70	257
0610	3-1/2" pipe size		2.80	2.857		1.29	205	23	229.29	330
0630	4" pipe size		2.50	3.200		1.29	229	25.50	255.79	370
0650	16" thick, 1/2" pipe size		7.60	1.053		.67	75.50	8.40	84.57	122
0670	3/4" pipe size		7	1.143		.67	82	9.10	91.77	132
0690	1" pipe size		6	1.333		.91	95.50	10.65	107.06	155
0710	1-1/4" pipe size		5.50	1.455		.91	104	11.60	116.51	169
0730	1-1/2" pipe size		5.50	1.455		.91	104	11.60	116.51	169
0750	2" pipe size		3	2.667		1.34	191	21.50	213.84	310
0770	2-1/2" pipe size		2.70	2.963		1.34	212	23.50	236.84	340
0790	3" pipe size		2.50	3.200		1.34	229	25.50	255.84	370
0810	3-1/2" pipe size		2.30	3.478		1.72	249	27.50	278.22	400
0830	4" pipe size		2	4		1.72	287	32	320.72	460
0850	20" thick, 1/2" pipe size		6.40	1.250		.83	89.50	9.95	100.28	145
0870	3/4" pipe size		6	1.333		.83	95.50	10.65	106.98	155
0890	1" pipe size		5	1.600		1.14	115	12.75	128.89	185
0910	1-1/4" pipe size		4.80	1.667		1.14	120	13.30	134.44	193
0930	1-1/2" pipe size		4.60	1.739		1.14	125	13.85	139.99	202
0950	2" pipe size		2.70	2.963		1.67	212	23.50	237.17	345
0970	2-1/2" pipe size		2.40	3.333		1.67	239	26.50	267.17	385
0990	3" pipe size		2.20	3.636		1.67	261	29	291.67	420
1010	3-1/2" pipe size		2	4		2.15	287	32	321.15	460
1030	4" pipe size		1.70	4.706		2.15	335	37.50	374.65	545
1050	24" thick, 1/2" pipe size		5.50	1.455		1	104	11.60	116.60	169
1070	3/4" pipe size		5.10	1.569		1	112	12.50	125.50	182
1090	1" pipe size		4.30	1.860		1.37	133	14.85	149.22	216
1110	1-1/4" pipe size		4	2		1.37	143	15.95	160.32	232
1130	1-1/2" pipe size		4	2		1.37	143	15.95	160.32	232
1150	2" pipe size		2.40	3.333		2.01	239	26.50	267.51	385
1170	2-1/2" pipe size		2.20	3.636		2.01	261	29	292.01	420
1190	3" pipe size		2	4		2.01	287	32	321.01	460
1210	3-1/2" pipe size		1.80	4.444		2.59	320	35.50	358.09	510
1230	4" pipe size		1.50	5.333		2.59	380	42.50	425.09	615
1500	Brick wall, 8" thick, 1/2" pipe size		18	.444		.33	32	3.54	35.87	51.50

For customer support on your Plumbing Costs with RSMeans Data call 800.448.8182.

26 05 Common Work Results for Electrical

26 05 33 – Raceway and Boxes for Electrical Systems

26 05 33.95 Cutting and Drilling		Crew	Daily Output	Labor-Hours	Unit	Material	2024 Bare Costs Labor	Equipment	Total	Total Incl O&P
1520	3/4" pipe size	R-31	18	.444	Ea.	.33	32	3.54	35.87	51.50
1540	1" pipe size		13.30	.602		.46	43	4.79	48.25	70
1560	1-1/4" pipe size		13.30	.602		.46	43	4.79	48.25	70
1580	1-1/2" pipe size		13.30	.602		.46	43	4.79	48.25	70
1600	2" pipe size		5.70	1.404		.67	101	11.20	112.87	162
1620	2-1/2" pipe size		5.70	1.404		.67	101	11.20	112.87	162
1640	3" pipe size		5.70	1.404		.67	101	11.20	112.87	162
1660	3-1/2" pipe size		4.40	1.818		.86	130	14.50	145.36	210
1680	4" pipe size		4	2		.86	143	15.95	159.81	232
1700	12" thick, 1/2" pipe size		14.50	.552		.50	39.50	4.40	44.40	64
1720	3/4" pipe size		14.50	.552		.50	39.50	4.40	44.40	64
1740	1" pipe size		11	.727		.69	52	5.80	58.49	84.50
1760	1-1/4" pipe size		11	.727		.69	52	5.80	58.49	84.50
1780	1-1/2" pipe size		11	.727		.69	52	5.80	58.49	84.50
1800	2" pipe size		5	1.600		1	115	12.75	128.75	185
1820	2-1/2" pipe size		5	1.600		1	115	12.75	128.75	185
1840	3" pipe size		5	1.600		1	115	12.75	128.75	185
1860	3-1/2" pipe size		3.80	2.105		1.29	151	16.80	169.09	244
1880	4" pipe size		3.30	2.424		1.29	174	19.30	194.59	281
1900	16" thick, 1/2" pipe size		12.30	.650		.67	46.50	5.20	52.37	75.50
1920	3/4" pipe size		12.30	.650		.67	46.50	5.20	52.37	75.50
1940	1" pipe size		9.30	.860		.91	61.50	6.85	69.26	100
1960	1-1/4" pipe size		9.30	.860		.91	61.50	6.85	69.26	100
1980	1-1/2" pipe size		9.30	.860		.91	61.50	6.85	69.26	100
2000	2" pipe size		4.40	1.818		1.34	130	14.50	145.84	210
2010	2-1/2" pipe size		4.40	1.818		1.34	130	14.50	145.84	210
2030	3" pipe size		4.40	1.818		1.34	130	14.50	145.84	210
2050	3-1/2" pipe size		3.30	2.424		1.72	174	19.30	195.02	281
2070	4" pipe size		3	2.667		1.72	191	21.50	214.22	310
2090	20" thick, 1/2" pipe size		10.70	.748		.83	53.50	5.95	60.28	87
2110	3/4" pipe size		10.70	.748		.83	53.50	5.95	60.28	87
2130	1" pipe size		8	1		1.14	71.50	7.95	80.59	116
2150	1-1/4" pipe size		8	1		1.14	71.50	7.95	80.59	116
2170	1-1/2" pipe size		8	1		1.14	71.50	7.95	80.59	116
2190	2" pipe size		4	2		1.67	143	15.95	160.62	232
2210	2-1/2" pipe size		4	2		1.67	143	15.95	160.62	232
2230	3" pipe size		4	2		1.67	143	15.95	160.62	232
2250	3-1/2" pipe size		3	2.667		2.15	191	21.50	214.65	310
2270	4" pipe size		2.70	2.963		2.15	212	23.50	237.65	345
2290	24" thick, 1/2" pipe size		9.40	.851		1	61	6.80	68.80	99
2310	3/4" pipe size		9.40	.851		1	61	6.80	68.80	99
2330	1" pipe size		7.10	1.127		1.37	81	9	91.37	131
2350	1-1/4" pipe size		7.10	1.127		1.37	81	9	91.37	131
2370	1-1/2" pipe size		7.10	1.127		1.37	81	9	91.37	131
2390	2" pipe size		3.60	2.222		2.01	159	17.70	178.71	258
2410	2-1/2" pipe size		3.60	2.222		2.01	159	17.70	178.71	258
2430	3" pipe size		3.60	2.222		2.01	159	17.70	178.71	258
2450	3-1/2" pipe size		2.80	2.857		2.59	205	23	230.59	335
2470	4" pipe size		2.50	3.200		2.59	229	25.50	257.09	370
3000	Knockouts to 8' high, metal boxes & enclosures									
3020	With hole saw, 1/2" pipe size	1 Elec	53	.151	Ea.		10.80		10.80	16.05
3040	3/4" pipe size		47	.170			12.20		12.20	18.10
3050	1" pipe size		40	.200			14.35		14.35	21.50

26 05 Common Work Results for Electrical

26 05 33 – Raceway and Boxes for Electrical Systems

26 05 33.95 Cutting and Drilling		Crew	Daily Output	Labor-Hours	Unit	Material	2024 Bare Costs Labor	Equipment	Total	Total Incl O&P
3060	1-1/4" pipe size	1 Elec	36	.222	Ea.		15.95		15.95	23.50
3070	1-1/2" pipe size		32	.250			17.95		17.95	26.50
3080	2" pipe size		27	.296			21		21	31.50
3090	2-1/2" pipe size		20	.400			28.50		28.50	42.50
4010	3" pipe size		16	.500			36		36	53
4030	3-1/2" pipe size		13	.615			44		44	65.50
4050	4" pipe size		11	.727			52		52	77.50

26 05 83 – Wiring Connections

26 05 83.10 Motor Connections

		Crew	Daily Output	Labor-Hours	Unit	Material	Labor	Equipment	Total	Total Incl O&P
0010	**MOTOR CONNECTIONS**									
0020	Flexible conduit and fittings, 115 volt, 1 phase, up to 1 HP motor	1 Elec	8	1	Ea.	7.85	71.50		79.35	115
0050	2 HP motor		6.50	1.231		15.95	88.50		104.45	149
0100	3 HP motor		5.50	1.455		14.10	104		118.10	171
0110	230 volt, 3 phase, 3 HP motor		6.78	1.180		9.20	84.50		93.70	135
0112	5 HP motor		5.47	1.463		8.10	105		113.10	164
0114	7-1/2 HP motor		4.61	1.735		13.50	124		137.50	199
0120	10 HP motor		4.20	1.905		23.50	137		160.50	228
0150	15 HP motor		3.30	2.424		23.50	174		197.50	284
0200	25 HP motor		2.70	2.963		37	212		249	355
0400	50 HP motor		2.20	3.636		74.50	261		335.50	465
0600	100 HP motor		1.50	5.333		169	380		549	750

26 05 90 – Residential Applications

26 05 90.10 Residential Wiring

		Crew	Daily Output	Labor-Hours	Unit	Material	Labor	Equipment	Total	Total Incl O&P
0010	**RESIDENTIAL WIRING**									
0020	20' avg. runs and #14/2 wiring incl. unless otherwise noted									
1000	Service & panel, includes 24' SE-AL cable, service eye, meter,									
1010	Socket, panel board, main bkr., ground rod, 15 or 20 amp									
1020	1-pole circuit breakers, and misc. hardware									
1100	100 amp, with 10 branch breakers	1 Elec	1.19	6.723	Ea.	510	480		990	1,275
1110	With PVC conduit and wire		.92	8.696		605	625		1,230	1,600
1120	With RGS conduit and wire		.73	10.959		895	785		1,680	2,150
1150	150 amp, with 14 branch breakers		1.03	7.767		795	555		1,350	1,700
1170	With PVC conduit and wire		.82	9.756		965	700		1,665	2,100
1180	With RGS conduit and wire		.67	11.940		1,325	855		2,180	2,750
1200	200 amp, with 18 branch breakers	2 Elec	1.80	8.889		1,375	635		2,010	2,475
1220	With PVC conduit and wire		1.46	10.959		1,550	785		2,335	2,900
1230	With RGS conduit and wire		1.24	12.903		2,275	925		3,200	3,875
1800	Lightning surge suppressor	1 Elec	32	.250		87	17.95		104.95	122
2000	Switch devices									
2100	Single pole, 15 amp, ivory, with a 1-gang box, cover plate,									
2110	Type NM (Romex) cable	1 Elec	17.10	.468	Ea.	14.10	33.50		47.60	65
2120	Type MC cable		14.30	.559		28	40		68	90.50
2130	EMT & wire		5.71	1.401		58.50	100		158.50	214
2150	3-way, #14/3, type NM cable		14.55	.550		17.55	39.50		57.05	78
2170	Type MC cable		12.31	.650		38.50	46.50		85	112
2180	EMT & wire		5	1.600		64	115		179	241
2200	4-way, #14/3, type NM cable		14.55	.550		27.50	39.50		67	88.50
2220	Type MC cable		12.31	.650		48.50	46.50		95	123
2230	EMT & wire		5	1.600		74	115		189	252
2250	S.P., 20 amp, #12/2, type NM cable		13.33	.600		21	43		64	87
2270	Type MC cable		11.43	.700		28.50	50		78.50	106
2280	EMT & wire		4.85	1.649		63.50	118		181.50	245

26 05 Common Work Results for Electrical

26 05 90 – Residential Applications

26 05 90.10 Residential Wiring		Crew	Daily Output	Labor-Hours	Unit	Material	2024 Bare Costs Labor	Equipment	Total	Total Incl O&P
2290	S.P. rotary dimmer, 600 W, no wiring	1 Elec	17	.471	Ea.	36.50	33.50		70	90.50
2300	S.P. rotary dimmer, 600 W, type NM cable		14.55	.550		47	39.50		86.50	110
2320	Type MC cable		12.31	.650		60.50	46.50		107	136
2330	EMT & wire		5	1.600		96	115		211	275
2350	3-way rotary dimmer, type NM cable		13.33	.600		45	43		88	114
2370	Type MC cable		11.43	.700		59	50		109	140
2380	EMT & wire		4.85	1.649		94.50	118		212.50	279
2400	Interval timer wall switch, 20 amp, 1-30 min., #12/2									
2410	Type NM cable	1 Elec	14.55	.550	Ea.	102	39.50		141.50	171
2420	Type MC cable		12.31	.650		101	46.50		147.50	180
2430	EMT & wire		5	1.600		144	115		259	330
2500	Decorator style									
2510	S.P., 15 amp, type NM cable	1 Elec	17.10	.468	Ea.	21	33.50		54.50	72.50
2520	Type MC cable		14.30	.559		35	40		75	98
2530	EMT & wire		5.71	1.401		65.50	100		165.50	221
2550	3-way, #14/3, type NM cable		14.55	.550		24.50	39.50		64	85.50
2570	Type MC cable		12.31	.650		45.50	46.50		92	120
2580	EMT & wire		5	1.600		71	115		186	248
2600	4-way, #14/3, type NM cable		14.55	.550		34.50	39.50		74	96.50
2620	Type MC cable		12.31	.650		55.50	46.50		102	130
2630	EMT & wire		5	1.600		81	115		196	259
2650	S.P., 20 amp, #12/2, type NM cable		13.33	.600		28	43		71	94.50
2670	Type MC cable		11.43	.700		35.50	50		85.50	114
2680	EMT & wire		4.85	1.649		70.50	118		188.50	253
2700	S.P., slide dimmer, type NM cable		17.10	.468		46.50	33.50		80	101
2720	Type MC cable		14.30	.559		60.50	40		100.50	126
2730	EMT & wire		5.71	1.401		95.50	100		195.50	254
2750	S.P., touch dimmer, type NM cable		17.10	.468		36.50	33.50		70	89.50
2770	Type MC cable		14.30	.559		50	40		90	115
2780	EMT & wire		5.71	1.401		85.50	100		185.50	243
2800	3-way touch dimmer, type NM cable		13.33	.600		41	43		84	110
2820	Type MC cable		11.43	.700		55	50		105	135
2830	EMT & wire		4.85	1.649		90.50	118		208.50	275
3000	Combination devices									
3100	S.P. switch/15 amp recpt., ivory, 1-gang box, plate									
3110	Type NM cable	1 Elec	11.43	.700	Ea.	30	50		80	108
3120	Type MC cable		10	.800		44	57.50		101.50	133
3130	EMT & wire		4.40	1.818		79	130		209	280
3150	S.P. switch/pilot light, type NM cable		11.43	.700		31.50	50		81.50	109
3170	Type MC cable		10	.800		45.50	57.50		103	135
3180	EMT & wire		4.43	1.806		80.50	129		209.50	281
3190	2-S.P. switches, 2-#14/2, no wiring		14	.571		5.65	41		46.65	66.50
3200	2-S.P. switches, 2-#14/2, type NM cables		10	.800		36.50	57.50		94	125
3220	Type MC cable		8.89	.900		51.50	64.50		116	153
3230	EMT & wire		4.10	1.951		90	140		230	305
3250	3-way switch/15 amp recpt., #14/3, type NM cable		10	.800		40	57.50		97.50	129
3270	Type MC cable		8.89	.900		61	64.50		125.50	163
3280	EMT & wire		4.10	1.951		86.50	140		226.50	300
3300	2-3 way switches, 2-#14/3, type NM cables		8.89	.900		52.50	64.50		117	153
3320	Type MC cable		8	1		82	71.50		153.50	196
3330	EMT & wire		4	2		100	143		243	325
3350	S.P. switch/20 amp recpt., #12/2, type NM cable		10	.800		48.50	57.50		106	138
3370	Type MC cable		8.89	.900		47.50	64.50		112	148

26 05 Common Work Results for Electrical

26 05 90 – Residential Applications

26 05 90.10 Residential Wiring		Crew	Daily Output	Labor-Hours	Unit	Material	2024 Bare Costs Labor	Equipment	Total	Total Incl O&P
3380	EMT & wire	1 Elec	4.10	1.951	Ea.	91	140		231	305
3400	Decorator style									
3410	S.P. switch/15 amp recpt., type NM cable	1 Elec	11.43	.700	Ea.	37	50		87	115
3420	Type MC cable		10	.800		51	57.50		108.50	141
3430	EMT & wire		4.40	1.818		86	130		216	288
3450	S.P. switch/pilot light, type NM cable		11.43	.700		38.50	50		88.50	117
3470	Type MC cable		10	.800		52.50	57.50		110	143
3480	EMT & wire		4.40	1.818		87.50	130		217.50	290
3500	2-S.P. switches, 2-#14/2, type NM cables		10	.800		43.50	57.50		101	133
3520	Type MC cable		8.89	.900		58.50	64.50		123	160
3530	EMT & wire		4.10	1.951		96.50	140		236.50	315
3550	3-way/15 amp recpt., #14/3, type NM cable		10	.800		47	57.50		104.50	137
3570	Type MC cable		8.89	.900		68	64.50		132.50	171
3580	EMT & wire		4.10	1.951		93.50	140		233.50	310
3650	2-3 way switches, 2-#14/3, type NM cables		8.89	.900		59.50	64.50		124	161
3670	Type MC cable		8	1		89	71.50		160.50	204
3680	EMT & wire		4	2		107	143		250	330
3700	S.P. switch/20 amp recpt., #12/2, type NM cable		10	.800		55.50	57.50		113	146
3720	Type MC cable		8.89	.900		54.50	64.50		119	156
3730	EMT & wire		4.10	1.951		98	140		238	315
4000	Receptacle devices									
4010	Duplex outlet, 15 amp recpt., ivory, 1-gang box, plate									
4015	Type NM cable	1 Elec	14.55	.550	Ea.	14.50	39.50		54	74.50
4020	Type MC cable		12.31	.650		28.50	46.50		75	101
4030	EMT & wire		5.33	1.501		59	108		167	225
4050	With #12/2, type NM cable		12.31	.650		17.85	46.50		64.35	88.50
4070	Type MC cable		10.67	.750		25.50	54		79.50	108
4080	EMT & wire		4.71	1.699		60.50	122		182.50	248
4100	20 amp recpt., #12/2, type NM cable		12.31	.650		31.50	46.50		78	104
4120	Type MC cable		10.67	.750		39	54		93	123
4130	EMT & wire		4.71	1.699		74	122		196	263
4140	For GFI see Section 26 05 90.10 line 4300 below									
4150	Decorator style, 15 amp recpt., type NM cable	1 Elec	14.55	.550	Ea.	21.50	39.50		61	82
4170	Type MC cable		12.31	.650		35.50	46.50		82	108
4180	EMT & wire		5.33	1.501		66	108		174	233
4200	With #12/2, type NM cable		12.31	.650		25	46.50		71.50	96.50
4220	Type MC cable		10.67	.750		32	54		86	115
4230	EMT & wire		4.71	1.699		67.50	122		189.50	255
4250	20 amp recpt., #12/2, type NM cable		12.31	.650		38.50	46.50		85	112
4270	Type MC cable		10.67	.750		46	54		100	130
4280	EMT & wire		4.71	1.699		81	122		203	270
4300	GFI, 15 amp recpt., type NM cable		12.31	.650		35	46.50		81.50	108
4320	Type MC cable		10.67	.750		49	54		103	134
4330	EMT & wire		4.71	1.699		79.50	122		201.50	269
4350	GFI with #12/2, type NM cable		10.67	.750		38.50	54		92.50	122
4370	Type MC cable		9.20	.870		46	62.50		108.50	143
4380	EMT & wire		4.21	1.900		81	136		217	291
4400	20 amp recpt., #12/2, type NM cable		10.67	.750		55	54		109	140
4420	Type MC cable		9.20	.870		62.50	62.50		125	161
4430	EMT & wire		4.21	1.900		97.50	136		233.50	310
4500	Weather-proof cover for above receptacles, add		32	.250		4.80	17.95		22.75	32
4550	Air conditioner outlet, 20 amp-240 volt recpt.									
4560	30' of #12/2, 2 pole circuit breaker									

26 05 Common Work Results for Electrical

26 05 90 – Residential Applications

26 05 90.10 Residential Wiring		Crew	Daily Output	Labor-Hours	Unit	Material	2024 Bare Costs Labor	Equipment	Total	Total Incl O&P
4570	Type NM cable	1 Elec	10	.800	Ea.	80.50	57.50		138	174
4580	Type MC cable		9	.889		85.50	63.50		149	189
4590	EMT & wire		4	2		122	143		265	345
4600	Decorator style, type NM cable		10	.800		88	57.50		145.50	182
4620	Type MC cable		9	.889		92.50	63.50		156	197
4630	EMT & wire	▼	4	2	▼	129	143		272	355
4650	Dryer outlet, 30 amp-240 volt recpt., 20' of #10/3									
4660	2 pole circuit breaker									
4670	Type NM cable	1 Elec	6.41	1.248	Ea.	78.50	89.50		168	219
4680	Type MC cable		5.71	1.401		66.50	100		166.50	222
4690	EMT & wire		3.48	2.299	▼	118	165		283	375
4700	Range outlet, 50 amp-240 volt recpt., 30' of #8/3									
4710	Type NM cable	1 Elec	4.21	1.900	Ea.	151	136		287	370
4720	Type MC cable		4	2		126	143		269	350
4730	EMT & wire		2.96	2.703		163	194		357	465
4750	Central vacuum outlet, type NM cable		6.40	1.250		91	89.50		180.50	233
4770	Type MC cable		5.71	1.401		87.50	100		187.50	245
4780	EMT & wire	▼	3.48	2.299	▼	145	165		310	405
4800	30 amp-110 volt locking recpt., #10/2 circ. bkr.									
4810	Type NM cable	1 Elec	6.20	1.290	Ea.	113	92.50		205.50	261
4830	EMT & wire	"	3.20	2.500	"	175	179		354	460
4900	Low voltage outlets									
4910	Telephone recpt., 20' of 4/C phone wire	1 Elec	26	.308	Ea.	13.35	22		35.35	47
4920	TV recpt., 20' of RG59U coax wire, F type connector	"	16	.500	"	18.15	36		54.15	73
4950	Door bell chime, transformer, 2 buttons, 60' of bellwire									
4970	Economy model	1 Elec	11.50	.696	Ea.	71	50		121	152
4980	Custom model		11.50	.696		116	50		166	202
4990	Luxury model, 3 buttons	▼	9.50	.842	▼	209	60.50		269.50	320
6000	Lighting outlets									
6050	Wire only (for fixture), type NM cable	1 Elec	32	.250	Ea.	13.95	17.95		31.90	42
6070	Type MC cable		24	.333		16.90	24		40.90	54
6080	EMT & wire		10	.800		46	57.50		103.50	136
6100	Box (4") and wire (for fixture), type NM cable		25	.320		23.50	23		46.50	60
6120	Type MC cable		20	.400		26.50	28.50		55	72
6130	EMT & wire	▼	11	.727	▼	56	52		108	139
6200	Fixtures (use with line 6050 or 6100 above)									
6210	Canopy style, economy grade	1 Elec	40	.200	Ea.	26.50	14.35		40.85	50.50
6220	Custom grade		40	.200		68	14.35		82.35	96
6250	Dining room chandelier, economy grade		19	.421		90	30		120	144
6260	Custom grade		19	.421		410	30		440	495
6270	Luxury grade		15	.533		3,425	38		3,463	3,825
6310	Kitchen fixture (fluorescent), economy grade		30	.267		97	19.10		116.10	136
6320	Custom grade		25	.320		220	23		243	276
6350	Outdoor, wall mounted, economy grade		30	.267		44	19.10		63.10	77
6360	Custom grade		30	.267		149	19.10		168.10	193
6370	Luxury grade		25	.320		266	23		289	325
6410	Outdoor PAR floodlights, 1 lamp, 150 watt		20	.400		19.15	28.50		47.65	63.50
6420	2 lamp, 150 watt each		20	.400		37	28.50		65.50	83.50
6430	For infrared security sensor, add		32	.250		114	17.95		131.95	152
6450	Outdoor, quartz-halogen, 300 watt flood		20	.400		51.50	28.50		80	99
6600	Recessed downlight, round, pre-wired, 50 or 75 watt trim		30	.267		59.50	19.10		78.60	94
6610	With shower light trim		30	.267		91.50	19.10		110.60	130
6620	With wall washer trim		28	.286		92	20.50		112.50	132

26 05 Common Work Results for Electrical

26 05 90 – Residential Applications

26 05 90.10 Residential Wiring

		Crew	Daily Output	Labor-Hours	Unit	Material	2024 Bare Costs Labor	Equipment	Total	Total Incl O&P
6630	With eye-ball trim	1 Elec	28	.286	Ea.	43.50	20.50		64	78
6700	Porcelain lamp holder		40	.200		3.40	14.35		17.75	25
6710	With pull switch		40	.200		14.50	14.35		28.85	37.50
6750	Fluorescent strip, 2-20 watt tube, wrap around diffuser, 24"		24	.333		55.50	24		79.50	97
6770	2-34 watt tubes, 48"		20	.400		160	28.50		188.50	219
6800	Bathroom heat lamp, 1-250 watt		28	.286		43	20.50		63.50	78
6810	2-250 watt lamps		28	.286		74	20.50		94.50	112
6820	For timer switch, see Section 26 05 90.10 line 2400									
6900	Outdoor post lamp, incl. post, fixture, 35' of #14/2									
6910	Type NM cable	1 Elec	3.50	2.286	Ea.	410	164		574	695
6920	Photo-eye, add		27	.296		15.20	21		36.20	48
6950	Clock dial time switch, 24 hr., w/enclosure, type NM cable		11.43	.700		98.50	50		148.50	183
6970	Type MC cable		11	.727		112	52		164	202
6980	EMT & wire		4.85	1.649		143	118		261	330
7000	Alarm systems									
7050	Smoke detectors, box, #14/3, type NM cable	1 Elec	14.55	.550	Ea.	44	39.50		83.50	107
7070	Type MC cable		12.31	.650		57	46.50		103.50	132
7080	EMT & wire		5	1.600		82.50	115		197.50	261
7090	For relay output to security system, add					10.80			10.80	11.90
8000	Residential equipment									
8050	Disposal hook-up, incl. switch, outlet box, 3' of flex									
8060	20 amp-1 pole circ. bkr., and 25' of #12/2									
8070	Type NM cable	1 Elec	10	.800	Ea.	35	57.50		92.50	124
8080	Type MC cable		8	1		41	71.50		112.50	151
8090	EMT & wire		5	1.600		84	115		199	262
8100	Trash compactor or dishwasher hook-up, incl. outlet box,									
8110	3' of flex, 15 amp-1 pole circ. bkr., and 25' of #14/2									
8120	Type NM cable	1 Elec	10	.800	Ea.	27.50	57.50		85	115
8130	Type MC cable		8	1		37.50	71.50		109	148
8140	EMT & wire		5	1.600		76	115		191	254
8150	Hot water sink dispenser hook-up, use line 8100									
8200	Vent/exhaust fan hook-up, type NM cable	1 Elec	32	.250	Ea.	13.95	17.95		31.90	42
8220	Type MC cable		24	.333		16.90	24		40.90	54
8230	EMT & wire		10	.800		46	57.50		103.50	136
8250	Bathroom vent fan, 50 CFM (use with above hook-up)									
8260	Economy model	1 Elec	15	.533	Ea.	24.50	38		62.50	83.50
8270	Low noise model		15	.533		56	38		94	119
8280	Custom model		12	.667		129	48		177	212
8300	Bathroom or kitchen vent fan, 110 CFM									
8310	Economy model	1 Elec	15	.533	Ea.	80.50	38		118.50	145
8320	Low noise model	"	15	.533	"	129	38		167	199
8350	Paddle fan, variable speed (w/o lights)									
8360	Economy model (AC motor)	1 Elec	10	.800	Ea.	168	57.50		225.50	270
8362	With light kit		10	.800		214	57.50		271.50	320
8370	Custom model (AC motor)		10	.800		410	57.50		467.50	535
8372	With light kit		10	.800		455	57.50		512.50	585
8380	Luxury model (DC motor)		8	1		299	71.50		370.50	435
8382	With light kit		8	1		345	71.50		416.50	485
8390	Remote speed switch for above, add		12	.667		52	48		100	129
8500	Whole house exhaust fan, ceiling mount, 36", variable speed									
8510	Remote switch, incl. shutters, 20 amp-1 pole circ. bkr.									
8520	30' of #12/2, type NM cable	1 Elec	4	2	Ea.	1,750	143		1,893	2,150
8530	Type MC cable		3.50	2.286		1,750	164		1,914	2,175

26 05 Common Work Results for Electrical

26 05 90 – Residential Applications

26 05 90.10 Residential Wiring

		Crew	Daily Output	Labor-Hours	Unit	Material	2024 Bare Costs Labor	Equipment	Total	Total Incl O&P
8540	EMT & wire	1 Elec	3	2.667	Ea.	1,800	191		1,991	2,250
8600	Whirlpool tub hook-up, incl. timer switch, outlet box									
8610	3' of flex, 20 amp-1 pole GFI circ. bkr.									
8620	30' of #12/2, type NM cable	1 Elec	5	1.600	Ea.	270	115		385	465
8630	Type MC cable		4.20	1.905		271	137		408	500
8640	EMT & wire	↓	3.40	2.353	↓	305	169		474	585
8650	Hot water heater hook-up, incl. 1-2 pole circ. bkr., box;									
8660	3' of flex, 20' of #10/2, type NM cable	1 Elec	5	1.600	Ea.	41.50	115		156.50	216
8670	Type MC cable		4.20	1.905		44.50	137		181.50	251
8680	EMT & wire	↓	3.40	2.353	↓	73.50	169		242.50	330
9000	Heating/air conditioning									
9050	Furnace/boiler hook-up, incl. firestat, local on-off switch									
9060	Emergency switch, and 40' of type NM cable	1 Elec	4	2	Ea.	86.50	143		229.50	310
9070	Type MC cable		3.50	2.286		102	164		266	355
9080	EMT & wire		1.50	5.333		164	380		544	745
9100	Air conditioner hook-up, incl. local 60 amp disc. switch									
9110	3' sealtite, 40 amp, 2 pole circuit breaker									
9130	40' of #8/2, type NM cable	1 Elec	3.50	2.286	Ea.	234	164		398	500
9140	Type MC cable		3	2.667		215	191		406	520
9150	EMT & wire	↓	1.30	6.154	↓	282	440		722	965
9200	Heat pump hook-up, 1-40 & 1-100 amp 2 pole circ. bkr.									
9210	Local disconnect switch, 3' sealtite									
9220	40' of #8/2 & 30' of #3/2									
9230	Type NM cable	1 Elec	1.30	6.154	Ea.	845	440		1,285	1,575
9240	Type MC cable		1.08	7.407		540	530		1,070	1,375
9250	EMT & wire	↓	.94	8.511	↓	795	610		1,405	1,775
9500	Thermostat hook-up, using low voltage wire									
9520	Heating only, 25' of #18-3	1 Elec	24	.333	Ea.	15	24		39	52
9530	Heating/cooling, 25' of #18-4	"	20	.400	"	12.90	28.50		41.40	56.50

26 24 Switchboards and Panelboards

26 24 19 – Motor-Control Centers

26 24 19.40 Motor Starters and Controls

		Crew	Daily Output	Labor-Hours	Unit	Material	Labor	Equipment	Total	Total Incl O&P
0010	**MOTOR STARTERS AND CONTROLS**									
0050	Magnetic, FVNR, with enclosure and heaters, 480 volt									
0080	2 HP, size 00	1 Elec	3.50	2.286	Ea.	181	164		345	440
0100	5 HP, size 0		2.30	3.478		385	249		634	795
0200	10 HP, size 1	↓	1.60	5		530	360		890	1,100
0300	25 HP, size 2	2 Elec	2.20	7.273		560	520		1,080	1,400
0400	50 HP, size 3		1.80	8.889		775	635		1,410	1,800
0500	100 HP, size 4		1.20	13.333		1,750	955		2,705	3,350
0600	200 HP, size 5		.90	17.778		4,175	1,275		5,450	6,500
0610	400 HP, size 6	↓	.80	20		10,600	1,425		12,025	13,700
0620	NEMA 7, 5 HP, size 0	1 Elec	1.60	5		2,600	360		2,960	3,375
0630	10 HP, size 1	"	1.10	7.273		2,700	520		3,220	3,750
0640	25 HP, size 2	2 Elec	1.80	8.889		4,350	635		4,985	5,750
0650	50 HP, size 3		1.20	13.333		6,550	955		7,505	8,625
0660	100 HP, size 4		.90	17.778		8,450	1,275		9,725	11,200
0670	200 HP, size 5	↓	.50	32		13,700	2,300		16,000	18,500
0700	Combination, with motor circuit protectors, 5 HP, size 0	1 Elec	1.80	4.444		1,475	320		1,795	2,100
0800	10 HP, size 1	"	1.30	6.154		1,550	440		1,990	2,350

26 24 Switchboards and Panelboards

26 24 19 – Motor-Control Centers

26 24 19.40 Motor Starters and Controls		Crew	Daily Output	Labor-Hours	Unit	Material	2024 Bare Costs Labor	Equipment	Total	Total Incl O&P
0900	25 HP, size 2	2 Elec	2	8	Ea.	2,150	575		2,725	3,225
1000	50 HP, size 3		1.32	12.121		3,125	870		3,995	4,725
1200	100 HP, size 4	↓	.80	20		6,850	1,425		8,275	9,650
1220	NEMA 7, 5 HP, size 0	1 Elec	1.30	6.154		3,450	440		3,890	4,450
1230	10 HP, size 1	"	1	8		3,550	575		4,125	4,750
1240	25 HP, size 2	2 Elec	1.32	12.121		4,725	870		5,595	6,500
1250	50 HP, size 3		.80	20		7,800	1,425		9,225	10,700
1260	100 HP, size 4		.60	26.667		12,200	1,900		14,100	16,200
1270	200 HP, size 5	↓	.40	40		26,400	2,875		29,275	33,400
1400	Combination, with fused switch, 5 HP, size 0	1 Elec	1.80	4.444		1,250	320		1,570	1,850
1600	10 HP, size 1	"	1.30	6.154		1,325	440		1,765	2,100
1800	25 HP, size 2	2 Elec	2	8		2,050	575		2,625	3,125
2000	50 HP, size 3		1.32	12.121		3,675	870		4,545	5,325
2200	100 HP, size 4	↓	.80	20	↓	7,400	1,425		8,825	10,300
3500	Magnetic FVNR with NEMA 12, enclosure & heaters, 480 volt									
3600	5 HP, size 0	1 Elec	2.20	3.636	Ea.	260	261		521	670
3700	10 HP, size 1	"	1.50	5.333		390	380		770	995
3800	25 HP, size 2	2 Elec	2	8		735	575		1,310	1,650
3900	50 HP, size 3		1.60	10		1,125	715		1,840	2,325
4000	100 HP, size 4		1	16		2,700	1,150		3,850	4,675
4100	200 HP, size 5	↓	.80	20		6,475	1,425		7,900	9,250
4200	Combination, with motor circuit protectors, 5 HP, size 0	1 Elec	1.70	4.706		865	335		1,200	1,450
4300	10 HP, size 1	"	1.20	6.667		895	480		1,375	1,700
4400	25 HP, size 2	2 Elec	1.80	8.889		1,350	635		1,985	2,425
4500	50 HP, size 3		1.20	13.333		2,175	955		3,130	3,825
4600	100 HP, size 4	↓	.74	21.622		4,925	1,550		6,475	7,725
4700	Combination, with fused switch, 5 HP, size 0	1 Elec	1.70	4.706		710	335		1,045	1,275
4800	10 HP, size 1	"	1.20	6.667		735	480		1,215	1,525
4900	25 HP, size 2	2 Elec	1.80	8.889		1,125	635		1,760	2,175
5000	50 HP, size 3		1.20	13.333		1,800	955		2,755	3,400
5100	100 HP, size 4	↓	.74	21.622	↓	3,650	1,550		5,200	6,325
5200	Factory installed controls, adders to size 0 thru 5									
5300	Start-stop push button	1 Elec	32	.250	Ea.	54.50	17.95		72.45	86.50
5400	Hand-off-auto-selector switch		32	.250		54.50	17.95		72.45	86.50
5500	Pilot light		32	.250		102	17.95		119.95	140
5600	Start-stop-pilot		32	.250		157	17.95		174.95	200
5700	Auxiliary contact, NO or NC		32	.250		75	17.95		92.95	109
5800	NO-NC	↓	32	.250	↓	150	17.95		167.95	192

26 29 Low-Voltage Controllers

26 29 13 – Enclosed Controllers

26 29 13.20 Control Stations

		Crew	Daily Output	Labor-Hours	Unit	Material	Labor	Equipment	Total	Total Incl O&P
0010	**CONTROL STATIONS**									
0050	NEMA 1, heavy duty, stop/start	1 Elec	8	1	Ea.	365	71.50		436.50	505
0100	Stop/start, pilot light		6.20	1.290		415	92.50		507.50	595
0200	Hand/off/automatic		6.20	1.290		375	92.50		467.50	550
0400	Stop/start/reverse		5.30	1.509		525	108		633	740
0500	NEMA 7, heavy duty, stop/start		6	1.333		515	95.50		610.50	710
0600	Stop/start, pilot light	↓	4	2	↓	750	143		893	1,050

Estimating Tips

- When estimating material costs for electronic safety and security systems, it is always prudent to obtain manufacturers' quotations for equipment prices and special installation requirements that may affect the total cost.

- Fire alarm systems consist of control panels, annunciator panels, batteries with rack, charger, and fire alarm actuating and indicating devices. Some fire alarm systems include speakers, telephone lines, door closer controls, and other components. Be careful not to overlook the costs related to installation for these items. Also be aware of costs for integrated automation instrumentation and terminal devices, control equipment, control wiring, and programming. Insurance underwriters may have specific requirements for the type of materials to be installed or design requirements based on the hazard to be protected. Local jurisdictions may have requirements not covered by code. It is advisable to be aware of any special conditions.

- Security equipment includes items such as CCTV, access control, and other detection and identification systems to perform alert and alarm functions. Be sure to consider the costs related to installation for this security equipment, such as for integrated automation instrumentation and terminal devices, control equipment, control wiring, and programming.

Reference Numbers

Reference numbers are shown at the beginning of some major classifications. These numbers refer to related items in the Reference Section. The reference information may be an estimating procedure, an alternate pricing method, or technical information.

Same Data. Simplified.

Enjoy the convenience and efficiency of accessing your costs anywhere:
- **Skip the multiplier** by setting your location
- **Quickly search**, edit, favorite and share costs
- **Stay on top of price changes** with automatic updates

Discover more at rsmeans.com/online

No part of this cost data may be reproduced, stored in a retrieval system, or transmitted in any form or by any means without prior written permission of Gordian.

Note: Trade Service, in part, has been used as a reference source for some of the material prices used in Division 28.

28 31 Intrusion Detection

28 31 16 – Intrusion Detection Systems Infrastructure

28 31 16.50 Intrusion Detection	Crew	Daily Output	Labor-Hours	Unit	Material	2024 Bare Costs Labor	Equipment	Total	Total Incl O&P
0010 **INTRUSION DETECTION**, not including wires & conduits									
0100 Burglar alarm, battery operated, mechanical trigger	1 Elec	4	2	Ea.	293	143		436	540
0200 Electrical trigger		4	2		350	143		493	600
0400 For outside key control, add		8	1		90.50	71.50		162	206
0600 For remote signaling circuitry, add		8	1		149	71.50		220.50	270
0800 Card reader, flush type, standard		2.70	2.963		705	212		917	1,100
1000 Multi-code		2.70	2.963		640	212		852	1,025

28 42 Gas Detection and Alarm

28 42 15 – Gas Detection Sensors

28 42 15.50 Tank Leak Detection Systems

	Crew	Daily Output	Labor-Hours	Unit	Material	Labor	Equipment	Total	Total Incl O&P
0010 **TANK LEAK DETECTION SYSTEMS** Liquid and vapor									
0100 For hydrocarbons and hazardous liquids/vapors									
0120 Controller, data acquisition, incl. printer, modem, RS232 port									
0140 24 channel, for use with all probes				Ea.	6,850			6,850	7,525
0160 9 channel, for external monitoring				"	2,275			2,275	2,525
0200 Probes									
0210 Well monitoring									
0220 Liquid phase detection				Ea.	870			870	960
0230 Hydrocarbon vapor, fixed position					1,075			1,075	1,175
0240 Hydrocarbon vapor, float mounted					800			800	880
0250 Both liquid and vapor hydrocarbon					1,075			1,075	1,175
0300 Secondary containment, liquid phase									
0310 Pipe trench/manway sump				Ea.	905			905	995
0320 Double wall pipe and manual sump					760			760	835
0330 Double wall fiberglass annular space					545			545	595
0340 Double wall steel tank annular space					330			330	360
0500 Accessories									
0510 Modem, non-dedicated phone line				Ea.	420			420	460
0600 Monitoring, internal									
0610 Automatic tank gauge, incl. overfill				Ea.	1,625			1,625	1,800
0620 Product line				"	1,700			1,700	1,875
0700 Monitoring, special									
0710 Cathodic protection				Ea.	925			925	1,025
0720 Annular space chemical monitor				"	1,250			1,250	1,375

28 46 Fire Detection and Alarm

28 46 11 – Fire Sensors and Detectors

28 46 11.27 Other Sensors

	Crew	Daily Output	Labor-Hours	Unit	Material	Labor	Equipment	Total	Total Incl O&P
0010 **OTHER SENSORS**									
5200 Smoke detector, ceiling type	1 Elec	6.20	1.290	Ea.	168	92.50		260.50	320
5240 Smoke detector, addressable type		6	1.333		265	95.50		360.50	435
5400 Duct type		3.20	2.500		365	179		544	665
5420 Duct addressable type		3.20	2.500		223	179		402	510

28 46 11.50 Fire and Heat Detectors

	Crew	Daily Output	Labor-Hours	Unit	Material	Labor	Equipment	Total	Total Incl O&P
0010 **FIRE & HEAT DETECTORS**									
5000 Detector, rate of rise	1 Elec	8	1	Ea.	36.50	71.50		108	146
5100 Fixed temp fire alarm	"	7	1.143	"	48.50	82		130.50	174

28 46 Fire Detection and Alarm

28 46 20 – Fire Alarm

28 46 20.50 Alarm Panels and Devices

		Crew	Daily Output	Labor-Hours	Unit	Material	2024 Bare Costs Labor	Equipment	Total	Total Incl O&P
0010	**ALARM PANELS AND DEVICES**, not including wires & conduits									
3600	4 zone	2 Elec	2	8	Ea.	540	575		1,115	1,450
3700	5 zone		1.50	10.667		710	765		1,475	1,900
3800	8 zone		1	16		680	1,150		1,830	2,450
3900	10 zone		1.25	12.800		980	920		1,900	2,425
4000	12 zone		.67	23.988		3,175	1,725		4,900	6,025
4020	Alarm device, tamper, flow	1 Elec	8	1		253	71.50		324.50	385
4025	Fire alarm, loop expander card		16	.500		915	36		951	1,050
4050	Actuating device		8	1		405	71.50		476.50	550
4200	Battery and rack		4	2		575	143		718	845
4400	Automatic charger		8	1		650	71.50		721.50	820
4600	Signal bell		8	1		66.50	71.50		138	179
4610	Fire alarm signal bell 10" red 20-24 V P		8	1		232	71.50		303.50	360
4800	Trouble buzzer or manual station		8	1		93.50	71.50		165	209
5425	Duct smoke and heat detector 2 wire		8	1		222	71.50		293.50	350
5430	Fire alarm duct detector controller		3	2.667		262	191		453	570
5435	Fire alarm duct detector sensor kit		8	1		115	71.50		186.50	232
5440	Remote test station for smoke detector duct type		5.30	1.509		62.50	108		170.50	229
5460	Remote fire alarm indicator light		5.30	1.509		34.50	108		142.50	198
5600	Strobe and horn		5.30	1.509		120	108		228	292
5610	Strobe and horn (ADA type)		5.30	1.509		145	108		253	320
5620	Visual alarm (ADA type)		6.70	1.194		128	85.50		213.50	267
5800	electric bell		6.70	1.194		62.50	85.50		148	196
6000	Door holder, electro-magnetic		4	2		99	143		242	320
6200	Combination holder and closer		3.20	2.500		194	179		373	480
6600	Drill switch		8	1		600	71.50		671.50	765
6800	Master box		2.70	2.963		7,250	212		7,462	8,300
7000	Break glass station		8	1		66	71.50		137.50	179
7800	Remote annunciator, 8 zone lamp		1.80	4.444		465	320		785	980
8000	12 zone lamp	2 Elec	2.60	6.154		510	440		950	1,225
8200	16 zone lamp	"	2.20	7.273		475	520		995	1,300

Division Notes

	CREW	DAILY OUTPUT	LABOR-HOURS	UNIT	BARE COSTS				TOTAL INCL O&P
					MAT.	LABOR	EQUIP.	TOTAL	

Estimating Tips
31 05 00 Common Work Results for Earthwork

- Estimating the actual cost of performing earthwork requires careful consideration of the variables involved. This includes items such as type of soil, whether water will be encountered, dewatering, whether banks need bracing, disposal of excavated earth, and length of haul to fill or spoil sites, etc. If the project has large quantities of cut or fill, consider raising or lowering the site to reduce costs, while paying close attention to the effect on site drainage and utilities.
- If the project has large quantities of fill, creating a borrow pit on the site can significantly lower the costs.
- It is very important to consider what time of year the project is scheduled for completion. Bad weather can create large cost overruns from dewatering, site repair, and lost productivity from cold weather.

Reference Numbers

Reference numbers are shown at the beginning of some major classifications. These numbers refer to related items in the Reference Section. The reference information may be an estimating procedure, an alternate pricing method, or technical information.

Note: Not all subdivisions listed here necessarily appear. ■

Same Data. Simplified.

Enjoy the convenience and efficiency of accessing your costs anywhere:

- **Skip the multiplier** by setting your location
- **Quickly search**, edit, favorite and share costs
- **Stay on top of price changes** with automatic updates

Discover more at rsmeans.com/online

No part of this cost data may be reproduced, stored in a retrieval system, or transmitted in any form or by any means without prior written permission of Gordian.

31 23 Excavation and Fill

31 23 16 – Excavation

31 23 16.13 Excavating, Trench

		Crew	Daily Output	Labor-Hours	Unit	Material	2024 Bare Costs Labor	Equipment	Total	Total Incl O&P
0010	**EXCAVATING, TRENCH** G1030-805									
0011	Or continuous footing									
0020	Common earth with no sheeting or dewatering included									
0050	1' to 4' deep, 3/8 C.Y. excavator	B-11C	150	.107	B.C.Y.		6.10	1.94	8.04	11.15
0060	1/2 C.Y. excavator	B-11M	200	.080			4.56	2.28	6.84	9.25
0090	4' to 6' deep, 1/2 C.Y. excavator	"	200	.080			4.56	2.28	6.84	9.25
0100	5/8 C.Y. excavator	B-12Q	250	.064			3.76	3.09	6.85	9
0300	1/2 C.Y. excavator, truck mounted	B-12J	200	.080			4.70	4.60	9.30	12
0500	6' to 10' deep, 3/4 C.Y. excavator	B-12F	225	.071			4.18	3.95	8.13	10.55
0600	1 C.Y. excavator, truck mounted	B-12K	400	.040			2.35	3.96	6.31	7.85
0900	10' to 14' deep, 3/4 C.Y. excavator	B-12F	200	.080			4.70	4.44	9.14	11.85
1000	1-1/2 C.Y. excavator	B-12B	540	.030			1.74	2.21	3.95	5
1300	14' to 20' deep, 1 C.Y. excavator	B-12A	320	.050			2.94	3.03	5.97	7.70
1340	20' to 24' deep, 1 C.Y. excavator	"	288	.056			3.27	3.37	6.64	8.55
1352	4' to 6' deep, 1/2 C.Y. excavator w/trench box	B-13H	188	.085			5	5.60	10.60	13.60
1354	5/8 C.Y. excavator	"	235	.068			4	4.49	8.49	10.90
1362	6' to 10' deep, 3/4 C.Y. excavator w/trench box	B-13G	212	.075			4.44	4.83	9.27	11.90
1374	10' to 14' deep, 3/4 C.Y. excavator w/trench box	"	188	.085			5	5.45	10.45	13.40
1376	1-1/2 C.Y. excavator	B-13E	508	.032			1.85	2.62	4.47	5.60
1381	14' to 20' deep, 1 C.Y. excavator w/trench box	B-13D	301	.053			3.13	3.68	6.81	8.65
1386	20' to 24' deep, 1 C.Y. excavator w/trench box	"	271	.059			3.47	4.08	7.55	9.65
1400	By hand with pick and shovel 2' to 6' deep, light soil	1 Clab	8	1			49		49	72.50
1500	Heavy soil	"	4	2			98		98	145
1700	For tamping backfilled trenches, air tamp, add	A-1G	100	.080			3.92	1.14	5.06	7.05
1900	Vibrating plate, add	B-18	180	.133			6.60	.85	7.45	10.75
2100	Trim sides and bottom for concrete pours, common earth		1500	.016	S.F.		.79	.10	.89	1.29
2300	Hardpan		600	.040	"		1.99	.25	2.24	3.22
5020	Loam & sandy clay with no sheeting or dewatering included									
5050	1' to 4' deep, 3/8 C.Y. tractor loader/backhoe	B-11C	162	.099	B.C.Y.		5.65	1.80	7.45	10.35
5060	1/2 C.Y. excavator	B-11M	216	.074			4.22	2.11	6.33	8.55
5080	4' to 6' deep, 1/2 C.Y. excavator	"	216	.074			4.22	2.11	6.33	8.55
5090	5/8 C.Y. excavator	B-12Q	276	.058			3.41	2.80	6.21	8.15
5130	1/2 C.Y. excavator, truck mounted	B-12J	216	.074			4.36	4.26	8.62	11.15
5140	6' to 10' deep, 3/4 C.Y. excavator	B-12F	243	.066			3.87	3.65	7.52	9.75
5160	1 C.Y. excavator, truck mounted	B-12K	432	.037			2.18	3.67	5.85	7.25
5190	10' to 14' deep, 3/4 C.Y. excavator	B-12F	216	.074			4.36	4.11	8.47	10.95
5210	1-1/2 C.Y. excavator	B-12B	583	.027			1.61	2.05	3.66	4.64
5250	14' to 20' deep, 1 C.Y. excavator	B-12A	346	.046			2.72	2.81	5.53	7.10
5300	20' to 24' deep, 1 C.Y. excavator	"	311	.051			3.03	3.12	6.15	7.90
5352	4' to 6' deep, 1/2 C.Y. excavator w/trench box	B-13H	205	.078			4.59	5.15	9.74	12.45
5354	5/8 C.Y. excavator	"	257	.062			3.66	4.11	7.77	9.95
5362	6' to 10' deep, 3/4 C.Y. excavator w/trench box	B-13G	231	.069			4.07	4.43	8.50	10.90
5370	10' to 14' deep, 3/4 C.Y. excavator w/trench box	"	205	.078			4.59	4.99	9.58	12.30
5374	1-1/2 C.Y. excavator	B-13E	554	.029			1.70	2.40	4.10	5.15
5382	14' to 20' deep, 1 C.Y. excavator w/trench box	B-13D	329	.049			2.86	3.36	6.22	7.95
5392	20' to 24' deep, 1 C.Y. excavator w/trench box	"	295	.054			3.19	3.75	6.94	8.85
6020	Sand & gravel with no sheeting or dewatering included									
6050	1' to 4' deep, 3/8 C.Y. excavator	B-11C	165	.097	B.C.Y.		5.55	1.76	7.31	10.15
6060	1/2 C.Y. excavator	B-11M	220	.073			4.15	2.07	6.22	8.45
6080	4' to 6' deep, 1/2 C.Y. excavator	"	220	.073			4.15	2.07	6.22	8.45
6090	5/8 C.Y. excavator	B-12Q	275	.058			3.42	2.81	6.23	8.15
6130	1/2 C.Y. excavator, truck mounted	B-12J	220	.073			4.28	4.18	8.46	10.95
6140	6' to 10' deep, 3/4 C.Y. excavator	B-12F	248	.065			3.79	3.58	7.37	9.55

31 23 Excavation and Fill

31 23 16 – Excavation

31 23 16.13 Excavating, Trench

		Crew	Daily Output	Labor-Hours	Unit	Material	2024 Bare Costs Labor	2024 Bare Costs Equipment	Total	Total Incl O&P
6160	1 C.Y. excavator, truck mounted	B-12K	440	.036	B.C.Y.		2.14	3.60	5.74	7.15
6190	10' to 14' deep, 3/4 C.Y. excavator	B-12F	220	.073			4.28	4.04	8.32	10.80
6210	1-1/2 C.Y. excavator	B-12B	594	.027			1.58	2.01	3.59	4.56
6250	14' to 20' deep, 1 C.Y. excavator	B-12A	352	.045			2.67	2.76	5.43	7
6300	20' to 24' deep, 1 C.Y. excavator	"	317	.050			2.97	3.06	6.03	7.75
6352	4' to 6' deep, 1/2 C.Y. excavator w/trench box	B-13H	209	.077			4.50	5.05	9.55	12.20
6354	5/8 C.Y. excavator	"	261	.061			3.60	4.05	7.65	9.80
6362	6' to 10' deep, 3/4 C.Y. excavator w/trench box	B-13G	236	.068			3.99	4.34	8.33	10.65
6370	10' to 14' deep, 3/4 C.Y. excavator w/trench box	"	209	.077			4.50	4.90	9.40	12.05
6374	1-1/2 C.Y. excavator	B-13E	564	.028			1.67	2.36	4.03	5.05
6382	14' to 20' deep, 1 C.Y. excavator w/trench box	B-13D	334	.048			2.82	3.31	6.13	7.80
6392	20' to 24' deep, 1 C.Y. excavator w/trench box	"	301	.053			3.13	3.68	6.81	8.65
7020	Dense hard clay with no sheeting or dewatering included									
7050	1' to 4' deep, 3/8 C.Y. excavator	B-11C	132	.121	B.C.Y.		6.90	2.20	9.10	12.70
7060	1/2 C.Y. excavator	B-11M	176	.091			5.20	2.59	7.79	10.55
7080	4' to 6' deep, 1/2 C.Y. excavator	"	176	.091			5.20	2.59	7.79	10.55
7090	5/8 C.Y. excavator	B-12Q	220	.073			4.28	3.51	7.79	10.20
7130	1/2 C.Y. excavator, truck mounted	B-12J	176	.091			5.35	5.25	10.60	13.65
7140	6' to 10' deep, 3/4 C.Y. excavator	B-12F	198	.081			4.75	4.48	9.23	12
7160	1 C.Y. excavator, truck mounted	B-12K	352	.045			2.67	4.50	7.17	8.90
7190	10' to 14' deep, 3/4 C.Y. excavator	B-12F	176	.091			5.35	5.05	10.40	13.45
7210	1-1/2 C.Y. excavator	B-12B	475	.034			1.98	2.51	4.49	5.70
7250	14' to 20' deep, 1 C.Y. excavator	B-12A	282	.057			3.34	3.44	6.78	8.75
7300	20' to 24' deep, 1 C.Y. excavator	"	254	.063			3.70	3.82	7.52	9.70

31 23 16.14 Excavating, Utility Trench

		Crew	Daily Output	Labor-Hours	Unit	Material	2024 Bare Costs Labor	2024 Bare Costs Equipment	Total	Total Incl O&P
0010	**EXCAVATING, UTILITY TRENCH** G1030-805									
0011	Common earth									
0050	Trenching with chain trencher, 12 HP, operator walking									
0100	4" wide trench, 12" deep	B-53	800	.010	L.F.		.62	.26	.88	1.21
0150	18" deep		750	.011			.66	.28	.94	1.29
0200	24" deep		700	.011			.71	.30	1.01	1.38
0300	6" wide trench, 12" deep		650	.012			.76	.32	1.08	1.49
0350	18" deep		600	.013			.83	.35	1.18	1.62
0400	24" deep		550	.015			.90	.38	1.28	1.76
0450	36" deep		450	.018			1.10	.47	1.57	2.15
0600	8" wide trench, 12" deep		475	.017			1.04	.44	1.48	2.04
0650	18" deep		400	.020			1.24	.53	1.77	2.42
0700	24" deep		350	.023			1.42	.60	2.02	2.76
0750	36" deep		300	.027			1.65	.70	2.35	3.22
1000	Backfill by hand including compaction, add									
1050	4" wide trench, 12" deep	A-1G	800	.010	L.F.		.49	.14	.63	.89
1100	18" deep		530	.015			.74	.21	.95	1.34
1150	24" deep		400	.020			.98	.28	1.26	1.76
1300	6" wide trench, 12" deep		540	.015			.73	.21	.94	1.30
1350	18" deep		405	.020			.97	.28	1.25	1.74
1400	24" deep		270	.030			1.45	.42	1.87	2.61
1450	36" deep		180	.044			2.18	.63	2.81	3.91
1600	8" wide trench, 12" deep		400	.020			.98	.28	1.26	1.76
1650	18" deep		265	.030			1.48	.43	1.91	2.66
1700	24" deep		200	.040			1.96	.57	2.53	3.52
1750	36" deep		135	.059			2.90	.84	3.74	5.25
2000	Chain trencher, 40 HP operator riding									

31 23 Excavation and Fill

31 23 16 – Excavation

31 23 16.14 Excavating, Utility Trench

		Crew	Daily Output	Labor-Hours	Unit	Material	2024 Bare Costs Labor	2024 Bare Costs Equipment	Total	Total Incl O&P
2050	6" wide trench and backfill, 12" deep	B-54	1200	.007	L.F.		.41	.34	.75	.98
2100	18" deep		1000	.008			.50	.40	.90	1.18
2150	24" deep		975	.008			.51	.41	.92	1.20
2200	36" deep		900	.009			.55	.45	1	1.31
2250	48" deep		750	.011			.66	.54	1.20	1.57
2300	60" deep		650	.012			.76	.62	1.38	1.81
2400	8" wide trench and backfill, 12" deep		1000	.008			.50	.40	.90	1.18
2450	18" deep		950	.008			.52	.42	.94	1.24
2500	24" deep		900	.009			.55	.45	1	1.31
2550	36" deep		800	.010			.62	.50	1.12	1.47
2600	48" deep		650	.012			.76	.62	1.38	1.81
2700	12" wide trench and backfill, 12" deep		975	.008			.51	.41	.92	1.20
2750	18" deep		860	.009			.58	.47	1.05	1.38
2800	24" deep		800	.010			.62	.50	1.12	1.47
2850	36" deep		725	.011			.68	.56	1.24	1.62
3000	16" wide trench and backfill, 12" deep		835	.010			.59	.48	1.07	1.41
3050	18" deep		750	.011			.66	.54	1.20	1.57
3100	24" deep	↓	700	.011	↓		.71	.58	1.29	1.68
3200	Compaction with vibratory plate, add								35%	35%
5100	Hand excavate and trim for pipe bells after trench excavation									
5200	8" pipe	1 Clab	155	.052	L.F.		2.53		2.53	3.74
5300	18" pipe	"	130	.062	"		3.02		3.02	4.46

31 23 19 – Dewatering

31 23 19.20 Dewatering Systems

		Crew	Daily Output	Labor-Hours	Unit	Material	Labor	Equipment	Total	Total Incl O&P
0010	**DEWATERING SYSTEMS**									
0020	Excavate drainage trench, 2' wide, 2' deep	B-11C	90	.178	C.Y.		10.15	3.23	13.38	18.55
0100	2' wide, 3' deep, with backhoe loader	"	135	.119			6.75	2.16	8.91	12.35
0200	Excavate sump pits by hand, light soil	1 Clab	7.10	1.127			55		55	82
0300	Heavy soil	"	3.50	2.286	↓		112		112	166
0500	Pumping 8 hrs., attended 2 hrs./day, incl. 20 L.F.									
0550	of suction hose & 100 L.F. discharge hose									
0600	2" diaphragm pump used for 8 hrs.	B-10H	4	3	Day		179	19.70	198.70	287
0650	4" diaphragm pump used for 8 hrs.	B-10I	4	3			179	51.50	230.50	320
0800	8 hrs. attended, 2" diaphragm pump	B-10H	1	12			715	78.50	793.50	1,125
0900	3" centrifugal pump	B-10J	1	12			715	107	822	1,175
1000	4" diaphragm pump	B-10I	1	12			715	206	921	1,275
1100	6" centrifugal pump	B-10K	1	12	↓		715	480	1,195	1,575
1300	CMP, incl. excavation 3' deep, 12" diameter	B-6	115	.209	L.F.	14.95	11.15	2.53	28.63	35.50
1400	18" diameter		100	.240	"	23.50	12.80	2.91	39.21	47.50
1600	Sump hole construction, incl. excavation and gravel, pit		1250	.019	C.F.	1.08	1.02	.23	2.33	2.97
1700	With 12" gravel collar, 12" pipe, corrugated, 16 ga.		70	.343	L.F.	22.50	18.30	4.16	44.96	56.50
1800	15" pipe, corrugated, 16 ga.		55	.436		29.50	23.50	5.30	58.30	73
1900	18" pipe, corrugated, 16 ga.		50	.480		34.50	25.50	5.80	65.80	82.50
2000	24" pipe, corrugated, 14 ga.		40	.600	↓	41	32	7.30	80.30	101
2200	Wood lining, up to 4' x 4', add	↓	300	.080	SFCA	15.30	4.27	.97	20.54	24
9950	See Section 31 23 19.40 for wellpoints									
9960	See Section 31 23 19.30 for deep well systems									

31 23 19.30 Wells

		Crew	Daily Output	Labor-Hours	Unit	Material	Labor	Equipment	Total	Total Incl O&P
0010	**WELLS**									
0011	For dewatering 10' to 20' deep, 2' diameter									
0020	with steel casing, minimum	B-6	165	.145	V.L.F.	36	7.75	1.76	45.51	53.50
0050	Average	↓	98	.245	↓	44	13.05	2.97	60.02	71

31 23 Excavation and Fill

31 23 19 – Dewatering

31 23 19.30 Wells

		Crew	Daily Output	Labor-Hours	Unit	Material	2024 Bare Costs Labor	Equipment	Total	Total Incl O&P
0100	Maximum	B-6	49	.490	V.L.F.	50	26	5.95	81.95	100
0300	For dewatering pumps see 01 54 33 in Reference Section									
0500	For domestic water wells, see Section 33 21 13.10									

31 23 19.40 Wellpoints

		Crew	Daily Output	Labor-Hours	Unit	Material	Labor	Equipment	Total	Total Incl O&P
0010	**WELLPOINTS** R312319-90									
0011	For equipment rental, see 01 54 33 in Reference Section									
0100	Installation and removal of single stage system									
0110	Labor only, 0.75 labor-hours per L.F.	1 Clab	10.70	.748	LF Hdr		36.50		36.50	54
0200	2.0 labor-hours per L.F.	"	4	2	"		98		98	145
0400	Pump operation, 4 @ 6 hr. shifts									
0410	Per 24 hr. day	4 Eqlt	1.27	25.197	Day		1,550		1,550	2,325
0500	Per 168 hr. week, 160 hr. straight, 8 hr. double time		.18	178	Week		11,000		11,000	16,300
0550	Per 4.3 week month		.04	800	Month		49,600		49,600	73,500
0600	Complete installation, operation, equipment rental, fuel &									
0610	removal of system with 2" wellpoints 5' OC									
0700	100' long header, 6" diameter, first month	4 Eqlt	3.23	9.907	LF Hdr	154	615		769	1,075
0800	Thereafter, per month		4.13	7.748		123	480		603	845
1000	200' long header, 8" diameter, first month		6	5.333		147	330		477	650
1100	Thereafter, per month		8.39	3.814		69	236		305	425
1300	500' long header, 8" diameter, first month		10.63	3.010		54	187		241	335
1400	Thereafter, per month		20.91	1.530		38.50	95		133.50	184
1600	1,000' long header, 10" diameter, first month		11.62	2.754		46	171		217	305
1700	Thereafter, per month		41.81	.765		23	47.50		70.50	96
1900	Note: above figures include pumping 168 hrs. per week,									
1910	the pump operator, and one stand-by pump.									

31 23 23 – Fill

31 23 23.15 Borrow, Loading and/or Spreading

		Crew	Daily Output	Labor-Hours	Unit	Material	Labor	Equipment	Total	Total Incl O&P
0010	**BORROW, LOADING AND/OR SPREADING**									
0020	Material only, bank run gravel				Ton	10.75			10.75	11.85
0500	Haul 2 mi. spread, 200 HP dozer, bank run gravel	B-15	1100	.025			1.48	3.11	4.59	5.60
1000	Hand spread, bank run gravel	A-5	33	.545			27	3.19	30.19	43.50
1800	Delivery charge, minimum 20 tons, 1 hr. round trip, add	B-34B	130	.062			3.52	7.60	11.12	13.60
1820	1-1/2 hr. round trip, add		93	.086			4.92	10.60	15.52	18.95
1840	2 hr. round trip, add		65	.123			7.05	15.20	22.25	27

31 23 23.16 Fill By Borrow and Utility Bedding

		Crew	Daily Output	Labor-Hours	Unit	Material	Labor	Equipment	Total	Total Incl O&P
0010	**FILL BY BORROW AND UTILITY BEDDING**									
0049	Utility bedding, for pipe & conduit, not incl. compaction G1030-805									
0050	Crushed or screened bank run gravel	B-6	150	.160	L.C.Y.	17.10	8.55	1.94	27.59	33.50
0100	Crushed stone 3/4" to 1/2"		150	.160		34	8.55	1.94	44.49	52.50
0200	Sand, dead or bank		150	.160		15.40	8.55	1.94	25.89	31.50
0500	Compacting bedding in trench	A-1D	90	.089	B.C.Y.		4.36	1.47	5.83	8.05
0600	If material source exceeds 2 miles, add for extra mileage.									
0610	See Section 31 23 23.20 for hauling mileage add.									

31 23 23.17 General Fill

		Crew	Daily Output	Labor-Hours	Unit	Material	Labor	Equipment	Total	Total Incl O&P
0010	**GENERAL FILL**									
0011	Spread dumped material, no compaction									
0020	By dozer	B-10B	1000	.012	L.C.Y.		.72	1.44	2.16	2.65
0100	By hand	1 Clab	12	.667	"		32.50		32.50	48.50
0500	Gravel fill, compacted, under floor slabs, 4" deep	B-37	10000	.005	S.F.	.34	.25	.03	.62	.77
0600	6" deep		8600	.006		.51	.29	.03	.83	1.02
0700	9" deep		7200	.007		.84	.34	.04	1.22	1.48

31 23 Excavation and Fill

31 23 23 – Fill

31 23 23.17 General Fill		Crew	Daily Output	Labor-Hours	Unit	Material	2024 Bare Costs Labor	2024 Bare Costs Equipment	Total	Total Incl O&P
0800	12" deep	B-37	6000	.008	S.F.	1.18	.41	.04	1.63	1.96
1000	Alternate pricing method, 4" deep		120	.400	B.C.Y.	25.50	20.50	2.20	48.20	61
1100	6" deep		160	.300		25.50	15.45	1.65	42.60	53
1200	9" deep		200	.240		25.50	12.35	1.32	39.17	48
1300	12" deep		220	.218		25.50	11.25	1.20	37.95	46
1400	Granular fill				L.C.Y.	16.85			16.85	18.55

31 23 23.20 Hauling		Crew	Daily Output	Labor-Hours	Unit	Material	2024 Bare Costs Labor	2024 Bare Costs Equipment	Total	Total Incl O&P
0010	**HAULING**									
0011	Excavated or borrow, loose cubic yards									
0012	no loading equipment, including hauling, waiting, loading/dumping									
0013	time per cycle (wait, load, travel, unload or dump & return)									
0014	8 C.Y. truck, 15 MPH avg., cycle 0.5 miles, 10 min. wait/ld./uld.	B-34A	320	.025	L.C.Y.		1.43	1.58	3.01	3.87
0016	cycle 1 mile		272	.029			1.68	1.86	3.54	4.55
0018	cycle 2 miles		208	.038			2.20	2.43	4.63	5.95
0020	cycle 4 miles		144	.056			3.18	3.52	6.70	8.60
0022	cycle 6 miles		112	.071			4.09	4.52	8.61	11.05
0024	cycle 8 miles		88	.091			5.20	5.75	10.95	14.10
0026	20 MPH avg., cycle 0.5 mile		336	.024			1.36	1.51	2.87	3.69
0028	cycle 1 mile		296	.027			1.55	1.71	3.26	4.18
0030	cycle 2 miles		240	.033			1.91	2.11	4.02	5.15
0032	cycle 4 miles		176	.045			2.60	2.88	5.48	7.05
0034	cycle 6 miles		136	.059			3.37	3.72	7.09	9.10
0036	cycle 8 miles		112	.071			4.09	4.52	8.61	11.05
0044	25 MPH avg., cycle 4 miles		192	.042			2.39	2.64	5.03	6.45
0046	cycle 6 miles		160	.050			2.86	3.16	6.02	7.75
0048	cycle 8 miles		128	.063			3.58	3.96	7.54	9.65
0050	30 MPH avg., cycle 4 miles		216	.037			2.12	2.34	4.46	5.75
0052	cycle 6 miles		176	.045			2.60	2.88	5.48	7.05
0054	cycle 8 miles		144	.056			3.18	3.52	6.70	8.60
0114	15 MPH avg., cycle 0.5 mile, 15 min. wait/ld./uld.		224	.036			2.04	2.26	4.30	5.55
0116	cycle 1 mile		200	.040			2.29	2.53	4.82	6.20
0118	cycle 2 miles		168	.048			2.73	3.01	5.74	7.35
0120	cycle 4 miles		120	.067			3.82	4.22	8.04	10.30
0122	cycle 6 miles		96	.083			4.77	5.25	10.02	12.90
0124	cycle 8 miles		80	.100			5.75	6.35	12.10	15.45
0126	20 MPH avg., cycle 0.5 mile		232	.034			1.97	2.18	4.15	5.35
0128	cycle 1 mile		208	.038			2.20	2.43	4.63	5.95
0130	cycle 2 miles		184	.043			2.49	2.75	5.24	6.75
0132	cycle 4 miles		144	.056			3.18	3.52	6.70	8.60
0134	cycle 6 miles		112	.071			4.09	4.52	8.61	11.05
0136	cycle 8 miles		96	.083			4.77	5.25	10.02	12.90
0144	25 MPH avg., cycle 4 miles		152	.053			3.01	3.33	6.34	8.15
0146	cycle 6 miles		128	.063			3.58	3.96	7.54	9.65
0148	cycle 8 miles		112	.071			4.09	4.52	8.61	11.05
0150	30 MPH avg., cycle 4 miles		168	.048			2.73	3.01	5.74	7.35
0152	cycle 6 miles		144	.056			3.18	3.52	6.70	8.60
0154	cycle 8 miles		120	.067			3.82	4.22	8.04	10.30
0214	15 MPH avg., cycle 0.5 mile, 20 min. wait/ld./uld.		176	.045			2.60	2.88	5.48	7.05
0216	cycle 1 mile		160	.050			2.86	3.16	6.02	7.75
0218	cycle 2 miles		136	.059			3.37	3.72	7.09	9.10
0220	cycle 4 miles		104	.077			4.40	4.87	9.27	11.90
0222	cycle 6 miles		88	.091			5.20	5.75	10.95	14.10

31 23 Excavation and Fill

31 23 23 – Fill

31 23 23.20 Hauling		Crew	Daily Output	Labor-Hours	Unit	Material	2024 Bare Costs Labor	Equipment	Total	Total Incl O&P
0224	cycle 8 miles	B-34A	72	.111	L.C.Y.		6.35	7.05	13.40	17.20
0226	20 MPH avg., cycle 0.5 mile		176	.045			2.60	2.88	5.48	7.05
0228	cycle 1 mile		168	.048			2.73	3.01	5.74	7.35
0230	cycle 2 miles		144	.056			3.18	3.52	6.70	8.60
0232	cycle 4 miles		120	.067			3.82	4.22	8.04	10.30
0234	cycle 6 miles		96	.083			4.77	5.25	10.02	12.90
0236	cycle 8 miles		88	.091			5.20	5.75	10.95	14.10
0244	25 MPH avg., cycle 4 miles		128	.063			3.58	3.96	7.54	9.65
0246	cycle 6 miles		112	.071			4.09	4.52	8.61	11.05
0248	cycle 8 miles		96	.083			4.77	5.25	10.02	12.90
0250	30 MPH avg., cycle 4 miles		136	.059			3.37	3.72	7.09	9.10
0252	cycle 6 miles		120	.067			3.82	4.22	8.04	10.30
0254	cycle 8 miles		104	.077			4.40	4.87	9.27	11.90
0314	15 MPH avg., cycle 0.5 mile, 25 min. wait/ld./uld.		144	.056			3.18	3.52	6.70	8.60
0316	cycle 1 mile		128	.063			3.58	3.96	7.54	9.65
0318	cycle 2 miles		112	.071			4.09	4.52	8.61	11.05
0320	cycle 4 miles		96	.083			4.77	5.25	10.02	12.90
0322	cycle 6 miles		80	.100			5.75	6.35	12.10	15.45
0324	cycle 8 miles		64	.125			7.15	7.90	15.05	19.35
0326	20 MPH avg., cycle 0.5 mile		144	.056			3.18	3.52	6.70	8.60
0328	cycle 1 mile		136	.059			3.37	3.72	7.09	9.10
0330	cycle 2 miles		120	.067			3.82	4.22	8.04	10.30
0332	cycle 4 miles		104	.077			4.40	4.87	9.27	11.90
0334	cycle 6 miles		88	.091			5.20	5.75	10.95	14.10
0336	cycle 8 miles		80	.100			5.75	6.35	12.10	15.45
0344	25 MPH avg., cycle 4 miles		112	.071			4.09	4.52	8.61	11.05
0346	cycle 6 miles		96	.083			4.77	5.25	10.02	12.90
0348	cycle 8 miles		88	.091			5.20	5.75	10.95	14.10
0350	30 MPH avg., cycle 4 miles		112	.071			4.09	4.52	8.61	11.05
0352	cycle 6 miles		104	.077			4.40	4.87	9.27	11.90
0354	cycle 8 miles		96	.083			4.77	5.25	10.02	12.90
0414	15 MPH avg., cycle 0.5 mile, 30 min. wait/ld./uld.		120	.067			3.82	4.22	8.04	10.30
0416	cycle 1 mile		112	.071			4.09	4.52	8.61	11.05
0418	cycle 2 miles		96	.083			4.77	5.25	10.02	12.90
0420	cycle 4 miles		80	.100			5.75	6.35	12.10	15.45
0422	cycle 6 miles		72	.111			6.35	7.05	13.40	17.20
0424	cycle 8 miles		64	.125			7.15	7.90	15.05	19.35
0426	20 MPH avg., cycle 0.5 mile		120	.067			3.82	4.22	8.04	10.30
0428	cycle 1 mile		112	.071			4.09	4.52	8.61	11.05
0430	cycle 2 miles		104	.077			4.40	4.87	9.27	11.90
0432	cycle 4 miles		88	.091			5.20	5.75	10.95	14.10
0434	cycle 6 miles		80	.100			5.75	6.35	12.10	15.45
0436	cycle 8 miles		72	.111			6.35	7.05	13.40	17.20
0444	25 MPH avg., cycle 4 miles		96	.083			4.77	5.25	10.02	12.90
0446	cycle 6 miles		88	.091			5.20	5.75	10.95	14.10
0448	cycle 8 miles		80	.100			5.75	6.35	12.10	15.45
0450	30 MPH avg., cycle 4 miles		96	.083			4.77	5.25	10.02	12.90
0452	cycle 6 miles		88	.091			5.20	5.75	10.95	14.10
0454	cycle 8 miles		80	.100			5.75	6.35	12.10	15.45
0514	15 MPH avg., cycle 0.5 mile, 35 min. wait/ld./uld.		104	.077			4.40	4.87	9.27	11.90
0516	cycle 1 mile		96	.083			4.77	5.25	10.02	12.90
0518	cycle 2 miles		88	.091			5.20	5.75	10.95	14.10
0520	cycle 4 miles		72	.111			6.35	7.05	13.40	17.20

31 23 Excavation and Fill

31 23 23 – Fill

31 23 23.20 Hauling		Crew	Daily Output	Labor-Hours	Unit	Material	2024 Bare Costs Labor	2024 Bare Costs Equipment	Total	Total Incl O&P
0522	cycle 6 miles	B-34A	64	.125	L.C.Y.		7.15	7.90	15.05	19.35
0524	cycle 8 miles		56	.143			8.20	9.05	17.25	22
0526	20 MPH avg., cycle 0.5 mile		104	.077			4.40	4.87	9.27	11.90
0528	cycle 1 mile		96	.083			4.77	5.25	10.02	12.90
0530	cycle 2 miles		96	.083			4.77	5.25	10.02	12.90
0532	cycle 4 miles		80	.100			5.75	6.35	12.10	15.45
0534	cycle 6 miles		72	.111			6.35	7.05	13.40	17.20
0536	cycle 8 miles		64	.125			7.15	7.90	15.05	19.35
0544	25 MPH avg., cycle 4 miles		88	.091			5.20	5.75	10.95	14.10
0546	cycle 6 miles		80	.100			5.75	6.35	12.10	15.45
0548	cycle 8 miles		72	.111			6.35	7.05	13.40	17.20
0550	30 MPH avg., cycle 4 miles		88	.091			5.20	5.75	10.95	14.10
0552	cycle 6 miles		80	.100			5.75	6.35	12.10	15.45
0554	cycle 8 miles		72	.111			6.35	7.05	13.40	17.20
1014	12 C.Y. truck, cycle 0.5 mile, 15 MPH avg., 15 min. wait/ld./uld.	B-34B	336	.024			1.36	2.94	4.30	5.25
1016	cycle 1 mile		300	.027			1.53	3.29	4.82	5.90
1018	cycle 2 miles		252	.032			1.82	3.92	5.74	7
1020	cycle 4 miles		180	.044			2.54	5.50	8.04	9.85
1022	cycle 6 miles		144	.056			3.18	6.85	10.03	12.30
1024	cycle 8 miles		120	.067			3.82	8.25	12.07	14.70
1025	cycle 10 miles		96	.083			4.77	10.30	15.07	18.40
1026	20 MPH avg., cycle 0.5 mile		348	.023			1.32	2.84	4.16	5.10
1028	cycle 1 mile		312	.026			1.47	3.16	4.63	5.65
1030	cycle 2 miles		276	.029			1.66	3.58	5.24	6.40
1032	cycle 4 miles		216	.037			2.12	4.57	6.69	8.20
1034	cycle 6 miles		168	.048			2.73	5.90	8.63	10.50
1036	cycle 8 miles		144	.056			3.18	6.85	10.03	12.30
1038	cycle 10 miles		120	.067			3.82	8.25	12.07	14.70
1040	25 MPH avg., cycle 4 miles		228	.035			2.01	4.33	6.34	7.75
1042	cycle 6 miles		192	.042			2.39	5.15	7.54	9.20
1044	cycle 8 miles		168	.048			2.73	5.90	8.63	10.50
1046	cycle 10 miles		144	.056			3.18	6.85	10.03	12.30
1050	30 MPH avg., cycle 4 miles		252	.032			1.82	3.92	5.74	7
1052	cycle 6 miles		216	.037			2.12	4.57	6.69	8.20
1054	cycle 8 miles		180	.044			2.54	5.50	8.04	9.85
1056	cycle 10 miles		156	.051			2.94	6.35	9.29	11.30
1060	35 MPH avg., cycle 4 miles		264	.030			1.73	3.74	5.47	6.70
1062	cycle 6 miles		228	.035			2.01	4.33	6.34	7.75
1064	cycle 8 miles		204	.039			2.25	4.84	7.09	8.65
1066	cycle 10 miles		180	.044			2.54	5.50	8.04	9.85
1068	cycle 20 miles		120	.067			3.82	8.25	12.07	14.70
1069	cycle 30 miles		84	.095			5.45	11.75	17.20	21
1070	cycle 40 miles		72	.111			6.35	13.70	20.05	24.50
1072	40 MPH avg., cycle 6 miles		240	.033			1.91	4.11	6.02	7.35
1074	cycle 8 miles		216	.037			2.12	4.57	6.69	8.20
1076	cycle 10 miles		192	.042			2.39	5.15	7.54	9.20
1078	cycle 20 miles		120	.067			3.82	8.25	12.07	14.70
1080	cycle 30 miles		96	.083			4.77	10.30	15.07	18.40
1082	cycle 40 miles		72	.111			6.35	13.70	20.05	24.50
1084	cycle 50 miles		60	.133			7.65	16.45	24.10	29.50
1094	45 MPH avg., cycle 8 miles		216	.037			2.12	4.57	6.69	8.20
1096	cycle 10 miles		204	.039			2.25	4.84	7.09	8.65
1098	cycle 20 miles		132	.061			3.47	7.50	10.97	13.40

31 23 Excavation and Fill

31 23 23 – Fill

31 23 23.20 Hauling

		Crew	Daily Output	Labor-Hours	Unit	Material	2024 Bare Costs Labor	Equipment	Total	Total Incl O&P
1100	cycle 30 miles	B-34B	108	.074	L.C.Y.		4.24	9.15	13.39	16.35
1102	cycle 40 miles		84	.095			5.45	11.75	17.20	21
1104	cycle 50 miles		72	.111			6.35	13.70	20.05	24.50
1106	50 MPH avg., cycle 10 miles		216	.037			2.12	4.57	6.69	8.20
1108	cycle 20 miles		144	.056			3.18	6.85	10.03	12.30
1110	cycle 30 miles		108	.074			4.24	9.15	13.39	16.35
1112	cycle 40 miles		84	.095			5.45	11.75	17.20	21
1114	cycle 50 miles		72	.111			6.35	13.70	20.05	24.50
1214	15 MPH avg., cycle 0.5 mile, 20 min. wait/ld./uld.		264	.030			1.73	3.74	5.47	6.70
1216	cycle 1 mile		240	.033			1.91	4.11	6.02	7.35
1218	cycle 2 miles		204	.039			2.25	4.84	7.09	8.65
1220	cycle 4 miles		156	.051			2.94	6.35	9.29	11.30
1222	cycle 6 miles		132	.061			3.47	7.50	10.97	13.40
1224	cycle 8 miles		108	.074			4.24	9.15	13.39	16.35
1225	cycle 10 miles		96	.083			4.77	10.30	15.07	18.40
1226	20 MPH avg., cycle 0.5 mile		264	.030			1.73	3.74	5.47	6.70
1228	cycle 1 mile		252	.032			1.82	3.92	5.74	7
1230	cycle 2 miles		216	.037			2.12	4.57	6.69	8.20
1232	cycle 4 miles		180	.044			2.54	5.50	8.04	9.85
1234	cycle 6 miles		144	.056			3.18	6.85	10.03	12.30
1236	cycle 8 miles		132	.061			3.47	7.50	10.97	13.40
1238	cycle 10 miles		108	.074			4.24	9.15	13.39	16.35
1240	25 MPH avg., cycle 4 miles		192	.042			2.39	5.15	7.54	9.20
1242	cycle 6 miles		168	.048			2.73	5.90	8.63	10.50
1244	cycle 8 miles		144	.056			3.18	6.85	10.03	12.30
1246	cycle 10 miles		132	.061			3.47	7.50	10.97	13.40
1250	30 MPH avg., cycle 4 miles		204	.039			2.25	4.84	7.09	8.65
1252	cycle 6 miles		180	.044			2.54	5.50	8.04	9.85
1254	cycle 8 miles		156	.051			2.94	6.35	9.29	11.30
1256	cycle 10 miles		144	.056			3.18	6.85	10.03	12.30
1260	35 MPH avg., cycle 4 miles		216	.037			2.12	4.57	6.69	8.20
1262	cycle 6 miles		192	.042			2.39	5.15	7.54	9.20
1264	cycle 8 miles		168	.048			2.73	5.90	8.63	10.50
1266	cycle 10 miles		156	.051			2.94	6.35	9.29	11.30
1268	cycle 20 miles		108	.074			4.24	9.15	13.39	16.35
1269	cycle 30 miles		72	.111			6.35	13.70	20.05	24.50
1270	cycle 40 miles		60	.133			7.65	16.45	24.10	29.50
1272	40 MPH avg., cycle 6 miles		192	.042			2.39	5.15	7.54	9.20
1274	cycle 8 miles		180	.044			2.54	5.50	8.04	9.85
1276	cycle 10 miles		156	.051			2.94	6.35	9.29	11.30
1278	cycle 20 miles		108	.074			4.24	9.15	13.39	16.35
1280	cycle 30 miles		84	.095			5.45	11.75	17.20	21
1282	cycle 40 miles		72	.111			6.35	13.70	20.05	24.50
1284	cycle 50 miles		60	.133			7.65	16.45	24.10	29.50
1294	45 MPH avg., cycle 8 miles		180	.044			2.54	5.50	8.04	9.85
1296	cycle 10 miles		168	.048			2.73	5.90	8.63	10.50
1298	cycle 20 miles		120	.067			3.82	8.25	12.07	14.70
1300	cycle 30 miles		96	.083			4.77	10.30	15.07	18.40
1302	cycle 40 miles		72	.111			6.35	13.70	20.05	24.50
1304	cycle 50 miles		60	.133			7.65	16.45	24.10	29.50
1306	50 MPH avg., cycle 10 miles		180	.044			2.54	5.50	8.04	9.85
1308	cycle 20 miles		132	.061			3.47	7.50	10.97	13.40
1310	cycle 30 miles		96	.083			4.77	10.30	15.07	18.40

For customer support on your Plumbing Costs with RSMeans Data call 800.448.8182.

31 23 Excavation and Fill

31 23 23 – Fill

31 23 23.20 Hauling

		Crew	Daily Output	Labor-Hours	Unit	Material	2024 Bare Costs Labor	Equipment	Total	Total Incl O&P
1312	cycle 40 miles	B-34B	84	.095	L.C.Y.		5.45	11.75	17.20	21
1314	cycle 50 miles		72	.111			6.35	13.70	20.05	24.50
1414	15 MPH avg., cycle 0.5 mile, 25 min. wait/ld./uld.		204	.039			2.25	4.84	7.09	8.65
1416	cycle 1 mile		192	.042			2.39	5.15	7.54	9.20
1418	cycle 2 miles		168	.048			2.73	5.90	8.63	10.50
1420	cycle 4 miles		132	.061			3.47	7.50	10.97	13.40
1422	cycle 6 miles		120	.067			3.82	8.25	12.07	14.70
1424	cycle 8 miles		96	.083			4.77	10.30	15.07	18.40
1425	cycle 10 miles		84	.095			5.45	11.75	17.20	21
1426	20 MPH avg., cycle 0.5 mile		216	.037			2.12	4.57	6.69	8.20
1428	cycle 1 mile		204	.039			2.25	4.84	7.09	8.65
1430	cycle 2 miles		180	.044			2.54	5.50	8.04	9.85
1432	cycle 4 miles		156	.051			2.94	6.35	9.29	11.30
1434	cycle 6 miles		132	.061			3.47	7.50	10.97	13.40
1436	cycle 8 miles		120	.067			3.82	8.25	12.07	14.70
1438	cycle 10 miles		96	.083			4.77	10.30	15.07	18.40
1440	25 MPH avg., cycle 4 miles		168	.048			2.73	5.90	8.63	10.50
1442	cycle 6 miles		144	.056			3.18	6.85	10.03	12.30
1444	cycle 8 miles		132	.061			3.47	7.50	10.97	13.40
1446	cycle 10 miles		108	.074			4.24	9.15	13.39	16.35
1450	30 MPH avg., cycle 4 miles		168	.048			2.73	5.90	8.63	10.50
1452	cycle 6 miles		156	.051			2.94	6.35	9.29	11.30
1454	cycle 8 miles		132	.061			3.47	7.50	10.97	13.40
1456	cycle 10 miles		120	.067			3.82	8.25	12.07	14.70
1460	35 MPH avg., cycle 4 miles		180	.044			2.54	5.50	8.04	9.85
1462	cycle 6 miles		156	.051			2.94	6.35	9.29	11.30
1464	cycle 8 miles		144	.056			3.18	6.85	10.03	12.30
1466	cycle 10 miles		132	.061			3.47	7.50	10.97	13.40
1468	cycle 20 miles		96	.083			4.77	10.30	15.07	18.40
1469	cycle 30 miles		72	.111			6.35	13.70	20.05	24.50
1470	cycle 40 miles		60	.133			7.65	16.45	24.10	29.50
1472	40 MPH avg., cycle 6 miles		168	.048			2.73	5.90	8.63	10.50
1474	cycle 8 miles		156	.051			2.94	6.35	9.29	11.30
1476	cycle 10 miles		144	.056			3.18	6.85	10.03	12.30
1478	cycle 20 miles		96	.083			4.77	10.30	15.07	18.40
1480	cycle 30 miles		84	.095			5.45	11.75	17.20	21
1482	cycle 40 miles		60	.133			7.65	16.45	24.10	29.50
1484	cycle 50 miles		60	.133			7.65	16.45	24.10	29.50
1494	45 MPH avg., cycle 8 miles		156	.051			2.94	6.35	9.29	11.30
1496	cycle 10 miles		144	.056			3.18	6.85	10.03	12.30
1498	cycle 20 miles		108	.074			4.24	9.15	13.39	16.35
1500	cycle 30 miles		84	.095			5.45	11.75	17.20	21
1502	cycle 40 miles		72	.111			6.35	13.70	20.05	24.50
1504	cycle 50 miles		60	.133			7.65	16.45	24.10	29.50
1506	50 MPH avg., cycle 10 miles		156	.051			2.94	6.35	9.29	11.30
1508	cycle 20 miles		120	.067			3.82	8.25	12.07	14.70
1510	cycle 30 miles		96	.083			4.77	10.30	15.07	18.40
1512	cycle 40 miles		72	.111			6.35	13.70	20.05	24.50
1514	cycle 50 miles		60	.133			7.65	16.45	24.10	29.50
1614	15 MPH avg., cycle 0.5 mile, 30 min. wait/ld./uld.		180	.044			2.54	5.50	8.04	9.85
1616	cycle 1 mile		168	.048			2.73	5.90	8.63	10.50
1618	cycle 2 miles		144	.056			3.18	6.85	10.03	12.30
1620	cycle 4 miles		120	.067			3.82	8.25	12.07	14.70

31 23 Excavation and Fill

31 23 23 – Fill

31 23 23.20 Hauling

		Crew	Daily Output	Labor-Hours	Unit	Material	2024 Bare Costs Labor	Equipment	Total	Total Incl O&P
1622	cycle 6 miles	B-34B	108	.074	L.C.Y.		4.24	9.15	13.39	16.35
1624	cycle 8 miles		84	.095			5.45	11.75	17.20	21
1625	cycle 10 miles		84	.095			5.45	11.75	17.20	21
1626	20 MPH avg., cycle 0.5 mile		180	.044			2.54	5.50	8.04	9.85
1628	cycle 1 mile		168	.048			2.73	5.90	8.63	10.50
1630	cycle 2 miles		156	.051			2.94	6.35	9.29	11.30
1632	cycle 4 miles		132	.061			3.47	7.50	10.97	13.40
1634	cycle 6 miles		120	.067			3.82	8.25	12.07	14.70
1636	cycle 8 miles		108	.074			4.24	9.15	13.39	16.35
1638	cycle 10 miles		96	.083			4.77	10.30	15.07	18.40
1640	25 MPH avg., cycle 4 miles		144	.056			3.18	6.85	10.03	12.30
1642	cycle 6 miles		132	.061			3.47	7.50	10.97	13.40
1644	cycle 8 miles		108	.074			4.24	9.15	13.39	16.35
1646	cycle 10 miles		108	.074			4.24	9.15	13.39	16.35
1650	30 MPH avg., cycle 4 miles		144	.056			3.18	6.85	10.03	12.30
1652	cycle 6 miles		132	.061			3.47	7.50	10.97	13.40
1654	cycle 8 miles		120	.067			3.82	8.25	12.07	14.70
1656	cycle 10 miles		108	.074			4.24	9.15	13.39	16.35
1660	35 MPH avg., cycle 4 miles		156	.051			2.94	6.35	9.29	11.30
1662	cycle 6 miles		144	.056			3.18	6.85	10.03	12.30
1664	cycle 8 miles		132	.061			3.47	7.50	10.97	13.40
1666	cycle 10 miles		120	.067			3.82	8.25	12.07	14.70
1668	cycle 20 miles		84	.095			5.45	11.75	17.20	21
1669	cycle 30 miles		72	.111			6.35	13.70	20.05	24.50
1670	cycle 40 miles		60	.133			7.65	16.45	24.10	29.50
1672	40 MPH avg., cycle 6 miles		144	.056			3.18	6.85	10.03	12.30
1674	cycle 8 miles		132	.061			3.47	7.50	10.97	13.40
1676	cycle 10 miles		120	.067			3.82	8.25	12.07	14.70
1678	cycle 20 miles		96	.083			4.77	10.30	15.07	18.40
1680	cycle 30 miles		72	.111			6.35	13.70	20.05	24.50
1682	cycle 40 miles		60	.133			7.65	16.45	24.10	29.50
1684	cycle 50 miles		48	.167			9.55	20.50	30.05	36.50
1694	45 MPH avg., cycle 8 miles		144	.056			3.18	6.85	10.03	12.30
1696	cycle 10 miles		132	.061			3.47	7.50	10.97	13.40
1698	cycle 20 miles		96	.083			4.77	10.30	15.07	18.40
1700	cycle 30 miles		84	.095			5.45	11.75	17.20	21
1702	cycle 40 miles		60	.133			7.65	16.45	24.10	29.50
1704	cycle 50 miles		60	.133			7.65	16.45	24.10	29.50
1706	50 MPH avg., cycle 10 miles		132	.061			3.47	7.50	10.97	13.40
1708	cycle 20 miles		108	.074			4.24	9.15	13.39	16.35
1710	cycle 30 miles		84	.095			5.45	11.75	17.20	21
1712	cycle 40 miles		72	.111			6.35	13.70	20.05	24.50
1714	cycle 50 miles		60	.133			7.65	16.45	24.10	29.50
2000	Hauling, 8 C.Y. truck, small project cost per hour	B-34A	8	1	Hr.		57.50	63.50	121	155
2100	12 C.Y. truck	B-34B	8	1			57.50	123	180.50	221
2150	16.5 C.Y. truck	B-34C	8	1			57.50	91.50	149	186
2175	18 C.Y. 8 wheel truck	B-34I	8	1			57.50	103	160.50	199
2200	20 C.Y. truck	B-34D	8	1			57.50	93.50	151	188
2300	Grading at dump, or embankment if required, by dozer	B-10B	1000	.012	L.C.Y.		.72	1.44	2.16	2.65
2310	Spotter at fill or cut, if required	1 Clab	8	1	Hr.		49		49	72.50
9014	18 C.Y. truck, 8 wheels,15 min. wait/ld./uld.,15 MPH, cycle 0.5 mi.	B-34I	504	.016	L.C.Y.		.91	1.64	2.55	3.16
9016	cycle 1 mile		450	.018			1.02	1.84	2.86	3.53
9018	cycle 2 miles		378	.021			1.21	2.19	3.40	4.21

31 23 Excavation and Fill

31 23 23 – Fill

31 23 23.20 Hauling

		Crew	Daily Output	Labor-Hours	Unit	Material	2024 Bare Costs Labor	2024 Bare Costs Equipment	Total	Total Incl O&P
9020	cycle 4 miles	B-34I	270	.030	L.C.Y.		1.70	3.06	4.76	5.90
9022	cycle 6 miles		216	.037			2.12	3.83	5.95	7.35
9024	cycle 8 miles		180	.044			2.54	4.60	7.14	8.85
9025	cycle 10 miles		144	.056			3.18	5.75	8.93	11.05
9026	20 MPH avg., cycle 0.5 mile		522	.015			.88	1.59	2.47	3.04
9028	cycle 1 mile		468	.017			.98	1.77	2.75	3.39
9030	cycle 2 miles		414	.019			1.11	2	3.11	3.84
9032	cycle 4 miles		324	.025			1.41	2.55	3.96	4.91
9034	cycle 6 miles		252	.032			1.82	3.28	5.10	6.30
9036	cycle 8 miles		216	.037			2.12	3.83	5.95	7.35
9038	cycle 10 miles		180	.044			2.54	4.60	7.14	8.85
9040	25 MPH avg., cycle 4 miles		342	.023			1.34	2.42	3.76	4.65
9042	cycle 6 miles		288	.028			1.59	2.87	4.46	5.50
9044	cycle 8 miles		252	.032			1.82	3.28	5.10	6.30
9046	cycle 10 miles		216	.037			2.12	3.83	5.95	7.35
9050	30 MPH avg., cycle 4 miles		378	.021			1.21	2.19	3.40	4.21
9052	cycle 6 miles		324	.025			1.41	2.55	3.96	4.91
9054	cycle 8 miles		270	.030			1.70	3.06	4.76	5.90
9056	cycle 10 miles		234	.034			1.96	3.54	5.50	6.80
9060	35 MPH avg., cycle 4 miles		396	.020			1.16	2.09	3.25	4.02
9062	cycle 6 miles		342	.023			1.34	2.42	3.76	4.65
9064	cycle 8 miles		288	.028			1.59	2.87	4.46	5.50
9066	cycle 10 miles		270	.030			1.70	3.06	4.76	5.90
9068	cycle 20 miles		162	.049			2.83	5.10	7.93	9.80
9070	cycle 30 miles		126	.063			3.63	6.55	10.18	12.60
9072	cycle 40 miles		90	.089			5.10	9.20	14.30	17.65
9074	40 MPH avg., cycle 6 miles		360	.022			1.27	2.30	3.57	4.42
9076	cycle 8 miles		324	.025			1.41	2.55	3.96	4.91
9078	cycle 10 miles		288	.028			1.59	2.87	4.46	5.50
9080	cycle 20 miles		180	.044			2.54	4.60	7.14	8.85
9082	cycle 30 miles		144	.056			3.18	5.75	8.93	11.05
9084	cycle 40 miles		108	.074			4.24	7.65	11.89	14.75
9086	cycle 50 miles		90	.089			5.10	9.20	14.30	17.65
9094	45 MPH avg., cycle 8 miles		324	.025			1.41	2.55	3.96	4.91
9096	cycle 10 miles		306	.026			1.50	2.70	4.20	5.20
9098	cycle 20 miles		198	.040			2.31	4.18	6.49	8.05
9100	cycle 30 miles		144	.056			3.18	5.75	8.93	11.05
9102	cycle 40 miles		126	.063			3.63	6.55	10.18	12.60
9104	cycle 50 miles		108	.074			4.24	7.65	11.89	14.75
9106	50 MPH avg., cycle 10 miles		324	.025			1.41	2.55	3.96	4.91
9108	cycle 20 miles		216	.037			2.12	3.83	5.95	7.35
9110	cycle 30 miles		162	.049			2.83	5.10	7.93	9.80
9112	cycle 40 miles		126	.063			3.63	6.55	10.18	12.60
9114	cycle 50 miles		108	.074			4.24	7.65	11.89	14.75
9214	20 min. wait/ld./uld.,15 MPH, cycle 0.5 mi.		396	.020			1.16	2.09	3.25	4.02
9216	cycle 1 mile		360	.022			1.27	2.30	3.57	4.42
9218	cycle 2 miles		306	.026			1.50	2.70	4.20	5.20
9220	cycle 4 miles		234	.034			1.96	3.54	5.50	6.80
9222	cycle 6 miles		198	.040			2.31	4.18	6.49	8.05
9224	cycle 8 miles		162	.049			2.83	5.10	7.93	9.80
9225	cycle 10 miles		144	.056			3.18	5.75	8.93	11.05
9226	20 MPH avg., cycle 0.5 mile		396	.020			1.16	2.09	3.25	4.02
9228	cycle 1 mile		378	.021			1.21	2.19	3.40	4.21

31 23 Excavation and Fill

31 23 23 – Fill

31 23 23.20 Hauling

		Crew	Daily Output	Labor-Hours	Unit	Material	2024 Bare Costs Labor	2024 Bare Costs Equipment	Total	Total Incl O&P
9230	cycle 2 miles	B-34I	324	.025	L.C.Y.		1.41	2.55	3.96	4.91
9232	cycle 4 miles		270	.030			1.70	3.06	4.76	5.90
9234	cycle 6 miles		216	.037			2.12	3.83	5.95	7.35
9236	cycle 8 miles		198	.040			2.31	4.18	6.49	8.05
9238	cycle 10 miles		162	.049			2.83	5.10	7.93	9.80
9240	25 MPH avg., cycle 4 miles		288	.028			1.59	2.87	4.46	5.50
9242	cycle 6 miles		252	.032			1.82	3.28	5.10	6.30
9244	cycle 8 miles		216	.037			2.12	3.83	5.95	7.35
9246	cycle 10 miles		198	.040			2.31	4.18	6.49	8.05
9250	30 MPH avg., cycle 4 miles		306	.026			1.50	2.70	4.20	5.20
9252	cycle 6 miles		270	.030			1.70	3.06	4.76	5.90
9254	cycle 8 miles		234	.034			1.96	3.54	5.50	6.80
9256	cycle 10 miles		216	.037			2.12	3.83	5.95	7.35
9260	35 MPH avg., cycle 4 miles		324	.025			1.41	2.55	3.96	4.91
9262	cycle 6 miles		288	.028			1.59	2.87	4.46	5.50
9264	cycle 8 miles		252	.032			1.82	3.28	5.10	6.30
9266	cycle 10 miles		234	.034			1.96	3.54	5.50	6.80
9268	cycle 20 miles		162	.049			2.83	5.10	7.93	9.80
9270	cycle 30 miles		108	.074			4.24	7.65	11.89	14.75
9272	cycle 40 miles		90	.089			5.10	9.20	14.30	17.65
9274	40 MPH avg., cycle 6 miles		288	.028			1.59	2.87	4.46	5.50
9276	cycle 8 miles		270	.030			1.70	3.06	4.76	5.90
9278	cycle 10 miles		234	.034			1.96	3.54	5.50	6.80
9280	cycle 20 miles		162	.049			2.83	5.10	7.93	9.80
9282	cycle 30 miles		126	.063			3.63	6.55	10.18	12.60
9284	cycle 40 miles		108	.074			4.24	7.65	11.89	14.75
9286	cycle 50 miles		90	.089			5.10	9.20	14.30	17.65
9294	45 MPH avg., cycle 8 miles		270	.030			1.70	3.06	4.76	5.90
9296	cycle 10 miles		252	.032			1.82	3.28	5.10	6.30
9298	cycle 20 miles		180	.044			2.54	4.60	7.14	8.85
9300	cycle 30 miles		144	.056			3.18	5.75	8.93	11.05
9302	cycle 40 miles		108	.074			4.24	7.65	11.89	14.75
9304	cycle 50 miles		90	.089			5.10	9.20	14.30	17.65
9306	50 MPH avg., cycle 10 miles		270	.030			1.70	3.06	4.76	5.90
9308	cycle 20 miles		198	.040			2.31	4.18	6.49	8.05
9310	cycle 30 miles		144	.056			3.18	5.75	8.93	11.05
9312	cycle 40 miles		126	.063			3.63	6.55	10.18	12.60
9314	cycle 50 miles		108	.074			4.24	7.65	11.89	14.75
9414	25 min. wait/ld./uld.,15 MPH, cycle 0.5 mi.		306	.026			1.50	2.70	4.20	5.20
9416	cycle 1 mile		288	.028			1.59	2.87	4.46	5.50
9418	cycle 2 miles		252	.032			1.82	3.28	5.10	6.30
9420	cycle 4 miles		198	.040			2.31	4.18	6.49	8.05
9422	cycle 6 miles		180	.044			2.54	4.60	7.14	8.85
9424	cycle 8 miles		144	.056			3.18	5.75	8.93	11.05
9425	cycle 10 miles		126	.063			3.63	6.55	10.18	12.60
9426	20 MPH avg., cycle 0.5 mile		324	.025			1.41	2.55	3.96	4.91
9428	cycle 1 mile		306	.026			1.50	2.70	4.20	5.20
9430	cycle 2 miles		270	.030			1.70	3.06	4.76	5.90
9432	cycle 4 miles		234	.034			1.96	3.54	5.50	6.80
9434	cycle 6 miles		198	.040			2.31	4.18	6.49	8.05
9436	cycle 8 miles		180	.044			2.54	4.60	7.14	8.85
9438	cycle 10 miles		144	.056			3.18	5.75	8.93	11.05
9440	25 MPH avg., cycle 4 miles		252	.032			1.82	3.28	5.10	6.30

31 23 Excavation and Fill

31 23 23 – Fill

31 23 23.20 Hauling

		Crew	Daily Output	Labor-Hours	Unit	Material	2024 Bare Costs Labor	Equipment	Total	Total Incl O&P
9442	cycle 6 miles	B-34I	216	.037	L.C.Y.		2.12	3.83	5.95	7.35
9444	cycle 8 miles		198	.040			2.31	4.18	6.49	8.05
9446	cycle 10 miles		180	.044			2.54	4.60	7.14	8.85
9450	30 MPH avg., cycle 4 miles		252	.032			1.82	3.28	5.10	6.30
9452	cycle 6 miles		234	.034			1.96	3.54	5.50	6.80
9454	cycle 8 miles		198	.040			2.31	4.18	6.49	8.05
9456	cycle 10 miles		180	.044			2.54	4.60	7.14	8.85
9460	35 MPH avg., cycle 4 miles		270	.030			1.70	3.06	4.76	5.90
9462	cycle 6 miles		234	.034			1.96	3.54	5.50	6.80
9464	cycle 8 miles		216	.037			2.12	3.83	5.95	7.35
9466	cycle 10 miles		198	.040			2.31	4.18	6.49	8.05
9468	cycle 20 miles		144	.056			3.18	5.75	8.93	11.05
9470	cycle 30 miles		108	.074			4.24	7.65	11.89	14.75
9472	cycle 40 miles		90	.089			5.10	9.20	14.30	17.65
9474	40 MPH avg., cycle 6 miles		252	.032			1.82	3.28	5.10	6.30
9476	cycle 8 miles		234	.034			1.96	3.54	5.50	6.80
9478	cycle 10 miles		216	.037			2.12	3.83	5.95	7.35
9480	cycle 20 miles		144	.056			3.18	5.75	8.93	11.05
9482	cycle 30 miles		126	.063			3.63	6.55	10.18	12.60
9484	cycle 40 miles		90	.089			5.10	9.20	14.30	17.65
9486	cycle 50 miles		90	.089			5.10	9.20	14.30	17.65
9494	45 MPH avg., cycle 8 miles		234	.034			1.96	3.54	5.50	6.80
9496	cycle 10 miles		216	.037			2.12	3.83	5.95	7.35
9498	cycle 20 miles		162	.049			2.83	5.10	7.93	9.80
9500	cycle 30 miles		126	.063			3.63	6.55	10.18	12.60
9502	cycle 40 miles		108	.074			4.24	7.65	11.89	14.75
9504	cycle 50 miles		90	.089			5.10	9.20	14.30	17.65
9506	50 MPH avg., cycle 10 miles		234	.034			1.96	3.54	5.50	6.80
9508	cycle 20 miles		180	.044			2.54	4.60	7.14	8.85
9510	cycle 30 miles		144	.056			3.18	5.75	8.93	11.05
9512	cycle 40 miles		108	.074			4.24	7.65	11.89	14.75
9514	cycle 50 miles		90	.089			5.10	9.20	14.30	17.65
9614	30 min. wait/ld./uld.,15 MPH, cycle 0.5 mi.		270	.030			1.70	3.06	4.76	5.90
9616	cycle 1 mile		252	.032			1.82	3.28	5.10	6.30
9618	cycle 2 miles		216	.037			2.12	3.83	5.95	7.35
9620	cycle 4 miles		180	.044			2.54	4.60	7.14	8.85
9622	cycle 6 miles		162	.049			2.83	5.10	7.93	9.80
9624	cycle 8 miles		126	.063			3.63	6.55	10.18	12.60
9625	cycle 10 miles		126	.063			3.63	6.55	10.18	12.60
9626	20 MPH avg., cycle 0.5 mile		270	.030			1.70	3.06	4.76	5.90
9628	cycle 1 mile		252	.032			1.82	3.28	5.10	6.30
9630	cycle 2 miles		234	.034			1.96	3.54	5.50	6.80
9632	cycle 4 miles		198	.040			2.31	4.18	6.49	8.05
9634	cycle 6 miles		180	.044			2.54	4.60	7.14	8.85
9636	cycle 8 miles		162	.049			2.83	5.10	7.93	9.80
9638	cycle 10 miles		144	.056			3.18	5.75	8.93	11.05
9640	25 MPH avg., cycle 4 miles		216	.037			2.12	3.83	5.95	7.35
9642	cycle 6 miles		198	.040			2.31	4.18	6.49	8.05
9644	cycle 8 miles		180	.044			2.54	4.60	7.14	8.85
9646	cycle 10 miles		162	.049			2.83	5.10	7.93	9.80
9650	30 MPH avg., cycle 4 miles		216	.037			2.12	3.83	5.95	7.35
9652	cycle 6 miles		198	.040			2.31	4.18	6.49	8.05
9654	cycle 8 miles		180	.044			2.54	4.60	7.14	8.85

31 23 Excavation and Fill

31 23 23 – Fill

31 23 23.20 Hauling

		Crew	Daily Output	Labor-Hours	Unit	Material	2024 Bare Costs Labor	2024 Bare Costs Equipment	Total	Total Incl O&P
9656	cycle 10 miles	B-34I	162	.049	L.C.Y.		2.83	5.10	7.93	9.80
9660	35 MPH avg., cycle 4 miles		234	.034			1.96	3.54	5.50	6.80
9662	cycle 6 miles		216	.037			2.12	3.83	5.95	7.35
9664	cycle 8 miles		198	.040			2.31	4.18	6.49	8.05
9666	cycle 10 miles		180	.044			2.54	4.60	7.14	8.85
9668	cycle 20 miles		126	.063			3.63	6.55	10.18	12.60
9670	cycle 30 miles		108	.074			4.24	7.65	11.89	14.75
9672	cycle 40 miles		90	.089			5.10	9.20	14.30	17.65
9674	40 MPH avg., cycle 6 miles		216	.037			2.12	3.83	5.95	7.35
9676	cycle 8 miles		198	.040			2.31	4.18	6.49	8.05
9678	cycle 10 miles		180	.044			2.54	4.60	7.14	8.85
9680	cycle 20 miles		144	.056			3.18	5.75	8.93	11.05
9682	cycle 30 miles		108	.074			4.24	7.65	11.89	14.75
9684	cycle 40 miles		90	.089			5.10	9.20	14.30	17.65
9686	cycle 50 miles		72	.111			6.35	11.50	17.85	22
9694	45 MPH avg., cycle 8 miles		216	.037			2.12	3.83	5.95	7.35
9696	cycle 10 miles		198	.040			2.31	4.18	6.49	8.05
9698	cycle 20 miles		144	.056			3.18	5.75	8.93	11.05
9700	cycle 30 miles		126	.063			3.63	6.55	10.18	12.60
9702	cycle 40 miles		108	.074			4.24	7.65	11.89	14.75
9704	cycle 50 miles		90	.089			5.10	9.20	14.30	17.65
9706	50 MPH avg., cycle 10 miles		198	.040			2.31	4.18	6.49	8.05
9708	cycle 20 miles		162	.049			2.83	5.10	7.93	9.80
9710	cycle 30 miles		126	.063			3.63	6.55	10.18	12.60
9712	cycle 40 miles		108	.074			4.24	7.65	11.89	14.75
9714	cycle 50 miles		90	.089			5.10	9.20	14.30	17.65

Division Notes

	CREW	DAILY OUTPUT	LABOR-HOURS	UNIT	BARE COSTS				TOTAL INCL O&P
					MAT.	LABOR	EQUIP.	TOTAL	

Division 32 — Exterior Improvements

Estimating Tips

32 01 00 Operations and Maintenance of Exterior Improvements

- Recycling of asphalt pavement is becoming very popular and is an alternative to removal and replacement. It can be a good value engineering proposal if removed pavement can be recycled, either at the project site or at another site that is reasonably close to the project site. Sections on repair of flexible and rigid pavement are included.

32 10 00 Bases, Ballasts, and Paving

- When estimating paving, keep in mind the project schedule. Also note that prices for asphalt and concrete are generally higher in the cold seasons. Lines for pavement markings, including tactile warning systems and fence lines, are included.

32 90 00 Planting

- The timing of planting and guarantee specifications often dictate the costs for establishing tree and shrub growth and a stand of grass or ground cover. Establish the work performance schedule to coincide with the local planting season. Maintenance and growth guarantees can add 20–100% to the total landscaping cost and can be contractually cumbersome. The cost to replace trees and shrubs can be as high as 5% of the total cost, depending on the planting zone, soil conditions, and time of year.

Reference Numbers

Reference numbers are shown at the beginning of some major classifications. These numbers refer to related items in the Reference Section. The reference information may be an estimating procedure, an alternate pricing method, or technical information.

Note: Not all subdivisions listed here necessarily appear. ■

Same Data. Simplified.

Enjoy the convenience and efficiency of accessing your costs anywhere:

- **Skip the multiplier** by setting your location
- **Quickly search,** edit, favorite and share costs
- **Stay on top of price changes** with automatic updates

Discover more at rsmeans.com/online

No part of this cost data may be reproduced, stored in a retrieval system, or transmitted in any form or by any means without prior written permission of Gordian.

32 12 Flexible Paving

32 12 16 – Asphalt Paving

32 12 16.13 Plant-Mix Asphalt Paving

		Crew	Daily Output	Labor-Hours	Unit	Material	2024 Bare Costs Labor	Equipment	Total	Total Incl O&P
0010	**PLANT-MIX ASPHALT PAVING**									
0020	For highways and large paved areas, excludes hauling									
0025	See Section 31 23 23.20 for hauling costs									
0080	Binder course, 1-1/2" thick	B-25	7725	.011	S.Y.	6.60	.61	.42	7.63	8.65
0120	2" thick		6345	.014		8.80	.74	.51	10.05	11.35
0130	2-1/2" thick		5620	.016		11	.84	.58	12.42	13.95
0160	3" thick		4905	.018		13.20	.96	.66	14.82	16.65
0170	3-1/2" thick		4520	.019		15.40	1.04	.72	17.16	19.30
0200	4" thick		4140	.021		17.60	1.14	.78	19.52	22
0300	Wearing course, 1" thick	B-25B	10575	.009		4.37	.49	.34	5.20	5.90
0340	1-1/2" thick		7725	.012		7.35	.68	.46	8.49	9.55
0380	2" thick		6345	.015		9.85	.82	.56	11.23	12.70
0420	2-1/2" thick		5480	.018		12.15	.95	.65	13.75	15.45
0460	3" thick		4900	.020		14.50	1.07	.73	16.30	18.35
0470	3-1/2" thick		4520	.021		17	1.16	.79	18.95	21.50
0480	4" thick		4140	.023		19.45	1.26	.86	21.57	24.50
0600	Porous pavement, 1-1/2" open graded friction course	B-25	7725	.011		20.50	.61	.42	21.53	24
0800	Alternate method of figuring paving costs									
0810	Binder course, 1-1/2" thick	B-25	630	.140	Ton	81	7.50	5.15	93.65	106
0811	2" thick		690	.128		81	6.85	4.69	92.54	104
0812	3" thick		800	.110		81	5.90	4.05	90.95	102
0813	4" thick		900	.098		81	5.25	3.60	89.85	101
0850	Wearing course, 1" thick	B-25B	575	.167		82.50	9.10	6.20	97.80	111
0851	1-1/2" thick		630	.152		82.50	8.30	5.65	96.45	110
0852	2" thick		690	.139		82.50	7.60	5.15	95.25	108
0853	2-1/2" thick		765	.125		82.50	6.85	4.65	94	106
0854	3" thick		800	.120		82.50	6.55	4.45	93.50	106
1000	Pavement replacement over trench, 2" thick	B-17C	90	.533	S.Y.	9.10	29	29	67.10	84.50
1050	4" thick		70	.686		18	37	37.50	92.50	116
1080	6" thick		55	.873		28.50	47	47.50	123	154

32 12 16.14 Asphaltic Concrete Paving

		Crew	Daily Output	Labor-Hours	Unit	Material	2024 Bare Costs Labor	Equipment	Total	Total Incl O&P
0011	**ASPHALTIC CONCRETE PAVING**, parking lots & driveways									
0015	No asphalt hauling included									
0018	Use 6.05 C.Y. per inch per M.S.F. for hauling									
0020	6" stone base, 2" binder course, 1" topping	B-25C	9000	.005	S.F.	2.20	.29	.31	2.80	3.19
0025	2" binder course, 2" topping		9000	.005		2.70	.29	.31	3.30	3.74
0030	3" binder course, 2" topping		9000	.005		3.19	.29	.31	3.79	4.28
0035	4" binder course, 2" topping		9000	.005		3.68	.29	.31	4.28	4.81
0040	1-1/2" binder course, 1" topping		9000	.005		1.95	.29	.31	2.55	2.92
0042	3" binder course, 1" topping		9000	.005		2.69	.29	.31	3.29	3.73
0045	3" binder course, 3" topping		9000	.005		3.69	.29	.31	4.29	4.83
0050	4" binder course, 3" topping		9000	.005		4.18	.29	.31	4.78	5.35
0055	4" binder course, 4" topping		9000	.005		4.68	.29	.31	5.28	5.90
0300	Binder course, 1-1/2" thick		35000	.001		.74	.07	.08	.89	1.01
0400	2" thick		25000	.002		.95	.10	.11	1.16	1.33
0500	3" thick		15000	.003		1.47	.17	.18	1.82	2.08
0600	4" thick		10800	.004		1.93	.24	.26	2.43	2.76
0800	Sand finish course, 3/4" thick		41000	.001		.40	.06	.07	.53	.60
0900	1" thick		34000	.001		.49	.08	.08	.65	.74
1000	Fill pot holes, hot mix, 2" thick	B-16	4200	.008		.98	.39	.24	1.61	1.92
1100	4" thick		3500	.009		1.43	.47	.28	2.18	2.59
1120	6" thick		3100	.010		1.92	.53	.32	2.77	3.26

32 12 Flexible Paving

32 12 16 – Asphalt Paving

32 12 16.14 Asphaltic Concrete Paving

		Crew	Daily Output	Labor-Hours	Unit	Material	2024 Bare Costs Labor	Equipment	Total	Total Incl O&P
1140	Cold patch, 2" thick	B-51	3000	.016	S.F.	1.15	.81	.14	2.10	2.61
1160	4" thick		2700	.018		2.20	.90	.16	3.26	3.92
1180	6" thick		1900	.025		3.42	1.27	.22	4.91	5.90

32 84 Planting Irrigation

32 84 13 – Drip Irrigation

32 84 13.10 Subsurface Drip Irrigation

			Crew	Daily Output	Labor-Hours	Unit	Material	Labor	Equipment	Total	Total Incl O&P
0010	**SUBSURFACE DRIP IRRIGATION**										
0011	Looped grid, pressure compensating										
0100	Preinserted PE emitter, line, hand bury, irregular area, small	G	3 Skwk	1200	.020	L.F.	.31	1.27		1.58	2.24
0150	Medium	G		1800	.013		.31	.85		1.16	1.61
0200	Large	G		2520	.010		.31	.60		.91	1.24
0250	Rectangular area, small	G		2040	.012		.31	.75		1.06	1.46
0300	Medium	G		2640	.009		.31	.58		.89	1.20
0350	Large	G		3600	.007		.31	.42		.73	.97
0400	Install in trench, irregular area, small	G		4050	.006		.31	.38		.69	.90
0450	Medium	G		7488	.003		.31	.20		.51	.64
0500	Large	G		16560	.001		.31	.09		.40	.48
0550	Rectangular area, small	G		8100	.003		.31	.19		.50	.62
0600	Medium	G		21960	.001		.31	.07		.38	.44
0650	Large	G		33264	.001		.31	.05		.36	.41
0700	Trenching and backfill	G	B-53	500	.016			.99	.42	1.41	1.93
0800	Vinyl tubing, 1/4", material only	G					.08			.08	.09
0850	Supply tubing, 1/2", material only, 100' coil	G					.17			.17	.19
0900	500' coil	G					.15			.15	.17
0950	Compression fittings	G	1 Skwk	90	.089	Ea.	1.89	5.65		7.54	10.55
1000	Barbed fittings, 1/4"	G		360	.022		.16	1.41		1.57	2.29
1100	Flush risers	G		60	.133		5.15	8.45		13.60	18.35
1150	Flush ends, figure eight	G		180	.044		.75	2.82		3.57	5.05
1300	Auto flush, spring loaded	G		90	.089		2.80	5.65		8.45	11.55
1350	Volumetric	G		90	.089		9.85	5.65		15.50	19.25
1400	Air relief valve, inline with compensation tee, 1/2"	G		45	.178		20.50	11.30		31.80	39.50
1450	1"	G		30	.267		21.50	16.95		38.45	49
1500	Round box for flush ends, 6"	G		30	.267		9.75	16.95		26.70	36
1600	Screen filter, 3/4" screen	G		12	.667		11.15	42.50		53.65	76
1650	1" disk	G		8	1		34	63.50		97.50	133
1700	1-1/2" disk	G		4	2		137	127		264	340
1750	2" disk	G		3	2.667		185	169		354	455
1800	Typical installation 18" OC, small, minimum					S.F.				1.53	2.35
1850	Maximum									1.78	2.75
1900	Large, minimum									1.48	2.28
2000	Maximum									1.71	2.64
2100	For non-pressure compensating systems, deduct						10%	10%			

32 84 23 – Underground Sprinklers

32 84 23.10 Sprinkler Irrigation System

			Crew	Daily Output	Labor-Hours	Unit	Material	Labor	Equipment	Total	Total Incl O&P
0010	**SPRINKLER IRRIGATION SYSTEM**	G2050-710									
0011	For lawns										
0800	Residential system, custom, 1" supply		B-20	2000	.012	S.F.	.33	.65		.98	1.33
0900	1-1/2" supply		"	1800	.013	"	.49	.73		1.22	1.62
1020	Pop up spray head w/risers, hi-pop, full circle pattern, 4"		2 Skwk	76	.211	Ea.	10.85	13.35		24.20	32

32 84 Planting Irrigation

32 84 23 – Underground Sprinklers

32 84 23.10 Sprinkler Irrigation System		Crew	Daily Output	Labor-Hours	Unit	Material	2024 Bare Costs Labor	Equipment	Total	Total Incl O&P
1030	1/2 circle pattern, 4"	2 Skwk	76	.211	Ea.	12.90	13.35		26.25	34
1040	6", full circle pattern		76	.211		15.35	13.35		28.70	37
1050	1/2 circle pattern, 6"		76	.211		16.55	13.35		29.90	38
1060	12", full circle pattern		76	.211		21.50	13.35		34.85	43.50
1070	1/2 circle pattern, 12"		76	.211		24.50	13.35		37.85	47
1080	Pop up bubbler head w/risers, hi-pop bubbler head, 4"		76	.211		5.65	13.35		19	26.50
1110	Impact full/part circle sprinklers, 28'-54' @ 25-60 psi		37	.432		27	27.50		54.50	71
1120	Spaced 37'-49' @ 25-50 psi		37	.432		22.50	27.50		50	66
1130	Spaced 43'-61' @ 30-60 psi		37	.432		76	27.50		103.50	125
1140	Spaced 54'-78' @ 40-80 psi		37	.432		129	27.50		156.50	183
1145	Impact rotor pop-up full/part commercial circle sprinklers									
1150	Spaced 42'-65' @ 35-80 psi	2 Skwk	25	.640	Ea.	30.50	40.50		71	94.50
1160	Spaced 48'-76' @ 45-85 psi	"	25	.640	"	22.50	40.50		63	85.50
1165	Impact rotor pop-up part. circle comm., 53'-75', 55-100 psi, w/accessories									
1180	Sprinkler, premium, pop-up rotator, 50'-100'	2 Skwk	25	.640	Ea.	113	40.50		153.50	185
1250	Plastic case, 2 nozzle, metal cover		25	.640		137	40.50		177.50	211
1260	Rubber cover		25	.640		119	40.50		159.50	192
1270	Iron case, 2 nozzle, metal cover		22	.727		172	46		218	258
1280	Rubber cover		22	.727		171	46		217	257
1282	Impact rotor pop-up full circle commercial, 39'-99', 30-100 psi									
1284	Plastic case, metal cover	2 Skwk	25	.640	Ea.	143	40.50		183.50	218
1286	Rubber cover		25	.640		159	40.50		199.50	236
1288	Iron case, metal cover		22	.727		211	46		257	300
1290	Rubber cover		22	.727		214	46		260	305
1292	Plastic case, 2 nozzle, metal cover		22	.727		157	46		203	242
1294	Rubber cover		22	.727		161	46		207	246
1296	Iron case, 2 nozzle, metal cover		20	.800		185	51		236	279
1298	Rubber cover		20	.800		219	51		270	315
1305	Electric remote control valve, plastic, 3/4"		18	.889		22	56.50		78.50	109
1310	1"		18	.889		23	56.50		79.50	110
1320	1-1/2"		18	.889		127	56.50		183.50	225
1330	2"		18	.889		178	56.50		234.50	281
1335	Quick coupling valves, brass, locking cover									
1340	Inlet coupling valve, 3/4"	2 Skwk	18.75	.853	Ea.	101	54		155	192
1350	1"		18.75	.853		141	54		195	236
1360	Controller valve boxes, 6" round boxes		18.75	.853		10.95	54		64.95	93
1370	10" round boxes		14.25	1.123		23.50	71.50		95	133
1380	12" square box		9.75	1.641		52.50	104		156.50	214
1388	Electromech. control, 14 day 3-60 min., auto start to 23/day									
1390	4 station	2 Skwk	1.04	15.385	Ea.	85	975		1,060	1,550
1400	7 station		.64	25		178	1,600		1,778	2,575
1410	12 station		.40	40		405	2,550		2,955	4,250
1420	Dual programs, 18 station		.24	66.667		350	4,225		4,575	6,700
1430	23 station		.16	100		955	6,350		7,305	10,600
1435	Backflow preventer, bronze, 0-175 psi, w/valves, test cocks									
1440	3/4"	2 Skwk	6	2.667	Ea.	450	169		619	750
1450	1"		6	2.667		265	169		434	545
1460	1-1/2"		6	2.667		935	169		1,104	1,275
1470	2"		6	2.667		505	169		674	810
1475	Pressure vacuum breaker, brass, 15-150 psi									
1480	3/4"	2 Skwk	6	2.667	Ea.	121	169		290	385
1490	1"		6	2.667		122	169		291	385
1500	1-1/2"		6	2.667		760	169		929	1,100

32 84 Planting Irrigation

32 84 23 – Underground Sprinklers

32 84 23.10 Sprinkler Irrigation System		Crew	Daily Output	Labor-Hours	Unit	Material	2024 Bare Costs Labor	Equipment	Total	Total Incl O&P
1510	2"	2 Skwk	6	2.667	Ea.	870	169		1,039	1,200
6000	Riser mounted gear drive sprinkler, nozzle and case									
6200	Plastic, medium volume	1 Skwk	30	.267	Ea.	23.50	16.95		40.45	51
7000	Riser mounted impact sprinkler, body, part or full circle									
7200	Full circle plastic, low/medium volume	1 Skwk	25	.320	Ea.	23	20.50		43.50	56
7400	Brass, low/medium volume		25	.320		52	20.50		72.50	88
7600	Medium volume		25	.320		69.50	20.50		90	107
7800	Female thread		25	.320		124	20.50		144.50	167
8000	Riser mounted impact sprinkler, body, full circle only									
8200	Plastic, low/medium volume	1 Skwk	25	.320	Ea.	12.50	20.50		33	44.50
8400	Brass, low/medium volume		25	.320		60	20.50		80.50	96.50
8600	High volume		25	.320		107	20.50		127.50	148
8800	Very high volume		25	.320		198	20.50		218.50	249

Division Notes

	CREW	DAILY OUTPUT	LABOR-HOURS	UNIT	BARE COSTS				TOTAL INCL O&P
					MAT.	LABOR	EQUIP.	TOTAL	

Estimating Tips
33 10 00 Water Utilities
33 30 00 Sanitary Sewerage Utilities
33 40 00 Storm Drainage Utilities

- Never assume that the water, sewer, and drainage lines will go in at the early stages of the project — both site and project specific conditions must be taken into consideration when assessing the cost implications for utility work, with particular attention paid to the scheduling of works. Consider the site access needs before dividing the site in half with open trenches, loose pipe, and machinery obstructions. Always inspect the site to establish that the site drawings are complete. Check off all existing utilities on your drawings as you locate them. Be especially careful with underground utilities because appurtenances are sometimes buried during regrading or repaving operations. If you find any discrepancies, mark up the site plan for further research. Differing site conditions can be very costly if discovered later in the project.

- See also Section 33 01 00 for restoration of pipe where removal/replacement may be undesirable. Use of new types of piping materials can reduce the overall project cost.

Owners/design engineers should consider the installing contractor as a valuable source of current information on utility products and local conditions that could lead to significant cost savings.

Reference Numbers
Reference numbers are shown at the beginning of some major classifications. These numbers refer to related items in the Reference Section. The reference information may be an estimating procedure, an alternate pricing method, or technical information.

Note: Not all subdivisions listed here necessarily appear. ■

Same Data. Simplified.
Enjoy the convenience and efficiency of accessing your costs anywhere:

- **Skip the multiplier** by setting your location
- **Quickly search,** edit, favorite and share costs
- **Stay on top of price changes** with automatic updates

Discover more at rsmeans.com/online

No part of this cost data may be reproduced, stored in a retrieval system, or transmitted in any form or by any means without prior written permission of Gordian.

Note: "Powered in part by CINX™, based on licensed proprietary information of Harrison Publishing House, Inc."

Note: Trade Service, in part, has been used as a reference source for some of the material prices used in Division 33

33 01 Operation and Maintenance of Utilities

33 01 10 – Operation and Maintenance of Water Utilities

33 01 10.10 Corrosion Resistance		Crew	Daily Output	Labor-Hours	Unit	Material	2024 Bare Costs Labor	Equipment	Total	Total Incl O&P
0010	**CORROSION RESISTANCE**									
0012	Wrap & coat, add to pipe, 4" diameter	1 Stpi	292	.027	L.F.	.60	2.07		2.67	3.74
0020	5" diameter		197	.041		.74	3.07		3.81	5.35
0040	6" diameter		171	.047		.88	3.53		4.41	6.20
0060	8" diameter		158	.051		1.15	3.83		4.98	6.95
0080	10" diameter		140	.057		1.43	4.32		5.75	7.95
0100	12" diameter		120	.067		1.70	5.05		6.75	9.35
0120	14" diameter		108	.074		1.70	5.60		7.30	10.20
0140	16" diameter		96	.083		2.13	6.30		8.43	11.70
0160	18" diameter		86	.093		2.40	7.05		9.45	13.10
0180	20" diameter		78	.103		2.66	7.75		10.41	14.50
0200	24" diameter		68	.118		3.20	8.90		12.10	16.70
0220	Small diameter pipe, 1" diameter, add		292	.027		.18	2.07		2.25	3.27
0240	2" diameter		292	.027		.32	2.07		2.39	3.43
0260	2-1/2" diameter		292	.027		.38	2.07		2.45	3.50
0280	3" diameter		292	.027		.47	2.07		2.54	3.59
0300	Fittings, field covered, add				S.F.	15.50			15.50	17.05
0500	Coating, bituminous, per diameter inch, 1 coat, add	1 Stpi	10200	.001	L.F.	.03	.06		.09	.12
0540	3 coat					.98			.98	1.08
0560	Coal tar epoxy, per diameter inch, 1 coat, add					.40			.40	.44
0600	3 coat					1.10			1.10	1.21
1000	Polyethylene H.D. extruded, 0.025" thk., 1/2" diameter, add					.16			.16	.18
1020	0.025" thick, 3/4" diameter					.27			.27	.30
1040	0.025" thick, 1" diameter					.31			.31	.34
1060	0.025" thick, 1-1/4" diameter					.41			.41	.45
1080	0.025" thick, 1-1/2" diameter					.46			.46	.51
1100	0.030" thick, 2" diameter					.63			.63	.69
1120	0.030" thick, 2-1/2" diameter					.81			.81	.89
1140	0.035" thk., 3" diameter					.87			.87	.96
1160	0.035" thick, 3-1/2" diameter					1			1	1.10
1180	0.035" thick, 4" diameter					1.18			1.18	1.30
1200	0.040" thk., 5" diameter					1.45			1.45	1.60
1220	6" diameter					1.73			1.73	1.90
1240	8" diameter					2.21			2.21	2.43
1260	10" diameter					2.84			2.84	3.12
1280	12" diameter					3.40			3.40	3.74
1300	0.060" thk., 14" diameter					4.49			4.49	4.94
1320	16" diameter					5.15			5.15	5.65
1340	18" diameter					5.60			5.60	6.20
1360	20" diameter					6.25			6.25	6.90
1380	Fittings, field wrapped, add				S.F.	2.79			2.79	3.07

33 01 10.20 Pipe Repair

		Crew	Daily Output	Labor-Hours	Unit	Material	Labor	Equipment	Total	Total Incl O&P
0010	**PIPE REPAIR**									
0020	Not including excavation or backfill									
0100	Clamp, stainless steel, lightweight, for steel pipe									
0110	3" long, 1/2" diameter pipe	1 Plum	34	.235	Ea.	24.50	17.55		42.05	53
0120	3/4" diameter pipe		32	.250		24	18.65		42.65	54.50
0130	1" diameter pipe		30	.267		26.50	19.90		46.40	59
0140	1-1/4" diameter pipe		28	.286		29.50	21.50		51	64
0150	1-1/2" diameter pipe		26	.308		31	23		54	68
0160	2" diameter pipe		24	.333		33	25		58	73.50
0170	2-1/2" diameter pipe		23	.348		33.50	26		59.50	75.50

33 01 Operation and Maintenance of Utilities

33 01 10 – Operation and Maintenance of Water Utilities

33 01 10.20 Pipe Repair		Crew	Daily Output	Labor-Hours	Unit	Material	2024 Bare Costs Labor	2024 Bare Costs Equipment	Total	Total Incl O&P
0180	3" diameter pipe	1 Plum	22	.364	Ea.	35	27		62	79
0190	3-1/2" diameter pipe	↓	21	.381		40	28.50		68.50	86.50
0200	4" diameter pipe	B-20	44	.545		40.50	29.50		70	88.50
0210	5" diameter pipe		42	.571		43	31		74	93.50
0220	6" diameter pipe		38	.632		50	34.50		84.50	106
0230	8" diameter pipe		30	.800		58.50	43.50		102	130
0240	10" diameter pipe		28	.857		385	46.50		431.50	495
0250	12" diameter pipe		24	1		405	54.50		459.50	525
0260	14" diameter pipe		22	1.091		445	59.50		504.50	580
0270	16" diameter pipe		20	1.200		480	65.50		545.50	625
0280	18" diameter pipe		18	1.333		505	72.50		577.50	665
0290	20" diameter pipe		16	1.500		535	82		617	710
0300	24" diameter pipe	↓	14	1.714		595	93.50		688.50	795
0360	For 6" long, add					100%	40%			
0370	For 9" long, add					200%	100%			
0380	For 12" long, add					300%	150%			
0390	For 18" long, add					500%	200%			
0400	Pipe freezing for live repairs of systems 3/8" to 6"									
0410	Note: Pipe freezing can also be used to install a valve into a live system									
0420	Pipe freezing each side 3/8"	2 Skwk	8	2	Ea.	675	127		802	930
0425	Pipe freezing each side 3/8", second location same kit		8	2		35	127		162	229
0430	Pipe freezing each side 3/4"		8	2		675	127		802	930
0435	Pipe freezing each side 3/4", second location same kit		8	2		35	127		162	229
0440	Pipe freezing each side 1-1/2"		6	2.667		675	169		844	995
0445	Pipe freezing each side 1-1/2", second location same kit		6	2.667		35	169		204	292
0450	Pipe freezing each side 2"		6	2.667		665	169		834	990
0455	Pipe freezing each side 2", second location same kit		6	2.667		35	169		204	292
0460	Pipe freezing each side 2-1/2" to 3"		6	2.667		1,050	169		1,219	1,400
0465	Pipe freezing each side 2-1/2" to 3", second location same kit		6	2.667		70	169		239	330
0470	Pipe freezing each side 4"		4	4		1,200	254		1,454	1,700
0475	Pipe freezing each side 4", second location same kit		4	4		111	254		365	500
0480	Pipe freezing each side 5" to 6"		4	4		5,050	254		5,304	5,950
0485	Pipe freezing each side 5" to 6", second location same kit	↓	4	4		335	254		589	745
0490	Pipe freezing extra 20 lb.CO_2 cylinders (3/8" to 2" - 1 ea, 3" - 2 ea)					271			271	298
0500	Pipe freezing extra 50 lb.CO_2 cylinders (4" - 2 ea, 5"-6" - 6 ea)				↓	845			845	930
1000	Clamp, stainless steel, with threaded service tap									
1040	Full seal for iron, steel, PVC pipe									
1100	6" long, 2" diameter pipe	1 Plum	17	.471	Ea.	150	35		185	218
1110	2-1/2" diameter pipe		16	.500		146	37.50		183.50	217
1120	3" diameter pipe		15.60	.513		165	38.50		203.50	238
1130	3-1/2" diameter pipe	↓	15	.533		178	40		218	254
1140	4" diameter pipe	B-20	32	.750		190	41		231	270
1150	6" diameter pipe		28	.857		232	46.50		278.50	325
1160	8" diameter pipe		21	1.143		274	62.50		336.50	395
1170	10" diameter pipe		20	1.200		350	65.50		415.50	480
1180	12" diameter pipe	↓	17	1.412		400	77		477	555
1200	8" long, 2" diameter pipe	1 Plum	11.72	.683		236	51		287	335
1210	2-1/2" diameter pipe		11	.727		249	54.50		303.50	355
1220	3" diameter pipe		10.75	.744		260	55.50		315.50	370
1230	3-1/2" diameter pipe	↓	10.34	.774		273	58		331	385
1240	4" diameter pipe	B-20	22	1.091		287	59.50		346.50	405
1250	6" diameter pipe		19.31	1.243		340	67.50		407.50	475
1260	8" diameter pipe	↓	14.48	1.657		395	90.50		485.50	570

33 01 Operation and Maintenance of Utilities

33 01 10 – Operation and Maintenance of Water Utilities

33 01 10.20 Pipe Repair

		Crew	Daily Output	Labor-Hours	Unit	Material	2024 Bare Costs Labor	Equipment	Total	Total Incl O&P
1270	10" diameter pipe	B-20	13.80	1.739	Ea.	475	95		570	665
1280	12" diameter pipe	↓	11.72	2.048		540	112		652	760
1300	12" long, 2" diameter pipe	1 Plum	9.44	.847		345	63.50		408.50	475
1310	2-1/2" diameter pipe		8.89	.900		350	67		417	485
1320	3" diameter pipe		8.67	.923		365	69		434	500
1330	3-1/2" diameter pipe	↓	8.33	.960		385	71.50		456.50	530
1340	4" diameter pipe	B-20	17.78	1.350		405	73.50		478.50	555
1350	6" diameter pipe		15.56	1.542		485	84		569	660
1360	8" diameter pipe		11.67	2.057		575	112		687	795
1370	10" diameter pipe		11.11	2.160		745	118		863	995
1380	12" diameter pipe	↓	9.44	2.542		865	139		1,004	1,150
1400	20" long, 2" diameter pipe	1 Plum	8.10	.988		420	73.50		493.50	570
1410	2-1/2" diameter pipe		7.62	1.050		460	78.50		538.50	625
1420	3" diameter pipe		7.43	1.077		530	80.50		610.50	700
1430	3-1/2" diameter pipe	↓	7.14	1.120		560	83.50		643.50	740
1440	4" diameter pipe	B-20	15.24	1.575		680	86		766	880
1450	6" diameter pipe		13.33	1.800		690	98		788	905
1460	8" diameter pipe		10	2.400		925	131		1,056	1,225
1470	10" diameter pipe		9.52	2.521		1,150	137		1,287	1,450
1480	12" diameter pipe	↓	8.10	2.963	↓	1,350	161		1,511	1,750
1600	Clamp, stainless steel, single section									
1640	Full seal for iron, steel, PVC pipe									
1700	6" long, 2" diameter pipe	1 Plum	17	.471	Ea.	143	35		178	211
1710	2-1/2" diameter pipe		16	.500		152	37.50		189.50	223
1720	3" diameter pipe		15.60	.513		160	38.50		198.50	234
1730	3-1/2" diameter pipe		15	.533		192	40		232	270
1740	4" diameter pipe	B-20	32	.750		204	41		245	285
1750	6" diameter pipe		27	.889		254	48.50		302.50	350
1760	8" diameter pipe		21	1.143		298	62.50		360.50	425
1770	10" diameter pipe		20	1.200		390	65.50		455.50	525
1780	12" diameter pipe		17	1.412		455	77		532	615
1800	8" long, 2" diameter pipe	1 Plum	11.72	.683		193	51		244	288
1805	2-1/2" diameter pipe		11.03	.725		205	54		259	305
1810	3" diameter pipe		10.76	.743		222	55.50		277.50	325
1815	3-1/2" diameter pipe		10.34	.774		229	58		287	335
1820	4" diameter pipe	B-20	22.07	1.087		245	59.50		304.50	355
1825	6" diameter pipe		19.31	1.243		291	67.50		358.50	420
1830	8" diameter pipe		14.48	1.657		340	90.50		430.50	510
1835	10" diameter pipe		13.79	1.740		450	95		545	635
1840	12" diameter pipe		11.72	2.048		510	112		622	725
1850	12" long, 2" diameter pipe	1 Plum	9.44	.847		320	63.50		383.50	450
1855	2-1/2" diameter pipe		8.89	.900		345	67		412	475
1860	3" diameter pipe		8.67	.923		365	69		434	500
1865	3-1/2" diameter pipe		8.33	.960		375	71.50		446.50	515
1870	4" diameter pipe	B-20	17.78	1.350		400	73.50		473.50	550
1875	6" diameter pipe		15.56	1.542		465	84		549	635
1880	8" diameter pipe		11.67	2.057		545	112		657	765
1885	10" diameter pipe		11.11	2.160		705	118		823	950
1890	12" diameter pipe		9.44	2.542		820	139		959	1,100
1900	20" long, 2" diameter pipe	1 Plum	8.10	.988		375	73.50		448.50	520
1905	2-1/2" diameter pipe		7.62	1.050		415	78.50		493.50	570
1910	3" diameter pipe		7.43	1.077		475	80.50		555.50	640
1915	3-1/2" diameter pipe	↓	7.14	1.120		490	83.50		573.50	660

33 01 Operation and Maintenance of Utilities

33 01 10 – Operation and Maintenance of Water Utilities

33 01 10.20 Pipe Repair

		Crew	Daily Output	Labor-Hours	Unit	Material	2024 Bare Costs Labor	Equipment	Total	Total Incl O&P
1920	4" diameter pipe	B-20	15.24	1.575	Ea.	650	86		736	850
1925	6" diameter pipe		13.33	1.800		775	98		873	1,000
1930	8" diameter pipe		10	2.400		895	131		1,026	1,175
1935	10" diameter pipe		9.52	2.521		1,125	137		1,262	1,450
1940	12" diameter pipe		8.10	2.963		1,325	161		1,486	1,700
2000	Clamp, stainless steel, two section									
2040	Full seal, for iron, steel, PVC pipe									
2100	8" long, 4" diameter pipe	B-20	24	1	Ea.	400	54.50		454.50	520
2110	6" diameter pipe		20	1.200		460	65.50		525.50	605
2120	8" diameter pipe		13	1.846		540	101		641	745
2130	10" diameter pipe		12	2		550	109		659	760
2140	12" diameter pipe		10	2.400		685	131		816	950
2200	10" long, 4" diameter pipe		16	1.500		510	82		592	685
2210	6" diameter pipe		13	1.846		595	101		696	805
2220	8" diameter pipe		9	2.667		660	145		805	940
2230	10" diameter pipe		8	3		865	164		1,029	1,200
2240	12" diameter pipe		7	3.429		990	187		1,177	1,375
2242	Clamp, stainless steel, three section									
2244	Full seal, for iron, steel, PVC pipe									
2250	10" long, 14" diameter pipe	B-20	6.40	3.750	Ea.	1,475	204		1,679	1,900
2260	16" diameter pipe		6	4		1,325	218		1,543	1,800
2270	18" diameter pipe		5	4.800		1,825	262		2,087	2,400
2280	20" diameter pipe		4.60	5.217		2,075	284		2,359	2,700
2290	24" diameter pipe		4	6		2,350	325		2,675	3,050
2320	For 12" long, add to 10"					15%	25%			
2330	For 20" long, add to 10"					70%	55%			
8000	For internal cleaning and inspection, see Section 33 01 30.11									
8100	For pipe testing, see Section 23 05 93.50									

33 01 30 – Operation and Maintenance of Sewer Utilities

33 01 30.11 Television Inspection of Sewers

		Crew	Daily Output	Labor-Hours	Unit	Material	2024 Bare Costs Labor	Equipment	Total	Total Incl O&P
0010	**TELEVISION INSPECTION OF SEWERS**									
0100	Pipe internal cleaning & inspection, cleaning, pressure pipe systems									
0120	Pig method, lengths 1000' to 10,000'									
0140	4" diameter thru 24" diameter, minimum				L.F.				3.60	4.14
0160	Maximum				"				18	21
6000	Sewage/sanitary systems									
6100	Power rodder with header & cutters									
6110	Mobilization charge, minimum				Total				695	800
6120	Mobilization charge, maximum				"				9,125	10,600
6140	Cleaning 4"-12" diameter				L.F.				6.96	7.66
6190	14"-24" diameter								9.28	10.21
6240	30" diameter								11.14	12.18
6250	36" diameter								13.92	15.31
6260	48" diameter								18.56	20.42
6270	60" diameter								27.84	30.74
6280	72" diameter								55.68	61.48
9000	Inspection, television camera with video									
9060	up to 500 linear feet				Total				893.75	1,025
9220	up to 500 linear feet				"					

33 01 Operation and Maintenance of Utilities

33 01 30 – Operation and Maintenance of Sewer Utilities

33 01 30.23 Pipe Bursting		Crew	Daily Output	Labor-Hours	Unit	Material	2024 Bare Costs Labor	2024 Bare Costs Equipment	Total	Total Incl O&P
0010	**PIPE BURSTING**									
0011	300' runs, replace with HDPE pipe									
0020	Not including excavation, backfill, shoring, or dewatering									
0100	6" to 15" diameter, minimum				L.F.				232	255.20
0200	Maximum								638	701.80
0300	18" to 36" diameter, minimum								754	829.40
0400	Maximum								1,218	1,334
0500	Mobilize and demobilize, minimum				Job				3,000	3,300
0600	Maximum				"				40,125	44,250

33 01 30.72 Cured-In-Place Pipe Lining										
0010	**CURED-IN-PLACE PIPE LINING**									
0011	Not incl. bypass or cleaning									
0020	Less than 10,000 L.F., urban, 6" to 10"	C-17E	130	.615	L.F.	14.80	39.50	.33	54.63	75.50
0050	10" to 12"		125	.640		18.25	41	.34	59.59	81.50
0070	12" to 16"		115	.696		18.65	44.50	.37	63.52	87.50
0100	16" to 20"		95	.842		22	54	.45	76.45	105
0200	24" to 36"		90	.889		24	57	.47	81.47	112
0300	48" to 72"		80	1		37.50	64	.53	102.03	138

33 01 30.74 Sliplining, Excludes Cleaning										
0010	**SLIPLINING, excludes cleaning** and video inspection									
0020	Pipe relined with one pipe size smaller than original (4" for 6")									
0100	6" diameter, original size	B-6B	600	.080	L.F.	2.91	3.97	1.95	8.83	11.25
0150	8" diameter, original size		600	.080		4.94	3.97	1.95	10.86	13.50
0200	10" diameter, original size		600	.080		10	3.97	1.95	15.92	19.05
0250	12" diameter, original size		400	.120		11.75	5.95	2.92	20.62	25
0300	14" diameter, original size		400	.120		13.65	5.95	2.92	22.52	27
0350	16" diameter, original size	B-6C	300	.160		18.55	7.95	6.70	33.20	39.50
0400	18" diameter, original size	"	300	.160		23.50	7.95	6.70	38.15	45
1000	Pipe HDPE lining, make service line taps	B-6	4	6	Ea.	115	320	73	508	680

33 01 30.75 Cured-In-place Pipe Lining										
0010	**CURED-IN-PLACE PIPE LINING**									
0050	Bypass, Sewer	C-17E	500	.160	L.F.		10.20	.08	10.28	15.40
0090	Mobilize - (Any Size) 1 Mob per Job.		1	80	Job		5,100	42.50	5,142.50	7,700
0091	Relocate - (°12") (8hrs, 3 per day)		3	26.667	Ea.		1,700	14.15	1,714.15	2,575
0092	Relocate - (12" to 24") (8hrs, 2 per day)		2	40			2,550	21	2,571	3,850
0093	Relocate - (24" to 42") (8hrs, 1.5 per day)		1.50	53.333			3,400	28.50	3,428.50	5,125
0094	Relocate - (42") (8hrs, 1.5 per day)		1	80			5,100	42.50	5,142.50	7,700
0095	Additional Travel, $2.00 per Mile		3362.50	.024	Mile		1.52	.01	1.53	2.28
0096	Demobilize - (Any Size) 1 Demob per Job.		1	80	Job		5,100	42.50	5,142.50	7,700
0097	Refrigeration Truck (12", Cost per Each Location)		3	26.667	Ea.		1,700	14.15	1,714.15	2,575
0098	Refrigeration Truck (12"-24", Each Pipe/Location)		3	26.667			1,700	14.15	1,714.15	2,575
0099	Refrigeration Truck (24"-42", Each Pipe/Location)		1.50	53.333			3,400	28.50	3,428.50	5,125
0100	Refrigeration Truck (42", Each Pipe / Location)		1	80			5,100	42.50	5,142.50	7,700
1210	12", 6mm, Epoxy, 250k, 2ft		6	13.333	L.F.	72.50	850	7.05	929.55	1,375
1211	12", 6mm, Epoxy, 250k, 4ft		12	6.667		72.50	425	3.53	501.03	720
1212	12", 6mm, Epoxy, 250k, 10ft		30	2.667		72.50	170	1.41	243.91	335
1213	12", 6mm, Epoxy, 250k, 20ft		60	1.333		72.50	85	.71	158.21	208
1214	12", 6mm, Epoxy, 250k, 50ft		150	.533		72.50	34	.28	106.78	131
1215	12", 6mm, Epoxy, 250k, 100ft		300	.267		72.50	17.05	.14	89.69	106
1216	12", 6mm, Epoxy, 250k, 300ft		900	.089		72.50	5.70	.05	78.25	88.50
1217	12", 6mm, Epoxy, 250k, 328ft		1000	.080		72.50	5.10	.04	77.64	87.50

33 01 Operation and Maintenance of Utilities

33 01 30 – Operation and Maintenance of Sewer Utilities

33 01 30.75 Cured-In-place Pipe Lining

		Crew	Daily Output	Labor-Hours	Unit	Material	2024 Bare Costs Labor	Equipment	Total	Total Incl O&P
1218	12", 6mm, Epoxy, 250k, Transitions, add				L.F.	20%				
1219	12", 6mm, Epoxy, 250k, 45 and 90 deg, add					50%				
1230	12", 5mm, Epoxy, 400k, 2ft	C-17E	6	13.333		60.50	850	7.05	917.55	1,350
1231	12", 5mm, Epoxy, 400k, 4ft		12	6.667		60.50	425	3.53	489.03	705
1232	12", 5mm, Epoxy, 400k, 10ft		30	2.667		60.50	170	1.41	231.91	325
1233	12", 5mm, Epoxy, 400k, 20ft		60	1.333		60.50	85	.71	146.21	194
1234	12", 5mm, Epoxy, 400k, 50ft		150	.533		60.50	34	.28	94.78	118
1235	12", 5mm, Epoxy, 400k, 100ft		300	.267		60.50	17.05	.14	77.69	92
1236	12", 5mm, Epoxy, 400k, 300ft		900	.089		60.50	5.70	.05	66.25	75
1237	12", 5mm, Epoxy, 400k, 328ft		1000	.080		60.50	5.10	.04	65.64	74
1238	12", 5mm, Epoxy, 400k, Transitions, add					20%				
1239	12", 5mm, Epoxy, 400k, 45 and 90 deg, add					50%				
2410	24", 12mm, Epoxy, 250k, 2ft	C-17E	4	20		291	1,275	10.60	1,576.60	2,225
2411	24", 12mm, Epoxy, 250k, 4ft		8	10		291	640	5.30	936.30	1,275
2412	24", 12mm, Epoxy, 250k, 10ft		20	4		291	256	2.12	549.12	700
2413	24", 12mm, Epoxy, 250k, 20ft		40	2		291	128	1.06	420.06	510
2414	24", 12mm, Epoxy, 250k, 50ft		100	.800		291	51	.42	342.42	395
2415	24", 12mm, Epoxy, 250k, 100ft		200	.400		291	25.50	.21	316.71	360
2416	24", 12mm, Epoxy, 250k, 300ft		600	.133		291	8.50	.07	299.57	335
2417	24", 12mm, Epoxy, 250k, 328ft		656	.122		291	7.80	.06	298.86	330
2418	24", 12mm, Epoxy, 250k, Transitions, add					20%				
2419	24", 12mm, Epoxy, 250k, 45 and 90 deg, add					50%				
2430	24", 10.5mm, Epoxy, 400k, 2ft	C-17E	4	20		254	1,275	10.60	1,539.60	2,200
2431	24", 10.5mm, Epoxy, 400k, 4ft		8	10		254	640	5.30	899.30	1,250
2432	24", 10.5mm, Epoxy, 400k, 10ft		20	4		254	256	2.12	512.12	660
2433	24", 10.5mm, Epoxy, 400k, 20ft		40	2		254	128	1.06	383.06	470
2434	24", 10.5mm, Epoxy, 400k, 50ft		100	.800		254	51	.42	305.42	355
2435	24", 10.5mm, Epoxy, 400k, 100ft		200	.400		254	25.50	.21	279.71	320
2436	24", 10.5mm, Epoxy, 400k, 300ft		600	.133		254	8.50	.07	262.57	293
2437	24", 10.5mm, Epoxy, 400k, 328ft		656	.122		254	7.80	.06	261.86	292
2438	24", 10.5mm, Epoxy, 400k, Transitions, add					20%				
2439	24", 10.5mm, Epoxy, 400k, 45 and 90 deg, add					50%				

33 05 Common Work Results for Utilities

33 05 07 – Trenchless Installation of Utility Piping

33 05 07.23 Utility Boring and Jacking

		Crew	Daily Output	Labor-Hours	Unit	Material	2024 Bare Costs Labor	Equipment	Total	Total Incl O&P
0010	**UTILITY BORING AND JACKING**									
0011	Casing only, 100' minimum,									
0020	not incl. jacking pits or dewatering									
0100	Roadwork, 1/2" thick wall, 24" diameter casing	B-42	20	3.200	L.F.	172	176	148	496	615
0200	36" diameter		16	4		266	221	185	672	825
0300	48" diameter		15	4.267		370	235	197	802	975
0500	Railroad work, 24" diameter		15	4.267		172	235	197	604	755
0600	36" diameter		14	4.571		266	252	211	729	900
0700	48" diameter		12	5.333		370	294	247	911	1,125
0900	For ledge, add								20%	20%
1000	Small diameter boring, 3", sandy soil	B-82	900	.018		38	.99	.13	39.12	43.50
1040	Rocky soil	"	500	.032		38	1.78	.24	40.02	45
1100	Prepare jacking pits, incl. mobilization & demobilization, minimum				Ea.				3,225	3,700
1101	Maximum				"				22,000	25,500

For customer support on your Plumbing Costs with RSMeans Data call 800.448.8182.

33 05 Common Work Results for Utilities

33 05 07 – Trenchless Installation of Utility Piping

33 05 07.36 Microtunneling

		Crew	Daily Output	Labor-Hours	Unit	Material	2024 Bare Costs Labor	Equipment	Total	Total Incl O&P
0010	**MICROTUNNELING**									
0011	Not including excavation, backfill, shoring,									
0020	or dewatering, average 50'/day, slurry method									
0100	24" to 48" outside diameter, minimum					L.F.				965	965
0110	Adverse conditions, add					"				500	500
1000	Rent microtunneling machine, average monthly lease					Month				97,500	107,000
1010	Operating technician					Day				630	705
1100	Mobilization and demobilization, minimum					Job				41,200	45,900
1110	Maximum					"				445,500	490,500

33 05 61 – Concrete Manholes

33 05 61.10 Storm Drainage Manholes, Frames and Covers

		Crew	Daily Output	Labor-Hours	Unit	Material	Labor	Equipment	Total	Total Incl O&P
0010	**STORM DRAINAGE MANHOLES, FRAMES & COVERS**									
0020	Excludes footing, excavation, backfill (See line items for frame & cover)									
0050	Brick, 4' inside diameter, 4' deep	D-1	1	16	Ea.	1,025	865		1,890	2,425
0100	6' deep		.70	22.857		1,450	1,225		2,675	3,450
0150	8' deep		.50	32		1,875	1,725		3,600	4,650
0200	Add for 1' depth increase		4	4	V.L.F.	256	216		472	605
0400	Concrete blocks (radial), 4' ID, 4' deep		1.50	10.667	Ea.	505	575		1,080	1,425
0500	6' deep		1	16		650	865		1,515	2,025
0600	8' deep		.70	22.857		795	1,225		2,020	2,725
0700	For depths over 8', add		5.50	2.909	V.L.F.	74.50	157		231.50	315
0800	Concrete, cast in place, 4' x 4', 8" thick, 4' deep	C-14H	2	24	Ea.	865	1,425	15.60	2,305.60	3,075
0900	6' deep		1.50	32		1,250	1,900	21	3,171	4,200
1000	8' deep		1	48		1,800	2,850	31	4,681	6,225
1100	For depths over 8', add		8	6	V.L.F.	208	355	3.90	566.90	755
1110	Precast, 4' ID, 4' deep	B-22	4.10	7.317	Ea.	1,300	420	73.50	1,793.50	2,150
1120	6' deep		3	10		1,600	575	101	2,276	2,700
1130	8' deep		2	15		2,025	860	151	3,036	3,675
1140	For depths over 8', add		16	1.875	V.L.F.	181	107	18.85	306.85	380
1150	5' ID, 4' deep	B-6	3	8	Ea.	2,500	425	97	3,022	3,475
1160	6' deep		2	12		3,075	640	146	3,861	4,475
1170	8' deep		1.50	16		3,650	855	194	4,699	5,500
1180	For depths over 8', add		12	2	V.L.F.	365	107	24.50	496.50	590
1190	6' ID, 4' deep		2	12	Ea.	4,425	640	146	5,211	5,975
1200	6' deep		1.50	16		4,425	855	194	5,474	6,375
1210	8' deep		1	24		5,175	1,275	291	6,741	7,925
1220	For depths over 8', add		8	3	V.L.F.	475	160	36.50	671.50	800
1250	Slab tops, precast, 8" thick									
1300	4' diameter manhole	B-6	8	3	Ea.	285	160	36.50	481.50	590
1400	5' diameter manhole		7.50	3.200		540	171	39	750	890
1500	6' diameter manhole		7	3.429		925	183	41.50	1,149.50	1,350
3800	Steps, heavyweight cast iron, 7" x 9"	1 Bric	40	.200		23.50	11.95		35.45	43.50
3900	8" x 9"		40	.200		28	11.95		39.95	49
3928	12" x 10-1/2"		40	.200		103	11.95		114.95	131
4000	Standard sizes, galvanized steel		40	.200		32.50	11.95		44.45	54
4100	Aluminum		40	.200		41.50	11.95		53.45	64
4150	Polyethylene		40	.200		40.50	11.95		52.45	62.50

33 05 Common Work Results for Utilities

33 05 63 – Concrete Vaults and Chambers

33 05 63.13 Precast Concrete Utility Structures

		Crew	Daily Output	Labor-Hours	Unit	Material	2024 Bare Costs Labor	Equipment	Total	Total Incl O&P
0010	**PRECAST CONCRETE UTILITY STRUCTURES**, 6" thick									
0050	5' x 10' x 6' high, ID	B-13	2	28	Ea.	2,225	1,500	1,175	4,900	5,925
0100	6' x 10' x 6' high, ID		2	28		2,300	1,500	1,175	4,975	6,025
0150	5' x 12' x 6' high, ID		2	28		2,425	1,500	1,175	5,100	6,175
0200	6' x 12' x 6' high, ID		1.80	31.111		2,725	1,650	1,300	5,675	6,875
0250	6' x 13' x 6' high, ID		1.50	37.333		3,575	2,000	1,550	7,125	8,600
0300	8' x 14' x 7' high, ID		1	56		3,875	3,000	2,325	9,200	11,300
0350	Hand hole, precast concrete, 1-1/2" thick									
0400	1'-0" x 2'-0" x 1'-9", ID, light duty	B-1	4	6	Ea.	880	298		1,178	1,400
0450	4'-6" x 3'-2" x 2'-0", OD, heavy duty	B-6	3	8	"	4,025	425	97	4,547	5,150

33 05 71 – Cleanouts

0300	Cleanout Access Housing, X-Hvy Dty, Ductile Iron	B-20	10	2.400	Ea.	2,050	131		2,181	2,475
0306	Vandal Proof, Add					117			117	129
0313	Galvanized, Add					940			940	1,025

33 05 97 – Identification and Signage for Utilities

33 05 97.05 Utility Connection

0010	**UTILITY CONNECTION**									
0020	Water, sanitary, stormwater, gas, single connection	B-14	1	48	Ea.	4,325	2,475	291	7,091	8,750
0030	Telecommunication	"	3	16	"	465	825	97	1,387	1,850

33 05 97.10 Utility Accessories

0010	**UTILITY ACCESSORIES**									
0400	Underground tape, detectable, reinforced, alum. foil core, 2"	1 Clab	150	.053	C.L.F.	2	2.61		4.61	6.05

33 11 Groundwater Sources

33 11 13 – Potable Water Supply Wells

33 11 13.10 Wells and Accessories

		Crew	Daily Output	Labor-Hours	Unit	Material	Labor	Equipment	Total	Total Incl O&P
0010	**WELLS & ACCESSORIES**									
0011	Domestic									
0100	Drilled, 4" to 6" diameter	B-23	120	.333	L.F.		16.45	11.90	28.35	37.50
0200	8" diameter	"	95.20	.420	"		21	15	36	47
0400	Gravel pack well, 40' deep, incl. gravel & casing, complete									
0500	24" diameter casing x 18" diameter screen	B-23	.13	308	Total	52,500	15,200	11,000	78,700	92,000
0600	36" diameter casing x 18" diameter screen		.12	333	"	54,000	16,500	11,900	82,400	97,000
0800	Observation wells, 1-1/4" riser pipe		163	.245	V.L.F.	4.17	12.10	8.75	25.02	32
0900	For flush Buffalo roadway box, add	1 Skwk	16.60	.482	Ea.	70.50	30.50		101	124
1200	Test well, 2-1/2" diameter, up to 50' deep (15 to 50 GPM)	B-23	1.51	26.490	"	1,200	1,300	945	3,445	4,300
1300	Over 50' deep, add	"	121.80	.328	L.F.	32.50	16.20	11.70	60.40	72.50
1500	Pumps, installed in wells to 100' deep, 4" submersible									
1510	1/2 HP	Q-1	3.22	4.969	Ea.	1,125	335		1,460	1,725
1520	3/4 HP		2.66	6.015		1,600	405		2,005	2,350
1600	1 HP		2.29	6.987		1,800	470		2,270	2,700
1700	1-1/2 HP	Q-22	1.60	10		2,425	670	1,400	4,495	5,200
1800	2 HP		1.33	12.030		2,475	810	1,675	4,960	5,750
1900	3 HP		1.14	14.035		3,100	945	1,950	5,995	6,950
2000	5 HP		1.14	14.035		3,450	945	1,950	6,345	7,325
3000	Pump, 6" submersible, 25' to 150' deep, 25 HP, 103 to 400 GPM		.89	17.978		17,600	1,200	2,500	21,300	24,000
3100	25' to 500' deep, 30 HP, 104 to 400 GPM		.73	21.918		18,000	1,475	3,050	22,525	25,400
8000	Steel well casing	B-23A	3020	.008	Lb.	1.75	.44	.38	2.57	3
8110	Well screen assembly, stainless steel, 2" diameter		273	.088	L.F.	129	4.84	4.18	138.02	154

For customer support on your Plumbing Costs with RSMeans Data call 800.448.8182.

33 11 Groundwater Sources

33 11 13 – Potable Water Supply Wells

33 11 13.10 Wells and Accessories		Crew	Daily Output	Labor-Hours	Unit	Material	2024 Bare Costs Labor	Equipment	Total	Total Incl O&P
8120	3" diameter	B-23A	253	.095	L.F.	190	5.20	4.51	199.71	222
8130	4" diameter		200	.120		221	6.60	5.70	233.30	259
8140	5" diameter		168	.143		230	7.85	6.80	244.65	271
8150	6" diameter		126	.190		257	10.50	9.05	276.55	310
8160	8" diameter		98.50	.244		345	13.40	11.60	370	410
8170	10" diameter		73	.329		430	18.10	15.65	463.75	515
8180	12" diameter		62.50	.384		500	21	18.25	539.25	600
8190	14" diameter		54.30	.442		565	24.50	21	610.50	680
8200	16" diameter		48.30	.497		620	27.50	23.50	671	745
8210	18" diameter		39.20	.612		785	33.50	29	847.50	940
8220	20" diameter		31.20	.769		890	42.50	36.50	969	1,075
8230	24" diameter		23.80	1.008		1,100	55.50	48	1,203.50	1,325
8240	26" diameter		21	1.143		1,400	63	54.50	1,517.50	1,675
8244	Well casing or drop pipe, PVC, 1/2" diameter		550	.044		1.76	2.40	2.08	6.24	7.80
8245	3/4" diameter		550	.044		1.78	2.40	2.08	6.26	7.80
8246	1" diameter		550	.044		1.83	2.40	2.08	6.31	7.85
8247	1-1/4" diameter		520	.046		2.29	2.54	2.20	7.03	8.70
8248	1-1/2" diameter		490	.049		2.44	2.69	2.33	7.46	9.25
8249	1-3/4" diameter		380	.063		2.49	3.47	3	8.96	11.20
8250	2" diameter		280	.086		2.85	4.71	4.08	11.64	14.65
8252	3" diameter		260	.092		5.65	5.10	4.39	15.14	18.55
8254	4" diameter		205	.117		6	6.45	5.55	18	22.50
8255	5" diameter		170	.141		6	7.75	6.70	20.45	25.50
8256	6" diameter		130	.185		11.50	10.15	8.80	30.45	37.50
8258	8" diameter		100	.240		17.55	13.20	11.40	42.15	51.50
8260	10" diameter		73	.329		28	18.10	15.65	61.75	75
8262	12" diameter		62	.387		32	21.50	18.40	71.90	87
8300	Slotted PVC, 1-1/4" diameter		521	.046		3.89	2.53	2.19	8.61	10.45
8310	1-1/2" diameter		488	.049		4.03	2.70	2.34	9.07	11
8320	2" diameter		273	.088		5.20	4.84	4.18	14.22	17.50
8330	3" diameter		253	.095		9.15	5.20	4.51	18.86	23
8340	4" diameter		200	.120		9.80	6.60	5.70	22.10	27
8350	5" diameter		168	.143		21	7.85	6.80	35.65	42.50
8360	6" diameter		126	.190		22.50	10.50	9.05	42.05	50.50
8370	8" diameter		98.50	.244		33.50	13.40	11.60	58.50	69
8400	Artificial gravel pack, 2" screen, 6" casing	B-23B	174	.138		6.10	7.60	8.90	22.60	28
8405	8" casing		111	.216		8.35	11.90	14	34.25	42
8410	10" casing		74.50	.322		11.50	17.70	21	50.20	62
8415	12" casing		60	.400		18.40	22	26	66.40	81
8420	14" casing		50.20	.478		18.80	26.50	31	76.30	93.50
8425	16" casing		40.70	.590		24.50	32.50	38	95	117
8430	18" casing		36	.667		30.50	36.50	43	110	136
8435	20" casing		29.50	.814		33.50	45	52.50	131	162
8440	24" casing		25.70	.934		38	51.50	60.50	150	185
8445	26" casing		24.60	.976		42.50	53.50	63	159	196
8450	30" casing		20	1.200		48.50	66	77.50	192	237
8455	36" casing		16.40	1.463		53	80.50	94.50	228	282
8500	Develop well		8	3	Hr.	410	165	194	769	910
8550	Pump test well		8	3		130	165	194	489	600
8560	Standby well	B-23A	8	3		134	165	143	442	550
8570	Standby, drill rig		8	3			165	143	308	400
8580	Surface seal well, concrete filled		1	24	Ea.	1,450	1,325	1,150	3,925	4,800
8590	Well test pump, install & remove	B-23	1	40			1,975	1,425	3,400	4,500

33 11 Groundwater Sources

33 11 13 – Potable Water Supply Wells

33 11 13.10 Wells and Accessories		Crew	Daily Output	Labor-Hours	Unit	Material	2024 Bare Costs Labor	Equipment	Total	Total Incl O&P
8600	Well sterilization, chlorine	2 Clab	1	16	Ea.	82	785		867	1,250
8610	Well water pressure switch	1 Clab	12	.667		132	32.50		164.50	194
8630	Well water pressure switch with manual reset	"	12	.667	↓	175	32.50		207.50	242
9950	See Section 31 23 19.40 for wellpoints									
9960	See Section 31 23 19.30 for drainage wells									

33 11 13.20 Water Supply Wells, Pumps

		Crew	Daily Output	Labor-Hours	Unit	Material	Labor	Equipment	Total	Total Incl O&P
0010	**WATER SUPPLY WELLS, PUMPS**									
0011	With pressure control									
1000	Deep well, jet, 42 gal. galvanized tank									
1040	3/4 HP	1 Plum	.80	10	Ea.	1,525	745		2,270	2,775
3000	Shallow well, jet, 30 gal. galvanized tank									
3040	1/2 HP	1 Plum	2	4	Ea.	1,225	299		1,524	1,800

33 14 Water Utility Transmission and Distribution

33 14 13 – Public Water Utility Distribution Piping

33 14 13.15 Water Supply, Ductile Iron Pipe

		Crew	Daily Output	Labor-Hours	Unit	Material	Labor	Equipment	Total	Total Incl O&P
0010	**WATER SUPPLY, DUCTILE IRON PIPE** R331113-80									
0020	Not including excavation or backfill									
2000	Pipe, class 50 water piping, 18' lengths									
2020	Mechanical joint, 4" diameter	B-21	200	.140	L.F.	114	7.90	1.01	122.91	138
2040	6" diameter		160	.175		136	9.90	1.26	147.16	166
2060	8" diameter		133.33	.210		150	11.85	1.51	163.36	184
2080	10" diameter		114.29	.245		196	13.85	1.76	211.61	238
2100	12" diameter		105.26	.266		242	15.05	1.91	258.96	292
2120	14" diameter		100	.280		126	15.80	2.01	143.81	164
2140	16" diameter		72.73	.385		128	22	2.76	152.76	176
2160	18" diameter		68.97	.406		171	23	2.91	196.91	225
2170	20" diameter		57.14	.490		172	27.50	3.52	203.02	235
2180	24" diameter		47.06	.595		190	33.50	4.27	227.77	264
3000	Push-on joint, 4" diameter		400	.070		24	3.96	.50	28.46	33
3020	6" diameter		333.33	.084		23.50	4.75	.60	28.85	33.50
3040	8" diameter		200	.140		33	7.90	1.01	41.91	49.50
3060	10" diameter		181.82	.154		51	8.70	1.11	60.81	70.50
3080	12" diameter		160	.175		54	9.90	1.26	65.16	75.50
3100	14" diameter		133.33	.210		54	11.85	1.51	67.36	79
3120	16" diameter		114.29	.245		57.50	13.85	1.76	73.11	85.50
3140	18" diameter		100	.280		64	15.80	2.01	81.81	95.50
3160	20" diameter		88.89	.315		66.50	17.80	2.26	86.56	102
3180	24" diameter	↓	76.92	.364	↓	92.50	20.50	2.61	115.61	135
8000	Piping, fittings, mechanical joint, AWWA C110									
8006	90° bend, 4" diameter	B-20	16	1.500	Ea.	257	82		339	405
8020	6" diameter	"	12.80	1.875		435	102		537	625
8040	8" diameter	B-21	10.67	2.624		650	148	18.85	816.85	955
8060	10" diameter		11.43	2.450		1,075	138	17.60	1,230.60	1,425
8080	12" diameter		10.53	2.659		1,725	150	19.10	1,894.10	2,150
8100	14" diameter		10	2.800		2,075	158	20	2,253	2,550
8120	16" diameter		7.27	3.851		3,025	218	27.50	3,270.50	3,675
8140	18" diameter		6.90	4.058		4,075	229	29	4,333	4,875
8160	20" diameter		5.71	4.904		5,100	277	35	5,412	6,050
8180	24" diameter		4.70	5.957		7,725	335	43	8,103	9,050
8200	Wye or tee, 4" diameter	B-20	10.67	2.249		570	123		693	805

33 14 Water Utility Transmission and Distribution

33 14 13 – Public Water Utility Distribution Piping

33 14 13.15 Water Supply, Ductile Iron Pipe		Crew	Daily Output	Labor-Hours	Unit	Material	2024 Bare Costs Labor	Equipment	Total	Total Incl O&P
8220	6" diameter	B-20	8.53	2.814	Ea.	900	153		1,053	1,225
8240	8" diameter	B-21	7.11	3.938		1,475	223	28.50	1,726.50	1,975
8260	10" diameter		7.62	3.675		2,800	208	26.50	3,034.50	3,425
8280	12" diameter		7.02	3.989		2,875	225	28.50	3,128.50	3,550
8300	14" diameter		6.67	4.198		8,250	237	30	8,517	9,475
8320	16" diameter		4.85	5.773		8,475	325	41.50	8,841.50	9,850
8340	18" diameter		4.60	6.087		9,850	345	43.50	10,238.50	11,400
8360	20" diameter		3.81	7.349		10,800	415	53	11,268	12,600
8380	24" diameter		3.14	8.917		17,800	505	64	18,369	20,300
8398	45° bend, 4" diameter	B-20	16	1.500		269	82		351	420
8400	6" diameter	"	12.80	1.875		410	102		512	600
8405	8" diameter	B-21	10.67	2.624		600	148	18.85	766.85	900
8410	12" diameter		10.53	2.659		1,175	150	19.10	1,344.10	1,550
8420	16" diameter		7.27	3.851		2,375	218	27.50	2,620.50	2,950
8430	20" diameter		5.71	4.904		3,350	277	35	3,662	4,125
8440	24" diameter		4.70	5.957		4,700	335	43	5,078	5,700
8450	Decreaser, 6" x 4" diameter	B-20	14.22	1.688		305	92		397	470
8460	8" x 6" diameter	B-21	11.64	2.406		460	136	17.25	613.25	725
8470	10" x 6" diameter		13.33	2.101		605	119	15.10	739.10	860
8480	12" x 6" diameter		12.70	2.205		1,075	125	15.85	1,215.85	1,375
8490	16" x 6" diameter		10	2.800		1,375	158	20	1,553	1,750
8500	20" x 6" diameter		8.42	3.325		4,700	188	24	4,912	5,475
8552	For water utility valves see Section 33 14 19									
8700	Joint restraint, ductile iron mechanical joints									
8710	4" diameter	B-20	32	.750	Ea.	32.50	41		73.50	96.50
8720	6" diameter	"	25.60	.938		40	51		91	120
8730	8" diameter	B-21	21.33	1.313		61	74	9.40	144.40	187
8740	10" diameter		18.28	1.532		111	86.50	11	208.50	263
8750	12" diameter		16.84	1.663		119	94	11.95	224.95	284
8760	14" diameter		16	1.750		188	99	12.55	299.55	370
8770	16" diameter		11.64	2.406		192	136	17.25	345.25	430
8780	18" diameter		11.03	2.539		270	143	18.25	431.25	530
8785	20" diameter		9.14	3.063		335	173	22	530	650
8790	24" diameter		7.53	3.718		465	210	26.50	701.50	850
9600	Steel sleeve with tap, 4" diameter	B-20	3	8		550	435		985	1,250
9620	6" diameter		2	12		590	655		1,245	1,625
9630	8" diameter		2	12		750	655		1,405	1,800

33 14 13.20 Water Supply, Polyethylene Pipe, C901

		Crew	Daily Output	Labor-Hours	Unit	Material	Labor	Equipment	Total	Total Incl O&P
0010	**WATER SUPPLY, POLYETHYLENE PIPE, C901**									
0020	Not including excavation or backfill									
1000	Piping, 160 psi, 3/4" diameter	Q-1A	525	.019	L.F.	.44	1.43		1.87	2.61
1120	1" diameter		485	.021		.74	1.55		2.29	3.11
1140	1-1/2" diameter		450	.022		1.89	1.67		3.56	4.54
1160	2" diameter		365	.027		2.02	2.06		4.08	5.30
2000	Fittings, insert type, nylon, 160 & 250 psi, cold water									
2220	Clamp ring, stainless steel, 3/4" diameter	Q-1A	345	.029	Ea.	1.97	2.18		4.15	5.40
2240	1" diameter		321	.031		3.82	2.34		6.16	7.70
2260	1-1/2" diameter		285	.035		3.96	2.63		6.59	8.30
2280	2" diameter		255	.039		5.35	2.94		8.29	10.30
2300	Coupling, 3/4" diameter		66	.152		1.76	11.35		13.11	18.85
2320	1" diameter		57	.175		2.36	13.15		15.51	22
2340	1-1/2" diameter		51	.196		5.75	14.70		20.45	28.50

33 14 Water Utility Transmission and Distribution

33 14 13 – Public Water Utility Distribution Piping

	33 14 13.20 Water Supply, Polyethylene Pipe, C901	Crew	Daily Output	Labor-Hours	Unit	Material	2024 Bare Costs Labor	Equipment	Total	Total Incl O&P
2360	2" diameter	Q-1A	48	.208	Ea.	7.25	15.65		22.90	31.50
2400	Elbow, 90°, 3/4" diameter		66	.152		2.89	11.35		14.24	20
2420	1" diameter		57	.175		3.47	13.15		16.62	23.50
2440	1-1/2" diameter		51	.196		8.95	14.70		23.65	32
2460	2" diameter		48	.208		11.95	15.65		27.60	36.50

33 14 13.25 Water Supply, Polyvinyl Chloride Pipe

		Crew	Daily Output	Labor-Hours	Unit	Material	Labor	Equipment	Total	Total Incl O&P
0010	**WATER SUPPLY, POLYVINYL CHLORIDE PIPE** R331113-80									
0020	Not including excavation or backfill, unless specified									
2100	PVC pipe, Class 150, 1-1/2" diameter	Q-1A	750	.013	L.F.	1.28	1		2.28	2.90
2120	2" diameter		686	.015		1.77	1.09		2.86	3.58
2140	2-1/2" diameter		500	.020		3.10	1.50		4.60	5.65
2160	3" diameter	B-20	430	.056		2.83	3.04		5.87	7.65
3010	AWWA C905, PR 100, DR 25									
3030	14" diameter	B-21	213	.131	L.F.	17.85	7.45	.94	26.24	31.50
3040	16" diameter		200	.140		24.50	7.90	1.01	33.41	40
3050	18" diameter		160	.175		29.50	9.90	1.26	40.66	48.50
3060	20" diameter		133	.211		36.50	11.90	1.51	49.91	60
3070	24" diameter		107	.262		54.50	14.80	1.88	71.18	84
3080	30" diameter		80	.350		92	19.80	2.51	114.31	133
3090	36" diameter		80	.350		142	19.80	2.51	164.31	188
3100	42" diameter		60	.467		192	26.50	3.35	221.85	254
3200	48" diameter		60	.467		245	26.50	3.35	274.85	310
3960	Pressure pipe, class 200, ASTM 2241, SDR 21, 3/4" diameter	Q-1A	1000	.010		.46	.75		1.21	1.63
3980	1" diameter		900	.011		1	.83		1.83	2.34
4000	1-1/2" diameter		750	.013		2.74	1		3.74	4.50
4010	2" diameter		686	.015		3.02	1.09		4.11	4.95
4020	2-1/2" diameter		500	.020		4.38	1.50		5.88	7.05
4030	3" diameter	B-20	430	.056		6.50	3.04		9.54	11.65
4040	4" diameter		375	.064		12.75	3.49		16.24	19.20
4050	6" diameter		316	.076		29.50	4.14		33.64	38.50
4060	8" diameter		260	.092		10.95	5.05		16	19.55
4090	Including trenching to 3' deep, 3/4" diameter	Q-1C	300	.080		.46	5.30	7.25	13.01	16.35
4100	1" diameter		280	.086		1	5.70	7.75	14.45	18.05
4110	1-1/2" diameter		260	.092		2.74	6.15	8.35	17.24	21.50
4120	2" diameter		220	.109		3.02	7.25	9.85	20.12	25
4130	2-1/2" diameter		200	.120		4.38	7.95	10.85	23.18	28.50
4140	3" diameter		175	.137		6.50	9.10	12.40	28	34.50
4150	4" diameter		150	.160		12.75	10.65	14.45	37.85	45.50
4160	6" diameter		125	.192		29.50	12.75	17.35	59.60	70.50
4165	Fittings									
4170	Elbow, 90°, 3/4"	Q-1A	114	.088	Ea.	.68	6.60		7.28	10.55
4180	1"		100	.100		4.14	7.50		11.64	15.70
4190	1-1/2"		80	.125		25.50	9.40		34.90	42.50
4200	2"		72	.139		4.58	10.40		14.98	20.50
4210	3"	B-20	46	.522		80	28.50		108.50	131
4220	4"		36	.667		65	36.50		101.50	125
4230	6"		24	1		224	54.50		278.50	325
4240	8"		14	1.714		140	93.50		233.50	293
4250	Elbow, 45°, 3/4"	Q-1A	114	.088		.95	6.60		7.55	10.85
4260	1"		100	.100		21	7.50		28.50	34
4270	1-1/2"		80	.125		25.50	9.40		34.90	42.50
4280	2"		72	.139		25.50	10.40		35.90	43.50

33 14 Water Utility Transmission and Distribution

33 14 13 – Public Water Utility Distribution Piping

33 14 13.25 Water Supply, Polyvinyl Chloride Pipe		Crew	Daily Output	Labor-Hours	Unit	Material	2024 Bare Costs Labor	Equipment	Total	Total Incl O&P
4290	2-1/2"	Q-1A	54	.185	Ea.	29	13.90		42.90	52.50
4300	3"	B-20	46	.522		37	28.50		65.50	83
4310	4"		36	.667		63	36.50		99.50	124
4320	6"		24	1		116	54.50		170.50	208
4330	8"		14	1.714		163	93.50		256.50	320
4340	Tee, 3/4"	Q-1A	76	.132		4.22	9.90		14.12	19.35
4350	1"		66	.152		8.40	11.35		19.75	26
4360	1-1/2"		54	.185		43	13.90		56.90	67.50
4370	2"		48	.208		53	15.65		68.65	82
4380	2-1/2"		36	.278		59	21		80	96
4390	3"	B-20	30	.800		59.50	43.50		103	131
4400	4"		24	1		31.50	54.50		86	116
4410	6"		14.80	1.622		69	88.50		157.50	207
4420	8"		9	2.667		122	145		267	350
4430	Coupling, 3/4"	Q-1A	114	.088		1.95	6.60		8.55	11.95
4440	1"		100	.100		6.15	7.50		13.65	17.90
4450	1-1/2"		80	.125		29.50	9.40		38.90	46.50
4460	2"		72	.139		30	10.40		40.40	48.50
4470	2-1/2"		54	.185		37.50	13.90		51.40	61.50
4480	3"	B-20	46	.522		41.50	28.50		70	88
4490	4"		36	.667		75	36.50		111.50	137
4500	6"		24	1		58.50	54.50		113	145
4510	8"		14	1.714		65	93.50		158.50	211
4520	Pressure pipe Class 150, SDR 18, AWWA C900, 4" diameter		380	.063	L.F.	4.93	3.44		8.37	10.50
4530	6" diameter		316	.076		7.15	4.14		11.29	14
4540	8" diameter	B-21	264	.106		9.10	6	.76	15.86	19.80
4550	10" diameter		220	.127		12.40	7.20	.91	20.51	25.50
4560	12" diameter		186	.151		16.90	8.50	1.08	26.48	32.50
8000	Fittings with rubber gasket									
8003	Class 150, DR 18									
8006	90° bend, 4" diameter	B-20	100	.240	Ea.	54.50	13.10		67.60	79.50
8020	6" diameter	"	90	.267		97	14.55		111.55	129
8040	8" diameter	B-21	80	.350		187	19.80	2.51	209.31	238
8060	10" diameter		50	.560		365	31.50	4.02	400.52	450
8080	12" diameter		30	.933		570	52.50	6.70	629.20	710
8100	Tee, 4" diameter		90	.311		165	17.60	2.23	184.83	210
8120	6" diameter		80	.350		269	19.80	2.51	291.31	330
8140	8" diameter		70	.400		490	22.50	2.87	515.37	575
8160	10" diameter		40	.700		1,450	39.50	5.05	1,494.55	1,675
8180	12" diameter		20	1.400		2,075	79	10.05	2,164.05	2,400
8200	45° bend, 4" diameter	B-20	100	.240		73	13.10		86.10	100
8220	6" diameter	"	90	.267		132	14.55		146.55	168
8240	8" diameter	B-21	50	.560		246	31.50	4.02	281.52	320
8260	10" diameter		50	.560		450	31.50	4.02	485.52	550
8280	12" diameter		30	.933		1,025	52.50	6.70	1,084.20	1,200
8300	Reducing tee 6" x 4"		100	.280		163	15.80	2.01	180.81	205
8320	8" x 6"		90	.311		290	17.60	2.23	309.83	350
8330	10" x 6"		90	.311		254	17.60	2.23	273.83	305
8340	10" x 8"		90	.311		272	17.60	2.23	291.83	325
8350	12" x 6"		90	.311		340	17.60	2.23	359.83	405
8360	12" x 8"		90	.311		380	17.60	2.23	399.83	445
8400	Tapped service tee (threaded type) 6" x 6" x 3/4"		100	.280		123	15.80	2.01	140.81	162
8430	6" x 6" x 1"		90	.311		123	17.60	2.23	142.83	164

33 14 Water Utility Transmission and Distribution

33 14 13 – Public Water Utility Distribution Piping

33 14 13.25 Water Supply, Polyvinyl Chloride Pipe		Crew	Daily Output	Labor-Hours	Unit	Material	2024 Bare Costs Labor	Equipment	Total	Total Incl O&P
8440	6" x 6" x 1-1/2"	B-21	90	.311	Ea.	123	17.60	2.23	142.83	164
8450	6" x 6" x 2"		90	.311		123	17.60	2.23	142.83	164
8460	8" x 8" x 3/4"		90	.311		182	17.60	2.23	201.83	228
8470	8" x 8" x 1"		90	.311		182	17.60	2.23	201.83	228
8480	8" x 8" x 1-1/2"		90	.311		182	17.60	2.23	201.83	228
8490	8" x 8" x 2"		90	.311		182	17.60	2.23	201.83	228
8500	Repair coupling 4"	B-20	100	.240		33.50	13.10		46.60	56.50
8520	6" diameter		90	.267		51.50	14.55		66.05	78.50
8540	8" diameter		50	.480		125	26		151	176
8560	10" diameter		50	.480		262	26		288	325
8580	12" diameter		50	.480		335	26		361	405
8600	Plug end 4"		100	.240		29	13.10		42.10	51.50
8620	6" diameter		90	.267		52.50	14.55		67.05	79.50
8640	8" diameter		50	.480		89.50	26		115.50	138
8660	10" diameter		50	.480		143	26		169	196
8680	12" diameter		50	.480		192	26		218	251
8700	PVC pipe, joint restraint									
8710	4" diameter	B-20	32	.750	Ea.	46.50	41		87.50	113
8720	6" diameter		25.60	.938		57.50	51		108.50	140
8730	8" diameter		21.33	1.125		83.50	61.50		145	183
8740	10" diameter		18.28	1.313		133	71.50		204.50	252
8750	12" diameter		16.84	1.425		140	77.50		217.50	269
8760	14" diameter		16	1.500		190	82		272	330
8770	16" diameter		11.64	2.062		256	112		368	450
8780	18" diameter		11.03	2.176		315	119		434	520
8785	20" diameter		9.14	2.626		445	143		588	705
8790	24" diameter		7.53	3.187		515	174		689	825
33 14 13.35 Water Supply, HDPE										
0010	**WATER SUPPLY, HDPE**									
0011	Butt fusion joints, SDR 21 40' lengths not including excavation or backfill									
0100	4" diameter	B-22A	400	.100	L.F.	1.34	5.60	1.87	8.81	11.90
0200	6" diameter		380	.105		2.91	5.90	1.97	10.78	14.15
0300	8" diameter		320	.125		4.94	7.05	2.34	14.33	18.45
0400	10" diameter		300	.133		10	7.50	2.49	19.99	25
0500	12" diameter		260	.154		11.75	8.65	2.88	23.28	29
0600	14" diameter	B-22B	220	.182		13.65	10.20	5.60	29.45	36.50
0700	16" diameter		180	.222		18.55	12.50	6.85	37.90	46.50
0800	18" diameter		140	.286		23.50	16.05	8.80	48.35	59.50
0850	20" diameter		130	.308		25.50	17.30	9.45	52.25	64
0900	24" diameter		100	.400		41.50	22.50	12.30	76.30	93
1000	Fittings									
1100	Elbows, 90 degrees									
1200	4" diameter	B-22A	32	1.250	Ea.	41	70.50	23.50	135	175
1300	6" diameter		28	1.429		35.50	80.50	26.50	142.50	188
1400	8" diameter		24	1.667		71.50	93.50	31	196	252
1500	10" diameter		18	2.222		106	125	41.50	272.50	350
1600	12" diameter		12	3.333		142	187	62.50	391.50	505
1700	14" diameter	B-22B	9	4.444		222	250	137	609	765
1800	16" diameter		6	6.667		695	375	205	1,275	1,550
1900	18" diameter		4	10		430	560	305	1,295	1,650
2000	24" diameter		3	13.333		890	750	410	2,050	2,550
2100	Tees									

33 14 Water Utility Transmission and Distribution

33 14 13 – Public Water Utility Distribution Piping

33 14 13.35 Water Supply, HDPE

		Crew	Daily Output	Labor-Hours	Unit	Material	2024 Bare Costs Labor	Equipment	Total	Total Incl O&P
2200	4" diameter	B-22A	30	1.333	Ea.	24	75	25	124	165
2300	6" diameter		26	1.538		41	86.50	29	156.50	205
2400	8" diameter		22	1.818		61.50	102	34	197.50	257
2500	10" diameter		15	2.667		81	150	50	281	365
2600	12" diameter		10	4		340	225	75	640	790
2700	14" diameter	B-22B	8	5		400	281	154	835	1,025
2800	16" diameter		6	6.667		470	375	205	1,050	1,300
2900	18" diameter		4	10		580	560	305	1,445	1,800
3000	24" diameter		2	20		705	1,125	615	2,445	3,125
4100	Caps									
4110	4" diameter	B-22A	34	1.176	Ea.	3.67	66	22	91.67	126
4120	6" diameter		30	1.333		26.50	75	25	126.50	168
4130	8" diameter		26	1.538		44.50	86.50	29	160	208
4150	10" diameter		20	2		110	112	37.50	259.50	330
4160	12" diameter		14	2.857		132	161	53.50	346.50	445

33 14 13.45 Water Supply, Copper Pipe

		Crew	Daily Output	Labor-Hours	Unit	Material	2024 Bare Costs Labor	Equipment	Total	Total Incl O&P
0010	**WATER SUPPLY, COPPER PIPE**									
0020	Not including excavation or backfill									
2000	Tubing, type K, 20' joints, 3/4" diameter	Q-1	400	.040	L.F.	5.50	2.69		8.19	10.05
2200	1" diameter		320	.050		7.15	3.36		10.51	12.90
3000	1-1/2" diameter		265	.060		11.55	4.06		15.61	18.75
3020	2" diameter		230	.070		17.40	4.67		22.07	26
3040	2-1/2" diameter		146	.110		23.50	7.35		30.85	36.50
3060	3" diameter		134	.119		36	8		44	51.50
4012	4" diameter		95	.168		62.50	11.30		73.80	86
4016	6" diameter	Q-2	80	.300		111	21		132	153
4018	8" diameter	"	80	.300		260	21		281	315
5000	Tubing, type L									
5108	2" diameter	Q-1	230	.070	L.F.	15	4.67		19.67	23.50
6010	3" diameter		134	.119		29.50	8		37.50	44.50
6012	4" diameter		95	.168		49.50	11.30		60.80	71.50
6016	6" diameter	Q-2	80	.300		99.50	21		120.50	141
7165	Fittings, brass, corporation stops, no lead, 3/4" diameter	1 Plum	19	.421	Ea.	92.50	31.50		124	149
7166	1" diameter		16	.500		123	37.50		160.50	191
7167	1-1/2" diameter		13	.615		305	46		351	410
7168	2" diameter		11	.727		495	54.50		549.50	625
7170	Curb stops, no lead, 3/4" diameter		19	.421		136	31.50		167.50	196
7171	1" diameter		16	.500		198	37.50		235.50	274
7172	1-1/2" diameter		13	.615		400	46		446	510
7173	2" diameter		11	.727		310	54.50		364.50	420

33 14 17 – Site Water Utility Service Laterals

33 14 17.15 Tapping, Crosses and Sleeves

		Crew	Daily Output	Labor-Hours	Unit	Material	2024 Bare Costs Labor	Equipment	Total	Total Incl O&P
0010	**TAPPING, CROSSES AND SLEEVES**									
4000	Drill and tap pressurized main (labor only)									
4100	6" main, 1" to 2" service	Q-1	3	5.333	Ea.		360		360	535
4150	8" main, 1" to 2" service	"	2.75	5.818	"		390		390	580
4500	Tap and insert gate valve									
4600	8" main, 4" branch	B-21	3.20	8.750	Ea.		495	63	558	805
4650	6" branch		2.70	10.370			585	74.50	659.50	950
4700	10" main, 4" branch		2.70	10.370			585	74.50	659.50	950
4750	6" branch		2.35	11.915			675	85.50	760.50	1,100
4800	12" main, 6" branch		2.35	11.915			675	85.50	760.50	1,100

33 14 Water Utility Transmission and Distribution

33 14 17 – Site Water Utility Service Laterals

33 14 17.15 Tapping, Crosses and Sleeves

		Crew	Daily Output	Labor-Hours	Unit	Material	2024 Bare Costs Labor	Equipment	Total	Total Incl O&P
4850	8" branch	B-21	2.35	11.915	Ea.		675	85.50	760.50	1,100
7020	Crosses, 4" x 4"		37	.757		1,400	43	5.45	1,448.45	1,625
7030	6" x 4"		25	1.120		1,675	63.50	8.05	1,746.55	1,950
7040	6" x 6"		25	1.120		1,675	63.50	8.05	1,746.55	1,950
7060	8" x 6"		21	1.333		2,050	75.50	9.55	2,135.05	2,375
7080	8" x 8"		21	1.333		2,225	75.50	9.55	2,310.05	2,575
7100	10" x 6"		21	1.333		4,050	75.50	9.55	4,135.05	4,600
7120	10" x 10"		21	1.333		4,400	75.50	9.55	4,485.05	4,950
7140	12" x 6"		18	1.556		4,050	88	11.15	4,149.15	4,625
7160	12" x 12"		18	1.556		5,125	88	11.15	5,224.15	5,800
7180	14" x 6"		16	1.750		10,100	99	12.55	10,211.55	11,300
7200	14" x 14"		16	1.750		10,700	99	12.55	10,811.55	12,000
7220	16" x 6"		14	2		10,900	113	14.35	11,027.35	12,100
7240	16" x 10"		14	2		11,000	113	14.35	11,127.35	12,300
7260	16" x 16"		14	2		11,600	113	14.35	11,727.35	12,900
7280	18" x 6"		10	2.800		16,200	158	20	16,378	18,200
7300	18" x 12"		10	2.800		16,400	158	20	16,578	18,300
7320	18" x 18"		10	2.800		16,800	158	20	16,978	18,800
7340	20" x 6"		8	3.500		13,100	198	25	13,323	14,800
7360	20" x 12"		8	3.500		14,100	198	25	14,323	15,800
7380	20" x 20"		8	3.500		20,600	198	25	20,823	22,900
7400	24" x 6"		6	4.667		17,000	264	33.50	17,297.50	19,100
7420	24" x 12"		6	4.667		17,200	264	33.50	17,497.50	19,300
7440	24" x 18"		6	4.667		26,100	264	33.50	26,397.50	29,100
7460	24" x 24"		6	4.667		26,700	264	33.50	26,997.50	29,800
7600	Cut-in sleeves with rubber gaskets, 4"		18	1.556		810	88	11.15	909.15	1,025
7620	6"		12	2.333		940	132	16.75	1,088.75	1,250
7640	8"		10	2.800		1,200	158	20	1,378	1,575
7660	10"		10	2.800		1,675	158	20	1,853	2,100
7680	12"		9	3.111		2,250	176	22.50	2,448.50	2,750
7800	Cut-in valves with rubber gaskets, 4"		18	1.556		460	88	11.15	559.15	655
7820	6"		12	2.333		600	132	16.75	748.75	875
7840	8"		10	2.800		910	158	20	1,088	1,250
7860	10"		10	2.800		1,375	158	20	1,553	1,750
7880	12"		9	3.111		1,725	176	22.50	1,923.50	2,150
7900	Tapping valve 4", MJ, ductile iron		18	1.556		670	88	11.15	769.15	880
7920	6", MJ, ductile iron		12	2.333		885	132	16.75	1,033.75	1,200
7940	Tapping valve 8", MJ, ductile iron		10	2.800		1,500	158	20	1,678	1,900
7960	Tapping valve 10", MJ, ductile iron		10	2.800		2,150	158	20	2,328	2,600
7980	Tapping valve 12", MJ, ductile iron		8	3.500		2,925	198	25	3,148	3,525
8000	Sleeves with rubber gaskets, 4" x 4"		37	.757		1,125	43	5.45	1,173.45	1,300
8010	6" x 4"		25	1.120		1,325	63.50	8.05	1,396.55	1,575
8020	6" x 6"		25	1.120		1,325	63.50	8.05	1,396.55	1,575
8030	8" x 4"		21	1.333		1,650	75.50	9.55	1,735.05	1,925
8040	8" x 6"		21	1.333		1,650	75.50	9.55	1,735.05	1,925
8060	8" x 8"		21	1.333		1,775	75.50	9.55	1,860.05	2,075
8070	10" x 4"		21	1.333		1,400	75.50	9.55	1,485.05	1,675
8080	10" x 6"		21	1.333		1,500	75.50	9.55	1,585.05	1,775
8090	10" x 8"		21	1.333		1,875	75.50	9.55	1,960.05	2,200
8100	10" x 10"		21	1.333		2,200	75.50	9.55	2,285.05	2,550
8110	12" x 4"		18	1.556		1,225	88	11.15	1,324.15	1,500
8120	12" x 6"		18	1.556		1,625	88	11.15	1,724.15	1,925
8130	12" x 8"		18	1.556		2,000	88	11.15	2,099.15	2,350

33 14 Water Utility Transmission and Distribution

33 14 17 – Site Water Utility Service Laterals

33 14 17.15 Tapping, Crosses and Sleeves		Crew	Daily Output	Labor-Hours	Unit	Material	2024 Bare Costs Labor	Equipment	Total	Total Incl O&P
8135	12" x 10"	B-21	18	1.556	Ea.	2,150	88	11.15	2,249.15	2,525
8140	12" x 12"		18	1.556		3,275	88	11.15	3,374.15	3,750
8160	14" x 6"		16	1.750		1,250	99	12.55	1,361.55	1,525
8180	14" x 14"		16	1.750		4,900	99	12.55	5,011.55	5,550
8200	16" x 6"		14	2		2,650	113	14.35	2,777.35	3,100
8220	16" x 10"		14	2		2,900	113	14.35	3,027.35	3,375
8240	16" x 16"		14	2		5,325	113	14.35	5,452.35	6,025
8260	18" x 6"		10	2.800		1,050	158	20	1,228	1,400
8280	18" x 12"		10	2.800		3,725	158	20	3,903	4,350
8300	18" x 18"		10	2.800		5,875	158	20	6,053	6,700
8320	20" x 6"		8	3.500		2,050	198	25	2,273	2,575
8340	20" x 12"		8	3.500		3,475	198	25	3,698	4,150
8360	20" x 20"		8	3.500		6,375	198	25	6,598	7,325
8380	24" x 6"		6	4.667		2,350	264	33.50	2,647.50	3,025
8400	24" x 12"		6	4.667		3,950	264	33.50	4,247.50	4,775
8420	24" x 18"		6	4.667		6,725	264	33.50	7,022.50	7,825
8440	24" x 24"		6	4.667		10,200	264	33.50	10,497.50	11,700
8800	Hydrant valve box, 6' long	B-20	20	1.200		355	65.50		420.50	485
8820	8' long		18	1.333		410	72.50		482.50	560
8830	Valve box w/lid 4' deep		14	1.714		107	93.50		200.50	256
8840	Valve box and large base w/lid		14	1.714		355	93.50		448.50	530

33 14 19 – Valves and Hydrants for Water Utility Service

33 14 19.10 Valves

		Crew	Daily Output	Labor-Hours	Unit	Material	2024 Bare Costs Labor	Equipment	Total	Total Incl O&P
0010	**VALVES**, water distribution									
0011	See Sections 22 05 23.20 and 22 05 23.60									
3000	Butterfly valves with boxes, cast iron, mechanical joint									
3100	4" diameter	B-6	6	4	Ea.	945	213	48.50	1,206.50	1,425
3140	6" diameter		6	4		1,475	213	48.50	1,736.50	2,000
3180	8" diameter		6	4		1,900	213	48.50	2,161.50	2,450
3300	10" diameter		6	4		2,875	213	48.50	3,136.50	3,550
3340	12" diameter		6	4		3,775	213	48.50	4,036.50	4,525
3400	14" diameter		4	6		6,550	320	73	6,943	7,750
3440	16" diameter		4	6		10,400	320	73	10,793	12,000
3460	18" diameter		4	6		10,900	320	73	11,293	12,500
3480	20" diameter		4	6		14,400	320	73	14,793	16,400
3500	24" diameter		4	6		24,200	320	73	24,593	27,200
3510	30" diameter		4	6		21,300	320	73	21,693	24,000
3520	36" diameter		4	6		26,400	320	73	26,793	29,700
3530	42" diameter		4	6		33,600	320	73	33,993	37,600
3540	48" diameter		4	6		43,300	320	73	43,693	48,200
3600	With lever operator									
3610	4" diameter	B-6	6	4	Ea.	835	213	48.50	1,096.50	1,300
3614	6" diameter		6	4		1,375	213	48.50	1,636.50	1,875
3616	8" diameter		6	4		1,775	213	48.50	2,036.50	2,325
3618	10" diameter		6	4		2,775	213	48.50	3,036.50	3,425
3620	12" diameter		6	4		3,675	213	48.50	3,936.50	4,400
3622	14" diameter		4	6		6,200	320	73	6,593	7,375
3624	16" diameter		4	6		10,000	320	73	10,393	11,600
3626	18" diameter		4	6		10,500	320	73	10,893	12,200
3628	20" diameter		4	6		14,000	320	73	14,393	16,000
3630	24" diameter		4	6		23,800	320	73	24,193	26,800
3700	Check valves, flanged									

33 14 Water Utility Transmission and Distribution

33 14 19 – Valves and Hydrants for Water Utility Service

33 14 19.10 Valves

		Crew	Daily Output	Labor-Hours	Unit	Material	2024 Bare Costs Labor	Equipment	Total	Total Incl O&P
3710	4" diameter	B-6	6	4	Ea.	1,675	213	48.50	1,936.50	2,225
3714	6" diameter		6	4		2,875	213	48.50	3,136.50	3,525
3716	8" diameter		6	4		5,400	213	48.50	5,661.50	6,325
3718	10" diameter		6	4		9,225	213	48.50	9,486.50	10,500
3720	12" diameter		6	4		12,500	213	48.50	12,761.50	14,100
3726	18" diameter		4	6		47,300	320	73	47,693	52,500
3730	24" diameter		4	6		60,000	320	73	60,393	66,500
3800	Gate valves, C.I., 125 psi, mechanical joint, w/boxes									
3810	4" diameter	B-6	6	4	Ea.	1,900	213	48.50	2,161.50	2,475
3814	6" diameter		6	4		3,075	213	48.50	3,336.50	3,750
3816	8" diameter		6	4		5,375	213	48.50	5,636.50	6,300
3818	10" diameter		6	4		9,750	213	48.50	10,011.50	11,100
3820	12" diameter		6	4		13,200	213	48.50	13,461.50	15,000
3822	14" diameter		4	6		27,200	320	73	27,593	30,500
3824	16" diameter		4	6		38,400	320	73	38,793	42,900
3826	18" diameter		4	6		39,200	320	73	39,593	43,700
3828	20" diameter		4	6		54,500	320	73	54,893	60,500
3830	24" diameter		4	6		28,800	320	73	29,193	32,300
3831	30" diameter		4	6		55,000	320	73	55,393	61,500
3832	36" diameter		4	6		91,500	320	73	91,893	101,000
3880	Sleeve, for tapping mains, 8" x 4", add					1,650			1,650	1,800
3884	10" x 6", add					1,500			1,500	1,650
3888	12" x 6", add					1,625			1,625	1,775
3892	12" x 8", add					2,000			2,000	2,200

33 14 19.20 Valves

		Crew	Daily Output	Labor-Hours	Unit	Material	2024 Bare Costs Labor	Equipment	Total	Total Incl O&P
0010	**VALVES**									
0011	Special trim or use									
9000	Valves, gate valve, N.R.S. PIV with post, 4" diameter	B-6	6	4	Ea.	3,650	213	48.50	3,911.50	4,400
9020	6" diameter		6	4		4,825	213	48.50	5,086.50	5,675
9040	8" diameter		6	4		7,125	213	48.50	7,386.50	8,225
9060	10" diameter		6	4		11,500	213	48.50	11,761.50	13,000
9080	12" diameter		6	4		15,000	213	48.50	15,261.50	16,900
9100	14" diameter		6	4		28,700	213	48.50	28,961.50	31,900
9120	OS&Y, 4" diameter		6	4		1,350	213	48.50	1,611.50	1,850
9140	6" diameter		6	4		1,825	213	48.50	2,086.50	2,400
9160	8" diameter		6	4		1,850	213	48.50	2,111.50	2,400
9180	10" diameter		6	4		5,125	213	48.50	5,386.50	6,000
9200	12" diameter		6	4		3,675	213	48.50	3,936.50	4,425
9220	14" diameter		4	6		5,800	320	73	6,193	6,925
9400	Check valves, rubber disc, 2-1/2" diameter		6	4		430	213	48.50	691.50	840
9420	3" diameter		6	4		590	213	48.50	851.50	1,025
9440	4" diameter		6	4		1,675	213	48.50	1,936.50	2,225
9480	6" diameter		6	4		2,875	213	48.50	3,136.50	3,525
9500	8" diameter		6	4		5,400	213	48.50	5,661.50	6,325
9520	10" diameter		6	4		9,225	213	48.50	9,486.50	10,500
9540	12" diameter		6	4		12,500	213	48.50	12,761.50	14,100
9542	14" diameter		4	6		8,525	320	73	8,918	9,925
9700	Detector check valves, reducing, 4" diameter		6	4		2,650	213	48.50	2,911.50	3,300
9720	6" diameter		6	4		4,250	213	48.50	4,511.50	5,050
9740	8" diameter		6	4		5,875	213	48.50	6,136.50	6,850
9760	10" diameter		6	4		8,600	213	48.50	8,861.50	9,850
9800	Galvanized, 4" diameter		6	4		2,675	213	48.50	2,936.50	3,325

33 14 Water Utility Transmission and Distribution

33 14 19 – Valves and Hydrants for Water Utility Service

33 14 19.20 Valves

		Crew	Daily Output	Labor-Hours	Unit	Material	2024 Bare Costs Labor	2024 Bare Costs Equipment	Total	Total Incl O&P
9820	6" diameter	B-6	6	4	Ea.	3,575	213	48.50	3,836.50	4,325
9840	8" diameter		6	4		7,575	213	48.50	7,836.50	8,725
9860	10" diameter	↓	6	4	↓	11,800	213	48.50	12,061.50	13,400

33 14 19.30 Fire Hydrants

		Crew	Daily Output	Labor-Hours	Unit	Material	Labor	Equipment	Total	Total Incl O&P
0010	**FIRE HYDRANTS** G3010-410									
0020	Mechanical joints unless otherwise noted									
1000	Fire hydrants, two way; excavation and backfill not incl.									
1100	4-1/2" valve size, depth 2'-0"	B-21	10	2.800	Ea.	3,075	158	20	3,253	3,650
1200	4'-6"		9	3.111		3,325	176	22.50	3,523.50	3,950
1260	6'-0"		7	4		3,575	226	28.50	3,829.50	4,325
1340	8'-0"		6	4.667		3,725	264	33.50	4,022.50	4,525
1420	10'-0"		5	5.600		3,975	315	40	4,330	4,900
2000	5-1/4" valve size, depth 2'-0"		10	2.800		3,325	158	20	3,503	3,925
2080	4'-0"		9	3.111		3,650	176	22.50	3,848.50	4,300
2160	6'-0"		7	4		3,975	226	28.50	4,229.50	4,750
2240	8'-0"		6	4.667		4,350	264	33.50	4,647.50	5,225
2320	10'-0"	↓	5	5.600		4,675	315	40	5,030	5,675
2350	For threeway valves, add					7%				
2400	Lower barrel extensions with stems, 1'-0"	B-20	14	1.714		655	93.50		748.50	860
2440	2'-0"		13	1.846		800	101		901	1,025
2480	3'-0"		12	2		1,375	109		1,484	1,650
2520	4'-0"	↓	10	2.400	↓	1,500	131		1,631	1,875
5000	Indicator post									
5020	Adjustable, valve size 4" to 14", 4' bury	B-21	10	2.800	Ea.	1,625	158	20	1,803	2,050
5060	8' bury		7	4		1,875	226	28.50	2,129.50	2,425
5080	10' bury		6	4.667		2,475	264	33.50	2,772.50	3,125
5100	12' bury		5	5.600		2,025	315	40	2,380	2,750
5120	14' bury		4	7		1,925	395	50.50	2,370.50	2,775
5500	Non-adjustable, valve size 4" to 14", 3' bury		10	2.800		1,000	158	20	1,178	1,350
5520	3'-6" bury		10	2.800		1,000	158	20	1,178	1,350
5540	4' bury	↓	9	3.111	↓	1,000	176	22.50	1,198.50	1,375

33 16 Water Utility Storage Tanks

33 16 36 – Ground-Level Reinforced Concrete Water Storage Tanks

33 16 36.16 Prestressed Conc. Water Storage Tanks

		Crew	Daily Output	Labor-Hours	Unit	Material	Labor	Equipment	Total	Total Incl O&P
0010	**PRESTRESSED CONC. WATER STORAGE TANKS**									
0020	Not including fdn., pipe or pumps, 250,000 gallons				Ea.				299,000	329,500

33 31 Sanitary Sewerage Piping

33 31 11 – Public Sanitary Sewerage Gravity Piping

33 31 11.10 Sewage Collection, Valves

		Crew	Daily Output	Labor-Hours	Unit	Material	2024 Bare Costs Labor	Equipment	Total	Total Incl O&P
0010	**SEWAGE COLLECTION, VALVES**									
1000	Backwater sewer line valve									
1010	Offset type, bronze swing check assy and bronze cover									
1020	B&S connections									
1040	2" size	2 Skwk	14	1.143	Ea.	1,075	72.50		1,147.50	1,275
1050	3" size		12.50	1.280		2,750	81.50		2,831.50	3,125
1060	4" size		11	1.455		1,525	92.50		1,617.50	1,825
1070	6" size	3 Skwk	15	1.600		2,450	102		2,552	2,850
1080	8" size	"	7.50	3.200		5,550	203		5,753	6,425
1110	Backwater drainage control									
1120	Offset type, w/bronze manually operated shear gate									
1130	B&S connections									
1160	4" size	2 Skwk	11	1.455	Ea.	4,425	92.50		4,517.50	5,025
1170	6" size	3 Skwk	15	1.600	"	6,025	102		6,127	6,775

33 31 11.25 Sewage Collection, Polyvinyl Chloride Pipe

		Crew	Daily Output	Labor-Hours	Unit	Material	Labor	Equipment	Total	Total Incl O&P
0010	**SEWAGE COLLECTION, POLYVINYL CHLORIDE PIPE**									
0020	Not including excavation or backfill									
2000	20' lengths, SDR 35, B&S, 4" diameter	B-20	375	.064	L.F.	5	3.49		8.49	10.70
2040	6" diameter	"	350	.069		9.75	3.74		13.49	16.30
2120	10" diameter	B-21	330	.085		12.45	4.79	.61	17.85	21.50
2160	12" diameter		320	.088		17.55	4.94	.63	23.12	27.50
2170	14" diameter		280	.100		34.50	5.65	.72	40.87	47
2200	15" diameter		240	.117		57	6.60	.84	64.44	73
2250	16" diameter		220	.127		51	7.20	.91	59.11	68
4000	Piping, DWV PVC, no exc./bkfill., 10' L, Sch 40, 4" diameter	B-20	375	.064		12.70	3.49		16.19	19.15
4010	6" diameter		350	.069		31.50	3.74		35.24	40.50
4020	8" diameter		335	.072		53.50	3.90		57.40	65

33 31 11.37 Centrif. Cst. Fbgs-Reinf. Polymer Mort. Util. Pipe

		Crew	Daily Output	Labor-Hours	Unit	Material	Labor	Equipment	Total	Total Incl O&P
0010	**CENTRIF. CST. FBGS-REINF. POLYMER MORT. UTIL. PIPE**									
0020	Not including excavation or backfill									
3348	48" diameter, SN 46, 25psi	B-13B	40	1.400	L.F.	220	75	64	359	425
3354	54" diameter		40	1.400		360	75	64	499	575
3363	63" diameter		20	2.800		445	150	128	723	845
3418	18" diameter, 100psi		60	.933		155	50	42.50	247.50	292
3424	24" diameter		60	.933		171	50	42.50	263.50	310
3436	36" diameter		40	1.400		193	75	64	332	395
3444	44" diameter		40	1.400		212	75	64	351	415
3448	48" diameter		40	1.400		237	75	64	376	440

33 34 Onsite Wastewater Disposal

33 34 13 – Septic Tanks

33 34 13.13 Concrete Septic Tanks

			Crew	Daily Output	Labor-Hours	Unit	Material	Labor	Equipment	Total	Total Incl O&P
0010	**CONCRETE SEPTIC TANKS**	G3020-300									
0011	Not including excavation or piping										
0015	Septic tanks, precast, 1,000 gallon		B-21	8	3.500	Ea.	985	198	25	1,208	1,400
0060	1,500 gallon			7	4		1,700	226	28.50	1,954.50	2,250
0100	2,000 gallon			5	5.600		2,400	315	40	2,755	3,150
0200	5,000 gallon		B-13	3.50	16		7,450	855	665	8,970	10,200
0300	15,000 gallon, 4 piece		B-13B	1.70	32.941		20,200	1,750	1,500	23,450	26,500
0400	25,000 gallon, 4 piece			1.10	50.909		37,300	2,725	2,325	42,350	47,700

33 34 Onsite Wastewater Disposal

33 34 13 – Septic Tanks

33 34 13.13 Concrete Septic Tanks

		Crew	Daily Output	Labor-Hours	Unit	Material	2024 Bare Costs Labor	2024 Bare Costs Equipment	Total	Total Incl O&P
0500	40,000 gallon, 4 piece	B-13B	.80	70	Ea.	59,500	3,750	3,200	66,450	74,500
0520	50,000 gallon, 5 piece	B-13C	.60	93.333		68,500	4,975	2,700	76,175	86,000
0640	75,000 gallon, cast in place	C-14C	.25	448		83,500	26,000	125	109,625	130,500
0660	100,000 gallon	"	.15	747		103,500	43,300	209	147,009	178,000
1150	Leaching field chambers, 13' x 3'-7" x 1'-4", standard	B-13	16	3.500		480	187	146	813	965
1200	Heavy duty, 8' x 4' x 1'-6"		14	4		283	214	167	664	810
1300	13' x 3'-9" x 1'-6"		12	4.667		1,400	249	195	1,844	2,100
1350	20' x 4' x 1'-6"		5	11.200		1,250	600	465	2,315	2,775
1400	Leaching pit, precast concrete, 3' diameter, 3' deep	B-21	8	3.500		710	198	25	933	1,100
1500	6' diameter, 3' section		4.70	5.957		1,125	335	43	1,503	1,775
2000	Velocity reducing pit, precast conc., 6' diameter, 3' deep		4.70	5.957		1,875	335	43	2,253	2,625

33 34 13.33 Polyethylene Septic Tanks

		Crew	Daily Output	Labor-Hours	Unit	Material	Labor	Equipment	Total	Total Incl O&P
0010	**POLYETHYLENE SEPTIC TANKS**									
0011	High density polyethylene, 300 gallon	B-21	9.50	2.947	Ea.	800	167	21	988	1,150
0012	High density polyethylene, 500 gallon		9	3.111		1,000	176	22.50	1,198.50	1,375
0014	High density polyethylene, 750 gallon		8.50	3.294		1,275	186	23.50	1,484.50	1,700
0015	High density polyethylene, 1,000 gallon		8	3.500		1,775	198	25	1,998	2,275
0020	1,250 gallon		8	3.500		2,275	198	25	2,498	2,825
0025	1,500 gallon		7	4		2,675	226	28.50	2,929.50	3,325
0030	2,500 gallon		6	4.667		4,725	264	33.50	5,022.50	5,625
0035	3,000 gallon		5.50	5.091		6,475	288	36.50	6,799.50	7,600
0040	3,500 gallon		5	5.600		7,725	315	40	8,080	9,025

33 34 16 – Septic Tank Effluent Filters

33 34 16.13 Septic Tank Gravity Effluent Filters

		Crew	Daily Output	Labor-Hours	Unit	Material	Labor	Equipment	Total	Total Incl O&P
0010	**SEPTIC TANK GRAVITY EFFLUENT FILTERS**									
3000	Effluent filter, 4" diameter	1 Skwk	8	1	Ea.	36	63.50		99.50	135
3020	6" diameter		7	1.143		43.50	72.50		116	157
3030	8" diameter		7	1.143		254	72.50		326.50	390
3040	8" diameter, very fine		7	1.143		505	72.50		577.50	665
3050	10" diameter, very fine		6	1.333		240	84.50		324.50	390
3060	10" diameter		6	1.333		275	84.50		359.50	425
3080	12" diameter		6	1.333		660	84.50		744.50	850
3090	15" diameter		5	1.600		1,100	102		1,202	1,350

33 34 51 – Drainage Field Systems

33 34 51.10 Drainage Field Excavation and Fill

		Crew	Daily Output	Labor-Hours	Unit	Material	Labor	Equipment	Total	Total Incl O&P
0010	**DRAINAGE FIELD EXCAVATION AND FILL**									
2200	Septic tank & drainage field excavation with 3/4 C.Y. backhoe	B-12F	145	.110	C.Y.		6.50	6.10	12.60	16.35
2400	4' trench for disposal field, 3/4 C.Y. backhoe	"	335	.048	L.F.		2.81	2.65	5.46	7.10
2600	Gravel fill, run of bank	B-6	150	.160	C.Y.	13.65	8.55	1.94	24.14	30
2800	Crushed stone, 3/4"	"	150	.160	"	37.50	8.55	1.94	47.99	56.50

33 34 51.13 Utility Septic Tank Tile Drainage Field

		Crew	Daily Output	Labor-Hours	Unit	Material	Labor	Equipment	Total	Total Incl O&P
0010	**UTILITY SEPTIC TANK TILE DRAINAGE FIELD**									
0015	Distribution box, concrete, 5 outlets	2 Clab	20	.800	Ea.	90	39		129	157
0020	7 outlets		16	1		93.50	49		142.50	176
0025	9 outlets		8	2		530	98		628	730
0115	Distribution boxes, HDPE, 5 outlets		20	.800		75	39		114	141
0117	6 outlets		15	1.067		75	52.50		127.50	160
0118	7 outlets		15	1.067		75	52.50		127.50	160
0120	8 outlets		10	1.600		79	78.50		157.50	203
0240	Distribution boxes, outlet flow leveler	1 Clab	50	.160		3	7.85		10.85	14.90
0300	Precast concrete, galley, 4' x 4' x 4'	B-21	16	1.750		247	99	12.55	358.55	430

33 34 Onsite Wastewater Disposal

33 34 51 – Drainage Field Systems

33 34 51.13 Utility Septic Tank Tile Drainage Field	Crew	Daily Output	Labor-Hours	Unit	Material	2024 Bare Costs Labor	Equipment	Total	Total Incl O&P
0350 HDPE infiltration chamber 12" H x 15" W	2 Clab	300	.053	L.F.	7.05	2.61		9.66	11.65
0351 12" H x 15" W end cap	1 Clab	32	.250	Ea.	19.10	12.25		31.35	39
0355 chamber 12" H x 22" W	2 Clab	300	.053	L.F.	6.70	2.61		9.31	11.25
0356 12" H x 22" W end cap	1 Clab	32	.250	Ea.	23.50	12.25		35.75	43.50
0360 chamber 13" H x 34" W	2 Clab	300	.053	L.F.	14.45	2.61		17.06	19.75
0361 13" H x 34" W end cap	1 Clab	32	.250	Ea.	51.50	12.25		63.75	74.50
0365 chamber 16" H x 34" W	2 Clab	300	.053	L.F.	14.90	2.61		17.51	20.50
0366 16" H x 34" W end cap	1 Clab	32	.250	Ea.	16.95	12.25		29.20	37
0370 chamber 8" H x 16" W	2 Clab	300	.053	L.F.	11.35	2.61		13.96	16.35
0371 8" H x 16" W end cap	1 Clab	32	.250	Ea.	11.15	12.25		23.40	30.50

33 41 Subdrainage

33 41 16 – Subdrainage Piping

33 41 16.25 Piping, Subdrainage, Corrugated Metal

	Crew	Daily Output	Labor-Hours	Unit	Material	Labor	Equipment	Total	Total Incl O&P
0010 **PIPING, SUBDRAINAGE, CORRUGATED METAL** G1030-805									
0021 Not including excavation and backfill									
2010 Aluminum, perforated									
2020 6" diameter, 18 ga.	B-20	380	.063	L.F.	8.70	3.44		12.14	14.70
2200 8" diameter, 16 ga.	"	370	.065		14.30	3.54		17.84	21
2220 10" diameter, 16 ga.	B-21	360	.078		17.90	4.40	.56	22.86	27
2240 12" diameter, 16 ga.		285	.098		20	5.55	.71	26.26	31
2260 18" diameter, 16 ga.		205	.137		30	7.70	.98	38.68	45.50
3000 Uncoated galvanized, perforated									
3020 6" diameter, 18 ga.	B-20	380	.063	L.F.	9.25	3.44		12.69	15.25
3200 8" diameter, 16 ga.	"	370	.065		11.10	3.54		14.64	17.50
3220 10" diameter, 16 ga.	B-21	360	.078		11.80	4.40	.56	16.76	20
3240 12" diameter, 16 ga.		285	.098		13.10	5.55	.71	19.36	23.50
3260 18" diameter, 16 ga.		205	.137		20	7.70	.98	28.68	34.50
4000 Steel, perforated, asphalt coated									
4020 6" diameter, 18 ga.	B-20	380	.063	L.F.	8.20	3.44		11.64	14.15
4030 8" diameter, 18 ga.	"	370	.065		12.75	3.54		16.29	19.25
4040 10" diameter, 16 ga.	B-21	360	.078		12.90	4.40	.56	17.86	21.50
4050 12" diameter, 16 ga.		285	.098		12.90	5.55	.71	19.16	23
4060 18" diameter, 16 ga.		205	.137		23	7.70	.98	31.68	38

33 41 16.30 Piping, Subdrainage, Plastic

	Crew	Daily Output	Labor-Hours	Unit	Material	Labor	Equipment	Total	Total Incl O&P
0010 **PIPING, SUBDRAINAGE, PLASTIC**									
0020 Not including excavation and backfill									
2100 Perforated PVC, 4" diameter	B-14	314	.153	L.F.	5	7.85	.93	13.78	18.15
2110 6" diameter		300	.160		9.75	8.25	.97	18.97	24
2120 8" diameter		290	.166		10.90	8.50	1	20.40	26
2130 10" diameter		280	.171		11.55	8.85	1.04	21.44	27
2140 12" diameter		270	.178		16.25	9.15	1.08	26.48	32.50

33 42 Stormwater Conveyance

33 42 11 – Stormwater Gravity Piping

33 42 11.40 Piping, Storm Drainage, Corrugated Metal		Crew	Daily Output	Labor-Hours	Unit	Material	2024 Bare Costs Labor	Equipment	Total	Total Incl O&P
0010	**PIPING, STORM DRAINAGE, CORRUGATED METAL**									
0020	Not including excavation or backfill									
2000	Corrugated metal pipe, galvanized									
2040	8" diameter, 16 ga.	B-14	330	.145	L.F.	9.05	7.50	.88	17.43	22
2060	10" diameter, 16 ga.		260	.185		9.40	9.50	1.12	20.02	25.50
2080	12" diameter, 16 ga.		210	.229		14.95	11.75	1.39	28.09	35.50
2100	15" diameter, 16 ga.		200	.240		15.80	12.35	1.45	29.60	37.50
2120	18" diameter, 16 ga.		190	.253		23.50	13	1.53	38.03	46.50
2140	24" diameter, 14 ga.		160	.300		26	15.45	1.82	43.27	53.50
2160	30" diameter, 14 ga.	B-13	120	.467		33	25	19.45	77.45	94.50
2180	36" diameter, 12 ga.		120	.467		36.50	25	19.45	80.95	99
2200	48" diameter, 12 ga.		100	.560		49.50	30	23.50	103	125
2220	60" diameter, 10 ga.	B-13B	75	.747		87	40	34	161	193
2240	72" diameter, 8 ga.	"	45	1.244		90.50	66.50	56.50	213.50	261
2250	End sections, 8" diameter, 16 ga.	B-14	20	2.400	Ea.	54.50	124	14.55	193.05	259
2255	10" diameter, 16 ga.		20	2.400		64	124	14.55	202.55	270
2260	12" diameter, 16 ga.		18	2.667		131	137	16.15	284.15	365
2265	15" diameter, 16 ga.		18	2.667		259	137	16.15	412.15	505
2270	18" diameter, 16 ga.		16	3		300	155	18.20	473.20	580
2275	24" diameter, 16 ga.	B-13	16	3.500		395	187	146	728	875
2280	30" diameter, 16 ga.		14	4		650	214	167	1,031	1,225
2285	36" diameter, 14 ga.		14	4		810	214	167	1,191	1,400
2290	48" diameter, 14 ga.		10	5.600		2,325	299	234	2,858	3,275
2292	60" diameter, 14 ga.		6	9.333		2,325	500	390	3,215	3,725
2294	72" diameter, 14 ga.	B-13B	5	11.200		3,525	600	510	4,635	5,350
2300	Bends or elbows, 8" diameter	B-14	28	1.714		129	88.50	10.40	227.90	284
2320	10" diameter		25	1.920		160	99	11.65	270.65	335
2340	12" diameter, 16 ga.		23	2.087		188	107	12.65	307.65	380
2342	18" diameter, 16 ga.		20	2.400		269	124	14.55	407.55	495
2344	24" diameter, 14 ga.		16	3		450	155	18.20	623.20	745
2346	30" diameter, 14 ga.		15	3.200		550	165	19.40	734.40	870
2348	36" diameter, 14 ga.	B-13	15	3.733		720	199	156	1,075	1,250
2350	48" diameter, 12 ga.	"	12	4.667		925	249	195	1,369	1,600
2352	60" diameter, 10 ga.	B-13B	10	5.600		1,225	299	255	1,779	2,075
2354	72" diameter, 10 ga.	"	6	9.333		1,525	500	425	2,450	2,900
2360	Wyes or tees, 8" diameter	B-14	25	1.920		182	99	11.65	292.65	360
2380	10" diameter		21	2.286		227	118	13.85	358.85	440
2400	12" diameter, 16 ga.		19	2.526		259	130	15.30	404.30	495
2410	18" diameter, 16 ga.		16	3		360	155	18.20	533.20	645
2412	24" diameter, 14 ga.		16	3		650	155	18.20	823.20	965
2414	30" diameter, 14 ga.	B-13	12	4.667		855	249	195	1,299	1,525
2416	36" diameter, 14 ga.		11	5.091		990	272	212	1,474	1,750
2418	48" diameter, 12 ga.		10	5.600		1,350	299	234	1,883	2,175
2420	60" diameter, 10 ga.	B-13B	8	7		1,950	375	320	2,645	3,050
2422	72" diameter, 10 ga.	"	5	11.200		2,350	600	510	3,460	4,050
2500	Galvanized, uncoated, 20' lengths									
2520	8" diameter, 16 ga.	B-14	355	.135	L.F.	10.20	6.95	.82	17.97	22.50
2540	10" diameter, 16 ga.		280	.171		10.15	8.85	1.04	20.04	25.50
2560	12" diameter, 16 ga.		220	.218		33.50	11.25	1.32	46.07	54.50
2580	15" diameter, 16 ga.		220	.218		34	11.25	1.32	46.57	55.50
2600	18" diameter, 16 ga.		205	.234		35	12.05	1.42	48.47	58.50
2620	24" diameter, 14 ga.		175	.274		50	14.15	1.66	65.81	78
2640	30" diameter, 14 ga.	B-13	130	.431		35	23	17.95	75.95	92.50

33 42 Stormwater Conveyance

33 42 11 – Stormwater Gravity Piping

33 42 11.40 Piping, Storm Drainage, Corrugated Metal

		Crew	Daily Output	Labor-Hours	Unit	Material	2024 Bare Costs Labor	Equipment	Total	Total Incl O&P
2660	36" diameter, 12 ga.	B-13	130	.431	L.F.	39.50	23	17.95	80.45	97.50
2680	48" diameter, 12 ga.	↓	110	.509		59	27	21	107	129
2690	60" diameter, 10 ga.	B-13B	78	.718		97	38.50	32.50	168	200
2695	72" diameter, 10 ga.	"	60	.933	↓	112	50	42.50	204.50	244
2711	Bends or elbows, 12" diameter, 16 ga.	B-14	30	1.600	Ea.	153	82.50	9.70	245.20	300
2712	15" diameter, 16 ga.		25.04	1.917		195	98.50	11.60	305.10	375
2714	18" diameter, 16 ga.		20	2.400		218	124	14.55	356.55	440
2716	24" diameter, 14 ga.		16	3		330	155	18.20	503.20	615
2718	30" diameter, 14 ga.	↓	15	3.200		440	165	19.40	624.40	750
2720	36" diameter, 14 ga.	B-13	15	3.733		590	199	156	945	1,125
2722	48" diameter, 12 ga.		12	4.667		795	249	195	1,239	1,450
2724	60" diameter, 10 ga.		10	5.600		1,250	299	234	1,783	2,075
2726	72" diameter, 10 ga.	↓	6	9.333		1,575	500	390	2,465	2,900
2728	Wyes or tees, 12" diameter, 16 ga.	B-14	22.48	2.135		196	110	12.95	318.95	395
2730	18" diameter, 16 ga.		15	3.200		305	165	19.40	489.40	600
2732	24" diameter, 14 ga.		15	3.200		530	165	19.40	714.40	850
2734	30" diameter, 14 ga.		14	3.429		685	177	21	883	1,025
2736	36" diameter, 14 ga.	B-13	14	4		870	214	167	1,251	1,450
2738	48" diameter, 12 ga.		12	4.667		1,275	249	195	1,719	1,975
2740	60" diameter, 10 ga.		10	5.600		1,825	299	234	2,358	2,725
2742	72" diameter, 10 ga.	↓	6	9.333		2,200	500	390	3,090	3,600
2780	End sections, 8" diameter	B-14	35	1.371		102	70.50	8.30	180.80	227
2785	10" diameter		35	1.371		100	70.50	8.30	178.80	224
2790	12" diameter		35	1.371		119	70.50	8.30	197.80	245
2800	18" diameter	↓	30	1.600		139	82.50	9.70	231.20	286
2810	24" diameter	B-13	25	2.240		235	120	93.50	448.50	540
2820	30" diameter		25	2.240		425	120	93.50	638.50	750
2825	36" diameter		20	2.800		565	150	117	832	970
2830	48" diameter	↓	10	5.600		1,225	299	234	1,758	2,050
2835	60" diameter	B-13B	5	11.200		2,425	600	510	3,535	4,100
2840	72" diameter	"	4	14		2,800	750	640	4,190	4,875
2850	Couplings, 12" diameter					39.50			39.50	43.50
2855	18" diameter					52.50			52.50	57.50
2860	24" diameter					48			48	53
2865	30" diameter					33.50			33.50	36.50
2870	36" diameter					50.50			50.50	56
2875	48" diameter					74			74	81.50
2880	60" diameter					70.50			70.50	77.50
2885	72" diameter				↓	79.50			79.50	87.50

33 42 11.60 Sewage/Drainage Collection, Concrete Pipe

		Crew	Daily Output	Labor-Hours	Unit	Material	2024 Bare Costs Labor	Equipment	Total	Total Incl O&P
0010	**SEWAGE/DRAINAGE COLLECTION, CONCRETE PIPE**									
0020	Not including excavation or backfill									
1000	Non-reinforced pipe, extra strength, B&S or T&G joints									
1010	6" diameter	B-14	265.04	.181	L.F.	12.85	9.35	1.10	23.30	29
1020	8" diameter		224	.214		14.15	11.05	1.30	26.50	33.50
1030	10" diameter		216	.222		15.70	11.45	1.35	28.50	35.50
1040	12" diameter		200	.240		16.35	12.35	1.45	30.15	38
1050	15" diameter		180	.267		23.50	13.75	1.62	38.87	48.50
1060	18" diameter		144	.333		29.50	17.15	2.02	48.67	60
1070	21" diameter		112	.429		31	22	2.60	55.60	69.50
1080	24" diameter	↓	100	.480	↓	35.50	24.50	2.91	62.91	78.50
2000	Reinforced culvert, class 3, no gaskets									

33 42 Stormwater Conveyance

33 42 11 – Stormwater Gravity Piping

33 42 11.60 Sewage/Drainage Collection, Concrete Pipe		Crew	Daily Output	Labor-Hours	Unit	Material	2024 Bare Costs Labor	Equipment	Total	Total Incl O&P
2010	12" diameter	B-14	150	.320	L.F.	24	16.50	1.94	42.44	52.50
2020	15" diameter		150	.320		28.50	16.50	1.94	46.94	57.50
2030	18" diameter		132	.364		33	18.75	2.20	53.95	66
2035	21" diameter		120	.400		38.50	20.50	2.42	61.42	75.50
2040	24" diameter		100	.480		47.50	24.50	2.91	74.91	92
2045	27" diameter	B-13	92	.609		54.50	32.50	25.50	112.50	136
2050	30" diameter		88	.636		65.50	34	26.50	126	152
2060	36" diameter		72	.778		112	41.50	32.50	186	220
2070	42" diameter	B-13B	68	.824		158	44	37.50	239.50	281
2080	48" diameter		64	.875		198	47	40	285	330
2085	54" diameter		56	1		216	53.50	45.50	315	365
2090	60" diameter		48	1.167		255	62.50	53	370.50	430
2100	72" diameter		40	1.400		365	75	64	504	580
2120	84" diameter		32	1.750		595	93.50	79.50	768	880
2140	96" diameter		24	2.333		715	125	106	946	1,075
2200	With gaskets, class 3, 12" diameter	B-21	168	.167		26	9.40	1.20	36.60	44.50
2220	15" diameter		160	.175		31	9.90	1.26	42.16	50
2230	18" diameter		152	.184		36	10.40	1.32	47.72	56.50
2235	21" diameter		152	.184		42.50	10.40	1.32	54.22	63.50
2240	24" diameter		136	.206		58.50	11.65	1.48	71.63	83
2260	30" diameter	B-13	88	.636		78.50	34	26.50	139	166
2270	36" diameter	"	72	.778		128	41.50	32.50	202	237
2290	48" diameter	B-13B	64	.875		219	47	40	306	355
2310	72" diameter	"	40	1.400		400	75	64	539	620
2330	Flared ends, 12" diameter	B-21	31	.903	Ea.	71	51	6.50	128.50	161
2340	15" diameter		25	1.120		76.50	63.50	8.05	148.05	187
2400	18" diameter		20	1.400		84.50	79	10.05	173.55	222
2420	24" diameter		14	2		101	113	14.35	228.35	295
2440	36" diameter	B-13	10	5.600		176	299	234	709	895
3080	Radius pipe, add to pipe prices, 12" to 60" diameter				L.F.	50%				
3090	Over 60" diameter, add				"	20%				
3500	Reinforced elliptical, 8' lengths, C507 class 3									
3520	14" x 23" inside, round equivalent 18" diameter	B-21	82	.341	L.F.	47	19.30	2.45	68.75	82.50
3524	18" x 29" inside, round equivalent 30" diameter	B-13	58	.966		61.50	51.50	40.50	153.50	189
3525	22" x 36" inside, round equivalent 30" diameter		58	.966		81	51.50	40.50	173	210
3530	24" x 38" inside, round equivalent 30" diameter		58	.966		87	51.50	40.50	179	217
3540	29" x 45" inside, round equivalent 36" diameter		52	1.077		120	57.50	45	222.50	267
3550	38" x 60" inside, round equivalent 48" diameter		38	1.474		246	78.50	61.50	386	455
3560	48" x 76" inside, round equivalent 60" diameter		26	2.154		320	115	90	525	620
3570	58" x 91" inside, round equivalent 72" diameter		22	2.545		450	136	106	692	815
3780	Concrete slotted pipe, class 4 mortar joint									
3800	12" diameter	B-21	168	.167	L.F.	39.50	9.40	1.20	50.10	59
3840	18" diameter	"	152	.184	"	49	10.40	1.32	60.72	71
3900	Concrete slotted pipe, Class 4 O-ring joint									
3940	12" diameter	B-21	168	.167	L.F.	31.50	9.40	1.20	42.10	50.50
3960	18" diameter	"	152	.184	"	51	10.40	1.32	62.72	73

33 42 13 – Stormwater Culverts

33 42 13.15 Oval Arch Culverts

		Crew	Daily Output	Labor-Hours	Unit	Material	Labor	Equipment	Total	Total Incl O&P
0010	**OVAL ARCH CULVERTS**									
3000	Corrugated galvanized or aluminum, coated & paved									
3020	17" x 13", 16 ga., 15" equivalent	B-14	200	.240	L.F.	14	12.35	1.45	27.80	35.50
3040	21" x 15", 16 ga., 18" equivalent		150	.320		14.30	16.50	1.94	32.74	42.50

33 42 Stormwater Conveyance

33 42 13 – Stormwater Culverts

33 42 13.15 Oval Arch Culverts

		Crew	Daily Output	Labor-Hours	Unit	Material	2024 Bare Costs Labor	Equipment	Total	Total Incl O&P
3060	28" x 20", 14 ga., 24" equivalent	B-14	125	.384	L.F.	22	19.80	2.33	44.13	56
3080	35" x 24", 14 ga., 30" equivalent	↓	100	.480		27	24.50	2.91	54.41	69
3100	42" x 29", 12 ga., 36" equivalent	B-13	100	.560		25	30	23.50	78.50	97.50
3120	49" x 33", 12 ga., 42" equivalent		90	.622		32	33.50	26	91.50	114
3140	57" x 38", 12 ga., 48" equivalent		75	.747	↓	42.50	40	31	113.50	140
3160	Steel, plain oval arch culverts, plain									
3180	17" x 13", 16 ga., 15" equivalent	B-14	225	.213	L.F.	33.50	11	1.29	45.79	54.50
3200	21" x 15", 16 ga., 18" equivalent		175	.274		36.50	14.15	1.66	52.31	63
3220	28" x 20", 14 ga., 24" equivalent	↓	150	.320		16.70	16.50	1.94	35.14	45
3240	35" x 24", 14 ga., 30" equivalent	B-13	108	.519		21.50	27.50	21.50	70.50	89
3260	42" x 29", 12 ga., 36" equivalent		108	.519		38.50	27.50	21.50	87.50	108
3280	49" x 33", 12 ga., 42" equivalent		92	.609		46.50	32.50	25.50	104.50	127
3300	57" x 38", 12 ga., 48" equivalent		75	.747	↓	46.50	40	31	117.50	145
3320	End sections, 17" x 13"		22	2.545	Ea.	430	136	106	672	795
3340	42" x 29"	↓	17	3.294	"	450	176	137	763	905
3360	Multi-plate arch, steel	B-20	1690	.014	Lb.	1.06	.77		1.83	2.32

33 42 33 – Stormwater Curbside Drains and Inlets

33 42 33.13 Catch Basins

		Crew	Daily Output	Labor-Hours	Unit	Material	2024 Bare Costs Labor	Equipment	Total	Total Incl O&P
0010	**CATCH BASINS**									
0011	Not including footing & excavation									
1600	Frames & grates, C.I., 24" square, 500 lb.	B-6	7.80	3.077	Ea.	1,175	164	37.50	1,376.50	1,575
1700	26" D shape, 600 lb.		7	3.429		2,200	183	41.50	2,424.50	2,725
1800	Light traffic, 18" diameter, 100 lb.		10	2.400		1,175	128	29	1,332	1,525
1900	24" diameter, 300 lb.		8.70	2.759		1,025	147	33.50	1,205.50	1,375
2000	36" diameter, 900 lb.		5.80	4.138		1,600	221	50	1,871	2,150
2100	Heavy traffic, 24" diameter, 400 lb.		7.80	3.077		1,125	164	37.50	1,326.50	1,500
2200	36" diameter, 1,150 lb.		3	8		1,875	425	97	2,397	2,775
2300	Mass. State standard, 26" diameter, 475 lb.		7	3.429		1,225	183	41.50	1,449.50	1,675
2400	30" diameter, 620 lb.		7	3.429		510	183	41.50	734.50	880
2500	Watertight, 24" diameter, 350 lb.		7.80	3.077		2,000	164	37.50	2,201.50	2,475
2600	26" diameter, 500 lb.		7	3.429		1,600	183	41.50	1,824.50	2,075
2700	32" diameter, 575 lb.	↓	6	4	↓	1,225	213	48.50	1,486.50	1,725
2800	3 piece cover & frame, 10" deep,									
2900	1,200 lb., for heavy equipment	B-6	3	8	Ea.	1,475	425	97	1,997	2,350
3000	Raised for paving 1-1/4" to 2" high									
3100	4 piece expansion ring									
3200	20" to 26" diameter	1 Clab	3	2.667	Ea.	300	131		431	525
3300	30" to 36" diameter	"	3	2.667	"	485	131		616	725
3320	Frames and covers, existing, raised for paving, 2", including									
3340	row of brick, concrete collar, up to 12" wide frame	B-6	18	1.333	Ea.	70.50	71	16.15	157.65	200
3360	20" to 26" wide frame		11	2.182		106	116	26.50	248.50	320
3380	30" to 36" wide frame	↓	9	2.667		132	142	32.50	306.50	390
3400	Inverts, single channel brick	D-1	3	5.333		153	288		441	600
3500	Concrete		5	3.200		185	173		358	460
3600	Triple channel, brick		2	8		250	435		685	920
3700	Concrete	↓	3	5.333	↓	210	288		498	660

33 52 Hydrocarbon Transmission and Distribution

33 52 13 – Liquid Hydrocarbon Piping

33 52 13.16 Gasoline Piping		Crew	Daily Output	Labor-Hours	Unit	Material	2024 Bare Costs Labor	2024 Bare Costs Equipment	Total	Total Incl O&P
0010	**GASOLINE PIPING**									
0020	Primary containment pipe, fiberglass-reinforced									
0030	Plastic pipe 15' & 30' lengths									
0040	2" diameter	Q-6	425	.056	L.F.	6.75	3.98		10.73	13.30
0050	3" diameter		400	.060		9.15	4.23		13.38	16.40
0060	4" diameter	↓	375	.064	↓	11.85	4.51		16.36	19.75
0100	Fittings									
0110	Elbows, 90° & 45°, bell ends, 2"	Q-6	24	1	Ea.	40.50	70.50		111	150
0120	3" diameter		22	1.091		53	77		130	173
0130	4" diameter		20	1.200		66.50	84.50		151	199
0200	Tees, bell ends, 2"		21	1.143		53.50	80.50		134	179
0210	3" diameter		18	1.333		61	94		155	207
0230	Flanges bell ends, 2"		24	1		29	70.50		99.50	137
0240	3" diameter		22	1.091		36	77		113	154
0250	4" diameter		20	1.200		40	84.50		124.50	170
0260	Sleeve couplings, 2"		21	1.143		11.10	80.50		91.60	132
0270	3" diameter		18	1.333		17.50	94		111.50	159
0280	4" diameter		15	1.600		19.45	113		132.45	190
0290	Threaded adapters, 2"		21	1.143		18.20	80.50		98.70	140
0300	3" diameter		18	1.333		23.50	94		117.50	166
0310	4" diameter		15	1.600		34	113		147	205
0320	Reducers, 2"		27	.889		25	62.50		87.50	121
0330	3" diameter		22	1.091		24.50	77		101.50	141
0340	4" diameter		20	1.200		33	84.50		117.50	163
1010	Gas station product line for secondary containment (double wall)									
1100	Fiberglass reinforced plastic pipe 25' lengths									
1120	Pipe, plain end, 3" diameter	Q-6	375	.064	L.F.	33.50	4.51		38.01	43
1130	4" diameter		350	.069		27	4.84		31.84	37
1140	5" diameter		325	.074		30.50	5.20		35.70	41.50
1150	6" diameter	↓	300	.080	↓	34	5.65		39.65	46
1200	Fittings									
1230	Elbows, 90° & 45°, 3" diameter	Q-6	18	1.333	Ea.	141	94		235	295
1240	4" diameter		16	1.500		170	106		276	345
1250	5" diameter		14	1.714		163	121		284	360
1260	6" diameter		12	2		203	141		344	435
1270	Tees, 3" diameter		15	1.600		176	113		289	360
1280	4" diameter		12	2		167	141		308	395
1290	5" diameter		9	2.667		219	188		407	520
1300	6" diameter		6	4		310	282		592	760
1310	Couplings, 3" diameter		18	1.333		50	94		144	195
1320	4" diameter		16	1.500		113	106		219	282
1330	5" diameter		14	1.714		202	121		323	405
1340	6" diameter		12	2		315	141		456	560
1350	Cross-over nipples, 3" diameter		18	1.333		9.50	94		103.50	150
1360	4" diameter		16	1.500		11.55	106		117.55	170
1370	5" diameter		14	1.714		16	121		137	198
1380	6" diameter		12	2		16.75	141		157.75	228
1400	Telescoping, reducers, concentric 4" x 3"		18	1.333		40.50	94		134.50	185
1410	5" x 4"		17	1.412		86.50	99.50		186	243
1420	6" x 5"	↓	16	1.500	↓	243	106		349	425

33 52 Hydrocarbon Transmission and Distribution

33 52 16 – Gas Hydrocarbon Piping

33 52 16.20 Piping, Gas Service and Distribution, P.E.

		Crew	Daily Output	Labor-Hours	Unit	Material	2024 Bare Costs Labor	Equipment	Total	Total Incl O&P
0010	**PIPING, GAS SERVICE AND DISTRIBUTION, POLYETHYLENE**									
0020	Not including excavation or backfill									
1000	60 psi coils, compression coupling @ 100', 1/2" diameter, SDR 11	B-20A	608	.053	L.F.	.47	3.08		3.55	5.10
1010	1" diameter, SDR 11		544	.059		2.18	3.45		5.63	7.50
1040	1-1/4" diameter, SDR 11		544	.059		3.41	3.45		6.86	8.85
1100	2" diameter, SDR 11		488	.066		5.65	3.84		9.49	11.90
1160	3" diameter, SDR 11		408	.078		10.85	4.60		15.45	18.70
1500	60 psi 40' joints with coupling, 3" diameter, SDR 11	B-21A	408	.098		10.75	5.95	1.63	18.33	22.50
1540	4" diameter, SDR 11		352	.114		10.85	6.90	1.89	19.64	24
1600	6" diameter, SDR 11		328	.122		53	7.40	2.02	62.42	71
1640	8" diameter, SDR 11		272	.147		88.50	8.90	2.44	99.84	113

33 52 16.23 Medium Density Polyethylene Piping

		Crew	Daily Output	Labor-Hours	Unit	Material	2024 Bare Costs Labor	Equipment	Total	Total Incl O&P
2010	**MEDIUM DENSITY POLYETHYLENE PIPING**									
2020	ASTM D2513, not including excavation or backfill									
2200	Butt fused pipe									
2205	80psi coils, butt fusion joint @ 100', 1/2" CTS diameter, SDR 7	B-22C	2050	.008	L.F.	.33	.44	.14	.91	1.17
2210	1" CTS diameter, SDR 11.5		1900	.008		.91	.47	.15	1.53	1.88
2215	80psi coils, butt fusion joint @ 100', IPS 1/2" diameter, SDR 9.3		1950	.008		.37	.46	.15	.98	1.26
2220	3/4" diameter, SDR 11		1950	.008		.73	.46	.15	1.34	1.65
2225	1" diameter, SDR 11		1850	.009		.96	.49	.16	1.61	1.95
2230	1-1/4" diameter, SDR 11		1850	.009		1.85	.49	.16	2.50	2.93
2235	1-1/2" diameter, SDR 11		1750	.009		2.47	.51	.17	3.15	3.67
2240	2" diameter, SDR 11		1750	.009		3.46	.51	.17	4.14	4.76
2245	80psi 40' lengths, butt fusion joint, IPS 3" diameter, SDR 11.5	B-22A	660	.061		3.62	3.41	1.13	8.16	10.30
2250	4" diameter, SDR 11.5	"	500	.080		2	4.50	1.50	8	10.55
2400	Socket fused pipe									
2405	80psi coils, socket fusion coupling @ 100', 1/2" CTS diameter, SDR 7	B-20	1050	.023	L.F.	.36	1.25		1.61	2.24
2410	1" CTS diameter, SDR 11.5		1000	.024		.94	1.31		2.25	2.97
2415	80psi coils, socket fusion coupling @ 100', IPS 1/2" diameter, SDR 9.3		1000	.024		.39	1.31		1.70	2.37
2420	3/4" diameter, SDR 11		1000	.024		.75	1.31		2.06	2.77
2425	1" diameter, SDR 11		950	.025		.99	1.38		2.37	3.13
2430	1-1/4" diameter, SDR 11		950	.025		1.88	1.38		3.26	4.12
2435	1-1/2" diameter, SDR 11		900	.027		2.51	1.45		3.96	4.92
2440	2" diameter, SDR 11		850	.028		3.49	1.54		5.03	6.15
2445	80psi 40' lengths, socket fusion coupling, IPS 3" diameter, SDR 11.5	B-21A	340	.118		3.84	7.15	1.95	12.94	16.95
2450	4" diameter, SDR 11.5	"	260	.154		2.90	9.30	2.55	14.75	19.85
2600	Compression coupled pipe									
2605	80psi coils, compression coupling @ 100', 1/2" CTS diameter, SDR 7	B-20	2250	.011	L.F.	.52	.58		1.10	1.43
2610	1" CTS diameter, SDR 11.5		2175	.011		1.27	.60		1.87	2.29
2615	80psi coils, compression coupling @ 100', IPS 1/2" diameter, SDR 9.3		2175	.011		.80	.60		1.40	1.77
2620	3/4" diameter, SDR 11		2100	.011		1.02	.62		1.64	2.06
2625	1" diameter, SDR 11		2025	.012		1.35	.65		2	2.45
3000	Fittings, butt fusion									
3010	SDR 11, IPS unless noted CTS									
3100	Caps, 3/4" diameter	B-22C	28.50	.561	Ea.	4.73	31.50	10.15	46.38	63.50
3105	1" diameter		27	.593		4.35	33.50	10.75	48.60	66
3110	1-1/4" diameter		27	.593		6.95	33.50	10.75	51.20	69
3115	1-1/2" diameter		25.50	.627		4.03	35.50	11.35	50.88	69.50
3120	2" diameter		24	.667		13.90	37.50	12.05	63.45	84.50
3125	3" diameter		24	.667		19.75	37.50	12.05	69.30	91
3130	4" diameter		18	.889		35.50	50	16.10	101.60	131
3200	Reducers, 1" x 3/4" diameters		13.50	1.185		16.80	66.50	21.50	104.80	141

33 52 Hydrocarbon Transmission and Distribution
33 52 16 – Gas Hydrocarbon Piping

33 52 16.23 Medium Density Polyethylene Piping		Crew	Daily Output	Labor-Hours	Unit	Material	2024 Bare Costs Labor	Equipment	Total	Total Incl O&P
3205	1-1/4" x 1" diameters	B-22C	13.50	1.185	Ea.	18.70	66.50	21.50	106.70	144
3210	1-1/2" x 3/4" diameters		12.75	1.255		24.50	70.50	22.50	117.50	157
3215	1-1/2" x 1" diameters		12.75	1.255		20.50	70.50	22.50	113.50	153
3220	1-1/2" x 1-1/4" diameters		12.75	1.255		20.50	70.50	22.50	113.50	153
3225	2" x 1" diameters		12	1.333		21	75	24	120	162
3230	2" x 1-1/4" diameters		12	1.333		21	75	24	120	162
3235	2" x 1-1/2" diameters		12	1.333		25	75	24	124	166
3240	3" x 2" diameters		12	1.333		25	75	24	124	166
3245	4" x 2" diameters		9	1.778		39.50	100	32	171.50	228
3250	4" x 3" diameters		9	1.778		35.50	100	32	167.50	224
3300	Elbows, 90°, 3/4" diameter		14.25	1.123		5.90	63	20.50	89.40	123
3302	1" diameter		13.50	1.185		7.20	66.50	21.50	95.20	131
3304	1-1/4" diameter		13.50	1.185		13.85	66.50	21.50	101.85	138
3306	1-1/2" diameter		12.75	1.255		12.05	70.50	22.50	105.05	143
3308	2" diameter		12	1.333		15.25	75	24	114.25	155
3310	3" diameter		12	1.333		28.50	75	24	127.50	170
3312	4" diameter		9	1.778		48	100	32	180	238
3350	45°, 3" diameter		12	1.333		39	75	24	138	181
3352	4" diameter		9	1.778		48	100	32	180	238
3400	Tees, 3/4" diameter		9.50	1.684		24	94.50	30.50	149	201
3405	1" diameter		9	1.778		7.25	100	32	139.25	193
3410	1-1/4" diameter		9	1.778		18.70	100	32	150.70	205
3415	1-1/2" diameter		8.50	1.882		22.50	106	34	162.50	221
3420	2" diameter		8	2		24	113	36	173	235
3425	3" diameter		8	2		43.50	113	36	192.50	256
3430	4" diameter		6	2.667		67.50	150	48.50	266	350
3500	Tapping tees, high volume, butt fusion outlets									
3505	1-1/2" punch, 2" x 2" outlet	B-22C	11	1.455	Ea.	160	82	26.50	268.50	325
3510	1-7/8" punch, 3" x 2" outlet		11	1.455		160	82	26.50	268.50	325
3515	4" x 2" outlet		9	1.778		160	100	32	292	360
3550	For protective sleeves, add					4.14			4.14	4.55
3600	Service saddles, saddle contour x outlet, butt fusion outlets									
3602	1-1/4" x 3/4" outlet	B-22C	17	.941	Ea.	26.50	53	17.05	96.55	127
3604	1-1/4" x 1" outlet		17	.941		9.70	53	17.05	79.75	108
3606	1-1/4" x 1-1/4" outlet		16	1		9.70	56.50	18.10	84.30	115
3608	1-1/2" x 3/4" outlet		16	1		9.70	56.50	18.10	84.30	115
3610	1-1/2" x 1-1/4" outlet		15	1.067		26	60	19.30	105.30	140
3612	2" x 3/4" outlet		12	1.333		9.70	75	24	108.70	149
3614	2" x 1" outlet		12	1.333		9.70	75	24	108.70	149
3616	2" x 1-1/4" outlet		11	1.455		9.70	82	26.50	118.20	162
3618	3" x 3/4" outlet		12	1.333		9.70	75	24	108.70	149
3620	3" x 1" outlet		12	1.333		9.70	75	24	108.70	149
3622	3" x 1-1/4" outlet		11	1.455		9.70	82	26.50	118.20	162
3624	4" x 3/4" outlet		10	1.600		9.70	90	29	128.70	177
3626	4" x 1" outlet		10	1.600		9.70	90	29	128.70	177
3628	4" x 1-1/4" outlet		9	1.778		26.50	100	32	158.50	214
3685	For protective sleeves, 3/4" diameter outlets, add					1.23			1.23	1.35
3690	1" diameter outlets, add					2.06			2.06	2.27
3695	1-1/4" diameter outlets, add					3.55			3.55	3.91
3700	Branch saddles, contour x outlet, butt outlets, round base									
3702	2" x 2" outlet	B-22C	11	1.455	Ea.	25	82	26.50	133.50	179
3704	3" x 2" outlet		11	1.455		48	82	26.50	156.50	204
3706	3" x 3" outlet		11	1.455		39.50	82	26.50	148	194

33 52 Hydrocarbon Transmission and Distribution

33 52 16 – Gas Hydrocarbon Piping

33 52 16.23 Medium Density Polyethylene Piping

		Crew	Daily Output	Labor-Hours	Unit	Material	2024 Bare Costs Labor	Equipment	Total	Total Incl O&P
3708	4" x 2" outlet	B-22C	9	1.778	Ea.	48	100	32	180	237
3710	4" x 3" outlet		9	1.778		90	100	32	222	284
3712	4" x 4" outlet		9	1.778		52.50	100	32	184.50	243
3750	Rectangular base, 2" x 2" outlet		11	1.455		25	82	26.50	133.50	179
3752	3" x 2" outlet		11	1.455		27.50	82	26.50	136	181
3754	3" x 3" outlet		11	1.455		39.50	82	26.50	148	194
3756	4" x 2" outlet		9	1.778		31	100	32	163	219
3758	4" x 3" outlet		9	1.778		37.50	100	32	169.50	226
3760	4" x 4" outlet	↓	9	1.778	↓	45.50	100	32	177.50	235
4000	Fittings, socket fusion									
4010	SDR 11, IPS unless noted CTS									
4100	Caps, 1/2" CTS diameter	B-20	30	.800	Ea.	3.46	43.50		46.96	69
4105	1/2" diameter		28.50	.842		3.46	46		49.46	72
4110	3/4" diameter		28.50	.842		5.20	46		51.20	73.50
4115	1" CTS diameter		28	.857		5.70	46.50		52.20	76
4120	1" diameter		27	.889		5.70	48.50		54.20	78.50
4125	1-1/4" diameter		27	.889		6.95	48.50		55.45	79.50
4130	1-1/2" diameter		25.50	.941		8.95	51.50		60.45	86.50
4135	2" diameter		24	1		8.85	54.50		63.35	90.50
4140	3" diameter		24	1		20.50	54.50		75	104
4145	4" diameter		18	1.333		30	72.50		102.50	141
4200	Reducers, 1/2" x 1/2" CTS diameters		14.25	1.684		9	92		101	146
4202	3/4" x 1/2" CTS diameters		14.25	1.684		8.30	92		100.30	145
4204	3/4" x 1/2" diameters		14.25	1.684		8.90	92		100.90	146
4206	1" CTS x 1/2" diameters		14	1.714		8.65	93.50		102.15	149
4208	1" CTS x 3/4" diameters		13.50	1.778		8.80	97		105.80	154
4210	1" x 1/2" CTS diameters		13.50	1.778		8.25	97		105.25	153
4212	1" x 1/2" diameters		13.50	1.778		9.20	97		106.20	154
4214	1" x 3/4" diameters		13.50	1.778		12.80	97		109.80	158
4216	1" x 1" CTS diameters		13.50	1.778		7.50	97		104.50	152
4218	1-1/4" x 1/2" CTS diameters		13.50	1.778		8.65	97		105.65	154
4220	1-1/4" x 1/2" diameters		13.50	1.778		12.65	97		109.65	158
4222	1-1/4" x 3/4" diameters		13.50	1.778		18.15	97		115.15	164
4224	1-1/4" x 1" CTS diameters		13.50	1.778		12.65	97		109.65	158
4226	1-1/4" x 1" diameters		13.50	1.778		15.50	97		112.50	161
4228	1-1/2" x 3/4" diameters		12.75	1.882		13.85	103		116.85	168
4230	1-1/2" x 1" diameters		12.75	1.882		11.75	103		114.75	166
4232	1-1/2" x 1-1/4" diameters		12.75	1.882		13.25	103		116.25	168
4234	2" x 3/4" diameters		12	2		14.50	109		123.50	178
4236	2" x 1" CTS diameters		12	2		14.35	109		123.35	178
4238	2" x 1" diameters		12	2		15.65	109		124.65	179
4240	2" x 1-1/4" diameters		12	2		14.20	109		123.20	178
4242	2" x 1-1/2" diameters		12	2		12.40	109		121.40	176
4244	3" x 2" diameters		12	2		13.30	109		122.30	177
4246	4" x 2" diameters		9	2.667		36	145		181	256
4248	4" x 3" diameters		9	2.667		40.50	145		185.50	261
4300	Couplings, 1/2" CTS diameter		15	1.600		2.83	87		89.83	133
4305	1/2" diameter		14.25	1.684		2.19	92		94.19	138
4310	3/4" diameter		14.25	1.684		2.45	92		94.45	139
4315	1" CTS diameter		14	1.714		2.96	93.50		96.46	142
4320	1" diameter		13.50	1.778		2.50	97		99.50	147
4325	1-1/4" diameter		13.50	1.778		3	97		100	147
4330	1-1/2" diameter		12.75	1.882		3.55	103		106.55	157

For customer support on your Plumbing Costs with RSMeans Data call 800.448.8182.

33 52 Hydrocarbon Transmission and Distribution

33 52 16 – Gas Hydrocarbon Piping

33 52 16.23 Medium Density Polyethylene Piping		Crew	Daily Output	Labor-Hours	Unit	Material	2024 Bare Costs Labor	Equipment	Total	Total Incl O&P
4335	2" diameter	B-20	12	2	Ea.	3.09	109		112.09	165
4340	3" diameter		12	2		8.65	109		117.65	172
4345	4" diameter		9	2.667		36	145		181	256
4400	Elbows, 90°, 1/2" CTS diameter		15	1.600		4.98	87		91.98	136
4405	1/2" diameter		14.25	1.684		4.89	92		96.89	141
4410	3/4" diameter		14.25	1.684		5.80	92		97.80	142
4415	1" CTS diameter		14	1.714		5.55	93.50		99.05	145
4420	1" diameter		13.50	1.778		6.20	97		103.20	151
4425	1-1/4" diameter		13.50	1.778		5.90	97		102.90	151
4430	1-1/2" diameter		12.75	1.882		7.45	103		110.45	161
4435	2" diameter		12	2		6.10	109		115.10	169
4440	3" diameter		12	2		32	109		141	198
4445	4" diameter		9	2.667		83	145		228	305
4460	45°, 1" diameter		13.50	1.778		9.90	97		106.90	155
4465	2" diameter		12	2		13.30	109		122.30	177
4500	Tees, 1/2" CTS diameter		10	2.400		4.76	131		135.76	199
4505	1/2" diameter		9.50	2.526		4.22	138		142.22	210
4510	3/4" diameter		9.50	2.526		5.70	138		143.70	211
4515	1" CTS diameter		9.33	2.571		5.55	140		145.55	214
4520	1" diameter		9	2.667		6.95	145		151.95	224
4525	1-1/4" diameter		9	2.667		7.70	145		152.70	224
4530	1-1/2" diameter		8.50	2.824		12.70	154		166.70	243
4535	2" diameter		8	3		15.20	164		179.20	260
4540	3" diameter		8	3		66	164		230	315
4545	4" diameter		6	4		87	218		305	420
4600	Tapping tees, type II, 3/4" punch, socket fusion outlets									
4601	Saddle contour x outlet diameter, IPS unless noted CTS									
4602	1-1/4" x 1/2" CTS outlet	B-20	17	1.412	Ea.	17.45	77		94.45	133
4604	1-1/4" x 1/2" outlet		17	1.412		17.45	77		94.45	133
4606	1-1/4" x 3/4" outlet		17	1.412		17.45	77		94.45	133
4608	1-1/4" x 1" CTS outlet		17	1.412		19.05	77		96.05	135
4610	1-1/4" x 1" outlet		17	1.412		19.05	77		96.05	135
4612	1-1/4" x 1-1/4" outlet		16	1.500		32	82		114	158
4614	1-1/2" x 1/2" CTS outlet		16	1.500		17.45	82		99.45	141
4616	1-1/2" x 1/2" outlet		16	1.500		17.45	82		99.45	141
4618	1-1/2" x 3/4" outlet		16	1.500		17.45	82		99.45	141
4620	1-1/2" x 1" CTS outlet		16	1.500		19.05	82		101.05	143
4622	1-1/2" x 1" outlet		16	1.500		19.05	82		101.05	143
4624	1-1/2" x 1-1/4" outlet		15	1.600		32	87		119	166
4626	2" x 1/2" CTS outlet		12	2		17.45	109		126.45	181
4628	2" x 1/2" outlet		12	2		17.45	109		126.45	181
4630	2" x 3/4" outlet		12	2		17.45	109		126.45	181
4632	2" x 1" CTS outlet		12	2		19.05	109		128.05	183
4634	2" x 1" outlet		12	2		19.05	109		128.05	183
4636	2" x 1-1/4" outlet		11	2.182		32	119		151	213
4638	3" x 1/2" CTS outlet		12	2		17.45	109		126.45	181
4640	3" x 1/2" outlet		12	2		17.45	109		126.45	181
4642	3" x 3/4" outlet		12	2		17.45	109		126.45	181
4644	3" x 1" CTS outlet		12	2		19.05	109		128.05	183
4646	3" x 1" outlet		12	2		19.05	109		128.05	183
4648	3" x 1-1/4" outlet		11	2.182		32	119		151	213
4650	4" x 1/2" CTS outlet		10	2.400		17.45	131		148.45	213
4652	4" x 1/2" outlet		10	2.400		17.45	131		148.45	213

33 52 Hydrocarbon Transmission and Distribution

33 52 16 – Gas Hydrocarbon Piping

33 52 16.23 Medium Density Polyethylene Piping		Crew	Daily Output	Labor-Hours	Unit	Material	2024 Bare Costs Labor	Equipment	Total	Total Incl O&P
4654	4" x 3/4" outlet	B-20	10	2.400	Ea.	17.45	131		148.45	213
4656	4" x 1" CTS outlet		10	2.400		19.05	131		150.05	215
4658	4" x 1" outlet		10	2.400		19.05	131		150.05	215
4660	4" x 1-1/4" outlet		9	2.667		32	145		177	252
4685	For protective sleeves, 1/2" CTS to 3/4" diameter outlets, add					1.23			1.23	1.35
4690	1" CTS & IPS diameter outlets, add					2.06			2.06	2.27
4695	1-1/4" diameter outlets, add					3.55			3.55	3.91
4700	Tapping tees, high volume, socket fusion outlets									
4705	1-1/2" punch, 2" x 1-1/4" outlet	B-20	11	2.182	Ea.	160	119		279	355
4710	1-7/8" punch, 3" x 1-1/4" outlet		11	2.182		160	119		279	355
4715	4" x 1-1/4" outlet		9	2.667		160	145		305	390
4750	For protective sleeves, add					4.14			4.14	4.55
4800	Service saddles, saddle contour x outlet, socket fusion outlets									
4801	IPS unless noted CTS									
4802	1-1/4" x 1/2" CTS outlet	B-20	17	1.412	Ea.	5.40	77		82.40	120
4804	1-1/4" x 1/2" outlet		17	1.412		5.40	77		82.40	120
4806	1-1/4" x 3/4" outlet		17	1.412		5.40	77		82.40	120
4808	1-1/4" x 1" CTS outlet		17	1.412		8.95	77		85.95	124
4810	1-1/4" x 1" outlet		17	1.412		26.50	77		103.50	144
4812	1-1/4" x 1-1/4" outlet		16	1.500		14.35	82		96.35	138
4814	1-1/2" x 1/2" CTS outlet		16	1.500		5.40	82		87.40	128
4816	1-1/2" x 1/2" outlet		16	1.500		5.40	82		87.40	128
4818	1-1/2" x 3/4" outlet		16	1.500		26.50	82		108.50	152
4820	1-1/2" x 1-1/4" outlet		15	1.600		14.35	87		101.35	146
4822	2" x 1/2" CTS outlet		12	2		5.40	109		114.40	168
4824	2" x 1/2" outlet		12	2		5.40	109		114.40	168
4826	2" x 3/4" outlet		12	2		5.40	109		114.40	168
4828	2" x 1" CTS outlet		12	2		8.95	109		117.95	172
4830	2" x 1" outlet		12	2		8.95	109		117.95	172
4832	2" x 1-1/4" outlet		11	2.182		26.50	119		145.50	207
4834	3" x 1/2" CTS outlet		12	2		5.40	109		114.40	168
4836	3" x 1/2" outlet		12	2		5.40	109		114.40	168
4838	3" x 3/4" outlet		12	2		5.40	109		114.40	168
4840	3" x 1" CTS outlet		12	2		8.95	109		117.95	172
4842	3" x 1" outlet		12	2		8.95	109		117.95	172
4844	3" x 1-1/4" outlet		11	2.182		23	119		142	202
4846	4" x 1/2" CTS outlet		10	2.400		5.40	131		136.40	200
4848	4" x 1/2" outlet		10	2.400		5.40	131		136.40	200
4850	4" x 3/4" outlet		10	2.400		5.40	131		136.40	200
4852	4" x 1" CTS outlet		10	2.400		8.95	131		139.95	204
4854	4" x 1" outlet		10	2.400		8.95	131		139.95	204
4856	4" x 1-1/4" outlet		9	2.667		23.50	145		168.50	242
4885	For protective sleeves, 1/2" CTS to 3/4" diameter outlets, add					1.23			1.23	1.35
4890	1" CTS & IPS diameter outlets, add					2.06			2.06	2.27
4895	1-1/4" diameter outlets, add					3.55			3.55	3.91
4900	Spigot fittings, tees, SDR 7, 1/2" CTS diameter	B-20	10	2.400		37.50	131		168.50	235
4901	SDR 9.3, 1/2" diameter		9.50	2.526		16.45	138		154.45	223
4902	SDR 10, 1-1/4" diameter		9	2.667		16.45	145		161.45	234
4903	SDR 11, 3/4" diameter		9.50	2.526		34.50	138		172.50	243
4904	2" diameter		8	3		31.50	164		195.50	278
4906	SDR 11.5, 1" CTS diameter		9.33	2.571		87.50	140		227.50	305
4907	3" diameter		8	3		89	164		253	340
4908	4" diameter		6	4		230	218		448	580

33 52 Hydrocarbon Transmission and Distribution

33 52 16 – Gas Hydrocarbon Piping

33 52 16.23 Medium Density Polyethylene Piping		Crew	Daily Output	Labor-Hours	Unit	Material	2024 Bare Costs Labor	Equipment	Total	Total Incl O&P
4921	90° elbows, SDR 7, 1/2" CTS diameter	B-20	15	1.600	Ea.	19.60	87		106.60	152
4922	SDR 9.3, 1/2" diameter		14.25	1.684		8.45	92		100.45	145
4923	SDR 10, 1-1/4" diameter		13.50	1.778		8.60	97		105.60	154
4924	SDR 11, 3/4" diameter		14.25	1.684		9.65	92		101.65	147
4925	2" diameter		12	2		36.50	109		145.50	202
4927	SDR 11.5, 1" CTS diameter		14	1.714		33	93.50		126.50	176
4928	3" diameter		12	2		82.50	109		191.50	253
4929	4" diameter		9	2.667		176	145		321	410
4935	Caps, SDR 7, 1/2" CTS diameter		30	.800		6.50	43.50		50	72
4936	SDR 9.3, 1/2" diameter		28.50	.842		6.50	46		52.50	75
4937	SDR 10, 1-1/4" diameter		27	.889		6.75	48.50		55.25	79.50
4938	SDR 11, 3/4" diameter		28.50	.842		6.95	46		52.95	75.50
4939	1" diameter		27	.889		7.75	48.50		56.25	80.50
4940	2" diameter		24	1		8.30	54.50		62.80	90
4942	SDR 11.5, 1" CTS diameter		28	.857		27.50	46.50		74	99.50
4943	3" diameter		24	1		44	54.50		98.50	130
4944	4" diameter		18	1.333		42.50	72.50		115	155
4946	SDR 13.5, 4" diameter		18	1.333		107	72.50		179.50	226
4950	Reducers, SDR 10 x SDR 11, 1-1/4" x 3/4" diameters		13.50	1.778		22.50	97		119.50	169
4951	1-1/4" x 1" diameters		13.50	1.778		22.50	97		119.50	169
4952	SDR 10 x SDR 11.5, 1-1/4" x 1" CTS diameters		13.50	1.778		22.50	97		119.50	169
4953	SDR 11 x SDR 7, 3/4" x 1/2" CTS diameters		14.25	1.684		9.95	92		101.95	147
4954	SDR 11 x SDR 9.3, 3/4" x 1/2" diameters		14.25	1.684		9.95	92		101.95	147
4955	SDR 11 x SDR 10, 2" x 1-1/4" diameters		12	2		23	109		132	188
4956	SDR 11 x SDR 11, 1" x 3/4" diameters		13.50	1.778		11.45	97		108.45	157
4957	2" x 3/4" diameters		12	2		23	109		132	187
4958	2" x 1" diameters		12	2		23	109		132	187
4959	SDR 11 x SDR 11.5, 1" x 1" CTS diameters		13.50	1.778		11.65	97		108.65	157
4960	2" x 1" CTS diameters		12	2		23	109		132	187
4962	SDR 11.5 x SDR 11, 3" x 2" diameters		12	2		30.50	109		139.50	196
4963	4" x 2" diameters		9	2.667		46.50	145		191.50	267
4964	SDR 11.5 x SDR 11.5, 4" x 3" diameters		9	2.667		50	145		195	271
6100	Fittings, compression									
6101	MDPE gas pipe, ASTM D2513/ASTM F1924-98									
6102	Caps, SDR 7, 1/2" CTS diameter	B-20	60	.400	Ea.	18.75	22		40.75	53
6104	SDR 9.3, 1/2" IPS diameter		58	.414		32.50	22.50		55	69.50
6106	SDR 10, 1/2" CTS diameter		60	.400		16.55	22		38.55	50.50
6108	1-1/4" IPS diameter		54	.444		109	24		133	156
6110	SDR 11, 3/4" IPS diameter		58	.414		29.50	22.50		52	66
6112	1" IPS diameter		54	.444		47.50	24		71.50	88
6114	1-1/4" IPS diameter		54	.444		114	24		138	162
6116	1-1/2" IPS diameter		52	.462		139	25		164	191
6118	2" IPS diameter		50	.480		122	26		148	173
6120	SDR 11.5, 1" CTS diameter		56	.429		30	23.50		53.50	67.50
6122	SDR 12.5, 1" CTS diameter		56	.429		35	23.50		58.50	73
6202	Reducers, SDR 7 x SDR 10, 1/2" CTS x 1/2" CTS diameters		30	.800		25.50	43.50		69	93
6204	SDR 9.3 x SDR 7, 1/2" IPS x 1/2" CTS diameters		29	.828		73	45		118	148
6206	SDR 11 x SDR 7, 3/4" IPS x 1/2" CTS diameters		29	.828		72.50	45		117.50	147
6208	1" IPS x 1/2" CTS diameters		27	.889		87.50	48.50		136	169
6210	SDR 11 x SDR 9.3, 3/4" IPS x 1/2" IPS diameters		29	.828		71	45		116	146
6212	1" IPS x 1/2" IPS diameters		27	.889		90.50	48.50		139	172
6214	SDR 11 x SDR 10, 2" IPS x 1-1/4" IPS diameters		25	.960		139	52.50		191.50	231
6216	SDR 11 x SDR 11, 1" IPS x 3/4" IPS diameters		27	.889		87.50	48.50		136	169

33 52 Hydrocarbon Transmission and Distribution
33 52 16 – Gas Hydrocarbon Piping

33 52 16.23 Medium Density Polyethylene Piping

		Crew	Daily Output	Labor-Hours	Unit	Material	2024 Bare Costs Labor	Equipment	Total	Total Incl O&P
6218	1-1/4" IPS x 1" IPS diameters	B-20	27	.889	Ea.	83	48.50		131.50	164
6220	2" IPS x 1-1/4" IPS diameters		25	.960		139	52.50		191.50	231
6222	SDR 11 x SDR 11.5, 1" IPS x 1" CTS diameters		27	.889		67.50	48.50		116	146
6224	SDR 11 x SDR 12.5, 1" IPS x 1" CTS diameters		27	.889		82	48.50		130.50	162
6226	SDR 11.5 x SDR 7, 1" CTS x 1/2" CTS diameters		28	.857		50	46.50		96.50	125
6228	SDR 11.5 x SDR 9.3, 1" CTS x 1/2" IPS diameters		28	.857		57.50	46.50		104	133
6230	SDR 11.5 x SDR 11, 1" CTS x 3/4" IPS diameters		28	.857		80	46.50		126.50	158
6232	SDR 12.5 x SDR 7, 1" CTS x 1/2" CTS diameters		28	.857		52.50	46.50		99	127
6234	SDR 12.5 x SDR 9.3, 1" CTS x 1/2" IPS diameters		28	.857		59	46.50		105.50	135
6236	SDR 12.5 x SDR 11, 1" CTS x 3/4" IPS diameters		28	.857		50.50	46.50		97	125
6302	Couplings, SDR 7, 1/2" CTS diameter		30	.800		19.10	43.50		62.60	86
6304	SDR 9.3, 1/2" IPS diameter		29	.828		42.50	45		87.50	114
6306	SDR 10, 1/2" CTS diameter		30	.800		18.15	43.50		61.65	85
6308	SDR 11, 3/4" IPS diameter		29	.828		29.50	45		74.50	99.50
6310	1" IPS diameter		27	.889		39.50	48.50		88	115
6312	SDR 11.5, 1" CTS diameter		28	.857		36	46.50		82.50	109
6314	SDR 12.5, 1" CTS diameter		28	.857		40.50	46.50		87	114
6402	Repair couplings, SDR 10, 1-1/4" IPS diameter		27	.889		104	48.50		152.50	187
6404	SDR 11, 1-1/4" IPS diameter		27	.889		107	48.50		155.50	189
6406	1-1/2" IPS diameter		26	.923		115	50.50		165.50	201
6408	2" IPS diameter		25	.960		134	52.50		186.50	225
6502	Elbows, 90°, SDR 7, 1/2" CTS diameter		30	.800		33.50	43.50		77	102
6504	SDR 9.3, 1/2" IPS diameter		29	.828		58	45		103	131
6506	SDR 10, 1-1/4" IPS diameter		27	.889		143	48.50		191.50	229
6508	SDR 11, 3/4" IPS diameter		29	.828		53	45		98	126
6510	1" IPS diameter		27	.889		53	48.50		101.50	131
6512	1-1/4" IPS diameter		27	.889		142	48.50		190.50	229
6514	1-1/2" IPS diameter		26	.923		213	50.50		263.50	310
6516	2" IPS diameter		25	.960		181	52.50		233.50	278
6518	SDR 11.5, 1" CTS diameter		28	.857		53.50	46.50		100	129
6520	SDR 12.5, 1" CTS diameter		28	.857		78.50	46.50		125	156
6602	Tees, SDR 7, 1/2" CTS diameter		20	1.200		59	65.50		124.50	162
6604	SDR 9.3, 1/2" IPS diameter		19.33	1.241		65.50	67.50		133	173
6606	SDR 10, 1-1/4" IPS diameter		18	1.333		185	72.50		257.50	310
6608	SDR 11, 3/4" IPS diameter		19.33	1.241		82.50	67.50		150	192
6610	1" IPS diameter		18	1.333		90.50	72.50		163	208
6612	1-1/4" IPS diameter		18	1.333		152	72.50		224.50	276
6614	1-1/2" IPS diameter		17.33	1.385		315	75.50		390.50	455
6616	2" IPS diameter		16.67	1.440		209	78.50		287.50	345
6618	SDR 11.5, 1" CTS diameter		18.67	1.286		83	70		153	196
6620	SDR 12.5, 1" CTS diameter	↓	18.67	1.286	↓	86.50	70		156.50	199
8100	Fittings, accessories									
8105	SDR 11, IPS unless noted CTS									
8110	Protective sleeves, for high volume tapping tees, butt fusion outlets	1 Skwk	16	.500	Ea.	7.95	32		39.95	56.50
8120	For tapping tees, socket outlets, CTS, 1/2" diameter		18	.444		2.07	28		30.07	44.50
8122	1" diameter		18	.444		3.66	28		31.66	46
8124	IPS, 1/2" diameter		18	.444		2.86	28		30.86	45
8126	3/4" diameter		18	.444		3.66	28		31.66	46
8128	1" diameter		18	.444		4.99	28		32.99	47.50
8130	1-1/4" diameter		18	.444		6.30	28		34.30	49
8205	Tapping tee test caps, type I, yellow PE cap, "aldyl style"		45	.178		64.50	11.30		75.80	88
8210	Type II, yellow polyethylene cap		45	.178		63	11.30		74.30	86.50
8215	High volume, yellow polyethylene cap	↓	45	.178	↓	83	11.30		94.30	108

33 52 Hydrocarbon Transmission and Distribution

33 52 16 – Gas Hydrocarbon Piping

33 52 16.23 Medium Density Polyethylene Piping

		Crew	Daily Output	Labor-Hours	Unit	Material	2024 Bare Costs Labor	Equipment	Total	Total Incl O&P
8250	Quick connector, female x female inlets, 1/4" N.P.T.	1 Skwk	50	.160	Ea.	26	10.15		36.15	44
8255	Test hose, 24" length, 3/8" ID, male outlets, 1/4" N.P.T.		50	.160		35.50	10.15		45.65	54.50
8260	Quick connector and test hose assembly	▼	50	.160		62	10.15		72.15	83
8305	Purge point caps, butt fusion, SDR 10, 1-1/4" diameter	B-22C	27	.593		46.50	33.50	10.75	90.75	112
8310	SDR 11, 1-1/4" diameter		27	.593		46.50	33.50	10.75	90.75	112
8315	2" diameter		24	.667		47	37.50	12.05	96.55	121
8320	3" diameter		24	.667		65.50	37.50	12.05	115.05	141
8325	4" diameter		18	.889		64	50	16.10	130.10	163
8340	Socket fusion, SDR 11, 1-1/4" diameter		27	.593		11.65	33.50	10.75	55.90	74
8345	2" diameter		24	.667		14	37.50	12.05	63.55	84.50
8350	3" diameter		24	.667		85.50	37.50	12.05	135.05	164
8355	4" diameter		18	.889		63	50	16.10	129.10	162
8360	Purge test quick connector, female x female inlets, 1/4" N.P.T.	1 Skwk	50	.160		26	10.15		36.15	44
8365	Purge test hose, 24" length, 3/8" ID, male outlets, 1/4" N.P.T.		50	.160		35.50	10.15		45.65	54.50
8370	Purge test quick connector and test hose assembly	▼	50	.160		62	10.15		72.15	83
8405	Transition fittings, MDPE x zinc plated steel, SDR 7, 1/2" CTS x 1/2" MPT	B-22C	30	.533		35.50	30	9.65	75.15	94.50
8410	SDR 9.3, 1/2" IPS x 3/4" MPT		28.50	.561		56	31.50	10.15	97.65	120
8415	SDR 10, 1-1/4" IPS x 1-1/4" MPT		27	.593		53.50	33.50	10.75	97.75	120
8420	SDR 11, 3/4" IPS x 3/4" MPT		28.50	.561		28.50	31.50	10.15	70.15	89
8425	1" IPS x 1" MPT		27	.593		34.50	33.50	10.75	78.75	99.50
8430	1-1/4" IPS x 1-1/4" MPT		17	.941		64.50	53	17.05	134.55	169
8435	1-1/2" IPS x 1-1/2" MPT		25.50	.627		66	35.50	11.35	112.85	138
8440	2" IPS x 2" MPT		24	.667		75.50	37.50	12.05	125.05	152
8445	SDR 11.5, 1" CTS x 1" MPT	▼	28	.571	▼	46.50	32	10.35	88.85	110

33 52 16.26 High Density Polyethylene Piping

		Crew	Daily Output	Labor-Hours	Unit	Material	2024 Bare Costs Labor	Equipment	Total	Total Incl O&P
2010	**HIGH DENSITY POLYETHYLENE PIPING**									
2020	ASTM D2513, not including excavation or backfill									
2200	Butt fused pipe									
2205	125psi coils, butt fusion joint @ 100', 1/2" CTS diameter, SDR 7	B-22C	2050	.008	L.F.	.20	.44	.14	.78	1.03
2210	160psi coils, butt fusion joint @ 100', IPS 1/2" diameter, SDR 9		1950	.008		.27	.46	.15	.88	1.15
2215	3/4" diameter, SDR 11		1950	.008		.40	.46	.15	1.01	1.29
2220	1" diameter, SDR 11		1850	.009		.82	.49	.16	1.47	1.79
2225	1-1/4" diameter, SDR 11		1850	.009		.97	.49	.16	1.62	1.96
2230	1-1/2" diameter, SDR 11		1750	.009		2.11	.51	.17	2.79	3.27
2235	2" diameter, SDR 11		1750	.009		1.47	.51	.17	2.15	2.57
2240	3" diameter, SDR 11	▼	1650	.010		2.42	.55	.18	3.15	3.66
2245	160psi 40' lengths, butt fusion joint, IPS 3" diameter, SDR 11	B-22A	660	.061		2.63	3.41	1.13	7.17	9.20
2250	4" diameter, SDR 11		500	.080		5.35	4.50	1.50	11.35	14.25
2255	6" diameter, SDR 11		500	.080		10.50	4.50	1.50	16.50	19.90
2260	8" diameter, SDR 11		420	.095		15.90	5.35	1.78	23.03	27.50
2265	10" diameter, SDR 11		340	.118		36.50	6.60	2.20	45.30	52.50
2270	12" diameter, SDR 11	▼	300	.133	▼	51	7.50	2.49	60.99	70
2400	Socket fused pipe									
2405	125psi coils, socket fusion coupling @ 100', 1/2" CTS diameter, SDR 7	B-20	1050	.023	L.F.	.23	1.25		1.48	2.10
2410	160psi coils, socket fusion coupling @ 100', IPS 1/2" diameter, SDR 9		1000	.024		.30	1.31		1.61	2.27
2415	3/4" diameter, SDR 11		1000	.024		.42	1.31		1.73	2.41
2420	1" diameter, SDR 11		950	.025		.84	1.38		2.22	2.98
2425	1-1/4" diameter, SDR 11		950	.025		1	1.38		2.38	3.15
2430	1-1/2" diameter, SDR 11		900	.027		2.14	1.45		3.59	4.51
2435	2" diameter, SDR 11		850	.028		1.51	1.54		3.05	3.95
2440	3" diameter, SDR 11	▼	850	.028		2.51	1.54		4.05	5.05
2445	160psi 40' lengths, socket fusion coupling, IPS 3" diameter, SDR 11	B-21A	340	.118		2.85	7.15	1.95	11.95	15.90

33 52 Hydrocarbon Transmission and Distribution

33 52 16 – Gas Hydrocarbon Piping

33 52 16.26 High Density Polyethylene Piping		Crew	Daily Output	Labor-Hours	Unit	Material	2024 Bare Costs Labor	2024 Bare Costs Equipment	Total	Total Incl O&P
2450	4" diameter, SDR 11	B-21A	260	.154	L.F.	6.25	9.30	2.55	18.10	23.50
2600	Compression coupled pipe									
2610	160psi coils, compression coupling @ 100', IPS 1/2" diameter, SDR 9	B-20	1000	.024	L.F.	.70	1.31		2.01	2.71
2615	3/4" diameter, SDR 11		1000	.024		.69	1.31		2	2.70
2620	1" diameter, SDR 11		950	.025		1.21	1.38		2.59	3.38
2625	1-1/4" diameter, SDR 11		950	.025		2.04	1.38		3.42	4.29
2630	1-1/2" diameter, SDR 11		900	.027		3.26	1.45		4.71	5.75
2635	2" diameter, SDR 11		850	.028		2.81	1.54		4.35	5.40
3000	Fittings, butt fusion									
3010	SDR 11, IPS unless noted CTS									
3105	Caps, 1/2" diameter	B-22C	28.50	.561	Ea.	10.55	31.50	10.15	52.20	70
3110	3/4" diameter		28.50	.561		5.50	31.50	10.15	47.15	64.50
3115	1" diameter		27	.593		6	33.50	10.75	50.25	68
3120	1-1/4" diameter		27	.593		9.90	33.50	10.75	54.15	72
3125	1-1/2" diameter		25.50	.627		7.20	35.50	11.35	54.05	73
3130	2" diameter		24	.667		15	37.50	12.05	64.55	86
3135	3" diameter		24	.667		21.50	37.50	12.05	71.05	93
3140	4" diameter		18	.889		38.50	50	16.10	104.60	134
3145	6" diameter	B-22A	18	2.222		113	125	41.50	279.50	355
3150	8" diameter		15	2.667		177	150	50	377	475
3155	10" diameter		12	3.333		525	187	62.50	774.50	925
3160	12" diameter		10.50	3.810		560	214	71	845	1,025
3205	Reducers, 1/2" x 1/2" CTS diameters	B-22C	14.25	1.123		19.60	63	20.50	103.10	138
3210	3/4" x 1/2" CTS diameters		14.25	1.123		14.05	63	20.50	97.55	132
3215	1" x 1/2" CTS diameters		13.50	1.185		22	66.50	21.50	110	147
3220	1" x 1/2" diameters		13.50	1.185		27	66.50	21.50	115	153
3225	1" x 3/4" diameters		13.50	1.185		18.05	66.50	21.50	106.05	143
3230	1-1/4" x 1" diameters		13.50	1.185		20	66.50	21.50	108	145
3232	1-1/2" x 3/4" diameters		12.75	1.255		12.65	70.50	22.50	105.65	144
3233	1-1/2" x 1" diameters		12.75	1.255		12.65	70.50	22.50	105.65	144
3234	1-1/2" x 1-1/4" diameters		12.75	1.255		12.65	70.50	22.50	105.65	144
3235	2" x 1" diameters		12	1.333		23	75	24	122	164
3240	2" x 1-1/4" diameters		12	1.333		23	75	24	122	164
3245	2" x 1-1/2" diameters		12	1.333		14.45	75	24	113.45	154
3250	3" x 2" diameters		12	1.333		16.85	75	24	115.85	157
3255	4" x 2" diameters		9	1.778		23	100	32	155	210
3260	4" x 3" diameters		9	1.778		24.50	100	32	156.50	212
3262	6" x 3" diameters	B-22A	9	4.444		56.50	250	83	389.50	525
3265	6" x 4" diameters		9	4.444		75.50	250	83	408.50	545
3270	8" x 6" diameters		7.50	5.333		130	300	99.50	529.50	700
3275	10" x 8" diameters		6	6.667		271	375	125	771	990
3280	12" x 8" diameters		5.25	7.619		400	430	142	972	1,225
3285	12" x 10" diameters		5.25	7.619		186	430	142	758	995
3305	Elbows, 90°, 3/4" diameter	B-22C	14.25	1.123		9.35	63	20.50	92.85	127
3310	1" diameter		13.50	1.185		9.20	66.50	21.50	97.20	133
3315	1-1/4" diameter		13.50	1.185		10.70	66.50	21.50	98.70	135
3320	1-1/2" diameter		12.75	1.255		12.15	70.50	22.50	105.15	143
3325	2" diameter		12	1.333		13.15	75	24	112.15	153
3330	3" diameter		12	1.333		25.50	75	24	124.50	167
3335	4" diameter		9	1.778		33.50	100	32	165.50	222
3340	6" diameter	B-22A	9	4.444		88	250	83	421	560
3345	8" diameter		7.50	5.333		263	300	99.50	662.50	845
3350	10" diameter		6	6.667		635	375	125	1,135	1,375

33 52 Hydrocarbon Transmission and Distribution

33 52 16 – Gas Hydrocarbon Piping

33 52 16.26 High Density Polyethylene Piping		Crew	Daily Output	Labor-Hours	Unit	Material	2024 Bare Costs Labor	Equipment	Total	Total Incl O&P
3355	12" diameter	B-22A	5.25	7.619	Ea.	590	430	142	1,162	1,450
3380	45°, 3/4" diameter	B-22C	14.25	1.123		10.35	63	20.50	93.85	128
3385	1" diameter		13.50	1.185		10.35	66.50	21.50	98.35	134
3390	1-1/4" diameter		13.50	1.185		10.65	66.50	21.50	98.65	135
3395	1-1/2" diameter		12.75	1.255		13.85	70.50	22.50	106.85	145
3400	2" diameter		12	1.333		15.50	75	24	114.50	156
3405	3" diameter		12	1.333		26.50	75	24	125.50	168
3410	4" diameter		9	1.778		33	100	32	165	221
3415	6" diameter	B-22A	9	4.444		88	250	83	421	560
3420	8" diameter		7.50	5.333		273	300	99.50	672.50	855
3425	10" diameter		6	6.667		600	375	125	1,100	1,350
3430	12" diameter		5.25	7.619		1,175	430	142	1,747	2,100
3505	Tees, 1/2" CTS diameter	B-22C	10	1.600		12.75	90	29	131.75	180
3510	1/2" diameter		9.50	1.684		14.10	94.50	30.50	139.10	190
3515	3/4" diameter		9.50	1.684		10.45	94.50	30.50	135.45	186
3520	1" diameter		9	1.778		11.30	100	32	143.30	197
3525	1-1/4" diameter		9	1.778		8.70	100	32	140.70	194
3530	1-1/2" diameter		8.50	1.882		19.70	106	34	159.70	217
3535	2" diameter		8	2		15.60	113	36	164.60	225
3540	3" diameter		8	2		29	113	36	178	240
3545	4" diameter		6	2.667		42	150	48.50	240.50	325
3550	6" diameter	B-22A	6	6.667		104	375	125	604	805
3555	8" diameter		5	8		420	450	150	1,020	1,300
3560	10" diameter		4	10		780	560	187	1,527	1,900
3565	12" diameter		3.50	11.429		1,050	645	214	1,909	2,350
3600	Tapping tees, type II, 3/4" punch, butt fusion outlets									
3601	Saddle contour x outlet diameter, IPS unless noted CTS									
3602	1-1/4" x 1/2" CTS outlet	B-22C	17	.941	Ea.	17.90	53	17.05	87.95	117
3604	1-1/4" x 1/2" outlet		17	.941		17.90	53	17.05	87.95	117
3606	1-1/4" x 3/4" outlet		17	.941		17.90	53	17.05	87.95	117
3608	1-1/4" x 1" outlet		17	.941		21	53	17.05	91.05	121
3610	1-1/4" x 1-1/4" outlet		16	1		37.50	56.50	18.10	112.10	145
3612	1-1/2" x 1/2" CTS outlet		16	1		17.90	56.50	18.10	92.50	124
3614	1-1/2" x 1/2" outlet		16	1		17.90	56.50	18.10	92.50	124
3616	1-1/2" x 3/4" outlet		16	1		17.90	56.50	18.10	92.50	124
3618	1-1/2" x 1" outlet		16	1		21	56.50	18.10	95.60	127
3620	1-1/2" x 1-1/4" outlet		15	1.067		37.50	60	19.30	116.80	152
3622	2" x 1/2" CTS outlet		12	1.333		17.90	75	24	116.90	158
3624	2" x 1/2" outlet		12	1.333		17.90	75	24	116.90	158
3626	2" x 3/4" outlet		12	1.333		17.90	75	24	116.90	158
3628	2" x 1" outlet		12	1.333		21	75	24	120	162
3630	2" x 1-1/4" outlet		11	1.455		37.50	82	26.50	146	192
3632	3" x 1/2" CTS outlet		12	1.333		17.90	75	24	116.90	158
3634	3" x 1/2" outlet		12	1.333		17.90	75	24	116.90	158
3636	3" x 3/4" outlet		12	1.333		17.90	75	24	116.90	158
3638	3" x 1" outlet		12	1.333		21	75	24	120	162
3640	3" x 1-1/4" outlet		11	1.455		21	82	26.50	129.50	174
3642	4" x 1/2" CTS outlet		10	1.600		17.90	90	29	136.90	186
3644	4" x 1/2" outlet		10	1.600		17.90	90	29	136.90	186
3646	4" x 3/4" outlet		10	1.600		17.90	90	29	136.90	186
3648	4" x 1" outlet		10	1.600		21	90	29	140	189
3650	4" x 1-1/4" outlet		9	1.778		37.50	100	32	169.50	226
3652	6" x 1/2" CTS outlet	B-22A	10	4		17.90	225	75	317.90	435

33 52 Hydrocarbon Transmission and Distribution

33 52 16 – Gas Hydrocarbon Piping

33 52 16.26 High Density Polyethylene Piping		Crew	Daily Output	Labor-Hours	Unit	Material	2024 Bare Costs Labor	Equipment	Total	Total Incl O&P
3654	6" x 1/2" outlet	B-22A	10	4	Ea.	17.90	225	75	317.90	435
3656	6" x 3/4" outlet		10	4		17.90	225	75	317.90	435
3658	6" x 1" outlet		10	4		21	225	75	321	440
3660	6" x 1-1/4" outlet		9	4.444		37.50	250	83	370.50	505
3662	8" x 1/2" CTS outlet		8	5		17.90	281	93.50	392.40	540
3664	8" x 1/2" outlet		8	5		17.90	281	93.50	392.40	540
3666	8" x 3/4" outlet		8	5		17.90	281	93.50	392.40	540
3668	8" x 1" outlet		8	5		21	281	93.50	395.50	540
3670	8" x 1-1/4" outlet	↓	7	5.714		37.50	320	107	464.50	635
3675	For protective sleeves, 1/2" to 3/4" diameter outlets, add					1.23			1.23	1.35
3680	1" diameter outlets, add					2.06			2.06	2.27
3685	1-1/4" diameter outlets, add				↓	3.55			3.55	3.91
3700	Tapping tees, high volume, butt fusion outlets									
3705	1-1/2" punch, 2" x 2" outlet	B-22C	11	1.455	Ea.	176	82	26.50	284.50	345
3710	1-7/8" punch, 3" x 2" outlet		11	1.455		176	82	26.50	284.50	345
3715	4" x 2" outlet	↓	9	1.778		176	100	32	308	380
3720	6" x 2" outlet	B-22A	9	4.444		214	250	83	547	695
3725	8" x 2" outlet		7	5.714		176	320	107	603	785
3730	10" x 2" outlet		6	6.667		176	375	125	676	885
3735	12" x 2" outlet	↓	5	8		246	450	150	846	1,100
3750	For protective sleeves, add				↓	4.14			4.14	4.55
3800	Service saddles, saddle contour x outlet, butt fusion outlets									
3801	IPS unless noted CTS									
3802	1-1/4" x 3/4" outlet	B-22C	17	.941	Ea.	10.65	53	17.05	80.70	109
3804	1-1/4" x 1" outlet		16	1		10.65	56.50	18.10	85.25	116
3806	1-1/4" x 1-1/4" outlet		16	1		11.10	56.50	18.10	85.70	116
3808	1-1/2" x 3/4" outlet		16	1		28.50	56.50	18.10	103.10	135
3810	1-1/2" x 1-1/4" outlet		15	1.067		28.50	60	19.30	107.80	143
3812	2" x 3/4" outlet		12	1.333		28.50	75	24	127.50	170
3814	2" x 1" outlet		11	1.455		10.65	82	26.50	119.15	163
3816	2" x 1-1/4" outlet		11	1.455		11.10	82	26.50	119.60	163
3818	3" x 3/4" outlet		12	1.333		28.50	75	24	127.50	170
3820	3" x 1" outlet		11	1.455		28.50	82	26.50	137	183
3822	3" x 1-1/4" outlet		11	1.455		11.10	82	26.50	119.60	163
3824	4" x 3/4" outlet		10	1.600		28.50	90	29	147.50	198
3826	4" x 1" outlet		9	1.778		28.50	100	32	160.50	216
3828	4" x 1-1/4" outlet	↓	9	1.778		28.50	100	32	160.50	216
3830	6" x 3/4" outlet	B-22A	10	4		10.65	225	75	310.65	430
3832	6" x 1" outlet		9	4.444		10.65	250	83	343.65	475
3834	6" x 1-1/4" outlet		9	4.444		11.10	250	83	344.10	475
3836	8" x 3/4" outlet		8	5		28.50	281	93.50	403	550
3838	8" x 1" outlet		7	5.714		10.65	320	107	437.65	605
3840	8" x 1-1/4" outlet	↓	7	5.714		11.10	320	107	438.10	605
3880	For protective sleeves, 3/4" diameter outlets, add					1.23			1.23	1.35
3885	1" diameter outlets, add					2.06			2.06	2.27
3890	1-1/4" diameter outlets, add					3.55			3.55	3.91
3905	Branch saddles, contour x outlet, 2" x 2" outlet	B-22C	11	1.455		30	82	26.50	138.50	184
3910	3" x 2" outlet		11	1.455		30	82	26.50	138.50	184
3915	3" x 3" outlet		11	1.455		40	82	26.50	148.50	195
3920	4" x 2" outlet		9	1.778		30	100	32	162	218
3925	4" x 3" outlet		9	1.778		40	100	32	172	229
3930	4" x 4" outlet		9	1.778		54.50	100	32	186.50	245
3935	6" x 2" outlet	B-22A	9	4.444		30	250	83	363	495

33 52 Hydrocarbon Transmission and Distribution

33 52 16 – Gas Hydrocarbon Piping

33 52 16.26 High Density Polyethylene Piping		Crew	Daily Output	Labor-Hours	Unit	Material	2024 Bare Costs Labor	Equipment	Total	Total Incl O&P
3940	6" x 3" outlet	B-22A	9	4.444	Ea.	40	250	83	373	505
3945	6" x 4" outlet		9	4.444		54.50	250	83	387.50	520
3950	6" x 6" outlet		9	4.444		131	250	83	464	605
3955	8" x 2" outlet		7	5.714		30	320	107	457	625
3960	8" x 3" outlet		7	5.714		40	320	107	467	635
3965	8" x 4" outlet		7	5.714		54.50	320	107	481.50	650
3970	8" x 6" outlet	↓	7	5.714		131	320	107	558	735
3980	Ball valves, full port, 3/4" diameter	B-22C	14.25	1.123		91.50	63	20.50	175	218
3982	1" diameter		13.50	1.185		91.50	66.50	21.50	179.50	224
3984	1-1/4" diameter		13.50	1.185		92.50	66.50	21.50	180.50	225
3986	1-1/2" diameter		12.75	1.255		135	70.50	22.50	228	278
3988	2" diameter		12	1.333		211	75	24	310	370
3990	3" diameter		12	1.333		495	75	24	594	685
3992	4" diameter	↓	9	1.778		650	100	32	782	905
3994	6" diameter	B-22A	9	4.444		1,725	250	83	2,058	2,350
3996	8" diameter	"	7.50	5.333	↓	2,825	300	99.50	3,224.50	3,650
4000	Fittings, socket fusion									
4010	SDR 11, IPS unless noted CTS									
4105	Caps, 1/2" CTS diameter	B-20	30	.800	Ea.	3.79	43.50		47.29	69
4110	1/2" diameter		28.50	.842		3.81	46		49.81	72
4115	3/4" diameter		28.50	.842		4.16	46		50.16	72.50
4120	1" diameter		27	.889		5.25	48.50		53.75	78
4125	1-1/4" diameter		27	.889		5.50	48.50		54	78
4130	1-1/2" diameter		25.50	.941		6.10	51.50		57.60	83
4135	2" diameter		24	1		6.40	54.50		60.90	88
4140	3" diameter		24	1		39	54.50		93.50	124
4145	4" diameter		18	1.333		64	72.50		136.50	179
4205	Reducers, 1/2" x 1/2" CTS diameters		14.25	1.684		9.55	92		101.55	147
4210	3/4" x 1/2" CTS diameters		14.25	1.684		9.85	92		101.85	147
4215	3/4" x 1/2" diameters		14.25	1.684		9.85	92		101.85	147
4220	1" x 1/2" CTS diameters		13.50	1.778		9.50	97		106.50	154
4225	1" x 1/2" diameters		13.50	1.778		10.10	97		107.10	155
4230	1" x 3/4" diameters		13.50	1.778		8.25	97		105.25	153
4235	1-1/4" x 1/2" CTS diameters		13.50	1.778		9.50	97		106.50	154
4240	1-1/4" x 3/4" diameters		13.50	1.778		9.50	97		106.50	154
4245	1-1/4" x 1" diameters		13.50	1.778		9	97		106	154
4250	1-1/2" x 3/4" diameters		12.75	1.882		10.35	103		113.35	164
4252	1-1/2" x 1" diameters		12.75	1.882		12.85	103		115.85	167
4255	1-1/2" x 1-1/4" diameters		12.75	1.882		10.55	103		113.55	165
4260	2" x 3/4" diameters		12	2		13.10	109		122.10	176
4265	2" x 1" diameters		12	2		13.35	109		122.35	177
4270	2" x 1-1/4" diameters		12	2		13.75	109		122.75	177
4275	3" x 2" diameters		12	2		18.95	109		127.95	183
4280	4" x 2" diameters		9	2.667		45	145		190	266
4285	4" x 3" diameters		9	2.667		41.50	145		186.50	262
4305	Couplings, 1/2" CTS diameter		15	1.600		3.11	87		90.11	133
4310	1/2" diameter		14.25	1.684		3.11	92		95.11	139
4315	3/4" diameter		14.25	1.684		2.46	92		94.46	139
4320	1" diameter		13.50	1.778		2.43	97		99.43	147
4325	1-1/4" diameter		13.50	1.778		2.78	97		99.78	147
4330	1-1/2" diameter		12.75	1.882		3.04	103		106.04	156
4335	2" diameter		12	2		4.02	109		113.02	166
4340	3" diameter	↓	12	2	↓	8.65	109		117.65	172

33 52 Hydrocarbon Transmission and Distribution

33 52 16 – Gas Hydrocarbon Piping

33 52 16.26 High Density Polyethylene Piping		Crew	Daily Output	Labor-Hours	Unit	Material	2024 Bare Costs Labor	Equipment	Total	Total Incl O&P
4345	4" diameter	B-20	9	2.667	Ea.	36	145		181	256
4405	Elbows, 90°, 1/2" CTS diameter		15	1.600		5.35	87		92.35	136
4410	1/2" diameter		14.25	1.684		5.40	92		97.40	142
4415	3/4" diameter		14.25	1.684		4.44	92		96.44	141
4420	1" diameter		13.50	1.778		5.35	97		102.35	150
4425	1-1/4" diameter		13.50	1.778		7.40	97		104.40	152
4430	1-1/2" diameter		12.75	1.882		10.75	103		113.75	165
4435	2" diameter		12	2		10.95	109		119.95	174
4440	3" diameter		12	2		40	109		149	206
4445	4" diameter		9	2.667		160	145		305	390
4450	45°, 3/4" diameter		14.25	1.684		10.90	92		102.90	148
4455	1" diameter		13.50	1.778		12.20	97		109.20	157
4460	1-1/4" diameter		13.50	1.778		10.25	97		107.25	155
4465	1-1/2" diameter		12.75	1.882		16.10	103		119.10	171
4470	2" diameter		12	2		11.95	109		120.95	175
4475	3" diameter		12	2		66	109		175	235
4480	4" diameter		9	2.667		86	145		231	310
4505	Tees, 1/2" CTS diameter		10	2.400		4.63	131		135.63	199
4510	1/2" diameter		9.50	2.526		4.59	138		142.59	210
4515	3/4" diameter		9.50	2.526		4.58	138		142.58	210
4520	1" diameter		9	2.667		5.65	145		150.65	222
4525	1-1/4" diameter		9	2.667		7.85	145		152.85	225
4530	1-1/2" diameter		8.50	2.824		13.50	154		167.50	244
4535	2" diameter		8	3		14.45	164		178.45	259
4540	3" diameter		8	3		59.50	164		223.50	310
4545	4" diameter		6	4		116	218		334	450
4600	Tapping tees, type II, 3/4" punch, socket fusion outlets									
4601	Saddle countour x outlet diameter, IPS unless noted CTS									
4602	1-1/4" x 1/2" CTS outlet	B-20	17	1.412	Ea.	17.90	77		94.90	134
4604	1-1/4" x 1/2" outlet		17	1.412		17.90	77		94.90	134
4606	1-1/4" x 3/4" outlet		17	1.412		17.90	77		94.90	134
4608	1-1/4" x 1" outlet		17	1.412		21	77		98	137
4610	1-1/4" x 1-1/4" outlet		16	1.500		37.50	82		119.50	163
4612	1-1/2" x 1/2" CTS outlet		16	1.500		17.90	82		99.90	142
4614	1-1/2" x 1/2" outlet		16	1.500		17.90	82		99.90	142
4616	1-1/2" x 3/4" outlet		16	1.500		17.90	82		99.90	142
4618	1-1/2" x 1" outlet		16	1.500		21	82		103	145
4620	1-1/2" x 1-1/4" outlet		15	1.600		37.50	87		124.50	171
4622	2" x 1/2" CTS outlet		12	2		17.90	109		126.90	182
4624	2" x 1/2" outlet		12	2		17.90	109		126.90	182
4626	2" x 3/4" outlet		12	2		17.90	109		126.90	182
4628	2" x 1" outlet		12	2		21	109		130	185
4630	2" x 1-1/4" outlet		11	2.182		37.50	119		156.50	218
4632	3" x 1/2" CTS outlet		12	2		17.90	109		126.90	182
4634	3" x 1/2" outlet		12	2		17.90	109		126.90	182
4636	3" x 3/4" outlet		12	2		17.90	109		126.90	182
4638	3" x 1" outlet		12	2		21	109		130	185
4640	3" x 1-1/4" outlet		11	2.182		37.50	119		156.50	218
4642	4" x 1/2" CTS outlet		10	2.400		17.90	131		148.90	214
4644	4" x 1/2" outlet		10	2.400		17.90	131		148.90	214
4646	4" x 3/4" outlet		10	2.400		17.90	131		148.90	214
4648	4" x 1" outlet		10	2.400		21	131		152	217
4650	4" x 1-1/4" outlet		9	2.667		37.50	145		182.50	257

33 52 Hydrocarbon Transmission and Distribution

33 52 16 – Gas Hydrocarbon Piping

33 52 16.26 High Density Polyethylene Piping

		Crew	Daily Output	Labor-Hours	Unit	Material	2024 Bare Costs Labor	Equipment	Total	Total Incl O&P
4652	6" x 1/2" CTS outlet	B-21A	10	4	Ea.	17.90	242	66.50	326.40	455
4654	6" x 1/2" outlet	B-20	10	2.400		17.90	131		148.90	214
4656	6" x 3/4" outlet	B-21A	10	4		17.90	242	66.50	326.40	455
4658	6" x 1" outlet		10	4		21	242	66.50	329.50	455
4660	6" x 1-1/4" outlet		9	4.444		37.50	269	73.50	380	520
4662	8" x 1/2" CTS outlet		8	5		17.90	305	83	405.90	560
4664	8" x 1/2" outlet		8	5		17.90	305	83	405.90	560
4666	8" x 3/4" outlet		8	5		17.90	305	83	405.90	560
4668	8" x 1" outlet		8	5		21	305	83	409	565
4670	8" x 1-1/4" outlet		7	5.714		37.50	345	95	477.50	660
4675	For protective sleeves, 1/2" to 3/4" diameter outlets, add					1.23			1.23	1.35
4680	1" diameter outlets, add					2.06			2.06	2.27
4685	1-1/4" diameter outlets, add					3.55			3.55	3.91
4700	Tapping tees, high volume, socket fusion outlets									
4705	1-1/2" punch, 2" x 1-1/4" outlet	B-20	11	2.182	Ea.	176	119		295	370
4710	1-7/8" punch, 3" x 1-1/4" outlet		11	2.182		176	119		295	370
4715	4" x 1-1/4" outlet		9	2.667		176	145		321	410
4720	6" x 1-1/4" outlet	B-21A	9	4.444		176	269	73.50	518.50	675
4725	8" x 1-1/4" outlet		7	5.714		176	345	95	616	810
4730	10" x 1-1/4" outlet		6	6.667		176	405	111	692	915
4735	12" x 1-1/4" outlet		5	8		176	485	133	794	1,050
4750	For protective sleeves, add					4.14			4.14	4.55
4800	Service saddles, saddle contour x outlet, socket fusion outlets									
4801	IPS unless noted CTS									
4802	1-1/4" x 1/2" CTS outlet	B-20	17	1.412	Ea.	9.40	77		86.40	124
4804	1-1/4" x 1/2" outlet		17	1.412		9.40	77		86.40	124
4806	1-1/4" x 3/4" outlet		17	1.412		9.40	77		86.40	124
4808	1-1/4" x 1" outlet		16	1.500		11.10	82		93.10	134
4810	1-1/4" x 1-1/4" outlet		16	1.500		15.70	82		97.70	139
4812	1-1/2" x 1/2" CTS outlet		16	1.500		9.40	82		91.40	132
4814	1-1/2" x 1/2" outlet		16	1.500		9.40	82		91.40	132
4816	1-1/2" x 3/4" outlet		16	1.500		9.40	82		91.40	132
4818	1-1/2" x 1-1/4" outlet		15	1.600		15.70	87		102.70	147
4820	2" x 1/2" CTS outlet		12	2		9.40	109		118.40	172
4822	2" x 1/2" outlet		12	2		9.40	109		118.40	172
4824	2" x 3/4" outlet		12	2		9.40	109		118.40	172
4826	2" x 1" outlet		11	2.182		11.10	119		130.10	189
4828	2" x 1-1/4" outlet		11	2.182		15.70	119		134.70	194
4830	3" x 1/2" CTS outlet		12	2		9.40	109		118.40	172
4832	3" x 1/2" outlet		12	2		9.40	109		118.40	172
4834	3" x 3/4" outlet		12	2		9.40	109		118.40	172
4836	3" x 1" outlet		11	2.182		11.10	119		130.10	189
4838	3" x 1-1/4" outlet		11	2.182		15.70	119		134.70	194
4840	4" x 1/2" CTS outlet		10	2.400		9.40	131		140.40	204
4842	4" x 1/2" outlet		10	2.400		9.40	131		140.40	204
4844	4" x 3/4" outlet		10	2.400		9.40	131		140.40	204
4846	4" x 1" outlet		9	2.667		11.10	145		156.10	228
4848	4" x 1-1/4" outlet		9	2.667		15.70	145		160.70	233
4850	6" x 1/2" CTS outlet	B-21A	10	4		9.40	242	66.50	317.90	445
4852	6" x 1/2" outlet		10	4		9.40	242	66.50	317.90	445
4854	6" x 3/4" outlet		10	4		9.40	242	66.50	317.90	445
4856	6" x 1" outlet		9	4.444		11.10	269	73.50	353.60	495
4858	6" x 1-1/4" outlet		9	4.444		15.70	269	73.50	358.20	500

33 52 Hydrocarbon Transmission and Distribution
33 52 16 – Gas Hydrocarbon Piping

33 52 16.26 High Density Polyethylene Piping		Crew	Daily Output	Labor-Hours	Unit	Material	2024 Bare Costs Labor	2024 Bare Costs Equipment	Total	Total Incl O&P
4860	8" x 1/2" CTS outlet	B-21A	8	5	Ea.	9.40	305	83	397.40	550
4862	8" x 1/2" outlet		8	5		9.40	305	83	397.40	550
4864	8" x 3/4" outlet		8	5		9.40	305	83	397.40	550
4866	8" x 1" outlet		7	5.714		11.30	345	95	451.30	630
4868	8" x 1-1/4" outlet	↓	7	5.714		16	345	95	456	635
4880	For protective sleeves, 1/2" to 3/4" diameter outlets, add					1.23			1.23	1.35
4885	1" diameter outlets, add					2.06			2.06	2.27
4890	1-1/4" diameter outlets, add					3.55			3.55	3.91
4900	Reducer tees, 1-1/4" x 3/4" x 3/4" diameters	B-20	9	2.667		11.95	145		156.95	229
4902	1-1/4" x 3/4" x 1" diameters		9	2.667		15.50	145		160.50	233
4904	1-1/4" x 3/4" x 1-1/4" diameters		9	2.667		15.50	145		160.50	233
4906	1-1/4" x 1" x 3/4" diameters		9	2.667		15.50	145		160.50	233
4908	1-1/4" x 1" x 1" diameters		9	2.667		11.85	145		156.85	229
4910	1-1/4" x 1" x 1-1/4" diameters		9	2.667		15.50	145		160.50	233
4912	1-1/4" x 1-1/4" x 3/4" diameters		9	2.667		11.15	145		156.15	228
4914	1-1/4" x 1-1/4" x 1" diameters		9	2.667		11.85	145		156.85	229
4916	1-1/2" x 3/4" x 3/4" diameters		8.50	2.824		19.70	154		173.70	251
4918	1-1/2" x 3/4" x 1" diameters		8.50	2.824		19.70	154		173.70	251
4920	1-1/2" x 3/4" x 1-1/4" diameters		8.50	2.824		19.70	154		173.70	251
4922	1-1/2" x 3/4" x 1-1/2" diameters		8.50	2.824		19.70	154		173.70	251
4924	1-1/2" x 1" x 3/4" diameters		8.50	2.824		19.70	154		173.70	251
4926	1-1/2" x 1" x 1" diameters		8.50	2.824		19.70	154		173.70	251
4928	1-1/2" x 1" x 1-1/4" diameters		8.50	2.824		19.70	154		173.70	251
4930	1-1/2" x 1" x 1-1/2" diameters		8.50	2.824		19.70	154		173.70	251
4932	1-1/2" x 1-1/4" x 3/4" diameters		8.50	2.824		16.55	154		170.55	247
4934	1-1/2" x 1-1/4" x 1" diameters		8.50	2.824		16.35	154		170.35	247
4936	1-1/2" x 1-1/4" x 1-1/4" diameters		8.50	2.824		16.55	154		170.55	247
4938	1-1/2" x 1-1/4" x 1-1/2" diameters		8.50	2.824		19.70	154		173.70	251
4940	1-1/2" x 1-1/2" x 3/4" diameters		8.50	2.824		15.40	154		169.40	246
4942	1-1/2" x 1-1/2" x 1" diameters		8.50	2.824		15.40	154		169.40	246
4944	1-1/2" x 1-1/2" x 1-1/4" diameters		8.50	2.824		15.40	154		169.40	246
4946	2" x 1-1/4" x 3/4" diameters		8	3		17.90	164		181.90	263
4948	2" x 1-1/4" x 1" diameters		8	3		17.35	164		181.35	262
4950	2" x 1-1/4" x 1-1/4" diameters		8	3		18.05	164		182.05	263
4952	2" x 1-1/2" x 3/4" diameters		8	3		17.90	164		181.90	263
4954	2" x 1-1/2" x 1" diameters		8	3		17.35	164		181.35	262
4956	2" x 1-1/2" x 1-1/4" diameters		8	3		17.35	164		181.35	262
4958	2" x 2" x 3/4" diameters		8	3		17.85	164		181.85	263
4960	2" x 2" x 1" diameters		8	3		17.50	164		181.50	262
4962	2" x 2" x 1-1/4" diameters	↓	8	3	↓	17.95	164		181.95	263
8100	Fittings, accessories									
8105	SDR 11, IPS unless noted CTS									
8110	Flange adapters, 2" x 6" long	1 Skwk	32	.250	Ea.	25	15.90		40.90	51.50
8115	3" x 6" long		32	.250		30.50	15.90		46.40	58
8120	4" x 6" long	↓	24	.333		38.50	21		59.50	74
8125	6" x 8" long	2 Skwk	24	.667		60.50	42.50		103	131
8130	8" x 9" long	"	20	.800		85	51		136	170
8135	Backup flanges, 2" diameter	1 Skwk	32	.250		31.50	15.90		47.40	59
8140	3" diameter		32	.250		42.50	15.90		58.40	71
8145	4" diameter	↓	24	.333		84	21		105	124
8150	6" diameter	2 Skwk	24	.667		86	42.50		128.50	159
8155	8" diameter	"	20	.800	↓	147	51		198	238
8200	Tapping tees, test caps									

33 52 Hydrocarbon Transmission and Distribution

33 52 16 – Gas Hydrocarbon Piping

33 52 16.26 High Density Polyethylene Piping		Crew	Daily Output	Labor-Hours	Unit	Material	2024 Bare Costs Labor	Equipment	Total	Total Incl O&P
8205	Type II, yellow polyethylene cap	1 Skwk	45	.178	Ea.	63	11.30		74.30	86.50
8210	High volume, black polyethylene cap		45	.178		81	11.30		92.30	106
8215	Quick connector, female x female inlets, 1/4" N.P.T.		50	.160		26	10.15		36.15	44
8220	Test hose, 24" length, 3/8" ID, male outlets, 1/4" N.P.T.		50	.160		35.50	10.15		45.65	54.50
8225	Quick connector and test hose assembly		50	.160		62	10.15		72.15	83
8300	Threaded transition fittings									
8302	HDPE x MPT zinc plated steel, SDR 7, 1/2" CTS x 1/2" MPT	B-22C	30	.533	Ea.	48.50	30	9.65	88.15	108
8304	SDR 9.3, 1/2" IPS x 3/4" MPT		28.50	.561		64	31.50	10.15	105.65	129
8306	SDR 11, 3/4" IPS x 3/4" MPT		28.50	.561		31.50	31.50	10.15	73.15	92.50
8308	1" IPS x 1" MPT		27	.593		41	33.50	10.75	85.25	107
8310	1-1/4" IPS x 1-1/4" MPT		27	.593		65.50	33.50	10.75	109.75	133
8312	1-1/2" IPS x 1-1/2" MPT		25.50	.627		76	35.50	11.35	122.85	149
8314	2" IPS x 2" MPT		24	.667		87	37.50	12.05	136.55	165
8322	HDPE x MPT 316 stainless steel, SDR 11, 3/4" IPS x 3/4" MPT		28.50	.561		42	31.50	10.15	83.65	104
8324	1" IPS x 1" MPT		27	.593		43	33.50	10.75	87.25	109
8326	1-1/4" IPS x 1-1/4" MPT		27	.593		53	33.50	10.75	97.25	120
8328	2" IPS x 2" MPT		24	.667		63.50	37.50	12.05	113.05	139
8330	3" IPS x 3" MPT		24	.667		127	37.50	12.05	176.55	209
8332	4" IPS x 4" MPT		18	.889		175	50	16.10	241.10	284
8334	6" IPS x 6" MPT	B-22A	18	2.222		325	125	41.50	491.50	585
8342	HDPE x FPT 316 stainless steel, SDR 11, 3/4" IPS x 3/4" FPT	B-22C	28.50	.561		54.50	31.50	10.15	96.15	118
8344	1" IPS x 1" FPT		27	.593		73	33.50	10.75	117.25	142
8346	1-1/4" IPS x 1-1/4" FPT		27	.593		118	33.50	10.75	162.25	191
8348	1-1/2" IPS x 1-1/2" FPT		25.50	.627		112	35.50	11.35	158.85	189
8350	2" IPS x 2" FPT		24	.667		149	37.50	12.05	198.55	233
8352	3" IPS x 3" FPT		24	.667		288	37.50	12.05	337.55	385
8354	4" IPS x 4" FPT		18	.889		415	50	16.10	481.10	545
8362	HDPE x MPT epoxy carbon steel, SDR 11, 3/4" IPS x 3/4" MPT		28.50	.561		31.50	31.50	10.15	73.15	93
8364	1" IPS x 1" MPT		27	.593		35	33.50	10.75	79.25	100
8366	1-1/4" IPS x 1-1/4" MPT		27	.593		37	33.50	10.75	81.25	102
8368	1-1/2" IPS x 1-1/2" MPT		25.50	.627		40.50	35.50	11.35	87.35	110
8370	2" IPS x 2" MPT		24	.667		43.50	37.50	12.05	93.05	117
8372	3" IPS x 3" MPT		24	.667		67.50	37.50	12.05	117.05	143
8374	4" IPS x 4" MPT		18	.889		91.50	50	16.10	157.60	192
8382	HDPE x FPT epoxy carbon steel, SDR 11, 3/4" IPS x 3/4" FPT		28.50	.561		38.50	31.50	10.15	80.15	101
8384	1" IPS x 1" FPT		27	.593		42.50	33.50	10.75	86.75	108
8386	1-1/4" IPS x 1-1/4" FPT		27	.593		90.50	33.50	10.75	134.75	161
8388	1-1/2" IPS x 1-1/2" FPT		25.50	.627		91.50	35.50	11.35	138.35	165
8390	2" IPS x 2" FPT		24	.667		97	37.50	12.05	146.55	176
8392	3" IPS x 3" FPT		24	.667		165	37.50	12.05	214.55	250
8394	4" IPS x 4" FPT		18	.889		206	50	16.10	272.10	320
8402	HDPE x MPT poly coated carbon steel, SDR 11, 1" IPS x 1" MPT		27	.593		34	33.50	10.75	78.25	99
8404	1-1/4" IPS x 1-1/4" MPT		27	.593		44.50	33.50	10.75	88.75	110
8406	1-1/2" IPS x 1-1/2" MPT		25.50	.627		53	35.50	11.35	99.85	124
8408	2" IPS x 2" MPT		24	.667		60	37.50	12.05	109.55	135
8410	3" IPS x 3" MPT		24	.667		116	37.50	12.05	165.55	196
8412	4" IPS x 4" MPT		18	.889		180	50	16.10	246.10	290
8414	6" IPS x 6" MPT	B-22A	18	2.222		420	125	41.50	586.50	690
8602	Socket fused HDPE x MPT brass, SDR 11, 3/4" IPS x 3/4" MPT	B-20	28.50	.842		18.65	46		64.65	88.50
8604	1" IPS x 3/4" MPT		27	.889		22.50	48.50		71	97
8606	1" IPS x 1" MPT		27	.889		22	48.50		70.50	96
8608	1-1/4" IPS x 3/4" MPT		27	.889		23.50	48.50		72	97.50
8610	1-1/4" IPS x 1" MPT		27	.889		23.50	48.50		72	97.50

33 52 Hydrocarbon Transmission and Distribution

33 52 16 – Gas Hydrocarbon Piping

33 52 16.26 High Density Polyethylene Piping		Crew	Daily Output	Labor-Hours	Unit	Material	2024 Bare Costs Labor	Equipment	Total	Total Incl O&P
8612	1-1/4" IPS x 1-1/4" MPT	B-20	27	.889	Ea.	33.50	48.50		82	109
8614	1-1/2" IPS x 1-1/2" MPT		25.50	.941		46	51.50		97.50	127
8616	2" IPS x 2" MPT		24	1		46.50	54.50		101	133
8618	Socket fused HDPE x FPT brass, SDR 11, 3/4" IPS x 3/4" FPT		28.50	.842		18.65	46		64.65	88.50
8620	1" IPS x 1/2" FPT		27	.889		18.65	48.50		67.15	92.50
8622	1" IPS x 3/4" FPT		27	.889		22.50	48.50		71	97
8624	1" IPS x 1" FPT		27	.889		22	48.50		70.50	96
8626	1-1/4" IPS x 3/4" FPT		27	.889		23.50	48.50		72	97.50
8628	1-1/4" IPS x 1" FPT		27	.889		22.50	48.50		71	97
8630	1-1/4" IPS x 1-1/4" FPT		27	.889		33.50	48.50		82	109
8632	1-1/2" IPS x 1-1/2" FPT		25.50	.941		46.50	51.50		98	128
8634	2" IPS x 1-1/2" FPT		24	1		47.50	54.50		102	133
8636	2" IPS x 2" FPT		24	1		50	54.50		104.50	136

33 61 Hydronic Energy Distribution

33 61 13 – Underground Hydronic Energy Distribution

33 61 13.20 Pipe Conduit, Prefabricated/Preinsulated		Crew	Daily Output	Labor-Hours	Unit	Material	2024 Bare Costs Labor	Equipment	Total	Total Incl O&P
0010	**PIPE CONDUIT, PREFABRICATED/PREINSULATED** R221113-70									
0020	Does not include trenching, fittings or crane.									
0300	For cathodic protection, add 12 to 14%									
0310	of total built-up price (casing plus service pipe)									
0580	Polyurethane insulated system, 250°F max. temp.									
0620	Black steel service pipe, standard wt., 1/2" insulation									
0660	3/4" diam. pipe size	Q-17	54	.296	L.F.	132	20	1.33	153.33	177
0670	1" diam. pipe size		50	.320		146	22	1.44	169.44	194
0680	1-1/4" diam. pipe size		47	.340		162	23	1.53	186.53	215
0690	1-1/2" diam. pipe size		45	.356		176	24	1.60	201.60	232
0700	2" diam. pipe size		42	.381		183	26	1.71	210.71	241
0710	2-1/2" diam. pipe size		34	.471		186	32	2.11	220.11	254
0720	3" diam. pipe size		28	.571		215	39	2.57	256.57	298
0730	4" diam. pipe size		22	.727		271	49.50	3.27	323.77	375
0740	5" diam. pipe size		18	.889		345	60.50	3.99	409.49	475
0750	6" diam. pipe size	Q-18	23	1.043		400	73.50	3.12	476.62	550
0760	8" diam. pipe size		19	1.263		590	89	3.78	682.78	785
0770	10" diam. pipe size		16	1.500		745	106	4.49	855.49	980
0780	12" diam. pipe size		13	1.846		925	130	5.50	1,060.50	1,225
0790	14" diam. pipe size		11	2.182		1,025	154	6.50	1,185.50	1,350
0800	16" diam. pipe size		10	2.400		1,175	169	7.20	1,351.20	1,550
0810	18" diam. pipe size		8	3		1,375	212	8.95	1,595.95	1,825
0820	20" diam. pipe size		7	3.429		1,525	242	10.25	1,777.25	2,050
0830	24" diam. pipe size		6	4		1,850	282	11.95	2,143.95	2,475
0900	For 1" thick insulation, add					10%				
0940	For 1-1/2" thick insulation, add					13%				
0980	For 2" thick insulation, add					20%				
1500	Gland seal for system, 3/4" diam. pipe size	Q-17	32	.500	Ea.	1,525	34	2.25	1,561.25	1,725
1510	1" diam. pipe size		32	.500		1,525	34	2.25	1,561.25	1,725
1540	1-1/4" diam. pipe size		30	.533		1,625	36.50	2.39	1,663.89	1,850
1550	1-1/2" diam. pipe size		30	.533		1,625	36.50	2.39	1,663.89	1,850
1560	2" diam. pipe size		28	.571		1,950	39	2.57	1,991.57	2,175
1570	2-1/2" diam. pipe size		26	.615		2,100	42	2.76	2,144.76	2,375
1580	3" diam. pipe size		24	.667		2,250	45.50	2.99	2,298.49	2,550

33 61 Hydronic Energy Distribution

33 61 13 – Underground Hydronic Energy Distribution

33 61 13.20 Pipe Conduit, Prefabricated/Preinsulated		Crew	Daily Output	Labor-Hours	Unit	Material	2024 Bare Costs Labor	Equipment	Total	Total Incl O&P
1590	4" diam. pipe size	Q-17	22	.727	Ea.	2,650	49.50	3.27	2,702.77	3,000
1600	5" diam. pipe size	↓	19	.842		3,275	57.50	3.78	3,336.28	3,700
1610	6" diam. pipe size	Q-18	26	.923		3,475	65	2.76	3,542.76	3,925
1620	8" diam. pipe size		25	.960		4,025	67.50	2.87	4,095.37	4,525
1630	10" diam. pipe size		23	1.043		4,700	73.50	3.12	4,776.62	5,275
1640	12" diam. pipe size		21	1.143		5,200	80.50	3.42	5,283.92	5,825
1650	14" diam. pipe size		19	1.263		5,825	89	3.78	5,917.78	6,525
1660	16" diam. pipe size		18	1.333		6,875	94	3.99	6,972.99	7,725
1670	18" diam. pipe size		16	1.500		7,300	106	4.49	7,410.49	8,175
1680	20" diam. pipe size		14	1.714		8,300	121	5.15	8,426.15	9,300
1690	24" diam. pipe size	↓	12	2	↓	9,200	141	6	9,347	10,300
2000	Elbow, 45° for system									
2020	3/4" diam. pipe size	Q-17	14	1.143	Ea.	1,000	77.50	5.15	1,082.65	1,225
2040	1" diam. pipe size		13	1.231		1,025	83.50	5.55	1,114.05	1,250
2050	1-1/4" diam. pipe size		11	1.455		1,175	99	6.55	1,280.55	1,450
2060	1-1/2" diam. pipe size		9	1.778		1,175	121	8	1,304	1,500
2070	2" diam. pipe size		6	2.667		1,275	181	11.95	1,467.95	1,675
2080	2-1/2" diam. pipe size		4	4		1,375	272	17.95	1,664.95	1,950
2090	3" diam. pipe size		3.50	4.571		1,600	310	20.50	1,930.50	2,250
2100	4" diam. pipe size		3	5.333		1,875	365	24	2,264	2,625
2110	5" diam. pipe size	↓	2.80	5.714		2,400	390	25.50	2,815.50	3,225
2120	6" diam. pipe size	Q-18	4	6		2,725	425	17.95	3,167.95	3,650
2130	8" diam. pipe size		3	8		3,950	565	24	4,539	5,225
2140	10" diam. pipe size		2.40	10		4,825	705	30	5,560	6,375
2150	12" diam. pipe size		2	12		6,350	845	36	7,231	8,275
2160	14" diam. pipe size		1.80	13.333		7,875	940	40	8,855	10,100
2170	16" diam. pipe size		1.60	15		9,375	1,050	45	10,470	11,900
2180	18" diam. pipe size		1.30	18.462		11,800	1,300	55	13,155	14,900
2190	20" diam. pipe size		1	24		14,800	1,700	72	16,572	18,900
2200	24" diam. pipe size	↓	.70	34.286	↓	18,600	2,425	103	21,128	24,200
2260	For elbow, 90°, add					25%				
2300	For tee, straight, add					85%	30%			
2340	For tee, reducing, add					170%	30%			
2380	For weldolet, straight, add					50%				
2400	Polyurethane insulation, 1"									
2410	FRP carrier and casing									
2420	4"	Q-5	18	.889	L.F.	77.50	60.50		138	176
2422	6"	Q-6	23	1.043		135	73.50		208.50	257
2424	8"		19	1.263		219	89		308	375
2426	10"		16	1.500		296	106		402	480
2428	12"	↓	13	1.846	↓	385	130		515	620
2430	FRP carrier and PVC casing									
2440	4"	Q-5	18	.889	L.F.	32.50	60.50		93	126
2444	8"	Q-6	19	1.263		69	89		158	209
2446	10"		16	1.500		100	106		206	267
2448	12"	↓	13	1.846		136	130		266	345
2450	PVC carrier and casing									
2460	4"	Q-1	36	.444	L.F.	16.60	30		46.60	63
2462	6"	"	29	.552		23.50	37		60.50	81
2464	8"	Q-2	36	.667		33.50	46.50		80	106
2466	10"		32	.750		44	52.50		96.50	126
2468	12"	↓	31	.774	↓	52.50	54		106.50	138

33 63 Steam Energy Distribution

33 63 13 – Underground Steam and Condensate Distribution Piping

33 63 13.10 Calcium Silicate Insulated System		Crew	Daily Output	Labor-Hours	Unit	Material	2024 Bare Costs Labor	Equipment	Total	Total Incl O&P
0010	**CALCIUM SILICATE INSULATED SYSTEM**									
0011	High temp. (1200 degrees F)									
2840	Steel casing with protective exterior coating									
2850	6-5/8" diameter	Q-18	52	.462	L.F.	193	32.50	1.38	226.88	262
2860	8-5/8" diameter		50	.480		209	34	1.44	244.44	282
2870	10-3/4" diameter		47	.511		245	36	1.53	282.53	325
2880	12-3/4" diameter		44	.545		267	38.50	1.63	307.13	355
2890	14" diameter		41	.585		300	41.50	1.75	343.25	395
2900	16" diameter		39	.615		325	43.50	1.84	370.34	420
2910	18" diameter		36	.667		355	47	1.99	403.99	460
2920	20" diameter		34	.706		400	50	2.11	452.11	515
2930	22" diameter		32	.750		555	53	2.24	610.24	690
2940	24" diameter		29	.828		635	58.50	2.47	695.97	790
2950	26" diameter		26	.923		725	65	2.76	792.76	900
2960	28" diameter		23	1.043		900	73.50	3.12	976.62	1,100
2970	30" diameter		21	1.143		965	80.50	3.42	1,048.92	1,175
2980	32" diameter		19	1.263		1,075	89	3.78	1,167.78	1,325
2990	34" diameter		18	1.333		1,100	94	3.99	1,197.99	1,350
3000	36" diameter		16	1.500		1,175	106	4.49	1,285.49	1,450
3040	For multi-pipe casings, add					10%				
3060	For oversize casings, add					2%				
3400	Steel casing gland seal, single pipe									
3420	6-5/8" diameter	Q-18	25	.960	Ea.	2,925	67.50	2.87	2,995.37	3,325
3440	8-5/8" diameter		23	1.043		3,425	73.50	3.12	3,501.62	3,875
3450	10-3/4" diameter		21	1.143		3,825	80.50	3.42	3,908.92	4,325
3460	12-3/4" diameter		19	1.263		4,525	89	3.78	4,617.78	5,100
3470	14" diameter		17	1.412		5,025	99.50	4.22	5,128.72	5,675
3480	16" diameter		16	1.500		5,875	106	4.49	5,985.49	6,600
3490	18" diameter		15	1.600		6,500	113	4.78	6,617.78	7,325
3500	20" diameter		13	1.846		7,200	130	5.50	7,335.50	8,125
3510	22" diameter		12	2		8,100	141	6	8,247	9,125
3520	24" diameter		11	2.182		9,100	154	6.50	9,260.50	10,200
3530	26" diameter		10	2.400		10,400	169	7.20	10,576.20	11,700
3540	28" diameter		9.50	2.526		11,700	178	7.55	11,885.55	13,200
3550	30" diameter		9	2.667		11,900	188	7.95	12,095.95	13,400
3560	32" diameter		8.50	2.824		13,400	199	8.45	13,607.45	15,100
3570	34" diameter		8	3		14,600	212	8.95	14,820.95	16,400
3580	36" diameter		7	3.429		15,600	242	10.25	15,852.25	17,500
3620	For multi-pipe casings, add					5%				
4000	Steel casing anchors, single pipe									
4020	6-5/8" diameter	Q-18	8	3	Ea.	2,625	212	8.95	2,845.95	3,225
4040	8-5/8" diameter		7.50	3.200		2,725	226	9.55	2,960.55	3,350
4050	10-3/4" diameter		7	3.429		3,575	242	10.25	3,827.25	4,300
4060	12-3/4" diameter		6.50	3.692		3,825	260	11.05	4,096.05	4,600
4070	14" diameter		6	4		4,525	282	11.95	4,818.95	5,400
4080	16" diameter		5.50	4.364		5,225	310	13.05	5,548.05	6,225
4090	18" diameter		5	4.800		5,925	340	14.35	6,279.35	7,025
4100	20" diameter		4.50	5.333		6,500	375	15.95	6,890.95	7,725
4110	22" diameter		4	6		7,250	425	17.95	7,692.95	8,625
4120	24" diameter		3.50	6.857		7,900	485	20.50	8,405.50	9,450
4130	26" diameter		3	8		8,950	565	24	9,539	10,700
4140	28" diameter		2.50	9.600		9,850	675	28.50	10,553.50	11,800
4150	30" diameter		2	12		10,400	845	36	11,281	12,800

33 63 Steam Energy Distribution

33 63 13 – Underground Steam and Condensate Distribution Piping

33 63 13.10 Calcium Silicate Insulated System		Crew	Daily Output	Labor-Hours	Unit	Material	2024 Bare Costs Labor	Equipment	Total	Total Incl O&P
4160	32" diameter	Q-18	1.50	16	Ea.	12,500	1,125	48	13,673	15,400
4170	34" diameter		1	24		14,000	1,700	72	15,772	18,000
4180	36" diameter	↓	1	24		15,300	1,700	72	17,072	19,400
4220	For multi-pipe, add				↓	5%	20%			
4800	Steel casing elbow									
4820	6-5/8" diameter	Q-18	15	1.600	Ea.	3,725	113	4.78	3,842.78	4,275
4830	8-5/8" diameter		15	1.600		4,000	113	4.78	4,117.78	4,575
4850	10-3/4" diameter		14	1.714		4,825	121	5.15	4,951.15	5,475
4860	12-3/4" diameter		13	1.846		5,700	130	5.50	5,835.50	6,475
4870	14" diameter		12	2		6,125	141	6	6,272	6,950
4880	16" diameter		11	2.182		6,700	154	6.50	6,860.50	7,575
4890	18" diameter		10	2.400		7,625	169	7.20	7,801.20	8,625
4900	20" diameter		9	2.667		8,150	188	7.95	8,345.95	9,250
4910	22" diameter		8	3		8,775	212	8.95	8,995.95	9,975
4920	24" diameter		7	3.429		9,650	242	10.25	9,902.25	11,000
4930	26" diameter		6	4		10,600	282	11.95	10,893.95	12,000
4940	28" diameter		5	4.800		11,400	340	14.35	11,754.35	13,100
4950	30" diameter		4	6		11,500	425	17.95	11,942.95	13,200
4960	32" diameter		3	8		13,000	565	24	13,589	15,200
4970	34" diameter		2	12		14,300	845	36	15,181	17,000
4980	36" diameter	↓	2	12	↓	15,200	845	36	16,081	18,100
5500	Black steel service pipe, std. wt., 1" thick insulation									
5510	3/4" diameter pipe size	Q-17	54	.296	L.F.	120	20	1.33	141.33	163
5540	1" diameter pipe size		50	.320		124	22	1.44	147.44	170
5550	1-1/4" diameter pipe size		47	.340		156	23	1.53	180.53	208
5560	1-1/2" diameter pipe size		45	.356		163	24	1.60	188.60	217
5570	2" diameter pipe size		42	.381		177	26	1.71	204.71	235
5580	2-1/2" diameter pipe size		34	.471		186	32	2.11	220.11	254
5590	3" diameter pipe size		28	.571		162	39	2.57	203.57	239
5600	4" diameter pipe size		22	.727		170	49.50	3.27	222.77	264
5610	5" diameter pipe size	↓	18	.889		233	60.50	3.99	297.49	350
5620	6" diameter pipe size	Q-18	23	1.043	↓	251	73.50	3.12	327.62	390
6000	Black steel service pipe, std. wt., 1-1/2" thick insul.									
6010	3/4" diameter pipe size	Q-17	54	.296	L.F.	142	20	1.33	163.33	187
6040	1" diameter pipe size		50	.320		149	22	1.44	172.44	198
6050	1-1/4" diameter pipe size		47	.340		160	23	1.53	184.53	212
6060	1-1/2" diameter pipe size		45	.356		158	24	1.60	183.60	212
6070	2" diameter pipe size		42	.381		170	26	1.71	197.71	227
6080	2-1/2" diameter pipe size		34	.471		155	32	2.11	189.11	220
6090	3" diameter pipe size		28	.571		172	39	2.57	213.57	250
6100	4" diameter pipe size		22	.727		197	49.50	3.27	249.77	294
6110	5" diameter pipe size	↓	18	.889		264	60.50	3.99	328.49	385
6120	6" diameter pipe size	Q-18	23	1.043		276	73.50	3.12	352.62	415
6130	8" diameter pipe size		19	1.263		355	89	3.78	447.78	525
6140	10" diameter pipe size		16	1.500		460	106	4.49	570.49	665
6150	12" diameter pipe size	↓	13	1.846		525	130	5.50	660.50	775
6190	For 2" thick insulation, add					15%				
6220	For 2-1/2" thick insulation, add					25%				
6260	For 3" thick insulation, add				↓	30%				
6800	Black steel service pipe, ex. hvy. wt., 1" thick insul.									
6820	3/4" diameter pipe size	Q-17	50	.320	L.F.	144	22	1.44	167.44	192
6840	1" diameter pipe size		47	.340		153	23	1.53	177.53	204
6850	1-1/4" diameter pipe size		44	.364		168	24.50	1.63	194.13	224

33 63 Steam Energy Distribution

33 63 13 – Underground Steam and Condensate Distribution Piping

33 63 13.10 Calcium Silicate Insulated System

		Crew	Daily Output	Labor-Hours	Unit	Material	2024 Bare Costs Labor	Equipment	Total	Total Incl O&P
6860	1-1/2" diameter pipe size	Q-17	42	.381	L.F.	170	26	1.71	197.71	227
6870	2" diameter pipe size		40	.400		188	27	1.80	216.80	248
6880	2-1/2" diameter pipe size		31	.516		153	35	2.32	190.32	223
6890	3" diameter pipe size		27	.593		177	40.50	2.66	220.16	257
6900	4" diameter pipe size		21	.762		218	52	3.42	273.42	320
6910	5" diameter pipe size		17	.941		205	64	4.23	273.23	325
6920	6" diameter pipe size	Q-18	22	1.091		198	77	3.26	278.26	335
7400	Black steel service pipe, ex. hvy. wt., 1-1/2" thick insul.									
7420	3/4" diameter pipe size	Q-17	50	.320	L.F.	106	22	1.44	129.44	151
7440	1" diameter pipe size		47	.340		133	23	1.53	157.53	182
7450	1-1/4" diameter pipe size		44	.364		147	24.50	1.63	173.13	200
7460	1-1/2" diameter pipe size		42	.381		144	26	1.71	171.71	198
7470	2" diameter pipe size		40	.400		153	27	1.80	181.80	211
7480	2-1/2" diameter pipe size		31	.516		142	35	2.32	179.32	212
7490	3" diameter pipe size		27	.593		158	40.50	2.66	201.16	236
7500	4" diameter pipe size		21	.762		200	52	3.42	255.42	300
7510	5" diameter pipe size		17	.941		277	64	4.23	345.23	405
7520	6" diameter pipe size	Q-18	22	1.091		277	77	3.26	357.26	425
7530	8" diameter pipe size		18	1.333		450	94	3.99	547.99	640
7540	10" diameter pipe size		15	1.600		425	113	4.78	542.78	640
7550	12" diameter pipe size		13	1.846		510	130	5.50	645.50	760
7590	For 2" thick insulation, add					13%				
7640	For 2-1/2" thick insulation, add					18%				
7680	For 3" thick insulation, add					24%				

33 63 13.20 Combined Steam Pipe With Condensate Return

		Crew	Daily Output	Labor-Hours	Unit	Material	2024 Bare Costs Labor	Equipment	Total	Total Incl O&P
0010	**COMBINED STEAM PIPE WITH CONDENSATE RETURN**									
9010	8" and 4" in 24" case	Q-18	100	.240	L.F.	650	16.90	.72	667.62	740
9020	6" and 3" in 20" case		104	.231		545	16.25	.69	561.94	625
9030	3" and 1-1/2" in 16" case		110	.218		410	15.40	.65	426.05	475
9040	2" and 1-1/4" in 12-3/4" case		114	.211		345	14.85	.63	360.48	405
9050	1-1/2" and 1-1/4" in 10-3/4" case		116	.207		410	14.60	.62	425.22	470
9100	Steam pipe only (no return)									
9110	6" in 18" case	Q-18	108	.222	L.F.	445	15.65	.66	461.31	515
9120	4" in 14" case		112	.214		345	15.10	.64	360.74	405
9130	3" in 14" case		114	.211		325	14.85	.63	340.48	385
9140	2-1/2" in 12-3/4" case		118	.203		305	14.35	.61	319.96	355
9150	2" in 12-3/4" case		122	.197		288	13.85	.59	302.44	335

Division Notes

	CREW	DAILY OUTPUT	LABOR-HOURS	UNIT	BARE COSTS				TOTAL INCL O&P
					MAT.	LABOR	EQUIP.	TOTAL	

Division 41 — Material Processing & Handling Equipment

Estimating Tips

Products such as conveyors, material handling cranes and hoists, and other items specified in this division require trained installers. The general contractor may not have any choice as to who will perform the installation or when it will be performed. Long lead times are often required for these products, making early decisions in purchasing and scheduling necessary. The installation of this type of equipment may require the embedment of mounting hardware during the construction of floors, structural walls, or interior walls/partitions. Electrical connections will require coordination with the electrical contractor.

Reference Numbers

Reference numbers are shown at the beginning of some major classifications. These numbers refer to related items in the Reference Section. The reference information may be an estimating procedure, an alternate pricing method, or technical information.

Same Data. Simplified.

Enjoy the convenience and efficiency of accessing your costs anywhere:

- **Skip the multiplier** by setting your location
- **Quickly search,** edit, favorite and share costs
- **Stay on top of price changes** with automatic updates

Discover more at rsmeans.com/online

No part of this cost data may be reproduced, stored in a retrieval system, or transmitted in any form or by any means without prior written permission of Gordian.

41 22 Cranes and Hoists

41 22 23 – Hoists

41 22 23.10 Material Handling

		Daily	Labor-			2024 Bare Costs			Total
		Crew	Output	Hours	Unit	Material	Labor	Equipment	Total	Incl O&P
0010	**MATERIAL HANDLING**, cranes, hoists and lifts									
1500	Cranes, portable hydraulic, floor type, 2,000 lb. capacity				Ea.	5,675			5,675	6,225
1600	4,000 lb. capacity					6,225			6,225	6,850
1800	Movable gantry type, 12' to 15' range, 2,000 lb. capacity					4,700			4,700	5,150
1900	6,000 lb. capacity					8,675			8,675	9,525
2100	Hoists, electric overhead, chain, hook hung, 15' lift, 1 ton cap.					3,900			3,900	4,275
2200	3 ton capacity					3,500			3,500	3,850
2500	5 ton capacity					5,650			5,650	6,225
2600	For hand-pushed trolley, add					15%				
2700	For geared trolley, add					30%				
2800	For motor trolley, add					75%				
3000	For lifts over 15', 1 ton, add				L.F.	34.50			34.50	38
3100	5 ton, add				"	127			127	140
3300	Lifts, scissor type, portable, electric, 36" high, 2,000 lb.				Ea.	4,600			4,600	5,050
3400	48" high, 4,000 lb.				"	8,875			8,875	9,750

Estimating Tips

This section involves equipment and construction costs for air, noise, and odor pollution control systems. These systems may be interrelated and care must be taken that the complete systems are estimated. For example, air pollution equipment may include dust and air-entrained particles that have to be collected. The vacuum systems could be noisy, requiring silencers to reduce noise pollution, and the collected solids have to be disposed of to prevent solid pollution.

Reference Numbers

Reference numbers are shown at the beginning of some major classifications. These numbers refer to related items in the Reference Section. The reference information may be an estimating procedure, an alternate pricing method, or technical information.

Division 44
Pollution & Waste Control Equipment

Same Data. Simplified.

Enjoy the convenience and efficiency of accessing your costs anywhere:

- **Skip the multiplier** by setting your location
- **Quickly search,** edit, favorite and share costs
- **Stay on top of price changes** with automatic updates

Discover more at rsmeans.com/online

No part of this cost data may be reproduced, stored in a retrieval system, or transmitted in any form or by any means without prior written permission of Gordian.

44 11 Particulate Control Equipment

44 11 16 – Fugitive Dust Barrier Systems

44 11 16.10 Dust Collection Systems		Crew	Daily Output	Labor-Hours	Unit	Material	2024 Bare Costs Labor	2024 Bare Costs Equipment	Total	Total Incl O&P
0010	**DUST COLLECTION SYSTEMS** Commercial/Industrial									
0120	Central vacuum units									
0130	Includes stand, filters and motorized shaker									
0200	500 CFM, 10" inlet, 2 HP	Q-20	2.40	8.333	Ea.	4,075	555		4,630	5,300
0220	1,000 CFM, 10" inlet, 3 HP		2.20	9.091		5,325	605		5,930	6,750
0240	1,500 CFM, 10" inlet, 5 HP		2	10		5,500	665		6,165	7,050
0260	3,000 CFM, 13" inlet, 10 HP		1.50	13.333		5,000	885		5,885	6,825
0280	5,000 CFM, 16" inlet, 2 @ 10 HP		1	20		15,000	1,325		16,325	18,500
1000	Vacuum tubing, galvanized									
1100	2-1/8" OD, 16 ga.	Q-9	440	.036	L.F.	3.65	2.36		6.01	7.60
1110	2-1/2" OD, 16 ga.		420	.038		3.95	2.48		6.43	8.10
1120	3" OD, 16 ga.		400	.040		4.03	2.60		6.63	8.35
1130	3-1/2" OD, 16 ga.		380	.042		6.15	2.74		8.89	10.90
1140	4" OD, 16 ga.		360	.044		7.05	2.89		9.94	12.10
1150	5" OD, 14 ga.		320	.050		10	3.25		13.25	15.90
1160	6" OD, 14 ga.		280	.057		12.15	3.72		15.87	18.95
1170	8" OD, 14 ga.		200	.080		18.75	5.20		23.95	28.50
1180	10" OD, 12 ga.		160	.100		55	6.50		61.50	70
1190	12" OD, 12 ga.		120	.133		51.50	8.65		60.15	69.50
1200	14" OD, 12 ga.		80	.200		58	13		71	83.50
1940	Hose, flexible wire reinforced rubber									
1956	3" diam.	Q-9	400	.040	L.F.	8.05	2.60		10.65	12.75
1960	4" diam.		360	.044		8.50	2.89		11.39	13.70
1970	5" diam.		320	.050		12.25	3.25		15.50	18.40
1980	6" diam.		280	.057		12.50	3.72		16.22	19.35
2000	90° elbow, slip fit									
2110	2-1/8" diam.	Q-9	70	.229	Ea.	13.70	14.85		28.55	37.50
2120	2-1/2" diam.		65	.246		24	16		40	50
2130	3" diam.		60	.267		26	17.35		43.35	54.50
2140	3-1/2" diam.		55	.291		37.50	18.90		56.40	70
2150	4" diam.		50	.320		35	21		56	70
2160	5" diam.		45	.356		78	23		101	121
2170	6" diam.		40	.400		89.50	26		115.50	138
2180	8" diam.		30	.533		234	34.50		268.50	310
2400	45° elbow, slip fit									
2410	2-1/8" diam.	Q-9	70	.229	Ea.	14.35	14.85		29.20	38.50
2420	2-1/2" diam.		65	.246		24	16		40	50.50
2430	3" diam.		60	.267		30	17.35		47.35	59
2440	3-1/2" diam.		55	.291		32	18.90		50.90	63.50
2450	4" diam.		50	.320		41	21		62	77
2460	5" diam.		45	.356		72	23		95	115
2470	6" diam.		40	.400		94	26		120	142
2480	8" diam.		35	.457		184	29.50		213.50	248
2800	90° TY, slip fit thru 6" diam.									
2810	2-1/8" diam.	Q-9	42	.381	Ea.	34.50	25		59.50	75.50
2820	2-1/2" diam.		39	.410		46.50	26.50		73	91.50
2830	3" diam.		36	.444		62.50	29		91.50	113
2840	3-1/2" diam.		33	.485		78	31.50		109.50	133
2850	4" diam.		30	.533		101	34.50		135.50	163
2860	5" diam.		27	.593		192	38.50		230.50	269
2870	6" diam.		24	.667		261	43.50		304.50	350
2880	8" diam., butt end					570			570	630
2890	10" diam., butt end					210			210	231

44 11 Particulate Control Equipment

44 11 16 – Fugitive Dust Barrier Systems

44 11 16.10 Dust Collection Systems		Crew	Daily Output	Labor-Hours	Unit	Material	2024 Bare Costs Labor	Equipment	Total	Total Incl O&P
2900	12" diam., butt end				Ea.	210			210	231
2910	14" diam., butt end					2,250			2,250	2,475
2920	6" x 4" diam., butt end					159			159	175
2930	8" x 4" diam., butt end					300			300	330
2940	10" x 4" diam., butt end					405			405	450
2950	12" x 4" diam., butt end					460			460	505
3100	90° elbow, butt end, segmented									
3110	8" diam., butt end, segmented				Ea.	635			635	695
3120	10" diam., butt end, segmented					233			233	256
3130	12" diam., butt end, segmented					201			201	221
3140	14" diam., butt end, segmented					310			310	340
3200	45° elbow, butt end, segmented									
3210	8" diam., butt end, segmented				Ea.	153			153	168
3220	10" diam., butt end, segmented					162			162	178
3230	12" diam., butt end, segmented					171			171	188
3240	14" diam., butt end, segmented					820			820	900
3400	All butt end fittings require one coupling per joint.									
3410	Labor for fitting included with couplings.									
3460	Compression coupling, galvanized, neoprene gasket									
3470	2-1/8" diam.	Q-9	44	.364	Ea.	15.45	23.50		38.95	52.50
3480	2-1/2" diam.		44	.364		15.45	23.50		38.95	52.50
3490	3" diam.		38	.421		17.90	27.50		45.40	60.50
3500	3-1/2" diam.		35	.457		18.75	29.50		48.25	65
3510	4" diam.		33	.485		20	31.50		51.50	70
3520	5" diam.		29	.552		24.50	36		60.50	81
3530	6" diam.		26	.615		28.50	40		68.50	91.50
3540	8" diam.		22	.727		51.50	47.50		99	128
3550	10" diam.		20	.800		65.50	52		117.50	151
3560	12" diam.		18	.889		73	58		131	168
3570	14" diam.		16	1		109	65		174	218
3800	Air gate valves, galvanized									
3810	2-1/8" diam.	Q-9	30	.533	Ea.	107	34.50		141.50	169
3820	2-1/2" diam.		28	.571		116	37		153	183
3830	3" diam.		26	.615		123	40		163	196
3840	4" diam.		23	.696		143	45		188	225
3850	6" diam.		18	.889		199	58		257	305

Division Notes

	CREW	DAILY OUTPUT	LABOR-HOURS	UNIT	BARE COSTS				TOTAL INCL O&P
					MAT.	LABOR	EQUIP.	TOTAL	

Estimating Tips

This division contains information about water and wastewater equipment and systems, which was formerly located in Division 44. The main areas of focus are total wastewater treatment plants and components of wastewater treatment plants. Also included in this section are oil/water separators for wastewater treatment.

Reference Numbers

Reference numbers are shown at the beginning of some major classifications. These numbers refer to related items in the Reference Section. The reference information may be an estimating procedure, an alternate pricing method, or technical information.

Division 46
Water & Wastewater Equipment

Same Data. Simplified.

Enjoy the convenience and efficiency of accessing your costs anywhere:
- **Skip the multiplier** by setting your location
- **Quickly search,** edit, favorite and share costs
- **Stay on top of price changes** with automatic updates

Discover more at rsmeans.com/online

No part of this cost data may be reproduced, stored in a retrieval system, or transmitted in any form or by any means without prior written permission of Gordian.

46 07 Packaged Water and Wastewater Treatment Equipment

46 07 53 – Packaged Wastewater Treatment Equipment

46 07 53.10 Biological Pkg. Wastewater Treatment Plants		Crew	Daily Output	Labor-Hours	Unit	Material	2024 Bare Costs Labor	Equipment	Total	Total Incl O&P
0010	**BIOLOGICAL PACKAGED WASTEWATER TREATMENT PLANTS**									
0011	Not including fencing or external piping									
0020	Steel packaged, blown air aeration plants									
0100	1,000 GPD				Gal.				55	60.50
0200	5,000 GPD								22	24
0300	15,000 GPD								22	24
0400	30,000 GPD								15.40	16.95
0500	50,000 GPD								11	12.10
0600	100,000 GPD								9.90	10.90
0700	200,000 GPD								8.80	9.70
0800	500,000 GPD				▼				7.70	8.45
1000	Concrete, extended aeration, primary and secondary treatment									
1010	10,000 GPD				Gal.				22	24
1100	30,000 GPD								15.40	16.95
1200	50,000 GPD								11	12.10
1400	100,000 GPD								9.90	10.90
1500	500,000 GPD				▼				7.70	8.45
1700	Municipal wastewater treatment facility									
1720	1.0 MGD				Gal.				11	12.10
1740	1.5 MGD								10.60	11.65
1760	2.0 MGD								10	11
1780	3.0 MGD								7.80	8.60
1800	5.0 MGD				▼				5.80	6.70
2000	Holding tank system, not incl. excavation or backfill									
2010	Recirculating chemical water closet	2 Plum	4	4	Ea.	525	299		824	1,025
2100	For voltage converter, add	"	16	1		263	74.50		337.50	400
2200	For high level alarm, add	1 Plum	7.80	1.026		165	76.50		241.50	296

46 07 53.20 Wastewater Treatment System

		Crew	Daily Output	Labor-Hours	Unit	Material	Labor	Equipment	Total	Total Incl O&P
0010	**WASTEWATER TREATMENT SYSTEM**									
0020	Fiberglass, 1,000 gallon	B-21	1.29	21.705	Ea.	4,100	1,225	156	5,481	6,500
0100	1,500 gallon	"	1.03	27.184	"	8,775	1,525	195	10,495	12,100

46 23 Grit Removal And Handling Equipment

46 23 23 – Vortex Grit Removal Equipment

46 23 23.10 Rainwater Filters

		Crew	Daily Output	Labor-Hours	Unit	Material	Labor	Equipment	Total	Total Incl O&P
0010	**RAINWATER FILTERS**									
0100	42 gal./min	B-21	3.50	8	Ea.	60,000	450	57.50	60,507.50	66,500
0200	65 gal./min		3.50	8		60,000	450	57.50	60,507.50	66,500
0300	208 gal./min	▼	3.50	8	▼	60,000	450	57.50	60,507.50	66,500

46 25 Oil and Grease Separation and Removal Equipment

46 25 13 – Coalescing Oil-Water Separators

46 25 13.20 Oil/Water Separators		Crew	Daily Output	Labor-Hours	Unit	Material	2024 Bare Costs Labor	Equipment	Total	Total Incl O&P
0010	**OIL/WATER SEPARATORS**									
0020	Underground, tank only									
0030	Excludes excavation, backfill & piping									
0100	200 GPM	B-21	3.50	8	Ea.	60,000	450	57.50	60,507.50	66,500
0110	400 GPM		3.25	8.615		74,000	485	62	74,547	82,000
0120	600 GPM		2.75	10.182		109,000	575	73	109,648	121,000
0130	800 GPM		2.50	11.200		132,500	635	80.50	133,215.50	147,000
0140	1,000 GPM		2	14		138,500	790	101	139,391	154,000
0150	1,200 GPM		1.50	18.667		164,000	1,050	134	165,184	182,000
0160	1,500 GPM	B-21	1	28	Ea.	199,500	1,575	201	201,276	222,000

Assemblies Section

Table of Contents

Table No.	Page

D SERVICES

D2010 Plumbing Fixtures
- D2010 110 Water Closet Systems 478
- D2010 120 Water Closets, Group 479
- D2010 210 Urinal Systems 480
- D2010 220 Urinal Systems, Battery Mount 481
- D2010 310 Lavatory Systems 482
- D2010 320 Lavatory Systems, Battery Mount 483
- D2010 410 Kitchen Sink Systems 484
- D2010 420 Laundry Sink Systems 485
- D2010 430 Laboratory Sink Systems 486
- D2010 440 Service Sink Systems 487
- D2010 510 Bathtub Systems 488
- D2010 610 Group Wash Fountain Systems 489
- D2010 710 Shower Systems 490
- D2010 810 Drinking Fountain Systems 491
- D2010 820 Water Cooler Systems 492
- D2010 920 Two Fixture Bathroom, Two Wall Plumbing 493
- D2010 922 Two Fixture Bathroom, One Wall Plumbing 493
- D2010 924 Three Fixture Bathroom, One Wall Plumbing 494
- D2010 926 Three Fixture Bathroom, Two Wall Plumbing 494
- D2010 928 Four Fixture Bathroom, Two Wall Plumbing 495
- D2010 930 Four Fixture Bathroom, Three Wall Plumbing 495
- D2010 932 Five Fixture Bathroom, Two Wall Plumbing 496
- D2010 934 Five Fixture Bathroom, Three Wall Plumbing 496
- D2010 936 Five Fixture Bathroom, One Wall Plumbing 496
- D2010 951 Plumbing Systems 20 Unit, 2 Story Apartment Building 497

D2020 Domestic Water Distribution
- D2020 210 Electric Water Heaters - Residential Systems 498
- D2020 220 Gas Fired Water Heaters - Residential Systems 499
- D2020 230 Oil Fired Water Heaters - Residential Systems 500
- D2020 240 Electric Water Heaters - Commercial Systems 501
- D2020 250 Gas Fired Water Heaters - Commercial Systems 502
- D2020 260 Oil Fired Water Heaters - Commercial Systems 503
- D2020 265 Solar, Closed Loop, Add-On Hot Water Systems 505
- D2020 270 Solar, Drainback, Hot Water Systems 507
- D2020 275 Solar, Draindown, Hot Water Systems 509
- D2020 280 Solar, Recirculation, Domestic Hot Water Systems 511
- D2020 285 Thermosyphon, Hot Water 513
- D2020 290 Solar, Hot Water, Air To Water Heat Exchange 515
- D2020 295 Solar, Closed Loop, Hot Water Systems 517

D2040 Rain Water Drainage
- D2040 210 Roof Drain Systems 518

D3010 Energy Supply
- D3010 510 Apartment Building Heating - Fin Tube Radiation 520
- D3010 650 Solar, Closed Loop, Space/Hot Water Systems 523
- D3010 660 Solar Swimming Pool Heater Systems 525
- D3010 675 Air To Water Heat Exchange 527

D3020 Heat Generating Systems
- D3020 102 Small Heating Systems, Hydronic, Electric Boilers 528

D3090 Other HVAC Systems/Equip
- D3090 320 Garage Exhaust Systems 529

D4010 Sprinklers
- D4010 310 Dry Pipe Sprinkler Systems 530
- D4010 350 Preaction Sprinkler Systems 533
- D4010 370 Deluge Sprinkler Systems 536
- D4010 390 On-off multicycle Sprinkler Systems 539
- D4010 410 Wet Pipe Sprinkler Systems 542
- D4010 412 Wet Sprinkler Seismic Components 545
- D4010 413 Seismic Wet Pipe Flexible Feed Sprinkler Systems 548
- D4010 414 Seismic Wet Pipe Flexible Feed Sprinkler Systems 550

D4020 Standpipes
- D4020 310 Wet Standpipe Risers, Class I 552
- Wet Standpipe Risers, Class II 552
- Wet Standpipe Risers, Class III 553
- D4020 330 Dry Standpipe Risers, Class I 554
- Dry Standpipe Risers, Class II 554
- Dry Standpipe Risers, Class III 555
- D4020 410 Fire Hose Equipment 556

D4090 Other Fire Protection Systems
- D4090 910 Fire Suppression Unit Components 557
- D4090 920 FM200 Systems 557

G BUILDING SITEWORK

G1030 Site Earthwork
- G1030 805 Trenching Common Earth 560
- G1030 806 Trenching Loam & Sandy Clay 562
- G1030 807 Trenching Sand & Gravel 564
- G1030 815 Pipe Bedding 566

G2040 Site Development
- G2040 920 Swimming Pools 568

G2050 Landscaping
- G2050 710 Site Irrigation 569
- G2050 720 Site Irrigation 572

G3010 Water Supply
- G3010 121 Water Service, Lead Free 573
- G3010 410 Fire Hydrants 575

G3020 Sanitary Sewer
- G3020 302 Septic Systems 577

G3030 Storm Sewer
- G3030 210 Manholes & Catch Basins 579

RSMeans Data: Assemblies— How They Work

Assemblies estimating provides a fast and reasonably accurate way to develop construction costs. An assembly is the grouping of individual work items — with appropriate quantities — to provide a cost for a major construction component in a convenient unit of measure.

An assemblies estimate is often used during early stages of design development to compare the cost impact of various design alternatives on total building cost.

Assemblies estimates are also used as an efficient tool to verify construction estimates.

Assemblies estimates do not require a completed design or detailed drawings. Instead, they are based on the general size of the structure and other known parameters of the project. The degree of accuracy of an assemblies estimate is generally within +/- 15%.

Most assemblies consist of three major elements: a graphic, the system components, and the cost data itself. The **graphic** is a visual representation showing the typical appearance of the assembly

❶ Unique 12-Character Identifier

Our assemblies are identified by a **unique 12-character identifier**. The assemblies are numbered using UNIFORMAT II, ASTM Standard E1557. The first five characters represent this system to level three. The last seven characters represent further breakdown in order to arrange items in understandable groups of similar tasks. Line numbers are consistent across all of our publications, so a line number in any assemblies data set will always refer to the same item.

❷ Reference Box

Information is available in the Reference Section to assist the estimator with estimating procedures, alternate pricing methods, and additional technical information.

The **Reference Box** indicates the exact location of this information in the Reference Section. The "R" stands for "reference," and the remaining characters are the line numbers.

❸ Narrative Descriptions

Our assemblies descriptions appear in two formats: narrative and table. **Narrative descriptions** are shown in a hierarchical structure to make them readable. In order to read a complete description, read up through the indents to the top of the section. Include everything that is above and to the left that is not contradicted by information below.

❹ System Components

System Components are listed separately to detail what is included in the development of the total system price.

Narrative Format

D40 Fire Protection
D4020 Standpipes

System Components

SYSTEM D4020 310 0560
WET STANDPIPE RISER, CLASS I, STEEL, BLACK, SCH. 40 PIPE, 10' HEIGHT
4" DIAMETER PIPE, ONE FLOOR

System Components	QUANTITY	UNIT	MAT.	INST.	TOTAL
Pipe, steel, black, schedule 40, threaded, 4" diam.	20.000	L.F.	1,470	890	2,360
Pipe, Tee, malleable iron, black, 150 lb. threaded, 4" pipe size	2.000	Ea.	1,200	800	2,000
Pipe, 90" elbow, malleable iron, black, 150 lb threaded, 4" pipe size	1.000	Ea.	380	266	646
Pipe, nipple, steel, black, schedule 40, 2-1/2" pipe size x 3" long	2.000	Ea.	50	200	250
Fire valve, gate, 300 lb., brass w/handwheel, 2-1/2" pipe size	1.000	Ea.	279	127	406
Fire valve, pressure reducing rgh brs, 2-1/2" pipe size	1.000	Ea.	1,730	254	1,984
Valve, swing check, w/ball drip, CI w/brs. ftngs., 4" pipe size	1.000	Ea.	505	535	1,040
Standpipe conn wall dble. flush brs. w/plugs & chains 2-1/2"x2-1/2"x4"	1.000	Ea.	900	320	1,220
Valve, swing check, bronze, 125 lb, regrinding disc, 2-1/2" pipe size	1.000	Ea.	1,700	107	1,807
Roof manifold, fire, w/valves & caps, horiz/vert brs 2-1/2"x2-1/2"x4"	1.000	Ea.	277	335	612
Fire, hydrolator, vent & drain, 2-1/2" pipe size	1.000	Ea.	182	74	256
Valve, gate, iron body 125 lb., OS&Y, threaded, 4" pipe size	1.000	Ea.	1,975	535	2,510
Tamper switch (valve supervisory switch)	1.000	Ea.	294	55.50	349.50
TOTAL			10,942	4,498.50	15,440.50

D4020 310	Wet Standpipe Risers, Class I		COST PER FLOOR	
		MAT.	INST.	TOTAL
0550	Wet standpipe risers, Class I, steel, black, sch. 40, 10' height			
0560	4" diameter pipe, one floor	10,900	4,500	15,400
0580	Additional floors	2,700	1,375	4,075
0600	6" diameter pipe, one floor	14,500	7,750	22,250
0620	Additional floors	3,450	2,175	5,625
0640	8" diameter pipe, one floor	21,600	9,350	30,950
0660	Additional floors	4,450	2,625	7,075
0680				

Reference boxes: R211226-10, R211226-20

For supplemental customizable square foot estimating forms, visit: RSMeans.com/2024books in question. It is frequently accompanied by additional explanatory technical information describing the class of items. The **System Components** is a listing of the individual tasks that make up the assembly, including the quantity and unit of measure for each item, along with the cost of material and installation. The **Assemblies data** below lists prices for other similar systems with dimensional and/or size variations.

All of our assemblies costs represent the cost for the installing contractor. An allowance for profit has been added to all material, labor, and equipment rental costs. A markup for labor burdens, including workers' compensation, fixed overhead, and business overhead, is included with installation costs.

The information in RSMeans cost data represents a "national average" cost. This data should be modified to the project location using the **City Cost Indexes** or **Location Factors** tables found in the Reference Section.

Table Format

D20 Plumbing
D2010 Plumbing Fixtures

Example of Plumbing Cost Calculations: The bathroom system includes the individual fixtures such as bathtub, lavatory, shower and water closet. These fixtures are listed below as separate items merely as a checklist.

⑤ Unit of Measure

All RSMeans data: Assemblies include a typical **Unit of Measure** used for estimating that item. For instance, for continuous footings or foundation walls the unit is linear feet (L.F.). For spread footings the unit is each (Ea.). The estimator needs to take special care that the unit in the data matches the unit in the takeoff. Abbreviations and unit conversions can be found in the Reference Section.

⑥ Table Descriptions

Table descriptions work similar to Narrative Descriptions, except that if there is a blank in the column at a particular line number, read up to the description above in the same column.

D2010 951 — Plumbing Systems 20 Unit, 2 Story Apartment Building

	FIXTURE	SYSTEM	LINE	QUANTITY	UNIT	COST EACH MAT.	COST EACH INST.	COST EACH TOTAL
0440	Bathroom	D2010 926	3640	20	Ea.	97,000	63,500	160,500
0480	Bathtub							
0520	Booster pump[1]	not req'd.						
0560	Drinking fountain							
0600	Garbage disposal[1]	not incl.						
0660								
0680	Grease interceptor							
0720	Water heater	D2020 250	2140	1	Ea.	14,300	4,325	18,625
0760	Kitchen sink	D2010 410	1960	20	Ea.	36,500	22,400	58,900
0800	Laundry sink	D2010 420	1840	4	Ea.	6,450	4,425	10,875
0840	Lavatory							
0900								
0920	Roof drain, 1 floor	D2040 210	4200	2	Ea.	3,425	2,300	5,725
0960	Roof drain, add'l floor	D2040 210	4240	20	L.F.	410	580	990
1000	Service sink	D2010 440	4300	1	Ea.	4,850	1,550	6,400
1040	Sewage ejector[1]	not req'd.						
1080	Shower							
1100								
1160	Sump pump							
1200	Urinal							
1240	Water closet							
1320								
1360	SUB TOTAL					163,000	99,000	262,000
1481	Water controls	R221113-40		10%[2]		16,300	9,900	26,200
1521	Pipe & fittings[3]	R221113-40		30%[2]		48,900	29,700	78,600
1560	Other							
1601	Quality/complexity	R221113-40		15%[2]		24,400	14,900	39,300
1680								
1720	TOTAL					253,000	153,500	406,500
1741								

[1]**Note:** Cost for items such as booster pumps, backflow preventers, sewage ejectors, water meters, etc., may be obtained from the unit price section in the front of this data set.

Water controls, pipe and fittings, and the Quality/Complexity factors come from Table R221113-40.

[2]Percentage of subtotal.

[3]Long, easily discernable runs of pipe would be more accurately priced from Unit Price Section 22 11 13. If this is done, reduce the miscellaneous percentage in proportion.

RSMeans Data: Assemblies—How They Work (Continued)

Sample Estimate

This sample demonstrates the elements of an estimate, including a tally of the RSMeans Data lines. Published assemblies costs include all markups for labor burden and profit for the installing contractor. This estimate adds a summary of the markups applied by a general contractor on the installing contractor's work. These figures represent the total cost to the owner. The location factor with RSMeans Data is applied at the bottom of the estimate to adjust the cost of the work to a specific location.

Project Name:	Interior Fit-out, ABC Office			
Location:	Anywhere, USA		Date: 1/1/2024	STD
Assembly Number	Description	Qty.	Unit	Subtotal
❶ C1010 124 1200	Wood partition, 2 x 4 @ 16" OC w/5/8" FR gypsum board	560	S.F.	$3,802.40
C1020 114 1800	Metal door & frame, flush hollow core, 3'-0" x 7'-0"	2	Ea.	$3,200.00
C3010 230 0080	Painting, brushwork, primer & 2 coats	1,120	S.F.	$1,904.00
C3020 410 0140	Carpet, tufted, nylon, roll goods, 12' wide, 26 oz	240	S.F.	$715.20
C3030 210 6000	Acoustic ceilings, 24" x 48" tile, tee grid suspension	200	S.F.	$2,342.00
D5020 125 0560	Receptacles incl plate, box, conduit, wire, 20 A duplex	8	Ea.	$3,044.00
D5020 125 0720	Light switch incl plate, box, conduit, wire, 20 A single pole	2	Ea.	$737.00
D5020 210 0560	Fluorescent fixtures, recess mounted, 20 per 1000 SF	200	S.F.	$3,450.00
	Assembly Subtotal			**$19,194.60**
	Sales Tax @ ❷	5 %		$ 479.87
	General Requirements @ ❸	7 %		$ 1,343.62
	Subtotal A			**$21,018.09**
	GC Overhead @ ❹	5 %		$ 1,050.90
	Subtotal B			**$22,068.99**
	GC Profit @ ❺	5 %		$ 1,103.45
	Subtotal C			**$23,172.44**
	Adjusted by Location Factor ❻	112.4		$ 26,045.82
	Architects Fee @ ❼	8 %		$ 2,083.67
	Contingency @ ❽	15 %		$ 3,906.87
	Project Total Cost			**$ 32,036.36**

This estimate is based on an interactive spreadsheet. You are free to download it and adjust it to your methodology. A copy of this spreadsheet is available at **RSMeans.com/2024books**.

① Work Performed
The body of the estimate shows the RSMeans Data selected, including line numbers, a brief description of each item, its takeoff quantity and unit, and the total installed cost, including the installing contractor's overhead and profit.

② Sales Tax
If the work is subject to state or local sales taxes, the amount must be added to the estimate. In a conceptual estimate, it can be assumed that one half of the total represents material costs. Therefore, apply the sales tax rate to 50% of the assembly subtotal.

③ General Requirements
This item covers project-wide needs provided by the general contractor. These items vary by project but may include temporary facilities and utilities, security, testing, project cleanup, etc. In assemblies estimates a percentage is used—typically between 5% and 15% of project cost.

④ General Contractor Overhead
This entry represents the general contractor's markup on all work to cover project administration costs.

⑤ General Contractor Profit
This entry represents the General Contractor's profit on all work performed. The value included here can vary widely by project and is influenced by the General Contractor's perception of the project's financial risk and market conditions.

⑥ Location Factor
RSMeans published data are based on national average costs. If necessary, adjust the total cost of the project using a location factor from the "Location Factor" table or the "City Cost Indexes" table found in the Reference Section. Use location factors if the work is general, covering the work of multiple trades. If the work is by a single trade (e.g., masonry), use the more specific data found in the City Cost Indexes.

To adjust costs by location factors, multiply the base cost by the factor and divide by 100.

⑦ Architect's Fee
If appropriate, add the design cost to the project estimate. These fees vary based on project complexity and size. Typical design and engineering fees can be found in the Reference Section.

⑧ Contingency
A factor for contingency may be added to any estimate to represent the cost of unknowns that may occur between the time that the estimate is performed and the time the project is constructed. The amount of the allowance will depend on the stage of design at which the estimate is done, as well as the contractor's assessment of the risk involved.

D Services

Same Data. Simplified.

Enjoy the convenience and efficiency of accessing your costs anywhere:
- **Skip the multiplier** by setting your location
- **Quickly search**, edit, favorite and share costs
- **Stay on top of price changes** with automatic updates

Discover more at rsmeans.com/online

No part of this cost data may be reproduced, stored in a retrieval system, or transmitted in any form or by any means without prior written permission of Gordian.

D20 Plumbing

D2010 Plumbing Fixtures

Systems are complete with trim seat and rough-in (supply, waste and vent) for connection to supply branches and waste mains.

One Piece Wall Hung | Supply | Waste/Vent | Floor Mount

System Components	QUANTITY	UNIT	MAT.	INST.	TOTAL
SYSTEM D2010 110 1880					
WATER CLOSET, VITREOUS CHINA					
TANK TYPE, WALL HUNG, TWO PIECE					
Water closet, tank type vit china wall hung 2 pc. w/seat supply & stop	1.000	Ea.	510	300	810
Pipe Steel galvanized, schedule 40, threaded, 2" diam.	4.000	L.F.	108	100	208
Pipe, CI soil, no hub, cplg 10' OC, hanger 5' OC, 4" diam.	2.000	L.F.	57	55	112
Pipe, coupling, standard coupling, CI soil, no hub, 4" diam.	2.000	Ea.	61	97	158
Copper tubing type L solder joint, hangar 10' O.C., 1/2" diam.	6.000	L.F.	24.36	65.70	90.06
Wrought copper 90° elbow for solder joints 1/2" diam.	2.000	Ea.	5.48	89	94.48
Wrought copper Tee for solder joints 1/2" diam.	1.000	Ea.	3.82	68.50	72.32
Supports/carrier, water closet, siphon jet, horiz, single, 4" waste	1.000	Ea.	1,575	167	1,742
TOTAL			2,344.66	942.20	3,286.86

D2010 110	Water Closet Systems		MAT.	INST.	TOTAL
1800	Water closet, vitreous china				
1840	Tank type, wall hung				
1880	Close coupled two piece	R221113 -40	2,350	940	3,290
1920	Floor mount, one piece		1,700	1,000	2,700
1960	One piece low profile	R224000 -30	1,675	1,000	2,675
2000	Two piece close coupled		965	1,000	1,965
2040	Bowl only with flush valve				
2080	Wall hung		3,200	1,075	4,275
2120	Floor mount		1,150	1,025	2,175
2160	Floor mount, ADA compliant with 18" high bowl		1,200	1,050	2,250

D20 Plumbing

D2010 Plumbing Fixtures

Systems are complete with trim, seat, flush valve and rough-in (supply, waste and vent) for connection to supply branches and waste mains.

System Components	QUANTITY	UNIT	COST EACH MAT.	COST EACH INST.	COST EACH TOTAL
SYSTEM D2010 120 1760					
WATER CLOSETS, BATTERY MOUNT, WALL HUNG, SIDE BY SIDE, FIRST CLOSET					
Water closet, bowl only w/flush valve, seat, wall hung	1.000	Ea.	1,175	276	1,451
Pipe, Cl soil, no hub, cplg 10' OC, hanger 5' OC, 4" diam.	3.000	L.F.	85.50	82.50	168
Coupling, standard, Cl, soil, no hub, 4" diam.	2.000	Ea.	61	97	158
Copper tubing, type L, solder joints, hangers 10' OC, 1" diam.	6.000	L.F.	51.60	78.30	129.90
Copper tubing, type DWV, solder joints, hangers 10'OC, 2" diam.	6.000	L.F.	123	120	243
Wrought copper 90° elbow for solder joints 1" diam.	1.000	Ea.	14.80	55.50	70.30
Wrought copper Tee for solder joints 1" diam.	1.000	Ea.	16	89	105
Support/carrier, siphon jet, horiz, adjustable single, 4" pipe	1.000	Ea.	1,575	167	1,742
Valve, gate, bronze, 125 lb, NRS, soldered 1" diam.	1.000	Ea.	194	47	241
Wrought copper, DWV, 90° elbow, 2" diam.	1.000	Ea.	129	89	218
TOTAL			3,424.90	1,101.30	4,526.20

D2010 120	Water Closets, Group		MAT.	INST.	TOTAL
1760	Water closets, battery mount, wall hung, side by side, first closet	R221113 -40	3,425	1,100	4,525
1800	Each additional water closet, add		3,250	1,050	4,300
3000	Back to back, first pair of closets	R224000 -30	6,025	1,475	7,500
3100	Each additional pair of closets, back to back		5,850	1,450	7,300
9000	Back to back, first pair of closets, auto sensor flush valve, 1.28 gpf		6,525	1,575	8,100
9100	Ea additional pair of cls, back to back, auto sensor flush valve, 1.28 gpf		6,275	1,475	7,750

D20 Plumbing

D2010 Plumbing Fixtures

Systems are complete with trim, flush valve and rough-in (supply, waste and vent) for connection to supply branches and waste mains.

Stall Type

Supply   Waste/Vent

Wall Hung

System Components	QUANTITY	UNIT	COST EACH		
			MAT.	INST.	TOTAL
SYSTEM D2010 210 2000					
URINAL, VITREOUS CHINA, WALL HUNG					
Urinal, wall hung, vitreous china, incl. hanger	1.000	Ea.	475	535	1,010
Pipe, steel, galvanized, schedule 40, threaded, 1-1/2" diam.	5.000	L.F.	100	100	200
Copper tubing type DWV, solder joint, hangers 10' OC, 2" diam.	3.000	L.F.	61.50	60	121.50
Combination Y & 1/8 bend for CI soil pipe, no hub, 3" diam.	1.000	Ea.	45		45
Pipe, cast iron soil, no hub, 3" diameter, includes couplings 10' OC, clevi	4.000	L.F.	88	100	188
Pipe coupling standard, CI soil, no hub, 3" diam.	2.000	Ea.	46	84	130
Copper tubing type L, solder joint, hanger 10' OC 3/4" diam.	5.000	L.F.	29.75	58.50	88.25
Wrought copper 90° elbow for solder joints 3/4" diam.	1.000	Ea.	6.05	47	53.05
Wrought copper Tee for solder joints, 3/4" diam.	1.000	Ea.	11.10	74	85.10
TOTAL			862.40	1,058.50	1,920.90

D2010 210	Urinal Systems		COST EACH		
			MAT.	INST.	TOTAL
2000	Urinal, vitreous china, wall hung	R224000 -30	860	1,050	1,910
2001	Urinal, vitreous china, wall hung	R224000 -30	860	1,050	1,910
2040	Stall type		1,900	1,275	3,175

D20 Plumbing

D2010 Plumbing Fixtures

Systems are complete with trim, flush valve and rough-in (supply, waste and vent) for connection to supply branches and waste mains.

Side by Side   Back to Back

  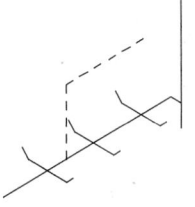

Waste/Vent   Supply   Supply   Waste/Vent

System Components	QUANTITY	UNIT	COST EACH MAT.	COST EACH INST.	COST EACH TOTAL
SYSTEM D2010 220 1760					
URINALS, BATTERY MOUNT, WALL HUNG, SIDE BY SIDE, FIRST URINAL					
Urinal, wall hung, vitreous china, with hanger & trim	1.000	Ea.	475	535	1,010
No hub cast iron soil pipe, 3" diameter	4.000	L.F.	88	100	188
No hub cast iron sanitary tee, 3" diameter	1.000	Ea.	45		45
No hub coupling, 3" diameter	2.000	Ea.	46	84	130
Copper tubing, type L, 3/4" diameter	5.000	L.F.	29.75	58.50	88.25
Copper tubing, type DWV, 2" diameter	2.000	L.F.	41	40	81
Copper 90° elbow, 3/4" diameter	2.000	Ea.	12.10	94	106.10
Copper 90° elbow, type DWV, 2" diameter	2.000	Ea.	258	178	436
Galvanized steel pipe, 1-1/2" diameter	5.000	L.F.	100	100	200
Cast iron drainage elbow, 90°, 1-1/2" diameter	1.000	Ea.	11.10	74	85.10
TOTAL			1,105.95	1,263.50	2,369.45

D2010 220	Urinal Systems, Battery Mount		MAT.	INST.	TOTAL
1760	Urinals, battery mount, side by side, first urinal	R221113 -40	1,100	1,275	2,375
1800	Each additional urinal, add		1,050	1,150	2,200
2000	Back to back, first pair of urinals	R224000 -30	1,875	1,925	3,800
2100	Each additional pair of urinals, back to back		1,300	1,525	2,825

For customer support on your Plumbing Costs with RSMeans Data call 800.448.8182

D20 Plumbing

D2010 Plumbing Fixtures

Systems are complete with trim and rough-in (supply, waste and vent) to connect to supply branches and waste mains.

Vanity Top

Supply   Waste/Vent

Wall Hung

System Components	QUANTITY	UNIT	COST EACH MAT.	COST EACH INST.	COST EACH TOTAL
SYSTEM D2010 310 1560					
LAVATORY W/TRIM, VANITY TOP, P.E. ON C.I., 20" X 18"					
Lavatory w/trim, PE on Cl, white, vanity top, 20" x 18" oval	1.000	Ea.	490	250	740
Pipe, steel, galvanized, schedule 40, threaded, 1-1/4" diam.	4.000	L.F.	68.20	71.80	140
Copper tubing type DWV, solder joint, hanger 10' OC 1-1/4" diam.	4.000	L.F.	46.60	59.20	105.80
Wrought copper DWV, Tee, sanitary, 1-1/4" diam.	1.000	Ea.	107	98.50	205.50
P trap w/cleanout, 20 ga., 1-1/4" diam.	1.000	Ea.	294	49.50	343.50
Copper tubing type L, solder joint, hanger 10' OC 1/2" diam.	10.000	L.F.	40.60	109.50	150.10
Wrought copper 90° elbow for solder joints 1/2" diam.	2.000	Ea.	5.48	89	94.48
Wrought copper Tee for solder joints, 1/2" diam.	2.000	Ea.	7.64	137	144.64
Stop, chrome, angle supply, 1/2" diam.	2.000	Ea.	32.20	81	113.20
TOTAL			1,091.72	945.50	2,037.22

D2010 310	Lavatory Systems		COST EACH MAT.	COST EACH INST.	COST EACH TOTAL
1560	Lavatory w/trim, vanity top, PE on Cl, 20" x 18", Vanity top by others.	R221113-40	1,100	945	2,045
1600	19" x 16" oval		910	945	1,855
1640	18" round		1,375	945	2,320
1680	Cultured marble, 19" x 17"		815	945	1,760
1720	25" x 19"		845	945	1,790
1760	Stainless, self-rimming, 25" x 22"		840	945	1,785
1800	17" x 22"	R224000-30	960	945	1,905
1840	Steel enameled, 20" x 17"		780	970	1,750
1880	19" round		775	970	1,745
1920	Vitreous china, 20" x 16"		825	990	1,815
1960	19" x 16"		765	990	1,755
2000	22" x 13"		835	990	1,825
2040	Wall hung, PE on Cl, 18" x 15"		1,100	1,050	2,150
2080	19" x 17"		1,200	1,050	2,250
2120	20" x 18"		1,225	1,050	2,275
2160	Vitreous china, 18" x 15"		965	1,075	2,040
2200	19" x 17"		895	1,075	1,970
2240	24" x 20"		905	1,075	1,980
2300	20" x 27", handicap		1,325	1,150	2,475

D20 Plumbing

D2010 Plumbing Fixtures

Systems are complete with trim, flush valve and rough-in (supply, waste and vent) for connection to supply branches and waste mains.

Side by Side

Back to Back

Waste/Vent

Supply
(Two supply systems required)

Supply
(Two supply systems required)

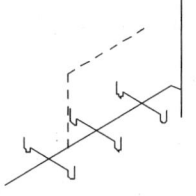
Waste/Vent

System Components	QUANTITY	UNIT	COST EACH MAT.	COST EACH INST.	COST EACH TOTAL
SYSTEM D2010 320 1760					
LAVATORIES, BATTERY MOUNT, WALL HUNG, SIDE BY SIDE, FIRST LAVATORY					
Lavatory w/trim wall hung PE on CI 20" x 18"	1.000	Ea.	525	200	725
Stop, chrome, angle supply, 3/8" diameter	2.000	Ea.	28.20	74	102.20
Concealed arm support	1.000	Ea.	2,075	148	2,223
P trap w/cleanout, 20 ga. C.P., 1-1/4" diameter	1.000	Ea.	39	49.50	88.50
Copper tubing, type L, 1/2" diameter	10.000	L.F.	40.60	109.50	150.10
Copper tubing, type DWV, 1-1/4" diameter	4.000	L.F.	46.60	59.20	105.80
Copper 90° elbow, 1/2" diameter	2.000	Ea.	5.48	89	94.48
Copper tee, 1/2" diameter	2.000	Ea.	7.64	137	144.64
DWV copper sanitary tee, 1-1/4" diameter	2.000	Ea.	214	197	411
Galvanized steel pipe, 1-1/4" diameter	4.000	L.F.	68.20	71.80	140
Black cast iron 90° elbow, 1-1/4" diameter	1.000	Ea.	9.20	72.50	81.70
TOTAL			3,058.92	1,207.50	4,266.42

D2010 320	Lavatory Systems, Battery Mount		COST EACH MAT.	COST EACH INST.	COST EACH TOTAL
1760	Lavatories, battery mount, side by side, first lavatory	R221113 -40	3,050	1,200	4,250
1800	Each additional lavatory, add		2,875	840	3,715
2000	Back to back, first pair of lavatories		2,975	1,925	4,900
2100	Each additional pair of lavatories, back to back		2,825	1,575	4,400

For customer support on your Plumbing Costs with RSMeans Data call 800.448.8182.

D20 Plumbing

D2010 Plumbing Fixtures

Systems are complete with trim and rough-in (supply, waste and vent) to connect to supply branches and waste mains.

Countertop Single Bowl

Supply

Waste/Vent

Countertop Double Bowl

System Components	QUANTITY	UNIT	COST EACH		
			MAT.	INST.	TOTAL
SYSTEM D2010 410 1720					
KITCHEN SINK W/TRIM, COUNTERTOP, P.E. ON C.I., 24" X 21", SINGLE BOWL					
Kitchen sink, counter top style, PE on CI, 24" x 21" single bowl	1.000	Ea.	610	286	896
Pipe, steel, galvanized, schedule 40, threaded, 1-1/4" diam.	4.000	L.F.	68.20	71.80	140
Copper tubing, type DWV, solder, hangers 10' OC 1-1/2" diam.	6.000	L.F.	87	98.70	185.70
Wrought copper, DWV, Tee, sanitary, 1-1/2" diam.	1.000	Ea.	133	111	244
P trap, standard, copper, 1-1/2" diam.	1.000	Ea.	224	52.50	276.50
Copper tubing, type L, solder joints, hangers 10' OC 1/2" diam.	10.000	L.F.	40.60	109.50	150.10
Wrought copper 90° elbow for solder joints 1/2" diam.	2.000	Ea.	5.48	89	94.48
Wrought copper Tee for solder joints, 1/2" diam.	2.000	Ea.	7.64	137	144.64
Stop, angle supply, chrome, 1/2" CTS	2.000	Ea.	32.20	81	113.20
TOTAL			1,208.12	1,036.50	2,244.62

D2010 410	Kitchen Sink Systems	COST EACH		
		MAT.	INST.	TOTAL
1720	Kitchen sink w/trim, countertop, PE on CI, 24"x21", single bowl	1,200	1,025	2,225
1760	30" x 21" single bowl	1,750	1,025	2,775
1800	32" x 21" double bowl	1,100	1,125	2,225
1880	Stainless steel, 19" x 18" single bowl	1,350	1,025	2,375
1920	25" x 22" single bowl	1,450	1,025	2,475
1960	33" x 22" double bowl	1,825	1,125	2,950
2000	43" x 22" double bowl	2,050	1,125	3,175
2040	44" x 22" triple bowl	1,950	1,175	3,125
2080	44" x 24" corner double bowl	1,575	1,125	2,700
2120	Steel, enameled, 24" x 21" single bowl	1,175	1,025	2,200
2160	32" x 21" double bowl	1,200	1,125	2,325
2240	Raised deck, PE on CI, 32" x 21", dual level, double bowl	1,225	1,425	2,650
2280	42" x 21" dual level, triple bowl	1,850	1,550	3,400

D20 Plumbing

D2010 Plumbing Fixtures

Single Compartment Sink

Supply Waste/Vent

Double Compartment Sink

Systems are complete with trim and rough-in (supply, waste and vent) to connect to supply branches and waste mains.

System Components	QUANTITY	UNIT	COST EACH		
			MAT.	INST.	TOTAL
SYSTEM D2010 420 1760					
LAUNDRY SINK W/TRIM, PE ON CI, BLACK IRON FRAME					
24" X 20" OD, SINGLE COMPARTMENT					
Laundry sink PE on CI w/trim & frame, 24" x 21" OD, 1 compartment	1.000	Ea.	765	266	1,031
Pipe, steel, galvanized, schedule 40, threaded, 1-1/4" diam	4.000	L.F.	68.20	71.80	140
Copper tubing, type DWV, solder joint, hanger 10' OC 1-1/2"diam	6.000	L.F.	87	98.70	185.70
Wrought copper, DWV, Tee, sanitary, 1-1/2" diam	1.000	Ea.	133	111	244
P trap, standard, copper, 1-1/2" diam	1.000	Ea.	224	52.50	276.50
Copper tubing type L, solder joints, hangers 10' OC, 1/2" diam	10.000	L.F.	40.60	109.50	150.10
Wrought copper 90° elbow for solder joints 1/2" diam	2.000	Ea.	5.48	89	94.48
Wrought copper Tee for solder joints, 1/2" diam	2.000	Ea.	7.64	137	144.64
Stop, angle supply, 1/2" diam	2.000	Ea.	32.20	81	113.20
TOTAL			1,363.12	1,016.50	2,379.62

D2010 420		Laundry Sink Systems		COST EACH		
				MAT.	INST.	TOTAL
1740	Laundry sink w/trim, PE on CI, black iron frame		R221113 -40			
1760		24" x 20", single compartment		1,375	1,025	2,400
1800		24" x 23" single compartment	R224000 -30	1,450	1,025	2,475
1840		48" x 21" double compartment		1,600	1,100	2,700
1920	Molded stone, on wall, 22" x 21" single compartment			815	1,025	1,840
1960		45"x 21" double compartment		1,075	1,100	2,175
2040	Plastic, on wall or legs, 18" x 23" single compartment			775	995	1,770
2080		20" x 24" single compartment		800	995	1,795
2120		36" x 23" double compartment		895	1,075	1,970
2160		40" x 24" double compartment		975	1,075	2,050

D20 Plumbing

D2010 Plumbing Fixtures

Corrosion resistant laboratory sink systems are complete with trim and rough-in (supply, waste and vent) to connect to supply branches and waste mains.

Laboratory Sink

Supply

Waste/Vent

Polypropylene Cup Sink

System Components	QUANTITY	UNIT	COST EACH		
			MAT.	INST.	TOTAL
SYSTEM D2010 430 1600					
LABORATORY SINK W/TRIM, STAINLESS STEEL, SINGLE BOWL					
DOUBLE DRAINBOARD, 54" X 24" O.D.					
Sink w/trim, stainless steel, 1 bowl, 2 drainboards, 54" x 24" OD	1.000	Ea.	1,600	535	2,135
Pipe, polypropylene, schedule 40, acid resistant 1-1/2" diam.	10.000	L.F.	181.50	235	416.50
Tee, sanitary, polypropylene, acid resistant, non-pressure, electrofusion j	1.000	Ea.	55.50	89	144.50
P trap, polypropylene, acid resistant, 1-1/2" diam.	1.000	Ea.	109	52.50	161.50
Copper tubing type L, solder joint, hanger 10' O.C. 1/2" diam.	10.000	L.F.	40.60	109.50	150.10
Wrought copper 90° elbow for solder joints 1/2" diam.	2.000	Ea.	5.48	89	94.48
Wrought copper Tee for solder joints, 1/2" diam.	2.000	Ea.	7.64	137	144.64
Stop, angle supply, chrome, 1/2" diam.	2.000	Ea.	32.20	81	113.20
TOTAL			2,031.92	1,328	3,359.92

D2010 430	Laboratory Sink Systems	COST EACH		
		MAT.	INST.	TOTAL
1580	Laboratory sink w/trim,			
1590	Stainless steel, single bowl,			
1600	Double drainboard, 54" x 24" O.D.	2,025	1,325	3,350
1640	Single drainboard, 47" x 24"O.D.	1,600	1,325	2,925
1670	Stainless steel, double bowl,			
1680	70" x 24" O.D.	2,200	1,325	3,525
1750	Polyethylene, single bowl,			
1760	Flanged, 14-1/2" x 14-1/2" O.D.	755	1,200	1,955
1800	18-1/2" x 18-1/2" O.D.	885	1,200	2,085
1840	23-1/2" x 20-1/2" O.D.	900	1,200	2,100
1920	Polypropylene, cup sink, oval, 7" x 4" O.D.	655	1,050	1,705
1960	10" x 4-1/2" O.D.	695	1,050	1,745

D20 Plumbing

D2010 Plumbing Fixtures

Wall Hung

Supply Waste/Vent

Corrosion resistant laboratory sink systems are complete with trim and rough-in (supply, waste and vent) to connect to supply branches and waste mains.

Corner, Floor

System Components	QUANTITY	UNIT	COST EACH		
			MAT.	INST.	TOTAL
SYSTEM D2010 440 4260					
SERVICE SINK, PE ON CI, CORNER FLOOR, 28"X28", W/RIM GUARD & TRIM					
Service sink, corner floor, PE on CI, 28" x 28", w/rim guard & trim	1.000	Ea.	1,750	365	2,115
Copper tubing type DWV, solder joint, hanger 10'OC 3" diam.	6.000	L.F.	252	165	417
Copper tubing type DWV, solder joint, hanger 10'OC 2" diam	4.000	L.F.	82	80	162
Wrought copper DWV, Tee, sanitary, 3" diam.	1.000	Ea.	765	228	993
P trap with cleanout & slip joint, copper 3" diam	1.000	Ea.	985	81	1,066
Copper tubing, type L, solder joints, hangers 10' OC, 1/2" diam	10.000	L.F.	40.60	109.50	150.10
Wrought copper 90° elbow for solder joints 1/2" diam	2.000	Ea.	5.48	89	94.48
Wrought copper Tee for solder joints, 1/2" diam	2.000	Ea.	7.64	137	144.64
Stop, angle supply, chrome, 1/2" diam	2.000	Ea.	32.20	81	113.20
TOTAL			3,919.92	1,335.50	5,255.42

D2010 440		Service Sink Systems		COST EACH		
				MAT.	INST.	TOTAL
4260	Service sink w/trim, PE on CI, corner floor, 28" x 28", w/rim guard		R221113 -40	3,925	1,325	5,250
4300	Wall hung w/rim guard, 22" x 18"			4,850	1,550	6,400
4340	24" x 20"		R224000 -30	5,400	1,550	6,950
4380	Vitreous china, wall hung 22" x 20"			4,850	1,550	6,400

D20 Plumbing

D2010 Plumbing Fixtures

Systems are complete with trim and rough-in (supply, waste and vent) to connect to supply branches and waste mains.

Recessed Bathtub   Supply   Waste/Vent   Corner Bathtub

System Components	QUANTITY	UNIT	COST EACH		
			MAT.	INST.	TOTAL
SYSTEM D2010 510 2000					
BATHTUB, RECESSED, PORCELAIN ENAMEL ON CAST IRON,, 48" x 42"					
Bath tub, porcelain enamel on cast iron, w/fittings, 48" x 42"	1.000	Ea.	4,200	400	4,600
Pipe, steel, galvanized, schedule 40, threaded, 1-1/4" diam.	4.000	L.F.	68.20	71.80	140
Pipe, CI no hub soil w/couplings 10' OC, hangers 5' OC, 4" diam.	3.000	L.F.	85.50	82.50	168
Combination Y and 1/8 bend for C.I. soil pipe, no hub, 4" pipe size	1.000	Ea.	117		117
Drum trap, 3" x 5", copper, 1-1/2" diam.	1.000	Ea.	445	55.50	500.50
Copper tubing type L, solder joints, hangers 10' OC 1/2" diam.	10.000	L.F.	40.60	109.50	150.10
Wrought copper 90° elbow, solder joints, 1/2" diam.	2.000	Ea.	5.48	89	94.48
Wrought copper Tee, solder joints, 1/2" diam.	2.000	Ea.	7.64	137	144.64
Stop, angle supply, 1/2" diameter	2.000	Ea.	32.20	81	113.20
Copper tubing type DWV, solder joints, hanger 10' OC 1-1/2" diam.	3.000	L.F.	43.50	49.35	92.85
Pipe coupling, standard, C.I. soil no hub, 4" pipe size	2.000	Ea.	61	97	158
TOTAL			5,106.12	1,172.65	6,278.77

D2010 510	Bathtub Systems		COST EACH		
			MAT.	INST.	TOTAL
2000	Bathtub, recessed, P.E. on CI., 48" x 42"	R224000 -30	5,100	1,175	6,275
2040	72" x 36"		6,800	1,300	8,100
2080	Mat bottom, 5' long	R221113 -40	2,875	1,150	4,025
2120	5'-6" long		3,325	1,175	4,500
2160	Corner, 48" x 42"		4,725	1,150	5,875
2200	Formed steel, enameled, 4'-6" long		1,750	1,050	2,800

D20 Plumbing

D2010 Plumbing Fixtures

Circular Fountain

Supply

Semi-Circular Fountain

Waste/Vent

Systems are complete with trim, flush valve and rough-in (supply, waste and vent) for connection to supply branches and waste mains.

System Components	QUANTITY	UNIT	COST EACH		
			MAT.	INST.	TOTAL
SYSTEM D2010 610 1760					
GROUP WASH FOUNTAIN, PRECAST TERRAZZO					
CIRCULAR, 36" DIAMETER					
Wash fountain, group, precast terrazzo, foot control 36" diam.	1.000	Ea.	8,975	830	9,805
Copper tubing type DWV, solder joint, hanger 10' OC, 2" diam.	10.000	L.F.	205	200	405
P trap, standard, copper, 2" diam.	1.000	Ea.	345	59	404
Wrought copper, Tee, sanitary, 2" diam.	1.000	Ea.	182	127	309
Copper tubing type L, solder joint, hanger 10' OC 1/2" diam.	20.000	L.F.	81.20	219	300.20
Wrought copper 90° elbow for solder joints 1/2" diam.	3.000	Ea.	8.22	133.50	141.72
Wrought copper Tee for solder joints, 1/2" diam.	2.000	Ea.	7.64	137	144.64
TOTAL			9,804.06	1,705.50	11,509.56

D2010 610	Group Wash Fountain Systems	COST EACH		
		MAT.	INST.	TOTAL
1740	Group wash fountain, precast terrazzo			
1760	Circular, 36" diameter	9,800	1,700	11,500
1800	54" diameter	13,900	1,875	15,775
1840	Semi-circular, 36" diameter	8,150	1,700	9,850
1880	54" diameter	14,300	1,875	16,175
1960	Stainless steel, circular, 36" diameter	8,725	1,575	10,300
2000	54" diameter	10,700	1,775	12,475
2040	Semi-circular, 36" diameter	7,275	1,575	8,850
2080	54" diameter	7,750	1,775	9,525
2160	Thermoplastic, circular, 36" diameter	6,325	1,300	7,625
2200	54" diameter	6,100	1,500	7,600
2240	Semi-circular, 36" diameter	6,775	1,300	8,075
2280	54" diameter	6,850	1,500	8,350

D20 Plumbing

D2010 Plumbing Fixtures

Systems are complete with trim and rough-in (supply, waste and vent) for connection to supply branches and waste mains.

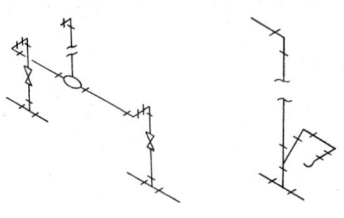

Three Wall   Supply   Waste/Vent   Corner Angle

System Components	QUANTITY	UNIT	COST EACH MAT.	COST EACH INST.	COST EACH TOTAL
SYSTEM D2010 710 1560					
SHOWER, STALL, BAKED ENAMEL, MOLDED STONE RECEPTOR, 30" SQUARE					
Shower stall, enameled steel, molded stone receptor, 30" square	1.000	Ea.	1,700	305	2,005
Copper tubing type DWV, solder joints, hangers 10' OC, 2" diam.	6.000	L.F.	87	98.70	185.70
Wrought copper DWV, Tee, sanitary, 2" diam.	1.000	Ea.	133	111	244
Trap, standard, copper, 2" diam.	1.000	Ea.	224	52.50	276.50
Copper tubing type L, solder joint, hanger 10' OC 1/2" diam.	16.000	L.F.	64.96	175.20	240.16
Wrought copper 90° elbow for solder joints 1/2" diam.	3.000	Ea.	8.22	133.50	141.72
Wrought copper Tee for solder joints, 1/2" diam.	2.000	Ea.	7.64	137	144.64
Stop and waste, straightway, bronze, solder joint 1/2" diam.	2.000	Ea.	52	74	126
TOTAL			2,276.82	1,086.90	3,363.72

D2010 710	Shower Systems		COST EACH MAT.	COST EACH INST.	COST EACH TOTAL
1560	Shower, stall, baked enamel, molded stone receptor, 30" square	R221113-40	2,275	1,075	3,350
1600	32" square		2,025	1,100	3,125
1640	Terrazzo receptor, 32" square	R224000-30	2,250	1,100	3,350
1680	36" square		2,775	1,125	3,900
1720	36" corner angle		3,025	460	3,485
1800	Fiberglass one piece, three walls, 32" square		1,200	1,075	2,275
1840	36" square		1,250	1,075	2,325
1880	Polypropylene, molded stone receptor, 30" square		1,525	1,575	3,100
1920	32" square		1,550	1,575	3,125
1960	Built-in head, arm, bypass, stops and handles		145	410	555
2050	Shower, stainless steel panels, handicap				
2100	w/fixed and handheld head, control valves, grab bar, and seat		6,025	4,900	10,925
2500	Shower, group with six heads, thermostatic mix valves & balancing valve		14,800	1,200	16,000
2520	Five heads		10,500	1,100	11,600

D20 Plumbing

D2010 Plumbing Fixtures

Wall Mounted, No Back

Supply   Waste/Vent

Wall Mounted, Low Back

Systems are complete with trim and rough-in (supply, waste and vent) to connect to supply branches and waste mains.

System Components	QUANTITY	UNIT	COST EACH MAT.	COST EACH INST.	COST EACH TOTAL
SYSTEM D2010 810 1800 DRINKING FOUNTAIN, ONE BUBBLER, WALL MOUNTED NON RECESSED, BRONZE, NO BACK					
Drinking fountain, wall mount, bronze, 1 bubbler	1.000	Ea.	3,725	222	3,947
Copper tubing, type L, solder joint, hanger 10' OC 3/8" diam.	5.000	L.F.	16.35	53	69.35
Stop, supply, straight, chrome, 3/8" diam.	1.000	Ea.	24	37	61
Wrought copper 90° elbow for solder joints 3/8" diam.	1.000	Ea.	7.60	40.50	48.10
Wrought copper Tee for solder joints, 3/8" diam.	1.000	Ea.	12.55	63.50	76.05
Copper tubing, type DWV, solder joint, hanger 10' OC 1-1/4" diam.	4.000	L.F.	46.60	59.20	105.80
P trap, standard, copper drainage, 1-1/4" diam.	1.000	Ea.	294	49.50	343.50
Wrought copper, DWV, Tee, sanitary, 1-1/4" diam.	1.000	Ea.	107	98.50	205.50
TOTAL			4,233.10	623.20	4,856.30

D2010 810	Drinking Fountain Systems		MAT.	INST.	TOTAL
1740	Drinking fountain, one bubbler, wall mounted				
1760	Non recessed	R221113-40			
1800	Bronze, no back	R224000-30	4,225	625	4,850
1840	Cast iron, enameled, low back		2,225	625	2,850
1880	Fiberglass, 12" back		4,250	625	4,875
1920	Stainless steel, no back		1,625	625	2,250
1960	Semi-recessed, poly marble		1,975	625	2,600
2040	Stainless steel		2,700	625	3,325
2080	Vitreous china		2,150	625	2,775
2120	Full recessed, poly marble		3,225	625	3,850
2200	Stainless steel		2,575	625	3,200
2240	Floor mounted, pedestal type, aluminum		4,150	845	4,995
2320	Bronze		4,850	845	5,695
2360	Stainless steel		3,575	845	4,420

For customer support on your Plumbing Costs with RSMeans Data call 800.448.8182.

D20 Plumbing

D2010 Plumbing Fixtures

Systems are complete with trim and rough-in (supply, waste and vent) for connection to supply branches and waste mains.

Wall Hung | Supply | Waste/Vent | Floor Mounted

System Components	QUANTITY	UNIT	COST EACH MAT.	COST EACH INST.	TOTAL
SYSTEM D2010 820 1840					
WATER COOLER, ELECTRIC, SELF CONTAINED, WALL HUNG, 8.2 G.P.H.					
Water cooler, wall mounted, non-recessed, 8.2 GPH	1.000	Ea.	1,425	400	1,825
Copper tubing type DWV, solder joint, hanger 10' OC 1-1/4" diam.	4.000	L.F.	46.60	59.20	105.80
Wrought copper DWV, Tee, sanitary 1-1/4" diam.	1.000	Ea.	107	98.50	205.50
P trap, copper drainage, 1-1/4" diam.	1.000	Ea.	294	49.50	343.50
Copper tubing type L, solder joint, hanger 10' OC 3/8" diam.	5.000	L.F.	16.35	53	69.35
Wrought copper 90° elbow for solder joints 3/8" diam.	1.000	Ea.	7.60	40.50	48.10
Tee, copper, wrought, copper x copper, 3/8"	1.000	Ea.	12.55	63.50	76.05
Stop and waste, straightway, bronze, solder, 3/8" diam.	1.000	Ea.	24	37	61
TOTAL			1,933.10	801.20	2,734.30

D2010 820	Water Cooler Systems		COST EACH MAT.	INST.	TOTAL
1840	Water cooler, electric, wall hung, 8.2 G.P.H.		1,925	800	2,725
1880	Dual height, 14.3 G.P.H.	R221113 -40	3,650	820	4,470
1920	Wheelchair type, 7.5 G.P.H.		1,975	800	2,775
1960	Semi recessed, 8.1 G.P.H.	R224000 -30	1,800	800	2,600
2000	Full recessed, 8 G.P.H.		3,675	855	4,530
2040	Floor mounted, 14.3 G.P.H.		2,025	695	2,720
2080	Dual height, 14.3 G.P.H.		2,425	845	3,270
2120	Refrigerated compartment type, 1.5 G.P.H.		2,875	695	3,570

D20 Plumbing

D2010 Plumbing Fixtures

Two Fixture Bathroom Systems consisting of a lavatory, water closet, and rough-in service piping.
- Prices for plumbing and fixtures only.

*Common wall is with an adjacent bathroom.

System Components	QUANTITY	UNIT	COST EACH MAT.	INST.	TOTAL
SYSTEM D2010 920 1180					
BATHROOM, LAVATORY & WATER CLOSET, 2 WALL PLUMBING, STAND ALONE					
Water closet, two piece, close coupled	1.000	Ea.	276	300	576
Water closet, rough-in waste & vent	1.000	Set	625	525	1,150
Lavatory w/ftngs., wall hung, white, PE on CI, 20" x 18"	1.000	Ea.	525	200	725
Lavatory, rough-in waste & vent	1.000	Set	695	965	1,660
Copper tubing type L, solder joint, hanger 10' OC 1/2" diam.	10.000	L.F.	40.60	109.50	150.10
Pipe, steel, galvanized, schedule 40, threaded, 2" diam.	12.000	L.F.	324	300	624
Pipe, CI soil, no hub, coupling 10' OC, hanger 5' OC, 4" diam.	7.000	L.F.	143.50	203	346.50
TOTAL			2,629.10	2,602.50	5,231.60

D2010 920	Two Fixture Bathroom, Two Wall Plumbing		COST EACH MAT.	INST.	TOTAL
1180	Bathroom, lavatory & water closet, 2 wall plumbing, stand alone	R221113 -40	2,625	2,600	5,225
1200	Share common plumbing wall*		2,325	2,250	4,575

D2010 922	Two Fixture Bathroom, One Wall Plumbing		COST EACH MAT.	INST.	TOTAL
2220	Bathroom, lavatory & water closet, one wall plumbing, stand alone	R221113 -40	2,425	2,350	4,775
2240	Share common plumbing wall*		2,125	2,000	4,125
2260		R224000 -30			
2280					

For customer support on your Plumbing Costs with RSMeans Data call 800.448.8182.

D20 Plumbing

D2010 Plumbing Fixtures

Three Fixture Bathroom Systems consisting of a lavatory, water closet, bathtub or shower and rough-in service piping.

- Prices for plumbing and fixtures only.

*Common wall is with an adjacent bathroom.

System Components	QUANTITY	UNIT	COST EACH		
			MAT.	INST.	TOTAL
SYSTEM D2010 924 1170					
BATHROOM, LAVATORY, WATER CLOSET & BATHTUB					
ONE WALL PLUMBING, STAND ALONE					
Wtr closet, rough-in, supply, waste and vent	1.000	Set	625	525	1,150
Wtr closet, 2 pc close cpld vit china flr mntd w/seat supply & stop	1.000	Ea.	276	300	576
Lavatory w/ftngs, wall hung, white, PE on CI, 20" x 18"	1.000	Ea.	525	200	725
Lavatory, rough-in waste & vent	1.000	Set	695	965	1,660
Bathtub, white PE on CI, w/ftgs, mat bottom, recessed, 5' long	1.000	Ea.	1,975	365	2,340
Baths, rough-in waste and vent	1.000	Set	700	770	1,470
TOTAL			4,796	3,125	7,921

D2010 924	Three Fixture Bathroom, One Wall Plumbing		COST EACH		
			MAT.	INST.	TOTAL
1150	Bathroom, three fixture, one wall plumbing	R221113 -40			
1160	Lavatory, water closet & bathtub				
1170	Stand alone	R224000 -30	4,800	3,125	7,925
1180	Share common plumbing wall *		4,125	2,200	6,325

D2010 926	Three Fixture Bathroom, Two Wall Plumbing		COST EACH		
			MAT.	INST.	TOTAL
2130	Bathroom, three fixture, two wall plumbing	R221113 -40			
2140	Lavatory, water closet & bathtub				
2160	Stand alone		4,750	3,075	7,825
2180	Long plumbing wall common *		4,300	2,450	6,750
3610	Lavatory, bathtub & water closet				
3620	Stand alone		5,200	3,525	8,725
3640	Long plumbing wall common *		4,850	3,175	8,025
4660	Water closet, corner bathtub & lavatory				
4680	Stand alone		6,650	3,125	9,775
4700	Long plumbing wall common *		5,950	2,350	8,300
6100	Water closet, stall shower & lavatory				
6120	Stand alone		4,600	3,500	8,100
6140	Long plumbing wall common *		4,350	3,225	7,575
7060	Lavatory, corner stall shower & water closet				
7080	Stand alone		5,550	3,100	8,650
7100	Short plumbing wall common *		4,700	2,075	6,775

D20 Plumbing

D2010 Plumbing Fixtures

Four Fixture Bathroom Systems consisting of a lavatory, water closet, bathtub, shower and rough-in service piping.

- Prices for plumbing and fixtures only.

*Common wall is with an adjacent bathroom.

System Components	QUANTITY	UNIT	COST EACH MAT.	COST EACH INST.	COST EACH TOTAL
SYSTEM D2010 928 1160					
BATHROOM, BATHTUB, WATER CLOSET, STALL SHOWER & LAVATORY					
TWO WALL PLUMBING, STAND ALONE					
Wtr closet, 2 pc close cpld vit china flr mntd w/seat supply & stop	1.000	Ea.	276	300	576
Water closet, rough-in waste & vent	1.000	Set	625	525	1,150
Lavatory w/ftngs, wall hung, white PE on CI, 20" x 18"	1.000	Ea.	525	200	725
Lavatory, rough-in waste & vent	1.000	Set	695	965	1,660
Bathtub, white PE on CI, w/ftgs, mat bottom, recessed, 5' long	1.000	Ea.	1,975	365	2,340
Baths, rough-in waste and vent	1.000	Set	700	770	1,470
Shower stall, bkd enam, molded stone receptor, door & trim 32" sq.	1.000	Ea.	1,450	320	1,770
Shower stall, rough-in supply, waste & vent	1.000	Set	675	780	1,455
TOTAL			6,921	4,225	11,146

D2010 928	Four Fixture Bathroom, Two Wall Plumbing		COST EACH MAT.	COST EACH INST.	COST EACH TOTAL
1140	Bathroom, four fixture, two wall plumbing	R221113 -40			
1150	Bathtub, water closet, stall shower & lavatory				
1160	Stand alone	R224000 -30	6,925	4,225	11,150
1180	Long plumbing wall common *		5,600	2,575	8,175
2260	Bathtub, lavatory, corner stall shower & water closet				
2280	Stand alone		7,600	3,375	10,975
2320	Long plumbing wall common *		6,900	2,600	9,500
3620	Bathtub, stall shower, lavatory & water closet				
3640	Stand alone		6,925	4,225	11,150
3660	Long plumbing wall (opp. door) common *		6,225	3,450	9,675

D2010 930	Four Fixture Bathroom, Three Wall Plumbing		COST EACH MAT.	COST EACH INST.	COST EACH TOTAL
4680	Bathroom, four fixture, three wall plumbing	R221113 -40			
4700	Bathtub, stall shower, lavatory & water closet				
4720	Stand alone		8,575	4,650	13,225
4760	Long plumbing wall (opposite door) common *		8,275	4,300	12,575

D20 Plumbing

D2010 Plumbing Fixtures

Five Fixture Bathroom Systems consisting of two lavatories, a water closet, bathtub, shower and rough-in service piping.

- Prices for plumbing and fixtures only.

*Common wall is with an adjacent bathroom.

System Components	QUANTITY	UNIT	COST EACH		
			MAT.	INST.	TOTAL
SYSTEM D2010 932 1360					
BATHROOM, BATHTUB, WATER CLOSET, STALL SHOWER & TWO LAVATORIES					
TWO WALL PLUMBING, STAND ALONE					
Wtr closet, 2 pc close cpld vit china flr mntd incl seat, supply & stop	1.000	Ea.	276	300	576
Water closet, rough-in waste & vent	1.000	Set	625	525	1,150
Lavatory w/ftngs, wall hung, white PE on CI, 20" x 18"	2.000	Ea.	1,050	400	1,450
Lavatory, rough-in waste & vent	2.000	Set	1,390	1,930	3,320
Bathtub, white PE on CI, w/ftgs, mat bottom, recessed, 5' long	1.000	Ea.	1,975	365	2,340
Baths, rough-in waste and vent	1.000	Set	700	770	1,470
Shower stall, bkd enam molded stone receptor, door & ftng, 32" sq.	1.000	Ea.	1,450	320	1,770
Shower stall, rough-in supply, waste & vent	1.000	Set	675	780	1,455
TOTAL			8,141	5,390	13,531

D2010 932	Five Fixture Bathroom, Two Wall Plumbing	COST EACH		
		MAT.	INST.	TOTAL
1320	Bathroom, five fixture, two wall plumbing			
1340	Bathtub, water closet, stall shower & two lavatories			
1360	Stand alone	8,150	5,400	13,550
1400	One short plumbing wall common *	7,450	4,625	12,075
1500	Bathtub, two lavatories, corner stall shower & water closet			
1520	Stand alone	9,450	5,400	14,850
1540	Long plumbing wall common*	8,575	4,200	12,775

D2010 934	Five Fixture Bathroom, Three Wall Plumbing	COST EACH		
		MAT.	INST.	TOTAL
2360	Bathroom, five fixture, three wall plumbing			
2380	Water closet, bathtub, two lavatories & stall shower			
2400	Stand alone	9,450	5,400	14,850
2440	One short plumbing wall common *	8,750	4,625	13,375

D2010 936	Five Fixture Bathroom, One Wall Plumbing	COST EACH		
		MAT.	INST.	TOTAL
4080	Bathroom, five fixture, one wall plumbing			
4100	Bathtub, two lavatories, corner stall shower & water closet			
4120	Stand alone	9,025	4,825	13,850
4160	Share common wall *	7,625	3,125	10,750

For customer support on your Plumbing Costs with RSMeans Data call 800.448.8182.

D20 Plumbing

D2010 Plumbing Fixtures

Example of Plumbing Cost Calculations: The bathroom system includes the individual fixtures such as bathtub, lavatory, shower and water closet. These fixtures are listed below as separate items merely as a checklist.

D2010 951 Plumbing Systems 20 Unit, 2 Story Apartment Building

	FIXTURE	SYSTEM	LINE	QUANTITY	UNIT	COST EACH MAT.	COST EACH INST.	COST EACH TOTAL
0440	Bathroom	D2010 926	3640	20	Ea.	97,000	63,500	160,500
0480	Bathtub							
0520	Booster pump[1]	not req'd.						
0560	Drinking fountain							
0600	Garbage disposal[1]	not incl.						
0660								
0680	Grease interceptor							
0720	Water heater	D2020 250	2140	1	Ea.	14,300	4,325	18,625
0760	Kitchen sink	D2010 410	1960	20	Ea.	36,500	22,400	58,900
0800	Laundry sink	D2010 420	1840	4	Ea.	6,450	4,425	10,875
0840	Lavatory							
0900								
0920	Roof drain, 1 floor	D2040 210	4200	2	Ea.	3,425	2,300	5,725
0960	Roof drain, add'l floor	D2040 210	4240	20	L.F.	410	580	990
1000	Service sink	D2010 440	4300	1	Ea.	4,850	1,550	6,400
1040	Sewage ejector[1]	not req'd.						
1080	Shower							
1100								
1160	Sump pump							
1200	Urinal							
1240	Water closet							
1320								
1360	SUB TOTAL					163,000	99,000	262,000
1481	Water controls	R221113-40		10%[2]		16,300	9,900	26,200
1521	Pipe & fittings[3]	R221113-40		30%[2]		48,900	29,700	78,600
1560	Other							
1601	Quality/complexity	R221113-40		15%[2]		24,400	14,900	39,300
1680								
1720	TOTAL					253,000	153,500	406,500
1741								

[1]**Note:** Cost for items such as booster pumps, backflow preventers, sewage ejectors, water meters, etc., may be obtained from the unit price section in the front of this data set.

Water controls, pipe and fittings, and the Quality/Complexity factors come from Table R221113-40.

[2]Percentage of subtotal.

[3]Long, easily discernable runs of pipe would be more accurately priced from Unit Price Section 22 11 13. If this is done, reduce the miscellaneous percentage in proportion.

D20 Plumbing

D2020 Domestic Water Distribution

Installation includes piping and fittings within 10' of heater. Electric water heaters do not require venting.

1 Kilowatt hour will raise:			
Gallons of Water	Degrees F	Gallons of Water	Degrees F
4.1	100°	6.8	60°
4.5	90°	8.2	50°
5.1	80°	10.0	40°
5.9	70°		

System Components	QUANTITY	UNIT	COST EACH		
			MAT.	INST.	TOTAL
SYSTEM D2020 210 1780					
ELECTRIC WATER HEATER, RESIDENTIAL, 100°F RISE					
10 GALLON TANK, 7 GPH					
Water heater, residential electric, glass lined tank, 10 gal.	1.000	Ea.	535	385	920
Copper tubing, type L, solder joint, hanger 10' OC 1/2" diam.	30.000	L.F.	121.80	328.50	450.30
Wrought copper 90° elbow for solder joints 1/2" diam.	4.000	Ea.	10.96	178	188.96
Wrought copper Tee for solder joints, 1/2" diam.	2.000	Ea.	7.64	137	144.64
Union, wrought copper, 1/2" diam.	2.000	Ea.	154	94	248
Valve, gate, bronze, 125 lb, NRS, soldered 1/2" diam.	2.000	Ea.	244	74	318
Relief valve, bronze, press & temp, self-close, 3/4" IPS	1.000	Ea.	297	31.50	328.50
Wrought copper adapter, CTS to MPT 3/4" IPS	1.000	Ea.	19.75	52.50	72.25
Copper tubing, type L, solder joints, 3/4" diam.	1.000	L.F.	5.95	11.70	17.65
Wrought copper 90° elbow for solder joints 3/4" diam.	1.000	Ea.	6.05	47	53.05
TOTAL			1,402.15	1,339.20	2,741.35

D2020 210	Electric Water Heaters - Residential Systems		COST EACH		
			MAT.	INST.	TOTAL
1760	Electric water heater, residential, 100°F rise				
1780	10 gallon tank, 7 GPH	R224000-10	1,400	1,350	2,750
1820	20 gallon tank, 7 GPH		1,600	1,425	3,025
1860	30 gallon tank, 7 GPH	R224000-20	2,150	1,500	3,650
1900	40 gallon tank, 8 GPH		2,400	1,650	4,050
1940	52 gallon tank, 10 GPH		2,625	1,675	4,300
1980	66 gallon tank, 13 GPH		4,825	1,900	6,725
2020	80 gallon tank, 16 GPH		4,925	1,975	6,900
2060	120 gallon tank, 23 GPH		7,150	2,325	9,475

D20 Plumbing

D2020 Domestic Water Distribution

Installation includes piping and fittings within 10' of heater. Gas heaters require vent piping (not included with these units).

System Components	QUANTITY	UNIT	COST EACH MAT.	COST EACH INST.	COST EACH TOTAL
SYSTEM D2020 220 2260					
GAS FIRED WATER HEATER, RESIDENTIAL, 100°F RISE					
30 GALLON TANK, 32 GPH					
Water heater, residential, gas, glass lined tank, 30 gallon	1.000	Ea.	1,150	445	1,595
Copper tubing, type L, solder joint, hanger 10' OC, 3/4" diam	33.000	L.F.	196.35	386.10	582.45
Wrought copper 90° elbow for solder joints, 3/4" diam	5.000	Ea.	30.25	235	265.25
Wrought copper Tee for solder joints, 3/4" diam	2.000	Ea.	22.20	148	170.20
Union, copper, cast, copper x copper, 3/4"	2.000	Ea.	193	99	292
Valve bronze, 125 lb., NRS, soldered 3/4" diam	2.000	Ea.	270	89	359
Relief valve, press & temp, bronze, self-close, 3/4" diam	1.000	Ea.	297	31.50	328.50
Wrought copper, adapter, CTS to MPT 3/4" IPS	1.000	Ea.	19.75	52.50	72.25
Pipe steel black, schedule 40, threaded, 1/2" diam	10.000	L.F.	66	141	207
Pipe, 90° elbow, malleable iron black, 150 lb., threaded, 1/2" diam	2.000	Ea.	13.80	118	131.80
Pipe, union with brass seat, malleable iron black, 1/2" diam	1.000	Ea.	32.50	63.50	96
Valve, gas stop w/o check, brass, 1/2" IPS	1.000	Ea.	36	37	73
TOTAL			2,326.85	1,845.60	4,172.45

D2020 220	Gas Fired Water Heaters - Residential Systems		COST EACH MAT.	COST EACH INST.	COST EACH TOTAL
2200	Gas fired water heater, residential, 100°F rise				
2260	30 gallon tank, 32 GPH	R224000-10	2,325	1,850	4,175
2300	40 gallon tank, 32 GPH		2,625	2,075	4,700
2340	50 gallon tank, 63 GPH	R224000-20	2,675	2,075	4,750
2380	75 gallon tank, 63 GPH		3,875	2,300	6,175
2420	100 gallon tank, 63 GPH		5,575	2,425	8,000

D20 Plumbing

D2020 Domestic Water Distribution

Installation includes piping and fittings within 10' of heater. Oil fired heaters require vent piping (not included in these prices).

System Components	QUANTITY	UNIT	MAT.	INST.	TOTAL
SYSTEM D2020 230 2220					
OIL FIRED WATER HEATER, RESIDENTIAL, 100°F RISE					
30 GALLON TANK, 103 GPH					
Water heater, residential, oil glass lined tank, 30 Gal	1.000	Ea.	2,525	445	2,970
Copper tubing, type L, solder joint, hanger 10' O.C. 3/4" diam.	33.000	L.F.	196.35	386.10	582.45
Wrought copper 90° elbow for solder joints 3/4" diam.	5.000	Ea.	30.25	235	265.25
Wrought copper Tee for solder joints, 3/4" diam.	2.000	Ea.	22.20	148	170.20
Wrought copper union for soldered joints, 3/4" diam.	2.000	Ea.	193	99	292
Valve, gate, bronze, 125 lb, NRS, soldered 3/4" diam.	2.000	Ea.	270	89	359
Relief valve, bronze, press & temp, self-close, 3/4" IPS	1.000	Ea.	297	31.50	328.50
Wrought copper adapter, CTS to MPT, 3/4" IPS	1.000	Ea.	19.75	52.50	72.25
Copper tubing, type L, solder joint, hanger 10' OC 3/8" diam.	10.000	L.F.	32.70	106	138.70
Wrought copper 90° elbow for solder joints 3/8" diam.	2.000	Ea.	15.20	81	96.20
Valve, globe, fusible, 3/8" diam.	1.000	Ea.	38.50	37.50	76
TOTAL			3,639.95	1,710.60	5,350.55

D2020 230	Oil Fired Water Heaters - Residential Systems		MAT.	INST.	TOTAL
2200	Oil fired water heater, residential, 100°F rise				
2220	30 gallon tank, 103 GPH		3,650	1,700	5,350
2260	50 gallon tank, 145 GPH		4,700	1,925	6,625
2300	70 gallon tank, 164 GPH	R224000 -20	6,900	2,150	9,050
2340	85 gallon tank, 181 GPH		11,800	2,200	14,000

D20 Plumbing

D2020 Domestic Water Distribution

Systems below include piping and fittings within 10' of heater. Electric water heaters do not require venting.

System Components	QUANTITY	UNIT	COST EACH MAT.	COST EACH INST.	COST EACH TOTAL
SYSTEM D2020 240 1820 ELECTRIC WATER HEATER, COMMERCIAL, 100°F RISE 50 GALLON TANK, 9 KW, 37 GPH					
Copper tubing, type L, solder joint, hanger 10' OC, 3/4" diam	34.000	L.F.	202.30	397.80	600.10
Wrought copper 90° elbow for solder joints 3/4" diam	5.000	Ea.	30.25	235	265.25
Wrought copper Tee for solder joints, 3/4" diam	2.000	Ea.	22.20	148	170.20
Union, copper, cast, copper x copper, 3/4"	2.000	Ea.	193	99	292
Valve, gate, bronze, 125 lb, NRS, soldered 3/4" diam	2.000	Ea.	270	89	359
Relief valve, bronze, press & temp, self-close, 3/4" IPS	1.000	Ea.	297	31.50	328.50
Wrought copper adapter, copper tubing to male, 3/4" IPS	1.000	Ea.	19.75	52.50	72.25
TOTAL			1,034.50	1,052.80	2,087.30

D2020 240	Electric Water Heaters - Commercial Systems		COST EACH MAT.	COST EACH INST.	COST EACH TOTAL
1800	Electric water heater, commercial, 100°F rise				
1820	50 gallon tank, 9 KW 37 GPH		6,850	1,550	8,400
1860	80 gal, 12 KW 49 GPH	R224000-10	9,150	1,900	11,050
1864	50 gal, 9 KW 49 GPH		7,800	1,800	9,600
1900	36 KW 147 GPH		16,100	2,050	18,150
1940	120 gal, 36 KW 147 GPH	R224000-20	17,700	2,225	19,925
1980	150 gal, 120 KW 490 GPH		56,500	2,375	58,875
2020	200 gal, 120 KW 490 GPH		59,500	2,450	61,950
2060	250 gal, 150 KW 615 GPH		57,500	2,875	60,375
2100	300 gal, 180 KW 738 GPH		87,000	3,000	90,000
2140	350 gal, 30 KW 123 GPH		46,500	3,250	49,750
2180	180 KW 738 GPH		64,000	3,250	67,250
2220	500 gal, 30 KW 123 GPH		72,500	3,825	76,325
2260	240 KW 984 GPH		118,000	3,825	121,825
2300	700 gal, 30 KW 123 GPH		73,000	4,350	77,350
2340	300 KW 1230 GPH		107,000	4,350	111,350
2380	1000 gal, 60 KW 245 GPH		90,500	6,075	96,575
2420	480 KW 1970 GPH		143,500	6,100	149,600
2460	1500 gal, 60 KW 245 GPH		130,000	7,525	137,525
2500	480 KW 1970 GPH		176,000	7,525	183,525

D20 Plumbing

D2020 Domestic Water Distribution

Units may be installed in multiples for increased capacity.

Included below is the heater with self-energizing gas controls, safety pilots, insulated jacket, hi-limit aquastat and pressure relief valve.

Installation includes piping and fittings within 10′ of heater. Gas heaters require vent piping (not included in these prices).

System Components	QUANTITY	UNIT	COST EACH		
			MAT.	INST.	TOTAL
SYSTEM D2020 250 1780					
GAS FIRED WATER HEATER, COMMERCIAL, 100°F RISE					
75.5 MBH INPUT, 63 GPH					
Water heater, gas fired, 75 MBH input, 73 GPH, includes standard controls,	1.000	Ea.	3,300	635	3,935
Copper tubing, type L, solder joint, hanger 10′ OC, 1-1/4″ diam	30.000	L.F.	360	459	819
Wrought copper 90° elbow for solder joints 1-1/4″ diam	4.000	Ea.	88	236	324
Wrought copper tee for solder joints, 1-1/4″ diam	2.000	Ea.	92	197	289
Wrought copper union for soldered joints, 1-1/4″ diam	2.000	Ea.	496	127	623
Valve, gate, bronze, 125 lb, NRS, soldered 1-1/4″ diam	2.000	Ea.	596	118	714
Relief valve, bronze, press & temp, self-close, 3/4″ IPS	1.000	Ea.	297	31.50	328.50
Copper tubing, type L, solder joints, 3/4″ diam	8.000	L.F.	47.60	93.60	141.20
Wrought copper 90° elbow for solder joints 3/4″ diam	1.000	Ea.	6.05	47	53.05
Wrought copper, adapter, CTS to MPT, 3/4″ IPS	1.000	Ea.	19.75	52.50	72.25
Pipe steel black, schedule 40, threaded, 3/4″ diam	10.000	L.F.	81.50	145.50	227
Pipe, 90° elbow, malleable iron black, 150 lb threaded, 3/4″ diam	2.000	Ea.	16.70	127	143.70
Pipe, union with brass seat, malleable iron black, 3/4″ diam	1.000	Ea.	37	68.50	105.50
Valve, gas stop w/o check, brass, 3/4″ IPS	1.000	Ea.	41.50	40.50	82
TOTAL			5,479.10	2,378.10	7,857.20

D2020 250	Gas Fired Water Heaters - Commercial Systems		COST EACH		
			MAT.	INST.	TOTAL
1760	Gas fired water heater, commercial, 100°F rise				
1780	75.5 MBH input, 63 GPH		5,475	2,375	7,850
1820	95 MBH input, 86 GPH	R224000	7,875	2,375	10,250
1860	100 MBH input, 91 GPH	-10	8,925	2,475	11,400
1900	115 MBH input, 110 GPH		8,825	2,575	11,400
1980	155 MBH input, 150 GPH		9,975	2,875	12,850
2020	175 MBH input, 168 GPH	R224000	11,500	3,075	14,575
2060	200 MBH input, 192 GPH	-20	12,400	3,475	15,875
2100	240 MBH input, 230 GPH		12,900	3,775	16,675
2140	300 MBH input, 278 GPH		14,300	4,325	18,625
2180	390 MBH input, 374 GPH		16,700	4,375	21,075
2220	500 MBH input, 480 GPH		21,600	4,700	26,300
2260	600 MBH input, 576 GPH		29,400	5,100	34,500

D20 Plumbing

D2020 Domestic Water Distribution

Units may be installed in multiples for increased capacity.

Included below is the heater, wired-in flame retention burners, cadmium cell primary controls, hi-limit controls, ASME pressure relief valves, draft controls, and insulated jacket.

Oil fired water heater systems include piping and fittings within 10' of heater. Oil fired heaters require vent piping (not included in these systems).

System Components	QUANTITY	UNIT	COST EACH		
			MAT.	INST.	TOTAL
SYSTEM D2020 260 1820					
OIL FIRED WATER HEATER, COMMERCIAL, 100°F RISE					
140 GAL., 140 MBH INPUT, 134 GPH					
Water heater, commercial, oil, 140 gal., 140 MBH input, 134 GPH	1.000	Ea.	26,200	750	26,950
Copper tubing, type L, solder joint, hanger 10' OC, 3/4" diam.	34.000	L.F.	202.30	397.80	600.10
Wrought copper 90° elbow for solder joints 3/4" diam.	5.000	Ea.	30.25	235	265.25
Wrought copper Tee for solder joints, 3/4" diam.	2.000	Ea.	22.20	148	170.20
Wrought copper union for soldered joints, 3/4" diam.	2.000	Ea.	193	99	292
Valve, bronze, 125 lb, NRS, soldered 3/4" diam.	2.000	Ea.	270	89	359
Relief valve, bronze, press & temp, self-close, 3/4" IPS	1.000	Ea.	297	31.50	328.50
Wrought copper adapter, copper tubing to male, 3/4" IPS	1.000	Ea.	19.75	52.50	72.25
Copper tubing, type L, solder joint, hanger 10' OC, 3/8" diam.	10.000	L.F.	32.70	106	138.70
Wrought copper 90° elbow for solder joints 3/8" diam.	2.000	Ea.	15.20	81	96.20
Valve, globe, fusible, 3/8" IPS	1.000	Ea.	38.50	37.50	76
TOTAL			27,320.90	2,027.30	29,348.20

D2020 260	Oil Fired Water Heaters - Commercial Systems	COST EACH		
		MAT.	INST.	TOTAL
1800	Oil fired water heater, commercial, 100°F rise			
1820	140 gal., 140 MBH input, 134 GPH	27,300	2,025	29,325
1900	140 gal., 255 MBH input, 247 GPH	30,000	2,550	32,550
1940	140 gal., 270 MBH input, 259 GPH	36,600	2,900	39,500
1980	140 gal., 400 MBH input, 384 GPH	38,300	3,350	41,650
2060	140 gal., 720 MBH input, 691 GPH	40,500	3,500	44,000
2100	221 gal., 300 MBH input, 288 GPH	54,000	3,850	57,850
2140	221 gal., 600 MBH input, 576 GPH	69,000	3,875	72,875
2180	221 gal., 800 MBH input, 768 GPH	61,000	4,025	65,025
2220	201 gal., 1000 MBH input, 960 GPH	62,500	4,050	66,550
2260	201 gal., 1250 MBH input, 1200 GPH	65,000	4,175	69,175
2300	201 gal., 1500 MBH input, 1441 GPH	69,500	4,275	73,775
2340	411 gal., 600 MBH input, 576 GPH	70,000	4,350	74,350
2380	411 gal., 800 MBH input, 768 GPH	73,000	4,475	77,475
2420	411 gal., 1000 MBH input, 960 GPH	78,000	5,175	83,175
2460	411 gal., 1250 MBH input, 1200 GPH	79,500	5,325	84,825
2500	397 gal., 1500 MBH input, 1441 GPH	83,500	5,475	88,975

For customer support on your Plumbing Costs with RSMeans Data call 800.448.8182.

D20 Plumbing

D2020 Domestic Water Distribution

In this closed-loop indirect collection system, fluid with a low freezing temperature, such as propylene glycol, transports heat from the collectors to water storage. The transfer fluid is contained in a closed-loop consisting of collectors, supply and return piping, and a remote heat exchanger. The heat exchanger transfers heat energy from the fluid in the collector loop to potable water circulated in a storage loop. A typical two-or-three panel system contains 5 to 6 gallons of heat transfer fluid.

When the collectors become approximately 20°F warmer than the storage temperature, a controller activates the circulator on the collector and storage loops. The circulators will move the fluid and potable water through the heat exchanger until heat collection no longer occurs. At that point, the system shuts down. Since the heat transfer medium is a fluid with a very low freezing temperature, there is no need for it to be drained from the system between periods of collection.

D20 Plumbing

D2020 Domestic Water Distribution

System Components	QUANTITY	UNIT	MAT.	INST.	TOTAL
SYSTEM D2020 265 2760					
SOLAR, CLOSED LOOP, ADD-ON HOT WATER SYS., EXTERNAL HEAT EXCHANGER					
3/4" TUBING, TWO 3'X7' BLACK CHROME COLLECTORS					
A,B,G,L,K,M Heat exchanger fluid-fluid pkg incl 2 circulators, expansion tank, Check valve, relief valve, controller, hi temp cutoff, & 2 sensors	1.000	Ea.	890	640	1,530
C Thermometer, 2" dial	3.000	Ea.	78	166.50	244.50
D, T Fill & drain valve, brass, 3/4" connection	1.000	Ea.	22	37	59
E Air vent, manual, 1/8" fitting	2.000	Ea.	7.50	56	63.50
F Air purger	1.000	Ea.	59.50	74	133.50
H Strainer, Y type, bronze body, 3/4" IPS	1.000	Ea.	102	47.50	149.50
I Valve, gate, bronze, NRS, soldered 3/4" diam	6.000	Ea.	810	267	1,077
J Neoprene vent flashing	2.000	Ea.	22.10	89	111.10
N, N-1 Relief valve temp & press, 150 psi 210°F self-closing 3/4" IPS	1.000	Ea.	30	29.50	59.50
O Pipe covering, urethane, ultraviolet cover, 1" wall 3/4" diam	20.000	L.F.	66.40	160	226.40
P Pipe covering, fiberglass, all service jacket, 1" wall, 3/4" diam	50.000	L.F.	139.50	320	459.50
Q Collector panel solar energy blk chrome on copper, 1/8" temp glass 3'x7'	2.000	Ea.	2,400	336	2,736
Roof clamps for solar energy collector panels	2.000	Set	8.10	46	54.10
R Valve, swing check, bronze, regrinding disc, 3/4" diam	2.000	Ea.	426	89	515
S Pressure gauge, 60 psi, 2" dial	1.000	Ea.	28.50	28	56.50
U Valve, water tempering, bronze, sweat connections, 3/4" diam	1.000	Ea.	246	44.50	290.50
W-2, V Tank water storage w/heating element, drain, relief valve, existing	1.000	Ea.			
Copper tubing type L, solder joint, hanger 10' OC 3/4" diam	20.000	L.F.	119	234	353
Copper tubing, type M, solder joint, hanger 10' OC 3/4" diam	70.000	L.F.	338.10	798	1,136.10
Sensor wire, #22-2 conductor multistranded	.500	C.L.F.	10.75	42.50	53.25
Solar energy heat transfer fluid, propylene glycol anti-freeze	6.000	Gal.	180	189	369
Wrought copper fittings & solder, 3/4" diam	76.000	Ea.	459.80	3,572	4,031.80
TOTAL			6,443.25	7,265.50	13,708.75

D2020 265	Solar, Closed Loop, Add-On Hot Water Systems		MAT.	INST.	TOTAL
2550	Solar, closed loop, add-on hot water system, external heat exchanger				
2570	3/8" tubing, 3 ea. 4' x 4'-4" vacuum tube collectors		6,900	6,800	13,700
2580	1/2" tubing, 4 ea. 4 x 4'-4" vacuum tube collectors	R235616 -60	7,625	7,350	14,975
2600	2 ea. 3'x7' black chrome collectors		5,725	6,925	12,650
2620	3 ea. 3'x7' black chrome collectors		6,925	7,100	14,025
2640	2 ea. 3'x7' flat black collectors		5,050	6,950	12,000
2660	3 ea. 3'x7' flat black collectors		5,925	7,150	13,075
2700	3/4" tubing, 3 ea. 3'x7' black chrome collectors		7,650	7,450	15,100
2720	3 ea. 3'x7' flat black absorber plate collectors		6,650	7,475	14,125
2740	2 ea. 4'x9' flat black w/plastic glazing collectors		6,150	7,500	13,650
2760	2 ea. 3'x7' black chrome collectors		6,450	7,275	13,725
2780	1" tubing, 4 ea 2'x9' plastic absorber & glazing collectors		8,175	8,425	16,600
2800	4 ea. 3'x7' black chrome absorber collectors		10,300	8,450	18,750
2820	4 ea. 3'x7' flat black absorber collectors		9,000	8,500	17,500

D20 Plumbing

D2020 Domestic Water Distribution

In the drainback indirect-collection system, the heat transfer fluid is distilled water contained in a loop consisting of collectors, supply and return piping, and an unpressurized holding tank. A large heat exchanger containing incoming potable water is immersed in the holding tank. When a controller activates solar collection, the distilled water is pumped through the collectors and heated and pumped back down to the holding tank. When the temperature differential between the water in the collectors and water in storage is such that collection no longer occurs, the pump turns off and gravity causes the distilled water in the collector loop to drain back to the holding tank. All the loop piping is pitched so that the water can drain out of the collectors and piping and not freeze there. As hot water is needed in the home, incoming water first flows through the holding tank with the immersed heat exchanger and is warmed and then flows through a conventional heater for any supplemental heating that is necessary.

D20 Plumbing

D2020 Domestic Water Distribution

System Components	QUANTITY	UNIT	COST EACH		
			MAT.	INST.	TOTAL
SYSTEM D2020 270 2760 SOLAR, DRAINBACK, ADD ON, HOT WATER, IMMERSED HEAT EXCHANGER 3/4" TUBING, THREE EA 3'X7' BLACK CHROME COLLECTOR					
A, B Differential controller 2 sensors, thermostat, solar energy system	1.000	Ea.	274	74	348
C Thermometer 2" dial	3.000	Ea.	78	166.50	244.50
D, T Fill & drain valve, brass, 3/4" connection	1.000	Ea.	22	37	59
E-1 Automatic air vent 1/8" fitting	1.000	Ea.	18.10	28	46.10
H Strainer, Y type, bronze body, 3/4" IPS	1.000	Ea.	102	47.50	149.50
I Valve, gate, bronze, NRS, soldered 3/4" diam	2.000	Ea.	270	89	359
J Neoprene vent flashing	2.000	Ea.	22.10	89	111.10
L Circulator, solar heated liquid, 1/20 HP	1.000	Ea.	350	133	483
N Relief valve temp. & press. 150 psi 210°F self-closing 3/4" IPS	1.000	Ea.	30	29.50	59.50
O Pipe covering, urethane, ultraviolet cover, 1" wall, 3/4" diam	20.000	L.F.	66.40	160	226.40
P Pipe covering, fiberglass, all service jacket, 1" wall, 3/4" diam	50.000	L.F.	139.50	320	459.50
Q Collector panel solar energy blk chrome on copper, 1/8" temp glas 3'x7'	3.000	Ea.	3,600	504	4,104
Roof clamps for solar energy collector panels	3.000	Set	12.15	69	81.15
R Valve, swing check, bronze, regrinding disc, 3/4" diam	1.000	Ea.	213	44.50	257.50
U Valve, water tempering, bronze sweat connections, 3/4" diam	1.000	Ea.	246	44.50	290.50
V Tank, water storage w/heating element, drain, relief valve, existing	1.000	Ea.			
W Tank, water storage immersed heat exchr elec 2"x1/2# insul 120 gal	1.000	Ea.	1,975	635	2,610
X Valve, globe, bronze, rising stem, 3/4" diam, soldered	3.000	Ea.	900	133.50	1,033.50
Y Flow control valve	1.000	Ea.	162	40.50	202.50
Z Valve, ball, bronze, solder 3/4" diam, solar loop flow control	1.000	Ea.	41	44.50	85.50
Copper tubing, type L, solder joint, hanger 10' OC 3/4" diam	20.000	L.F.	119	234	353
Copper tubing, type M, solder joint, hanger 10' OC 3/4" diam	70.000	L.F.	338.10	798	1,136.10
Sensor wire, #22-2 conductor, multistranded	.500	C.L.F.	10.75	42.50	53.25
Wrought copper fittings & solder, 3/4" diam	76.000	Ea.	459.80	3,572	4,031.80
TOTAL			9,448.90	7,335.50	16,784.40

D2020 270	Solar, Drainback, Hot Water Systems		COST EACH		
			MAT.	INST.	TOTAL
2550	Solar, drainback, hot water, immersed heat exchanger				
2560	3/8" tubing, 3 ea. 4' x 4'-4" vacuum tube collectors		8,625	6,600	15,225
2580	1/2" tubing, 4 ea 4' x 4'-4" vacuum tube collectors, 80 gal tank	R235616	9,350	7,150	16,500
2600	120 gal tank	-60	9,300	7,225	16,525
2640	2 ea. 3'x7' blk chrome collectors, 80 gal tank		7,425	6,725	14,150
2660	3 ea. 3'x7' blk chrome collectors, 120 gal tank		8,575	7,000	15,575
2700	2 ea. 3'x7' flat blk collectors, 120 gal tank		6,700	6,825	13,525
2720	3 ea. 3'x7' flat blk collectors, 120 gal tank		7,575	7,025	14,600
2760	3/4" tubing, 3 ea 3'x7' black chrome collectors, 120 gal tank		9,450	7,325	16,775
2780	3 ea. 3'x7' flat black absorber collectors, 120 gal tank		8,450	7,375	15,825
2800	2 ea. 4'x9' flat blk w/plastic glazing collectors 120 gal tank		7,950	7,400	15,350
2840	1" tubing, 4 ea. 2'x9' plastic absorber & glazing collectors, 120 gal tank		10,200	8,300	18,500
2860	4 ea. 3'x7' black chrome absorber collectors, 120 gal tank		12,400	8,325	20,725
2880	4 ea. 3'x7' flat black absorber collectors, 120 gal tank		11,000	8,375	19,375

D20 Plumbing

D2020 Domestic Water Distribution

In the draindown direct-collection system, incoming domestic water is heated in the collectors. When the controller activates solar collection, domestic water is first heated as it flows through the collectors and is then pumped to storage. When conditions are no longer suitable for heat collection, the pump shuts off and the water in the loop drains down and out of the system by means of solenoid valves and properly pitched piping.

D20 Plumbing

D2020 Domestic Water Distribution

System Components		QUANTITY	UNIT	COST EACH		
				MAT.	INST.	TOTAL
SYSTEM D2020 275 2760						
SOLAR, DRAINDOWN, HOT WATER, DIRECT COLLECTION						
3/4" TUBING, THREE 3'X7' BLACK CHROME COLLECTORS						
A, B	Differential controller, 2 sensors, thermostat, solar energy system	1.000	Ea.	274	74	348
A-1	Solenoid valve, solar heating loop, brass, 3/4" diam, 24 volts	3.000	Ea.	588	295.50	883.50
B-1	Solar energy sensor, freeze prevention	1.000	Ea.	29.50	28	57.50
C	Thermometer, 2" dial	3.000	Ea.	78	166.50	244.50
E-1	Vacuum relief valve, 3/4" diam	1.000	Ea.	35	28	63
F-1	Air vent, automatic, 1/8" fitting	1.000	Ea.	18.10	28	46.10
H	Strainer, Y type, bronze body, 3/4" IPS	1.000	Ea.	102	47.50	149.50
I	Valve, gate, bronze, NRS, soldered, 3/4" diam	2.000	Ea.	270	89	359
J	Vent flashing neoprene	2.000	Ea.	22.10	89	111.10
K	Circulator, solar heated liquid, 1/25 HP	1.000	Ea.	236	114	350
N	Relief valve temp & press 150 psi 210°F self-closing 3/4" IPS	1.000	Ea.	30	29.50	59.50
O	Pipe covering, urethane, ultraviolet cover, 1" wall, 3/4" diam	20.000	L.F.	66.40	160	226.40
P	Pipe covering, fiberglass, all service jacket, 1" wall, 3/4" diam	50.000	L.F.	139.50	320	459.50
	Roof clamps for solar energy collector panels	3.000	Set	12.15	69	81.15
Q	Collector panel solar energy blk chrome on copper, 1/8" temp glass 3'x7'	3.000	Ea.	3,600	504	4,104
R	Valve, swing check, bronze, regrinding disc, 3/4" diam, soldered	2.000	Ea.	426	89	515
T	Drain valve, brass, 3/4" connection	2.000	Ea.	44	74	118
U	Valve, water tempering, bronze, sweat connections, 3/4" diam	1.000	Ea.	246	44.50	290.50
W, W-2	Tank, water storage elec elem 2"x1/2# insul 120 gal	1.000	Ea.	1,975	635	2,610
X	Valve, globe, bronze, rising stem, 3/4" diam, soldered	1.000	Ea.	300	44.50	344.50
	Copper tubing, type L, solder joints, hangers 10' OC 3/4" diam	20.000	L.F.	119	234	353
	Copper tubing, type M, solder joints, hangers 10' OC 3/4" diam	70.000	L.F.	338.10	798	1,136.10
	Sensor wire, #22-2 conductor, multistranded	.500	C.L.F.	10.75	42.50	53.25
	Wrought copper fittings & solder, 3/4" diam	76.000	Ea.	459.80	3,572	4,031.80
	TOTAL			9,419.40	7,575.50	16,994.90

D2020 275	Solar, Draindown, Hot Water Systems		COST EACH		
			MAT.	INST.	TOTAL
2550	Solar, draindown, hot water				
2560	3/8" tubing, 3 ea. 4' x 4'-4" vacuum tube collectors, 80 gal tank		8,350	7,200	15,550
2580	1/2" tubing, 4 ea. 4' x 4'-4" vacuum tube collectors, 80 gal tank	R235616 -60	9,425	7,400	16,825
2600	120 gal tank		9,375	7,475	16,850
2640	2 ea. 3'x7' black chrome collectors, 80 gal tank		7,525	6,975	14,500
2660	3 ea. 3'x7' black chrome collectors, 120 gal tank		8,675	7,250	15,925
2700	2 ea. 3'x7' flat black collectors, 120 gal tank		6,800	7,075	13,875
2720	3 ea. 3'x7' flat black collectors, 120 gal tank		7,500	7,250	14,750
2760	3/4" tubing, 3 ea. 3'x7' black chrome collectors, 120 gal tank		9,425	7,575	17,000
2780	3 ea. 3'x7' flat collectors, 120 gal tank		8,425	7,600	16,025
2800	2 ea. 4'x9' flat black & plastic glazing collectors, 120 gal tank		7,925	7,625	15,550
2840	1" tubing, 4 ea. 2'x9' plastic absorber & glazing collectors, 120 gal tank		14,000	10,000	24,000
2860	4 ea. 3'x7' black chrome absorber collectors, 120 gal tank		13,600	9,475	23,075
2880	4 ea. 3'x7' flat black absorber collectors, 120 gal tank		11,100	8,600	19,700

D20 Plumbing

D2020 Domestic Water Distribution

In the recirculation system, (a direct-collection system), incoming domestic water is heated in the collectors. When the controller activates solar collection, domestic water is heated as it flows through the collectors and then it flows back to storage. When conditions are not suitable for heat collection, the pump shuts off and the flow of the water stops. In this type of system, water remains in the collector loop at all times. A "frost sensor" at the collector activates the circulation of warm water from storage through the collectors when protection from freezing is required.

D20 Plumbing

D2020 Domestic Water Distribution

System Components		QUANTITY	UNIT	COST EACH		
				MAT.	INST.	TOTAL
SYSTEM D2020 280 2820						
SOLAR, RECIRCULATION, HOT WATER						
3/4" TUBING, TWO 3'X7' BLACK CHROME COLLECTORS						
A, B	Differential controller 2 sensors, thermostat, for solar energy system	1.000	Ea.	274	74	348
A-1	Solenoid valve, solar heating loop, brass, 3/4" IPS, 24 volts	2.000	Ea.	392	197	589
B-1	Solar energy sensor freeze prevention	1.000	Ea.	29.50	28	57.50
C	Thermometer, 2" dial	3.000	Ea.	78	166.50	244.50
D	Drain valve, brass, 3/4" connection	1.000	Ea.	22	37	59
F-1	Air vent, automatic, 1/8" fitting	1.000	Ea.	18.10	28	46.10
H	Strainer, Y type, bronze body, 3/4" IPS	1.000	Ea.	102	47.50	149.50
I	Valve, gate, bronze, 125 lb, soldered 3/4" diam	3.000	Ea.	405	133.50	538.50
J	Vent flashing, neoprene	2.000	Ea.	22.10	89	111.10
L	Circulator, solar heated liquid, 1/20 HP	1.000	Ea.	350	133	483
N	Relief valve, temp & press 150 psi 210° F self-closing 3/4" IPS	2.000	Ea.	60	59	119
O	Pipe covering, urethane, ultraviolet cover, 1" wall, 3/4" diam	20.000	L.F.	66.40	160	226.40
P	Pipe covering, fiberglass, all service jacket, 1" wall 3/4" diam	50.000	L.F.	139.50	320	459.50
Q	Collector panel solar energy blk chrome on copper, 1/8" temp glass 3'x7'	2.000	Ea.	2,400	336	2,736
	Roof clamps for solar energy collector panels	2.000	Set	8.10	46	54.10
R	Valve, swing check, bronze, 125 lb, regrinding disc, soldered 3/4" diam	2.000	Ea.	426	89	515
U	Valve, water tempering, bronze, sweat connections, 3/4" diam	1.000	Ea.	246	44.50	290.50
V	Tank, water storage, w/heating element, drain, relief valve, existing	1.000	Ea.			
X	Valve, globe, bronze, 125 lb, 3/4" diam	2.000	Ea.	600	89	689
	Copper tubing, type L, solder joints, hangers 10' OC 3/4" diam	20.000	L.F.	119	234	353
	Copper tubing, type M, solder joints, hangers 10' OC 3/4" diam	70.000	L.F.	338.10	798	1,136.10
	Wrought copper fittings & solder, 3/4" diam	76.000	Ea.	459.80	3,572	4,031.80
	Sensor wire, #22-2 conductor, multistranded	.500	C.L.F.	10.75	42.50	53.25
	TOTAL			**6,566.35**	**6,723.50**	**13,289.85**

D2020 280	Solar, Recirculation, Domestic Hot Water Systems	COST EACH		
		MAT.	INST.	TOTAL
2550	Solar, recirculation, hot water			
2560	3/8" tubing, 3 ea. 4' x 4'-4" vacuum tube collectors	6,900	6,250	13,150
2580	1/2" tubing, 4 ea. 4' x 4'-4" vacuum tube collectors	7,650	6,800	14,450
2640	2 ea. 3'x7' black chrome collectors	5,725	6,375	12,100
2660	3 ea. 3'x7' black chrome collectors	6,925	6,575	13,500
2700	2 ea. 3'x7' flat black collectors	5,050	6,400	11,450
2720	3 ea. 3'x7' flat black collectors	5,925	6,600	12,525
2760	3/4" tubing, 3 ea. 3'x7' black chrome collectors	7,775	6,925	14,700
2780	3 ea. 3'x7' flat black absorber plate collectors	6,775	6,950	13,725
2800	2 ea. 4'x9' flat black w/plastic glazing collectors	6,275	6,975	13,250
2820	2 ea. 3'x7' black chrome collectors	6,575	6,725	13,300
2840	1" tubing, 4 ea. 2'x9' black plastic absorber & glazing collectors	8,700	7,875	16,575
2860	4 ea. 3'x7' black chrome absorber collectors	10,900	7,900	18,800
2880	4 ea. 3'x7' flat black absorber collectors	9,525	7,950	17,475

D20 Plumbing

D2020 Domestic Water Distribution

The thermosyphon domestic hot water system, a direct collection system, operates under city water pressure and does not require pumps for system operation. An insulated water storage tank is located above the collectors. As the sun heats the collectors, warm water in them rises by means of natural convection; the colder water in the storage tank flows into the collectors by means of gravity. As long as the sun is shining the water continues to flow through the collectors and to become warmer.

To prevent freezing, the system must be drained or the collectors covered with an insulated lid when the temperature drops below 32°F.

D20 Plumbing

D2020 Domestic Water Distribution

System Components	QUANTITY	UNIT	COST EACH MAT.	COST EACH INST.	TOTAL
SYSTEM D2020 285 0960					
SOLAR, THERMOSYPHON, WATER HEATER					
3/4" TUBING, TWO 3'X7' BLACK CHROME COLLECTORS					
D-1 Framing lumber, fir, 2" x 6" x 8', tank cradle	.008	M.B.F.	13.40	9.20	22.60
F-1 Framing lumber, fir, 2" x 4" x 24', sleepers	.016	M.B.F.	26.80	27.60	54.40
I Valve, gate, bronze, 125 lb, soldered 1/2" diam	2.000	Ea.	244	74	318
J Vent flashing, neoprene	4.000	Ea.	44.20	178	222.20
O Pipe covering, urethane, ultraviolet cover, 1" wall, 1/2"diam	40.000	L.F.	95.20	314	409.20
P Pipe covering fiberglass all service jacket 1" wall 1/2" diam	160.000	L.F.	406.40	984	1,390.40
Q Collector panel solar, blk chrome on copper, 3/16" temp glass 3'-6" x 7.5'	2.000	Ea.	1,730	356	2,086
Y Flow control valve, globe, bronze, 125#, soldered, 1/2" diam	1.000	Ea.	226	37	263
U Valve, water tempering, bronze, sweat connections, 1/2" diam	1.000	Ea.	173	37	210
W Tank, water storage, solar energy system, 80 Gal, 2" x 1/2 lb insul	1.000	Ea.	2,025	555	2,580
Copper tubing type L, solder joints, hangers 10' OC 1/2" diam	150.000	L.F.	609	1,642.50	2,251.50
Copper tubing type M, solder joints, hangers 10' OC 1/2" diam	50.000	L.F.	162.50	530	692.50
Sensor wire, #22-2 gauge multistranded	.500	C.L.F.	10.75	42.50	53.25
Wrought copper fittings & solder, 1/2" diam	75.000	Ea.	205.50	3,337.50	3,543
TOTAL			5,971.75	8,124.30	14,096.05

D2020 285	Thermosyphon, Hot Water		COST EACH MAT.	COST EACH INST.	TOTAL
0960	Solar, thermosyphon, hot water, two collector system	R235616 -60	5,975	8,125	14,100
0970					

D20 Plumbing

D2020 Domestic Water Distribution

This domestic hot water pre-heat system includes heat exchanger with a circulating pump, blower, air-to-water, coil and controls, mounted in the upper collector manifold. Heat from the hot air coming out of the collectors is transferred through the heat exchanger. For each degree of DHW preheating gained, one degree less heating is needed from the fuel fired water heater. The system is simple, inexpensive to operate and can provide a substantial portion of DHW requirements for modest additional cost.

D20 Plumbing

D2020 Domestic Water Distribution

System Components

	System Components	QUANTITY	UNIT	MAT.	INST.	TOTAL
	SYSTEM D2020 290 2560					
	SOLAR, HOT WATER, AIR TO WATER HEAT EXCHANGE					
	THREE COLLECTORS, OPTICAL BLACK ON ALUM., 7.5' x 3.5', 80 GAL TANK					
A, B	Differential controller, 2 sensors, thermostat, solar energy system	1.000	Ea.	274	74	348
C	Thermometer, 2" dial	2.000	Ea.	52	111	163
C-1	Heat exchanger, air to fluid, up flow 70 MBH	1.000	Ea.	430	455	885
E	Air vent, manual, for solar energy system 1/8" fitting	1.000	Ea.	3.75	28	31.75
F	Air purger	1.000	Ea.	59.50	74	133.50
G	Expansion tank	1.000	Ea.	74.50	28	102.50
H	Strainer, Y type, bronze body, 1/2" IPS	1.000	Ea.	60.50	45	105.50
I	Valve, gate, bronze, 125 lb, NRS, soldered 1/2" diam	5.000	Ea.	610	185	795
N	Relief valve, temp & pressure solar 150 psi 210°F self-closing	1.000	Ea.	30	29.50	59.50
P	Pipe covering, fiberglass, all service jacket, 1" wall, 1/2" diam	60.000	L.F.	152.40	369	521.40
Q	Collector panel solar energy, air, black on alum plate, 7.5' x 3.5'	3.000	Ea.	2,595	534	3,129
B-1, R-1	Shutter damper for solar heater circulator	1.000	Ea.	67	130	197
B-1, R-1	Shutter motor for solar heater circulator	1.000	Ea.	167	98	265
R	Backflow preventer, 1/2" pipe size	2.000	Ea.	202	111	313
T	Drain valve, brass, 3/4" connection	1.000	Ea.	22	37	59
U	Valve, water tempering, bronze, sweat connections, 1/2" diam	1.000	Ea.	173	37	210
W	Tank, water storage, solar energy system, 80 Gal, 2" x 2 lb insul	1.000	Ea.	2,025	555	2,580
V	Tank, water storage, w/heating element, drain, relief valve, existing	1.000	System			
X	Valve, globe, bronze, 125 lb, rising stem, 1/2" diam	1.000	Ea.	226	37	263
	Copper tubing type M, solder joints, hangers 10' OC, 1/2" diam	50.000	L.F.	162.50	530	692.50
	Copper tubing type L, solder joints, hangers 10' OC 1/2" diam	10.000	L.F.	40.60	109.50	150.10
	Wrought copper fittings & solder, 1/2" diam	10.000	Ea.	27.40	445	472.40
	Sensor wire, #22-2 conductor multistranded	.500	C.L.F.	10.75	42.50	53.25
Q-1, Q-2	Ductwork, fiberglass, aluminized jacket, 1-1/2" thick, 8" diam	32.000	S.F.	294.40	278.40	572.80
Q-3	Manifold for flush mount solar energy collector panels, air	6.000	L.F.	1,026	58.80	1,084.80
	TOTAL			8,785.30	4,401.70	13,187

D2020 290	Solar, Hot Water, Air To Water Heat Exchange		MAT.	INST.	TOTAL
2550	Solar, hot water, air to water heat exchange				
2560	Three collectors, optical black on aluminum, 7.5' x 3.5', 80 Gal tank		8,775	4,400	13,175
2580	Four collectors, optical black on aluminum, 7.5' x 3.5', 80 Gal tank	R235616 -60	10,100	4,650	14,750
2600	Four collectors, optical black on aluminum, 7.5' x 3.5', 120 Gal tank		10,000	4,750	14,750

D20 Plumbing

D2020 Domestic Water Distribution

In this closed-loop indirect collection system, fluid with a low freezing temperature, such as propylene glycol, transports heat from the collectors to water storage. The transfer fluid is contained in a closed-loop consisting of collectors, supply and return piping, and a heat exchanger immersed in the storage tank. A typical two-or-three panel system contains 5 to 6 gallons of heat transfer fluid.

When the collectors become approximately 20°F warmer than the storage temperature, a controller activates the circulator. The circulator moves the fluid continuously through the collectors until the temperature difference between the collectors and storage is such that heat collection no longer occurs; at that point, the circulator shuts off. Since the heat transfer fluid has a very low freezing temperature, there is no need for it to be drained from the collectors between periods of collection.

D20 Plumbing

D2020 Domestic Water Distribution

System Components	QUANTITY	UNIT	MAT.	INST.	TOTAL
SYSTEM D2020 295 2760					
SOLAR, CLOSED LOOP, HOT WATER SYSTEM, IMMERSED HEAT EXCHANGER					
3/4" TUBING, THREE 3' X 7' BLACK CHROME COLLECTORS					
A, B Differential controller, 2 sensors, thermostat, solar energy system	1.000	Ea.	274	74	348
C Thermometer 2" dial	3.000	Ea.	78	166.50	244.50
A, D, T Fill & drain valves, brass, 3/4" connection	3.000	Ea.	66	111	177
E Air vent, manual, 1/8" fitting	1.000	Ea.	3.75	28	31.75
F Air purger	1.000	Ea.	59.50	74	133.50
G Expansion tank	1.000	Ea.	74.50	28	102.50
I Valve, gate, bronze, NRS, soldered 3/4" diam	3.000	Ea.	405	133.50	538.50
J Neoprene vent flashing	2.000	Ea.	22.10	89	111.10
K Circulator, solar heated liquid, 1/25 HP	1.000	Ea.	236	114	350
N, N-1 Relief valve, temp & press 150 psi 210°F self-closing 3/4" IPS	2.000	Ea.	60	59	119
O Pipe covering, urethane ultraviolet cover, 1" wall, 3/4" diam	20.000	L.F.	66.40	160	226.40
P Pipe covering, fiberglass, all service jacket, 1" wall, 3/4" diam	50.000	L.F.	139.50	320	459.50
Roof clamps for solar energy collector panel	3.000	Set	12.15	69	81.15
Q Collector panel solar blk chrome on copper, 1/8" temp glass, 3'x7'	3.000	Ea.	3,600	504	4,104
R-1 Valve, swing check, bronze, regrinding disc, 3/4" diam, soldered	1.000	Ea.	213	44.50	257.50
S Pressure gauge, 60 psi, 2-1/2" dial	1.000	Ea.	28.50	28	56.50
U Valve, water tempering, bronze, sweat connections, 3/4" diam	1.000	Ea.	246	44.50	290.50
W, W-2 Tank, water storage immersed heat exchr elec elem 2"x2# insul 120 Gal	1.000	Ea.	1,975	635	2,610
X Valve, globe, bronze, rising stem, 3/4" diam, soldered	1.000	Ea.	300	44.50	344.50
Copper tubing type L, solder joint, hanger 10' OC 3/4" diam	20.000	L.F.	119	234	353
Copper tubing, type M, solder joint, hanger 10' OC 3/4" diam	70.000	L.F.	338.10	798	1,136.10
Sensor wire, #22-2 conductor multistranded	.500	C.L.F.	10.75	42.50	53.25
Solar energy heat transfer fluid, propylene glycol, anti-freeze	6.000	Gal.	180	189	369
Wrought copper fittings & solder, 3/4" diam	76.000	Ea.	459.80	3,572	4,031.80
TOTAL			**8,967.05**	**7,562**	**16,529.05**

D2020 295	Solar, Closed Loop, Hot Water Systems		MAT.	INST.	TOTAL
2550	Solar, closed loop, hot water system, immersed heat exchanger				
2560	3/8" tubing, 3 ea. 4' x 4'-4" vacuum tube collectors, 80 gal. tank		8,300	6,850	15,150
2580	1/2" tubing, 4 ea. 4' x 4'-4" vacuum tube collectors, 80 gal. tank		9,050	7,400	16,450
2600	120 gal. tank		9,000	7,475	16,475
2640	2 ea. 3'x7' black chrome collectors, 80 gal. tank	R235616 -60	7,125	7,050	14,175
2660	120 gal. tank		7,100	7,050	14,150
2700	2 ea. 3'x7' flat black collectors, 120 gal. tank		6,425	7,075	13,500
2720	3 ea. 3'x7' flat black collectors, 120 gal. tank		7,300	7,275	14,575
2760	3/4" tubing, 3 ea. 3'x7' black chrome collectors, 120 gal. tank		8,975	7,550	16,525
2780	3 ea. 3'x7' flat black collectors, 120 gal. tank		7,950	7,600	15,550
2800	2 ea. 4'x9' flat black w/plastic glazing collectors 120 gal. tank		7,475	7,625	15,100
2840	1" tubing, 4 ea. 2'x9' plastic absorber & glazing collectors 120 gal. tank		9,300	8,500	17,800
2860	4 ea. 3'x7' black chrome collectors, 120 gal. tank		11,500	8,525	20,025
2880	4 ea. 3'x7' flat black absorber collectors, 120 gal. tank		10,100	8,550	18,650

D20 Plumbing

D2040 Rain Water Drainage

Design Assumptions: Vertical conductor size is based on a maximum rate of rainfall of 4″ per hour. To convert roof area to other rates multiply "Max. S.F. Roof Area" shown by four and divide the result by desired local rate. The answer is the local roof area that may be handled by the indicated pipe diameter.

Basic cost is for roof drain, 10′ of vertical leader and 10′ of horizontal, plus connection to the main.

Pipe Dia.	Max. S.F. Roof Area	Gallons per Min.
2″	544	23
3″	1610	67
4″	3460	144
5″	6280	261
6″	10,200	424
8″	22,000	913

System Components	QUANTITY	UNIT	COST EACH MAT.	COST EACH INST.	COST EACH TOTAL
SYSTEM D2040 210 1880					
ROOF DRAIN, DWV PVC PIPE, 2″ DIAM., 10′ HIGH					
Drain, roof, main, ABS, dome type 2″ pipe size	1.000	Ea.	182	114	296
Clamp, roof drain, underdeck	1.000	Ea.	68	66.50	134.50
Pipe, Tee, PVC DWV, schedule 40, 2″ pipe size	1.000	Ea.	45.50	80	125.50
Pipe, PVC, DWV, schedule 40, 2″ diam.	20.000	L.F.	139	540	679
Pipe, elbow, PVC schedule 40, 2″ diam.	2.000	Ea.	6.16	88	94.16
TOTAL			440.66	888.50	1,329.16

D2040 210	Roof Drain Systems	COST EACH MAT.	COST EACH INST.	COST EACH TOTAL
1880	Roof drain, DWV PVC, 2″ diam., piping, 10′ high	440	890	1,330
1920	For each additional foot add	6.95	27	33.95
1960	3″ diam., 10′ high	675	1,025	1,700
2000	For each additional foot add	13.70	30	43.70
2040	4″ diam., 10′ high	895	1,175	2,070
2080	For each additional foot add	19.40	33.50	52.90
2120	5″ diam., 10′ high	2,150	1,350	3,500
2160	For each additional foot add	42	37	79
2200	6″ diam., 10′ high	2,500	1,500	4,000
2240	For each additional foot add	42.50	41	83.50
2280	8″ diam., 10′ high	4,700	2,550	7,250
2320	For each additional foot add	72.50	52	124.50
3940	C.I., soil, single hub, service wt., 2″ diam. piping, 10′ high	835	975	1,810
3980	For each additional foot add	12.10	25.50	37.60
4120	3″ diam., 10′ high	1,175	1,050	2,225
4160	For each additional foot add	15.90	26.50	42.40
4200	4″ diam., 10′ high	1,700	1,150	2,850
4240	For each additional foot add	20.50	29	49.50
4280	5″ diam., 10′ high	2,300	1,275	3,575
4320	For each additional foot add	41	32.50	73.50
4360	6″ diam., 10′ high	2,600	1,350	3,950
4400	For each additional foot add	34.50	34	68.50
4440	8″ diam., 10′ high	5,100	2,775	7,875
4480	For each additional foot add	53	57.50	110.50
6040	Steel galv. sch 40 threaded, 2″ diam. piping, 10′ high	1,250	945	2,195
6080	For each additional foot add	27	25	52
6120	3″ diam., 10′ high	2,525	1,350	3,875
6160	For each additional foot add	57.50	37	94.50

D20 Plumbing

D2040 Rain Water Drainage

D2040 210	Roof Drain Systems	MAT.	INST.	TOTAL
6200	4" diam., 10' high	3,875	1,750	5,625
6240	For each additional foot add	78.50	44.50	123
6280	5" diam., 10' high	3,800	1,450	5,250
6320	For each additional foot add	77	43	120
6360	6" diam., 10' high	4,775	1,875	6,650
6400	For each additional foot add	97.50	59	156.50
6440	8" diam., 10' high	8,500	2,725	11,225
6480	For each additional foot add	155	67	222

(COST EACH)

D30 HVAC

D3010 Energy Supply

Basis for Heat Loss Estimate, Apartment Type Structures:

1. Masonry walls and flat roof are insulated. U factor is assumed at .08.
2. Window glass area taken as BOCA minimum, 1/10th of floor area. Double insulating glass with 1/4" air space, U = .65.
3. Infiltration = 0.3 C.F. per hour per S.F. of net wall.
4. Concrete floor loss is 2 BTUH per S.F.
5. Temperature difference taken as 70°F.
6. Ventilating or makeup air has not been included and must be added if desired. Air shafts are not used.

System Components	QUANTITY	UNIT	COST EACH		
			MAT.	INST.	TOTAL
SYSTEM D3010 510 1760					
HEATING SYSTEM, FIN TUBE RADIATION, FORCED HOT WATER					
1,000 S.F. AREA, 10,000 C.F. VOLUME					
Boiler, oil fired, CI, burner, ctrls/insul/breech/pipe/ftng/valves, 109 MBH	1.000	Ea.	4,900	4,987.50	9,887.50
Circulating pump, CI flange connection, 1/12 HP	1.000	Ea.	805	266	1,071
Expansion tank, painted steel, ASME 18 Gal capacity	1.000	Ea.	900	116	1,016
Storage tank, steel, above ground, 275 Gal capacity w/supports	1.000	Ea.	1,600	325	1,925
Copper tubing type L, solder joint, hanger 10' OC, 3/4" diam	100.000	L.F.	595	1,170	1,765
Radiation, 3/4" copper tube w/alum fin baseboard pkg, 7" high	30.000	L.F.	273	840	1,113
Pipe covering, calcium silicate w/cover, 1' wall, 3/4' diam	100.000	L.F.	343	865	1,208
TOTAL			9,416	8,569.50	17,985.50
COST PER S.F.			9.42	8.57	17.99

D3010 510	Apartment Building Heating - Fin Tube Radiation	COST PER S.F.		
		MAT.	INST.	TOTAL
1740	Heating systems, fin tube radiation, forced hot water			
1760	1,000 S.F. area, 10,000 C.F. volume	9.43	8.58	18.01
1800	10,000 S.F. area, 100,000 C.F. volume	4.20	5.15	9.35
1840	20,000 S.F. area, 200,000 C.F. volume	4.02	5.80	9.82
1880	30,000 S.F. area, 300,000 C.F. volume	3.93	5.60	9.53

D30 HVAC

D3010 Energy Supply

Many styles of active solar energy systems exist. Those shown on the following page represent the majority of systems now being installed in different regions of the country.

The five active domestic hot water (DHW) systems which follow are typically specified as two or three panel systems with additional variations being the type of glazing and size of the storage tanks. Various combinations have been costed for the user's evaluation and comparison. The basic specifications from which the following systems were developed satisfy the construction detail requirements specified in the HUD Intermediate Minimum Property Standards (IMPS). If these standards are not complied with, the renewable energy system's costs could be significantly lower than shown.

To develop the system's specifications and costs it was necessary to make a number of assumptions about the systems. Certain systems are more appropriate to one climatic region than another or the systems may require modifications to be usable in particular locations. Specific instances in which the systems are not appropriate throughout the country as specified, or in which modification will be needed include the following:

- The freeze protection mechanisms provided in the DHW systems vary greatly. In harsh climates, where freeze is a major concern, a closed-loop indirect collection system may be more appropriate than a direct collection system.
- The thermosyphon water heater system described cannot be used when temperatures drop below 32°F.
- In warm climates it may be necessary to modify the systems installed to prevent overheating.

For each renewable resource (solar) system a schematic diagram and descriptive summary of the system is provided along with a list of all the components priced as part of the system. The costs were developed based on these specifications.

Considerations affecting costs which may increase or decrease beyond the estimates presented here include the following:

- Special structural qualities (allowance for earthquake, future expansion, high winds, and unusual spans or shapes);
- Isolated building site or rough terrain that would affect the transportation of personnel, material, or equipment;
- Unusual climatic conditions during the construction process;
- Substitution of other materials or system components for those used in the system specifications.

D30 HVAC

D3010 Energy Supply

In this closed-loop indirect collection system, fluid with a low freezing temperature, propylene glycol, transports heat from the collectors to water storage. The transfer fluid is contained in a closed loop consisting of collectors, supply and return piping, and a heat exchanger immersed in the storage tank.

When the collectors become approximately 20°F warmer than the storage temperature, the controller activates the circulator. The circulator moves the fluid continuously until the temperature difference between fluid in the collectors and storage is such that the collection will no longer occur and then the circulator turns off. Since the heat transfer fluid has a very low freezing temperature, there is no need for it to be drained from the collectors between periods of collection.

D30 HVAC

D3010 Energy Supply

System Components	QUANTITY	UNIT	COST EACH MAT.	COST EACH INST.	TOTAL
SYSTEM D3010 650 2750					
SOLAR, CLOSED LOOP, SPACE/HOT WATER					
1" TUBING, TEN 3'X7' BLK CHROME ON COPPER ABSORBER COLLECTORS					
A, B Differential controller 2 sensors, thermostat, solar energy system	2.000	Ea.	548	148	696
C Thermometer, 2" dial	10.000	Ea.	260	555	815
C-1 Heat exchanger, solar energy system, fluid to air, up flow, 80 MBH	1.000	Ea.	570	535	1,105
D, T Fill & drain valves, brass, 3/4" connection	5.000	Ea.	110	185	295
D-1 Fan center	1.000	Ea.	212	189	401
E Air vent, manual, 1/8" fitting	1.000	Ea.	3.75	28	31.75
E-2 Thermostat, 2 stage for sensing room temperature	1.000	Ea.	355	112	467
F Air purger	2.000	Ea.	119	148	267
F-1 Controller, liquid temperature, solar energy system	1.000	Ea.	135	178	313
G Expansion tank	2.000	Ea.	149	56	205
I Valve, gate, bronze, 125 lb, soldered, 1" diam	5.000	Ea.	970	235	1,205
J Vent flashing, neoprene	2.000	Ea.	22.10	89	111.10
K Circulator, solar heated liquid, 1/25 HP	2.000	Ea.	472	228	700
L Circulator, solar heated liquid, 1/20 HP	1.000	Ea.	350	133	483
N Relief valve, temp & pressure 150 psi 210°F self-closing	4.000	Ea.	120	118	238
N-1 Relief valve, pressure poppet, bronze, 30 psi, 3/4" IPS	3.000	Ea.	366	94.50	460.50
O Pipe covering, urethane, ultraviolet cover, 1" wall, 1" diam	50.000	L.F.	166	400	566
P Pipe covering, fiberglass, all service jacket, 1" wall, 1" diam	60.000	L.F.	167.40	384	551.40
Q Collector panel solar energy blk chrome on copper 1/8" temp glass 3'x7'	10.000	Ea.	12,000	1,680	13,680
Roof clamps for solar energy collector panel	10.000	Set	40.50	230	270.50
R Valve, swing check, bronze, 125 lb, regrinding disc, 3/4" & 1" diam	4.000	Ea.	1,220	188	1,408
S Pressure gage, 0-60 psi, for solar energy system	2.000	Ea.	57	56	113
U Valve, water tempering, bronze, sweat connections, 3/4" diam	1.000	Ea.	246	44.50	290.50
W, W-1, W-2 Tank, water storage immersed heat xchr elec elem 2"x1/2# ins 120 gal	4.000	Ea.	7,900	2,540	10,440
X Valve, globe, bronze, 125 lb, rising stem, 1" diam	3.000	Ea.	1,425	141	1,566
Y Valve, flow control	1.000	Ea.	162	40.50	202.50
Copper tubing, type M, solder joint, hanger 10' OC 1" diam	110.000	L.F.	797.50	1,397	2,194.50
Copper tubing, type L, solder joint, hanger 10' OC 3/4" diam	20.000	L.F.	119	234	353
Wrought copper fittings & solder, 3/4" & 1" diam	121.000	Ea.	1,790.80	6,715.50	8,506.30
Sensor, wire, #22-2 conductor, multistranded	.700	C.L.F.	15.05	59.50	74.55
Ductwork, galvanized steel, for heat exchanger	8.000	Lb.	50.80	82.80	133.60
Solar energy heat transfer fluid propylene glycol, anti-freeze	25.000	Gal.	750	787.50	1,537.50
TOTAL			31,668.90	18,011.80	49,680.70

D3010 650	Solar, Closed Loop, Space/Hot Water Systems		COST EACH MAT.	COST EACH INST.	TOTAL
2540	Solar, closed loop, space/hot water				
2550	1/2" tubing, 12 ea. 4'x4'4" vacuum tube collectors		28,800	16,800	45,600
2600	3/4" tubing, 12 ea. 4'x4'4" vacuum tube collectors	R235616 -60	30,800	17,300	48,100
2650	10 ea. 3' x 7' black chrome absorber collectors		29,900	16,800	46,700
2700	10 ea. 3' x 7' flat black absorber collectors		26,500	16,900	43,400
2750	1" tubing, 10 ea. 3' x 7' black chrome absorber collectors		31,700	18,000	49,700
2800	10 ea. 3' x 7' flat black absorber collectors		28,600	18,100	46,700
2850	6 ea. 4' x 9' flat black w/plastic glazing collectors		26,200	18,000	44,200
2900	12 ea. 2' x 9' plastic absorber and glazing collectors		27,900	18,300	46,200

D30 HVAC

D3010 Energy Supply

This draindown pool system uses a differential thermostat similar to those used in solar domestic hot water and space heating applications. To heat the pool, the pool water passes through the conventional pump-filter loop and then flows through the collectors. When collection is not possible, or when the pool temperature is reached, all water drains from the solar loop back to the pool through the existing piping. The modes are controlled by solenoid valves or other automatic valves in conjunction with a vacuum breaker relief valve, which facilitates draindown.

D30 HVAC

D3010 Energy Supply

System Components	QUANTITY	UNIT	COST EACH		
			MAT.	INST.	TOTAL
SYSTEM D3010 660 2640 SOLAR SWIMMING POOL HEATER, ROOF MOUNTED COLLECTORS TEN 4' X 10' FULLY WETTED UNGLAZED PLASTIC ABSORBERS					
A Differential thermostat/controller, 110V, adj pool pump system	1.000	Ea.	375	445	820
A-1 Solenoid valve, PVC, normally 1 open 1 closed (included)	2.000	Ea.			
B Sensor, thermistor type (included)	2.000	Ea.			
E-1 Valve, vacuum relief	1.000	Ea.	35	28	63
Q Collector panel, solar energy, plastic, liquid full wetted, 4' x 10'	10.000	Ea.	3,750	3,200	6,950
R Valve, ball check, PVC, socket, 1-1/2" diam	1.000	Ea.	177	44.50	221.50
Z Valve, ball, PVC, socket, 1-1/2" diam	3.000	Ea.	333	133.50	466.50
Pipe, PVC, sch 40, 1-1/2" diam	80.000	L.F.	724	1,960	2,684
Pipe fittings, PVC sch 40, socket joint, 1-1/2" diam	10.000	Ea.	22	445	467
Sensor wire, #22-2 conductor, multistranded	.500	C.L.F.	10.75	42.50	53.25
Roof clamps for solar energy collector panels	10.000	Set	40.50	230	270.50
Roof strap, Teflon for solar energy collector panels	26.000	L.F.	1,001	112.58	1,113.58
TOTAL			6,468.25	6,641.08	13,109.33

D3010 660	Solar Swimming Pool Heater Systems		COST EACH		
			MAT.	INST.	TOTAL
2530	Solar swimming pool heater systems, roof mounted collectors				
2540	10 ea. 3'x7' black chrome absorber, 1/8" temp. glass		14,700	5,125	19,825
2560	10 ea. 4'x8' black chrome absorber, 3/16" temp. glass	R235616 -60	16,500	6,100	22,600
2580	10 ea. 3'8"x6' flat black absorber, 3/16" temp. glass		11,400	5,225	16,625
2600	10 ea. 4'x9' flat black absorber, plastic glazing		13,200	6,350	19,550
2620	10 ea. 2'x9' rubber absorber, plastic glazing		16,000	6,875	22,875
2640	10 ea. 4'x10' fully wetted unglazed plastic absorber		6,475	6,650	13,125
2660	Ground mounted collectors				
2680	10 ea. 3'x7' black chrome absorber, 1/8" temp. glass		14,700	5,725	20,425
2700	10 ea. 4'x8' black chrome absorber, 3/16" temp. glass		16,400	6,700	23,100
2720	10 ea. 3'8"x6' flat blk absorber, 3/16" temp. glass		11,300	5,825	17,125
2740	10 ea. 4'x9' flat blk absorber, plastic glazing		13,200	6,950	20,150
2760	10 ea. 2'x9' rubber absorber, plastic glazing		15,900	7,225	23,125
2780	10 ea. 4'x10' fully wetted unglazed plastic absorber		6,425	7,225	13,650

D30 HVAC

D3010 Energy Supply

The complete Solar Air Heating System provides maximum savings of conventional fuel with both space heating and year-round domestic hot water heating. It allows for the home air conditioning to operate simultaneously and independently from the solar domestic water heating in summer. The system's modes of operation are:

Mode 1: The building is heated directly from the collectors with air circulated by the Solar Air Mover.

Mode 2: When heat is not needed in the building, the dampers change within the air mover to circulate the air from the collectors to the rock storage bin.

Mode 3: When heat is not available from the collector array and is available in rock storage, the air mover draws heated air from rock storage and directs it into the building. When heat is not available from the collectors or the rock storage bin, the auxiliary heating unit will provide heat for the building. The size of the collector array is typically 25% the size of the main floor area.

D30 HVAC

D3010 Energy Supply

System Components		QUANTITY	UNIT	COST EACH		
				MAT.	INST.	TOTAL
	SYSTEM D3010 675 1210					
	SOLAR, SPACE/HOT WATER, AIR TO WATER HEAT EXCHANGE					
A, B	Differential controller 2 sensors thermos., solar energy sys liquid loop	1.000	Ea.	274	74	348
A-1, B	Differential controller 2 sensors 6 station solar energy sys air loop	1.000	Ea.	315	296	611
B-1	Solar energy sensor, freeze prevention	1.000	Ea.	29.50	28	57.50
C	Thermometer for solar energy system, 2" dial	2.000	Ea.	52	111	163
C-1	Heat exchanger, solar energy system, air to fluid, up flow, 70 MBH	1.000	Ea.	430	455	885
D	Drain valve, brass, 3/4" connection	2.000	Ea.	44	74	118
E	Air vent, manual, for solar energy system 1/8" fitting	1.000	Ea.	3.75	28	31.75
E-1	Thermostat, 2 stage for sensing room temperature	1.000	Ea.	355	112	467
F	Air purger	1.000	Ea.	59.50	74	133.50
G	Expansion tank, for solar energy system	1.000	Ea.	74.50	28	102.50
I	Valve, gate, bronze, 125 lb, NRS, soldered 3/4" diam	2.000	Ea.	270	89	359
K	Circulator, solar heated liquid, 1/25 HP	1.000	Ea.	236	114	350
N	Relief valve temp & press 150 psi 210°F self-closing, 3/4" IPS	1.000	Ea.	30	29.50	59.50
N-1	Relief valve, pressure, poppet, bronze, 30 psi, 3/4" IPS	1.000	Ea.	122	31.50	153.50
P	Pipe covering, fiberglass, all service jacket, 1" wall, 3/4" diam	60.000	L.F.	167.40	384	551.40
Q-3	Manifold for flush mount solar energy collector panels	20.000	L.F.	3,420	196	3,616
Q	Collector panel solar energy, air, black on alum. plate, 7.5' x 3.5'	10.000	Ea.	8,650	1,780	10,430
R	Valve, swing check, bronze, 125 lb, regrinding disc, 3/4" diam	2.000	Ea.	426	89	515
S	Pressure gage, 2" dial, for solar energy system	1.000	Ea.	28.50	28	56.50
U	Valve, water tempering, bronze, sweat connections, 3/4" diam	1.000	Ea.	246	44.50	290.50
W, W-2	Tank, water storage, solar, elec element 2"x1/2# insul, 80 Gal	1.000	Ea.	2,025	555	2,580
X	Valve, globe, bronze, 125 lb, soldered, 3/4" diam	1.000	Ea.	300	44.50	344.50
	Copper tubing type L, solder joints, hangers 10' OC 3/4" diam	10.000	L.F.	59.50	117	176.50
	Copper tubing type M, solder joints, hangers 10' OC 3/4" diam	60.000	L.F.	289.80	684	973.80
	Wrought copper fittings & solder, 3/4" diam	26.000	Ea.	157.30	1,222	1,379.30
	Sensor wire, #22-2 conductor multistranded	1.200	C.L.F.	25.80	102	127.80
Q-1	Duct work, rigid fiberglass, rectangular	400.000	S.F.	556	2,780	3,336
	Duct work, spiral preformed, steel, PVC coated both sides, 12" x 10"	8.000	Ea.	244	520	764
R-2	Shutter/damper for solar heater circulator	9.000	Ea.	603	1,170	1,773
K-1	Shutter motor for solar heater circulator blower	9.000	Ea.	1,503	882	2,385
K-1	Fan, solar energy heated air circulator, space & DHW system	1.000	Ea.	1,825	3,125	4,950
R-3, R-4, V	Tank, solar energy air storage, 6'-3"H 7'x7' = 306 CF/2000 Gal	1.000	Ea.	15,800	2,025	17,825
Z-2	Crushed stone 1-1/2"	11.000	C.Y.	291.50	113.19	404.69
C-2	Thermometer, remote probe, 2" dial	1.000	Ea.	39.50	111	150.50
R-1	Solenoid valve	1.000	Ea.	196	98.50	294.50
Z-1	Furnace, supply diffusers, return grilles, existing	1.000	Ea.	15,800	2,025	17,825
	TOTAL			54,948.55	19,639.69	74,588.24

D3010 675		Air To Water Heat Exchange	COST EACH		
			MAT.	INST.	TOTAL
1210	Solar, air to water heat exchange, for space/hot water heating	R235616 -60	55,000	19,600	74,600
1220					

D30 HVAC

D3020 Heat Generating Systems

Boiler Baseboard Radiation

Small Electric Boiler
System Considerations:
1. Terminal units are fin tube baseboard radiation rated at 720 BTU/hr with 200° water temperature or 820 BTU/hr steam.
2. Primary use being for residential or smaller supplementary areas, the floor levels are based on 7-1/2' ceiling heights.
3. All distribution piping is copper for boilers through 205 MBH. All piping for larger systems is steel pipe.

System Components	QUANTITY	UNIT	COST EACH MAT.	COST EACH INST.	COST EACH TOTAL
SYSTEM D3020 102 1120					
SMALL HEATING SYSTEM, HYDRONIC, ELECTRIC BOILER					
1,480 S.F., 61 MBH, STEAM, 1 FLOOR					
Boiler, electric steam, std cntrls, trim, ftngs and valves, 18 KW, 61.4 MBH	1.000	Ea.	5,527.50	2,255	7,782.50
Copper tubing type L, solder joint, hanger 10'OC, 1-1/4" diam	160.000	L.F.	1,920	2,448	4,368
Radiation, 3/4" copper tube w/alum fin baseboard pkg 7" high	60.000	L.F.	546	1,680	2,226
Rough in baseboard panel or fin tube with valves & traps	10.000	Set	4,500	8,500	13,000
Pipe covering, calcium silicate w/cover, 1" wall 1-1/4" diam	160.000	L.F.	534.40	1,424	1,958.40
Low water cut-off, quick hookup, in gage glass tappings	1.000	Ea.	645	56	701
TOTAL			13,672.90	16,363	30,035.90
COST PER S.F.			9.57	11.45	21.02

D3020 102	Small Heating Systems, Hydronic, Electric Boilers	COST PER S.F. MAT.	COST PER S.F. INST.	COST PER S.F. TOTAL
1100	Small heating systems, hydronic, electric boilers			
1120	Steam, 1 floor, 1480 S.F., 61 M.B.H.	9.59	11.48	21.07
1160	3,000 S.F., 123 M.B.H.	7.25	9.70	16.95
1200	5,000 S.F., 205 M.B.H.	6.40	8.95	15.35
1240	2 floors, 12,400 S.F., 512 M.B.H.	5.85	8.90	14.75
1280	3 floors, 24,800 S.F., 1023 M.B.H.	6.35	8.80	15.15
1360	Hot water, 1 floor, 1,000 S.F., 41 M.B.H.	14.95	6.15	21.10
1400	2,500 S.F., 103 M.B.H.	11.10	11.05	22.15
1440	2 floors, 4,850 S.F., 205 M.B.H.	10.75	13.25	24
1480	3 floors, 9,700 S.F., 410 M.B.H.	11.30	13.70	25

D30 HVAC

D3090 Other HVAC Systems/Equip

Cast Iron Garage Exhaust System

Dual Exhaust System

System Components	QUANTITY	UNIT	COST EACH		
			MAT.	INST.	TOTAL
SYSTEM D3090 320 1040					
GARAGE, EXHAUST, SINGLE 3" EXHAUST OUTLET, CARS & LIGHT TRUCKS					
A Outlet top assy, for engine exhaust system with adapters and ftngs, 3" diam	1.000	Ea.	350	54.50	404.50
F Bullnose (guide) for engine exhaust system, 3" diam	1.000	Ea.	41		41
G Galvanized flexible tubing for engine exhaust system, 3" diam	8.000	L.F.	110.80		110.80
H Adapter for metal tubing end of engine exhaust system, 3" tail pipe	1.000	Ea.	68.50		68.50
J Pipe, sewer, cast iron, push-on joint, 8" diam.	18.000	L.F.	1,098	981	2,079
Excavating utility trench, chain trencher, 8" wide, 24" deep	18.000	L.F.		49.68	49.68
Backfill utility trench by hand, incl. compaction, 8" wide 24" deep	18.000	L.F.		63.36	63.36
Stand for blower, concrete over polystyrene core, 6" high	1.000	Ea.	9.20	27	36.20
AC&V duct spiral reducer 10"x8"	1.000	Ea.	66	49	115
AC&V duct spiral reducer 12"x10"	1.000	Ea.	77.50	65	142.50
AC&V duct spiral preformed 45° elbow, 8" diam	1.000	Ea.	47.50	56	103.50
AC&V utility fan, belt drive, 3 phase, 2000 CFM, 1 HP	2.000	Ea.	3,600	870	4,470
Safety switch, heavy duty fused, 240V, 3 pole, 30 amp	1.000	Ea.	170	266	436
TOTAL			5,638.50	2,481.54	8,120.04

D3090 320	Garage Exhaust Systems	COST PER BAY		
		MAT.	INST.	TOTAL
1040	Garage, single 3" exhaust outlet, cars & light trucks, one bay	5,650	2,475	8,125
1060	Additional bays up to seven bays	1,175	660	1,835
1500	4" outlet, trucks, one bay	5,675	2,475	8,150
1520	Additional bays up to six bays	1,225	660	1,885
1600	5" outlet, diesel trucks, one bay	6,050	2,475	8,525
1650	Additional single bays up to six bays	1,700	785	2,485
1700	Two adjoining bays	6,050	2,475	8,525
2000	Dual exhaust, 3" outlets, pair of adjoining bays	6,825	3,100	9,925
2100	Additional pairs of adjoining bays	1,875	785	2,660

D40 Fire Protection

D4010 Sprinklers

Dry Pipe System: A system employing automatic sprinklers attached to a piping system containing air under pressure, the release of which from the opening of sprinklers permits the water pressure to open a valve known as a "dry pipe valve". The water then flows into the piping system and out the opened sprinklers.

All areas are assumed to be open.

System Components	QUANTITY	UNIT	COST EACH		
			MAT.	INST.	TOTAL
SYSTEM D4010 310 0580					
DRY PIPE SPRINKLER, STEEL, BLACK, SCH. 40 PIPE					
LIGHT HAZARD, ONE FLOOR, 2000 S.F.					
Valve, gate, iron body 125 lb., OS&Y, flanged, 4" pipe size	1.000	Ea.	1,975	535	2,510
4" pipe size	1.000	Ea.	4,100	535	4,635
Tamper switch (valve supervisory switch)	3.000	Ea.	882	166.50	1,048.50
Valve, swing check, bronze, 125 lb, regrinding disc, 2-1/2" pipe size	1.000	Ea.	1,700	107	1,807
Valve, angle, bronze, 150 lb., rising stem, threaded, 2" pipe size	1.000	Ea.	1,450	81	1,531
*Alarm valve, 2-1/2" pipe size	1.000	Ea.	2,950	535	3,485
Alarm, water motor, complete with gong	1.000	Ea.	555	222	777
Fire alarm horn, electric	1.000	Ea.	68.50	127	195.50
Valve swing check w/balldrip CI with brass trim, 4" pipe size	1.000	Ea.	505	535	1,040
Pipe, steel, black, schedule 40, 4" diam.	8.000	L.F.	480	361.04	841.04
Dry pipe valve, trim & gauges, 4" pipe size	1.000	Ea.	4,250	1,600	5,850
Pipe, steel, black, schedule 40, threaded, cplg & hngr 10'OC 2-1/2" diam.	15.000	L.F.	577.50	480	1,057.50
Pipe, steel, black, schedule 40, threaded, cplg & hngr 10'OC 2" diam.	9.375	L.F.	215.63	234.38	450.01
Pipe, steel, black, schedule 40, threaded, cplg & hngr 10'OC 1-1/4" diam.	28.125	L.F.	410.63	504.84	915.47
Pipe, steel, black, schedule 40, threaded, cplg & hngr 10'OC 1" diam.	84.000	L.F.	932.40	1,407	2,339.40
Pipe Tee, malleable iron black, 150 lb. threaded, 4" pipe size	2.000	Ea.	1,200	800	2,000
Pipe Tee, malleable iron black, 150 lb. threaded, 2-1/2" pipe size	2.000	Ea.	336	356	692
Pipe Tee, malleable iron black, 150 lb. threaded, 2" pipe size	1.000	Ea.	78	145	223
Pipe Tee, malleable iron black, 150 lb. threaded, 1-1/4" pipe size	4.000	Ea.	148	456	604
Pipe Tee, malleable iron black, 150 lb. threaded, 1" pipe size	3.000	Ea.	67.50	333	400.50
Pipe 90° elbow malleable iron black, 150 lb. threaded, 1" pipe size	5.000	Ea.	72.50	342.50	415
Sprinkler head dry K5.6, 1" NPT, 3" to 6" length	12.000	Ea.	1,740	762	2,502
Air compressor, 200 Gal sprinkler system capacity, 1/3 HP	1.000	Ea.	2,275	685	2,960
*Standpipe connection, wall, flush, brs. w/plug & chain 2-1/2"x2-1/2"	1.000	Ea.	231	320	551
Valve gate bronze, 300 psi, NRS, class 150, threaded, 1" pipe size	1.000	Ea.	272	47	319
TOTAL			27,471.66	11,677.26	39,148.92
COST PER S.F.			10.99	4.67	15.66

*Not included in systems under 2000 S.F.

D4010 310	Dry Pipe Sprinkler Systems		COST PER S.F.		
			MAT.	INST.	TOTAL
0520	Dry pipe sprinkler systems, steel, black, sch. 40 pipe				
0530	Light hazard, one floor, 500 S.F.		20.50	8.35	28.85
0560	1000 S.F.	R211313	13.70	4.90	18.60
0580	2000 S.F.	-10	11	4.68	15.68

D40 Fire Protection

D4010 Sprinklers

D4010 310	Dry Pipe Sprinkler Systems		COST PER S.F.		
			MAT.	INST.	TOTAL
0600	5000 S.F.	R211313	5.45	3.29	8.74
0620	10,000 S.F.	-20	3.75	2.68	6.43
0640	50,000 S.F.		2.86	2.35	5.21
0660	Each additional floor, 500 S.F.		4.07	3.93	8
0680	1000 S.F.		3.62	3.20	6.82
0700	2000 S.F.		3.36	2.95	6.31
0720	5000 S.F.		2.56	2.53	5.09
0740	10,000 S.F.		2.38	2.32	4.70
0760	50,000 S.F.		2.14	2.07	4.21
1000	Ordinary hazard, one floor, 500 S.F.		21	8.40	29.40
1020	1000 S.F.		13.85	4.94	18.79
1040	2000 S.F.		10.85	5.15	16
1060	5000 S.F.		5.80	3.51	9.31
1080	10,000 S.F.		4.56	3.50	8.06
1100	50,000 S.F.		3.73	3.27	7
1140	Each additional floor, 500 S.F.		4.29	4.02	8.31
1160	1000 S.F.		4.06	3.59	7.65
1180	2000 S.F.		3.58	3.26	6.84
1200	5000 S.F.		3.05	2.80	5.85
1220	10,000 S.F.		2.83	2.72	5.55
1240	50,000 S.F.		2.70	2.35	5.05
1500	Extra hazard, one floor, 500 S.F.		26.50	10.45	36.95
1520	1000 S.F.		18.90	7.60	26.50
1540	2000 S.F.		12.10	6.55	18.65
1560	5000 S.F.		7.05	4.84	11.89
1580	10,000 S.F.		6.20	4.58	10.78
1600	50,000 S.F.		6.20	4.40	10.60
1660	Each additional floor, 500 S.F.		6.35	4.96	11.31
1680	1000 S.F.		5.75	4.64	10.39
1700	2000 S.F.		5.15	4.65	9.80
1720	5000 S.F.		4.29	4.07	8.36
1740	10,000 S.F.		4.08	3.72	7.80
1760	50,000 S.F.		4	3.58	7.58
2020	Grooved steel, black, sch. 40 pipe, light hazard, one floor, 2000 S.F.		11	4.29	15.29
2060	10,000 S.F.		4.03	2.33	6.36
2100	Each additional floor, 2000 S.F.		3.73	2.39	6.12
2150	10,000 S.F.		2.67	1.97	4.64
2200	Ordinary hazard, one floor, 2000 S.F.		11.40	4.53	15.93
2250	10,000 S.F.		4.91	2.97	7.88
2300	Each additional floor, 2000 S.F.		4.12	2.63	6.75
2350	10,000 S.F.		3.84	2.64	6.48
2400	Extra hazard, one floor, 2000 S.F.		12.70	5.65	18.35
2450	10,000 S.F.		6.90	3.84	10.74
2500	Each additional floor, 2000 S.F.		5.85	3.85	9.70
2550	10,000 S.F.		5	3.28	8.28
3050	Grooved steel, black, sch. 10 pipe, light hazard, one floor, 2000 S.F.		10.60	4.26	14.86
3100	10,000 S.F.		3.68	2.29	5.97
3150	Each additional floor, 2000 S.F.		3.32	2.35	5.67
3200	10,000 S.F.		2.31	1.94	4.25
3250	Ordinary hazard, one floor, 2000 S.F.		11	4.50	15.50
3300	10,000 S.F.		4.30	2.90	7.20
3350	Each additional floor, 2000 S.F.		3.72	2.60	6.32
3400	10,000 S.F.		3.02	2.56	5.58
3450	Extra hazard, one floor, 2000 S.F.		12.35	5.60	17.95
3500	10,000 S.F.		6.25	3.78	10.03
3550	Each additional floor, 2000 S.F.		5.55	3.82	9.37
3600	10,000 S.F.		4.64	3.24	7.88
4050	Copper tubing, type L, light hazard, one floor, 2000 S.F.		10.50	4.29	14.79

D40 Fire Protection

D4010 Sprinklers

D4010 310	Dry Pipe Sprinkler Systems	COST PER S.F.		
		MAT.	INST.	TOTAL
4100	10,000 S.F.	3.77	2.37	6.14
4150	Each additional floor, 2000 S.F.	3.25	2.43	5.68
4200	10,000 S.F.	2.41	2.02	4.43
4250	Ordinary hazard, one floor, 2000 S.F.	11	4.75	15.75
4300	10,000 S.F.	4.30	2.73	7.03
4350	Each additional floor, 2000 S.F.	4.09	2.76	6.85
4400	10,000 S.F.	2.85	2.33	5.18
4450	Extra hazard, one floor, 2000 S.F.	12.15	5.75	17.90
4500	10,000 S.F.	7.85	4.13	11.98
4550	Each additional floor, 2000 S.F.	5.20	3.89	9.09
4600	10,000 S.F.	5.30	3.54	8.84
5050	Copper tubing, type L, T-drill system, light hazard, one floor			
5060	2000 S.F.	10.45	4.04	14.49
5100	10,000 S.F.	3.49	1.99	5.48
5150	Each additional floor, 2000 S.F.	3.17	2.18	5.35
5200	10,000 S.F.	2.13	1.65	3.78
5250	Ordinary hazard, one floor, 2000 S.F.	10.55	4.12	14.67
5300	10,000 S.F.	4.20	2.50	6.70
5350	Each additional floor, 2000 S.F.	3.26	2.22	5.48
5400	10,000 S.F.	2.72	2.04	4.76
5450	Extra hazard, one floor, 2000 S.F.	11.25	4.81	16.06
5500	10,000 S.F.	6.45	3.13	9.58
5550	Each additional floor, 2000 S.F.	4.40	3.03	7.43
5600	10,000 S.F.	3.90	2.53	6.43

D40 Fire Protection

D4010 Sprinklers

Pre-Action System: A system employing automatic sprinklers attached to a piping system containing air that may or may not be under pressure, with a supplemental heat responsive system of generally more sensitive characteristics than the automatic sprinklers themselves, installed in the same areas as the sprinklers. Actuation of the heat responsive system, as from a fire, opens a valve which permits water to flow into the sprinkler piping system and to be discharged from those sprinklers which were opened by heat from the fire.

All areas are assumed to be open.

System Components	QUANTITY	UNIT	COST EACH MAT.	COST EACH INST.	COST EACH TOTAL
SYSTEM D4010 350 0580 PREACTION SPRINKLER SYSTEM, STEEL, BLACK, SCH. 40 PIPE LIGHT HAZARD, 1 FLOOR, 2000 S.F.					
Valve, gate, iron body 125 lb., OS&Y, flanged, 4" pipe size	1.000	Ea.	1,975	535	2,510
4" pipe size	1.000	Ea.	4,100	535	4,635
Tamper switch (valve supervisory switch)	3.000	Ea.	882	166.50	1,048.50
*Valve, swing check w/ball drip CI with brass trim 4" pipe size	1.000	Ea.	505	535	1,040
Valve, swing check, bronze, 125 lb, regrinding disc, 2-1/2" pipe size	1.000	Ea.	1,700	107	1,807
Valve, angle, bronze, 150 lb., rising stem, threaded, 2" pipe size	1.000	Ea.	1,450	81	1,531
*Alarm valve, 2-1/2" pipe size	1.000	Ea.	2,950	535	3,485
Alarm, water motor, complete with gong	1.000	Ea.	555	222	777
Fire alarm horn, electric	1.000	Ea.	68.50	127	195.50
Thermostatic release for release line	2.000	Ea.	2,500	89	2,589
Pipe, steel, black, schedule 40, 4" diam.	8.000	L.F.	480	361.04	841.04
Dry pipe valve, trim & gauges, 4" pipe size	1.000	Ea.	4,250	1,600	5,850
Pipe, steel, black, schedule 40, threaded, cplg. & hngr. 10'OC 2-1/2" diam.	15.000	L.F.	577.50	480	1,057.50
Pipe steel black, schedule 40, threaded, cplg. & hngr. 10'OC 2" diam.	9.375	L.F.	215.63	234.38	450.01
Pipe, steel, black, schedule 40, threaded, cplg. & hngr. 10'OC 1-1/4" diam.	28.125	L.F.	410.63	504.84	915.47
Pipe, steel, black, schedule 40, threaded, cplg. & hngr. 10'OC 1" diam.	84.000	L.F.	932.40	1,407	2,339.40
Pipe, Tee, malleable iron, black, 150 lb. threaded, 4" diam.	2.000	Ea.	1,200	800	2,000
Pipe, Tee, malleable iron, black, 150 lb. threaded, 2-1/2" pipe size	2.000	Ea.	336	356	692
Pipe, Tee, malleable iron, black, 150 lb. threaded, 2" pipe size	1.000	Ea.	78	145	223
Pipe, Tee, malleable iron, black, 150 lb. threaded, 1-1/4" pipe size	4.000	Ea.	148	456	604
Pipe, Tee, malleable iron, black, 150 lb. threaded, 1" pipe size	3.000	Ea.	67.50	333	400.50
Pipe, 90° elbow, malleable iron, blk., 150 lb. threaded, 1" pipe size	5.000	Ea.	72.50	342.50	415
Sprinkler head, std. spray, brass 135°-286°F 1/2" NPT, 3/8" orifice	12.000	Ea.	522	666	1,188
Air compressor auto complete 200 Gal sprinkler sys. cap., 1/3 HP	1.000	Ea.	2,275	685	2,960
*Standpipe conn.,wall, flush, brass w/plug & chain 2-1/2" x 2-1/2"	1.000	Ea.	231	320	551
Valve, gate, bronze, 300 psi, NRS, class 150, threaded, 1" pipe size	1.000	Ea.	272	47	319
TOTAL			28,753.66	11,670.26	40,423.92
COST PER S.F.			11.50	4.67	16.17

*Not included in systems under 2000 S.F.

D4010 350	Preaction Sprinkler Systems	COST PER S.F. MAT.	COST PER S.F. INST.	COST PER S.F. TOTAL
0520	Preaction sprinkler systems, steel, black, sch. 40 pipe			
0530	Light hazard, one floor, 500 S.F.	21.50	6.70	28.20

D40 Fire Protection

D4010 Sprinklers

D4010 350	Preaction Sprinkler Systems		COST PER S.F.		
			MAT.	INST.	TOTAL
0560	1000 S.F.	R211313 -10	12.10	4.96	17.06
0580	2000 S.F.		11.52	4.68	16.20
0600	5000 S.F.	R211313 -20	5.75	3.27	9.02
0620	10,000 S.F.		3.98	2.67	6.65
0640	50,000 S.F.		3.07	2.34	5.41
0660	Each additional floor, 500 S.F.		5.45	3.51	8.96
0680	1000 S.F.		4.10	3.20	7.30
0700	2000 S.F.		3.84	2.95	6.79
0720	5000 S.F.		3.75	2.58	6.33
0740	10,000 S.F.		3.09	2.35	5.44
0760	50,000 S.F.		2.60	2.14	4.74
1000	Ordinary hazard, one floor, 500 S.F.		22.50	7.25	29.75
1020	1000 S.F.		14.15	4.93	19.08
1040	2000 S.F.		11.65	5.15	16.80
1060	5000 S.F.		5.90	3.49	9.39
1080	10,000 S.F.		4.61	3.47	8.08
1100	50,000 S.F.		3.79	3.23	7.02
1140	Each additional floor, 500 S.F.		5.55	4.04	9.59
1160	1000 S.F.		4.08	3.23	7.31
1180	2000 S.F.		3.44	3.22	6.66
1200	5000 S.F.		3.45	3.01	6.46
1220	10,000 S.F.		3.27	3.12	6.39
1240	50,000 S.F.		3.07	2.77	5.84
1500	Extra hazard, one floor, 500 S.F.		32	9.35	41.35
1520	1000 S.F.		19.15	6.95	26.10
1540	2000 S.F.		12.10	6.50	18.60
1560	5000 S.F.		7.70	5.20	12.90
1580	10,000 S.F.		6.40	5.05	11.45
1600	50,000 S.F.		6.30	4.87	11.17
1660	Each additional floor, 500 S.F.		7.30	4.96	12.26
1680	1000 S.F.		6	4.64	10.64
1700	2000 S.F.		5.25	4.64	9.89
1720	5000 S.F.		4.35	4.09	8.44
1740	10,000 S.F.		3.91	3.76	7.67
1760	50,000 S.F.		3.64	3.52	7.16
2020	Grooved steel, black, sch. 40 pipe, light hazard, one floor, 2000 S.F.		11.50	4.29	15.79
2060			4.26	2.32	6.58
2100	Each additional floor of 2000 S.F.		4.21	2.38	6.59
2150	10,000 S.F.		2.90	1.96	4.86
2200	Ordinary hazard, one floor, 2000 S.F.		11.75	4.52	16.27
2250	10,000 S.F.		4.95	2.95	7.90
2300	Each additional floor, 2000 S.F.		4.44	2.62	7.06
2350	10,000 S.F.		3.61	2.60	6.21
2400	Extra hazard, one floor, 2000 S.F.		12.70	5.60	18.30
2450	10,000 S.F.		6.75	3.80	10.55
2500	Each additional floor, 2000 S.F.		5.90	3.81	9.71
2550	10,000 S.F.		4.75	3.24	7.99
3050	Grooved steel, black, sch. 10 pipe light hazard, one floor, 2000 S.F.		11.10	4.25	15.35
3100	10,000 S.F.		3.91	2.28	6.19
3150	Each additional floor, 2000 S.F.		3.80	2.35	6.15
3200	10,000 S.F.		2.54	1.93	4.47
3250	Ordinary hazard, one floor, 2000 S.F.		11.15	4.22	15.37
3300	10,000 S.F.		3.94	2.87	6.81
3350	Each additional floor, 2000 S.F.		4.05	2.58	6.63
3400	10,000 S.F.		3.06	2.53	5.59
3450	Extra hazard, one floor, 2000 S.F.		12.40	5.55	17.95
3500	10,000 S.F.		5.95	3.73	9.68
3550	Each additional floor, 2000 S.F.		5.55	3.79	9.34

D40 Fire Protection

D4010 Sprinklers

D4010 350	Preaction Sprinkler Systems	COST PER S.F.		
		MAT.	INST.	TOTAL
3600	10,000 S.F.	4.38	3.19	7.57
4050	Copper tubing, type L, light hazard, one floor, 2000 S.F.	11	4.29	15.29
4100	10,000 S.F.	4.01	2.36	6.37
4150	Each additional floor, 2000 S.F.	3.76	2.43	6.19
4200	10,000 S.F.	2.17	2	4.17
4250	Ordinary hazard, one floor, 2000 S.F.	11.20	4.69	15.89
4300	10,000 S.F.	4.34	2.71	7.05
4350	Each additional floor, 2000 S.F.	3.72	2.45	6.17
4400	10,000 S.F.	2.70	2.13	4.83
4450	Extra hazard, one floor, 2000 S.F.	12.05	5.65	17.70
4500	10,000 S.F.	7.45	4.07	11.52
4550	Each additional floor, 2000 S.F.	5.20	3.85	9.05
4600	10,000 S.F.	5.05	3.49	8.54
5050	Copper tubing, type L, T-drill system, light hazard, one floor			
5060	2000 S.F.	10.90	4.04	14.94
5100	10,000 S.F.	3.72	1.98	5.70
5150	Each additional floor, 2000 S.F.	3.65	2.18	5.83
5200	10,000 S.F.	2.36	1.63	3.99
5250	Ordinary hazard, one floor, 2000 S.F.	10.85	4.11	14.96
5300	10,000 S.F.	4.24	2.47	6.71
5350	Each additional floor, 2000 S.F.	3.61	2.22	5.83
5400	10,000 S.F.	2.90	2.12	5.02
5450	Extra hazard, one floor, 2000 S.F.	11.25	4.78	16.03
5500	10,000 S.F.	6.05	3.07	9.12
5550	Each additional floor, 2000 S.F.	4.43	2.99	7.42
5600	10,000 S.F.	3.64	2.48	6.12

D40 Fire Protection

D4010 Sprinklers

Deluge System: A system employing open sprinklers attached to a piping system connected to a water supply through a valve which is opened by the operation of a heat responsive system installed in the same areas as the sprinklers. When this valve opens, water flows into the piping system and discharges from all sprinklers attached thereto.

All areas are assumed to be open.

System Components	QUANTITY	UNIT	COST EACH		
			MAT.	INST.	TOTAL
SYSTEM D4010 370 0580					
DELUGE SPRINKLER SYSTEM, STEEL BLACK SCH. 40 PIPE					
LIGHT HAZARD, 1 FLOOR, 2000 S.F.					
Valve, gate, iron body 125 lb., OS&Y, flanged, 4" pipe size	1.000	Ea.	1,975	535	2,510
4" pipe size	1.000	Ea.	4,100	535	4,635
Tamper switch (valve supervisory switch)	3.000	Ea.	882	166.50	1,048.50
Valve, swing check w/ball drip, CI w/brass ftngs., 4" pipe size	1.000	Ea.	505	535	1,040
Valve, swing check, bronze, 125 lb, regrinding disc, 2-1/2" pipe size	1.000	Ea.	1,700	107	1,807
Valve, angle, bronze, 150 lb., rising stem, threaded, 2" pipe size	1.000	Ea.	1,450	81	1,531
*Alarm valve, 2-1/2" pipe size	1.000	Ea.	2,950	535	3,485
Alarm, water motor, complete with gong	1.000	Ea.	555	222	777
Fire alarm horn, electric	1.000	Ea.	68.50	127	195.50
Thermostatic release for release line	2.000	Ea.	2,500	89	2,589
Pipe, steel, black, schedule 40, 4" diam.	8.000	L.F.	480	361.04	841.04
Deluge valve trim, pressure relief, emergency release, gauge, 4" pipe size	1.000	Ea.	8,350	1,600	9,950
Deluge system, monitoring panel w/deluge valve & trim	1.000	Ea.	28,700	49.50	28,749.50
Pipe, steel, black, schedule 40, threaded, cplg & hngr 10' OC 2-1/2" diam.	15.000	L.F.	577.50	480	1,057.50
Pipe, steel, black, schedule 40, threaded, cplg & hngr 10' OC 2" diam.	9.375	L.F.	215.63	234.38	450.01
Pipe, steel, black, schedule 40, threaded, cplg & hngr 10' OC 1-1/4" diam.	28.125	L.F.	410.63	504.84	915.47
Pipe, steel, black, schedule 40, threaded, cplg & hngr 10' OC 1" diam.	84.000	L.F.	932.40	1,407	2,339.40
Pipe, Tee, malleable iron, black, 150 lb. threaded, 4" pipe size	2.000	Ea.	1,200	800	2,000
Pipe, Tee, malleable iron, black, 150 lb. threaded, 2-1/2" pipe size	2.000	Ea.	336	356	692
Pipe, Tee, malleable iron, black, 150 lb. threaded, 2" pipe size	1.000	Ea.	78	145	223
Pipe, Tee, malleable iron, black, 150 lb. threaded, 1-1/4" pipe size	4.000	Ea.	148	456	604
Pipe, Tee, malleable iron, black, 150 lb. threaded, 1" pipe size	3.000	Ea.	67.50	333	400.50
Pipe, 90° elbow, malleable iron, black, 150 lb. threaded 1" pipe size	5.000	Ea.	72.50	342.50	415
Sprinkler head, std spray, brass 135°-286°F 1/2" NPT, 3/8" orifice	12.000	Ea.	522	666	1,188
Air compressor, auto, complete, 200 Gal sprinkler sys. cap., 1/3 HP	1.000	Ea.	2,275	685	2,960
*Standpipe connection, wall, flush w/plug & chain 2-1/2" x 2-1/2"	1.000	Ea.	231	320	551
Valve, gate, bronze, 300 psi, NRS, class 150, threaded, 1" pipe size	1.000	Ea.	272	47	319
TOTAL			61,553.66	11,719.76	73,273.42
COST PER S.F.			24.62	4.69	29.31

*Not included in systems under 2000 S.F.

D4010 370		Deluge Sprinkler Systems	COST PER S.F.		
			MAT.	INST.	TOTAL
0520	Deluge sprinkler systems, steel, black, sch. 40 pipe				
0530	Light hazard, one floor, 500 S.F.		67.50	6.80	74.30

D40 Fire Protection

D4010 Sprinklers

D4010 370	Deluge Sprinkler Systems		COST PER S.F.		
			MAT.	INST.	TOTAL
0560	1000 S.F.	R211313-10	37	4.82	41.82
0580	2000 S.F.		24.60	4.68	29.28
0600	5000 S.F.	R211313-20	10.65	3.28	13.93
0620	10,000 S.F.		6.45	2.67	9.12
0640	50,000 S.F.		3.56	2.34	5.90
0660	Each additional floor, 500 S.F.		4.69	3.51	8.20
0680	1000 S.F.		4.10	3.20	7.30
0700	2000 S.F.		3.84	2.95	6.79
0720	5000 S.F.		2.82	2.51	5.33
0740	10,000 S.F.		2.61	2.31	4.92
0760	50,000 S.F.		2.58	2.13	4.71
1000	Ordinary hazard, one floor, 500 S.F.		70	7.75	77.75
1020	1000 S.F.		37	4.96	41.96
1040	2000 S.F.		24	5.20	29.20
1060	5000 S.F.		10.85	3.50	14.35
1080	10,000 S.F.		7.05	3.48	10.53
1100	50,000 S.F.		4.32	3.29	7.61
1140	Each additional floor, 500 S.F.		5.55	4.04	9.59
1160	1000 S.F.		4.08	3.23	7.31
1180	2000 S.F.		3.44	3.22	6.66
1200	5000 S.F.		3.19	2.78	5.97
1220	10,000 S.F.		3.14	2.76	5.90
1240	50,000 S.F.		2.88	2.53	5.41
1500	Extra hazard, one floor, 500 S.F.		77.50	9.45	86.95
1520	1000 S.F.		43	7.20	50.20
1540	2000 S.F.		24.50	6.50	31
1560	5000 S.F.		11.90	4.81	16.71
1580	10,000 S.F.		8.40	4.64	13.04
1600	50,000 S.F.		7.85	4.48	12.33
1660	Each additional floor, 500 S.F.		7.30	4.96	12.26
1680	1000 S.F.		6	4.64	10.64
1700	2000 S.F.		5.25	4.64	9.89
1720	5000 S.F.		4.35	4.09	8.44
1740	10,000 S.F.		4.03	3.90	7.93
1760	50,000 S.F.		3.87	3.76	7.63
2000	Grooved steel, black, sch. 40 pipe, light hazard, one floor				
2020	2000 S.F.		24	4.31	28.31
2060	10,000 S.F.		6.75	2.34	9.09
2100	Each additional floor, 2,000 S.F.		4.21	2.38	6.59
2150	10,000 S.F.		2.90	1.96	4.86
2200	Ordinary hazard, one floor, 2000 S.F.		11.75	4.52	16.27
2250	10,000 S.F.		7.40	2.95	10.35
2300	Each additional floor, 2000 S.F.		4.44	2.62	7.06
2350	10,000 S.F.		3.61	2.60	6.21
2400	Extra hazard, one floor, 2000 S.F.		25	5.60	30.60
2450	10,000 S.F.		9.15	3.82	12.97
2500	Each additional floor, 2000 S.F.		5.90	3.81	9.71
2550	10,000 S.F.		4.75	3.24	7.99
3000	Grooved steel, black, sch. 10 pipe, light hazard, one floor				
3050	2000 S.F.		22.50	4.09	26.59
3100	10,000 S.F.		6.35	2.29	8.64
3150	Each additional floor, 2000 S.F.		3.80	2.35	6.15
3200	10,000 S.F.		2.54	1.93	4.47
3250	Ordinary hazard, one floor, 2000 S.F.		23.50	4.50	28
3300	10,000 S.F.		6.40	2.87	9.27
3350	Each additional floor, 2000 S.F.		4.05	2.58	6.63
3400	10,000 S.F.		3.06	2.53	5.59
3450	Extra hazard, one floor, 2000 S.F.		24.50	5.60	30.10

D40 Fire Protection

D4010 Sprinklers

D4010 370	Deluge Sprinkler Systems	COST PER S.F.		
		MAT.	INST.	TOTAL
3500	10,000 S.F.	8.45	3.73	12.18
3550	Each additional floor, 2000 S.F.	5.55	3.79	9.34
3600	10,000 S.F.	4.38	3.19	7.57
4000	Copper tubing, type L, light hazard, one floor			
4050	2000 S.F.	23.50	4.30	27.80
4100	10,000 S.F.	6.40	2.36	8.76
4150	Each additional floor, 2000 S.F.	3.73	2.43	6.16
4200	10,000 S.F.	2.17	2	4.17
4250	Ordinary hazard, one floor, 2000 S.F.	23.50	4.75	28.25
4300	10,000 S.F.	6.85	2.76	9.61
4350	Each additional floor, 2000 S.F.	3.79	2.48	6.27
4400	10,000 S.F.	2.81	2.17	4.98
4450	Extra hazard, one floor, 2000 S.F.	24.50	5.70	30.20
4500	10,000 S.F.	10	4.16	14.16
4550	Each additional floor, 2000 S.F.	5.35	3.91	9.26
4600	10,000 S.F.	5.15	3.54	8.69
5000	Copper tubing, type L, T-drill system, light hazard, one floor			
5050	2000 S.F.	23	4.06	27.06
5100	10,000 S.F.	6.20	1.99	8.19
5150	Each additional floor, 2000 S.F.	3.76	2.21	5.97
5200	10,000 S.F.	2.36	1.63	3.99
5250	Ordinary hazard, one floor, 2000 S.F.	21.50	3.86	25.36
5300	10,000 S.F.	6.70	2.48	9.18
5350	Each additional floor, 2000 S.F.	3.58	2.20	5.78
5400	10,000 S.F.	2.90	2.12	5.02
5450	Extra hazard, one floor, 2000 S.F.	21.50	4.53	26.03
5500	10,000 S.F.	8.55	3.08	11.63
5550	Each additional floor, 2000 S.F.	4.43	2.99	7.42
5600	10,000 S.F.	3.64	2.48	6.12

D40 Fire Protection

D4010 Sprinklers

On-off multicycle sprinkler system is a fixed fire protection system utilizing water as its extinguishing agent. It is a time delayed, recycling, preaction type which automatically shuts the water off when heat is reduced below the detector operating temperature and turns the water back on when that temperature is exceeded.

The system senses a fire condition through a closed circuit electrical detector system which controls water flow to the fire automatically. Batteries supply up to 90 hour emergency power supply for system operation. The piping system is dry (until water is required) and is monitored with pressurized air. Should any leak in the system piping occur, an alarm will sound, but water will not enter the system until heat is sensed by a Firecycle detector.

All areas are assumed to be open.

System Components	QUANTITY	UNIT	COST EACH MAT.	INST.	TOTAL
SYSTEM D4010 390 0580					
ON-OFF MULTICYCLE SPRINKLER SYSTEM, STEEL, BLACK, SCH. 40 PIPE					
LIGHT HAZARD, ONE FLOOR, 2000 S.F.					
Valve, gate, iron body 125 lb., OS&Y, flanged, 4" pipe size	1.000	Ea.	1,975	535	2,510
4" pipe size	1.000	Ea.	4,100	535	4,635
Tamper switch (valve supervisory switch)	3.000	Ea.	882	166.50	1,048.50
Valve, angle, bronze, 150 lb., rising stem, threaded, 2" pipe size	1.000	Ea.	1,450	81	1,531
Valve, swing check, bronze, 125 lb, regrinding disc, 2-1/2" pipe size	1.000	Ea.	1,700	107	1,807
*Alarm valve, 2-1/2" pipe size	1.000	Ea.	2,950	535	3,485
Alarm, water motor, complete with gong	1.000	Ea.	555	222	777
Pipe, steel, black, schedule 40, 4" diam.	8.000	L.F.	480	361.04	841.04
Fire alarm, horn, electric	1.000	Ea.	68.50	127	195.50
Pipe, steel, black, schedule 40, threaded, cplg & hngr 10' OC 2-1/2" diam.	15.000	L.F.	577.50	480	1,057.50
Pipe, steel, black, schedule 40, threaded, cplg & hngr 10' OC 2" diam.	9.375	L.F.	215.63	234.38	450.01
Pipe, steel, black, schedule 40, threaded, cplg & hngr 10' OC 1-1/4" diam.	28.125	L.F.	410.63	504.84	915.47
Pipe, steel, black, schedule 40, threaded, cplg & hngr 10' OC 1" diam.	84.000	L.F.	932.40	1,407	2,339.40
Pipe, Tee, malleable iron, black, 150 lb. threaded, 4" pipe size	2.000	Ea.	1,200	800	2,000
Pipe, Tee, malleable iron, black, 150 lb. threaded, 2-1/2" pipe size	2.000	Ea.	336	356	692
Pipe, Tee, malleable iron, black, 150 lb. threaded, 2" pipe size	1.000	Ea.	78	145	223
Pipe, Tee, malleable iron, black, 150 lb. threaded, 1-1/4" pipe size	4.000	Ea.	148	456	604
Pipe, Tee, malleable iron, black, 150 lb. threaded, 1" pipe size	3.000	Ea.	67.50	333	400.50
Pipe, 90° elbow, malleable iron, black, 150 lb. threaded, 1" pipe size	5.000	Ea.	72.50	342.50	415
Sprinkler head std spray, brass 135°-286°F 1/2" NPT, 3/8" orifice	12.000	Ea.	522	666	1,188
Firecycle controls, incls panel, battery, solenoid valves, press switches	1.000	Ea.	40,900	3,375	44,275
Detector, firecycle system	2.000	Ea.	2,650	111	2,761
Firecycle pkg, swing check & flow control valves w/trim 4" pipe size	1.000	Ea.	8,625	1,600	10,225
Air compressor, auto, complete, 200 Gal sprinkler sys. cap., 1/3 HP	1.000	Ea.	2,275	685	2,960
*Standpipe connection, wall, flush, brass w/plug & chain 2-1/2"x2-1/2"	1.000	Ea.	231	320	551
Valve, gate, bronze 300 psi, NRS, class 150, threaded, 1" diam.	1.000	Ea.	272	47	319
TOTAL			73,673.66	14,532.26	88,205.92
COST PER S.F.			29.47	5.81	35.28

*Not included in systems under 2000 S.F.

D4010 390	On-off multicycle Sprinkler Systems	COST PER S.F. MAT.	INST.	TOTAL
0520	On-off multicycle sprinkler systems, steel, black, sch. 40 pipe			
0530	Light hazard, one floor, 500 S.F.	88.50	12.90	101.40

D40 Fire Protection

D4010 Sprinklers

D4010 390	On-off multicycle Sprinkler Systems		COST PER S.F.		
			MAT.	INST.	TOTAL
0560	1000 S.F.	R211313 -10	47.50	8.10	55.60
0580	2000 S.F.		29.40	5.80	35.20
0600	5000 S.F.	R211313 -20	12.50	3.71	16.21
0620	10,000 S.F.		7.45	2.89	10.34
0640	50,000 S.F.		3.85	2.38	6.23
0660	Each additional floor of 500 S.F.		4.80	3.53	8.33
0680	1000 S.F.		4.15	3.21	7.36
0700	2000 S.F.		3.40	2.93	6.33
0720	5000 S.F.		2.87	2.52	5.39
0740	10,000 S.F.		2.75	2.32	5.07
0760	50,000 S.F.		2.66	2.13	4.79
1000	Ordinary hazard, one floor, 500 S.F.		84.50	13.05	97.55
1020	1000 S.F.		47.50	8	55.50
1040	2000 S.F.		28	6.20	34.20
1060	5000 S.F.		12.70	3.92	16.62
1080	10,000 S.F.		8.10	3.70	11.80
1100	50,000 S.F.		4.85	3.67	8.52
1140	Each additional floor, 500 S.F.		5.65	4.06	9.71
1160	1000 S.F.		4.14	3.24	7.38
1180	2000 S.F.		3.78	2.97	6.75
1200	5000 S.F.		3.24	2.78	6.02
1220	10,000 S.F.		3.01	2.70	5.71
1240	50,000 S.F.		2.92	2.41	5.33
1500	Extra hazard, one floor, 500 S.F.		98.50	15.50	114
1520	1000 S.F.		51.50	10	61.50
1540	2000 S.F.		29	7.55	36.55
1560	5000 S.F.		13.70	5.25	18.95
1580	10,000 S.F.		9.75	5.25	15
1600	50,000 S.F.		7.65	5.75	13.40
1660	Each additional floor, 500 S.F.		7.40	4.98	12.38
1680	1000 S.F.		6.05	4.65	10.70
1700	2000 S.F.		5.35	4.64	9.99
1720	5000 S.F.		4.40	4.10	8.50
1740	10,000 S.F.		4.05	3.77	7.82
1760	50,000 S.F.		3.87	3.63	7.50
2020	Grooved steel, black, sch. 40 pipe, light hazard, one floor				
2030	2000 S.F.		26.50	5.10	31.60
2060	10,000 S.F.		8.55	3.51	12.06
2100	Each additional floor, 2000 S.F.		4.27	2.39	6.66
2150	10,000 S.F.		3.04	1.97	5.01
2200	Ordinary hazard, one floor, 2000 S.F.		28.50	5.60	34.10
2250	10,000 S.F.		9.10	3.34	12.44
2300	Each additional floor, 2000 S.F.		4.50	2.62	7.12
2350	10,000 S.F.		3.75	2.61	6.36
2400	Extra hazard, one floor, 2000 S.F.		27.50	6.40	33.90
2450	10,000 S.F.		10.10	3.99	14.09
2500	Each additional floor, 2000 S.F.		5.95	3.82	9.77
2550	10,000 S.F.		4.89	3.25	8.14
3050	Grooved steel, black, sch. 10 pipe, light hazard, one floor,				
3060	2000 S.F.		28	5.35	33.35
3100	10,000 S.F.		7.40	2.50	9.90
3150	Each additional floor, 2000 S.F.		3.86	2.36	6.22
3200	10,000 S.F.		2.68	1.94	4.62
3250	Ordinary hazard, one floor, 2000 S.F.		28	5.55	33.55
3300	10,000 S.F.		7.90	3.11	11.01
3350	Each additional floor, 2000 S.F.		4.11	2.59	6.70
3400	10,000 S.F.		3.20	2.54	5.74
3450	Extra hazard, one floor, 2000 S.F.		29	6.65	35.65

D40 Fire Protection

D4010 Sprinklers

D4010 390	On-off multicycle Sprinkler Systems	COST PER S.F.		
		MAT.	INST.	TOTAL
3500	10,000 S.F.	9.45	3.93	13.38
3550	Each additional floor, 2000 S.F.	5.60	3.79	9.39
3600	10,000 S.F.	4.52	3.20	7.72
4060	Copper tubing, type L, light hazard, one floor, 2000 S.F.	28	5.35	33.35
4100	10,000 S.F.	7.50	2.58	10.08
4150	Each additional floor, 2000 S.F.	3.78	2.44	6.22
4200	10,000 S.F.	2.78	2.02	4.80
4250	Ordinary hazard, one floor, 2000 S.F.	28	5.75	33.75
4300	10,000 S.F.	7.85	2.93	10.78
4350	Each additional floor, 2000 S.F.	3.77	2.45	6.22
4400	10,000 S.F.	2.80	2.11	4.91
4450	Extra hazard, one floor, 2000 S.F.	29	6.70	35.70
4500	10,000 S.F.	11.05	4.33	15.38
4550	Each additional floor, 2000 S.F.	5.25	3.86	9.11
4600	10,000 S.F.	5.20	3.50	8.70
5060	Copper tubing, type L, T-drill system, light hazard, one floor 2000 S.F.	28	5.10	33.10
5100	10,000 S.F.	7.20	2.19	9.39
5150	Each additional floor, 2000 S.F.	4.10	2.28	6.38
5200	10,000 S.F.	2.49	1.64	4.13
5250	Ordinary hazard, one floor, 2000 S.F.	27.50	5.15	32.65
5300	10,000 S.F.	7.60	2.64	10.24
5350	Each additional floor, 2000 S.F.	3.54	2.17	5.71
5400	10,000 S.F.	2.91	2.08	4.99
5450	Extra hazard, one floor, 2000 S.F.	28	5.80	33.80
5500	10,000 S.F.	9.40	3.21	12.61
5550	Each additional floor, 2000 S.F.	4.37	2.94	7.31
5600	10,000 S.F.	3.65	2.44	6.09

D40 Fire Protection

D4010 Sprinklers

Wet Pipe System. A system employing automatic sprinklers attached to a piping system containing water and connected to a water supply so that water discharges immediately from sprinklers opened by heat from a fire.

All areas are assumed to be open.

System Components	QUANTITY	UNIT	COST EACH MAT.	INST.	TOTAL
SYSTEM D4010 410 0580					
WET PIPE SPRINKLER, STEEL, BLACK, SCH. 40 PIPE					
LIGHT HAZARD, ONE FLOOR, 2000 S.F.	1.000	S.F.			
Valve, gate, iron body, 125 lb., OS&Y, flanged, 4" diam.	1.000	Ea.	.99	.27	1.26
4" pipe size	1.000	Ea.	2.05	.27	2.32
Tamper switch (valve supervisory switch)	3.000	Ea.	.44	.08	.52
Valve, swing check, bronze, 125 lb, regrinding disc, 2-1/2" pipe size	1.000	Ea.	.85	.05	.90
Valve, angle, bronze, 150 lb., rising stem, threaded, 2" diam.	1.000	Ea.	.73	.04	.77
*Alarm valve, 2-1/2" pipe size	1.000	Ea.	1.48	.27	1.75
Alarm, water motor, complete with gong	1.000	Ea.	.28	.11	.39
Valve, swing check, w/balldrip CI with brass trim 4" pipe size	1.000	Ea.	.25	.27	.52
Pipe, steel, black, schedule 40, 4" diam.	8.000	L.F.	.24	.18	.42
Fire alarm horn, electric	1.000	Ea.	.03	.06	.09
Pipe, steel, black, schedule 40, threaded, cplg & hngr 10' OC, 2-1/2" diam.	15.000	L.F.	.29	.24	.53
Pipe, steel, black, schedule 40, threaded, cplg & hngr 10' OC, 2" diam.	9.375	L.F.	.11	.12	.23
Pipe, steel, black, schedule 40, threaded, cplg & hngr 10' OC, 1-1/4" diam.	28.125	L.F.	.21	.25	.46
Pipe, steel, black, schedule 40, threaded cplg & hngr 10' OC, 1" diam.	84.000	L.F.	.47	.70	1.17
Pipe Tee, malleable iron black, 150 lb.threaded, 4" pipe size	2.000	Ea.	.60	.40	1
Pipe Tee, malleable iron black, 150 lb.threaded, 2-1/2" pipe size	2.000	Ea.	.17	.18	.35
Pipe Tee, malleable iron black, 150 lb.threaded, 2" pipe size	1.000	Ea.	.04	.07	.11
Pipe Tee, malleable iron black, 150 lb.threaded, 1-1/4" pipe size	4.000	Ea.	.07	.23	.30
Pipe Tee, malleable iron black, 150 lb.threaded, 1" pipe size	3.000	Ea.	.03	.17	.20
Pipe 90° elbow, malleable iron black, 150 lb.threaded, 1" pipe size	5.000	Ea.	.04	.17	.21
Sprinkler head, standard spray, brass 135°-286°F 1/2" NPT, 3/8" orifice	12.000	Ea.	.26	.33	.59
Valve, gate, bronze, NRS, class 150, threaded, 1" pipe size	1.000	Ea.	.14	.02	.16
*Standpipe connection, wall, single, flush w/plug & chain 2-1/2"x2-1/2"	1.000	Ea.	.12	.16	.28
TOTAL	1.000		9.89	4.64	14.53
COST PER S.F.	1.000	S.F.	9.89	4.64	14.53

*Not included in systems under 2000 S.F.

D4010 410	Wet Pipe Sprinkler Systems		COST PER S.F. MAT.	INST.	TOTAL
0520	Wet pipe sprinkler systems, steel, black, sch. 40 pipe				
0530	Light hazard, one floor, 500 S.F.		9.65	4.42	14.07
0560	1000 S.F.		8.20	3.86	12.06
0580	2000 S.F.	R211313 -10	9.85	4.65	14.50
0600	5000 S.F.		4.01	2.91	6.92
0620	10,000 S.F.	R211313 -20	2.83	2.47	5.30

D40 Fire Protection

D4010 Sprinklers

D4010 410	Wet Pipe Sprinkler Systems		COST PER S.F.		
			MAT.	INST.	TOTAL
0640	50,000 S.F.		2.37	2.28	4.65
0660	Each additional floor, 500 S.F.		2.88	3.53	6.41
0680	1000 S.F.	R211313	3.23	3.25	6.48
0700	2000 S.F.	-40	2.90	2.91	5.81
0720	5000 S.F.		2.07	2.49	4.56
0740	10,000 S.F.		1.96	2.29	4.25
0760	50,000 S.F.		1.64	1.80	3.44
1000	Ordinary hazard, one floor, 500 S.F.		10.25	4.71	14.96
1020	1000 S.F.		8.10	3.78	11.88
1040	2000 S.F.		7.80	4.25	12.05
1060	5000 S.F.		4.20	3.12	7.32
1080	10,000 S.F.		3.47	3.28	6.75
1100	50,000 S.F.		3.04	3.14	6.18
1140	Each additional floor, 500 S.F.		3.68	3.98	7.66
1160	1000 S.F.		3.14	3.20	6.34
1180	2000 S.F.		2.97	3.21	6.18
1200	5000 S.F.		2.75	3.03	5.78
1220	10,000 S.F.		2.61	3.10	5.71
1240	50,000 S.F.		2.47	2.74	5.21
1500	Extra hazard, one floor, 500 S.F.		15.35	6.05	21.40
1520	1000 S.F.		10.90	5.40	16.30
1540	2000 S.F.		8.80	5.80	14.60
1560	5000 S.F.		6.50	5.15	11.65
1580	10,000 S.F.		5.10	4.91	10.01
1600	50,000 S.F.		5.25	4.71	9.96
1660	Each additional floor, 500 S.F.		5.40	4.89	10.29
1680	1000 S.F.		5.05	4.61	9.66
1700	2000 S.F.		4.34	4.60	8.94
1720	5000 S.F.		3.60	4.07	7.67
1740	10,000 S.F.		3.26	3.74	7
1760	50,000 S.F.		3.12	3.56	6.68
2020	Grooved steel, black sch. 40 pipe, light hazard, one floor, 2000 S.F.		8.10	3.40	11.50
2060	10,000 S.F.		3.12	2.12	5.24
2100	Each additional floor, 2000 S.F.		3.27	2.35	5.62
2150	10,000 S.F.		2.24	1.94	4.18
2200	Ordinary hazard, one floor, 2000 S.F.		8.35	3.63	11.98
2250	10,000 S.F.		3.81	2.75	6.56
2300	Each additional floor, 2000 S.F.		3.51	2.58	6.09
2350	10,000 S.F.		2.95	2.57	5.52
2400	Extra hazard, one floor, 2000 S.F.		7.45	4.44	11.89
2450	10,000 S.F.		4.98	3.53	8.51
2500	Each additional floor, 2000 S.F.		4.95	3.78	8.73
2550	10,000 S.F.		4.10	3.21	7.31
3050	Grooved steel, black sch. 10 pipe, light hazard, one floor, 2000 S.F.		5.85	3.10	8.95
3100	10,000 S.F.		2.76	2.09	4.85
3150	Each additional floor, 2000 S.F.		2.87	2.32	5.19
3200	10,000 S.F.		1.89	1.90	3.79
3250	Ordinary hazard, one floor, 2000 S.F.		7.95	3.60	11.55
3300	10,000 S.F.		3.20	2.68	5.88
3350	Each additional floor, 2000 S.F.		3.12	2.55	5.67
3400	10,000 S.F.		2.41	2.51	4.92
3450	Extra hazard, one floor, 2000 S.F.		9	4.68	13.68
3500	10,000 S.F.		4.83	3.54	8.37
3550	Each additional floor, 2000 S.F.		4.63	3.75	8.38
3600	10,000 S.F.		3.72	3.17	6.89
4050	Copper tubing, type L, light hazard, one floor, 2000 S.F.		7.60	3.40	11
4100	10,000 S.F.		2.85	2.17	5.02
4150	Each additional floor, 2000 S.F.		2.79	2.40	5.19

D40 Fire Protection

D4010 Sprinklers

D4010 410	Wet Pipe Sprinkler Systems	COST PER S.F.		
		MAT.	INST.	TOTAL
4200	10,000 S.F.	1.98	1.99	3.97
4250	Ordinary hazard, one floor, 2000 S.F.	7.90	3.84	11.74
4300	10,000 S.F.	3.32	2.57	5.89
4350	Each additional floor, 2000 S.F.	3.17	2.66	5.83
4400	10,000 S.F.	2.37	2.34	4.71
4450	Extra hazard, one floor, 2000 S.F.	8.80	4.80	13.60
4500	10,000 S.F.	6.45	3.94	10.39
4550	Each additional floor, 2000 S.F.	4.41	3.88	8.29
4600	10,000 S.F.	4.52	3.52	8.04
5050	Copper tubing, type L, T-drill system, light hazard, one floor			
5060	2000 S.F.	7.55	3.15	10.70
5100	10,000 S.F.	2.57	1.79	4.36
5150	Each additional floor, 2000 S.F.	2.72	2.15	4.87
5200	10,000 S.F.	1.70	1.61	3.31
5250	Ordinary hazard, one floor, 2000 S.F.	5.60	2.95	8.55
5300	10,000 S.F.	3.10	2.28	5.38
5350	Each additional floor, 2000 S.F.	2.66	2.17	4.83
5400	10,000 S.F.	2.24	2.10	4.34
5450	Extra hazard, one floor, 2000 S.F.	7.85	3.89	11.74
5500	10,000 S.F.	4.92	2.88	7.80
5550	Each additional floor, 2000 S.F.	5.95	3.31	9.26
5600	10,000 S.F.	2.98	2.46	5.44

D40 Fire Protection

D4010 Sprinklers

Plan

Longitudinal Movement

Elevation

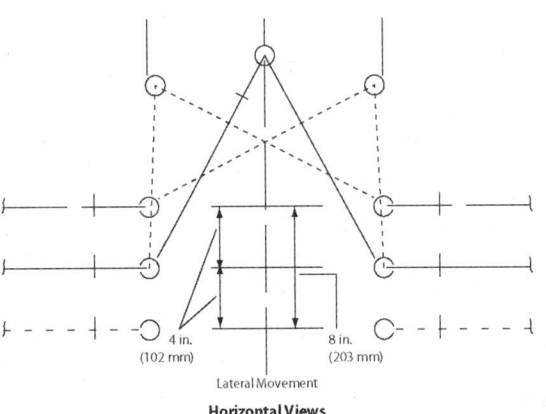

Horizontal Views

System Components	QUANTITY	UNIT	COST PER EACH		
			MAT.	INST.	TOTAL
SYSTEM D4010 412 1000					
WET SPRINKLER SYSTEM, SCHEDULE 10 BLACK STEEL GROOVED PIPE					
SEPARATION ASSEMBLY, 2 INCH DIAMETER					
Hanger support for 2 inch pipe	2.000	Ea.	145	97	242
Pipe roller support yoke	2.000	Ea.	36.10	22.80	58.90
Spool pieces 2 inch	3.000	Ea.	36.90	61.50	98.40
2 inch grooved elbows	6.000	Ea.	456	213	669
Coupling grooved joint 2 inch pipe	10.000	Ea.	755	177.50	932.50
Roll grooved joint labor only	8.000	Ea.		110.40	110.40
TOTAL			1,429	682.20	2,111.20

D4010 412	Wet Sprinkler Seismic Components	COST PER EACH		
		MAT.	INST.	TOTAL
1000	Wet sprinkler sys, Sch. 10, blk steel grooved, separation assembly, 2 inch	1,425	680	2,105
1100	2-1/2 inch	1,550	760	2,310
1200	3 inch	2,075	875	2,950
1300	4 inch	2,575	1,075	3,650
1400	6 inch	5,200	1,550	6,750
1500	8 inch	9,275	1,825	11,100
2000	Wet sprinkler sys, Sch. 10, blk steel grooved, flexible coupling, 2-1/2 inch	1,025	380	1,405
2100	3 inch	1,100	445	1,545
2200	4 inch	1,475	590	2,065
2300	6 inch	2,150	830	2,980

D40 Fire Protection

D4010 Sprinklers

D4010 412	Wet Sprinkler Seismic Components	COST PER EACH		
		MAT.	INST.	TOTAL
2400	8 inch	2,825	1,050	3,875
2990	Allowance for seismic movement by providing annular space in concrete wall			
2995	If additional cores are performed for the same size and at the same time reduce			
2996	price of additional cores by 50 %. If different size cores reduce by 30 %.			
3000	Wet pipe sprinkler systems, 2 inch black steel, annular space 6 inch wall	12.95	800	812.95
3010	8 inch wall	13.25	810	823.25
3020	10 inch wall	13.55	815	828.55
3030	12 inch wall	13.90	825	838.90
3100	Wet pipe sprinkler systems, 2-1/2/3 inch black steel, annular space 6" wall	12.95	825	837.95
3110	8 inch wall	13.25	830	843.25
3120	10 inch wall	13.55	840	853.55
3130	12 inch wall	13.90	850	863.90
3200	Wet pipe sprinkler systems, 4 inch black steel, annular space 6" wall	12.95	915	927.95
3210	8 inch wall	13.25	925	938.25
3220	10 inch wall	13.55	930	943.55
3230	12 inch wall	13.90	940	953.90
3300	Wet pipe sprinkler systems, 6 inch black steel, annular space 6" wall	12.95	950	962.95
3310	8 inch wall	13.25	960	973.25
3320	10 inch wall	13.55	970	983.55
3330	12 inch wall	13.90	975	988.90
3400	Wet pipe sprinkler systems, 8 inch black steel, annular space 6" wall	12.95	990	1,002.95
3410	8 inch wall	13.25	1,000	1,013.25
3420	10 inch wall	13.55	1,000	1,013.55
3430	12 inch wall	13.90	1,025	1,038.90
3996	Lateral, longitudinal and 4-way seismic strut braces			
4000	Wet pipe sprinkler systems, 2 inch pipe double lateral strut brace	223	370	593
4010	2-1/2 inch	233	370	603
4020	3 inch	240	370	610
4030	4 inch	260	375	635
4040	6 inch	395	375	770
4050	8 inch	475	375	850
4100	Wet pipe sprinkler systems, 2 inch pipe longitudinal strut brace	223	370	593
4110	2-1/2 inch	233	370	603
4120	3 inch	240	370	610
4130	4 inch	260	375	635
4140	6 inch	395	375	770
4150	8 inch	475	375	850
4200	Wet pipe sprinkler systems, 2 inch pipe single lateral strut brace	153	243	396
4210	2-1/2 inch	162	244	406
4220	3 inch	170	244	414
4230	4 inch	186	248	434
4240	6 inch	320	249	569
4250	8 inch	400	250	650
4300	Wet pipe sprinkler systems, 2 inch pipe longitudinal wire brace	157	255	412
4310	2-1/2 inch	166	255	421
4320	3 inch	174	256	430
4330	4 inch	190	264	454
4340	6 inch	325	261	586
4350	8 inch	410	262	672
4400	Wet pipe sprinkler systems, 2 inch pipe 4-way wire brace	231	390	621
4410	2-1/2 inch	241	395	636
4420	3 inch	248	395	643
4430	4 inch	268	405	673
4440	6 inch	410	400	810
4450	8 inch	490	400	890
4500	Wet pipe sprinkler systems, 2 inch pipe 4-way strut brace	365	620	985
4510	2-1/2 inch	375	620	995
4520	3 inch	380	620	1,000

D40 Fire Protection

D4010 Sprinklers

D4010 412	Wet Sprinkler Seismic Components	COST PER EACH		
		MAT.	INST.	TOTAL
4530	4 inch	405	630	1,035
4540	6 inch	540	630	1,170
4550	8 inch	620	630	1,250

D40 Fire Protection

D4010 Sprinklers

Wet Pipe System. A system employing automatic sprinklers attached to a piping system containing water and connected to a water supply so that water discharges immediately from sprinklers opened by heat from a fire.

All areas are assumed to be open.

System Components	QUANTITY	UNIT	COST PER S.F. MAT.	COST PER S.F. INST.	COST PER S.F. TOTAL
SYSTEM D4010 413 0580					
SEISMIC WET PIPE SPRINKLER, STEEL, BLACK, SCH. 40 PIPE					
LIGHT HAZARD, ONE FLOOR, 3' FLEXIBLE FEED, 2000 S.F.					
Valve, gate, iron body, 125 lb., OS&Y, flanged, 4" diam.	1.000	Ea.	.74	.20	.94
4" pipe size	1.000	Ea.	1.54	.20	1.74
Tamper switch (valve supervisory switch)	3.000	Ea.	.33	.06	.39
Valve, swing check, bronze, 125 lb, regrinding disc, 2-1/2" pipe size	1.000	Ea.	.64	.04	.68
Valve, angle, bronze, 150 lb., rising stem, threaded, 2" diam.	1.000	Ea.	.54	.03	.57
*Alarm valve, 2-1/2" pipe size	1.000	Ea.	1.11	.20	1.31
Alarm, water motor, complete with gong	1.000	Ea.	.21	.08	.29
Valve, swing check, w/balldrip CI with brass trim 4" pipe size	1.000	Ea.	.19	.20	.39
Pipe, steel, black, schedule 40, 4" diam.	8.000	L.F.	.18	.14	.32
Fire alarm horn, electric	1.000	Ea.	.03	.05	.08
Pipe, steel, black, schedule 40, threaded, cplg & hngr 10' OC, 2-1/2" diam.	15.000	L.F.	.22	.18	.40
Pipe, steel, black, schedule 40, threaded, cplg & hngr 10' OC, 2" diam.	9.375	L.F.	.08	.09	.17
Pipe, steel, black, schedule 40, threaded, cplg & hngr 10' OC, 1-1/4" diam.	28.125	L.F.	.15	.19	.34
Pipe Tee, malleable iron black, 150 lb. threaded, 4" pipe size	2.000	Ea.	.45	.30	.75
Pipe Tee, malleable iron black, 150 lb. threaded, 2-1/2" pipe size	2.000	Ea.	.13	.13	.26
Pipe Tee, malleable iron black, 150 lb. threaded, 2" pipe size	1.000	Ea.	.03	.05	.08
Pipe Tee, malleable iron black, 150 lb. threaded, 1-1/4" pipe size	4.000	Ea.	.06	.17	.23
Pipe Tee, malleable iron black, 150 lb. threaded, 1" pipe size	3.000	Ea.	.03	.12	.15
Pipe 90° elbow, malleable iron black, 150 lb. threaded, 1" pipe size	5.000	Ea.	.03	.13	.16
Sprinkler head, standard spray, brass 135°-286°F 1/2" NPT, 3/8" orifice	12.000	Ea.	.20	.25	.45
Valve, gate, bronze, NRS, class 150, threaded, 1" pipe size	1.000	Ea.	.10	.02	.12
*Standpipe connection, wall, single, flush w/plug & chain 2-1/2"x2-1/2"	1.000	Ea.	.09	.12	.21
Flexible connector 36 inches long	12.000	Ea.	.22	.13	.35
TOTAL			7.30	3.08	10.38

*Not included in systems under 2000 S.F.

D4010 413	Seismic Wet Pipe Flexible Feed Sprinkler Systems	COST PER S.F. MAT.	COST PER S.F. INST.	COST PER S.F. TOTAL
0520	Seismic wet pipe 3' flexible feed sprinkler systems, steel, black, sch. 40 pipe			
0525	Note: See D4010-412 for strut braces, flexible joints and separation assemblies			
0530	Light hazard, one floor, 3' flexible feed, 500 S.F.	9.25	3.64	12.89
0560	1000 S.F.	8	3.36	11.36
0580	2000 S.F.	7.25	3.09	10.34
0600	5000 S.F.	3.91	2.54	6.45

D40 Fire Protection

D4010 Sprinklers

D4010 413	Seismic Wet Pipe Flexible Feed Sprinkler Systems	COST PER S.F.		
		MAT.	INST.	TOTAL
0620	10,000 S.F.	2.84	2.31	5.15
0640	50,000 S.F.	2.29	1.99	4.28
0660	Each additional floor, 500 S.F.	2.57	2.80	5.37
0680	1000 S.F.	3.10	2.80	5.90
0700	2000 S.F.	2.65	2.34	4.99
0720	5000 S.F.	1.97	2.13	4.10
0740	10,000 S.F.	1.99	2.13	4.12
0760	50,000 S.F.	1.69	1.69	3.38
1000	Ordinary hazard, one floor, 500 S.F.	9.95	3.98	13.93
1020	1000 S.F.	7.95	3.24	11.19
1040	2000 S.F.	7.75	3.93	11.68
1060	5000 S.F.	4.22	2.90	7.12
1080	10,000 S.F.	3.54	3.13	6.67
1100	50,000 S.F.	3.01	2.84	5.85
1140	Each additional floor, 500 S.F.	7.75	3.53	11.28
1160	1000 S.F.	2.96	2.66	5.62
1180	2000 S.F.	2.93	2.88	5.81
1200	5000 S.F.	2.82	2.81	5.63
1220	10,000 S.F.	2.71	2.95	5.66
1240	50,000 S.F.	2.46	2.45	4.91
1500	Extra hazard, one floor, 500 S.F.	14.80	4.92	19.72
1520	1000 S.F.	10.30	4.29	14.59
1540	2000 S.F.	8.65	5.25	13.90
1560	5000 S.F.	6.45	4.80	11.25
1580	10,000 S.F.	5.15	4.67	9.82
1600	50,000 S.F.	5.30	4.43	9.73
1660	Each additional floor, 500 S.F.	4.39	3.68	8.07
1680	1000 S.F.	4.69	3.55	8.24
1700	2000 S.F.	4.30	4.11	8.41
1720	5000 S.F.	3.62	3.75	7.37
1740	10,000 S.F.	3.34	3.49	6.83
1760	50,000 S.F.	3.19	3.28	6.47
2020	Grooved steel, black sch. 40 pipe, light hazard, one floor, 2000 S.F.	5.85	2.67	8.52
2060	10,000 S.F.	2.93	1.91	4.84
2100	Each additional floor, 2000 S.F.	2.90	1.89	4.79
2150	10,000 S.F.	2.08	1.73	3.81
2200	Ordinary hazard, one floor, 2000 S.F.	8.20	3.38	11.58
2250	10,000 S.F.	3.82	2.65	6.47
2300	Each additional floor, 2000 S.F.	3.37	2.34	5.71
2350	10,000 S.F.	2.99	2.48	5.47
2400	Extra hazard, one floor, 2000 S.F.	9	4.31	13.31
2450	10,000 S.F.	5.45	3.43	8.88
2500	Each additional floor, 2000 S.F.	4.76	3.40	8.16
2550	10,000 S.F.	4.07	3.05	7.12
3050	Grooved steel black sch. 10 pipe, light hazard, one floor, 2000 S.F.	7.35	2.90	10.25
3100	10,000 S.F.	2.72	1.97	4.69
3150	Each additional floor, 2000 S.F.	2.49	1.86	4.35
3200	10,000 S.F.	1.72	1.70	3.42
3250	Ordinary hazard, one floor, 2000 S.F.	7.80	3.35	11.15
3300	10,000 S.F.	3.28	2.59	5.87
3350	Each additional floor, 2000 S.F.	2.87	2.28	5.15
3400	10,000 S.F.	2.40	2.41	4.81
3450	Extra hazard, one floor, 2000 S.F.	8.70	4.28	12.98
3500	10,000 S.F.	4.78	3.37	8.15
3550	Each additional floor, 2000 S.F.	4.44	3.38	7.82
3600	10,000 S.F.	3.70	3	6.70

D40 Fire Protection

D4010 Sprinklers

Wet Pipe System. A system employing automatic sprinklers attached to a piping system containing water and connected to a water supply so that water discharges immediately from sprinklers opened by heat from a fire.

All areas are assumed to be open.

System Components	QUANTITY	UNIT	COST PER S.F. MAT.	INST.	TOTAL
SYSTEM D4010 414 0580					
SEISMIC WET PIPE SPRINKLER, STEEL, BLACK, SCH. 40 PIPE					
LIGHT HAZARD, ONE FLOOR, 4' FLEXIBLE FEED, 2000 S.F.					
Valve, gate, iron body, 125 lb., OS&Y, flanged, 4" diam.	1.000	Ea.	.74	.20	.94
4" pipe size	1.000	Ea.	1.54	.20	1.74
Tamper switch (valve supervisory switch)	3.000	Ea.	.33	.06	.39
Valve, swing check, bronze, 125 lb, regrinding disc, 2-1/2" pipe size	1.000	Ea.	.64	.04	.68
Valve, angle, bronze, 150 lb., rising stem, threaded, 2" diam.	1.000	Ea.	.54	.03	.57
*Alarm valve, 2-1/2" pipe size	1.000	Ea.	1.11	.20	1.31
Alarm, water motor, complete with gong	1.000	Ea.	.21	.08	.29
Valve, swing check, w/balldrip CI with brass trim 4" pipe size	1.000	Ea.	.19	.20	.39
Pipe, steel, black, schedule 40, 4" diam.	8.000	L.F.	.18	.14	.32
Fire alarm horn, electric	1.000	Ea.	.03	.05	.08
Pipe, steel, black, schedule 40, threaded, cplg & hngr 10' OC, 2-1/2" diam.	15.000	L.F.	.22	.18	.40
Pipe, steel, black, schedule 40, threaded, cplg & hngr 10' OC, 2" diam.	9.375	L.F.	.08	.09	.17
Pipe, steel, black, schedule 40, threaded, cplg & hngr 10' OC, 1-1/4" diam.	28.125	L.F.	.15	.19	.34
Pipe Tee, malleable iron black, 150 lb. threaded, 4" pipe size	2.000	Ea.	.45	.30	.75
Pipe Tee, malleable iron black, 150 lb. threaded, 2-1/2" pipe size	2.000	Ea.	.13	.13	.26
Pipe Tee, malleable iron black, 150 lb. threaded, 2" pipe size	1.000	Ea.	.03	.05	.08
Pipe Tee, malleable iron black, 150 lb. threaded, 1-1/4" pipe size	4.000	Ea.	.06	.17	.23
Pipe Tee, malleable iron black, 150 lb. threaded, 1" pipe size	3.000	Ea.	.03	.12	.15
Pipe 90° elbow, malleable iron black, 150 lb. threaded, 1" pipe size	5.000	Ea.	.03	.13	.16
Sprinkler head, standard spray, brass 135°-286°F 1/2" NPT, 3/8" orifice	12.000	Ea.	.20	.25	.45
Valve, gate, bronze, NRS, class 150, threaded, 1" pipe size	1.000	Ea.	.10	.02	.12
*Standpipe connection, wall, single, flush w/plug & chain 2-1/2"x2-1/2"	1.000	Ea.	.09	.12	.21
Flexible connector 48 inches long	12.000	Ea.	.34	.18	.52
TOTAL			7.42	3.13	10.55

*Not included in systems under 2000 S.F.

D4010 414	Seismic Wet Pipe Flexible Feed Sprinkler Systems	COST PER S.F. MAT.	INST.	TOTAL
0520	Seismic wet pipe 4' flexible feed sprinkler systems, steel, black, sch. 40 pipe			
0525	Note: See D4010-412 for strut braces, flexible joints and separation assemblies			
0530	Light hazard, one floor, 4' flexible feed, 500 S.F.	9.35	3.69	13.04
0560	1000 S.F.	8.10	3.41	11.51
0580	2000 S.F.	7.40	3.14	10.54
0600	5000 S.F.	4.04	2.60	6.64
0620	10,000 S.F.	2.95	2.36	5.31
0640	50,000 S.F.	2.40	2.03	4.43

D40 Fire Protection

D4010 Sprinklers

D4010 414 Seismic Wet Pipe Flexible Feed Sprinkler Systems

		COST PER S.F.		
		MAT.	INST.	TOTAL
0660	Each additional floor, 500 S.F.	2.73	2.86	5.59
0680	1000 S.F.	3.26	2.86	6.12
0700	2000 S.F.	2.77	2.39	5.16
0720	5000 S.F.	2.10	2.18	4.28
0740	10,000 S.F.	2.10	2.17	4.27
0760	50,000 S.F.	1.80	1.73	3.53
1000	Ordinary hazard, one floor, 500 S.F.	10.10	4.04	14.14
1020	1000 S.F.	8.10	3.31	11.41
1040	2000 S.F.	7.90	3.99	11.89
1060	5000 S.F.	4.38	2.96	7.34
1080	10,000 S.F.	3.70	3.20	6.90
1100	50,000 S.F.	3.17	2.91	6.08
1140	Each additional floor, 500 S.F.	3.53	3.31	6.84
1160	1000 S.F.	3.12	2.73	5.85
1180	2000 S.F.	3.09	2.95	6.04
1200	5000 S.F.	2.98	2.88	5.86
1220	10,000 S.F.	2.87	3.02	5.89
1240	50,000 S.F.	2.61	2.51	5.12
1500	Extra hazard, one floor, 500 S.F.	15	5	20
1520	1000 S.F.	10.55	4.39	14.94
1540	2000 S.F.	8.90	5.35	14.25
1560	5000 S.F.	6.65	4.89	11.54
1580	10,000 S.F.	5.40	4.77	10.17
1600	50,000 S.F.	5.55	4.53	10.08
1660	Each additional floor, 500 S.F.	4.62	3.77	8.39
1680	1000 S.F.	4.93	3.64	8.57
1700	2000 S.F.	4.54	4.21	8.75
1720	5000 S.F.	3.84	3.84	7.68
1740	10,000 S.F.	3.58	3.59	7.17
1760	50,000 S.F.	3.44	3.39	6.83
2020	Grooved steel, black sch. 40 pipe, light hazard, one floor, 2000 S.F.	7.85	2.99	10.84
2060	10,000 S.F.	2.96	1.93	4.89
2100	Each additional floor, 2000 S.F.	3.02	1.94	4.96
2150	10,000 S.F.	2.11	1.75	3.86
2200	Ordinary hazard, one floor, 2000 S.F.	8.35	3.45	11.80
2250	10,000 S.F.	3.98	2.72	6.70
2300	Each additional floor, 2000 S.F.	3.53	2.40	5.93
2350	10,000 S.F.	3.15	2.55	5.70
2400	Extra hazard, one floor, 2000 S.F.	9.25	4.41	13.66
2450	10,000 S.F.	5.70	3.53	9.23
2500	Each additional floor, 2000 S.F.	5	3.50	8.50
2550	10,000 S.F.	4.31	3.15	7.46
3050	Grooved steel black sch. 10 pipe, light hazard, one floor, 2000 S.F.	7.45	2.95	10.40
3100	10,000 S.F.	2.83	2.02	4.85
3150	Each additional floor, 2000 S.F.	2.61	1.91	4.52
3200	10,000 S.F.	1.75	1.71	3.46
3250	Ordinary hazard, one floor, 2000 S.F.	8	3.42	11.42
3300	10,000 S.F.	3.44	2.66	6.10
3350	Each additional floor, 2000 S.F.	3.14	2.37	5.51
3400	10,000 S.F.	2.60	2.48	5.08
3450	Extra hazard, one floor, 2000 S.F.	8.95	4.38	13.33
3500	10,000 S.F.	5	3.47	8.47
3550	Each additional floor, 2000 S.F.	4.68	3.48	8.16
3600	10,000 S.F.	3.94	3.10	7.04

D40 Fire Protection

D4020 Standpipes

- Roof — Roof connections with hose gate valves (for combustible roof)
- Hose connections on each floor (size based on class of service)
- Check Valve
- Siamese inlet connections (for fire department use)

System Components	QUANTITY	UNIT	COST PER FLOOR		
			MAT.	INST.	TOTAL
SYSTEM D4020 310 0560 WET STANDPIPE RISER, CLASS I, STEEL, BLACK, SCH. 40 PIPE, 10' HEIGHT 4" DIAMETER PIPE, ONE FLOOR					
Pipe, steel, black, schedule 40, threaded, 4" diam.	20.000	L.F.	1,470	890	2,360
Pipe, Tee, malleable iron, black, 150 lb. threaded, 4" pipe size	2.000	Ea.	1,200	800	2,000
Pipe, 90° elbow, malleable iron, black, 150 lb threaded, 4" pipe size	1.000	Ea.	380	266	646
Pipe, nipple, steel, black, schedule 40, 2-1/2" pipe size x 3" long	2.000	Ea.	50	200	250
Fire valve, gate, 300 lb., brass w/handwheel, 2-1/2" pipe size	1.000	Ea.	279	127	406
Fire valve, pressure reducing rgh brs, 2-1/2" pipe size	1.000	Ea.	1,730	254	1,984
Valve, swing check, w/ball drip, CI w/brs. ftngs., 4" pipe size	1.000	Ea.	505	535	1,040
Standpipe conn wall dble. flush brs. w/plugs & chains 2-1/2"x2-1/2"x4"	1.000	Ea.	900	320	1,220
Valve, swing check, bronze, 125 lb, regrinding disc, 2-1/2" pipe size	1.000	Ea.	1,700	107	1,807
Roof manifold, fire, w/valves & caps, horiz/vert brs 2-1/2"x2-1/2"x4"	1.000	Ea.	277	335	612
Fire, hydrolator, vent & drain, 2-1/2" pipe size	1.000	Ea.	182	74	256
Valve, gate, iron body 125 lb., OS&Y, threaded, 4" pipe size	1.000	Ea.	1,975	535	2,510
Tamper switch (valve supervisory switch)	1.000	Ea.	294	55.50	349.50
TOTAL			10,942	4,498.50	15,440.50

D4020 310	Wet Standpipe Risers, Class I		COST PER FLOOR		
			MAT.	INST.	TOTAL
0550	Wet standpipe risers, Class I, steel, black, sch. 40, 10' height				
0560	4" diameter pipe, one floor		10,900	4,500	15,400
0580	Additional floors		2,700	1,375	4,075
0600	6" diameter pipe, one floor		14,500	7,750	22,250
0620	Additional floors	R211226 -10	3,450	2,175	5,625
0640	8" diameter pipe, one floor		21,600	9,350	30,950
0660	Additional floors		4,450	2,625	7,075
0680		R211226 -20			

D4020 310	Wet Standpipe Risers, Class II	COST PER FLOOR		
		MAT.	INST.	TOTAL
1030	Wet standpipe risers, Class II, steel black sch. 40, 10' height			
1040	2" diameter pipe, one floor	4,750	1,650	6,400
1060	Additional floors	1,375	615	1,990
1080	2-1/2" diameter pipe, one floor	6,375	2,350	8,725
1100	Additional floors	1,650	720	2,370
1120				

D40 Fire Protection

D4020 Standpipes

D4020 310	Wet Standpipe Risers, Class III	COST PER FLOOR		
		MAT.	INST.	TOTAL
1530	Wet standpipe risers, Class III, steel, black, sch. 40, 10' height			
1540	4" diameter pipe, one floor	11,200	4,500	15,700
1560	Additional floors	2,550	1,150	3,700
1580	6" diameter pipe, one floor	14,800	7,750	22,550
1600	Additional floors	3,600	2,175	5,775
1620	8" diameter pipe, one floor	21,900	9,350	31,250
1640	Additional floors	4,575	2,625	7,200

For customer support on your Plumbing Costs with RSMeans Data call 800.448.8182.

D40 Fire Protection

D4020 Standpipes

System Components	QUANTITY	UNIT	COST PER FLOOR		
			MAT.	INST.	TOTAL
SYSTEM D4020 330 0540					
DRY STANDPIPE RISER, CLASS I, PIPE, STEEL, BLACK, SCH 40, 10' HEIGHT					
4" DIAMETER PIPE, ONE FLOOR					
Pipe, steel, black, schedule 40, threaded, 4" diam.	20.000	L.F.	1,470	890	2,360
Pipe, Tee, malleable iron, black, 150 lb. threaded, 4" pipe size	2.000	Ea.	1,200	800	2,000
Pipe, 90° elbow, malleable iron, black, 150 lb threaded, 4" pipe size	1.000	Ea.	380	266	646
Pipe, nipple, steel, black, schedule 40, 2-1/2" pipe size x 3" long	2.000	Ea.	50	200	250
Fire valve gate NRS 300 lb., brass w/handwheel, 2-1/2" pipe size	1.000	Ea.	279	127	406
Tamper switch (valve supervisory switch)	1.000	Ea.	294	55.50	349.50
Fire valve, pressure reducing rgh brs, 2-1/2" pipe size	1.000	Ea.	865	127	992
Standpipe conn wall dble. flush brs. w/plugs & chains 2-1/2"x2-1/2"x4"	1.000	Ea.	900	320	1,220
Valve swing check w/ball drip Cl w/brs. ftngs., 4"pipe size	1.000	Ea.	505	535	1,040
Roof manifold, fire, w/valves & caps, horiz/vert brs 2-1/2"x2-1/2"x4"	1.000	Ea.	277	335	612
TOTAL			6,220	3,655.50	9,875.50

D4020 330	Dry Standpipe Risers, Class I		COST PER FLOOR		
			MAT.	INST.	TOTAL
0530	Dry standpipe riser, Class I, steel, black, sch. 40, 10' height				
0540	4" diameter pipe, one floor		6,225	3,650	9,875
0560	Additional floors		2,525	1,300	3,825
0580	6" diameter pipe, one floor		9,250	6,150	15,400
0600	Additional floors	R211226-10	3,275	2,100	5,375
0620	8" diameter pipe, one floor		13,800	7,475	21,275
0640	Additional floors		4,250	2,550	6,800
0660		R211226-20			

D4020 330	Dry Standpipe Risers, Class II	COST PER FLOOR		
		MAT.	INST.	TOTAL
1030	Dry standpipe risers, Class II, steel, black, sch. 40, 10' height			
1040	2" diameter pipe, one floor	3,400	1,675	5,075
1060	Additional floors	1,175	545	1,720
1080	2-1/2" diameter pipe, one floor	4,975	1,950	6,925
1100	Additional floors	1,475	645	2,120
1120				

D40 Fire Protection

D4020 Standpipes

D4020 330	Dry Standpipe Risers, Class III	COST PER FLOOR		
		MAT.	INST.	TOTAL
1530	Dry standpipe risers, Class III, steel, black, sch. 40, 10' height			
1540	4" diameter pipe, one floor	6,025	3,525	9,550
1560	Additional floors	2,400	1,175	3,575
1580	6" diameter pipe, one floor	9,400	6,150	15,550
1600	Additional floors	3,425	2,100	5,525
1620	8" diameter pipe, one floor	13,900	7,475	21,375
1640	Additional floors	4,400	2,550	6,950

D40 Fire Protection

D4020 Standpipes

D4020 410	Fire Hose Equipment	COST EACH		
		MAT.	INST.	TOTAL
0100	Adapters, reducing, 1 piece, FxM, hexagon, cast brass, 2-1/2" x 1-1/2"	84.50		84.50
0200	Pin lug, 1-1/2" x 1"	49		49
0250	3" x 2-1/2"	101		101
0300	For polished chrome, add 75% mat.			
0400	Cabinets, D.S. glass in door, recessed, steel box, not equipped			
0500	Single extinguisher, steel door & frame	131	200	331
0550	Stainless steel door & frame	211	200	411
0600	Valve, 2-1/2" angle, steel door & frame	450	133	583
0650	Aluminum door & frame	505	133	638
0700	Stainless steel door & frame	560	133	693
0750	Hose rack assy, 2-1/2" x 1-1/2" valve & 100' hose, steel door & frame	1,250	267	1,517
0800	Aluminum door & frame	1,225	267	1,492
0850	Stainless steel door & frame	1,750	267	2,017
0900	Hose rack assy & extinguisher, 2-1/2"x1-1/2" valve & hose, steel door & frame	515	320	835
0950	Aluminum	515	320	835
1000	Stainless steel	1,125	320	1,445
1550	Compressor, air, dry pipe system, automatic, 200 gal., 3/4 H.P.	2,275	685	2,960
1600	520 gal., 1 H.P.	1,825	685	2,510
1650	Alarm, electric pressure switch (circuit closer)	176	34	210
2500	Couplings, hose, rocker lug, cast brass, 1-1/2"	71.50		71.50
2550	2-1/2"	206		206
3000	Escutcheon plate, for angle valves, polished brass, 1-1/2"	24.50		24.50
3050	2-1/2"	41		41
3500	Fire pump, electric, w/controller, fittings, relief valve			
3550	4" pump, 30 HP, 500 GPM	24,400	4,975	29,375
3600	5" pump, 40 H.P., 1000 G.P.M.	35,700	5,650	41,350
3650	5" pump, 100 H.P., 1000 G.P.M.	40,000	6,275	46,275
3700	For jockey pump system, add	4,625	800	5,425
5000	Hose, per linear foot, synthetic jacket, lined,			
5100	300 lb. test, 1-1/2" diameter	2.41	.62	3.03
5150	2-1/2" diameter	4.49	.73	5.22
5200	500 lb. test, 1-1/2" diameter	3.98	.62	4.60
5250	2-1/2" diameter	6.70	.73	7.43
5500	Nozzle, plain stream, polished brass, 1-1/2" x 10"	64.50		64.50
5550	2-1/2" x 15" x 13/16" or 1-1/2"	180		180
5600	Heavy duty combination adjustable fog and straight stream w/handle 1-1/2"	805		805
5650	2-1/2" direct connection	730		730
6000	Rack, for 1-1/2" diameter hose 100 ft. long, steel	92	80	172
6050	Brass	194	80	274
6500	Reel, steel, for 50 ft. long 1-1/2" diameter hose	199	114	313
6550	For 75 ft. long 2-1/2" diameter hose	285	114	399
7050	Siamese, w/plugs & chains, polished brass, sidewalk, 4" x 2-1/2" x 2-1/2"	930	640	1,570
7100	6" x 2-1/2" x 2-1/2"	1,475	800	2,275
7200	Wall type, flush, 4" x 2-1/2" x 2-1/2"	900	320	1,220
7250	6" x 2-1/2" x 2-1/2"	1,150	350	1,500
7300	Projecting, 4" x 2-1/2" x 2-1/2"	475	320	795
7350	6" x 2-1/2" x 2-1/2"	1,075	350	1,425
7400	For chrome plate, add 15% mat.			
8000	Valves, angle, wheel handle, 300 Lb., rough brass, 1-1/2"	111	74	185
8050	2-1/2"	214	127	341
8100	Combination pressure restricting, 1-1/2"	157	74	231
8150	2-1/2"	258	127	385
8200	Pressure restricting, adjustable, satin brass, 1-1/2"	575	74	649
8250	2-1/2"	865	127	992
8300	Hydrolator, vent and drain, rough brass, 1-1/2"	182	74	256
8350	2-1/2"	182	74	256
8400	Cabinet assy, incls. adapter, rack, hose, and nozzle	2,025	485	2,510

D40 Fire Protection

D4090 Other Fire Protection Systems

General: Automatic fire protection (suppression) systems other than water sprinklers may be desired for special environments, high risk areas, isolated locations or unusual hazards. Some typical applications would include:

Paint dip tanks
Securities vaults
Electronic data processing
Tape and data storage
Transformer rooms
Spray booths
Petroleum storage
High rack storage

Piping and wiring costs are dependent on the individual application and must be added to the component costs shown below.

All areas are assumed to be open.

D4090 910	Fire Suppression Unit Components	MAT.	INST.	TOTAL
0020	Detectors with brackets			
0040	Fixed temperature heat detector	53	121	174
0060	Rate of temperature rise detector	40	106	146
0080	Ion detector (smoke) detector	185	137	322
0200	Extinguisher agent			
0240	200 lb FM200, container	9,725	400	10,125
0280	75 lb carbon dioxide cylinder	1,800	266	2,066
0320	Dispersion nozzle			
0340	FM200 1-1/2" dispersion nozzle	325	63.50	388.50
0380	Carbon dioxide 3" x 5" dispersion nozzle	203	49.50	252.50
0420	Control station			
0440	Single zone control station with batteries	2,025	850	2,875
0470	Multizone (4) control station with batteries	3,925	1,700	5,625
0490				
0500	Electric mechanical release	1,350	435	1,785
0520				
0550	Manual pull station	129	148	277
0570				
0640	Battery standby power 10" x 10" x 17"	630	213	843
0700				
0740	Bell signaling device	73	106	179

D4090 920	FM200 Systems	MAT.	INST.	TOTAL
0820	Average FM200 system, minimum			2.64
0840	Maximum			5.25

G Building Sitework

Same Data. Simplified.

Enjoy the convenience and efficiency of accessing your costs anywhere:
- **Skip the multiplier** by setting your location
- **Quickly search,** edit, favorite and share costs
- **Stay on top of price changes** with automatic updates

Discover more at rsmeans.com/online

No part of this cost data may be reproduced, stored in a retrieval system, or transmitted in any form or by any means without prior written permission of Gordian.

G10 Site Preparation

G1030 Site Earthwork

Trenching Systems are shown on a cost per linear foot basis. The systems include: excavation; backfill and removal of spoil; and compaction for various depths and trench bottom widths. The backfill has been reduced to accommodate a pipe of suitable diameter and bedding.

The slope for trench sides varies from none to 1:1.

The Expanded System Listing shows Trenching Systems that range from 2' to 12' in width. Depths range from 2' to 25'.

System Components	QUANTITY	UNIT	COST PER L.F.		
			EQUIP.	LABOR	TOTAL
SYSTEM G1030 805 1310					
TRENCHING, COMMON EARTH, NO SLOPE, 2' WIDE, 2' DP, 3/8 C.Y. BUCKET					
Excavation, trench, hyd. backhoe, track mtd., 3/8 C.Y. bucket	.148	C.Y.	.32	1.33	1.65
Backfill and load spoil, from stockpile	.153	L.C.Y.	.15	.41	.56
Compaction by vibrating plate, 6" lifts, 4 passes	.118	C.Y.	.12	.49	.61
Remove excess spoil, 8 C.Y. dump truck, 2 mile roundtrip	.040	L.C.Y.	.19	.23	.42
TOTAL			.78	2.46	3.24

G1030 805	Trenching Common Earth	COST PER L.F.		
		EQUIP.	LABOR	TOTAL
1310	Trenching, common earth, no slope, 2' wide, 2' deep, 3/8 C.Y. bucket	.78	2.45	3.23
1320	3' deep, 3/8 C.Y. bucket	1.11	3.68	4.79
1330	4' deep, 3/8 C.Y. bucket	1.44	4.91	6.35
1340	6' deep, 3/8 C.Y. bucket	2.27	6.35	8.62
1350	8' deep, 1/2 C.Y. bucket	3.06	8.45	11.51
1360	10' deep, 1 C.Y. bucket	5	10.10	15.10
1400	4' wide, 2' deep, 3/8 C.Y. bucket	1.75	4.88	6.63
1410	3' deep, 3/8 C.Y. bucket	2.42	7.35	9.77
1420	4' deep, 1/2 C.Y. bucket	3.52	8.20	11.72
1430	6' deep, 1/2 C.Y. bucket	4.88	13.15	18.03
1440	8' deep, 1/2 C.Y. bucket	8.50	17.10	25.60
1450	10' deep, 1 C.Y. bucket	9.95	21	30.95
1460	12' deep, 1 C.Y. bucket	12.90	27	39.90
1470	15' deep, 1-1/2 C.Y. bucket	10.60	24	34.60
1480	18' deep, 2-1/2 C.Y. bucket	15.05	33.50	48.55
1520	6' wide, 6' deep, 5/8 C.Y. bucket w/trench box	11	19.80	30.80
1530	8' deep, 3/4 C.Y. bucket	14.90	26	40.90
1540	10' deep, 1 C.Y. bucket	13.50	27	40.50
1550	12' deep, 1-1/2 C.Y. bucket	14.15	28.50	42.65
1560	16' deep, 2-1/2 C.Y. bucket	19	36	55
1570	20' deep, 3-1/2 C.Y. bucket	21.50	42.50	64
1580	24' deep, 3-1/2 C.Y. bucket	26	51.50	77.50
1640	8' wide, 12' deep, 1-1/2 C.Y. bucket w/trench box	19.65	36.50	56.15
1650	15' deep, 1-1/2 C.Y. bucket	26	48	74
1660	18' deep, 2-1/2 C.Y. bucket	27.50	48	75.50
1680	24' deep, 3-1/2 C.Y. bucket	35	66.50	101.50
1730	10' wide, 20' deep, 3-1/2 C.Y. bucket w/trench box	29	63	92
1740	24' deep, 3-1/2 C.Y. bucket	41.50	76	117.50
1780	12' wide, 20' deep, 3-1/2 C.Y. bucket w/trench box	44.50	80	124.50
1790	25' deep, bucket	55	102	157
1800	1/2 to 1 slope, 2' wide, 2' deep, 3/8 C.Y. bucket	1.11	3.68	4.79
1810	3' deep, 3/8 C.Y. bucket	1.86	6.45	8.31
1820	4' deep, 3/8 C.Y. bucket	2.77	9.85	12.62
1840	6' deep, 3/8 C.Y. bucket	5.50	15.95	21.45

G10 Site Preparation

G1030 Site Earthwork

G1030 805	Trenching Common Earth	COST PER L.F.		
		EQUIP.	LABOR	TOTAL
1860	8' deep, 1/2 C.Y. bucket	8.80	25.50	34.30
1880	10' deep, 1 C.Y. bucket	17.40	35.50	52.90
2300	4' wide, 2' deep, 3/8 C.Y. bucket	2.09	6.10	8.19
2310	3' deep, 3/8 C.Y. bucket	3.17	10.10	13.27
2320	4' deep, 1/2 C.Y. bucket	4.97	12.45	17.42
2340	6' deep, 1/2 C.Y. bucket	8.05	23.50	31.55
2360	8' deep, 1/2 C.Y. bucket	16.25	34.50	50.75
2380	10' deep, 1 C.Y. bucket	22	48.50	70.50
2400	12' deep, 1 C.Y. bucket	28	65.50	93.50
2430	15' deep, 1-1/2 C.Y. bucket	30	70	100
2460	18' deep, 2-1/2 C.Y. bucket	51.50	109	160.50
2840	6' wide, 6' deep, 5/8 C.Y. bucket w/trench box	16.55	29.50	46.05
2860	8' deep, 3/4 C.Y. bucket	24	44	68
2880	10' deep, 1 C.Y. bucket	21.50	44.50	66
2900	12' deep, 1-1/2 C.Y. bucket	27	58	85
2940	16' deep, 2-1/2 C.Y. bucket	43.50	85.50	129
2980	20' deep, 3-1/2 C.Y. bucket	54.50	115	169.50
3020	24' deep, 3-1/2 C.Y. bucket	77	157	234
3100	8' wide, 12' deep, 1-1/2 C.Y. bucket w/trench box	33.50	66.50	100
3120	15' deep, 1-1/2 C.Y. bucket	48.50	96	144.50
3140	18' deep, 2-1/2 C.Y. bucket	60	114	174
3180	24' deep, 3-1/2 C.Y. bucket	86	172	258
3270	10' wide, 20' deep, 3-1/2 C.Y. bucket w/trench box	56.50	132	188.50
3280	24' deep, 3-1/2 C.Y. bucket	95	188	283
3370	12' wide, 20' deep, 3-1/2 C.Y. bucket w/trench box	80	154	234
3380	25' deep, 3-1/2 C.Y. bucket	111	219	330
3500	1 to 1 slope, 2' wide, 2' deep, 3/8 C.Y. bucket	1.44	4.92	6.36
3520	3' deep, 3/8 C.Y. bucket	4.28	11.25	15.53
3540	4' deep, 3/8 C.Y. bucket	4.10	14.75	18.85
3560	6' deep, 1/2 C.Y. bucket	5.50	15.95	21.45
3580	8' deep, 1/2 C.Y. bucket	10.95	32	42.95
3600	10' deep, 1 C.Y. bucket	30	61	91
3800	4' wide, 2' deep, 3/8 C.Y. bucket	2.42	7.35	9.77
3820	3' deep, 3/8 C.Y. bucket	3.91	12.85	16.76
3840	4' deep, 1/2 C.Y. bucket	6.40	16.70	23.10
3860	6' deep, 1/2 C.Y. bucket	11.20	33.50	44.70
3880	8' deep, 1/2 C.Y. bucket	24	52	76
3900	10' deep, 1 C.Y. bucket	34.50	75.50	110
3920	12' deep, 1 C.Y. bucket	51	109	160
3940	15' deep, 1-1/2 C.Y. bucket	49.50	116	165.50
3960	18' deep, 2-1/2 C.Y. bucket	71	151	222
4030	6' wide, 6' deep, 5/8 C.Y. bucket w/trench box	21.50	39.50	61
4040	8' deep, 3/4 C.Y. bucket	31.50	54	85.50
4050	10' deep, 1 C.Y. bucket	31	65.50	96.50
4060	12' deep, 1-1/2 C.Y. bucket	41.50	88.50	130
4070	16' deep, 2-1/2 C.Y. bucket	68	135	203
4080	20' deep, 3-1/2 C.Y. bucket	88	187	275
4090	24' deep, 3-1/2 C.Y. bucket	128	263	391
4500	8' wide, 12' deep, 1-1/2 C.Y. bucket w/trench box	47	96.50	143.50
4550	15' deep, 1-1/2 C.Y. bucket	71.50	144	215.50
4600	18' deep, 2-1/2 C.Y. bucket	91	177	268
4650	24' deep, 3-1/2 C.Y. bucket	137	278	415
4800	10' wide, 20' deep, 3-1/2 C.Y. bucket w/trench box	84	201	285
4850	24' deep, 3-1/2 C.Y. bucket	146	294	440
4950	12' wide, 20' deep, 3-1/2 C.Y. bucket w/trench box	115	227	342
4980	25' deep, 3-1/2 C.Y. bucket	166	330	496

For customer support on your Plumbing Costs with RSMeans Data call 800.448.8182.

G10 Site Preparation

G1030 Site Earthwork

Trenching Systems are shown on a cost per linear foot basis. The systems include: excavation; backfill and removal of spoil; and compaction for various depths and trench bottom widths. The backfill has been reduced to accommodate a pipe of suitable diameter and bedding.

The slope for trench sides varies from none to 1:1.

The Expanded System Listing shows Trenching Systems that range from 2' to 12' in width. Depths range from 2' to 25'.

System Components	QUANTITY	UNIT	COST PER L.F.		
			EQUIP.	LABOR	TOTAL
SYSTEM G1030 806 1310					
TRENCHING, LOAM & SANDY CLAY, NO SLOPE, 2' WIDE, 2' DP, 3/8 C.Y. BUCKET					
Excavation, trench, hyd. backhoe, track mtd., 3/8 C.Y. bucket	.148	C.Y.	.29	1.24	1.53
Backfill and load spoil, from stockpile	.165	L.C.Y.	.17	.44	.61
Compaction by vibrating plate 18" wide, 6" lifts, 4 passes	.118	C.Y.	.12	.49	.61
Remove excess spoil, 8 C.Y. dump truck, 2 mile roundtrip	.042	L.C.Y.	.19	.24	.43
TOTAL			.77	2.41	3.18

G1030 806	Trenching Loam & Sandy Clay	COST PER L.F.		
		EQUIP.	LABOR	TOTAL
1310	Trenching, loam & sandy clay, no slope, 2' wide, 2' deep, 3/8 C.Y. bucket	.78	2.40	3.18
1320	3' deep, 3/8 C.Y. bucket	1.18	3.94	5.10
1330	4' deep, 3/8 C.Y. bucket	1.43	4.80	6.25
1340	6' deep, 3/8 C.Y. bucket	2.58	5.75	8.30
1350	8' deep, 1/2 C.Y. bucket	3.46	7.60	11.05
1360	10' deep, 1 C.Y. bucket	3.71	8.10	11.80
1400	4' wide, 2' deep, 3/8 C.Y. bucket	1.78	4.80	6.60
1410	3' deep, 3/8 C.Y. bucket	2.44	7.20	9.65
1420	4' deep, 1/2 C.Y. bucket	3.53	8.05	11.60
1430	6' deep, 1/2 C.Y. bucket	5.50	11.85	17.40
1440	8' deep, 1/2 C.Y. bucket	8.25	16.85	25
1450	10' deep, 1 C.Y. bucket	7.35	17.20	24.50
1460	12' deep, 1 C.Y. bucket	9.30	21.50	30.50
1470	15' deep, 1-1/2 C.Y. bucket	11.10	25	36
1480	18' deep, 2-1/2 C.Y. bucket	12.80	27	40
1520	6' wide, 6' deep, 5/8 C.Y. bucket w/trench box	10.65	19.45	30
1530	8' deep, 3/4 C.Y. bucket	14.35	25.50	40
1540	10' deep, 1 C.Y. bucket	12.30	25.50	38
1550	12' deep, 1-1/2 C.Y. bucket	13.80	29	42.50
1560	16' deep, 2-1/2 C.Y. bucket	18.55	36	55
1570	20' deep, 3-1/2 C.Y. bucket	20	42.50	63
1580	24' deep, 3-1/2 C.Y. bucket	25.50	52	77.50
1640	8' wide, 12' deep, 1-1/4 C.Y. bucket w/trench box	19.30	36.50	56
1650	15' deep, 1-1/2 C.Y. bucket	23.50	46.50	70
1660	18' deep, 2-1/2 C.Y. bucket	28	52	80.50
1680	24' deep, 3-1/2 C.Y. bucket	34.50	67.50	102
1730	10' wide, 20' deep, 3-1/2 C.Y. bucket w/trench box	34.50	68	102
1740	24' deep, 3-1/2 C.Y. bucket	43	83.50	127
1780	12' wide, 20' deep, 3-1/2 C.Y. bucket w/trench box	42	80.50	122
1790	25' deep, 3-1/2 C.Y. bucket	54	104	158
1800	1/2:1 slope, 2' wide, 2' deep, 3/8 C.Y. bucket	1.11	3.60	4.71
1810	3' deep, 3/8 C.Y. bucket	1.85	6.30	8.15
1820	4' deep, 3/8 C.Y. bucket	2.75	9.60	12.35
1840	6' deep, 3/8 C.Y. bucket	6.25	14.35	20.50

G10 Site Preparation

G1030 Site Earthwork

G1030 806	Trenching Loam & Sandy Clay	COST PER L.F.		
		EQUIP.	LABOR	TOTAL
1860	8' deep, 1/2 C.Y. bucket	10.05	23	33
1880	10' deep, 1 C.Y. bucket	12.85	28.50	41.50
2300	4' wide, 2' deep, 3/8 C.Y. bucket	2.11	6	8.10
2310	3' deep, 3/8 C.Y. bucket	3.18	9.90	13.10
2320	4' deep, 1/2 C.Y. bucket	4.94	12.25	17.20
2340	6' deep, 1/2 C.Y. bucket	9.15	21	30
2360	8' deep, 1/2 C.Y. bucket	15.75	34	50
2380	10' deep, 1 C.Y. bucket	16.25	39.50	55.50
2400	12' deep, 1 C.Y. bucket	27.50	65	92.50
2430	15' deep, 1-1/2 C.Y. bucket	31.50	72.50	104
2460	18' deep, 2-1/2 C.Y. bucket	50.50	111	161
2840	6' wide, 6' deep, 5/8 C.Y. bucket w/trench box	15.45	29.50	45
2860	8' deep, 3/4 C.Y. bucket	23	43	66
2880	10' deep, 1 C.Y. bucket	22	48	70.50
2900	12' deep, 1-1/2 C.Y. bucket	27	59	86
2940	16' deep, 2-1/2 C.Y. bucket	42.50	86	129
2980	20' deep, 3-1/2 C.Y. bucket	53.50	116	170
3020	24' deep, 3-1/2 C.Y. bucket	75	159	234
3100	8' wide, 12' deep, 1-1/2 C.Y. bucket w/trench box	32.50	66.50	99
3120	15' deep, 1-1/2 C.Y. bucket	44.50	93.50	138
3140	18' deep, 2-1/2 C.Y. bucket	58.50	116	174
3180	24' deep, 3-1/2 C.Y. bucket	84	175	259
3270	10' wide, 20' deep, 3-1/2 C.Y. bucket w/trench box	67.50	141	209
3280	24' deep, 3-1/2 C.Y. bucket	93	191	284
3320	12' wide, 20' deep, 3-1/2 C.Y. bucket w/trench box	75	154	229
3380	25' deep, 3-1/2 C.Y. bucket w/trench box	102	206	310
3500	1:1 slope, 2' wide, 2' deep, 3/8 C.Y. bucket	1.44	4.80	6.25
3520	3' deep, 3/8 C.Y. bucket	2.59	9	11.60
3540	4' deep, 3/8 C.Y. bucket	4.06	14.40	18.45
3560	6' deep, 1/2 C.Y. bucket	6.25	14.35	20.50
3580	8' deep, 1/2 C.Y. bucket	16.60	38	55
3600	10' deep, 1 C.Y. bucket	22	49	71
3800	4' wide, 2' deep, 3/8 C.Y. bucket	2.44	7.20	9.65
3820	3' deep, 1/2 C.Y. bucket	3.92	12.60	16.55
3840	4' deep, 1/2 C.Y. bucket	6.35	16.40	23
3860	6' deep, 1/2 C.Y. bucket	12.75	30.50	43
3880	8' deep, 1/2 C.Y. bucket	23.50	51	74.50
3900	10' deep, 1 C.Y. bucket	25	61.50	87
3920	12' deep, 1 C.Y. bucket	36.50	87	124
3940	15' deep, 1-1/2 C.Y. bucket	51.50	120	172
3960	18' deep, 2-1/2 C.Y. bucket	69.50	153	222
4030	6' wide, 6' deep, 5/8 C.Y. bucket w/trench box	20.50	39	59.50
4040	8' deep, 3/4 C.Y. bucket	31.50	60.50	92
4050	10' deep, 1 C.Y. bucket	32	71	103
4060	12' deep, 1-1/2 C.Y. bucket	40.50	89	129
4070	16' deep, 2-1/2 C.Y. bucket	66.50	136	203
4080	20' deep, 3-1/2 C.Y. bucket	86.50	190	276
4090	24' deep, 3-1/2 C.Y. bucket	125	267	390
4500	8' wide, 12' deep, 1-1/4 C.Y. bucket w/trench box	46	96.50	143
4550	15' deep, 1-1/2 C.Y. bucket	65	141	206
4600	18' deep, 2-1/2 C.Y. bucket	89	179	268
4650	24' deep, 3-1/2 C.Y. bucket	134	282	415
4800	10' wide, 20' deep, 3-1/2 C.Y. bucket w/trench box	101	215	315
4850	24' deep, 3-1/2 C.Y. bucket	143	298	440
4950	12' wide, 20' deep, 3-1/2 C.Y. bucket w/trench box	108	228	335
4980	25' deep, 3-1/2 C.Y. bucket	162	335	500

G10 Site Preparation

G1030 Site Earthwork

Trenching Systems are shown on a cost per linear foot basis. The systems include: excavation; backfill and removal of spoil; and compaction for various depths and trench bottom widths. The backfill has been reduced to accommodate a pipe of suitable diameter and bedding.

The slope for trench sides varies from none to 1:1.

The Expanded System Listing shows Trenching Systems that range from 2' to 12' in width. Depths range from 2' to 25'.

System Components	QUANTITY	UNIT	COST PER L.F.		
			EQUIP.	LABOR	TOTAL
SYSTEM G1030 807 1310					
TRENCHING, SAND & GRAVEL, NO SLOPE, 2' WIDE, 2' DEEP, 3/8 C.Y. BUCKET					
Excavation, trench, hyd. backhoe, track mtd., 3/8 C.Y. bucket	.148	C.Y.	.29	1.21	1.50
Backfill and load spoil, from stockpile	.140	L.C.Y.	.14	.37	.51
Compaction by vibrating plate 18" wide, 6" lifts, 4 passes	.118	C.Y.	.12	.49	.61
Remove excess spoil, 8 C.Y. dump truck, 2 mile roundtrip	.035	L.C.Y.	.16	.20	.36
TOTAL			.71	2.27	2.98

G1030 807	Trenching Sand & Gravel	COST PER L.F.		
		EQUIP.	LABOR	TOTAL
1310	Trenching, sand & gravel, no slope, 2' wide, 2' deep, 3/8 C.Y. bucket	.72	2.27	2.99
1320	3' deep, 3/8 C.Y. bucket	1.11	3.79	4.90
1330	4' deep, 3/8 C.Y. bucket	1.33	4.56	5.90
1340	6' deep, 3/8 C.Y. bucket	2.46	5.45	7.90
1350	8' deep, 1/2 C.Y. bucket	3.30	7.20	10.55
1360	10' deep, 1 C.Y. bucket	3.50	7.60	11.10
1400	4' wide, 2' deep, 3/8 C.Y. bucket	1.61	4.51	6.10
1410	3' deep, 3/8 C.Y. bucket	2.23	6.80	9.05
1420	4' deep, 1/2 C.Y. bucket	3.24	7.65	10.90
1430	6' deep, 1/2 C.Y. bucket	5.20	11.35	16.55
1440	8' deep, 1/2 C.Y. bucket	7.80	15.95	23.50
1450	10' deep, 1 C.Y. bucket	6.90	16.25	23
1460	12' deep, 1 C.Y. bucket	8.75	20	29
1470	15' deep, 1-1/2 C.Y. bucket	10.40	23.50	34
1480	18' deep, 2-1/2 C.Y. bucket	12.05	25.50	37.50
1520	6' wide, 6' deep, 5/8 C.Y. bucket w/trench box	10.05	18.35	28.50
1530	8' deep, 3/4 C.Y. bucket	13.55	24	37.50
1540	10' deep, 1 C.Y. bucket	11.60	24.50	36
1550	12' deep, 1-1/2 C.Y. bucket	13	27	40
1560	16' deep, 2 C.Y. bucket	17.70	34	52
1570	20' deep, 3-1/2 C.Y. bucket	19	40	59
1580	24' deep, 3-1/2 C.Y. bucket	24	49	72.50
1640	8' wide, 12' deep, 1-1/2 C.Y. bucket w/trench box	18.15	34.50	52.50
1650	15' deep, 1-1/2 C.Y. bucket	22	43.50	66
1660	18' deep, 2-1/2 C.Y. bucket	26.50	49	75.50
1680	24' deep, 3-1/2 C.Y. bucket	32	63	95.50
1730	10' wide, 20' deep, 3-1/2 C.Y. bucket w/trench box	32.50	63.50	95.50
1740	24' deep, 3-1/2 C.Y. bucket	40.50	78	119
1780	12' wide, 20' deep, 3-1/2 C.Y. bucket w/trench box	39	75	114
1790	25' deep, 3-1/2 C.Y. bucket	50.50	97	148
1800	1/2:1 slope, 2' wide, 2' deep, 3/8 C.Y. bucket	1.02	3.42	4.45
1810	3' deep, 3/8 C.Y. bucket	1.72	6	7.70
1820	4' deep, 3/8 C.Y. bucket	2.57	9.15	11.70
1840	6' deep, 3/8 C.Y. bucket	6	13.65	19.70

G10 Site Preparation

G1030 Site Earthwork

G1030 807	Trenching Sand & Gravel	COST PER L.F.		
		EQUIP.	LABOR	TOTAL
1860	8' deep, 1/2 C.Y. bucket	9.60	22	31.50
1880	10' deep, 1 C.Y. bucket	12.15	27	39
2300	4' wide, 2' deep, 3/8 C.Y. bucket	1.92	5.65	7.60
2310	3' deep, 3/8 C.Y. bucket	2.93	9.40	12.30
2320	4' deep, 1/2 C.Y. bucket	4.58	11.60	16.20
2340	6' deep, 1/2 C.Y. bucket	8.70	20	29
2360	8' deep, 1/2 C.Y. bucket	14.95	32	47
2380	10' deep, 1 C.Y. bucket	15.35	37.50	52.50
2400	12' deep, 1 C.Y. bucket	26	62	87.50
2430	15' deep, 1-1/2 C.Y. bucket	29.50	68.50	98
2460	18' deep, 2-1/2 C.Y. bucket	48	104	152
2840	6' wide, 6' deep, 5/8 C.Y. bucket w/trench box	14.65	28	42.50
2860	8' deep, 3/4 C.Y. bucket	21.50	40.50	62.50
2880	10' deep, 1 C.Y. bucket	21	45.50	66.50
2900	12' deep, 1-1/2 C.Y. bucket	25.50	55.50	81
2940	16' deep, 2 C.Y. bucket	40.50	81.50	122
2980	20' deep, 3-1/2 C.Y. bucket	50	109	159
3020	24' deep, 3-1/2 C.Y. bucket	70.50	150	220
3100	8' wide, 12' deep, 1-1/4 C.Y. bucket w/trench box	31	63	94
3120	15' deep, 1-1/2 C.Y. bucket	41.50	88	130
3140	18' deep, 2-1/2 C.Y. bucket	55.50	109	164
3180	24' deep, 3-1/2 C.Y. bucket	79	164	243
3270	10' wide, 20' deep, 3-1/2 C.Y. bucket w/trench box	63.50	133	196
3280	24' deep, 3-1/2 C.Y. bucket	87.50	179	266
3370	12' wide, 20' deep, 3-1/2 C.Y. bucket w/trench box	71	147	218
3380	25' deep, 3-1/2 C.Y. bucket	101	206	310
3500	1:1 slope, 2' wide, 2' deep, 3/8 C.Y. bucket	2.45	5.75	8.20
3520	3' deep, 3/8 C.Y. bucket	2.42	8.60	11
3540	4' deep, 3/8 C.Y. bucket	3.81	13.75	17.55
3560	6' deep, 3/8 C.Y. bucket	6	13.70	19.70
3580	8' deep, 1/2 C.Y. bucket	15.90	36.50	52.50
3600	10' deep, 1 C.Y. bucket	21	46.50	67
3800	4' wide, 2' deep, 3/8 C.Y. bucket	2.23	6.80	9.05
3820	3' deep, 3/8 C.Y. bucket	3.62	11.95	15.60
3840	4' deep, 1/2 C.Y. bucket	5.90	15.60	21.50
3860	6' deep, 1/2 C.Y. bucket	12.15	29	41
3880	8' deep, 1/2 C.Y. bucket	22	48.50	70.50
3900	10' deep, 1 C.Y. bucket	24	58.50	82
3920	12' deep, 1 C.Y. bucket	34.50	82.50	117
3940	15' deep, 1-1/2 C.Y. bucket	49	114	162
3960	18' deep, 2-1/2 C.Y. bucket	65.50	144	209
4030	6' wide, 6' deep, 5/8 C.Y. bucket w/trench box	19.25	37	56.50
4040	8' deep, 3/4 C.Y. bucket	30	57.50	87.50
4050	10' deep, 1 C.Y. bucket	30	67	97
4060	12' deep, 1-1/2 C.Y. bucket	38	84	122
4070	16' deep, 2 C.Y. bucket	63.50	129	192
4080	20' deep, 3-1/2 C.Y. bucket	81	178	260
4090	24' deep, 3-1/2 C.Y. bucket	118	250	370
4500	8' wide, 12' deep, 1-1/2 C.Y. bucket w/trench box	43.50	91.50	135
4550	15' deep, 1-1/2 C.Y. bucket	61.50	132	194
4600	18' deep, 2-1/2 C.Y. bucket	84	168	253
4650	24' deep, 3-1/2 C.Y. bucket	126	265	390
4800	10' wide, 20' deep, 3-1/2 C.Y. bucket w/trench box	94.50	202	296
4850	24' deep, 3-1/2 C.Y. bucket	134	280	415
4950	12' wide, 20' deep, 3-1/2 C.Y. bucket w/trench box	101	213	315
4980	25' deep, 3-1/2 C.Y. bucket	152	315	470

G10 Site Preparation

G1030 Site Earthwork

The Pipe Bedding System is shown for various pipe diameters. Compacted bank sand is used for pipe bedding and to fill 12" over the pipe. No backfill is included. Various side slopes are shown to accommodate different soil conditions. Pipe sizes vary from 6" to 84" diameter.

System Components	QUANTITY	UNIT	COST PER L.F.		
			MAT.	INST.	TOTAL
SYSTEM G1030 815 1440 PIPE BEDDING, SIDE SLOPE 0 TO 1, 1' WIDE, PIPE SIZE 6" DIAMETER					
Borrow, bank sand, 2 mile haul, machine spread	.086	C.Y.	1.45	.88	2.33
Compaction, vibrating plate	.086	C.Y.		.31	.31
TOTAL			1.45	1.19	2.64

G1030 815	Pipe Bedding	COST PER L.F.		
		MAT.	INST.	TOTAL
1440	Pipe bedding, side slope 0 to 1, 1' wide, pipe size 6" diameter	1.45	1.19	2.64
1460	2' wide, pipe size 8" diameter	3.14	2.58	5.72
1480	Pipe size 10" diameter	3.20	2.63	5.83
1500	Pipe size 12" diameter	3.27	2.69	5.96
1520	3' wide, pipe size 14" diameter	5.30	4.36	9.66
1540	Pipe size 15" diameter	5.35	4.40	9.75
1560	Pipe size 16" diameter	5.40	4.44	9.84
1580	Pipe size 18" diameter	5.50	4.52	10.02
1600	4' wide, pipe size 20" diameter	7.85	6.45	14.30
1620	Pipe size 21" diameter	7.90	6.50	14.40
1640	Pipe size 24" diameter	8.05	6.65	14.70
1660	Pipe size 30" diameter	8.20	6.75	14.95
1680	6' wide, pipe size 32" diameter	14.05	11.55	25.60
1700	Pipe size 36" diameter	14.40	11.80	26.20
1720	7' wide, pipe size 48" diameter	23	18.80	41.80
1740	8' wide, pipe size 60" diameter	28	23	51
1760	10' wide, pipe size 72" diameter	39	32	71
1780	12' wide, pipe size 84" diameter	51	42	93
2140	Side slope 1/2 to 1, 1' wide, pipe size 6" diameter	2.70	2.22	4.92
2160	2' wide, pipe size 8" diameter	4.59	3.77	8.36
2180	Pipe size 10" diameter	4.93	4.05	8.98
2200	Pipe size 12" diameter	5.20	4.29	9.49
2220	3' wide, pipe size 14" diameter	7.55	6.20	13.75
2240	Pipe size 15" diameter	7.70	6.35	14.05
2260	Pipe size 16" diameter	7.90	6.50	14.40
2280	Pipe size 18" diameter	8.30	6.85	15.15
2300	4' wide, pipe size 20" diameter	11	9	20
2320	Pipe size 21" diameter	11.20	9.20	20.40
2340	Pipe size 24" diameter	11.95	9.80	21.75
2360	Pipe size 30" diameter	13.25	10.85	24.10
2380	6' wide, pipe size 32" diameter	19.55	16.05	35.60
2400	Pipe size 36" diameter	21	17.05	38.05
2420	7' wide, pipe size 48" diameter	32.50	26.50	59
2440	8' wide, pipe size 60" diameter	41	34	75
2460	10' wide, pipe size 72" diameter	56.50	46.50	103
2480	12' wide, pipe size 84" diameter	74	60.50	134.50
2620	Side slope 1 to 1, 1' wide, pipe size 6" diameter	3.96	3.25	7.21
2640	2' wide, pipe size 8" diameter	6.10	5	11.10

G10 Site Preparation

G1030 Site Earthwork

G1030 815	Pipe Bedding	COST PER L.F.		
		MAT.	INST.	TOTAL
2660	Pipe size 10" diameter	6.65	5.45	12.10
2680	Pipe size 12" diameter	7.20	5.95	13.15
2700	3' wide, pipe size 14" diameter	9.80	8.05	17.85
2720	Pipe size 15" diameter	10.10	8.30	18.40
2740	Pipe size 16" diameter	10.40	8.55	18.95
2760	Pipe size 18" diameter	11.15	9.15	20.30
2780	4' wide, pipe size 20" diameter	14.15	11.60	25.75
2800	Pipe size 21" diameter	14.55	11.95	26.50
2820	Pipe size 24" diameter	15.75	12.95	28.70
2840	Pipe size 30" diameter	18.20	14.95	33.15
2860	6' wide, pipe size 32" diameter	25	20.50	45.50
2880	Pipe size 36" diameter	27	22.50	49.50
2900	7' wide, pipe size 48" diameter	42	34.50	76.50
2920	8' wide, pipe size 60" diameter	54.50	44.50	99
2940	10' wide, pipe size 72" diameter	74	61	135
2960	12' wide, pipe size 84" diameter	96.50	79.50	176

G20 Site Improvements

G2040 Site Development

- Chain Link Fence
- Concrete Sidewalk
- Pool Equipment (Building not included in price)
- 12' x 30' Swimming Pool
- Fence Gate

The Swimming Pool System is a complete package. Everything from excavation to deck hardware is included in system costs. Below are three basic types of pool systems: residential, motel, and municipal. Systems elements include: excavation, pool materials, installation, deck hardware, pumps and filters, sidewalk, and fencing.

The Expanded System Listing shows three basic types of pools with a variety of finishes and basic materials. These systems are either vinyl lined with metal sides; gunite shell with a cement plaster finish or tile finish; or concrete sided with vinyl lining. Pool sizes listed here vary from 12' x 30' to 60' x 82.5'. All costs are on a per unit basis.

System Components	QUANTITY	UNIT	COST EACH		
			MAT.	INST.	TOTAL
SYSTEM G2040 920 1000					
SWIMMING POOL, RESIDENTIAL, CONC. SIDES, VINYL LINED, 12' X 30'					
Swimming pool, residential, in-ground including equipment	360.000	S.F.	17,460	6,447.60	23,907.60
4" thick reinforced concrete sidewalk, broom finish, no base	400.000	S.F.	1,500	1,308	2,808
Chain link fence, residential, 4' high	124.000	L.F.	1,202.80	725.40	1,928.20
Fence gate, chain link, 4' high	1.000	Ea.	127	234.50	361.50
TOTAL			20,289.80	8,715.50	29,005.30

G2040 920	Swimming Pools	COST EACH		
		MAT.	INST.	TOTAL
1000	Swimming pool, residential class, concrete sides, vinyl lined, 12' x 30'	20,300	8,725	29,025
1100	16' x 32'	23,000	9,850	32,850
1200	20' x 40'	29,700	12,500	42,200
1500	Tile finish, 12' x 30'	37,500	36,500	74,000
1600	16' x 32'	38,300	38,500	76,800
1700	20' x 40'	57,000	54,500	111,500
2000	Metal sides, vinyl lined, 12' x 30'	39,200	5,775	44,975
2100	16' x 32'	44,500	6,475	50,975
2200	20' x 40'	58,000	8,150	66,150
3000	Gunite shell, cement plaster finish, 12' x 30'	30,000	15,600	45,600
3100	16' x 32'	37,900	20,200	58,100
3200	20' x 40'	52,500	20,100	72,600
4000	Motel class, concrete sides, vinyl lined, 20' x 40'	42,500	17,300	59,800
4100	28' x 60'	59,500	24,200	83,700
4500	Tile finish, 20' x 40'	67,000	62,500	129,500
4600	28' x 60'	106,000	102,000	208,000
5000	Metal sides, vinyl lined, 20' x 40'	104,500	12,700	117,200
5100	28' x 60'	140,500	17,000	157,500
6000	Gunite shell, cement plaster finish, 20' x 40'	96,500	49,700	146,200
6100	28' x 60'	144,500	74,000	218,500
7000	Municipal class, Gunite shell, cement plaster finish, 42' x 75'	384,500	174,500	559,000
7100	60' x 82.5'	494,000	223,500	717,500
7500	Concrete walls, tile finish, 42' x 75'	429,500	236,500	666,000
7600	60' x 82.5'	559,000	313,500	872,500
7700	Tile finish and concrete gutter, 42' x 75'	471,000	236,500	707,500
7800	60' x 82.5'	609,500	313,500	923,000
7900	Tile finish and stainless gutter, 42' x 75'	553,000	236,500	789,500
8000	60' x 82.5'	816,500	362,000	1,178,500

G20 Site Improvements

G2050 Landscaping

There are three basic types of Site Irrigation Systems: pop-up, riser mounted and quick coupling. Sprinkler heads are spray, impact or gear driven. Each system includes: the hardware for spraying the water; the pipe and fittings needed to deliver the water; and all other accessory equipment such as valves, couplings, nipples, and nozzles. Excavation heads and backfill costs are also included in the system.
The Expanded System Listing shows a wide variety of Site Irrigation Systems.

System Components	QUANTITY	UNIT	COST PER S.F.		
			MAT.	INST.	TOTAL
SYSTEM G2050 710 1000 SITE IRRIGATION, POP UP SPRAY, PLASTIC, 10' RADIUS, 1000 S.F., PVC PIPE					
Excavation, chain trencher	54.000	L.F.		65.34	65.34
Pipe, fittings & nipples, PVC Schedule 40, 1" diameter	5.000	Ea.	3.80	140	143.80
Fittings, bends or elbows, 4" diameter	5.000	Ea.	89.50	317.50	407
Couplings PVC plastic, high pressure, 1" diameter	5.000	Ea.	3.80	177.50	181.30
Valves, bronze, globe, 125 lb. rising stem, threaded, 1" diameter	1.000	Ea.	475	47	522
Head & nozzle, pop-up spray, PVC plastic	5.000	Ea.	27.75	127.50	155.25
Backfill by hand with compaction	54.000	L.F.		48.06	48.06
Total cost per 1,000 S.F.			599.85	922.90	1,522.75
Total cost per S.F.			.60	.92	1.52

G2050 710	Site Irrigation	COST PER S.F.		
		MAT.	INST.	TOTAL
1000	Site irrigation, pop up spray, 10' radius, 1000 S.F., PVC pipe	.60	.93	1.53
1100	Polyethylene pipe	.65	.80	1.45
1200	14' radius, 8000 S.F., PVC pipe	.22	.40	.62
1300	Polyethylene pipe	.20	.37	.57
1400	18' square, 1000 S.F. PVC pipe	.64	.63	1.27
1500	Polyethylene pipe	.59	.55	1.14
1600	24' square, 8000 S.F., PVC pipe	.17	.26	.43
1700	Polyethylene pipe	.17	.25	.42
1800	4' x 30' strip, 200 S.F., PVC pipe	2.96	2.60	5.56
1900	Polyethylene pipe	2.86	2.42	5.28
2000	6' x 40' strip, 800 S.F., PVC pipe	.80	.87	1.67
2200	Economy brass, 11' radius, 1000 S.F., PVC pipe	.77	.88	1.65
2300	Polyethylene pipe	.73	.80	1.53
2400	14' radius, 8000 S.F., PVC pipe	.26	.40	.66
2500	Polyethylene pipe	.24	.37	.61
2600	3' x 28' strip, 200 S.F., PVC pipe	3.20	2.60	5.80
2700	Polyethylene pipe	3.10	2.42	5.52
2800	7' x 36' strip, 1000 S.F., PVC pipe	.70	.69	1.39
2900	Polyethylene pipe	.67	.64	1.31
3000	Hd brass, 11' radius, 1000 S.F., PVC pipe	.82	.88	1.70
3100	Polyethylene pipe	.78	.80	1.58
3200	14' radius, 8000 S.F., PVC pipe	.28	.40	.68
3300	Polyethylene pipe	.26	.37	.63
3400	Riser mounted spray, plastic, 10' radius, 1000 S.F., PVC pipe	.69	.88	1.57
3500	Polyethylene pipe	.65	.80	1.45
3600	12' radius, 5000 S.F., PVC pipe	.32	.52	.84

For customer support on your Plumbing Costs with RSMeans Data call 800.448.8182.

G20 Site Improvements

G2050 Landscaping

G2050 710	Site Irrigation	COST PER S.F.		
		MAT.	INST.	TOTAL
3700	Polyethylene pipe	.29	.48	.77
3800	19' square, 2000 S.F., PVC pipe	.31	.29	.60
3900	Polyethylene pipe	.29	.26	.55
4000	24' square, 8000 S.F., PVC pipe	.18	.26	.44
4100	Polyethylene pipe	.17	.25	.42
4200	5' x 32' strip, 300 S.F., PVC pipe	1.98	1.75	3.73
4300	Polyethylene pipe	1.91	1.62	3.53
4400	6' x 40' strip, 800 S.F., PVC pipe	.80	.87	1.67
4500	Polyethylene pipe	.76	.80	1.56
4600	Brass, 11' radius, 1000 S.F., PVC pipe	.74	.88	1.62
4700	Polyethylene pipe	.70	.80	1.50
4800	14' radius, 8000 S.F., PVC pipe	.24	.40	.64
4900	Polythylene pipe	.22	.37	.59
5000	Pop up gear drive stream type, plastic, 30' radius, 10,000 S.F., PVC pipe	.42	.76	1.18
5020	Polyethylene pipe	.21	.23	.44
5040	40,000 S.F., PVC pipe	.35	.76	1.11
5060	Polyethylene pipe	.17	.22	.39
5080	Riser mounted gear drive stream type, plas., 30' rad., 10,000 S.F.,PVC pipe	.40	.76	1.16
5100	Polyethylene pipe	.20	.23	.43
5120	40,000 S.F., PVC pipe	.34	.76	1.10
5140	Polyethylene pipe	.16	.22	.38
5200	Q.C. valve thread type w/impact head, brass, 75' rad 20,000 S.F., PVC pipe	.16	.30	.46
5250	Polyethylene pipe	.07	.08	.15
5300	100,000 S.F., PVC pipe	.23	.48	.71
5350	Polyethylene pipe	.11	.12	.23
5400	Q.C. valve lug type w/impact head, brass, 75' rad, 20,000 S.F., PVC pipe	.16	.30	.46
5450	Polyethylene pipe	.08	.08	.16
5500	100,000 S.F. PVC pipe	.23	.48	.71
5550	Polyethylene pipe	.11	.12	.23
6000	Site irrigation, pop up impact type, plastic, 40' rad.,10000 S.F., PVC pipe	.25	.49	.74
6100	Polyethylene pipe	.12	.14	.26
6200	45,000 S.F., PVC pipe	.23	.54	.77
6300	Polyethylene pipe	.09	.14	.23
6400	High medium volume brass, 40' radius, 10000 S.F., PVC pipe	.26	.49	.75
6500	Polyethylene pipe	.12	.14	.26
6600	45,000 S.F. PVC pipe	.23	.54	.77
6700	Polyethylene pipe	.10	.14	.24
6800	High volume brass, 60' radius, 25,000 S.F., PVC pipe	.19	.38	.57
6900	Polyethylene pipe	.08	.10	.18
7000	100,000 S.F., PVC pipe	.20	.38	.58
7100	Polyethylene pipe	.10	.09	.19
7200	Riser mounted part/full impact type, plas., 40' rad., 10,000 S.F., PVC pipe	.24	.49	.73
7300	Polyethylene pipe	.11	.28	.39
7400	45,000 S.F., PVC pipe	.22	.54	.76
7500	Polyethylene pipe	.08	.14	.22
7600	Low medium volume brass, 40' radius, 10,000 S.F., PVC pipe	.25	.49	.74
7700	Polyethylene pipe	.12	.14	.26
7800	45,000 S.F., PVC pipe	.23	.54	.77
7900	Polyethylene pipe	.09	.14	.23
8000	Medium volume brass, 50' radius, 30,000 S.F., PVC pipe	.20	.40	.60
8100	Polyethylene pipe	.09	.11	.20
8200	70,000 S.F., PVC pipe	.29	.66	.95
8300	Polyethylene pipe	.12	.17	.29
8400	Riser mounted full only impact type, plas., 40' rad., 10,000 S.F., PVC pipe	.24	.49	.73
8500	Polyethylene pipe	.10	.14	.24
8600	45,000 S.F., PVC pipe	.22	.54	.76
8700	Polyethylene pipe	.08	.14	.22
8800	Low medium volume brass, 40' radius, 10,000 S.F., PVC pipe	.26	.49	.75

G20 Site Improvements

G2050 Landscaping

G2050 710	Site Irrigation	COST PER S.F.		
		MAT.	INST.	TOTAL
8900	Polyethylene pipe	.12	.14	.26
9000	45,000 S.F., PVC pipe	.23	.54	.77
9100	Polyethylene pipe	.10	.14	.24
9200	High volume brass, 80' radius, 75,000 S.F., PVC pipe	.14	.29	.43
9300	Polyethylene pipe	.01	.02	.03
9400	150,000 S.F., PVC pipe	.14	.26	.40
9500	Polyethylene pipe	.01	.02	.03
9600	Very high volume brass, 100' radius, 100,000 S.F., PVC pipe	.13	.22	.35
9700	Polyethylene pipe	.01	.02	.03
9800	200,000 S.F., PVC pipe	.13	.22	.35
9900	Polyethylene pipe	.01	.02	.03

For customer support on your Plumbing Costs with RSMeans Data call 800.448.8182.

G20 Site Improvements

G2050 Landscaping

Drip irrigation systems can be for either lawns or individual plants. Shown below are drip irrigation systems for lawns. These drip type systems are most cost effective where there are water restrictions on use or the cost of water is very high. The supply uses PVC piping with the laterals polyethylene drip lines.

System Components	QUANTITY	UNIT	COST PER S.F.		
			MAT.	INST.	TOTAL
SYSTEM G2050 720 1000					
SITE IRRIGATION, DRIP SYSTEM, 800 S.F. (20' X 40')					
Excavate supply and header lines 4" x 18" deep	50.000	L.F.		64.50	64.50
Excavate drip lines 4" x 4" deep	560.000	L.F.		1,080.80	1,080.80
Install supply manifold (stop valve, strainer, PRV, adapters)	1.000	Ea.	28.50	190	218.50
Install 3/4" PVC supply line and risers to 4" drip level	75.000	L.F.	30.75	189.75	220.50
Install 3/4" PVC fittings for supply line	33.000	Ea.	73.59	627	700.59
Install PVC to drip line adapters	14.000	Ea.	32.20	266	298.20
Install 1/4 inch drip lines with hose clamps	560.000	L.F.	78.40	352.80	431.20
Backfill trenches	3.180	C.Y.		168.54	168.54
Cleanup area when completed	1.000	Ea.		145	145
Total cost per 800 S.F.			243.44	3,084.39	3,327.83
Total cost per S.F.			.32	4.01	4.33

G2050 720	Site Irrigation	COST PER S.F.		
		MAT.	INST.	TOTAL
1000	Site irrigation, drip lawn watering system, 800 S.F. (20' x 40' area)	.32	4	4.32
1100	1000 S.F. (20' x 50' area)	.26	3.47	3.73
1200	1600 S.F. (40' x 40' area), 2 zone	.33	3.71	4.04
1300	2000 S.F. (40' x 50' area), 2 zone	.28	3.35	3.63
1400	2400 S.F. (60' x 40' area), 3 zone	.31	3.66	3.97
1500	3000 S.F. (60' x 50' area), 3 zone	.27	3.30	3.57
1600	3200 S.F. (2 x 40' x 40'), 4 zone	.32	3.64	3.96
1700	4000 S.F. (2 x 40' x 50'), 4 zone	.27	3.30	3.57
1800	4800 S.F. (2 x 60' x 40'), 6 zone with control	.34	3.61	3.95
1900	6000 S.F. (2 x 60' x 50'), 6 zone with control	.29	3.26	3.55
2000	6400 S.F. (4 x 40' x 40'), 8 zone with control	.33	3.66	3.99
2100	8000 S.F. (4 x 40' x 50'), 8 zone with control	.28	3.32	3.60
2200	3200 S.F. (2 x 40' x 40'), 4 zone with control	.34	3.72	4.06
2300	4000 S.F. (2 x 40' x 50'), 4 zone with control	.29	3.36	3.65
2400	2400 S.F. (60' x 40'), 3 zone with control	.34	3.77	4.11
2500	3000 S.F. (60' x 50'), 3 zone with control	.29	3.38	3.67
2600	4800 S.F. (2 x 60' x 40'), 6 zone, manual	.31	3.57	3.88
2700	6000 S.F. (2 x 60' x 50'), 6 zone, manual	.26	3.22	3.48
2800	1000 S.F. (10' x 100' area)	.16	2.16	2.32
2900	2000 S.F. (2 x 10' x 100' area)	.18	2.08	2.26

G30 Site Mechanical Utilities

G3010 Water Supply

The Water Service Systems are for copper service taps from 1" to 2" diameter into pressurized mains from 6" to 8" diameter. Costs are given for two offsets with depths varying from 2' to 10'. Included in system components are excavation and backfill and required curb stops with boxes.

System Components	QUANTITY	UNIT	COST EACH		
			MAT.	INST.	TOTAL
SYSTEM G3010 121 1000					
WATER SERVICE, LEAD FREE, 6" MAIN, 1" COPPER SERVICE, 10' OFFSET, 2' DEEP					
Trench excavation, 1/2 C.Y. backhoe, 1 laborer	2.220	C.Y.		20.56	20.56
Drill & tap pressurized main, 6", 1" to 2" service	1.000	Ea.		535	535
Corporation stop, 1" diameter	1.000	Ea.	135	55.50	190.50
Saddles, 3/4" & 1" diameter, add	1.000	Ea.	80		80
Copper tubing, type K, 1" diameter	12.000	L.F.	94.80	60	154.80
Piping, curb stops, no lead, 1" diameter	1.000	Ea.	218	55.50	273.50
Curb box, cast iron, 1/2" to 1" curb stops	1.000	Ea.	44.50	74	118.50
Backfill by hand, no compaction, heavy soil	2.890	C.Y.		8.50	8.50
Compaction, vibrating plate	2.220	C.Y.		23.82	23.82
TOTAL			572.30	832.88	1,405.18

G3010 121	Water Service, Lead Free	COST EACH		
		MAT.	INST.	TOTAL
1000	Water service, Lead Free, 6" main, 1" copper service, 10' offset, 2' deep	570	835	1,405
1040	4' deep	570	885	1,455
1060	6' deep	570	1,125	1,695
1080	8' deep	570	1,250	1,820
1100	10' deep	570	1,375	1,945
1200	20' offset, 2' deep	570	885	1,455
1240	4' deep	570	990	1,560
1260	6' deep	570	1,475	2,045
1280	8' deep	570	1,725	2,295
1300	10' deep	570	1,950	2,520
1400	1-1/2" copper service, 10' offset, 2' deep	1,200	910	2,110
1440	4' deep	1,200	960	2,160
1460	6' deep	1,200	1,200	2,400
1480	8' deep	1,200	1,325	2,525
1500	10' deep	1,200	1,450	2,650
1520	20' offset, 2' deep	1,200	960	2,160
1530	4' deep	1,200	1,075	2,275
1540	6' deep	1,200	1,550	2,750
1560	8' deep	1,200	1,800	3,000
1580	10' deep	1,200	2,025	3,225
1600	2" copper service, 10' offset, 2' deep	1,575	945	2,520
1610	4' deep	1,375	995	2,370
1620	6' deep	1,375	1,250	2,625
1630	8' deep	1,375	1,350	2,725
1650	10' deep	1,375	1,475	2,850
1660	20' offset, 2' deep	1,375	995	2,370
1670	4' deep	1,375	1,100	2,475
1680	6' deep	1,375	1,600	2,975

G30 Site Mechanical Utilities

G3010 Water Supply

G3010 121	Water Service, Lead Free	COST EACH		
		MAT.	INST.	TOTAL
1690	8' deep	1,375	1,825	3,200
1695	10' deep	1,375	2,075	3,450
1700	8" main, 1" copper service, 10' offset, 2' deep	570	880	1,450
1710	4' deep	570	930	1,500
1720	6' deep	570	1,175	1,745
1730	8' deep	570	1,300	1,870
1740	10' deep	570	1,425	1,995
1750	20' offset, 2' deep	570	930	1,500
1760	4' deep	570	1,025	1,595
1770	6' deep	570	1,525	2,095
1780	8' deep	570	1,775	2,345
1790	10' deep	570	2,000	2,570
1800	1-1/2" copper service, 10' offset, 2' deep	1,200	955	2,155
1810	4' deep	1,200	1,000	2,200
1820	6' deep	1,200	1,250	2,450
1830	8' deep	1,200	1,825	3,025
1840	10' deep	1,200	1,500	2,700
1850	20' offset, 2' deep	1,200	1,000	2,200
1860	4' deep	1,200	1,000	2,200
1870	6' deep	1,200	1,600	2,800
1880	8' deep	1,200	1,825	3,025
1890	10' deep	1,200	2,075	3,275
1900	2" copper service, 10' offset, 2' deep	1,575	990	2,565
1910	4' deep	1,375	1,050	2,425
1920	6' deep	1,375	1,300	2,675
1930	8' deep	1,375	1,400	2,775
1940	10' deep	1,375	1,525	2,900
1950	20' offset, 2' deep	1,375	1,050	2,425
1960	4' deep	1,375	1,150	2,525
1970	6' deep	1,375	1,650	3,025
1980	8' deep	1,375	1,875	3,250
1990	10' deep	1,375	2,100	3,475

G30 Site Mechanical Utilities

G3010 Water Supply

The Fire Hydrant Systems include: four different hydrants with three different lengths of offsets, at several depths of trenching. Excavation and backfill is included with each system as well as thrust blocks as necessary and pipe bedding. Finally spreading of excess material and fine grading complete the components.

System Components	QUANTITY	UNIT	COST PER EACH		
			MAT.	INST.	TOTAL
SYSTEM G3010 410 1500					
HYDRANT, 4-1/2" VALVE SIZE, TWO WAY, 10' OFFSET, 2' DEEP					
Excavation, trench, 1 C.Y. hydraulic backhoe	3.556	C.Y.		37.48	37.48
Sleeve, 12" x 6"	1.000	Ea.	1,775	143.30	1,918.30
Ductile iron pipe, 6" diameter	8.000	L.F.	1,200	128.64	1,328.64
Gate valve, 6"	1.000	Ea.	5,300	368.50	5,668.50
Hydrant valve box, 6' long	1.000	Ea.	390	97	487
4-1/2" valve size, depth 2'-0"	1.000	Ea.	3,400	257	3,657
Thrust blocks, at valve, shoe and sleeve	1.600	C.Y.	496	553.98	1,049.98
Borrow, crushed stone, 3/8"	4.089	C.Y.	171.74	42.08	213.82
Backfill and compact, dozer, air tamped	4.089	C.Y.		92.20	92.20
Spread excess excavated material	.204	C.Y.		10.81	10.81
Fine grade, hand	400.000	S.F.		339.50	339.50
TOTAL			12,732.74	2,070.49	14,803.23

G3010 410	Fire Hydrants	COST PER EACH		
		MAT.	INST.	TOTAL
1000	Hydrant, 4-1/2" valve size, two way, 0' offset, 2' deep	11,500	1,450	12,950
1100	4' deep	11,800	1,500	13,300
1200	6' deep	12,100	1,575	13,675
1300	8' deep	12,300	1,650	13,950
1400	10' deep	12,600	1,725	14,325
1500	10' offset, 2' deep	12,700	2,075	14,775
1600	4' deep	13,000	2,450	15,450
1700	6' deep	13,300	3,175	16,475
1800	8' deep	13,500	4,225	17,725
1900	10' deep	13,800	6,425	20,225
2000	20' offset, 2' deep	14,200	2,675	16,875
2100	4' deep	14,500	3,300	17,800
2200	6' deep	14,800	4,375	19,175
2300	8' deep	15,000	5,900	20,900
2400	10' deep	15,300	7,975	23,275
2500	Hydrant, 4-1/2" valve size, three way, 0' offset, 2' deep	11,800	1,475	13,275
2600	4' deep	12,100	1,500	13,600
2700	6' deep	12,400	1,600	14,000
2800	8' deep	12,600	1,675	14,275
2900	10' deep	12,900	1,775	14,675
3000	10' offset, 2' deep	13,000	2,100	15,100
3100	4' deep	13,300	2,475	15,775
3200	6' deep	13,600	3,200	16,800
3300	8' deep	13,800	4,250	18,050

G30 Site Mechanical Utilities

G3010 Water Supply

G3010 410	Fire Hydrants	COST PER EACH		
		MAT.	INST.	TOTAL
3400	10' deep	14,100	6,450	20,550
3500	20' offset, 2' deep	14,500	2,700	17,200
3600	4' deep	14,800	3,325	18,125
3700	6' deep	15,100	4,400	19,500
3800	8' deep	15,300	5,925	21,225
3900	10' deep	15,600	8,000	23,600
5000	5-1/4" valve size, two way, 0' offset, 2' deep	11,800	1,450	13,250
5100	4' deep	12,200	1,500	13,700
5200	6' deep	12,500	1,575	14,075
5300	8' deep	13,000	1,650	14,650
5400	10' deep	13,300	1,725	15,025
5500	10' offset, 2' deep	13,000	2,075	15,075
5600	4' deep	13,400	2,450	15,850
5700	6' deep	13,700	3,175	16,875
5800	8' deep	14,200	4,225	18,425
5900	10' deep	14,500	6,425	20,925
6000	20' offset, 2' deep	14,500	2,675	17,175
6100	4' deep	14,900	3,300	18,200
6200	6' deep	15,200	4,375	19,575
6300	8' deep	15,700	5,900	21,600
6400	10' deep	16,000	7,975	23,975
6500	Three way, 0' offset, 2' deep	12,100	1,475	13,575
6600	4' deep	12,400	1,500	13,900
6700	6' deep	12,800	1,600	14,400
6800	8' deep	13,300	1,675	14,975
6900	10' deep	13,700	1,775	15,475
7000	10' offset, 2' deep	13,300	2,100	15,400
7100	4' deep	13,600	2,475	16,075
7200	6' deep	14,000	3,200	17,200
7300	8' deep	14,500	4,250	18,750
7400	10' deep	14,900	6,450	21,350
7500	20' offset, 2' deep	14,800	2,700	17,500
7600	4' deep	15,100	2,975	18,075
7700	6' deep	15,500	4,400	19,900

G30 Site Mechanical Utilities

G3020 Sanitary Sewer

The Septic System includes: a septic tank; leaching field; concrete distribution boxes; plus excavation and gravel backfill.

The Expanded System Listing shows systems with tanks ranging from 1000 gallons to 2000 gallons. Tanks are either concrete or fiberglass. Cost is on a complete unit basis.

System Components	QUANTITY	UNIT	COST EACH		
			MAT.	INST.	TOTAL
SYSTEM G3020 302 0300					
1000 GALLON TANK, LEACHING FIELD, 600 S.F., 50' FROM BLDG.					
Mobilization	2.000	Ea.		1,986	1,986
Septic tank, precast, 1000 gallon	1.000	Ea.	1,075	321.50	1,396.50
Effluent filter	1.000	Ea.	39.50	95	134.50
Distribution box, precast, 5 outlets	1.000	Ea.	103	72.50	175.50
Flow leveler	3.000	Ea.	9.90	34.80	44.70
Sewer pipe, PVC, SDR 35, 4" diameter	160.000	L.F.	880	832	1,712
Tee	1.000	Ea.	21	95	116
Elbow	2.000	Ea.	35.80	127	162.80
Viewport cap	1.000	Ea.	10.45	31.50	41.95
Filter fabric	67.000	S.Y.	148.74	32.16	180.90
Detectable marking tape	1.600	C.L.F.	3.52	6.19	9.71
Excavation	160.000	C.Y.		2,616	2,616
Backfill	133.000	L.C.Y.		486.78	486.78
Spoil	55.000	L.C.Y.		473	473
Compaction	113.000	C.Y.		1,365.04	1,365.04
Stone fill, 3/4" to 1-1/2"	39.000	C.Y.	1,618.50	576.42	2,194.92
TOTAL			3,945.41	9,150.89	13,096.30

G3020 302	Septic Systems	COST EACH		
		MAT.	INST.	TOTAL
0300	1000 gal. concrete septic tank, 600 S.F. leaching field, 50 feet from bldg.	3,950	9,150	13,100
0301	200 feet from building	4,775	11,400	16,175
0305	750 S.F. leaching field, 50 feet from building	4,525	9,950	14,475
0306	200 feet from building	5,350	12,200	17,550
0400	1250 gal. concrete septic tank, 600 S.F. leaching field, 50 feet from bldg.	4,175	9,500	13,675
0401	200 feet from building	5,000	11,800	16,800
0405	750 S.F. leaching field, 50 feet from building	4,750	10,300	15,050
0406	200 feet from building	5,575	12,600	18,175
0410	1000 S.F. leaching field, 50 feet from building	5,775	11,800	17,575
0411	200 feet from building	6,625	14,100	20,725
0500	1500 gal. concrete septic tank, 600 S.F. leaching field, 50 feet from bldg.	4,775	9,875	14,650
0501	200 feet from building	5,575	12,100	17,675
0505	750 S.F. leaching field, 50 feet from building	5,350	10,700	16,050
0506	200 feet from building	6,175	14,100	20,275
0510	1000 S.F. leaching field, 50 feet from building	6,350	12,200	18,550
0511	200 feet from building	7,200	14,400	21,600
0515	1100 S.F. leaching field, 50 feet from building	6,750	12,800	19,550
0516	200 feet from building	7,575	15,100	22,675
0600	2000 gal concrete tank, 1200 S.F. leaching field, 50 feet from building	7,925	13,500	21,425
0601	200 feet from building	8,750	15,700	24,450

For customer support on your Plumbing Costs with RSMeans Data call 800.448.8182.

G30 Site Mechanical Utilities

G3020 Sanitary Sewer

G3020 302	Septic Systems	COST EACH		
		MAT.	INST.	TOTAL
0605	1500 S.F. leaching field, 50 feet from building	9,125	15,200	24,325
0606	200 feet from building	9,950	17,500	27,450
0710	2500 gal concrete tank, 1500 S.F. leaching field, 50 feet from building	9,075	16,200	25,275
0711	200 feet from building	9,900	18,400	28,300
0715	1600 S.F. leaching field, 50 feet from building	9,500	16,800	26,300
0716	200 feet from building	10,300	19,000	29,300
0720	1800 S.F. leaching field, 50 feet from building	10,300	18,000	28,300
0721	200 feet from building	11,100	20,200	31,300
1300	1000 gal. 2 compartment tank, 600 S.F. leaching field, 50 feet from bldg.	3,650	9,150	12,800
1301	200 feet from building	4,475	11,400	15,875
1305	750 S.F. leaching field, 50 feet from building	4,225	9,950	14,175
1306	200 feet from building	5,050	12,200	17,250
1400	1250 gal. 2 compartment tank, 600 S.F. leaching field, 50 feet from bldg.	4,050	9,500	13,550
1401	200 feet from building	4,875	11,800	16,675
1405	750 S.F. leaching field, 50 feet from building	4,625	10,300	14,925
1406	200 feet from building	5,450	12,600	18,050
1410	1000 S.F. leaching field, 50 feet from building	5,650	11,800	17,450
1411	200 feet from building	6,500	14,100	20,600
1500	1500 gal. 2 compartment tank, 600 S.F. leaching field, 50 feet from bldg.	4,975	9,875	14,850
1501	200 feet from building	5,775	12,100	17,875
1505	750 S.F. leaching field, 50 feet from building	5,550	10,700	16,250
1506	200 feet from building	6,375	14,100	20,475
1510	1000 S.F. leaching field, 50 feet from building	6,550	12,200	18,750
1511	200 feet from building	7,400	14,400	21,800
1515	1100 S.F. leaching field, 50 feet from building	6,950	12,800	19,750
1516	200 feet from building	7,775	15,100	22,875
1600	2000 gal 2 compartment tank, 1200 S.F. leaching field, 50 feet from bldg.	8,125	13,500	21,625
1601	200 feet from building	8,950	15,700	24,650
1605	1500 S.F. leaching field, 50 feet from building	9,325	15,200	24,525
1606	200 feet from building	10,100	17,500	27,600
1710	2500 gal 2 compartment tank, 1500 S.F. leaching field, 50 feet from bldg.	10,400	16,200	26,600
1711	200 feet from building	11,200	18,400	29,600
1715	1600 S.F. leaching field, 50 feet from building	10,800	16,800	27,600
1716	200 feet from building	11,600	19,000	30,600
1720	1800 S.F. leaching field, 50 feet from building	11,600	18,000	29,600
1721	200 feet from building	12,500	20,200	32,700

G30 Site Mechanical Utilities

G3030 Storm Sewer

Manhole   Catch Basin

The Manhole and Catch Basin System includes: excavation with a backhoe; a formed concrete footing; frame and cover; cast iron steps and compacted backfill.

The Expanded System Listing shows manholes that have a 4', 5' and 6' inside diameter riser. Depths range from 4' to 14'. Construction material shown is either concrete, concrete block, precast concrete, or brick.

System Components			COST PER EACH		
	QUANTITY	UNIT	MAT.	INST.	TOTAL
SYSTEM G3030 210 1920					
MANHOLE/CATCH BASIN, BRICK, 4' I.D. RISER, 4' DEEP					
Excavation, hydraulic backhoe, 3/8 C.Y. bucket	14.815	C.Y.		156.15	156.15
Trim sides and bottom of excavation	64.000	S.F.		82.56	82.56
Forms in place, manhole base, 4 uses	20.000	SFCA	34.40	132	166.40
Reinforcing in place footings, #4 to #7	.019	Ton	28.98	28.98	57.96
Concrete, 3000 psi	.925	C.Y.	186.85		186.85
Place and vibrate concrete, footing, direct chute	.925	C.Y.		61.29	61.29
Catch basin or MH, brick, 4' ID, 4' deep	1.000	Ea.	1,125	1,300	2,425
Catch basin or MH steps; heavy galvanized cast iron	1.000	Ea.	25.50	17.80	43.30
Catch basin or MH frame and cover	1.000	Ea.	1,225	284	1,509
Fill, granular	12.954	L.C.Y.	240.30		240.30
Backfill, spread with wheeled front end loader	12.954	L.C.Y.		38.09	38.09
Backfill compaction, 12" lifts, air tamp	12.954	C.Y.		150.53	150.53
TOTAL			2,866.03	2,251.40	5,117.43

G3030 210	Manholes & Catch Basins	COST PER EACH		
		MAT.	INST.	TOTAL
1920	Manhole/catch basin, brick, 4' I.D. riser, 4' deep	2,875	2,250	5,125
1940	6' deep	3,600	3,125	6,725
1960	8' deep	4,400	4,275	8,675
1980	10' deep	5,175	5,300	10,475
3000	12' deep	6,200	5,750	11,950
3020	14' deep	7,300	8,100	15,400
3200	Block, 4' I.D. riser, 4' deep	2,300	1,800	4,100
3220	6' deep	2,725	2,575	5,300
3240	8' deep	3,200	3,550	6,750
3260	10' deep	3,575	4,400	7,975
3280	12' deep	4,200	5,575	9,775
3300	14' deep	4,900	6,825	11,725
4620	Concrete, cast-in-place, 4' I.D. riser, 4' deep	2,700	3,075	5,775
4640	6' deep	3,375	4,100	7,475
4660	8' deep	4,300	5,950	10,250
4680	10' deep	4,975	7,400	12,375
4700	12' deep	5,875	9,175	15,050
4720	14' deep	6,875	11,000	17,875
5820	Concrete, precast, 4' I.D. riser, 4' deep	3,200	1,650	4,850
5840	6' deep	3,750	2,225	5,975

G30 Site Mechanical Utilities

G3030 Storm Sewer

G3030 210	Manholes & Catch Basins	COST PER EACH		
		MAT.	INST.	TOTAL
5860	8' deep	4,550	3,125	7,675
5880	10' deep	5,175	3,875	9,050
5900	12' deep	6,025	4,725	10,750
5920	14' deep	6,950	6,100	13,050
6000	5' I.D. riser, 4' deep	4,600	1,825	6,425
6020	6' deep	5,500	2,550	8,050
6040	8' deep	6,475	3,375	9,850
6060	10' deep	7,700	4,325	12,025
6080	12' deep	9,025	5,500	14,525
6100	14' deep	10,500	6,725	17,225
6200	6' I.D. riser, 4' deep	6,900	2,375	9,275
6220	6' deep	7,225	3,150	10,375
6240	8' deep	8,450	4,425	12,875
6260	10' deep	9,975	5,600	15,575
6280	12' deep	11,600	7,075	18,675
6300	14' deep	13,300	8,575	21,875

Reference Section

All the reference information is in one section, making it easy to find what you need to know and easy to use the data set on a daily basis. This section is visually identified by a vertical black bar on the page edges.

In this Reference Section, we've included Equipment Rental Costs, a listing of rental and operating costs; Crew Listings, a full listing of all crews and equipment, and their costs; Historical Cost Indexes for cost comparisons over time; City Cost Indexes and Location Factors for adjusting costs to the region you are in; Reference Tables, where you will find explanations, estimating information and procedures, and technical data; Change Orders, information on pricing changes to contract documents; and an explanation of all the Abbreviations in the data set.

Table of Contents

Construction Equipment Rental Costs	583
Crew Listings	595
Historical Cost Indexes	632
City Cost Indexes	633
Location Factors	676
Reference Tables	682
R01 General Requirements	682
R02 Existing Conditions	697
R03 Concrete	698
R05 Metals	699
R13 Special Construction	699
R21 Fire Suppression	699

Reference Tables (cont.)

R22 Plumbing	703
R23 Heating, Ventilating & Air Conditioning	713
R26 Electrical	716
R31 Earthwork	717
R33 Utilities	719
Change Orders	720
Project Costs	723
Abbreviations	728

Equipment Rental Costs

Estimating Tips
- This section contains the average costs to rent and operate hundreds of pieces of construction equipment. This is useful information when one is estimating the time and material requirements of any particular operation in order to establish a unit or total cost. Bare equipment costs shown on a unit cost line include, not only rental, but also operating costs for equipment under normal use.

Rental Costs
- Equipment rental rates are obtained from the following industry sources throughout North America: contractors, suppliers, dealers, manufacturers, and distributors.
- Rental rates vary throughout the country, with larger cities generally having lower rates. Lease plans for new equipment are available for periods in excess of six months, with a percentage of payments applying toward purchase.
- Monthly rental rates vary from 2% to 5% of the purchase price of the equipment depending on the anticipated life of the equipment and its wearing parts.
- Rental rates can also be treated as reimbursement costs for contractor-owned equipment. Owned equipment costs include depreciation, loan payments, interest, taxes, insurance, storage, and major repairs.

Operating Costs
- The operating costs include parts and labor for routine servicing, such as the repair and replacement of pumps, filters, and worn lines. Normal operating expendables, such as fuel, lubricants, tires, and electricity (where applicable), are also included.
- Extraordinary operating expendables with highly variable wear patterns, such as diamond bits and blades, are excluded. These costs can be found as material costs in the Unit Price section.
- The hourly operating costs listed do not include the operator's wages.

Equipment Cost/Day
- Any power equipment required by a crew is shown in the Crew Listings with a daily cost.
- This daily cost of equipment needed by a crew includes both the rental cost and the operating cost and is based on dividing the weekly rental rate by 5 (the number of working days in the week), then adding the hourly operating cost multiplied by 8 (the number of hours in a day). This "Equipment Cost/Day" is shown in the far right column of the Equipment Rental section.
- If equipment is needed for only one or two days, it is best to develop your own cost by including components for daily rent and hourly operating costs. This is important when the listed Crew for a task does not contain the equipment needed, such as a crane for lifting mechanical heating/cooling equipment up onto a roof.
- If the quantity of work is less than the crew's Daily Output shown for a Unit Price line item that includes a bare unit equipment cost, the recommendation is to estimate one day's rental cost and operating cost for equipment shown in the Crew Listing for that line item.
- Please note, in some cases the equipment description in the crew is followed by a time period in parenthesis. For example: (daily) or (monthly). In these cases the equipment cost/day is calculated by adding the rental cost per time period to the hourly operating cost multiplied by 8.

Mobilization, Demobilization Costs
- The cost to move construction equipment from an equipment yard or rental company to the job site and back again is not included in equipment rental costs listed in the Reference Section. It is also not included in the bare equipment cost of any Unit Price line item or in any equipment costs shown in the Crew Listings.
- Mobilization (to the site) and demobilization (from the site) costs can be found in the Unit Price section.
- If a piece of equipment is already at the job site, it is not appropriate to utilize mobilization or demobilization costs again in an estimate. ∎

Same Data. Simplified.

Enjoy the convenience and efficiency of accessing your costs anywhere:
- **Skip the multiplier** by setting your location
- **Quickly search,** edit, favorite and share costs
- **Stay on top of price changes** with automatic updates

Discover more at rsmeans.com/online

No part of this cost data may be reproduced, stored in a retrieval system, or transmitted in any form or by any means without prior written permission of Gordian.

01 54 | Construction Aids

01 54 33 | Equipment Rental

		UNIT	HOURLY OPER. COST	RENT PER DAY	RENT PER WEEK	RENT PER MONTH	EQUIPMENT COST/DAY	
10 0010	**CONCRETE EQUIPMENT RENTAL** without operators R015433-10							10
0200	Bucket, concrete lightweight, 1/2 C.Y.	Ea.	.88	60.34	181	543	43.27	
0300	1 C.Y.		1.15	72.73	218.17	654.52	52.84	
0400	1-1/2 C.Y.		1.49	94.86	284.60	853.80	68.85	
0500	2 C.Y.		1.62	110.47	331.41	994.24	79.23	
0580	8 C.Y.		8.10	138.95	416.84	1,250.52	148.21	
0600	Cart, concrete, self-propelled, operator walking, 10 C.F.		3.33	214.36	643.08	1,929.24	155.28	
0700	Operator riding, 18 C.F.		5.61	148.60	429	973.71	130.70	
0800	Conveyer for concrete, portable, gas, 16" wide, 26' long		12.40	117.42	352.26	1,056.78	169.62	
0900	46' long		12.83	159.65	478.95	1,436.85	198.46	
1000	56' long		13.03	166.38	499.12	1,497.34	204.02	
1100	Core drill, electric, 2-1/2 H.P., 1" to 8" bit diameter		1.83	77.25	245.48	585.38	63.75	
1150	11 H.P., 8" to 18" cores		6.30	149.79	527.46	1,137.88	155.93	
1200	Finisher, concrete floor, gas, riding trowel, 96" wide		11.28	250	793.33	2,155	248.89	
1300	Gas, walk-behind, 3 blade, 36" trowel		2.38	120	390	840	97	
1400	4 blade, 48" trowel		3.59	129.67	472.43	937.41	123.20	
1500	Float, hand-operated (Bull float), 48" wide		.10	14.27	44.36	128.35	9.64	
1570	Curb builder, 14 H.P., gas, single screw		16.36	164.80	494.40	1,483.20	229.75	
1590	Double screw		14.46	300	825	2,000	280.70	
1600	Floor grinder, concrete and terrazzo, electric, 22" path		3.55	141.56	410.33	1,028.57	110.44	
1700	Edger, concrete, electric, 7" path		1.38	160.58	519.62	1,095	115	
1750	Vacuum pick-up system for floor grinders, wet/dry		1.90	113	362.88	907.19	87.74	
1800	Mixer, powered, mortar and concrete, gas, 6 C.F., 18 H.P.		8.66	87.71	241.14	728.75	117.50	
1900	10 C.F., 25 H.P.		10.50	124.63	432.17	940	170.44	
2000	16 C.F.		10.93	177.08	774.51	1,212.49	242.32	
2100	Concrete, stationary, tilt drum, 2 C.Y.		9.23	86.52	256.86	706.84	125.24	
2120	Pump, concrete, truck mounted, 4" line, 80' boom		36.15	954.47	2,863.40	8,590.20	861.85	
2140	5" line, 110' boom		46.26	1,239.43	3,718.30	11,154.90	1,113.77	
2160	Mud jack, 50 C.F. per hr.		7.52	175.10	525.30	1,575.90	165.21	
2180	225 C.F. per hr.		9.96	207.72	623.15	1,869.45	204.29	
2190	Shotcrete pump rig, 12 C.Y./hr.		19.35	868.29	2,604.87	7,814.61	675.78	
2200	35 C.Y./hr.		18.40	1,131.28	3,393.85	10,181.55	826	
2600	Saw, concrete, manual, gas, 18 H.P.		6.46	189.60	338	1,239.91	119.32	
2650	Self-propelled, gas, 30 H.P.		9.21	197.18	605	1,570	194.70	
2675	V-groove crack chaser, manual, gas, 6 H.P.		1.92	137.50	362.50	962.50	87.84	
2700	Vibrators, concrete, electric, 60 cycle, 2 H.P.		.54	84.40	196	542	43.55	
2800	3 H.P.		.66	95	257	638	56.68	
2900	Gas engine, 5 H.P.		1.80	18.70	58.26	168.93	26.05	
3000	8 H.P.		2.43	18.92	58.85	170.03	31.20	
3050	Vibrating screed, gas engine, 8 H.P.		3.28	119.11	313.11	784.29	88.86	
3120	Concrete transit mixer, 6 x 4, 250 H.P., 8 C.Y., rear discharge		59.10	172.01	516.03	1,548.09	575.98	
3200	Front discharge		68.61	105.63	316.87	950.61	612.23	
3300	6 x 6, 285 H.P., 12 C.Y., rear discharge		67.74	343.33	1,030	3,090	747.96	
3400	Front discharge		70.59	291.83	875.50	2,626.50	739.81	
20 0010	**EARTHWORK EQUIPMENT RENTAL** without operators R015433-10							20
0040	Aggregate spreader, push type, 8' to 12' wide	Ea.	3.02	76.79	230.36	691.08	70.27	
0045	Tailgate type, 8' wide		2.97	57.77	173.32	519.95	58.43	
0055	Earth auger, truck mounted, for fence & sign posts, utility poles		16.15	68.25	168.75	461.25	162.91	
0060	For borings and monitoring wells		49.69	126.38	379.13	1,137.40	473.37	
0070	Portable, trailer mounted		2.68	120.24	457.02	990	112.87	
0075	Truck mounted, for caissons, water wells		99.49	186.91	560.73	1,682.20	908.08	
0080	Horizontal boring machine, 12" to 36" diameter, 45 H.P.		26.53	238.62	715.85	2,147.55	355.40	
0090	12" to 48" diameter, 65 H.P.		36.41	281.53	844.60	2,533.80	460.22	
0095	Auger, for fence posts, gas engine, hand held		.52	85.75	256	640	55.37	
0100	Excavator, diesel hydraulic, crawler mounted, 1/2 C.Y. cap.		25.36	709.38	2,113.13	5,700.63	625.49	
0120	5/8 C.Y. capacity		33.90	916.28	2,506.95	6,890.74	772.58	
0140	3/4 C.Y. capacity		38.13	1,200.58	2,914.03	7,935.40	887.82	
0150	1 C.Y. capacity		48.11	1,214.43	2,929.05	7,953.81	970.66	

For customer support on your Plumbing Costs with RSMeans Data call 800.448.8182.

01 54 | Construction Aids

01 54 33 | Equipment Rental

		UNIT	HOURLY OPER. COST	RENT PER DAY	RENT PER WEEK	RENT PER MONTH	EQUIPMENT COST/DAY
0200	1-1/2 C.Y. capacity	Ea.	56.71	1,425.67	3,700.81	9,354.76	1,193.85
0300	2 C.Y. capacity		66.05	1,673.65	4,675.92	11,002.47	1,463.59
0320	2-1/2 C.Y. capacity		96.46	1,846.43	5,144.41	12,997.45	1,800.54
0325	3-1/2 C.Y. capacity		140.22	1,850.90	5,152.48	13,006.19	2,152.24
0330	4-1/2 C.Y. capacity		176.99	4,058.72	12,663.06	36,638.13	3,948.55
0335	6 C.Y. capacity		224.57	3,565.09	11,108.95	32,140.64	4,018.32
0340	7 C.Y. capacity		204.51	4,583.50	13,750.50	41,251.50	4,386.20
0342	Excavator attachments, bucket thumbs		3.97	286.31	891.71	2,577.83	210.12
0345	Grapples		3.66	246.82	766.87	2,221.33	182.68
0346	Hydraulic hammer for boom mounting, 4000 ft lb.		15.73	987.26	3,073.67	8,885.30	740.58
0347	5000 ft lb.		18.62	1,095.52	3,201.52	7,503.57	789.23
0348	8000 ft lb.		27.48	1,343.77	4,144.28	11,956.76	1,048.67
0349	12,000 ft lb.		31.60	1,500.32	4,627.11	13,349.78	1,178.21
0350	Gradall type, truck mounted, 3 ton @ 15' radius, 5/8 C.Y.		50.70	858.33	2,575	7,725	920.64
0370	1 C.Y. capacity		69.34	1,716.67	5,150	15,450	1,584.74
0400	Backhoe-loader, 40 to 45 H.P., 5/8 C.Y. capacity		13.89	217.72	607.32	1,565.73	232.56
0450	45 H.P. to 60 H.P., 3/4 C.Y. capacity		21.03	221	613.65	1,612.64	291
0460	80 H.P., 1-1/4 C.Y. capacity		23.76	475.24	1,327.14	2,929.57	455.51
0470	112 H.P., 1-1/2 C.Y. capacity		38.50	610.52	1,864.71	4,902.33	680.94
0482	Backhoe-loader attachment, compactor, 20,000 lb.		7.52	335	935	2,635	247.15
0485	Hydraulic hammer, 750 ft lb.		4.29	118.47	368.58	1,064.04	108.05
0486	Hydraulic hammer, 1200 ft lb.		7.65	227.07	707.42	2,056.79	202.66
0500	Brush chipper, gas engine, 6" cutter head, 35 H.P.		10.70	329.57	949.76	2,145.29	275.58
0550	Diesel engine, 12" cutter head, 130 H.P.		27.64	550.22	1,431.72	3,762.65	507.44
0600	15" cutter head, 165 H.P.		31.03	564.93	1,757.50	5,073.40	599.77
0750	Bucket, clamshell, general purpose, 3/8 C.Y.		1.63	41.20	123.60	370.80	37.76
0800	1/2 C.Y.		1.77	41.20	123.60	370.80	38.86
0850	3/4 C.Y.		1.92	44.98	134.93	404.79	42.32
0900	1 C.Y.		1.98	54.93	164.80	494.40	48.81
0950	1-1/2 C.Y.		3.25	50.65	151.93	455.78	56.37
1000	2 C.Y.		3.41	173.38	520.15	1,560.45	131.29
1010	Bucket, dragline, medium duty, 1/2 C.Y.		.96	36	101	285	27.87
1020	3/4 C.Y.		.91	39	112	316	29.64
1030	1 C.Y.		.93	44	117	336	30.81
1040	1-1/2 C.Y.		1.47	52	149	452	41.56
1050	2 C.Y.		1.81	54.75	160.76	484.79	46.64
1070	3 C.Y.		2.43	57.50	172.53	517.58	53.93
1200	Compactor, manually guided 2-drum vibratory smooth roller, 7.5 H.P.		8.42	203	539	1,478	175.19
1250	Rammer/tamper, gas, 8"		2.58	119.71	393.77	873.76	99.37
1260	15"		3.07	130	445	965	113.54
1300	Vibratory plate, gas, 18" plate, 3000 lb. blow		2.48	179.70	563.40	1,398.75	132.53
1350	21" plate, 5000 lb. blow		3.06	242.88	641.75	1,665.88	152.80
1370	Curb builder/extruder, 14 H.P., gas, single screw		14.46	1,096.95	3,290.85	9,872.55	773.87
1390	Double screw		17.35	1,278	3,834	11,502	905.59
1500	Disc harrow attachment, for tractor		.55	383.93	1,206.65	3,619.94	245.76
1810	Feller buncher, shearing & accumulating trees, 100 H.P.		50.62	1,200	3,600	8,500	1,124.96
1860	Grader, self-propelled, 25,000 lb.		38.93	1,120	3,770	7,750	1,065.41
1910	30,000 lb.		49.75	1,195.83	3,587.50	10,762.50	1,115.47
1920	40,000 lb.		60.57	1,254.92	3,800.75	11,491.25	1,244.68
1930	55,000 lb.		78.13	1,314	4,014	12,220	1,427.83
1950	Hammer, pavement breaker, self-propelled, diesel, 1000 to 1250 lb.		33.15	618	1,854	5,562	636.03
2000	1300 to 1500 lb.		49.96	618	1,854	5,562	770.47
2050	Pile driving hammer, steam or air, 4150 ft lb. @ 225 bpm		14.19	553.96	1,726.78	4,991.12	458.84
2100	8750 ft lb. @ 145 bpm		16.74	778.83	2,417.49	6,993.06	617.43
2150	15,000 ft lb. @ 60 bpm		17.13	926.93	2,877.96	8,336.82	712.59
2200	24,450 ft lb. @ 111 bpm		18.31	1,075.01	3,338.45	9,653.16	814.15
2250	Leads, 60' high for pile driving hammers up to 20,000 ft lb.		4.28	334.57	1,036.07	2,989.19	241.46
2300	90' high for hammers over 20,000 ft lb.		6.36	597.84	1,864.93	5,402.48	423.85

For customer support on your Plumbing Costs with RSMeans Data call 800.448.8182.

01 54 | Construction Aids

01 54 33 | Equipment Rental

		Description	UNIT	HOURLY OPER. COST	RENT PER DAY	RENT PER WEEK	RENT PER MONTH	EQUIPMENT COST/DAY
20	2350	Diesel type hammer, 22,400 ft lb.	Ea.	20.80	543	1,694.25	4,908.86	505.25
	2400	41,300 ft lb.		29.98	685.60	2,140.10	6,197.77	667.86
	2450	141,000 ft lb.		48.24	1,091.47	3,388.50	9,790.28	1,063.66
	2500	Vib. elec. hammer/extractor, 200 kW diesel generator, 34 H.P.		48.29	795.29	2,467.07	7,130.18	879.71
	2550	80 H.P.		85.24	1,151.80	3,566.84	10,311.33	1,395.31
	2600	150 H.P.		157.75	2,193.90	6,866.17	19,854.80	2,635.22
	2700	Hydro Excavator w/EXT boom 12 C.Y., 1200 gallons		44.13	1,782.55	5,525.70	16,015.47	1,458.21
	2800	Log chipper, up to 22" diameter, 600 H.P.		52.06	507.28	1,521.83	4,565.48	720.82
	2850	Logger, for skidding & stacking logs, 150 H.P.		50.72	145.92	437.75	1,313.25	493.27
	2860	Mulcher, diesel powered, trailer mounted		23.21	788.47	2,365.40	7,096.19	658.73
	2900	Rake, spring tooth, with tractor		17.18	178.65	451.64	1,141.43	227.75
	3000	Roller, vibratory, tandem, smooth drum, 20 H.P.		9.12	400.23	957.21	1,988.73	264.37
	3050	35 H.P.		11.83	453.65	1,125.91	2,927.94	319.84
	3100	Towed type vibratory compactor, smooth drum, 50 H.P.		29.50	575	2,300	6,900	696
	3150	Sheepsfoot, 50 H.P.		29.93	448	1,385	4,001	516.41
	3170	Landfill compactor, 220 H.P.		81.57	2,896.50	7,919	18,725	2,236.35
	3200	Pneumatic tire roller, 80 H.P.		15.08	608.43	1,731.81	3,928.29	467.01
	3250	120 H.P.		22.63	715.81	2,027.95	5,293.24	586.64
	3300	Sheepsfoot vibratory roller, 240 H.P.		72.61	377.67	1,133	3,399	807.49
	3320	340 H.P.		97.84	1,545	4,635	13,905	1,709.73
	3350	Smooth drum vibratory roller, 75 H.P.		27.24	276.38	733.02	2,072.59	364.55
	3400	125 H.P.		32.24	493.63	1,480.88	4,332.95	554.08
	3410	Rotary mower, brush, 60", with tractor		21.93	126.43	380	942.86	251.43
	3420	Rototiller, walk-behind, gas, 5 H.P.		2.49	90.29	291.66	695	78.27
	3422	8 H.P.		3.28	105.14	345.57	863.93	95.36
	3440	Scrapers, towed type, 7 C.Y. capacity		7.52	141.51	439.91	1,261.49	148.13
	3450	10 C.Y. capacity		8.41	188.68	588.52	1,700.27	185.01
	3500	15 C.Y. capacity		8.64	218.30	677.70	1,947.09	204.64
	3525	Self-propelled, single engine, 14 C.Y. capacity		155.59	1,716.67	5,150	15,450	2,274.69
	3550	Dual engine, 21 C.Y. capacity		165.02	3,329	9,771	28,681	3,274.37
	3600	31 C.Y. capacity		219.27	3,721	10,869	31,856	3,927.98
	3640	44 C.Y. capacity		271.60	2,403.33	7,210	21,630	3,614.77
	3650	Elevating type, single engine, 11 C.Y. capacity		72.22	824	2,472	7,416	1,072.14
	3700	22 C.Y. capacity		133.80	1,716.67	5,150	15,450	2,100.37
	3710	Screening plant, 110 H.P. w/5' x 10' screen		24.67	713.02	2,221.11	6,417.16	641.55
	3720	5' x 16' screen		31.14	1,258.89	3,776.67	11,330	1,004.46
	3850	Shovel, crawler-mounted, front-loading, 7 C.Y. capacity		255.23	4,360.38	13,553.99	39,161.12	4,752.62
	3855	12 C.Y. capacity		393.25	6,033.23	18,785.36	54,299.03	6,903.08
	3860	Shovel/backhoe bucket, 1/2 C.Y.		3.14	81.17	252.06	729.48	75.55
	3870	3/4 C.Y.		3.11	91.05	282.97	817.23	81.47
	3880	1 C.Y.		3.22	102.13	317.67	915.55	89.26
	3890	1-1/2 C.Y.		3.45	118.47	368.58	1,064.04	101.32
	3910	3 C.Y.		4.02	160.15	499.35	1,453.46	131.99
	3950	Stump chipper, 18" deep, 30 H.P.		8.04	335.37	978.52	2,206.22	260.03
	4110	Dozer, crawler, torque converter, diesel 80 H.P.		29.48	699.45	1,995.19	5,254.53	634.87
	4150	105 H.P.		40.08	850.43	2,351.14	6,253	790.84
	4200	140 H.P.		48.18	679.80	2,039.40	6,118.20	793.32
	4260	200 H.P.		73.72	1,422.43	4,267.29	12,801.87	1,443.21
	4310	300 H.P.		94.23	2,370	8,200	20,890	2,393.85
	4360	410 H.P.		124.61	3,290	9,865	29,580	2,969.84
	4370	500 H.P.		155.69	3,800	11,395	34,170	3,524.54
	4380	700 H.P.		268.67	4,310	12,925	38,760	4,734.34
	4400	Loader, crawler, torque conv., diesel 1-1/2 C.Y., 80 H.P.		34.48	541.24	1,432.19	3,406.43	562.32
	4450	1-1/2 to 1-3/4 C.Y., 95 H.P.		35.34	773.35	2,411.58	6,965.63	765.01
	4510	1-3/4 to 2-1/4 C.Y., 130 H.P.		55.74	1,615	3,670	9,235	1,179.94
	4530	2-1/2 to 3-1/4 C.Y., 190 H.P.		67.46	1,234.07	3,867.63	11,188.89	1,313.18
	4560	3-1/2 to 5 C.Y., 275 H.P.		83.35	1,990	5,965	17,850	1,859.78
	4610	Front end loader, 4WD, articulated frame, diesel, 1 to 1-1/4 C.Y., 70 H.P.		19.40	313.75	1,065.63	3,165.63	368.36

01 54 | Construction Aids

01 54 33 | Equipment Rental

			UNIT	HOURLY OPER. COST	RENT PER DAY	RENT PER WEEK	RENT PER MONTH	EQUIPMENT COST/DAY	
20	4620	1-1/2 to 1-3/4 C.Y., 95 H.P.	Ea.	23.34	660	1,980	3,705	582.76	20
	4650	1-3/4 to 2 C.Y., 130 H.P.		24.59	808.69	2,338.52	5,158.86	664.43	
	4710	2-1/2 to 3-1/2 C.Y., 145 H.P.		34.46	957.38	2,697.05	6,612.71	815.12	
	4730	3 to 4-1/2 C.Y., 185 H.P.		37.46	1,041.94	2,834.74	6,978.49	866.60	
	4760	5-1/4 to 5-3/4 C.Y., 270 H.P.		62.09	1,350.67	3,693.24	10,004.76	1,235.36	
	4810	7 to 9 C.Y., 475 H.P.		106.43	3,080	9,230	28,950	2,697.40	
	4870	9 to 11 C.Y., 620 H.P.		153.99	3,470	8,530	21,500	2,937.91	
	4880	Skid-steer loader, wheeled, 10 C.F., 30 H.P. gas		11.17	302	895.17	1,968.68	268.41	
	4890	1 C.Y., 78 H.P., diesel		21.52	383.30	1,112.23	2,432.72	394.64	
	4892	Skid-steer attachment, auger		.87	120.44	345.17	870.57	76.02	
	4893	Backhoe		.86	92	254	692	57.70	
	4894	Broom		.83	141.22	426.42	986.52	91.93	
	4895	Forks		.18	54.89	144.56	325.14	30.36	
	4896	Grapple		.84	99.89	289.51	664.92	64.63	
	4897	Concrete hammer		1.22	215	603.56	1,539	130.51	
	4898	Tree spade		.70	345.54	1,036.62	2,487.88	212.95	
	4899	Trencher		.77	179.65	542.69	1,379.71	114.67	
	4900	Trencher, chain, boom type, gas, operator walking, 12 H.P.		4.88	289.90	859.81	1,760.87	210.98	
	4910	Operator riding, 40 H.P.		19.48	442.38	1,235.55	2,951.47	402.94	
	5000	Wheel type, diesel, 4' deep, 12" wide		80.21	1,069.53	3,329.04	9,625.74	1,307.45	
	5100	6' deep, 20" wide		102.23	1,306.81	2,938.08	6,790.28	1,405.45	
	5150	Chain type, diesel, 5' deep, 8" wide		19.03	400.39	1,248.39	3,619.94	401.93	
	5200	Diesel, 8' deep, 16" wide		104.66	2,139.05	6,658.11	19,306.32	2,168.88	
	5202	Rock trencher, wheel type, 6" wide x 18" deep		54.90	1,306.81	2,987	6,790.28	1,036.61	
	5206	Chain type, 18" wide x 7' deep		121.99	279.82	839.45	2,518.35	1,143.77	
	5210	Tree spade, self-propelled		15.95	425	1,275	3,060	382.63	
	5250	Truck, dump, 2-axle, 12 ton, 8 C.Y. payload, 220 H.P.		27.96	498.64	1,413.25	3,511.62	506.30	
	5300	Three axle dump, 16 ton, 12 C.Y. payload, 400 H.P.		52.10	775.38	2,851.38	7,003.33	987.07	
	5310	Four axle dump, 25 ton, 18 C.Y. payload, 450 H.P.		58.36	600.83	1,802.50	5,407.50	827.40	
	5350	Dump trailer only, rear dump, 16-1/2 C.Y.		6.71	167.84	523.14	1,508.31	158.30	
	5400	20 C.Y.		7.24	188.68	588.52	1,700.27	175.64	
	5450	Flatbed, single axle, 1-1/2 ton rating		22.24	374.26	1,214.68	3,317.31	420.83	
	5500	3 ton rating		30.02	430.40	1,396.88	3,814.91	519.55	
	5550	Off highway rear dump, 25 ton capacity		73.37	1,579.33	4,738	14,214	1,534.54	
	5600	35 ton capacity		78.33	1,579.33	4,738	14,214	1,574.25	
	5610	50 ton capacity		98.19	2,569	7,624	19,811	2,310.34	
	5620	65 ton capacity		104.86	2,916.22	8,894.75	24,604.63	2,617.83	
	5630	100 ton capacity		141.95	3,263.43	10,165.49	29,398.26	3,168.73	
	6000	Vibratory plow, 25 H.P., walking		7.91	354.68	1,064.04	3,192.12	276.11	
40	0010	**GENERAL EQUIPMENT RENTAL** without operators	R015433-10						40
	0020	Aerial lift, scissor type, to 20' high, 1200 lb. capacity, electric		Ea.	4.08	187.68	391.74	756.73	110.98
	0030	To 30' high, 1200 lb. capacity			4.42	232.08	481.53	980.53	131.66
	0040	Over 30' high, 1500 lb. capacity			6.01	386.56	779	1,622	203.85
	0070	Articulating boom, to 45' high, 500 lb. capacity, diesel	R015433-15		14.39	561.06	1,309.50	2,950.56	377.01
	0075	To 60' high, 500 lb. capacity			16.00	638.46	1,575.42	3,311.82	443.05
	0080	To 80' high, 500 lb. capacity			18.80	1,050.93	2,761.39	5,823.75	702.66
	0085	To 125' high, 500 lb. capacity			21.48	1,904.93	4,805.68	11,079.81	1,132.98
	0100	Telescoping boom to 40' high, 500 lb. capacity, diesel			13.15	517.26	1,195.42	2,582.74	344.31
	0105	To 45' high, 500 lb. capacity			14.64	535.60	1,245.27	2,659.46	366.20
	0110	To 60' high, 500 lb. capacity			19.15	635.81	1,572.05	3,301.14	467.60
	0115	To 80' high, 500 lb. capacity			24.90	1,048.49	2,754.57	5,831.76	750.11
	0120	To 100' high, 500 lb. capacity			33.62	1,082.48	2,886.86	5,943.14	846.35
	0125	To 120' high, 500 lb. capacity			34.14	1,902.38	4,794.08	11,081.99	1,231.97
	0195	Air compressor, portable, 6.5 CFM, electric			1.05	57.56	140.78	351.94	36.59
	0196	Gasoline			.77	52.80	155.60	377.29	37.25
	0200	Towed type, gas engine, 60 CFM			11.04	199.50	578.33	1,024.17	204.02
	0300	160 CFM			12.26	220.43	558.98	1,167.91	209.86

01 54 | Construction Aids

01 54 33 | Equipment Rental

		UNIT	HOURLY OPER. COST	RENT PER DAY	RENT PER WEEK	RENT PER MONTH	EQUIPMENT COST/DAY	
0400	Diesel engine, rotary screw, 250 CFM	Ea.	14.15	220	568.33	1,045	226.90	40
0500	365 CFM		18.73	357.41	973.79	2,425.47	344.62	
0550	450 CFM		23.36	371.25	963.75	2,783.75	379.59	
0600	600 CFM		39.93	275.34	856.03	2,468.14	490.62	
0700	750 CFM		40.53	892.71	2,392.45	5,879.31	802.76	
0915	Air purifier		.82	9.80	20.40	58.50	10.64	
0917	Air scrubber, 500 - 700 CFM, 110 V		.81	89.40	278.70	806.26	62.21	
0919	200 - 1200 CFM, 110 V		.81	105.85	329.89	954.35	72.45	
0930	Air tools, breaker, pavement, 60 lb.		.66	60.80	173.40	434	39.96	
0940	80 lb.		.66	65.50	190.40	452	43.36	
0950	Drills, hand (jackhammer), 65 lb.		.79	65.04	229.47	495.53	52.20	
0960	Track or wagon, swing boom, 4" drifter		72.30	1,112.40	3,337.20	10,011.60	1,245.86	
0970	5" drifter		72.30	1,112.40	3,337.20	10,011.60	1,245.86	
0975	Track mounted quarry drill, 6" diameter drill		119.10	822.28	2,466.85	7,400.55	1,446.16	
0980	Dust control per drill		1.21	10.99	32.96	98.88	16.30	
0990	Hammer, chipping, 12 lb.		.70	44.50	119	295.50	29.42	
1000	Hose, air with couplings, 50' long, 3/4" diameter		.07	12.60	32.50	78.22	7.10	
1100	1" diameter		.10	16.40	41.30	118.70	9.03	
1200	1-1/2" diameter		.26	43	107.60	290.80	23.56	
1300	2" diameter		.28	61.60	148.50	411	31.92	
1400	2-1/2" diameter		.42	64.70	184	524	40.12	
1410	3" diameter		.49	81.30	209	619	45.72	
1450	Drill, steel, 7/8" x 2'		.10	12.80	29.90	80.70	6.75	
1460	7/8" x 6'		.14	21.77	67.77	196.36	14.66	
1520	Moil points		.03	10.20	22.60	60.56	4.78	
1525	Pneumatic nailer w/accessories		.55	29	116	255.20	27.63	
1530	Sheeting driver for 60 lb. breaker		.05	8.61	26.76	77.33	5.78	
1540	For 90 lb. breaker		.15	11.68	36.27	104.76	8.45	
1550	Spade, 25 lb.		.59	8.23	25.55	74.05	9.80	
1560	Tamper, single, 35 lb.		.69	65	240	525	53.54	
1570	Triple, 140 lb.		1.03	53.20	147	404.17	37.66	
1580	Wrenches, impact, air powered, up to 3/4" bolt		.50	59.68	183.80	432.89	40.76	
1590	Up to 1-1/4" bolt		.67	95	245	645	54.37	
1600	Barricades, barrels, reflectorized, 1 to 99 barrels		.04	5.60	12.20	35	2.78	
1610	100 to 200 barrels		.03	5.40	12.70	37.30	2.80	
1620	Barrels with flashers, 1 to 99 barrels		.04	5.49	13.05	41.31	2.95	
1630	100 to 200 barrels		.03	5.71	13.83	44.62	3.02	
1640	Barrels with steady burn type C lights		.05	5.49	13.05	41.31	3.04	
1650	Illuminated board, trailer mounted, with generator		3.83	93.73	297.23	756.16	90.12	
1670	Portable barricade, stock, with flashers, 1 to 6 units		.04	5.30	12.70	38.57	2.88	
1680	25 to 50 units		.04	5.70	13.46	40.50	3.03	
1685	Butt fusion machine, wheeled, 1.5 HP electric, 2" - 8" diameter pipe		3.08	441.87	1,325.61	3,976.83	289.74	
1690	Tracked, 20 HP diesel, 4"-12" diameter pipe		11.62	420.58	1,261.75	3,785.25	345.30	
1695	83 HP diesel, 8" - 24" diameter pipe		59.97	578.52	1,735.55	5,206.65	826.87	
1700	Carts, brick, gas engine, 1000 lb. capacity		3.44	33.89	83.33	208.89	44.19	
1800	1500 lb., 7-1/2' lift		3.42	76.79	239.44	691.08	75.24	
1822	Dehumidifier, medium, 6 lb./hr., 150 CFM		1.40	46	164.10	480.78	43.98	
1824	Large, 18 lb./hr., 600 CFM		2.57	220.11	1,321.24	3,963.69	284.78	
1830	Distributor, asphalt, trailer mounted, 2000 gal., 38 H.P. diesel		12.88	389.42	1,218.67	3,537.67	346.74	
1840	3000 gal., 38 H.P. diesel		15.06	422.33	1,307.84	3,784.48	382.04	
1850	Drill, rotary hammer, electric		1.30	79.41	230.08	495	56.41	
1860	Carbide bit, 1-1/2" diameter, add to electric rotary hammer		.03	53.54	135.65	397.07	27.39	
1865	Rotary, crawler, 250 H.P.		158.96	2,532.08	7,596.25	22,788.75	2,790.95	
1870	Emulsion sprayer, 65 gal., 5 H.P. gas engine		3.24	118.47	368.58	1,064.04	99.62	
1880	200 gal., 5 H.P. engine		8.46	198.55	618.25	1,782.55	191.30	
1900	Floor auto-scrubbing machine, walk-behind, 28" path		6.58	310.40	933.10	2,252.55	239.27	
1930	Floodlight, mercury vapor, or quartz, on tripod, 1000 watt		.53	45.17	119.17	313.33	28.09	
1940	2000 watt		.69	46.97	128.24	353.29	31.19	

For customer support on your Plumbing Costs with RSMeans Data call 800.448.8182.

01 54 | Construction Aids

01 54 33 | Equipment Rental

			UNIT	HOURLY OPER. COST	RENT PER DAY	RENT PER WEEK	RENT PER MONTH	EQUIPMENT COST/DAY
40	1950	Floodlights, trailer mounted with generator, 1 - 300 watt light	Ea.	4.15	196.28	499.38	1,179.82	133.10
	1960	2 - 1000 watt lights		5.25	229.65	584.28	1,380.39	158.86
	2000	4 - 300 watt lights		4.97	175.10	418.62	864.05	123.51
	2005	Foam spray rig, incl. box trailer, compressor, generator, proportioner		29.81	592.35	1,842.87	5,320.21	607.05
	2015	Forklift, pneumatic tire, rough terr, straight mast, 5000 lb, 12' lift, gas		21.77	650.56	1,511.94	3,265	476.54
	2025	8000 lb, 12' lift		26.55	812.78	1,919.72	4,002.78	596.35
	2030	5000 lb, 12' lift, diesel		18.04	458.99	1,160.09	2,634.78	376.35
	2035	8000 lb, 12' lift, diesel		19.55	708.41	1,728.68	3,662.79	502.16
	2045	All terrain, telescoping boom, diesel, 5000 lb, 10' reach, 19' lift		20.14	462.38	1,202.29	2,684.29	401.57
	2055	6600 lb, 29' reach, 42' lift		24.63	534.64	1,325.47	3,114.66	462.16
	2065	10,000 lb, 31' reach, 45' lift		26.96	752.66	2,084.41	4,885.47	632.52
	2070	Cushion tire, smooth floor, gas, 5000 lb capacity		9.63	304.42	752.94	1,814.24	227.61
	2075	8000 lb capacity		13.27	451.86	1,101.97	2,615.06	326.55
	2085	Diesel, 5000 lb capacity		9.04	326.11	797.41	1,902.70	231.82
	2090	12,000 lb capacity		14.07	690.33	2,080.57	4,161.10	528.66
	2095	20,000 lb capacity		20.14	1,150.57	3,201.52	7,903.76	801.42
	2100	Generator, electric, gas engine, 1.5 kW to 3 kW		3.00	74.91	270.97	625	78.22
	2200	5 kW		3.76	89.74	297.95	673.32	89.67
	2300	10 kW		6.92	163.68	518.99	1,173.06	159.18
	2400	25 kW		8.65	354	928.67	2,102.56	254.92
	2500	Diesel engine, 20 kW		10.75	294.62	724.93	1,555.70	230.95
	2600	50 kW		18.62	449.75	1,245.03	2,971.63	397.94
	2700	100 kW		33.38	646.39	1,736.30	4,133.60	614.28
	2800	250 kW		63.44	1,038.61	2,578.28	6,711.31	1,023.19
	2850	Hammer, hydraulic, for mounting on boom, to 500 ft lb.		3.39	103.66	322.20	932.41	91.53
	2860	1000 ft lb.		5.38	154.68	481.53	1,398.62	139.33
	2900	Heaters, space, oil or electric, 50 MBH		1.70	91.74	243.04	609.61	62.24
	3000	100 MBH		3.17	94.24	248.67	617.25	75.12
	3100	300 MBH		9.25	154.27	442.20	904.45	162.48
	3150	500 MBH		15.36	222.56	587.60	1,500.71	240.38
	3200	Hose, water, suction with coupling, 20' long, 2" diameter		.02	8.50	22.20	60.33	4.61
	3210	3" diameter		.03	17.30	48	134.13	9.86
	3220	4" diameter		.03	31.26	96.70	279.73	19.59
	3230	6" diameter		.13	44.98	139.87	405.87	29
	3240	8" diameter		.32	59.24	184.18	532.03	39.39
	3250	Discharge hose with coupling, 50' long, 2" diameter		.01	8.70	22.20	55.20	4.53
	3260	3" diameter		.01	10.90	26	74.11	5.29
	3270	4" diameter		.02	23.04	71.95	208.42	14.56
	3280	6" diameter		.07	32.36	100.15	289.59	20.63
	3290	8" diameter		.28	41.68	129.50	372.96	28.12
	3295	Insulation blower		.97	129.44	402.16	1,151.80	88.19
	3300	Ladders, extension type, 16' to 36' long		.21	53	115.80	289.50	24.86
	3400	40' to 60' long		.75	127.50	345.17	848.33	75
	3405	Lance for cutting concrete		2.58	106.43	319.30	957.90	84.48
	3407	Lawn mower, rotary, 22", 5 H.P.		1.24	59.56	227.94	440	55.47
	3408	48" self-propelled		3.39	199.44	566.22	1,110	140.34
	3410	Level, electronic, automatic, with tripod and leveling rod		1.22	48.86	133	383	36.40
	3430	Laser type, for pipe and sewer line and grade		2.53	151	391.83	1,088.67	98.64
	3440	Rotating beam for interior control		1.05	85.67	210.17	622.67	50.47
	3460	Builder's optical transit, with tripod and rod		.12	48.79	125.48	354.84	26.03
	3500	Light towers, towable, with diesel generator, 2000 watt		4.98	185.10	475.24	988.67	134.92
	3600	4000 watt		5.27	214.18	478.52	1,061.25	137.88
	3700	Mixer, powered, plaster and mortar, 6 C.F., 7 H.P.		2.41	91.97	265.60	668.03	72.37
	3800	10 C.F., 9 H.P.		2.62	120	435	940	107.96
	3850	Nailer, pneumatic		.56	25.75	77.25	154.50	19.97
	3900	Paint sprayers complete, 8 CFM		1.02	93.16	222.09	619.25	52.60
	4000	17 CFM		1.86	174.46	415.91	1,159.68	98.09
	4020	Pavers, bituminous, rubber tires, 8' wide, 50 H.P., diesel		37.38	630.75	1,961.76	5,676.72	691.40

For customer support on your Plumbing Costs with RSMeans Data call 800.448.8182.

01 54 | Construction Aids

01 54 33 | Equipment Rental

			UNIT	HOURLY OPER. COST	RENT PER DAY	RENT PER WEEK	RENT PER MONTH	EQUIPMENT COST/DAY	
40	4030	10' wide, 150 H.P.	Ea.	111.95	2,166.48	6,717.55	19,416.02	2,239.13	40
	4050	Crawler, 8' wide, 100 H.P., diesel		102.55	1,200	3,560	9,240	1,532.39	
	4060	10' wide, 150 H.P.		121.72	1,425	4,225	10,975	1,818.75	
	4070	Concrete paver, 12' to 24' wide, 250 H.P.		102.58	1,864.82	5,825.83	16,893.03	1,985.81	
	4080	Placer-spreader-trimmer, 24' wide, 300 H.P.		137.59	2,824.65	8,827.92	25,558.94	2,866.28	
	4100	Pump, centrifugal gas pump, 1-1/2" diam., 65 GPM		4.59	59.78	186.67	537.51	74.05	
	4200	2" diameter, 130 GPM		5.83	45.77	144.20	379.86	75.44	
	4300	3" diameter, 250 GPM		5.99	64.83	192.61	536.63	86.40	
	4400	6" diameter, 1500 GPM		25.99	390	1,015	2,405	410.89	
	4500	Submersible electric pump, 1-1/4" diameter, 55 GPM		.47	49.13	128.93	341.45	29.53	
	4600	1-1/2" diameter, 83 GPM		.52	61.01	165.24	441.43	37.22	
	4700	2" diameter, 120 GPM		1.93	70	200	530	55.42	
	4800	3" diameter, 300 GPM		3.55	125	295	860	87.37	
	4900	4" diameter, 560 GPM		17.24	135	345	970	206.94	
	5000	6" diameter, 1590 GPM		25.79	232.19	696.57	2,089.69	345.67	
	5100	Diaphragm pump, gas, single, 1-1/2" diameter		1.32	41.20	123.60	370.80	35.28	
	5200	2" diameter		4.65	46.35	139.05	417.15	65.04	
	5300	3" diameter		4.73	79.33	234.67	589	84.76	
	5400	Double, 4" diameter		7.05	224.74	503.43	1,284.32	157.09	
	5450	Pressure washer 5 GPM, 3000 psi		4.53	129.51	496.88	1,038.10	135.59	
	5460	7 GPM, 3000 psi		5.78	115.36	360.50	872.41	118.36	
	5470	High Pressure Water Jet 10 KSI		46.31	800.77	2,486.56	7,185.02	867.76	
	5480	40 KSI		32.64	1,085.98	3,384.50	9,790.28	938.04	
	5500	Trash pump, self-priming, gas, 2" diameter		4.46	95	270	635	89.70	
	5600	Diesel, 4" diameter		7.81	270	695	1,850	201.45	
	5650	Diesel, 6" diameter		19.69	400	1,200	3,500	397.53	
	5655	Grout Pump		21.89	311.53	968.99	2,797.22	368.88	
	5700	Salamanders, L.P. gas fired, 100,000 Btu		3.38	80	230	580	73.01	
	5705	50,000 Btu		1.95	29.05	74.47	197.76	30.49	
	5720	Sandblaster, portable, open top, 3 C.F. capacity		.70	135.62	406.85	1,220.55	86.99	
	5730	6 C.F. capacity		1.17	271.23	813.70	2,441.10	172.11	
	5740	Accessories for above		.16	26.33	82.04	236.94	17.69	
	5750	Sander, floor		.89	85	300	645	67.16	
	5760	Edger		.61	59.64	227.54	495	50.37	
	5800	Saw, chain, gas engine, 18" long		2.06	84.23	297.04	640.80	75.85	
	5900	Hydraulic powered, 36" long		.92	80.26	240.78	722.34	55.48	
	5950	60" long		.92	89.59	268.76	806.26	61.08	
	6000	Masonry, table mounted, 14" diameter, 5 H.P.		1.54	108.79	408.14	890	93.98	
	6050	Portable cut-off, 8 H.P.		2.12	95.15	340.97	745	85.15	
	6100	Circular, hand held, electric, 7-1/4" diameter		.27	25	90.57	226.43	20.24	
	6200	12" diameter		.28	49	137.20	365	29.66	
	6250	Wall saw, w/hydraulic power, 10 H.P.		3.84	141.87	425.62	1,276.85	115.88	
	6275	Shot blaster, walk-behind, 20" wide		5.54	311.53	968.99	2,797.22	238.10	
	6280	Sidewalk broom, walk-behind		2.62	91.60	285.35	828.20	78.03	
	6300	Steam cleaner, 100 gallons per hour		3.91	91.60	285.35	828.20	88.34	
	6310	200 gallons per hour		5.07	110.80	344.79	998.22	109.51	
	6340	Tar Kettle/Pot, 400 gallons		19.26	130.47	391.40	1,174.20	232.32	
	6350	Torch, cutting, acetylene-oxygen, 150' hose, excludes gases		.53	17.01	52.90	153.57	14.84	
	6360	Hourly operating cost includes tips and gas		24.50	7.79	24.15	69.66	200.79	
	6410	Toilet, portable chemical		.15	25.78	79.66	230.36	17.12	
	6420	Recycle flush type		.19	31.82	98.68	285.21	21.27	
	6430	Toilet, fresh water flush, garden hose,		.22	37.84	117.70	340.05	25.33	
	6440	Hoisted, non-flush, for high rise		.18	30.71	96.31	278.63	20.71	
	6465	Tractor, farm with attachment		20.33	343.85	1,015.07	2,271.13	365.66	
	6480	Trailers, platform, flush deck, 2 axle, 3 ton capacity		1.98	105.31	326.93	943.38	81.23	
	6500	25 ton capacity		7.30	159.06	493.41	1,426.04	157.04	
	6600	40 ton capacity		9.41	225.97	701.48	2,029.36	215.61	
	6700	3 axle, 50 ton capacity		10.21	446.33	1,339	4,017	349.51	

01 54 | Construction Aids

01 54 33 | Equipment Rental

		UNIT	HOURLY OPER. COST	RENT PER DAY	RENT PER WEEK	RENT PER MONTH	EQUIPMENT COST/DAY	
40	6800	75 ton capacity	Ea.	12.97	634.08	1,903.65	5,716.50	484.50	40
	6810	Trailer mounted cable reel for high voltage line work		6.88	260.25	780.74	2,342.22	211.19	
	6820	Trailer mounted cable tensioning rig		13.64	85.83	257.50	772.50	160.64	
	6830	Cable pulling rig		86.21	161.37	484.10	1,452.30	786.51	
	6850	Portable cable/wire puller, 8000 lb max pulling capacity		4.32	192.45	476.50	1,210.33	129.89	
	6900	Water tank trailer, engine driven discharge, 5000 gallons		8.38	175.51	546.92	1,590.58	176.44	
	6925	10,000 gallons		11.42	239.14	743.09	2,139.05	239.95	
	6950	Water truck, off highway, 6000 gallons		84.01	1,600.76	4,001.90	10,004.76	1,472.44	
	7010	Tram car for high voltage line work, powered, 2 conductor		8.04	32.27	96.82	290.46	83.69	
	7020	Transit (builder's level) with tripod		.12	48.79	125.48	354.84	26.03	
	7030	Trench box, 3000 lb., 6' x 8'		.65	106.96	333.47	965.32	71.89	
	7040	7200 lb., 6' x 20'		.84	207.33	644.67	1,864.82	135.66	
	7050	8000 lb., 8' x 16'		1.26	224.88	699.59	2,029.36	149.97	
	7060	9500 lb., 8' x 20'		1.41	257.79	802.53	2,331.02	171.75	
	7065	11,000 lb., 8' x 24'		1.48	275.34	856.04	2,481.85	183.05	
	7070	12,000 lb., 10' x 20'		1.75	292.89	909.55	2,632.68	195.88	
	7100	Truck, pickup, 3/4 ton, 2 wheel drive		10.81	215.10	735.62	2,101	233.60	
	7200	4 wheel drive		11.10	215.10	735.62	2,101	235.90	
	7250	Crew carrier, 9 passenger		14.81	240.10	895.43	2,496.19	297.60	
	7290	Flat bed truck, 20,000 lb. GVW		17.87	146.99	457.74	1,316.34	234.51	
	7300	Tractor, 4 x 2, 220 H.P.		26.05	239.14	743.09	2,139.05	357.02	
	7410	330 H.P.		37.85	326.89	1,016.56	2,934.35	506.11	
	7500	6 x 4, 380 H.P.		42.26	378.45	1,177.06	3,400.55	573.49	
	7600	450 H.P.		51.79	460.72	1,426.74	4,140.99	699.67	
	7610	Tractor, with A frame, boom and winch, 225 H.P.		28.97	324.70	1,008.72	2,906.92	433.49	
	7620	Vacuum truck, hazardous material, 2500 gallons		14.97	345.54	1,070.06	3,098.89	333.80	
	7625	5,000 gallons		15.25	488.15	1,515.91	4,387.80	425.19	
	7650	Vacuum, HEPA, 16 gallon, wet/dry		.99	150	365	970	80.92	
	7655	55 gallon, wet/dry		.99	159.75	386.90	1,018.50	85.30	
	7660	Water tank, portable		.85	165	497	1,246	106.22	
	7690	Sewer/catch basin vacuum, 14 C.Y., 1500 gallons		20.27	734.96	2,288.72	6,609.13	619.88	
	7700	Welder, electric, 200 amp		4.46	48.75	105	273.75	56.70	
	7800	300 amp		6.50	39	99	245	71.77	
	7900	Gas engine, 200 amp		10.47	134.90	344.80	823.76	152.71	
	8000	300 amp		11.85	135.05	345.14	825.38	163.86	
	8100	Wheelbarrow, any size		.07	15.80	36.30	93	7.86	
	8200	Wrecking ball, 4000 lb.		2.93	70.38	211.15	633.45	65.66	
50	0010	**HIGHWAY EQUIPMENT RENTAL** without operators							50
	0050	Asphalt batch plant, portable drum mixer, 100 ton/hr.	Ea.	103.51	1,700.27	5,320.54	15,357.30	1,892.17	
	0060	200 ton/hr.		119.41	1,837.40	5,677.22	16,454.25	2,090.71	
	0070	300 ton/hr.		140.32	2,139.05	6,658.11	19,306.32	2,454.22	
	0100	Backhoe attachment, long stick, up to 185 H.P., 10.5' long		.44	28.52	87.98	254.49	21.09	
	0140	Up to 250 H.P., 12' long		.48	31.82	98.68	285.21	23.57	
	0180	Over 250 H.P., 15' long		.66	43.33	134.35	389.42	32.15	
	0200	Special dipper arm, up to 100 H.P., 32' long		1.35	88.30	274.64	795.29	65.75	
	0240	Over 100 H.P., 33' long		1.69	110.80	344.79	998.22	82.51	
	0280	Catch basin/sewer cleaning truck, 3 ton, 9 C.Y., 1000 gal.		41.43	466.21	1,456.46	4,223.26	622.72	
	0300	Concrete batch plant, portable, electric, 200 C.Y./hr.		28.32	619.78	1,932.03	5,594.45	612.95	
	0520	Grader/dozer attachment, ripper/scarifier, rear mounted, up to 135 H.P.		3.68	70.20	218.76	630.75	73.23	
	0540	Up to 180 H.P.		4.85	106.41	330.53	954.35	104.87	
	0580	Up to 250 H.P.		6.85	170.03	529.08	1,535.73	160.60	
	0700	Pvmt. removal bucket, for hyd. excavator, up to 90 H.P.		2.52	64.73	200.93	581.38	60.38	
	0740	Up to 200 H.P.		2.69	82.82	256.81	740.45	72.92	
	0780	Over 200 H.P.		2.95	101.47	315.07	910.47	86.61	
	0900	Aggregate spreader, self-propelled, 187 H.P.		59.25	822.71	2,556.23	7,404.41	985.21	
	1000	Chemical spreader, 3 C.Y.		3.71	102.66	307.97	923.91	91.24	
	1900	Hammermill, traveling, 250 H.P.		78.70	369.43	1,108.28	3,324.84	851.28	

01 54 | Construction Aids

01 54 33 | Equipment Rental

		UNIT	HOURLY OPER. COST	RENT PER DAY	RENT PER WEEK	RENT PER MONTH	EQUIPMENT COST/DAY	
50	2000	Horizontal borer, 3" diameter, 13 H.P. gas driven	Ea.	6.33	115.02	345.05	1,035.15	119.62	50
	2150	Horizontal directional drill, 20,000 lb. thrust, 78 H.P. diesel		32.23	760.83	2,282.48	6,847.44	714.31	
	2160	30,000 lb. thrust, 115 H.P.		39.62	760.83	2,282.48	6,847.44	773.44	
	2170	50,000 lb. thrust, 170 H.P.		56.80	760.83	2,282.48	6,847.44	910.87	
	2190	Mud trailer for HDD, 1500 gallons, 175 H.P., gas		29.80	810.79	2,432.35	7,297.04	724.86	
	2200	Hydromulcher, diesel, 3000 gallon, for truck mounting		20.37	1,016.51	3,049.52	9,148.56	772.89	
	2300	Gas, 600 gallon		8.75	290.12	870.35	2,611.05	244.10	
	2400	Joint & crack cleaner, walk behind, 25 H.P.		3.70	239.65	718.94	2,156.82	173.35	
	2500	Filler, trailer mounted, 400 gallons, 20 H.P.		9.76	219.73	659.20	1,977.60	209.88	
	3000	Paint striper, self-propelled, 40 gallon, 22 H.P.		7.90	24.72	74.16	222.48	78.05	
	3100	120 gallon, 120 H.P.		20.62	159.65	478.95	1,436.85	260.74	
	3200	Post drivers, 6" I-Beam frame, for truck mounting		14.51	128.75	386.25	1,158.75	193.29	
	3400	Road sweeper, self-propelled, 8' wide, 90 H.P.		42.04	464.25	1,225.22	2,963.41	581.33	
	3450	Road sweeper, vacuum assisted, 4 C.Y., 220 gallons		68.23	3,329.25	7,146.63	13,761.24	1,975.20	
	4000	Road mixer, self-propelled, 130 H.P.		54.13	915.96	2,853.47	8,254.55	1,003.77	
	4100	310 H.P.		87.82	2,385.87	7,460.64	21,609.92	2,194.69	
	4220	Cold mix paver, incl. pug mill and bitumen tank, 165 H.P.		111.19	738.17	2,214.50	6,643.50	1,332.39	
	4240	Pavement brush, towed		4.02	110.80	344.79	998.22	101.08	
	4250	Paver, asphalt, wheel or crawler, 130 H.P., diesel		110.33	2,522.99	7,847.04	22,706.87	2,452.08	
	4300	Paver, road widener, gas, 1' to 6', 67 H.P.		54.62	1,080.50	3,358.77	9,708.01	1,108.74	
	4400	Diesel, 2' to 14', 88 H.P.		66.01	1,288.92	3,982.97	11,517.98	1,324.66	
	4600	Slipform pavers, curb and gutter, 2 track, 75 H.P.		67.71	910.58	2,828.08	8,173.88	1,107.32	
	4700	4 track, 165 H.P.		41.78	1,357.88	4,213.26	12,141	1,176.89	
	4800	Median barrier, 215 H.P.		68.41	1,480.88	4,636.90	13,382.79	1,474.62	
	4901	Trailer, low bed, 75 ton capacity		12.54	313.73	974.94	2,824.65	295.27	
	5000	Road planer, walk behind, 10" cutting width, 10 H.P.		2.86	321.27	1,128.36	2,653.57	248.59	
	5100	Self-propelled, 12" cutting width, 64 H.P.		9.65	357.73	962.89	2,665.59	269.77	
	5120	Traffic line remover, metal ball blaster, truck mounted, 115 H.P.		54.41	2,128.67	6,386	19,158	1,712.49	
	5140	Grinder, truck mounted, 115 H.P.		59.47	2,128.67	6,386	19,158	1,752.96	
	5160	Walk-behind, 11 H.P.		4.15	333	828.50	2,480.50	198.93	
	5200	Pavement profiler, 4' to 6' wide, 450 H.P.		253.10	1,158.75	3,476.25	10,428.75	2,720.03	
	5300	8' to 10' wide, 750 H.P.		387.49	1,321.83	3,965.50	11,896.50	3,893.02	
	5400	Roadway plate, steel, 1" x 8' x 20'		.10	67.47	210.09	608.81	42.78	
	5600	Stabilizer, self-propelled, 150 H.P.		48.07	259.22	777.65	2,332.95	540.12	
	5700	310 H.P.		89.02	322.73	968.20	2,904.60	905.83	
	5800	Striper, truck mounted, 120 gallon paint, 460 H.P.		56.97	422.30	1,266.90	3,800.70	709.11	
	5900	Thermal paint heating kettle, 115 gallons		9.01	175.10	525.30	1,575.90	177.14	
	6000	Tar kettle, 330 gallon, trailer mounted		14.35	157.59	472.77	1,418.31	209.32	
	7000	Tunnel locomotive, diesel, 8 to 12 ton		34.84	685.60	2,140.10	6,197.77	706.71	
	7005	Electric, 10 ton		34.24	784.32	2,437.33	7,047.91	761.38	
	7010	Muck cars, 1/2 C.Y. capacity		2.69	29.62	92.14	266.56	39.98	
	7020	1 C.Y. capacity		2.94	38.40	120.09	345.54	47.53	
	7030	2 C.Y. capacity		3.11	43.33	134.35	389.42	51.75	
	7040	Side dump, 2 C.Y. capacity		3.37	53.76	166.45	482.66	60.21	
	7050	3 C.Y. capacity		4.52	58.69	183.10	532.03	72.75	
	7060	5 C.Y. capacity		6.58	76.24	236.60	685.60	99.97	
	7100	Ventilating blower for tunnel, 7-1/2 H.P.		2.50	58.69	181.91	526.54	56.40	
	7110	10 H.P.		2.83	60.88	190.23	548.48	60.71	
	7120	20 H.P.		4.14	79.53	247.29	713.02	82.60	
	7140	40 H.P.		7.19	105.31	326.95	943.38	122.90	
	7160	60 H.P.		10.17	112.99	350.74	1,014.68	151.51	
	7175	75 H.P.		12.14	175.51	546.92	1,590.58	206.51	
	7180	200 H.P.		24.34	345.54	1,076	3,126.31	409.88	
	7800	Windrow loader, elevating		63.04	1,716.67	5,150	15,450	1,534.30	
60	0010	**LIFTING AND HOISTING EQUIPMENT RENTAL** without operators							60
	0150	Crane, flatbed mounted, 3 ton capacity	Ea.	16.87	796.74	2,231.19	5,243.45	581.20	
	0200	Crane, climbing, 106' jib, 6000 lb. capacity, 410 fpm		46.42	3,096.79	9,290.36	27,871.10	2,229.46	
	0300	101' jib, 10,250 lb. capacity, 270 fpm		54.26	3,260.61	9,781.83	29,345.48	2,390.46	

R015433-10

R312316-45

01 54 | Construction Aids

01 54 33 | Equipment Rental

		UNIT	HOURLY OPER. COST	RENT PER DAY	RENT PER WEEK	RENT PER MONTH	EQUIPMENT COST/DAY
0500	Tower, static, 130' high, 106' jib, 6200 lb. capacity at 400 fpm	Ea.	52.77	2,665.85	7,997.53	23,992.59	2,021.67
0520	Mini crawler spider crane, up to 24" wide, 1990 lb. lifting capacity		14.63	608.81	1,902.32	5,512.18	497.53
0525	Up to 30" wide, 6450 lb. lifting capacity		17.01	723.99	2,259	6,526.85	587.86
0530	Up to 52" wide, 6680 lb. lifting capacity		27.05	888.53	2,764.30	8,007.74	769.27
0535	Up to 55" wide, 8920 lb. lifting capacity		30.20	981.78	3,061.53	8,857.88	853.93
0540	Up to 66" wide, 13,350 lb. lifting capacity		40.89	1,535.73	4,755.78	13,711.88	1,278.24
0600	Crawler mounted, lattice boom, 1/2 C.Y., 15 tons at 12' radius		43.20	986.01	2,958.03	8,874.07	937.18
0700	3/4 C.Y., 20 tons at 12' radius		63.30	1,107.82	3,323.44	9,970.32	1,171.12
0800	1 C.Y., 25 tons at 12' radius		78.79	1,171.03	3,513.08	10,539.26	1,332.93
0900	1-1/2 C.Y., 40 tons at 12' radius		77.50	1,339.87	4,019.59	12,058.75	1,423.92
1000	2 C.Y., 50 tons at 12' radius		103.73	1,588.10	4,764.29	14,292.87	1,782.71
1100	3 C.Y., 75 tons at 12' radius		75.96	2,779.17	8,337.51	25,012.52	2,275.15
1200	100 ton capacity, 60' boom		100.40	1,369.90	4,109.70	12,329.10	1,625.12
1300	165 ton capacity, 60' boom		124.00	1,641.13	4,923.40	14,770.20	1,976.66
1400	200 ton capacity, 70' boom		161.52	1,828.25	5,484.75	16,454.25	2,389.09
1500	350 ton capacity, 80' boom		212.91	3,836.75	11,510.25	34,530.75	4,005.37
1600	Truck mounted, lattice boom, 6 x 4, 20 tons at 10' radius		46.46	1,057.04	2,673.41	7,892.91	906.32
1700	25 tons at 10' radius		49.93	2,779.05	8,337.17	25,011.51	2,066.85
1800	8 x 4, 30 tons at 10' radius		63.29	2,977.77	8,933.32	26,799.97	2,293.01
1900	40 tons at 12' radius		63.29	3,255.46	9,766.37	29,299.10	2,459.62
2000	60 tons at 15' radius		62.74	3,414.50	10,243.51	30,730.54	2,550.62
2050	82 tons at 15' radius		69.45	3,513.68	10,541.03	31,623.09	2,663.80
2100	90 tons at 15' radius		77.59	3,616.59	10,849.77	32,549.32	2,790.64
2200	115 tons at 15' radius		87.52	3,724	11,171.99	33,515.96	2,934.57
2300	150 tons at 18' radius		94.76	3,215.78	9,647.36	28,942.08	2,687.58
2350	165 tons at 18' radius		101.71	3,275.67	9,826.99	29,480.98	2,779.06
2400	Truck mounted, hydraulic, 12 ton capacity		34.47	3,247.36	9,742.09	29,226.28	2,224.21
2500	25 ton capacity		42.48	3,325.23	9,975.72	29,927.16	2,335.01
2550	33 ton capacity		63.29	3,354.66	10,063.99	30,191.95	2,519.14
2560	40 ton capacity		63.29	3,384.34	10,153.03	30,459.08	2,536.95
2600	55 ton capacity		62.85	3,414.41	10,243.23	30,729.67	2,551.41
2700	80 ton capacity		82.29	3,473.77	10,421.30	31,263.92	2,742.60
2720	100 ton capacity		87.60	3,622.55	10,867.66	32,603	2,874.30
2740	120 ton capacity		123.03	3,672.67	11,018	33,054	3,187.83
2760	150 ton capacity		131.66	3,905.11	11,715.33	35,145.99	3,396.31
2800	Self-propelled, 4 x 4, with telescoping boom, 5 ton		17.69	434.32	1,302.95	3,908.85	402.11
2900	12-1/2 ton capacity		25.03	772.50	2,317.50	6,952.50	663.72
3000	15 ton capacity		40.23	880.65	2,641.95	7,925.85	850.19
3050	20 ton capacity		26.09	969.92	2,909.75	8,729.25	790.69
3100	25 ton capacity		42.88	1,038.58	3,115.75	9,347.25	966.17
3150	40 ton capacity		52.47	1,278.92	3,836.75	11,510.25	1,187.13
3200	Derricks, guy, 20 ton capacity, 60' boom, 75' mast		26.58	1,687.54	5,062.64	15,187.91	1,225.19
3300	100' boom, 115' mast		42.12	2,382.14	7,146.44	21,439.31	1,766.55
3400	Stiffleg, 20 ton capacity, 70' boom, 37' mast		29.69	734.69	2,204.07	6,612.19	678.35
3500	100' boom, 47' mast		45.94	794.05	2,382.14	7,146.44	843.98
3550	Helicopter, small, lift to 1250 lb. maximum, w/pilot		115.86	8,480.33	25,441	76,323	6,015.09
3600	Hoists, chain type, overhead, manual, 3/4 ton		.17	25	64	182	14.16
3900	10 ton		.92	127.72	319.30	638.60	71.19
4000	Hoist and tower, 5000 lb. cap., portable electric, 40' high		5.58	168.83	506.49	1,519.49	145.94
4100	For each added 10' section, add		.14	37.77	113.32	339.97	23.77
4200	Hoist and single tubular tower, 5000 lb. electric, 100' high		8.13	125.28	375.83	1,127.47	140.17
4300	For each added 6'-6" section, add		.25	45.48	136.45	409.36	29.25
4400	Hoist and double tubular tower, 5000 lb., 100' high		8.85	144.08	432.24	1,296.72	157.25
4500	For each added 6'-6" section, add		.27	45.66	136.97	410.91	29.52
4550	Hoist and tower, mast type, 6000 lb., 100' high		10.78	534.80	1,604.40	4,813.20	407.10
4570	For each added 10' section, add		.15	37.77	113.32	339.97	23.86
4600	Hoist and tower, personnel, electric, 2000 lb., 100' @ 125 fpm		20.45	593.61	1,780.83	5,342.48	519.75
4700	3000 lb., 100' @ 200 fpm		23.40	623.29	1,869.87	5,609.61	561.16

01 54 | Construction Aids

01 54 33 | Equipment Rental

		UNIT	HOURLY OPER. COST	RENT PER DAY	RENT PER WEEK	RENT PER MONTH	EQUIPMENT COST/DAY	
60	4800	3000 lb., 150' @ 300 fpm	Ea.	25.96	841.85	2,525.54	7,576.61	712.83	60
	4900	4000 lb., 100' @ 300 fpm		26.86	871.14	2,613.42	7,840.27	737.56	
	5000	6000 lb., 100' @ 275 fpm		28.86	901.21	2,703.62	8,110.86	771.62	
	5100	For added heights up to 500', add	L.F.	.01	3.85	11.57	34.69	2.40	
	5200	Jacks, hydraulic, 20 ton	Ea.	.05	25.71	62.14	111.43	12.85	
	5500	100 ton		.47	30	70	140	17.75	
	6100	Jacks, hydraulic, climbing w/50' jackrods, control console, 30 ton cap.		2.53	37.01	111.01	333.04	42.48	
	6150	For each added 10' jackrod section, add		.05	5.78	17.35	52.04	3.90	
	6300	50 ton capacity		4.07	39.71	119.11	357.32	56.37	
	6350	For each added 10' jackrod section, add		.07	5.78	17.35	52.04	4.07	
	6500	125 ton capacity		10.64	39.71	119.11	357.32	108.94	
	6550	For each added 10' jackrod section, add		.72	5.78	17.35	52.04	9.26	
	6600	Cable jack, 10 ton capacity with 200' cable		1.85	42.41	127.21	381.60	40.27	
	6650	For each added 50' of cable, add		.26	17.73	53.19	159.58	12.68	
70	0010	**WELLPOINT EQUIPMENT RENTAL** without operators	R015433 -10						70
	0020	Based on 2 months rental							
	0100	Combination jetting & wellpoint pump, 60 H.P. diesel	Ea.	18.32	355.39	1,066.18	3,198.55	359.78	
	0200	High pressure gas jet pump, 200 H.P., 300 psi	"	39.53	197.76	593.28	1,779.84	434.92	
	0300	Discharge pipe, 8" diameter	L.F.	.01	54.85	164.54	493.63	32.99	
	0350	12" diameter		.01	58.50	175.51	526.54	35.19	
	0400	Header pipe, flows up to 150 GPM, 4" diameter		.01	32.27	96.82	290.46	19.45	
	0500	400 GPM, 6" diameter		.01	42.57	127.72	383.16	25.63	
	0600	800 GPM, 8" diameter		.01	47.04	141.11	423.33	28.31	
	0700	1500 GPM, 10" diameter		.01	59.24	177.71	533.12	35.63	
	0800	2500 GPM, 12" diameter		.03	67.28	201.84	605.52	40.62	
	0900	4500 GPM, 16" diameter		.04	76.42	229.25	687.75	46.19	
	0950	For quick coupling aluminum and plastic pipe, add		.04	10.87	32.59	97.76	6.86	
	1100	Wellpoint, 25' long, with fittings & riser pipe, 1-1/2" or 2" diameter	Ea.	.07	84.74	254.21	762.65	51.44	
	1200	Wellpoint pump, diesel powered, 4" suction, 20 H.P.		8.18	166.52	499.55	1,498.65	165.34	
	1300	6" suction, 30 H.P.		10.98	305.57	916.70	2,750.10	271.18	
	1400	8" suction, 40 H.P.		14.87	266.08	798.25	2,394.75	278.59	
	1500	10" suction, 75 H.P.		21.69	299.39	898.16	2,694.48	353.18	
	1600	12" suction, 100 H.P.		31.83	307.28	921.85	2,765.55	439.03	
	1700	12" suction, 175 H.P.		45.55	315.87	947.60	2,842.80	553.92	
80	0010	**MARINE EQUIPMENT RENTAL** without operators	R015433 -10						80
	0200	Barge, 400 Ton, 30' wide x 90' long	Ea.	20.64	1,316.34	4,131.59	11,956.76	991.44	
	0240	800 Ton, 45' wide x 90' long		25.92	1,645.43	5,082.75	14,699.13	1,223.93	
	2000	Tugboat, diesel, 100 H.P.		34.62	263.27	820.37	2,385.87	441.06	
	2040	250 H.P.		67.21	477.18	1,486.18	4,305.53	834.93	
	2080	380 H.P.		146.33	1,426.04	4,458.55	12,944.01	2,062.36	
	3000	Small work boat, gas, 16-foot, 50 H.P.		13.28	53.20	164.95	477.18	139.24	
	4000	Large, diesel, 48-foot, 200 H.P.		87.43	1,508.31	4,726.06	13,711.88	1,644.62	

Crews - Standard

Crew No.	Bare Costs		Incl. Subs O&P		Cost Per Labor-Hour	
Crew A-1	Hr.	Daily	Hr.	Daily	Bare Costs	Incl. O&P
1 Building Laborer	$49.00	$392.00	$72.55	$580.40	$49.00	$72.55
1 Concrete Saw, Gas Manual		119.32		131.25	14.91	16.41
8 L.H., Daily Totals		$511.32		$711.65	$63.91	$88.96
Crew A-1A	Hr.	Daily	Hr.	Daily	Bare Costs	Incl. O&P
1 Skilled Worker	$63.50	$508.00	$95.00	$760.00	$63.50	$95.00
1 Shot Blaster, 20"		238.10		261.91	29.76	32.74
8 L.H., Daily Totals		$746.10		$1021.91	$93.26	$127.74
Crew A-1B	Hr.	Daily	Hr.	Daily	Bare Costs	Incl. O&P
1 Building Laborer	$49.00	$392.00	$72.55	$580.40	$49.00	$72.55
1 Concrete Saw		194.70		214.17	24.34	26.77
8 L.H., Daily Totals		$586.70		$794.57	$73.34	$99.32
Crew A-1C	Hr.	Daily	Hr.	Daily	Bare Costs	Incl. O&P
1 Building Laborer	$49.00	$392.00	$72.55	$580.40	$49.00	$72.55
1 Chain Saw, Gas, 18"		75.85		83.44	9.48	10.43
8 L.H., Daily Totals		$467.85		$663.84	$58.48	$82.98
Crew A-1D	Hr.	Daily	Hr.	Daily	Bare Costs	Incl. O&P
1 Building Laborer	$49.00	$392.00	$72.55	$580.40	$49.00	$72.55
1 Vibrating Plate, Gas, 18"		132.53		145.78	16.57	18.22
8 L.H., Daily Totals		$524.53		$726.18	$65.57	$90.77
Crew A-1E	Hr.	Daily	Hr.	Daily	Bare Costs	Incl. O&P
1 Building Laborer	$49.00	$392.00	$72.55	$580.40	$49.00	$72.55
1 Vibrating Plate, Gas, 21"		152.80		168.08	19.10	21.01
8 L.H., Daily Totals		$544.80		$748.48	$68.10	$93.56
Crew A-1F	Hr.	Daily	Hr.	Daily	Bare Costs	Incl. O&P
1 Building Laborer	$49.00	$392.00	$72.55	$580.40	$49.00	$72.55
1 Rammer/Tamper, Gas, 8"		99.37		109.31	12.42	13.66
8 L.H., Daily Totals		$491.37		$689.71	$61.42	$86.21
Crew A-1G	Hr.	Daily	Hr.	Daily	Bare Costs	Incl. O&P
1 Building Laborer	$49.00	$392.00	$72.55	$580.40	$49.00	$72.55
1 Rammer/Tamper, Gas, 15"		113.54		124.89	14.19	15.61
8 L.H., Daily Totals		$505.54		$705.29	$63.19	$88.16
Crew A-1H	Hr.	Daily	Hr.	Daily	Bare Costs	Incl. O&P
1 Building Laborer	$49.00	$392.00	$72.55	$580.40	$49.00	$72.55
1 Exterior Steam Cleaner		88.34		97.17	11.04	12.15
8 L.H., Daily Totals		$480.34		$677.57	$60.04	$84.70
Crew A-1J	Hr.	Daily	Hr.	Daily	Bare Costs	Incl. O&P
1 Building Laborer	$49.00	$392.00	$72.55	$580.40	$49.00	$72.55
1 Cultivator, Walk-Behind, 5 H.P.		78.27		86.10	9.78	10.76
8 L.H., Daily Totals		$470.27		$666.50	$58.78	$83.31
Crew A-1K	Hr.	Daily	Hr.	Daily	Bare Costs	Incl. O&P
1 Building Laborer	$49.00	$392.00	$72.55	$580.40	$49.00	$72.55
1 Cultivator, Walk-Behind, 8 H.P.		95.36		104.89	11.92	13.11
8 L.H., Daily Totals		$487.36		$685.29	$60.92	$85.66
Crew A-1M	Hr.	Daily	Hr.	Daily	Bare Costs	Incl. O&P
1 Building Laborer	$49.00	$392.00	$72.55	$580.40	$49.00	$72.55
1 Snow Blower, Walk-Behind		78.03		85.83	9.75	10.73
8 L.H., Daily Totals		$470.03		$666.23	$58.75	$83.28

Crew No.	Bare Costs		Incl. Subs O&P		Cost Per Labor-Hour	
Crew A-2	Hr.	Daily	Hr.	Daily	Bare Costs	Incl. O&P
2 Laborers	$49.00	$784.00	$72.55	$1160.80	$51.05	$75.70
1 Truck Driver (light)	55.15	441.20	82.00	656.00		
1 Flatbed Truck, Gas, 1.5 Ton		420.83		462.92	17.53	19.29
24 L.H., Daily Totals		$1646.03		$2279.72	$68.58	$94.99
Crew A-2A	Hr.	Daily	Hr.	Daily	Bare Costs	Incl. O&P
2 Laborers	$49.00	$784.00	$72.55	$1160.80	$51.05	$75.70
1 Truck Driver (light)	55.15	441.20	82.00	656.00		
1 Flatbed Truck, Gas, 1.5 Ton		420.83		462.92		
1 Concrete Saw		194.70		214.17	25.65	28.21
24 L.H., Daily Totals		$1840.73		$2493.88	$76.70	$103.91
Crew A-2B	Hr.	Daily	Hr.	Daily	Bare Costs	Incl. O&P
1 Truck Driver (light)	$55.15	$441.20	$82.00	$656.00	$55.15	$82.00
1 Flatbed Truck, Gas, 1.5 Ton		420.83		462.92	52.60	57.86
8 L.H., Daily Totals		$862.03		$1118.92	$107.75	$139.86
Crew A-3A	Hr.	Daily	Hr.	Daily	Bare Costs	Incl. O&P
1 Equip. Oper. (light)	$62.00	$496.00	$91.95	$735.60	$62.00	$91.95
1 Pickup Truck, 4x4, 3/4 Ton		235.90		259.49	29.49	32.44
8 L.H., Daily Totals		$731.90		$995.09	$91.49	$124.39
Crew A-3B	Hr.	Daily	Hr.	Daily	Bare Costs	Incl. O&P
1 Equip. Oper. (medium)	$65.00	$520.00	$96.40	$771.20	$61.13	$90.75
1 Truck Driver (heavy)	57.25	458.00	85.10	680.80		
1 Dump Truck, 12 C.Y., 400 H.P.		987.07		1085.78		
1 F.E. Loader, W.M., 2.5 C.Y.		815.12		896.63	112.64	123.90
16 L.H., Daily Totals		$2780.19		$3434.41	$173.76	$214.65
Crew A-3C	Hr.	Daily	Hr.	Daily	Bare Costs	Incl. O&P
1 Equip. Oper. (light)	$62.00	$496.00	$91.95	$735.60	$62.00	$91.95
1 Loader, Skid Steer, 78 H.P.		394.64		434.10	49.33	54.26
8 L.H., Daily Totals		$890.64		$1169.70	$111.33	$146.21
Crew A-3D	Hr.	Daily	Hr.	Daily	Bare Costs	Incl. O&P
1 Truck Driver (light)	$55.15	$441.20	$82.00	$656.00	$55.15	$82.00
1 Pickup Truck, 4x4, 3/4 Ton		235.90		259.49		
1 Flatbed Trailer, 25 Ton		157.04		172.75	49.12	54.03
8 L.H., Daily Totals		$834.15		$1088.24	$104.27	$136.03
Crew A-3E	Hr.	Daily	Hr.	Daily	Bare Costs	Incl. O&P
1 Equip. Oper. (crane)	$68.60	$548.80	$101.75	$814.00	$62.92	$93.42
1 Truck Driver (heavy)	57.25	458.00	85.10	680.80		
1 Pickup Truck, 4x4, 3/4 Ton		235.90		259.49	14.74	16.22
16 L.H., Daily Totals		$1242.70		$1754.29	$77.67	$109.64
Crew A-3F	Hr.	Daily	Hr.	Daily	Bare Costs	Incl. O&P
1 Equip. Oper. (crane)	$68.60	$548.80	$101.75	$814.00	$62.92	$93.42
1 Truck Driver (heavy)	57.25	458.00	85.10	680.80		
1 Pickup Truck, 4x4, 3/4 Ton		235.90		259.49		
1 Truck Tractor, 6x4, 380 H.P.		573.49		630.83		
1 Lowbed Trailer, 75 Ton		295.27		324.79	69.04	75.95
16 L.H., Daily Totals		$2111.46		$2709.92	$131.97	$169.37

Crews - Standard

Crew No.	Bare Costs		Incl. Subs O&P		Cost Per Labor-Hour	
Crew A-3G	Hr.	Daily	Hr.	Daily	Bare Costs	Incl. O&P
1 Equip. Oper. (crane)	$68.60	$548.80	$101.75	$814.00	$62.92	$93.42
1 Truck Driver (heavy)	57.25	458.00	85.10	680.80		
1 Pickup Truck, 4x4, 3/4 Ton		235.90		259.49		
1 Truck Tractor, 6x4, 450 H.P.		699.67		769.64		
1 Lowbed Trailer, 75 Ton		295.27		324.79	76.93	84.62
16 L.H., Daily Totals		$2237.64		$2848.73	$139.85	$178.05

Crew A-3H	Hr.	Daily	Hr.	Daily	Bare Costs	Incl. O&P
1 Equip. Oper. (crane)	$68.60	$548.80	$101.75	$814.00	$68.60	$101.75
1 Hyd. Crane, 12 Ton (Daily)		2167.46		2384.21	270.93	298.03
8 L.H., Daily Totals		$2716.26		$3198.21	$339.53	$399.78

Crew A-3I	Hr.	Daily	Hr.	Daily	Bare Costs	Incl. O&P
1 Equip. Oper. (crane)	$68.60	$548.80	$101.75	$814.00	$68.60	$101.75
1 Hyd. Crane, 25 Ton (Daily)		2294.03		2523.44	286.75	315.43
8 L.H., Daily Totals		$2842.83		$3337.44	$355.35	$417.18

Crew A-3J	Hr.	Daily	Hr.	Daily	Bare Costs	Incl. O&P
1 Equip. Oper. (crane)	$68.60	$548.80	$101.75	$814.00	$68.60	$101.75
1 Hyd. Crane, 40 Ton (Daily)		2477.80		2725.59	309.73	340.70
8 L.H., Daily Totals		$3026.60		$3539.59	$378.33	$442.45

Crew A-3K	Hr.	Daily	Hr.	Daily	Bare Costs	Incl. O&P
1 Equip. Oper. (crane)	$68.60	$548.80	$101.75	$814.00	$63.50	$94.17
1 Equip. Oper. (oiler)	58.40	467.20	86.60	692.80		
1 Hyd. Crane, 55 Ton (Daily)		2491.74		2740.91		
1 P/U Truck, 3/4 Ton (Daily)		165.25		181.77	166.06	182.67
16 L.H., Daily Totals		$3672.99		$4429.49	$229.56	$276.84

Crew A-3L	Hr.	Daily	Hr.	Daily	Bare Costs	Incl. O&P
1 Equip. Oper. (crane)	$68.60	$548.80	$101.75	$814.00	$63.50	$94.17
1 Equip. Oper. (oiler)	58.40	467.20	86.60	692.80		
1 Hyd. Crane, 80 Ton (Daily)		2681.89		2950.08		
1 P/U Truck, 3/4 Ton (Daily)		165.25		181.77	177.95	195.74
16 L.H., Daily Totals		$3863.14		$4638.66	$241.45	$289.92

Crew A-3M	Hr.	Daily	Hr.	Daily	Bare Costs	Incl. O&P
1 Equip. Oper. (crane)	$68.60	$548.80	$101.75	$814.00	$63.50	$94.17
1 Equip. Oper. (oiler)	58.40	467.20	86.60	692.80		
1 Hyd. Crane, 100 Ton (Daily)		2811.00		3092.10		
1 P/U Truck, 3/4 Ton (Daily)		165.25		181.77	186.02	204.62
16 L.H., Daily Totals		$3992.24		$4780.67	$249.52	$298.79

Crew A-3N	Hr.	Daily	Hr.	Daily	Bare Costs	Incl. O&P
1 Equip. Oper. (crane)	$68.60	$548.80	$101.75	$814.00	$68.60	$101.75
1 Tower Crane (monthly)		1961.62		2157.79	245.20	269.72
8 L.H., Daily Totals		$2510.42		$2971.79	$313.80	$371.47

Crew A-3P	Hr.	Daily	Hr.	Daily	Bare Costs	Incl. O&P
1 Equip. Oper. (light)	$62.00	$496.00	$91.95	$735.60	$62.00	$91.95
1 A.T. Forklift, 31' reach, 45' lift		632.52		695.77	79.07	86.97
8 L.H., Daily Totals		$1128.52		$1431.37	$141.07	$178.92

Crew A-3Q	Hr.	Daily	Hr.	Daily	Bare Costs	Incl. O&P
1 Equip. Oper. (light)	$62.00	$496.00	$91.95	$735.60	$62.00	$91.95
1 Pickup Truck, 4x4, 3/4 Ton		235.90		259.49		
1 Flatbed Trailer, 3 Ton		81.23		89.36	39.64	43.61
8 L.H., Daily Totals		$813.14		$1084.45	$101.64	$135.56

Crew No.	Bare Costs		Incl. Subs O&P		Cost Per Labor-Hour	
Crew A-3R	Hr.	Daily	Hr.	Daily	Bare Costs	Incl. O&P
1 Equip. Oper. (light)	$62.00	$496.00	$91.95	$735.60	$62.00	$91.95
1 Forklift, Smooth Floor, 8,000 Lb.		326.55		359.21	40.82	44.90
8 L.H., Daily Totals		$822.55		$1094.81	$102.82	$136.85

Crew A-4	Hr.	Daily	Hr.	Daily	Bare Costs	Incl. O&P
2 Carpenters	$60.55	$968.80	$89.65	$1434.40	$57.60	$85.20
1 Painter, Ordinary	51.70	413.60	76.30	610.40		
24 L.H., Daily Totals		$1382.40		$2044.80	$57.60	$85.20

Crew A-5	Hr.	Daily	Hr.	Daily	Bare Costs	Incl. O&P
2 Laborers	$49.00	$784.00	$72.55	$1160.80	$49.68	$73.60
.25 Truck Driver (light)	55.15	110.30	82.00	164.00		
.25 Flatbed Truck, Gas, 1.5 Ton		105.21		115.73	5.84	6.43
18 L.H., Daily Totals		$999.51		$1440.53	$55.53	$80.03

Crew A-6	Hr.	Daily	Hr.	Daily	Bare Costs	Incl. O&P
1 Instrument Man	$63.50	$508.00	$95.00	$760.00	$60.85	$90.47
1 Rodman/Chainman	58.20	465.60	85.95	687.60		
1 Level, Electronic		36.40		40.04	2.27	2.50
16 L.H., Daily Totals		$1010.00		$1487.64	$63.12	$92.98

Crew A-7	Hr.	Daily	Hr.	Daily	Bare Costs	Incl. O&P
1 Chief of Party	$74.00	$592.00	$110.20	$881.60	$65.23	$97.05
1 Instrument Man	63.50	508.00	95.00	760.00		
1 Rodman/Chainman	58.20	465.60	85.95	687.60		
1 Level, Electronic		36.40		40.04	1.52	1.67
24 L.H., Daily Totals		$1602.00		$2369.24	$66.75	$98.72

Crew A-8	Hr.	Daily	Hr.	Daily	Bare Costs	Incl. O&P
1 Chief of Party	$74.00	$592.00	$110.20	$881.60	$63.48	$94.28
1 Instrument Man	63.50	508.00	95.00	760.00		
2 Rodmen/Chainmen	58.20	931.20	85.95	1375.20		
1 Level, Electronic		36.40		40.04	1.14	1.25
32 L.H., Daily Totals		$2067.60		$3056.84	$64.61	$95.53

Crew A-9	Hr.	Daily	Hr.	Daily	Bare Costs	Incl. O&P
1 Asbestos Foreman	$67.60	$540.80	$103.00	$824.00	$67.16	$102.34
7 Asbestos Workers	67.10	3757.60	102.25	5726.00		
64 L.H., Daily Totals		$4298.40		$6550.00	$67.16	$102.34

Crew A-10A	Hr.	Daily	Hr.	Daily	Bare Costs	Incl. O&P
1 Asbestos Foreman	$67.60	$540.80	$103.00	$824.00	$67.27	$102.50
2 Asbestos Workers	67.10	1073.60	102.25	1636.00		
24 L.H., Daily Totals		$1614.40		$2460.00	$67.27	$102.50

Crew A-10B	Hr.	Daily	Hr.	Daily	Bare Costs	Incl. O&P
1 Asbestos Foreman	$67.60	$540.80	$103.00	$824.00	$67.22	$102.44
3 Asbestos Workers	67.10	1610.40	102.25	2454.00		
32 L.H., Daily Totals		$2151.20		$3278.00	$67.22	$102.44

Crew A-10C	Hr.	Daily	Hr.	Daily	Bare Costs	Incl. O&P
3 Asbestos Workers	$67.10	$1610.40	$102.25	$2454.00	$67.10	$102.25
1 Flatbed Truck, Gas, 1.5 Ton		420.83		462.92	17.53	19.29
24 L.H., Daily Totals		$2031.23		$2916.92	$84.63	$121.54

Crews - Standard

Crew No.		Bare Costs		Incl. Subs O&P		Cost Per Labor-Hour	
Crew A-10D	Hr.	Daily	Hr.	Daily	Bare Costs	Incl. O&P
2 Asbestos Workers	$67.10	$1073.60	$102.25	$1636.00	$65.30	$98.21
1 Equip. Oper. (crane)	68.60	548.80	101.75	814.00		
1 Equip. Oper. (oiler)	58.40	467.20	86.60	692.80		
1 Hydraulic Crane, 33 Ton		2519.14		2771.05	78.72	86.60
32 L.H., Daily Totals		$4608.74		$5913.85	$144.02	$184.81

Crew A-11	Hr.	Daily	Hr.	Daily	Bare Costs	Incl. O&P
1 Asbestos Foreman	$67.60	$540.80	$103.00	$824.00	$67.16	$102.34
7 Asbestos Workers	67.10	3757.60	102.25	5726.00		
2 Chip. Hammers, 12 Lb., Elec.		58.85		64.73	.92	1.01
64 L.H., Daily Totals		$4357.25		$6614.73	$68.08	$103.36

Crew A-12	Hr.	Daily	Hr.	Daily	Bare Costs	Incl. O&P
1 Asbestos Foreman	$67.60	$540.80	$103.00	$824.00	$67.16	$102.34
7 Asbestos Workers	67.10	3757.60	102.25	5726.00		
1 Trk-Mtd Vac, 14 CY, 1500 Gal.		619.88		681.87		
1 Flatbed Truck, 20,000 GVW		234.51		257.97	13.35	14.68
64 L.H., Daily Totals		$5152.79		$7489.83	$80.51	$117.03

Crew A-13	Hr.	Daily	Hr.	Daily	Bare Costs	Incl. O&P
1 Equip. Oper. (light)	$62.00	$496.00	$91.95	$735.60	$62.00	$91.95
1 Trk-Mtd Vac, 14 CY, 1500 Gal.		619.88		681.87		
1 Flatbed Truck, 20,000 GVW		234.51		257.97	106.80	117.48
8 L.H., Daily Totals		$1350.39		$1675.43	$168.80	$209.43

Crew B-1	Hr.	Daily	Hr.	Daily	Bare Costs	Incl. O&P
1 Labor Foreman (outside)	$51.00	$408.00	$75.50	$604.00	$49.67	$73.53
2 Laborers	49.00	784.00	72.55	1160.80		
24 L.H., Daily Totals		$1192.00		$1764.80	$49.67	$73.53

Crew B-1A	Hr.	Daily	Hr.	Daily	Bare Costs	Incl. O&P
1 Labor Foreman (outside)	$51.00	$408.00	$75.50	$604.00	$49.67	$73.53
2 Laborers	49.00	784.00	72.55	1160.80		
2 Cutting Torches		29.68		32.65		
2 Sets of Gases		401.58		441.74	17.97	19.77
24 L.H., Daily Totals		$1623.26		$2239.19	$67.64	$93.30

Crew B-1B	Hr.	Daily	Hr.	Daily	Bare Costs	Incl. O&P
1 Labor Foreman (outside)	$51.00	$408.00	$75.50	$604.00	$54.40	$80.59
2 Laborers	49.00	784.00	72.55	1160.80		
1 Equip. Oper. (crane)	68.60	548.80	101.75	814.00		
2 Cutting Torches		29.68		32.65		
2 Sets of Gases		401.58		441.74		
1 Hyd. Crane, 12 Ton		2224.21		2446.63	82.98	91.28
32 L.H., Daily Totals		$4396.27		$5499.82	$137.38	$171.87

Crew B-1C	Hr.	Daily	Hr.	Daily	Bare Costs	Incl. O&P
1 Labor Foreman (outside)	$51.00	$408.00	$75.50	$604.00	$49.67	$73.53
2 Laborers	49.00	784.00	72.55	1160.80		
1 Telescoping Boom Lift, to 60'		467.60		514.36	19.48	21.43
24 L.H., Daily Totals		$1659.60		$2279.16	$69.15	$94.96

Crew B-1D	Hr.	Daily	Hr.	Daily	Bare Costs	Incl. O&P
2 Laborers	$49.00	$784.00	$72.55	$1160.80	$49.00	$72.55
1 Small Work Boat, Gas, 50 H.P.		139.24		153.16		
1 Pressure Washer, 7 GPM		118.36		130.20	16.10	17.71
16 L.H., Daily Totals		$1041.60		$1444.16	$65.10	$90.26

Crew B-1E	Hr.	Daily	Hr.	Daily	Bare Costs	Incl. O&P
1 Labor Foreman (outside)	$51.00	$408.00	$75.50	$604.00	$49.50	$73.29
3 Laborers	49.00	1176.00	72.55	1741.20		
1 Work Boat, Diesel, 200 H.P.		1644.62		1809.08		
2 Pressure Washers, 7 GPM		236.73		260.40	58.79	64.67
32 L.H., Daily Totals		$3465.35		$4414.68	$108.29	$137.96

Crew B-1F	Hr.	Daily	Hr.	Daily	Bare Costs	Incl. O&P
2 Skilled Workers	$63.50	$1016.00	$95.00	$1520.00	$58.67	$87.52
1 Laborer	49.00	392.00	72.55	580.40		
1 Small Work Boat, Gas, 50 H.P.		139.24		153.16		
1 Pressure Washer, 7 GPM		118.36		130.20	10.73	11.81
24 L.H., Daily Totals		$1665.60		$2383.76	$69.40	$99.32

Crew B-1G	Hr.	Daily	Hr.	Daily	Bare Costs	Incl. O&P
2 Laborers	$49.00	$784.00	$72.55	$1160.80	$49.00	$72.55
1 Small Work Boat, Gas, 50 H.P.		139.24		153.16	8.70	9.57
16 L.H., Daily Totals		$923.24		$1313.96	$57.70	$82.12

Crew B-1H	Hr.	Daily	Hr.	Daily	Bare Costs	Incl. O&P
2 Skilled Workers	$63.50	$1016.00	$95.00	$1520.00	$58.67	$87.52
1 Laborer	49.00	392.00	72.55	580.40		
1 Small Work Boat, Gas, 50 H.P.		139.24		153.16	5.80	6.38
24 L.H., Daily Totals		$1547.24		$2253.56	$64.47	$93.90

Crew B-1J	Hr.	Daily	Hr.	Daily	Bare Costs	Incl. O&P
1 Labor Foreman (inside)	$49.50	$396.00	$73.30	$586.40	$49.25	$72.92
1 Laborer	49.00	392.00	72.55	580.40		
16 L.H., Daily Totals		$788.00		$1166.80	$49.25	$72.92

Crew B-1K	Hr.	Daily	Hr.	Daily	Bare Costs	Incl. O&P
1 Carpenter Foreman (inside)	$61.05	$488.40	$90.40	$723.20	$60.80	$90.03
1 Carpenter	60.55	484.40	89.65	717.20		
16 L.H., Daily Totals		$972.80		$1440.40	$60.80	$90.03

Crew B-2	Hr.	Daily	Hr.	Daily	Bare Costs	Incl. O&P
1 Labor Foreman (outside)	$51.00	$408.00	$75.50	$604.00	$49.40	$73.14
4 Laborers	49.00	1568.00	72.55	2321.60		
40 L.H., Daily Totals		$1976.00		$2925.60	$49.40	$73.14

Crew B-2A	Hr.	Daily	Hr.	Daily	Bare Costs	Incl. O&P
1 Labor Foreman (outside)	$51.00	$408.00	$75.50	$604.00	$49.67	$73.53
2 Laborers	49.00	784.00	72.55	1160.80		
1 Telescoping Boom Lift, to 60'		467.60		514.36	19.48	21.43
24 L.H., Daily Totals		$1659.60		$2279.16	$69.15	$94.96

Crew B-3	Hr.	Daily	Hr.	Daily	Bare Costs	Incl. O&P
1 Labor Foreman (outside)	$51.00	$408.00	$75.50	$604.00	$54.75	$81.20
2 Laborers	49.00	784.00	72.55	1160.80		
1 Equip. Oper. (medium)	65.00	520.00	96.40	771.20		
2 Truck Drivers (heavy)	57.25	916.00	85.10	1361.60		
1 Crawler Loader, 3 C.Y.		1313.18		1444.50		
2 Dump Trucks, 12 C.Y., 400 H.P.		1974.15		2171.56	68.49	75.33
48 L.H., Daily Totals		$5915.33		$7513.67	$123.24	$156.53

Crew B-3A	Hr.	Daily	Hr.	Daily	Bare Costs	Incl. O&P
4 Laborers	$49.00	$1568.00	$72.55	$2321.60	$52.20	$77.32
1 Equip. Oper. (medium)	65.00	520.00	96.40	771.20		
1 Hyd. Excavator, 1.5 C.Y.		1193.85		1313.24	29.85	32.83
40 L.H., Daily Totals		$3281.85		$4406.04	$82.05	$110.15

Crews - Standard

Crew No.		Bare Costs		Incl. Subs O&P		Cost Per Labor-Hour	
Crew B-3B	Hr.	Daily	Hr.	Daily	Bare Costs	Incl. O&P
2 Laborers	$49.00	$784.00	$72.55	$1160.80	$55.06	$81.65
1 Equip. Oper. (medium)	65.00	520.00	96.40	771.20		
1 Truck Driver (heavy)	57.25	458.00	85.10	680.80		
1 Backhoe Loader, 80 H.P.		455.51		501.06		
1 Dump Truck, 12 C.Y., 400 H.P.		987.07		1085.78	45.08	49.59
32 L.H., Daily Totals		$3204.58		$4199.64	$100.14	$131.24
Crew B-3C	Hr.	Daily	Hr.	Daily	Bare Costs	Incl. O&P
3 Laborers	$49.00	$1176.00	$72.55	$1741.20	$53.00	$78.51
1 Equip. Oper. (medium)	65.00	520.00	96.40	771.20		
1 Crawler Loader, 4 C.Y.		1859.78		2045.75	58.12	63.93
32 L.H., Daily Totals		$3555.78		$4558.15	$111.12	$142.44
Crew B-4	Hr.	Daily	Hr.	Daily	Bare Costs	Incl. O&P
1 Labor Foreman (outside)	$51.00	$408.00	$75.50	$604.00	$50.71	$75.13
4 Laborers	49.00	1568.00	72.55	2321.60		
1 Truck Driver (heavy)	57.25	458.00	85.10	680.80		
1 Truck Tractor, 220 H.P.		357.02		392.72		
1 Flatbed Trailer, 40 Ton		215.61		237.17	11.93	13.12
48 L.H., Daily Totals		$3006.63		$4236.29	$62.64	$88.26
Crew B-5	Hr.	Daily	Hr.	Daily	Bare Costs	Incl. O&P
1 Labor Foreman (outside)	$51.00	$408.00	$75.50	$604.00	$53.86	$79.79
4 Laborers	49.00	1568.00	72.55	2321.60		
2 Equip. Oper. (medium)	65.00	1040.00	96.40	1542.40		
1 Air Compressor, 250 cfm		226.90		249.59		
2 Breakers, Pavement, 60 lb.		79.92		87.92		
2 -50' Air Hoses, 1.5"		47.13		51.84		
1 Crawler Loader, 3 C.Y.		1313.18		1444.50	29.77	32.75
56 L.H., Daily Totals		$4683.13		$6301.85	$83.63	$112.53
Crew B-5A	Hr.	Daily	Hr.	Daily	Bare Costs	Incl. O&P
1 Labor Foreman (outside)	$51.00	$408.00	$75.50	$604.00	$54.29	$80.48
6 Laborers	49.00	2352.00	72.55	3482.40		
2 Equip. Oper. (medium)	65.00	1040.00	96.40	1542.40		
1 Equip. Oper. (light)	62.00	496.00	91.95	735.60		
2 Truck Drivers (heavy)	57.25	916.00	85.10	1361.60		
1 Air Compressor, 365 cfm		344.62		379.09		
2 Breakers, Pavement, 60 lb.		79.92		87.92		
8 -50' Air Hoses, 1"		72.21		79.44		
2 Dump Trucks, 8 C.Y., 220 H.P.		1012.60		1113.86	15.72	17.29
96 L.H., Daily Totals		$6721.36		$9386.30	$70.01	$97.77
Crew B-5B	Hr.	Daily	Hr.	Daily	Bare Costs	Incl. O&P
1 Powderman	$63.50	$508.00	$95.00	$760.00	$60.88	$90.52
2 Equip. Oper. (medium)	65.00	1040.00	96.40	1542.40		
3 Truck Drivers (heavy)	57.25	1374.00	85.10	2042.40		
1 F.E. Loader, W.M., 2.5 C.Y.		815.12		896.63		
3 Dump Trucks, 12 C.Y., 400 H.P.		2961.22		3257.35		
1 Air Compressor, 365 cfm		344.62		379.09	85.85	94.44
48 L.H., Daily Totals		$7042.96		$8877.86	$146.73	$184.96

Crew No.		Bare Costs		Incl. Subs O&P		Cost Per Labor-Hour	
Crew B-5C	Hr.	Daily	Hr.	Daily	Bare Costs	Incl. O&P
3 Laborers	$49.00	$1176.00	$72.55	$1741.20	$56.69	$84.08
1 Equip. Oper. (medium)	65.00	520.00	96.40	771.20		
2 Truck Drivers (heavy)	57.25	916.00	85.10	1361.60		
1 Equip. Oper. (crane)	68.60	548.80	101.75	814.00		
1 Equip. Oper. (oiler)	58.40	467.20	86.60	692.80		
2 Dump Trucks, 12 C.Y., 400 H.P.		1974.15		2171.56		
1 Crawler Loader, 4 C.Y.		1859.78		2045.75		
1 S.P. Crane, 4x4, 25 Ton		966.17		1062.78	75.00	82.50
64 L.H., Daily Totals		$8428.09		$10660.90	$131.69	$166.58
Crew B-5D	Hr.	Daily	Hr.	Daily	Bare Costs	Incl. O&P
1 Labor Foreman (outside)	$51.00	$408.00	$75.50	$604.00	$54.28	$80.45
4 Laborers	49.00	1568.00	72.55	2321.60		
2 Equip. Oper. (medium)	65.00	1040.00	96.40	1542.40		
1 Truck Driver (heavy)	57.25	458.00	85.10	680.80		
1 Air Compressor, 250 cfm		226.90		249.59		
2 Breakers, Pavement, 60 lb.		79.92		87.92		
2 -50' Air Hoses, 1.5"		47.13		51.84		
1 Crawler Loader, 3 C.Y.		1313.18		1444.50		
1 Dump Truck, 12 C.Y., 400 H.P.		987.07		1085.78	41.47	45.62
64 L.H., Daily Totals		$6128.21		$8068.43	$95.75	$126.07
Crew B-5E	Hr.	Daily	Hr.	Daily	Bare Costs	Incl. O&P
1 Labor Foreman (outside)	$51.00	$408.00	$75.50	$604.00	$54.28	$80.45
4 Laborers	49.00	1568.00	72.55	2321.60		
2 Equip. Oper. (medium)	65.00	1040.00	96.40	1542.40		
1 Truck Driver (heavy)	57.25	458.00	85.10	680.80		
1 Water Tank Trailer, 5000 Gal.		176.44		194.08		
1 High Pressure Water Jet 40 KSI		938.04		1031.84		
2 -50' Air Hoses, 1.5"		47.13		51.84		
1 Crawler Loader, 3 C.Y.		1313.18		1444.50		
1 Dump Truck, 12 C.Y., 400 H.P.		987.07		1085.78	54.09	59.50
64 L.H., Daily Totals		$6935.86		$8956.85	$108.37	$139.95
Crew B-6	Hr.	Daily	Hr.	Daily	Bare Costs	Incl. O&P
2 Laborers	$49.00	$784.00	$72.55	$1160.80	$53.33	$79.02
1 Equip. Oper. (light)	62.00	496.00	91.95	735.60		
1 Backhoe Loader, 48 H.P.		291.00		320.10	12.13	13.34
24 L.H., Daily Totals		$1571.00		$2216.50	$65.46	$92.35
Crew B-6A	Hr.	Daily	Hr.	Daily	Bare Costs	Incl. O&P
.5 Labor Foreman (outside)	$51.00	$204.00	$75.50	$302.00	$55.80	$82.68
1 Laborer	49.00	392.00	72.55	580.40		
1 Equip. Oper. (medium)	65.00	520.00	96.40	771.20		
1 Vacuum Truck, 5000 Gal.		425.19		467.71	21.26	23.39
20 L.H., Daily Totals		$1541.19		$2121.31	$77.06	$106.07
Crew B-6B	Hr.	Daily	Hr.	Daily	Bare Costs	Incl. O&P
2 Labor Foremen (outside)	$51.00	$816.00	$75.50	$1208.00	$49.67	$73.53
4 Laborers	49.00	1568.00	72.55	2321.60		
1 S.P. Crane, 4x4, 5 Ton		402.11		442.32		
1 Flatbed Truck, Gas, 1.5 Ton		420.83		462.92		
1 Butt Fusion Mach., 4"-12" diam.		345.30		379.83	24.34	26.77
48 L.H., Daily Totals		$3552.24		$4814.67	$74.01	$100.31

Crews - Standard

Crew No.		Bare Costs		Incl. Subs O&P		Cost Per Labor-Hour	
Crew B-6C	Hr.	Daily	Hr.	Daily	Bare Costs	Incl. O&P
2 Labor Foremen (outside)	$51.00	$816.00	$75.50	$1208.00	$49.67	$73.53
4 Laborers	49.00	1568.00	72.55	2321.60		
1 S.P. Crane, 4x4, 12 Ton		663.72		730.09		
1 Flatbed Truck, Gas, 3 Ton		519.55		571.51		
1 Butt Fusion Mach., 8"-24" diam.		826.87		909.56	41.88	46.07
48 L.H., Daily Totals		$4394.15		$5740.76	$91.54	$119.60
Crew B-6D	Hr.	Daily	Hr.	Daily	Bare Costs	Incl. O&P
.5 Labor Foreman (outside)	$51.00	$204.00	$75.50	$302.00	$55.80	$82.68
1 Laborer	49.00	392.00	72.55	580.40		
1 Equip. Oper. (medium)	65.00	520.00	96.40	771.20		
1 Hydro Excavator, 12 C.Y.		1458.21		1604.03	72.91	80.20
20 L.H., Daily Totals		$2574.21		$3257.63	$128.71	$162.88
Crew B-7	Hr.	Daily	Hr.	Daily	Bare Costs	Incl. O&P
1 Labor Foreman (outside)	$51.00	$408.00	$75.50	$604.00	$52.00	$77.02
4 Laborers	49.00	1568.00	72.55	2321.60		
1 Equip. Oper. (medium)	65.00	520.00	96.40	771.20		
1 Brush Chipper, 12", 130 H.P.		507.44		558.18		
1 Crawler Loader, 3 C.Y.		1313.18		1444.50		
2 Chain Saws, Gas, 36" Long		110.97		122.06	40.24	44.27
48 L.H., Daily Totals		$4427.59		$5821.55	$92.24	$121.28
Crew B-7A	Hr.	Daily	Hr.	Daily	Bare Costs	Incl. O&P
2 Laborers	$49.00	$784.00	$72.55	$1160.80	$53.33	$79.02
1 Equip. Oper. (light)	62.00	496.00	91.95	735.60		
1 Rake w/Tractor		227.75		250.53		
2 Chain Saws, Gas, 18"		151.70		166.87	15.81	17.39
24 L.H., Daily Totals		$1659.46		$2313.80	$69.14	$96.41
Crew B-7B	Hr.	Daily	Hr.	Daily	Bare Costs	Incl. O&P
1 Labor Foreman (outside)	$51.00	$408.00	$75.50	$604.00	$52.75	$78.17
4 Laborers	49.00	1568.00	72.55	2321.60		
1 Equip. Oper. (medium)	65.00	520.00	96.40	771.20		
1 Truck Driver (heavy)	57.25	458.00	85.10	680.80		
1 Brush Chipper, 12", 130 H.P.		507.44		558.18		
1 Crawler Loader, 3 C.Y.		1313.18		1444.50		
2 Chain Saws, Gas, 36" Long		110.97		122.06		
1 Dump Truck, 8 C.Y., 220 H.P.		506.30		556.93	43.53	47.89
56 L.H., Daily Totals		$5391.89		$7059.28	$96.28	$126.06
Crew B-7C	Hr.	Daily	Hr.	Daily	Bare Costs	Incl. O&P
1 Labor Foreman (outside)	$51.00	$408.00	$75.50	$604.00	$52.75	$78.17
4 Laborers	49.00	1568.00	72.55	2321.60		
1 Equip. Oper. (medium)	65.00	520.00	96.40	771.20		
1 Truck Driver (heavy)	57.25	458.00	85.10	680.80		
1 Brush Chipper, 12", 130 H.P.		507.44		558.18		
1 Crawler Loader, 3 C.Y.		1313.18		1444.50		
2 Chain Saws, Gas, 36" Long		110.97		122.06		
1 Dump Truck, 12 C.Y., 400 H.P.		987.07		1085.78	52.12	57.33
56 L.H., Daily Totals		$5872.66		$7588.13	$104.87	$135.50

Crew No.		Bare Costs		Incl. Subs O&P		Cost Per Labor-Hour	
Crew B-8	Hr.	Daily	Hr.	Daily	Bare Costs	Incl. O&P
1 Labor Foreman (outside)	$51.00	$408.00	$75.50	$604.00	$56.49	$83.78
2 Laborers	49.00	784.00	72.55	1160.80		
2 Equip. Oper. (medium)	65.00	1040.00	96.40	1542.40		
1 Equip. Oper. (oiler)	58.40	467.20	86.60	692.80		
2 Truck Drivers (heavy)	57.25	916.00	85.10	1361.60		
1 Hyd. Crane, 25 Ton		2335.01		2568.51		
1 Crawler Loader, 3 C.Y.		1313.18		1444.50		
2 Dump Trucks, 12 C.Y., 400 H.P.		1974.15		2171.56	87.85	96.63
64 L.H., Daily Totals		$9237.54		$11546.17	$144.34	$180.41
Crew B-9	Hr.	Daily	Hr.	Daily	Bare Costs	Incl. O&P
1 Labor Foreman (outside)	$51.00	$408.00	$75.50	$604.00	$49.40	$73.14
4 Laborers	49.00	1568.00	72.55	2321.60		
1 Air Compressor, 250 cfm		226.90		249.59		
2 Breakers, Pavement, 60 lb.		79.92		87.92		
2 -50' Air Hoses, 1.5"		47.13		51.84	8.85	9.73
40 L.H., Daily Totals		$2329.95		$3314.95	$58.25	$82.87
Crew B-9A	Hr.	Daily	Hr.	Daily	Bare Costs	Incl. O&P
2 Laborers	$49.00	$784.00	$72.55	$1160.80	$51.75	$76.73
1 Truck Driver (heavy)	57.25	458.00	85.10	680.80		
1 Water Tank Trailer, 5000 Gal.		176.44		194.08		
1 Truck Tractor, 220 H.P.		357.02		392.72		
2 -50' Discharge Hoses, 3"		10.57		11.63	22.67	24.93
24 L.H., Daily Totals		$1786.02		$2440.03	$74.42	$101.67
Crew B-9B	Hr.	Daily	Hr.	Daily	Bare Costs	Incl. O&P
2 Laborers	$49.00	$784.00	$72.55	$1160.80	$51.75	$76.73
1 Truck Driver (heavy)	57.25	458.00	85.10	680.80		
2 -50' Discharge Hoses, 3"		10.57		11.63		
1 Water Tank Trailer, 5000 Gal.		176.44		194.08		
1 Truck Tractor, 220 H.P.		357.02		392.72		
1 Pressure Washer		135.59		149.14	28.32	31.15
24 L.H., Daily Totals		$1921.61		$2589.17	$80.07	$107.88
Crew B-9D	Hr.	Daily	Hr.	Daily	Bare Costs	Incl. O&P
1 Labor Foreman (outside)	$51.00	$408.00	$75.50	$604.00	$49.40	$73.14
4 Common Laborers	49.00	1568.00	72.55	2321.60		
1 Air Compressor, 250 cfm		226.90		249.59		
2 -50' Air Hoses, 1.5"		47.13		51.84		
2 Air Powered Tampers		107.08		117.78	9.53	10.48
40 L.H., Daily Totals		$2357.10		$3344.81	$58.93	$83.62
Crew B-9E	Hr.	Daily	Hr.	Daily	Bare Costs	Incl. O&P
1 Cement Finisher	$56.80	$454.40	$82.80	$662.40	$52.90	$77.67
1 Laborer	49.00	392.00	72.55	580.40		
1 Chip. Hammers, 12 Lb., Elec.		29.42		32.37	1.84	2.02
16 L.H., Daily Totals		$875.82		$1275.17	$54.74	$79.70
Crew B-10	Hr.	Daily	Hr.	Daily	Bare Costs	Incl. O&P
1 Equip. Oper. (medium)	$65.00	$520.00	$96.40	$771.20	$59.67	$88.45
.5 Laborer	49.00	196.00	72.55	290.20		
12 L.H., Daily Totals		$716.00		$1061.40	$59.67	$88.45
Crew B-10A	Hr.	Daily	Hr.	Daily	Bare Costs	Incl. O&P
1 Equip. Oper. (medium)	$65.00	$520.00	$96.40	$771.20	$59.67	$88.45
.5 Laborer	49.00	196.00	72.55	290.20		
1 Roller, 2-Drum, W.B., 7.5 H.P.		175.19		192.71	14.60	16.06
12 L.H., Daily Totals		$891.19		$1254.11	$74.27	$104.51

Crews - Standard

Crew No.	Bare Costs		Incl. Subs O&P		Cost Per Labor-Hour	

Crew B-10B	Hr.	Daily	Hr.	Daily	Bare Costs	Incl. O&P
1 Equip. Oper. (medium)	$65.00	$520.00	$96.40	$771.20	$59.67	$88.45
.5 Laborer	49.00	196.00	72.55	290.20		
1 Dozer, 200 H.P.		1443.21		1587.53	120.27	132.29
12 L.H., Daily Totals		$2159.21		$2648.93	$179.93	$220.74

Crew B-10C	Hr.	Daily	Hr.	Daily	Bare Costs	Incl. O&P
1 Equip. Oper. (medium)	$65.00	$520.00	$96.40	$771.20	$59.67	$88.45
.5 Laborer	49.00	196.00	72.55	290.20		
1 Dozer, 200 H.P.		1443.21		1587.53		
1 Vibratory Roller, Towed, 23 Ton		696.00		765.60	178.27	196.09
12 L.H., Daily Totals		$2855.22		$3414.54	$237.93	$284.54

Crew B-10D	Hr.	Daily	Hr.	Daily	Bare Costs	Incl. O&P
1 Equip. Oper. (medium)	$65.00	$520.00	$96.40	$771.20	$59.67	$88.45
.5 Laborer	49.00	196.00	72.55	290.20		
1 Dozer, 200 H.P.		1443.21		1587.53		
1 Sheepsft. Roller, Towed		516.41		568.05	163.30	179.63
12 L.H., Daily Totals		$2675.62		$3216.99	$222.97	$268.08

Crew B-10E	Hr.	Daily	Hr.	Daily	Bare Costs	Incl. O&P
1 Equip. Oper. (medium)	$65.00	$520.00	$96.40	$771.20	$59.67	$88.45
.5 Laborer	49.00	196.00	72.55	290.20		
1 Tandem Roller, 5 Ton		264.37		290.81	22.03	24.23
12 L.H., Daily Totals		$980.37		$1352.21	$81.70	$112.68

Crew B-10F	Hr.	Daily	Hr.	Daily	Bare Costs	Incl. O&P
1 Equip. Oper. (medium)	$65.00	$520.00	$96.40	$771.20	$59.67	$88.45
.5 Laborer	49.00	196.00	72.55	290.20		
1 Tandem Roller, 10 Ton		319.84		351.82	26.65	29.32
12 L.H., Daily Totals		$1035.84		$1413.22	$86.32	$117.77

Crew B-10G	Hr.	Daily	Hr.	Daily	Bare Costs	Incl. O&P
1 Equip. Oper. (medium)	$65.00	$520.00	$96.40	$771.20	$59.67	$88.45
.5 Laborer	49.00	196.00	72.55	290.20		
1 Sheepsfoot Roller, 240 H.P.		807.49		888.24	67.29	74.02
12 L.H., Daily Totals		$1523.49		$1949.64	$126.96	$162.47

Crew B-10H	Hr.	Daily	Hr.	Daily	Bare Costs	Incl. O&P
1 Equip. Oper. (medium)	$65.00	$520.00	$96.40	$771.20	$59.67	$88.45
.5 Laborer	49.00	196.00	72.55	290.20		
1 Diaphragm Water Pump, 2"		65.04		71.55		
1 -20' Suction Hose, 2"		4.61		5.07		
2 -50' Discharge Hoses, 2"		9.05		9.96	6.56	7.21
12 L.H., Daily Totals		$794.70		$1147.97	$66.23	$95.66

Crew B-10I	Hr.	Daily	Hr.	Daily	Bare Costs	Incl. O&P
1 Equip. Oper. (medium)	$65.00	$520.00	$96.40	$771.20	$59.67	$88.45
.5 Laborer	49.00	196.00	72.55	290.20		
1 Diaphragm Water Pump, 4"		157.09		172.80		
1 -20' Suction Hose, 4"		19.59		21.55		
2 -50' Discharge Hoses, 4"		29.12		32.03	17.15	18.87
12 L.H., Daily Totals		$921.80		$1287.78	$76.82	$107.32

Crew B-10J	Hr.	Daily	Hr.	Daily	Bare Costs	Incl. O&P
1 Equip. Oper. (medium)	$65.00	$520.00	$96.40	$771.20	$59.67	$88.45
.5 Laborer	49.00	196.00	72.55	290.20		
1 Centrifugal Water Pump, 3"		86.40		95.04		
1 -20' Suction Hose, 3"		9.86		10.84		
2 -50' Discharge Hoses, 3"		10.57		11.63	8.90	9.79
12 L.H., Daily Totals		$822.83		$1178.91	$68.57	$98.24

Crew B-10K	Hr.	Daily	Hr.	Daily	Bare Costs	Incl. O&P
1 Equip. Oper. (medium)	$65.00	$520.00	$96.40	$771.20	$59.67	$88.45
.5 Laborer	49.00	196.00	72.55	290.20		
1 Centr. Water Pump, 6"		410.89		451.98		
1 -20' Suction Hose, 6"		29.00		31.90		
2 -50' Discharge Hoses, 6"		41.25		45.38	40.09	44.10
12 L.H., Daily Totals		$1197.14		$1590.65	$99.76	$132.55

Crew B-10L	Hr.	Daily	Hr.	Daily	Bare Costs	Incl. O&P
1 Equip. Oper. (medium)	$65.00	$520.00	$96.40	$771.20	$59.67	$88.45
.5 Laborer	49.00	196.00	72.55	290.20		
1 Dozer, 80 H.P.		634.87		698.36	52.91	58.20
12 L.H., Daily Totals		$1350.87		$1759.76	$112.57	$146.65

Crew B-10M	Hr.	Daily	Hr.	Daily	Bare Costs	Incl. O&P
1 Equip. Oper. (medium)	$65.00	$520.00	$96.40	$771.20	$59.67	$88.45
.5 Laborer	49.00	196.00	72.55	290.20		
1 Dozer, 300 H.P.		2393.85		2633.23	199.49	219.44
12 L.H., Daily Totals		$3109.85		$3694.63	$259.15	$307.89

Crew B-10N	Hr.	Daily	Hr.	Daily	Bare Costs	Incl. O&P
1 Equip. Oper. (medium)	$65.00	$520.00	$96.40	$771.20	$59.67	$88.45
.5 Laborer	49.00	196.00	72.55	290.20		
1 F.E. Loader, T.M., 1.5 C.Y.		562.32		618.55	46.86	51.55
12 L.H., Daily Totals		$1278.32		$1679.95	$106.53	$140.00

Crew B-10O	Hr.	Daily	Hr.	Daily	Bare Costs	Incl. O&P
1 Equip. Oper. (medium)	$65.00	$520.00	$96.40	$771.20	$59.67	$88.45
.5 Laborer	49.00	196.00	72.55	290.20		
1 F.E. Loader, T.M., 2.25 C.Y.		1179.94		1297.93	98.33	108.16
12 L.H., Daily Totals		$1895.94		$2359.33	$157.99	$196.61

Crew B-10P	Hr.	Daily	Hr.	Daily	Bare Costs	Incl. O&P
1 Equip. Oper. (medium)	$65.00	$520.00	$96.40	$771.20	$59.67	$88.45
.5 Laborer	49.00	196.00	72.55	290.20		
1 Crawler Loader, 3 C.Y.		1313.18		1444.50	109.43	120.38
12 L.H., Daily Totals		$2029.18		$2505.90	$169.10	$208.83

Crew B-10Q	Hr.	Daily	Hr.	Daily	Bare Costs	Incl. O&P
1 Equip. Oper. (medium)	$65.00	$520.00	$96.40	$771.20	$59.67	$88.45
.5 Laborer	49.00	196.00	72.55	290.20		
1 Crawler Loader, 4 C.Y.		1859.78		2045.75	154.98	170.48
12 L.H., Daily Totals		$2575.78		$3107.15	$214.65	$258.93

Crew B-10R	Hr.	Daily	Hr.	Daily	Bare Costs	Incl. O&P
1 Equip. Oper. (medium)	$65.00	$520.00	$96.40	$771.20	$59.67	$88.45
.5 Laborer	49.00	196.00	72.55	290.20		
1 F.E. Loader, W.M., 1 C.Y.		368.36		405.20	30.70	33.77
12 L.H., Daily Totals		$1084.36		$1466.60	$90.36	$122.22

Crew B-10S	Hr.	Daily	Hr.	Daily	Bare Costs	Incl. O&P
1 Equip. Oper. (medium)	$65.00	$520.00	$96.40	$771.20	$59.67	$88.45
.5 Laborer	49.00	196.00	72.55	290.20		
1 F.E. Loader, W.M., 1.5 C.Y.		582.76		641.03	48.56	53.42
12 L.H., Daily Totals		$1298.76		$1702.43	$108.23	$141.87

Crew B-10T	Hr.	Daily	Hr.	Daily	Bare Costs	Incl. O&P
1 Equip. Oper. (medium)	$65.00	$520.00	$96.40	$771.20	$59.67	$88.45
.5 Laborer	49.00	196.00	72.55	290.20		
1 F.E. Loader, W.M., 2.5 C.Y.		815.12		896.63	67.93	74.72
12 L.H., Daily Totals		$1531.12		$1958.03	$127.59	$163.17

Crews - Standard

Crew No.	Bare Costs		Incl. Subs O&P		Cost Per Labor-Hour	
Crew B-10U	Hr.	Daily	Hr.	Daily	Bare Costs	Incl. O&P
1 Equip. Oper. (medium)	$65.00	$520.00	$96.40	$771.20	$59.67	$88.45
.5 Laborer	49.00	196.00	72.55	290.20		
1 F.E. Loader, W.M., 5.5 C.Y.		1235.36		1358.90	102.95	113.24
12 L.H., Daily Totals		$1951.36		$2420.30	$162.61	$201.69
Crew B-10V	Hr.	Daily	Hr.	Daily	Bare Costs	Incl. O&P
1 Equip. Oper. (medium)	$65.00	$520.00	$96.40	$771.20	$59.67	$88.45
.5 Laborer	49.00	196.00	72.55	290.20		
1 Dozer, 700 H.P.		4734.34		5207.77	394.53	433.98
12 L.H., Daily Totals		$5450.34		$6269.17	$454.20	$522.43
Crew B-10W	Hr.	Daily	Hr.	Daily	Bare Costs	Incl. O&P
1 Equip. Oper. (medium)	$65.00	$520.00	$96.40	$771.20	$59.67	$88.45
.5 Laborer	49.00	196.00	72.55	290.20		
1 Dozer, 105 H.P.		790.84		869.92	65.90	72.49
12 L.H., Daily Totals		$1506.84		$1931.32	$125.57	$160.94
Crew B-10X	Hr.	Daily	Hr.	Daily	Bare Costs	Incl. O&P
1 Equip. Oper. (medium)	$65.00	$520.00	$96.40	$771.20	$59.67	$88.45
.5 Laborer	49.00	196.00	72.55	290.20		
1 Dozer, 410 H.P.		2969.84		3266.82	247.49	272.24
12 L.H., Daily Totals		$3685.84		$4328.22	$307.15	$360.69
Crew B-10Y	Hr.	Daily	Hr.	Daily	Bare Costs	Incl. O&P
1 Equip. Oper. (medium)	$65.00	$520.00	$96.40	$771.20	$59.67	$88.45
.5 Laborer	49.00	196.00	72.55	290.20		
1 Vibr. Roller, Towed, 12 Ton		364.55		401.00	30.38	33.42
12 L.H., Daily Totals		$1080.55		$1462.40	$90.05	$121.87
Crew B-11A	Hr.	Daily	Hr.	Daily	Bare Costs	Incl. O&P
1 Equipment Oper. (med.)	$65.00	$520.00	$96.40	$771.20	$57.00	$84.47
1 Laborer	49.00	392.00	72.55	580.40		
1 Dozer, 200 H.P.		1443.21		1587.53	90.20	99.22
16 L.H., Daily Totals		$2355.21		$2939.13	$147.20	$183.70
Crew B-11B	Hr.	Daily	Hr.	Daily	Bare Costs	Incl. O&P
1 Equipment Oper. (light)	$62.00	$496.00	$91.95	$735.60	$55.50	$82.25
1 Laborer	49.00	392.00	72.55	580.40		
1 Air Powered Tamper		53.54		58.89		
1 Air Compressor, 365 cfm		344.62		379.09		
2 -50' Air Hoses, 1.5"		47.13		51.84	27.83	30.61
16 L.H., Daily Totals		$1333.29		$1805.82	$83.33	$112.86
Crew B-11C	Hr.	Daily	Hr.	Daily	Bare Costs	Incl. O&P
1 Equipment Oper. (med.)	$65.00	$520.00	$96.40	$771.20	$57.00	$84.47
1 Laborer	49.00	392.00	72.55	580.40		
1 Backhoe Loader, 48 H.P.		291.00		320.10	18.19	20.01
16 L.H., Daily Totals		$1203.00		$1671.70	$75.19	$104.48
Crew B-11J	Hr.	Daily	Hr.	Daily	Bare Costs	Incl. O&P
1 Equipment Oper. (med.)	$65.00	$520.00	$96.40	$771.20	$57.00	$84.47
1 Laborer	49.00	392.00	72.55	580.40		
1 Grader, 30,000 Lbs.		1115.47		1227.02		
1 Ripper, Beam & 1 Shank		104.87		115.36	76.27	83.90
16 L.H., Daily Totals		$2132.34		$2693.97	$133.27	$168.37

Crew No.	Bare Costs		Incl. Subs O&P		Cost Per Labor-Hour	
Crew B-11K	Hr.	Daily	Hr.	Daily	Bare Costs	Incl. O&P
1 Equipment Oper. (med.)	$65.00	$520.00	$96.40	$771.20	$57.00	$84.47
1 Laborer	49.00	392.00	72.55	580.40		
1 Trencher, Chain Type, 8' D		2168.88		2385.77	135.56	149.11
16 L.H., Daily Totals		$3080.88		$3737.37	$192.56	$233.59
Crew B-11L	Hr.	Daily	Hr.	Daily	Bare Costs	Incl. O&P
1 Equipment Oper. (med.)	$65.00	$520.00	$96.40	$771.20	$57.00	$84.47
1 Laborer	49.00	392.00	72.55	580.40		
1 Grader, 30,000 Lbs.		1115.47		1227.02	69.72	76.69
16 L.H., Daily Totals		$2027.47		$2578.62	$126.72	$161.16
Crew B-11M	Hr.	Daily	Hr.	Daily	Bare Costs	Incl. O&P
1 Equipment Oper. (med.)	$65.00	$520.00	$96.40	$771.20	$57.00	$84.47
1 Laborer	49.00	392.00	72.55	580.40		
1 Backhoe Loader, 80 H.P.		455.51		501.06	28.47	31.32
16 L.H., Daily Totals		$1367.51		$1852.66	$85.47	$115.79
Crew B-11N	Hr.	Daily	Hr.	Daily	Bare Costs	Incl. O&P
1 Labor Foreman (outside)	$51.00	$408.00	$75.50	$604.00	$58.28	$86.54
2 Equipment Operators (med.)	65.00	1040.00	96.40	1542.40		
6 Truck Drivers (heavy)	57.25	2748.00	85.10	4084.80		
1 F.E. Loader, W.M., 5.5 C.Y.		1235.36		1358.90		
1 Dozer, 410 H.P.		2969.84		3266.82		
6 Dump Trucks, Off Hwy., 50 Ton		13862.06		15248.27	250.93	276.03
72 L.H., Daily Totals		$22263.27		$26105.19	$309.21	$362.57
Crew B-11Q	Hr.	Daily	Hr.	Daily	Bare Costs	Incl. O&P
1 Equipment Operator (med.)	$65.00	$520.00	$96.40	$771.20	$59.67	$88.45
.5 Laborer	49.00	196.00	72.55	290.20		
1 Dozer, 140 H.P.		793.32		872.66	66.11	72.72
12 L.H., Daily Totals		$1509.32		$1934.06	$125.78	$161.17
Crew B-11R	Hr.	Daily	Hr.	Daily	Bare Costs	Incl. O&P
1 Equipment Operator (med.)	$65.00	$520.00	$96.40	$771.20	$59.67	$88.45
.5 Laborer	49.00	196.00	72.55	290.20		
1 Dozer, 200 H.P.		1443.21		1587.53	120.27	132.29
12 L.H., Daily Totals		$2159.21		$2648.93	$179.93	$220.74
Crew B-11S	Hr.	Daily	Hr.	Daily	Bare Costs	Incl. O&P
1 Equipment Operator (med.)	$65.00	$520.00	$96.40	$771.20	$59.67	$88.45
.5 Laborer	49.00	196.00	72.55	290.20		
1 Dozer, 300 H.P.		2393.85		2633.23		
1 Ripper, Beam & 1 Shank		104.87		115.36	208.23	229.05
12 L.H., Daily Totals		$3214.72		$3809.99	$267.89	$317.50
Crew B-11T	Hr.	Daily	Hr.	Daily	Bare Costs	Incl. O&P
1 Equipment Operator (med.)	$65.00	$520.00	$96.40	$771.20	$59.67	$88.45
.5 Laborer	49.00	196.00	72.55	290.20		
1 Dozer, 410 H.P.		2969.84		3266.82		
1 Ripper, Beam & 2 Shanks		160.60		176.66	260.87	286.96
12 L.H., Daily Totals		$3846.44		$4504.88	$320.54	$375.41
Crew B-11U	Hr.	Daily	Hr.	Daily	Bare Costs	Incl. O&P
1 Equipment Operator (med.)	$65.00	$520.00	$96.40	$771.20	$59.67	$88.45
.5 Laborer	49.00	196.00	72.55	290.20		
1 Dozer, 520 H.P.		3524.54		3876.99	293.71	323.08
12 L.H., Daily Totals		$4240.54		$4938.39	$353.38	$411.53

Crews - Standard

Crew No.	Bare Costs		Incl. Subs O&P		Cost Per Labor-Hour	
	Hr.	Daily	Hr.	Daily	Bare Costs	Incl. O&P
Crew B-11V						
3 Laborers	$49.00	$1176.00	$72.55	$1741.20	$49.00	$72.55
1 Roller, 2-Drum, W.B., 7.5 H.P.		175.19		192.71	7.30	8.03
24 L.H., Daily Totals		$1351.19		$1933.91	$56.30	$80.58
Crew B-11W	Hr.	Daily	Hr.	Daily	Bare Costs	Incl. O&P
1 Equipment Operator (med.)	$65.00	$520.00	$96.40	$771.20	$57.21	$85.00
1 Common Laborer	49.00	392.00	72.55	580.40		
10 Truck Drivers (heavy)	57.25	4580.00	85.10	6808.00		
1 Dozer, 200 H.P.		1443.21		1587.53		
1 Vibratory Roller, Towed, 23 Ton		696.00		765.60		
10 Dump Trucks, 8 C.Y., 220 H.P.		5062.99		5569.29	75.02	82.53
96 L.H., Daily Totals		$12694.21		$16082.03	$132.23	$167.52
Crew B-11Y	Hr.	Daily	Hr.	Daily	Bare Costs	Incl. O&P
1 Labor Foreman (outside)	$51.00	$408.00	$75.50	$604.00	$54.56	$80.83
5 Common Laborers	49.00	1960.00	72.55	2902.00		
3 Equipment Operators (med.)	65.00	1560.00	96.40	2313.60		
1 Dozer, 80 H.P.		634.87		698.36		
2 Rollers, 2-Drum, W.B., 7.5 H.P.		350.39		385.43		
4 Vibrating Plates, Gas, 21"		611.21		672.33	22.17	24.39
72 L.H., Daily Totals		$5524.47		$7575.71	$76.73	$105.22
Crew B-12A	Hr.	Daily	Hr.	Daily	Bare Costs	Incl. O&P
1 Equip. Oper. (crane)	$68.60	$548.80	$101.75	$814.00	$58.80	$87.15
1 Laborer	49.00	392.00	72.55	580.40		
1 Hyd. Excavator, 1 C.Y.		970.66		1067.72	60.67	66.73
16 L.H., Daily Totals		$1911.46		$2462.12	$119.47	$153.88
Crew B-12B	Hr.	Daily	Hr.	Daily	Bare Costs	Incl. O&P
1 Equip. Oper. (crane)	$68.60	$548.80	$101.75	$814.00	$58.80	$87.15
1 Laborer	49.00	392.00	72.55	580.40		
1 Hyd. Excavator, 1.5 C.Y.		1193.85		1313.24	74.62	82.08
16 L.H., Daily Totals		$2134.65		$2707.64	$133.42	$169.23
Crew B-12C	Hr.	Daily	Hr.	Daily	Bare Costs	Incl. O&P
1 Equip. Oper. (crane)	$68.60	$548.80	$101.75	$814.00	$58.80	$87.15
1 Laborer	49.00	392.00	72.55	580.40		
1 Hyd. Excavator, 2 C.Y.		1463.59		1609.95	91.47	100.62
16 L.H., Daily Totals		$2404.39		$3004.35	$150.27	$187.77
Crew B-12D	Hr.	Daily	Hr.	Daily	Bare Costs	Incl. O&P
1 Equip. Oper. (crane)	$68.60	$548.80	$101.75	$814.00	$58.80	$87.15
1 Laborer	49.00	392.00	72.55	580.40		
1 Hyd. Excavator, 3.5 C.Y.		2152.24		2367.46	134.51	147.97
16 L.H., Daily Totals		$3093.04		$3761.86	$193.31	$235.12
Crew B-12E	Hr.	Daily	Hr.	Daily	Bare Costs	Incl. O&P
1 Equip. Oper. (crane)	$68.60	$548.80	$101.75	$814.00	$58.80	$87.15
1 Laborer	49.00	392.00	72.55	580.40		
1 Hyd. Excavator, .5 C.Y.		625.49		688.03	39.09	43.00
16 L.H., Daily Totals		$1566.29		$2082.43	$97.89	$130.15
Crew B-12F	Hr.	Daily	Hr.	Daily	Bare Costs	Incl. O&P
1 Equip. Oper. (crane)	$68.60	$548.80	$101.75	$814.00	$58.80	$87.15
1 Laborer	49.00	392.00	72.55	580.40		
1 Hyd. Excavator, .75 C.Y.		887.82		976.60	55.49	61.04
16 L.H., Daily Totals		$1828.62		$2371.00	$114.29	$148.19
Crew B-12G	Hr.	Daily	Hr.	Daily	Bare Costs	Incl. O&P
1 Equip. Oper. (crane)	$68.60	$548.80	$101.75	$814.00	$58.80	$87.15
1 Laborer	49.00	392.00	72.55	580.40		
1 Crawler Crane, 15 Ton		937.18		1030.89		
1 Clamshell Bucket, .5 C.Y.		38.86		42.75	61.00	67.10
16 L.H., Daily Totals		$1916.84		$2468.04	$119.80	$154.25
Crew B-12H	Hr.	Daily	Hr.	Daily	Bare Costs	Incl. O&P
1 Equip. Oper. (crane)	$68.60	$548.80	$101.75	$814.00	$58.80	$87.15
1 Laborer	49.00	392.00	72.55	580.40		
1 Crawler Crane, 25 Ton		1332.93		1466.22		
1 Clamshell Bucket, 1 C.Y.		48.81		53.69	86.36	94.99
16 L.H., Daily Totals		$2322.53		$2914.31	$145.16	$182.14
Crew B-12I	Hr.	Daily	Hr.	Daily	Bare Costs	Incl. O&P
1 Equip. Oper. (crane)	$68.60	$548.80	$101.75	$814.00	$58.80	$87.15
1 Laborer	49.00	392.00	72.55	580.40		
1 Crawler Crane, 20 Ton		1171.12		1288.23		
1 Dragline Bucket, .75 C.Y.		29.64		32.61	75.05	82.55
16 L.H., Daily Totals		$2141.56		$2715.23	$133.85	$169.70
Crew B-12J	Hr.	Daily	Hr.	Daily	Bare Costs	Incl. O&P
1 Equip. Oper. (crane)	$68.60	$548.80	$101.75	$814.00	$58.80	$87.15
1 Laborer	49.00	392.00	72.55	580.40		
1 Gradall, 5/8 C.Y.		920.64		1012.70	57.54	63.29
16 L.H., Daily Totals		$1861.44		$2407.10	$116.34	$150.44
Crew B-12K	Hr.	Daily	Hr.	Daily	Bare Costs	Incl. O&P
1 Equip. Oper. (crane)	$68.60	$548.80	$101.75	$814.00	$58.80	$87.15
1 Laborer	49.00	392.00	72.55	580.40		
1 Gradall, 3 Ton, 1 C.Y.		1584.74		1743.21	99.05	108.95
16 L.H., Daily Totals		$2525.54		$3137.61	$157.85	$196.10
Crew B-12L	Hr.	Daily	Hr.	Daily	Bare Costs	Incl. O&P
1 Equip. Oper. (crane)	$68.60	$548.80	$101.75	$814.00	$58.80	$87.15
1 Laborer	49.00	392.00	72.55	580.40		
1 Crawler Crane, 15 Ton		937.18		1030.89		
1 F.E. Attachment, .5 C.Y.		75.55		83.10	63.30	69.62
16 L.H., Daily Totals		$1953.52		$2508.39	$122.10	$156.77
Crew B-12M	Hr.	Daily	Hr.	Daily	Bare Costs	Incl. O&P
1 Equip. Oper. (crane)	$68.60	$548.80	$101.75	$814.00	$58.80	$87.15
1 Laborer	49.00	392.00	72.55	580.40		
1 Crawler Crane, 20 Ton		1171.12		1288.23		
1 F.E. Attachment, .75 C.Y.		81.47		89.62	78.29	86.12
16 L.H., Daily Totals		$2193.39		$2772.25	$137.09	$173.27
Crew B-12N	Hr.	Daily	Hr.	Daily	Bare Costs	Incl. O&P
1 Equip. Oper. (crane)	$68.60	$548.80	$101.75	$814.00	$58.80	$87.15
1 Laborer	49.00	392.00	72.55	580.40		
1 Crawler Crane, 25 Ton		1332.93		1466.22		
1 F.E. Attachment, 1 C.Y.		89.26		98.19	88.89	97.78
16 L.H., Daily Totals		$2362.99		$2958.81	$147.69	$184.93
Crew B-12O	Hr.	Daily	Hr.	Daily	Bare Costs	Incl. O&P
1 Equip. Oper. (crane)	$68.60	$548.80	$101.75	$814.00	$58.80	$87.15
1 Laborer	49.00	392.00	72.55	580.40		
1 Crawler Crane, 40 Ton		1423.92		1566.31		
1 F.E. Attachment, 1.5 C.Y.		101.32		111.45	95.33	104.86
16 L.H., Daily Totals		$2466.04		$3072.16	$154.13	$192.01

Crews - Standard

Crew No.		Bare Costs		Incl. Subs O&P		Cost Per Labor-Hour	
Crew B-12P	Hr.	Daily	Hr.	Daily	Bare Costs	Incl. O&P
1 Equip. Oper. (crane)	$68.60	$548.80	$101.75	$814.00	$58.80	$87.15
1 Laborer	49.00	392.00	72.55	580.40		
1 Crawler Crane, 40 Ton		1423.92		1566.31		
1 Dragline Bucket, 1.5 C.Y.		41.56		45.71	91.59	100.75
16 L.H., Daily Totals		$2406.28		$3006.42	$150.39	$187.90
Crew B-12Q	Hr.	Daily	Hr.	Daily	Bare Costs	Incl. O&P
1 Equip. Oper. (crane)	$68.60	$548.80	$101.75	$814.00	$58.80	$87.15
1 Laborer	49.00	392.00	72.55	580.40		
1 Hyd. Excavator, 5/8 C.Y.		772.58		849.84	48.29	53.12
16 L.H., Daily Totals		$1713.38		$2244.24	$107.09	$140.26
Crew B-12S	Hr.	Daily	Hr.	Daily	Bare Costs	Incl. O&P
1 Equip. Oper. (crane)	$68.60	$548.80	$101.75	$814.00	$58.80	$87.15
1 Laborer	49.00	392.00	72.55	580.40		
1 Hyd. Excavator, 2.5 C.Y.		1800.54		1980.59	112.53	123.79
16 L.H., Daily Totals		$2741.34		$3374.99	$171.33	$210.94
Crew B-12T	Hr.	Daily	Hr.	Daily	Bare Costs	Incl. O&P
1 Equip. Oper. (crane)	$68.60	$548.80	$101.75	$814.00	$58.80	$87.15
1 Laborer	49.00	392.00	72.55	580.40		
1 Crawler Crane, 75 Ton		2275.15		2502.66		
1 F.E. Attachment, 3 C.Y.		131.99		145.19	150.45	165.49
16 L.H., Daily Totals		$3347.94		$4042.25	$209.25	$252.64
Crew B-12V	Hr.	Daily	Hr.	Daily	Bare Costs	Incl. O&P
1 Equip. Oper. (crane)	$68.60	$548.80	$101.75	$814.00	$58.80	$87.15
1 Laborer	49.00	392.00	72.55	580.40		
1 Crawler Crane, 75 Ton		2275.15		2502.66		
1 Dragline Bucket, 3 C.Y.		53.93		59.32	145.57	160.12
16 L.H., Daily Totals		$3269.88		$3956.39	$204.37	$247.27
Crew B-12Y	Hr.	Daily	Hr.	Daily	Bare Costs	Incl. O&P
1 Equip. Oper. (crane)	$68.60	$548.80	$101.75	$814.00	$55.53	$82.28
2 Laborers	49.00	784.00	72.55	1160.80		
1 Hyd. Excavator, 3.5 C.Y.		2152.24		2367.46	89.68	98.64
24 L.H., Daily Totals		$3485.04		$4342.26	$145.21	$180.93
Crew B-12Z	Hr.	Daily	Hr.	Daily	Bare Costs	Incl. O&P
1 Equip. Oper. (crane)	$68.60	$548.80	$101.75	$814.00	$55.53	$82.28
2 Laborers	49.00	784.00	72.55	1160.80		
1 Hyd. Excavator, 2.5 C.Y.		1800.54		1980.59	75.02	82.52
24 L.H., Daily Totals		$3133.34		$3955.39	$130.56	$164.81
Crew B-13	Hr.	Daily	Hr.	Daily	Bare Costs	Incl. O&P
1 Labor Foreman (outside)	$51.00	$408.00	$75.50	$604.00	$53.43	$79.15
4 Laborers	49.00	1568.00	72.55	2321.60		
1 Equip. Oper. (crane)	68.60	548.80	101.75	814.00		
1 Equip. Oper. (oiler)	58.40	467.20	86.60	692.80		
1 Hyd. Crane, 25 Ton		2335.01		2568.51	41.70	45.87
56 L.H., Daily Totals		$5327.01		$7000.91	$95.13	$125.02

Crew No.		Bare Costs		Incl. Subs O&P		Cost Per Labor-Hour	
Crew B-13A	Hr.	Daily	Hr.	Daily	Bare Costs	Incl. O&P
1 Labor Foreman (outside)	$51.00	$408.00	$75.50	$604.00	$56.21	$83.37
2 Laborers	49.00	784.00	72.55	1160.80		
2 Equipment Operators (med.)	65.00	1040.00	96.40	1542.40		
2 Truck Drivers (heavy)	57.25	916.00	85.10	1361.60		
1 Crawler Crane, 75 Ton		2275.15		2502.66		
1 Crawler Loader, 4 C.Y.		1859.78		2045.75		
2 Dump Trucks, 8 C.Y., 220 H.P.		1012.60		1113.86	91.92	101.11
56 L.H., Daily Totals		$8295.52		$10331.07	$148.13	$184.48
Crew B-13B	Hr.	Daily	Hr.	Daily	Bare Costs	Incl. O&P
1 Labor Foreman (outside)	$51.00	$408.00	$75.50	$604.00	$53.43	$79.15
4 Laborers	49.00	1568.00	72.55	2321.60		
1 Equip. Oper. (crane)	68.60	548.80	101.75	814.00		
1 Equip. Oper. (oiler)	58.40	467.20	86.60	692.80		
1 Hyd. Crane, 55 Ton		2551.41		2806.55	45.56	50.12
56 L.H., Daily Totals		$5543.41		$7238.95	$98.99	$129.27
Crew B-13C	Hr.	Daily	Hr.	Daily	Bare Costs	Incl. O&P
1 Labor Foreman (outside)	$51.00	$408.00	$75.50	$604.00	$53.43	$79.15
4 Laborers	49.00	1568.00	72.55	2321.60		
1 Equip. Oper. (crane)	68.60	548.80	101.75	814.00		
1 Equip. Oper. (oiler)	58.40	467.20	86.60	692.80		
1 Crawler Crane, 100 Ton		1625.12		1787.63	29.02	31.92
56 L.H., Daily Totals		$4617.12		$6220.03	$82.45	$111.07
Crew B-13D	Hr.	Daily	Hr.	Daily	Bare Costs	Incl. O&P
1 Laborer	$49.00	$392.00	$72.55	$580.40	$58.80	$87.15
1 Equip. Oper. (crane)	68.60	548.80	101.75	814.00		
1 Hyd. Excavator, 1 C.Y.		970.66		1067.72		
1 Trench Box		135.66		149.23	69.15	76.06
16 L.H., Daily Totals		$2047.12		$2611.35	$127.95	$163.21
Crew B-13E	Hr.	Daily	Hr.	Daily	Bare Costs	Incl. O&P
1 Laborer	$49.00	$392.00	$72.55	$580.40	$58.80	$87.15
1 Equip. Oper. (crane)	68.60	548.80	101.75	814.00		
1 Hyd. Excavator, 1.5 C.Y.		1193.85		1313.24		
1 Trench Box		135.66		149.23	83.09	91.40
16 L.H., Daily Totals		$2270.32		$2856.87	$141.89	$178.55
Crew B-13F	Hr.	Daily	Hr.	Daily	Bare Costs	Incl. O&P
1 Laborer	$49.00	$392.00	$72.55	$580.40	$58.80	$87.15
1 Equip. Oper. (crane)	68.60	548.80	101.75	814.00		
1 Hyd. Excavator, 3.5 C.Y.		2152.24		2367.46		
1 Trench Box		135.66		149.23	142.99	157.29
16 L.H., Daily Totals		$3228.70		$3911.09	$201.79	$244.44
Crew B-13G	Hr.	Daily	Hr.	Daily	Bare Costs	Incl. O&P
1 Laborer	$49.00	$392.00	$72.55	$580.40	$58.80	$87.15
1 Equip. Oper. (crane)	68.60	548.80	101.75	814.00		
1 Hyd. Excavator, .75 C.Y.		887.82		976.60		
1 Trench Box		135.66		149.23	63.97	70.36
16 L.H., Daily Totals		$1964.29		$2520.24	$122.77	$157.51
Crew B-13H	Hr.	Daily	Hr.	Daily	Bare Costs	Incl. O&P
1 Laborer	$49.00	$392.00	$72.55	$580.40	$58.80	$87.15
1 Equip. Oper. (crane)	68.60	548.80	101.75	814.00		
1 Gradall, 5/8 C.Y.		920.64		1012.70		
1 Trench Box		135.66		149.23	66.02	72.62
16 L.H., Daily Totals		$1997.10		$2556.33	$124.82	$159.77

Crews - Standard

Crew No.	Bare Costs		Incl. Subs O&P		Cost Per Labor-Hour	
Crew B-13I	Hr.	Daily	Hr.	Daily	Bare Costs	Incl. O&P
1 Laborer	$49.00	$392.00	$72.55	$580.40	$58.80	$87.15
1 Equip. Oper. (crane)	68.60	548.80	101.75	814.00		
1 Gradall, 3 Ton, 1 C.Y.		1584.74		1743.21		
1 Trench Box		135.66		149.23	107.53	118.28
16 L.H., Daily Totals		$2661.20		$3286.84	$166.33	$205.43
Crew B-13J	Hr.	Daily	Hr.	Daily	Bare Costs	Incl. O&P
1 Laborer	$49.00	$392.00	$72.55	$580.40	$58.80	$87.15
1 Equip. Oper. (crane)	68.60	548.80	101.75	814.00		
1 Hyd. Excavator, 2.5 C.Y.		1800.54		1980.59		
1 Trench Box		135.66		149.23	121.01	133.11
16 L.H., Daily Totals		$2877.00		$3524.22	$179.81	$220.26
Crew B-13K	Hr.	Daily	Hr.	Daily	Bare Costs	Incl. O&P
2 Equip. Opers. (crane)	$68.60	$1097.60	$101.75	$1628.00	$68.60	$101.75
1 Hyd. Excavator, .75 C.Y.		887.82		976.60		
1 Hyd. Hammer, 4000 ft-lb		740.58		814.63		
1 Hyd. Excavator, .75 C.Y.		887.82		976.60	157.26	172.99
16 L.H., Daily Totals		$3613.82		$4395.84	$225.86	$274.74
Crew B-13L	Hr.	Daily	Hr.	Daily	Bare Costs	Incl. O&P
2 Equip. Opers. (crane)	$68.60	$1097.60	$101.75	$1628.00	$68.60	$101.75
1 Hyd. Excavator, 1.5 C.Y.		1193.85		1313.24		
1 Hyd. Hammer, 5000 ft-lb		789.23		868.16		
1 Hyd. Excavator, .75 C.Y.		887.82		976.60	179.43	197.38
16 L.H., Daily Totals		$3968.51		$4786.00	$248.03	$299.13
Crew B-13M	Hr.	Daily	Hr.	Daily	Bare Costs	Incl. O&P
2 Equip. Opers. (crane)	$68.60	$1097.60	$101.75	$1628.00	$68.60	$101.75
1 Hyd. Excavator, 2.5 C.Y.		1800.54		1980.59		
1 Hyd. Hammer, 8000 ft-lb		1048.67		1153.54		
1 Hyd. Excavator, 1.5 C.Y.		1193.85		1313.24	252.69	277.96
16 L.H., Daily Totals		$5140.66		$6075.37	$321.29	$379.71
Crew B-13N	Hr.	Daily	Hr.	Daily	Bare Costs	Incl. O&P
2 Equip. Opers. (crane)	$68.60	$1097.60	$101.75	$1628.00	$68.60	$101.75
1 Hyd. Excavator, 3.5 C.Y.		2152.24		2367.46		
1 Hyd. Hammer, 12,000 ft-lb		1178.21		1296.03		
1 Hyd. Excavator, 1.5 C.Y.		1193.85		1313.24	282.77	311.05
16 L.H., Daily Totals		$5621.90		$6604.73	$351.37	$412.80
Crew B-14	Hr.	Daily	Hr.	Daily	Bare Costs	Incl. O&P
1 Labor Foreman (outside)	$51.00	$408.00	$75.50	$604.00	$51.50	$76.28
4 Laborers	49.00	1568.00	72.55	2321.60		
1 Equip. Oper. (light)	62.00	496.00	91.95	735.60		
1 Backhoe Loader, 48 H.P.		291.00		320.10	6.06	6.67
48 L.H., Daily Totals		$2763.00		$3981.30	$57.56	$82.94
Crew B-14A	Hr.	Daily	Hr.	Daily	Bare Costs	Incl. O&P
1 Equip. Oper. (crane)	$68.60	$548.80	$101.75	$814.00	$62.07	$92.02
.5 Laborer	49.00	196.00	72.55	290.20		
1 Hyd. Excavator, 4.5 C.Y.		3948.55		4343.41	329.05	361.95
12 L.H., Daily Totals		$4693.35		$5447.61	$391.11	$453.97
Crew B-14B	Hr.	Daily	Hr.	Daily	Bare Costs	Incl. O&P
1 Equip. Oper. (crane)	$68.60	$548.80	$101.75	$814.00	$62.07	$92.02
.5 Laborer	49.00	196.00	72.55	290.20		
1 Hyd. Excavator, 6 C.Y.		4018.32		4420.15	334.86	368.35
12 L.H., Daily Totals		$4763.12		$5524.35	$396.93	$460.36

Crew No.	Bare Costs		Incl. Subs O&P		Cost Per Labor-Hour	
Crew B-14C	Hr.	Daily	Hr.	Daily	Bare Costs	Incl. O&P
1 Equip. Oper. (crane)	$68.60	$548.80	$101.75	$814.00	$62.07	$92.02
.5 Laborer	49.00	196.00	72.55	290.20		
1 Hyd. Excavator, 7 C.Y.		4386.20		4824.82	365.52	402.07
12 L.H., Daily Totals		$5131.00		$5929.02	$427.58	$494.08
Crew B-14F	Hr.	Daily	Hr.	Daily	Bare Costs	Incl. O&P
1 Equip. Oper. (crane)	$68.60	$548.80	$101.75	$814.00	$62.07	$92.02
.5 Laborer	49.00	196.00	72.55	290.20		
1 Hyd. Shovel, 7 C.Y.		4752.62		5227.88	396.05	435.66
12 L.H., Daily Totals		$5497.42		$6332.08	$458.12	$527.67
Crew B-14G	Hr.	Daily	Hr.	Daily	Bare Costs	Incl. O&P
1 Equip. Oper. (crane)	$68.60	$548.80	$101.75	$814.00	$62.07	$92.02
.5 Laborer	49.00	196.00	72.55	290.20		
1 Hyd. Shovel, 12 C.Y.		6903.08		7593.39	575.26	632.78
12 L.H., Daily Totals		$7647.88		$8697.59	$637.32	$724.80
Crew B-14J	Hr.	Daily	Hr.	Daily	Bare Costs	Incl. O&P
1 Equip. Oper. (medium)	$65.00	$520.00	$96.40	$771.20	$59.67	$88.45
.5 Laborer	49.00	196.00	72.55	290.20		
1 F.E. Loader, 8 C.Y.		2697.40		2967.14	224.78	247.26
12 L.H., Daily Totals		$3413.40		$4028.54	$284.45	$335.71
Crew B-14K	Hr.	Daily	Hr.	Daily	Bare Costs	Incl. O&P
1 Equip. Oper. (medium)	$65.00	$520.00	$96.40	$771.20	$59.67	$88.45
.5 Laborer	49.00	196.00	72.55	290.20		
1 F.E. Loader, 10 C.Y.		2937.91		3231.70	244.83	269.31
12 L.H., Daily Totals		$3653.91		$4293.10	$304.49	$357.76
Crew B-15	Hr.	Daily	Hr.	Daily	Bare Costs	Incl. O&P
1 Equipment Oper. (med.)	$65.00	$520.00	$96.40	$771.20	$58.29	$86.54
.5 Laborer	49.00	196.00	72.55	290.20		
2 Truck Drivers (heavy)	57.25	916.00	85.10	1361.60		
2 Dump Trucks, 12 C.Y., 400 H.P.		1974.15		2171.56		
1 Dozer, 200 H.P.		1443.21		1587.53	122.05	134.25
28 L.H., Daily Totals		$5049.36		$6182.10	$180.33	$220.79
Crew B-16	Hr.	Daily	Hr.	Daily	Bare Costs	Incl. O&P
1 Labor Foreman (outside)	$51.00	$408.00	$75.50	$604.00	$51.56	$76.42
2 Laborers	49.00	784.00	72.55	1160.80		
1 Truck Driver (heavy)	57.25	458.00	85.10	680.80		
1 Dump Truck, 12 C.Y., 400 H.P.		987.07		1085.78	30.85	33.93
32 L.H., Daily Totals		$2637.07		$3531.38	$82.41	$110.36
Crew B-17	Hr.	Daily	Hr.	Daily	Bare Costs	Incl. O&P
2 Laborers	$49.00	$784.00	$72.55	$1160.80	$54.31	$80.54
1 Equip. Oper. (light)	62.00	496.00	91.95	735.60		
1 Truck Driver (heavy)	57.25	458.00	85.10	680.80		
1 Backhoe Loader, 48 H.P.		291.00		320.10		
1 Dump Truck, 8 C.Y., 220 H.P.		506.30		556.93	24.92	27.41
32 L.H., Daily Totals		$2535.30		$3454.23	$79.23	$107.94
Crew B-17A	Hr.	Daily	Hr.	Daily	Bare Costs	Incl. O&P
2 Labor Foremen (outside)	$51.00	$816.00	$75.50	$1208.00	$52.50	$77.93
6 Laborers	49.00	2352.00	72.55	3482.40		
1 Skilled Worker Foreman (out)	65.50	524.00	98.00	784.00		
1 Skilled Worker	63.50	508.00	95.00	760.00		
80 L.H., Daily Totals		$4200.00		$6234.40	$52.50	$77.93

Crews - Standard

Crew No.		Bare Costs		Incl. Subs O&P		Cost Per Labor-Hour	
Crew B-17B	Hr.	Daily	Hr.	Daily	Bare Costs	Incl. O&P	
2 Laborers	$49.00	$784.00	$72.55	$1160.80	$54.31	$80.54	
1 Equip. Oper. (light)	62.00	496.00	91.95	735.60			
1 Truck Driver (heavy)	57.25	458.00	85.10	680.80			
1 Backhoe Loader, 48 H.P.		291.00		320.10			
1 Dump Truck, 12 C.Y., 400 H.P.		987.07		1085.78	39.94	43.93	
32 L.H., Daily Totals		$3016.08		$3983.08	$94.25	$124.47	
Crew B-17C	Hr.	Daily	Hr.	Daily	Bare Costs	Incl. O&P	
1 Labor Foreman (outside)	$51.00	$408.00	$75.50	$604.00	$53.98	$80.00	
3 Laborers	49.00	1176.00	72.55	1741.20			
1 Equip. Oper. (heavy)	68.60	548.80	101.75	814.00			
1 Truck Driver (heavy)	57.25	458.00	85.10	680.80			
1 Hyd. Excavator, 2 C.Y.		1463.59		1609.95			
1 Dump Truck, 12 C.Y., 400 H.P.		987.07		1085.78			
1 P/U, 3/4 ton, Tool Truck		165.25		181.77	54.50	59.95	
48 L.H., Daily Totals		$5206.72		$6717.51	$108.47	$139.95	
Crew B-18	Hr.	Daily	Hr.	Daily	Bare Costs	Incl. O&P	
1 Labor Foreman (outside)	$51.00	$408.00	$75.50	$604.00	$49.67	$73.53	
2 Laborers	49.00	784.00	72.55	1160.80			
1 Vibrating Plate, Gas, 21"		152.80		168.08	6.37	7.00	
24 L.H., Daily Totals		$1344.80		$1932.88	$56.03	$80.54	
Crew B-19	Hr.	Daily	Hr.	Daily	Bare Costs	Incl. O&P	
1 Pile Driver Foreman (outside)	$64.75	$518.00	$99.40	$795.20	$63.92	$96.84	
4 Pile Drivers	62.75	2008.00	96.30	3081.60			
2 Equip. Oper. (crane)	68.60	1097.60	101.75	1628.00			
1 Equip. Oper. (oiler)	58.40	467.20	86.60	692.80			
1 Crawler Crane, 40 Ton		1423.92		1566.31			
1 Lead, 90' High		423.85		466.24			
1 Hammer, Diesel, 22k ft-lb		505.25		555.77	36.77	40.44	
64 L.H., Daily Totals		$6443.81		$8785.91	$100.68	$137.28	
Crew B-19A	Hr.	Daily	Hr.	Daily	Bare Costs	Incl. O&P	
1 Pile Driver Foreman (outside)	$64.75	$518.00	$99.40	$795.20	$63.92	$96.84	
4 Pile Drivers	62.75	2008.00	96.30	3081.60			
2 Equip. Oper. (crane)	68.60	1097.60	101.75	1628.00			
1 Equip. Oper. (oiler)	58.40	467.20	86.60	692.80			
1 Crawler Crane, 75 Ton		2275.15		2502.66			
1 Lead, 90' High		423.85		466.24			
1 Hammer, Diesel, 41k ft-lb		667.86		734.64	52.61	57.87	
64 L.H., Daily Totals		$7457.66		$9901.14	$116.53	$154.71	
Crew B-19B	Hr.	Daily	Hr.	Daily	Bare Costs	Incl. O&P	
1 Pile Driver Foreman (outside)	$64.75	$518.00	$99.40	$795.20	$63.92	$96.84	
4 Pile Drivers	62.75	2008.00	96.30	3081.60			
2 Equip. Oper. (crane)	68.60	1097.60	101.75	1628.00			
1 Equip. Oper. (oiler)	58.40	467.20	86.60	692.80			
1 Crawler Crane, 40 Ton		1423.92		1566.31			
1 Lead, 90' High		423.85		466.24			
1 Hammer, Diesel, 22k ft-lb		505.25		555.77			
1 Barge, 400 Ton		991.44		1090.58	52.26	57.48	
64 L.H., Daily Totals		$7435.25		$9876.49	$116.18	$154.32	

Crew No.		Bare Costs		Incl. Subs O&P		Cost Per Labor-Hour	
Crew B-19C	Hr.	Daily	Hr.	Daily	Bare Costs	Incl. O&P	
1 Pile Driver Foreman (outside)	$64.75	$518.00	$99.40	$795.20	$63.92	$96.84	
4 Pile Drivers	62.75	2008.00	96.30	3081.60			
2 Equip. Oper. (crane)	68.60	1097.60	101.75	1628.00			
1 Equip. Oper. (oiler)	58.40	467.20	86.60	692.80			
1 Crawler Crane, 75 Ton		2275.15		2502.66			
1 Lead, 90' High		423.85		466.24			
1 Hammer, Diesel, 41k ft-lb		667.86		734.64			
1 Barge, 400 Ton		991.44		1090.58	68.10	74.91	
64 L.H., Daily Totals		$8449.09		$10991.72	$132.02	$171.75	
Crew B-20	Hr.	Daily	Hr.	Daily	Bare Costs	Incl. O&P	
1 Labor Foreman (outside)	$51.00	$408.00	$75.50	$604.00	$54.50	$81.02	
1 Skilled Worker	63.50	508.00	95.00	760.00			
1 Laborer	49.00	392.00	72.55	580.40			
24 L.H., Daily Totals		$1308.00		$1944.40	$54.50	$81.02	
Crew B-20A	Hr.	Daily	Hr.	Daily	Bare Costs	Incl. O&P	
1 Labor Foreman (outside)	$51.00	$408.00	$75.50	$604.00	$58.59	$86.97	
1 Laborer	49.00	392.00	72.55	580.40			
1 Plumber	74.65	597.20	111.05	888.40			
1 Plumber Apprentice	59.70	477.60	88.80	710.40			
32 L.H., Daily Totals		$1874.80		$2783.20	$58.59	$86.97	
Crew B-21	Hr.	Daily	Hr.	Daily	Bare Costs	Incl. O&P	
1 Labor Foreman (outside)	$51.00	$408.00	$75.50	$604.00	$56.51	$83.98	
1 Skilled Worker	63.50	508.00	95.00	760.00			
1 Laborer	49.00	392.00	72.55	580.40			
.5 Equip. Oper. (crane)	68.60	274.40	101.75	407.00			
.5 S.P. Crane, 4x4, 5 Ton		201.05		221.16	7.18	7.90	
28 L.H., Daily Totals		$1783.45		$2572.56	$63.69	$91.88	
Crew B-21A	Hr.	Daily	Hr.	Daily	Bare Costs	Incl. O&P	
1 Labor Foreman (outside)	$51.00	$408.00	$75.50	$604.00	$60.59	$89.93	
1 Laborer	49.00	392.00	72.55	580.40			
1 Plumber	74.65	597.20	111.05	888.40			
1 Plumber Apprentice	59.70	477.60	88.80	710.40			
1 Equip. Oper. (crane)	68.60	548.80	101.75	814.00			
1 S.P. Crane, 4x4, 12 Ton		663.72		730.09	16.59	18.25	
40 L.H., Daily Totals		$3087.32		$4327.29	$77.18	$108.18	
Crew B-21B	Hr.	Daily	Hr.	Daily	Bare Costs	Incl. O&P	
1 Labor Foreman (outside)	$51.00	$408.00	$75.50	$604.00	$53.32	$78.98	
3 Laborers	49.00	1176.00	72.55	1741.20			
1 Equip. Oper. (crane)	68.60	548.80	101.75	814.00			
1 Hyd. Crane, 12 Ton		2224.21		2446.63	55.61	61.17	
40 L.H., Daily Totals		$4357.01		$5605.83	$108.93	$140.15	
Crew B-21C	Hr.	Daily	Hr.	Daily	Bare Costs	Incl. O&P	
1 Labor Foreman (outside)	$51.00	$408.00	$75.50	$604.00	$53.43	$79.15	
4 Laborers	49.00	1568.00	72.55	2321.60			
1 Equip. Oper. (crane)	68.60	548.80	101.75	814.00			
1 Equip. Oper. (oiler)	58.40	467.20	86.60	692.80			
2 Cutting Torches		29.68		32.65			
2 Sets of Gases		401.58		441.74			
1 Lattice Boom Crane, 90 Ton		2790.64		3069.70	57.53	63.29	
56 L.H., Daily Totals		$6213.90		$7976.49	$110.96	$142.44	

Crews - Standard

Crew No.	Bare Costs		Incl. Subs O&P		Cost Per Labor-Hour	
Crew B-22	Hr.	Daily	Hr.	Daily	Bare Costs	Incl. O&P
1 Labor Foreman (outside)	$51.00	$408.00	$75.50	$604.00	$57.32	$85.16
1 Skilled Worker	63.50	508.00	95.00	760.00		
1 Laborer	49.00	392.00	72.55	580.40		
.75 Equip. Oper. (crane)	68.60	411.60	101.75	610.50		
.75 S.P. Crane, 4x4, 5 Ton		301.58		331.74	10.05	11.06
30 L.H., Daily Totals		$2021.18		$2886.64	$67.37	$96.22

Crew B-22A	Hr.	Daily	Hr.	Daily	Bare Costs	Incl. O&P
1 Labor Foreman (outside)	$51.00	$408.00	$75.50	$604.00	$56.22	$83.47
1 Skilled Worker	63.50	508.00	95.00	760.00		
2 Laborers	49.00	784.00	72.55	1160.80		
1 Equipment Operator, Crane	68.60	548.80	101.75	814.00		
1 S.P. Crane, 4x4, 5 Ton		402.11		442.32		
1 Butt Fusion Mach., 4"-12" diam.		345.30		379.83	18.69	20.55
40 L.H., Daily Totals		$2996.21		$4160.95	$74.91	$104.02

Crew B-22B	Hr.	Daily	Hr.	Daily	Bare Costs	Incl. O&P
1 Labor Foreman (outside)	$51.00	$408.00	$75.50	$604.00	$56.22	$83.47
1 Skilled Worker	63.50	508.00	95.00	760.00		
2 Laborers	49.00	784.00	72.55	1160.80		
1 Equip. Oper. (crane)	68.60	548.80	101.75	814.00		
1 S.P. Crane, 4x4, 5 Ton		402.11		442.32		
1 Butt Fusion Mach., 8"-24" diam.		826.87		909.56	30.72	33.80
40 L.H., Daily Totals		$3477.78		$4690.68	$86.94	$117.27

Crew B-22C	Hr.	Daily	Hr.	Daily	Bare Costs	Incl. O&P
1 Skilled Worker	$63.50	$508.00	$95.00	$760.00	$56.25	$83.78
1 Laborer	49.00	392.00	72.55	580.40		
1 Butt Fusion Mach., 2"-8" diam.		289.74		318.72	18.11	19.92
16 L.H., Daily Totals		$1189.74		$1659.12	$74.36	$103.69

Crew B-23	Hr.	Daily	Hr.	Daily	Bare Costs	Incl. O&P
1 Labor Foreman (outside)	$51.00	$408.00	$75.50	$604.00	$49.40	$73.14
4 Laborers	49.00	1568.00	72.55	2321.60		
1 Drill Rig, Truck-Mounted		908.08		998.89		
1 Flatbed Truck, Gas, 3 Ton		519.55		571.51	35.69	39.26
40 L.H., Daily Totals		$3403.64		$4496.00	$85.09	$112.40

Crew B-23A	Hr.	Daily	Hr.	Daily	Bare Costs	Incl. O&P
1 Labor Foreman (outside)	$51.00	$408.00	$75.50	$604.00	$55.00	$81.48
1 Laborer	49.00	392.00	72.55	580.40		
1 Equip. Oper. (medium)	65.00	520.00	96.40	771.20		
1 Drill Rig, Truck-Mounted		908.08		998.89		
1 Pickup Truck, 3/4 Ton		233.60		256.96	47.57	52.33
24 L.H., Daily Totals		$2461.69		$3211.46	$102.57	$133.81

Crew B-23B	Hr.	Daily	Hr.	Daily	Bare Costs	Incl. O&P
1 Labor Foreman (outside)	$51.00	$408.00	$75.50	$604.00	$55.00	$81.48
1 Laborer	49.00	392.00	72.55	580.40		
1 Equip. Oper. (medium)	65.00	520.00	96.40	771.20		
1 Drill Rig, Truck-Mounted		908.08		998.89		
1 Pickup Truck, 3/4 Ton		233.60		256.96		
1 Centr. Water Pump, 6"		410.89		451.98	64.69	71.16
24 L.H., Daily Totals		$2872.57		$3663.43	$119.69	$152.64

Crew B-24	Hr.	Daily	Hr.	Daily	Bare Costs	Incl. O&P
1 Cement Finisher	$56.80	$454.40	$82.80	$662.40	$55.45	$81.67
1 Laborer	49.00	392.00	72.55	580.40		
1 Carpenter	60.55	484.40	89.65	717.20		
24 L.H., Daily Totals		$1330.80		$1960.00	$55.45	$81.67

Crew B-25	Hr.	Daily	Hr.	Daily	Bare Costs	Incl. O&P
1 Labor Foreman (outside)	$51.00	$408.00	$75.50	$604.00	$53.55	$79.32
7 Laborers	49.00	2744.00	72.55	4062.80		
3 Equip. Oper. (medium)	65.00	1560.00	96.40	2313.60		
1 Asphalt Paver, 130 H.P.		2452.08		2697.29		
1 Tandem Roller, 10 Ton		319.84		351.82		
1 Roller, Pneum. Whl., 12 Ton		467.01		513.71	36.81	40.49
88 L.H., Daily Totals		$7950.92		$10543.22	$90.35	$119.81

Crew B-25B	Hr.	Daily	Hr.	Daily	Bare Costs	Incl. O&P
1 Labor Foreman (outside)	$51.00	$408.00	$75.50	$604.00	$54.50	$80.75
7 Laborers	49.00	2744.00	72.55	4062.80		
4 Equip. Oper. (medium)	65.00	2080.00	96.40	3084.80		
1 Asphalt Paver, 130 H.P.		2452.08		2697.29		
2 Tandem Rollers, 10 Ton		639.68		703.64		
1 Roller, Pneum. Whl., 12 Ton		467.01		513.71	37.07	40.78
96 L.H., Daily Totals		$8790.76		$11666.24	$91.57	$121.52

Crew B-25C	Hr.	Daily	Hr.	Daily	Bare Costs	Incl. O&P
1 Labor Foreman (outside)	$51.00	$408.00	$75.50	$604.00	$54.67	$80.99
3 Laborers	49.00	1176.00	72.55	1741.20		
2 Equip. Oper. (medium)	65.00	1040.00	96.40	1542.40		
1 Asphalt Paver, 130 H.P.		2452.08		2697.29		
1 Tandem Roller, 10 Ton		319.84		351.82	57.75	63.52
48 L.H., Daily Totals		$5395.92		$6936.71	$112.42	$144.51

Crew B-25D	Hr.	Daily	Hr.	Daily	Bare Costs	Incl. O&P
1 Labor Foreman (outside)	$51.00	$408.00	$75.50	$604.00	$54.93	$81.40
3 Laborers	49.00	1176.00	72.55	1741.20		
2.130 Equip. Oper. (medium)	65.00	1107.60	96.40	1642.66		
.13 Truck Driver (heavy)	57.25	59.54	85.10	88.50		
.13 Truck Tractor, 6x4, 380 H.P.		74.55		82.01		
.13 Dist. Tanker, 3000 Gallon		49.67		54.63		
1 Asphalt Paver, 130 H.P.		2452.08		2697.29		
1 Tandem Roller, 10 Ton		319.84		351.82	57.83	63.61
50.08 L.H., Daily Totals		$5647.28		$7262.11	$112.77	$145.01

Crew B-25E	Hr.	Daily	Hr.	Daily	Bare Costs	Incl. O&P
1 Labor Foreman (outside)	$51.00	$408.00	$75.50	$604.00	$55.16	$81.74
3 Laborers	49.00	1176.00	72.55	1741.20		
2.250 Equip. Oper. (medium)	65.00	1170.00	96.40	1735.20		
.25 Truck Driver (heavy)	57.25	114.50	85.10	170.20		
.25 Truck Tractor, 6x4, 380 H.P.		143.37		157.71		
.25 Dist. Tanker, 3000 Gallon		95.51		105.06		
1 Asphalt Paver, 130 H.P.		2452.08		2697.29		
1 Tandem Roller, 10 Ton		319.84		351.82	57.90	63.69
52 L.H., Daily Totals		$5879.30		$7562.48	$113.06	$145.43

Crew B-26	Hr.	Daily	Hr.	Daily	Bare Costs	Incl. O&P
1 Labor Foreman (outside)	$51.00	$408.00	$75.50	$604.00	$54.44	$80.58
6 Laborers	49.00	2352.00	72.55	3482.40		
2 Equip. Oper. (medium)	65.00	1040.00	96.40	1542.40		
1 Rodman (reinf.)	67.05	536.40	100.00	800.00		
1 Cement Finisher	56.80	454.40	82.80	662.40		
1 Grader, 30,000 Lbs.		1115.47		1227.02		
1 Paving Mach. & Equip.		2866.28		3152.91	45.25	49.77
88 L.H., Daily Totals		$8772.55		$11471.13	$99.69	$130.35

Crews - Standard

Crew No.	Bare Costs		Incl. Subs O&P		Cost Per Labor-Hour	
Crew B-26A	Hr.	Daily	Hr.	Daily	Bare Costs	Incl. O&P
1 Labor Foreman (outside)	$51.00	$408.00	$75.50	$604.00	$54.44	$80.58
6 Laborers	49.00	2352.00	72.55	3482.40		
2 Equip. Oper. (medium)	65.00	1040.00	96.40	1542.40		
1 Rodman (reinf.)	67.05	536.40	100.00	800.00		
1 Cement Finisher	56.80	454.40	82.80	662.40		
1 Grader, 30,000 Lbs.		1115.47		1227.02		
1 Paving Mach. & Equip.		2866.28		3152.91		
1 Concrete Saw		194.70		214.17	47.46	52.21
88 L.H., Daily Totals		$8967.25		$11685.30	$101.90	$132.79
Crew B-26B	Hr.	Daily	Hr.	Daily	Bare Costs	Incl. O&P
1 Labor Foreman (outside)	$51.00	$408.00	$75.50	$604.00	$55.32	$81.90
6 Laborers	49.00	2352.00	72.55	3482.40		
3 Equip. Oper. (medium)	65.00	1560.00	96.40	2313.60		
1 Rodman (reinf.)	67.05	536.40	100.00	800.00		
1 Cement Finisher	56.80	454.40	82.80	662.40		
1 Grader, 30,000 Lbs.		1115.47		1227.02		
1 Paving Mach. & Equip.		2866.28		3152.91		
1 Concrete Pump, 110' Boom		1113.77		1225.15	53.08	58.39
96 L.H., Daily Totals		$10406.32		$13467.47	$108.40	$140.29
Crew B-26C	Hr.	Daily	Hr.	Daily	Bare Costs	Incl. O&P
1 Labor Foreman (outside)	$51.00	$408.00	$75.50	$604.00	$53.38	$79.00
6 Laborers	49.00	2352.00	72.55	3482.40		
1 Equip. Oper. (medium)	65.00	520.00	96.40	771.20		
1 Rodman (reinf.)	67.05	536.40	100.00	800.00		
1 Cement Finisher	56.80	454.40	82.80	662.40		
1 Paving Mach. & Equip.		2866.28		3152.91		
1 Concrete Saw		194.70		214.17	38.26	42.09
80 L.H., Daily Totals		$7331.78		$9687.08	$91.65	$121.09
Crew B-27	Hr.	Daily	Hr.	Daily	Bare Costs	Incl. O&P
1 Labor Foreman (outside)	$51.00	$408.00	$75.50	$604.00	$49.50	$73.29
3 Laborers	49.00	1176.00	72.55	1741.20		
1 Berm Machine		905.59		996.15	28.30	31.13
32 L.H., Daily Totals		$2489.59		$3341.35	$77.80	$104.42
Crew B-28	Hr.	Daily	Hr.	Daily	Bare Costs	Incl. O&P
2 Carpenters	$60.55	$968.80	$89.65	$1434.40	$56.70	$83.95
1 Laborer	49.00	392.00	72.55	580.40		
24 L.H., Daily Totals		$1360.80		$2014.80	$56.70	$83.95
Crew B-29	Hr.	Daily	Hr.	Daily	Bare Costs	Incl. O&P
1 Labor Foreman (outside)	$51.00	$408.00	$75.50	$604.00	$53.43	$79.15
4 Laborers	49.00	1568.00	72.55	2321.60		
1 Equip. Oper. (crane)	68.60	548.80	101.75	814.00		
1 Equip. Oper. (oiler)	58.40	467.20	86.60	692.80		
1 Gradall, 5/8 C.Y.		920.64		1012.70	16.44	18.08
56 L.H., Daily Totals		$3912.64		$5445.10	$69.87	$97.23
Crew B-30	Hr.	Daily	Hr.	Daily	Bare Costs	Incl. O&P
1 Equip. Oper. (medium)	$65.00	$520.00	$96.40	$771.20	$59.83	$88.87
2 Truck Drivers (heavy)	57.25	916.00	85.10	1361.60		
1 Hyd. Excavator, 1.5 C.Y.		1193.85		1313.24		
2 Dump Trucks, 12 C.Y., 400 H.P.		1974.15		2171.56	132.00	145.20
24 L.H., Daily Totals		$4604.00		$5617.60	$191.83	$234.07

Crew No.	Bare Costs		Incl. Subs O&P		Cost Per Labor-Hour	
Crew B-31	Hr.	Daily	Hr.	Daily	Bare Costs	Incl. O&P
1 Labor Foreman (outside)	$51.00	$408.00	$75.50	$604.00	$51.71	$76.56
3 Laborers	49.00	1176.00	72.55	1741.20		
1 Carpenter	60.55	484.40	89.65	717.20		
1 Air Compressor, 250 cfm		226.90		249.59		
1 Sheeting Driver		8.45		9.29		
2 -50' Air Hoses, 1.5"		47.13		51.84	7.06	7.77
40 L.H., Daily Totals		$2350.87		$3373.12	$58.77	$84.33
Crew B-32	Hr.	Daily	Hr.	Daily	Bare Costs	Incl. O&P
1 Laborer	$49.00	$392.00	$72.55	$580.40	$61.00	$90.44
3 Equip. Oper. (medium)	65.00	1560.00	96.40	2313.60		
1 Grader, 30,000 Lbs.		1115.47		1227.02		
1 Tandem Roller, 10 Ton		319.84		351.82		
1 Dozer, 200 H.P.		1443.21		1587.53	89.95	98.95
32 L.H., Daily Totals		$4830.52		$6060.37	$150.95	$189.39
Crew B-32A	Hr.	Daily	Hr.	Daily	Bare Costs	Incl. O&P
1 Laborer	$49.00	$392.00	$72.55	$580.40	$59.67	$88.45
2 Equip. Oper. (medium)	65.00	1040.00	96.40	1542.40		
1 Grader, 30,000 Lbs.		1115.47		1227.02		
1 Roller, Vibratory, 25 Ton		554.08		609.48	69.56	76.52
24 L.H., Daily Totals		$3101.55		$3959.30	$129.23	$164.97
Crew B-32B	Hr.	Daily	Hr.	Daily	Bare Costs	Incl. O&P
1 Laborer	$49.00	$392.00	$72.55	$580.40	$59.67	$88.45
2 Equip. Oper. (medium)	65.00	1040.00	96.40	1542.40		
1 Dozer, 200 H.P.		1443.21		1587.53		
1 Roller, Vibratory, 25 Ton		554.08		609.48	83.22	91.54
24 L.H., Daily Totals		$3429.29		$4319.82	$142.89	$179.99
Crew B-32C	Hr.	Daily	Hr.	Daily	Bare Costs	Incl. O&P
1 Labor Foreman (outside)	$51.00	$408.00	$75.50	$604.00	$57.33	$84.97
2 Laborers	49.00	784.00	72.55	1160.80		
3 Equip. Oper. (medium)	65.00	1560.00	96.40	2313.60		
1 Grader, 30,000 Lbs.		1115.47		1227.02		
1 Tandem Roller, 10 Ton		319.84		351.82		
1 Dozer, 200 H.P.		1443.21		1587.53	59.97	65.97
48 L.H., Daily Totals		$5630.52		$7244.77	$117.30	$150.93
Crew B-33A	Hr.	Daily	Hr.	Daily	Bare Costs	Incl. O&P
1 Equip. Oper. (medium)	$65.00	$520.00	$96.40	$771.20	$60.43	$89.59
.5 Laborer	49.00	196.00	72.55	290.20		
.25 Equip. Oper. (medium)	65.00	130.00	96.40	192.80		
1 Scraper, Towed, 7 C.Y.		148.13		162.95		
1.25 Dozers, 300 H.P.		2992.31		3291.54	224.32	246.75
14 L.H., Daily Totals		$3986.45		$4708.69	$284.75	$336.33
Crew B-33B	Hr.	Daily	Hr.	Daily	Bare Costs	Incl. O&P
1 Equip. Oper. (medium)	$65.00	$520.00	$96.40	$771.20	$60.43	$89.59
.5 Laborer	49.00	196.00	72.55	290.20		
.25 Equip. Oper. (medium)	65.00	130.00	96.40	192.80		
1 Scraper, Towed, 10 C.Y.		185.01		203.51		
1.25 Dozers, 300 H.P.		2992.31		3291.54	226.95	249.65
14 L.H., Daily Totals		$4023.32		$4749.26	$287.38	$339.23

Crews - Standard

Crew No.	Bare Costs		Incl. Subs O&P		Cost Per Labor-Hour	
Crew B-33C	Hr.	Daily	Hr.	Daily	Bare Costs	Incl. O&P
1 Equip. Oper. (medium)	$65.00	$520.00	$96.40	$771.20	$60.43	$89.59
.5 Laborer	49.00	196.00	72.55	290.20		
.25 Equip. Oper. (medium)	65.00	130.00	96.40	192.80		
1 Scraper, Towed, 15 C.Y.		204.64		225.10		
1.25 Dozers, 300 H.P.		2992.31		3291.54	228.35	251.19
14 L.H., Daily Totals		$4042.95		$4770.84	$288.78	$340.77
Crew B-33D	Hr.	Daily	Hr.	Daily	Bare Costs	Incl. O&P
1 Equip. Oper. (medium)	$65.00	$520.00	$96.40	$771.20	$60.43	$89.59
.5 Laborer	49.00	196.00	72.55	290.20		
.25 Equip. Oper. (medium)	65.00	130.00	96.40	192.80		
1 S.P. Scraper, 14 C.Y.		2274.69		2502.16		
.25 Dozer, 300 H.P.		598.46		658.31	205.22	225.75
14 L.H., Daily Totals		$3719.15		$4414.66	$265.65	$315.33
Crew B-33E	Hr.	Daily	Hr.	Daily	Bare Costs	Incl. O&P
1 Equip. Oper. (medium)	$65.00	$520.00	$96.40	$771.20	$60.43	$89.59
.5 Laborer	49.00	196.00	72.55	290.20		
.25 Equip. Oper. (medium)	65.00	130.00	96.40	192.80		
1 S.P. Scraper, 21 C.Y.		3274.37		3601.81		
.25 Dozer, 300 H.P.		598.46		658.31	276.63	304.29
14 L.H., Daily Totals		$4718.84		$5514.32	$337.06	$393.88
Crew B-33F	Hr.	Daily	Hr.	Daily	Bare Costs	Incl. O&P
1 Equip. Oper. (medium)	$65.00	$520.00	$96.40	$771.20	$60.43	$89.59
.5 Laborer	49.00	196.00	72.55	290.20		
.25 Equip. Oper. (medium)	65.00	130.00	96.40	192.80		
1 Elev. Scraper, 11 C.Y.		1072.14		1179.36		
.25 Dozer, 300 H.P.		598.46		658.31	119.33	131.26
14 L.H., Daily Totals		$2516.60		$3091.86	$179.76	$220.85
Crew B-33G	Hr.	Daily	Hr.	Daily	Bare Costs	Incl. O&P
1 Equip. Oper. (medium)	$65.00	$520.00	$96.40	$771.20	$60.43	$89.59
.5 Laborer	49.00	196.00	72.55	290.20		
.25 Equip. Oper. (medium)	65.00	130.00	96.40	192.80		
1 Elev. Scraper, 22 C.Y.		2100.37		2310.40		
.25 Dozer, 300 H.P.		598.46		658.31	192.77	212.05
14 L.H., Daily Totals		$3544.83		$4222.91	$253.20	$301.64
Crew B-33H	Hr.	Daily	Hr.	Daily	Bare Costs	Incl. O&P
.5 Laborer	$49.00	$196.00	$72.55	$290.20	$60.43	$89.59
1 Equipment Operator (med.)	65.00	520.00	96.40	771.20		
.25 Equipment Operator (med.)	65.00	130.00	96.40	192.80		
1 S.P. Scraper, 44 C.Y.		3614.77		3976.25		
.25 Dozer, 410 H.P.		742.46		816.71	311.23	342.35
14 L.H., Daily Totals		$5203.23		$6047.15	$371.66	$431.94
Crew B-33J	Hr.	Daily	Hr.	Daily	Bare Costs	Incl. O&P
1 Equipment Operator (med.)	$65.00	$520.00	$96.40	$771.20	$65.00	$96.40
1 S.P. Scraper, 14 C.Y.		2274.69		2502.16	284.34	312.77
8 L.H., Daily Totals		$2794.69		$3273.36	$349.34	$409.17
Crew B-33K	Hr.	Daily	Hr.	Daily	Bare Costs	Incl. O&P
1 Equipment Operator (med.)	$65.00	$520.00	$96.40	$771.20	$60.43	$89.59
.25 Equipment Operator (med.)	65.00	130.00	96.40	192.80		
.5 Laborer	49.00	196.00	72.55	290.20		
1 S.P. Scraper, 31 C.Y.		3927.98		4320.78		
.25 Dozer, 410 H.P.		742.46		816.71	333.60	366.96
14 L.H., Daily Totals		$5516.44		$6391.69	$394.03	$456.55

Crew No.	Bare Costs		Incl. Subs O&P		Cost Per Labor-Hour	
Crew B-34A	Hr.	Daily	Hr.	Daily	Bare Costs	Incl. O&P
1 Truck Driver (heavy)	$57.25	$458.00	$85.10	$680.80	$57.25	$85.10
1 Dump Truck, 8 C.Y., 220 H.P.		506.30		556.93	63.29	69.62
8 L.H., Daily Totals		$964.30		$1237.73	$120.54	$154.72
Crew B-34B	Hr.	Daily	Hr.	Daily	Bare Costs	Incl. O&P
1 Truck Driver (heavy)	$57.25	$458.00	$85.10	$680.80	$57.25	$85.10
1 Dump Truck, 12 C.Y., 400 H.P.		987.07		1085.78	123.38	135.72
8 L.H., Daily Totals		$1445.07		$1766.58	$180.63	$220.82
Crew B-34C	Hr.	Daily	Hr.	Daily	Bare Costs	Incl. O&P
1 Truck Driver (heavy)	$57.25	$458.00	$85.10	$680.80	$57.25	$85.10
1 Truck Tractor, 6x4, 380 H.P.		573.49		630.83		
1 Dump Trailer, 16.5 C.Y.		158.30		174.13	91.47	100.62
8 L.H., Daily Totals		$1189.79		$1485.77	$148.72	$185.72
Crew B-34D	Hr.	Daily	Hr.	Daily	Bare Costs	Incl. O&P
1 Truck Driver (heavy)	$57.25	$458.00	$85.10	$680.80	$57.25	$85.10
1 Truck Tractor, 6x4, 380 H.P.		573.49		630.83		
1 Dump Trailer, 20 C.Y.		175.64		193.20	93.64	103.00
8 L.H., Daily Totals		$1207.13		$1504.84	$150.89	$188.10
Crew B-34E	Hr.	Daily	Hr.	Daily	Bare Costs	Incl. O&P
1 Truck Driver (heavy)	$57.25	$458.00	$85.10	$680.80	$57.25	$85.10
1 Dump Truck, Off Hwy., 25 Ton		1534.54		1688.00	191.82	211.00
8 L.H., Daily Totals		$1992.54		$2368.80	$249.07	$296.10
Crew B-34F	Hr.	Daily	Hr.	Daily	Bare Costs	Incl. O&P
1 Truck Driver (heavy)	$57.25	$458.00	$85.10	$680.80	$57.25	$85.10
1 Dump Truck, Off Hwy., 35 Ton		1574.25		1731.67	196.78	216.46
8 L.H., Daily Totals		$2032.25		$2412.47	$254.03	$301.56
Crew B-34G	Hr.	Daily	Hr.	Daily	Bare Costs	Incl. O&P
1 Truck Driver (heavy)	$57.25	$458.00	$85.10	$680.80	$57.25	$85.10
1 Dump Truck, Off Hwy., 50 Ton		2310.34		2541.38	288.79	317.67
8 L.H., Daily Totals		$2768.34		$3222.18	$346.04	$402.77
Crew B-34H	Hr.	Daily	Hr.	Daily	Bare Costs	Incl. O&P
1 Truck Driver (heavy)	$57.25	$458.00	$85.10	$680.80	$57.25	$85.10
1 Dump Truck, Off Hwy., 65 Ton		2617.83		2879.61	327.23	359.95
8 L.H., Daily Totals		$3075.83		$3560.41	$384.48	$445.05
Crew B-34I	Hr.	Daily	Hr.	Daily	Bare Costs	Incl. O&P
1 Truck Driver (heavy)	$57.25	$458.00	$85.10	$680.80	$57.25	$85.10
1 Dump Truck, 18 C.Y., 450 H.P.		827.40		910.14	103.42	113.77
8 L.H., Daily Totals		$1285.40		$1590.94	$160.67	$198.87
Crew B-34J	Hr.	Daily	Hr.	Daily	Bare Costs	Incl. O&P
1 Truck Driver (heavy)	$57.25	$458.00	$85.10	$680.80	$57.25	$85.10
1 Dump Truck, Off Hwy., 100 Ton		3168.73		3485.60	396.09	435.70
8 L.H., Daily Totals		$3626.73		$4166.40	$453.34	$520.80
Crew B-34K	Hr.	Daily	Hr.	Daily	Bare Costs	Incl. O&P
1 Truck Driver (heavy)	$57.25	$458.00	$85.10	$680.80	$57.25	$85.10
1 Truck Tractor, 6x4, 450 H.P.		699.67		769.64		
1 Lowbed Trailer, 75 Ton		295.27		324.79	124.37	136.80
8 L.H., Daily Totals		$1452.94		$1775.24	$181.62	$221.90

Crews - Standard

Crew B-34L

	Hr.	Bare Costs Daily	Hr.	Incl. Subs O&P Daily	Bare Costs	Incl. O&P
1 Equip. Oper. (light)	$62.00	$496.00	$91.95	$735.60	$62.00	$91.95
1 Flatbed Truck, Gas, 1.5 Ton		420.83		462.92	52.60	57.86
8 L.H., Daily Totals		$916.83		$1198.52	$114.60	$149.81

Crew B-34M

	Hr.	Daily	Hr.	Daily	Bare Costs	Incl. O&P
1 Equip. Oper. (light)	$62.00	$496.00	$91.95	$735.60	$62.00	$91.95
1 Flatbed Truck, Gas, 3 Ton		519.55		571.51	64.94	71.44
8 L.H., Daily Totals		$1015.55		$1307.11	$126.94	$163.39

Crew B-34N

	Hr.	Daily	Hr.	Daily	Bare Costs	Incl. O&P
1 Truck Driver (heavy)	$57.25	$458.00	$85.10	$680.80	$61.13	$90.75
1 Equip. Oper. (medium)	65.00	520.00	96.40	771.20		
1 Truck Tractor, 6x4, 380 H.P.		573.49		630.83		
1 Flatbed Trailer, 40 Ton		215.61		237.17	49.32	54.25
16 L.H., Daily Totals		$1767.10		$2320.01	$110.44	$145.00

Crew B-34P

	Hr.	Daily	Hr.	Daily	Bare Costs	Incl. O&P
1 Pipe Fitter	$75.55	$604.40	$112.40	$899.20	$65.23	$96.93
1 Truck Driver (light)	55.15	441.20	82.00	656.00		
1 Equip. Oper. (medium)	65.00	520.00	96.40	771.20		
1 Flatbed Truck, Gas, 3 Ton		519.55		571.51		
1 Backhoe Loader, 48 H.P.		291.00		320.10	33.77	37.15
24 L.H., Daily Totals		$2376.16		$3218.01	$99.01	$134.08

Crew B-34Q

	Hr.	Daily	Hr.	Daily	Bare Costs	Incl. O&P
1 Pipe Fitter	$75.55	$604.40	$112.40	$899.20	$66.43	$98.72
1 Truck Driver (light)	55.15	441.20	82.00	656.00		
1 Equip. Oper. (crane)	68.60	548.80	101.75	814.00		
1 Flatbed Trailer, 25 Ton		157.04		172.75		
1 Dump Truck, 8 C.Y., 220 H.P.		506.30		556.93		
1 Hyd. Crane, 25 Ton		2335.01		2568.51	124.93	137.42
24 L.H., Daily Totals		$4592.75		$5667.39	$191.36	$236.14

Crew B-34R

	Hr.	Daily	Hr.	Daily	Bare Costs	Incl. O&P
1 Pipe Fitter	$75.55	$604.40	$112.40	$899.20	$66.43	$98.72
1 Truck Driver (light)	55.15	441.20	82.00	656.00		
1 Equip. Oper. (crane)	68.60	548.80	101.75	814.00		
1 Flatbed Trailer, 25 Ton		157.04		172.75		
1 Dump Truck, 8 C.Y., 220 H.P.		506.30		556.93		
1 Hyd. Crane, 25 Ton		2335.01		2568.51		
1 Hyd. Excavator, 1 C.Y.		970.66		1067.72	165.38	181.91
24 L.H., Daily Totals		$5563.41		$6735.11	$231.81	$280.63

Crew B-34S

	Hr.	Daily	Hr.	Daily	Bare Costs	Incl. O&P
2 Pipe Fitters	$75.55	$1208.80	$112.40	$1798.40	$69.24	$102.91
1 Truck Driver (heavy)	57.25	458.00	85.10	680.80		
1 Equip. Oper. (crane)	68.60	548.80	101.75	814.00		
1 Flatbed Trailer, 40 Ton		215.61		237.17		
1 Truck Tractor, 6x4, 380 H.P.		573.49		630.83		
1 Hyd. Crane, 80 Ton		2742.60		3016.86		
1 Hyd. Excavator, 2 C.Y.		1463.59		1609.95	156.10	171.71
32 L.H., Daily Totals		$7210.89		$8788.02	$225.34	$274.63

Crew B-34T

	Hr.	Daily	Hr.	Daily	Bare Costs	Incl. O&P
2 Pipe Fitters	$75.55	$1208.80	$112.40	$1798.40	$69.24	$102.91
1 Truck Driver (heavy)	57.25	458.00	85.10	680.80		
1 Equip. Oper. (crane)	68.60	548.80	101.75	814.00		
1 Flatbed Trailer, 40 Ton		215.61		237.17		
1 Truck Tractor, 6x4, 380 H.P.		573.49		630.83		
1 Hyd. Crane, 80 Ton		2742.60		3016.86	110.37	121.40
32 L.H., Daily Totals		$5747.30		$7178.07	$179.60	$224.31

Crew B-34U

	Hr.	Daily	Hr.	Daily	Bare Costs	Incl. O&P
1 Truck Driver (heavy)	$57.25	$458.00	$85.10	$680.80	$59.63	$88.53
1 Equip. Oper. (light)	62.00	496.00	91.95	735.60		
1 Truck Tractor, 220 H.P.		357.02		392.72		
1 Flatbed Trailer, 25 Ton		157.04		172.75	32.13	35.34
16 L.H., Daily Totals		$1468.06		$1981.87	$91.75	$123.87

Crew B-34V

	Hr.	Daily	Hr.	Daily	Bare Costs	Incl. O&P
1 Truck Driver (heavy)	$57.25	$458.00	$85.10	$680.80	$62.62	$92.93
1 Equip. Oper. (crane)	68.60	548.80	101.75	814.00		
1 Equip. Oper. (light)	62.00	496.00	91.95	735.60		
1 Truck Tractor, 6x4, 450 H.P.		699.67		769.64		
1 Equipment Trailer, 50 Ton		349.51		384.46		
1 Pickup Truck, 4x4, 3/4 Ton		235.90		259.49	53.55	58.90
24 L.H., Daily Totals		$2787.88		$3643.99	$116.16	$151.83

Crew B-34W

	Hr.	Daily	Hr.	Daily	Bare Costs	Incl. O&P
5 Truck Drivers (heavy)	$57.25	$2290.00	$85.10	$3404.00	$60.13	$89.28
2 Equip. Opers. (crane)	68.60	1097.60	101.75	1628.00		
1 Equip. Oper. (mechanic)	68.75	550.00	101.95	815.60		
1 Laborer	49.00	392.00	72.55	580.40		
4 Truck Tractors, 6x4, 380 H.P.		2293.95		2523.34		
2 Equipment Trailers, 50 Ton		699.01		768.91		
2 Flatbed Trailers, 40 Ton		431.23		474.35		
1 Pickup Truck, 4x4, 3/4 Ton		235.90		259.49		
1 S.P. Crane, 4x4, 20 Ton		790.69		869.76	61.82	68.00
72 L.H., Daily Totals		$8780.38		$11323.85	$121.95	$157.28

Crew B-35

	Hr.	Daily	Hr.	Daily	Bare Costs	Incl. O&P
1 Labor Foreman (outside)	$51.00	$408.00	$75.50	$604.00	$62.83	$93.36
1 Skilled Worker	63.50	508.00	95.00	760.00		
2 Welders	74.65	1194.40	111.05	1776.80		
1 Laborer	49.00	392.00	72.55	580.40		
1 Equip. Oper. (crane)	68.60	548.80	101.75	814.00		
1 Equip. Oper. (oiler)	58.40	467.20	86.60	692.80		
2 Welder, Electric, 300 amp		143.54		157.90		
1 Hyd. Excavator, .75 C.Y.		887.82		976.60	18.42	20.26
56 L.H., Daily Totals		$4549.77		$6362.50	$81.25	$113.62

Crew B-35A

	Hr.	Daily	Hr.	Daily	Bare Costs	Incl. O&P
1 Labor Foreman (outside)	$51.00	$408.00	$75.50	$604.00	$59.16	$87.86
2 Laborers	49.00	784.00	72.55	1160.80		
1 Skilled Worker	63.50	508.00	95.00	760.00		
1 Welder (plumber)	74.65	597.20	111.05	888.40		
1 Equip. Oper. (crane)	68.60	548.80	101.75	814.00		
1 Equip. Oper. (oiler)	58.40	467.20	86.60	692.80		
1 Welder, Gas Engine, 300 amp		163.86		180.24		
1 Crawler Crane, 75 Ton		2275.15		2502.66	43.55	47.91
56 L.H., Daily Totals		$5752.20		$7602.90	$102.72	$135.77

Crew B-36

	Hr.	Daily	Hr.	Daily	Bare Costs	Incl. O&P
1 Labor Foreman (outside)	$51.00	$408.00	$75.50	$604.00	$55.80	$82.68
2 Laborers	49.00	784.00	72.55	1160.80		
2 Equip. Oper. (medium)	65.00	1040.00	96.40	1542.40		
1 Dozer, 200 H.P.		1443.21		1587.53		
1 Aggregate Spreader		70.27		77.30		
1 Tandem Roller, 10 Ton		319.84		351.82	45.83	50.42
40 L.H., Daily Totals		$4065.32		$5323.85	$101.63	$133.10

Crews - Standard

Crew No.		Bare Costs		Incl. Subs O&P	Cost Per Labor-Hour	
Crew B-36A	Hr.	Daily	Hr.	Daily	Bare Costs	Incl. O&P
1 Labor Foreman (outside)	$51.00	$408.00	$75.50	$604.00	$58.43	$86.60
2 Laborers	49.00	784.00	72.55	1160.80		
4 Equip. Oper. (medium)	65.00	2080.00	96.40	3084.80		
1 Dozer, 200 H.P.		1443.21		1587.53		
1 Aggregate Spreader		70.27		77.30		
1 Tandem Roller, 10 Ton		319.84		351.82		
1 Roller, Pneum. Whl., 12 Ton		467.01		513.71	41.08	45.19
56 L.H., Daily Totals		$5572.32		$7379.96	$99.51	$131.79
Crew B-36B	Hr.	Daily	Hr.	Daily	Bare Costs	Incl. O&P
1 Labor Foreman (outside)	$51.00	$408.00	$75.50	$604.00	$58.28	$86.41
2 Laborers	49.00	784.00	72.55	1160.80		
4 Equip. Oper. (medium)	65.00	2080.00	96.40	3084.80		
1 Truck Driver (heavy)	57.25	458.00	85.10	680.80		
1 Grader, 30,000 Lbs.		1115.47		1227.02		
1 F.E. Loader, Crl, 1.5 C.Y.		765.01		841.51		
1 Dozer, 300 H.P.		2393.85		2633.23		
1 Roller, Vibratory, 25 Ton		554.08		609.48		
1 Truck Tractor, 6x4, 450 H.P.		699.67		769.64		
1 Water Tank Trailer, 5000 Gal.		176.44		194.08	89.13	98.05
64 L.H., Daily Totals		$9434.52		$11805.37	$147.41	$184.46
Crew B-36C	Hr.	Daily	Hr.	Daily	Bare Costs	Incl. O&P
1 Labor Foreman (outside)	$51.00	$408.00	$75.50	$604.00	$60.65	$89.96
3 Equip. Oper. (medium)	65.00	1560.00	96.40	2313.60		
1 Truck Driver (heavy)	57.25	458.00	85.10	680.80		
1 Grader, 30,000 Lbs.		1115.47		1227.02		
1 Dozer, 300 H.P.		2393.85		2633.23		
1 Roller, Vibratory, 25 Ton		554.08		609.48		
1 Truck Tractor, 6x4, 450 H.P.		699.67		769.64		
1 Water Tank Trailer, 5000 Gal.		176.44		194.08	123.49	135.84
40 L.H., Daily Totals		$7365.51		$9031.86	$184.14	$225.80
Crew B-36D	Hr.	Daily	Hr.	Daily	Bare Costs	Incl. O&P
1 Labor Foreman (outside)	$51.00	$408.00	$75.50	$604.00	$61.50	$91.17
3 Equip. Oper. (medium)	65.00	1560.00	96.40	2313.60		
1 Grader, 30,000 Lbs.		1115.47		1227.02		
1 Dozer, 300 H.P.		2393.85		2633.23		
1 Roller, Vibratory, 25 Ton		554.08		609.48	126.98	139.68
32 L.H., Daily Totals		$6031.40		$7387.34	$188.48	$230.85
Crew B-37	Hr.	Daily	Hr.	Daily	Bare Costs	Incl. O&P
1 Labor Foreman (outside)	$51.00	$408.00	$75.50	$604.00	$51.50	$76.28
4 Laborers	49.00	1568.00	72.55	2321.60		
1 Equip. Oper. (light)	62.00	496.00	91.95	735.60		
1 Tandem Roller, 5 Ton		264.37		290.81	5.51	6.06
48 L.H., Daily Totals		$2736.37		$3952.01	$57.01	$82.33
Crew B-37A	Hr.	Daily	Hr.	Daily	Bare Costs	Incl. O&P
2 Laborers	$49.00	$784.00	$72.55	$1160.80	$51.05	$75.70
1 Truck Driver (light)	55.15	441.20	82.00	656.00		
1 Flatbed Truck, Gas, 1.5 Ton		420.83		462.92		
1 Tar Kettle, T.M.		209.32		230.25	26.26	28.88
24 L.H., Daily Totals		$1855.35		$2509.97	$77.31	$104.58
Crew B-37B	Hr.	Daily	Hr.	Daily	Bare Costs	Incl. O&P
3 Laborers	$49.00	$1176.00	$72.55	$1741.20	$50.54	$74.91
1 Truck Driver (light)	55.15	441.20	82.00	656.00		
1 Flatbed Truck, Gas, 1.5 Ton		420.83		462.92		
1 Tar Kettle, T.M.		209.32		230.25	19.69	21.66
32 L.H., Daily Totals		$2247.35		$3090.37	$70.23	$96.57

Crew No.		Bare Costs		Incl. Subs O&P	Cost Per Labor-Hour	
Crew B-37C	Hr.	Daily	Hr.	Daily	Bare Costs	Incl. O&P
2 Laborers	$49.00	$784.00	$72.55	$1160.80	$52.08	$77.28
2 Truck Drivers (light)	55.15	882.40	82.00	1312.00		
2 Flatbed Trucks, Gas, 1.5 Ton		841.67		925.83		
1 Tar Kettle, T.M.		209.32		230.25	32.84	36.13
32 L.H., Daily Totals		$2717.38		$3628.88	$84.92	$113.40
Crew B-37D	Hr.	Daily	Hr.	Daily	Bare Costs	Incl. O&P
1 Laborer	$49.00	$392.00	$72.55	$580.40	$52.08	$77.28
1 Truck Driver (light)	55.15	441.20	82.00	656.00		
1 Pickup Truck, 3/4 Ton		233.60		256.96	14.60	16.06
16 L.H., Daily Totals		$1066.80		$1493.36	$66.68	$93.34
Crew B-37E	Hr.	Daily	Hr.	Daily	Bare Costs	Incl. O&P
3 Laborers	$49.00	$1176.00	$72.55	$1741.20	$54.90	$81.43
1 Equip. Oper. (light)	62.00	496.00	91.95	735.60		
1 Equip. Oper. (medium)	65.00	520.00	96.40	771.20		
2 Truck Drivers (light)	55.15	882.40	82.00	1312.00		
4 Barrels w/ Flasher		11.80		12.98		
1 Concrete Saw		194.70		214.17		
1 Rotary Hammer Drill		56.41		62.05		
1 Hammer Drill Bit		27.39		30.12		
1 Loader, Skid Steer, 30 H.P.		268.41		295.25		
1 Conc. Hammer Attach.		130.51		143.56		
1 Vibrating Plate, Gas, 18"		132.53		145.78		
2 Flatbed Trucks, Gas, 1.5 Ton		841.67		925.83	29.70	32.67
56 L.H., Daily Totals		$4737.81		$6389.75	$84.60	$114.10
Crew B-37F	Hr.	Daily	Hr.	Daily	Bare Costs	Incl. O&P
3 Laborers	$49.00	$1176.00	$72.55	$1741.20	$50.54	$74.91
1 Truck Driver (light)	55.15	441.20	82.00	656.00		
4 Barrels w/ Flasher		11.80		12.98		
1 Concrete Mixer, 10 C.F.		170.44		187.48		
1 Air Compressor, 60 cfm		204.02		224.42		
1 -50' Air Hose, 3/4"		7.10		7.81		
1 Spade (Chipper)		9.80		10.78		
1 Flatbed Truck, Gas, 1.5 Ton		420.83		462.92	25.75	28.32
32 L.H., Daily Totals		$2441.19		$3303.59	$76.29	$103.24
Crew B-37G	Hr.	Daily	Hr.	Daily	Bare Costs	Incl. O&P
1 Labor Foreman (outside)	$51.00	$408.00	$75.50	$604.00	$51.50	$76.28
4 Laborers	49.00	1568.00	72.55	2321.60		
1 Equip. Oper. (light)	62.00	496.00	91.95	735.60		
1 Berm Machine		905.59		996.15		
1 Tandem Roller, 5 Ton		264.37		290.81	24.37	26.81
48 L.H., Daily Totals		$3641.96		$4948.16	$75.87	$103.09
Crew B-37H	Hr.	Daily	Hr.	Daily	Bare Costs	Incl. O&P
1 Labor Foreman (outside)	$51.00	$408.00	$75.50	$604.00	$51.50	$76.28
4 Laborers	49.00	1568.00	72.55	2321.60		
1 Equip. Oper. (light)	62.00	496.00	91.95	735.60		
1 Tandem Roller, 5 Ton		264.37		290.81		
1 Flatbed Truck, Gas, 1.5 Ton		420.83		462.92		
1 Tar Kettle, T.M.		209.32		230.25	18.64	20.50
48 L.H., Daily Totals		$3366.52		$4645.18	$70.14	$96.77

Crews - Standard

Crew No.		Bare Costs		Incl. Subs O&P	Cost Per Labor-Hour	
Crew B-37I	Hr.	Daily	Hr.	Daily	Bare Costs	Incl. O&P
3 Laborers	$49.00	$1176.00	$72.55	$1741.20	$54.90	$81.43
1 Equip. Oper. (light)	62.00	496.00	91.95	735.60		
1 Equip. Oper. (medium)	65.00	520.00	96.40	771.20		
2 Truck Drivers (light)	55.15	882.40	82.00	1312.00		
4 Barrels w/ Flasher		11.80		12.98		
1 Concrete Saw		194.70		214.17		
1 Rotary Hammer Drill		56.41		62.05		
1 Hammer Drill Bit		27.39		30.12		
1 Air Compressor, 60 cfm		204.02		224.42		
1 -50' Air Hose, 3/4"		7.10		7.81		
1 Spade (Chipper)		9.80		10.78		
1 Loader, Skid Steer, 30 H.P.		268.41		295.25		
1 Conc. Hammer Attach.		130.51		143.56		
1 Concrete Mixer, 10 C.F.		170.44		187.48		
1 Vibrating Plate, Gas, 18"		132.53		145.78		
2 Flatbed Trucks, Gas, 1.5 Ton		841.67		925.83	36.69	40.36
56 L.H., Daily Totals		$5129.16		$6820.24	$91.59	$121.79
Crew B-37J	Hr.	Daily	Hr.	Daily	Bare Costs	Incl. O&P
1 Labor Foreman (outside)	$51.00	$408.00	$75.50	$604.00	$51.50	$76.28
4 Laborers	49.00	1568.00	72.55	2321.60		
1 Equip. Oper. (light)	62.00	496.00	91.95	735.60		
1 Air Compressor, 60 cfm		204.02		224.42		
1 -50' Air Hose, 3/4"		7.10		7.81		
2 Concrete Mixers, 10 C.F.		340.88		374.97		
2 Flatbed Trucks, Gas, 1.5 Ton		841.67		925.83		
1 Shot Blaster, 20"		238.10		261.91	34.00	37.39
48 L.H., Daily Totals		$4103.76		$5456.14	$85.50	$113.67
Crew B-37K	Hr.	Daily	Hr.	Daily	Bare Costs	Incl. O&P
1 Labor Foreman (outside)	$51.00	$408.00	$75.50	$604.00	$51.50	$76.28
4 Laborers	49.00	1568.00	72.55	2321.60		
1 Equip. Oper. (light)	62.00	496.00	91.95	735.60		
1 Air Compressor, 60 cfm		204.02		224.42		
1 -50' Air Hose, 3/4"		7.10		7.81		
2 Flatbed Trucks, Gas, 1.5 Ton		841.67		925.83		
1 Shot Blaster, 20"		238.10		261.91	26.89	29.58
48 L.H., Daily Totals		$3762.88		$5081.17	$78.39	$105.86
Crew B-38	Hr.	Daily	Hr.	Daily	Bare Costs	Incl. O&P
1 Labor Foreman (outside)	$51.00	$408.00	$75.50	$604.00	$55.20	$81.79
2 Laborers	49.00	784.00	72.55	1160.80		
1 Equip. Oper. (light)	62.00	496.00	91.95	735.60		
1 Equip. Oper. (medium)	65.00	520.00	96.40	771.20		
1 Backhoe Loader, 48 H.P.		291.00		320.10		
1 Hyd. Hammer (1200 lb.)		202.66		222.92		
1 F.E. Loader, W.M., 4 C.Y.		866.60		953.26		
1 Pvmt. Rem. Bucket		72.92		80.21	35.83	39.41
40 L.H., Daily Totals		$3641.17		$4848.09	$91.03	$121.20
Crew B-39	Hr.	Daily	Hr.	Daily	Bare Costs	Incl. O&P
1 Labor Foreman (outside)	$51.00	$408.00	$75.50	$604.00	$51.50	$76.28
4 Laborers	49.00	1568.00	72.55	2321.60		
1 Equip. Oper. (light)	62.00	496.00	91.95	735.60		
1 Air Compressor, 250 cfm		226.90		249.59		
2 Breakers, Pavement, 60 lb.		79.92		87.92		
2 -50' Air Hoses, 1.5"		47.13		51.84	7.37	8.11
48 L.H., Daily Totals		$2825.95		$4050.55	$58.87	$84.39

Crew No.		Bare Costs		Incl. Subs O&P	Cost Per Labor-Hour	
Crew B-40	Hr.	Daily	Hr.	Daily	Bare Costs	Incl. O&P
1 Pile Driver Foreman (outside)	$64.75	$518.00	$99.40	$795.20	$63.92	$96.84
4 Pile Drivers	62.75	2008.00	96.30	3081.60		
2 Equip. Oper. (crane)	68.60	1097.60	101.75	1628.00		
1 Equip. Oper. (oiler)	58.40	467.20	86.60	692.80		
1 Crawler Crane, 40 Ton		1423.92		1566.31		
1 Vibratory Hammer & Gen.		2635.22		2898.74	63.42	69.77
64 L.H., Daily Totals		$8149.93		$10662.65	$127.34	$166.60
Crew B-40B	Hr.	Daily	Hr.	Daily	Bare Costs	Incl. O&P
1 Labor Foreman (outside)	$51.00	$408.00	$75.50	$604.00	$54.17	$80.25
3 Laborers	49.00	1176.00	72.55	1741.20		
1 Equip. Oper. (crane)	68.60	548.80	101.75	814.00		
1 Equip. Oper. (oiler)	58.40	467.20	86.60	692.80		
1 Lattice Boom Crane, 40 Ton		2459.62		2705.58	51.24	56.37
48 L.H., Daily Totals		$5059.62		$6557.58	$105.41	$136.62
Crew B-41	Hr.	Daily	Hr.	Daily	Bare Costs	Incl. O&P
1 Labor Foreman (outside)	$51.00	$408.00	$75.50	$604.00	$50.68	$75.05
4 Laborers	49.00	1568.00	72.55	2321.60		
.25 Equip. Oper. (crane)	68.60	137.20	101.75	203.50		
.25 Equip. Oper. (oiler)	58.40	116.80	86.60	173.20		
.25 Crawler Crane, 40 Ton		355.98		391.58	8.09	8.90
44 L.H., Daily Totals		$2585.98		$3693.88	$58.77	$83.95
Crew B-42	Hr.	Daily	Hr.	Daily	Bare Costs	Incl. O&P
1 Labor Foreman (outside)	$51.00	$408.00	$75.50	$604.00	$55.13	$82.11
4 Laborers	49.00	1568.00	72.55	2321.60		
1 Equip. Oper. (crane)	68.60	548.80	101.75	814.00		
1 Equip. Oper. (oiler)	58.40	467.20	86.60	692.80		
1 Welder	67.05	536.40	102.80	822.40		
1 Hyd. Crane, 25 Ton		2335.01		2568.51		
1 Welder, Gas Engine, 300 amp		163.86		180.24		
1 Horz. Boring Csg. Mch.		460.22		506.24	46.24	50.86
64 L.H., Daily Totals		$6487.48		$8509.79	$101.37	$132.97
Crew B-43	Hr.	Daily	Hr.	Daily	Bare Costs	Incl. O&P
1 Labor Foreman (outside)	$51.00	$408.00	$75.50	$604.00	$54.17	$80.25
3 Laborers	49.00	1176.00	72.55	1741.20		
1 Equip. Oper. (crane)	68.60	548.80	101.75	814.00		
1 Equip. Oper. (oiler)	58.40	467.20	86.60	692.80		
1 Drill Rig, Truck-Mounted		908.08		998.89	18.92	20.81
48 L.H., Daily Totals		$3508.08		$4850.89	$73.09	$101.06
Crew B-44	Hr.	Daily	Hr.	Daily	Bare Costs	Incl. O&P
1 Pile Driver Foreman (outside)	$64.75	$518.00	$99.40	$795.20	$62.74	$95.08
4 Pile Drivers	62.75	2008.00	96.30	3081.60		
2 Equip. Oper. (crane)	68.60	1097.60	101.75	1628.00		
1 Laborer	49.00	392.00	72.55	580.40		
1 Crawler Crane, 40 Ton		1423.92		1566.31		
1 Lead, 60' High		241.46		265.61		
1 Hammer, Diesel, 15K ft.-lbs.		712.59		783.85	37.16	40.87
64 L.H., Daily Totals		$6393.58		$8700.97	$99.90	$135.95
Crew B-45	Hr.	Daily	Hr.	Daily	Bare Costs	Incl. O&P
1 Equip. Oper. (medium)	$65.00	$520.00	$96.40	$771.20	$61.13	$90.75
1 Truck Driver (heavy)	57.25	458.00	85.10	680.80		
1 Dist. Tanker, 3000 Gallon		382.04		420.25		
1 Truck Tractor, 6x4, 380 H.P.		573.49		630.83	59.72	65.69
16 L.H., Daily Totals		$1933.53		$2503.08	$120.85	$156.44

Crews - Standard

Crew No.	Bare Costs		Incl. Subs O&P		Cost Per Labor-Hour	
Crew B-46	Hr.	Daily	Hr.	Daily	Bare Costs	Incl. O&P
1 Pile Driver Foreman (outside)	$64.75	$518.00	$99.40	$795.20	$56.21	$84.94
2 Pile Drivers	62.75	1004.00	96.30	1540.80		
3 Laborers	49.00	1176.00	72.55	1741.20		
1 Chain Saw, Gas, 36" Long		55.48		61.03	1.16	1.27
48 L.H., Daily Totals		$2753.48		$4138.23	$57.36	$86.21
Crew B-47	Hr.	Daily	Hr.	Daily	Bare Costs	Incl. O&P
1 Blast Foreman (outside)	$51.00	$408.00	$75.50	$604.00	$54.00	$80.00
1 Driller	49.00	392.00	72.55	580.40		
1 Equip. Oper. (light)	62.00	496.00	91.95	735.60		
1 Air Track Drill, 4"		1245.86		1370.45		
1 Air Compressor, 600 cfm		490.62		539.68		
2 -50' Air Hoses, 3"		91.44		100.58	76.16	83.78
24 L.H., Daily Totals		$3123.92		$3930.71	$130.16	$163.78
Crew B-47A	Hr.	Daily	Hr.	Daily	Bare Costs	Incl. O&P
1 Drilling Foreman (outside)	$51.00	$408.00	$75.50	$604.00	$59.33	$87.95
1 Equip. Oper. (heavy)	68.60	548.80	101.75	814.00		
1 Equip. Oper. (oiler)	58.40	467.20	86.60	692.80		
1 Air Track Drill, 5"		1245.86		1370.45	51.91	57.10
24 L.H., Daily Totals		$2669.86		$3481.25	$111.24	$145.05
Crew B-47C	Hr.	Daily	Hr.	Daily	Bare Costs	Incl. O&P
1 Laborer	$49.00	$392.00	$72.55	$580.40	$55.50	$82.25
1 Equip. Oper. (light)	62.00	496.00	91.95	735.60		
1 Air Compressor, 750 C.F.M.		802.76		883.04		
2 -50' Air Hoses, 3"		91.44		100.58		
1 Air Track Drill, 4"		1245.86		1370.45	133.75	147.13
16 L.H., Daily Totals		$3028.06		$3670.07	$189.25	$229.38
Crew B-47E	Hr.	Daily	Hr.	Daily	Bare Costs	Incl. O&P
1 Labor Foreman (outside)	$51.00	$408.00	$75.50	$604.00	$49.50	$73.29
3 Laborers	49.00	1176.00	72.55	1741.20		
1 Flatbed Truck, Gas, 3 Ton		519.55		571.51	16.24	17.86
32 L.H., Daily Totals		$2103.55		$2916.71	$65.74	$91.15
Crew B-47G	Hr.	Daily	Hr.	Daily	Bare Costs	Incl. O&P
1 Labor Foreman (outside)	$51.00	$408.00	$75.50	$604.00	$52.75	$78.14
2 Laborers	49.00	784.00	72.55	1160.80		
1 Equip. Oper. (light)	62.00	496.00	91.95	735.60		
1 Air Track Drill, 4"		1245.86		1370.45		
1 Air Compressor, 600 cfm		490.62		539.68		
2 -50' Air Hoses, 3"		91.44		100.58		
1 Gunite Pump Rig		368.88		405.77	68.65	75.52
32 L.H., Daily Totals		$3884.81		$4916.89	$121.40	$153.65
Crew B-47H	Hr.	Daily	Hr.	Daily	Bare Costs	Incl. O&P
1 Skilled Worker Foreman (out)	$65.50	$524.00	$98.00	$784.00	$64.00	$95.75
3 Skilled Workers	63.50	1524.00	95.00	2280.00		
1 Flatbed Truck, Gas, 3 Ton		519.55		571.51	16.24	17.86
32 L.H., Daily Totals		$2567.55		$3635.51	$80.24	$113.61

Crew No.	Bare Costs		Incl. Subs O&P		Cost Per Labor-Hour	
Crew B-48	Hr.	Daily	Hr.	Daily	Bare Costs	Incl. O&P
1 Labor Foreman (outside)	$51.00	$408.00	$75.50	$604.00	$55.29	$81.92
3 Laborers	49.00	1176.00	72.55	1741.20		
1 Equip. Oper. (crane)	68.60	548.80	101.75	814.00		
1 Equip. Oper. (oiler)	58.40	467.20	86.60	692.80		
1 Equip. Oper. (light)	62.00	496.00	91.95	735.60		
1 Centr. Water Pump, 6"		410.89		451.98		
1 -20' Suction Hose, 6"		29.00		31.90		
1 -50' Discharge Hose, 6"		20.63		22.69		
1 Drill Rig, Truck-Mounted		908.08		998.89	24.44	26.88
56 L.H., Daily Totals		$4464.60		$6093.06	$79.72	$108.80
Crew B-49	Hr.	Daily	Hr.	Daily	Bare Costs	Incl. O&P
1 Labor Foreman (outside)	$51.00	$408.00	$75.50	$604.00	$58.14	$86.76
3 Laborers	49.00	1176.00	72.55	1741.20		
2 Equip. Oper. (crane)	68.60	1097.60	101.75	1628.00		
2 Equip. Oper. (oilers)	58.40	934.40	86.60	1385.60		
1 Equip. Oper. (light)	62.00	496.00	91.95	735.60		
2 Pile Drivers	62.75	1004.00	96.30	1540.80		
1 Hyd. Crane, 25 Ton		2335.01		2568.51		
1 Centr. Water Pump, 6"		410.89		451.98		
1 -20' Suction Hose, 6"		29.00		31.90		
1 -50' Discharge Hose, 6"		20.63		22.69		
1 Drill Rig, Truck-Mounted		908.08		998.89	42.09	46.30
88 L.H., Daily Totals		$8819.60		$11709.16	$100.22	$133.06
Crew B-50	Hr.	Daily	Hr.	Daily	Bare Costs	Incl. O&P
2 Pile Driver Foremen (outside)	$64.75	$1036.00	$99.40	$1590.40	$60.61	$91.74
6 Pile Drivers	62.75	3012.00	96.30	4622.40		
2 Equip. Oper. (crane)	68.60	1097.60	101.75	1628.00		
1 Equip. Oper. (oiler)	58.40	467.20	86.60	692.80		
3 Laborers	49.00	1176.00	72.55	1741.20		
1 Crawler Crane, 40 Ton		1423.92		1566.31		
1 Lead, 60' High		241.46		265.61		
1 Hammer, Diesel, 15K ft.-lbs.		712.59		783.85		
1 Air Compressor, 600 cfm		490.62		539.68		
2 -50' Air Hoses, 3"		91.44		100.58		
1 Chain Saw, Gas, 36" Long		55.48		61.03	26.92	29.62
112 L.H., Daily Totals		$9804.32		$13591.87	$87.54	$121.36
Crew B-51	Hr.	Daily	Hr.	Daily	Bare Costs	Incl. O&P
1 Labor Foreman (outside)	$51.00	$408.00	$75.50	$604.00	$50.36	$74.62
4 Laborers	49.00	1568.00	72.55	2321.60		
1 Truck Driver (light)	55.15	441.20	82.00	656.00		
1 Flatbed Truck, Gas, 1.5 Ton		420.83		462.92	8.77	9.64
48 L.H., Daily Totals		$2838.03		$4044.52	$59.13	$84.26
Crew B-52	Hr.	Daily	Hr.	Daily	Bare Costs	Incl. O&P
1 Carpenter Foreman (outside)	$62.55	$500.40	$92.60	$740.80	$56.13	$82.99
1 Carpenter	60.55	484.40	89.65	717.20		
3 Laborers	49.00	1176.00	72.55	1741.20		
1 Cement Finisher	56.80	454.40	82.80	662.40		
.5 Rodman (reinf.)	67.05	268.20	100.00	400.00		
.5 Equip. Oper. (medium)	65.00	260.00	96.40	385.60		
.5 Crawler Loader, 3 C.Y.		656.59		722.25	11.72	12.90
56 L.H., Daily Totals		$3799.99		$5369.45	$67.86	$95.88
Crew B-53	Hr.	Daily	Hr.	Daily	Bare Costs	Incl. O&P
1 Equip. Oper. (light)	$62.00	$496.00	$91.95	$735.60	$62.00	$91.95
1 Trencher, Chain, 12 H.P.		210.98		232.08	26.37	29.01
8 L.H., Daily Totals		$706.98		$967.68	$88.37	$120.96

Crews - Standard

Crew No.	Bare Costs		Incl. Subs O&P		Cost Per Labor-Hour	
Crew B-54	Hr.	Daily	Hr.	Daily	Bare Costs	Incl. O&P
1 Equip. Oper. (light)	$62.00	$496.00	$91.95	$735.60	$62.00	$91.95
1 Trencher, Chain, 40 H.P.		402.94		443.23	50.37	55.40
8 L.H., Daily Totals		$898.94		$1178.83	$112.37	$147.35
Crew B-54A	Hr.	Daily	Hr.	Daily	Bare Costs	Incl. O&P
.17 Labor Foreman (outside)	$51.00	$69.36	$75.50	$102.68	$62.97	$93.36
1 Equipment Operator (med.)	65.00	520.00	96.40	771.20		
1 Wheel Trencher, 67 H.P.		1307.45		1438.19	139.68	153.65
9.36 L.H., Daily Totals		$1896.81		$2312.07	$202.65	$247.02
Crew B-54B	Hr.	Daily	Hr.	Daily	Bare Costs	Incl. O&P
.25 Labor Foreman (outside)	$51.00	$102.00	$75.50	$151.00	$62.20	$92.22
1 Equipment Operator (med.)	65.00	520.00	96.40	771.20		
1 Wheel Trencher, 150 H.P.		1405.45		1545.99	140.54	154.60
10 L.H., Daily Totals		$2027.45		$2468.19	$202.75	$246.82
Crew B-54C	Hr.	Daily	Hr.	Daily	Bare Costs	Incl. O&P
1 Laborer	$49.00	$392.00	$72.55	$580.40	$57.00	$84.47
1 Equipment Operator (med.)	65.00	520.00	96.40	771.20		
1 Wheel Trencher, 67 H.P.		1307.45		1438.19	81.72	89.89
16 L.H., Daily Totals		$2219.45		$2789.79	$138.72	$174.36
Crew B-54D	Hr.	Daily	Hr.	Daily	Bare Costs	Incl. O&P
1 Laborer	$49.00	$392.00	$72.55	$580.40	$57.00	$84.47
1 Equipment Operator (med.)	65.00	520.00	96.40	771.20		
1 Rock Trencher, 6" Width		1036.61		1140.27	64.79	71.27
16 L.H., Daily Totals		$1948.61		$2491.87	$121.79	$155.74
Crew B-54E	Hr.	Daily	Hr.	Daily	Bare Costs	Incl. O&P
1 Laborer	$49.00	$392.00	$72.55	$580.40	$57.00	$84.47
1 Equipment Operator (med.)	65.00	520.00	96.40	771.20		
1 Rock Trencher, 18" Width		1143.77		1258.15	71.49	78.63
16 L.H., Daily Totals		$2055.77		$2609.75	$128.49	$163.11
Crew B-55	Hr.	Daily	Hr.	Daily	Bare Costs	Incl. O&P
2 Laborers	$49.00	$784.00	$72.55	$1160.80	$51.05	$75.70
1 Truck Driver (light)	55.15	441.20	82.00	656.00		
1 Truck-Mounted Earth Auger		473.37		520.71		
1 Flatbed Truck, Gas, 3 Ton		519.55		571.51	41.37	45.51
24 L.H., Daily Totals		$2218.12		$2909.02	$92.42	$121.21
Crew B-56	Hr.	Daily	Hr.	Daily	Bare Costs	Incl. O&P
1 Laborer	$49.00	$392.00	$72.55	$580.40	$55.50	$82.25
1 Equip. Oper. (light)	62.00	496.00	91.95	735.60		
1 Air Track Drill, 4"		1245.86		1370.45		
1 Air Compressor, 600 cfm		490.62		539.68		
1 -50' Air Hose, 3"		45.72		50.29	111.39	122.53
16 L.H., Daily Totals		$2670.20		$3276.42	$166.89	$204.78

Crew No.	Bare Costs		Incl. Subs O&P		Cost Per Labor-Hour	
Crew B-57	Hr.	Daily	Hr.	Daily	Bare Costs	Incl. O&P
1 Labor Foreman (outside)	$51.00	$408.00	$75.50	$604.00	$56.33	$83.48
2 Laborers	49.00	784.00	72.55	1160.80		
1 Equip. Oper. (crane)	68.60	548.80	101.75	814.00		
1 Equip. Oper. (light)	62.00	496.00	91.95	735.60		
1 Equip. Oper. (oiler)	58.40	467.20	86.60	692.80		
1 Crawler Crane, 25 Ton		1332.93		1466.22		
1 Clamshell Bucket, 1 C.Y.		48.81		53.69		
1 Centr. Water Pump, 6"		410.89		451.98		
1 -20' Suction Hose, 6"		29.00		31.90		
20 -50' Discharge Hoses, 6"		412.52		453.77	46.54	51.20
48 L.H., Daily Totals		$4938.13		$6464.75	$102.88	$134.68
Crew B-58	Hr.	Daily	Hr.	Daily	Bare Costs	Incl. O&P
2 Laborers	$49.00	$784.00	$72.55	$1160.80	$53.33	$79.02
1 Equip. Oper. (light)	62.00	496.00	91.95	735.60		
1 Backhoe Loader, 48 H.P.		291.00		320.10		
1 Small Helicopter, w/ Pilot		6015.09		6616.60	262.75	289.03
24 L.H., Daily Totals		$7586.09		$8833.10	$316.09	$368.05
Crew B-59	Hr.	Daily	Hr.	Daily	Bare Costs	Incl. O&P
1 Truck Driver (heavy)	$57.25	$458.00	$85.10	$680.80	$57.25	$85.10
1 Truck Tractor, 220 H.P.		357.02		392.72		
1 Water Tank Trailer, 5000 Gal.		176.44		194.08	66.68	73.35
8 L.H., Daily Totals		$991.45		$1267.60	$123.93	$158.45
Crew B-59A	Hr.	Daily	Hr.	Daily	Bare Costs	Incl. O&P
2 Laborers	$49.00	$784.00	$72.55	$1160.80	$51.75	$76.73
1 Truck Driver (heavy)	57.25	458.00	85.10	680.80		
1 Water Tank Trailer, 5000 Gal.		176.44		194.08		
1 Truck Tractor, 220 H.P.		357.02		392.72	22.23	24.45
24 L.H., Daily Totals		$1775.45		$2428.40	$73.98	$101.18
Crew B-60	Hr.	Daily	Hr.	Daily	Bare Costs	Incl. O&P
1 Labor Foreman (outside)	$51.00	$408.00	$75.50	$604.00	$57.14	$84.69
2 Laborers	49.00	784.00	72.55	1160.80		
1 Equip. Oper. (crane)	68.60	548.80	101.75	814.00		
2 Equip. Oper. (light)	62.00	992.00	91.95	1471.20		
1 Equip. Oper. (oiler)	58.40	467.20	86.60	692.80		
1 Crawler Crane, 40 Ton		1423.92		1566.31		
1 Lead, 60' High		241.46		265.61		
1 Hammer, Diesel, 15K ft.-lbs.		712.59		783.85		
1 Backhoe Loader, 48 H.P.		291.00		320.10	47.66	52.43
56 L.H., Daily Totals		$5868.98		$7678.67	$104.80	$137.12
Crew B-61	Hr.	Daily	Hr.	Daily	Bare Costs	Incl. O&P
1 Labor Foreman (outside)	$51.00	$408.00	$75.50	$604.00	$52.00	$77.02
3 Laborers	49.00	1176.00	72.55	1741.20		
1 Equip. Oper. (light)	62.00	496.00	91.95	735.60		
1 Cement Mixer, 2 C.Y.		125.24		137.76		
1 Air Compressor, 160 cfm		209.86		230.85	8.38	9.22
40 L.H., Daily Totals		$2415.10		$3449.41	$60.38	$86.24
Crew B-62	Hr.	Daily	Hr.	Daily	Bare Costs	Incl. O&P
2 Laborers	$49.00	$784.00	$72.55	$1160.80	$53.33	$79.02
1 Equip. Oper. (light)	62.00	496.00	91.95	735.60		
1 Loader, Skid Steer, 30 H.P.		268.41		295.25	11.18	12.30
24 L.H., Daily Totals		$1548.41		$2191.65	$64.52	$91.32

Crews - Standard

Crew No.	Bare Costs		Incl. Subs O&P		Cost Per Labor-Hour	
	Hr.	Daily	Hr.	Daily	Bare Costs	Incl. O&P
Crew B-62A						
2 Laborers	$49.00	$784.00	$72.55	$1160.80	$53.33	$79.02
1 Equip. Oper. (light)	62.00	496.00	91.95	735.60		
1 Loader, Skid Steer, 30 H.P.		268.41		295.25		
1 Trencher Attachment		114.67		126.14	15.96	17.56
24 L.H., Daily Totals		$1663.08		$2317.79	$69.30	$96.57
Crew B-63						
4 Laborers	$49.00	$1568.00	$72.55	$2321.60	$51.60	$76.43
1 Equip. Oper. (light)	62.00	496.00	91.95	735.60		
1 Loader, Skid Steer, 30 H.P.		268.41		295.25	6.71	7.38
40 L.H., Daily Totals		$2332.41		$3352.45	$58.31	$83.81
Crew B-63B						
1 Labor Foreman (inside)	$49.50	$396.00	$73.30	$586.40	$52.38	$77.59
2 Laborers	49.00	784.00	72.55	1160.80		
1 Equip. Oper. (light)	62.00	496.00	91.95	735.60		
1 Loader, Skid Steer, 78 H.P.		394.64		434.10	12.33	13.57
32 L.H., Daily Totals		$2070.64		$2916.90	$64.71	$91.15
Crew B-64						
1 Laborer	$49.00	$392.00	$72.55	$580.40	$52.08	$77.28
1 Truck Driver (light)	55.15	441.20	82.00	656.00		
1 Power Mulcher (small)		275.58		303.13		
1 Flatbed Truck, Gas, 1.5 Ton		420.83		462.92	43.53	47.88
16 L.H., Daily Totals		$1529.61		$2002.45	$95.60	$125.15
Crew B-65						
1 Laborer	$49.00	$392.00	$72.55	$580.40	$52.08	$77.28
1 Truck Driver (light)	55.15	441.20	82.00	656.00		
1 Power Mulcher (Large)		658.73		724.60		
1 Flatbed Truck, Gas, 1.5 Ton		420.83		462.92	67.47	74.22
16 L.H., Daily Totals		$1912.76		$2423.92	$119.55	$151.49
Crew B-66						
1 Equip. Oper. (light)	$62.00	$496.00	$91.95	$735.60	$62.00	$91.95
1 Loader-Backhoe, 40 H.P.		232.56		255.82	29.07	31.98
8 L.H., Daily Totals		$728.56		$991.42	$91.07	$123.93
Crew B-67						
1 Millwright	$64.95	$519.60	$93.75	$750.00	$63.48	$92.85
1 Equip. Oper. (light)	62.00	496.00	91.95	735.60		
1 R.T. Forklift, 5,000 Lb., diesel		376.35		413.98	23.52	25.87
16 L.H., Daily Totals		$1391.95		$1899.58	$87.00	$118.72
Crew B-67B						
1 Millwright Foreman (inside)	$65.45	$523.60	$94.45	$755.60	$65.20	$94.10
1 Millwright	64.95	519.60	93.75	750.00		
16 L.H., Daily Totals		$1043.20		$1505.60	$65.20	$94.10
Crew B-68						
2 Millwrights	$64.95	$1039.20	$93.75	$1500.00	$63.97	$93.15
1 Equip. Oper. (light)	62.00	496.00	91.95	735.60		
1 R.T. Forklift, 5,000 Lb., diesel		376.35		413.98	15.68	17.25
24 L.H., Daily Totals		$1911.55		$2649.58	$79.65	$110.40
Crew B-68A						
1 Millwright Foreman (inside)	$65.45	$523.60	$94.45	$755.60	$65.12	$93.98
2 Millwrights	64.95	1039.20	93.75	1500.00		
1 Forklift, Smooth Floor, 8,000 Lb.		326.55		359.21	13.61	14.97
24 L.H., Daily Totals		$1889.35		$2614.81	$78.72	$108.95

Crew No.	Bare Costs		Incl. Subs O&P		Cost Per Labor-Hour	
	Hr.	Daily	Hr.	Daily	Bare Costs	Incl. O&P
Crew B-68B						
1 Millwright Foreman (inside)	$65.45	$523.60	$94.45	$755.60	$69.72	$102.38
2 Millwrights	64.95	1039.20	93.75	1500.00		
2 Electricians	71.70	1147.20	106.30	1700.80		
2 Plumbers	74.65	1194.40	111.05	1776.80		
1 R.T. Forklift, 5,000 Lb., gas		476.54		524.19	8.51	9.36
56 L.H., Daily Totals		$4380.94		$6257.39	$78.23	$111.74
Crew B-68C						
1 Millwright Foreman (inside)	$65.45	$523.60	$94.45	$755.60	$69.19	$101.39
1 Millwright	64.95	519.60	93.75	750.00		
1 Electrician	71.70	573.60	106.30	850.40		
1 Plumber	74.65	597.20	111.05	888.40		
1 R.T. Forklift, 5,000 Lb., gas		476.54		524.19	14.89	16.38
32 L.H., Daily Totals		$2690.54		$3768.59	$84.08	$117.77
Crew B-68D						
1 Labor Foreman (inside)	$49.50	$396.00	$73.30	$586.40	$53.50	$79.27
1 Laborer	49.00	392.00	72.55	580.40		
1 Equip. Oper. (light)	62.00	496.00	91.95	735.60		
1 R.T. Forklift, 5,000 Lb., gas		476.54		524.19	19.86	21.84
24 L.H., Daily Totals		$1760.54		$2426.59	$73.36	$101.11
Crew B-68E						
1 Struc. Steel Foreman (inside)	$67.55	$540.40	$103.55	$828.40	$67.15	$102.95
3 Struc. Steel Workers	67.05	1609.20	102.80	2467.20		
1 Welder	67.05	536.40	102.80	822.40		
1 Forklift, Smooth Floor, 8,000 Lb.		326.55		359.21	8.16	8.98
40 L.H., Daily Totals		$3012.55		$4477.21	$75.31	$111.93
Crew B-68F						
1 Skilled Worker Foreman (out)	$65.50	$524.00	$98.00	$784.00	$64.17	$96.00
2 Skilled Workers	63.50	1016.00	95.00	1520.00		
1 R.T. Forklift, 5,000 Lb., gas		476.54		524.19	19.86	21.84
24 L.H., Daily Totals		$2016.54		$2828.19	$84.02	$117.84
Crew B-68G						
2 Structural Steel Workers	$67.05	$1072.80	$102.80	$1644.80	$67.05	$102.80
1 R.T. Forklift, 5,000 Lb., gas		476.54		524.19	29.78	32.76
16 L.H., Daily Totals		$1549.34		$2168.99	$96.83	$135.56
Crew B-69						
1 Labor Foreman (outside)	$51.00	$408.00	$75.50	$604.00	$54.17	$80.25
3 Laborers	49.00	1176.00	72.55	1741.20		
1 Equip. Oper. (crane)	68.60	548.80	101.75	814.00		
1 Equip. Oper. (oiler)	58.40	467.20	86.60	692.80		
1 Hyd. Crane, 80 Ton		2742.60		3016.86	57.14	62.85
48 L.H., Daily Totals		$5342.60		$6868.86	$111.30	$143.10
Crew B-69A						
1 Labor Foreman (outside)	$51.00	$408.00	$75.50	$604.00	$53.30	$78.72
3 Laborers	49.00	1176.00	72.55	1741.20		
1 Equip. Oper. (medium)	65.00	520.00	96.40	771.20		
1 Concrete Finisher	56.80	454.40	82.80	662.40		
1 Curb/Gutter Paver, 2-Track		1107.32		1218.05	23.07	25.38
48 L.H., Daily Totals		$3665.72		$4996.85	$76.37	$104.10

For customer support on your Plumbing Costs with RSMeans Data call 800.448.8182.

Crews - Standard

Crew No.	Bare Costs		Incl. Subs O&P		Cost Per Labor-Hour	
Crew B-69B	Hr.	Daily	Hr.	Daily	Bare Costs	Incl. O&P
1 Labor Foreman (outside)	$51.00	$408.00	$75.50	$604.00	$53.30	$78.72
3 Laborers	49.00	1176.00	72.55	1741.20		
1 Equip. Oper. (medium)	65.00	520.00	96.40	771.20		
1 Cement Finisher	56.80	454.40	82.80	662.40		
1 Curb/Gutter Paver, 4-Track		1176.89		1294.58	24.52	26.97
48 L.H., Daily Totals		$3735.29		$5073.38	$77.82	$105.70
Crew B-70	Hr.	Daily	Hr.	Daily	Bare Costs	Incl. O&P
1 Labor Foreman (outside)	$51.00	$408.00	$75.50	$604.00	$56.14	$83.19
3 Laborers	49.00	1176.00	72.55	1741.20		
3 Equip. Oper. (medium)	65.00	1560.00	96.40	2313.60		
1 Grader, 30,000 Lbs.		1115.47		1227.02		
1 Ripper, Beam & 1 Shank		104.87		115.36		
1 Road Sweeper, S.P., 8' wide		581.33		639.46		
1 F.E. Loader, W.M., 1.5 C.Y.		582.76		641.03	42.58	46.84
56 L.H., Daily Totals		$5528.43		$7281.67	$98.72	$130.03
Crew B-70A	Hr.	Daily	Hr.	Daily	Bare Costs	Incl. O&P
1 Laborer	$49.00	$392.00	$72.55	$580.40	$61.80	$91.63
4 Equip. Oper. (medium)	65.00	2080.00	96.40	3084.80		
1 Grader, 40,000 Lbs.		1244.68		1369.15		
1 F.E. Loader, W.M., 2.5 C.Y.		815.12		896.63		
1 Dozer, 80 H.P.		634.87		698.36		
1 Roller, Pneum. Whl., 12 Ton		467.01		513.71	79.04	86.95
40 L.H., Daily Totals		$5633.68		$7143.04	$140.84	$178.58
Crew B-71	Hr.	Daily	Hr.	Daily	Bare Costs	Incl. O&P
1 Labor Foreman (outside)	$51.00	$408.00	$75.50	$604.00	$56.14	$83.19
3 Laborers	49.00	1176.00	72.55	1741.20		
3 Equip. Oper. (medium)	65.00	1560.00	96.40	2313.60		
1 Pvmt. Profiler, 750 H.P.		3893.02		4282.32		
1 Road Sweeper, S.P., 8' wide		581.33		639.46		
1 F.E. Loader, W.M., 1.5 C.Y.		582.76		641.03	90.31	99.34
56 L.H., Daily Totals		$8201.10		$10221.61	$146.45	$182.53
Crew B-72	Hr.	Daily	Hr.	Daily	Bare Costs	Incl. O&P
1 Labor Foreman (outside)	$51.00	$408.00	$75.50	$604.00	$57.25	$84.84
3 Laborers	49.00	1176.00	72.55	1741.20		
4 Equip. Oper. (medium)	65.00	2080.00	96.40	3084.80		
1 Pvmt. Profiler, 750 H.P.		3893.02		4282.32		
1 Hammermill, 250 H.P.		851.28		936.41		
1 Windrow Loader		1534.30		1687.73		
1 Mix Paver, 165 H.P.		1332.39		1465.63		
1 Roller, Pneum. Whl., 12 Ton		467.01		513.71	126.22	138.84
64 L.H., Daily Totals		$11741.99		$14315.79	$183.47	$223.68
Crew B-73	Hr.	Daily	Hr.	Daily	Bare Costs	Incl. O&P
1 Labor Foreman (outside)	$51.00	$408.00	$75.50	$604.00	$59.25	$87.83
2 Laborers	49.00	784.00	72.55	1160.80		
5 Equip. Oper. (medium)	65.00	2600.00	96.40	3856.00		
1 Road Mixer, 310 H.P.		2194.69		2414.16		
1 Tandem Roller, 10 Ton		319.84		351.82		
1 Hammermill, 250 H.P.		851.28		936.41		
1 Grader, 30,000 Lbs.		1115.47		1227.02		
.5 F.E. Loader, W.M., 1.5 C.Y.		291.38		320.52		
.5 Truck Tractor, 220 H.P.		178.51		196.36		
.5 Water Tank Trailer, 5000 Gal.		88.22		97.04	78.74	86.61
64 L.H., Daily Totals		$8831.39		$11164.12	$137.99	$174.44

Crew No.	Bare Costs		Incl. Subs O&P		Cost Per Labor-Hour	
Crew B-74	Hr.	Daily	Hr.	Daily	Bare Costs	Incl. O&P
1 Labor Foreman (outside)	$51.00	$408.00	$75.50	$604.00	$59.31	$87.98
1 Laborer	49.00	392.00	72.55	580.40		
4 Equip. Oper. (medium)	65.00	2080.00	96.40	3084.80		
2 Truck Drivers (heavy)	57.25	916.00	85.10	1361.60		
1 Grader, 30,000 Lbs.		1115.47		1227.02		
1 Ripper, Beam & 1 Shank		104.87		115.36		
2 Stabilizers, 310 H.P.		1811.65		1992.82		
1 Flatbed Truck, Gas, 3 Ton		519.55		571.51		
1 Chem. Spreader, Towed		91.24		100.37		
1 Roller, Vibratory, 25 Ton		554.08		609.48		
1 Water Tank Trailer, 5000 Gal.		176.44		194.08		
1 Truck Tractor, 220 H.P.		357.02		392.72	73.91	81.30
64 L.H., Daily Totals		$8526.32		$10834.16	$133.22	$169.28
Crew B-75	Hr.	Daily	Hr.	Daily	Bare Costs	Incl. O&P
1 Labor Foreman (outside)	$51.00	$408.00	$75.50	$604.00	$59.61	$88.39
1 Laborer	49.00	392.00	72.55	580.40		
4 Equip. Oper. (medium)	65.00	2080.00	96.40	3084.80		
1 Truck Driver (heavy)	57.25	458.00	85.10	680.80		
1 Grader, 30,000 Lbs.		1115.47		1227.02		
1 Ripper, Beam & 1 Shank		104.87		115.36		
2 Stabilizers, 310 H.P.		1811.65		1992.82		
1 Dist. Tanker, 3000 Gallon		382.04		420.25		
1 Truck Tractor, 6x4, 380 H.P.		573.49		630.83		
1 Roller, Vibratory, 25 Ton		554.08		609.48	81.10	89.21
56 L.H., Daily Totals		$7879.60		$9945.76	$140.71	$177.60
Crew B-76	Hr.	Daily	Hr.	Daily	Bare Costs	Incl. O&P
1 Dock Builder Foreman (outside)	$64.75	$518.00	$99.40	$795.20	$63.79	$96.78
5 Dock Builders	62.75	2510.00	96.30	3852.00		
2 Equip. Oper. (crane)	68.60	1097.60	101.75	1628.00		
1 Equip. Oper. (oiler)	58.40	467.20	86.60	692.80		
1 Crawler Crane, 50 Ton		1782.71		1960.98		
1 Barge, 400 Ton		991.44		1090.58		
1 Hammer, Diesel, 15K ft.-lbs.		712.59		783.85		
1 Lead, 60' High		241.46		265.61		
1 Air Compressor, 600 cfm		490.62		539.68		
2 -50' Air Hoses, 3"		91.44		100.58	59.86	65.85
72 L.H., Daily Totals		$8903.06		$11709.28	$123.65	$162.63
Crew B-76A	Hr.	Daily	Hr.	Daily	Bare Costs	Incl. O&P
1 Labor Foreman (outside)	$51.00	$408.00	$75.50	$604.00	$52.88	$78.33
5 Laborers	49.00	1960.00	72.55	2902.00		
1 Equip. Oper. (crane)	68.60	548.80	101.75	814.00		
1 Equip. Oper. (oiler)	58.40	467.20	86.60	692.80		
1 Crawler Crane, 50 Ton		1782.71		1960.98		
1 Barge, 400 Ton		991.44		1090.58	43.35	47.68
64 L.H., Daily Totals		$6158.14		$8064.35	$96.22	$126.01
Crew B-77	Hr.	Daily	Hr.	Daily	Bare Costs	Incl. O&P
1 Labor Foreman (outside)	$51.00	$408.00	$75.50	$604.00	$50.63	$75.03
3 Laborers	49.00	1176.00	72.55	1741.20		
1 Truck Driver (light)	55.15	441.20	82.00	656.00		
1 Crack Cleaner, 25 H.P.		173.35		190.69		
1 Crack Filler, Trailer Mtd.		209.88		230.87		
1 Flatbed Truck, Gas, 3 Ton		519.55		571.51	22.57	24.83
40 L.H., Daily Totals		$2927.99		$3994.27	$73.20	$99.86

Crews - Standard

Crew No.	Bare Costs		Incl. Subs O&P		Cost Per Labor-Hour	
Crew B-78	Hr.	Daily	Hr.	Daily	Bare Costs	Incl. O&P
1 Labor Foreman (outside)	$51.00	$408.00	$75.50	$604.00	$50.36	$74.62
4 Laborers	49.00	1568.00	72.55	2321.60		
1 Truck Driver (light)	55.15	441.20	82.00	656.00		
1 Paint Striper, S.P., 40 Gallon		78.05		85.86		
1 Flatbed Truck, Gas, 3 Ton		519.55		571.51		
1 Pickup Truck, 3/4 Ton		233.60		256.96	17.32	19.05
48 L.H., Daily Totals		$3248.41		$4495.93	$67.68	$93.67
Crew B-78A	Hr.	Daily	Hr.	Daily	Bare Costs	Incl. O&P
1 Equip. Oper. (light)	$62.00	$496.00	$91.95	$735.60	$62.00	$91.95
1 Line Rem. (Metal Balls) 115 H.P.		1712.49		1883.74	214.06	235.47
8 L.H., Daily Totals		$2208.49		$2619.34	$276.06	$327.42
Crew B-78B	Hr.	Daily	Hr.	Daily	Bare Costs	Incl. O&P
2 Laborers	$49.00	$784.00	$72.55	$1160.80	$50.44	$74.71
.25 Equip. Oper. (light)	62.00	124.00	91.95	183.90		
1 Pickup Truck, 3/4 Ton		233.60		256.96		
1 Line Rem.,11 H.P.,Walk Behind		198.93		218.82		
.25 Road Sweeper, S.P., 8' wide		145.33		159.87	32.10	35.31
18 L.H., Daily Totals		$1485.86		$1980.35	$82.55	$110.02
Crew B-78C	Hr.	Daily	Hr.	Daily	Bare Costs	Incl. O&P
1 Labor Foreman (outside)	$51.00	$408.00	$75.50	$604.00	$50.36	$74.62
4 Laborers	49.00	1568.00	72.55	2321.60		
1 Truck Driver (light)	55.15	441.20	82.00	656.00		
1 Paint Striper, T.M., 120 Gal.		709.11		780.03		
1 Flatbed Truck, Gas, 3 Ton		519.55		571.51		
1 Pickup Truck, 3/4 Ton		233.60		256.96	30.46	33.51
48 L.H., Daily Totals		$3879.47		$5190.10	$80.82	$108.13
Crew B-78D	Hr.	Daily	Hr.	Daily	Bare Costs	Incl. O&P
2 Labor Foremen (outside)	$51.00	$816.00	$75.50	$1208.00	$50.02	$74.08
7 Laborers	49.00	2744.00	72.55	4062.80		
1 Truck Driver (light)	55.15	441.20	82.00	656.00		
1 Paint Striper, T.M., 120 Gal.		709.11		780.03		
1 Flatbed Truck, Gas, 3 Ton		519.55		571.51		
3 Pickup Trucks, 3/4 Ton		700.81		770.89		
1 Air Compressor, 60 cfm		204.02		224.42		
1 -50' Air Hose, 3/4"		7.10		7.81		
1 Breaker, Pavement, 60 lb.		39.96		43.96	27.26	29.98
80 L.H., Daily Totals		$6181.75		$8325.41	$77.27	$104.07
Crew B-78E	Hr.	Daily	Hr.	Daily	Bare Costs	Incl. O&P
2 Labor Foremen (outside)	$51.00	$816.00	$75.50	$1208.00	$49.85	$73.83
9 Laborers	49.00	3528.00	72.55	5223.60		
1 Truck Driver (light)	55.15	441.20	82.00	656.00		
1 Paint Striper, T.M., 120 Gal.		709.11		780.03		
1 Flatbed Truck, Gas, 3 Ton		519.55		571.51		
4 Pickup Trucks, 3/4 Ton		934.41		1027.85		
2 Air Compressors, 60 cfm		408.04		448.84		
2 -50' Air Hoses, 3/4"		14.19		15.61		
2 Breakers, Pavement, 60 lb.		79.92		87.92	27.76	30.54
96 L.H., Daily Totals		$7450.43		$10019.36	$77.61	$104.37
Crew B-78F	Hr.	Daily	Hr.	Daily	Bare Costs	Incl. O&P
2 Labor Foremen (outside)	$51.00	$816.00	$75.50	$1208.00	$49.73	$73.65
11 Laborers	49.00	4312.00	72.55	6384.40		
1 Truck Driver (light)	55.15	441.20	82.00	656.00		
1 Paint Striper, T.M., 120 Gal.		709.11		780.03		
1 Flatbed Truck, Gas, 3 Ton		519.55		571.51		
7 Pickup Trucks, 3/4 Ton		1635.21		1798.73		
3 Air Compressors, 60 cfm		612.06		673.26		
3 -50' Air Hoses, 3/4"		21.29		23.42		
3 Breakers, Pavement, 60 lb.		119.89		131.88	32.30	35.53
112 L.H., Daily Totals		$9186.32		$12227.23	$82.02	$109.17
Crew B-79	Hr.	Daily	Hr.	Daily	Bare Costs	Incl. O&P
1 Labor Foreman (outside)	$51.00	$408.00	$75.50	$604.00	$50.63	$75.03
3 Laborers	49.00	1176.00	72.55	1741.20		
1 Truck Driver (light)	55.15	441.20	82.00	656.00		
1 Paint Striper, T.M., 120 Gal.		709.11		780.03		
1 Heating Kettle, 115 Gallon		177.14		194.85		
1 Flatbed Truck, Gas, 3 Ton		519.55		571.51		
2 Pickup Trucks, 3/4 Ton		467.20		513.92	46.83	51.51
40 L.H., Daily Totals		$3898.21		$5061.51	$97.46	$126.54
Crew B-79A	Hr.	Daily	Hr.	Daily	Bare Costs	Incl. O&P
1.5 Equip. Oper. (light)	$62.00	$744.00	$91.95	$1103.40	$62.00	$91.95
.5 Line Remov. (Grinder) 115 H.P.		876.48		964.13		
1 Line Rem. (Metal Balls) 115 H.P.		1712.49		1883.74	215.75	237.32
12 L.H., Daily Totals		$3332.97		$3951.26	$277.75	$329.27
Crew B-79B	Hr.	Daily	Hr.	Daily	Bare Costs	Incl. O&P
1 Laborer	$49.00	$392.00	$72.55	$580.40	$49.00	$72.55
1 Set of Gases		200.79		220.87	25.10	27.61
8 L.H., Daily Totals		$592.79		$801.27	$74.10	$100.16
Crew B-79C	Hr.	Daily	Hr.	Daily	Bare Costs	Incl. O&P
1 Labor Foreman (outside)	$51.00	$408.00	$75.50	$604.00	$50.16	$74.32
5 Laborers	49.00	1960.00	72.55	2902.00		
1 Truck Driver (light)	55.15	441.20	82.00	656.00		
1 Paint Striper, T.M., 120 Gal.		709.11		780.03		
1 Heating Kettle, 115 Gallon		177.14		194.85		
1 Flatbed Truck, Gas, 3 Ton		519.55		571.51		
3 Pickup Trucks, 3/4 Ton		700.81		770.89		
1 Air Compressor, 60 cfm		204.02		224.42		
1 -50' Air Hose, 3/4"		7.10		7.81		
1 Breaker, Pavement, 60 lb.		39.96		43.96	42.10	46.31
56 L.H., Daily Totals		$5166.89		$6755.46	$92.27	$120.63
Crew B-79D	Hr.	Daily	Hr.	Daily	Bare Costs	Incl. O&P
2 Labor Foremen (outside)	$51.00	$816.00	$75.50	$1208.00	$50.27	$74.47
5 Laborers	49.00	1960.00	72.55	2902.00		
1 Truck Driver (light)	55.15	441.20	82.00	656.00		
1 Paint Striper, T.M., 120 Gal.		709.11		780.03		
1 Heating Kettle, 115 Gallon		177.14		194.85		
1 Flatbed Truck, Gas, 3 Ton		519.55		571.51		
4 Pickup Trucks, 3/4 Ton		934.41		1027.85		
1 Air Compressor, 60 cfm		204.02		224.42		
1 -50' Air Hose, 3/4"		7.10		7.81		
1 Breaker, Pavement, 60 lb.		39.96		43.96	40.49	44.54
64 L.H., Daily Totals		$5808.49		$7616.42	$90.76	$119.01

Crews - Standard

Crew No.		Bare Costs		Incl. Subs O&P		Cost Per Labor-Hour	
Crew B-79E	Hr.	Daily	Hr.	Daily	Bare Costs	Incl. O&P
2 Labor Foremen (outside)	$51.00	$816.00	$75.50	$1208.00	$50.02	$74.08
7 Laborers	49.00	2744.00	72.55	4062.80		
1 Truck Driver (light)	55.15	441.20	82.00	656.00		
1 Paint Striper, T.M., 120 Gal.		709.11		780.03		
1 Heating Kettle, 115 Gallon		177.14		194.85		
1 Flatbed Truck, Gas, 3 Ton		519.55		571.51		
5 Pickup Trucks, 3/4 Ton		1168.01		1284.81		
2 Air Compressors, 60 cfm		408.04		448.84		
2 -50' Air Hoses, 3/4"		14.19		15.61		
2 Breakers, Pavement, 60 lb.		79.92		87.92	38.45	42.29
80 L.H., Daily Totals		$7077.17		$9310.37	$88.46	$116.38
Crew B-80	Hr.	Daily	Hr.	Daily	Bare Costs	Incl. O&P
1 Labor Foreman (outside)	$51.00	$408.00	$75.50	$604.00	$54.29	$80.50
1 Laborer	49.00	392.00	72.55	580.40		
1 Truck Driver (light)	55.15	441.20	82.00	656.00		
1 Equip. Oper. (light)	62.00	496.00	91.95	735.60		
1 Flatbed Truck, Gas, 3 Ton		519.55		571.51		
1 Earth Auger, Truck-Mtd.		162.91		179.20	21.33	23.46
32 L.H., Daily Totals		$2419.67		$3326.71	$75.61	$103.96
Crew B-80A	Hr.	Daily	Hr.	Daily	Bare Costs	Incl. O&P
3 Laborers	$49.00	$1176.00	$72.55	$1741.20	$49.00	$72.55
1 Flatbed Truck, Gas, 3 Ton		519.55		571.51	21.65	23.81
24 L.H., Daily Totals		$1695.55		$2312.71	$70.65	$96.36
Crew B-80B	Hr.	Daily	Hr.	Daily	Bare Costs	Incl. O&P
3 Laborers	$49.00	$1176.00	$72.55	$1741.20	$52.25	$77.40
1 Equip. Oper. (light)	62.00	496.00	91.95	735.60		
1 Crane, Flatbed Mounted, 3 Ton		581.20		639.32	18.16	19.98
32 L.H., Daily Totals		$2253.20		$3116.12	$70.41	$97.38
Crew B-80C	Hr.	Daily	Hr.	Daily	Bare Costs	Incl. O&P
2 Laborers	$49.00	$784.00	$72.55	$1160.80	$51.05	$75.70
1 Truck Driver (light)	55.15	441.20	82.00	656.00		
1 Flatbed Truck, Gas, 1.5 Ton		420.83		462.92		
1 Manual Fence Post Auger, Gas		55.37		60.91	19.84	21.83
24 L.H., Daily Totals		$1701.41		$2340.63	$70.89	$97.53
Crew B-81	Hr.	Daily	Hr.	Daily	Bare Costs	Incl. O&P
1 Laborer	$49.00	$392.00	$72.55	$580.40	$57.08	$84.68
1 Equip. Oper. (medium)	65.00	520.00	96.40	771.20		
1 Truck Driver (heavy)	57.25	458.00	85.10	680.80		
1 Hydromulcher, T.M., 3000 Gal.		772.89		850.18		
1 Truck Tractor, 220 H.P.		357.02		392.72	47.08	51.79
24 L.H., Daily Totals		$2499.91		$3275.30	$104.16	$136.47
Crew B-81A	Hr.	Daily	Hr.	Daily	Bare Costs	Incl. O&P
1 Laborer	$49.00	$392.00	$72.55	$580.40	$52.08	$77.28
1 Truck Driver (light)	55.15	441.20	82.00	656.00		
1 Hydromulcher, T.M., 600 Gal.		244.10		268.51		
1 Flatbed Truck, Gas, 3 Ton		519.55		571.51	47.73	52.50
16 L.H., Daily Totals		$1596.86		$2076.42	$99.80	$129.78
Crew B-82	Hr.	Daily	Hr.	Daily	Bare Costs	Incl. O&P
1 Laborer	$49.00	$392.00	$72.55	$580.40	$55.50	$82.25
1 Equip. Oper. (light)	62.00	496.00	91.95	735.60		
1 Horiz. Borer, 6 H.P.		119.62		131.58	7.48	8.22
16 L.H., Daily Totals		$1007.62		$1447.58	$62.98	$90.47

Crew No.		Bare Costs		Incl. Subs O&P		Cost Per Labor-Hour	
Crew B-82A	Hr.	Daily	Hr.	Daily	Bare Costs	Incl. O&P
2 Laborers	$49.00	$784.00	$72.55	$1160.80	$55.50	$82.25
2 Equip. Opers. (light)	62.00	992.00	91.95	1471.20		
2 Dump Truck, 8 C.Y., 220 H.P.		1012.60		1113.86		
1 Flatbed Trailer, 25 Ton		157.04		172.75		
1 Horiz. Dir. Drill, 20k lb. Thrust		714.31		785.74		
1 Mud Trailer for HDD, 1500 Gal.		724.86		797.34		
1 Pickup Truck, 4x4, 3/4 Ton		235.90		259.49		
1 Flatbed Trailer, 3 Ton		81.23		89.36		
1 Loader, Skid Steer, 78 H.P.		394.64		434.10	103.77	114.15
32 L.H., Daily Totals		$5096.58		$6284.64	$159.27	$196.40
Crew B-82B	Hr.	Daily	Hr.	Daily	Bare Costs	Incl. O&P
2 Laborers	$49.00	$784.00	$72.55	$1160.80	$55.50	$82.25
2 Equip. Opers. (light)	62.00	992.00	91.95	1471.20		
2 Dump Truck, 8 C.Y., 220 H.P.		1012.60		1113.86		
1 Flatbed Trailer, 25 Ton		157.04		172.75		
1 Horiz. Dir. Drill, 30k lb. Thrust		773.44		850.78		
1 Mud Trailer for HDD, 1500 Gal.		724.86		797.34		
1 Pickup Truck, 4x4, 3/4 Ton		235.90		259.49		
1 Flatbed Trailer, 3 Ton		81.23		89.36		
1 Loader, Skid Steer, 78 H.P.		394.64		434.10	105.62	116.18
32 L.H., Daily Totals		$5155.71		$6349.68	$161.12	$198.43
Crew B-82C	Hr.	Daily	Hr.	Daily	Bare Costs	Incl. O&P
2 Laborers	$49.00	$784.00	$72.55	$1160.80	$55.50	$82.25
2 Equip. Opers. (light)	62.00	992.00	91.95	1471.20		
2 Dump Truck, 8 C.Y., 220 H.P.		1012.60		1113.86		
1 Flatbed Trailer, 25 Ton		157.04		172.75		
1 Horiz. Dir. Drill, 50k lb. Thrust		910.87		1001.95		
1 Mud Trailer for HDD, 1500 Gal.		724.86		797.34		
1 Pickup Truck, 4x4, 3/4 Ton		235.90		259.49		
1 Flatbed Trailer, 3 Ton		81.23		89.36		
1 Loader, Skid Steer, 78 H.P.		394.64		434.10	109.91	120.90
32 L.H., Daily Totals		$5293.14		$6500.85	$165.41	$203.15
Crew B-82D	Hr.	Daily	Hr.	Daily	Bare Costs	Incl. O&P
1 Equip. Oper. (light)	$62.00	$496.00	$91.95	$735.60	$62.00	$91.95
1 Mud Trailer for HDD, 1500 Gal.		724.86		797.34	90.61	99.67
8 L.H., Daily Totals		$1220.86		$1532.94	$152.61	$191.62
Crew B-83	Hr.	Daily	Hr.	Daily	Bare Costs	Incl. O&P
1 Tugboat Captain	$65.00	$520.00	$96.40	$771.20	$57.00	$84.47
1 Tugboat Hand	49.00	392.00	72.55	580.40		
1 Tugboat, 250 H.P.		834.93		918.43	52.18	57.40
16 L.H., Daily Totals		$1746.93		$2270.03	$109.18	$141.88
Crew B-84	Hr.	Daily	Hr.	Daily	Bare Costs	Incl. O&P
1 Equip. Oper. (medium)	$65.00	$520.00	$96.40	$771.20	$65.00	$96.40
1 Rotary Mower/Tractor		251.43		276.57	31.43	34.57
8 L.H., Daily Totals		$771.43		$1047.77	$96.43	$130.97
Crew B-85	Hr.	Daily	Hr.	Daily	Bare Costs	Incl. O&P
3 Laborers	$49.00	$1176.00	$72.55	$1741.20	$53.85	$79.83
1 Equip. Oper. (medium)	65.00	520.00	96.40	771.20		
1 Truck Driver (heavy)	57.25	458.00	85.10	680.80		
1 Telescoping Boom Lift, to 80'		750.11		825.12		
1 Brush Chipper, 12", 130 H.P.		507.44		558.18		
1 Pruning Saw, Rotary		29.66		32.62	32.18	35.40
40 L.H., Daily Totals		$3441.20		$4609.12	$86.03	$115.23

Crews - Standard

Crew No.		Bare Costs		Incl. Subs O&P		Cost Per Labor-Hour	
Crew B-86	Hr.	Daily	Hr.	Daily	Bare Costs	Incl. O&P	
1 Equip. Oper. (medium)	$65.00	$520.00	$96.40	$771.20	$65.00	$96.40	
1 Stump Chipper, S.P.		260.03		286.03	32.50	35.75	
8 L.H., Daily Totals		$780.03		$1057.23	$97.50	$132.15	
Crew B-86A	Hr.	Daily	Hr.	Daily	Bare Costs	Incl. O&P	
1 Equip. Oper. (medium)	$65.00	$520.00	$96.40	$771.20	$65.00	$96.40	
1 Grader, 30,000 Lbs.		1115.47		1227.02	139.43	153.38	
8 L.H., Daily Totals		$1635.47		$1998.22	$204.43	$249.78	
Crew B-86B	Hr.	Daily	Hr.	Daily	Bare Costs	Incl. O&P	
1 Equip. Oper. (medium)	$65.00	$520.00	$96.40	$771.20	$65.00	$96.40	
1 Dozer, 200 H.P.		1443.21		1587.53	180.40	198.44	
8 L.H., Daily Totals		$1963.21		$2358.73	$245.40	$294.84	
Crew B-87	Hr.	Daily	Hr.	Daily	Bare Costs	Incl. O&P	
1 Laborer	$49.00	$392.00	$72.55	$580.40	$61.80	$91.63	
4 Equip. Oper. (medium)	65.00	2080.00	96.40	3084.80			
2 Feller Bunchers, 100 H.P.		2249.91		2474.90			
1 Log Chipper, 22" Tree		720.82		792.90			
1 Dozer, 105 H.P.		790.84		869.92			
1 Chain Saw, Gas, 36" Long		55.48		61.03	95.43	104.97	
40 L.H., Daily Totals		$6289.05		$7863.96	$157.23	$196.60	
Crew B-88	Hr.	Daily	Hr.	Daily	Bare Costs	Incl. O&P	
1 Laborer	$49.00	$392.00	$72.55	$580.40	$62.71	$92.99	
6 Equip. Oper. (medium)	65.00	3120.00	96.40	4627.20			
2 Feller Bunchers, 100 H.P.		2249.91		2474.90			
1 Log Chipper, 22" Tree		720.82		792.90			
2 Log Skidders, 50 H.P.		986.54		1085.20			
1 Dozer, 105 H.P.		790.84		869.92			
1 Chain Saw, Gas, 36" Long		55.48		61.03	85.78	94.36	
56 L.H., Daily Totals		$8315.60		$10491.56	$148.49	$187.35	
Crew B-89	Hr.	Daily	Hr.	Daily	Bare Costs	Incl. O&P	
1 Equip. Oper. (light)	$62.00	$496.00	$91.95	$735.60	$58.58	$86.97	
1 Truck Driver (light)	55.15	441.20	82.00	656.00			
1 Flatbed Truck, Gas, 3 Ton		519.55		571.51			
1 Concrete Saw		194.70		214.17			
1 Water Tank, 65 Gal.		106.22		116.84	51.28	56.41	
16 L.H., Daily Totals		$1757.67		$2294.12	$109.85	$143.38	
Crew B-89A	Hr.	Daily	Hr.	Daily	Bare Costs	Incl. O&P	
1 Skilled Worker	$63.50	$508.00	$95.00	$760.00	$56.25	$83.78	
1 Laborer	49.00	392.00	72.55	580.40			
1 Core Drill (Large)		155.93		171.52	9.75	10.72	
16 L.H., Daily Totals		$1055.93		$1511.92	$66.00	$94.50	
Crew B-89B	Hr.	Daily	Hr.	Daily	Bare Costs	Incl. O&P	
1 Equip. Oper. (light)	$62.00	$496.00	$91.95	$735.60	$58.58	$86.97	
1 Truck Driver (light)	55.15	441.20	82.00	656.00			
1 Wall Saw, Hydraulic, 10 H.P.		115.88		127.47			
1 Generator, Diesel, 100 kW		614.28		675.70			
1 Water Tank, 65 Gal.		106.22		116.84			
1 Flatbed Truck, Gas, 3 Ton		519.55		571.51	84.75	93.22	
16 L.H., Daily Totals		$2293.13		$2883.12	$143.32	$180.19	
Crew B-89C	Hr.	Daily	Hr.	Daily	Bare Costs	Incl. O&P	
1 Cement Finisher	$56.80	$454.40	$82.80	$662.40	$56.80	$82.80	
1 Masonry cut-off saw, gas		85.15		93.66	10.64	11.71	
8 L.H., Daily Totals		$539.55		$756.06	$67.44	$94.51	

Crew No.		Bare Costs		Incl. Subs O&P		Cost Per Labor-Hour	
Crew B-90	Hr.	Daily	Hr.	Daily	Bare Costs	Incl. O&P	
1 Labor Foreman (outside)	$51.00	$408.00	$75.50	$604.00	$54.56	$80.91	
3 Laborers	49.00	1176.00	72.55	1741.20			
2 Equip. Oper. (light)	62.00	992.00	91.95	1471.20			
2 Truck Drivers (heavy)	57.25	916.00	85.10	1361.60			
1 Road Mixer, 310 H.P.		2194.69		2414.16			
1 Dist. Truck, 2000 Gal.		346.74		381.41	39.71	43.68	
64 L.H., Daily Totals		$6033.43		$7973.57	$94.27	$124.59	
Crew B-90A	Hr.	Daily	Hr.	Daily	Bare Costs	Incl. O&P	
1 Labor Foreman (outside)	$51.00	$408.00	$75.50	$604.00	$58.43	$86.60	
2 Laborers	49.00	784.00	72.55	1160.80			
4 Equip. Oper. (medium)	65.00	2080.00	96.40	3084.80			
2 Graders, 30,000 Lbs.		2230.94		2454.03			
1 Tandem Roller, 10 Ton		319.84		351.82			
1 Roller, Pneum. Whl., 12 Ton		467.01		513.71	53.89	59.28	
56 L.H., Daily Totals		$6289.78		$8169.16	$112.32	$145.88	
Crew B-90B	Hr.	Daily	Hr.	Daily	Bare Costs	Incl. O&P	
1 Labor Foreman (outside)	$51.00	$408.00	$75.50	$604.00	$57.33	$84.97	
2 Laborers	49.00	784.00	72.55	1160.80			
3 Equip. Oper. (medium)	65.00	1560.00	96.40	2313.60			
1 Roller, Pneum. Whl., 12 Ton		467.01		513.71			
1 Road Mixer, 310 H.P.		2194.69		2414.16	55.45	61.00	
48 L.H., Daily Totals		$5413.69		$7006.26	$112.79	$145.96	
Crew B-90C	Hr.	Daily	Hr.	Daily	Bare Costs	Incl. O&P	
1 Labor Foreman (outside)	$51.00	$408.00	$75.50	$604.00	$55.80	$82.75	
4 Laborers	49.00	1568.00	72.55	2321.60			
3 Equip. Oper. (medium)	65.00	1560.00	96.40	2313.60			
3 Truck Drivers (heavy)	57.25	1374.00	85.10	2042.40			
3 Road Mixers, 310 H.P.		6584.06		7242.47	74.82	82.30	
88 L.H., Daily Totals		$11494.06		$14524.07	$130.61	$165.05	
Crew B-90D	Hr.	Daily	Hr.	Daily	Bare Costs	Incl. O&P	
1 Labor Foreman (outside)	$51.00	$408.00	$75.50	$604.00	$54.75	$81.18	
6 Laborers	49.00	2352.00	72.55	3482.40			
3 Equip. Oper. (medium)	65.00	1560.00	96.40	2313.60			
3 Truck Drivers (heavy)	57.25	1374.00	85.10	2042.40			
3 Road Mixers, 310 H.P.		6584.06		7242.47	63.31	69.64	
104 L.H., Daily Totals		$12278.06		$15684.87	$118.06	$150.82	
Crew B-90E	Hr.	Daily	Hr.	Daily	Bare Costs	Incl. O&P	
1 Labor Foreman (outside)	$51.00	$408.00	$75.50	$604.00	$55.47	$82.22	
4 Laborers	49.00	1568.00	72.55	2321.60			
3 Equip. Oper. (medium)	65.00	1560.00	96.40	2313.60			
1 Truck Driver (heavy)	57.25	458.00	85.10	680.80			
1 Road Mixer, 310 H.P.		2194.69		2414.16	30.48	33.53	
72 L.H., Daily Totals		$6188.69		$8334.16	$85.95	$115.75	
Crew B-91	Hr.	Daily	Hr.	Daily	Bare Costs	Incl. O&P	
1 Labor Foreman (outside)	$51.00	$408.00	$75.50	$604.00	$58.28	$86.41	
2 Laborers	49.00	784.00	72.55	1160.80			
4 Equip. Oper. (medium)	65.00	2080.00	96.40	3084.80			
1 Truck Driver (heavy)	57.25	458.00	85.10	680.80			
1 Dist. Tanker, 3000 Gallon		382.04		420.25			
1 Truck Tractor, 6x4, 380 H.P.		573.49		630.83			
1 Aggreg. Spreader, S.P.		985.21		1083.74			
1 Roller, Pneum. Whl., 12 Ton		467.01		513.71			
1 Tandem Roller, 10 Ton		319.84		351.82	42.62	46.88	
64 L.H., Daily Totals		$6457.59		$8530.74	$100.90	$133.29	

Crews - Standard

Crew No.		Bare Costs		Incl. Subs O&P		Cost Per Labor-Hour	
Crew B-91B	Hr.	Daily	Hr.	Daily	Bare Costs	Incl. O&P
1 Laborer	$49.00	$392.00	$72.55	$580.40	$57.00	$84.47
1 Equipment Oper. (med.)	65.00	520.00	96.40	771.20		
1 Road Sweeper, Vac. Assist.		1975.20		2172.72	123.45	135.80
16 L.H., Daily Totals		$2887.20		$3524.32	$180.45	$220.27
Crew B-91C	Hr.	Daily	Hr.	Daily	Bare Costs	Incl. O&P
1 Laborer	$49.00	$392.00	$72.55	$580.40	$52.08	$77.28
1 Truck Driver (light)	55.15	441.20	82.00	656.00		
1 Catch Basin Cleaning Truck		622.72		684.99	38.92	42.81
16 L.H., Daily Totals		$1455.92		$1921.39	$91.00	$120.09
Crew B-91D	Hr.	Daily	Hr.	Daily	Bare Costs	Incl. O&P
1 Labor Foreman (outside)	$51.00	$408.00	$75.50	$604.00	$56.58	$83.88
5 Laborers	49.00	1960.00	72.55	2902.00		
5 Equip. Oper. (medium)	65.00	2600.00	96.40	3856.00		
2 Truck Drivers (heavy)	57.25	916.00	85.10	1361.60		
1 Aggreg. Spreader, S.P.		985.21		1083.74		
2 Truck Tractors, 6x4, 380 H.P.		1146.97		1261.67		
2 Dist. Tankers, 3000 Gallon		764.08		840.49		
2 Pavement Brushes, Towed		202.16		222.37		
2 Rollers Pneum. Whl., 12 Ton		934.01		1027.41	38.77	42.65
104 L.H., Daily Totals		$9916.44		$13159.28	$95.35	$126.53
Crew B-92	Hr.	Daily	Hr.	Daily	Bare Costs	Incl. O&P
1 Labor Foreman (outside)	$51.00	$408.00	$75.50	$604.00	$49.50	$73.29
3 Laborers	49.00	1176.00	72.55	1741.20		
1 Crack Cleaner, 25 H.P.		173.35		190.69		
1 Air Compressor, 60 cfm		204.02		224.42		
1 Tar Kettle, T.M.		209.32		230.25		
1 Flatbed Truck, Gas, 3 Ton		519.55		571.51	34.57	38.03
32 L.H., Daily Totals		$2690.24		$3562.07	$84.07	$111.31
Crew B-93	Hr.	Daily	Hr.	Daily	Bare Costs	Incl. O&P
1 Equip. Oper. (medium)	$65.00	$520.00	$96.40	$771.20	$65.00	$96.40
1 Feller Buncher, 100 H.P.		1124.96		1237.45	140.62	154.68
8 L.H., Daily Totals		$1644.96		$2008.65	$205.62	$251.08
Crew B-94A	Hr.	Daily	Hr.	Daily	Bare Costs	Incl. O&P
1 Laborer	$49.00	$392.00	$72.55	$580.40	$49.00	$72.55
1 Diaphragm Water Pump, 2"		65.04		71.55		
1 -20' Suction Hose, 2"		4.61		5.07		
2 -50' Discharge Hoses, 2"		9.05		9.96	9.84	10.82
8 L.H., Daily Totals		$470.70		$666.97	$58.84	$83.37
Crew B-94B	Hr.	Daily	Hr.	Daily	Bare Costs	Incl. O&P
1 Laborer	$49.00	$392.00	$72.55	$580.40	$49.00	$72.55
1 Diaphragm Water Pump, 4"		157.09		172.80		
1 -20' Suction Hose, 4"		19.59		21.55		
2 -50' Discharge Hoses, 4"		29.12		32.03	25.73	28.30
8 L.H., Daily Totals		$597.80		$806.78	$74.73	$100.85
Crew B-94C	Hr.	Daily	Hr.	Daily	Bare Costs	Incl. O&P
1 Laborer	$49.00	$392.00	$72.55	$580.40	$49.00	$72.55
1 Centrifugal Water Pump, 3"		86.40		95.04		
1 -20' Suction Hose, 3"		9.86		10.84		
2 -50' Discharge Hoses, 3"		10.57		11.63	13.35	14.69
8 L.H., Daily Totals		$498.83		$697.91	$62.35	$87.24

Crew No.		Bare Costs		Incl. Subs O&P		Cost Per Labor-Hour	
Crew B-94D	Hr.	Daily	Hr.	Daily	Bare Costs	Incl. O&P
1 Laborer	$49.00	$392.00	$72.55	$580.40	$49.00	$72.55
1 Centr. Water Pump, 6"		410.89		451.98		
1 -20' Suction Hose, 6"		29.00		31.90		
2 -50' Discharge Hoses, 6"		41.25		45.38	60.14	66.16
8 L.H., Daily Totals		$873.14		$1109.65	$109.14	$138.71
Crew C-1	Hr.	Daily	Hr.	Daily	Bare Costs	Incl. O&P
3 Carpenters	$60.55	$1453.20	$89.65	$2151.60	$57.66	$85.38
1 Laborer	49.00	392.00	72.55	580.40		
32 L.H., Daily Totals		$1845.20		$2732.00	$57.66	$85.38
Crew C-2	Hr.	Daily	Hr.	Daily	Bare Costs	Incl. O&P
1 Carpenter Foreman (outside)	$62.55	$500.40	$92.60	$740.80	$58.96	$87.29
4 Carpenters	60.55	1937.60	89.65	2868.80		
1 Laborer	49.00	392.00	72.55	580.40		
48 L.H., Daily Totals		$2830.00		$4190.00	$58.96	$87.29
Crew C-2A	Hr.	Daily	Hr.	Daily	Bare Costs	Incl. O&P
1 Carpenter Foreman (outside)	$62.55	$500.40	$92.60	$740.80	$58.33	$86.15
3 Carpenters	60.55	1453.20	89.65	2151.60		
1 Cement Finisher	56.80	454.40	82.80	662.40		
1 Laborer	49.00	392.00	72.55	580.40		
48 L.H., Daily Totals		$2800.00		$4135.20	$58.33	$86.15
Crew C-3	Hr.	Daily	Hr.	Daily	Bare Costs	Incl. O&P
1 Rodman Foreman (outside)	$69.05	$552.40	$102.95	$823.60	$62.16	$92.50
4 Rodmen (reinf.)	67.05	2145.60	100.00	3200.00		
1 Equip. Oper. (light)	62.00	496.00	91.95	735.60		
2 Laborers	49.00	784.00	72.55	1160.80		
3 Stressing Equipment		53.25		58.57		
.5 Grouting Equipment		102.15		112.36	2.43	2.67
64 L.H., Daily Totals		$4133.39		$6090.93	$64.58	$95.17
Crew C-4	Hr.	Daily	Hr.	Daily	Bare Costs	Incl. O&P
1 Rodman Foreman (outside)	$69.05	$552.40	$102.95	$823.60	$67.55	$100.74
3 Rodmen (reinf.)	67.05	1609.20	100.00	2400.00		
3 Stressing Equipment		53.25		58.57	1.66	1.83
32 L.H., Daily Totals		$2214.85		$3282.17	$69.21	$102.57
Crew C-4A	Hr.	Daily	Hr.	Daily	Bare Costs	Incl. O&P
2 Rodmen (reinf.)	$67.05	$1072.80	$100.00	$1600.00	$67.05	$100.00
4 Stressing Equipment		71.00		78.09	4.44	4.88
16 L.H., Daily Totals		$1143.80		$1678.09	$71.49	$104.88
Crew C-5	Hr.	Daily	Hr.	Daily	Bare Costs	Incl. O&P
1 Rodman Foreman (outside)	$69.05	$552.40	$102.95	$823.60	$66.32	$98.76
4 Rodmen (reinf.)	67.05	2145.60	100.00	3200.00		
1 Equip. Oper. (crane)	68.60	548.80	101.75	814.00		
1 Equip. Oper. (oiler)	58.40	467.20	86.60	692.80		
1 Hyd. Crane, 25 Ton		2335.01		2568.51	41.70	45.87
56 L.H., Daily Totals		$6049.01		$8098.91	$108.02	$144.62
Crew C-6	Hr.	Daily	Hr.	Daily	Bare Costs	Incl. O&P
1 Labor Foreman (outside)	$51.00	$408.00	$75.50	$604.00	$50.63	$74.75
4 Laborers	49.00	1568.00	72.55	2321.60		
1 Cement Finisher	56.80	454.40	82.80	662.40		
2 Gas Engine Vibrators		62.39		68.63	1.30	1.43
48 L.H., Daily Totals		$2492.79		$3656.63	$51.93	$76.18

Crews - Standard

Crew No.	Bare Costs		Incl. Subs O&P		Cost Per Labor-Hour	
Crew C-6A	Hr.	Daily	Hr.	Daily	Bare Costs	Incl. O&P
2 Cement Finishers	$56.80	$908.80	$82.80	$1324.80	$56.80	$82.80
1 Concrete Vibrator, Elec, 2 HP		43.55		47.90	2.72	2.99
16 L.H., Daily Totals		$952.35		$1372.70	$59.52	$85.79
Crew C-7	Hr.	Daily	Hr.	Daily	Bare Costs	Incl. O&P
1 Labor Foreman (outside)	$51.00	$408.00	$75.50	$604.00	$52.91	$78.23
5 Laborers	49.00	1960.00	72.55	2902.00		
1 Cement Finisher	56.80	454.40	82.80	662.40		
1 Equip. Oper. (medium)	65.00	520.00	96.40	771.20		
1 Equip. Oper. (oiler)	58.40	467.20	86.60	692.80		
2 Gas Engine Vibrators		62.39		68.63		
1 Concrete Bucket, 1 C.Y.		52.84		58.12		
1 Hyd. Crane, 55 Ton		2551.41		2806.55	37.04	40.74
72 L.H., Daily Totals		$6476.24		$8565.70	$89.95	$118.97
Crew C-7A	Hr.	Daily	Hr.	Daily	Bare Costs	Incl. O&P
1 Labor Foreman (outside)	$51.00	$408.00	$75.50	$604.00	$51.31	$76.06
5 Laborers	49.00	1960.00	72.55	2902.00		
2 Truck Drivers (heavy)	57.25	916.00	85.10	1361.60		
2 Conc. Transit Mixers		1479.61		1627.57	23.12	25.43
64 L.H., Daily Totals		$4763.61		$6495.17	$74.43	$101.49
Crew C-7B	Hr.	Daily	Hr.	Daily	Bare Costs	Incl. O&P
1 Labor Foreman (outside)	$51.00	$408.00	$75.50	$604.00	$52.88	$78.33
5 Laborers	49.00	1960.00	72.55	2902.00		
1 Equipment Operator, Crane	68.60	548.80	101.75	814.00		
1 Equipment Oiler	58.40	467.20	86.60	692.80		
1 Conc. Bucket, 2 C.Y.		79.23		87.16		
1 Lattice Boom Crane, 165 Ton		2779.06		3056.96	44.66	49.13
64 L.H., Daily Totals		$6242.29		$8156.92	$97.54	$127.45
Crew C-7C	Hr.	Daily	Hr.	Daily	Bare Costs	Incl. O&P
1 Labor Foreman (outside)	$51.00	$408.00	$75.50	$604.00	$53.25	$78.88
5 Laborers	49.00	1960.00	72.55	2902.00		
2 Equipment Operators (med.)	65.00	1040.00	96.40	1542.40		
2 F.E. Loaders, W.M., 4 C.Y.		1733.19		1906.51	27.08	29.79
64 L.H., Daily Totals		$5141.19		$6954.91	$80.33	$108.67
Crew C-7D	Hr.	Daily	Hr.	Daily	Bare Costs	Incl. O&P
1 Labor Foreman (outside)	$51.00	$408.00	$75.50	$604.00	$51.57	$76.38
5 Laborers	49.00	1960.00	72.55	2902.00		
1 Equip. Oper. (medium)	65.00	520.00	96.40	771.20		
1 Concrete Conveyer		204.02		224.43	3.64	4.01
56 L.H., Daily Totals		$3092.02		$4501.63	$55.21	$80.39
Crew C-8	Hr.	Daily	Hr.	Daily	Bare Costs	Incl. O&P
1 Labor Foreman (outside)	$51.00	$408.00	$75.50	$604.00	$53.80	$79.31
3 Laborers	49.00	1176.00	72.55	1741.20		
2 Cement Finishers	56.80	908.80	82.80	1324.80		
1 Equip. Oper. (medium)	65.00	520.00	96.40	771.20		
1 Concrete Pump (Small)		861.85		948.03	15.39	16.93
56 L.H., Daily Totals		$3874.65		$5389.23	$69.19	$96.24
Crew C-8A	Hr.	Daily	Hr.	Daily	Bare Costs	Incl. O&P
1 Labor Foreman (outside)	$51.00	$408.00	$75.50	$604.00	$51.93	$76.46
3 Laborers	49.00	1176.00	72.55	1741.20		
2 Cement Finishers	56.80	908.80	82.80	1324.80		
48 L.H., Daily Totals		$2492.80		$3670.00	$51.93	$76.46

Crew No.	Bare Costs		Incl. Subs O&P		Cost Per Labor-Hour	
Crew C-8B	Hr.	Daily	Hr.	Daily	Bare Costs	Incl. O&P
1 Labor Foreman (outside)	$51.00	$408.00	$75.50	$604.00	$52.60	$77.91
3 Laborers	49.00	1176.00	72.55	1741.20		
1 Equip. Oper. (medium)	65.00	520.00	96.40	771.20		
1 Vibrating Power Screed		88.86		97.75		
1 Roller, Vibratory, 25 Ton		554.08		609.48		
1 Dozer, 200 H.P.		1443.21		1587.53	52.15	57.37
40 L.H., Daily Totals		$4190.15		$5411.17	$104.75	$135.28
Crew C-8C	Hr.	Daily	Hr.	Daily	Bare Costs	Incl. O&P
1 Labor Foreman (outside)	$51.00	$408.00	$75.50	$604.00	$53.30	$78.72
3 Laborers	49.00	1176.00	72.55	1741.20		
1 Cement Finisher	56.80	454.40	82.80	662.40		
1 Equip. Oper. (medium)	65.00	520.00	96.40	771.20		
1 Shotcrete Pump Rig, 12 C.Y./hr		675.78		743.36		
1 Air Compressor, 160 cfm		209.86		230.85		
4 -50' Air Hoses, 1"		36.11		39.72		
4 -50' Air Hoses, 2"		127.66		140.43	21.86	24.05
48 L.H., Daily Totals		$3607.81		$4933.15	$75.16	$102.77
Crew C-8D	Hr.	Daily	Hr.	Daily	Bare Costs	Incl. O&P
1 Labor Foreman (outside)	$51.00	$408.00	$75.50	$604.00	$54.70	$80.70
1 Laborer	49.00	392.00	72.55	580.40		
1 Cement Finisher	56.80	454.40	82.80	662.40		
1 Equipment Oper. (light)	62.00	496.00	91.95	735.60		
1 Air Compressor, 250 cfm		226.90		249.59		
2 -50' Air Hoses, 1"		18.05		19.86	7.65	8.42
32 L.H., Daily Totals		$1995.35		$2851.85	$62.35	$89.12
Crew C-8E	Hr.	Daily	Hr.	Daily	Bare Costs	Incl. O&P
1 Labor Foreman (outside)	$51.00	$408.00	$75.50	$604.00	$52.80	$77.98
3 Laborers	49.00	1176.00	72.55	1741.20		
1 Cement Finisher	56.80	454.40	82.80	662.40		
1 Equipment Oper. (light)	62.00	496.00	91.95	735.60		
1 Shotcrete Rig, 35 C.Y./hr		826.00		908.60		
1 Air Compressor, 250 cfm		226.90		249.59		
4 -50' Air Hoses, 1"		36.11		39.72		
4 -50' Air Hoses, 2"		127.66		140.43	25.35	27.88
48 L.H., Daily Totals		$3751.06		$5081.53	$78.15	$105.87
Crew C-9	Hr.	Daily	Hr.	Daily	Bare Costs	Incl. O&P
1 Cement Finisher	$56.80	$454.40	$82.80	$662.40	$54.20	$79.96
2 Laborers	49.00	784.00	72.55	1160.80		
1 Equipment Oper. (light)	62.00	496.00	91.95	735.60		
1 Grout Pump, 50 C.F./hr.		165.21		181.73		
1 Air Compressor, 160 cfm		209.86		230.85		
2 -50' Air Hoses, 1"		18.05		19.86		
2 -50' Air Hoses, 2"		63.83		70.21	14.28	15.71
32 L.H., Daily Totals		$2191.36		$3061.45	$68.48	$95.67
Crew C-10	Hr.	Daily	Hr.	Daily	Bare Costs	Incl. O&P
1 Laborer	$49.00	$392.00	$72.55	$580.40	$54.20	$79.38
2 Cement Finishers	56.80	908.80	82.80	1324.80		
24 L.H., Daily Totals		$1300.80		$1905.20	$54.20	$79.38
Crew C-10B	Hr.	Daily	Hr.	Daily	Bare Costs	Incl. O&P
3 Laborers	$49.00	$1176.00	$72.55	$1741.20	$52.12	$76.65
2 Cement Finishers	56.80	908.80	82.80	1324.80		
1 Concrete Mixer, 10 C.F.		170.44		187.48		
2 Trowels, 48" Walk-Behind		246.40		271.04	10.42	11.46
40 L.H., Daily Totals		$2501.64		$3524.52	$62.54	$88.11

Crews - Standard

Crew No.		Bare Costs		Incl. Subs O&P		Cost Per Labor-Hour	
Crew C-10C	Hr.	Daily	Hr.	Daily	Bare Costs	Incl. O&P
1 Laborer	$49.00	$392.00	$72.55	$580.40	$54.20	$79.38
2 Cement Finishers	56.80	908.80	82.80	1324.80		
1 Trowel, 48" Walk-Behind		123.20		135.52	5.13	5.65
24 L.H., Daily Totals		$1424.00		$2040.72	$59.33	$85.03
Crew C-10D	Hr.	Daily	Hr.	Daily	Bare Costs	Incl. O&P
1 Laborer	$49.00	$392.00	$72.55	$580.40	$54.20	$79.38
2 Cement Finishers	56.80	908.80	82.80	1324.80		
1 Vibrating Power Screed		88.86		97.75		
1 Trowel, 48" Walk-Behind		123.20		135.52	8.84	9.72
24 L.H., Daily Totals		$1512.86		$2138.47	$63.04	$89.10
Crew C-10E	Hr.	Daily	Hr.	Daily	Bare Costs	Incl. O&P
1 Laborer	$49.00	$392.00	$72.55	$580.40	$54.20	$79.38
2 Cement Finishers	56.80	908.80	82.80	1324.80		
1 Vibrating Power Screed		88.86		97.75		
1 Cement Trowel, 96" Ride-On		248.89		273.78	14.07	15.48
24 L.H., Daily Totals		$1638.56		$2276.73	$68.27	$94.86
Crew C-10F	Hr.	Daily	Hr.	Daily	Bare Costs	Incl. O&P
1 Laborer	$49.00	$392.00	$72.55	$580.40	$54.20	$79.38
2 Cement Finishers	56.80	908.80	82.80	1324.80		
1 Telescoping Boom Lift, to 60'		467.60		514.36	19.48	21.43
24 L.H., Daily Totals		$1768.40		$2419.56	$73.68	$100.81
Crew C-11	Hr.	Daily	Hr.	Daily	Bare Costs	Incl. O&P
1 Struc. Steel Foreman (outside)	$69.05	$552.40	$105.85	$846.80	$66.48	$101.22
6 Struc. Steel Workers	67.05	3218.40	102.80	4934.40		
1 Equip. Oper. (crane)	68.60	548.80	101.75	814.00		
1 Equip. Oper. (oiler)	58.40	467.20	86.60	692.80		
1 Lattice Boom Crane, 150 Ton		2687.58		2956.34	37.33	41.06
72 L.H., Daily Totals		$7474.38		$10244.34	$103.81	$142.28
Crew C-12	Hr.	Daily	Hr.	Daily	Bare Costs	Incl. O&P
1 Carpenter Foreman (outside)	$62.55	$500.40	$92.60	$740.80	$60.30	$89.31
3 Carpenters	60.55	1453.20	89.65	2151.60		
1 Laborer	49.00	392.00	72.55	580.40		
1 Equip. Oper. (crane)	68.60	548.80	101.75	814.00		
1 Hyd. Crane, 12 Ton		2224.21		2446.63	46.34	50.97
48 L.H., Daily Totals		$5118.61		$6733.43	$106.64	$140.28
Crew C-13	Hr.	Daily	Hr.	Daily	Bare Costs	Incl. O&P
1 Struc. Steel Worker	$67.05	$536.40	$102.80	$822.40	$64.88	$98.42
1 Welder	67.05	536.40	102.80	822.40		
1 Carpenter	60.55	484.40	89.65	717.20		
1 Welder, Gas Engine, 300 amp		163.86		180.24	6.83	7.51
24 L.H., Daily Totals		$1721.06		$2542.24	$71.71	$105.93
Crew C-14	Hr.	Daily	Hr.	Daily	Bare Costs	Incl. O&P
1 Carpenter Foreman (outside)	$62.55	$500.40	$92.60	$740.80	$59.45	$88.06
5 Carpenters	60.55	2422.00	89.65	3586.00		
4 Laborers	49.00	1568.00	72.55	2321.60		
4 Rodmen (reinf.)	67.05	2145.60	100.00	3200.00		
2 Cement Finishers	56.80	908.80	82.80	1324.80		
1 Equip. Oper. (crane)	68.60	548.80	101.75	814.00		
1 Equip. Oper. (oiler)	58.40	467.20	86.60	692.80		
1 Hyd. Crane, 80 Ton		2742.60		3016.86	19.05	20.95
144 L.H., Daily Totals		$11303.40		$15696.86	$78.50	$109.01

Crew No.		Bare Costs		Incl. Subs O&P		Cost Per Labor-Hour	
Crew C-14A	Hr.	Daily	Hr.	Daily	Bare Costs	Incl. O&P
1 Carpenter Foreman (outside)	$62.55	$500.40	$92.60	$740.80	$60.77	$90.05
16 Carpenters	60.55	7750.40	89.65	11475.20		
4 Rodmen (reinf.)	67.05	2145.60	100.00	3200.00		
2 Laborers	49.00	784.00	72.55	1160.80		
1 Cement Finisher	56.80	454.40	82.80	662.40		
1 Equip. Oper. (medium)	65.00	520.00	96.40	771.20		
1 Gas Engine Vibrator		31.20		34.32		
1 Concrete Pump (Small)		861.85		948.03	4.47	4.91
200 L.H., Daily Totals		$13047.85		$18992.75	$65.24	$94.96
Crew C-14B	Hr.	Daily	Hr.	Daily	Bare Costs	Incl. O&P
1 Carpenter Foreman (outside)	$62.55	$500.40	$92.60	$740.80	$60.62	$89.77
16 Carpenters	60.55	7750.40	89.65	11475.20		
4 Rodmen (reinf.)	67.05	2145.60	100.00	3200.00		
2 Laborers	49.00	784.00	72.55	1160.80		
2 Cement Finishers	56.80	908.80	82.80	1324.80		
1 Equip. Oper. (medium)	65.00	520.00	96.40	771.20		
1 Gas Engine Vibrator		31.20		34.32		
1 Concrete Pump (Small)		861.85		948.03	4.29	4.72
208 L.H., Daily Totals		$13502.25		$19655.15	$64.91	$94.50
Crew C-14C	Hr.	Daily	Hr.	Daily	Bare Costs	Incl. O&P
1 Carpenter Foreman (outside)	$62.55	$500.40	$92.60	$740.80	$58.05	$85.96
6 Carpenters	60.55	2906.40	89.65	4303.20		
2 Rodmen (reinf.)	67.05	1072.80	100.00	1600.00		
4 Laborers	49.00	1568.00	72.55	2321.60		
1 Cement Finisher	56.80	454.40	82.80	662.40		
1 Gas Engine Vibrator		31.20		34.32	.28	.31
112 L.H., Daily Totals		$6533.20		$9662.32	$58.33	$86.27
Crew C-14D	Hr.	Daily	Hr.	Daily	Bare Costs	Incl. O&P
1 Carpenter Foreman (outside)	$62.55	$500.40	$92.60	$740.80	$60.25	$89.22
18 Carpenters	60.55	8719.20	89.65	12909.60		
2 Rodmen (reinf.)	67.05	1072.80	100.00	1600.00		
2 Laborers	49.00	784.00	72.55	1160.80		
1 Cement Finisher	56.80	454.40	82.80	662.40		
1 Equip. Oper. (medium)	65.00	520.00	96.40	771.20		
1 Gas Engine Vibrator		31.20		34.32		
1 Concrete Pump (Small)		861.85		948.03	4.47	4.91
200 L.H., Daily Totals		$12943.85		$18827.15	$64.72	$94.14
Crew C-14E	Hr.	Daily	Hr.	Daily	Bare Costs	Incl. O&P
1 Carpenter Foreman (outside)	$62.55	$500.40	$92.60	$740.80	$59.60	$88.40
2 Carpenters	60.55	968.80	89.65	1434.40		
4 Rodmen (reinf.)	67.05	2145.60	100.00	3200.00		
3 Laborers	49.00	1176.00	72.55	1741.20		
1 Cement Finisher	56.80	454.40	82.80	662.40		
1 Gas Engine Vibrator		31.20		34.32	.35	.39
88 L.H., Daily Totals		$5276.40		$7813.12	$59.96	$88.79
Crew C-14F	Hr.	Daily	Hr.	Daily	Bare Costs	Incl. O&P
1 Labor Foreman (outside)	$51.00	$408.00	$75.50	$604.00	$54.42	$79.71
2 Laborers	49.00	784.00	72.55	1160.80		
6 Cement Finishers	56.80	2726.40	82.80	3974.40		
1 Gas Engine Vibrator		31.20		34.32	.43	.48
72 L.H., Daily Totals		$3949.60		$5773.52	$54.86	$80.19

Crews - Standard

Crew No.	Bare Costs		Incl. Subs O&P		Cost Per Labor-Hour	
					Bare Costs	Incl. O&P
Crew C-14G	**Hr.**	**Daily**	**Hr.**	**Daily**		
1 Labor Foreman (outside)	$51.00	$408.00	$75.50	$604.00	$53.74	$78.83
2 Laborers	49.00	784.00	72.55	1160.80		
4 Cement Finishers	56.80	1817.60	82.80	2649.60		
1 Gas Engine Vibrator		31.20		34.32	.56	.61
56 L.H., Daily Totals		$3040.80		$4448.72	$54.30	$79.44
Crew C-14H	**Hr.**	**Daily**	**Hr.**	**Daily**	Bare Costs	Incl. O&P
1 Carpenter Foreman (outside)	$62.55	$500.40	$92.60	$740.80	$59.42	$87.88
2 Carpenters	60.55	968.80	89.65	1434.40		
1 Rodman (reinf.)	67.05	536.40	100.00	800.00		
1 Laborer	49.00	392.00	72.55	580.40		
1 Cement Finisher	56.80	454.40	82.80	662.40		
1 Gas Engine Vibrator		31.20		34.32	.65	.71
48 L.H., Daily Totals		$2883.20		$4252.32	$60.07	$88.59
Crew C-14L	**Hr.**	**Daily**	**Hr.**	**Daily**	Bare Costs	Incl. O&P
1 Carpenter Foreman (outside)	$62.55	$500.40	$92.60	$740.80	$56.55	$83.63
6 Carpenters	60.55	2906.40	89.65	4303.20		
4 Laborers	49.00	1568.00	72.55	2321.60		
1 Cement Finisher	56.80	454.40	82.80	662.40		
1 Gas Engine Vibrator		31.20		34.32	.33	.36
96 L.H., Daily Totals		$5460.40		$8062.32	$56.88	$83.98
Crew C-14M	**Hr.**	**Daily**	**Hr.**	**Daily**	Bare Costs	Incl. O&P
1 Carpenter Foreman (outside)	$62.55	$500.40	$92.60	$740.80	$58.81	$87.03
2 Carpenters	60.55	968.80	89.65	1434.40		
1 Rodman (reinf.)	67.05	536.40	100.00	800.00		
2 Laborers	49.00	784.00	72.55	1160.80		
1 Cement Finisher	56.80	454.40	82.80	662.40		
1 Equip. Oper. (medium)	65.00	520.00	96.40	771.20		
1 Gas Engine Vibrator		31.20		34.32		
1 Concrete Pump (Small)		861.85		948.03	13.95	15.35
64 L.H., Daily Totals		$4657.05		$6551.95	$72.77	$102.37
Crew C-15	**Hr.**	**Daily**	**Hr.**	**Daily**	Bare Costs	Incl. O&P
1 Carpenter Foreman (outside)	$62.55	$500.40	$92.60	$740.80	$56.81	$83.91
2 Carpenters	60.55	968.80	89.65	1434.40		
3 Laborers	49.00	1176.00	72.55	1741.20		
2 Cement Finishers	56.80	908.80	82.80	1324.80		
1 Rodman (reinf.)	67.05	536.40	100.00	800.00		
72 L.H., Daily Totals		$4090.40		$6041.20	$56.81	$83.91
Crew C-16	**Hr.**	**Daily**	**Hr.**	**Daily**	Bare Costs	Incl. O&P
1 Labor Foreman (outside)	$51.00	$408.00	$75.50	$604.00	$53.80	$79.31
3 Laborers	49.00	1176.00	72.55	1741.20		
2 Cement Finishers	56.80	908.80	82.80	1324.80		
1 Equip. Oper. (medium)	65.00	520.00	96.40	771.20		
1 Gunite Pump Rig		368.88		405.77		
2 -50' Air Hoses, 3/4"		14.19		15.61		
2 -50' Air Hoses, 2"		63.83		70.21	7.98	8.78
56 L.H., Daily Totals		$3459.71		$4932.80	$61.78	$88.09
Crew C-16A	**Hr.**	**Daily**	**Hr.**	**Daily**	Bare Costs	Incl. O&P
1 Laborer	$49.00	$392.00	$72.55	$580.40	$56.90	$83.64
2 Cement Finishers	56.80	908.80	82.80	1324.80		
1 Equip. Oper. (medium)	65.00	520.00	96.40	771.20		
1 Gunite Pump Rig		368.88		405.77		
2 -50' Air Hoses, 3/4"		14.19		15.61		
2 -50' Air Hoses, 2"		63.83		70.21		
1 Telescoping Boom Lift, to 60'		467.60		514.36	28.58	31.44
32 L.H., Daily Totals		$2735.31		$3682.36	$85.48	$115.07

Crew No.	Bare Costs		Incl. Subs O&P		Cost Per Labor-Hour	
Crew C-17	**Hr.**	**Daily**	**Hr.**	**Daily**	Bare Costs	Incl. O&P
2 Skilled Worker Foremen (out)	$65.50	$1048.00	$98.00	$1568.00	$63.90	$95.60
8 Skilled Workers	63.50	4064.00	95.00	6080.00		
80 L.H., Daily Totals		$5112.00		$7648.00	$63.90	$95.60
Crew C-17A	**Hr.**	**Daily**	**Hr.**	**Daily**	Bare Costs	Incl. O&P
2 Skilled Worker Foremen (out)	$65.50	$1048.00	$98.00	$1568.00	$63.96	$95.68
8 Skilled Workers	63.50	4064.00	95.00	6080.00		
.13 Equip. Oper. (crane)	68.60	71.34	101.75	105.82		
.13 Hyd. Crane, 80 Ton		356.54		392.19	4.40	4.84
81.04 L.H., Daily Totals		$5539.88		$8146.01	$68.36	$100.52
Crew C-17B	**Hr.**	**Daily**	**Hr.**	**Daily**	Bare Costs	Incl. O&P
2 Skilled Worker Foremen (out)	$65.50	$1048.00	$98.00	$1568.00	$64.01	$95.75
8 Skilled Workers	63.50	4064.00	95.00	6080.00		
.25 Equip. Oper. (crane)	68.60	137.20	101.75	203.50		
.25 Hyd. Crane, 80 Ton		685.65		754.22		
.25 Trowel, 48" Walk-Behind		30.80		33.88	8.74	9.61
82 L.H., Daily Totals		$5965.65		$8639.60	$72.75	$105.36
Crew C-17C	**Hr.**	**Daily**	**Hr.**	**Daily**	Bare Costs	Incl. O&P
2 Skilled Worker Foremen (out)	$65.50	$1048.00	$98.00	$1568.00	$64.07	$95.83
8 Skilled Workers	63.50	4064.00	95.00	6080.00		
.38 Equip. Oper. (crane)	68.60	208.54	101.75	309.32		
.38 Hyd. Crane, 80 Ton		1042.19		1146.41	12.55	13.81
83.04 L.H., Daily Totals		$6362.73		$9103.73	$76.62	$109.63
Crew C-17D	**Hr.**	**Daily**	**Hr.**	**Daily**	Bare Costs	Incl. O&P
2 Skilled Worker Foremen (out)	$65.50	$1048.00	$98.00	$1568.00	$64.12	$95.89
8 Skilled Workers	63.50	4064.00	95.00	6080.00		
.5 Equip. Oper. (crane)	68.60	274.40	101.75	407.00		
.5 Hyd. Crane, 80 Ton		1371.30		1508.43	16.32	17.96
84 L.H., Daily Totals		$6757.70		$9563.43	$80.45	$113.85
Crew C-17E	**Hr.**	**Daily**	**Hr.**	**Daily**	Bare Costs	Incl. O&P
2 Skilled Worker Foremen (out)	$65.50	$1048.00	$98.00	$1568.00	$63.90	$95.60
8 Skilled Workers	63.50	4064.00	95.00	6080.00		
1 Hyd. Jack with Rods		42.48		46.73	.53	.58
80 L.H., Daily Totals		$5154.48		$7694.73	$64.43	$96.18
Crew C-18	**Hr.**	**Daily**	**Hr.**	**Daily**	Bare Costs	Incl. O&P
.13 Labor Foreman (outside)	$51.00	$53.04	$75.50	$78.52	$49.23	$72.89
1 Laborer	49.00	392.00	72.55	580.40		
1 Concrete Cart, 10 C.F.		155.28		170.81	17.18	18.90
9.04 L.H., Daily Totals		$600.32		$829.73	$66.41	$91.78
Crew C-19	**Hr.**	**Daily**	**Hr.**	**Daily**	Bare Costs	Incl. O&P
.13 Labor Foreman (outside)	$51.00	$53.04	$75.50	$78.52	$49.23	$72.89
1 Laborer	49.00	392.00	72.55	580.40		
1 Concrete Cart, 18 C.F.		130.70		143.77	14.46	15.90
9.04 L.H., Daily Totals		$575.74		$802.69	$63.69	$88.79
Crew C-20	**Hr.**	**Daily**	**Hr.**	**Daily**	Bare Costs	Incl. O&P
1 Labor Foreman (outside)	$51.00	$408.00	$75.50	$604.00	$52.23	$77.18
5 Laborers	49.00	1960.00	72.55	2902.00		
1 Cement Finisher	56.80	454.40	82.80	662.40		
1 Equip. Oper. (medium)	65.00	520.00	96.40	771.20		
2 Gas Engine Vibrators		62.39		68.63		
1 Concrete Pump (Small)		861.85		948.03	14.44	15.89
64 L.H., Daily Totals		$4266.64		$5956.27	$66.67	$93.07

Crews - Standard

Crew No.		Bare Costs		Incl. Subs O&P		Cost Per Labor-Hour	
Crew C-21	**Hr.**	**Daily**	**Hr.**	**Daily**	**Bare Costs**	**Incl. O&P**	
1 Labor Foreman (outside)	$51.00	$408.00	$75.50	$604.00	$52.23	$77.18	
5 Laborers	49.00	1960.00	72.55	2902.00			
1 Cement Finisher	56.80	454.40	82.80	662.40			
1 Equip. Oper. (medium)	65.00	520.00	96.40	771.20			
2 Gas Engine Vibrators		62.39		68.63			
1 Concrete Conveyer		204.02		224.43	4.16	4.58	
64 L.H., Daily Totals		$3608.82		$5232.66	$56.39	$81.76	
Crew C-22	**Hr.**	**Daily**	**Hr.**	**Daily**	**Bare Costs**	**Incl. O&P**	
1 Rodman Foreman (outside)	$69.05	$552.40	$102.95	$823.60	$67.25	$100.27	
4 Rodmen (reinf.)	67.05	2145.60	100.00	3200.00			
.13 Equip. Oper. (crane)	68.60	71.34	101.75	105.82			
.13 Equip. Oper. (oiler)	58.40	60.74	86.60	90.06			
.13 Hyd. Crane, 25 Ton		303.55		333.91	7.21	7.93	
42.08 L.H., Daily Totals		$3133.63		$4553.39	$74.47	$108.21	
Crew C-23	**Hr.**	**Daily**	**Hr.**	**Daily**	**Bare Costs**	**Incl. O&P**	
2 Skilled Worker Foremen (out)	$65.50	$1048.00	$98.00	$1568.00	$63.90	$95.44	
6 Skilled Workers	63.50	3048.00	95.00	4560.00			
1 Equip. Oper. (crane)	68.60	548.80	101.75	814.00			
1 Equip. Oper. (oiler)	58.40	467.20	86.60	692.80			
1 Lattice Boom Crane, 90 Ton		2790.64		3069.70	34.88	38.37	
80 L.H., Daily Totals		$7902.64		$10704.50	$98.78	$133.81	
Crew C-23A	**Hr.**	**Daily**	**Hr.**	**Daily**	**Bare Costs**	**Incl. O&P**	
1 Labor Foreman (outside)	$51.00	$408.00	$75.50	$604.00	$55.20	$81.79	
2 Laborers	49.00	784.00	72.55	1160.80			
1 Equip. Oper. (crane)	68.60	548.80	101.75	814.00			
1 Equip. Oper. (oiler)	58.40	467.20	86.60	692.80			
1 Crawler Crane, 100 Ton		1625.12		1787.63			
3 Conc. Buckets, 8 C.Y.		444.62		489.08	51.74	56.92	
40 L.H., Daily Totals		$4277.74		$5548.31	$106.94	$138.71	
Crew C-24	**Hr.**	**Daily**	**Hr.**	**Daily**	**Bare Costs**	**Incl. O&P**	
2 Skilled Worker Foremen (out)	$65.50	$1048.00	$98.00	$1568.00	$63.90	$95.44	
6 Skilled Workers	63.50	3048.00	95.00	4560.00			
1 Equip. Oper. (crane)	68.60	548.80	101.75	814.00			
1 Equip. Oper. (oiler)	58.40	467.20	86.60	692.80			
1 Lattice Boom Crane, 150 Ton		2687.58		2956.34	33.59	36.95	
80 L.H., Daily Totals		$7799.58		$10591.14	$97.49	$132.39	
Crew C-25	**Hr.**	**Daily**	**Hr.**	**Daily**	**Bare Costs**	**Incl. O&P**	
2 Rodmen (reinf.)	$67.05	$1072.80	$100.00	$1600.00	$54.02	$83.03	
2 Rodmen Helpers	41.00	656.00	66.05	1056.80			
32 L.H., Daily Totals		$1728.80		$2656.80	$54.02	$83.03	
Crew C-27	**Hr.**	**Daily**	**Hr.**	**Daily**	**Bare Costs**	**Incl. O&P**	
2 Cement Finishers	$56.80	$908.80	$82.80	$1324.80	$56.80	$82.80	
1 Concrete Saw		194.70		214.17	12.17	13.39	
16 L.H., Daily Totals		$1103.50		$1538.97	$68.97	$96.19	
Crew C-28	**Hr.**	**Daily**	**Hr.**	**Daily**	**Bare Costs**	**Incl. O&P**	
1 Cement Finisher	$56.80	$454.40	$82.80	$662.40	$56.80	$82.80	
1 Portable Air Compressor, Gas		37.25		40.98	4.66	5.12	
8 L.H., Daily Totals		$491.65		$703.38	$61.46	$87.92	
Crew C-29	**Hr.**	**Daily**	**Hr.**	**Daily**	**Bare Costs**	**Incl. O&P**	
1 Laborer	$49.00	$392.00	$72.55	$580.40	$49.00	$72.55	
1 Pressure Washer		135.59		149.14	16.95	18.64	
8 L.H., Daily Totals		$527.59		$729.54	$65.95	$91.19	

Crew No.		Bare Costs		Incl. Subs O&P		Cost Per Labor-Hour	
Crew C-30	**Hr.**	**Daily**	**Hr.**	**Daily**	**Bare Costs**	**Incl. O&P**	
1 Laborer	$49.00	$392.00	$72.55	$580.40	$49.00	$72.55	
1 Concrete Mixer, 10 C.F.		170.44		187.48	21.31	23.44	
8 L.H., Daily Totals		$562.44		$767.88	$70.31	$95.99	
Crew C-31	**Hr.**	**Daily**	**Hr.**	**Daily**	**Bare Costs**	**Incl. O&P**	
1 Cement Finisher	$56.80	$454.40	$82.80	$662.40	$56.80	$82.80	
1 Grout Pump		368.88		405.77	46.11	50.72	
8 L.H., Daily Totals		$823.28		$1068.17	$102.91	$133.52	
Crew C-32	**Hr.**	**Daily**	**Hr.**	**Daily**	**Bare Costs**	**Incl. O&P**	
1 Cement Finisher	$56.80	$454.40	$82.80	$662.40	$52.90	$77.67	
1 Laborer	49.00	392.00	72.55	580.40			
1 Crack Chaser Saw, Gas, 6 H.P.		87.84		96.62			
1 Vacuum Pick-Up System		87.74		96.51	10.97	12.07	
16 L.H., Daily Totals		$1021.98		$1435.93	$63.87	$89.75	
Crew D-1	**Hr.**	**Daily**	**Hr.**	**Daily**	**Bare Costs**	**Incl. O&P**	
1 Bricklayer	$59.65	$477.20	$89.10	$712.80	$54.08	$80.78	
1 Bricklayer Helper	48.50	388.00	72.45	579.60			
16 L.H., Daily Totals		$865.20		$1292.40	$54.08	$80.78	
Crew D-2	**Hr.**	**Daily**	**Hr.**	**Daily**	**Bare Costs**	**Incl. O&P**	
3 Bricklayers	$59.65	$1431.60	$89.10	$2138.40	$55.68	$83.10	
2 Bricklayer Helpers	48.50	776.00	72.45	1159.20			
.5 Carpenter	60.55	242.20	89.65	358.60			
44 L.H., Daily Totals		$2449.80		$3656.20	$55.68	$83.10	
Crew D-3	**Hr.**	**Daily**	**Hr.**	**Daily**	**Bare Costs**	**Incl. O&P**	
3 Bricklayers	$59.65	$1431.60	$89.10	$2138.40	$55.45	$82.78	
2 Bricklayer Helpers	48.50	776.00	72.45	1159.20			
.25 Carpenter	60.55	121.10	89.65	179.30			
42 L.H., Daily Totals		$2328.70		$3476.90	$55.45	$82.78	
Crew D-4	**Hr.**	**Daily**	**Hr.**	**Daily**	**Bare Costs**	**Incl. O&P**	
1 Bricklayer	$59.65	$477.20	$89.10	$712.80	$54.66	$81.49	
2 Bricklayer Helpers	48.50	776.00	72.45	1159.20			
1 Equip. Oper. (light)	62.00	496.00	91.95	735.60			
1 Grout Pump, 50 C.F./hr.		165.21		181.73	5.16	5.68	
32 L.H., Daily Totals		$1914.41		$2789.33	$59.83	$87.17	
Crew D-5	**Hr.**	**Daily**	**Hr.**	**Daily**	**Bare Costs**	**Incl. O&P**	
1 Bricklayer	59.65	477.20	89.10	712.80	59.65	89.10	
8 L.H., Daily Totals		$477.20		$712.80	$59.65	$89.10	
Crew D-6	**Hr.**	**Daily**	**Hr.**	**Daily**	**Bare Costs**	**Incl. O&P**	
3 Bricklayers	$59.65	$1431.60	$89.10	$2138.40	$54.33	$81.13	
3 Bricklayer Helpers	48.50	1164.00	72.45	1738.80			
.25 Carpenter	60.55	121.10	89.65	179.30			
50 L.H., Daily Totals		$2716.70		$4056.50	$54.33	$81.13	
Crew D-7	**Hr.**	**Daily**	**Hr.**	**Daily**	**Bare Costs**	**Incl. O&P**	
1 Tile Layer	$57.20	$457.60	$83.25	$666.00	$51.65	$75.17	
1 Tile Layer Helper	46.10	368.80	67.10	536.80			
16 L.H., Daily Totals		$826.40		$1202.80	$51.65	$75.17	
Crew D-8	**Hr.**	**Daily**	**Hr.**	**Daily**	**Bare Costs**	**Incl. O&P**	
3 Bricklayers	$59.65	$1431.60	$89.10	$2138.40	$55.19	$82.44	
2 Bricklayer Helpers	48.50	776.00	72.45	1159.20			
40 L.H., Daily Totals		$2207.60		$3297.60	$55.19	$82.44	

Crews - Standard

Crew No.	Hr.	Bare Costs Daily	Hr.	Incl. Subs O&P Daily	Bare Costs	Incl. O&P
Crew D-9						
3 Bricklayers	$59.65	$1431.60	$89.10	$2138.40	$54.08	$80.78
3 Bricklayer Helpers	48.50	1164.00	72.45	1738.80		
48 L.H., Daily Totals		$2595.60		$3877.20	$54.08	$80.78
Crew D-10						
1 Bricklayer Foreman (outside)	$61.65	$493.20	$92.10	$736.80	$59.60	$88.85
1 Bricklayer	59.65	477.20	89.10	712.80		
1 Bricklayer Helper	48.50	388.00	72.45	579.60		
1 Equip. Oper. (crane)	68.60	548.80	101.75	814.00		
1 S.P. Crane, 4x4, 12 Ton		663.72		730.09	20.74	22.82
32 L.H., Daily Totals		$2570.92		$3573.29	$80.34	$111.67
Crew D-11						
1 Bricklayer Foreman (outside)	$61.65	$493.20	$92.10	$736.80	$56.60	$84.55
1 Bricklayer	59.65	477.20	89.10	712.80		
1 Bricklayer Helper	48.50	388.00	72.45	579.60		
24 L.H., Daily Totals		$1358.40		$2029.20	$56.60	$84.55
Crew D-12						
1 Bricklayer Foreman (outside)	$61.65	$493.20	$92.10	$736.80	$54.58	$81.53
1 Bricklayer	59.65	477.20	89.10	712.80		
2 Bricklayer Helpers	48.50	776.00	72.45	1159.20		
32 L.H., Daily Totals		$1746.40		$2608.80	$54.58	$81.53
Crew D-13						
1 Bricklayer Foreman (outside)	$61.65	$493.20	$92.10	$736.80	$57.91	$86.25
1 Bricklayer	59.65	477.20	89.10	712.80		
2 Bricklayer Helpers	48.50	776.00	72.45	1159.20		
1 Carpenter	60.55	484.40	89.65	717.20		
1 Equip. Oper. (crane)	68.60	548.80	101.75	814.00		
1 S.P. Crane, 4x4, 12 Ton		663.72		730.09	13.83	15.21
48 L.H., Daily Totals		$3443.32		$4870.09	$71.74	$101.46
Crew D-14						
3 Bricklayers	$59.65	$1431.60	$89.10	$2138.40	$56.86	$84.94
1 Bricklayer Helper	48.50	388.00	72.45	579.60		
32 L.H., Daily Totals		$1819.60		$2718.00	$56.86	$84.94
Crew E-1						
1 Welder Foreman (outside)	$69.05	$552.40	$105.85	$846.80	$66.03	$100.20
1 Welder	67.05	536.40	102.80	822.40		
1 Equip. Oper. (light)	62.00	496.00	91.95	735.60		
1 Welder, Gas Engine, 300 amp		163.86		180.24	6.83	7.51
24 L.H., Daily Totals		$1748.66		$2585.04	$72.86	$107.71
Crew E-2						
1 Struc. Steel Foreman (outside)	$69.05	$552.40	$105.85	$846.80	$66.32	$100.77
4 Struc. Steel Workers	67.05	2145.60	102.80	3289.60		
1 Equip. Oper. (crane)	68.60	548.80	101.75	814.00		
1 Equip. Oper. (oiler)	58.40	467.20	86.60	692.80		
1 Lattice Boom Crane, 90 Ton		2790.64		3069.70	49.83	54.82
56 L.H., Daily Totals		$6504.64		$8712.90	$116.15	$155.59
Crew E-3						
1 Struc. Steel Foreman (outside)	$69.05	$552.40	$105.85	$846.80	$67.72	$103.82
1 Struc. Steel Worker	67.05	536.40	102.80	822.40		
1 Welder	67.05	536.40	102.80	822.40		
1 Welder, Gas Engine, 300 amp		163.86		180.24	6.83	7.51
24 L.H., Daily Totals		$1789.06		$2671.84	$74.54	$111.33

Crew No.	Hr.	Bare Costs Daily	Hr.	Incl. Subs O&P Daily	Bare Costs	Incl. O&P
Crew E-3A						
1 Struc. Steel Foreman (outside)	$69.05	$552.40	$105.85	$846.80	$67.72	$103.82
1 Struc. Steel Worker	67.05	536.40	102.80	822.40		
1 Welder	67.05	536.40	102.80	822.40		
1 Welder, Gas Engine, 300 amp		163.86		180.24		
1 Telescoping Boom Lift, to 40'		344.31		378.74	21.17	23.29
24 L.H., Daily Totals		$2133.36		$3050.58	$88.89	$127.11
Crew E-4						
1 Struc. Steel Foreman (outside)	$69.05	$552.40	$105.85	$846.80	$67.55	$103.56
3 Struc. Steel Workers	67.05	1609.20	102.80	2467.20		
1 Welder, Gas Engine, 300 amp		163.86		180.24	5.12	5.63
32 L.H., Daily Totals		$2325.46		$3494.24	$72.67	$109.20
Crew E-5						
2 Struc. Steel Foremen (outside)	$69.05	$1104.80	$105.85	$1693.60	$66.74	$101.69
5 Struc. Steel Workers	67.05	2682.00	102.80	4112.00		
1 Equip. Oper. (crane)	68.60	548.80	101.75	814.00		
1 Welder	67.05	536.40	102.80	822.40		
1 Equip. Oper. (oiler)	58.40	467.20	86.60	692.80		
1 Lattice Boom Crane, 90 Ton		2790.64		3069.70		
1 Welder, Gas Engine, 300 amp		163.86		180.24	36.93	40.62
80 L.H., Daily Totals		$8293.69		$11384.74	$103.67	$142.31
Crew E-6						
3 Struc. Steel Foremen (outside)	$69.05	$1657.20	$105.85	$2540.40	$66.67	$101.62
9 Struc. Steel Workers	67.05	4827.60	102.80	7401.60		
1 Equip. Oper. (crane)	68.60	548.80	101.75	814.00		
1 Welder	67.05	536.40	102.80	822.40		
1 Equip. Oper. (oiler)	58.40	467.20	86.60	692.80		
1 Equip. Oper. (light)	62.00	496.00	91.95	735.60		
1 Lattice Boom Crane, 90 Ton		2790.64		3069.70		
1 Welder, Gas Engine, 300 amp		163.86		180.24	13.83	15.21
1 Air Compressor, 160 cfm		209.86		230.85		
2 Impact Wrenches		108.74		119.61	25.57	28.13
128 L.H., Daily Totals		$11806.29		$16607.20	$92.24	$129.74
Crew E-7						
1 Struc. Steel Foreman (outside)	$69.05	$552.40	$105.85	$846.80	$66.74	$101.69
4 Struc. Steel Workers	67.05	2145.60	102.80	3289.60		
1 Equip. Oper. (crane)	68.60	548.80	101.75	814.00		
1 Equip. Oper. (oiler)	58.40	467.20	86.60	692.80		
1 Welder Foreman (outside)	69.05	552.40	105.85	846.80		
2 Welders	67.05	1072.80	102.80	1644.80		
1 Lattice Boom Crane, 90 Ton		2790.64		3069.70		
2 Welder, Gas Engine, 300 amp		327.71		360.48	38.98	42.88
80 L.H., Daily Totals		$8457.55		$11564.98	$105.72	$144.56
Crew E-8						
1 Struc. Steel Foreman (outside)	$69.05	$552.40	$105.85	$846.80	$66.42	$101.11
4 Struc. Steel Workers	67.05	2145.60	102.80	3289.60		
1 Welder Foreman (outside)	69.05	552.40	105.85	846.80		
4 Welders	67.05	2145.60	102.80	3289.60		
1 Equip. Oper. (crane)	68.60	548.80	101.75	814.00		
1 Equip. Oper. (oiler)	58.40	467.20	86.60	692.80		
1 Equip. Oper. (light)	62.00	496.00	91.95	735.60		
1 Lattice Boom Crane, 90 Ton		2790.64		3069.70		
4 Welder, Gas Engine, 300 amp		655.42		720.97	33.14	36.45
104 L.H., Daily Totals		$10354.06		$14305.87	$99.56	$137.56

Crews - Standard

Crew No.		Bare Costs		Incl. Subs O&P		Cost Per Labor-Hour	
Crew E-9	Hr.	Daily	Hr.	Daily	Bare Costs	Incl. O&P
2 Struc. Steel Foremen (outside)	$69.05	$1104.80	$105.85	$1693.60	$66.67	$101.62
5 Struc. Steel Workers	67.05	2682.00	102.80	4112.00		
1 Welder Foreman (outside)	69.05	552.40	105.85	846.80		
5 Welders	67.05	2682.00	102.80	4112.00		
1 Equip. Oper. (crane)	68.60	548.80	101.75	814.00		
1 Equip. Oper. (oiler)	58.40	467.20	86.60	692.80		
1 Equip. Oper. (light)	62.00	496.00	91.95	735.60		
1 Lattice Boom Crane, 90 Ton		2790.64		3069.70		
5 Welder, Gas Engine, 300 amp		819.28		901.21	28.20	31.02
128 L.H., Daily Totals		$12143.12		$16977.71	$94.87	$132.64
Crew E-10	Hr.	Daily	Hr.	Daily	Bare Costs	Incl. O&P
1 Welder Foreman (outside)	$69.05	$552.40	$105.85	$846.80	$68.05	$104.33
1 Welder	67.05	536.40	102.80	822.40		
1 Welder, Gas Engine, 300 amp		163.86		180.24		
1 Flatbed Truck, Gas, 3 Ton		519.55		571.51	42.71	46.98
16 L.H., Daily Totals		$1772.21		$2420.95	$110.76	$151.31
Crew E-11	Hr.	Daily	Hr.	Daily	Bare Costs	Incl. O&P
2 Painters, Struc. Steel	$53.00	$848.00	$83.40	$1334.40	$54.25	$82.83
1 Building Laborer	49.00	392.00	72.55	580.40		
1 Equip. Oper. (light)	62.00	496.00	91.95	735.60		
1 Air Compressor, 250 cfm		226.90		249.59		
1 Sandblaster, Portable, 3 C.F.		86.99		95.69		
1 Set Sand Blasting Accessories		17.69		19.45	10.36	11.40
32 L.H., Daily Totals		$2067.58		$3015.13	$64.61	$94.22
Crew E-11A	Hr.	Daily	Hr.	Daily	Bare Costs	Incl. O&P
2 Painters, Struc. Steel	$53.00	$848.00	$83.40	$1334.40	$54.25	$82.83
1 Building Laborer	49.00	392.00	72.55	580.40		
1 Equip. Oper. (light)	62.00	496.00	91.95	735.60		
1 Air Compressor, 250 cfm		226.90		249.59		
1 Sandblaster, Portable, 3 C.F.		86.99		95.69		
1 Set Sand Blasting Accessories		17.69		19.45		
1 Telescoping Boom Lift, to 60'		467.60		514.36	24.97	27.47
32 L.H., Daily Totals		$2535.18		$3529.49	$79.22	$110.30
Crew E-11B	Hr.	Daily	Hr.	Daily	Bare Costs	Incl. O&P
2 Painters, Struc. Steel	$53.00	$848.00	$83.40	$1334.40	$51.67	$79.78
1 Building Laborer	49.00	392.00	72.55	580.40		
2 Paint Sprayer, 8 C.F.M.		105.19		115.71		
1 Telescoping Boom Lift, to 60'		467.60		514.36	23.87	26.25
24 L.H., Daily Totals		$1812.79		$2544.87	$75.53	$106.04
Crew E-12	Hr.	Daily	Hr.	Daily	Bare Costs	Incl. O&P
1 Welder Foreman (outside)	$69.05	$552.40	$105.85	$846.80	$65.53	$98.90
1 Equip. Oper. (light)	62.00	496.00	91.95	735.60		
1 Welder, Gas Engine, 300 amp		163.86		180.24	10.24	11.27
16 L.H., Daily Totals		$1212.26		$1762.64	$75.77	$110.17
Crew E-13	Hr.	Daily	Hr.	Daily	Bare Costs	Incl. O&P
1 Welder Foreman (outside)	$69.05	$552.40	$105.85	$846.80	$66.70	$101.22
.5 Equip. Oper. (light)	62.00	248.00	91.95	367.80		
1 Welder, Gas Engine, 300 amp		163.86		180.24	13.65	15.02
12 L.H., Daily Totals		$964.26		$1394.84	$80.35	$116.24
Crew E-14	Hr.	Daily	Hr.	Daily	Bare Costs	Incl. O&P
1 Welder Foreman (outside)	$69.05	$552.40	$105.85	$846.80	$69.05	$105.85
1 Welder, Gas Engine, 300 amp		163.86		180.24	20.48	22.53
8 L.H., Daily Totals		$716.26		$1027.04	$89.53	$128.38

Crew No.		Bare Costs		Incl. Subs O&P		Cost Per Labor-Hour	
Crew E-16	Hr.	Daily	Hr.	Daily	Bare Costs	Incl. O&P
1 Welder Foreman (outside)	$69.05	$552.40	$105.85	$846.80	$68.05	$104.33
1 Welder	67.05	536.40	102.80	822.40		
1 Welder, Gas Engine, 300 amp		163.86		180.24	10.24	11.27
16 L.H., Daily Totals		$1252.66		$1849.44	$78.29	$115.59
Crew E-17	Hr.	Daily	Hr.	Daily	Bare Costs	Incl. O&P
1 Struc. Steel Foreman (outside)	$69.05	$552.40	$105.85	$846.80	$68.05	$104.33
1 Structural Steel Worker	67.05	536.40	102.80	822.40		
16 L.H., Daily Totals		$1088.80		$1669.20	$68.05	$104.33
Crew E-18	Hr.	Daily	Hr.	Daily	Bare Costs	Incl. O&P
1 Struc. Steel Foreman (outside)	$69.05	$552.40	$105.85	$846.80	$67.04	$102.13
3 Structural Steel Workers	67.05	1609.20	102.80	2467.20		
1 Equipment Operator (med.)	65.00	520.00	96.40	771.20		
1 Lattice Boom Crane, 20 Ton		906.32		996.96	22.66	24.92
40 L.H., Daily Totals		$3587.92		$5082.16	$89.70	$127.05
Crew E-19	Hr.	Daily	Hr.	Daily	Bare Costs	Incl. O&P
1 Struc. Steel Foreman (outside)	$69.05	$552.40	$105.85	$846.80	$66.03	$100.20
1 Structural Steel Worker	67.05	536.40	102.80	822.40		
1 Equip. Oper. (light)	62.00	496.00	91.95	735.60		
1 Lattice Boom Crane, 20 Ton		906.32		996.96	37.76	41.54
24 L.H., Daily Totals		$2491.12		$3401.76	$103.80	$141.74
Crew E-20	Hr.	Daily	Hr.	Daily	Bare Costs	Incl. O&P
1 Struc. Steel Foreman (outside)	$69.05	$552.40	$105.85	$846.80	$66.41	$101.03
5 Structural Steel Workers	67.05	2682.00	102.80	4112.00		
1 Equip. Oper. (crane)	68.60	548.80	101.75	814.00		
1 Equip. Oper. (oiler)	58.40	467.20	86.60	692.80		
1 Lattice Boom Crane, 40 Ton		2459.62		2705.58	38.43	42.27
64 L.H., Daily Totals		$6710.02		$9171.18	$104.84	$143.30
Crew E-22	Hr.	Daily	Hr.	Daily	Bare Costs	Incl. O&P
1 Skilled Worker Foreman (out)	$65.50	$524.00	$98.00	$784.00	$64.17	$96.00
2 Skilled Workers	63.50	1016.00	95.00	1520.00		
24 L.H., Daily Totals		$1540.00		$2304.00	$64.17	$96.00
Crew E-24	Hr.	Daily	Hr.	Daily	Bare Costs	Incl. O&P
3 Structural Steel Workers	$67.05	$1609.20	$102.80	$2467.20	$66.54	$101.01
1 Equipment Operator (med.)	65.00	520.00	96.40	771.20		
1 Hyd. Crane, 25 Ton		2335.01		2568.51	72.97	80.27
32 L.H., Daily Totals		$4464.21		$5806.91	$139.51	$181.47
Crew E-25	Hr.	Daily	Hr.	Daily	Bare Costs	Incl. O&P
1 Welder Foreman (outside)	$69.05	$552.40	$105.85	$846.80	$69.05	$105.85
1 Cutting Torch		14.84		16.32	1.86	2.04
8 L.H., Daily Totals		$567.24		$863.12	$70.91	$107.89
Crew E-26	Hr.	Daily	Hr.	Daily	Bare Costs	Incl. O&P
1 Struc. Steel Foreman (outside)	$69.05	$552.40	$105.85	$846.80	$68.50	$104.51
1 Struc. Steel Worker	67.05	536.40	102.80	822.40		
1 Welder	67.05	536.40	102.80	822.40		
.25 Electrician	71.70	143.40	106.30	212.60		
.25 Plumber	74.65	149.30	111.05	222.10		
1 Welder, Gas Engine, 300 amp		163.86		180.24	5.85	6.44
28 L.H., Daily Totals		$2081.76		$3106.54	$74.35	$110.95

Crews - Standard

Crew No.		Bare Costs		Incl. Subs O&P		Cost Per Labor-Hour	
Crew E-27	Hr.	Daily	Hr.	Daily	Bare Costs	Incl. O&P
1 Struc. Steel Foreman (outside)	$69.05	$552.40	$105.85	$846.80	$66.41	$101.03
5 Struc. Steel Workers	67.05	2682.00	102.80	4112.00		
1 Equip. Oper. (crane)	68.60	548.80	101.75	814.00		
1 Equip. Oper. (oiler)	58.40	467.20	86.60	692.80		
1 Hyd. Crane, 12 Ton		2224.21		2446.63		
1 Hyd. Crane, 80 Ton		2742.60		3016.86	77.61	85.37
64 L.H., Daily Totals		$9217.21		$11929.09	$144.02	$186.39
Crew F-3	Hr.	Daily	Hr.	Daily	Bare Costs	Incl. O&P
4 Carpenters	$60.55	$1937.60	$89.65	$2868.80	$62.16	$92.07
1 Equip. Oper. (crane)	68.60	548.80	101.75	814.00		
1 Hyd. Crane, 12 Ton		2224.21		2446.63	55.61	61.17
40 L.H., Daily Totals		$4710.61		$6129.43	$117.77	$153.24
Crew F-4	Hr.	Daily	Hr.	Daily	Bare Costs	Incl. O&P
4 Carpenters	$60.55	$1937.60	$89.65	$2868.80	$61.53	$91.16
1 Equip. Oper. (crane)	68.60	548.80	101.75	814.00		
1 Equip. Oper. (oiler)	58.40	467.20	86.60	692.80		
1 Hyd. Crane, 55 Ton		2551.41		2806.55	53.15	58.47
48 L.H., Daily Totals		$5505.01		$7182.15	$114.69	$149.63
Crew F-5	Hr.	Daily	Hr.	Daily	Bare Costs	Incl. O&P
1 Carpenter Foreman (outside)	$62.55	$500.40	$92.60	$740.80	$61.05	$90.39
3 Carpenters	60.55	1453.20	89.65	2151.60		
32 L.H., Daily Totals		$1953.60		$2892.40	$61.05	$90.39
Crew F-6	Hr.	Daily	Hr.	Daily	Bare Costs	Incl. O&P
2 Carpenters	$60.55	$968.80	$89.65	$1434.40	$57.54	$85.23
2 Building Laborers	49.00	784.00	72.55	1160.80		
1 Equip. Oper. (crane)	68.60	548.80	101.75	814.00		
1 Hyd. Crane, 12 Ton		2224.21		2446.63	55.61	61.17
40 L.H., Daily Totals		$4525.81		$5855.83	$113.15	$146.40
Crew F-7	Hr.	Daily	Hr.	Daily	Bare Costs	Incl. O&P
2 Carpenters	$60.55	$968.80	$89.65	$1434.40	$54.77	$81.10
2 Building Laborers	49.00	784.00	72.55	1160.80		
32 L.H., Daily Totals		$1752.80		$2595.20	$54.77	$81.10
Crew G-1	Hr.	Daily	Hr.	Daily	Bare Costs	Incl. O&P
1 Roofer Foreman (outside)	$55.70	$445.60	$89.75	$718.00	$50.36	$81.15
4 Roofers Composition	53.70	1718.40	86.55	2769.60		
2 Roofer Helpers	41.00	656.00	66.05	1056.80		
1 Application Equipment		198.46		218.30		
1 Tar Kettle/Pot		232.32		255.55		
1 Crew Truck		297.60		327.36	13.01	14.31
56 L.H., Daily Totals		$3548.38		$5345.61	$63.36	$95.46
Crew G-2	Hr.	Daily	Hr.	Daily	Bare Costs	Incl. O&P
1 Plasterer	$55.20	$441.60	$81.75	$654.00	$51.20	$75.82
1 Plasterer Helper	49.40	395.20	73.15	585.20		
1 Building Laborer	49.00	392.00	72.55	580.40		
1 Grout Pump, 50 C.F./hr.		165.21		181.73	6.88	7.57
24 L.H., Daily Totals		$1394.01		$2001.33	$58.08	$83.39

Crew No.		Bare Costs		Incl. Subs O&P		Cost Per Labor-Hour	
Crew G-2A	Hr.	Daily	Hr.	Daily	Bare Costs	Incl. O&P
1 Roofer Composition	$53.70	$429.60	$86.55	$692.40	$47.90	$75.05
1 Roofer Helper	41.00	328.00	66.05	528.40		
1 Building Laborer	49.00	392.00	72.55	580.40		
1 Foam Spray Rig, Trailer-Mtd.		607.05		667.75		
1 Pickup Truck, 3/4 Ton		233.60		256.96	35.03	38.53
24 L.H., Daily Totals		$1990.25		$2725.91	$82.93	$113.58
Crew G-3	Hr.	Daily	Hr.	Daily	Bare Costs	Incl. O&P
2 Sheet Metal Workers	$72.25	$1156.00	$108.70	$1739.20	$60.63	$90.63
2 Building Laborers	49.00	784.00	72.55	1160.80		
32 L.H., Daily Totals		$1940.00		$2900.00	$60.63	$90.63
Crew G-4	Hr.	Daily	Hr.	Daily	Bare Costs	Incl. O&P
1 Labor Foreman (outside)	$51.00	$408.00	$75.50	$604.00	$49.67	$73.53
2 Building Laborers	49.00	784.00	72.55	1160.80		
1 Flatbed Truck, Gas, 1.5 Ton		420.83		462.92		
1 Air Compressor, 160 cfm		209.86		230.85	26.28	28.91
24 L.H., Daily Totals		$1822.69		$2458.56	$75.95	$102.44
Crew G-5	Hr.	Daily	Hr.	Daily	Bare Costs	Incl. O&P
1 Roofer Foreman (outside)	$55.70	$445.60	$89.75	$718.00	$49.02	$78.99
2 Roofers Composition	53.70	859.20	86.55	1384.80		
2 Roofer Helpers	41.00	656.00	66.05	1056.80		
1 Application Equipment		198.46		218.30	4.96	5.46
40 L.H., Daily Totals		$2159.26		$3377.90	$53.98	$84.45
Crew G-6A	Hr.	Daily	Hr.	Daily	Bare Costs	Incl. O&P
2 Roofers Composition	$53.70	$859.20	$86.55	$1384.80	$53.70	$86.55
1 Small Compressor, Electric		36.59		40.25		
2 Pneumatic Nailers		55.26		60.79	5.74	6.31
16 L.H., Daily Totals		$951.05		$1485.84	$59.44	$92.86
Crew G-7	Hr.	Daily	Hr.	Daily	Bare Costs	Incl. O&P
1 Carpenter	$60.55	$484.40	$89.65	$717.20	$60.55	$89.65
1 Small Compressor, Electric		36.59		40.25		
1 Pneumatic Nailer		27.63		30.39	8.03	8.83
8 L.H., Daily Totals		$548.62		$787.84	$68.58	$98.48
Crew H-1	Hr.	Daily	Hr.	Daily	Bare Costs	Incl. O&P
2 Glaziers	$58.20	$931.20	$85.95	$1375.20	$62.63	$94.38
2 Struc. Steel Workers	67.05	1072.80	102.80	1644.80		
32 L.H., Daily Totals		$2004.00		$3020.00	$62.63	$94.38
Crew H-2	Hr.	Daily	Hr.	Daily	Bare Costs	Incl. O&P
2 Glaziers	$58.20	$931.20	$85.95	$1375.20	$55.13	$81.48
1 Building Laborer	49.00	392.00	72.55	580.40		
24 L.H., Daily Totals		$1323.20		$1955.60	$55.13	$81.48
Crew H-3	Hr.	Daily	Hr.	Daily	Bare Costs	Incl. O&P
1 Glazier	$58.20	$465.60	$85.95	$687.60	$52.50	$78.17
1 Helper	46.80	374.40	70.40	563.20		
16 L.H., Daily Totals		$840.00		$1250.80	$52.50	$78.17
Crew H-4	Hr.	Daily	Hr.	Daily	Bare Costs	Incl. O&P
1 Carpenter	$60.55	$484.40	$89.65	$717.20	$57.28	$85.28
1 Carpenter Helper	46.80	374.40	70.40	563.20		
.5 Electrician	71.70	286.80	106.30	425.20		
20 L.H., Daily Totals		$1145.60		$1705.60	$57.28	$85.28

Crews - Standard

Crew No.	Bare Costs		Incl. Subs O&P		Cost Per Labor-Hour	
Crew J-1	Hr.	Daily	Hr.	Daily	Bare Costs	Incl. O&P
3 Plasterers	$55.20	$1324.80	$81.75	$1962.00	$52.88	$78.31
2 Plasterer Helpers	49.40	790.40	73.15	1170.40		
1 Mixing Machine, 6 C.F.		117.50		129.25	2.94	3.23
40 L.H., Daily Totals		$2232.70		$3261.65	$55.82	$81.54
Crew J-2	Hr.	Daily	Hr.	Daily	Bare Costs	Incl. O&P
3 Plasterers	$55.20	$1324.80	$81.75	$1962.00	$54.19	$79.98
2 Plasterer Helpers	49.40	790.40	73.15	1170.40		
1 Lather	60.75	486.00	88.35	706.80		
1 Mixing Machine, 6 C.F.		117.50		129.25	2.45	2.69
48 L.H., Daily Totals		$2718.70		$3968.45	$56.64	$82.68
Crew J-3	Hr.	Daily	Hr.	Daily	Bare Costs	Incl. O&P
1 Terrazzo Worker	$57.30	$458.40	$83.40	$667.20	$52.85	$77.00
1 Terrazzo Helper	48.40	387.20	70.60	564.80		
1 Floor Grinder, 22" Path		110.44		121.48		
1 Terrazzo Mixer		242.32		266.55	22.05	24.25
16 L.H., Daily Totals		$1198.35		$1620.03	$74.90	$101.25
Crew J-4	Hr.	Daily	Hr.	Daily	Bare Costs	Incl. O&P
2 Cement Finishers	$56.80	$908.80	$82.80	$1324.80	$54.20	$79.38
1 Laborer	49.00	392.00	72.55	580.40		
1 Floor Grinder, 22" Path		110.44		121.48		
1 Floor Edger, 7" Path		115.00		126.50		
1 Vacuum Pick-Up System		87.74		96.51	13.05	14.35
24 L.H., Daily Totals		$1613.98		$2249.70	$67.25	$93.74
Crew J-4A	Hr.	Daily	Hr.	Daily	Bare Costs	Incl. O&P
2 Cement Finishers	$56.80	$908.80	$82.80	$1324.80	$52.90	$77.67
2 Laborers	49.00	784.00	72.55	1160.80		
1 Floor Grinder, 22" Path		110.44		121.48		
1 Floor Edger, 7" Path		115.00		126.50		
1 Vacuum Pick-Up System		87.74		96.51		
1 Floor Auto Scrubber		239.27		263.20	17.26	18.99
32 L.H., Daily Totals		$2245.25		$3093.30	$70.16	$96.67
Crew J-4B	Hr.	Daily	Hr.	Daily	Bare Costs	Incl. O&P
1 Laborer	$49.00	$392.00	$72.55	$580.40	$49.00	$72.55
1 Floor Auto Scrubber		239.27		263.20	29.91	32.90
8 L.H., Daily Totals		$631.27		$843.60	$78.91	$105.45
Crew J-6	Hr.	Daily	Hr.	Daily	Bare Costs	Incl. O&P
2 Painters	$51.70	$827.20	$76.30	$1220.80	$53.60	$79.28
1 Building Laborer	49.00	392.00	72.55	580.40		
1 Equip. Oper. (light)	62.00	496.00	91.95	735.60		
1 Air Compressor, 250 cfm		226.90		249.59		
1 Sandblaster, Portable, 3 C.F.		86.99		95.69		
1 Set Sand Blasting Accessories		17.69		19.45	10.36	11.40
32 L.H., Daily Totals		$2046.78		$2901.53	$63.96	$90.67
Crew J-7	Hr.	Daily	Hr.	Daily	Bare Costs	Incl. O&P
2 Painters	$51.70	$827.20	$76.30	$1220.80	$51.70	$76.30
1 Floor Belt Sander		67.16		73.87		
1 Floor Sanding Edger		50.37		55.40	7.35	8.08
16 L.H., Daily Totals		$944.72		$1350.07	$59.05	$84.38

Crew No.	Bare Costs		Incl. Subs O&P		Cost Per Labor-Hour	
Crew K-1	Hr.	Daily	Hr.	Daily	Bare Costs	Incl. O&P
1 Carpenter	$60.55	$484.40	$89.65	$717.20	$57.85	$85.83
1 Truck Driver (light)	55.15	441.20	82.00	656.00		
1 Flatbed Truck, Gas, 3 Ton		519.55		571.51	32.47	35.72
16 L.H., Daily Totals		$1445.15		$1944.71	$90.32	$121.54
Crew K-2	Hr.	Daily	Hr.	Daily	Bare Costs	Incl. O&P
1 Struc. Steel Foreman (outside)	$69.05	$552.40	$105.85	$846.80	$63.75	$96.88
1 Struc. Steel Worker	67.05	536.40	102.80	822.40		
1 Truck Driver (light)	55.15	441.20	82.00	656.00		
1 Flatbed Truck, Gas, 3 Ton		519.55		571.51	21.65	23.81
24 L.H., Daily Totals		$2049.55		$2896.71	$85.40	$120.70
Crew L-1	Hr.	Daily	Hr.	Daily	Bare Costs	Incl. O&P
1 Electrician	$71.70	$573.60	$106.30	$850.40	$73.17	$108.68
1 Plumber	74.65	597.20	111.05	888.40		
16 L.H., Daily Totals		$1170.80		$1738.80	$73.17	$108.68
Crew L-2	Hr.	Daily	Hr.	Daily	Bare Costs	Incl. O&P
1 Carpenter	$60.55	$484.40	$89.65	$717.20	$53.67	$80.03
1 Carpenter Helper	46.80	374.40	70.40	563.20		
16 L.H., Daily Totals		$858.80		$1280.40	$53.67	$80.03
Crew L-3	Hr.	Daily	Hr.	Daily	Bare Costs	Incl. O&P
1 Carpenter	$60.55	$484.40	$89.65	$717.20	$66.26	$98.58
.5 Electrician	71.70	286.80	106.30	425.20		
.5 Sheet Metal Worker	72.25	289.00	108.70	434.80		
16 L.H., Daily Totals		$1060.20		$1577.20	$66.26	$98.58
Crew L-3A	Hr.	Daily	Hr.	Daily	Bare Costs	Incl. O&P
1 Carpenter Foreman (outside)	$62.55	$500.40	$92.60	$740.80	$65.78	$97.97
.5 Sheet Metal Worker	72.25	289.00	108.70	434.80		
12 L.H., Daily Totals		$789.40		$1175.60	$65.78	$97.97
Crew L-4	Hr.	Daily	Hr.	Daily	Bare Costs	Incl. O&P
2 Skilled Workers	$63.50	$1016.00	$95.00	$1520.00	$57.93	$86.80
1 Helper	46.80	374.40	70.40	563.20		
24 L.H., Daily Totals		$1390.40		$2083.20	$57.93	$86.80
Crew L-5	Hr.	Daily	Hr.	Daily	Bare Costs	Incl. O&P
1 Struc. Steel Foreman (outside)	$69.05	$552.40	$105.85	$846.80	$67.56	$103.09
5 Struc. Steel Workers	67.05	2682.00	102.80	4112.00		
1 Equip. Oper. (crane)	68.60	548.80	101.75	814.00		
1 Hyd. Crane, 25 Ton		2335.01		2568.51	41.70	45.87
56 L.H., Daily Totals		$6118.21		$8341.31	$109.25	$148.95
Crew L-5A	Hr.	Daily	Hr.	Daily	Bare Costs	Incl. O&P
1 Struc. Steel Foreman (outside)	$69.05	$552.40	$105.85	$846.80	$67.94	$103.30
2 Structural Steel Workers	67.05	1072.80	102.80	1644.80		
1 Equip. Oper. (crane)	68.60	548.80	101.75	814.00		
1 S.P. Crane, 4x4, 25 Ton		966.17		1062.78	30.19	33.21
32 L.H., Daily Totals		$3140.17		$4368.38	$98.13	$136.51

Crews - Standard

Crew No.		Bare Costs		Incl. Subs O&P	Cost Per Labor-Hour	
Crew L-5B	Hr.	Daily	Hr.	Daily	Bare Costs	Incl. O&P
1 Struc. Steel Foreman (outside)	$69.05	$552.40	$105.85	$846.80	$69.41	$104.13
2 Structural Steel Workers	67.05	1072.80	102.80	1644.80		
2 Electricians	71.70	1147.20	106.30	1700.80		
2 Steamfitters/Pipefitters	75.55	1208.80	112.40	1798.40		
1 Equip. Oper. (crane)	68.60	548.80	101.75	814.00		
1 Equip. Oper. (oiler)	58.40	467.20	86.60	692.80		
1 Hyd. Crane, 80 Ton		2742.60		3016.86	38.09	41.90
72 L.H., Daily Totals		$7739.80		$10514.46	$107.50	$146.03
Crew L-6	Hr.	Daily	Hr.	Daily	Bare Costs	Incl. O&P
1 Plumber	$74.65	$597.20	$111.05	$888.40	$73.67	$109.47
.5 Electrician	71.70	286.80	106.30	425.20		
12 L.H., Daily Totals		$884.00		$1313.60	$73.67	$109.47
Crew L-7	Hr.	Daily	Hr.	Daily	Bare Costs	Incl. O&P
2 Carpenters	$60.55	$968.80	$89.65	$1434.40	$58.84	$87.14
1 Building Laborer	49.00	392.00	72.55	580.40		
.5 Electrician	71.70	286.80	106.30	425.20		
28 L.H., Daily Totals		$1647.60		$2440.00	$58.84	$87.14
Crew L-8	Hr.	Daily	Hr.	Daily	Bare Costs	Incl. O&P
2 Carpenters	$60.55	$968.80	$89.65	$1434.40	$63.37	$93.93
.5 Plumber	74.65	298.60	111.05	444.20		
20 L.H., Daily Totals		$1267.40		$1878.60	$63.37	$93.93
Crew L-9	Hr.	Daily	Hr.	Daily	Bare Costs	Incl. O&P
1 Labor Foreman (inside)	$49.50	$396.00	$73.30	$586.40	$55.64	$83.19
2 Building Laborers	49.00	784.00	72.55	1160.80		
1 Struc. Steel Worker	67.05	536.40	102.80	822.40		
.5 Electrician	71.70	286.80	106.30	425.20		
36 L.H., Daily Totals		$2003.20		$2994.80	$55.64	$83.19
Crew L-10	Hr.	Daily	Hr.	Daily	Bare Costs	Incl. O&P
1 Struc. Steel Foreman (outside)	$69.05	$552.40	$105.85	$846.80	$68.23	$103.47
1 Structural Steel Worker	67.05	536.40	102.80	822.40		
1 Equip. Oper. (crane)	68.60	548.80	101.75	814.00		
1 Hyd. Crane, 12 Ton		2224.21		2446.63	92.68	101.94
24 L.H., Daily Totals		$3861.81		$4929.83	$160.91	$205.41
Crew L-11	Hr.	Daily	Hr.	Daily	Bare Costs	Incl. O&P
2 Wreckers	$49.00	$784.00	$73.75	$1180.00	$57.15	$85.30
1 Equip. Oper. (crane)	68.60	548.80	101.75	814.00		
1 Equip. Oper. (light)	62.00	496.00	91.95	735.60		
1 Hyd. Excavator, 2.5 C.Y.		1800.54		1980.59		
1 Loader, Skid Steer, 78 H.P.		394.64		434.10	68.60	75.46
32 L.H., Daily Totals		$4023.97		$5144.29	$125.75	$160.76
Crew M-1	Hr.	Daily	Hr.	Daily	Bare Costs	Incl. O&P
3 Elevator Constructors	$100.00	$2400.00	$147.70	$3544.80	$95.00	$140.32
1 Elevator Apprentice	80.00	640.00	118.20	945.60		
5 Hand Tools		355.94		391.53	11.12	12.24
32 L.H., Daily Totals		$3395.94		$4881.93	$106.12	$152.56
Crew M-3	Hr.	Daily	Hr.	Daily	Bare Costs	Incl. O&P
1 Electrician Foreman (outside)	$73.70	$589.60	$109.25	$874.00	$75.05	$111.01
1 Common Laborer	49.00	392.00	72.55	580.40		
.25 Equipment Operator (med.)	65.00	130.00	96.40	192.80		
1 Elevator Constructor	100.00	800.00	147.70	1181.60		
1 Elevator Apprentice	80.00	640.00	118.20	945.60		
.25 S.P. Crane, 4x4, 20 Ton		197.67		217.44	5.81	6.40
34 L.H., Daily Totals		$2749.27		$3991.84	$80.86	$117.41
Crew M-4	Hr.	Daily	Hr.	Daily	Bare Costs	Incl. O&P
1 Electrician Foreman (outside)	$73.70	$589.60	$109.25	$874.00	$74.32	$109.95
1 Common Laborer	49.00	392.00	72.55	580.40		
.25 Equipment Operator, Crane	68.60	137.20	101.75	203.50		
.25 Equip. Oper. (oiler)	58.40	116.80	86.60	173.20		
1 Elevator Constructor	100.00	800.00	147.70	1181.60		
1 Elevator Apprentice	80.00	640.00	118.20	945.60		
.25 S.P. Crane, 4x4, 40 Ton		296.78		326.46	8.24	9.07
36 L.H., Daily Totals		$2972.38		$4284.76	$82.57	$119.02
Crew Q-1	Hr.	Daily	Hr.	Daily	Bare Costs	Incl. O&P
1 Plumber	$74.65	$597.20	$111.05	$888.40	$67.17	$99.92
1 Plumber Apprentice	59.70	477.60	88.80	710.40		
16 L.H., Daily Totals		$1074.80		$1598.80	$67.17	$99.92
Crew Q-1A	Hr.	Daily	Hr.	Daily	Bare Costs	Incl. O&P
.25 Plumber Foreman (outside)	$76.65	$153.30	$114.05	$228.10	$75.05	$111.65
1 Plumber	74.65	597.20	111.05	888.40		
10 L.H., Daily Totals		$750.50		$1116.50	$75.05	$111.65
Crew Q-1C	Hr.	Daily	Hr.	Daily	Bare Costs	Incl. O&P
1 Plumber	$74.65	$597.20	$111.05	$888.40	$66.45	$98.75
1 Plumber Apprentice	59.70	477.60	88.80	710.40		
1 Equip. Oper. (medium)	65.00	520.00	96.40	771.20		
1 Trencher, Chain Type, 8' D		2168.88		2385.77	90.37	99.41
24 L.H., Daily Totals		$3763.68		$4755.77	$156.82	$198.16
Crew Q-2	Hr.	Daily	Hr.	Daily	Bare Costs	Incl. O&P
2 Plumbers	$74.65	$1194.40	$111.05	$1776.80	$69.67	$103.63
1 Plumber Apprentice	59.70	477.60	88.80	710.40		
24 L.H., Daily Totals		$1672.00		$2487.20	$69.67	$103.63
Crew Q-3	Hr.	Daily	Hr.	Daily	Bare Costs	Incl. O&P
1 Plumber Foreman (inside)	$75.15	$601.20	$111.80	$894.40	$71.04	$105.68
2 Plumbers	74.65	1194.40	111.05	1776.80		
1 Plumber Apprentice	59.70	477.60	88.80	710.40		
32 L.H., Daily Totals		$2273.20		$3381.60	$71.04	$105.68
Crew Q-4	Hr.	Daily	Hr.	Daily	Bare Costs	Incl. O&P
1 Plumber Foreman (inside)	$75.15	$601.20	$111.80	$894.40	$71.04	$105.68
1 Plumber	74.65	597.20	111.05	888.40		
1 Welder (plumber)	74.65	597.20	111.05	888.40		
1 Plumber Apprentice	59.70	477.60	88.80	710.40		
1 Welder, Electric, 300 amp		71.77		78.95	2.24	2.47
32 L.H., Daily Totals		$2344.97		$3460.55	$73.28	$108.14
Crew Q-5	Hr.	Daily	Hr.	Daily	Bare Costs	Incl. O&P
1 Steamfitter	$75.55	$604.40	$112.40	$899.20	$68.00	$101.18
1 Steamfitter Apprentice	60.45	483.60	89.95	719.60		
16 L.H., Daily Totals		$1088.00		$1618.80	$68.00	$101.18

Crews - Standard

Crew Q-6	Hr.	Daily	Hr.	Daily	Bare Costs	Incl. O&P
2 Steamfitters	$75.55	$1208.80	$112.40	$1798.40	$70.52	$104.92
1 Steamfitter Apprentice	60.45	483.60	89.95	719.60		
24 L.H., Daily Totals		$1692.40		$2518.00	$70.52	$104.92

Crew Q-7	Hr.	Daily	Hr.	Daily	Bare Costs	Incl. O&P
1 Steamfitter Foreman (inside)	$76.05	$608.40	$113.15	$905.20	$71.90	$106.97
2 Steamfitters	75.55	1208.80	112.40	1798.40		
1 Steamfitter Apprentice	60.45	483.60	89.95	719.60		
32 L.H., Daily Totals		$2300.80		$3423.20	$71.90	$106.97

Crew Q-8	Hr.	Daily	Hr.	Daily	Bare Costs	Incl. O&P
1 Steamfitter Foreman (inside)	$76.05	$608.40	$113.15	$905.20	$71.90	$106.97
1 Steamfitter	75.55	604.40	112.40	899.20		
1 Welder (steamfitter)	75.55	604.40	112.40	899.20		
1 Steamfitter Apprentice	60.45	483.60	89.95	719.60		
1 Welder, Electric, 300 amp		71.77		78.95	2.24	2.47
32 L.H., Daily Totals		$2372.57		$3502.15	$74.14	$109.44

Crew Q-9	Hr.	Daily	Hr.	Daily	Bare Costs	Incl. O&P
1 Sheet Metal Worker	$72.25	$578.00	$108.70	$869.60	$65.03	$97.83
1 Sheet Metal Apprentice	57.80	462.40	86.95	695.60		
16 L.H., Daily Totals		$1040.40		$1565.20	$65.03	$97.83

Crew Q-10	Hr.	Daily	Hr.	Daily	Bare Costs	Incl. O&P
2 Sheet Metal Workers	$72.25	$1156.00	$108.70	$1739.20	$67.43	$101.45
1 Sheet Metal Apprentice	57.80	462.40	86.95	695.60		
24 L.H., Daily Totals		$1618.40		$2434.80	$67.43	$101.45

Crew Q-11	Hr.	Daily	Hr.	Daily	Bare Costs	Incl. O&P
1 Sheet Metal Foreman (inside)	$72.75	$582.00	$109.45	$875.60	$68.76	$103.45
2 Sheet Metal Workers	72.25	1156.00	108.70	1739.20		
1 Sheet Metal Apprentice	57.80	462.40	86.95	695.60		
32 L.H., Daily Totals		$2200.40		$3310.40	$68.76	$103.45

Crew Q-12	Hr.	Daily	Hr.	Daily	Bare Costs	Incl. O&P
1 Sprinkler Installer	$74.65	$597.20	$111.10	$888.80	$67.17	$99.97
1 Sprinkler Apprentice	59.70	477.60	88.85	710.80		
16 L.H., Daily Totals		$1074.80		$1599.60	$67.17	$99.97

Crew Q-13	Hr.	Daily	Hr.	Daily	Bare Costs	Incl. O&P
1 Sprinkler Foreman (inside)	$75.15	$601.20	$111.85	$894.80	$71.04	$105.72
2 Sprinkler Installers	74.65	1194.40	111.10	1777.60		
1 Sprinkler Apprentice	59.70	477.60	88.85	710.80		
32 L.H., Daily Totals		$2273.20		$3383.20	$71.04	$105.72

Crew Q-14	Hr.	Daily	Hr.	Daily	Bare Costs	Incl. O&P
1 Asbestos Worker	$67.10	$536.80	$102.25	$818.00	$60.40	$92.03
1 Asbestos Apprentice	53.70	429.60	81.80	654.40		
16 L.H., Daily Totals		$966.40		$1472.40	$60.40	$92.03

Crew Q-15	Hr.	Daily	Hr.	Daily	Bare Costs	Incl. O&P
1 Plumber	$74.65	$597.20	$111.05	$888.40	$67.17	$99.92
1 Plumber Apprentice	59.70	477.60	88.80	710.40		
1 Welder, Electric, 300 amp		71.77		78.95	4.49	4.93
16 L.H., Daily Totals		$1146.57		$1677.75	$71.66	$104.86

Crew Q-16	Hr.	Daily	Hr.	Daily	Bare Costs	Incl. O&P
2 Plumbers	$74.65	$1194.40	$111.05	$1776.80	$69.67	$103.63
1 Plumber Apprentice	59.70	477.60	88.80	710.40		
1 Welder, Electric, 300 amp		71.77		78.95	2.99	3.29
24 L.H., Daily Totals		$1743.77		$2566.15	$72.66	$106.92

Crew Q-17	Hr.	Daily	Hr.	Daily	Bare Costs	Incl. O&P
1 Steamfitter	$75.55	$604.40	$112.40	$899.20	$68.00	$101.18
1 Steamfitter Apprentice	60.45	483.60	89.95	719.60		
1 Welder, Electric, 300 amp		71.77		78.95	4.49	4.93
16 L.H., Daily Totals		$1159.77		$1697.75	$72.49	$106.11

Crew Q-17A	Hr.	Daily	Hr.	Daily	Bare Costs	Incl. O&P
1 Steamfitter	$75.55	$604.40	$112.40	$899.20	$68.20	$101.37
1 Steamfitter Apprentice	60.45	483.60	89.95	719.60		
1 Equip. Oper. (crane)	68.60	548.80	101.75	814.00		
1 Hyd. Crane, 12 Ton		2224.21		2446.63		
1 Welder, Electric, 300 amp		71.77		78.95	95.67	105.23
24 L.H., Daily Totals		$3932.78		$4958.38	$163.87	$206.60

Crew Q-18	Hr.	Daily	Hr.	Daily	Bare Costs	Incl. O&P
2 Steamfitters	$75.55	$1208.80	$112.40	$1798.40	$70.52	$104.92
1 Steamfitter Apprentice	60.45	483.60	89.95	719.60		
1 Welder, Electric, 300 amp		71.77		78.95	2.99	3.29
24 L.H., Daily Totals		$1764.17		$2596.95	$73.51	$108.21

Crew Q-19	Hr.	Daily	Hr.	Daily	Bare Costs	Incl. O&P
1 Steamfitter	$75.55	$604.40	$112.40	$899.20	$69.23	$102.88
1 Steamfitter Apprentice	60.45	483.60	89.95	719.60		
1 Electrician	71.70	573.60	106.30	850.40		
24 L.H., Daily Totals		$1661.60		$2469.20	$69.23	$102.88

Crew Q-20	Hr.	Daily	Hr.	Daily	Bare Costs	Incl. O&P
1 Sheet Metal Worker	$72.25	$578.00	$108.70	$869.60	$66.36	$99.52
1 Sheet Metal Apprentice	57.80	462.40	86.95	695.60		
.5 Electrician	71.70	286.80	106.30	425.20		
20 L.H., Daily Totals		$1327.20		$1990.40	$66.36	$99.52

Crew Q-21	Hr.	Daily	Hr.	Daily	Bare Costs	Incl. O&P
2 Steamfitters	$75.55	$1208.80	$112.40	$1798.40	$70.81	$105.26
1 Steamfitter Apprentice	60.45	483.60	89.95	719.60		
1 Electrician	71.70	573.60	106.30	850.40		
32 L.H., Daily Totals		$2266.00		$3368.40	$70.81	$105.26

Crew Q-22	Hr.	Daily	Hr.	Daily	Bare Costs	Incl. O&P
1 Plumber	$74.65	$597.20	$111.05	$888.40	$67.17	$99.92
1 Plumber Apprentice	59.70	477.60	88.80	710.40		
1 Hyd. Crane, 12 Ton		2224.21		2446.63	139.01	152.91
16 L.H., Daily Totals		$3299.01		$4045.43	$206.19	$252.84

Crew Q-22A	Hr.	Daily	Hr.	Daily	Bare Costs	Incl. O&P
1 Plumber	$74.65	$597.20	$111.05	$888.40	$62.99	$93.54
1 Plumber Apprentice	59.70	477.60	88.80	710.40		
1 Laborer	49.00	392.00	72.55	580.40		
1 Equip. Oper. (crane)	68.60	548.80	101.75	814.00		
1 Hyd. Crane, 12 Ton		2224.21		2446.63	69.51	76.46
32 L.H., Daily Totals		$4239.81		$5439.83	$132.49	$169.99

Crews - Standard

Crew Q-23

Crew Q-23	Hr.	Daily	Hr.	Daily	Bare Costs	Incl. O&P
1 Plumber Foreman (outside)	$76.65	$613.20	$114.05	$912.40	$72.10	$107.17
1 Plumber	74.65	597.20	111.05	888.40		
1 Equip. Oper. (medium)	65.00	520.00	96.40	771.20		
1 Lattice Boom Crane, 20 Ton		906.32		996.96	37.76	41.54
24 L.H., Daily Totals		$2636.72		$3568.96	$109.86	$148.71

Crew R-1

Crew R-1	Hr.	Daily	Hr.	Daily	Bare Costs	Incl. O&P
1 Electrician Foreman	$72.20	$577.60	$107.05	$856.40	$67.00	$99.33
3 Electricians	71.70	1720.80	106.30	2551.20		
2 Electrician Apprentices	57.35	917.60	85.00	1360.00		
48 L.H., Daily Totals		$3216.00		$4767.60	$67.00	$99.33

Crew R-1A

Crew R-1A	Hr.	Daily	Hr.	Daily	Bare Costs	Incl. O&P
1 Electrician	$71.70	$573.60	$106.30	$850.40	$64.53	$95.65
1 Electrician Apprentice	57.35	458.80	85.00	680.00		
16 L.H., Daily Totals		$1032.40		$1530.40	$64.53	$95.65

Crew R-1B

Crew R-1B	Hr.	Daily	Hr.	Daily	Bare Costs	Incl. O&P
1 Electrician	$71.70	$573.60	$106.30	$850.40	$62.13	$92.10
2 Electrician Apprentices	57.35	917.60	85.00	1360.00		
24 L.H., Daily Totals		$1491.20		$2210.40	$62.13	$92.10

Crew R-1C

Crew R-1C	Hr.	Daily	Hr.	Daily	Bare Costs	Incl. O&P
2 Electricians	$71.70	$1147.20	$106.30	$1700.80	$64.53	$95.65
2 Electrician Apprentices	57.35	917.60	85.00	1360.00		
1 Portable cable puller, 8000 lb.		129.89		142.88	4.06	4.46
32 L.H., Daily Totals		$2194.69		$3203.68	$68.58	$100.11

Crew R-2

Crew R-2	Hr.	Daily	Hr.	Daily	Bare Costs	Incl. O&P
1 Electrician Foreman	$72.20	$577.60	$107.05	$856.40	$67.23	$99.67
3 Electricians	71.70	1720.80	106.30	2551.20		
2 Electrician Apprentices	57.35	917.60	85.00	1360.00		
1 Equip. Oper. (crane)	68.60	548.80	101.75	814.00		
1 S.P. Crane, 4x4, 5 Ton		402.11		442.32	7.18	7.90
56 L.H., Daily Totals		$4166.91		$6023.92	$74.41	$107.57

Crew R-3

Crew R-3	Hr.	Daily	Hr.	Daily	Bare Costs	Incl. O&P
1 Electrician Foreman	$72.20	$577.60	$107.05	$856.40	$71.28	$105.69
1 Electrician	71.70	573.60	106.30	850.40		
.5 Equip. Oper. (crane)	68.60	274.40	101.75	407.00		
.5 S.P. Crane, 4x4, 5 Ton		201.05		221.16	10.05	11.06
20 L.H., Daily Totals		$1626.65		$2334.96	$81.33	$116.75

Crew R-4

Crew R-4	Hr.	Daily	Hr.	Daily	Bare Costs	Incl. O&P
1 Struc. Steel Foreman (outside)	$69.05	$552.40	$105.85	$846.80	$68.38	$104.11
3 Struc. Steel Workers	67.05	1609.20	102.80	2467.20		
1 Electrician	71.70	573.60	106.30	850.40		
1 Welder, Gas Engine, 300 amp		163.86		180.24	4.10	4.51
40 L.H., Daily Totals		$2899.06		$4344.64	$72.48	$108.62

Crew R-5

Crew R-5	Hr.	Daily	Hr.	Daily	Bare Costs	Incl. O&P
1 Electrician Foreman	$72.20	$577.60	$107.05	$856.40	$62.69	$93.31
4 Electrician Linemen	71.70	2294.40	106.30	3401.60		
2 Electrician Operators	71.70	1147.20	106.30	1700.80		
4 Electrician Groundmen	46.80	1497.60	70.40	2252.80		
1 Crew Truck		297.60		327.36		
1 Flatbed Truck, 20,000 GVW		234.51		257.97		
1 Pickup Truck, 3/4 Ton		233.60		256.96		
.2 Hyd. Crane, 55 Ton		510.28		561.31		
.2 Hyd. Crane, 12 Ton		444.84		489.33		
.2 Earth Auger, Truck-Mtd.		32.58		35.84		
1 Tractor w/Winch		433.49		476.84	24.85	27.34
88 L.H., Daily Totals		$7703.71		$10617.20	$87.54	$120.65

Crew R-6

Crew R-6	Hr.	Daily	Hr.	Daily	Bare Costs	Incl. O&P
1 Electrician Foreman	$72.20	$577.60	$107.05	$856.40	$62.69	$93.31
4 Electrician Linemen	71.70	2294.40	106.30	3401.60		
2 Electrician Operators	71.70	1147.20	106.30	1700.80		
4 Electrician Groundmen	46.80	1497.60	70.40	2252.80		
1 Crew Truck		297.60		327.36		
1 Flatbed Truck, 20,000 GVW		234.51		257.97		
1 Pickup Truck, 3/4 Ton		233.60		256.96		
.2 Hyd. Crane, 55 Ton		510.28		561.31		
.2 Hyd. Crane, 12 Ton		444.84		489.33		
.2 Earth Auger, Truck-Mtd.		32.58		35.84		
1 Tractor w/Winch		433.49		476.84		
3 Cable Trailers		633.56		696.92		
.5 Tensioning Rig		80.32		88.35		
.5 Cable Pulling Rig		393.26		432.58	37.43	41.18
88 L.H., Daily Totals		$8810.85		$11835.05	$100.12	$134.49

Crew R-7

Crew R-7	Hr.	Daily	Hr.	Daily	Bare Costs	Incl. O&P
1 Electrician Foreman	$72.20	$577.60	$107.05	$856.40	$51.03	$76.51
5 Electrician Groundmen	46.80	1872.00	70.40	2816.00		
1 Crew Truck		297.60		327.36	6.20	6.82
48 L.H., Daily Totals		$2747.20		$3999.76	$57.23	$83.33

Crew R-8

Crew R-8	Hr.	Daily	Hr.	Daily	Bare Costs	Incl. O&P
1 Electrician Foreman	$72.20	$577.60	$107.05	$856.40	$63.48	$94.46
3 Electrician Linemen	71.70	1720.80	106.30	2551.20		
2 Electrician Groundmen	46.80	748.80	70.40	1126.40		
1 Pickup Truck, 3/4 Ton		233.60		256.96		
1 Crew Truck		297.60		327.36	11.07	12.17
48 L.H., Daily Totals		$3578.40		$5118.32	$74.55	$106.63

Crew R-9

Crew R-9	Hr.	Daily	Hr.	Daily	Bare Costs	Incl. O&P
1 Electrician Foreman	$72.20	$577.60	$107.05	$856.40	$59.31	$88.44
1 Electrician Lineman	71.70	573.60	106.30	850.40		
2 Electrician Operators	71.70	1147.20	106.30	1700.80		
4 Electrician Groundmen	46.80	1497.60	70.40	2252.80		
1 Pickup Truck, 3/4 Ton		233.60		256.96		
1 Crew Truck		297.60		327.36	8.30	9.13
64 L.H., Daily Totals		$4327.20		$6244.72	$67.61	$97.57

Crew R-10

Crew R-10	Hr.	Daily	Hr.	Daily	Bare Costs	Incl. O&P
1 Electrician Foreman	$72.20	$577.60	$107.05	$856.40	$67.63	$100.44
4 Electrician Linemen	71.70	2294.40	106.30	3401.60		
1 Electrician Groundman	46.80	374.40	70.40	563.20		
1 Crew Truck		297.60		327.36		
3 Tram Cars		251.07		276.18	11.43	12.57
48 L.H., Daily Totals		$3795.07		$5424.74	$79.06	$113.02

Crews - Standard

Crew No.		Bare Costs		Incl. Subs O&P		Cost Per Labor-Hour	
Crew R-11	Hr.	Daily	Hr.	Daily	Bare Costs	Incl. O&P
1 Electrician Foreman	$72.20	$577.60	$107.05	$856.40	$68.09	$100.94
4 Electricians	71.70	2294.40	106.30	3401.60		
1 Equip. Oper. (crane)	68.60	548.80	101.75	814.00		
1 Common Laborer	49.00	392.00	72.55	580.40		
1 Crew Truck		297.60		327.36		
1 Hyd. Crane, 12 Ton		2224.21		2446.63	45.03	49.54
56 L.H., Daily Totals		$6334.61		$8426.39	$113.12	$150.47
Crew R-12	Hr.	Daily	Hr.	Daily	Bare Costs	Incl. O&P
1 Carpenter Foreman (inside)	$61.05	$488.40	$90.40	$723.20	$57.39	$85.31
4 Carpenters	60.55	1937.60	89.65	2868.80		
4 Common Laborers	49.00	1568.00	72.55	2321.60		
1 Equip. Oper. (medium)	65.00	520.00	96.40	771.20		
1 Steel Worker	67.05	536.40	102.80	822.40		
1 Dozer, 200 H.P.		1443.21		1587.53		
1 Pickup Truck, 3/4 Ton		233.60		256.96	19.05	20.96
88 L.H., Daily Totals		$6727.21		$9351.70	$76.45	$106.27
Crew R-13	Hr.	Daily	Hr.	Daily	Bare Costs	Incl. O&P
1 Electrician Foreman	$72.20	$577.60	$107.05	$856.40	$69.11	$102.47
3 Electricians	71.70	1720.80	106.30	2551.20		
.25 Equip. Oper. (crane)	68.60	137.20	101.75	203.50		
1 Equipment Oiler	58.40	467.20	86.60	692.80		
.25 Hydraulic Crane, 33 Ton		629.79		692.76	14.99	16.49
42 L.H., Daily Totals		$3532.59		$4996.66	$84.11	$118.97
Crew R-15	Hr.	Daily	Hr.	Daily	Bare Costs	Incl. O&P
1 Electrician Foreman	$72.20	$577.60	$107.05	$856.40	$70.17	$104.03
4 Electricians	71.70	2294.40	106.30	3401.60		
1 Equipment Oper. (light)	62.00	496.00	91.95	735.60		
1 Telescoping Boom Lift, to 40'		344.31		378.74	7.17	7.89
48 L.H., Daily Totals		$3712.31		$5372.34	$77.34	$111.92
Crew R-15A	Hr.	Daily	Hr.	Daily	Bare Costs	Incl. O&P
1 Electrician Foreman	$72.20	$577.60	$107.05	$856.40	$62.60	$92.78
2 Electricians	71.70	1147.20	106.30	1700.80		
2 Common Laborers	49.00	784.00	72.55	1160.80		
1 Equip. Oper. (light)	62.00	496.00	91.95	735.60		
1 Telescoping Boom Lift, to 40'		344.31		378.74	7.17	7.89
48 L.H., Daily Totals		$3349.11		$4832.34	$69.77	$100.67
Crew R-18	Hr.	Daily	Hr.	Daily	Bare Costs	Incl. O&P
.25 Electrician Foreman	$72.20	$144.40	$107.05	$214.10	$62.91	$93.25
1 Electrician	71.70	573.60	106.30	850.40		
2 Electrician Apprentices	57.35	917.60	85.00	1360.00		
26 L.H., Daily Totals		$1635.60		$2424.50	$62.91	$93.25
Crew R-19	Hr.	Daily	Hr.	Daily	Bare Costs	Incl. O&P
.5 Electrician Foreman	$72.20	$288.80	$107.05	$428.20	$71.80	$106.45
2 Electricians	71.70	1147.20	106.30	1700.80		
20 L.H., Daily Totals		$1436.00		$2129.00	$71.80	$106.45
Crew R-21	Hr.	Daily	Hr.	Daily	Bare Costs	Incl. O&P
1 Electrician Foreman	$72.20	$577.60	$107.05	$856.40	$71.66	$106.24
3 Electricians	71.70	1720.80	106.30	2551.20		
.1 Equip. Oper. (medium)	65.00	52.00	96.40	77.12		
.1 S.P. Crane, 4x4, 25 Ton		96.62		106.28	2.95	3.24
32.8 L.H., Daily Totals		$2447.02		$3591.00	$74.60	$109.48

Crew No.		Bare Costs		Incl. Subs O&P		Cost Per Labor-Hour	
Crew R-22	Hr.	Daily	Hr.	Daily	Bare Costs	Incl. O&P
.66 Electrician Foreman	$72.20	$381.22	$107.05	$565.22	$65.61	$97.26
2 Electricians	71.70	1147.20	106.30	1700.80		
2 Electrician Apprentices	57.35	917.60	85.00	1360.00		
37.28 L.H., Daily Totals		$2446.02		$3626.02	$65.61	$97.26
Crew R-30	Hr.	Daily	Hr.	Daily	Bare Costs	Incl. O&P
.25 Electrician Foreman (outside)	$73.70	$147.40	$109.25	$218.50	$57.88	$85.76
1 Electrician	71.70	573.60	106.30	850.40		
2 Laborers (Semi-Skilled)	49.00	784.00	72.55	1160.80		
26 L.H., Daily Totals		$1505.00		$2229.70	$57.88	$85.76
Crew R-31	Hr.	Daily	Hr.	Daily	Bare Costs	Incl. O&P
1 Electrician	$71.70	$573.60	$106.30	$850.40	$71.70	$106.30
1 Core Drill, Electric, 2.5 H.P.		63.75		70.13	7.97	8.77
8 L.H., Daily Totals		$637.35		$920.53	$79.67	$115.07
Crew W-41E	Hr.	Daily	Hr.	Daily	Bare Costs	Incl. O&P
.5 Plumber Foreman (outside)	$76.65	$306.60	$114.05	$456.20	$64.79	$96.25
1 Plumber	74.65	597.20	111.05	888.40		
1 Laborer	49.00	392.00	72.55	580.40		
20 L.H., Daily Totals		$1295.80		$1925.00	$64.79	$96.25

Historical Cost Indexes

The table below lists both the RSMeans® historical cost index based on Jan. 1, 1993 = 100 as well as the computed value of an index based on Jan. 1, 2024 costs. Since the Jan. 1, 2024 figure is estimated, space is left to write in the actual index figures as they become available through the quarterly *RSMeans Construction Cost Indexes*.

To compute the actual index based on Jan. 1, 2024 = 100, divide the historical cost index for a particular year by the actual Jan. 1, 2024 construction cost index. Space has been left to advance the index figures as the year progresses.

Year	Historical Cost Index Jan. 1, 1993 = 100		Current Index Based on Jan. 1, 2024 = 100		Year	Historical Cost Index Jan. 1, 1993 = 100	Current Index Based on Jan. 1, 2024 = 100		Year	Historical Cost Index Jan. 1, 1993 = 100	Current Index Based on Jan. 1, 2024 = 100	
	Est.	Actual	Est.	Actual		Actual	Est.	Actual		Actual	Est.	Actual
Oct 2024					July 2007	169.4	58.8		July 1987	87.7	30.4	
July 2024					2006	162.0	56.2		1986	84.2	26.4	
April 2024					2005	151.6	52.6		1985	82.6	28.7	
Jan 2024	288.1		100.0		2004	143.7	49.9		1984	82.0	28.4	
July 2023		293.7	101.9		2003	132.0	45.8		1983	80.2	27.8	
2022		297.1	103.1		2002	128.7	44.7		1982	76.1	26.4	
2021		257.5	89.4		2001	125.1	43.4		1981	70.0	24.3	
2020		234.6	81.4		2000	120.9	42.0		1980	62.9	21.8	
2019		232.2	80.6		1999	117.6	40.8		1979	57.8	20.1	
2018		222.9	77.4		1998	115.1	40.0		1978	53.5	18.6	
2017		213.6	74.1		1997	112.8	39.2		1977	49.5	17.2	
2016		207.3	72.0		1996	110.2	38.3		1976	46.9	16.3	
2015		206.2	71.6		1995	107.6	37.3		1975	44.8	15.6	
2014		204.9	71.1		1994	104.4	36.2		1974	41.4	14.4	
2013		201.2	69.8		1993	101.7	35.3		1973	37.7	13.1	
2012		194.6	67.5		1992	99.4	34.5		1972	34.8	12.1	
2011		191.2	66.4		1991	96.8	33.6					
2010		183.5	63.7		1990	94.3	32.7					
2009		180.1	62.5		1989	92.1	32.0					
2008		180.4	62.6		1988	89.9	31.2					

Adjustments to Costs

The "Historical Cost Index" can be used to convert national average building costs at a particular time to the approximate building costs for some other time.

Example:

Estimate and compare construction costs for different years in the same city.
To estimate the national average construction cost of a building in 1971, knowing that it cost $900,000 in 2024:

INDEX in 1970 = 32.1
INDEX in 2024 = 288.1

Note: The city cost indexes for Canada can be used to convert U.S. national averages to local costs in Canadian dollars.

Time Adjustment Using the Historical Cost Indexes:

$$\frac{\text{Index for Year A}}{\text{Index for Year B}} \times \text{Cost in Year B} = \text{Cost in Year A}$$

$$\frac{\text{INDEX 1971}}{\text{INDEX 2024}} \times \text{Cost 2024} = \text{Cost 1971}$$

$$\frac{32.1}{288.1} \times \$900{,}000 = .111 \times \$900{,}000 = \$99{,}900$$

The construction cost of the building in 1971 was $90,000.

Example:

To estimate and compare the cost of a building in Toronto, ON in 2024 with the known cost of $600,000 (US$) in New York, NY in 2024:

INDEX Toronto = 132.1
INDEX New York = 139.6

$$\frac{\text{INDEX Toronto}}{\text{INDEX New York}} \times \text{Cost New York} = \text{Cost Toronto}$$

$$\frac{132.1}{139.6} \times \$600{,}000 = .946 \times \$600{,}000 = \$567{,}600$$

The construction cost of the building in Toronto is $567,600 (CN$).

*Historical Cost Index updates and other resources are provided on the following website:
rsmeans.com/2024books

City Cost Indexes

How to Use the City Cost Indexes

What you should know before you begin

RSMeans City Cost Indexes (CCI) are an extremely useful tool for when you want to compare costs from city to city and region to region.

This publication contains average construction cost indexes for 731 U.S. and Canadian cities covering over 930 three-digit zip code locations, as listed directly under each city.

Keep in mind that a City Cost Index number is a percentage ratio of a specific city's cost to the national average cost of the same item at a stated time period.

In other words, these index figures represent relative construction factors (or, if you prefer, multipliers) for material and installation costs, as well as the weighted average for Total In Place costs for each CSI MasterFormat division. Installation costs include both labor and equipment rental costs. When estimating equipment rental rates only for a specific location, use 01 54 33 EQUIPMENT RENTAL COSTS in the Reference Section.

The 30 City Average Index is the average of 30 major U.S. cities and serves as a national average. This national average represents the baseline from which all locations are calculated.

Index figures for both material and installation are based on the 30 major city average of 100 and represent the cost relationship as of July 1, 2023. The index for each division is computed from representative material and labor quantities for that division. The weighted average for each city is a weighted total of the components listed above it. It does not include relative productivity between trades or cities.

As changes occur in local material prices, labor rates, and equipment rental rates (including fuel costs), the impact of these changes should be accurately measured by the change in the City Cost Index for each particular city (as compared to the 30 city average).

Therefore, if you know (or have estimated) building costs in one city today, you can easily convert those costs to expected building costs in another city.

In addition, by using the Historical Cost Index, you can easily convert national average building costs at a particular time to the approximate building costs for some other time. The City Cost Indexes can then be applied to calculate the costs for a particular city.

Quick calculations

Location Adjustment Using the City Cost Indexes:

$$\frac{\text{Index for City A}}{\text{Index for City B}} \times \text{Cost in City B} = \text{Cost in City A}$$

Time Adjustment for the National Average Using the Historical Cost Index:

$$\frac{\text{Index for Year A}}{\text{Index for Year B}} \times \text{Cost in Year B} = \text{Cost in Year A}$$

Adjustment from the National Average:

$$\frac{\text{Index for City A}}{100} \times \text{National Average Cost} = \text{Cost in City A}$$

Since each of the other RSMeans data sets contains many different items, any *one* item multiplied by the particular city index may give incorrect results. However, the larger the number of items compiled, the closer the results should be to actual costs for that particular city.

The City Cost Indexes for Canadian cities are calculated using Canadian material and equipment prices and labor rates in Canadian dollars. When compared to the baseline mentioned previously, the resulting index enables the user to convert baseline costs to local costs. Therefore, indexes for Canadian cities can be used to convert U.S. national average prices to local costs in Canadian dollars.

How to use this section

1. Compare costs from city to city.

In using the RSMeans Indexes, remember that an index number is not a fixed number but a ratio: It's a percentage ratio of a building component's cost at any stated time to the national average cost of that same component at the same time period. Put in the form of an equation:

$$\frac{\text{Specific City Cost}}{\text{National Average Cost}} \times 100 = \text{City Index Number}$$

Therefore, when making cost comparisons between cities, do not subtract one city's index number from the index number of another city and read the result as a percentage difference. Instead, divide one city's index number by that of the other city. The resulting number may then be used as a multiplier to calculate cost differences from city to city.

The formula used to find cost differences between cities for the purpose of comparison is as follows:

$$\frac{\text{City A Index}}{\text{City B Index}} \times \text{City B Cost (Known)} = \text{City A Cost (Unknown)}$$

In addition, you can use RSMeans CCI to calculate and compare costs division by division between cities using the same basic formula. (Just be sure that you're comparing similar divisions.)

2. Compare a specific city's construction costs with the national average.

When you're studying construction location feasibility, it's advisable to compare a prospective project's cost index with an index of the national average cost.

For example, divide the weighted average index of construction costs of a specific city by that of the 30 City Average, which = 100.

$$\frac{\text{City Index}}{100} = \% \text{ of National Average}$$

As a result, you get a ratio that indicates the relative cost of construction in that city in comparison with the national average.

3. Convert U.S. national average to actual costs in Canadian City.

$$\frac{\text{Index for Canadian City}}{100} \times \text{National Average Cost} = \text{Cost in Canadian City in \$ CAN}$$

4. Adjust construction cost data based on a national average.
When you use a source of construction cost data which is based on a national average (such as RSMeans cost data), it is necessary to adjust those costs to a specific location.

$$\frac{\text{City Index}}{100} \times \text{Cost Based on National Average Costs} = \text{City Cost (Unknown)}$$

5. When applying the City Cost Indexes to demolition projects, use the **appropriate division installation index.** For example, for removal of existing doors and windows, use the Division 8 (Openings) index.

What you might like to know about how we developed the Indexes

The information presented in the CCI is organized according to the Construction Specifications Institute (CSI) MasterFormat 2018 classification system.

To create a reliable index, RSMeans researched the building type most often constructed in the United States and Canada. Because it was concluded that no one type of building completely represented the building construction industry, nine different types of buildings were combined to create a composite model.

The exact material, labor, and equipment quantities are based on detailed analyses of these nine building types, and then each quantity is weighted in proportion to expected usage. These various material items, labor hours, and equipment rental rates are thus combined to form a composite building representing as closely as possible the actual usage of materials, labor, and equipment in the North American building construction industry.

The following structures were chosen to make up that composite model:

1. Factory, 1 story
2. Office, 2-4 stories
3. Store, Retail
4. Town Hall, 2-3 stories
5. High School, 2-3 stories
6. Hospital, 4-8 stories
7. Garage, Parking
8. Apartment, 1-3 stories
9. Hotel/Motel, 2-3 stories

For the purposes of ensuring the timeliness of the data, the components of the index for the composite model have been streamlined. They currently consist of:

- specific quantities of 66 commonly used construction materials;
- specific labor-hours for 21 building construction trades; and
- specific days of equipment rental for 6 types of construction equipment (normally used to install the 66 material items by the 21 trades.) Fuel costs and routine maintenance costs are included in the equipment cost.

Material and equipment price quotations are gathered quarterly from cities in the United States and Canada. These prices and the latest negotiated labor wage rates for 21 different building trades are used to compile the quarterly update of the City Cost Index.

The 30 major U.S. cities used to calculate the national average are:

Atlanta, GA
Baltimore, MD
Boston, MA
Buffalo, NY
Chicago, IL
Cincinnati, OH
Cleveland, OH
Columbus, OH
Dallas, TX
Denver, CO
Detroit, MI
Houston, TX
Indianapolis, IN
Kansas City, MO
Los Angeles, CA

Memphis, TN
Milwaukee, WI
Minneapolis, MN
Nashville, TN
New Orleans, LA
New York, NY
Philadelphia, PA
Phoenix, AZ
Pittsburgh, PA
St. Louis, MO
San Antonio, TX
San Diego, CA
San Francisco, CA
Seattle, WA
Washington, DC

What the CCI does not indicate

The weighted average for each city is a total of the divisional components weighted to reflect typical usage. It does not include the productivity variations between trades or cities.

In addition, the CCI does not take into consideration factors such as the following:

- managerial efficiency
- competitive conditions
- automation
- restrictive union practices
- unique local requirements
- regional variations due to specific building codes

City Cost Indexes

DIVISION		UNITED STATES 30 CITY AVERAGE			ALABAMA ANNISTON 362			ALABAMA BIRMINGHAM 350 - 352			ALABAMA BUTLER 369			ALABAMA DECATUR 356			ALABAMA DOTHAN 363		
		MAT.	INST.	TOTAL	MAT.	INST.	TOTAL	MAT.	INST.	TOTAL	MAT.	INST.	TOTAL	MAT.	INST.	TOTAL	MAT.	INST.	TOTAL
015433	CONTRACTOR EQUIPMENT		100.0	100.0		94.4	94.4		105.9	105.9		92.4	92.4		97.6	97.6		92.4	92.4
0241, 31 - 34	SITE & INFRASTRUCTURE, DEMOLITION	100.0	100.0	100.0	98.0	87.5	91.2	96.1	102.8	100.4	102.4	84.3	90.6	89.2	92.2	91.1	100.4	84.4	90.0
0310	Concrete Forming & Accessories	100.0	100.0	100.0	98.3	62.2	68.5	107.8	68.3	75.2	95.1	64.3	69.7	107.0	60.7	68.9	102.5	67.8	73.9
0320	Concrete Reinforcing	100.0	100.0	100.0	150.2	67.6	116.5	151.7	68.0	117.5	158.3	65.3	120.3	141.6	62.4	109.3	158.3	67.6	121.3
0330	Cast-in-Place Concrete	100.0	100.0	100.0	99.2	66.8	88.4	109.5	74.1	97.7	96.8	69.6	87.7	101.7	66.2	89.8	96.8	70.6	88.0
03	CONCRETE	100.0	100.0	100.0	107.2	65.8	90.2	109.4	71.0	93.7	108.4	67.3	91.5	102.4	64.0	86.6	107.8	69.7	92.1
04	MASONRY	100.0	100.0	100.0	84.1	58.4	69.1	85.3	62.8	72.2	85.1	58.5	69.6	81.2	57.5	67.4	86.9	61.7	72.2
05	METALS	100.0	100.0	100.0	97.9	82.3	94.6	97.6	81.9	94.3	96.9	81.7	93.7	99.4	79.2	95.0	93.8	83.6	94.1
06	WOOD, PLASTICS & COMPOSITES	100.0	100.0	100.0	97.9	62.2	80.4	108.0	68.5	88.6	93.9	64.6	79.5	114.5	60.5	87.9	103.3	68.2	86.1
07	THERMAL & MOISTURE PROTECTION	100.0	100.0	100.0	98.9	60.1	85.9	102.0	69.8	91.2	99.0	64.3	87.3	99.9	63.3	87.6	98.9	65.7	87.8
08	OPENINGS	100.0	100.0	100.0	100.6	63.9	91.7	107.6	68.0	97.9	100.6	65.0	92.0	109.9	62.0	98.2	100.7	68.4	92.8
0920	Plaster & Gypsum Board	100.0	100.0	100.0	104.7	61.5	77.2	104.4	67.5	80.9	103.0	63.9	78.2	103.8	59.7	75.7	111.1	67.7	83.5
0950, 0980	Ceilings & Acoustic Treatment	100.0	100.0	100.0	85.6	61.5	72.1	71.6	67.5	69.3	85.6	63.9	73.5	69.8	59.7	64.1	85.6	67.7	75.6
0960	Flooring	100.0	100.0	100.0	74.8	62.4	71.6	107.6	69.6	97.8	78.2	62.4	74.2	101.1	62.4	91.1	81.9	66.9	78.1
0970, 0990	Wall Finishes & Painting/Coating	100.0	100.0	100.0	95.6	49.1	68.2	99.9	51.5	71.5	95.6	41.6	63.8	89.4	55.3	69.3	95.6	80.3	86.6
09	FINISHES	100.0	100.0	100.0	87.0	60.7	74.0	95.2	66.6	81.1	89.5	61.3	75.5	90.1	61.1	75.3	91.3	68.8	80.2
COVERS	DIVS. 10 - 14, 25, 28, 41, 43, 44, 46	100.0	100.0	100.0	100.0	83.8	96.5	100.0	86.0	97.0	100.0	82.7	96.3	100.0	77.3	95.2	100.0	85.6	96.9
21, 22, 23	FIRE SUPPRESSION, PLUMBING & HVAC	100.0	100.0	100.0	105.5	48.6	85.0	100.0	63.9	87.0	96.0	60.0	83.0	100.1	60.0	85.6	96.0	61.9	83.7
26, 27, 3370	ELECTRICAL, COMMUNICATIONS & UTIL.	100.0	100.0	100.0	98.9	51.7	78.4	101.6	64.1	85.3	100.2	51.9	79.2	98.5	58.4	81.1	99.4	73.3	88.1
MF2018	WEIGHTED AVERAGE	100.0	100.0	100.0	99.8	62.0	85.5	100.4	70.7	89.2	98.0	64.6	85.4	99.0	64.9	86.1	98.1	70.2	87.6

DIVISION		ALABAMA EVERGREEN 364			ALABAMA GADSDEN 359			ALABAMA HUNTSVILLE 357 - 358			ALABAMA JASPER 355			ALABAMA MOBILE 365 - 366			ALABAMA MONTGOMERY 360 - 361		
		MAT.	INST.	TOTAL	MAT.	INST.	TOTAL	MAT.	INST.	TOTAL	MAT.	INST.	TOTAL	MAT.	INST.	TOTAL	MAT.	INST.	TOTAL
015433	CONTRACTOR EQUIPMENT		92.4	92.4		97.6	97.6		97.6	97.6		97.6	97.6		92.4	92.4		103.3	103.3
0241, 31 - 34	SITE & INFRASTRUCTURE, DEMOLITION	102.8	84.3	90.7	99.1	92.7	95.0	88.9	92.6	91.3	99.4	92.7	95.0	98.6	84.3	89.3	96.7	98.7	98.0
0310	Concrete Forming & Accessories	92.6	62.3	67.6	99.9	66.6	72.2	107.0	70.7	77.1	104.6	62.9	70.2	101.8	67.0	73.1	105.9	70.5	74.3
0320	Concrete Reinforcing	158.4	65.3	120.4	149.8	67.9	116.3	141.6	75.8	114.7	141.6	67.7	111.4	155.4	68.6	119.9	170.8	67.9	128.8
0330	Cast-in-Place Concrete	96.8	66.9	86.8	101.7	70.5	91.3	99.0	70.0	89.3	112.7	67.6	97.6	101.5	70.1	91.0	101.4	73.1	91.9
03	CONCRETE	108.7	65.5	90.9	106.7	69.0	91.2	101.1	72.1	89.2	110.2	66.4	92.2	105.2	69.3	90.4	108.3	70.3	92.7
04	MASONRY	85.1	58.5	69.6	79.6	62.2	69.5	82.0	61.2	69.9	77.2	59.4	66.8	87.1	60.6	71.7	83.8	60.8	70.4
05	METALS	96.9	81.4	93.7	97.9	83.2	94.8	99.4	86.3	96.7	97.9	82.7	94.7	98.4	83.3	95.2	97.6	81.8	94.3
06	WOOD, PLASTICS & COMPOSITES	91.1	62.2	76.9	105.9	66.3	86.4	114.5	72.6	93.9	112.0	62.2	87.5	102.2	68.1	85.4	105.9	68.5	87.5
07	THERMAL & MOISTURE PROTECTION	99.0	62.9	86.9	100.1	66.6	88.9	99.9	66.9	88.8	100.1	63.2	87.8	98.5	63.2	87.4	97.9	68.5	88.0
08	OPENINGS	100.6	63.7	91.7	106.1	66.5	96.5	109.5	72.3	100.5	106.1	64.3	95.9	103.7	67.7	94.9	103.9	68.0	95.1
0920	Plaster & Gypsum Board	102.8	61.5	76.5	96.9	65.7	77.0	103.8	72.2	83.7	100.5	61.5	75.7	110.1	67.5	83.0	112.5	67.5	83.8
0950, 0980	Ceilings & Acoustic Treatment	85.6	61.5	72.1	65.4	65.7	65.6	71.3	72.2	71.8	65.4	61.5	63.2	95.0	67.5	79.6	97.7	67.5	80.8
0960	Flooring	76.6	62.4	73.0	98.2	66.9	90.2	101.1	66.9	92.3	99.7	62.4	90.2	82.1	65.6	77.9	80.9	65.6	77.0
0970, 0990	Wall Finishes & Painting/Coating	95.6	41.6	63.8	89.4	49.1	65.7	89.4	59.3	71.7	89.4	49.1	65.7	99.6	41.6	65.5	99.9	49.1	70.0
09	FINISHES	89.0	59.9	74.6	87.7	64.3	76.2	90.6	68.9	79.9	88.5	61.0	74.9	93.4	64.0	78.8	96.1	65.1	80.8
COVERS	DIVS. 10 - 14, 25, 28, 41, 43, 44, 46	100.0	82.4	96.3	100.0	84.7	96.7	100.0	82.8	96.3	100.0	84.1	96.6	100.0	83.0	96.4	100.0	85.5	96.9
21, 22, 23	FIRE SUPPRESSION, PLUMBING & HVAC	96.0	54.2	81.0	107.0	64.1	91.6	100.0	63.4	86.9	107.0	63.4	91.3	100.0	60.3	85.7	100.0	60.3	85.8
26, 27, 3370	ELECTRICAL, COMMUNICATIONS & UTIL.	98.5	51.9	78.2	98.8	64.2	83.7	99.4	64.0	84.0	98.3	51.7	78.0	100.9	56.8	81.7	101.6	69.0	87.4
MF2018	WEIGHTED AVERAGE	97.8	62.8	84.6	100.5	69.3	88.7	99.0	70.5	88.2	100.9	66.0	87.7	99.5	66.6	87.1	99.9	69.8	88.5

DIVISION		ALABAMA PHENIX CITY 368			ALABAMA SELMA 367			ALABAMA TUSCALOOSA 354			ALASKA ANCHORAGE 995 - 996			ALASKA FAIRBANKS 997			ALASKA JUNEAU 998		
		MAT.	INST.	TOTAL	MAT.	INST.	TOTAL	MAT.	INST.	TOTAL	MAT.	INST.	TOTAL	MAT.	INST.	TOTAL	MAT.	INST.	TOTAL
015433	CONTRACTOR EQUIPMENT		92.4	92.4		92.4	92.4		97.6	97.6		104.7	104.7		101.8	101.8		98.4	98.4
0241, 31 - 34	SITE & INFRASTRUCTURE, DEMOLITION	105.8	84.3	91.8	100.3	84.3	89.9	89.5	92.6	91.5	108.4	105.2	106.3	106.9	108.4	107.9	119.9	102.8	108.7
0310	Concrete Forming & Accessories	98.2	66.9	72.4	96.1	62.7	68.5	106.9	67.2	74.2	99.2	115.4	112.5	101.0	113.4	111.2	98.8	115.4	112.4
0320	Concrete Reinforcing	158.3	66.0	120.6	158.3	67.7	121.3	141.6	67.9	111.5	174.6	116.0	150.6	165.3	115.9	145.1	160.6	115.9	142.4
0330	Cast-in-Place Concrete	96.8	69.7	87.7	96.8	67.0	86.8	103.2	69.2	92.0	92.5	118.6	101.2	99.8	109.1	102.9	109.0	118.5	112.2
03	CONCRETE	111.1	68.7	93.7	107.4	66.1	90.4	103.1	69.2	89.2	133.0	116.1	126.1	110.9	117.8	111.3	117.0	115.7	116.4
04	MASONRY	85.1	61.6	71.4	90.5	58.4	71.8	81.4	61.0	69.5	279.9	113.2	182.9	242.7	110.1	165.5	188.7	113.3	144.7
05	METALS	96.9	82.4	93.8	96.9	82.8	93.9	98.6	83.2	95.4	143.7	103.9	135.4	141.5	102.1	133.2	143.8	97.7	134.2
06	WOOD, PLASTICS & COMPOSITES	97.7	67.9	83.0	95.3	62.2	79.0	114.5	68.1	91.6	96.6	113.1	104.7	108.1	111.9	110.0	104.9	113.1	108.9
07	THERMAL & MOISTURE PROTECTION	99.3	66.3	88.2	98.8	63.6	87.1	99.9	66.3	88.6	119.2	112.3	116.9	119.8	107.9	115.8	113.2	112.2	112.9
08	OPENINGS	100.6	67.2	92.5	100.6	64.3	91.8	109.5	67.8	99.4	130.9	113.3	126.6	132.8	112.6	127.9	131.6	113.3	127.1
0920	Plaster & Gypsum Board	105.9	67.3	81.4	104.5	61.5	77.1	103.8	67.5	80.7	115.1	113.1	113.9	144.3	112.3	123.9	137.0	113.1	121.8
0950, 0980	Ceilings & Acoustic Treatment	85.6	67.3	75.4	85.6	61.5	72.1	71.3	67.5	69.2	88.4	113.1	102.2	78.0	113.2	97.2	87.4	113.1	101.8
0960	Flooring	79.5	62.4	75.1	78.4	62.4	74.3	101.1	66.9	92.3	123.4	106.4	119.0	113.6	106.4	111.8	119.0	106.4	115.8
0970, 0990	Wall Finishes & Painting/Coating	95.6	72.9	82.2	95.6	49.1	68.2	89.4	49.1	65.7	99.9	113.6	107.9	100.4	117.4	110.4	99.9	113.6	107.9
09	FINISHES	90.6	66.6	78.7	89.5	60.7	75.2	90.5	65.1	77.9	106.1	113.8	109.9	104.4	112.7	108.8	107.1	113.8	110.4
COVERS	DIVS. 10 - 14, 25, 28, 41, 43, 44, 46	100.0	79.0	95.5	100.0	83.8	96.6	100.0	84.5	96.7	100.0	112.8	102.7	100.0	110.9	102.3	100.0	112.8	102.7
21, 22, 23	FIRE SUPPRESSION, PLUMBING & HVAC	96.0	60.2	83.1	96.0	59.5	82.9	100.1	63.3	86.8	100.3	102.1	100.9	100.0	107.5	102.7	100.1	102.1	100.8
26, 27, 3370	ELECTRICAL, COMMUNICATIONS & UTIL.	99.8	61.1	83.0	99.3	65.7	84.6	99.1	64.2	83.9	104.6	102.4	103.6	113.3	102.3	108.5	93.7	102.3	97.5
MF2018	WEIGHTED AVERAGE	98.5	67.3	86.7	98.0	66.3	86.0	99.0	69.2	87.7	124.9	108.3	118.6	121.2	108.3	116.3	117.9	107.5	114.0

City Cost Indexes

DIVISION		ALASKA KETCHIKAN 999			ARIZONA													
					CHAMBERS 865			FLAGSTAFF 860			GLOBE 855			KINGMAN 864			MESA/TEMPE 852		
		MAT.	INST.	TOTAL	MAT.	INST.	TOTAL	MAT.	INST.	TOTAL	MAT.	INST.	TOTAL	MAT.	INST.	TOTAL	MAT.	INST.	TOTAL
015433	CONTRACTOR EQUIPMENT		101.8	101.8		92.1	92.1		92.1	92.1		95.0	95.0		92.1	92.1		95.0	95.0
0241, 31 - 34	SITE & INFRASTRUCTURE, DEMOLITION	140.6	108.6	119.8	73.9	90.7	84.9	93.5	91.1	91.9	117.9	90.7	100.2	73.9	91.1	85.1	110.1	91.1	97.7
0310	Concrete Forming & Accessories	96.0	115.0	111.6	93.8	64.5	69.6	97.7	71.8	76.4	91.4	64.6	69.3	92.6	61.0	66.5	93.3	69.3	73.5
0320	Concrete Reinforcing	126.2	115.9	122.0	116.8	71.4	98.3	116.6	71.1	98.1	116.0	71.4	97.8	117.0	71.4	98.4	116.8	71.5	98.3
0330	Cast-in-Place Concrete	202.2	114.8	173.0	83.8	66.8	78.1	83.9	67.2	78.3	88.7	67.1	81.5	83.5	67.2	78.0	89.4	67.6	82.1
03	CONCRETE	182.7	114.5	154.7	96.4	66.8	84.3	116.0	70.3	97.2	117.4	67.2	96.8	96.1	65.4	83.5	107.3	69.5	91.8
04	MASONRY	248.4	112.9	169.6	99.0	64.2	78.7	99.1	59.0	75.8	107.7	64.2	82.3	99.0	64.3	78.8	107.9	64.3	82.5
05	METALS	141.4	101.9	133.2	100.0	73.5	94.5	100.4	74.5	95.0	89.1	76.8	86.5	100.6	74.7	95.2	89.3	78.1	86.9
06	WOOD, PLASTICS & COMPOSITES	102.9	112.7	107.7	94.0	64.8	79.6	98.0	74.4	86.4	84.0	64.9	74.6	90.7	59.9	75.5	86.4	71.0	78.8
07	THERMAL & MOISTURE PROTECTION	131.6	108.7	123.9	91.2	67.7	83.3	92.8	68.5	84.7	102.0	67.6	90.5	91.2	67.7	83.3	101.9	68.8	90.8
08	OPENINGS	126.2	113.1	123.0	98.5	62.1	89.6	98.6	71.2	91.9	89.8	62.2	83.1	98.6	60.9	89.4	89.9	66.3	84.1
0920	Plaster & Gypsum Board	133.1	113.1	120.4	93.7	64.1	74.8	96.2	74.0	82.1	94.8	64.1	75.2	88.1	58.9	69.5	97.2	70.3	80.1
0950, 0980	Ceilings & Acoustic Treatment	75.0	113.1	96.3	107.7	64.1	83.3	108.1	74.0	89.0	94.7	64.1	77.6	108.1	58.9	80.6	94.7	70.3	81.1
0960	Flooring	113.0	106.4	111.4	90.6	56.1	81.8	92.2	61.0	84.2	95.7	56.1	85.5	89.7	56.1	81.1	96.8	60.0	87.3
0970, 0990	Wall Finishes & Painting/Coating	100.4	113.6	108.1	84.0	55.1	67.1	84.0	55.1	67.1	92.2	55.1	70.4	84.0	55.1	67.1	92.2	55.1	70.4
09	FINISHES	104.9	113.5	109.1	96.0	61.5	78.9	98.3	68.1	83.4	98.4	61.6	80.2	95.1	58.6	77.0	97.9	65.9	82.1
COVERS	DIVS. 10 - 14, 25, 28, 41, 43, 44, 46	100.0	111.9	102.5	100.0	83.7	96.5	100.0	84.7	96.7	100.0	83.9	96.6	100.0	83.2	96.4	100.0	84.6	96.7
21, 22, 23	FIRE SUPPRESSION, PLUMBING & HVAC	93.5	102.0	96.6	94.3	76.7	88.0	100.4	76.7	91.9	93.1	76.7	87.2	94.3	76.7	88.0	100.4	76.7	91.9
26, 27, 3370	ELECTRICAL, COMMUNICATIONS & UTIL.	113.3	102.3	108.5	100.4	63.7	84.4	99.8	61.9	83.3	97.9	63.7	83.0	100.4	63.7	84.4	96.0	63.7	82.0
MF2018	WEIGHTED AVERAGE	129.1	107.9	121.1	96.8	70.3	86.8	101.3	71.5	90.0	97.9	70.6	87.6	96.8	69.7	86.6	98.0	71.9	88.2

DIVISION		ARIZONA											ARKANSAS					
		PHOENIX 850,853			PRESCOTT 863			SHOW LOW 859			TUCSON 856 - 857			BATESVILLE 725			CAMDEN 717		
		MAT.	INST.	TOTAL	MAT.	INST.	TOTAL	MAT.	INST.	TOTAL	MAT.	INST.	TOTAL	MAT.	INST.	TOTAL	MAT.	INST.	TOTAL
015433	CONTRACTOR EQUIPMENT		101.7	101.7		92.1	92.1		95.0	95.0		106.9	106.9		87.7	87.7		90.0	90.0
0241, 31 - 34	SITE & INFRASTRUCTURE, DEMOLITION	111.3	97.7	102.4	83.0	91.1	88.3	120.3	90.7	101.0	106.2	103.2	104.2	72.0	79.7	77.1	85.1	80.6	82.2
0310	Concrete Forming & Accessories	98.1	73.0	77.4	94.9	67.5	72.3	96.1	64.6	70.1	93.7	78.5	81.2	92.2	55.9	62.3	89.6	56.2	62.0
0320	Concrete Reinforcing	110.1	67.5	92.7	116.6	71.4	98.2	116.8	71.4	98.3	97.2	71.2	86.6	93.4	61.6	80.4	149.0	62.6	113.7
0330	Cast-in-Place Concrete	94.1	72.2	86.8	83.8	67.2	78.3	88.7	67.2	81.5	92.0	70.1	84.7	74.5	72.2	73.8	82.9	71.3	79.0
03	CONCRETE	109.3	72.1	94.0	101.7	68.4	88.0	119.9	67.2	98.2	105.3	74.6	92.7	77.7	63.4	71.8	89.1	63.5	78.6
04	MASONRY	100.0	66.0	80.2	99.1	64.3	78.8	107.7	64.2	82.3	92.0	59.1	72.9	87.8	56.8	69.7	101.8	56.6	75.5
05	METALS	96.1	77.1	92.1	100.4	74.8	95.1	88.9	76.9	86.4	90.0	80.4	88.0	95.4	72.7	90.7	108.4	75.7	101.6
06	WOOD, PLASTICS & COMPOSITES	96.4	75.1	85.9	95.0	68.6	82.0	89.1	64.9	77.2	86.6	83.2	85.0	100.4	56.7	78.9	96.6	57.2	77.2
07	THERMAL & MOISTURE PROTECTION	102.9	72.9	92.8	91.7	69.2	84.1	102.2	67.6	90.6	102.7	70.5	91.9	105.2	59.3	89.8	103.9	58.2	88.6
08	OPENINGS	97.9	70.4	91.2	98.6	64.7	90.3	89.1	63.7	82.9	87.0	76.1	84.3	102.6	54.6	91.0	96.9	55.2	86.8
0920	Plaster & Gypsum Board	106.3	74.2	85.9	93.5	68.0	77.3	98.8	64.1	76.7	101.7	82.4	89.5	87.7	55.7	67.3	90.9	56.1	68.8
0950, 0980	Ceilings & Acoustic Treatment	109.9	74.2	89.9	105.5	68.0	84.5	94.7	64.1	77.6	97.8	82.4	89.2	88.9	55.7	70.3	85.4	56.1	69.0
0960	Flooring	102.0	66.4	92.9	91.2	60.1	83.3	97.9	56.1	87.1	87.7	64.4	81.7	98.5	64.2	89.7	102.8	65.5	93.2
0970, 0990	Wall Finishes & Painting/Coating	99.9	55.5	73.8	84.0	55.1	67.1	92.2	55.1	70.4	91.8	55.1	70.3	97.8	47.8	68.5	99.7	49.3	70.1
09	FINISHES	104.8	70.1	87.6	96.0	64.5	80.4	99.8	61.6	80.9	96.6	74.1	85.4	88.5	56.4	72.6	91.5	57.0	74.4
COVERS	DIVS. 10 - 14, 25, 28, 41, 43, 44, 46	100.0	86.1	97.0	100.0	84.1	96.6	100.0	83.9	96.6	100.0	86.8	97.2	100.0	76.9	95.1	100.0	76.8	95.1
21, 22, 23	FIRE SUPPRESSION, PLUMBING & HVAC	100.1	77.6	92.0	100.4	76.7	91.9	93.1	76.7	87.2	100.3	75.9	91.5	93.0	48.2	76.9	92.7	52.9	78.4
26, 27, 3370	ELECTRICAL, COMMUNICATIONS & UTIL.	100.1	63.7	84.2	99.7	63.7	84.0	96.3	63.7	82.1	97.4	58.4	80.4	93.3	52.2	75.5	96.1	50.2	76.1
MF2018	WEIGHTED AVERAGE	100.9	74.0	90.8	99.1	71.2	88.6	98.1	70.7	87.7	96.9	74.0	88.3	92.3	58.9	79.7	97.1	60.0	83.1

DIVISION		ARKANSAS																
		FAYETTEVILLE 727			FORT SMITH 729			HARRISON 726			HOT SPRINGS 719			JONESBORO 724			LITTLE ROCK 720 - 722		
		MAT.	INST.	TOTAL	MAT.	INST.	TOTAL	MAT.	INST.	TOTAL	MAT.	INST.	TOTAL	MAT.	INST.	TOTAL	MAT.	INST.	TOTAL
015433	CONTRACTOR EQUIPMENT		87.7	87.7		87.7	87.7		87.7	87.7		90.0	90.0		109.3	109.3		100.1	100.1
0241, 31 - 34	SITE & INFRASTRUCTURE, DEMOLITION	71.8	79.7	76.9	79.5	79.9	79.8	75.8	79.7	78.3	88.3	80.7	83.3	93.1	98.1	96.4	84.4	96.4	92.2
0310	Concrete Forming & Accessories	88.6	56.1	61.8	103.7	58.6	66.5	95.8	55.9	62.9	87.4	56.5	61.9	95.3	56.8	63.5	102.4	59.5	67.0
0320	Concrete Reinforcing	93.5	59.5	79.6	94.6	63.4	81.9	93.1	62.6	80.6	146.3	62.5	112.0	90.2	67.2	80.8	96.0	66.2	83.8
0330	Cast-in-Place Concrete	74.5	71.8	73.6	85.3	74.7	81.8	82.7	71.8	79.0	84.8	72.0	80.5	81.2	73.7	78.7	82.7	78.3	81.2
03	CONCRETE	77.4	63.0	71.5	84.9	65.8	77.1	84.1	63.4	75.6	91.6	63.9	80.2	88.1	65.9	75.3	87.9	67.9	79.7
04	MASONRY	79.8	56.7	66.4	88.4	58.9	71.2	88.3	56.7	69.9	76.9	55.9	64.7	81.5	58.3	68.0	85.5	61.9	71.8
05	METALS	95.4	71.8	90.5	97.2	73.7	92.2	96.1	72.8	91.2	108.4	75.3	101.5	91.5	86.2	90.4	97.4	74.5	92.6
06	WOOD, PLASTICS & COMPOSITES	97.4	57.1	77.6	114.0	59.9	87.4	105.3	57.1	81.6	94.6	57.2	76.2	104.1	57.5	81.2	104.9	60.4	83.0
07	THERMAL & MOISTURE PROTECTION	106.0	59.0	90.4	106.3	60.9	91.1	105.5	59.6	90.1	104.1	57.5	88.5	110.7	60.1	93.7	100.0	63.6	87.8
08	OPENINGS	102.6	54.4	90.9	104.9	56.7	93.1	103.4	55.1	91.6	96.9	54.7	86.6	108.3	56.4	95.6	98.7	57.7	88.8
0920	Plaster & Gypsum Board	87.0	56.1	67.3	93.3	59.0	71.4	93.0	56.1	69.5	90.0	56.1	68.4	98.5	56.1	71.5	107.1	59.0	76.4
0950, 0980	Ceilings & Acoustic Treatment	88.9	56.1	70.6	91.6	59.0	73.3	91.6	56.1	71.7	85.4	56.1	69.0	91.3	56.1	71.6	97.5	59.0	75.9
0960	Flooring	96.3	65.5	88.4	103.5	72.6	95.6	100.2	65.5	91.3	101.9	61.8	91.6	69.2	72.6	70.0	106.5	80.2	99.7
0970, 0990	Wall Finishes & Painting/Coating	97.8	49.3	69.3	97.8	49.1	69.2	97.8	49.3	69.3	99.7	47.4	69.0	85.6	48.5	63.8	99.9	50.0	70.6
09	FINISHES	87.8	56.9	72.5	91.5	60.3	76.0	90.5	56.9	73.9	91.5	56.4	74.1	84.4	58.7	71.7	101.2	62.3	82.0
COVERS	DIVS. 10 - 14, 25, 28, 41, 43, 44, 46	100.0	76.6	95.0	100.0	79.5	95.6	100.0	76.6	95.0	100.0	77.4	95.2	100.0	77.8	95.3	100.0	80.6	95.9
21, 22, 23	FIRE SUPPRESSION, PLUMBING & HVAC	93.1	56.9	80.1	100.4	47.7	81.5	93.0	45.8	76.0	92.7	46.7	76.2	101.1	47.7	81.8	100.0	50.5	82.2
26, 27, 3370	ELECTRICAL, COMMUNICATIONS & UTIL.	90.2	46.5	71.2	92.0	55.1	75.9	92.6	49.7	73.9	97.3	56.3	79.5	99.5	56.6	80.8	100.1	58.4	82.0
MF2018	WEIGHTED AVERAGE	91.6	59.8	79.6	95.9	60.6	82.5	93.5	58.1	80.1	96.5	59.4	82.5	95.2	62.9	83.0	97.1	64.0	84.6

City Cost Indexes

		ARKANSAS												CALIFORNIA					
		PINE BLUFF			RUSSELLVILLE			TEXARKANA			WEST MEMPHIS			ALHAMBRA			ANAHEIM		
DIVISION		716			728			718			723			917 - 918			928		
		MAT.	INST.	TOTAL	MAT.	INST.	TOTAL	MAT.	INST.	TOTAL	MAT.	INST.	TOTAL	MAT.	INST.	TOTAL	MAT.	INST.	TOTAL
015433	CONTRACTOR EQUIPMENT		90.0	90.0		87.7	87.7		91.8	91.8		109.3	109.3		96.1	96.1		95.4	95.4
0241, 31 - 34	SITE & INFRASTRUCTURE, DEMOLITION	93.6	80.7	85.2	73.2	79.8	77.5	104.9	83.6	91.0	94.4	98.0	96.8	94.8	103.9	100.7	95.9	95.5	95.6
0310	Concrete Forming & Accessories	87.2	56.9	62.2	92.6	56.3	62.7	91.8	56.4	62.6	99.6	56.8	64.3	91.6	141.3	132.6	91.5	141.6	132.8
0320	Concrete Reinforcing	148.9	65.9	115.0	94.0	62.4	81.1	148.2	64.1	113.8	90.2	55.2	75.9	107.9	131.5	117.6	113.8	131.6	121.1
0330	Cast-in-Place Concrete	84.8	72.1	80.6	78.1	72.5	76.2	92.5	71.5	85.5	85.2	73.9	81.4	88.0	126.6	100.9	83.5	131.8	99.6
03	CONCRETE	92.5	64.7	81.0	80.5	63.8	73.7	92.1	64.0	80.6	87.8	64.0	78.0	95.1	133.7	111.0	104.4	135.6	117.2
04	MASONRY	110.6	59.1	80.7	87.5	56.0	69.2	88.5	58.1	70.8	73.2	55.9	63.2	114.8	139.8	129.4	91.9	140.7	120.3
05	METALS	108.4	77.2	101.9	95.4	72.4	90.6	100.2	76.5	95.3	91.5	81.1	89.3	92.2	120.3	98.1	108.3	119.6	110.7
06	WOOD, PLASTICS & COMPOSITES	94.3	57.2	76.1	101.5	57.1	79.7	99.8	57.2	78.9	108.9	57.5	83.6	84.7	139.8	111.8	83.5	140.4	111.5
07	THERMAL & MOISTURE PROTECTION	104.2	59.5	89.2	106.2	58.9	90.3	104.6	58.6	89.2	111.1	58.8	93.6	114.5	129.9	119.7	88.0	134.8	103.7
08	OPENINGS	98.4	55.8	88.0	102.6	54.7	91.0	102.8	55.6	91.3	105.2	53.2	92.5	95.5	138.0	105.8	103.5	136.7	111.6
0920	Plaster & Gypsum Board	89.8	56.1	68.3	87.7	56.1	67.6	93.2	56.1	69.6	100.7	56.1	72.3	117.5	141.7	132.9	109.4	141.7	130.0
0950, 0980	Ceilings & Acoustic Treatment	85.4	56.1	69.0	88.9	56.1	70.6	92.5	56.1	72.1	90.8	56.1	71.4	90.0	141.7	118.9	91.0	141.7	119.3
0960	Flooring	101.8	72.6	94.3	98.0	61.8	88.7	103.4	73.6	95.7	71.0	61.8	68.6	101.0	118.5	105.6	99.0	120.7	104.6
0970, 0990	Wall Finishes & Painting/Coating	99.7	50.1	70.5	97.8	47.4	68.2	99.7	49.3	70.1	85.6	47.4	63.2	104.9	134.8	122.5	87.8	124.5	109.3
09	FINISHES	91.5	58.8	75.3	88.5	56.3	72.6	94.7	58.7	76.9	85.6	56.6	71.2	97.9	136.5	117.0	95.0	136.1	115.3
COVERS	DIVS. 10 - 14, 25, 28, 41, 43, 44, 46	100.0	79.4	95.6	100.0	77.1	95.1	100.0	77.0	95.1	100.0	80.4	95.8	100.0	117.3	103.7	100.0	118.5	104.0
21, 22, 23	FIRE SUPPRESSION, PLUMBING & HVAC	100.2	51.1	82.5	93.1	46.2	76.3	100.2	53.7	83.4	93.7	58.2	80.9	92.9	129.6	106.1	99.9	129.8	110.7
26, 27, 3370	ELECTRICAL, COMMUNICATIONS & UTIL.	96.2	54.9	78.2	92.0	49.7	73.6	97.2	51.7	77.4	100.3	56.4	81.2	106.0	137.3	119.6	85.7	113.7	97.9
MF2018	WEIGHTED AVERAGE	100.0	61.2	85.3	92.6	58.0	79.6	98.4	61.1	84.3	93.9	63.8	82.5	97.3	130.6	109.9	99.4	126.9	109.8

		CALIFORNIA																	
		BAKERSFIELD			BERKELEY			EUREKA			FRESNO			INGLEWOOD			LONG BEACH		
DIVISION		932 - 933			947			955			936 - 938			903 - 905			906 - 908		
		MAT.	INST.	TOTAL	MAT.	INST.	TOTAL	MAT.	INST.	TOTAL	MAT.	INST.	TOTAL	MAT.	INST.	TOTAL	MAT.	INST.	TOTAL
015433	CONTRACTOR EQUIPMENT		105.9	105.9		92.0	92.0		95.1	95.1		100.4	100.4		93.3	93.3		93.3	93.3
0241, 31 - 34	SITE & INFRASTRUCTURE, DEMOLITION	109.2	111.1	110.9	98.3	97.2	97.6	100.1	96.4	97.7	112.8	102.7	106.2	103.1	93.1	96.6	111.4	91.9	99.5
0310	Concrete Forming & Accessories	95.2	141.6	133.5	99.8	169.7	157.4	96.9	157.0	146.5	92.4	156.8	145.5	99.0	141.9	134.4	95.5	141.9	133.8
0320	Concrete Reinforcing	156.0	131.6	146.1	88.8	138.6	109.1	123.9	129.9	126.3	129.9	132.2	130.9	92.9	131.6	108.7	92.1	131.6	108.2
0330	Cast-in-Place Concrete	86.5	132.2	101.8	128.0	131.6	129.2	90.6	129.6	103.6	93.7	129.8	105.8	90.7	130.4	104.0	103.3	130.4	112.4
03	CONCRETE	106.4	135.7	118.5	122.3	149.1	133.3	115.7	141.5	126.3	105.0	142.0	120.1	92.7	135.3	110.2	102.4	135.3	115.9
04	MASONRY	109.7	140.6	127.7	103.5	152.1	131.8	113.7	151.6	135.7	114.8	144.7	132.2	71.8	140.0	111.5	80.2	140.0	115.0
05	METALS	101.6	119.2	105.3	96.4	120.3	101.4	108.1	120.0	110.5	102.3	122.0	106.4	87.0	120.6	94.0	86.9	120.6	93.9
06	WOOD, PLASTICS & COMPOSITES	81.2	140.6	110.4	100.3	175.8	137.5	94.1	161.7	127.4	83.5	161.8	122.0	84.2	140.4	111.9	80.3	140.4	109.9
07	THERMAL & MOISTURE PROTECTION	101.0	128.6	110.2	83.4	152.5	106.5	90.3	146.8	109.2	91.3	135.4	106.1	93.6	132.2	106.5	93.8	132.2	106.7
08	OPENINGS	100.1	136.6	109.0	91.9	163.6	109.3	102.6	143.3	112.5	103.0	148.3	114.0	94.5	138.4	105.2	94.5	138.4	105.1
0920	Plaster & Gypsum Board	106.1	141.7	128.7	92.1	178.0	146.8	113.5	163.6	145.4	102.0	163.6	141.2	121.5	141.7	134.3	118.2	141.7	133.1
0950, 0980	Ceilings & Acoustic Treatment	79.5	141.7	114.3	73.5	178.0	132.0	96.3	163.6	134.0	71.2	163.6	122.9	106.3	141.7	126.1	106.3	141.7	126.1
0960	Flooring	108.9	120.7	111.9	115.8	142.9	122.8	103.5	139.2	112.7	109.5	123.9	113.2	104.5	118.8	108.2	102.4	118.8	106.6
0970, 0990	Wall Finishes & Painting/Coating	99.9	113.6	107.9	100.1	171.3	142.0	89.1	134.8	116.0	112.3	124.9	119.7	100.9	134.8	120.9	100.9	134.8	120.9
09	FINISHES	99.5	135.1	117.1	97.4	166.5	131.5	100.4	153.3	126.6	97.7	149.8	123.4	106.6	136.9	121.6	106.1	136.9	121.3
COVERS	DIVS. 10 - 14, 25, 28, 41, 43, 44, 46	100.0	119.0	104.1	100.0	131.0	106.6	100.0	128.7	106.1	100.0	128.8	106.1	100.0	118.7	104.0	100.0	118.7	104.0
21, 22, 23	FIRE SUPPRESSION, PLUMBING & HVAC	100.0	129.8	110.7	93.0	169.0	120.3	92.6	128.2	105.4	100.0	134.4	112.4	91.9	129.8	105.5	91.9	129.8	105.5
26, 27, 3370	ELECTRICAL, COMMUNICATIONS & UTIL.	101.2	108.8	104.5	102.4	160.3	127.6	92.5	122.0	105.3	90.1	108.5	98.1	103.4	137.3	118.1	103.2	137.3	118.0
MF2018	WEIGHTED AVERAGE	101.7	127.2	111.3	99.3	151.5	119.0	101.4	133.2	113.4	100.5	132.0	112.4	93.7	130.2	107.5	95.3	130.2	108.5

		CALIFORNIA																	
		LOS ANGELES			MARYSVILLE			MODESTO			MOJAVE			OAKLAND			OXNARD		
DIVISION		900 - 902			959			953			935			946			930		
		MAT.	INST.	TOTAL	MAT.	INST.	TOTAL	MAT.	INST.	TOTAL	MAT.	INST.	TOTAL	MAT.	INST.	TOTAL	MAT.	INST.	TOTAL
015433	CONTRACTOR EQUIPMENT		101.1	101.1		95.1	95.1		95.1	95.1		100.4	100.4		92.0	92.0		99.4	99.4
0241, 31 - 34	SITE & INFRASTRUCTURE, DEMOLITION	114.0	102.7	106.6	97.9	96.6	97.1	97.2	96.8	97.0	102.4	103.2	102.9	105.5	97.2	100.1	113.1	101.4	105.5
0310	Concrete Forming & Accessories	97.2	142.0	134.2	90.8	156.8	145.2	88.9	157.0	145.1	101.3	141.4	134.3	92.0	169.7	156.1	94.9	141.9	133.6
0320	Concrete Reinforcing	91.0	134.0	108.6	123.9	132.1	127.2	128.3	132.3	130.0	157.4	131.6	146.8	90.8	138.6	110.3	154.5	131.7	145.2
0330	Cast-in-Place Concrete	93.8	132.3	106.7	101.2	129.7	110.8	90.6	129.8	103.7	81.0	130.2	97.5	121.4	131.6	124.8	94.4	130.5	106.5
03	CONCRETE	100.1	136.5	115.0	116.2	141.8	126.7	107.2	142.0	121.5	98.8	135.0	113.7	123.3	149.1	133.9	107.0	135.4	118.6
04	MASONRY	87.5	140.7	118.4	114.6	142.5	130.9	118.7	145.7	134.4	112.1	140.4	128.6	109.7	152.1	134.4	116.2	140.5	130.3
05	METALS	99.1	121.9	103.8	107.5	120.5	110.2	102.4	121.1	106.3	100.9	121.0	105.1	90.4	120.3	96.6	97.8	121.6	102.8
06	WOOD, PLASTICS & COMPOSITES	96.0	140.5	117.9	86.8	161.7	123.7	84.4	161.7	122.5	81.8	140.5	110.7	92.6	175.8	133.6	78.6	140.5	109.1
07	THERMAL & MOISTURE PROTECTION	91.2	135.0	105.9	89.9	137.4	105.8	89.5	138.6	106.0	95.9	124.2	105.4	82.9	152.5	106.2	98.7	132.6	110.1
08	OPENINGS	108.9	139.0	116.2	101.8	148.2	113.1	100.9	149.9	112.8	97.1	136.6	106.7	91.9	163.6	109.3	100.0	138.4	109.4
0920	Plaster & Gypsum Board	120.7	141.7	134.0	108.6	163.6	143.6	109.4	163.6	143.9	109.4	141.7	129.9	87.9	178.0	145.3	104.5	141.7	128.2
0950, 0980	Ceilings & Acoustic Treatment	119.6	141.7	131.9	95.8	163.6	133.8	91.0	163.6	131.6	74.2	141.7	112.0	75.0	178.0	132.6	73.7	141.7	111.7
0960	Flooring	106.5	120.7	110.1	100.6	126.5	107.3	100.8	133.9	109.3	72.0	120.7	84.5	111.7	142.9	119.7	101.1	120.7	106.2
0970, 0990	Wall Finishes & Painting/Coating	99.9	130.6	117.9	89.1	134.8	116.0	89.1	143.7	121.2	93.2	113.6	105.2	100.1	171.3	142.0	93.2	130.6	115.1
09	FINISHES	111.2	136.9	123.9	98.5	151.1	124.5	97.0	153.6	124.9	97.1	135.1	115.9	96.4	166.5	131.1	94.8	136.9	115.6
COVERS	DIVS. 10 - 14, 25, 28, 41, 43, 44, 46	100.0	118.9	104.0	100.0	128.6	106.1	100.0	128.6	106.1	100.0	116.0	103.4	100.0	131.0	106.6	100.0	118.8	104.0
21, 22, 23	FIRE SUPPRESSION, PLUMBING & HVAC	100.0	129.8	110.8	92.6	129.1	105.7	99.9	133.7	112.1	92.7	127.1	105.0	100.3	169.0	125.0	99.9	129.8	110.7
26, 27, 3370	ELECTRICAL, COMMUNICATIONS & UTIL.	102.2	135.8	116.8	90.7	115.0	101.3	92.3	108.9	99.6	88.5	104.9	95.6	101.9	160.3	127.3	96.8	115.0	104.7
MF2018	WEIGHTED AVERAGE	101.1	131.2	112.5	100.8	131.2	112.3	100.5	132.2	112.5	96.9	125.2	107.6	100.2	151.5	119.6	100.4	127.8	110.8

City Cost Indexes

CALIFORNIA

DIVISION		PALM SPRINGS 922			PALO ALTO 943			PASADENA 910 - 912			REDDING 960			RICHMOND 948			RIVERSIDE 925		
		MAT.	INST.	TOTAL	MAT.	INST.	TOTAL	MAT.	INST.	TOTAL	MAT.	INST.	TOTAL	MAT.	INST.	TOTAL	MAT.	INST.	TOTAL
015433	CONTRACTOR EQUIPMENT		94.4	94.4		92.0	92.0		96.1	96.1		102.7	102.7		92.0	92.0		103.8	103.8
0241, 31 - 34	SITE & INFRASTRUCTURE, DEMOLITION	85.9	93.9	91.1	94.4	97.2	96.2	92.0	103.9	99.7	101.1	104.6	103.4	101.5	97.2	98.7	95.0	106.2	102.3
0310	Concrete Forming & Accessories	89.5	137.1	128.8	90.8	169.8	156.0	89.7	141.3	132.2	89.0	152.8	141.6	101.4	169.2	157.3	91.9	142.0	133.2
0320	Concrete Reinforcing	130.3	131.3	130.7	88.8	138.5	109.1	109.7	131.5	118.6	157.3	132.1	147.0	88.8	138.4	109.0	126.6	131.7	128.6
0330	Cast-in-Place Concrete	79.5	131.7	97.0	108.2	131.7	116.1	83.4	126.6	97.9	83.3	130.6	99.2	124.6	131.4	126.9	86.6	132.7	102.0
03	CONCRETE	99.2	133.5	113.3	110.6	149.1	126.4	91.5	133.7	108.9	138.5	140.4	139.3	125.2	148.7	134.8	105.2	136.1	117.9
04	MASONRY	88.8	136.8	116.7	86.8	149.8	123.5	97.2	139.8	122.0	176.5	142.5	156.7	103.2	149.8	130.4	89.9	140.6	119.4
05	METALS	108.9	118.9	111.0	89.8	120.2	96.2	84.3	120.3	91.8	111.8	122.6	114.1	89.8	119.5	96.1	107.4	120.6	110.2
06	WOOD, PLASTICS & COMPOSITES	80.2	134.6	107.0	91.0	175.8	132.8	80.1	139.3	109.5	95.4	156.3	125.4	102.3	175.8	138.5	83.5	140.7	111.6
07	THERMAL & MOISTURE PROTECTION	87.3	129.7	101.5	82.2	152.8	105.9	102.6	129.9	111.7	97.2	136.5	110.3	82.7	150.3	105.4	88.0	134.4	103.6
08	OPENINGS	99.4	133.5	107.7	91.9	161.9	108.9	91.1	138.0	102.5	111.8	145.2	119.9	91.9	162.8	109.2	102.2	138.5	111.0
0920	Plaster & Gypsum Board	104.8	135.7	124.5	86.7	178.0	144.8	98.8	141.7	126.1	114.3	157.7	141.9	92.4	178.0	146.9	108.3	141.7	129.5
0950, 0980	Ceilings & Acoustic Treatment	87.4	135.7	114.5	74.0	178.0	132.2	84.7	141.7	116.6	142.0	157.7	150.8	74.0	178.0	132.2	91.4	141.7	119.5
0960	Flooring	103.0	115.0	106.1	110.9	142.9	119.1	97.8	118.8	103.2	81.4	115.6	90.2	117.3	142.9	123.9	103.9	120.7	108.2
0970, 0990	Wall Finishes & Painting/Coating	86.5	124.5	108.8	100.1	171.3	142.0	104.3	134.8	122.2	94.6	134.8	118.2	100.1	171.3	142.0	86.5	130.6	112.4
09	FINISHES	94.0	131.6	112.6	95.2	166.5	130.5	92.7	136.5	114.3	106.6	146.1	126.1	98.3	166.5	132.0	96.0	136.9	116.2
COVERS	DIVS. 10 - 14, 25, 28, 41, 43, 44, 46	100.0	117.9	103.8	100.0	131.0	106.6	100.0	117.3	103.7	100.0	128.7	106.1	100.0	130.9	106.6	100.0	116.6	103.5
21, 22, 23	FIRE SUPPRESSION, PLUMBING & HVAC	92.6	127.1	105.0	93.0	171.0	121.0	92.9	129.6	106.1	100.0	129.1	110.5	93.0	155.2	115.4	99.9	129.8	110.7
26, 27, 3370	ELECTRICAL, COMMUNICATIONS & UTIL.	87.2	114.9	99.2	101.8	176.2	134.2	114.0	137.3	124.1	95.6	115.0	104.0	102.1	135.1	116.4	85.4	114.9	98.2
MF2018	WEIGHTED AVERAGE	96.5	124.7	107.2	95.4	154.0	117.5	94.2	130.6	107.9	111.1	131.0	118.6	98.4	144.5	115.9	99.1	128.2	110.1

CALIFORNIA

DIVISION		SACRAMENTO 942,956 - 958			SALINAS 939			SAN BERNARDINO 923 - 924			SAN DIEGO 919 - 921			SAN FRANCISCO 940 - 941			SAN JOSE 951		
		MAT.	INST.	TOTAL	MAT.	INST.	TOTAL	MAT.	INST.	TOTAL	MAT.	INST.	TOTAL	MAT.	INST.	TOTAL	MAT.	INST.	TOTAL
015433	CONTRACTOR EQUIPMENT		91.1	91.1		100.4	100.4		94.4	94.4		104.4	104.4		103.9	103.9		96.6	96.6
0241, 31 - 34	SITE & INFRASTRUCTURE, DEMOLITION	91.5	101.8	98.2	124.5	103.0	110.5	75.0	93.9	87.3	103.9	111.5	108.9	107.9	108.3	108.2	118.8	92.7	101.8
0310	Concrete Forming & Accessories	90.9	159.1	147.1	97.1	159.7	148.7	94.3	141.6	133.3	96.5	140.2	132.6	95.0	170.1	157.0	92.4	169.9	156.3
0320	Concrete Reinforcing	84.6	132.3	104.1	155.4	132.7	146.2	126.6	131.6	128.6	105.8	131.4	116.2	100.1	139.7	116.3	113.2	138.7	123.6
0330	Cast-in-Place Concrete	102.6	128.7	111.3	93.3	130.4	105.7	59.7	131.8	83.8	95.6	130.4	107.3	135.7	132.7	134.7	105.3	133.1	114.6
03	CONCRETE	113.0	142.0	124.9	116.6	143.5	127.7	78.8	135.6	102.1	103.2	134.4	116.0	135.7	150.2	141.7	112.3	150.3	127.9
04	MASONRY	87.6	145.5	121.3	113.3	150.7	135.1	100.4	140.7	123.8	93.4	136.0	118.2	112.8	155.9	137.9	150.8	153.2	152.2
05	METALS	86.4	112.4	91.9	103.7	123.9	108.0	107.4	119.5	110.0	97.7	118.4	102.0	98.9	127.6	104.9	101.3	129.7	107.2
06	WOOD, PLASTICS & COMPOSITES	84.9	164.4	124.0	81.6	164.4	122.3	85.6	140.4	112.5	96.0	140.1	117.7	96.0	175.7	135.2	95.4	175.8	135.0
07	THERMAL & MOISTURE PROTECTION	91.5	140.1	107.8	96.9	144.3	112.8	86.5	134.8	102.7	97.1	126.4	106.9	87.5	156.2	110.5	87.1	155.7	110.1
08	OPENINGS	101.2	151.3	113.4	101.3	156.0	114.6	99.5	138.3	108.9	101.5	134.6	109.6	102.0	163.7	117.0	95.0	163.6	111.7
0920	Plaster & Gypsum Board	81.7	166.3	135.5	105.8	166.3	144.3	109.9	141.7	130.1	90.9	141.7	123.2	83.9	178.0	143.8	104.5	178.0	151.3
0950, 0980	Ceilings & Acoustic Treatment	74.0	166.3	125.6	74.2	166.3	125.7	91.0	141.7	119.3	90.7	141.7	119.2	88.4	178.0	138.5	87.0	178.0	137.9
0960	Flooring	110.3	131.2	115.6	103.4	142.9	113.6	105.3	118.8	108.8	107.4	120.7	110.8	108.7	142.9	117.5	93.7	142.9	106.3
0970, 0990	Wall Finishes & Painting/Coating	96.5	139.3	121.7	94.0	166.8	136.8	86.5	124.5	108.8	104.8	123.8	116.0	99.9	174.9	144.0	89.3	171.3	137.5
09	FINISHES	93.6	154.1	123.5	97.8	159.1	128.1	95.3	135.7	115.2	96.8	135.4	115.9	98.3	167.0	132.2	94.3	166.6	130.1
COVERS	DIVS. 10 - 14, 25, 28, 41, 43, 44, 46	100.0	129.0	106.2	100.0	129.2	106.2	100.0	115.5	103.4	100.0	117.3	103.7	100.0	130.8	106.6	100.0	131.0	106.6
21, 22, 23	FIRE SUPPRESSION, PLUMBING & HVAC	100.1	132.7	111.8	92.7	139.8	109.6	92.6	129.8	106.0	100.2	128.5	110.4	100.1	182.2	129.7	99.9	171.0	125.5
26, 27, 3370	ELECTRICAL, COMMUNICATIONS & UTIL.	96.8	121.9	107.7	89.5	137.6	110.5	87.2	115.0	99.3	105.6	103.3	104.6	102.2	192.7	141.6	96.6	184.9	135.0
MF2018	WEIGHTED AVERAGE	97.0	133.7	110.8	100.7	140.2	115.6	94.2	126.9	106.6	100.1	125.2	109.6	104.6	161.2	126.0	102.7	156.4	123.0

CALIFORNIA

DIVISION		SAN LUIS OBISPO 934			SAN MATEO 944			SAN RAFAEL 949			SANTA ANA 926 - 927			SANTA BARBARA 931			SANTA CRUZ 950		
		MAT.	INST.	TOTAL	MAT.	INST.	TOTAL	MAT.	INST.	TOTAL	MAT.	INST.	TOTAL	MAT.	INST.	TOTAL	MAT.	INST.	TOTAL
015433	CONTRACTOR EQUIPMENT		100.4	100.4		92.0	92.0		91.4	91.4		94.4	94.4		100.4	100.4		96.6	96.6
0241, 31 - 34	SITE & INFRASTRUCTURE, DEMOLITION	115.9	103.2	107.6	99.6	97.2	98.0	101.4	101.4	101.4	84.7	93.9	90.7	113.0	103.2	106.6	118.7	92.5	101.6
0310	Concrete Forming & Accessories	102.4	141.9	135.0	94.9	169.6	156.5	98.7	169.2	156.9	94.3	141.8	133.4	95.4	141.6	133.5	92.4	159.8	148.0
0320	Concrete Reinforcing	157.4	131.7	146.9	88.8	138.5	109.1	89.5	132.9	107.2	130.9	131.6	131.2	154.5	131.7	145.2	139.9	132.8	137.0
0330	Cast-in-Place Concrete	100.3	130.4	110.3	120.5	131.8	124.2	140.4	130.8	137.2	76.3	131.8	94.9	94.1	130.3	106.2	104.6	132.0	113.8
03	CONCRETE	114.7	135.3	123.2	121.4	149.0	132.8	148.2	147.4	147.9	95.5	135.7	112.6	106.8	135.2	116.5	116.1	144.3	127.7
04	MASONRY	113.8	140.5	129.3	102.9	152.5	131.8	85.5	152.6	124.5	86.2	140.7	117.9	112.5	144.1	128.8	155.9	150.9	153.0
05	METALS	102.0	121.6	106.1	89.7	120.2	96.1	90.0	115.1	95.3	107.5	119.7	110.1	98.9	121.3	103.6	108.3	125.8	111.9
06	WOOD, PLASTICS & COMPOSITES	83.1	140.5	111.4	96.1	175.8	135.3	87.6	175.6	130.9	86.7	140.4	113.1	78.6	140.5	109.1	95.4	164.4	129.4
07	THERMAL & MOISTURE PROTECTION	96.7	132.1	108.6	82.6	152.7	106.1	86.0	152.4	108.2	87.6	135.3	103.6	96.3	131.8	108.2	86.8	147.7	107.2
08	OPENINGS	99.2	136.6	108.3	91.9	162.8	109.1	98.8	160.5	113.8	98.7	138.3	108.4	101.2	136.8	109.9	95.9	156.0	110.5
0920	Plaster & Gypsum Board	109.8	141.7	130.1	91.0	178.0	146.4	92.0	178.0	146.7	110.9	141.7	130.5	104.5	141.7	128.2	113.6	166.3	147.1
0950, 0980	Ceilings & Acoustic Treatment	74.2	141.7	112.0	74.0	178.0	132.2	83.2	178.0	136.3	91.0	141.7	119.3	73.7	141.7	111.7	91.9	166.3	133.5
0960	Flooring	108.2	120.7	111.4	113.2	142.9	120.8	122.7	139.2	127.0	105.7	120.7	109.5	102.8	115.0	105.9	97.5	142.9	109.2
0970, 0990	Wall Finishes & Painting/Coating	93.2	119.0	108.4	100.1	171.3	142.0	96.2	166.8	137.7	86.5	130.6	112.4	88.0	130.6	115.1	89.1	171.3	137.4
09	FINISHES	98.5	135.7	116.9	96.9	166.5	131.3	100.3	165.2	132.4	96.5	136.8	116.4	95.5	135.8	115.4	97.8	159.7	128.4
COVERS	DIVS. 10 - 14, 25, 28, 41, 43, 44, 46	100.0	127.7	105.9	100.0	131.0	106.6	100.0	130.4	106.5	100.0	118.6	104.0	100.0	116.1	103.4	100.0	129.3	106.2
21, 22, 23	FIRE SUPPRESSION, PLUMBING & HVAC	92.7	129.8	106.0	93.0	162.6	118.0	93.0	177.2	123.3	92.6	129.8	106.0	99.9	129.8	110.7	99.9	139.9	114.3
26, 27, 3370	ELECTRICAL, COMMUNICATIONS & UTIL.	88.5	112.9	99.1	101.8	169.4	131.2	94.8	122.0	106.6	87.2	118.7	100.9	87.9	104.4	95.1	96.2	137.6	114.2
MF2018	WEIGHTED AVERAGE	99.7	127.7	110.3	97.7	151.5	118.0	100.3	147.2	118.0	96.0	127.7	108.0	99.5	126.0	109.5	105.1	139.9	118.2

City Cost Indexes

		CALIFORNIA															COLORADO		
	DIVISION	SANTA ROSA			STOCKTON			SUSANVILLE			VALLEJO			VAN NUYS			ALAMOSA		
		954			952			961			945			913 - 916			811		
		MAT.	INST.	TOTAL	MAT.	INST.	TOTAL	MAT.	INST.	TOTAL	MAT.	INST.	TOTAL	MAT.	INST.	TOTAL	MAT.	INST.	TOTAL
015433	CONTRACTOR EQUIPMENT		95.7	95.7		95.1	95.1		102.7	102.7		91.4	91.4		96.1	96.1		91.7	91.7
0241, 31 - 34	SITE & INFRASTRUCTURE, DEMOLITION	96.0	96.8	96.5	97.0	96.8	96.9	101.4	104.6	103.5	93.3	101.5	98.7	104.2	103.9	104.0	128.7	82.7	98.7
0310	Concrete Forming & Accessories	90.1	168.9	155.1	91.1	158.8	147.0	89.6	152.9	141.8	92.2	168.4	155.1	93.5	141.3	132.9	99.9	67.8	73.4
0320	Concrete Reinforcing	124.9	133.1	128.3	128.3	132.3	129.9	157.3	132.1	147.0	90.6	133.0	108.0	109.7	131.5	118.6	126.4	68.3	102.6
0330	Cast-in-Place Concrete	99.5	131.4	110.2	88.3	129.7	102.2	75.8	130.7	94.2	111.7	130.1	117.9	88.0	126.6	100.9	93.5	69.2	85.4
03	CONCRETE	116.3	148.1	129.3	106.2	142.8	121.2	147.0	140.5	144.3	118.5	146.9	130.2	104.0	133.7	116.2	115.4	69.1	96.4
04	MASONRY	114.7	155.0	138.1	118.7	145.7	134.4	175.2	142.5	156.2	65.6	154.8	117.5	115.3	139.8	129.6	134.3	66.9	95.1
05	METALS	107.8	123.8	111.1	102.8	121.0	106.6	109.8	122.7	112.5	89.9	114.9	95.1	83.7	120.3	91.3	102.2	81.8	97.9
06	WOOD, PLASTICS & COMPOSITES	81.2	175.6	127.6	87.6	164.3	125.3	96.3	156.3	125.8	80.8	175.6	127.4	84.7	139.8	111.8	94.5	69.5	82.2
07	THERMAL & MOISTURE PROTECTION	88.0	154.3	110.2	89.9	138.3	106.1	97.6	136.5	110.6	84.5	153.0	107.4	103.7	129.9	112.4	101.6	66.3	89.8
08	OPENINGS	100.3	162.1	115.4	100.9	150.5	112.9	111.7	146.1	120.0	100.6	160.5	115.2	91.0	138.0	102.4	90.9	68.0	85.4
0920	Plaster & Gypsum Board	107.1	178.0	152.2	109.4	166.3	145.6	114.2	157.7	141.9	88.0	178.0	145.3	101.0	141.7	126.9	84.4	68.6	74.4
0950, 0980	Ceilings & Acoustic Treatment	91.0	178.0	139.7	94.9	166.3	134.9	136.8	157.7	148.5	84.2	178.0	136.7	82.1	141.7	115.4	102.4	68.6	83.5
0960	Flooring	103.4	130.0	110.2	100.8	133.9	109.3	81.7	115.6	90.4	119.0	142.9	125.1	99.8	118.8	104.7	111.8	77.4	103.0
0970, 0990	Wall Finishes & Painting/Coating	86.5	157.9	128.5	89.1	135.7	116.5	94.6	134.8	118.2	97.0	166.6	138.0	104.3	134.8	122.2	100.6	69.6	82.4
09	FINISHES	96.0	162.4	128.8	98.0	154.2	125.8	105.8	146.1	125.7	97.8	165.6	131.3	94.1	136.5	115.1	103.6	69.9	86.9
COVERS	DIVS. 10 - 14, 25, 28, 41, 43, 44, 46	100.0	130.0	106.4	100.0	126.0	105.5	100.0	128.7	106.1	100.0	130.1	106.4	100.0	117.3	103.7	100.0	85.3	96.9
21, 22, 23	FIRE SUPPRESSION, PLUMBING & HVAC	92.6	181.6	124.6	99.9	132.6	111.7	92.7	130.9	106.4	100.0	148.0	117.4	92.9	129.0	106.1	92.7	66.0	83.1
26, 27, 3370	ELECTRICAL, COMMUNICATIONS & UTIL.	87.3	117.4	100.4	92.3	113.0	101.3	95.7	117.3	105.1	92.5	121.3	105.1	114.0	137.3	124.1	91.8	54.6	75.6
MF2018	WEIGHTED AVERAGE	100.0	147.9	118.1	100.6	132.7	112.7	110.0	131.7	118.2	96.9	141.1	113.6	96.8	130.6	109.6	101.5	68.8	89.1

		COLORADO																	
	DIVISION	BOULDER			COLORADO SPRINGS			DENVER			DURANGO			FORT COLLINS			FORT MORGAN		
		803			808 - 809			800 - 802			813			805			807		
		MAT.	INST.	TOTAL	MAT.	INST.	TOTAL	MAT.	INST.	TOTAL	MAT.	INST.	TOTAL	MAT.	INST.	TOTAL	MAT.	INST.	TOTAL
015433	CONTRACTOR EQUIPMENT		95.1	95.1		93.1	93.1		97.2	97.2		91.7	91.7		95.1	95.1		95.1	95.1
0241, 31 - 34	SITE & INFRASTRUCTURE, DEMOLITION	99.3	88.0	91.9	104.6	83.3	90.7	108.4	93.0	98.4	123.9	82.7	97.0	114.2	87.6	96.9	101.7	87.0	92.1
0310	Concrete Forming & Accessories	97.7	72.4	76.9	91.6	68.0	72.2	95.8	70.8	75.2	104.1	67.5	73.9	96.0	68.0	72.9	98.1	67.7	73.1
0320	Concrete Reinforcing	91.2	68.3	81.8	90.3	69.4	81.8	94.0	81.4	88.8	126.4	68.2	102.6	91.2	63.9	80.0	91.4	68.3	82.0
0330	Cast-in-Place Concrete	99.6	75.4	91.5	102.3	73.9	92.8	103.5	74.9	94.0	107.6	69.1	94.7	112.5	72.1	99.0	97.7	70.3	88.5
03	CONCRETE	93.2	73.4	85.0	96.0	71.1	85.7	101.3	74.5	90.3	117.3	68.9	97.5	102.6	69.4	89.0	91.8	69.5	82.6
04	MASONRY	98.6	68.4	81.0	102.0	60.9	78.1	108.7	65.7	83.7	121.2	66.9	89.6	114.3	67.0	86.8	113.3	67.0	86.4
05	METALS	88.2	82.1	86.9	90.2	82.3	88.5	98.9	84.5	95.9	102.2	81.5	97.8	88.1	80.1	86.4	88.0	81.6	86.7
06	WOOD, PLASTICS & COMPOSITES	92.2	74.1	83.3	87.2	69.6	78.5	96.0	73.4	84.9	100.7	69.5	85.4	90.3	69.4	80.0	92.2	69.4	81.0
07	THERMAL & MOISTURE PROTECTION	99.4	72.0	90.2	100.2	69.5	89.9	98.6	73.1	90.1	101.4	66.3	89.6	99.6	69.6	89.6	99.3	68.4	89.0
08	OPENINGS	90.7	71.8	86.1	94.3	69.3	88.3	98.4	74.0	92.5	97.5	68.0	90.4	90.6	67.7	85.1	90.6	68.0	85.1
0920	Plaster & Gypsum Board	97.9	73.5	82.4	90.4	68.6	76.5	96.8	72.7	81.5	94.4	68.6	78.0	92.9	68.6	77.4	97.9	68.6	79.3
0950, 0980	Ceilings & Acoustic Treatment	93.6	73.5	82.4	105.9	68.6	85.1	109.7	72.7	89.0	102.4	68.6	83.5	93.6	68.6	79.6	93.6	68.6	79.6
0960	Flooring	118.2	77.4	107.7	109.6	77.4	101.3	115.1	77.4	105.4	115.5	77.4	105.7	115.2	77.4	105.5	118.5	77.4	107.9
0970, 0990	Wall Finishes & Painting/Coating	91.8	73.8	81.2	91.5	76.7	82.8	99.9	73.8	84.6	100.6	69.6	82.4	91.8	69.6	78.7	91.8	69.6	78.7
09	FINISHES	103.2	73.5	88.6	103.1	70.6	87.0	107.0	72.2	89.8	105.3	69.9	87.8	102.3	69.8	86.2	103.3	69.8	86.7
COVERS	DIVS. 10 - 14, 25, 28, 41, 43, 44, 46	100.0	86.3	97.1	100.0	85.3	96.9	100.0	85.2	96.8	100.0	85.2	96.9	100.0	85.2	96.8	100.0	85.1	96.8
21, 22, 23	FIRE SUPPRESSION, PLUMBING & HVAC	92.7	73.0	85.6	100.2	68.1	88.6	100.0	73.9	90.6	92.7	53.9	78.7	100.0	70.9	89.5	92.7	67.0	83.5
26, 27, 3370	ELECTRICAL, COMMUNICATIONS & UTIL.	98.3	77.5	89.2	100.0	67.9	86.1	101.1	80.4	92.1	91.5	48.0	72.5	98.3	74.7	88.0	98.8	67.5	85.2
MF2018	WEIGHTED AVERAGE	94.4	75.6	87.3	97.6	71.1	87.6	101.0	76.6	91.8	101.7	65.2	87.9	98.1	73.0	88.7	94.9	71.2	86.0

		COLORADO																	
	DIVISION	GLENWOOD SPRINGS			GOLDEN			GRAND JUNCTION			GREELEY			MONTROSE			PUEBLO		
		816			804			815			806			814			810		
		MAT.	INST.	TOTAL	MAT.	INST.	TOTAL	MAT.	INST.	TOTAL	MAT.	INST.	TOTAL	MAT.	INST.	TOTAL	MAT.	INST.	TOTAL
015433	CONTRACTOR EQUIPMENT		95.4	95.4		95.1	95.1		95.4	95.4		95.1	95.1		93.6	93.6		91.7	91.7
0241, 31 - 34	SITE & INFRASTRUCTURE, DEMOLITION	135.9	91.1	106.7	110.9	87.1	95.4	126.8	91.6	103.9	101.5	87.7	92.5	130.8	87.2	102.4	120.1	83.3	96.1
0310	Concrete Forming & Accessories	97.7	67.2	72.6	92.9	67.0	71.6	103.2	67.7	73.9	94.6	68.0	72.6	97.5	67.4	72.7	101.5	67.9	73.8
0320	Concrete Reinforcing	125.1	68.2	101.9	91.4	61.4	79.1	125.5	63.6	100.2	91.2	63.9	80.0	125.0	68.2	101.8	120.9	69.6	99.9
0330	Cast-in-Place Concrete	93.5	68.1	85.0	97.8	74.0	89.8	103.5	73.1	93.3	93.9	72.1	86.6	93.5	68.6	85.1	92.8	72.3	85.9
03	CONCRETE	120.5	68.4	99.1	99.4	69.3	87.0	113.8	69.7	95.7	88.9	69.5	80.9	111.5	68.7	93.9	104.0	70.5	90.3
04	MASONRY	106.5	66.9	83.4	116.2	62.4	84.9	142.7	64.0	96.9	107.4	67.0	86.3	113.3	66.9	86.3	102.8	63.3	79.8
05	METALS	101.9	81.0	97.5	88.1	78.7	86.2	102.2	79.5	97.5	88.1	80.1	86.4	100.5	81.3	96.4	104.4	82.5	99.8
06	WOOD, PLASTICS & COMPOSITES	90.4	69.2	80.0	87.0	69.4	78.4	98.4	69.2	84.1	88.8	69.4	79.3	92.1	69.4	80.9	96.3	69.5	83.1
07	THERMAL & MOISTURE PROTECTION	101.4	66.2	89.6	100.4	67.7	89.4	100.5	67.2	89.3	99.0	69.6	89.1	101.5	66.2	89.7	100.2	68.0	89.4
08	OPENINGS	96.7	67.9	89.7	90.7	66.4	84.7	97.4	67.4	90.1	90.6	67.7	85.0	97.7	68.0	90.5	92.5	69.3	86.8
0920	Plaster & Gypsum Board	126.0	68.6	89.5	90.5	68.6	76.6	136.0	68.6	93.1	92.2	68.6	77.2	83.9	68.6	74.2	89.5	68.6	76.2
0950, 0980	Ceilings & Acoustic Treatment	101.9	68.6	83.3	93.6	68.6	79.6	101.9	68.6	83.3	93.6	68.6	79.6	102.4	68.6	83.5	112.5	68.6	88.0
0960	Flooring	111.2	77.4	102.5	113.5	77.4	104.2	115.0	77.4	105.4	114.3	77.4	104.9	113.6	77.4	104.3	112.7	77.4	103.6
0970, 0990	Wall Finishes & Painting/Coating	100.6	69.6	82.4	91.8	69.6	78.7	100.6	69.6	82.4	91.8	69.6	78.7	100.6	69.6	82.4	100.6	69.6	82.4
09	FINISHES	108.9	69.7	89.5	102.2	69.3	85.9	109.9	69.7	90.0	101.2	69.8	85.7	104.1	69.8	87.1	105.8	69.7	87.9
COVERS	DIVS. 10 - 14, 25, 28, 41, 43, 44, 46	100.0	84.6	96.7	100.0	84.5	96.7	100.0	84.7	96.7	100.0	85.2	96.8	100.0	84.9	96.8	100.0	85.1	96.8
21, 22, 23	FIRE SUPPRESSION, PLUMBING & HVAC	92.7	53.9	78.7	92.7	65.9	83.1	100.0	69.7	89.1	100.0	70.9	89.5	92.7	54.0	78.7	100.0	68.0	88.5
26, 27, 3370	ELECTRICAL, COMMUNICATIONS & UTIL.	90.1	48.0	71.8	98.8	69.6	86.1	91.3	52.4	74.4	98.3	74.7	88.0	91.3	48.0	72.5	91.8	60.9	78.4
MF2018	WEIGHTED AVERAGE	101.6	65.6	88.0	96.1	70.4	86.4	104.2	69.4	91.1	95.8	73.0	87.2	100.3	65.5	87.1	100.9	70.1	89.2

City Cost Indexes

		COLORADO			CONNECTICUT															
	DIVISION	SALIDA 812			BRIDGEPORT 066			BRISTOL 060			HARTFORD 061			MERIDEN 064			NEW BRITAIN 060		
		MAT.	INST.	TOTAL	MAT.	INST.	TOTAL	MAT.	INST.	TOTAL	MAT.	INST.	TOTAL	MAT.	INST.	TOTAL	MAT.	INST.	TOTAL
015433	CONTRACTOR EQUIPMENT		93.6	93.6		102.9	102.9		102.9	102.9		109.0	109.0		103.3	103.3		102.9	102.9
0241, 31 - 34	SITE & INFRASTRUCTURE, DEMOLITION	123.6	86.9	99.7	90.3	102.3	98.1	89.4	102.3	97.8	90.0	111.2	103.8	84.1	102.9	96.4	89.6	102.3	97.9
0310	Concrete Forming & Accessories	103.2	67.7	73.9	100.7	112.3	110.2	100.7	112.2	110.2	101.0	112.5	110.4	100.3	112.1	110.0	101.1	112.2	110.2
0320	Concrete Reinforcing	124.7	68.2	101.6	181.2	139.6	164.2	181.2	139.5	164.2	172.8	139.6	159.2	181.2	139.5	164.2	181.2	139.5	164.2
0330	Cast-in-Place Concrete	107.2	68.7	94.3	95.5	124.8	105.3	89.5	124.8	101.3	91.1	126.9	103.1	86.1	124.7	99.0	90.9	124.7	102.2
03	CONCRETE	112.4	68.9	94.5	105.8	121.4	112.2	102.8	121.3	110.4	103.3	122.1	111.0	101.1	121.2	109.4	103.5	121.3	110.8
04	MASONRY	142.7	66.9	98.6	116.4	129.9	124.3	108.1	129.9	120.8	111.7	130.1	122.4	107.7	129.9	120.7	110.2	129.9	121.7
05	METALS	100.2	81.6	96.3	102.1	123.6	106.6	102.1	123.5	106.6	106.1	121.8	109.4	98.1	123.3	103.4	98.0	123.4	103.3
06	WOOD, PLASTICS & COMPOSITES	96.9	69.4	83.3	109.0	108.4	108.7	109.0	108.4	108.7	97.6	108.4	103.0	109.0	108.4	108.7	109.0	108.4	108.7
07	THERMAL & MOISTURE PROTECTION	100.6	66.3	89.1	95.3	120.1	103.6	95.5	117.5	102.8	99.4	120.3	106.4	95.5	117.4	102.8	95.5	116.4	102.5
08	OPENINGS	91.0	68.0	85.4	96.6	115.7	101.3	96.6	115.7	101.3	98.3	115.8	102.6	98.6	115.7	102.8	96.6	115.7	101.3
0920	Plaster & Gypsum Board	83.9	68.6	74.2	134.5	108.6	118.0	134.5	108.6	118.0	120.7	108.6	113.0	138.1	108.6	119.3	134.5	108.6	118.0
0950, 0980	Ceilings & Acoustic Treatment	102.4	68.6	83.5	99.3	108.6	104.5	99.3	108.6	104.5	100.6	108.6	105.1	110.3	108.6	109.3	99.3	108.6	104.5
0960	Flooring	117.5	77.4	107.2	100.9	118.5	105.4	100.9	118.5	105.4	108.9	125.1	113.1	100.9	108.4	102.9	100.9	118.5	105.4
0970, 0990	Wall Finishes & Painting/Coating	100.6	69.6	82.4	92.8	124.3	111.3	92.8	124.9	111.6	99.9	124.9	114.6	92.8	124.3	111.3	92.8	124.9	111.6
09	FINISHES	104.3	69.8	87.2	100.8	114.3	107.5	100.8	114.4	107.5	104.4	115.7	110.0	104.2	112.6	108.3	100.8	114.4	107.5
COVERS	DIVS. 10 - 14, 25, 28, 41, 43, 44, 46	100.0	85.0	96.8	100.0	111.5	102.5	100.0	111.6	102.5	100.0	112.0	102.6	100.0	111.5	102.5	100.0	111.6	102.5
21, 22, 23	FIRE SUPPRESSION, PLUMBING & HVAC	92.7	67.0	83.4	100.3	115.8	105.9	100.3	115.8	105.9	100.2	115.8	105.9	93.0	115.8	101.2	100.3	115.8	105.9
26, 27, 3370	ELECTRICAL, COMMUNICATIONS & UTIL.	91.4	54.6	75.4	98.0	98.4	98.2	98.0	104.9	101.0	101.2	104.8	102.8	98.0	91.5	95.2	98.1	104.9	101.0
MF2018	WEIGHTED AVERAGE	101.0	69.2	89.0	101.1	114.8	106.3	100.4	115.7	106.2	102.2	116.6	107.7	98.0	113.6	103.9	99.8	115.7	105.8

		CONNECTICUT																	
	DIVISION	NEW HAVEN 065			NEW LONDON 063			NORWALK 068			STAMFORD 069			WATERBURY 067			WILLIMANTIC 062		
		MAT.	INST.	TOTAL	MAT.	INST.	TOTAL	MAT.	INST.	TOTAL	MAT.	INST.	TOTAL	MAT.	INST.	TOTAL	MAT.	INST.	TOTAL
015433	CONTRACTOR EQUIPMENT		103.3	103.3		103.3	103.3		102.9	102.9		102.9	102.9		102.9	102.9		102.9	102.9
0241, 31 - 34	SITE & INFRASTRUCTURE, DEMOLITION	89.6	102.4	97.9	80.6	102.4	94.8	90.1	101.7	97.7	90.5	101.7	97.8	90.5	102.3	98.2	89.6	101.6	97.4
0310	Concrete Forming & Accessories	100.3	112.1	110.0	100.3	112.0	109.9	100.7	112.2	110.2	100.6	112.2	110.2	100.7	112.2	110.2	100.7	111.8	109.9
0320	Concrete Reinforcing	181.2	139.5	164.2	142.0	139.5	141.0	181.2	139.5	164.2	181.2	139.5	164.2	181.2	139.5	164.2	181.2	139.5	164.1
0330	Cast-in-Place Concrete	92.5	124.5	103.2	78.7	124.5	94.0	94.0	125.6	104.5	95.5	125.6	105.6	95.5	124.7	105.3	89.2	118.1	98.8
03	CONCRETE	114.4	121.2	117.2	89.3	121.1	102.4	105.0	121.6	111.8	105.8	121.6	112.3	105.8	121.3	112.1	102.6	118.7	109.3
04	MASONRY	108.3	129.9	120.9	106.5	129.9	120.1	107.7	129.9	120.7	108.6	129.9	121.0	108.6	129.9	121.0	107.9	129.9	120.7
05	METALS	98.2	123.3	103.5	97.9	123.2	103.2	102.1	123.5	106.6	102.1	123.5	106.6	102.1	123.4	106.6	101.9	123.0	106.3
06	WOOD, PLASTICS & COMPOSITES	109.0	108.4	108.7	109.0	108.4	108.7	109.0	108.4	108.7	109.0	108.4	108.7	109.0	108.4	108.7	109.0	108.4	108.7
07	THERMAL & MOISTURE PROTECTION	95.5	117.6	102.9	95.3	117.4	102.7	95.5	120.2	103.8	95.5	120.2	103.7	95.5	117.7	102.9	95.6	116.3	102.5
08	OPENINGS	96.6	115.7	101.3	99.2	115.3	103.1	96.6	115.7	101.3	96.6	115.7	101.3	96.6	115.7	101.3	99.3	115.7	103.3
0920	Plaster & Gypsum Board	134.5	108.6	118.0	134.5	108.6	118.0	134.5	108.6	118.0	134.5	108.6	118.0	134.5	108.6	118.0	134.5	108.6	118.0
0950, 0980	Ceilings & Acoustic Treatment	99.3	108.6	104.5	98.9	108.6	104.3	99.3	108.6	104.5	99.3	108.6	104.5	99.3	108.6	104.5	98.9	108.6	104.3
0960	Flooring	100.9	118.5	105.4	100.9	110.5	103.4	100.9	118.5	105.4	100.9	118.5	105.4	100.9	118.5	105.4	100.9	105.4	102.1
0970, 0990	Wall Finishes & Painting/Coating	92.8	119.5	108.5	92.8	115.9	106.4	92.8	124.3	111.3	92.8	124.3	111.3	92.8	124.3	111.3	92.8	124.3	111.3
09	FINISHES	100.9	113.8	107.3	100.5	112.0	106.2	100.9	114.3	107.5	100.9	114.3	107.5	100.8	114.3	107.5	100.8	112.1	106.3
COVERS	DIVS. 10 - 14, 25, 28, 41, 43, 44, 46	100.0	111.5	102.5	100.0	111.5	102.5	100.0	111.5	102.5	100.0	111.6	102.5	100.0	111.5	102.5	100.0	111.5	102.5
21, 22, 23	FIRE SUPPRESSION, PLUMBING & HVAC	100.3	115.8	105.9	93.0	115.8	101.2	100.3	115.8	105.9	100.3	115.8	105.9	100.3	115.8	105.9	100.3	115.7	105.8
26, 27, 3370	ELECTRICAL, COMMUNICATIONS & UTIL.	98.0	98.7	98.3	96.2	93.3	94.9	98.0	98.4	98.2	98.0	100.9	99.3	97.8	98.7	98.2	98.0	96.1	97.2
MF2018	WEIGHTED AVERAGE	101.0	114.7	106.2	96.0	113.7	102.7	100.7	114.8	106.0	100.8	115.2	106.3	100.8	114.8	106.1	100.5	113.6	105.5

		D.C.			DELAWARE									FLORIDA					
	DIVISION	WASHINGTON 200 - 205			DOVER 199			NEWARK 197			WILMINGTON 198			DAYTONA BEACH 321			FORT LAUDERDALE 333		
		MAT.	INST.	TOTAL	MAT.	INST.	TOTAL	MAT.	INST.	TOTAL	MAT.	INST.	TOTAL	MAT.	INST.	TOTAL	MAT.	INST.	TOTAL
015433	CONTRACTOR EQUIPMENT		101.3	101.3		107.6	107.6		108.2	108.2		111.0	111.0		91.2	91.2		95.2	95.2
0241, 31 - 34	SITE & INFRASTRUCTURE, DEMOLITION	112.4	99.2	103.8	113.5	102.7	106.4	109.3	102.7	105.0	112.8	109.4	110.5	113.2	84.2	94.3	100.2	85.9	90.9
0310	Concrete Forming & Accessories	104.1	75.1	80.2	107.0	96.1	98.0	99.8	95.8	96.5	99.9	96.3	96.9	100.2	64.5	70.8	97.6	63.3	69.3
0320	Concrete Reinforcing	131.0	89.4	114.0	176.2	114.4	151.0	153.6	114.4	137.6	176.2	114.5	151.0	106.4	58.1	86.6	75.9	61.3	69.9
0330	Cast-in-Place Concrete	109.5	79.7	99.5	96.0	110.5	100.8	84.8	107.2	92.3	96.0	110.6	100.9	107.7	69.9	95.1	92.5	68.1	84.3
03	CONCRETE	108.4	79.5	96.6	109.0	104.7	107.2	99.2	103.7	101.0	108.5	104.8	107.0	100.3	66.0	86.2	90.8	65.6	80.5
04	MASONRY	105.7	87.0	94.8	99.2	102.3	101.0	104.0	102.1	102.9	102.3	102.3	102.3	88.5	62.7	73.5	115.9	56.6	81.4
05	METALS	105.2	88.9	101.8	107.5	111.2	108.3	107.1	116.3	109.0	106.1	111.3	107.2	102.2	73.7	96.2	99.5	79.7	95.3
06	WOOD, PLASTICS & COMPOSITES	102.9	73.8	88.6	106.7	92.6	99.8	95.6	92.2	93.9	97.0	92.6	94.8	100.4	63.5	82.2	84.6	64.2	74.6
07	THERMAL & MOISTURE PROTECTION	99.0	86.9	95.0	99.7	113.3	104.2	102.4	110.5	105.1	98.6	113.3	103.5	88.5	68.2	81.7	90.1	62.3	80.8
08	OPENINGS	107.9	76.3	100.3	97.8	104.4	99.4	95.8	104.1	97.8	97.8	104.4	99.4	92.6	60.8	84.9	94.8	61.9	86.8
0920	Plaster & Gypsum Board	116.5	72.9	88.7	110.4	91.9	98.7	99.3	91.9	94.6	106.8	91.9	97.3	101.4	62.7	76.8	108.9	63.3	79.9
0950, 0980	Ceilings & Acoustic Treatment	111.6	72.9	90.0	103.7	91.9	97.1	99.8	91.9	95.4	100.6	91.9	95.8	76.0	62.7	68.5	85.3	63.3	73.0
0960	Flooring	104.1	78.0	97.4	109.7	109.6	109.7	101.5	109.6	103.6	110.7	109.6	110.4	109.6	55.7	95.8	112.0	60.9	98.9
0970, 0990	Wall Finishes & Painting/Coating	99.9	69.6	82.1	99.9	117.8	110.4	92.6	117.8	107.4	99.9	117.8	110.4	102.8	56.7	75.7	94.7	57.8	73.0
09	FINISHES	107.3	74.1	90.9	106.8	99.7	103.3	96.5	99.4	97.9	105.9	99.7	102.8	95.9	61.7	79.0	99.2	61.8	80.7
COVERS	DIVS. 10 - 14, 25, 28, 41, 43, 44, 46	100.0	95.5	99.0	100.0	99.3	99.8	100.0	107.7	101.6	100.0	106.0	101.3	100.0	83.6	96.5	100.0	83.6	96.5
21, 22, 23	FIRE SUPPRESSION, PLUMBING & HVAC	100.0	93.5	97.7	100.1	119.0	106.9	100.4	118.9	107.0	100.0	119.0	106.9	99.9	75.7	91.2	99.9	70.2	89.2
26, 27, 3370	ELECTRICAL, COMMUNICATIONS & UTIL.	99.8	100.6	100.1	101.6	109.0	104.8	102.2	109.0	105.2	100.2	109.0	104.0	98.1	57.8	80.6	98.5	67.2	84.9
MF2018	WEIGHTED AVERAGE	103.8	88.0	98.0	103.4	107.8	105.1	101.5	108.2	104.0	102.9	108.5	105.0	98.7	68.4	87.3	98.4	68.4	87.1

City Cost Indexes

		\multicolumn{18}{c}{FLORIDA}
\multicolumn{2}{c}{DIVISION}	\multicolumn{3}{c}{FORT MYERS 339,341}	\multicolumn{3}{c}{GAINESVILLE 326,344}	\multicolumn{3}{c}{JACKSONVILLE 320,322}	\multicolumn{3}{c}{LAKELAND 338}	\multicolumn{3}{c}{MELBOURNE 329}	\multicolumn{3}{c}{MIAMI 330-332,340}
		MAT.	INST.	TOTAL	MAT.	INST.	TOTAL	MAT.	INST.	TOTAL	MAT.	INST.	TOTAL	MAT.	INST.	TOTAL	MAT.	INST.	TOTAL
015433	CONTRACTOR EQUIPMENT		103.6	103.6		91.2	91.2		91.2	91.2		103.5	103.5		91.2	91.2		107.6	107.6
0241, 31-34	SITE & INFRASTRUCTURE, DEMOLITION	108.2	99.9	102.8	117.6	84.5	96.0	113.2	84.0	94.2	109.9	99.7	103.2	120.2	84.2	96.7	102.2	102.5	102.4
0310	Concrete Forming & Accessories	94.3	66.0	70.9	96.4	64.2	69.9	100.0	64.1	70.4	91.6	63.3	68.3	97.3	64.8	70.5	103.9	65.6	72.3
0320	Concrete Reinforcing	76.7	71.4	74.6	112.8	60.7	91.5	106.4	60.6	87.7	78.7	72.1	76.0	107.6	65.4	90.3	83.7	61.3	74.5
0330	Cast-in-Place Concrete	96.4	72.6	88.5	123.9	69.1	105.5	108.8	69.6	95.7	98.6	69.0	88.7	130.1	70.0	110.0	89.5	74.1	84.3
03	CONCRETE	91.6	69.9	82.7	112.5	66.1	93.4	100.8	66.1	86.6	93.3	67.8	82.8	113.6	67.4	94.6	91.7	68.6	82.2
04	MASONRY	109.8	59.2	80.4	97.5	61.1	76.3	88.1	58.5	70.9	130.9	59.7	89.4	80.2	62.7	70.0	122.2	61.7	87.0
05	METALS	102.3	79.7	97.6	101.8	75.5	96.3	100.7	73.7	95.1	102.3	83.7	98.4	110.2	76.8	103.2	99.8	77.1	95.0
06	WOOD, PLASTICS & COMPOSITES	82.4	65.2	73.9	95.9	63.3	79.9	100.4	63.3	82.2	79.1	63.6	71.5	97.2	63.5	80.6	101.6	64.6	83.4
07	THERMAL & MOISTURE PROTECTION	89.9	66.9	82.2	88.9	65.9	81.2	88.8	65.4	80.9	89.8	65.0	81.5	89.0	66.4	81.4	91.5	68.3	83.7
08	OPENINGS	96.8	64.8	89.0	92.6	61.4	85.0	92.6	61.4	85.0	96.7	64.1	88.8	92.0	62.5	84.8	97.7	62.2	89.1
0920	Plaster & Gypsum Board	104.8	63.9	78.8	98.7	62.6	75.7	101.4	62.6	76.7	102.7	62.7	77.2	98.7	62.7	75.8	97.1	63.3	75.6
0950, 0980	Ceilings & Acoustic Treatment	79.9	63.9	70.9	72.6	62.6	67.0	76.0	62.6	68.5	79.9	62.7	70.3	75.1	62.7	68.1	85.7	63.3	73.2
0960	Flooring	109.7	67.2	98.8	107.8	59.7	95.4	109.6	62.1	97.4	108.2	65.9	97.4	108.0	62.7	96.4	110.3	60.3	97.5
0970, 0990	Wall Finishes & Painting/Coating	98.5	64.1	78.3	102.8	59.9	77.6	102.8	59.9	77.6	98.5	64.1	78.3	102.8	80.5	89.7	99.9	57.8	75.1
09	FINISHES	98.3	65.8	82.2	95.0	62.6	79.0	96.0	63.1	79.7	97.7	63.6	80.9	95.4	65.6	80.7	99.2	63.5	81.5
COVERS	DIVS. 10-14, 25, 28, 41, 43, 44, 46	100.0	81.6	96.1	100.0	79.7	95.7	100.0	81.8	96.1	100.0	82.6	96.3	100.0	83.6	96.5	100.0	86.5	97.1
21, 22, 23	FIRE SUPPRESSION, PLUMBING & HVAC	95.9	59.4	82.8	95.7	64.0	84.3	99.9	65.1	87.4	95.9	57.0	81.9	99.9	76.0	91.3	100.0	65.2	87.5
26, 27, 3370	ELECTRICAL, COMMUNICATIONS & UTIL.	99.7	58.3	81.7	98.3	58.1	80.8	98.0	64.3	83.3	98.7	50.6	77.7	99.1	67.8	85.5	101.6	72.7	89.0
MF2018	WEIGHTED AVERAGE	98.2	67.5	86.6	99.6	66.0	86.9	98.5	66.7	86.5	99.2	65.6	86.5	101.7	70.9	90.1	99.7	70.6	88.7

		\multicolumn{18}{c}{FLORIDA}
\multicolumn{2}{c}{DIVISION}	\multicolumn{3}{c}{ORLANDO 327-328,347}	\multicolumn{3}{c}{PANAMA CITY 324}	\multicolumn{3}{c}{PENSACOLA 325}	\multicolumn{3}{c}{SARASOTA 342}	\multicolumn{3}{c}{ST. PETERSBURG 337}	\multicolumn{3}{c}{TALLAHASSEE 323}
		MAT.	INST.	TOTAL	MAT.	INST.	TOTAL	MAT.	INST.	TOTAL	MAT.	INST.	TOTAL	MAT.	INST.	TOTAL	MAT.	INST.	TOTAL
015433	CONTRACTOR EQUIPMENT		104.1	104.1		91.2	91.2		91.2	91.2		94.4	94.4		103.5	103.5		100.7	100.7
0241, 31-34	SITE & INFRASTRUCTURE, DEMOLITION	111.7	101.8	105.2	123.3	84.4	97.9	124.9	84.0	98.2	119.8	87.2	98.5	113.2	99.3	104.1	111.4	95.9	101.0
0310	Concrete Forming & Accessories	104.1	64.9	71.8	99.5	70.6	75.6	97.6	69.4	74.3	102.8	63.0	70.0	97.1	63.0	69.0	105.3	64.6	71.7
0320	Concrete Reinforcing	84.4	61.4	75.0	111.1	65.6	92.5	113.9	65.3	94.0	116.8	66.7	96.3	78.7	68.6	74.6	151.4	60.8	114.4
0330	Cast-in-Place Concrete	148.4	73.5	123.4	114.4	69.7	99.5	141.6	68.1	117.0	112.7	68.0	97.7	99.7	67.8	89.0	96.8	72.9	88.8
03	CONCRETE	120.7	67.8	99.0	109.4	70.0	93.2	122.1	68.8	100.2	104.2	66.3	88.7	94.8	66.6	83.2	103.0	67.5	88.4
04	MASONRY	96.5	62.9	77.0	91.5	59.8	73.0	117.0	58.6	83.0	93.4	59.7	73.7	182.4	56.1	108.9	80.3	61.6	69.4
05	METALS	99.8	73.0	94.2	101.7	77.2	96.6	102.9	76.1	97.3	101.8	80.1	97.2	102.3	80.6	97.7	99.8	73.9	94.4
06	WOOD, PLASTICS & COMPOSITES	101.6	64.0	83.1	99.5	72.1	86.0	98.4	72.1	85.4	100.6	63.4	82.3	85.7	63.6	74.8	103.4	63.7	83.9
07	THERMAL & MOISTURE PROTECTION	92.8	70.7	85.4	89.0	65.3	81.1	89.0	64.0	80.6	100.5	64.5	88.5	90.0	61.0	80.3	91.2	68.2	83.5
08	OPENINGS	97.8	61.8	89.1	90.8	67.3	85.1	90.8	67.2	85.1	99.2	62.4	90.2	95.3	63.3	87.5	96.8	61.6	88.2
0920	Plaster & Gypsum Board	110.5	62.7	80.1	100.4	71.6	82.1	122.0	71.6	89.9	107.1	62.7	78.9	106.7	62.7	78.7	116.0	62.6	82.0
0950, 0980	Ceilings & Acoustic Treatment	80.0	62.7	70.3	75.1	71.6	73.1	75.1	71.6	73.1	89.1	62.7	74.3	80.9	62.7	70.7	101.6	62.6	79.8
0960	Flooring	108.9	57.9	95.8	109.4	71.8	99.7	106.3	59.1	94.2	111.4	47.8	95.1	111.1	52.4	96.1	109.1	59.9	96.5
0970, 0990	Wall Finishes & Painting/Coating	99.9	81.7	89.2	102.8	59.9	77.6	102.8	61.6	78.6	102.6	64.1	80.0	98.5	59.9	75.8	99.9	59.9	76.4
09	FINISHES	99.8	65.2	82.7	96.6	69.7	83.3	98.2	67.1	82.8	102.6	60.4	81.7	99.4	60.7	80.3	106.2	63.0	84.8
COVERS	DIVS. 10-14, 25, 28, 41, 43, 44, 46	100.0	84.8	96.8	100.0	83.3	96.4	100.0	80.4	95.8	100.0	78.9	95.5	100.0	79.5	95.6	100.0	82.7	96.3
21, 22, 23	FIRE SUPPRESSION, PLUMBING & HVAC	100.2	55.4	84.1	99.9	64.8	87.3	99.9	61.4	86.1	99.6	59.5	85.2	99.9	54.4	83.5	100.1	65.3	87.6
26, 27, 3370	ELECTRICAL, COMMUNICATIONS & UTIL.	101.2	60.4	83.4	97.3	55.2	79.0	99.8	48.3	77.4	98.9	50.5	77.8	98.7	57.2	80.6	101.8	54.2	81.0
MF2018	WEIGHTED AVERAGE	102.3	66.6	88.8	99.9	67.6	87.7	103.3	65.0	88.8	101.0	64.1	87.0	100.8	64.6	88.3	99.9	66.8	87.4

		\multicolumn{6}{c}{FLORIDA}	\multicolumn{12}{c}{GEORGIA}
\multicolumn{2}{c}{DIVISION}	\multicolumn{3}{c}{TAMPA 335-336,346}	\multicolumn{3}{c}{WEST PALM BEACH 334,349}	\multicolumn{3}{c}{ALBANY 317,398}	\multicolumn{3}{c}{ATHENS 306}	\multicolumn{3}{c}{ATLANTA 300-303,399}	\multicolumn{3}{c}{AUGUSTA 308-309}
		MAT.	INST.	TOTAL	MAT.	INST.	TOTAL	MAT.	INST.	TOTAL	MAT.	INST.	TOTAL	MAT.	INST.	TOTAL	MAT.	INST.	TOTAL
015433	CONTRACTOR EQUIPMENT		103.5	103.5		95.2	95.2		92.2	92.2		91.0	91.0		96.4	96.4		91.0	91.0
0241, 31-34	SITE & INFRASTRUCTURE, DEMOLITION	113.5	99.9	104.6	95.3	85.9	89.2	130.3	86.6	101.8	122.3	85.2	98.1	121.8	94.2	103.8	117.2	85.9	96.8
0310	Concrete Forming & Accessories	99.2	64.5	70.6	100.5	62.9	69.5	100.7	71.3	76.4	98.4	69.0	74.2	102.3	75.6	80.3	99.2	74.7	79.0
0320	Concrete Reinforcing	75.9	72.1	74.3	78.0	55.4	68.8	139.1	69.4	110.6	91.3	55.0	76.5	99.1	70.3	87.3	91.7	70.4	83.0
0330	Cast-in-Place Concrete	97.4	70.6	88.5	87.9	67.9	81.2	108.5	72.2	96.3	104.7	68.1	92.5	108.1	73.2	96.4	98.9	71.3	89.7
03	CONCRETE	93.4	68.9	83.3	87.7	64.3	78.1	106.8	72.0	92.5	97.6	67.0	85.0	100.3	74.2	89.6	91.2	73.4	83.9
04	MASONRY	116.7	62.6	85.2	115.4	56.9	81.3	92.7	67.4	78.0	94.4	62.5	75.8	109.3	67.9	85.2	111.5	69.1	86.8
05	METALS	101.4	83.8	97.7	99.0	77.0	94.4	103.4	83.8	99.2	90.0	75.5	87.0	95.9	81.8	93.0	89.7	84.9	88.7
06	WOOD, PLASTICS & COMPOSITES	88.7	63.6	76.3	88.3	64.2	76.4	92.6	72.7	82.8	94.3	72.5	83.6	103.1	78.8	91.1	95.5	77.8	86.8
07	THERMAL & MOISTURE PROTECTION	90.2	66.3	82.2	89.8	64.0	81.2	101.4	69.8	90.8	101.6	65.2	89.4	102.3	72.3	92.3	101.4	70.6	91.1
08	OPENINGS	96.3	64.1	88.5	94.5	60.6	86.3	87.4	72.1	83.7	91.3	68.0	85.6	101.5	75.8	95.3	91.4	75.3	87.4
0920	Plaster & Gypsum Board	109.8	62.7	79.8	111.7	63.3	80.9	95.7	72.1	80.7	98.2	72.1	81.6	104.6	78.2	87.8	99.4	77.5	85.5
0950, 0980	Ceilings & Acoustic Treatment	85.3	62.7	72.6	79.9	63.3	70.6	81.3	72.1	76.2	111.9	72.1	89.6	102.4	78.2	88.9	112.8	77.5	93.1
0960	Flooring	112.0	65.9	100.2	113.4	47.8	96.5	115.9	64.9	102.8	99.3	64.9	90.5	104.8	70.3	96.0	99.3	72.3	92.4
0970, 0990	Wall Finishes & Painting/Coating	98.5	64.1	78.3	94.7	55.9	71.9	100.1	94.8	97.0	94.0	81.8	86.8	99.9	96.5	97.9	94.0	82.4	87.2
09	FINISHES	101.3	64.3	83.0	98.4	58.9	78.9	100.1	72.4	86.4	104.8	70.0	87.6	105.0	77.0	91.1	104.3	75.3	90.0
COVERS	DIVS. 10-14, 25, 28, 41, 43, 44, 46	100.0	82.3	96.2	100.0	83.6	96.5	100.0	85.9	97.0	100.0	82.2	96.2	100.0	86.5	97.1	100.0	85.7	97.0
21, 22, 23	FIRE SUPPRESSION, PLUMBING & HVAC	99.9	58.5	85.0	95.9	60.3	83.1	100.1	70.3	89.4	92.8	58.3	80.4	100.0	71.9	89.9	100.1	66.1	87.8
26, 27, 3370	ELECTRICAL, COMMUNICATIONS & UTIL.	98.1	66.3	84.2	99.5	58.2	81.5	98.8	55.6	80.0	101.0	55.2	81.1	101.0	67.7	86.5	101.4	64.5	85.3
MF2018	WEIGHTED AVERAGE	99.7	68.8	88.0	96.9	64.3	84.6	100.8	71.4	89.7	96.2	66.0	84.8	100.9	75.1	91.2	97.7	72.8	88.3

City Cost Indexes

		GEORGIA																	
	DIVISION	COLUMBUS 318 - 319			DALTON 307			GAINESVILLE 305			MACON 310 - 312			SAVANNAH 313 - 314			STATESBORO 304		
		MAT.	INST.	TOTAL	MAT.	INST.	TOTAL	MAT.	INST.	TOTAL	MAT.	INST.	TOTAL	MAT.	INST.	TOTAL	MAT.	INST.	TOTAL
015433	CONTRACTOR EQUIPMENT		92.2	92.2		103.2	103.2		91.0	91.0		104.6	104.6		105.0	105.0		91.8	91.8
0241, 31 - 34	SITE & INFRASTRUCTURE, DEMOLITION	130.2	87.0	102.1	120.3	89.9	100.5	121.6	85.0	97.7	131.9	104.3	113.9	133.3	103.5	113.9	123.0	72.8	90.3
0310	Concrete Forming & Accessories	100.6	71.0	76.2	93.4	66.9	71.6	101.3	51.3	60.1	99.9	69.0	74.4	105.7	71.0	77.1	89.5	68.3	72.0
0320	Concrete Reinforcing	140.1	70.9	111.8	90.8	52.7	75.2	91.1	55.0	76.4	141.9	69.6	112.4	151.0	70.3	118.0	90.4	61.7	78.7
0330	Cast-in-Place Concrete	108.1	73.8	96.6	101.8	66.6	90.0	110.1	67.7	95.9	106.6	73.1	95.4	109.5	76.7	98.5	104.6	67.0	92.0
03	CONCRETE	106.7	72.7	92.8	96.7	65.9	84.1	99.7	58.8	82.9	106.2	71.4	91.9	107.6	73.5	93.6	97.2	68.2	85.3
04	MASONRY	92.0	71.1	79.8	94.2	61.0	74.9	105.8	61.6	80.1	105.8	67.9	83.7	86.4	69.3	76.5	97.7	62.4	77.1
05	METALS	102.9	86.0	99.4	92.1	87.0	91.0	89.4	75.4	86.4	98.3	85.3	95.6	99.8	83.1	96.3	94.4	91.9	93.8
06	WOOD, PLASTICS & COMPOSITES	92.6	71.8	82.3	77.2	70.8	74.1	97.2	49.0	73.5	103.7	70.5	87.4	105.8	72.1	89.2	72.6	71.4	72.0
07	THERMAL & MOISTURE PROTECTION	101.4	71.8	91.5	103.6	63.5	90.2	101.6	62.3	88.4	100.0	72.6	90.8	98.5	73.8	90.2	102.3	62.5	88.9
08	OPENINGS	87.4	72.8	83.9	94.4	66.5	87.6	91.3	55.1	82.5	87.2	70.6	83.1	96.4	72.6	90.6	95.0	69.2	88.7
0920	Plaster & Gypsum Board	95.7	71.2	80.1	86.7	70.3	76.3	100.2	47.8	66.8	102.3	69.8	81.6	100.6	71.0	81.8	87.6	71.0	77.1
0950, 0980	Ceilings & Acoustic Treatment	81.3	71.2	75.7	117.6	70.3	91.1	111.9	47.8	76.0	78.7	69.8	73.7	101.6	71.0	84.5	118.0	71.0	91.7
0960	Flooring	115.9	72.3	104.7	98.8	64.9	90.1	100.5	64.9	91.4	92.9	64.9	85.7	108.9	69.5	98.8	118.7	64.9	104.9
0970, 0990	Wall Finishes & Painting/Coating	100.1	85.7	91.7	83.6	61.0	70.3	94.0	81.8	86.8	101.8	94.8	97.7	99.9	82.7	89.8	92.4	61.0	73.9
09	FINISHES	100.0	72.4	86.4	112.4	66.4	89.7	105.1	56.0	80.8	89.2	70.5	80.0	104.6	71.8	88.4	116.9	67.1	92.3
COVERS	DIVS. 10 - 14, 25, 28, 41, 43, 44, 46	100.0	85.9	97.0	100.0	75.8	94.8	100.0	79.5	95.6	100.0	85.0	96.8	100.0	86.9	97.2	100.0	82.0	96.2
21, 22, 23	FIRE SUPPRESSION, PLUMBING & HVAC	100.2	66.8	88.2	92.8	53.5	78.7	92.8	57.8	80.2	100.2	70.2	89.4	100.3	66.2	88.0	94.7	61.2	82.6
26, 27, 3370	ELECTRICAL, COMMUNICATIONS & UTIL.	98.6	70.1	86.2	113.8	53.8	87.7	101.0	63.5	84.6	96.4	56.3	78.9	101.6	61.2	84.0	102.2	56.9	82.5
MF2018	WEIGHTED AVERAGE	100.6	73.5	90.4	98.7	65.0	86.0	96.9	63.1	84.1	99.2	72.6	89.2	101.4	73.0	90.7	98.9	67.1	86.9

		GEORGIA						HAWAII									IDAHO		
	DIVISION	VALDOSTA 316			WAYCROSS 315			HILO 967			HONOLULU 968			STATES & POSS., GUAM 969			BOISE 836 - 837		
		MAT.	INST.	TOTAL	MAT.	INST.	TOTAL	MAT.	INST.	TOTAL	MAT.	INST.	TOTAL	MAT.	INST.	TOTAL	MAT.	INST.	TOTAL
015433	CONTRACTOR EQUIPMENT		92.2	92.2		92.2	92.2		103.7	103.7		111.1	111.1		180.1	180.1		109.6	109.6
0241, 31 - 34	SITE & INFRASTRUCTURE, DEMOLITION	143.1	86.6	106.2	137.3	86.0	103.8	115.5	104.9	108.6	120.4	117.2	118.3	136.6	103.7	115.1	90.0	110.1	103.1
0310	Concrete Forming & Accessories	92.7	70.4	74.3	94.1	68.1	72.7	91.0	123.4	117.7	98.3	123.4	119.0	92.9	61.2	66.8	96.2	80.1	82.9
0320	Concrete Reinforcing	142.7	58.9	108.5	142.7	51.7	105.5	163.7	124.1	147.5	187.0	124.1	161.3	283.2	40.4	184.0	119.2	74.0	100.8
0330	Cast-in-Place Concrete	106.2	72.1	94.8	120.0	69.5	103.1	140.3	123.4	134.6	109.5	125.0	114.7	121.6	110.3	117.8	84.6	99.1	89.4
03	CONCRETE	111.0	69.7	94.0	115.7	66.3	95.4	161.5	123.1	145.7	166.7	123.5	149.0	170.9	75.9	131.9	100.7	86.0	94.7
04	MASONRY	97.3	70.0	81.4	98.4	62.6	77.5	217.3	121.9	161.8	211.2	122.0	159.3	330.8	45.1	164.5	130.5	82.5	102.5
05	METALS	102.1	79.2	97.3	102.1	70.1	95.4	118.6	114.1	117.6	134.5	112.0	129.8	152.1	85.3	138.1	107.5	81.9	102.2
06	WOOD, PLASTICS & COMPOSITES	83.1	71.6	77.5	84.5	71.6	78.2	97.7	124.1	110.7	112.5	124.1	118.2	103.7	61.4	82.9	88.0	78.2	83.2
07	THERMAL & MOISTURE PROTECTION	101.7	71.5	91.6	101.5	65.5	89.5	96.8	115.9	103.2	107.4	118.3	111.1	112.7	69.1	98.1	92.8	85.1	90.2
08	OPENINGS	84.0	68.4	80.2	84.4	64.6	79.6	109.2	122.8	112.5	121.0	122.8	121.4	113.8	50.0	98.3	91.2	73.1	86.8
0920	Plaster & Gypsum Board	90.4	71.0	78.1	90.4	71.0	78.1	113.7	124.5	120.6	151.4	124.5	134.3	243.9	48.5	119.5	96.5	77.3	84.3
0950, 0980	Ceilings & Acoustic Treatment	79.5	71.0	74.8	78.6	71.0	74.3	129.3	124.5	126.6	143.5	124.5	132.9	304.2	48.5	161.1	108.6	77.3	91.1
0960	Flooring	111.3	70.9	100.9	112.3	64.9	100.1	90.2	137.9	102.5	112.1	137.9	118.7	108.1	43.1	91.5	94.3	82.3	91.2
0970, 0990	Wall Finishes & Painting/Coating	100.1	94.8	97.0	100.1	61.0	77.1	88.8	130.5	113.3	99.9	130.5	117.9	94.6	36.2	60.3	90.1	60.2	72.5
09	FINISHES	98.6	73.0	86.0	98.2	67.2	82.9	105.8	127.3	116.5	121.6	127.4	124.4	199.1	55.6	128.1	98.8	78.4	88.7
COVERS	DIVS. 10 - 14, 25, 28, 41, 43, 44, 46	100.0	85.8	97.0	100.0	76.7	95.0	100.0	112.4	102.6	100.0	112.5	102.7	100.0	91.4	98.2	100.0	90.8	98.0
21, 22, 23	FIRE SUPPRESSION, PLUMBING & HVAC	100.2	69.9	89.3	95.8	56.0	81.5	100.0	111.6	104.2	100.0	111.6	104.2	102.8	49.2	83.5	100.1	72.6	90.2
26, 27, 3370	ELECTRICAL, COMMUNICATIONS & UTIL.	97.6	50.9	77.2	100.0	56.8	81.2	103.7	115.8	109.0	104.5	115.8	109.4	145.8	44.2	101.5	98.2	71.0	86.3
MF2018	WEIGHTED AVERAGE	101.0	70.1	89.3	100.7	64.6	87.1	118.0	117.3	117.8	124.4	118.2	122.0	145.0	61.8	113.6	101.4	80.6	93.5

		IDAHO															ILLINOIS		
	DIVISION	COEUR D'ALENE 838			IDAHO FALLS 834			LEWISTON 835			POCATELLO 832			TWIN FALLS 833			BLOOMINGTON 617		
		MAT.	INST.	TOTAL	MAT.	INST.	TOTAL	MAT.	INST.	TOTAL	MAT.	INST.	TOTAL	MAT.	INST.	TOTAL	MAT.	INST.	TOTAL
015433	CONTRACTOR EQUIPMENT		94.1	94.1		99.0	99.0		94.1	94.1		99.0	99.0		99.0	99.0		99.7	99.7
0241, 31 - 34	SITE & INFRASTRUCTURE, DEMOLITION	90.7	91.5	91.2	90.8	94.7	93.4	99.8	90.8	94.0	91.0	94.6	93.4	96.8	94.1	95.0	85.7	98.1	93.8
0310	Concrete Forming & Accessories	107.4	80.4	85.1	92.1	76.7	79.4	110.9	87.4	91.5	96.3	79.2	82.2	97.3	75.1	79.0	90.9	117.1	112.5
0320	Concrete Reinforcing	127.9	98.5	115.9	121.4	74.6	102.3	127.9	98.6	115.9	119.7	74.0	101.0	121.8	70.8	100.9	86.7	102.6	93.2
0330	Cast-in-Place Concrete	91.5	79.3	87.4	80.5	92.3	84.5	95.1	83.4	91.2	87.0	96.3	90.1	89.3	91.7	90.1	88.4	112.2	96.4
03	CONCRETE	107.4	83.5	97.6	93.1	82.3	88.6	110.9	88.1	101.5	99.9	84.8	93.7	107.5	80.8	96.5	90.8	113.4	100.1
04	MASONRY	132.9	82.5	103.6	125.8	85.4	102.3	133.3	87.3	106.6	128.1	84.1	102.5	131.4	77.0	99.7	110.9	122.1	117.4
05	METALS	99.5	93.2	98.2	114.9	83.9	108.4	99.4	93.5	98.2	115.3	83.3	108.6	115.0	81.9	108.0	93.8	121.3	99.5
06	WOOD, PLASTICS & COMPOSITES	97.6	79.3	88.6	84.1	74.9	79.6	101.3	86.4	94.0	88.0	77.9	83.0	88.9	73.6	81.3	87.1	115.5	101.1
07	THERMAL & MOISTURE PROTECTION	140.8	79.0	120.1	92.0	76.0	86.6	141.1	80.7	120.9	92.5	73.3	86.1	93.1	78.0	88.1	101.5	111.5	104.9
08	OPENINGS	110.7	74.9	102.0	93.8	69.9	88.0	101.8	82.3	97.1	91.8	66.2	85.6	94.8	69.1	88.6	87.7	118.6	95.2
0920	Plaster & Gypsum Board	167.2	78.8	110.0	84.5	74.3	78.0	168.4	86.1	116.1	87.2	77.3	80.9	88.0	72.8	78.3	88.1	116.1	105.9
0950, 0980	Ceilings & Acoustic Treatment	127.3	78.8	100.2	104.1	74.3	87.4	127.3	86.1	104.3	112.5	77.3	92.8	107.7	72.8	88.2	87.6	116.1	103.5
0960	Flooring	138.9	87.5	125.7	95.0	74.1	89.6	141.3	72.6	123.7	97.5	72.6	91.1	98.3	77.5	93.0	85.4	123.9	95.3
0970, 0990	Wall Finishes & Painting/Coating	112.4	66.8	85.6	90.1	41.0	61.3	112.4	80.1	93.5	90.0	56.7	70.5	90.1	56.7	70.5	88.0	117.3	105.2
09	FINISHES	165.0	80.1	123.0	95.9	72.2	84.2	166.0	83.7	125.3	99.5	75.8	87.8	99.1	73.6	86.5	88.5	118.7	103.5
COVERS	DIVS. 10 - 14, 25, 28, 41, 43, 44, 46	100.0	95.1	99.0	100.0	89.2	97.7	100.0	102.3	100.5	100.0	90.1	97.9	100.0	86.6	97.1	100.0	106.8	101.4
21, 22, 23	FIRE SUPPRESSION, PLUMBING & HVAC	96.9	84.8	92.5	103.5	75.5	93.4	101.3	93.9	98.7	100.0	75.5	91.2	100.0	67.5	88.3	92.5	105.3	97.1
26, 27, 3370	ELECTRICAL, COMMUNICATIONS & UTIL.	83.6	76.1	80.3	83.4	65.9	75.8	82.6	85.1	83.6	93.9	65.9	81.7	84.1	68.1	77.1	87.5	90.0	88.6
MF2018	WEIGHTED AVERAGE	106.8	83.4	98.0	100.7	78.0	92.1	107.8	88.9	100.7	102.3	78.5	93.3	102.5	75.4	92.3	92.7	109.4	99.0

City Cost Indexes

ILLINOIS

DIVISION		CARBONDALE 629			CENTRALIA 628			CHAMPAIGN 618 - 619			CHICAGO 606 - 608			DECATUR 625			EAST ST. LOUIS 620 - 622		
		MAT.	INST.	TOTAL	MAT.	INST.	TOTAL	MAT.	INST.	TOTAL	MAT.	INST.	TOTAL	MAT.	INST.	TOTAL	MAT.	INST.	TOTAL
015433	CONTRACTOR EQUIPMENT		106.3	106.3		106.3	106.3		100.8	100.8		101.3	101.3		101.9	101.9		106.3	106.3
0241, 31 - 34	SITE & INFRASTRUCTURE, DEMOLITION	91.1	100.7	97.4	91.4	101.9	98.2	91.8	99.2	96.6	102.3	104.2	103.5	91.5	101.4	98.0	96.4	101.6	99.8
0310	Concrete Forming & Accessories	100.1	105.5	104.5	101.5	111.2	109.5	95.9	115.2	111.8	98.3	159.3	148.6	101.7	115.0	112.6	98.0	111.4	109.1
0320	Concrete Reinforcing	95.1	96.4	95.6	95.1	101.3	97.6	86.7	97.8	91.2	90.8	149.5	114.8	93.4	97.8	95.2	95.0	101.2	97.5
0330	Cast-in-Place Concrete	81.0	100.7	87.6	81.4	110.4	91.1	102.5	109.8	105.0	119.0	153.9	130.7	88.5	111.9	96.3	82.8	114.2	93.3
03	CONCRETE	80.2	103.2	89.6	80.6	110.2	92.8	102.4	110.8	105.8	114.4	155.5	131.3	89.4	111.4	98.4	81.5	111.7	93.9
04	MASONRY	92.1	109.2	102.0	92.1	120.1	108.4	133.4	119.7	125.4	95.4	164.2	135.4	87.2	119.3	105.9	92.3	118.8	107.7
05	METALS	99.3	119.4	103.5	99.3	124.5	104.6	93.8	116.0	98.4	99.9	151.1	110.6	103.5	116.2	106.2	99.3	124.9	104.8
06	WOOD, PLASTICS & COMPOSITES	101.2	103.7	102.4	103.4	108.4	105.9	92.4	114.3	103.1	100.6	158.5	129.1	100.1	114.1	107.0	98.8	108.4	103.6
07	THERMAL & MOISTURE PROTECTION	93.2	96.8	94.4	93.2	108.3	98.3	102.2	110.8	105.0	101.0	149.2	117.2	98.0	110.8	102.3	93.2	107.2	97.9
08	OPENINGS	88.0	108.3	92.9	88.0	112.3	93.9	88.2	115.4	94.8	100.8	168.0	117.2	97.0	115.3	101.5	88.0	115.6	94.7
0920	Plaster & Gypsum Board	91.9	104.1	99.7	92.9	109.0	103.1	89.6	114.8	105.6	92.2	160.3	135.5	96.5	114.8	108.2	91.0	109.0	102.4
0950, 0980	Ceilings & Acoustic Treatment	91.0	104.1	98.4	91.0	109.0	101.1	87.6	114.8	102.8	87.4	160.3	128.2	102.5	114.8	109.4	91.0	109.0	101.1
0960	Flooring	104.5	102.4	103.9	105.2	99.7	103.7	87.9	111.4	93.9	90.8	162.3	109.2	94.9	120.1	101.4	103.6	99.7	102.6
0970, 0990	Wall Finishes & Painting/Coating	104.8	103.2	103.9	104.8	106.1	105.6	88.0	109.0	100.4	99.9	163.2	137.1	97.7	106.0	102.6	104.8	108.6	107.0
09	FINISHES	99.3	104.8	99.0	93.6	108.7	101.1	89.9	114.4	102.0	93.2	161.1	126.8	95.8	115.6	105.6	93.0	108.9	100.9
COVERS	DIVS. 10 - 14, 25, 28, 41, 43, 44, 46	100.0	102.2	100.5	100.0	104.3	100.9	100.0	106.0	101.4	100.0	127.2	105.8	100.0	106.0	101.3	100.0	107.1	101.5
21, 22, 23	FIRE SUPPRESSION, PLUMBING & HVAC	92.4	97.7	94.3	92.4	93.5	92.8	92.5	104.3	96.7	99.8	136.1	112.9	99.8	96.1	98.5	99.7	94.0	97.7
26, 27, 3370	ELECTRICAL, COMMUNICATIONS & UTIL.	79.9	103.9	90.3	80.5	91.8	85.4	89.1	92.9	90.7	95.7	131.1	111.1	81.7	88.7	84.8	80.3	100.2	88.9
MF2018	WEIGHTED AVERAGE	91.2	104.1	96.1	91.4	105.2	96.6	95.7	107.9	100.3	100.6	144.7	117.2	95.9	105.9	99.7	93.2	106.8	98.4

ILLINOIS

DIVISION		EFFINGHAM 624			GALESBURG 614			JOLIET 604			KANKAKEE 609			LA SALLE 613			NORTH SUBURBAN 600 - 603		
		MAT.	INST.	TOTAL	MAT.	INST.	TOTAL	MAT.	INST.	TOTAL	MAT.	INST.	TOTAL	MAT.	INST.	TOTAL	MAT.	INST.	TOTAL
015433	CONTRACTOR EQUIPMENT		101.9	101.9		99.7	99.7		95.6	95.6		95.6	95.6		99.7	99.7		95.6	95.6
0241, 31 - 34	SITE & INFRASTRUCTURE, DEMOLITION	90.1	101.0	97.2	87.4	97.8	94.2	98.1	96.2	96.9	90.8	94.6	93.3	86.9	99.1	94.9	97.3	158.6	147.8
0310	Concrete Forming & Accessories	105.3	113.9	112.4	95.8	116.3	112.7	97.7	162.1	150.8	93.3	145.1	136.0	106.6	125.5	122.2	97.3	158.6	147.8
0320	Concrete Reinforcing	96.8	82.0	90.8	86.1	102.4	92.8	98.3	138.8	114.8	99.3	130.5	112.1	86.3	129.0	103.7	98.3	149.2	119.1
0330	Cast-in-Place Concrete	88.2	106.7	94.4	91.0	107.5	96.5	108.2	149.4	121.9	100.8	130.5	110.7	90.9	126.7	102.9	108.2	141.6	119.4
03	CONCRETE	90.2	106.3	96.8	93.4	111.3	100.8	107.1	153.4	126.1	101.0	137.4	115.9	94.1	127.2	107.7	107.1	150.7	125.0
04	MASONRY	96.0	112.7	105.7	111.0	120.1	116.3	95.0	164.1	135.2	91.5	143.1	121.5	111.1	133.2	123.9	92.0	161.6	132.5
05	METALS	101.4	106.2	102.4	93.8	120.3	99.3	91.7	147.2	103.3	91.7	137.7	101.4	93.8	140.0	103.5	92.9	149.9	104.8
06	WOOD, PLASTICS & COMPOSITES	102.1	114.1	108.0	92.3	115.5	103.7	88.8	162.7	125.2	84.4	144.7	114.1	104.4	122.6	113.4	87.4	158.3	122.3
07	THERMAL & MOISTURE PROTECTION	97.6	102.2	99.2	101.7	107.7	103.7	107.5	145.6	120.2	106.8	135.7	116.5	101.8	120.3	108.0	108.0	145.6	120.6
08	OPENINGS	92.4	109.4	96.5	87.7	114.4	94.2	95.7	166.9	113.0	88.4	153.7	104.3	87.7	130.8	98.1	95.7	166.9	113.0
0920	Plaster & Gypsum Board	94.1	114.8	107.3	89.6	116.1	106.5	88.2	164.8	137.0	87.9	146.3	125.1	95.3	123.5	113.2	91.3	160.3	135.2
0950, 0980	Ceilings & Acoustic Treatment	91.0	114.8	104.3	87.6	116.1	103.6	89.4	164.8	131.6	89.4	146.3	121.3	87.6	123.5	107.7	89.4	160.3	129.1
0960	Flooring	95.8	111.4	99.8	87.7	123.9	97.0	88.7	156.4	106.1	86.4	140.4	100.2	92.8	125.2	101.1	89.6	156.4	106.7
0970, 0990	Wall Finishes & Painting/Coating	97.7	107.0	103.1	88.0	95.4	92.4	88.2	163.2	132.3	88.2	130.5	113.1	88.0	126.7	110.8	91.3	163.2	133.5
09	FINISHES	92.7	113.7	103.1	89.4	116.3	102.7	90.5	162.5	126.1	89.6	143.5	116.3	91.6	125.2	108.2	91.3	159.9	125.2
COVERS	DIVS. 10 - 14, 25, 28, 41, 43, 44, 46	100.0	103.2	100.7	100.0	104.3	100.9	100.0	127.1	105.8	100.0	111.2	102.4	100.0	106.5	101.4	100.0	123.9	105.1
21, 22, 23	FIRE SUPPRESSION, PLUMBING & HVAC	92.5	103.1	96.3	92.5	99.2	94.9	99.8	135.7	112.7	92.5	127.6	105.2	92.5	125.8	104.5	99.8	133.4	111.9
26, 27, 3370	ELECTRICAL, COMMUNICATIONS & UTIL.	80.8	103.9	90.9	87.9	89.9	88.8	94.4	130.6	110.1	91.4	134.0	110.0	86.5	134.1	107.2	94.6	129.3	109.7
MF2018	WEIGHTED AVERAGE	93.6	106.5	98.4	93.3	106.8	98.4	97.4	143.3	114.7	93.6	132.9	108.4	93.5	126.4	105.9	97.5	141.7	114.2

ILLINOIS

DIVISION		PEORIA 615 - 616			QUINCY 623			ROCK ISLAND 612			ROCKFORD 610 - 611			SOUTH SUBURBAN 605			SPRINGFIELD 626 - 627		
		MAT.	INST.	TOTAL	MAT.	INST.	TOTAL	MAT.	INST.	TOTAL	MAT.	INST.	TOTAL	MAT.	INST.	TOTAL	MAT.	INST.	TOTAL
015433	CONTRACTOR EQUIPMENT		99.7	99.7		101.9	101.9		99.7	99.7		99.7	99.7		95.6	95.6		110.2	110.2
0241, 31 - 34	SITE & INFRASTRUCTURE, DEMOLITION	91.3	97.9	95.6	89.1	101.8	97.4	86.1	96.7	93.0	91.1	99.5	96.6	97.8	95.3	96.2	93.9	112.6	106.1
0310	Concrete Forming & Accessories	98.3	117.0	113.8	103.4	114.8	112.8	97.1	103.6	102.4	101.4	134.6	128.8	97.3	158.6	147.8	101.6	115.5	113.1
0320	Concrete Reinforcing	83.9	102.6	91.6	96.3	83.7	91.2	86.1	98.5	91.2	79.7	134.9	102.3	98.3	149.2	119.1	92.2	98.0	94.6
0330	Cast-in-Place Concrete	88.3	114.3	97.0	88.3	114.2	97.0	89.0	100.6	92.9	90.4	130.3	103.7	108.2	148.5	121.7	84.1	111.2	93.1
03	CONCRETE	90.8	114.1	100.4	89.9	109.8	98.1	91.4	102.4	95.9	91.4	133.6	108.7	107.1	153.2	126.0	87.9	111.3	97.5
04	MASONRY	110.4	122.8	117.6	124.3	114.6	118.6	110.9	105.7	107.9	86.0	143.4	119.4	92.0	161.5	132.5	100.7	120.2	112.0
05	METALS	95.5	121.3	100.9	101.4	110.1	103.2	93.8	114.7	98.2	95.5	143.3	105.5	92.9	149.8	104.8	100.7	114.6	103.6
06	WOOD, PLASTICS & COMPOSITES	98.8	115.1	106.8	100.0	114.1	106.9	93.6	102.7	98.1	98.7	132.1	115.2	87.4	158.3	122.3	102.8	114.5	108.6
07	THERMAL & MOISTURE PROTECTION	102.2	111.4	105.3	97.6	103.6	99.6	101.6	99.3	100.9	104.7	131.3	113.6	108.0	144.7	120.3	102.4	113.5	106.1
08	OPENINGS	93.0	118.4	99.2	93.1	109.9	97.2	87.7	106.2	92.2	93.0	140.2	104.5	95.7	166.9	113.0	98.9	115.6	103.0
0920	Plaster & Gypsum Board	94.9	115.7	108.1	92.9	114.8	106.9	89.6	102.9	98.0	94.9	133.3	119.3	91.3	160.3	135.2	97.9	114.8	108.7
0950, 0980	Ceilings & Acoustic Treatment	95.6	115.7	106.8	91.0	114.8	104.3	87.6	102.9	96.2	95.6	133.3	116.7	89.4	160.3	129.1	105.6	114.8	110.8
0960	Flooring	90.4	123.9	99.0	94.9	99.7	96.1	88.5	96.9	90.7	90.4	129.2	100.4	89.6	156.4	106.7	94.6	111.4	98.9
0970, 0990	Wall Finishes & Painting/Coating	88.0	130.5	113.0	97.7	108.8	104.2	88.0	95.4	92.4	88.0	141.2	119.3	91.3	163.2	133.5	99.9	108.8	105.1
09	FINISHES	93.0	120.1	106.4	92.3	111.9	102.0	89.6	101.7	95.6	93.0	134.4	113.5	91.3	159.9	125.2	100.0	114.6	107.2
COVERS	DIVS. 10 - 14, 25, 28, 41, 43, 44, 46	100.0	107.0	101.5	100.0	103.8	100.8	100.0	97.0	99.4	100.0	111.6	102.5	100.0	123.9	105.1	100.0	107.0	101.5
21, 22, 23	FIRE SUPPRESSION, PLUMBING & HVAC	99.8	98.3	99.2	92.5	100.2	95.3	92.5	97.0	94.1	99.9	119.6	107.0	99.8	133.4	111.9	99.8	100.9	100.2
26, 27, 3370	ELECTRICAL, COMMUNICATIONS & UTIL.	88.3	89.4	88.8	79.8	100.2	88.7	83.9	88.9	86.1	88.6	127.1	105.4	94.6	129.2	109.7	86.8	86.7	86.8
MF2018	WEIGHTED AVERAGE	95.9	108.1	100.5	94.7	106.2	99.0	92.6	100.1	95.4	95.0	128.5	107.7	97.5	142.0	114.3	97.1	107.4	101.0

City Cost Indexes

		\multicolumn{18}{c}{INDIANA}															
	DIVISION	\multicolumn{3}{c}{ANDERSON 460}	\multicolumn{3}{c}{BLOOMINGTON 474}	\multicolumn{3}{c}{COLUMBUS 472}	\multicolumn{3}{c}{EVANSVILLE 476 - 477}	\multicolumn{3}{c}{FORT WAYNE 467 - 468}	\multicolumn{3}{c}{GARY 463 - 464}
		MAT.	INST.	TOTAL	MAT.	INST.	TOTAL	MAT.	INST.	TOTAL	MAT.	INST.	TOTAL	MAT.	INST.	TOTAL	MAT.	INST.	TOTAL
015433	CONTRACTOR EQUIPMENT		97.4	97.4		87.1	87.1		87.1	87.1		114.7	114.7		97.4	97.4		97.4	97.4
0241, 31 - 34	SITE & INFRASTRUCTURE, DEMOLITION	97.6	90.1	92.7	82.7	87.9	86.1	76.7	87.6	83.8	86.3	114.5	104.7	99.5	89.4	92.9	98.2	92.9	94.8
0310	Concrete Forming & Accessories	97.0	73.8	77.9	101.8	77.0	81.4	97.4	73.6	77.8	97.1	80.4	83.3	95.7	78.2	81.3	97.1	111.4	108.9
0320	Concrete Reinforcing	85.8	79.3	83.1	80.2	82.9	81.3	80.6	82.7	81.5	87.9	81.5	85.3	85.8	79.4	83.2	85.8	110.1	95.7
0330	Cast-in-Place Concrete	95.0	73.3	87.8	102.6	73.6	92.9	102.2	70.4	91.5	98.0	81.3	92.4	101.0	78.0	93.3	99.3	113.2	104.0
03	CONCRETE	90.7	75.4	84.4	100.8	77.0	91.0	100.2	74.2	89.5	100.9	81.4	92.9	93.5	79.0	87.6	92.8	111.9	100.6
04	MASONRY	99.7	74.9	85.2	98.7	70.4	82.2	98.6	67.9	80.7	93.9	77.5	84.4	103.4	76.6	87.8	101.1	105.7	103.8
05	METALS	98.0	90.1	96.3	98.9	80.7	95.1	99.0	79.1	94.8	93.4	89.7	92.6	98.0	90.0	96.3	98.0	108.9	100.3
06	WOOD, PLASTICS & COMPOSITES	93.1	73.1	83.3	115.5	77.7	96.9	111.3	73.5	92.7	94.8	80.5	87.7	93.1	78.4	85.9	91.3	109.9	100.5
07	THERMAL & MOISTURE PROTECTION	108.5	74.2	97.0	95.8	75.4	89.0	95.4	72.6	87.8	100.0	81.3	93.7	108.2	80.3	98.9	107.2	103.5	106.0
08	OPENINGS	92.0	71.5	87.1	96.6	75.3	91.4	92.8	72.7	87.9	89.7	77.8	86.9	92.0	74.6	87.8	92.0	114.3	97.4
0920	Plaster & Gypsum Board	113.0	72.5	87.2	92.0	77.8	83.0	89.3	73.5	79.3	88.4	79.7	82.8	112.8	78.0	90.6	107.8	110.4	109.5
0950, 0980	Ceilings & Acoustic Treatment	99.5	72.5	84.4	84.2	77.8	80.6	84.2	73.5	78.2	87.2	79.7	83.0	99.5	78.0	87.5	99.5	110.4	105.6
0960	Flooring	93.5	75.7	88.9	94.9	74.6	89.7	91.0	74.6	86.8	92.3	69.3	86.4	93.5	74.3	88.6	93.5	110.5	97.8
0970, 0990	Wall Finishes & Painting/Coating	97.4	69.8	81.2	84.8	75.1	79.1	84.8	72.8	77.8	92.5	86.8	89.2	97.4	69.2	80.8	97.4	116.4	108.6
09	FINISHES	97.6	73.2	85.5	92.0	76.4	84.3	90.6	73.7	82.2	91.6	78.9	85.4	97.5	76.7	87.2	96.9	111.9	104.3
COVERS	DIVS. 10 - 14, 25, 28, 41, 43, 44, 46	100.0	89.3	97.7	100.0	88.6	97.6	100.0	88.1	97.5	100.0	93.5	98.6	100.0	91.7	98.2	100.0	106.8	101.4
21, 22, 23	FIRE SUPPRESSION, PLUMBING & HVAC	99.9	76.4	91.4	99.5	77.3	91.5	92.2	76.3	86.5	99.8	78.8	92.3	99.9	73.6	90.4	99.9	97.1	98.9
26, 27, 3370	ELECTRICAL, COMMUNICATIONS & UTIL.	81.6	76.2	79.3	97.2	80.3	89.9	96.8	78.2	88.7	91.8	77.7	85.7	82.6	74.7	79.2	91.8	101.9	96.2
MF2018	WEIGHTED AVERAGE	95.7	78.0	89.0	98.1	78.2	90.6	95.6	76.3	88.3	95.7	83.0	90.9	96.4	78.7	89.7	97.1	104.6	100.0

		\multicolumn{18}{c}{INDIANA}															
	DIVISION	\multicolumn{3}{c}{INDIANAPOLIS 461 - 462}	\multicolumn{3}{c}{KOKOMO 469}	\multicolumn{3}{c}{LAFAYETTE 479}	\multicolumn{3}{c}{LAWRENCEBURG 470}	\multicolumn{3}{c}{MUNCIE 473}	\multicolumn{3}{c}{NEW ALBANY 471}
		MAT.	INST.	TOTAL	MAT.	INST.	TOTAL	MAT.	INST.	TOTAL	MAT.	INST.	TOTAL	MAT.	INST.	TOTAL	MAT.	INST.	TOTAL
015433	CONTRACTOR EQUIPMENT		101.4	101.4		97.4	97.4		87.1	87.1		102.9	102.9		96.6	96.6		94.1	94.1
0241, 31 - 34	SITE & INFRASTRUCTURE, DEMOLITION	98.4	97.2	97.6	91.2	88.6	89.5	77.1	87.7	84.0	77.4	99.6	91.8	83.6	89.6	87.5	72.8	88.6	83.1
0310	Concrete Forming & Accessories	99.8	78.3	82.0	99.3	72.0	76.8	95.5	81.1	83.6	94.5	72.4	76.3	95.6	73.1	77.0	92.2	71.1	74.8
0320	Concrete Reinforcing	88.6	83.4	86.5	77.5	83.3	79.9	80.2	83.2	81.4	79.3	71.4	76.1	88.8	79.2	84.9	80.8	78.7	79.9
0330	Cast-in-Place Concrete	88.7	87.2	88.2	94.1	78.0	88.7	102.7	74.6	93.3	96.0	70.2	87.4	107.9	71.8	95.8	99.2	70.2	89.5
03	CONCRETE	90.6	82.7	87.4	87.7	76.9	83.2	100.4	79.2	91.7	93.6	72.5	84.9	99.9	74.7	89.6	98.7	72.8	88.1
04	MASONRY	90.9	79.3	84.2	99.3	74.4	84.8	104.4	74.0	86.7	82.9	73.0	77.1	100.2	75.0	85.5	89.7	66.8	76.4
05	METALS	100.4	87.2	97.7	94.8	91.1	94.1	98.2	80.7	94.5	94.7	88.3	93.4	100.9	91.6	99.0	96.7	84.7	94.2
06	WOOD, PLASTICS & COMPOSITES	100.4	76.4	88.6	95.3	70.7	83.2	109.2	83.7	96.7	94.0	71.5	82.9	112.0	72.5	92.6	95.0	70.9	83.1
07	THERMAL & MOISTURE PROTECTION	102.0	81.9	95.2	107.6	73.9	96.3	95.4	75.6	88.8	100.2	75.0	91.8	98.2	75.7	90.7	89.1	70.6	82.9
08	OPENINGS	97.1	75.7	91.9	87.4	71.2	83.4	91.5	78.4	88.3	90.3	70.7	85.5	92.1	71.2	87.0	89.5	68.3	84.3
0920	Plaster & Gypsum Board	94.8	75.6	82.6	117.0	70.0	87.1	86.7	84.1	85.0	74.3	71.4	72.4	88.4	72.5	78.3	86.3	70.5	76.2
0950, 0980	Ceilings & Acoustic Treatment	94.9	75.6	84.1	100.8	70.0	83.6	78.9	84.1	81.8	94.2	71.4	81.4	84.2	72.5	77.7	87.2	70.5	77.9
0960	Flooring	94.6	81.6	91.3	96.5	87.7	94.3	90.1	81.6	87.9	68.0	74.6	69.7	91.6	75.7	87.5	89.4	47.0	78.5
0970, 0990	Wall Finishes & Painting/Coating	99.9	78.9	87.5	97.4	61.4	76.3	84.8	80.1	82.0	85.1	65.6	73.6	84.8	69.8	76.0	92.5	58.9	72.8
09	FINISHES	96.7	78.6	87.8	99.2	73.3	86.4	88.6	81.4	85.0	84.6	72.1	78.4	90.3	72.7	81.6	90.7	65.0	78.0
COVERS	DIVS. 10 - 14, 25, 28, 41, 43, 44, 46	100.0	91.7	98.2	100.0	89.1	97.7	100.0	88.8	97.6	100.0	82.1	96.2	100.0	87.9	97.4	100.0	81.9	96.1
21, 22, 23	FIRE SUPPRESSION, PLUMBING & HVAC	99.9	78.9	92.3	92.6	76.6	86.8	92.2	76.0	86.4	93.4	69.4	84.8	99.5	76.2	91.1	92.5	72.0	85.2
26, 27, 3370	ELECTRICAL, COMMUNICATIONS & UTIL.	95.7	86.2	91.5	83.9	69.5	77.7	96.5	72.1	85.9	90.0	66.4	79.7	87.9	67.9	79.2	91.2	67.1	80.7
MF2018	WEIGHTED AVERAGE	97.6	82.9	92.0	92.9	77.1	87.0	95.5	78.2	89.0	92.2	74.6	85.6	96.9	76.7	89.3	93.4	72.4	85.5

		\multicolumn{9}{c}{INDIANA}	\multicolumn{9}{c}{IOWA}
	DIVISION	\multicolumn{3}{c}{SOUTH BEND 465 - 466}	\multicolumn{3}{c}{TERRE HAUTE 478}	\multicolumn{3}{c}{WASHINGTON 475}	\multicolumn{3}{c}{BURLINGTON 526}	\multicolumn{3}{c}{CARROLL 514}	\multicolumn{3}{c}{CEDAR RAPIDS 522 - 524}
		MAT.	INST.	TOTAL	MAT.	INST.	TOTAL	MAT.	INST.	TOTAL	MAT.	INST.	TOTAL	MAT.	INST.	TOTAL	MAT.	INST.	TOTAL
015433	CONTRACTOR EQUIPMENT		106.5	106.5		114.7	114.7		114.7	114.7		98.7	98.7		98.7	98.7		95.0	95.0
0241, 31 - 34	SITE & INFRASTRUCTURE, DEMOLITION	94.7	100.4	98.4	87.4	114.6	105.1	83.1	114.5	103.6	80.3	90.4	86.9	74.9	91.1	85.5	84.9	90.6	88.6
0310	Concrete Forming & Accessories	99.3	81.0	84.2	97.7	76.4	80.2	98.2	75.2	79.2	97.1	83.7	86.0	87.8	74.6	76.9	101.7	86.6	89.2
0320	Concrete Reinforcing	82.6	81.3	82.1	87.9	83.3	86.0	81.3	77.6	79.8	90.8	85.1	88.4	91.4	74.7	84.6	91.4	98.8	94.4
0330	Cast-in-Place Concrete	98.7	80.6	92.6	94.9	75.9	88.5	103.3	81.1	95.9	102.2	52.1	85.5	102.2	75.6	93.3	102.5	80.1	95.0
03	CONCRETE	103.2	81.4	94.3	103.3	78.0	92.9	109.1	78.4	96.5	96.6	73.2	87.0	95.6	75.7	87.4	96.6	86.9	92.6
04	MASONRY	118.5	75.7	93.5	101.8	74.2	85.8	94.1	71.8	81.1	106.3	63.2	81.2	107.7	63.7	82.1	112.1	79.2	93.0
05	METALS	100.4	89.9	98.2	94.0	90.1	93.2	88.5	87.6	88.3	88.1	91.2	88.8	88.2	87.7	88.1	90.1	100.3	92.2
06	WOOD, PLASTICS & COMPOSITES	102.5	81.0	91.9	96.4	76.5	86.6	96.7	74.3	85.7	94.8	87.3	91.1	84.6	78.7	81.7	100.3	88.4	94.4
07	THERMAL & MOISTURE PROTECTION	100.9	78.8	93.5	100.0	77.5	92.5	100.0	77.6	92.5	104.4	68.7	92.4	104.6	70.2	93.1	105.2	78.8	96.3
08	OPENINGS	98.1	76.9	93.0	90.3	74.0	86.3	87.6	73.9	84.3	89.6	84.7	88.4	93.9	74.5	89.2	94.2	87.9	92.6
0920	Plaster & Gypsum Board	101.0	80.1	87.7	88.4	75.6	80.3	87.5	73.3	78.5	104.0	86.9	93.1	101.1	78.1	86.5	108.7	88.3	95.7
0950, 0980	Ceilings & Acoustic Treatment	103.7	80.1	90.5	87.2	75.6	80.7	81.4	73.3	76.9	106.6	86.9	95.6	106.6	78.1	90.6	109.7	88.3	97.7
0960	Flooring	94.6	87.0	92.7	92.3	76.4	88.2	93.0	74.6	88.3	96.4	60.2	87.1	91.8	69.2	86.0	110.8	80.2	102.9
0970, 0990	Wall Finishes & Painting/Coating	99.9	81.1	88.8	92.5	72.2	80.6	92.5	84.7	87.9	93.5	73.6	81.8	93.5	73.6	81.8	94.6	66.0	78.6
09	FINISHES	100.5	82.1	91.4	91.6	75.6	83.7	90.4	75.8	83.2	99.0	79.3	89.2	96.6	73.9	85.4	104.7	83.5	94.2
COVERS	DIVS. 10 - 14, 25, 28, 41, 43, 44, 46	100.0	91.3	98.2	100.0	90.6	98.0	100.0	92.4	98.4	100.0	92.8	98.5	100.0	89.1	97.7	100.0	92.2	98.3
21, 22, 23	FIRE SUPPRESSION, PLUMBING & HVAC	99.8	77.9	91.9	99.8	76.8	91.5	92.5	73.8	85.8	92.8	73.7	85.9	92.8	68.5	84.0	100.1	82.3	93.7
26, 27, 3370	ELECTRICAL, COMMUNICATIONS & UTIL.	95.9	79.7	88.8	91.0	76.6	84.7	91.3	75.2	84.3	90.5	62.4	78.3	90.8	66.5	80.2	89.3	72.0	81.8
MF2018	WEIGHTED AVERAGE	100.6	82.1	93.6	96.5	80.9	90.6	93.7	79.7	88.4	93.5	75.5	86.7	93.5	73.8	86.1	96.7	84.0	91.9

City Cost Indexes

		IOWA																
	DIVISION	COUNCIL BLUFFS 515			CRESTON 508			DAVENPORT 527 - 528			DECORAH 521			DES MOINES 500 - 503,509			DUBUQUE 520		
		MAT.	INST.	TOTAL	MAT.	INST.	TOTAL	MAT.	INST.	TOTAL	MAT.	INST.	TOTAL	MAT.	INST.	TOTAL	MAT.	INST.	TOTAL
015433	CONTRACTOR EQUIPMENT		94.3	94.3		101.8	101.8		98.7	98.7		98.7	98.7		110.4	110.4		93.9	93.9
0241, 31 - 34	SITE & INFRASTRUCTURE, DEMOLITION	84.8	87.4	86.5	87.6	97.6	94.1	84.3	94.1	90.6	79.4	90.2	86.4	95.4	110.3	105.1	83.3	88.3	86.6
0310	Concrete Forming & Accessories	87.2	77.9	79.5	88.3	77.0	79.0	101.2	92.8	94.3	95.3	64.0	69.5	104.4	89.9	92.5	88.4	77.4	79.3
0320	Concrete Reinforcing	93.3	82.3	88.8	75.4	74.7	75.1	91.4	91.4	91.4	90.8	74.1	84.0	82.8	99.2	89.5	90.2	98.2	93.4
0330	Cast-in-Place Concrete	106.6	85.2	99.4	99.9	79.5	93.1	98.7	91.4	96.3	99.4	70.3	89.7	85.2	96.3	88.9	100.4	79.8	93.5
03	CONCRETE	99.0	81.9	92.0	92.4	78.1	86.5	94.7	92.7	93.9	94.6	68.9	84.1	91.1	94.1	92.4	93.7	82.6	89.1
04	MASONRY	112.4	76.6	91.6	135.0	70.3	97.3	107.5	90.2	97.4	128.5	60.8	89.1	117.3	88.5	100.5	113.2	66.4	85.9
05	METALS	93.4	92.5	93.3	90.1	86.8	89.4	90.1	102.5	92.7	88.3	86.5	87.9	94.9	100.5	96.1	88.2	99.8	90.6
06	WOOD, PLASTICS & COMPOSITES	83.7	77.6	80.7	89.6	78.7	84.2	100.3	92.3	96.3	92.6	63.2	78.1	108.6	89.0	99.0	85.0	77.5	81.3
07	THERMAL & MOISTURE PROTECTION	104.7	74.4	94.6	111.8	74.6	99.4	104.7	87.5	98.9	104.5	72.1	90.5	103.6	90.5	98.2	104.9	73.3	94.3
08	OPENINGS	93.4	80.4	90.3	107.4	76.0	99.8	94.2	93.4	94.0	92.5	68.9	86.8	98.3	94.3	97.3	93.4	83.6	91.0
0920	Plaster & Gypsum Board	101.1	77.2	85.9	117.6	78.1	92.5	108.7	92.1	98.1	103.2	62.1	77.1	104.1	88.4	94.1	101.1	77.1	85.8
0950, 0980	Ceilings & Acoustic Treatment	106.6	77.2	90.1	99.3	78.1	87.4	109.7	92.1	99.8	106.6	62.1	81.7	103.7	88.4	95.2	106.6	77.1	90.1
0960	Flooring	90.8	75.1	86.8	84.4	60.2	78.2	98.4	82.6	94.3	96.3	60.2	87.0	94.6	89.9	93.4	103.4	71.2	95.1
0970, 0990	Wall Finishes & Painting/Coating	90.2	58.0	71.3	88.8	73.6	79.9	93.5	95.7	94.8	93.5	73.6	81.8	99.9	82.9	89.9	95.9	72.5	82.1
09	FINISHES	96.8	75.1	86.1	95.2	73.7	84.5	100.9	91.1	96.1	98.8	64.0	81.6	101.3	89.0	95.3	100.7	75.4	88.2
COVERS	DIVS. 10 - 14, 25, 28, 41, 43, 44, 46	100.0	91.4	98.2	100.0	91.2	98.1	100.0	95.1	99.0	100.0	88.7	97.6	100.0	95.1	99.0	100.0	90.2	97.9
21, 22, 23	FIRE SUPPRESSION, PLUMBING & HVAC	100.1	74.9	91.0	92.8	70.2	84.7	100.1	96.5	98.8	92.8	65.5	83.0	100.0	85.7	94.8	100.1	77.4	91.9
26, 27, 3370	ELECTRICAL, COMMUNICATIONS & UTIL.	91.9	81.6	87.4	87.2	66.5	78.2	86.9	79.1	83.5	89.3	40.8	68.2	95.8	89.6	93.1	91.2	69.1	81.6
MF2018	WEIGHTED AVERAGE	97.1	80.3	90.8	95.9	75.8	88.3	95.7	92.0	94.3	94.4	66.2	83.7	98.3	92.1	96.0	95.7	78.8	89.3

		IOWA																
	DIVISION	FORT DODGE 505			MASON CITY 504			OTTUMWA 525			SHENANDOAH 516			SIBLEY 512			SIOUX CITY 510 - 511		
		MAT.	INST.	TOTAL	MAT.	INST.	TOTAL	MAT.	INST.	TOTAL	MAT.	INST.	TOTAL	MAT.	INST.	TOTAL	MAT.	INST.	TOTAL
015433	CONTRACTOR EQUIPMENT		101.8	101.8		101.8	101.8		93.9	93.9		94.3	94.3		98.7	98.7		98.7	98.7
0241, 31 - 34	SITE & INFRASTRUCTURE, DEMOLITION	96.7	94.8	95.4	96.8	95.7	96.1	79.9	85.7	83.7	80.5	86.8	84.6	85.3	90.1	88.5	90.3	92.2	91.5
0310	Concrete Forming & Accessories	88.8	69.4	72.8	92.1	63.7	68.7	93.6	77.5	80.3	88.6	68.7	72.2	89.0	34.2	43.8	101.7	76.3	80.8
0320	Concrete Reinforcing	75.4	74.1	74.9	75.3	81.3	77.8	90.8	85.2	88.5	93.3	74.7	85.7	93.3	74.0	85.4	91.4	98.2	94.2
0330	Cast-in-Place Concrete	93.8	41.9	76.4	93.8	67.2	84.9	102.9	59.5	88.4	103.0	76.0	94.0	100.9	52.7	84.8	101.6	83.3	95.5
03	CONCRETE	88.1	61.2	77.1	88.3	68.8	80.3	96.2	73.1	86.7	96.6	73.2	87.0	95.6	49.2	76.6	96.0	83.3	90.8
04	MASONRY	133.8	45.8	82.6	151.5	59.9	98.2	109.1	48.6	73.9	112.0	65.5	84.9	132.3	45.9	82.0	105.8	65.0	82.1
05	METALS	90.1	84.8	89.0	90.2	88.3	89.8	88.1	92.4	89.0	93.4	88.4	92.4	88.4	85.7	87.8	90.1	99.4	92.0
06	WOOD, PLASTICS & COMPOSITES	90.0	78.7	84.4	93.7	63.2	78.7	90.4	87.1	88.8	85.0	69.9	77.6	85.6	30.9	58.7	100.3	77.6	89.1
07	THERMAL & MOISTURE PROTECTION	111.3	60.2	94.2	111.0	64.7	95.5	105.0	62.3	90.7	104.2	65.5	91.2	104.4	50.1	86.2	104.7	70.3	93.2
08	OPENINGS	101.0	67.2	92.7	92.7	70.8	87.4	93.9	82.0	91.0	85.3	67.6	81.0	90.7	40.8	78.6	94.2	81.4	91.0
0920	Plaster & Gypsum Board	117.6	78.1	92.5	117.6	62.1	82.3	101.3	86.9	92.2	101.1	69.2	80.8	101.1	28.8	55.1	108.7	77.0	88.5
0950, 0980	Ceilings & Acoustic Treatment	99.3	78.1	87.4	99.3	62.1	78.5	106.6	86.9	95.6	106.6	69.2	85.7	106.6	28.8	63.0	109.7	77.0	91.4
0960	Flooring	85.5	60.2	79.0	87.1	60.2	80.2	105.9	60.2	94.2	91.4	64.4	84.5	92.6	60.2	84.3	98.4	69.1	90.9
0970, 0990	Wall Finishes & Painting/Coating	88.8	70.7	78.2	88.8	73.6	79.9	95.9	73.6	82.8	90.2	73.6	80.4	93.5	72.7	81.3	93.5	69.7	79.5
09	FINISHES	96.9	69.0	83.1	97.3	63.8	80.7	101.5	74.9	88.4	96.9	68.2	82.7	98.2	41.2	70.0	101.6	74.2	88.1
COVERS	DIVS. 10 - 14, 25, 28, 41, 43, 44, 46	100.0	85.4	96.9	100.0	88.3	97.5	100.0	86.8	97.2	100.0	88.0	97.4	100.0	80.4	95.8	100.0	89.9	97.9
21, 22, 23	FIRE SUPPRESSION, PLUMBING & HVAC	92.8	62.8	82.0	92.8	68.4	84.0	92.8	64.3	82.5	92.8	73.8	85.9	92.8	62.9	82.0	100.1	77.6	92.0
26, 27, 3370	ELECTRICAL, COMMUNICATIONS & UTIL.	90.4	59.9	77.1	89.9	40.8	68.5	90.4	61.3	77.7	89.3	67.8	79.9	89.3	40.8	68.2	89.3	66.5	79.4
MF2018	WEIGHTED AVERAGE	95.5	66.6	84.6	95.7	67.4	85.0	94.1	70.5	85.2	94.1	73.4	86.3	94.6	56.2	80.1	96.3	78.4	89.5

		IOWA						KANSAS										
	DIVISION	SPENCER 513			WATERLOO 506 - 507			BELLEVILLE 669			COLBY 677			DODGE CITY 678			EMPORIA 668		
		MAT.	INST.	TOTAL	MAT.	INST.	TOTAL	MAT.	INST.	TOTAL	MAT.	INST.	TOTAL	MAT.	INST.	TOTAL	MAT.	INST.	TOTAL
015433	CONTRACTOR EQUIPMENT		98.7	98.7		101.8	101.8		105.0	105.0		103.1	103.1		103.1	103.1		102.9	102.9
0241, 31 - 34	SITE & INFRASTRUCTURE, DEMOLITION	85.3	89.0	87.7	104.7	97.7	100.1	91.6	96.9	95.0	85.7	93.7	90.9	90.9	94.3	93.1	87.0	94.0	91.5
0310	Concrete Forming & Accessories	93.6	33.9	44.3	101.7	70.8	76.2	101.0	49.3	58.3	105.4	54.8	63.6	99.6	56.5	64.0	93.7	62.4	67.9
0320	Concrete Reinforcing	93.3	74.0	85.4	75.9	98.6	85.2	88.1	99.5	92.7	91.7	99.5	94.9	89.4	99.4	93.4	86.9	99.6	92.1
0330	Cast-in-Place Concrete	100.9	61.3	87.7	100.5	82.2	94.4	97.9	77.2	91.0	89.0	79.6	85.8	90.6	83.7	88.3	94.6	79.4	89.5
03	CONCRETE	95.9	52.1	77.9	93.6	80.5	88.2	104.8	69.0	90.1	99.8	72.4	88.6	101.0	74.6	90.1	97.7	75.8	88.7
04	MASONRY	132.5	45.9	82.0	134.6	74.0	99.3	100.7	53.3	73.1	86.8	56.8	69.4	94.8	55.0	71.6	107.1	58.1	78.6
05	METALS	88.3	85.3	87.7	92.0	99.2	93.5	94.5	93.5	94.3	94.8	94.4	94.7	94.6	94.9	94.6	94.2	94.5	94.3
06	WOOD, PLASTICS & COMPOSITES	90.3	30.9	61.1	105.2	68.1	86.9	100.1	45.6	73.3	100.2	51.2	76.1	93.3	51.9	73.0	92.3	61.2	77.0
07	THERMAL & MOISTURE PROTECTION	105.0	50.6	86.7	111.2	77.1	99.8	100.4	58.3	86.3	105.4	60.3	90.3	105.4	63.8	91.5	98.9	67.6	88.4
08	OPENINGS	101.8	40.8	87.0	92.8	78.8	89.4	89.6	57.5	81.8	94.1	60.6	86.0	94.1	61.0	86.0	87.7	68.0	82.9
0920	Plaster & Gypsum Board	101.3	28.8	55.1	123.9	67.1	87.8	91.1	44.2	61.2	102.6	49.8	69.0	97.6	50.6	67.7	88.4	60.2	70.5
0950, 0980	Ceilings & Acoustic Treatment	106.6	28.8	63.0	101.9	67.1	82.5	71.3	44.2	56.1	88.6	49.8	66.9	88.6	50.6	67.3	71.3	60.2	65.1
0960	Flooring	94.7	60.2	85.8	91.2	75.1	87.1	92.5	59.5	84.0	88.7	59.5	81.2	85.9	60.7	79.4	89.0	59.5	81.4
0970, 0990	Wall Finishes & Painting/Coating	93.5	49.8	67.8	88.8	87.0	87.7	94.4	99.1	97.2	98.6	99.1	98.9	98.6	99.1	98.9	94.4	99.1	97.2
09	FINISHES	98.8	37.7	68.6	100.2	72.4	86.5	86.6	55.0	71.0	91.7	59.1	75.6	90.0	60.3	75.5	84.5	65.0	74.9
COVERS	DIVS. 10 - 14, 25, 28, 41, 43, 44, 46	100.0	80.3	95.8	100.0	89.8	97.8	100.0	73.2	94.3	100.0	75.1	94.7	100.0	78.7	95.5	100.0	74.8	94.6
21, 22, 23	FIRE SUPPRESSION, PLUMBING & HVAC	92.8	62.9	82.0	100.1	79.7	92.8	92.3	62.8	81.7	92.7	62.6	81.9	100.0	70.5	89.4	92.3	64.7	82.4
26, 27, 3370	ELECTRICAL, COMMUNICATIONS & UTIL.	90.2	40.8	68.7	88.2	57.6	74.9	93.4	54.2	76.3	95.0	58.6	79.2	93.6	63.9	80.6	92.0	57.8	77.1
MF2018	WEIGHTED AVERAGE	95.7	56.1	80.7	97.9	78.2	90.5	94.9	65.4	83.8	94.9	67.5	84.5	96.8	70.5	86.9	93.6	69.8	84.6

City Cost Indexes

KANSAS

DIVISION		FORT SCOTT 667			HAYS 676			HUTCHINSON 675			INDEPENDENCE 673			KANSAS CITY 660 - 662			LIBERAL 679		
		MAT.	INST.	TOTAL	MAT.	INST.	TOTAL	MAT.	INST.	TOTAL	MAT.	INST.	TOTAL	MAT.	INST.	TOTAL	MAT.	INST.	TOTAL
015433	CONTRACTOR EQUIPMENT		103.9	103.9		103.1	103.1		103.1	103.1		103.1	103.1		101.4	101.4		103.1	103.1
0241, 31 - 34	SITE & INFRASTRUCTURE, DEMOLITION	84.9	94.5	91.1	88.0	93.6	91.7	76.2	94.1	87.9	88.0	94.2	92.0	86.5	95.6	92.4	87.4	93.8	91.6
0310	Concrete Forming & Accessories	108.0	73.7	79.7	103.2	53.5	62.2	94.9	50.9	58.6	112.5	60.6	69.7	105.2	96.6	98.1	99.9	52.8	61.1
0320	Concrete Reinforcing	86.3	87.6	86.9	89.4	99.5	93.5	89.4	99.5	93.5	88.8	87.7	88.4	83.7	101.1	90.8	90.7	99.2	94.2
0330	Cast-in-Place Concrete	87.8	75.5	83.7	70.2	77.8	72.7	65.0	79.7	69.9	90.9	79.8	87.2	75.1	97.0	82.4	70.2	76.8	72.4
03	CONCRETE	93.5	77.5	86.9	93.7	71.1	84.4	77.6	70.7	74.7	102.0	73.1	90.1	86.7	97.8	91.2	95.6	70.5	85.3
04	MASONRY	109.6	49.5	74.6	93.8	53.4	70.3	87.6	56.9	69.7	84.0	56.9	68.2	109.3	98.1	102.8	92.9	47.3	66.3
05	METALS	94.2	90.5	93.4	94.4	94.4	94.4	94.3	94.7	94.4	94.2	90.6	93.4	101.9	102.3	102.0	94.7	94.4	94.6
06	WOOD, PLASTICS & COMPOSITES	109.1	80.3	94.9	97.8	51.2	74.8	99.3	45.7	67.8	109.3	58.6	84.4	105.2	95.6	100.5	93.8	51.2	72.8
07	THERMAL & MOISTURE PROTECTION	99.7	69.9	89.7	105.8	58.9	90.1	104.3	59.4	89.3	105.5	71.7	94.2	99.4	98.1	99.0	106.0	56.5	89.4
08	OPENINGS	87.7	75.8	84.8	94.1	60.6	85.9	94.0	57.7	85.2	92.1	62.0	84.7	88.7	95.5	90.4	94.1	60.6	86.0
0920	Plaster & Gypsum Board	93.2	79.9	84.8	101.0	49.8	68.4	96.9	44.4	63.5	109.5	57.5	76.4	86.6	95.7	92.4	98.1	49.8	67.4
0950, 0980	Ceilings & Acoustic Treatment	71.3	79.9	76.1	88.6	49.8	66.9	88.6	44.4	63.8	88.6	57.5	71.2	71.3	95.7	84.9	88.6	49.8	66.9
0960	Flooring	101.3	58.2	90.2	87.8	59.5	80.6	83.8	59.5	77.6	91.9	58.2	83.3	82.0	95.7	85.5	86.1	59.5	79.3
0970, 0990	Wall Finishes & Painting/Coating	96.1	67.4	79.3	98.6	99.1	98.9	98.6	99.1	98.9	98.6	99.1	98.9	103.3	106.2	105.0	98.6	99.1	98.9
09	FINISHES	88.9	71.1	80.1	91.6	58.3	75.1	88.5	56.0	72.5	93.6	63.7	78.8	85.4	97.3	91.3	91.0	57.8	74.6
COVERS	DIVS. 10 - 14, 25, 28, 41, 43, 44, 46	100.0	75.6	94.8	100.0	73.9	94.4	100.0	74.5	94.6	100.0	75.9	94.9	100.0	96.2	99.2	100.0	73.3	94.3
21, 22, 23	FIRE SUPPRESSION, PLUMBING & HVAC	92.3	59.3	80.4	92.7	60.4	81.1	92.7	62.6	81.9	92.7	62.0	81.7	99.5	100.1	99.8	92.7	61.1	81.3
26, 27, 3370	ELECTRICAL, COMMUNICATIONS & UTIL.	91.6	58.6	77.2	94.5	58.6	78.9	92.2	52.7	75.0	93.2	62.9	80.0	94.3	92.2	93.4	93.6	58.6	78.4
MF2018	WEIGHTED AVERAGE	93.6	69.3	84.4	94.3	66.3	83.8	91.2	65.8	81.6	94.8	68.9	85.0	96.1	97.5	96.6	94.4	65.6	83.5

KANSAS / KENTUCKY

DIVISION		SALINA 674			TOPEKA 664 - 666			WICHITA 670 - 672			ASHLAND 411 - 412			BOWLING GREEN 421 - 422			CAMPTON 413 - 414		
		MAT.	INST.	TOTAL	MAT.	INST.	TOTAL	MAT.	INST.	TOTAL	MAT.	INST.	TOTAL	MAT.	INST.	TOTAL	MAT.	INST.	TOTAL
015433	CONTRACTOR EQUIPMENT		103.1	103.1		112.3	112.3		110.3	110.3		99.4	99.4		94.1	94.1		100.9	100.9
0241, 31 - 34	SITE & INFRASTRUCTURE, DEMOLITION	85.0	93.9	90.8	88.0	107.9	100.9	84.1	104.2	97.2	102.9	78.2	86.8	76.2	89.6	84.9	80.8	89.7	86.6
0310	Concrete Forming & Accessories	96.6	57.3	64.2	102.6	68.6	74.6	103.0	57.7	65.6	92.3	79.7	81.9	89.5	79.2	81.0	93.2	72.2	75.8
0320	Concrete Reinforcing	88.8	91.1	89.8	84.9	92.5	88.0	83.0	100.7	90.2	82.7	93.2	87.0	79.7	81.2	80.3	80.5	80.9	80.6
0330	Cast-in-Place Concrete	78.6	80.5	79.3	83.3	86.1	84.2	73.5	79.4	75.5	90.2	85.2	88.6	89.5	69.8	82.9	99.9	62.8	87.4
03	CONCRETE	89.6	72.5	82.6	91.3	79.7	86.5	86.2	73.7	81.1	94.5	85.4	90.8	92.8	76.9	86.3	96.9	71.1	86.3
04	MASONRY	106.8	52.6	75.3	103.1	62.2	79.3	85.2	54.3	67.2	99.5	80.8	88.6	101.4	69.3	82.7	99.2	48.2	69.5
05	METALS	94.4	92.7	94.0	96.8	92.7	95.9	96.8	94.6	96.3	96.1	108.8	98.7	96.5	91.0	95.3	96.7	89.0	95.1
06	WOOD, PLASTICS & COMPOSITES	90.4	56.0	73.5	106.1	69.0	87.8	106.0	54.8	80.8	77.1	77.8	77.4	91.0	80.2	85.7	89.9	78.4	84.2
07	THERMAL & MOISTURE PROTECTION	104.9	60.1	89.9	102.5	81.3	95.4	102.6	63.8	89.6	92.0	80.2	88.0	89.1	79.7	86.0	100.1	61.0	87.0
08	OPENINGS	94.1	61.7	86.2	97.1	72.7	91.2	97.1	64.1	89.1	87.4	81.2	85.9	89.5	78.0	86.7	90.8	77.1	87.5
0920	Plaster & Gypsum Board	96.9	54.8	70.1	98.9	67.8	79.1	103.6	53.1	71.5	61.7	77.5	71.7	83.2	80.1	81.2	83.2	77.5	79.6
0950, 0980	Ceilings & Acoustic Treatment	88.6	54.8	69.7	86.2	67.8	75.9	107.2	53.1	76.9	84.2	77.5	80.5	87.2	80.1	83.2	87.2	77.5	81.8
0960	Flooring	84.7	60.7	78.6	94.6	68.3	87.9	94.9	92.3	94.2	73.7	70.8	72.9	87.8	61.9	81.1	90.3	56.0	81.5
0970, 0990	Wall Finishes & Painting/Coating	98.6	99.1	98.9	99.9	99.1	99.4	100.5	96.2	98.0	95.6	96.7	96.3	92.5	66.8	77.4	92.5	46.9	65.7
09	FINISHES	89.4	61.2	75.4	95.1	71.0	83.2	101.5	67.1	84.5	80.7	79.6	80.1	89.5	74.5	82.2	90.6	66.9	78.9
COVERS	DIVS. 10 - 14, 25, 28, 41, 43, 44, 46	100.0	85.4	96.9	100.0	80.2	95.8	100.0	86.9	97.2	100.0	76.6	95.0	100.0	89.4	97.7	100.0	84.3	96.6
21, 22, 23	FIRE SUPPRESSION, PLUMBING & HVAC	100.0	67.4	88.3	99.7	72.0	89.8	99.7	68.5	88.5	92.2	81.6	88.4	99.8	78.1	92.0	92.5	67.2	83.4
26, 27, 3370	ELECTRICAL, COMMUNICATIONS & UTIL.	93.4	71.3	83.8	95.6	64.6	82.1	95.8	71.3	85.2	89.2	76.3	83.6	91.5	74.9	84.3	90.1	76.2	84.0
MF2018	WEIGHTED AVERAGE	95.6	70.5	86.1	97.1	75.8	89.1	96.2	73.0	87.4	92.6	82.8	88.9	94.9	78.5	88.7	94.1	71.5	85.6

KENTUCKY

DIVISION		CORBIN 407 - 409			COVINGTON 410			ELIZABETHTOWN 427			FRANKFORT 406			HAZARD 417 - 418			HENDERSON 424		
		MAT.	INST.	TOTAL	MAT.	INST.	TOTAL	MAT.	INST.	TOTAL	MAT.	INST.	TOTAL	MAT.	INST.	TOTAL	MAT.	INST.	TOTAL
015433	CONTRACTOR EQUIPMENT		103.4	103.4		102.9	102.9		94.1	94.1		105.3	105.3		100.9	100.9		114.7	114.7
0241, 31 - 34	SITE & INFRASTRUCTURE, DEMOLITION	80.8	92.5	88.4	78.2	99.5	92.0	68.7	87.9	81.2	80.4	98.4	92.1	79.2	90.7	86.7	74.9	112.9	99.7
0310	Concrete Forming & Accessories	94.8	67.6	72.3	89.5	73.6	76.4	85.6	64.3	68.0	106.3	69.9	76.2	90.5	72.9	76.0	95.4	68.3	73.0
0320	Concrete Reinforcing	76.9	80.2	78.3	79.0	78.1	78.6	80.1	72.8	77.1	85.0	73.1	80.1	80.8	80.5	80.7	79.8	73.3	77.2
0330	Cast-in-Place Concrete	91.1	68.2	83.5	95.5	79.7	90.2	80.8	62.3	74.6	89.5	72.0	83.6	96.0	64.1	85.3	79.0	76.9	78.3
03	CONCRETE	86.7	70.8	80.2	95.0	77.5	87.8	84.9	66.1	77.2	90.9	71.8	83.1	93.7	71.9	84.7	89.4	73.0	82.7
04	MASONRY	94.6	52.9	70.3	114.3	69.2	88.1	84.7	54.5	67.1	92.0	65.5	76.5	96.6	49.9	69.4	104.3	69.2	83.9
05	METALS	99.9	87.2	97.3	94.7	91.6	94.0	96.5	85.6	94.3	103.0	83.3	98.9	96.7	88.9	95.1	88.4	85.8	87.8
06	WOOD, PLASTICS & COMPOSITES	86.1	69.1	77.7	88.5	74.0	81.4	87.1	65.6	76.5	109.7	68.9	89.6	87.3	78.4	82.9	92.9	67.3	80.3
07	THERMAL & MOISTURE PROTECTION	105.5	64.0	91.6	100.4	69.3	90.0	88.8	61.3	79.5	103.1	70.8	92.3	100.0	62.4	87.4	99.4	73.9	90.8
08	OPENINGS	91.0	62.3	84.0	91.2	75.0	87.3	89.5	64.4	83.4	97.1	71.1	90.8	91.2	77.0	87.7	88.0	69.3	83.5
0920	Plaster & Gypsum Board	99.3	67.7	79.2	71.7	74.0	73.2	82.0	65.1	71.3	107.1	67.7	82.0	82.0	77.5	79.1	84.4	66.1	72.8
0950, 0980	Ceilings & Acoustic Treatment	90.2	67.7	77.6	94.2	74.0	82.9	87.2	65.1	74.8	127.5	67.7	94.1	87.2	77.5	81.8	81.4	66.1	72.9
0960	Flooring	87.4	56.0	79.3	66.1	82.1	70.2	85.7	64.3	80.2	94.6	68.4	87.9	89.0	56.0	80.6	91.5	66.2	85.0
0970, 0990	Wall Finishes & Painting/Coating	91.8	53.9	69.6	85.1	61.9	71.5	92.5	59.3	73.0	99.9	79.8	88.1	92.5	46.9	65.7	92.5	75.5	82.5
09	FINISHES	90.3	64.1	77.3	83.9	73.8	78.9	88.8	63.1	76.1	106.7	70.6	88.9	90.0	67.4	78.8	89.1	67.8	79.0
COVERS	DIVS. 10 - 14, 25, 28, 41, 43, 44, 46	100.0	86.0	97.0	100.0	88.1	97.5	100.0	82.8	96.3	100.0	87.3	97.3	100.0	80.9	95.9	100.0	49.0	89.1
21, 22, 23	FIRE SUPPRESSION, PLUMBING & HVAC	92.8	65.3	82.9	93.4	78.1	87.9	92.8	68.5	84.1	99.8	71.2	89.6	92.5	68.2	83.8	92.8	69.7	84.5
26, 27, 3370	ELECTRICAL, COMMUNICATIONS & UTIL.	89.9	76.2	84.0	91.4	76.9	85.1	90.0	67.3	80.1	96.9	67.3	84.0	90.1	76.2	84.0	91.2	67.3	80.8
MF2018	WEIGHTED AVERAGE	93.5	70.7	84.9	93.9	79.0	88.3	91.1	68.9	82.7	98.8	73.6	89.3	93.5	72.1	85.4	91.5	73.7	84.8

City Cost Indexes

KENTUCKY

DIVISION		LEXINGTON 403-405			LOUISVILLE 400-402			OWENSBORO 423			PADUCAH 420			PIKEVILLE 415-416			SOMERSET 425-426		
		MAT.	INST.	TOTAL	MAT.	INST.	TOTAL	MAT.	INST.	TOTAL	MAT.	INST.	TOTAL	MAT.	INST.	TOTAL	MAT.	INST.	TOTAL
015433	CONTRACTOR EQUIPMENT		103.4	103.4		110.7	110.7		114.7	114.7		114.7	114.7		99.4	99.4		100.9	100.9
0241, 31-34	SITE & INFRASTRUCTURE, DEMOLITION	86.1	95.7	92.4	80.6	110.1	99.8	85.5	115.0	104.7	76.5	113.0	100.3	109.9	77.5	88.8	74.0	90.2	84.6
0310	Concrete Forming & Accessories	105.1	78.3	83.0	105.7	78.8	83.5	94.1	80.5	82.9	92.7	71.9	75.6	98.9	75.9	79.9	91.3	68.0	72.0
0320	Concrete Reinforcing	84.5	80.0	82.6	85.0	80.0	82.9	79.8	81.7	80.6	80.3	71.7	76.8	83.1	93.1	87.2	80.1	80.4	80.2
0330	Cast-in-Place Concrete	93.3	89.0	91.8	89.5	74.8	84.6	92.3	85.4	90.0	84.2	73.9	80.8	99.3	80.7	93.0	79.0	79.7	79.2
03	CONCRETE	89.6	83.0	86.9	90.8	78.1	85.6	101.3	83.1	93.9	94.0	73.4	85.5	107.5	82.1	97.1	80.4	75.1	78.2
04	MASONRY	94.4	71.7	81.2	92.0	68.4	78.2	97.1	79.6	86.9	101.0	69.6	82.7	98.7	73.1	83.8	91.9	55.6	70.8
05	METALS	102.0	90.2	99.5	103.0	87.7	99.8	88.4	92.9	89.3	88.2	86.3	87.8	96.0	108.3	98.5	96.6	88.8	95.0
06	WOOD, PLASTICS & COMPOSITES	98.9	77.1	88.2	109.3	80.9	95.3	91.3	79.8	85.7	89.6	72.3	81.1	84.5	77.8	81.2	87.7	68.9	78.5
07	THERMAL & MOISTURE PROTECTION	105.8	81.8	97.7	103.2	78.8	95.0	100.0	83.8	94.6	99.5	73.8	90.9	92.6	71.4	85.5	99.4	65.0	87.9
08	OPENINGS	91.0	77.4	87.7	97.1	76.1	92.0	88.0	80.2	86.1	87.3	71.6	83.5	88.0	78.3	85.6	90.2	68.0	84.8
0920	Plaster & Gypsum Board	107.8	76.0	87.6	101.9	80.1	88.1	83.5	79.0	80.6	82.8	71.3	75.4	64.8	77.5	72.9	82.0	67.7	72.9
0950, 0980	Ceilings & Acoustic Treatment	95.0	76.0	84.4	108.6	80.1	92.7	81.4	79.0	80.1	81.4	71.3	75.7	84.2	77.5	80.5	87.2	67.7	76.3
0960	Flooring	91.1	65.5	84.5	94.6	60.0	85.7	91.1	61.9	83.6	90.3	66.2	84.1	76.9	56.0	71.5	89.2	56.0	80.7
0970, 0990	Wall Finishes & Painting/Coating	91.8	82.8	86.5	99.9	68.7	81.6	92.5	89.2	90.6	92.5	63.8	75.6	95.6	79.8	86.3	92.5	59.3	73.0
09	FINISHES	93.8	76.0	85.0	100.0	74.2	87.2	89.2	77.6	83.5	88.7	70.0	79.4	82.5	72.8	77.7	89.6	64.6	77.2
COVERS	DIVS. 10-14, 25, 28, 41, 43, 44, 46	100.0	91.9	98.3	100.0	90.2	97.9	100.0	96.3	99.2	100.0	79.3	95.6	100.0	42.4	87.7	100.0	85.7	97.0
21, 22, 23	FIRE SUPPRESSION, PLUMBING & HVAC	100.1	75.9	91.4	99.9	78.5	92.2	99.8	72.9	90.2	92.8	68.8	84.1	92.2	72.4	85.1	92.8	65.0	82.8
26, 27, 3370	ELECTRICAL, COMMUNICATIONS & UTIL.	91.4	74.9	84.2	96.9	74.9	87.3	91.2	72.0	82.9	92.5	66.8	81.3	90.8	76.3	84.5	90.3	76.2	84.2
MF2018	WEIGHTED AVERAGE	96.6	79.8	90.3	98.3	79.8	91.3	94.5	81.8	89.7	91.9	74.9	85.5	94.7	77.1	88.1	91.5	71.8	84.1

LOUISIANA

DIVISION		ALEXANDRIA 713-714			BATON ROUGE 707-708			HAMMOND 704			LAFAYETTE 705			LAKE CHARLES 706			MONROE 712		
		MAT.	INST.	TOTAL	MAT.	INST.	TOTAL	MAT.	INST.	TOTAL	MAT.	INST.	TOTAL	MAT.	INST.	TOTAL	MAT.	INST.	TOTAL
015433	CONTRACTOR EQUIPMENT		91.8	91.8		105.9	105.9		96.3	96.3		96.3	96.3		96.0	96.0		91.8	91.8
0241, 31-34	SITE & INFRASTRUCTURE, DEMOLITION	111.1	84.7	93.9	92.3	106.0	101.2	98.9	88.4	92.1	103.2	88.6	93.7	104.0	88.1	93.6	111.1	84.5	93.7
0310	Concrete Forming & Accessories	88.4	63.4	67.8	106.0	72.7	78.5	84.8	50.7	56.7	97.6	71.1	75.7	99.1	70.1	75.2	88.1	61.8	66.5
0320	Concrete Reinforcing	151.1	70.0	118.0	152.5	69.9	118.7	119.7	47.4	90.2	121.5	69.8	100.4	121.5	70.0	100.5	149.4	70.0	117.0
0330	Cast-in-Place Concrete	96.7	66.6	86.7	93.0	68.9	84.9	85.8	63.9	78.4	85.4	65.7	78.8	89.9	66.4	82.0	96.7	64.5	85.9
03	CONCRETE	97.0	66.4	84.4	99.5	71.2	87.9	88.0	56.1	74.9	88.9	69.7	81.0	91.2	69.6	82.3	96.7	65.0	83.7
04	MASONRY	104.9	64.1	81.2	92.2	57.4	71.9	107.4	57.2	78.1	107.3	60.1	79.8	106.5	64.4	82.0	100.6	61.0	77.6
05	METALS	98.5	79.8	94.6	100.4	77.4	95.6	87.8	73.1	84.7	87.0	82.4	86.0	87.0	82.7	86.1	98.5	79.8	94.5
06	WOOD, PLASTICS & COMPOSITES	96.6	62.3	79.8	102.7	77.3	90.2	83.2	48.4	66.1	98.2	73.9	86.2	96.9	71.8	84.5	96.2	62.3	79.5
07	THERMAL & MOISTURE PROTECTION	105.1	66.7	92.2	95.0	70.0	86.6	97.8	61.8	85.8	98.2	67.9	88.0	98.0	68.4	88.1	105.0	64.6	91.5
08	OPENINGS	104.3	64.3	94.3	98.6	72.1	92.2	94.3	48.6	83.2	98.0	67.6	90.6	98.0	67.1	90.5	104.3	61.9	94.0
0920	Plaster & Gypsum Board	90.3	61.4	71.9	99.0	76.8	84.9	99.8	47.2	66.4	105.4	73.5	85.1	105.4	71.4	83.7	90.0	61.4	71.8
0950, 0980	Ceilings & Acoustic Treatment	86.3	61.4	72.4	99.6	76.8	86.9	105.6	47.2	72.9	100.7	73.5	85.5	101.2	71.4	84.5	86.3	61.4	72.4
0960	Flooring	101.9	65.4	92.6	110.0	61.6	97.6	99.5	61.6	89.8	105.7	61.6	94.4	105.7	61.6	94.4	101.7	61.6	91.4
0970, 0990	Wall Finishes & Painting/Coating	99.7	62.5	77.8	99.9	55.2	73.6	98.8	52.1	71.3	98.8	63.9	78.3	98.8	55.2	73.2	99.7	63.5	78.5
09	FINISHES	92.8	63.3	78.3	102.8	69.4	86.3	99.1	52.0	75.8	100.3	69.0	84.8	100.4	67.2	84.0	92.8	62.0	77.5
COVERS	DIVS. 10-14, 25, 28, 41, 43, 44, 46	100.0	78.2	95.4	100.0	85.5	96.9	100.0	79.7	95.7	100.0	85.5	96.9	100.0	85.8	97.0	100.0	76.9	95.1
21, 22, 23	FIRE SUPPRESSION, PLUMBING & HVAC	100.2	62.0	86.4	100.3	60.6	86.0	93.2	55.4	79.6	100.5	56.9	84.8	100.5	61.7	86.5	100.2	60.0	85.7
26, 27, 3370	ELECTRICAL, COMMUNICATIONS & UTIL.	93.6	53.1	76.0	101.8	53.2	80.6	97.1	60.2	81.0	97.8	55.5	79.2	97.4	59.3	80.8	94.6	52.5	76.3
MF2018	WEIGHTED AVERAGE	99.1	65.7	86.5	99.7	68.4	87.9	93.9	60.5	81.3	96.2	66.7	85.1	96.4	68.5	85.9	98.9	64.3	85.8

LOUISIANA / MAINE

DIVISION		NEW ORLEANS 700-701			SHREVEPORT 710-711			THIBODAUX 703			AUGUSTA 043			BANGOR 044			BATH 045		
		MAT.	INST.	TOTAL	MAT.	INST.	TOTAL	MAT.	INST.	TOTAL	MAT.	INST.	TOTAL	MAT.	INST.	TOTAL	MAT.	INST.	TOTAL
015433	CONTRACTOR EQUIPMENT		98.3	98.3		102.6	102.6		96.3	96.3		109.1	109.1		101.0	101.0		101.0	101.0
0241, 31-34	SITE & INFRASTRUCTURE, DEMOLITION	114.6	95.0	101.8	114.0	98.4	103.8	100.7	88.4	92.7	86.2	108.4	100.7	87.4	99.3	95.1	82.3	97.6	92.3
0310	Concrete Forming & Accessories	100.0	71.6	76.6	101.5	63.9	70.5	95.1	57.8	64.3	106.4	73.6	79.4	98.7	77.0	80.8	95.4	72.8	76.8
0320	Concrete Reinforcing	100.8	70.2	88.3	152.8	70.1	119.0	119.7	47.4	90.2	173.6	82.5	136.4	149.3	82.7	122.1	147.7	82.2	121.0
0330	Cast-in-Place Concrete	80.5	73.5	78.1	100.0	67.9	89.3	92.2	63.6	82.6	74.0	107.1	85.1	59.7	110.0	76.5	59.7	103.3	74.3
03	CONCRETE	85.0	72.3	79.8	102.7	67.0	88.0	92.6	59.2	78.9	99.7	87.9	94.8	89.8	90.6	90.1	89.7	86.3	88.3
04	MASONRY	118.8	63.7	86.8	87.7	61.4	72.4	129.0	56.8	86.9	116.4	88.1	99.9	129.1	91.4	107.2	136.4	85.6	106.8
05	METALS	98.3	76.6	93.7	100.6	78.5	95.9	87.8	73.1	84.7	103.9	97.6	102.6	94.7	99.5	95.7	94.6	98.3	95.4
06	WOOD, PLASTICS & COMPOSITES	98.4	74.3	86.5	99.9	64.8	82.6	88.8	58.4	73.8	107.7	69.9	89.1	99.6	74.0	87.0	95.3	69.4	82.5
07	THERMAL & MOISTURE PROTECTION	97.9	70.2	88.6	102.2	67.0	90.4	97.7	62.1	85.8	94.7	97.0	95.5	94.5	100.2	96.4	94.5	93.5	94.2
08	OPENINGS	98.8	70.2	91.8	98.9	62.1	90.0	98.9	50.4	87.1	98.3	74.9	92.6	95.3	81.0	91.8	95.3	73.8	90.0
0920	Plaster & Gypsum Board	95.9	73.4	81.6	106.3	63.4	79.0	100.8	57.5	73.2	81.6	68.6	73.4	88.1	73.3	78.7	84.5	68.6	74.4
0950, 0980	Ceilings & Acoustic Treatment	107.7	73.4	88.5	97.2	63.4	78.3	105.6	57.5	78.7	76.1	68.6	71.9	71.5	73.3	72.6	71.5	68.6	69.9
0960	Flooring	105.4	68.7	96.0	108.9	61.6	96.8	103.6	61.1	92.7	107.9	100.2	105.9	102.6	100.2	102.0	101.3	96.3	100.0
0970, 0990	Wall Finishes & Painting/Coating	103.1	60.4	78.0	99.9	63.9	78.8	98.8	52.1	71.3	104.8	82.1	91.5	97.1	94.5	95.5	97.1	77.4	85.5
09	FINISHES	101.7	70.2	86.2	103.7	63.4	83.8	100.5	57.7	79.3	89.8	78.3	84.1	86.2	82.0	84.1	85.4	76.6	81.0
COVERS	DIVS. 10-14, 25, 28, 41, 43, 44, 46	100.0	86.4	97.1	100.0	78.4	95.4	100.0	82.8	96.3	100.0	93.1	98.5	100.0	102.1	100.4	100.0	88.2	97.5
21, 22, 23	FIRE SUPPRESSION, PLUMBING & HVAC	100.2	60.8	86.0	100.0	60.2	85.7	93.2	55.1	79.5	100.1	74.9	91.0	100.5	75.9	91.6	93.2	74.7	86.6
26, 27, 3370	ELECTRICAL, COMMUNICATIONS & UTIL.	104.9	67.5	88.6	102.1	58.9	83.3	96.3	60.2	80.6	105.3	74.7	92.0	102.7	63.6	85.7	101.1	74.7	89.8
MF2018	WEIGHTED AVERAGE	99.6	70.4	88.6	100.7	66.9	87.9	95.9	61.9	83.0	100.7	84.1	94.4	97.5	84.0	92.4	95.8	82.3	90.7

For customer support on your Plumbing Costs with RSMeans Data call 800.448.8182.

City Cost Indexes

DIVISION		MAINE																	
		HOULTON 047			KITTERY 039			LEWISTON 042			MACHIAS 046			PORTLAND 040 - 041			ROCKLAND 048		
		MAT.	INST.	TOTAL	MAT.	INST.	TOTAL	MAT.	INST.	TOTAL	MAT.	INST.	TOTAL	MAT.	INST.	TOTAL	MAT.	INST.	TOTAL
015433	CONTRACTOR EQUIPMENT		101.0	101.0		94.5	94.5		101.0	101.0		101.0	101.0		108.7	108.7		101.0	101.0
0241, 31 - 34	SITE & INFRASTRUCTURE, DEMOLITION	83.7	97.6	92.8	68.0	89.5	82.0	86.1	99.3	94.7	83.3	97.6	92.6	88.6	108.4	101.5	80.9	97.6	91.8
0310	Concrete Forming & Accessories	101.7	72.8	77.9	94.9	72.6	76.5	102.9	77.1	81.6	99.3	72.8	77.4	100.7	78.3	82.2	100.1	72.8	77.6
0320	Concrete Reinforcing	149.3	82.2	121.9	152.6	82.2	123.8	183.4	82.7	142.3	149.3	82.2	121.9	173.6	82.9	136.6	149.3	82.2	121.9
0330	Cast-in-Place Concrete	59.7	102.4	74.0	56.1	102.2	71.6	60.9	110.0	77.4	59.7	103.3	74.3	74.0	113.4	87.2	61.0	103.3	75.1
03	CONCRETE	90.7	85.9	88.7	83.9	85.8	84.7	92.7	90.7	91.9	90.2	86.3	88.6	99.3	92.3	96.4	87.9	86.3	87.2
04	MASONRY	107.9	85.6	94.9	142.1	85.6	109.2	108.6	91.4	98.6	107.9	85.6	94.9	107.2	91.6	98.1	101.1	85.6	92.1
05	METALS	94.9	98.3	95.6	91.9	97.9	93.2	99.3	99.6	99.4	94.9	98.3	95.6	109.9	99.1	107.6	94.7	98.3	95.5
06	WOOD, PLASTICS & COMPOSITES	102.5	69.4	86.2	97.4	69.2	83.5	103.9	74.0	89.2	100.3	69.4	85.1	96.9	74.5	85.8	101.0	69.4	85.4
07	THERMAL & MOISTURE PROTECTION	94.6	93.5	94.2	92.1	93.4	92.5	94.3	100.2	96.3	94.5	93.5	94.2	97.5	102.2	99.1	94.3	93.5	94.0
08	OPENINGS	95.3	73.8	90.1	97.4	76.7	92.4	98.3	81.0	94.1	95.3	73.8	90.1	98.4	81.3	94.2	95.3	73.8	90.0
0920	Plaster & Gypsum Board	89.5	68.6	76.2	105.4	68.6	82.0	93.3	73.3	80.6	88.8	68.6	76.0	98.3	73.3	82.4	88.8	68.6	76.0
0950, 0980	Ceilings & Acoustic Treatment	71.5	68.6	69.9	97.2	68.6	81.2	82.1	73.3	77.2	71.5	68.6	69.9	100.6	73.3	85.4	71.5	68.6	69.9
0960	Flooring	103.6	96.3	101.7	103.5	96.3	101.7	104.7	100.2	103.6	103.0	96.3	101.3	107.9	166.7	123.0	103.3	96.3	101.5
0970, 0990	Wall Finishes & Painting/Coating	97.1	77.4	85.5	83.8	88.9	86.8	97.1	94.5	95.5	97.1	77.4	85.5	104.8	94.5	98.7	97.1	77.4	85.5
09	FINISHES	86.7	76.6	81.7	98.7	77.7	88.3	90.0	82.0	86.0	86.4	76.6	81.6	98.5	96.0	97.2	86.3	76.6	81.5
COVERS	DIVS. 10 - 14, 25, 28, 41, 43, 44, 46	100.0	85.4	96.9	100.0	87.6	97.3	100.0	102.1	100.4	100.0	85.4	96.9	100.0	103.2	100.7	100.0	88.2	97.5
21, 22, 23	FIRE SUPPRESSION, PLUMBING & HVAC	93.2	74.8	86.6	93.1	70.4	84.9	100.5	75.9	91.6	93.2	74.8	86.6	100.2	76.1	91.5	93.2	74.8	86.6
26, 27, 3370	ELECTRICAL, COMMUNICATIONS & UTIL.	103.8	74.7	91.1	100.3	74.7	89.1	103.9	77.0	92.2	103.8	74.7	91.1	105.7	77.0	93.2	103.8	74.7	91.1
MF2018	WEIGHTED AVERAGE	95.1	82.1	90.2	95.4	80.9	89.9	98.5	86.0	93.8	95.0	82.2	90.2	102.2	88.8	97.1	94.3	82.3	89.8

DIVISION		MAINE			MARYLAND														
		WATERVILLE 049			ANNAPOLIS 214			BALTIMORE 210 - 212			COLLEGE PARK 207 - 208			CUMBERLAND 215			EASTON 216		
		MAT.	INST.	TOTAL	MAT.	INST.	TOTAL	MAT.	INST.	TOTAL	MAT.	INST.	TOTAL	MAT.	INST.	TOTAL	MAT.	INST.	TOTAL
015433	CONTRACTOR EQUIPMENT		101.0	101.0		117.7	117.7		100.9	100.9		103.4	103.4		101.3	101.3		101.3	101.3
0241, 31 - 34	SITE & INFRASTRUCTURE, DEMOLITION	83.4	97.6	92.6	104.2	107.4	106.3	113.8	97.7	103.3	106.5	92.3	97.2	97.0	93.0	94.4	103.4	91.0	95.3
0310	Concrete Forming & Accessories	95.1	72.8	76.7	99.4	74.0	78.5	104.3	75.4	80.5	93.7	68.3	72.8	96.3	82.9	85.3	95.0	65.9	71.0
0320	Concrete Reinforcing	149.3	82.2	121.9	131.0	91.1	114.7	131.0	87.9	113.4	127.3	96.9	114.8	115.2	83.8	102.4	114.2	75.8	98.5
0330	Cast-in-Place Concrete	59.7	103.3	74.3	105.1	78.3	96.2	109.5	77.9	98.9	115.6	70.7	100.6	85.8	84.3	85.3	95.4	60.9	83.8
03	CONCRETE	91.2	86.3	89.2	106.0	79.3	95.0	108.4	79.0	96.3	109.9	75.2	95.7	90.9	84.4	88.2	98.2	67.0	85.4
04	MASONRY	119.0	85.6	99.6	110.2	69.7	86.6	105.6	75.2	87.9	119.1	72.5	92.0	106.0	87.0	94.9	121.9	51.8	81.1
05	METALS	94.8	98.3	95.6	106.0	97.5	104.3	105.3	91.5	102.4	88.3	103.0	91.4	100.2	98.1	99.7	100.4	91.7	98.6
06	WOOD, PLASTICS & COMPOSITES	94.8	69.4	82.3	94.6	74.9	84.9	102.9	74.8	89.1	79.0	67.6	73.4	86.0	81.3	83.7	84.6	72.0	78.4
07	THERMAL & MOISTURE PROTECTION	94.6	93.5	94.2	102.3	78.8	94.4	98.4	81.6	92.8	98.8	74.5	90.7	97.4	83.4	92.7	97.5	66.0	87.0
08	OPENINGS	95.3	73.8	90.1	97.8	82.1	94.0	107.9	81.7	101.6	97.1	77.3	92.3	97.9	81.8	94.0	96.1	74.3	90.8
0920	Plaster & Gypsum Board	84.5	68.6	74.4	113.5	73.7	88.2	113.0	74.0	88.2	108.5	66.5	81.7	120.3	80.9	95.2	120.3	71.3	89.1
0950, 0980	Ceilings & Acoustic Treatment	71.5	68.6	69.9	102.4	73.7	86.4	100.6	74.0	85.7	112.3	66.5	86.6	106.4	80.9	92.1	106.4	71.3	86.8
0960	Flooring	101.1	96.3	99.9	112.6	77.9	103.7	99.8	77.2	94.0	98.4	68.3	90.7	100.6	90.7	98.0	99.9	65.9	91.2
0970, 0990	Wall Finishes & Painting/Coating	97.1	77.4	85.5	99.9	69.1	81.8	97.2	67.8	79.9	98.9	63.4	78.1	94.6	86.5	89.8	94.6	63.4	76.3
09	FINISHES	85.4	76.6	81.1	106.1	73.7	90.1	102.3	74.3	88.5	103.8	67.0	85.6	105.7	84.8	95.4	105.9	65.8	86.1
COVERS	DIVS. 10 - 14, 25, 28, 41, 43, 44, 46	100.0	85.2	96.9	100.0	89.2	97.7	100.0	89.8	97.8	100.0	76.3	95.0	100.0	92.5	98.4	100.0	77.3	95.2
21, 22, 23	FIRE SUPPRESSION, PLUMBING & HVAC	93.2	74.8	86.6	100.0	81.5	93.4	100.0	85.7	94.9	92.9	77.2	87.2	92.5	74.8	86.2	92.5	64.1	82.3
26, 27, 3370	ELECTRICAL, COMMUNICATIONS & UTIL.	103.8	74.7	91.1	99.8	85.9	93.7	99.8	86.3	93.9	100.2	96.0	98.4	99.3	77.4	89.7	99.0	53.8	79.3
MF2018	WEIGHTED AVERAGE	95.5	82.2	90.5	102.8	83.1	95.3	103.4	83.5	95.9	98.2	81.0	91.7	97.4	83.6	92.2	99.1	67.4	87.1

DIVISION		MARYLAND														MASSACHUSETTS		
		ELKTON 219			HAGERSTOWN 217			SALISBURY 218			SILVER SPRING 209			WALDORF 206			BOSTON 020 - 022, 024		
		MAT.	INST.	TOTAL	MAT.	INST.	TOTAL	MAT.	INST.	TOTAL	MAT.	INST.	TOTAL	MAT.	INST.	TOTAL	MAT.	INST.	TOTAL
015433	CONTRACTOR EQUIPMENT		101.3	101.3		101.3	101.3		101.3	101.3		95.7	95.7		95.7	95.7		99.1	99.1
0241, 31 - 34	SITE & INFRASTRUCTURE, DEMOLITION	91.6	91.5	91.5	98.8	93.3	95.2	103.4	90.7	95.1	95.5	84.4	88.3	101.5	84.2	90.2	94.2	101.2	98.8
0310	Concrete Forming & Accessories	99.2	82.0	85.1	95.7	83.0	85.2	105.2	45.3	55.8	101.3	67.4	73.4	107.1	67.3	74.3	100.4	133.8	128.0
0320	Concrete Reinforcing	114.2	102.0	109.2	115.2	83.8	102.4	114.2	56.8	90.7	125.9	96.9	114.0	126.7	96.7	114.5	109.0	157.2	128.7
0330	Cast-in-Place Concrete	77.2	66.5	73.6	81.8	84.3	82.6	95.4	59.1	83.2	118.3	70.9	102.5	132.6	70.8	111.9	89.2	139.3	105.9
03	CONCRETE	84.0	80.8	82.7	87.5	84.5	86.3	98.9	53.8	80.4	108.5	74.8	94.7	118.9	74.7	100.8	92.5	139.4	111.7
04	MASONRY	106.1	58.9	78.6	112.6	87.0	97.7	120.4	48.7	78.7	118.0	72.9	91.8	101.9	72.9	85.0	98.7	144.4	125.3
05	METALS	100.4	103.3	101.0	100.3	98.2	99.8	100.4	82.7	96.7	91.7	99.7	93.4	91.7	99.1	93.3	105.7	136.7	112.2
06	WOOD, PLASTICS & COMPOSITES	89.8	90.0	89.6	85.5	81.3	83.4	96.5	46.0	71.6	84.7	66.8	75.9	89.7	66.8	78.4	96.0	132.2	113.9
07	THERMAL & MOISTURE PROTECTION	97.1	71.2	88.4	97.7	83.1	92.8	97.7	61.9	85.7	102.4	79.8	94.8	102.9	79.8	95.2	95.9	137.0	109.7
08	OPENINGS	96.1	91.2	94.9	96.1	81.7	92.6	96.4	54.8	86.3	91.5	76.9	87.9	92.3	76.9	88.5	101.3	143.2	111.5
0920	Plaster & Gypsum Board	121.7	89.9	101.5	120.3	80.9	95.2	127.6	44.5	74.7	115.9	66.5	84.4	117.3	66.5	84.9	99.8	133.2	121.1
0950, 0980	Ceilings & Acoustic Treatment	106.4	89.9	97.2	107.9	80.9	92.8	106.4	44.5	71.8	122.9	66.5	91.3	122.9	66.5	91.3	78.6	133.2	109.1
0960	Flooring	101.8	65.9	92.6	100.2	90.7	97.7	104.7	65.9	94.7	104.1	68.3	94.9	106.9	68.3	97.0	108.6	158.7	121.4
0970, 0990	Wall Finishes & Painting/Coating	94.6	63.4	76.3	94.6	69.1	79.6	94.6	63.4	76.3	105.2	63.4	80.6	105.2	63.4	80.6	99.9	156.0	132.9
09	FINISHES	105.9	78.2	92.2	105.8	82.9	94.5	108.2	49.8	79.3	105.1	66.3	85.9	106.4	66.4	86.6	96.7	140.9	118.6
COVERS	DIVS. 10 - 14, 25, 28, 41, 43, 44, 46	100.0	50.2	89.4	100.0	92.5	98.4	100.0	73.6	94.4	100.0	74.6	94.6	100.0	72.8	94.2	100.0	115.9	103.4
21, 22, 23	FIRE SUPPRESSION, PLUMBING & HVAC	92.5	69.3	84.2	99.8	90.9	96.6	92.5	62.3	81.7	92.9	77.5	87.4	92.9	77.4	87.3	100.2	131.8	111.5
26, 27, 3370	ELECTRICAL, COMMUNICATIONS & UTIL.	100.0	75.1	89.1	99.1	77.4	89.7	98.3	51.9	78.1	96.0	96.0	96.0	94.7	96.0	95.2	102.2	128.1	113.5
MF2018	WEIGHTED AVERAGE	96.5	77.0	89.1	98.9	86.8	94.3	99.3	60.4	84.6	97.7	80.1	91.1	98.4	80.0	91.4	100.0	133.0	112.4

City Cost Indexes

		MASSACHUSETTS																	
		BROCKTON			BUZZARDS BAY			FALL RIVER			FITCHBURG			FRAMINGHAM			GREENFIELD		
	DIVISION	023			025			027			014			017			013		
		MAT.	INST.	TOTAL	MAT.	INST.	TOTAL	MAT.	INST.	TOTAL	MAT.	INST.	TOTAL	MAT.	INST.	TOTAL	MAT.	INST.	TOTAL
015433	CONTRACTOR EQUIPMENT		97.2	97.2		97.2	97.2		97.9	97.9		99.3	99.3		100.9	100.9		99.3	99.3
0241, 31 - 34	SITE & INFRASTRUCTURE, DEMOLITION	90.0	94.9	93.2	79.0	94.4	89.0	89.1	95.0	92.9	77.9	98.8	91.5	75.9	98.1	90.4	80.7	97.0	91.3
0310	Concrete Forming & Accessories	98.7	125.3	120.6	97.2	124.4	119.6	98.7	125.1	120.5	96.6	108.3	106.2	102.0	124.9	120.9	95.4	113.8	110.6
0320	Concrete Reinforcing	107.1	148.3	123.9	85.9	121.2	100.3	107.1	121.3	112.9	123.4	147.1	133.1	123.4	147.8	133.4	128.0	119.0	124.3
0330	Cast-in-Place Concrete	76.7	125.8	93.1	63.7	129.9	85.8	74.1	130.4	93.0	66.3	125.5	86.1	66.3	126.0	86.3	68.1	109.7	82.1
03	CONCRETE	83.8	129.4	102.5	70.9	125.7	93.4	81.6	126.2	99.9	77.8	121.4	95.7	79.9	129.4	100.2	81.0	113.3	94.3
04	MASONRY	113.0	131.8	123.9	104.7	134.3	121.9	113.7	134.2	125.6	111.7	121.9	117.6	119.1	125.6	122.9	117.3	111.9	114.1
05	METALS	101.9	134.4	108.7	96.7	121.4	101.9	101.9	122.4	106.2	99.1	132.6	106.1	99.1	135.8	106.8	101.0	117.7	104.5
06	WOOD, PLASTICS & COMPOSITES	94.4	125.6	109.7	92.0	125.6	108.6	94.4	125.9	109.9	98.8	103.2	100.9	103.4	125.3	114.2	97.4	117.4	107.3
07	THERMAL & MOISTURE PROTECTION	92.7	123.6	103.0	91.7	121.5	101.7	92.5	124.1	103.1	92.5	116.6	100.6	92.6	121.5	102.3	92.5	104.8	96.7
08	OPENINGS	96.9	134.3	106.0	92.9	119.5	99.4	96.9	120.5	102.7	98.3	121.8	104.0	90.6	134.1	101.2	98.3	117.2	102.9
0920	Plaster & Gypsum Board	89.8	126.3	113.0	83.5	126.3	110.7	89.8	126.3	113.0	107.2	103.2	104.6	109.6	126.3	120.2	109.9	117.5	115.0
0950, 0980	Ceilings & Acoustic Treatment	88.1	126.3	109.5	73.0	126.3	102.8	88.1	126.3	109.5	86.3	103.2	95.7	86.3	126.3	108.6	97.7	117.9	109.0
0960	Flooring	105.6	152.7	117.7	103.2	152.7	115.9	104.1	152.7	116.5	102.4	152.7	115.3	103.6	152.7	116.2	101.8	130.3	109.1
0970, 0990	Wall Finishes & Painting/Coating	88.7	142.8	120.5	88.7	142.8	120.5	88.7	142.8	120.5	89.1	142.8	120.7	90.2	142.8	121.1	89.1	114.7	104.2
09	FINISHES	94.6	132.9	113.5	88.7	132.9	110.6	94.2	133.0	113.4	93.5	119.6	106.4	94.1	132.6	113.1	96.8	117.9	107.2
COVERS	DIVS. 10 - 14, 25, 28, 41, 43, 44, 46	100.0	113.2	102.8	100.0	113.2	102.8	100.0	113.7	102.9	100.0	98.5	99.7	100.0	112.6	102.7	100.0	108.8	101.9
21, 22, 23	FIRE SUPPRESSION, PLUMBING & HVAC	100.6	107.6	103.1	93.3	94.3	93.7	100.6	104.3	101.9	99.3	108.3	98.7	93.3	110.0	99.3	93.3	96.3	94.4
26, 27, 3370	ELECTRICAL, COMMUNICATIONS & UTIL.	102.1	89.6	96.7	100.4	86.6	94.4	101.7	90.8	96.9	99.6	90.0	95.4	97.7	107.5	101.9	99.6	97.5	98.7
MF2018	WEIGHTED AVERAGE	98.2	117.0	105.3	92.3	111.6	99.6	97.9	114.7	104.2	94.7	112.1	101.2	94.5	119.7	104.0	96.0	106.8	100.1

		MASSACHUSETTS																	
		HYANNIS			LAWRENCE			LOWELL			NEW BEDFORD			PITTSFIELD			SPRINGFIELD		
	DIVISION	026			019			018			027			012			010 - 011		
		MAT.	INST.	TOTAL	MAT.	INST.	TOTAL	MAT.	INST.	TOTAL	MAT.	INST.	TOTAL	MAT.	INST.	TOTAL	MAT.	INST.	TOTAL
015433	CONTRACTOR EQUIPMENT		97.2	97.2		101.2	101.2		99.3	99.3		97.9	97.9		99.3	99.3		99.3	99.3
0241, 31 - 34	SITE & INFRASTRUCTURE, DEMOLITION	86.9	94.6	91.9	88.2	98.9	95.2	87.1	98.9	94.8	88.0	95.0	92.5	88.0	97.5	94.2	87.5	97.6	94.1
0310	Concrete Forming & Accessories	93.2	124.8	119.2	102.8	125.8	121.8	100.2	125.8	121.3	98.7	125.1	120.5	100.1	99.8	99.9	100.5	114.9	112.4
0320	Concrete Reinforcing	85.9	121.3	100.3	152.7	141.7	148.2	154.0	141.2	148.8	107.1	121.0	112.8	127.0	107.7	119.1	154.0	119.0	139.7
0330	Cast-in-Place Concrete	69.9	130.0	90.0	76.7	130.4	94.7	69.7	130.5	90.1	65.3	130.4	87.1	76.1	112.5	88.3	72.6	111.4	85.6
03	CONCRETE	75.8	125.9	96.4	93.7	130.2	108.7	87.1	130.0	104.7	78.2	126.2	97.9	86.1	106.0	94.3	88.6	114.4	99.2
04	MASONRY	111.9	134.3	124.9	125.8	138.5	133.2	110.6	131.5	122.7	111.9	128.0	121.3	111.2	113.4	112.5	110.9	114.9	113.2
05	METALS	96.8	121.8	102.0	101.5	134.8	108.4	101.4	131.5	107.7	101.9	121.9	106.1	101.2	112.5	103.6	104.6	117.7	107.3
06	WOOD, PLASTICS & COMPOSITES	88.3	125.6	106.7	102.9	125.5	114.0	103.1	125.5	114.1	94.4	125.9	109.9	103.1	98.1	100.6	103.1	117.4	110.1
07	THERMAL & MOISTURE PROTECTION	92.2	123.7	102.7	93.0	127.1	104.5	92.8	123.9	103.3	92.4	122.4	102.5	92.9	113.4	99.7	92.8	106.1	97.3
08	OPENINGS	93.5	120.6	100.1	94.1	132.3	103.4	99.4	132.3	107.4	96.9	124.5	103.6	99.4	103.4	100.4	99.4	117.2	103.7
0920	Plaster & Gypsum Board	81.3	126.3	109.9	113.7	126.3	121.7	113.7	126.3	121.7	89.8	126.3	113.0	113.7	97.9	103.7	113.7	117.9	116.4
0950, 0980	Ceilings & Acoustic Treatment	78.0	126.3	105.0	97.7	126.3	113.7	97.7	126.3	113.7	88.1	126.3	109.5	97.7	97.9	97.9	97.7	117.9	109.0
0960	Flooring	101.2	152.7	114.4	104.1	152.7	116.6	104.1	152.7	116.6	104.1	152.7	116.5	104.4	131.1	111.2	103.7	130.3	110.5
0970, 0990	Wall Finishes & Painting/Coating	88.7	142.8	120.5	89.2	142.8	120.7	89.1	142.8	120.7	88.7	142.8	120.5	89.1	114.7	104.2	90.1	114.7	104.6
09	FINISHES	89.5	132.9	110.9	98.1	132.8	115.3	98.1	132.9	115.3	94.1	133.0	113.4	98.1	106.9	102.5	98.0	118.6	108.2
COVERS	DIVS. 10 - 14, 25, 28, 41, 43, 44, 46	100.0	113.2	102.8	100.0	113.1	102.8	100.0	113.2	102.8	100.0	113.7	102.9	100.0	107.1	101.5	100.0	109.8	102.1
21, 22, 23	FIRE SUPPRESSION, PLUMBING & HVAC	100.6	102.7	101.4	100.1	127.7	110.0	100.1	128.0	110.1	100.6	104.2	101.9	100.1	95.7	98.5	100.1	97.9	99.3
26, 27, 3370	ELECTRICAL, COMMUNICATIONS & UTIL.	101.1	90.8	96.6	99.1	112.7	105.0	99.3	111.6	104.7	103.1	92.6	98.5	99.3	97.5	98.5	99.4	92.4	96.3
MF2018	WEIGHTED AVERAGE	95.3	114.2	102.4	99.5	125.8	109.4	98.4	124.5	108.3	97.5	114.4	103.9	98.3	103.1	100.1	99.2	107.1	102.2

		MASSACHUSETTS			MICHIGAN													
		WORCESTER			ANN ARBOR			BATTLE CREEK			BAY CITY			DEARBORN			DETROIT		
	DIVISION	015 - 016			481			490			487			481			482		
		MAT.	INST.	TOTAL	MAT.	INST.	TOTAL	MAT.	INST.	TOTAL	MAT.	INST.	TOTAL	MAT.	INST.	TOTAL	MAT.	INST.	TOTAL
015433	CONTRACTOR EQUIPMENT		99.3	99.3		105.8	105.8		97.3	97.3		105.8	105.8		105.8	105.8		100.1	100.1
0241, 31 - 34	SITE & INFRASTRUCTURE, DEMOLITION	87.5	98.8	94.9	73.8	88.8	83.6	94.6	86.0	89.0	70.6	88.1	82.0	73.5	88.9	83.5	83.7	96.1	91.8
0310	Concrete Forming & Accessories	100.7	116.2	113.5	96.7	102.4	101.4	101.8	75.7	80.3	96.8	75.2	79.0	96.6	102.9	101.8	94.7	102.1	100.8
0320	Concrete Reinforcing	154.0	147.8	151.5	91.5	104.4	96.8	80.7	71.4	76.9	91.5	103.7	96.5	91.5	105.5	97.2	102.4	103.1	102.7
0330	Cast-in-Place Concrete	72.2	125.6	90.1	85.1	93.3	87.9	132.8	81.3	115.6	81.4	87.2	83.4	83.2	98.2	88.2	94.1	99.0	95.7
03	CONCRETE	88.4	125.1	103.5	91.5	100.3	95.1	113.6	77.7	98.9	89.7	85.7	88.1	90.6	102.4	95.4	95.6	101.1	97.9
04	MASONRY	110.6	132.8	123.5	114.2	97.4	104.4	106.0	73.6	87.1	113.8	81.3	94.9	114.1	115.2	114.7	120.2	97.8	107.2
05	METALS	104.6	133.8	110.7	96.0	114.7	99.9	106.1	88.0	102.3	96.7	112.6	100.0	96.1	116.5	100.4	96.6	101.1	97.6
06	WOOD, PLASTICS & COMPOSITES	103.4	113.6	108.4	94.8	105.4	100.0	100.9	74.5	87.9	94.8	72.9	84.0	94.8	105.4	100.0	96.0	104.3	100.1
07	THERMAL & MOISTURE PROTECTION	92.8	120.7	102.2	104.0	95.1	101.0	99.6	78.2	92.5	101.8	82.6	95.4	102.6	103.4	102.9	102.0	103.0	102.3
08	OPENINGS	99.4	127.5	106.2	90.4	99.5	92.6	84.0	69.8	80.6	90.4	80.1	87.9	90.4	99.4	92.6	98.0	100.1	98.5
0920	Plaster & Gypsum Board	113.7	113.9	113.8	100.5	105.2	103.5	93.7	73.2	80.7	100.5	71.7	82.2	100.5	105.2	103.5	95.3	104.4	101.1
0950, 0980	Ceilings & Acoustic Treatment	97.7	113.9	106.8	95.6	105.2	100.9	93.9	73.2	82.3	96.5	71.7	82.6	95.6	105.2	100.9	103.7	104.4	104.1
0960	Flooring	104.1	159.5	118.4	88.9	111.6	94.7	92.5	61.3	84.5	88.9	87.8	88.6	87.5	104.6	91.9	89.4	106.6	93.8
0970, 0990	Wall Finishes & Painting/Coating	89.1	142.8	120.7	81.8	99.5	92.2	90.9	66.4	76.5	81.8	86.7	84.7	81.8	99.5	92.2	99.9	99.5	99.6
09	FINISHES	98.1	127.2	112.5	94.4	104.1	99.2	94.1	71.5	82.9	94.5	77.8	86.2	94.0	103.3	98.6	96.6	103.1	99.8
COVERS	DIVS. 10 - 14, 25, 28, 41, 43, 44, 46	100.0	111.8	102.5	100.0	101.1	100.2	100.0	93.9	98.7	100.0	95.4	99.0	100.0	101.2	100.3	100.0	98.3	99.6
21, 22, 23	FIRE SUPPRESSION, PLUMBING & HVAC	100.1	99.5	99.9	100.1	91.5	97.0	99.9	85.4	94.6	100.1	83.4	94.1	100.1	93.2	97.6	99.9	94.8	98.1
26, 27, 3370	ELECTRICAL, COMMUNICATIONS & UTIL.	99.4	95.5	97.7	94.3	94.4	94.4	90.9	67.2	80.6	93.3	71.3	83.7	94.3	101.9	97.6	99.6	101.8	100.6
MF2018	WEIGHTED AVERAGE	99.2	114.6	105.0	96.5	98.0	97.1	100.1	78.3	91.9	96.1	84.0	91.5	96.3	101.9	98.4	98.9	99.4	99.1

City Cost Indexes

		MICHIGAN																	
		FLINT			GAYLORD			GRAND RAPIDS			IRON MOUNTAIN			JACKSON			KALAMAZOO		
	DIVISION	484 - 485			497			493,495			498 - 499			492			491		
		MAT.	INST.	TOTAL	MAT.	INST.	TOTAL	MAT.	INST.	TOTAL	MAT.	INST.	TOTAL	MAT.	INST.	TOTAL	MAT.	INST.	TOTAL
015433	CONTRACTOR EQUIPMENT		105.8	105.8		114.8	114.8		105.0	105.0		105.5	105.5		114.8	114.8		97.3	97.3
0241, 31 - 34	SITE & INFRASTRUCTURE, DEMOLITION	70.1	88.3	81.9	89.2	85.3	86.7	93.9	100.0	97.9	95.4	96.5	96.1	102.5	87.4	92.7	95.0	86.0	89.1
0310	Concrete Forming & Accessories	98.9	86.3	88.5	100.0	64.4	70.7	99.6	77.4	81.3	93.1	69.1	73.3	97.3	77.0	80.5	101.8	76.0	80.5
0320	Concrete Reinforcing	91.5	104.1	96.6	75.2	80.7	77.4	83.4	72.2	78.8	75.4	73.8	74.7	73.0	103.5	85.5	80.7	73.2	77.6
0330	Cast-in-Place Concrete	85.7	86.9	86.1	132.5	67.5	110.7	139.5	84.0	120.9	157.2	59.9	124.7	132.3	80.8	115.1	135.5	81.4	117.4
03	CONCRETE	91.9	90.7	91.4	110.2	71.1	94.2	123.4	79.4	105.3	123.7	68.4	101.0	105.2	85.3	97.0	117.4	78.1	101.3
04	MASONRY	114.3	89.1	99.6	117.5	64.0	86.4	104.0	84.3	92.6	103.3	70.1	84.0	96.1	80.3	86.9	104.6	83.8	92.5
05	METALS	96.1	113.2	99.7	107.6	120.0	110.2	102.3	87.8	99.2	107.3	99.2	105.6	107.7	128.7	112.0	106.1	89.5	102.6
06	WOOD, PLASTICS & COMPOSITES	97.5	86.8	92.2	92.8	63.9	78.6	102.5	76.6	89.7	88.3	69.4	79.0	92.0	75.8	84.0	100.9	74.5	87.9
07	THERMAL & MOISTURE PROTECTION	102.0	88.0	97.3	98.2	68.2	88.2	101.1	78.2	93.4	101.5	67.5	90.1	97.6	82.9	92.7	99.6	81.2	93.5
08	OPENINGS	90.4	86.9	89.6	85.0	68.8	81.0	97.4	73.9	91.6	88.0	61.3	81.5	84.2	81.4	83.5	84.0	71.6	81.0
0920	Plaster & Gypsum Board	102.4	86.0	91.9	92.8	63.5	74.2	101.0	75.6	84.8	62.1	69.8	67.0	92.1	75.7	81.6	93.7	73.2	80.7
0950, 0980	Ceilings & Acoustic Treatment	95.6	86.0	90.2	91.3	63.5	75.7	103.7	75.6	88.0	92.4	69.8	79.8	91.3	75.7	82.5	93.9	73.2	82.3
0960	Flooring	88.9	82.8	87.3	85.1	74.5	82.4	94.6	87.7	92.9	107.1	79.2	100.0	84.2	77.1	82.4	92.5	68.7	86.4
0970, 0990	Wall Finishes & Painting/Coating	81.8	78.5	79.8	88.5	71.0	77.0	99.9	74.9	85.2	110.8	60.6	81.3	85.5	81.6	83.2	90.9	71.9	79.7
09	FINISHES	94.3	84.6	89.5	93.4	66.2	80.0	100.6	78.8	89.8	96.8	70.0	83.6	94.3	76.6	85.5	94.1	73.6	83.9
COVERS	DIVS. 10 - 14, 25, 28, 41, 43, 44, 46	100.0	97.6	99.5	100.0	88.0	97.5	100.0	95.6	99.1	100.0	87.9	97.4	100.0	93.5	98.6	100.0	93.9	98.7
21, 22, 23	FIRE SUPPRESSION, PLUMBING & HVAC	100.1	84.2	94.4	93.0	69.1	84.4	99.8	83.5	93.9	92.7	73.6	85.8	93.0	85.0	90.1	99.9	81.6	93.3
26, 27, 3370	ELECTRICAL, COMMUNICATIONS & UTIL.	94.3	88.8	91.9	90.1	66.0	79.6	95.9	84.8	91.0	94.1	69.7	83.5	92.2	89.1	90.8	90.7	74.4	83.6
MF2018	WEIGHTED AVERAGE	96.4	89.8	93.9	98.7	74.1	89.4	102.6	84.0	95.6	100.7	75.1	91.0	97.7	87.9	94.0	100.5	80.2	92.8

		MICHIGAN																MINNESOTA		
		LANSING			MUSKEGON			ROYAL OAK			SAGINAW			TRAVERSE CITY			BEMIDJI		
	DIVISION	488 - 489			494			480,483			486			496			566		
		MAT.	INST.	TOTAL	MAT.	INST.	TOTAL	MAT.	INST.	TOTAL	MAT.	INST.	TOTAL	MAT.	INST.	TOTAL	MAT.	INST.	TOTAL
015433	CONTRACTOR EQUIPMENT		105.8	105.8		97.3	97.3		91.6	91.6		105.8	105.8		105.5	105.5		97.3	97.3
0241, 31 - 34	SITE & INFRASTRUCTURE, DEMOLITION	74.8	99.9	91.1	93.1	86.0	88.5	70.0	87.6	81.5	71.3	88.1	82.3	82.5	96.5	91.7	78.1	94.8	89.0
0310	Concrete Forming & Accessories	99.2	85.0	87.5	102.0	74.8	79.6	93.8	101.1	99.8	96.7	79.5	82.6	93.1	73.2	76.7	90.3	94.2	93.5
0320	Concrete Reinforcing	87.6	104.0	94.3	81.2	71.9	77.4	82.9	91.1	86.3	91.5	103.7	96.5	76.5	71.9	74.6	93.5	106.7	98.9
0330	Cast-in-Place Concrete	101.1	89.2	97.1	132.4	80.1	114.9	74.4	88.5	79.1	84.1	87.2	85.1	122.4	76.8	107.1	97.0	100.1	98.0
03	CONCRETE	105.2	90.3	99.0	112.0	76.9	97.6	78.8	94.5	85.3	91.0	87.7	89.6	100.4	75.9	90.4	92.1	99.6	95.2
04	MASONRY	104.0	90.1	95.9	103.3	81.3	90.5	106.5	87.4	95.4	115.8	81.3	95.7	100.3	82.2	89.8	105.6	103.5	104.4
05	METALS	98.5	102.6	99.3	104.3	88.8	101.1	98.9	89.2	96.9	96.1	112.5	99.6	107.2	99.8	105.7	90.5	122.9	97.3
06	WOOD, PLASTICS & COMPOSITES	102.5	85.0	93.9	96.7	73.0	85.1	90.5	105.4	97.8	90.1	78.9	84.6	88.3	73.0	80.8	70.8	91.7	81.1
07	THERMAL & MOISTURE PROTECTION	100.5	87.6	96.2	98.7	74.9	90.7	100.5	89.9	96.9	102.8	83.2	96.2	100.7	79.5	93.6	106.2	95.3	102.6
08	OPENINGS	97.4	85.6	94.5	83.1	70.7	80.0	90.3	95.4	91.6	88.6	83.4	87.4	88.0	66.1	82.7	94.3	111.2	98.4
0920	Plaster & Gypsum Board	93.6	84.3	87.7	74.2	71.7	72.6	98.1	105.2	102.6	100.5	77.9	86.1	62.1	73.6	69.4	102.1	91.7	95.2
0950, 0980	Ceilings & Acoustic Treatment	100.2	84.3	91.3	93.9	71.7	81.5	95.2	105.2	100.8	95.6	77.9	85.6	92.4	73.6	81.9	119.2	91.7	103.8
0960	Flooring	94.6	87.7	92.9	91.3	80.3	88.5	87.1	92.9	88.6	88.9	87.8	88.6	107.1	91.6	103.2	93.8	104.4	96.5
0970, 0990	Wall Finishes & Painting/Coating	88.0	74.9	80.3	88.7	72.1	79.0	84.2	81.6	82.7	81.8	86.7	84.7	110.8	48.9	74.5	90.2	103.7	98.1
09	FINISHES	96.7	84.1	90.4	90.5	75.1	82.9	93.6	98.2	95.9	94.3	81.3	87.8	95.9	73.9	85.0	100.9	97.0	99.0
COVERS	DIVS. 10 - 14, 25, 28, 41, 43, 44, 46	100.0	96.6	99.3	100.0	95.8	99.1	100.0	98.2	99.6	100.0	96.1	99.2	100.0	91.3	98.2	100.0	100.3	100.1
21, 22, 23	FIRE SUPPRESSION, PLUMBING & HVAC	99.8	87.6	95.4	99.7	83.8	94.0	93.2	89.1	91.7	100.1	83.1	93.9	92.7	79.8	88.1	93.0	89.0	91.6
26, 27, 3370	ELECTRICAL, COMMUNICATIONS & UTIL.	96.1	92.6	94.6	91.2	71.0	82.4	95.5	89.1	92.8	92.9	78.4	86.6	91.6	74.5	84.1	94.1	79.9	87.9
MF2018	WEIGHTED AVERAGE	99.0	90.9	95.9	99.0	79.7	91.7	93.4	91.5	92.7	96.0	85.9	92.2	97.1	80.7	90.9	94.2	96.5	95.1

		MINNESOTA																	
		BRAINERD			DETROIT LAKES			DULUTH			MANKATO			MINNEAPOLIS			ROCHESTER		
	DIVISION	564			565			556 - 558			560			553 - 555			559		
		MAT.	INST.	TOTAL	MAT.	INST.	TOTAL	MAT.	INST.	TOTAL	MAT.	INST.	TOTAL	MAT.	INST.	TOTAL	MAT.	INST.	TOTAL
015433	CONTRACTOR EQUIPMENT		100.0	100.0		97.3	97.3		107.5	107.5		100.0	100.0		104.2	104.2		100.1	100.1
0241, 31 - 34	SITE & INFRASTRUCTURE, DEMOLITION	81.2	99.6	93.2	77.0	94.2	88.2	74.3	108.5	96.6	79.2	98.6	91.9	79.5	106.5	97.1	76.6	99.3	91.4
0310	Concrete Forming & Accessories	91.9	94.5	94.1	87.9	75.5	77.6	100.8	102.7	102.4	98.1	99.4	99.1	100.9	124.6	120.4	101.7	106.6	105.7
0320	Concrete Reinforcing	92.0	106.8	98.1	93.5	106.3	98.8	88.4	107.3	96.1	91.9	108.0	98.5	90.3	112.8	99.5	86.0	108.4	95.1
0330	Cast-in-Place Concrete	105.5	105.1	105.4	94.2	100.1	96.2	90.3	107.1	95.9	97.1	101.0	98.4	120.6	119.2	120.1	108.5	101.3	106.1
03	CONCRETE	95.9	101.5	98.2	89.8	91.0	90.3	94.0	105.8	98.8	91.5	102.4	96.0	109.1	120.9	113.9	95.6	105.9	99.8
04	MASONRY	131.7	112.5	120.5	130.8	99.7	112.7	118.7	115.3	116.7	119.3	107.9	112.6	88.1	123.0	108.4	102.7	113.4	108.9
05	METALS	91.8	122.8	98.3	90.4	120.7	96.8	102.1	122.2	106.3	91.7	123.1	98.2	99.9	125.6	105.3	99.1	124.9	104.5
06	WOOD, PLASTICS & COMPOSITES	93.4	88.1	90.8	68.7	66.3	67.6	102.6	100.5	101.6	100.4	97.8	99.1	102.9	124.0	113.3	101.7	106.4	104.0
07	THERMAL & MOISTURE PROTECTION	104.2	100.7	103.0	106.1	93.5	101.9	102.9	104.2	103.4	104.4	93.0	100.6	102.9	119.5	108.5	108.6	98.3	105.1
08	OPENINGS	83.8	109.2	90.0	94.3	97.2	95.0	97.1	112.5	100.9	88.0	114.4	94.4	96.8	131.4	105.3	94.1	119.7	100.3
0920	Plaster & Gypsum Board	82.0	88.2	86.0	101.0	65.5	78.4	98.1	100.3	99.5	84.9	98.2	93.4	97.6	124.6	114.8	103.8	106.9	105.8
0950, 0980	Ceilings & Acoustic Treatment	62.7	88.2	77.0	119.2	65.5	89.2	103.7	100.3	101.8	62.7	98.2	82.6	103.7	124.6	115.4	97.8	106.9	102.9
0960	Flooring	92.8	104.0	95.7	92.8	74.5	88.1	94.6	104.0	97.0	94.1	91.4	93.4	89.4	126.6	98.9	95.2	93.2	94.7
0970, 0990	Wall Finishes & Painting/Coating	85.2	103.7	96.1	90.2	103.7	98.1	99.9	112.4	107.2	95.0	127.3	114.0	99.9	133.4	119.6	91.4	101.2	97.1
09	FINISHES	83.0	96.7	89.8	100.5	77.2	89.0	98.7	104.0	101.3	84.2	103.7	93.8	97.3	126.1	111.5	95.3	104.2	99.7
COVERS	DIVS. 10 - 14, 25, 28, 41, 43, 44, 46	100.0	102.1	100.4	100.0	97.9	99.5	100.0	103.7	100.8	100.0	101.2	100.3	100.0	108.8	101.9	100.0	102.8	100.6
21, 22, 23	FIRE SUPPRESSION, PLUMBING & HVAC	92.0	93.0	92.3	93.0	89.7	91.8	99.8	96.4	98.6	92.0	89.3	91.0	99.8	115.5	105.4	99.9	97.9	99.2
26, 27, 3370	ELECTRICAL, COMMUNICATIONS & UTIL.	93.2	101.7	96.9	93.8	70.0	83.5	96.3	101.7	98.7	96.4	97.0	96.6	95.9	114.6	104.0	95.3	97.0	96.0
MF2018	WEIGHTED AVERAGE	93.7	102.0	96.9	95.0	89.9	93.0	99.2	105.6	101.7	93.4	100.8	96.2	99.2	119.1	106.7	97.8	104.8	100.4

City Cost Indexes

		MINNESOTA																	MISSISSIPPI		
DIVISION		SAINT PAUL			ST. CLOUD			THIEF RIVER FALLS			WILLMAR			WINDOM			BILOXI		
		550 - 551			563			567			562			561			395		
		MAT.	INST.	TOTAL	MAT.	INST.	TOTAL	MAT.	INST.	TOTAL	MAT.	INST.	TOTAL	MAT.	INST.	TOTAL	MAT.	INST.	TOTAL
015433	CONTRACTOR EQUIPMENT		108.6	108.6		100.0	100.0		97.3	97.3		100.0	100.0		100.0	100.0		96.8	96.8
0241, 31 - 34	SITE & INFRASTRUCTURE, DEMOLITION	76.3	109.3	97.9	81.8	100.4	93.9	77.5	94.4	88.5	77.7	98.9	91.5	73.7	97.7	89.3	95.9	93.9	94.6
0310	Concrete Forming & Accessories	100.4	118.0	114.9	89.9	119.9	114.6	90.8	93.7	93.2	89.8	95.3	94.3	93.0	75.4	78.4	101.5	67.1	73.1
0320	Concrete Reinforcing	90.3	108.7	97.8	92.1	108.4	98.7	94.0	106.3	99.0	91.6	108.2	98.4	91.6	106.7	97.7	150.6	64.8	115.6
0330	Cast-in-Place Concrete	117.6	121.9	119.0	93.0	117.2	101.1	96.2	90.1	94.1	94.5	109.7	99.6	81.7	79.5	80.9	100.3	68.9	89.8
03	CONCRETE	107.6	118.3	112.0	87.7	117.5	99.9	90.9	95.6	92.8	87.7	103.7	94.2	79.0	83.7	80.9	100.0	68.1	86.9
04	MASONRY	106.7	125.9	117.9	115.0	120.7	118.4	105.6	98.8	101.6	118.7	113.7	115.8	130.5	81.7	102.1	79.7	59.3	67.8
05	METALS	102.1	125.5	107.0	91.7	125.3	98.7	90.6	120.7	96.9	91.6	123.8	98.4	91.6	119.1	97.3	94.1	78.3	90.8
06	WOOD, PLASTICS & COMPOSITES	102.5	114.0	108.2	91.3	118.3	104.6	71.7	91.7	81.6	91.0	89.7	90.4	94.4	71.1	82.9	95.6	68.2	82.1
07	THERMAL & MOISTURE PROTECTION	102.8	119.0	108.2	104.3	114.5	107.7	107.0	91.9	102.0	104.1	103.5	103.9	104.0	76.5	94.8	96.5	62.6	85.2
08	OPENINGS	97.1	123.9	103.6	88.5	126.2	97.7	94.3	111.2	98.4	85.8	110.0	91.7	89.4	95.0	90.7	94.3	62.3	86.6
0920	Plaster & Gypsum Board	97.8	114.2	108.2	82.0	119.4	105.8	101.2	91.7	95.2	82.0	89.9	87.0	82.0	70.7	74.8	121.2	67.6	87.1
0950, 0980	Ceilings & Acoustic Treatment	101.2	114.2	108.5	62.7	119.4	94.4	119.2	91.7	103.8	62.7	89.9	77.9	62.7	70.7	67.2	96.3	67.6	80.3
0960	Flooring	110.2	117.4	112.1	90.1	90.7	90.3	93.5	74.5	88.6	91.4	87.7	90.5	93.5	74.5	88.6	112.1	58.7	98.4
0970, 0990	Wall Finishes & Painting/Coating	99.9	127.3	116.0	95.0	129.0	114.9	90.2	103.7	98.1	90.2	99.9	95.9	90.2	127.3	112.0	93.6	45.1	65.1
09	FINISHES	102.6	118.8	110.6	82.6	116.1	99.2	100.8	91.8	96.4	82.7	93.8	88.2	82.9	80.0	81.5	102.6	63.4	83.2
COVERS	DIVS. 10 - 14, 25, 28, 41, 43, 44, 46	100.0	109.0	101.9	100.0	107.0	101.5	100.0	100.3	100.1	100.0	101.5	100.3	100.0	95.7	99.1	100.0	82.9	96.3
21, 22, 23	FIRE SUPPRESSION, PLUMBING & HVAC	99.8	115.9	105.6	99.3	116.4	105.4	93.0	89.2	91.6	92.0	108.7	97.8	92.0	78.0	86.9	99.8	54.8	83.6
26, 27, 3370	ELECTRICAL, COMMUNICATIONS & UTIL.	95.7	114.6	103.9	93.2	114.6	102.5	92.9	70.0	82.9	93.2	96.2	94.5	96.4	96.9	96.6	99.7	50.3	78.2
MF2018	WEIGHTED AVERAGE	100.6	117.9	107.1	94.0	116.3	102.4	94.0	93.1	93.7	92.2	104.7	96.9	92.2	88.3	90.7	97.4	64.1	84.8

		MISSISSIPPI																		
DIVISION		CLARKSDALE			COLUMBUS			GREENVILLE			GREENWOOD			JACKSON			LAUREL		
		386			397			387			389			390 - 392			394		
		MAT.	INST.	TOTAL	MAT.	INST.	TOTAL	MAT.	INST.	TOTAL	MAT.	INST.	TOTAL	MAT.	INST.	TOTAL	MAT.	INST.	TOTAL
015433	CONTRACTOR EQUIPMENT		95.0	95.0		96.8	96.8		95.0	95.0		95.0	95.0		105.7	105.7		96.8	96.8
0241, 31 - 34	SITE & INFRASTRUCTURE, DEMOLITION	104.0	86.4	92.5	92.8	92.7	92.7	111.3	88.5	96.4	107.0	86.1	93.4	92.1	105.1	100.6	96.6	92.0	93.6
0310	Concrete Forming & Accessories	93.6	39.6	49.1	92.4	41.6	50.5	91.1	58.6	64.3	101.3	39.8	50.5	102.2	68.0	74.0	92.5	53.3	60.2
0320	Concrete Reinforcing	126.0	57.9	98.2	161.2	58.1	119.1	126.7	65.9	101.8	126.0	57.9	98.2	169.9	65.2	127.1	162.2	28.6	107.6
0330	Cast-in-Place Concrete	111.7	56.6	93.2	102.3	58.2	87.6	115.0	66.0	98.6	120.1	56.4	98.8	86.5	73.3	82.1	100.1	57.4	85.8
03	CONCRETE	103.4	50.1	81.5	102.2	51.6	81.4	108.4	63.5	90.0	109.8	50.0	85.3	98.8	70.0	86.9	104.0	51.5	82.4
04	MASONRY	94.0	46.0	66.1	98.0	50.5	70.3	136.7	60.6	92.4	94.7	45.9	66.3	84.9	64.6	73.1	94.9	48.3	67.8
05	METALS	93.3	72.4	88.9	91.7	73.2	87.8	93.3	80.4	90.6	93.3	72.2	88.8	100.4	77.7	95.6	91.8	59.5	85.0
06	WOOD, PLASTICS & COMPOSITES	89.8	39.8	65.2	83.9	40.5	62.6	86.9	56.0	71.7	100.1	39.8	70.4	103.7	68.2	86.3	84.8	57.5	71.4
07	THERMAL & MOISTURE PROTECTION	98.7	48.6	81.9	96.5	51.7	81.5	99.1	62.3	86.7	99.0	50.5	82.7	94.2	67.1	85.2	96.7	53.0	82.1
08	OPENINGS	95.7	42.7	82.8	94.2	43.1	81.8	95.4	54.1	85.3	95.7	42.7	82.8	97.7	60.6	88.7	91.7	45.9	80.5
0920	Plaster & Gypsum Board	101.1	38.3	61.2	111.3	39.1	65.3	100.4	55.1	71.6	110.1	38.3	64.4	106.9	67.2	81.6	111.3	76.6	76.5
0950, 0980	Ceilings & Acoustic Treatment	87.4	38.3	59.9	89.2	39.1	61.2	89.4	55.1	70.2	87.4	38.3	59.9	101.6	67.2	82.3	89.2	56.6	71.0
0960	Flooring	107.2	58.7	94.7	107.3	62.3	95.8	105.9	58.7	93.8	111.4	58.7	97.9	109.1	65.4	97.9	106.3	58.7	94.1
0970, 0990	Wall Finishes & Painting/Coating	98.8	40.8	64.7	93.6	40.8	62.6	98.8	55.0	73.0	98.8	40.8	64.7	99.9	55.0	73.5	93.6	40.8	62.6
09	FINISHES	98.1	43.0	70.8	98.2	44.7	71.7	98.6	57.6	78.4	100.7	43.0	72.2	103.9	66.2	85.3	98.3	54.0	76.4
COVERS	DIVS. 10 - 14, 25, 28, 41, 43, 44, 46	100.0	42.6	87.8	100.0	43.5	87.9	100.0	82.0	96.2	100.0	42.6	87.8	100.0	84.3	96.7	100.0	30.8	85.3
21, 22, 23	FIRE SUPPRESSION, PLUMBING & HVAC	96.4	45.2	78.0	95.7	47.0	78.2	100.1	53.5	83.3	96.4	45.5	78.1	99.9	60.2	85.6	95.8	42.0	76.4
26, 27, 3370	ELECTRICAL, COMMUNICATIONS & UTIL.	99.0	35.9	71.6	98.2	47.5	76.1	99.0	56.0	80.3	99.0	33.6	70.6	102.1	56.0	82.1	99.1	50.0	77.7
MF2018	WEIGHTED AVERAGE	97.4	49.6	79.3	96.3	53.2	80.0	100.9	62.7	86.5	98.5	49.4	80.0	99.2	68.2	87.5	96.5	52.2	79.7

		MISSISSIPPI									MISSOURI								
DIVISION		MCCOMB			MERIDIAN			TUPELO			BOWLING GREEN			CAPE GIRARDEAU			CHILLICOTHE		
		396			393			388			633			637			646		
		MAT.	INST.	TOTAL	MAT.	INST.	TOTAL	MAT.	INST.	TOTAL	MAT.	INST.	TOTAL	MAT.	INST.	TOTAL	MAT.	INST.	TOTAL
015433	CONTRACTOR EQUIPMENT		96.8	96.8		96.8	96.8		95.0	95.0		94.6	94.6		94.6	94.6		100.8	100.8
0241, 31 - 34	SITE & INFRASTRUCTURE, DEMOLITION	87.3	91.8	90.2	92.5	94.0	93.5	102.0	86.3	91.8	77.2	87.3	83.8	82.3	87.1	85.4	100.5	91.1	94.4
0310	Concrete Forming & Accessories	92.4	40.8	49.8	90.4	67.8	71.7	91.4	41.0	49.8	95.9	85.4	87.2	90.9	79.6	81.6	94.2	85.0	86.6
0320	Concrete Reinforcing	163.2	29.9	108.8	161.2	64.9	121.8	123.3	57.8	96.5	85.7	93.5	88.9	86.8	77.5	83.0	91.0	89.2	90.3
0330	Cast-in-Place Concrete	88.8	55.9	77.8	95.0	69.1	86.3	111.7	57.4	93.5	77.9	89.4	81.7	77.1	81.2	78.4	88.3	77.4	84.6
03	CONCRETE	93.3	45.4	73.7	97.0	68.5	85.3	102.9	50.9	81.6	83.8	88.7	85.8	83.1	80.5	82.0	96.8	83.8	91.5
04	MASONRY	98.9	45.5	67.8	79.3	59.5	67.8	124.9	46.9	79.5	128.7	89.7	106.0	126.9	73.4	95.8	93.7	80.9	86.2
05	METALS	91.9	58.5	84.9	91.8	78.5	89.0	93.2	71.9	88.7	86.1	99.2	88.9	86.1	91.3	87.2	83.6	101.1	87.3
06	WOOD, PLASTICS & COMPOSITES	83.9	41.9	63.2	81.8	68.8	75.4	87.4	40.5	64.3	97.7	84.1	91.0	92.5	79.4	86.0	101.1	86.1	93.7
07	THERMAL & MOISTURE PROTECTION	96.1	50.1	80.7	96.3	63.4	85.2	98.6	48.9	82.0	98.0	88.9	95.0	97.6	77.4	90.8	101.9	82.3	95.3
08	OPENINGS	94.2	36.6	80.2	93.9	63.7	86.5	95.7	45.5	83.5	92.5	89.3	91.7	92.5	74.9	88.2	82.9	84.8	83.4
0920	Plaster & Gypsum Board	111.3	40.5	66.2	111.3	68.3	83.9	100.4	39.1	61.4	88.5	83.7	85.4	88.0	78.8	82.2	95.7	85.7	89.3
0950, 0980	Ceilings & Acoustic Treatment	89.2	40.5	61.9	89.7	68.3	77.7	87.4	39.1	60.4	99.1	83.7	90.5	99.1	78.8	87.8	98.6	85.7	91.4
0960	Flooring	107.3	58.7	94.8	106.3	58.7	94.1	106.1	58.7	93.9	88.1	84.4	87.1	85.4	77.2	83.3	89.7	86.8	88.9
0970, 0990	Wall Finishes & Painting/Coating	93.6	40.8	62.6	93.6	52.4	69.4	98.8	39.4	63.8	97.3	92.5	94.4	97.3	70.1	81.3	95.0	89.8	92.0
09	FINISHES	97.7	44.1	71.2	97.8	64.6	81.4	97.7	43.7	71.0	94.6	85.5	90.1	93.8	77.8	85.9	97.4	86.0	91.8
COVERS	DIVS. 10 - 14, 25, 28, 41, 43, 44, 46	100.0	45.1	88.3	100.0	83.0	96.4	100.0	43.5	88.0	100.0	97.4	99.4	100.0	95.6	99.1	100.0	92.8	98.5
21, 22, 23	FIRE SUPPRESSION, PLUMBING & HVAC	95.7	44.7	77.3	99.8	56.8	84.3	96.6	46.4	78.5	92.5	96.3	93.9	99.8	90.7	96.5	92.6	87.8	90.9
26, 27, 3370	ELECTRICAL, COMMUNICATIONS & UTIL.	97.3	48.3	76.0	99.1	52.1	78.6	98.9	47.5	76.5	92.4	66.3	81.0	92.3	85.0	89.2	90.4	65.5	79.5
MF2018	WEIGHTED AVERAGE	95.1	49.9	78.0	95.8	65.1	84.2	98.6	52.0	81.0	92.4	87.8	90.7	93.9	83.8	90.1	91.9	84.4	89.0

City Cost Indexes

		MISSOURI																
		COLUMBIA 652			FLAT RIVER 636			HANNIBAL 634			HARRISONVILLE 647			JEFFERSON CITY 650 - 651			JOPLIN 648		
DIVISION		MAT.	INST.	TOTAL	MAT.	INST.	TOTAL	MAT.	INST.	TOTAL	MAT.	INST.	TOTAL	MAT.	INST.	TOTAL	MAT.	INST.	TOTAL
015433	CONTRACTOR EQUIPMENT		99.0	99.0		94.6	94.6		94.6	94.6		100.8	100.8		108.8	108.8		104.8	104.8
0241, 31 - 34	SITE & INFRASTRUCTURE, DEMOLITION	81.0	94.8	90.0	79.2	87.2	84.4	76.2	86.8	83.1	93.9	92.5	93.0	81.8	107.4	98.5	104.1	97.2	99.6
0310	Concrete Forming & Accessories	89.7	83.1	84.3	100.6	81.7	85.0	94.9	74.0	77.7	91.9	98.0	96.9	100.2	80.0	83.5	103.3	71.2	76.8
0320	Concrete Reinforcing	86.1	105.0	93.8	86.8	89.5	87.9	85.3	99.2	91.0	90.4	96.5	92.9	89.8	96.1	92.4	94.0	96.2	94.9
0330	Cast-in-Place Concrete	74.9	83.2	77.7	80.4	87.2	82.7	73.7	85.6	77.7	90.4	91.9	90.9	79.5	86.5	81.8	95.6	72.3	87.8
03	CONCRETE	77.6	87.7	81.8	86.3	85.6	86.0	80.6	83.2	81.7	93.1	96.1	94.3	85.2	85.8	85.4	96.0	76.9	88.2
04	MASONRY	119.8	85.8	100.0	126.2	75.0	96.4	117.4	83.0	97.4	88.7	92.2	90.7	84.9	86.0	85.5	87.5	80.5	83.4
05	METALS	95.7	107.9	98.3	86.0	96.3	88.2	86.1	101.4	89.3	83.9	105.7	88.5	96.8	102.7	98.0	84.5	100.6	87.9
06	WOOD, PLASTICS & COMPOSITES	84.9	81.5	83.2	103.7	79.8	91.9	96.4	72.4	84.6	97.8	98.5	98.1	101.1	77.0	89.2	110.8	69.2	90.3
07	THERMAL & MOISTURE PROTECTION	97.4	84.6	93.1	98.2	86.8	94.3	97.9	85.1	93.6	101.2	93.3	98.5	103.0	86.8	97.5	101.2	76.0	92.8
08	OPENINGS	96.4	87.0	94.1	92.5	86.1	90.9	92.5	78.1	89.0	83.1	97.1	86.5	96.6	82.2	93.1	83.8	72.6	81.1
0920	Plaster & Gypsum Board	83.8	81.2	82.1	93.3	79.3	84.4	88.3	71.6	77.7	94.1	98.5	96.9	91.1	76.1	81.5	101.1	68.2	80.2
0950, 0980	Ceilings & Acoustic Treatment	77.2	81.5	79.4	99.1	79.3	88.0	99.1	71.6	83.7	98.6	98.5	98.5	82.5	76.1	78.9	99.9	68.2	82.2
0960	Flooring	90.3	96.3	91.9	90.7	73.6	86.3	87.6	84.4	86.7	85.8	97.5	88.8	94.9	92.6	94.3	111.1	65.3	99.4
0970, 0990	Wall Finishes & Painting/Coating	88.3	81.9	84.5	97.3	62.4	76.8	97.3	81.9	88.2	99.8	93.8	96.3	88.0	81.9	84.4	94.7	66.0	77.8
09	FINISHES	84.1	84.9	84.5	96.1	77.2	86.8	94.4	75.4	85.0	95.8	97.9	96.9	91.9	81.6	86.8	102.8	69.5	86.3
COVERS	DIVS. 10 - 14, 25, 28, 41, 43, 44, 46	100.0	94.9	98.9	100.0	90.1	97.9	100.0	94.0	98.7	100.0	96.9	99.3	100.0	97.0	99.4	100.0	91.0	98.1
21, 22, 23	FIRE SUPPRESSION, PLUMBING & HVAC	99.7	88.8	95.8	92.5	96.0	93.8	92.5	92.9	92.6	92.5	91.2	92.1	99.8	95.9	98.4	99.9	66.3	87.8
26, 27, 3370	ELECTRICAL, COMMUNICATIONS & UTIL.	81.7	80.8	81.3	94.8	85.0	90.5	91.7	66.3	80.6	93.8	87.4	91.0	86.0	80.8	83.7	89.2	67.1	79.5
MF2018	WEIGHTED AVERAGE	93.1	88.7	91.4	93.1	86.7	90.7	91.4	83.7	88.5	91.3	94.2	92.4	94.1	89.9	92.5	93.9	76.4	87.3

		MISSOURI																
		KANSAS CITY 640 - 641			KIRKSVILLE 635			POPLAR BLUFF 639			ROLLA 654 - 655			SEDALIA 653			SIKESTON 638		
DIVISION		MAT.	INST.	TOTAL	MAT.	INST.	TOTAL	MAT.	INST.	TOTAL	MAT.	INST.	TOTAL	MAT.	INST.	TOTAL	MAT.	INST.	TOTAL
015433	CONTRACTOR EQUIPMENT		104.7	104.7		88.3	88.3		90.9	90.9		99.0	99.0		93.5	93.5		90.9	90.9
0241, 31 - 34	SITE & INFRASTRUCTURE, DEMOLITION	99.3	104.4	102.6	78.4	80.9	80.0	69.5	85.6	80.0	76.4	94.0	87.9	78.4	90.1	86.0	71.7	86.2	81.1
0310	Concrete Forming & Accessories	103.6	101.8	102.1	89.0	70.4	73.6	89.4	74.6	77.2	95.3	90.2	91.1	93.2	72.2	75.8	89.8	74.8	77.4
0320	Concrete Reinforcing	89.8	106.5	96.6	86.0	82.3	84.5	88.6	68.0	80.2	86.5	92.3	88.9	85.7	105.4	93.7	88.0	86.3	87.3
0330	Cast-in-Place Concrete	93.8	99.7	95.8	80.4	76.1	78.9	61.8	82.5	68.7	76.6	90.8	81.4	80.1	77.9	79.4	66.0	82.5	71.6
03	CONCRETE	97.3	102.0	99.2	96.6	75.0	87.8	75.1	76.7	75.8	79.2	91.4	84.2	91.0	80.6	86.8	78.3	80.0	79.0
04	MASONRY	94.2	98.9	96.9	133.8	74.5	99.3	124.6	75.0	95.7	97.8	81.3	88.2	103.1	78.5	88.8	123.6	74.9	95.3
05	METALS	98.2	106.4	99.9	86.8	88.1	87.1	87.2	81.3	86.0	96.2	100.9	97.2	97.5	100.2	98.1	88.1	89.4	88.3
06	WOOD, PLASTICS & COMPOSITES	108.1	102.3	105.3	85.1	68.3	76.8	84.4	71.4	78.0	90.2	91.9	91.0	83.4	68.1	75.9	85.6	71.4	78.6
07	THERMAL & MOISTURE PROTECTION	102.7	102.2	102.5	103.2	82.4	96.2	101.9	79.8	94.5	97.6	88.7	94.6	102.8	83.3	96.3	102.0	79.3	94.4
08	OPENINGS	96.6	100.5	97.5	95.6	72.3	89.9	96.4	67.1	89.3	84.4	88.3	94.4	100.2	79.2	95.1	96.4	71.9	90.4
0920	Plaster & Gypsum Board	102.7	102.4	102.5	83.6	67.4	73.3	84.5	70.6	75.6	84.8	91.9	89.3	80.7	67.4	72.2	85.9	70.6	76.1
0950, 0980	Ceilings & Acoustic Treatment	106.8	102.4	104.4	96.4	67.4	80.2	99.1	70.6	83.1	77.2	91.9	85.4	77.2	67.4	71.7	99.1	70.6	83.1
0960	Flooring	89.4	100.4	92.2	69.9	84.0	73.5	80.9	73.6	79.1	93.1	88.1	91.8	73.6	63.5	71.0	81.4	73.6	79.4
0970, 0990	Wall Finishes & Painting/Coating	100.3	110.2	106.1	92.6	68.1	78.2	91.9	58.4	72.2	88.3	85.4	86.6	88.3	89.8	89.2	91.9	58.4	72.2
09	FINISHES	99.7	102.5	101.1	93.8	71.7	82.9	93.6	71.8	82.8	85.1	89.2	87.1	83.9	71.4	77.8	94.1	72.1	83.2
COVERS	DIVS. 10 - 14, 25, 28, 41, 43, 44, 46	100.0	99.7	99.9	100.0	93.5	98.6	100.0	96.0	99.1	100.0	96.9	99.3	100.0	90.8	98.0	100.0	89.3	97.7
21, 22, 23	FIRE SUPPRESSION, PLUMBING & HVAC	99.7	100.9	100.1	92.5	92.4	92.5	92.5	95.4	93.6	92.4	94.9	93.3	92.4	87.1	90.5	92.5	95.6	93.6
26, 27, 3370	ELECTRICAL, COMMUNICATIONS & UTIL.	95.8	97.2	96.4	90.9	66.3	80.2	91.5	85.0	88.7	81.0	73.9	77.9	81.1	87.4	83.9	91.0	85.0	88.4
MF2018	WEIGHTED AVERAGE	98.4	101.2	99.5	94.4	79.2	88.7	91.4	82.4	88.0	90.6	89.3	90.1	92.9	84.1	89.6	91.9	83.6	88.8

		MISSOURI									MONTANA								
		SPRINGFIELD 656 - 658			ST. JOSEPH 644 - 645			ST. LOUIS 630 - 631			BILLINGS 590 - 591			BUTTE 597			GREAT FALLS 594		
DIVISION		MAT.	INST.	TOTAL	MAT.	INST.	TOTAL	MAT.	INST.	TOTAL	MAT.	INST.	TOTAL	MAT.	INST.	TOTAL	MAT.	INST.	TOTAL
015433	CONTRACTOR EQUIPMENT		95.5	95.5		100.8	100.8		96.7	96.7		98.6	98.6		98.4	98.4		98.4	98.4
0241, 31 - 34	SITE & INFRASTRUCTURE, DEMOLITION	82.0	93.6	89.6	100.9	90.7	94.3	86.8	97.1	93.5	74.7	92.3	86.2	76.5	91.5	86.3	78.8	91.8	87.3
0310	Concrete Forming & Accessories	99.6	78.4	82.1	102.3	88.3	90.8	98.0	103.7	102.7	95.1	68.4	73.0	86.4	68.5	71.6	94.8	64.4	69.7
0320	Concrete Reinforcing	83.5	104.6	92.1	88.1	106.2	95.5	83.8	103.4	91.8	162.4	83.9	130.3	176.4	83.3	138.3	162.6	83.6	130.3
0330	Cast-in-Place Concrete	81.4	77.5	80.1	88.8	94.3	90.7	87.1	103.2	92.4	98.3	73.3	90.0	108.2	68.9	95.1	114.4	70.4	99.7
03	CONCRETE	87.8	83.0	85.8	92.2	94.3	93.1	87.8	103.4	94.2	105.1	73.6	92.2	109.4	72.0	94.1	112.8	70.7	95.5
04	MASONRY	79.6	81.6	80.8	89.2	89.7	89.5	97.9	103.2	101.0	163.1	83.9	117.0	158.4	71.7	107.9	164.4	74.8	112.2
05	METALS	102.9	98.3	101.9	89.5	110.8	93.9	96.7	102.7	97.9	98.7	90.4	97.0	92.7	89.1	92.0	95.8	89.7	94.5
06	WOOD, PLASTICS & COMPOSITES	89.1	77.2	83.2	110.8	88.4	99.8	100.9	103.3	102.1	89.7	64.5	77.3	82.2	66.9	74.6	90.4	61.4	76.1
07	THERMAL & MOISTURE PROTECTION	101.3	78.5	93.7	101.5	87.3	96.7	98.3	103.1	99.9	96.5	75.4	89.4	96.3	70.8	87.7	96.7	70.2	87.8
08	OPENINGS	102.2	89.7	99.2	87.3	95.6	89.4	96.6	106.5	99.0	102.2	65.8	93.3	100.4	66.2	92.0	103.4	67.3	94.6
0920	Plaster & Gypsum Board	85.7	76.7	80.0	104.2	88.0	93.9	89.3	103.5	98.3	98.2	63.6	76.2	97.6	66.1	77.6	104.5	60.5	76.5
0950, 0980	Ceilings & Acoustic Treatment	77.2	76.7	76.9	109.6	88.0	97.5	95.5	103.5	100.0	98.9	63.6	79.2	103.1	66.1	82.4	105.3	60.5	80.2
0960	Flooring	91.5	73.5	86.4	93.3	91.1	92.8	89.4	92.5	90.2	98.2	77.6	92.9	97.2	72.5	90.8	102.4	70.3	94.2
0970, 0990	Wall Finishes & Painting/Coating	82.7	101.4	93.7	95.0	107.6	102.4	99.9	104.5	102.6	98.3	86.4	91.3	95.7	80.7	86.9	95.7	83.2	88.4
09	FINISHES	87.2	80.0	83.7	101.8	91.0	96.5	94.4	101.5	97.9	92.0	71.2	81.7	92.5	70.1	81.4	95.6	66.5	81.2
COVERS	DIVS. 10 - 14, 25, 28, 41, 43, 44, 46	100.0	94.0	98.7	100.0	96.0	99.2	100.0	102.0	100.4	100.0	94.8	98.9	100.0	94.0	98.7	100.0	93.1	98.5
21, 22, 23	FIRE SUPPRESSION, PLUMBING & HVAC	99.8	72.0	89.8	99.9	89.3	96.1	99.8	102.2	100.7	100.0	76.0	91.4	100.1	67.2	88.2	100.1	72.8	90.3
26, 27, 3370	ELECTRICAL, COMMUNICATIONS & UTIL.	83.2	67.8	76.5	93.8	71.8	84.2	95.6	101.9	98.4	84.7	75.1	80.5	87.5	63.2	76.9	84.2	65.8	76.2
MF2018	WEIGHTED AVERAGE	94.9	80.5	89.5	95.1	90.1	93.2	96.2	102.2	98.5	100.2	78.2	91.9	99.5	72.7	89.4	101.0	74.0	90.8

City Cost Indexes

		\multicolumn{18}{c}{MONTANA}
		\multicolumn{3}{c}{HAVRE}	\multicolumn{3}{c}{HELENA}	\multicolumn{3}{c}{KALISPELL}	\multicolumn{3}{c}{MILES CITY}	\multicolumn{3}{c}{MISSOULA}	\multicolumn{3}{c}{WOLF POINT}
	DIVISION	\multicolumn{3}{c}{595}	\multicolumn{3}{c}{596}	\multicolumn{3}{c}{599}	\multicolumn{3}{c}{593}	\multicolumn{3}{c}{598}	\multicolumn{3}{c}{592}
		MAT.	INST.	TOTAL	MAT.	INST.	TOTAL	MAT.	INST.	TOTAL	MAT.	INST.	TOTAL	MAT.	INST.	TOTAL	MAT.	INST.	TOTAL
---	---	---	---	---	---	---	---	---	---	---	---	---	---	---	---	---	---	---	---
015433	CONTRACTOR EQUIPMENT		98.4	98.4		107.5	107.5		98.4	98.4		98.4	98.4		98.4	98.4		98.4	98.4
0241, 31 - 34	SITE & INFRASTRUCTURE, DEMOLITION	76.3	90.9	85.8	73.1	103.0	92.6	67.4	91.0	82.8	70.5	90.9	83.8	67.1	91.1	82.7	78.7	90.9	86.6
0310	Concrete Forming & Accessories	82.0	62.6	66.0	97.5	63.9	69.8	88.3	63.6	67.9	93.9	62.8	68.2	88.3	64.0	68.3	89.2	62.8	67.4
0320	Concrete Reinforcing	177.7	77.9	136.9	181.3	77.7	139.0	181.0	83.6	141.2	176.9	77.9	136.4	179.4	83.4	140.2	179.4	77.9	137.9
0330	Cast-in-Place Concrete	116.6	66.7	99.9	83.5	70.9	79.3	94.0	67.9	85.2	102.9	66.8	90.8	79.8	68.4	75.9	115.3	65.9	98.7
03	CONCRETE	117.1	67.6	96.8	107.4	69.5	91.8	100.4	69.4	87.7	106.5	67.7	90.6	90.1	69.7	81.7	120.5	67.4	98.7
04	MASONRY	159.5	70.9	107.9	142.8	69.1	99.9	157.5	72.7	108.1	167.2	70.9	111.1	194.2	69.7	121.7	168.3	70.9	111.6
05	METALS	89.6	85.2	88.6	93.9	83.5	91.7	89.4	87.6	89.1	89.3	85.3	88.5	89.4	87.4	89.0	89.4	85.3	88.5
06	WOOD, PLASTICS & COMPOSITES	77.3	61.4	69.5	96.0	61.8	79.2	84.0	61.4	72.9	88.7	61.4	75.3	84.0	61.4	72.9	83.7	61.4	72.7
07	THERMAL & MOISTURE PROTECTION	96.7	61.2	84.8	96.6	68.7	87.3	95.9	67.5	86.4	96.2	62.4	84.9	95.5	68.6	86.5	97.1	62.3	85.4
08	OPENINGS	101.0	61.9	91.5	100.5	62.2	91.2	101.0	63.3	91.8	100.5	61.9	91.1	100.4	63.3	91.4	100.5	61.9	91.1
0920	Plaster & Gypsum Board	94.5	60.5	72.9	95.9	60.5	73.4	97.6	60.5	74.0	102.3	60.5	75.7	97.6	60.5	74.0	98.3	60.5	74.3
0950, 0980	Ceilings & Acoustic Treatment	103.1	60.5	79.3	106.5	60.5	80.8	103.1	60.5	79.3	98.7	60.5	77.3	103.1	60.5	79.3	98.7	60.5	77.3
0960	Flooring	95.4	79.2	91.2	109.6	72.5	100.1	98.5	79.2	93.6	102.3	79.2	96.4	98.5	72.5	91.9	99.6	79.2	94.3
0970, 0990	Wall Finishes & Painting/Coating	95.7	59.0	74.1	105.2	52.3	74.1	95.7	79.2	86.0	95.7	59.0	74.1	95.7	79.2	86.0	95.7	59.0	74.1
09	FINISHES	91.9	65.2	78.7	100.0	63.9	82.1	92.6	67.9	80.4	93.3	65.2	79.4	92.3	66.7	79.7	92.7	65.2	79.1
COVERS	DIVS. 10 - 14, 25, 28, 41, 43, 44, 46	100.0	78.1	95.3	100.0	85.5	96.9	100.0	78.7	95.5	100.0	78.1	95.3	100.0	84.9	96.8	100.0	78.1	95.3
21, 22, 23	FIRE SUPPRESSION, PLUMBING & HVAC	92.8	60.7	81.2	100.2	62.8	86.7	92.8	61.1	81.4	92.8	66.3	83.2	100.1	63.2	86.8	92.8	66.3	83.2
26, 27, 3370	ELECTRICAL, COMMUNICATIONS & UTIL.	84.2	59.8	73.6	89.6	63.6	78.3	86.0	58.8	74.2	84.2	64.3	75.6	86.5	62.0	75.8	84.2	64.3	75.6
MF2018	WEIGHTED AVERAGE	97.8	68.1	86.6	99.7	70.3	88.6	95.7	69.3	85.8	96.8	70.0	86.7	97.8	70.1	87.3	98.7	70.0	87.9

		\multicolumn{18}{c}{NEBRASKA}
		\multicolumn{3}{c}{ALLIANCE}	\multicolumn{3}{c}{COLUMBUS}	\multicolumn{3}{c}{GRAND ISLAND}	\multicolumn{3}{c}{HASTINGS}	\multicolumn{3}{c}{LINCOLN}	\multicolumn{3}{c}{MCCOOK}
	DIVISION	\multicolumn{3}{c}{693}	\multicolumn{3}{c}{686}	\multicolumn{3}{c}{688}	\multicolumn{3}{c}{689}	\multicolumn{3}{c}{683 - 685}	\multicolumn{3}{c}{690}
		MAT.	INST.	TOTAL	MAT.	INST.	TOTAL	MAT.	INST.	TOTAL	MAT.	INST.	TOTAL	MAT.	INST.	TOTAL	MAT.	INST.	TOTAL
---	---	---	---	---	---	---	---	---	---	---	---	---	---	---	---	---	---	---	---
015433	CONTRACTOR EQUIPMENT		96.8	96.8		102.1	102.1		102.1	102.1		102.1	102.1		107.3	107.3		99.7	99.7
0241, 31 - 34	SITE & INFRASTRUCTURE, DEMOLITION	92.7	97.2	95.7	94.5	93.1	93.6	101.7	94.3	96.9	97.3	93.1	94.5	92.7	106.3	101.6	90.7	91.7	91.3
0310	Concrete Forming & Accessories	92.9	49.4	57.0	101.1	66.8	72.8	100.8	80.8	84.3	103.4	64.7	71.5	100.5	69.8	75.2	97.6	49.9	58.2
0320	Concrete Reinforcing	101.7	76.0	91.2	85.5	74.7	81.1	85.0	79.5	82.8	85.0	66.3	77.3	84.5	79.7	82.5	93.2	66.4	82.2
0330	Cast-in-Place Concrete	97.1	74.7	89.6	111.9	75.0	99.5	118.5	74.5	103.8	118.5	68.2	101.7	92.7	80.1	88.5	105.5	67.9	92.9
03	CONCRETE	112.3	63.7	92.3	103.4	72.0	90.6	108.2	79.1	96.3	108.4	67.2	91.5	94.8	75.8	87.0	102.2	60.4	85.0
04	MASONRY	106.4	68.1	84.1	108.9	68.0	85.1	101.4	75.3	86.2	107.7	65.0	82.8	88.4	78.7	82.8	102.5	68.0	82.4
05	METALS	97.0	78.5	93.1	90.2	88.4	89.8	90.2	92.5	90.7	92.3	84.3	90.6	99.1	87.6	96.7	92.6	82.7	90.5
06	WOOD, PLASTICS & COMPOSITES	85.3	43.6	64.7	96.5	66.7	81.9	95.9	81.8	89.0	98.8	64.3	81.8	101.2	66.9	84.3	94.0	44.4	69.6
07	THERMAL & MOISTURE PROTECTION	106.1	67.7	93.3	106.4	71.1	94.5	106.5	82.1	98.3	106.5	68.8	93.9	102.9	80.9	95.5	102.0	67.7	90.5
08	OPENINGS	89.0	51.4	79.8	87.9	65.2	82.4	87.9	78.3	85.6	87.9	61.7	81.6	98.0	64.1	89.7	87.9	49.4	78.6
0920	Plaster & Gypsum Board	79.4	42.0	55.6	92.9	65.7	75.6	92.2	81.2	85.2	93.6	63.2	74.2	101.2	65.7	78.6	89.6	42.8	59.8
0950, 0980	Ceilings & Acoustic Treatment	90.2	42.0	63.2	87.1	65.7	75.1	87.1	81.2	83.8	87.1	63.2	73.7	103.7	65.7	82.4	87.6	42.8	62.5
0960	Flooring	90.7	76.0	87.0	83.7	76.0	81.7	83.4	68.7	79.7	84.5	70.8	81.0	94.6	90.0	93.4	88.4	76.0	85.2
0970, 0990	Wall Finishes & Painting/Coating	146.1	44.9	86.7	72.5	52.3	60.6	72.5	71.8	72.1	72.5	52.3	60.6	89.1	69.0	77.3	88.0	39.2	59.3
09	FINISHES	91.4	52.4	72.1	87.3	66.8	77.2	87.4	77.6	82.5	87.8	64.2	76.2	99.3	73.0	86.3	90.0	52.2	71.3
COVERS	DIVS. 10 - 14, 25, 28, 41, 43, 44, 46	100.0	84.5	96.7	100.0	87.4	97.3	100.0	90.8	98.0	100.0	87.1	97.3	100.0	89.5	97.8	100.0	84.7	96.7
21, 22, 23	FIRE SUPPRESSION, PLUMBING & HVAC	93.8	66.0	83.8	92.8	66.3	83.3	100.1	76.5	91.6	92.8	65.6	83.0	99.9	76.5	91.5	92.5	66.2	83.0
26, 27, 3370	ELECTRICAL, COMMUNICATIONS & UTIL.	85.5	56.7	73.0	88.2	70.3	80.4	87.5	67.1	78.6	87.2	68.6	79.1	95.8	67.0	83.3	86.6	56.7	73.6
MF2018	WEIGHTED AVERAGE	96.5	66.0	85.0	94.0	72.6	85.9	96.0	79.0	89.6	95.0	70.3	85.6	97.9	77.9	90.4	93.7	65.4	83.0

		\multicolumn{12}{c}{NEBRASKA}	\multicolumn{6}{c}{NEVADA}
		\multicolumn{3}{c}{NORFOLK}	\multicolumn{3}{c}{NORTH PLATTE}	\multicolumn{3}{c}{OMAHA}	\multicolumn{3}{c}{VALENTINE}	\multicolumn{3}{c}{CARSON CITY}	\multicolumn{3}{c}{ELKO}
	DIVISION	\multicolumn{3}{c}{687}	\multicolumn{3}{c}{691}	\multicolumn{3}{c}{680 - 681}	\multicolumn{3}{c}{692}	\multicolumn{3}{c}{897}	\multicolumn{3}{c}{898}
		MAT.	INST.	TOTAL	MAT.	INST.	TOTAL	MAT.	INST.	TOTAL	MAT.	INST.	TOTAL	MAT.	INST.	TOTAL	MAT.	INST.	TOTAL
---	---	---	---	---	---	---	---	---	---	---	---	---	---	---	---	---	---	---	---
015433	CONTRACTOR EQUIPMENT		93.6	93.6		99.7	99.7		107.5	107.5		95.8	95.8		104.8	104.8		99.9	99.9
0241, 31 - 34	SITE & INFRASTRUCTURE, DEMOLITION	80.1	92.1	87.9	95.2	91.5	92.8	89.9	106.5	100.8	80.2	97.4	91.4	81.6	104.2	96.3	72.0	94.9	86.9
0310	Concrete Forming & Accessories	89.5	65.9	70.1	99.5	67.7	73.3	100.4	78.1	82.0	89.8	47.6	55.0	97.8	86.4	88.4	98.2	85.1	87.4
0320	Concrete Reinforcing	85.6	57.8	74.3	92.7	71.1	83.8	84.5	79.9	82.6	93.2	57.7	78.7	155.3	119.2	140.5	156.7	82.4	126.4
0330	Cast-in-Place Concrete	112.0	65.3	96.4	105.5	63.5	91.4	93.0	85.4	90.5	92.7	50.5	78.6	93.0	88.6	91.5	87.1	65.1	79.7
03	CONCRETE	102.0	64.9	86.8	102.2	67.6	88.0	95.0	81.5	89.4	99.5	51.3	79.7	123.5	93.0	111.0	109.7	77.8	96.6
04	MASONRY	112.4	67.9	86.5	91.3	66.9	77.5	96.9	81.2	87.7	101.4	67.5	81.8	140.1	72.6	100.8	150.2	59.3	97.3
05	METALS	92.7	73.6	88.7	90.5	85.0	89.4	96.9	88.3	95.1	102.2	71.8	95.8	100.0	100.9	100.2	104.1	84.6	100.0
06	WOOD, PLASTICS & COMPOSITES	79.8	66.2	73.1	95.6	68.4	82.2	101.0	77.7	89.4	79.4	42.3	61.1	91.1	85.2	88.2	95.9	90.8	93.4
07	THERMAL & MOISTURE PROTECTION	105.2	69.2	93.1	101.9	71.1	91.6	103.2	83.5	96.6	101.6	65.7	89.6	95.0	84.6	91.5	91.6	63.4	82.2
08	OPENINGS	88.5	60.7	81.7	87.3	68.2	82.7	98.0	78.4	93.2	88.9	47.2	78.8	96.7	82.9	93.3	98.5	78.0	93.5
0920	Plaster & Gypsum Board	93.6	65.7	75.9	89.6	67.6	75.6	103.1	76.7	86.3	92.2	41.2	59.7	115.1	84.7	95.8	110.8	90.6	97.9
0950, 0980	Ceilings & Acoustic Treatment	99.9	65.7	80.8	87.6	67.6	76.4	111.2	76.7	91.9	102.4	41.2	68.2	87.4	84.7	85.9	83.7	90.6	87.6
0960	Flooring	105.0	76.0	97.6	89.3	68.7	84.0	94.6	90.1	93.5	114.1	76.0	104.4	110.2	58.4	96.9	107.9	58.4	95.2
0970, 0990	Wall Finishes & Painting/Coating	123.6	52.3	81.7	88.0	67.6	76.1	99.9	59.1	75.9	148.9	53.1	92.6	99.9	87.4	92.5	95.9	69.0	80.1
09	FINISHES	104.6	66.4	85.7	90.3	67.8	79.2	102.3	78.1	90.4	110.0	52.4	81.5	100.3	81.0	90.8	95.5	79.7	87.7
COVERS	DIVS. 10 - 14, 25, 28, 41, 43, 44, 46	100.0	86.3	97.1	100.0	87.1	97.3	100.0	90.7	98.0	100.0	83.3	96.4	100.0	110.4	102.2	100.0	79.3	95.6
21, 22, 23	FIRE SUPPRESSION, PLUMBING & HVAC	92.4	65.4	82.6	99.8	68.1	88.4	99.8	75.9	91.2	91.9	64.7	82.1	100.1	90.0	96.5	96.3	67.5	85.9
26, 27, 3370	ELECTRICAL, COMMUNICATIONS & UTIL.	87.5	70.3	80.0	85.7	59.3	74.2	95.6	82.6	90.0	84.0	56.7	72.1	101.2	90.1	96.3	97.5	76.3	88.2
MF2018	WEIGHTED AVERAGE	95.2	69.8	85.6	94.5	70.6	85.5	98.0	82.6	92.2	96.1	63.1	83.6	103.8	89.6	98.4	101.6	75.4	91.7

City Cost Indexes

DIVISION		NEVADA									NEW HAMPSHIRE					
		ELY 893			LAS VEGAS 889 - 891			RENO 894 - 895			CHARLESTON 036			CLAREMONT 037			CONCORD 032 - 033		
		MAT.	INST.	TOTAL	MAT.	INST.	TOTAL	MAT.	INST.	TOTAL	MAT.	INST.	TOTAL	MAT.	INST.	TOTAL	MAT.	INST.	TOTAL
015433	CONTRACTOR EQUIPMENT		99.9	99.9		109.3	109.3		99.9	99.9		94.5	94.5		94.5	94.5		99.6	99.6
0241, 31 - 34	SITE & INFRASTRUCTURE, DEMOLITION	77.0	96.0	89.4	80.1	114.0	102.2	78.8	98.1	91.4	71.9	90.7	84.1	68.1	90.7	82.8	80.8	101.1	94.1
0310	Concrete Forming & Accessories	93.5	89.7	90.4	94.5	109.8	107.2	91.3	86.3	87.2	93.1	75.8	78.8	97.5	75.8	79.6	105.2	90.0	92.6
0320	Concrete Reinforcing	154.9	82.6	125.3	143.2	124.1	135.4	146.5	122.4	136.6	152.6	86.2	125.4	152.6	86.2	125.5	178.2	86.8	140.8
0330	Cast-in-Place Concrete	93.5	84.6	90.5	90.5	110.6	97.3	98.9	85.8	94.5	67.2	101.7	78.8	61.7	101.8	75.1	79.5	112.1	90.4
03	CONCRETE	119.4	86.9	106.1	113.5	112.3	113.0	118.0	92.6	107.5	90.8	87.5	89.4	84.6	87.5	85.8	103.0	97.5	100.7
04	MASONRY	156.7	65.6	103.7	139.7	106.9	120.6	148.6	72.4	104.2	116.7	87.4	99.6	117.6	87.4	100.0	141.7	100.0	117.4
05	METALS	104.1	87.4	100.6	112.1	109.3	111.5	105.2	103.8	104.9	99.4	94.3	98.3	99.4	94.3	98.3	106.1	94.3	103.7
06	WOOD, PLASTICS & COMPOSITES	89.9	92.6	91.3	88.6	107.1	97.7	86.2	85.1	85.6	96.1	73.4	85.0	100.5	73.4	87.2	105.0	88.2	96.7
07	THERMAL & MOISTURE PROTECTION	92.1	79.2	87.8	100.7	103.0	101.5	91.7	81.2	88.2	91.7	95.1	92.9	91.5	95.1	92.7	93.4	107.9	98.3
08	OPENINGS	98.4	79.1	93.7	97.4	112.8	101.1	96.2	83.5	93.1	97.3	75.1	91.9	98.5	75.1	92.8	98.0	86.8	95.3
0920	Plaster & Gypsum Board	107.2	92.5	97.9	108.6	107.1	107.6	100.0	84.7	90.3	105.4	73.1	84.8	105.9	73.1	85.0	102.3	88.3	93.4
0950, 0980	Ceilings & Acoustic Treatment	83.7	92.5	88.7	89.0	107.1	99.1	86.4	84.7	85.4	97.2	73.1	83.7	97.2	73.1	83.7	103.7	88.3	95.1
0960	Flooring	106.1	58.4	93.9	97.9	105.9	100.0	103.9	58.4	92.2	102.4	98.5	101.4	104.3	98.5	102.8	109.7	102.4	107.8
0970, 0990	Wall Finishes & Painting/Coating	95.9	97.5	96.8	98.2	122.8	112.6	95.9	87.4	90.9	83.8	78.3	80.6	83.8	78.3	80.6	99.9	98.1	98.8
09	FINISHES	94.8	85.5	90.2	94.0	110.3	102.1	93.8	80.8	87.4	98.0	79.6	88.9	98.3	79.6	89.1	102.7	92.6	97.7
COVERS	DIVS. 10 - 14, 25, 28, 41, 43, 44, 46	100.0	62.0	91.9	100.0	107.4	101.6	100.0	110.0	102.1	100.0	76.1	94.9	100.0	76.1	94.9	100.0	105.4	101.1
21, 22, 23	FIRE SUPPRESSION, PLUMBING & HVAC	96.3	84.4	92.0	100.3	106.9	102.7	100.1	90.0	96.5	93.1	72.2	85.6	93.1	72.2	85.6	100.1	88.1	95.8
26, 27, 3370	ELECTRICAL, COMMUNICATIONS & UTIL.	97.7	80.3	90.2	103.5	110.4	106.5	97.8	90.1	94.5	101.0	65.0	85.4	101.0	65.0	85.4	101.6	75.4	90.2
MF2018	WEIGHTED AVERAGE	103.1	82.5	95.3	105.0	109.5	106.7	103.4	89.2	98.0	96.7	80.0	90.4	96.0	80.0	90.0	103.0	91.9	98.8

DIVISION		NEW HAMPSHIRE															NEW JERSEY		
		KEENE 034			LITTLETON 035			MANCHESTER 031			NASHUA 030			PORTSMOUTH 038			ATLANTIC CITY 082, 084		
		MAT.	INST.	TOTAL	MAT.	INST.	TOTAL	MAT.	INST.	TOTAL	MAT.	INST.	TOTAL	MAT.	INST.	TOTAL	MAT.	INST.	TOTAL
015433	CONTRACTOR EQUIPMENT		94.5	94.5		94.5	94.5		99.6	99.6		94.5	94.5		94.5	94.5		99.5	99.5
0241, 31 - 34	SITE & INFRASTRUCTURE, DEMOLITION	74.4	90.9	85.1	68.3	89.8	82.3	81.2	101.4	94.4	79.6	92.5	88.0	75.1	92.5	86.5	92.4	97.3	95.6
0310	Concrete Forming & Accessories	96.5	76.0	79.6	106.0	70.7	76.9	100.6	90.4	92.2	102.8	90.2	92.4	94.1	88.4	89.4	106.0	142.2	135.8
0320	Concrete Reinforcing	152.6	86.2	125.5	153.9	86.2	126.2	178.2	86.9	140.9	190.6	86.9	148.2	152.6	86.8	125.7	89.1	138.6	109.3
0330	Cast-in-Place Concrete	67.5	102.0	79.0	60.6	94.3	71.8	79.5	114.6	91.2	63.9	113.2	80.4	60.6	111.6	77.7	77.9	135.0	97.0
03	CONCRETE	90.5	87.7	89.4	84.3	82.5	83.6	102.7	98.7	101.0	94.1	98.2	95.8	84.2	96.9	89.4	83.0	138.4	105.8
04	MASONRY	119.7	87.4	100.9	133.4	73.9	98.8	117.9	100.0	107.5	123.9	99.9	109.9	118.0	96.1	105.3	110.9	138.4	126.9
05	METALS	99.4	95.0	98.5	99.4	94.3	98.4	106.1	95.6	103.9	105.0	97.4	103.4	99.5	98.5	99.3	102.4	126.8	107.5
06	WOOD, PLASTICS & COMPOSITES	99.5	73.4	86.7	107.5	73.4	90.8	96.9	88.2	92.6	106.5	88.2	97.5	97.1	88.2	92.7	111.7	143.0	127.1
07	THERMAL & MOISTURE PROTECTION	92.2	95.1	93.2	91.6	89.1	90.8	97.1	108.2	100.8	92.5	106.1	97.0	92.1	103.2	95.8	96.3	133.9	108.9
08	OPENINGS	96.0	78.2	91.6	99.4	75.1	93.5	98.0	90.9	96.3	100.4	85.7	96.9	101.0	77.5	95.3	97.7	138.9	107.7
0920	Plaster & Gypsum Board	105.6	73.1	84.9	116.3	73.1	88.8	103.0	88.3	93.6	115.6	88.3	98.2	105.4	88.3	94.5	114.9	144.1	133.5
0950, 0980	Ceilings & Acoustic Treatment	97.2	73.1	83.7	97.2	73.1	83.7	100.6	88.3	93.7	112.2	88.3	98.8	97.2	88.3	92.2	99.8	144.1	124.6
0960	Flooring	104.1	98.5	102.6	112.8	98.5	109.1	109.7	110.8	110.0	107.1	100.4	105.4	102.5	100.4	101.9	108.4	150.3	119.2
0970, 0990	Wall Finishes & Painting/Coating	83.8	89.0	87.4	83.8	78.3	80.6	99.9	120.6	112.0	83.8	117.8	103.8	83.8	89.0	86.8	84.4	150.3	123.1
09	FINISHES	99.0	80.9	90.1	102.1	76.2	89.3	102.0	96.7	99.4	105.1	94.3	99.8	98.3	90.2	94.3	99.6	145.9	122.5
COVERS	DIVS. 10 - 14, 25, 28, 41, 43, 44, 46	100.0	81.4	96.0	100.0	82.2	96.2	100.0	105.4	101.1	100.0	105.4	101.2	100.0	104.1	100.9	100.0	118.3	103.9
21, 22, 23	FIRE SUPPRESSION, PLUMBING & HVAC	93.1	72.2	85.6	93.1	65.1	83.0	100.3	88.2	95.9	100.4	88.3	96.0	100.4	85.9	95.2	99.4	133.7	111.8
26, 27, 3370	ELECTRICAL, COMMUNICATIONS & UTIL.	101.0	65.0	85.4	101.7	42.5	75.9	102.3	76.6	91.1	102.4	76.6	91.2	101.3	69.6	87.5	93.9	137.7	113.0
MF2018	WEIGHTED AVERAGE	96.9	80.5	90.7	97.2	72.9	88.0	102.0	93.2	98.7	101.4	91.9	97.9	98.1	89.0	94.7	97.7	133.4	111.2

DIVISION		NEW JERSEY																	
		CAMDEN 081			DOVER 078			ELIZABETH 072			HACKENSACK 076			JERSEY CITY 073			LONG BRANCH 077		
		MAT.	INST.	TOTAL	MAT.	INST.	TOTAL	MAT.	INST.	TOTAL	MAT.	INST.	TOTAL	MAT.	INST.	TOTAL	MAT.	INST.	TOTAL
015433	CONTRACTOR EQUIPMENT		99.5	99.5		99.2	99.2		99.2	99.2		99.2	99.2		97.6	97.6		97.2	97.2
0241, 31 - 34	SITE & INFRASTRUCTURE, DEMOLITION	93.7	97.5	96.2	101.5	105.6	104.2	105.2	105.7	105.5	102.5	105.6	104.6	93.6	105.6	101.4	96.6	105.4	102.4
0310	Concrete Forming & Accessories	100.2	142.2	134.8	95.2	142.9	134.6	102.3	143.0	135.9	95.2	142.9	134.5	98.3	142.9	135.1	98.5	142.4	134.7
0320	Concrete Reinforcing	117.0	134.3	124.1	61.3	146.8	96.2	61.3	146.8	96.2	61.3	146.8	96.2	79.6	146.8	107.1	61.3	146.8	96.2
0330	Cast-in-Place Concrete	75.5	135.0	95.4	64.3	134.0	87.6	55.3	134.9	81.9	52.2	134.8	86.9	50.2	134.0	78.2	55.8	134.1	82.0
03	CONCRETE	85.1	137.7	106.7	70.7	139.5	98.9	67.9	139.8	97.4	69.4	139.7	98.3	66.8	139.3	96.6	69.3	139.1	98.0
04	MASONRY	98.8	138.4	121.8	115.3	138.9	129.0	138.1	138.9	138.6	120.6	138.9	131.3	111.0	138.9	127.2	128.6	138.3	134.2
05	METALS	107.9	125.2	111.5	99.0	125.3	104.5	99.0	125.4	104.6	99.1	125.2	104.6	104.6	123.2	108.5	99.2	122.8	104.1
06	WOOD, PLASTICS & COMPOSITES	104.7	143.0	123.5	96.3	143.0	119.3	104.9	143.0	123.6	96.3	143.0	119.3	96.1	143.0	119.2	96.7	142.9	119.5
07	THERMAL & MOISTURE PROTECTION	96.2	134.5	109.1	95.1	134.2	108.2	95.2	137.4	109.3	94.7	132.7	107.6	94.6	137.2	108.9	94.8	131.7	107.1
08	OPENINGS	99.7	137.9	109.0	98.5	139.6	108.5	96.7	139.6	107.1	96.0	139.6	106.6	96.5	139.6	107.0	92.7	139.6	104.1
0920	Plaster & Gypsum Board	115.9	144.1	133.8	110.3	144.1	131.8	115.5	144.1	133.7	110.3	144.1	131.8	116.1	144.1	133.9	111.7	144.1	132.3
0950, 0980	Ceilings & Acoustic Treatment	117.1	144.1	132.2	95.9	144.1	123.0	96.4	144.1	123.1	95.9	144.1	122.9	111.9	144.1	129.9	95.9	144.1	122.9
0960	Flooring	105.5	150.3	117.0	93.1	181.9	115.8	97.1	181.9	118.9	93.1	181.9	115.8	93.9	181.9	116.4	94.1	181.9	116.6
0970, 0990	Wall Finishes & Painting/Coating	84.4	150.3	123.1	87.3	141.7	119.3	87.3	141.7	119.3	87.3	141.7	119.3	87.4	141.7	119.3	87.4	150.3	124.4
09	FINISHES	103.4	145.9	124.4	96.1	150.6	123.1	98.4	150.6	124.2	96.0	150.6	123.0	101.0	150.6	125.5	96.7	151.3	123.7
COVERS	DIVS. 10 - 14, 25, 28, 41, 43, 44, 46	100.0	118.3	103.9	100.0	127.7	105.9	100.0	127.7	105.9	100.0	127.7	105.9	100.0	127.7	105.9	100.0	118.0	103.8
21, 22, 23	FIRE SUPPRESSION, PLUMBING & HVAC	100.0	133.8	112.2	99.3	134.9	112.1	99.9	134.9	112.5	99.9	134.9	112.1	99.9	134.9	112.5	99.3	133.5	111.6
26, 27, 3370	ELECTRICAL, COMMUNICATIONS & UTIL.	96.6	137.7	114.5	93.2	141.6	114.2	93.5	141.6	114.4	93.2	136.0	111.8	95.9	136.0	113.4	93.0	130.5	109.3
MF2018	WEIGHTED AVERAGE	99.3	133.2	112.1	95.5	135.9	110.8	96.6	136.1	111.5	95.4	135.1	110.4	96.4	135.0	111.0	95.4	133.4	109.7

City Cost Indexes

DIVISION		NEW JERSEY																	
		NEW BRUNSWICK 088 - 089			NEWARK 070 - 071			PATERSON 074 - 075			POINT PLEASANT 087			SUMMIT 079			TRENTON 085 - 086		
		MAT.	INST.	TOTAL	MAT.	INST.	TOTAL	MAT.	INST.	TOTAL	MAT.	INST.	TOTAL	MAT.	INST.	TOTAL	MAT.	INST.	TOTAL
015433	CONTRACTOR EQUIPMENT		99.1	99.1		106.4	106.4		99.2	99.2		99.1	99.1		99.2	99.2		105.6	105.6
0241, 31 - 34	SITE & INFRASTRUCTURE, DEMOLITION	103.5	98.5	100.2	110.0	115.1	113.3	104.6	105.6	105.3	104.7	98.4	100.6	103.0	105.7	104.7	95.0	107.6	103.2
0310	Concrete Forming & Accessories	102.1	142.9	135.8	97.7	143.3	135.3	96.5	142.9	134.8	98.3	142.3	134.6	96.8	143.0	134.9	99.6	142.3	134.8
0320	Concrete Reinforcing	90.2	146.8	113.3	82.9	146.9	109.1	79.6	146.8	107.1	90.2	146.8	113.3	61.3	146.8	96.2	117.7	134.3	124.5
0330	Cast-in-Place Concrete	96.4	135.2	109.4	72.7	137.4	94.4	64.0	134.8	87.7	96.4	134.8	109.2	53.4	134.9	80.7	92.2	136.4	107.0
03	CONCRETE	97.8	140.2	115.2	79.3	140.7	104.5	73.4	139.7	100.6	97.6	139.7	114.9	65.9	139.8	96.2	94.3	138.2	112.3
04	MASONRY	107.9	138.9	126.0	120.5	139.0	131.3	116.1	138.9	129.4	95.5	138.3	120.4	119.9	138.9	131.0	106.7	138.0	124.9
05	METALS	102.5	130.5	108.3	106.0	124.3	109.8	100.0	125.3	105.3	102.5	130.0	108.2	99.0	125.4	104.6	107.2	124.4	110.8
06	WOOD, PLASTICS & COMPOSITES	107.9	143.0	125.2	96.4	143.3	119.5	97.8	143.0	120.0	103.1	143.0	122.7	98.5	143.0	120.4	96.4	143.0	119.4
07	THERMAL & MOISTURE PROTECTION	96.8	137.0	110.2	96.9	139.4	111.1	95.1	132.7	107.7	96.8	133.7	109.2	95.3	137.4	109.4	97.3	136.9	110.6
08	OPENINGS	92.4	139.6	103.9	98.2	139.8	108.3	101.2	139.6	110.5	94.4	140.8	105.7	103.0	139.6	111.9	97.9	136.7	107.3
0920	Plaster & Gypsum Board	113.7	144.1	133.0	108.1	144.1	131.0	116.1	144.1	133.9	109.9	144.1	131.6	111.7	144.1	132.3	108.1	144.1	131.0
0950, 0980	Ceilings & Acoustic Treatment	99.8	144.1	124.6	112.2	144.1	130.1	111.9	144.1	129.9	99.8	144.1	124.6	95.9	144.1	122.9	110.8	144.1	129.4
0960	Flooring	106.6	181.9	125.9	110.8	181.9	129.0	93.9	181.9	116.4	104.4	150.3	116.2	94.1	181.9	116.6	110.8	177.3	127.9
0970, 0990	Wall Finishes & Painting/Coating	84.4	141.7	118.1	99.9	141.7	124.5	87.3	141.7	119.3	84.4	150.3	123.1	87.3	141.7	119.3	99.9	150.3	129.5
09	FINISHES	99.7	150.6	124.8	107.3	150.8	128.8	101.2	150.6	125.6	98.6	145.9	121.9	96.8	150.6	123.4	106.2	150.6	128.2
COVERS	DIVS. 10 - 14, 25, 28, 41, 43, 44, 46	100.0	127.7	105.9	100.0	128.4	106.1	100.0	127.7	105.9	100.0	118.1	103.9	100.0	127.7	105.9	100.0	118.3	103.9
21, 22, 23	FIRE SUPPRESSION, PLUMBING & HVAC	99.4	133.9	111.8	99.9	134.9	112.5	99.9	134.9	112.5	99.4	133.4	111.7	99.4	134.9	112.2	100.0	133.4	112.0
26, 27, 3370	ELECTRICAL, COMMUNICATIONS & UTIL.	94.3	141.1	114.7	101.2	136.0	116.3	95.9	141.6	115.8	93.9	130.5	109.8	93.5	141.6	114.4	101.2	126.6	112.2
MF2018	WEIGHTED AVERAGE	99.2	135.7	113.0	100.3	136.1	113.8	97.2	135.9	111.8	98.6	132.9	111.6	95.7	136.1	110.9	101.2	132.9	113.2

DIVISION		NEW JERSEY			NEW MEXICO														
		VINELAND 080,083			ALBUQUERQUE 870 - 872			CARRIZOZO 883			CLOVIS 881			FARMINGTON 874			GALLUP 873		
		MAT.	INST.	TOTAL	MAT.	INST.	TOTAL	MAT.	INST.	TOTAL	MAT.	INST.	TOTAL	MAT.	INST.	TOTAL	MAT.	INST.	TOTAL
015433	CONTRACTOR EQUIPMENT		99.5	99.5		102.5	102.5		108.9	108.9		108.9	108.9		102.5	102.5		102.5	102.5
0241, 31 - 34	SITE & INFRASTRUCTURE, DEMOLITION	96.2	97.5	97.0	89.6	96.2	93.9	106.2	97.0	100.2	95.6	97.0	96.5	94.4	96.2	95.6	98.4	96.2	97.0
0310	Concrete Forming & Accessories	96.3	142.1	134.1	97.0	67.0	72.2	95.1	66.9	71.8	95.1	66.9	71.8	97.0	67.0	72.2	97.0	67.0	72.2
0320	Concrete Reinforcing	89.1	134.3	107.6	163.7	67.6	124.4	128.6	67.6	103.7	130.1	67.6	104.6	178.9	67.6	133.4	171.2	67.6	128.9
0330	Cast-in-Place Concrete	84.0	135.0	101.1	90.5	67.1	82.7	88.5	68.4	81.8	88.5	68.4	81.7	91.4	67.1	83.3	86.0	67.1	79.7
03	CONCRETE	87.2	137.6	107.9	109.1	68.1	92.3	119.3	68.9	98.6	107.7	68.9	91.8	113.9	68.1	95.1	120.2	68.1	98.8
04	MASONRY	98.7	138.4	121.8	103.9	57.6	76.9	112.1	57.8	80.5	112.2	57.8	80.5	110.3	57.6	79.6	100.1	57.6	75.3
05	METALS	102.3	125.1	107.1	119.5	85.6	112.4	103.9	92.0	101.4	103.6	92.0	101.2	115.6	85.6	109.3	115.7	85.6	109.4
06	WOOD, PLASTICS & COMPOSITES	101.1	143.0	121.7	92.7	68.0	80.6	88.0	68.0	78.2	88.0	68.0	78.2	92.8	68.0	80.6	92.8	68.0	80.6
07	THERMAL & MOISTURE PROTECTION	96.3	133.9	108.9	90.8	67.3	82.9	96.6	69.6	87.5	95.5	69.6	86.9	91.1	67.3	83.1	92.1	67.3	83.8
08	OPENINGS	93.9	137.9	104.6	97.8	66.3	90.1	90.8	66.3	84.8	91.0	66.3	85.0	100.3	66.3	92.0	100.3	66.3	92.0
0920	Plaster & Gypsum Board	108.5	144.1	131.1	99.8	66.9	78.9	83.9	66.9	73.1	83.9	66.9	73.1	86.1	66.9	73.9	86.1	66.9	73.9
0950, 0980	Ceilings & Acoustic Treatment	99.8	144.1	124.6	108.3	66.9	85.1	102.4	66.9	82.5	102.4	66.9	82.5	101.5	66.9	82.1	101.5	66.9	82.1
0960	Flooring	103.9	150.3	115.8	98.3	66.8	90.2	99.4	66.8	91.0	99.4	66.8	91.0	99.6	66.8	91.2	99.6	66.8	91.2
0970, 0990	Wall Finishes & Painting/Coating	84.4	150.3	123.1	95.6	52.6	70.3	90.1	52.6	68.1	90.1	52.6	68.1	89.2	52.6	67.7	89.2	52.6	67.7
09	FINISHES	97.8	145.9	121.6	99.0	65.4	82.4	98.4	65.3	82.0	97.3	65.3	81.5	95.6	65.4	80.7	96.6	65.4	81.2
COVERS	DIVS. 10 - 14, 25, 28, 41, 43, 44, 46	100.0	118.3	103.9	100.0	86.8	97.2	100.0	86.6	97.2	100.0	86.6	97.2	100.0	86.8	97.2	100.0	86.8	97.2
21, 22, 23	FIRE SUPPRESSION, PLUMBING & HVAC	99.4	133.7	111.8	100.3	66.4	88.1	95.5	66.4	85.1	95.5	66.4	85.1	100.2	66.4	88.0	95.7	66.4	85.1
26, 27, 3370	ELECTRICAL, COMMUNICATIONS & UTIL.	93.9	137.7	113.0	76.1	68.9	73.0	85.1	68.9	78.1	83.8	68.9	77.4	74.9	68.9	72.3	74.6	68.9	72.1
MF2018	WEIGHTED AVERAGE	97.2	133.1	110.8	101.5	70.6	89.8	100.0	71.3	89.1	98.0	71.3	87.9	101.5	70.6	89.8	101.0	70.6	89.5

DIVISION		NEW MEXICO																	
		LAS CRUCES 880			LAS VEGAS 877			ROSWELL 882			SANTA FE 875			SOCORRO 878			TRUTH/CONSEQUENCES 879		
		MAT.	INST.	TOTAL	MAT.	INST.	TOTAL	MAT.	INST.	TOTAL	MAT.	INST.	TOTAL	MAT.	INST.	TOTAL	MAT.	INST.	TOTAL
015433	CONTRACTOR EQUIPMENT		84.3	84.3		102.5	102.5		108.9	108.9		108.2	108.2		102.5	102.5		79.2	79.2
0241, 31 - 34	SITE & INFRASTRUCTURE, DEMOLITION	98.1	76.6	84.1	91.4	96.2	94.6	99.7	97.0	98.0	95.1	104.0	100.9	88.7	96.2	93.6	101.9	75.9	84.9
0310	Concrete Forming & Accessories	92.5	65.8	70.5	97.0	67.0	72.2	95.1	66.9	71.8	97.6	67.2	72.5	97.0	67.0	72.2	94.6	65.9	70.9
0320	Concrete Reinforcing	125.7	67.5	101.9	174.2	67.6	130.6	130.1	67.6	104.6	174.3	67.7	130.7	177.5	67.6	132.6	170.1	67.5	128.2
0330	Cast-in-Place Concrete	83.6	61.4	76.2	88.8	67.1	81.6	88.5	68.4	81.8	94.4	69.4	86.0	87.0	67.1	80.4	95.5	66.6	83.8
03	CONCRETE	86.3	65.6	77.8	111.1	68.1	93.4	108.5	68.9	92.2	118.0	68.9	97.8	110.2	68.1	92.9	103.1	65.0	87.5
04	MASONRY	107.7	57.4	78.4	100.4	57.6	75.5	123.4	57.8	85.2	97.1	57.7	74.2	100.3	57.6	75.4	96.9	57.3	73.9
05	METALS	100.9	85.1	97.6	115.4	85.6	109.2	103.8	92.0	101.3	113.2	84.0	107.1	115.7	85.6	109.4	114.6	79.7	107.3
06	WOOD, PLASTICS & COMPOSITES	76.4	66.9	71.7	92.8	68.0	80.6	88.0	68.0	78.2	91.5	68.3	80.1	92.8	68.0	80.6	81.9	66.9	74.6
07	THERMAL & MOISTURE PROTECTION	86.4	65.0	79.2	90.8	67.3	82.9	95.6	69.6	86.9	93.0	69.3	85.0	90.8	67.3	82.9	83.3	63.6	76.7
08	OPENINGS	87.2	65.7	82.0	96.8	66.3	89.4	90.8	66.3	84.8	98.1	66.5	90.4	96.7	66.3	89.3	89.6	65.8	84.0
0920	Plaster & Gypsum Board	83.6	66.9	72.9	86.1	66.9	73.9	83.9	66.9	73.1	96.7	66.9	77.7	86.1	66.9	73.9	88.9	66.9	74.9
0950, 0980	Ceilings & Acoustic Treatment	99.2	66.9	81.1	101.5	66.9	82.1	102.4	66.9	82.5	100.3	66.9	81.6	101.5	66.9	82.1	100.4	66.9	81.7
0960	Flooring	127.6	66.8	112.0	99.6	66.8	91.2	99.4	66.8	91.0	109.7	66.8	98.7	99.6	66.8	91.2	128.3	66.8	112.5
0970, 0990	Wall Finishes & Painting/Coating	80.9	52.6	64.2	89.2	52.6	67.7	90.1	52.6	68.1	99.9	52.6	72.1	89.2	52.6	67.7	83.4	52.6	65.3
09	FINISHES	109.1	64.4	87.0	95.5	65.4	80.6	97.4	65.3	81.6	102.1	65.6	84.1	95.5	65.4	80.6	109.7	64.6	87.4
COVERS	DIVS. 10 - 14, 25, 28, 41, 43, 44, 46	100.0	84.3	96.6	100.0	86.8	97.2	100.0	86.6	97.2	100.0	87.4	97.3	100.0	86.8	97.2	100.0	84.3	96.7
21, 22, 23	FIRE SUPPRESSION, PLUMBING & HVAC	100.7	66.1	88.3	95.7	66.4	85.1	100.0	66.4	87.9	100.1	66.5	88.0	95.7	66.4	85.1	94.6	66.1	84.3
26, 27, 3370	ELECTRICAL, COMMUNICATIONS & UTIL.	87.1	73.7	81.2	75.7	68.9	72.7	84.6	68.9	77.8	90.1	68.9	80.9	74.8	68.9	72.2	77.9	68.9	74.0
MF2018	WEIGHTED AVERAGE	96.6	69.0	86.2	99.4	70.6	88.5	99.9	71.3	89.1	103.1	71.3	91.1	99.2	70.6	88.4	98.6	67.7	86.9

City Cost Indexes

		NEW MEXICO			NEW YORK														
		TUCUMCARI			ALBANY			BINGHAMTON			BRONX			BROOKLYN			BUFFALO		
	DIVISION	884			120 - 122			137 - 139			104			112			140 - 142		
		MAT.	INST.	TOTAL	MAT.	INST.	TOTAL	MAT.	INST.	TOTAL	MAT.	INST.	TOTAL	MAT.	INST.	TOTAL	MAT.	INST.	TOTAL
015433	CONTRACTOR EQUIPMENT		108.9	108.9		108.3	108.3		107.7	107.7		102.6	102.6		106.2	106.2		107.9	107.9
0241, 31 - 34	SITE & INFRASTRUCTURE, DEMOLITION	95.3	97.0	96.4	80.1	113.6	102.0	93.2	92.9	93.0	100.0	113.4	108.8	111.3	120.3	117.2	95.2	111.2	105.6
0310	Concrete Forming & Accessories	95.1	66.9	71.8	106.9	102.5	103.3	102.8	89.8	92.1	101.7	176.7	163.5	107.6	176.1	164.1	107.9	109.0	108.8
0320	Concrete Reinforcing	127.5	67.6	103.0	152.5	109.4	134.9	121.9	105.4	115.1	77.2	237.2	142.6	123.3	231.6	167.5	100.9	108.7	104.1
0330	Cast-in-Place Concrete	88.5	68.4	81.7	74.1	113.2	87.2	98.7	104.0	100.5	90.1	159.1	113.2	100.4	158.1	119.7	113.0	117.7	114.6
03	CONCRETE	106.8	68.9	91.3	92.3	107.7	98.6	94.8	98.8	96.5	83.3	179.5	122.8	104.3	178.0	134.5	105.6	111.9	108.2
04	MASONRY	124.2	57.8	85.5	99.6	115.3	108.8	110.9	102.1	105.8	100.0	181.4	147.4	125.0	181.5	157.9	99.4	120.3	111.6
05	METALS	103.6	92.0	101.2	103.8	108.8	104.9	95.5	119.4	100.5	89.5	173.9	107.2	104.4	172.5	118.6	103.7	106.6	104.3
06	WOOD, PLASTICS & COMPOSITES	88.0	68.0	78.2	100.4	98.0	99.2	100.3	85.9	93.2	95.1	173.7	133.8	99.6	173.2	135.8	106.7	106.9	106.8
07	THERMAL & MOISTURE PROTECTION	95.4	69.6	86.8	95.3	109.0	99.9	106.4	92.6	101.8	92.1	156.6	113.7	104.3	157.9	122.3	96.9	108.3	100.8
08	OPENINGS	90.7	66.3	84.8	98.7	101.0	99.3	90.0	91.7	90.4	90.5	187.9	114.2	89.7	186.3	113.2	100.3	104.1	101.2
0920	Plaster & Gypsum Board	83.9	66.9	73.1	108.2	98.3	101.9	114.4	85.2	95.9	98.2	175.6	147.4	106.4	175.6	150.5	117.8	106.9	110.9
0950, 0980	Ceilings & Acoustic Treatment	102.4	66.9	82.5	100.6	98.3	99.3	111.1	85.2	96.6	83.6	175.6	135.1	102.3	175.6	143.3	127.5	106.9	116.0
0960	Flooring	99.4	66.8	91.0	108.7	103.0	107.2	112.6	97.9	108.8	98.9	175.8	118.6	119.3	175.8	133.8	106.8	117.1	109.5
0970, 0990	Wall Finishes & Painting/Coating	90.1	52.6	68.1	97.2	101.1	99.5	92.1	99.5	96.4	101.0	163.0	137.5	114.4	163.0	143.0	88.0	110.3	101.1
09	FINISHES	97.3	65.3	81.5	102.9	101.7	102.3	102.8	91.4	97.2	94.9	175.1	134.6	113.0	174.7	143.5	109.9	110.9	110.4
COVERS	DIVS. 10 - 14, 25, 28, 41, 43, 44, 46	100.0	86.6	97.2	100.0	100.7	100.2	100.0	98.3	99.6	100.0	139.8	108.5	100.0	138.8	108.3	100.0	103.7	100.8
21, 22, 23	FIRE SUPPRESSION, PLUMBING & HVAC	95.5	66.4	85.1	100.1	111.9	104.3	100.8	100.0	100.5	100.2	170.3	125.4	99.6	170.1	125.0	100.1	98.7	99.6
26, 27, 3370	ELECTRICAL, COMMUNICATIONS & UTIL.	85.1	68.9	78.1	101.7	111.1	105.8	101.5	96.0	99.1	97.9	171.9	130.1	104.1	171.9	133.6	101.3	100.9	101.1
MF2018	WEIGHTED AVERAGE	98.6	71.3	88.3	99.5	109.0	103.1	98.9	98.7	98.8	94.3	168.9	122.5	103.5	169.0	128.2	102.2	107.0	104.0

		NEW YORK																	
		ELMIRA			FAR ROCKAWAY			FLUSHING			GLENS FALLS			HICKSVILLE			JAMAICA		
	DIVISION	148 - 149			116			113			128			115, 117, 118			114		
		MAT.	INST.	TOTAL	MAT.	INST.	TOTAL	MAT.	INST.	TOTAL	MAT.	INST.	TOTAL	MAT.	INST.	TOTAL	MAT.	INST.	TOTAL
015433	CONTRACTOR EQUIPMENT		114.0	114.0		106.2	106.2		106.2	106.2		102.1	102.1		106.2	106.2		106.2	106.2
0241, 31 - 34	SITE & INFRASTRUCTURE, DEMOLITION	90.3	99.3	96.2	110.2	120.3	116.8	110.3	120.3	116.8	70.4	104.4	92.5	106.0	118.8	114.3	105.8	120.3	115.3
0310	Concrete Forming & Accessories	91.7	91.8	91.8	97.8	176.1	162.4	100.6	176.1	162.9	93.4	95.9	95.5	95.1	146.2	137.2	100.6	176.1	162.9
0320	Concrete Reinforcing	125.7	104.4	117.0	123.3	231.6	167.5	125.4	231.6	168.8	147.6	113.0	132.0	123.3	237.0	169.7	123.3	231.6	167.5
0330	Cast-in-Place Concrete	95.7	103.9	98.4	108.7	158.1	125.2	108.7	158.1	125.2	71.4	107.5	83.5	92.2	148.5	111.1	100.4	158.1	119.7
03	CONCRETE	92.9	99.6	95.7	110.0	178.0	137.9	110.6	178.0	138.2	82.1	102.8	90.6	97.0	161.9	123.7	103.8	178.0	134.3
04	MASONRY	113.2	102.1	106.8	126.8	181.5	158.7	120.4	181.5	156.0	103.9	109.2	106.9	116.8	164.9	144.8	127.0	181.5	158.7
05	METALS	95.8	120.7	101.0	104.5	172.3	118.7	104.5	172.3	118.7	98.6	110.3	101.0	104.5	171.9	118.6	104.5	172.3	118.7
06	WOOD, PLASTICS & COMPOSITES	92.0	89.4	90.8	87.9	173.6	129.9	91.3	173.2	131.6	92.4	92.6	92.5	85.6	141.8	113.3	91.3	173.2	131.6
07	THERMAL & MOISTURE PROTECTION	96.0	92.8	94.9	104.3	157.9	122.3	104.4	157.9	122.3	89.7	103.5	94.3	104.1	145.9	118.1	104.2	157.9	122.2
08	OPENINGS	95.8	93.4	95.2	88.4	186.3	112.2	88.4	186.3	112.2	91.8	96.5	92.9	88.8	170.3	108.7	88.4	186.3	112.2
0920	Plaster & Gypsum Board	115.2	88.9	98.4	92.8	175.6	145.5	95.2	175.6	146.4	94.5	92.8	93.4	92.8	143.2	124.9	95.2	175.6	146.4
0950, 0980	Ceilings & Acoustic Treatment	119.0	88.9	102.2	83.3	175.6	134.9	83.3	175.6	134.9	88.8	92.8	91.0	82.8	143.2	116.6	83.3	175.6	134.9
0960	Flooring	104.7	97.9	103.0	115.2	175.8	130.8	116.3	175.8	131.6	98.0	103.0	99.2	114.4	174.7	129.8	116.3	175.8	131.6
0970, 0990	Wall Finishes & Painting/Coating	92.9	91.9	92.3	114.4	163.0	143.0	114.4	163.0	143.0	91.0	99.6	96.0	114.4	163.0	143.0	114.4	163.0	143.0
09	FINISHES	105.2	92.4	98.9	105.4	174.7	139.7	106.1	174.7	140.0	93.9	96.7	95.3	104.4	152.0	127.9	105.7	174.7	139.9
COVERS	DIVS. 10 - 14, 25, 28, 41, 43, 44, 46	100.0	97.0	99.4	100.0	138.8	108.3	100.0	138.8	108.3	100.0	93.9	98.7	100.0	129.8	106.4	100.0	138.8	108.3
21, 22, 23	FIRE SUPPRESSION, PLUMBING & HVAC	93.0	93.4	93.1	92.1	170.1	120.1	92.1	170.1	120.1	92.9	101.9	96.1	99.6	156.8	120.2	92.1	170.1	120.1
26, 27, 3370	ELECTRICAL, COMMUNICATIONS & UTIL.	98.5	96.8	97.8	108.0	171.9	135.8	108.0	171.9	135.8	96.3	110.3	102.4	103.4	145.9	121.9	102.8	171.9	132.9
MF2018	WEIGHTED AVERAGE	96.8	98.3	97.4	102.2	169.0	127.4	102.0	169.0	127.3	93.4	103.7	97.3	101.2	153.7	121.1	100.8	169.0	126.5

		NEW YORK																	
		JAMESTOWN			KINGSTON			LONG ISLAND CITY			MONTICELLO			MOUNT VERNON			NEW ROCHELLE		
	DIVISION	147			124			111			127			105			108		
		MAT.	INST.	TOTAL	MAT.	INST.	TOTAL	MAT.	INST.	TOTAL	MAT.	INST.	TOTAL	MAT.	INST.	TOTAL	MAT.	INST.	TOTAL
015433	CONTRACTOR EQUIPMENT		97.0	97.0		104.1	104.1		106.2	106.2		104.1	104.1		102.6	102.6		102.6	102.6
0241, 31 - 34	SITE & INFRASTRUCTURE, DEMOLITION	91.7	99.6	96.8	123.1	120.8	121.6	112.2	120.3	117.5	119.6	121.1	120.6	100.8	109.6	106.5	100.4	109.6	106.4
0310	Concrete Forming & Accessories	91.7	89.6	90.0	94.7	129.4	123.4	103.9	176.1	163.5	100.8	127.0	122.4	94.4	168.7	155.7	106.0	168.8	157.8
0320	Concrete Reinforcing	125.8	108.1	118.6	148.4	158.1	152.4	123.3	231.6	167.5	147.2	158.1	151.6	75.6	167.4	113.1	75.7	167.4	113.1
0330	Cast-in-Place Concrete	99.3	103.2	100.6	96.3	140.7	111.2	103.6	158.1	121.9	90.2	141.1	107.2	100.6	144.1	115.2	100.6	144.1	115.2
03	CONCRETE	95.7	97.7	96.5	100.0	137.8	115.5	106.6	178.0	135.9	95.7	136.9	112.6	91.3	159.6	119.4	91.0	159.6	119.2
04	MASONRY	121.3	100.7	109.3	120.2	152.7	139.1	121.9	181.5	156.6	114.2	152.9	136.7	105.2	151.7	132.3	105.2	151.7	132.3
05	METALS	93.5	102.2	95.3	106.2	130.7	111.3	104.4	172.3	118.6	106.2	131.5	111.5	89.3	166.9	105.5	89.6	166.9	105.8
06	WOOD, PLASTICS & COMPOSITES	90.4	86.3	88.4	93.5	121.8	107.4	95.6	173.2	133.8	99.7	118.3	108.9	90.0	173.7	131.2	100.5	173.7	136.5
07	THERMAL & MOISTURE PROTECTION	95.5	91.3	94.1	107.5	140.9	118.6	104.3	157.9	122.2	107.2	140.5	118.3	92.8	144.3	110.1	92.8	144.3	110.0
08	OPENINGS	95.6	92.7	94.9	101.3	140.2	110.8	88.4	186.3	112.2	97.1	138.3	107.1	90.6	187.9	114.3	90.7	187.9	114.3
0920	Plaster & Gypsum Board	99.4	85.6	90.6	92.5	123.1	112.0	99.2	175.6	147.8	93.2	119.5	109.9	94.2	175.6	146.0	103.7	175.6	149.5
0950, 0980	Ceilings & Acoustic Treatment	113.3	85.6	97.8	72.4	123.1	100.8	83.3	175.6	134.9	72.4	119.5	98.8	80.1	175.6	133.5	80.1	175.6	133.5
0960	Flooring	108.1	97.9	105.5	119.4	155.9	128.8	117.7	175.8	132.6	121.3	155.9	130.2	91.1	169.2	111.1	97.4	172.1	116.6
0970, 0990	Wall Finishes & Painting/Coating	95.3	110.3	104.1	115.6	123.5	120.3	114.4	163.0	143.0	115.6	123.5	120.3	99.0	163.0	136.6	99.0	163.0	136.6
09	FINISHES	102.9	92.4	97.7	105.2	132.7	118.8	106.8	174.7	140.4	105.5	130.7	118.0	91.6	169.9	130.3	94.5	170.4	132.0
COVERS	DIVS. 10 - 14, 25, 28, 41, 43, 44, 46	100.0	97.0	99.4	100.0	117.1	103.7	100.0	138.8	108.3	100.0	114.0	103.0	100.0	134.3	107.3	100.0	134.3	107.3
21, 22, 23	FIRE SUPPRESSION, PLUMBING & HVAC	92.8	93.5	93.1	92.6	138.7	109.2	99.6	170.1	125.0	92.6	137.3	108.7	92.7	143.8	111.1	92.7	143.8	111.1
26, 27, 3370	ELECTRICAL, COMMUNICATIONS & UTIL.	97.2	96.8	97.0	98.1	126.9	110.6	103.1	171.9	133.1	98.1	153.5	122.2	95.1	154.3	120.8	95.1	158.5	122.7
MF2018	WEIGHTED AVERAGE	96.7	96.3	96.5	101.5	134.7	114.0	102.9	169.0	127.9	100.3	137.7	114.5	93.2	152.9	115.7	93.5	153.6	116.2

City Cost Indexes

NEW YORK

DIVISION		NEW YORK 100-102 MAT.	INST.	TOTAL	NIAGARA FALLS 143 MAT.	INST.	TOTAL	PLATTSBURGH 129 MAT.	INST.	TOTAL	POUGHKEEPSIE 125-126 MAT.	INST.	TOTAL	QUEENS 110 MAT.	INST.	TOTAL	RIVERHEAD 119 MAT.	INST.	TOTAL
015433	CONTRACTOR EQUIPMENT		100.3	100.3		97.0	97.0		94.3	94.3		104.1	104.1		106.2	106.2		106.2	106.2
0241, 31-34	SITE & INFRASTRUCTURE, DEMOLITION	108.3	114.4	112.3	93.2	100.9	98.2	104.4	103.7	104.0	120.5	120.0	120.2	108.4	120.4	116.2	106.8	118.8	114.6
0310	Concrete Forming & Accessories	109.0	177.0	165.0	91.6	109.2	106.1	97.5	92.7	93.6	94.7	153.0	142.8	95.3	176.2	162.0	98.6	146.2	137.9
0320	Concrete Reinforcing	86.3	166.2	119.0	124.1	109.1	118.0	152.6	108.9	134.7	148.4	158.0	152.4	125.4	237.1	171.1	125.6	237.0	171.1
0330	Cast-in-Place Concrete	104.4	161.2	123.4	102.7	124.1	109.9	87.2	102.5	92.3	93.3	133.7	106.8	95.4	158.1	116.4	93.7	148.5	112.1
03	CONCRETE	96.1	169.0	126.0	97.7	114.1	104.4	93.6	98.8	95.7	97.7	145.9	117.5	100.1	179.0	132.5	97.8	162.0	124.2
04	MASONRY	121.3	185.9	158.9	129.8	129.7	129.7	99.0	102.9	101.3	112.5	141.5	129.4	116.2	181.5	154.2	122.3	164.9	147.1
05	METALS	104.9	165.9	117.7	96.0	103.2	97.5	102.1	97.6	101.2	106.3	130.4	111.3	104.4	174.6	119.1	105.1	173.3	119.3
06	WOOD, PLASTICS & COMPOSITES	100.6	173.7	136.6	90.4	102.3	96.2	97.3	88.6	93.0	93.5	158.2	125.4	85.7	173.2	128.8	89.0	141.8	115.0
07	THERMAL & MOISTURE PROTECTION	96.3	160.5	117.8	95.6	109.5	100.2	104.5	100.1	103.0	107.4	139.9	118.3	104.0	157.9	122.0	105.4	148.3	119.8
08	OPENINGS	97.9	187.2	119.6	95.6	101.6	97.0	102.1	94.4	100.2	101.3	160.3	115.7	88.4	187.6	112.5	88.9	171.1	108.9
0920	Plaster & Gypsum Board	110.5	175.6	151.9	99.4	102.1	101.1	111.4	88.5	96.8	92.5	160.6	135.9	92.8	175.6	145.5	93.8	143.2	125.2
0950, 0980	Ceilings & Acoustic Treatment	114.3	175.6	148.6	113.3	102.1	107.0	101.1	88.5	94.0	72.4	160.6	121.8	83.3	175.6	134.9	84.6	143.2	117.4
0960	Flooring	98.8	175.8	118.6	108.1	117.1	110.4	124.4	103.0	118.9	119.4	140.1	124.7	114.4	175.8	130.1	115.2	174.7	130.5
0970, 0990	Wall Finishes & Painting/Coating	99.7	163.0	136.9	95.3	110.3	104.1	109.9	101.6	105.0	115.6	123.5	120.3	114.4	163.0	143.0	114.4	163.0	143.0
09	FINISHES	104.7	175.6	139.8	102.9	110.6	106.7	104.1	94.7	99.4	105.0	148.6	126.6	104.7	174.7	139.3	105.2	152.0	128.3
COVERS	DIVS. 10-14, 25, 28, 41, 43, 44, 46	100.0	140.3	108.6	100.0	105.1	101.1	100.0	94.1	98.7	100.0	119.0	104.1	100.0	138.8	108.3	100.0	129.8	106.4
21, 22, 23	FIRE SUPPRESSION, PLUMBING & HVAC	100.1	171.2	125.7	92.8	103.7	96.7	92.8	101.8	96.0	92.6	134.6	107.7	99.6	170.2	125.0	100.0	156.9	120.5
26, 27, 3370	ELECTRICAL, COMMUNICATIONS & UTIL.	101.6	183.5	137.2	96.4	98.9	97.5	90.7	89.5	90.2	98.1	126.9	110.6	103.4	171.9	133.2	104.4	145.9	122.5
MF2018	WEIGHTED AVERAGE	101.9	169.4	127.4	97.7	107.8	101.5	97.6	97.8	97.7	100.8	137.1	114.5	101.6	169.4	127.2	102.0	154.0	121.6

NEW YORK

DIVISION		ROCHESTER 144-146 MAT.	INST.	TOTAL	SCHENECTADY 123 MAT.	INST.	TOTAL	STATEN ISLAND 103 MAT.	INST.	TOTAL	SUFFERN 109 MAT.	INST.	TOTAL	SYRACUSE 130-132 MAT.	INST.	TOTAL	UTICA 133-135 MAT.	INST.	TOTAL
015433	CONTRACTOR EQUIPMENT		112.4	112.4		102.1	102.1		102.6	102.6		102.6	102.6		105.9	105.9		105.9	105.9
0241, 31-34	SITE & INFRASTRUCTURE, DEMOLITION	86.4	113.1	103.8	82.0	104.8	96.8	107.6	113.4	111.4	98.2	109.8	105.8	91.9	100.7	97.6	75.1	100.6	91.7
0310	Concrete Forming & Accessories	105.0	96.8	98.2	107.0	102.2	103.0	94.0	176.7	162.2	100.5	158.6	148.4	101.9	91.6	93.5	103.2	91.9	93.9
0320	Concrete Reinforcing	151.8	104.4	132.5	146.0	109.4	131.1	77.2	237.2	142.6	75.7	162.2	111.0	123.2	105.4	115.9	123.2	104.4	115.5
0330	Cast-in-Place Concrete	87.6	108.2	94.5	86.2	110.8	94.5	100.7	159.1	120.2	97.6	145.3	113.5	91.6	106.1	96.4	83.8	106.0	91.2
03	CONCRETE	100.8	102.4	101.4	93.5	106.8	99.0	92.7	179.5	128.3	88.5	153.3	115.1	96.6	99.9	97.9	94.3	99.7	96.6
04	MASONRY	130.6	105.4	116.0	101.6	115.2	109.5	114.7	181.4	153.5	106.8	154.0	134.2	104.8	106.3	105.7	94.4	106.6	101.5
05	METALS	103.1	105.1	103.5	102.1	110.4	103.8	87.8	173.9	105.8	87.8	136.7	98.0	99.9	111.2	102.3	97.9	110.8	100.6
06	WOOD, PLASTICS & COMPOSITES	107.1	94.3	100.8	108.5	97.8	103.3	88.5	173.7	130.4	95.6	160.0	127.3	96.2	87.3	91.8	96.2	87.1	91.7
07	THERMAL & MOISTURE PROTECTION	94.2	101.8	96.8	91.1	106.7	96.3	92.5	156.6	114.0	92.7	143.8	109.8	100.7	98.1	99.8	90.8	98.2	93.3
08	OPENINGS	98.7	96.3	98.1	97.1	99.0	97.5	90.5	187.9	114.2	90.7	162.2	108.0	92.5	90.8	92.1	93.8	90.5	93.0
0920	Plaster & Gypsum Board	111.4	93.7	100.1	106.1	98.3	101.1	95.1	175.6	146.3	96.8	161.5	138.0	103.5	86.8	92.9	103.5	86.6	92.7
0950, 0980	Ceilings & Acoustic Treatment	103.7	93.7	98.1	102.8	98.3	100.3	83.6	175.6	135.1	80.1	161.5	125.6	111.1	86.8	97.5	111.1	86.6	97.4
0960	Flooring	109.7	105.0	108.5	103.6	103.0	103.5	95.0	175.8	115.7	94.0	174.7	114.7	97.9	94.2	96.9	94.8	94.3	94.7
0970, 0990	Wall Finishes & Painting/Coating	99.9	96.3	97.8	91.0	101.1	96.9	101.0	163.0	137.5	99.0	129.8	117.1	91.6	99.7	96.3	86.2	99.7	94.1
09	FINISHES	104.6	98.0	101.4	101.2	101.5	101.3	94.1	175.1	134.1	92.6	159.8	125.8	100.5	92.1	96.3	98.9	92.2	95.6
COVERS	DIVS. 10-14, 25, 28, 41, 43, 44, 46	100.0	98.9	99.8	100.0	100.2	100.0	100.0	139.8	108.5	100.0	133.4	107.1	100.0	99.0	99.8	100.0	95.0	98.9
21, 22, 23	FIRE SUPPRESSION, PLUMBING & HVAC	100.0	90.8	96.7	100.2	108.8	103.3	100.2	170.3	125.4	92.7	138.2	109.1	100.4	95.1	98.5	100.4	100.7	100.5
26, 27, 3370	ELECTRICAL, COMMUNICATIONS & UTIL.	101.3	96.2	99.1	99.1	107.9	102.9	97.9	171.9	130.1	99.2	113.8	105.5	101.4	102.8	102.0	98.4	102.8	100.3
MF2018	WEIGHTED AVERAGE	102.0	99.3	101.0	98.8	107.1	101.9	95.8	168.9	123.4	93.1	140.1	110.9	99.3	99.4	99.3	97.0	100.4	98.3

NEW YORK / NORTH CAROLINA

DIVISION		WATERTOWN 136 MAT.	INST.	TOTAL	WHITE PLAINS 106 MAT.	INST.	TOTAL	YONKERS 107 MAT.	INST.	TOTAL	ASHEVILLE 287-288 MAT.	INST.	TOTAL	CHARLOTTE 281-282 MAT.	INST.	TOTAL	DURHAM 277 MAT.	INST.	TOTAL
015433	CONTRACTOR EQUIPMENT		105.9	105.9		102.6	102.6		102.6	102.6		95.7	95.7		104.0	104.0		96.9	96.9
0241, 31-34	SITE & INFRASTRUCTURE, DEMOLITION	81.4	100.3	93.7	99.7	109.6	106.1	106.6	109.6	108.5	110.2	84.3	93.3	114.1	96.9	102.9	108.4	85.7	93.6
0310	Concrete Forming & Accessories	92.1	93.4	93.2	104.6	139.0	133.0	104.8	140.6	134.3	103.1	58.7	66.5	105.5	62.9	70.3	108.2	59.1	67.7
0320	Concrete Reinforcing	124.0	105.4	116.4	75.7	167.3	113.1	78.7	167.4	114.9	146.7	57.6	110.3	150.4	67.5	116.5	150.4	58.3	112.7
0330	Cast-in-Place Concrete	97.6	107.2	100.8	89.3	144.0	107.6	100.0	144.0	114.7	83.0	72.0	79.3	84.7	74.5	81.2	90.3	71.9	84.2
03	CONCRETE	105.8	101.1	103.9	82.8	146.2	108.8	91.0	146.9	114.0	93.2	64.1	81.3	95.3	68.5	84.3	100.1	64.5	85.5
04	MASONRY	95.7	107.8	102.8	106.1	151.7	132.6	112.5	151.7	135.3	102.9	60.6	78.3	105.0	62.2	80.1	83.7	60.6	70.3
05	METALS	98.0	111.2	100.8	87.9	166.6	104.3	97.1	166.6	111.6	95.0	75.7	91.0	96.0	78.3	92.3	110.7	76.6	103.6
06	WOOD, PLASTICS & COMPOSITES	83.8	89.4	86.5	99.0	133.5	116.0	99.0	135.6	117.0	108.2	56.3	82.7	103.8	61.0	82.8	106.7	56.8	82.2
07	THERMAL & MOISTURE PROTECTION	91.2	99.0	93.8	92.5	140.0	108.4	92.8	140.3	108.7	106.3	60.0	90.8	98.6	65.6	87.6	104.4	60.3	89.6
08	OPENINGS	93.8	93.9	93.8	90.7	165.8	108.9	93.8	166.9	111.6	89.8	54.9	81.3	98.3	62.0	89.5	96.9	58.1	87.4
0920	Plaster & Gypsum Board	96.4	89.0	91.7	99.4	134.2	121.5	110.9	136.3	127.1	106.5	54.8	73.6	94.6	59.5	72.3	95.1	55.3	69.8
0950, 0980	Ceilings & Acoustic Treatment	111.1	89.0	98.7	80.1	134.2	110.4	116.3	136.3	127.5	101.2	54.8	75.2	103.7	59.5	79.0	77.3	55.3	65.0
0960	Flooring	89.5	94.3	90.7	96.0	173.4	115.8	95.5	175.8	116.1	108.5	58.1	95.6	110.2	63.6	98.3	119.8	58.1	104.0
0970, 0990	Wall Finishes & Painting/Coating	86.2	103.2	96.2	99.0	163.0	136.6	99.0	163.0	136.6	104.1	49.7	72.2	99.9	63.0	78.2	115.1	49.7	72.6
09	FINISHES	97.0	93.9	95.5	93.2	147.0	119.8	104.4	148.7	126.3	105.0	57.2	81.3	104.6	62.6	83.8	97.8	57.5	77.9
COVERS	DIVS. 10-14, 25, 28, 41, 43, 44, 46	100.0	99.4	99.9	100.0	130.0	106.4	100.0	130.3	106.4	100.0	84.5	96.7	100.0	85.6	96.9	100.0	84.5	96.7
21, 22, 23	FIRE SUPPRESSION, PLUMBING & HVAC	100.4	94.2	98.1	100.3	143.8	115.9	100.3	143.8	115.9	100.9	59.3	85.9	100.0	62.5	86.5	101.0	59.4	86.0
26, 27, 3370	ELECTRICAL, COMMUNICATIONS & UTIL.	101.3	89.5	96.2	95.1	154.3	120.8	99.2	154.3	123.2	100.4	49.9	78.4	101.3	78.8	91.5	95.7	49.5	75.6
MF2018	WEIGHTED AVERAGE	98.7	98.0	98.4	93.8	146.4	113.7	98.7	146.8	116.9	98.7	62.4	85.0	99.6	70.4	88.6	101.1	62.8	86.6

City Cost Indexes

		\multicolumn{18}{c}{NORTH CAROLINA}

		ELIZABETH CITY 279			FAYETTEVILLE 283			GASTONIA 280			GREENSBORO 270,272 - 274			HICKORY 286			KINSTON 285		
DIVISION		MAT.	INST.	TOTAL	MAT.	INST.	TOTAL	MAT.	INST.	TOTAL	MAT.	INST.	TOTAL	MAT.	INST.	TOTAL	MAT.	INST.	TOTAL
015433	CONTRACTOR EQUIPMENT		101.0	101.0		101.2	101.2		95.7	95.7		96.9	96.9		101.2	101.2		101.2	101.2
0241, 31 - 34	SITE & INFRASTRUCTURE, DEMOLITION	109.9	86.7	94.8	109.0	92.9	98.5	109.7	84.3	93.1	108.2	85.7	93.6	105.9	92.9	97.4	104.4	92.9	96.9
0310	Concrete Forming & Accessories	96.0	57.2	64.0	103.0	57.4	65.4	108.4	59.3	67.9	107.9	59.1	67.7	99.9	59.2	66.3	96.8	57.1	64.1
0320	Concrete Reinforcing	147.9	60.9	112.3	151.8	67.3	117.3	147.3	58.3	110.9	149.2	58.3	112.1	146.7	58.3	110.6	146.0	58.3	110.1
0330	Cast-in-Place Concrete	90.5	71.4	84.1	87.0	69.2	81.1	81.1	72.1	78.1	89.7	71.9	83.7	83.0	71.7	79.2	80.1	69.1	76.4
03	CONCRETE	100.0	63.9	85.1	95.2	64.3	82.5	92.2	64.6	80.8	99.5	64.5	85.1	93.0	64.3	81.2	90.5	62.5	79.0
04	MASONRY	95.3	55.4	72.1	110.3	55.4	78.4	112.6	60.6	82.4	82.3	60.6	69.7	89.3	60.5	72.5	99.0	55.4	73.6
05	METALS	97.1	78.7	93.2	113.9	79.7	106.8	95.7	76.2	91.6	102.9	76.6	97.4	95.8	75.1	91.5	94.6	75.9	90.7
06	WOOD, PLASTICS & COMPOSITES	92.5	56.6	74.9	107.1	56.8	82.4	115.0	56.8	86.4	105.6	56.8	82.0	103.5	56.8	80.6	100.7	56.8	79.1
07	THERMAL & MOISTURE PROTECTION	103.5	57.5	88.1	105.9	57.9	89.8	106.4	60.0	90.9	103.9	60.3	89.3	106.7	60.0	91.1	106.6	57.7	90.2
08	OPENINGS	93.9	55.8	84.7	89.9	60.1	82.6	93.2	55.4	84.0	96.9	58.1	87.4	89.8	55.4	81.4	89.9	55.4	81.5
0920	Plaster & Gypsum Board	90.5	54.5	67.6	108.4	55.3	74.6	112.4	55.3	76.1	96.0	55.3	70.1	106.5	55.3	73.9	108.1	55.3	74.5
0950, 0980	Ceilings & Acoustic Treatment	77.3	54.5	64.5	105.6	55.3	77.5	109.2	55.3	79.0	77.3	55.3	65.0	101.2	55.3	75.5	109.2	55.3	79.0
0960	Flooring	113.4	58.1	99.2	108.6	58.1	95.6	111.1	58.1	97.5	119.8	58.1	104.0	108.4	58.1	95.5	106.1	58.1	93.8
0970, 0990	Wall Finishes & Painting/Coating	105.1	49.7	72.6	104.1	49.7	72.2	104.1	49.7	72.2	105.1	49.7	72.6	104.1	49.7	72.2	104.1	49.7	72.2
09	FINISHES	95.7	56.2	76.2	106.3	56.2	81.6	108.4	57.5	83.2	98.0	57.5	77.9	105.2	57.5	81.6	106.6	56.2	81.7
COVERS	DIVS. 10 - 14, 25, 28, 41, 43, 44, 46	100.0	84.8	96.8	100.0	82.9	96.4	100.0	84.7	96.7	100.0	82.3	96.2	100.0	84.7	96.7	100.0	82.9	96.4
21, 22, 23	FIRE SUPPRESSION, PLUMBING & HVAC	93.5	56.8	80.3	100.7	60.4	86.2	100.9	59.4	86.0	100.8	59.4	85.9	93.6	59.3	81.3	93.6	56.6	80.3
26, 27, 3370	ELECTRICAL, COMMUNICATIONS & UTIL.	95.0	59.7	79.6	102.2	49.5	79.3	100.1	79.0	90.9	94.9	50.0	75.4	99.1	79.0	90.3	98.9	48.2	76.8
MF2018	WEIGHTED AVERAGE	96.6	63.0	83.9	103.2	63.0	88.0	99.7	66.8	87.3	99.3	62.8	85.5	96.3	67.3	85.3	96.3	61.3	83.0

		\multicolumn{15}{c}{NORTH CAROLINA}	\multicolumn{3}{c}{NORTH DAKOTA}

		MURPHY 289			RALEIGH 275 - 276			ROCKY MOUNT 278			WILMINGTON 284			WINSTON-SALEM 271			BISMARCK 585		
DIVISION		MAT.	INST.	TOTAL	MAT.	INST.	TOTAL	MAT.	INST.	TOTAL	MAT.	INST.	TOTAL	MAT.	INST.	TOTAL	MAT.	INST.	TOTAL
015433	CONTRACTOR EQUIPMENT		95.7	95.7		105.4	105.4		96.9	96.9		95.7	95.7		96.9	96.9		102.4	102.4
0241, 31 - 34	SITE & INFRASTRUCTURE, DEMOLITION	108.2	83.9	92.4	108.3	98.5	101.9	107.8	85.3	93.1	110.9	83.9	93.3	108.6	85.7	93.7	85.8	98.7	94.2
0310	Concrete Forming & Accessories	108.9	54.0	63.6	105.8	58.8	67.0	101.4	55.5	66.0	104.2	57.2	65.4	109.3	59.1	67.9	106.1	78.1	83.0
0320	Concrete Reinforcing	146.0	56.1	109.3	151.2	58.3	113.2	147.9	58.2	111.3	147.9	58.3	111.3	149.2	58.3	112.1	91.4	102.7	96.0
0330	Cast-in-Place Concrete	85.9	69.1	80.2	93.0	73.5	86.5	88.5	70.9	82.6	82.7	69.1	78.1	91.9	71.9	85.2	98.5	92.0	96.3
03	CONCRETE	95.6	60.7	81.3	99.5	64.8	85.3	100.5	63.8	85.4	93.3	62.6	80.7	100.7	64.5	85.8	102.0	87.5	96.0
04	MASONRY	91.7	55.4	70.6	83.5	59.6	69.6	74.0	59.3	65.5	90.0	55.4	69.9	82.5	60.4	69.8	96.2	83.0	88.5
05	METALS	93.8	75.1	89.9	96.0	74.7	91.6	96.9	75.5	92.4	94.6	76.0	90.7	100.3	76.6	95.3	95.1	93.5	94.8
06	WOOD, PLASTICS & COMPOSITES	115.6	52.6	84.6	104.0	57.0	80.9	98.8	56.8	78.1	109.5	56.8	83.6	106.5	56.8	82.0	108.9	73.8	91.6
07	THERMAL & MOISTURE PROTECTION	106.5	57.3	90.0	98.5	61.9	86.3	103.9	59.6	89.1	106.2	57.9	90.0	103.9	60.3	89.3	106.1	86.4	99.5
08	OPENINGS	89.8	52.6	80.7	98.1	55.7	87.7	93.3	55.4	84.1	89.9	55.4	81.5	96.9	58.1	87.4	94.7	83.4	91.9
0920	Plaster & Gypsum Board	109.8	51.0	72.4	91.5	55.3	68.5	91.0	55.3	68.3	108.4	55.3	74.6	96.0	55.3	70.1	97.0	72.7	81.6
0950, 0980	Ceilings & Acoustic Treatment	101.2	51.0	73.1	73.8	55.3	63.5	75.1	55.3	64.0	105.6	55.3	77.5	77.3	55.3	65.0	113.3	72.7	90.6
0960	Flooring	111.4	58.1	97.7	109.1	58.1	96.1	116.2	58.1	101.3	109.0	58.1	96.0	119.8	58.1	104.0	95.3	53.2	84.5
0970, 0990	Wall Finishes & Painting/Coating	104.1	49.7	72.2	99.9	49.7	70.4	105.1	49.7	72.6	104.1	49.7	72.2	105.1	49.7	72.6	87.1	58.6	70.3
09	FINISHES	106.4	53.7	80.3	95.7	57.3	76.5	96.1	57.2	76.9	106.4	56.2	81.6	98.0	57.5	77.9	103.6	71.9	87.9
COVERS	DIVS. 10 - 14, 25, 28, 41, 43, 44, 46	100.0	82.4	96.3	100.0	84.6	96.7	100.0	84.1	96.6	100.0	82.9	96.4	100.0	84.5	96.7	100.0	95.5	99.0
21, 22, 23	FIRE SUPPRESSION, PLUMBING & HVAC	93.6	56.6	80.3	100.0	58.8	85.2	93.5	58.7	81.0	100.9	56.7	85.0	100.8	59.4	85.9	100.1	77.6	92.0
26, 27, 3370	ELECTRICAL, COMMUNICATIONS & UTIL.	100.9	48.2	78.0	101.1	48.6	78.3	96.2	49.5	75.9	100.9	48.2	78.0	94.9	50.0	75.4	84.4	86.1	85.1
MF2018	WEIGHTED AVERAGE	96.8	59.8	82.8	98.2	63.2	85.0	95.9	62.1	83.1	98.3	60.6	84.1	99.0	62.8	85.3	97.2	84.0	92.2

		\multicolumn{18}{c}{NORTH DAKOTA}

		DEVILS LAKE 583			DICKINSON 586			FARGO 580 - 581			GRAND FORKS 582			JAMESTOWN 584			MINOT 587		
DIVISION		MAT.	INST.	TOTAL	MAT.	INST.	TOTAL	MAT.	INST.	TOTAL	MAT.	INST.	TOTAL	MAT.	INST.	TOTAL	MAT.	INST.	TOTAL
015433	CONTRACTOR EQUIPMENT		94.6	94.6		94.6	94.6		103.3	103.3		94.6	94.6		94.6	94.6		94.6	94.6
0241, 31 - 34	SITE & INFRASTRUCTURE, DEMOLITION	85.9	88.0	87.3	89.8	87.9	88.6	86.3	99.3	94.8	91.2	88.7	89.5	85.3	88.0	87.0	89.8	89.0	89.3
0310	Concrete Forming & Accessories	104.6	64.2	71.3	95.9	64.1	69.7	100.6	65.3	71.5	99.1	70.6	75.6	97.3	64.1	69.9	95.6	64.7	70.1
0320	Concrete Reinforcing	91.1	102.7	95.8	92.0	102.5	96.3	90.0	103.0	95.3	89.8	102.7	95.1	91.7	102.8	96.2	92.9	102.5	96.8
0330	Cast-in-Place Concrete	115.0	75.5	101.8	104.0	75.4	94.5	94.6	83.5	90.9	104.0	81.3	96.4	113.6	75.5	100.8	104.0	76.1	94.6
03	CONCRETE	102.1	75.5	91.2	100.9	75.4	90.4	96.3	78.8	89.1	98.5	80.4	91.1	100.8	75.4	90.4	97.4	75.9	88.6
04	MASONRY	115.0	78.4	93.7	115.0	75.4	91.9	103.0	81.4	90.4	108.3	81.1	92.5	127.1	81.1	100.3	107.6	73.9	87.9
05	METALS	91.3	92.7	91.6	91.2	92.2	91.4	95.0	93.6	94.7	91.3	93.5	91.7	91.3	92.8	91.6	91.6	94.1	92.1
06	WOOD, PLASTICS & COMPOSITES	100.9	60.2	80.9	91.0	60.2	75.9	102.6	60.7	82.0	94.7	67.0	81.0	92.6	60.2	76.7	90.7	60.2	75.7
07	THERMAL & MOISTURE PROTECTION	106.6	77.7	97.0	107.1	79.1	97.7	102.9	82.2	96.0	106.8	80.6	98.0	106.5	78.8	97.2	106.6	79.2	97.4
08	OPENINGS	94.7	75.9	90.1	94.7	75.9	90.1	96.2	76.2	91.3	93.0	79.6	89.7	94.7	75.9	90.1	93.1	75.9	88.9
0920	Plaster & Gypsum Board	106.9	59.2	76.6	100.0	59.2	74.1	98.1	59.2	73.4	101.2	66.2	78.9	100.9	59.2	74.4	100.0	59.2	74.1
0950, 0980	Ceilings & Acoustic Treatment	102.5	59.2	78.3	102.5	59.2	78.3	103.7	59.2	78.8	102.5	66.2	82.2	102.5	59.2	78.3	102.5	59.2	78.3
0960	Flooring	103.9	53.2	90.9	98.4	53.2	86.8	109.7	53.2	95.2	100.0	53.2	88.0	99.0	53.2	87.3	98.2	53.2	86.6
0970, 0990	Wall Finishes & Painting/Coating	86.6	49.0	64.5	86.6	49.0	64.5	99.9	58.6	75.6	86.6	57.5	69.5	86.6	49.0	64.5	86.6	50.0	65.1
09	FINISHES	99.7	60.6	80.4	97.9	60.6	79.5	103.7	62.0	83.1	98.1	66.2	82.3	97.6	60.6	79.3	97.3	60.7	79.2
COVERS	DIVS. 10 - 14, 25, 28, 41, 43, 44, 46	100.0	76.5	95.0	100.0	76.5	95.0	100.0	91.6	98.2	100.0	83.7	96.5	100.0	76.4	95.0	100.0	90.5	98.0
21, 22, 23	FIRE SUPPRESSION, PLUMBING & HVAC	92.8	69.2	84.3	92.8	64.6	82.6	99.8	72.5	90.0	100.1	72.1	90.0	92.8	63.8	82.3	100.1	71.1	89.6
26, 27, 3370	ELECTRICAL, COMMUNICATIONS & UTIL.	84.9	62.8	75.3	88.9	62.6	77.4	95.9	60.0	80.2	86.5	62.8	76.2	84.9	59.0	73.6	87.9	63.3	77.2
MF2018	WEIGHTED AVERAGE	95.3	73.1	86.9	95.5	71.7	86.5	98.0	75.9	89.6	96.2	76.1	88.6	95.4	71.7	86.4	96.2	73.8	87.7

City Cost Indexes

DIVISION		NORTH DAKOTA WILLISTON 588			OHIO AKRON 442-443			OHIO ATHENS 457			OHIO CANTON 446-447			OHIO CHILLICOTHE 456			OHIO CINCINNATI 451-452		
		MAT.	INST.	TOTAL	MAT.	INST.	TOTAL	MAT.	INST.	TOTAL	MAT.	INST.	TOTAL	MAT.	INST.	TOTAL	MAT.	INST.	TOTAL
015433	CONTRACTOR EQUIPMENT		94.6	94.6		99.6	99.6		89.6	89.6		99.6	99.6		96.3	96.3		96.0	96.0
0241, 31 - 34	SITE & INFRASTRUCTURE, DEMOLITION	86.2	88.7	87.9	92.3	94.7	93.9	99.3	83.3	88.9	92.4	94.6	93.9	90.4	89.5	89.8	92.9	94.5	94.0
0310	Concrete Forming & Accessories	100.6	70.5	75.8	99.2	83.3	86.1	94.3	83.4	85.3	99.2	78.1	81.8	95.7	72.7	76.7	98.6	75.1	79.2
0320	Concrete Reinforcing	93.8	102.4	97.3	88.3	86.7	87.7	89.5	85.8	88.0	88.3	78.5	84.3	85.3	77.5	82.1	90.0	79.0	85.5
0330	Cast-in-Place Concrete	104.0	81.3	96.4	87.3	90.9	88.5	106.1	90.7	100.9	88.1	89.6	88.6	96.3	84.3	92.3	91.9	81.7	88.5
03	CONCRETE	98.6	80.4	91.1	90.8	86.9	89.2	99.9	86.3	94.3	91.2	82.7	87.7	94.1	78.4	87.6	92.3	78.4	86.6
04	MASONRY	102.3	76.6	87.3	97.8	90.0	93.3	78.7	89.5	85.0	98.4	88.4	92.6	84.8	85.4	85.2	90.0	83.4	86.1
05	METALS	91.4	93.1	91.8	93.5	91.3	93.0	97.9	84.1	95.0	93.5	87.7	92.3	91.5	88.2	90.8	99.8	82.3	96.1
06	WOOD, PLASTICS & COMPOSITES	96.0	67.0	81.7	102.5	81.7	92.3	81.3	81.5	81.4	102.9	76.4	89.9	94.1	69.4	81.9	100.4	73.0	86.9
07	THERMAL & MOISTURE PROTECTION	106.8	80.5	98.0	104.0	86.6	98.2	100.5	85.9	95.6	104.9	85.3	98.3	102.4	80.9	95.2	102.0	82.6	95.5
08	OPENINGS	94.8	79.6	91.1	99.9	81.0	95.3	94.1	78.1	90.2	95.0	73.1	89.7	84.5	69.3	80.8	97.2	73.1	91.4
0920	Plaster & Gypsum Board	101.2	66.2	78.9	95.3	81.0	86.2	95.8	80.7	86.2	96.5	75.5	83.1	97.7	68.8	79.3	94.8	72.3	80.5
0950, 0980	Ceilings & Acoustic Treatment	102.5	66.2	82.2	96.3	81.0	87.7	106.4	80.7	92.0	96.3	75.5	84.6	101.6	68.8	83.3	90.9	72.3	80.5
0960	Flooring	100.7	53.2	88.5	90.2	75.3	86.4	111.1	74.5	101.7	90.5	70.0	85.3	91.3	74.5	87.0	94.6	77.2	90.2
0970, 0990	Wall Finishes & Painting/Coating	86.6	55.2	68.2	95.5	89.9	92.2	104.2	83.7	92.1	95.5	75.0	83.5	100.5	76.4	86.4	99.9	74.1	84.7
09	FINISHES	98.3	66.1	82.4	95.7	82.5	89.2	99.9	81.6	90.9	96.0	75.6	85.9	98.6	72.7	85.8	96.0	74.9	85.6
COVERS	DIVS. 10 - 14, 25, 28, 41, 43, 44, 46	100.0	85.7	96.9	100.0	93.7	98.7	100.0	92.0	98.3	100.0	92.5	98.4	100.0	88.3	97.5	100.0	88.9	97.6
21, 22, 23	FIRE SUPPRESSION, PLUMBING & HVAC	92.8	69.1	84.3	99.8	88.0	95.6	92.6	80.3	88.2	99.8	78.5	92.1	93.2	81.1	88.9	99.8	82.4	93.5
26, 27, 3370	ELECTRICAL, COMMUNICATIONS & UTIL.	86.7	63.3	76.5	95.6	82.2	89.8	98.6	86.9	93.5	95.3	85.6	91.1	95.7	77.6	87.8	95.7	75.7	87.0
MF2018	WEIGHTED AVERAGE	94.4	75.0	87.1	96.6	87.1	93.0	96.1	84.2	91.6	96.3	83.1	91.3	93.4	80.4	88.5	97.4	80.6	91.1

DIVISION		OHIO CLEVELAND 441			OHIO COLUMBUS 430-432			OHIO DAYTON 453-454			OHIO HAMILTON 450			OHIO LIMA 458			OHIO LORAIN 440		
		MAT.	INST.	TOTAL	MAT.	INST.	TOTAL	MAT.	INST.	TOTAL	MAT.	INST.	TOTAL	MAT.	INST.	TOTAL	MAT.	INST.	TOTAL
015433	CONTRACTOR EQUIPMENT		98.0	98.0		97.7	97.7		91.0	91.0		96.3	96.3		92.3	92.3		99.6	99.6
0241, 31 - 34	SITE & INFRASTRUCTURE, DEMOLITION	91.5	96.3	94.6	92.8	94.9	94.2	90.8	89.5	90.0	90.8	89.1	89.7	94.5	82.4	86.6	91.7	94.4	93.5
0310	Concrete Forming & Accessories	99.1	86.5	88.7	96.7	80.2	83.1	97.1	81.5	84.2	97.1	81.2	84.0	94.2	75.5	78.8	99.3	81.7	84.8
0320	Concrete Reinforcing	88.4	88.8	88.6	87.1	77.6	83.2	90.5	77.2	85.0	90.5	76.9	84.9	89.5	77.4	84.5	88.3	86.8	87.7
0330	Cast-in-Place Concrete	87.0	94.9	89.7	114.4	88.3	105.6	82.4	78.2	81.0	88.3	81.7	86.1	97.4	83.1	92.6	83.1	88.0	84.7
03	CONCRETE	90.3	90.0	90.2	102.8	82.8	94.6	86.0	79.7	83.4	88.9	81.2	85.7	93.2	78.9	87.3	88.7	85.2	87.3
04	MASONRY	102.1	95.4	98.2	88.6	86.7	87.5	83.9	78.3	80.6	84.3	76.6	79.8	106.2	76.8	89.0	94.9	88.6	91.2
05	METALS	99.9	90.1	97.8	97.9	83.4	94.9	93.0	80.9	90.5	92.9	87.5	91.8	98.0	83.9	95.0	94.2	91.5	93.6
06	WOOD, PLASTICS & COMPOSITES	100.6	84.3	92.6	100.7	78.6	89.9	97.3	82.8	90.2	95.8	84.4	90.2	81.3	75.8	78.6	102.5	81.9	92.3
07	THERMAL & MOISTURE PROTECTION	102.7	94.5	100.0	99.6	84.2	94.4	105.8	78.7	96.7	102.4	76.8	93.8	100.1	81.8	94.0	104.9	84.0	97.9
08	OPENINGS	97.7	83.3	94.2	97.2	74.7	91.7	91.9	77.4	88.4	89.6	78.2	86.8	94.1	71.9	88.7	95.0	81.1	91.6
0920	Plaster & Gypsum Board	95.5	83.9	88.1	95.5	77.9	84.3	98.6	82.7	88.5	98.6	84.2	89.5	95.8	74.9	82.5	95.3	81.1	86.3
0950, 0980	Ceilings & Acoustic Treatment	94.9	83.9	88.7	84.1	77.9	80.6	101.6	82.7	91.0	101.6	84.2	91.9	106.4	74.9	88.8	96.3	81.1	87.8
0960	Flooring	94.6	93.3	94.3	94.6	77.5	90.2	94.5	71.9	88.7	92.2	77.2	88.3	111.0	78.5	102.6	90.5	85.8	89.3
0970, 0990	Wall Finishes & Painting/Coating	99.9	87.3	92.5	99.9	78.5	87.3	100.5	69.2	82.1	100.5	62.1	77.9	104.2	66.6	82.1	95.5	85.6	89.7
09	FINISHES	96.7	87.5	92.2	94.0	79.2	86.6	99.4	78.6	89.1	98.7	79.0	89.0	99.6	74.9	87.4	95.8	83.0	89.5
COVERS	DIVS. 10 - 14, 25, 28, 41, 43, 44, 46	100.0	96.2	99.2	100.0	90.5	98.0	100.0	88.9	97.6	100.0	85.7	97.0	100.0	89.3	97.7	100.0	94.2	98.8
21, 22, 23	FIRE SUPPRESSION, PLUMBING & HVAC	99.8	89.3	96.1	99.7	89.1	95.9	100.7	80.9	93.6	105.5	76.9	92.0	92.6	88.4	91.1	99.8	77.5	91.8
26, 27, 3370	ELECTRICAL, COMMUNICATIONS & UTIL.	95.7	86.0	91.5	95.9	83.0	90.3	94.1	75.1	85.8	94.4	65.2	81.7	98.8	65.4	84.3	95.4	71.7	85.1
MF2018	WEIGHTED AVERAGE	97.8	90.0	94.9	98.0	82.6	93.1	95.0	80.1	89.4	96.0	78.3	88.7	96.4	79.0	89.9	96.0	83.0	91.1

DIVISION		OHIO MANSFIELD 448-449			OHIO MARION 433			OHIO SPRINGFIELD 455			OHIO STEUBENVILLE 439			OHIO TOLEDO 434-436			OHIO YOUNGSTOWN 444-445		
		MAT.	INST.	TOTAL	MAT.	INST.	TOTAL	MAT.	INST.	TOTAL	MAT.	INST.	TOTAL	MAT.	INST.	TOTAL	MAT.	INST.	TOTAL
015433	CONTRACTOR EQUIPMENT		99.6	99.6		95.9	95.9		91.0	91.0		100.1	100.1		99.3	99.3		99.6	99.6
0241, 31 - 34	SITE & INFRASTRUCTURE, DEMOLITION	86.1	94.1	91.3	83.7	89.5	87.5	91.2	89.3	90.0	112.4	97.5	102.7	89.6	90.4	90.1	92.2	94.0	93.4
0310	Concrete Forming & Accessories	91.9	81.7	83.5	95.4	83.7	85.7	97.1	74.4	78.4	97.5	79.6	82.7	98.0	88.7	90.3	99.2	73.8	78.2
0320	Concrete Reinforcing	80.5	69.3	75.9	82.8	77.9	80.8	90.5	77.2	85.0	80.2	91.8	85.0	89.8	84.6	87.7	88.3	74.7	82.8
0330	Cast-in-Place Concrete	80.8	86.0	82.6	98.9	84.2	93.9	84.6	77.8	82.3	107.4	82.8	99.2	108.3	90.2	102.3	86.5	83.8	85.6
03	CONCRETE	83.8	81.5	82.8	90.0	83.2	87.2	87.1	76.4	82.7	94.5	83.0	89.8	98.2	89.0	94.4	90.4	78.0	85.3
04	MASONRY	96.9	88.8	92.2	91.6	87.1	89.0	84.1	77.6	80.3	81.2	86.3	84.2	97.9	90.1	93.4	98.1	84.3	90.1
05	METALS	94.7	84.1	92.4	93.3	87.0	92.0	93.0	80.8	90.5	90.6	90.2	90.5	93.8	95.1	94.1	93.6	85.5	91.9
06	WOOD, PLASTICS & COMPOSITES	93.8	81.9	87.9	89.9	85.4	87.7	99.0	73.7	86.6	85.9	78.5	82.3	92.8	89.8	91.3	102.5	72.1	87.6
07	THERMAL & MOISTURE PROTECTION	103.5	84.2	97.0	95.2	82.4	90.9	105.7	77.4	96.2	106.7	82.9	98.8	95.6	88.6	93.2	105.0	84.4	98.1
08	OPENINGS	94.6	73.5	89.4	86.2	77.4	84.0	90.1	72.1	85.7	86.0	77.8	84.0	88.8	84.1	87.7	95.0	71.7	89.3
0920	Plaster & Gypsum Board	90.4	81.1	84.5	95.0	84.9	88.6	98.6	73.3	82.5	93.2	77.3	83.1	96.5	89.4	92.0	95.3	71.1	79.9
0950, 0980	Ceilings & Acoustic Treatment	98.1	81.1	88.6	88.3	84.9	86.4	101.6	73.3	85.8	86.8	77.3	81.5	88.3	89.4	88.9	96.3	71.1	82.2
0960	Flooring	86.5	81.8	87.8	92.1	91.8	92.0	94.5	71.9	88.7	121.9	82.9	111.9	92.6	84.4	90.5	90.5	79.0	87.6
0970, 0990	Wall Finishes & Painting/Coating	95.5	67.7	79.2	102.6	67.7	82.1	100.5	69.2	82.1	118.9	75.8	93.5	102.7	89.3	94.8	95.5	73.7	82.7
09	FINISHES	94.3	82.3	88.4	95.0	83.9	89.5	99.4	73.1	86.4	112.4	79.3	96.0	95.5	88.0	91.8	95.9	74.1	85.1
COVERS	DIVS. 10 - 14, 25, 28, 41, 43, 44, 46	100.0	92.8	98.5	100.0	89.8	97.8	100.0	87.6	97.4	100.0	86.6	97.2	100.0	94.5	98.8	100.0	91.1	98.1
21, 22, 23	FIRE SUPPRESSION, PLUMBING & HVAC	92.5	78.1	87.3	92.4	85.3	89.9	100.7	78.4	92.7	93.1	87.4	91.0	99.7	91.6	96.8	99.8	80.8	93.0
26, 27, 3370	ELECTRICAL, COMMUNICATIONS & UTIL.	94.1	73.2	85.0	93.7	73.2	84.8	94.1	80.6	88.2	87.3	92.0	89.4	97.4	92.5	95.3	95.4	78.3	88.0
MF2018	WEIGHTED AVERAGE	93.4	81.7	89.0	92.5	83.5	89.1	95.0	78.7	88.8	93.9	86.7	91.2	96.4	90.6	94.2	96.2	80.9	90.4

659

City Cost Indexes

Ohio / Oklahoma (Zanesville, Ardmore, Clinton, Durant, Enid, Guymon)

DIVISION		OHIO ZANESVILLE 437-438			OKLAHOMA ARDMORE 734			OKLAHOMA CLINTON 736			OKLAHOMA DURANT 747			OKLAHOMA ENID 737			OKLAHOMA GUYMON 739		
		MAT.	INST.	TOTAL	MAT.	INST.	TOTAL	MAT.	INST.	TOTAL	MAT.	INST.	TOTAL	MAT.	INST.	TOTAL	MAT.	INST.	TOTAL
015433	CONTRACTOR EQUIPMENT		95.9	95.9		90.1	90.1		89.2	89.2		86.5	86.5		89.2	89.2		89.2	89.2
0241, 31 - 34	SITE & INFRASTRUCTURE, DEMOLITION	85.7	89.7	88.3	71.7	97.8	88.7	72.1	96.3	87.9	89.4	94.4	92.7	76.6	96.4	89.5	73.6	95.4	87.8
0310	Concrete Forming & Accessories	93.4	82.4	84.3	94.0	51.9	59.3	92.9	51.9	59.1	90.2	51.3	58.1	95.5	52.2	59.8	97.3	49.6	58.0
0320	Concrete Reinforcing	82.3	80.6	81.6	134.6	64.9	106.1	135.3	64.9	106.5	119.8	64.4	97.2	134.5	65.0	106.1	135.3	55.1	102.5
0330	Cast-in-Place Concrete	104.2	82.4	96.9	87.0	72.8	82.2	84.1	72.8	80.3	89.8	69.5	83.0	84.1	75.4	81.2	84.1	69.4	79.2
03	CONCRETE	93.9	82.6	89.3	96.6	61.8	82.3	96.2	61.8	82.1	92.0	60.3	79.0	96.6	62.8	82.8	99.4	57.8	82.3
04	MASONRY	89.8	76.7	82.2	90.5	60.2	72.9	113.5	60.2	82.5	90.3	57.7	71.3	96.3	60.2	75.3	92.0	48.9	66.9
05	METALS	94.5	91.6	93.9	101.4	64.7	93.7	101.5	64.7	93.8	88.9	65.3	84.0	101.4	65.0	93.8	101.9	58.3	92.8
06	WOOD, PLASTICS & COMPOSITES	86.5	85.4	85.9	103.8	48.8	76.7	103.3	48.8	76.4	91.5	48.6	70.4	105.3	48.8	77.5	107.3	48.8	78.5
07	THERMAL & MOISTURE PROTECTION	95.3	78.9	89.8	112.7	65.2	96.8	112.8	65.2	96.9	104.2	61.5	89.9	112.9	65.6	97.1	113.2	58.1	94.7
08	OPENINGS	86.2	81.3	85.0	103.0	50.1	90.1	103.0	50.1	90.1	94.0	49.9	83.3	104.5	51.9	91.7	103.1	47.9	89.7
0920	Plaster & Gypsum Board	91.5	84.9	87.3	92.1	47.5	63.7	91.9	47.5	63.7	79.5	47.5	59.1	92.9	47.5	64.0	92.9	47.5	64.0
0950, 0980	Ceilings & Acoustic Treatment	88.3	84.9	86.4	91.3	47.5	66.8	91.3	47.5	66.8	80.2	47.5	61.9	91.3	47.5	66.8	91.3	47.5	66.8
0960	Flooring	90.7	61.8	83.3	103.9	49.9	90.0	103.1	49.9	89.4	103.2	70.1	94.7	104.3	69.3	95.3	105.6	49.9	91.3
0970, 0990	Wall Finishes & Painting/Coating	102.6	76.4	87.2	94.1	42.7	63.9	94.1	42.7	63.9	94.9	42.7	64.2	94.1	42.7	63.9	94.1	36.8	60.4
09	FINISHES	94.3	78.0	86.2	93.5	49.0	71.5	93.3	49.0	71.4	88.7	52.7	70.9	93.8	53.0	73.6	94.3	48.4	71.6
COVERS	DIVS. 10 - 14, 25, 28, 41, 43, 44, 46	100.0	88.7	97.6	100.0	79.3	95.6	100.0	79.3	95.6	100.0	78.4	95.4	100.0	79.3	95.6	100.0	77.7	95.3
21, 22, 23	FIRE SUPPRESSION, PLUMBING & HVAC	92.4	84.7	89.7	93.1	66.7	83.6	93.1	66.7	83.6	93.1	65.9	83.3	100.4	66.7	88.3	93.1	60.5	81.4
26, 27, 3370	ELECTRICAL, COMMUNICATIONS & UTIL.	94.1	77.6	86.9	93.5	70.4	83.4	94.0	70.4	83.8	98.5	59.8	81.7	94.0	70.4	83.8	94.9	56.7	78.3
MF2018	WEIGHTED AVERAGE	93.2	82.5	89.1	96.6	65.3	84.8	97.7	65.2	85.4	93.1	63.2	81.8	98.9	65.9	86.4	97.4	59.1	83.0

Oklahoma (Lawton, McAlester, Miami, Muskogee, Oklahoma City, Ponca City)

DIVISION		LAWTON 735			MCALESTER 745			MIAMI 743			MUSKOGEE 744			OKLAHOMA CITY 730-731			PONCA CITY 746		
		MAT.	INST.	TOTAL	MAT.	INST.	TOTAL	MAT.	INST.	TOTAL	MAT.	INST.	TOTAL	MAT.	INST.	TOTAL	MAT.	INST.	TOTAL
015433	CONTRACTOR EQUIPMENT		90.1	90.1		86.5	86.5		95.1	95.1		95.1	95.1		109.3	109.3		86.5	86.5
0241, 31 - 34	SITE & INFRASTRUCTURE, DEMOLITION	75.5	97.9	90.1	84.2	94.2	90.7	85.3	91.3	89.2	89.0	90.9	90.3	75.9	107.9	96.8	89.8	94.4	92.8
0310	Concrete Forming & Accessories	97.5	56.9	64.0	88.9	54.4	60.4	97.8	51.3	59.5	100.9	53.1	61.5	98.7	62.9	69.2	94.7	51.0	58.7
0320	Concrete Reinforcing	134.8	65.0	106.3	119.4	66.1	97.7	117.6	64.9	96.1	118.7	60.8	95.1	151.7	65.1	116.3	118.7	64.9	96.7
0330	Cast-in-Place Concrete	81.3	75.4	79.3	78.7	70.5	76.0	82.5	70.6	78.5	83.5	69.2	78.7	85.4	78.0	82.9	92.3	69.5	84.6
03	CONCRETE	93.0	64.9	81.5	83.2	62.3	74.7	87.2	61.5	76.7	88.8	61.1	77.4	102.4	69.3	88.8	93.9	60.2	80.1
04	MASONRY	92.0	60.2	73.5	106.4	57.3	77.8	93.0	58.5	72.9	106.4	56.2	77.2	91.2	57.8	71.7	84.5	58.4	69.3
05	METALS	105.7	65.0	97.2	88.8	65.8	84.0	88.8	77.8	86.5	88.8	75.2	85.9	99.1	76.9	94.5	88.8	65.2	83.9
06	WOOD, PLASTICS & COMPOSITES	106.8	55.1	81.3	90.1	53.5	72.1	99.8	48.8	74.7	102.7	52.6	78.0	94.9	64.4	79.9	96.8	48.6	73.1
07	THERMAL & MOISTURE PROTECTION	112.7	66.3	97.1	103.8	61.9	89.8	104.2	62.6	90.2	104.5	59.3	89.3	103.1	69.1	91.7	104.3	61.6	90.0
08	OPENINGS	105.8	55.4	93.6	94.0	54.4	84.3	94.0	50.1	83.3	95.4	51.2	84.7	98.7	60.5	89.4	94.0	50.0	83.3
0920	Plaster & Gypsum Board	97.2	54.0	69.7	79.3	52.5	62.2	84.0	47.5	60.8	88.7	51.4	65.0	97.2	63.1	75.5	83.1	47.5	60.4
0950, 0980	Ceilings & Acoustic Treatment	104.9	54.0	76.4	80.2	52.5	64.7	80.2	47.5	61.9	94.8	51.4	70.5	94.2	63.1	76.8	80.2	47.5	61.9
0960	Flooring	105.7	69.3	96.4	102.5	63.8	92.5	107.8	70.1	98.1	109.7	59.2	96.8	109.1	69.3	98.9	105.6	49.9	91.3
0970, 0990	Wall Finishes & Painting/Coating	94.1	42.7	63.9	94.9	45.2	65.7	94.9	42.2	64.0	94.9	36.8	60.8	99.9	42.7	66.2	94.9	42.7	64.2
09	FINISHES	98.1	56.8	77.7	88.0	54.3	71.3	90.1	52.8	71.6	95.1	51.6	73.6	99.4	61.6	80.7	89.9	49.4	69.9
COVERS	DIVS. 10 - 14, 25, 28, 41, 43, 44, 46	100.0	80.0	95.7	100.0	78.6	95.4	100.0	78.8	95.5	100.0	78.5	95.4	100.0	81.3	96.0	100.0	78.4	95.4
21, 22, 23	FIRE SUPPRESSION, PLUMBING & HVAC	100.4	66.7	88.3	93.1	61.2	81.7	93.1	62.4	82.1	100.4	59.3	85.6	100.3	65.5	87.8	93.1	60.6	81.4
26, 27, 3370	ELECTRICAL, COMMUNICATIONS & UTIL.	95.0	67.6	83.1	97.6	65.8	83.8	98.4	65.8	84.2	97.4	80.2	89.9	100.4	70.5	87.4	97.4	56.7	79.7
MF2018	WEIGHTED AVERAGE	99.6	66.7	87.2	92.5	63.8	81.7	92.8	64.5	82.1	95.7	65.2	84.2	99.1	70.0	88.1	93.1	61.3	81.1

Oklahoma / Oregon (Poteau, Shawnee, Tulsa, Woodward, Bend, Eugene)

DIVISION		POTEAU 749			SHAWNEE 748			TULSA 740-741			WOODWARD 738			BEND 977			EUGENE 974		
		MAT.	INST.	TOTAL	MAT.	INST.	TOTAL	MAT.	INST.	TOTAL	MAT.	INST.	TOTAL	MAT.	INST.	TOTAL	MAT.	INST.	TOTAL
015433	CONTRACTOR EQUIPMENT		93.2	93.2		86.5	86.5		106.9	106.9		89.2	89.2		95.8	95.8		95.8	95.8
0241, 31 - 34	SITE & INFRASTRUCTURE, DEMOLITION	76.9	88.2	84.3	92.2	94.2	93.5	94.1	107.6	102.9	72.1	96.4	87.9	92.1	91.9	92.0	89.7	91.9	91.2
0310	Concrete Forming & Accessories	93.4	51.2	58.6	90.1	49.8	56.9	101.1	55.0	63.1	93.0	57.4	63.6	101.5	99.7	100.0	99.2	99.9	99.8
0320	Concrete Reinforcing	120.1	64.9	97.5	118.7	57.3	93.6	119.0	65.0	96.9	134.5	65.0	106.1	143.5	108.7	129.3	149.5	108.7	132.9
0330	Cast-in-Place Concrete	82.5	70.6	78.5	95.2	67.8	86.0	79.7	75.6	85.8	84.1	74.5	80.9	99.6	102.1	100.4	96.4	102.1	98.3
03	CONCRETE	89.4	61.5	77.9	95.6	57.8	80.1	93.8	64.8	81.9	96.5	64.9	83.5	112.2	102.0	108.0	104.5	102.1	103.5
04	MASONRY	93.2	58.5	73.0	107.8	55.3	77.3	94.0	57.7	72.7	86.2	60.2	71.1	143.3	103.9	120.4	137.7	103.9	118.0
05	METALS	88.9	77.7	86.5	88.8	62.2	83.2	92.4	75.2	88.8	101.5	65.0	93.9	93.4	100.0	94.8	93.8	100.2	95.1
06	WOOD, PLASTICS & COMPOSITES	94.7	48.8	72.1	91.4	48.6	70.4	102.2	54.1	78.5	103.3	55.8	80.0	90.9	99.7	95.2	88.0	99.7	93.8
07	THERMAL & MOISTURE PROTECTION	104.3	62.6	90.3	104.3	58.0	88.8	104.5	66.9	91.9	112.9	66.2	97.2	93.4	101.3	96.0	92.6	102.4	95.9
08	OPENINGS	94.0	50.1	83.3	93.9	48.2	82.8	96.8	54.6	86.6	103.0	55.4	91.4	96.1	102.1	97.5	96.3	102.1	97.7
0920	Plaster & Gypsum Board	81.9	47.5	60.0	79.5	47.5	59.1	88.7	52.5	65.6	91.9	54.8	68.3	111.5	99.9	104.1	109.3	99.9	103.3
0950, 0980	Ceilings & Acoustic Treatment	80.2	47.5	61.9	80.2	47.5	61.9	94.8	52.5	71.1	91.3	54.8	70.9	72.3	99.9	87.8	72.3	99.9	87.8
0960	Flooring	105.1	70.1	96.1	103.2	49.9	89.5	108.8	60.1	96.3	103.1	65.9	93.5	111.8	103.8	109.7	110.6	103.8	108.8
0970, 0990	Wall Finishes & Painting/Coating	94.9	42.7	64.2	94.9	36.8	60.8	94.9	54.8	71.4	94.1	42.7	63.9	100.3	85.2	91.4	100.3	60.9	77.1
09	FINISHES	88.6	52.8	70.9	88.9	47.1	68.2	94.9	55.0	75.2	93.3	56.5	75.1	98.9	99.0	98.9	97.6	96.3	96.9
COVERS	DIVS. 10 - 14, 25, 28, 41, 43, 44, 46	100.0	78.8	95.5	100.0	77.4	95.2	100.0	80.1	95.8	100.0	80.1	95.8	100.0	101.9	100.4	100.0	101.9	100.4
21, 22, 23	FIRE SUPPRESSION, PLUMBING & HVAC	93.1	57.8	80.4	93.1	64.2	82.7	100.4	60.8	86.2	93.1	66.7	83.6	92.8	96.2	94.0	100.1	109.8	103.6
26, 27, 3370	ELECTRICAL, COMMUNICATIONS & UTIL.	97.4	65.8	83.7	98.6	70.4	86.3	98.5	64.7	83.8	94.4	70.4	84.2	95.3	86.8	91.6	94.5	86.8	91.1
MF2018	WEIGHTED AVERAGE	92.5	63.3	81.5	94.4	62.6	82.4	96.8	66.1	85.2	96.6	66.9	85.4	99.0	97.4	98.4	99.3	100.0	99.6

City Cost Indexes

OREGON

DIVISION		KLAMATH FALLS 976			MEDFORD 975			PENDLETON 978			PORTLAND 970-972			SALEM 973			VALE 979		
		MAT.	INST.	TOTAL	MAT.	INST.	TOTAL	MAT.	INST.	TOTAL	MAT.	INST.	TOTAL	MAT.	INST.	TOTAL	MAT.	INST.	TOTAL
015433	CONTRACTOR EQUIPMENT		95.8	95.8		95.8	95.8		93.5	93.5		95.8	95.8		101.1	101.1		93.5	93.5
0241, 31 - 34	SITE & INFRASTRUCTURE, DEMOLITION	94.5	91.9	92.8	94.5	91.9	92.8	98.1	85.6	90.0	91.9	92.0	91.9	88.0	99.1	95.2	89.1	85.6	86.8
0310	Concrete Forming & Accessories	96.6	99.5	99.0	95.8	99.6	99.0	96.5	99.5	98.9	99.9	100.1	100.1	99.4	100.1	100.0	101.1	98.4	98.8
0320	Concrete Reinforcing	143.5	108.7	129.2	145.9	108.7	130.7	142.7	108.6	128.8	150.7	108.8	133.6	161.6	108.8	140.0	139.3	108.5	126.7
0330	Cast-in-Place Concrete	99.6	91.0	96.7	99.5	102.0	100.4	100.2	91.6	97.3	99.1	102.2	100.1	91.1	104.6	95.6	78.8	91.8	83.2
03	CONCRETE	115.0	97.9	108.0	110.1	101.9	106.7	97.1	98.1	97.5	106.0	102.2	104.5	105.5	102.9	104.4	82.5	97.7	88.7
04	MASONRY	159.4	103.9	127.1	130.9	103.9	115.2	145.6	104.0	121.4	139.0	103.9	118.6	142.8	104.1	120.3	143.6	104.0	120.6
05	METALS	93.4	99.7	94.7	93.4	99.8	94.7	99.8	100.0	99.8	95.0	100.4	96.1	99.8	98.4	99.5	99.7	98.8	99.5
06	WOOD, PLASTICS & COMPOSITES	84.6	99.7	92.1	84.1	99.7	91.8	84.6	99.8	92.1	88.6	99.7	94.1	81.8	99.9	90.7	90.3	99.8	95.0
07	THERMAL & MOISTURE PROTECTION	93.6	97.4	94.9	93.2	96.7	94.4	89.9	92.3	90.7	92.6	101.3	95.5	89.2	102.6	93.7	89.3	92.8	90.5
08	OPENINGS	96.1	102.1	97.5	98.9	102.1	99.6	93.5	102.1	95.6	94.3	102.1	96.2	100.6	102.2	100.9	93.4	88.7	92.3
0920	Plaster & Gypsum Board	107.4	99.9	102.6	107.4	99.9	102.6	94.1	99.9	97.8	110.8	99.9	103.9	107.4	99.9	102.6	99.6	99.9	99.8
0950, 0980	Ceilings & Acoustic Treatment	79.8	99.9	91.1	82.8	99.9	92.4	54.5	99.9	79.9	74.3	99.9	88.6	87.4	99.9	94.4	54.5	99.9	79.9
0960	Flooring	109.6	103.8	108.1	109.1	103.8	107.8	74.3	103.8	81.8	107.6	103.8	106.6	110.2	103.8	108.6	75.9	103.8	83.0
0970, 0990	Wall Finishes & Painting/Coating	100.3	85.2	91.4	100.3	85.2	91.4	86.3	85.2	85.7	89.2	85.2	91.0	99.9	68.0	81.2	86.3	85.2	85.7
09	FINISHES	100.0	99.0	99.5	100.1	99.0	99.6	69.0	99.0	83.8	97.4	99.0	98.2	99.8	97.2	98.6	69.5	99.0	84.1
COVERS	DIVS. 10 - 14, 25, 28, 41, 43, 44, 46	100.0	101.9	100.4	100.0	101.9	100.4	100.0	97.5	99.5	100.0	102.0	100.4	100.0	102.4	100.5	100.0	102.0	100.4
21, 22, 23	FIRE SUPPRESSION, PLUMBING & HVAC	92.8	96.2	94.0	100.1	101.5	100.6	100.0	102.1	100.8	100.1	109.8	103.6	100.1	112.3	104.5	100.0	66.2	87.9
26, 27, 3370	ELECTRICAL, COMMUNICATIONS & UTIL.	94.6	86.8	91.2	96.5	86.8	92.3	88.0	83.7	86.1	95.2	112.1	102.5	102.2	86.8	95.5	88.0	58.8	75.3
MF2018	WEIGHTED AVERAGE	100.1	96.7	98.8	100.3	98.4	99.6	96.8	96.8	96.8	99.8	104.0	101.4	102.0	101.2	101.7	94.8	85.0	91.1

PENNSYLVANIA

DIVISION		ALLENTOWN 181			ALTOONA 166			BEDFORD 155			BRADFORD 167			BUTLER 160			CHAMBERSBURG 172		
		MAT.	INST.	TOTAL	MAT.	INST.	TOTAL	MAT.	INST.	TOTAL	MAT.	INST.	TOTAL	MAT.	INST.	TOTAL	MAT.	INST.	TOTAL
015433	CONTRACTOR EQUIPMENT		105.9	105.9		105.9	105.9		112.4	112.4		105.9	105.9		105.9	105.9		100.5	100.5
0241, 31 - 34	SITE & INFRASTRUCTURE, DEMOLITION	90.5	99.3	96.2	91.8	99.5	96.8	89.8	99.8	96.3	86.2	96.7	93.0	81.6	98.7	92.7	80.4	90.6	87.0
0310	Concrete Forming & Accessories	101.4	102.5	102.3	90.7	86.4	87.1	87.3	72.6	75.1	92.0	85.9	87.0	91.7	86.6	87.5	89.2	68.3	72.0
0320	Concrete Reinforcing	123.2	107.2	116.6	119.4	105.0	113.5	98.9	92.0	96.1	121.9	92.0	109.7	120.1	118.2	119.3	87.1	95.7	91.4
0330	Cast-in-Place Concrete	82.9	99.3	88.4	92.4	89.5	91.4	110.3	78.7	99.7	88.3	82.3	86.3	81.6	97.8	87.0	87.8	85.3	87.0
03	CONCRETE	91.5	102.6	96.1	88.6	91.3	89.7	102.8	79.3	93.2	93.4	86.3	90.5	81.4	96.6	87.6	96.4	80.3	89.8
04	MASONRY	99.3	95.9	97.3	101.5	87.0	93.1	109.3	70.5	86.7	98.8	72.0	83.2	103.4	88.2	94.5	105.5	69.5	84.6
05	METALS	99.6	110.6	101.9	94.0	106.0	96.5	97.7	103.7	99.0	98.7	97.2	98.4	93.9	110.8	97.4	99.9	99.2	99.7
06	WOOD, PLASTICS & COMPOSITES	95.8	103.3	99.5	79.5	84.3	81.9	77.8	72.7	75.3	85.3	89.9	87.6	80.5	83.6	82.0	77.2	67.4	72.4
07	THERMAL & MOISTURE PROTECTION	100.7	108.1	103.2	99.2	93.2	97.2	111.1	81.2	101.1	100.6	79.8	93.6	98.7	91.3	96.2	108.6	73.6	96.9
08	OPENINGS	92.5	103.2	95.1	87.2	87.7	87.3	90.7	78.3	87.7	92.8	86.8	91.3	87.2	94.0	88.8	87.3	72.0	83.5
0920	Plaster & Gypsum Board	99.2	103.3	101.8	93.4	83.8	87.3	105.4	71.8	84.0	93.8	89.5	91.1	93.4	83.0	86.8	101.7	66.2	79.1
0950, 0980	Ceilings & Acoustic Treatment	97.4	103.3	100.7	101.8	83.8	91.7	115.9	71.8	91.2	101.8	89.5	94.9	102.3	83.0	91.5	96.9	66.2	79.7
0960	Flooring	97.9	91.0	96.1	91.0	97.4	92.7	90.8	90.3	90.7	93.4	90.3	92.6	91.8	91.7	91.8	88.4	67.9	83.1
0970, 0990	Wall Finishes & Painting/Coating	91.6	107.8	101.1	86.5	107.5	98.9	94.6	91.9	93.1	91.6	91.9	91.8	86.5	92.4	90.0	95.7	87.6	91.0
09	FINISHES	96.4	100.8	98.5	95.0	90.0	92.5	101.8	77.1	89.6	95.6	87.6	91.6	94.9	87.3	91.2	92.9	69.6	81.4
COVERS	DIVS. 10 - 14, 25, 28, 41, 43, 44, 46	100.0	102.3	100.5	100.0	99.1	99.8	100.0	94.1	98.7	100.0	96.6	99.3	100.0	99.7	99.9	100.0	91.9	98.3
21, 22, 23	FIRE SUPPRESSION, PLUMBING & HVAC	100.4	111.1	104.2	99.6	87.0	95.1	92.8	74.5	86.2	93.0	79.7	88.2	92.4	87.7	90.7	92.9	78.9	87.8
26, 27, 3370	ELECTRICAL, COMMUNICATIONS & UTIL.	100.5	91.4	96.6	92.1	111.2	100.4	100.7	111.2	105.3	96.8	111.2	103.1	92.4	93.0	92.7	93.7	74.1	85.2
MF2018	WEIGHTED AVERAGE	97.9	102.5	99.6	94.8	94.6	94.7	98.1	85.7	93.4	95.6	89.1	93.1	92.1	93.2	92.5	95.5	78.7	89.2

PENNSYLVANIA

DIVISION		DOYLESTOWN 189			DUBOIS 158			ERIE 164 - 165			GREENSBURG 156			HARRISBURG 170 - 171			HAZLETON 182		
		MAT.	INST.	TOTAL	MAT.	INST.	TOTAL	MAT.	INST.	TOTAL	MAT.	INST.	TOTAL	MAT.	INST.	TOTAL	MAT.	INST.	TOTAL
015433	CONTRACTOR EQUIPMENT		90.3	90.3		112.4	112.4		105.9	105.9		112.4	112.4		106.9	106.9		105.9	105.9
0241, 31 - 34	SITE & INFRASTRUCTURE, DEMOLITION	98.8	86.7	90.9	92.4	100.6	97.8	89.6	98.7	95.5	87.1	102.4	97.0	85.9	101.5	96.1	82.0	97.5	92.1
0310	Concrete Forming & Accessories	89.7	112.2	108.3	87.0	75.1	77.2	101.2	89.2	91.3	91.4	81.9	83.6	99.8	92.3	93.6	88.1	78.8	80.5
0320	Concrete Reinforcing	119.1	131.1	124.0	98.2	103.9	100.5	121.9	106.8	115.7	98.2	118.0	106.2	91.9	110.1	99.4	119.6	98.3	110.9
0330	Cast-in-Place Concrete	78.3	115.7	90.8	106.3	93.2	101.9	90.9	89.1	90.3	102.3	98.3	100.9	86.5	103.2	92.1	78.3	86.4	81.0
03	CONCRETE	87.4	116.3	99.3	104.0	87.7	97.3	87.9	92.7	89.9	97.8	95.0	96.7	90.8	99.6	94.4	85.1	85.7	85.4
04	MASONRY	102.2	118.4	111.6	109.5	82.2	93.6	92.7	89.4	90.8	118.4	85.0	98.9	100.8	96.6	98.3	110.7	78.6	92.0
05	METALS	97.3	112.8	100.6	97.7	110.6	100.4	94.3	105.9	96.7	97.7	116.7	101.7	105.3	107.3	105.8	99.4	102.4	100.0
06	WOOD, PLASTICS & COMPOSITES	82.3	111.5	96.7	77.2	72.7	75.0	91.5	88.9	90.3	81.4	77.4	79.5	90.0	89.3	89.7	81.5	77.4	79.5
07	THERMAL & MOISTURE PROTECTION	97.7	114.7	103.4	111.4	87.6	103.4	99.6	90.2	96.5	110.9	90.0	103.9	113.0	109.6	111.9	100.1	88.4	96.2
08	OPENINGS	94.2	117.4	99.9	90.7	81.0	88.3	87.4	90.9	88.2	90.7	90.6	90.6	97.9	92.8	96.6	93.1	82.4	90.5
0920	Plaster & Gypsum Board	91.5	111.8	104.4	104.7	71.8	83.8	99.2	88.5	92.4	106.1	76.7	87.4	108.8	88.6	95.9	92.0	76.6	82.2
0950, 0980	Ceilings & Acoustic Treatment	96.1	111.8	104.9	115.9	71.8	91.2	97.4	88.5	92.4	115.9	76.7	94.0	106.8	88.6	96.6	97.9	76.6	86.0
0960	Flooring	83.1	121.3	92.9	90.6	90.3	90.5	95.5	98.6	96.3	93.3	67.9	86.8	94.6	96.5	95.1	91.2	77.8	87.7
0970, 0990	Wall Finishes & Painting/Coating	91.6	125.0	111.2	94.6	107.5	102.2	99.7	88.5	93.1	94.6	92.4	93.3	99.9	91.6	95.0	91.6	90.6	91.0
09	FINISHES	88.6	114.9	101.6	102.0	80.1	91.1	96.6	90.7	93.7	102.4	79.4	91.0	100.4	92.3	96.4	93.3	79.6	86.5
COVERS	DIVS. 10 - 14, 25, 28, 41, 43, 44, 46	100.0	112.7	102.7	100.0	95.7	99.1	100.0	99.2	99.8	100.0	99.0	99.8	100.0	99.9	100.0	100.0	94.8	98.9
21, 22, 23	FIRE SUPPRESSION, PLUMBING & HVAC	92.4	116.5	101.0	92.8	77.2	87.2	99.6	94.8	97.9	92.8	80.6	88.4	100.0	98.7	99.6	93.0	84.0	89.8
26, 27, 3370	ELECTRICAL, COMMUNICATIONS & UTIL.	95.6	114.4	103.8	101.0	111.2	105.5	93.3	86.2	90.2	101.0	111.2	105.5	100.4	91.3	96.4	97.3	77.7	88.8
MF2018	WEIGHTED AVERAGE	94.2	113.4	101.4	98.4	90.0	95.2	94.7	93.2	94.1	98.0	93.2	96.2	99.9	97.7	99.1	95.0	85.1	91.3

City Cost Indexes

PENNSYLVANIA

DIVISION		INDIANA 157			JOHNSTOWN 159			KITTANNING 162			LANCASTER 175 - 176			LEHIGH VALLEY 180			MONTROSE 188		
		MAT.	INST.	TOTAL	MAT.	INST.	TOTAL	MAT.	INST.	TOTAL	MAT.	INST.	TOTAL	MAT.	INST.	TOTAL	MAT.	INST.	TOTAL
015433	CONTRACTOR EQUIPMENT		112.4	112.4		112.4	112.4		105.9	105.9		100.5	100.5		105.9	105.9		105.9	105.9
0241, 31 - 34	SITE & INFRASTRUCTURE, DEMOLITION	85.7	101.3	95.9	90.1	102.6	98.2	83.6	99.3	93.8	74.4	93.7	87.0	85.1	105.9	98.7	83.9	97.6	92.8
0310	Concrete Forming & Accessories	87.7	86.3	86.5	87.0	84.8	85.2	91.7	83.5	85.0	90.4	90.1	90.1	96.5	97.7	97.5	88.7	79.3	80.9
0320	Concrete Reinforcing	97.5	118.3	106.0	98.9	118.6	106.9	120.1	118.1	119.3	86.7	103.0	93.4	119.6	93.9	109.1	125.3	101.0	115.4
0330	Cast-in-Place Concrete	100.3	97.7	99.4	111.3	87.3	103.2	84.8	97.5	89.1	74.6	97.6	82.3	84.8	89.5	86.4	83.1	84.2	83.5
03	CONCRETE	95.5	96.8	96.1	103.8	92.5	99.1	83.7	95.1	88.4	84.8	95.6	89.3	90.7	94.6	92.3	90.0	85.6	88.2
04	MASONRY	105.6	90.4	96.7	106.6	88.4	96.0	106.3	86.2	94.6	112.4	89.9	99.3	99.3	84.7	90.8	99.3	80.4	88.3
05	METALS	97.8	115.9	101.6	97.8	117.3	101.9	93.9	109.8	97.3	99.9	108.2	101.6	99.4	101.8	99.9	98.8	103.1	99.7
06	WOOD, PLASTICS & COMPOSITES	78.2	83.5	80.8	77.2	84.3	80.7	80.5	79.4	79.9	79.0	89.0	84.0	89.7	99.9	94.7	82.0	77.4	79.7
07	THERMAL & MOISTURE PROTECTION	110.9	92.4	104.7	111.1	90.5	104.2	98.8	90.3	96.0	108.0	104.0	106.7	100.4	97.9	99.6	100.2	80.1	93.5
08	OPENINGS	90.7	90.4	90.6	90.7	90.8	90.7	87.2	91.7	88.3	87.3	87.3	87.3	93.1	94.1	93.3	89.9	81.1	87.8
0920	Plaster & Gypsum Board	105.7	83.0	91.2	104.7	83.8	91.4	93.4	78.7	84.1	103.8	88.1	94.1	93.2	99.9	97.4	93.3	76.6	82.7
0950, 0980	Ceilings & Acoustic Treatment	115.9	83.0	97.5	115.9	83.8	97.9	102.3	78.7	89.1	96.9	88.6	92.2	97.9	99.8	98.9	101.8	76.6	87.7
0960	Flooring	91.2	90.3	90.9	90.6	94.6	91.6	91.8	90.3	91.4	89.2	96.5	91.1	95.5	81.9	92.1	91.8	90.3	91.4
0970, 0990	Wall Finishes & Painting/Coating	94.6	107.5	102.2	94.6	107.5	102.2	86.5	107.5	98.9	95.7	81.8	87.5	91.6	87.9	89.4	91.6	90.6	91.0
09	FINISHES	101.7	88.5	95.2	101.7	88.3	95.1	95.0	86.1	90.6	92.9	89.9	91.4	95.0	93.9	94.4	94.9	81.8	88.4
COVERS	DIVS. 10 - 14, 25, 28, 41, 43, 44, 46	100.0	99.6	99.9	100.0	97.6	99.5	100.0	99.3	99.9	100.0	97.6	99.5	100.0	98.6	99.7	100.0	95.4	99.0
21, 22, 23	FIRE SUPPRESSION, PLUMBING & HVAC	92.8	79.8	88.1	92.8	85.9	90.3	92.4	84.5	89.5	92.9	96.2	94.1	93.0	103.3	96.7	93.0	83.3	89.5
26, 27, 3370	ELECTRICAL, COMMUNICATIONS & UTIL.	101.0	111.2	105.5	101.0	111.2	105.5	92.1	111.2	100.4	94.5	86.5	91.0	97.3	111.7	103.6	96.8	82.2	90.5
MF2018	WEIGHTED AVERAGE	97.0	95.0	96.3	98.1	95.6	97.2	92.5	94.3	93.2	94.4	93.9	94.2	95.4	98.9	96.8	94.8	85.9	91.5

PENNSYLVANIA

DIVISION		NEW CASTLE 161			NORRISTOWN 194			OIL CITY 163			PHILADELPHIA 190 - 191			PITTSBURGH 150 - 152			POTTSVILLE 179		
		MAT.	INST.	TOTAL	MAT.	INST.	TOTAL	MAT.	INST.	TOTAL	MAT.	INST.	TOTAL	MAT.	INST.	TOTAL	MAT.	INST.	TOTAL
015433	CONTRACTOR EQUIPMENT		105.9	105.9		92.8	92.8		105.9	105.9		97.4	97.4		102.3	102.3		100.5	100.5
0241, 31 - 34	SITE & INFRASTRUCTURE, DEMOLITION	82.0	99.5	93.4	99.5	89.9	93.3	80.8	96.8	91.2	97.7	98.3	98.1	94.5	103.4	100.3	76.6	91.1	86.0
0310	Concrete Forming & Accessories	91.7	90.2	90.4	89.8	116.5	111.8	91.7	82.6	84.2	98.4	132.8	126.8	99.6	98.3	98.5	85.1	78.0	79.2
0320	Concrete Reinforcing	118.8	96.6	109.7	151.5	131.1	143.2	120.1	96.0	110.3	117.7	148.0	130.1	105.0	121.0	111.6	86.1	99.2	91.4
0330	Cast-in-Place Concrete	82.4	93.4	86.0	80.0	113.7	91.3	80.0	85.5	81.8	98.3	130.4	109.1	109.8	99.2	106.2	79.5	94.4	84.5
03	CONCRETE	81.6	93.0	86.3	94.1	117.5	103.7	80.3	86.6	82.9	100.5	133.8	114.2	104.1	102.4	103.4	88.4	88.2	88.3
04	MASONRY	102.7	93.7	97.4	110.3	115.1	113.1	102.6	77.9	88.2	108.1	129.5	120.6	94.6	98.9	97.1	105.6	76.9	88.9
05	METALS	93.9	102.7	95.8	102.2	113.3	104.5	93.9	99.9	95.2	105.3	124.9	109.4	106.2	105.5	106.1	100.1	100.9	100.3
06	WOOD, PLASTICS & COMPOSITES	80.5	88.6	84.5	85.3	118.9	101.8	80.5	83.6	82.0	96.0	132.9	114.2	97.3	98.9	98.1	73.1	75.8	74.4
07	THERMAL & MOISTURE PROTECTION	98.7	90.6	96.0	101.3	114.0	105.6	98.6	81.7	92.9	95.9	131.8	107.9	113.3	99.6	108.7	108.2	88.7	101.7
08	OPENINGS	87.2	87.9	87.4	90.4	121.5	97.9	87.2	85.9	86.9	98.1	136.7	107.5	98.1	103.7	99.4	87.3	82.2	86.1
0920	Plaster & Gypsum Board	93.4	88.2	90.1	86.8	119.5	107.6	93.4	83.0	86.8	86.0	133.9	116.5	107.3	98.9	101.9	99.5	74.9	83.8
0950, 0980	Ceilings & Acoustic Treatment	102.3	88.2	94.4	93.2	119.5	107.9	102.3	83.0	91.5	97.3	133.9	118.1	110.3	98.9	103.9	96.9	74.9	84.6
0960	Flooring	91.8	94.3	92.4	98.8	121.3	104.6	91.8	90.3	91.4	107.4	143.8	116.8	96.2	105.6	98.6	86.0	90.3	87.1
0970, 0990	Wall Finishes & Painting/Coating	86.5	105.9	97.9	94.3	125.0	112.4	86.5	107.5	98.9	104.8	167.1	141.4	99.9	107.5	104.4	95.7	90.6	92.7
09	FINISHES	94.9	92.3	93.6	92.1	118.5	105.1	94.8	86.4	90.7	96.9	138.3	117.3	102.3	100.3	101.3	91.6	80.5	86.2
COVERS	DIVS. 10 - 14, 25, 28, 41, 43, 44, 46	100.0	100.2	100.0	100.0	112.3	102.6	100.0	96.9	99.3	100.0	117.2	103.7	100.0	100.8	100.2	100.0	94.7	98.9
21, 22, 23	FIRE SUPPRESSION, PLUMBING & HVAC	92.4	97.3	94.1	92.8	114.8	100.7	92.4	82.9	89.0	100.1	141.7	115.0	100.0	97.3	99.1	92.9	84.2	89.7
26, 27, 3370	ELECTRICAL, COMMUNICATIONS & UTIL.	92.4	90.4	91.5	99.3	122.7	109.5	93.7	93.0	93.4	105.3	161.2	129.6	101.4	111.2	105.7	93.5	78.8	87.1
MF2018	WEIGHTED AVERAGE	92.1	94.7	93.1	97.0	115.0	103.8	92.0	87.9	90.4	101.4	135.6	114.3	101.9	102.2	102.0	94.3	85.0	90.8

PENNSYLVANIA

DIVISION		READING 195 - 196			SCRANTON 184 - 185			STATE COLLEGE 168			STROUDSBURG 183			SUNBURY 178			UNIONTOWN 154		
		MAT.	INST.	TOTAL	MAT.	INST.	TOTAL	MAT.	INST.	TOTAL	MAT.	INST.	TOTAL	MAT.	INST.	TOTAL	MAT.	INST.	TOTAL
015433	CONTRACTOR EQUIPMENT		108.2	108.2		105.9	105.9		105.0	105.0		105.9	105.9		101.7	101.7		112.4	112.4
0241, 31 - 34	SITE & INFRASTRUCTURE, DEMOLITION	106.7	101.9	103.6	91.1	98.6	96.0	80.4	97.9	91.8	83.3	97.8	92.7	83.2	92.5	89.3	86.1	101.8	96.4
0310	Concrete Forming & Accessories	101.0	88.1	90.4	101.6	87.8	90.2	89.2	86.6	87.2	92.5	80.4	82.5	94.9	75.3	78.8	83.4	86.6	86.0
0320	Concrete Reinforcing	153.6	107.0	134.6	123.2	106.9	116.5	121.0	105.3	114.6	123.6	101.2	114.4	88.5	97.6	92.2	98.2	118.3	106.4
0330	Cast-in-Place Concrete	71.7	93.1	78.8	86.6	89.8	87.6	83.5	90.3	85.8	81.6	85.5	82.9	87.0	86.2	86.7	100.3	97.8	99.5
03	CONCRETE	92.8	93.9	93.3	93.4	92.5	93.0	93.0	91.8	92.5	88.6	86.6	87.8	91.9	83.8	88.5	95.4	97.0	96.0
04	MASONRY	100.4	89.5	94.1	99.7	91.6	95.0	104.1	91.1	96.5	96.1	84.5	89.4	105.3	71.1	85.4	122.2	90.4	103.7
05	METALS	102.5	111.1	104.3	101.7	108.3	103.0	98.5	106.7	100.3	99.4	103.6	100.3	99.8	99.8	99.8	97.6	116.5	101.6
06	WOOD, PLASTICS & COMPOSITES	97.4	86.5	92.0	95.8	86.9	91.4	86.4	84.3	85.4	85.9	77.4	81.7	77.5	75.8	76.7	73.5	83.5	78.6
07	THERMAL & MOISTURE PROTECTION	102.3	103.3	102.6	100.6	89.5	96.9	99.8	101.2	100.3	100.3	80.4	93.7	109.2	81.8	100.0	110.8	92.4	104.7
08	OPENINGS	95.5	94.0	95.1	92.5	89.3	91.7	89.7	87.7	89.2	93.1	83.5	90.8	87.4	79.4	85.5	90.6	91.0	90.7
0920	Plaster & Gypsum Board	93.7	86.0	88.8	103.5	86.4	92.6	93.1	83.8	87.1	92.2	76.6	82.3	98.0	74.9	83.3	102.6	83.0	90.1
0950, 0980	Ceilings & Acoustic Treatment	82.2	86.0	84.3	111.1	86.4	97.3	97.4	83.8	89.8	96.1	76.6	85.2	92.0	74.9	82.4	115.9	83.0	97.5
0960	Flooring	101.5	88.0	98.1	97.9	98.8	98.1	96.1	89.8	94.5	93.8	81.9	90.8	86.4	90.3	87.4	88.4	103.8	92.4
0970, 0990	Wall Finishes & Painting/Coating	92.6	101.4	97.8	91.6	101.4	97.4	91.6	107.5	101.0	91.6	90.6	91.0	95.7	90.6	92.7	94.6	107.5	102.2
09	FINISHES	91.1	88.5	89.8	100.4	91.0	95.7	94.5	88.8	91.7	93.8	81.0	87.4	90.9	79.1	85.1	100.0	90.8	95.7
COVERS	DIVS. 10 - 14, 25, 28, 41, 43, 44, 46	100.0	98.7	99.7	100.0	99.2	99.8	100.0	97.4	99.4	100.0	96.2	99.2	100.0	90.9	98.1	100.0	99.6	99.9
21, 22, 23	FIRE SUPPRESSION, PLUMBING & HVAC	100.4	108.8	103.4	100.4	93.9	98.0	93.1	96.7	94.4	93.0	86.1	90.5	92.8	76.8	87.1	92.8	84.4	89.8
26, 27, 3370	ELECTRICAL, COMMUNICATIONS & UTIL.	103.8	90.5	98.0	100.5	87.1	94.7	95.9	111.2	102.6	97.3	122.5	108.2	94.1	79.3	87.7	99.2	111.2	104.4
MF2018	WEIGHTED AVERAGE	99.3	97.9	98.8	98.9	93.5	96.8	95.2	97.1	95.9	94.9	92.9	94.1	94.9	81.7	89.9	97.3	96.5	97.0

City Cost Indexes

DIVISION		PENNSYLVANIA																	
		WASHINGTON 153			WELLSBORO 169			WESTCHESTER 193			WILKES-BARRE 186 - 187			WILLIAMSPORT 177			YORK 173 - 174		
		MAT.	INST.	TOTAL	MAT.	INST.	TOTAL	MAT.	INST.	TOTAL	MAT.	INST.	TOTAL	MAT.	INST.	TOTAL	MAT.	INST.	TOTAL
015433	CONTRACTOR EQUIPMENT		112.4	112.4		105.9	105.9		92.8	92.8		105.9	105.9		101.7	101.7		100.5	100.5
0241, 31 - 34	SITE & INFRASTRUCTURE, DEMOLITION	86.2	102.6	96.9	88.7	97.1	94.2	105.2	90.8	95.8	81.5	98.2	92.4	76.8	93.8	87.9	80.8	93.7	89.2
0310	Concrete Forming & Accessories	87.9	92.3	91.6	91.5	74.7	77.6	94.3	112.0	108.9	94.6	83.3	85.2	92.8	80.7	82.8	87.1	88.4	88.1
0320	Concrete Reinforcing	98.2	118.5	106.5	121.0	100.9	112.8	150.2	131.1	142.4	121.9	108.9	116.6	87.8	108.8	96.4	88.5	108.9	96.8
0330	Cast-in-Place Concrete	100.3	98.4	99.6	87.5	80.0	85.0	88.7	115.4	97.6	78.3	88.1	81.6	73.6	87.2	78.1	79.9	97.7	85.9
03	CONCRETE	95.7	99.9	97.4	95.3	82.0	89.8	101.1	116.1	107.3	85.9	90.2	87.6	80.4	88.6	83.8	89.5	95.8	92.0
04	MASONRY	103.7	92.7	97.3	106.9	71.5	86.3	104.4	118.4	112.5	111.2	90.5	99.2	96.8	86.6	90.9	106.4	89.9	96.8
05	METALS	97.6	117.8	101.8	98.6	102.3	99.4	102.2	113.2	104.5	98.7	108.7	100.8	99.9	107.3	101.4	99.9	108.3	101.7
06	WOOD, PLASTICS & COMPOSITES	78.3	90.8	84.4	84.9	75.0	80.0	89.8	111.5	100.4	87.5	81.4	84.5	75.7	79.3	77.5	74.9	86.6	80.7
07	THERMAL & MOISTURE PROTECTION	110.9	94.5	105.4	100.8	75.9	92.5	101.7	110.7	104.7	100.1	89.3	96.5	108.6	87.7	101.6	108.2	103.2	106.5
08	OPENINGS	90.6	97.9	92.4	92.8	79.5	89.5	90.4	117.4	96.9	89.9	86.3	89.1	87.4	85.2	86.9	87.3	91.0	88.2
0920	Plaster & Gypsum Board	105.7	90.5	96.0	92.4	74.2	80.8	87.3	111.8	102.9	94.0	80.7	85.5	99.5	78.6	86.2	99.5	86.0	90.9
0950, 0980	Ceilings & Acoustic Treatment	115.9	90.5	101.7	97.4	74.2	84.4	93.2	111.8	103.6	101.8	80.7	90.0	96.9	78.6	86.6	95.9	86.0	90.4
0960	Flooring	91.2	103.8	94.4	93.1	90.3	92.4	101.1	121.3	106.3	94.5	98.8	95.6	85.6	86.2	85.8	87.1	96.5	89.5
0970, 0990	Wall Finishes & Painting/Coating	94.6	107.5	102.2	91.6	90.6	91.0	94.3	125.0	112.4	91.6	106.9	100.6	95.7	106.9	102.3	95.7	84.9	89.3
09	FINISHES	101.7	95.4	98.6	94.5	79.1	86.9	93.3	114.9	104.0	95.6	88.0	91.8	91.7	83.9	87.8	91.7	88.8	90.3
COVERS	DIVS. 10 - 14, 25, 28, 41, 43, 44, 46	100.0	100.4	100.1	100.0	90.7	98.0	100.0	112.6	102.7	100.0	98.3	99.6	100.0	95.3	99.0	100.0	97.3	99.4
21, 22, 23	FIRE SUPPRESSION, PLUMBING & HVAC	92.8	87.7	91.0	93.0	76.8	87.2	92.8	116.5	101.3	93.0	94.2	93.5	92.8	91.6	92.4	100.1	96.2	98.7
26, 27, 3370	ELECTRICAL, COMMUNICATIONS & UTIL.	100.7	111.2	105.3	96.8	82.2	90.5	99.2	114.4	105.8	97.3	82.5	90.9	94.4	76.4	86.6	94.5	76.8	86.8
MF2018	WEIGHTED AVERAGE	96.9	99.0	97.7	96.1	82.3	90.9	97.8	113.6	103.8	95.0	91.8	93.8	93.1	88.6	91.4	96.4	92.5	94.9

DIVISION		PUERTO RICO			RHODE ISLAND						SOUTH CAROLINA								
		SAN JUAN 009			NEWPORT 028			PROVIDENCE 029			AIKEN 298			BEAUFORT 299			CHARLESTON 294		
		MAT.	INST.	TOTAL	MAT.	INST.	TOTAL	MAT.	INST.	TOTAL	MAT.	INST.	TOTAL	MAT.	INST.	TOTAL	MAT.	INST.	TOTAL
015433	CONTRACTOR EQUIPMENT		96.2	96.2		96.9	96.9		103.0	103.0		96.8	96.8		96.8	96.8		105.9	105.9
0241, 31 - 34	SITE & INFRASTRUCTURE, DEMOLITION	115.8	93.6	101.3	85.8	94.5	91.5	87.7	102.5	97.4	137.1	82.6	101.6	132.2	82.6	99.9	119.6	101.8	108.0
0310	Concrete Forming & Accessories	104.0	28.2	41.5	98.6	117.6	114.3	100.8	117.7	114.7	97.5	64.8	70.6	97.0	61.2	67.5	96.5	66.3	71.6
0320	Concrete Reinforcing	137.9	24.3	91.5	107.1	116.1	110.8	109.0	116.1	111.9	150.0	52.6	110.2	148.6	57.9	111.5	148.3	66.6	114.9
0330	Cast-in-Place Concrete	82.4	41.2	68.6	62.3	112.1	79.0	85.4	114.4	95.1	87.6	67.5	80.9	87.6	67.5	80.9	102.8	71.5	92.3
03	CONCRETE	95.6	33.0	69.9	76.8	115.4	92.6	90.7	116.1	101.1	110.2	64.5	91.5	107.7	63.8	89.7	105.1	68.7	90.2
04	MASONRY	112.8	27.9	63.4	105.8	118.7	113.3	134.0	118.9	125.2	77.6	52.6	63.1	92.8	52.6	69.5	94.4	64.8	77.2
05	METALS	124.9	44.6	108.1	101.8	115.9	104.8	108.5	114.9	109.8	97.0	74.7	92.3	97.0	76.7	92.8	98.3	76.9	93.8
06	WOOD, PLASTICS & COMPOSITES	88.0	27.1	58.1	94.3	116.8	105.4	106.2	116.8	111.4	94.5	68.8	81.9	93.8	63.8	79.0	93.0	68.7	81.1
07	THERMAL & MOISTURE PROTECTION	134.7	33.7	100.9	92.2	113.6	99.3	95.7	116.6	102.8	106.8	58.4	90.6	106.5	58.5	90.4	105.4	68.2	92.9
08	OPENINGS	176.2	25.2	139.5	96.9	117.0	101.8	97.9	117.0	102.6	92.7	60.4	84.8	92.7	58.8	84.5	96.3	65.7	88.9
0920	Plaster & Gypsum Board	155.1	24.8	72.2	87.8	117.1	106.5	108.5	117.1	114.0	75.6	67.5	70.4	80.9	62.3	69.1	80.2	67.5	72.1
0950, 0980	Ceilings & Acoustic Treatment	234.1	24.8	117.0	77.0	117.1	99.5	100.6	117.1	109.8	96.2	67.5	80.1	105.9	62.3	81.5	105.9	67.5	84.4
0960	Flooring	200.0	27.6	155.8	104.1	126.5	109.8	110.2	126.5	114.4	115.5	78.2	105.9	116.7	66.0	103.7	116.5	79.8	107.1
0970, 0990	Wall Finishes & Painting/Coating	182.7	29.9	92.9	88.7	118.8	106.4	99.9	118.8	111.0	100.4	57.5	75.2	100.4	49.5	70.5	100.4	65.9	80.1
09	FINISHES	204.2	28.3	117.2	91.1	119.8	105.3	103.6	119.9	111.6	99.6	67.0	83.5	102.7	61.1	82.1	100.6	69.1	85.0
COVERS	DIVS. 10 - 14, 25, 28, 41, 43, 44, 46	105.0	26.8	88.3	100.0	106.6	101.4	100.0	106.7	101.4	100.0	85.0	96.8	100.0	74.5	94.6	100.0	85.6	96.9
21, 22, 23	FIRE SUPPRESSION, PLUMBING & HVAC	114.2	24.3	81.9	100.6	112.2	104.8	100.2	112.2	104.5	93.1	48.8	77.2	93.1	53.8	79.0	100.4	57.9	85.1
26, 27, 3370	ELECTRICAL, COMMUNICATIONS & UTIL.	122.8	22.6	79.2	103.1	96.9	100.4	102.3	96.9	99.9	96.9	53.4	78.0	99.0	57.3	80.8	98.1	63.1	82.9
MF2018	WEIGHTED AVERAGE	126.9	33.5	91.6	96.7	111.2	102.2	102.1	111.9	105.8	98.2	61.3	84.2	98.9	61.8	84.9	100.3	68.9	88.4

DIVISION		SOUTH CAROLINA														SOUTH DAKOTA		
		COLUMBIA 290 - 292			FLORENCE 295			GREENVILLE 296			ROCK HILL 297			SPARTANBURG 293			ABERDEEN 574		
		MAT.	INST.	TOTAL	MAT.	INST.	TOTAL	MAT.	INST.	TOTAL	MAT.	INST.	TOTAL	MAT.	INST.	TOTAL	MAT.	INST.	TOTAL
015433	CONTRACTOR EQUIPMENT		105.0	105.0		96.8	96.8		96.8	96.8		96.8	96.8		96.8	96.8		96.3	96.3
0241, 31 - 34	SITE & INFRASTRUCTURE, DEMOLITION	119.9	96.5	104.7	129.3	83.0	99.1	124.2	83.0	97.3	118.3	82.6	95.0	124.1	83.0	97.3	90.5	90.4	90.4
0310	Concrete Forming & Accessories	96.5	66.5	71.8	88.6	66.3	70.2	96.0	66.5	71.7	94.7	64.6	69.9	97.8	66.4	71.9	101.0	62.9	69.6
0320	Concrete Reinforcing	152.5	66.8	117.5	147.7	66.7	114.6	147.5	66.5	114.4	148.8	57.1	111.3	147.5	58.9	111.3	88.0	67.9	79.8
0330	Cast-in-Place Concrete	104.1	71.0	93.0	87.5	70.1	81.7	87.5	70.1	81.7	87.5	67.1	80.7	87.5	70.1	81.7	105.9	76.4	96.1
03	CONCRETE	104.6	68.9	89.9	103.0	68.5	88.9	101.7	68.6	88.1	100.1	65.0	85.7	101.8	67.2	87.6	100.5	69.3	87.7
04	MASONRY	86.8	67.4	75.5	77.7	64.6	70.1	76.2	64.6	69.4	98.7	52.0	71.5	77.7	64.6	70.1	112.8	68.9	87.3
05	METALS	95.7	80.9	92.6	97.0	81.8	93.8	97.0	81.9	93.8	97.0	76.4	92.7	97.0	79.0	93.2	95.1	78.6	91.6
06	WOOD, PLASTICS & COMPOSITES	92.4	68.8	80.8	84.9	68.8	77.0	92.5	68.8	80.9	91.7	68.8	80.4	95.0	68.8	82.1	99.9	58.0	79.3
07	THERMAL & MOISTURE PROTECTION	101.3	67.9	90.1	106.0	65.6	92.4	105.8	65.6	92.3	105.6	54.1	88.4	105.8	65.6	92.3	104.1	71.0	93.0
08	OPENINGS	97.5	65.7	89.8	92.8	65.7	86.2	92.7	65.6	86.1	92.7	61.4	85.1	92.7	63.9	85.7	90.9	69.2	85.6
0920	Plaster & Gypsum Board	80.3	67.5	72.1	72.2	67.5	69.2	74.2	67.5	69.9	74.2	67.5	69.9	76.1	67.5	70.6	106.9	56.9	75.1
0950, 0980	Ceilings & Acoustic Treatment	107.0	67.5	84.9	98.9	67.5	81.3	96.2	67.5	80.1	96.2	67.5	80.1	96.2	67.5	80.1	105.8	56.9	78.4
0960	Flooring	109.1	82.2	102.2	109.6	73.0	100.2	114.6	82.2	106.3	113.8	66.0	101.5	115.7	82.2	107.1	90.0	63.2	83.1
0970, 0990	Wall Finishes & Painting/Coating	99.9	65.9	79.9	100.4	65.9	80.1	100.4	65.9	80.1	100.4	57.5	75.2	100.4	65.9	80.1	82.4	72.8	76.8
09	FINISHES	100.2	69.6	85.1	97.0	68.0	82.6	97.6	69.6	83.7	97.1	64.8	81.1	98.1	69.6	84.0	96.8	64.1	80.7
COVERS	DIVS. 10 - 14, 25, 28, 41, 43, 44, 46	100.0	85.6	96.9	100.0	85.6	96.9	100.0	85.8	97.0	100.0	84.9	96.8	100.0	85.8	97.0	100.0	79.4	95.6
21, 22, 23	FIRE SUPPRESSION, PLUMBING & HVAC	99.9	58.2	84.9	100.4	57.9	85.1	100.4	57.9	85.1	93.1	48.5	77.1	100.4	57.9	85.1	100.0	75.5	91.2
26, 27, 3370	ELECTRICAL, COMMUNICATIONS & UTIL.	103.1	63.3	85.8	96.8	54.2	78.3	98.1	81.0	90.7	98.1	78.3	89.5	98.1	81.0	90.7	84.9	65.2	76.4
MF2018	WEIGHTED AVERAGE	99.7	69.2	88.2	98.5	66.3	86.3	98.4	70.4	87.8	97.4	64.6	85.0	98.5	69.9	87.7	96.9	72.0	87.5

City Cost Indexes

DIVISION		SOUTH DAKOTA																	
		MITCHELL			MOBRIDGE			PIERRE			RAPID CITY			SIOUX FALLS			WATERTOWN		
		573			576			575			577			570 - 571			572		
		MAT.	INST.	TOTAL	MAT.	INST.	TOTAL	MAT.	INST.	TOTAL	MAT.	INST.	TOTAL	MAT.	INST.	TOTAL	MAT.	INST.	TOTAL
015433	CONTRACTOR EQUIPMENT		96.3	96.3		96.3	96.3		101.6	101.6		96.3	96.3		107.8	107.8		96.3	96.3
0241, 31 - 34	SITE & INFRASTRUCTURE, DEMOLITION	84.6	89.7	87.9	84.6	89.8	88.0	81.3	95.5	90.6	89.4	90.5	90.1	94.3	106.4	102.2	84.5	89.7	87.9
0310	Concrete Forming & Accessories	100.2	40.7	51.1	92.7	41.2	50.2	105.9	84.5	88.2	107.0	54.8	64.0	100.4	83.1	86.1	90.0	67.0	71.0
0320	Concrete Reinforcing	87.5	67.7	79.4	89.7	67.6	80.7	93.1	70.3	83.8	82.3	69.8	77.2	90.3	95.8	92.5	85.0	67.6	77.9
0330	Cast-in-Place Concrete	102.9	50.5	85.4	102.9	75.0	93.6	99.3	82.6	93.7	102.1	77.3	93.8	92.7	84.3	89.9	102.9	74.8	93.5
03	CONCRETE	98.2	50.1	78.4	98.0	59.0	82.0	102.6	81.4	93.9	97.4	66.2	84.6	95.7	85.8	91.7	97.1	70.5	86.2
04	MASONRY	100.8	68.1	81.7	110.0	64.0	83.2	93.5	77.0	83.9	109.3	67.9	85.2	117.6	76.8	93.9	136.8	64.8	94.9
05	METALS	95.1	77.3	91.4	95.1	77.8	91.4	98.6	78.7	94.4	97.3	78.9	93.5	98.5	89.4	96.6	95.1	77.1	91.3
06	WOOD, PLASTICS & COMPOSITES	99.2	30.4	65.4	90.1	30.2	60.6	108.9	84.7	97.0	103.6	46.7	75.6	102.4	82.1	92.4	87.0	66.2	76.8
07	THERMAL & MOISTURE PROTECTION	103.9	66.1	91.2	103.9	68.9	92.2	106.1	81.9	98.0	104.4	74.3	94.3	103.0	85.9	97.3	103.8	70.2	92.5
08	OPENINGS	90.1	54.0	81.3	92.6	53.9	83.2	94.2	85.0	92.0	94.5	64.1	87.1	96.3	89.1	94.5	90.1	55.8	81.8
0920	Plaster & Gypsum Board	105.6	28.5	56.5	101.6	28.3	54.9	99.8	84.0	89.7	107.0	45.3	68.0	100.7	81.3	88.4	99.7	65.3	77.8
0950, 0980	Ceilings & Acoustic Treatment	101.8	28.5	60.8	105.8	28.3	62.4	122.1	84.0	100.8	108.9	45.3	73.3	103.7	81.3	91.2	101.8	65.3	81.4
0960	Flooring	89.7	68.3	84.2	85.4	40.4	74.1	99.0	67.6	91.0	89.3	65.0	83.1	94.6	74.3	89.4	84.5	38.1	72.6
0970, 0990	Wall Finishes & Painting/Coating	82.4	72.8	76.8	82.4	72.8	76.8	87.1	115.7	103.9	82.4	115.7	101.9	99.9	115.7	109.1	82.4	72.8	76.8
09	FINISHES	95.4	47.3	71.6	94.8	43.4	69.4	106.6	86.5	96.7	97.5	62.5	80.2	100.9	84.9	93.0	93.2	64.1	78.8
COVERS	DIVS. 10 - 14, 25, 28, 41, 43, 44, 46	100.0	72.0	94.0	100.0	71.9	94.0	100.0	92.3	98.4	100.0	86.0	97.0	100.0	92.1	98.3	100.0	75.2	94.7
21, 22, 23	FIRE SUPPRESSION, PLUMBING & HVAC	92.7	43.3	75.0	92.7	67.0	83.5	100.1	71.5	89.8	100.0	69.5	89.1	99.8	72.7	90.1	92.7	46.0	75.9
26, 27, 3370	ELECTRICAL, COMMUNICATIONS & UTIL.	84.2	65.2	75.9	84.9	34.3	62.9	84.4	52.2	70.4	83.4	52.2	69.8	95.8	67.2	83.4	83.8	65.2	75.7
MF2018	WEIGHTED AVERAGE	94.0	58.7	80.7	94.6	59.7	81.4	97.9	76.7	89.9	97.0	68.1	86.1	99.2	81.5	92.5	95.2	64.6	83.6

DIVISION		TENNESSEE																	
		CHATTANOOGA			COLUMBIA			COOKEVILLE			JACKSON			JOHNSON CITY			KNOXVILLE		
		373 - 374			384			385			383			376			377 - 379		
		MAT.	INST.	TOTAL	MAT.	INST.	TOTAL	MAT.	INST.	TOTAL	MAT.	INST.	TOTAL	MAT.	INST.	TOTAL	MAT.	INST.	TOTAL
015433	CONTRACTOR EQUIPMENT		97.8	97.8		94.4	94.4		94.4	94.4		100.8	100.8		91.8	91.8		102.3	102.3
0241, 31 - 34	SITE & INFRASTRUCTURE, DEMOLITION	105.3	92.5	97.0	94.1	86.3	89.0	99.8	85.6	90.5	105.5	97.3	100.1	110.2	82.1	91.9	96.3	98.3	97.6
0310	Concrete Forming & Accessories	107.9	58.9	67.5	91.4	55.9	62.1	91.6	29.6	40.5	97.1	65.4	70.9	96.0	55.4	62.5	106.9	64.4	71.8
0320	Concrete Reinforcing	97.9	67.4	85.4	110.2	55.3	88.2	110.2	56.3	88.2	110.2	63.2	91.0	98.8	58.7	82.4	97.9	67.4	85.5
0330	Cast-in-Place Concrete	110.4	61.8	94.1	99.6	61.7	86.9	112.9	55.6	93.7	124.0	64.7	95.0	88.7	56.6	77.9	103.7	70.6	92.6
03	CONCRETE	99.6	62.4	84.3	99.4	59.0	82.9	109.6	45.0	83.1	101.6	65.5	86.8	103.2	57.5	84.4	96.5	67.7	84.7
04	MASONRY	105.7	53.3	75.2	113.6	48.9	75.9	109.3	34.8	65.9	114.1	54.3	79.3	122.6	40.4	74.8	83.3	55.7	67.3
05	METALS	95.4	80.2	92.2	94.5	73.4	90.0	94.5	72.7	90.0	95.7	76.4	91.7	92.0	76.1	88.7	95.7	76.5	91.6
06	WOOD, PLASTICS & COMPOSITES	114.5	59.4	87.4	75.3	56.5	66.1	75.5	26.6	51.4	92.3	66.4	79.6	85.5	60.1	73.0	98.4	65.1	82.0
07	THERMAL & MOISTURE PROTECTION	115.0	60.2	96.6	97.1	57.6	83.9	97.5	48.9	81.2	98.9	62.6	86.8	110.2	54.5	91.6	108.3	67.2	94.6
08	OPENINGS	100.9	58.3	90.5	91.1	47.2	80.4	91.1	31.6	76.6	98.6	60.1	89.3	96.4	57.0	86.8	93.7	58.0	85.0
0920	Plaster & Gypsum Board	93.6	58.7	71.4	96.6	55.6	70.5	96.6	24.7	50.9	97.3	65.7	77.2	116.3	59.4	80.1	123.9	64.0	85.8
0950, 0980	Ceilings & Acoustic Treatment	100.9	58.7	77.3	76.8	55.6	64.9	76.8	24.7	47.7	82.1	65.7	73.0	96.7	59.4	75.9	98.9	64.0	79.4
0960	Flooring	93.3	59.5	84.7	91.8	47.0	80.3	91.8	43.5	79.4	88.1	51.2	78.6	91.4	51.2	81.1	95.3	56.4	85.3
0970, 0990	Wall Finishes & Painting/Coating	99.1	55.0	73.2	88.2	49.1	65.3	88.2	49.1	65.3	90.7	55.3	69.9	96.2	51.8	70.1	96.2	54.5	71.7
09	FINISHES	96.3	58.1	77.4	93.3	53.2	73.5	93.7	32.2	63.3	91.4	61.8	76.8	101.3	54.2	78.0	94.8	61.6	78.4
COVERS	DIVS. 10 - 14, 25, 28, 41, 43, 44, 46	100.0	80.8	95.9	100.0	80.6	95.9	100.0	73.9	94.4	100.0	83.3	96.4	100.0	77.7	95.3	100.0	83.6	96.5
21, 22, 23	FIRE SUPPRESSION, PLUMBING & HVAC	100.2	59.0	85.4	94.5	64.8	83.8	94.5	59.1	81.8	100.1	61.7	86.3	100.0	49.0	81.7	100.0	63.2	86.8
26, 27, 3370	ELECTRICAL, COMMUNICATIONS & UTIL.	103.5	71.6	89.6	96.8	43.6	73.7	97.8	52.9	78.3	104.7	56.7	83.8	93.4	45.3	72.5	96.8	56.7	79.3
MF2018	WEIGHTED AVERAGE	100.3	65.6	87.2	96.2	59.7	82.4	97.5	52.1	80.4	99.8	65.4	86.8	99.4	55.8	82.9	96.9	66.3	85.3

DIVISION		TENNESSEE						TEXAS											
		MCKENZIE			MEMPHIS			NASHVILLE			ABILENE			AMARILLO			AUSTIN		
		382			375,380 - 381			370 - 372			795 - 796			790 - 791			786 - 787		
		MAT.	INST.	TOTAL	MAT.	INST.	TOTAL	MAT.	INST.	TOTAL	MAT.	INST.	TOTAL	MAT.	INST.	TOTAL	MAT.	INST.	TOTAL
015433	CONTRACTOR EQUIPMENT		94.4	94.4		95.6	95.6		96.0	96.0		94.6	94.6		102.6	102.6		105.7	105.7
0241, 31 - 34	SITE & INFRASTRUCTURE, DEMOLITION	99.3	85.8	90.5	91.6	95.4	94.1	105.2	94.2	98.0	91.8	88.5	89.6	91.7	97.6	95.5	88.5	102.8	97.8
0310	Concrete Forming & Accessories	97.9	31.6	43.2	107.7	68.0	75.0	107.5	71.2	77.6	98.7	58.4	65.4	100.3	57.4	64.9	97.5	56.7	63.8
0320	Concrete Reinforcing	110.4	57.1	88.6	105.7	67.4	90.0	105.7	67.7	90.2	150.3	50.5	109.5	151.2	50.5	110.0	151.3	50.6	110.2
0330	Cast-in-Place Concrete	110.5	56.5	92.4	114.6	70.5	99.9	93.3	71.1	85.9	90.3	67.8	82.8	92.2	73.5	85.9	101.4	71.6	91.4
03	CONCRETE	108.1	46.4	82.8	105.4	69.1	90.5	96.0	70.9	85.7	103.9	61.2	86.4	113.5	62.7	92.6	104.0	61.6	86.6
04	MASONRY	112.6	39.8	70.2	99.4	59.0	75.9	97.5	63.4	77.7	103.8	60.6	78.6	104.5	62.6	80.1	94.1	63.0	76.0
05	METALS	94.5	73.2	90.1	99.2	72.3	93.6	99.4	74.4	94.1	90.6	72.0	86.7	88.0	70.7	84.4	97.0	69.2	91.2
06	WOOD, PLASTICS & COMPOSITES	82.8	28.6	56.1	110.2	67.6	89.2	109.9	71.9	91.2	103.5	59.6	81.9	99.7	56.6	78.4	96.3	56.7	76.8
07	THERMAL & MOISTURE PROTECTION	97.5	49.7	81.5	112.8	68.7	98.0	112.4	70.3	98.3	98.4	63.4	86.7	97.8	66.1	87.2	99.5	69.6	89.5
08	OPENINGS	91.1	33.0	77.0	101.2	63.4	92.0	101.1	68.0	93.0	100.2	56.1	89.5	98.1	54.3	87.4	98.0	53.4	87.1
0920	Plaster & Gypsum Board	99.6	26.8	53.3	108.3	66.8	81.9	104.2	71.2	83.2	95.6	58.5	72.0	101.1	54.7	71.6	98.2	55.2	70.9
0950, 0980	Ceilings & Acoustic Treatment	76.8	26.8	48.8	103.7	66.8	83.0	103.7	71.2	85.5	89.4	58.5	72.1	87.5	54.7	69.2	102.1	55.2	75.9
0960	Flooring	93.9	47.0	81.8	94.6	57.1	85.0	94.6	64.2	86.8	106.9	69.0	97.2	109.2	65.0	97.8	109.7	64.4	98.1
0970, 0990	Wall Finishes & Painting/Coating	88.2	38.4	59.0	99.9	72.5	83.8	99.9	65.9	79.9	95.5	55.3	71.9	99.9	52.2	71.8	99.9	47.8	69.3
09	FINISHES	94.6	33.4	64.3	99.5	66.1	83.0	102.4	69.3	86.1	93.6	60.0	77.0	99.1	57.8	78.7	102.2	57.1	79.9
COVERS	DIVS. 10 - 14, 25, 28, 41, 43, 44, 46	100.0	72.4	94.1	100.0	84.6	96.7	100.0	85.1	96.8	100.0	80.2	95.8	100.0	82.0	96.2	100.0	81.9	96.2
21, 22, 23	FIRE SUPPRESSION, PLUMBING & HVAC	94.5	51.6	79.1	100.1	75.7	91.3	100.0	72.9	90.3	100.4	50.0	82.2	100.1	53.7	83.4	100.1	60.8	86.0
26, 27, 3370	ELECTRICAL, COMMUNICATIONS & UTIL.	97.7	47.8	76.0	101.3	63.2	84.7	101.3	62.3	84.3	99.1	52.5	78.8	102.2	58.2	83.1	101.1	57.6	82.2
MF2018	WEIGHTED AVERAGE	97.6	50.8	79.9	101.0	70.7	89.6	100.4	71.5	89.5	98.1	60.8	84.0	99.2	63.1	85.6	99.5	64.7	86.3

City Cost Indexes

TEXAS

DIVISION		BEAUMONT 776-777			BROWNWOOD 768			BRYAN 778			CHILDRESS 792			CORPUS CHRISTI 783-784			DALLAS 752-753		
		MAT.	INST.	TOTAL	MAT.	INST.	TOTAL	MAT.	INST.	TOTAL	MAT.	INST.	TOTAL	MAT.	INST.	TOTAL	MAT.	INST.	TOTAL
015433	CONTRACTOR EQUIPMENT		90.3	90.3		92.3	92.3		90.3	90.3		94.6	94.6		104.3	104.3		98.9	98.9
0241, 31-34	SITE & INFRASTRUCTURE, DEMOLITION	104.4	87.5	93.4	97.6	85.7	89.9	91.6	87.7	89.1	96.3	88.3	91.1	107.3	86.3	93.6	91.2	97.6	95.4
0310	Concrete Forming & Accessories	102.2	53.8	62.3	96.7	54.4	61.8	86.0	53.8	59.5	97.4	54.7	62.2	101.2	53.6	61.9	96.5	61.7	67.8
0320	Concrete Reinforcing	81.2	72.4	77.6	93.7	44.6	73.6	83.4	50.4	69.9	150.5	44.6	107.2	107.2	50.7	84.0	103.6	52.0	82.5
0330	Cast-in-Place Concrete	85.5	66.0	78.9	110.2	56.4	92.2	68.4	66.0	67.6	92.6	56.1	80.4	120.5	68.2	103.0	85.1	69.0	79.7
03	CONCRETE	86.3	62.1	76.4	100.2	54.3	81.4	72.6	58.4	66.8	113.3	54.4	89.1	104.8	60.0	86.4	88.6	63.1	78.2
04	MASONRY	101.0	61.8	78.1	120.3	53.6	81.5	140.4	61.0	94.2	106.6	53.1	75.4	83.2	60.0	69.7	99.4	58.2	75.4
05	METALS	91.8	76.8	88.6	96.1	67.2	90.0	92.1	68.3	87.1	88.7	68.6	84.4	91.2	84.2	89.8	97.5	68.5	91.4
06	WOOD, PLASTICS & COMPOSITES	102.1	52.9	77.9	102.4	56.3	79.7	71.7	52.8	62.4	103.1	56.5	80.1	119.3	53.4	86.9	96.2	63.5	80.1
07	THERMAL & MOISTURE PROTECTION	107.4	63.9	92.9	105.9	59.2	90.2	98.9	62.5	86.7	99.0	57.8	85.2	103.6	63.3	92.7	96.6	65.8	86.3
08	OPENINGS	89.3	57.9	81.7	93.7	51.2	83.4	87.0	52.8	78.7	94.0	51.3	83.6	98.4	51.1	86.9	101.0	59.4	90.9
0920	Plaster & Gypsum Board	102.2	52.0	70.2	83.3	55.3	65.5	89.2	51.9	65.5	94.2	55.3	69.5	99.4	52.3	69.4	91.7	62.4	73.0
0950, 0980	Ceilings & Acoustic Treatment	116.6	52.0	80.4	81.6	55.3	66.9	105.7	51.9	75.6	84.9	55.3	68.4	108.1	52.3	76.9	77.4	62.4	69.0
0960	Flooring	114.2	74.6	104.1	87.5	47.5	77.3	89.0	71.7	84.6	105.6	47.5	90.7	121.6	72.8	109.1	108.7	67.6	98.1
0970, 0990	Wall Finishes & Painting/Coating	94.8	54.3	71.0	90.7	44.9	63.8	91.4	61.5	73.8	95.5	44.9	65.8	111.6	44.2	72.0	99.9	52.7	72.1
09	FINISHES	99.4	57.1	78.5	84.6	52.1	68.5	87.3	56.7	72.2	92.8	52.2	72.7	105.2	55.7	80.7	94.8	61.8	78.5
COVERS	DIVS. 10-14, 25, 28, 41, 43, 44, 46	100.0	74.0	94.5	100.0	76.8	95.1	100.0	80.3	95.8	100.0	77.1	95.1	100.0	78.6	95.4	100.0	81.2	96.0
21, 22, 23	FIRE SUPPRESSION, PLUMBING & HVAC	100.1	62.3	86.5	92.9	43.9	75.2	92.8	62.5	81.9	93.1	47.8	76.8	100.2	60.5	86.0	100.1	60.6	85.9
26, 27, 3370	ELECTRICAL, COMMUNICATIONS & UTIL.	102.2	63.2	85.2	101.8	39.9	74.8	103.1	62.9	85.6	99.0	48.2	76.9	98.8	62.9	83.2	99.9	60.4	82.7
MF2018	WEIGHTED AVERAGE	96.6	64.9	84.6	97.2	53.9	80.8	93.2	63.5	82.0	96.8	56.2	81.5	98.9	64.3	85.8	97.5	65.1	85.2

TEXAS

DIVISION		DEL RIO 788			DENTON 762			EASTLAND 764			EL PASO 798-799,885			FORT WORTH 760-761			GALVESTON 775		
		MAT.	INST.	TOTAL	MAT.	INST.	TOTAL	MAT.	INST.	TOTAL	MAT.	INST.	TOTAL	MAT.	INST.	TOTAL	MAT.	INST.	TOTAL
015433	CONTRACTOR EQUIPMENT		95.3	95.3		99.6	99.6		92.3	92.3		106.5	106.5		101.5	101.5		99.3	99.3
0241, 31-34	SITE & INFRASTRUCTURE, DEMOLITION	97.5	88.7	91.8	95.4	80.8	85.9	99.9	85.7	90.7	87.9	103.8	98.3	96.2	96.0	96.1	120.1	86.6	98.3
0310	Concrete Forming & Accessories	98.9	45.8	55.1	100.4	54.8	62.8	96.9	54.5	61.9	98.9	59.2	66.2	97.4	59.1	65.8	92.9	58.2	64.3
0320	Concrete Reinforcing	107.7	41.4	80.6	95.2	45.0	74.7	94.0	44.6	73.8	152.5	50.7	110.9	103.6	50.6	82.0	82.9	50.4	69.6
0330	Cast-in-Place Concrete	129.8	55.1	104.8	85.1	57.8	76.0	116.5	56.4	96.4	75.7	67.9	73.8	98.9	67.7	88.5	96.7	67.0	82.9
03	CONCRETE	123.4	49.4	93.0	79.6	55.8	69.8	104.9	54.4	84.2	105.5	62.3	87.8	95.5	61.5	81.5	87.9	61.3	77.0
04	MASONRY	96.9	53.3	71.5	126.9	59.7	87.8	93.3	53.6	70.4	94.3	63.6	76.5	93.8	62.0	75.2	97.3	61.0	76.2
05	METALS	91.1	65.0	85.6	95.4	79.9	92.2	95.9	67.3	89.9	85.9	71.1	82.8	97.6	72.0	92.3	93.7	79.5	90.7
06	WOOD, PLASTICS & COMPOSITES	96.3	45.1	71.1	110.1	56.5	83.7	110.5	56.3	83.9	95.3	59.7	77.8	94.7	60.0	77.6	88.2	58.9	73.8
07	THERMAL & MOISTURE PROTECTION	104.0	57.6	88.4	103.4	62.0	89.6	106.2	59.2	90.4	96.8	66.6	86.7	101.8	66.5	90.0	98.0	64.8	86.8
08	OPENINGS	92.9	42.3	80.6	111.1	51.0	96.4	73.8	51.2	68.3	98.3	54.2	87.6	98.0	56.7	87.9	92.1	56.2	83.4
0920	Plaster & Gypsum Board	95.4	43.8	62.5	87.8	55.3	67.1	83.3	55.3	65.5	105.5	58.1	75.4	93.5	58.5	71.2	96.1	58.0	71.9
0950, 0980	Ceilings & Acoustic Treatment	102.7	43.8	69.7	86.0	55.3	68.8	81.6	55.3	66.9	89.6	58.1	72.0	93.2	58.5	73.8	111.4	58.0	81.6
0960	Flooring	102.3	47.5	88.3	83.3	47.5	74.1	110.5	47.5	94.3	109.1	75.7	100.6	109.7	69.0	99.3	103.7	71.7	95.5
0970, 0990	Wall Finishes & Painting/Coating	98.7	37.0	62.4	101.5	42.5	66.9	91.8	44.9	64.3	99.9	49.1	70.0	99.9	49.7	70.4	105.5	46.7	70.9
09	FINISHES	98.0	44.6	71.6	82.6	51.9	67.4	91.4	52.1	72.0	100.7	61.0	81.1	100.4	59.8	80.3	97.7	58.7	78.4
COVERS	DIVS. 10-14, 25, 28, 41, 43, 44, 46	100.0	71.3	93.9	100.0	77.2	95.1	100.0	76.9	95.1	100.0	80.5	95.9	100.0	81.2	96.0	100.0	75.2	94.7
21, 22, 23	FIRE SUPPRESSION, PLUMBING & HVAC	92.9	52.5	78.4	92.9	49.4	77.2	92.9	43.9	75.2	100.1	62.4	86.5	100.1	58.8	85.3	92.8	62.5	81.9
26, 27, 3370	ELECTRICAL, COMMUNICATIONS & UTIL.	99.9	51.7	78.9	105.0	50.7	81.3	101.6	50.6	79.4	101.7	46.1	77.5	101.4	53.7	80.7	103.6	54.8	82.3
MF2018	WEIGHTED AVERAGE	98.6	55.1	82.1	96.4	58.2	82.0	95.6	55.5	80.4	97.3	64.2	84.8	98.7	63.7	85.4	95.5	64.0	83.6

TEXAS

DIVISION		GIDDINGS 789			GREENVILLE 754			HOUSTON 770-772			HUNTSVILLE 773			LAREDO 780			LONGVIEW 756		
		MAT.	INST.	TOTAL	MAT.	INST.	TOTAL	MAT.	INST.	TOTAL	MAT.	INST.	TOTAL	MAT.	INST.	TOTAL	MAT.	INST.	TOTAL
015433	CONTRACTOR EQUIPMENT		95.3	95.3		89.5	89.5		97.3	97.3		90.3	90.3		95.3	95.3		85.5	85.5
0241, 31-34	SITE & INFRASTRUCTURE, DEMOLITION	87.6	89.0	88.5	82.3	81.6	81.8	122.3	92.1	102.6	107.0	87.1	94.0	86.9	89.5	88.6	85.2	87.3	86.6
0310	Concrete Forming & Accessories	97.0	46.1	55.0	89.3	51.4	58.0	96.4	60.2	66.6	90.5	48.4	55.8	98.9	54.1	61.9	87.6	54.3	60.1
0320	Concrete Reinforcing	108.3	42.2	81.3	103.9	45.0	79.8	82.2	50.5	69.2	83.6	44.5	67.7	107.7	50.7	84.3	103.0	44.2	79.0
0330	Cast-in-Place Concrete	109.9	55.4	91.6	87.2	54.8	76.4	84.5	70.6	79.9	94.2	54.3	80.9	92.6	66.8	84.0	101.5	53.7	85.5
03	CONCRETE	101.4	49.9	80.2	86.2	52.6	72.4	85.0	62.8	75.9	93.3	50.7	75.8	94.7	58.9	80.0	100.2	52.9	80.8
04	MASONRY	102.6	53.4	74.0	154.3	59.5	99.1	95.6	64.3	77.4	138.3	53.3	88.8	90.2	61.7	73.6	150.3	52.1	93.2
05	METALS	90.7	66.2	85.5	91.7	69.7	87.1	98.9	68.4	92.5	92.0	64.1	85.2	93.2	71.3	88.6	84.8	60.2	79.6
06	WOOD, PLASTICS & COMPOSITES	95.4	45.1	70.6	80.3	51.9	66.4	96.3	59.8	78.4	77.2	48.1	62.9	96.3	53.3	75.2	76.4	56.1	66.4
07	THERMAL & MOISTURE PROTECTION	104.5	60.0	89.6	96.4	58.3	83.7	98.7	70.0	89.1	99.8	58.7	86.0	103.4	65.7	90.8	98.4	55.9	84.2
08	OPENINGS	92.2	43.1	80.3	93.6	48.9	82.7	98.2	56.4	88.1	87.0	46.4	77.1	92.8	50.3	82.5	85.4	50.7	76.9
0920	Plaster & Gypsum Board	94.7	43.8	62.3	77.8	50.9	60.7	96.6	58.6	72.4	92.3	47.1	63.5	97.5	52.3	68.7	76.3	55.3	62.9
0950, 0980	Ceilings & Acoustic Treatment	102.7	43.8	69.7	71.9	50.9	60.1	106.5	58.6	79.7	105.7	47.1	72.9	109.3	52.3	77.4	67.1	55.3	60.5
0960	Flooring	103.6	47.5	89.2	100.1	47.5	86.6	107.4	72.8	98.5	91.9	47.5	80.5	102.2	62.5	92.0	104.8	47.5	90.1
0970, 0990	Wall Finishes & Painting/Coating	98.7	38.5	63.3	91.8	44.9	64.2	104.8	57.9	77.3	91.4	50.0	67.0	98.7	46.9	68.2	82.5	42.5	59.0
09	FINISHES	97.6	44.7	71.4	88.5	49.5	69.2	102.9	62.1	82.7	89.5	47.8	68.9	98.9	54.3	76.8	93.9	51.6	73.0
COVERS	DIVS. 10-14, 25, 28, 41, 43, 44, 46	100.0	76.6	95.0	100.0	76.2	94.9	100.0	83.1	96.4	100.0	72.8	94.2	100.0	78.9	95.5	100.0	76.3	95.0
21, 22, 23	FIRE SUPPRESSION, PLUMBING & HVAC	92.9	57.1	80.1	92.9	51.2	77.9	100.1	63.5	86.9	92.8	57.9	80.3	100.2	63.2	86.9	92.8	50.8	77.7
26, 27, 3370	ELECTRICAL, COMMUNICATIONS & UTIL.	98.0	48.0	76.3	98.1	50.7	77.4	105.3	62.5	86.6	103.1	51.1	80.4	100.1	54.1	80.0	96.6	43.9	73.7
MF2018	WEIGHTED AVERAGE	95.6	56.0	80.7	95.2	56.7	80.7	99.0	66.2	86.6	96.8	56.8	81.3	96.8	62.6	83.9	95.0	55.0	79.9

City Cost Indexes

		TEXAS																	
	DIVISION	LUBBOCK			LUFKIN			MCALLEN			MCKINNEY			MIDLAND			ODESSA		
		793 - 794			759			785			750			797			797		
		MAT.	INST.	TOTAL	MAT.	INST.	TOTAL	MAT.	INST.	TOTAL	MAT.	INST.	TOTAL	MAT.	INST.	TOTAL	MAT.	INST.	TOTAL
015433	CONTRACTOR EQUIPMENT		105.2	105.2		85.5	85.5		104.5	104.5		89.5	89.5		105.2	105.2		94.6	94.6
0241, 31 - 34	SITE & INFRASTRUCTURE, DEMOLITION	108.9	88.6	95.6	82.1	86.5	85.0	106.3	86.5	93.4	80.4	81.6	81.2	107.7	88.5	95.2	92.1	88.5	89.8
0310	Concrete Forming & Accessories	96.1	54.7	62.0	89.5	48.5	55.7	103.2	47.5	57.2	88.7	51.4	57.9	98.6	61.4	68.0	98.7	61.0	67.6
0320	Concrete Reinforcing	151.5	50.5	110.2	104.9	58.1	85.7	107.3	50.4	84.1	103.9	45.0	79.8	152.5	50.5	110.8	150.3	50.4	109.5
0330	Cast-in-Place Concrete	90.4	70.7	83.8	90.7	53.0	78.1	131.0	63.0	108.2	81.8	54.8	72.7	96.1	70.8	87.7	90.3	65.5	82.0
03	CONCRETE	102.4	61.3	85.5	93.2	52.2	76.4	112.7	55.3	89.1	82.0	52.6	69.9	106.8	64.4	89.4	103.9	61.6	86.5
04	MASONRY	103.0	62.5	79.5	116.1	53.1	79.4	96.5	61.8	76.3	165.6	59.5	103.8	119.2	61.2	85.4	103.8	61.5	79.2
05	METALS	93.5	84.3	91.6	92.1	63.6	86.1	90.8	83.4	89.3	91.6	69.7	87.0	92.5	84.5	90.8	89.9	71.8	86.1
06	WOOD, PLASTICS & COMPOSITES	100.1	53.0	77.0	83.6	48.1	66.1	118.5	45.2	82.4	79.7	51.9	66.0	103.1	62.9	83.3	103.5	62.7	83.4
07	THERMAL & MOISTURE PROTECTION	88.2	64.4	80.2	98.2	55.4	83.8	107.3	63.4	92.6	96.2	58.3	83.5	88.4	64.8	80.5	98.4	63.4	86.7
08	OPENINGS	105.9	53.4	93.1	70.5	49.9	65.5	98.5	44.4	85.4	93.6	48.8	82.7	108.2	58.2	96.0	100.2	58.1	89.9
0920	Plaster & Gypsum Board	96.1	51.6	67.8	74.9	47.1	57.2	100.4	43.8	64.3	77.8	50.9	60.7	96.1	61.8	74.3	95.6	61.8	74.1
0950, 0980	Ceilings & Acoustic Treatment	90.7	51.6	68.8	62.7	47.1	53.9	109.3	43.8	72.6	71.9	50.9	60.1	87.1	61.8	72.9	89.4	61.8	73.9
0960	Flooring	101.4	67.6	92.7	139.7	47.5	116.1	121.2	72.8	108.8	99.7	47.5	86.3	102.2	66.9	93.1	106.9	60.7	95.1
0970, 0990	Wall Finishes & Painting/Coating	107.4	52.1	74.9	82.5	44.9	60.4	111.6	37.0	67.8	91.8	44.9	64.2	107.4	53.2	75.5	95.5	51.6	69.7
09	FINISHES	95.9	56.3	76.3	102.3	47.6	75.2	105.7	50.6	78.4	88.3	49.5	69.1	95.5	61.6	78.7	93.6	60.1	77.0
COVERS	DIVS. 10 - 14, 25, 28, 41, 43, 44, 46	100.0	80.9	95.9	100.0	72.8	94.2	100.0	78.2	95.4	100.0	76.2	94.9	100.0	81.3	96.0	100.0	81.0	95.9
21, 22, 23	FIRE SUPPRESSION, PLUMBING & HVAC	99.6	50.7	82.0	92.8	56.3	79.7	92.9	44.7	75.6	92.9	53.2	78.6	92.3	54.0	78.5	100.4	47.9	81.5
26, 27, 3370	ELECTRICAL, COMMUNICATIONS & UTIL.	97.7	53.8	78.6	97.4	53.0	78.1	98.6	27.3	67.6	98.2	50.7	77.5	97.7	58.4	80.6	99.2	58.3	81.4
MF2018	WEIGHTED AVERAGE	98.7	61.8	84.8	93.6	56.9	79.8	98.7	54.3	81.9	95.1	57.2	80.8	98.3	64.5	85.5	97.9	61.5	84.2

		TEXAS																	
	DIVISION	PALESTINE			SAN ANGELO			SAN ANTONIO			TEMPLE			TEXARKANA			TYLER		
		758			769			781 - 782			765			755			757		
		MAT.	INST.	TOTAL	MAT.	INST.	TOTAL	MAT.	INST.	TOTAL	MAT.	INST.	TOTAL	MAT.	INST.	TOTAL	MAT.	INST.	TOTAL
015433	CONTRACTOR EQUIPMENT		85.5	85.5		92.3	92.3		100.4	100.4		92.3	92.3		85.5	85.5		85.5	85.5
0241, 31 - 34	SITE & INFRASTRUCTURE, DEMOLITION	83.9	87.3	86.1	94.6	85.8	88.8	81.8	98.7	92.8	85.2	85.1	85.2	78.4	87.7	84.4	84.5	87.6	86.5
0310	Concrete Forming & Accessories	84.0	54.3	59.5	96.9	46.8	55.6	98.2	56.2	63.6	98.9	46.1	55.3	94.3	59.2	65.4	90.6	61.5	66.6
0320	Concrete Reinforcing	102.2	44.5	78.6	93.6	50.6	76.0	93.8	52.0	76.7	93.7	50.0	75.9	102.1	50.8	81.1	103.0	50.4	81.5
0330	Cast-in-Place Concrete	82.9	53.7	73.1	104.0	68.1	92.0	85.7	72.1	81.1	85.1	55.9	75.3	83.5	66.5	77.8	99.7	56.2	85.1
03	CONCRETE	93.7	52.9	76.9	95.7	56.1	79.4	87.5	61.7	76.9	81.9	51.2	69.3	86.6	60.8	76.0	99.7	58.0	82.6
04	MASONRY	110.2	52.1	76.4	117.2	62.0	85.1	95.8	64.6	77.7	125.9	53.4	83.7	169.6	67.3	110.1	159.2	62.9	103.2
05	METALS	91.9	60.3	85.3	96.2	70.7	90.9	97.6	67.7	91.3	95.9	67.6	90.0	84.7	64.7	80.5	91.8	63.8	85.9
06	WOOD, PLASTICS & COMPOSITES	78.6	56.1	67.5	102.6	45.1	74.3	96.3	55.2	76.0	112.1	45.1	79.2	84.1	59.3	71.9	84.5	62.9	73.9
07	THERMAL & MOISTURE PROTECTION	98.7	55.6	84.2	105.2	63.1	91.4	99.5	69.4	89.4	105.2	57.8	89.3	97.9	67.6	87.7	98.4	63.0	86.6
08	OPENINGS	70.5	51.1	65.8	93.7	46.4	82.2	98.0	53.0	87.1	70.8	46.4	64.8	85.3	58.2	78.7	70.4	60.2	67.9
0920	Plaster & Gypsum Board	74.9	55.3	62.4	83.3	43.8	58.1	98.2	53.8	70.0	80.3	43.8	58.1	80.8	58.5	66.6	74.9	62.2	66.8
0950, 0980	Ceilings & Acoustic Treatment	62.7	55.3	58.5	81.6	43.8	60.4	102.1	53.8	75.1	81.6	43.8	60.4	67.1	58.5	62.3	62.7	62.2	62.4
0960	Flooring	133.1	47.5	111.2	87.7	62.0	81.1	108.7	75.5	100.2	111.7	47.5	95.2	110.8	64.1	98.8	141.4	62.0	121.0
0970, 0990	Wall Finishes & Painting/Coating	82.5	44.9	60.4	90.7	44.9	63.8	99.9	45.5	67.9	91.8	38.5	60.5	82.5	62.3	70.6	82.5	62.3	70.6
09	FINISHES	100.8	51.9	76.6	84.4	48.5	66.6	101.7	58.2	80.2	90.6	44.8	68.0	95.8	60.0	78.1	103.0	61.7	82.6
COVERS	DIVS. 10 - 14, 25, 28, 41, 43, 44, 46	100.0	76.3	95.0	100.0	76.8	95.1	100.0	80.2	95.8	100.0	75.7	94.8	100.0	80.1	95.8	100.0	80.5	95.8
21, 22, 23	FIRE SUPPRESSION, PLUMBING & HVAC	92.8	50.1	77.4	92.9	49.0	77.1	100.1	63.2	86.8	92.9	47.1	76.4	92.8	61.0	81.4	92.8	58.7	80.6
26, 27, 3370	ELECTRICAL, COMMUNICATIONS & UTIL.	95.1	41.8	71.9	104.4	47.2	79.5	100.4	61.6	83.5	102.4	44.9	77.4	97.3	54.6	78.8	96.6	46.4	74.8
MF2018	WEIGHTED AVERAGE	93.0	54.5	78.5	96.7	56.7	81.6	97.4	65.6	85.4	93.7	53.5	78.5	94.4	63.6	82.7	96.3	61.3	83.1

		TEXAS																UTAH		
	DIVISION	VICTORIA			WACO			WAXAHACHIE			WHARTON			WICHITA FALLS			LOGAN		
		779			766 - 767			751			774			763			843		
		MAT.	INST.	TOTAL	MAT.	INST.	TOTAL	MAT.	INST.	TOTAL	MAT.	INST.	TOTAL	MAT.	INST.	TOTAL	MAT.	INST.	TOTAL
015433	CONTRACTOR EQUIPMENT		98.0	98.0		92.3	92.3		89.5	89.5		99.3	99.3		92.3	92.3		89.8	89.8
0241, 31 - 34	SITE & INFRASTRUCTURE, DEMOLITION	125.2	83.9	98.3	95.3	85.6	89.0	80.7	81.9	81.5	130.7	85.9	101.5	96.3	85.9	89.5	100.0	83.2	89.0
0310	Concrete Forming & Accessories	93.0	46.0	54.2	98.0	59.8	66.5	88.7	61.2	66.0	89.6	47.5	54.9	98.0	58.1	65.1	99.5	68.7	74.1
0320	Concrete Reinforcing	79.6	44.3	65.2	93.4	49.7	75.5	103.9	51.6	82.6	82.8	44.3	67.1	93.4	50.5	75.8	119.7	82.3	104.4
0330	Cast-in-Place Concrete	102.1	55.4	86.5	92.1	67.2	83.8	86.3	63.4	78.6	105.0	54.5	88.1	98.4	70.1	88.9	80.6	71.8	77.7
03	CONCRETE	94.9	50.7	76.7	88.3	61.4	77.3	85.3	61.2	75.4	98.5	51.0	79.0	91.4	61.8	79.3	108.0	72.8	93.5
04	MASONRY	115.1	53.3	79.1	91.7	62.0	74.4	154.9	62.0	100.8	98.6	53.2	72.2	92.3	60.3	73.7	113.1	60.6	82.5
05	METALS	92.0	75.3	88.5	97.7	69.5	91.8	91.7	73.3	87.9	93.7	74.8	89.7	97.7	70.8	92.0	106.0	85.0	101.6
06	WOOD, PLASTICS & COMPOSITES	91.2	45.0	68.5	111.1	61.2	86.5	79.7	63.0	71.5	83.9	47.0	65.7	111.1	59.2	85.5	78.3	69.0	73.7
07	THERMAL & MOISTURE PROTECTION	101.9	55.3	86.3	105.9	65.6	92.4	96.4	62.8	85.1	98.3	59.3	85.2	105.9	63.7	91.8	93.7	66.9	84.7
08	OPENINGS	92.1	45.1	80.7	82.0	57.4	76.0	93.6	58.9	85.1	92.1	46.2	80.9	82.0	56.3	75.8	86.8	70.2	82.8
0920	Plaster & Gypsum Board	92.7	43.8	61.6	83.6	60.3	68.8	78.4	62.2	68.1	92.0	45.7	62.6	83.6	58.2	67.4	84.5	68.8	74.5
0950, 0980	Ceilings & Acoustic Treatment	113.6	43.8	74.5	82.5	60.3	70.1	73.7	62.2	67.3	111.4	45.7	74.7	82.5	58.2	68.9	104.1	68.8	84.4
0960	Flooring	104.2	47.5	89.7	111.2	67.4	100.0	99.7	60.2	89.6	101.8	58.0	90.6	112.1	71.9	101.8	99.4	62.2	89.8
0970, 0990	Wall Finishes & Painting/Coating	105.7	50.0	72.9	91.8	57.0	71.3	91.8	55.3	70.3	105.5	48.5	72.0	94.5	49.7	68.2	90.1	60.8	72.9
09	FINISHES	96.5	46.0	71.5	91.2	60.8	76.2	88.9	60.3	74.8	97.5	48.7	73.4	91.6	59.7	75.8	98.3	66.4	82.5
COVERS	DIVS. 10 - 14, 25, 28, 41, 43, 44, 46	100.0	72.7	94.2	100.0	80.3	95.8	100.0	78.2	95.4	100.0	72.9	94.2	100.0	79.9	95.7	100.0	84.4	96.7
21, 22, 23	FIRE SUPPRESSION, PLUMBING & HVAC	92.8	57.9	80.3	100.2	61.6	86.3	92.9	61.7	81.7	92.8	54.6	79.1	100.2	54.0	83.6	100.0	72.3	90.0
26, 27, 3370	ELECTRICAL, COMMUNICATIONS & UTIL.	107.3	46.6	80.9	104.5	53.8	82.4	98.2	60.7	81.8	105.9	51.1	82.0	107.5	50.2	82.6	92.1	71.6	83.1
MF2018	WEIGHTED AVERAGE	97.4	56.9	81.9	96.4	63.4	83.9	95.1	64.3	83.5	97.3	57.1	82.1	97.1	61.0	83.5	100.2	72.3	89.7

City Cost Indexes

		UTAH											VERMONT					
	DIVISION	OGDEN 842,844			PRICE 845			PROVO 846 - 847			SALT LAKE CITY 840 - 841			BELLOWS FALLS 051			BENNINGTON 052		
		MAT.	INST.	TOTAL	MAT.	INST.	TOTAL	MAT.	INST.	TOTAL	MAT.	INST.	TOTAL	MAT.	INST.	TOTAL	MAT.	INST.	TOTAL
015433	CONTRACTOR EQUIPMENT		89.8	89.8		88.9	88.9		99.1	99.1		89.7	89.7		104.9	104.9		104.9	104.9
0241, 31 - 34	SITE & INFRASTRUCTURE, DEMOLITION	90.1	83.2	85.6	95.9	80.6	85.9	96.9	98.2	97.7	90.0	83.1	85.5	79.1	102.0	94.0	78.6	102.0	93.8
0310	Concrete Forming & Accessories	99.6	68.7	74.1	101.3	58.0	65.6	100.9	68.9	74.5	101.3	68.7	74.4	101.3	113.7	111.5	99.4	95.7	96.3
0320	Concrete Reinforcing	119.3	82.3	104.2	128.4	77.8	107.7	129.5	82.3	110.2	122.0	82.3	105.8	146.3	83.0	120.4	146.3	82.9	120.4
0330	Cast-in-Place Concrete	81.9	71.8	78.5	80.7	64.7	75.4	80.7	73.5	78.3	89.5	71.8	83.6	73.9	118.8	88.9	73.9	118.7	88.9
03	CONCRETE	97.5	72.8	87.4	109.5	64.6	91.1	108.0	73.4	93.8	116.7	72.8	98.7	88.6	110.2	97.4	88.4	102.0	94.0
04	MASONRY	107.1	60.6	80.0	119.0	60.7	85.1	119.2	60.7	85.1	121.8	60.6	86.2	106.2	100.9	103.1	119.5	100.9	108.7
05	METALS	106.5	85.0	102.0	104.0	81.4	99.2	104.0	83.0	99.6	110.3	85.0	105.0	99.2	97.1	98.8	99.2	96.8	98.7
06	WOOD, PLASTICS & COMPOSITES	78.3	69.0	73.7	80.5	56.4	68.7	79.3	69.2	74.3	79.5	69.0	74.3	107.2	118.9	112.9	105.2	94.8	100.1
07	THERMAL & MOISTURE PROTECTION	92.7	66.9	84.1	95.2	61.5	83.9	95.3	68.2	86.2	99.6	66.9	88.7	92.1	92.0	92.1	92.1	89.5	91.2
08	OPENINGS	86.8	70.2	82.8	90.7	68.2	85.2	90.7	70.3	85.8	88.5	70.2	84.0	97.5	101.0	98.4	97.5	87.7	95.1
0920	Plaster & Gypsum Board	84.5	68.8	74.5	86.9	55.8	67.1	85.0	68.8	74.7	93.9	68.8	77.9	117.2	119.2	118.4	116.5	94.3	102.4
0950, 0980	Ceilings & Acoustic Treatment	104.1	68.8	84.4	104.1	55.8	77.1	104.1	68.8	84.4	100.2	68.8	82.6	87.7	119.2	105.3	87.7	94.3	91.4
0960	Flooring	97.1	62.2	88.1	100.1	48.8	86.9	100.0	62.2	90.3	101.5	62.2	91.4	101.4	109.3	103.4	100.6	109.3	102.8
0970, 0990	Wall Finishes & Painting/Coating	90.1	60.8	72.9	90.1	52.8	68.2	90.1	57.3	70.8	92.4	60.2	73.5	83.0	105.5	96.2	83.0	105.5	96.2
09	FINISHES	96.7	66.4	81.7	99.3	55.0	77.4	99.0	66.1	82.7	98.7	66.3	82.7	92.6	113.5	102.9	92.2	99.4	95.8
COVERS	DIVS. 10 - 14, 25, 28, 41, 43, 44, 46	100.0	84.4	96.7	100.0	80.3	95.8	100.0	84.8	96.8	100.0	84.4	96.7	100.0	105.6	101.2	100.0	100.8	100.6
21, 22, 23	FIRE SUPPRESSION, PLUMBING & HVAC	100.0	72.3	90.0	96.0	57.3	82.1	100.0	72.4	90.1	100.2	72.3	90.2	93.2	95.2	94.0	93.2	95.2	94.0
26, 27, 3370	ELECTRICAL, COMMUNICATIONS & UTIL.	92.5	71.6	83.4	94.9	59.4	79.4	92.4	64.2	80.1	95.3	71.6	85.0	90.7	68.8	81.1	90.7	47.1	71.7
MF2018	WEIGHTED AVERAGE	98.5	72.3	88.6	100.0	63.8	86.3	100.5	72.4	89.9	103.0	72.3	91.4	94.6	97.8	95.9	95.2	90.8	93.5

		VERMONT																	
	DIVISION	BRATTLEBORO 053			BURLINGTON 054			GUILDHALL 059			MONTPELIER 056			RUTLAND 057			ST. JOHNSBURY 058		
		MAT.	INST.	TOTAL	MAT.	INST.	TOTAL	MAT.	INST.	TOTAL	MAT.	INST.	TOTAL	MAT.	INST.	TOTAL	MAT.	INST.	TOTAL
015433	CONTRACTOR EQUIPMENT		104.9	104.9		111.4	111.4		104.9	104.9		111.4	111.4		104.9	104.9		104.9	104.9
0241, 31 - 34	SITE & INFRASTRUCTURE, DEMOLITION	79.5	102.0	94.2	87.6	113.2	104.3	78.5	100.9	93.1	82.8	112.4	102.1	85.2	102.4	96.4	78.6	100.3	92.7
0310	Concrete Forming & Accessories	101.4	113.7	111.5	100.5	83.4	86.4	99.9	103.9	103.2	106.9	111.1	110.3	101.8	83.4	86.6	99.2	113.9	111.3
0320	Concrete Reinforcing	144.6	83.0	119.4	179.6	82.9	140.1	147.6	82.9	121.1	179.8	82.9	140.1	182.9	82.9	142.1	144.6	82.9	119.4
0330	Cast-in-Place Concrete	76.2	118.8	90.5	88.4	116.7	97.9	71.6	105.0	82.8	88.2	116.7	97.7	72.4	115.1	86.7	71.6	105.0	82.8
03	CONCRETE	90.1	110.2	98.3	107.3	95.6	102.5	86.7	100.8	92.5	103.4	108.1	105.3	94.1	95.2	94.6	86.2	100.8	92.2
04	MASONRY	119.3	100.9	108.6	119.3	94.5	104.8	119.3	76.3	94.4	119.0	94.5	104.7	97.3	94.3	95.6	152.0	76.3	107.9
05	METALS	99.2	97.1	98.8	106.0	94.8	103.6	99.2	96.6	98.7	106.0	94.9	103.7	104.4	96.8	102.8	99.2	96.5	98.7
06	WOOD, PLASTICS & COMPOSITES	107.4	118.9	113.1	96.9	81.5	89.3	104.7	118.9	111.7	105.6	118.9	112.1	107.5	81.4	94.7	101.2	118.9	109.9
07	THERMAL & MOISTURE PROTECTION	92.1	92.0	92.1	96.0	99.6	97.2	91.9	81.1	88.3	96.6	103.5	98.9	92.2	97.3	93.9	91.9	81.1	88.3
08	OPENINGS	97.5	101.2	98.4	99.9	82.1	95.6	97.5	102.7	98.8	99.9	102.7	100.6	100.4	82.1	95.9	97.5	102.7	98.8
0920	Plaster & Gypsum Board	117.2	119.2	118.4	117.1	80.6	93.8	122.9	119.2	120.5	124.8	119.2	121.2	118.0	80.6	94.2	124.5	119.2	121.1
0950, 0980	Ceilings & Acoustic Treatment	87.7	119.2	105.3	86.1	80.6	83.0	87.7	119.2	105.3	109.8	119.2	115.1	93.8	80.6	86.4	87.7	119.2	105.3
0960	Flooring	101.5	109.3	103.5	109.7	109.3	109.6	103.8	109.3	105.2	109.7	109.3	109.6	101.4	109.3	103.4	106.4	109.3	107.2
0970, 0990	Wall Finishes & Painting/Coating	83.0	105.5	96.2	99.9	98.9	99.3	83.0	98.9	92.3	91.5	98.9	95.8	83.0	98.9	92.3	83.0	98.9	92.3
09	FINISHES	92.7	113.5	103.0	100.0	89.2	94.7	93.9	106.6	100.2	103.7	111.2	107.4	94.3	89.2	91.8	94.9	106.6	100.7
COVERS	DIVS. 10 - 14, 25, 28, 41, 43, 44, 46	100.0	105.6	101.2	100.0	99.4	99.9	100.0	97.3	99.4	100.0	103.4	100.7	100.0	99.4	99.9	100.0	97.3	99.4
21, 22, 23	FIRE SUPPRESSION, PLUMBING & HVAC	93.2	95.2	94.0	100.3	69.2	89.1	93.2	59.7	81.2	93.1	69.2	84.5	100.5	69.2	89.3	93.2	59.7	81.2
26, 27, 3370	ELECTRICAL, COMMUNICATIONS & UTIL.	90.7	68.8	81.1	90.8	51.9	73.9	90.7	47.1	71.7	89.6	51.9	73.2	90.7	51.9	73.8	90.7	47.1	71.7
MF2018	WEIGHTED AVERAGE	95.4	97.9	96.3	101.4	83.5	94.7	95.1	81.8	90.1	99.4	89.6	95.7	98.1	82.7	92.3	96.5	81.8	91.0

		VERMONT			VIRGINIA														
	DIVISION	WHITE RIVER JCT. 050			ALEXANDRIA 223			ARLINGTON 222			BRISTOL 242			CHARLOTTESVILLE 229			CULPEPER 227		
		MAT.	INST.	TOTAL	MAT.	INST.	TOTAL	MAT.	INST.	TOTAL	MAT.	INST.	TOTAL	MAT.	INST.	TOTAL	MAT.	INST.	TOTAL
015433	CONTRACTOR EQUIPMENT		104.9	104.9		101.8	101.8		100.5	100.5		100.5	100.5		105.0	105.0		100.5	100.5
0241, 31 - 34	SITE & INFRASTRUCTURE, DEMOLITION	81.0	100.4	93.6	123.1	92.7	103.3	133.6	90.2	105.3	115.7	90.4	99.2	120.2	92.1	101.9	118.0	89.6	99.5
0310	Concrete Forming & Accessories	97.4	104.3	103.1	98.5	69.2	74.3	98.1	60.6	67.1	95.2	56.3	63.1	93.9	62.1	67.7	91.5	63.7	68.6
0320	Concrete Reinforcing	146.3	82.9	120.4	112.1	87.6	102.1	126.6	85.0	109.6	126.7	83.6	109.1	125.9	67.8	102.1	126.6	87.3	110.5
0330	Cast-in-Place Concrete	76.2	105.6	86.1	103.7	76.9	94.7	100.9	75.7	92.5	100.6	56.3	85.8	104.7	71.9	93.7	103.3	71.3	92.6
03	CONCRETE	91.6	101.2	95.6	103.2	75.9	92.0	108.0	71.2	92.9	104.9	62.2	87.3	105.6	67.6	90.0	103.0	71.3	90.0
04	MASONRY	135.1	77.5	101.5	90.4	73.6	80.6	100.0	70.2	82.6	91.3	51.9	68.4	115.6	52.8	79.0	106.0	64.5	81.8
05	METALS	99.2	96.5	98.7	102.1	93.5	100.3	100.5	91.9	98.7	100.1	89.9	98.0	100.3	85.2	97.2	100.4	90.8	98.4
06	WOOD, PLASTICS & COMPOSITES	103.0	118.9	110.8	97.2	66.2	81.9	94.7	56.6	75.9	89.0	53.4	71.5	87.8	60.3	74.3	86.8	62.5	74.9
07	THERMAL & MOISTURE PROTECTION	92.2	81.6	88.7	101.4	80.1	94.3	103.4	75.7	94.1	102.9	59.8	88.4	102.5	67.6	90.8	102.6	71.8	92.3
08	OPENINGS	97.5	102.7	98.8	96.3	73.2	90.7	94.5	66.8	87.8	97.5	65.5	89.7	95.7	65.0	88.2	96.0	69.3	89.5
0920	Plaster & Gypsum Board	115.7	119.2	117.9	100.6	64.9	77.9	97.5	55.1	70.5	94.5	51.8	67.3	94.5	58.2	71.4	94.9	61.2	73.5
0950, 0980	Ceilings & Acoustic Treatment	87.7	119.2	105.3	102.5	64.9	81.5	98.9	55.1	74.4	97.6	51.8	72.0	97.6	58.2	75.6	98.9	61.2	77.8
0960	Flooring	99.9	109.3	102.3	109.3	77.4	101.1	108.1	71.4	98.7	105.5	56.5	92.9	104.2	54.9	91.6	104.2	64.8	94.1
0970, 0990	Wall Finishes & Painting/Coating	83.0	98.9	92.3	114.8	64.0	85.0	114.8	69.7	88.3	102.9	74.9	86.4	102.9	76.6	87.4	114.8	63.8	84.9
09	FINISHES	92.1	106.9	99.4	104.1	69.0	86.8	103.7	62.0	83.1	100.9	57.5	79.4	100.5	59.4	80.2	101.2	63.0	82.3
COVERS	DIVS. 10 - 14, 25, 28, 41, 43, 44, 46	100.0	97.7	99.5	100.0	89.1	97.7	100.0	84.7	96.7	100.0	82.2	96.2	100.0	84.0	96.6	100.0	84.7	96.7
21, 22, 23	FIRE SUPPRESSION, PLUMBING & HVAC	93.2	60.4	81.4	100.6	88.8	96.1	100.6	84.2	94.7	93.3	64.6	83.0	93.3	67.4	84.0	93.3	76.9	87.4
26, 27, 3370	ELECTRICAL, COMMUNICATIONS & UTIL.	90.7	47.0	71.7	96.6	101.7	98.8	95.0	96.1	95.5	96.1	31.4	67.9	96.1	68.4	84.0	97.4	87.3	93.0
MF2018	WEIGHTED AVERAGE	96.3	82.2	91.0	100.8	84.2	94.5	101.4	79.7	93.2	98.5	61.2	84.6	99.6	68.8	88.0	99.1	76.3	90.5

City Cost Indexes

		VIRGINIA																
	DIVISION	FAIRFAX 220 - 221			FARMVILLE 239			FREDERICKSBURG 224 - 225			GRUNDY 246			HARRISONBURG 228			LYNCHBURG 245		
		MAT.	INST.	TOTAL	MAT.	INST.	TOTAL	MAT.	INST.	TOTAL	MAT.	INST.	TOTAL	MAT.	INST.	TOTAL	MAT.	INST.	TOTAL
015433	CONTRACTOR EQUIPMENT		100.5	100.5		106.9	106.9		100.5	100.5		100.5	100.5		100.5	100.5		100.5	100.5
0241, 31 - 34	SITE & INFRASTRUCTURE, DEMOLITION	129.1	90.3	103.8	120.7	97.5	105.6	117.5	89.5	99.3	113.4	88.8	97.4	125.9	90.2	102.7	114.2	90.5	98.7
0310	Concrete Forming & Accessories	93.9	62.1	67.7	107.4	56.1	65.1	93.9	58.6	64.8	97.7	54.5	62.1	90.8	60.1	65.5	95.2	60.7	66.8
0320	Concrete Reinforcing	126.6	87.6	110.6	137.5	59.3	105.6	127.5	70.7	104.3	124.9	38.6	89.6	126.6	84.9	109.6	125.9	84.0	108.8
0330	Cast-in-Place Concrete	100.9	75.9	92.5	108.4	79.8	98.8	102.5	69.5	91.4	100.6	49.6	83.5	100.9	75.4	92.4	100.6	72.4	91.2
03	CONCRETE	107.7	72.4	93.2	110.5	66.0	92.2	102.7	65.6	87.5	103.5	50.9	81.9	105.8	70.8	91.4	103.5	70.0	89.7
04	MASONRY	99.8	72.5	83.9	85.4	52.9	66.5	104.7	74.7	87.3	97.0	52.8	71.3	100.1	69.4	82.2	109.0	55.2	77.6
05	METALS	100.5	92.8	98.9	95.2	75.4	91.0	100.4	85.0	97.2	100.1	61.9	92.1	100.3	91.6	98.5	100.3	91.4	98.4
06	WOOD, PLASTICS & COMPOSITES	89.0	57.5	73.5	101.7	53.8	78.1	89.0	57.7	73.6	91.3	53.4	72.6	86.0	56.6	71.5	89.0	58.2	73.8
07	THERMAL & MOISTURE PROTECTION	103.2	77.0	94.4	99.1	65.6	87.9	102.6	73.5	92.8	102.8	56.0	87.1	103.0	76.5	94.1	102.7	68.2	91.1
08	OPENINGS	94.5	66.4	87.6	94.7	48.9	83.6	95.7	62.0	87.5	97.5	41.0	83.8	96.0	66.8	88.9	96.0	68.2	89.2
0920	Plaster & Gypsum Board	94.9	56.0	70.1	100.2	51.8	69.4	94.9	56.2	70.3	94.5	51.8	67.3	94.5	55.1	69.4	94.5	56.7	70.5
0950, 0980	Ceilings & Acoustic Treatment	98.9	56.0	74.9	84.8	51.8	66.3	98.9	56.2	75.0	97.6	51.8	72.0	97.6	55.1	73.8	97.6	56.7	74.7
0960	Flooring	105.6	75.9	98.0	109.7	50.2	94.4	105.6	63.0	94.7	106.4	50.2	92.0	104.0	74.4	96.4	105.5	50.2	91.3
0970, 0990	Wall Finishes & Painting/Coating	114.8	69.7	88.3	99.5	49.8	70.3	114.8	49.6	76.5	102.9	27.2	58.4	114.8	54.9	79.6	102.9	74.9	86.4
09	FINISHES	102.6	64.0	83.5	98.8	53.8	76.5	101.5	57.5	79.8	101.0	51.0	76.3	101.4	60.9	81.4	100.7	59.0	80.1
COVERS	DIVS. 10 - 14, 25, 28, 41, 43, 44, 46	100.0	85.6	96.9	100.0	77.4	95.2	100.0	68.8	93.3	100.0	76.5	95.0	100.0	82.7	96.3	100.0	82.8	96.3
21, 22, 23	FIRE SUPPRESSION, PLUMBING & HVAC	93.3	87.0	91.0	93.4	49.6	77.7	93.3	70.3	85.0	93.3	59.0	80.9	93.3	72.2	85.7	93.3	67.5	84.0
26, 27, 3370	ELECTRICAL, COMMUNICATIONS & UTIL.	96.7	96.1	96.4	93.0	62.6	79.8	95.1	94.4	94.8	96.1	62.6	81.5	96.2	74.5	86.8	96.7	74.1	86.9
MF2018	WEIGHTED AVERAGE	99.6	81.1	92.6	97.3	61.8	83.9	98.7	74.2	89.5	98.5	58.9	83.6	99.2	73.7	89.6	99.0	70.6	88.3

		VIRGINIA																
	DIVISION	NEWPORT NEWS 236			NORFOLK 233 - 235			PETERSBURG 238			PORTSMOUTH 237			PULASKI 243			RICHMOND 230 - 232		
		MAT.	INST.	TOTAL	MAT.	INST.	TOTAL	MAT.	INST.	TOTAL	MAT.	INST.	TOTAL	MAT.	INST.	TOTAL	MAT.	INST.	TOTAL
015433	CONTRACTOR EQUIPMENT		107.0	107.0		109.1	109.1		106.9	106.9		106.8	106.8		100.5	100.5		109.7	109.7
0241, 31 - 34	SITE & INFRASTRUCTURE, DEMOLITION	122.4	98.9	107.1	125.2	104.6	111.8	123.6	98.8	107.4	121.2	98.2	106.3	112.9	88.9	97.3	114.1	106.5	109.2
0310	Concrete Forming & Accessories	106.7	62.1	70.0	106.0	62.1	69.8	101.1	61.9	68.8	97.6	56.2	63.5	97.7	54.7	62.2	105.7	61.0	68.8
0320	Concrete Reinforcing	137.3	66.0	108.2	150.5	66.0	116.0	136.7	66.0	108.6	136.7	61.0	105.8	124.9	73.0	103.7	151.1	67.9	117.1
0330	Cast-in-Place Concrete	105.3	73.7	94.7	103.0	78.0	94.6	111.9	73.8	99.1	104.3	62.9	90.4	124.9	76.4	92.5	103.0	76.9	94.3
03	CONCRETE	107.7	67.9	91.3	108.4	69.3	92.3	113.0	68.1	94.6	106.5	60.5	87.6	103.5	66.6	88.3	108.5	68.7	92.1
04	MASONRY	82.9	55.5	66.9	83.6	55.7	67.3	91.6	55.4	70.6	87.0	52.0	66.6	86.9	49.1	64.9	83.4	55.6	67.2
05	METALS	97.0	82.7	94.0	98.6	80.8	94.9	95.3	83.7	92.8	95.9	79.4	92.5	100.1	82.0	96.3	98.4	80.8	94.7
06	WOOD, PLASTICS & COMPOSITES	100.6	60.8	81.0	104.0	60.6	82.6	93.4	60.1	77.0	90.2	53.8	72.3	91.3	53.4	72.6	104.0	58.9	81.8
07	THERMAL & MOISTURE PROTECTION	99.1	66.6	88.2	94.5	70.7	86.6	99.1	68.8	88.8	99.1	62.8	87.0	102.8	63.8	89.7	97.8	71.0	88.8
08	OPENINGS	94.9	63.5	87.3	98.5	65.2	90.4	94.4	64.9	87.2	95.0	58.5	86.1	97.5	51.5	86.3	98.4	64.2	90.1
0920	Plaster & Gypsum Board	102.3	59.0	74.7	100.9	59.0	74.2	96.0	58.2	72.0	97.5	51.8	68.4	94.5	51.8	67.3	91.5	57.3	69.7
0950, 0980	Ceilings & Acoustic Treatment	91.4	59.0	73.3	99.0	59.0	76.6	86.5	58.2	70.7	91.4	51.8	69.2	97.6	51.8	72.0	73.8	57.3	64.5
0960	Flooring	109.7	54.3	95.5	109.1	54.3	95.1	106.5	54.9	93.3	104.2	50.2	90.3	106.4	50.2	92.0	109.1	54.9	95.2
0970, 0990	Wall Finishes & Painting/Coating	99.5	53.0	72.2	99.9	58.8	75.7	99.5	58.2	75.2	99.5	58.8	75.5	102.9	42.0	67.1	99.9	58.2	75.4
09	FINISHES	100.6	59.0	80.0	103.8	59.4	81.9	98.0	59.2	78.8	98.5	54.5	76.7	101.0	51.7	76.6	95.4	58.5	77.1
COVERS	DIVS. 10 - 14, 25, 28, 41, 43, 44, 46	100.0	84.3	96.7	100.0	83.8	96.6	100.0	83.5	96.5	100.0	81.2	96.0	100.0	79.0	95.5	100.0	83.7	96.5
21, 22, 23	FIRE SUPPRESSION, PLUMBING & HVAC	100.7	64.7	87.8	100.0	64.6	87.3	93.4	67.3	84.0	100.7	61.2	86.5	93.3	59.0	81.0	100.0	67.3	88.2
26, 27, 3370	ELECTRICAL, COMMUNICATIONS & UTIL.	94.5	62.5	80.6	100.2	63.5	84.2	94.6	68.4	83.2	93.6	63.5	80.5	96.1	72.0	85.6	101.3	68.4	87.0
MF2018	WEIGHTED AVERAGE	99.3	67.8	87.4	100.7	68.7	88.6	98.0	69.5	87.2	98.7	64.5	85.8	98.1	64.6	85.4	99.9	69.8	88.6

		VIRGINIA									WASHINGTON								
	DIVISION	ROANOKE 240 - 241			STAUNTON 244			WINCHESTER 226			CLARKSTON 994			EVERETT 982			OLYMPIA 985		
		MAT.	INST.	TOTAL	MAT.	INST.	TOTAL	MAT.	INST.	TOTAL	MAT.	INST.	TOTAL	MAT.	INST.	TOTAL	MAT.	INST.	TOTAL
015433	CONTRACTOR EQUIPMENT		100.5	100.5		105.0	105.0		100.5	100.5		82.9	82.9		102.2	102.2		105.6	105.6
0241, 31 - 34	SITE & INFRASTRUCTURE, DEMOLITION	116.4	90.6	99.6	116.9	90.7	99.8	124.7	89.6	101.8	90.8	75.5	80.8	90.4	102.2	98.1	86.4	105.1	98.6
0310	Concrete Forming & Accessories	102.6	61.0	68.3	97.4	56.0	63.5	92.7	59.2	65.1	90.3	57.3	63.1	106.5	109.3	108.8	100.3	110.3	108.5
0320	Concrete Reinforcing	126.3	84.1	109.0	125.9	63.3	100.3	125.7	69.6	102.8	122.2	97.6	112.1	135.8	118.0	128.5	160.2	118.2	143.0
0330	Cast-in-Place Concrete	114.3	86.2	104.9	104.6	80.5	96.6	100.9	59.5	87.0	74.8	74.9	74.8	100.0	111.2	103.8	87.9	114.2	96.7
03	CONCRETE	108.3	75.0	94.6	105.0	67.1	89.4	105.3	62.1	87.6	97.1	70.8	86.3	100.4	111.3	104.9	103.7	112.8	107.4
04	MASONRY	98.4	55.6	73.5	106.3	52.8	75.2	97.5	61.3	76.4	125.7	80.5	99.4	111.0	102.8	106.2	138.1	107.4	120.2
05	METALS	102.0	91.5	99.8	100.3	78.2	95.7	100.4	83.3	96.8	109.6	84.8	104.4	99.2	107.8	101.0	99.8	107.6	101.5
06	WOOD, PLASTICS & COMPOSITES	97.9	58.2	78.3	91.3	54.0	73.0	87.8	57.8	73.1	95.7	52.1	74.2	92.8	110.2	101.4	78.2	110.4	94.1
07	THERMAL & MOISTURE PROTECTION	102.6	68.5	91.2	102.4	65.3	90.0	103.0	68.8	91.6	99.1	74.6	90.9	95.0	106.5	98.8	92.4	109.1	98.0
08	OPENINGS	96.3	68.2	89.5	96.0	49.8	84.8	97.6	60.4	88.5	113.4	60.5	100.5	100.3	111.5	103.0	99.3	112.9	102.6
0920	Plaster & Gypsum Board	100.6	56.7	72.7	94.5	51.8	67.3	94.9	56.4	70.4	128.5	50.6	78.9	111.4	110.5	110.8	110.6	110.5	110.6
0950, 0980	Ceilings & Acoustic Treatment	102.5	56.7	76.9	97.6	51.8	72.0	98.9	56.4	75.1	65.7	50.6	57.3	91.6	110.5	102.2	103.7	110.5	107.5
0960	Flooring	109.3	54.9	95.4	106.0	50.2	91.7	105.1	64.8	94.8	90.5	67.5	84.6	110.8	98.8	107.7	110.8	103.3	108.9
0970, 0990	Wall Finishes & Painting/Coating	102.9	74.9	86.4	102.9	26.7	58.1	114.8	67.5	87.0	74.1	62.8	67.4	93.6	93.5	93.6	99.9	97.0	98.2
09	FINISHES	103.4	60.0	81.9	100.8	51.4	76.4	102.0	60.5	81.5	90.2	58.0	74.3	103.4	105.5	104.5	104.9	107.4	106.1
COVERS	DIVS. 10 - 14, 25, 28, 41, 43, 44, 46	100.0	82.8	96.3	100.0	78.0	95.3	100.0	72.5	94.1	100.0	89.8	97.8	100.0	100.9	100.2	100.0	104.4	100.9
21, 22, 23	FIRE SUPPRESSION, PLUMBING & HVAC	100.6	67.4	88.7	93.3	53.3	78.9	93.3	71.7	85.5	92.6	70.9	84.8	100.3	105.9	102.3	100.1	110.5	103.9
26, 27, 3370	ELECTRICAL, COMMUNICATIONS & UTIL.	96.1	53.5	77.6	95.5	72.7	85.6	95.3	79.3	88.3	81.1	82.6	81.8	105.2	100.5	103.1	101.6	106.5	103.7
MF2018	WEIGHTED AVERAGE	101.4	68.5	89.0	99.1	63.6	85.7	99.1	70.6	88.3	98.8	73.5	89.3	100.9	105.5	102.6	101.9	108.7	104.5

City Cost Indexes

WASHINGTON

DIVISION		RICHLAND 993			SEATTLE 980 - 981,987			SPOKANE 990 - 992			TACOMA 983 - 984			VANCOUVER 986			WENATCHEE 988		
		MAT.	INST.	TOTAL	MAT.	INST.	TOTAL	MAT.	INST.	TOTAL	MAT.	INST.	TOTAL	MAT.	INST.	TOTAL	MAT.	INST.	TOTAL
015433	CONTRACTOR EQUIPMENT		82.9	82.9		103.1	103.1		82.9	82.9		102.2	102.2		98.7	98.7		102.2	102.2
0241, 31 - 34	SITE & INFRASTRUCTURE, DEMOLITION	96.0	77.7	84.0	98.6	103.8	102.0	95.5	77.6	83.9	93.0	102.2	99.0	100.4	90.0	93.6	96.0	98.9	97.9
0310	Concrete Forming & Accessories	90.4	85.3	86.2	98.1	110.8	108.6	93.3	85.0	86.5	99.8	110.1	108.3	100.4	94.5	95.5	101.0	73.7	78.5
0320	Concrete Reinforcing	117.2	97.9	109.3	125.9	120.7	123.8	117.9	97.9	109.7	133.9	118.2	127.5	135.2	118.0	128.2	135.2	97.8	119.9
0330	Cast-in-Place Concrete	75.0	90.8	80.3	105.7	114.1	108.5	77.9	90.7	82.2	102.9	112.0	106.0	115.0	102.6	110.9	105.1	83.8	97.9
03	CONCRETE	96.5	89.3	93.6	107.0	113.4	109.6	98.4	89.1	94.6	102.2	112.0	106.2	112.2	101.7	107.8	109.6	82.1	98.3
04	MASONRY	126.6	89.7	105.1	86.5	107.5	98.7	127.4	89.7	105.4	111.8	107.3	109.1	111.8	105.2	108.0	115.5	82.9	96.5
05	METALS	109.6	88.0	105.1	99.9	108.2	101.6	111.5	87.7	106.5	101.3	108.1	102.7	100.0	107.4	101.5	99.2	96.7	98.7
06	WOOD, PLASTICS & COMPOSITES	95.8	82.9	89.5	96.0	110.3	103.0	100.5	82.9	91.9	85.1	110.2	97.4	76.9	92.7	84.7	86.4	71.8	79.2
07	THERMAL & MOISTURE PROTECTION	99.2	86.0	94.7	93.6	111.1	99.5	97.2	86.1	93.5	95.0	109.1	99.7	94.7	101.6	97.0	94.6	79.7	89.6
08	OPENINGS	109.2	78.8	101.8	106.0	113.3	107.8	109.8	77.7	102.0	100.7	112.8	103.6	97.8	100.0	98.4	100.3	71.2	93.2
0920	Plaster & Gypsum Board	128.5	82.5	99.2	104.2	110.5	108.2	118.2	82.5	95.5	109	110.5	110.0	105.9	92.8	97.6	110.1	71.0	85.2
0950, 0980	Ceilings & Acoustic Treatment	68.7	82.5	76.4	88.4	110.5	100.8	66.7	82.5	75.5	95.6	110.5	104.0	89.2	92.8	91.2	87.1	71.0	78.1
0960	Flooring	90.7	75.0	86.6	102.7	103.3	102.8	89.0	101.1	92.1	105.8	92.5	102.4	113.8	95.9	109.2	107.8	67.5	97.4
0970, 0990	Wall Finishes & Painting/Coating	74.1	84.3	80.1	99.9	97.0	98.2	74.2	84.3	80.2	93.6	97.0	95.6	98.6	79.2	87.2	93.6	98.7	96.6
09	FINISHES	91.2	82.4	86.8	98.8	107.3	103.0	88.9	87.7	88.3	102.9	105.0	103.9	100.1	92.5	96.3	102.1	74.0	88.3
COVERS	DIVS. 10 - 14, 25, 28, 41, 43, 44, 46	100.0	101.3	100.3	100.0	105.6	101.2	100.0	101.3	100.3	100.0	103.9	100.8	100.0	93.6	98.6	100.0	92.7	98.4
21, 22, 23	FIRE SUPPRESSION, PLUMBING & HVAC	100.1	109.9	103.6	100.1	122.5	108.2	100.1	92.3	97.3	100.4	110.5	104.0	100.4	106.6	102.6	93.1	81.1	88.8
26, 27, 3370	ELECTRICAL, COMMUNICATIONS & UTIL.	77.7	99.5	87.1	102.2	129.9	114.3	78.7	83.8	81.0	105.1	106.5	105.7	114.2	97.9	107.1	105.6	81.7	95.2
MF2018	WEIGHTED AVERAGE	100.0	93.1	97.4	100.6	114.8	105.9	100.6	87.7	95.7	101.5	108.1	104.0	103.1	100.5	102.1	100.5	83.1	93.9

WASHINGTON / WEST VIRGINIA

DIVISION		YAKIMA 989			BECKLEY 258 - 259			BLUEFIELD 247 - 248			BUCKHANNON 262			CHARLESTON 250 - 253			CLARKSBURG 263 - 264		
		MAT.	INST.	TOTAL	MAT.	INST.	TOTAL	MAT.	INST.	TOTAL	MAT.	INST.	TOTAL	MAT.	INST.	TOTAL	MAT.	INST.	TOTAL
015433	CONTRACTOR EQUIPMENT		102.2	102.2		105.3	105.3		100.5	100.5		100.5	100.5		111.3	111.3		100.5	100.5
0241, 31 - 34	SITE & INFRASTRUCTURE, DEMOLITION	94.9	101.4	99.1	104.7	101.7	102.7	107.4	90.9	96.7	113.5	91.0	98.8	107.0	112.5	110.6	114.3	91.0	99.1
0310	Concrete Forming & Accessories	100.0	77.1	81.1	92.8	88.4	89.2	95.2	88.4	89.6	94.6	87.4	88.7	100.9	88.7	90.8	92.8	87.6	88.5
0320	Concrete Reinforcing	134.6	94.2	118.1	81.8	78.1	80.3	124.5	78.1	105.5	125.3	85.7	109.1	87.2	78.4	83.6	125.3	92.3	111.8
0330	Cast-in-Place Concrete	109.9	91.1	103.6	109.7	93.9	104.4	98.4	94.1	96.9	98.1	87.6	94.6	106.2	91.1	101.1	107.5	83.9	99.6
03	CONCRETE	106.9	85.6	98.2	98.3	88.9	94.4	99.7	89.1	95.3	102.3	87.7	96.3	99.1	88.0	94.5	106.5	87.5	98.7
04	MASONRY	105.4	94.4	99.0	83.1	83.7	83.5	88.1	83.7	85.5	98.5	86.3	91.4	82.7	85.9	84.6	101.3	86.3	92.6
05	METALS	99.1	97.8	98.8	100.4	88.8	98.0	100.3	90.7	98.3	100.5	94.0	99.1	98.4	87.7	96.1	100.5	96.6	99.6
06	WOOD, PLASTICS & COMPOSITES	85.4	71.8	78.7	94.8	88.8	91.9	90.7	88.9	89.8	90.1	87.3	88.7	99.1	89.3	94.3	87.6	87.3	87.4
07	THERMAL & MOISTURE PROTECTION	95.2	88.2	92.8	108.5	85.3	100.7	102.6	85.3	96.8	102.9	84.3	96.7	104.7	86.2	98.5	102.8	84.1	96.5
08	OPENINGS	100.3	81.9	95.8	96.3	81.4	92.7	97.8	81.4	93.8	97.8	82.2	94.0	96.5	81.6	92.9	97.8	85.5	94.8
0920	Plaster & Gypsum Board	107.5	71.0	84.3	89.9	88.3	88.9	92.7	88.3	89.9	93.8	86.7	89.3	98.9	88.8	92.5	92.4	86.7	88.8
0950, 0980	Ceilings & Acoustic Treatment	88.1	71.0	78.5	93.3	88.3	90.5	94.1	88.3	90.9	97.6	86.7	91.5	107.0	88.8	96.8	97.6	86.7	91.5
0960	Flooring	106.4	94.9	103.4	86.8	98.1	89.7	103.6	98.1	102.2	103.3	90.8	100.1	88.1	98.1	90.7	102.5	90.8	99.5
0970, 0990	Wall Finishes & Painting/Coating	93.6	84.3	88.2	103.2	80.2	89.7	102.9	78.2	88.4	102.9	85.5	92.7	104.8	87.4	94.6	102.9	85.5	92.7
09	FINISHES	101.0	79.2	90.2	92.3	89.9	91.1	98.6	89.7	94.2	100.1	88.1	94.2	99.3	90.6	95.0	99.6	88.1	93.9
COVERS	DIVS. 10 - 14, 25, 28, 41, 43, 44, 46	100.0	96.6	99.3	100.0	87.2	97.3	100.0	93.6	98.6	100.0	93.5	98.6	100.0	93.3	98.6	100.0	93.5	98.6
21, 22, 23	FIRE SUPPRESSION, PLUMBING & HVAC	100.4	108.8	103.4	93.2	88.7	91.6	93.3	76.9	87.4	93.3	90.5	92.3	99.9	88.3	95.7	93.3	90.7	92.4
26, 27, 3370	ELECTRICAL, COMMUNICATIONS & UTIL.	106.8	99.5	103.6	91.1	72.6	83.1	95.5	81.8	89.5	96.3	85.8	91.7	97.6	81.8	90.7	96.3	85.8	91.7
MF2018	WEIGHTED AVERAGE	101.4	95.0	99.0	96.0	86.6	92.5	97.3	85.0	92.7	98.5	88.5	94.7	98.5	89.0	94.9	99.1	88.9	95.3

WEST VIRGINIA

DIVISION		GASSAWAY 266			HUNTINGTON 255 - 257			LEWISBURG 249			MARTINSBURG 254			MORGANTOWN 265			PARKERSBURG 261		
		MAT.	INST.	TOTAL	MAT.	INST.	TOTAL	MAT.	INST.	TOTAL	MAT.	INST.	TOTAL	MAT.	INST.	TOTAL	MAT.	INST.	TOTAL
015433	CONTRACTOR EQUIPMENT		100.5	100.5		105.3	105.3		100.5	100.5		105.3	105.3		100.5	100.5		100.5	100.5
0241, 31 - 34	SITE & INFRASTRUCTURE, DEMOLITION	111.0	91.0	97.9	112.4	102.8	106.2	123.1	91.0	102.2	108.3	101.5	103.9	108.3	92.2	97.8	119.7	92.4	101.9
0310	Concrete Forming & Accessories	94.3	79.5	82.1	101.9	83.1	86.4	93.0	88.5	89.3	92.8	70.9	74.7	93.0	88.0	88.9	96.3	87.6	89.2
0320	Concrete Reinforcing	125.3	78.2	106.0	83.0	92.2	86.8	125.3	78.2	106.0	81.8	82.7	82.2	125.3	92.3	111.8	124.5	85.5	108.6
0330	Cast-in-Place Concrete	102.7	90.1	98.5	119.7	91.0	110.1	98.4	94.1	97.0	115.0	80.3	103.3	98.1	93.8	96.7	100.3	88.9	96.5
03	CONCRETE	103.1	83.7	95.1	104.0	87.9	97.4	108.3	89.1	100.4	102.0	76.9	91.7	99.5	91.3	96.1	104.2	88.2	97.6
04	MASONRY	102.2	83.7	91.4	87.2	88.4	87.9	96.5	83.7	89.1	85.7	73.7	78.7	120.3	86.3	100.5	90.8	79.0	79.8
05	METALS	100.4	90.8	98.4	102.7	94.6	101.0	100.4	90.9	98.4	100.8	87.8	98.0	100.5	97.0	99.7	100.4	93.9	99.0
06	WOOD, PLASTICS & COMPOSITES	89.5	76.7	83.2	102.7	80.3	91.7	87.9	88.9	88.4	94.8	70.0	82.6	87.9	87.3	87.6	90.1	88.6	89.4
07	THERMAL & MOISTURE PROTECTION	102.6	83.4	96.2	108.6	84.7	100.6	103.5	85.3	97.4	108.7	72.8	96.7	102.6	85.5	96.9	102.9	82.7	96.1
08	OPENINGS	95.9	74.7	90.7	95.6	79.8	91.8	97.8	81.4	93.8	98.2	65.3	90.2	99.1	85.5	95.8	96.9	81.7	93.2
0920	Plaster & Gypsum Board	93.3	75.8	82.2	94.9	79.6	85.2	92.4	88.3	89.8	89.9	68.9	76.5	92.4	86.7	88.8	94.5	88.1	90.4
0950, 0980	Ceilings & Acoustic Treatment	97.6	75.8	85.4	93.3	79.6	85.6	97.6	88.3	92.4	93.3	68.9	79.6	97.6	86.7	91.5	97.6	88.1	92.3
0960	Flooring	103.2	98.1	101.9	92.7	94.4	93.1	102.7	98.1	101.5	86.8	86.1	86.6	102.7	90.8	99.6	105.7	94.3	102.8
0970, 0990	Wall Finishes & Painting/Coating	102.9	87.4	93.8	103.2	81.5	90.4	102.9	56.1	75.4	103.2	72.9	85.4	102.9	85.5	92.7	102.9	87.4	93.8
09	FINISHES	99.7	83.6	91.7	94.5	84.7	89.7	100.7	87.3	94.1	92.5	73.3	83.0	99.2	88.1	93.7	100.9	89.1	95.1
COVERS	DIVS. 10 - 14, 25, 28, 41, 43, 44, 46	100.0	92.3	98.4	100.0	93.1	98.5	100.0	93.6	98.6	100.0	89.1	97.7	100.0	93.5	98.6	100.0	92.7	98.4
21, 22, 23	FIRE SUPPRESSION, PLUMBING & HVAC	93.3	87.7	91.3	100.5	90.6	97.0	93.3	88.7	91.6	93.2	71.3	85.3	93.3	90.9	92.4	100.5	87.7	95.9
26, 27, 3370	ELECTRICAL, COMMUNICATIONS & UTIL.	96.3	81.8	90.0	93.0	80.5	87.6	94.1	81.8	88.7	94.1	66.4	82.0	96.4	85.8	91.8	96.3	81.8	90.0
MF2018	WEIGHTED AVERAGE	98.5	85.2	93.5	99.6	88.4	95.4	99.2	87.2	94.6	97.3	75.9	89.2	99.1	89.7	95.5	99.7	86.9	94.9

City Cost Indexes

DIVISION		WEST VIRGINIA									WISCONSIN								
		PETERSBURG			ROMNEY			WHEELING			BELOIT			EAU CLAIRE			GREEN BAY		
		268			267			260			535			547			541 - 543		
		MAT.	INST.	TOTAL	MAT.	INST.	TOTAL	MAT.	INST.	TOTAL	MAT.	INST.	TOTAL	MAT.	INST.	TOTAL	MAT.	INST.	TOTAL
015433	CONTRACTOR EQUIPMENT		100.5	100.5		100.5	100.5		100.5	100.5		101.6	101.6		100.0	100.0		107.3	107.3
0241, 31 - 34	SITE & INFRASTRUCTURE, DEMOLITION	107.7	92.3	97.7	110.6	92.3	98.7	120.3	91.9	101.8	89.1	100.5	96.5	82.7	103.3	96.1	84.4	110.9	101.7
0310	Concrete Forming & Accessories	95.5	91.1	91.9	92.5	91.0	91.2	97.8	87.2	89.0	94.6	101.7	100.5	99.3	100.6	100.4	105.1	101.3	102.0
0320	Concrete Reinforcing	124.5	78.3	105.6	125.3	85.6	109.1	123.7	92.1	110.8	88.7	138.2	108.9	91.0	105.8	97.0	88.6	110.7	97.6
0330	Cast-in-Place Concrete	98.1	87.7	94.6	102.7	80.3	95.2	100.3	89.6	96.7	98.9	93.8	97.2	95.2	98.7	96.3	98.4	104.0	100.3
03	CONCRETE	99.6	88.1	94.9	103.0	86.7	96.3	104.2	89.3	98.1	99.5	105.4	102.0	93.9	100.8	96.7	96.6	103.8	99.5
04	MASONRY	94.7	86.3	89.8	96.9	84.7	89.8	100.8	82.3	90.0	97.4	103.6	101.0	96.8	100.3	98.8	129.2	98.6	111.4
05	METALS	100.5	91.3	98.6	100.6	93.7	99.1	100.5	96.6	99.7	95.1	119.3	100.1	90.5	101.9	92.9	95.3	103.1	96.9
06	WOOD, PLASTICS & COMPOSITES	90.9	92.2	91.6	87.2	92.2	89.7	91.3	87.3	89.3	93.6	101.4	97.4	106.5	101.5	104.1	105.4	102.0	103.7
07	THERMAL & MOISTURE PROTECTION	102.6	80.5	95.2	102.8	80.0	95.1	103.0	84.5	96.8	102.7	103.3	102.9	103.7	100.9	102.8	105.8	101.9	104.5
08	OPENINGS	99.1	84.2	95.5	99.0	85.9	95.8	97.7	85.5	94.7	91.3	109.5	95.7	96.4	97.2	96.6	93.9	100.8	95.6
0920	Plaster & Gypsum Board	93.8	91.8	92.5	92.1	91.8	91.9	94.5	86.7	89.5	86.9	101.9	96.5	102.8	101.9	102.3	93.6	102.0	98.9
0950, 0980	Ceilings & Acoustic Treatment	97.6	91.8	94.4	97.6	91.8	94.4	97.6	86.7	91.5	87.5	101.9	95.6	92.5	101.9	97.8	86.1	102.0	95.0
0960	Flooring	104.0	90.8	100.6	102.5	87.9	98.7	106.4	90.8	102.4	84.0	123.8	94.2	83.0	111.9	90.4	98.3	113.5	102.2
0970, 0990	Wall Finishes & Painting/Coating	102.9	85.5	92.7	102.9	85.5	92.7	102.9	85.5	92.7	92.3	90.1	91.0	83.4	85.1	84.4	92.9	126.2	112.4
09	FINISHES	99.8	91.0	95.4	99.3	90.4	94.9	101.1	87.7	94.5	89.8	104.6	97.1	90.6	101.5	96.0	93.0	106.3	99.6
COVERS	DIVS. 10 - 14, 25, 28, 41, 43, 44, 46	100.0	91.7	98.2	100.0	94.0	98.7	100.0	86.1	97.0	100.0	97.8	99.5	100.0	92.5	98.4	100.0	98.6	99.7
21, 22, 23	FIRE SUPPRESSION, PLUMBING & HVAC	93.3	88.2	91.5	93.3	88.0	91.4	100.6	89.9	96.7	99.9	104.0	101.4	99.9	91.3	96.8	100.3	97.2	99.2
26, 27, 3370	ELECTRICAL, COMMUNICATIONS & UTIL.	98.1	75.2	88.1	97.7	75.2	87.9	94.8	85.8	90.9	96.2	72.8	86.0	91.7	95.4	93.3	89.6	97.3	93.0
MF2018	WEIGHTED AVERAGE	98.2	86.8	93.9	98.6	86.7	94.1	100.6	88.4	96.0	96.7	100.8	98.2	95.1	97.9	96.1	97.7	101.4	99.1

DIVISION		WISCONSIN																	
		KENOSHA			LA CROSSE			LANCASTER			MADISON			MILWAUKEE			NEW RICHMOND		
		531			546			538			537			530,532			540		
		MAT.	INST.	TOTAL	MAT.	INST.	TOTAL	MAT.	INST.	TOTAL	MAT.	INST.	TOTAL	MAT.	INST.	TOTAL	MAT.	INST.	TOTAL
015433	CONTRACTOR EQUIPMENT		99.3	99.3		100.0	100.0		101.6	101.6		102.1	102.1		96.5	96.5		100.8	100.8
0241, 31 - 34	SITE & INFRASTRUCTURE, DEMOLITION	92.5	97.7	95.9	78.7	103.3	94.7	84.8	99.6	94.4	90.0	102.1	97.9	84.2	99.2	93.9	79.6	102.3	94.4
0310	Concrete Forming & Accessories	99.4	114.2	111.6	89.2	100.7	98.6	94.1	84.7	86.4	100.2	102.7	102.2	97.1	115.5	112.3	95.6	82.1	84.5
0320	Concrete Reinforcing	88.5	115.8	99.6	90.6	107.1	97.3	90.4	93.2	91.5	88.4	107.4	96.1	89.8	112.8	99.2	87.5	100.1	92.6
0330	Cast-in-Place Concrete	107.7	108.4	107.9	85.5	98.7	90.0	98.3	90.4	95.6	93.0	110.6	98.9	89.6	110.9	96.8	99.0	93.7	97.2
03	CONCRETE	104.1	112.4	107.5	85.7	101.1	92.0	99.3	88.8	95.0	101.4	106.2	103.4	99.7	112.9	105.1	91.8	89.7	90.9
04	MASONRY	95.6	111.0	104.6	95.9	100.3	98.4	97.5	100.6	99.3	104.0	104.2	104.2	94.5	114.1	105.9	123.2	100.8	110.2
05	METALS	97.1	111.4	100.1	90.4	102.5	92.9	93.1	99.8	94.5	102.4	103.2	102.6	97.2	102.6	98.3	93.1	97.9	94.1
06	WOOD, PLASTICS & COMPOSITES	92.1	115.5	103.6	95.2	101.5	98.3	93.1	83.5	88.4	102.6	101.9	102.3	100.1	115.8	107.9	96.7	80.0	88.5
07	THERMAL & MOISTURE PROTECTION	103.3	107.3	104.7	103.3	100.3	102.3	102.5	85.9	97.0	101.8	106.3	103.3	99.9	112.9	104.3	104.3	93.3	100.6
08	OPENINGS	87.0	113.3	93.4	96.4	96.4	96.4	87.5	81.1	85.9	96.4	104.4	98.3	95.8	112.7	99.9	85.6	79.7	84.2
0920	Plaster & Gypsum Board	75.2	116.5	101.5	99.2	101.9	100.9	84.5	83.5	83.9	95.3	101.9	99.5	89.3	116.5	106.6	81.8	80.0	80.7
0950, 0980	Ceilings & Acoustic Treatment	87.5	116.5	103.7	90.7	101.9	97.0	80.0	83.5	82.0	103.7	101.9	102.7	87.1	116.5	103.6	61.4	80.0	71.8
0960	Flooring	100.2	117.9	104.7	78.3	113.5	87.3	83.7	96.6	87.0	89.4	117.6	96.6	84.6	118.5	93.3	92.8	99.7	94.6
0970, 0990	Wall Finishes & Painting/Coating	105.8	120.4	114.4	83.4	115.1	102.0	92.3	85.0	88.0	99.9	104.5	102.6	99.9	122.1	112.9	95.0	71.1	80.9
09	FINISHES	93.6	116.3	104.8	88.1	105.1	96.5	87.4	86.7	87.1	98.0	105.7	101.8	90.6	117.4	103.8	83.1	83.9	83.5
COVERS	DIVS. 10 - 14, 25, 28, 41, 43, 44, 46	100.0	101.2	100.3	100.0	97.6	99.5	100.0	94.3	98.8	100.0	101.7	100.4	100.0	102.7	100.6	100.0	82.8	96.3
21, 22, 23	FIRE SUPPRESSION, PLUMBING & HVAC	100.1	100.9	100.4	99.9	84.1	94.2	92.6	78.5	87.5	99.8	105.3	101.8	99.8	107.8	102.7	92.0	78.2	87.0
26, 27, 3370	ELECTRICAL, COMMUNICATIONS & UTIL.	96.3	92.5	94.6	91.9	97.3	94.2	95.8	73.3	86.0	95.9	97.6	96.6	95.5	99.8	97.4	91.1	73.3	83.4
MF2018	WEIGHTED AVERAGE	97.7	105.8	100.7	93.6	97.3	95.0	94.0	86.8	91.2	99.7	103.7	101.2	97.1	108.4	101.4	93.0	86.3	90.5

DIVISION		WISCONSIN																	
		OSHKOSH			PORTAGE			RACINE			RHINELANDER			SUPERIOR			WAUSAU		
		549			539			534			545			548			544		
		MAT.	INST.	TOTAL	MAT.	INST.	TOTAL	MAT.	INST.	TOTAL	MAT.	INST.	TOTAL	MAT.	INST.	TOTAL	MAT.	INST.	TOTAL
015433	CONTRACTOR EQUIPMENT		97.8	97.8		101.6	101.6		101.6	101.6		97.8	97.8		100.8	100.8		97.8	97.8
0241, 31 - 34	SITE & INFRASTRUCTURE, DEMOLITION	75.5	98.1	90.3	78.6	100.3	92.8	88.9	101.8	97.3	82.8	97.7	92.5	77.4	102.4	93.7	72.8	98.9	89.8
0310	Concrete Forming & Accessories	92.0	85.3	86.5	88.8	85.4	86.0	94.9	110.9	108.1	90.2	84.3	85.3	94.1	108.0	105.5	91.6	89.4	89.8
0320	Concrete Reinforcing	88.8	96.4	91.9	90.5	93.3	91.6	88.7	115.8	99.8	89.0	93.4	90.8	87.5	115.8	99.0	89.0	107.0	96.3
0330	Cast-in-Place Concrete	91.2	90.4	90.9	84.4	89.2	86.0	97.0	108.1	100.7	103.5	89.2	98.7	93.4	93.3	93.4	85.0	87.7	85.9
03	CONCRETE	87.2	89.4	88.1	87.1	88.9	87.8	98.6	110.8	103.6	98.6	88.0	94.2	86.7	104.0	93.8	82.5	92.1	86.4
04	MASONRY	110.6	102.0	105.6	96.3	100.6	98.9	97.4	111.0	105.3	130.8	100.1	112.9	122.5	107.5	113.7	110.1	102.0	105.4
05	METALS	93.6	96.8	94.2	93.7	103.8	95.9	96.8	111.4	99.8	93.0	95.3	93.5	94.0	105.3	96.3	92.9	101.6	94.7
06	WOOD, PLASTICS & COMPOSITES	89.9	83.7	86.8	86.5	83.5	85.0	93.8	111.1	102.3	87.9	83.7	85.8	95.5	112.0	103.6	89.4	86.3	87.9
07	THERMAL & MOISTURE PROTECTION	105.1	79.3	96.5	102.1	91.4	98.5	102.7	107.0	104.1	105.9	77.8	96.5	104.0	101.0	103.0	104.9	93.5	101.1
08	OPENINGS	90.6	85.0	89.2	87.6	87.9	87.7	91.3	110.8	96.0	90.6	81.1	88.3	85.4	108.9	91.1	90.8	88.9	90.3
0920	Plaster & Gypsum Board	84.1	83.5	83.7	81.2	83.5	82.7	86.9	112.0	102.8	84.1	83.5	83.7	82.3	113.0	101.8	84.1	86.2	85.5
0950, 0980	Ceilings & Acoustic Treatment	86.1	83.5	84.6	85.3	83.5	84.3	87.5	112.0	101.2	86.1	83.5	84.6	62.7	113.0	90.8	86.1	86.2	86.2
0960	Flooring	91.4	99.9	93.6	80.9	99.7	85.8	84.0	117.9	92.7	91.0	99.7	93.2	93.9	107.2	97.3	91.4	99.7	93.6
0970, 0990	Wall Finishes & Painting/Coating	90.2	97.1	94.2	92.3	85.0	88.0	92.3	124.0	110.9	90.2	69.6	78.1	85.2	92.0	89.2	90.2	105.1	99.0
09	FINISHES	89.3	89.3	89.3	87.2	87.6	87.4	89.8	114.1	101.8	89.9	85.7	87.8	83.1	107.3	95.1	89.2	92.9	91.0
COVERS	DIVS. 10 - 14, 25, 28, 41, 43, 44, 46	100.0	92.9	98.5	100.0	94.4	98.8	100.0	100.7	100.2	100.0	92.2	98.3	100.0	87.4	97.3	100.0	96.6	99.3
21, 22, 23	FIRE SUPPRESSION, PLUMBING & HVAC	93.0	77.9	87.6	92.6	84.3	89.6	99.9	100.8	100.2	93.0	77.9	87.6	92.0	83.4	88.9	93.0	92.2	92.7
26, 27, 3370	ELECTRICAL, COMMUNICATIONS & UTIL.	91.3	72.8	83.3	98.1	81.3	90.8	96.2	89.6	93.3	91.0	67.5	80.8	93.5	85.2	89.9	91.9	67.5	81.3
MF2018	WEIGHTED AVERAGE	93.0	86.7	90.6	92.6	90.1	91.7	96.9	105.0	100.4	95.4	84.7	91.3	92.7	97.4	94.5	92.3	91.0	91.8

670

City Cost Indexes

		WYOMING																	
	DIVISION	CASPER 826			CHEYENNE 820			NEWCASTLE 827			RAWLINS 823			RIVERTON 825			ROCK SPRINGS 829 - 831		
		MAT.	INST.	TOTAL	MAT.	INST.	TOTAL	MAT.	INST.	TOTAL	MAT.	INST.	TOTAL	MAT.	INST.	TOTAL	MAT.	INST.	TOTAL
015433	CONTRACTOR EQUIPMENT		106.3	106.3		98.1	98.1		98.1	98.1		98.1	98.1		98.1	98.1		98.1	98.1
0241, 31 - 34	SITE & INFRASTRUCTURE, DEMOLITION	90.1	101.7	97.7	84.6	89.0	87.5	78.4	88.5	85.0	87.6	88.5	88.1	83.3	88.4	86.6	83.2	88.5	86.6
0310	Concrete Forming & Accessories	105.0	62.1	69.6	107.5	70.2	76.7	99.3	59.5	66.5	102.7	59.5	67.1	98.3	59.4	66.2	104.4	62.6	70.0
0320	Concrete Reinforcing	90.5	86.9	89.0	83.5	87.1	85.0	89.4	86.9	88.4	89.1	86.9	88.2	89.9	86.9	88.7	89.9	76.6	84.5
0330	Cast-in-Place Concrete	87.6	80.8	85.3	82.5	79.1	81.4	83.4	75.6	80.8	83.5	75.6	80.9	83.5	75.6	80.8	83.4	76.1	81.0
03	CONCRETE	93.5	73.7	85.4	88.2	76.9	83.5	88.4	70.8	81.2	99.8	70.8	87.9	95.3	70.7	85.2	88.8	70.6	81.4
04	MASONRY	97.3	63.8	77.8	98.9	68.3	81.1	95.5	62.4	76.2	95.5	62.4	76.2	95.5	62.4	76.2	152.8	57.7	97.4
05	METALS	112.7	85.5	107.0	115.1	87.9	109.4	112.0	87.0	106.8	112.1	87.0	106.8	112.1	86.9	106.9	112.1	82.9	106.0
06	WOOD, PLASTICS & COMPOSITES	103.7	58.3	81.4	99.9	69.3	84.8	91.2	57.0	74.4	94.6	57.0	76.1	90.2	57.0	73.9	98.3	60.9	79.9
07	THERMAL & MOISTURE PROTECTION	103.0	68.3	91.4	98.0	69.4	88.4	98.9	63.6	87.1	100.2	63.6	87.9	99.7	66.4	88.5	99.0	66.6	88.2
08	OPENINGS	94.0	65.9	87.2	92.5	71.9	87.5	96.2	62.8	88.1	95.9	62.8	87.8	96.1	62.8	88.0	96.5	63.8	88.6
0920	Plaster & Gypsum Board	120.6	57.0	80.1	103.1	68.5	81.1	100.9	55.9	72.2	100.9	55.9	72.2	100.9	55.9	72.2	110.1	59.9	78.2
0950, 0980	Ceilings & Acoustic Treatment	127.1	57.0	87.9	104.8	68.5	84.5	105.3	55.9	77.7	105.3	55.9	77.7	105.3	55.9	77.7	105.3	59.9	79.9
0960	Flooring	89.9	75.4	86.2	89.6	75.4	86.0	84.7	61.7	78.8	86.7	61.7	80.3	84.2	61.7	78.5	88.3	54.3	79.6
0970, 0990	Wall Finishes & Painting/Coating	88.7	56.9	70.0	89.2	56.9	70.3	86.1	68.2	75.6	86.1	68.2	75.6	86.1	52.6	66.4	86.1	69.6	76.4
09	FINISHES	108.4	63.1	86.0	101.0	69.5	85.4	96.8	59.9	78.6	98.3	59.9	79.3	97.3	58.2	78.0	99.1	61.2	80.3
COVERS	DIVS. 10 - 14, 25, 28, 41, 43, 44, 46	100.0	88.7	97.6	100.0	89.4	97.7	100.0	90.1	97.9	100.0	90.1	97.9	100.0	80.0	95.7	100.0	84.6	96.7
21, 22, 23	FIRE SUPPRESSION, PLUMBING & HVAC	99.8	75.5	91.0	100.1	75.4	91.2	96.0	73.6	87.9	96.0	73.6	87.9	96.0	73.5	87.9	99.9	74.0	90.6
26, 27, 3370	ELECTRICAL, COMMUNICATIONS & UTIL.	98.6	57.6	80.8	96.2	65.1	82.7	94.4	53.9	76.7	94.4	53.9	76.7	94.4	57.6	78.4	93.4	62.4	79.9
MF2018	WEIGHTED AVERAGE	101.5	72.3	90.5	100.1	74.8	90.6	98.0	69.3	87.2	99.8	69.3	88.3	99.0	69.4	87.8	101.8	70.0	89.8

		WYOMING												CANADA					
	DIVISION	SHERIDAN 828			WHEATLAND 822			WORLAND 824			YELLOWSTONE NAT'L PA 821			BARRIE, ONTARIO			BATHURST, NEW BRUNSWICK		
		MAT.	INST.	TOTAL	MAT.	INST.	TOTAL	MAT.	INST.	TOTAL	MAT.	INST.	TOTAL	MAT.	INST.	TOTAL	MAT.	INST.	TOTAL
015433	CONTRACTOR EQUIPMENT		98.1	98.1		98.1	98.1		98.1	98.1		98.1	98.1		100.7	100.7		101.3	101.3
0241, 31 - 34	SITE & INFRASTRUCTURE, DEMOLITION	83.2	89.0	87.0	81.6	88.4	86.1	79.7	88.5	85.4	79.8	88.4	85.4	123.4	94.7	104.7	121.6	91.3	101.9
0310	Concrete Forming & Accessories	105.9	60.9	68.8	100.9	59.3	66.6	100.9	59.6	66.8	101.0	59.4	66.7	129.0	76.3	85.5	115.8	53.8	64.7
0320	Concrete Reinforcing	89.9	87.0	88.7	89.4	86.2	88.1	89.9	86.9	88.7	91.5	76.9	85.5	195.3	79.2	147.9	139.0	52.4	103.6
0330	Cast-in-Place Concrete	86.3	78.9	83.8	87.1	75.5	83.2	83.4	75.6	80.8	83.4	75.5	80.8	160.6	77.9	133.0	107.8	54.8	90.0
03	CONCRETE	95.5	72.6	86.1	92.7	70.5	83.6	88.6	70.8	81.3	88.8	69.0	80.7	156.7	77.9	124.3	120.0	54.8	93.2
04	MASONRY	95.8	67.3	79.2	95.8	51.7	70.1	95.5	62.4	76.2	95.6	62.4	76.3	176.6	82.2	121.6	149.9	53.0	93.5
05	METALS	115.7	87.5	109.8	112.0	85.9	106.5	112.1	87.1	106.9	112.6	83.3	106.5	110.9	86.5	105.8	95.4	68.7	89.8
06	WOOD, PLASTICS & COMPOSITES	101.2	57.0	79.5	92.8	57.0	75.2	92.9	57.0	75.2	92.9	57.0	75.2	107.4	75.2	91.6	106.2	54.0	80.5
07	THERMAL & MOISTURE PROTECTION	100.2	67.8	89.3	99.2	60.6	86.3	99.0	63.6	87.1	98.7	63.6	86.9	110.3	79.7	100.1	103.5	55.1	87.3
08	OPENINGS	96.8	62.8	88.5	94.9	62.8	87.1	96.4	62.8	88.2	90.2	60.6	83.0	87.6	74.8	84.5	91.6	47.5	80.9
0920	Plaster & Gypsum Board	126.7	55.9	81.6	100.9	55.9	72.2	100.9	55.9	72.2	101.3	55.9	72.4	148.0	74.5	101.2	118.0	52.6	76.3
0950, 0980	Ceilings & Acoustic Treatment	108.3	55.9	79.0	105.3	55.9	77.7	105.3	55.9	77.7	106.6	55.9	78.2	93.6	74.5	82.9	89.1	52.6	68.7
0960	Flooring	90.0	52.5	80.4	85.7	61.7	79.6	85.7	61.7	79.6	85.7	61.7	79.6	122.8	99.7	111.7	102.9	37.9	86.2
0970, 0990	Wall Finishes & Painting/Coating	87.7	56.9	69.6	86.1	50.8	65.4	86.1	68.2	75.6	86.1	52.6	66.4	106.1	76.5	88.7	106.2	43.7	69.5
09	FINISHES	105.0	58.3	81.9	97.3	58.0	77.9	97.1	59.9	78.7	97.5	58.2	78.1	111.3	77.1	94.4	94.4	49.9	72.4
COVERS	DIVS. 10 - 14, 25, 28, 41, 43, 44, 46	100.0	88.0	97.5	100.0	80.6	95.9	100.0	90.1	97.9	100.0	90.1	97.9	131.1	59.6	115.9	131.1	53.2	114.5
21, 22, 23	FIRE SUPPRESSION, PLUMBING & HVAC	96.0	75.4	88.6	96.0	73.6	87.9	96.0	73.6	87.9	96.0	73.5	87.9	109.8	86.2	101.3	109.8	59.7	91.8
26, 27, 3370	ELECTRICAL, COMMUNICATIONS & UTIL.	96.3	57.7	79.5	94.4	57.6	78.4	94.4	57.6	78.4	93.8	57.6	78.1	124.4	75.1	103.0	123.8	50.6	91.9
MF2018	WEIGHTED AVERAGE	100.7	70.9	89.5	98.6	68.0	87.0	98.1	69.9	87.5	97.7	69.0	86.9	120.5	80.9	105.5	110.5	58.0	90.7

		CANADA																	
	DIVISION	BRANDON, MANITOBA			BRANTFORD, ONTARIO			BRIDGEWATER, NOVA SCOTIA			CALGARY, ALBERTA			CAP-DE-LA-MADELEINE, QUEBEC			CHARLESBOURG, QUEBEC		
		MAT.	INST.	TOTAL	MAT.	INST.	TOTAL	MAT.	INST.	TOTAL	MAT.	INST.	TOTAL	MAT.	INST.	TOTAL	MAT.	INST.	TOTAL
015433	CONTRACTOR EQUIPMENT		100.6	100.6		100.6	100.6		100.8	100.8		119.0	119.0		101.8	101.8		101.8	101.8
0241, 31 - 34	SITE & INFRASTRUCTURE, DEMOLITION	139.1	91.8	108.3	137.1	94.9	109.6	121.0	92.8	102.6	156.2	110.3	126.3	116.4	94.3	102.0	116.4	94.3	102.0
0310	Concrete Forming & Accessories	166.7	61.4	79.8	137.2	82.6	92.2	105.6	63.1	70.5	136.3	84.5	93.6	143.4	73.5	85.8	143.4	73.5	85.8
0320	Concrete Reinforcing	147.6	49.7	107.6	149.5	78.0	120.3	129.2	43.4	94.1	115.5	74.7	98.8	129.2	66.0	103.4	129.2	66.0	103.4
0330	Cast-in-Place Concrete	109.3	67.0	95.2	144.7	95.7	128.3	148.7	64.3	120.5	176.1	93.2	148.4	116.7	83.0	105.4	116.7	83.0	105.4
03	CONCRETE	136.2	62.2	105.8	148.2	86.8	123.0	146.8	61.0	111.6	195.2	86.4	150.5	131.7	76.1	108.9	131.7	76.1	108.9
04	MASONRY	200.4	55.9	116.3	168.5	86.0	120.4	163.6	60.4	103.6	202.7	79.5	131.0	164.0	70.3	109.5	164.0	70.3	109.5
05	METALS	150.9	72.1	134.4	100.6	87.1	97.7	99.9	71.1	93.9	117.7	88.8	111.6	99.1	80.3	95.2	99.1	80.3	95.2
06	WOOD, PLASTICS & COMPOSITES	157.8	62.2	110.8	122.8	81.6	102.5	90.0	62.9	76.6	96.0	84.4	90.3	134.8	73.6	104.7	134.8	73.6	104.7
07	THERMAL & MOISTURE PROTECTION	115.6	64.2	98.4	111.3	84.5	102.3	107.0	63.3	92.4	130.4	89.9	116.8	106.0	78.0	96.6	106.0	78.0	96.6
08	OPENINGS	111.0	55.4	97.5	95.4	80.1	91.7	91.3	56.8	82.9	101.6	74.8	95.1	97.7	66.9	90.2	97.7	66.9	90.2
0920	Plaster & Gypsum Board	99.1	60.8	74.7	114.1	81.1	93.1	117.0	61.7	81.8	133.8	83.1	101.5	144.1	72.6	98.6	144.1	72.6	98.6
0950, 0980	Ceilings & Acoustic Treatment	91.4	60.8	74.3	85.4	81.1	82.9	85.4	61.7	72.1	129.3	83.1	103.4	85.4	72.6	78.2	85.4	72.6	78.2
0960	Flooring	123.4	56.5	106.3	113.4	79.7	104.8	99.7	53.8	87.9	131.6	76.1	117.4	113.4	78.5	104.5	113.4	78.5	104.5
0970, 0990	Wall Finishes & Painting/Coating	111.6	49.3	75.0	114.0	83.9	96.3	114.0	54.1	78.8	125.0	92.7	106.0	114.0	76.3	91.8	114.0	76.3	91.8
09	FINISHES	103.6	59.5	81.8	98.1	82.5	90.4	94.1	60.7	77.6	126.3	84.3	105.5	101.4	75.0	88.4	101.4	75.0	88.4
COVERS	DIVS. 10 - 14, 25, 28, 41, 43, 44, 46	131.1	55.1	114.9	131.1	61.3	116.3	131.1	55.9	115.1	131.1	82.4	120.7	131.1	69.2	117.9	131.1	69.2	117.9
21, 22, 23	FIRE SUPPRESSION, PLUMBING & HVAC	116.3	72.7	100.6	109.7	88.7	102.2	109.7	73.3	96.6	108.8	79.7	98.3	109.5	77.6	98.0	109.5	77.6	98.0
26, 27, 3370	ELECTRICAL, COMMUNICATIONS & UTIL.	128.4	57.1	97.4	139.1	74.7	111.1	140.5	53.1	102.5	153.3	81.1	121.9	134.4	59.1	101.6	134.4	59.1	101.6
MF2018	WEIGHTED AVERAGE	131.1	65.3	106.2	118.8	84.2	105.7	117.0	65.4	97.5	134.3	84.7	115.5	115.6	74.4	100.0	115.6	74.4	100.0

City Cost Indexes

CANADA

DIVISION		CHARLOTTETOWN, PRINCE EDWARD ISLAND			CHICOUTIMI, QUEBEC			CORNER BROOK, NEWFOUNDLAND			CORNWALL, ONTARIO			DALHOUSIE, NEW BRUNSWICK			DARTMOUTH, NOVA SCOTIA		
		MAT.	INST.	TOTAL	MAT.	INST.	TOTAL	MAT.	INST.	TOTAL	MAT.	INST.	TOTAL	MAT.	INST.	TOTAL	MAT.	INST.	TOTAL
015433	CONTRACTOR EQUIPMENT		118.6	118.6		102.0	102.0		99.5	99.5		100.6	100.6		100.6	100.6		98.1	98.1
0241, 31 - 34	SITE & INFRASTRUCTURE, DEMOLITION	170.9	107.8	129.8	118.9	95.0	103.4	144.0	89.9	108.7	135.0	94.4	108.5	121.6	90.9	101.6	134.2	91.0	106.1
0310	Concrete Forming & Accessories	143.6	49.5	66.0	151.0	88.4	99.4	135.4	69.9	81.4	134.6	76.5	86.7	111.6	54.0	64.1	122.2	63.0	73.3
0320	Concrete Reinforcing	127.0	42.5	92.5	104.8	91.3	99.3	136.0	44.5	98.6	149.5	77.7	120.1	131.6	52.5	99.3	141.7	43.4	101.6
0330	Cast-in-Place Concrete	122.0	57.4	100.4	101.5	94.4	99.1	127.3	61.0	105.1	130.1	87.6	115.9	135.8	54.7	108.7	122.9	63.8	103.1
03	CONCRETE	134.8	52.3	100.9	110.6	91.2	102.6	175.2	63.0	129.1	140.9	81.1	116.3	149.4	54.8	110.6	152.8	60.7	115.0
04	MASONRY	161.6	50.8	97.1	151.4	88.3	114.7	196.0	68.3	121.7	167.2	78.8	115.8	162.7	53.0	98.8	209.7	60.1	122.8
05	METALS	101.2	68.9	94.4	95.1	90.5	94.1	151.4	69.3	134.2	100.3	85.8	97.2	99.8	68.5	93.3	152.8	69.6	135.4
06	WOOD, PLASTICS & COMPOSITES	128.3	49.1	89.3	146.0	89.0	117.9	132.5	75.5	104.4	120.9	75.9	98.8	100.6	54.0	77.7	118.9	62.7	91.2
07	THERMAL & MOISTURE PROTECTION	127.7	55.9	103.7	103.9	94.0	100.6	118.4	61.7	99.4	111.0	79.8	100.5	109.2	55.1	91.1	116.6	63.2	98.7
08	OPENINGS	99.0	42.5	85.3	95.4	74.5	90.3	116.7	61.5	103.3	97.7	74.6	92.1	96.8	47.5	84.8	102.6	56.7	91.4
0920	Plaster & Gypsum Board	151.9	46.9	85.0	144.8	88.5	108.9	127.8	74.7	94.0	172.4	75.2	110.5	125.9	52.6	79.2	124.9	61.7	84.7
0950, 0980	Ceilings & Acoustic Treatment	104.0	46.9	72.0	88.3	88.5	88.4	91.4	74.7	82.1	88.4	75.2	81.0	87.0	52.6	67.7	98.0	61.7	77.7
0960	Flooring	131.4	50.4	110.6	115.2	78.5	105.8	109.3	45.2	92.8	113.4	78.5	104.5	108.2	57.9	95.3	105.3	53.8	92.1
0970, 0990	Wall Finishes & Painting/Coating	106.7	36.4	65.4	106.2	101.1	103.2	111.5	51.5	76.2	114.0	78.5	93.0	120.0	43.7	75.2	111.5	54.1	77.8
09	FINISHES	121.3	48.6	85.3	100.9	89.0	95.0	103.6	64.7	84.4	106.4	77.2	92.0	100.6	53.9	77.5	102.7	60.6	81.9
COVERS	DIVS. 10 - 14, 25, 28, 41, 43, 44, 46	131.1	53.9	114.7	131.1	75.0	119.2	131.1	55.5	115.0	131.1	59.2	115.8	131.1	53.2	114.5	131.1	55.6	115.0
21, 22, 23	FIRE SUPPRESSION, PLUMBING & HVAC	116.1	54.4	93.9	109.8	79.6	98.9	116.3	60.7	96.3	109.5	86.9	101.4	110.4	59.7	92.1	116.3	73.2	100.8
26, 27, 3370	ELECTRICAL, COMMUNICATIONS & UTIL.	145.4	43.0	100.8	118.2	80.8	101.9	122.8	46.7	89.6	137.5	75.5	110.5	142.8	47.8	101.5	125.4	53.1	93.9
MF2018	WEIGHTED AVERAGE	122.8	56.1	97.6	109.8	85.7	100.7	135.4	63.3	108.2	118.3	81.1	104.3	118.8	58.1	95.9	132.3	65.1	106.9

CANADA

DIVISION		EDMONTON, ALBERTA			FORT MCMURRAY, ALBERTA			FREDERICTON, NEW BRUNSWICK			GATINEAU, QUEBEC			GRANBY, QUEBEC			HALIFAX, NOVA SCOTIA		
		MAT.	INST.	TOTAL	MAT.	INST.	TOTAL	MAT.	INST.	TOTAL	MAT.	INST.	TOTAL	MAT.	INST.	TOTAL	MAT.	INST.	TOTAL
015433	CONTRACTOR EQUIPMENT		119.1	119.1		103.0	103.0		118.2	118.2		101.8	101.8		101.8	101.8		116.7	116.7
0241, 31 - 34	SITE & INFRASTRUCTURE, DEMOLITION	137.9	111.3	120.6	142.0	95.5	111.7	136.3	108.5	118.2	116.2	94.3	101.9	116.7	94.3	102.1	114.9	108.8	110.9
0310	Concrete Forming & Accessories	136.3	84.5	93.6	134.7	81.1	90.5	143.6	54.8	70.4	143.4	73.4	85.7	143.5	73.3	85.6	143.6	80.7	91.8
0320	Concrete Reinforcing	115.5	74.7	98.8	139.3	74.7	112.9	136.7	52.7	102.4	135.8	66.0	107.3	135.8	66.0	107.3	140.4	71.9	112.4
0330	Cast-in-Place Concrete	179.9	93.0	150.8	192.2	87.4	157.1	148.3	57.8	118.0	115.1	82.9	104.4	119.0	82.9	106.9	109.5	77.0	98.6
03	CONCRETE	197.0	86.3	151.6	169.7	82.6	134.0	149.2	56.6	111.2	132.0	76.1	109.0	133.9	76.0	110.1	130.7	78.6	109.3
04	MASONRY	208.1	79.5	133.2	208.8	77.7	132.5	163.6	54.3	100.0	163.9	70.3	109.4	164.2	70.3	109.5	158.6	79.2	112.4
05	METALS	117.7	88.4	111.5	124.6	84.9	116.3	140.6	74.0	126.7	99.1	80.2	95.2	99.4	80.1	95.4	100.8	89.1	98.4
06	WOOD, PLASTICS & COMPOSITES	96.0	84.3	90.3	116.4	80.7	98.8	118.0	54.6	86.8	134.8	73.6	104.7	134.8	73.6	104.7	118.0	81.0	99.8
07	THERMAL & MOISTURE PROTECTION	130.6	89.8	116.9	118.4	84.3	107.0	127.6	57.4	104.1	106.0	78.0	96.6	106.2	76.7	96.3	130.8	83.4	114.9
08	OPENINGS	101.6	74.8	95.1	97.7	72.8	91.6	97.4	46.8	85.1	97.7	62.9	89.2	97.7	62.9	89.2	98.9	72.8	92.5
0920	Plaster & Gypsum Board	133.8	83.1	101.5	114.3	79.8	92.3	121.9	52.6	77.8	116.0	72.6	88.4	116.0	72.6	88.4	121.8	79.8	95.1
0950, 0980	Ceilings & Acoustic Treatment	129.3	83.1	103.4	92.0	79.8	85.2	96.5	52.6	71.9	85.4	72.6	78.2	85.4	72.6	78.2	98.1	79.8	87.9
0960	Flooring	133.7	76.1	118.9	113.4	76.1	103.9	128.9	60.5	111.4	113.4	78.5	104.5	113.4	78.5	104.5	124.2	73.1	111.1
0970, 0990	Wall Finishes & Painting/Coating	125.0	92.6	105.9	114.2	80.6	94.4	107.5	55.7	77.1	114.0	76.3	91.8	114.0	76.3	91.8	107.3	84.1	93.6
09	FINISHES	125.3	84.3	105.0	100.9	80.4	90.8	107.7	56.1	82.2	97.8	75.0	86.5	97.8	75.0	86.5	105.5	80.2	93.0
COVERS	DIVS. 10 - 14, 25, 28, 41, 43, 44, 46	131.1	83.4	121.0	131.1	81.5	120.6	131.1	54.4	114.8	131.1	69.2	117.9	131.1	69.2	117.9	131.1	62.6	116.5
21, 22, 23	FIRE SUPPRESSION, PLUMBING & HVAC	108.8	79.7	98.3	110.1	85.8	101.4	116.1	68.0	98.8	109.5	77.6	98.0	109.7	77.6	98.2	109.6	76.0	97.5
26, 27, 3370	ELECTRICAL, COMMUNICATIONS & UTIL.	153.6	81.1	122.0	129.6	70.2	103.7	145.6	63.1	109.7	134.4	59.1	101.6	136.0	59.1	102.5	122.7	82.0	105.0
MF2018	WEIGHTED AVERAGE	134.2	84.8	115.5	127.6	81.5	110.2	130.1	64.6	105.4	115.3	74.2	99.8	115.9	74.2	100.1	115.4	81.4	102.5

CANADA

DIVISION		HAMILTON, ONTARIO			HULL, QUEBEC			JOLIETTE, QUEBEC			KAMLOOPS, BRITISH COLUMBIA			KINGSTON, ONTARIO			KITCHENER, ONTARIO		
		MAT.	INST.	TOTAL	MAT.	INST.	TOTAL	MAT.	INST.	TOTAL	MAT.	INST.	TOTAL	MAT.	INST.	TOTAL	MAT.	INST.	TOTAL
015433	CONTRACTOR EQUIPMENT		112.5	112.5		101.8	101.8		101.8	101.8		105.1	105.1		102.9	102.9		104.0	104.0
0241, 31 - 34	SITE & INFRASTRUCTURE, DEMOLITION	128.5	106.1	113.9	116.1	94.3	101.9	116.8	94.3	102.1	137.8	97.5	111.5	135.0	98.1	110.9	115.3	101.0	106.0
0310	Concrete Forming & Accessories	140.0	86.7	96.1	143.5	73.4	85.7	143.5	73.3	85.8	131.4	76.4	86.0	134.8	76.5	86.7	121.8	82.9	89.7
0320	Concrete Reinforcing	113.7	93.7	105.5	135.8	66.0	107.3	129.2	66.0	103.4	100.5	69.2	87.7	149.5	77.7	120.1	82.4	93.6	87.0
0330	Cast-in-Place Concrete	127.4	98.4	117.7	115.1	82.9	104.4	119.9	83.0	107.6	103.8	87.1	98.2	130.1	87.6	115.9	125.9	92.8	114.9
03	CONCRETE	145.6	92.4	123.8	132.0	76.1	109.0	133.3	76.1	109.8	146.5	79.5	119.0	143.4	81.1	117.8	118.8	86.8	106.4
04	MASONRY	203.5	94.3	139.9	163.8	70.3	109.4	164.2	70.3	109.6	171.1	77.3	116.5	174.3	78.9	118.7	166.5	91.9	123.1
05	METALS	108.9	96.9	106.4	99.4	80.2	95.4	99.4	80.3	95.4	100.9	82.5	97.1	101.4	85.8	98.2	101.5	94.7	100.1
06	WOOD, PLASTICS & COMPOSITES	98.4	85.4	92.0	134.8	73.6	104.7	134.8	73.6	104.7	103.5	75.1	89.5	120.9	76.0	98.8	95.0	81.2	88.2
07	THERMAL & MOISTURE PROTECTION	131.2	96.4	119.5	106.2	78.0	96.8	106.2	78.0	96.8	120.6	76.2	105.7	111.0	80.8	100.8	112.6	92.3	105.8
08	OPENINGS	96.1	84.8	93.4	97.7	62.9	89.2	97.7	66.9	90.2	94.8	72.7	89.4	97.7	74.3	92.0	85.3	80.9	84.3
0920	Plaster & Gypsum Board	129.8	84.4	100.9	116.0	72.6	88.4	144.1	72.6	98.6	98.1	74.0	82.7	175.8	75.3	111.8	109.2	80.6	91.0
0950, 0980	Ceilings & Acoustic Treatment	132.3	84.4	105.5	85.4	72.6	78.2	85.4	72.6	78.2	85.4	74.0	79.0	99.0	75.3	85.8	100.5	80.6	89.4
0960	Flooring	128.1	85.2	117.1	113.4	78.5	104.5	113.4	78.5	104.5	116.3	44.9	98.0	113.4	78.5	104.5	131.6	85.7	119.8
0970, 0990	Wall Finishes & Painting/Coating	125.0	95.6	107.7	114.0	76.3	91.8	114.0	76.3	91.8	114.0	69.7	88.0	114.0	72.2	89.5	118.6	86.5	99.7
09	FINISHES	119.2	87.1	103.3	97.8	75.0	86.5	101.4	75.0	88.4	98.3	70.1	84.4	109.6	76.6	93.3	96.6	83.2	90.0
COVERS	DIVS. 10 - 14, 25, 28, 41, 43, 44, 46	131.1	83.2	120.9	131.1	69.2	117.9	131.1	69.2	117.9	131.1	77.2	119.6	131.1	59.2	115.8	131.1	81.1	120.5
21, 22, 23	FIRE SUPPRESSION, PLUMBING & HVAC	108.9	86.5	100.8	109.7	77.6	98.2	109.7	77.6	98.2	109.7	80.7	99.3	109.5	87.0	101.4	108.1	86.2	100.2
26, 27, 3370	ELECTRICAL, COMMUNICATIONS & UTIL.	153.9	95.3	128.4	139.2	59.1	104.3	136.0	59.1	102.5	141.6	67.2	109.2	137.5	74.4	110.1	162.1	93.3	132.1
MF2018	WEIGHTED AVERAGE	125.2	91.9	112.6	116.0	74.2	100.2	116.1	74.4	100.4	119.2	77.7	103.5	119.4	81.2	105.0	116.0	89.3	105.9

672

City Cost Indexes

CANADA

DIVISION		LAVAL, QUEBEC			LETHBRIDGE, ALBERTA			LLOYDMINSTER, ALBERTA			LONDON, ONTARIO			MEDICINE HAT, ALBERTA			MONCTON, NEW BRUNSWICK		
		MAT.	INST.	TOTAL	MAT.	INST.	TOTAL	MAT.	INST.	TOTAL	MAT.	INST.	TOTAL	MAT.	INST.	TOTAL	MAT.	INST.	TOTAL
015433	CONTRACTOR EQUIPMENT		101.8	101.8		103.0	103.0		103.0	103.0		113.2	113.2		103.0	103.0		101.3	101.3
0241, 31 - 34	SITE & INFRASTRUCTURE, DEMOLITION	116.7	94.3	102.1	134.0	96.0	109.3	133.6	95.5	108.8	135.4	105.9	116.2	132.5	95.5	108.4	121.1	93.8	103.3
0310	Concrete Forming & Accessories	143.7	74.0	86.2	136.3	81.1	90.8	134.2	72.5	83.4	140.0	83.1	93.1	136.3	72.5	83.7	115.8	63.5	72.7
0320	Concrete Reinforcing	135.8	66.7	107.6	139.3	74.7	112.9	139.3	74.6	112.9	113.7	92.6	105.1	139.3	74.6	112.9	139.0	63.5	108.1
0330	Cast-in-Place Concrete	119.0	83.5	107.1	144.1	87.5	125.1	133.7	84.3	117.1	130.7	96.6	119.3	133.7	84.3	117.1	103.8	66.2	91.2
03	CONCRETE	133.9	76.7	110.4	146.3	82.6	120.1	141.0	77.6	115.0	147.2	90.0	123.7	141.1	77.6	115.1	118.0	65.4	96.4
04	MASONRY	164.2	70.9	109.9	182.7	77.7	121.6	163.9	72.0	110.4	203.8	92.8	139.2	163.9	72.0	110.4	149.5	71.6	104.2
05	METALS	98.8	80.6	95.0	119.8	84.9	112.5	100.8	84.8	97.5	108.9	95.9	106.2	101.1	84.7	97.7	95.4	83.0	92.8
06	WOOD, PLASTICS & COMPOSITES	134.8	74.2	105.0	120.2	80.7	100.7	116.4	72.1	94.6	98.4	81.2	89.9	120.2	72.1	96.5	106.2	61.6	84.2
07	THERMAL & MOISTURE PROTECTION	107.6	78.5	97.8	116.6	84.3	105.8	113.8	80.4	102.6	131.2	94.3	118.8	118.6	80.4	105.8	106.6	69.7	94.3
08	OPENINGS	97.7	63.5	89.4	97.7	72.8	91.6	97.7	68.1	90.5	96.1	80.6	92.4	97.7	68.1	90.5	91.6	57.8	83.4
0920	Plaster & Gypsum Board	116.0	73.3	88.8	105.9	79.8	89.3	101.2	71.0	82.0	129.8	80.0	98.1	103.8	71.0	82.9	118.0	60.3	81.3
0950, 0980	Ceilings & Acoustic Treatment	85.4	73.3	78.6	92.0	79.8	85.2	85.4	71.0	77.3	132.3	80.0	103.1	85.4	71.0	77.3	89.1	63.0	73.0
0960	Flooring	113.4	79.3	104.7	113.4	76.1	103.9	113.4	76.1	103.9	108.0	85.3	102.2	113.4	76.1	103.9	102.9	59.2	91.7
0970, 0990	Wall Finishes & Painting/Coating	114.0	77.0	92.2	114.0	88.0	98.7	114.2	68.5	87.3	124.6	92.6	105.8	114.0	68.5	87.3	106.2	79.4	90.4
09	FINISHES	97.8	75.6	86.8	99.1	81.2	90.3	96.9	72.6	84.9	113.8	84.1	99.1	97.1	72.6	85.0	94.4	64.0	79.4
COVERS	DIVS. 10 - 14, 25, 28, 41, 43, 44, 46	131.1	69.8	118.1	131.1	80.5	120.3	131.1	78.8	120.0	131.1	82.6	120.8	131.1	77.7	119.7	131.1	56.8	115.3
21, 22, 23	FIRE SUPPRESSION, PLUMBING & HVAC	108.3	78.3	97.5	110.0	82.9	100.3	109.5	82.8	99.9	108.9	84.6	100.1	109.7	79.9	99.0	109.9	74.8	97.2
26, 27, 3370	ELECTRICAL, COMMUNICATIONS & UTIL.	136.5	59.6	103.0	133.5	70.2	106.0	128.3	70.2	103.0	177.8	93.1	140.9	128.3	70.2	103.0	125.2	84.6	107.5
MF2018	WEIGHTED AVERAGE	115.6	74.8	100.1	122.7	81.0	106.9	116.6	78.1	102.0	127.8	89.9	113.5	116.9	77.4	102.0	110.5	73.8	96.6

CANADA

DIVISION		MONTREAL, QUEBEC			MOOSE JAW, SASKATCHEWAN			NEW GLASGOW, NOVA SCOTIA			NEWCASTLE, NEW BRUNSWICK			NORTH BAY, ONTARIO			OSHAWA, ONTARIO		
		MAT.	INST.	TOTAL	MAT.	INST.	TOTAL	MAT.	INST.	TOTAL	MAT.	INST.	TOTAL	MAT.	INST.	TOTAL	MAT.	INST.	TOTAL
015433	CONTRACTOR EQUIPMENT		116.0	116.0		99.2	99.2		98.1	98.1		101.3	101.3		98.1	98.1		104.0	104.0
0241, 31 - 34	SITE & INFRASTRUCTURE, DEMOLITION	119.4	106.5	111.0	133.1	90.2	105.2	126.5	91.0	103.4	121.6	91.4	101.9	141.1	92.4	109.3	126.0	101.1	109.7
0310	Concrete Forming & Accessories	143.6	89.0	98.6	117.0	50.8	62.4	122.1	63.0	73.3	115.8	54.0	64.8	167.7	74.2	90.5	127.0	86.0	93.2
0320	Concrete Reinforcing	142.2	91.4	121.5	98.3	56.0	81.0	136.0	43.4	98.2	139.0	52.5	103.6	159.5	77.3	125.9	130.5	95.9	116.4
0330	Cast-in-Place Concrete	131.6	98.1	120.4	129.7	61.3	106.8	122.9	63.8	103.1	107.8	54.8	90.0	118.3	75.8	104.1	145.7	101.6	130.9
03	CONCRETE	150.9	93.0	127.1	123.5	56.3	95.9	151.9	60.7	114.5	120.0	54.9	93.3	153.8	75.7	121.7	144.1	93.6	123.4
04	MASONRY	179.4	88.5	126.5	162.1	52.0	98.0	195.6	60.4	116.9	149.9	53.0	93.5	201.8	75.4	128.2	169.8	95.0	126.3
05	METALS	109.5	94.9	106.5	98.0	69.8	92.1	149.4	69.6	132.7	95.4	68.9	89.9	150.2	84.2	136.4	93.4	96.1	93.9
06	WOOD, PLASTICS & COMPOSITES	115.8	89.5	102.8	100.5	49.7	75.5	118.9	62.7	91.2	106.2	54.0	80.5	160.9	74.6	118.5	101.4	84.6	93.1
07	THERMAL & MOISTURE PROTECTION	126.3	96.5	116.3	105.5	56.5	89.1	116.6	63.2	98.7	106.6	55.1	89.4	121.5	76.6	106.5	113.2	97.2	107.9
08	OPENINGS	96.8	76.5	91.9	93.9	47.6	82.6	102.6	56.7	91.4	91.6	47.5	80.9	107.8	72.3	99.2	89.8	84.2	88.4
0920	Plaster & Gypsum Board	120.9	88.5	100.3	96.4	48.1	65.7	122.8	61.7	83.9	118.0	52.6	76.3	120.6	74.0	90.9	112.5	84.1	94.4
0950, 0980	Ceilings & Acoustic Treatment	110.0	88.5	97.9	85.4	48.1	64.5	91.4	61.7	74.7	89.1	52.6	68.7	91.4	74.0	81.6	97.5	84.1	90.0
0960	Flooring	111.2	81.2	103.5	105.8	49.0	91.2	105.3	53.8	92.1	102.9	57.9	91.3	123.4	78.5	111.9	103.5	87.2	99.3
0970, 0990	Wall Finishes & Painting/Coating	112.8	101.1	105.9	114.0	55.7	79.7	111.5	54.1	77.8	106.2	43.7	69.5	111.5	77.6	91.6	118.6	99.3	107.2
09	FINISHES	105.4	89.9	97.7	93.9	50.7	72.6	100.7	60.6	80.9	94.4	54.0	74.4	106.1	75.6	91.1	97.3	87.2	92.3
COVERS	DIVS. 10 - 14, 25, 28, 41, 43, 44, 46	131.1	76.3	119.4	131.1	52.8	114.4	131.1	55.6	115.0	131.1	53.2	114.5	131.1	57.9	115.5	131.1	81.8	120.6
21, 22, 23	FIRE SUPPRESSION, PLUMBING & HVAC	108.2	79.7	98.0	109.5	64.8	93.4	116.3	73.2	100.8	109.8	59.7	91.8	116.3	85.1	105.1	108.1	86.0	100.2
26, 27, 3370	ELECTRICAL, COMMUNICATIONS & UTIL.	122.7	80.8	104.4	141.6	51.0	102.2	123.5	53.1	92.9	123.5	50.6	91.8	127.6	75.4	104.9	162.4	95.5	133.3
MF2018	WEIGHTED AVERAGE	119.9	87.6	107.7	114.4	59.4	93.6	130.4	65.1	105.7	110.6	58.6	91.0	133.2	78.9	112.7	118.3	91.6	108.2

CANADA

DIVISION		OTTAWA, ONTARIO			OWEN SOUND, ONTARIO			PETERBOROUGH, ONTARIO			PORTAGE LA PRAIRIE, MANITOBA			PRINCE ALBERT, SASKATCHEWAN			PRINCE GEORGE, BRITISH COLUMBIA		
		MAT.	INST.	TOTAL	MAT.	INST.	TOTAL	MAT.	INST.	TOTAL	MAT.	INST.	TOTAL	MAT.	INST.	TOTAL	MAT.	INST.	TOTAL
015433	CONTRACTOR EQUIPMENT		114.7	114.7		100.7	100.7		100.6	100.6		103.1	103.1		99.2	99.2		105.1	105.1
0241, 31 - 34	SITE & INFRASTRUCTURE, DEMOLITION	119.7	106.6	111.1	123.4	94.5	104.6	137.1	94.3	109.2	134.1	93.4	107.6	128.0	90.4	103.5	141.6	97.5	112.9
0310	Concrete Forming & Accessories	131.7	87.3	95.1	129.0	73.0	82.8	137.2	75.2	86.0	136.5	61.1	74.3	117.0	50.6	62.3	123.5	72.0	81.0
0320	Concrete Reinforcing	113.7	92.6	105.1	195.3	79.2	147.9	149.5	77.8	120.2	139.3	49.7	102.7	102.7	55.9	83.6	100.5	69.1	87.7
0330	Cast-in-Place Concrete	130.7	99.7	120.3	160.6	72.9	131.3	144.7	77.6	122.2	133.7	67.0	111.4	117.5	61.3	98.7	130.1	87.2	115.8
03	CONCRETE	146.7	93.1	124.7	156.7	74.6	123.0	148.2	77.0	119.0	132.8	62.1	103.8	118.3	56.2	92.8	158.9	77.5	125.5
04	MASONRY	204.1	93.6	139.8	176.8	80.2	120.4	168.5	81.1	117.6	167.1	55.1	101.9	161.2	52.0	97.6	173.4	77.3	117.5
05	METALS	106.5	98.5	104.8	110.9	86.3	105.8	100.6	85.9	97.5	101.1	73.4	95.3	98.1	69.7	92.1	100.9	82.6	97.1
06	WOOD, PLASTICS & COMPOSITES	98.4	86.5	92.5	107.4	71.9	89.9	122.8	73.6	98.6	120.2	62.3	91.7	100.5	49.7	75.5	103.5	69.1	86.5
07	THERMAL & MOISTURE PROTECTION	128.5	95.9	117.6	110.3	77.4	99.3	111.3	81.5	101.3	106.1	63.9	91.9	105.4	55.6	88.7	115.7	75.6	102.3
08	OPENINGS	96.0	84.4	93.2	87.6	71.8	83.8	95.4	73.9	90.2	97.7	55.5	87.4	93.0	47.6	81.9	94.8	69.3	88.6
0920	Plaster & Gypsum Board	129.8	85.4	101.6	148.0	71.1	99.0	114.1	72.8	87.8	103.6	60.8	76.4	96.4	48.1	65.7	98.1	67.7	78.7
0950, 0980	Ceilings & Acoustic Treatment	132.3	85.4	106.1	93.6	71.1	81.0	85.4	72.8	78.3	85.4	60.8	71.6	85.4	48.1	64.5	85.4	67.7	75.5
0960	Flooring	107.9	81.3	101.1	122.8	79.7	111.7	113.4	78.5	104.5	113.4	56.5	98.8	105.8	49.0	91.2	109.9	61.5	97.5
0970, 0990	Wall Finishes & Painting/Coating	124.3	87.9	102.9	106.1	76.5	88.7	114.0	79.5	93.7	114.2	49.3	76.1	114.0	47.5	74.9	114.0	69.7	88.0
09	FINISHES	112.5	86.2	99.5	111.3	74.7	93.2	98.1	76.3	87.3	97.0	59.3	78.4	93.9	49.8	72.1	96.5	69.4	83.1
COVERS	DIVS. 10 - 14, 25, 28, 41, 43, 44, 46	131.1	81.6	120.6	131.1	58.8	115.7	131.1	59.4	115.8	131.1	55.0	114.9	131.1	52.8	114.4	131.1	76.5	119.5
21, 22, 23	FIRE SUPPRESSION, PLUMBING & HVAC	108.9	85.3	100.4	109.8	85.1	100.9	109.7	88.2	102.0	109.7	72.2	96.2	109.5	58.4	91.1	109.7	80.7	99.3
26, 27, 3370	ELECTRICAL, COMMUNICATIONS & UTIL.	153.9	93.7	127.5	126.6	74.4	103.9	139.1	75.1	111.2	140.9	49.3	101.0	141.6	51.0	102.2	138.8	67.2	107.6
MF2018	WEIGHTED AVERAGE	124.0	91.4	111.7	120.7	79.3	105.1	118.8	80.9	104.5	117.0	64.2	97.1	113.5	57.9	92.5	120.3	77.1	103.9

City Cost Indexes

CANADA

DIVISION		QUEBEC CITY, QUEBEC			RED DEER, ALBERTA			REGINA, SASKATCHEWAN			RIMOUSKI, QUEBEC			ROUYN-NORANDA, QUEBEC			SAINT HYACINTHE, QUEBEC		
		MAT.	INST.	TOTAL	MAT.	INST.	TOTAL	MAT.	INST.	TOTAL	MAT.	INST.	TOTAL	MAT.	INST.	TOTAL	MAT.	INST.	TOTAL
015433	CONTRACTOR EQUIPMENT		117.4	117.4		103.0	103.0		126.1	126.1		101.8	101.8		101.8	101.8		101.8	101.8
0241, 31 - 34	SITE & INFRASTRUCTURE, DEMOLITION	136.3	106.9	117.2	132.5	95.5	108.4	148.2	119.5	129.5	116.3	94.9	102.4	116.1	94.3	101.9	116.6	94.3	102.0
0310	Concrete Forming & Accessories	143.6	89.2	98.7	147.8	72.5	85.7	153.8	81.5	94.1	143.5	88.4	98.0	143.5	73.4	85.7	143.5	73.4	85.7
0320	Concrete Reinforcing	143.6	91.4	122.3	139.3	74.6	112.9	119.4	77.3	102.2	97.5	91.3	94.9	135.8	66.0	107.3	135.8	66.0	107.3
0330	Cast-in-Place Concrete	120.7	98.3	113.2	133.7	84.3	117.1	172.4	91.5	145.3	121.1	94.3	112.2	115.1	82.9	104.4	119.0	82.9	106.9
03	CONCRETE	145.8	93.2	124.2	141.9	77.6	115.5	169.2	84.9	134.6	129.0	91.1	113.5	132.0	76.1	109.0	133.9	76.1	110.2
04	MASONRY	182.8	88.5	127.9	163.9	72.0	110.4	206.2	77.6	131.4	163.2	88.3	119.6	163.8	70.3	109.4	164.1	70.3	109.5
05	METALS	108.5	96.5	106.0	101.1	84.7	97.7	118.1	90.6	112.4	98.9	90.4	97.1	99.4	80.2	95.4	99.4	80.2	95.4
06	WOOD, PLASTICS & COMPOSITES	116.6	89.5	103.3	120.2	72.1	96.5	142.4	82.0	112.7	134.8	88.9	112.3	134.8	73.6	104.7	134.8	73.6	104.7
07	THERMAL & MOISTURE PROTECTION	125.4	96.6	115.8	126.1	80.4	110.8	128.3	79.6	112.0	106.2	94.0	102.1	106.2	78.0	96.8	107.6	78.0	97.7
08	OPENINGS	98.9	83.2	95.1	97.7	68.1	90.5	101.9	70.8	94.4	97.2	74.4	91.7	97.7	62.9	89.2	97.7	62.9	89.2
0920	Plaster & Gypsum Board	116.7	88.5	98.7	103.8	71.0	82.9	132.8	80.6	99.6	143.9	88.5	108.6	115.8	72.6	88.3	115.8	72.6	88.3
0950, 0980	Ceilings & Acoustic Treatment	104.5	88.5	95.5	85.4	71.0	77.3	110.6	80.6	93.8	84.9	88.5	86.9	84.9	72.6	78.0	84.9	72.6	78.0
0960	Flooring	111.0	81.2	103.4	118.2	76.1	107.4	128.9	85.3	117.7	114.5	78.5	105.3	113.4	78.5	104.5	113.4	78.5	104.5
0970, 0990	Wall Finishes & Painting/Coating	113.7	101.1	106.3	114.0	68.5	87.3	107.3	77.5	89.8	117.1	101.1	107.7	114.0	76.3	91.8	114.0	76.3	91.8
09	FINISHES	104.4	89.9	97.2	98.4	72.6	85.7	113.6	82.5	98.2	101.8	89.0	95.5	97.7	75.0	86.5	97.7	75.0	86.5
COVERS	DIVS. 10 - 14, 25, 28, 41, 43, 44, 46	131.1	76.3	119.5	131.1	77.7	119.7	131.1	63.5	116.7	131.1	75.0	119.2	131.1	69.2	117.9	131.1	69.2	117.9
21, 22, 23	FIRE SUPPRESSION, PLUMBING & HVAC	107.9	79.7	97.8	109.7	79.9	99.0	108.5	78.0	97.7	109.7	79.6	98.9	109.7	77.6	98.2	105.6	77.6	95.5
26, 27, 3370	ELECTRICAL, COMMUNICATIONS & UTIL.	122.7	80.8	104.4	128.3	70.2	103.0	119.2	79.1	101.7	136.0	80.0	112.0	136.0	59.1	102.5	136.8	59.1	103.0
MF2018	WEIGHTED AVERAGE	119.6	88.1	107.7	117.3	77.4	102.2	126.7	83.2	110.3	115.4	85.7	104.2	115.6	74.2	100.0	115.1	74.2	99.6

CANADA

DIVISION		SAINT JOHN, NEW BRUNSWICK			SARNIA, ONTARIO			SASKATOON, SASKATCHEWAN			SAULT STE MARIE, ONTARIO			SHERBROOKE, QUEBEC			SOREL, QUEBEC		
		MAT.	INST.	TOTAL	MAT.	INST.	TOTAL	MAT.	INST.	TOTAL	MAT.	INST.	TOTAL	MAT.	INST.	TOTAL	MAT.	INST.	TOTAL
015433	CONTRACTOR EQUIPMENT		101.3	101.3		100.6	100.6		98.8	98.8		100.6	100.6		101.8	101.8		101.8	101.8
0241, 31 - 34	SITE & INFRASTRUCTURE, DEMOLITION	121.7	93.8	103.5	135.4	94.4	108.7	132.4	93.2	106.8	125.8	94.0	105.1	116.7	94.3	102.1	116.8	94.3	102.1
0310	Concrete Forming & Accessories	140.5	65.8	78.9	135.7	81.3	90.8	116.1	80.6	86.8	123.3	80.9	88.3	143.4	73.4	85.7	143.5	73.5	85.8
0320	Concrete Reinforcing	139.0	63.5	108.1	110.2	79.0	97.4	104.3	77.2	93.2	95.9	78.0	88.6	135.8	66.0	107.3	129.2	66.0	103.4
0330	Cast-in-Place Concrete	106.2	66.2	92.8	133.5	88.8	118.5	139.5	85.7	121.5	119.9	76.5	105.4	119.0	82.9	106.9	119.0	83.0	107.6
03	CONCRETE	121.0	66.5	98.6	136.5	83.9	114.9	133.2	82.1	112.2	118.8	79.4	102.6	133.8	76.1	110.2	133.3	76.1	109.8
04	MASONRY	170.3	71.6	112.8	180.0	83.4	123.8	170.9	77.3	116.4	164.3	85.8	118.6	164.2	70.3	109.6	164.2	70.3	109.6
05	METALS	95.3	83.0	92.8	100.5	86.3	97.5	100.8	83.4	97.1	99.6	91.3	97.9	99.1	80.2	95.2	99.4	80.3	95.4
06	WOOD, PLASTICS & COMPOSITES	133.2	64.7	99.5	121.8	80.7	101.6	101.0	81.1	91.2	108.2	82.9	95.7	134.8	73.6	104.7	134.8	73.6	104.7
07	THERMAL & MOISTURE PROTECTION	106.9	69.9	94.5	111.4	84.5	102.4	107.5	75.6	96.9	110.5	81.7	100.9	106.0	78.0	96.6	106.2	78.0	96.8
08	OPENINGS	91.5	58.6	83.5	99.9	77.3	94.4	96.5	70.4	90.2	90.1	80.7	87.8	97.7	62.9	89.2	97.7	66.9	90.2
0920	Plaster & Gypsum Board	136.7	63.6	90.2	138.8	80.1	101.5	113.6	80.6	92.6	105.2	82.4	90.7	115.8	72.6	88.3	143.9	72.6	98.6
0950, 0980	Ceilings & Acoustic Treatment	92.7	63.6	76.4	89.8	80.1	84.4	101.1	80.6	89.6	85.4	82.4	83.7	84.9	72.6	78.0	84.9	72.6	78.0
0960	Flooring	111.9	59.2	98.4	113.4	85.9	106.4	111.7	85.3	104.9	108.0	92.0	103.9	113.4	78.5	104.5	113.4	78.5	104.5
0970, 0990	Wall Finishes & Painting/Coating	106.2	79.4	90.4	114.0	89.9	99.9	120.0	77.5	95.0	114.0	83.3	96.0	114.0	76.3	91.8	114.0	76.3	91.8
09	FINISHES	100.3	65.8	83.3	102.5	83.4	93.0	104.3	81.9	93.2	94.9	82.0	88.5	97.7	75.0	86.5	101.3	75.0	88.3
COVERS	DIVS. 10 - 14, 25, 28, 41, 43, 44, 46	131.1	57.4	115.4	131.1	60.6	116.1	131.1	61.8	116.4	131.1	79.3	120.1	131.1	69.2	117.9	131.1	69.2	117.9
21, 22, 23	FIRE SUPPRESSION, PLUMBING & HVAC	109.8	74.8	97.2	109.7	93.5	103.9	108.5	77.8	97.5	109.7	83.7	100.4	109.5	77.6	98.0	109.7	77.6	98.2
26, 27, 3370	ELECTRICAL, COMMUNICATIONS & UTIL.	126.4	84.6	108.2	146.4	77.0	116.2	144.4	79.0	115.9	143.1	75.4	113.6	136.0	59.1	102.5	136.0	59.1	102.5
MF2018	WEIGHTED AVERAGE	112.6	74.2	98.1	119.4	84.8	106.3	117.6	79.8	103.4	114.3	83.0	102.5	115.8	74.2	100.1	116.1	74.4	100.4

CANADA

DIVISION		ST CATHARINES, ONTARIO			ST JEROME, QUEBEC			ST JOHNS, NEWFOUNDLAND			SUDBURY, ONTARIO			SUMMERSIDE, PRINCE EDWARD ISLAND			SYDNEY, NOVA SCOTIA		
		MAT.	INST.	TOTAL	MAT.	INST.	TOTAL	MAT.	INST.	TOTAL	MAT.	INST.	TOTAL	MAT.	INST.	TOTAL	MAT.	INST.	TOTAL
015433	CONTRACTOR EQUIPMENT		101.9	101.9		101.8	101.8		120.2	120.2		101.9	101.9		98.0	98.0		98.1	98.1
0241, 31 - 34	SITE & INFRASTRUCTURE, DEMOLITION	115.6	97.5	103.8	116.1	94.3	101.9	119.7	113.2	115.4	115.7	97.3	103.7	135.3	88.6	104.9	122.5	91.0	102.0
0310	Concrete Forming & Accessories	119.8	87.8	93.4	143.5	73.4	85.7	143.7	77.6	89.2	115.7	83.7	89.3	122.4	48.8	61.7	122.1	63.0	73.3
0320	Concrete Reinforcing	83.1	93.6	87.4	135.8	66.0	107.3	165.0	75.1	128.3	83.7	94.0	87.9	133.9	42.4	96.5	136.0	43.4	98.2
0330	Cast-in-Place Concrete	120.3	94.3	111.6	115.1	82.9	104.4	124.8	93.6	114.4	121.3	91.3	111.2	116.6	52.9	95.3	94.7	63.8	84.4
03	CONCRETE	116.0	91.4	105.9	132.0	76.1	109.0	142.0	83.5	118.0	116.4	85.7	103.7	163.2	50.1	116.8	138.1	60.7	106.3
04	MASONRY	166.0	93.9	124.0	163.8	70.3	109.4	184.8	83.0	125.6	166.0	90.8	122.2	194.8	50.6	110.8	193.1	60.4	115.8
05	METALS	93.3	94.6	93.6	99.4	80.2	95.4	141.6	87.5	130.3	93.1	94.8	93.4	149.4	63.0	131.3	149.4	69.6	132.7
06	WOOD, PLASTICS & COMPOSITES	92.9	87.4	90.2	134.8	73.6	104.7	118.7	75.7	97.6	89.1	83.0	86.1	119.5	48.4	84.5	118.9	62.7	91.2
07	THERMAL & MOISTURE PROTECTION	112.6	95.1	106.7	106.2	78.0	96.8	127.8	88.9	114.7	111.0	90.8	104.2	116.1	54.0	95.3	116.6	63.2	98.7
08	OPENINGS	84.7	84.6	84.7	97.7	62.9	89.2	98.1	67.1	90.6	85.2	81.1	84.2	113.0	42.1	95.8	102.6	56.7	91.4
0920	Plaster & Gypsum Board	104.1	87.0	93.2	115.8	72.6	88.3	144.2	74.3	99.7	102.6	82.4	89.8	124.0	46.9	74.9	122.8	61.7	83.9
0950, 0980	Ceilings & Acoustic Treatment	97.5	87.0	91.6	84.9	72.6	78.0	108.2	74.3	89.2	93.0	82.4	87.1	91.4	46.9	66.5	91.4	61.7	74.7
0960	Flooring	100.4	82.4	95.8	113.4	78.5	104.5	127.7	46.9	107.0	99.0	82.4	94.7	105.3	53.8	91.2	105.3	53.8	92.1
0970, 0990	Wall Finishes & Painting/Coating	118.6	95.6	105.1	114.0	76.3	91.8	109.0	89.8	97.7	118.6	87.4	100.3	111.5	36.4	67.3	111.5	54.1	77.7
09	FINISHES	94.9	87.7	91.3	97.7	75.0	86.5	112.4	73.0	92.9	93.2	83.7	88.5	101.7	48.0	75.2	100.7	60.6	80.9
COVERS	DIVS. 10 - 14, 25, 28, 41, 43, 44, 46	131.1	63.5	116.7	131.1	69.2	117.9	131.1	61.8	116.4	131.1	81.0	120.5	131.1	52.2	114.3	131.1	55.6	115.0
21, 22, 23	FIRE SUPPRESSION, PLUMBING & HVAC	108.1	85.4	99.9	109.7	77.6	98.2	108.5	76.3	97.0	108.6	83.6	99.6	116.3	54.3	94.0	116.3	73.2	100.8
26, 27, 3370	ELECTRICAL, COMMUNICATIONS & UTIL.	167.0	94.0	135.2	137.0	59.1	103.4	122.8	70.3	100.0	161.1	94.1	131.9	121.0	42.9	87.2	123.5	53.1	92.9
MF2018	WEIGHTED AVERAGE	114.4	89.9	105.1	115.8	74.2	100.1	126.1	79.9	108.7	113.7	88.0	104.0	132.5	53.6	102.7	128.5	65.1	104.6

City Cost Indexes

		\multicolumn{18}{c}{CANADA}
	DIVISION	THUNDER BAY, ONTARIO			TIMMINS, ONTARIO			TORONTO, ONTARIO			TROIS RIVIERES, QUEBEC			TRURO, NOVA SCOTIA			VANCOUVER, BRITISH COLUMBIA		
		MAT.	INST.	TOTAL	MAT.	INST.	TOTAL	MAT.	INST.	TOTAL	MAT.	INST.	TOTAL	MAT.	INST.	TOTAL	MAT.	INST.	TOTAL
015433	CONTRACTOR EQUIPMENT		101.9	101.9		100.6	100.6		113.4	113.4		99.0	99.0		100.8	100.8		131.6	131.6
0241, 31 - 34	SITE & INFRASTRUCTURE, DEMOLITION	119.9	97.4	105.2	137.1	94.0	109.0	128.5	106.7	114.3	122.8	92.5	103.0	121.2	92.8	102.7	143.2	122.2	129.6
0310	Concrete Forming & Accessories	127.0	85.8	93.0	137.2	74.3	85.3	140.0	96.1	103.8	176.9	73.4	91.5	105.6	63.1	70.5	138.9	83.9	93.6
0320	Concrete Reinforcing	74.3	93.1	82.0	149.5	77.3	120.0	113.7	96.0	106.5	136.0	66.0	107.4	129.2	43.4	94.1	132.9	87.5	114.4
0330	Cast-in-Place Concrete	132.4	93.7	119.4	144.7	76.3	121.8	127.4	109.0	121.3	98.1	82.4	92.9	150.3	64.3	121.5	157.7	95.8	137.0
03	CONCRETE	125.3	90.1	110.9	148.2	76.0	118.6	145.6	100.9	127.3	140.8	75.8	114.2	147.6	61.0	112.1	164.8	89.6	133.9
04	MASONRY	166.8	92.3	123.4	168.5	75.4	114.3	208.8	101.6	146.4	197.0	70.3	123.2	163.8	60.4	103.6	209.3	87.1	138.2
05	METALS	93.3	93.7	93.4	100.6	85.5	97.4	100.3	99.7	100.2	148.7	78.9	134.1	99.9	71.1	93.9	106.0	100.0	104.7
06	WOOD, PLASTICS & COMPOSITES	101.4	85.3	93.5	122.8	74.7	99.1	98.4	94.5	96.5	177.1	73.5	126.1	90.0	62.9	76.6	117.4	83.1	100.5
07	THERMAL & MOISTURE PROTECTION	112.8	92.2	105.9	111.3	76.7	99.7	131.2	103.8	122.0	115.8	77.9	103.1	107.0	63.3	92.4	131.0	87.5	116.5
08	OPENINGS	84.0	82.9	83.8	95.4	72.4	89.8	95.7	92.0	94.8	111.0	66.9	100.2	91.3	56.8	82.9	102.9	80.9	97.6
0920	Plaster & Gypsum Board	129.8	84.8	101.2	114.1	74.0	88.6	129.8	93.8	106.9	148.3	72.6	100.1	117.0	61.7	81.8	138.6	81.5	102.3
0950, 0980	Ceilings & Acoustic Treatment	93.0	84.8	88.4	85.4	74.0	79.0	132.3	93.8	110.8	90.0	72.6	80.3	85.4	61.7	72.1	131.9	81.5	103.7
0960	Flooring	103.5	88.3	99.6	113.4	78.5	104.5	127.9	90.4	118.3	123.4	78.5	111.9	99.7	53.8	87.9	120.0	79.4	109.6
0970, 0990	Wall Finishes & Painting/Coating	118.6	88.3	100.8	114.0	77.6	92.6	124.3	99.3	109.6	111.5	76.3	90.8	114.0	54.1	78.8	123.3	93.1	105.5
09	FINISHES	98.2	86.4	92.4	98.1	75.7	87.1	119.1	95.4	107.4	108.7	74.9	92.0	94.1	60.7	77.6	118.1	83.8	101.1
COVERS	DIVS. 10 - 14, 25, 28, 41, 43, 44, 46	131.1	63.0	116.6	131.1	58.2	115.6	131.1	86.1	121.5	131.1	68.9	117.9	131.1	55.9	115.1	131.1	81.5	120.6
21, 22, 23	FIRE SUPPRESSION, PLUMBING & HVAC	108.1	84.7	99.7	109.7	85.1	100.9	108.9	95.4	104.0	116.3	77.6	102.3	109.7	73.3	96.6	108.9	83.0	99.6
26, 27, 3370	ELECTRICAL, COMMUNICATIONS & UTIL.	162.0	93.2	132.1	143.1	75.4	113.6	153.6	95.5	128.3	124.2	59.1	95.8	135.2	53.1	99.5	153.9	73.2	118.8
MF2018	WEIGHTED AVERAGE	115.4	88.8	105.3	119.2	79.2	104.1	123.7	97.8	113.9	130.7	74.1	109.3	116.5	65.4	97.2	128.1	87.4	112.7

		\multicolumn{18}{c}{CANADA}
	DIVISION	VICTORIA, BRITISH COLUMBIA			WHITEHORSE, YUKON			WINDSOR, ONTARIO			WINNIPEG, MANITOBA			YARMOUTH, NOVA SCOTIA			YELLOWKNIFE, NWT		
		MAT.	INST.	TOTAL	MAT.	INST.	TOTAL	MAT.	INST.	TOTAL	MAT.	INST.	TOTAL	MAT.	INST.	TOTAL	MAT.	INST.	TOTAL
015433	CONTRACTOR EQUIPMENT		107.6	107.6		133.0	133.0		101.9	101.9		124.2	124.2		98.1	98.1		126.7	126.7
0241, 31 - 34	SITE & INFRASTRUCTURE, DEMOLITION	144.3	102.4	117.0	151.8	120.4	131.3	110.8	97.6	102.2	143.0	115.5	125.1	126.3	91.0	103.3	159.6	116.8	131.7
0310	Concrete Forming & Accessories	122.1	81.6	88.7	147.3	52.9	69.4	127.0	84.3	91.8	138.8	59.8	73.7	122.1	63.0	73.3	155.9	70.5	85.5
0320	Concrete Reinforcing	102.0	87.3	96.0	135.4	57.7	103.6	81.4	92.5	86.0	116.2	54.6	91.0	136.0	43.4	98.2	126.5	60.0	99.4
0330	Cast-in-Place Concrete	144.6	91.1	126.7	156.6	70.5	127.8	123.2	95.1	113.8	199.4	69.4	155.9	121.6	63.8	102.2	174.9	85.4	144.9
03	CONCRETE	173.9	86.3	137.9	183.9	61.3	133.6	117.7	89.9	106.3	180.9	63.3	132.6	151.2	60.7	114.1	178.0	74.9	135.7
04	MASONRY	173.8	86.8	123.2	238.1	53.7	130.8	166.2	93.3	123.7	208.5	59.2	121.6	195.5	60.4	116.9	225.5	63.8	131.4
05	METALS	101.5	89.6	99.0	160.3	80.6	143.6	93.3	94.2	93.5	118.1	77.0	109.5	149.4	69.6	132.7	164.4	83.4	147.4
06	WOOD, PLASTICS & COMPOSITES	105.6	80.7	93.3	128.2	51.8	90.6	101.4	82.8	92.3	117.4	60.6	89.4	118.9	62.7	91.2	136.3	72.0	104.6
07	THERMAL & MOISTURE PROTECTION	116.3	85.5	106.0	129.8	62.5	107.2	112.7	92.4	105.9	131.4	66.7	109.7	116.6	63.2	98.7	131.6	76.3	113.1
08	OPENINGS	98.0	75.9	92.6	114.1	49.2	98.3	83.9	82.0	83.4	101.5	54.4	90.0	102.6	56.7	91.4	105.0	60.8	94.2
0920	Plaster & Gypsum Board	107.3	79.7	89.8	157.1	49.2	88.4	114.2	82.2	93.9	138.6	58.4	87.6	122.8	61.7	83.9	160.4	70.0	102.9
0950, 0980	Ceilings & Acoustic Treatment	86.5	79.7	82.7	127.5	49.2	83.7	93.0	82.2	87.0	131.9	58.4	90.8	91.4	61.7	74.7	125.4	70.0	94.4
0960	Flooring	115.9	61.5	102.0	125.9	50.3	106.5	103.5	85.9	99.0	147.6	61.4	125.5	105.3	53.8	92.1	121.1	75.7	109.5
0970, 0990	Wall Finishes & Painting/Coating	120.0	89.9	102.3	114.5	48.5	75.7	118.6	89.1	101.3	123.3	47.9	79.0	111.5	54.1	77.8	118.2	69.3	89.5
09	FINISHES	102.1	78.9	90.6	128.1	51.8	90.3	95.9	84.9	90.5	125.9	59.2	92.9	100.7	60.6	80.9	125.3	70.9	98.4
COVERS	DIVS. 10 - 14, 25, 28, 41, 43, 44, 46	131.1	59.9	116.0	131.1	55.9	115.1	131.1	63.0	116.6	131.1	57.8	115.5	131.1	55.6	115.0	131.1	58.9	115.8
21, 22, 23	FIRE SUPPRESSION, PLUMBING & HVAC	110.4	80.8	99.7	116.7	66.0	98.5	108.1	86.1	100.2	109.0	58.5	90.8	116.3	73.2	100.8	117.2	81.6	104.4
26, 27, 3370	ELECTRICAL, COMMUNICATIONS & UTIL.	140.9	73.9	111.7	162.7	51.7	114.4	176.2	93.8	140.3	153.9	56.7	111.6	123.5	53.1	92.9	154.1	70.2	117.6
MF2018	WEIGHTED AVERAGE	123.3	82.6	107.9	147.0	64.3	115.7	115.6	89.1	105.6	132.9	65.0	107.2	130.3	65.1	105.7	145.0	76.8	119.2

Location Factors - Commercial

Costs shown in RSMeans cost data publications are based on national averages for materials and installation. To adjust these costs to a specific location, simply multiply the base cost by the factor and divide by 100 for that city. The data is arranged alphabetically by state and postal zip code numbers. For a city not listed, use the factor for a nearby city with similar economic characteristics.

STATE/ZIP	CITY	MAT.	INST.	TOTAL
ALABAMA				
350-352	Birmingham	100.4	70.7	89.2
354	Tuscaloosa	99.0	69.2	87.7
355	Jasper	100.9	66.0	87.7
356	Decatur	99.0	64.9	86.1
357-358	Huntsville	99.0	70.5	88.2
359	Gadsden	100.5	69.3	88.7
360-361	Montgomery	99.9	69.8	88.5
362	Anniston	99.8	62.0	85.5
363	Dothan	98.1	70.2	87.6
364	Evergreen	97.8	62.8	84.6
365-366	Mobile	99.5	66.6	87.1
367	Selma	98.0	66.3	86.0
368	Phenix City	98.5	67.3	86.7
369	Butler	98.0	64.6	85.4
ALASKA				
995-996	Anchorage	124.9	108.3	118.6
997	Fairbanks	121.2	108.3	116.3
998	Juneau	117.9	107.5	114.0
999	Ketchikan	129.1	107.9	121.1
ARIZONA				
850,853	Phoenix	100.9	74.0	90.8
851,852	Mesa/Tempe	98.0	71.9	88.2
855	Globe	97.9	70.6	87.6
856-857	Tucson	96.9	74.0	88.3
859	Show Low	98.1	70.7	87.7
860	Flagstaff	101.3	71.5	90.0
863	Prescott	99.1	71.2	88.6
864	Kingman	96.8	69.7	86.6
865	Chambers	96.8	70.3	86.8
ARKANSAS				
716	Pine Bluff	100.0	61.2	85.3
717	Camden	97.1	60.0	83.1
718	Texarkana	98.4	61.1	84.3
719	Hot Springs	96.5	59.4	82.5
720-722	Little Rock	97.1	64.0	84.6
723	West Memphis	93.9	63.8	82.5
724	Jonesboro	95.2	62.9	83.0
725	Batesville	92.3	58.9	79.7
726	Harrison	93.5	58.1	80.1
727	Fayetteville	91.6	59.8	79.6
728	Russellville	92.6	58.0	79.6
729	Fort Smith	95.9	60.6	82.5
CALIFORNIA				
900-902	Los Angeles	101.1	131.2	112.5
903-905	Inglewood	93.7	130.2	107.5
906-908	Long Beach	95.3	130.2	108.5
910-912	Pasadena	94.2	130.6	107.9
913-916	Van Nuys	96.8	130.6	109.6
917-918	Alhambra	97.3	130.6	109.9
919-921	San Diego	100.1	125.2	109.6
922	Palm Springs	96.5	124.7	107.2
923-924	San Bernardino	94.2	126.9	106.6
925	Riverside	99.1	128.2	110.1
926-927	Santa Ana	96.0	127.7	108.0
928	Anaheim	99.4	126.9	109.8
930	Oxnard	100.4	127.8	110.8
931	Santa Barbara	99.5	126.0	109.5
932-933	Bakersfield	101.7	127.2	111.3
934	San Luis Obispo	99.7	127.7	110.3
935	Mojave	96.9	125.2	107.6
936-938	Fresno	100.5	132.0	112.4
939	Salinas	100.7	140.2	115.6
940-941	San Francisco	104.6	161.2	126.0
942,956-958	Sacramento	97.0	133.7	110.8
943	Palo Alto	95.4	154.0	117.5
944	San Mateo	97.7	151.5	118.0
945	Vallejo	96.9	141.1	113.6
946	Oakland	100.2	151.5	119.6
947	Berkeley	99.3	151.5	119.0
948	Richmond	98.4	144.5	115.9
949	San Rafael	100.3	147.2	118.0
950	Santa Cruz	105.1	139.9	118.2

STATE/ZIP	CITY	MAT.	INST.	TOTAL
CALIFORNIA (CONT'D)				
951	San Jose	102.7	156.4	123.0
952	Stockton	100.6	132.7	112.7
953	Modesto	100.5	132.2	112.5
954	Santa Rosa	100.0	147.9	118.1
955	Eureka	101.4	133.2	113.4
959	Marysville	100.8	131.2	112.3
960	Redding	111.1	131.0	118.6
961	Susanville	110.0	131.7	118.2
COLORADO				
800-802	Denver	101.0	76.6	91.8
803	Boulder	94.4	75.6	87.3
804	Golden	96.1	70.4	86.4
805	Fort Collins	98.1	73.0	88.7
806	Greeley	95.8	73.0	87.2
807	Fort Morgan	94.9	71.2	86.0
808-809	Colorado Springs	97.6	71.1	87.6
810	Pueblo	100.9	70.1	89.2
811	Alamosa	101.5	68.8	89.1
812	Salida	101.0	69.2	89.0
813	Durango	101.7	65.2	87.9
814	Montrose	100.3	65.5	87.1
815	Grand Junction	104.2	69.4	91.1
816	Glenwood Springs	101.6	65.6	88.0
CONNECTICUT				
060	New Britain	99.8	115.7	105.8
061	Hartford	102.2	116.6	107.7
062	Willimantic	100.5	113.6	105.5
063	New London	96.0	113.7	102.7
064	Meriden	98.0	113.6	103.9
065	New Haven	101.0	114.7	106.2
066	Bridgeport	101.1	114.8	106.3
067	Waterbury	100.8	114.8	106.1
068	Norwalk	100.7	114.8	106.0
069	Stamford	100.8	115.2	106.3
D.C.				
200-205	Washington	103.8	88.4	98.0
DELAWARE				
197	Newark	101.5	108.2	104.0
198	Wilmington	102.9	108.5	105.0
199	Dover	103.4	107.8	105.1
FLORIDA				
320,322	Jacksonville	98.5	66.7	86.5
321	Daytona Beach	98.7	68.4	87.3
323	Tallahassee	99.9	66.8	87.4
324	Panama City	99.9	67.6	87.7
325	Pensacola	103.3	65.0	88.8
326,344	Gainesville	99.6	66.0	86.9
327-328,347	Orlando	102.3	66.6	88.8
329	Melbourne	101.7	70.9	90.1
330-332,340	Miami	99.7	70.6	88.7
333	Fort Lauderdale	98.4	68.4	87.1
334,349	West Palm Beach	96.9	64.3	84.6
335-336,346	Tampa	99.7	68.8	88.0
337	St. Petersburg	102.8	64.6	88.3
338	Lakeland	99.2	65.6	86.5
339,341	Fort Myers	98.2	67.5	86.6
342	Sarasota	101.0	64.1	87.0
GEORGIA				
300-303,399	Atlanta	100.9	75.1	91.2
304	Statesboro	98.9	67.1	86.9
305	Gainesville	96.9	63.1	84.1
306	Athens	96.2	66.0	84.8
307	Dalton	98.7	65.0	86.0
308-309	Augusta	97.7	72.8	88.3
310-312	Macon	99.2	72.6	89.2
313-314	Savannah	101.4	73.0	90.7
315	Waycross	100.7	64.6	87.1
316	Valdosta	101.0	70.1	89.3
317,398	Albany	100.8	71.4	89.7
318-319	Columbus	100.6	73.5	90.4

Location Factors - Commercial

STATE/ZIP	CITY	MAT.	INST.	TOTAL
HAWAII				
967	Hilo	118.0	117.3	117.8
968	Honolulu	124.4	118.2	122.0
STATES & POSS.				
969	Guam	145.0	61.8	113.6
IDAHO				
832	Pocatello	102.3	78.5	93.3
833	Twin Falls	102.5	75.4	92.3
834	Idaho Falls	100.7	78.0	92.1
835	Lewiston	107.8	88.9	100.7
836-837	Boise	101.4	80.6	93.5
838	Coeur d'Alene	106.8	83.4	98.0
ILLINOIS				
600-603	North Suburban	97.5	141.7	114.2
604	Joliet	97.4	143.3	114.7
605	South Suburban	97.5	142.0	114.3
606-608	Chicago	100.6	144.7	117.2
609	Kankakee	93.6	132.9	108.4
610-611	Rockford	95.0	128.5	107.7
612	Rock Island	92.6	100.1	95.4
613	La Salle	93.5	126.4	105.9
614	Galesburg	93.3	106.8	98.4
615-616	Peoria	95.9	108.1	100.5
617	Bloomington	92.7	109.4	99.0
618-619	Champaign	95.7	107.9	100.3
620-622	East St. Louis	93.2	106.8	98.4
623	Quincy	94.7	106.2	99.0
624	Effingham	93.6	106.5	98.4
625	Decatur	95.9	105.9	99.7
626-627	Springfield	97.1	107.4	101.0
628	Centralia	91.4	105.2	96.6
629	Carbondale	91.2	104.1	96.1
INDIANA				
460	Anderson	95.7	78.0	89.0
461-462	Indianapolis	97.6	82.9	92.0
463-464	Gary	97.1	104.6	100.0
465-466	South Bend	100.6	82.1	93.6
467-468	Fort Wayne	96.4	78.7	89.7
469	Kokomo	92.9	77.1	87.0
470	Lawrenceburg	92.2	74.6	85.6
471	New Albany	93.4	72.4	85.5
472	Columbus	95.6	76.3	88.3
473	Muncie	96.9	76.7	89.3
474	Bloomington	98.1	78.2	90.6
475	Washington	93.7	79.7	88.4
476-477	Evansville	95.7	83.0	90.9
478	Terre Haute	96.5	80.9	90.6
479	Lafayette	95.5	78.2	89.0
IOWA				
500-503,509	Des Moines	98.3	92.1	96.0
504	Mason City	95.7	67.4	85.0
505	Fort Dodge	95.5	66.6	84.6
506-507	Waterloo	97.9	78.2	90.5
508	Creston	95.9	75.8	88.3
510-511	Sioux City	96.3	78.4	89.5
512	Sibley	94.6	56.2	80.1
513	Spencer	95.7	56.1	80.7
514	Carroll	93.5	73.8	86.1
515	Council Bluffs	97.1	80.3	90.8
516	Shenandoah	94.1	73.4	86.3
520	Dubuque	95.7	78.8	89.3
521	Decorah	94.4	66.2	83.7
522-524	Cedar Rapids	96.7	84.0	91.9
525	Ottumwa	94.1	70.5	85.2
526	Burlington	93.5	75.5	86.7
527-528	Davenport	95.7	92.0	94.3
KANSAS				
660-662	Kansas City	96.1	97.5	96.6
664-666	Topeka	97.1	75.8	89.1
667	Fort Scott	93.6	69.3	84.4
668	Emporia	93.6	69.8	84.6
669	Belleville	94.9	65.4	83.8
670-672	Wichita	96.2	73.0	87.4
673	Independence	94.8	68.9	85.0
674	Salina	95.6	70.5	86.1
675	Hutchinson	91.2	65.8	81.6
676	Hays	94.3	66.3	83.8
677	Colby	94.9	67.5	84.5

STATE/ZIP	CITY	MAT.	INST.	TOTAL
KANSAS (CONT'D)				
678	Dodge City	96.8	70.5	86.9
679	Liberal	94.4	65.6	83.5
KENTUCKY				
400-402	Louisville	98.3	79.8	91.3
403-405	Lexington	96.6	79.8	90.3
406	Frankfort	98.8	73.6	89.3
407-409	Corbin	93.5	70.7	84.9
410	Covington	93.9	79.0	88.3
411-412	Ashland	92.6	82.8	88.9
413-414	Campton	94.1	71.5	85.6
415-416	Pikeville	94.7	77.1	88.1
417-418	Hazard	93.5	72.1	85.4
420	Paducah	91.9	74.9	85.5
421-422	Bowling Green	94.9	78.5	88.7
423	Owensboro	94.5	81.8	89.7
424	Henderson	91.5	73.7	84.8
425-426	Somerset	91.5	71.8	84.1
427	Elizabethtown	91.1	68.9	82.7
LOUISIANA				
700-701	New Orleans	99.6	70.4	88.6
703	Thibodaux	95.9	61.9	83.0
704	Hammond	93.9	60.5	81.3
705	Lafayette	96.2	66.7	85.1
706	Lake Charles	96.4	68.5	85.9
707-708	Baton Rouge	99.7	68.4	87.9
710-711	Shreveport	100.7	66.9	87.9
712	Monroe	98.9	64.3	85.8
713-714	Alexandria	99.1	65.7	86.5
MAINE				
039	Kittery	95.4	80.9	89.9
040-041	Portland	102.2	88.8	97.1
042	Lewiston	98.5	86.0	93.8
043	Augusta	100.7	84.1	94.4
044	Bangor	97.5	84.0	92.4
045	Bath	95.8	82.3	90.7
046	Machias	95.0	82.2	90.2
047	Houlton	95.1	82.1	90.2
048	Rockland	94.3	82.3	89.8
049	Waterville	95.5	82.2	90.5
MARYLAND				
206	Waldorf	98.4	80.0	91.4
207-208	College Park	98.2	81.0	91.7
209	Silver Spring	97.7	80.1	91.1
210-212	Baltimore	103.4	83.5	95.9
214	Annapolis	102.8	83.1	95.3
215	Cumberland	97.4	83.6	92.2
216	Easton	99.1	67.4	87.1
217	Hagerstown	98.9	86.8	94.3
218	Salisbury	99.3	60.4	84.6
219	Elkton	96.5	77.0	89.1
MASSACHUSETTS				
010-011	Springfield	99.2	107.1	102.2
012	Pittsfield	98.3	103.1	100.1
013	Greenfield	96.0	106.8	100.1
014	Fitchburg	94.7	112.1	101.2
015-016	Worcester	99.2	114.6	105.0
017	Framingham	94.5	119.7	104.0
018	Lowell	98.4	124.5	108.3
019	Lawrence	99.5	125.8	109.4
020-022, 024	Boston	100.0	133.0	112.4
023	Brockton	98.2	117.0	105.3
025	Buzzards Bay	92.3	111.6	99.6
026	Hyannis	95.3	114.2	102.4
027	New Bedford	97.5	114.4	103.9
MICHIGAN				
480,483	Royal Oak	93.4	91.5	92.7
481	Ann Arbor	96.5	98.0	97.1
482	Detroit	98.9	99.4	99.1
484-485	Flint	96.4	89.8	93.9
486	Saginaw	96.0	85.9	92.2
487	Bay City	96.1	84.0	91.5
488-489	Lansing	99.0	90.9	95.9
490	Battle Creek	100.1	78.3	91.9
491	Kalamazoo	100.5	80.2	92.8
492	Jackson	97.7	87.9	94.0
493,495	Grand Rapids	102.6	84.0	95.6
494	Muskegon	99.0	79.7	91.7

Location Factors - Commercial

STATE/ZIP	CITY	MAT.	INST.	TOTAL
MICHIGAN (CONT'D)				
496	Traverse City	97.1	80.7	90.9
497	Gaylord	98.7	74.1	89.4
498-499	Iron Mountain	100.7	75.1	91.0
MINNESOTA				
550-551	Saint Paul	100.6	117.9	107.1
553-555	Minneapolis	99.2	119.1	106.7
556-558	Duluth	99.2	105.6	101.7
559	Rochester	97.8	104.8	100.4
560	Mankato	93.4	100.8	96.2
561	Windom	92.2	88.3	90.7
562	Willmar	92.2	104.7	96.9
563	St. Cloud	94.0	116.3	102.4
564	Brainerd	93.7	102.0	96.9
565	Detroit Lakes	95.0	89.9	93.0
566	Bemidji	94.2	96.5	95.1
567	Thief River Falls	94.0	93.1	93.7
MISSISSIPPI				
386	Clarksdale	97.4	49.6	79.3
387	Greenville	100.9	62.7	86.5
388	Tupelo	98.6	52.0	81.0
389	Greenwood	98.5	49.4	80.0
390-392	Jackson	99.2	68.2	87.5
393	Meridian	95.8	65.1	84.2
394	Laurel	96.5	52.2	79.7
395	Biloxi	97.4	64.1	84.8
396	McComb	95.1	49.9	78.0
397	Columbus	96.3	53.2	80.0
MISSOURI				
630-631	St. Louis	96.2	102.2	98.5
633	Bowling Green	92.4	87.8	90.7
634	Hannibal	91.4	83.7	88.5
635	Kirksville	94.4	79.2	88.7
636	Flat River	93.1	86.7	90.7
637	Cape Girardeau	93.9	83.8	90.1
638	Sikeston	91.9	83.6	88.8
639	Poplar Bluff	91.4	82.4	88.0
640-641	Kansas City	98.4	101.2	99.5
644-645	St. Joseph	95.1	90.1	93.2
646	Chillicothe	91.9	84.4	89.0
647	Harrisonville	91.3	94.2	92.4
648	Joplin	93.9	76.4	87.3
650-651	Jefferson City	94.1	89.9	92.5
652	Columbia	93.1	88.7	91.4
653	Sedalia	92.9	84.1	89.6
654-655	Rolla	90.6	89.3	90.1
656-658	Springfield	94.9	80.5	89.5
MONTANA				
590-591	Billings	100.2	78.2	91.9
592	Wolf Point	98.7	70.0	87.9
593	Miles City	96.8	70.0	86.7
594	Great Falls	101.0	74.0	90.8
595	Havre	97.8	68.1	86.6
596	Helena	99.7	70.3	88.6
597	Butte	99.5	72.7	89.4
598	Missoula	97.8	70.1	87.3
599	Kalispell	95.7	69.3	85.8
NEBRASKA				
680-681	Omaha	98.0	82.6	92.2
683-685	Lincoln	97.9	77.9	90.4
686	Columbus	94.0	72.6	85.9
687	Norfolk	95.2	69.8	85.6
688	Grand Island	96.0	79.0	89.6
689	Hastings	95.0	70.3	85.6
690	McCook	93.7	65.4	83.0
691	North Platte	94.5	70.6	85.5
692	Valentine	96.1	63.1	83.6
693	Alliance	96.5	66.0	85.0
NEVADA				
889-891	Las Vegas	105.0	109.5	106.7
893	Ely	103.1	82.5	95.3
894-895	Reno	103.4	89.2	98.0
897	Carson City	103.8	89.6	98.4
898	Elko	101.6	75.4	91.7
NEW HAMPSHIRE				
030	Nashua	101.4	91.9	97.9
031	Manchester	102.0	93.2	98.7

STATE/ZIP	CITY	MAT.	INST.	TOTAL
NEW HAMPSHIRE (CONT'D)				
032-033	Concord	103.0	91.9	98.8
034	Keene	96.9	80.5	90.7
035	Littleton	97.2	72.7	88.0
036	Charleston	96.7	80.0	90.4
037	Claremont	96.0	80.0	90.0
038	Portsmouth	98.1	89.0	94.7
NEW JERSEY				
070-071	Newark	100.3	136.1	113.8
072	Elizabeth	96.6	136.1	111.5
073	Jersey City	96.4	135.0	111.0
074-075	Paterson	97.2	135.9	111.8
076	Hackensack	95.4	135.1	110.4
077	Long Branch	95.4	133.4	109.7
078	Dover	95.5	135.9	110.8
079	Summit	95.7	136.1	110.9
080,083	Vineland	97.2	133.1	110.8
081	Camden	99.3	133.2	112.1
082,084	Atlantic City	97.7	133.4	111.2
085-086	Trenton	101.2	132.9	113.2
087	Point Pleasant	98.6	132.9	111.6
088-089	New Brunswick	99.2	135.7	113.0
NEW MEXICO				
870-872	Albuquerque	101.5	70.6	89.8
873	Gallup	101.0	70.6	89.5
874	Farmington	101.5	70.6	89.8
875	Santa Fe	103.1	71.3	91.1
877	Las Vegas	99.4	70.6	88.5
878	Socorro	99.2	70.6	88.4
879	Truth/Consequences	98.6	67.7	86.9
880	Las Cruces	96.6	69.0	86.2
881	Clovis	98.0	71.3	87.9
882	Roswell	99.9	71.3	89.1
883	Carrizozo	100.0	71.3	89.1
884	Tucumcari	98.6	71.3	88.3
NEW YORK				
100-102	New York	101.9	169.4	127.4
103	Staten Island	95.8	168.9	123.4
104	Bronx	94.3	168.9	122.5
105	Mount Vernon	93.2	152.9	115.7
106	White Plains	93.8	146.4	113.7
107	Yonkers	98.7	146.8	116.9
108	New Rochelle	93.5	153.6	116.2
109	Suffern	93.1	140.1	110.9
110	Queens	101.6	169.4	127.2
111	Long Island City	102.9	169.0	127.9
112	Brooklyn	103.5	169.0	128.2
113	Flushing	102.0	169.0	127.3
114	Jamaica	100.8	169.0	126.5
115,117,118	Hicksville	101.2	153.7	121.1
116	Far Rockaway	102.2	169.0	127.4
119	Riverhead	102.0	154.0	121.6
120-122	Albany	99.5	109.0	103.1
123	Schenectady	98.8	107.1	101.9
124	Kingston	101.5	134.7	114.0
125-126	Poughkeepsie	100.8	137.1	114.5
127	Monticello	100.3	137.7	114.5
128	Glens Falls	93.4	103.7	97.3
129	Plattsburgh	97.6	97.8	97.7
130-132	Syracuse	99.3	99.4	99.3
133-135	Utica	97.0	100.4	98.3
136	Watertown	98.7	98.0	98.4
137-139	Binghamton	98.9	98.7	98.8
140-142	Buffalo	102.2	107.0	104.0
143	Niagara Falls	97.7	107.8	101.5
144-146	Rochester	102.0	99.3	101.0
147	Jamestown	96.7	96.3	96.5
148-149	Elmira	96.8	98.3	97.4
NORTH CAROLINA				
270,272-274	Greensboro	99.3	62.8	85.5
271	Winston-Salem	99.0	62.8	85.3
275-276	Raleigh	98.2	63.2	85.0
277	Durham	101.1	62.8	86.6
278	Rocky Mount	95.9	62.1	83.1
279	Elizabeth City	96.6	63.0	83.9
280	Gastonia	99.7	66.8	87.3
281-282	Charlotte	99.6	70.4	88.6
283	Fayetteville	103.2	63.0	88.0
284	Wilmington	98.3	60.6	84.1
285	Kinston	96.3	61.3	83.0

Location Factors - Commercial

STATE/ZIP	CITY	MAT.	INST.	TOTAL	STATE/ZIP	CITY	MAT.	INST.	TOTAL
NORTH CAROLINA (CONT'D)					**PENNSYLVANIA (CONT'D)**				
286	Hickory	96.3	67.3	85.3	177	Williamsport	93.1	88.6	91.4
287-288	Asheville	98.7	62.4	85.0	178	Sunbury	94.9	81.7	89.9
289	Murphy	96.8	59.8	82.8	179	Pottsville	94.3	85.0	90.8
NORTH DAKOTA					180	Lehigh Valley	95.4	98.9	96.8
580-581	Fargo	98.0	75.9	89.6	181	Allentown	97.9	102.5	99.6
582	Grand Forks	96.2	76.1	88.6	182	Hazleton	95.0	85.1	91.3
583	Devils Lake	95.3	73.1	86.9	183	Stroudsburg	94.9	92.9	94.1
584	Jamestown	95.4	71.7	86.4	184-185	Scranton	98.9	93.5	96.8
585	Bismarck	97.2	84.0	92.2	186-187	Wilkes-Barre	95.0	91.8	93.8
586	Dickinson	95.5	71.7	86.5	188	Montrose	94.8	85.9	91.5
587	Minot	96.2	73.8	87.7	189	Doylestown	94.2	113.4	101.4
588	Williston	94.4	75.0	87.1	190-191	Philadelphia	101.4	135.6	114.3
OHIO					193	Westchester	97.8	113.6	103.8
430-432	Columbus	98.0	85.0	93.1	194	Norristown	97.0	115.0	103.8
433	Marion	92.5	83.5	89.1	195-196	Reading	99.3	97.9	98.8
434-436	Toledo	96.4	90.6	94.2	**PUERTO RICO**				
437-438	Zanesville	93.2	82.5	89.1	009	San Juan	126.9	33.5	91.6
439	Steubenville	93.9	86.7	91.2	**RHODE ISLAND**				
440	Lorain	96.0	83.0	91.1	028	Newport	96.7	111.2	102.2
441	Cleveland	97.8	90.0	94.9	029	Providence	102.1	111.9	105.8
442-443	Akron	96.6	87.1	93.0	**SOUTH CAROLINA**				
444-445	Youngstown	96.2	80.9	90.4	290-292	Columbia	99.7	69.2	88.2
446-447	Canton	96.3	83.1	91.3	293	Spartanburg	98.5	69.9	87.7
448-449	Mansfield	93.4	81.7	89.0	294	Charleston	100.3	68.9	88.4
450	Hamilton	95.0	78.3	88.7	295	Florence	98.5	66.3	86.3
451-452	Cincinnati	97.4	80.6	91.1	296	Greenville	98.4	70.4	87.8
453-454	Dayton	95.0	80.1	89.4	297	Rock Hill	97.4	64.6	85.0
455	Springfield	95.0	78.7	88.8	298	Aiken	98.2	61.3	84.2
456	Chillicothe	93.4	80.4	88.5	299	Beaufort	98.9	61.8	84.9
457	Athens	96.1	84.2	91.6	**SOUTH DAKOTA**				
458	Lima	96.4	79.0	89.9	570-571	Sioux Falls	99.2	81.5	92.5
OKLAHOMA					572	Watertown	95.2	64.6	83.6
730-731	Oklahoma City	99.1	70.0	88.1	573	Mitchell	94.0	58.7	80.7
734	Ardmore	96.6	65.3	84.8	574	Aberdeen	96.9	72.0	87.5
735	Lawton	99.6	66.7	87.2	575	Pierre	97.9	76.7	89.9
736	Clinton	97.7	65.2	85.4	576	Mobridge	94.6	59.7	81.4
737	Enid	98.9	65.9	86.4	577	Rapid City	97.0	68.1	86.1
738	Woodward	96.6	66.9	85.4	**TENNESSEE**				
739	Guymon	97.4	59.1	83.0	370-372	Nashville	100.4	71.5	89.5
740-741	Tulsa	96.8	66.1	85.2	373-374	Chattanooga	100.3	65.6	87.2
743	Miami	92.8	64.5	82.1	375,380-381	Memphis	101.0	70.7	89.6
744	Muskogee	95.7	65.2	84.2	376	Johnson City	99.4	55.8	82.9
745	McAlester	92.5	63.8	81.7	377-379	Knoxville	96.9	66.3	85.3
746	Ponca City	93.1	61.3	81.1	382	McKenzie	97.6	50.8	79.9
747	Durant	93.1	63.2	81.8	383	Jackson	99.8	65.4	86.8
748	Shawnee	94.4	62.6	82.4	384	Columbia	96.2	59.7	82.4
749	Poteau	92.5	63.3	81.5	385	Cookeville	97.5	52.1	80.4
OREGON					**TEXAS**				
970-972	Portland	99.8	104.0	101.4	750	McKinney	95.1	57.2	80.8
973	Salem	102.0	101.2	101.7	751	Waxahachie	95.1	64.3	83.5
974	Eugene	99.3	100.0	99.6	752-753	Dallas	97.5	65.1	85.2
975	Medford	100.3	98.4	99.6	754	Greenville	95.2	56.7	80.7
976	Klamath Falls	100.1	96.7	98.8	755	Texarkana	94.4	63.6	82.7
977	Bend	99.0	97.4	98.4	756	Longview	95.0	55.0	79.9
978	Pendleton	96.8	96.8	96.8	757	Tyler	96.3	61.3	83.1
979	Vale	94.8	85.0	91.1	758	Palestine	93.0	54.5	78.5
PENNSYLVANIA					759	Lufkin	93.6	56.9	79.8
150-152	Pittsburgh	101.9	102.2	102.0	760-761	Fort Worth	98.7	63.7	85.5
153	Washington	96.9	99.0	97.7	762	Denton	96.4	58.2	82.0
154	Uniontown	97.3	96.5	97.0	763	Wichita Falls	97.2	61.0	83.5
155	Bedford	98.1	85.7	93.4	764	Eastland	95.6	55.5	80.4
156	Greensburg	98.0	93.2	96.2	765	Temple	93.7	53.5	78.5
157	Indiana	97.0	95.0	96.3	766-767	Waco	96.4	63.4	83.9
158	Dubois	98.4	90.0	95.2	768	Brownwood	97.2	53.9	80.8
159	Johnstown	98.1	95.6	97.2	769	San Angelo	96.7	56.7	81.6
160	Butler	92.1	93.2	92.5	770-772	Houston	99.0	66.2	86.6
161	New Castle	92.1	94.7	93.1	773	Huntsville	96.2	56.8	81.3
162	Kittanning	92.5	94.3	93.2	774	Wharton	97.3	57.1	82.1
163	Oil City	92.0	87.9	90.4	775	Galveston	95.5	64.0	83.6
164-165	Erie	94.7	93.2	94.1	776-777	Beaumont	96.6	64.9	84.6
166	Altoona	94.8	94.6	94.7	778	Bryan	93.2	63.5	82.0
167	Bradford	95.6	89.1	93.1	779	Victoria	97.4	56.5	81.9
168	State College	95.2	97.1	95.9	780	Laredo	96.8	62.6	83.9
169	Wellsboro	96.1	82.3	90.9	781-782	San Antonio	97.4	65.6	85.4
170-171	Harrisburg	99.9	97.7	99.1	783-784	Corpus Christi	98.9	64.3	85.8
172	Chambersburg	95.5	78.7	89.2	785	McAllen	98.7	54.3	81.9
173-174	York	96.4	92.5	94.9	786-787	Austin	99.5	64.7	86.3
175-176	Lancaster	94.4	93.9	94.2					

For customer support on your Plumbing Costs with RSMeans Data call 800.448.8182.

Location Factors - Commercial

STATE/ZIP	CITY	MAT.	INST.	TOTAL	STATE/ZIP	CITY	MAT.	INST.	TOTAL
TEXAS (CONT'D)					**WISCONSIN (CONT'D)**				
788	Del Rio	98.6	55.1	82.1	538	Lancaster	94.0	86.8	91.2
789	Giddings	95.6	56.0	80.7	539	Portage	92.6	90.1	91.7
790-791	Amarillo	99.2	63.1	85.6	540	New Richmond	93.0	86.3	90.5
792	Childress	96.8	56.2	81.5	541-543	Green Bay	97.7	101.4	99.1
793-794	Lubbock	98.7	61.8	84.8	544	Wausau	92.3	91.0	91.8
795-796	Abilene	98.1	60.8	84.0	545	Rhinelander	95.4	84.7	91.3
797	Midland	98.3	64.5	85.5	546	La Crosse	93.6	97.3	95.0
798-799,885	El Paso	97.3	64.2	84.8	547	Eau Claire	95.1	97.9	96.1
UTAH					548	Superior	92.7	97.4	94.5
840-841	Salt Lake City	103.0	72.3	91.4	549	Oshkosh	93.0	86.7	90.6
842,844	Ogden	98.5	72.3	88.6	**WYOMING**				
843	Logan	100.2	72.3	89.7	820	Cheyenne	100.1	74.8	90.6
845	Price	100.0	63.8	86.3	821	Yellowstone Nat'l Park	97.7	69.0	86.9
846-847	Provo	100.5	72.4	89.9	822	Wheatland	98.6	68.0	87.0
VERMONT					823	Rawlins	99.8	69.3	88.3
050	White River Jct.	96.3	82.2	91.0	824	Worland	98.1	69.9	87.5
051	Bellows Falls	94.6	97.8	95.9	825	Riverton	99.0	69.4	87.8
052	Bennington	95.2	90.8	93.5	826	Casper	101.5	72.3	90.5
053	Brattleboro	95.4	97.9	96.3	827	Newcastle	98.0	69.3	87.2
054	Burlington	101.4	83.5	94.7	828	Sheridan	100.7	70.9	89.5
056	Montpelier	99.4	89.6	95.7	829-831	Rock Springs	101.8	70.0	89.8
057	Rutland	98.1	82.7	92.3	**CANADIAN FACTORS (reflect Canadian currency)**				
058	St. Johnsbury	96.5	81.8	91.0	**ALBERTA**				
059	Guildhall	95.1	81.8	90.1		Calgary	134.3	84.7	115.5
VIRGINIA						Edmonton	134.2	84.8	115.5
220-221	Fairfax	99.6	81.1	92.6		Fort McMurray	127.6	81.5	110.2
222	Arlington	101.4	79.7	93.2		Lethbridge	122.7	81.0	106.9
223	Alexandria	100.8	84.2	94.5		Lloydminster	116.6	78.1	102.0
224-225	Fredericksburg	98.7	74.2	89.5		Medicine Hat	116.9	77.4	102.0
226	Winchester	99.1	70.6	88.3		Red Deer	117.3	77.4	102.2
227	Culpeper	99.1	76.3	90.5	**BRITISH COLUMBIA**				
228	Harrisonburg	99.2	73.7	89.6		Kamloops	119.2	77.7	103.5
229	Charlottesville	99.6	68.8	88.0		Prince George	120.3	77.1	103.9
230-232	Richmond	99.9	69.8	88.6		Vancouver	128.1	87.4	112.7
233-235	Norfolk	100.7	68.7	88.6		Victoria	123.3	82.6	107.9
236	Newport News	99.3	67.8	87.4	**MANITOBA**				
237	Portsmouth	98.7	64.5	85.8		Brandon	131.1	65.3	106.2
238	Petersburg	98.0	69.5	87.2		Portage la Prairie	117.0	64.2	97.1
239	Farmville	97.3	61.8	83.9		Winnipeg	132.9	65.0	107.2
240-241	Roanoke	101.4	68.5	89.0	**NEW BRUNSWICK**				
242	Bristol	98.5	61.7	84.6		Bathurst	110.5	58.0	90.7
243	Pulaski	98.1	64.6	85.4		Dalhousie	118.8	58.1	95.9
244	Staunton	99.1	63.6	85.7		Fredericton	130.1	64.6	105.4
245	Lynchburg	99.0	70.6	88.3		Moncton	110.5	73.8	96.6
246	Grundy	98.5	58.9	83.6		Newcastle	110.6	58.6	91.0
WASHINGTON						St. John	112.6	74.2	98.1
980-981,987	Seattle	100.6	114.8	105.9	**NEWFOUNDLAND**				
982	Everett	100.9	105.5	102.6		Corner Brook	135.4	63.3	108.2
983-984	Tacoma	101.5	108.1	104.0		St. Johns	126.1	79.9	108.7
985	Olympia	101.9	108.7	104.5	**NORTHWEST TERRITORIES**				
986	Vancouver	103.1	100.5	102.1		Yellowknife	145.0	76.8	119.2
988	Wenatchee	100.5	83.1	93.9	**NOVA SCOTIA**				
989	Yakima	101.4	95.0	99.0		Bridgewater	117.0	65.4	97.5
990-992	Spokane	100.6	87.7	95.7		Dartmouth	132.3	65.1	106.9
993	Richland	100.0	93.1	97.4		Halifax	115.4	81.4	102.5
994	Clarkston	98.8	73.5	89.3		New Glasgow	130.4	65.1	105.7
WEST VIRGINIA						Sydney	128.5	65.1	104.6
247-248	Bluefield	97.3	85.0	92.7		Truro	116.5	65.4	97.2
249	Lewisburg	99.2	87.2	94.6		Yarmouth	130.3	65.1	105.7
250-253	Charleston	98.5	89.0	94.9	**ONTARIO**				
254	Martinsburg	97.3	75.9	89.2		Barrie	120.5	80.9	105.5
255-257	Huntington	99.6	88.4	95.4		Brantford	118.8	84.2	105.7
258-259	Beckley	96.0	86.6	92.5		Cornwall	118.3	81.1	104.3
260	Wheeling	100.6	88.4	96.0		Hamilton	125.2	91.9	112.6
261	Parkersburg	99.7	86.9	94.9		Kingston	119.4	81.2	105.0
262	Buckhannon	98.5	88.5	94.7		Kitchener	116.0	89.3	105.9
263-264	Clarksburg	99.1	88.9	95.3		London	127.8	89.9	113.5
265	Morgantown	99.1	89.7	95.5		North Bay	133.2	78.9	112.7
266	Gassaway	98.5	85.2	93.5		Oshawa	118.3	91.6	108.2
267	Romney	98.6	86.7	94.1		Ottawa	124.0	91.4	111.7
268	Petersburg	98.2	86.8	93.9		Owen Sound	120.7	79.3	105.1
WISCONSIN						Peterborough	118.8	80.9	104.5
530,532	Milwaukee	97.1	108.4	101.4		Sarnia	119.4	84.8	106.3
531	Kenosha	97.7	105.8	100.7					
534	Racine	96.9	105.0	100.0					
535	Beloit	96.7	100.8	98.2					
537	Madison	99.7	103.7	101.2					

Location Factors - Commercial

STATE/ZIP	CITY	MAT.	INST.	TOTAL
ONTARIO (CONT'D)				
	Sault Ste. Marie	114.3	83.0	102.5
	St. Catharines	114.4	89.9	105.1
	Sudbury	113.7	88.5	104.2
	Thunder Bay	115.4	88.8	105.3
	Timmins	119.2	79.2	104.1
	Toronto	123.7	97.8	113.9
	Windsor	115.6	89.1	105.6
PRINCE EDWARD ISLAND				
	Charlottetown	122.8	56.1	97.6
	Summerside	132.5	53.6	102.7
QUEBEC				
	Cap-de-la-Madeleine	115.6	74.4	100.0
	Charlesbourg	115.6	74.4	100.0
	Chicoutimi	109.9	85.7	100.7
	Gatineau	115.3	74.2	99.8
	Granby	115.9	74.2	100.1
	Hull	116.0	74.2	100.2
	Joliette	116.1	74.4	100.4
	Laval	115.6	74.8	100.1
	Montreal	119.9	87.6	107.7
	Quebec City	119.6	88.1	107.7
	Rimouski	115.4	85.7	104.2
	Rouyn-Noranda	115.6	74.2	100.0
	Saint-Hyacinthe	115.1	74.2	99.6
	Sherbrooke	115.8	74.2	100.1
	Sorel	116.1	74.4	100.4
	Saint-Jerome	115.8	74.2	100.1
	Trois-Rivieres	130.7	74.1	109.3
SASKATCHEWAN				
	Moose Jaw	114.4	59.4	93.6
	Prince Albert	113.5	57.9	92.5
	Regina	126.7	83.2	110.3
	Saskatoon	117.6	79.8	103.4
YUKON				
	Whitehorse	147.0	64.3	115.7

General Requirements — R0111 Summary of Work

R011105-05 Tips for Accurate Estimating

1. Use computer applications or pre-printed forms for orderly sequence of dimensions and locations. Keep track of phone conversations by recording (with permission) or note taking on computer applications or pre-printed forms.
2. Use only the front side if pre-printed forms are necessary. Label all pre-printed forms with the same convention.
3. Be consistent in listing dimensions: For example, length x width x height. This helps in rechecking to ensure that, the total length of partitions is appropriate for the building area.
4. Use printed (rather than measured) dimensions where given.
5. Add up multiple printed dimensions for a single entry where possible.
6. Measure all other dimensions carefully.
7. Use each set of dimensions to calculate multiple related quantities.
8. Convert foot and inch measurements to decimal feet when listing. Memorize decimal equivalents to .01 parts of a foot (1/8" equals approximately .01').
9. Do not "round off" quantities until the final summary.
10. Mark drawings with different colors as items are taken off.
11. Keep similar items together, different items separate.
12. Identify location and drawing numbers to aid in future checking for completeness.
13. Measure or list everything on the drawings or mentioned in the specifications.
14. It may be necessary to list items not called for to make the job complete.
15. Be alert for: Notes on plans such as N.T.S. (not to scale); changes in scale throughout the drawings; reduced size drawings; discrepancies between the specifications and the drawings.
16. Develop a consistent pattern of performing an estimate. For example:
    a. Start the quantity takeoff at the lower floor and move to the next higher floor.
    b. Proceed from the main section of the building to the wings.
    c. Proceed from south to north or vice versa, clockwise or counterclockwise.
    d. Take off floor plan quantities first, elevations next, then detail drawings.
17. List all gross dimensions that can be either used again for different quantities, or used as a rough check of other quantities for verification (exterior perimeter, gross floor area, individual floor areas, etc.).
18. Utilize design symmetry or repetition (repetitive floors, repetitive wings, symmetrical design around a center line, similar room layouts, etc.). Note: Extreme caution is needed here so as not to omit or duplicate an area.
19. Do not convert units until the final total is obtained. For instance, when estimating concrete work, keep all units to the nearest cubic foot, then summarize and convert to cubic yards.
20. When figuring alternatives, it is best to total all items involved in the basic system, then total all items involved in the alternates. Therefore you work with positive numbers in all cases. When adds and deducts are used, it is often confusing whether to add or subtract a portion of an item; especially on a complicated or involved alternate.

R011105-10 Unit Gross Area Requirements

The figures in the table below indicate typical ranges in square feet as a function of the "occupant" unit. This table is best used in the preliminary design stages to help determine the probable size requirement for the total project.

Building Type	Unit	Gross Area in S.F.		
		1/4	Median	3/4
Apartments	Unit	660	860	1,100
Auditorium & Play Theaters	Seat	18	25	38
Bowling Alleys	Lane		940	
Churches & Synagogues	Seat	20	28	39
Dormitories	Bed	200	230	275
Fraternity & Sorority Houses	Bed	220	315	370
Garages, Parking	Car	325	355	385
Hospitals	Bed	685	850	1,075
Hotels	Rental Unit	475	600	710
Housing for the elderly	Unit	515	635	755
Housing, Public	Unit	700	875	1,030
Ice Skating Rinks	Total	27,000	30,000	36,000
Motels	Rental Unit	360	465	620
Nursing Homes	Bed	290	350	450
Restaurants	Seat	23	29	39
Schools, Elementary	Pupil	65	77	90
Junior High & Middle	↓	85	110	129
Senior High		102	130	145
Vocational		110	135	195
Shooting Ranges	Point		450	
Theaters & Movies	Seat		15	

General Requirements — R0111 Summary of Work

R011105-20 Floor Area Ratios

Table below lists commonly used gross to net area and net to gross area ratios expressed in % for various building types.

Building Type	Gross to Net Ratio	Net to Gross Ratio	Building Type	Gross to Net Ratio	Net to Gross Ratio
Apartment	156	64	School Buildings (campus type)		
Bank	140	72	Administrative	150	67
Church	142	70	Auditorium	142	70
Courthouse	162	61	Biology	161	62
Department Store	123	81	Chemistry	170	59
Garage	118	85	Classroom	152	66
Hospital	183	55	Dining Hall	138	72
Hotel	158	63	Dormitory	154	65
Laboratory	171	58	Engineering	164	61
Library	132	76	Fraternity	160	63
Office	135	75	Gymnasium	142	70
Restaurant	141	70	Science	167	60
Warehouse	108	93	Service	120	83
			Student Union	172	59

The gross area of a building is the total floor area based on outside dimensions.

The net area of a building is the usable floor area for the function intended and excludes such items as stairways, corridors and mechanical rooms. In the case of a commercial building, it might be considered as the "leasable area."

General Requirements — R0111 Summary of Work

R011105-30 Occupancy Determinations

Function of Space	SF/Person Required
Accessory storage areas, mechanical equipment rooms	300
Agriculture Building	300
Aircraft Hangars	500
Airport Terminal	
Baggage claim	20
Baggage handling	300
Concourse	100
Waiting areas	15
Assembly	
Gaming floors (keno, slots, etc.)	11
Exhibit Gallery and Museum	30
Assembly w/ fixed seats	load determined by seat number
Assembly w/o fixed seats	
Concentrated (chairs only-not fixed)	7
Standing space	5
Unconcentrated (tables and chairs)	15
Bowling centers, allow 5 persons for each lane including 15 feet of runway, and for additional areas	7
Business areas	100
Courtrooms-other than fixed seating areas	40
Day care	35
Dormitories	50
Educational	
Classroom areas	20
Shops and other vocational room areas	50
Exercise rooms	50
Fabrication and Manufacturing areas where hazardous materials are used	200
Industrial areas	100
Institutional areas	
Inpatient treatment areas	240
Outpatient areas	100
Sleeping areas	120
Kitchens commercial	200
Library	
Reading rooms	50
Stack area	100
Mercantile	
Areas on other floors	60
Basement and grade floor areas	30
Storage, stock, shipping areas	300
Parking garages	200
Residential	200
Skating rinks, swimming pools	
Rink and pool	50
Decks	15
Stages and platforms	15
Warehouses	500

Excerpted from the 2012 *International Building Code*, Copyright 2011. Washington, D.C.: International Code Council. Reproduced with permission. All rights reserved. www.ICCSAFE.org

General Requirements R0111 Summary of Work

R011105-40 Weather Data and Design Conditions

City	Latitude (1) 0	1'	Winter Temperatures (1) Med. of Annual Extremes	99%	97½%	Winter Degree Days (2)	Summer (Design Dry Bulb) Temperatures and Relative Humidity 1%	2½%	5%
UNITED STATES									
Albuquerque, NM	35	0	5.1	12	16	4,400	96/61	94/61	92/61
Atlanta, GA	33	4	11.9	17	22	3,000	94/74	92/74	90/73
Baltimore, MD	39	2	7	14	17	4,600	94/75	91/75	89/74
Birmingham, AL	33	3	13	17	21	2,600	96/74	94/75	92/74
Bismarck, ND	46	5	-32	-23	-19	8,800	95/68	91/68	88/67
Boise, ID	43	3	1	3	10	5,800	96/65	94/64	91/64
Boston, MA	42	2	-1	6	9	5,600	91/73	88/71	85/70
Burlington, VT	44	3	-17	-12	-7	8,200	88/72	85/70	82/69
Charleston, WV	38	2	3	7	11	4,400	92/74	90/73	87/72
Charlotte, NC	35	1	13	18	22	3,200	95/74	93/74	91/74
Casper, WY	42	5	-21	-11	-5	7,400	92/58	90/57	87/57
Chicago, IL	41	5	-8	-3	2	6,600	94/75	91/74	88/73
Cincinnati, OH	39	1	0	1	6	4,400	92/73	90/72	88/72
Cleveland, OH	41	2	-3	1	5	6,400	91/73	88/72	86/71
Columbia, SC	34	0	16	20	24	2,400	97/76	95/75	93/75
Dallas, TX	32	5	14	18	22	2,400	102/75	100/75	97/75
Denver, CO	39	5	-10	-5	1	6,200	93/59	91/59	89/59
Des Moines, IA	41	3	-14	-10	-5	6,600	94/75	91/74	88/73
Detroit, MI	42	2	-3	3	6	6,200	91/73	88/72	86/71
Great Falls, MT	47	3	-25	-21	-15	7,800	91/60	88/60	85/59
Hartford, CT	41	5	-4	3	7	6,200	91/74	88/73	85/72
Houston, TX	29	5	24	28	33	1,400	97/77	95/77	93/77
Indianapolis, IN	39	4	-7	-2	2	5,600	92/74	90/74	87/73
Jackson, MS	32	2	16	21	25	2,200	97/76	95/76	93/76
Kansas City, MO	39	1	-4	2	6	4,800	99/75	96/74	93/74
Las Vegas, NV	36	1	18	25	28	2,800	108/66	106/65	104/65
Lexington, KY	38	0	-1	3	8	4,600	93/73	91/73	88/72
Little Rock, AR	34	4	11	15	20	3,200	99/76	96/77	94/77
Los Angeles, CA	34	0	36	41	43	2,000	93/70	89/70	86/69
Memphis, TN	35	0	10	13	18	3,200	98/77	95/76	93/76
Miami, FL	25	5	39	44	47	200	91/77	90/77	89/77
Milwaukee, WI	43	0	-11	-8	-4	7,600	90/74	87/73	84/71
Minneapolis, MN	44	5	-22	-16	-12	8,400	92/75	89/73	86/71
New Orleans, LA	30	0	28	29	33	1,400	93/78	92/77	90/77
New York, NY	40	5	6	11	15	5,000	92/74	89/73	87/72
Norfolk, VA	36	5	15	20	22	3,400	93/77	91/76	89/76
Oklahoma City, OK	35	2	4	9	13	3,200	100/74	97/74	95/73
Omaha, NE	41	2	-13	-8	-3	6,600	94/76	91/75	88/74
Philadelphia, PA	39	5	6	10	14	4,400	93/75	90/74	87/72
Phoenix, AZ	33	3	27	31	34	1,800	109/71	107/71	105/71
Pittsburgh, PA	40	3	-1	3	7	6,000	91/72	88/71	86/70
Portland, ME	43	4	-10	-6	-1	7,600	87/72	84/71	81/69
Portland, OR	45	4	18	17	23	4,600	89/68	85/67	81/65
Portsmouth, NH	43	1	-8	-2	2	7,200	89/73	85/71	83/70
Providence, RI	41	4	-1	5	9	6,000	89/73	86/72	83/70
Rochester, NY	43	1	-5	1	5	6,800	91/73	88/71	85/70
Salt Lake City, UT	40	5	0	3	8	6,000	97/62	95/62	92/61
San Francisco, CA	37	5	36	38	40	3,000	74/63	71/62	69/61
Seattle, WA	47	4	22	22	27	5,200	85/68	82/66	78/65
Sioux Falls, SD	43	4	-21	-15	-11	7,800	94/73	91/72	88/71
St. Louis, MO	38	4	-3	3	8	5,000	98/75	94/75	91/75
Tampa, FL	28	0	32	36	40	680	92/77	91/77	90/76
Trenton, NJ	40	1	4	11	14	5,000	91/75	88/74	85/73
Washington, DC	38	5	7	14	17	4,200	93/75	91/74	89/74
Wichita, KS	37	4	-3	3	7	4,600	101/72	98/73	96/73
Wilmington, DE	39	4	5	10	14	5,000	92/74	89/74	87/73
ALASKA									
Anchorage	61	1	-29	-23	-18	10,800	71/59	68/58	66/56
Fairbanks	64	5	-59	-51	-47	14,280	82/62	78/60	75/59
CANADA									
Edmonton, Alta.	53	3	-30	-29	-25	11,000	85/66	82/65	79/63
Halifax, N.S.	44	4	-4	1	5	8,000	79/66	76/65	74/64
Montreal, Que.	45	3	-20	-16	-10	9,000	88/73	85/72	83/71
Saskatoon, Sask.	52	1	-35	-35	-31	11,000	89/68	86/66	83/65
St. John's, N.F.	47	4	1	3	7	8,600	77/66	75/65	73/64
Saint John, N.B.	45	2	-15	-12	-8	8,200	80/67	77/65	75/64
Toronto, Ont.	43	4	-10	-5	-1	7,000	90/73	87/72	85/71
Vancouver, B.C.	49	1	13	15	19	6,000	79/67	77/66	74/65
Winnipeg, Man.	49	5	-31	-30	-27	10,800	89/73	86/71	84/70

(1) Handbook of Fundamentals, ASHRAE, Inc., NY 1989
(2) Local Climatological Annual Survey, USDC Env. Science Services Administration, Asheville, NC

General Requirements — R0111 Summary of Work

R011105-50 Metric Conversion Factors

Description: This table is primarily for converting customary U.S. units in the left hand column to SI metric units in the right hand column. In addition, conversion factors for some commonly encountered Canadian and non-SI metric units are included.

	If You Know		Multiply By		To Find
Length	Inches	x	25.4[a]	=	Millimeters
	Feet	x	0.3048[a]	=	Meters
	Yards	x	0.9144[a]	=	Meters
	Miles (statute)	x	1.609	=	Kilometers
Area	Square inches	x	645.2	=	Square millimeters
	Square feet	x	0.0929	=	Square meters
	Square yards	x	0.8361	=	Square meters
Volume (Capacity)	Cubic inches	x	16,387	=	Cubic millimeters
	Cubic feet	x	0.02832	=	Cubic meters
	Cubic yards	x	0.7646	=	Cubic meters
	Gallons (U.S. liquids)[b]	x	0.003785	=	Cubic meters[c]
	Gallons (Canadian liquid)[b]	x	0.004546	=	Cubic meters[c]
	Ounces (U.S. liquid)[b]	x	29.57	=	Milliliters[c,d]
	Quarts (U.S. liquid)[b]	x	0.9464	=	Liters[c,d]
	Gallons (U.S. liquid)[b]	x	3.785	=	Liters[c,d]
Force	Kilograms force[d]	x	9.807	=	Newtons
	Pounds force	x	4.448	=	Newtons
	Pounds force	x	0.4536	=	Kilograms force[d]
	Kips	x	4448	=	Newtons
	Kips	x	453.6	=	Kilograms force[d]
Pressure, Stress, Strength (Force per unit area)	Kilograms force per square centimeter[d]	x	0.09807	=	Megapascals
	Pounds force per square inch (psi)	x	0.006895	=	Megapascals
	Kips per square inch	x	6.895	=	Megapascals
	Pounds force per square inch (psi)	x	0.07031	=	Kilograms force per square centimeter[d]
	Pounds force per square foot	x	47.88	=	Pascals
	Pounds force per square foot	x	4.882	=	Kilograms force per square meter[d]
Flow	Cubic feet per minute	x	0.4719	=	Liters per second
	Gallons per minute	x	0.0631	=	Liters per second
	Gallons per hour	x	1.05	=	Milliliters per second
Bending Moment Or Torque	Inch-pounds force	x	0.01152	=	Meter-kilograms force[d]
	Inch-pounds force	x	0.1130	=	Newton-meters
	Foot-pounds force	x	0.1383	=	Meter-kilograms force[d]
	Foot-pounds force	x	1.356	=	Newton-meters
	Meter-kilograms force[d]	x	9.807	=	Newton-meters
Mass	Ounces (avoirdupois)	x	28.35	=	Grams
	Pounds (avoirdupois)	x	0.4536	=	Kilograms
	Tons (metric)	x	1000	=	Kilograms
	Tons, short (2000 pounds)	x	907.2	=	Kilograms
	Tons, short (2000 pounds)	x	0.9072	=	Megagrams[e]
Mass per Unit Volume	Pounds mass per cubic foot	x	16.02	=	Kilograms per cubic meter
	Pounds mass per cubic yard	x	0.5933	=	Kilograms per cubic meter
	Pounds mass per gallon (U.S. liquid)[b]	x	119.8	=	Kilograms per cubic meter
	Pounds mass per gallon (Canadian liquid)[b]	x	99.78	=	Kilograms per cubic meter
Temperature	Degrees Fahrenheit	(F-32)/1.8		=	Degrees Celsius
	Degrees Fahrenheit	(F+459.67)/1.8		=	Degrees Kelvin
	Degrees Celsius	C+273.15		=	Degrees Kelvin

[a] The factor given is exact
[b] One U.S. gallon = 0.8327 Canadian gallon
[c] 1 liter = 1000 milliliters = 1000 cubic centimeters
  1 cubic decimeter = 0.001 cubic meter
[d] Metric but not SI unit
[e] Called "tonne" in England and "metric ton" in other metric countries

General Requirements — R0111 Summary of Work

R011105-60 Weights and Measures

Measures of Length
1 Mile = 1760 Yards = 5280 Feet
1 Yard = 3 Feet = 36 inches
1 Foot = 12 Inches
1 Mil = 0.001 Inch
1 Fathom = 2 Yards = 6 Feet
1 Rod = 5.5 Yards = 16.5 Feet
1 Hand = 4 Inches
1 Span = 9 Inches
1 Micro-inch = One Millionth Inch or 0.000001 Inch
1 Micron = One Millionth Meter + 0.00003937 Inch

Surveyor's Measure
1 Mile = 8 Furlongs = 80 Chains
1 Furlong = 10 Chains = 220 Yards
1 Chain = 4 Rods = 22 Yards = 66 Feet = 100 Links
1 Link = 7.92 Inches

Square Measure
1 Square Mile = 640 Acres = 6400 Square Chains
1 Acre = 10 Square Chains = 4840 Square Yards = 43,560 Sq. Ft.
1 Square Chain = 16 Square Rods = 484 Square Yards = 4356 Sq. Ft.
1 Square Rod = 30.25 Square Yards = 272.25 Square Feet = 625 Square Lines
1 Square Yard = 9 Square Feet
1 Square Foot = 144 Square Inches
An Acre equals a Square 208.7 Feet per Side

Cubic Measure
1 Cubic Yard = 27 Cubic Feet
1 Cubic Foot = 1728 Cubic Inches
1 Cord of Wood = 4 x 4 x 8 Feet = 128 Cubic Feet
1 Perch of Masonry = 16½ x 1½ x 1 Foot = 24.75 Cubic Feet

Avoirdupois or Commercial Weight
1 Gross or Long Ton = 2240 Pounds
1 Net or Short Ton = 2000 Pounds
1 Pound = 16 Ounces = 7000 Grains
1 Ounce = 16 Drachms = 437.5 Grains
1 Stone = 14 Pounds

Power
1 British Thermal Unit per Hour = 0.2931 Watts
1 Ton (Refrigeration) = 3.517 Kilowatts
1 Horsepower (Boiler) = 9.81 Kilowatts
1 Horsepower (550 ft-lb/s) = 0.746 Kilowatts

Shipping Measure
For Measuring Internal Capacity of a Vessel:
    1 Register Ton = 100 Cubic Feet

For Measurement of Cargo:
    Approximately 40 Cubic Feet of Merchandise is considered a Shipping Ton, unless that bulk would weigh more than 2000 Pounds, in which case Freight Charge may be based upon weight.

40 Cubic Feet = 32.143 U.S. Bushels = 31.16 Imp. Bushels

Liquid Measure
1 Imperial Gallon = 1.2009 U.S. Gallon = 277.42 Cu. In.
1 Cubic Foot = 7.48 U.S. Gallons

General Requirements — R0111 Summary of Work

R011110-30 Engineering Fees

Typical **Structural Engineering Fees** based on type of construction and total project size. These fees are included in Architectural Fees.

Type of Construction	Total Project Size (in thousands of dollars)			
	$500	$500-$1,000	$1,000-$5,000	Over $5000
Industrial buildings, factories & warehouses	Technical payroll times 2.0 to 2.5	1.60%	1.25%	1.00%
Hotels, apartments, offices, dormitories, hospitals, public buildings, food stores		2.00%	1.70%	1.20%
Museums, banks, churches and cathedrals		2.00%	1.75%	1.25%
Thin shells, prestressed concrete, earthquake resistive		2.00%	1.75%	1.50%
Parking ramps, auditoriums, stadiums, convention halls, hangars & boiler houses		2.50%	2.00%	1.75%
Special buildings, major alterations, underpinning & future expansion	↓	Add to above 0.5%	Add to above 0.5%	Add to above 0.5%

For complex reinforced concrete or unusually complicated structures, add 20% to 50%.

Typical **Mechanical and Electrical Engineering Fees** are based on the size of the subcontract. The fee structure for both is shown below. These fees are included in Architectural Fees.

Type of Construction	Subcontract Size							
	$25,000	$50,000	$100,000	$225,000	$350,000	$500,000	$750,000	$1,000,000
Simple structures	6.4%	5.7%	4.8%	4.5%	4.4%	4.3%	4.2%	4.1%
Intermediate structures	8.0	7.3	6.5	5.6	5.1	5.0	4.9	4.8
Complex structures	10.1	9.0	9.0	8.0	7.5	7.5	7.0	7.0

For renovations, add 15% to 25% to applicable fee.

General Requirements — R0121 Allowances

R012153-10 Repair and Remodeling

Cost figures are based on new construction utilizing the most cost-effective combination of labor, equipment and material with the work scheduled in proper sequence to allow the various trades to accomplish their work in an efficient manner.

The costs for repair and remodeling work must be modified due to the following factors that may be present in any given repair and remodeling project.

1. Equipment usage curtailment due to the physical limitations of the project, with only hand-operated equipment being used.
2. Increased requirement for shoring and bracing to hold up the building while structural changes are being made and to allow for temporary storage of construction materials on above-grade floors.
3. Material handling becomes more costly due to having to move within the confines of an enclosed building. For multi-story construction, low capacity elevators and stairwells may be the only access to the upper floors.
4. Large amount of cutting and patching and attempting to match the existing construction is required. It is often more economical to remove entire walls rather than create many new door and window openings. This sort of trade-off has to be carefully analyzed.
5. Cost of protection of completed work is increased since the usual sequence of construction usually cannot be accomplished.
6. Economies of scale usually associated with new construction may not be present. If small quantities of components must be custom fabricated due to job requirements, unit costs will naturally increase. Also, if only small work areas are available at a given time, job scheduling between trades becomes difficult and subcontractor quotations may reflect the excessive start-up and shut-down phases of the job.
7. Work may have to be done on other than normal shifts and may have to be done around an existing production facility which has to stay in production during the course of the repair and remodeling.
8. Dust and noise protection of adjoining non-construction areas can involve substantial special protection and alter usual construction methods.
9. Job may be delayed due to unexpected conditions discovered during demolition or removal. These delays ultimately increase construction costs.
10. Piping and ductwork runs may not be as simple as for new construction. Wiring may have to be snaked through walls and floors.
11. Matching "existing construction" may be impossible because materials may no longer be manufactured. Substitutions may be expensive.
12. Weather protection of existing structure requires additional temporary structures to protect building at openings.
13. On small projects, because of local conditions, it may be necessary to pay a tradesman for a minimum of four hours for a task that is completed in one hour.

All of the above areas can contribute to increased costs for a repair and remodeling project. Each of the above factors should be considered in the planning, bidding and construction stage in order to minimize the increased costs associated with repair and remodeling jobs.

General Requirements R0121 Allowances

R012153-60 Security Factors

Contractors entering, working in, and exiting secure facilities often lose productive time during a normal workday. The recommended allowances in this section are intended to provide for the loss of productivity by increasing labor costs. Note that different costs are associated with searches upon entry only and searches upon entry and exit. Time spent in a queue is unpredictable and not part of these allowances. Contractors should plan ahead for this situation.

Security checkpoints are designed to reflect the level of security required to gain access or egress. An extreme example is when contractors, along with any materials, tools, equipment, and vehicles, must be physically searched and have all materials, tools, equipment, and vehicles inventoried and documented prior to both entry and exit.

Physical searches without going through the documentation process represent the next level and take up less time.

Electronic searches—passing through a detector or x-ray machine with no documentation of materials, tools, equipment, and vehicles—take less time than physical searches.

Visual searches of materials, tools, equipment, and vehicles represent the next level of security.

Finally, access by means of an ID card or displayed sticker takes the least amount of time.

Another consideration is if the searches described above are performed each and every day, or if they are performed only on the first day with access granted by ID card or displayed sticker for the remainder of the project. The figures for this situation have been calculated to represent the initial check-in as described and subsequent entry by ID card or displayed sticker for up to 20 days on site. For the situation described above, where the time period is beyond 20 days, the impact on labor cost is negligible.

There are situations where tradespeople must be accompanied by an escort and observed during the work day. The loss of freedom of movement will slow down productivity for the tradesperson. Costs for the observer have not been included. Those costs are normally born by the owner.

R012153-65 Infectious Disease Precautions

Contractors entering and working on job sites may be required to take precautions to prevent the spread of infectious diseases. Those precautions will reduce the amount of productive time during a normal workday. The recommended allowances in this section are intended to provide for the loss of productive time by increasing labor costs.

The estimator should be aware that one, many or none of these precautions apply to the line items in an estimate. Job site requirements and sound judgement must be applied.

Labor cost implications are based upon:

Temperature checks	Once per day
Donning/doffing masks and gloves	Four times per day (2 times each)
Washing hands (additional over normal)	Eight times per day
Informational meetings	Once per day
Maintaining social distance	Throughout the day
Disinfecting tools or equipment	Throughout the day

General Requirements — R0129 Payment Procedures

R012909-80 Sales Tax by State

State sales tax on materials is tabulated below (5 states have no sales tax). Many states allow local jurisdictions, such as a county or city, to levy additional sales tax.

Some projects may be sales tax exempt, particularly those constructed with public funds.

State	Tax (%)	State	Tax (%)	State	Tax (%)	State	Tax (%)
Alabama	4	Illinois	6.25	Montana	0	Rhode Island	7
Alaska	0	Indiana	7	Nebraska	5.5	South Carolina	6
Arizona	5.6	Iowa	6	Nevada	6.85	South Dakota	4.5
Arkansas	6.5	Kansas	6.5	New Hampshire	0	Tennessee	7
California	7.25	Kentucky	6	New Jersey	6.625	Texas	6.25
Colorado	2.9	Louisiana	4.45	New Mexico	5.000	Utah	6.10
Connecticut	6.35	Maine	5.5	New York	4	Vermont	6
Delaware	0	Maryland	6	North Carolina	4.75	Virginia	5.3
District of Columbia	6	Massachusetts	6.25	North Dakota	5	Washington	6.5
Florida	6	Michigan	6	Ohio	5.75	West Virginia	6
Georgia	4	Minnesota	6.875	Oklahoma	4.5	Wisconsin	5
Hawaii	4	Mississippi	7	Oregon	0	Wyoming	4
Idaho	6	Missouri	4.225	Pennsylvania	6	Average	5.10%

Sales Tax by Province (Canada)

GST - a value-added tax, which the government imposes on most goods and services provided in or imported into Canada. PST - a retail sales tax, which five of the provinces impose on the prices of most goods and some services. QST - a value-added tax, similar to the federal GST, which Quebec imposes. HST - Three provinces have combined their retail sales taxes with the federal GST into one harmonized tax.

Province	PST (%)	QST (%)	GST (%)	HST (%)
Alberta	0	0	5	0
British Columbia	7	0	5	0
Manitoba	7	0	5	0
New Brunswick	0	0	0	15
Newfoundland	0	0	0	15
Northwest Territories	0	0	5	0
Nova Scotia	0	0	0	15
Ontario	8	0	0	13
Prince Edward Island	0	0	0	15
Quebec	9.975	0	5	0
Saskatchewan	6	0	5	0
Yukon	0	0	5	0

General Requirements   R0129 Payment Procedures

R012909-85 Unemployment Taxes and Social Security Taxes

State unemployment tax rates vary not only from state to state, but also with the experience rating of the contractor. The federal unemployment tax rate is 6.0% of the first $7,000 of wages. This is reduced by a credit of up to 5.4% for timely payment to the state. The minimum federal unemployment tax is 0.6% after all credits.

Social security (FICA) for 2024 is estimated at time of publication to be 7.65% of wages up to $160,200.

R012909-86 Unemployment Tax by State

Information is from the U.S. Department of Labor, state unemployment tax rates.

State	Tax (%)	State	Tax (%)	State	Tax (%)	State	Tax (%)
Alabama	5.34	Illinois	8.65	Montana	6.12	Rhode Island	5.40
Alaska	5.4	Indiana	7.4	Nebraska	5.4	South Carolina	5.46
Arizona	18.78	Iowa	7	Nevada	5.4	South Dakota	9.3
Arkansas	14.2	Kansas	6.4	New Hampshire	8.5	Tennessee	10.0
California	6.2	Kentucky	9.0	New Jersey	6.4	Texas	6.2
Colorado	10.39	Louisiana	6.2	New Mexico	6.4	Utah	7.3
Connecticut	6.8	Maine	5.47	New York	9.82	Vermont	5.4
Delaware	8.20	Maryland	10.50	North Carolina	5.76	Virginia	6.43
District of Columbia	7.4	Massachusetts	8.62	North Dakota	9.97	Washington	5.78
Florida	5.4	Michigan	10.3	Ohio	10.3	West Virginia	8.5
Georgia	8.1	Minnesota	8.9	Oklahoma	9.2	Wisconsin	12.0
Hawaii	6.2	Mississippi	5.4	Oregon	5.4	Wyoming	10.0
Idaho	5.4	Missouri	5.4	Pennsylvania	10.37	Median	7.00%

R012909-90 Overtime

One way to improve the completion date of a project or eliminate negative float from a schedule is to compress activity duration times. This can be achieved by increasing the crew size or working overtime with the proposed crew.

To determine the costs of working overtime to compress activity duration times, consider the following examples. Below is an overtime efficiency and cost chart based on a five, six, or seven day week with an eight through twelve hour day. Payroll percentage increases for time and one half and double times are shown for the various working days.

Days per Week	Hours per Day	Production Efficiency					Payroll Cost Factors	
		1st Week	2nd Week	3rd Week	4th Week	Average 4 Weeks	@ 1-1/2 Times	@ 2 Times
5	8	100%	100%	100%	100%	100%	1.000	1.000
	9	100	100	95	90	96	1.056	1.111
	10	100	95	90	85	93	1.100	1.200
	11	95	90	75	65	81	1.136	1.273
	12	90	85	70	60	76	1.167	1.333
6	8	100	100	95	90	96	1.083	1.167
	9	100	95	90	85	93	1.130	1.259
	10	95	90	85	80	88	1.167	1.333
	11	95	85	70	65	79	1.197	1.394
	12	90	80	65	60	74	1.222	1.444
7	8	100	95	85	75	89	1.143	1.286
	9	95	90	80	70	84	1.183	1.365
	10	90	85	75	65	79	1.214	1.429
	11	85	80	65	60	73	1.240	1.481
	12	85	75	60	55	69	1.262	1.524

General Requirements — R0131 Project Management & Coordination

R013113-40 Builder's Risk Insurance

Builder's risk insurance is insurance on a building during construction. Premiums are paid by the owner or the contractor. Blasting, collapse and underground insurance would raise total insurance costs.

R013113-50 General Contractor's Overhead

There are two distinct types of overhead on a construction project: Project overhead and main office overhead. Project overhead includes those costs at a construction site not directly associated with the installation of construction materials. Examples of project overhead costs include the following:

1. Superintendent
2. Construction office and storage trailers
3. Temporary sanitary facilities
4. Temporary utilities
5. Security fencing
6. Photographs
7. Cleanup
8. Performance and payment bonds

The above project overhead items are also referred to as general requirements and therefore are estimated in Division 1. Division 1 is the first division listed in the CSI MasterFormat but it is usually the last division estimated. The sum of the costs in Divisions 1 through 49 is referred to as the sum of the direct costs.

All construction projects also include indirect costs. The primary components of indirect costs are the contractor's main office overhead and profit. The amount of the main office overhead expense varies depending on the following:

1. Owner's compensation
2. Project managers' and estimators' wages
3. Clerical support wages
4. Office rent and utilities
5. Corporate legal and accounting costs
6. Advertising
7. Automobile expenses
8. Association dues
9. Travel and entertainment expenses

These costs are usually calculated as a percentage of annual sales volume. This percentage can range from 35% for a small contractor doing less than $500,000 to 5% for a large contractor with sales in excess of $100 million.

R013113-55 Installing Contractor's Overhead

Installing contractors (subcontractors) also incur costs for general requirements and main office overhead.

Included within the total incl. overhead and profit costs is a percent mark-up for overhead that includes:

1. Compensation and benefits for office staff and project managers
2. Office rent, utilities, business equipment, and maintenance
3. Corporate legal and accounting costs
4. Advertising
5. Vehicle expenses (for office staff and project managers)
6. Association dues
7. Travel, entertainment
8. Insurance
9. Small tools and equipment

General Requirements   R0131 Project Management & Coordination

R013113-60   Workers' Compensation Insurance Rates by Trade

The table below tabulates the national averages for Workers' Compensation insurance rates by trade and type of building. The average "Insurance Rate" is multiplied by the "% of Building Cost" for each trade. This produces the "Workers' Compensation Cost" by % of total labor cost, to be added for each trade by building type to determine the weighted average Workers' Compensation rate for the building types analyzed.

Trade	Insurance Rate (% Labor Cost) Range	Insurance Rate (% Labor Cost) Average	% of Building Cost Office Bldgs.	% of Building Cost Schools & Apts.	% of Building Cost Mfg.	Workers' Compensation Office Bldgs.	Workers' Compensation Schools & Apts.	Workers' Compensation Mfg.
Excavation, Grading, etc.	1.9% to 14.7%	8.3%	4.8%	4.9%	4.5%	0.40%	0.41%	0.37%
Piles & Foundations	1.9 to 26.7	14.3	7.1	5.2	8.7	1.02	0.74	1.25
Concrete	2.6 to 24.2	13.4	5.0	14.8	3.7	0.67	1.99	0.50
Masonry	2.6 to 48.0	25.3	6.9	7.5	1.9	1.75	1.90	0.48
Structural Steel	1.9 to 30.9	16.4	10.7	3.9	17.6	1.76	0.64	2.89
Miscellaneous & Ornamental Metals	1.9 to 22.6	12.3	2.8	4.0	3.6	0.34	0.49	0.44
Carpentry & Millwork	2.2 to 29.2	15.7	3.7	4.0	0.5	0.58	0.63	0.08
Metal or Composition Siding	3.8 to 127.0	65.4	2.3	0.3	4.3	1.50	0.20	2.81
Roofing	4.1 to 101.9	53.0	2.3	2.6	3.1	1.22	1.38	1.64
Doors & Hardware	2.6 to 29.2	15.9	0.9	1.4	0.4	0.14	0.22	0.06
Sash & Glazing	3.1 to 17.6	10.3	3.5	4.0	1.0	0.36	0.41	0.10
Lath & Plaster	2.1 to 32.4	17.3	3.3	6.9	0.8	0.57	1.19	0.14
Tile, Marble & Floors	2.0 to 19.2	10.6	2.6	3.0	0.5	0.28	0.32	0.05
Acoustical Ceilings	1.7 to 18.9	10.3	2.4	0.2	0.3	0.25	0.02	0.03
Painting	2.7 to 35.8	19.2	1.5	1.6	1.6	0.29	0.31	0.31
Interior Partitions	2.2 to 29.2	15.7	3.9	4.3	4.4	0.61	0.68	0.69
Miscellaneous Items	1.2 to 97.7	49.4	5.2	3.7	9.7	2.57	1.83	4.80
Elevators	1.2 to 8.3	4.7	2.1	1.1	2.2	0.10	0.05	0.10
Sprinklers	1.5 to 13.2	7.3	0.5	—	2.0	0.04	—	0.15
Plumbing	1.2 to 14.1	7.6	4.9	7.2	5.2	0.37	0.55	0.40
Heat., Vent., Air Conditioning	1.9 to 27.2	14.5	13.5	11.0	12.9	1.96	1.60	1.87
Electrical	1.3 to 9.5	5.4	10.1	8.4	11.1	0.54	0.45	0.60
Total	4.1% to 127.0%	65.52	100.0%	100.0%	100.0%	17.32%	16.01%	19.76%
		Overall Weighted Average	17.70%					

Workers' Compensation Insurance Rates by States

The table below lists the weighted average Workers' Compensation base rate for each state with a factor comparing this with the national average of 17.7%.

State	Weighted Average	Factor	State	Weighted Average	Factor	State	Weighted Average	Factor
Alabama	22.7%	280	Kentucky	22.6%	279	North Dakota	7.3%	90
Alaska	14.3	177	Louisiana	27.0	333	Ohio	8.4	104
Arizona	12.5	154	Maine	13.5	167	Oklahoma	13.0	160
Arkansas	9.0	111	Maryland	15.9	196	Oregon	13.5	167
California	44.2	546	Massachusetts	14.7	181	Pennsylvania	36.3	448
Colorado	8.2	101	Michigan	8.7	107	Rhode Island	13.6	168
Connecticut	25.7	317	Minnesota	22.9	283	South Carolina	33.9	419
Delaware	13.9	172	Mississippi	16.3	201	South Dakota	14.3	177
District of Columbia	13.8	170	Missouri	24.8	306	Tennessee	10.3	127
Florida	12.7	157	Montana	11.9	147	Texas	8.4	104
Georgia	59.1	730	Nebraska	18.2	225	Utah	8.5	105
Hawaii	18.0	222	Nevada	14.5	179	Vermont	16.7	206
Idaho	13.2	163	New Hampshire	16.0	198	Virginia	11.0	136
Illinois	37.1	458	New Jersey	22.7	280	Washington	12.7	157
Indiana	6.2	77	New Mexico	25.4	314	West Virginia	6.2	77
Iowa	18.5	228	New York	27.2	336	Wisconsin	16.4	202
Kansas	11.1	137	North Carolina	21.1	260	Wyoming	8.7	107
			Weighted Average for U.S. is	17.7% of payroll = 100%				

The weighted average skilled worker rate for 35 trades is 17.7%. For bidding purposes, apply the full value of Workers' Compensation directly to total labor costs, or if labor is 38%, materials 42% and overhead and profit 20% of total cost, carry 38/80 x 17.12% = 8.13% of cost (before overhead and profit) into overhead. Rates vary not only from state to state but also with the experience rating of the contractor.

Rates are the most current available at the time of publication.

General Requirements   R0131 Project Management & Coordination

R013113-80   Performance Bond

This table shows the cost of a Performance Bond for a construction job scheduled to be completed in 12 months. Add 1% of the premium cost per month for jobs requiring more than 12 months to complete. The rates are "standard" rates offered to contractors that the bonding company considers financially sound and capable of doing the work. Preferred rates are offered by some bonding companies based upon financial strength of the contractor. Actual rates vary from contractor to contractor and from bonding company to bonding company. Contractors should prequalify through a bonding agency before submitting a bid on a contract that requires a bond.

Contract Amount	Building Construction Class B Projects	Highways & Bridges Class A New Construction	Class A-1 Highway Resurfacing
	$25.00 per M	$15.00 per M	$9.40 per M
First $ 100,000 bid			
Next 400,000 bid	$ 2,500 plus $15.00 per M	$ 1,500 plus $10.00 per M	$ 940 plus $7.20 per M
Next 2,000,000 bid	8,500 plus 10.00 per M	5,500 plus 7.00 per M	3,820 plus 5.00 per M
Next 2,500,000 bid	28,500 plus 7.50 per M	19,500 plus 5.50 per M	15,820 plus 4.50 per M
Next 2,500,000 bid	47,250 plus 7.00 per M	33,250 plus 5.00 per M	28,320 plus 4.50 per M
Over 7,500,000 bid	64,750 plus 6.00 per M	45,750 plus 4.50 per M	39,570 plus 4.00 per M

General Requirements   R0154 Construction Aids

R015423-10   Steel Tubular Scaffolding

On new construction, tubular scaffolding is efficient up to 60' high or five stories. Above this it is usually better to use a hung scaffolding if construction permits. Swing scaffolding operations may interfere with tenants. In this case, the tubular is more practical at all heights.

In repairing or cleaning the front of an existing building the cost of tubular scaffolding per S.F. of building front increases as the height increases above the first tier. The first tier cost is relatively high due to leveling and alignment.

The minimum efficient crew for erecting and dismantling is three workers. They can set up and remove 18 frame sections per day up to 5 stories high. For 6 to 12 stories high, a crew of four is most efficient. Use two or more on top and two on the bottom for handing up or hoisting. They can also set up and remove 18 frame sections per day. At 7' horizontal spacing, this will run about 800 S.F. per day of erecting and dismantling. Time for placing and removing planks must be added to the above. A crew of three can place and remove 72 planks per day up to 5 stories. For over 5 stories, a crew of four can place and remove 80 planks per day.

The table below shows the number of pieces required to erect tubular steel scaffolding for 1000 S.F. of building frontage. This area is made up of a scaffolding system that is 12 frames (11 bays) long by 2 frames high.

For jobs under twenty-five frames, add 50% to rental cost. Rental rates will be lower for jobs over three months duration. Large quantities for long periods can reduce rental rates by 20%.

Description of Component	Number of Pieces for 1000 S.F. of Building Front	Unit
5' Wide Standard Frame, 6'-4" High	24	Ea.
Leveling Jack & Plate	24	
Cross Brace	44	
Side Arm Bracket, 21"	12	
Guardrail Post	12	
Guardrail, 7' section	22	
Stairway Section	2	
Stairway Starter Bar	1	
Stairway Inside Handrail	2	
Stairway Outside Handrail	2	
Walk-Thru Frame Guardrail	2	

Scaffolding is often used as falsework over 15' high during construction of cast-in-place concrete beams and slabs. Two foot wide scaffolding is generally used for heavy beam construction. The span between frames depends upon the load to be carried with a maximum span of 5'.

Heavy duty shoring frames with a capacity of 10,000#/leg can be spaced up to 10' O.C. depending upon form support design and loading.

Scaffolding used as horizontal shoring requires less than half the material required with conventional shoring.

On new construction, erection is done by carpenters.

Rolling towers supporting horizontal shores can reduce labor and speed the job. For maintenance work, catwalks with spans up to 70' can be supported by the rolling towers.

General Requirements R0154 Construction Aids

R015433-10 Contractor Equipment

Rental Rates shown elsewhere in the data set pertain to late model high quality machines in excellent working condition, rented from equipment dealers. Rental rates from contractors may be substantially lower than the rental rates from equipment dealers depending upon economic conditions; for older, less productive machines, reduce rates by a maximum of 15%. Any overtime must be added to the base rates. For shift work, rates are lower. Usual rule of thumb is 150% of one shift rate for two shifts; 200% for three shifts.

For periods of less than one week, operated equipment is usually more economical to rent than renting bare equipment and hiring an operator.

Costs to move equipment to a job site (mobilization) or from a job site (demobilization) are not included in rental rates, nor in any Equipment costs on any Unit Price line items or crew listings. These costs can be found elsewhere. If a piece of equipment is already at a job site, it is not appropriate to utilize mob/demob costs in an estimate again.

Rental rates vary throughout the country with larger cities generally having lower rates. Lease plans for new equipment are available for periods in excess of six months with a percentage of payments applying toward purchase.

Rental rates can also be treated as reimbursement costs for contractor-owned equipment. Owned equipment costs include depreciation, loan payments, interest, taxes, insurance, storage, and major repairs.

Monthly rental rates vary from 2% to 5% of the cost of the equipment depending on the anticipated life of the equipment and its wearing parts. Weekly rates are about 1/3 the monthly rates and daily rental rates are about 1/3 the weekly rates.

The hourly operating costs for each piece of equipment include costs to the user such as fuel, oil, lubrication, normal expendables for the equipment, and a percentage of the mechanic's wages chargeable to maintenance. The hourly operating costs listed do not include the operator's wages.

The daily cost for equipment used in the standard crews is figured by dividing the weekly rate by five, then adding eight times the hourly operating cost to give the total daily equipment cost, not including the operator. This figure is in the right hand column of the Equipment listings under Equipment Cost/Day.

Pile Driving rates shown for the pile hammer and extractor do not include leads, cranes, boilers or compressors. Vibratory pile driving requires an added field specialist during set-up and pile driving operation for the electric model. The hydraulic model requires a field specialist for set-up only. Up to 125 reuses of sheet piling are possible using vibratory drivers. For normal conditions, crane capacity for hammer type and size is as follows.

Crane Capacity	Hammer Type and Size		
	Air or Steam	Diesel	Vibratory
25 ton	to 8,750 ft.-lb.		70 H.P.
40 ton	15,000 ft.-lb.	to 32,000 ft.-lb.	170 H.P.
60 ton	25,000 ft.-lb.		300 H.P.
100 ton		112,000 ft.-lb.	

Cranes should be specified for the job by size, building and site characteristics, availability, performance characteristics, and duration of time required.

Backhoes & Shovels rent for about the same as equivalent size cranes but maintenance and operating expenses are higher. The crane operator's rate must be adjusted for high boom heights. Average adjustments: for 150' boom add 2% per hour; over 185', add 4% per hour; over 210', add 6% per hour; over 250', add 8% per hour and over 295', add 12% per hour.

Tower Cranes of the climbing or static type have jibs from 50' to 200' and capacities at maximum reach range from 4,000 to 14,000 pounds. Lifting capacities increase up to maximum load as the hook radius decreases.

Typical rental rates, based on purchase price, are about 2% to 3% per month.

Erection and dismantling run between 500 and 2000 labor hours. Climbing operation takes 10 labor hours per 20' climb. Crane dead time is about 5 hours per 40' climb. If crane is bolted to side of the building add cost of ties and extra mast sections. Climbing cranes have from 80' to 180' of mast while static cranes have 80' to 800' of mast.

Truck Cranes can be converted to tower cranes by using tower attachments. Mast heights over 400' have been used.

A single 100' high material **Hoist and Tower** can be erected and dismantled in about 400 labor hours; a double 100' high hoist and tower in about 600 labor hours. Erection times for additional heights are 3 and 4 labor hours per vertical foot respectively up to 150', and 4 to 5 labor hours per vertical foot over 150' high. A 40' high portable Buck hoist takes about 160 labor hours to erect and dismantle. Additional heights take 2 labor hours per vertical foot to 80' and 3 labor hours per vertical foot for the next 100'. Most material hoists do not meet local code requirements for carrying personnel.

A 150' high **Personnel Hoist** requires about 500 to 800 labor hours to erect and dismantle. Budget erection time at 5 labor hours per vertical foot for all trades. Local code requirements or labor scarcity requiring overtime can add up to 50% to any of the above erection costs.

Earthmoving Equipment: The selection of earthmoving equipment depends upon the type and quantity of material, moisture content, haul distance, haul road, time available, and equipment available. Short haul cut and fill operations may require dozers only, while another operation may require excavators, a fleet of trucks, and spreading and compaction equipment. Stockpiled material and granular material are easily excavated with front end loaders. Scrapers are most economically used with hauls between 300' and 1-1/2 miles if adequate haul roads can be maintained. Shovels are often used for blasted rock and any material where a vertical face of 8' or more can be excavated. Special conditions may dictate the use of draglines, clamshells, or backhoes. Spreading and compaction equipment must be matched to the soil characteristics, the compaction required and the rate the fill is being supplied.

R015433-15 Heavy Lifting

Hydraulic Climbing Jacks

The use of hydraulic heavy lift systems is an alternative to conventional type crane equipment. The lifting, lowering, pushing, or pulling mechanism is a hydraulic climbing jack moving on a square steel jackrod from 1-5/8" to 4" square, or a steel cable. The jackrod or cable can be vertical or horizontal, stationary or movable, depending on the individual application. When the jackrod is stationary, the climbing jack will climb the rod and push or pull the load along with itself. When the climbing jack is stationary, the jackrod is movable with the load attached to the end and the climbing jack will lift or lower the jackrod with the attached load. The heavy lift system is normally operated by a single control lever located at the hydraulic pump.

The system is flexible in that one or more climbing jacks can be applied wherever a load support point is required, and the rate of lift synchronized.

Economic benefits have been demonstrated on projects such as: erection of ground assembled roofs and floors, complete bridge spans, girders and trusses, towers, chimney liners and steel vessels, storage tanks, and heavy machinery. Other uses are raising and lowering offshore work platforms, caissons, tunnel sections and pipelines.

General Requirements — R0154 Construction Aids

R015436-50 Mobilization

Costs to move rented construction equipment to a job site from an equipment dealer's or contractor's yard (mobilization) or off the job site (demobilization) are not included in the rental or operating rates, nor in the equipment cost on a unit price line or in a crew listing. These costs can be found consolidated in the Mobilization section of the data and elsewhere in particular site work sections. If a piece of equipment is already on the job site, it is not appropriate to include mob/demob costs in a new estimate that requires use of that equipment. The following table identifies approximate sizes of rented construction equipment that would be hauled on a towed trailer. Because this listing is not all-encompassing, the user can infer as to what size trailer might be required for a piece of equipment not listed.

3-ton Trailer	20-ton Trailer	40-ton Trailer	50-ton Trailer
20 H.P. Excavator	110 H.P. Excavator	200 H.P. Excavator	270 H.P. Excavator
50 H.P. Skid Steer	165 H.P. Dozer	300 H.P. Dozer	Small Crawler Crane
35 H.P. Roller	150 H.P. Roller	400 H.P. Scraper	500 H.P. Scraper
40 H.P. Trencher	Backhoe	450 H.P. Art. Dump Truck	500 H.P. Art. Dump Truck

Existing Conditions — R0241 Demolition

R024119-10 Demolition Defined

Whole Building Demolition - Demolition of the whole building with no concern for any particular building element, component, or material type being demolished. This type of demolition is accomplished with large pieces of construction equipment that break up the structure, load it into trucks and haul it to a disposal site, but disposal or dump fees are not included. Demolition of below-grade foundation elements, such as footings, foundation walls, grade beams, slabs on grade, etc., is not included. Certain mechanical equipment containing flammable liquids or ozone-depleting refrigerants, electric lighting elements, communication equipment components, and other building elements may contain hazardous waste, and must be removed, either selectively or carefully, as hazardous waste before the building can be demolished.

Foundation Demolition - Demolition of below-grade foundation footings, foundation walls, grade beams, and slabs on grade. This type of demolition is accomplished by hand or pneumatic hand tools, and does not include saw cutting, or handling, loading, hauling, or disposal of the debris.

Gutting - Removal of building interior finishes and electrical/mechanical systems down to the load-bearing and sub-floor elements of the rough building frame, with no concern for any particular building element, component, or material type being demolished. This type of demolition is accomplished by hand or pneumatic hand tools, and includes loading into trucks, but not hauling, disposal or dump fees, scaffolding, or shoring. Certain mechanical equipment containing flammable liquids or ozone-depleting refrigerants, electric lighting elements, communication equipment components, and other building elements may contain hazardous waste, and must be removed, either selectively or carefully, as hazardous waste, before the building is gutted.

Selective Demolition - Demolition of a selected building element, component, or finish, with some concern for surrounding or adjacent elements, components, or finishes (see the first Subdivision (s) at the beginning of appropriate Divisions). This type of demolition is accomplished by hand or pneumatic hand tools, and does not include handling, loading, storing, hauling, or disposal of the debris, scaffolding, or shoring. "Gutting" methods may be used in order to save time, but damage that is caused to surrounding or adjacent elements, components, or finishes may have to be repaired at a later time.

Careful Removal - Removal of a piece of service equipment, building element or component, or material type, with great concern for both the removed item and surrounding or adjacent elements, components or finishes. The purpose of careful removal may be to protect the removed item for later re-use, preserve a higher salvage value of the removed item, or replace an item while taking care to protect surrounding or adjacent elements, components, connections, or finishes from cosmetic and/or structural damage. An approximation of the time required to perform this type of removal is 1/3 to 1/2 the time it would take to install a new item of like kind (see Reference Number R220105-10). This type of removal is accomplished by hand or pneumatic hand tools, and does not include loading, hauling, or storing the removed item, scaffolding, shoring, or lifting equipment.

Cutout Demolition - Demolition of a small quantity of floor, wall, roof, or other assembly, with concern for the appearance and structural integrity of the surrounding materials. This type of demolition is accomplished by hand or pneumatic hand tools, and does not include saw cutting, handling, loading, hauling, or disposal of debris, scaffolding, or shoring.

Rubbish Handling - Work activities that involve handling, loading or hauling of debris. Generally, the cost of rubbish handling must be added to the cost of all types of demolition, with the exception of whole building demolition.

Minor Site Demolition - Demolition of site elements outside the footprint of a building. This type of demolition is accomplished by hand or pneumatic hand tools, or with larger pieces of construction equipment, and may include loading a removed item onto a truck (check the Crew for equipment used). It does not include saw cutting, hauling or disposal of debris, and, sometimes, handling or loading.

R024119-20 Dumpsters

Dumpster rental costs on construction sites are presented in two ways.

The cost per week rental includes the delivery of the dumpster; its pulling or emptying once per week, and its final removal. The assumption is made that the dumpster contractor could choose to empty a dumpster by simply bringing in an empty unit and removing the full one. These costs also include the disposal of the materials in the dumpster.

The Alternate Pricing can be used when actual planned conditions are not approximated by the weekly numbers. For example, these lines can be used when a dumpster is needed for 4 weeks and will need to be emptied 2 or 3 times per week. Conversely the Alternate Pricing lines can be used when a dumpster will be rented for several weeks or months but needs to be emptied only a few times over this period.

Existing Conditions — R0265 Underground Storage Tank Removal

R026510-20 Underground Storage Tank Removal

Underground Storage Tank Removal can be divided into two categories: Non-Leaking and Leaking. Prior to removing an underground storage tank, tests should be made, with the proper authorities present, to determine whether a tank has been leaking or the surrounding soil has been contaminated.

To safely remove Liquid Underground Storage Tanks:
1. Excavate to the top of the tank.
2. Disconnect all piping.
3. Open all tank vents and access ports.
4. Remove all liquids and/or sludge.
5. Purge the tank with an inert gas.
6. Provide access to the inside of the tank and clean out the interior using proper personal protective equipment (PPE).
7. Excavate soil surrounding the tank using proper PPE for on-site personnel.
8. Pull and properly dispose of the tank.
9. Clean up the site of all contaminated material.
10. Install new tanks or close the excavation.

Existing Conditions — R0282 Asbestos Remediation

R028213-20 Asbestos Removal Process

Asbestos removal is accomplished by a specialty contractor who understands the federal and state regulations regarding the handling and disposal of the material. The process of asbestos removal is divided into many individual steps. An accurate estimate can be calculated only after all the steps have been priced.

The steps are generally as follows:

1. Obtain an asbestos abatement plan from an industrial hygienist.
2. Monitor the air quality in and around the removal area and along the path of travel between the removal area and transport area. This establishes the background contamination.
3. Construct a two part decontamination chamber at entrance to removal area.
4. Install a HEPA filter to create a negative pressure in the removal area.
5. Install wall, floor and ceiling protection as required by the plan, usually 2 layers of fireproof 6 mil polyethylene.
6. Industrial hygienist visually inspects work area to verify compliance with plan.
7. Provide temporary supports for conduit and piping affected by the removal process.
8. Proceed with asbestos removal and bagging process. Monitor air quality as described in Step #2. Discontinue operations when contaminate levels exceed applicable standards.
9. Document the legal disposal of materials in accordance with EPA standards.
10. Thoroughly clean removal area including all ledges, crevices and surfaces.
11. Post abatement inspection by industrial hygienist to verify plan compliance.
12. Provide a certificate from a licensed industrial hygienist attesting that contaminate levels are within acceptable standards before returning area to regular use.

Concrete — R0330 Cast-In-Place Concrete

R033053-60 Maximum Depth of Frost Penetration in Inches

THIS MAP IS REASONABLY ACCURATE FOR MOST PARTS OF THE UNITED STATES BUT IS NECESSARILY HIGHLY GENERALIZED, AND CONSEQUENTLY NOT TOO ACCURATE IN MOUNTAINOUS REGIONS, PARTICULARLY IN THE ROCKIES.

Metals — R0505 Common Work Results for Metals

R050521-20 Welded Structural Steel

Usual weight reductions with welded design run 10% to 20% compared with bolted or riveted connections. This amounts to about the same total cost compared with bolted structures since field welding is more expensive than bolts. For normal spans of 18' to 24' figure 6 to 7 connections per ton.

Trusses — For welded trusses add 4% to weight of main members for connections. Up to 15% less steel can be expected in a welded truss compared to one that is shop bolted. Cost of erection is the same whether shop bolted or welded.

General — Typical electrodes for structural steel welding are E6010, E6011, E60T and E70T. Typical buildings vary between 2# to 8# of weld rod per ton of steel. Buildings utilizing continuous design require about three times as much welding as conventional welded structures. In estimating field erection by welding, it is best to use the average linear feet of weld per ton to arrive at the welding cost per ton. The type, size and position of the weld will have a direct bearing on the cost per linear foot. A typical field welder will deposit 1.8# to 2# of weld rod per hour manually. Using semiautomatic methods can increase production by as much as 50% to 75%.

Special Construction — R1311 Swimming Pools

R131113-20 Swimming Pools

Pool prices given per square foot of surface area include pool structure, filter and chlorination equipment, pumps, related piping, ladders/steps, maintenance kit, skimmer and vacuum system. Decks and electrical service to equipment are not included.

Residential in-ground pool construction can be divided into two categories: vinyl lined and gunite. Vinyl lined pool walls are constructed of different materials including wood, concrete, plastic or metal. The bottom is often graded with sand over which the vinyl liner is installed. Vermiculite or soil cement bottoms may be substituted for an added cost.

Gunite pool construction is used both in residential and municipal installations. These structures are steel reinforced for strength and finished with a white cement limestone plaster.

Municipal pools will have a higher cost because plumbing codes require more expensive materials, chlorination equipment and higher filtration rates.

Municipal pools greater than 1,800 S.F. require gutter systems to control waves. This gutter may be formed into the concrete wall. Often a vinyl/stainless steel gutter or gutter/wall system is specified, which will raise the pool cost.

Competition pools usually require tile bottoms and sides with contrasting lane striping, which will also raise the pool cost.

Fire Suppression — R2112 Fire-Suppression Standpipes

R211226-10 Standpipe Systems

The basis for standpipe system design is National Fire Protection Association NFPA 14. However, the authority having jurisdiction should be consulted for special conditions, local requirements, and approval.

Standpipe systems, properly designed and maintained, are an effective and valuable time saving aid for extinguishing fires, especially in the upper stories of tall buildings, the interior of large commercial or industrial malls, or other areas where construction features or access make the laying of temporary hose lines time consuming and/or hazardous. Standpipes are frequently installed with automatic sprinkler systems for maximum protection.

There are three general classes of service for standpipe systems:
Class I A system with 2-1/2" (65 mm) hose connections for Fire Department use and those trained in handling heavy fire streams.
Class II A system with either 1-1/2" (40 mm) hose stations for use by trained personnel or a hose connection for the fire department's use.
Class III A system with 1-1/2" (40 mm) hose stations for trained personnel and 2-1/2" (65 mm) hose connections for fire department use.

Standpipe systems are also classified by the way water is supplied to the system. The following are the types of systems:
Automatic Dry Standpipe A system containing air or nitrogen under pressure, with a water supply capable of meeting water demands at all times. Opening of a valve allows the air/nitrogen to dissipate, releasing the pressurized dry valve's clapper to open and fill the system with water.
Automatic Wet Standpipe A system containing water with a water supply capable of meeting system demands at all times. Open a valve or connection and water will immediately flow.
Combination Standpipe A system that supplies both sprinkler systems and fire department/hose connections. Manual operation of approved remote control devices located at each hose station.
Manual Dry Standpipe A system not containing water. Water is manually pumped into the system by means of a fire department connection attached to a water supply.
Semiautomatic Dry Standpipe A system with an attached water supply held back at a valve which requires remote activation to open and allow flow of water into the system.
Wet Standpipe A system containing water at all times.

Reprinted with permission from NFPA 14-2013, *Installation of Standpipe and Hose Systems*, Copyright © 2013, National Fire Protection Association, Quincy, MA. This reprinted material is not the complete and official position of the NFPA on the referenced subject, which is represented only by the standard in its entirety.

Fire Suppression — R2112 Fire-Suppression Standpipes

R211226-20 NFPA 14 Basic Standpipe Design

Class	Design-Use	Pipe Size Minimums	Water Supply Minimums
Class I	2 1/2" hose connection on each floor. All areas within 150' of an exit in every exit stairway. Fire Department Trained Personnel	Height to 100', 4" dia. Heights above 100', 6" dia. (275' max. except with pressure regulators 400' max.)	For each standpipe riser 500 GPM flow. For common supply pipe allow 500 GPM for first standpipe plus 250 GPM for each additional standpipe (2500 GPM max. total). 30 min. duration 65 PSI at 500 GPM
Class II	1 1/2" hose connection with hose on each floor. All areas within 130' of hose connection measured along path of hose travel. Occupant personnel	Height to 50', 2" dia. Height above 50', 2 1/2" dia.	For each standpipe riser 100 GPM flow. For multiple riser common supply pipe 100 GPM. 300 min. duration, 65 PSI at 100 GPM
Class III	Both of above. Class I valved connections will meet Class III with additional 2 1/2" by 1 1/2" adapter and 1 1/2" hose.	Same as Class I	Same as Class I

*Note: Where 2 or more standpipes are installed in the same building or section of building they shall be interconnected at the bottom.

Combined Systems

Combined systems are systems where the risers supply both automatic sprinklers and 2-1/2" hose connection outlets for fire department use. In such a system the sprinkler spacing pattern shall be in accordance with NFPA 13 while the risers and supply piping will be sized in accordance with NFPA 14. When the building is completely sprinklered the risers may be sized by hydraulic calculation. The minimum size riser for buildings not completely sprinklered is 6".

The minimum water supply of a completely sprinklered, light hazard, high-rise occupancy building will be 500 GPM while the supply required for other types of completely sprinklered high-rise buildings is 1000 GPM.

General System Requirements

1. Approved valves will be provided at the riser for controlling branch lines to hose outlets.
2. A hose valve will be provided at each outlet for attachment of hose.
3. Where pressure at any standpipe outlet exceeds 100 PSI a pressure reducer must be installed to limit the pressure to 100 PSI. Note that the pressure head due to gravity in 100' of riser is 43.4 PSI. This must be overcome by city pressure, fire pumps, or gravity tanks to provide adequate pressure at the top of the riser.
4. Each hose valve on a wet system having linen hose shall have an automatic drip connection to prevent valve leakage from entering the hose.
5. Each riser will have a valve to isolate it from the rest of the system.
6. One or more fire department connections as an auxiliary supply shall be provided for each Class I or Class III standpipe system. In buildings having two or more zones, a connection will be provided for each zone.
7. There will be no shutoff valve in the fire department connection, but a check valve will be located in the line before it joins the system.
8. All hose connections street side will be identified on a cast plate or fitting as to purpose.

Reprinted with permission from NFPA 14-2013, *Installation of Standpipe and Hose Systems*, Copyright © 2013, National Fire Protection Association, Quincy, MA. This reprinted material is not the complete and official position of the NFPA on the referenced subject, which is represented only by the standard in its entirety.

Fire Suppression

R2113 Fire-Suppression Sprinkler Systems

R211313-10 Sprinkler Systems (Automatic)

Sprinkler systems may be classified by type as follows:

1. **Wet Pipe System.** A system employing automatic sprinklers attached to a piping system containing water and connected to a water supply so that water discharges immediately from sprinklers opened by a fire.
2. **Dry Pipe System.** A system employing automatic sprinklers attached to a piping system containing air under pressure, the release of which as from the opening of sprinklers permits the water pressure to open a valve known as a "dry pipe valve". The water then flows into the piping system and out the opened sprinklers.
3. **Pre-Action System.** A system employing automatic sprinklers attached to a piping system containing air that may or may not be under pressure, with a supplemental heat responsive system of generally more sensitive characteristics than the automatic sprinklers themselves, installed in the same areas as the sprinklers; actuation of the heat responsive system, as from a fire, opens a valve which permits water to flow into the sprinkler piping system and to be discharged from any sprinklers which may be open.
4. **Deluge System.** A system employing open sprinklers attached to a piping system connected to a water supply through a valve which is opened by the operation of a heat responsive system installed in the same areas as the sprinklers. When this valve opens, water flows into the piping system and discharges from all sprinklers attached thereto.
5. **Combined Dry Pipe and Pre-Action Sprinkler System.** A system employing automatic sprinklers attached to a piping system containing air under pressure with a supplemental heat responsive system of generally more sensitive characteristics than the automatic sprinklers themselves, installed in the same areas as the sprinklers; operation of the heat responsive system, as from a fire, actuates tripping devices which open dry pipe valves simultaneously and without loss of air pressure in the system. Operation of the heat responsive system also opens approved air exhaust valves at the end of the feed main which facilitates the filling of the system with water which usually precedes the opening of sprinklers. The heat responsive system also serves as an automatic fire alarm system.
6. **Limited Water Supply System.** A system employing automatic sprinklers and conforming to these standards but supplied by a pressure tank of limited capacity.
7. **Chemical Systems.** Systems using halon, carbon dioxide, dry chemical or high expansion foam as selected for special requirements. Agent may extinguish flames by chemically inhibiting flame propagation, suffocate flames by excluding oxygen, interrupting chemical action of oxygen uniting with fuel or sealing and cooling the combustion center.
8. **Firecycle System.** Firecycle is a fixed fire protection sprinkler system utilizing water as its extinguishing agent. It is a time delayed, recycling, preaction type which automatically shuts the water off when heat is reduced below the detector operating temperature and turns the water back on when that temperature is exceeded. The system senses a fire condition through a closed circuit electrical detector system which controls water flow to the fire automatically. Batteries supply up to 90 hour emergency power supply for system operation. The piping system is dry (until water is required) and is monitored with pressurized air. Should any leak in the system piping occur, an alarm will sound, but water will not enter the system until heat is sensed by a firecycle detector.

Area coverage sprinkler systems may be laid out and fed from the supply in any one of several patterns as shown below. It is desirable, if possible, to utilize a central feed and achieve a shorter flow path from the riser to the furthest sprinkler. This permits use of the smallest sizes of pipe possible with resulting savings.

Reprinted with permission from NFPA 13-2013, *Installation of Sprinkler Systems,* Copyright © 2012, National Fire Protection Association, Quincy, MA. This reprinted material is not the complete and official position of the NFPA on the referenced subject, which is represented only by the standard in its entirety.

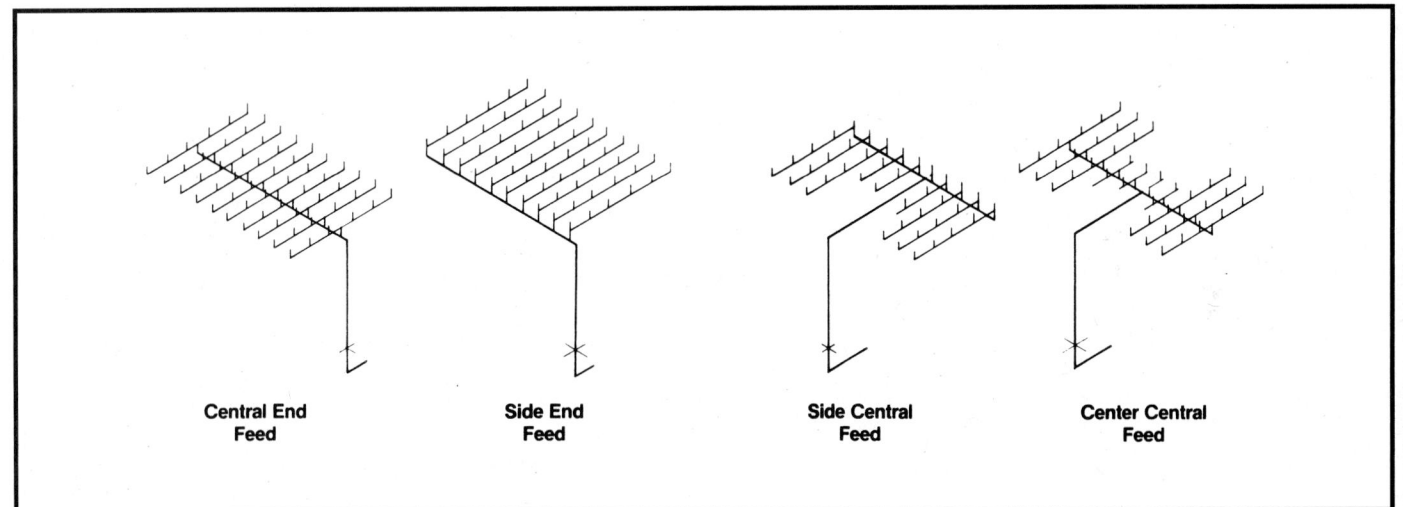

Central End Feed | Side End Feed | Side Central Feed | Center Central Feed

Fire Suppression
R2113 Fire-Suppression Sprinkler Systems

R211313-20 System Classification

System Classification

Rules for installation of sprinkler systems vary depending on the classification of occupancy falling into one of three categories as follows:

Light Hazard Occupancy

The protection area allotted per sprinkler should not exceed 225 S.F., with the maximum distance between lines and sprinklers on lines being 15'. The sprinklers do not need to be staggered. Branch lines should not exceed eight sprinklers on either side of a cross main. Each large area requiring more than 100 sprinklers and without a sub-dividing partition should be supplied by feed mains or risers sized for ordinary hazard occupancy.
Maximum system area = 52,000 S.F.

Included in this group are:

Churches
Clubs
Educational
Hospitals
Institutional
Libraries
(except large stack rooms)
Museums

Nursing Homes
Offices
Residential
Restaurants
Theaters and Auditoriums
(except stages and prosceniums)
Unused Attics

Ordinary Hazard Occupancy

The protection area allotted per sprinkler shall not exceed 130 S.F. of noncombustible ceiling and 130 S.F. of combustible ceiling. The maximum allowable distance between sprinkler lines and sprinklers on line is 15'. Sprinklers shall be staggered if the distance between heads exceeds 12'. Branch lines should not exceed eight sprinklers on either side of a cross main.
Maximum system area = 52,000 S.F.

Included in this group are:

Group 1
Automotive Parking and Showrooms
Bakeries
Beverage manufacturing
Canneries
Dairy Products Manufacturing/Processing
Electronic Plans
Glass and Glass Products Manufacturing
Laundries
Restaurant Service Areas

Group 2
Cereal Mills
Chemical Plants—Ordinary
Confectionery Products
Distilleries
Dry Cleaners
Feed Mills
Horse Stables
Leather Goods Manufacturing
Libraries—Large Stack Room Areas
Machine Shops
Metal Working
Mercantile
Paper and Pulp Mills
Paper Process Plants
Piers and Wharves
Post Offices
Printing and Publishing
Repair Garages
Stages
Textile Manufacturing
Tire Manufacturing
Tobacco Products Manufacturing
Wood Machining
Wood Product Assembly

Extra Hazard Occupancy

The protection area allotted per sprinkler shall not exceed 100 S.F. of noncombustible ceiling and 100 S.F. of combustible ceiling. The maximum allowable distance between lines and between sprinklers on lines is 12'. Sprinklers on alternate lines shall be staggered if the distance between sprinklers on lines exceeds 8'. Branch lines should not exceed six sprinklers on either side of a cross main.
Maximum system area:
   Design by pipe schedule = 25,000 S.F.
   Design by hydraulic calculation = 40,000 S.F.

Included in this group are:

Group 1
Aircraft hangars
Combustible Hydraulic Fluid Use Area
Die Casting
Metal Extruding
Plywood/Particle Board Manufacturing
Printing (inks with flash points < 100 degrees F
Rubber Reclaiming, Compounding, Drying, Milling, Vulcanizing
Saw Mills
Textile Picking, Opening, Blending, Garnetting, Carding, Combing of Cotton, Synthetics, Wood Shoddy, or Burlap
Upholstering with Plastic Foams

Group 2
Asphalt Saturating
Flammable Liquids Spraying
Flow Coating
Manufactured/Modular Home Building Assemblies (where finished enclosure is present and has combustible interiors)
Open Oil Quenching
Plastics Processing
Solvent Cleaning
Varnish and Paint Dipping

Reprinted with permission from NFPA 13-2013, *Installation of Sprinkler Systems*, Copyright © 2012, National Fire Protection Association, Quincy, MA. This reprinted material is not the complete and official position of the NFPA on the referenced subject, which is represented only by the standard in its entirety.

Fire Suppression — R2113 Fire-Suppression Sprinkler Systems

R211313-40 Adjustment for Sprinkler/Standpipe Installations

Quality/Complexity Multiplier (For all installations)

Economy installation, add	0 to 5%
Good quality, medium complexity, add	5 to 15%
Above average quality and complexity, add	15 to 25%

Plumbing — R2201 Operation & Maintenance of Plumbing

R220102-20 Labor Adjustment Factors

Labor Adjustment Factors are provided for Divisions 21, 22, and 23 to assist the mechanical estimator account for the various complexities and special conditions of any particular project. While a single percentage has been entered on each line of Division 22 01 02.20, it should be understood that these are just suggested midpoints of ranges of values commonly used by mechanical estimators. They may be increased or decreased depending on the severity of the special conditions.

The group for "existing occupied buildings" has been the subject of requests for explanation. Actually there are two stages to this group: buildings that are existing and "finished" but unoccupied, and those that also are occupied. Buildings that are "finished" may result in higher labor costs due to the workers having to be more careful not to damage finished walls, ceilings, floors, etc. and may necessitate special protective coverings and barriers. Also corridor bends and doorways may not accommodate long pieces of pipe or larger pieces of equipment. Work above an already hung ceiling can be very time consuming. The addition of occupants may force the work to be done on premium time (nights and/or weekends), eliminate the possible use of some preferred tools such as pneumatic drivers, powder charged drivers etc. The estimator should evaluate the access to the work area and just how the work is going to be accomplished to arrive at an increase in labor costs over "normal" new construction productivity.

R220105-10 Demolition (Selective vs. Removal for Replacement)

Demolition can be divided into two basic categories.

One type of demolition involves the removal of material with no concern for its replacement. The labor-hours to estimate this work are found under "Selective Demolition" in the Fire Protection, Plumbing and HVAC Divisions. It is selective in that individual items or all the material installed as a system or trade grouping such as plumbing or heating systems are removed. This may be accomplished by the easiest way possible, such as sawing, torch cutting, or sledge hammering as well as simple unbolting.

The second type of demolition is the removal of some items for repair or replacement. This removal may involve careful draining, opening of unions, disconnecting and tagging electrical connections, capping pipes/ducts to prevent entry of debris or leakage of the material contained as well as transporting the item away from its in-place location to a truck/dumpster. An approximation of the time required to accomplish this type of demolition is to use half of the time indicated as necessary to install a new unit. For example: installation of a new pump might be listed as requiring 6 labor-hours so if we had to estimate the removal of the old pump we would allow an additional 3 hours for a total of 9 hours. That is, the complete replacement of a defective pump with a new pump would be estimated to take 9 labor-hours.

Plumbing — R2205 Common Work Results for Plumbing

R220523-80 Valve Materials

VALVE MATERIALS

Bronze:
Bronze is one of the oldest materials used to make valves. It is most commonly used in hot and cold water systems and other non-corrosive services. It is often used as a seating surface in larger iron body valves to ensure tight closure.

Carbon Steel:
Carbon steel is a high strength material. Therefore, valves made from this metal are used in higher pressure services, such as steam lines up to 600 psi at 850°F. Many steel valves are available with butt-weld ends for economy and are generally used in high pressure steam service as well as other higher pressure non-corrosive services.

Forged Steel:
Valves from tough carbon steel are used in service up to 2000 psi and temperatures up to 1000°F in Gate, Globe and Check valves.

Iron:
Valves are normally used in medium to large pipe lines to control non-corrosive fluid and gases, where pressures do not exceed 250 psi at 450° or 500 psi cold water, oil or gas.

Stainless Steel:
Developed steel alloys can be used in over 90% corrosive services.

Plastic PVC:
This is used in a great variety of valves generally in high corrosive service with lower temperatures and pressures.

VALVE SERVICE PRESSURES

Pressure ratings on valves provide an indication of the safe operating pressure for a valve at some elevated temperature. This temperature is dependent upon the materials used and the fabrication of the valve. When specific data is not available, a good "rule-of-thumb" to follow is the temperature of saturated steam on the primary rating indicated on the valve body. Example: The valve has the number 150S printed on the side indicating 150 psi and hence, a maximum operating temperature of 367°F (temperature of saturated steam and 150 psi).

DEFINITIONS

1. "WOG" – Water, oil, gas (cold working pressures).
2. "SWP" – Steam working pressure.
3. 100% area (full port) – means the area through the valve is equal to or greater than the area of standard pipe.
4. "Standard Opening" – means that the area through the valve is less than the area of standard pipe and therefore these valves should be used only where restriction of flow is unimportant.
5. "Round Port" – means the valve has a full round opening through the plug and body, of the same size and area as standard pipe.
6. "Rectangular Port" – valves have rectangular shaped ports through the plug body. The area of the port is either equal to 100% of the area of standard pipe, or restricted (standard opening). In either case it is clearly marked.
7. "ANSI" – American National Standards Institute.

R220523-90 Valve Selection Considerations

INTRODUCTION: In any piping application, valve performance is critical. Valves should be selected to give the best performance at the lowest cost.

The following is a list of performance characteristics generally expected of valves.

1. Stopping flow or starting it.
2. Throttling flow (Modulation).
3. Flow direction changing.
4. Checking backflow (Permitting flow in only one direction).
5. Relieving or regulating pressure.

In order to properly select the right valve, some facts must be determined.

A. What liquid or gas will flow through the valve?
B. Does the fluid contain suspended particles?
C. Does the fluid remain in liquid form at all times?
D. Which metals does fluid corrode?
E. What are the pressure and temperature limits? (As temperature and pressure rise, so will the price of the valve.)
F. Is there constant line pressure?
G. Is the valve merely an on-off valve?
H. Will checking of backflow be required?
I. Will the valve operate frequently or infrequently?

Valves are classified by design type into such classifications as Gate, Globe, Angle, Check, Ball, Butterfly and Plug. They are also classified by end connection, stem, pressure restrictions and material such as bronze, cast iron, etc. Each valve has a specific use. A quality valve used correctly will provide a lifetime of trouble-free service, but a high quality valve installed in the wrong service may require frequent attention.

STEM TYPES
(OS & Y)—Rising Stem-Outside Screw and Yoke

Offers a visual indication of whether the valve is open or closed. Recommended where high temperatures, corrosives, and solids in the line might cause damage to inside-valve stem threads. The stem threads are engaged by the yoke bushing so the stem rises through the hand wheel as it is turned.

(R.S.)—Rising Stem-Inside Screw

Adequate clearance for operation must be provided because both the hand wheel and the stem rise.
The valve wedge position is indicated by the position of the stem and hand wheel.

(N.R.S.)—Non-Rising Stem-Inside Screw

A minimum clearance is required for operating this type of valve. Excessive wear or damage to stem threads inside the valve may be caused by heat, corrosion, and solids. Because the hand wheel and stem do not rise, wedge position cannot be visually determined.

VALVE TYPES
Gate Valves

Provide full flow, minute pressure drop, minimum turbulence and minimum fluid trapped in the line.
They are normally used where operation is infrequent.

Globe Valves

Globe valves are designed for throttling and/or frequent operation with positive shut-off. Particular attention must be paid to the several types of seating materials available to avoid unnecessary wear. The seats must be compatible with the fluid in service and may be composition or metal. The configuration of the Globe valve opening causes turbulence which results in increased resistance. Most bronze Globe valves are rising stem-inside screw, but they are also available on O.S. & Y.

Angle Valves

The fundamental difference between the Angle valve and the Globe valve is the fluid flow through the Angle valve. It makes a 90° turn and offers less resistance to flow than the Globe valve while replacing an elbow. An Angle valve thus reduces the number of joints and installation time.

Plumbing — R2205 Common Work Results for Plumbing

Check Valves

Check valves are designed to prevent backflow by automatically seating when the direction of fluid is reversed.
Swing Check valves are generally installed with Gate-valves, as they provide comparable full flow. Usually recommended for lines where flow velocities are low and should not be used on lines with pulsating flow. Recommended for horizontal installation, or in vertical lines only where flow is upward.

Lift Check Valves

These are commonly used with Globe and Angle valves since they have similar diaphragm seating arrangements and are recommended for preventing backflow of steam, air, gas and water, and on vapor lines with high flow velocities. For horizontal lines, horizontal lift checks should be used and vertical lift checks for vertical lines.

Ball Valves

Ball valves are light and easily installed, yet because of modern elastomeric seats, provide tight closure. Flow is controlled by rotating up to 90° a drilled ball which fits tightly against resilient seals. This ball seats with flow in either direction, and valve handle indicates the degree of opening. Recommended for frequent operation readily adaptable to automation, ideal for installation where space is limited.

Butterfly Valves

Butterfly valves provide bubble-tight closure with excellent throttling characteristics. They can be used for full-open, closed and for throttling applications.

The Butterfly valve consists of a disc within the valve body which is controlled by a shaft. In its closed position, the valve disc seals against a resilient seat. The disc position throughout the full 90° rotation is visually indicated by the position of the operator.

A Butterfly valve is only a fraction of the weight of a Gate valve and requires no gaskets between flanges in most cases. Recommended for frequent operation and adaptable to automation where space is limited.

Wafer and Lug type bodies when installed between two pipe flanges, can be easily removed from the line. The pressure of the bolted flanges holds the valve in place.
Locating lugs makes installation easier.

Plug Valves

Lubricated plug valves, because of the wide range of service to which they are adapted, may be classified as all purpose valves. They can be safely used at all pressure and vacuums, and at all temperatures up to the limits of available lubricants. They are the most satisfactory valves for the handling of gritty suspensions and many other destructive, erosive, corrosive and chemical solutions.

Plumbing — R2211 Facility Water Distribution

R221113-40 Plumbing Approximations for Quick Estimating

Water Control
Water Meter; Backflow Preventer, ... 10 to 15% of Fixtures
Shock Absorbers; Vacuum Breakers;
Mixer.

Pipe And Fittings .... 30 to 60% of Fixtures

  Note: Lower percentage for compact buildings or larger buildings with plumbing in one area.
    Larger percentage for large buildings with plumbing spread out.
    In extreme cases pipe may be more than 100% of fixtures.
    Percentages **do not** include special purpose or process piping.

Plumbing Labor
1 & 2 Story Residential .... Rough-in Labor = 80% of Materials
Apartment Buildings .... Rough-in Labor = 90 to 100% of Materials
Labor for handling and placing fixtures is approximately 25 to 30% of fixtures

Quality/Complexity Multiplier (for all installations)
Economy installation, add. .... 0 to 5%
Good quality, medium complexity, add .... 5 to 15%
Above average quality and complexity, add .... 15 to 25%

R221113-50 Pipe Material Considerations

1. Malleable fittings should be used for gas service.
2. Malleable fittings are used where there are stresses/strains due to expansion and vibration.
3. Cast fittings may be broken as an aid to disassembling heating lines frozen by long use, temperature and minerals.
4. A cast iron pipe is extensively used for underground and submerged service.
5. Type M (light wall) copper tubing is available in hard temper only and is used for nonpressure and less severe applications than K and L.
6. Type L (medium wall) copper tubing, available hard or soft for interior service.
7. Type K (heavy wall) copper tubing, available in hard or soft temper for use where conditions are severe. For underground and interior service.
8. Hard drawn tubing requires fewer hangers or supports but should not be bent. Silver brazed fittings are recommended, but soft solder is normally used.
9. Type DMV (very light wall) copper tubing designed for drainage, waste and vent plus other non-critical pressure services.

Domestic/Imported Pipe and Fittings Costs

The prices shown in this publication for steel/cast iron pipe and steel, cast iron, and malleable iron fittings are based on domestic production sold at the normal trade discounts. The above listed items of foreign manufacture may be available at prices 1/3 to 1/2 of those shown. Some imported items after minor machining or finishing operations are being sold as domestic to further complicate the system.

Caution: Most pipe prices in this data set also include a coupling and pipe hangers which for the larger sizes can add significantly to the per foot cost and should be taken into account when comparing "book cost" with the quoted supplier's cost.

Plumbing — R2211 Facility Water Distribution

R221113-70 Piping to 10' High

When taking off pipe, it is important to identify the different material types and joining procedures, as well as distances between supports and components required for proper support.

During the takeoff, measure through all fittings. Do not subtract the lengths of the fittings, valves, or strainers, etc. This added length plus the final rounding of the totals will compensate for nipples and waste.

When rounding off totals always increase the actual amount to correspond with manufacturer's shipping lengths.

A. Both red brass and yellow brass pipe are normally furnished in 12' lengths, plain end. The Unit Price section includes in the linear foot costs two field threads and one coupling per 10' length. A carbon steel clevis type hanger assembly every 10' is also prorated into the linear foot costs, including both material and labor.

B. Cast iron soil pipe is furnished in either 5' or 10' lengths. For pricing purposes, the Unit Price section features 10' lengths with a joint and a carbon steel clevis hanger assembly every 5' prorated into the per foot costs of both material and labor.

   Three methods of joining are considered: lead and oakum poured joints or push-on gasket type joints for the bell and spigot pipe and a joint clamp for the no-hub soil pipe. The labor and material costs for each of these individual joining procedures are also prorated into the linear costs per foot.

C. Copper tubing covers types K, L, M, and DWV which are furnished in 20' lengths. Means pricing data is based on a tubing cut each length and a coupling and two soft soldered joints every 10'. A carbon steel, clevis type hanger assembly every 10' is also prorated into the per foot costs. The prices for refrigeration tubing are for materials only. Labor for full lengths may be based on the type L labor but short cut measures in tight areas can increase the installation labor-hours from 20 to 40%.

D. Corrosion-resistant piping does not lend itself to one particular standard of hanging or support assembly due to its diversity of application and placement. The several varieties of corrosion-resistant piping do not include any material or labor costs for hanger assemblies (See the Unit Price section for appropriate selection).

E. Glass pipe is furnished in standard lengths either 5' or 10' long, beaded on one end. Special orders for diverse lengths beaded on both ends are also available. For pricing purposes, R.S. Means features 10' lengths with a coupling and a carbon steel band hanger assembly every 10' prorated into the per foot linear costs.

   Glass pipe is also available with conical ends and standard lengths ranging from 6" through 3' in 6" increments, then up to 10' in 12" increments. Special lengths can be customized for particular installation requirements.

   For pricing purposes, Means has based the labor and material pricing on 10' lengths. Included in these costs per linear foot are the prorated costs for a flanged assembly every 10' consisting of two flanges, a gasket, two insertable seals, and the required number of bolts and nuts. A carbon steel band hanger assembly based on 10' center lines has also been prorated into the costs per foot for labor and materials.

F. Plastic pipe of several compositions and joining methods are considered. Fiberglass reinforced pipe (FRP) is priced, based on 10' lengths (20' lengths are also available), with coupling and epoxy joints every 10'. FRP is furnished in both "General Service" and "High Strength." A carbon steel clevis hanger assembly, 3 for every 10', is built into the prorated labor and material costs on a per foot basis.

   The PVC and CPVC pipe schedules 40, 80 and 120, plus SDR ratings are all based on 20' lengths with a coupling installed every 10', as well as a carbon steel clevis hanger assembly every 3'. The PVC and ABS type DWV piping is based on 10' lengths with solvent weld couplings every 10', and with carbon steel clevis hanger assemblies, 3 for every 10'. The rest of the plastic piping in this section is based on flexible 100' coils and does not include any coupling or supports.

   This section ends with PVC drain and sewer piping based on 10' lengths with bell and spigot ends and O-ring type, push-on joints.

G. Stainless steel piping includes both weld end and threaded piping, both in the type 304 and 316 specification and in the following schedules, 5, 10, 40, 80, and 160. Although this piping is usually furnished in 20' lengths, this cost grouping has a joint (either heli-arc butt-welded or threads and coupling) every 10'. A carbon steel clevis type hanger assembly is also included at 10' intervals and prorated into the linear foot costs.

H. Carbon steel pipe includes both black and galvanized. This section encompasses schedules 40 (standard) and 80 (extra heavy).

   Several common methods of joining steel pipe — such as thread and coupled, butt welded, and flanged (150 lb. weld neck flanges) are also included.

   For estimating purposes, it is assumed that the piping is purchased in 20' lengths and that a compatible joint is made up every 10'. These joints are prorated into the labor and material costs per linear foot. The following hanger and support assemblies every 10' are also included: carbon steel clevis for the T & C pipe, and single rod roll type for both the welded and flanged piping. All of these hangers are oversized to accommodate pipe insulation 3/4" thick through 5" pipe size and 1-1/2" thick from 6" through 12" pipe size.

I. Grooved joint steel pipe is priced both black and galvanized, in schedules 10, 40, and 80, furnished in 20' lengths. This section describes two joining methods: cut groove and roll groove. The schedule 10 piping is roll-grooved, while the heavier schedules are cut-grooved. The labor and material costs are prorated into per linear foot prices, including a coupled joint every 10', as well as a carbon steel clevis hanger assembly.

Notes:

The pipe hanger assemblies mentioned in the preceding paragraphs include the described hanger; appropriately sized steel, box-type insert and nut; plus 18" of threaded hanger rod.

C clamps are used when the pipe is to be supported from steel shapes rather than anchored in the slab. C clamps are slightly less costly than inserts. However, to save time in estimating, it is advisable to use the given line number cost, rather than substituting a C clamp for the insert.

Add to piping labor for elevated installation:

10' to 14.5' high	10%	30' to 34.5' high	40%
15' to 19.5' high	20%	35' to 39.5' high	50%
20' to 24.5' high	25%	40' and higher	55%
25' to 29.5' high	35%		

When using the percentage adds for elevated piping installations as shown above, bear in mind that the given heights are for the pipe supports, even though the insert, anchor, or clamp may be several feet higher than the pipe itself.

An allowance has been included in the piping installation time for testing and minor tightening of leaking joints, fittings, stuffing boxes, packing glands, etc. For extraordinary test requirements such as x-rays, prolonged pressure or demonstration tests, a percentage of the piping labor, based on the estimator's experience, must be added to the labor total. A testing service specializing in weld x-rays should be consulted for pricing if it is an estimate requirement. Equipment installation time includes start-up with associated adjustments.

Plumbing — R2213 Facility Sanitary Sewerage

R221316-10 Drainage Fixture Units for Fixtures and Groups

Fixture Type	Drainage Fixture Unit Value as Load Factors	Minimum Size of Trap (inches)
Automatic Clothes Washer, commercial (Note A)	3.0	2.0
Automatic Clothes Washer, residential	2.0	2.0
Full Bathroom Group w/bathtub or shower stall (1.6 gpf WC)	5.0	-
Full Bathroom Group w/bathtub or shower stall (WC flushing greater than 1.6 gpf) (Note D)	6.0	-
Bathtub (with or without overhead shower)	2.0	1.5
Bidet	1.0	1.25
Drinking Fountain	0.5	1025
Dishwasher, domestic	2.0	1.5
Emergency floor drains	0.0	2
Floor drains	2.0	2
Kitchen sinks, domestic	2.0	1.5
Lavatory	1.0	1.25
Shower (5.7 gpm or less flow rate)	2.0	1.5
Shower (5.7 gpm - 12.3 gpm flow rate)	3.0	2
Shower (12.3 gpm - 25.8 gpm flow rate)	5.0	3
Shower (25.8 gpm to 55.6 gpm flow rate)	6.0	4
Service Sink	2.0	1.5
Urinal	4.0	Note C
Urinal (1.0 gpf or less)	2.0	Note C
Urinal (nonwater supplied)	0.5	Note C
Water closet, flushometer tank, public or private	4.0	Note C
Water closet, private (1.6 gpf)	3.0	Note C
Water closet, private (flushing greater than 1.6 gpf)	4.0	Note C
Water closet, public (1.6 gpf)	4.0	Note C
Water closet, public (flushing greater than 1.6 gpf)	6.0	Note C

Notes:
A. A showerhead over a bathtub or whirlpool tub attachment does not increase the drainage fixture unit value.
B. Trap size shall be consistent with the fixture outlet size.
C. For fixtures added to a bathroom group, add the DFU value to those additional fixtures to the bathroom group fixture count.

Excerpted from the 2012 *International Plumbing Code*, Copyright 2011. Washington, D.C.: International Code Council. Reproduced with permission. All rights reserved. www.ICCSAFE.org

R221316-15 Drainage Fixture Units for Fixture Drains or Traps

Fixture Drain or Trap Size (inches)	Drainage Fixture Unit Value
1.25	1.0
1.5	2.0
2.0	3.0
2.5	4.0
3.0	5.0
4.0	6.0

Notes:
Drainage Fixture Unit values designate the relative load weight or different kinds of fixtures that shall be emplored in estimating the total load carried by a soil or waste pipe.

Excerpted from the 2012 *International Plumbing Code*, Copyright 2011. Washington, D.C.: International Code Council. Reproduced with permission. All rights reserved. www.ICCSAFE.org

Plumbing — R2213 Facility Sanitary Sewerage

R221316-20 Allowable Fixture Units (d.f.u.) for Branches and Stacks

Pipe Diam.	Horiz. Branch (not incl. drains)	Stack Size for 3 Stories or 3 Levels	Stack size for Over 3 levels	Maximum for 1 Story building Stack
1-1/2"	3	4	8	2
2"	6	10	24	6
2-1/2"	12	20	42	9
3"	20*	48*	72*	20*
4"	160	240	500	90
5"	360	540	1100	200
6"	620	960	1900	350
8"	1400	2200	3600	600
10"	2500	3800	5600	1000
12"	3900	6000	8400	1500
15"	7000			

*Not more than two water closets or bathroom groups within each branch interval nor more than six water closets or bathroom groups on the stack.

Stacks sized for the total may be reduced as load decreases at each story to a minimum diameter of 1/2 the maximum diameter.

Plumbing — R2240 Plumbing Fixtures

R224000-10 Water Consumption Rates

Fixture Type	Water Supply Fixture Unit Value		
	Hot Water	Cold Water	Combined
Bathtub	1.0	1.0	1.4
Clothes Washer	1.0	1.0	1.4
Dishwasher	1.4	0.0	1.4
Kitchen Sink	1.0	1.0	1.4
Laundry Tub	1.0	1.0	1.4
Lavatory	0.5	0.5	0.7
Shower Stall	1.0	1.0	1.4
Water Closet (tank type)	0.0	2.2	2.2
Full Bath Group			
w/bathtub or shower stall	1.5	2.7	3.6
Half Bath Group			
w/W.C. and Lavatory	0.5	2.5	2.6
Kitchen Group			
w/Dishwasher and Sink	1.9	1.0	2.5
Laundry Group			
w/Clothes Washer and Laundry Tub	1.8	1.8	2.5
Hose bibb (sillcock)	0.0	2.5	2.5

Notes:
Typically, WSFU = 1GPM

Supply loads in the building water-distribution system shall be determined by total load on the pipe being sized, in terms of water supply fixture units (WSFU) and gallons per minute (GPM) flow rates. For fixtures not listed, choose a WSFU value of a fixture with similar flow characteristics. Water Fixture Supply Units determined the required water supply to fixtures and their service systems. Fixture units are equal to (1) cubic foot of water drained in a 1-1/4" pipe per minute. It is not a flow rate unit but a design factor.

Excerpted from the 2012 *International Plumbing Code,* Copyright 2011.
Washington, D.C.: International Code Council. Reproduced with permission.
All rights reserved. www.ICCSAFE.org

Plumbing — R2240 Plumbing Fixtures

R224000-20 Fixture Demands in Gallons per Fixture per Hour

Table below is based on 140°F final temperature except for dishwashers in public places (*) where 180°F water is mandatory.

Supply Systems for Flush Tanks			Supply Systems for Flushometer Valves		
Load	Demand		Load	Demand	
WSFU	GPM	CU. FT.	WSFU	GPM	CU. FT.
1.0	3.0	0.041040	-	-	-
2.0	5.0	0.068400	-	-	-
3.0	6.5	0.868920	-	-	-
4.0	8.0	1.069440	-	-	-
5.0	9.4	1.256592	5.0	15	2.0052
6.0	10.7	1.430376	6.0	17.4	2.326032
7.0	11.8	1.577424	7.0	19.8	2.646364
8.0	12.8	1.711104	8.0	22.2	2.967696
9.0	13.7	1.831416	9.0	24.6	3.288528
10.0	14.6	1.951728	10.0	27	3.60936
11.0	15.4	2.058672	11.0	27.8	3.716304
12.0	16.0	2.138880	12.0	28.6	3.823248
13.0	16.5	2.205720	13.0	29.4	3.930192
14.0	17.0	2.272560	14.0	30.2	4.037136
15.0	17.5	2.339400	15.0	31	4.14408
16.0	18.0	2.906240	16.0	31.8	4.241024
17.0	18.4	2.459712	17.0	32.6	4.357968
18.0	18.8	2.513184	18.0	33.4	4.464912
19.0	19.2	2.566656	19.0	34.2	4.571856
20.0	19.6	2.620218	20.0	35.0	4.678800
25.0	21.5	2.874120	25.0	38.0	5.079840
30.0	23.3	3.114744	30.0	42.0	5.611356
35.0	24.9	3.328632	35.0	44.0	5.881920
40.0	26.3	3.515784	40.0	46.0	6.149280
45.0	27.7	3.702936	45.0	48.0	6.416640
50.0	29.1	3.890088	50.0	50.0	6.684000

Notes:
When designing a plumbing system that utilizes fixtures other than, or in addition to, water closets, use the data provided in the Supply Systems for Flush Tanks section of the above table.

To obtain the probable maximum demand, multiply the total demands for the fixtures (gal./fixture/hour) by the demand factor. The heater should have a heating capacity in gallons per hour equal to this maximum. The storage tank should have a capacity in gallons equal to the probable maximum demand multiplied by the storage capacity factor.

Excerpted from the 2012 *International Residential Code*, Copyright 2011. Washington, D.C.: International Code Council. Reproduced with permission. All rights reserved. www.ICCSAFE.org

Plumbing

R2240 Plumbing Fixtures

R224000-30 Minimum Plumbing Fixture Requirements

Classification	Occupancy	Description	Water Closet Male	Water Closet Female	Lavatories Male	Lavatories Female	Bathtubs/Showers	Drinking Fountains	Other
Assembly	A-1	Theaters and other buildings for the performing arts and motion pictures	1:125	1:65	1:200			1:500	1 Service Sink
	A-2	Nightclubs, bars, taverns dance halls	1:40		1:75			1:500	1 Service Sink
		Restaurants, banquet halls, food courts	1:75		1:200			1:500	1 Service Sink
	A-3	Auditorium w/o permanent seating, art galleries, exhibition halls, museums, lecture halls, libraries, arcades & gymnasiums	1:125	1:65	1:200			1:500	1 Service Sink
		Passenger terminals and transportation facilities	1:500		1:750			1:1000	1 Service Sink
		Places of worship and other religious services	1:150	1:75	1:200			1:1000	1 Service Sink
	A-4	Indoor sporting events and activities, coliseums, arenas, skating rinks, pools, and tennis courts	1:75 for the first 1500, then 1:120 for the remainder	1:40 for the first 1520, then 1:60 for the remainder	1:200	1:150		1:1000	1 Service Sink
	A-5	Outdoor sporting events and activities, stadiums, amusement parks, bleachers, grandstands	1:75 for the first 1500, then 1:120 for the remainder	1:40 for the first 1520, then 1:60 for the remainder	1:200	1:150		1:1000	1 Service Sink
Business	B	Buildings for the transaction of business, professional services, other services involving merchandise, office buildings, banks, light industrial	1:25 for the first 50, then 1:50 for the remainder		1:40 for the first 80, then 1:80 for the remainder			1:100	1 Service Sink
Educational	E	Educational Facilities	1:50		1:50			1:100	1 Service Sink
Factory and industrial	F-1 and F-2	Structures in which occupants are engaged in work fabricating, assembly or processing of products or materials	1:100		1:100		See International Plumbing Code	1:400	1 Service Sink
Institutional	I-1	Residential Care	1:10		1:10		1:8	1:100	1 Service Sink
	I-2	Hospitals, ambulatory nursing home care recipient	1 per room		1 per room		1:15	1:100	1 Service Sink
		Employees, other than residential care	1:25		1:35			1:100	
		Visitors, other than residential care	1:75		1:100			1:500	
	I-3	Prisons	1 per cell		1 per cell		1:15	1:100	1 Service Sink
		Reformatories, detention and correction centers	1:15		1:15		1:15	1:100	1 Service Sink
		Employees	1:25		1:35			1:100	
	I-4	Adult and child day care	1:15		1:15		1	1:100	1 Service Sink
Mercantile	M	Retail stores, service stations, shops, salesrooms, markets and shopping centers	1:500		1:750			1:1000	1 Service Sink
Residential	R-1	Hotels, Motels, boarding houses (transient)	1 per sleeping unit		1 per sleeping unit		1 per sleeping unit		1 Service Sink
	R-2	Dormitories, fraternities, sororities and boarding houses (not transient)	1:10		1:10		1:8	1:100	1 Service Sink
		Apartment House	1 per dwelling unit		1 per dwelling unit		1 per dwelling unit		1 Kitchen sink per dwelling; 1 clothes washer connection per 20 dwellings
	R-3	1 and 2 Family Dwellings	1 per dwelling unit		1:10		1 per dwelling unit		1 Kitchen sink per dwelling; 1 clothes washer connection per dwelling
	R-3	Congregate living facilities w/<16 people	1:10		1:10		1:8	1:100	1 Service Sink
	R-4	Congregate living facilities w/<16 people	1:10		1:10		1:8	1:100	1 Service Sink
Storage	S-1 and S-2	Structures for the storage of good, warehouses, storehouses and freight depots, low and moderate hazard	1:100		1:100		See International Plumbing Code	1:1000	1 Service Sink

Table 2902.1

Excerpted from the 2012 *International Building Code*, Copyright 2011. Washington, D.C.: International Code Council. Reproduced with permission. All rights reserved. www.ICCSAFE.org

Heating, Ventilating & A.C. R2305 Common Work Results for HVAC

Fig. R238313-11

R230500-10 Subcontractors

On the unit cost pages of the R.S. Means Cost Data data set, the last column is entitled "Total Incl. O&P". This is normally the cost of the installing contractor. In the HVAC Division, this is the cost of the mechanical contractor. If the particular work being estimated is to be performed by a sub to the mechanical contractor, the mechanical's profit and handling charge (usually 10%) is added to the total of the last column.

Heating, Ventilating & A.C. R2356 Solar Energy Heating Equipment

R235616-60 Solar Heating (Space and Hot Water)

Collectors should face as close to due South as possible, but variations of up to 20 degrees on either side of true South are acceptable. Local climate and collector type may influence the choice between east or west deviations. Obviously they should be located so they are not shaded from the sun's rays. Incline collectors at a slope of latitude minus 5 degrees for domestic hot water and latitude plus 15 degrees for space heating.

Flat plate collectors consist of a number of components as follows: Insulation to reduce heat loss through the bottom and sides of the collector. The enclosure which contains all the components in this assembly is usually weatherproof and prevents dust, wind and water from coming in contact with the absorber plate. The cover plate usually consists of one or more layers of a variety of glass or plastic and reduces the reradiation by creating an air space which traps the heat between the cover and the absorber plates.

The absorber plate must have a good thermal bond with the fluid passages. The absorber plate is usually metallic and treated with a surface coating which improves absorptivity. Black or dark paints or selective coatings are used for this purpose, and the design of this passage and plate combination helps determine a solar system's effectiveness.

Heat transfer fluid passage tubes are attached above and below or integral with an absorber plate for the purpose of transferring thermal energy from the absorber plate to a heat transfer medium. The heat exchanger is a device for transferring thermal energy from one fluid to another.

Piping and storage tanks should be well insulated to minimize heat losses.

Size domestic water heating storage tanks to hold 20 gallons of water per user, minimum, plus 10 gallons per dishwasher or washing machine. For domestic water heating an optimum collector size is approximately 3/4 square foot of area per gallon of water storage. For space heating of residences and small commercial applications the collector is commonly sized between 30% and 50% of the internal floor area. For space heating of large commercial applications, collector areas less than 30% of the internal floor area can still provide significant heat reductions.

A supplementary heat source is recommended for Northern states for December through February.

The solar energy transmission per square foot of collector surface varies greatly with the material used. Initial cost, heat transmittance and useful life are obviously interrelated.

Heating, Ventilating & A.C. R2383 Radiant Heating Units

R238313-10 Heat Trace Systems

Before you can determine the cost of a HEAT TRACE installation, the method of attachment must be established. There are (4) common methods:
1. Cable is simply attached to the pipe with polyester tape every 12'.
2. Cable is attached with a continuous cover of 2" wide aluminum tape.
3. Cable is attached with factory extruded heat transfer cement and covered with metallic raceway with clips every 10'.
4. Cable is attached between layers of pipe insulation using either clips or polyester tape.

In all of the above methods each component of the system must be priced individually.

Example: Components for method 3 must include:
- A. Heat trace cable by voltage and watts per linear foot.
- B. Heat transfer cement, 1 gallon per 60 linear feet of cover.
- C. Metallic raceway by size and type.
- D. Raceway clips by size of pipe.

When taking off linear foot lengths of cable add the following for each valve in the system. (E)

SCREWED OR WELDED VALVE:			FLANGED VALVE:			BUTTERFLY VALVES:		
1/2"	=	6"	1/2"	=	1'-0"	1/2"	=	0'
3/4"	=	9"	3/4"	=	1'-6"	3/4"	=	0'
1"	=	1'-0"	1"	=	2'-0"	1"	=	1'-0"
1-1/2"	=	1'-6"	1-1/2"	=	2'-6"	1-1/2"	=	1'-6"
2"	=	2'	2"	=	2'-6"	2"	=	2'-0"
2-1/2"	=	2'-6"	2-1/2"	=	3'-0"	2-1/2"	=	2'-6"
3"	=	2'-6"	3"	=	3'-6"	3"	=	2'-6"
4"	=	4'-0"	4"	=	4'-0"	4"	=	3'-0"
6"	=	7'-0"	6"	=	8'-0"	6"	=	3'-6"
8"	=	9'-6"	8"	=	11'-0"	8"	=	4'-0"
10"	=	12'-6"	10"	=	14'-0"	10"	=	4'-0"
12"	=	15'-0"	12"	=	16'-6"	12"	=	5'-0"
14"	=	18'-0"	14"	=	19'-6"	14"	=	5'-6"
16"	=	21'-6"	16"	=	23'-0"	16"	=	6'-0"
18"	=	25'-6"	18"	=	27'-0"	18"	=	6'-6"
20"	=	28'-6"	20"	=	30'-0"	20"	=	7'-0"
24"	=	34'-0"	24"	=	36'-0"	24"	=	8'-0"
30"	=	40'-0"	30"	=	42'-0"	30"	=	10'-0"

Heating, Ventilating & A.C. — R2383 Radiant Heating Units

R238313-10 Heat Trace Systems (cont.)

Add the following quantities of heat transfer cement to linear foot totals for each valve:

Nominal Valve Size	Gallons of Cement per Valve
1/2"	0.14
3/4"	0.21
1"	0.29
1-1/2"	0.36
2"	0.43
2-1/2"	0.70
3"	0.71
4"	1.00
6"	1.43
8"	1.48
10"	1.50
12"	1.60
14"	1.75
16"	2.00
18"	2.25
20"	2.50
24"	3.00
30"	3.75

The following must be added to the list of components to accurately price HEAT TRACE systems:
1. Expediter fitting and clamp fasteners (F)
2. Junction box and nipple connected to expediter fitting (G)
3. Field installed terminal blocks within junction box
4. Ground lugs
5. Piping from power source to expediter fitting
6. Controls
7. Thermostats
8. Branch wiring
9. Cable splices
10. End of cable terminations
11. Branch piping fittings and boxes

Deduct the following percentages from labor if cable lengths in the same area exceed:

150' to 250' 10%   351' to 500' 20%
251' to 350' 15%   Over 500'   25%

Add the following percentages to labor for elevated installations:

15' to 20' high 10%   31' to 35' high 40%
21' to 25' high 20%   36' to 40' high 50%
26' to 30' high 30%   Over 40' high   60%

R238313-20 Spiral-Wrapped Heat Trace Cable (Pitch Table)

In order to increase the amount of heat, occasionally heat trace cable is wrapped in a spiral fashion around a pipe; increasing the number of feet of heater cable per linear foot of pipe.

$$\text{Feet of Heat Trace per Foot of Pipe} = \frac{\text{Watts/Foot of Heat Loss}}{\text{Watts/Foot of the Cable}}$$

The linear distance between wraps (pitch) is then taken from a chart or table. Generally, the pitch is listed on a drawing leaving the estimator to calculate the total length of heat tape required. An approximation may be taken from this table.

Engineers first determine the heat loss per foot of pipe (based on the insulating material, its thickness, and the temperature differential across it). A ratio is then calculated by the formula:

Feet of Heat Trace Per Foot of Pipe

Pitch In Inches	1	1¼	1½	2	2½	3	4	6	8	10	12	14	16	18	20	24
3.5	1.80															
4	1.65															
5	1.46	1.60	1.80													
6	1.34	1.45	1.55	1.75												
7	1.25	1.35	1.43	1.57	1.75											
8	1.20	1.28	1.34	1.45	1.60	1.80										
9	1.16	1.23	1.28	1.37	1.51	1.68										
10	1.13	1.19	1.24	1.32	1.44	1.57	1.82									
15	1.06	1.08	1.10	1.15	1.21	1.29	1.42	1.78								
20	1.04	1.05	1.06	1.08	1.13	1.17	1.25	1.49	1.73							
25		1.04	1.04	1.06	1.08	1.11	1.17	1.33	1.51	1.72						
30				1.04	1.05	1.07	1.12	1.24	1.37	1.54	1.70					
35					1.06	1.06	1.09	1.17	1.28	1.42	1.54	1.80				
40						1.05	1.07	1.14	1.22	1.33	1.44	1.64	1.78			
50							1.05	1.09	1.15	1.22	1.29	1.52	1.64	1.75		
60								1.06	1.11	1.16	1.21	1.35	1.44	1.53	1.64	1.83
70								1.05	1.08	1.12	1.17	1.25	1.31	1.39	1.46	1.62
80									1.06	1.09	1.13	1.19	1.24	1.30	1.35	1.47
90									1.04	1.06	1.10	1.15	1.19	1.24	1.28	1.38
100										1.05	1.08	1.13	1.16	1.19	1.23	1.32
												1.10	1.13	1.15	1.19	1.23

Note: Common practice would normally limit the lower end of the table to 5% of additional heat and above 80% an engineer would likely opt for two (2) parallel cables.

Electrical — R2605 Common Work Results for Electrical

R260519-90 Wire

Wire quantities are taken off by either measuring each cable run or by extending the conduit and raceway quantities times the number of conductors in the raceway. Ten percent should be added for waste and tie-ins. Keep in mind that the unit of measure of wire is C.L.F. not L.F. as in raceways so the formula would read:

$$\frac{(\text{L.F. Raceway} \times \text{No. of Conductors}) \times 1.10}{100} = \text{C.L.F.}$$

Price per C.L.F. of wire includes:
1. Setting up wire coils or spools on racks
2. Attaching wire to pull in means
3. Measuring and cutting wire
4. Pulling wire into a raceway
5. Identifying and tagging

Price does not include:
1. Connections to breakers, panelboards, or equipment
2. Splices

Job Conditions: Productivity is based on new construction to a height of 15' using rolling staging in an unobstructed area. Material staging is assumed to be within 100' of work being performed.

Economy of Scale: If more than three wires at a time are being pulled, deduct the following percentages from the labor of that grouping:

4-5 wires	25%
6-10 wires	30%
11-15 wires	35%
over 15	40%

If a wire pull is less than 100' in length and is interrupted several times by boxes, lighting outlets, etc., it may be necessary to add the following lengths to each wire being pulled:

Junction box to junction box	2 L.F.
Lighting panel to junction box	6 L.F.
Distribution panel to sub panel	8 L.F.
Switchboard to distribution panel	12 L.F.
Switchboard to motor control center	20 L.F.
Switchboard to cable tray	40 L.F.

Measure of Drops and Riser: It is important when taking off wire quantities to include the wire for drops to electrical equipment. If heights of electrical equipment are not clearly stated, use the following guide:

	Bottom A.F.F.	Top A.F.F.	Inside Cabinet
Safety switch to 100A	5'	6'	2'
Safety switch 400 to 600A	4'	6'	3'
100A panel 12 to 30 circuit	4'	6'	3'
42 circuit panel	3'	6'	4'
Switch box	3'	3'6"	1'
Switchgear	0'	8'	8'
Motor control centers	0'	8'	8'
Transformers - wall mount	4'	8'	2'
Transformers - floor mount	0'	12'	4'

EARTHWORK

R3123 Excavation & Fill

R312316-45 Excavating Equipment

The table below lists theoretical hourly production in C.Y./hr. bank measure for some typical excavation equipment. Figures assume 50 minute hours, 83% job efficiency, 100% operator efficiency, 90° swing and properly sized hauling units, which must be modified for adverse digging and loading conditions. Actual production costs in the front of the data set average about 50% of the theoretical values listed here.

Equipment	Soil Type	B.C.Y. Weight	% Swell	1 C.Y.	1-1/2 C.Y.	2 C.Y.	2-1/2 C.Y.	3 C.Y.	3-1/2 C.Y.	4 C.Y.
Hydraulic Excavator "Backhoe" 15' Deep Cut	Moist loam, sandy clay	3400 lb.	40%	165	195	200	275	330	385	440
	Sand and gravel	3100	18	140	170	225	240	285	330	380
	Common earth	2800	30	150	180	230	250	300	350	400
	Clay, hard, dense	3000	33	120	140	190	200	240	260	320
Power Shovel Optimum Cut (Ft.)	Moist loam, sandy clay	3400	40	170 (6.0)	245 (7.0)	295 (7.8)	335 (8.4)	385 (8.8)	435 (9.1)	475 (9.4)
	Sand and gravel	3100	18	165 (6.0)	225 (7.0)	275 (7.8)	325 (8.4)	375 (8.8)	420 (9.1)	460 (9.4)
	Common earth	2800	30	145 (7.8)	200 (9.2)	250 (10.2)	295 (11.2)	335 (12.1)	375 (13.0)	425 (13.8)
	Clay, hard, dense	3000	33	120 (9.0)	175 (10.7)	220 (12.2)	255 (13.3)	300 (14.2)	335 (15.1)	375 (16.0)
Drag Line Optimum Cut (Ft.)	Moist loam, sandy clay	3400	40	130 (6.6)	180 (7.4)	220 (8.0)	250 (8.5)	290 (9.0)	325 (9.5)	385 (10.0)
	Sand and gravel	3100	18	130 (6.6)	175 (7.4)	210 (8.0)	245 (8.5)	280 (9.0)	315 (9.5)	375 (10.0)
	Common earth	2800	30	110 (8.0)	160 (9.0)	190 (9.9)	220 (10.5)	250 (11.0)	280 (11.5)	310 (12.0)
	Clay, hard, dense	3000	33	90 (9.3)	130 (10.7)	160 (11.8)	190 (12.3)	225 (12.8)	250 (13.3)	280 (12.0)

Equipment	Soil Type	B.C.Y. Weight	% Swell	Wheel Loaders				Track Loaders		
				3 C.Y.	4 C.Y.	6 C.Y.	8 C.Y.	2-1/4 C.Y.	3 C.Y.	4 C.Y.
Loading Tractors	Moist loam, sandy clay	3400	40	260	340	510	690	135	180	250
	Sand and gravel	3100	18	245	320	480	650	130	170	235
	Common earth	2800	30	230	300	460	620	120	155	220
	Clay, hard, dense	3000	33	200	270	415	560	110	145	200
	Rock, well-blasted	4000	50	180	245	380	520	100	130	180

EARTHWORK — R3123 Excavation & Fill

R312319-90 Wellpoints

A single stage wellpoint system is usually limited to dewatering an average 15' depth below normal ground water level. Multi-stage systems are employed for greater depth with the pumping equipment installed only at the lowest header level. Ejectors with unlimited lift capacity can be economical when two or more stages of wellpoints can be replaced or when horizontal clearance is restricted, such as in deep trenches or tunneling projects, and where low water flows are expected. Wellpoints are usually spaced on 2-1/2' to 10' centers along a header pipe. Wellpoint spacing, header size, and pump size are all determined by the expected flow as dictated by soil conditions.

In almost all soils encountered in wellpoint dewatering, the wellpoints may be jetted into place. Cemented soils and stiff clays may require sand wicks about 12" in diameter around each wellpoint to increase efficiency and eliminate weeping into the excavation. These sand wicks require 1/2 to 3 C.Y. of washed filter sand and are installed by using a 12" diameter steel casing and hole puncher jetted into the ground 2' deeper than the wellpoint. Rock may require predrilled holes.

Labor required for the complete installation and removal of a single stage wellpoint system is in the range of 3/4 to 2 labor-hours per linear foot of header, depending upon jetting conditions, wellpoint spacing, etc.

Continuous pumping is necessary except in some free draining soil where temporary flooding is permissible (as in trenches which are backfilled after each day's work). Good practice requires provision of a stand-by pump during the continuous pumping operation.

Systems for continuous trenching below the water table should be installed three to four times the length of expected daily progress to ensure uninterrupted digging, and header pipe size should not be changed during the job.

For pervious free draining soils, deep wells in place of wellpoints may be economical because of lower installation and maintenance costs. Daily production ranges between two to three wells per day, for 25' to 40' depths, to one well per day for depths over 50'.

Detailed analysis and estimating for any dewatering problem is available at no cost from wellpoint manufacturers. Major firms will quote "sufficient equipment" quotes or their affiliates will offer lump sum proposals to cover complete dewatering responsibility.

	Description for 200' System with 8" Header	Quantities
Equipment & Material	Wellpoints 25' long, 2" diameter @ 5' O.C.	40 Each
	Header pipe, 8" diameter	200 L.F.
	Discharge pipe, 8" diameter	100 L.F.
	8" valves	3 Each
	Combination jetting & wellpoint pump (standby)	1 Each
	Wellpoint pump, 8" diameter	1 Each
	Transportation to and from site	1 Day
	Fuel for 30 days x 60 gal./day	1800 Gallons
	Lubricants for 30 days x 16 lbs./day	480 Lbs.
	Sand for points	40 C.Y.
Labor	Technician to supervise installation	1 Week
	Labor for installation and removal of system	300 Labor-hours
	4 Operators straight time 40 hrs./wk. for 4.33 wks.	693 Hrs.
	4 Operators overtime 2 hrs./wk. for 4.33 wks.	35 Hrs.

Earthwork — R3141 Shoring

R314116-40 Wood Sheet Piling

Wood sheet piling may be used for depths to 20' where there is no ground water. If moderate ground water is encountered Tongue & Groove sheeting will help to keep it out. When considerable ground water is present, steel sheeting must be used.

For estimating purposes on trench excavation, sizes are as follows:

Depth	Sheeting	Wales	Braces	B.F. per S.F.
To 8'	3 x 12's	6 x 8's, 2 line	6 x 8's, @ 10'	4.0 @ 8'
8' x 12'	3 x 12's	10 x 10's, 2 line	10 x 10's, @ 9'	5.0 average
12' to 20'	3 x 12's	12 x 12's, 3 line	12 x 12's, @ 8'	7.0 average

Sheeting to be toed in at least 2' depending upon soil conditions. A five person crew with an air compressor and sheeting driver can drive and brace 440 SF/day at 8' deep, 360 SF/day at 12' deep, and 320 SF/day at 16' deep.

For normal soils, piling can be pulled in 1/3 the time to install. Pulling difficulty increases with the time in the ground. Production can be increased by high pressure jetting.

R314116-45 Steel Sheet Piling

Limiting weights are 22 to 38#/S.F. of wall surface with 27#/S.F. average for usual types and sizes. (Weights of piles themselves are from 30.7#/L.F. to 57#/L.F. but they are 15" to 21" wide.) Lightweight sections 12" to 28" wide from 3 ga. to 12 ga. thick are also available for shallow excavations. Piles may be driven two at a time with an impact or vibratory hammer (use vibratory to pull) hung from a crane without leads. A reasonable estimate of the life of steel sheet piling is 10 uses with up to 125 uses possible if a vibratory hammer is used. Used piling costs from 50% to 80% of new piling depending on location and market conditions. Sheet piling and H piles can be rented for about 30% of the delivered mill price for the first month and 5% per month thereafter. Allow 1 labor-hour per pile for cleaning and trimming after driving. These costs increase with depth and hydrostatic head. Vibratory drivers are faster in wet granular soils and are excellent for pile extraction. Pulling difficulty increases with the time in the ground and may cost more than driving. It is often economical to abandon the sheet piling, especially if it can be used as the outer wall form. Allow about 1/3 additional length or more for toeing into ground. Add bracing, waler and strut costs. Waler costs can equal the cost per ton of sheeting.

Utilities — R3311 Water Utility Distribution Piping

R331113-80 Piping Designations

There are several systems currently in use to describe pipe and fittings. The following paragraphs will help to identify and clarify classifications of piping systems used for water distribution.

Piping may be classified by schedule. Piping schedules include 5S, 10S, 10, 20, 30, Standard, 40, 60, Extra Strong, 80, 100, 120, 140, 160 and Double Extra Strong. These schedules are dependent upon the pipe wall thickness. The wall thickness of a particular schedule may vary with pipe size.

Ductile iron pipe for water distribution is classified by Pressure Classes such as Class 150, 200, 250, 300 and 350. These classes are actually the rated water working pressure of the pipe in pounds per square inch (psi). The pipe in these pressure classes is designed to withstand the rated water working pressure plus a surge allowance of 100 psi.

The American Water Works Association (AWWA) provides standards for various types of **plastic pipe.** C-900 is the specification for polyvinyl chloride (PVC) piping used for water distribution in sizes ranging from 4" through 12". C-901 is the specification for polyethylene (PE) pressure pipe, tubing and fittings used for water distribution in sizes ranging from 1/2" through 3". C-905 is the specification for PVC piping sizes 14" and greater.

PVC pressure-rated pipe is identified using the standard dimensional ratio (SDR) method. This method is defined by the American Society for Testing and Materials (ASTM) Standard D 2241. This pipe is available in SDR numbers 64, 41, 32.5, 26, 21, 17, and 13.5. Pipe with an SDR of 64 will have the thinnest wall while pipe with an SDR of 13.5 will have the thickest wall. When the pressure rating (PR) of a pipe is given in psi, it is based on a line supplying water at 73 degrees F.

The National Sanitation Foundation (NSF) seal of approval is applied to products that can be used with potable water. These products have been tested to ANSI/NSF Standard 14.

Valves and strainers are classified by American National Standards Institute (ANSI) Classes. These Classes are 125, 150, 200, 250, 300, 400, 600, 900, 1500 and 2500. Within each class there is an operating pressure range dependent upon temperature. Design parameters should be compared to the appropriate material dependent, pressure-temperature rating chart for accurate valve selection.

Change Orders

Change Order Considerations

A change order is a written document usually prepared by the design professional and signed by the owner, the architect/engineer, and the contractor. A change order states the agreement of the parties to: an addition, deletion, or revision in the work; an adjustment in the contract sum, if any; or an adjustment in the contract time, if any. Change orders, or "extras", in the construction process occur after execution of the construction contract and impact architects/engineers, contractors, and owners.

Change orders that are properly recognized and managed can ensure orderly, professional, and profitable progress for everyone involved in the project. There are many causes for change orders and change order requests. In all cases, change orders or change order requests should be addressed promptly and in a precise and prescribed manner. The following paragraphs include information regarding change order pricing and procedures.

The Causes of Change Orders

Reasons for issuing change orders include:

- Unforeseen field conditions that require a change in the work
- Correction of design discrepancies, errors, or omissions in the contract documents
- Owner-requested changes, either by design criteria, scope of work, or project objectives
- Completion date changes for reasons unrelated to the construction process
- Changes in building code interpretations, or other public authority requirements that require a change in the work
- Changes in availability of existing or new materials and products

Procedures

Properly written contract documents must include the correct change order procedures for all parties—owners, design professionals, and contractors—to follow in order to avoid costly delays and litigation.

Being "in the right" is not always a sufficient or acceptable defense. The contract provisions requiring notification and documentation must be adhered to within a defined or reasonable time frame.

The appropriate method of handling change orders is by a written proposal and acceptance by all parties involved. Prior to starting work on a project, all parties should identify their authorized agents who may sign and accept change orders, as well as any limits placed on their authority.

Time may be a critical factor when the need for a change arises. For such cases, the contractor might be directed to proceed on a "time and materials" basis, rather than wait for all paperwork to be processed—a delay that could impede progress. In this situation, the contractor must still follow the prescribed change order procedures including, but not limited to, notification and documentation.

Lack of documentation can be very costly, especially if legal judgments are to be made, and if certain field personnel are no longer available. For time and material change orders, the contractor should keep accurate daily records of all labor and material allocated to the change.

Owners or awarding authorities who do considerable and continual building construction (such as the federal government) realize the inevitability of change orders for numerous reasons, both predictable and unpredictable. As a result, the federal government, the American Institute of Architects (AIA), the Engineers Joint Contract Documents Committee (EJCDC), and other contractor, legal, and technical organizations have developed standards and procedures to be followed by all parties to achieve contract continuance and timely completion, while being financially fair to all concerned.

Pricing Change Orders

When pricing change orders, regardless of their cause, the most significant factor is when the change occurs. The need for a change may be perceived in the field or requested by the architect/engineer *before* any of the actual installation has begun, or may evolve or appear *during* construction when the item of work in question is partially installed. In the latter cases, the original sequence of construction is disrupted, along with all contiguous and supporting systems. Change orders cause the greatest impact when they occur *after* the installation has been completed and must be uncovered, or even replaced. Post-completion changes may be caused by necessary design changes, product failure, or changes in the owner's requirements that are not discovered until the building or the systems begin to function.

Specified procedures of notification and record keeping must be adhered to and enforced regardless of the stage of construction: *before*, *during*, or *after* installation. Some bidding documents anticipate change orders by requiring that unit prices including overhead and profit percentages—for additional as well as deductible changes—be listed. Generally these unit prices do not fully take into account the ripple effect, or impact on other trades, and should be used for general guidance only.

When pricing change orders, it is important to classify the time frame in which the change occurs. There are two basic time frames for change orders: *pre-installation change orders*, which occur before the start of construction, and *post-installation change orders*, which involve reworking after the original installation. Change orders that occur between these stages may be priced according to the extent of work completed using a combination of techniques developed for pricing *pre-* and *post-installation* changes.

Factors To Consider When Pricing Change Orders

As an estimator begins to prepare a change order, the following questions should be reviewed to determine their impact on the final price.

General

- *Is the change order work* pre-installation *or* post-installation?

  Change order work costs vary according to how much of the installation has been completed. Once workers have the project scoped in their minds, even though they have not started, it can be difficult to refocus. Consequently they may spend more than the normal amount of time understanding the change. Also, modifications to work in place, such as trimming or refitting, usually take more time than was initially estimated. The greater the amount of work in place, the more reluctant workers are to change it. Psychologically they may resent the change and as a result the rework takes longer than normal. Post-installation change order estimates must include demolition of existing work as required to accomplish the change. If the work is performed at a later time, additional obstacles, such as building finishes, may be present which must be protected. Regardless of whether the change occurs pre-installation or post-installation, attempt to isolate the identifiable factors and price them separately. For example, add shipping costs that may be required pre-installation or any demolition required post-installation. Then analyze the potential impact on productivity of psychological and/or learning curve factors and adjust the output rates accordingly. One approach is to break down the typical workday into segments and quantify the impact on each segment.

Change Order Installation Efficiency

The labor-hours expressed (for new construction) are based on average installation time, using an efficiency level. For change order situations, adjustments to this efficiency level should reflect the daily labor-hour allocation for that particular occurrence.

- *Will the change substantially delay the original completion date?*

    A significant change in the project may cause the original completion date to be extended. The extended schedule may subject the contractor to new wage rates dictated by relevant labor contracts. Project supervision and other project overhead must also be extended beyond the original completion date. The schedule extension may also put installation into a new weather season. For example, underground piping scheduled for October installation was delayed until January. As a result, frost penetrated the trench area, thereby changing the degree of difficulty of the task. Changes and delays may have a ripple effect throughout the project. This effect must be analyzed and negotiated with the owner.

- *What is the net effect of a deduct change order?*

    In most cases, change orders resulting in a deduction or credit reflect only bare costs. The contractor may retain the overhead and profit based on the original bid.

Materials

- *Will you have to pay more or less for the new material, required by the change order, than you paid for the original purchase?*

    The same material prices or discounts will usually apply to materials purchased for change orders as new construction. In some instances, however, the contractor may forfeit the advantages of competitive pricing for change orders. Consider the following example:

    A contractor purchased over $20,000 worth of fan coil units for an installation and obtained the maximum discount. Some time later it was determined the project required an additional matching unit. The contractor has to purchase this unit from the original supplier to ensure a match. The supplier at this time may not discount the unit because of the small quantity, and he is no longer in a competitive situation. The impact of quantity on purchase can add between 0% and 25% to material prices and/or subcontractor quotes.

- *If materials have been ordered or delivered to the job site, will they be subject to a cancellation charge or restocking fee?*

    Check with the supplier to determine if ordered materials are subject to a cancellation charge. Delivered materials not used as a result of a change order may be subject to a restocking fee if returned to the supplier. Common restocking charges run between 20% and 40%. Also, delivery charges to return the goods to the supplier must be added.

Labor

- *How efficient is the existing crew at the actual installation?*

    Is the same crew that performed the initial work going to do the change order? Possibly the change consists of the installation of a unit identical to one already installed; therefore, the change should take less time. Be sure to consider this potential productivity increase and modify the productivity rates accordingly.

- *If the crew size is increased, what impact will that have on supervision requirements?*

    Under most bargaining agreements or management practices, there is a point at which a working foreperson is replaced by a nonworking foreperson. This replacement increases project overhead by adding a nonproductive worker. If additional workers are added to accelerate the project or to perform changes while maintaining the schedule, be sure to add additional supervision time if warranted. Calculate the hours involved and the additional cost directly if possible.

- *What are the other impacts of increased crew size?*

    The larger the crew, the greater the potential for productivity to decrease. Some of the factors that cause this productivity loss are: overcrowding (producing restrictive conditions in the working space) and possibly a shortage of any special tools and equipment required. Such factors affect not only the crew working on the elements directly involved in the change order, but other crews whose movements may also be hampered. As the crew increases, check its basic composition for changes by the addition or deletion of apprentices or nonworking foreperson, and quantify the potential effects of equipment shortages or other logistical factors.

- *As new crews, unfamiliar with the project, are brought onto the site, how long will it take them to become oriented to the project requirements?*

    The orientation time for a new crew to become 100% effective varies with the site and type of project. Orientation is easiest at a new construction site and most difficult at existing, very restrictive renovation sites. The type of work also affects orientation time. When all elements of the work are exposed, such as concrete or masonry work, orientation is decreased. When the work is concealed or less visible, such as existing electrical systems, orientation takes longer. Usually orientation can be accomplished in one day or less. Costs for added orientation should be itemized and added to the total estimated cost.

- *How much actual production can be gained by working overtime?*

    Short term overtime can be used effectively to accomplish more work in a day. However, as overtime is scheduled to run beyond several weeks, studies have shown marked decreases in output. The following chart shows the effect of long term overtime on worker efficiency. If the anticipated change requires extended overtime to keep the job on schedule, these factors can be used as a guide to predict the impact on time and cost. Add project overhead, particularly supervision, that may also be incurred.

Days per Week	Hours per Day	Production Efficiency					Payroll Cost Factors	
		1st Week	2nd Week	3rd Week	4th Week	Average 4 Weeks	@ 1-1/2 Times	@ 2 Times
5	8	100%	100%	100%	100%	100%	100%	100%
	9	100	100	95	90	96	1.056	1.111
	10	100	95	90	85	93	1.100	1.200
	11	95	90	75	65	81	1.136	1.273
	12	90	85	70	60	76	1.167	1.333
6	8	100	100	95	90	96	1.083	1.167
	9	100	95	90	85	93	1.130	1.259
	10	95	90	85	80	88	1.167	1.333
	11	95	85	70	65	79	1.197	1.394
	12	90	80	65	60	74	1.222	1.444
7	8	100	95	85	75	89	1.143	1.286
	9	95	90	80	70	84	1.183	1.365
	10	90	85	75	65	79	1.214	1.429
	11	85	80	65	60	73	1.240	1.481
	12	85	75	60	55	69	1.262	1.524

Effects of Overtime

Caution: Under many labor agreements, Sundays and holidays are paid at a higher premium than the normal overtime rate.

The use of long-term overtime is counterproductive on almost any construction job; that is, the longer the period of overtime, the lower the actual production rate. Numerous studies have been conducted, and while they have resulted in slightly different numbers, all reach the same conclusion. The figure above tabulates the effects of overtime work on efficiency.

As illustrated, there can be a difference between the *actual* payroll cost per hour and the *effective* cost per hour for overtime work. This is due to the reduced production efficiency with the increase in weekly hours beyond 40. This difference between actual and effective cost results from overtime work over a prolonged period. Short-term overtime work does not result in as great a reduction in efficiency and, in such cases, effective cost may not vary significantly from the actual payroll cost. As the total hours per week are increased on a regular basis, more time is lost due to fatigue, lowered morale, and an increased accident rate.

As an example, assume a project where workers are working 6 days a week, 10 hours per day. From the figure above (based on productivity studies), the average effective productive hours over a 4-week period are:

$$0.875 \times 60 = 52.5$$

Depending upon the locale and day of week, overtime hours may be paid at time and a half or double time. For time and a half, the overall (average) *actual* payroll cost (including regular and overtime hours) is determined as follows:

$$\frac{40 \text{ reg. hrs.} + (20 \text{ overtime hrs.} \times 1.5)}{60 \text{ hrs.}} = 1.167$$

Based on 60 hours, the payroll cost per hour will be 116.7% of the normal rate at 40 hours per week. However, because the effective production (efficiency) for 60 hours is reduced to the equivalent of 52.5 hours, the effective cost of overtime is calculated as follows:

For time and a half:

$$\frac{40 \text{ reg. hrs.} + (20 \text{ overtime hrs.} \times 1.5)}{52.5 \text{ hrs.}} = 1.33$$

The installed cost will be 133% of the normal rate (for labor).

Thus, when figuring overtime, the actual cost per unit of work will be higher than the apparent overtime payroll dollar increase, due to the reduced productivity of the longer work week. These efficiency calculations are true only for those cost factors determined by hours worked. Costs that are applied weekly or monthly, such as equipment rentals, will not be similarly affected.

Equipment

- What equipment is required to complete the change order?

Change orders may require extending the rental period of equipment already on the job site, or the addition of special equipment brought in to accomplish the change work. In either case, the additional rental charges and operator labor charges must be added.

Summary

The preceding considerations and others you deem appropriate should be analyzed and applied to a change order estimate. The impact of each should be quantified and listed on the estimate to form an audit trail.

Change orders that are properly identified, documented, and managed help to ensure the orderly, professional, and profitable progress of the work. They also minimize potential claims or disputes at the end of the project.

Project Costs

Back by customer demand!

You asked and we listened. For customer convenience and estimating ease, we have made the 2024 Project Costs available for download at **RSMeans.com/2024books**. You will also find sample estimates, an RSMeans data overview video, and a book registration form to receive quarterly data updates throughout 2024.

Estimating Tips

- The cost figures available in the download were derived from hundreds of projects contained in the RSMeans database of completed construction projects. They include the contractor's overhead and profit. The figures have been adjusted to January of the current year.

- These projects were located throughout the U.S. and reflect a tremendous variation in square foot (S.F.) costs. This is due to differences, not only in labor and material costs, but also in individual owners' requirements. For instance, a bank in a large city would have different features than one in a rural area. This is true of all the different types of buildings analyzed. Therefore, caution should be exercised when using these Project Costs. For example, for courthouses, costs in the database are local courthouse costs and will not apply to the larger, more elaborate federal courthouses.

- None of the figures "go with" any others. All individual cost items were computed and tabulated separately. Thus, the sum of the median figures for plumbing, HVAC, and electrical will not normally total up to the total mechanical and electrical costs arrived at by separate analysis and tabulation of the projects.

- Each building was analyzed as to total and component costs and percentages. The figures were arranged in ascending order with the results tabulated as shown. The 1/4 column shows that 25% of the projects had lower costs and 75% had higher. The 3/4 column shows that 75% of the projects had lower costs and 25% had higher. The median column shows that 50% of the projects had lower costs and 50% had higher.

- Project Costs are useful in the conceptual stage when no details are available. As soon as details become available in the project design, the square foot approach should be discontinued and the project should be priced as to its particular components. When more precision is required, or for estimating the replacement cost of specific buildings, the current edition of *Square Foot Costs with RSMeans data* should be used.

- In using the figures in this section, it is recommended that the median column be used for preliminary figures if no additional information is available. The median figures, when multiplied by the total city construction cost index figures (see City Cost Indexes) and then multiplied by the project size modifier at the end of this section, should present a fairly accurate base figure, which would then have to be adjusted in view of the estimator's experience, local economic conditions, code requirements, and the owner's particular requirements. There is no need to factor in the percentage figures, as these should remain constant from city to city.

- The editors of this data would greatly appreciate receiving cost figures on one or more of your recent projects, which would then be included in the averages for next year. All cost figures received will be kept confidential, except that they will be averaged with other similar projects to arrive at square foot cost figures for next year.

See the website above for details and the discount available for submitting one or more of your projects.

Same Data. Simplified.

Enjoy the convenience and efficiency of accessing your costs anywhere:

- **Skip the multiplier** by setting your location
- **Quickly search,** edit, favorite and share costs
- **Stay on top of price changes** with automatic updates

Discover more at rsmeans.com/online

No part of this cost data may be reproduced, stored in a retrieval system, or transmitted in any form or by any means without prior written permission of Gordian.

50 17 | Project Costs

50 17 00 | Project Costs

			UNIT	UNIT COSTS			% OF TOTAL		
				1/4	MEDIAN	3/4	1/4	MEDIAN	3/4
01	**0000**	**Auto Sales with Repair**	S.F.						
	0100	Architectural		132	147	159	58%	64%	67%
	0200	Plumbing		11	11.55	15.40	4.84%	5.20%	6.80%
	0300	Mechanical		14.75	19.75	22	6.40%	8.70%	10.15%
	0400	Electrical		22.50	28	35	9.05%	11.70%	15.90%
	0500	Total Project Costs		221	230	237			
02	**0000**	**Banking Institutions**	S.F.						
	0100	Architectural		199	244	297	59%	65%	69%
	0200	Plumbing		8	11.15	15.50	2.12%	3.39%	4.19%
	0300	Mechanical		15.90	22	26	4.41%	5.10%	10.75%
	0400	Electrical		39	47	72	10.45%	13.05%	15.90%
	0500	Total Project Costs		330	370	455			
03	**0000**	**Court House**	S.F.						
	0100	Architectural		105	206	287	54.50%	58.50%	61%
	0200	Plumbing		3.96	14.75	14.75	2.07%	3.13%	3.13%
	0300	Mechanical		24.50	29.50	29.50	6.25%	12.95%	12.95%
	0400	Electrical		31.50	36	36	7.65%	16.60%	16.60%
	0500	Total Project Costs		191	350	470			
04	**0000**	**Data Centers**	S.F.						
	0100	Architectural		237	237	237	68%	68%	68%
	0200	Plumbing		12.95	12.95	12.95	3.71%	3.71%	3.71%
	0300	Mechanical		33	33	33	9.45%	9.45%	9.45%
	0400	Electrical		31.50	31.50	31.50	9%	9%	9%
	0500	Total Project Costs		350	350	350			
05	**0000**	**Detention Centers**	S.F.						
	0100	Architectural		219	232	246	52%	53%	60.50%
	0200	Plumbing		23	28	34	5.15%	7.10%	7.25%
	0300	Mechanical		29.50	42	50	7.55%	9.50%	13.80%
	0400	Electrical		48	57	74	10.90%	14.85%	17.95%
	0500	Total Project Costs		370	390	460			
06	**0000**	**Fire Stations**	S.F.						
	0100	Architectural		127	162	256	46%	54.50%	61%
	0200	Plumbing		13.30	17.80	22.50	4.67%	5.60%	6.30%
	0300	Mechanical		19.70	28	36.50	6.10%	8.25%	10.20%
	0400	Electrical		30	37	50	10.75%	12.15%	14.70%
	0500	Total Project Costs		264	320	420			
07	**0000**	**Gymnasium**	S.F.						
	0100	Architectural		110	145	145	57%	64.50%	64.50%
	0200	Plumbing		2.69	8.80	8.80	1.58%	3.48%	3.48%
	0300	Mechanical		4.12	37	37	2.42%	14.65%	14.65%
	0400	Electrical		13.50	26	26	7.95%	10.35%	10.35%
	0500	Total Project Costs		170	253	253			
08	**0000**	**Hospitals**	S.F.						
	0100	Architectural		133	204	237	40.50%	47%	48%
	0200	Plumbing		9.75	40.50	48	6%	7.65%	10.35%
	0300	Mechanical		53	66	94.50	12.55%	17.85%	23.50%
	0400	Electrical		29.50	59	76.50	10.95%	13.75%	16.85%
	0500	Total Project Costs		310	465	500			
09	**0000**	**Industrial Buildings**	S.F.						
	0100	Architectural		56	88.50	167	49%	56%	74.50%
	0200	Plumbing		2.09	3.62	8.15	2%	2.80%	3.71%
	0300	Mechanical		5.95	6.90	17.25	4.81%	5.55%	10.10%
	0400	Electrical		7.40	10.40	49.50	4.95%	12.05%	13.75%
	0500	Total Project Costs		99	129	360			
10	**0000**	**Medical Clinics & Offices**	S.F.						
	0100	Architectural		121	150	197	48.50%	54%	62%
	0200	Plumbing		11.10	16.75	27.50	4.50%	6.65%	8.75%
	0300	Mechanical		18	27.50	49.50	7.80%	10.85%	15.75%
	0400	Electrical		24.50	30	46	8.90%	11.20%	13.85%
	0500	Total Project Costs		209	278	365			

50 17 | Project Costs

50 17 00 | Project Costs

			UNIT	UNIT COSTS 1/4	UNIT COSTS MEDIAN	UNIT COSTS 3/4	% OF TOTAL 1/4	% OF TOTAL MEDIAN	% OF TOTAL 3/4
11	0000	**Mixed Use**	S.F.						
	0100	Architectural		136	188	250	45.50%	52.50%	60.50%
	0200	Plumbing		7.70	14.05	14.95	3.31%	3.47%	4.18%
	0300	Mechanical		20.50	30.50	57	4.70%	12.85%	16.05%
	0400	Electrical		27	44	65.50	8.30%	11.40%	14%
	0500	Total Project Costs		238	415	425			
12	0000	**Multi-Family Housing**	S.F.						
	0100	Architectural		95	129	211	54.50%	62%	69%
	0200	Plumbing		8.50	13.65	18.60	5.25%	6.65%	8%
	0300	Mechanical		8.70	11.75	33.50	4.41%	6.05%	10.25%
	0400	Electrical		11.45	19.30	28	5.65%	7.90%	10.25%
	0500	Total Project Costs		157	258	335			
13	0000	**Nursing Home & Assisted Living**	S.F.						
	0100	Architectural		89.50	129	147	51.50%	55.50%	63.50%
	0200	Plumbing		9.60	14.40	17.15	6.25%	7.40%	9.20%
	0300	Mechanical		7.85	11.60	22.50	4.04%	6.70%	9.55%
	0400	Electrical		13.20	23	30.50	7.25%	11%	13.10%
	0500	Total Project Costs		157	202	267			
14	0000	**Office Buildings**	S.F.						
	0100	Architectural		118	160	220	54.50%	61%	69%
	0200	Plumbing		6.35	9.95	18.65	2.70%	3.78%	5.20%
	0300	Mechanical		12.40	21	32.50	5.55%	8.15%	11.10%
	0400	Electrical		16.60	27	43	7.80%	10.10%	12.90%
	0500	Total Project Costs		200	263	360			
15	0000	**Parking Garage**	S.F.						
	0100	Architectural		39	48	50	70%	79%	88%
	0200	Plumbing		1.30	1.35	2.53	2.05%	2.70%	2.83%
	0300	Mechanical		1.01	1.54	5.85	2.11%	3.62%	3.81%
	0400	Electrical		3.45	3.78	7.90	5.30%	6.35%	7.95%
	0500	Total Project Costs		47.50	58.50	63			
16	0000	**Parking Garage/Mixed Use**	S.F.						
	0100	Architectural		127	139	142	61%	62%	65.50%
	0200	Plumbing		4.09	5.35	8.20	2.47%	2.72%	3.66%
	0300	Mechanical		17.50	19.70	28.50	7.80%	13.10%	13.60%
	0400	Electrical		18.30	26.50	27.50	8.20%	12.65%	18.15%
	0500	Total Project Costs		208	217	224			
17	0000	**Police Stations**	S.F.						
	0100	Architectural		144	203	250	49%	61%	61.50%
	0200	Plumbing		19	23	23	5.05%	5.55%	7.70%
	0300	Mechanical		43	60	62.50	12.35%	14.55%	16.55%
	0400	Electrical		32.50	37.50	55.50	9.15%	12.10%	14%
	0500	Total Project Costs		269	375	410			
18	0000	**Police/Fire**	S.F.						
	0100	Architectural		140	140	430	55.50%	66%	68%
	0200	Plumbing		11.20	11.65	43	5.45%	5.50%	5.55%
	0300	Mechanical		17.15	27	98	8.35%	12.70%	12.80%
	0400	Electrical		19.55	25	112	9.50%	11.75%	14.55%
	0500	Total Project Costs		206	212	775			
19	0000	**Public Assembly Buildings**	S.F.						
	0100	Architectural		142	186	290	56.50%	61%	64%
	0200	Plumbing		7.55	11.05	16.35	2.63%	3.36%	4.39%
	0300	Mechanical		15.90	27.50	44	6.45%	8.75%	12.45%
	0400	Electrical		23.50	32	50.50	8.60%	10.70%	12.80%
	0500	Total Project Costs		229	305	455			
20	0000	**Recreational**	S.F.						
	0100	Architectural		137	208	292	49.50%	59%	64.50%
	0200	Plumbing		10.25	16.55	27	3.08%	4.67%	7.40%
	0300	Mechanical		16.35	25	37	5.15%	6.65%	11.35%
	0400	Electrical		20	34	49	7.10%	8.95%	10.80%
	0500	Total Project Costs		244	350	550			

For customer support on your Plumbing Costs with RSMeans Data call 800.448.8182.

50 17 | Project Costs

50 17 00	Project Costs	UNIT	UNIT COSTS			% OF TOTAL		
			1/4	MEDIAN	3/4	1/4	MEDIAN	3/4
21 0000	**Restaurants**	S.F.						
0100	Architectural		156	244	310	57.50%	60%	63.50%
0200	Plumbing		17.10	34.50	45	7.35%	7.70%	8.75%
0300	Mechanical		18.45	24.50	46	6.50%	8.15%	11.15%
0400	Electrical		18.35	30	60	6.75%	10.30%	11.60%
0500	Total Project Costs		258	425	515			
22 0000	**Retail**	S.F.						
0100	Architectural		71.50	109	224	54.50%	60%	64.50%
0200	Plumbing		8.70	12.15	15.05	4.18%	5.45%	8.45%
0300	Mechanical		8.15	11.50	23	4.98%	6.15%	10.20%
0400	Electrical		12.95	23.50	39	7.90%	10.15%	12.45%
0500	Total Project Costs		116	210	360			
23 0000	**Schools**	S.F.						
0100	Architectural		120	152	204	50.50%	55.50%	60.50%
0200	Plumbing		9.50	13.15	19.20	3.61%	4.57%	6.95%
0300	Mechanical		22.50	32.50	47.50	8.60%	11.85%	14.55%
0400	Electrical		22.50	31	40.50	9.25%	11.25%	13.30%
0500	Total Project Costs		219	279	380			
24 0000	**University, College & Private School Classroom & Admin Buildings**	S.F.						
0100	Architectural		155	209	276	50%	53.50%	58.50%
0200	Plumbing		10.60	14.85	29.50	3.04%	4.28%	6.35%
0300	Mechanical		33	47.50	57	9.20%	10.95%	12.95%
0400	Electrical		26	38	50	7.70%	9.95%	12.55%
0500	Total Project Costs		269	380	505			
25 0000	**University, College & Private School Dormitories**	S.F.						
0100	Architectural		101	187	380	51.50%	58%	68%
0200	Plumbing		16.50	20	28	3.41%	6.45%	8.95%
0300	Mechanical		17.70	40	60	5.80%	8.95%	11.80%
0400	Electrical		15.75	37.50	78.50	6.95%	10.60%	12.60%
0500	Total Project Costs		227	335	740			
26 0000	**University, College & Private School Science, Eng. & Lab Buildings**	S.F.						
0100	Architectural		172	204	300	48%	54.50%	58%
0200	Plumbing		11.90	18	30.50	3.29%	3.77%	5%
0300	Mechanical		45.50	85	87	11.70%	19.40%	23.50%
0400	Electrical		35.50	46.50	47.50	9%	12.05%	13.15%
0500	Total Project Costs		360	390	525			
27 0000	**University, College & Private School Student Union Buildings**	S.F.						
0100	Architectural		136	360	365	48%	51%	54.50%
0200	Plumbing		20.50	24	30.50	3.13%	3.36%	4.52%
0300	Mechanical		39	53.50	63.50	7.35%	9.60%	9.60%
0400	Electrical		34.50	60	85.50	9.05%	10.10%	12.80%
0500	Total Project Costs		269	660	880			
28 0000	**Warehouses**	S.F.						
0100	Architectural		58.50	91	207	58%	67%	71.50%
0200	Plumbing		3.04	6.50	13.45	2.82%	3.58%	5%
0300	Mechanical		6.85	20.50	32	4.56%	8.15%	10.70%
0400	Electrical	S.F.	7.60	18.10	38.50	7.50%	10.10%	15.35%
0500	Total Project Costs	S.F.	87	155	300			

Square Foot Project Size Modifier

One factor that affects the S.F. cost of a particular building is the size. In general, for buildings built to the same specifications in the same locality, the larger building will have the lower S.F. cost. This is due mainly to the decreasing contribution of the exterior walls plus the economy of scale usually achievable in larger buildings. The Area Conversion Scale shown below will give a factor to convert costs for the typical size building to an adjusted cost for the particular project.

The Square Foot Base Size lists the median costs, most typical project size in our accumulated data, and the range in size of the projects.

The Size Factor for your project is determined by dividing your project area in S.F. by the typical project size for the particular Building Type. With this factor, enter the Area Conversion Scale at the appropriate Size Factor and determine the appropriate Cost Multiplier for your building size.

Example: Determine the cost per S.F. for a 107,200 S.F. Multi-family housing.

$$\frac{\text{Proposed building area} = 107{,}200 \text{ S.F.}}{\text{Typical size from below} = 53{,}600 \text{ S.F.}} = 2.00$$

Enter Area Conversion Scale at 2.0, intersect curve, read horizontally the appropriate cost multiplier of .94. Size adjusted cost becomes .94 x $258.00 = $242.52 based on national average costs.

Note: For Size Factors less than .50, the Cost Multiplier is 1.1
For Size Factors greater than 3.5, the Cost Multiplier is .90

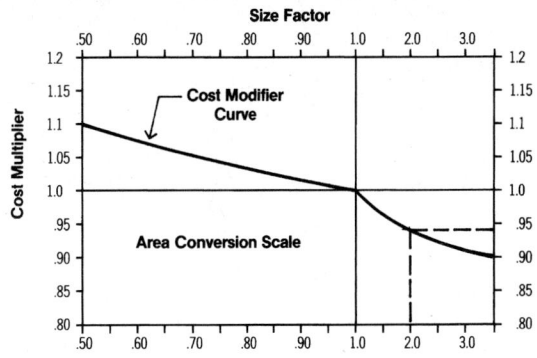

System	Median Cost (Total Project Costs)	Typical Size Gross S.F. (Median of Projects)	Typical Range (Low – High) (Projects)
Auto Sales with Repair	$230.00	24,900	4,700 – 29,300
Banking Institutions	370.00	9,300	3,300 – 38,100
Courthouse	350.00	56,000	24,700 – 70,500
Data Centers	350.00	14,400	14,400 – 14,400
Detention Centers	390.00	37,800	12,300 – 183,330
Fire Stations	320.00	12,600	6,300 – 49,600
Gymnasium	253.00	52,400	22,800 – 82,000
Hospitals	465.00	63,600	12,700 – 410,300
Industrial Buildings	129.00	21,100	5,100 – 200,600
Medical Clinics & Offices	278.00	24,200	2,300 – 327,000
Mixed Use	415.00	29,800	7,200 – 188,900
Multi-Family Housing	258.00	53,600	2,500 – 1,161,500
Nursing Home & Assisted Living	202.00	38,700	1,500 – 242,600
Office Buildings	263.00	21,000	1,100 – 930,000
Parking Garage	58.50	151,800	99,900 – 287,000
Parking Garage/Mixed Use	217.00	254,200	5,300 – 318,000
Police Stations	375.00	25,200	12,700 – 88,600
Police/Fire	212.00	44,300	8,600 – 50,300
Public Assembly Buildings	305.00	20,800	2,200 – 235,300
Recreational	350.00	27,700	1,000 – 223,800
Restaurants	425.00	5,900	2,100 – 42,000
Retail	210.00	22,000	4,000 – 84,300
Schools	279.00	69,900	1,300 – 410,800
University, College & Private School Classroom & Admin Buildings	380.00	48,400	2,400 – 196,200
University, College & Private School Dormitories	335.00	44,200	1,500 – 134,800
University, College & Private School Science, Eng. & Lab Buildings	390.00	60,000	5,300 – 117,600
University, College & Private School Student Union Buildings	660.00	48,400	23,000 – 82,100
Warehouses	155.00	10,400	600 – 303,800

Abbreviations

A	Area Square Feet; Ampere	Brk., brk	Brick	Csc	Cosecant
AAFES	Army and Air Force Exchange Service	brkt	Bracket	C.S.F.	Hundred Square Feet
		Brs.	Brass	CSI	Construction Specifications Institute
ABS	Acrylonitrile Butadiene Stryrene; Asbestos Bonded Steel	Brz.	Bronze		
		Bsn.	Basin	CT	Current Transformer
A.C., AC	Alternating Current; Air-Conditioning; Asbestos Cement; Plywood Grade A & C	Btr.	Better	CTS	Copper Tube Size
		BTU	British Thermal Unit	Cu	Copper, Cubic
		BTUH	BTU per Hour	Cu. Ft.	Cubic Foot
		Bu.	Bushels	cw	Continuous Wave
ACI	American Concrete Institute	BUR	Built-up Roofing	C.W.	Cool White; Cold Water
ACR	Air Conditioning Refrigeration	BX	Interlocked Armored Cable	Cwt.	100 Pounds
ADA	Americans with Disabilities Act	°C	Degree Centigrade	C.W.X.	Cool White Deluxe
AD	Plywood, Grade A & D	c	Conductivity, Copper Sweat	C.Y.	Cubic Yard (27 cubic feet)
Addit.	Additional	C	Hundred; Centigrade	C.Y./Hr.	Cubic Yard per Hour
Adh.	Adhesive	C/C	Center to Center, Cedar on Cedar	Cyl.	Cylinder
Adj.	Adjustable	C-C	Center to Center	d	Penny (nail size)
af	Audio-frequency	Cab	Cabinet	D	Deep; Depth; Discharge
AFFF	Aqueous Film Forming Foam	Cair.	Air Tool Laborer	Dis., Disch.	Discharge
AFUE	Annual Fuel Utilization Efficiency	Cal.	Caliper	Db	Decibel
AGA	American Gas Association	Calc	Calculated	Dbl.	Double
Agg.	Aggregate	Cap.	Capacity	DC	Direct Current
A.H., Ah	Ampere Hours	Carp.	Carpenter	DDC	Direct Digital Control
A hr.	Ampere-hour	C.B.	Circuit Breaker	Demob.	Demobilization
A.H.U., AHU	Air Handling Unit	C.C.A.	Chromate Copper Arsenate	d.f.t.	Dry Film Thickness
A.I.A.	American Institute of Architects	C.C.F.	Hundred Cubic Feet	d.f.u.	Drainage Fixture Units
AIC	Ampere Interrupting Capacity	cd	Candela	D.H.	Double Hung
Allow.	Allowance	cd/sf	Candela per Square Foot	DHW	Domestic Hot Water
alt., alt	Alternate	CD	Grade of Plywood Face & Back	DI	Ductile Iron
Alum.	Aluminum	CDX	Plywood, Grade C & D, exterior glue	Diag.	Diagonal
a.m.	Ante Meridiem			Diam., Dia	Diameter
Amp.	Ampere	Cefi.	Cement Finisher	Distrib.	Distribution
Anod.	Anodized	Cem.	Cement	Div.	Division
ANSI	American National Standards Institute	CF	Hundred Feet	Dk.	Deck
		C.F.	Cubic Feet	D.L.	Dead Load; Diesel
APA	American Plywood Association	CFM	Cubic Feet per Minute	DLH	Deep Long Span Bar Joist
Approx.	Approximate	CFRP	Carbon Fiber Reinforced Plastic	dlx	Deluxe
Apt.	Apartment	c.g.	Center of Gravity	Do.	Ditto
Asb.	Asbestos	CHW	Chilled Water; Commercial Hot Water	DOP	Dioctyl Phthalate Penetration Test (Air Filters)
A.S.B.C.	American Standard Building Code				
Asbe.	Asbestos Worker	C.I., CI	Cast Iron	Dp., dp	Depth
ASCE	American Society of Civil Engineers	C.I.P., CIP	Cast in Place	D.P.S.T.	Double Pole, Single Throw
A.S.H.R.A.E.	American Society of Heating, Refrig. & AC Engineers	Circ.	Circuit	Dr.	Drive
		C.L.	Carload Lot	DR	Dimension Ratio
ASME	American Society of Mechanical Engineers	CL	Chain Link	Drink.	Drinking
		Clab.	Common Laborer	D.S.	Double Strength
ASTM	American Society for Testing and Materials	Clam	Common Maintenance Laborer	D.S.A.	Double Strength A Grade
		C.L.F.	Hundred Linear Feet	D.S.B.	Double Strength B Grade
Attchmt.	Attachment	CLF	Current Limiting Fuse	Dty.	Duty
Avg., Ave.	Average	CLP	Cross Linked Polyethylene	DWV	Drain Waste Vent
AWG	American Wire Gauge	cm	Centimeter	DX	Deluxe White, Direct Expansion
AWWA	American Water Works Assoc.	CMP	Corr. Metal Pipe	dyn	Dyne
Bbl.	Barrel	CMU	Concrete Masonry Unit	e	Eccentricity
B&B, BB	Grade B and Better; Balled & Burlapped	CN	Change Notice	E	Equipment Only; East; Emissivity
		Col.	Column	Ea.	Each
B&S	Bell and Spigot	CO_2	Carbon Dioxide	EB	Encased Burial
B.&W.	Black and White	Comb.	Combination	Econ.	Economy
b.c.c.	Body-centered Cubic	comm.	Commercial, Communication	E.C.Y	Embankment Cubic Yards
B.C.Y.	Bank Cubic Yards	Compr.	Compressor	EDP	Electronic Data Processing
BE	Bevel End	Conc.	Concrete	EIFS	Exterior Insulation Finish System
B.F.	Board Feet	Cont., cont	Continuous; Continued, Container	E.D.R.	Equiv. Direct Radiation
Bg. cem.	Bag of Cement	Corkbd.	Cork Board	Eq.	Equation
BHP	Boiler Horsepower; Brake Horsepower	Corr.	Corrugated	EL	Elevation
		Cos	Cosine	Elec.	Electrician; Electrical
B.I.	Black Iron	Cot	Cotangent	Elev.	Elevator; Elevating
bidir.	bidirectional	Cov.	Cover	EMT	Electrical Metallic Conduit; Thin Wall Conduit
Bit., Bitum.	Bituminous	C/P	Cedar on Paneling		
Bit., Conc.	Bituminous Concrete	CPA	Control Point Adjustment	Eng.	Engine, Engineered
Bk.	Backed	Cplg.	Coupling	EPDM	Ethylene Propylene Diene Monomer
Bkrs.	Breakers	CPM	Critical Path Method		
Bldg., bldg	Building	CPVC	Chlorinated Polyvinyl Chloride	EPS	Expanded Polystyrene
Blk.	Block	C.Pr.	Hundred Pair	Eqhv.	Equip. Oper., Heavy
Bm.	Beam	CRC	Cold Rolled Channel	Eqlt.	Equip. Oper., Light
Boil.	Boilermaker	Creos.	Creosote	Eqmd.	Equip. Oper., Medium
bpm	Blows per Minute	Crpt.	Carpet & Linoleum Layer	Eqmm.	Equip. Oper., Master Mechanic
BR	Bedroom	CRT	Cathode-ray Tube	Eqol.	Equip. Oper., Oilers
Brg., brng.	Bearing	CS	Carbon Steel, Constant Shear Bar Joist	Equip.	Equipment
Brhe.	Bricklayer Helper			ERW	Electric Resistance Welded
Bric.	Bricklayer				

Abbreviations

E.S.	Energy Saver	H	High Henry	Lath.	Lather
Est.	Estimated	HC	High Capacity	Lav.	Lavatory
esu	Electrostatic Units	H.D., HD	Heavy Duty; High Density	lb.; #	Pound
E.W.	Each Way	H.D.O.	High Density Overlaid	L.B., LB	Load Bearing; L Conduit Body
EWT	Entering Water Temperature	HDPE	High Density Polyethylene Plastic	L. & E.	Labor & Equipment
Excav.	Excavation	Hdr.	Header	lb./hr.	Pounds per Hour
excl	Excluding	Hdwe.	Hardware	lb./L.F.	Pounds per Linear Foot
Exp., exp	Expansion, Exposure	H.I.D., HID	High Intensity Discharge	lbf/sq.in.	Pound-force per Square Inch
Ext., ext	Exterior; Extension	Help.	Helper Average	L.C.L.	Less than Carload Lot
Extru.	Extrusion	HEPA	High Efficiency Particulate Air Filter	L.C.Y.	Loose Cubic Yard
f.	Fiber Stress	Hg	Mercury	Ld.	Load
F	Fahrenheit; Female; Fill	HIC	High Interrupting Capacity	LE	Lead Equivalent
Fab., fab	Fabricated; Fabric	HM	Hollow Metal	LED	Light Emitting Diode
FBGS	Fiberglass	HMWPE	High Molecular Weight Polyethylene	L.F.	Linear Foot
F.C.	Footcandles			L.F. Hdr	Linear Feet of Header
f.c.c.	Face-centered Cubic	HO	High Output	L.F. Nose	Linear Foot of Stair Nosing
f'c.	Compressive Stress in Concrete; Extreme Compressive Stress	Horiz.	Horizontal	L.F. Rsr	Linear Foot of Stair Riser
		H.P., HP	Horsepower; High Pressure	Lg.	Long; Length; Large
F.E.	Front End	H.P.F.	High Power Factor	L & H	Light and Heat
FEP	Fluorinated Ethylene Propylene (Teflon)	Hr.	Hour	LH	Long Span Bar Joist
		Hrs./Day	Hours per Day	L.H.	Labor Hours
F.G.	Flat Grain	HSC	High Short Circuit	L.L., LL	Live Load
F.H.A.	Federal Housing Administration	Ht.	Height	L.L.D.	Lamp Lumen Depreciation
Fig.	Figure	Htg.	Heating	lm	Lumen
Fin.	Finished	Htrs.	Heaters	lm/sf	Lumen per Square Foot
FIPS	Female Iron Pipe Size	HVAC	Heating, Ventilation & Air-Conditioning	lm/W	Lumen per Watt
Fixt.	Fixture			LOA	Length Over All
FJP	Finger jointed and primed	Hvy.	Heavy	log	Logarithm
Fl. Oz.	Fluid Ounces	HW	Hot Water	L-O-L	Lateralolet
Flr.	Floor	Hyd.; Hydr.	Hydraulic	long.	Longitude
Flrs.	Floors	Hz	Hertz (cycles)	L.P., LP	Liquefied Petroleum; Low Pressure
FM	Frequency Modulation; Factory Mutual	I.	Moment of Inertia	L.P.F.	Low Power Factor
		IBC	International Building Code	LR	Long Radius
Fmg.	Framing	I.C.	Interrupting Capacity	L.S.	Lump Sum
FM/UL	Factory Mutual/Underwriters Labs	ID	Inside Diameter	Lt.	Light
Fdn.	Foundation	I.D.	Inside Dimension; Identification	Lt. Ga.	Light Gauge
FNPT	Female National Pipe Thread	I.F.	Inside Frosted	L.T.L.	Less than Truckload Lot
Fori.	Foreman, Inside	I.M.C.	Intermediate Metal Conduit	Lt. Wt.	Lightweight
Foro.	Foreman, Outside	In.	Inch	L.V.	Low Voltage
Fount.	Fountain	Incan.	Incandescent	M	Thousand; Material; Male; Light Wall Copper Tubing
fpm	Feet per Minute	Incl.	Included; Including		
FPT	Female Pipe Thread	Int.	Interior	M^2CA	Meters Squared Contact Area
Fr	Frame	Inst.	Installation	m/hr.; M.H.	Man-hour
F.R.	Fire Rating	Insul., insul	Insulation/Insulated	mA	Milliampere
FRK	Foil Reinforced Kraft	I.P.	Iron Pipe	Mach.	Machine
FSK	Foil/Scrim/Kraft	I.P.S., IPS	Iron Pipe Size	Mag. Str.	Magnetic Starter
FRP	Fiberglass Reinforced Plastic	IPT	Iron Pipe Threaded	Maint.	Maintenance
FS	Forged Steel	I.W.	Indirect Waste	Marb.	Marble Setter
FSC	Cast Body; Cast Switch Box	J	Joule	Mat; Mat'l.	Material
Ft., ft	Foot; Feet	J.I.C.	Joint Industrial Council	Max.	Maximum
Ftng.	Fitting	K	Thousand; Thousand Pounds; Heavy Wall Copper Tubing, Kelvin	MBF	Thousand Board Feet
Ftg.	Footing			MBH	Thousand BTU's per hr.
Ft lb.	Foot Pound			MC	Metal Clad Cable
Furn.	Furniture	K.A.H.	Thousand Amp. Hours	MCC	Motor Control Center
FVNR	Full Voltage Non-Reversing	kcmil	Thousand Circular Mils	M.C.F.	Thousand Cubic Feet
FVR	Full Voltage Reversing	KD	Knock Down	MCFM	Thousand Cubic Feet per Minute
FXM	Female by Male	K.D.A.T.	Kiln Dried After Treatment	M.C.M.	Thousand Circular Mils
Fy.	Minimum Yield Stress of Steel	kg	Kilogram	MCP	Motor Circuit Protector
g	Gram	kG	Kilogauss	MD	Medium Duty
G	Gauss	kgf	Kilogram Force	MDF	Medium-density fibreboard
Ga.	Gauge	kHz	Kilohertz	M.D.O.	Medium Density Overlaid
Gal., gal.	Gallon	Kip	1000 Pounds	Med.	Medium
Galv., galv	Galvanized	KJ	Kilojoule	MF	Thousand Feet
GC/MS	Gas Chromatograph/Mass Spectrometer	K.L.	Effective Length Factor	M.F.B.M.	Thousand Feet Board Measure
		K.L.F.	Kips per Linear Foot	Mfg.	Manufacturing
Gen.	General	Km	Kilometer	Mfrs.	Manufacturers
GFI	Ground Fault Interrupter	KO	Knock Out	mg	Milligram
GFRC	Glass Fiber Reinforced Concrete	K.S.F.	Kips per Square Foot	MGD	Million Gallons per Day
Glaz.	Glazier	K.S.I.	Kips per Square Inch	MGPH	Million Gallons per Hour
GPD	Gallons per Day	kV	Kilovolt	MH, M.H.	Manhole; Metal Halide; Man-Hour
gpf	Gallon per Flush	kVA	Kilovolt Ampere	MHz	Megahertz
GPH	Gallons per Hour	kVAR	Kilovar (Reactance)	Mi.	Mile
gpm, GPM	Gallons per Minute	KW	Kilowatt	MI	Malleable Iron; Mineral Insulated
GR	Grade	KWh	Kilowatt-hour	MIPS	Male Iron Pipe Size
Gran.	Granular	L	Labor Only; Length; Long; Medium Wall Copper Tubing	mj	Mechanical Joint
Grnd.	Ground			m	Meter
GVW	Gross Vehicle Weight	Lab.	Labor	mm	Millimeter
GWB	Gypsum Wall Board	lat	Latitude	Mill.	Millwright
				Min., min.	Minimum, Minute

Abbreviations

Misc.	Miscellaneous	PCM	Phase Contrast Microscopy	SBS	Styrene Butadiere Styrene
ml	Milliliter, Mainline	PDCA	Painting and Decorating Contractors of America	SC	Screw Cover
M.L.F.	Thousand Linear Feet			SCFM	Standard Cubic Feet per Minute
Mo.	Month	P.E., PE	Professional Engineer; Porcelain Enamel; Polyethylene; Plain End	Scaf.	Scaffold
Mobil.	Mobilization			Sch., Sched.	Schedule
Mog.	Mogul Base			S.C.R.	Modular Brick
MPH	Miles per Hour	P.E.C.I.	Porcelain Enamel on Cast Iron	S.D.	Sound Deadening
MPT	Male Pipe Thread	Perf.	Perforated	SDR	Standard Dimension Ratio
MRGWB	Moisture Resistant Gypsum Wallboard	PEX	Cross Linked Polyethylene	S.E.	Surfaced Edge
		Ph.	Phase	Sel.	Select
MRT	Mile Round Trip	P.I.	Pressure Injected	SER, SEU	Service Entrance Cable
ms	Millisecond	Pile.	Pile Driver	S.F.	Square Foot
M.S.F.	Thousand Square Feet	Pkg.	Package	S.F.C.A.	Square Foot Contact Area
Mstz.	Mosaic & Terrazzo Worker	Pl.	Plate	S.F. Flr.	Square Foot of Floor
M.S.Y.	Thousand Square Yards	Plah.	Plasterer Helper	S.F.G.	Square Foot of Ground
Mtd., mtd., mtd	Mounted	Plas.	Plasterer	S.F. Hor.	Square Foot Horizontal
Mthe.	Mosaic & Terrazzo Helper	plf	Pounds Per Linear Foot	SFR	Square Feet of Radiation
Mtng.	Mounting	Pluh.	Plumber Helper	S.F. Shlf.	Square Foot of Shelf
Mult.	Multi; Multiply	Plum.	Plumber	S4S	Surface 4 Sides
MUTCD	Manual on Uniform Traffic Control Devices	Ply.	Plywood	Shee.	Sheet Metal Worker
		p.m.	Post Meridiem	Sin.	Sine
M.V.A.	Million Volt Amperes	Pntd.	Painted	Skwk.	Skilled Worker
M.V.A.R.	Million Volt Amperes Reactance	Pord.	Painter, Ordinary	SL	Saran Lined
MV	Megavolt	pp	Pages	S.L.	Slimline
MW	Megawatt	PP, PPL	Polypropylene	Sldr.	Solder
MXM	Male by Male	P.P.M.	Parts per Million	SLH	Super Long Span Bar Joist
MYD	Thousand Yards	Pr.	Pair	S.N.	Solid Neutral
N	Natural; North	P.E.S.B.	Pre-engineered Steel Building	SO	Stranded with oil resistant inside insulation
nA	Nanoampere	Prefab.	Prefabricated		
NA	Not Available; Not Applicable	Prefin.	Prefinished	S-O-L	Socketolet
N.B.C.	National Building Code	Prop.	Propelled	sp	Standpipe
NC	Normally Closed	PSF, psf	Pounds per Square Foot	S.P.	Static Pressure; Single Pole; Self-Propelled
NEMA	National Electrical Manufacturers Assoc.	PSI, psi	Pounds per Square Inch		
		PSIG	Pounds per Square Inch Gauge	Spri.	Sprinkler Installer
NEHB	Bolted Circuit Breaker to 600V.	PSP	Plastic Sewer Pipe	spwg	Static Pressure Water Gauge
NFPA	National Fire Protection Association	Pspr.	Painter, Spray	S.P.D.T.	Single Pole, Double Throw
NLB	Non-Load-Bearing	Psst.	Painter, Structural Steel	SPF	Spruce Pine Fir; Sprayed Polyurethane Foam
NM	Non-Metallic Cable	P.T.	Potential Transformer		
nm	Nanometer	P. & T.	Pressure & Temperature	S.P.S.T.	Single Pole, Single Throw
No.	Number	Ptd.	Painted	SPT	Standard Pipe Thread
NO	Normally Open	Ptns.	Partitions	Sq.	Square; 100 Square Feet
N.O.C.	Not Otherwise Classified	Pu	Ultimate Load	Sq. Hd.	Square Head
Nose.	Nosing	PVC	Polyvinyl Chloride	Sq. In.	Square Inch
NPT	National Pipe Thread	Pvmt.	Pavement	S.S.	Single Strength; Stainless Steel
NQOD	Combination Plug-on/Bolt on Circuit Breaker to 240V.	PRV	Pressure Relief Valve	S.S.B.	Single Strength B Grade
		Pwr.	Power	sst, ss	Stainless Steel
N.R.C., NRC	Noise Reduction Coefficient/ Nuclear Regulator Commission	Q	Quantity Heat Flow	Sswk.	Structural Steel Worker
		Qt.	Quart	Sswl.	Structural Steel Welder
N.R.S.	Non Rising Stem	Quan., Qty.	Quantity	St.; Stl.	Steel
ns	Nanosecond	Q.C.	Quick Coupling	STC	Sound Transmission Coefficient
NTP	Notice to Proceed	r	Radius of Gyration	Std.	Standard
nW	Nanowatt	R	Resistance	Stg.	Staging
OB	Opposing Blade	R.C.P.	Reinforced Concrete Pipe	STK	Select Tight Knot
OC	On Center	Rect.	Rectangle	STP	Standard Temperature & Pressure
OD	Outside Diameter	recpt.	Receptacle	Stpi.	Steamfitter, Pipefitter
O.D.	Outside Dimension	Reg.	Regular	Str.	Strength; Starter; Straight
ODS	Overhead Distribution System	Reinf.	Reinforced	Strd.	Stranded
O.G.	Ogee	Req'd.	Required	Struct.	Structural
O.H.	Overhead	Res.	Resistant	Sty.	Story
O&P	Overhead and Profit	Resi.	Residential	Subj.	Subject
Oper.	Operator	RF	Radio Frequency	Subs.	Subcontractors
Opng.	Opening	RFID	Radio-frequency Identification	Surf.	Surface
Orna.	Ornamental	Rgh.	Rough	Sw.	Switch
OSB	Oriented Strand Board	RGS	Rigid Galvanized Steel	Swbd.	Switchboard
OS&Y	Outside Screw and Yoke	RHW	Rubber, Heat & Water Resistant; Residential Hot Water	S.Y.	Square Yard
OSHA	Occupational Safety and Health Act			Syn.	Synthetic
		rms	Root Mean Square	S.Y.P.	Southern Yellow Pine
Ovhd.	Overhead	Rnd.	Round	Sys.	System
OWG	Oil, Water or Gas	Rodm.	Rodman	t.	Thickness
Oz.	Ounce	Rofc.	Roofer, Composition	T	Temperature; Ton
P.	Pole; Applied Load; Projection	Rofp.	Roofer, Precast	Tan	Tangent
p.	Page	Rohe.	Roofer Helpers (Composition)	T.C.	Terra Cotta
Pape.	Paperhanger	Rots.	Roofer, Tile & Slate	T & C	Threaded and Coupled
P.A.P.R.	Powered Air Purifying Respirator	R.O.W.	Right of Way	T.D.	Temperature Difference
PAR	Parabolic Reflector	RPM	Revolutions per Minute	TDD	Telecommunications Device for the Deaf
P.B., PB	Push Button	R.S.	Rapid Start		
Pc., Pcs.	Piece, Pieces	Rsr	Riser	T.E.M.	Transmission Electron Microscopy
P.C.	Portland Cement; Power Connector	RT	Round Trip	temp	Temperature, Tempered, Temporary
P.C.F.	Pounds per Cubic Foot	S.	Suction; Single Entrance; South	TFFN	Nylon Jacketed Wire

Abbreviations

TFE	Tetrafluoroethylene (Teflon)	U.L., UL	Underwriters Laboratory	w/	With
T. & G.	Tongue & Groove; Tar & Gravel	Uld.	Unloading	W.C., WC	Water Column; Water Closet
Th., Thk.	Thick	Unfin.	Unfinished	W.F.	Wide Flange
Thn.	Thin	UPS	Uninterruptible Power Supply	W.G.	Water Gauge
Thrded	Threaded	URD	Underground Residential Distribution	Wldg.	Welding
Tilf.	Tile Layer, Floor	US	United States	W. Mile	Wire Mile
Tilh.	Tile Layer, Helper	USGBC	U.S. Green Building Council	W-O-L	Weldolet
THHN	Nylon Jacketed Wire	USP	United States Primed	W.R.	Water Resistant
THW.	Insulated Strand Wire	UTMCD	Uniform Traffic Manual For Control Devices	Wrck.	Wrecker
THWN	Nylon Jacketed Wire			WSFU	Water Supply Fixture Unit
T.L., TL	Truckload	UTP	Unshielded Twisted Pair	W.S.P.	Water, Steam, Petroleum
T.M.	Track Mounted	V	Volt	WT., Wt.	Weight
Tot.	Total	VA	Volt Amperes	WWF	Welded Wire Fabric
T-O-L	Threadolet	VAT	Vinyl Asbestos Tile	XFER	Transfer
tmpd	Tempered	V.C.T.	Vinyl Composition Tile	XFMR	Transformer
TPO	Thermoplastic Polyolefin	VAV	Variable Air Volume	XHD	Extra Heavy Duty
T.S.	Trigger Start	VC	Veneer Core	XHHW	Cross-Linked Polyethylene Wire
Tr.	Trade	VDC	Volts Direct Current	XLPE	Insulation
Transf.	Transformer	Vent.	Ventilation	XLP	Cross-linked Polyethylene
Trhv.	Truck Driver, Heavy	Vert.	Vertical	Xport	Transport
Trlr	Trailer	V.F.	Vinyl Faced	Y	Wye
Trlt.	Truck Driver, Light	V.G.	Vertical Grain	yd	Yard
TTY	Teletypewriter	VHF	Very High Frequency	yr	Year
TV	Television	VHO	Very High Output	Δ	Delta
T.W.	Thermoplastic Water Resistant Wire	Vib.	Vibrating	%	Percent
		VLF	Vertical Linear Foot	~	Approximately
UCI	Uniform Construction Index	VOC	Volatile Organic Compound	Ø	Phase; diameter
UF	Underground Feeder	Vol.	Volume	@	At
UGND	Underground Feeder	VRP	Vinyl Reinforced Polyester	#	Pound; Number
UHF	Ultra High Frequency	W	Wire; Watt; Wide; West	<	Less Than
U.I.	United Inch			>	Greater Than
				Z	Zone

Index

A

Abandon catch basin	22
Abatement asbestos	26
equipment asbestos	25
ABC extinguisher portable	67
extinguisher wheeled	67
Aboveground storage	
tank concrete	340
ABS DWV pipe	222
Absorber shock	256
vibration	129
A/C packaged terminal	366
removal fan-coil	323
removal rooftop	324
removal thru-the-wall	324
removal window	324
Accelerator sprinkler system	101
Access road and parking area	16
Accessory bathroom	64, 65
compressor	286
fuel oil	335
polypropylene	238
toilet	64
Acid resistant drain	279
resistant pipe	316
Acoustical sealant	55
ACR tubing copper	155
ADA compliant drinking	
fountain	307
compliant fixture support	302
compliant lavatory	305
compliant shower	296, 305
compliant water cooler	308
Adapter fire hose swivel	97
polybutylene	237
Adjustment factor	8
factor labor	108
for sprinkler/standpipe	
installations	703
Aeration sewage	468
Aerator	309
Aerial survey	22
After cooler medical	313
Aggregate spreader	584, 591
Air automatic vent	341
balancing	329
cock	341
compressor	286, 587
compressor dental	75
compressor medical	313
compressor package	286
compressor portable	587
compressor removal	109
compressor sprinkler system	101
conditioner cooling & heating	366
conditioner direct expansion	368
conditioner general	322
conditioner maintenance	19
conditioner packaged term.	366
conditioner portable	366
conditioner receptacle	380
conditioner removal	322
conditioner thru-wall	366
conditioner window	366
conditioner wiring	383
conditioning ventilating	366
control	340
curtain removal	322
deaerator	340
dryer system	313
eliminator	340
filter regulator lubricator	286
filter removal	322
filtration	25
gap fitting	256
hose	588
line coupler	286
purging scoop	340
quality	72
sampling	25
scoop	340
scrubber	588
separator	340
spade	588
unit removal make-up	323
vent automatic	341
vent convector or baseboard	368
Airless sprayer	25
Air-source heat pump	367
Alarm device	387
dry	88
fire	100
panel and device	387
panel module	312
residential	382
standpipe	100
system medical	312
transducer medical	312
valve sprinkler	88
vent	335
water motor	100
All fuel chimney	356, 358
service jacket insulation	133, 138
Alteration fee	8
Aluminum flashing	50, 278
insulation jacketing	146
pipe	433, 434
rivet	44
salvage	110
weld rod	45
Anchor bolt	33
chemical	38, 42
epoxy	38, 42
expansion	42
hollow wall	42
lead screw	43
machinery	35
metal nailing	42
nailing	42
nylon nailing	42
pipe conduit casing	457
plastic screw	43
screw	42
toggle bolt	42
wedge	43
Angle valve bronze	111
valve plastic	116
Anti-freeze inhibited	349
Anti-siphon device	256
Appliance	71
plumbing	287, 289, 308, 309
residential	71, 382
Arch culvert oval	436
Architectural fee	8
Area clean-up	27
Articulating boom lift	587
Asbestos abatement	26
abatement equipment	25
area decontamination	27
demolition	27
disposal	28
encapsulation	28
remediation plan/method	25
removal	26
removal process	698
Asphalt distributor	588
paver	590
paving	406
plant portable	591
Asphaltic binder	406
concrete	406
concrete paving	406
pavement	406
wearing course	406
Aspirator dental	75
Atomizer water	25
Attachment ripper	591
Attachments skidsteer	587
Auger earth	584
Auto park drain	278
Automatic fire-suppression	103
flush	302
washing machine	71
Automotive equipment	70
exhaust system	529
lift	86
spray painting booth	70
Autopsy equipment	76
Autoscrub machine	588
Axe fire	98

B

B and S pipe gasket	270
Backer rod	54
Backfill	393
trench	391
Backflow preventer	255
preventer removal	109
preventer solar	364
Backhoe	585
bucket	586
extension	591
trenching	560, 562, 564
Backwater drainage control	431
sewer valve	431
valve	283
Bag disposable	25, 30
glove	26
Balance valve circuit setter	341
Balancing air	329
hydronic	347
water	330
Ball check valve	117
check valve plastic	117
valve brass	324
valve bronze	111, 112
valve for medical gas	312
valve grooved joint	203
valve plastic	116
valve polypropylene	117
valve slow close	99
wrecking	591
Baptistry	76
Bar front	82
grab	64
towel	64
tub	64
Barber chair	70
equipment	70
Barge construction	594
Barometric damper	353
Barrels flasher	588
reflectorized	588
Barricade	17
flasher	588
tape	17
Barrier and enclosure	16
dust	16
separation	26, 28, 29
slipform paver	592
Base cabinet	78
sink	78
stabilizer	592
vanity	78
Baseboard heat	368
heat electric	370
heater electric	370
removal hydronic	323
Base plate scaffold	14
shoring	14
Basket type strainer	344
Bath hospital	305
paraffin	75
perineal	305
redwood	81
spa	81
steam	82
whirlpool	75, 81
Bathroom	295
accessory	64, 65
exhaust fan	350
faucet	297
five fixture	496
fixture	292, 293, 295, 296
four fixture	495
heater & fan	350
soaking	295
system	494-496
three fixture	494
two fixture	493
Bathtub	488
bar	64
enclosure	66
removal	109
residential	295
Beam attachment welded	119
clamp	119
flange clip	128
Bedding pipe	393
Bedpan cleanser	305
Bell & spigot pipe	261
signal	387
Bellow expansion joint	342
Bibb hose	341
Bidet	292
removal	109
rough-in	293
Bimodal MDPE, ASTM D2513	439
Binder asphaltic	406
Bituminous coating	412
paver	589
Blaster shot	590
Blind flange	186
structural bolt	45
Block manhole	418
manhole/catch basin	579
Blood bank refrigeration	74
Blowdown removal boiler	322
Blower insulation	589
Board insulation	331
mineral wool	331
Boat work	594
Boiler	359
blowdown removal	322
condensing	359
cut off low water	332
demolition	322
drain	341
electric	359
electric steam	359
gas fired	360
gas pulse	359
general	108
hot water	359, 360
insulation	332
oil-fired	360
removal	322
steam	360
steam electric	528
Bolt & gasket set	185
anchor	33

Index

blind structural 45
Bond performance 11, 694
Boom lift articulating 587
    lift telescoping 587
Booster system water pressure .. 260
Booth painting 70
Borer horizontal 592
Boring horizontal 417
    machine horizontal 584
    service 417
Borosilicate pipe 314
Borrow fill 393
    loading and/or spreading 393
Bottled water cooler 309
Boundary and survey marker 22
Bowl toilet 292
Box Buffalo 419
    distribution 432
    flow leveler distribution 432
    storage 13
    trench 591
    utility 419
Brace cross 46
Bracing shoring 14
Bracket pipe 119
    scaffold 14
Braided bronze hose 250
    steel hose 250
Brass pipe 151
    pipe fitting 152
    salvage 110
    valve 111
Break glass station 387
Breaker air gap vacuum 256
    pavement 588
    vacuum 256
Breeching insulation 332
Brick cart 588
    catch basin 418
    manhole 418
Bridge sidewalk 15
Bronze angle valve 111
    ball valve 112
    body strainer 346
    butterfly valve 112
    globe valve 113
    swing check valve 112
    valve 111
Bronze/brass valve 324
Broom finish concrete 38
    sidewalk 590
Brush chipper 585
    cutter 585, 586
Bubbler 307
    drinking 308
Bucket backhoe 586
    clamshell 585
    concrete 584
    dragline 585
    excavator 591
    pavement 591
Buffalo box 419
Buggy concrete 584
Builder's risk insurance 692
Building permit 12
    portable 13
    sprinkler 102
    temporary 13
Built-in range 71
    shower 296
Bulldozer 586
Bull float concrete 584
Buncher feller 585
Bunk house trailer 13
Burner gas conversion 361
    gun type 361

oil 361
residential 361
Butt fusion machine 588
Butterfly valve 325, 428
    valve bronze 112
    valve grooved joint 204
Butyl caulking 55
    rubber 54
Bypass pipe 416

C

Cabinet base 78
    convector heater 372
    fire equipment 66, 98
    hardboard 78
    heater electric 372
    hose rack 66
    hotel 65
    kitchen 78
    medicine 65
    shower 65
    unit heater 372
    valve 67
Cable hanger 128
    jack 594
    pulling 591
    tensioning 591
    trailer 591
Cable/wire puller 591
Calcium silicate insulated system . 457
    silicate insulation 332, 457
    silicate pipe covering 135
Cap HDPE piping 426
    vent 277, 335
Car tram 591
Carbon dioxide extinguisher 103
Carrier and support removal 109
    fixture support 302
    pipe 120, 124
Carrier/support fixture 302
Cart brick 588
    concrete 584
    mounted extinguisher 67
Cartridge style water filter 288
Casework custom 78
Casing anchor pipe conduit 457
Cast in place concrete 36, 37
    iron cleanout 131
    iron fitting 184, 262
    iron manhole cover 437
    iron pipe 261
    iron pipe fitting 173, 262
    iron pipe gasket 270
    iron radiator 368
    iron trap 275
    iron vent cap 277
Caster scaffold 14
Cast-iron weld rod 45
Catch basin 437
    basin and manhole 580
    basin brick 418
    basin cleaner 591
    basin precast 418
    basin removal 22
    basin vacuum 591
    basin/manhole 579
Cathodic protection 83
Catwalk scaffold 15
Caulking 55
    lead 262
    oakum 262
    polyurethane 55
    sealant 54
Ceiling fan 349

heater 72
Cell equipment 76
    prison 82
Cellular glass insulation 134
Cement liner 416
Central station AHU removal ... 322
    vacuum 76
    vacuum unit 464
Centrifugal in-line motor 259
    pump 258, 590
Chain fall hoist 593
    hoist 462
    link fence 17
    saw 590
    trencher 391, 587
Chair barber 70
    dental 75
    hydraulic 75
    pipe support 124
Chamber decontamination 26, 28
    infiltration 433
Channel steel 122
Charge disposal 28
    powder 44
Check lift valve 115
    swing valve 112
    valve 88, 429
    valve ball 117
    valve flanged cast iron 428
    valve grooved joint 204
    valve silent 114, 327
    valve stainless steel 328
    valve wafer 115, 327
Checkered plate 46
    plate cover 46
    plate platform 46
Chemical anchor 38, 42
    dilution tank 319
    dry extinguisher 67
    spreader 591
    storage tank 319
    toilet 590
    water closet 468
Chemical-waste dilution tank ... 319
Chilled water pipe underground . 455
Chiller remote water 309
    removal water 324
Chimney all fuel 356, 358
    all fuel vent 358
    positive pressure 356, 358
    prefabricated metal 356
    vent 353
    vent fitting 358
    vent oval 355
Chipper brush 585
    log 586
    stump 586
Chipping hammer 588
Chloride accelerator concrete ... 37
Chlorination system 309
Church equipment 76
CI acid resistant drain 279
    roof drain system 518
Circuit setter 341
Circular saw 590
Circulating pump 348
Clamp beam 119
    pipe 119, 412
    pipe repair 413
    ring 422
    riser 120
    valve 116
Clamshell bucket 585
Classroom sink 300
    sink rough-in 300
Clean control joint 33

ductwork 19
    tank 24
Cleaner catch basin 591
    crack 592
    steam 590
Cleaning & disposal equipment .. 73
    duct 19
    internal pipe 415
    up 18
Cleanout and drain removal 109
    cast iron 131
    floor 130
    pipe 130
    polypropylene 132
    PVC 132
    tee 131
    wall type 131
Cleanouts 419
Clean-up area 27
Clevis pipe hanger 121
Climbing crane 592
    hydraulic jack 594
Clinic service sink 305
Clock timer 382
Closet water 292, 299
Clothes dryer commercial 70
Coat hook 64
Coating bituminous 412
    epoxy 412
    polyethylene 412
Cock air 341
    drain and specialty 341
    gas 111
    gauge 341
    pet 341
CO_2 extinguisher 67
    fire extinguishing system ... 103
Cold mix paver 592
Collection sewage/drainage 435
    system dust 464
Collector solar energy system ... 363
Combination ball valve 324
    device 379
Comfort station 82
Command dog 18
Commercial dishwasher 73
    gas water heater 290
    lavatory 300
    oil-fired water heater 291
    sink 300
    toilet accessory 64
    water heater 289, 291
    water heater electric 289
    water-heater 501-503
Commissioning 19
Compact fill 393
Compactor earth 585
    landfill 586
Companion flange 186
Compartment toilet 62
Compensation workers 11
Compliant drinking
    fountain ADA 307
    fixture support ADA 302
    lavatory ADA 305
    shower ADA 296, 305
    water cooler ADA 308
Component control 333, 334
Component/DDC sys. control ... 332
Compressed air equipment
    automotive 70
Compression joint fitting 160
    seal 53
    tank 343
Compressor accessory 286
    air 286, 587

Index

air package 286
  reciprocating 286
  reciprocating hermetic 286
  removal air 109
  removal refrigerant 324
Computer room unit removal ... 322
Concrete asphaltic 406
  broom finish 38
  bucket 584
  buggy 584
  bull float 584
  cart 584
  cast in place 36, 37
  catch basin 418
  chloride accelerator 37
  conveyer 584
  core drilling 39
  direct chute 37
  distribution box 432
  drill 376
  drilling 39
  equipment rental 584
  fiber reinforcing 37
  float finish 38
  floor edger 584
  floor grinder 584
  hand trowel finish 38
  hole cutting 377
  hole drilling 376
  impact drilling 39
  insert hanger 120
  lance 589
  machine trowel finish 38
  manhole 418
  mixer 584
  non-chloride accelerator ... 37
  paver 590
  pipe 435
  pipe removal 22
  placement footing 37
  placing 37
  pump 584
  ready mix 37
  reinforcing 35
  retarder 37
  saw 584
  septic tank 431
  short load 37
  spreader 590
  tank aboveground storage ... 340
  trowel 584
  truck 584
  truck holding 37
  utility vault 419
  vibrator 584
  water reducer 37
  water storage tank 430
  winter 37
Condensate meter rem. steam .. 324
  removal pump 349
Condenser removal 322
Condensing boiler 359
  furnace 361
  unit removal 322
Conditioner general air 322
  maintenance air 19
  portable air 366
Conditioning ventilating air . 366
Conduit & fitting flexible ... 378
  fitting pipe 456
  pipe prefabricated 458
  prefabricated pipe 455, 457
  preinsulated pipe 455
Connection fire-department ... 95
  motor 378
  standpipe 95

Storz type 95
utility 419
Connector flexible 249
  gas 249
  water copper tubing 250
Construction barge 594
  management fee 8
  photography 12
  sump hole 392
  temporary 16
  time 8, 689
Contained pipe 245
Containment unit dust 17, 29
Contaminated soil 24
Contingency 8
Contractor overhead 18
Control & motor starter 383
  air 340
  component 333, 334
  component/DDC system 332
  DDC 332
  DDC system 333
  draft 353
  flow check 344
  hand/off/automatic 384
  joint 32
  joint clean 33
  joint sawn 32
  joint sealant 33
  pressure sprinkler 101
  station 384
  station stop/start 384
  system 332
  valve heating 335, 344
  water level 332
Control-component 335
Convector cabinet heater 372
  hydronic heating 368
Cooking equipment 73
  range 71
Cooler beverage 73
  removal evaporative 323
  water 308
Cooling tower removal 322
Copper ACR tubing 155
  drum trap 276
  DWV tubing 154
  fitting 156
  flashing 50, 278
  grooved joint 164
  pipe 153, 426
  rivet 44
  salvage 110
  tube 153, 426
  tube fitting 156
  tubing oxygen class 154
Core drill 584
  drilling concrete 39
Cornice drain 283
Corrosion monitor 89
  resistance 412
  resistant fitting 316
  resistant lab equipment 319
  resistant pipe 314, 315
  resistant pipe fitting 316
  resistant trap 276
Corrosion-resistant sink 300
Corrugated metal pipe ... 433, 434
  pipe 433
  steel pipe 433
Cost mark-up 11
Countertop sink 295
Coupler air line 286
Coupling fire hose 97
  mechanical 196
  plastic 234

polypropylene 238
Course wearing 406
Cover checkered plate 46
  manhole 437
  stair tread 18
Covering calcium silicate pipe .. 135
  protection saddle 125
CPVC pipe 223
  valve 117
Crack cleaner 592
  filler 592
Crane 462
  climbing 592
  crawler 593
  crew daily 13
  hydraulic 462, 593
  material handling 462
  tower 13, 593
  truck mounted 593
Crawler crane 593
  drill rotary 588
  shovel 586
Crew daily crane 13
  forklift 13
Cross 427
  brace 46
Crowbar fire 98
Cubicle shower 296
  toilet 63
Culvert end 436
  pipe 436
  reinforced 435
Cup sink 301, 486
Curb builder 584
  extruder 585
  prefabricated 374
  slipform paver 592
Cured in place pipe liner ... 416, 417
Curtain removal air 322
  rod 64
Custom casework 78
Cut in sleeve 427
  in valve 427
  off low water boiler 332
  pipe groove 204
Cutter brush 585, 586
Cutting and drilling 376
  steel pipe labor 172
  torch 590

D

Daily crane crew 13
Damper barometric 353
Darkroom equipment 71
DDC control 332
Deaerator 340
  air 340
Deck drain 278
  roof 48
Decontamination asbestos area .. 27
  chamber 26, 28
  enclosure 26-28
  equipment 25
Decorator device 379
  switch 379
Deep seal trap 276
Dehumidifier 588
  removal 322
Dehydrator package sprinkler . 101
Delivery charge 15
Deluge sprinkler 536, 538
  sprinkler monitoring panel . 103
  valve assembly sprinkler ... 103

Demo hydronic convector
  & radiator 323
Demolish remove pavement
  and curb 22
Demolition 697
  asbestos 27
  boiler 322
  furnace 323
  hammer 585
  HVAC 322
  mold contaminated area 29
  pavement 22
  plumbing 109
  site 22
  torch cutting 23
Dental chair 75
  equipment 75
  metal interceptor 281
  office equipment 75
Derrick crane guyed 593
  crane stifleg 593
Detection intrusion 386
  leak 386
  probe leak 386
  system 386
Detector check valve 429
  meter water supply 254
  smoke 386
  temperature rise 386
Detention equipment 76
Detour sign 17
Device alarm 387
  anti-siphon 256
  combination 379
  decorator 379
  GFI 380
  receptacle 380
  residential 378
Dew point monitor 313
Dewater 392, 393
  pumping 392
Dewatering 392, 718
  equipment 594
Diaphragm pump 590
  valve 116
Dielectric union 342
Diesel hammer 586
  tugboat 594
Diffuser pump suction 347
  suction 347
Dilution tank chemical 319
  tank chemical-waste 319
Dimmer switch 379
Direct chute concrete 37
Directional drill horizontal . 592
Disc harrow 585
Discharge hose 589
Disease infectious 9
Dishwasher commercial 73
  residential 71
Dispenser hot water 288
  napkin 64
  soap 64
  towel 64
Dispersion nozzle 103
Disposable bag 25, 30
Disposal asbestos 28
  charge 28
  field 432
  garbage 71
Distiller water 74
Distribution box 432
  box concrete 432
  box flow leveler 432
  box HDPE 432
  pipe water 421, 423

Index

Distributor asphalt 588
Ditching 392
Diving stand 80
Dog command 18
Dome drain 283
Domestic hot water temp maint . 128
   hot-water 498-500
   water booster system 260
Door bell residential 381
   fire 387
   shower 65
Double wall pipe 241, 438
Dozer 586
Draft control 353
   damper vent 353
Dragline bucket 585
Drain 275, 283
   acid resistant 279
   boiler 341
   ci acid resistant 279
   deck 278
   dome 283
   expansion joint roof 283
   facility trench 284
   floor 279
   main 283
   pipe 392
   PVC acid resistant 279
   roof 283
   sanitary 278
   scupper 284
   sediment bucket 279
   shower 275
   terrace 283
   trap seal floor 280
   trench 284
Drainage control backwater 431
   field 432
   fitting 273
   fixture units 709, 710
   pipe 314, 315, 431, 435
   trap 275, 276
Draindown valve 365
Drainwater heat recovery 292
Drill concrete 376
   core 584
   main 426
   quarry 588
   steel 588
   tap main 426
   track 588
Drilling concrete 39
   concrete impact 39
   horizontal 417
   plaster 58
   rig 584
   steel 43
Drinking bubbler 308
   fountain 307, 308
   fountain deck rough-in 308
   fountain floor rough-in 308
   fountain support 302
   fountain wall rough-in 307
Drip irrigation 407
   irrigation subsurface 407
   pan elbow 275
Driver post 592
   sheeting 588
Drum trap copper 276
Dry alarm 88
   pipe sprinkler head 101
   standpipe riser 554
Dryer accessory washer 298
   commercial clothes 70
   hand 64
   industrial 70

receptacle 381
residential 71
system air 313
vent 71, 299
Dry-pipe sprinkler system 101
Dual flush flushometer 298, 302
   flush valve toilet 302
Duck tarpaulin 16
Duct cleaning 19
   insulation 331
Ductile iron fitting 421
   iron fitting mech joint 422
   iron grooved joint 90, 199, 203
   iron pipe 421
Ductless removal split 324
Ductwork clean 19
Dump charge 23
   truck 587
Dumpster 23
Dumpsters 697
Dump truck off highway 587
Duplex style strainer 345
Dust barrier 16
   collection system 464
   containment unit 17, 29
DWV pipe ABS 222
   PVC pipe 222, 431
   tubing copper 154

E

Earth auger 584
   compactor 585
   scraper 586
   vibrator 390
Earthquake shutoff gas 361
   valve gas 361
Earthwork equipment rental 584
Ecclesiastical equipment 76
Economizer shower-head water . 296
Edger concrete floor 584
Efficiency flush valve high 302
Effluent-filter septic system 432
Ejector pump 282
Elbow drip pan 275
   HDPE piping 425
   pipe 199
Electric baseboard heater 370
   boiler 359, 528
   boiler small hydronic 528
   cabinet heater 372
   commercial water heater .. 289
   fire pump 556
   generator 589
   heater 72
   heater removal 323
   heating 370
   hoist 462
   hot air heater 372
   pool heater 361
   unit heater 371
   water cooler 308
   water heater 289
   water heater residential ... 289
   water heater tankless 288
   water-heater commercial .. 501
   water-heater residential ... 498
Electrical fee 8
   installation drilling 376
   knockout 377
   laboratory 74
Electricity temporary 12
Electrofusion welded PP pipe .. 317
Elevated installation add 108
   pipe add 108

Elevator fee 8
   sump pump 285
Eliminator air 340
Emergency equipment laboratory . 74
   eyewash 306
   shower 305
Employer liability 11
Emulsion sprayer 588
Encapsulation asbestos 28
   pipe 28
Enclosure bathtub 66
   decontamination 26-28
   shower 66
End culvert 436
Energy circulator air solar 363
   distribution pipe steam ... 457
   system air purger solar 364
   system air vent solar 364
   system balancing valve solar . 365
   system control valve solar .. 364
   system controller solar 364
   system expansion tank solar . 365
   system gauge pressure solar . 365
   system heat exchanger solar . 364
   system storage tank solar .. 364
   system vacuum relief solar . 365
Engine exhaust elimination ... 350
Engineering fee 8, 688
Entrainment eliminator 281
Entrance screen 62
Epoxy anchor 38, 42
   coating 412
   fiberglass wound pipe 315
   resin fitting 226
   welded wire 36
Equipment 70, 584
   automotive 70
   barber 70
   cell 76
   cleaning & disposal 73
   darkroom 71
   dental 75
   dental office 75
   detention 76
   ecclesiastical 76
   fire 556
   fire hose 96, 556
   fire-extinguishing 103
   foundation formwork 32
   hospital 74
   insulation 332
   insurance 11
   laboratory emergency 74
   laundry 70
   lubrication 70
   medical 74-76
   medical sterilizing 74
   pad 36
   refrigerated storage 73
   rental 584, 695, 696
   rental concrete 584
   rental earthwork 584
   rental general 587
   rental highway 591
   rental lifting 592
   rental marine 594
   rental wellpoint 594
   roof support 127
   safety eye/face 306
   swimming pool 80
Escutcheon 254
   plate 99, 100
   sprinkler 100
Estimate electrical heating 370
   plumbing 497
Estimating 682

Ethylene glycol 349
Evaporative cooler removal 323
Evaporator removal 323
Excavating equipment 717
   trench 390
   utility trench 391
Excavation 390
   hand 390, 392
   septic tank 432
   tractor 390
   trench 390, 391, 560-562, 564
Excavator bucket 591
   hydraulic 584
Excavator hydro 586
Exchanger heat 365
   removal heat 323
Exhaust elimination engine ... 350
   elimination garage 350
   hood 71
   system 351
   system removal 323
Expansion anchor 42
   joint 342
   joint bellow 342
   joint grooved joint 203
   joint roof drain 283
   shield 42
   tank 343
   tank steel 343
Extension backhoe 591
   ladder 589
Extinguisher cart mounted 67
   chemical dry 67
   CO_2 67
   fire 67, 103
   FM200 fire 103
   installation 67
   portable ABC 67
   pressurized fire 67
   standard 67
   wheeled ABC 67
Extra work 11
Extruder curb 585
Eye wash fountain 306
   wash portable 306
Eye/face wash safety equipment . 306
Eyewash emergency 306
   safety equipment 306

F

Fabric-backed flashing 50
Face wash fountain 305
Facility trench drain 284
Factor 8
   security 9
Fan bathroom exhaust 350
   ceiling 349
   paddle 382
   removal 323
   residential 382
   ventilation 382
   wiring 382
Fan-coil A/C removal 323
Faucet & fitting 297, 302, 305
   bathroom 297
   gooseneck 305
   laundry 297
   lavatory 297
   medical 305
F&C plate 254
Fee architectural 8
   engineering 8
Feller buncher 585
Fence chain link 17

Index

plywood 17
   temporary 17
   wire 18
Fiber reinforcing concrete 37
Fiberglass panel 16
   pipe covering 137
   rainwater storage tank 285
   tank 338
   trench drain 284
   underground storage tank 261
Field disposal 432
   drainage 432
   office 13
   personnel 10, 11
Fill 393
   borrow 393
   by borrow & utility bedding . . 393
   gravel 393
Filler crack 592
   joint 54
Fillet welding 44
Film equipment 71
Filter iron removal 288
   oil 335
   rainwater 468
   removal air 322
   swimming pool 309
   water 288
Filtration air 25
   equipment 80
Finishing floor concrete 38
Fin-tube radiation
   apartment bldg 520
Fire alarm 100
   axe 98
   call pullbox 387
   crowbar 98
   door 387
   equipment cabinet 66, 98
   extinguisher 67, 103
   extinguisher portable 66, 67
   extinguisher . . 531, 532, 534, 535,
       537, 538, 540, 541, 543, 544,
       548, 550, 552, 554-557
   extinguishing system . 96, 97, 103,
       105
   horn 387
   hose 97
   hose adapter 96
   hose coupling 97
   hose equipment 96
   hose gate valve 99
   hose nipple 97
   hose nozzle 97
   hose rack 98
   hose reel 98
   hose storage cabinet 66
   hose storage house 98
   hose valve 99
   hose wye 100
   hydrant 430, 575
   hydrant building 95
   hydrant remove 22
   protection 66
fire protection, cost per square . . 542

F

Fire protection system
   classification 702
      pump 104, 105
      retardant pipe 316
      sprinkler head 101
      suppression 557
      suppression valve 91

tool 98
valve hydrant 99
Fire-department connection 95
Fire-extinguishing equipment . . . 103
Firestop wood 48
Firestopping 52
Fire-suppression automatic 103
   grooved joint 90, 92
   hose reel 98
   pipe fitting 93
   plastic pipe 93
Fitting adapter pipe 158
   cast iron 184, 262
   cast iron pipe 173, 262
   compression joint 160
   copper 156
   copper pipe 156, 166
   corrosion resistant 316
   drainage 273
   drainage special pipe 273
   ductile iron 421
   DWV pipe 231
   epoxy resin 226
   flanged 185
   flanged cast iron pipe 184
   flare joint 161
   flexible gas pipe 336
   forged steel pipe 191
   galvanized 274
   gas vent 353
   glass 314
   grooved joint 165, 197
   grooved joint pipe 90, 199
   grooved unit 164, 201
   HDPE 242
   insert pipe 237
   malleable iron 177
   malleable iron pipe 178, 194
   mechanical joint pipe 194
   monoflow 344
   pipe 184, 273, 423, 455, 457
   pipe conduit 456
   plastic 231
   plastic pipe 93
   polybutylene pipe 236
   polypropylene 238, 317
   PVC 228, 424
   PVC pipe 238
   refrigeration 161
   removal piping 109
   stainless steel pipe 212
   steel 173, 184
   steel carbon pipe 187
   steel pipe 187
   tube 206
   vent chimney 353, 358
   weld 190
   weld joint pipe 191
   welded steel pipe 195
Fixture bathroom . 292, 293, 295, 296
   carrier/support 302
   institution 306
   plumbing . 280, 281, 288, 292, 294,
       301, 307, 348, 421
   prison 306
   removal 109
   removal prison 110
   residential 381
Flange blind 186
   clip beam 128
   companion 186
   gasket 185
   grooved joint 202
   PVC 236
   slip on escutcheon 254
   stainless steel 217

steel 193, 202
steel weld-on 193
threaded 186
Flanged fitting 185
   pipe 170
Flare joint fitting 161
Flasher barrels 588
   barricade 588
Flashing 50
   aluminum 50, 278
   copper 50, 278
   fabric-backed 50
   galvanized 278
   laminated sheet 50
   lead 278
   masonry 50
   mastic-backed 50
   neoprene 278
   paperbacked 50
   plastic sheet 51
   PVC 51
   sheet metal 50
   stainless 50
   vent 277
   vent chimney 354, 359
Flatbed truck 587, 591
   truck crane 592
Flexible conduit & fitting 378
   connector 249
   gas pipe fitting 336
   metal hose 250
   sprinkler connector 100
Float finish concrete 38
   valve 343
Floater equipment 11
Floodlight trailer 589
   tripod 588
Floor cleaning 18
   cleanout 130
   concrete finishing 38
   drain 279
   drain removal 109
   drain trap seal 280
   heating radiant 369
   heating removal radiant 323
   receptor 279
   sander 590
   scupper 284
Flow check control 344
   fitting hydronic 344
   meter 348
Flue chimney metal 353
   prefab metal 353
   shutter damper removal 323
Fluid heat transfer 364
Flush automatic 302
   flushometer dual 298, 302
   high efficiency toilet (HET) . . . 302
   valve 302
FM200 fire extinguisher 103
   fire suppression 557
   system 557
Foam core DWV ABS pipe 222
   core DWV PVC pipe 222
   pipe covering 140
   rubber pipe covering 140
   spray rig 589
Foam-water system component . . 103
Folding door shower 65
Food service equipment 73
Foot valve 118
   valve oil 335
Footing concrete placement 37
   formwork continuous 32
   formwork spread 32
   reinforcing 35

spread 36
Forklift 589
   crew 13
Formwork continuous footing . . . 32
   equipment foundation 32
   slab edge 32
   slab haunch 37
   slab on grade 32
   slab thickened edge 37
   slab trench 32
   slab turndown 37
   sleeve 32
   spread footing 32
Foundation mat 36
   mat concrete placement 38
Fountain 81
   drinking 307, 308
   eye wash 306
   face wash 305
   indoor 81
   lighting 310
   outdoor 81
   pump 309
   wash 301
   water pump 309
   yard 81
Frame scaffold 14
Framing lightweight 46
   lightweight angle 46
   lightweight channel 46
   miscellaneous wood 48
   pipe support 46
   slotted channel 46
   wood 48
Freezer 73
Frost penetration 698
Fuel oil gauge 335
   oil pump 337
   oil pump & motor set 337
   oil specialty 335
   oil valve 335
   tank 338
Fume elimination welding 352
   hood removal weld 323
Furnace condensing 361
   demolition 323
Fused pipe 425
Fusible oil valve 335
Fusion machine butt 588
   welded pipe fitting 317

G

Galley septic 432
Galvanized fitting 274
   flashing 278
   pipe fitting 275
   welded wire 36
Gantry crane 462
Gap fitting air 256
Garage exhaust elimination 350
   exhaust system 529
   ventilation 350
Garbage disposal 71
Gas cock 111
   connector 249
   conversion burner 361
   earthquake valve 361
   fired boiler 360
   fired infrared heater 362
   fired water-heater commercial . . 502
   fired water-heater residential . . 499
   meter 335
   meter residential 335
   pipe 439

Index

piping flexible (CSST) 335
piping medical 311
pressure regulator 252
pulse combustion 359
regulator 252
safety valve 361
station tank 338
stop valve 111
tubing (CSST) 335
vent 353
vent fitting 353
water heater commercial 290
water heater instantaneous ... 290
water heater residential 290
water heater tankless 290
Gasket & bolt set 185
  B and S pipe 270
  cast iron pipe 270
  flange 185
  joint 53
  joint pipe 262
  joint pipe fitting 266
  neoprene 53
  toilet 298
Gasoline piping 438
Gate box 429
  valve 325, 328, 429
  valve grooved joint 204
  valve soldered 112
Gauge cock 341
  fuel oil 335
  pressure 334
  pressure/vacuum 334
  vacuum 334
General air conditioner 322
  boiler 108
  contractor's overhead 692
  equipment rental 587
  fill 393
  maintenance 19
Generator electric 589
  steam 74
GFI receptacle 380
Gland seal pipe conduit 455
Glass door shower 65
  filler 308
  fitting 314
  insulation cellular 134
  lined water heater 72
  mirror 64
  P trap 276
  pipe 109, 314
  pipe fitting 314
  pipe removal 109
  process supply pipe 314
  shower stall 65
Glassware sterilizer 74
  washer 74
Globe valve 326, 328
  valve bronze 113
Glove bag 26
Glycol ethylene 349
  propylene 349
Gooseneck faucet 305
Grab bar 64
Gradall 585
Grader motorized 585
Grading 399
Gravel fill 393
  pack well 419
Grease interceptor 280
  trap 280
Grille painting 58
Grinder concrete floor 584
  pump/sewage ejector removal . 109
  system pump 281

Grit removal and handling
  equipment 468
Groove cut labor steel 205
  roll labor steel 205
Grooved joint check valve 204
  joint copper 164
  joint ductile iron ... 199, 203
  joint fire-suppression . 90, 92
  joint fitting 165, 197
  joint flange 202
  joint pipe 197
  joint plug valve 204
  joint reducer 164
  joint strainer 203
  joint suction diffuser 203
  joint valve 91
  reducer 201
  unit fitting 164, 201
Ground box hydrant 257
  hydrant removal 109
  post hydrant 258
Group shower 301
  wash fountain 301, 489
Grout pump 590
Guard service 18
  snow 51
  sprinkler head 101
Guardrail scaffold 14
  temporary 17
Guide pipe 121
Gun type burner 361
Guyed derrick crane 593

H

Hair interceptor 280
Hammer chipping 588
  demolition 585
  diesel 586
  drill rotary 588
  hydraulic 585, 589
  pile 585
  vibratory 586
Hammermill 591
Hand dryer 64
  excavation 390, 392
  hole 419
  trowel finish concrete 38
Handicap tub shower 295
Handling material 18, 462
Hand/off/automatic control ... 384
Hanger & support pipe 119
  assembly pipe 123
  cable 128
  clevis 121
  pipe 119
  plastic pipe 127
  rod coupling 123
  rod pipe 123
  rod socket 126
  roll 124
  split ring 122
  trapeze 124
  U-bolt pipe 126
  U-hook 127
  vibration absorbing 129
Hanger/support removal pipe .. 109
Hanging lintel 46
Hardboard cabinet 78
Harrow disc 585
Hat and coat strip 64
Hauling 394
  cycle 394
Haunch slab 37
Hazardous waste cleanup 24

waste disposal 24
HDPE distribution box 432
  fitting 242
  infiltration chamber 433
  pipe 241
  pipe dual wall 245
  pipe liner 416
  piping 425
  piping cap 426
  piping elbow 425
  piping tee 425
Head sprinkler 100
Header pipe wellpoint 594
Heat baseboard 368
  electric baseboard 370
  exchanger 365
  exchanger plate-type 365
  exchanger removal 323
  exchanger shell-type 366
  pipe 366
  pump 367
  pump air-source 367
  pump removal 323
  pump residential 383
  pump water heater 367
  pump water-source 367
  recovery drainwater 292
  recovery package removal .. 323
  therapy 75
  trace system 370
  transfer fluid 364
  transfer package 291
Heater & fan bathroom 350
  cabinet convector 372
  ceiling mount unit 372
  electric 72
  electric hot air 372
  gas fired infrared 362
  gas residential water 290
  gas water 290
  infrared 362
  infrared quartz 371
  quartz 371
  removal electric 323
  removal space 324
  sauna 82
  space 589
  swimming pool 360
  swimming pool solar 525
  terminal 362
  tubular infrared 362
  vertical discharge 372
  wall mounted 372
  water 72, 383
  water residential electric . 289
Heating 335
  & ventilating unit removal . 323
  control valve 344
  electric 370
  estimate electrical 370
  fin-tube residential 520
  hot water solar 507
  hydronic 359, 360, 368
  industrial 359
  insulation 133, 136, 137, 332
  kettle 592
  panel radiant 371
  solar 363
  solar-energy 515, 525
  steam-to-water 365
Heavy duty shoring 14
  lifting 695
Helicopter 593
High efficiency flush valve .. 302
  efficiency toilet (HET) flush .. 302
  efficiency urinal 302

impact pipe 220
  pressure HDPE, ASTM D2513 . 446
Highway equipment rental 591
Hoist 462
  chain 462
  chain fall 593
  electric 462
  overhead 462
  personnel 593
  tower 593
Holding tank 468
Hole cutting electrical 377
  drilling electrical 376
Hollow wall anchor 42
Hood and ventilation equip. .. 352
  exhaust 71
  fire protection 352
  range 71
Hook coat 64
  robe 64
  type pipe outlet 196
Horizontal borer 592
  boring 417
  boring machine 584
  directional drill 592
  drilling 417
Horn fire 387
Hose & hydrant house 98
  adapter fire 96
  air 588
  bibb 341
  bibb sillcock 298
  braided bronze 250
  braided stainless steel ... 250
  braided steel 250
  discharge 589
  equipment 96
  fire 97
  metal flexible 250
  nozzle 98
  rack 98
  rack cabinet 66
  reel fire 98
  reel fire-suppression 98
  suction 589
  valve cabinet 67
  water 589
Hospital bath 305
  equipment 74
  sink 305
  type valve 329
  water closet 304
  whirlpool 305
Hot air heater electric 372
  tub 81
  water boiler 359, 360
  water dispenser 288
  water dispenser removal ... 109
  water heating 359, 368
  water temp maint domestic ... 128
  water-steam exchange 291
  water-water exchange 366
Hotel cabinet 65
Hot-water commercial 501-503
  heating forced 520
  solar-energy ... 505, 507, 509, 511,
                  513, 517, 523
  system 498, 500-503
House fire hose storage 98
  hose & hydrant 98
  safety flood shut-off 115
Hubbard tank 75
Humidifier 72
  removal 323
HVAC demolition 322
  equipment insulation 332

Index

piping specialty 250, 252, 281,
    332, 343, 345, 347
Hydrant building fire 95
    fire 430
    ground box 257
    ground post 258
    removal 22
    removal ground 109
    removal wall 109
    remove fire 22
    screw type valve 99
    tool 98
    wall 257
    water 257
Hydraulic chair 75
    crane 462, 593
    excavator 584
    hammer 585, 589
    jack 594
    jack climbing 594
    jacking 695
    lift 86
    pressure test 330
Hydro excavator 586
Hydrocumulator 260
Hydromulcher 592
Hydronic balancing 347
    baseboard removal 323
    convector & radiator demo ... 323
    energy underground 457
    flow fitting 344
    heating 359, 360, 368
    heating control valve 344
    heating convector 368
    unit heater removal 323

I

Ice machine 73
Icemaker 71, 73
Impact sprinkler 409
    wrench 588
In place pipe liner cured ... 416, 417
Indicator thermoflo 347
    valve post 430
Indoor fountain 81
    water storage tank 261
Induced draft fan removal 323
Industrial dryer 70
    heating 359
    safety fixture 305
    safety fixture removal 109
Inert gas 24
Infectious disease 9
    disease precautions 689
Infiltration chamber 433
    chamber HDPE 433
Infrared heater 362
    heater gas fired 362
    heater tubular 362
    quartz heater 371
Insert fitting PVC 238
    hanger concrete 120
Inspection internal pipe 415
Installation add elevated 108
    extinguisher 67
Instantaneous gas water heater .. 290
    water heater 288
Institution fixture 306
Insulated protector ADA 132
Insulation 137
    all service jacket 133, 138
    blower 589
    board 331
    boiler 332

breeching 332
calcium silicate 332
duct 331
equipment 332
heating 133, 136, 137, 332
HVAC equipment 332
jacket stainless-steel 150
jacketing 142
jacketing aluminum 146
jacketing protective 142
pipe 132
polyethylene 140, 331
polyolefin 141
removal 26
vapor proof 134, 141
water heater 132
Insurance 11, 692
    builder risk 11
    equipment 11
    public liability 11
Intake filter medical 311
Interceptor 280
    drain oil 279
    grease 280
    hair 280
    lint 280
    metal recovery 281
    oil 281
    sand 281
Internal cleaning pipe 415
Interval timer 379
Intrusion detection 386
    system 386
Invert manhole 437
Iron alloy mechanical joint pipe . 315
    body valve 325
    removal filter 288
Irrigation drip 407
    system sprinkler 407

J

J hook clamp w/nail 128
Jack cable 594
    hydraulic 594
Jacketing insulation 142
Jackhammer 588
Jacking 417
Jet water system 421
Job condition 10
Jockey pump fire 105
Joint control 32
    expansion 342
    filler 54
    gasket 53
    grooved joint expansion 203
    push-on 421
    restraint 422, 425
    sealer 53, 54

K

Kettle 73
    heating 592
    tar 590, 592
Kitchen cabinet 78
    equipment 73
    equipment fee 8
    sink 295, 484
    sink faucet 297
    sink residential 295
    unit commercial 72
Knee action mixing valve 305
Knockout electrical 377

L

Label pipe & valve 130
Labor adjustment factor 108
    modifier 108
    pipe cutting steel 172
    pipe groove roll 205
    pipe threading st steel ... 211
    pipe threading steel 171
    pipe weld stainless steel .. 211
    pipe weld steel 172
Laboratory safety equipment 74
    sink 73, 74, 300, 486
Ladder extension 589
    rolling 15
    towel 65
Lag screw 44
    screw shield 42
Laminated sheet flashing 50
Lance concrete 589
Landfill compactor 586
Landscape fee 8
Laser level 589
Latex caulking 54
Laundry equipment 70
    faucet 297
    sink 296, 485
Lavatory 482
    commercial 300
    faucet 297
    pedestal type 294
    prison/institution 306
    removal 109
    residential 293
    sink 293
    support 302
    system battery mount 483
    vanity top 293
    wall hung 294
Lawn mower 589
    sprinkler 569
Leaching field 577
    field chamber 432
    pit 432
Lead caulking 262
    flashing 50, 278
    salvage 110
    screw anchor 43
Leader line wye 100
Leads pile 585
Leak detection 386
    detection probe 386
    detection tank 386
Level laser 589
Leveling jack shoring 14
Liability employer 11
    insurance 692
Lift automotive 86
    hydraulic 86
    scissor 462, 587
Lifting equipment rental 592
Light dental 75
    hazard, one floor, 2000 s.m. . 542
    stand 25
    temporary 12
    tower 589
    underwater 80
Lighting fountain 310
    outlet 381
    residential 381
    temporary 12
Lightning suppressor 378
Lightweight angle framing 46
    channel framing 46
    framing 46
Line remover traffic 592

Lined valve 115
Liner cement 416
    pipe 416
Link seal pipe 253
Lint interceptor 280
Lintel hanging 46
Loader skidsteer 587
    tractor 586
    vacuum 25
    wheeled 586
    windrow 592
Locking receptacle 381
Locomotive tunnel 592
Log chipper 586
    skidder 586
Low bed trailer 592
Lubricated plug valve 327
Lubrication equipment 70
Lubricator air filter regulator 286

M

Machine autoscrub 588
    screw 44
    trowel finish concrete 38
    welding 591
Machinery anchor 35
Magnetic motor starter 383
Main drain 283
Maintenance cable temperature . 128
    general 19
    mechanical 19
Make-up air unit removal 323
Malleable iron fitting 177
    iron pipe fitting 177
Management fee construction 8
Manhole 418
    brick 418
    concrete 418
    cover 437
    frame and cover 437
    invert 437
    raise 437
    removal 22
    step 418
Manifold medical gas 313
    roof fire valve 95
Marble screen 63
    shower stall 65
    sink 482
Marine equipment rental 594
Marker boundary and survey 22
    pipe 130
Mark-up cost 11
Mason scaffold 13
Masonry flashing 50
    manhole 418
    saw 590
Mastic-backed flashing 50
Mat concrete placement
    foundation 38
    foundation 36
Material handling 18, 462
Mechanical 703
    coupling 196
    equipment demolition 323
    fee 8
    maintenance 19
    roof support 127
    tee 197
Medical after cooler 313
    air compressor 313
    alarm system 312
    alarm transducer 312
    clean copper tubing 153

Index

equipment 74-76
faucet 305
gas manifold 313
gas piping 311
gas specialty removal 109
intake filter 311
nitrogen or oxygen 311
sterilizer 74
sterilizing equipment 74
vacuum pump 310
vacuum system 310
Medicine cabinet 65
Metal flexible hose 250
   flue chimney 353
   interceptor dental 281
   nailing anchor 42
   pipe 434
   pipe removal 109
   recovery interceptor 281
   support assembly 58
   toilet partition 62
   valve removal 110
Meter 335
   flow 348
   gas 335
   Venturi flow 347
   water supply 254
   water supply detector 254
   water supply domestic 254
Metric conversion factors 686
Microtunneling 417, 418
Mineral wool board 331
   wool pipe covering 132
Minor site demolition 22
Mirror 64
   glass 64
Miscellaneous painting 58
   pump 259
Mixer concrete 584
   mortar 584, 589
   plaster 589
   road 592
Mixing shower valve 296
   valve 251, 298
   valve shower 296
Mobilization or demobilization . . . 15
Modification to cost 10
Modifier labor 108
Module alarm panel 312
   tub-shower 295
Moil point 588
Mold abatement work area . . . 28
   contaminated area demolition . . 29
Monitor corrosion 89
   dew point 313
Monoflow fitting 344
   tee fitting 344
Monument survey 22
Mop holder strip 64
   sink 301
Mortar mixer 584, 589
Mortuary equipment 76
Motor centrifugal in-line 259
   connection 378
   starter 383
   starter & control 383
   starter enclosed & heated . . 383
   starter magnetic 383
   starter w/circuit protector . . 383
   starter w/fused switch 384
Motorized grader 585
   zone valve 335
Mount vibration absorbing . . . 129
Mounting board plywood 48
Mower lawn 589
Muck car tunnel 592

Mud pump 584
   trailer 592
Mulcher power 586
Multicycle valve package on-off . . 102
Mylar tarpaulin 16

N

Nailer pneumatic 588, 589
   wood 48
Nailing anchor 42
Napkin dispenser 64
Needle valve 118
Neoprene flashing 278
   gasket 53
Nipple fire hose 97
   pipe 177
Nitrogen or oxygen medical . . . 311
No hub pipe 262
   hub pipe fitting 271
Non-chloride accelerator conc. . . 37
Nondestructive pipe testing . . . 330
Nonfusible oil valve 335
Nozzle dispersion 103
   fire hose 97
   fog 98
   playpipe 98
Nut threaded 123
Nylon nailing anchor 42

O

Oakum caulking 262
Observation well 419
Off highway dump truck 587
Office & storage space 13
   field 13
   trailer 13
Oil burner 361
   filter 335
   fired boiler 360
   fired water-heater commercial . 503
   fired water-heater residential . 500
   interceptor 281
   interceptor drain 279
   shut-off valve 335
   specialty fuel 335
   valve fuel 335
Oil-fired boiler 360
   water heater 291
   water heater commercial . . 291
   water heater residential . . . 291
Oil/water separator 469
Omitted work 11
On-off multicycle sprinkler . . . 540
   multicycle valve package . . . 102
Opening roof frame 46
Operating room equipment . . . 75
OSHA testing 27
Outdoor fountain 81
Outlet lighting 381
Oval arch culvert 436
   chimney vent 355
Oven 71, 73
Overhaul 23
Overhead & profit 11
   contractor 18, 692
   hoist 462
Overtime 10, 11
Oxygen lance cutting 24
   vaporizer 311

P

P trap 276
   trap glass 276
   trap running 275
Packaged terminal A/C removal . 324
   terminal air conditioner . . . 366
Packaging waste 28
Pad equipment 36
   prefabricated 374
   vibration absorbing 129
Paddle fan 382
Paint & coating 58
   interior miscellaneous 58
   sprayer 589
   striper 592
Painting booth 70
   grille 58
   miscellaneous 58
   pipe 58
   swimming pool 80
Panel and device alarm 387
   board residential 378
   fiberglass 16
   radiant heat 371
Paperbacked flashing 50
Paperholder 64
Paraffin bath 75
Parking lot paving 406
Partition shower 65
   toilet 62, 63
   toilet stone 63
Patient care equipment 75
Pavement asphaltic 406
   breaker 588
   bucket 591
   demolition 22
   planer 592
   profiler 592
   replacement 406
   widener 592
Paver asphalt 590
   bituminous 589
   cold mix 592
   concrete 590
   roof 51
   shoulder 592
Paving asphalt 406
   asphaltic concrete 406
   parking lot 406
Pedestal type lavatory 294
Perforated aluminum pipe . . . 433
   pipe 433
   PVC pipe 433
Performance bond 11, 694
Perineal bath 305
Permit building 12
Personal respirator 25
Personnel field 10, 11
   hoist 593
Pet cock 341
Pete's plug 253
PEX pipe 225
   tubing 225, 369
   tubing fitting 369
Photography 12
   construction 12
   time lapse 12
Pickup truck 591
Pick-up vacuum 584
Pigtail steam syphon 341
Pilaster toilet partition 63
Pile driving 695, 696
   hammer 585
   leads 585
Piling sheet 719

Pin powder 44
Pipe & fitting 119, 303
   & fitting backflow preventer . . 255
   & fitting backwater valve . . 283
   & fitting borosilicate 314
   & fitting brass 111, 153
   & fitting bronze 114
   & fitting carbon steel 187
   & fitting cast iron 131, 263
   & fitting copper . 153, 154, 156, 166
   & fitting corrosion resistant . . 317
   & fitting drain 283
   & fitting DWV 231
   & fitting faucet 297
   & fitting grooved joint 198
   & fitting hydrant 257
   & fitting iron body 326
   & fitting malleable iron 178
   & fitting polypropylene . 117, 316
   & fitting PVC 220
   & fitting sanitary drain 278
   & fitting semi-steel 328
   & fitting stainless steel . 207, 213, 328
   & fitting steel 168
   & fitting steel cast iron 176
   & fitting trap 276
   & fitting turbine water meter . 255
   & valve label 130
   acid resistant 316
   add elevated 108
   aluminum 433, 434
   and fittings 707
   bedding 393, 566, 567
   bedding trench 392
   bracket 119
   brass 151
   bursting 416
Pipe bypass 416
Pipe carrier 120, 124
   cast iron 261
   clamp 119, 412
   clamp plastic 127
   cleaning internal 415
   cleanout 130
   concrete 435
   conduit gland seal 455
   conduit prefabricated . . 455, 457
   conduit preinsulated 455
   conduit system 455, 458
   contained 245
   copper 153, 426
   corrosion resistant 315
   corrugated 433
   corrugated metal 433, 434
   covering 132
   covering calcium silicate . . 135
   covering fiberglass 137
   covering foam 140
   covering mineral wool 132
   CPVC 223
   culvert 436
   cutting steel labor 172
   double wall 241, 438
   drain 392
   drainage 314, 315, 431, 435
   dual wall HDPE 245
   ductile iron 421
   DWV PVC 222, 431
   elbow 199
   encapsulation 28
   epoxy fiberglass wound . . . 315
   fire retardant 316
   fire-suppression plastic 93
   fitting 184, 273, 423, 455, 457
   fitting adapter 158

Index

fitting brass 152
fitting cast iron 173, 262
fitting copper 156, 166
fitting corrosion resistant 316
fitting drainage special 273
fitting DWV 231
fitting fire-suppression 93
fitting flanged cast iron 184
fitting forged steel 191
fitting galvanized 275
fitting gasket joint 266
fitting glass 314
fitting grooved joint 90, 199
fitting insert 237
ftg. malleable iron . . . 177, 178, 194
fitting mechanical joint 194
fitting no hub 270
fitting pitched 273
fitting plastic . . . 93, 226, 234, 235, 422
fitting polybutylene 236
fitting polypropylene 238
fitting PVC 238
fitting soil 262
fitting stainless steel 212
fitting steel 173, 187
fitting steel carbon 187
fitting weld joint 191
fitting weld steel 187
fitting welded steel 195
flanged 170
foam core DWV ABS 222
foam core DWV PVC 222
freezing 413
fused 425
gas 439
glass 109, 314
groove cut 204
groove roll labor 205
grooved joint 197
guide 121
hanger 119
hanger & support 119
hanger assembly 123
hanger clevis 121
hanger plastic 127
hanger rod 123
hanger strap 126
hanger U-bolt 126
hanger/support removal 109
HDPE 241
heat 366
high impact 220
inspection internal 415
insulation 132
insulation removal 26
internal cleaning 415
iron alloy mechanical joint 315
liner 416
liner HDPE 416
lining 416
link seal 253
marker 130
metal 434
nipple 177
nipple steel 177
no hub 262
painting 58
perforated aluminum 433
PEX 225
plastic 93, 220, 223
plastic FRP 220
polyethylene 422, 439
polypropylene 225, 316
prefabricated 455, 457
preinsulated 455, 457

pressed joint 165
process pressure 314
proxylene 316
PVC 220, 423, 431
PVC pressure 221
reinforced concrete 436
relay 392
removal 22
removal glass 109
removal metal 109
removal plastic 110
repair 412
repair clamp 413
residential PVC 224
ring hanger 121
rodding 415
roll single 124
roof support 127
seal 253
sewage 431, 434, 435
sewage collection PVC 431
shock absorber 257
single hub 261
sleeve 253
sleeve plastic 32
sleeve sheet metal 32
sleeve steel 32
soil 261
stainless steel 207
steam 459
steel 168, 434
subdrainage 433
subdrainage plastic 433
support 119
support chair 124
support framing 46
support saddle 124
tee 199
testing 330
testing nondestructive 330
threading st steel labor 211
threading steel labor 171
water 421
water distribution 426
weld joint 169, 207
weld stainless steel labor 211
weld steel labor 172
wrapping 412
X-ray 330
Pipe bursting 416
Piping designations 719
Piping excavation 560, 562, 564
   fitting removal 109
   flexible (CSST) gas 335
   gas service polyethylene 439
   gasoline 438
   HDPE 425
   specialty HVAC 250, 252, 281, 332, 343, 345, 347
   storm drainage 434
   to 10' high 708
Pit leaching 432
   sump 392
Pitch pocket 51
Pitched pipe fitting 273
Placing concrete 37
Plan remediation 25
Planer pavement 592
Plank scaffolding 14
Plant screening 586
Plant-mix asphalt paving 406
Plaster drilling 58
   mixer 589
Plastic angle valve 116
   ball check valve 117
   ball valve 116

coupling 234
fitting 231
FRP pipe 220
pipe 93, 220, 223
pipe clamp 127
pipe fire-suppression 93
pipe fitting 226, 234, 235, 422
pipe hanger 127
pipe polyethylene 241
pipe removal 110
pipe weld 244
screw anchor 43
sheet flashing 51
toilet partition 63
trap 277
trench drain 284
valve 116
valve removal 111
vent cap 278
Plastic-laminate toilet
   compartment 62
Plate checkered 46
   escutcheon 99, 100
   F&C 254
   roadway 592
Plate-type heat exchanger 365
Platform checkered plate 46
   trailer 590
Playpipe fire hose 98
Plow vibrator 587
Plug Pete's 253
   pressure/temperature safety . . . 253
   p/t 253
   p/t probe 253
   valve 327
   valve grooved joint 204
Plumbing 255
   appliance 287, 289, 308, 309
   approximations for quick
   estimating 707
   demolition 109
   fixture 280, 281, 288, 292, 294, 301, 307, 348, 421, 484, 491
   fixture removal 109
   fixture requirements 712
   laboratory 74
   system estimate 497
Plywood fence 17
   mounting board 48
   sheathing roof & wall 48
   sidewalk 18
Pneumatic nailer 588, 589
Pocket pitch 51
Point moil 588
   of use water heater 288
Polybutylene adapter 237
Polyethylene coating 412
   insulation 140, 331
   pipe 422, 439, 569, 572
   plastic pipe 241
   septic tank 432
   tarpaulin 16
Polymer trench drain 284
Polyolefin insulation 141
Polypropylene accessory 238
   cleanout 132
   coupling 238
   fitting 238, 317
   pipe 225, 316
   pipe fitting 238
   shower 296
   sink 300
   tool 240
   trap 277
   tubing 225
   valve 117

Polysulfide caulking 55
Polyurethane caulking 55
Polyvinyl tarpaulin 16
Pool concrete side/vinyl lined . . . 568
   filtration swimming 309
   gunite shell 568
   heater electric 361
   heater swimming 361
   swimming 80
Porcelain enamel sink 482
Portable air compressor 587
   asphalt plant 591
   building 13
   eye wash 306
   fire extinguisher 66, 67
Positive pressure chimney . . 356, 358
Post driver 592
   indicator valve 430
Potable water softener 287
   water treatment 287
Potable-water storage 261
   storage tank 261
Powder actuated tool 44
   charge 44
   pin 44
Power mulcher 586
   temporary 12
   trowel 584
Preaction valve cabinet 102
Precast catch basin 418
   receptor 65
   septic tank 431
Prefab metal flue 353
Prefabricated comfort station . . . 82
   metal chimney 356
   pad 374
   pipe 455, 457
Preinsulated pipe 455, 457
Pressed joint pipe 165
Pressure & temperature
   measurement 253
   booster package water 260
   booster pump 260
   booster system water 260
   gauge 334
   pipe 222
   pipe process 314
   pipe PVC 221
   reducing valve steam 252
   reducing valve water 114
   regulator 252
   regulator gas 252
   regulator oil 252
   relief valve 114
   restricting valve 100
   switch well water 421
   test 330
   test hydraulic 330
   valve relief 114
   washer 590
Pressure/temp. safety plug . . . 253
Pressure/vacuum gauge 334
Pressurized fire extinguisher . . . 67
Preventer backflow 255
   removal backflow 109
Primer trap 277
Prison cell 82
   fixture 306
   fixture removal 110
   toilet 76
Prison/institution lavatory 306
   shower 307
   sink 307
Probe plug p/t 253
Process supply pipe glass 314
Product piping 438

Index

Profiler pavement 592
Project overhead 11
   sign 18
Promenade drain 278
Property line survey 22
Propylene glycol 349
Protection fire 66
   winter 16
   worker 25
Protective insulation jacketing . . . 142
Protector ADA insulated 132
Proxylene pipe 316
P/t plug 253
P&T relief valve 114
PTAC unit 366
Pulse boiler gas 359
   combustion gas 359
Pump 348, 419
   and motor set 337
   centrifugal 258, 590
   circulating 348
   concrete 584
   condensate removal 349
   contractor 392
   diaphragm 590
   fire 104, 105
   fire jockey 105
   fountain 309
   fuel oil 337
   general utility 258
   grinder system 281
   grout 590
   heat 367
   in-line centrifugal 348
   medical vacuum 310
   miscellaneous 259
   mud 584
   operator 393
   pressure booster 260
   removal 110
   removal heat 323
   rotary 259
   sewage ejector 282
   shallow well 421
   shotcrete 584
   submersible 285, 419, 590
   sump 72, 284
   trash 590
   turbine 259
   vacuum 310
   water 348, 419, 590
   water supply well 421
   wellpoint 594
Pumping 392
   dewater 392
Push-on joint 421
Putlog scaffold 15
PVC acid resistant drain 279
   cleanout 132
   fitting 228, 424
   flange 236
   flashing 51
   insert fitting 238
   pipe 220, 423, 431, 569, 572
   pipe perforated 433
   pipe residential 224
   roof drain system 518
   trap 277
   union 236
   valve 116
   well casing 420

Q

Quarry drill 588

Quartz heater 371

R

Raceway 376, 377
Rack hose 98
Radiant floor heating 369
   floor heating removal 323
   heating panel 371
Radiator air vent 341
   cast iron 368
   supply valve 344
   valve 344
Rainwater filter 468
   storage tank fiberglass 285
Raise manhole 437
   manhole frame 437
Rake tractor 586
Rammer/tamper 585
Ramp temporary 16
Range cooking 71
   hood 71
   receptacle 381
Ready mix concrete 37, 688
Receptacle air conditioner 381
   device 380
   dryer 381
   GFI 380
   locking 381
   range 381
   telephone 381
   television 381
   waste 65
   weatherproof 380
Receptor & interceptor removal . 110
   floor 279
   precast 65
   shower 65, 280, 296, 301
   terrazzo 65
Reciprocating compressor 286
   hermetic compressor 286
Recirculating chemical toilet 468
Recovery package removal heat . 323
Reducer grooved 201
   grooved joint 164
Reducing tee 174
Redwood bath 81
   tub 81
Reflectorized barrels 588
Refrigerant compressor removal . 324
   removal 324
Refrigerated storage equipment . . . 73
Refrigeration blood bank 74
   fitting 161
   tubing 155
Refrigerator compartment cooler . 309
Regulator gas 252
   lubricator air filter 286
   oil pressure 252
   pressure 252
Reinforced concrete pipe 436
   culvert 435
Reinforcing concrete 35
   footing 35
Relay pipe 392
Release emergency sprinkler 100
Relief valve P&T 114
   valve self-closing 114
   valve temperature 114
   vent removal 324
Relining sewer 416
Remediation plan 25
   plan/method asbestos 25
Removal air conditioner 322
   asbestos 26

bathtub 109
bidet 109
boiler 322
catch basin 22
concrete pipe 22
condenser 322
dehumidifier 322
evaporator 323
fan 323
fixture 109
heating & ventilating unit 323
humidifier 323
hydrant 22
insulation 26
lavatory 109
pipe 22
pipe insulation 26
plumbing fixture 109
pump 110
refrigerant 324
shower 109
sidewalk 22
sink 109
solar heating system 110
sprinkler system 110
steel pipe 22
tank 24
urinal 109
utility line 22
ventilator 324
wash fountain 109
water closet 109
water fountain 109
water heater 110
water softener 111
whirlpool/hot tub 109
Rental equipment 584
Repair pipe 412
Replacement pavement 406
Residential alarm 382
appliance 71, 382
application 378
bathtub 295
burner 361
device 378
dishwasher 71
door bell 381
dryer 71
fan 382
fin-tube heating 520
fixture 381
gas meter 335
gas water heater 290
heat pump 383
kitchen sink 295
lavatory 293
lighting 381
oil-fired water heater 291
panel board 378
pool 568
PVC pipe 224
roof jack 350
service 378
sink 295
smoke detector 382
sprinkler 101
switch 378
transition 350
wall cap 350
wash bowl 293
washer 71
water heater 72, 291, 383, 499
water heater electric 289
water-heater 498, 500
wiring 378, 382
Resistance corrosion 412

Resistant trap corrosion 276
Respirator 25
   personal 25
Retarder concrete 37
Rigid joint sealant 55
Ring clamp 422
   hanger pipe 121
Ripper attachment 591
Riser clamp 120
   pipe wellpoint 594
   standpipe 552, 555
Rivet 44
   aluminum 44
   copper 44
   stainless 45
   steel 45
   tool 45
Road mixer 592
   sweeper 592
   temporary 16
Roadway plate 592
Robe hook 64
Rock trencher 587
Rod backer 54
   coupling hanger 123
   curtain 64
   pipe hanger 123
   socket 126
   threaded 123
   tie 46
   weld 45
Roll hanger 124
Roller sheepsfoot 586
   tandem 586
   vibratory 586
Rolling ladder 15
   tower scaffold 15
Roof drain 283
   drain removal 109
   drain system 518, 519
   fire valve manifold 95
   flashing vent chimney 359
   frame opening 46
   jack residential 350
   paver 51
   paver and support 51
   sheathing 48
   support equipment 127
   support mechanical 127
   support pipe 127
Rooftop A/C removal 324
Room unit removal computer . . . 322
Rotary crawler drill 588
   hammer drill 588
   pump 259
Rototiller 586
Rough-in bidet 293
   classroom sink 300
   drinking fountain deck 308
   drinking fountain floor 308
   drinking fountain wall 307
   sink corrosion resistant 301
   sink countertop 295
   sink cup 301
   sink raised deck 295
   sink service floor 301
   sink service wall 301
   tub 296
Rubber pipe insulation 140
Rubbish handling 23
Running trap 275

S

S trap 276

Index

Saddle covering protection 125
    pipe support 124
Safety equipment laboratory 74
    eye/face equipment 306
    fixture industrial 305
    fixture removal industrial 109
    flood shut-off house 115
    plug pressure/temperature 253
    shower 305
    shut-off flood whole house 115
    valve gas 361
    water and gas shut-off 115
Salamander 590
Sales tax 10, 690, 691
Sampling air 25
Sand backfill 566
    interceptor 281
Sandblasting equipment 590
Sander floor 590
Sanitary drain 278
    tee 271
Sauna 81
Saw chain 590
    circular 590
    concrete 584
    masonry 590
Sawn control joint 32
Scaffold base plate 14
    bracket 14
    caster 14
    catwalk 15
    frame 14
    guardrail 14
    mason 13
    putlog 15
    rolling tower 15
    specialty 15
    stairway 14
    wood plank 14
Scaffolding 694
    plank 14
    tubular 13
Scissor lift 462, 587
Scoop air 340
    air purging 340
Scraper earth 586
Screed, gas engine,
8HP vibrating 584
Screen entrance 62
    urinal 63
Screening plant 586
Screw anchor 42
    lag 44
    machine 44
Scrub station 75
Scrubber air 588
Scupper drain 284
    floor 284
Seal compression 53
    floor drain trap 280
    pipe 253
Sealant acoustical 55
    caulking 54
    control joint 33
    rigid joint 55
    tape 55
Sealer joint 53, 54
Seat toilet 293
    water closet 293
Secondary treatment plant 468
Security factor 9
    shower 307
Sediment bucket drain 279
    strainer trap 277
    strainer Y valve 118
Seismic fire extinguishing 545

wet pipe system 548, 549
Self-closing relief valve 114
Self-contained single
pkg A/C rmvl 324
Semi-steel valve 327
Separation barrier 26, 28, 29
Separator 281
    air 340
    oil/water 469
Septic galley 432
    system 431, 577
Septic system, 1000
gallon, (5) 4" 578
Septic system chamber 433
    system effluent-filter 432
    tank 431, 577
    tank concrete 431
    tank polyethylene 432
    tank precast 431
    trench 577
Service boring 417
    residential 378
    sink 301, 487
    sink clinic 305
    sink faucet 302
    station equipment 70
    tap 573
Setter circuit 341
Sewage aeration 468
    collection PVC pipe 431
    collection valve 431
    collection vent 431
    ejector pump 282
    municipal waste water 468
    pipe 431, 434, 435
    treatment plant 468
Sewage/drainage collection 435
Sewer relining 416
    valve backwater 431
Sheathing 48
    roof 48
    roof & wall plywood 48
    wall 48
Sheepsfoot roller 586
Sheet metal flashing 50
    piling 719
Sheeting driver 588
    wood 392, 719
Shelf bathroom 64
Shell-type heat exchanger 366
Shield expansion 42
    lag screw 42
Shift work 10
Shock absorber 256
    absorber pipe 257
Shoring base plate 14
    bracing 14
    heavy duty 14
    leveling jack 14
    slab 15
Short load concrete 37
Shot blaster 590
Shotcrete pump 584
Shoulder paver 592
Shovel crawler 586
Shower arm 296
    built-in 296
    by-pass valve 297
    cabinet 65
    cubicle 296
    door 65
    drain 275
    emergency 305
    enclosure 66
    glass door 65
    group 301

    partition 65
    polypropylene 296
    prison/institution 307
    receptor 65, 280, 296, 301
    removal 109
    safety 305
    security 307
    spray 298
    stall 296
    surround 66
    system 490
Shower-head water economizer 296
Shower/tub control set 298
Shower-tub valve spout set 298
Shut-off flood whole
house safety 115
Shutoff gas earthquake 361
Shut-off safety water and gas 115
    valve oil 335
    water heater safety 115
Shutter damper removal flue 323
Sidewalk bridge 15
    broom 590
    removal 22
    temporary 18
Sign 18
    detour 17
    project 18
Signal bell 387
Silent check valve 114, 327
Silicone 54
    caulking 55
Sillcock hose bibb 298
Simplex style strainer 344
Single hub pipe 261
    pipe roll 124
    pkg A/C rmvl self-contained 324
Sink barber 70
    base 78
    classroom 300
    commercial 300
    corrosion resistant rough-in 301
    corrosion-resistant 300
    countertop 295
    countertop rough-in 295
    cup 301
    cup rough-in 301
    faucet kitchen 297
    hospital 305
    kitchen 295
    laboratory 73, 74, 300
    laundry 296
    lavatory 293
    mop 301
    polypropylene 300
    prison/institution 307
    raised deck rough-in 295
    removal 109
    residential 295
    service 301
    service floor rough-in 301
    service wall rough-in 301
    slop 301
    stainless steel 300
    support 303
    waste treatment 280
Site demolition 22
    improvement 407
    irrigation 569, 572
    utility 566
Sitework manhole 579
Skidder log 586
Skidsteer attachments 587
    loader 587
Slab edge formwork 32
    haunch 37

    haunch formwork 37
    on grade 36
    on grade formwork 32
    shoring 15
    thickened edge 37
    thickened edge formwork 37
    trench formwork 32
    turndown 37
    turndown formwork 37
Sleeve 253, 427
    and tap 422
    cut in 427
    formwork 32
    pipe 253
    plastic pipe 32
    sheet metal pipe 32
    steel pipe 32
    wall 254
Sliding door shower 65
    mirror 65
Slip on escutcheon flange 254
Slipform paver barrier 592
    paver curb 592
Slop sink 301
Slotted channel framing 46
    pipe 436
Slow close ball valve 99
Smoke detector 386
    vent chimney 353
Snow guard 51
Snubber valve 341
Soaking bathroom 295
    tub 295
Soap dispenser 64
    holder 65
Socket hanger rod 126
Socket-O-Let 193
Softener water 287
Soil decontamination 24
    pipe 261
Solar air to water heat exchange 527
    backflow preventer 364
    closed loop add-on hot water 505
    closed loop hot water system 517
    closed loop space/hot water 523
    drainback hot water 506
    draindown hot-water 509
    energy 364
    energy circulator air 363
    energy system . 505, 511, 513, 517, 523
    energy system air purger 364
    energy system air vent 364
    energy system balancing valve 365
    energy system collector 363
    energy system control valve 364
    energy system controller 364
    energy system expansion tank 365
    energy sys. gauge pressure 365
    energy sys. heat exchanger 364
    energy system storage tank 364
    energy system thermometer 365
    energy system vacuum relief 365
    heating 363, 713
    heating system 363
    heating system removal 110
    hot water 515
    recirculation hot water 511
    swimming pool heater 525
    system solenoid valve 365
Solar-energy pool heater 525
    water-heater 515
Solder 153
Source heat pump water 367
Spa bath 81
Space heater 589

Index

heater removal 324
   office & storage 13
Spade air 588
   tree 587
Specialty 64
   piping HVAC .. 250, 281, 342, 345, 347
   scaffold 15
Split ductless removal 324
   ring hanger 122
Spotter 399
Spray painting booth automotive . 70
   rig foam 589
   shower 298
   substrate 27
Sprayer airless 25
   emulsion 588
   paint 589
Spread footing 36
   footing formwork 32
Spreader aggregate 584, 591
   chemical 591
   concrete 590
Sprinkler ball valve 99
   cabinet 100
   connector flexible 100
   control pressure 101
   dehydrator package 101
   deluge system 537, 538
   dry pipe 530
   dry pipe system 530, 532
   escutcheon 100
   floor control valve 88
   head 100
   head guard 101
   head wrench 101
   irrigation system 407
   line tester 95
   monitoring panel deluge 103
   on-off multicycle system . 540, 541
   preaction system 533
   quantities 703
   release emergency 100
   residential 101
   system 100, 701
   system accelerator 101
   system dry-pipe 101
   system removal 110
   trim valve 99
   underground 407
   valve 88, 101
   wet pipe system ... 543, 544, 548, 550
Stabilizer base 592
Stainless flashing 50
   rivet 45
   screen 62
   steel fitting 212
   steel flange 217
   steel globe valve 329
   steel pipe 207
   steel shelf 64
   steel sink 300, 482, 484
   steel tubing 205, 206
   steel valve 328
   weld rod 45
Stainless-steel insulation jacket ... 150
Stair temporary protection 18
Stairway scaffold 14
Stall shower 296
   toilet 62, 63
   type urinal 299
   urinal 299, 300
Standard extinguisher 67
Standpipe alarm 100
   connection 95

equipment 556
   systems 699
Starter board & switch 384
   motor 383
Station AHU removal central ... 322
   control 384
   hospital 75
Steam bath 82
   bath residential 82
   boiler 360
   boiler electric 359
   cleaner 590
   condensate meter removal 324
   energy distribution pipe 457
   jacketed kettle 73
   pipe 459
   pipe underground 455
   pressure reducing valve 252
   radiator valve 344
   syphon pigtail 341
Steam-to-water heating 365
Steel channel 122
   drill 588
   drilling 43
   expansion tank 343
   fitting 173, 184
   flange 193, 202
   pipe 168, 434
   pipe corrugated 433
   pipe fitting 173, 187
   pipe labor cutting 172
   pipe nipple 177
   pipe removal 22
   rivet 45
   roof drain system 518
   salvage 110
   sink 482, 484
   tank 343
   tank above ground 339
   underground storage tank 337
   weld rod 45
   well casing 419
   well screen 419
Step manhole 418
Sterilizer barber 70
   dental 75
   glassware 74
   medical 74
Stiffleg derrick crane 593
Stone toilet compartment 63
Stop valve 298
   water supply 298
Stop/start control station 384
Storage box 13
   potable-water 261
   tank 338
   tank chemical 319
   tank concrete aboveground ... 340
   tank fiberglass rainwater 285
   tank fiberglass underground .. 261
   tank potable-water 261
   tank steel underground 337
   tank underground 338
Storm drainage manhole frame . 418
   drainage piping 434
   drainage system 519
Storz type connection 95
Strainer basket type 344
   bronze body 346
   duplex style 345
   grooved joint 203
   simplex style 344
   Y type bronze body 346
   Y type iron body 346
Strap pipe hanger 126
Strapless outlet 196, 197

Strap-on T outlet 202
Strip footing 36
Striper paint 592
Structural fee 8
   welding 44
Stump chipper 586
Subcontractor O&P 11
Subcontractors 713
Subdrainage pipe 433
   plastic pipe 433
   system 433
Submersible pump 285, 419, 590
   sump pump 285
Subsurface drip irrigation 407
Suction diffuser 347
   diffuser grooved joint 203
   diffuser pump 347
   hose 589
Sump hole construction 392
   pit 392
   pump 72, 284
   pump elevator 285
   pump submersible 285
Supply copper pipe water 426
   ductile iron pipe water 421
   HDPE water 425
   polyethylene pipe water 422
Support carrier fixture 302
   drinking fountain 302
   framing pipe 46
   lavatory 302
   pipe 119
   sink 303
   urinal 303
   water closet 303
   water cooler 304
Suppression valve fire 91
Suppressor lightning 378
Surfactant 27
Surround shower 66
   tub 66
Survey aerial 22
   monument 22
   property line 22
   topographic 22
Sweeper road 592
Swimming pool 80
   pool equipment 80
   pool filter 309
   pool filtration 309
   pool heater 361
   pool painting 80
   pool residential 568
   pools 699
Swing check valve 112, 326
   check valve bronze 112
Switch decorator 379
   dimmer 379
   residential 378
   tamper 101
   well water pressure 421
Switchboard electric 384
Swivel adapter fire hose 97
System boiler steam 528
   chamber septic 433
   component foam-water 103
   control 332
   deluge sprinkler 537, 538
   drinking fountain 491
   dry pipe sprinkler 530-532
   exhaust 351
   fire extinguishing . 96, 97, 103, 105
   fire sprinkler .. 531, 532, 534, 535, 537, 538, 540, 541, 543, 544, 548, 550
   FM200 fire suppression 557

grinder pump 281
heat trace 370
on-off multicycle sprinkler . 539-541
pipe conduit 455, 458
plumbing estimate 497
preaction sprinkler 533-535
removal exhaust 323
riser dry standpipe 555
septic 431
sitework catch basin 579
sitework swimming pool ... 568
sitework trenching .. 560, 562, 564
solar-energy 511, 525
solenoid valve solar 365
sprinkler 100, 101, 103
standpipe riser dry 554, 555
standpipe riser wet 552
storm drainage 518
subdrainage 433
wet pipe sprinkler 542-544

T

T outlet strap-on 202
Tag valve 130
Tamper 390, 588
   switch 101
Tandem roller 586
Tank above ground steel 339
   aboveground storage conc. ... 340
   chemical-waste dilution 319
   clean 24
   compression 343
   darkroom 71
   disposal 24
   expansion 343
   fiberglass 338
   fiberglass rainwater storage .. 285
   fiberglass underground storage 261
   holding 468
   horizontal above ground 339
   Hubbard 75
   leak detection 386
   potable-water storage 261
   removal 24
   septic 431
   steel 343
   steel underground storage .. 337
   storage 338
   water 338, 430, 591
   water heater storage 261
   water htr liquid container ... 110
   water storage solar 365
Tankless electric water heater ... 288
   gas water heater 290
Tank/wtr htr liquid ctnr removal . 110
Tap and sleeve 422
Tape barricade 17
   sealant 55
   underground 419
Tapping cross and sleeve 426
   main 426
   valve 427
Tar kettle 590, 592
Tarpaulin 16
   duck 16
   Mylar 16
   polyethylene 16
   polyvinyl 16
Tax 10
   sales 10
   Social Security 10
   unemployment 10
Taxes 691

Index

Tee cleanout 131
   fitting monoflow 344
   HDPE piping 425
   mechanical 197
   pipe 199
   reducing 174
Telephone receptacle 381
Telescoping boom lift 587
Television receptacle 381
Temperature maintenance cable . 128
   relief valve 114
   rise detector 386
Tempering valve 115
   valve water 115, 251
Temporary barricade 17
   building 13
   construction 12, 16
   electricity 12
   facility 17
   fence 17
   guardrail 17
   light 12
   lighting 12
   power 12
   ramp 16
   road 16
   toilet 590
   utility 12
Terminal A/C packaged 366
   A/C removal packaged 324
   air conditioner packaged ... 366
   heater 362
Terne coated flashing 50
Terrace drain 283
Terrazzo receptor 65
Test pressure 330
   well 419
Tester sprinkler line 95
Testing OSHA 27
   pipe 330
Thermoflo indicator 347
Thermometer 334
   solar energy system 365
   well 197
Thermostat contactor
combination 371
   integral 370
   wire 383
Thermosyphon hot-water 513
Thickened edge slab 37
Threaded flange 186
   nut 123
   rod 123
Threading labor st steel 211
   labor steel 171
Thread-O-Let 192
Thru-the-wall A/C removal 324
Thru-wall air conditioner 366
Tie rod 46
Time lapse photography 12
Timer clock 382
   interval 379
Toggle-bolt anchor 42
Toilet 468
   accessory 64
   accessory commercial 64
   bowl 292
   chemical 590
   compartment 62
   compartment plastic-laminate . 62
   compartment stone 63
   dual flush valve 302
   gasket 298
   partition 62, 63
   prison 76
   seat 293

stall 62, 63
stone partition 63
temporary 590
Tool fire 98
   hydrant 98
   polypropylene 240
   powder actuated 44
   rivet 45
Topographical survey 22
Torch cutting 590
   cutting demolition 23
Total 542
Towel bar 64
   dispenser 64
Tower crane 13, 593, 695, 696
   hoist 593
   light 589
   removal cooling 322
Track drill 588
Tractor loader 586
   rake 586
   truck 591
Traffic line remover 592
Trailer bunk house 13
   floodlight 589
   low bed 592
   mud 592
   office 13
   platform 590
   truck 590
   water 591
Tram car 591
Transition residential 350
Transparent pipe 314
Trap cast iron 275
   deep seal 276
   drainage 275, 276
   grease 280
   plastic 277
   polypropylene 277
   primer 277
   PVC 277
   seal floor drain 280
   sediment strainer 277
Trapeze hanger 124
Trash pump 590
Treatment plant secondary 468
   plant sewage 468
   potable water 287
   salt water 287
Tree spade 587
Trench backfill 391, 566, 567
   box 591
   disposal field 432
   drain 284
   drain fiberglass 284
   drain plastic 284
   drain polymer 284
   excavating 390
   excavation 390, 391
   utility 391
Trencher chain 391, 587
   rock 587
   wheel 587
Trenching 392, 561
   common earth 560, 561
   loam & sandy clay 562, 563
   sand & gravel 564, 565
Tripod floodlight 588
Trowel concrete 584
   power 584
Truck concrete 584
   crane flatbed 592
   dump 587
   flatbed 587, 591
   holding concrete 37

mounted crane 593
pickup 591
tractor 591
trailer 590
vacuum 591
winch 591
Tub bar 64
   hot 81
   redwood 81
   rough-in 296
   shower handicap 295
   soaking 295
   surround 66
Tube copper 153, 426
   fitting 206
   fitting copper 156
Tubing copper 153
   (CSST) gas 335
   fitting PEX 369
   oxygen class copper 154
   PEX 225, 369
   polypropylene 225
   refrigeration 155
   stainless steel 205, 206
Tub-shower module 295
Tubular scaffolding 13
Tugboat diesel 594
Tumbler holder 65
Tunnel locomotive 592
   muck car 592
   ventilator 592
Turbine pump 259
   water meter 255
Turnbuckle 123
Turndown slab 37
TV inspection sewer pipeline .. 415

U

U-bolt pipe hanger 126
U-hook hanger 127
Underdrain 418
Underground chilled water pipe . 455
   hydronic energy 457
   piping 566
   sprinkler 407
   steam pipe 455
   storage tank 338
   storage tank fiberglass ... 261
   storage tank removal 697
   storage tank steel 337
   tape 419
Underwater light 80
Unemployment tax 10
Union dielectric 342
   PVC 236
Unit commercial kitchen 72
   gross area requirements .. 682
   heater cabinet 372
   heater electric 371
   heater removal hydronic .. 323
   removal condensing 322
   removal valance 323
Urinal 299
   high efficiency 302
   removal 109
   screen 63
   stall 299, 300
   stall type 299
   support 303
   system 480
   system battery mount ... 481
   wall hung 299
   waterless 300
   watersaving 299

Utensil washer medical 74
   washer-sanitizer 74
Utility accessory 419
   box 419
   connection 419
   excavation 560, 562, 564
   line removal 22
   structure 579
   temporary 12
   trench 391
   trench excavating 391

V

Vacuum breaker 256
   breaker air gap 256
   catch basin 591
   central 76
   cleaning 76
   gauge 334
   loader 25
   pick-up 584
   pump 310
   pump medical 310
   system medical 310
   truck 591
   unit central 464
   wet/dry 591
Valance unit removal 323
Valve 324, 429
   assembly dry pipe sprinkler . 102
   assembly sprinkler deluge .. 103
   backwater 283
   balancing & shut-off 344
   ball check 117
   box 428
   brass 111
   brass ball 324
   bronze 111
   bronze angle 111
   bronze butterfly 112
   bronze/brass 324
   butterfly 325, 428
   cabinet 67
   cap fire 99
   check 88, 429
   check lift 115
   circuit setter balance 341
   clamp 116
   control solar energy system . 364
   CPVC 117
   cut in 427
   diaphragm 116
   draindown 365
   fire hose 99
   fire suppression 91
   float 343
   flush 302
   foot 118
   foot oil 335
   for medical gas ball 312
   fusible oil 335
   gas stop 111
   gate 325, 328, 429
   gauge zone 312
   globe 326, 328
   grooved joint 91
   grooved joint butterfly .. 204
   grooved joint gate 204
   heating control 344
   hospital type 329
   hot water radiator 344
   hydrant fire 99
   hydrant screw type 99
   iron body 325

Index

lined ... 115
lubricated plug ... 327
materials ... 704-706
mixing ... 251, 298
mixing shower ... 296
motorized zone ... 335
needle ... 118
nonfusible oil ... 335
oil shut-off ... 335
plastic ... 116
plastic angle ... 116
plug ... 327
polypropylene ... 117
polypropylene ball ... 117
PVC ... 116
radiator ... 344
radiator supply ... 344
relief pressure ... 114
removal metal ... 110
removal plastic ... 111
selection considerations ... 704
semi-steel ... 327
sewage collection ... 431
shower by-pass ... 297
shower mixing ... 296
slow close ball ... 99
snubber ... 341
soldered gate ... 112
spout set shower-tub ... 298
sprinkler ... 88, 101
sprinkler alarm ... 88
sprinkler ball ... 99
sprinkler floor control ... 88
sprinkler trim ... 99
stainless steel ... 328
stainless steel globe ... 329
steam radiator ... 344
stop ... 298
swing check ... 112, 326
tag ... 130
tapping ... 427
tempering ... 115
washing machine ... 298
water pressure ... 114
water supply ... 298
water tempering ... 251
water utility distribution ... 428
with box zone ... 312
Y sediment strainer ... 118
Y-check ... 118
Valves grooved joint ... 91
Vanity base ... 78
  top lavatory ... 293, 482
Vapor proof insulation ... 134
Vaporizer oxygen ... 311
Vaporproof insulation ... 141
Vent air automatic ... 341
  alarm ... 335
  automatic air ... 341
  cap ... 277, 335
  cap cast iron ... 277
  cap plastic ... 278
  chimney ... 353
  chimney all fuel ... 358
  chimney fitting ... 353, 358
  chimney flashing ... 354, 359
  chimney prefabricated
    removal ... 324
  convector or baseboard air ... 368
  draft damper ... 353
  dryer ... 71, 299
  flashing ... 277
  flashing and cap removal ... 111
  gas ... 353
  metal chimney ... 353
  radiator air ... 341

removal relief ... 324
sewage collection ... 431
Ventilation equip. and hood ... 352
  fan ... 382
  garage ... 350
Ventilator removal ... 324
  tunnel ... 592
Venturi flow meter ... 347
Vertical discharge heater ... 372
Vibrating screed,
  gas engine, 8HP ... 584
Vibration absorber ... 129
  absorbing hanger ... 129
  absorbing mount ... 129
  absorbing pad ... 129
Vibrator concrete ... 584
  earth ... 390
  plow ... 587
Vibratory hammer ... 586
  roller ... 586
Vitreous china lavatory ... 482
Vitreous-china service sink ... 487

W

Wafer check valve ... 115, 327
Wall cap residential ... 350
  heater ... 72
  hung lavatory ... 294
  hung urinal ... 299
  hydrant ... 257
  hydrant removal ... 109
  sheathing ... 48
  sleeve ... 254
  type cleanout ... 131
Wash bowl residential ... 293
  fountain ... 301
  fountain group ... 301
  fountain removal ... 109
  safety equipment eye/face ... 306
Washer ... 122
  and extractor ... 70
  commercial ... 70
  dryer accessory ... 298
  pressure ... 590
  residential ... 71
Washer-sanitizer utensil ... 74
Washing machine automatic ... 71
  machine valve ... 298
Waste cleanup hazardous ... 24
  disposal hazardous ... 24
  packaging ... 28
  receptacle ... 65
  treatment sink ... 280
Wastewater treatment system ... 468
Watchman service ... 18
Water atomizer ... 25
  balancing ... 330
  booster system domestic ... 260
  bubbler ... 491
  chiller remote ... 309
  chiller removal ... 324
  closet ... 292, 299
  closet chemical ... 468
  closet healthcare ... 304
  closet hospital ... 304
  closet removal ... 109
  closet seat ... 293
  closet support ... 303, 304
  cooler ... 308, 492
  cooler bottled ... 309
  cooler electric ... 308
  cooler support ... 304
  copper tubing connector ... 250
  dispenser hot ... 288

distiller ... 74
distribution pipe ... 421, 423, 426
filter ... 288
filter commercial removal ... 111
filter dirt and rust ... 288
flow indicator ... 88
fountain removal ... 109
hammer arrester ... 256
heater ... 72, 383
heater commercial ... 289, 291
heater electric ... 289
heater gas ... 290
heater gas residential ... 290
heater heat pump ... 367
heater instantaneous ... 288
heater insulation ... 132
heater oil-fired ... 291
heater point of use ... 288
heater removal ... 110
heater residential ... 72, 291, 383
heater residential electric ... 289
heater safety shut-off ... 115
heater storage tank ... 261
heater under the sink ... 289
heater wrap kit ... 132
heating hot ... 359, 368
hose ... 589
hydrant ... 257
level control ... 332
meter turbine ... 255
motor alarm ... 100
pipe ... 421
pressure booster package ... 260
pressure booster system ... 260
pressure reducing valve ... 114
pressure relief valve ... 114
pressure switch well ... 421
pressure valve ... 114
pump ... 348, 419, 590
pump fire ... 105
pump fountain ... 309
pumping ... 392
purification ... 288
reducer concrete ... 37
service lead free ... 573
softener ... 287
softener potable ... 287
softener removal ... 111
source heat pump ... 367
storage solar tank ... 365
storage tank indoor ... 261
supply copper pipe ... 426
supply detector meter ... 254
supply domestic meter ... 254
supply ductile iron pipe ... 421
supply HDPE ... 425
supply meter ... 254
supply polyethylene pipe ... 422
supply PVC pipe ... 423
supply stop ... 298
supply valve ... 298
supply well pump ... 421
tank ... 338, 430, 591
tempering valve ... 115, 251
trailer ... 591
treatment ... 468
treatment potable ... 288
treatment salt ... 287
utility distribution valve ... 428
well ... 419
Water-closet ... 479
  battery mount ... 479
  system ... 478
Water-heater electric ... 498, 501
  gas-fired ... 499, 502
  oil-fired ... 500, 503

solar-energy ... 507, 509, 511, 513, 517, 523
Waterless urinal ... 300
Watersaving urinal ... 299
Water-source heat pump ... 367
Water-water exchange hot ... 366
Wearing course ... 406
Weather data and design
  conditions ... 685
Weatherproof receptacle ... 380
Wedge anchor ... 43
Weights and measures ... 687
Weld fitting ... 190
  fume hood removal ... 323
  joint pipe ... 169, 207
  plastic pipe ... 244
  rod ... 45
  rod aluminum ... 45
  rod cast-iron ... 45
  rod stainless ... 45
  rod steel ... 45
Welded beam attachment ... 119
  structural steel ... 699
  wire epoxy ... 36
  wire fabric ... 36
  wire galvanized ... 36
Welding fillet ... 44
  fume elimination ... 352
  labor stainless-steel ... 211
  labor steel ... 172
  machine ... 591
  structural ... 44
Weld-O-Let ... 193
Weld-on flange steel ... 193
Well ... 392
  & accessory ... 419
  casing PVC ... 420
  casing steel ... 419
  gravel pack ... 419
  pump ... 419
  pump shallow ... 421
  screen steel ... 419
  thermometer ... 197
  water ... 419
  water pressure switch ... 421
Wellpoint ... 393
  discharge pipe ... 594
  equipment rental ... 594
  header pipe ... 594
  pump ... 594
  riser pipe ... 594
Wellpoints ... 718
Wet pipe sprinkler systems ... 542
Wet sprinkler seismic
  component ... 545-547
  sprinkler system ... 545
  standpipe riser ... 552
Wet/dry vacuum ... 591
Wheel trencher ... 587
Wheelbarrow ... 591
Wheeled loader ... 586
Whirlpool bath ... 75, 81
  hospital ... 305
Whirlpool/hot tub removal ... 109
Widener pavement ... 592
Winch truck ... 591
Window A/C removal ... 324
  air conditioner ... 366
Windrow loader ... 592
Winter concrete ... 37
  protection ... 16
Wire ... 716
  fence ... 18
  thermostat ... 383
Wiring air conditioner ... 383
  fan ... 382

Index

residential 378, 382
Wood firestop 48
    framing 48
    framing miscellaneous 48
    nailer 48
    plank scaffold 14
    sheet piling 719
    sheeting 392, 719
Work boat 594
    extra 11
Worker protection 25
Workers' compensation 11, 693
Wrapping pipe 412
Wrecking ball 591
Wrench impact 588
    sprinkler head 101
Wye fire hose 100

X

X-ray pipe 330

Y

Y sediment strainer valve 118
    type bronze body strainer 346
    type iron body strainer 346
Yard fountain 81
Y-check valve 118

Z

Zone valve gauge 312
    valve with box 312

Notes

Notes

Notes

Division Notes

		CREW	DAILY OUTPUT	LABOR-HOURS	UNIT	BARE COSTS				TOTAL INCL O&P
						MAT.	LABOR	EQUIP.	TOTAL	

Division Notes

	CREW	DAILY OUTPUT	LABOR-HOURS	UNIT	BARE COSTS				TOTAL INCL O&P
					MAT.	LABOR	EQUIP.	TOTAL	

Division Notes

		CREW	DAILY OUTPUT	LABOR-HOURS	UNIT	BARE COSTS				TOTAL INCL O&P
						MAT.	LABOR	EQUIP.	TOTAL	

Division Notes

	CREW	DAILY OUTPUT	LABOR-HOURS	UNIT	BARE COSTS				TOTAL INCL O&P
					MAT.	LABOR	EQUIP.	TOTAL	

2024 Training Class Options
A tradition of excellence in construction cost information and services since 1942

Virtual and in person classes offered monthly. Call for the schedule. ☎ 877.620.6245

Gordian offers educational content in a variety of formats — including self-paced training modules, live virtual seminars, and in-person classes. We also offer customized private training solutions to meet your organization's unique continuing education needs. Please visit our website at https://www.rsmeans.com/products/services/training for our current schedule of offerings.

Seminars include: Introduction to Cost Estimating, Advanced Cost Estimating, Facilities Estimating, Maintenance & Repair Estimating, Mechanical & Electrical Estimating, and RSMeans Online Training.

Registration Information

How to register

By Phone
Register by phone at 877.620.6245

Online
Register online at rsmeans.com/products/services/training

Note: Purchase orders or credits cards are required to register.

Instructor-led Government Pricing

All federal government employees are eligible for discounted training. Other promotional discounts cannot be combined with the government discount. Call 877.620.6245 for government pricing.

If you have any questions or you would like to register for any class or purchase a training module, call us at 877.620.6245.

Become an RSMeans Data Certified Professional

Gordian's RSMeans Data Certification program allows you to differentiate yourself and your organization when it comes to demonstrating your mastery of RSMeans Data, the construction industry standard for reliable costs. Visit https://www.rsmeans.com/landing-pages/rsmeans-data-certification to learn more.

Introduction to Cost Estimating

This one-day introductory course to improve estimating skills and effectiveness starts with the details of interpreting bid documents and ends with the summary of the estimate and bid submission.

Topics include:
- Using plans and specifications to create estimates
- The takeoff process — deriving all tasks with correct quantities
- Summarizing the estimate to arrive at the final number
- Formulas for area and cubic measure, adding waste and adjusting productivity to specific projects
- Evaluating subcontractors' proposals and prices
- Adding insurance and bonds
- Understanding how labor costs are calculated
- Submitting bids and proposals

Who should attend: novice estimators, project managers, architects, engineers, owners' representatives, contractors, and anyone responsible for budgeting or estimating construction projects.

Advanced Cost Estimating

This three-day practical training program addresses the vital importance of understanding the scope of projects in order to produce accurate cost estimates for facilities repair and remodeling.

Topics include:
- Discussions of site visits, plans/specs, record drawings of facilities and site-specific lists
- Review of CSI divisions, including means, methods, materials and the challenges of scoping each topic
- Exercises in scope identification and scope writing for accurate estimating of projects
- Hands-on exercises that require scope, takeoff and pricing

Who should attend: corporate and government estimators, planners, facility managers and others who need to produce accurate project estimates.

isit rsmeans.com for more details.

Mechanical & Electrical Estimating

This three-day course teaches attendees how to prepare more accurate and complete mechanical/electrical estimates, avoid the pitfalls of omission and double-counting, and understand the composition and rationale within the RSMeans Data mechanical/electrical database.

Topics include:
- The unique way mechanical and electrical systems are interrelated
- M&E estimates — conceptual, planning, budgeting, and bidding stages
- Order of magnitude, square foot, assemblies and unit price estimating
- Comparative cost analysis of equipment and design alternatives

Who should attend: architects, engineers, facilities managers, mechanical and electrical contractors, and others who need a highly reliable method for developing, understanding, and evaluating mechanical and electrical contracts.

Facilities Estimating

In this three-day course, professionals working in facilities management can get help with their daily challenges to establish budgets for all phases of a project.

Topics include:
- Determining the full scope of a project
- Understanding of RSMeans Data and what is included in prices
- Identifying appropriate factors to be included in your estimate
- Creative solutions to estimating issues
- Organizing estimates for presentation and discussion
- Special estimating techniques for repair/remodel and maintenance projects
- Appropriate use of contingency, city cost indexes and reference notes
- Techniques to get to the correct estimate quickly

Who should attend: facility managers, engineers, contractors, facility tradespeople, planners and project managers.

Maintenance & Repair Estimating

This three-day course teaches attendees how to plan, budget and estimate the cost of ongoing and preventive maintenance and repair for existing buildings and grounds.

Topics include:
- The most financially favorable maintenance, repair, and replacement scheduling and estimating
- Preventive planning and facilities upgrading
- Determining both in-house and contract-out service costs
- Annual asset-protecting M&R plan

Who should attend: facility managers, maintenance supervisors, buildings and grounds superintendents, plant managers, planners, estimators, and others involved in facilities planning and budgeting.

RSMeans Online Training

Construction estimating is vital to the decision-making process at each state of every project. Our online solution works the way you do. It's systematic, flexible and intuitive. In this two-day course you will see how you can estimate any phase of any project faster and better.

Topics include:
- Customizing our online estimating solution
- Making the most of RSMeans Data "Circle Reference" numbers
- How to integrate your cost data
- Generating reports, exporting estimates to MS Excel, sharing, collaborating and more

Also offered as a self-paced or on-site training program!

Visit rsmeans.com for more details.

RSMeans Data Training Cancellation Policy

Virtual Training (Individual)
If you are unable to attend a training class, a colleague may substitute at any time before the session starts by notifying the training registrar at 877.620.6245 or your sales representative. Gordian is not responsible for sending duplicate materials to the substitute colleague.

If you are unable to find a substitute and cancel fewer than ten (10) business days prior to the training class, you will either forfeit the registration fee or be allowed to apply your registration fee to the same class only once within the same calendar year. No-shows will forfeit their registration fees and no rescheduling is permitted. In the unfortunate circumstance that Gordian must cancel your event, Gordian will work with you to reschedule your attendance in the same training class at a later date or will fully refund your registration fee.

Any on-demand (self-paced) training modules are not eligible for cancellation, substitution, transfer, return or refund.

Virtual Training (Private Group)
If you provide notice more than ten (10) business days prior to the training class, Gordian will work to reschedule your event. If you cancel your event fewer than ten (10) business days prior to the training class, you are responsible for paying for the trainer's time for the cancelled training, as well as the full cost of materials and shipping. In the unfortunate circumstance that Gordian must cancel your event, Gordian will work with you to reschedule your attendance in the same training class at a later date or will fully refund your registration fee.

Public Training Events (Individual)
If you are unable to attend a training conference, a colleague may substitute no fewer than ten (10) business days before the session starts by notifying the training registrar at 877.620.6245 or your sales representative. Gordian is not responsible for sending duplicate materials to the substitute colleague.

If you are unable to find a substitute and cancel fewer than ten (10) business days prior to the conference, you will forfeit the registration fee. No-shows will forfeit their registration fees and no rescheduling is permitted. In the unfortunate circumstance that Gordian must cancel your event, Gordian will fully refund your registration fee.

On-Site Training (Private Group)
If you provide notice more than ten (10) business days prior to the training class, Gordian will work with you to reschedule your event, but you are responsible for rescheduling fees associated with the trainer's time, airfare and lodging. If you cancel fewer than ten (10) business days before your event, you are responsible for the full cost of the event. In the unfortunate event that Gordian must cancel your event, Gordian will work with you to reschedule your attendance at a later date or will fully refund your registration fee.

AACE Approved Courses
The AACE recognizes .1 CEUs per hour of training attended for all of Gordian's virtual training courses and public training events.

Important
Class sizes are limited, so please register as soon as possible.